# WEBSTER'S NEW WORLD™

---

# ROGET'S A–Z THESAURUS

# WEBSTER'S NEW WORLD™

# ROGET'S A–Z THESAURUS

## Charlton Laird
*and the Editors of*
Webster's New World Dictionaries

## Michael Agnes
*Editor in Chief*

**WILEY**

Wiley Publishing, Inc.

For general information on our other products and services please contact our Customer Care Department within the U.S. at 800-762-2974, outside the U.S. at 317-572-3993 or fax 317-572-4002.

Wiley also publishes its books in a variety of electronic formats. Some content that appears in print may not be available in electronic books. For more information about Wiley products, visit our web site at www.wiley.com.

*Library of Congress Cataloging-in-Publication Data:*
Laird, Charlton Grant, 1901-84
    Webster's New World Roget's A–Z thesaurus / Charlton Laird and the
  editors of Webster's New World dictionaries ; Michael Agnes, editor in chief.
     p.    cm.
    Rev. ed of: Webster's New World thesaurus. c1997.
    "A Webster's New World book"—T.p. verso.
    ISBN 978-0-02-863122-6 (thumb-indexed). — ISBN
  978-0-02-863281-0 (leatherkraft). — ISBN 978-0-02-863123-3 (pbk.)
    1. English language—Synonyms and antonyms.  I. Agnes, Michael.
  II. Laird, Charlton Grant, 1901-84. Webster's New World thesaurus.
  III. Title.
  PE1591.L27  1999
  423′.1—dc21                         99-13475
                                             CIP

Manufactured in the United States of America

10

# CONTENTS

# WEBSTER'S NEW WORLD®
# ROGET'S A–Z THESAURUS

*Editor in Chief*
Michael Agnes

*Contributing Editors*
Frank R. Abate, Supervising Editor
John K. Bollard, Editor
Sharon Goldstein, Editor
Lois Principe, Associate Editor
Barbara Ann Kipfer, Editor, Roget's Index

*Managing Editor*
James J. Heaney

*Senior Editors*
Andrew N. Sparks
Jonathan L. Goldman

*Editor and Database Administrator*
Donald Stewart

*Editors*
James E. Naso
Katherine Soltis
Stephen P. Teresi
Laura Borovac Walker

*Production Coordinator*
Barbara Apanites

*Administrative and Data Processing Staff*
Alisa Murray Davis
Cynthia M. Sadonick
Betty Dziedzic Thompson

*Proofreading and Data Inputting*
Joan Carlson
Elaine Chasse
Jacquelyn Goodwin
Paulette Kovelan

*Citation Readers*
Batya Jundef
Joan Komic

*Manufacturing Coordinator*
Andrew Stone

*Front and Back Matter
Typesetting and Design*
Otto H. Barz,
Publishing Synthesis Ltd., New York

# FOREWORD

This fourth edition of Webster's New World's college thesaurus is the latest incarnation of the eminently successful work originally created by Charlton Laird. Professor Laird's thesaurus, first published in 1971 and revised in 1985 and 1997, has over the years proved itself to be the most usable and the most useful thesaurus available. These two qualities match perfectly the guiding principles of its acclaimed companion volume, the fourth edition of *Webster's New World College Dictionary*.

A thesaurus is designed to function as a "treasure house" of possibilities. The entries in this thesaurus have been chosen from the 30,000 most commonly used words in American English. Matched with them are over 300,000 alternate terms that are potentially usable in their place. Entries in the main section of the thesaurus appear in alphabetical order, a sensible format that has proved popular because it offers the convenience of immediate access to the wealth of synonyms, antonyms, related terms, and discussions of comparative meaning and usage.

The main entry list includes synonym studies adapted from the *Webster's New World College Dictionary* and integrated into the text, a feature not found in most thesauruses. The useful distinctions made in previous editions between main entries, brief entries, and cross-referring entries remain. Both the choice of entries overall and the order of synonyms within entries are intended to reflect the frequency with which the terms are used in our language. The user of this book is more likely to need an alternate for a commonly used expression than for one of greater rarity. Further delving into an entry, however, will lead the user away from the familiar toward more colorful, specific, or appropriate vocabulary. Users of the thesaurus are urged to read the user's guide, beginning on page ix, in order to get the most out of this edition.

The new title gracing this fourth edition, *Webster's New World Roget's A-Z Thesaurus*, denotes the inclusion of a schematic outline of language that offers readers a choice in how they can use the work. The outline offered is drawn from the original plan of Peter Roget that was published in his ground-breaking thesaurus of 1852. The editors wish to thank Mrs. Evelyn Ward, head of the Literature Department of the Cleveland Public Library, for her assistance in researching Roget's original plan. The version presented here has been ably prepared by Barbara Ann Kipfer especially for Webster's New World. Dr. Kipfer also compiled the word lists given in the back of the book. The schematic outline enables users to explore language by using broad concepts rather than by searching for a single synonym for a specific word. It thus functions as a thematic index of and a gateway to the main entries in their alphabetical order. In offering both a thematic outline and an alphabetical listing in a single volume, the editors hope to serve readers who may find one or the other method of searching preferable at any given time.

The editors of Webster's New World proudly present this fourth edition with the confidence that it will provide inspiration and worthwhile assistance to writers, speakers, students, editors, and professionals everywhere.

Michael Agnes
Editor in Chief

# GUIDE TO THE USE OF THE THESAURUS

This book has two principal sections. You are invited to begin your search for words in either section. The introductory thematic outline is designed to assist in exploring language by starting from a list of broad *concepts,* organized into one thousand entries. The main body of the book has about 50,000 entries that are specific *words* listed with their synonyms. Additional word lists are given at the end of the main A–Z section.

## THEMATIC INDEX

The thematic entries in the first section of the book represent a division of language into concept groups and subgroups. There are six principal divisions:

Abstract Concepts
Spatial Concepts
Physical and Material Concepts
Human Intellect
Human Personality and Actions
Human Emotions and Beliefs

Each of these principal divisions has subgroups. Many of the entries exist in pairs of opposite concepts, such as *wholeness* and *incomplete state* or *forerunner* and *sequel,* and are arranged facing each other on the page. These entries, in turn, are cross-referenced to one or several word entries in the main section of the book. By starting with the thematic entries, you can thus proceed from a general idea to the specific expression of some aspect of that idea. The emphasis in the thematic section is not on listing comprehensive synonym entries but rather on providing two, three, or four possible gateways for exploration. Where such exploration will lead depends on what specific aspect you are interested in.

There are one thousand thematic entries. They are printed in regular type, and a colon separates them from the boldface cross-references that follow. Where necessary, parts of speech and sense numbers are given so that the reader can quickly find the specific group of synonyms recommended.

11. Related by family: **related** 3; **parentage; family** 1
21. Copy: **copy** *n., v.;* **duplicate** *n., v.*

## MAIN A–Z SECTION

Entries in the main A–Z section, by contrast, are arranged alphabetically by boldface headword, just as entries are arranged in a dictionary. This section is designed to help you find a new way to say what you want to say when, for any of a variety of reasons, you do not want to use the specific word that you have in mind. You may, for instance, have used that word too often and feel you need a substitute for it. More likely, you may have found that the supply of words at your disposal has become uncomfortably small for your liking. What you need is not just one word to use in place of another, but access to a broader vocabulary, where greater possibilities for expression can be found.

## Entries

The main entries offer you several different means to extend your reach in writing. Every boldface entry is accompanied by synonyms. Commonly used terms have the greatest number of synonyms. Those less frequently used have a smaller number but will include at least one cross-reference to a more common term. Antonyms are provided where appropriate. A variety of examples listed under general terms offers you additional vocabulary rich in concreteness and specificity. And, finally, terms with synonyms that call for special care in use are followed by synonym studies containing usage information and illustrative examples.

The following guide sets out in detail the features you will find in the thesaurus's main section.

***Order of Entries.*** All headwords in this book are listed in strict alphabetical order and set in boldface type. Headwords may be single words, hyphenated compounds, unhyphenated compounds, abbreviations, or phrases:

> **able** . . .
> **able-bodied** . . .
> **account** . . .
> **accountant** . . .
> **account for** . . .
> **acquaintance** . . .
> **acquainted (with)** . . .
> **all right** . . .
> **A.M.** . . . .
> **amass** . . .

***Parts of Speech and Other Information.*** Labels are given for all headwords, including single words, compounds, and phrases. The parts of speech identified in this thesaurus are:

> *conj.*—conjunction
> *interj.*—interjection
> *modif.*—modifier (adjective or adverb)
> *n.*—noun
> *prep.*—preposition
> *pron.*—pronoun
> *v.*—verb

Labels are also used at headwords for the following:

> *abbr.*—abbreviation
> *pl.n.* —plural noun

*interrog.*—interrogative
*—asterisk indicating archaic, colloquial, dialect, slang, or other unusual usage

> **add up***, *v.* —*Syn.* be plausible, seem reasonable, . . .

Foreign terms appear in boldface, italic type. Their language of origin is given in parentheses:

> ***au courant*** (French), *modif.* —*Syn.* up-to-date, well-informed, . . .

Generally, a word having more than one part of speech is given a separate entry block for each part of speech:

> **abuse,** *n.* **1.** [Misuse] —*Syn.* misuse, misapplication, . . .
> **abuse,** *v.* **1.** [To treat badly] —*Syn.* misuse, mistreat, insult, . . .

An entry may carry more than one label:

> **why,** *modif., conj. & interrog.* —*Syn.* for what reason?, how so?, . . .


## Synonyms: Main Entries and Brief Entries

Entries in this book list synonyms (words or phrases that are similar in meaning):

> **why,** *modif., conj. & interrog.* —*Syn.* for what reason?, how so?, how?, how is it that?, on whose account?, . . .

Synonyms are listed by approximate frequency of use, from the most common to the least common:

> **celebration,** *n.* **1.** [An act or instance of recognizing an occasion] —*Syn.* commemoration, observance, honoring, keeping, . . . centennial, . . . bicentennial, . . . tercentenary, millennium, . . .

An asterisk beside a synonym indicates an archaic, colloquial, dialect, slang, or other unusual usage:

> **walk,** *v.* **1.** [To move on foot] —*Syn.* step, pace, march, . . . hoof it*, . . . locomote*, cruise*.

***Main entries.*** Because it would be impractical for reasons of space to list every possible synonym at every entry block, certain entry blocks or numbered senses have been chosen to be the primary location of synonyms belonging to a particular family of meanings. These primary locations are "main entries." Main entries always contain either more than four synonyms or a list of examples:

> **dwell,** *v.* —*Syn.* live, reside, inhabit, stay, lodge, room, abide, sojourn, stop, settle, . . .

*Brief entries.* Entry blocks or numbered senses containing up to four synonyms are "brief entries." Brief entries always refer you to at least one main entry:

> **able-bodied,** *modif.* —*Syn.* fit, powerful, sturdy, healthy; see **healthy** 1, **strong** 1.

## The Main Entry Block

*Numbered Senses and Definitions.* Different senses of a word given in a single entry block are numbered consecutively in boldface numerals and may be further distinguished by brief definitions or explanatory notes in brackets:

> **capital,** *n.* **1.** [A seat of government] . . .
> **2.** [Money and property] . . .
> **3.** [A letter usually used initially] . . .

An asterisk beside a definition signals that the headword in this particular sense may be archaic, colloquial, dialect, slang, or in some other way unusual in usage:

> **acid,** *n.* **1.** [A sour substance] . . .
> **2.** [\*A drug] —*Syn.* LSD, D-lysergic acid diethylamide, . . .

*Idioms.* Idiomatic phrases under a headword are listed in alphabetical order after the headword's numbered senses:

> **action,** *n.* **1.** [Any state opposed to rest and quiet] . . .
> **2.** [An individual deed] . . .
> **3.** [A process at law] . . .
> **4.** [Military activity] . . .
> **5.** [The plot or events in a creative work] . . .
> **bring action** . . .
> **see action** . . .
> **take action** . . .

*Antonyms.* Antonyms (words that are opposite or nearly opposite in meaning) are listed after the synonyms. Antonyms given in small capitals are entries the user is especially advised to consult:

> **insulted,** *modif.* —*Syn.* offended, affronted, slighted, slandered, libeled, vilified, . . . cut to the quick; see also **disgraced.** —*Ant.* flattered, complimented, PRAISED.

> **a,** *modif. & prep.* **1.** [The indefinite article; *before vowels, written "an"*] . . . —*Ant.* THE, this, that.

*Lists of Examples.* Often, a writer or speaker is helped by being able to browse through the variety of things that may fall under one general heading. Some main entries include such lists of examples:

> **boat,** *n.* —*Syn.* vessel, bark, sailboat, yacht, steamboat, craft, watercraft, bottom, hulk; see also **ship.**
> Types of small boats include: rowboat, shell, scull, kayak, dugout, canoe, . . .

When a term applies to several different things but itself has no close synonymies, only a selected list of those things is given:

> **varnish,** *n.*
> Colors of varnish include: light oak, dark oak, golden oak, mahogany, . . .

*Cross-references.*   When it is appropriate to call the user's attention to another closely related family of synonyms, a cross-reference is made from one entry to another:

> **settle,** *v.* . . .
> 7. [To establish residence] —*Syn.* locate, lodge, become a citizen, reside, fix one's residence, abide, . . . establish a home, keep house; see also **dwell.**

*Synonym Studies.*  Although synonyms are words with similar or closely related meanings, they are not normally interchangeable with one another. When the synonyms of a main entry need further explanation, synonym studies with usage information and illustrative examples are provided:

> *SYN.*—**will,** the more inclusive term here, basically denotes the power of choice and deliberate action or the intention resulting from the exercise of this power [freedom of the *will,* the *will* to succeed]; **volition** stresses the exercise of the will in making a choice or decision [he came of his own *volition*]

Cross-references to a synonym study always give in small capitals the headword at which it will be found:

> **cabal,** *n.* —*Syn.* plot, scheme, conspiracy, junta; see **intrigue** 1, **plot** 1, **ring** 3, **trick** 1.
> *See Synonym Study at* PLOT.

# WORD LISTS

Additional lists of words are given in the back of the book, following the main A–Z section. The word groups given are similar to the lists of examples offered in entries in the A–Z section.

# ROGET'S THEMATIC INDEX

## I. ABSTRACT CONCEPTS

### Existence

Existence: **reality** 1; **alive** 1; **real**
Physical being: **person** 1; **animal** 1, 2; **thing** 1
Inherent by nature: **essence** 1; **inherent**
State: **state** 2

Non-existence: **nothingness**; **oblivion** 2
Nothingness: **nothing**; **blank** 1
Non-inherent: objective 1; **accidental**

### Relation

Related in general: **relationship**; **related** 2
Related by family: **related** 3; **parentage**; **family** 1
Mutual relation: **mutual** 1; **exchange** 2
Identical: **equal**; **same**; **identical**
Difference: **different**; **difference** 2
Uniformity: **uniform** 1; **consistency** 1
Dissimilarity: **difference**
Imitation: **imitation**
Variation: **variation** 1
Copy: **copy**; **duplicate**
Agreement: **agreement** 2; **agree**; **harmonious** 2

Unrelated: **separate**; **separated**; **irrelevant**


Opposite: **opposite**; **contrast**; **contrary** 1, 2

Similarity: **similarity**; **likeness**; **resemble**

Non-imitation: **original** 3; **unique** 1

Item copied: **model** 2; **original** 3
Disagreement: **clash** 2

### Quantity

Quantity: **quantity**; **size** 2
Equal quantity: **parity**
Mean: **average**; **center** 1
Compensation: **offset** 3
Great amount: **quantity**; **lot** 4
Superiority: **perfection** 3; **advantage** 2
Increased amount: **increase**; **growth** 1; **intensify**

Addition: **addition** 1; **plus**
Amount added: **addition** 2; **adjunct** 1

Relative quantity: **degree** 2; **extent**
Unequal quantity: **unequal** 2; **irregular**


Small amount: **minimum**; **small** 1, 2
Inferiority: **second**; **inferior**
Decreased amount: **decrease**; **reduction**; **diminish**
Subtraction: **deduction** 3; **removal** 1
Amount subtracted: **decrease** n; **diminution**

Mix: **mixture** 1; **adulterate**; **compound** *n.*
Complexity: **complicate**; **complex**
Connection: **junction**; **fastener**; **bind** 1
Bond: **bond** 1; **link**; **tie** 1
Sticking together: **coherence** 1; **tenacious** 1;
 **adhesive**
Combination: **union**; **combination**; **associate** 1
Whole: **whole**; **totality**; **entirety**
Wholeness: **unity** 1; **plenty**
Composition: **composition** 1, 2; **constituent**;
 **construction**

Remains: **remainder; residue**
Simplicity: **simple** 1; **simplicity** 1

Disconnection: **separated**; **break** *v.* 1; **division** 1

Unbound: **loose** 1; **slack** 1

Disintegration: **dissolution** 1; **decay**
Part: **part**; **portion** 1; **piece** 1
Incomplete state: **deficiency**; **lack**
Component: **part** 1; **element** 1

# Order

Order: **order** 2, 3; **orderly** 1, 2; **system** 1

Arrangement: **arrangement** 1, 2; **organization** 1,
 2; **system**
In order: **precedence**; **precede**; **former**
Forerunner: **precursor**; **pioneer** 1, 2; **prelude** 1
Beginning: **start**; **open** *v.* 1; **originate**; **first** 1
Middle: **middle**; **median**; **midway**
Uninterrupted sequence: **continuity** 1;
 **progressive** 1; **endless**
Accompaniment: **accompaniment** 1; **following** *n;*
 **escort**
Assemblage: **assemble** 2; **gathering**; **collection**
Classification: **class** 1; **division** 2; **category**
Inclusion: **inclusion**; **include** 1; **involve**
General quality: **generality**; **prevalent**;
 **extensive** 1, 2
Rule: **custom** *n.* 1, 2; **practice** *n.* 1
Conformity: **conformity**; **adapt** 2; **accommodate** 2

Normality: **normal**; **normality**; **common** 1, 2, 3;
 **natural** 2

Disorder: **disorder** 1, 2; **disorganize**; **jumble**;
 **confusion**
Disarrangement: **derange** 1; **jumble**

Succession: **sequence**; **progression**
Sequel: **sequel**; **appendix**
End: **end**; **final**; **conclude** 1; **finish** 1

Interrupted sequence: **interruption**;
 **discontinued**

Dispersion: **distribution**; **scatter** 1, 2; **spread** 1, 2

Exclusion: **exclusion**; **exclude** 1; **bar** *v.* 2
Special quality: **special** 1; **characteristic**;
 **specification**

Unconformity: **unconformity**; **inconsistency**;
 **unconventional**
Abnormality: **abnormal**; **abnormality**; **unusual**

# Number

Number: **number** 2; **numerical**; **sum**; **percentage**
Counting: **numerate**; **number** *v;* **calculate** 1;
 **mathematics**
Listing: **list**; **table** 2; **enumeration**; **inventory**
Aloneness: **unity** 1; **oneness**; **singular** 1
Two: **dualism**; **two**; **pair**; **couple**
Doubling: **duplicate**; **reproduction** 2; **increase** 1
Dividing in halves: **bisect**; **half**; **halve**; **divide** 1
Three: **trio**; **three**; **triple**
Tripling: **triple**; **three**
Dividing in thirds: **third**; **three**
Four: **fourfold**; **foursquare** 1; **foursome**
Quadrupling: **fourfold**
Plurality: **plural** 1; **plurality**; **majority** 2;
 **multiply** 1
Fraction: **fraction**; **part** 1; **division** 2

Accompaniment: **together** 1; **accompaniment** 1

Zero: **zero; blank** 1; **null** 1, 2
Numerousness: **numerous; multiple** 2; **abundance**
Repetition: **repetition; iteration; repeat**
Infinity: **infinite; infinity; inclusive; comprehensive**

Fewness: **few; sparse; infrequent; minority** 1

# Time

Time: **time; duration; term** 2
Spell in time: **spell** *n.* 2; **shift** *n.* 2; **tour** *n.* 3

Interim: **interim; interval; transient**
Endlessness: **perpetual; perpetuity; eternity** 1

Chronology: **chronological; time** 1, 9; **calendar; clock**
Previous time: **previous; precede; priority**
Later time: **posterior** 1; **later; subsequent; following**
Present time: **present** *n.* 1; **now** 1
Past: **past** *n.* 1; **antiquity** 3; **former**
Future: **future; coming** 1; **tomorrow; hereafter**
Simultaneousness: **simultaneous; contemporary** 1; **synchronous**
Newness: **newness; novelty** 1; **fresh** 1, 2

Morning: **morning; noon**
Youth: **youth; young** 1; **childhood**
Infancy: **baby** 1, 2; **child; infancy**
Adolescence: **adolescence; youth** 1; **teens; puberty**
Earliness: **early** 2; **premature; prompt**
Timeliness: **timely; timeliness; opportune**

Frequency: **frequency; frequent; often**
Regularity: **regularity; periodic; systematic**

Point in time: **period** 1; **age** 3; **juncture; time** 2
Durability: **durability; endurance** 2; **permanence**

Instantaneousness: **instantaneous; suddenly; momentary**
Anachronism: **anachronism; misdate**

Oldness: **ancient; antiquated; old** 2, 3; **old-fashioned**
Evening: **night; evening; dusky**
Oldness: **age** 2; **old; antiquated**
Maturity: **maturity** 3; **mature** 1; **senior; old age**

Lateness: **late** 1; **delay; postponed**
Untimeliness: **untimely; inopportune; unfavorable** 2
Infrequency: **infrequent; rare** 2; **occasional** 1
Irregularity: **irregularity; variation** 1, 2; **fluctuation**

# Change

Change: **change** 1, 2; **variety** 1; **alteration; innovation**
Stopping: **cessation; end** 2; **pause** 1, 2; **halt**

Conversion: **conversion** 1; **transformation** 1; **rehabilitation; transition**
Radical change: **revolution** 2, 3; **radical** 2; **overthrow; overturn**
Substitution: **substitute; exchange** 1, 3; **replace** 1, 2; **relieve** 1
Changeability: **changeable; inconstant; uncertainty** 2, 3; **fickle**
Regularity: **regularly; methodical; uniform** *modif.*
Destiny: **eventual; future; happen**

Permanence: **permanent; stability** 1; **perpetual** 1; **conservation**
Continuing: **continuity** 1; **persistence; persevere** 1
Reversion: **revert; retrogression** 1; **regress**

Mutual change: **interchange** 1, 2; **reciprocate; trade** *v.* 2
Stability: **stability** 1; **reliable** 1; **steady** 1

# Causation

Cause: **cause 1-4; reason 3; basis 1; source 1**

Attribution: **attribute** v; **imputation; accusation** 2

Potency: **potent; forceful; powerful; omnipotence**

Strength: **strength 1; might; vigor 2; brawn**

Productivity: **productivity; fruitful 2; prolific; proliferate**

Product: **product; result; handiwork; workmanship**

Reproduction: **reproduction 1; reconstruct; procreation; generation 1, 2**

Ancestry: **ancestry; family 1; paternity 1; maternity**

Destroyer: **destroyer; killer**

Functioning: **operation 1, 2; perform 1; operate 2; procedure 1**

Energy: **energy; vitality; force 1, 3; invigorate**

Violence: **violence 2; vehemence; intensity 1**

Influence: **influence; impact 2; power 2; weight 3**

Tendency: **tendency 1; inclination 1; propensity; trend 1**

Liability: **liability 1; likelihood; probability; susceptibility**

Concurrence: **concurrent; cooperation**

Effect: **effect; result; consequence; impact** n. 2

Unassignable cause: **chance** modif.; **fortuitous; accidental; haphazard**

Impotency: **impotent 1; weakness 1; inability; helpless 1**

Weakness: **weakness 1; feeble 1; frailty 1; delicate 1**

Non-productiveness: **unproductive; waste** modif.; **sterile 1, 2, 5; fruitless**

Posterity: **progeny; offspring, posterity; descendants**

Inertia: **inertia; laziness; idleness**

Moderation: **moderation 1; restraint 1; temper** v. 1

Absence of Influence: **ineffective; useless 1; powerless**

Counteraction: **counteraction; opposition 1; cancellation; neutralize**

# II. SPATIAL CONCEPTS

## Space in General

Indefinite space: **space 1, 2; expanse; range 2; latitude 1**

Place: **country; town 1, 2; city; district**

Location: **location; situation 2; place 3; position 1**

Presence: **presence 1; attendance; frequent** v.

Inhabitant: **inhabitant; resident; native 2; aboriginal**

Habitation: **habitation; inhabited; dwell**

Abode: **abode; dwelling; home 1**

Room: **room 2, 4; compartment; chamber 1; cell 3**

Receptacle: **container; receptacle; repository**

Region: **region 1; area 2; zone 2**

Displacement: **dislocation 1; displace**

Absence: **absence 1; vacancy; void 2; vacant 2**

## Dimensions

Large size: **size 2; measurement 2; largeness; capacity 1**

Size increase: **expansion; increase 1; growth 1; development 2**

Distance: **distance 2; far 1; remote 1; isolated**

Small size: **littleness; smallness; diminutive; little 1**

Size decrease: **contraction 1; reduction 1; decrease; compress**

Nearness: **nearness 1; proximity; vicinity; contiguous**

Interval: **interval; pause** 1, 2; **hiatus; gap** 2
Length: **length** 1; **extent; reach** *n.*; **long** 1

Thickness: **breadth** 1; **width; diameter; thickness**
Layer: **layer; stratum; stratification**
Height: **height** 1; **tall** 1; **high** 1; **altitude**
Depth: **depth** 1, 2; **deep** 1, 2; **profound** 1; **abysmal** 1
Top: **summit; top** 1; **pinnacle; head** 3

Vertical: **vertical; upright** 1; **erected** 1; **perpendicular**
Hanging: **pendent; hanging; suspended; overhang** 1
Shaft: **shaft** 1; **post** 1; **pole; rod** 1
Parallelism: **parallel** 1; **collateral** *modif.*
Inversion: **inverse; opposite** 1; **overturn; upset** 1
Crossing: **crossing** 1; **intersection; junction** 2; **transverse**
Exterior: **exterior; external; outside** 1; **outdoors**
Centrality: **center** 1; **inside** *n.*; **middle; centrally**
Covering: **cover** 1, 2; **covering; shelter; wrap** 2
Clothing: **clothes; costume; uniform**
Environment: **environment; surroundings; circumstance** 1
Boundaries: **boundary; limitation** 2; **border; outline** 3
Circumscription: **circumscribe; demarcation** 1; **restraint** 2; **edge** 1
Enclosure: **enclosure; package** 1; **confine** 2; **fence** 1
In between: **interpose** 2; **interposition; interpolation; insertion**
Intrusion: **intrusion; interference** 2; **encroachment**
Front: **front** 1; **fore; primary** 1
Side: **lateral; side; flank; beside**
Opposite: **oppose** 1; **face** 1; **antithesis; contrast** 2
Right side: **right** *modif.* 7; **right** *n.* 4

Shortness: **shortness; brevity; abridgment; curtail**
Narrowness: **thinness; narrow** 1; **taper; decrease** 1, 2
Filament: **fiber** 1; **filament; thread; stringy** 1
Lowness: **low** 1; **squat** *modif.;* **short** 1
Shallowness: **shallow** 1; **cursory; superficial**

Bottom: **base** 3; **foundation** 2; **bottom** 1, 2; **underside**
Horizontal: **horizontal; level** 3; **flatten; plane** 1

Supporting: **support** *v.* 1, 2; **backing** 2; **mainstay; foothold**

Obliquity: **oblique** 1; **deviate; declivity; diagonal**

Interior: **interior** 1; **internal** 1, 2; **inside** 1, 2

Lining: **lining; insulation** 2; **membrane; skin**
No clothing: **divest** 1; **strip; undress**

Rear: **rear n; posterior** 2; **behind** 1; **back** 1, 2

Left side: **left** *modif.* 1; **left** *n.*

# Form

Form: **shape** 1; **form** 1; **physique; configuration**
Symmetry: **balance** 2; **symmetry; proportion**
Angularity: **angular** 1; **crooked** 1; **bent**
Curvature: **curve** 1; **bent; arc**
Circularity: **circular** 1; **round** 1, 2; **circle; coil**
Roundness: **rotund** 1; **sphere** 1; **orb**
Convex: **convex; bulge; protuberance**
Flatness: **flat** 1; **level** 2; **horizontal**
Sharpness: **sharp** 1, 2; **point** *n.* 2; **spike** 1
Smoothness: **smooth** 1; **level** 1; **flat** 1
Notched: **notch; dent; indent**
Folded: **fold** *n.* 1; **fold** *v.* 2; **pleat**
Furrowed: **furrow; groove; wrinkle**

Formlessness: **formless; shapeless** 1; **indefinite** 1
Asymmetry: **contortion** 1, 2; **change** 4; **distortion** 1

Straightness: **straight** 1; **direct** 1; **vertical**

Concave: **concave; hole** 2; **hollow** 2; **depression** 1

Bluntness: **blunt** 1; **dull** 1; **obtuse** 2
Roughness: **rough** 1; **uneven** 1; **bumpy**

Opening: **opening** *n*. 1; **hole** 1, 2; **aperture**; **perforation**

Closing: **closure**; **shut**; **obstruct**; **stopped**

# Motion

Motion: **motion** 1, 2; **movement** 1, 2; **stir** 1

Quiet: **quiescent**; **resting** 1; **peaceful** 1

Transfer: **transferred**; **shipped**; **transmit**

Land travel: **journey**; **travel** 1; **passage** 1; **traveler**

Water travel: **navigation**; **navigator**; **boating**; **mariner**

Air travel: **aeronautics**; **flying**; **pilot** 1; **astronaut**

Vehicle: **conveyance** 2; **vehicle** 1; **automobile**

Ship: **ship**; **boat**; **vessel** 2; **yacht**

Aircraft: **plane** 3; **airplane**; **airship**; **spacecraft**

Fastness: **velocity**; **speed**; **swiftness**

Slowness: **slow** *modif*. 1; **sluggish**; **plod**; **brake**

Driving force: **momentum**; **impulse**; **energy** 3

Reaction: **recoil**; **reflex**; **react**

Direction: **direction** 1; **way** 2; **point** 1

Indirect course: **deviate**; **wandering** 1; **departure** 2

Preceding: **before**; **precede**; **lead** *n*. 1

Following: **after**; **succeed** 2; **follower**

Progressing: **progress** *v*. 1; **advance** 1; **further** *v*.

Regressing: **regress**; **lapse**; **setback**

Propelling: **propulsion**; **thrust** 3; **pushing**

Pulling: **pull** 1, 2; **traction**; **stress** 2

Approaching: **approach** 2; **nearing**; **coming** 1

Receding: **recede** 1; **withdrawal**; **retreat** *v*. 1, *n*. 1

Attracting: **draw** *v*. 1; **attract** *v*. 1; **magnetic**

Repelling: **repulse** 1; **rebuff**; **repel** 1

Converging: **convergent**; **meeting** 1; **congregate**

Diverging: **divergent**; **centrifugal**; **radiate** 1

Arriving: **arrive** 1; **landing** 1, 3; **entrance** 1

Departing: **departure** 1; **leave** *v*. 1; **retreat** 1

Entering: **ingress**; **entrance**; **entry** 1

Going out: **egress**; **exit** 1; **emerge**

Taking in: **reception** 1, 2; **admission** 2; **receive** 4

Letting out: **ejection**; **expel** 1; **discharge** *n*. 1

Eating: **eating**; **digestion**; **dine**

Excreting: **excretion**; **eliminate** 2

Secreting: **secretion**; **gland**

Overrunning: **overrun** 2; **infest**; **trespass** 2

Shortcoming: **default**; **wanting** 1; **shortcoming**

Ascending: **ascend**; **rise** 1; **mount** 1, 2

Descending: **descend** 1; **drop** 1; **sink** 1

Elevating: **elevate** 1; **raise** 1; **lift**

Lowering: **lower**; **decrease** 1, 2; **depress** 1

Leap: **leap**; **jump** 1

Plunge: **plunge**; **dive** 1

Circuitous: **circuit**; **circuitous**; **circular** 2

Rotation: **rotate** 1; **rotation**; **revolution** 1

Evolution: **evolution**; **unfold**; **development** 2

Oscillation: **oscillation**; **sway** 1; **vibration**

Agitation: **agitation**; **disturbance** 2; **shake**

# III. PHYSICAL AND MATERIAL CONCEPTS

## Matter in General

Material world: **material** *n*. 1; **matter** 1; **object** *n*. 1

Immaterial world: **immaterial** 2; **incorporeal**; **insubstantial**

Chemicals: **element** 2; **chemical**

Oils: **oil**; **lubricant**; **grease**

Resins: **resin**; **gum**

## Inorganic Matter

Weight: **weight** 1; **gravity** 1; **heaviness**

Density: **density** 1; **compact** *modif.*; **weight** 1

Lightness: **lightness** 2; **buoyancy** 1; **light** *modif.* 5

Flimsiness: **rare** 4; **tenuous**; **light** 5

Hardness: **hard** 1; **solid** 2; **rigid** 1

Softness: **soft** 1, 2; **flexible** 1; **pliant** 2

Elasticity: **elastic**; **resilient**; **flexibility** 1

Inelasticity: **inelastic**; **stiff** 1

Toughness: **tough** 1, 2, 3; **unbreakable**; **tenacious** 1

Brittleness: **fragile**; **brittle**; **crumbly**

Powdery: **powdery; pulverize; gritty**
Texture: **texture; form** 2
Friction: **friction** 1; **rub** 1 — Lubrication: **lubrication; grease**
Pulpiness: **pulp** 2; **mash; mush** 2
Semiliquid: **creamy; viscid; syrup**
Fluid: **liquid, fluid**
Gas: **gas, fumes**
Solid: **solid, body** 7
Melting: **liquefy, melt** 1 — Vaporizing: **vaporize, evaporate** 1
Water: **rain** 1; **water; precipitation** 2 — Air: **air** 1; **atmosphere** 1; **sky**
Moisture: **moisture; damp; wet** 1, 2 — Dryness: **dryness; drought; arid** 1; **dry** 1
Ocean: **ocean; sea** — Land: **land** 1; **earth** 2; **ground** 1
Lake: **pool** 1; **gulf** 2; **lake; pond** — Plain: **plain; steppe; prairie; field** 1
River: **stream; river** 1; **channel** 2 — Wind: **wind** 1; **draft** 3; **breeze**
Cloud: **bubble; cloud**
Body of land: **continent; island** 1; **region** 1 — Marsh: **marsh; swamp**
Inorganic Matter: **inorganic; artificial; inanimate** 1
Minerals: **mineral; rock** 1; **stone**
Metals: **metal; ore**

# Living Matter

Organic Matter: **organic** 1; **animate** *modif.;* **organism**
Mankind: **mankind; man** 1; **human**
Man: **masculine; male; virile** 1; **man** 2 — Woman: **feminine; female; woman** 1
Life: **life** 1; **living a**1; **vitality** — Death: **dying** 1; **die** 1; **extinction**
Birth: **birth** 1; **childbirth**
Killing: **kill** 1; **slay; fatal**
Corpse: **body** 2; **corpse; cadaver**
Burial: **interment; burial; funeral** 1
Animal Kingdom: **animal** *modif.* 1 — Plant Kingdom: **planting**
Animals: **animal** *n.* 2; **creature** 1; **beast** 1 — Vegetation: **plant** 1; **vegetation; grass** 1
Zoology: **zoology; life** 1 — Botany: **botany**
Animal Care: **husbandry** 1; **breeder** — Plant Care: **agriculture; farming; cultivation** 1
Food: **meat** 1; **vegetable** 1; **fruit** 1; **food**
Senses: **sensation; sense** 1; **feeling** 1
Physical feeling: **sensibility; awareness** — Physical insensitivity: **unfeeling** 1; **insensible** 1; **unconscious** 1

Physical pleasure: **satisfaction** 2; **comfort** 1 — Physical pain: **suffering; pain** 2; **hurt** 1
Touch: **touch** 1; **tactile; feel** *v.* 1 — Numbness: **numb; unfeeling**
Touches: **tingle; tickle** 1; **sting** *v.*
Heat: **heat** 1; **warmth** 3; **tepid** — Cold: **cold** 1; **chilly** 1; **cool** 1
Taste: **taste** 2; **lick** 1; **sip**
Weak taste: **insipid** 1; **tasteless** 1; **unsavory** 1 — Strong taste: **pungent; piquant** 2
Tasting good: **tasty; savory; delicious; palatable** — Tasting bad: **distasteful; bitter** 1
Sweet taste: **sweet** 1; **sugary** 1 — Sour taste: **sour; acid** 1; **tart**
Condiment: **condiment; seasoning; flavoring**
Smell: **smell** 3; **scent**
Odor: **odor; smell** 1, 2 — Non-odor: **odorless; deodorize; fumigate**
Good smell: **perfume; aromatic; fragrant** — Bad smell: **stink; stench; fetid**
Sound: **sound** 1, 2; **noise** 1 — Silence: **silence; mute**
Hearing: **hearing; listening; heed** — Deafness: **deaf** 1
Loudness: **loud** 1, 2; **noisy; sonorous** — Quietness: **faint** 3; **quiet** 2; **low** 2

Resonance: **resonance; reverberation; rumble; vibrant** 1

Violent sound: **report** 3; **thunder; whack**

Harsh sound: **shrill; harsh** 1; **hoarse**

Hissing sound: **hiss; buzz**

Shout: **cry** 1; **call** 1; **shout; yell** 1

Music: **music** 1; **melody** 2; **tune; song**

Harmony: **melody** 1; **harmony** 1; **concord** 1

Sight: **seeing; vision** 1; **eyesight**

Visibility: **perceivable; perceptible; visible**

Light: **light** 1; **illumination** 1; **luminous**

Dimness: **dim; fading; hazy** 1

Shade: **shade; gloom** 1; **shadow**

Transparency: **transparent** 1; **lucid** 1; **clear** 2

Semitransparency: **opalescent; iridescent; pearly**

Color: **color** 1; **hue** 1, 2; **tint; stain** *v.* 2

Multicolored: **variegation; rainbow; multicolored**

White: **white** 1; **ivory; blond**

Gray: **gray** 1; **dusky** 2; **ashen**

Brown: **brown; tan; ecru; sand**

Red: **red; rose; pink; crimson**

Yellow: **yellow** 1; **gold** 2; **tawny; amber**

Blue: **blue** 1; **azure; turquoise; bluish**

Green: **green** 1; **olive; emerald**

Purple: **purple; violet; lavender; mauve**

Orange: **orange; rust; auburn; russet**

Repeated sound: **tick** 1; **beat** 2; **throb**

Howl: **howl; cry** 2; **warble**

Disharmony: **discord** 2; **noise** 2; **cacophony**

Blindness: **sightless; blind** 1; **eyeless**

Invisibility: **invisible** 1; **fuzzy** 2; **obscure** 1

Darkness: **dark** 1; **darkness** 1; **blackness**

Opaqueness: **opaque; impervious** 2

No color: **colorless; pale** 1; **neutral** 3; **white** 2

Black: **black** 1; **jet; ebony**

# IV. HUMAN INTELLECT

## Formation of Ideas

Intellect: **faculty** 1; **mentality; intellect**

Thought: **thought** 1; **cogitation; consideration** 1

Idea: **idea** 1; **thought** 2; **concept; notion** 2

Knowledge: **knowledge** 1; **awareness; familiarity** 2

Intellectual: **intellectual; scholar** 2; **intelligentsia; learned**

Wisdom: **intelligence** 1, 2; **wisdom** 1; **comprehension** 1; **sense** 2

Wise person: **sage; master** 3; **savant; wise** 1, 4

Sanity: **sanity; reason** 1; **judgment** 1; **understanding** 1

Eccentricity: **eccentric; idiosyncrasy; quirk**

Question: **inquiry** 1; **question** 1; **query; quest**

Solution: **solution** 1; **answer** 2; **explanation** 2

Discovery: **discovery** 1; **find out; expose** 1

Experiment: **experiment** 1; **trial** *modif.*; **testing; probe**

Measurement: **measurement** 1; **assessment** 1; **estimate** 1

Comparison: **compare** 2; **check** 3; **weigh** 4

Unintelligence: **unintelligent; uneducated; dumb** 3; **ignorant** 2

Unthinking: **thoughtless** 1; **vacant** 3; **vacuous** 2; **blank** 3

Topic: **topic; theme** 1; **subject** *n.* 1

Ignorance: **ignorance** 1; **unaware; unmindful**

Idiocy: **imbecile; idiot**

Idiot: **stupid** 1; **subnormal; ignorant** 1; **fool** 1

Insanity: **insanity** 1; **mania; obsession; crazy**

Answer: **answer** 1; **reply; respond**

Discrimination: **discrimination** 1, 2; **distinction** 1, 2; **differentiate** 1; **discretion** 2

Attitude: **attitude** 2; **feeling** 3; **outlook** 1

Curiosity: **curiosity** 1; **inquisitive**; **wonder** 2

Attention: **attentive** 1; **mindful**; **interest** *n.* 1

Care: **care** 1; **attention** 2; **prudence**

Proof: **evidence**; **proof** 1; **grounds** 2; **fact**

Qualification: **qualification** 1, 3; **limitation** 2; **stipulation**; **requirement** 1

Possibility: **possibility**; **likelihood**; **imaginable**; **conceivable**

Probability: **feasible** 3; **probability**; **liable** 2; **inclination** 1

Certainty: **certainty**; **precision**; **accuracy** 2; **definite** 3

Gamble: **gamble** *n.*; **chance** 1; **risk** 2

Judgment: **judgment** 1, 2; **judicial**; **criticism** 1

Prejudgment: **prejudge**; **prejudiced**; **assume** 1; **presume**

Misjudgment: **misjudgment**; **miscalculate**; **misunderstand**

Overestimation: **overestimate**; **exaggerate**; **overrate**

Theory: **theory**; **supposition** 2; **conjecture**; **hypothesis**

Philosophy: **philosophy** 1, 3; **school** 2; **idealism** 2

Belief: **belief**; **faith** 2; **conviction** 1

Doubt: **disbelief**; **doubt**; **dubious** 1; **suspicious** 2

Intuition: **intuition**; **hunch** 2; **feeling** 4

Reasoning: **logic**; **reasoning**; **rationale**; **rationalize** 2

Gullible: **credulous**; **naïve**; **trusting** 1

Skepticism: **skeptical**; **incredulous**

Truth: **truth** 1; **verity**; **right** *modif.* 1

Maxim: **maxim**; **proverb**; **saying**

Illusion: **illusion** 2; **misconception**; **misunderstanding** 1

Disenchantment: **disillusion**; **disappoint**

Assent: **assent**; **agree**; **acquiesce**

Affirmation: **affirmation**; **declaration**; **oath**

Memory: **remembrance** 1; **recollection**; **memory** 1

Imagination: **fancy** *n.* 1, 2; **invention** 1; **dream** *v.* 2, 3; **imagination**

Guess: **guess**; **notion** 2; **supposition** 1

Expectation: **anticipation** 1; **expectation**; **await**; **imminent**

Surprise: **revelation** 1; **unforeseen**; **unexpected**; **startle**

Disappointment: **let down**; **dash** *v.* 2; **disappointment** 1

Foresight: **foresight** 1; **anticipation** 2; **foreknowledge**

Prediction: **prophecy**; **prognosis**; **prediction**

Omen: **portent**; **sign** 1; **omen**; **oracle**

Lack of discrimination: **indiscriminate**; **uncritical**; **imprudent**

Lack of curiosity: **incurious**; **indifferent** 1; **apathetic**

Inattention: **inattentive**; **absent-minded**; **distracted** 2

Neglect: **remiss**; **neglect**; **negligent**

Lack of proof: **disprove**; **invalidate**; **annul**

Absoluteness: **unqualified** 1; **unconditional**; **absolute** 1; **utter**

Impossibility: **impossibility**; **unimaginable**; **inconceivable**

Improbability: **improbable**; **remote** 4; **unlikely** 1

Uncertainty: **uncertainty** 1, 2; **incertitude**; **indecision**

Underestimation: **underestimate**; **depreciate** 2; **minimize**

Mistake: **error** 1, 2; **mistake** 2; **wrong** *modif.* 2; **fallacy**

Dissent: **dissent**; **difference** 3; **dispute**

Denial: **denial**; **rejection**; **negation** 2

Forgetfulness: **oblivion** 1; **forgetfulness**; **forget** 1

Unimaginativeness: **prosaic**; **staid**; **unimaginative**

# Communication of Ideas

Meaning: **definition** 1; **signify**; **imply** 2; **meaning**

Meaningless: **nonsense** 1; **trivial**; **meaningless**

Implied meaning: **imply** 1; **undercurrent** 3; **hint** 1; **latent**

Intelligibility: **understandable**; **explainable**; **intelligible**; **comprehensible**

Unintelligibility: **imperceptible**; **unfathomable** 2; **inexplicable**; **unintelligible**

Ambiguity: **equivocal**; **ambiguous**; **double-entendre**

Figure of speech: **metaphor**; **simile**; **allegory**; **figure of speech**

Interpretation: **interpretation** 1, 2; **rendition**; **translation**

Misinterpretation: **misinterpret**; **misconceive**; **misunderstand**

Information: **inform** 1; **report** 2; **information** 1; **enlightenment**

Misinformation: **misinform**; **misdirect**; **misguided**; **propaganda**;

News: **intelligence** 3; **information** 2; **message** 1; **news**

Publication: **broadcast**; **circulation** 2; **announcement**; **publication**

Manifestation: **appearance** 3; **display** v. 1; **manifest** v. 1; **expose** v. 2

Disclosure: **revelation** 1; **exposé**; **disclosure**

Concealment: **conceal, secret** n.; **confidence** 3; **private**

Transmission: **transmit**; **carry** 2; **dispatch** v1; **messenger**

Teaching: **teach** 1; **schooling**; **instruction**; **lesson** 2

Truth: **truth**; **honesty**; **honor** 3

Falsity: **falsehood**; **dishonesty**; **falsely**; **untruth**

Exaggeration: **dramatize** 2; **magnify** 2; **exaggeration**

Deception: **deceit**; **sham**; **fake**

Deceiver: **cheat** 1; **swindler**; **deceiver**

Gullible person: **naïve**; **trustful**; **fool** 2

Learning: **learn** 1; **study** v. 1, 2; **knowledge** 2; **educated** 1

Teacher: **teacher**; **instructor**; **mentor**

Student: **learner**; **student**; **pupil**

School: **academy** 1; **school**; **college**

# Means of Communication

Indication: **signify**; **mark** 6; **indication**

Insignia: **emblem**; **regalia** 2; **insignia**

Record: **record** n. 1; **recording** 1; **memo**; **chronicle**

Destruction of record: **obliterate**; **erase** 1; **cancel** 1

Recorder: **clerk** 2; **registrar**; **recorder**

Representation: **representation**; **portrayal**; **description** 1

Misrepresentation: **misrepresentation**; **perversion** 1; **falsify**

Art: **art**; **design** v. 2; **artistry**; **talent** 1

Sculpture: **sculpture**; **statue**; **bust** 2; **sculptor**

Ceramics: **ceramics**; **pottery**; **porcelain**

Painting: **paint** 1; **painting** 1

Drawing: **illustrator**; **draftsman**; **draw** v. 2

Photography: **photograph**; **photography**; **camera**

Engraving: **engraving**; **printing**; **etching**

Artist: **artist** 1; **artistic** 2; **painter** 2; **photographer**

Language: **tongue** 2; **parlance**; **language** 1

Letter: **letter** 1; **character** 3; **symbol**; **sign** 3

Word: **term** 1; **expression** 3; **word** 1

Phrase: **phrase**; **expression** 3; **express** 1; **sentence** 2

Terminology: **nomenclature**; **name** 1; **terminology**

Anonymity: **anonymous**; **unknown** 2; **nameless** 1

Grammatical: **syntax**; **language** 2; **grammar**; **grammatical**

Style of speech: **style**; **wording**; **diction**; **usage** 2

Clear speech: **perspicuity**; **clarity**; **plain** 5

Concise speech: **concise**; **brevity**; **laconic**; **succinct**

Elegant speech: **elegant** 3; **affected** 2; **euphonious**; **mannered**

Excited speech: **loquacious**; **fluent**; **talkative**

Imperfect speech: **stammer**; **stutter**; **impediment** 2; **mispronunciation**

Public speaking: **elocution**; **speech** 2; **delivery** 3

Address: **soliloquy**; **speech** 3; **address** 1; **oration**

Eloquence: **eloquence** 1, 2; **fluency**; **articulate**

Grandiloquence: **grandiloquent**; **bombastic**; **oratorical**

Conversation: **discuss**; **talk** v. 1; **chat**; **conversation**

Printing: **printing** 1; **presswork**; **copy**; **press** 3

Correspondence: **correspond** 2; **write** 1; **mail**; **letter** 2

Book: **book** 1; **periodical**; **volume** 3; **edition**

Description: **portrayal**; **description**; **sketch** 2; **narration**

Dissertation: **thesis** 2; **treatise**; **exposition**; **dissertation**

Summary: **compendium**; **abstract**; **synopsis**; **summary**

Poetry: **poem**; **verse** 1; **sonnet**; **poet**

Drama: **play** 4; **scenario**; **drama** 1; **dramatist**

New word: **neologism**; **jargon** 2, 3; **coin** v. 2

Incorrect terminology: **misname**; **miscall**

Ungrammatical: **solecism**; **misusage**; **ungrammatical**

Obscure speech: **obscurity**; **impediment** 2; **inarticulate** 2

Profuse speech: **verbosity**; **profuseness** 2; **wordiness**

Inelegant speech: **inelegant**; **vulgar** 2, 3; **colloquial**

Weak speech: **feeble** 2; **ineffective**; **uncommunicative**; **taciturn**

Response: **response**; **answer** 1

Written Language: **writing** 2, 3; **write** 2; **composition** 4; **authorship**

Prose: **prose**; **matter-of-fact**; **literature** 2

# V. HUMAN PERSONALITY AND ACTIONS

## Individual

Will: **will** 3; **volition**; **inclination** 1

Willingness: **willing**; **compliant**; **submissive**; **volunteer**

Strong will: **resolution** 1; **determination** 2; **firmness** 3

Perseverance: **persevere** 2; **persistent**; **endure** 1; **unfaltering**

Obstinance: **obstinate**; **headstrong**; **pertinacious** 2; **pigheaded**

Fate: **predetermine**; **foreordain**; **fate**; **fortune** 1

Whim: **caprice**; **whim**; **impulse** 2; **fickle** 1

Necessity: **necessity**; **need** 3; **requirement** 2; **obligation**

Unwillingness: **unwilling**; **indisposed** 2; **demur**; **reluctant**

Weak will: **irresolute**; **undecided**; **vacillate** 2; **hesitate**

Changing of mind: **backslide**; **about-face**; **recant**; **apostate**

Impulse: **impulse** 2; **inspiration** 1; **improvise**

Avoidance: **avoid; shun; elude; shirk**
Escape: **escape** *n.* **1; loophole** 1
Abandonment: **abandon** *v.* **2; forsake** 1; **desertion**
Desire: **desire** 1, 2; **wish** *n.* 1; **yearning; appetite** 2
Eagerness: **enthusiasm** 1; **zest** 1; **eager; keen** 4

Indifference: **indifferent** 1; **halfhearted; unconcern; aloof**
Rejection: **reject; repudiate; denial**

Choice: **choice** *n.* 1, 3; **selection** 1; **pick** *v.* 1; **preference** 1
Habit: **custom** 1, 2; **habit** 1, 2; **wont; routine**
Convention: **conventional** 1; **orthodox; custom** 3
Formality: **formal** 2; **conventional** 2; **ceremonious**

Without habit: **unaccustomed; unfamiliar** 2

Informality: **informal; unceremonious** 1; **casual** 5

Motivation: **motive; motivation; inducement; grounds** 2
Pretext: **pretense** 1; **pretext**
Enticement: **entice; allure; lure; inveigle**
Bribery: **bribe; corruption** 2
Good: **good** 1; **goodness; virtue** 1, 2
Plan: **plan** 2; **scheme; design** 2
Intention: **intention; purpose** 1
Pursuit: **pursuing; hunting; chase; pursuit**
Occupation: **business** 2, 3; **occupation** 2; **job** 1; **stint** 2
Method: **way** 3; **method** 2; **technique**
Equipment: **equipment; device** 1
Means: **instrumentality; means** 1; **resource**
Instrument: **instrument; tool** 1
Supply: **store** 2; **supply** 1; **stock** 1; **provision** 2
Materials: **material** 2; **commodity; thing** 1
Waste: **waste** *n.* 2; **refuse; trash** 1, 3; **wasteful**
Sufficiency: **plenty; sufficient**
Excess: **excess** 1; **inordinate; excessive**
Redundancy: **redundant; superfluous**
Satisfaction: **satisfaction** 2; **satiate**
Substitute: **substitute; makeshift; temporary**
Importance: **important** 1; **significant; urgent** 1; **big shot**
Use: **utility** 1; **useful; helpful** 1; **functional**
Disuse: **disuse** 1; **obsolete**
Misuse: **misuse; abuse** 1
Expedience: **expedient** 2; **advisability; appropriate**
Perfection: **perfection; flawless; faultless**
Curse: **curse** 2; **affliction; poison**
Blemish: **scar; blemish; defect** 2
Mediocrity: **mediocre; second-rate; inferior** 2
Cleanness: **clean** 1; **pure** 2; **sterile** 3
Health: **condition** 4; **health**
Healthfulness: **healthful; nutritious; salutary; salubrious**
Improvement: **betterment; improvement** 1; **progress** 2
Restoration: **rehabilitate; recovery** 2; **restoration** 1
Damage: **harm** 1; **injury** 1; **impaired**
Relapse: **relapse; reversion; backslide**
Remedy: **remedy** 2; **cure; nostrum; medicine** 2

Dissuasion: **deter; discourage** 1, 3

Evil: **evil; bad** 1; **wickedness**

Insufficiency: **inadequacy** 1; **insufficient**

Unimportance: **unimportant; insignificance; trivial**
Not using: **useless** 1; **unnecessary; in vain**

Inexpedience: **inexpedient; impropriety; injudicious**
Imperfection: **imperfection; faulty; flaw**

Dirtiness: **dirty** 1; **impure** 1; **filth**
Disease: **illness** 1; **ailment; disease**
Unhealthfulness: **unhealthful; harmful; toxic**

Deterioration: **deteriorate; decay** *n.* 1; **worsen**

Medicine: **medicine** 1, 3; **therapy; doctor** 1;
  **therapeutic**

Psychology: **psychology; psychiatry;
  psychoanalysis**

Safety: **safety** 1; **security** 1; **safe** 1, 2

Danger: **danger; peril; threat; jeopardize**

Protection: **refuge** 1; **protection** 2; **safekeeping;
  guardian** 1

Preservation: **saving** 1; **preservative; secure** v. 3;
  **preservation**

Pitfall: **trap** 1; **pitfall**

Warning: **warning; caution** 2; **caveat; notify** 2

Apprehension: **alarm** 2; **apprehension** 1;
  **trepidation** 2

Rescue: **deliverance; freeing; rescue** 1

Preparation: **ready** 2; **arrange** 2; **preparatory;
  preparation**

Lack of preparedness: **undeveloped** 1; **immature;
  lazy** 1; **unprepared**

Endeavor: **essay** 2; **effort** 1, 2; **endeavor**

Undertaking: **enterprise** 1; **venture;
  undertaking**

Action: **action** 1; **operation** 2; **practice** 1;
  **exercise** 1

Inaction: **inactive** 1; **passive** 2; **do-nothing**

Activity: **doing; action** 2; **activity** 1; **active** 2;
  **busy**

Inactivity: **inactive** 2; **indolent; quiescence;
  idleness**

Hurry: **haste** 1; **hurry** n. 3, v. 1, 2; **hasten; dispatch** 1

Leisure: **ease** 1; **leisure**

Exertion: **exertion; effort** 1; **work** 2

Rest: **repose; rest** 1; **relaxation; vacation**

Wakefulness: **awake; awaken** 1; **get up** 2

Sleep: **slumber; doze; sleep**

Invigoration: **refresh; invigorate; exhilarating;
  stimulating**

Worker: **doer; laborer; worker; craftsman**

Workplace: **office** 3; **workshop** 1; **factory; plant** 2

Government: **government** 1; **regulation** 1;
  **politics** 1

Supervision: **direction** 2; **management;
  supervision**

Advice: **advice; counsel** 1; **guidance**

Precept: **precept; doctrine** 1; **law** 2, 4

Command: **order** 1; **decree; command** 1

Demand: **demand** v. 1; **requisition; order** 5; **claim**

Behavior: **conduct** 1; **behavior** 1; **deportment;
  manner** 1

Misbehavior: **transgression; misconduct;
  naughty; misbehavior**

Skilled: **skill; proficient; expert; skillful**

Unskilled: **unskilled; incompetent;
  inexperienced; bungler**

Clever: **shrewd; calculating; cunning** 2; **clever**

Unsophisticated: **artless; naïve; ingenuous** 2;
  **unsophisticated** 1

Accomplishment: **achieve** 1; **consummate** v.;
  **accomplish; complete** 1

Nonaccomplishment: **unaccomplished** 1;
  **incomplete** 1; **undone** 1

Success: **pull off** 2; **make good** 4; **success**

Failure: **fail** 1; **flop** 4; **botch; failure**

Victory: **triumph** 1; **winning** 2; **champion** 1;
  **victory**

Defeat: **beat** v. 4; **vanquish; lose** 1, 2, 3; **defeat**

Prosperity: **thrive** 2; **succeed** 1; **good fortune;
  prosper**

Adversity: **hardship; trouble** 1; **misfortune;
  adverse** 2

Difficulty: **difficulty** 1, 2, 3; **predicament; hard** 2;
  **arduous**

Easiness: **effortless; easy** 2; **facility** 1; **facilitate**

Hindrance: **thwart; prevent; impediment** 1;
  **hinder**

Help: **help** v. 1; **aid** n. 1; **support** 1; **patronage** 1

Opposition: **oppose** 1; **resist** 2; **contradict** 1

Cooperation: **cooperate** 1, 2; **collaborate;
  alliance** 1; **side with**

Opponent: **adversary; foe; opponent; enemy** 1, 2

Auxiliary: **auxiliary** 2, 3; **accessory; abet** 1

Participant: **confederate** *n.*; **associate** *n.*; **party** 4

Associates: **association** 3; **alliance** 3; **fellowship** 3

Discord: **contention** 1; **conflict** 2; **opposition** 1; **discord** 1

Accord: **agreement** 2, 3; **rapport; congenial** 1; **accord**

Defiance: **insubordination; insurgence; rebellion; defiance**

War: **battle** 1, 2; **combat; make war; fight** *v.* 2

Peace: **harmony** 2; **pacifist; peace** 1; **peaceable**

Attack: **attack** 1; **assault** 1; **offensive** 1; **raid** 1

Defense: **defense** 1, 2; **guard** 1; **champion** 2; **self-defense**

Retaliation: **revenge; vindictive; vengeful; retaliate**

Resistance: **resist; withstand; hold out** 2; **repulse**

Creating conflict: **contention** 1; **contest** 2; **rival; strife**

Making peace: **pacification; conciliate; pacify** 1; **peace offering**

Mediation: **intervention** 1; **intercede; arbitrate; mediation**

Neutrality: **neutral** 1; **impartial; disengaged; disinterested**

Compromise: **work out** 1; **concession** 1; **adjust** 1; **compromise**

Resignation: **docility; resignation** 1

Fighter: **combatant; fighter** 1; **soldier; army**

Weapons: **arms** 1; **weapon** 1; **munitions; arsenal**

Battlefield: **arena; scene** 3; **theater** 3; **battlefield**

# Social

Authority: **authority** 1, 2, 3; **power** 2; **lead** *v.* 2

Lack of authority: **lawless** 1; **anarchy** 2; **disorder** 2

Strictness: **stringent** 1; **rigid** 2; **strict**

Lenience: **lenient; mildness; tolerance** 1; **lax** 4

Freedom: **liberty** 1, 3; **license** 1; **independence** 1; **freedom** 1, 2,

Servitude: **subjection; servitude; slavery** 1

Liberation: **freeing; emancipation; freedom** 1; **set free**

Submission: **submit** 2; **capitulate; yielding** 4; **compliant**

Obedience: **obedient** 1; **dutiful; obey** 1

Disobedience: **disobedient; unruly; uncontrollable**

Restraint: **restraint** 2; **constraint** 1; **coercion; suppress**

Confinement: **prison; confine** 1; **custody** 2; **jail**

Deputized authority: **commission** 3; **deputation; appointment**

Promotion: **promote** 2; **advance** *v.* 4; **upgrade**

Demotion: **demote; downgrade; humble** *v.*

Removal from office: **depose; dethrone; oust; sack** 2

Deputy: **deputy; proxy; agent** 1; **delegate**

Master: **master** 1; **boss; administrator; mistress** 1

Employee: **servant; employee; worker; assistant**

Permitting: **permission; leave** *n.* 1; **authorize; permissible**

Prohibiting: **prohibition** 1; **forbid; veto; ban**

Consenting: **consent; assent; approve** 1; **yes**

Rescinding: **repeal; rescind; revoke**

Offering: **offer; tender** *v.*; **propose** 1; **bid** 1

Refusing: **refusal; reject** 1; **noncompliance; rebuff**

Requesting: **request; petition; invite** 1; **entreat**

Objecting: **deprecate; disapprove** 2; **object** *v.*; **oppose** 1

Promise: **promise** 1; **assurance** 1; **oath** 1

Contract: **compact** *n.* 2; **contract; covenant; treaty**

Security: **security** 2; **guarantee** 2; **pledge; lien**

Keeping promise: **observe** 5; **keep** 9; **follow** 2 | Disregarding promise: **nonobservance; breach** 2; **disregard**

Acquisition: **acquire** 1; **obtain** 1; **profit** 2; **procure** | Loss: **loss** 3; **deprivation; need** 1; **forfeiture**

Possession: **possession** 1; **ownership; have** 1; **belong to**

Possessor: **owner; proprietor; possessor; holder** 2

Property: **holdings; property** 1; **possession** 2; **belongings**

Retention: **keeping** 1; **maintenance** 1; **retention** 1 | Relinquishment: **relinquish; waive; let go; riddance**

Transferring property: **consign** 1; **hand over; hand down; transferable**

Giving: **giving; donation; bestow; gift** 1 | Receiving: **receiving; inherit; receipt** 1; **come into** 1

Allotting: **apportion; distribute** 1; **allot**

Lending: **lend** 1; **loan; advance** *n.* 4 | Borrowing: **borrow** 1; **borrowing; debt**

Taking: **take** 1, 5; **seize** 2; **appropriate** 1; **deprive**

Stealing: **theft; thief; steal; plunder** | Restitution; **reparation** 2; **compensation; restitution; remunerate**

Commerce: **trade** *n.* 1; **commerce; traffic** 2

Buying: **purchase; buy** 1; **shopping; marketing** | Selling: **sale** 1, 2; **sell** 1; **retail; auction**

Merchant: **businessperson; merchant; seller; vendor**

Merchandise: **wares; goods** 1; **product** 2; **merchandise**

Market: **market; store** 1; **shop n; mart**

Barter: **barter; trade** *v.* 2; **exchange** 2

Illicit purchase: **racket** 3; **bootleg; contraband; smuggle**

Stock market: **stock market; stock** 4; **bond** 3; **investment**

Financing: **finance; economics**

Financial institution: **treasury; bank** 4; **depository**

Money: **money** 1; **currency; cash** 1; **coin**

Wealth: **wealth** 2; **riches; affluent; rich** 1 | Poverty: **poverty** 1; **indigence; penury; poor** 1

Credit: **credit** 2; **assets; wealth** 1; **creditor** | Debt: **debt** 2; **arrears; liability** 2; **debtor**

Payment: **compensation; payment; settlement** 2; **fee** | Nonpayment: **default; deficit; delinquent** 2; **nonpayment**

Expenditure: **expense** 1; **expenses; outgo; expenditure**

Receipts: **receipts; profit** 2; **net** *modif.;* **income** | Bills: **bill** 1; **tally** 1; **reckoning** 2; **statement** 3

Price: **cost** 1; **rate** 2; **quote** 2; **price**

Discount: **deduction** 3; **rebate; cut** *v.* 2; **discount**

Expensiveness: **dear** *modif.* 2; **exorbitant; costly; expensive** | Inexpensiveness: **cheap** 1; **bargain** *n.* 2; **moderate; inexpensive**

Tipping: **gratuity; tip** 2; **complimentary** 2

Giving freely: **liberality** 2; **largess** 2; **donation; gift** 2 | Giving carefully: **economy** 2; **thrifty; economical** 1; **frugal** 1

Spending freely: **prodigality** 2; **extravagance; indulgence** 3; **waste** 1 | Spending almost nothing: **parsimony; stingy; miser** 2; **penurious**

# VI.  HUMAN EMOTIONS AND BELIEFS

## Emotions In General

Feelings: **emotion; sentiment** 1; **feeling** 4; **thought** 2

Sensitiveness: **sensibility; responsive; sensitive** 4

Excitement: **excitable; exhilarate; thrill; excitement**

Weariness: **weary; exhausted; tired; beat** 1

Lack of feelings: **unemotional; apathy; indifference** 1; **unfeeling**

Insensitiveness: **insensibility; insensitive; callous**

Inexcitability: **disinterested; unperturbed; dispassionate**

## Personal Emotions

Pleasure: **enjoyment; pleasure** 1; **gratify; happiness** 2

Pleasantness: **pleasant** 2; **pleasing; cheerful; delightful**

Dislike: **dislike; aversion; objection** 1

Discontent: **discontent; dissatisfied; disappointed** 1

Cheerfulness: **cheerful; happy** 1; **good humor; cheer up**

Dejection: **solemn** 1; **solemnity; depression** 2; **dejection**

Regret: **regret** 1; **remorse; sorrow** 1

Lamenting: **lament** 1; **mourn** 1; **grieve**

Celebration: **celebrate** 1, 3; **observe** 4; **commemorate**

Amusement: **diversion** 2; **entertainment** 1, 2; **amusement; festivity**

Humor: **humor** 3; **funny** 1; **amusing** 2; **joke** 1, 2

Tedium: **boring; dull** 3, 4; **tedious; monotonous** 1

Aggravation: **aggravation** 1; **intensify; worse**

Beauty: **beauty** 1; **pretty** 1; **handsome** 1, 2; **gorgeous**

Taste: **taste** 3; **tact; elegance; decorum**

Fashionableness: **fashionable**

Ornamentation: **decoration** 1; **adornment; embellish; ornamentation**

Affectation: **affectation; ostentatious; pretentious; showy**

Pride: **pride** 1, 3; **self-esteem; dignity** 1; **self-respect**

Hope: **hope; optimism** 2; **promising; belief** 1

Fear: **dread; fright** 1; **fear** 2

Cowardice: **timidity** 1; **cowardice; fainthearted; cowardly** 1, 2

Rashness: **foolhardy; reckless; rash; rashness**

Fastidiousness: **particular** 3; **perfection** 1, 3; **fussy; fastidious**

Wonder: **marvel; wonder** 2; **phenomenon**

Expectancy: **anticipation** 1; **prospect** 3; **expectancy**

Displeasure: **upset; pain** 1, 3; **discomposure; displeasure**

Unpleasantness: **unpleasant** 2; **disagreeable** 2; **undesirable; horrible** 1

Contentment: **content; satisfied; complacent**

Sadness: **sad** 1; **heavy-hearted; melancholy** 1; **gloomy** 2

Non-regret: **remorseless** 1; **impenitent; hardened** 3

Rejoicing: **rejoice; exult; celebrate** 3

Seriousness: **serious** 2; **dry** 4

Relief: **relief** 1; **palliate; mollify** 2; **alleviate**

Ugliness: **ugliness; homely** 2; **ugly** 1; **eyesore**

Vulgarity: **indecorum; rudeness; inelegant; vulgarity**

Unfashionableness: **unfashionable**

Simplicity: **unaffected** 1; **natural** 3; **unpretentious; simplicity** 2

Hopelessness: **futility; pessimism; cynicism; hopeless** 1

Courage: **bravery; valor; courage** 1

Caution: **mindful; prudent** 1; **wary; caution** n. 1

Miracle: **prodigy** 1; **miracle**; **revelation** 2, 3

Good reputation: **repute**; **reputation** 1, 2; **standing**; **esteem**

Bad reputation: **disrepute**; **disgrace** 1; **dishonor** 1; **infamy**

Honor: **award**; **prize**; **honor** 1; **trophy**

Nobility: **noble** 3; **aristocracy**; **royalty**; **nobility** 2

Common man: **populace**; **proletariat**; **masses**; **rank and file** 2

Title: **title** 3; **handle** 2; **degree** 3

Humility: **humility**; **mortification**; **obsequious**; **condescension**

Modesty: **modesty** 1, 2; **unassuming**; **humble** 1

Vanity: **vanity** 1; **pride** 1; **vain** 1; **conceit**

Boasting: **bluster**; **boast** 1; **brag**; **swagger** 2

Arrogance: **insolence**; **arrogance**; **audacity** 2; **haughty**

Sociableness: **sociability**; **social** 3; **affable**; **amiable**

Unsociableness: **unsociable**; **aloof**; **standoffish**; **reserved** 3

Seclusion: **exclusion**; **loner**; **seclusion**; **retreat**

Hospitality: **welcome**; **hospitality**; **guest** 1; **visitor**

Lack of hospitality: **inhospitable**; **ostracize**; **blacklist**; **unwelcome**

Friendliness: **friendship**; **friend** 1, 2; **kind**; **acquaintance** 1, 2

Unfriendliness: **enmity**; **antagonism**; **malice**; **estrangement**

Love: **amour**; **affection** 1; **favorite**; **love** 2, 3

Hate: **hatred**; **detest**; **abhor**; **hate**

Courtesy: **courteous**; **gracious** 1; **polite** 1; **cultured**

Discourtesy: **discourteous**; **rudeness**; **uncivil**; **rude** 2

Resentment: **rancor**; **vexed**; **resentment**; **resent**;

Irritation: **irascible**; **irritable**; **irritation** 2; **stress** *n*. 3

Ill humor: **sullen**; **ill-humored**; **cross**; **angry**

Romance: **romance** 1, 2; **endearment**; **courtship**; **love** 1

Marriage: **wedlock**; **union** 3; **wedding**; **marriage** 2

Unmarried state: **celibate**; **unmarried**; **bachelor**; **spinster**

Divorce: **separation** 3; **estrangement**; **alienation**; **divorce**

Widowhood: **widow**; **widower**; **dowager**

Kindness: **benevolence**; **kindness** 1; **kindhearted**; **good-natured**

Unkindness: **malevolence**; **unkind**; **nasty** 4; **mean** 3

Curse: **curse** 1; **malediction**; **damnation**; **condemnation**

Threat: **menace** 1; **intimidate**; **threat**

Philanthropy: **philanthropic**; **patronage** 1; **philanthropy**; **generosity** 1

Misanthropy: **misanthropic**; **misanthropy**; **antisocial** 1

Patriotism: **patriot**; **public-spirited**; **humanitarian**

Benefactor: **patron** 1; **benefactor**

Evildoer: **malefactor**; **evildoer**; **criminal**

Pity: **pity** 1; **sympathy** 1, 2; **compassion**

Pitilessness: **pitiless**; **unfeeling** 2; **heartless**

Condolence: **comfort** 2; **solace**; **condole**; **condolence**

Congratulating: **congratulate**; **salute** *v*. 2; **felicitation**

Gratitude: **thankful**; **grateful** 1; **gratitude**; **appreciation** 1

Ingratitude: **ungrateful**; **thankless** 1; **ingratitude**; **ingrate**

Forgiving: **forgiving**; **forgiveness**; **pardon** 2

Unforgiving: **unforgiving**; **uncharitable**; **unmerciful**

Jealousy: **jealous**; **jealousy**; **envy**; **envious** 1

# Morality

Ethics: **ethics; morals; ideals; principles**

Right: **right** 2; **propriety** 2; **decorum; decency**

Entitlement: **due** 2; **deserved; entitle** 2

Moral obligation: **duty** 1; **responsibility** 2; **behoove**

Imposition: **impose; imposition** 1; **pressure** 2

Respect: **esteem; respect; regard** 2

Contempt: **scorn; disdain; contempt** 1

Ridicule: **derision; mockery** 1; **ridicule; teasing**

Approval: **approbation; endorse** 2; **O.K.; approval** 2

Flattery: **flatter** 1, 2; **adulation; worship** 1; **praise**

Blame: **blame** 1; **accusation** 1; **indict**

Honesty: **honesty** 1; **probity; honorable; integrity**

Justice: **justice** 1; **fairness; equity** 2; **impartial**

Selfishness: **selfish** 1; **self-seeking; egoistic**

Virtue: **virtue** 1, 2; **goodness; righteous** 1; **moral** 1

Innocence: **innocence** 1; **guiltless; harmless** 1; **faultless**

Good people: **hero** 1; **heroine** 1; **model** 1; **paragon**

Temperance: **temperance; moderation; self-control; sobriety** 1

Gluttony: **glutton; voracious; epicure; overeat**

Self-denying: **ascetic; austere; rigorous** 1

Legality: **legal; legality; lawful; legalize**

Jurisdiction: **jurisdiction; law** 1; **jurisprudence**

Court of law: **tribunal; court** 2; **bar** 3; **forum**

Judge: **magistrate; judge** 1; **justice** 4

Lawyer: **lawyer; attorney; counsel** 2; **solicitor**

Lawsuit: **lawsuit; prosecute** 2; **litigation; trial** 2

Acquittal: **acquit** 1; **exculpate; exonerate**

Condemnation: **condemn** 1; **damn** 1; **denounce; sentence** 1

Punishment: **discipline** 2; **chastise; punishment**

Penalty: **penalty; fine** 3; **damages; retribution**

Atonement: **atonement; amends; penance** 1

Wrong: **wrong** 3; **impropriety; indecency** 2

Undeservedness: **undue; improper** 1; **supposed**

Dereliction of duty: **dereliction** 2; **forsake** 1

Exemption: **exempt; exemption; immunity** 1

Disrespect: **rudeness; disrespect; discourtesy**

Disapproval: **disapproval** 2; **censure; berate; criticize** 2

Detraction: **detraction; discredit; reproach; defame**

Dishonesty: **dishonest; unscrupulous; knave; untruthful** 2

Injustice: **iniquity; unjust; wrong** n. 1; **injustice** 1

Unselfishness: **unselfish; altruistic; magnanimous**

Vice: **vice** 1; **immorality; criminality** 2

Guilt: **guilt; culpability; guilty** 1

Bad people: **disreputable; wretch** 2; **villain**

Intemperance: **intemperance; drunkenness; indulgence** 3

Fasting: **fast** n.; **starve** 2

Illegality: **illegal; illicit; unlawful; illegitimate** 1

# Religion

Deity: **deity; god** 1, 2, 3; **divinity**

Angel: **angel** 1; **cherub**

Mythical being: **myth; goddess; spirit** 3

Ghost: **specter; ghost** 1; **phantom**

Heaven: **heaven** 2; **paradise** 1; **eternity** 2; **hereafter**

Theology: **theology; religion** 1; **doctrine** 2; **faith** 2

Orthodox beliefs: **orthodox; conservative; orthodoxy**

Scripture: **bible** 2; **scripture** 3; **revelation** 3; **sacred** 1

Devil: **devil** 1; **satan; evil** 2

Evil spirit: **demon** 1; **imp; fiend** 1

Hell: **hell** 1; **perdition; doom** 1; **infernal** 1

Unorthodox beliefs: **heterodox; skeptic; atheist; agnostic**

Religious founders: **prophet**; **evangelist**;
  **missionary**; **apostle**

Piety: **devout**; **reverent**; **believer**; **piety**          Impiety: **blasphemy**; **irreverent**; **impiety**;
                                                                   **unbeliever**

Worship: **worship** 2; **church** 2; **homage**; **prayer** 2     Idol worship: **idolatry** 1; **worship** 1; **adoration** 1;
                                                                   **venerate**

Occultism: **occult**; **mysticism**; **occultism**;
  **spiritualism** 1

Witchcraft: **sorcery**; **witchcraft**; **magic** 1;
  **exorcism** 1; **wizard** 1

Spell: **charm** 3; **spell** 1; **bewitch** 2; **incantation** 2

Religion: **religion** 3; **cult** 1, **sect**; **church** 3

Church: **church** 1; **temple**; **chapel**; **shrine**

Clergy: **clergy**; **ministry** 2; **priesthood**; **minister** 1   Lay people: **laity**; **laymen**; **congregation**; **parish**

Rite: **rite**; **sacrament** 1; **ritual**; **ceremony** 2

Church attire: **clerical** 2; **vestments**; **canonical**

# A

**a,** *modif. & prep.* **1.** [The indefinite article; *before vowels, written "an"*] — *Syn.* some, one, any, each, some kind of, some particular, any of, any one of, a certain. — *Ant.* THE, this, that.
**2.** [An indication of frequency] — *Syn.* per, in a, on a, each, every, to the, by the, at the rate of.

**abandon,** *n.* — *Syn.* unrestraint, spontaneity, freedom, impetuosity, exuberance, uninhibitedness, spirit, verve, enthusiasm, dash, vigor, animation, élan, recklessness.

**abandon,** *v.* **1.** [To give up] — *Syn.* relinquish, leave off, withdraw from, discontinue, quit, give over, break off, throw over, throw off, let go, cease, desist, renounce, forgo, forswear, dispense with, lay down, cast aside, cast off, cast away, discard, give away, hand over, part with, surrender, forfeit, yield, deliver, cede, lay aside, concede, waive, abdicate, resign, disclaim, back down from, back out of, go back on, break with, break, drop, lose hope of, despair of, have done with, be done with, secede from, bow out, pull out, apostatize, quitclaim, break the pattern, break the habit, chuck*, throw in the towel, throw in the sponge*, cop out*, hang up the fiddle*.
**2.** [To leave a person, place, or thing in trouble] — *Syn.* desert, forsake, leave, quit, back out on, run away, break with, break up with, defect, reject, disown, cast off, ostracize, maroon, strand, have done with, be done with, depart from, flee, vacate, evacuate, throw over, throw overboard, jettison, leave behind, slip away from, turn one's back on, stand up*, leave in the lurch*, leave high and dry*, walk out on*, run out on*, skip out on*, fink out*, take a powder*, duck out*, bolt*, bail out*, turn tail*, leave flat*, leave in the cold*, drop*, ditch*, bid a long farewell*. — *Ant.* CHERISH, uphold, protect.

---

SYN. — **abandon** implies leaving a person or thing, either as a final, necessary measure /to *abandon* a drought area/ or as a complete rejection of one's responsibilities, claims, etc. /she *abandoned* her child/; **desert** emphasizes leaving in willful violation, as of one's obligation or oath /the soldier *deserted* his post/; **forsake** stresses renouncing a person or thing formerly dear to one /to *forsake* one's friends or ideals/; **quit**, meaning to leave or give up /I *quit* my job/, is also commonly used now simply to mean stop

---

**abandoned,** *modif.* **1.** [Left uninhabited or unsupported] — *Syn.* deserted, desolate, forsaken, desperate, surrendered, empty, given up, unused, vacated, left, vacant, neglected, relinquished, lonely, solitary, hopeless, cast aside, cast off, cast away, forgotten, repudiated, derelict, shunned, adrift, at the mercy of the elements, forlorn, at the mercy of one's enemies, mournful, avoided, rejected, helpless, unfortunate, alone, lorn, discarded, scorned, lost, doomed, friendless, wretched, in the hands of fate, eliminated, in the wastebasket*, thrown overboard*, out on a limb*, waiting at the church*, left hanging*, left in the lurch*, left in

the cold*, left holding the bag*. — *Ant.* INHABITED, used, cared for.
**2.** [Having lost one's self-respect] — *Syn.* immoral, debased, dissolute, unrestrained; see **lewd** 2, **wicked** 1.

**abase,** *v.* — *Syn.* humiliate, humble, debase; see **humble**.
See Synonym Study at HUMBLE.

**abasement,** *n.* — *Syn.* dishonor, deterioration, shame; see **disgrace** 1.

**abash,** *v.* embarrass, disconcert, rattle*; see **embarrass** 1.
See Synonym Study at EMBARRASS.

**abate,** *v.* **1.** [To make less] — *Syn.* reduce, lower, lighten; see **decrease** 2.
**2.** [To grow less] — *Syn.* lessen, decline, diminish; see **decrease** 1, **wane**.
See Synonym Study at WANE.

**abatement,** *n.* — *Syn.* lessening, decrease, decline; see **discount, reduction** 1.

**abbey,** *n.* — *Syn.* monastery, convent, cloister; see **cloister** 1.
See Synonym Study at CLOISTER.

**abbot,** *n.* — *Syn.* prior, rector, archabbot, abbot-general; see **friar, monk, minister** 1.

**abbreviate,** *v.* — *Syn.* shorten, cut, condense, abridge; see **decrease** 2, **shorten**.
See Synonym Study at SHORTEN.

**abbreviation,** *n.* **1.** [An abbreviated form] — *Syn.* acronym, initialism, contraction, abridgment, shortening, sketch, précis, brief, abstract, curtailment, reduction, abstraction, condensation, outline, summary, elision, short form, clipped form, clipping, abbreviated version; see also **abridgment** 2, **summary**. — *Ant.* expansion, enlargement, full form.
**2.** [The act of abbreviating] — *Syn.* reducing, shortening, truncating, reduction, contraction, condensing, abridgment, cutting, clipping, cutting out, cutting down, restriction, constriction, removing, taking out, truncation, editing, censoring, reshaping, pruning, lopping off, paring down, trimming, retrenchment, compression, foreshortening, telescoping, apocope, syncope, elision. — *Ant.* ADDITION, augmenting, expanding.

**abdicate,** *v.* — *Syn.* relinquish, give up, renounce, withdraw; see **abandon** 1, **resign** 2.

**abdomen,** *n.* — *Syn.* stomach, midsection, belly, paunch, middle, epigastrium, belly cavity, venter, visceral region, ventral region, bowels, intestines, viscera, epigastric region, hypogastric region, umbilical region, entrails, insides*, gut*, guts*, breadbasket*, bay window*, tummy*, pot*, pot belly*, spare tire*, corporation*.

**abdominal,** *modif.* — *Syn.* ventral, visceral, intestinal, alvine, uterine, celiac, gastric, stomachic, duodenal, in the solar plexus, belly plexus*, inside*.

**abduct,** *v.* — *Syn.* kidnap, seize, carry off; see **kidnap**.

**aberrant,** *modif.* — *Syn.* deviant, anomalous, errant, strange; see **unusual** 2, **wrong** 2.

1

**aberration,** *n.* **1.** [Deviation] — *Syn.* irregularity, lapse, wandering; see **difference** 2.
**2.** [Abnormality] — *Syn.* strangeness, peculiarity, derangement; see **characteristic, irregularity** 2, **quirk**.
**abet,** *v.* **1.** [To help] — *Syn.* assist, befriend, support, sanction; see **approve** 1, **help** 1.
**2.** [To incite] — *Syn.* forward, encourage, inspire; see **incite, promote** 1.
**abhor,** *v.* — *Syn.* detest, abominate, loathe; see **hate** 1.
*See Synonym Study at* HATE.
**abhorrence,** *n.* — *Syn.* hatred, loathing, aversion, repugnance; see **aversion, hatred** 1.
*See Synonym Study at* AVERSION.
**abhorrent,** *modif.* — *Syn.* disgusting, shocking, revolting; see **offensive** 2.
*See Synonym Study at* OFFENSIVE.
**abide,** *v.* **1.** [To submit to] — *Syn.* put up with, bear, bear with, withstand; see **endure** 2.
**2.** [To reside or stay] — *Syn.* live, remain, tarry, dwell; see **dwell, lodge** 2, **remain** 1.
**3.** [To remain] — *Syn.* continue, keep on, last; see **continue** 1, **endure** 1.
**4.** [To wait for] — *Syn.* expect, anticipate, be in readiness; see **wait** 1.
*See Synonym Study at* CONTINUE, STAY.
**abide by,** *v.* **1.** [To adhere to] — *Syn.* follow, observe, comply with; see **follow** 2.
**2.** [To accept] — *Syn.* submit to, consent to, acknowledge, concede; see **agree to**.
**abiding,** *modif.* — *Syn.* enduring, lasting, tenacious; see **permanent** 2.
**ability,** *n.* **1.** [Capacity to act] — *Syn.* aptitude, intelligence, innate qualities, capacity, sense, powers, potency, worth, talent, gift, genius, flair, mind for, ingenuity, bent, strength, understanding, faculty, comprehension, knack, makings, brains, head, what it takes*, the stuff*, the right stuff*, hang of*. — *Ant.* INABILITY, ineptitude, awkwardness.
**2.** [Power that results from capacity] — *Syn.* capability, eligibility, competence, proficiency, adeptness, qualification(s), knowledge, strength, sufficiency, self-sufficiency, efficacy, expertise, tact, finish, technique, craft, skill, artistry, cunning, expertness, skillfulness, aptness, dexterity, facility, finesse, mastery, quickness, cleverness, deftness, handiness, experience, readiness, adroitness, artifice, energy, background, know-how*, savvy*, touch*, the goods*. — *Ant.* IGNORANCE, incompetence, inexperience.
**abject,** *modif.* — *Syn.* miserable, wretched, degraded, servile; see **humble** 2, **mean** 1, **obsequious**.
*See Synonym Study at* MEAN.
**ablaze,** *modif.* **1.** [Burning] — *Syn.* blazing, lighted, aflame; see **burning** 1.
**2.** [Excited] — *Syn.* intense, vehement, heated; see **excited**.
**able,** *modif.* **1.** [Showing superior innate capacity] — *Syn.* talented, gifted, intelligent, ingenious, clever, smart, bright, canny, apt, ready, well-fitted, well-suited, worthy, capable, endowed, dexterous, handy, agile, nimble, nimble-fingered, strong, powerful, versatile, well-rounded, capacitated, cut out for*, having what it takes*, having the right stuff*. — *Ant.* stupid, bungling, unadaptable.
**2.** [Showing superior proven skill] — *Syn.* competent, capable, effective, efficient, qualified, well-qualified, fit, accomplished, proficient, skillful, skilled, adept, deft, adroit, clever, artful, masterly, masterful, expert, practiced, experienced, workmanlike, versatile, well-rounded, well-versed, conversant, knowledgeable,

*au fait* (French), responsible, enterprising, resourceful, inventive, dexterous, strong, superior, first-rate, top-notch*, top-flight*, crack*, crackerjack*, slick*, smooth*, all-around*, an old dog at*, up on*, hotshot*, up to snuff*, up to the mark*, on the ball*. — *Ant.* inexperienced, inefficient, unskillful.
**3.** [Having the necessary power, skill, or resources] — *Syn.* capable of, qualified, fit for, fitted, well-fitted, equipped, well-equipped, equal to, suited to, competent to, having the ability, having the capability, having the capacity, cut out for*, up to*, up on*, conversant with, proficient, at home in, adequate, suitable, prepared, ready, endowed, authorized, empowered.

---

**SYN. — able** means having the power or capacity to do something [*able* to make payments] but when used before a noun implies superior power or skill [an *able* administrator]; **capable** usually implies the satisfactory meeting of ordinary requirements [a *capable* machinist]; **competent** and **qualified** both imply the possession of the requisite qualifications or skills for the specified work, situation, etc., but **qualified** stresses compliance with specified requirements [a *competent* critic of modern art, a *qualified* voter]

---

**able-bodied,** *modif.* — *Syn.* fit, powerful, sturdy, healthy; see **healthy** 1, **strong** 1.
**abnormal,** *modif.* — *Syn.* strange, irregular, unnatural; see **irregular** 2, **unusual** 2.
*See Synonym Study at* IRREGULAR.
**abnormality,** *n.* **1.** [Irregularity] — *Syn.* peculiarity, singularity, aberration; see **irregularity** 2, **strangeness**.
**2.** [Something abnormal] — *Syn.* malformation, deformity, anomaly, rarity; see **contortion** 1, **freak** 2, **irregularity** 2.
**aboard,** *modif.* — *Syn.* on board, on ship, shipped, loaded, on board ship, freight on board, F.O.B., being shipped, en route, consigned, in the hold, in transit, being transported, embarked, afloat, at sea, on deck, topside, *en voyage* (French), traveling, at point of entry. — *Ant.* ASHORE, disembarked, on land.
**abode,** *n.* — *Syn.* house, dwelling, residence; see **home** 1.
**abolish,** *v.* — *Syn.* suppress, eradicate, terminate, exterminate, obliterate, do away with, eliminate, remove, revoke, annul, abrogate, put an end to, end, finish, extirpate, nullify, set aside, repeal, rescind, reverse, annihilate, abate, supplant, prohibit, quash, squelch, extinguish, cancel, erase, wipe out, disannul, root out, pull up, uproot, disestablish, demolish, invalidate, overturn, overthrow, declare null and void, make null and void, stamp out, crush, undo, throw out, supersede, deprive of force, vitiate, inhibit, make void, dispense with, subvert, vacate, repudiate, make an end of, cut out, batter down, raze; see also **destroy** 1.

---

**SYN. — abolish** denotes a complete doing away with something, as a practice, institution, or condition [to *abolish* slavery, to *abolish* bias]; **annul** and **abrogate** stress a canceling by authority or formal action [the marriage was *annulled*; the law *abrogated* certain privileges]; **rescind, revoke,** and **repeal** all describe the setting aside of laws, orders, etc. [to *rescind* an order, *revoke* a charter, *repeal* a law]

---

**abolition,** *n.* **1.** [The act of abolishing] — *Syn.* annulment, eradication, overthrow; see **cancellation, destruction** 1, **repeal**.

**2.** [The abolition of slavery; *sometimes capitalized*] — *Syn.* emancipation, manumission, enfranchisement; see **freeing**.

**abominable,** *modif.* — *Syn.* offensive, odious, loathsome, nauseating; see **offensive** 2.

*See Synonym Study at* OFFENSIVE.

**abominate,** *v.* — *Syn.* abhor, despise, loathe; see **hate** 1.

**abomination,** *n.* **1.** [Detestation] — *Syn.* aversion, loathing, repugnance; see **hatred** 1.

**2.** [Something hateful or disgusting] — *Syn.* atrocity, horror, offense; see **bugbear, crime** 1, **evil** 1.

**aboriginal,** *modif.* — *Syn.* indigenous, autochthonous, original, earliest; see **native** 2.

*See Synonym Study at* NATIVE.

**abort,** *v.* **1.** [To fail] — *Syn.* miscarry, fall short, miss; see **fail** 1.

**2.** [To cancel] — *Syn.* stop, cut short, nullify; see **cancel** 2.

**abortion,** *n.* **1.** [Expulsion of a fetus from the womb] — *Syn.* unnatural birth, arrested development, termination of pregnancy, miscarriage, premature birth, premature labor, premature delivery, casting, aborting, untimely birth, forced birth.

**2.** [Something malformed or incomplete] — *Syn.* abnormality, malformation, monstrosity; see **freak** 2.

**3.** [A failure] — *Syn.* fiasco, total loss, disaster; see **failure** 1.

**abortive,** *modif.* — *Syn.* vain, failing, fruitless; see **futile** 1.

*See Synonym Study at* FUTILE.

**abound,** *v.* — *Syn.* overflow, swarm, be plentiful; see **teem**.

**abounding,** *modif.* — *Syn.* teeming, flowing, overflowing; see **plentiful** 1.

**about,** *modif. & prep.* **1.** [Approximately] — *Syn.* roughly, nearly, around; see **approximately**.

**2.** [Concerning] — *Syn.* regarding, respecting, concerning, touching, of, on, in relation to, relative to, relating to, as regards, with regard to, with respect to, in the matter of, in reference to, with reference to, referring to, as concerns, so far as (something) is concerned, in connection with, apropos of, connected with, concerned with, dealing with, thereunto, *in re* (Latin), thereby, hereof, wherein, with a view toward, as to, as for, anent.

**3.** [Around] — *Syn.* surrounding, round about, on all sides; see **around** 1.

**4.** [Active] — *Syn.* astir, in motion, alert; see **active** 1, 2.

**about-face,** *n.* **1.** reversal, reverse, turnabout, turnaround, rightabout-face, switch, shift, U-turn, rightabout, *volte-face* (French), change of heart, 180-degree turn, flip-flop*.

**about to,** *modif. & prep.* — *Syn.* not quite, on the verge of, at the point of, ready, set, intending, willing to, fixing to*; see also **almost**.

**above,** *modif. & prep.* **1.** [High in position] — *Syn.* over, high, higher, superior, beyond, up, high up, on high, raised, above one's head, in a higher place, aloft, into the firmament, overhead, in the celestial heights, toward the sky, in the heavens. — *Ant.* BELOW, beneath, low.

**2.** [Referring to something earlier] — *Syn.* before, foregoing, earlier; see **preceding**.

**3.** [Higher] — *Syn.* larger than, more advanced than, greater than; see **higher, superior**.

**4.** [Directly over] — *Syn.* just over, overhead, up from; see **over** 1.

**above,** *n.* — *Syn.* firmament, sky, heights; see **heaven** 1.

**aboveboard,** *modif.* **1.** [Characterized by being candid] — *Syn.* honest, open, straightforward; see **frank**.

**2.** [In a candid manner] — *Syn.* candidly, honestly, frankly; see **openly** 1.

**abrasive,** *modif.* **1.** [Causing abrasion] — *Syn.* grinding, sharpening, cutting, abrading, abradant, rasping, rough, harsh, coarse, scratchy, sandpapery; see also **rough** 1.

**2.** [Aggressively annoying] — *Syn.* irritating, grating, caustic; see **disturbing, harsh** 1.

**abrasive,** *n.* — *Syn.* sharpener, cutter, grinder, grindstone, scarifier, polisher, grater, rasp, file, millstone, sander, sandpaper, sharpening stone, whetstone, brush. Types of abrasives include: file, sandstone, pumice, carborundum (trademark for silicon carbide), corundum, diamond, emery, emery cloth, emery paper, oil stone, chalk, salt, sanddust, sandpaper, shagreen, steel wool, tripoli.

**abreast,** *modif.* **1.** [Side by side] — *Syn.* level, equal, side by side, abeam of, against, off, stem to stem, bow to bow, over against, on a line with, by the side of, alongside, beside, next to, in one line, in alignment, shoulder to shoulder, in line; see also **beside, next** 2.

**2.** [Acquainted with recent developments] — *Syn.* informed, knowledgeable, up-to-date, *au courant* (French); see **knowledgeable**.

**abridge,** *v.* — *Syn.* digest, condense, compress, shorten; see **decrease** 2, **shorten**.

*See Synonym Study at* SHORTEN.

**abridgment,** *n.* **1.** [The act of reducing or shortening] — *Syn.* shortening, reduction, cutting; see **abbreviation** 2.

**2.** [A shortened form of a work] — *Syn.* digest, condensation, compendium, summary, epitome, précis, abstract, brief, synopsis, outline, condensed version, condensed form, concise edition, cut version, edited version, short form, encapsulation, abbreviation, reduction, capsule form, thumbnail sketch; see also **abbreviation** 1, **summary**.

---

*SYN.* — **abridgment** describes a work condensed from a larger work by omitting the less important parts, but keeping the main contents more or less unaltered; an **abstract** is a short statement of the essential contents of a book, article, speech, court record, etc. often used as an index to the original material; **brief** is applied to a concise statement of the main points of a law case; a **summary** is a brief statement of the main points of the matter under consideration and especially connotes a recapitulating statement; a **synopsis** is a condensed, orderly treatment, as of the plot of a novel, that permits a quick general view of the whole; **digest** is applied either to a concise, systematic treatment, generally more comprehensive in scope than a synopsis, and, in the case of technical material, often arranged under titles for quick reference or to a collection of articles, stories, etc. condensed from other publications; an **epitome** is a statement of the essence of a subject in the shortest possible form

---

**abroad,** *modif.* — *Syn.* away, overseas, out of the country, at large, adrift, wandering, elsewhere, traveling, touring, outside, at some remove, afar off, distant, in a foreign land, in foreign parts, far away, gone, removed, in Europe, on the Continent, beyond seas, on one's travels. — *Ant.* at home, HERE, domestic.

**abrogate,** *v.* — *Syn.* revoke, repeal, annul; see **abolish, cancel** 2.

*See Synonym Study at* ABOLISH.

**abrupt,** *modif.* **1.** [Said of things, usually landscape] — *Syn.* steep, precipitate, sheer, precipitous, sudden, sharp, angular, craggy, unexpected, uneven, rough, rugged, irregular, jagged, perpendicular, straight up, straight down, without a break, vertical, headlong, zigzag, broken, uphill, downhill, falling, bluffy.— *Ant.* LEVEL, flat, horizontal.

**2.** [*Said of people or acts of people*] — *Syn.* rough, blunt, short, terse, brusque, unceremonious, sudden, hasty, hurried, precipitate, impetuous, uncivil, gruff, impolite, curt, bluff, ungracious, rude, crude, uncomplaisant, downright, outspoken, direct, unexpected, to the point, matter-of-fact, discourteous, sharp, snippy*; see also **blunt** 2.— *Ant.* POLITE, ceremonious, gracious.

*SYN.* — **abrupt** implies a sharp degree of inclination in a surface breaking off suddenly from the level /an *abrupt* bank at the river's edge/; **steep** suggests such sharpness of rise or slope as to make ascent or descent very difficult /a *steep* hill/; **precipitous** suggests the sudden and headlong drop of a precipice /a *precipitous* height/; **sheer** applies to that which is perpendicular, or almost so, and unbroken throughout its length /cliffs falling *sheer* to the sea, a *sheer* drop from the sixth floor/ See also Synonym Study at SUDDEN.

**abscess,** *n.*— *Syn.* ulcer, boil, canker; see **sore**.

**abscond,** *v.*— *Syn.* flee, steal off, slip away; see **escape**.

**absence,** *n.* **1.** [The state of being elsewhere] — *Syn.* truancy, nonattendance, nonappearance, nonresidence, nonexistence, loss, vacancy, inattentiveness, absenteeism, cut*, hooky*.— *Ant.* presence, APPEARANCE, attendance.

**2.** [The state of lacking something] — *Syn.* deficiency, need, lack, inadequacy; see **lack** 1.

**absent,** *modif.* **1.** [Not present] — *Syn.* away, missing, elsewhere, gone, gone out, vanished, moved, removed, flown, not at home, not present, out, wanting, lacking, nonexistent, nonattendant, abroad, lost, overseas, out of sight, nowhere to be found, on leave, astray, on vacation, *in absentia* (Latin), on tour, engaged elsewhere, taken, omitted, truant, on French leave*, AWOL*, playing hooky*, split*.— *Ant.* HERE, present, at home.

**2.** [Inattentive] — *Syn.* dreamy, faraway, blank, vacant; see **absent-minded**.

**absentee,** *modif.*— *Syn.* remote, absent, at a distance; see **away** 1.

**absenteeism,** *n.*— *Syn.* truancy, defection, sneaking out; see **desertion**.

**absent-minded,** *modif.*— *Syn.* abstracted, preoccupied, lost in thought, forgetful, distracted, dreamy, inattentive, lost, unmindful, absent, unheeding, heedless, oblivious, distrait, daydreaming, napping, unconscious, unaware, inadvertent, withdrawn, removed, faraway, musing, bemused, woolgathering, stargazing, remote, scatterbrained, vacant, blank, nobody home*, mooning*, not all there*, moony*, in a brown study*, in the clouds*, with one's head in the clouds*, out of it*, spacey*, spaced out*.— *Ant.* attentive, OBSERVANT, alert.

*SYN.* — **absent-minded** suggests an aimless wandering of the mind away from the immediate situation, often implying a habitual tendency of this kind /the *absent-minded* professor/; **abstracted** suggests a withdrawal of the mind from the immediate present and a serious concern with some other subject; **preoccupied** implies that the attention cannot be readily turned to something new because of its concern with a present matter; **distrait** suggests inability to concentrate, often emphasizing such a condition as a mood; **distraught** connotes agitation along with an inability to concentrate, specifically because of worry, grief, etc.; **inattentive** implies a failure to pay attention, emphasizing such behavior as a lack of discipline

**absolute,** *modif.* **1.** [Without limitation] — *Syn.* total, complete, entire, utter, perfect, infinite, unalloyed, fixed, settled, supreme, full, self-sufficing, unconditioned, unrestricted, unlimited, unconditional, unconstrained, unrestrained, unequivocal, independent, self-existent, unmixed, unqualified, categorical, without reserve, wholehearted, sheer, unstinted, unbounded, self-determined, pure, unmitigated, unabridged, thorough, clean, outright, downright, thoroughgoing, ideal, inalienable, free, simple, all-out, hard and fast, blanket, out-and-out; see also **comprehensive**.— *Ant.* RESTRICTED, limited, qualified.

**2.** [Perfect] — *Syn.* pure, faultless, unblemished, untarnished; see **perfect** 2.

**3.** [Without limit in authority] — *Syn.* authoritarian, domineering, supreme, arbitrary, official, authoritative, suppressive, highhanded, autocratic, tyrannous, tyrannical, fascist, fascistic, absolutist, absolutistic, autarchic, overbearing, czarist, nazi, totalitarian, communistic, inquisitorial, oppressive, undemocratic, antidemocratic, imperious, imperative, dogmatic, commanding, controlling, compelling, despotic, lordly, intimidating, fanatic, dictatorial, peremptory, arrogant, with an iron hand; see also **autocratic** 1.— *Ant.* DEMOCRATIC, constitutional, lenient.

**4.** [Pure] — *Syn.* unadulterated, unmixed, unalloyed; see **pure** 1.

**5.** [Certain] — *Syn.* positive, unquestionable, undeniable; see **certain** 3.

**absolutely,** *modif.* **1.** [Completely] — *Syn.* utterly, unconditionally, thoroughly; see **completely**.

**2.** [Positively] — *Syn.* unquestionably, certainly, definitely; see **surely**.

**absolve,** *v.*— *Syn.* acquit, exonerate, vindicate, clear, forgive, pardon, excuse, exculpate, remit, grant absolution, shrive, release, exempt, set free, let off; see also **excuse**.

*SYN.* — **absolve** implies a setting free from responsibilities or obligation /*absolved* from her promise/ or from the penalties for their violation; **acquit** means to clear of a specific charge by a judicial decision, usually for lack of evidence; to **exonerate** is to relieve of all blame for a wrongdoing; to **pardon** is to release from punishment for an offense /the prisoner was *pardoned* by the governor/; **forgive** implies giving up all claim that an offense be punished as well as any resentment or vengeful feelings; to **vindicate** is to clear (a person or thing under attack) through evidence of the unfairness of the charge, criticism, etc.

**absorb,** *v.* **1.** [To take in by absorption] — *Syn.* digest, suck up, suck in, take in, take up, drink in, drink up, receive, ingest, intercept, appropriate, embody, use up, assimilate, osmose, blot, imbibe, swallow, consume, ingurgitate, incorporate, sop up, soak up, sponge up, get by osmosis.— *Ant.* EJECT, expel, discharge.

**2.** [To occupy completely] — *Syn.* engage, engross, employ; see **occupy** 3.

**3.** [To take in mentally] — *Syn.* grasp, learn, sense, assimilate; see **learn** 1, **understand** 1.

**absorbed,** *modif.* **1.** [Soaked up] — *Syn.* assimilated, taken in, taken into, taken up, soaked up, swallowed up, consumed, lost, drunk, imbibed, dissolved, fused, united, vaporized, incorporated into, amalgamated, interfused, impregnated into, digested. — *Ant.* RE-MOVED, unassimilated, unconsumed.

**2.** [Occupied mentally] — *Syn.* engrossed, intent, pre-occupied, immersed; see **rapt** 2.

**absorbent,** *modif.* — *Syn.* porous, absorptive, spongy, permeable, dry, soft, pervious, pregnable, assimilative, imbibing, penetrable, receptive, retentive, spongiose, thirsty. — *Ant.* impermeable, impervious, solid.

**absorbing,** *modif.* — *Syn.* engaging, engrossing, enthralling; see **interesting.**

**absorption,** *n.* **1.** [The process of absorbing or being absorbed] — *Syn.* assimilation, digestion, osmosis, saturation, conversion, impregnation, penetration, fusion, intake, union, engorgement, consumption, ingestion, blending, swallowing up, taking in, imbibing, reception, retention, incorporation, appropriation, merging, ingurgitation, engulfment, bibulation, drinking in, suction, sopping up, soaking up, drying up, blotting up, sponging up, inhalation. — *Ant.* REMOVAL, ejection, discharge.

**2.** [Engrossment] — *Syn.* preoccupation, engrossment, immersion; see **reflection** 1.

**abstain,** *v.* — *Syn.* refrain, forbear, renounce, desist, forgo, withhold, avoid, stop, deny oneself, hold aloof from, keep aloof from, eschew, refuse, decline, spare, hold back, shun, evade, cease, dispense with, do without, go without, fast, starve oneself, teetotal, not touch, have nothing to do with, let alone, let well enough alone, do nothing, keep from, keep one's hands off, stay one's hand, withhold oneself from, restrain oneself, exercise self-restraint, turn aside from, abjure, swear off\*, lay off\*, pass up\*, turn over a new leaf\*, have no hand in\*, take the pledge\*, get on the water wagon\*, (just) say no\*. — *Ant.* indulge, JOIN, gorge.

---

**SYN.** — **abstain** implies voluntary self-denial or the deliberate giving up of something /to *abstain* from alcohol/; **refrain** usually suggests the curbing of a passing impulse in keeping oneself from saying or doing something /although provoked, she *refrained* from answering/; **forbear** suggests self-restraint manifesting a patient endurance under provocation /to *forbear* venting one's wrath/

---

**abstainer,** *n.* — *Syn.* teetotaler, prohibitionist, abstinent, teetotalist, nondrinker, temperance advocate, puritan, ascetic, water-drinker, Calvinist, member of the WCTU, one who is on the wagon\*, bluenose\*, dry\*.

**abstemious,** *modif.* — *Syn.* abstinent, temperate, sober; see **moderate** 5.

**abstemiousness,** *n.* — *Syn.* sobriety, self-denial, abstinence; see **abstinence, moderation** 1, **restraint** 1.

**abstinence,** *n.* — *Syn.* abstaining, abstention, abstemiousness, temperance, forbearance, denial, self-denial, self-control, self-restraint, continence, fasting, frugality, abnegation, renunciation, avoidance, sobriety, desistance, austerity, withholding, refraining, keeping aloof, nonindulgence, asceticism, moderation, soberness, chastity, Puritanism, teetotalism. — *Ant.* INDULGENCE, overindulgence, intemperance.

**abstract,** *modif.* **1.** [Theoretical] — *Syn.* general, conceptual, intellectual, ideal; see **theoretical.**

**2.** [Abstruse] — *Syn.* complex, involved, obscure; see **difficult** 2.

**3.** [Nonrealistic] — *Syn.* nonrepresentational, geometric, symbolic, biomorphic, abstract expressionist, cubist; see also **painting** 1.

**abstract,** *n.* — *Syn.* synopsis, outline, résumé; see **abridgment, summary.**

*See Synonym Study at* ABRIDGMENT.

**abstract,** *v.* **1.** [To take away] — *Syn.* withdraw, separate, extract; see **remove** 1.

**2.** [To prepare an abstract] — *Syn.* digest, summarize, condense; see **decrease** 2, **summarize.**

**abstracted,** *modif.* **1.** [Absent-minded] — *Syn.* preoccupied, dreaming, absorbed; see **absent-minded.**

**2.** [Removed] — *Syn.* apart, separated, disassociated; see **separated.**

*See Synonym Study at* ABSENT-MINDED.

**abstraction,** *n.* **1.** [The state of being absorbed] — *Syn.* deliberation, absorption, preoccupation, speculation, absent-mindedness, musing, thinking, reflecting, rumination, reflection, self-communing, reverie, daydreaming, engrossment, cogitation, contemplation, brooding, brown study, cerebration, detachment, aloofness, distraction, consideration, pondering, remoteness, inattention. — *Ant.* alertness, AWARENESS, attention.

**2.** [An abstract idea] — *Syn.* concept, idea, notion, generality; see **thought** 2.

**abstruse,** *modif.* — *Syn.* recondite, deep, obscure, complex; see **difficult** 2.

**absurd,** *modif.* — *Syn.* preposterous, ridiculous, ludicrous, foolish, silly, laughable, crazy, irrational, senseless, pointless, meaningless, nonsensical, illogical, unreasonable, self-contradictory, impossible, implausible, outlandish, untenable, unsound, incongruous, risible, mad, loony\*; see also **stupid** 1. — *Ant.* sensible, logical, rational.

---

**SYN.** — **absurd** means laughably inconsistent with what is judged as true or reasonable /an *absurd* conclusion/; **ludicrous** is applied to something that provokes laughter or scorn because of incongruity or exaggeration /a *ludicrous* facial expression, a *ludicrous* suggestion/; **preposterous** is used to describe anything flagrantly absurd or ludicrous; **foolish** describes that which shows lack of good judgment or of common sense /don't take *foolish* chances/; **silly** and **ridiculous** apply to whatever excites amusement or contempt by reason of extreme foolishness, **silly** often indicating an utterly nonsensical quality

---

**absurdity,** *n.* — *Syn.* improbability, foolishness, senselessness; see **nonsense** 1, 2, **stupidity** 2.

**abundance,** *n.* — *Syn.* bounty, copiousness, profusion, affluence; see **excess** 1, **plenty, wealth** 2.

**abundant,** *modif.* **1.** [Copious] — *Syn.* sufficient, ample, plentiful, copious; see **plentiful** 2.

**2.** [Well-supplied] — *Syn.* abounding, rich, overflowing, teeming; see **plentiful** 1.

*See Synonym Study at* PLENTIFUL.

**abundantly,** *modif.* — *Syn.* plentifully, lavishly, fulsomely, satisfactorily, richly, handsomely, in large measure, profusely, amply, sufficiently, copiously, generously, luxuriantly, affluently, inexhaustibly, many times over, to one's heart's content, on the fat of the land, so that one's cup runneth over. — *Ant.* meagerly, POORLY, meanly.

**abuse,** *n.* **1.** [Misuse] — *Syn.* misuse, misapplication, perversion, debasement, degradation, ill-usage, misemployment, desecration, misappropriation, mishandling, mismanagement, pollution, improper use, exploitation, profanation, defilement, prostitution. — *Ant.* respect, CARE, veneration.

**2.** [Insulting language] — *Syn.* invective, revilement, vituperation; see **blame** 1, **insult.**

**3.** [Ill-treatment] — *Syn.* injury, mistreatment, damage, harm, hurt, maltreatment, ill-usage, ill-treatment, molestation, molesting, battering, battery, outrage, impairment, wrong, injustice, violation, persecution, harassment. — *Ant.* HELP, defense, benefit.

**abuse,** *v.* **1.** [To treat badly] — *Syn.* misuse, mistreat, insult, injure, hurt, harm, damage, impair, aggrieve, ill-treat, ill-use, batter, molest, maltreat, misemploy, misapply, misappropriate, wrong, persecute, torment, nag, victimize, oppress, ruin, mar, spoil, vulgarize, outrage, do wrong by, do wrong to, mishandle, pervert, profane, prostitute, desecrate, pollute, harass, manhandle, do an injustice to, take advantage of, exploit, overstrain, overwork, overtax, overdrive, overburden, violate, defile, impose upon, deprave, taint, debase, corrupt, squander, waste, dissipate, exhaust, do one's worst*, knock about*. — *Ant.* DEFEND, protect, befriend.
**2.** [To hurt with words] — *Syn.* revile, malign, vilify, berate; see **censure, scold, slander**.

**abused,** *modif.* — *Syn.* maltreated, hurt, reviled, wronged, injured, insulted, harmed, offended, illtreated, ill-used, misused, battered, molested, disparaged, persecuted, oppressed, exploited, mishandled, harassed, victimized, manhandled, violated, debased. — *Ant.* PRAISED, admired, aided.

**abusive,** *modif.* **1.** [Harshly insulting] — *Syn.* offensive, scurrilous, insulting, sharp-tongued; see **opprobrious, rude** 2.
**2.** [Treating badly] — *Syn.* brutal, sadistic, injurious, corrupt; see **cruel** 1.

**abut,** *v.* — *Syn.* border on, adjoin, be adjacent to; see **join** 3.

**abysmal,** *modif.* **1.** [Like an abyss] — *Syn.* profound, bottomless, unfathomable; see **deep** 1.
**2.** [Immeasurably bad] — *Syn.* wretched, appalling, hopelessly bad; see **poor** 2.

**abyss,** *n.* — *Syn.* pit, chasm, void, depths; see **depth** 2, **hole** 2.

**academic,** *modif.* **1.** [Referring to learned matters] — *Syn.* scholastic, erudite, scholarly; see **educational** 1, **learned** 1, 2.
**2.** [Of philosophic interest, but having little practical importance] — *Syn.* formalistic, hypothetical, speculative; see **theoretical**.

**academy,** *n.* **1.** [A private institution for secondary or specialized education] — *Syn.* preparatory school, boarding school, secondary school, military school, military academy, Latin school, day school, seminary, institute, conservatory, finishing school, prep school*.
**2.** [A learned society] — *Syn.* association, institute, league, fraternity, federation, alliance, foundation, council, society, institution, scientific body, circle, salon.

**accede,** *v.* — *Syn.* consent, comply, acquiesce, give in; see **agree, consent**.
*See Synonym Study at* CONSENT.

**accelerate,** *v.* — *Syn.* quicken, stimulate, expedite, speed up; see **hasten** 2.

**acceleration,** *n.* — *Syn.* speeding up, speedup, hastening, increase of speed, dispatch, quickening, hurrying, expedition, stepping up, picking up speed.

**accelerator,** *n.* — *Syn.* atomic accelerator, particle accelerator, atom smasher.
Types of (particle) accelerators include: Bevatron, Cosmotron, cyclotron, electron accelerator, linear accelerator, linac, positive-ion accelerator, superconducting super collider, SSC, synchrotron, synchrocyclotron, Tevatron.

**accent,** *n.* **1.** [Importance] — *Syn.* emphasis, stress, weight, significance; see **importance** 1.
**2.** [Stress] — *Syn.* stress, prominence, emphasis, beat,

stroke, pitch, modulation, accentuation, rhythm, meter, cadence, accent mark, diacritic.
**3.** [Manner of pronunciation] — *Syn.* pronunciation, speech pattern, inflection, intonation, articulation, enunciation, dialect, twang, drawl, brogue, burr; see also **dialect**.

**accent,** *v.* — *Syn.* accentuate, stress, intensify; see **emphasize**.

**accentuate,** *v.* — *Syn.* stress, accent, strengthen; see **emphasize**.

**accept,** *v.* **1.** [To receive] — *Syn.* take, acquire, admit, allow; see **receive** 1, 4.
**2.** [To assent] — *Syn.* admit, consent to, acquiesce in, submit to; see **agree to, endure** 2.
**3.** [To believe] — *Syn.* hold, trust, affirm; see **believe** 1.
*See Synonym Study at* RECEIVE.

**acceptable,** *modif.* — *Syn.* satisfactory, tolerable, adequate, agreeable; see **admissible, fair** 2, **pleasant** 2.

**acceptance,** *n.* **1.** [The act of accepting] — *Syn.* reception, taking, receiving; see **receipt** 1.
**2.** [An expression of acceptance] — *Syn.* recognition, assent, approval; see **agreement** 3, **permission**.

**accepted,** *modif.* — *Syn.* taken, received, assumed, approved, adopted, recognized, endorsed, verified, acclaimed, welcomed, engaged, hired, claimed, delivered, used, employed, affirmed, upheld, authorized, preferred, acknowledged, accredited, allowed, settled, established, customary, sanctioned, unopposed, authentic, confirmed, time-honored, fashionable, favorably received, chosen, acceptable, popular, formally admitted, stereotyped, orthodox, standard, conventional, in vogue, current, taken for granted, credited, OK'd. — *Ant.* REFUSED, denied, nullified.

**access,** *n.* **1.** [Admission] — *Syn.* admittance, entree, introduction; see **entrance** 1.
**2.** [A means of admission] — *Syn.* path, passage, way; see **entrance** 2.

**access*,** *v.* — *Syn.* gain access to, get at, reach, locate see **enter** 1, **locate** 1, **obtain** 1.

**accessibility,** *n.* — *Syn.* approachability, receptiveness, openness; see **convenience** 1.

**accessible,** *modif.* — *Syn.* approachable, open, obtainable, attainable; see **available, convenient** 2, **easy** 2, **friendly** 1.

**accession,** *n.* **1.** [Coming into office or power] — *Syn.* induction, investment, inauguration; see **installation** 1.
**2.** [Addition] — *Syn.* increase, addition, enlargement, augmentation; see **addition** 2, **increase** 1.
**3.** [Agreement] — *Syn.* assent, acceptance, consent; see **agreement** 1.

**accessories,** *pl.n.* — *Syn.* appurtenances, frills, ornaments, adornments, decorations, additions, attachments, extras, embellishments, trimmings, gimmicks*, doodads*, bells and whistles*; see also **equipment**. For specific kinds of accessories: see also **bag, band** 1, **decoration** 2, **glove, hat, jewelry, muffler, necktie, scarf, shoe**.

**accessory,** *n.* — *Syn.* accomplice, confederate, abettor, assistant; see **associate**.

**accident,** *n.* **1.** [An unexpected misfortune] — *Syn.* mishap, mischance, setback, collision; see **collision** 1, **disaster, misfortune** 2.
**2.** [Chance, or a chance happening] — *Syn.* fortune, chance, luck, adventure, contingency, occurrence, happening, circumstance, turn, unforeseen occurrence, fortuity, event, occasion, befalling, fluke*; see also **chance** 1.

**accidental,** *modif.* **1.** [Happening by chance] — *Syn.*

chance, fortuitous, coincidental, unintentional, inadvertent, unplanned, unpremeditated, undesigned, unwitting, uncalculated, unintended, unanticipated, unforeseen, unexpected, casual, adventitious, random, haphazard, involuntary, lucky, unlucky, serendipitous, fluky*; see also **unexpected**.

**2.** [Incidental] — *Syn.* incidental, secondary, nonessential, adventitious; see **subordinate, under** 3.

---

*SYN.* — **accidental** describes that which occurs by chance [an *accidental* encounter] or outside the normal course of events [an *accidental* attribute]; **fortuitous**, which frequently suggests a complete absence of cause, now usually refers to chance events of a fortunate nature; **casual** describes the unpremeditated, random, or irregular quality of something [a *casual* remark, a *casual* visit] or its informality [*casual* clothes]; **incidental** emphasizes the nonessential or secondary nature of something [*incidental* expenses]; **adventitious** refers to that which is added extrinsically and connotes a lack of essential connection

---

**accidentally,** *modif.* — *Syn.* unintentionally, involuntarily, unwittingly, unexpectedly, inadvertently, casually, fortuitously, by accident, by chance, haphazardly, incidentally, randomly, undesignedly, adventitiously, not purposely, by a fluke*. — *Ant.* DELIBERATELY, voluntarily, intentionally.

**acclaim,** *n.* — *Syn.* approval, recognition, plaudits; see **praise** 1, 2.

**acclaim,** *v.* — *Syn.* laud, commend, celebrate; see **praise** 1.

*See Synonym Study at* PRAISE.

**acclamation,** *n.* — *Syn.* applause, acclaim, approval; see **praise** 1, 2.

**acclimate,** *v.* — *Syn.* adapt, accommodate, adjust, become accustomed to; see **adjust** 1, **conform**.

**accommodate,** *v.* **1.** [To render a service] — *Syn.* help, aid, comfort, make comfortable, oblige, suit, serve, gratify, please, favor, arrange, settle, provide, convenience, benefit, tender, supply, furnish, assist, support, sustain, do a favor, do a favor for, profit, avail, indebt, indulge, humor, pamper, yield, bow, defer, submit, attend to the convenience of, accept, put oneself out for, do a service for, meet the wants of. — *Ant.* inconvenience, discommode, refuse.

**2.** [To suit one thing to another] — *Syn.* adjust, adapt, fit, suit, harmonize, conform, modify, attune, reconcile, settle, agree, accord, correspond, acclimate, accustom, compose, make suitable, make correspond, make conform, bring into consistency; see also **adjust** 1. — *Ant.* disrupt, CONFUSE, derange.

**3.** [To provide lodging] — *Syn.* house, quarter, lodge, rent to, put up, receive, take in, serve as host, entertain, welcome, board, shelter, billet, supply accommodations, furnish accommodations, entertain comfortably, host. — *Ant.* BAR, turn out, refuse entrance.

**4.** [To hold] — *Syn.* hold, contain, have room for; see **contain** 1, **include** 1.

*See Synonym Study at* ADJUST, CONTAIN.

**accommodating,** *modif.* — *Syn.* obliging, helpful, neighborly; see **kind** 1.

**accommodation,** *n.* **1.** [Adjustment] — *Syn.* compromise, reconciliation, settlement, adaptation; see **adjustment** 1, **agreement** 2, 3.

**2.** [Convenience] — *Syn.* ease, comfort, luxury; see **convenience** 2.

**3.** [Favor] — *Syn.* service, benevolence, aid; see **kindness** 2.

**accommodations,** *pl.n.* — *Syn.* quarters, rooms, lodging, maintenance, housing, apartment, hotel, room and board, bunk, bed, board, place, place to stay, roof over one's head, facilities, seat, berth, digs*.

For kinds of accommodations; see also **apartment, apartment house, dormitory, home** 1, **hotel, motel, room** 4.

**accompaniment,** *n.* **1.** [That which accompanies as a necessary part of another] — *Syn.* accessory, adjunct, concomitant, consequence, necessary circumstance, appurtenance, attribute, context, appendage, necessary link, attendant condition, attachment, attendant, complement, coexistence, supplement.

**2.** [Incidental music] — *Syn.* accompanying instrument, backup, orchestral part, obbligato, piano part, instrumental music, chords, background music, harmony, minor harmony, subsidiary part, supplementary part, continuo; see also **music** 1.

**accompany,** *v.* **1.** [To go with] — *Syn.* escort, attend, chaperon, be a companion to, tend, be with, go with, keep one company, follow, guard, guide, usher, lead (in), show around, show in, show the way, conduct, squire, bring, convoy, go along with, associate with, consort with, go around with, go out with, take out*, keep company with, give safe conduct, look after, hang around with, hang out with*, hang out together*, band together, bear one company, tag along with*, be by one's side.

**2.** [To supplement] — *Syn.* add to, complete, append; see **supplement**.

**3.** [To occur with] — *Syn.* occur with, happen with, coexist with, appear with, be connected with, go hand in hand with, go together with, take place with, go hand in glove with, occur in association with, characterize, co-occur.

---

*SYN.* — **accompany** means to go or be together with as a companion, associate, attribute, etc., and usually connotes equality of relationship [he *accompanied* her to the theater]; **attend** implies presence either in a subordinate position or to render services [Dr. Jones *attended* the patient]; **escort** and **convoy** are both applied to the accompanying, as by an armed guard, of persons or things needing protection (**convoy**, esp. in the case of sea travel and **escort**, in the case of land travel); **escort** also implies accompanying as a mark of honor or an act of courtesy; **chaperon** implies accompaniment, for reasons of propriety, of young unmarried people by an older or married person

---

**accomplice,** *n.* — *Syn.* confederate, accessory, helper, partner in crime; see **assistant, associate**.

*See Synonym Study at* ASSOCIATE.

**accomplish,** *v.* — *Syn.* fulfill, perform, finish, achieve; see **achieve** 1, 2, **perform** 1, **succeed** 1.

*See Synonym Study at* ACHIEVE, PERFORM.

**accomplished,** *modif.* **1.** [Done] — *Syn.* completed, consummated, concluded; see **finished** 1.

**2.** [Skilled] — *Syn.* proficient, expert, skillful; see **able** 2.

**3.** [Polished] — *Syn.* cultured, cultivated, finished; see **cultured, refined** 2.

**accomplishment,** *n.* **1.** [The act of accomplishing] — *Syn.* completion, fulfillment, realization, finishing; see **success** 1.

**2.** [A completed action] — *Syn.* achievement, feat, attainment; see **achievement** 2.

**accord,** *n.* — *Syn.* harmony, understanding, reconciliation, agreement; see **agreement** 2, 3.

**accord,** *v.* **1.** [To be in agreement] — *Syn.* agree, concur, correspond; see **agree.**
*See Synonym Study at* AGREE.
**2.** [To grant] — *Syn.* bestow, grant, concede, allow; see **admit 3, give 1.**

**accordingly,** *modif.* — *Syn.* in consequence, consequently, equally, respectively, proportionately, duly, correspondingly, in accordance, subsequently, in respect to, thus, hence, therefore, as a result, resultantly, as a consequence, as the case may be, on the ground, under the circumstances, as things go, to that end, in that event, as an outgrowth.

**according to,** *prep.* — *Syn.* in accordance with, as, to the degree that, in consonance with, conforming to, just as, in keeping with, in line with, in agreement with, consistent with, congruent with, pursuant to, in proportion to, commensurate with, on the authority of, as reported by, as stated in.

**accost,** *v.* **1.** [To greet] — *Syn.* address, hail, call to; see **greet.**
**2.** [To solicit] — *Syn.* approach, waylay, confront, proposition*; see **approach 1, solicit 3.**

**account,** *n.* **1.** [A narrative] — *Syn.* tale, recital, report, chronicle; see **description 1, story.**
**2.** [A record] — *Syn.* statement, reckoning, record; see **record 1, statement 3.**
**call to account** — *Syn.* demand an explanation, reprimand, censure; see **accuse.**
**give a good account of oneself** — *Syn.* acquit oneself well, do well, perform creditably; see **succeed 1.**
**on account** — *Syn.* charged, in *or* on layaway, on credit; see **bought, charged 1, due.**
**on account of** — *Syn.* because of, by virtue of, since, for the sake of; see **because.**
**on no account** — *Syn.* for no reason, no way, under no circumstances; see **never.**
**on someone's account** — *Syn.* because of, for someone's sake, in someone's behalf, in someone's interest; see **because, for.**
**take account of** — *Syn.* take into account, take into consideration, take notice of; see **consider 1.**
**take into account** — *Syn.* take into consideration, judge, allow for, weigh; see **consider 1.**
**turn to account** — *Syn.* utilize, exploit, profit by; see **profit 2, use 1.**

**account,** *v.* — *Syn.* value, judge, reckon, deem; see **consider 2, estimate 1.**

**accountability,** *n.* — *Syn.* culpability, liability, answerability; see **responsibility 2.**

**accountable,** *modif.* — *Syn.* liable, culpable, answerable; see **responsible 1.**
*See Synonym Study at* RESPONSIBLE.

**accountant,** *n.* — *Syn.* bookkeeper, auditor, actuary, bookkeeping expert, examiner of business accounts, expert in accounts, clerk, inspector of accounts, comptroller, controller, calculator, reckoner, analyst, chartered accountant, certified public accountant, C.P.A. *or* CPA, inventory expert, bean counter*.

**account for,** *v.* — *Syn.* clarify, resolve, elucidate, show grounds; see **explain, justify 2.**

**accredit,** *v.* **1.** [To authorize] — *Syn.* authorize, give credentials to, certify, sanction; see **approve 1, commission.**
**2.** [To attribute] — *Syn.* credit, impute, ascribe; see **attribute.**
*See Synonym Study at* COMMISSION

**accredited,** *modif.* — *Syn.* vouched for, certified, authorized; see **approved.**

**accretion,** *n.* — *Syn.* accumulation, growth, addition, buildup; see **addition 2, increase 1.**

**accrue,** *v.* — *Syn.* increase, collect, gather; see **accumulate 1.**

**accumulate,** *v.* **1.** [To amass] — *Syn.* gather, collect, amass, mass, hoard, get together, pile up, heap, store, assemble, cache, muster, aggregate, cumulate, concentrate, compile, agglomerate, accrue, pile, scrape together, scrape up, stack up, stockpile, store up, garner, heap up, heap together, procure, acquire, gain, load up, attach, draw together, bring together, rake up, lump together, amalgamate, unite, incorporate, add to, save, bank, profit, make money, build up, gain control of, drag in*, haul in*, rake in*, roll in*, squirrel away*. — *Ant.* SCATTER, squander, distribute.
**2.** [To increase] — *Syn.* swell, build up, expand, mount up; see **grow 1.**

**accumulation,** *n.* **1.** [The act of amassing] — *Syn.* collection, buildup, amassing, accretion, aggregation, augmentation, inflation, addition, enlargement, multiplication, intensification, accession, agglomeration, growth, collecting, amassment, gathering, hoarding, growth by addition, increase, conglomeration. — *Ant.* REDUCTION, dispersal, diminution.
**2.** [A heap] — *Syn.* mass, pile, quantity; see **heap.**

**accuracy,** *n.* **1.** [The state of being without error] — *Syn.* exactness, exactitude, correctness; see **truth 1.**
**2.** [The quality of precision or deftness] — *Syn.* precision, preciseness, exactness, skill, efficiency, one-for-one targeting, correctness, skillfulness, sharpness, mastery, dependability, strictness, certainty, sureness, dotting the *i*'s and crossing the *t*'s*. — *Ant.* imprecision, sloppiness, incompetence.

**accurate,** *modif.* **1.** [Free from error] — *Syn.* correct, exact, right, precise, infallible, perfect, nice, faultless, flawless, errorless, just, factual, true, unquestionable, veracious, unquestioned, unerring, unimpeachable, authoritative, authentic, valid, undisputed, undeniable, unrefuted, irrefutable, conclusive, absolute, final, certain, unambiguous, straight, proper, strict, undeviating, not amiss, definite, actual, definitive, fundamental, clear-cut, genuine, official, OK, checked and double-checked*, dead right*, on target*, on the nose*, on the button*, on the money*, right on*; see also sense 2. — *Ant.* erroneous, FALSE, questionable.
**2.** [Characterized by precision] — *Syn.* careful, meticulous, precise, deft, reliable, trustworthy, true, correct, exact, well-defined, specific, dependable, skillful, methodical, systematic, discriminative, nice, distinct, particular, well-drawn, realistic, authentic, genuine, close, critical, detailed, factual, severe, rigorous, literal, word-for-word, rigid, scrupulous, strict, exacting, punctilious, discriminating, faithful, punctual, scientific, objective, detached, unprejudiced, unbiased, disinterested, veracious, matter-of-fact, rational, unmistakable, reasonable, judicious, right, explicit, mathematically precise, mathematically exact, ultraprecise, definite, religiously exact, unerring, concrete, defined, sharp, sound, solid, like clockwork, on the spot*, on the dot*. — *Ant.* inaccurate, CARELESS, faulty.

---

**SYN. — accurate** implies a positive exercise of care to obtain conformity with fact or truth /an *accurate* account of the events/; **correct** connotes little more than absence of error /a *correct* answer/ or adherence to a conventional standard /*correct* behavior/; **exact** stresses perfect conformity to fact, truth, or some standard /the *exact* time, an *exact* quotation/; **precise**

suggests minute accuracy of detail and often connotes a finicky or overly fastidious attitude [*precise* in all his habits]

**accurately,** *modif.* — *Syn.* correctly, precisely, exactly, certainly, truly, truthfully, justly, rightly, carefully, perfectly, invariably, in detail, strictly, unerringly, unmistakenly, infallibly, rigorously, scrupulously, literally, verbatim, squarely, explicitly, word for word, to a nicety, just so, as is just, like clockwork, to a hair*, to a turn*, on the button*, on the nose*, within an inch*.

**accursed,** *modif.* 1. [Detestable] — *Syn.* hateful, loathsome, abhorrent; see **offensive** 2.
2. [Doomed] — *Syn.* ill-fated, cursed, damned; see **doomed.**

**accusation,** *n.* 1. [The act of accusing] — *Syn.* arraignment, indictment, prosecution, accusal, impeachment, denunciation, incrimination, bringing of charges, finger-pointing*; see also **blame** 1.
2. [A charge] — *Syn.* charge, indictment, allegation, imputation, denunciation, slur, exposé, complaint, citation, censure, insinuation, count, rap*, beef*, smear*, frame-up*.

**accuse,** *v.* — *Syn.* charge with, blame, censure, hold responsible, arraign, indict, impeach, prefer charges, file a claim, challenge, denounce, fault, find fault, attack, brand, impute, involve, inculpate, incriminate, implicate, summon, litigate, arrest, apprehend, sue, bring up on charges, press charges, prosecute, slander, libel, betray, tax, slur, cite, reprove, reproach, haul into court, bring into court, have the law on, inform against, hold accountable, bring proceedings against, bring charges against, appeal to law, bring to trial, serve with a summons, complain against, lodge a complaint, charge to, declaim against, recriminate, fix the responsibility for, connect with, cast blame upon, place to one's account, hall into court, hang something on*, pin something on*, put the finger on*, put the screws on*, smear*, pin the blame on*, hold against*, point the finger at*, fasten on*, lay at one's door*, throw in one's teeth*, bring home to*. — *Ant.* VINDICATE, exonerate, pardon.

**SYN.** — **accuse** means to find fault for offenses of varying gravity [to *accuse* someone of murder, to *accuse* someone of carelessness]; to **charge** is to make an accusation of a legal or formal nature [the police *charged* her with jaywalking]; **indict** describes the action of a grand jury and means to find a case against a person and order the person to be brought to trial; **arraign** means to call a person before a court to be informed of pending charges; **impeach** means to charge a public official with misconduct in office, but in nonlegal usage means to challenge a person's motives, credibility, etc.

**accused,** *modif.* — *Syn.* arraigned, indicted, incriminated, charged with, blamed, under suspicion, under indictment, supposedly guilty, alleged to be guilty, on the police blotter, apprehended, held for questioning, liable, implicated, in danger, subject to accusation, under attack, under fire, on the docket, given the blame, taxed with, under a cloud, up for*. — *Ant.* DISCHARGED, acquitted, cleared.

**accuser,** *n.* — *Syn.* prosecutor, plaintiff, objector, complainant, libelant, informant, district attorney, court, law, judicial party, suitor, petitioner, litigant, delator, adversary, opposer, opponent, informer, government witness, state witness, rat*, stool pigeon*, fink*. — *Ant.* DEFENDANT, accused, prisoner.

**accustomed,** *modif.* — *Syn.* usual, customary, habitual;

see **conventional** 1, **usual** 2.
*See Synonym Study at* USUAL.

**accustomed to,** *modif.* in the habit of, used to, habituated to, wont to, acclimated to, acclimatized to, adjusted to, adapted to, inured to, familiar with, conditioned to; see also **addicted to.**

**ace*,** *modif.* — *Syn.* expert, first-rate, outstanding; see **able** 2, **distinguished** 2.

**ace,** *n.* 1. [A pilot who has shot down five planes or more] — *Syn.* veteran, combat pilot, fighter pilot, expert, seasoned aviator, dogfighter*.
2. [An expert in an activity] — *Syn.* expert, master, champion; see **specialist.**

**acerbic,** *modif.* 1. [Sour in taste] — *Syn.* sour, acidic, tart; see **sour** 1.
2. [Sharp or harsh in temper or language] — *Syn.* biting, severe, caustic; see **abrupt** 2, **sarcastic, severe** 2.

**acerbity,** *n.* 1. [Sourness] — *Syn.* astringency, tartness, acidity; see **bitterness** 1.
2. [Harshness] — *Syn.* irritability, asperity, mordancy; see **roughness** 2, **rudeness, sarcasm.**

**acetic,** *modif.* — *Syn.* tart, acid, biting; see **sour** 1.

**ache,** *n.* — *Syn.* dull pain, throbbing, twinge, pang; see **pain** 2.

**ache,** *v.* — *Syn.* pain, throb, be sore; see **hurt** 4.

**achievable,** *modif.* — *Syn.* obtainable, attainable, feasible; see **available, possible** 2.

**achieve,** *v.* 1. [To succeed in carrying out] — *Syn.* complete, end, terminate, conclude, finish, finish up, finish off, do, perform, execute, fulfill, consummate, perfect, cap, carry off, carry out, carry through, turn out, bring about, bring off, make happen, settle, effect, bring to an end, bring to a conclusion, close, stop, encompass, produce, realize, effectuate, actualize, discharge, make work out, wind up, work out, adjust, resolve, solve, accomplish, dispose of, dispatch, make an end of, enact, manage, contrive, negotiate, sign, seal, bring to pass, do the job, have effect, see to, see it through, get done, close up, put the lid on, carry to completion, follow through, take measures, deliver, knock off*, fill the bill*, round out*, come through*, polish off*, score*, clean up*, mop up*, put across*, pull off*, swing*, hack it*, make short work of*, do up brown*, put through*, go whole hog*, go all the way*, go the limit*, sew up*, button up*, do oneself proud*, call it a day*, put the finishing touch on*, turn the trick*, do the trick*, wrap up*; see also **perform** 1. — *Ant.* ABANDON, fail, give up.
2. [To reach a goal] — *Syn.* accomplish, attain, reach, gain, succeed (in), realize, obtain, gain one's end, make it*; see also sense 1, **succeed** 1.

**SYN.** — **achieve** suggests exertion and the use of skill in reaching or getting something [we've *achieved* a great victory]; **attain** adds an implication of being goaded on by great ambition to gain an end regarded as beyond the reach of most people [she has *attained* great fame in her profession]; **accomplish** implies success in completing a set task [to *accomplish* an end]; **gain** suggests the exertion of considerable effort to reach some goal [they *gained* the top of the hill] *See also Synonym Study at* PERFORM.

**achievement,** *n.* 1. [The act of reaching a goal] — *Syn.* attainment, accomplishment, fulfillment, realization, actualization, effectuation, encompassment, execution; see also **success** 1.
2. [A creditable action completed] — *Syn.* accomplishment, feat, exploit, contrivance, triumph, hit, success, realization, acquirement, creation, completion,

consummation, masterwork, masterpiece, performance, deed, act, enactment, victory, conquest, *chef d'oeuvre* (French), tour de force, coup, attainment, rendition, action, stunt, feather in one's cap*. — *Ant.* FAILURE, blunder, collapse.

**acid,** *modif.* **1.** [Having the characteristics of an acid] — *Syn.* sharp, tart, biting; see **sour** 1.
**2.** [Having the properties of an acid] — *Syn.* corrosive, erosive, eroding, corroding, oxidizing, rusting, eating away, biting, disinfectant, disintegrative, dissolvent, bleaching, acidic, anti-alkaline.
**3.** [Cutting or sarcastic] — *Syn.* biting, sharp, barbed, astringent; see **sarcastic.**
*See Synonym Study at* SOUR.

**acid,** *n.* **1.** [A sour substance] — *Syn.* acidulous compound, corrosive, Lewis acid, hydrogen-ion concentration.
**2.** [*A drug] — *Syn.* LSD, D-lysergic acid diethylamide, hallucinogen, psychedelic; see **drug** 2.
Common acids include: vinegar, acetic acid, verjuice, lemon juice; citric, ascorbic, lactic, malic, formic, tannic, tartaric, nicotinic, boric, acetic, sulfuric, muriatic, hydrochloric, hydrosulfurous, hydrobromic, hydrofluoric, hydrocyanic, hydroferrocyanic, hydriodic, hyponitrous, sulfonic, phosphoric, carbolic, nitric, benzoic, amino, monobasic, dibasic, polybasic acid, aqua regia (Latin).

**acidity,** *n.* — *Syn.* sourness, bitterness, acridity, acidosis, acidulousness, hyperacidity, tartness, sharpness, acridness, pungency, fermentation, vinegariness, harshness, causticity, astringency, keenness. — *Ant.* SWEETNESS, alkalinity, sugariness.

**acidulous,** *modif.* **1.** [Acid] — *Syn.* bitter, piquant, sharp, subacid; see **sour** 1.
**2.** [Sarcastic] — *Syn.* satirical, ironical, mocking; see **sarcastic.**
*See Synonym Study at* SOUR.

**acknowledge,** *v.* **1.** [To admit] — *Syn.* concede, admit, confess, declare; see **admit** 2, 3.
**2.** [To recognize the authority of] — *Syn.* recognize, accept, endorse, certify, confirm, uphold, support, ratify, approve, defend, subscribe to, acquiesce in, accede to, make legal, attest to, take an oath by, defer to, have to hand it to*.
**3.** [To answer] — *Syn.* respond to, reply to, answer, thank, recognize, make acknowledgment, notice, R.S.V.P.; see also **greet, thank.**
*See Synonym Study at* ADMIT.

**acknowledged,** *modif.* — *Syn.* recognized, accepted, admitted, confessed, unquestioned, authorized, confirmed, received, sanctioned, accredited, approved, receipted, professed, avowed.

**acknowledgment,** *n.* **1.** [The act of acknowledging] — *Syn.* acceptance, declaration, compliance, affirmation, corroboration, avowal, recognition, confession, admission, admitting, conceding, concession, concurrence, assent, confirmation, accession, profession, allowance, ratification, acquiescence, assertion, asseveration, owning up*. — *Ant.* DENIAL, confutation, refutation.
**2.** [Something intended to acknowledge] — *Syn.* greeting, reply, answer, response, nod, confession, statement, apology, thanks, guarantee, return, support, signature, receipt, letter, card, contract, acclamation, applause, bow, token, bestowal, gift, bouquet, vote of thanks, IOU, R.S.V.P.; see also **thanks.**

**acme,** *n.* — *Syn.* zenith, summit, highest point; see **summit, top** 1.
*See Synonym Study at* SUMMIT.

**acolyte,** *n.* — *Syn.* helper, attendant, follower; see **assistant, follower.**

**acquaint,** *v.* **1.** [To let know] — *Syn.* tell, advise, inform; see **notify** 1, **tell** 1.
**2.** [To make familiar with] — *Syn.* familiarize, make acquainted, introduce; see **familiarize with.**
*See Synonym Study at* NOTIFY.

**acquaintance,** *n.* **1.** [The state of being acquainted] — *Syn.* association, companionship, relationship, knowledge; see **friendship** 1.
**2.** [A person with whom one is acquainted] — *Syn.* colleague, associate, bowing acquaintance, speaking acquaintance, escort, neighbor; see also **associate, friend** 1.
**3.** [Knowledge gained through personal experience or study] — *Syn.* familiarity, conversance, awareness; see **awareness, experience** 3.

**acquainted (with),** *modif.* — *Syn.* introduced, on speaking terms, conversant with; see **conscious** 1, **familiar with, knowledgeable.**

**acquiesce,** *v.* — *Syn.* consent, comply, submit; see **agree, consent.**

**acquiescence,** *n.* — *Syn.* passive consent, quiet submission, resignation; see **permission.**

**acquire,** *v.* **1.** [To obtain] — *Syn.* take, get, earn, procure; see **obtain** 1.
**2.** [To receive] — *Syn.* get, gain, take possession, collect; see **receive** 1.
*See Synonym Study at* OBTAIN.

**acquired,** *modif.* **1.** [Gained by personal exertion] — *Syn.* reached, attained, gained, won, accomplished, learned, adopted, earned, collected, gathered, secured, procured, obtained, captured, seized, drawn, harvested, regained, retrieved, realized, got by the sweat of one's brow, dug out, raked in, cornered, netted, grabbed; see also **won.**
**2.** [Gained without special exertion] — *Syn.* given, accrued, derived, granted, endowed, transmitted, adapted to, conveyed to, inherited, handed down, bequeathed, ceded, allowed, awarded, passed on, willed to. — *Ant.* forfeited, deprived, lost.

**acquisition,** *n.* **1.** [The act of acquiring] — *Syn.* acquirement, acquiring, obtainment, attainment, procuring, procurement, procuration, purchase, recovery, retrieval, redemption, takeover, appropriation, accretion, addition, inheriting, winning, gaining.
**2.** [Anything acquired] — *Syn.* purchase, addition, inheritance, gift, donation, grant, gain, possession, property, belonging, asset, accomplishment, achievement, acquirement, accession, increment, profit, income, winnings, booty, proceeds, benefit, prize, reward, award, premium, bonus, fee, allowance, benefaction, patrimony, dividend, find*, catch*, buy*. — *Ant.* LOSS, expenditure, penalty.

**acquisitive,** *modif.* — *Syn.* greedy, grasping, avaricious, rapacious; see **greedy** 1.
*See Synonym Study at* GREEDY.

**acquit,** *v.* **1.** [To exonerate] — *Syn.* clear, absolve, vindicate; see **absolve, excuse.**
**2.** [To behave] — *Syn.* comport, conduct, bear, act; see **behave** 2.
*See Synonym Study at* ABSOLVE, BEHAVE.

**acquittal,** *n.* — *Syn.* absolution, acquitting, suspended sentence, clearance, quittance, exoneration, dismissal, dismissing, deliverance, amnesty, discharge, discharging, pardon, reprieve, exemption, liberation, release, releasing, freeing, vindication, exculpation, remission, relief from, letting off, springing*. — *Ant.* PUNISHMENT, sentence, imprisonment.

**acre,** *n.* — *Syn.* plot, acreage, bit of land, estate; see **area** 2, **property** 2.

**acreage,** *n.* — *Syn.* land, grounds, acres, real estate; see **area** 2, **property** 2.

**acrid,** *modif.* **1.** [Harsh in taste or smell] — *Syn.* bitter, sharp, stinging, irritating; see **sour** 1.
**2.** [Caustic] — *Syn.* acrimonious, bitter, caustic, sarcastic; see **sarcastic.**

**acrimonious,** *modif.* — *Syn.* sharp, bitter, caustic, rancorous; see **angry, sarcastic.**

**acrimony,** *n.* — *Syn.* bitterness, asperity, harshness, rancor; see **anger, bitterness** 2, **hatred** 2, **rudeness.**

**acrobat,** *n.* — *Syn.* tumbler, gymnast, trampolinist, aerial artist, aerialist, equilibrist, trapeze artist, contortionist, circus, performer, tightrope walker, high-vaulter, somersaulter, bar swinger, ropewalker, ropedancer, flying trapezist, circus athlete, aerosaltant, stuntman, stuntwoman, figure skater, ballet dancer, aerial gymnast, funambulist, clown, balancer, trap man*, dangler*, stunter*, mat worker*, flier*, tramper*.

**acrobatics,** *pl.n.* — *Syn.* gymnastics, tumbling, calisthenics, aerobatics; see **gymnastics.**

**across,** *modif.* and *prep.* — *Syn.* crosswise, crossed, athwart, to the opposite side of, over, over against, opposite, directly opposite, on the other side, from side to side of, from one side to another, in a crossing position, transversely, contrariwise, in front of, beyond.

**across-the-board,** *modif.* — *Syn.* general, universal, blanket, affecting everyone; see **general** 1.

**act,** *n.* **1.** [An action] — *Syn.* action, deed, performance, exploit; see **action** 2.
**2.** [An official or legal statement] — *Syn.* law, proposal, judgment, commitment, verdict, amendment, order, announcement, edict, ordinance, decree, statute, writ, bull, warrant, summons, subpoena, document, bill, code, clause, law of the land*.
**3.** [A division of a play] — *Syn.* scene, curtain, prologue, epilogue, introduction, entr'acte, interlude, finale, unit of dramatic action.
**4.** [A short performance in a show] — *Syn.* routine, performance, number, bit, sketch, skit, monologue, curtain raiser, appearance, turn, stand-up routine, shtick*.
**5.** [A pose] — *Syn.* falsification, feigning, affectation, pose; see **pose, pretense** 1.

**act,** *v.* **1.** [To perform an action] — *Syn.* do, execute, carry out, carry on, perform, operate, transact, accomplish, achieve, consummate, carry into effect, perpetrate, persevere, persist, labor, work, run, function, officiate, preside, serve, go ahead, take action, go about, step into, take steps, play a part, take a part, begin, move, proceed, enforce, maneuver, be in process, be in action, create, practice, deal in, prosecute, develop, make progress, be active, take effect, produce an effect, commit, fight, combat, respond, keep going, answer, pursue, put forth energy, hustle*, get going*, pull*, do one's stuff*, get down to brass tacks*; see also **perform** 1. — *Ant.* WAIT, await, rest.
**2.** [To conduct oneself] — *Syn.* behave, seem, appear, carry oneself, acquit oneself, comport oneself, bear oneself, handle oneself, demean oneself, give the appearance of, represent oneself as, take on, play one's part, impress one as, cut a figure*; see also **behave** 2.
**3.** [To play a role in or as if in a play] — *Syn.* perform, play, playact, impersonate, personate, represent, enact, act out, simulate, live over, pretend, mimic, mime, pantomime, burlesque, parody, feign, fake, portray, render the role of, create a role, rehearse, take a part, dramatize, star, spout, rant, declaim, overact, play the part of, act the part of, make one's debut, masquerade as, put

on airs*, put on an act*, tread the boards*, strut one's stuff*, ham*, emote*, mug*, chew the scenery*, throw a performance*; see also **pretend** 1, 2.

**act for,** *v.* — *Syn.* do the work of, replace, fill in for; see **substitute** 2.

**acting,** *modif.* — *Syn.* substitute, substituting, temporary, alternate, deputy, officiating, interim, delegated, assistant, adjutant, surrogate, pro tem; see also **temporary.** — *Ant.* OFFICIAL, confirmed, regular.
*See Synonym Study at* TEMPORARY.

**acting,** *n.* — *Syn.* pretending, feigning, simulating, gesturing, ranting, spouting, orating, dramatizing, performing, behaving, playing, showing off, posturing, enactment, impersonation, depiction, portrayal, pantomime, rendition, dramatics, histrionic art, stage playing, stagecraft, simulation, theatricals, performance, dramatic action, mimicry, histrionics, mime, playacting.

**action,** *n.* **1.** [Any state opposed to rest and quiet] — *Syn.* activity, movement, operation, performance, business, occupation, work, functioning, performing, behavior, response, reaction, execution, commission, manipulation, industry, bustle, turmoil, conflict, stir, flurry, animation, vivacity, enterprise, energy, drive, liveliness, alacrity, alertness, readiness, quickness, keenness, vigor, life, dash, commotion, rush, motion, mobility, haste, speed, activism, go*, doings*, snap*. — *Ant.* REST, quiet, inaction.
**2.** [An individual deed] — *Syn.* act, deed, feat, exploit, performance, accomplishment, something done, maneuver, step, achievement, thing, blow, stroke, thrust, stratagem, effort, enterprise, endeavor, move, movement, doing, effect, transaction, exertion, operation, bout, handiwork, dealings, procedure, stunt, trick.
**3.** [A process at law] — *Syn.* suit, claim, litigation, lawsuit; see **trial** 2.
**4.** [Military activity] — *Syn.* battle, engagement, combat, fighting; see **battle** 1, 2.
**5.** [The plot or events in a creative work] — *Syn.* plot, development, progress, unfolding; see **plot** 2.
*See Synonym Study at* BATTLE.

**bring action** — *Syn.* accuse, start a lawsuit, take to court; see **sue.**

**see action** — *Syn.* do battle, engage in combat, fight; see **fight** 2.

**take action** — *Syn.* become active, do, initiate activity; see **act** 1.

**actions,** *pl.n.* — *Syn.* behavior, conduct, manner(s); see **behavior** 1.

**activate,** *v.* — *Syn.* stimulate, initiate, arouse, actuate; see **animate** 1, **begin** 1.

**active,** *modif.* **1.** [Engaged in or capable of action] — *Syn.* functioning, acting, working, moving, going, operative, in effect, in action, operating, in force, live, alive, dynamic, running, mobile, busy, bustling, rushing, astir, stirring, humming, in operation, current, actual, participating, engaged, practicing, effective, effectual, productive, powerful, efficacious, serviceable, impelling, ongoing, going on, existing, in process, in progress, progressive, in a state of action, activated, volatile, restless, in play, at work, up and about, up and around, at it*, on the go*, on the move*, hopping*, ticking*, going full blast*, in high gear*. — *Ant.* quiet, inactive, MOTIONLESS.
**2.** [Notable for activity] — *Syn.* energetic, lively, busy, eventful, brisk, dynamic, agile, quick, nimble, spry, rapid, dexterous, fresh, frisky, sprightly, alert, alive, ready, sharp, keen, wide-awake, animated, spirited, vital, full of life, enlivened, vibrant, kinetic, vigorous, strenuous, bustling, industrious, persevering, enthusias-

tic, ardent, unfaltering, purposeful, resolute, pushing, aggressive, forceful, intense, forcible, determined, unwearied, diligent, hard-working, assiduous, enterprising, activist, eager, zealous, dashing, bold, daring, high-spirited, overactive, hyperactive, hyper*, hectic, frenetic, frenzied, chipper*, snappy*, peppy*, zippy*, full of pep*, on the ball*, on one's toes*, with plenty of go*, rarin' to go*, up and coming*, on the job*, on the stick*, full of pizazz*, hot*, hyped up*, pumped up*, charged up*, turned on (to)*. — *Ant.* LAZY, lethargic, sluggish.

---

**SYN.** — **active** implies a state of motion, operation, etc. ranging from cases of normal functioning to instances of quickened activity /he's still *active* at eighty; an *active* market/; **energetic** suggests a concentrated exertion of energy or effort /an *energetic* workout/; **vigorous** implies forcefulness, robustness, and strength as an inherent quality /a *vigorous* plant/; **strenuous** is applied to things that make trying demands on one's strength or energy /*strenuous* exercise/; **brisk** implies liveliness and vigor of motion /a *brisk* walk/

---

**activity,** *n.* 1. [The state of being active] — *Syn.* motion, movement, exercise, liveliness; see **action** 1.
2. [A pursuit] — *Syn.* pursuit, exercise, project, venture; see **enterprise** 1, **exercise** 2.
**act on** *or* **upon,** *v.* 1. [To act in accordance with] — *Syn.* heed, follow, attend to; see **follow** 2, **obey** 1.
2. [To influence] — *Syn.* affect, sway, impress; see **influence.**
**actor,** *n.* 1. [A theatrical performer] — *Syn.* player, performer, star, character, comedian, tragedian, member of the cast, thespian, leading man, leading woman, leading lady, lead, entertainer, artist, movie star, film star, television star, character actor, character actress, supporting actor, supporting actress, featured player, costar, superstar, principal, protagonist, deuteragonist, hero, heroine, villain, antihero, bad guy, juvenile, ingénue, soubrette, motion picture actor, stage actor, trouper, impersonator, mimic, mime, clown, comic, ventriloquist, pantomimist, monologist, performance artist, mummer, masker, heavy lead, heavy, romantic lead, matinee idol, theatrical performer, dramatic artist, artiste, headliner, understudy, stand-in, personator, *histrio* (Latin), extra, bit player, walk-on, supernumerary, spear carrier*, ham*, straight man, straight person, barnstormer, gallery player, scene stealer, punchinello, harlequin, *farceur* (French), vaudevillian, song and dance man, top banana, second banana; see also **actress, cast** 2.
2. [A person who does or participates in something] — *Syn.* participant, doer, performer; see **doer, participant.**
**actress,** *n.* — *Syn.* actor, female performer, member of the cast, ingénue, comedienne, tragedienne, prima donna, leading woman, leading lady, heroine, star, starlet, supporting actress, character actress, soubrette, chorus girl, showgirl; see also **actor** 1, **cast** 2.
**actual,** *modif.* 1. [True] — *Syn.* original, real, exact; see **genuine** 1.
2. [Existent] — *Syn.* concrete, present, tangible, substantive; see **real** 2.
*See Synonym Study at* REAL.
**actuality,** *n.* — *Syn.* materiality, substance, substantiality, fact; see **fact** 1, **reality** 1.
**actualize,** *v.* — *Syn.* realize, bring about, make real, make good; see **achieve** 1, **complete** 1.
**actually,** *modif.* — *Syn.* truly, in fact, as a matter of fact; see **really** 1.
**act up,** *v.* — *Syn.* carry on, create a disturbance, cause

trouble, malfunction; see **break down** 3, **hurt** 4, **misbehave.**
**acumen,** *n.* — *Syn.* keenness, insight, penetration, perspicacity, percipience, discernment, sharpness, acuteness, astuteness, sagacity, cleverness, shrewdness, accuracy, intelligence, wisdom, long-headedness, understanding, comprehension, intuition, sensitivity, vision, grasp, perception, smartness, brilliance, farsightedness, keensightedness, awareness, cunning, guile, acuity, wit, quickness of perception, perspicuity, mental acuteness, mother wit, *esprit* (French), foresightedness, quick sense, quickness, intellect, discrimination, judgment, good taste, refinement, brains*, horse sense*, know-how*, high I.Q.*, smarts*. — *Ant.* STUPIDITY, dullness, obtuseness.
**acute,** *modif.* 1. [Pointed] — *Syn.* sharp-pointed, spiked, keen; see **sharp** 2.
2. [Crucial] — *Syn.* critical, crucial, decisive, severe, serious, grave, dangerous, important, vital, intense, pressing, urgent, desperate, dire, drastic; see also **crucial.**
3. [Shrewd] — *Syn.* clever, astute, penetrating; see **intelligent** 1, **judicious.**
4. [Sharp] — *Syn.* severe, keen, cutting; see **intense, painful** 1.
5. [Discerning] — *Syn.* discriminating, penetrating, sensitive, perceptive, keen, sharp; see also **observant** 1.

---

**SYN.** — **acute** suggests severe intensification of a condition that is sharply approaching a climax /an *acute* shortage of workers/; **critical** is applied to a crisis or a turning point that will decisively determine an outcome /the situation was *critical*; a *critical* point in the negotiations/; **crucial** comes into contrast with **critical** where a trial determining a course of action rather than a decisive turning point is involved /a *crucial* debate on foreign policy/ *See also Synonym Study at* SHARP.

---

**acutely,** *modif.* — *Syn.* keenly, sharply, severely; see **very.**
**acuteness,** *n.* 1. [Intensity] — *Syn.* forcefulness, severity, fierceness; see **intensity** 1.
2. [Shrewdness] — *Syn.* cleverness, keenness, astuteness; see **acumen.**
**A.D.,** *abbr.* — *Syn. anno Domini* (Latin), in the year of our Lord, after the birth of Christ, Christian Era, C.E., Common Era, modern times.
**ad*,** *n.* — *Syn.* advertisement, commercial, announcement, notice; see **advertisement** 1, 2.
**adage,** *n.* — *Syn.* aphorism, saying, maxim; see **proverb, saying.**
*See Synonym Study at* SAYING.
**adamant,** *modif.* — *Syn.* fixed, inflexible, set, settled; see **inflexible, resolute** 2.
*See Synonym Study at* INFLEXIBLE.
**adapt,** *v.* 1. [To alter or adjust] — *Syn.* modify, adjust, readjust; see **accommodate** 2, **change** 1.
2. [To adapt oneself] — *Syn.* accustom, acclimate, accommodate; see **change** 4, **conform.**
*See Synonym Study at* ADJUST.
**adaptability,** *n.* — *Syn.* changeability, flexibility, versatility, adjustability, ambidexterity, many-sidedness, tractability, conformability, ductility, accommodativeness, pliableness, pliancy, malleability, amenability, docility, compliancy, pliability, plasticity.
**adaptable,** *modif.* — *Syn.* pliant, tractable, pliable, versatile; see **docile, flexible** 1, **pliable** 2.
**adaptation,** *n.* 1. [The state or process of being adapted] — *Syn.* adjustment, conversion, adoption, reworking, revision, arrangement, modification, altera-

tion, change, accommodation, acclimatization, familiarization, acculturation, habituation, conditioning, fitting, realignment, natural selection, evolution; see also **adjustment** 1, **change** 1.

**2.** [Condition resulting from adaptation, sense 1] — *Syn.* acclimatization, correspondence, compliance; see **agreement** 2, **change** 2.

**adapted,** *modif.* — *Syn.* suitable, becoming, fitting; see **fit** 1, 2.

**add,** *v.* **1.** [To combine numbers into a sum] — *Syn.* total, sum, sum up, figure, figure up, compute, calculate, do a sum, tally, count up, foot up, cipher up, add up, cast up, do simple addition, run over, enumerate, reckon, tell off, score, tote up★. — *Ant.* subtract, DECREASE, take away.

**2.** [To join so as to increase] — *Syn.* append, annex, supplement, affix, attach, unite, combine, superimpose, tack on, hitch on, clap on★; see also **join** 1.

**3.** [To make a further remark] — *Syn.* say further, continue, write further, append, add a postscript, reply, go on.

**adder,** *n.* — *Syn.* viper, asp, snake.
Adders include: European, spotted, puff adder, hognose snake, dwarf puff, night adder, milk adder, milk snake; see also **snake.**

**addict,** *n.* — *Syn.* habitué, devotee, fan, enthusiast, fanatic, adherent, practitioner, drug abuser, user, substance abuser, alcoholic, chain smoker, junkie★, fiend★, nut★, freak★, regular★, -aholic (*used in combination*), druggie★, pill popper★, hophead★, customer★, head★, dope fiend★, drug fiend★, cokey★, mainliner★, crackhead★, snowbird★, tripper★, acidhead★, pothead★, speed freak★.

**addicted (to),** *modif.* — *Syn.* given over, given up to, dependent on, disposed to, inclined, habituated, prone, accustomed, attached, abandoned, wedded, devoted, predisposed, used to, imbued with, fanatic about, obsessed with, wont to, in the habit of, under the influence of, in favor of, hooked on★, strung out★. — *Ant.* UNACCUSTOMED, disinclined, averse to.

**addiction,** *n.* — *Syn.* dependence, habit, fixation, craving, compulsion, habituation, inclination, bent, enslavement, substance abuse, alcoholism, monkey on one's back★, jones★; see also **habit** 1, **obsession.**

**addition,** *n.* **1.** [The process of adding] — *Syn.* reckoning, computing, totaling, summing up, summation, enlarging, accruing, increasing, expanding, tabulating, counting, accretion, joining, uniting, appending, annexing. — *Ant.* subtraction, REDUCTION, lessening.

**2.** [That which has been added] — *Syn.* interest, raise, additive, adjunct, augmentation, addendum, profit, profits, dividend, dividends, bonus, commission, increment, supplement, gain, insert, accretion, accession, accrual, subordinate part, enhancement, aggrandizement, reinforcement, appendage, appendix, accessory, appurtenance, attachment, extension, increase, annex, affix, appreciation. — *Ant.* LOSS, REDUCTION, shrinkage.

**3.** [An architectural extension] — *Syn.* wing, ell, annex, spare room, extension; see also **room** 2.

**additional,** *modif.* — *Syn.* supplementary, new, further, added; see **extra.**

**addleheaded,** *modif.* — *Syn.* addlebrained, muddled, confused, idiotic; see **stupid** 1.

**address,** *n.* **1.** [A formal speech] — *Syn.* oration, lecture, speech, sermon; see **speech** 3.

**2.** [Place at which one may be reached] — *Syn.* residence, home, quarters, dwelling, headquarters, place of business, location, box number; street, number, and zip code; see also **business** 4, **home** 1, **hotel.**

**3.** [Directions for delivery] — *Syn.* inscription, label, superscription, directions.

**4.** [Behavior] — *Syn.* delivery, manner(s), bearing, habit(s), approach; see also **behavior** 1.

**5.** [Storage place in a computer] — *Syn.* source of output, position of input, data storage; see **place** 3, **position** 1.

*See Synonym Study at* SPEECH.

**address,** *v.* **1.** [To provide directions for delivery] — *Syn.* inscribe, label, mark, direct, prepare for mailing, superscribe; see also **write** 2.

**2.** [To speak formally to an assemblage] — *Syn.* lecture, discourse on, discuss, give a talk, make a speech, deliver an address, speak, take the floor, orate, pontificate, declaim, harangue, rant, expatiate on, sermonize, speechify★, spout★, spout off★, spiel★, take the stump★, take the soapbox★, take the platform★, do a spellbinder★.

**3.** [To communicate in a formal way] — *Syn.* petition, appeal to, write to, speak to, lay a matter before someone, plead, enter a plea for, seek redress for, enter a suit for, approach, greet; see also **ask** 1, **greet.**

**address (oneself) to,** *v.* — *Syn.* devote (oneself) to, turn to, apply (oneself) to, direct one's energies to; see **try** 1, **undertake.**

**add to,** *v.* — *Syn.* augment, amplify, expand; see **increase** 1.

**add up★,** *v.* — *Syn.* be plausible, seem reasonable, stand to reason, hold water★; see **make sense.**

**add up to,** *v.* — *Syn.* indicate, signify, imply; see **mean** 1.

**adept,** *modif.* — *Syn.* skilled, skillful, proficient, capable; see **able** 1, 2.

**adequacy,** *n.* — *Syn.* capacity, sufficiency, enough, competence; see **fitness** 1, **plenty.**

**adequate,** *modif.* — *Syn.* sufficient, equal to the need, satisfactory; see **enough** 1, **fair** 2, **fit** 1, 2, **sufficient.**

*See Synonym Study at* SUFFICIENT.

**adequately,** *modif.* **1.** [Enough] — *Syn.* sufficiently, enough, appropriately, suitably, fittingly, satisfactorily, amply, abundantly, copiously, capably, competently; see also **well** 2, 3. — *Ant.* INADEQUATELY, badly, insufficiently.

**2.** [Passably] — *Syn.* acceptably, passably, tolerably, decently, presentably, modestly, not too badly, fairly well, well enough, up to a standard, up to a minimal standard, up to code, satisfying the code, not so badly as it might be, pleasantly enough, not disgracefully, to an acceptable degree, in an ordinary way, in an ordinary manner, all right. — *Ant.* BADLY, poorly, unsatisfactorily.

**adherent,** *n.* — *Syn.* follower, partisan, disciple, backer; see **follower.**

*See Synonym Study at* FOLLOWER.

**adhere (to),** *v.* **1.** [To serve] — *Syn.* follow, be devoted to, practice; see **obey** 2.

**2.** [To conform to] — *Syn.* observe, abide by, comply with; see **follow** 2.

**3.** [To stick to] — *Syn.* stay attached, cling, hold fast; see **stick** 1.

*See Synonym Study at* STICK.

**adhesive,** *modif.* — *Syn.* adhering, adherent, sticking, sticky, glutinous, resinous, gummy, viscid, viscous, gluey, gelatinous, waxy, gummed, pasty, clinging, agglutinant, tenacious, hugging, conformable, sticking fast, tending to adhere, emplastic, mucilaginous. — *Ant.* LOOSE, inadhesive, slippery.

**adhesive**, *n.* Varieties include: paste, glue, mucilage, cement, epoxy, cyanocrylate, rubber cement, library paste, gluten, Scotch tape (trademark), adhesive tape, masking tape, draftsman's tape, duct tape.

**adieu**, *n.* — *Syn.* goodbye, farewell, so long*, see you later*; see **goodbye**.

**ad infinitum**, *modif.* — *Syn.* endlessly, forever, ceaselessly; see **forever** 1, **regularly** 2.

**ad interim**, *modif.* — *Syn.* temporary, interim, acting; see **temporary**.

*See Synonym Study at* TEMPORARY.

**adjacent**, *modif.* — *Syn.* nearby, neighboring, adjoining, contiguous, bordering, abutting, tangent, juxtaposed, proximate, next, beside, alongside, facing, conterminous, coterminous, close by; see also **near** 1.

*SYN.* — **adjacent** things may or may not be in actual contact with each other, but they are not separated by things of the same kind [*adjacent* angles, *adjacent* farmhouses]; that which is **adjoining** something else touches it at some point or along a line [*adjoining* rooms]; things are **contiguous** when they touch along the whole or most of one side [*contiguous* farms]; **tangent** implies contact at a single, nonintersecting point with a curved line or surface [a line *tangent* to a circle]; **neighboring** things lie near to each other [*neighboring* villages]

**adjective**, *n.* — *Syn.* modifier, article, determiner, attribute, attributive, qualifier, adjectival, descriptive word, descriptive term, limiting word, limiter, dependent, adjectival construction, identifier, qualifying word, qualifying term, attributive name, adjunct, adnoun.

**adjoin**, *v.* 1. [To be close to] — *Syn.* abut, lie beside, be adjacent to; see **join** 3.
2. [To join] — *Syn.* unite, append, annex; see **join** 1.

**adjoining**, *modif.* — *Syn.* adjacent, neighboring, connecting, bordering; see **adjacent**.

*See Synonym Study at* ADJACENT.

**adjourn**, *v.* — *Syn.* postpone, dismiss, recess, prorogue; see **suspend** 2.

*See Synonym Study at* SUSPEND.

**adjournment**, *n.* 1. [Recess] — *Syn.* intermission, pause, break; see **recess** 1.
2. [Delay] — *Syn.* postponement, putting off, deferment; see **delay** 1.

**adjudicate**, *v.* — *Syn.* mediate, settle, adjudge, arbitrate; see **decide**.

**adjunct**, *n.* 1. [Something added] — *Syn.* supplement, subordinate part, minor detail; see **addition** 2.
2. [Assistant] — *Syn.* auxiliary, aide, associate, collaborator; see **assistant**.

**adjust**, *v.* 1. [To bring into agreement] — *Syn.* change, modify, alter, adapt, accommodate, settle, arrange, reconcile, conform, resolve, coordinate, regulate, harmonize, acclimate, accustom, get used to, acclimatize, habituate, accord, attune, rectify, patch up, arbitrate, mediate, redress, set right, put to rights, straighten, standardize, make correspond, gear to, make jibe*; see also **accommodate** 2.
2. [To settle a claim] — *Syn.* make an adjustment, make payment, arrange a settlement; see **settle** 9.
3. [To place or regulate parts] — *Syn.* regulate, set, repair, fix, put in order, tune, tune up, fine-tune, calibrate, synchronize, customize, connect, square, balance, stabilize, tighten, fit, focus, tailor, readjust, rectify, correct, mend, improve, overhaul, grind, sharpen, renovate, collate, bring into line, align, put in working order, temper,

service, do a repair job, trouble-shoot, tweak*, revamp*, put in A-1 condition*.

*SYN.* — **adjust** implies the bringing of things into proper relation through the use of skill or judgment [to *adjust* brakes, to *adjust* differences]; **adapt** implies a modification to suit new conditions and suggests flexibility [to *adapt* oneself to a new environment]; **accommodate** implies a subordinating of one thing to the needs of another and suggests concession or compromise [he *accommodated* his walk to the halting steps of his friend]; **conform** means to bring into or act in harmony with some standard pattern, principle, etc. [to *conform* to specifications]

**adjustable**, *modif.* — *Syn.* adaptable, alterable, stretchable, tractable; see **flexible** 1, **movable**.

**adjustment**, *n.* 1. [The act of adjusting] — *Syn.* alteration, modification, fixing, mending, repairing, improvement, balancing, adaptation, acclimation, orientation, shaping, readjustment, tuning, fine-tuning, fitting, alignment, calibration, organization, standardization, conformance, alleviation, regulating, regulation, arrangement, correcting, correction, tweak*; see also **adaptation** 1, **change** 2. — *Ant.* DISTURBANCE, derangement, demolishing.
2. [The settlement of a claim] — *Syn.* settlement, arrangement, payment, pay, remuneration, reimbursement, stipulation, compensation, compromise, reconciliation, agreement, apportionment, allotment, share, benefit, stake, making up, mutual understanding.

**adjutant**, *n.* — *Syn.* helper, aide, auxiliary; see **assistant**.

**ad-lib***, *v.* — *Syn.* improvise, extemporize, make up; see **invent** 1.

**administer**, *v.* 1. [To manage] — *Syn.* conduct, direct, control, govern; see **command** 2, **govern**, **manage** 1.
2. [To apply or dispense] — *Syn.* provide with, give, bring in, furnish, dispense, regulate, apply, authorize, determine, administer to, minister to, serve, give out, mete out, serve out, measure out, deal out, supply, tender, offer, proffer, distribute, make application of, impose, contribute, disburse; see also **offer** 1.
3. [To inflict] — *Syn.* deal out, strike, deliver; see **inflict** 1.

*See Synonym Study at* GOVERN.

**administration**, *n.* 1. [The direction of affairs] — *Syn.* management, government, supervision, command, superintendence, guidance, surveillance, conduct, conducting, directing, direction, decision making, decision theory, oversight, organization, agency, authority, disposition, policing, treatment, handling, strategy, policy, ordering, legislation, jurisdiction, execution, regulation, performance, rule, order, enforcement, charge, control, power, husbandry, housekeeping, stewardship.
2. [Those who direct affairs] — *Syn.* directors, administrators, officers, supervisors, executives, superintendents, advisers, command, stewards, strategists, officials, committee, board, board of directors, board of governors, board of overseers, executive, executive office, executive branch, legislature, office of the president, president, presidency, chief executive, cabinet, ministry, commander, chair, chairman, general, admiral, commander in chief, central office, headquarters, the management, executive committee, bureau, consulate, consulate general, embassy, legation, department, Washington, chargé d'affaires, governmental power, party in power, brass*; front office*, the powers that be*, (insider's) insider*, the man*.

**3.** [The period in which an administration, sense 2, is operative] — *Syn.* term, term of office, tenure, presidency, regime, reign, dynasty, incumbency, power, stay.

**administrative,** *modif.* — *Syn.* executive, managerial, supervisory, controlling, deciding, jurisdictional, decisive, commanding, directing, directorial, regulatory, organizational, presiding, official, central, governmental, gubernatorial, directive, supervising, superintending, managing, magisterial, lawgiving, governing, legislative, ruling, authoritative, departmental, bureaucratic, determining, in control, in charge, policy-making.

**administrator,** *n.* — *Syn.* executive, director, manager, head, supervisor, president, vice-president, secretary, treasurer, executive secretary, head of the department, department head, chief executive, CEO, Chief Executive Officer, supervising director, chairman of the board of directors, director-general, vice-president in charge, person in authority, divisional supervisor, district manager, chair, chairman, dean, registrar, bursar, provost, principal, boss, chief, person in charge, superintendent, minister, bureaucrat, ambassador, leader, governor, controller, chief controller, consul, comptroller, commissar, premier, mayor, organizer, official, master, commander, captain, guardian, custodian, trustee, overseer, leader, inspector, impresario, producer, judge, key person, pencil pusher★, the brains★, big shot★, front office★, the guv'nor★.

**admirable,** *modif.* — *Syn.* praiseworthy, commendable, splendid, good; see **excellent, worthy.**

**admiral,** *n.* — *Syn.* commander of the fleet, commander in chief, naval officer, chief of naval operations, admiralty, office of the admiral; see also **officer** 3.
Admirals include: fleet admiral, admiral of the fleet, vice-admiral, rear admiral.

**admiration,** *n.* — *Syn.* esteem, respect, regard, appreciation, praise, deference, approbation, approval, estimation, encomium, fondness, favor, pleasurable contemplation, adoration, applause, glorification, idolization, idolatry, honor, recognition, prizing, valuing, liking, love, high regard, high opinion, great respect, reverence, veneration, homage, obeisance, kneeling, wonder, wonderment, awe. — *Ant.* contempt, condemnation, disregard.

**admire,** *v.* **1.** [To have regard for] — *Syn.* esteem, honor, applaud, praise, extol, respect, approve, revere, venerate, eulogize, panegyrize, laud, boost, glorify, reverence, hold dear, appreciate, credit, commend, favor, value, treasure, prize, look up to, rate highly, pay homage to, idolize, adore, worship, hail, put a high price on, regard with approbation, have a high opinion of, regard highly, wonder at, marvel at, think highly of, value highly, esteem highly, regard as fine, consider brilliant, think wonderful, hold in esteem, hold in respect, think well of, show deference to, set store by★, put on a pedestal★, make an ado about★, think the world of★. — *Ant.* CENSURE, deride, deprecate.
**2.** [To be fond of or delighted with] — *Syn.* cherish, contemplate pleasurably, delight in, relish; see **like** 1, 2.
*See Synonym Study at* REGARD.

**admirer,** *n.* **1.** [One who admires a person or thing] — *Syn.* fan, devotee, fancier, supporter; see **enthusiast** 1, **follower.**
**2.** [A suitor] — *Syn.* wooer, adorer, sweetheart, suitor; see **lover** 1.

**admissible,** *modif.* — *Syn.* allowable, allowed, permissible, permitted, acceptable, proper, suitable, right, just, fair, passable, probable, possible, tolerable, fit, approvable, reasonable, justifiable, rational, logical, warranted, legal, lawful, licit, legitimate, not impossible,

warrantable, considerable, concedable, not unlikely, worthy, unprohibited, relevant, appropriate, likely, applicable, pertinent, all right, okay★. — *Ant.* unfair, banned, inadmissible.

**admission,** *n.* **1.** [The act of entering] — *Syn.* admittance, entry, ingress, access; see **entrance** 1.
**2.** [The act of granting entrance] — *Syn.* acceptance, admittance, permission, reception, welcome, recognition, acknowledgment, certification, confirmation, designation, selection, initiation, induction, entree. — *Ant.* REMOVAL, rejection, expulsion.
**3.** [The entrance fee] — *Syn.* charge, cover charge, fee, entrance fee, ticket, price, check, dues, charges, demand, toll, tax, minimum, donation, cover★, gate★, tariff★.
**4.** [Something acknowledged] — *Syn.* statement, disclosure, confession, profession, avowal, acknowledgment, concession, allowance, divulgence, declaration, affirmation, confirmation, assertion, accession, testimony, attestation, testimonial, averment, allegation, deposition, affidavit. — *Ant.* DENIAL, disallowance, repudiation.
**5.** [The act of admitting] — *Syn.* acknowledgment, concession, granting, confession; see **acknowledgment** 1.

**admit,** *v.* **1.** [To grant entrance] — *Syn.* receive, give access to, allow entrance to; see **receive** 4.
**2.** [To confess] — *Syn.* acknowledge, confess, own, indicate, disclose, divulge, reveal, avow, declare, proclaim, communicate, make known, confide, open up, unbosom oneself, bare, uncover, expose, bring to light, tell, relate, narrate, go into details, make a clean breast of, break down and confess, plead guilty, tell all★, own up★, fess up★, come clean★, level with★, make no bones about★, let slip★, talk★, sing★, cough up★, spill the beans★, spill★, let on★, let one's hair down★, let it all hang out★, come out into the open★, come out of the closet★. — *Ant.* HIDE, cover up, obscure.
**3.** [To acknowledge] — *Syn.* concede, allow, acknowledge, grant, accept, agree, confess, realize, indicate, concur, avow, consent, accede, acquiesce, yield, tolerate, recognize, declare, profess, adopt, assent, accord, confirm, affirm, approve, subscribe to, go along with, coincide, assume, make way for, credit, give credence to, fall in with. — *Ant.* DENY, differ, disagree.
**4.** [To permit] — *Syn.* let, allow, grant; see **allow** 1.

*SYN.* — **admit** is applied to assent that has been elicited by persuasion and implies a conceding of a fact or point of view [I'll *admit* you're right]; **acknowledge** implies the reluctant disclosure of something one might have kept secret [he *acknowledged* the child as his]; **own** denotes an informal acknowledgment of something in connection with oneself [to *own* to a liking for turnips]; **avow** implies an open, emphatic declaration, often as an act of affirmation; **confess** is applied to a formal acknowledgment of a sin, crime, etc., but in a weakened sense is used in making simple declarations, esp. of something about oneself felt to be shameful, awkward, or damaging [I *confess* I've never understood it] *See also Synonym Study at* RECEIVE.

**admonish,** *v.* **1.** [To reprimand] — *Syn.* reprove, chide, rebuke; see **scold.**
**2.** [To exhort] — *Syn.* advise, counsel, caution; see **advise** 1, **warn.**
*See Synonym Study at* ADVISE.

**admonition,** *n.* — *Syn.* advice, caution, exhortation, reproof; see **rebuke, warning.**

**adolescence,** *n.* — *Syn.* minority, puberty, teens, youth; see **youth** 1.

**adolescent,** *modif.* — *Syn.* teenage, pubescent, juvenile, youthful, young, growing, underage, half-grown, in one's teens, immature, unsettled, callow, puerile, sophomoric, sweet sixteen*; see also **young** 1, 2.
*See Synonym Study at* YOUNG.

**adolescent,** *n.* — *Syn.* teenager, youngster, minor; see **youth** 3.

**adopt,** *v.* **1.** [To take as a son or daughter] — *Syn.* take in, raise, take from an orphanage, sign adoption papers for, take into one's family, make one's heir, take as one's own, foster, rear, bring up, mother, father, parent, give one's name to. — *Ant.* give up, DISINHERIT, cast out.
**2.** [To take as one's own] — *Syn.* embrace, appropriate, seize, take up, take over, choose, select, assume, use, take to oneself, utilize, imitate, borrow, adapt for use, make one's own, espouse, affiliate, mimic. — *Ant.* DENY, repudiate, reject.
**3.** [To vote acceptance] — *Syn.* affirm, assent (to), ratify; see **approve** 1.

**adoption,** *n.* **1.** [Selection] — *Syn.* choosing, appropriation, choice; see **selection** 1.
**2.** [Acceptance] — *Syn.* confirmation, enactment, approval; see **permission.**

**adorable*,** *modif.* — *Syn.* delightful, lovable, cute, appealing; see **charming.**

**adoration,** *n.* **1.** [Worship] — *Syn.* devotion, homage, veneration; see **worship** 1.
**2.** [Love] — *Syn.* ardor, affection, devotion; see **love** 1.

**adore,** *v.* **1.** [To worship] — *Syn.* venerate, revere, glorify; see **revere, worship** 2.
**2.** [To love] — *Syn.* cherish, treasure, love, prize; see **love** 1.
*See Synonym Study at* REVERE.

**adorn,** *v.* — *Syn.* beautify, embellish, ornament, enhance; see **decorate.**
*See Synonym Study at* DECORATE.

**adorned,** *modif.* — *Syn.* trimmed, decked, garnished, decorated; see **ornate** 1.

**adornment,** *n.* **1.** [The act of decorating] — *Syn.* ornamentation, embellishment, gilding; see **decoration** 1.
**2.** [A decoration] — *Syn.* ornament, trimming, frill, accessory; see **decoration** 1.

**adrift,** *modif.* — *Syn.* loose, drifting, directionless; see **afloat, bewildered, uncertain** 2.

**adroit,** *modif.* — *Syn.* dexterous, clever, skillful, adept; see **able** 1, 2, **dexterous.**
*See Synonym Study at* DEXTEROUS.

**adroitness,** *n.* — *Syn.* deftness, dexterity, skill, cleverness; see **ability** 2.

**adulation,** *n.* — *Syn.* idolization, hero worship, applause, laudation; see **admiration, flattery, praise** 1, 2, **worship** 1.

**adult,** *modif.* — *Syn.* of age, mature, grown, developed; see **mature** 1, **ripe** 2.
*See Synonym Study at* RIPE.

**adult,** *n.* — *Syn.* mature person, grown-up, fully developed member of a species; see **man** 2, **woman** 1.

**adulterate,** *v.* — *Syn.* weaken, mix with, intermix, alloy, amalgamate, dilute, water down, water, infiltrate, infect, lessen, reduce, concoct, infuse, mingle with, commingle, blend, taint, pollute, debase, corrupt, contaminate, depreciate, cheapen, devalue, vitiate, muddle, impair, make lower in quality, thin out, defile, denature, degrade, deteriorate, dissolve, make impure, tamper with, simplify, falsify, cut*, doctor*. — *Ant.* PURIFY, cleanse, maintain.

**adulterated,** *modif.* — *Syn.* diluted, mixed, contaminated; see **impure** 1.

**adulteration,** *n.* — *Syn.* corruption, deterioration, contamination; see **pollution.**

**adulterous,** *modif.* — *Syn.* illicit, extramarital, unfaithful, unchaste, philandering, promiscuous, immoral, extracurricular*; see also **lewd** 2.

**adultery,** *n.* — *Syn.* unlicensed intercourse, infidelity, cuckoldry, extramarital affair; see **fornication.**

**advance,** *n.* **1.** [The act of moving forward] — *Syn.* progression, motion, approach; see **progress** 1.
**2.** [Improvement] — *Syn.* progress, advancement, new development, stride; see **improvement** 1, 2.
**3.** [Increase] — *Syn.* rise, progress, boost; see **increase** 1.
**4.** [Loan] — *Syn.* accommodation, allowance, credit; see **loan.**
**5.** [Suggestion; *usually plural*] — *Syn.* overture, approach, proposal; see **proposal** 1, **suggestion** 1.
**in advance** — *Syn.* ahead of time, beforehand, up front, earlier; see **ahead** 2, **before** 1.

**advance,** *v.* **1.** [To move forward] — *Syn.* progress, proceed, move on, forge ahead, press on, stride forward, push ahead, go on, go forth, gain ground, speed on, make headway, storm across, step forward, come to the front, conquer territory, march on, get on, move onward, continue ahead, push on, press on, eat up ground*, tear ahead*. — *Ant.* HALT, stop, stand still.
**2.** [To cause to move forward] — *Syn.* launch, propel, drive; see **push** 2.
**3.** [To propose] — *Syn.* set forth, introduce, suggest; see **propose** 1.
**4.** [To promote] — *Syn.* further, promote, forward, encourage; see **promote** 1.
**5.** [To promote in rank or station] — *Syn.* raise, graduate, elevate; see **promote** 2.
**6.** [To accelerate] — *Syn.* dispatch, speed up, move up, quicken; see **hasten** 2.
**7.** [To lend] — *Syn.* loan, provide with, furnish; see **lend** 1.
**8.** [To pay] — *Syn.* make payment, prepay, pay up; see **pay** 1.
**9.** [To improve] — *Syn.* develop, make progress, get better; see **improve** 2.
*See Synonym Study at* PROMOTE.

**advanced,** *modif.* **1.** [Ahead in progress or complexity] — *Syn.* precocious, exceptional, high-level, upper-level; see **difficult** 1, 2, **excellent, superior.**
**2.** [Aged] — *Syn.* seasoned, venerable, far along in life; see **old** 1, 3.
**3.** [Progressive] — *Syn.* radical, unconventional, ahead of the times, forward-looking; see **liberal** 2.
**4.** [In front] — *Syn.* forward, in advance, first; see **ahead** 2.
*See Synonym Study at* LIBERAL.

**advancement,** *n.* **1.** [Promotion in rank] — *Syn.* preferment, elevation, raise; see **promotion** 1.
**2.** [Progress] — *Syn.* gain, headway, progression; see **improvement** 1, **progress** 1.

**advantage,** *n.* **1.** [Preferred condition or circumstance] — *Syn.* luck, favor, approval, help, aid, sanction, leeway, good, patronage, support, preference, choice, odds, protection, start, leg up, helping hand, upper hand, leverage, purchase, hold, favoring circumstance, dominating position, favorable opportunity, superior situation, best estate, vantage, ground, play point, pull*, edge*, ace in the hole*, whip hand*, card up one's sleeve*, drop*, jump*. — *Ant.* handicap, DISADVANTAGE, drawback.
**2.** [The result of having an advantage, sense 1] — *Syn.*

dominance, superiority, supremacy, lead, influence, vantage, upper hand, power, resources, wealth, mastery, profit, gain, authority, prestige, recognition, position, eminence, preeminence, primacy, hold, sway, precedence, ascendancy, prevalence. — *Ant.* FAILURE, hindrance, impotence.

**3.** [Benefit] — *Syn.* good, gain, benefit, profit, welfare, avail, interest, expediency, improvement, return, behalf, account, sake, worth, comfort, gratification, convenience, help, utility, use, success, emolument, windfall, satisfaction, consolation, enjoyment, pleasure, solace, bounty, favor, boon, weal, blessing, service, compensation, asset, prize, mileage*. — *Ant.* MISFORTUNE, calamity, catastrophe.

**have the advantage of**— *Syn.* be superior, have the opportunity, be privileged; see **succeed** 1.

**take advantage of 1.** [To make use of] — *Syn.* avail oneself of, profit by, make the most of; see **use** 1.

**2.** [To make unfair use of] — *Syn.* impose upon, exploit, abuse; see **abuse** 1, **deceive**.

**to advantage**— *Syn.* successfully, advantageously, well; see **helpfully**.

**advantageous,** *modif.* — *Syn.* beneficial, favorable, profitable, worthwhile; see **helpful** 1, **profitable**.

**advent,** *n.* — *Syn.* approach, coming, appearance; see **arrival** 1.

**adventure,** *n.* — *Syn.* exploit, venture, escapade, experience; see **enterprise** 1, **event** 1, 2, **venture**.

**adventurer,** *n.* **1.** [One who seeks adventure] — *Syn.* explorer, pirate, globe-trotter, traveler, free lance, soldier of fortune, knight-errant, daredevil, swashbuckler, hero, heroine, pioneer, mountain climber, wild game hunter, record breaker, stunt flyer, Don Quixote, Robin Hood, romantic, dragonslayer, entrepreneur; see also **pioneer** 2, **traveler.**

**2.** [One who seeks wealth or power by dubious schemes] — *Syn.* charlatan, opportunist, rogue, adventuress; see **opportunist, rascal.**

**adventurous,** *modif.* — *Syn.* bold, adventuresome, courageous; see **brave** 1.

**adverb,** *n.* — *Syn.* qualifier, modifier, adverbial modifier, adverbial, qualifying construction, limiting word, intensifier, intensive.

**adversary,** *n.* — *Syn.* opponent, rival, enemy, foe; see **enemy** 1, 2, **opponent** 1, 2, 3.

See Synonym Study at OPPONENT.

**adverse,** *modif.* **1.** [Hostile] — *Syn.* antagonistic, conflicting, inimical; see **opposing** 2, **unfriendly** 1.

**2.** [Unfavorable] — *Syn.* unpropitious, inopportune, disadvantageous; see **unfavorable** 2.

**adversely,** *modif.* — *Syn.* unfavorably, negatively, with prejudice, skeptically, resentfully, with scarce sympathy, without sympathy, unsympathetically, coolly, with a jaundiced eye, with a cold eye; see also **unfavorably.**

**adversity,** *n.* — *Syn.* misfortune, reverse, trouble; see **affliction, difficulty** 1, 2, **misfortune** 1.

**advertise,** *v.* **1.** [To make public] — *Syn.* publicize, proclaim, herald, announce, broadcast, blazon, declare, notify, promulgate, display, exhibit, show, reveal, expose, disclose, unmask, divulge, uncover, communicate, publish abroad, issue, print, circulate, placard, show off, parade, flaunt, vent, post, propagate, disseminate, inform, celebrate, propagandize, spread, splash, put on display, unveil, air, acquaint, apprise, noise abroad, make known, announce publicly, make a public announcement of, lay before the public, call public attention to, give public notice of, go public, bruit about, blaze abroad, trumpet, give out;

press-agent*, plug*, play up*. — *Ant.* HIDE, conceal, cover.

**2.** [To solicit business] — *Syn.* promote, praise, publicize, cry up, sell, build up, vaunt, commend to the public, display, exhibit, circularize, advance, give samples, sponsor, endorse, ballyhoo*, boost*, push*, plug*, tout*, hype*, puff*, press-agent*, beat the drum for*, make a pitch for*.

**advertised,** *modif.* — *Syn.* announced, posted, noted, publicized, promoted, celebrated, heralded, billed, published, printed, pasted up, made public, broadcast, emphasized, pointed out, built up, told of, displayed, exhibited, shown, offered, presented, put on sale, up for sale, flaunted, plugged*, boosted*, ballyhooed*, pushed*, touted*. — *Ant.* unannounced, forgotten, suppressed.

**advertisement,** *n.* **1.** [A public notice] — *Syn.* proclamation, notification, declaration, broadcast, propaganda sheet, communication, publication, display, bill, placard, poster, billboard, printed public notice; see also **announcement** 2, 3.

**2.** [Anything intended to promote a sale] — *Syn.* commercial, announcement, notice, publicity, display, window display, circular, flier, handbill, broadside, billboard, display advertisement, classified advertisement, sample, endorsement, ad*, want ad*, plug*, ballyhoo*, blurb*, pitch*, spot*, trailer*, throwaway*, spread*, color spread*, classified*, promo*, hype*, puffery*.

**advertiser,** *n.* — *Syn.* dealer, merchant, peddler, hawker, sponsor, promoter, adman, pitchman*, huckster*; see also **businessperson, publicist.**

**advertising,** *n.* **1.** [Calling goods to public attention] — *Syn.* promotion, promoting, publicity, publicizing, circularization, billing, posting, placarding, announcing, displaying, broadcasting, advocacy, Madison Avenue, ballyhooing*, plugging*, pushing*, buildup*, drumbeating*, puffery*, hype*, hucksterism*; see also **publicity** 3.

**2.** [Anything intended to advertise] — *Syn.* announcement, window display, exhibit; see **advertisement** 1, 2.

**advice,** *n.* — *Syn.* guidance, counsel, recommendation, instruction(s), consultation, suggestion(s), preaching, information, admonition, exhortation, forewarning, warning, caution, a word to the wise, injunction, charge, lesson, directions, advocacy, opinion, recommendation regarding a course of action, advisement, encouragement, persuasion, dissuasion, prescription, urging, proposition, proposal, view, help, aid, judgment, word, input, pointer*, tip*.

**advisability,** *n.* — *Syn.* recommendability, suitability, fitness; see **propriety** 1.

**advisable,** *modif.* — *Syn.* fitting, prudent, expedient, desirable; see **fit** 1.

**advise,** *v.* **1.** [To give advice] — *Syn.* recommend, counsel, prescribe, exhort, direct, admonish, warn, caution, suggest, guide, steer, instruct, advocate, urge, prompt, encourage, coax, persuade, induce, charge, enjoin, dissuade, teach, propose, tell, preach, give advice to, give counsel to, forewarn, entreat, hint, point out, opine, seek to persuade, wise up*, straighten out*, give the facts*, put one's two cents worth in*.

**2.** [To give information] — *Syn.* notify, inform, apprise, make known; see **notify** 1.

---

SYN. — **advise** means simply to recommend a course of action and implies that the giver of the advice has knowledge or experience; **counsel** implies serious deliberation of weighty matters; **admonish** suggests earnest, gently reproving advice concerning a fault, error, etc., given by someone fitted to do so by age or position; to **caution** or **warn** is to give advice that puts one on guard against possible danger, failure, etc.; **warn** is used especially when a serious danger is involved

---

**advised,** *modif.* — *Syn.* thought out, prudent, considered, well-considered; see **deliberate** 1.

**advisedly,** *modif.* — *Syn.* consciously, thoughtfully, intentionally, after due consideration; see **deliberately**.

**adviser,** *n.* — *Syn.* counselor, consultant, guide, mentor, counsel, lawyer, attorney, solicitor, instructor, preceptor, tutor, teacher, coach, therapist, monitor, admonitor, back-seat driver, Solon, Nestor, doctor, judge, priest, confessor, confidant, informant, helper, partner, referee, director, prompter, expert, authority, cabinet, right-hand man*; see also **friend** 1, **specialist**, **teacher** 1.

**advisory,** *modif.* — *Syn.* consulting, consultative, consultatory, having power to advise, giving advice, deliberative, admonitory, monitory, counseling, instructive, instructional, prudential.

**advisory,** *n.* — *Syn.* report, warning, bulletin; see **announcement** 2, **warning**.

**advocacy,** *n.* — *Syn.* support, promotion, backing, espousal; see **aid** 1.

**advocate,** *v.* 1. [To defend] — *Syn.* vindicate, plead for, uphold; see **defend** 3.
2. [To promote] — *Syn.* bolster, push, further, advance; see **promote** 1, **support** 2.
*See Synonym Study at* SUPPORT.

**aerial,** *modif.* — *Syn.* in the air, flying, aeronautical, birdlike, atmospheric, aeriform, air-minded, airy, ethereal, unsubstantial, fanciful, up above, lofty, elevated, highflying, airborne, on the ether waves*; see also **high** 2. — *Ant.* terrestrial, EARTHLY, on the ground.

**aeronautics,** *pl.n.* — *Syn.* aviation, air transportation, flight, flying, theory of flight, pneumatics, aerodynamics, aeromechanics, aerostatics, aerial navigation, airmanship, ballooning, gliding, aerodonetics, science of flight in aircraft, art of navigation in the air, volitation, aerial studies, aerial maneuvers, aerobatics, avigation.

**aesthete,** *n.* — *Syn.* connoisseur, person of good taste, dilettante; see **connoisseur**.
*See Synonym Study at* CONNOISSEUR.

**aesthetic,** *modif.* — *Syn.* artistic, aesthetically pleasing, tasteful, appreciative; see **artistic** 1, 2, **beautiful** 1.

**aesthetics,** *n.* — *Syn.* philosophy of art, principles of art, theory of art, study of beauty, the nature of beauty, philosophy of beauty, philosophy of the fine arts, philosophy of taste, artistic taste.

**afar,** *modif.* — *Syn.* far off, remote, far away; see **distant** 1.

**affable,** *modif.* — *Syn.* sociable, courteous, approachable, friendly; see **amiable**, **friendly** 1.
*See Synonym Study at* AMIABLE.

**affair,** *n.* 1. [Business; *often plural*] — *Syn.* concern, business, responsibility, matter, duty, topic, subject, case, circumstance, thing, question, office, function, transaction, proceeding, operation, activity, private concern, personal business, calling, employment, occupation, profession, pursuit, obligation, job, province, realm, interest, mission, assignment, task, undertaking.
2. [An illicit love affair] — *Syn.* liaison, rendezvous, intrigue, amour, affaire, intimacy, romance, relationship, love affair, affair of the heart, *affaire d'amour, affaire de coeur* (*both* French), entanglement, dalliance, fling*.
3. [Party] — *Syn.* entertainment, gathering, function, occasion; see **party** 1.

4. [A thing or event] — *Syn.* occurrence, matter, case, incident; see **event** 1, **thing** 8.

**affect,** *v.* 1. [To have an effect upon] — *Syn.* influence, sway, impress, alter, modify, change, transform, act on, work on, induce, move, be of importance to, concern, interest, be of interest to, impact on, hit, impair, harm, attack, afflict, strike, grip, seize; see also **influence**.
2. [To pretend] — *Syn.* assume, take on, feign, put on; see **pretend** 1.
3. [To move emotionally] — *Syn.* touch, stir, sway; see **move** 3.

---

**SYN.** — **affect** implies the producing of an effect strong enough to evoke a reaction /interest rates *affect* housing sales; her death *affected* us deeply/; to **influence** is to affect in such a way as to produce a change in action, thought, nature, or behavior /to *influence* legislation/; **impress** is used of that which produces a deep or lasting effect on the mind; **touch** and the stronger **move**, as considered here, are both applied to the arousing of sympathy or other emotion, but **move** also denotes influencing so as to bring about a change or a show of feeling /his story *moved* me to tears/; **sway** emphasizes influence intended to turn a person from a given course /threats will not *sway* us/ *See also Synonym Study at* PRETEND.

---

**affectation,** *n.* — *Syn.* pose, mannerism, simulation; see **pose, pretense** 1, 2.
*See Synonym Study at* POSE.

**affected,** *modif.* 1. [Being subject to influence] — *Syn.* moved, touched, melted, influenced, sympathetic, stirred, grieved, overwhelmed, moved to tears, hurt, injured, wakened, struck, impressed, brought to a realization of, overwrought, imbued with, devoured by, acted upon, worked upon, changed, altered, concerned, involved, interested, afflicted, attacked, stricken, compassionate, tender, sorry, troubled, distressed. — *Ant.* INDIFFERENT, unmoved, untouched.
2. [Full of affectation] — *Syn.* insincere, pretentious, pedantic, melodramatic, self-conscious, starchy, stagy, unnatural, histrionic, stilted, overprecise, superficial, mannered, precious, theatrical, stiff, strained, mincing, overdone, apish, ostentatious, showy, exhibitionistic, hollow, shallow, highfalutin*, arty*, too-too*, stuck-up*, la-di-da*. — *Ant.* SIMPLE, natural, genuine.
3. [Feigned] — *Syn.* simulated, imitated, faked, unnatural, counterfeited, falsified, shammed, studied, artificial, pretended, bogus, phony*, put-on*.

**affecting,** *modif.* — *Syn.* moving, touching, pathetic; see **moving** 2, **pitiful** 1.
*See Synonym Study at* MOVING.

**affection,** *n.* 1. [Warm liking] — *Syn.* love, fondness, friendship, liking, attachment, good will, predilection, warm feeling, warmth, heart, endearment, partiality, passion, ardor, attachment, friendliness, concern, regard, caring, desire, closeness, kindness, devotion, tenderness, solicitude, soft spot*; see also **love** 1. — *Ant.* HATRED, dislike, enmity.
2. [Disease] — *Syn.* disease, ailment, malady; see **disease**.
*See Synonym Study at* DISEASE, LOVE.

**affectionate,** *modif.* — *Syn.* loving, tender, fond, devoted; see **loving**.

**affidavit,** *n.* — *Syn.* testimony, sworn statement, affirmation; see **oath** 1.

**affiliate,** *n.* — *Syn.* subsidiary, branch, associate, member; see **branch** 1, **member** 1.

**affiliated,** *modif.* — *Syn.* associated, connected, united, hooked up with*; see **joined, related** 2, **united**.

See *Synonym Study* at RELATED.

**affiliation,** *n.* — *Syn.* association, connection, alliance; see **association** 1.

**affinity,** *n.* **1.** [Natural liking or attraction] — *Syn.* fondness, liking, sympathy, proclivity; see **affection** 1, **agreement** 2, **inclination** 1.

**2.** [Family relationship] — *Syn.* kinship, relation, relationship, bond, tie, connection, consanguinity, alliance, blood tie, association, attachment, union, propinquity, relationship by marriage, interconnection, parentage, fraternity, strain, lineage, heritage, agnation, cognation, breed, stock, affiliation.

**3.** [Attractive force] — *Syn.* attraction, magnetism, magnetization, ionization, appetency, combining power, instability, susceptibility, attractivity, elective affinity, chemical affinity, valence.

**4.** [Similarity] — *Syn.* likeness, resemblance, correspondence; see **similarity.**

**affirm,** *v.* — *Syn.* assert, repeat, insist; see **assert** 1, **declare** 1.

See *Synonym Study* at ASSERT.

**affirmation,** *n.* **1.** [An assertion] — *Syn.* statement, avowal, attestation; see **declaration** 1.

**2.** [A solemn declaration] — *Syn.* testimony, affidavit, sworn statement; see **oath** 1.

**3.** [Ratification] — *Syn.* confirmation, sanction, acceptance; see **confirmation** 1.

**affirmative,** *modif.* — *Syn.* agreeing, affirming, affirmatory, positive, consenting, concurring, approving, ratifying, assenting, supporting, complying, endorsing, acknowledging, acquiescent, establishing, corroborative, confirmatory, confirming. — *Ant.* NEGATIVE, contradictory, noncommittal.

**in the affirmative** — *Syn.* favorably, in assent, in agreement, with an affirmative answer; see **yes.**

**affix,** *v.* — *Syn.* fasten, attach, append; see **join** 1.

**afflict,** *v.* — *Syn.* try, torment, trouble, distress; see **bother** 2, 3, **hurt** 1.

**affliction,** *n.* — *Syn.* suffering, pain, distress, trouble, misfortune, tribulation, trial, hardship, adversity, misery, wretchedness, calamity, catastrophe, disaster, ailment, infirmity, sickness, disease, disorder, grief, woe, sorrow, care, unhappiness, heartache, cross, cross to bear, ordeal, torment, scourge, plight, difficulty, burden, curse, bane, visitation, tsoris*; see also **difficulty** 1, 2, **pain** 1, 2.

---

*SYN.* — **affliction** implies pain, suffering, or distress imposed by illness, loss, misfortune, etc.; **trial** suggests suffering that tries one's endurance, but in a weaker sense refers to annoyance that tries one's patience; **tribulation** connotes severe affliction continuing over a long and trying period; **misfortune** is applied to a circumstance or event involving adverse fortune or to the suffering or distress occasioned by it

---

**affluent,** *modif.* — *Syn.* wealthy, prosperous, well-to-do; see **rich** 1.

See *Synonym Study* at RICH.

**afford,** *v.* **1.** [To give] — *Syn.* provide, furnish, yield; see **produce** 1.

**2.** [To be in a position to buy or bear] — *Syn.* have enough for, spare the money for, allow, be able to, be disposed to, have the means for, be financially able, have sufficient means for, sustain, bear, manage, support, stand, spare the price of, be able to meet the expense of, incur without detriment to financial condition, bear the expense, bear the cost of, have the wherewithal, swing*.

**affront,** *n.* — *Syn.* insult, indignity, offense; see **insult.**

**affront,** *v.* — *Syn.* offend, insult, slight, provoke; see **insult, offend.**

See *Synonym Study* at OFFEND.

**afire,** *modif.* — *Syn.* on fire, aflame, burning, excited; see **burning** 1, **excited.**

**afloat,** *modif.* — *Syn.* adrift, drifting, floating, unfastened, loose, untied, unfixed, on the seas, at sea, on board ship, sailing, seaworthy, flooded, on the high seas, in service, commissioned. — *Ant.* ASHORE, docked, beached.

**afoot,** *modif.* **1.** [Walking] — *Syn.* on foot, hiking, marching, on shank's mare*; see **walking.**

**2.** [In preparation] — *Syn.* in progress, stirring, going on, brewing, forthcoming, hatching, advancing, being prepared, in its first stages, being born, in embryo, astir, abroad, in action, getting ready, in the air, in the cards*, cooking*, up*. — *Ant.* FINISHED, completed, ended.

**aforesaid,** *modif.* — *Syn.* previous, above-mentioned, foregoing; see **preceding.**

**afraid,** *modif.* **1.** [Apprehensive of the future] — *Syn.* hesitant, anxious, apprehensive, disturbed, frightened, fearful, scared, nervous, timorous, cautious, uneasy, timid, jittery, fidgety, alarmed, cowed, intimidated, cowardly, dismayed, daunted, disheartened, disquieted, discouraged, perplexed, worried, perturbed, upset, distressed, fainthearted, jumpy*, leery*, chicken*, shaky*, shook-up*. — *Ant.* CONFIDENT, self-assured, fearless.

**2.** [Gripped by fear] — *Syn.* scared, frightened, terrified, panic-stricken, in a fright, terror-stricken, terrorized, petrified, shocked, frozen, aghast, nerves all shot, alarmed, startled, aroused, horrified, stunned, rattled, unnerved, affrighted, struck dumb, trembling, in awe, in consternation, as though looking into an abyss, blanched, ashen, white as a sheet*, frightened to death*, scared to death*, scared stiff*, out of one's wits*, out of one's senses*, in a funk*. — *Ant.* BRAVE, unafraid, bold.

---

*SYN.* — **afraid** is applied to a general feeling of fear or disquiet and is the broadest in application of all the words considered here /to be *afraid* of the dark, to be *afraid* to die/; **frightened** implies a sudden, usually temporary seizure of fear / the child was *frightened* by the dog/; **timid** implies a lack of courage or self-confidence and suggests overcautiousness or shyness /too *timid* to ask for an explanation/; **fearful** suggests a feeling of disquiet and a tendency to worry rather than an alarming fear /*fearful* of making an error/; **timorous** suggests fearfulness and lack of confidence as a habitual state of mind /raised a *timorous* objection/; **terrified** implies intense, overwhelming fear /he stood *terrified* as the tiger charged/

---

**afresh,** *modif.* — *Syn.* anew, newly, once more, over again; see **again.**

**Africa,** *n.* — *Syn.* the Dark Continent, land of the Niger, equatorial Africa, land of the Sahara, South of the Sahara, savannas, the veld, the high veld.

Countries in Africa include: Senegal, Chad, Congo, Gabon, Benin, Ivory Coast (Cote d'Ivoire), Madagascar, Seychelles, Rwanda, Togo, Algeria, Libya, Mauritania, Mali, Guinea, Guinea-Bissau, Liberia, Nigeria, Niger, Egypt, Sudan, Ethiopia, Zambia, Mozambique, Kenya, Tanzania, Burundi, Angola, Eritrea, Mauritius, São Tomé and Principe, Uganda, Central African Republic, Cameroon, Ghana, Zaire, Morocco, Tunisia, Gambia, Somalia, Zimbabwe, South Africa, Namibia, Sierra Leone, Equatorial Guinea,

Malawi, Botswana, Lesotho, Swaziland, Djibouti, Burkina Faso, Cape Verde, Comoros.

**African,** *modif.* **1.** [Concerning the inhabitants of Africa] — *Syn.* Negro, negroid, black.

Terms for specific peoples include: Bantu, Zulu, Swazi, Hutu, Tutsi, Ubangi, Watusi, Dinka, Mandingo, Matabele, Khoikhoi, Hottentot, San, Bushman, Pygmy, Afrikaaner, Boer, Yoruba, Ibo, Hausa, Ashanti, Masai, Kikuyu, Somali, Ethiopian, Egyptian, Nilotic, Nubian, Hamite, Berber, Bedouin, Arab, Moor.

**African-American,** *n.* — *Syn.* black American, person of color, Afro-American; see **black** 2.

**aft,** *modif.* — *Syn.* abaft, rearward, behind; see **back.**

**after,** *modif.* and *prep.* **1.** [Behind in space] — *Syn.* back of, in the rear, behind; see **back.**

**2.** [Following] — *Syn.* next, later, subsequent; see **following.**

**afterlife,** *n.* — *Syn.* life after death, eternity, heaven, the hereafter; see **immortality** 2.

**aftermath,** *n.* — *Syn.* consequence, outcome, aftereffect, sequel; see **result.**

**afternoon,** *n.* — *Syn.* post meridian, P.M., midday, lunchtime, teatime, cocktail hour, siesta hour, evening.

**afterthought,** *n.* — *Syn.* second thought, reconsideration, review; see **review** 1.

**afterward,** *modif.* — *Syn.* later, after, subsequently, in a while, a while later, afterwards, by and by, eventually, soon, on the next day, ultimately, in subsequent time, another time, in aftertime, thereon, thereafter, then, latterly, thereupon, posteriorly, in the sequel, ensuingly, at a later time.

**again,** *modif.* — *Syn.* anew, afresh, newly, once more, once again, repeatedly, over, over and over, from the beginning, again and again, on and on, encore, another time, bis, over again, a second time, anon, freshly, *de novo* (Latin), *da capo* (Italian), reiteratively, recurrently, ditto*, repeat*. — *Ant.* ONCE, once only, at first.

**as much again** — *Syn.* doubled, twice as much, multiplied; see **double.**

**again and again,** *modif.* — *Syn.* repeatedly, once again, continuously; see **again, frequently, regularly** 1, 2.

**against,** *modif.* and *prep.* **1.** [Counter to] — *Syn.* in the face of, into, toward, opposite to, facing.

**2.** [In contact with] — *Syn.* on, upon, in collision with, in contact with; see **next** 2.

**3.** [Contrary to] — *Syn.* in opposition to, opposed to, counter to, adverse to, in violation of, versus, in contrariety to, over against.

**4.** [Opposite] — *Syn.* facing, fronting, abreast, corresponding; see **opposite** 3.

**age,** *n.* **1.** [The period of one's existence] — *Syn.* span, lifetime, duration, time of life; see **life** 4.

Particular stages of life include: infancy, childhood, girlhood, boyhood, adolescence, teens, youth, adulthood, middle age, old age, dotage, sweet sixteen*, flaming youth*, anecdotage*.

**2.** [Old age] — *Syn.* old age, advanced years, elderliness, senescence, antiquity, oldness, ancientness, decrepitude, superannuation, seniority, maturity, golden years, declining years, sunset years, winter of life, senectitude; see also **sense** 1.

**3.** [A period of time] — *Syn.* epoch, era, period, time, century, decade, eon, generation, interval, interim, term, days (*of someone* or *something*); see also **life** 4, **period** 1.

**4.** [*A long time; often plural*] — *Syn.* eon, eternity, years, dog's age*, coon's age*, donkey's years*, month of Sundays*.

*See Synonym Study at* PERIOD.

**of age** — *Syn.* adult, mature, eighteen, twenty-one, having attained one's majority; see also **mature** 1.

**age,** *v.* **1.** [To grow old] — *Syn.* grow old, get on, get on in years, grow feeble, decline, wane, advance in years, wrinkle, deteriorate, fail, waste away, turn gray, turn white, show one's years, show one's age, have one foot in the grave*, go downhill*, be over the hill*.

**2.** [To mature] — *Syn.* ripen, develop, mellow, mature; see **grow** 2.

**aged,** *modif.* — *Syn.* old, gray, elderly, worn; see **old** 1, 2.

**agency,** *n.* **1.** [Place where business is transacted] — *Syn.* firm, bureau, company; see **business** 4, **office** 3.

**2.** [An instrumentality] — *Syn.* power, auspices, action; see **means** 1.

**agenda,** *n.* — *Syn.* program, list, plan, schedule; see **program** 2.

**agent,** *n.* **1.** [One who acts for another] — *Syn.* representative, deputy, broker, promoter, operator, salesperson, salesman, assistant, emissary, appointee, proxy, intermediary, executor, attorney, lawyer, go-between, surrogate, procurator, principal, factor, minister, envoy, delegate, spokesperson, spokesman, canvasser, middleman, commissioner, regent, consignee, commissary, syndic, substitute, factotum, steward, functionary, servant, assignee, solicitor, ambassador, diplomat, *chargé d'affaires* (French), attaché, comprador, proctor, negotiator, advocate, coagent, instrument, tool, cat's paw, press agent, publicity agent, claim agent, employment agent, headhunter*, literary agent, actor's agent, booking agent, flesh peddler*, ten percenter*, handler, secret agent, spy, operative, double agent, FBI agent, G-man*, treasury agent, T-man*, narcotics agent, narc*.

**2.** [An instrumentality] — *Syn.* active force, cause, means, agency; see **doer, means** 1.

---

*SYN.* — **agent** is, generally, a person or thing that acts or is capable of acting, or, in this comparison, one who is empowered to act for another [*a literary agent*]; **factor,** a less common term, now usually denotes an agent for the sale of goods; a **deputy** is a public official to whom certain authority has been delegated by superiors; **proxy** implies the delegation of power to substitute for another in some formal or ceremonial act [*some stockholders vote by proxy*]

---

**aggrandize,** *v.* **1.** [To exalt] — *Syn.* acclaim, applaud, glorify; see **praise** 1.

**2.** [To increase] — *Syn.* enlarge, intensify, extend; see **increase** 1.

**aggravate,** *v.* **1.** [To irritate] — *Syn.* exasperate, annoy, provoke; see **bother** 2.

**2.** [To make worse] — *Syn.* worsen, exacerbate, complicate; see **increase** 1, **intensify.**

*See Synonym Study at* INTENSIFY.

**aggravation,** *n.* **1.** [Intensification] — *Syn.* heightening, worsening, exacerbation, intensification, sharpening, inflammation, deepening, strengthening, exaggeration, magnification.

**2.** [A cause of aggravation] — *Syn.* worry, affliction, irritant, nuisance; see **difficulty** 1, 2, **trouble** 2.

**3.** [*Annoyance] — *Syn.* irritation, provocation, exasperation; see **annoyance** 1.

**aggregate,** *n.* — *Syn.* sum, gross, total, whole; see **all** 1, **sum, whole.**

*See Synonym Study at* SUM.

**aggregation,** *n.* — *Syn.* collection, aggregate, gathering; see **all** 1, **collection** 2, **whole.**

**aggression,** *n.* **1.** [An attack] — *Syn.* offensive, assault, invasion; see **attack** 1.
**2.** [Aggressive behavior] — *Syn.* aggressiveness, belligerence, hostility, combativeness, pugnacity, militancy, bellicosity, quarrelsomeness, militarism, warmongering, drive, forcefulness, fight\*, push\*, pushiness\*, feistiness\*, killer instinct\*.

**aggressive,** *modif.* **1.** [Energetic and forceful] — *Syn.* assertive, forward, pushing, enterprising, forceful, domineering, self-assertive, outspoken, bold, energetic, vigorous, dynamic, driving, determined, competitive, activist, proactive, pushy\*, hard-hitting\*, hustling\*, take-charge\*, go-ahead\*, go-getter\*, Type A\*. — *Ant.* submissive, retiring, passive.
**2.** [Combative] — *Syn.* belligerent, combative, pugnacious, militant, martial, encroaching, warlike, attacking, bellicose, threatening, advancing, offensive, antagonistic, disruptive, truculent, hostile, intrusive, destructive, warmongering, hawkish, onrushing, contentious, quarrelsome, intruding, battering, rapacious, invading, on the offensive, guilty of aggression, up in arms\*, on the warpath\*, feisty\*, scrappy\*, trigger-happy\*. — *Ant.* PEACEFUL, peace-loving, dovish.

---

**SYN.** — **aggressive** implies a bold and energetic pursuit of one's ends, connoting, in derogatory usage, a ruthless desire to dominate and, in a favorable sense, enterprise or initiative; **militant** implies a vigorous, unrelenting espousal of a cause, movement, etc. and rarely suggests the furthering of one's own ends; **assertive** emphasizes self-confidence and a persistent determination to express oneself or one's opinions; **pushing** is applied derogatorily to a forwardness of personality that manifests itself in officiousness or rudeness

---

**aggressor,** *n.* — *Syn.* assailant, invader, offender; see **attacker.**
**aggrieve,** *v.* — *Syn.* wrong, oppress, abuse; see **wrong.**
*See Synonym Study at* WRONG.
**aghast,** *modif.* — *Syn.* horrified, alarmed, appalled, dismayed; see **afraid** 2, **bewildered, shocked.**
**agile,** *modif.* — *Syn.* nimble, quick, spry, deft, lithe, sprightly, supple, dexterous, limber, athletic, easy-moving, well-coordinated, graceful, vigorous, frisky, spirited, rapid, prompt, tripping, active, ready, winged, swift-footed, alive, buoyant, energetic, brisk, lively, swift, alert, keen, sharp, flexible, resourceful, fleet, sure-footed, light-footed, nimble-footed, mercurial, light-fingered, nimble-fingered. — *Ant.* AWKWARD, slow, clumsy.

---

**SYN.** — **agile** and **nimble** both imply rapidity, ease, and lightness of movement, **agile** emphasizing dexterity in the use of the limbs and **nimble**, deftness in the performance of some act; **quick** implies rapidity and promptness, seldom indicating, out of context, the degree of skillfulness; **spry** suggests nimbleness or alacrity, esp. as displayed by vigorous elderly people; **sprightly** implies animation or vivacity and suggests lightheartedness

---

**agility,** *n.* — *Syn.* nimbleness, dexterity, spryness, quickness, deftness, briskness, swiftness, sprightliness, friskiness, rapidity, readiness, liveliness, promptitude, alacrity, promptness, alertness, dispatch, expedition, litheness, activity, fleetness, suppleness, celerity, adroitness, coordination. — *Ant.* AWKWARDNESS, slowness, clumsiness.
**aging,** *modif.* — *Syn.* declining, waning, failing, falling,

sinking, mellowing, getting on, getting along, maturing, senescent, developing, fermenting, wasting away, wearing out, growing old, graying, lapsing, outworn, fading, crumbling, decaying, deteriorating, moldering, falling apart, doddering, one foot in the grave\*, over the hill\*, stale\*. — *Ant.* youthful, FRESH, vigorous.
**agitate,** *v.* — *Syn.* stir, move, arouse, disturb; see **disturb** 2, **excite** 1, 2.
*See Synonym Study at* DISTURB.
**agitated,** *modif.* — *Syn.* disturbed, moved, upset, aroused; see **excited, troubled** 1.
**agitation,** *n.* — *Syn.* stir, unrest, tumult, disquiet; see **anxiety, confusion** 2, **disturbance** 2, **excitement.**
**agitator,** *n.* — *Syn.* instigator, fomenter, reformer, revolutionary, radical, revisionist, anarchist, rabble-rouser, demagogue, dogmatist, malcontent, disrupter, heretic, fighter, propagandist, ringleader, stormy petrel, zealous advocate, firebrand, incendiary, soapbox orator, active supporter, active partisan, ardent champion, exciter of public debate, troublemaker, agent, *provocateur, agent provocateur* (*both* French), organizer, sans-culotte, dissident, fifth columnist\*; see also **conservative, radical, rebel** 1.
**agnostic,** *n.* — *Syn.* freethinker, unbeliever, skeptic, doubter; see **skeptic.**
*See Synonym Study at* ATHEIST.
**ago,** *modif.* — *Syn.* gone, since, past; see **before** 1.
**agonize,** *v.* — *Syn.* anguish, struggle, writhe; see **suffer** 1, **worry** 2.
**agonizing,** *modif.* — *Syn.* excruciating, tormenting, torturous, distressing; see **disturbing, painful** 1.
**agony,** *n.* — *Syn.* suffering, torture, anguish, distress; see **distress** 1, **pain** 1, 2.
*See Synonym Study at* DISTRESS.
**agree,** *v.* — *Syn.* harmonize, coincide, concur, assent, consent, say yes, go along with, side with, accept, accede, allow, grant, acquiesce, concede, come to an agreement, reach an agreement, come to terms, reach an understanding, get along with, be of one mind, accord, conform, tally, correspond, match, match up, fit in, be consistent, go well with, go together, fall in with, recognize, admit, acknowledge, approve of, be in favor of, subscribe to, favor, hold with, come around, be agreeable to, suit, be in harmony, chime, attune, parallel, equal, synchronize, square with, jibe\*, check out\*, see eye to eye\*, click\*, hit it off\*, have no problem with\*, buy\*, call it a go\*, get together\*; see also **agree on, agree to, agree with.** — *Ant.* DIFFER, disagree, refuse.

---

**SYN.** — **agree** implies being or going together without conflict and is the general term used in expressing an absence of inconsistencies, inequalities, etc.; **conform** emphasizes agreement in form or basic character; **accord** emphasizes fitness for each other of things that are being considered together; **harmonize** implies a combination or association of different things in a proportionate or pleasing arrangement [*harmonizing* colors]; **correspond** is applied to that which matches, complements, or is analogous to something else [their Foreign Office *corresponds* to our State Department]; **coincide** stresses the identical character of the things considered [their needs *coincide*]; **tally** implies exact correspondence of one thing to another [their accounts of the incident did not *tally*] *See also Synonym Study at* CONSENT.

---

**agreeable,** *modif.* — *Syn.* pleasing, pleasant, congenial, amenable; see **friendly** 1, **harmonious** 2, **kind, pleasant** 1, 2.
*See Synonym Study at* PLEASANT.

**agreeably,** *modif.* — *Syn.* well, appropriately, happily, good-humoredly, good-naturedly, kindly, politely, graciously, pleasantly, pleasingly, satisfactorily, affably, charmingly, sympathetically, convivially, benevolently, frankly, affirmatively, obligingly, genially, amicably, amiably, welcomely, cheerfully, mutually, peacefully, favorably. — *Ant.* DISAGREEABLY, negatively, antagonistically.

**agreement,** *n.* **1.** [The act of agreeing] — *Syn.* understanding, complying, compromise, assenting, accession, ratifying, authorizing, granting, adjustment, concession, arbitration, mediation, negotiation, bargaining, arrangement, acknowledging, verifying, approving, acceding, endorsing, finding a middle course, find a middle ground, finding common ground, ironing out the difficulties, supporting, concurring, dealing. — *Ant.* DISAGREEING, disrupting, disputing.
**2.** [The state of being in accord] — *Syn.* conformity, friendship, accord, accordance, accommodation, congruity, concordance, correspondence, harmony, consensus, concord, unison, concert, common view, understanding, meeting of minds, amity, sympathy, brotherhood, reconciliation, affiliation, détente, entente, alliance, intimacy, fellowship, companionship, goodwill, cooperation, satisfaction, concurrence, compliance, fraternity, brotherliness, affinity, rapport, closeness, balance, congruousness, equality, kinship, comity, peace, love, unity, uniformity, union, unanimity, acclimation, conjunction, adjustment, equalization, consonance, tie. — *Ant.* DISAGREEMENT, enmity, disunity.
**3.** [An expression of agreement, sense 1] — *Syn.* recognition, assent, approval, concurrence, avowal, confirmation, acknowledgment, adjustment, okay*, reconciliation, compromise, treaty, pact, contract, indenture, bargain, compact, accord, adjudication, covenant, cartel, arrangement, gentleman's agreement, note, writ, oath, affidavit, settlement, stipulation, bond, charter, protocol, convention, codicil, lease, transaction, interchange, exchange, meeting of minds, deal.

**agree on,** *v.* — *Syn.* come to terms, settle, make an arrangement, come to an understanding, arrange, close a deal, make a bargain, strike a bargain, see eye to eye*; see also **agree.**

**agree to,** *v.* — *Syn.* consent to, approve, endorse, accept, settle for, support, allow, ratify, comply with, acquiesce in, assent to, confirm, go along with, abide by, affirm, acknowledge, defer to, concede, accede, verify, yield, permit, let, suffer, promise, contract, engage to, submit to, give in, sanction, authorize, OK, sign on, sign up, give ones word, shake on*; see also **agree.** — *Ant.* REFUSE, dispute, dissent.

**agree with,** *v.* **1.** [To concur] — *Syn.* concur, coincide, accord, harmonize; see **agree.**
**2.** [To suit] — *Syn.* be suitable, be favorable, be agreeable, be healthful, be good for, suit, be appropriate to, satisfy, be acceptable, please, fit, befit, sit well with.

**agricultural,** *modif.* — *Syn.* rural, farm, farming, agrarian, rustic, gardening, horticultural, floricultural, arboricultural, agronomical; see also **rural.**

**agriculture,** *n.* — *Syn.* farming, tillage, cultivation, horticulture; see **farming.**

**agriculturist,** *n.* — *Syn.* farmer, agronomist, farm expert; see **farmer.**

**aground,** *modif.* — *Syn.* on the ground, washed ashore, beached, foundered, grounded, stranded, swamped, shipwrecked, reefed, disabled, marooned, on the shore, resting on the bottom, on a rock, stuck in the mud, stuck, stuck fast, not afloat, cast away, wrecked, shoaled, piled up.

**ahead,** *modif.* **1.** [Going forward] — *Syn.* advancing, progressing, onward, leading; see **forward** 1.
**2.** [To the fore] — *Syn.* before, earlier than, in advance, ahead of, advanced, preceding, precedent, antecedent, foremost, leading, in the lead, at the head of, in the foreground, in lee of, to the fore, in the van, first, in front of, a jump ahead of, in the front line, winning, victorious, before one's path, in the direct line of one's course, triumphant, preliminary. — *Ant.* behind, BACK, toward the end.

**get ahead** — *Syn.* advance, prosper, progress; see **succeed** 1.

**get ahead of** — *Syn.* outdo, excel, subordinate; see **surpass.**

**ahead of,** *modif.* — *Syn.* in advance of, before, above, beyond; see **ahead** 2.

**aid,** *n.* **1.** [Assistance] — *Syn.* help, assistance, support, comfort, benefit, favor, benevolence, patronage, cooperation, giving, gift, subsidy, financial support, relief, welfare, bounty, compensation, allowance, charity, benefaction, succor, alleviation, mitigation, ministry, ministration, reinforcement, advocacy, promotion, subvention, encouragement, treatment, furtherance, advancement, backing, advice, guidance, service, sustenance, grant, funding, honorarium, endowment, rescue, deliverance, attention, care, first aid, lift*, hand*, helping hand*, boost*, leg up*. — *Ant.* hindrance, BARRIER, obstacle.
**2.** [One appointed to give assistance] — *Syn.* aide, deputy, lieutenant; see **assistant.**

**aid,** *v.* — *Syn.* help, support, assist, serve; see **help** 1.
*See Synonym Study at* HELP.

**ailing,** *modif.* — *Syn.* ill, sickly, feeble, weak; see **sick.**
*See Synonym Study at* SICK.

**ailment,** *n.* — *Syn.* disease, illness, sickness, infirmity; see **disease.**
*See Synonym Study at* DISEASE.

**aim,** *n.* — *Syn.* intention, object, plan; see **purpose** 1.
*See Synonym Study at* PURPOSE.

**take aim** — *Syn.* sight, level at, train on; see **aim** 2.

**aim,** *v.* **1.** [To direct one's effort] — *Syn.* endeavor, strive, propose; see **intend** 1, **try** 1.
**2.** [To point a weapon] — *Syn.* train, point, direct, steer, level at, beam, cock, set up, look through the gunsight, set the sights, sight, take aim, hold to a target, bracket, zero in on, draw a bead on.

**aimed,** *modif.* — *Syn.* proposed, marked, intended, directed, designed, calculated, leveled, trained, steered, set, planned, anticipated.

**aimless,** *modif.* — *Syn.* purposeless, pointless, erratic, unavailing, thoughtless, careless, heedless, rambling, wandering, blind, random, indiscriminate, unsettled, flighty, capricious, wayward, dissolute, without aim, without end, chance, haphazard, desultory, fortuitous, to no purpose, rudderless, drifting, stray, accidental, undirected, objectless, casual, indecisive, irresolute, fitful, fanciful, fickle, eccentric, unplanned, planless, helpless, unpredictable, shiftless, unfruitful, wanton. — *Ant.* purposeful, systematic, planned.

**air,** *n.* **1.** [The gaseous envelope of the earth] — *Syn.* atmosphere, stratosphere, troposphere, wind, breeze, draft, breath, fresh air, the open air, ozone, ether, sky, space, oxygen, the open, ventilation, the out of doors.
**2.** [The apparent quality] — *Syn.* look, mien, demeanor, atmosphere; see **appearance** 1, **character** 1.
**3.** [A tune] — *Syn.* theme, melody, strain; see **melody** 2, **song, tune.**
*See Synonym Study at* MELODY.

**in the air** — *Syn.* prevalent, abroad, current, in circulation; see **fashionable, popular** 3.

**off the air** — *Syn.* not broadcasting, not being broadcast, closed, signed off; see **quiet** 2.

**on the air** — *Syn.* broadcasting, transmitting, reporting, going on, televising, in progress, speaking, performing, telecasting, being telecast, live.

**up in the air 1.** [Not certain] — *Syn.* undecided, unsettled, unsure; see **uncertain** 2.

**2.** [Agitated] — *Syn.* angry, excited, annoyed; see **angry, excited.**

**walk on air** — *Syn.* feel good, feel happy, be exultant, be lively; see **enjoy oneself, exult.**

**air,** *v.* **1.** [To introduce air] — *Syn.* ventilate, open, freshen, aerate, air out, air-condition, circulate air, change the air, expel air, eject air, aerify, expose to air, draw in air, fan, refresh, cool, purify, oxygenate, revivify. — *Ant.* CLOSE, keep in, stifle.

**2.** [To expose to the air] — *Syn.* expose, hang out, sun, dry, spread (out).

**3.** [To speak publicly; *often derogatory*] — *Syn.* express, proclaim, vent; see **advertise** 1, **display** 1, **utter.**

**4.** [To broadcast] — *Syn.* put on the air, transmit, televise; see **broadcast** 2.

**aired,** *modif.* **1.** [Exposed to the air] — *Syn.* ventilated, opened, freshened, purified, oxygenated, exposed, aerated, hung out, sunned, dried, spread out. — *Ant.* CLOSED, stuffy, dark.

**2.** [Exposed to public attention] — *Syn.* exposed, disclosed, bruited about, discussed, revealed, told, expressed, unveiled, publicized, brought to light, advertised, propagated, made known, made public, published, broadcast, divulged, voiced, promulgated, spread abroad, disseminated. — *Ant.* SECRET, undisclosed, concealed.

**air force,** *n.* — *Syn.* air fleet, flying force, flying corps, aviation service, air power, air cover, aerospace team, air arm, air service, U.S. Air Force, USAF, Strategic Air Command, SAC, Tactical Air Command, TAC, Navy Air Force, Marine Corps Air Force, Royal Air Force, R.A.F., air cadets, *Luftwaffe* (German).

Types of crewmen include: pilot, copilot, fighter pilot, bomber pilot, electronic countermeasures man, radar man, bombardier, radar operator, radio operator, flight engineer, navigator.

**airlift,** *n.* — *Syn.* transit, airdrop, air jump, air freight; see **transportation.**

**airlift,** *v.* — *Syn.* transport, convey, fly, airdrop; see **carry** 1.

**airline,** *n.* — *Syn.* air carrier, commercial airline, air passenger carrier, air freight carrier, air service, scheduled airline, commuter airline, air shuttle, shuttle, air taxi, charter airline, nonscheduled airline, nonsked*.

Specific airlines include: American, Air Canada, Air France, Alitalia, British Airways, Continental, Delta, El Al, Icelandair, KLM, Royal Dutch Airlines, Lufthansa German Airlines, Northwest Airlines, Sabena-Belgian World Airlines, US Air, Qantas Airways Ltd., Trans World Airlines (TWA), United.

**airplane,** *n.* — *Syn.* aircraft, airliner, aeroplane, glider; see **plane** 3.

**airport,** *n.* — *Syn.* airfield, airdrome, aerodrome, jetport, spaceport, airstrip, flying field, landing field, landing zone, landing strip, air base, hangar, air terminal, terminal, runway, heliport, helipad, dock, installations.

Noted U.S. airports include: John F. Kennedy (JFK; New York), La Guardia (New York), O'Hare (Chicago), LAX (Los Angeles International), National (Washington, D.C.), Dulles (Washington, D.C.), Hartsfield (Atlanta), Logan (Boston), Stapleton (Denver), McCarran (Las Vegas), Sky Harbor (Phoenix), Lambert (St. Louis).

**airs,** *pl.n.* — *Syn.* affectation, affectedness, pretense, show; see **pose, pretense** 2.

*See Synonym Study at* POSE.

**airship,** *n.* — *Syn.* dirigible, zeppelin, lighter-than-air craft; see **balloon, plane** 3.

**airtight,** *modif.* **1.** [Not allowing air to enter] — *Syn.* impermeable to air, sealed, shut tight; see **tight** 2.

**2.** [Incontestable] — *Syn.* unassailable, indisputable, irrefutable, invulnerable; see **accurate** 1, **certain** 3.

**airy,** *modif.* **1.** [Open to the breeze] — *Syn.* windy, breezy, draughty, exposed, ventilated, open, spacious, lofty, well-ventilated, atmospheric, aerial, out-of-doors, pneumatic, climatic, outdoors, in the open, fluttering. — *Ant.* stifling, CLOSED, confined.

**2.** [Light and gay] — *Syn.* flippant, sprightly, whimsical; see **happy** 1, **sprightly.**

**3.** [Immaterial] — *Syn.* unsubstantial, intangible, ethereal, visionary; see **imaginary, immaterial** 2.

**4.** [Delicate] — *Syn.* fragile, frail, thin; see **dainty** 1.

**aisle,** *n.* — *Syn.* passageway, walkway, opening, way, walk, path, course, artery, clearing, avenue, corridor, passage, gangway, alley, lane, ingress, egress.

**ajar,** *modif.* — *Syn.* half-open, unshut, unclosed, unlatched; see **open** 1, 2.

**akin,** *modif.* — *Syn.* cognate, kindred, affiliated, similar; see **alike** 2, **related** 2, 3.

**alacrity,** *n.* — *Syn.* alertness, promptness, readiness, quickness; see **action** 1, **willingness.**

**alarm,** *n.* **1.** [Anything that gives a warning] — *Syn.* bell, siren, horn, signal, tocsin, buzzer, beeper, call, alarm clock, burglar alarm, fire alarm, fire bell, foghorn, gong, whistle, drum, trumpet, distress signal, SOS, Mayday, red light, hoot, blast, shout, alarm bell, call to arms, summons to arms, warning sound, sound of trumpet, beat of drum, war cry, hue and cry, danger signal, signal of distress, cry, squeal, yell, scream, air raid siren, panic button*, escape button*, chicken switch*.

**2.** [Apprehension of danger] — *Syn.* fear, dread, fright, trepidation; see **fear** 1, 2.

**3.** [A warning] — *Syn.* alert, notification, caution; see **warning.**

*See Synonym Study at* FEAR.

**alarm,** *v.* — *Syn.* frighten, scare, terrify; see **frighten.**

*See Synonym Study at* FRIGHTEN.

**alarmed,** *modif.* — *Syn.* frightened, fearful, anxious, aroused; see **afraid** 2.

**alarming,** *modif.* — *Syn.* frightening, distressing, disquieting, startling; see **dangerous** 1, **disturbing, frightful** 1.

**alarmist,** *n.* — *Syn.* scaremonger, panicmonger, doomsayer, prophet of doom, voice of doom, Chicken Little, the boy who cried wolf, worrywart*; see also **pessimist.**

**alas,** *interj.* — *Syn.* dear, dear me, oh, lackaday, alack, woe, woe is me, too bad, my God, gracious me, gee, tsk-tsk.

**Alaska,** *n.* — *Syn.* the Klondike, the 49th state, the frozen North, the gold country, land of the sourdoughs*, Seward's Folly*, Uncle Sam's Attic*, America's Icebox*, the Last Frontier.

**albeit,** *conj.* — *Syn.* even though, admitting, even if; see **although.**

**album,** *n.* **1.** [A blank book for collecting photographs, stamps, or autographs] — *Syn.* collection, stamp book, register, registry, index, autograph book, visitor's book,

memento, snapshots, scrapbook, notebook, photograph album, bride's book, portfolio, commonplace book, visitor's register, memorandum book, memory book.
**2.** [A recording] — *Syn.* record, LP, compact disk; see **record** 3.

**alcohol,** *n.* — *Syn.* spirits, liquor, drink, intoxicant, palliative, methanol, ethanol, wood alcohol, grain alcohol, rubbing alcohol, ethyl alcohol, amyl alcohol, methyl alcohol, booze★, alky★, hard stuff★, the sauce★, the bottle★, juice★, hooch★; see also **drink** 2, **whiskey**.

**alcoholic,** *modif.* — *Syn.* spirituous, fermented, distilled; see **strong** 8.

**alcoholic,** *n.* — *Syn.* addict, heavy drinker, dipsomaniac, sot; see **drunkard**.

**alcoholism,** *n.* — *Syn.* problem drinking, heavy drinking, insobriety, dipsomania; see **addiction, drunkenness**.

**alcove,** *n.* — *Syn.* niche, anteroom, nook, corner, recess, bay, cubicle, study; see also **recess** 3, **room** 2.

**alderman,** *n.* — *Syn.* councilman, council member, councilwoman, selectman, magistrate, ward officer, representative, district representative, borough elector, municipal legislator, member of the board of aldermen, assemblyman, city father★.

**ale,** *n.* — *Syn.* malt, tap-fermented ale, brew; see **beer**.

**alert,** *modif.* **1.** [Watchful] — *Syn.* wary, on guard, wideawake; see **observant** 2.
**2.** [Intelligent] — *Syn.* bright, clever, quick, sharp; see **intelligent** 1, **observant** 1.
*See Synonym Study at* INTELLIGENT, WATCHFUL.

**alert,** *n.* — *Syn.* signal, alarm, warning; see **alarm** 1, **warning**.
**on the alert** — *Syn.* watchful, aware, vigilant, on guard; see **observant** 1, 2.

**alert,** *v.* — *Syn.* inform, put on guard, warn, signal; see **warn**.

**alertness,** *n.* — *Syn.* sharpness, readiness, attentiveness, vigilance; see **watchfulness**.

**alfalfa,** *n.* — *Syn.* fodder, feed, legume; see **hay**.

**algae,** *pl.n.* — *Syn.* seaweed, rockweed, scum, stonewort, dulse, sea lettuce, pond life, kelp, blue-green algae; see also **seaweed**.

**alias,** *n.* — *Syn.* pseudonym, false name, assumed name, pen name, nom de plume, incognito, nom de guerre, stage name, anonym, sobriquet, nickname, moniker★.

---

*SYN.* — **alias** refers to an assumed name and, in popular use, is specifically applied to one taken by a criminal to disguise identity; a **pseudonym** is a fictitious name assumed, esp. by a writer, for anonymity, for effect, etc.; **pen name** and **nom de plume** are applied specifically to the pseudonym of a writer; **incognito**, often used as an adverb or adjective, implies a fictitious name or identity temporarily assumed by a famous person, as in traveling, to avoid being recognized

---

**alibi,** *n.* **1.** [A legal defense] — *Syn.* proof of absence, plea, explanation, defense, declaration, statement, case, defense of being elsewhere, allegation, affirmation, avowal, assurance, profession, plausible excuse, assertion, justification, answer, reply, retort, pretext, vindication, puncture-proof, alibi, airtight alibi★, out★, cover story★.
**2.** [★An excuse] — *Syn.* defense, account, excuse, reason; see **explanation** 2.

**alien,** *modif.* **1.** [Of foreign extraction] — *Syn.* exotic, strange, unknown; see **foreign** 1, 2.
**2.** [Unlike] — *Syn.* different, dissimilar, outlandish, opposed; see **repugnant** 1, **unusual** 2.

*See Synonym Study at* FOREIGN.

**alien,** *n.* — *Syn.* foreigner, stranger, nonnative, refugee, outsider, outlander, migrant, émigré, immigrant, emigrant, expatriate, displaced person, D.P., guest, visitor, newcomer, space creature, extraterrestrial, Martian, barbarian, Ishmael, outcast, settler, tenderfoot, stateless person, foreign national, migratory worker, intruder, squatter, interloper, noncitizen, man without a country, tramontane, auslander, *gringo*★ (Spanish), *gaijin*★ (Japanese). — *Ant.* native, CITIZEN, local.

*SYN.* — **alien** is applied to a resident who bears political allegiance to another country; **foreigner,** to a visitor or resident from another country, esp. one with a different language, cultural pattern, etc.; **stranger,** to a person from another region who is unacquainted with local people, customs, etc.; **immigrant,** to a person who comes to another country to settle; **émigré,** to a citizen of one country who has left it to take political refuge in another

---

**alienate,** *v.* — *Syn.* estrange, turn away, set against, disaffect, distance, withdraw the affections of, antagonize, make unfriendly, come between, disunite, make inimical, separate, divide, part, wean away, make indifferent *or* averse, turn off★. — *Ant.* UNITE, reconcile, acclimate.

**alienation,** *n.* — *Syn.* estrangement, disaffection, withdrawal, isolation, separation, deflection, variance, coolness, breach, rupture, falling out, weaning away, disengagement, division.

**align,** *v.* **1.** [To adjust] — *Syn.* arrange, straighten, regulate; see **adjust** 1, 3.
**2.** [To join] — *Syn.* associate (with), enlist (with), follow; see **join** 2.

**alignment,** *n.* — *Syn.* adjustment, arrangement, allying, association; see **alliance** 1, **order** 3.
**out of alignment** — *Syn.* misaligned, out of adjustment, twisted; see **crooked** 1, **wrong** 2.

**alike,** *modif.* **1.** [With the same qualities] — *Syn.* like, same, self-same, neither more nor less, without distinction or difference, twin, one, indistinguishable, copied, facsimile, duplicate, consubstantial, matched, mated, equal, matching, identical, one and the same, all one, chip off the old block★, in the same boat★, on all fours with★, the very image of★. — *Ant.* distinct, INCONGRUOUS, heterogeneous.
**2.** [With similar qualities] — *Syn.* analogous, akin, kindred, like, similar, much the same, comparable, homologous, parallel, correspondent, resembling, related, cognate, approximate, proximate, proportionate, equivalent, allied, associated, corresponding, of that kind, of a kind, congeneric, concurrent, nearly the same, of the same kidney★, same but different★, the same more or less★. — *Ant.* DIFFERENT, dissimilar, unlike.
**3.** [In like manner] — *Syn.* similarly, equally, likewise, in common, in the same manner, to the same degree, comparably, consonantly, answerable to, analogously, comparatively, in accordance with, correspondently, the same way. — *Ant.* DIFFERENTLY, dissimilarly, divergently.

**alimentary,** *modif.* — *Syn.* alimental, wholesome, supplying sustenance, nutritious, salutary, nourishing, nutrient, sustaining, nutritive, sustentative, digestive, digestible, succulent, food-taking, invigorating, food-carrying, comestible, dietary, dietetic, providing maintenance, eutropic, esculent, absorptive, eupeptic, peptic.

**alimony,** *n.* — *Syn.* support, divorce settlement, maintenance, provision; see **support** 3.

**alive,** *modif.* **1.** [Having life] — *Syn.* living, live, animate, animated, breathing, existing, existent, subsisting, vital, not dead, mortal, organic, extant, viable, growing, inspirited, in existence, quick, having life, vivified, conscious, alive and kicking*, above ground*, among the living*, this side of the grave*, with us*, in the flesh*. — *Ant.* DEAD, lifeless, inanimate.

2. [Alert] — *Syn.* quick, sharp, ready; see **active** 2.

3. [Active] — *Syn.* swarming, bustling, stirring, lively; see **active** 1, 2.

*SYN.* — **alive** and **living**, the former usually a predicate adjective, are the simple, basic terms for organisms having life at the time of reference, **alive** figuratively connoting full force or vigor /prejudices kept *alive* by ignorance/ and **living**, continued existence or activity; **animate**, opposed to *inanimate}*, *is applied to living organisms as distinguished from lifeless ones or inorganic objects;* **animated**, in this connection, is applied to inanimate things to which life or, in extended use, motion has been imparted /*animated* cartoons/; **vital**, in this connection, is applied to that which is essential to organic life /*vital* functions/ or to the energy, force, etc. manifested by living things

**alkali,** *n.* — *Syn.* salt, antacid, base, caustic soda.
Varieties include: lye, salt, soda, ammonia, ammonium hydroxide, potassium hydrate, sodium hydrate, lithium hydrate, caesium hydrate, rubidium hydrate, ammonium hydrate, lime, magnesia, sodium carbonate, potassium carbonate.

**alkaline,** *modif.* — *Syn.* alkali, alkalescent, basic, caustic, salty, bitter, acrid, soluble, chemical, antacid, neutralizing.

**all,** *modif.* **1.** [Completely] — *Syn.* totally, wholly, entirely; see **completely.**

**2.** [Every] — *Syn.* every one of, every, any, each, each and every, any and every, every member of, the entire number of, without exception, barring no one, bar none, from A to Z. — *Ant.* NO, not any, none.

**3.** [Exclusively] — *Syn.* alone, nothing but, solely; see **only** 1.

**4.** [The whole of] — *Syn.* complete, total, full; see **whole** 1.

**all,** *n. & pron.* — *Syn.* everything, everyone, everybody, every person, sum, sum total, aggregate, aggregation, collection, group, accumulation, ensemble, total, totality, whole, entirety, mass, quantity, unit, the whole number, the whole amount, every one, every part, every bit, the whole affair, the beginning and end, A to Z, the alpha and omega, the whole kit and caboodle*, lock, stock, and barrel*, the works*, the whole schmear*, the devil and all*; see also **everybody, everything, whole.** — *Ant.* NONE, nobody, nothing.

**above all**— *Syn.* in the first place, chiefly, especially, most important; see **principally.**

**after all**— *Syn.* nevertheless, in spite of everything, when all is said and done; see **although, finally** 2.

**at all**— *Syn.* to the slightest degree, in the least, anyhow, ever, in any way, in any wise, in any case, in any respect, under any condition, under any circumstances, anywise, in any manner, in any degree, to any extent, in the least degree, anyway.

**for all**— *Syn.* after all, nevertheless, despite; see **although.**

**in all**— *Syn.* all told, collectively, on the whole; see **altogether** 2.

**allay,** *v.* **1.** [To lessen] — *Syn.* reduce, relieve, alleviate, moderate; see **decrease** 2, **relieve** 2.

**2.** [To soothe] — *Syn.* mollify, pacify, ease; see **quiet** 1.

*See Synonym Study at* RELIEVE.

**allegation,** *n.* — *Syn.* assertion, affirmation, charge, imputation; see **accusation** 2, **contention** 2, **declaration** 1.

**allege,** *v.* — *Syn.* assert, affirm, testify, claim; see **declare** 1.

**allegedly,** *modif.* — *Syn.* assertedly, by allegation, by declaration, according to affirmation, professedly, avowedly, according to the statement, as stated, by deposition, according to an affidavit, supposedly, purportedly, ostensibly.

**allegiance,** *n.* — *Syn.* loyalty, fidelity, fealty, devotion; see **loyalty.**

*See Synonym Study at* LOYALTY.

**allegorical,** *modif.* — *Syn.* figurative, symbolic, metaphorical; see **illustrative.**

**allegory,** *n.* — *Syn.* moral story, allegorical representation, parable, fable; see **story.**

**allergic to,** *modif.* — *Syn.* sensitive to, affected by, subject to, susceptible to, repelled by, oversensitive to, hypersensitive to, responsive to. — *Ant.* IMMUNE, unaffected by, hardened to.

**allergy,** *n.* — *Syn.* hypersensitivity, sensitivity, hay fever, anaphylaxis; see **disease.**

**alleviate,** *v.* — *Syn.* lighten, mitigate, ease; see **relieve** 2.

*See Synonym Study at* RELIEVE.

**alley,** *n.* — *Syn.* back street, lane, rear way; see **road** 1.

**up** or **down one's alley**— *Syn.* suited to one's abilities, suited to one's tastes, suited to one's interests, enjoyable; see **fit** 1.

**alliance,** *n.* **1.** [The state of being allied] — *Syn.* connection, adherence, membership, affinity, concurrence, participation, cooperation, support, collusion, union, interrelation, concord, agreement, common understanding, marriage, matrimony, betrothal, kinship, relation, collaboration, fraternization, consanguinity, federation, communion, entente, engagement, friendship, partnership, coalition, association, affiliation, alignment, confederation, implication, bond, accord, congruity, mutuality, tie. — *Ant.* SEPARATION, rupture, repudiation.

**2.** [The act of joining] — *Syn.* fusion, combination, coupling; see **union** 1.

**3.** [A union] — *Syn.* league, union, federation, coalition, confederacy, confederation, bloc, bund, association, partnership, community, pact, treaty, entente, compact, cooperative, co-op, consortium, syndicate, corporation, company, combination, merger, conglomerate, cartel, trust, combine, conspiracy, network, ring, party, band, group, consociation; see also **organization** 3.

*SYN.* — **alliance** refers to any association entered into for mutual benefit; **league**, often interchangeable with **alliance**, stresses formality of organization and definiteness of purpose; **coalition** implies a temporary alliance of opposing parties, factions, etc., as in times of emergency; **confederacy** and **confederation** in political usage refer to a combination of independent states for the joint exercise of certain governmental functions, as defense or customs; **union** implies a close, permanent alliance and suggests complete unity of purpose and interest

**allied,** *modif.* **1.** [United] — *Syn.* unified, confederated, associated; see **united** 2.

**2.** [Related] — *Syn.* associated, connected, linked; see **related** 2.

*See Synonym Study at* RELATED.

**all-inclusive,** *modif.* — *Syn.* comprehensive, encircling, complete, extensive; see **comprehensive.**

**allocate,** *v.* — *Syn.* allot, designate, earmark; see **allot.** See Synonym Study at ALLOT.

**allot,** *v.* — *Syn.* apportion, allocate, assign, mete out, distribute, dispense, parcel out, divide up, share, allow, bestow, grant, give, dole out, set apart, set aside, designate, earmark, appropriate; see also **assign** 1, **distribute** 1.

*SYN.* — **allot** and **assign** both imply the giving of a share or portion with no indication of uniform distribution, **assign** having the extra connotation of authoritativeness /I was *assigned* the task of *allotting* the seats/; **apportion** connotes the just, proportionate, often uniform distribution of a fixed number of portions; **allocate** usually implies the allowance of a fixed amount for a specific purpose /to *allocate* $50 for books/

**allotment,** *n.* **1.** [A portion allotted] — *Syn.* portion, lot, part; see **share.**
**2.** [Distribution] — *Syn.* allocation, apportionment, allotting; see **distribution** 1.

**all-out,** *modif.* — *Syn.* total, complete, full-scale; see **absolute** 1.

**allow,** *v.* **1.** [To permit an action] — *Syn.* permit, let, sanction, grant, consent to, grant permission, give permission, suffer, tolerate, favor, be favorable to, agree to, yield, acquiesce, stand for, bear, privilege, accord, approve, approve of, give leave, accredit, endorse, certify, commission, humor, put no obstacles in the way of, gratify, have no objection, release, pass, indulge, be indulgent of, be permissive, oblige, authorize, license, warrant, empower, enable, entitle, put up with, brook, countenance, go along with, OK, leave*, give the green light*, give the go-ahead*, blink at*, give the reins to*, give free rein to*, grin and bear it*, leave the door open to*, hear of*, give one one's head*, give one leeway*, not blink an eye*, not bat an eye*; give carte blanche*, give a free hand*, let things take their course*, give one rope, give one line*, open the door to*, open the floodgates*. — *Ant.* DENY, forbid, prohibit.
**2.** [To grant a request or assertion] — *Syn.* recognize, concede, acknowledge, support; see **admit** 3.
**3.** [To include in an estimate] — *Syn.* provide, set aside, allot, concede, subtract, deduct, make allowance, give an allowance for, give at lower rates, add to, raise assessment.

*SYN.* — **allow** and **permit** imply power or authority to give or deny consent, **allow** connoting a refraining from the enforcement of usual requirements /honor students were *allowed* to miss the examinations/, and **permit** more positively suggesting formal consent or authorization /she was *permitted* to talk to the prisoner/; **let** may imply positive consent but more often stresses the offering of no opposition or resistance, sometimes connoting negligence, lack of power, etc. /don't *let* this happen again/; **suffer,** now somewhat rare in this sense, is closely synonymous with **allow** and may connote passive consent or reluctant tolerance

**allowable,** *modif.* — *Syn.* permissible, proper, legal; see **admissible.**

**allowance,** *n.* **1.** [Portion] — *Syn.* quantity, quota, ration; see **share.**
**2.** [A periodic gratuity] — *Syn.* stipend, salary, wage, commission, fee, recompense, hire, quarterage, pittance, remittance, gift, grant, travel grant, pension, alimony, annuity, stated maintenance, settled rate, en-

dowment, scholarship, fellowship, prize, bounty, interest, subsidy, honorarium, pay, viaticum, stint, bequest, legacy, inheritance, grant for support, contribution, aid, subvention, pocket money, dole*, handout*, pin money*.
**3.** [Discount] — *Syn.* reduction, deduction, cut, adjustment; see **discount.**
**make allowances (for)** — *Syn.* weigh, excuse, rationalize; see **allow for, consider** 1, **justify** 2.

**allow for,** *v.* — *Syn.* take into account, take into consideration, provide for, consider, make allowance for, make concession for, make provision for, make up for, set apart, set aside. — *Ant.* NEGLECT, ignore, reject.

**alloy,** *n.* — *Syn.* amalgam, admixture, compound, composite, fusion, mixture, intermixture, combination, debasement, adulteration, reduction; see also **metal.**
Common metal alloys include: steel, ferromanganese, ferrosilicon, cast iron, pewter, type metal, chromesteel, nichrome, vanadium-steel, tungsten-steel, ferro-magnetic manganese, chrome-vanadium-steel, titanium-steel, uranium-steel, austenitic steel, stainless steel, nonmagnetic steel, chromium steel, chrome-nickel steel, high tensile steel, cobalt-steel, tungsten-chromium-cobalt, carbide of tungsten-cobalt, Widia (trademark), Carboloy (trademark), finishing steel, high speed steel, high tungsten steel, low tungsten steel, structural steel, carbon steel, brass, bronze, Muntz metal, green gold, white gold, electrum, magnanin, iridium, Wood's metal, sterling silver, nickel-silver, magnalium, zinc-aluminum, aluminum-bronze, boron bronze, copper-aluminum, cupronickel, Duralumin (trademark), aluminum-manganese-copper, manganese-copper, tin-manganese, tin-copper, molybdenum-chromium-nickel, Monel metal (trademark), R-301, babbitt metal, bell metal, britannia metal, Dutch metal, gunmetal, osmiridium, pinchbeck, spiegeleisen.

**alloy,** *v.* **1.** [To mix metals] — *Syn.* mix, amalgamate, combine, compound, blend, adulterate, fuse.
Metals are alloyed to produce qualities which include: hardness, brittleness, resistance to heat, resistance to acids, resistance to wear, resistance to stain, resistance to rust, light weight, tensile strength, malleability, lack of magnetism, conductivity, etc.
**2.** [To devaluate] — *Syn.* debase, devalue, admix; see **adulterate.**

**all right,** *modif.* **1.** [Adequately] — *Syn.* tolerably, acceptably, passably; see **adequately** 2.
**2.** [Yes] — *Syn.* agreed, very well, of course, OK; see **yes.**
**3.** [Suitable] — *Syn.* proper, appropriate, fitting, allowable; see **admissible, fit** 1, 2.
**4.** [Adequate] — *Syn.* satisfactory, acceptable, satisfying; see **enough** 1.
**5.** [Uninjured] — *Syn.* safe, well, unhurt; see **healthy** 1, **whole** 2.
**6.** [Certainly] — *Syn.* without a doubt, definitely, positively; see **surely.**
**7.** [Correct] — *Syn.* exact, precise, right; see **accurate** 1.
**8.** [*Reliable] — *Syn.* honest, dependable, trustworthy; see **reliable** 1.
**9.** [*Excellent] — *Syn.* first-class, great, good; see **excellent.**

**all-time,** *modif.* — *Syn.* champion, record-breaking, unsurpassed, to the greatest extent, never surpassed, never greater, unequaled; see also **best** 1.

**all told,** *modif.* — *Syn.* in all, in toto, on the whole; see **altogether** 2.

**allude to,** *v.* — *Syn.* imply, suggest, insinuate, refer to; see **hint, refer** 2.

See Synonym Study at REFER.

**allure,** *n.* — *Syn.* attraction, charm, lure, fascination; see **appeal** 3, **attraction** 2.

**allure,** *v.* — *Syn.* attract, entice, intrigue, lure; see **attract** 2, **fascinate.**

See Synonym Study at ATTRACT.

**allusion,** *n.* — *Syn.* reference, mention, hint, suggestion, inference, quotation, citation, remark, statement, connection, implication, indication, connotation, casual reference, indirect reference, denotation, intimation, insinuation, innuendo, implied indication, implied reference, charge, imputation, incidental mention, subtext. — *Ant.* EXPLANATION, delineation, specification.

**ally,** *n.* — *Syn.* confederate, partner, collaborator; see **associate.**

See Synonym Study at ASSOCIATE.

**alma mater,** *n.* — *Syn.* place of matriculation, place of graduation, institution; see **college, school** 1, **university.**

**almanac,** *n.* — *Syn.* calendar, yearbook, annual, ephemeris, astronomical table, register, registry, Whitaker, farmer's almanac, world almanac, nautical almanac, statistical almanac, chronicle, journal, record, register of the year, *fasti* (Latin).

**almighty,** *modif.* **1.** [Omnipotent] — *Syn.* invincible, all-powerful, mighty, supreme; see **powerful.**
**2.** [Omnipresent] — *Syn.* infinite, eternal, godlike, omnipresent, all-knowing, all-seeing, omniscient, deathless, immortal, deific, celestial, divine, godly, heavenly, enduring, pervading, all-pervading, boundless, illimitable, uncircumscribed, everlasting. — *Ant.* MORTAL, transient, finite.
**3.** [*Great] — *Syn.* intense, extreme, terrible, severe; see **extreme** 2.
**4.** [*Exceedingly] — *Syn.* extremely, greatly, acutely; see **very.**

**Almighty,** *n.* — *Syn.* All-ruling, Omnipotent, All-powerful; see **god** 2.

**almost,** *modif.* — *Syn.* all but, very nearly, nearly, well-nigh, nigh, for the greatest part, approximately, roughly, about, just about, practically, for ordinary purposes, to all intents, near upon, as good as, near to, substantially, tantamount to, essentially, in effect, on the edge of, on the brink of, on the point of, on the verge of, on the eve of, relatively, for all practical purposes, for all intents and purposes, virtually, in a general way, to that effect, not quite, about to, with some exceptions, in the vicinity of, bordering on, within sight of, with little tolerance, close upon, with small probability of error, in the neighborhood of, most*, around*, pretty near*, nigh unto*, within a hair of*, within an ace of*.

**alms,** *n.* — *Syn.* charity, relief, donation, handout*; see **gift** 1.

**aloft,** *modif.* — *Syn.* on high, overhead, up; see **over** 1.

**alone,** *modif.* **1.** [Separate from others] — *Syn.* lone, lonely, solitary, separate, lonesome, deserted, forlorn, lorn, isolated, individual, forsaken, desolate, detached, companionless, friendless, unaccompanied, unescorted, abandoned, secluded, apart, by oneself, under one's own power, unassisted, unaided, single-handed, single, widowed, unmarried, unattached, solo, *solus* (Latin), in solitude, by one's lonesome*. — *Ant.* accompanied, attended, escorted.
**2.** [Exclusive of others] — *Syn.* solely, singly, simply; see **only** 1.
**3.** [Unique] — *Syn.* unparalleled, unexampled, unequaled; see **unique** 1.

**let alone**— *Syn.* **1.** not to mention, not to speak of, also, in addition to; see **besides.**
**2.** ignore, leave to oneself, isolate, refrain from disturbing; see **leave** 3, **neglect** 1, 2.

**let well enough alone**— *Syn.* forget, ignore, let alone; see **neglect** 1.

---

**SYN. — alone,** unqualified, denotes the simple fact of being by oneself or itself; **solitary** and the more poetic **lone** convey the same sense but suggest more strongly the lack of companionship or association [a *solitary* tree in the meadow a *lone* wanderer]; **lonely** conveys a heightened sense of solitude and gloom [the *lonely* sentinel walks his post]; **lonesome** suggests a longing or yearning for companionship, often for a particular person [the child is *lonesome* for her mother]

---

**along,** *modif. & prep.* **1.** [Near] — *Syn.* by, at, adjacent, parallel with; see **beside, near** 1.
**2.** [Ahead] — *Syn.* on, onward, forward; see **forward** 1.
**3.** [Together with] — *Syn.* with, accompanying, in addition to, in company with, as a companion, side by side, by the side of, in conformity with, in accordance with, coupled with, at the same time, simultaneously.

**all along**— *Syn.* all the time, from the beginning, all the while, throughout; see **regularly** 2, **throughout.**

**alongside,** *modif. & prep.* — *Syn.* parallel to, close by, close at hand, by *or* at the side of, along the side, close to the side, side by side, equal with, in company with, apace with, on the same plane with, almost touching, shoulder to shoulder*, neck and neck*; see also **adjacent, beside.** — *Ant.* BEYOND, ahead, behind.

**aloof,** *modif.* — *Syn.* remote, reserved, distant, detached, unapproachable, standoffish, cool, removed, apart, at a distance, separate, unresponsive, indifferent, disinterested; see also **indifferent** 1.

**aloud,** *modif.* — *Syn.* audibly, out loud, above a whisper, distinctly, intelligibly, plainly, clearly, vociferously, lustily, noisily; see also **loudly.**

**alphabet,** *n.* **1.** [Linguistic symbols] — *Syn.* letters, syllabary, pictographs, ideographs, graphic representation, characters, symbols, signs, runes, futhark, writing system, script, ABC's, system of characters, hieroglyphs, cryptographs, phonemes, sounds, phonetic alphabet, phonetic notation, International Phonetic Alphabet, IPA; see also **letter** 1.
Alphabets include: Greek, Arabic, Sanskrit, Devanagari, Latin, Roman, Russian, Cyrillic, Hebrew.
**2.** [Elements] — *Syn.* fundamentals, first principles, rudiments, ABC's; see **elements.**

**alphabetical,** *modif.* — *Syn.* alphabetic, systematic, consecutive, progressive, one after another, step by step, graded, planned, ordered, letter by letter, from A to Z, indexed, in order of cataloging.

**alphabetize,** *v.* — *Syn.* arrange alphabetically, index, systematize; see **order** 3.

**alpine,** *modif.* — *Syn.* mountainous, high, lofty, snow-capped, rocky, in the clouds, high-reaching, soaring, rangy, snow-clad, heaven-kissing, cloud-capped, aerial, ice-peaked, elevated, breathlessly high, rarified, towering, alpestrine, subalpine; see also **high** 1, 2.

**Alps,** *n.*
Major divisions of the Alps include: Swiss, Italian, Austrian, Jurian, Cottian, Graian, Liqurian, Maritime, Bernese, Pennine, Lepontine, Rhaetian, Bavarian, Carnic; see also **mountain** 1.

**already,** *modif.* — *Syn.* previously, by now, now, even now, by this time, at present, but now, just now, by the time mentioned, even then, in the past, up to now, by that time, then, so soon, so early.

**also,** *modif.* — *Syn.* too, likewise, besides, as well, in addition, additionally, withal, similarly, in like manner (with), along with, more than that, conjointly, *au reste* (French), over and above, in conjunction with, therewithal, thereto, together with, ditto, more, moreover, further, furthermore, including, plus, to boot*. — *Ant.* excluding, WITHOUT, otherwise.

**altar,** *n.* — *Syn.* altar table, Communion table, shrine, chantry, tabernacle, baptismal font, reredos, sacrificial stone, platform, elevation for offerings, retable, scroll box.

**alter,** *v.* **1.** [To change for a purpose] — *Syn.* modify, adjust, remodel, reconstruct; see **change** 1.
**2.** [To castrate or spay] — *Syn.* castrate, spay, neuter, desex, geld, sterilize, asexualize, emasculate, caponize, mutilate, fix*.
**3.** [To become different] — *Syn.* change, develop, decay; see **change** 4.
*See Synonym Study at* CHANGE.

**alteration,** *n.* **1.** [The act of altering] — *Syn.* exchange, modification, revision, remodeling; see **change** 1.
**2.** [A modification] — *Syn.* qualification, correction, adjustment; see **change** 2.

**altercation,** *n.* — *Syn.* wrangle, argument, quarrel, squabble, row; see **dispute, fight** 1.
*See Synonym Study at* QUARREL.

**altered,** *modif.* **1.** [Changed] — *Syn.* modified, qualified, changed, revised; see **changed** 2.
**2.** [Recut] — *Syn.* fitted, refitted, renovated, adjusted, remade, reconstructed, redone, remodeled, retailored, taken in, let out, made fashionable, updated.

**alternate,** *modif.* **1.** [Alternative] — *Syn.* alternative, substitute, makeshift, other; see **temporary.**
**2.** [Recurrent] — *Syn.* intermittent, alternating, every other, every second; see **intermittent.**
*See Synonym Study at* INTERMITTENT.

**alternate,** *n.* — *Syn.* replacement, equivalent, double; see **substitute.**

**alternate,** *v.* **1.** [To take or do by turns] — *Syn.* rotate, substitute, follow in turn, follow successively, happen by turns, follow one another, do by turns, act reciprocally, do one then the other, act alternately, relieve, fill in for, exchange, take turns, reciprocate, interchange, transpose, change off, spell*.
**2.** [To fluctuate] — *Syn.* vary, fluctuate, vacillate, oscillate, waver, seesaw, rise and fall, blow hot and cold, teeter, shift, sway, totter, come and go, ebb and flow, shuffle, go to and fro, ride and tie*, back and fill*, teeter-totter*.

**alternation,** *n.* — *Syn.* variation, rotation, transposition, shift; see **interchange** 2.

**alternative,** *n.* **1.** [A choice between things] — *Syn.* option, choice, dilemma; see **choice** 1.
**2.** [A thing to be chosen] — *Syn.* option, choice, remaining choice, Plan B*; see **option** 1.
*See Synonym Study at* CHOICE.

**although,** *conj.* — *Syn.* though, even though, despite, still, despite the fact that, even supposing, be it that, in spite of, in spite of the fact that, granting all this, even if, while, however that may be, for all that, admitting that, granting that, supposing that, notwithstanding that, albeit.

**altitude,** *n.* — *Syn.* height, elevation, loftiness, eminence; see **height** 1.
*See Synonym Study at* HEIGHT.

**altogether,** *modif.* **1.** [Completely] — *Syn.* entirely, wholly, fully; see **completely.**

**2.** [In all] — *Syn.* all told, in all, collectively, on the whole, with everything included, in the aggregate, in sum total, bodily, everything being considered, all in all, all things considered, by and large, in a mass, in a body, all, conjointly, taking all things together, as a whole, for the most part; *en bloc, tout ensemble, en masse* (all French), in the lump*.

**altruistic,** *modif.* — *Syn.* unselfish, benevolent, charitable, selfless; see **generous** 1, **humane** 1, **kind, philanthropic, unselfish.**
*See Synonym Study at* PHILANTHROPIC.

**alumni** or **alumnae,** *pl.n.* — *Syn.* graduates, postgraduates, former students, Class of ..., postgrads*, old grads*, Old Boys*.

**always,** *modif.* **1.** [Constantly] — *Syn.* at all times, all the time, invariably, without exception, on all occasions, constantly, continuously, periodically, continually, incessantly, ceaselessly, unfailingly; see also **regularly** 2.
**2.** [Forever] — *Syn.* ever, perpetually, eternally, evermore; see **forever** 1.

**A.M.,** *abbr.* — *Syn.* after midnight, morning, early hours, wee hours, before noon, forenoon, antemeridian, dawn, early morning, late morning, sunup, matins, lauds, prime. — *Ant.* AFTERNOON, P.M., evening.

**amass,** *v.* — *Syn.* gather, hoard, store up, garner; see **accumulate** 1.

**amateur,** *modif.* — *Syn.* nonprofessional, lay, unpaid, inexperienced, avocational, dilettantish, amateurish, unskilled, inexpert, sandlot*; see also **inexperienced.**

**amateur,** *n.* — *Syn.* nonprofessional, layman, layperson, beginner, novice, learner, dabbler, recruit, dilettante, probationer, aspirant, hopeful, tyro, abecedarian, neophyte, initiate, apprentice, do-it-yourselfer, hobbyist, putterer, freshman*, tenderfoot*, ham*, rookie*, greenhorn*, cub*, fumbler*, bungler*, clod*; see also **beginner.** — *Ant.* VETERAN, professional, expert.

---

**SYN. — amateur** refers to one who does something for the pleasure of it rather than for pay and often implies a relative lack of skill; a **dilettante** is an amateur in the arts, usually applied disparagingly to a superficial dabbler; **novice** and **neophyte** refer to one who is a beginner, hence inexperienced, in some activity, **neophyte** carrying additional connotations of youthful enthusiasm; **tyro** refers to an inexperienced but self-assertive beginner and generally connotes incompetence

---

**amateurish,** *modif.* — *Syn.* crude, unskilled, unprofessional, bush-league*; see **incompetent.**

**amatory,** *modif.* — *Syn.* amorous, passionate, erotic, loving; see **amorous.**

**amaze,** *v.* — *Syn.* astonish, perplex, astound; see **surprise** 1.
*See Synonym Study at* SURPRISE.

**amazement,** *n.* — *Syn.* astonishment, surprise, awe, bewilderment; see **wonder** 1.

**amazing,** *modif.* — *Syn.* astonishing, astounding, marvelous; see **unusual** 1, **wondrous.**

**amazon,** *n.* — *Syn.* female warrior, virago, giantess, woman athlete, fury.

**ambassador,** *n.* — *Syn.* representative, envoy, minister; see **diplomat** 1.

**amber,** *modif.* — *Syn.* amber-colored, yellowish, golden; see **brown, tan, yellow** 1.

**ambience,** *n.* — *Syn.* atmosphere, environment, milieu, climate; see **character** 1, **environment.**

**ambiguity,** *n.* — *Syn.* doubtfulness, incertitude, vagueness, double meaning; see **uncertainty** 2.

**ambiguous,** *modif.* — *Syn.* equivocal, enigmatic, vague, amphibolic; see **obscure** 1.
*See Synonym Study at* OBSCURE.

**ambition,** *n.* **1.** [Eager desire] — *Syn.* aspiration, ambitiousness, drive, enterprise, hope, earnestness, appetite for fame, yearning, eagerness, longing, hankering, craving, passion, lust, itch, hunger, thirst, appetite, avidity, energy, ardor, zeal, enthusiasm, spirit, vigor, hunger for power, love of glory, eagerness for distinction, emulation, get-up-and-go★, push★, what it takes★. — *Ant.* INDIFFERENCE, apathy, laziness.
**2.** [The object of desire] — *Syn.* aim, goal, objective, dream; see **purpose** 1.

**ambitious,** *modif.* **1.** [Characterized by ambition] — *Syn.* aspiring, enterprising, emulous, hopeful, zealous, high-reaching, climbing, eager, aggressive, earnest, determined, industrious, driven, goal-oriented, hungry, thirsty, itching, designing, scheming, pushing, emulous of fame, anxious for power, resourceful, opportunistic, energetic, enthusiastic, driving, striving, avid, sharp, intent, vaulting, up and coming, upwardly mobile, careerist, power-hungry, overambitious, predatory, hustling★, pushy★, high-flying★, on the fast track★, on the make★. — *Ant.* unambitious, lackadaisical, indolent.
**2.** [Challenging] — *Syn.* arduous, formidable, lofty, pretentious; see **difficult** 1, **grand** 2.

---

**SYN.** — **ambitious** implies a striving for advancement, wealth, fame, etc., and is used with both favorable and unfavorable connotations; **aspiring** suggests a striving to reach some lofty end regarded as somewhat beyond one's normal expectations *[an aspiring young poet]*; **enterprising** implies an energetic readiness to take risks or undertake new projects in order to succeed; **emulous** suggests ambition characterized by a competitive desire to equal or surpass another

---

**ambivalence,** *n.* — *Syn.* uncertainty, vacillation, conflicting feelings; see **doubt** 2.

**ambivalent,** *modif.* — *Syn.* uncertain, irresolute, of two minds, conflicted; see **doubtful** 2.

**amble,** *v.* — *Syn.* saunter, stroll, wander; see **walk** 1.

**ambrosia,** *n.* — *Syn.* nectar, immortal food, food of the gods, milk and honey, amrita, delectable sustenance, heavenly food, savory fare, delicacy.

**ambulance,** *n.* — *Syn.* hospital wagon, mobile hospital, Red Cross truck, rescue squad, field wagon, hospital plane, sick transport, meat wagon★.

**ambulatory,** *modif.* — *Syn.* mobile, wandering, walking, able to walk; see **itinerant, wandering.**
*See Synonym Study at* ITINERANT.

**ambush,** *n.* — *Syn.* hiding place, pitfall, snare, camouflage, ambuscade, deception, cover, blind; see also **trap** 1, **trick** 1.

**ambush,** *v.* — *Syn.* waylay, ensnare, ambuscade, lie in wait for, set a trap, attack from a concealed position, keep out of sight, lie concealed, wait in ambuscade, bait the hook, decoy, entrap, hook in, skulk, lurk, surround, hem in, surprise, lay for★; see also **attack** 1.

**ameliorate,** *v.* — *Syn.* improve, better, enhance; see **improve** 1, 2.
*See Synonym Study at* IMPROVE.

**amenable,** *modif.* — *Syn.* tractable, manageable, agreeable, responsive; see **docile.**
*See Synonym Study at* DOCILE.

**amend,** *v.* — *Syn.* correct, mend, revise, alter; see **change** 1, **correct** 1, **improve** 1.

**amendment,** *n.* **1.** [The act of amending] — *Syn.* alteration, reformation, correction, revision; see **improvement** 1, **revision.**
**2.** [A proposal to amend] — *Syn.* bill, measure, act, clause, motion, revision, modification of the law, legislative addition, supplement, rider, committee suggestion, redefinition, addendum, reform, substitute motion, codicil.

**amends,** *pl.n.* — *Syn.* compensation, indemnity, reparation, restitution; see **reparation** 2.

**amenities** *pl.n.* — *Syn.* civilities, courtesies, etiquette; see **behavior** 1, **courtesy** 1.

**amenity,** *n.* **1.** [A desirable feature; *often plural*] — *Syn.* convenience, facility, comfort, creature comfort; see **convenience** 2.
**2.** [Pleasantness] — *Syn.* agreeableness, mildness, charity; see **kindness** 1.

**America,** *n.* **1.** [One or both of the continents of the Western Hemisphere] — *Syn.* North America, Latin America, South America, Central America, the New World, this side of the Atlantic, the Western Hemisphere, Organization of American States.
**2.** [The United States of America] — *Syn.* United States, U.S., the States, Uncle Sam★; see **United States.**

**American,** *modif.* **1.** [Related to the Western Hemisphere] — *Syn.* hemispheric, continental, Western, North American, Latin American, South American, Central American, Pan-American, inter-American.
In reference to specific countries: Canadian, Mexican, Belizean, Nicaraguan, Costa Rican, Guatemalan, Honduran, Salvadoran, Salvadorian, Panamanian, Cuban, Haitian, Puerto Rican, Colombian, Venezuelan, Guianan, Brazilian, Peruvian, Ecuadorian, Chilean, Argentinian, Uruguayan, Paraguayan, Bolivian, Surinamese.
In reference to the native peoples: Indian, American Indian, Amerindian, Native American, Aztec, Mayan, Incan, Araucanian, Algonquian, Apache, Arawakan, Athabaskan, Carib, Cherokee, Chinookan, Choctaw, Cree, Creek, Dakota, Lakota, Hopi, Inuit, Iroquoian, Miskito, Nahuatl, Navajo, Olmec, Quechua, Seminole, Sioux, Siouan, Taino, Tanoan, Ute.
**2.** [Related to the United States of America] — *Syn.* republican, constitutional, democratic, patriotic, freedom-loving, Yankee.

**American,** *n.* **1.** [A citizen of the United States] — *Syn.* citizen of the United States, United States national, Yankee, Westerner, Northerner, Southerner, Native American, American Indian, pioneer, Yank★, gringo★.
**2.** [An inhabitant of the Western Hemisphere] — *Syn.* North American, South American, Latin American, Western; see **American** (*modif.*) 1.

**Americana,** *n.* — *Syn.* American history, local history, Indian lore, regional folklore, pioneer stories, American materials.

**Americanism,** *n.* **1.** [Attachment to America as a place or a way of life] — *Syn.* patriotism, nationalism, provincialism, isolationism, flag waving, chauvinism, jingoism, America for Americans, America first.
**2.** [Anything thought of as characteristic of the United States] — *Syn.* mannerism, habit, custom, trick of speech, American slang, Yankeeism, free enterprise, spirit of '76★.

**Americanize,** *v.* — *Syn.* naturalize, enfranchise, assimilate, level, melt, make into an American, introduce to American ways, indoctrinate, acculturate.

**amiable,** *modif.* — *Syn.* pleasant, affable, genial, good-natured, obliging, friendly, cordial, agreeable, likable, congenial, gracious, good-tempered, sweet-tempered, sweet, easygoing, amicable, sociable, easy to get along with; see also **friendly** 1, **kind**.

---

*SYN.* — **amiable** and **affable** suggest qualities of friendliness, easy temper, etc. that make one likable, **affable** also implying a readiness to be approached or to converse; a **good-natured** person is one who is disposed to like as well as be liked and is sometimes easily imposed on; **obliging** implies a ready, often cheerful, desire to be helpful *[the obliging clerk took my order]*; **genial** suggests good cheer and sociability *[our genial host]*; **cordial** suggests graciousness and warmth *[a cordial greeting]*

---

**amicable,** *modif.* — *Syn.* peaceable, friendly, neighborly, genial; see **friendly** 1.

**amid,** *prep.* — *Syn.* between, in the midst of, in the middle of; see **among**.

**amiss,** *modif.* — *Syn.* erring, improper, astray, awry; see **wrong** 2.

**ammonia,** *n.* — *Syn.* gas, vapor, alkali, ammonia water, sal volatile, smelling salts, spirits of hartshorn.

**ammunition,** *n.* ammo*, munitions, materiel, resources.
Types of ammunition include: buckshot, gunpowder, cartridge, bullet, round, clip, napalm, bomb, missile, projectile, charge, depth charge, grenade, hand grenade, fuse, torpedo, shell, ball, cannonball, shot, gunpowder, rocket; see also **bomb, bullet, mine** 2, **munitions, shell** 2, **shot** 2.
Materials used in ammunition include: dynamite, trotyl, trinitrotoluene (TNT); nitrocotton, melinite, gelignite, cordite, trinitrocresol, poison gas, tear gas, nerve gas, nitroglycerine, nitrate compound, gun cotton, lyddite; see also **explosive**.

**amnesty,** *n.* — *Syn.* pardon, reprieve, absolution, immunity; see **acquittal, pardon** 1, 3.

**among,** *prep.* — *Syn.* between, in between, in the midst of, in the middle of, with, mingled with, surrounded by, in connection with, in association with, betwixt, encompassed by, in dispersion through, amid, amongst, amidst, in the company of, betwixt and between. — *Ant.* BEYOND, away from, outside of.

**amorous,** *modif.* — *Syn.* passionate, affectionate, loving, amatory, erotic, sexual, romantic, ardent, fervent, tender, devoted, fond, enamored, rapturous, lovesick, languishing, impassioned, desirous, sentimental, wooing, amative, Anacreontic.

**amount,** *n.* **1.** [The total of several quantities] — *Syn.* sum, product, sum total; see **all** 1, **sum, whole**.
**2.** [Price] — *Syn.* expense, cost, outlay; see **price**.
**3.** [Quantity] — *Syn.* volume, measure, mass, number; see **quantity**.
**4.** [The combined effect] — *Syn.* substance, value, significance; see **result**.
*See Synonym Study at* SUM.

**amount to,** *v.* — *Syn.* add up to, equal, total, come to, reach, extend to, mount up to, run to, effect, aggregate, be equal to, be equivalent to, be tantamount to, approximate, check with, be equal in quantity to, total up to, sum up to, foot up to, be in all, be in the whole, tally with, develop into, become.

**amour,** *n.* — *Syn.* romance, liaison, relationship, love affair; see **affair** 2.

**ample,** *modif.* **1.** [Enough or more than enough] — *Syn.* sufficient, adequate, abundant, plentiful; see **enough** 1, **plentiful** 2.
**2.** [Large in size or scope] — *Syn.* spacious, roomy, extensive; see **broad** 1, **large** 1.

*See Synonym Study at* PLENTIFUL.

**amplification,** *n.* — *Syn.* addition, augmentation, elaboration, intensification; see **increase** 1.

**amplifier,** *n.* — *Syn.* speaker, loudspeaker, bullhorn, amplifying device, amplifying mechanism, microphone, high-fidelity speaker, stereo speaker, woofer, tweeter, hearing aid, echo chamber, megaphone, amp*.

**amplify,** *v.* — *Syn.* expand, augment, magnify, elaborate; see **increase** 1.

**amply,** *modif.* — *Syn.* enough, sufficiently, abundantly, fully; see **adequately** 1.

**amputate,** *v.* — *Syn.* cut off, sever, operate on, eliminate, cut away, separate, excise, dismember, remove, lop off, truncate.

**amulet,** *n.* — *Syn.* talisman, fetish, ornament; see **charm** 2.

**amuse,** *v.* — *Syn.* divert, entertain, cheer, beguile, occupy, interest, delight, regale, make laugh, strike as funny, recreate, tickle, tickle one's fancy, raise a laugh, convulse, crack up*, break up*, have rolling in the aisles*, have in stitches*, kill*, slay*, fracture*, tickle silly*; see also **entertain** 1.

---

*SYN.* — **amuse** suggests the agreeable occupation of the mind, esp. by something that is light or appeals to the sense of humor *[we amused ourselves with a game of cards; the monkey's antics amused him]*; to **divert** is to take the attention from serious thought or worry to something that amuses; **entertain** implies planned amusement or diversion, often with some intellectual appeal *[another guest entertained us with folk songs]*; **beguile** suggests the occupation of time with an agreeable activity, largely to dispel boredom or tedium

---

**amusement,** *n.* — *Syn.* recreation, pastime, diversion; see **entertainment** 1, 2.

**amusement park,** *n.* — *Syn.* carnival, fair, fun fair, theme park, safari park, water park, Disneyland, Disneyworld, Tivoli.

**amusing,** *modif.* **1.** [Entertaining] — *Syn.* engaging, diverting, enjoyable, beguiling; see **entertaining, pleasant** 2.
**2.** [Funny] — *Syn.* humorous, funny, comical; see **funny** 1.
*See Synonym Study at* FUNNY.

**anachronism,** *n.* — *Syn.* misdate, misdating, antedate, postdate, prochronism, chronological error, misplacement in time, prolepsis, metachronism.

**analogous,** *modif.* — *Syn.* comparable, like, similar; see **alike** 2.

**analogy,** *n.* — *Syn.* relationship, similarity, resemblance, parallel; see **similarity**.
*See Synonym Study at* LIKENESS.

**analysis,** *n.* **1.** [The process of logical division] — *Syn.* separation, breakdown, dissection, subdivision; see **division** 1.
**2.** [Examination] — *Syn.* study, investigation, inquiry, interpretation; see **examination** 1, **judgment** 2.
**3.** [A statement employing analysis, sense 1 or 2] — *Syn.* outline, report, commentary, critique; see **exposition** 2, **review** 2, **summary**.
**4.** [Psychoanalysis] — *Syn.* psychotherapy, depth psychiatry, dream analysis; see **psychoanalysis**.
**in the last** or **final analysis** — *Syn.* lastly, everything considered, in conclusion; see **finally** 2.

**analyst,** *n.* **1.** [Examiner] — *Syn.* questioner, investigator, inquisitor, interpreter; see **critic** 2, **examiner**.
**2.** [Psychoanalyst] — *Syn.* psychiatrist, neuropsychiatrist, psychotherapist; see **psychoanalyst**.

**analytical,** *modif.* **1.** [*Said of persons*] — *Syn.* logical, probing, penetrating; see **judicious, rational** 1.
**2.** [*Said of written or spoken work*] — *Syn.* analytic, systematic, well-organized, precise, scientific, reasonable, rational, well-grounded, well-thought-out, logical, sound, solid, cogent, perspicuous, perceptive, penetrating, searching, thorough, conclusive. — *Ant.* ILLOGICAL, unreasonable, unsound.
**analyze,** *v.* **1.** [To subject to analysis] — *Syn.* dissect, examine, investigate, separate, decompose, break down, break up, take apart, disintegrate, resolve into elements, determine the essential features of, decentralize, decompose into constituent parts, examine minutely, hydrolyze, anatomize, cut up, lay bare, electrolyze, dissolve, decompound, parse, X-ray, put under the microscope. — *Ant.* synthesize, COMPOUND, fuse.
**2.** [To study carefully] — *Syn.* probe, scrutinize, investigate, interpret; see **examine** 1, **explain**.
**anarchist,** *n.* — *Syn.* insurgent, rebel, revolutionary; see **agitator**.
**anarchy,** *n.* **1.** [Disorder] — *Syn.* turmoil, chaos, mob rule; see **disorder** 2.
**2.** [Absence of government] — *Syn.* political nihilism, disregard for law, lawlessness, avowed hostility to government.
**anatomize,** *v.* — *Syn.* dissect, cut up, lay bare, examine; see **analyze** 1.
**anatomy,** *n.* **1.** [The study of living organisms, especially of the body] — *Syn.* medicine, biology, zoology, histology, cytology, embryology, comparative anatomy, morphology, physiology, zootomy, genetics, etiology, ontogeny, morphography.
**2.** [The body or its structure] — *Syn.* bone structure, frame, physique, body, physical structure, skeleton, form, figure, shape, build, carcass*, bone house*, body beautiful*, chassis*.
**3.** [The act of dividing or separating for examination] — *Syn.* dissection, analysis, diagnosis; see **division** 1.
**ancestor,** *n.* — *Syn.* progenitor, forebear, founder of the family, forefather, parent, father, mother, sire, grandsire, forerunner, author, predecessor, originator, precursor, prototype, primogenitor, grandfather, grandmother, procreator, matriarch, patriarch, paterfamilias, materfamilias, relative, begetter, founder, kinsman, kinswoman, grandpa*, grandma*.
**ancestral,** *modif.* — *Syn.* hereditary, familial, parental, paternal, maternal, genealogical, patrimonial, family, inborn, innate, inbred, congenital, genetic, running in the family*, lineal, belonging to the family, tribal, totemic, consanguineous, affiliated, past, old, atavistic, inherited, bequeathed, handed down, transmissible, in the family.
**ancestry,** *n.* — *Syn.* lineage, heritage, parentage, pedigree; see **family** 1.
**anchor,** *n.* **1.** [A device to keep a vessel from drifting] — *Syn.* stay, tie, cramp, killick, grapnel, kedge, bower, mooring, drag anchor, sea anchor, bow anchor, waist anchor, mushroom anchor, stockless anchor, grappling iron, hook*.
**2.** [Anything that holds] — *Syn.* support, mainstay, ballast, safeguard, stay, security, protection, hold, tie, pillar, staff, fastener, grip, defense, protection, foothold, belay.
**3.** [A person who coordinates a newscast] — *Syn.* newscaster, commentator, anchorman, anchorwoman; see **reporter**.
**cast** or **drop anchor** — *Syn.* stay, dock, stop, stopover; see **anchor** 1, **stop** 1.
**weigh anchor** — *Syn.* depart, embark, set out; see **leave** 1, **sail** 1.
**anchor,** *v.* **1.** [To drop an anchor] — *Syn.* make port, tie up, moor, berth, bring a ship in, drop anchor, cast anchor, heave the hook*, lay anchor*, foul the anchor*, carry out the anchor*. — *Ant.* SAIL, weigh anchor, set out for sea.
**2.** [To make fast] — *Syn.* tie, secure, attach; see **fasten** 1.
**anchorage,** *n.* — *Syn.* roadstead, port, harbor, harborage, wharf, dock, jetty, pier, mooring, safety, resting place, berth, refuge, facilities, amphibious installation, haven, quay, embankment, landing place, breakwater, embarcadero.
**ancient,** *modif.* **1.** [Very old] — *Syn.* antique, antiquated, aged; see **old** 1, 2, 3, **old-fashioned**.
**2.** [Belonging to the early history of the world] — *Syn.* classical, Biblical, early; see **classical** 2, **old** 3. Ancient cultures of the Western world include: Roman, Greek, Sumerian, Akkadian, Hittite, Israelite, Egyptian, Hebrew, Chinese, Chaldean, Etruscan, Carthaginian, Babylonian, Phoenician, Mesopotamian, Assyrian, Persian.
*See Synonym Study at* OLD.
**anciently,** *modif.* — *Syn.* long ago, of old, in ancient times, in days of yore, since Adam*.
**and,** *conj.* — *Syn.* in addition to, also, including, plus, together with, as well as, furthermore, moreover.
**Andes,** *n.* — *Syn.* Cordilleras, Andean range, Andean chain, Ecuadorean Andes, Peruvian Andes, Bolivian Andes, Chilean Andes, land of the condor*; see also **mountain** 1.
**andiron,** *n.* — *Syn.* firedog, dog, metal hearth support, fireplace lift.
**androgynous,** *modif.* — *Syn.* hermaphroditic, epicene, unisex, gynandrous; see **bisexual**.
**anecdote,** *n.* — *Syn.* tale, incident, episode; see **story**.
*See Synonym Study at* STORY.
**anemic,** *modif.* **1.** [Pale] — *Syn.* pallid, wan, sickly; see **pale** 1.
**2.** [Weak] — *Syn.* frail, feeble, infirm, lifeless; see **listless** 1, **weak** 1.
**anesthesia,** *n.* — *Syn.* insentience, unconsciousness, numbness, insensibility; see **stupor**.
**anesthetic,** *n.* — *Syn.* sedative, analgesic, painkiller, anodyne, soporific, hypnosis, inhalant, gas, hypodermic injection, drops, opiate, narcotic, dope*.
Specific anesthetics include: benzocaine, lidocaine, Novocain (trademark), methyl chloride, oil of clove, ether, chloroform, cocaine, sodium pentothal, truth serum, chloral hydrate, nitrous oxide, laughing gas, morphine, procaine, alcohol, scopolamine; see also **drug** 2.
**anew,** *modif.* — *Syn.* again, once more, from the beginning, *de novo* (Latin), once again, afresh, newly, in a new or different manner, over again, over, in a different way, as a new act*.
**angel,** *n.* **1.** [A heavenly messenger] — *Syn.* seraph, supernatural being, God's messenger, Angel of Death, good angel, dark angel, archangel, guardian angel, spirit, sprite, cherub, ministering spirit, celestial spirit, winged being, glorified spirit, attendant of God, invisible helper, heavenly spirit, saint, host of heaven. — *Ant.* DEVIL, demon, fiend.
**2.** [*A financial supporter] — *Syn.* benefactor, supporter, backer of theatrical performances; see **patron** 1, **sponsor**.
*See Synonym Study at* SPONSOR.
**angelic,** *modif.* — *Syn.* saintly, beneficent, good, otherworldly, humble, heavenly, ethereal, spiritual, celestial, kind, radiant, beautiful, divine, holy, pure, lovely, innocent, devout, archangelic, virtuous, above reproach, se-

raphic, righteous, self-sacrificing, cherubic. — *Ant.* diabolic, demonic, fiendish.

**anger,** *n.* — *Syn.* wrath, rage, fury, passion, choler, temper, bad *or* ill temper, ire, indignation, acrimony, animosity, hostility, hatred, resentment, outrage, vengeful passion, revengeful passion, hot temper, irascibility, displeasure, irritation, impatience, vexation, annoyance, antagonism, hot blood, violence, agitation, excitement, frenzy, umbrage, disapprobation, tantrum, temper tantrum, petulance, dudgeon, high dudgeon, fretfulness, rankling, peevishness, exasperation, spleen, huff, gall, pique, black mood, aggravation*, fit*, conniption fit*, conniption*, slow burn*, bile*, dander*, snit*, distemper*; see also **rage** 2. — *Ant.* PATIENCE, mildness, calm.

**anger,** *v.* **1.** [To arouse (someone) to anger] — *Syn.* infuriate, madden, enrage, arouse, annoy, get on one's nerves, irritate, agitate, affront, bait, cross, put out of humor, incense, fret, rankle, put into a temper, drive into a rage, vex, gall, goad, chafe, nettle, excite, work up, arouse resentment, provoke ire, arouse ire, ruffle, exasperate, embitter, goad into a frenzy, craze, provoke, make angry, stir up, outrage, offend, inflame, pique, rile, enkindle, exacerbate, burn up*, make all hot and bothered*, get one's back up*, get one's goat*, get in one's hair*, make the fur fly*, get one's dander up*, put one's dander up*, make bad blood*, make one's blood boil*, stir up a hornet's nest*, make sore*, make one blow one's top*, make one blow one's stack*, steam up*, miff*, tick off*, tee off*. — *Ant.* CALM, soothe, placate.
**2.** [To become angry] — *Syn.* lose one's temper, forget oneself, get mad; see **fume, rage** 1.

---

**SYN.** — **anger** is broadly applicable to feelings of resentful or revengeful displeasure; **indignation** implies righteous anger aroused by what seems unjust, mean, or insulting; **rage** suggests a violent outburst of anger in which self-control is lost; **fury** implies a frenzied rage that borders on madness; **ire**, chiefly a literary word, suggests a show of great anger in acts, words, looks, etc.; **wrath** implies deep indignation expressing itself in a desire to punish or get revenge

---

**angle,** *n.* **1.** [Figure or plane formed at an intersection] — *Syn.* notch, flare, crotch, elbow, fork, cusp, incline, obliquity, decline, Y, V, right angle, acute angle, divergence, obtuse angle, point where two lines meet. — *Ant.* CURVE, arc, oval.
**2.** [A projecting corner] — *Syn.* corner, end, point, bend; see **edge** 1, **turn** 2.
**3.** [Point of view] — *Syn.* standpoint, outlook, perspective; see **viewpoint.**
**4.** [An aspect] — *Syn.* phase, aspect, side; see **phase.**
**5.** [*Purpose] — *Syn.* intention, aim, plan, motive; see **purpose** 1, **reason** 3.
*See Synonym Study at* PHASE.

**angle for,** *v.* — *Syn.* plot for, scheme for, maneuver for, fish for, be after, cast about for, hunt for, look for, seek, try for, hint at, be out for, conspire for, try by artful means to get, try to attain by artifice.

**angler,** *n.* — *Syn.* fisher, fisherman, Waltonian, sportsman; see **fisherman.**

**Anglo-Saxon,** *modif.* — *Syn.* Old English, A.S., early English, early British, Germanic, Alfredian, Northumbrian, East Anglian, West Saxon, Anglian, Beowulfian; see also **English.**

**angrily,** *modif.* — *Syn.* heatedly, indignantly, testily, irately, grouchily, crisply, sharply, infuriatedly, savagely, hotly, fiercely, tartly, bitterly, acidly, furiously, wildly,

violently, in anger, crossly, irritably, in the heat of passion. — *Ant.* CALMLY, softly, quietly.

**angry,** *modif.* — *Syn.* enraged, furious, irate, infuriated, mad, fuming, fierce, fiery, raging, convulsed, wrathful, stormy, indignant, cross, vexed, exasperated, resentful, irritated, bitter, ferocious, turbulent, nettled, incensed, piqued, offended, outraged, sullen, irascible, inflamed, annoyed, provoked, galled, chafed, exacerbated, displeased, riled, affronted, wroth, storming, raving, impassioned, sulky, splenetic, choleric, huffy, hostile, rabid, livid, out of humor, out of temper, sore*, peeved*, in a passion*, flown off the handle*, in a pet*, in high dudgeon*, up in the air*, hot under the collar*, boiling*, seething*, burned up*, steamed up*, at the boiling point*, purple in the face*, with one's back up*, all worked up*, seeing red*, het up*, teed off*, ticked off*, miffed*, in a huff*, foaming at the mouth, frothing at the mouth*, wrought up*, up in arms*, fit to be tied*, bent out of shape*. — *Ant.* CALM, pleased, restrained.

**angst,** *n.* — *Syn.* anxiety, apprehension, dread, anguish; see **anxiety.**

**anguish,** *n.* — *Syn.* wretchedness, pain, agony, distress; see **distress** 1, **pain** 1.
*See Synonym Study at* DISTRESS.

**angular,** *modif.* **1.** [Coming to an angle] — *Syn.* sharp-cornered, intersecting, crossing, oblique, divaricate, with corners, V-shaped, Y-shaped, crotched, forked, bent, akimbo, bifurcate(d), crooked, pointed, triangular, rectangular, scraggy, jagged, staggered, zigzag. — *Ant.* ROUND, parallel, side-by-side.
**2.** [Tall and bony] — *Syn.* lank, lean, gaunt, rawboned, bony, awkward, ungainly, lanky, stiff, spindly, spare, gangling, gawky, scrawny, clumsy. — *Ant.* ROUND, plump, fleshy.

**animal,** *modif.* **1.** [Referring to characteristics of the animal kingdom] — *Syn.* animalistic, bestial, beastly, swinish, brutish, wild, beastlike, feral, untamed, instinctual, zoological.
Terms referring to specific animals include: vertebrate, invertebrate, mammalian, ruminant, ungulate, bovine, canine, equine, feline, leonine, lupine, vulpine, ursine, porcine, caprine, ovine, pachydermal, lagomorphic, rodent, marsupial, piscatorial, crustacean, cetacean, amphibian, avian, serpentine, ophidian, reptilian.
**2.** [Referring to the bodily characteristics of humans] — *Syn.* corporeal, physical, bodily, muscular, fleshly, sensual, carnal, earthy, earthly, natural; see also **sensual** 2. — *Ant.* SPIRITUAL, intellectual, supernatural.
*See Synonym Study at* SENSUAL.

**animal,** *n.* **1.** [A mobile organism] — *Syn.* living thing, creature, human being, primate, mammal, beast, being, vertebrate, invertebrate, quadruped, biped, carnivore, herbivore, insectivore, scavenger, omnivore, a representative of the fauna.
**2.** [A nonhuman creature] — *Syn.* creature, beast, beast of burden, brute, domestic animal, wild animal, lower animal, quadruped, beast of the field, creeping thing, varmint, pet, farm animal, dumb animal, wild thing, one of God's creatures, monster, critter*.
**3.** [A brutish human] — *Syn.* brute, savage, monster; see **beast** 2.

**animate,** *modif.* — *Syn.* alive, breathing, moving, animated; see **alive** 1.
*See Synonym Study at* ALIVE.

**animate,** *v.* **1.** [To give life or spirit to] — *Syn.* activate, enliven, vitalize, vivify, stimulate, quicken, energize, invigorate, arouse, exhilarate, liven up, charge, charge up, inspirit, encourage, spark, galvanize, stir, inform, put life into, breathe new life into, bring to life, revive, revitalize,

revivify, endow with life, imbue with life, furnish with vital principle, perk up.
**2.** [To incite] — *Syn.* inspire, arouse, excite, motivate; see **encourage** 2, **incite**.

---

*SYN.* — **animate** implies making alive or lively /an *animated* conversation/ or the imparting of motion or activity /an *animated* doll/; to **quicken** is to rouse to action that which is lifeless or inert /the rebuff *quickened* my resolution/; **exhilarate** implies an enlivening or elevation of the spirits; **stimulate** implies a rousing from inertia, inactivity, or lethargy, as if by goading; **invigorate** means to fill with vigor or energy in a physical sense /an *invigorating* walk/; **vitalize** implies the imparting of vigor or animation in a nonphysical sense /to *vitalize* a dull story/

---

**animated,** *modif.* — *Syn.* spirited, lively, alive, vigorous, vivacious, moving, lifelike; see also **active** 2, **alive** 1, **happy** 1, **lively** 2.
*See Synonym Study at* ALIVE, LIVELY.
**animosity,** *n.* — *Syn.* dislike, enmity, ill will, hostility; see **emnity, hatred** 1, 2.
*See Synonym Study at* ENMITY.
**ankle,** *n.* — *Syn.* anklebone, joint, tarsus, astragalus, talus; see also **bone**.
**annals,** *pl.n.* — *Syn.* chronicles, records, archives; see **history** 2, **journal** 1.
**anneal,** *v.* — *Syn.* toughen, temper, subject to high heat; see **strengthen**.
**annex,** *n.* — *Syn.* addition, additional quarters, new wing; see **addition** 2, 3.
**annex,** *v.* — *Syn.* append, attach, affix; see **add** 2, **join** 1.
**annexation,** *n.* — *Syn.* attachment, incorporation, expansion, occupation; see **addition** 1, **capture, increase** 1.
**annihilate,** *v.* — *Syn.* destroy, demolish, exterminate, obliterate; see **destroy** 1.
*See Synonym Study at* DESTROY.
**anniversary,** *modif.* — *Syn.* yearly, recurrent, once a year; see **annual**.
**anniversary,** *n.* — *Syn.* commemoration (of a past event), yearly celebration, wedding anniversary, birthday, birth date, holiday, saint's day, yearly observance of an event, feast day, ceremony, memorable date, day of annual celebration, celebration of a date, natal day, annual meeting, biennial, triennial, quadrennial, quinquennial, sextennial, septennial, octennial, novennial, decennial, silver anniversary, golden anniversary, diamond jubilee, yearly commemoration, jubilee, festival, fiesta, centenary, centennial, sesquicentennial, bicentenary, bicentennial, tercentenary, tricentennial, red-letter day*.
**annotate,** *v.* — *Syn.* comment, gloss, expound, interpret; see **explain**.
**annotation,** *n.* — *Syn.* footnotes, glossary, notes, commentary; see **explanation** 2.
**announce,** *v.* — *Syn.* declare, proclaim, publish, state; see **advertise** 1, **declare** 1.
*See Synonym Study at* DECLARE.
**announced,** *modif.* — *Syn.* reported, given out, promulgated, told, broadcast, issued, circulated, proclaimed, declared, published, disclosed, divulged, released, made known, disseminated, revealed, publicized, made public, heralded. — *Ant.* HIDDEN, unannounced, suppressed.
**announcement,** *n.* **1.** [The act of announcing] — *Syn.* declaration, notification, prediction, proclamation, communication, publication, broadcasting, expression,

exposition, narration, retailing, reporting, exposing, briefing, promulgation, dissemination, pronouncement, disclosure. — *Ant.* ban, SECRET, silence.
**2.** [The thing announced] — *Syn.* report, statement, advertisement, commercial, decision, news, tidings, returns, brief, bulletin, edict, dictum, white paper, message, notice, advisory, interim report, survey, advice, item, detail, communiqué, speech, release; see also sense 1.
**3.** [A printed announcement] — *Syn.* handbill, poster, pamphlet, flier, circular, broadside, placard, billboard, brochure, form letter, telegram, wire, cable, letter, card, fax, prospectus, leaflet, third-class mail, junk mail.
**announcer,** *n.* — *Syn.* program announcer, broadcaster, telecaster, commentator, sportscaster, weather announcer, weatherman, newscaster, anchor, communicator, disk jockey, DJ*, master of ceremonies, MC, emcee*, moderator, host.
**annoy,** *v.* — *Syn.* pester, irritate, harass, disturb; see **bother** 2, 3.
*See Synonym Study at* BOTHER.
**annoyance,** *n.* **1.** [A feeling of annoyance] — *Syn.* vexation, irritation, pique, uneasiness, disgust, displeasure, provocation, nervousness, irascibility, exasperation, ferment, indignation, sullenness, sulkiness, bad humor, touchiness, perturbation, moodiness, mortification, worry, distress, unhappiness, discontent, heartache, misery, aches and pains, dissatisfaction, impatience, peevishness, aggravation*. — *Ant.* PLEASURE, joy, delight.
**2.** [A source of annoyance] — *Syn.* irritant, inconvenience, nuisance; see **difficulty** 1, 2, **trouble** 2.
**annoying,** *modif.* — *Syn.* irritating, bothersome, vexatious; see **disturbing**.
**annual,** *modif.* — *Syn.* yearly, each year, every year, once a year, year-end, occurring every year, lasting a year, year-long, anniversary, twelvemonth, seasonal, recurring once a year, reckoned by the term of a year, living only one growing season, performed in a year, valid for one year.
**annually,** *modif.* — *Syn.* by the year, each year, per year, once a year, periodically, every year, seasonally, once every twelve months, yearly, *per annum* (Latin), year after year. — *Ant.* DAILY, weekly, monthly.
**annul,** *v.* — *Syn.* invalidate, render void, repeal, revoke; see **abolish, cancel** 2.
*See Synonym Study at* ABOLISH.
**annulment,** *n.* — *Syn.* invalidation, nullification, dissolution, divorce; see **cancellation**.
**anomalous,** *modif.* — *Syn.* atypical, irregular, abnormal, exceptional; see **irregular** 2, **unusual** 2.
*See Synonym Study at* IRREGULAR.
**anomaly,** *n.* — *Syn.* peculiarity, aberration, exception, oddity; see **exception** 2, **freak** 2, **irregularity** 2.
**anonymous,** *modif.* — *Syn.* unsigned, nameless, unknown, unacknowledged, uncredited, pseudonymous, unnamed, authorless, unavowed, unclaimed, unidentified, secret, with the name withheld, of unknown authorship, without a name, bearing no name, incognito, anon., faceless, undifferentiated, indistinguishable, nondescript. — *Ant.* NAMED, signed, acknowledged.
**another,** *modif.* **1.** [Additional] — *Syn.* one more, a further, added; see **extra**.
**2.** [Different] — *Syn.* a separate, a distinct, some other; see **different** 1.
**another,** *pron.* — *Syn.* someone else, a different person, one more, an additional one, something else, a different one.
**answer,** *n.* **1.** [A reply] — *Syn.* response, reply, return,

statement, antiphon, retort, riposte, echo, reverberation, reaction, retaliation, repartee, password, rebuttal, approval, replication, acknowledgment, sign, rejoinder, comeback, back talk*.— *Ant.* QUESTION, query, request.
**2.** [A solution] — *Syn.* discovery, find, solution, result, disclosure, revelation, explanation, interpretation, clue, resolution, elucidation, key, the why and the wherefore*, the idea*, the dope*.
**3.** [A defense] — *Syn.* plea, counterclaim, rebuttal; see **defense** 3.
**answer,** *v.* **1.** [To reply] — *Syn.* reply, respond, rejoin, retort, acknowledge, give answer, field questions, say, echo, return, remark, make reply, return for answer, talk back*, answer back*, come back with*, flash back*, shoot back*.— *Ant.* ask, QUESTION, inquire.
**2.** [To be sufficient] — *Syn.* fill, satisfy, fulfill; see **satisfy** 3.
**3.** [To move in response] — *Syn.* return, refute, retaliate, react, deny, dispute, rebut, parry, argue, plead, defend, contest, rejoin, claim, quash, counterclaim, crush, strike back, backfire*, squelch*, smash*, squash*. — *Ant.* admit, agree, take.
**4.** [To provide a solution] — *Syn.* solve, elucidate, clarify; see **explain, solve.**

*SYN.* — **answer** implies saying, writing, or acting in return, as required by the situation or by courtesy [to *answer* a letter, to *answer* the phone]; **respond** implies an appropriate reaction, either in words or action, made voluntarily or spontaneously to that which serves as a stimulus [to *respond* to an appeal]; **reply** in its strictest application refers to an answer that directly or in detail satisfies a question, charge, etc.; **retort** suggests a reply, esp. one that is sharp or witty, provoked by a charge or criticism; **rejoin** implies an answer, originally to a reply, now often to an objection

**answerable,** *modif.* — *Syn.* responsible, liable, accountable; see **responsible** 1.
*See Synonym Study at* RESPONSIBLE.
**answer for,** *v.* — *Syn.* be responsible for, take the blame for, be accountable for, accept the responsibility for, be liable for, pay for, atone for, make amends for, take upon oneself, sponsor, do at one's own risk, take the rap for*.
**answer to,** *v.* — *Syn.* be responsible for, to be ruled by, respect the authority of; see **obey** 1, **respect** 2.
**ant,** *n.* — *Syn.* emmet, pismire, insect.
Types of ants include: worker, neuter, replete, queen, male.
Antlike insects include: termite, white ant, army ant, legionary ant, fire ant, Texas red ant, black ant, visiting ant, agricultural ant, slave-making ant, slave ant, soldier ant, carpenter ant, mining ant, European ant, pharaoh ant, velvet ant.
**antagonism,** *n.* — *Syn.* enmity, hostility, opposition; see **enmity, hatred** 1, 2.
*See Synonym Study at* ENMITY.
**antagonist,** *n.* — *Syn.* opponent, adversary, opposition, competitor; see **enemy** 1, 2, **opponent** 1, 2, 3.
*See Synonym Study at* OPPONENT.
**antagonistic,** *modif.* — *Syn.* opposing, hostile, inimical; see **unfriendly** 1.
**antagonize,** *v.* — *Syn.* alienate, offend, set against; see **alienate, anger** 1.
**ante-bellum,** *modif.* — *Syn.* before the war, prewar, prior to the war, pre-Civil War.
**antecedent,** *modif.* — *Syn.* preliminary, previous, prior; see **preceding.**
*See Synonym Study at* PREVIOUS.

**antecedent,** *n.* — *Syn.* predecessor, precursor, forerunner; see **forerunner.**
*See Synonym Study at* CAUSE.
**antedate,** *v.* **1.** [To give an earlier date to] — *Syn.* date back, predate, backdate, anachronize, misdate, date before the true date, date earlier than the fact, transfer to an earlier date, accelerate, cause to happen sooner.
**2.** [To precede in time] — *Syn.* come before, precede, antecede; see **precede.**
**antediluvian,** *modif.* — *Syn.* before the Flood, antiquated, out-of-date; see **old** 3, **old-fashioned.**
**antelope,** *n.* — *Syn.* gazelle, eland, addix, dik-dik.
Animals commonly called antelopes include: American antelope, pronghorn, impala, Indian antelope, sasin, algazel, duiker, impoon, tumogo, waterbuck, roodebok, redgazel, korin of Senegal, Indian gazelle, muscat, agacella, blackbuck, bongo, bontebok, bushbuck, gemsbok, gnu, chamois, nilgai, steenbok, Persian gazelle; see also **deer.**
**antenna,** *n.* — *Syn.* aerial, wire, receiving wire, radiating wire, rabbit ears*.
**anteroom,** *n.* — *Syn.* waiting room, antechamber, outer office; see **room** 2.
**anthem,** *n.* — *Syn.* hymn, paean, song of devotion, song of praise; see **hymn, song.**
**anthology,** *n.* — *Syn.* collection, compilation, miscellany, treasury; see **collection** 2.
**anthropology,** *n.* — *Syn.* science of humans, study of humans, study of culture.
Branches of anthropology include: anthropometry, anthropography, anthropogeography, ethnography, ethnology, demography, sociology, prehistoric anthropology, linguistics, cultural anthropology, human paleontology, archaeology, folklore, eugenics, criminology, psychology; see also **social science, sociology.**
**antibiotic,** *n.* — *Syn.* antimicrobial, antitoxin, wonder drug, miracle drug, bacteriostat; see also **medicine** 2.
Common antibiotics include: bacitracin, chlortetracycline, erythromycin, mycomycin, neomycin, nystatin, penicillin, amoxicillin, ampicillin, tetracycline, streptomycin
**antibody,** *n.* — *Syn.* immunizer, neutralizer, immune response *or* defense, immunoglobulin, gamma globulin.
**anticipate,** *v.* **1.** [To foresee] — *Syn.* expect, foresee, look forward to, predict, forecast, prophesy, prognosticate, hope for, look for, look ahead, wait for, count on, plan on, contemplate, have a hunch, bargain for, hold in view, have in prospect, assume, suppose, divine, conjecture, promise oneself, lean upon, entertain the hope, await, surmise, have a presentiment of, reckon on, envision, look into the future, intuit, feel in one's bones*, have a funny feeling*, champ at the bit*, hold one's breath*. — *Ant.* FEAR, be surprised, be caught unawares.
**2.** [To forestall] — *Syn.* prepare for, provide against, forestall, delay, hold back, preclude, hinder, intercept, apprehend, block, be ready, be early, precede, be one step ahead*. — *Ant.* NEGLECT, be caught, ignore.
**3.** [To foretaste] — *Syn.* experience beforehand, have a taste of, look forward to, have an introduction to, have foreknowledge of, take a vicarious pleasure in, thrill to*, know what's coming*.

*SYN.* — **anticipate** implies a looking forward to something with a foretaste of the pleasure or distress it promises, or a realizing of something in advance, and a taking of steps to meet it [*anticipating* her visit, to *anticipate* trouble]; **expect** implies a considerable degree of confidence that a particular event will happen [to *expect* guests for dinner]; **hope** implies a desire for something, accompanied by some confidence in the belief that it can be realized /to *hope* for a raise/; **await** implies a waiting for, or a being ready for, a person or thing /a hearty welcome *awaits* you/

---

**anticipated,** *modif.* — *Syn.* foreseen, predictable, prepared for; see **expected** 2, **likely** 1.

**anticipation,** *n.* **1.** [Expectation] — *Syn.* expectancy, expectation, looking forward, outlook, trust, confident expectation, eager expectation, contemplation, promise, prospect, awaiting, joy, impatience, preoccupation, hope, high hopes. — *Ant.* FEAR, dread, surprise.
**2.** [Presentiment] — *Syn.* prevision, presentiment, intuition, foresight, inkling, premonition, apprehension, foreboding, foreseeing, envisioning, awareness, experience beforehand, foretaste, foreknowledge, forethought, forefeeling, preassurance, forecast, prior realization, obsession, fixation, preconception, preoccupation, a priori knowledge, realization in advance, prescience, hunch, a feeling in one's bones*. — *Ant.* SURPRISE, shock, wonder.

**anticlimax,** *n.* — *Syn.* disappointment, bathos, drop, descent, decline, letdown, comedown, deflation.

**antics,** *pl.n.* — *Syn.* capers, frolics, tricks; see **joke** 1.

**antidote,** *n.* — *Syn.* antitoxin, counteractant, remedy; see **medicine** 2, **remedy** 2.

**antipathetic,** *modif.* — *Syn.* hostile, averse, antagonistic; see **unfriendly** 1.

**antipathy,** *n.* — *Syn.* hostility, abhorrence, aversion; see **aversion** 1, **hatred** 1.
*See Synonym Study at* AVERSION.

**antiquarian,** *modif.* — *Syn.* archaic, ancient, antique; see **old** 3.

**antiquarian,** *n.* — *Syn.* antiquary, student of antiquity, collector, savant, archaeologist, anthropologist, historian, paleologist, medievalist, classicist, archaist, paleographer, bibliophile, archivist, curator.

**antiquated,** *modif.* — *Syn.* old-fashioned, outmoded, out-of-date, obsolescent; see **old** 2, 3, **old-fashioned.**
*See Synonym Study at* OLD.

**antique,** *modif.* **1.** [Old] — *Syn.* ancient, archaic, old; see **old** 3.
**2.** [Old-fashioned] — *Syn.* obsolete, obsolescent, out-of-date; see **old-fashioned.**
*See Synonym Study at* OLD.

**antique,** *n.* — *Syn.* relic, artifact, heirloom, curio, bibelot, collectible, collector's item, old example, early example, ancient evidence, ancient representative, outmoded example, survival, rarity, monument, vestige, *objet d'art* (French), ruin, Rosetta stone; *used in pl.:* antiquities, reliques; see also **art** 3, **furniture, manuscript.**

**antiquity,** *n.* **1.** [The quality of being old] — *Syn.* antiqueness, ancientness, oldness, elderliness, age, old age, great age, venerableness, hoariness, archaism, archaicism, obsolescence. — *Ant.* NEWNESS, modernity, youthfulness.
**2.** [An object out of the past; *used in plural*] — *Syn.* artifact, monument, relic; see **antique, relic** 1.
**3.** [Ancient times] — *Syn.* remote times, ancient times, old days, former ages, the olden time, days of old, days of yore, distant past, ancient history, classical times, Homeric age, Athens, Etruscan period, ancient Egypt, Chou Dynasty, Roman era, era before Christ, pagan times, Babylon, Biblical days, Hellenistic period, Dark Ages, early ages, the time before the Middle Ages. — *Ant.* PRESENT, modern times, contemporary times.

**antiseptic,** *modif.* **1.** [Free of germs] — *Syn.* clean, germ-free, sterile; see **pure** 2.

**2.** [Destructive of germs] — *Syn.* prophylactic, aseptic, purifying, hygienic, antibacterial, medicated, germ-destroying, germicidal, disinfectant, bactericidal, sterilizing, antibiotic.

**antiseptic,** *n.* — *Syn.* disinfectant, germicide, cleanser, detergent, prophylactic, preservative, preventive, preventative, counterirritant, sterilizer, immunizing agent, bactericide, microbicide, insecticide, fumigant; see also **medicine** 2.
Antiseptics include: iodine, boric acid, creosote, guaiacol, hexylresorcinol, sulfanilamide, sulfathiazole, Lysol (trademark), Listerine (trademark), Mercurochrome (trademark), hydrogen peroxide, salt solution, carbolic acid, phenol, alcohol, boiling water, soap, boracic acid, silver vitellin, mycozol, merthiolate, iodoform, triiodomethane; see also **sulfa drug.**

**antisocial,** *modif.* **1.** [Unfriendly] — *Syn.* unsociable, reclusive, retiring, misanthropic; see **misanthropic, unfriendly** 2.
**2.** [Harmful to society] — *Syn.* hostile, alienated, asocial, rebellious; see **rebellious** 2, 3, **unfriendly** 1.

**antithesis,** *n.* **1.** [Opposition] — *Syn.* contrast, contradiction, contraposition, contrariety; see **contrast** 2.
**2.** [Opposite] — *Syn.* direct opposite, reverse, converse; see **opposite.**

**antithetical,** *modif.* — *Syn.* opposite, antithetic, diametrically opposed; see **opposite** 1.
*See Synonym Study at* OPPOSITE.

**antitoxin,** *n.* — *Syn.* vaccine, antibody, immunizing agent, serum, antiserum, counteragent, antidote, antivenin, defensive protein, preventive, toxin neutralizer, neutralizing agent, counteractant, counterpoison, antivenom, antibiotic, antiseptic, alexipharmic; see also **medicine** 2.

**antlers,** *pl.n.* — *Syn.* horns, tusks, excrescences.
Prongs of an antler include: brow antler, bez *or* bay antler, royal antler, surroyal *or* crown antler; see also **horn** 2.

**anxiety,** *n.* — *Syn.* worry, uneasiness, apprehension, disquiet, nervousness, anxiousness, concern, misgiving, foreboding, fear, dread, agitation, inquietude, unease, distress, angst, stress, tension, strain, neurosis, butterflies*; see also **care** 2, **nervousness** 1.
*See Synonym Study at* CARE.

**anxious,** *modif.* **1.** [Disturbed in mind] — *Syn.* apprehensive, concerned, uneasy, worried; see **afraid** 1, **troubled** 1, **uneasy** 1.
**2.** [Eager] — *Syn.* desirous, zealous, eager, fervent; see **eager, enthusiastic** 1, 2.
*See Synonym Study at* EAGER.

**any,** *modif.* **1.** [Without discrimination] — *Syn.* either, whatever, whichever, a, an, one, any sort, any kind, any one, in general, each, one or more, even one.
**2.** [Every] — *Syn.* every, all, each and every, one and all, several, unspecified; see also **all** 2, **each** 1.
**3.** [Some] — *Syn.* some, a little, part of, a bit; see **some** 1.

**anybody,** *pron.* — *Syn.* anyone, any person, whoever, whomever, everyone, everybody, all, the whole world, each and every one, any of them, anyone at all; see also **everybody.**

**anyhow,** *modif.* **1.** [In any event] — *Syn.* at any rate, in any event, at all events, anyway, nevertheless, nonetheless, in spite of, however, in any case, regardless, and so, whatever happens, under any circumstances, irregardless*, somehow or other*.
**2.** [In any manner] — *Syn.* anyway, in any way, in whatever way, however, in one way or the other, in any respect, in either way, at all, haphazardly, carelessly,

anywhichway★, nohow★. — *Ant.* EXACTLY, in one way, in a certain way.

**anyone,** pron. — *Syn.* a person, one, anyone at all; see **anybody.**

**anyplace★,** *modif.* — *Syn.* everywhere, wherever, in any place; see **anywhere.**

**anything,** pron. — *Syn.* something, everything, all, anything at all, anything whatever, aught, any, any one thing, whatever one wants, you name it★.

**any time,** *modif.* — *Syn.* whenever, at your convenience, when you will, no matter when, any time when, at any moment, anytime★.

**anyway,** *modif.* — *Syn.* in any event, nevertheless, in any manner; see **anyhow** 1, 2.

**anywhere,** *modif.* — *Syn.* wherever, in any place, to any place, all over, everywhere, in whatever place, wherever you go★, anyplace★.

   **get anywhere** — *Syn.* prosper, thrive, advance, make headway; see **succeed** 1.

**apart,** *modif.* **1.** [Separated] — *Syn.* disconnected, distant, disassociated; see **separated.**

   **2.** [Aside] — *Syn.* to one side, at one side, at a distance, aloof; see **aside.**

   **3.** [Distinct] — *Syn.* separate, special, alone, isolated; see **individual** 1.

   **4.** [Separately] — *Syn.* freely, exclusively, singly, alone; see **independently, individually.**

   **5.** [Into pieces] — *Syn.* asunder, to pieces, in two, to bits; see **asunder** 1.

   **take apart** — *Syn.* disassemble, dismember, dissect, reduce; see **analyze** 1, **dismantle, divide** 1.

   **tell apart** — *Syn.* distinguish, characterize, discriminate, differentiate; see **distinguish** 1.

**apartment,** *n.* — *Syn.* rooms, quarters, flat, suite, cooperative apartment, condominium apartment, penthouse, residence, home, duplex, studio, efficiency, floor-through, railroad flat, walk-up, loft, townhouse, lodgings, pied-à-terre, bed-sitter, bed-sit (*both* British), bachelor apartment★, digs★, bachelor pad★, pad★, co-op★, condo★.

**apartment house,** *n.* — *Syn.* apartment building, apartment complex, tenement, hotel, condominium, condo★, high-rise apartments, high-rise, apartment hotel, court, co-op★.

**apathetic,** *modif.* — *Syn.* unemotional, impassive, unresponsive, unconcerned; see **indifferent** 1, **listless** 1, **unconcerned.**

*See Synonym Study at* IMPASSIVE.

**apathy,** *n.* — *Syn.* dullness, impassivity, indifference, unconcern; see **indifference** 1.

**ape,** *n.* — *Syn.* anthropoid ape, great ape, primate, simian, gorilla, chimpanzee, orangutan, baboon, gibbon, siamang; see also **monkey.**

**ape,** *v.* — *Syn.* imitate, copy, mimic, impersonate; see **imitate** 2.

*See Synonym Study at* IMITATE.

**aperture,** *n.* — *Syn.* opening, fissure, gap; see **hole** 1, 2.

**apex,** *n.* — *Syn.* summit, top, zenith; see **summit, top** 1.

*See Synonym Study at* SUMMIT.

**aphorism,** *n.* — *Syn.* saying, proverb, adage; see **proverb, saying.**

*See Synonym Study at* SAYING.

**aphrodisiac,** *n.* — *Syn.* love potion, philter, turn-on★.

**apiece,** *modif.* — *Syn.* each, respectively, separately, individually; see **each** 2.

**apocryphal,** *modif.* — *Syn.* spurious, unauthenticated, fictitious, doubtful; see **false** 2, **legendary** 2.

*See Synonym Study at* LEGENDARY.

**apologetic,** *modif.* — *Syn.* contrite, remorseful, sorry,

penitent, repentant, regretful, supplicating, retracting, self-effacing, self-reproachful, self-condemnatory, self-incriminating, explanatory, extenuating, atoning, expiatory, rueful, expressing regret, regretfully acknowledging, compunctious, penitential, propitiatory, conciliatory, conscience-stricken, down on one's knees★. — *Ant.* stubborn, unrepentant, unregenerate.

**apologize,** *v.* — *Syn.* beg pardon, ask pardon, excuse oneself, offer an excuse, atone, ask forgiveness, make amends, make apology for, regret, express regret, give satisfaction, clear oneself, make up, bow to, make reparations for, confess, offer compensation, admit one's guilt, retract, withdraw, eat crow★, eat one's words★; see also **excuse.** — *Ant.* INSULT, offend, hurt.

**apology,** *n.* — *Syn.* excuse, regrets, plea, justification; see **acknowledgment** 1, 2, **explanation** 2, **regret** 1.

**apoplexy,** *n.* — *Syn.* breaking a blood vessel, thrombosis, occlusion, circulatory trouble, stroke, seizure; see also **disease.**

**apostate,** *n.* — *Syn.* renegade, one of little faith, backslider, defector; see **deserter, traitor.**

**apostle,** *n.* — *Syn.* messenger, witness, disciple, evangelist; see **disciple** 2, **follower, missionary.**

**apostrophe,** *n.* **1.** [A punctuation mark] — *Syn.* pause, contraction mark, sign of omission, plural mark, sign of possession.

   **2.** [An appeal] — *Syn.* invocation, address, soliloquy, supplication; see **appeal** 1, **speech** 3.

**appall,** *v.* — *Syn.* shock, amaze, horrify, dismay; see **dismay, shock** 2.

*See Synonym Study at* DISMAY.

**appalling,** *modif.* — *Syn.* horrifying, shocking, dreadful; see **frightful** 1.

**apparatus,** *n.* — *Syn.* appliance, machinery, contrivance, paraphernalia; see **device** 1, **equipment.**

**apparel,** *n.* — *Syn.* clothes, attire, garments; see **clothes**

**apparent,** *modif.* **1.** [Open to view] — *Syn.* visible, clear, obvious, manifest; see **obvious** 1.

   **2.** [Obvious] — *Syn.* obvious, self-evident, glaring, patent; see **obvious** 2.

   **3.** [Seeming, but not actual] — *Syn.* ostensible, seeming, possible, plausible; see **likely** 1.

*See Synonym Study at* OBVIOUS.

**apparently,** *modif.* — *Syn.* evidently, obviously, at first sight, at first view, in plain sight, unmistakably, at a glance, indubitably, expressly, transparently, perceptibly, plainly, patently, clearly, openly, overtly, conspicuously, evident to the senses, palpably, tangibly, presumably, possibly, supposedly, manifestly, most likely, ostensibly, reasonably, intuitively, seemingly, assumably, reputedly, as if, as though, if one may judge, to all appearances, in almost every way, allegedly, as far as it is possible to assume, in all likelihood, as it seems, as it were, on the face of it, at first blush, to the eye. — *Ant.* SURELY, genuinely, truly.

**apparition,** *n.* — *Syn.* phantom, specter, spirit; see **ghost** 1.

**appeal,** *n.* **1.** [A plea] — *Syn.* request, plea, bid, claim, suit, submission, solicitation, petition, question, imploring, recourse, entreaty, prayer, invocation, supplication, address, demand, importunity, call, requisition, application, overture, proposition, proposal, call for aid, earnest request, adjuration. — *Ant.* DENIAL, refusal, renunciation.

   **2.** [Action to carry a case to a higher court] — *Syn.* petition, motion, application, request for retrial, request for review.

   **3.** [Attractiveness] — *Syn.* attractiveness, attraction, charm, glamour, interest, allure, charmingness, seductiveness, engagingness, winsomeness, desirability, fascination, magnetism, charisma, sex appeal.

**appeal,** *v.* **1.** [To ask another seriously] — *Syn.* entreat, request, petition, implore, beseech, plead, solicit, beg, supplicate, importune, urge, adjure, pray, sue; see also **beg** 1.
**2.** [To carry a case to a higher court] — *Syn.* apply for a retrial, retry, contest, bring new evidence, advance, reopen, refer to, review.
**3.** [To attract] — *Syn.* interest, attract, engage, fascinate, tempt, tantalize, awaken a response, invite, entice, allure, captivate, intrigue, attract one's interest, enchant, beguile, please, catch one's eye; see also **fascinate.**

*SYN.* — **appeal** implies an earnest, sometimes urgent request and in legal usage connotes resort to a higher court or authority; **plead,** applied to formal statements in court answering to allegations or charges, carries into general usage the implication of entreaty by argument *[she pleaded for tolerance];* **sue** implies respectful or formal solicitation for redress, a favor, etc.; **petition** implies a formal request, usually in writing and in accordance with established rights; **pray** and **supplicate** suggest humility in entreaty and imply that the request is addressed to God or to a superior authority, **supplicate** in addition suggesting a kneeling or other abjectly prayerful attitude

**appear,** *v.* **1.** [To come into sight or being] — *Syn.* emerge, arise, come into view, come forth, come out, come forward, be within view, be in sight, present itself, show itself, expose itself, discover itself, betray itself, manifest itself, rise, come into sight, surface, become plain, issue, come into being, be published, loom, arrive, come to light, enter the picture, recur, materialize, become visible, loom up, develop, break through, show up, crop up, crop out, burst forth, look forth, turn up, stand out, come onto the horizon, meet the eye, catch the eye, spring up, pop up*, bob up*, poke up*, cut a figure*, heave in sight*, see the light of day*, peep out*, break cover*, rear its head*. — *Ant.* depart, DISAPPEAR, vanish.
**2.** [To seem] — *Syn.* look, seem, have the appearance, resemble; see **seem.**
**3.** [To present oneself publicly] — *Syn.* be in attendance, put in an appearance, make an appearance, answer a summons, present oneself, be present, submit oneself, arrive, stand before, obey an order, oblige, come into public notice, come before the public, be placed before the public, come upon the stage, perform, turn up, be there, show up*, show one's face*, show one's mug*. — *Ant.* be absent, LEAVE, be missing.

**appearance,** *n.* **1.** [Looks] — *Syn.* look, looks, aspect, features, exterior, countenance, face, bearing, demeanor, mien, manner, condition, presentation, carriage, cast, air, fashion, attitude, stamp, expression, lineaments, guise, dress, outline, contour, visage, form, shape, semblance, color, port, presence, posture, pose, figure, outward form, character, makeup, cut of one's jib*. — *Ant.* MIND, personality, soul.
**2.** [Outward show] — *Syn.* show, pretense, façade, semblance, guise, impression, idea, image, mask, surface, mirage, illusion, seeming, surface show, false front, exterior, pose, face, veneer, vision, aura, shadow, simulacrum, front*, window dressing*. — *Ant.* reality, FACT, substance.
**3.** [The act of appearing] — *Syn.* arrival, advent, coming, presentation, representation, exhibition, unveil-

ing, display, emergence, rise, introduction, occurrence, manifestation, actualization, materialization, debut, entrance, publication. — *Ant.* DEPARTURE, going, vanishing.
**keep up appearances** — *Syn.* be outwardly proper, hide one's faults *or* failures, put up a front*, keep up with the Joneses*; see **deceive, pretend** 1.
**make** *or* **put in an appearance** — *Syn.* appear, appear publicly, come, show up*; see **appear** 3, **arrive** 1.

*SYN.* — **appearance** and **look** refer generally to the outward impression of a person or thing, but the former often implies mere show or pretense *[gave an appearance of honesty],* and the latter (often in the plural) refers specifically to physical details *[the forlorn look of an abandoned house, good looks];* **aspect,** in this comparison, also refers to physical features, esp. to facial expression *[a man of morose aspect]* or to visual effect at a given time or place *[in spring the yard had a refreshing aspect];* **semblance,** which refers to the outward impression as contrasted with the inner reality, usually does not imply deception *[a semblance of order],* while **guise** is usually used of a deliberately misleading appearance *[under the guise of patriotism]*

**appease,** *v.* **1.** [To satisfy] — *Syn.* allay, relieve, satisfy, assuage; see **relieve** 2, **satisfy** 1, 3.
**2.** [To calm] — *Syn.* soothe, pacify, conciliate, give in to; see **pacify** 1, **quiet** 1, **yield** 1.
*See Synonym Study at* PACIFY.
**appeasement,** *n.* — *Syn.* moderation, satisfaction, peace offering, settlement, amends, accommodation, assuagement, submission, yielding, adjustment, reparation, pacification, alleviation, mollification, conciliation, propitiation, placation, reconciliation, restoration of harmony, mitigation, compromise, grant, giving in. — *Ant.* IRRITATION, excitation, fomentation.
**append,** *v.* **1.** [To add] — *Syn.* affix, supplement, annex; see **add** 2.
**2.** [To attach] — *Syn.* fasten, fix, conjoin; see **join** 1.
**appendage,** *n.* **1.** [An addition] — *Syn.* attachment, appendix, accessory; see **addition** 2.
**2.** [A bodily extension] — *Syn.* arm, leg, limb, external organ, feeler, tentacle, tail, extremity, member, flipper, fin*, shank*, stem*, dog*.
**appendicitis,** *n.* — *Syn.* diseased appendix, ruptured appendix, inflamed appendix, case for an appendectomy; see **disease.**
**appendix,** *n.* — *Syn.* addendum, supplement, codicil, excursus, attachment, addition, bibliography, tables, notes, index, samples, quotations, verification, proof, letters, documents, postscript; see also **addition** 2.
Anatomical appendices include: vermiform appendix, appendix vermiformis, appendix caeci, appendices epiploicae, appendix auriculae, appendix vesicae (*all* Latin).
**appetite,** *n.* **1.** [A craving for food or drink] — *Syn.* hunger, thirst, craving, longing, urge, taste, dryness, dehydration, starvation, empty stomach, thirstiness, ravenousness, voracity, desire. — *Ant.* INDIFFERENCE, satiety, surfeit.
**2.** [Desire] — *Syn.* longing, craving, hankering, taste; see **desire** 1, 3.
**appetizer,** *n.* — *Syn.* hors d'oeuvre, antipasto, canapé, aperitif, cocktail, tidbit, delicacy, relish; see also **hors d'oeuvre.**
**appetizing,** *modif.* — *Syn.* savory, tasty, tantalizing, delicious, appealing, mouth-watering, tempting, inviting,

luscious, delectable; see also **delicious** 1.— *Ant.* TASTE-LESS, uninteresting, unappealing.

**applaud,** *v.* — *Syn.* cheer, clap, give an ovation to, acclaim; see **praise** 1.

**applause,** *n.* — *Syn.* clapping, ovation, cheers, acclaim; see **praise** 1, 2.

**apple,** *n.* **1.** Varieties of apples include: MacIntosh, Baldwin, Delicious, Russet, Northern Spy, Snow, crab, Jonathan, Rome Beauty, Albermarle pippin, Missouri pippin, Newtown pippin, yellow Newtown, Rhode Island Greening, Arkansas Black, Wolf River, Fameuse, Gravenstein, Wealthy, Ben Davis, Granny Smith, Grimes Golden, Oldenburg, red Astrakhan, white Astrakhan, Russian Astrakhan, Winesap, Stayman Winesap, yellow transparent, York Imperial, Janet, king, Lawyer, Maiden's Blush, Shockley, Twenty-ounce, Peck's Pleasant, Pennock, Willow Twig, red June, Early Harvest, early Redbird, Cortland.
**2.** [Something suggesting an apple] — *Syn.* oak apple, gall, gallnut, nutgall, custard apple, fir apple, balsam apple, May apple, love apple, egg apple, hawthorn berry, Dead Sea apple, apple of Sodom, mad apple, rose apple, hip, haw.

**apple of one's eye,** *n.* — *Syn.* pet, idol, darling, ideal; see **favorite.**

**apple polisher\*,** *n.* — *Syn.* flatterer, toady, flunkey; see **sycophant.**

**appliance,** *n.* — *Syn.* instrument, machine, apparatus; see **device** 1, **tool** 1.
Common household appliances include: broiler, deep-fryer, broom, floor waxer, can opener, carving knife, coffee maker, blender, food processor, microwave oven, hair dryer, popcorn popper, toaster, toothbrush, waffle iron, griddle, warming tray, iron, sewing machine, vacuum cleaner, dishwasher, rotisserie, disposal, clothes dryer, clothes washer, washing machine, stove, oven, refrigerator, freezer, barbecue, water heater, air conditioner, air purifier; see also **radio** 2, **record player, television.**
*See Synonym Study at* TOOL.

**applicable,** *modif.* — *Syn.* suitable, appropriate, relevant; see **fit** 1, 2, **relevant.**
*See Synonym Study at* RELEVANT.

**applicant,** *n.* — *Syn.* petitioner, aspirant, claimant, appellant; see **candidate.**

**application,** *n.* **1.** [Use] — *Syn.* employment, utilization, use, purpose; see **use** 1, 2.
**2.** [Close attention] — *Syn.* devotion, assiduousness, diligence; see **attention** 2, **diligence.**
**3.** [That which is applied] — *Syn.* lotion, balm, wash, ointment, salve, face cream, mud pack, ice bag, bandage, compress, dressing, tourniquet, alcohol, alcohol rub, stimulant, rubefacient, emollient, pomade, poultice, talcum powder, unguent, plaster, heating pad; see also **cosmetic, lotion, medicine** 2, **salve.**
**4.** [Putting one thing on another] — *Syn.* administering, administration, applying, laying on, piling on, cementing, oiling, dosing, rubbing, reinforcement, creaming, treatment, massaging, bringing into contact, juxtaposing, juxtaposition.
**5.** [A request] — *Syn.* petition, entreaty, demand; see **appeal** 1, **request.**
**6.** [The instrument by which a request is made] — *Syn.* petition, form, questionnaire, blank, paper, letter, credentials, certificate, statement, requisition, bill, formal application, letter of application; see also **form** 5.
**7.** [Relevance] — *Syn.* applicability, relevance, pertinence, relationship; see **fitness** 1, **importance** 1.

**applied,** *modif.* **1.** [Put to use] — *Syn.* used, employed, related, correlated, enforced, practiced, utilized, brought to bear, adapted, shaped, exercised, devoted, tested, adjusted, activated.
**2.** [*Said of theoretical knowledge that can be used*] — *Syn.* practical, pragmatic, utilitarian, practicable; see **practical.**

**apply,** *v.* **1.** [To make a request] — *Syn.* petition, demand, appeal, put in for; see **ask** 1, **beg** 1, **try out for.**
**2.** [To make use of] — *Syn.* utilize, employ, practice, implement; see **use** 1.
**3.** [To place upon] — *Syn.* affix, fasten, stamp, administer, lay on, put on, spread on, place on, touch, bestow, rub in, massage in; see also **fasten** 1, **join** 1.
**4.** [To be relevant] — *Syn.* be pertinent, pertain, bear on, have bearing on, relate to, be applicable to, be adapted to, be suitable to, allude to, concern, touch, touch on, involve, affect, regard, have reference to, connect, refer, fit, fit the case, have some connection with, suit, be in relationship, hold good, hold true, come into play.

**apply (oneself),** *v.* — *Syn.* attend to, dedicate oneself, devote oneself, address oneself, be occupied with, keep one's mind on, direct oneself to, concentrate on, persevere in, persist in, give oneself wholly to, be industrious, work at, buckle down\*, keep one's nose to the grindstone\*.

**appoint,** *v.* **1.** [To designate] — *Syn.* select, designate, elect, name; see **delegate** 1, 2.
**2.** [To furnish] — *Syn.* furnish, equip, outfit; see **furnish** 1, 2.
*See Synonym Study at* FURNISH.

**appointed,** *modif.* — *Syn.* selected, chosen, delegated; see **named** 2.

**appointee,** *n.* — *Syn.* nominee, deputy, representative; see **delegate.**

**appointment,** *n.* **1.** [The act of appointing] — *Syn.* designation, election, selection, nomination, approval, choice, promotion, placing in office, ordination, assignment, assigning, commissioning, authorization, installation, deputation, delegation, delegating, certification, empowering.
**2.** [An engagement] — *Syn.* interview, meeting, arrangement, engagement, rendezvous, assignment, invitation, errand, date, assignation, tryst.
**3.** [A position] — *Syn.* office, post, employment, placement; see **job** 1, **profession** 1.

**apportion,** *v.* — *Syn.* allot, portion out, allocate, distribute; see **allot, distribute** 1.
*See Synonym Study at* ALLOT.

**apportionment,** *n.* — *Syn.* partition, allotment, division; see **distribution** 1.

**appraisal,** *n.* — *Syn.* examination, evaluation, assessment; see **estimate** 1, **judgment** 2.

**appraise,** *v.* **1.** [To set a price on] — *Syn.* assess, price, assay; see **value** 2.
**2.** [To judge] — *Syn.* estimate, evaluate, calculate, size up\*; see **estimate** 1.
*See Synonym Study at* ESTIMATE.

**appreciable,** *modif.* — *Syn.* recognizable, considerable, perceptible, discernible, measurable, sizable, goodly, good-sized, substantial, tangible, definite, estimable, ascertainable, calculable, visible, apparent, distinguishable, sensible, material, perceivable, evident, detectable, noticeable, significant, fairish\*, not inconsiderable\*, healthy\*. — *Ant.* imperceptible, slight, inconsiderable.
*See Synonym Study at* TANGIBLE.

**appreciate,** *v.* **1.** [To be grateful] — *Syn.* welcome, thank, enjoy, pay respects to, be obliged, feel obliged, be indebted, feel obligated, be obligated, be appreciative, acknowledge, never forget, give thanks, overflow with gratitude; see also **thank.** — *Ant.* find fault with, minimize, COMPLAIN, object.

**2.** [To recognize worth] — *Syn.* esteem, prize, value, treasure, cherish, honor, extol, praise, applaud, admire, look up to; see also **admire** 1.

**3.** [To enjoy, as art] — *Syn.* be sensitive to, have a taste for, have a faculty for, respond to, enjoy, relish; see also **like** 1.

**4.** [To be aware of] — *Syn.* comprehend, understand, apprehend, recognize; see **understand** 1.

---

*SYN.* — **appreciate**, in this comparison, implies sufficient critical judgment to see the value of or to enjoy [to *appreciate* good music]; to **value** is to rate highly because of worth [I *value* your friendship]; to **prize** is to value highly or take great satisfaction in [a *prized* possession]; to **treasure** is to regard as precious and implies special care to protect from loss; to **esteem** is to hold in high regard and implies warm attachment or respect [an *esteemed* statesman]; to **cherish** is to prize or treasure, but connotes greater affection for or attachment to the thing cherished [she *cherished* her friends] See also Synonym Study at UNDERSTAND.

---

**appreciation,** *n.* **1.** [Sense of gratitude] — *Syn.* thankfulness, recognition, gratefulness; see **gratitude.**
**2.** [Favorable opinion] — *Syn.* esteem, commendation, high regard; see **admiration.**
**3.** [Enjoyment, as of art] — *Syn.* aesthetic sense, appreciativeness, taste, love, affection, sensitivity, relish, enjoyment, sensibility, sensitiveness, attraction.
**4.** [Realization] — *Syn.* recognition, grasp, visualization; see **judgment** 1, 2.
**appreciative,** *modif.* — *Syn.* thankful, appreciatory, grateful, obliged, indebted, responsive, keen, alive to, sensitive to, understanding, sympathetic, generous, cooperative, enlightened, aware, perceptive, favorable, satisfied, cordial, considerate, friendly, affectionate, entertained, gladdened, sensible of, cognizant of, conscious of, capable of appreciating, under obligation, beholden, enthusiastic, receptive. — *Ant.* UNFRIENDLY, cold, hostile.
**apprehend,** *v.* **1.** [To understand] — *Syn.* perceive, comprehend, grasp; see **understand** 1.
**2.** [To arrest] — *Syn.* seize, place under arrest, take into custody; see **arrest** 1.
**apprehension,** *n.* **1.** [Foreboding] — *Syn.* trepidation, dread, misgiving; see **anxiety, fear** 2.
**2.** [Understanding] — *Syn.* comprehension, grasp, perception, perspicacity; see **judgment** 1.
**3.** [Arrest] — *Syn.* capture, seizure, detention; see **arrest** 1.
**4.** [Estimate] — *Syn.* opinion, conclusion, belief; see **judgment** 3.
**apprehensive,** *modif.* — *Syn.* fearful, worried, anxious, uncertain; see **afraid** 1, **troubled** 1, **uneasy** 1.
**apprentice,** *n.* — *Syn.* trainee, novice, beginner, learner; see **amateur, assistant, student.**
**apprise,** *v.* — *Syn.* notify, inform, advise; see **notify** 1.
*See Synonym Study at* NOTIFY.
**approach,** *n.* **1.** [A means of access] — *Syn.* path, way, road, passageway; see **entrance** 2, **road** 1.
**2.** [Plan of action] — *Syn.* method, program, procedure, strategy; see **method** 2, **plan** 2.
**3.** [The act of coming near or on] — *Syn.* coming, advance, advent, arrival, access, appearance, oncoming,

reaching, landing, approaching, nearing, act of drawing near, coming nearer, accession.
**4.** [Overture; *usually plural*] — *Syn.* proposal, offer, proposition; see **proposal** 1, **suggestion** 1.
**approach,** *v.* **1.** [To approach personally] — *Syn.* appeal to, apply to, address, speak to, talk to, propose, request, accost, direct oneself to, make advances to, make overtures to, take aside, talk to in private, buttonhole*, corner*, descend on, descend upon*, sound out*. — *Ant.* AVOID, shun, turn away.
**2.** [To come near in space] — *Syn.* near, come near, come nearer, go toward, move toward, drift toward, come up to, step up to, roll up to, advance, loom up, creep up, drive up, verge upon, draw near, go near, converge on, advance on, gain on, come into sight, progress, close in, surround, come forward, come closer, catch up to, overtake, bear down on, edge up to, ease up to, head into. — *Ant.* LEAVE, recede, depart.
**3.** [To come near in time] — *Syn.* be imminent, be forthcoming, threaten, slip by, loom (up), await, near, draw near, impend, diminish, decrease, grow short, stare one in the face*, be around the corner*. — *Ant.* recede, extend, stretch out.
**4.** [To approximate] — *Syn.* come close to, approximate, compare; see **equal, resemble.**
**approachable,** *modif.* **1.** [Accessible] — *Syn.* convenient, attainable, obtainable; see **available.**
**2.** [Sociable] — *Syn.* agreeable, receptive, congenial; see **friendly** 1.
**approaching,** *modif.* — *Syn.* nearing, advancing, convergent, impending, oncoming, impinging, touching, approximating, coming, looming up, drawing near, to come, next to come, threatening, emergent, rising, moving closer, gaining. — *Ant.* PASSING, receding, diminishing.
**approbation,** *n.* **1.** [Approval] — *Syn.* high regard, esteem, favor; see **admiration.**
**2.** [Sanction] — *Syn.* consent, support, endorsement; see **permission.**
**appropriate,** *modif.* — *Syn.* proper, suitable, suited, fitting; see **fit** 1, 2, **relevant.**
*See Synonym Study at* FIT.
**appropriate,** *v.* **1.** [To seize] — *Syn.* secure, usurp, take possession of; see **seize** 2.
**2.** [To provide money] — *Syn.* set aside, set apart, allocate, assign (to a particular use), reserve, apportion, devote, appoint, allow, allow for, disburse, budget, allot, earmark.
**appropriately,** *modif.* — *Syn.* fittingly, suitably, judiciously, justly, aptly, fitly, relevantly, decorously, rightly, properly, duly, becomingly, seasonably, competently, agreeably, happily. — *Ant.* BADLY, inappropriately, improperly.
**appropriateness,** *n.* — *Syn.* aptness, propriety, suitability; see **fitness** 1.
**appropriation,** *n.* **1.** [The act of providing money] — *Syn.* allocation, allotment, donation, funding, sponsoring, sponsorship, grant, bestowal, giving, endowing, budgeting, provision, allowance, concession, apportionment, stipulation, shelling out*. — *Ant.* REDUCTION, curtailment, stoppage.
**2.** [Money provided] — *Syn.* stipend, grant, fund, allotment, allowance, allocation, contribution, cash, budget, subscription, benefit, relief, remittance, gift, remuneration, donation, support, subsidy, subvention, pay, the wherewithal.
**approval,** *n.* **1.** [Favorable opinion] — *Syn.* regard, esteem, favor; see **admiration.**

2. [Sanction] — *Syn.* endorsement, support, consent; see **permission.**

**on approval** — *Syn.* on trial, subject to refusal, on probation, on examination, guaranteed; see also **temporarily.**

**approve,** *v.* 1. [To give approval] — *Syn.* ratify, affirm, support, countenance, endorse, sign, countersign, confirm, license, consent to, agree to, assent to, sanction, empower, charter, validate, seal, legalize, recognize, accredit, certify, give one's blessing, recommend, make law, pronounce legal, authorize, second, subscribe to, adopt, make valid, sustain, uphold, concur in, allow, permit, go along with, maintain, vote for, accede to, corroborate, acquiesce in, establish, homologate, pass, OK, give the go-ahead*, give the green light*, give one's imprimatur*, rubber-stamp*, come around*. — *Ant.* reject, veto, DENY.

2. [To favor] — *Syn.* encourage, be in favor of, favor, support, recommend, make allowances for, subscribe to, advocate, accept, tolerate, condone, appreciate, acclaim, applaud, take kindly to, go for*, hold with*; see also sense 1, **praise** 1.

**SYN.** — **approve,** the most general of the following terms, means simply to regard as good or satisfactory; **endorse** adds the further implication of active support or advocacy /to *endorse* a candidate for office/; **sanction** implies authoritative approval /a practice *sanctioned* by the charter/; **certify** implies official approval because of compliance with the requirements or standards /a *certified* public accountant/; **ratify** implies official approval of that which has been done by one's representative /to *ratify* a peace treaty/

**approved,** *modif.* — *Syn.* certified, authorized, validated, passed, affirmed, legalized, ratified, sanctioned, permitted, endorsed, vouched for, praised, canonical, recognized, recommended, backed, supported, upheld, made official, agreed to, allowed, inspected, audited, proven, ordered, commanded, established, ordained, accredited, OK'd*. — *Ant.* REFUSED, censured, disapproved.

**approximate,** *modif.* — *Syn.* rough, inexact, estimated, uncertain, guessed, imprecise, unprecise, proximate, imperfect, close, near, by rule of thumb, surmised, unscientific, by means of trial and error, more or less, not quite, coming close, approaching, fair, nearly exact, nearly correct, nearly perfect, comparative, relative, ballpark*.

**approximately,** *modif.* — *Syn.* nearly, closely, roughly, close to, near to, almost, around, about, circa, well-nigh, very near, approaching, close upon, proximately, in general, in round numbers, not quite, not far from, more or less, practically, just about, on the edge of, for all practical purposes, bordering on, generally, comparatively, relatively, in the neighborhood of, pretty nearly*, in the ballpark*.

**approximation,** *n.* 1. [Closeness] — *Syn.* resemblance, likeness, approach; see **nearness** 1, **similarity.**
2. [An estimate] — *Syn.* estimate, conjecture, rough idea; see **guess.**

**April,** *n.* — *Syn.* spring, springtime, planting time, fourth month, month of rain, the cruelest month*; see also **spring** 2.

**apron,** *n.* — *Syn.* cover, smock, bib, overskirt.

**apropos,** *modif.* — *Syn.* pertinent, apt, opportune; see **relevant.**

**apropos of** — *Syn.* with regard to, in connection with, concerning; see **about** 2, **regarding.**

See Synonym Study at RELEVANT.

**apt,** *modif.* 1. [Quick to learn] — *Syn.* adept, quick, clever, bright; see **able** 1, **clever** 1, **intelligent** 1, **quick** 4.
2. [Inclined] — *Syn.* prone, tending, liable; see **likely** 4.
3. [Well-suited] — *Syn.* appropriate, suitable, proper; see **fit** 1, 2.
See Synonym Study at FIT, LIKELY, QUICK.

**aptitude,** *n.* 1. [Inclination] — *Syn.* bent, tendency, propensity; see **inclination** 1.
2. [Natural ability] — *Syn.* capacity, talent, gift, quickness; see **ability** 1, **talent** 1.
See Synonym Study at TALENT.

**Aqua-lung,** *n.* — *Syn.* self-contained underwater breathing apparatus, scuba, diving lung, compressed air tank; see **skin diving.**

**aquarium,** *n.* — *Syn.* artificial pond, fishbowl, fish tank, aquatic museum, marine exhibit.

**aquatic,** *modif.* — *Syn.* swimming, amphibian, amphibious, natatory, oceanic, of the sea, watery, water, floating, maritime, marine, fishlike, sea, deep-sea.

**aqueduct,** *n.* — *Syn.* conduit, water system, water passage, canal, duct, channel, artificial watercourse, waterworks, water bridge, pipeline, culvert.

**aquiline,** *modif.* — *Syn.* hooked, beaklike, eaglelike, curved, beaked, Roman-nosed, angular, resembling an eagle, bent, curving, prominent. — *Ant.* STRAIGHT, snubnosed, pug.

**Arab,** *n.* — *Syn.* Bedouin, Arabian, Saudi, Yemenite, Syrian, Iraqi, Jordanian, Lebanese, Egyptian, Tunisian, Libyan, Algerian, Moroccan, Kuwaiti, Omani, Muslim, Moor, nomad, Ishmaelite*.

**Arabia,** *n.* — *Syn.* Arabian Peninsula, Arabistan, Saudi Arabia, Yemen, Oman, Arabia Deserta, Arabia Felix, United Arab Republic, UAR, Arabia Petraea, Araby*.

**Arabian,** *modif.* — *Syn.* Arabic, Semitic, from Arabia, Saudi Arabian, Yemenite, Omani, Kuwaiti, Bedouin, Middle Eastern, near Eastern.

**arbiter,** *n.* — *Syn.* judge, referee, arbitrator, authority; see **judge** 2.
See Synonym Study at JUDGE.

**arbitrary,** *modif.* 1. [Capricious; *said of people*] — *Syn.* willful, capricious, self-assertive, frivolous, injudicious, wayward, offhand, erratic, impulsive, inconsistent, crotchety, irresponsible, opinionated, supercilious, self-willed, whimsical, unreasonable, irrational, toplofty*. — *Ant.* REASONABLE, consistent, rational.
2. [Without adequate determining principle: *said of actions or ideas*] — *Syn.* subjective, unscientific, unreasonable, unpredictable, capricious, random, chance, temporary, unpremeditated, irrational, motiveless, unaccountable, superficial, whimsical, fanciful, freakish, determined by no principle, depending on the will alone, optional, uncertain, inconsistent, discretionary, subject to individual will, half-baked*. — *Ant.* JUDICIOUS, scientific, considered.
3. [Despotic] — *Syn.* imperious, dictatorial, tyrannical, dogmatic; see **absolute** 3, **autocratic** 1.
See Synonym Study at DOGMATIC.

**arbitrate,** *v.* — *Syn.* settle peacefully, adjust differences, smooth out, reconcile, employ diplomacy, bring before a referee, hear both sides, act as arbiter, referee, parley, placate, bring to terms, decide between opposing parties, intervene, intercede, conciliate, step in, mediate, interpose, negotiate, come between, submit to arbitration, straighten out, meet halfway, come to terms, make an adjustment, pour oil on troubled waters*; see also **decide.**

**arbitration,** *n.* — *Syn.* mediation, negotiation, compromise, adjustment; see **agreement** 1, **intervention** 1.

**arbitrator,** *n.* — *Syn.* arbiter, referee, mediator; see **judge** 2.

**arc,** *n.* — *Syn.* arch, curve, segment of a circle; see **arch, curve** 1.

**Arcadia,** *n.* — *Syn.* paradise, utopia, Shangri-la, Arcady; see **paradise** 3, **utopia**.

**arch,** *modif.* **1.** [Main] — *Syn.* chief, main, principal; see **principal**.
**2.** [Playfully mischievous] — *Syn.* roguish, saucy, mischievous, waggish; see **jaunty**.

**arch,** *n.* — *Syn.* arc, curve, vault, dome, cupola, ogive, span, bend, archivolt, squinch, architrave, arching, archway, curvature, bend, cove, camber.
Arches include: round, horseshoe, lancet, ogee, trefoil, basket-handle, decorated, Tudor, Egyptian, Gothic, Ionian, flat, Roman.

**arch,** *v.* — *Syn.* extend, round, stretch, camber, curve, bend, form, shape, hunch, hump, hook, arch over. — *Ant.* STRAIGHTEN, unbend, smooth.

**archaeologist,** *n.* — *Syn.* paleontologist, paleologist, excavator, prehistorian, classicist, Egyptologist, Americanist, archaeologian, student of antiquity, paleographer, epigraphist, antiquarian; see also **scientist**.

**archaeology,** *n.* — *Syn.* antiquarianism, prehistory, paleethnology, paleology, paleontology, study of archaic cultures, study of antiquity, paleohistory, paleography, epigraphy, digging*.

**archaic,** *modif.* — *Syn.* antiquated, old, obsolete; see **old** 3, **old-fashioned**.
*See Synonym Study at* OLD.

**archbishop,** *n.* — *Syn.* chief bishop, prelate, head of an ecclesiastical province, church dignitary, primate, high churchman; see also **minister** 1, **priest**.

**archer,** *n.* — *Syn.* bowman, longbowman, toxophilite, member of an archery team, crossbowman, arbalester, Sagittarius, William Tell.

**archetype,** *n.* — *Syn.* prototype, ideal, pattern; see **model** 1, 2.
*See Synonym Study at* MODEL.

**architect,** *n.* **1.** [One who designs buildings] — *Syn.* planner, designer, draftsman, artist, engineer, structural engineer, architectural engineer, builder, director of construction, director of building, master builder, environmental engineer, civil architect, landscape architect, urban planner, designer of buildings.
**2.** [Author] — *Syn.* creator, originator, prime mover; see **author** 1.

**architectural,** *modif.* — *Syn.* structural, constructive, architectonic, building, compositional, design, lineal, developmental, engineered.

**architecture,** *n.* — *Syn.* construction, planning, design, building, structure, architectonics, ecclesiology, housebuilding, shipbuilding, bridge-building, environmental engineering.
Styles of architecture include — *Classic:* Ionian, Doric, Corinthian, Alexandrian, Greek, Egyptian, Etruscan, Roman; *Romanesque:* Norman, Rhenish; *Gothic:* Transitional, Lancet, Decorated, Flamboyant, Perpendicular; *Renaissance:* Italian, Jacobean. Elizabethan, Châteaux, English Classic, German Late; *Pseudo-Classic:* Rococo, Baroque, Georgian, Wren, Louis XIV; *Recent:* Pseudo-Gothic, Empire, Victorian, Colonial, Cape Cod, Georgian, Federal, Factory, Modernistic, Functional, Bauhaus, setback, skyscraper, Frank Lloyd Wright, Le Corbusier, Mies van der Rohe, futuristic; *misc.:* Mayan, Malayan, Hindu, Chinese, Japanese, Byzantine, Saracenic, Moresque.

**archives,** *pl.n.* **1.** [Place where documents are stored] — *Syn.* repository, library, vault, treasury; see **library, museum**.
**2.** [Documents] — *Syn.* chronicles, annals, public papers; see **records**.

**archivist,** *n.* — *Syn.* annalist, chronicler, librarian, curator; see **historian, librarian**.

**archway,** *n.* — *Syn.* entrance, passage, opening, arch; see **arch, entrance** 2.

**arctic,** *modif.* — *Syn.* polar, northern, in the Arctic Circle, in the tundra areas, frozen, icy, boreal, hyperborean, under the Bear*; see also **cold** 1.

**ardent,** *modif.* **1.** [Passionate] — *Syn.* passionate, fervent, impassioned, warm; see **passionate** 2.
**2.** [Eager] — *Syn.* zealous, fervent, fervid; see **enthusiastic** 2, 3.
**3.** [Devoted] — *Syn.* constant, loyal, true; see **faithful**.
*See Synonym Study at* PASSIONATE.

**ardor,** *n.* — *Syn.* zest, fervor, passion, warmth; see **enthusiasm** 1.
*See Synonym Study at* ENTHUSIASM.

**arduous,** *modif.* — *Syn.* difficult, severe, strenuous, laborious; see **difficult** 1.
*See Synonym Study at* DIFFICULT.

**area,** *n.* **1.** [An expanse] — *Syn.* stretch, distance, space; see **expanse**.
**2.** [A physical unit] — *Syn.* section, lot, neighborhood, plot, zone, sector, patch, square, quarter, block, precinct, ward, field, meridian, territory, district, locality, ghetto, township, region, tract, belt, enclosure, parcel, division, city, parish, diocese, principality, dominion, duchy, kingdom, empire, state; see also **measure** 1, **region** 1.
**3.** [Scope] — *Syn.* sphere, domain, range, operation; see **field** 4.

**arena,** *n.* — *Syn.* field, pit, ground, park, coliseum, square, football field, gridiron, stadium, athletic field, playing field, baseball field, amphitheater, boxing ring, hippodrome, circus, bowl, stage, platform, course, gymnasium, gym*, sphere, battlefield.

**argot,** *n.* — *Syn.* jargon, cant, dialect; see **dialect**.
*See Synonym Study at* DIALECT.

**argue,** *v.* **1.** [To endeavor to convince] — *Syn.* plead, appeal, assert, maintain, claim, hold, explain, justify, elucidate, present, show, support, reason with, dispute, contend, oppose, demonstrate, establish, join issue, make a case for, put up an argument*.
**2.** [To discuss] — *Syn.* debate, discuss, talk about, clarify; see sense 1, **discuss**.
**3.** [To quarrel] — *Syn.* dispute, contend, fight, bicker; see **quarrel**.
*See Synonym Study at* DISCUSS.

**argument,** *n.* **1.** [An effort to convince] — *Syn.* discussion, exchange, contention; see **discussion** 1, 2.
**2.** [Material intended to convince] — *Syn.* case, reasoning, evidence, reasons; see **proof** 1, **thought** 1.
**3.** [Verbal disagreement] — *Syn.* debate, quarrel, row; see **dispute**.
*See Synonym Study at* DISPUTE.

**argumentative,** *modif.* — *Syn.* disputatious, pugnacious, contentious, factious; see **quarrelsome** 1.

**arid,** *modif.* **1.** [Dry] — *Syn.* dry, parched, desert, dried; see **dry** 1.
**2.** [Barren] — *Syn.* desolate, waste, desert; see **sterile** 2.
**3.** [Dull] — *Syn.* uninteresting, flat, dry; see **dull** 4.
*See Synonym Study at* DRY.

**arise,** *v.* **1.** [To get up] — *Syn.* rise, get up, stand up, stand, wake up, awake, get out of bed, get out of a chair,

get to one's feet, jump up, turn out*; roll out*, hit the deck*. — *Ant.* FALL, SIT, LIE.
**2.** [To ascend] — *Syn.* mount, go up, climb; see **rise** 1.
**3.** [To come into being] — *Syn.* rise, spring, emanate, originate, issue, proceed, derive, stem, flow, begin, start, crop up, appear, emerge, occur, ensue, result; see also **begin** 2.

---

*SYN.* — **arise** and **rise** both imply a coming into being, action, notice, etc., but **arise** is often used to indicate a causal relationship [accidents *arise* from carelessness] and **rise** carries an implication of ascent [empires *rise* and fall]; **spring** implies sudden emergence [weeds *sprang* up in the garden]; **originate** is used in indicating a definite source, beginning, or prime cause [psychoanalysis *originated* with Freud]; **derive** implies a proceeding or developing from something else that is the source [this word *derives* from the Latin]; **flow** suggests a streaming from a source like water ["Praise God, from whom all blessings *flow*"]; **issue** suggests emergence through an outlet [not a word *issued* from his lips]; **emanate** implies the flowing forth from a source of something that is nonmaterial or intangible [rays of light *emanating* from the sun]; **stem** implies outgrowth as from a root or a main stalk [modern detective fiction *stems* from Poe]

---

**aristocracy,** *n.* — *Syn.* nobility, privileged class, peerage, patriciate, House of Lords, superior group, ruling class, noblemen, nobles, the elite, gentry, high society, upper class(es), persons of rank, patricians, optimates, gentility, fashionable world, class of hereditary nobility, body of nobles, royalty, *beau monde, haut monde, pur sang, noblesse* (all French), the Quality*, the upper ten*, high livers*, the four hundred*, the upper crust*, the social register*, the jet set*, the blue book crowd*; see also **society** 3. — *Ant.* PEOPLE, working class, peasantry.
**aristocrat,** *n.* — *Syn.* nobleman, noble, peer, patrician, lord, duke, baron, baronet, earl, count, viscount, marquess, marquis, prince, noblewoman, lady, peeress, duchess, marchioness, viscountess, countess, baroness, marquise, princess, knight, chevalier, titled person, person of fashion, member of the ruling class, thoroughbred, optimate, grandee, don, hidalgo, hereditary noble, king, duke, viscount, count, emperor, empress, *Graf* (German), magnifico, blue blood*, silkstocking*, swell*; see also **king** 1, **lady** 3, **lord** 2, **queen, royalty.** — *Ant.* CITIZEN, commoner, proletarian.
**aristocratic,** *modif.* **1.** [Belonging to the aristocracy] — *Syn.* noble, patrician, highborn, blue-blooded; see **noble** 3.
**2.** [Having qualities associated with the aristocracy] — *Syn.* refined, well-bred, aloof, snobbish; see **distinguished** 2, **proud** 2.
**arithmetic,** *n.* — *Syn.* mathematics, computation, addition, subtraction, multiplication, division, calculation, 'rithmetic*; see also **mathematics.**
**Arizona,** *n.* — *Syn.* Grand Canyon State, Apache State*, Sunset Land*, Valentine State*.
**Arkansas,** *n.* — *Syn.* Land of Opportunity, Ozark country, Bear State*, Razorback State*.
**arm,** *n.* **1.** [The upper human limb] — *Syn.* member, appendage, forelimb, forearm, fin*, soupbone*.
**2.** [Anything resembling an arm, sense 1] — *Syn.* bend, crook, projection, cylinder, sofa-end, branch, limb, appendage, rod, assembly, bough, offshoot, wing, prong, stump, hook, handle, bow, sleeve.
**3.** [A narrow stretch of water] — *Syn.* inlet, tributary,

subdivision, branch, stream, estuary, sound, creek, run, brook, rivulet; see also **bay.**
**4.** [A weapon] — *Syn.* implement of war, gun, firearm; see **arms** 1.
**5.** [A branch] — *Syn.* division, department, unit; see **branch** 1.
**at arm's length** — *Syn.* aloof, at a distance, haughty, remote; see **away** 1, **unfriendly** 2.
**with open arms** — *Syn.* warmly, affectionately, joyously, cordially; see **friendly** 1, **sympathetically.**
**arm,** *v.* **1.** [To equip] — *Syn.* supply, outfit, furnish; see **provide** 1.
**2.** [To equip with weapons] — *Syn.* furnish weapons, prepare for combat, load, give firearms, issue weapons, equip with arms, accouter, array, gird, outfit, fit out, supply with instruments of warfare, provide with arms, munition, fortify. — *Ant.* DISARM, demilitarize, deactivate.
*See Synonym Study at* FURNISH.
**armada,** *n.* — *Syn.* fleet, flotilla, task force, invasion force; see **fleet.**
**armaments,** *pl.n.* — *Syn.* combat equipment, deadly weapons, munitions; see **arms** 1.
**armchair,** *n.* — *Syn.* easy chair, wing chair, Morris chair, captain's chair, elbow chair, rocking chair, rocker, reclining chair, recliner, throne, *fauteuil* (French).
**armed,** *modif.* — *Syn.* equipped, outfitted, girded, in battle formation, under arms, loaded, provided with arms, accoutered, fortified, protected, fitted out, in arms, well-armed, heavily armed, armed to the teeth*. — *Ant.* UNARMED, vulnerable, unprotected.
**armistice,** *n.* — *Syn.* truce, cease-fire, temporary peace; see **truce.**
**armor,** *n.* **1.** [An armored protection] — *Syn.* shield, protection, covering, guard, armor plate, breastplate, protective covering, mail, steel sheet, helmet, heat sheath, reinforced helmet, cuirass, bulletproof vest, flak vest, tin hat, hard hat, sallet, armet, target, gauntlet, visor, morion, basinet, heaume, casquetel, casque, siege-cap, helm, steel helmet, headpiece, brigandine, jambeaux, greaves, defensive clothing, defensive equipment, leg armor, corset, chain mail, buckler, hauberk, coat of mail, panoply, habergeon, lorica, plastron, trench helmet.
**2.** [An armored force] — *Syn.* tanks, tank force, Panzer divisions, armored personnel carriers, APC's, armored column, gun carriers, armor divisions.
**armored,** *modif.* — *Syn.* heavily clad, steel-plated, bulletproof, ironclad, protected, shielded, invulnerable, bombproof, casemated. — *Ant.* UNARMED, unarmored, unprotected.
**armory,** *n.* **1.** [Place where arms are made or stored] — *Syn.* munitions plant, arsenal, arms factory, magazine; see **arsenal.**
**2.** [Building for military purposes] — *Syn.* ordnance headquarters, training center, drilling place, depot, gymnasium, drill center, shooting range, National Guard building, reserve corps headquarters.
**arms,** *pl.n.* **1.** [Weapons] — *Syn.* weapons, armament, armor, ammunition, firearms, munitions, panoply, guns, small arms, side arms, missiles, accouterments, instruments of war, harness, deadly weapons, lethal weapons, means of offense and defense, martial array, pistols, rifles, machine guns, equipment, supplies, ordnance, artillery, weaponry, materiel, hardware*, ammo*; see also **munitions.**
Arms include: MRV (multiple re-entry vehicle), MIRV (multiple independently targetable re-entry vehicle), ABM (anti-ballistic missile), ICBM (intercontinental

ballistic missile), sword, broadsword, foil, dagger, stiletto, bayonet, cutlass, scimitar, machete, saber, ax, halberd, partisan, bill, tomahawk, hatchet, spear, pike, javelin, lance, boomerang, arrow, cross-bow, missile, club, truncheon, bludgeon, cudgel, mace, sling, longbow, catapult, musket, blunderbuss, matchlock, breechloader, harquebus, pistol, cannon, BAR (Browning automatic rifle), machine gun, submachine gun, rifle, M1, M14, M16, AK47, Uzi, Thompson submachine gun (Tommy gun), carbine, bazooka, trench mortar, hand grenade, howitzer, antitank gun, antiaircraft gun, depth bomb, gun, revolver, shotgun, switchblade, blackjack, knife, Saturday night special.
**2.** [The design used by family, town, etc., as its sign] — *Syn.* coat of arms, ensign, crest, insignia, heraldic bearings, heraldic devices, heraldic emblems, armorial ensigns *or* bearings, shield, escutcheon, scutcheon, emblazonry, blazonry, blazon, official insignia, signet, pennon.
**bear arms** — *Syn.* carry weapons, be armed, be militant, serve in the military, see active duty, soldier; see also **arm** 2, **fight** 2.
**take up arms** — *Syn.* go to war, rebel, do battle; see **fight** 2.
**under arms** — *Syn.* outfitted, in battle formation, fortified; see **armed.**
**up in arms** — *Syn.* hostile, indignant, willing to fight; see **angry.**
**army,** *modif.* — *Syn.* military, regimental, combat, land, air, ground, commando, veteran, guerrilla, fighting, militant, belligerent, martial, regimented, under arms, in the army, under orders, drafted, volunteered, in service, serving one's country; see also **military.**
**army,** *n.* **1.** [Military land forces] — *Syn.* armed force, standing army, regulars, soldiery, soldiers, troops, men, cavalry, *force de frappe* (French), infantry, artillery, land forces, reserves, militia, the military; see also **air force, artillery** 2, **infantry.**
**2.** [A unit of an army, sense 1] — *Syn.* division, regiment, air mobile division, armored division, airborne division, infantry division, regiment, battalion, company, battery, corps, brigade, flight, wing, amphibious force, task force, detail, detachment, squad, troop, platoon, blocking force, patrol, unit, command, formation, point, squadron, maniple, cohort, decury, column, legion, platoon, outfit.
**3.** [Any large group] — *Syn.* host, throng, multitude; see **crowd** 1.
**aroma,** *n.* — *Syn.* smell, fragrance, perfume, odor; see **smell** 1, 2.
*See Synonym Study at* SMELL.
**aromatic,** *modif.* — *Syn.* pungent, fragrant, sweet-smelling; see **odorous** 2.
**around,** *modif. & prep.* **1.** [Surrounding] — *Syn.* about, in this area, on all sides, on every side, in circumference, neighboring, in the vicinity, all round, circuitously, round, round about, encompassing, in various directions, in every direction, nearby, proximately, in a sphere, in a circle, along a circuit, all about, close to, close by, nearly in a circle, on various sides, here and there, throughout, round and round*, right and left*.
**2.** [In size] — *Syn.* in circumference, in area, in size, in extent, in measure, in dimension, in bigness.
**3.** [Approximately] — *Syn.* almost, about, close to; see **approximately.**
**been around*** — *Syn.* worldly, sophisticated, knowledgeable; see **experienced.**
**arouse,** *v.* — *Syn.* move, stir, stir up, incite, stimulate; see also **animate** 1, **excite** 1, 2, **incite.**

*See Synonym Study at* INCITE, STIR.
**arraign,** *v.* — *Syn.* summon, charge, indict; see **accuse.**
*See Synonym Study at* ACCUSE.
**arrange,** *v.* **1.** [To put in order] — *Syn.* order, regulate, systematize, array; see **order** 3.
**2.** [To make arrangements] — *Syn.* determine, plan, devise, contrive, prepare for, get ready, make ready, set up, draft, scheme, design, project, concert, provide, make preparations, set the stage, prepare, put into shape, make plans for, line up, organize, adjust, adapt, manage, direct, establish, decide, resolve, settle. — *Ant.* BOTHER, disorganize, disturb.
**3.** [To adapt music] — *Syn.* orchestrate, score, adapt, instrument, harmonize, transcribe, transpose.
**arrangement,** *n.* **1.** [The act of arranging] — *Syn.* ordering, grouping, classification; see **classification** 1, **organization** 1.
**2.** [The result of arranging] — *Syn.* method, system, form; see **order** 3, **organization** 2.
**3.** [An agreement] — *Syn.* settlement, adjustment, compromise; see **agreement** 3.
**4.** [A design] — *Syn.* pattern, composition, combination; see **design** 1, **form** 1.
**5.** [An adaptation of a piece of music] — *Syn.* orchestration, score, transcription, instrumentation, harmonization, adaptation, composition, version.
**arrangements,** *pl.n.* — *Syn.* plans, preparations, preparatory measures, provisions, accommodations, groundwork.
**array,** *n.* **1.** [Formal order] — *Syn.* design, pattern, arrangement; see **order** 3.
**2.** [Relatively formal dress] — *Syn.* full dress, fashion, evening dress, apparel, attire, dress clothes, finery; see also **clothes.**
**3.** [An impressive grouping] — *Syn.* collection, assemblage, host; see **collection** 2, **crowd** 1, **display** 2.
**arrears,** *pl.n.* — *Syn.* back payments, overdue debts, unpaid debts, outstanding debts, unfinished work, obligations, deficiency, unpaid bills, deficit, debit, claim, arrearage, liability, balance due.
**in arrears** — *Syn.* behindhand, overdue, in debt, in default; see **due, indebted, late** 1, **unpaid** 1.
**arrest,** *n.* **1.** [Legal restraint] — *Syn.* apprehension, taking into custody, imprisonment, commitment, confinement, incarceration, capture, protective custody, preventive custody, restraining, taking by force, constraint, seizure, detention, pinch*, pickup*, bust*, collar*; see also **imprisonment** 1. — *Ant.* FREEING, acquittal, release.
**2.** [Act of stopping] — *Syn.* check, checking, stay, staying, stoppage, interruption, hindrance, obstruction, restraining, cessation, prevention, suspension, suppression, holdup*, letup*; see also **delay** 1, **restraint** 2. — *Ant.* ACTION, CONTINUATION, extension.
**under arrest** — *Syn.* arrested, in custody, caught, apprehended, taken into custody, seized, taken in, handcuffed, confined, jailed, imprisoned, detained, shut up, penned up, put in irons, sent to prison, busted, sent to jail, booked, pinched*, collared*, nabbed*, sent up the river*.
**arrest,** *v.* **1.** [To seize legally] — *Syn.* apprehend, take into custody, take charge of, take hold of, hold, place under arrest, take into protective custody, capture, seize by legal warrant, take by authority, imprison, jail, incarcerate, detain, secure, seize, get, catch, take prisoner, lay by the heels*, lay one's hands on*, nab*, collar*, grab*, run in*, pick up*, bust*, nail*. — *Ant.* FREE, liberate, parole.
**2.** [To stop] — *Syn.* restrain, restrict, slow down, check; see **halt** 2, **hinder, prevent.**

**arrested,** *modif.* — *Syn.* seized, taken into custody, jailed; see **under arrest, arrest**.

**arrival,** *n.* 1. [The act of arriving] — *Syn.* entrance, advent, coming, entry, appearance, landing, homecoming, debarkation, alighting, ingress, influx, landfall, inflow, approach, appearance, accession, dismounting, return, reaching one's destination, meeting, disembarkation. — *Ant.* DEPARTURE, leaving, leavetaking.
2. [That which has arrived] — *Syn.* passenger, visitor, tourist, guest, newcomer, delegate, representative, traveler, immigrant, envoy, conferee, cargo, freight, mail, shipment, package, parcel, addition.

**arrive,** *v.* 1. [To come to a place] — *Syn.* come, enter, get there, get here, get back, land, report, disembark, alight, dismount, halt, come in, show up, turn up, put in, drop in, roll in, roll up, reach, get to, get in, visit, make shore, cast anchor, drop anchor, come to hand, reach home, reach one's destination, appear, appear on the scene, sign in, hit★, blow in★, breeze in★, check in★, pull in★, pop in★, bob up★, hit town★, fetch up at★. — *Ant.* LEAVE, go, depart.
2. [★To obtain recognized success] — *Syn.* achieve success, grow famous, make it★; see **succeed** 1.

**arrogance,** *n.* — *Syn.* pride, self-importance, presumption, *hauteur* (French), disdain, hubris, swagger, pomposity, contemptuousness, reserve, overbearingness, domineeringness, insolence, priggishness, smugness, vanity, overconfidence, air of superiority, braggadocio, superciliousness, audacity, haughtiness, aloofness, display, ostentation, vainglory, vaingloriousness, egotism, ego, conceit, self-love, airs, pretension, pretense, snobbishness, patronization, nerve★, high-and-mightiness★, cheek★, stiff neck★, snootiness★, uppityness★, high horse★. — *Ant.* MODESTY, humility, shyness.

**arrogant,** *modif.* — *Syn.* self-important, domineering, overbearing, superior; see **egotistic** 2, **proud** 2.
*See Synonym Study at* PROUD.

**arrogantly,** *modif.* — *Syn.* proudly, haughtily, insolently, loftily, superciliously, imperiously, *de haut en bas* (French), with arms akimbo★, with one's nose in the air★.

**arrow,** *n.* — *Syn.* shaft, bolt, dart, barb, missile, sign, butt shaft, indicator, directive, pointer.

**arsenal,** *n.* — *Syn.* arms plant, military warehouse, armory, munitions factory, ammunition depot, magazine, ammunition dump, stockpile.

**arson,** *n.* — *Syn.* pyromania, firing, incendiarism, deliberate burning of property, willful burning of property, criminal setting of fires, set conflagration, malicious burning of other's property, torching★, torch job★.

**arsonist,** *n.* — *Syn.* incendiary, pyromaniac, firebug★, one who sets fires illegally, torch, *petroleur* (French); see also **criminal**.

**art,** *n.* 1. [Skill or creative power] — *Syn.* skill, craft, technique, artistry, craftsmanship, artisanship, trade, creativity, skillfulness, expertise, faculty, talent, knack, flair, ingenuity, inventiveness, imagination, adroitness, artifice, cunning, craftiness, artfulness, wiliness, finesse, facility, mastery, virtuosity, know-how★.
2. [The study and creation of beauty] — *Syn.* representation, illustration, delineation, abstraction, imitation, modeling, description, portrayal, pictorialization, design, simulation, performance, personification, drawing, sketching, molding, shaping, painting, symbolization, characterization, creating, creativity, sculpting, carving, fine art.
Styles or schools of art include: realist, naturalist, genre, abstract, representational, functional, organic, modernist, futurist, nonobjective, cubist, surrealist, dadaist, primitivist, impressionist, post-impressionist, expressionist, symbolist, constructivist, dynamic, vitalistic, abstract expressionist, op, pop, art nouveau, pre-Columbian, Pre-Raphaelite, Victorian, Greek, Roman, Japanese, classical, medieval, Renaissance, Restoration, grotesque, Mannerist, rococo, baroque, romantic, minimalist.
3. [The product of art, sense 2] — *Syn.* work of art, artwork, creation, masterpiece, *magnum opus* (Latin), *chef d'oeuvre, objet d'art* (*both* French); see also **architecture, dance** 1, **literature** 1, **music** 1, **painting** 1, **picture** 3, **sculpture** 2, **statue**.
4. [The study of humanities; *plural*] — *Syn.* liberal arts, humanities, philosophy, music, painting, history, literature, language; see also **history** 2, **language** 2, **literature** 1, **music** 1, **philosophy** 1, **science** 1.

---

*SYN.* — **art**, the word of widest application in this group, denotes in its broadest sense merely the ability to make or do something [the *art* of making friends], but in a narrower sense implies making or doing that displays creativity and unusual perception; **skill** implies expertness or great proficiency in doing something; **artifice** implies skill used as a means of trickery or deception; **craft** implies ingenuity in execution, sometimes even suggesting trickery or deception; in another sense, **craft** is distinguished from **art** in its application to a lesser skill involving little or no creative thought

---

**artery,** *n.* 1. [Main channel of communication or travel] — *Syn.* highway, main road, avenue, course, passage, thoroughfare, trunk line, supply route, track, pathway, corridor, conduit, duct, canal, river; see also **road** 1, **way** 2.
2. [Blood vessel] — *Syn.* tube, blood vessel, aorta, arterial passageway; see **vein** 2.
Important arteries include: aorta, pulmonary, carotid, axillary, brachial, coronary, nutrient, radial, intercostal, femoral, innominate, scapular, subclavian.

**artful,** *modif.* 1. [Crafty] — *Syn.* shrewd, cunning, wily; see **intelligent** 1, **sly** 1.
2. [Skillful] — *Syn.* clever, adroit, ingenious; see **able** 2.

**arthritis,** *n.* — *Syn.* inflammation of a joint, arthropathy, collagen disease, osteoarthritis, rheumatoid arthritis, gout; see also **disease**.

**article,** *n.* 1. [An individual thing] — *Syn.* item, object, substance, commodity; see **thing** 1.
2. [Nonfiction appearing in a periodical] — *Syn.* essay, editorial, commentary, news item, column, feature, piece, report, study; see also **exposition** 2.
3. [A division of a piece of writing] — *Syn.* portion, section, provision, item, clause, stipulation, chapter.

**articulate,** *modif.* — *Syn.* eloquent, well-spoken, lucid, clear; see **fluent** 2, **understandable**.

**articulate,** *v.* 1. [To speak clearly] — *Syn.* enunciate, pronounce, verbalize, put into words; see **explain, utter**.
2. [To join] — *Syn.* fit together, combine, connect, link; see **join** 1.

**articulation,** *n.* 1. [Pronunciation] — *Syn.* enunciation, utterance, vocalization; see **diction**.
2. [The act of joining] — *Syn.* unification, coupling, junction; see **union** 1.
3. [A joint] — *Syn.* union, connection, coupling; see **joint** 1.

**artifice,** *n.* 1. [Maneuver] — *Syn.* stratagem, trick, wile, ruse; see **trick** 1.
2. [Trickery] — *Syn.* guile, cunning, deceit; see **cunning, dishonesty**.

**3.** [Skill] — *Syn.* skill, ingenuity, inventiveness; see **ability** 2, **art** 1.
*See Synonym Study at* ART, TRICK.
**artificial,** *modif.* **1.** [*Said of things*] — *Syn.* synthetic, unreal, counterfeit, spurious, ersatz, fake, manufactured, man-made, imitation, mock, simulated, substitute, false, sham, fabricated, contrived, unnatural, plastic, pseudo, bogus, fictitious, make-believe, phony*; see also **false** 3. — *Ant.* natural, GENUINE, real.
**2.** [*Said of conduct*] — *Syn.* mannered, unnatural, feigned; see **affected** 2, 3.

SYN. — **artificial** is applied to anything made by human work, esp. if in imitation of something natural [*artificial* hair]; **synthetic** is applied to a substance that is produced by chemical synthesis and is used as a substitute for a natural substance which it resembles [*synthetic* dyes]; **ersatz**, which refers to an artificial substitute, always implies an inferior substance [*ersatz* coffee made from chicory]; **counterfeit** and **spurious** are applied to a careful imitation deliberately intended to deceive [*counterfeit* money, a *spurious* signature]

**artillery,** *n.* **1.** [Heavy ordnance] — *Syn.* gunnery, ordnance, mounted guns, cannons, missile launchers; see also **cannon, munitions.**
**2.** [The branch of the service that mans artillery, sense 1] — *Syn.* gun crew, field battery, field artillery, motorized units, antiaircraft units, armored force.
**artist,** *n.* **1.** [A creative worker in the fine arts] — *Syn.* creator, painter, sculptor, master, performing artist, artiste, maestro, virtuoso, musician, singer, performer, entertainer, actor, actress, limner, practitioner of the arts, art student, portraitist, watercolorist, landscapist, muralist, miniaturist, illustrator, caricaturist, cartoonist, etcher, engraver, ceramicist, ceramist, potter, photographer, commercial artist, graphic artist, calligrapher, colorist, writer, belletrist, composer, comedian, mime, performance artist, opera singer, prima donna, dancer, ballerina, interpreter, designer, architect.
**2.** [A highly skilled workman] — *Syn.* adept, expert, master, virtuoso, past master, artisan, craftsman, artificer, inventor, contriver, specialist, handicraftsman, professional, skilled hand, genius, proficient.
**3.** [A clever trickster] — *Syn.* sharper, crook, con man*; see **rascal.**
**artistic,** *modif.* **1.** [Pertaining to the fine arts] — *Syn.* aesthetic, decorative, picturesque, musical, pictorial, painterly, rhythmical, poetic, dramatic, compositional, patterned, studied, belletristic, photographic, arty*.
**2.** [Showing taste and skill] — *Syn.* inventive, skillful, artful, imaginative, discriminating, creative, graceful, talented, accomplished, aesthetic, aesthetically pleasing, well-turned, well-proportioned, well-executed, wellwrought, pleasing, selective, sublime, judicious, ideal, well-balanced, cultured, tasteful, exquisite, sensitive, fine, elegant, harmonious, grand, elevated, noble, beautiful. — *Ant.* TASTELESS, flat, inept.
**artistry,** *n.* — *Syn.* workmanship, skill, proficiency; see **ability** 2, **art** 1.
**artless,** *modif.* — *Syn.* simple, guileless, natural; see **naive, natural.**
*See Synonym Study at* NAIVE.
**artlessness,** *n.* **1.** [Simplicity] — *Syn.* ingenuousness, naiveté, candor; see **innocence** 2.
**2.** [Unskillfulness] — *Syn.* ineptitude, crudeness, clumsiness; see **awkwardness** 1.
**arty*,** *modif.* — *Syn.* artsy*, pretentious, imitative, dilet-

tantish, tasteless, pseudo, false, flaunting, without taste, artsy-craftsy*; see also **affected** 2, 3.
**as,** *conj., modif., & prep.* **1.** [While] — *Syn.* in the process of, in the act of, on the point of; see **while** 1.
**2.** [Because] — *Syn.* since, inasmuch as, for the reason that; see **because.**
**3.** [To the same degree] — *Syn.* in the same way, in the same manner, equally, comparatively, similarly.
**4.** [For a given purpose, end, use, etc] — *Syn.* just as, *qua* (Latin), just for, serving as, functioning as, acting as, in the capacity of, being, in and of itself, by its nature, essentially.
**ascend,** *v.* **1.** [To rise] — *Syn.* go up, move upward, sprout, soar; see **rise** 1.
**2.** [To climb] — *Syn.* mount, scale, work one's way up; see **climb** 2.
**ascendancy,** *n.* — *Syn.* authority, domination, sway, power; see **command** 2, **power** 2.
**ascension,** *n.* — *Syn.* ascent, rising, climbing; see **rise** 1.
**ascent,** *n.* **1.** [Rising] — *Syn.* climbing, mounting, ascension; see **rise** 1.
**2.** [Upgrade] — *Syn.* incline, slope, acclivity; see **grade** 1.
**ascertain,** *v.* — *Syn.* learn, find out, determine; see **discover, learn** 2.
*See Synonym Study at* LEARN.
**ascetic,** *modif.* — *Syn.* austere, self-denying, plain, rigorous; see **moderate** 5, **modest** 2, **severe** 2.
*See Synonym Study at* SEVERE.
**ascetic,** *n.* — *Syn.* holy man, monk, religious devotee, anchorite, self-denier, nun, self-tormenter, hermit, stylite, eremite, fakir, penitent, puritan, yogi, flagellant, mortifier of the flesh, recluse.
**ashamed,** *modif.* — *Syn.* embarrassed, shamed, chagrined, humiliated, mortified, abashed, discomfited, regretful, contrite, rueful, repentant, penitent, apologetic, demeaned, crestfallen, conscience-stricken, uncomfortable, discomforted, hesitant, perplexed, bewildered, shamefaced, sheepish, dashed, bowed down, disconcerted, sputtering, stammering, stuttering, gasping, floundering, rattled, muddled, confused, nonplused, blushing, flustered, self-conscious, meek, red-faced, hangdog, feeling like a jackass*, taken down a peg*, out of countenance*, looking silly *or* foolish*, at a loss, unable to show one's face*, with egg on one's face*. — *Ant.* PROUD, smug, brazen.

SYN. — **ashamed** implies embarrassment, and sometimes guilt, felt because of one's own or another's wrong or foolish behavior [*ashamed* of his tears]; **humiliated** implies a sense of being humbled or disgraced [*humiliated* by my failure]; **mortified** suggests humiliation so great as to seem almost fatal to one's pride or self-esteem [she was *mortified* by his rude behavior in front of her family]; **chagrined** suggests embarrassment coupled usually with regret over what might have been prevented [*chagrined* at her error]

**ashen,** *modif.* — *Syn.* pale, ashy, colorless, gray; see **pale** 1.
*See Synonym Study at* PALE.
**ashes,** *pl.n.* **1.** [Powdery remains after a fire] — *Syn.* dust, powder, cinders, slag, embers, charcoal, volcanic ash, soot, remains of what is burned, scoriae.
**2.** [Ruins] — *Syn.* remains, vestiges, remnants; see **destruction** 2.
**ashore,** *modif.* — *Syn.* on shore, on land, on dry land, on terra firma, beached, aground, on the beach. — *Ant.* AFLOAT, at sea, on board.

**Asia,** *n.* — *Syn.* the Orient, the East, the mysterious East*.

Countries and regions of Asia include — *Far East:* China, Taiwan, Japan, North Korea, South Korea, Mongolia, Tibet, Siberia, Vietnam, Laos, Cambodia, Kampuchea, Thailand, Burma, Myanmar, Singapore, India, Sri Lanka, Bangladesh, Bhutan, Nepal, Malaysia, Indonesia; *Near and Middle East:* Turkey, Georgia, Syria, Iraq, Iran, Jordan, Israel, Lebanon, Saudi Arabia, Yemen, Oman, United Arab Emirates, Kuwait, Qatar, Afghanistan, Pakistan, Turkmenistan, Uzbekistan, Kazakhstan, Tajikistan, Kyrgyzstan.

**Asian,** *modif.* **1.** [Said of people] — *Syn.* Oriental, Mongolian; see **sense** 2.
**2.** [Said of objects, culture, etc.] — *Syn.* Oriental, Far Eastern, Mongolian, East Asian, Middle Eastern, Near Eastern, Eastern, Confucian, Levantine, Chinese, Sinitic, Buddhist, Japanese, Nipponese, Korean, Thai, Vietnamese, Hindu, Indian, Brahman, Aryan, Cambodian, Chinese, Tibetan, Burmese, Asiatic.

**aside,** *modif.* — *Syn.* to the side, to one side, on one side, at rest, out, by oneself, away from some position, apart, by the side of, at one side, by itself, alone, alongside, out of the way, aloof, laterally, down, away, in isolation, afar, in safekeeping, in reserve, beside, sideways, sidewise, abreast, abeam, at a short distance, by.

**aside from,** *prep.* — *Syn.* apart from, beside, in addition to, excluding; see **besides.**

**as if,** *conj. & modif.* **1.** [As though] — *Syn.* just as, just as if, as though, just as though, as it were, in such a way that, as if it were, supposing, quasi, so to speak, as it would be if, as might be, like*, just like*.
**2.** [Seemingly] — *Syn.* manifestly, supposedly, presumably; see **apparently.**

**asinine,** *modif.* — *Syn.* silly, stupid, foolish, idiotic; see **silly, stupid** 1.
*See Synonym Study at* SILLY.

**as is*,** *modif.* — *Syn.* as it stands, just the same, the same way, just as it is, in its present condition.

**as it were,** *modif.* — *Syn.* so to speak, figuratively speaking, in a way, as it seems, as it would seem, in some sort, in a manner, so to say, in a manner of speaking, kind of*, sort of*.

**ask,** *v.* **1.** [To inquire] — *Syn.* request, query, question, inquire, interrogate, examine, cross-examine, demand, make a request, raise a question, pose a question, call for, apply for, file for, angle for, frame a question, require an answer, want to know, catechize, make inquiry, make application, apply to, order, command, requisition, direct, put questions to, institute an inquiry, enjoin, bid, charge, petition, call upon, invite, urge, pray, beg leave, challenge, pry into, probe, scour, investigate, quiz, sound out, draw out, grill*, dun*, put the screws on*, turn the heat on*, put the bite on*, put the bee on*, pump*, give the third degree*, worm out of*; see also **question** 1. — *Ant.* ANSWER, refute, deny.
**2.** [To solicit] — *Syn.* request, entreat, supplicate; see **beg** 1.
**3.** [To expect] — *Syn.* hope for, claim, demand, charge; see **require** 2, **value** 2.
**4.** [To invite] — *Syn.* propose, suggest, urge, summon; see **invite** 1, 2.

**SYN.** — **ask** and the more formal **inquire** and **query** usually denote no more than the seeking of an answer or information, but **query** also often implies doubt as to the correctness of something /the printer *queried* the spelling of several words/; **question** and **interrogate** imply the asking of a series of questions /to *question* a

witness/, **interrogate** adding the further implication of systematic, often extensive, official examination /to *interrogate* a prisoner of war/; **catechize** also denotes close questioning, but implies the expectation of certain fixed answers, esp. with reference to religious doctrine; **quiz,** used esp. in schools, implies a short, selective questioning to test factual knowledge of some subject

**askew,** *modif.* — *Syn.* awry, aslant, to one side; see **crooked** 1, **oblique** 1.

**asleep,** *modif.* — *Syn.* sleeping, dreaming, inert, quiet, resting, snoring, somnolent, in a state of sleep, in a sound sleep, sound asleep, fast asleep, dead asleep, comatose, in a torpor, slumbering, heavy with sleep, reposing, taking a siesta, in repose, hibernating, dozing, napping, drowsing, nodding, unconscious, abed, dormant, dead to the world*, in the arms of Morpheus*, in the Land of Nod*, asnore*, anesthetized*, snoozing*, conked out*, out like a light*, assuming the horizontal*, sacked out*, copping some Z's*. — *Ant.* AWAKE, waking, alert.

**aspect,** *n.* **1.** [Looks] — *Syn.* look, appearance, features, character; see **appearance** 1.
**2.** [View] — *Syn.* perspective, regard, slant, viewpoint; see **phase, viewpoint.**
*See Synonym Study at* APPEARANCE, PHASE.

**asperity,** *n.* **1.** [Acrimony] — *Syn.* bitterness, sharpness, ill temper; see **roughness** 2, **rudeness.**
**2.** [Hardship] — *Syn.* rigor, severity, difficulty; see **difficulty** 1, 2, **rigor.**
**3.** [Roughness] — *Syn.* harshness, unevenness, ruggedness; see **roughness** 1.

**aspersion,** *n.* — *Syn.* detraction, defamation, calumny, slur; see **accusation** 2, **lie** 1.

**asphalt,** *n.* — *Syn.* asphaltum, bitumen, pavement, roadbed, blacktop, macadam, speedway; see also **pavement** 1, **road** 1.

**aspirant,** *n.* — *Syn.* competitor, applicant, hopeful, wannabe*; see **candidate.**

**aspiration,** *n.* — *Syn.* yearning, eagerness, hope, goal; see **ambition** 1, **purpose** 1.

**aspire,** *v.* — *Syn.* yearn, seek, aim, strive; see **try** 1, **want** 1, **yearn.**

**aspiring,** *modif.* — *Syn.* hopeful, ambitious, striving, enthusiastic; see **ambitious** 1.
*See Synonym Study at* AMBITIOUS.

**ass,** *n.* **1.** [A stupid person] — *Syn.* dolt, dunce, blockhead; see **fool** 1.
**2.** [A donkey] — *Syn.* burro, jackass, jennet; see **donkey.**

**assail,** *v.* — *Syn.* attack, assault, beset, plague; see **attack** 2.
*See Synonym Study at* ATTACK.

**assailable,** *modif.* — *Syn.* vulnerable, defenseless, exposed; see **weak** 5.

**assailant,** *n.* — *Syn.* attacker, assaulter, antagonist, mugger; see **attacker.**

**assassin,** *n.* — *Syn.* murderer, slayer, butcher; see **killer.**

**assassinate,** *v.* — *Syn.* kill, slay, slaughter, do in*; see **kill** 1.
*See Synonym Study at* KILL.

**assassination,** *n.* — *Syn.* killing, shooting, slaying; see **murder.**

**assault,** *n.* **1.** [An attack] — *Syn.* charge, advance, onslaught; see **attack** 1.
**2.** [A physical attack on another person] — *Syn.* attack, mugging, assault and battery, rape; see **crime** 2, **rape.**

**assault,** *v.* **1.** [To attack] — *Syn.* attack, assail, set upon, strike; see **attack** 1, 2.
**2.** [To rape] — *Syn.* attack, violate, ravish; see **rape.**

*See Synonym Study at* ATTACK.

**assay,** *v.* — *Syn.* test, measure, run tests on; see **examine** 1.

**assemblage,** *n.* — *Syn.* assembly, collection, association; see **collection** 2, **gathering.**

**assemble,** *v.* **1.** [To come together] — *Syn.* meet, convene, congregate; see **gather** 1.
**2.** [To bring together] — *Syn.* collect, gather, rally, call, convoke, muster, round up, head up, group, convene, summon, mobilize, call together, accumulate, amass, compile, make up, reunite, form a whole, invite guests, hold a celebration, hold a meeting, unite, hold a convocation, herd together, lump together, pack them in*, throw a party*. — *Ant.* SCATTER, disperse, send away.
**3.** [To put together] — *Syn.* piece together, fit together, put together, set up, erect, construct, join, unite, solder, mold, weld, glue, model, throw together. — *Ant.* BREAK, disassemble, break down.
*See Synonym Study at* GATHER.

**assembly,** *n.* **1.** [A gathering of persons] — *Syn.* assemblage, meeting, association; see **gathering.**
**2.** [The process of bringing parts together] — *Syn.* construction, piecing together, putting together, fitting in, joining, modeling, assembling, attachment, adjustment, collection, welding, soldering, molding, fixing, setting up, manufacture. — *Ant.* SEPARATION, dismantling, wrecking.
**3.** [An assembled mechanism] — *Syn.* arrangement, parts, equipment; see **device** 1, **machine** 1.

**assent,** *n.* — *Syn.* approval, agreement, concurrence, consent; see **permission.**

**assent,** *v.* — *Syn.* agree to, concur, consent; see **agree, consent.**
*See Synonym Study at* CONSENT.

**assert,** *v.* **1.** [To state positively] — *Syn.* state, say, declare, affirm, aver, avow, avouch, attest, profess, asseverate, warrant*; see also **declare** 1.
**2.** [To maintain] — *Syn.* cite, allege, advance; see **support** 2.

---

**SYN.** — **assert** is to state positively with great confidence but with no objective proof *[to* assert *that human nature will never change]*; to **declare** is to assert openly or formally, often in the face of opposition *[they* declared *their independence]*; **affirm** implies deep conviction in one's statement or the unlikelihood of denial by another *[she* affirmed *her innocence]*; **aver** connotes implicit confidence in the truth of one's statement from one's own knowledge of the matter; **avouch** implies firsthand knowledge or authority on the part of the speaker; **warrant,** in this comparison, is colloquial, and implies positiveness by the speaker *[I* warrant *they'll be late again]* See also Synonym Study at DECLARE.

---

**assertion,** *n.* — *Syn.* affirmation, statement, contention; see **contention** 2, **declaration** 1.

**assertive,** *modif.* — *Syn.* confident, self-assured, positive, outspoken; see **aggressive** 1, **certain** 1.
*See Synonym Study at* AGGRESSIVE.

**assess,** *v.* **1.** [To tax] — *Syn.* charge, exact, impose; see **tax** 1.
**2.** [To estimate] — *Syn.* judge, appraise, evaluate; see **estimate** 1, **value** 2.

**assessment,** *n.* **1.** [Valuation] — *Syn.* appraisal, evaluation, estimation; see **estimate** 1.
**2.** [Tax] — *Syn.* levy, charge, fee; see **tax** 1.

**assets,** *pl.n.* — *Syn.* holdings, possessions, capital; see **property** 1, **wealth** 1.

**assiduous,** *modif.* — *Syn.* industrious, persevering, careful, attentive; see **careful, diligent.**
*See Synonym Study at* DILIGENT.

**assign,** *v.* **1.** [To delegate to a specific purpose] — *Syn.* commit, commission, authorize, hand over, earmark, allocate, detail, appoint, allot, prescribe, nominate, name, select, hold responsible, empower, entrust, allow, cast, deputize, attach, charge, accredit, hire, elect, ordain, enroll, relegate, draft. — *Ant.* MAINTAIN, dismiss, keep back.
**2.** [To distribute] — *Syn.* give out, consign, allot; see **allot, distribute** 1.
**3.** [To designate] — *Syn.* specify, indicate, set apart; see **designate** 1.
**4.** [To attribute] — *Syn.* ascribe, attribute, accredit; see **attribute.**
*See Synonym Study at* ALLOT, ATTRIBUTE.

**assignation,** *n.* — *Syn.* rendezvous, clandestine meeting, tryst; see **appointment** 2, **date** 2.

**assignee,** *n.* — *Syn.* guardian, appointee, administrator; see **trustee.**

**assignment,** *n.* **1.** [Appointment] — *Syn.* designation, allotment, authorization, nomination; see **appointment** 1, **distribution** 1.
**2.** [Something assigned] — *Syn.* job, responsibility, task, homework; see **duty** 2, **job** 2, 3.
*See Synonym Study at* TASK.

**assimilate,** *v.* **1.** [To absorb] — *Syn.* take up, digest, osmose; see **absorb** 1.
**2.** [To understand] — *Syn.* grasp, learn, sense; see **learn** 1, **understand** 1.
**3.** [To adjust] — *Syn.* adapt, acclimatize, accustom; see **conform.**

**assimilation,** *n.* **1.** [Absorption] — *Syn.* digestion, inhalation, soaking up; see **absorption** 1.
**2.** [Adjustment] — *Syn.* adaptation, acclimatization, conformity; see **adaptation** 1.

**assist,** *v.* — *Syn.* help, support, aid, serve; see **help** 1.
*See Synonym Study at* HELP.

**assistance,** *n.* — *Syn.* help, support, compensation; see **aid** 1.

**assistant,** *n.* — *Syn.* aide, deputy, henchman, friend, follower, adherent, auxiliary, lieutenant, associate, companion, colleague, partner, helper, acolyte, representative, second in command, apprentice, co-worker, fellow-worker, secretary, supporter, appointee, abettor, ancillary, standby, helping hand, patron, backer, bodyguard, aide-de-camp, ally, accessory, clerk, adjunct, collaborator, confederate, subaltern, mate, helpmate, adjutant, subordinate, coadjutor, attendant, accomplice, second, right hand, right-hand man, man Friday, gal Friday, underling, lackey, flunky*, sidekick*, yes-man*, stooge*, gofer*. — *Ant.* supervisor, rival, antagonist.

**associate,** *n.* — *Syn.* comrade, colleague, cohort, peer, partner, copartner, companion, friend, ally, buddy, crony, alter ego, accomplice, abettor, assistant, attendant, henchman, confederate, auxiliary, co-operator, co-worker, co-helper, co-conspirator, accessory, coadjutor, collaborator, confrere, fellow-worker, compatriot, comrade in arms, brother-in-arms, right hand, right-hand man, compeer, yokefellow, mate, teammate, partner in crime, sidekick*, stooge*, plant*, ringer*. — *Ant.* ENEMY, foe, antagonist.

---

**SYN.** — **associate** refers to a person who is frequently in one's company, usually because of shared work *[business* associates*]*; **colleague** denotes a co-worker, esp. in one of the professions, and may or may not imply a personal relationship *[one of my* colleagues *at the univer-*

sity*]*; **companion** always refers to a person who actually accompanies one and usually implies a close, personal relationship *[a dinner companion, the companions of one's youth]*; **comrade** refers to a close associate and implies a sharing in activities and fortunes *[comrades in arms]*; **ally** refers to one joined with another for a common purpose or for support and is applied esp. to a government joined with another or others in a common pursuit, as war; a **confederate** is one who joins with another or others for some common purpose, esp. in some unlawful act; an **accomplice** is one who unites with another or others in an unlawful act

**associate,** *v.* **1.** [To keep company with] — *Syn.* have relations with, be intimate with, fraternize with, join with, keep company with, consort with, mingle with, socialize with, be friendly with, get along with, hobnob with, mix with, work with, hang around with*, hang out with*, run around with*, take up with*, mess around with*, hook up with*, keep in with*, gang up with*, pal around with*; see also **join** 2.— *Ant.* LEAVE, break off relations with, sever a friendship.
**2.** [To relate] — *Syn.* correlate, link, connect; see **compare** 1.
**3.** [To form an organization] — *Syn.* incorporate, affiliate, ally, unite, federate, amalgamate, take out a charter; see also **unite** 1.— *Ant.* DISBAND, dissolve, break up.
**4.** [To combine] — *Syn.* unite, blend, connect; see **join** 1.
*See Synonym Study at* JOIN.
**association,** *n.* **1.** [The act of associating] — *Syn.* fraternization, socializing, friendship, acquaintanceship, cooperation, assistance, relationship, affiliation, agreement, participation, companionship, intercourse, intimacy, fellowship, familiarity, friendliness, camaraderie, membership, acquaintance, mingling, union, community, bond, connection.— *Ant.* DISAGREEMENT, severance, rupture.
**2.** [The process of intellectual comparison] — *Syn.* connection, relation, comparison, linking, correlation, identification, mental connection, train of thought, chain of ideas, free association, recollection, impression, remembrance, suggestibility.— *Ant.* SEPARATION, dissociation, segregation.
**3.** [An organization] — *Syn.* union, federation, corporation; see **organization** 3.
**4.** [Companionship] — *Syn.* alliance, partnership, friendship; see **fellowship** 2, **friendship** 1.
**assort,** *v.* — *Syn.* sort, arrange, group; see **classify.**
**assorted,** *modif.* — *Syn.* varied, miscellaneous, mixed; see **different** 2.
**assortment,** *n.* — *Syn.* variety, combination, group; see **collection** 2.
**assuage,** *v.* **1.** [To alleviate] — *Syn.* mitigate, lessen, soothe; see **relieve** 2.
**2.** [To satisfy] — *Syn.* appease, fill, surfeit; see **satisfy** 1, 3.
**3.** [To calm] — *Syn.* pacify, still, mollify; see **quiet** 1.
*See Synonym Study at* RELIEVE.
**assume,** *v.* **1.** [To take for granted] — *Syn.* suppose, presume, postulate, posit, presuppose, predicate, premise, take for granted, understand, gather, find, collect, theorize, ascertain, consider as true, draw the inference, judge, divine, get the idea, have an idea that, suspect, regard, consider, imply, hypothesize, guess, take without proof, treat as conceded, take it as given, conjecture, suppose as fact, deem, imagine, surmise, opine, estimate, speculate, fancy, take the liberty, be of the opinion, dare say, deduce, count upon, infer, conclude,

put two and two together, be inclined to think, hold the opinion, think, calculate, hope, feel, believe, have faith, be afraid*, take it*, expect*, allow*, reckon*.— *Ant.* DOUBT, be surprised that, know.
**2.** [To pretend] — *Syn.* feign, put on, affect; see **pretend** 1.
**3.** [To take] — *Syn.* seize, appropriate, arrogate; see **seize** 2.

*SYN.* — **assume** implies the supposition of something as the basis for argument or action *[let us assume her motives were good]*; **presume** implies the taking of something for granted or accepting it as true, usually on the basis of probable evidence in its favor and the absence of proof to the contrary *[the prisoner is presumed to be of sound mind]*; **presuppose** may imply taking something for granted without necessarily having good reason *[this writer presupposes an extensive vocabulary in children]* or, in another sense, may imply that something is required as a preceding condition *[brilliant technique in piano playing presupposes years of practice]*; **postulate** implies the assumption of something as an underlying factor, often one that is incapable of proof *[his argument postulates the inherent goodness of humanity]*; **premise** implies the setting forth of a proposition on which a conclusion can be based *See also Synonym Study at* PRETEND.

**assumed,** *modif.* **1.** [Taken for granted] — *Syn.* presumed, understood, presupposed, counted on, inferred, postulated, given, granted, taken for granted, taken as known, conjectured, accepted, supposed, suppositional, hypothetical, hypothesized.
**2.** [Fictitious] — *Syn.* pretended, counterfeit, spurious; see **false** 2, 3.
**assuming,** *modif.* — *Syn.* arrogant, presumptuous, bold; see **egotistic** 2.
**assumption,** *n.* **1.** [The act of taking for granted] — *Syn.* supposition, presupposition, presumption, supposal, conjecture, assuming, taking for granted, accepting, suspicion, surmise, theorization, hypothesization.— *Ant.* PROOF, demonstrating, establishing.
**2.** [Something assumed] — *Syn.* hypothesis, theory, postulate, premise; see **hypothesis, opinion** 1.
**3.** [The act of becoming responsible for] — *Syn.* accepting, assuming, taking on, shouldering, taking over, appropriation, usurpation, arrogation.
**assurance,** *n.* **1.** [A guaranty] — *Syn.* insurance, support, pledge; see **promise** 1.
**2.** [Confidence] — *Syn.* conviction, trust, certainty, certitude; see **certainty** 1, **faith** 1.
**3.** [Self-confidence or audacity] — *Syn.* self-confidence, self-reliance, coolness, poise, audacity, boldness, insolence, effrontery, presumption; see also **confidence** 2, **rudeness, temerity.**
*See Synonym Study at* CERTAINTY, CONFIDENCE.
**assure,** *v.* **1.** [To guarantee] — *Syn.* vouch for, ensure, confirm, secure; see **guarantee** 1.
**2.** [To convince] — *Syn.* prove, persuade, reassure; see **convince.**
**3.** [To promise] — *Syn.* pledge, affirm, swear; see **promise** 1.
**4.** [To encourage] — *Syn.* reassure, inspirit, hearten, comfort; see **comfort, encourage** 2.
**assured,** *modif.* **1.** [Certain] — *Syn.* sure, undoubted, guaranteed; see **certain** 3.
**2.** [Confident] — *Syn.* self-possessed, bold, unhesitating; see **confident** 2.

Pg 21

**assuredly,** *modif.* — *Syn.* positively, definitely, certainly; see **surely.**

**as though,** *conj. & modif.* **1.** [As if] — *Syn.* just as, just as if, just as though; see **as if** 1.
**2.** [Seemingly] — *Syn.* evidently, supposedly, presumably; see **apparently.**

**astonish,** *v.* — *Syn.* surprise, shock, amaze, astound; see **surprise** 1.
*See Synonym Study at* SURPRISE.

**astonishing,** *modif.* — *Syn.* surprising, startling, extraordinary; see **unusual** 1.

**astonishment,** *n.* — *Syn.* surprise, amazement, bewilderment; see **wonder** 1.

**astound,** *v.* — *Syn.* surprise, amaze, shock, startle; see **surprise** 1.
*See Synonym Study at* SURPRISE.

**astray,** *modif.* — *Syn.* straying, adrift, amiss, off the track; see **wandering** 1, **wrong** 2.

**astride,** *modif.* — *Syn.* with one leg on each side of, on the back of, sitting on, astraddle, straddling, piggyback.

**astrologer,** *n.* — *Syn.* soothsayer, horoscopist, stargazer, astromancer; see **prophet.**

**astronaut,** *n.* — *Syn.* space traveler, cosmonaut, spaceman, spacewoman, space pilot, rocket pilot, rocketeer, spacewalker, explorer.

**astronomer,** *n.* — *Syn.* stargazer, astrochemist, astrophysicist, astrophotographer, astrophotometrist, cosmologist, uranologist, uranographer; see also **scientist.**

**astronomical,** *modif.* **1.** [Pertaining to astronomy] — *Syn.* uranographical, uranological, cosmological, astrophotometric, astrophotographic, astrophysical, astrochemical, heavenly, celestial, cosmic, planetary, planetoidal, astral, solar, lunar, galactic, telescopic, four-dimensional.
**2.** [Of a magnitude suggesting distances in astronomy] — *Syn.* gigantic, enormous, immeasurable, infinite, ungraspable; see also **large** 1, **many.**

**astronomy,** *n.* — *Syn.* stargazing, astrochemistry, astrophysics, earth-space science, selenology, astrophotography, astrophotometry, uranology, uranography, uranometry, celestial mechanics, astrography, cosmology; see also **science** 1.

**astute,** *modif.* — *Syn.* keen, shrewd, clever; see **intelligent** 1, **shrewd.**
*See Synonym Study at* SHREWD.

**astuteness,** *n.* — *Syn.* sagacity, keenness, shrewdness; see **acumen.**

**asunder,** *modif.* **1.** [In pieces] — *Syn.* apart, in two, in half, in pieces, into pieces, to shreds, in bits and pieces, into bits and pieces, dismantled, sundered, dissected, in two parts, divided, into separate parts, separated, disjoined, rent, carved, dismembered, torn apart, broken apart, split; see also **broken** 1. — *Ant.* WHOLE, together, sound.
**2.** [Apart] — *Syn.* divided, disconnected, distant, divergent; see **separated.**

**asylum,** *n.* — *Syn.* shelter, refuge, safety; see **shelter.**
*See Synonym Study at* SHELTER.

**at,** *prep.* **1.** [Position] — *Syn.* on, by, near to, in, about, occupying the precise position of, in the vicinity of, placed at, situated at, found in, in front of, appearing in; see also **in** 1, **near** 1.
**2.** [Direction] — *Syn.* toward, in the direction of, through; see **to** 1.

**atheism,** *n.* — *Syn.* irreligion, heresy, agnosticism, ungodliness, godlessness, impiety, unbelief, positivism, denial of God, nihilism, iconoclasm, disbelief in God, irreverence, pyrrhonism, rationalism, dogmatic, atheism, skeptical atheism, infidelity, antichristianism, ma-

terialism, skepticism, freethinking, disbelief; see also **doubt** 1.

**atheist,** *n.* — *Syn.* freethinker, nonbeliever, disbeliever, unbeliever, agnostic, infidel, heathen, irreligionist, materialist, nihilist, nullifidian; see also **skeptic.**

---

*SYN.* — **atheist** rejects all religious belief and denies the existence of God; an **agnostic** questions the existence of God, heaven, etc. in the absence of material proof and in unwillingness to accept supernatural revelation; **deist,** a historical term, was applied to 18th-century rationalists who believed in God as a creative, moving force but who otherwise rejected formal religion and its doctrines of revelation, divine authority, etc.; **freethinker,** the current parallel term, similarly implies rejection of the tenets and traditions of formal religion as incompatible with reason; **unbeliever** is a more negative term, simply designating, without further qualification, one who does not accept any religious belief; **infidel** is applied to a person not believing in a certain religion or the prevailing religion

---

**atheistic,** *modif.* — *Syn.* freethinking, agnostic, skeptic, disbelieving, unbelieving, nonbelieving, irreligious, heretical, antichristian, unconverted, profane, impious, blasphemous, worldly, materialistic, nihilist, godless, irreverent, ungodly. — *Ant.* RELIGIOUS, God-fearing, devout.

**athlete,** *n.* — *Syn.* player, acrobat, gymnast, ballplayer, contestant, competitor, champion, sportsman, sportswoman, amateur, professional, semi-professional, contender, challenger, jock*, varsity man*, letterman*.
Athletes include: baseball player, football player, basketball player, soccer player, volleyball player, boxer, pugilist, wrestler, swimmer, diver, golfer, tennis player, badminton player, jockey, trackman, marathoner, javelin thrower, high-jumper, discus thrower, shot putter, weight lifter, skier, ski jumper, slalom racer, runner, jogger, long-jumper, pole vaulter, hurdler, bowler, polo player, hockey player, skater, bicyclist, fencer, swordsman.

**athletic,** *modif.* — *Syn.* muscular, fit, husky, wiry, springy, slim, fast, solid, strapping, hardy, robust, strong, vigorous, active, energetic, agile, well-knit, powerful, brawny, sinewy, sturdy, well-built, well-proportioned, Herculean*, Amazonian*, Titanic*, built like an ox*, muscle-bound*. — *Ant.* WEAK, sickly, flabby.

**athletics,** *pl.n.* — *Syn.* sports, games, gymnastics, acrobatics; see **sport** 3.

**Atlantic,** *modif.* — *Syn.* oceanic, transoceanic, transatlantic, eastern, coastal; see also **ocean.**

**atlas,** *n.* — *Syn.* book of maps, gazetteer, charts, tables; see **book** 1.

**atmosphere,** *n.* **1.** [The air] — *Syn.* layer of air, gaseous envelope, air pressure; see **air** 1.
**2.** [A pervading quality] — *Syn.* environment, ambience, climate, mood; see **character** 1, **characteristic.**

**atmospheric,** *modif.* **1.** [Of or in the atmosphere] — *Syn.* airy, climatic, barometrical, baroscopic, aeroscopic, meteorological, aerial.
**2.** [Having or giving an atmosphere] — *Syn.* hazy, misty, evocative, mysterious; see **hazy** 1.

**atom,** *n.* **1.** [Tiny particle] — *Syn.* fragment, mite, speck, particle, iota, mote, jot, grain, scintilla; see also **bit** 1.
**2.** [Particle in atomic physics] — *Syn.* the smallest particle of an element, molecule*, smallest quantity of a

radical, basic unit, basic constituent, irreducible unit, irreducible constituent, atomic mass unit.

Parts and forms of atoms include: electron, proton, neutron, positron, neutrino, positive electron, neutral electron, nuclide quark; see also **atomic energy, element** 2.

**atomic,** *modif.* **1.** [Minute] — *Syn.* microscopic, tiny, diminutive; see **minute** 1.

**2.** [Referring to atoms] — *Syn.* nuclear, thermonuclear, fissionable, atom-powered, nuclear-controlled.

**atomic bomb,** *n.* — *Syn.* atom bomb, A-bomb, nuclear weapon; see **nuclear bomb**.

**atomic energy,** *n.* — *Syn.* nuclear energy, nuclear power, thermonuclear power, energy from fission, energy from fusion, atomic chain discharge, power from the sun.

Possible sources of atomic energy include: uranium and uranium ores, isotopes of uranium, uranium 235, U-235, U-238, plutonium and plutonium ores, plutonium isotopes, plutonium 239, Pu-239, Pu-240, thorium.

**atom smasher,** *n.* — *Syn.* cyclotron, linear accelerator, atomic accelerator, particle accelerator; see **accelerator.**

**atone for,** *v.* — *Syn.* compensate for, do penance, make amends; see **pay for.**

**atonement,** *n.* — *Syn.* amends, satisfaction, expiation, penance; see **reparation** 1, 2.

**atrocious,** *modif.* — *Syn.* abominable, monstrous, appalling; see **cruel** 1, **frightful** 1, **outrageous**.

*See Synonym Study at* OUTRAGEOUS.

**atrocity,** *n.* **1.** [Brutality] — *Syn.* inhumanity, wickedness, barbarity; see **cruelty.**

**2.** [A cruel deed] — *Syn.* crime, offense, outrage, atrocious deed, horror, iniquity, enormity, abomination, slaughter, wrong; see also **crime** 1, 2, **murder.**

**attach,** *v.* **1.** [To join] — *Syn.* connect, append, add; see **fasten** 1, **join** 1.

**2.** [To seize; especially, to seize legally] — *Syn.* appropriate, take over, confiscate; see **seize** 2.

**3.** [To attribute] — *Syn.* associate, impute, ascribe; see **attribute.**

**4.** [To assign] — *Syn.* appoint, name, detail; see **assign** 1.

*See Synonym Study at* ATTRIBUTE, FASTEN.

**attachable,** *modif.* — *Syn.* adjustable, appendable, annexable, connective, portable, movable, detachable, separable, in sections, prefabricated, prefab*. — *Ant.* WHOLE, in one piece, inseparable.

**attachment,** *n.* **1.** [Affection] — *Syn.* fondness, liking, devotion; see **affection** 1, **love** 1.

**2.** [Something attached] — *Syn.* accessory, adjunct, appendage; see **addition** 2.

*See Synonym Study at* LOVE.

**attack,** *n.* **1.** [Offensive tactical action] — *Syn.* assault, raid, onslaught, advance, charge, thrust, lunge, offense, drive, strike, aggression, offensive, onset, irruption, outbreak, offensive military operation, push, storming, assailment, broadside, volley, sally, *coup de main* (French), shooting, barrage, bombardment, fusillade, cannonade, siege, firing, trespass, blockade, boarding, cross-fire, assailing, initiative, invasion, incursion, forced entrance, intrusion, intervention, increased presence, onrush, inroad, encroachment, counterattack.

Types of military attack include: commando raid, air strike, air raid, blitzkrieg, charge, sortie, foray, counterforce, siege, bombardment, bomb run, invasion, infiltration, encirclement, wave, pincer movement, strafing, fire mission, firing pass, low-level attack, mast-level attack, kamikaze, suicide attack, atomic thrust, nuclear armored thrust, torpedo attack, mechanized attack, amphibious landing, depth charge, shelling, banzai charge, mortar attack. — *Ant.* withdrawal, RETREAT, defense.

**2.** [Verbal attack] — *Syn.* libel, slander, denunciation, censure; see **blame** 1.

**3.** [Illness] — *Syn.* seizure, fit, bout, relapse; see **fit** 1, **illness** 1.

**4.** [Physical assault] — *Syn.* assault, mugging, rape; see **crime** 2, **rape.**

**attack,** *v.* **1.** [To fight offensively; *used of an army*] — *Syn.* assault, strike, invade, storm, advance, beset, besiege, beleaguer, infiltrate, take offensive action, raid, assail, encircle, march against, take the initiative, take the offensive, charge, fire at, shoot at, snipe at, come at, run at, shell, ambush, take by surprise, sally forth, make a push, bombard, bomb, go over the top, fall on, fall upon, burst upon, fire the first shot, fan out, mushroom out, lay siege to, open fire, bear down on, swoop down on, launch an attack, spring on, advance on, turn on, strafe, waylay, aggress, engage, tilt against, set upon, torpedo, stone, fire at, fire on, push, combat, attempt violence to, trespass against, launch an offensive, mount an offensive, begin hostilities against, take up arms against, rush, fusillade, barrage, strike the first blow, counterattack, enfilade, bayonet, saber, stab, pelt, blitz, pounce on, close with*, pepper*, rake*, light into*, sail into*, go for*, have at*, open up on*, let have it*. — *Ant.* RETREAT, fall back, defend.

**2.** [To assault; *used of an individual*] — *Syn.* assault, assail, combat, knock down, seduce, rape, punch, kick, molest, beat, hit, overwhelm, kidnap, strike, club, stab, knock unconscious, throw oneself on, throw oneself upon, lift a hand against, tackle, fly at, lay into*, tear into*, pitch into*, gang up on*, lower the boom on*, go for the jugular*, mug*, jump*; see also sense 1. — *Ant.* RETALIATE, resist, fight back.

**3.** [To assail with words] — *Syn.* revile, denounce, criticize, blindside*; see **censure.**

**4.** [To proceed vigorously] — *Syn.* take up, deal with, set to work, start in on, undertake, come to grips with, set to, buckle down, tackle, plunge into*, dive into*, wade into*, tear into*.

---

*SYN.* — **attack** implies vigorous, aggressive action, whether in actual combat or in an undertaking /to *attack* a city, to *attack* a problem/; **assail** means to attack by or as if by repeated blows or thrusts /assailed by reproaches/; **assault** implies a sudden, violent attack or onslaught and suggests direct contact and the use of force; **beset** implies an attack or onset from all sides /beset with fears/; **storm** suggests a rushing, powerful assault that is stormlike in its action and effect; **bombard** means to attack with artillery or bombs, and in figurative use suggests persistent, repetitious action /to *bombard* a speaker with questions/

---

**attacked,** *modif.* — *Syn.* assaulted, bombed, bombarded, assailed, stoned, torpedoed, fired upon, stormed, under attack, strafed, invaded, besieged.

**attacker,** *n.* — *Syn.* aggressor, assailant, antagonist, invader, foe, enemy, criminal, mugger, molester, rapist, assaulter, plunderer, intruder, trespasser, violator, ravager, spoiler, felon, vilifier, maligner, accuser; see also **critic** 1. — *Ant.* VICTIM, prey, martyr.

**attain,** *v.* — *Syn.* win, achieve, accomplish; see **achieve** 2, **succeed** 1.

*See Synonym Study at* ACHIEVE.

**attainable,** *modif.* — *Syn.* achievable, feasible, reachable; see **available.**

**attainment,** *n.* — *Syn.* accomplishment, fulfillment, feat; see **achievement** 1, 2.

**attempt,** *n.* — *Syn.* trial, try, struggle, endeavor; see **effort** 1, 2.

**attempt,** *v.* — *Syn.* try, endeavor, strive, venture; see **try** 1.

*See Synonym Study at* TRY.

**attend,** *v.* **1.** [To go with] — *Syn.* accompany, escort, chaperon; see **accompany** 1, 3.

**2.** [To go to] — *Syn.* be present at, go to, frequent, appear at, sit in on, visit, be a guest, revisit, haunt, be a member, be an habitué, make an appearance, audit. — *Ant.* LEAVE, be missing, absent oneself.

**3.** [To take care of] — *Syn.* minister to, serve, tend; see **tend** 1.

**attend school** — *Syn.* undergo schooling, study, go to school, be educated, receive instruction, matriculate, learn, take courses, register, enroll; see also **register** 1.

*See Synonym Study at* ACCOMPANY.

**attendance,** *n.* **1.** [The act of attending] — *Syn.* presence, participation, appearance, frequenting, being present, putting in an appearance, being in evidence, turning up*, showing up*. — *Ant.* ABSENCE, nonappearance, nonattendance.

**2.** [The persons attending] — *Syn.* audience, spectators, witnesses, hearers, patrons, onlookers, public, listeners, viewers, observers, house guests, company, assembly, assemblage, gathering, congregation, number present, number attending, turnout, gate*, crowd*, cash customers*, suckers*.

**attendant,** *n.* — *Syn.* aide, orderly, valet, nurse, usher, bellhop, servant, escort, companion, chaperon, caretaker, caregiver, warden, custodian, flight attendant, steward, stewardess, *valet de chambre* (French), maid, retainer, employee; see also **assistant.**

**attention,** *n.* **1.** [The state of giving heed] — *Syn.* observation, observance, regard, notice, mindfulness, inspection, study, heed, watching, listening, concentration, care, consideration. — *Ant.* INDIFFERENCE, abstraction, inattention.

**2.** [The power of giving heed] — *Syn.* concentration, attentiveness, intentness, alertness, thought, application, assiduousness, diligence, caution, preoccupation, thoroughness, recognition, regard, vigilance, mindfulness, watchfulness, heedfulness, awareness, consciousness. — *Ant.* INDIFFERENCE, inattentiveness, negligence.

**3.** [Courtesies; *usually plural*] — *Syn.* respects, civilities, gestures, mannerliness, attentiveness, deference, offerings, consideration, kindnesses, politeness, obeisance, genuflections. — *Ant.* RUDENESS, off-handedness, crudeness.

**call attention to** — *Syn.* point out, indicate, note, bring to one's notice; see **designate** 1, **remind** 2, **warn.**

**attentive,** *modif.* **1.** [Paying attention] — *Syn.* observant, mindful, alert, intent; see **observant** 2.

**2.** [Considerate] — *Syn.* considerate, thoughtful, courteous, solicitous; see **thoughtful** 2.

*See Synonym Study at* THOUGHTFUL.

**attic,** *n.* — *Syn.* garret, loft, dormer; see **garret.**

**attitude,** *n.* **1.** [Posture] — *Syn.* pose, posture, stance, stand; see **pose, position** 5, **posture.**

**2.** [State of mind] — *Syn.* mood, opinion, idea about, viewpoint, point of view, standpoint, outlook, perspective, belief, air, demeanor, manner, condition of mind, habitual mode of regarding something, disposition of mind, state of feeling, mindset, manner of thinking, way of looking at things, position, reaction, bias, slant,

set, leaning, proclivity, bent, inclination, propensity, cast, emotion, temper, temperament, sensibility, disposition, mental state, notion, philosophy, view, approach, stance, stand, orientation, nature, makeup, frame of mind, character.

**strike an attitude** — *Syn.* be theatrical, assume a posture *or* pose, be affected; see **pose** 2.

*See Synonym Study at* POSTURE.

**attorney,** *n.* — *Syn.* lawyer, attorney-at-law, solicitor; see **lawyer.**

*See Synonym Study at* LAWYER.

**attract,** *v.* **1.** [To draw] — *Syn.* pull, draw, drag, bring; see **draw** 1.

**2.** [To allure] — *Syn.* allure, charm, appeal to, interest, intrigue, lure, captivate, fascinate, enchant, invite, entice, draw, beguile, tempt, excite, strike one's fancy, catch one's eye, pique one's interest, turn one on*; see also **fascinate.**

---

**SYN.** — **attract** implies the exertion of a force such as magnetism to draw a person or thing and connotes susceptibility in the thing drawn; **allure** implies attraction by that which seductively offers pleasure, delight, reward, etc.; **charm** suggests the literal or figurative casting of a spell and implies very pleasing qualities in the agent; **fascinate** and **enchant** both also suggest a magical power, **fascinate** stressing an irresistible holding of interest and **enchant** the evoking of great delight; **captivate** implies a capturing of the attention or affection, but suggests a light, passing influence

---

**attraction,** *n.* **1.** [The act of drawing toward] — *Syn.* magnetism, allurement, fascination, captivation, temptation, pull, gravitation, affinity, inclination, tendency, enticement, draw. — *Ant.* repulsion, revulsion, alienation.

**2.** [That which draws toward itself] — *Syn.* gravity, magnet, lure, bait, decoy, blind, charm, appeal, allure, drawing power, pull*, glamour, sex appeal, spectacle, display, demonstration, performance, drawing card*, main event*, sucker bait*, plant*.

**attractive,** *modif.* — *Syn.* good-looking, winning, engaging; see **beautiful** 1, 2, **charming, handsome** 2.

**attribute,** *n.* — *Syn.* quality, trait, property; see **characteristic, quality** 1.

*See Synonym Study at* QUALITY.

**attribute,** *v.* — *Syn.* ascribe, credit, impute, assign, refer to, trace to, connect, give credit, accredit, associate, attach, put down to, set down to, lay to, apply to, fix upon, account for, point to, blame, chalk up to, lay at one's door*; see also **accuse.** — *Ant.* DENY, dissociate, absolve.

---

**SYN.** — **attribute** implies assignment of a quality, factor, or responsibility that may reasonably be regarded as applying or belonging to someone or something [to *attribute* an error to carelessness]; **ascribe** implies assignment of something that may reasonably be deduced [to *ascribe* a motive to someone]; **impute** usually implies the assignment of something unfavorable or accusatory [to *impute* evil to someone]; **assign**, in this comparison, implies the placement of something in a particular category because of some quality or characteristic attributed to it [to *assign* a poem to the 17th century]; **credit** implies belief in the possession of some quality or the responsibility for some action, often of a commendable nature [to *credit* someone with intelligence]; **attach** implies the connection of something with something else as being appropriate to it /different people *attach* different meanings to words/

---

**attrition,** *n.*— *Syn.* wearing down, wearing away, friction, rubbing, abrasion, weakening, grinding down, erosion, depreciation, gradual disintegration, reduction, decline; see also **reduction** 1.— *Ant.* INCREASE, appreciation, buildup.

**attune,** *v.* **1.** [To tune]— *Syn.* adjust the pitch, put in tune, tune up; see **tune.**
**2.** [To adjust]— *Syn.* bring into accord, make agree, harmonize; see **accommodate** 2, **adjust** 1.

**attuned (to),** *modif.*— *Syn.* receptive, responsive, perceptive, in harmony with; see **sensitive** 3, **sympathetic.**

**auburn,** *modif.*— *Syn.* reddish, coppery, reddish-brown, reddish-yellow, titian, copper, russet, rust, henna, chestnut; see also **brown, red.**

*au courant* (French), *modif.*— *Syn.* up-to-date, well-informed, fully acquainted with; see **cultured, knowledgeable.**

**auction,** *n.*— *Syn.* disposal, public sale, bankruptcy sale; see **sale** 2.

**auction,** *v.*— *Syn.* sell at auction, auctioneer, put on the block*, put under the hammer*; see **sell** 1.
*See Synonym Study at* SELL.

**auctioneer,** *n.*— *Syn.* salesman, salesperson, seller, vendor, barker, crier.

**audacious,** *modif.* **1.** [Daring]— *Syn.* bold, daring, reckless, rash; see **brave** 1, **rash.**
**2.** [Impudent]— *Syn.* brazen, presumptuous, unabashed; see **rude** 2.
*See Synonym Study at* BRAVE.

**audacity,** *n.* **1.** [Courage]— *Syn.* daring, boldness, valor; see **courage** 1.
**2.** [Impudence]— *Syn.* impertinence, temerity, brazenness, insolence; see **rudeness, temerity.**
*See Synonym Study at* TEMERITY.

**audible,** *modif.*— *Syn.* perceptible, discernible, auricular, distinct, actually heard, perceptible by the ear, loud enough to be heard, capable of being heard, within earshot, within hearing distance, hearable, sounding, resounding, loud, deafening, roaring, aloud, clear, plain, emphatic; see also **sensory** 2.

**audience,** *n.* **1.** [A group attending an event]— *Syn.* spectators, witnesses, patrons, viewers, listeners, public, theatergoers, moviegoers, concertgoers, attendees, readers, auditors, fans, following, house; see also **attendance** 2.
**2.** [An interview]— *Syn.* hearing, interview, conference; see **conversation.**

**audit,** *n.* **1.** [Examination]— *Syn.* checking, scrutiny, inspection, review; see **examination** 1.
**2.** [Statement]— *Syn.* record, account, report; see **statement** 3.

**audit,** *v.* **1.** [To examine accounts]— *Syn.* examine, check, inspect, review; see **examine** 1.
**2.** [To attend classes without receiving credit]— *Syn.* sit in, attend as an auditor, observe; see **attend school, attend.**

**audition,** *n.*— *Syn.* test, tryout*, trial; see **hearing** 1.

**auditor,** *n.* **1.** [One who listens]— *Syn.* listener, hearer, witness, spectator, eavesdropper, public, audience, patron, confessor, adviser, critic, judge.— *Ant.* ACTOR, entertainer, storyteller.
**2.** [One who audits accounts]— *Syn.* accountant, examiner, bookkeeper, actuary; see **accountant.**

**auditorium,** *n.*— *Syn.* hall, lecture hall, theater, playhouse, movie house, reception hall, amphitheater, assembly hall, opera house, music hall, odeum, concert hall, chapel, assembly room, auditory.
Sections of an auditorium include: stage, lodge, proscenium, orchestra, parquet, stalls, boxes, pit, orchestra circle, dress circle, balcony, gallery, top gallery, tiers, box office, mezzanine.

**auditory,** *modif.*— *Syn.* hearing, auricular, acoustic, aural, otic, auditive, audible; see also **sensory** 1.

**auger,** *n.*— *Syn.* bit, twist drill, screw auger; see **drill** 2.

**augment,** *v.*— *Syn.* increase, enlarge, expand, add to; see **grow** 1, **increase** 1.
*See Synonym Study at* INCREASE.

**augmentation,** *n.* **1.** [The act of augmenting]— *Syn.* development, growth, enlargement; see **increase** 1.
**2.** [An addition]— *Syn.* increment, accretion, gain; see **addition** 2.

**augur,** *v.*— *Syn.* predict, forecast, prognosticate, presage; see **anticipate** 1, **foretell.**

**august,** *modif.* **1.** [Noble]— *Syn.* eminent, venerable, regal; see **distinguished** 2, **noble** 1.
**2.** [Stately]— *Syn.* imposing, grand, majestic; see **grand** 2, **noble** 3.
*See Synonym Study at* GRAND.

**August,** *n.*— *Syn.* eighth month, midsummer, harvest time, vacation time, hottest season, driest season, height of a long, hot summer*, worst of a long, hot summer*; see also **summer.**

**aunt,** *n.*— *Syn.* mother's sister, father's sister, uncle's wife, grandaunt, great-aunt, auntie*, *tante* (French), *Tante* (German), *Tia* (Spanish); see also **relative.**

**aura,** *n.*— *Syn.* air, atmosphere, quality, emanation; see **character** 1, **characteristic.**

**auspices,** *pl.n.*— *Syn.* protection, aegis, support; see **patronage** 1.

**auspicious,** *modif.*— *Syn.* promising, propitious, favorable; see **hopeful** 2.
*See Synonym Study at* FAVORABLE.

**austere,** *modif.*— *Syn.* harsh, forbidding, ascetic, stark; see **modest** 2, **severe** 1, 2.
*See Synonym Study at* SEVERE.

**austerity,** *n.*— *Syn.* sternness, severity, strictness, harshness, asperity, hardness, grimness, stiffness, seriousness, rigidity, uncompromisingness, formality, gravity, rigor, asceticism, self-denial, self-discipline, abstemiousness, puritanism, plainness, simplicity, spareness, starkness, Spartanism, belt-tightening*.— *Ant.* MERCY, luxury, casualness.

**authentic,** *modif.* **1.** [Reliable]— *Syn.* trustworthy, authoritative, factual; see **authoritative** 1, **official** 3.
**2.** [Genuine]— *Syn.* real, true, actual; see **genuine** 1.
*See Synonym Study at* GENUINE.

**authenticate,** *v.*— *Syn.* verify, confirm, validate; see **prove, verify.**
*See Synonym Study at* VERIFY.

**author,** *n.* **1.** [One who originates]— *Syn.* inventor, originator, creator, architect, framer, artificer, discoverer, innovator, maker, planner, strategist, designer, projector, founder, father, organizer, prompter, producer, fabricator, artist, composer, begetter, prime mover, initiator, the brains*.
**2.** [One who writes]— *Syn.* writer, novelist, essayist, poet, short-story writer, dramatist, playwright, biographer, journalist, columnist, contributor, *littérateur* (French), belletrist, script writer, scenario writer, scenarist, screenwriter, librettist, scribe, penman, poetess, authoress, literary man, ghostwriter, encyclopedist, lexicographer, scholar, critic, annotator, hack, hack writer, scribbler, freelance writer, ghost*; see also **writer.**— *Ant.* READER, audience, publisher.

**authoritarian,** *modif.* — *Syn.* dictatorial, tyrannical, dogmatic, strict; see **absolute** 3, **autocratic** 1.

**authoritative,** *modif.* **1.** [Based on competent authority] — *Syn.* well-supported, well-documented, scholarly, reliable, trustworthy, authentic, dependable, definitive, sound; see also sense 2, **official** 3.
**2.** [Having authority] — *Syn.* official, executive, imperial, administrative, supreme, *ex cathedra* (Latin), dominant, lawful, legal, mandatory, impressive, imposing, orthodox, ruling, sovereign, having due authority, weighty, having the weight of authority, entitled to obedience, decisive, worthy of acceptance, canonical, valid, standard, authorized; see also **administrative, approved, governing, reigning.** — *Ant.* unauthorized, ILLEGAL, questionable.
**3.** [Suggestive of authority] — *Syn.* dogmatic, officious, domineering; see **absolute** 3, **autocratic** 1.

**authority,** *n.* **1.** [Power based on right] — *Syn.* right, authorization, jurisdiction; see **power** 2.
**2.** [The appearance of having authority, sense 1] — *Syn.* prestige, political influence, weight, self-assurance; see **influence** 2.
**3.** [A person or persons vested with authority, sense 1; *usually plural*] — *Syn.* officialdom, officials, judges, court, police, government, government agency, officeholders, administration, cabinet, executive, duly constituted representatives, ecclesiastics, the powers that be*; see also **bureaucracy** 1.
**4.** [One who knows] — *Syn.* expert, scholar, critic, professional; see **specialist.**
*See Synonym Study at* INFLUENCE, POWER.

**authorization,** *n.* — *Syn.* sanction, signature, support; see **permission.**

**authorize,** *v.* — *Syn.* empower, commission, sanction, entitle; see **allow** 1, **approve** 1, **commission.**
*See Synonym Study at* COMMISSION.

**authorized,** *modif.* — *Syn.* allowed, sanctioned, confirmed, accredited; see **approved.**

**authorship,** *n.* — *Syn.* origin, origination, initiation, invention, instigation, signature, creation, making, doing, production, writing, composition; see also **writing** 3.

**auto,** *n.* — *Syn.* car, vehicle, passenger car; see **automobile.**

**autobiography,** *n.* — *Syn.* memoirs, personal history, self-portrayal, confession, life, experiences, account of oneself, adventures, biography, life story, journal, letters, fortunes, diary.

**autocracy,** *n.* — *Syn.* absolute monarchy, dictatorship, totalitarian government, despotism, czarism, absolutism, tyranny, totalitarianism, autarchy, one-man rule; see also **fascism, government** 2.

**autocrat,** *n.* — *Syn.* absolute ruler, despot, tyrant; see **dictator.**

**autocratic,** *modif.* **1.** [*Said of persons*] — *Syn.* domineering, dictatorial, tyrannical, authoritarian, imperious, self-willed, officious, strict, severe, dogmatic, despotic, inquisitorial, authoritative, overbearing, peremptory, arrogant, repressive, harsh, inflexible, arbitrary, oppressive, cruel, grinding, exacting, unrelenting, heavy-handed, iron-handed, megalomaniacal, monomaniacal, power-crazed, power-mad, petulant, willful, headstrong, highhanded, bossy*, like godalmighty*, high-and-mighty*. — *Ant.* LENIENT, submissive, affable.
**2.** [*Said of governments*] — *Syn.* despotic, dictatorial, absolutistic; see **absolute** 3.

**autograph,** *n.* — *Syn.* signature, writing, handwriting, seal, token, memento, John Hancock*.

**automated,** *modif.* — *Syn.* mechanical, mechanized, motorized, computerized, automatic, electronic, mechano-electronic, programmed, cybernetic, untouched by human hands*; see also **automatic** 1.

**automatic,** *modif.* **1.** [Mechanical] — *Syn.* self-starting, motorized, self-regulating, automated, mechanized, electric, under its own power, under its own steam, cybernetic, self-operating, self-moving, self-acting, self-propelled, computerized, programmed, electronic, robotized, push-button*. — *Ant.* MANUAL, hand-operated, by hand.
**2.** [Habitual] — *Syn.* involuntary, unthinking, mechanical, instinctive, spontaneous, reflex, intuitive, unintentional, unforced, unconscious, unwilling, knee-jerk*; see also **habitual** 1, **spontaneous.** — *Ant.* DELIBERATE, willed, premeditated.
*See Synonym Study at* SPONTANEOUS.

**automation,** *n.* — *Syn.* mechanization, computerization, cybernation, robotization, industrialization, motorization, self-regulation.

**automaton,** *n.* — *Syn.* robot, humanoid, android; see **robot** 1.

**automobile,** *n.* — *Syn.* car, motorcar, vehicle, motor vehicle, auto, passenger car, machine, motor, wheels*.
Types of automobiles include: passenger car, limousine, sedan, coupe, saloon (British), hardtop, compact, subcompact, hatchback, notchback, sports car, stock car, convertible, station wagon, minivan, taxicab, squad car, dragster, funny car, lemon, clunker, jalopy.
Principal parts of an automobile include: wheels, ignition, battery, tires, fenders, chassis, headlight, taillight, hood, trunk, radiator, engine *or* motor, fan, cylinder, windshield, wipers, water pump, catalytic converter, fuel injector, carburetor, exhaust, muffler, throttle, gear, gear shift, clutch, steering wheel, transmission, universal joint, disc brake, brake pad, brake shoe, brake drum, alternator, generator, distributor, starter, speedometer, tachometer, spark plug, axles, emergency brake, heater, seat belt, airbag, filter, drive shaft, oil pan, hand brake, accelerator, MacPherson strut, shock absorber, radius rod, piston, intake and exhaust valves, fuel pump, gas tank, dashboard, glove compartment, turn signal, steering column.
Automobile makes include: Chrysler, Dodge, Plymouth, Jeep, Eagle, Cadillac, Oldsmobile, Buick, Pontiac, Chevrolet, Saturn, Geo, Ford, Lincoln, Mercury, Honda, Acura, Toyota, Lexus, Nissan (Datsun), Infiniti, Subaru, Mazda, Mitsubishi, Hyundai, Suzuki, Daihatsu, Isuzu, Mercedes-Benz, BMW (Bayerische Motoren-Werke), Porsche, Audi, Volkswagen, Volvo, Saab, Fiat, Alfa Romeo, Lancia, Lamborghini, Ferrari, Maserati, Bugatti, Rolls-Royce, Bentley, Jaguar, Rover, Triumph, MG (Morris Garage), Lotus, Aston Martin, Austin Healey, Hillman, Vauxhall, Sunbeam, Peugeot, Renault.
Former makes include: Avanti, Citroën, DeLorean, Yugo, Imperial, Checker, International, Rambler, Nash, Studebaker, De Soto, Edsel, Packard, Kaiser, Hudson, Duesenberg, Pierce-Arrow, Hupmobile, La Salle, Stutz, Reo, Cord, Crosley, Stanley, Daimler, Opel, Simca, Skoda, Zil.

**autonomous,** *modif.* — *Syn.* self-governing, self-ruling, independent, self-sufficient; see **free** 1.

**autonomy,** *n.* — *Syn.* liberty, independence, sovereignty; see **freedom** 1.

**autopsy,** *n.* — *Syn.* post-mortem examination, post-mortem, dissection, necropsy, pathological examination of the dead; see also **examination** 3.

**autumn,** *n.* — *Syn.* fall, harvest time, Indian summer, autumnal equinox, close of the year.

**autumnal,** *modif.* — *Syn.* fall, cool, brisk, windy, dry, sere, late, in the latter part of the year.

**auxiliary,** *modif.* **1.** [Helping] — *Syn.* aiding, assisting, supporting, collaborating, cooperating, sustaining, abetting, ancillary, serving, assistant, ministering.
**2.** [Subsidiary] — *Syn.* secondary, accessory, subsidiary, ancillary; see **subordinate.**
**3.** [Supplementary] — *Syn.* reserve, supplemental, spare, backup; see **extra.**

**auxiliary,** *n.* — *Syn.* helper, accessory, adjutant; see **assistant.**

**available,** *modif.* — *Syn.* accessible, usable, ready, convenient, serviceable, prepared, handy, on call, ready for use, open, obtainable, attainable, practicable, achievable, feasible, possible, procurable, realizable, reachable, within reach, at one's disposal, at one's beck and call, at hand, at one's elbow, free, at liberty, to be had, on tap*, on deck*. — *Ant.* OCCUPIED, unavailable, unobtainable.

**avalanche,** *n.* **1.** [A mass moving down a slope] — *Syn.* mudslide, snowslide, landslide, landslip, rockslide, icefall.
**2.** [Any overwhelming mass] — *Syn.* flood, deluge, torrent; see **plenty.**

**avant-garde,** *modif.* — *Syn.* new, progressive, unconventional, experimental; see **liberal** 2, **modern** 1, **unusual** 2.

**avant-garde,** *n.* — *Syn.* vanguard, cutting edge, advance guard; see **vanguard.**

**avarice,** *n.* — *Syn.* covetousness, cupidity, greediness; see **greed.**

**avaricious,** *modif.* — *Syn.* greedy, grasping, covetous, mercenary; see **greedy** 1.
*See Synonym Study at* GREEDY.

**avenge,** *v.* — *Syn.* retaliate, requite, punish for; see **revenge.**
*See Synonym Study at* REVENGE.

**avenue,** *n.* — *Syn.* street, boulevard, parkway, promenade; see **road** 1, **street.**

**average,** *modif.* — *Syn.* ordinary, normal, medium, mediocre; see **common** 1, **normal** 1.

**average,** *n.* **1.** [A mean] — *Syn.* mean, midpoint, standard, center, median, norm, middle, normal, the usual, typical kind, rule, par, common run, general run. — *Ant.* EXTREME, highest, lowest, exception.
**2.** [A score] — *Syn.* proportion, percentage, tally, aggregate; see **score** 1.

**on (the) average** — *Syn.* usually, generally, commonly, ordinarily; see **regularly** 1.

**SYN.** — **average** refers to the result obtained by dividing a sum by the number of quantities added /the *average* of 7, 9, 17 is 33 ÷ 3, or 11/ and in extended use is applied to the usual or ordinary kind, instance, etc.; **mean** commonly designates a figure intermediate between two extremes /the *mean* temperature for a day with a high of 56° and a low of 34° is 45°/ and figuratively implies moderation /the golden *mean*/; the **median** is the middle number or point in a series arranged in order of size /the *median* grade in the group 50, 55, 85, 88, 92 is 85; the average is 74/; **norm** implies a standard of average performance for a given group /a child below the *norm* for his age in reading comprehension/

**average,** *v.* — *Syn.* compute an average, take the average, strike a balance, reduce to a mean, split the difference, equate, equalize, pair off.

**average out** — *Syn.* stabilize, balance, arrive at an average; see **equalize.**

**averse,** *modif.* — *Syn.* disinclined, opposed, unwilling, loath; see **opposed, reluctant, unwilling.**
*See Synonym Study at* RELUCTANT.

**aversion,** *n.* — *Syn.* antipathy, dislike, repugnance, abhorrence, hatred, loathing, revulsion, antagonism, hostility, distaste, disinclination, reluctance, disrelish, disgust, detestation, abomination, horror, allergy*; see also **hatred** 1, **objection** 1. — *Ant.* attraction, AFFINITY, predilection.

**SYN.** — **aversion** and **antipathy** both imply an ingrained feeling against that which is disagreeable or offensive, **aversion** stressing avoidance or rejection, and **antipathy**, active hostility; **repugnance** emphasizes the emotional resistance or opposition one offers to that which is incompatible with one's ideas, tastes, etc.; **loathing** suggests a feeling of extreme disgust or intolerance; **revulsion** suggests a drawing back or away from in disgust, horror, etc.; **abhorrence** implies a feeling of extreme aversion or repugnance

**avert,** *v.* **1.** [To turn away] — *Syn.* turn aside, turn away, sidetrack, deflect, shove aside, shunt, look away, cock the eye, look another way, cast one's eyes down.
**2.** [To prevent] — *Syn.* ward off, thwart, avoid; see **prevent.**
*See Synonym Study at* PREVENT.

**aviation,** *n.* — *Syn.* flying, flight, aeronautics, theory of flight, aeronautical engineering, aeronautical navigation, piloting, aeromechanics, pneumatics, aerostatics, aerodynamics, aerodonetics, airmanship, aerodromics; see also **aeronautics.**

**aviator,** *n.* — *Syn.* pilot, flier, spotter, birdman, ace, flyboy*; see also **pilot** 1.

**avid,** *modif.* — *Syn.* eager, keen, greedy, desirous; see **enthusiastic** 2.
*See Synonym Study at* EAGER.

**avocation,** *n.* — *Syn.* side interest, pastime, diversion, sideline; see **hobby.**

**avoid,** *v.* — *Syn.* keep away from, abstain from, flee from, shrink from, escape from, evade, shun, elude, malinger, dodge, give one the slip, draw back, hold off, edge off, go off, turn aside, recoil from, keep at arm's length, desist, withdraw, stay off, stay back, stay away, stay out of, shirk, let alone, keep out of the way, keep clear of, keep oneself aloof, hold oneself aloof from, keep at a respectful distance, let well enough alone, avert the eyes, keep in the background, keep one's distance, refrain from, bypass, circumvent, sidestep, skirt, give a wide berth, steer clear of*, lay off*, pass up*, shake off*, fight shy of*, duck*. — *Ant.* FACE, meet, undertake.
*See Synonym Study at* ESCAPE.

**avoidance,** *n.* — *Syn.* evasion, delay, elusion, escape, retreat, abstention, restraint, refraining, forbearance, passive resistance, evasive action, temperance, flight, recoil, nonparticipation, shunning, shirking, sidestepping, eschewal, escape mechanism, slip*, go-by*, brush*, dodge*, duck*. — *Ant.* MEETING, encounter, participation.

**avow,** *v.* — *Syn.* declare, assert, profess, admit; see **declare** 1.
*See Synonym Study at* ADMIT.

**await,** *v.* — *Syn.* wait for, anticipate, expect, be in store for; see **anticipate** 1.
*See Synonym Study at* ANTICIPATE.

**awake,** *modif.* — *Syn.* waking, conscious, up, up and

about, stirring, astir, not sleeping, aroused, wakeful, sleepless, wide-awake, attentive, vigilant, alert, observant; see also **observant** 1, 2, **vigilant**.

**awake,** *v.* **1.** [To come out of sleep] — *Syn.* wake, wake up, get up, open one's eyes, become aware, gain consciousness, see the light, stir, rub one's eyes, rise, get out of bed, stretch one's limbs, show signs of life, awaken, arise, turn out\*, roll out\*, hit the deck\*, rise and shine\*. — *Ant.* SLEEP, doze off, slumber.

**2.** [To awaken another] — *Syn.* rouse, call, arouse; see **wake** 1.

**awaken,** *v.* **1.** [To arouse another] — *Syn.* awake, rouse, call, wake up; see **wake** 1.

**2.** [To excite] — *Syn.* stir up, stimulate, arouse, animate; see **excite** 1, 2, **stir** 1.

*See Synonym Study at* STIR.

**awakening,** *n.* — *Syn.* rebirth, arousal, renewal; see **revival** 1.

**award,** *n.* — *Syn.* citation, honor, scholarship, grant; see **prize**.

*See Synonym Study at* PRIZE.

**award,** *v.* — *Syn.* grant, confer, bestow; see **give** 1.

**aware,** *modif.* — *Syn.* conscious, knowledgeable, cognizant, informed; see **conscious** 1.

*See Synonym Study at* CONSCIOUS.

**awareness,** *n.* — *Syn.* consciousness, knowledge, sensibility, mindfulness, discernment, cognizance, alertness, keenness, attentiveness, aliveness, acquaintanceship, recognition, realization, comprehension, perception, information, apprehension, appreciation, experience; see also **knowledge** 1.

**away,** *modif.* **1.** [Removed] — *Syn.* absent, not present, gone, distant, at a distance, not here, elsewhere, far afield, at arm's length, remote, from home, out of, far off, apart, beyond, off, aside. — *Ant.* HERE, present, at hand.

**2.** [Continuously] — *Syn.* on, on and on, continuously, incessantly, without stopping, without rest, without end, without a break, tirelessly, endlessly. — *Ant.* BRIEFLY, momentarily, sporadically.

**do away with** — *Syn.* eliminate, get rid of, abolish, kill; see **abolish, discard, end** 1, **kill** 1.

**awe,** *n.* — *Syn.* reverence, wonder, reverential fear; see **fear** 2, **reverence** 1.

*See Synonym Study at* REVERENCE.

**awe-inspiring,** *modif.* — *Syn.* majestic, awesome, remarkable; see **grand** 2, **impressive** 1.

**awesome,** *modif.* **1.** [Inspiring awe] — *Syn.* awe-inspiring, formidable, imposing, exalted; see **grand** 2, **impressive** 1.

**2.** [\*Outstanding] — *Syn.* wonderful, remarkable, impressive, outstanding; see **excellent**.

**awful,** *modif.* **1.** [Very bad or unpleasant] — *Syn.* terrible, wretched, disagreeable, objectionable; see **offensive** 2, **poor** 2.

**2.** [Frightful] — *Syn.* terrible, dreadful, appalling, terrifying; see **frightful** 1, **terrible** 1.

**3.** [Impressive] — *Syn.* awe-inspiring, lofty, exalted, majestic; see **grand** 2.

**4.** [\*Very great] — *Syn.* great, colossal, tremendous, prodigious; see **large** 1.

**awfully,** *modif.* **1.** [Badly] — *Syn.* poorly, objectionably, horribly, outrageously; see **badly** 1.

**2.** [Very\*] — *Syn.* very much, very, extremely, indeed; see **very**.

**awhile,** *modif.* — *Syn.* for a moment, for the moment, briefly, momentarily, for a short time, for a brief respite, for some time, not for long, temporarily, for a little while,

for a spell\*. — *Ant.* FOREVER, permanently, for a long time.

**awkward,** *modif.* **1.** [Unskillful] — *Syn.* clumsy, inept, maladroit, ungainly, uncoordinated, gawky, ungraceful, unskillful, bungling, fumbling, floundering, stumbling, lacking dexterity, inexpert, unskilled, unhandy, unpolished, gauche, stiff, graceless, bumbling, blundering, uncouth, inexperienced, incompetent, rusty, unused to, green, amateurish, butterfingered\*, all thumbs\*, cloddish\*, clodhopping\*, botchy\*, with two left feet\*, left-handed\*, hamhanded\*, klutzy\*. — *Ant.* GRACEFUL, dexterous, smooth.

**2.** [Inconvenient] — *Syn.* unwieldy, cumbersome, ponderous, inconvenient, incommodious, disagreeable, cramped; see also **heavy** 1, **uncomfortable** 2.

**3.** [Embarrassing] — *Syn.* inconvenient, inopportune, touchy, delicate; see **embarrassing**.

**4.** [Uncomfortable] — *Syn.* ill at ease, embarrassed, out of place, self-conscious; see **ashamed, uncomfortable** 1.

---

*SYN.* — **awkward** implies unfitness for smooth, easy functioning and has the broadest application of the terms here, suggesting ungracefulness, unwieldiness, inconvenience or embarrassment [an *awkward* dancer, implement, step, position, silence]; **clumsy,** emphasizing stiffness or bulkiness, suggests a lack of flexibility, dexterity, or adroitness, unwieldiness or tactlessness [a *clumsy* build, *clumsy* galoshes, a *clumsy* apology]; **maladroit** and **inept** both imply tactlessness in social relations, **maladroit** often emphasizing this as a tendency and **inept** stressing inappropriateness of a particular act or remark [inept praise]; **inept** can also refer to general lack of skill or competence

---

**awkwardly,** *modif.* — *Syn.* clumsily, bunglingly, unskillfully, unadroitly, ineptly, maladroitly, undexterously, fumblingly, lumberingly, ponderously, gawkily, gauchely, uncouthly, gracelessly, inelegantly, incompetently, amateurishly, ungracefully, stiffly, woodenly, rigidly, with difficulty, with embarrassment, in an ungainly manner, with unaccustomed fingers. — *Ant.* GRACEFULLY, skillfully, adroitly.

**awkwardness,** *n.* **1.** [Clumsiness] — *Syn.* inaptitude, clumsiness, ineptitude, ineptness, inability, incompetence, botchery, gawkiness, maladroitness, crudeness, ignorance, heavy-handedness, unhandiness, ungainliness, ungracefulness, oafishness, gracelessness, butterfingers\*, handful of thumbs\*, klutziness\*. — *Ant.* ABILITY, GRACE, competence.

**2.** [Embarrassment] — *Syn.* embarrassment, discomfiture, gaucherie, tactlessness; see **embarrassment** 1, 2,.

**awl,** *n.* — *Syn.* bit, drill, pick, borer, bradawl, drawbore, punch, fid, needle.

**awning,** *n.* — *Syn.* canvas covering, canopy, shelter, sunshade, tent, tester, marquee; see also **cover** 1.

**awry,** *modif.* **1.** [Wrong] — *Syn.* amiss, astray, wrong; see **wrong** 2, 3.

**2.** [Askew] — *Syn.* aslant, crooked, to one side; see **crooked** 1, **oblique** 1.

**ax,** *n.* — *Syn.* hatchet, adz, mattock, tomahawk, battle-ax, poleax, pickax, cleaver, broadax, hand ax, single-bitted ax, double-bitted ax.

**get the ax\*** — *Syn.* be fired, be dismissed, be discharged, be dropped from the payroll, be let go, get the boot\*, get the sack\*.

**have an ax to grind\*** — *Syn.* have an ulterior motive, have a hidden agenda, have one's own agenda, have one's own ends to promote.

**axiom,** *n.* **1.** [A maxim] — *Syn.* maxim, saying, adage, aphorism; see **proverb.**

**2.** [A proposition assumed to be true] — *Syn.* premise, assumption, postulate; see **hypothesis**.

**axiomatic,** *modif.* — *Syn.* aphoristic, self-evident, taken for granted, proverbial; see **obvious** 2.

**axis,** *n.* — *Syn.* shaft, pivot, axle, pole, stem, support, dividing line, spindle, arbor, line of symmetry, line of rotation, line of revolution.

**axle,** *n.* — *Syn.* shaft, arbor, pivot, spindle, axis, pin, gudgeon; see also **axis.**

**azure,** *modif.* — *Syn.* cerulean, pale blue, sky-blue; see **blue** 1.

# B

**babble,** *n.* — *Syn.* jabber, chatter, twaddle; see **nonsense** 1.

**babble,** *v.* — *Syn.* talk incoherently, chatter, prattle, blab, rattle (on), talk nonsense, talk foolishly, rant, rave, drivel, mouth, gush, maunder, ramble on, run on, gossip, murmur, chat, prate, twaddle, gabble, tattle, jabber, blather, palaver, blurt, patter, clack, burble, gurgle, coo, sputter, gibber, beat one's gums*, run off at the mouth*, talk off the top of one's head*, shoot the breeze*, gab*, blabber*, clatter*, go on*, natter*; see also **talk** 1.

**baby,** *modif.* **1.** [Infantile] — *Syn.* youthful, babyish, juvenile; see **childish** 1.
**2.** [Small] — *Syn.* diminutive, miniature, tiny; see **little** 1.

**baby,** *n.* **1.** [An infant] — *Syn.* infant, newborn, babe, nursling, suckling, babe in arms, neonate, preemie*, child, toddler, tot, youngling, brat, bairn, young one, little one, papoose, *bambino* (Italian), *enfant* (French), kid*, cherub*, pledge of love*, little stranger*, little newcomer*, (little) accident*, bundle from heaven*, bundle of joy*, another mouth to feed*; see also **child.** — *Ant.* adult, adolescent, grown-up.
**2.** [The youngest or smallest of a group] — *Syn.* junior, youngest, the baby of the family*; see sense 1.
**3.** [A beginner] — *Syn.* learner, novice, apprentice; see **amateur.**
**4.** [A timid or helpless person] — *Syn.* crybaby, coward, sissy*, wimp*; see **coward, weakling.**

**baby,** *v.* — *Syn.* pamper, coddle, pet, spoil, dandle, nurse, cherish, foster, cuddle, make much of, cosset, humor, indulge, mollycoddle; see also **humor.**
*See synonym study at* HUMOR.

**baby carriage,** *n.* — *Syn.* carriage, (baby) buggy, stroller, walker, perambulator, pram.

**babyhood,** *n.* — *Syn.* infancy, cradle, diaper days*; see **childhood.**

**baby-sit,** *v.* — *Syn.* watch, mind, care for, sit*; see **guard** 2.

**baby-sitter,** *n.* — *Syn.* sitter, nanny, mother's helper, au pair, day-care provider, child-care worker, caregiver; see also **nurse** 2.

**bachelor,** *n.* — *Syn.* unmarried man, single man, celibate, misogamist, misogynist, bach*, lone wolf*. — *Ant.* married man, HUSBAND, benedict.

**back,** *modif.* — *Syn.* rear, hinder, after, in back of, in the wake of, backward, hindmost, behind, abaft, astern, hind, rearward, aback, aft, to *or* in the rear, dorsal, caudal, following, at the heels of, posterior, terminal, in the wake, in the background, final. — *Ant.* FRONT, forward, head.

**back,** *n.* **1.** [The rear part or side] — *Syn.* rear, hinder part, posterior, stern, poop, aft, tailpiece, tail, back end, end, reverse, flip side. — *Ant.* FRONT, fore part, fore.
**2.** [The rear of the torso] — *Syn.* posterior, dorsal aspect, tergum, dorsum, tergal portion, spinal portion, hindquarters, rump, backbone, spine; see also **rump.**
— *Ant.* CHEST, stomach, ventral aspect.

**3.** [One who plays behind the line, especially in football] — *Syn.* linebacker, fullback, halfback, quarterback, tailback, flanker back, wingback, running back, slot back, blocking back, cornerback, safety man, free safety, ball carrier, kicker, passer, pass receiver.

**behind one's back** — *Syn.* in secret, without one's knowledge, surreptitiously, underhandedly; see **secretly.**

**(flat) on one's back** — *Syn.* ill, bedridden, helpless, laid up; see **sick.**

**get off one's back*** — *Syn.* let alone, stop nagging, leave one in peace; see **neglect** 1.

**get one's back up*** — *Syn.* become angry, be stubborn, lose one's temper; see **rage** 1.

**in back of** — *Syn.* at the rear, behind, coming after; see **back** *modif.,* **following.**

**turn one's back on** — *Syn.* reject, desert, fail; see **abandon** 1.

**with one's back to the wall** — *Syn.* desperate, cornered, stopped; see **sad** 1, **trapped.**

**back,** *v.* **1.** [To move or cause to move backward] — *Syn.* back up, reverse, withdraw, drive backward; see **retreat** 1.
**2.** [To further] — *Syn.* support, uphold, stand behind, finance; see **support** 2, 5.
**3.** [To equip with a back] — *Syn.* stiffen, cane, line; see **strengthen.**
*See Synonym Study at* SUPPORT.

**back and forth,** *modif.* — *Syn.* zigzag, in and out, to and fro, from side to side; see **to and fro.**

**backbiting,** *n.* — *Syn.* slander, calumny, detraction; see **lie** 1.

**backbone,** *n.* **1.** [Line of bones in the back supporting the body] — *Syn.* spine, spinal column, vertebrae, chine.
**2.** [Determination] — *Syn.* firmness, fortitude, resolution; see **determination** 2.
*See Synonym Study at* FORTITUDE.

**back down,** *v.* — *Syn.* withdraw, recoil, back out; see **retreat** 1.

**backed,** *modif.* **1.** [Supported] — *Syn.* upheld, supported, encouraged, approved, aided, assisted, advanced, promoted, sustained, fostered, countenanced, favored, championed, advocated, supplied, maintained, established, helped, bolstered, propped, stayed, incited, furthered, seconded, prompted, served, endorsed, sponsored, subsidized, financed, underwritten, pushed*, boosted*, bankrolled*. — *Ant.* discouraged, OPPOSED, obstructed.
**2.** [Supplied with a back or backing] — *Syn.* stiffened, built up, strengthened; see **reinforced.**

**backer,** *n.* — *Syn.* sponsor, benefactor, supporter, follower; see **patron** 1, **sponsor.**
*See Synonym Study at* SPONSOR.

**backfire,** *v.* **1.** [To explode] — *Syn.* burst, erupt, detonate; see **explode** 1.
**2.** [To go awry] — *Syn.* boomerang, recoil, rebound,

ricochet, bounce back, strike back, kick back, fly back, spring back, miscarry; see also **fail** 1.

**background,** *n.* **1.** [Setting] — *Syn.* backdrop, framework, environment; see **setting.**

**2.** [The total of one's experiences] — *Syn.* education, experience, training, qualifications, preparation, grounding, upbringing, rearing, credentials, accomplishments, achievements, attainments, acquirements, history, past; see also **experience** 3, **knowledge** 1.

**in the background** — *Syn.* unobtrusive, retiring, unseen, out of sight; see **obscure** 3, **unnoticed, withdrawn.**

**backhanded,** *modif.* — *Syn.* oblique, ambiguous, equivocal, sarcastic; see **indirect, obscure** 1.

**backing,** *n.* **1.** [Assistance] — *Syn.* subsidy, encouragement, help, sponsorship; see **aid** 1.

**2.** [Support] — *Syn.* reinforcement, buttress, lining; see **support** 2.

**backlash,** *n.* — *Syn.* adverse reaction, repercussion, resentment; see **reaction** 1, 2.

**backlog,** *n.* — *Syn.* reserve, accumulation, supply, overload; see **excess** 1, **heap, reserve** 1.

**back off,** *v.* — *Syn.* withdraw, retire, recede, back down; see **retreat** 1, 2.

**back out of,** *v.* — *Syn.* withdraw, shrink from, escape; see **abandon** 1, **retreat** 1.

**backpack,** *n.* — *Syn.* knapsack, pack, rucksack; see **bag** 1.

**backslide,** *v.* — *Syn.* apostatize, break faith, fall from grace; see **relapse.**

**backstop,** *n.* — *Syn.* screen, net, barrier; see **fence** 1.

**back talk\*,** *n.* — *Syn.* insolence, impudence, sass\*, lip\*; see **answer** 1, **rudeness.**

**backup,** *n.* — *Syn.* auxiliary, reinforcement, alternate, reserve; see **substitute.**

**back up,** *v.* **1.** [To move backward] — *Syn.* fall back, withdraw, retrogress; see **retreat** 1.

**2.** [To support] — *Syn.* help, lend support, stand by, corroborate; see **support** 2.

*See Synonym Study at* SUPPORT.

**backward,** *modif.* **1.** [To the rear] — *Syn.* rearward, astern, behind, aback, retro-, retrograde, regressive, reflex, retrogressive. — *Ant.* FORWARD, progressive, onward.

**2.** [Dull] — *Syn.* stupid, slow-witted, dense; see **dull** 3.

**3.** [Retiring] — *Syn.* bashful, reserved, shy; see **humble** 1.

**4.** [Reversed] — *Syn.* turned around, counterclockwise, inverted; see **reversed.**

**5.** [Behind in development] — *Syn.* underdeveloped, slow, slow to develop, retarded, delayed, arrested, checked, behindhand, late, undeveloped, underprivileged, unenlightened.

**bend over backward\*** — *Syn.* try hard to please, conciliate, be fair; see **try** 1.

**backwash,** *n.* — *Syn.* wake, aftermath, repercussion; see **result.**

**backwoods,** *modif.* — *Syn.* rustic, secluded, remote, unsophisticated; see **isolated.**

**backwoods,** *pl.n.* — *Syn.* groves, woodlands, timberland, hinterland; see **country** 1, **forest.**

**backyard,** *n.* — *Syn.* yard, grounds, garden, patio, terrace, deck, enclosure, play area, lawn, grass, court; see also **garden, yard** 1.

**bacon,** *n.* — *Syn.* flitch, gammon, side pork, beef bacon, Danish bacon, Canadian bacon, breakfast meat, pancetta, side meat\*, sowbelly\*.

**bring home the bacon\*** — *Syn.* earn a living, provide for, triumph, achieve; see **succeed** 1, **support** 5.

**bacteria,** *pl.n.* — *Syn.* bacilli, microbes, microorganisms; see **germ** 3.

**bad,** *modif.* **1.** [Wicked] — *Syn.* immoral, evil, wrong, corrupt; see **wicked** 1, 2.

**2.** [Spoiled] — *Syn.* rotten, rancid, decayed, putrid; see **rotten** 1, 2.

**3.** [Below standard] — *Syn.* defective, inferior, inadequate; see **faulty, poor** 2, **unsatisfactory.**

**4.** [In poor health] — *Syn.* ill, diseased, ailing; see **sick.**

**5.** [Injurious] — *Syn.* hurtful, damaging, detrimental; see **harmful.**

**6.** [Not pleasant or opportune] — *Syn.* unfavorable, disagreeable, adverse, unfortunate; see **unfavorable** 2.

**7.** [Sorry] — *Syn.* regretful, contrite, distressed, dejected; see **sad** 1, **sorry** 1.

**8.** [Severe] — *Syn.* severe, serious, grave, critical; see **acute** 2, **dangerous** 1.

**9.** [Not behaving properly] — *Syn.* naughty, disobedient, mischievous; see **naughty.**

**10.** [\*Very good] — *Syn.* stylish, effective, sharp; see **excellent, fashionable.**

*See Synonym Study at* WICKED.

**in a bad way\*** — *Syn.* dangerously ill, in critical condition, in serious trouble; see **dying** 1, **sick, in trouble** 1 at **trouble.**

**in bad\*** — *Syn.* in difficulty, in disfavor, unwelcome; see **in trouble** 1 at **trouble.**

**not bad\*** — *Syn.* all right, pretty good, good, passable; see **excellent, fair** 2.

---

*SYN.* — **bad,** in this comparison, is the broadest term, ranging in implication from merely unsatisfactory to utterly depraved; **evil** and **wicked** connote willful violation of a moral code, but **evil** often has ominous or malevolent implications [an *evil* hour], and **wicked** is sometimes weakened in a playful way to mean merely mischievous [*wicked* wit]; **ill,** which is slightly weaker than **evil** in its implications of immorality, is now used chiefly in certain idiomatic phrases [*ill*-gotten gains]; **naughty** today implies mere mischievousness or disobedience [a *naughty* child]

---

**badge,** *n.* **1.** [Outward evidence] — *Syn.* marker, symbol, identification; see **emblem, identification** 2.

**2.** [A device worn as evidence] — *Syn.* pin, insignia, insigne (*plural:* insignia), cordon, shield, ribbon, device, medallion, escutcheon, brassard, brand, ensign, token of office, epaulet, cockade, motto, official star, marker, phylactery, feather, rosette, weeper, aiguillette, aglet, cuff band, clasp, button, emblem, signet, seal, sigil, crest, star, chevron, stripe, medal; see also **decoration** 3.

**badger,** *v.* — *Syn.* harass, annoy, pester; see **bait** 2, **bother** 2.

*See Synonym Study at* BAIT.

**badlands,** *n.* — *Syn.* waste, wilderness, desert; see **waste** 3.

*See Synonym Study at* WASTE.

**badly,** *modif.* **1.** [In an ineffectual or incompetent manner] — *Syn.* wrongly, imperfectly, ineffectively, inefficiently, poorly, unsatisfactorily, crudely, boorishly, unskillfully, defectively, weakly, haphazardly, clumsily, carelessly, negligently, incompetently, stupidly, blunderingly, mistakenly, bunglingly, awkwardly, maladroitly, unhandily, faultily, amiss, abominably, awfully, terribly. — *Ant.* CAREFULLY, competently, adequately.

**2.** [To a marked degree] — *Syn.* severely, seriously, greatly; see **very.**

**3.** [*Sorry] — *Syn.* bad, sorry, distressed; see **sad** 1, **sorry.**

**bad-mouth**★ — *Syn.* criticize, disparage, malign; see **censure.**

**baffle,** *v.* **1.** [To confuse] — *Syn.* perplex, puzzle, bewilder; see **confuse.**

**2.** [To hinder] — *Syn.* block, obstruct, frustrate, impede; see **frustrate, hinder.**

*See Synonym Study at* FRUSTRATE.

**bag,** *n.* **1.** [A container] — *Syn.* purse, sack, pouch, pocket, grip, handbag, shopping bag, tote bag, tote, ditty bag, kit bag, knapsack, haversack, rucksack, backpack, fanny pack, carpetbag, kit, satchel, saddlebag, gunny sack, grain sack, woolsack, sac, saccule, suitcase, briefcase, attaché case, *sacculus* (Latin), bursa, *poche, pochette* (both French), duffel bag, garment bag, mailbag, diplomatic pouch, pack, container, feedbag, quiver, portmanteau, packet, pocketbook, Gladstone, holster, vanity bag, valise, sabretache, case, wallet, reticule, poke★, holdall★, carryall★, bindle★, tuckerbag★; see also **purse.**

**2.** [*A specialty] — *Syn.* preference, (favorite) activity, one's thing★; see **specialty** 1.

**in the bag**★ — *Syn.* assured, sure, definite, clinched; see **certain** 3.

**left holding the bag**★ — *Syn.* deceived, tricked, deserted, left to face the consequences; see **abandoned** 1, **deserted** 1.

**bag,** *v.* — *Syn.* trap, seize, get; see **catch** 1.

**baggage,** *n.* — *Syn.* luggage, impedimenta, dunnage, gear, bags, trunks, valises, suitcases, steamer trunks, overnight cases, duffel bags, garment bags, packs, grips, parcels, paraphernalia, encumbrances, effects, equipment, accouterments, movables, freight, traps★, duffel★, things★, truck★.

**baggy,** *modif.* — *Syn.* slack, loose-fitting, shapeless, bulging; see **loose** 1.

**bail,** *n.* — *Syn.* bond, security, surety, recognizance, pledge, pawn, hostage, warrant, guaranty, collateral.

**bail,** *v.* **1.** [To dip] — *Syn.* scoop, spoon out, dredge; see **dip** 2.

**2.** [To empty] — *Syn.* clear, drain, deplete; see **empty** 2.

**out on bail** — *Syn.* bailed out, free on bail, released, out on bond; see **discharged** 1, **free** 2.

**bail out,** *v.* **1.** [To post bond for] — *Syn.* release, give security for, post bail for, assure, underwrite, guarantee, warrant, insure, deliver, go bail for★, spring★.

**2.** [To help in a crisis] — *Syn.* assist, relieve, give a helping hand; see **help** 1.

**3.** [*To retreat] — *Syn.* withdraw, flee, escape; see **abandon** 2, **retreat** 1, 2.

**bait,** *n.* — *Syn.* lure, inducement, bribe; see **attraction** 2.

**bait,** *v.* **1.** [To provide with a lure] — *Syn.* set, furnish, cover, charge.

**2.** [To torment] — *Syn.* badger, harass, goad, hound, nag, tease, torment, hector, heckle, worry, persecute, beleaguer, anger, ride★, needle★, pick on★; see also **bother** 2.

**3.** [To lure] — *Syn.* entice, attract, draw; see **deceive, fascinate, seduce, tempt.**

---

*SYN.* — **bait** is to harass or goad, as with repeated, unprovoked attacks, insults, or derision, and implies that the persecutor gets malicious pleasure from the act; to **badger** is to pester so persistently as to bring to a state of confusion or wear down; to **hound** is to pursue or attack relentlessly until the victim succumbs /he was *hounded* out of office/; **heckle** denotes the persistent questioning and taunting of a public speaker so as to annoy or con-

fuse; **hector** implies a continual bullying or nagging in order to intimidate or break down resistance; **torment**, in this comparison, suggests continued harassment so as to cause acute suffering /*tormented* by her memories/; **ride** is colloquial and implies harassment or teasing by ridiculing, criticizing, etc. /they were *riding* the rookie unmercifully from the dugout/

---

**bake,** *v.* **1.** [To cook] — *Syn.* roast, toast, warm; see **cook.**

**2.** [To harden] — *Syn.* temper, anneal, fire; see **harden** 1.

**baked,** *modif.* — *Syn.* parched, scorched, dried, toasted, warmed, heated, cooked, grilled, burned, charred, roasted, incinerated.

**baker,** *n.* — *Syn.* pastry cook, pastry chef, confectioner, *pâtissier, boulanger* (both French); see also **cook.**

**bakery,** *n.* — *Syn.* bakeshop, pastry shop, pastry kitchen, patisserie, boulangerie, confectionery, cook shop, bread *or* cake *or* biscuit factory, bread bakery, cake bakery, bakehouse, *Konditorei* (German).

**balance,** *n.* **1.** [Whatever remains] — *Syn.* remainder, excess, surplus, amount due; see **remainder.**

**2.** [An equilibrium] — *Syn.* equipoise, poise, counterpoise, equilibrium, symmetry, antithesis, offset, equivalence, counterbalance, tension, equalization, equality of weight, parity; see also **symmetry.** — *Ant.* IMBALANCE, lopsidedness, topheaviness.

**3.** [An excess of credits over debits] — *Syn.* credit balance, surplus, dividend, profit, cash on hand, available funds.

**4.** [A balance scale] — *Syn.* steelyard, spring balance, scales; see **scale** 3.

**5.** [Judgment] — *Syn.* perspective, discretion, insight, steadiness; see **judgment** 1, **stability** 1, 2.

*See Synonym Study at* REMAINDER, SYMMETRY.

**in the balance** — *Syn.* undetermined, undecided, critical; **uncertain** 2.

**off balance** — *Syn.* unbalanced, tipsy, eccentric; see **irregular** 1, 4, **unsteady** 1.

**balance,** *v.* **1.** [To offset] — *Syn.* equipoise, counterpoise, counterbalance; see **offset.**

**2.** [To place in balance] — *Syn.* poise, oppose, place in equilibrium, steady, stabilize, neutralize, set, level, equalize, support, equilibrate, even, weigh, counteract, make equal, make level, make steady, compensate, tie, adjust, square, nullify, parallel, cancel, coordinate, readjust, equate, trim, match, level off, pair off, restore, attune, harmonize, tune, countervail, accord, correspond. — *Ant.* topple, UPSET, turn over.

**3.** [To demonstrate that debits and credits are in balance] — *Syn.* estimate, compare, account (for), count, compute, prove, adjust, settle, make up, strike a balance, take a trial balance, tell, audit, calculate, enumerate, equate, square, tally, total, reckon, take stock, sum up; see also **check** 3.

**4.** [To compare as to relative importance or value] — *Syn.* weigh, evaluate, ponder; see **compare** 1, **consider** 1, 3.

**balanced,** *modif.* **1.** [Made even] — *Syn.* equalized, poised, offset, in equilibrium, even, equal, counterweighted, equivalent, stabilized, antithetic, symmetrical, counterpoised, counterbalanced, proportionate, harmonious, steady, stable, well-balanced, on an even keel★. — *Ant.* TOP-HEAVY, unbalanced, unequal.

**2.** [Fair] — *Syn.* equitable, just, evenhanded, impartial; see **fair** 1.

**balance of power,** *n.* — *Syn.* equilibrium, distribution, degree of power, apportionment; see **balance** 2.

**balance sheet,** *n.* — *Syn.* annual report, budget, liability and asset sheet; see **statement** 3.

**balcony,** *n.* — *Syn.* gallery, catwalk, mezzanine, loge, balustrade, loggia, veranda, terrace, stoop, piazza, portico, porch, deck, platform, parapet, box.

**bald,** *modif.* **1.** [Without natural covering; usually, without hair] — *Syn.* hairless, baldheaded, depilated, tonsured, shaven, shaved, bare, featherless, treeless, glabrous, shiny, smooth, baldpated, hairless as an egg*, like a billiard ball*; see also **naked** 1. — *Ant.* HAIRY, covered, hirsute.
**2.** [Not adorned, elaborated, or disguised] — *Syn.* plain, blunt, simple, forthright; see **abrupt** 2, **frank, modest** 2.
*See Synonym Study at* NAKED.

**balderdash,** *n.* — *Syn.* senseless talk, gibberish, bombast; see **nonsense** 1.

**baldness,** *n.* — *Syn.* hairlessness, lack *or* absence of hair, sparseness, alopecia.

**bale,** *n.* — *Syn.* bundle, bunch, parcel, package; see **package** 1.
*See Synonym Study at* PACKAGE.

**baleful,** *modif.* — *Syn.* deadly, noxious, sinister, injurious; see **harmful, sinister.**
*See Synonym Study at* SINISTER.

**balk,** *v.* **1.** [To refuse] — *Syn.* demur, resist, recoil, be unwilling; see **hesitate, refuse** 1.
**2.** [To frustrate] — *Syn.* thwart, hinder, check; see **frustrate, prevent.**
*See Synonym Study at* FRUSTRATE.

**balky,** *modif.* — *Syn.* contrary, stubborn, perverse, mulish; see **contrary** 4, **obstinate** 1.
*See Synonym Study at* CONTRARY.

**ball,** *n.* **1.** [A spherical body] — *Syn.* globe, spheroid, sphere, balloon, orb, perisphere, globule, globular *or* rounded *or* spherical *or* orbicular object, drop, knot, marble, pellet, glob, pill*.
**2.** [A game played with a ball] — *Syn.* baseball, football, catch; see **sport** 3.
**3.** [In baseball, a pitch that is not swung at and is not a strike] — *Syn.* wild pitch, inside pitch, outside pitch, wide one*, high baby*, duster*, insider*.
**4.** [Missile for a gun] — *Syn.* bullet, shell, lead; see **ammunition, shot** 2.
**5.** [A dance] — *Syn.* grand ball, dance, promenade, reception; see **dance** 2, **party** 1.
**carry the ball*** — *Syn.* assume responsibility, take command, take control, bear the burden; see **lead** 1, **manage** 1.
**get** *or* **keep the ball rolling*** — *Syn.* initiate action, get underway, maintain action, carry on; see **begin** 1, **continue** 1.
**have a ball** — *Syn.* revel, have fun, celebrate; see **enjoy oneself, play** 1.
**on the ball*** — *Syn.* skilled, alert, efficient, with-it*; see **able** 1, 2, **observant** 1, **responsible** 2.

**ballad,** *n.* — *Syn.* popular song, folk song, love song, narrative poem, lay; see also **poetry, song, story.**

**ballade,** *n.* — *Syn.* art song, ballad, lyric; see **poetry, song.**

**ballast,** *n.* — *Syn.* sandbags, counterbalance, counterweight; see **weight** 2.

**ballet,** *n.* — *Syn.* toe dancing, choreography, modern dance; see **dance** 1.

**ballet dancer,** *n.* — *Syn.* ballerina, prima ballerina, danseuse, danseur, figurante, figurant, coryphée, member of the chorus, student dancer; see also **dancer.**

**balloon,** *n.* — *Syn.* dirigible, aircraft, airship, weather balloon, nondirigible aerostat, montgolfier, free balloon, captive balloon, kite balloon, lighter-than-air craft, toy balloon, zeppelin, observation balloon, barrage balloon, radar balloon, blimp*, bag*, sausage*, gasbag*, zep*.

**balloon,** *v.* — *Syn.* bloat, swell up, expand; see **inflate** 2.

**ballot,** *n.* **1.** [A vote] — *Syn.* tally, ticket, poll; see **vote** 1.
**2.** [A list of candidates] — *Syn.* choice, slate, ticket, lineup; see **ticket** 2.

**ballroom,** *n.* — *Syn.* dance hall, dance floor, assembly hall, discotheque; see **hall** 1.

**ball up*,** *v.* — *Syn.* muddle, jumble, tangle; see **confuse.**

**balm,** *n.* **1.** [Anything healing and soothing] — *Syn.* solace, consolation, comfort, relief, easement, alleviation, refreshment, mitigation, remedy, assuagement, cure. — *Ant.* IRRITATION, vexation, irritant.
**2.** [An ointment of resin] — *Syn.* salve, ointment, unguent, lotion, liniment, potion, poultice, plaster, application, dressing, preparation, formula, compound, prescription, emollient, sweet oil, demulcent; see also **lotion, medicine** 2, **salve.**

**balmy,** *modif.* **1.** [Mild; *said of weather*] — *Syn.* warm, soothing, summerlike, gentle; see **mild** 2.
**2.** [*Crazy] — *Syn.* crazy, foolish, eccentric; see **insane** 1.

**bamboozle,** *v.* **1.** [To cheat] — *Syn.* swindle, trick, dupe, hoodwink; see **deceive.**
**2.** [To perplex] — *Syn.* puzzle, confound, baffle; see **confuse.**

**ban,** *n.* — *Syn.* interdiction, prohibition, limitation, embargo; see **refusal, taboo.**

**ban,** *v.* — *Syn.* forbid, outlaw, prevent, declare illegal; see **forbid, halt** 2, **prevent.**
*See Synonym Study at* FORBID.

**banal,** *modif.* — *Syn.* dull, trite, hackneyed; see **common** 1, **insipid.**
*See Synonym Study at* INSIPID.

**banality,** *n.* — *Syn.* commonplace, platitude, trite phrase; see **cliché.**

**band,** *n.* **1.** [A beltlike strip] — *Syn.* ribbon, belt, line, strip, tape, fillet, sash, twine, twist, riband, cingle, surcingle, girth, cincture, cinch, scarf, bandage, circuit, meridian, latitude, circle, ring, orbit, stripe, girdle, zodiac, zonule, circumference, border, cordon, zone, streak, thong, wristband, braid, ferrule, brace, strap, binding, hoop, waistband, cummerbund, obi, baldric, collar, hatband, headband; see also **stripe.**
**2.** [That which binds] — *Syn.* bond, tie, ligature, binding, binder, hoop, stay, truss, belt, shackle, cord, tendon, harness, cable, rope, link, chain, line, hawser, string, guy wire, guy, painter, strap, trace, thong, withe; see also sense 1, **dressing** 3, **rope, wire** 1.
**3.** [A company of people] — *Syn.* troop, group, collection, association; see **gathering, troop.**
**4.** [A group of musicians] — *Syn.* orchestra, company, ensemble, group, troupe, combo*.
Kinds of bands include: military, brass, street, skiffle, concert, parade, jazz, rock, electric, stage, dance, German, Dixieland, jug, swing*, sweet*.
*See Synonym Study at* TROOP.

**bandage,** *n.* — *Syn.* dressing, compress, gauze, Band-Aid (trademark); see **dressing** 3.

**bandage,** *v.* — *Syn.* dress, wrap, swathe, truss; see **bind** 1, **dress** 4, **wrap** 1.

**bandit,** *n.* — *Syn.* highwayman, thief, brigand; see **robber.**

**band together,** *v.* — *Syn.* ally, join, gather together, confederate; see **unite** 1.

**bang,** *n.* **1.** [A loud report] — *Syn.* crash, blast, roar, detonation; see **noise** 1.
**2.** [A blow] — *Syn.* hit, smack, whack; see **blow** 1.

**3.** [*A thrill] — *Syn.* enjoyment, pleasant feeling, excitement, kick*; see **thrill.**

**bang,** *v.* **1.** [To beat] — *Syn.* strike, slam, whack, pound; see **beat** 1, **crash** 4, **hit** 1.

**2.** [To make a noise] — *Syn.* crash, clatter, rattle; see **sound** 1.

**banish,** *v.* **1.** [To condemn to exile] — *Syn.* exile, expatriate, deport, transport, ostracize, excommunicate, proscribe, drive out, cast out, outlaw, extradite, sequester, isolate, relegate, expel, oust, dismiss, send to Coventry*, put a price on*. — *Ant.* RECEIVE, welcome, accept.

**2.** [To remove completely] — *Syn.* expel, evict, discharge; see **dismiss** 1, 2.

*SYN.* — **banish** implies removal from a country (not necessarily one's own) as a formal punishment; **exile** implies compulsion to leave one's own country, either because of a formal decree or through force of circumstance; **expatriate** suggests more strongly voluntary exile and often implies the acquiring of citizenship in another country; to **deport** is to send (an alien) out of the country, because the alien either entered unlawfully or is regarded as undesirable; to **transport**, in this connection, is to banish (a convict) to a penal colony; **ostracize**, which historically referred to temporary banishment of a citizen in ancient Greece by popular vote, today implies forced exclusion from society or a certain group by general consent [*ostracized* for scandalous behavior]

**banishment,** *n.* — *Syn.* expatriation, deportation, expulsion; see **exile** 1.

**banister,** *n.* — *Syn.* railing, baluster, balustrade; see **rail** 1.

**bank,** *n.* **1.** [A wall of earth] — *Syn.* levee, embankment, mound; see **ridge** 2.

**2.** [Ground rising above adjacent water] — *Syn.* ledge, cliff, edge, shore; see **shore.**

**3.** [Raised ground under water] — *Syn.* shoal, reef, bar; see **shoal.**

**4.** [A financial establishment] — *Syn.* savings bank, commercial bank, countinghouse, investment firm, banking house, financial custodian, credit union, trust company, treasury, exchequer, repository of funds, national bank, state bank, cooperative bank, savings and loan association, thrift (institution), Federal Reserve Bank, private bank, lending institution, depository, vault, automated teller machine *or* ATM, cash machine.

**5.** [A row of objects close together] — *Syn.* series, group, sequence; see **line** 1.

**6.** [The pitch in a turn] — *Syn.* slope, lean, incline; see **inclination** 5.

**7.** [A gambling establishment] — *Syn.* the house, cashier, club; see **casino.**

*See Synonym Study at* SHOAL, SHORE.

**bank,** *v.* **1.** [To deposit money] — *Syn.* save, deposit, put in the bank, enter an account; see **deposit** 2.

**2.** [To operate a bank] — *Syn.* lend money, hold money in trust, practice usury, speculate.

**3.** [To heap earth or similar material] — *Syn.* dike, pile, hill; see **heap** 1.

**4.** [To cover a fire for the night] — *Syn.* trim, build up, stoke, replenish, regulate, cover.

**5.** [To tilt on a curve] — *Syn.* lean, pitch, bend, slope; see **lean** 1.

**banker,** *n.* **1.** [One who owns or operates a bank] — *Syn.* steward, treasurer, teller, manager, bank officer, loan officer, broker, financier, capitalist, investment banker, moneylender, usurer.

**2.** [The holder of funds in a gambling game] — *Syn.* croupier, house, bank; see **dealer** 2.

**banking,** *n.* — *Syn.* investment, trading, funding, moneylending, usury, brokerage, speculation; see also **business** 1.

**bank on*,** *v.* — *Syn.* rely on, depend on, count on; see **count on, trust** 1.

*See Synonym Study at* TRUST.

**bankrupt,** *modif.* — *Syn.* failed, out of business, broke*; see **insolvent, ruined** 4.

**bankruptcy,** *n.* — *Syn.* insolvency, failure, financial loss *or* ruin, nonpayment, defaulting, repudiation, overdraft, defalcation, liquidation, chapter 11, economic death, pauperism, destitution, indigence, privation, distress, straitened circumstances, beggary, impecuniosity, ruin, ruination, going to the wall*. — *Ant.* solvency, PROSPERITY, soundness.

**banner,** *n.* — *Syn.* colors, pennant, standard; see **emblem, flag** 1.

**banquet,** *n.* — *Syn.* feast, repast, fete, festivity; see **dinner, feast.**

**bantam,** *modif.* — *Syn.* small, diminutive, tiny; see **little** 1.

**banter,** *n.* — *Syn.* teasing, joking, raillery, badinage; see **fun, ridicule, teasing.**

**banter,** *v.* — *Syn.* tease, jest (with), kid*; see **joke, ridicule.**

**baptism,** *n.* — *Syn.* immersion, dedication, christening, ablution, initiation, lustration, ritual, rite, baptismal regeneration, rebirth, sprinkling, infant baptism, dunking*; see also **sacrament** 1.

**Baptist,** *n.* — *Syn.* immersionist, baptizer, Anabaptist, Dunker*.

Baptist church bodies include: the Southern Baptist Convention, American Baptist Churches, National Baptist Convention; Baptist groups or types include: Regular, Six-principle, Free Original, Southern, Freewill, Seventh Day, General, Primitive, Separate, United.

**baptize,** *v.* **1.** [To cleanse sacramentally] — *Syn.* immerse, purify, regenerate, sprinkle, dip, dunk, asperse, administer baptism to, initiate.

**2.** [To give a name] — *Syn.* christen, name, denominate, dub; see **name** 1.

**baptized,** *modif.* — *Syn.* christened, purified, held at the font; see **named** 1.

**bar,** *n.* **1.** [A relatively long, narrow object] — *Syn.* strip, stake, rod, pole, stick, crossbar, boom, rib, jimmy, handspike, crosspiece, spar, pry, rail, ingot, block, cake, lever, pinch bar, wrecking bar, crowbar, shaft, slab, pig.

**2.** [A counter serving refreshments, especially drinks, or the accompanying establishment] — *Syn.* saloon, tavern, pub, public house, counter, buffet, barroom, cafe, bistro, cocktail lounge, beer parlor, beer garden, alehouse, fern bar, nightclub, cabaret, restaurant, inn, cafeteria, snack bar, canteen, grillroom, grill, taproom, tap, piano bar, wine bar, rathskeller, *brasserie* (French), brewery, speakeasy, roadhouse, watering hole*, booze joint*, dive*, barrelhouse*, gin mill*, honky-tonk*, after-hours joint*, local* (British).

**3.** [A court of law] — *Syn.* tribunal, judiciary, session; see **court** 2.

**4.** [The legal profession] — *Syn.* lawyers, advocates, counselors, barristers, judiciary, solicitors, jurists, body of lawyers, attorneys, the legal fraternity, bar association.

**5.** [An obstruction] — *Syn.* hindrance, obstacle, hurdle; see **barrier.**

**6.** [A relatively long, narrow area] — *Syn.* strip, stripe, ribbon; see **band** 1, **stripe.**

7. [Raised ground underwater] — *Syn.* shoal, bank, reef; see **shoal**.

*See Synonym Study at* SHOAL.

**bar,** *v.* **1.** [To raise a physical obstruction] — *Syn.* barricade, dam, dike, fence, wall, obstruct, erect a barrier, brick up, blockade, trammel, clog, exclude, shut, shut off, block, block off, block up, lock (out), keep out, debar, bolt, latch, cork, plug, seal, jam, caulk, stop, impede, (set up a) roadblock, raise the drawbridge*. — *Ant.* OPEN, free, clear.

**2.** [To obstruct by refusal] — *Syn.* interdict, ban, forbid, disallow, deny, refuse, debar, repudiate, suspend, segregate, boycott, ostracize, blackball, prevent, preclude, shut out, keep out, exclude, exile, reject, outlaw, condemn, prohibit, discourage, discountenance, interfere with, restrain, stop, frustrate, circumvent, override, except, blacklist, freeze out*. — *Ant.* ALLOW, admit, welcome.

**3.** [To hinder] — *Syn.* obstruct, impede, interfere with; see **hinder**.

*See Synonym Study at* HINDER.

**barb,** *n.* — *Syn.* arrow, thorn, spike; see **point** 2.

**barbarian,** *modif.* **1.** [Uncivilized] — *Syn.* primitive, uncivilized, barbaric, barbarous, rude, rough, savage, coarse, uncultivated, wild, crude, uncouth; see also **primitive** 3.

**2.** [Savage] — *Syn.* brutal, savage, barbarous, cruel; see **cruel** 1, 2.

---

**SYN. — barbarian** basically refers to a civilization or people regarded as primitive, either without further connotation [*barbarian* tribes] or with the implication of lack of cultivation and refinement or of brutishness; **barbaric** suggests crudeness and lack of restraint regarded as characteristic of primitive peoples [*barbaric* splendor]; **barbarous** connotes cruelty and brutality regarded as characteristic of primitive people; [*barbarous* warfare]; **savage** implies a more primitive civilization than **barbarian** and connotes great fierceness and cruelty [a *savage* inquisition]

---

**barbarian,** *n.* **1.** [An uncivilized person] — *Syn.* savage, brute, Hun, cannibal, Goth, yahoo, Philistine, troglodyte, boor, lout, clod.

**2.** [A brute] — *Syn.* rascal, ruffian, monster; see **beast** 2.

**3.** [A foreigner] — *Syn.* stranger, outsider, newcomer; see **alien**.

**barbaric,** *modif.* **1.** [Primitive] — *Syn.* uncivilized, wild, crude, unrestrained; see **barbarian** 1, **primitive** 3.

**2.** [Cruel] — *Syn.* inhuman, brutal, fierce, barbarous; see **cruel** 1.

*See Synonym Study at* BARBARIAN.

**barbarism,** *n.* — *Syn.* inhumanity, brutality, barbarity; see **cruelty**.

**barbarity,** *n.* **1.** [Savagery] — *Syn.* savageness, cruelty, brutality; see **cruelty**.

**2.** [Crudity] — *Syn.* boorishness, vulgarity, crudeness; see **rudeness**.

**barbarous,** *modif.* **1.** [Characterized by cruelty] — *Syn.* cruel, inhuman, brutal, fierce; see **cruel** 1.

**2.** [Uncivilized] — *Syn.* barbaric, rude, unsophisticated; see **barbarian** 1, **primitive** 3.

*See Synonym Study at* BARBARIAN.

**barbecue,** *n.* **1.** [A grill] — *Syn.* roaster, grill, hibachi, griddle; see **appliance, broiler**.

**2.** [A picnic] — *Syn.* cookout, picnic, wiener roast, clambake; see **picnic** 1.

**barbecue,** *v.* — *Syn.* grill, broil, roast; see **cook**.

**barbed,** *modif.* — *Syn.* pointed, spiked, piercing; see **sharp** 2.

**barbed wire,** *n.* — *Syn.* barbwire, fence wire, galvanized wire, fencing, wire fence, concertina wire; see also **fence** 1, 2.

**barber,** *n.* — *Syn.* hairdresser, haircutter, shaver, coiffeur, coiffeuse, cosmetologist, beautician, beauty parlor operator, hair stylist, tonsorial artist*.

**barber shop,** *n.* — *Syn.* tonsorium, tonsorial parlor, styling salon, beauty parlor, beauty salon, beauty shop.

**bard,** *n.* — *Syn.* troubadour, versifier, minstrel; see **poet**.

**bare,** *modif.* **1.** [Without covering] — *Syn.* exposed, uncovered, naked, stripped; see **naked** 1, **open** 4.

**2.** [Plain] — *Syn.* unadorned, simple, unornamented, stark; see **modest** 2.

**3.** [Without content] — *Syn.* barren, void, unfurnished; see **empty** 1.

**4.** [Without surplus] — *Syn.* scant, meager, insufficient; see **inadequate** 1.

*See Synonym Study at* NAKED.

**bare,** *v.* — *Syn.* reveal, uncover, expose, unveil, strip, lay bare, divulge, publish, disclose; see also **expose** 1, **reveal** 1, **strip** 1, **undress**.

*See Synonym Study at* STRIP.

**barefaced,** *modif.* **1.** [Open] — *Syn.* unconcealed, clear, apparent; see **obvious** 1.

**2.** [Impudent] — *Syn.* shameless, audacious, bold, brazen; see **rude** 2.

**barefoot,** *modif.* — *Syn.* shoeless, barefooted, unshod, discalced (*used of members of certain religious orders*).

**barely,** *modif.* — *Syn.* almost, scarcely, just; see **hardly**.

**bareness,** *n.* **1.** [Nakedness] — *Syn.* nudity, undress, déshabillé; see **nakedness**.

**2.** [Plainness] — *Syn.* unadornment, starkness, austerity; see **simplicity** 2.

**bargain,** *n.* **1.** [An agreement] — *Syn.* pact, compact, contract; see **agreement** 3.

**2.** [An advantageous purchase] — *Syn.* good value, good deal, discount, reduction, marked-down price, markdown, good buy, value*, buy*, steal*, giveaway*, deal*.

**into the bargain*** — *Syn.* in addition, too, additionally; see **also**.

**bargain,** *v.* **1.** [To trade] — *Syn.* barter, do business, merchandise; see **buy** 1, **sell** 1.

**2.** [To negotiate] — *Syn.* haggle, dicker, make terms, arrange; see **negotiate** 1.

**bargain for*,** *v.* — *Syn.* expect, plan on, foresee; see **anticipate** 1.

**bargaining,** *n.* — *Syn.* trade, transaction, haggling; see **agreement** 1, **business** 1.

**barge,** *n.* — *Syn.* scow, flatboat, canal boat, raft, pleasure barge, freight barge, lighter; see also **boat, ship**.

**bark,** *n.* **1.** [An outer covering, especially of trees] — *Syn.* rind, skin, peel, shell, case, crust, peeling, cork, husk, cortex, hide, pelt, coat; see also **skin**.

**2.** [A short, explosive sound] — *Syn.* yelp, yap, grunt; see **noise** 1.

**3.** [A ship] — *Syn.* vessel, sloop, brig; see **boat, ship**.

*See Synonym Study at* SKIN.

**bark,** *v.* **1.** [To emit a dog's characteristic sound] — *Syn.* yelp, yap, bay, howl, cry, growl, snarl, gnar, gnarl, yip, woof*, arf*.

**2.** [To speak as though barking] — *Syn.* snap, snarl, growl; see **yell**.

**bark at,** *v.* — *Syn.* shout at, scold, rebuke; see **censure, scold**.

**bark up the wrong tree*,** *v.* — *Syn.* miscalculate, mistake, misdirect one's efforts; see **misjudge** 2.

**barley,** *n.* — *Syn.* small grain, barleycorn, cereal; see **grain** 1.

**barn,** *n.* — *Syn.* outbuilding, shed, outhouse, shelter, lean-to.
Kinds of barns include: stable, chicken house, cow barn, coop, cote, hutch, sty, fold, pen, byre, kennel, mow; pad*, bullock lodge*, cow house*.

**barnstorm,** *v.* — *Syn.* tour, troupe, go on tour; see **act** 3, **campaign** 1, **travel** 2.

**barnyard,** *n.* — *Syn.* farmyard, feedyard, pen, corral, stableyard, lot, feedlot, run.

**barometer,** *n.* — *Syn.* glass, weather gauge, storm gauge, pressure indicator, weatherglass, aneroid barometer, mercury barometer, gauge.

**baron,** *n.* — *Syn.* peer, nobleman, noble; see aristocrat, **lord** 2.

**baroness,** *n.* — *Syn.* peeress, gentlewoman, noblewoman; see aristocrat, **lady** 3.

**baroque,** *modif.* — *Syn.* elaborate, rococo, extravagant, florid; see **ornate** 1.

**barracks,** *pl.n.* — *Syn.* encampment, shelters, military enclosure, tents, quarters, (field) headquarters, camp, bivouac, cantonment, garrison huts, Quonset huts (trademark), dormitory, billet, casern, prefabs*.

**barrage,** *n.* — *Syn.* bombardment, blast, volley, torrent; see **attack** 1, **fire** 2, **plenty.**

**barred,** *modif.* **1.** [Equipped or marked with bars] — *Syn.* striped, banded, stripped, streaked, twilled, pleated, pied, parti-colored, variegated, motley, tortoiseshell, calico, mottled, dappled, veined, brindled, tabby, ribbed, crosshatched, ridged, marked, piped, lined.
**2.** [Prohibited] — *Syn.* banned, outlawed, forbidden; see **illegal.**

**barrel,** *n.* — *Syn.* cask, keg, hogshead, stoup, vat, tub, puncheon, firkin, butt, carboy, cylinder, tun, receptacle, pipe, container, vessel.
**over a barrel** — *Syn.* at one's mercy, between a rock and a hard place*, in trouble; see **beaten** 1.

**barren,** *modif.* **1.** [Incapable of producing young] — *Syn.* sterile, impotent, infertile, childless; see **sterile** 1.
**2.** [Lacking vegetation] — *Syn.* fallow, unproductive, desolate, arid; see **sterile** 2.
**3.** [Without intellectual interest] — *Syn.* insipid, dry, boring, stupid; see **dull** 4.
**4.** [Unprofitable] — *Syn.* fruitless, unproductive, profitless; see **waste, worthless** 1.
*See Synonym Study at* NAKED, STERILE.

**barrenness,** *n.* — *Syn.* sterility, unproductiveness, infecundity, infertility, childlessness, effeteness, impotence, desolateness, unfruitfulness, bleakness, emptiness, aridness, aridity, agenesis, unfructuosity. — *Ant.* FERTILITY, fruitfulness, richness.

**barricade,** *n.* — *Syn.* obstacle, blockade, roadblock, obstruction; see **barrier.**

**barricade,** *v.* — *Syn.* obstruct, block, fortify; see **bar** 1.

**barrier,** *n.* — *Syn.* bar, obstruction, difficulty, hindrance, obstacle, hurdle, fortification, stumbling block, fence, sound *or* sonic *or* transonic barrier, restriction, limitation, restraint, impediment, let, drawback, check, preventive, encumbrance, stop, stopper, block, stay, bulwark, barricade, rampart, wall, palisade, picket, roadblock, earthwork, breastwork, outwork, embankment, parapet, blockade, moat, trench, barbed wire, entanglement, pale, limit, boundary, iron curtain, bamboo curtain. — *Ant.* WAY, passage, opening.
*See Synonym Study at* IMPEDIMENT.

**barrister,** *n.* — *Syn.* counselor, attorney, advocate; see **lawyer.**

*See Synonym Study at* LAWYER.

**barroom,** *n.* — *Syn.* tavern, saloon, pub*; see **bar** 2.

**barrow,** *n.* — *Syn.* wheelbarrow, pushcart, handbarrow, handtruck, carriage, cart, dumpcart, rickshaw, jinrikisha; see also **cart.**

**barter,** *n.* — *Syn.* trade, exchange, traffic; see **business** 1, **exchange** 2.

**barter,** *v.* — *Syn.* trade, bargain, swap*; see **exchange** 2, **sell** 1.
*See Synonym Study at* SELL.

**base,** *modif.* — *Syn.* low, ignoble, sordid; see **mean** 1, **vulgar** 1.
*See Synonym Study at* MEAN.

**base,** *n.* **1.** [A point from which action is initiated] — *Syn.* home, headquarters, camp, post, station, home base, base of operations, base camp, starting point, point of departure, field, landing field, strip, airport, airfield, airstrip, hangar, port, terminal, garrison, billet, center, depot, supply base, dock, harbor, anchorage, seat, base line.
**2.** [The principal or basic ingredient] — *Syn.* chief constituent, core, essence, filler; see **essence** 1.
**3.** [The bottom, thought of as a support] — *Syn.* foundation, support, bottom, pedestal, stand, bed, rest, foot, root, trunk, footing; see also **foundation** 2.
**4.** [Foundation of a belief or statement] — *Syn.* basis, groundwork, underpinning, principle, authority; see also **basis** 1.
**5.** [A goal, especially in baseball] — *Syn.* mark, bound, station, plate, post, goal, first base, first, second base, second, keystone*, third base, third, hot corner*, home plate, platter*, corner*, bag*, sack*.

**off base*** — *Syn.* erring, mistaken, incorrect; see **mistaken** 1, **wrong** 2.

**SYN.** — **base,** as compared here, refers to a part or thing at the bottom acting as a support or underlying structure [the *base* of a lamp]; **basis,** conveying the same idea, is the term preferred for nonphysical things [the *basis* of a theory]; **foundation** stresses solidity in the underlying or supporting thing and often suggests permanence and stability in that which is built on it [the *foundation* of a house]; **groundwork,** closely synonymous with **foundation,** is principally applied to nonphysical things [the *groundwork* of a good education]

**baseball,** *n.* — *Syn.* ball, the Major Leagues, Little League, the national pastime.
The major league teams in the United States include — *National League:* Los Angeles Dodgers, San Francisco Giants, Pittsburgh Pirates, Philadelphia Phillies, Atlanta Braves, St. Louis Cardinals, San Diego Padres, Cincinnati Reds, Houston Astros, Montreal Expos, New York Mets, Chicago Cubs, Florida Marlins, Colorado Rockies; *American League:* Baltimore Orioles, Minnesota Twins, Detroit Tigers, Chicago White Sox, Cleveland Indians, California Angels, Kansas City Royals, Oakland A's *or* Athletics, Milwaukee Brewers, Texas Rangers, Boston Red Sox, Toronto Blue Jays, Seattle Mariners, New York Yankees.

**based,** *modif.* — *Syn.* situated, stationed, planted, founded; see **established** 2, **placed.**

**baseman,** *n.* — *Syn.* first baseman, second baseman, third baseman, sacker*.

**basement,** *n.* **1.** [A story wholly or partly below ground] — *Syn.* cellar, excavation, storage room, root cellar, wine cellar, furnace room, vault, subterranean apartment, crypt, bunker, subbasement, subcellar, cyclone

cellar, storm cellar, cellarage.
**2.** [Foundation] — *Syn.* wall, footing, heavy construction; see **foundation** 2.

**baseness,** *n.* — *Syn.* meanness, debasement, degeneracy; see **evil** 1, **meanness** 1, **rudeness.**

**base on,** *v.* — *Syn.* establish, ground on, found on, depend on, stand on, settle on, form on, hinge on, place on, fasten on, rest on, predicate on, institute, build; see also **establish** 2, **organize** 2.

**bashful,** *modif.* — *Syn.* shy, retiring, reserved, timid; see **humble** 1, **modest** 2, **shy.**
*See Synonym Study at* SHY.

**bashfulness,** *n.* — *Syn.* modesty, timidity, reserve; see **shyness.**

**basic,** *modif.* — *Syn.* essential, central, primary, elementary; see **fundamental** 1, **necessary** 1.

**basically,** *modif.* — *Syn.* fundamentally, primarily, radically; see **essentially.**

**basics,** *pl.n.* — *Syn.* fundamentals, essentials, rudiments, ABC's, elements, principles, first steps, principia, nuts and bolts*, nitty-gritty*, brass tacks*, the three R's*; see **elements.**

**basin,** *n.* — *Syn.* sink, pan, ewer, bowl; see **container, sink.**

**basis,** *n.* **1.** [An intellectual foundation] — *Syn.* support, foundation, justification, grounds, reason, explanation, *raison d'être* (French), background, source, authority, principle, groundwork, underpinning, base, axiom, assumption, *point d'appui* (French), premise, postulate, antecedent, backing, proof, evidence, data, security, warrant, crux, nexus, nucleus, heart.
**2.** [A physical foundation] — *Syn.* base, foundation, footing, cornerstone; see **foundation** 2.
*See Synonym Study at* BASE.

**bask,** *v.* — *Syn.* loll, lounge, relax, luxuriate, revel, take comfort, enjoy, relish, wallow, laze, warm oneself, sun oneself, sunbathe.

**basket,** *n.* **1.** [A container] — *Syn.* bushel, crate, hamper, pannier, creel, bassinet, bin, box, cradle; see also **case** 7, **container.**
**2.** [The contents of a basket] — *Syn.* basketful, bushel, load; see **load** 1, **measure** 1.
**3.** [The goal in basketball] — *Syn.* net, hoop, bucket*, pot*, swisher*.

**basketball,** *n.* — *Syn.* court game, round ball, cage meet*, hoopfest*, hoop*, b-ball*; see also **sport** 3.

**bass,** *modif.* — *Syn.* deep, grave, low, sonorous, low-pitched, resonant, baritone, grave, sepulchral; see also **faint** 3.

**bass,** *n.* Varieties include: black, striped, sea, smallmouthed, large-mouthed, rock, red, calico, channel, white, yellow, brass; see also **fish.**

**bastard,** *modif.* **1.** [Born out of wedlock] — *Syn.* illegitimate, natural, fatherless; see **illegitimate** 2.
**2.** [Of dubious extraction] — *Syn.* false, adulterated, spurious; see **false** 3, **impure** 1, **mixed** 1.

**bastard,** *n.* **1.** [An illegitimate child] — *Syn.* illegitimate child, natural child, spurious issue, whoreson, love child, child born out of wedlock, *nullius filius* (Latin), Sunday's child*.
**2.** [A rascal] — *Syn.* scoundrel, ne'er-do-well, cheat, rascal, son of a bitch* or SOB*, stinker*, rat*, fink*, ratfink*, heel*; see also **rascal.**

**bastardize,** *v.* — *Syn.* debase, pervert, degrade, adulterate; see **corrupt** 1.

**baste,** *v.* **1.** [To sew temporarily] — *Syn.* stitch, catch, tack; see **sew.**
**2.** [To moisten cooking meat with fat or liquid] — *Syn.* lard, moisten, grease, drip, season; see also **cook.**

**3.** [To beat] — *Syn.* club, trounce, thrash; see **beat** 2.

**bat,** *n.* **1.** [A club, especially one used in sports] — *Syn.* ball bat, baseball bat, cricket bat, stick, club, racket, pole, mallet.
**2.** [*A blow] — *Syn.* hit, rap, knock; see **blow** 1.
**3.** [A turn at batting] — *Syn.* inning, round, trip to the plate, up, turn.

**blind as a bat*** — *Syn.* sightless, unseeing, blinded; see **blind** 1.

**go to bat for*** — *Syn.* intervene for, support, stand by, back up; see **defend** 3.

**have bats in one's belfry*** — *Syn.* be crazy, be mad, be eccentric, be peculiar, be out of one's mind, have a screw loose*; see also **insane** 1.

**not bat an eye** or **eyelash*** — *Syn.* not be surprised or shocked or amazed, ignore, remain unruffled, show no surprise, not turn a hair*, keep one's cool*; see also **neglect** 1.

**(right) off the bat*** — *Syn.* at once, without delay, instantly; see **immediately.**

**bat,** *v.* — *Syn.* strike, hit, whack, sock*; see **hit** 1.

**bat around*,** *v.* **1.** [To travel] — *Syn.* roam, cruise, tour; see **roam, travel** 2.
**2.** [To discuss] — *Syn.* talk over, consider, debate; see **discuss.**

**batch,** *n.* — *Syn.* bunch, group, shipment, quantity; see **lot** 2, **quantity.**

**bath,** *n.* **1.** [The act of cleansing the body] — *Syn.* bathing, washing, laving, sponge bath, shower, tub bath, steam bath, sauna, sauna bath, Turkish bath, Russian bath, sitz bath, whirlpool bath, soak, dip, soaking, rinsing, shampoo, immersion, ablutions.
**2.** [A liquid prepared for immersion] — *Syn.* wash, douche, spray, suds, shampoo, eyewash, rinse, tub, bath water.
**3.** [An enclosure prepared for bathing] — *Syn.* bathroom, bathtub, tub, shower, washroom, powder room, lavatory, bidet, steam room, Turkish bath, sauna, public baths, bathhouse, pumproom, sweat lodge, shower room, shower stall, sitz bath, hot tub, whirlpool bath, Jacuzzi (trademark), baths, spa, thermae, mikvah (Judaism).

**bathe,** *v.* **1.** [To take or give a bath] — *Syn.* soak, take a bath, soap, scrub; see **wash** 1.
**2.** [To immerse] — *Syn.* dip, submerge, dunk; see **immerse** 1.

**bathing suit,** *n.* — *Syn.* swimsuit, swimming suit, trunks, bikini, two-piece suit, tank suit, maillot, monokini, string bikini, bathing costume, beach costume, bathing dress, topless suit, wet suit, two-piece*.

**bathos,** *n.* — *Syn.* melodrama, maudlinness, triteness; see **pathos, sentimentality.**
*See Synonym Study at* PATHOS.

**bathrobe,** *n.* — *Syn.* robe, lounging robe, wrapper, housecoat, negligee, kimono, happi coat, peignoir, muumuu, duster, smock, wraparound, tunic, bed jacket, dressing gown, smoking jacket; see also **clothes.**

**bathroom,** *n.* — *Syn.* bath, shower, toilet, lavatory; see **bath** 3, **toilet** 2.

**baton,** *n.* — *Syn.* stick, rod, staff; see **club** 3, **rod** 1, **stick, wand.**

**battalion,** *n.* — *Syn.* unit, force, corps; see **army** 2.

**batten,** *v.* — *Syn.* board up, secure, tie; see **fasten** 1.

**batter,** *n.* **1.** [One who bats] — *Syn.* hitter, batsman, pinch-hitter, designated hitter, switch-hitter, player, man who is up, man at the plate, leadoff hitter or man, cleanup hitter or man, clouter*, slugger*, socker*, walloper*.
**2.** [A semifluid mixture for baking] — *Syn.* dough, mix,

paste, recipe, concoction, preparation, starter, mush; see also **mixture** 1.

**batter,** *v.* **1.** [To strike] — *Syn.* beat, pound, punish, maul; see **abuse** 1, **beat** 1, 2, **hit** 1.

**2.** [To damage] — *Syn.* wreck, smash, injure; see **damage** 1.

**battery,** *n.* **1.** [Cells that generate or store electricity] — *Syn.* dry cell, wet cell, storage cell, storage battery, flashlight battery, solar battery, atomic battery, electric cell, voltaic battery, alkaline battery.

**2.** [An organized unit of artillery] — *Syn.* gunnery unit, artillery corps, field guns, cannon, primary *or* main battery, secondary battery.

**3.** [In baseball, a pitching team] — *Syn.* pitcher and catcher, mound team, pitching combination.

**4.** [The act of beating] — *Syn.* assault, mayhem, attack, thumping, beating, physical violence, battering, pounding, mugging, slugging*.

**5.** [A group of similar things] — *Syn.* set, series, array; see **collection** 2.

**battle,** *n.* **1.** [An armed encounter] — *Syn.* engagement, fight, action, skirmish, encounter, contest, clash, brush, sortie, pitched battle, battle royal, confrontation, significant contact; see also sense 2, **fight** 1.

Famous battles include: Marathon, Salamis, Thermopylae, Syracuse, Plataea, Lake Trasimenus, Cannae, Pharsalus, Philippi, Actium, Hastings, Agincourt, St Albans, Tewkesbury, Bosworth Field, Blenheim, Marston Moor, Culloden Moor, Fontenoy, Austerlitz, Waterloo, Trafalgar, Solferino, Balaklava, Borodino, Sadowa, Plassey, Bunker Hill, Yorktown, New Orleans, First Bull Run (Manassas), Shiloh, Gettysburg, Vicksburg, Mukden, Jutland, First and Second Marne, First and Second Ypres, the Somme, Verdun, Chateau-Thierry, Saint-Mihiel, Meuse, Argonne, Battle of France, Battle of Britain, Siege of Leningrad, Stalingrad, Midway, El Alamein, Guadalcanal, Normandy, Battle of the Bulge, Okinawa, Battle of the Philippine Sea, Leyte Gulf, Iwo Jima, Inchon, Seoul, Chosin Reservoir, Heartbreak Ridge, Pork Chop Hill, Dienbienphu, Tet Offensive.

**2.** [The progress of a battle, sense 1] —- *Syn.* combat, fighting, action, strife, contention, struggle, hostilities, campaign, bombing, bloodshed, clash, onslaught, exchange of blows, onset, barrage, conflict, affray, warfare, fray, assault, human sea, press, crusade, pincer, havoc, carnage, ravage, rage of battle, blitz, blitzkrieg, retreat, tactical retreat, maneuver.

**3.** [Any fight or struggle] — *Syn.* conflict, struggle, contest, contention; see **dispute, fight** 1.

**give** *or* **do battle** — *Syn.* fight back, struggle, engage in a battle; see **attack** 1, 2, **fight** 2.

---

**SYN.** — **battle** denotes a conflict between armed forces in a war and implies a large-scale, prolonged contest over a particular area; **engagement**, a more formal term, stresses the actual meeting of opposing forces, with no restrictive connotation as to duration; a **campaign** is a series of military operations with a particular objective and may involve a number of battles; **encounter** usually suggests a chance meeting of hostile forces; **skirmish** refers to a brief encounter between small detachments; **action** stresses engagement in active fighting /killed in *action*/; **combat**, the most general of these terms, simply implies armed fighting, without further qualification

---

**battle cry,** *n.* — *Syn.* slogan, motto, war cry; see **motto.**
**battlefield,** *n.* — *Syn.* battleground, field of battle, field of war, the front, front line, battlefront, place of slaugh-

ter, scene of carnage, theater of war, area between the lines, area of confrontation, area of conflict, scene of battle, theater of operations, arena, killing field, combat zone, disputed territory, salient, no man's land*.

**battlement,** *n.* — *Syn.* parapet, tower, escarpment, bartizan, barbican, bastion, balcony; see also **fortification** 2.

**battleship,** *n.* — *Syn.* man-of-war, floating fortress, battlewagon*; see **warship.**

**bauble,** *n.* — *Syn.* trinket, trifle, gewgaw, knickknack; see **jewel** 1, **jewelry, trinket.**

**bawdy,** *modif.* — *Syn.* ribald, indecent, earthy, risqué; see **lewd** 1, 2.

**bawdyhouse,** *n.* — *Syn.* brothel, whorehouse, house of prostitution; see **brothel.**

**bawl,** *v.* **1.** [To make a bellowing sound] — *Syn.* roar, bellow, howl, shout; see **yell.**

**2.** [To cry] — *Syn.* weep, wail, shed tears, sob; see **cry** 1.

**bawl out*,** *v.* — *Syn.* reprimand, berate, upbraid, chew out*; see **scold.**

**bay,** *modif.* — *Syn.* reddish-brown, reddish, brownish-red, castaneous, chestnut, rufous, badeous, ruddy; see also **brown.**

**bay,** *n.* **1.** [Part of a sea or lake indenting the shoreline] — *Syn.* inlet, gulf, bayou, loch, bight, sound, fiord, firth, frith, estuary, strait, narrows, arm of the sea, mouth, lagoon, cove, anchorage, harbor.

**2.** [A recess] — *Syn.* alcove, nook, compartment, bay window; see **alcove, recess** 3, **window** 1.

**at bay** — *Syn.* cornered, caught, captured; see **trapped.**
**bring to bay** — *Syn.* corner, trap, catch; see **ambush.**

**bay,** *v.* — *Syn.* bellow, howl, cry; see **bark** 1.

**bayonet,** *n.* — *Syn.* blade, spike, lance, pike; see **knife.**

**bayonet,** *v.* — *Syn.* stab, spear, stick; see **penetrate** 1, **stab.**

**bay window,** *n.* — *Syn.* bow window, picture window, oriel, alcove; see **window** 1.

**bazaar,** *n.* — *Syn.* marketplace, fair, exchange, mart; see **market** 1.

**B.C.,** *abbr.* — *Syn.* before Christ, pre-Christian, B.C.E., before the Common Era, before the Christian Era, A.C., *ante Christum* (Latin); see also **ancient** 2.

**be,** *v.* **1.** [To have being] — *Syn.* live, stay, be alive, exist, remain, continue, rest, endure, go on, stand, subsist, breathe, last, prevail, abide, survive, obtain, move, act, do, hold, have place, be located, occupy a position. — *Ant.* DIE, disappear, stop.

**2.** [To happen] — *Syn.* take place, come about, transpire*; occur; see **happen** 2.

**3.** [To equal] — *Syn.* amount to, consist of, comprise; see **equal.**

**4.** [To mean] — *Syn.* signify, denote, imply; see **mean** 1.

**beach,** *n.* **1.** [The edge of the water] — *Syn.* shore, strand, shingle, bank; see **shore.**

**2.** [A waterside resort] — *Syn.* shore, seashore, bathing beach, boardwalk, seaside, lakefront, watering place, the sea, the ocean, the lake, the sands, the coast, lido, *plage* (French), *playa* (Spanish).

*See Synonym Study at* SHORE.

**beachcomber,** *n.* — *Syn.* drifter, wanderer, scavenger, beach bum*; see **loafer.**

**beached,** *modif.* — *Syn.* stranded, marooned, abandoned; see **aground.**

**beacon,** *n.* — *Syn.* flare, lantern, guide, signal, signal fire, signal light, signal beam, lighthouse, pharos, lamp, light, torch, rocket, heliograph, beam, radar, sonar, airline beacon, radio beacon, air control beacon.

**bead,** *n.* **1.** [A small globule] — *Syn.* drop, droplet, bubble, globule, pellet, grain, particle, speck, dot, dab, pea, shot, pill, spherule, driblet; see also **bean** 2.

**2.** [A small ornament] — *Syn.* pearl, gem, stone; see **jewel** 1.

**draw a bead on** — *Syn.* take aim at, train on, sight, get in the sights; see **aim** 2.

**beads,** *pl.n.* — *Syn.* necklace, pendant, pearls, string of beads, string of jewels, choker, necklet, rosary, chaplet, wampum, peag; see also **necklace.**

**beak,** *n.* — *Syn.* bill, nib, mandible, nose, prow, projection, proboscis, neb, rostrum, snout, nozzle.

**beaked,** *modif.* — *Syn.* curved, hooked, angled; see **bent.**

**beaker,** *n.* — *Syn.* goblet, stein, glass, measuring cup; see **cup.**

**beam,** *n.* **1.** [A relatively long, stout bar] — *Syn.* timber, brace, rafter, stringer, stud, two-by-four, scantling, strut, bolster, axle, reach, girder, sleeper, stay, crosspiece, prop, support, trestle, spar, transverse, pole, lath, furring strip, pile, balk, crossbar, T-beam, I-beam, steel beam, boom, post, kingpost, column, pillar, piling, stanchion, flitches, hammer beam, bail, joist, lintel, sill, jamb, cantilever, shaft, scaffolding, board, plank.

**2.** [A ray or rays] — *Syn.* ray, emission, shaft, bar, sparkle, twinkle, flicker, streak, laser, pencil, glitter, glare, stream of light, shimmer, glint, glow, chink, gleam, glimmer, finger, beacon.

**3.** [Radio waves intended as a guide] — *Syn.* direction finder, unidirectional radio signal, radar; see **beacon.**

**off the beam★** — *Syn.* in error, misdirected, incorrect, inaccurate; see **mistaken** 1, **wrong** 2.

**on the beam★** — *Syn.* on course, functioning well, alert, keen; see **accurate** 1, **intelligent** 1.

**beam,** *v.* **1.** [To emit] — *Syn.* transmit, broadcast, give out, direct; see **broadcast** 1, **radiate** 1, **send** 4.

**2.** [To shine] — *Syn.* radiate, glitter, gleam; see **radiate** 2, **shine** 1.

**3.** [To smile] — *Syn.* grin, laugh, smile radiantly, glow; see **smile.**

**beamed,** *modif.* — *Syn.* transmitted, aimed, pointed, channeled, broadcast, radiated; see also **sent.**

**beaming,** *modif.* **1.** [Giving forth beams] — *Syn.* radiant, glowing, gleaming; see **bright** 1.

**2.** [In very genial humor] — *Syn.* grinning, animated, radiant, sunny; see **happy** 1.

**bean,** *n.* **1.** [A leguminous plant] — *Syn.* legume, pulse, snap bean, shell bean, seed, pod, *frijol* (Spanish), haricot. Varieties include: kidney, navy, lima, soy, castor, black, pinto, lentil, mung, frijol, carob, goa, snap, string, black-eyed *or* black-eye pea, stringless, pole, bush, green, wax, fava, *haricot vert* (French), butter, Egyptian, hyacinth, Calabar *or* ordeal, coffee, cacao, jumping; see also **string bean.**

**2.** [A small hard pellet] — *Syn.* kernel, seed, berry, nugget, bullet, pill, grain, knot, node, nodule, nodosity.

**full of beans★** — *Syn.* **1.** lively, vital, energetic; see **active** 2.

**2.** mistaken, erring, incorrect; see **wrong** 2.

**spill the beans★** — *Syn.* divulge information, tell secrets, talk; see **reveal** 1, **tell** 1.

**bear,** *n.* **1.** [A bruin] — *Syn.* ursus, cub, bar★, brownie★. Varieties include: American black, cinnamon, grizzly, brown, polar, Syrian, sloth *or* honey, Russian, sun *or* bruang, moon, spectacled, Kodiak, Japanese, Himalayan, black

**2.** [An irritable person] — *Syn.* grumbler, growler, sourpuss★; see **grouch.**

**be a bear for punishment** — *Syn.* be rugged, be tough, be determined; see **endure** 2.

**bear,** *v.* **1.** [To carry] — *Syn.* transport, convey, transfer; see **carry** 1, 2.

**2.** [To support weight] — *Syn.* sustain, hold up, shoulder; see **support** 1.

**3.** [To bring forth] — *Syn.* give birth to, be delivered of, produce, yield; see **produce** 1.

**4.** [To suffer] — *Syn.* tolerate, stand, support, undergo; see **endure** 2.

**5.** [To possess as a mark or characteristic] — *Syn.* have, show, exhibit, carry; see **display** 1, **own** 1.

**6.** [To move in a given direction] — *Syn.* head, aim, turn, go; see **sail** 2, **turn** 6, **veer.**

*See Synonym Study at* CARRY, ENDURE.

**bring to bear (on** *or* **upon)** — *Syn.* exert, apply, pressure, have an effect (on); see **exercise** 2, **influence, use** 1.

**bearable,** *modif.* — *Syn.* endurable, tolerable, passable, admissible, supportable, sufferable.

**beard,** *n.* — *Syn.* whiskers, brush, Vandyke, chin whiskers, imperial, muttonchops, goatee, spade beard, full beard, forked beard, side whiskers, sideburns, burnsides, stubble, five o'clock shadow★.

**bearded,** *modif.* — *Syn.* bewhiskered, bushy, unshaven; see **hairy** 1.

**beardless,** *modif.* **1.** [Hairless] — *Syn.* clean-shaven, smooth-faced, smooth; see **hairless.**

**2.** [Inexperienced] — *Syn.* callow, fresh, immature; see **inexperienced.**

**bear down on** *or* **upon,** *v.* **1.** [To press down on] — *Syn.* squeeze, compress, push; see **press** 1.

**2.** [To try] — *Syn.* endeavor, strive, attempt, make a strong effort; see **try** 1.

**3.** [To approach] — *Syn.* draw near, converge on, close in on; see **approach** 2, 3.

**bearer,** *n.* **1.** [One who presents a draft for payment] — *Syn.* payee, consignee, beneficiary, casher, collector, endorsee.

**2.** [One who carries a burden] — *Syn.* porter, packman, carrier, transporter, conveyor, courier, pallbearer, messenger, beast of burden, coolie.

**bearing,** *n.* **1.** [A point of support] — *Syn.* block, frame, journal box, pivot, fulcrum, babbitted bearing, ball bearing, roller bearing.

**2.** [Manner of carriage] — *Syn.* mien, deportment, manner, carriage, posture, demeanor, presence, conduct, behavior, comportment, address, attitude, stance, aspect, port, body language; see also **behavior** 1.

**3.** [Relevance] — *Syn.* application, relation, pertinence, significance; see **importance** 1, **relationship.**

---

*SYN.* — **bearing,** denoting manner of carrying or conducting oneself, refers to characteristic physical and mental posture; **carriage,** also applied to posture, specif. stresses the physical aspects of a person's bearing [an erect *carriage*]; **demeanor** refers to behavior as expressing one's attitude or a specified personality trait [a demure *demeanor*]; **mien,** a literary word, refers to bearing and manner, esp. as reflective of one's character or emotional state [a man of melancholy *mien*]; **deportment** refers to one's behavior with reference to standards of conduct or social conventions; **manner** is applied to customary or distinctive attitude, actions, speech, etc. and, in the plural, refers to behavior conforming with polite conventions

---

**bearings,** *pl.n.* — *Syn.* orientation, relative position, location, direction, sense of direction, fix★; see also **position** 1.

**bear on, bear upon,** *v.* — *Syn.* pertain, refer to, relate to, regard; see **concern** 1.

**bear oneself,** *v.* — *Syn.* act, appear, conduct oneself, deport oneself; see **behave** 2.

**bear out,** *v.* — *Syn.* confirm, substantiate, support; see **prove.**

**bear up,** *v.* — *Syn.* withstand, persevere, carry on, keep one's chin up*; see **endure** 2.

**bear with,** *v.* — *Syn.* tolerate, be patient, suffer, put up with; see **endure** 2.

**beast,** *n.* 1. [A large animal] — *Syn.* brute, creature, lower animal; see **animal** 2.
   2. [A person of brutish nature] — *Syn.* monster, brute, degenerate, animal, fiend, ogre, swine, throwback, pervert, lout, hun, savage, barbarian, pig, satyr, goat, sensualist, seducer, libertine, hog, voluptuary, monstrosity, sadist, fornicator, glutton, lecher, gargoyle, Bluebeard, cur, skunk*.

**beastlike,** *modif.* — *Syn.* ferocious, barbaric, savage; see **fierce** 1.

**beastly,** *modif.* 1. [Bestial] — *Syn.* brutal, savage, cruel, coarse, swinish, repulsive, gluttonous, obscene, piggish, hoggish, irrational, prurient, boorish, carnal, brutish, depraved, abominable, loathsome, hateful, vile, low, degraded, sensual, foul, base, disgusting, inhuman, gross, unclean, vulgar. — *Ant.* REFINED, sweet, nice.
   2. [*Unpleasant] — *Syn.* nasty, disagreeable, odious, revolting; see **offensive** 2.

**beat,** *modif.* 1. [*Tired] — *Syn.* weary, fatigued, worn out; see **tired.**
   2. [Unconventional] — *Syn.* Bohemian, beatnik, Left Bank; see **unconventional.**

**beat,** *n.* 1. [A stroke] — *Syn.* thump, punch, strike, hit, lash, slap, swing, shake; see also **blow** 1.
   2. [A throb] — *Syn.* pulsation, pulse, cadence, vibration, drum, throb, pound, thump, tick, oscillation, flow, surge, ripple, impulse, undulation, palpitation, flutter, rhythm, tattoo, rat-a-tat, rat-a-tat-tat, pitapat, pitterpatter.
   3. [A unit of music] — *Syn.* accent, vibration, division, stress, measure, rhythm, meter, time, tempo, downbeat, upbeat, offbeat.

**beat,** *v.* 1. [To strike repeatedly] — *Syn.* pound, hammer, pummel, batter, whack, strike, hit, bang, drum, thump, knock, rap; see also sense 2, **hit** 1.
   2. [To thrash] — *Syn.* punish, whip, flog, castigate, drub, club, trounce, spank, smite, scourge, switch, lash, slap, smack, punch, cuff, box, pummel, strap, birch, cane, flagellate, horsewhip, pistol-whip, buffet, beat up, give a thumping, lay on blows, rap, strike, hit, knock, lambaste, ram, pound, cudgel, bludgeon, bastinado, bat, flail, batter, maul, maltreat, belabor, clout, clobber*, lace*, bang*, swat*, thump*, slug*, beat black and blue*, pound to a jelly, beat to a jelly, beat to a paste*, hide*, give it to*, let have it*, give a workout*, whale*, belt*, sock*, whack*, trim*, beat the tar out of*, knock the tar out of*, knock the daylights out of*, knock the hell out of*, knock the stuffing out of*, lick the pants off of*, larrup*, wallop*, lick*, paste*, bash*, whang*, lay into*, baste*, work over*, rough up*, thwack*, whop*, paddle*, crown*, lather*, leather*, tan*, tan one's hide*, knock one's block off*.
   3. [To pulsate] — *Syn.* pound, thump, strike, throb, hammer, tick, ripple, flutter, flap, undulate, ebb and flow, vibrate, swing, palpitate, rise and fall, fluctuate, flicker, oscillate, pulse, dash against, buffet, pitapat, go pitapat.
   4. [To worst] — *Syn.* overcome, surpass, conquer; see **defeat** 1, 2, 3.

5. [To mix] — *Syn.* stir, whip, whisk; see **mix** 1.
6. [*To perplex] — *Syn.* puzzle, baffle, befuddle; see **confuse.**
7. [*To swindle] — *Syn.* defraud, cheat, dupe; see **deceive.**

---

**SYN. — beat,** the most general word in this comparison, conveys the basic idea of hitting or striking repeatedly, whether with the hands, a stick, or other instrument; **pound** suggests heavier, more effective blows than beat [to *pound* with a hammer]; **pummel** implies the beating of a person with the fists and suggests a continuous, indiscriminate rain of damaging blows; **thrash,** originally referring to the beating of grain with a flail, suggests similar broad, swinging strokes, as in striking a person repeatedly with a stick or whip; **flog** implies punishment by the infliction of repeated blows with a strap, whip, stick, etc.; **whip,** often used as an equivalent of **flog,** specifically suggests lashing strokes or motions; **maul** implies the infliction of repeated heavy blows so as to bruise or lacerate: most of these terms are used loosely, esp. by journalists, in describing a decisive victory in a contest

---

**beaten,** *modif.* 1. [Defeated] — *Syn.* worsted, humbled, cowed, thwarted, bested, disappointed, frustrated, balked, circumvented, baffled, conquered, overthrown, subdued, subjugated, ruined, mastered, trounced, surmounted, undone, vanquished, discomfited, routed, crushed, overwhelmed, overpowered, licked*, done in*, done for*, kayoed*, skinned*, trimmed*, had it*, washed up*, thrown for a loss*, sunk*. — *Ant.* victorious, SUCCESSFUL, triumphant.
   2. [Made firm and hard] — *Syn.* hammered, tramped, stamped, rolled, milled, forged, trodden, pounded, tramped down, tamped. — *Ant.* SOFT, ductile, loose.
   3. [Made light by beating] — *Syn.* whipped, frothy, foamy, mixed, blended, whisked, aerated, churned, creamy, bubbly, meringued.
   4. [Thrashed] — *Syn.* pounded, battered, bruised; see **hit, hurt.**

**beater,** *n.* — *Syn.* whipper, mixer, eggbeater, electric beater, blender, whisk, churn; see also **mixer** 1.

**beatific,** *modif.* — *Syn.* blissful, joyful, heavenly, rapturous; see **divine** 1, **happy** 1.

**beatify,** *v.* — *Syn.* glorify, sanctify, consecrate; see **bless** 3.

**beating,** *n.* — *Syn.* thrashing, whipping, drubbing; see **defeat** 2, 3, **flogging.**

**beatitude,** *n.* — *Syn.* bliss, delight, joy, blessedness; see **happiness** 2.

**beatnik,** *n.* — *Syn.* Bohemian, beat, hippie-type, maverick, radical, iconoclast, hipster*, longhair*; see also **hippie, nonconformist.**

**beau,** *n.* — *Syn.* fiancé, escort, boyfriend; see **lover** 1.

**beautiful,** *modif.* 1. [Having qualities of beauty] — *Syn.* lovely, attractive, appealing, pleasing, pretty, fair, fine, nice, dainty, good-looking, delightful, charming, enticing, fascinating, admirable, rich, graceful, sightly, ideal, delicate, refined, elegant, symmetrical, well-formed, shapely, harmonious, well-made, aesthetic, splendid, gorgeous, brilliant, radiant, exquisite, dazzling, flowerlike, resplendent, magnificent, superb, ornamental, decorative, marvelous, wonderful, glorious, grand, awe-inspiring, imposing, majestic, august, wondrous, excellent, impressive, showy, sublime, heavenly*. — *Ant.* UGLY, hideous, unsightly.
   2. [Applied especially to human beings] — *Syn.* lovely, pretty, attractive, good-looking, comely, fair, handsome,

graceful, exquisite, gorgeous, refined, delicate, cute, divine, blooming, rosy, bonny, beauteous, statuesque, Junoesque, pulchritudinous, well-favored, bewitching, enchanting, appealing, ravishing, personable, pleasing, taking, winning, alluring, glamorous, shapely, voluptuous, svelte, lissome, radiant, stunning*, classy*, easy on the eyes*, long on looks*, eye-filling*, built*, well-built*, sexy*, looking good*, foxy*; see also **handsome** 2.— *Ant.* plain, unattractive, ill-favored.
**3.** [Applied especially to works of art] — *Syn.* aesthetically pleasing, fine, elegant; see **artistic** 2.

*SYN.* — **beautiful** is applied to that which gives the highest degree of aesthetic pleasure to the senses or to the mind and suggests that the object of delight approximates one's conception of an ideal; **lovely** refers to that which delights by inspiring affection or warm admiration; **handsome** implies attractiveness by reason of pleasing proportions, symmetry, elegance, etc. and carries connotations of masculinity, dignity, or impressiveness; **pretty** implies a dainty, delicate, or graceful quality in that which pleases and carries connotations of femininity or diminutiveness; **good-looking** is closely equivalent to **handsome** or **pretty**, suggesting a pleasing appearance but not expressing the fine distinctions of either word; **comely** applies to persons only and suggests a wholesome attractiveness of form and features rather than a high degree of beauty; **fair**, in this comparison, suggests beauty that is fresh, bright, or flawless and, when applied to persons, is used esp. of complexion and features; **beauteous**, equivalent to **beautiful** in poetry and lofty prose, is now sometimes used in humorously disparaging references to beauty

**beautifully**, *modif.* **1.** [In a beautiful manner] — *Syn.* gracefully, exquisitely, charmingly, attractively, prettily, delightfully, appealingly, seductively, alluringly, elegantly, gorgeously, splendidly, magnificently, ideally, tastefully, sublimely, bewitchingly, entrancingly, celestially, handsomely, superbly, divinely.— *Ant.* hideously, repulsively, foully.
**2.** [*Very well] — *Syn.* splendidly, wonderfully, superbly; see **excellently.**
**beautify**, *v.* **1.** [To make beautiful] — *Syn.* adorn, embellish, enhance, ornament; see **decorate.**
**2.** [To improve the grounds] — *Syn.* landscape, plant, garden; see **improve** 1.
*See Synonym Study at* DECORATE.
**beauty**, *n.* **1.** [A pleasing physical quality] — *Syn.* attractiveness, grace, loveliness, comeliness, fairness, prettiness, handsomeness, pulchritude, charm, delicacy, exquisiteness, elegance, harmony, attraction, appeal, fascination, allurement, shapeliness, majesty, magnificence, good looks, winsomeness, glamour, bloom, radiance, class*.— *Ant.* UGLINESS, homeliness, deformity.
**2.** [An exalted mental or moral quality] — *Syn.* value, merit, excellence; see **virtue** 1.
**3.** [Use or value] — *Syn.* advantage, attraction, excellence, worth; see **advantage** 3.
**4.** [A beautiful thing or person, particularly a woman] — *Syn.* goddess, belle, ornament, attraction, vision, picture, *belle chose* (French), siren, Circe, enchantress, seductress, Venus, femme fatale, charmer, angel, looker*, eyeful*, knockout*, dreamboat*, dish*, doll*, stunner*, good-looker*, sex goddess*, fox*, ten*.— *Ant.* WITCH, BLEMISH, fright.
**becalm**, *v.* — *Syn.* soothe, calm, pacify; see **quiet** 1.
**because**, *conj.* — *Syn.* on account of, in consequence of, in view of, by reason of, for the reason that, for the sake

of, in behalf of, on the grounds that, in the interest of, as a result of, as things go, by virtue of, in that, since, as, by the agency of, owing to, due to*, being as how*; see also **since** 1.
**beckon**, *v.* — *Syn.* signal, motion, sign, invite; see **summon** 1, **wave** 2.
**becloud**, *v.* — *Syn.* darken, obscure, cloud, overcast; see **confuse, shade** 2.
**become**, *v.* **1.** [To come to be] — *Syn.* develop into, change into, resolve into, turn into, pass into, grow into, evolve into, be metamorphosed, eventually be, emerge as, turn out to be, progress toward being, come to be, get to be, be transformed into, be translated into, shift, assume the form of, assume the shape of, be reformed to, be remodeled, be transmuted, be transfigured, be reduced to, be converted to, convert, mature, increasingly grow, shift toward, incline to, melt into*; see also **grow** 2.
**2.** [To be suitable] — *Syn.* enhance, set off, display, agree with, accord with, harmonize with, go with, make handsome, adorn, be appropriate, heighten, belong to, be consistent with, match, enrich, garnish, grace, befit, ornament, suit, fit, be fitting, behoove, flatter, embellish, put in the best light, reveal the charm of, augment the attraction of.— *Ant.* DISTORT, detract from, spoil.
**becoming**, *modif.* **1.** [Appropriate] — *Syn.* suitable, proper, fitting, seemly; see **fit** 1, 2.
**2.** [Pleasing] — *Syn.* attractive, flattering, agreeable, handsome, good-looking, seemly, comely, tasteful, well-chosen, fair, trim, graceful, flattering, spruce, effective, symmetrical, suitable, enhancing, fetching, good, nice; see also **beautiful** 1, **neat** 1.— *Ant.* UGLY, unattractive, unbecoming.
**bed**, *n.* **1.** [A place of rest] — *Syn.* couch, pallet, mattress, cot, bedstead, berth, chaise, bunk, roost, accommodations, lodging, flop*, hay*, sack*, rack*.
Beds include: single *or* double, davenport, cot, four-poster, canopy, trundle, twin, water, platform, fold-away, hammock, feather, double-deck, stretcher, folding, futon, bunk, litter, cradle, crib, bassinet, Murphy, Hollywood, king *or* king-size, queen *or* queen-size, hospital, gurney, circular, day.
**2.** [A foundation] — *Syn.* base, bottom, groundwork; see **foundation** 2.
**3.** [A garden plot] — *Syn.* patch, strip, plot, border, garden, area, row, planting, hotbed, cold frame, seedbed, flower bed, raised bed, island bed; see also **garden.**
**bed**, *v.* — *Syn.* embed, fix, implant; see **embed** 1, **fasten** 1.
**bedaub**, *v.* — *Syn.* smear, stain, soil; see **dirty.**
**bedbug**, *n.* — *Syn. Cimex lectularius* (Latin), bloodsucker, bug, kissing bug, conenose.
**bedding**, *n.* — *Syn.* bedclothes, bed linen, linens, covers, bedcovers.
Kinds of bedding include: blankets, thermal blankets, quilts, patchwork quilts, comforters, duvets, eiderdowns, pillows, sheets, pillowcases, pillowslips, pillow shams, comforter, covers, duvet covers, coverlets, bedspreads, spreads, mattresses, featherbeds, mattress pads, dust ruffles, bedskirts, counterpanes.
**bed down**, *v.* **1.** [To provide with accommodations] — *Syn.* put up, house, accommodate; see **accommodate** 3, **quarter** 2.
**2.** [To go to bed] — *Syn.* turn in, retire, hit the hay*; see **lie** 4, **rest** 1, **sleep.**
**bedeck**, *v.* — *Syn.* adorn, festoon, ornament; see **decorate.**
*See Synonym Study at* DECORATE.

**bedevil,** *v.* **1.** [To plague] — *Syn.* harass, torment, beset; see **bother** 2.
**2.** [To confuse completely] — *Syn.* baffle, bewilder, muddle; see **confuse.**
**bedlam,** *n.* **1.** [Uproar] — *Syn.* confusion, pandemonium, clamor, chaos; see **confusion** 2, **noise** 2.
**2.** [A lunatic asylum] — *Syn.* madhouse, insane asylum, sanitarium; see **hospital.**
**bedraggled,** *modif.* — *Syn.* wet, soiled, unkempt, messy; see **dirty** 1.
**bedridden,** *modif.* — *Syn.* incapacitated, confined to bed, laid up*; see **disabled, sick.**
**bedroom,** *n.* — *Syn.* bedchamber, dormitory, sleeping room, guest room, master bedroom, boudoir, chamber, bunk room, nursery; see also **room** 2.
**bedspread,** *n.* — *Syn.* coverlet, spread, cover, bedcover, quilt, comforter, blanket, counterpane; see also **bedding.**
**bedtime,** *n.* — *Syn.* slumbertime, time to retire, lights out, sleepy time*, time to hit the hay*, sack time*; see also **night** 1.
**bee,** *n.* **1.** [A stinging, honey-gathering insect] Social classes: queen, worker, drone (male).
Varieties include: domestic: Caucasian, Madagascar, three-banded, three-band golden, golden Caucasian, black, Italian, German, Carniolan, Africanized; wild: bumblebee, sweat bee, killer bee, carpenter bee.
**2.** [A communal gathering] — *Syn.* social, harvest home, work party, function; see **party** 1.
**have a bee in one's bonnet*** — be obsessed with, be fussy about, hound somebody, hound something, busy oneself with; see also **pursue** 1.
**beef,** *n.* **1.** [Bovine flesh used as food] — *Syn.* cow's flesh, steer beef, ox meat, red meat, cornfed beef, steak, hamburger, roast beef, pot roast, corned beef, pastrami, jerky, Kobe beef; see also **meat.**
**2.** [A grown animal of the genus *Bos*] — *Syn.* cow, bovine, bull, steer; see **cow.**
**3.** [*Human flesh] — *Syn.* flesh, brawn, meat*; see **muscle.**
**4.** [A complaint] — *Syn.* dispute, protestation, gripe*; see **objection** 2.
**beef up*,** *v.* — *Syn.* intensify, augment, increase, reinforce; see **strengthen.**
**beefy,** *modif.* — *Syn.* brawny, husky, burly, muscular; see **fat** 1, **strong** 1.
**beehive,** *n.* — *Syn.* hive, stand, apiary, colony, swarm, beehouse.
**beeline,** *n.* — *Syn.* direct route, straight line, air line, straightaway, shortcut, path as straight as the crow flies*.
**Beelzebub,** *n.* — *Syn.* Satan, fallen angel, Prince of Darkness; see **devil** 1.
**beer,** *n.* — *Syn.* malt beverage, malt liquor, brew, suds*, the amber brew*, slops*, brewskie*.
Varieties include: lager, bock, ale, stout, porter, light, dry, ice, heavy, dark, black, Danzig, Schenk, winter, Pilsener, bitter, Bavarian.
**beetle,** *n.* — *Syn.* insect, bug, scarab, crawling thing; see **insect.**
**befall,** *v.* — *Syn.* happen, occur, take place, come to pass; see **happen** 2.
**befog,** *v.* — *Syn.* obscure, blur, cloud; see **confuse, shade** 2.
**before,** *modif.* **1.** [In time] — *Syn.* previously, earlier, in the past, since, already, gone by, ago, in old days, heretofore, formerly, anteriorly, antecedently, in days of yore, back, sooner, up to now, ahead, in front, in advance, beforehand, afore, ere, facing, BP, before the present. — *Ant.* in the future, to come, NOW.

**2.** [In space] — *Syn.* ahead, in advance, in front, advanced; see **ahead** 2.
**before,** *prep.* — *Syn.* prior to, previous to, in front of, ahead of, ere, in the presence of, in the sight of, earlier than, anterior to, under jurisdiction of, antecedent to. — *Ant.* BEHIND, following, at the rear of.
**beforehand,** *modif.* — *Syn.* previously, already, in anticipation; see **before** 1.
**befriend,** *v.* — *Syn.* encourage, advise, stand by, make friends with; see **associate** 1, **help** 1.
**befuddle,** *v.* — *Syn.* bewilder, make drunk, inebriate, muddle; see **confuse, intoxicate** 1.
**befuddled,** *modif.* — *Syn.* confused, inebriated, intoxicated; see **doubtful** 2, **drunk.**
**beg,** *v.* **1.** [To ask earnestly or importunately] — *Syn.* entreat, implore, beseech, ask, supplicate, crave, solicit, pray for, urge, plead, sue, importune, petition, apply to, request, press, call on, call upon, appeal to, requisition, conjure, adjure, apostrophize, canvass; see also **ask** 1. — *Ant.* order, concede, accede.
**2.** [To ask alms] — *Syn.* appeal to, ask alms, live on charity, panhandle*, clamor for, solicit, seek alms, solicit charity, want, starve, go from door to door, live from hand to mouth, mendicate, cadge, mooch*, bum*, sponge*, scrounge*, chisel*, touch*, make a touch*, put the touch on*, hit*, hit up*, pass the hat, pass the cup*. — *Ant.* GIVE, bestow, endow.
**beg the question** — *Syn.* equivocate, dodge, hedge; see **evade** 1.
**go begging** — *Syn.* be unwanted, be unpopular, find no takers, be in little demand, be unneeded, be rejected, lose out; see also **fail** 1.

---

*SYN.* — **beg** implies humbleness or earnestness in asking for something and is now often used in polite formulas *[I beg to differ]*; **solicit** suggests courtesy and formality in petitioning for something *[we solicit your aid]* or a general canvassing *[to solicit donations]*; **entreat** implies the use of all the persuasive power at one's command; **beseech** suggests fervor or passion in the asking and connotes anxiety over the outcome; **implore** is stronger still, suggesting desperation or great distress; **importune** suggests persistence in entreating, often to the point of becoming troublesome or annoying

---

**beget,** *v.* — *Syn.* father, sire, generate; see **propagate** 1.
**beggar,** *n.* **1.** [One who begs] — *Syn.* mendicant, supplicant, suppliant, lazzarone, cadger, parasite, almsman, lazar, panhandler*, moocher*, touch artist*, bummer*, sponger*, freeloader*; see also **tramp** 1. — *Ant.* prodigal, DONOR, giver.
**2.** [An impoverished person] — *Syn.* pauper, poor person, indigent, poverty-stricken person, destitute person, bag lady, street person, homeless person, shopping-bag lady, dependent, derelict, poor relation, ward of the state, bankrupt, starveling, down-and-outer*, bum*. — *Ant.* FINANCIER, millionaire, landed proprietor.
**3.** [A rascal] — *Syn.* scamp, fellow, scoundrel; see **rascal.**
**beggarly,** *modif.* — *Syn.* destitute, poverty-stricken, mean, meager; see **inadequate** 1, **poor** 1.
**begging,** *modif.* — *Syn.* desirous, anxious, in need, imploring, supplicating.
**begin,** *v.* **1.** [To get under way] — *Syn.* start, cause, initiate, inaugurate, commence, occasion, impel, produce, effect, set in motion, launch, mount, start up, start off, start on, start in, take up, induce, create, bring about, get going, set going, set about, institute, lead up to, undertake, enter on, enter upon, embark on, embark upon, set

to, set to work, get to, fall to, open, animate, motivate, go into, go ahead, lead the way, give impulse to, bring in, bring on, bring to pass, activate, act on, generate, drive, actualize, eventuate, introduce, originate, found, establish, set up, trigger, spark, give birth to, raise, breed, work, necessitate, take the lead, pioneer, lay the foundation for, break ground, open up, tackle, plunge into, lead off, kick off*, get on the ball, get on the beam*, go to it*, get down to*, get moving*, get cracking*, put one's shoulder to the wheel*, open fire*, fire away*, scratch the surface*, open the door to*, touch a match to*, throw the first stone*, break the ice*, be in on the ground floor*, strike out*, strike up*, tee off*, jump off*, dig in*, get the show on the road*, start the ball rolling*, get the ball rolling, play ball*, dive in*, take the plunge*, get one's feet wet*. — *Ant.* END, finish, terminate.
**2.** [To come into being] — *Syn.* commence, get under way, start, start out, set out, set in, come out, arise, rise, proceed from, result from, enter, dawn, sprout, originate, spring, spring up, crop up, be born, come into the world, come to birth, emanate, come into existence, occur, burst forth, issue forth, come forth, bud, stem from, spring from, come from, derive from, grow out of, flower, blossom, break out, start up, have origin, lead out, take off, see the light of day*, raise its head*, rear its head*. — *Ant.* END, subside, terminate.

---

*SYN.* — **begin**, the most general of these terms, indicates merely a setting into motion of some action, process, or course /to *begin* eating/; **commence**, a more formal term, is used esp. with reference to a ceremony or an elaborate course of action /to *commence* a court action/; **start** is sometimes interchangeable with **begin**, but carries the particular implication of leaving a point of departure in any kind of progression /to *start* a journey, the boulder *started* a landslide/; **initiate**, in this connection, refers to the carrying out of the first steps in some course or process, with no indication of what is to follow /to *initiate* peace talks/; **inaugurate** suggests a formal or ceremonial beginning or opening /to *inaugurate* a new library/

---

**beginner,** *n.* — *Syn.* novice, freshman, apprentice, neophyte, abecedarian, tyro, initiate, newcomer, entrant, recruit, trainee, intern, fledgling, tenderfoot, novitiate, catechumen, rookie*, greenhorn*, boot*; see also **amateur.**
**beginning,** *n.* **1.** [The origin in point of time or place] — *Syn.* source, outset, day one*; see **origin** 2.
**2.** [The origin, thought of as the cause] — *Syn.* germ, heart, antecedent; see **origin** 3.
**3.** [The act of beginning] — *Syn.* start, opening, commencement, inception; see **origin** 1.
*See Synonym Study at* ORIGIN.
**begrudge,** *v.* — *Syn.* grudge, resent, be stingy, be reluctant; see **envy.**
*See Synonym Study at* ENVY.
**beguile,** *v.* **1.** [To deceive] — *Syn.* mislead, trick, delude, hoodwink; see **deceive, tempt.**
**2.** [To charm] — *Syn.* delight, divert, amuse, captivate; see **amuse, entertain** 1, **fascinate.**
*See Synonym Study at* AMUSE, DECEIVE, TEMPT.
**begun,** *modif.* — *Syn.* started, initiated, instituted, under way, in motion, in progress, on foot, inaugurated, happening, proceeding, going, active, existing, operational, operative, working, in force, advanced. — *Ant.* potential, LATENT, prospective.
**behalf,** *n.* — *Syn.* interest, part, welfare, sake, side, benefit, advantage, place, account, service, stead, profit,

concern, furtherance, recommendation, favor, encouragement, aid, help, assistance, representation, countenance, support. — *Ant.* OPPOSITION, derogation, detraction.
**on behalf of** — *Syn.* in the interest of, for the benefit of, speaking for, as a representative of; see **for, representing** 2.
**behave,** *v.* **1.** [To act] — *Syn.* perform, work, run, function; see **act** 1.
**2.** [To act in a specified or proper way] — *Syn.* conduct oneself, acquit oneself, deport oneself, comport oneself, handle oneself, demean oneself, acquit oneself well, act with decorum, observe the golden rule, be nice, be good, be civil, act properly, mind one's p's and q's, be orderly, obey, play one's part, observe the rules, observe the law, reform, mind one's manners, manage oneself, discipline oneself, be on one's best behavior, act one's age, avoid offense, keep the peace, toe the mark, toe the line*, shape up*, stay in line*, keep out of mischief*; see also **act** 2. — *Ant.* MISBEHAVE, be rude, offend.

---

*SYN.* — **behave**, used reflexively (as also the other words in this comparison), implies action in conformity with the required standards of decorum /did the children *behave* themselves?/; **conduct** implies the direction or guidance of one's actions in a specified way /she *conducted* herself well at the trial/; **comport** and esp. **deport** suggest behavior in accordance with the fixed rules of society /they *deported* themselves like gentlemen/; **acquit** suggests behavior in accordance with the duties of one's position or with one's obligations /the rookie *acquitted* himself like a major leaguer/; **demean** suggests behavior or appearance that is indicative of the specified character trait /she *demeaned* herself like a gracious hostess/

---

**behavior,** *n.* **1.** [Public manner(s)] — *Syn.* conduct, deportment, comportment, bearing, mien, demeanor, air, presence, carriage, manner(s), action(s), attitude(s), way of life, speech, talk, tone, morals, habits, tact, etiquette, protocol, social graces, seemliness, correctness, decorum, form, convention, propriety, management, mode, routine, practice, delivery, formality, style, expression, performance, front, code, role, observance, course, guise, act, deed, ethics, way, ways, dealings, what's done*.
**2.** [The action of an organism under given circumstances] — *Syn.* function, functioning, adaptation, operation, performance, action, counteraction, execution, act, adjustment, compliance, conduct, response, reaction, reflex, conditioned reflex, typical reaction.
**behead,** *v.* — *Syn.* decapitate, execute, guillotine; see **kill** 1.
**behest,** *n.* — *Syn.* direction, order, precept, injunction; see **command** 1.
**behind,** *modif.* and *prep.* **1.** [To the rear in space] — *Syn.* in back of, following, after; see **back.**
**2.** [Late in time] — *Syn.* tardy, dilatory, behind time; see **late** 1, **slow** 2.
**3.** [Slow in progress] — *Syn.* sluggish, slow-moving, delayed, backward, underdeveloped, retarded, behind schedule, in arrears, belated, laggard; see also **slow** 1, 3. — *Ant.* FAST, rapid, ahead of schedule.
**behindhand,** *modif.* **1.** [Late] — *Syn.* tardy, slow, behind time; see **late** 1, **slow** 2.
**2.** [Backward] — *Syn.* undeveloped, late, retarded, in arrears; see **backward** 5, **slow** 3.
**behold,** *v.* — *Syn.* observe, look at, see, view; see **see** 1.
*See Synonym Study at* SEE.

**beholden,** *modif.* — *Syn.* obligated, obliged, indebted, under obligation; see **indebted.**

**beholder,** *n.* — *Syn.* spectator, viewer, perceiver, onlooker; see **observer** 1.

**behoove,** *v.* — *Syn.* be incumbent upon, be necessary, be required, be expected, be requisite, be needful, be one's obligation, be right, be proper, owe it to, be fitting, become, be worthwhile, be advantageous, benefit, profit.

**being,** *n.* **1.** [Existence] — *Syn.* presence, actuality, animation; see **life** 1, **reality** 1.
**2.** [The essential part] — *Syn.* nature, quintessence, marrow; see **essence** 1.
**3.** [A living thing] — *Syn.* creature, conscious agent, individual, human; see **animal** 1, 2, **person** 1.
**for the time being** — *Syn.* temporarily, tentatively, for now, for the present; see **briefly** 2, **now** 1, **temporarily.**

**belabor,** *v.* — *Syn.* dwell on, harp on, overemphasize, run into the ground*; see **emphasize, repeat** 1, 3.

**belated,** *modif.* — *Syn.* late, remiss, tardy, overdue; see **late** 1, **slow** 3.

**belfry,** *n.* — *Syn.* steeple, cupola, bell tower, tower, spire, turret, dome, carillon, campanile, clocher, minaret; see also **tower.**

**belie,** *v.* **1.** [To mislead] — *Syn.* give the lie to, misrepresent, disguise; see **disguise, mislead.**
**2.** [To contradict] — *Syn.* prove false, repudiate, gainsay; see **deny, refute.**

**belief,** *n.* **1.** [Mental conviction] — *Syn.* credit, credence, acceptance, trust, avowal, conviction, confidence, profession, opinion, notion, persuasion, position, understanding, faith, assent, mindset, surmise, suspicion, thesis, knowledge, feeling, sentiment, conclusion, presumption, hypothesis, thinking, hope, intuition, assurance, expectation, axiom, deduction, judgment, certainty, mind, impression, assumption, conjecture, postulation, theorem, divination, fancy, presupposition, supposition, notion, apprehension, theory, view, viewpoint, guess, conception, reliance, dependence, idea, inference. [That which is believed] — *Syn.* creed, credo, tenet, dogma; see **faith** 2, **tenet.**

SYN. — **belief,** the term of broadest application in this comparison, implies mental acceptance of something as true, even though absolute certainty may be absent; **faith** implies complete, unquestioning acceptance of something, esp. something not supported by reason, even in the absence of proof; **trust** implies assurance, often apparently intuitive, in the reliability of someone or something; **confidence** also suggests such assurance, esp. when based on reason or evidence; **credence** suggests mere mental acceptance of something that may have no solid basis in fact *See also Synonym Study at* OPINION.

**believable,** *modif.* — *Syn.* credible, plausible, trustworthy; see **convincing** 2.

**believe,** *v.* **1.** [To accept as true] — *Syn.* accept, hold, think, conclude, have faith, be convinced, be certain, be confident, deem, understand, regard, take at one's word, consider, affirm, maintain, be of the opinion, postulate, opine, conceive, give credence to, credit, have no doubt, feel sure, rest assured, swear by, take one's word for, cherish a belief, nurture a belief, keep the faith, be credulous, entertain a belief, hold a belief, attach some weight to, take stock in, put stock in, take on faith, take as gospel, doubt not, buy*, swallow*. — *Ant.* doubt, DENY, suspect.

**2.** [To assume] — *Syn.* suppose, guess, gather; see **assume** 1.

**believe in,** *v.* — *Syn.* swear by, look to, put faith in, have faith in, have confidence in; see also **trust** 1.

**believer,** *n.* — *Syn.* convert, devotee, canonist, dogmatist, accepter, adherent, apostle, disciple, prophet, confirmed believer, one of the faithful, theist, religionist, doctrinaire; see also **follower.** — *Ant.* SKEPTIC, doubter, agnostic.

**believing,** *modif.* — *Syn.* maintaining, trusting, presuming, assuming, regarding, holding, accepting, impressed with, under the impression, having faith. — *Ant.* DOUBTFUL, mistrustful, rejecting.

**belittle,** *v.* — *Syn.* lower, disparage, decry, deprecate, depreciate; see also **depreciate** 2.
*See Synonym Study at* DEPRECIATE.

**bell,** *n.* **1.** [Device for signaling audibly] — *Syn.* chime(s), signal, gong, siren, carillon, angelus, tintinnabulum, buzzer, ding-dong*, ringer*; see also **alarm** 1.
**2.** [Sound made by a bell] — *Syn.* toll, carillon, gong, pealing, tocsin, buzz, chime, tintinnabulation, ringing, knell, tinkle, bong, ding-dong, ding; see also **sound** 2.

**belle,** *n.* — *Syn.* beauty, coquette, debutante, queen; see **beauty** 4, **girl** 1, **woman** 1.

**bellhop,** *n.* — *Syn.* steward, porter, bellboy, bellman, messenger, attendant; see also **assistant.**

**bellicose,** *modif.* — *Syn.* warlike, belligerent, hostile; see **aggressive** 2, **belligerent.**
*See Synonym Study at* BELLIGERENT.

**belligerent,** *modif.* — *Syn.* warlike, pugnacious, hostile, quarrelsome, contentious, bellicose, warring, militant, martial, warmongering, hawkish, combative, truculent, antagonistic, aggressive, full of fight*; see also **aggressive** 2, **quarrelsome** 1.

SYN. — **belligerent** implies engagement in war or fighting or in actions that are likely to provoke fighting *[belligerent* nations]; **bellicose** implies a warlike or hostile nature, suggesting a readiness to fight *[a bellicose* mood]; **pugnacious** and **quarrelsome** both connote aggressiveness and a willingness to initiate a fight, but **quarrelsome** more often suggests pettiness and eagerness to fight for little or no reason; **contentious** suggests an inclination to argue or quarrel, usually with annoying persistence

**bellow,** *n.* — *Syn.* howl, cry, roar; see **cry** 1, **yell** 1.

**bellow,** *v.* — *Syn.* howl, roar, shout; see **cry** 3, **yell.**

**bell tower,** *n.* — *Syn.* campanile, turret, belfry; see **belfry, tower.**

**belly,** *n.* — *Syn.* stomach, paunch, gut*; see **abdomen.**

**belly,** *v.* — *Syn.* swell, bulge *or* curve out, unfold; see **fill** 2, **spread** 3.

**bellyache*,** *v.* — *Syn.* whine, grumble, protest; see **complain** 1.

**belong,** *v.* **1.** [To be properly placed] — *Syn.* fit, go, reside, normally exist, have (its) place, pertain, appertain, bear, apply, relate, inhere, bear upon, regard, correlate with, go with, have to do with, be associated with, linked with, merge with, have respect to, have applicability to, be a part of, be a constituent of, be a component of, be an attribute of, be an adjunct of, permeate, touch, be linked, to be joined to, be allied to, be akin to, be related to, refer, concern, associate, be relevant. — *Ant.* DISTURB, intrude, be incongruous.
**2.** [To be accepted in a group; *said of persons*] — *Syn.* be a member, fit in, have a place, be one of, be born so, take one's place with, be associated with, be affiliated with, be classified among, be counted among, be included in,

be contained in, owe allegiance to, owe support to, be bound to, be a part of, be one of the family\*, be in with\*. — *Ant.* DIFFER, rebel, not fit in.

**belongings,** *pl. n.* — *Syn.* possessions, goods, things; see **property** 1.

**belong to,** *v.* — *Syn.* be owned by, be held by, be occupied by, be enjoyed by, be in the hands of, be in the possession of, be at the disposal of, be the property of, be the right of, pertain to, relate to, concern, come with, go with, be associated with, fall under, be classified under; see also **belong** 1, 2. — *Ant.* ESCAPE, be free, have no owner.

**beloved,** *modif.* — *Syn.* loved, adored, worshiped, cherished, dear, favorite, admired, highly regarded *or* valued, idolized, precious, prized, dearest, yearned for, hallowed, popular, revered, venerated, treasured, well-liked, cared for, respected, endeared, favored, esteemed, doted on, nearest to one's own heart, dearly beloved, pleasing, after one's own heart, darling, pet. — *Ant.* HATED, abhorred, disliked.

**beloved,** *n.* — *Syn.* fiancé, sweetheart, object of one's affection; see **lover** 1.

**below,** *modif. and prep.* **1.** [Lower in position] — *Syn.* beneath, underneath, down from; see **under** 1.
**2.** [Lower in rank or importance] — *Syn.* inferior, subject to, lesser; see **subordinate, under** 2.
**3.** [*In written work,* farther along] — *Syn.* following, later, on a following page, *infra, vide infra, v.i.* (all Latin), in a statement to be made, hereinafter, subsequently. — *Ant.* earlier, ABOVE, on a previous page.
**4.** [*In a ship,* on *or* to a lower deck] — *Syn.* between-decks, below-decks, in the hold, in steerage, in the engine room, below the waterline.
**5.** [On earth] — *Syn.* in this world, here below, under the sun, on the face of the earth, in mundane existence, in this period of earthly probation, in this our life, here.
**6.** [In hell] — *Syn.* in the underworld, with the fallen angels, in Pluto's realm, damned, condemned, in Inferno; see also **damned** 1.

**belt,** *n.* **1.** [A long flexible strip] — *Syn.* sash, cummerbund, obi, cincture, girdle; see also **band** 1.
**2.** [A distinctly defined area] — *Syn.* tract, region, zone; see **area** 2.

**below the belt** — *Syn.* unfair, unsporting, foul, unjust; see **unfair.**

**tighten one's belt** — *Syn.* endure hunger, endure privation, be more frugal, retrench, cut back; see also **economize, endure** 2.

**under one's belt\*** — *Syn.* past, achieved, completed; see **done** 1, **finished** 1.

**bemoan,** *v.* — *Syn.* lament, bewail, weep over, grieve for; see **mourn** 1, **regret** 1.

**bemuse,** *v.* — *Syn.* muddle, bewilder, daze, distract; see **confuse.**

**bench,** *n.* **1.** [A long seat] — *Syn.* settee, pew, form, lawn seat, settle, bank, stall, bleacher (*usually plural*); see also **chair** 1, **seat** 1.
**2.** [A long table] — *Syn.* workbench, worktable, desk, trestle, counter, board, shelf, ledge, stand, easel; see also **table** 1.
**3.** [Those who administer justice] — *Syn.* the bar, judges, tribunal; see **court** 2.

**bend,** *n.* — *Syn.* crook, bow, arch; see **curve** 1.

**bend,** *v.* **1.** [To force out of a straight line] — *Syn.* twist, turn, curve, warp, arch, round, crimp, flex, pervert, spiral, camber, coil, crinkle, curl, buckle, crook, bow, wind, incline, contort, deflect, deform, double, loop, twine, refract, angle, hook. — *Ant.* STRAIGHTEN, STIFFEN, SUPPORT.

**2.** [To be forced out of a straight line] — *Syn.* stoop, lean, buckle, bow, turn, zigzag, crumple, meander, circle, swerve, diverge, deviate, detour, veer, droop, angle off, angle away, wilt, sag, hunch, give; see also sense 1, **bow** 1, **deviate, turn** 6, **veer.** — *Ant.* stand up, EXTEND, straighten.
**3.** [To influence] — *Syn.* direct, persuade, mold; see **change** 1, **influence.**
**4.** [To yield] — *Syn.* submit, accede, give in; see **yield** 1.

---

*SYN.* — **bend** refers to the curving or crooking of something that is normally straight but that yields to pressure or tension /to *bend* a wire/; **twist,** in this connection, implies greater resistance in the object to be bent and often connotes a wrenching out of the normal line /to *twist* one's arm/; **turn,** in this comparison, suggests a change in direction, as a curving back of an object upon itself /to *turn* the sheet back/; **curve** suggests a swerving or deflection in a line that follows or approximates the arc of a circle /he *curved* the next pitch/

---

**bending,** *modif.* — *Syn.* turning, twisting, veering, curving, buckling, twining, spiraling, looping, doubling, drooping, leaning, inclining, bowing, arching, curling, warping, crooking, winding, stooping, crumpling, waving, wavering, yielding.

**beneath,** *modif. and prep.* **1.** [Under] — *Syn.* below, underneath, in a lower place; see **under** 1.
**2.** [Lower in rank or importance] — *Syn.* subject to, inferior, lesser; see **subordinate, under** 2.
**3.** [Unworthy of] — *Syn.* demeaning, unbefitting, beneath one's dignity, infra dig\*; see **unsuitable.**

**benediction,** *n.* — *Syn.* sanctification, blessing, good wishes; see **blessing** 1.

**benefaction,** *n.* **1.** [A gift] — *Syn.* donation, legacy, grant; see **gift** 1.
**2.** [A good deed] — *Syn.* favor, charity, good turn; see **kindness** 2.

**benefactor,** *n.* — *Syn.* helper, protector, angel\*; see **patron** 1.

**beneficent,** *modif.* — *Syn.* benign, salutary, benevolent; see **helpful** 1, **kind.**

**beneficial,** *modif.* — *Syn.* useful, propitious, salubrious, advantageous; see **helpful** 1, **profitable.**

**beneficiary,** *n.* — *Syn.* recipient, receiver, payee, legatee, heir, heiress, inheritor, possessor, successor, assignee, donee, stipendiary, pensioner, almsman, grantee, devisee, charity case\*. — *Ant.* DONOR, giver, testator.

**benefit,** *modif.* — *Syn.* (for) charity, for a good *or* worthy cause, in one's favor.

**benefit,** *n.* **1.** [Advantage] — *Syn.* gain, profit, good, interest; see **advantage** 3.
**2.** [Charitable affair] — *Syn.* charity ball, benefit performance, donor dinner, donor lunch, dance, fair, bazaar, exhibit, exhibition, raffle, concert.
**3.** [A payment or favor received in addition to wages; *often plural*] — *Syn.* fringe benefit, perquisite, extra, bonus, compensation, privilege, perk\*.

**benefit,** *v.* — *Syn.* serve, profit, avail; see **help** 1.

**benevolence,** *n.* — *Syn.* kindness, charity, altruism, good will; see **kindness** 1.

**benevolent,** *modif.* — *Syn.* kind, generous, altruistic, helpful; see **kind.**
*See Synonym Study at* KIND.

**benign,** *modif.* **1.** [Kind or beneficial] — *Syn.* good, gracious, kindly, favorable; see **kind.**

**2.** [Harmless] — *Syn.* mild, innocuous, not malignant; see **harmless** 2.

*See Synonym Study at* KIND.

**bent,** *modif.* — *Syn.* curved, warped, crooked, looped, twined, sinuous, bowed, flexed, contorted, stooped, doubled over, limp, wilted, drooping, humped, slumped, hunched, humpbacked, lordotic, bowlegged, hooked, beaked, inclined; see also **twisted** 1. — *Ant.* rigid, STRAIGHT, erect.

**bent,** *n.* — *Syn.* inclination, leaning, tendency, propensity; see **inclination** 1.

*See Synonym Study at* INCLINATION.

**bent on,** *modif.* — *Syn.* determined, set on, intent on, resolved; see **resolute** 2.

**benumb,** *v.* — *Syn.* dull, numb, stupefy, paralyze; see **deaden** 1.

**bequeath,** *v.* — *Syn.* grant, hand down, pass on, will; see **give** 1, **leave** 1.

**bequest,** *n.* — *Syn.* inheritance, estate, endowment, legacy; see **estate** 2, **gift** 1.

**berate,** *v.* — *Syn.* scold, chide, reprimand, rebuke; see **scold.**

*See Synonym Study at* SCOLD.

**bereavement,** *n.* — *Syn.* loss, deprivation, mourning, affliction; see **death** 1, **grief** 1, **loss** 1.

**bereft,** *modif.* — *Syn.* bereaved, deprived, cut off, dispossessed, forlorn of, wanting, divested, destitute, stripped, impoverished, beggared, left unprovided for, naked, left without, robbed, straitened; see also **poor** 1. — *Ant.* RICH, possessed, in enjoyment.

**berry,** *n.* **1.** [A small pulpy fruit] — *Syn.* drupe, hip, drupelet, haw, pome.

Common berries include: raspberry, blackberry, blueberry, loganberry, boysenberry, cranberry, huckleberry, whortleberry, bilberry, gooseberry, currant, strawberry, checkerberry, dewberry, hagberry, dogberry, bayberry, serviceberry, mulberry.

**2.** [A dry fruit] — *Syn.* seed, grain, kernel; see **bean** 1.

**berserk,** *modif.* — *Syn.* frenzied, crazed, wild, amok; see **insane** 1, **violent** 2.

**berth,** *n.* **1.** [A bed, especially in a conveyance] — *Syn.* bunk, deck, hammock, upper berth, lower berth, transom berth, bedroom, roomette, sleeping compartment, couchette, shakedown*.

**2.** [A position] — *Syn.* place, situation, job, employment; see **job** 1, **profession** 1.

**give a wide berth** — *Syn.* keep clear of, evade, stay away (from); see **avoid.**

**beseech,** *v.* — *Syn.* implore, importune, entreat; see **beg** 1.

*See Synonym Study at* BEG.

**beset,** *v.* — *Syn.* besiege, assail, plague, harass; see **attack** 1, 2.

*See Synonym Study at* ATTACK.

**beside,** *modif. & prep.* — *Syn.* by the side of, on the edge of, next to, adjacent to, contiguous to, parallel to, close to, adjoining, alongside, near, but a step from, close at hand, by, with, abreast, side by side, at one's elbow, bordering on, verging on, neighboring, overlooking, next door to, to one side, in juxtaposition, nearby, connected with, compared with, in comparison with, cheek by jowl*, close upon*.

**besides,** *modif.* — *Syn.* in addition to, additionally, moreover, over and above, supplementary to, added to, likewise, further, furthermore, beyond, exceeding, secondly, more than, apart from, aside from, extra, in distinction to, in excess of, plus, also, in other respects, exclusive of, with the exception of, as well as, not counting, other than, too, in conjunction with, conjointly, together with,

along with, else, to boot*, on top of that*, on the side*, and all*, into the bargain*.

**besiege,** *v.* — *Syn.* lay siege to, blockade, close in on, beset; see **attack** 1, 2.

**best,** *modif.* **1.** [Generally excellent] — *Syn.* choicest, finest, greatest, highest, first, transcendent, prime, premium, supreme, optimum, incomparable, culminating, preeminent, leading, crowning, *sans pareil* (French), paramount, matchless, nonpareil, unrivaled, unparalleled, unsurpassed, second to none, in a class by itself, nonesuch, unequaled, unexcelled, inimitable, beyond compare, superlative, foremost, peerless, champion, top, prize, most desirable, most suitable, most favorable, most advantageous, most outstanding, tip-top*. — *Ant.* WORST, poorest, lowest.

**2.** [Applied especially to things] — *Syn.* choice, premium, highest-quality, top-of-the-line*; see **excellent.**

**3.** [Applied especially to people] — *Syn.* of the elite, belonging to the upper classes, socially preferred, aristocratic; see **cultured, distinguished** 2, **noble** 3, **rich** 1.

**4.** [Applied especially to actions] — *Syn.* noblest, sincerest, most magnanimous, most creditable, most illustrious, most glorious, most honorable, most praiseworthy, greatest, kindest, nicest; see also sense 1. — *Ant.* WORST, meanest, lowest.

**5.** [Largest] — *Syn.* greatest, biggest, most; see **large** 1, **most.**

**best,** *n.* — *Syn.* first, favorite, choice, finest, top, pick, prime, flower, cream, elite, *crème de la crème* (French), utmost, salt of the earth*, pick of the crop*, cream of the crop*, tops*.

**all for the best** — *Syn.* favorable, fortunate, advantageous; see **helpful** 1, **hopeful** 2.

**as best one can** — *Syn.* skillfully, ably, capably, as well as one can; see **well** 2.

**at best** — *Syn.* at most, under the most favorable conditions, under the most favorable circumstances, according to the most favorable interpretation, at the outside*.

**at one's best** — *Syn.* well, in one's prime, at the top of one's form, in one's best mood; see **able** 2, **healthy** 1.

**get** or **have the best of** — *Syn.* outdo, overcome, defeat, outwit; see **defeat** 1, 2, 3, **surpass, win** 1.

**make the best of** — *Syn.* tolerate, get by, manage, make do; see **endure** 2.

**with the best** — *Syn.* excellently, well, ably; see **excellently, well** 2.

**best,** *v.* — *Syn.* worst, get the better of, overcome, outdo; see **defeat** 1, 2, 3, **surpass.**

**bestial,** *modif.* — *Syn.* brutish, brutal, savage, depraved; see **animal** 1, **beastly** 1, **cruel** 1.

**bestir,** *v.* — *Syn.* stir up, rouse, exert, exert oneself; see **excite** 1, 2, **incite, try** 1.

**bestow,** *v.* — *Syn.* give, bequeath, present, offer; see **give** 1.

*See Synonym Study at* GIVE.

**bestride,** *v.* — *Syn.* ride, mount, sit; see **straddle.**

**bestseller,** *n.* — *Syn.* hit, success, blockbuster*; see **hit** 2.

**bet,** *n.* — *Syn.* gamble, wager, venture, pot, ante, hazard, tossup, stake, speculation, betting, play, raffle, odds, uncertainty, tossup, chance, random shot, lottery, fortune, lot, game of chance, sweepstake(s), risk, flier*, long shot*, shot in the dark*, blind bargain*, roll of the dice*, plunge*, pig in a poke*, crapshoot*, piece of the action*.

**bet,** *v.* — *Syn.* wager, gamble, stake, bet on, back, bet against, venture, hazard, trust, play against, speculate, tempt fortune, play for, put money on, lay money down, dice, flip a coin, toss up, risk, game, chance, ante, make a bet, put up, take a chance, try one's luck, take a flier*, declare oneself in*, lay down*, buy in on*, plank down*, post*, punt*, play the ponies*, pony up*, lay odds*, lay even money*, make book*.

**you bet*** — *Syn.* certainly, by all means; yes, indeed; see **surely, yes.**

**betray,** *v.* **1.** [To deliver into the hands of an enemy] — *Syn.* play false, break faith (with), inform on, inform against, turn in, commit treason, turn informer, delude, break one's promise, be false to, be false-hearted to, be disloyal to, go over to the enemy, trick, let down, disappoint, deceive, sell down the river*, play Judas*, give the Judas kiss to*, double-cross*, deliver up*, sell out*, stab in the back*, bite the hand that feeds one*, cross up*, turn state's evidence; see also **deceive, inform** 2. — *Ant.* SUPPORT, adhere, stand firm.

**2.** [To lead astray] — *Syn.* seduce, misguide, corrupt; see **seduce.**

**3.** [To reveal] — *Syn.* divulge, disclose, uncover, make known; see **reveal** 1.

*See Synonym Study at* DECEIVE, REVEAL.

**betrayal,** *n.* — *Syn.* treason, treachery, disloyalty; see **deception** 1, **dishonesty.**

**betrayer,** *n.* — *Syn.* informer, renegade, deceiver, conspirator; see **informer, traitor.**

**betroth,** *v.* — *Syn.* publish the banns, become engaged, bestow one's hand, give one's hand, contract, pledge, promise, precontract, plight faith, plight troth, bind, engage, affiance, commit oneself to, undertake to marry, espouse.

**betrothal,** *n.* — *Syn.* engagement, espousal, betrothing; see **engagement** 2.

**better,** *modif.* **1.** [Superior] — *Syn.* greater, finer, preferred, preferable, surpassing, excelling, improved, more suitable, more desirable, more favorable, more virtuous; see also **best** 1, **excellent.**

**2.** [Thought of as somewhat exclusive] — *Syn.* more select, of higher quality, more refined, more aloof, more noteworthy, more distinguished, more sophisticated, politer, posher*, classier*. — *Ant.* COMMON, vulgar, popular.

**3.** [Recovering health] — *Syn.* convalescent, improved in health, stronger, recovering, convalescing, improving, on the road to recovery, mending, progressing, on the mend*. — *Ant.* SICK, failing, wasting away.

**4.** [Larger] — *Syn.* bigger, preponderant, weightier, more; see **large** 1, **more** 2.

**for better or worse** — *Syn.* regardless, in any event, no matter what happens; see **anyhow** 1, **notwithstanding.**

**for the better** — *Syn.* favorable, fortunate, resulting in improvement, to a better condition; see **helpful** 1, **hopeful** 2.

**get** or **have the better of** — *Syn.* outdo, overcome, defeat, outwit; see **defeat** 1, 2, 3, **surpass, win** 1.

**better,** *v.* **1.** [To improve] — *Syn.* ameliorate, revamp, refine; see **improve** 1.

**2.** [To surpass] — *Syn.* outdo, improve upon, top; see **exceed, surpass.**

**betterment,** *n.* — *Syn.* improvement, prosperity, upgrading, progress; see **improvement** 1, 2.

**between,** *prep.* — *Syn.* separating, within, enclosed by, bounded by, amidst, amid, among, in, in between, interpolated, mid, interjacent, intervening, inserted, in the midst of, in the middle, medially, centrally located, surrounded by, midway, halfway, intermediate to, linking, connecting, betwixt, in the thick of, betwixt and between, sandwichwise*; see also **among.**

**between you and me** — *Syn.* confidentially, privately, personally; see **secretly.**

**bevel,** *n.* — *Syn.* angle, slant, slope; see **inclination** 5.

**beverage,** *n.* — *Syn.* drink, liquor, refreshment, draft; see **drink** 1, 2, 3.

**bevy,** *n.* — *Syn.* flock, pack, group; see **gathering, herd** 1.

**bewilder,** *v.* — *Syn.* confound, upset, disconcert, puzzle; see **confuse.**

*See Synonym Study at* CONFUSE.

**bewildered,** *modif.* — *Syn.* confused, puzzled, perplexed, baffled, lost, amazed, astonished, thunderstruck, shocked, muddled, upset, dismayed, dazed, giddy, dizzy, reeling, vertiginous, misled, addled, mystified, uncertain, surprised, disconcerted, taken aback, nonplused, aghast, put out of countenance, adrift, at sea, off the track, awed, stupefied, astounded, struck speechless, agog, agape, breathless, befuddled, bemused, startled, struck dumb, dumbfounded, dazzled, stunned, confounded, staggered, awe-struck, flabbergasted, flustered, rattled, all balled up*, in a dither*, lost in the fog*, bowled over*, euchred*, fazed*, come unstuck*, at a loss*, all hot and bothered*, going around in circles*, in a stew*, up in the air*, stumped*, punchdrunk*. — *Ant.* self-possessed, RATIONAL, cool.

**bewitch,** *v.* **1.** [To fascinate] — *Syn.* enthrall, beguile, capture; see **fascinate.**

**2.** [To charm] — *Syn.* enchant, cast a spell over, control magically; see **charm** 1.

**bewitched,** *modif.* **1.** [Fascinated] — *Syn.* enraptured, entranced, captivated; see **fascinated.**

**2.** [Charmed] — *Syn.* enchanted, ensorcelled, controlled supernaturally; see **charmed.**

**beyond,** *modif. & prep.* — *Syn.* on the other side, on the far side, over there, beyond the bounds, in advance of, over the mark, above the mark, away, out of range, a long way off, over the border, yonder, past, free of, clear of, farther back, farther off, farther on, ahead, behind, more remote, wide of the mark, outside the reach of, exceeding, surpassing. — *Ant.* on this side, HERE, nearer.

**the great beyond** — *Syn.* the afterlife, the hereafter, heaven and hell, purgatory; see **heaven** 2, **hell** 1, **immortality** 2.

**biannual,** *modif.* — *Syn.* semiannual, occurring twice a year, half-yearly.

**bias,** *n.* — *Syn.* bent, preference, leaning; see **inclination** 1, **prejudice.**

*See Synonym Study at* PREJUDICE.

**bias,** *v.* — *Syn.* influence, prejudice, sway; see **influence.**

**bib,** *n.* — *Syn.* napkin, tucker, face cloth, chin-wiper, collar, dickey; see also **apron.**

**bible,** *n.* **1.** [Ultimate authority] — *Syn.* handbook, text, guidebook, manual, vade mecum, creed, accepted statement, authority, guide, unquestioned doctrine, court of final appeal, scripture, canon, the last word*, Hoyle*.

**2.** [Holy Scripture; *capitalized*] — *Syn.* Scripture, the Good Book, God's word, the Word, the Scriptures, the Holy Scriptures, the Old Testament, the New Testament, the Torah, the Canon, the Testaments, Sacred History, the Writings of the Apostles and Prophets, Holy Writ, the Holy Bible, the Word of God, Testament, the Book.

Famous Bibles include: Vulgate, Douay, King James *or* Authorized Version (KJV), Tyndale, Coverdale, Wycliffe, Revised Standard Version (RSV), Luther's, Wenzel, Mazarin, Wujek's, Gutenberg, Geneva *or* Breeches, Vinegar, Cicked, American *or* Revised, New English Bible (NEB).

Other sacred texts include: Koran, Veda, Masora, Alcoran, Tripitaka, Torah, Talmud, the Analects, Book of Mormon, the Eddas.

**bibliography,** *n.* — *Syn.* catalogue, compilation, list of books, list of sources, book list, index, annotated bibliography, list of publications, literature; see also **catalog, index** 2, **list.**

**bibliophile,** *n.* — *Syn.* booklover, reader, bookworm, bibliolater, bibliophilist, antiquarian, book collector, bibliomaniac, book nut*.

**bicker,** *v.* — *Syn.* wrangle, squabble, dispute, argue; see **quarrel.**

**bicycle,** *n.* — *Syn.* cycle, machine, velocipede, ten-speed, five-speed, three-speed, racer, tandem, bicycle built for two, stationary bicycle, Exercycle (trademark), bike*, two-wheeler*, mountain bike*; see also **tricycle.**

**bid,** *n.* **1.** [An offer] — *Syn.* proposal, proposition, declaration, tender; see **proposal** 1, **suggestion** 1.
**2.** [An effort to gain an end] — *Syn.* attempt, try, effort, gambit; see **effort** 2.
**3.** [*An invitation] — *Syn.* request, summons, proposal; see **invitation** 1, 2.

**bid,** *v.* **1.** [To propose a price for purchase] — *Syn.* offer, venture, proffer, tender, bid for, submit a bid, make an offer.
**2.** [To offer a commitment at cards] — *Syn.* declare, name a trump, bid in, name a suit, open, respond.
**3.** [To order] — *Syn.* demand, charge, direct, instruct; see **command** 1.
**4.** [To invite] — *Syn.* request, ask, solicit; see **invite** 1, 2.

**bidding,** *n.* **1.** [Order] — *Syn.* direction, demand, charge; see **command** 1.
**2.** [Invitation] — *Syn.* summons, call, request; see **invitation** 1.
**do the bidding of**— *Syn.* be obedient, obey, follow orders, submit; see **obey** 1, **serve** 2.

**bide one's time,** *v.* — *Syn.* await, watch for, lie in wait, play a waiting game; see **wait** 1.

**bier,** *n.* — *Syn.* coffin, pall, hearse, catafalque, casket, stretcher, barrow, litter, pyre, sarcophagus; see also **coffin, grave** 1.

**big,** *modif.* **1.** [Of great size] — *Syn.* large, huge, great; see **high** 1, **large** 1, **long** 1.
**2.** [Grown, or partially grown] — *Syn.* grown-up, full-grown, adult, elder; see **mature** 1.
**3.** [Important] — *Syn.* prominent, significant, influential, consequential; see **important** 1, 2.
**4.** [Pompous] — *Syn.* presumptuous, pretentious, boastful, imperious; see **egotistic** 2, **pompous, proud** 2.
**5.** [Loud] — *Syn.* roaring, deafening, heavy; see **loud** 1.
**6.** [Generous] — *Syn.* magnanimous, liberal, unselfish; see **generous** 1, 2.
**7.** [With child] — *Syn.* gravid, parturient, expecting*; see **pregnant** 1.
**8.** [*Pompously] — *Syn.* pretentiously, boastfully, ostentatiously, flamboyantly; see **pompously.**
*See Synonym Study at* LARGE.

**bigamy,** *n.* — *Syn.* polygamy, unlawful polygamy, plural marriage, real bigamy, interpretative bigamy; see also **polygamy.**

**bigot,** *n.* — *Syn.* dogmatist, doctrinaire, fanatic, extremist, zealot, radical, monomaniac, narrow-minded person, opinionated person, puritan, partisan, enthusiast, racist, white supremacist, chauvinist, sexist, male chauvinist, anti-Semite, xenophobe, hatemonger, die-hard, mule*, bitter-ender*, crank*, redneck*, Archie Bunker*; see also **radical, zealot.**
*See Synonym Study at* ZEALOT.

**bigoted,** *modif.* — *Syn.* biased, narrow-minded, intolerant, opinionated; see **prejudiced.**

**bigotry,** *n.* — *Syn.* dogmatism, narrow-mindedness, injustice; see **fanaticism, intolerance** 2, **prejudice.**

**big shot*,** *n.* — *Syn.* dignitary, big wheel*, big gun*, VIP*; see **administrator, chief** 1, **personage** 2.

**bilateral,** *modif.* — *Syn.* two-sided, respective, reciprocal; see **mutual** 1.

**bill,** *n.* **1.** [A statement of account] — *Syn.* invoice, itemized account, request for payment, check, tab*; see also **statement** 3.
**2.** [A piece of paper money] — *Syn.* bank note, note, Federal Reserve note, currency, paper money, gold certificate, silver certificate, dollar bill, long green*, greenback*, folding money*, skin*, one-spot*, fiver*, five-spot*, tenner*, ten-spot*, sawbuck*, C-note*; see also **dollar, money** 1.
**3.** [A statement prepared for enactment into law] — *Syn.* draft, measure, proposal, act, proposed act, piece of legislation; see also **law** 3.
**4.** [A handbill] — *Syn.* poster, circular, folder; see **advertisement** 1, 2.
**5.** [A formal statement, usually legal] — *Syn.* charge, allegation, indictment; see **declaration** 2.
**6.** [A beak] — *Syn.* nib, mandible, projection; see **beak.**
**fill the bill*** — *Syn.* meet requirements, be satisfactory, serve the purpose; see **satisfy** 3.

**bill,** *v.* **1.** [To request payment] — *Syn.* dun, solicit, charge, render *or* send account of indebtedness, draw upon, send a statement, invoice.
**2.** [To advertise, especially a coming attraction] — *Syn.* announce, book, give advance notice of; see **advertise** 1.

**billboard,** *n.* — *Syn.* signboard, bulletin board, display panel, poster board; see **advertisement** 1, 2, **announcement** 3.

**billed,** *modif.* — *Syn.* announced, publicized, published; see **advertised.**

**billfold,** *n.* — *Syn.* card case, wallet, pocketbook, purse; see **wallet.**

**billow,** *n.* — *Syn.* wave, surge, crest, tide; see **wave** 1, 2.
*See Synonym Study at* WAVE.

**billowy,** *modif.* — *Syn.* surging, swelling, rising, waving, rolling, rising and falling, heaving, undulating, ebbing and flowing, rippled, rippling, wavy, billowing, bulging; see also **rough** 1, **turbulent.**

**billy goat*,** *n.* — *Syn.* sire, he-goat, buck, billy*; see **goat.**

**bin,** *n.* — *Syn.* box, bunker, hopper, storeroom, crib, mow, granary, silo, locker, drawer, bay, canister; see also **case** 7, **container.**

**binary,** *modif.* — *Syn.* double, twofold, paired; see **double.**

**bind*,** *n.* — *Syn.* dilemma, tight situation, quandary, jam*; see **predicament.**

**bind,** *v.* **1.** [To constrain with bonds] — *Syn.* tie, tie up, truss, truss up, shackle, fetter, pinion, cinch, clamp, chain, leash, constrict, manacle, enchain, enfetter, lace, pin, restrict, restrain, moor, handcuff, hamper, muzzle, hitch, secure, yoke, pin down, peg down, fix, strap, tether, bind up, lash (down), hobble, trammel, hogtie.
**2.** [To hold together or in place] — *Syn.* secure, attach, adhere; see **fasten** 1.
**3.** [To obligate] — *Syn.* oblige, necessitate, compel; see **force** 1.
**4.** [To dress] — *Syn.* treat, wrap, bandage; see **dress** 4.
**5.** [To join] — *Syn.* unite, put together, connect; see **join** 1.

**binder,** *n.* **1.** [A person who binds] — *Syn.* tier, shackler, hobbler, coupler, grappler, bookbinder.

**2.** [A machine that binds] — *Syn.* reaper, harvester, harvesting machine; see **machine** 1.

**3.** [Anything used to bind] — *Syn.* tie, adhesive, fastener, ring binder; see **adhesive, band** 2, **cover** 1, **rope, wire** 1.

**binding,** *modif.* **1.** [Tying] — *Syn.* restraining, confining, limiting, restrictive; see **tying.**

**2.** [Imposing adherence] — *Syn.* obligatory, compulsory, requisite, required; see **necessary** 1.

**binding,** *n.* **1.** [The act of joining] — *Syn.* merging, coupling, junction; see **union** 1.

**2.** [Anything used to bind] — *Syn.* tie, adhesive, fastener; see **adhesive, band** 2, **rope, wire** 1.

**3.** [A cover] — *Syn.* wrapper, jacket, book cover; see **cover** 1, 2.

**binge\*,** *n.* — *Syn.* spree, fling, overeating, drinking bout; see **indulgence** 3, **orgy.**

**biography,** *n.* — *Syn.* life story, memoir, journal, experiences, autobiography, vita, life, adventures, saga, personal account, personal narrative, life history, confessions, fortunes, personal anecdote, recollections, profile, sketch, picture, portrait, biographical account, biographical sketch, psychobiography, bio\*; see also **autobiography, record** 1, 2.

**biological,** *modif.* — *Syn.* organic, life, living, zoological, botanical, concerning life, biotic, vital, physiological, anatomical, morphological, natural.

**biology,** *n.* — *Syn.* science of organisms, natural science, natural history, nature study, life science, study of living things.

Divisions of biology include: botany, zoology, physiology, genetics, ecology, microbiology, molecular biology, embryology, biochemistry, marine biology, oceanography, biotechnology, biostatistics, bioengineering, biomathematics; see also **botany, physiology, science** 1, **zoology.**

**birch,** *n.*

Popular classifications of birch include: paper, white, aspen-leaved, yellow, black, weeping; see also **tree, wood** 2.

**bird,** *n.* **1.** [Any warm-blooded vertebrate with feathers and wings] — *Syn.* fowl, feathered creature, *Avis* (Latin), songbird, passerine bird, oscine bird, bird of prey, raptor, shorebird, seabird, wader, wading bird, waterfowl, ratite, cageling, chick, nestling, fledgling, birdie\*.

Common birds include: sparrow, starling, robin, bluejay, crow, hawk, meadowlark, cowbird, hummingbird, finch, quail, partridge, pheasant, owl, vulture, buzzard, turkey buzzard, woodpecker, cardinal, oriole, bluebird, kingfisher, canary, parrot, chickadee, swallow, skylark, nightingale, nuthatch, whippoorwill, flycatcher, thrush, catbird, cuckoo, bobolink, titmouse, wren, gull, sandpiper, eagle, falcon, albatross, cormorant, osprey, cedarbird, ovenbird, blackbird, dove, duck, swan, goose, pigeon, brambling, bullfinch, parakeet *or* parrakeet, chat, creeper, crane, shitepoke, heron, pelican, loon, tern, goshawk, goatsucker, mockingbird, ostrich, emu, kestrel, petrel, auk; see also **hawk, owl, sparrow, thrush, woodpecker.**

**2.** [A game bird] — *Syn.* wildfowl, game, partridge, quail, woodcock, grouse; see also **duck, goose** 1, **pheasant.**

**3.** [\*A person; a mildly derogatory term] — *Syn.* person, fellow, guy\*, coot\*, duck\*, duffer\*.

**eat like a bird** — *Syn.* diet, starve, restrain one's appetite, pick; see **fast.**

**for the birds** — *Syn.* ridiculous, absurd, useless; see **absurd, stupid** 1, **useless** 1, **worthless** 1.

**bird dog,** *n.* — *Syn.* pointer, setter, hunting dog; see **dog** 1.

**birdhouse,** *n.* — *Syn.* aviary, bird cage, dovecote, roost, perch, roosting place, pigeon house, columbary, coop; see also **enclosure** 1.

**birth,** *n.* **1.** [The coming into life] — *Syn.* delivery, childbirth, parturition, nativity, beginning, blessed event\*, visit from the stork\*, act of God\*; see also **childbirth.** — *Ant.* DEATH, decease, demise.

**2.** [The origin] — *Syn.* commencement, source, start; see **origin** 1, 2, 3.

**3.** [One's origin or natal background] — *Syn.* background, lineage, extraction, descent; see **family** 1, **rank** 3.

**give birth to** — *Syn.* bring forth, have a child, bear a child, deliver; see **produce** 1.

**birthday,** *n.* — *Syn.* natal day, name day, date of birth; see **anniversary.**

**birthplace,** *n.* — *Syn.* place of origin, place of birth, place of nativity, one's country, home town, native home, native land; see also **country** 3.

**birthright,** *n.* — *Syn.* heritage, inheritance, patrimony; see **heritage** 1.

*See Synonym Study at* HERITAGE.

**biscuit,** *n.* — *Syn.* roll, scone, quick bread, cracker, wafer; see also **bread.**

Biscuits include the following types: beaten, soda, baking powder, cream, hot, sea, ship, Brussels, pilot, raised, rolled.

**bisect,** *v.* — *Syn.* cut in two, hemisect, halve; see **divide** 1.

**bisexual,** *modif.* — *Syn.* androgynous, hermaphroditic, gynandrous, epicene, monoclinous, intersexual, ambisexual, switch-hitting\*, AC-DC\*, swinging both ways\*.

**bishop,** *n.* — *Syn.* prelate, shepherd, diocesan, suffragan, archbishop, primate; see also **minister** 1, **priest.**

**bishopric,** *n.* — *Syn.* diocese, see, episcopate, episcopacy, prelacy, archbishopric, primacy, prelature, prelateship, archiepiscopacy, pontificate, bishopdom.

**bison,** *n.* — *Syn.* buffalo, American buffalo, wisent, European aurochs; see **buffalo.**

**bit,** *n.* **1.** [A small quantity] — *Syn.* piece, fragment, crumb, dot, particle, jot, trifle, mite, grain, iota, whit, tittle, scintilla, splinter, parcel, portion, drop, droplet, trickle, driblet, sprinkling, modicum, morsel, dollop, dab, dash, pinch, snippet, snip, shred, atom, speck, molecule, mote, shard, chip, fraction, sliver, segment, section, lump, slice, shaving, moiety, sample, specimen, scale, flake, collop, excerpt, scrap, part, division, share, trace, hint, touch, tad, item, chunk, paring, taste, lick, mouthful, bite, dose, dram, stub, butt, stump, snatch, a drop in the bucket\*, peanuts\*, chicken feed\*, smithereen\*, smidgen\*, flyspeck\*, spot\*; see also **division** 2, **part** 1, **piece** 1. — *Ant.* QUANTITY, LOT, excess.

**2.** [A brief time] — *Syn.* second, instant, minute, jiffy; see **moment** 1.

**3.** [A small degree] — *Syn.* little, jot, minimum, inch, tittle, modicum, hairbreadth, trifle, touch, tad, iota, mite, fraction, tolerance, margin, whisker\*, wink\*, hair\*, skin of one's teeth\*, skin of one's nose\*, eyelash\*. — *Ant.* infinitude, maximum, great deal.

**4.** [The mouthpiece of a bridle] — *Syn.* curb, curb bit, snaffle, gag; see **halter** 1.

**5.** [A boring or gouging implement] — *Syn.* rock drill, drift, auger; see **drill** 2.

Varieties of bits include: carpenter's, blacksmith's, drilling-machine, spiral, expanding, brace, expanding-center, German, half-round, plug-center, twisted, coal-boring, countersink.

**do one's bit** — *Syn.* participate, share, do one's share, contribute; see **join** 2, **participate** 1.

**every bit** — *Syn.* wholly, altogether, entirely; see **completely.**

**bite,** *n.* **1.** [What one takes in the mouth at one time] — *Syn.* mouthful, cud, chew, taste, spoonful, forkful, nip, morsel, nibble, bit, chaw*.

**2.** [The result of being bitten] — *Syn.* wound, sting, laceration; see **injury** 1.

**3.** [A sharp sensation] — *Syn.* sting, prick, burn; see **pain** 2.

**4.** [A quick meal] — *Syn.* snack, nibble, light meal, nosh*; see **meal** 2.

**put the bite on*** — *Syn.* pressure, ask for a loan, touch*; see **borrow** 1.

**bite,** *v.* **1.** [To seize or sever with the teeth] — *Syn.* snap, gnaw, sink one's teeth into, nip, lacerate, pierce, sting, nibble, chew, chew up, mouth, gulp, worry, taste, masticate, clamp, champ, chomp, munch, bite into, crunch, ruminate, mangle, chaw*; see also **eat** 1, **taste** 1.

**2.** [To be given to biting] — *Syn.* snap, be vicious, bare the teeth; see **attack** 2, **hurt** 1.

**3.** [To cut or corrode] — *Syn.* burn, sting, slash, smart, etch, eat away, wear away, sear, rot, rust, oxidize, erode, dissolve, deteriorate, decay, consume, decompose, engrave.

**4.** [To take bait] — *Syn.* rise to the bait, strike, nibble, get hooked; swallow hook, line, and sinker*.

**5.** [*To take a chance] — *Syn.* volunteer, risk, be a victim; see **chance** 2.

**bite the dust*,** *v.* — *Syn.* be fatally wounded, fall, drop; see **die** 1.

**biting,** *modif.* **1.** [Acidulous] — *Syn.* sharp, keen, tangy, stinging; see **acid** 2, **sour** 1.

**2.** [In the act of biting] — *Syn.* seizing, wounding, abrading, piercing, puncturing, incising, lacerating, holding, tasting, masticating, mangling, nipping, nibbling, snapping, gnawing, munching, crunching, gripping, chewing, worrying, in the mouth, with teeth in, sinking teeth into, champing, chomping.

**3.** [Sarcastic] — *Syn.* caustic, cutting, acrimonious, bitter; see **sarcastic.**

**bitten,** *modif.* — *Syn.* chewed, mouthed, torn, lacerated, slashed, gnawed, nibbled, nipped, seized, gripped, tasted, devoured, eaten, masticated, worried, tossed, stung, pierced, mangled, punctured, cut, ripped; see also **hurt.**

**bitter,** *modif.* **1.** [Acrid] — *Syn.* astringent, acid, tart, sharp; see **sour** 1.

**2.** [Intense] — *Syn.* sharp, harsh, severe; see **intense.**

**3.** [Sarcastic] — *Syn.* acrimonious, caustic, biting; see **sarcastic.**

**4.** [Painful] — *Syn.* grievous, hurtful, stinging, galling; see **disturbing, painful** 1.

**5.** [Embittered] — *Syn.* resentful, cynical, hostile, rancorous; see **angry, unfriendly** 2.

**bitterness,** *n.* **1.** [The quality of being bitter to the tongue] — *Syn.* tartness, piquancy, pungency, astringency, acidity, acerbity, sourness, acridity, brackishness, brininess, sharpness, harshness. — *Ant.* SWEETNESS, blandness, delectability.

**2.** [The quality of being bitter to the mind] — *Syn.* pain, painfulness, virulence, anguish, agony, grievousness, mordancy, venom, harshness, acrimony, rancor, resentment, gall, cynicism, acerbity, asperity, embitterment, hostility; see also **distress** 1, **rancor, resent-**

ment. — *Ant.* solace, BALM, enjoyment.

**biweekly,** *modif.* — *Syn.* semiweekly, twice monthly, once every two weeks, fortnightly.

**bizarre,** *modif.* — *Syn.* odd, strange, eccentric, grotesque; see **fantastic** 1, **unusual** 2.
*See Synonym Study at* FANTASTIC.

**blab,** *v.* **1.** [To reveal] — *Syn.* disclose, tell, divulge, give away; see **inform** 2, **reveal** 1.

**2.** [To chatter] — *Syn.* prattle, jabber, gab; see **babble.**

**blabber*,** *n.* — *Syn.* prattle, jabber, drivel; see **nonsense** 1.

**blabber*,** *v.* — *Syn.* chatter, prattle, gabble; see **babble.**

**blabbermouth*,** *n.* — *Syn.* chatterer, chatterbox, informer, motormouth*; see **gossip** 2, **tattletale.**

**black,** *modif.* **1.** [Opposite to white] — *Syn.* dark, blackish, ebony, jet, inky, raven, coal-black, dusky, dingy, murky, inklike, livid, somber, swarthy, swart, pitch-black, black as coal, black as pitch, black as jet, black as night, sooty, raven-hued, sable, somber, gun-metal, flat black, jet black, nigrous, nigrescent, atramentous, ebon-hued, black as the ace of spades*, black as a crow*. — *Ant.* WHITE, colored, colorful.

**2.** [Without light] — *Syn.* gloomy, shadowy, clouded, pitch-dark; see **dark** 1.

**3.** [Negroid; *often capitalized*] — *Syn.* Negro, African, African-American, colored, dark-skinned, black-skinned, dark-complexioned, Afro-American, Ethiopian, Nubian, Negrito, Melanesian, swarthy, dusky; see also **African** 2. — *Ant.* white, Caucasian, fair-skinned.

**4.** [Unpropitious] — *Syn.* threatening, foreboding, sinister; see **ominous.**

**5.** [Angry] — *Syn.* fierce, enraged, sour; see **angry.**

**6.** [Evil] — *Syn.* villainous, mean, diabolical; see **harmful, wicked** 1.

**7.** [Dirty] — *Syn.* soiled, stained, dingy; see **dirty** 1.

**8.** [Dismal] — *Syn.* melancholy, gloomy, somber, pessimistic; see **dismal** 1.

**black,** *n.* **1.** [A chromatic color least resembling white] — *Syn.* lampblack, carbon, jet, sable, ebony, darkest gray, charcoal, blackness, darkness. — *Ant.* WHITE, blond, brightness.

**2.** [A Negro; *often capitalized*] — *Syn.* black person, black man, black woman, African-American, person of color, Negro, African, colored person, colored man, colored woman, Afro-American, soul brother, soul sister, blood*; see also **Negro.**

**in the black** — *Syn.* successful, lucrative, gainful, operating at a profit; see **profitable.**

**black,** *v.* — *Syn.* darken, make black, blacken; see **shade** 2.

**blackball,** *v.* — *Syn.* ostracize, exclude, repudiate; see **bar** 2.

**blackbird,** *n.* Types of blackbirds include: (purple) grackle, (jack)daw, English thrush, red-winged blackbird, yellow-winged blackbird, rusty blackbird, yellow-headed blackbird, Brewer's blackbird; see also **bird** 1.

**blackboard,** *n.* — *Syn.* slate, board, chalkboard, wall-slate, greenboard.

**blacken,** *v.* **1.** [To make black] — *Syn.* darken, nigrify, make black, begrime; see **dirty, shade** 2.

**2.** [To smirch] — *Syn.* sully, tarnish, attack; see **slander.**

**3.** [To become black] — *Syn.* grow black, grow dark, dim, deepen; see **shade** 3.

**blackguard,** *n.* — *Syn.* villain, scoundrel, rogue; see **rascal.**

**blackjack,** *n.* — *Syn.* bat, stick, cudgel; see **club** 3.

**blacklist,** *v.* — *Syn.* bar, exclude, blackball; see **bar** 2, **denounce, ostracize.**

**black magic,** *n.* — *Syn.* sorcery, witchcraft, necromancy; see **magic** 1, 2.

**blackmail,** *n.* — *Syn.* hush money, protection*, extortion, shakedown*; see **bribe.**

**blackmail,** *v.* — *Syn.* extort, exact, coerce, shake down*; see **bribe, force** 1.

**blackness,** *n.* — *Syn.* gloom, duskiness, murkiness, negritude; see **darkness** 1.

**black out,** *v.* 1. [To delete] — *Syn.* rub out, eradicate, erase, obliterate; see **cancel** 1, **censor.**
2. [To faint] — *Syn.* pass out, lose consciousness, swoon; see **faint.**
3. [To darken] — *Syn.* put out the lights, make dark, batten, eclipse; see **shade** 2.

**black sheep,** *n.* — *Syn.* outcast, prodigal, reprobate; see **rascal, refugee.**

**blacksmith,** *n.* — *Syn.* metalworker, forger, smith, smithy; see **smith.**

**blade,** *n.* 1. [A cutting instrument] — *Syn.* edge, cutting edge, knife, sword; see **knife, razor, sword.**
2. [A relatively long leaf] — *Syn.* frond, spear, flag, shoot, lamina; see also **leaf** 1.

**blamable,** *modif.* — *Syn.* reprehensible, culpable, blameworthy; see **guilty** 2.

**blame,** *n.* 1. [Censure] — *Syn.* disapproval, condemnation, reprehension, castigation, remonstrance, denunciation, reprobation, disparagement, depreciation, animadversion, opposition, deprecation, abuse, opprobrium, contumely, objection, reproach, stricture, derogation, criticism, dispraise, disfavor, repudiation, disapprobation, reprimand, invective, slur, aspersion, accusation, reproof, attack, chiding, rebuke, vituperation, objurgation, impeachment, complaint, diatribe, tirade, charge, expostulation, indictment, recrimination, attribution, jeremiad, arraignment, implication, obloquy, imputation, exprobration, inculpation, incrimination, Philippic, reflection, discountenance, calumny, ascription, frowning upon. — *Ant.* PRAISE, commendation, appreciation.
2. [Responsibility] — *Syn.* culpability, answerability, liability, onus; see **guilt, responsibility** 2.
**to blame** — *Syn.* guilty, at fault, culpable, blamable; see **guilty** 2.

**blame,** *v.* 1. [To censure] — *Syn.* condemn, rebuke, criticize; see **censure.**
2. [To hold responsible for] — *Syn.* charge, indict, impute; see **accuse.**
See Synonym Study at CENSURE.

**blameless,** *modif.* — *Syn.* faultless, not guilty, inculpable; see **innocent** 1.

**blameworthy,** *modif.* — *Syn.* at fault, culpable, blamable, reprehensible; see **guilty** 2.

**blanch,** *v.* — *Syn.* whiten, etiolate, wash out, turn pale; see **bleach, whiten** 1.

**bland,** *modif.* 1. [Suave] — *Syn.* affable, agreeable, urbane; see **pleasant** 1, **suave.**
2. [Mild] — *Syn.* soothing, soft, smooth; see **mild** 4.
3. [Temperate; *said especially of weather*] — *Syn.* calm, clear, balmy; see **mild** 2.
4. [Flavorless] — *Syn.* flat, dull, insipid; see **tasteless** 1.
See Synonym Study at SOFT, SUAVE.

**blank,** *modif.* 1. [Without writing or other marks] — *Syn.* white, clear, virgin, fresh, unused, plain, empty, unmarked, untouched, pale, new, spotless, unadorned, bare; see also **clean** 1. — *Ant.* USED, inscribed, PRINTED.
2. [Without meaning or expression] — *Syn.* impassive, expressionless, vague, vacant, vacuous, dull, glazed, glassy-eyed, hollow, empty, meaningless, fruitless, noncommittal, uncommunicative, masklike, stiff, immobile, inscrutable, deadpan, poker-faced. — *Ant.* EXCITED, expressive, nervous.
3. [Without content] — *Syn.* void, barren, vacant, vacuous; see **empty** 1.
4. [Bewildered] — *Syn.* disconcerted, nonplused, confused, muddled; see **bewildered.**
5. [Complete] — *Syn.* utter, total, unconditional; see **absolute** 1.

**blank,** *n.* 1. [An empty space] — *Syn.* void, hollow, hole, cavity, vacancy, space, gulf, nothingness, emptiness, hollowness, vacuity, abyss, opening, vacuum, *tabula rasa* (Latin), hiatus, gap, interval, lacuna; see also **emptiness.**
2. [A form] — *Syn.* questionnaire, data sheet, information blank; see **form** 5.
**draw a blank*** — *Syn.* fail to remember, be unable to remember, lose one's memory, disremember*; see **forget** 1.

**blanket,** *modif.* — *Syn.* all-inclusive, sweeping, unconditional; see **absolute** 1, **comprehensive.**

**blanket,** *n.* 1. [A covering in the form of a layer] — *Syn.* sheet, sheath, strip, coating; see **cover** 2, **sheet** 2.
2. [Fabric used as a covering] — *Syn.* cover, quilt, plaid, fleece, lap robe, carriage robe, comforter, puff, featherbed, throw, afghan, stadium blanket, rug, mat, cloak; see also **bedding.**

**blanket,** *v.* — *Syn.* envelop, conceal, bury, overspread; see **cover** 1.

**blank out,** *v.* 1. [To cancel by covering over] — *Syn.* delete, erase, whiteout, cross out; see **cancel** 1.
2. [To become confused or forgetful] — *Syn.* lose one's memory, lose one's concentration, become abstracted, draw a blank*; see **forget** 1.

**blare,** *v.* — *Syn.* boom, trumpet, blast; see **sound** 1, **yell.**

**blarney,** *n.* — *Syn.* cajolery, blandishment, malarkey*; see **flattery, nonsense** 1.

**blasé,** *modif.* — *Syn.* unconcerned, unimpressed, nonchalant, jaded; see **bored, indifferent** 1.

**blaspheme,** *v.* — *Syn.* swear, revile, utter impieties; see **curse** 1, 2.

**blasphemous,** *modif.* — *Syn.* irreverent, profane, irreligious; see **impious.**

**blasphemy,** *n.* — *Syn.* impiety, sacrilege, profanity, irreverence, disrespect, swearing, cursing, obscenity, lewdness, reviling, scoffing, profanation, profaneness, desecration; see also **curse** 1, **heresy.** — *Ant.* worship, PIETY, prayer, reverence.

---

*SYN.* — **blasphemy,** the strongest of the following terms, is used of a remark deliberately mocking or contemptuous of God or something held as sacred; **profanity** applies to language that makes impious use of sacred names; **swearing** and **cursing,** in this connection, both refer to the utterance of profane oaths and imprecations, the latter more particularly to the calling down of evil upon someone or something

---

**blast,** *n.* 1. [An explosion] — *Syn.* burst, eruption, detonation; see **explosion** 1.
2. [A sudden force of wind] — *Syn.* gust, gale, draft, wind; see **wind** 1.
3. [A loud sound] — *Syn.* roar, din, bang, blare; see **noise** 1.
4. [An explosive charge] — *Syn.* gunpowder, TNT, explosive, dynamite; see **explosive.**
5. [*Fun] — *Syn.* excitement, amusement, good time; see **fun, thrill.**

*See Synonym Study at* WIND.

**(at) full blast**— *Syn.* at full speed, at full capacity, at full tilt, maximally, to the max\*; see also **completely, fast** 1.

**blast,** *v.* **1.** [To shatter by explosion] — *Syn.* blow up, dynamite, detonate; see **explode** 1.

**2.** [To ruin] — *Syn.* blight, shatter, annihilate, wreck; see **destroy** 1.

**3.** [To make a loud sound] — *Syn.* blare, boom, trumpet; see **sound** 1.

**blast off,** *v.* — *Syn.* take off, ascend, rocket, soar up; see **rise** 1.

**blatant,** *modif.* **1.** [Obvious] — *Syn.* obtrusive, glaring, plain, clear; see **obvious** 1, 2.

**2.** [Loud] — *Syn.* noisy, clamorous, vociferous, boisterous; see **loud** 2, **vociferous.**

*See Synonym Study at* VOCIFEROUS.

**blaze,** *n.* **1.** [Fire] — *Syn.* conflagration, flame, burning; see **fire** 1.

**2.** [Sudden or strong light] — *Syn.* burst, gleam, flash, beam; see **flash** 1.

*See Synonym Study at* FLAME.

**blaze,** *v.* — *Syn.* flame, flash, flare up; see **burn** 1.

**blaze away,** *v.* — *Syn.* shoot, fire away, discharge, blast; see **shoot** 1.

**bleach,** *v.* — *Syn.* blanch, fade, wash out, whiten, lighten, etiolate, achromatize, decolorize. — *Ant.* COLOR, dye, stain.

**bleachers,** *pl.n.* — *Syn.* grandstand, stands, seats, benches, boxes, tiers.

**bleak,** *modif.* **1.** [Applied to countryside or conditions] — *Syn.* dreary, desolate, bare, cheerless, wild, exposed, barren, blank, disheartening, weary, melancholy, lonely, flat, somber, grim, distressing, depressing, comfortless, hopeless, drear, joyless, uninviting, dull, sad, mournful, monotonous, waste, gloomy, dismal, unsheltered, windswept, treeless, frowning, blighted, blasted, unpopulated, desert, deserted, fog-hung, craggy, scorched, stony, burned (over), denuded, bombed, deforested, bulldozed, cleared, frozen. — *Ant.* verdant, GREEN, fruitful.

**2.** [Applied to atmosphere] — *Syn.* chill, windy, stormy, boisterous, cold, piercing, cutting, wintry, keen, biting, icy, hiemal, shivery, boreal, bitter, rigorous, chilly, nipping, severe, raw, freezing, inclement, frosty, pinching, glacial, polar, arctic, sharp, harsh, dank, foul, murky, misty, foggy, brumous. — *Ant.* MILD, pleasant, sunny.

**blear,** *v.* — *Syn.* dim, blur, obscure; see **shade** 2.

**bleary,** *modif.* **1.** [Blurry] — *Syn.* dim, blurred, indistinct; see **obscure** 1.

**2.** [Tired] — *Syn.* worn out, weary, bleary-eyed; see **tired.**

**bleed,** *v.* **1.** [To lose blood] — *Syn.* shed blood, be bleeding, have unstaunched wounds, hemorrhage, have a hemorrhage.

**2.** [To issue as blood] — *Syn.* fall drop by drop, gush, spurt, ooze; see **flow** 2.

**3.** [\*To extort money] — *Syn.* extort, impoverish, pauperize, exhaust one's resources, drain, bleed white\*, blackmail, confiscate, put the squeeze on\*, strong-arm\*, put the screws to\*; see also **steal.**

**4.** [To let blood] — *Syn.* cup, draw blood, take blood, open a vein, leech, phlebotomize.

**5.** [To suffer] — *Syn.* ache, agonize, grieve, be in pain; see **mourn** 1, **suffer** 1.

**6.** [To drain] — *Syn.* exhaust, reduce, get rid of, sap; see **drain** 1, 2, 3.

**blemish,** *n.* — *Syn.* flaw, defect, stain, spot, smudge,

imperfection, fault, shortcoming, disfigurement, defacement, blot, blur, chip, taint, tarnish, smirch, stigma, brand, deformity, dent, daub, discoloration, mole, nevus, pock, pockmark, blister, birthmark, wart, scar, impurity, speck, speckle, maculation, bruise, freckle, pimple, cicatrix, patch, blotch, lump, nodule, lentigo, smutch, zit\*, hickey\*; see also **lack** 2, **pimple.** — *Ant.* flawlessness, PERFECTION, purity.

*See Synonym Study at* DEFECT.

**blench,** *v.* — *Syn.* flinch, quail, shrink back; see **wince.**

**blend,** *n.* — *Syn.* combination, mixture, compound, amalgam, olio; see also **mixture** 1.

**blend,** *v.* — *Syn.* combine, mingle, compound, mix; see **mix** 1.

*See Synonym Study at* MIX.

**bless,** *v.* **1.** [To give] — *Syn.* endow, bestow, favor, grant, commend, endorse, approve, praise, extol, give one's blessing; see also **give** 1.

**2.** [To call the blessing of God upon] — *Syn.* commend to God, give benediction, pray for, make the sign of the cross, cross, sign, sprinkle with holy water, anoint, anoint with oil, invoke benefits upon, give a blessing, absolve. — *Ant.* CURSE, anathematize, imprecate.

**3.** [To make or pronounce holy] — *Syn.* baptize, canonize, glorify, honor, dedicate, dedicate to God, exalt, give benediction, absolve, anoint, ordain, hallow, consecrate, beatify, sanctify, enshrine, render acceptable to, sacrifice, confirm, laud. — *Ant.* sell to the devil, DAMN, condemn.

**blessed,** *modif.* **1.** [Joyful] — *Syn.* joyous, glad, content, blissful; see **happy** 1.

**2.** [Marked by God's favor, especially in heaven] — *Syn.* saved, redeemed, glorified, translated, exalted, rewarded, resurrected, enthroned among the angels, sanctified, glorious, beatified, holy, spiritual, religious. — *Ant.* lost, DOOMED, accursed.

**3.** [Consecrated] — *Syn.* sacred, dedicated, sanctified, holy; see **divine** 2.

**4.** [Fortunate] — *Syn.* favored, graced, lucky; see **fortunate** 1.

**5.** [\*Damned] — *Syn.* confounded\*, blamed\*, blasted\*, darned\*; see **damned** 2.

**blessing,** *n.* **1.** [An act or prayer of one who blesses] — *Syn.* benediction, benison, benedicite, commendation, sanctification, invocation, grace, laying on of hands, absolution, baptism, unction, consecration, Eucharist, divine approval, divine sanction, divine approbation. — *Ant.* damnation, CURSE, anathema.

**2.** [Anything that is very welcome] — *Syn.* boon, benefit, good, advantage, help, asset, good fortune, favor, stroke of luck, godsend, windfall, miracle, manna from heaven, break, lucky break; see also **advantage** 3, **aid** 1.

**3.** [Approval] — *Syn.* sanction, approbation, consent, good wishes; see **permission.** — *Ant.* OBSTACLE, disadvantage, nuisance.

**blight,** *n.* — *Syn.* disease, withering, mildew, scourge; see **affliction, decay** 1.

**blight,** *v.* — *Syn.* damage, spoil, ruin; see **decay.**

**blind,** *modif.* **1.** [Without sight] — *Syn.* sightless, unseeing, eyeless, blinded, visionless, in darkness, dim-sighted, visually impaired, groping (in the dark), deprived of sight, sun-blind, purblind, undiscerning, stone-blind, moon-blind, blind as a bat\*. — *Ant.* OBSERVANT, seeing, sighted, keen-sighted.

**2.** [Without thought or reason] — *Syn.* heedless, irrational, impetuous, unthinking; see **careless** 1, **rash.**

**3.** [Without perceiving or understanding] — *Syn.* obtuse, unseeing, unaware, oblivious, unconscious, imperceptive, undiscerning, by guesswork, by calculation, with instruments; see also **unaware**. — *Ant.* OBSERVANT, perceptive, discerning.

**4.** [Without passage] — *Syn.* obstructed, blocked, without egress; see **tight** 2.

**5.** [Concealed] — *Syn.* secluded, obscured, out of sight; see **hidden** 2.

**6.** [Random] — *Syn.* chance, accidental, unplanned; see **accidental** 1.

**blind**, *n.* **1.** [An obstruction to light or sight] — *Syn.* blindfold, blinder, blinker, shade, Venetian blind, window shade, mini-blind, vertical blind, shutter, screen; see also **curtain, veil** 2.

**2.** [Something intended to deceive] — *Syn.* front, cover, trap, decoy; see **camouflage** 1, **trick** 1.

**blind**, *v.* **1.** [To obscure] — *Syn.* darken, shadow, dim, blindfold; see **shade** 1, 2.

**2.** [To deceive] — *Syn.* conceal, delude, mislead, dazzle; see **deceive.**

**blindly**, *modif.* **1.** [Without direction] — *Syn.* at random, wildly, in all directions, frantically, instinctively, madly, purposelessly, aimlessly, confusedly, indiscriminately, pell-mell. — *Ant.* directly, PURPOSELY, straightforwardly.

**2.** [Without thought or judgment] — *Syn.* heedlessly, carelessly, recklessly, passionately, tumultuously, wildly, thoughtlessly, regardlessly, impulsively, inconsiderately, willfully, obtusely, purblindly, unreasonably, unreasoningly, without (rhyme or) reason, senselessly; see also **carelessly, foolishly.** — *Ant.* thoughtfully, CAREFULLY, prudently.

**blindness**, *n.* **1.** [Loss of vision] — *Syn.* sightlessness, stone blindness, purblindness, visual impairment, nearsightedness, myopia, astigmatism, night blindness, day blindness, snow blindness, moon blindness, color blindness, fairsightedness, presbyopia, amblyopia, tunnel vision, darkness. — *Ant.* SIGHT, VISION, seeing.

**2.** [Insensitivity] — *Syn.* obtuseness, unawareness, apathy, inattention; see **carelessness, ignorance** 1, 2, **indifference** 1, **stupidity** 2.

**blind spot**, *n.* — *Syn.* obstruction, lack of perception, mote in one's eye, oversight, failing, unseen area; see also **blindness** 1, **fault** 2, **weakness** 2.

**blink**, *v.* **1.** [To wink rapidly] — *Syn.* flicker, bat one's eyes, flutter one's eyelids, nictitate; see **wink** 1.

**2.** [To squint] — *Syn.* screw up the eyes, peek, peep; see **squint.**

**3.** [To twinkle] — *Syn.* glimmer, flicker, flash, glitter; see **shine** 1.

*See Synonym Study at* WINK.

**blink at**, *v.* — *Syn.* ignore, condone, disregard, wink at; see **approve** 1, **neglect** 1, **wink at.**

**bliss**, *n.* — *Syn.* joy, rapture, ecstasy; see **happiness** 2, **pleasure** 1, **rapture** 2.

*See Synonym Study at* RAPTURE.

**blissful**, *modif.* — *Syn.* joyful, delightful, ecstatic; see **happy** 1, **pleasant** 2.

**blister**, *n.* — *Syn.* vesicle, bleb, sac, bulla, wheal, wale, weal, welt, blood blister, water blister, second-degree burn; see also **injury** 1, **sore.**

**blister**, *v.* — *Syn.* scald, irritate, mark; see **burn** 2, 6, **hurt** 1.

**blithe**, *modif.* — *Syn.* gay, carefree, joyful, cheerful; see **happy** 1.

**blitz**, *n.* — *Syn.* blitzkrieg, lightning attack, barrage, onslaught; see **attack** 1.

**blitzkrieg**, *n.* — *Syn.* blitz, raid, assault, lightning attack; see **attack** 1.

**blizzard**, *n.* — *Syn.* snowstorm, snow squall, tempest, blast; see **storm** 1.

**bloc**, *n.* — *Syn.* coalition, alliance, cabal, ring; see **alliance** 3, **faction** 1.

**block**, *n.* **1.** [A mass, usually with flat surfaces] — *Syn.* slab, chunk, piece, square, cake, cube, slice, segment, loaf, clod, bar, ingot, oblong, section, mill end, hunk*; see also **brick, slab, stone.**

**2.** [The area between streets] — *Syn.* square, city square, lots, neighborhood; see **neighborhood.**

**3.** [The distance of the side of a block, sense 2] — *Syn.* street, city block, intersection; see **distance** 3.

**4.** [An obstruction] — *Syn.* hindrance, bar, obstacle; see **barrier.**

**5.** [In sports, an obstruction to a move or play] — *Syn.* charge, tackle, check, body check, body block, running block, cross-body block, downfield block, pick (*in basketball*).

**6.** [A massive object] — *Syn.* chunk, mass, impediment, solid, cylinder block, slab, base; see also sense 1.

**7.** [A pulley] — *Syn.* sheave, wheel, hoist, rope-block, chain-block, lift.

**8.** [A chunk used for chopping] — *Syn.* chopping block, slab, breadboard, cheeseboard, table, butcher block, cutting board.

**9.** [Place of execution] — *Syn.* headsman's block, guillotine, scaffold, stake, tree, cross, gibbet; see also **gallows.**

**knock someone's block off*** — *Syn.* thrash, hit, beat up; see **beat** 2.

**block**, *v.* **1.** [To impede] — *Syn.* obstruct, interfere with, prevent, close off; see **bar** 1, **hinder.**

**2.** [In sports, to impede a play] — *Syn.* throw a block, tackle, charge, check, block out, take out of play.

**3.** [To shape on or as if on a block] — *Syn.* press, shape, reshape, mold; see **form** 1.

*See Synonym Study at* HINDER.

**blockade**, *n.* — *Syn.* barricade, encirclement, bar, siege; see **barrier.**

**run the blockade** — *Syn.* break through (a blockade), go past, overcome an obstacle; see **penetrate** 1.

**blockhead**, *n.* — *Syn.* nitwit, fool, imbecile; see **fool** 1.

**blockhouse**, *n.* — *Syn.* stockade, fort, outpost; see **fortification** 2.

**block out**, *v.* **1.** [To obscure] — *Syn.* conceal, screen, cover; see **hide** 1.

**2.** [To plan] — *Syn.* outline, sketch, chart; see **plan** 2.

**block up**, *v.* — *Syn.* obstruct, barricade, dam; see **bar** 1.

**blond**, *modif.* — *Syn.* blonde, fair, fair-skinned, pale, light, ash-blond, platinum-blond, strawberry-blond, bleached, blanched, light-complexioned, washed-out, sallow, high in tone, pearly, platinum, towheaded, flaxen, snowy, ivory, creamy, whitish, milky, albino, lily-white, pallid, light-haired, golden-haired, fair-haired, yellow-haired, sandy-haired, faded, colorless, white-skinned, bleached-blond, natural-blond, peroxide blond, bottle-blond. — *Ant.* DARK, brunet, swarthy.

**blood**, *n.* **1.** [Fluid in the mammalian circulatory system] — *Syn.* lifeblood, heart's blood, vital fluid, vital juices, gore, sanguine fluid, hemoglobin, plasma, serum.

**2.** [Lineage] — *Syn.* stock, ancestry, descent, line; see **family** 1.

**bad blood** — *Syn.* malice, rancor, feud; see **anger, hatred** 2.

**have someone's blood on one's head** *or* **hands** — *Syn.* be blamable, be culpable, be responsible; see **guilty** 2.

**in cold blood** — *Syn.* deliberately, intentionally, willfully, dispassionately; see **deliberately.** — *Syn.* cruelly, heartlessly, ruthlessly; see **brutally.**

**make one's blood boil**— *Syn.* disturb, infuriate, agitate; see **anger** 1.

**make one's blood run cold**— *Syn.* terrify, horrify, scare; see **frighten** 1.

**blooded**, *modif.*— *Syn.* thoroughbred, pedigreed, choice, purebred, fullblooded, legitimate, fancy, highbred, aristocratic, patrician, highborn, registered, quality; see also **genuine** 1, **noble** 3.— *Ant.* BASTARD, mongrel, scrub.

**bloodless**, *modif.* **1.** [Pale]— *Syn.* pallid, wan, anemic; see **pale** 1.
**2.** [Coldhearted]— *Syn.* unemotional, unfeeling, unkind; see **indifferent** 1.
**3.** [Listless]— *Syn.* indolent, sluggish, lazy; see **slow** 2.

**bloodshed**, *n.*— *Syn.* slaughter, butchery, gore, killing; see **battle** 2, **carnage**, **murder**.

**bloodshot**, *modif.*— *Syn.* inflamed, bloody, streaked, red; see **inflamed** 2.

**bloodthirsty**, *modif.*— *Syn.* murderous, homicidal, savage, ruthless; see **cruel** 2, **ferocious, fierce** 1, **murderous, savage** 2.

**bloody**, *modif.* **1.** [Showing blood]— *Syn.* bleeding, bloodstained, blood-spattered, gory, gaping, unstaunched, grisly, crimson, open, wounded, dripping blood, hematic, raw, blood-soaked, hemorrhaging. — *Ant.* UNHURT, WHOLE, uninjured.
**2.** [Fiercely fought]— *Syn.* gory, sanguinary, savage, fierce, heavy, hand-to-hand, murderous, decimating, expensive, Pyrrhic, suicidal; see also **ferocious, fierce** 1, **savage** 2.— *Ant.* EASY, light, desultory.
**3.** [*British** Disapproved of]— *Syn.* rotten, vile, cursed; see **damned** 2.
**4.** [*British** Very]— *Syn.* extremely, exceedingly, excessively; see **very**.

**bloom**, *n.*— *Syn.* flower, blossom, floweret, efflorescence; see **flower** 1.

**bloom**, *v.*— *Syn.* flower, blossom, effloresce, burst into bloom, open, bud, sprout, burgeon, prosper, grow, develop, wax, bear fruit, thrive, germinate, flourish, be in health, fructify, tassel out, display petals, blow, come out in flower, put forth flowers, be in flower, be in the flowering stage.

**bloomers**, *pl.n.*— *Syn.* breeches, drawers, trunks; see **pants** 1, 2.

**blooming**, *modif.*— *Syn.* flowering, blossoming, in flower, efflorescent, opening, flourishing, thriving, glowing, radiant, sprouting, burgeoning, bearing fruit, budding, tasseling; see also **budding, growing**.

**blossom**, *n.*— *Syn.* bloom, flower, floweret, bud; see **flower** 1.

**blossom**, *v.*— *Syn.* flower, blow, burst into blossom; see **bloom**.

**blossoming**, *n.*— *Syn.* blooming, flowering, efflorescence, flourishing, budding, fructification, waxing, thriving, developing.

**blot**, *n.*— *Syn.* spot, stain, smudge, splotch; see **blemish, stain**.

**blot**, *v.* **1.** [To stain]— *Syn.* smudge, blotch, spatter, sully; see **dirty, disgrace**.
**2.** [To absorb]— *Syn.* soak up, dry, sponge; see **absorb** 1.

**blotch**, *n.*— *Syn.* blot, stain, spot; see **blemish, stain**.

**blot out**, *v.* **1.** [To mark out]— *Syn.* deface, cross out, scratch out, delete; see **cancel** 1.
**2.** [To obscure]— *Syn.* darken, blur, shroud, eclipse; see **shade** 2.

**blotter**, *n.*— *Syn.* blotting paper, (desk) pad, ink absorber, pen-wiper.

**blouse**, *n.*— *Syn.* shirt, shirtwaist, pullover, turtleneck,

shell, bodysuit, V-neck, man-tailored blouse, overblouse, peasant blouse, middy blouse, shirt, camp shirt, top, waist; see also **clothes, shirt**.

**blow**, *n.* **1.** [A heavy physical stroke]— *Syn.* hit, strike, punch, buffet, swing, bump, wallop, rap, bang, whack, thwack, cuff, box, uppercut, dint, knock, clout, slam, bruise, swipe, thump, kick, stroke, buck, rabbit punch, jab, gouge, lunge, thrust, swat, poke, prod, slap, smack, the old one-two*, bat*, sock*, clip*, belt*, slug*, cut*, bop*, bonk*, whop*, bash*, biff*, lick*, crack*, haymaker*, roundhouse*, a knuckle sandwich*, kayo* or K.O*.
**2.** [A catastrophe]— *Syn.* setback, calamity, tragedy, shock; see **disaster, surprise** 2.
**3.** [A heavy wind]— *Syn.* blast, gale, typhoon, hurricane; see **wind** 1.

**blow**, *v.* **1.** [To send forth air rapidly]— *Syn.* puff, blast, pant, exhale, fan, whiff, whisk, whisper, puff away, huff, waft, breathe, whistle, bluster.
**2.** [To move rapidly; *said of air*]— *Syn.* rush, whirl, stream, storm; see **flow** 1.
**3.** [To carry on the wind]— *Syn.* waft, flutter, bear, whisk, drive, fling, whirl, flap, flip, wave, buffet, sweep.
**4.** [To play a wind instrument]— *Syn.* pipe, toot, mouth; see **play** 3.
**5.** [To sound when blown]— *Syn.* trumpet, vibrate, blare, honk; see **sound** 1.
**6.** [To give form by inflation]— *Syn.* inflate, swell, puff up, pump up; see **fill** 1.
**7.** [*To leave suddenly]— *Syn.* go, depart, leave town; see **leave** 1.
**8.** [*To boast]— *Syn.* brag, swagger, bluster; see **boast** 1.
**9.** [*To fail]— *Syn.* miss, flounder, miscarry; see **fail** 1.
**10.** [*To spend]— *Syn.* lay out, pay out, waste, squander; see **spend** 1, **waste** 2.

**blow in***, *v.*— *Syn.* arrive, appear, reach, land; see **arrive** 1.

**blowing**, *modif.* **1.** [Agitating the air]— *Syn.* blasting, puffing, fanning, panting, whisking, breathing, gasping, whistling.
**2.** [Being agitated by the air]— *Syn.* fluttering, flapping, waving, streaming, flying, whipping, drifting, tumbling, gliding, straining, whirling; see also **flying**. — *Ant.* standing still, FALLING, hovering.

**blown**, *modif.*— *Syn.* buffeted, blasted, windblown, puffed, fluttered, flung, fanned, waved, flapped, whisked, whirled, flicked, wafted.— *Ant.* QUIET, still, sucked in.

**blowout**, *n.* **1.** [The result of bursting]— *Syn.* tear, break, puncture, rupture, leak, gap, seam, flat tire, flat*; see also **hole** 2.
**2.** [*A celebration or party]— *Syn.* riot, spree, bash*, binge*; see **party** 1.

**blow out**, *v.* **1.** [To extinguish]— *Syn.* put out, dampen, snuff; see **extinguish** 1.
**2.** [To burst]— *Syn.* shatter, erupt, rupture; see **explode** 1.

**blowup**, *n.* **1.** [An explosion]— *Syn.* eruption, blast, detonation; see **explosion** 1.
**2.** [*An angry outburst]— *Syn.* explosion, outburst, flareup; see **dispute, fit** 2.

**blow up**, *v.* **1.** [To fill]— *Syn.* pump up, puff up, swell, inflate; see **fill** 1.
**2.** [To explode]— *Syn.* erupt, rupture, burst, go off; see **explode** 1.
**3.** [To destroy with explosives]— *Syn.* bomb, dynamite, detonate; see **attack** 1, **bomb, destroy** 1.
**4.** [To magnify]— *Syn.* enlarge, enlarge on, exaggerate,

overstate; see **exaggerate, increase** 1.

**5.** [*To lose one's temper] — *Syn.* become angry *or* enraged, rave, lose self-control; see **rage** 1.

**blubber,** *n.* — *Syn.* suet, lard, tallow; see **fat.**

**blue,** *modif.* **1.** [One of the primary colors] — *Syn.* of the color of the sky, azure, cerulean, sky-blue.

Hues of blue include: indigo, watchet, sapphire, sapphirine, turquoise, smalt, lapis lazuli, aquamarine, aqua, blue-black, blue-green; royal, Prussian, navy, Dumont's, king's, starch, powder, baby, Paris, cobalt, Antwerp, Haarlem, mineral, Parma, Napoleon, Chinese, robin's egg, pale, teal, sky, slate, light, dark, deep, livid, electric, etc., blue.

**2.** [*Despondent] — *Syn.* depressed, moody, melancholy; see **sad** 1.

**once in a blue moon** — *Syn.* rarely, infrequently, once in a while; see **seldom.**

**blue,** *n.* **1.** [One of the primary colors] — *Syn.* blueness, bluing, azure, sky blue; see **blue** (*modif.*) 1, **color** 1.

**2.** [Heavens] — *Syn.* sky, vault of the sky, ether, the wild blue yonder*; see **heaven** 1, **sky, space** 1.

**out of the blue** — *Syn.* unforeseen, surprising, sudden, unanticipated; see **unexpected.**

**bluebell,** *n.* — *Syn.* harebell, bluebell of Scotland, campanula, bellflower, Virginia bluebell; see also **flower** 2.

**blue-blooded,** *modif.* — *Syn.* pedigreed, thoroughbred, purebred; see **blooded, genuine** 1, **noble** 3.

**bluejay,** *n.* — *Syn.* jay, common jay, jaybird; see **bird** 1.

**blueprint,** *n.* — *Syn.* plan, diagram, outline, draft; see **design** 1, **plan** 1, 2.

**blues,** *pl.n.* **1.** [A state of despondency; *often with* the] — *Syn.* depressed spirits, heaviness of heart, melancholy, dejection; see **gloom** 2.

**2.** [Rhythmic lamentation in a minor key] — *Syn.* dirge, lament, torch song, jazz, funk, soul music, rhythm and blues; see also **music** 1.

**bluff,** *modif.* — *Syn.* outspoken, crusty, hearty; see **abrupt** 2, **blunt** 2, **rude** 1.

*See Synonym Study at* BLUNT.

**bluff,** *n.* **1.** [A bank] — *Syn.* cliff, precipice, steep; see **hill, mountain** 1.

**2.** [A trick] — *Syn.* ruse, deception, delusion; see **trick** 1.

**bluff,** *v.* — *Syn.* fool, mislead, feign, four-flush*; see **deceive, pretend** 1.

**bluing,** *n.* — *Syn.* whitener, bleach, rinse, solution. See **solution** 2.

**bluish,** *modif.* — *Syn.* somewhat blue, pale blue, blue-gray; see **blue** 1.

**blunder,** *n.* — *Syn.* mistake, lapse, oversight, gaffe; see **error** 1.

*See Synonym Study at* ERROR.

**blunder,** *v.* — *Syn.* flounder, bumble, bungle, goof*; see **botch, fail** 1.

**blunt,** *modif.* **1.** [Dull] — *Syn.* dull, unsharpened, unpointed, round; see **dull** 1.

*See Synonym Study at* DULL.

**2.** [Abrupt] — *Syn.* brusque, curt, bluff, gruff, candid, frank, direct, forthright, plain-spoken, outspoken, straightforward, unceremonious, undiplomatic, inconsiderate, thoughtless, tactless, impolite, rough, short; see also **abrupt** 2, **frank.**

---

*SYN.* — **blunt** implies a candor and tactlessness that show little regard for another's feelings /"You're a fool," was his *blunt* reply/; **bluff** suggests a coarse heartiness of manner and a good nature that causes the candor to seem inoffensive /a *bluff* old gardener/; **brusque** implies apparent rudeness, as evidenced by abruptness of speech

or behavior /a *brusque* rejection/; **curt** suggests a terseness of expression that implies a lack of tact or courtesy /a *curt* dismissal/; **gruff** suggests bad temper and roughness of speech and manner, connoting, in addition, a harshness or throatiness in utterance /a *gruff* sergeant/ *See also Synonym Study at* DULL.

---

**blur,** *v.* **1.** [To dim] — *Syn.* obscure, blear, dim, cloud; see **shade** 2.

**2.** [To stain] — *Syn.* blemish, smudge, blot, smear; see **dirty.**

**blurt out,** *v.* — *Syn.* speak unthinkingly, divulge, burst out with, gush; see **exclaim, tell** 1, **utter.**

**blush,** *v.* — *Syn.* change color, flush, redden, turn red, turn scarlet, color, crimson, mantle, glow, have rosy cheeks, have heightened color.

**blushing,** *modif.* — *Syn.* coloring, reddening, turning red, turning scarlet, flushing, glowing, changing color, mantling, burning, red-faced, embarrassed, ashamed, rubescent, red as fire, red as a rose, rosy-red, with burning cheeks; see also **ashamed.**

**bluster,** *v.* — *Syn.* rant, rave, brag, boast, crow, gloat, swagger, swell, vapor, strut, roister, bully, brazen, hector, badger, bulldoze, talk big, give oneself airs, show off, shoot off one's mouth*, blow off*; see also **boast** 1.

**boar,** *n.* — *Syn.* male hog, sire, pig; see **hog** 1.

**board,** *n.* **1.** [A piece of thin lumber] — *Syn.* plank, lath, strip, slat; see **beam** 1, **lumber.**

**2.** [Meals] — *Syn.* food, mess, fare, provisions, keep, victuals, rations, eats*; see also **food, meal** 2.

**3.** [A body of men having specific responsibilities] — *Syn.* jury, council, cabinet; see **committee.**

**across the board** — *Syn.* equally, impartially, fairly; see **equally.**

**go by the board** — *Syn.* be lost, be ignored, go, vanish; see **fail** 1.

**on board** — *Syn.* present, in transit, loaded, en route; see **aboard, shipped.**

**board,** *v.* **1.** [To cover] — *Syn.* plank, tile, paper, batten; see **cover** 1.

**2.** [To go aboard] — *Syn.* mount, embark, embus, entrain, enplane, put to sea, cast off, go on board, get on; see also **climb** 2, **leave** 1. — *Ant.* disembark, get off, go ashore.

**3.** [To take care of] — *Syn.* lodge, room, put up, harbor, bed, accommodate, feed, house, care for, let crash*; see also **accommodate** 3, **feed.** — *Ant.* NEGLECT, reject, starve.

**boarder,** *n.* — *Syn.* guest, paying guest, lodger, roomer, diner, patron, resident, star boarder*.

**boast,** *n.* — *Syn.* brag, bragging, vaunt, source of pride, gasconade, pretension, self-satisfaction, avowal, bravado, bluster.

**boast,** *v.* **1.** [To brag] — *Syn.* gloat, triumph, brag, swagger, exult, crow, show off, vaunt, swell, strut, bluff, flaunt, bluster, bully, swash, vapor, gasconade, flourish, parade, congratulate oneself, plume oneself, flatter oneself, pat oneself on the back, sing one's own praises, talk big*, blow*, sound off*, mouth off*, hug oneself*, pat oneself on the back, puff oneself up*, blow one's own trumpet*, blow one's own horn*, draw the longbow*, give oneself airs*. — *Ant.* APOLOGIZE, humble oneself, be self-deprecating.

**2.** [To have to one's credit] — *Syn.* possess, pride oneself on, claim; see **own** 1.

---

*SYN.* — **boast,** the basic term in this list, may suggest either reasonable or excessive pride or satisfaction, as in one's deeds or abilities /you may well *boast* of your efficiency/; **brag** suggests greater ostentation and overstatement /always *bragging* about the famous people she knew/; **vaunt**, a formal, literary term, implies greater suavity but more vainglory than either of the preceding /*vaunting* of his prowess/; **swagger** suggests a proclaiming of one's superiority in an insolent or overbearing way; **crow** suggests loud boasting in exultation or triumph /*crowing* over their victory/

**boastful,** *modif.* — *Syn.* bragging, pretentious, bombastic, braggart; see **egotistic** 2, **proud** 2.

**boat,** *n.* — *Syn.* vessel, bark, sailboat, yacht, steamboat, craft, watercraft, bottom, hulk; see also **ship**.
Types of small boats include: rowboat, shell, scull, kayak, dugout, canoe, scow, jolly boat, raft, pinnace, launch, cockboat, motorboat, shallop, dory, Johnboat, galiot, catboat, tartan, sharp, pulk, hydrofoil, speedboat, sunfish, yawl, iceboat, sloop, cutter, ketch, schooner, gig, lifeboat, tugboat, barge, cockleshell, wherry, punt, outrigger, dinghy, pontoon, bateau, pirogue, racer, hydroplane, catamaran, trimaran, skiff, umiak, gondola, proa, longboat, coracle, war canoe, clam boat, Baltimore buckeye, settee, bombard, flatboat, junk, collapsible boat, sponson, sharpie, ferry, houseboat, river boat, canal boat.
**in the same boat\*** — *Syn.* in the same situation, in the same predicament, on the same footing, in the same fix\*; see **equal**.
**miss the boat\*** — *Syn.* miss, fall short, neglect, blow it\*; see **fail** 1.
**rock the boat\*** — *Syn.* upset, disturb, disrupt, make waves\*; see **confuse**.

**boating,** *n.* — *Syn.* rowing, sculling, canoeing, sailing, kayaking, rafting, paddling, drifting, trawling, yachting, cruising, navigation.

**bob,** *n.* — *Syn.* duck, nod, weave, bow, curtsey, genuflection, quaver, wobble, twist, inclination, jerk, motion, gesture, quiver, falter, sway, swing, fall.

**bob,** *v.* **1.** [To move jerkily down and up] — *Syn.* duck, bounce, curtsey; see **bounce** 1, **bow** 1.
**2.** [To cut short] — *Syn.* crop, dock, clip; see **cut** 1, **trim** 1.

**bobbed,** *modif.* — *Syn.* clipped, shortened, curtailed, cut, coiffed, cropped, docked, trimmed.

**bobcat,** *n.* — *Syn.* wildcat, lynx, *Lynx rufus* (Latin), catamount, mountain cat; see also **cat** 2.

**bobsled,** *n.* — *Syn.* sleigh, bobsleigh, coaster, toboggan; see **sled** 1, 2.

**bobwhite,** *n.* — *Syn.* quail, partridge, *Colinus* (Latin); see **bird** 1.

**bodiless,** *modif.* — *Syn.* incorporeal, insubstantial, spiritual; see **immaterial** 2.

**bodily,** *modif.* **1.** [Concerning the body] — *Syn.* corporeal, corporal, physical, carnal, fleshly, somatic, incarnate, mortal, gross, hylic, solid, unspiritual, worldly, tangible, material, substantial, human, animal, natural, constitutional, organic; see also **biological, physical** 1, **real** 2.
**2.** [As a whole] — *Syn.* entirely, totally, absolutely; see **completely**.

**SYN. — bodily** refers to the human body as distinct from the mind or spirit /*bodily* ills/; **physical**, while often interchangeable with **bodily**, suggests somewhat less directly the anatomy and physiology of the body /*physical* exercise/; **corporeal** refers to the material substance of the body and is opposed to *spiritual* /his *corporeal* remains/; **corporal** refers to the effect of something upon

the body /*corporal* punishment/; **somatic** is a scientific word and refers to the body as distinct from the psyche, with no philosophic or poetic overtones /the *somatic* differences between individuals/

**body,** *n.* **1.** [The physical structure of a human or animal] — *Syn.* frame, corporeal frame, physique, anatomy, form, figure, shape, make, mortal part, build, physical makeup, flesh and bones, carcass\*, tenement of clay\*.
**2.** [A corpse] — *Syn.* corpse, cadaver, dead body, remains, *corpus delicti* (Latin), dust, clay, carcass, relics, the dead, the deceased, the departed, mummy, skeleton, ashes, carrion, organic remains, mortal remains, bones, *reliquiae* (Latin), cold meat\*, stiff\*.
**3.** [The torso] — *Syn.* trunk, figure, form, shape, build.
**4.** [The central portion of an object] — *Syn.* chassis, basis, groundwork, frame, fuselage, assembly, trunk, hull, bed, box, substructure, skeleton, scaffold, anatomy, bones\*, guts\*; see **essence** 1, **foundation** 2.
**5.** [The central portion of a composition] — *Syn.* dissertation, discourse, thesis, treatise, argument, material, heart, evidence, demonstration, exposition, gist; see also **basis** 1, **essence** 1, **theory** 1. — *Ant.* INTRODUCTION, preface, preamble.
**6.** [Individuals having an organization] — *Syn.* society, group, party; see **organization** 3.
**7.** [A unified or organized mass] — *Syn.* aggregate, mass, bulk, variety; see **collection** 2, **whole**.
**8.** [Full consistency] — *Syn.* substance, fullness, richness, thickness; see **consistency** 2, **density** 1.
**keep body and soul together** — *Syn.* stay alive, endure, earn a living; see **survive** 1.
**over one's dead body** — *Syn.* not if one can help it, not on one's life, by no means, not at all, no way\*.

**SYN. — body** refers to the whole physical substance of a person or animal, whether dead or alive; **corpse** and the euphemistic **remains** refer to a dead human body; **carcass** is used of the dead body of an animal or, contemptuously or humorously, of the living or dead body of a human being; **cadaver** refers primarily to a dead human body used for medical dissection

**bog,** *n.* — *Syn.* marsh, lowland, peat bog; see **swamp**.

**bogus,** *modif.* — *Syn.* false, sham, counterfeit; see **false** 2, 3.
*See Synonym Study at* FALSE.

**bogy,** *n.* — *Syn.* goblin, spook, bogeyman, bugbear; see **bugbear, fairy, ghost** 1.

**Bohemian,** *modif.* — *Syn.* nonconformist, unorthodox, beat, hippie; see **unconventional**.

**Bohemian,** *n.* — *Syn.* beatnik, hippie, nonconformist, iconoclast; see **beatnik, nonconformist**.

**boil,** *v.* **1.** [To subject to or continue boiling] — *Syn.* seethe, simmer, bubble, stew, steam, parboil, blanch, poach, coddle, scald, heat, brew, steep, boil over, evaporate, sterilize, autoclave; see also **cook**.
**2.** [To seethe] — *Syn.* effervesce, gurgle, percolate, seethe, churn, froth, foam, ferment, surge, tumble, burble; see also **bubble**.
**3.** [To be angry] — *Syn.* fume, seethe, sputter, quiver with rage; see **fume, rage** 1.

**SYN. — boil,** the basic word, refers to the bubbling up and vaporization of a liquid over direct heat or, metaphorically, to great agitation, as with rage /it made my blood *boil*/; **seethe** suggests violent boiling with much bubbling and foaming or, in an extended sense, excitement /the country *seethed* with rebellion/; **simmer** implies a gentle, continuous cooking at or just below the boiling point or, metaphorically, imminence of eruption, as in anger or revolt; **stew** refers to slow, prolonged boiling or, in an extended colloquial sense, unrest caused by worry, anxiety, or resentment

**boil away,** *v.* — *Syn.* steam, vaporize, dissipate; see **evaporate** 1.

**boil down,** *v.* — *Syn.* condense, summarize, sum up; see **decrease** 2.

**boiler,** *n.* — *Syn.* double boiler, evaporator, hot-water cooker, kettle; see **pan, pot** 1.

**boiling,** *modif.* **1.** [Cooking] — *Syn.* stewing, steeping, percolating, steaming, bubbling, seething, simmering, evaporating, distilling, boiling over; see also **cooking** 1.
**2.** [Hot] — *Syn.* warm, scorching, torrid; see **hot** 1.
**3.** [Angry] — *Syn.* raging, fuming, infuriated; see **angry.**

**boisterous,** *modif.* — *Syn.* tumultuous, uproarious, noisy, rowdy; see **loud** 2, **rude** 2, **vociferous.**
*See Synonym Study at* VOCIFEROUS.

**bold,** *modif.* **1.** [Courageous] — *Syn.* intrepid, fearless, daring; see **brave** 1.
**2.** [Impertinent] — *Syn.* brazen, forward, audacious, presumptuous; see **rude** 2.
**3.** [Prominent] — *Syn.* strong, clear, plain, striking; see **bright** 2, **definite** 2.
*See Synonym Study at* BRAVE.

**boldly,** *modif.* **1.** [*Said of animate beings*] — *Syn.* impetuously, headlong, intrepidly, fearlessly, with hardihood, recklessly, courageously, bravely, dauntlessly, daringly, forwardly, venturesomely, valiantly, stoutly, resolutely, brazenly, audaciously, saucily, firmly. — *Ant.* COWARDLY, fearfully, cravenly, cautiously.
**2.** [*Said of inanimate objects*] — *Syn.* prominently, conspicuously, saliently, sharply, clearly, plainly, openly, abruptly, steeply, eminently, vividly, strongly, palpably, commandingly, compellingly, showily, strikingly. — *Ant.* OBSCURELY, inconspicuously, unobtrusively.

**boldness,** *n.* — *Syn.* audacity, hardihood, self-reliance; see **courage** 1, **rudeness.**

**Bolshevik,** *n.* **1.** [An adherent of the Bolsheviki] — *Syn.* Marxist, revolutionary, Soviet, Communist, Marxian socialist, Bolshevist, Commie*, Red*.
**2.** [A radical; *usually lower case*] — *Syn.* revolutionary, extremist, radical, anarchist; see **radical, rebel** 1.

**bolster,** *v.* — *Syn.* prop, hold up, reinforce, sustain; see **support** 1, 2.

**bolt,** *n.* **1.** [A rod used for fastening] — *Syn.* screw, brad, nut, skewer, peg, dowel, rivet, pin, spike, stud, coupling, kingbolt, key, lag screw, toggle bolt, pin, pipe, rod, bar, latch; see also **lock** 1, **nail, screw.**
**2.** [A roll of goods or paper] — *Syn.* cylinder, roll, length, package, spindle, curl, coil, spiral, twist.
**3.** [Lightning] — *Syn.* stroke of lightning, sheet of lightning, thunderbolt, flash, stroke, discharge, fulguration, shock.

**bomb,** *n.* — *Syn.* weapon, missile, high explosive, charge, bombshell, grenade; see also **explosive, mine** 2, **nuclear bomb, shell** 2.
Types of bombs include: incendiary, multiple warhead, nuclear warhead, magnesium, high explosive, demolition, glider, jet-propulsion, time, letter, pipe, smart, plastic, six-ton, chain detonation, smoke, delayed-action, cyanide, parachute, antipersonnel bomb; atom(ic) bomb *or* A-bomb, cobalt bomb *or* C-bomb, hydrogen bomb *or* H-bomb, neutron bomb, napalm bomb, rack of bombs, cluster bomb unit *or* CBU, salvo

of bombs, torpedo, depth charge, cherry bomb, hand grenade; blockbuster*, ash can*, pineapple*, potato masher*, Molotov cocktail*, stink bomb*.

**bomb,** *v.* — *Syn.* shell, bombard, torpedo, napalm, blow up, wipe out, subject to bombing runs, blast, attack from the air, zero in on*, rain destruction, raid, dive-bomb, skip-bomb, mass-bomb, precision-bomb, lay an egg*; see also **attack** 1, **destroy** 1.

**bombard,** *v.* — *Syn.* besiege, assault, blast, barrage; see **attack** 1, **bomb.**
*See Synonym Study at* ATTACK.

**bombardment,** *n.* — *Syn.* assault, shelling, barrage; see **attack** 1, **fire** 2.

**bombast,** *n.* — *Syn.* grandiloquence, rant, fustian, pomposity; see **nonsense** 1.

**bombastic,** *modif.* — *Syn.* pompous, declamatory, grandiloquent, orotund, lofty, inflated, grandiose, rhetorical, high-sounding, high-flown, fustian, flowery, florid, pretentious, ostentatious, overwrought, overblown, magniloquent, euphuistic, turgid, flatulent; see also **oratorical.**

---

*SYN.* — **bombastic** refers to speech or writing that is pompous and inflated and suggests extravagant verbal padding and little substance; **grandiloquent** suggests an overreaching eloquence and implies the use of grandiose, high-flown language and an oratorical tone; **flowery** language is full of figurative and ornate expressions and high-sounding words; **euphuistic** is applied to an extremely artificial style of writing in which there is a straining for effect at the expense of thought; **turgid** implies such inflation of style as to obscure meaning

---

**bomber,** *n.* — *Syn.* bombing plane, heavy bomber, medium bomber, light bomber, aerial attack plane, bombardier; see also **aviator, pilot** 1, **plane** 3.

**bombing,** *n.* — *Syn.* bombardment, shelling, air attack; see **attack** 1.
Methods of bombing include: air bombing, high-altitude bombing, precision bombing, saturation bombing, carpet bombing, wave bombing, dive bombing, skip bombing, low-level bombing, nuisance bombing, mass bombing, tactical bombing, pattern bombing, around-the-clock bombing, napalming, hedgehopping*.

**bona fide,** *modif.* — *Syn.* in good faith, genuine, real, sincere; see **genuine** 1, 2.
*See Synonym Study at* GENUINE.

**bond,** *n.* **1.** [A physical tie; *often plural*] — *Syn.* shackle, linkage, chain; see **band** 2, **link, rope, wire** 1.
**2.** [A mental or emotional tie] — *Syn.* attachment, link, tie, union, obligation, connection, relation, affinity, affiliation, bond of union, friendship, covenant, pact, restraint; see also **agreement** 3, **duty** 2, **friendship** 1, **marriage** 2, **relationship.**
**3.** [A secured debenture] — *Syn.* security, warranty, debenture, certificate, registered bond, bearer bond, coupon bond, zero coupon bond, gold bond, government bond, municipal bond, long *or* short term bond, junk bond*.
**4.** [Bail] — *Syn.* surety, guaranty, warrant; see **bail, pledge.**

**bondage,** *n.* — *Syn.* slavery, servitude, thralldom, subjugation; see **slavery** 1.
*See Synonym Study at* SLAVERY.

**bonded,** *modif.* **1.** [*Said of persons*] — *Syn.* shackled, fettered, manacled, chained, bound, confined, restrained, articled, debentured. — *Ant.* FREE, liberated, independent.
**2.** [*Said especially of stored goods or storehouses*] — *Syn.*

insured, certified, warranted; see **guaranteed, protected.**

**bone,** *n.* — *Syn.* skeletal substance, osseous matter, bony process, bone cartilage, ossein.

Bones of the human skeleton include: cranium *or* skull, frontal, temporal, parietal, occipital, zygomatic *or* cheekbone, sphenoid, ethmoid, vomer *or* nasal bones, mandible *or* jawbone, maxilla, malleus *or* hammer, incus *or* anvil, stapes *or* stirrup, spinal column *or* vertebral column *or* vertebrae *or* backbone, atlas, axis, coccyx, ribcage, sternum *or* breastbone, clavicle *or* collarbone, scapula *or* shoulder blade, humerus, radius, ulna, carpal, metacarpal, phalanges, pelvis, ischium, pubis, ilium *or* hipbone, femur *or* thighbone, patella *or* kneecap, tibia *or* shinbone, fibula, talus, tarsal, metatarsal.

**feel in one's bones** — *Syn.* be convinced, feel intuitively, have a presentiment, have a hunch; see **anticipate** 1, see **believe** 1, **feel** 2.

**have a bone to pick\*** — *Syn.* have a complaint, have a quarrel, be angry, express an objection; see **complain** 1, **oppose** 1.

**make no bones about\*** — *Syn.* confess, reveal, expose; see **admit** 2.

**boner\*,** *n.* — *Syn.* blunder, error, mistake; see **error** 1. *See Synonym Study at* ERROR.

**bonfire,** *n.* — *Syn.* campfire, blaze, signal fire; see **fire** 1.

**bonnet,** *n.* — *Syn.* hood, sunbonnet, cap; see **hat.**

**bonus,** *n.* — *Syn.* gratuity, reward, special compensation, additional compensation, token of appreciation; see also **gift** 1, **premium, tip** 2.

*See Synonym Study at* PREMIUM.

**bony,** *modif.* **1.** [Of or like bone] — *Syn.* skeletal, anatomical, osseous, ossified, formative, cartilaginous, horny, hard, osteal; see also **structural.**

**2.** [Thin] — *Syn.* emaciated, skinny, scrawny; see **angular** 2, **thin** 2.

**booboo\*,** *n.* — *Syn.* blunder, error, mistake; see **error** 1. *See Synonym Study at* ERROR.

**book,** *n.* **1.** [A bound volume] — *Syn.* publication, work, volume, booklet, paperback, tome, pamphlet, literary work, reprint, preprint, offprint, hardcover, softcover, text, edition, title, brochure, manual, album, folio, copy, opus, opuscule, vade mecum, monograph, writing, codex, scroll, incunabulum, periodical, octavo, magazine, quarto; see also **biography, dictionary, novel.**

Kinds of books include: fiction book, nonfiction book, manual, handbook, enchiridion, children's *or* juvenile book, primer, reader, grammar, novel, atlas, gazetteer, chapbook, cookbook, guidebook, story book, song book, trade book, reference book, logbook, textbook, workbook, hymnbook *or* hymnal, prayer book, audio book, catalog, bible *or* Bible, treatise, libretto, tract, thesis, portfolio, album, dissertation.

**2.** [A division of a literary composition] — *Syn.* canto, chapter, part, volume; see **division** 2.

**3.** [An account of transactions] — *Syn.* record, register, roster, ledger; see **list, record** 1.

**bring to book** — *Syn.* reprimand, call to account, demand an explanation; see **censure, examine** 2.

**by the book** — *Syn.* according to the rules, properly, correctly, strictly; see **accurately, legally** 1, **officially** 1.

**in one's book** — *Syn.* in one's opinion, for oneself, to one's mind; see **personally** 2.

**in one's good books** — *Syn.* in favor, in one's good graces, liked, favored; see **approved, favorite, honored.**

**in the book\*** — *Syn.* practiced, done, established, prevalent; see **known** 2.

**know like a book** — *Syn.* understand, comprehend, be familiar with; see **know** 1.

**make book\*** — *Syn.* bet, risk, wager; see **bet, gamble** 1.

**off the books** — *Syn.* unreported, unrecorded, undocumented; see **illegal, secret, secretly.**

**one for the books\*** — *Syn.* source of amazement, shock, novelty; see **surprise** 2.

**on the books** — *Syn.* listed, noted, set down; see **recorded.**

**throw the book at\*** — *Syn.* deal out the maximum punishment, charge with every possible offense, be overzealous with; see **accuse, punish.**

**book,** *v.* **1.** [To record charges against] — *Syn.* charge, take into custody, prefer charges; see **accuse, arrest** 1.

**2.** [To engage ahead of time] — *Syn.* engage, schedule, reserve; see **hire** 1, **maintain** 3, **program** 1.

**bookcase,** *n.* — *Syn.* bookshelf, cabinet, sectional bookcase, secretary, bookrack; see also **furniture.**

**booked,** *modif.* **1.** [Scheduled] — *Syn.* engaged, contracted, reserved, programmed, slated, billed, advertised, lined up\*; see also **proposed.**

**2.** [Arrested] — *Syn.* charged, taken into custody, jailed; see **accused, under arrest, arrest** *n.*

**bookish,** *modif.* — *Syn.* scholarly, academic, erudite, book-learned; see **learned** 1, **pedantic.**

**bookkeeper,** *n.* — *Syn.* clerk, accountant, actuary, auditor; see **accountant, clerk** 2.

**bookkeeping,** *n.* — *Syn.* accountancy, auditing, recording, accounting.

**book review,** *n.* — *Syn.* critical review, notice, blurb\*; see **review** 2.

**bookworm,** *n.* — *Syn.* savant, booklover, bibliophile, reader; see **bibliophile, reader** 1, **scholar** 2.

**boom,** *n.* **1.** [A loud noise] — *Syn.* roar, blast, blare; see **noise** 1.

**2.** [Sudden increase, especially sudden prosperity] — *Syn.* rush, growth, inflation; see **increase** 1.

**boom,** *v.* **1.** [To make a loud sound] — *Syn.* roar, reverberate, thunder; see **sound** 1.

**2.** [To increase rapidly] — *Syn.* prosper, expand, swell, flourish; see **grow** 1, **prosper.**

**lower the boom (on)\*** — *Syn.* take action against, move against, beat, overcome; see **attack** 2, **punish.**

**boon,** *n.* — *Syn.* benefit, good fortune, help; see **blessing** 2.

**boor,** *n.* — *Syn.* lout, oaf, churl, yokel, back countryman, rustic, peasant, clown, bumpkin, country bumpkin, lubber, bear, looby, vulgarian, Philistine, yahoo, barbarian, lumpkin, gaffer, cad, hick\*, rube\*, clodpole\*, hayseed\*, clod\*, clodhopper\*, lummox\*, slob\*, chuff\*; see also **barbarian** 1.

**boorish,** *modif.* — *Syn.* ill-mannered, clumsy, churlish, insensitive; see **rude** 1, 2. *See Synonym Study at* RUDE.

**boost,** *n.* **1.** [Aid] — *Syn.* assistance, help, helping hand, lift; see **aid** 1.

**2.** [An increase] — *Syn.* addition, advance, hike\*; see **increase** 1.

**boost,** *v.* **1.** [To raise] — *Syn.* push up, lift up, hoist, shove; see **raise** 1.

**2.** [To promote] — *Syn.* encourage, support, advance, advertise; see **promote** 1, 2.

**3.** [To increase] — *Syn.* raise, heighten, expand; see **increase** 1. *See Synonym Study at* LIFT.

**booster\*,** *n.* — *Syn.* supporter, promoter, sponsor; see **patron** 1, **supporter.**

**boot,** *n.* **1.** [High footwear, often of rubber] — *Syn.* overshoe, galosh, rubber, bootee, wader, hip-boot, laced boot, chukka boot, high shoe, jackboot, hiking boot, cowboy boot, climbing boot, riding boot, ski boot, combat boot, mukluk, gumshoe, Wellington, wellie*, wafflestomper*; see also **shoe.**

**2.** [A kick] — *Syn.* drive, shove, knock; see **kick** 1.

**bet your boots*** — *Syn.* be certain, rely on it, trust in it; see **trust** 1.

**die with one's boots on*** — *Syn.* die in action, keep going, die fighting; see **continue** 1, **die** 1.

**lick the boots of*** — *Syn.* fawn over, be a pawn for, be a lackey for, bootlick*; see **grovel, obey** 1.

**booth,** *n.* — *Syn.* stall, counter, nook, corner, carrel, pew, berth, cote, compartment, hutch, shed, manger, cubbyhole, coop, pen, hut, enclosure, stand, kiosk, dispensary, cubicle, repository, box.

**bootleg,** *modif.* — *Syn.* illegal, unlawful, contraband; see **illegal.**

**bootlegger,** *n.* — *Syn.* illicit liquor dealer, racketeer, whiskey peddler, moonshiner*, rumrunner*.

**booty,** *n.* — *Syn.* plunder, spoils, loot, winnings, stolen goods, prey, ill-gotten gains, seizure, prize, gift, pillage, takings, pickings, haul*, take*, swag*, boodle*, hot goods*.

---

*SYN.* — **booty** suggests property taken by a band or gang, to be divided among the members; **spoils** (occasionally **spoil**) refers to any property, territory, etc. taken in war by the conqueror; **pillage** suggests violence and destructiveness in the taking of spoils; **plunder** is equivalent to **pillage** but also applies to property taken by bandits, highwaymen, etc.; **prize** refers specifically to spoils taken at sea, esp. the taking of an enemy warship or its cargo; **loot,** a more derogatory equivalent for any of the preceding, emphasizes the immorality or predatory nature of the act

---

**booze*,** *n.* — *Syn.* liquor, alcohol, whiskey; see **alcohol, drink** 2, **whiskey.**

**border,** *n.* **1.** [Edge] — *Syn.* margin, hem, trim; see **decoration** 2, **edge** 1, **fringe** 2, **rim, trimming** 1.

**2.** [Boundary] — *Syn.* boundary, frontier, outpost, perimeter; see **boundary, edge** 1.

*See Synonym Study at* RIM.

**border,** *v.* — *Syn.* be adjacent to, adjoin, abut (on); see **join** 3.

**bordering,** *modif.* — *Syn.* rimming, bounding, neighboring, adjoining, fringing, edging, lining, conjoining, verging, skirting, flanking, connecting, on the edge of, on the confines of; see also **near** 1.

**borderline,** *modif.* — *Syn.* marginal, indeterminate, problematic, doubtful; see **questionable** 1, **uncertain** 2.

**border on,** *v.* — *Syn.* lie next to, abut, touch, verge on; see **join** 3.

**bore,** *n.* — *Syn.* nuisance, pest, tiresome person, tedious person, drag*; see **nuisance** 3, **trouble** 2.

**bore,** *v.* **1.** [To pierce by rotary motion] — *Syn.* drill, ream, perforate, tunnel; see **penetrate** 1.

**2.** [To weary] — *Syn.* fatigue, tire, put to sleep; see **weary** 1.

**bored,** *modif.* — *Syn.* wearied, fatigued, uninterested, jaded, dull, irked, annoyed, *ennuyé* (French), blasé, world-weary, bored to death, bored to tears*, in a rut*, sick and tired*, bored stiff*, fed up*; see also **tired.** — *Ant.* exhilarated, EXCITED, interested.

**boredom,** *n.* — *Syn.* ennui, lack of interest, weariness, world-weariness, *taedium vitae* (Latin), tedium, tiresomeness, apathy, wearisomeness, doldrums, listless-

ness, irksomeness, the blahs*; see also **dullness** 1, **indifference** 1, **monotony.**

**boring,** *modif.* — *Syn.* tedious, tiresome, monotonous; see **dull** 3, 4.

**born,** *modif.* — *Syn.* intrinsic, innate, inherent, by birth; see **native** 1, **natural** 1.

**borough,** *n.* — *Syn.* precinct, ward, district; see **area** 2, **division** 6, **government** 2.

**borrow,** *v.* **1.** [To receive temporarily] — *Syn.* accept the loan of, obtain the use of, negotiate a loan for, get a loan, go into debt, get temporary use of, use, pledge, rent, hire, acquire, obtain, give a note for, raise money, touch up for*, sponge*, sponge on, sponge off*, hit up for*, bum*, beg*, cadge*, chisel*, mooch*, scrounge*, borrow from Peter to pay Paul*. — *Ant.* LEND, loan, give back.

**2.** [To adopt] — *Syn.* appropriate, assume, make one's own, plagiarize; see **adopt** 2.

**borrowed,** *modif.* — *Syn.* appropriated, taken, acquired, assumed, adopted, hired, rented, plagiarized, imported, cultivated, imitated; see also **rented, stolen.** — *Ant.* OWNED, possessed, titular.

**borrowing,** *n.* — *Syn.* renting, hiring, accepting a loan, financing, assuming, taking, adopting, appropriating, imitating, plagiarizing, utilizing, importing, bumming*, cadging*, mooching*, freeloading*; see also **using.** — *Ant.* LOAN, loaning, pawning.

**bosom,** *n.* **1.** [The breast] — *Syn.* breasts, bust, teats; see **breast** 2.

**2.** [The chest] — *Syn.* breast, ribs, rib cage, thorax; see **chest** 2.

**3.** [One's inner self] — *Syn.* heart, intimate center, core; see **breast** 3, **center** 1, **mind** 1.

*See Synonym Study at* BREAST.

**boss,** *n.* — *Syn.* supervisor, manager, person in charge; see **administrator, chief** 1, **foreman.**

**Boston,** *n.* — *Syn.* capital of Massachusetts, the Hub, Hub of the Universe, Beantown*, Athens of America*, home of the bean and the cod*, cradle of liberty.

**botanical,** *modif.* — *Syn.* concerning plants, vegetable, floral, arboreal, herbaceous, herbal, horticultural, phytogenetic, paleobotanical, taxonomic, phytogeographical, agricultural, phytologic; see also **biological.**

**botany,** *n.* — *Syn.* natural history, study of flora, study of vegetation, study of plant life, phytology.

Divisions of botany include: morphology, anatomy, cytology, physiology, paleobotany, horticulture, ecology, taxonomy, phytogeography, pathology, (phyto-) genetics, applied *or* economic botany; see also **biology, science** 1.

**botch,** *v.* — *Syn.* bungle, spoil, mar, ruin, wreck, mutilate, fumble, distort, blunder, mishandle, do clumsily, muddle, make a mess of, trip up, flounder, err, fall down, be mistaken, misapply, misjudge, misconjecture, mismanage, miscalculate, misconstrue, misreckon, miscompute, misestimate, execute clumsily, do unskillfully, stumble, make a hash of*, put one's foot in it*, pull a boner*, goof up*, butcher*, screw up*, mess up*, foul up*, muff*, flub one's lines*, put out of whack*; see also **destroy** 1, **fail** 1. — *Ant.* SUCCEED, FIX, do well.

**both,** *modif. & pron.* — *Syn.* the two, both together, the one and the other, the pair, the couple, one as well as the other. — *Ant.* ONE, EITHER, each, each alone.

**bother,** *n.* **1.** [Trouble or worry] — *Syn.* vexation, fuss, inconvenience, anxiety; see **care** 2.

**2.** [A cause of trouble or worry] — *Syn.* nuisance, problem, concern, care; see **difficulty** 1, 2, **trouble** 2.

**bother,** *v.* **1.** [To take trouble] — *Syn.* put oneself out, fret, go out of one's way, make a fuss about, fuss (over), take pains, make an effort, exert oneself, trouble oneself, concern oneself, be concerned about, worry about; see also **try** 1, **worry** 2.
**2.** [To give trouble] — *Syn.* annoy, plague, vex, pester, molest, irritate, irk, disturb, provoke, harass, badger, hound, heckle, aggravate, tease, goad, pursue, torment, torture, taunt, try one's patience, carp at, nag, hector, harry, exasperate, nettle, cross, exacerbate, intrude upon, interrupt, discommode, inconvenience, hinder, impede, bore, afflict, grate on, bedevil, beset, browbeat, tantalize, bug★, peeve★, get on one's nerves★, give one a pain★, drive one nuts★, drive up a wall★, put out★, gripe★, get one's goat★, put one's nose out of joint★, get under one's skin★, ride★, pick on★, needle★, get in one's hair★, hassle★, get on one's back★, noodge★, give one a hard time★, get on one's case★; see also **disturb** 2. — *Ant.* help, please, delight.
**3.** [To be disturbing] — *Syn.* disturb, distress, upset, hurt, trouble, be the matter, displease, disconcert, worry, agitate, disquiet, perturb, discompose, embarrass, unsettle, discomfit, pain, grieve, bewilder, confuse, perplex, ruffle, mortify, chagrin, gnaw at, jar, make one lose sleep, discombobulate★, rub the wrong way★, go against the grain★, jangle the nerves★; see also sense 2.

---

*SYN.* — **bother** implies disturbance of one's peace of mind and may suggest mild perplexity or anxiety; **annoy** implies temporary disturbance of mind caused by something that displeases one or tries one's patience; **vex** implies a more serious source of irritation and greater disturbance, often intense worry; **irk** stresses a wearing down of one's patience by persistent annoyance; to **tease** is to annoy by persistent, irritating actions, remarks, or requests; **plague** suggests mental torment comparable to the physical suffering caused by an affliction

---

**bothered,** *modif.* — *Syn.* harassed, vexed, annoyed, troubled, irked, chagrined, agitated, disturbed, disconcerted, disquieted, bugged★, exercised★; see also **troubled** 1.
**bothersome,** *modif.* — *Syn.* vexatious, troublesome, annoying, irksome; see **disturbing.**
**bottle,** *n.* — *Syn.* container, flask, flagon, decanter, demijohn, cruet, jug, urn, canteen, cruse, jar, pitcher, ewer, gourd, carafe, hip flask, vial, phial, caster, vacuum bottle, glass, fiasco, dead soldier (empty liquor bottle)★; see also **flask, jar.**
**hit the bottle★** — *Syn.* get drunk, imbibe, become an alcoholic; see **drink** 2.
**bottle up,** *v.* — *Syn.* contain, check, curb, suppress; see **enclose** 1, **restrain** 1, **restrict** 2, **suppress.**
**bottom,** *n.* **1.** [The lowest part] — *Syn.* underside, nether portion, base, nadir, foot, pediment, depths, bed, floor, lowest part, deepest part, sole, ground, underpart. — *Ant.* TOP, peak, pinnacle.
**2.** [The foundation] — *Syn.* base, substructure, support; see **foundation** 2.
**3.** [The source] — *Syn.* cause, basis, origin, root; see **origin** 2, 3.
**4.** [★The buttocks] — *Syn.* behind, seat, rear; see **back** 2, **rump.**
**at bottom** — *Syn.* fundamentally, basically, actually; see **essentially, really** 1.
**be at the bottom of** — *Syn.* originate, be the reason for, activate, be responsible for; see **cause** 2.

**bet one's bottom dollar★** — *Syn.* bet everything one has, be certain, be assured; see **bet, trust** 1.
**bottomless,** *modif.* — *Syn.* deep, unfathomable, boundless; see **infinite** 1.
**bottom line★,** *n.* **1.** [Profits or losses] — *Syn.* net income, net loss, net profits; see **income, profit** 2, **loss** 3.
**2.** [Final result or decision] — *Syn.* conclusion, outcome, upshot, last word★; see **end** 2, **result.**
**bottoms,** *pl.n.* — *Syn.* low land, marsh, bottomland; see **swamp.**
**bough,** *n.* — *Syn.* branch, limb, arm; see **branch** 2.
**bought,** *modif.* — *Syn.* purchased, procured, acquired, budgeted for, requisitioned, paid for, on order, to be delivered, contracted for, included in the purchase, store-bought, ready-made; see also **acquired** 1, 2, **ordered** 1, **ready-made.** — *Ant.* SOLD, pawned, given away.
**boulder,** *n.* — *Syn.* stone, fieldstone, slab, crag; see **rock** 2.
**boulevard,** *n.* — *Syn.* street, avenue, highway; see **road** 1, **street.**
**bounce,** *v.* **1.** [To rebound] — *Syn.* ricochet, recoil, carom, glance off, spring back, leap, hop, skip, bob, buck, jump, bound, jerk up and down, snap back, fly back, bounce back, kick back, boomerang, backlash, jounce; see also **jump** 4.
**2.** [To move suddenly] — *Syn.* spring, hop, leap, jump, bolt, vault, bound; see also **jump** 1.
**3.** [★To discharge from one's employ *or* establishment] — *Syn.* eject, oust, fire; see **dismiss** 1, 2, **oust.**
**bound,** *modif.* **1.** [Literally confined in bonds] — *Syn.* fettered, shackled, trussed up, manacled, chained, enchained, handcuffed, hobbled, captive, confined, restrained, trammeled, pinioned, pilloried, muzzled, in leash, tied up, harnessed, bound hand and foot, lashed fast, swathed, pinned down, pegged down, tethered, picketed, secured, roped, gagged, hogtied, loaded with irons★. — *Ant.* FREE, unrestrained, loose.
**2.** [Figuratively constrained] — *Syn.* impelled, compelled, obliged, obligated, under compulsion, constrained, duty-bound, committed, sworn, pledged, forced, coerced, driven, necessitated, under necessity, made, having no alternative, required, bounden. — *Ant.* unconstrained, FREE, independent.
**bound,** *v.* **1.** [To move in leaps] — *Syn.* jump, spring, vault, skip; see **jump** 1, **skip.**
**2.** [To rebound] — *Syn.* bounce, ricochet, recoil; see **bounce** 1, **jump** 4.
**3.** [To set limits] — *Syn.* restrict, confine, circumscribe, border; see **define** 1, **limit, surround** 1.
*See Synonym Study at* LIMIT, SKIP.
**out of bounds** — *Syn.* off limits, not permitted, restricted, forbidden; see **illegal.**
**boundary,** *n.* — *Syn.* outline, border, verge, rim, beginning, end, terminal, confines, limit, limits, bounds, radius, terminus, landmark, march, extremity, fence, compass, side, purlieus, hem, frame, skirt, line of demarcation, termination, margin, line, barrier, frontier, outpost, perimeter, extent, circumference, horizon, periphery, fringe, pale, mark, borderland; see also **edge** 1. — *Ant.* surface, interior, center.
**bounded,** *modif.* — *Syn.* limited, edged, enclosed, defined, delimited, circumscribed, rimmed, encircled, hedged in, hemmed in, ringed, fenced in, walled in, bordered, confined, surrounded, brimmed, boundaried, enveloped, encompassed, compassed about, girdled, belted, girt, flanked, neighbored, adjacent, next to, contiguous, skirted, fringed, encroached upon, clasped, restricted. — *Ant.* UNLIMITED, ill-defined, unbounded.

**boundless,** *modif.* **1.** [Immense] — *Syn.* great, tremendous, vast; see **large** 1.
**2.** [Infinite] — *Syn.* limitless, endless, unlimited, illimitable; see **infinite** 1.
**bound to,** *v.* — *Syn.* certain to, sure to, destined to; see **doomed, inevitable.**
**bountiful,** *modif.* **1.** [Plentiful] — *Syn.* bounteous, abundant, lavish; see **plentiful** 1, 2.
**2.** [Generous] — *Syn.* munificent, liberal, openhanded; see **generous** 1, **philanthropic.**
**bounty,** *n.* **1.** [A recompense] — *Syn.* prize, premium, bonus; see **pay** 1, 2, **premium.**
**2.** [Liberality] — *Syn.* openhandedness, munificence, hospitality; see **generosity** 1.
*See Synonym Study at* PREMIUM.
**bouquet,** *n.* **1.** [Flowers] — *Syn.* nosegay, bunch of flowers, corsage, boutonniere, garland, vase of flowers, flower arrangement, wreath, spray, posy; see also **wreath.**
**2.** [Fragrance] — *Syn.* aroma, scent, odor, nose; see **perfume, smell** 1.
*See Synonym Study at* PERFUME.
**bourgeois,** *modif.* — *Syn.* middle-class, conventional, materialistic, white-bread*; see **common** 1, **materialistic, popular** 3, 4.
**bout,** *n.* — *Syn.* match, set-to, round, session; see **fight** 1, **period** 1.
**bovine,** *modif.* — *Syn.* slow, stolid, dense; see **dull** 3, **indifferent** 1.
**bovine,** *n.* — *Syn.* cow, bull, calf, ox; see **cow.**
**bow,** *n.* — *Syn.* longbow, self-bow, union bow, crossbow, single-piece bow, back bow, stone-bow, arbalest, arbalist; see also **weapon** 1.
**bow,** *n.* **1.** [Front of a boat] — *Syn.* forepart, bowsprit, prow, head, stem, fore, nose; see also **front** 1.
**2.** [A bend from the waist] — *Syn.* nod, bend, salaam, curtsey, obeisance, kowtow, genuflection, bowing and scraping, bob, dip.
**take a bow** — *Syn.* accept praise, be congratulated, feel honored, acknowledge applause, bow.
**bow,** *v.* **1.** [To bend] — *Syn.* curtsey, do obeisance, stoop, dip, nod, drop, hunch over, incline, bob, duck, cower, kowtow, salaam, kneel, genuflect, prostrate oneself, bow and scrape. — *Ant.* RISE, tower, become erect.
**2.** [To submit] — *Syn.* bend, surrender, acquiesce, capitulate; see **yield** 1, 3.
**bowels,** *pl.n.* — *Syn.* viscera, entrails, intestines, guts*; see **abdomen, insides, intestines.**
**bower,** *n.* — *Syn.* arbor, nook, grove, thicket, grotto, summerhouse, pergola, gazebo, shady retreat, shady lair, leafy den, recess, shelter, alcove; see also **forest, garden, refuge** 1, **retreat** 2.
**bowl,** *n.* — *Syn.* dish, vessel, tureen, pot, porringer, saucer, crock, jar, urn, pan, basin, casserole, boat, vase; see also **china, container, dish.**
**bowl,** *v.* — *Syn.* play ninepins, play tenpins, play duckpins, play candlepins, roll, play at bowling, play at bowls.
**bowl along,** *v.* — *Syn.* trundle, roll, wheel along; see **drive** 3, **move** 1.
**bowlegged,** *modif.* — *Syn.* bandylegged, pigeon-toed, bowed, misshapen; see **bent, deformed.**
**bowling,** *n.* — *Syn.* bowls, duckpins, candlepins, ninepins, tenpins, bocce ball, lawn bowling, skittles, American bowls, kegling*.
**bowl over,** *v.* — *Syn.* astonish, stagger, flabbergast; see **surprise** 1.
**bow out,** *v.* — *Syn.* withdraw, resign, quit, retire; see **abandon** 1, **resign** 2.

**box,** *n.* — *Syn.* carton, crate, case, receptacle; see **case** 7.
**in a box*** — *Syn.* in difficulty, in a predicament, at an impasse, in a fix*; see **in trouble** 1 at **trouble.**
**box,** *v.* **1.** [To enclose in a box] — *Syn.* pack, confine, package, crate; see **pack** 2, **wrap** 2.
**2.** [To fight for sport] — *Syn.* spar, punch, slug, hit, cuff, fight, cross gloves*, mix punches*, scrap*, swap punches*, duke*.
**boxcar,** *n.* — *Syn.* freight car, refrigerator car, automobile car, caboose, freighter; see also **car** 2.
**boxer,** *n.* — *Syn.* pugilist, fighter, prizefighter; see **fighter** 2.
**box in** *or* **up,** *v.* — *Syn.* confine, trap, block, hem in; see **enclose** 1, **hinder, surround** 1, 2.
**boxing,** *n.* — *Syn.* pugilism, fighting, prizefighting, fisticuffs, the manly art, the fights, the ring, sparring, fight racket*, glove game*.
**boy,** *n.* — *Syn.* lad, youth, youngster, young man, schoolboy, stripling, fellow, master, cadet, whippersnapper, son, male child, junior, little gentleman, tad, little guy*, small fry*, puppy*, shaver*; see also **child.**
**boycott,** *v.* — *Syn.* withhold patronage, hold aloof from, blacklist, avoid; see **bar** 2, **ostracize, strike** 2.
**boyfriend,** *n.* — *Syn.* date, young man, beau, escort, companion, gentleman friend, steady, lover, inamorato, sweetheart, man, gentleman caller, suitor, flame, paramour, truelove, admirer, wooer, fellow*, main man*, old man*.
**boyhood,** *n.* — *Syn.* schoolboy days, growing years, formative period, adolescence; see **childhood, youth** 1.
**boyish,** *modif.* — *Syn.* juvenile, youthful, boylike, adolescent; see **childish, juvenile** 1, **young** 1.
**boy scout,** *n.* — *Syn.* cub scout, explorer (scout), troop member; see **scout** 2.
**brace,** *n.* **1.** [A support] — *Syn.* prop, bolster, stay, support, lever, beam, truss, shore, girder, block, skid, rib, strut, buttress, splice, reinforcement, bearing, upholder, peg, bracket, strengthener, band, bracer, stave, guy, sustainer, stirrup, arm, splint, boom, bar, staff, plinth, stanchion, cantilever, rafter, round, mainstay, jack, crutch; see also **beam** 1, **support** 2.
**2.** [A pair] — *Syn.* pair, couple, two; see **pair.**
*See Synonym Study at* PAIR.
**brace,** *v.* **1.** [To give support] — *Syn.* prop, bolster, hold up; see **strengthen, support** 1.
**2.** [To encourage] — *Syn.* uphold, hearten, give new life; see **encourage** 1, 2, **support** 2.
**bracelet,** *n.* — *Syn.* bangle, armlet, wristlet, charm bracelet, circlet, ankle bracelet, wristband, chain, armband, ornament, trinket; see also **jewelry.**
**brace oneself,** *v.* — *Syn.* steady oneself, prepare oneself, steel oneself; see **prepare** 1.
**bracing,** *modif.* — *Syn.* invigorating, rousing, exhilarating; see **stimulating.**
**bracket,** *n.* — *Syn.* support, angle iron, brace, cantilever, console, corbel, strut, modillion wall bracket, section, L joint, hanging bracket, shelf bracket; see also **brace** 1.
**brackish,** *modif.* — *Syn.* somewhat salty, saline, undrinkable; see **salty.**
**brag,** *v.* — *Syn.* boast, swagger, exult, gloat; see **boast** 1.
*See Synonym Study at* BOAST.
**braggart,** *n.* — *Syn.* boaster, braggadocio, brag, big talker, self-promoter, trumpeter, swaggerer, strutter, exhibitionist, egotist, rodomont, peacock, blusterer, bragger, showoff, fanfaron, gascon, blowhard*, windbag*, hot dog*, know-it-all*, bull peddler*.
**braid,** *n.* — *Syn.* plait, pigtail, queue, twist, twine, mesh, net, wreath, knot, chain, filigree, weave, reticulation; see also **hairstyle, rope.**

**braid,** *v.* — *Syn.* twine, plait, interweave; see **weave** 1.

**brain,** *n.* **1.** [The organ of intelligence] — *Syn.* pons, cerebrum, cerebellum, medulla oblongata; encephalon, center of the nervous system, gray matter, cerebral matter, cortical substance, medullary substance, brain cells.
**2.** [The intelligence; *often plural*] — *Syn.* intellect, understanding, mental ability; see **genius** 1, **head** 1, **mind** 1.
**3.** [*A very intelligent person*] — *Syn.* genius, intellectual, scholar, mastermind; see **genius** 2, **intellectual.**
**have on the brain** — *Syn.* be obsessed with, be preoccupied by, think about obsessively, be fixated on; see **haunt** 3, **occupy** 3.

**brainwash,** *v.* — *Syn.* indoctrinate, instill, program, catechize; see **convince, influence, teach** 1, 2.

**brainwashing,** *n.* — *Syn.* indoctrination, implantation, conditioning; see **education** 1, **persuasion** 1.

**brake,** *n.* — *Syn.* check, curb, restraint, deterrent, obstacle, damper, hurdle, discouragement, hindrance, retarding device, governor, drag.
Types of brakes include: shoe, drum, band, catch, pawl, disk, disc, friction, webbing, ratchet, contracting, expanding, hand, compressed air, automatic, emergency, parking, four-wheel, hydraulic, power ABS, anti-lock braking system.

**bramble,** *n.* — *Syn.* blackberry, raspberry, brier, thorn, prickle, bur, gorse, furze, thistle sage, nettle, stinging nettle, prickly shrub, thistle, cleavers, shrub, bramble bush, hedge.

**branch,** *n.* **1.** [A part, usually of secondary importance] — *Syn.* tributary, outpost, chapter, member, part, office, bureau, division, subdivision, section, derivative, dependency, subsidiary, affiliate, arm, wing, classification, department, category, ramification, local office, branch office, branch factory, etc.; see also **division** 2.
**2.** [A secondary shoot] — *Syn.* bough, limb, offshoot, sprig, twig, sucker, scion, bud, arm, fork, growth.

**branch off,** *v.* — *Syn.* diverge, separate, part, fork; see **divide** 1, **veer.**

**branch out,** *v.* — *Syn.* expand, extend, add to, diversify; see **grow** 1, **increase** 1.

**brand,** *n.* **1.** [A trademark] — *Syn.* brand name, make, seal, mark; see **kind** 2, **label, name** 1, **trademark.**
**2.** [A mark indicating ownership] — *Syn.* stigma, scar, sear, welt, cauterization, range brand, mark of the branding iron, earmark, wattle, owner's sign, owner's mark, heraldry of the range*, the rancher's coat of arms*; see also **mark** 1.
Common branding terms include: circle, bar, cross, rocking, lazy, tumbling, swinging, flying, double; *letters*: A, J, X, etc.; *numbers*: 0, 1, 2, 3, etc.
Types of brands include: fast, slow, dewlap, overslope, underslope, crop, half crop, upperbit, underbit, jinglebob, wattle, earmark.
**3.** [A burning stick] — *Syn.* ember, live coal, spark, torch; see **embers.**

**brand,** *v.* — *Syn.* blaze, stamp, imprint, stigmatize; see **disgrace, mark** 1.

**brandish,** *v.* — *Syn.* wave, shake, wield, display threateningly; see **display** 1, **flourish** 1.

**brandy,** *n.* — *Syn.* cognac, *Schnaps* (German), *aguardiente* (Spanish), *eau-de-vie* (French), *aqua vitae* (Latin), slivovitz, Armagnac, applejack, Calvados, grappa, marc, kirsch, kirschwasser, framboise, mirabelle; see also **drink** 2.
Types of brandy include: apple, plum, prune, peach, cherry, apricot, grape.

**brass,** *n.* **1.** [An alloy of copper and zinc] — *Syn.* copper alloy, pinchbeck, Muntz's metal, orichalc, mosaic gold, yellow metal, prince's metal, brass foil, brass leaf, brass powder; see also **alloy.**
**2.** [*High-ranking officials*] — *Syn.* officers, executives, front office, brass hats*; see **administration** 2, **officer** 3.
**3.** [*Impudence*] — *Syn.* effrontery, impertinence, audacity; see **rudeness.**

**brasses,** *pl.n.*
Brasses include: trumpet, trombone, French horn, horn, B-flat cornet, fluegelhorn, sousaphone, bass tuba, helicon, bombardon, euphonium, serpent, E-flat cornet; see also **musical instrument.**

**brassy,** *modif.* — *Syn.* brazen, saucy, flirtatious, impudent, bold, pert, forward, brash; see also **rude** 2.

**brat*,** *n.* — *Syn.* impudent, child, unruly child, imp, whelp, urchin, rascal, terror*, whippersnapper, minx, *enfant terrible* (French), youngster, kid*; see also **boy, child, girl** 1.

**bravado,** *n.* — *Syn.* boasting, bluster, bold front, swagger, vaunting, bragging, gasconade, grandiosity, fanfaronade, bombast, rant, braggadocio, bullying, blowing, puffing, self-glorification, crowing, swaggering, bluff, pretended courage, bravura, daring, defiance, heroics, derring-do.

**brave,** *modif.* **1.** [Courageous] — *Syn.* fearless, courageous, daring, valiant, intrepid, bold, dauntless, undaunted, undismayed, confident, unafraid, plucky, unabashed, chivalrous, valorous, heroic, adventurous, dashing, venturesome, mettlesome, forward, audacious, reckless, foolhardy, gallant, resolute, militant, defiant, hardy, doughty, stout, stout-hearted, lion-hearted, greathearted, manful, manly, firm, high-spirited, unshrinking, unblenching, dreadless, unfearful, spirited, game, strong, stalwart, unflinching, unyielding, indomitable, unconquerable, soldierly, unappalled, spunky*, gritty*, full of guts*, nervy*, gutsy*, macho*, with heart of oak*. — *Ant.* COWARDLY, timid, craven, fearful.
**2.** [Making a good showing] — *Syn.* brilliant, colorful, high-colored, splendid; see **beautiful** 1, **bright** 1, 2.

**brave,** *v.* — *Syn.* confront, risk, court; see **dare** 1, 2, **face** 1.

---

**SYN. — brave** implies fearlessness in meeting danger or difficulty and has the broadest application of the words considered here; **courageous** suggests readiness to deal with things fearlessly by reason of a stout-hearted temperament or a resolute spirit; **bold** stresses a daring temperament, whether displayed courageously, presumptuously, or defiantly; **audacious** suggests an imprudent or reckless boldness; **valiant** emphasizes a heroic quality in the courage or fortitude shown; **intrepid** implies absolute fearlessness and esp. suggests dauntlessness in facing the new or unknown; **plucky** emphasizes gameness in fighting against something when one is at a decided disadvantage

---

**bravely,** *modif.* — *Syn.* courageously, fearlessly, valiantly, boldly, daringly, dauntlessly, intrepidly, heroically, gallantly, doughtily, hardily, stoutly, manfully, staunchly, pluckily, resolutely, valorously, spiritedly, firmly, audaciously, with fortitude, unabashedly, unflinchingly, chivalrously, indomitably, gamely, spunkily*, with plenty of guts*, like a man*, gutsily*. — *Ant.* cravenly, FEARFULLY, timidly.

**bravery,** *n.* — *Syn.* courage, valor, intrepidity, fearlessness; see **courage** 1.

**brawl,** *n.* — *Syn.* fracas, row, melee, riot; see **fight** 1.

**brawn,** *n.* — *Syn.* muscle, sinew, strength, power; see **muscle, strength** 1.

**brawny,** *modif.* — *Syn.* powerful, muscular, sturdy; see **strong** 1.

**bray,** *v.* — *Syn.* bawl, whinny, neigh; see **sound** 1, **yell.**

**brazen,** *modif.* **1.** [Impudent] — *Syn.* audacious, impertinent, forward, shameless; see **rude** 2.

**2.** [Made of brass] — *Syn.* brass, bronze, brassy, brassplated, of brass, brasslike; see also **metallic** 1.

**breach,** *n.* **1.** [An opening, especially in fortifications] — *Syn.* break, gap, rupture; see **break** 1, **hole** 1, 2.

**2.** [An infraction of law or custom] — *Syn.* violation, infringement, transgression; see **crime** 1, 2, **violation** 1.

**bread,** *n.* **1.** [Grain product] — *Syn.* loaf, baked goods, the staff of life.

Types of bread include: whole wheat, grain, oatmeal, graham, rye, leavened, unleavened, matzo, salt-rising, yeast, quick, flat, pita, baguette, corn, sourdough, Russian, raisin, pumpernickel, Vienna, French, Italian, white, black, dark brown, Boston brown, steamed, Swedish, potato, hardtack.

Breadlike foods include: Zwieback, spoon bread, cake, dumpling, turnover, rusk, gem, bun, cookie, English muffin, corn bread, bagel, biscuit, doughnut, muffin, popover, scone, shortbread, hoecake, pone, johnnycake, pancake, waffle, tortilla, Indian bread; see also **biscuit, roll** 4.

**2.** [Food] — *Syn.* meal, sustenance, livelihood, bed and board; see **food, subsistence** 1.

**3.** [*Money] — *Syn.* cash, dollars, dough*; see **money** 1.

**break bread** — *Syn.* partake of food, eat, have a meal; see **eat** 1.

**cast one's bread upon the waters** — *Syn.* grant, endow, be generous; see **give** 1, **help** 1.

**know which side one's bread is buttered on*** — *Syn.* be prudent, be shrewd, look out for number one*; see **prosper.**

**breadth,** *n.* **1.** [Width] — *Syn.* wideness, broadness, thickness, distance across; see **diameter, width.**

**2.** [Scope] — *Syn.* largeness, extent, vastness, compass, magnitude, inclusiveness, greatness, extensiveness, comprehensiveness, amplitude, latitude, liberality; see also **extent, size** 2. — *Ant.* SMALLNESS, narrowness, littleness.

**breadwinner,** *n.* — *Syn.* wage earner, jobholder, provider, producer, supporter, worker, laborer, toiler, workingman, workingwoman, meal ticket*.

**break,** *n.* **1.** [The act of breaking] — *Syn.* fracture, rift, split, schism, cleavage, dissevering, riving, breach, rupture, eruption, bursting, failure, collapse, disjunction; see also **division** 1, **fracture** 1, **parting** 2. — *Ant.* mending, REPAIR, maintenance.

**2.** [The effect of breaking] — *Syn.* crack, split, tear, separation; see **fracture** 2, 3, **hole** 1.

**3.** [A pause] — *Syn.* intermission, interim, lapse, rest; see **pause** 1, **recess** 1.

**4.** [Quarrel and separation] — *Syn.* rift, difference, difference of opinion, alteration, parting of the ways; see also sense 1, **disagreement** 1, **dispute.**

**5.** [Fortunate change or event: *often plural*] — *Syn.* good luck, accident, favorable circumstances, opportunity; see **luck** 1.

**break,** *v.* **1.** [To start a rupture] — *Syn.* crack, burst, split, rend, rupture, sunder, sever, fracture, tear, cleave, rive, break into, break through, force open, puncture, pierce, breach, snap, slash, gash, dissect, slice, detach, divide, separate, disjoin, bust*; see also **cut** 1, 2, **divide** 1.

**2.** [To shatter] — *Syn.* smash, shatter, crash, break up, crush, break to atoms, shiver, splinter, smash to flinders,

pull to pieces, break all to pieces, fragment, fragmentize, crumble, bust up*, break all to smithereens*.

**3.** [To fall apart] — *Syn.* disintegrate, fall apart, shiver, burst, shatter, fall to pieces, splinter, crumble, collapse, break down, come apart, come off, get loose, fall off, fall down, cave in, give way, dilapidate, go to wrack and ruin, get wrecked, break into flinders, split, be destroyed, get busted*, fold up*, come unstuck*, come unglued*, come apart at the seams*; see also **break down** 3, **disintegrate** 1.

**4.** [To bring to ruin or to an end] — *Syn.* demolish, annihilate, eradicate, crush; see **destroy** 1.

**5.** [To violate] — *Syn.* infringe, fail to observe, contravene; see **transgress, violate** 1.

**6.** [To interrupt] — *Syn.* disrupt, discontinue, suspend, recess; see **interrupt** 2, **suspend** 2.

**7.** [To make known] — *Syn.* disclose, tell, divulge; see **reveal** 1.

**8.** [To make tractable or spiritless] — *Syn.* subdue, tame, wear down; see **defeat** 1, **teach** 2.

**9.** [To happen] — *Syn.* come to pass, come into being, occur, develop; see **happen** 2.

*SYN.* — **break,** the most general of these terms, expresses their basic idea of separating into pieces as a result of impact, stress, etc.; **smash** and **crash** add connotations of suddenness, violence, and noise; **crush** suggests a crumpling or pulverizing pressure; **shatter,** sudden fragmentation and a scattering of pieces; **crack,** incomplete separation of parts or a sharp, snapping noise in breaking; **split,** separation lengthwise, as along the direction of the grain or layers; **fracture,** the breaking of a hard or rigid substance, as bone or rock; **splinter,** the splitting of wood, bone, etc. into long, thin, sharp pieces: all of these terms are used figuratively to imply great force or damage [to *break* one's heart, *smash* one's hopes, *crush* the opposition, *shatter* one's nerves, etc.]

**breakable,** *modif.* — *Syn.* fragile, delicate, frail, brittle; see **weak** 2.

**breakage,** *n.* — *Syn.* damage, harm, wreckage, ruined goods; see **damage** 2.

**breakdown,** *n.* **1.** [A failure to work or function properly] — *Syn.* stoppage, collapse, malfunction, disruption; see **failure** 1, **wreck** 1.

**2.** [A failure of mental or physical health] — *Syn.* collapse, nervous breakdown, decline, crackup*; see **decay** 1.

**3.** [A separation into parts] — *Syn.* analysis, categorization, itemization; see **division** 1.

**break down,** *v.* **1.** [To analyze] — *Syn.* examine, investigate, dissect; see **analyze** 1.

**2.** [To overcome] — *Syn.* surmount, overwhelm, conquer; see **defeat** 1, 2.

**3.** [To malfunction] — *Syn.* fail, stop, malfunction, go out of order, falter, misfire, give out, go down, crash, cease, die, collapse, succumb, backfire, conk out*, go kaput*, go on the blink*, go on the fritz*, go haywire*, go blooey*, go kerflooey*, crack up*, curl up*, roll up*, bomb*, run out of gas*, peter out*, fizzle out*, go out of commission*, get out of gear*, get out of whack*, get out of kilter*, flake out*.

**breaker,** *n.* — *Syn.* wave, comber, roller, surge; see **wave** 1.

*See Synonym Study at* WAVE.

**break free,** *v.* — *Syn.* get out, break out, escape, get loose, break one's bonds; see also **escape, fly** 1, **leave** 1.

**breakfast,** *n.* — *Syn.* morning meal, first meal of the day, early meal, brunch, continental breakfast, English breakfast, *petit déjeuner* (French), breaking the fast; see also **meal**.

**breakfast food,** *n.* — *Syn.* cereal, breakfast cereal, hot cereal, dry cereal, porridge.

Varieties of breakfast cereal include: rolled oats, oatmeal, oat bran, farina, corn flakes, shredded wheat, rice flakes, wheat flakes, puffed wheat, puffed rice, pearl barley, bran, bran flakes, wheat germ, grits, granola, muesli.

**break in,** *v.* **1.** [To train] — *Syn.* educate, instruct, prepare; see **teach** 1, 2.
**2.** [To intrude] — *Syn.* invade, burglarize, trespass; see **meddle** 1, **rob, steal.**

**breaking,** *modif.* — *Syn.* bursting, splitting, cracking, rending, riving, sundering, parting, severing, dissevering, exploding, erupting, shattering, splintering, fracturing, tearing, cleaving, snapping, separating, smashing, shivering, crashing, disintegrating, crumbling, collapsing, caving in, falling, dispersing, busting*, going to pot*. — *Ant.* enduring, STRONG, stable.

**breaking,** *n.* **1.** [A fracture] — *Syn.* cleavage, rupture, separating; see **division** 1, **fracture** 1.
**2.** [A violation] — *Syn.* transgressing, breach, shattering, violating; see **violation** 1.

**break in on** *or* **upon,** *v.* — *Syn.* cut in (on), intrude on, intervene; see **interrupt** 2, **meddle** 1.

**break off,** *v.* — *Syn.* stop abruptly, end, cease, discontinue; see **end** 1, **stop** 2.

**break out,** *v.* **1.** [To start suddenly] — *Syn.* begin, commence, arise, erupt; see **begin** 2.
**2.** [To escape] — *Syn.* burst out, flee, depart; see **escape, leave** 1.
**3.** [To erupt] — *Syn.* acquire blemishes, have acned skin, become diseased, get pimples, get a rash.

**breakthrough,** *n.* — *Syn.* discovery, finding, invention; see **discovery** 2.

**break through,** *v.* — *Syn.* penetrate, force a way, intrude; see **penetrate** 1.

**break up,** *v.* **1.** [To scatter] — *Syn.* disperse, disband, separate; see **divide** 1.
**2.** [To dismantle] — *Syn.* take apart, disassemble, break down; see **dismantle.**
**3.** [To stop] — *Syn.* put an end to, halt, terminate; see **stop** 2.
**4.** [*To distress] — *Syn.* hurt, sadden, upset; see **disturb** 2.
**5.** [*To end a relationship] — *Syn.* split up, part company, break off, drop; see **end** 1, **separate** 2.

**breakwater,** *n.* — *Syn.* jetty, sea wall, embankment, mole; see **barrier, dock** 1, **harbor** 2.

**breast,** *n.* **1.** [The forepart of the body above the abdomen] — *Syn.* chest, thorax, heart, bosom; see **chest** 2.
**2.** [A protuberant mammary gland] — *Syn.* bosom, mammary gland, teat, mammilla, nipple, bust, dug (*especially of animals*), udder (*especially of cows*), tit*, titty*, jug*, boobie*, boob*, knocker*.
**3.** [One's inner self] — *Syn.* mind, heart, bosom, thoughts, conscience, soul, feelings, psyche, spirit, essential nature, being, character, innermost being, heart of hearts, core; see also **mind** 1, **soul** 2.

**beat one's breast** — *Syn.* repent, humble oneself, be penitent, be remorseful; see **apologize, regret** 1.

**make a clean breast of** — *Syn.* confess, reveal, expose; see **admit** 2.

*SYN.* — **breast** refers to the front part of the human torso from the shoulders to the abdomen, or designates either of the female mammary glands; **bosom** refers to the entire human breast or to a woman's two breasts but, except in euphemistic applications [a big-*bosomed* ma-

tron], is now more common in figurative usage, where it implies the human breast as a source of feeling, a protective, loving enclosure, etc. [the *bosom* of his family]; **bust,** as considered here, almost always implies the female breasts and is the conventional term in referring to silhouette, form, etc., as in garment fitting or beauty contests

**breath,** *n.* **1.** [Respiration] — *Syn.* inhalation, exhalation, inspiration, expiration, breathing, gasp, sigh, pant, suspiration, wheeze.
**2.** [A very light wind] — *Syn.* whiff, flutter, puff; see **wind** 1.

**catch one's breath** — *Syn.* pause, rest, stop, slow down; see **pause.**

**in the same breath** — *Syn.* simultaneously, concurrently, at the same time; see **together** 2.

**out of breath** — *Syn.* gasping, winded, exhausted; see **breathless.**

**save one's breath*** — *Syn.* be quiet, refrain from talking, never mind; see **quiet** 2, **shut up** 1.

**take one's breath away** — *Syn.* thrill, stagger, stun; see **excite** 1, **surprise** 1.

**under one's breath** — *Syn.* quietly, muttering, murmuring, sotto voce; see **whispering.**

**breathe,** *v.* **1.** [To draw breath] — *Syn.* respire, use one's lungs, inhale, exhale, draw in, breathe in *or* out, gasp, pant, wheeze, snort, sigh, take air into one's lungs *or* nostrils, scent, sniff, smell, huff, puff, sniffle.
**2.** [To live] — *Syn.* move, exist, be alive; see **be** 1.
**3.** [To blow gently] — *Syn.* puff, fan, exhale; see **blow** 1.
**4.** [To pause] — *Syn.* take a breath, recuperate, take a breather*; see **pause, rest** 2.

**breathing,** *modif.* — *Syn.* respiring, inhaling, inspiring, gasping, panting, wheezing, sighing, smelling, sniffing, respiratory, living, sensitive, palpitant; see also **alive** 1.

**breathless,** *modif.* — *Syn.* out of breath, winded, gasping, panting, spent, exhausted, used up, choking, short of breath, windless, wheezing, blown, short-winded, asthmatic, emphysematous, puffing, broken-winded; see also **enthusiastic** 1, **excited, tired.** — *Ant.* FRESH, breathing freely, long-winded.

**bred,** *modif.* — *Syn.* developed, cultivated, cultured, raised, reared, bought up, trained, educated, refined, produced, propagated.

**breeches,** *pl.n.* — *Syn.* trousers, slacks, knickers; see **pants** 1.

**breed,** *n.* — *Syn.* strain, variety, kind; see **class** 1, **race** 1.

**breed,** *v.* **1.** [To produce young] — *Syn.* reproduce, give birth, procreate, beget; see **produce** 1, **propagate** 1, **reproduce** 3.
**2.** [To cause] — *Syn.* give rise to, engender, occasion, produce; see **begin** 1, **cause** 2, **produce** 1.
**3.** [To cause animals or plants to reproduce] — *Syn.* raise, grow, cultivate, develop, propagate, rear, keep, hybridize, crossbreed, clone.

**breeder,** *n.* — *Syn.* stock raiser, stockbreeder, stockman, herdsman, cattleman, sheepman, plantsman, grower, hybridizer; see also **farmer, rancher.**

**breeze,** *n.* — *Syn.* gentle wind, zephyr, flurry; see **wind** 1. *See Synonym Study at* WIND.

**in a breeze** — *Syn.* effortlessly, readily, jauntily; see **easily** 1.

**shoot the breeze** — *Syn.* converse, chat, chatter; see **talk** 1.

**breezy,** *modif.* **1.** [Said of weather] — *Syn.* gusty, blowy, stormy; see **windy** 1.

**2.** [*Said of people, talk, music, etc.*] — *Syn.* carefree, jaunty, sprightly, casual; see **happy** 1, **sprightly.**

**brevity,** *n.* — *Syn.* shortness, conciseness, concision, briefness, terseness, pointedness, pithiness, compression, succinctness, crispness, compactness, curtness, economy.

**brew,** *n.* — *Syn.* concoction, preparation, mixture, instillation, distillation, drink, liquor, compound, blend, infusion, broth, beer, home-brew, ale, stout; see also **beer, drink** 1, 2, 3.

**brew,** *v.* — *Syn.* concoct, ferment, mull, steep; see **cook.**

**brewery,** *n.* — *Syn.* still, distillery, microbrewery, bottling works, winery; see also **factory.**

**bribe,** *n.* — *Syn.* graft, fee, reward, hush money, sop, lure, gift, remuneration, corrupt money, tribute, perquisite, bait, inducement, tip, blackmail, price, gratuity, lagniappe, protection*, kickback*, payoff*, payola*, plugola*, boodle*.

**bribe,** *v.* — *Syn.* corrupt, pay off, buy, get at, get to, influence by a gift, pervert, reward, tip, give a bribe, give a sop to, give a price to, approach, lure, entice, tempt, influence, induce, seduce with money, suborn, buy off*, butter*, grease one's palm*, cross one's palm*, salve*, soap*, square*, fix*, take care of*.

**brick,** *n.* — *Syn.* cube, Roman brick, pressed brick, adobe, cement block, concrete block, cinder block, glass brick, masonry, chunk; see also **block** 1, **slab, stone.**

**bridal,** *modif.* — *Syn.* nuptial, marriage, wedding, hymeneal, matrimonial, marital, conjugal, connubial, nubile, wedded, epithalamic, prothalamic.

**bride,** *n.* — *Syn.* wife, spouse, partner, mate, helpmate, helpmeet, newly married woman; see also **wife.**

**bridegroom,** *n.* — *Syn.* groom, benedict, husband, spouse; see **husband.**

**bridge,** *n.* **1.** [An elevated structure] — *Syn.* viaduct, platform, pontoon, catwalk, gangplank, drawbridge, trestle, overpass, span, scaffold.
Types of bridges include: arch, pier, gantry, leg, suspension, truss, trestle, cantilever, bowstring, tubular, bascule, pontoon, swing, tubular-arch, turnpike, floating, steel arch, vertical lift, draw, box-girder, lattice, hoist, induction, bottom-road, arched-truss, panel-truss, covered, covered Bailey.
Famous bridges include: Alexander Hamilton, Ambassador, Bayonne, Bronx-Whitestone, Brooklyn, Carquinez Strait, Chesapeake Bay, Corpus Christi, Eads, Firth of Forth, Florianopolis, George Washington, Golden Gate, Henry Hudson, Iberville Memorial, Karlsbrücke, Kitchikas, Lake Pontchartrain, London, Mackinac, Oakland *or* Bay Bridge, Pont Neuf, Pont d'Avignon, Ponte Vecchio, Verrazano-Narrows, Bridge of Sighs, Bridge of St. Angelo.
**2.** [A game at cards] — *Syn.* whist, bridge-whist, contract bridge, auction bridge, duplicate bridge, rubber bridge, honeymoon bridge; see also **game** 1.
**3.** [A link] — *Syn.* connection, bond, tie; see **joint** 1, **link.**

**burn one's bridges** — *Syn.* commit oneself, be determined, go forward resolutely, cross the Rubicon; see **advance** 1.

**bridge,** *v.* — *Syn.* connect, span, link; see **join** 1.

**bridle,** *n.* — *Syn.* hackamore, headstall, leash, harness; see **halter** 1.

**bridle,** *v.* — *Syn.* check, curb, control; see **restrain** 1.
*See Synonym Study at* RESTRAIN.

**brief,** *modif.* **1.** [Short in time] — *Syn.* short, fleeting, concise; see **fleeting, short** 2.
**2.** [Short in space] — *Syn.* skimpy, scanty, slight, small; see **short** 1.

**3.** [Abrupt] — *Syn.* hasty, curt, brusque; see **abrupt** 2.
*See Synonym Study at* SHORT.

**brief,** *n.* **1.** [A summary] — *Syn.* digest, abstract, outline; see **summary.**
**2.** [A legal document] — *Syn.* brief, writ, deed, affidavit, summation, bill, claim, counterclaim, plea, declaration.
*See Synonym Study at* ABRIDGMENT.

**in brief** — *Syn.* in short, succinctly, in a few words, to put it briefly; see **briefly** 1.

**brief,** *v.* **1.** [To summarize] — *Syn.* epitomize, recapitulate, abridge; see **decrease** 2, **summarize.**
**2.** [To inform] — *Syn.* prime, advise, instruct; see **notify** 1, **prepare** 1.

**briefcase,** *n.* — *Syn.* attaché case, dispatch case, note case, folder, portfolio, satchel, book bag; see also **bag.**

**briefing,** *n.* — *Syn.* instructions, guidance, preparation; see **advice, announcement** 1, **directions.**

**briefly,** *modif.* **1.** [Concisely] — *Syn.* in a few words, in a word, succinctly, concisely, in brief, in short, in sum, in a nutshell, in capsule form, in outline, shortly, curtly, abruptly, brusquely, laconically, tersely, summarily, to be brief, to put it briefly, to cut the matter short, to sum things up, to sum up, to come to the point, to come straight to the point, to make a long story short*. — *Ant.* at length, verbosely, long-windedly.
**2.** [For a short time] — *Syn.* fleetingly, momentarily, temporarily, in passing, quickly, hastily, cursorily, hurriedly, casually, briskly, transiently, shortly, for a short time, for a little while.

**brigade,** *n.* — *Syn.* unit, detachment, force; see **army** 2.

**brigand,** *n.* — *Syn.* highwayman, thief, bandit; see **robber.**

**bright,** *modif.* **1.** [Shining] — *Syn.* shiny, shining, gleaming, glittering, luminous, lustrous, burnished, polished, sparkling, brilliant, dazzling, radiant, light, lit up, lighted, illuminated, full of light, glowing, mirrorlike, limpid, flashing, scintillating, coruscating, shimmering, incandescent, effulgent, fulgent, twinkling, illumined, relucent, argent, golden, nitid, silvery, lambent, refulgent, irradiated, glistening, glossy, auroral, burning, blazing, glaring, blinding, beaming, glimmering, splendid, resplendent, alight, aglow, ablaze, flamelike, moonlit, sunlit, starlit, lamplit, candlelit, floodlit, on fire, phosphorescent, luminescent. — *Ant.* dim, DULL, clouded, opaque.
**2.** [Vivid] — *Syn.* colored, colorful, tinted, vivid, intense, deep, sharp, rich, brilliant, gay, gorgeous, exotic, tinged, hued, touched with color, fresh, clear, florid, ruddy, bright-colored, full-colored, deep-colored, rich-colored, high-colored, fluorescent, Day-Glo (*trademark*), psychedelic.
**3.** [Intelligent] — *Syn.* clever, quick, alert, quick-witted; see **able** 1, **intelligent** 1.
**4.** [Not rainy] — *Syn.* clear, sunny, cloudless; see **fair** 3.
**5.** [Cheerful] — *Syn.* lively, vivacious, sunny, radiant; see **happy** 1.
**6.** [Splendid] — *Syn.* famous, illustrious, eminent; see **glorious** 1.
**7.** [Promising] — *Syn.* auspicious, favorable, propitious; see **hopeful** 2.

---

*SYN.* — **bright,** the most general term here, is applied to that which gives forth, reflects, or is filled with light [*a bright day, star, shield, etc.*]; **radiant** emphasizes the actual or apparent emission of rays of light; **shining** implies a steady, continuous brightness [*the shining sun*]; **brilliant** implies intense or flashing brightness [*brilliant sunlight, brilliant diamonds*]; **luminous** is applied to objects that are full of light or give off reflected or phosphorescent light; **lustrous** is applied to objects whose surfaces gleam by reflected light and emphasizes gloss or sheen *[lustrous* silk*] See also Synonym Study at* INTELLI-GENT.

**brighten,** *v.* **1.** [To become brighter] — *Syn.* clear up, lighten, grow calm, improve, grow sunny, become gentle, glow, kindle. — *Ant.* SHADE, grow dull, darken.
**2.** [To make brighter] — *Syn.* polish, burnish, lighten; see **intensify, shine** 3.
**3.** [To make more cheerful] — *Syn.* cheer, gladden, perk up; see **encourage** 2.
**brightly,** *modif.* — *Syn.* glitteringly, sparklingly, limpidly, lustrously, shiningly, glowingly, incandescently, luminously, effulgently, glisteningly, shimmeringly, radiantly, coruscatingly, glaringly, blindingly, gleamingly, splendidly, resplendently, brilliantly, dazzlingly, blazingly, glossily, lambently, shinily, scintillatingly, gaily, freshly, vividly, colorfully, cleverly, quickly, sunnily, phosphorescently. — *Ant.* DULLY, dingily, darkly.
**brightness,** *n.* — *Syn.* shine, luster, illumination; see **light** 1.
**brilliant,** *modif.* **1.** [Shining] — *Syn.* dazzling, gleaming, sparkling; see **bright** 1.
**2.** [Showing remarkable ability] — *Syn.* gifted, ingenious, profound, penetrating; see **intelligent** 1.
**3.** [Illustrious] — *Syn.* splendid, distinguished, excellent, eminent; see **excellent, glorious** 1.
*See Synonym Study at* BRIGHT.
**brilliantly,** *modif.* **1.** [Very brightly] — *Syn.* shiningly, radiantly, blazingly; see **brightly.**
**2.** [With superior intelligence] — *Syn.* cleverly, shrewdly, knowledgeably; see **intelligently.**
**brim,** *n.* — *Syn.* margin, rim, border; see **edge** 1, **rim.**
*See Synonym Study at* RIM.
**brindled,** *modif.* — *Syn.* streaked, spotted, mottled; see **barred** 1, **speckled.**
**brine,** *n.* — *Syn.* salt water, saline solution, sea water, pickling solution, saturated solution of salt, brackish water; see also **ocean.**
**bring,** *v.* **1.** [To transport] — *Syn.* convey, take along, carry, bear, fetch, deliver, transport, conduct, escort, lead, guide; see also **accompany** 1, **carry** 1, **pick up** 6.
**2.** [To be worth in sale] — *Syn.* sell for, command, fetch, produce, net, return, gross, earn, yield, afford, draw, bring in, realize, take; see also **pay** 2.
**3.** [To initiate legal action] — *Syn.* institute, declare, prefer, take (to court), appeal, serve, cite, arraign, summon, indict.
**4.** [To cause] — *Syn.* produce, effect, induce, make; see **begin** 1, **cause** 2.

---

**SYN.** — **bring** (in strict usage) implies a carrying or conducting to, and **take,** similar action away from, the place where the speaker is or will be or a place regarded as "here" *[bring* the book to me; I will *take* it back to the library*]*; **fetch** implies a going after something, getting it, and bringing it back

**bring about,** *v.* **1.** [To achieve] — *Syn.* do, accomplish, realize; see **achieve** 1, 2, **succeed** 1.
**2.** [To cause] — *Syn.* produce, effect, engender, make happen; see **begin** 1, **cause** 2, **manage** 1.
**bring around,** *v.* **1.** [To convince] — *Syn.* persuade, induce, argue into, win over; see **convince.**
**2.** [To revive] — *Syn.* restore, refresh, resuscitate, bring to; see **revive** 1.

**bring down,** *v.* **1.** [To kill] — *Syn.* slay, murder, cut down, mow down*; see **kill** 1.
**2.** [To cause to fall] — *Syn.* injure, wound, overthrow; see **fell, hurt** 1, **oust.**
**bring forth,** *v.* — *Syn.* deliver, bear, yield; see **produce** 1, 2.
**bring forward,** *v.* — *Syn.* present, give, introduce; see **contribute, display** 1, **offer** 1.
**bring in,** *v.* **1.** [To import] — *Syn.* ship in, introduce, buy abroad; see **import** 1.
**2.** [To produce] — *Syn.* yield, bear, earn, accrue; see **bring** 2, **produce** 1.
**bringing,** *n.* — *Syn.* fetching, carrying, transporting, importing, accompanying, conducting, introducing, shipping, bearing, hauling, ushering in, bringing in, conveying, delivering, procuring, getting, providing. — *Ant.* TAKING, deporting, sending.
**bring off,** *v.* — *Syn.* accomplish, realize, execute; see **achieve** 1, 2, **succeed** 1.
**bring on,** *v.* — *Syn.* cause, lead to, provoke; see **begin** 1, **cause** 2.
**bring out,** *v.* **1.** [To cause to appear] — *Syn.* elicit, arouse, evoke, reveal; see **excite** 2, **expose** 1.
**2.** [To publish] — *Syn.* print, issue, put out; see **publish** 1.
**3.** [To produce a play] — *Syn.* present, put on the stage, exhibit; see **perform** 2.
**4.** [To intensify] — *Syn.* heighten, sharpen, magnify, set off; see **emphasize, increase** 1, **intensify.**
**bring to,** *v.* — *Syn.* resuscitate, restore, reanimate, revivify; see **revive** 1.
**bring up,** *v.* **1.** [To rear] — *Syn.* raise, care for, nurture, teach; see **raise** 2, **support** 5, **train** 4.
**2.** [To mention] — *Syn.* tender, submit, advance, introduce; see **hint, mention, propose** 1.
**brink,** *n.* — *Syn.* edge, brim, rim, verge; see **edge** 1, **rim.**
*See Synonym Study at* RIM.
**brisk,** *modif.* **1.** [Active] — *Syn.* lively, energetic, quick; see **active** 2.
**2.** [Stimulating] — *Syn.* sharp, keen, invigorating, bracing; see **cool** 1, **stimulating.**
*See Synonym Study at* ACTIVE.
**briskly,** *modif.* — *Syn.* energetically, quickly, brusquely, rapidly, impulsively, nimbly, agilely, dexterously, decisively, firmly, actively, promptly, readily, vigorously, incisively, in a lively manner, bracingly; see also **emphatically.** — *Ant.* listlessly, SLOWLY, sluggishly.
**bristle,** *n.* — *Syn.* hair, fiber, quill, seta; see **hair** 2, **point** 2, **thorn.**
**bristle,** *v.* **1.** [To display in abundance] — *Syn.* swarm, be alive, abound, exuberate, be thick with, be covered with, thrust out, crawl with*; see also **teem.**
**2.** [To show sudden anger] — *Syn.* ruffle, bridle, get one's hackles up; see **rage** 1.
**Britain,** *n.* — *Syn.* Great Britain, United Kingdom, Albion; England, Scotland, and Wales; see also **England.**
**British,** *modif.* **1.** [English] — *Syn.* English, Anglian, Anglo-; see **Anglo-Saxon, English.**
**2.** [Celtic] — *Syn.* Gaelic, Cymric, Brythonic; see **Scots, Welsh.**
**brittle,** *modif.* — *Syn.* fragile, crisp, inelastic, breakable; see **crumbly.**
*See Synonym Study at* FRAGILE.
**broach,** *v.* **1.** [To mention] — *Syn.* suggest, introduce, bring up; see **ask** 1, **hint, propose** 1.
**2.** [To penetrate] — *Syn.* tap, pierce, puncture; see **open** 3, **penetrate** 1.
*See Synonym Study at* UTTER.

**broad,** *modif.* **1.** [Physically wide] — *Syn.* wide, extended, large, extensive, ample, spacious, deep, expansive, immense, roomy, outspread, capacious, outstretched, thick, widespread, broad-gauged, full; see also **deep** 2, **extensive** 1, **large** 1. — *Ant.* NARROW, THIN, slender, constricted.
**2.** [Extensive] — *Syn.* ubiquitous, all-inclusive, farflung; see **comprehensive, general** 1, **widespread.**
**3.** [Culturally wide] — *Syn.* cultivated, experienced, cosmopolitan; see **cultured.**
**4.** [Tolerant] — *Syn.* progressive, open-minded, unbiased; see **liberal** 2.
**5.** [Indelicate] — *Syn.* dirty, off-color, suggestive, smutty; see **lewd** 1.
**6.** [Clear] — *Syn.* unequivocal, explicit, apparent; see **obvious** 2.

*SYN.* — **broad** and **wide** both are applied to extent from side to side of surfaces having height or length, **wide** being preferred when the distance between limits is stressed /two feet *wide*, a *wide* aperture/, and **broad**, when the full extent of surface is considered /*broad* hips, *broad* plains/; **deep**, in this connection, refers to extent backward, as from the front or an opening /a *deep* lot, a *deep* cave/

**broadcast,** *n.* — *Syn.* television program, TV program, radio program, show, newscast, telecast, wireless transmission, radiocast, simulcast; see also **performance** 2, **show** 2.
**broadcast,** *v.* **1.** [To disperse] — *Syn.* spread, distribute, disseminate; see **scatter** 2, 3.
**2.** [To transmit electronically] — *Syn.* announce, relay, transmit, air, televise, telecast, radiobroadcast, simulcast, send out, cable, beam, narrowcast, put on the air.
**3.** [To announce] — *Syn.* publicize, blazon, proclaim; see **advertise** 1, **declare** 1.
**broadcasting,** *n.* — *Syn.* television, radio, radio transmission, television transmission, announcing, airing, performing before a camera, performing before a microphone, telecasting, cable television, network television, community antenna television, CATV, newscasting, transmitting, reporting, programming, video.
**broaden,** *v.* — *Syn.* widen, expand, increase; see **grow** 1, **increase** 1, **widen** 1, 2.
**broadening,** *modif.* — *Syn.* enlightening, refining, improving, cultivating; see **cultural.**
**broad hint,** *n.* — *Syn.* thinly veiled request, strong suggestion, allusion; see **hint** 1.
**broad-minded,** *modif.* — *Syn.* tolerant, progressive, unprejudiced; see **liberal** 2.
**brochure,** *n.* — *Syn.* handout, circular, pamphlet, leaflet; see **advertisement** 2, **announcement** 3, **book** 1, **folder** 1.
**broil,** *v.* — *Syn.* grill, sear, barbecue; see **cook.**
**broiler,** *n.* — *Syn.* oven, electric broiler, roaster-oven, charcoal broiler, grill, barbecue, hibachi, griddle, portable oven, rotisserie; see also **appliance.**
**broke\*,** *modif.* — *Syn.* bankrupt, out of money, indebted; see **insolvent, ruined** 4.
**go broke\*** — *Syn.* become penniless, become bankrupt, lose everything, be reduced to poverty; see **fail** 4, **lose** 2.
**go for broke\*** — *Syn.* gamble, risk everything, use all one's resources; see **chance** 2, **gamble** 1, **risk, try** 1.
**broken,** *modif.* **1.** [Fractured] — *Syn.* shattered, ruptured, burst, splintered, shivered, smashed, in pieces, collapsed, destroyed, gashed, pulverized, crumbled, mutilated, bruised, injured, lacerated, damaged, rent, split, torn, riven, cracked, mangled, fragmented, fragmentary,

defective, disintegrated, crippled, shredded, crushed, slivered, chipped, busted\*; see also **destroyed, hurt.** — *Ant.* sound, WHOLE, intact.
**2.** [Not functioning properly] — *Syn.* defective, inoperative, in need of repair, in disrepair, out of order, malfunctioning, down, fallen apart, busted\*, gone to pot\*, screwed up\*, shot\*, gone haywire\*, on the fritz\*, on the blink\*, gone to pieces\*, kaput\*, come unstuck, come unglued\*, out of gear\*, out of commission\*, out of whack\*, out of kilter\*, conked out\*, dead\*; see also **faulty.** — *Ant.* operative, USABLE, working.
**3.** [Discontinuous] — *Syn.* spasmodic, interrupted, disrupted, intermittent; see **irregular** 1, 4, **separated.**
**4.** [Not kept; *said especially of promises*] — *Syn.* violated, infringed, dishonored, traduced, forgotten, ignored, transgressed, retracted, disregarded, contravened, flouted. — *Ant.* KEPT, observed, performed.
**5.** [Incoherent; *said of speech*] — *Syn.* unintelligible, mumbled, jumbled; see **incoherent** 1.
**6.** [Infirm] — *Syn.* decrepit, frail, tottering; see **weak** 1.
**7.** [Bankrupt] — *Syn.* indebted, ruined, insolvent, broke\*; see **insolvent, ruined** 4.
**8.** [Disheartened] — *Syn.* discouraged, depressed, heartsick, defeated; see **beaten** 1, **sad** 1.
**broken-down,** *modif.* — *Syn.* dilapidated, battered, in disrepair; see **broken** 2, **old** 2.
**brokenhearted,** *modif.* — *Syn.* despondent, crushed, grieved, inconsolable; see **sad** 1.
**broker,** *n.* — *Syn.* stockbroker, agent, intermediary; see **agent** 1, **businessperson, financier, merchant.**
**bronco,** *n.* — *Syn.* mustang, cattle-pony, wild horse, range horse, fuzztail, broomtail, bronc\*, *cerrero* (Spanish); see also **horse** 1.
**bronze,** *modif.* **1.** [Made of bronze] — *Syn.* bell-metal, copper alloy, cast bronze; see **metallic** 1.
**2.** [Having the color of bronze] — *Syn.* coppercolored, reddish-brown, burnished, russet, rust; see also **brown, gold** 2.
**bronze,** *n.*
Varieties of bronze include: white, steel, phosphor, aluminum, manganese, malleable, Bavarian, ormolu, chemical; see also **alloy, metal.**
**brooch,** *n.* — *Syn.* bar pin, breastpin, clasp; see **jewelry, pin** 2.
**brood,** *n.* — *Syn.* flock, offspring, young; see **family** 1, **herd** 1, **litter** 2, **offspring.**
**brood,** *v.* **1.** [To hatch] — *Syn.* set, cover, incubate, warm, sit; see also **produce** 1.
**2.** [To nurse one's troubles] — *Syn.* mope, ruminate, ponder, repine, grieve, fret, sulk, cherish anxious thoughts, consider, muse, mull over, deliberate, dwell on, agonize, speculate, daydream, reflect, meditate, worry, chafe inwardly, give oneself over to reflections, be in a brown study\*, eat one's heart out\*; see also **meditate** 1, **think** 1, **worry** 2.
**brook,** *n.* — *Syn.* creek, stream, streamlet; see **river** 1.
**brook,** *v.* — *Syn.* tolerate, suffer, stand for, accept; see **endure** 2.
*See Synonym Study at* ENDURE.
**broom,** *n.* — *Syn.* sweeper, besom, whisk, whisk broom, mop, feather duster, brush, swab, floor brush, electric broom, carpet sweeper.
**broth,** *n.* — *Syn.* soup, stock, bouillon, consommé, brew, distillation, concoction, decoction, potage, pot liquor, purée, borscht, vichyssoise, pottage, chowder, gumbo; see also **food, soup, stew.**
**brothel,** *n.* — *Syn.* whorehouse, bordello, bawdyhouse, house of ill-fame, house of ill-repute, bagnio, house of prostitution, massage parlor, cathouse\*, stew\*, red-

light house*, house with red doors*, house*, sporting house*.

**brother,** *n.* **1.** [A male sibling] — *Syn.* sibling, male sibling, stepbrother, half brother, foster brother, kinsman, blood relative, sib, big brother, kid brother*, bro*; see also **relative.**
**2.** [A fellow member of a group] — *Syn.* associate, colleague, confrere, compatriot, fellow member, fellow human being, fellow creature, fellow man, soul brother, blood brother, buddy*; see also **associate, friar.**

**brotherhood,** *n.* **1.** [The quality or state of being brothers] — *Syn.* fellowship, consanguinity, fraternity, equality, kinship, intimacy, (blood) relationship, family connection, affiliation, association, society, common humanity, family, race, comradeship, camaraderie, friendship, amity, filiation, sibling rivalry.
**2.** [A fraternal organization] — *Syn.* fraternity, secret society, order; see **organization** 3.

**brotherly,** *modif.* — *Syn.* fraternal, solicitous, charitable, kindly, selfless, devoted, loyal, affectionate, fond, caring, loving, compassionate, humane, sympathetic, personal, tender, benevolent, forgiving, comradely; see also **friendly** 1, **kind, loving.** — *Ant.* UNFRIENDLY, hostile, aloof.

**brow,** *n.* — *Syn.* eyebrow, forehead, temples, front; see **forehead.**

**browbeat,** *v.* — *Syn.* bully, intimidate, frighten, cow; see **ride** 4, **threaten** 1.

**brown,** *modif.* — *Syn.* brownish, copper-colored, rust-colored, coffee-colored; see **brown** *n.*

**brown,** *n.*
Hues of brown include: tan, bay, chestnut, nutbrown, almond, copper-colored, mahogany, bronze, russet, chocolate, cinnamon, hazel, reddish-brown, roan, sorrel, sepia, tawny, ochre, rust, rust-colored, brownish, puce, terra-cotta, fawn, snuff-colored, liver-colored, beige, taupe, ecru, dust, drab, dun, henna, coffee, khaki, maroon, cocoa, umber, brick, ginger, light brown, dark brown, auburn, buff, Caledonia, Antwerp, burnt orange, burnt ochre, burnt russet; Vandyke brown, Rembrandt brown, Verona brown; see also **color** 1.

**brown,** *v.* — *Syn.* toast, scorch, sauté, tan; see **cook, fry.**

**brownie,** *n.* **1.** [Fairy] — *Syn.* spirit, sprite, goblin, elf; see **fairy.**
**2.** [Girl Scout] — *Syn.* explorer, tenderfoot, camper; see **scout** 3.

**browse,** *v.* — *Syn.* skim, peruse, scan, glance at, flip through, look through, run through, look over, glance over, check over, run over, survey, inspect loosely, pass the eye over, read here and there, examine cursorily, go through carelessly, go through in a desultory manner, leaf through, thumb through, dip into, shop around, window-shop.

**bruise,** *n.* — *Syn.* contusion, black-and-blue mark, discoloration, abrasion, wound, swelling, blister, black eye, shiner*, ecchymosis, petechia; see also **blemish, injury** 1.

**bruise,** *v.* — *Syn.* contuse, beat, injure, wound; see **damage** 1, **hurt** 1.

**brunet,** *modif.* — *Syn.* brunette, dark, dark-complexioned, tawny, dusky, brown, tanned, swarthy, dark-haired, dark-skinned, olive-skinned, brown-haired, black-haired, pigmented, Latin, Mediterranean. — *Ant.* FAIR, light, light-complexioned, blond.

**brush,** *n.* **1.** [A brushing instrument] Common types of brushes include: bristle, fiber, wire, nail, clothes, camel's hair, hydraulic, rotary, paint, tooth, scrubbing, bottle, floor, hair, bath, dust; see also **broom, mop.**

**2.** [A touch] — *Syn.* rub, tap, stroke, graze; see **touch** 2.
**3.** [A light encounter] — *Syn.* skirmish, scrap, patrol action; see **battle** 1, **fight** 1.
**4.** [Underbrush] — *Syn.* thicket, boscage, undergrowth, second growth, chaparral, cover, brushwood, shrubbery, canebrake, grove, hedge, underwood, gorse, bracken, sedge, scrub, copse, coppice, spinney, dingle, brake; see also **bush** 1.
**5.** [*The act of ignoring] — *Syn.* cut, slight, rebuff, brushoff*; see **insult, rudeness.**

**brush,** *v.* **1.** [To clean by brushing] — *Syn.* sweep, whisk, wipe; see **clean.**
**2.** [To touch lightly] — *Syn.* stroke, smooth, graze; see **touch.**

**brush aside,** *v.* — *Syn.* dismiss, ignore, disregard, discount; see **disregard.**

**brushfire,** *n.* — *Syn.* burning, conflagration, forest fire; see **fire** 1.

**brush off*,** *v.* — *Syn.* reject, get rid of, send away, rebuff; see **dismiss** 1, **refuse.**

**brush up,** *v.* **1.** [To study] — *Syn.* reread, look over, review; see **study** 1.
**2.** [To clean] — *Syn.* renovate, refurbish, clean up; see **clean.**

**brusque,** *modif.* — *Syn.* terse, blunt, abrupt, curt; see **abrupt** 2, **blunt** 2.
*See Synonym Study at* BLUNT.

**brutal,** *modif.* **1.** [Cruel] — *Syn.* pitiless, harsh, unmerciful; see **cruel** 1, 2.
**2.** [Crude] — *Syn.* coarse, unfeeling, rude; see **crude** 1.
*See Synonym Study at* CRUEL.

**brutality,** *n.* — *Syn.* savageness, ruthlessness, harshness, unfeelingness; see **cruelty.**

**brutally,** *modif.* — *Syn.* ruthlessly, cruelly, callously, relentlessly, mercilessly, heartlessly, unfeelingly, harshly, grimly, viciously, meanly, inhumanly, inhumanely, brutishly, savagely, in a ruthless manner, in a cruel manner, in a heartless manner, hellishly, pitilessly, barbarously, remorselessly, unkindly, unrelentingly, wildly, inexorably, fiercely, atrociously, hard-heartedly, murderously, ferociously, diabolically, ferally, barbarically, demoniacally, in cold blood, animalistically. — *Ant.* gently, KINDLY, mercifully.

**brute,** *n.* **1.** [An animal] — *Syn.* mammal, beast, creature; see **animal** 2, **monster** 1.
**2.** [A person lacking human feelings] — *Syn.* degenerate, monster, barbarian, lout; see **beast** 2.

**bubble,** *n.* — *Syn.* globule, sac, air bubble, soap bubble, balloon, droplet, foam, froth, effervescence, lather, carbonation, fizz; see also **froth.**

**bubble,** *v.* — *Syn.* froth, foam, gurgle, gush, well, trickle, effervesce, fizz, boil, seethe, percolate, spume, simmer, seep, work, eddy, ferment, erupt, issue, burble, fizzle, sparkle, lather.

**buccaneer,** *n.* — *Syn.* pirate, marauder, freebooter; see **criminal, robber.**

**buck,** *n.* **1.** [The male of certain animals] — *Syn.* sire, stag, bull; see **deer, goat.**
**pass the buck*** — *Syn.* avoid responsibility, shirk, shift the blame; see **delegate** 2, **evade** 1.

**buck,** *v.* **1.** [To attempt to throw a rider by jumping] — *Syn.* rear, plunge, buck off, unseat, unhorse, dislodge, throw off, eject; see also **jump** 1, **oust.**
**2.** [*To oppose] — *Syn.* resist, combat, counter; see **oppose** 1, **resist** 1.

**bucket,** *n.* — *Syn.* pail, canister, can, basin, cask, scuttle, kettle, hod; see also **can** 1, **container, pot** 1.
**kick the bucket*** — *Syn.* expire, lose one's life, pass away; see **die** 1.

**buckle,** n. — Syn. clasp, clamp, catch, fastening; see **fastener.**

**buckle down\*,** v. — Syn. apply oneself, attend to, set to work, keep one's mind on; see **apply (oneself), attack** 4, **concentrate** 2.

**buck up\*,** v. — Syn. cheer, comfort, hearten; see **encourage** 2.

**bucolic,** modif. — Syn. rural, rustic, pastoral; see **rural.** See Synonym Study at RURAL.

**bud,** n. — Syn. shoot, incipient flower, germ, embryo; see **flower** 1.

**nip in the bud** — Syn. check, halt, stop; see **halt** 2, **prevent.**

**Buddha,** n. — Syn. Siddhartha Gautama, Gautama Buddha, Prince Siddhartha, bodhisattva, the Lord Buddha.

**budding,** modif. — Syn. maturing, developing, growing, incipient, about to bloom, fresh, shooting up, burgeoning, opening, blossoming, bursting (forth), putting forth shoots, vegetating, beginning to grow or blossom or bloom, flowering, blooming, promising, aspiring, young, pubescent, sprouting, germinating, pullulating, immature, latent, embryonic, in bud; see also **growing.**

**buddy,** n. **1.** [\*A close friend] — Syn. intimate, friend, partner, mate, fellow, peer, companion, comrade, confidant, crony, chum\*, pal\*, sidekick\*; see also **associate, friend** 1. — Ant. stranger, ENEMY, alien.
**2.** [\*Used in informal address to a male] — Syn. excuse me, bud\*, you there\*, Mac\*, Jack\*, hey you, hey, brother\*, buster\*, bub\*, bro\*, yo\*.

**budge,** v. — Syn. stir, change position, yield; see **influence, move** 1, **push** 2, **shift** 1, **yield** 1.

**budget,** n. — Syn. estimates, estimated expenses, allocations, allowance, budgetary figures, accounts, financial statement, financial plan, cost of operation, cost of living, funds, resources, means, spending plan, planned disbursement; see also **statement** 3.

**budget,** v. **1.** [To estimate expenditures and income] — Syn. allocate expenditures, balance income and outgo, allow for, figure in, ration, figure on, cost out; see also **estimate** 1.
**2.** [To estimate time or rations or distance, etc.] — Syn. compute, predict, plan, schedule; see **estimate** 1, 2.

**buff,** modif. — Syn. tan, ocher, tawny, brownish yellow; see **brown, tan, yellow** 1.

**in the buff\*** — Syn. naked, nude, bare, unclothed; see **naked** 1.

**buff,** v. — Syn. polish, burnish, brush; see **polish, shine** 3. See Synonym Study at POLISH.

**buffalo,** n.
Types of buffalo include: common or water buffalo, Cape buffalo, American bison, wild ox, African buffalo, Forest buffalo, European bison or wisent; see also **animal** 2.

**buffer,** n. — Syn. cushion, shield, shock absorber, bumper; see **barrier, defense** 1, **fender, shield.**

**buffet,** n. **1.** [A cupboard or table] — Syn. cabinet, sideboard, counter, table; see **cupboard, furniture.**
**2.** [A meal at which guests serve themselves] — Syn. smorgasbord, potluck, self-service meal, stand-up dinner, all-you-can-eat; see also **meal** 2.

**buffet,** v. — Syn. slap, strike, pound, batter; see **beat** 1, 2, 3, **hit** 1, 2.

**buffoon,** n. — Syn. joker, clown, comedian; see **clown, fool** 1, 2.

**bug,** n. **1.** [An insect] — Syn. beetle, vermin, gnat, hemipteran; see **insect, pest** 1.

**2.** [\*A microbe] — Syn. bacillus, disease germ, virus; see **germ** 3.
**3.** [\*A defect] — Syn. flaw, fault, imperfection, glitch\*; see **blemish, defect** 2.
**4.** [\*An enthusiast] — Syn. devotee, zealot, fanatic, hobbyist; see **enthusiast** 1.

**bug,** v. **1.** [\*To annoy] — Syn. irritate, plague, bother, pester; see **bother** 2, 3, **disturb** 2.
**2.** [\*To install hidden microphones] — Syn. spy on, eavesdrop, overhear, listen in on, wiretap, tap, put under surveillance; see also **eavesdrop.**

**bugbear,** n. — Syn. horror, terror, dread, hate, bête noire, bugaboo, nightmare, phantom, specter, goblin, bogy, bogeyman, scarecrow, curse, anathema, bane, pet peeve; see also **care** 2, **difficulty** 1, 2, **fear** 2.

**buggy,** n. — Syn. carriage, buckboard, surrey; see **baby carriage, carriage** 2.

**bugle,** n. — Syn. clarion, trumpet, cornet; see **horn** 1.

**build,** v. **1.** [To construct] — Syn. erect, construct, frame, raise, rear, make, manufacture, put together, fit together, fabricate, contrive, carpenter, assemble, put up, set up, model, hammer together, knock together, throw together, throw up, pile stone on stone, sculpture, fashion, compose, evolve, develop, compile, cast, reconstruct, chisel, hew, mold, produce, forge, block out, bring about, create, devise, carve, weave; see also **create** 2, **form** 1. — Ant. DESTROY, demolish, wreck.
**2.** [To increase] — Syn. mount, wax, swell, intensify; see **grow** 1, 2, **increase** 1, **strengthen.**
**3.** [To found] — Syn. establish, formulate, institute, constitute; see **establish** 2, **organize** 2.

**builder,** n. **1.** [Craftsman] — Syn. manufacturer, contractor, developer, mason, fabricator, artisan, carpenter, lather, taper, plasterer, producer, construction worker; see also **architect** 1. — Ant. DESTROYER, wrecker, consumer.
**2.** [Creator] — Syn. maker, originator, inventor, constructor; see **author** 1.

**build in,** v. — Syn. incorporate, add, insert; see **include** 2.

**building,** n. **1.** [A structure] — Syn. edifice, structure, construction, erection, fabrication, fabric, house, framework, superstructure, frame, architectural construction, pile, outbuilding; see also **apartment house, architecture, barn, castle, church** 1, **factory, home** 1, **hotel, motel, palace, skyscraper, temple.**
**2.** [The act of building] — Syn. erection, raising, construction, fabricating; see **construction** 1.

---

SYN. — **building** is the general term applied to a fixed structure in which people dwell, work, etc.; **edifice** implies a large or stately building and is sometimes used figuratively /the edifice of democracy/; **structure** may also suggest an imposing building, or may be used when the material of construction is being stressed /a steel structure/; **pile** is applied in poetry and lofty prose to a very large building or mass of buildings

---

**build on,** v. — Syn. extend, enlarge, add (on) to, develop; see **develop** 1, **increase** 1.

**build up,** v. **1.** [To increase] — Syn. develop, strengthen, add to, expand; see **develop** 1, **grow** 1, **increase** 1, **strengthen.**
**2.** [To make more desirable or attractive] — Syn. promote, talk up, magnify, boost; see **advertise** 2, **exaggerate, praise** 1, **promote** 1.

**buildup\*,** n. **1.** [A gradual increase] — Syn. accumulation, accretion, amassing, development; see **accumulation** 1, **increase** 1.

**2.** [Favorable publicity] — *Syn.* promotion, praise, hype*; see **advertising** 1, **praise** 1, **publicity** 3.

**built,** *modif.* **1.** [Erected] — *Syn.* constructed, fabricated, manufactured, made, put together, produced, assembled, set up, contrived, reared, raised, remodeled, completed, joined, perfected, finished, realized, established, created, formed, cast, forged, framed; see also **formed.**

**2.** [*Buxom] — *Syn.* well-proportioned, shapely, stacked*; see **buxom** 2.

**built-up,** *modif.* — *Syn.* developed, overdeveloped, congested, overbuilt; see **full** 1, **growing.**

**bulb,** *n.* — *Syn.* globe, globule, ball, knob, nodule, corn, nub, tuber, bulbil, tubercle, corm, protuberance, head, bunch, swelling, bulge, tumor, tube.
Plant bulbs include: tulip, gladiolus, daffodil, jonquil, narcissus, amaryllis, anemone, crocus, hyacinth, snowdrop, spring-flowering, onion, camas, grape hyacinth; lilies: butterfly, tiger, Easter, spider, mariposa; see also **flower** 2, **plant.**
Types of electric light bulbs include: high-intensity, three-way, soft-white, two-way, flash bulb; fluorescent, halogen, incandescent, mercury-vapor, ultraviolet, infrared, sun lamp; floodlight, black light, strobe light *or* strobe*; see also **light** 3, **lamp.**

**bulge,** *n.* — *Syn.* swelling, lump, protrusion, protuberance, hump, bump, convexity, intumescence, bulb, bunching, outgrowth, superfluity, tumefaction, nodule, sagging, tuberosity, nodulation, growth, dilation, prominence, salience, excess, bagginess, appendage, projection, excrescence, tumor, gibbosity, boss, distention, salient, egg, sac, knob, horn, ridge, flange, rib, wart, promontory, hummock; see also **growth** 3, **point** 2, **projection** 1.
*See Synonym Study at* PROJECTION.

**bulge,** *v.* — *Syn.* puff out, distend, protrude; see **project** 1, **swell.**

**bulk,** *n.* **1.** [Size] — *Syn.* magnitude, mass, extent, size, volume, amount, quantity, weight, heft, largeness, thickness, substance, body; see also **quantity, size** 2.

**2.** [Major portion] — *Syn.* greater part, better part, main part, principal part, major part, best part, predominant part, most, majority, plurality, biggest share, greater number, nearly all, almost all, body, more than half, best, gross, staple, preponderance, lion's share. — *Ant.* BIT, remnant, fraction, minority.

---

**SYN.** — **bulk, mass,** and **volume** all refer to a quantity of matter or collection of units forming a body or whole, **bulk** implying a body of great size, weight, or numbers /the lumbering *bulk* of a hippopotamus, the *bulk* of humanity/, **mass,** an aggregate, often as expanse forming a cohesive, unified, or solid body /an egg-shaped *mass,* a *mass* of color, the *mass* of workers/, and **volume,** a moving or flowing mass, often of a fluctuating nature /*volumes* of smoke, the *volume* of production/

---

**bulky,** *modif.* — *Syn.* massive, big, cumbersome; see **fat** 1, **heavy** 1, **large** 1.

**bull,** *n.* **1.** [The male of the bovine species] — *Syn. Bos taurus* (Latin), herd leader, bullock, steer, sire, ox, male, male cow, top cow*, brute*, beast*, seed ox*, animal*; see also **calf, cow.**

**2.** [One who endeavors to profit from a rising market] — *Syn.* buyer, speculator, margin purchaser, long seller; see **businessperson, financier.** — *Ant.* seller, short seller, bear.

**3.** [*Nonsense] — *Syn.* rubbish, baloney*, bullshit*; see **nonsense** 1.

**bullet,** *n.* — *Syn.* shell, cartridge, shot, ball, bolt, projectile, missile, ammunition, slug, steel-jacketed bullet, soft-nosed bullet, dum-dum bullet, machine-gun bullet, ammo*; see also **shot** 2, **weapon** 1.

**bite the bullet*** — *Syn.* face up to, confront, bear up; see **endure** 2, **face** 1.

**bulletin,** *n.* **1.** [A brief notice] — *Syn.* release, notice, communiqué, news flash; see **announcement** 2, **news** 2.

**2.** [A published report] — *Syn.* summary, journal, digest, periodical; see **journal** 2, **record** 1.

**bully,** *n.* — *Syn.* tormentor, ruffian, tough, tyrant; see **rascal.**

**bully,** *v.* — *Syn.* browbeat, tyrannize, domineer, harass; see **dominate, ride** 4, **threaten** 1.

**bulwark,** *n.* — *Syn.* buttress, outwork, rampart; see **barrier, defense** 2, **fortification** 2, **support** 2.

**bum*,** *n.* — *Syn.* tramp, hobo, vagrant, derelict; see **beggar** 1, 2, **tramp** 1.
*See Synonym Study at* TRAMP.

**bump,** *n.* **1.** [A jarring collision] — *Syn.* knock, bang, bounce, jounce, jar, box, smash, pat, crack, jolt, crash, sideswipe, collision, blow, punch, hit, clap, push, shove, thrust, boost, shock, clash, impact, stroke, rap, tap, slap, smack, cuff, whack, thwack, clout, jab, jerk, crash, prod, jolt, slam, nudge, buffet, thud, swat*, bash*, wallop*, belt*, bat*, swipe*, thump*, poke*, clump*, plump*, clunk*, sock*, whop*, slug*; see also **blow** 1, **collision** 1.

**2.** [A swelling or bulge] — *Syn.* lump, projection, protuberance, knob; see **bulge, swelling.**

**bump,** *v.* **1.** [To collide with] — *Syn.* collide, knock against, run into, strike; see **crash** 4, **hit** 1, 2.

**2.** [To make a bumping sound] — *Syn.* thud, whack, pound, smack, thwack, rap, slap, punch, slam, plop, plunk, thump, clump, bang, knock, clatter, clap, crash, rattle, thunder, tramp.

**3.** [To move with jerks or jolts] — *Syn.* bounce, jolt, jounce; see **jar** 1.

**bumper,** *n.* — *Syn.* cover, guard, protector; see **defense** 1, **fender, shield.**

**bump into*,** *v.* — *Syn.* run into, meet unexpectedly, encounter; see **find** 1, **meet** 6.

**bumpkin,** *n.* — *Syn.* rustic, yokel, hick*; see **boor.**

**bump off*,** *v.* — *Syn.* murder, slay, rub out, assassinate; see **kill** 1.

**bumptious,** *modif.* — *Syn.* conceited, arrogant, forward, pushy*; see **aggressive** 1, **egotistic** 2.

**bumpy,** *modif.* — *Syn.* rough, uneven, lumpy, jolting; see **irregular** 4, **jarring** 2, **rough** 1.

**bun,** *n.* — *Syn.* roll, muffin, scone, hot cross bun; see **bread** 1, **pastry, roll** 4.

**bunch,** *n.* **1.** [A connected group of things] — *Syn.* cluster, clump, batch, spray, bouquet, sheaf, tuft, shock, stack, thicket, tussock, fascicle, pack, group, gathering, host, galaxy, faggot, bundle, knot, collection, agglomeration, mass, passel*, mess*, slew*, caboodle*, oodles*, shootin'-match*, shebang*; see also **collection** 2.

**2.** [*A group of people] — *Syn.* crowd, pack, band, assemblage; see **crowd** 1, **gathering.**

**bundle,** *n.* — *Syn.* packet, parcel, bunch; see **package** 1.
*See Synonym Study at* PACKAGE.

**bundle up,** *v.* — *Syn.* dress warmly, wrap up, clothe; see **dress** 1.

**bungalow,** *n.* — *Syn.* cottage, lodging, one-story dwelling; see **home** 1.

**bungle,** *v.* — *Syn.* botch, blunder, fumble, mishandle; see **botch, fail** 1.

**bungler,** *n.* — *Syn.* fumbler, botcher, blunderer, flounderer, mismanager, muddler, spoiler, incompetent, numskull, featherbrain, harebrain, dolt, blockhead, scatterbrain, airhead, dunce, clod, ignoramus, idiot, duffer, addlebrain, gawk, donkey, marplot, butterfingers, lubber, bumbler, bonehead*, screw-up*, rattlehead*, clumsy oaf*, lummox*, bull in a china shop*, butcher*, schlemiel*, blunderhead*, klutz*, block*, muffer*, hacker*, looby*, stumblebum*, turkey*, doofus*; see also **fool** 1.

**bungling,** *modif.* — *Syn.* clumsy, unskillful, inept; see **awkward** 1, **incompetent**.

**bunk,** *n.* **1.** [A bed] — *Syn.* bunk bed, berth, cot, pallet; see **bed** 1.
**2.** [*Empty or insincere talk] — *Syn.* rubbish, rot, bunkum*, hogwash*; see **nonsense** 1.

**bunker,** *n.* — *Syn.* bin, locker, shelter, dugout; see **bin, container, fortification** 2.

**bunt,** *v.* **1.** [To butt] — *Syn.* toss, gore, horn; see **butt** 1, **throw** 1, 2.
**2.** [In baseball, to meet the ball with a loosely held bat] — *Syn.* meet it*, lay it down*, lay it along the base line*, sacrifice*, bunt and run*; see also **hit** 4.

**buoy,** *n.* — *Syn.* float, drift, floating marker; see **float** 1. Types of buoys include: bell, can, life, nun, light, whistling.

**buoyancy,** *n.* **1.** [Lightness] — *Syn.* levity, ethereality, buoyance, airiness, weightlessness, floatability; see also **lightness** 2.
**2.** [Cheerfulness] — *Syn.* gaiety, good humor, resilience, lightheartedness; see **happiness** 1, 2.

**buoyant,** *modif.* **1.** [Light in weight] — *Syn.* floating, floatable, weightless, unsinkable; see **floating, light** 5.
**2.** [Light in spirits] — *Syn.* jaunty, jovial, cheerful, resilient; see **happy** 1, **lively** 2, **sprightly**.

**buoy (up),** *v.* — *Syn.* keep afloat, sustain, uplift, hearten; see **encourage** 2, **support** 1, 2.

**bur,** *n.* — *Syn.* prickly seedcase, nut, grain, acorn, pod, seed pod, boll; see also **bramble, seed** 1.

**burden,** *n.* **1.** [Something carried] — *Syn.* load, weight, freight, pack; see **freight** 1, **load** 1, **package** 1.
**2.** [Anything hard to support or endure] — *Syn.* encumbrance, trouble, thorn in the flesh, onus, weary load, heavy load, weight, millstone, albatross around one's neck, cross to bear, impediment, imposition, inconvenience, hardship, trial, strain, responsibility; see also **affliction, difficulty** 2, **duty** 2, **misfortune** 1.

**burden,** *v.* — *Syn.* weigh down, encumber, cumber, oppress, overwhelm, hinder, hamper, strain, load with, saddle with, task with, handicap, obligate, lade, tax, charge, overtask, afflict, vex, try, trouble, pile, overcharge, overburden, bear down, bog down, crush, depress, impede, overload, overtax, load down with, make heavy; see also **force** 1, **hinder, oppress.** — *Ant.* LIGHTEN, relieve, unload.

**burdensome,** *modif.* — *Syn.* heavy, oppressive, troublesome; see **difficult** 1, 2, **disturbing, onerous.**
*See Synonym Study at* ONEROUS.

**bureau,** *n.* **1.** [An office of division] — *Syn.* agency, department, authority, board; see **committee, department** 2, **office** 3.
**2.** [Chest of drawers] — *Syn.* highboy, dresser, chiffonier; see **chest** 1, **furniture.**

**bureaucracy,** *n.* **1.** [Government] — *Syn.* officialdom, administration, the Establishment, the authorities, apparatchiki, the powers that be, city hall, civil service, they, them, the system*; see also **authority** 3, **government** 1.
**2.** [Rigid routine] — *Syn.* red tape, official procedure, inflexible routine, strict procedure, officialism, bumbledom*.

**bureaucrat,** *n.* — *Syn.* functionary, official, apparatchik, mandarin, civil servant; see also **administrator.**

**burglar,** *n.* — *Syn.* thief, housebreaker, second-story man*; see **criminal, robber.**

**burglary,** *n.* — *Syn.* theft, housebreaking, stealing, robbery; see **crime** 2, **theft.**
*See Synonym Study at* THEFT.

**burial,** *n.* — *Syn.* last rites, interment, obsequies; see **funeral** 1.

**burial ground,** *n.* — *Syn.* cemetery, necropolis, graveyard, memorial park; see **cemetery.**

**burlesque,** *n.* **1.** [Anything intending to mock] — *Syn.* parody, travesty, caricature, lampoon; see **parody.**
**2.** [A bawdy stage show] — *Syn.* show, theatrical entertainment, revue, vaudeville, burleycue*, strip*, burly*, topless show*, nudie*, girlie show*; see also **performance** 2, **show** 2.
*See Synonym Study at* PARODY.

**burly,** *modif.* — *Syn.* husky, stout, beefy, brawny; see **fat** 1, **strong** 1.

**burn,** *n.* — *Syn.* blister, scorch, scald, wound, impairment, trauma, first-degree burn, second-degree burn, third-degree burn, sunburn, windburn, reddening; see also **blister, injury** 1.

**burn,** *v.* **1.** [To oxidize] — *Syn.* be on fire, catch on fire, consume, combust, burn up, burn down, incinerate, rage, blaze, flame, flash, glow, burn fiercely, flare up, flame up, flare up, burst into flame, grow bright, turn to ashes, smolder, smoke.
**2.** [To subject to fire] — *Syn.* set on fire, ignite, light, kindle, incinerate, enkindle, cremate, relight, conflagrate, consume with flames, rekindle, reduce to ashes, set a match to, set ablaze, set afire, torch, sear, singe, scorch, brand, char, cauterize, roast, toast, heat, bake, brown, blacken, overcook, carbonize, fire, consign to the flame; see also **cook.** — *Ant.* EXTINGUISH, put out, quench.
**3.** [To feel emotion suggestive of fire] — *Syn.* tingle, lust, desire, yearn, thirst, be excited, be inflamed, be aroused, be stirred up, breathe fire and fury*; see also **rage** 1.
**4.** [To feel or cause to feel a burning sensation] — *Syn.* smart, sting, bite, throb; see **hurt** 1, 4.
**5.** [*To cheat] — *Syn.* swindle, defraud, trick, rob; see **deceive.**
**6.** [To scorch] — *Syn.* char, sear, roast, toast, parch, bake, singe, scald, wither; see also sense 2.

---

**SYN.** — **burn** is the broadest term in this comparison, denoting injury to any extent by fire or something with the effect of fire, as intense heat, friction, or acid [a burnt log, sunburned, windburned]; **scorch** and **singe** both imply superficial burning, **scorch** emphasizing discoloration or damaging of texture [to scorch a shirt in ironing], and **singe**, the burning off, often intentional, of bristles, feathers, the ends of hair, etc.; **sear** implies the burning of animal tissue and is applied specifically to the quick browning of the outside of meat in cooking to seal in the juices [to sear a roast]; **char** implies a reduction by burning to charcoal or carbon: all of these terms have figurative applications [a burning desire, a scorching tirade, a singed reputation, a soul-searing experience, charred hopes]

---

**burned,** *modif.* **1.** [Marked by fire or intense heat] — *Syn.* scorched, charred, seared, burnt, singed, branded, cauterized, marked, blistered, sunburned, scalded.

**2.** [Consumed] — *Syn.* burned up, reduced to ashes, incinerated; see **destroyed.**

**burned up\***, *modif.* — *Syn.* angered, enraged, infuriated; see **angry.**

**burner,** *n.* — *Syn.* torch, jet, heat unit, heater, warmer, cooker, gas burner, surface element, heating element, lamp; see also **stove.**

**burning,** *modif.* **1.** [On fire] — *Syn.* flaming, fiery, blazing, glowing, ablaze, afire, on fire, smoking, in flames, aflame, inflamed, kindled, enkindled, ignited, lighted, lit, red, hot, scorching, incandescent, turning to ashes, aglow, searing, roasting, in a blaze, blistering, red-hot, white-hot, smoldering, oxidizing, being consumed, going up in smoke. — *Ant.* COLD, frozen, out.

**2.** [Fervent] — *Syn.* intense, ardent, impassioned; see **passionate** 4.

**3.** [Eager] — *Syn.* zealous, fervid, rapt, glowing; see **enthusiastic** 2, 3.

**4.** [Caustic] — *Syn.* sharp, biting, stinging; see **painful** 1, **sour** 1.

**burnish,** *v.* — *Syn.* polish, buff, shine; see **polish, shine** 3.

*See Synonym Study at* POLISH.

**burnt,** *modif.* — *Syn.* scorched, singed, charred; see **burned** 1.

**burrow,** *n.* — *Syn.* tunnel, den, lair; see **hole** 3, **retreat** 2.

**bursar,** *n.* — *Syn.* treasurer, controller, purser, cashier; see **accountant, treasurer.**

**burst,** *n.* **1.** [An act or result of bursting] — *Syn.* blowout, rupture, blast, blowup; see **blowout** 1, **explosion** 1.

**2.** [A sudden spurt] — *Syn.* rush, outburst, spate; see **fit** 2.

**3.** [A volley] — *Syn.* salvo, round, discharge; see **fire** 2, **volley.**

**burst,** *v.* **1.** [To explode] — *Syn.* blow up, rupture, shatter, fly apart; see **break** 2, 3, **disintegrate** 1, **explode** 1.

**2.** [To break] — *Syn.* crack, split, fracture; see **break** 1, **destroy** 1.

**3.** [To puncture] — *Syn.* pierce, prick, perforate; see **penetrate** 1.

**burst in,** *v.* — *Syn.* rush in, break in, barge in, invade, intrude; see also **enter** 1, **meddle** 1.

**bursting,** *modif.* **1.** [Breaking open] — *Syn.* exploding, erupting, shattering; see **breaking.**

**2.** [As full as possible] — *Syn.* full, filled, packed, at the bursting point; see **full** 1, **jammed** 2.

**burst into tears,** *v.* weep, start crying, break into tears, see **cry** 1.

**bury,** *v.* **1.** [To inter] — *Syn.* inhume, lay in the grave, lay to rest, entomb, consign to dust, enshrine, ensepulcher, deposit in the earth, embalm, give burial to, hold funeral services for, hold (the) last rites for, lay out, mummify, put six feet under\*. — *Ant.* EXHUME, disinter, dig up.

**2.** [To cover] — *Syn.* hide, conceal, secrete, stow away; see **hide** 1.

**3.** [To occupy] — *Syn.* engross, immerse, engage, inundate; see **occupy** 3.

**4.** [To embed] — *Syn.* sink, implant, drive in; see **embed** 1, **fasten** 1.

**5.** [To defeat] — *Syn.* overcome, win over, beat, conquer; see **defeat** 1, 2, 3.

*See Synonym Study at* HIDE.

**bus,** *n.* — *Syn.* motor coach, motorbus, autobus, omnibus, passenger bus, transit vehicle, tour bus, sightseeing bus, charabanc (British), shuttle bus, school bus, inter-

urban, limousine, common carrier, public conveyance, Greyhound (Trademark), minibus, jitney, van, double-decker, limo\*.

**bus\*,** *v.* — *Syn.* transport, integrate (by busing), redistrict; see **carry** 1.

**bush,** *n.* **1.** [A woody plant] — *Syn.* shrub, bramble, thicket, hedge, shrubbery; see also **hedge, plant.**

**2.** [A wild region] — *Syn.* hinterland, backcountry, backwoods; see **country** 1, **forest.**

**beat around the bush** — *Syn.* speak indirectly, speak evasively, avoid the subject, avoid the issue, be deceptive; see also **evade** 1.

**bushy,** *modif.* — *Syn.* fuzzy, disordered, thick, shaggy, rough, full, tufted, fringed, woolly, nappy, fluffy, furry, hairy, crinkly, stiff, wiry, rumpled, unkempt, prickly, feathery, leafy, bristly, unruly, spreading, heavy; see also **hairy** 1. — *Ant.* THIN, sleek, smooth.

**busily,** *modif.* — *Syn.* diligently, actively, energetically, strenuously, eagerly, earnestly, seriously, intently, determinedly, rapidly, dexterously, industriously, assiduously, sedulously, carefully, steadily, laboriously, painstakingly, unremittingly, studiously, perseveringly, hurriedly, briskly, vivaciously, animatedly, purposefully, ardently, arduously, fervently, spiritedly, nimbly, zealously, agilely, vigorously, drudgingly, indefatigably, restlessly, vigilantly, enthusiastically, speedily, hastily, persistently, expeditiously, unweariedly, with all dispatch, like hell, like the dickens, like the devil\*. — *Ant.* listlessly, idly, perfunctorily.

**business,** *modif.* — *Syn.* financial, monetary, commercial, trade; see **commercial** 1.

**business,** *n.* **1.** [Industry and trade] — *Syn.* commerce, exchange, trade, traffic, barter, industry, venture, commercial enterprise, gainful occupation, buying and selling, negotiation, production and distribution, dealings, affairs, sales, contracts, bargaining, trading, transaction, banking, marketing, merchandising, custom, undertaking, speculation, haggling, market, mercantilism, wholesale and retail, capital and labor, laissez-faire, free enterprise, game\*, racket\*, wheeling and dealing\*.

**2.** [Occupation] — *Syn.* trade, profession, vocation; see **job** 1, **profession** 1, **trade** 2.

**3.** [One's proper concerns] — *Syn.* affair, concern, interest; see **affair** 1.

**4.** [A commercial enterprise] — *Syn.* firm, company, factory, manufacturer, mill, store, shop, corporation, concern, combine, establishment, enterprise, partnership, institution, house, outfit, market, conglomerate, consortium, syndicate, cartel, trust, monopoly, holding company, mutual company, pool.

Some large well-known businesses include: Amoco, American Telephone and Telegraph (AT&T), Boeing Corporation, Chevron, Chrysler Corporation, Coca-Cola, ConAgra, Dow Chemical, Eastman Kodak, Exxon, Ford Motor Company, General Dynamics, General Electric, General Motors, DuPont, International Business Machines (IBM), Microsoft, Union Carbide, International Telephone and Telegraph (IT & T), Mobil Oil, PepsiCo, Philip Morris, Procter & Gamble, Shell Oil, Sony, Texaco, Xerox.

**5.** [The business cycle] — *Syn.* market, trade, volume of trade, patronage, upward trend, downward trend; see also sense 1.

**do business with** — *Syn.* deal with, trade with, patronize, employ; see **buy** 1, **sell** 1, **treat** 1.

**get the business\*** — *Syn.* be mistreated, be abused, be scolded; see **endure** 2, **suffer** 1.

**give the business\*** — *Syn.* mistreat, bother, victimize, give a tongue-lashing\*; see **abuse** 1, **bother** 2, **scold.**

**mean business** — *Syn.* be serious, be in earnest, stress, impress; see **emphasize, intend** 1, **resolve** 1.

*SYN.* — **business**, in this comparison, refers generally to the buying and selling of commodities and services and connotes a profit motive; **commerce** and **trade** both refer to the distribution or exchange of commodities, esp. as this involves their transportation, but **commerce** generally implies such activity on a large scale between cities, countries, etc.; **industry** refers chiefly to the large-scale manufacture of commodities

**businesslike**, *modif.* — *Syn.* purposeful, methodical, efficient, systematic, intent, earnest, serious, sedulous, energetic, hardworking, brisk, diligent, painstaking, careful, organized, professional, impersonal, matter-of-fact, vigorous, direct, orderly, skillful, dexterous, practiced, accustomed, thorough, accomplished, expeditious, prompt, industrious, assiduous, attentive, enterprising, resolute, careful, economical, disciplined, effective; see also **efficient** 1, **practical.** — *Ant.* AIMLESS, dilatory, inefficient.

**businessperson**, *n.* — *Syn.* businessman, businesswoman, industrialist, capitalist, employer, executive, entrepreneur, tycoon, magnate, broker, organization man, man in the gray flannel suit, retailer, wholesaler, stockbroker, manager, buyer, owner, operator, franchiser, speculator, purchasing agent, storekeeper, tradesman, middleman, suit*; see also **financier, manufacturer, merchant.**

**bust**, *n.* **1.** [Breast] — *Syn.* bosom, breasts, torso; see **breast** 2, **chest** 2.
**2.** [Figurehead] — *Syn.* carving, sculpture, model, head; see **image** 2, **statue.**
**3.** [*A total failure] — *Syn.* flop*, washout*, dud*; see **failure** 1.
*See Synonym Study at* BREAST.

**bust***, *v.* — *Syn.* break, smash, fracture, burst; see **break** 1, 2.

**bustle**, *v.* — *Syn.* move quickly, hasten, hustle; see **hurry** 1, **run** 2.

**busy**, *modif.* **1.** [Engaged] — *Syn.* occupied, diligent, working, employed, involved, tied up, in conference, in a meeting, in the field, on an assignment; with a customer, with a patient, etc.; on duty, on the job, at work, on the move, on the run, on the road, hardworking, industrious, buried in, busy as a bee*, hustling*, up to one's ears, up to one's neck, up to one's eyeballs*, on the go*, on the jump*, hard at it*, having many irons in the fire*, having other fish to fry*; see also **employed.** — *Ant.* idle, UNEMPLOYED, unoccupied, free.
**2.** [Active] — *Syn.* bustling, energetic, lively, hectic; see **active** 2.
**3.** [In use] — *Syn.* employed, occupied, in someone else's possession, unavailable, already taken, full; see also **rented.** — *Ant.* not in use, AVAILABLE, free.
**4.** [Officious] — *Syn.* meddlesome, curious, forward, intrusive, obtrusive, meddling, prying, interfering, butting in*, snoopy*, nosy*, pushy*; see also **meddlesome.**
**5.** [Too crowded with detail] — *Syn.* fussy, cluttered, overelaborate; see **elaborate** 1, **ornate** 1.
*See Synonym Study at* DILIGENT.

**busybody**, *n.* — *Syn.* snoop, meddler, pry, gossip, tattletale, eavesdropper, prier, intriguer, intruder, troublemaker, buttinsky*, kibitzer*, fink*, yenta*, rubberneck*, Nosy Parker*; see also **gossip** 2.

**but**, *conj. & prep.* **1.** [Indicating contrast] — *Syn.* how-

ever, on the other hand, in contrast, nevertheless, still, yet, though, on the contrary, but then, but as you see; see also **although.**
**2.** [Indicating an exception] — *Syn.* except, save, disregarding, without, not including, not taking into account, let alone, leaving out of consideration, aside from, with the exception of, not to mention, passing over, barring, setting aside, forgetting, omitting (to mention); see also **except.**
**3.** [Indicating a limitation] — *Syn.* only, only just, merely, simply, barely, solely, purely, just, no more, exactly, no other than, without.

**butcher**, *n.* **1.** [A meat dealer] — *Syn.* meat seller, meat vendor, slaughterer, processor, skinner, boner, cutter, proprietor of a meat market, pig-sticker*; see also **businessperson, merchant.**
**2.** [A killer] — *Syn.* murderer, slaughter, cutthroat, mass murderer; see **criminal, killer.**

**butcher**, *v.* **1.** [To prepare animals for human consumption] — *Syn.* slaughter, stick, pack, dress, clean, cure, smoke, salt, cut, put up, carve, trim.
**2.** [To kill inhumanly] — *Syn.* slaughter, slay, massacre; see **kill** 1.
**3.** [*To ruin] — *Syn.* botch, mutilate, spoil, wreck; see **botch, destroy** 1.

**butchery**, *n.* — *Syn.* slaughter, carnage, killing, massacre; see **carnage, murder.**
*See Synonym Study at* CARNAGE.

**butler**, *n.* — *Syn.* steward, head servant, manservant, major-domo; see **servant.**

**butt**, *n.* **1.** [The butt end] — *Syn.* base, tail end, bottom, hilt, extremity, tail, tip, fundament, stump, stub, end, fag end; see also **foundation** 2. — *Ant.* pinnacle, point, peak.
**2.** [A laughingstock] — *Syn.* sap, dupe, target, victim; see **fool** 2, **victim** 1, 2.
**3.** [*The buttocks] — *Syn.* bottom, seat, posterior; see **back** 2, **rump.**

**butt**, *v.* **1.** [To strike with the head] — *Syn.* ram, push headfirst, bump, batter, knock, collide with, run into, smack, buffet, strike, hook, gore, horn, buck, bunt, toss, crash into, collide; see also **crash** 4, **hit** 2.
**2.** [To abut] — *Syn.* adjoin, touch, bound; see **join** 3.

**butter**, *n.* Varieties of butter include the following: dairy, creamery, sweet, bulk, cube, country, tub, buffalo, ghee, yak, vegetable, soy, cacao, shea.

**butterfly**, *n.*
Common American butterflies include: Falcate Orangetip, Tiger Swallowtail, Mourning Cloak, Common Sulfur, American Copper, Cabbage, Colorado Parnassian, Great Spangled Fritillary, Tortoiseshell, Viceroy, Wood Nymph, Painted Lady, Monarch, Zebra, Buckeye, Skipper, Hairstreak, Red Admiral, Cloudless Sulfur, Grayling, Spicebush, Swallowtail, Ursula, Silverspot, Thecla, Blue, Violet; see also **insect.**

**butt in***, *v.* — *Syn.* interrupt, intrude, interface, horn in; see **interrupt** 2, **meddle** 1.

**buttocks**, *pl.n.* — *Syn.* backside, rump, behind*, rear end*; see **back** 2, **rump.**

**button**, *n.* — *Syn.* knob, catch, disk, badge, pin, snap, frog, clasp, switch, dial, key; see also **fastener.**
**on the button*** — *Syn.* exactly, precisely, squarely, on target*; see **accurate** 1, 2, **accurately.**

**button**, *v.* — *Syn.* close, clasp, fasten, snap; see **fasten** 1.

**buttress**, *v.* — *Syn.* prop (up), bolster, sustain; see **support** 1, 2.

**buxom**, *modif.* **1.** [Hearty] — *Syn.* plump, robust, vigorous; see **healthy** 1, **fat** 1.

**2.** [Large-breasted] — *Syn.* shapely, curvaceous, voluptuous, full-bosomed, bosomy, well-built, well-proportioned, comely, stacked\*, built\*, busty\*, chesty\*.

**buy\*,** *n.* — *Syn.* value, good deal, bargain, steal\*; see **bargain** 2.

**buy,** *v.* **1.** [To acquire by purchase] — *Syn.* purchase, acquire, get, pay for, bargain for, barter for, procure, gain, secure for a consideration, contract for, sign for, get in exchange, shop for, go marketing, buy and sell, order, invest in, make an investment, acquire ownership of, procure title to, pay cash for, redeem, hire, pay a price for, pick up, score\*, traffic in\*; see also **obtain** 1. — *Ant.* SELL, vend, auction.

**2.** [To bribe] — *Syn.* suborn, have in one's pay, corrupt, grease one's palm\*; see **bribe.**

**buyer,** *n.* — *Syn.* purchasing agent, purchaser, customer, consumer, shopper, client, prospect, representative, patron, user, emptor, bull\*. — *Ant.* SALESMAN, vendor, dealer.

**buyer's market,** *n.* — *Syn.* depression, recession, bargain prices; see **bargain** 2, **opportunity** 1, **sale** 3.

**buying,** *n.* — *Syn.* purchasing, getting, obtaining, acquiring, paying, shopping, marketing, investing, exchange, bartering, bargaining, procuring, ordering, trafficking, consumerism. — *Ant.* SELLING, vending, auctioning.

**buy off,** *v.* — *Syn.* corrupt, influence, fix\*; see **bribe.**

**buzz,** *n.* — *Syn.* murmur, buzzing, hum, drone; see **noise** 1.

**buzz,** *v.* drone, hum, whir; see **sound** 1.

**buzzard,** *n.* — *Syn.* bird of prey, *Buteo* (Latin), turkey vulture, carrion-eater; see **bird** 1.

**buzzer,** *n.* — *Syn.* siren, signal, electric bell; see **alarm** 1, **bell** 1, **sign** 1.

**by,** *prep.* **1.** [Near] — *Syn.* close to, next to, by the side of, at; see **near** 1, **next** 2.

**2.** [By stated means] — *Syn.* over, with, through, by means of, by the agency *or* intermediacy of, in the name of, at the hand of, along with, through the medium of, with the assistance *or* aid of, on, supported by, via.

**bygone,** *modif.* — *Syn.* former, olden, past, of old; see **former, old** 3, **past** 1.

**bylaw,** *n.* — *Syn.* ordinance, local law, standing rule, internal regulation; see **law** 3.

**bypass,** *n.* — *Syn.* detour, temporary route, side road; see **detour, road** 1.

**bypass,** *v.* — *Syn.* avoid, circumvent, skirt, detour; see **avoid, neglect** 1.

**bystander,** *n.* — *Syn.* onlooker, watcher, spectator, witness; see **observer** 1.

**byword,** *n.* — *Syn.* standing joke, axiom, gnomic saying, catchword; see **motto, proverb.**

# C

**cab,** *n.* — *Syn.* taxi, taxicab, limousine, hack\*; see **automobile, taxicab, vehicle** 1.

**cabal,** *n.* — *Syn.* plot, scheme, conspiracy, junta; see **intrigue** 1, **plot** 1, **ring** 3, **trick** 1.
*See Synonym Study at* PLOT.

**cabaret,** *n.* — *Syn.* café, nightclub, supper club, nightspot\*; see **bar** 2, **nightclub, restaurant.**

**cabin,** *n.* — *Syn.* log house, cottage, hut; see **home** 1, **shelter.**

**cabinet,** *n.* **1.** [A piece of furniture with shelves] — *Syn.* cupboard, closet, china closet, china cabinet, medicine chest; see also **chest** 1, **closet, cupboard, furniture.**
**2.** [An executive body] — *Syn.* council, advisory council, bureau, governing body, administrators, counselors, assembly, assistants, department heads, advisers, United States Cabinet, ministry, council of ministers, privy council, kitchen cabinet\*, brain trust\*; see also **authority** 3, **committee, government** 2.

**cable,** *n.* — *Syn.* cord, preformed cable, wire twist; see **chain** 1, **wire** 1.

**caboose,** *n.* — *Syn.* trainmen's car, rear car, crew car, boxcar, cab\*; see also **car** 2, **train** 2.

**cache,** *n.* — *Syn.* hoard, supplies, hidden reserve, stockpile; see **reserve** 1, **treasure, wealth** 2.

**cache,** *v.* — *Syn.* conceal, store, lay away, stash away\*; see **accumulate** 1, **hide** 1, **maintain** 3, **save** 3, **store.**
*See Synonym Study at* HIDE.

**cackle,** *v.* — *Syn.* cluck, gabble, chortle, chuckle, titter, snicker, quack, giggle, snigger; see also **laugh.**

**cacophonous,** *modif.* — *Syn.* ill-sounding, dissonant, discordant, raucous; see **harsh** 1.

**cacophony,** *n.* — *Syn.* dissonance, discord, harshness; see **noise** 1, 2.

**cactus,** *n.* — *Syn.* one of the *Cactaceae* (Latin), desert flora, desert vegetation, succulent; see **plant.**
Varieties of cactuses include: giant, saguaro, organ-pipe, barrel, hedgehog, cochineal, nipple, opuntia, cholla, prickly pear, night-blooming cereus, century plant, mescal, echinocactus, mammillaria.

**cad,** *n.* — *Syn.* rogue, scoundrel, rake; see **boor, rascal.**

**cadaver,** *n.* — *Syn.* corpse, dead body, remains; see **body** 2.
*See Synonym Study at* BODY.

**cadaverous,** *modif.* — *Syn.* ghostly, pallid, gaunt, haggard; see **ghastly** 1, **pale** 1, **sick, thin** 2.

**cadence,** *n.* — *Syn.* rhythm, meter, flow; see **beat** 2, 3, **measure** 3.

**cadre,** *n.* — *Syn.* staff officers, force, personnel, nucleus; see **organization** 3, **staff** 2.

**café,** *n.* — *Syn.* coffeehouse, bistro, lunchroom, coffee shop; see **restaurant.**

**cage,** *n.* — *Syn.* coop, pen, mew, crate; see **enclosure** 1, **jail, pen** 1.

**cajole,** *v.* — *Syn.* wheedle, coax, flatter; see **coax, influence, tempt, urge** 2.
*See Synonym Study at* COAX.

**cake,** *n.* **1.** [A flattish, compact mass] — *Syn.* cube, bar, block, loaf; see **block** 1, 6, **mass** 1, **slab.**
**2.** [Sweet baked goods]
Kinds of cake include: wedding, birthday, angel food, devil's-food, corn, sponge, fruit, burnt-sugar, caramel, chocolate, German chocolate, upside-down, tube, Bundt, pound, Martha Washington, maple, orange, coconut, white lemon, citron, walnut, almond, layer, chiffon, white mountain, spice, marble, Lady Baltimore, coffeecake, Kuchen; jellyroll, gingerbread, éclair, shortbread, cheesecake, fruitcake, cupcake, torte, petit four; see also **bread** 1, **pastry.**

**take the cake\*** — *Syn.* excel, outdo, win the prize; see **surpass.**

**cake,** *v.* — *Syn.* crust, solidify, pack; see **freeze** 1, **harden** 1, 2, **thicken** 1.

**calamitous,** *modif.* — *Syn.* disastrous, catastrophic, ruinous, unfortunate; see **harmful, unfavorable** 2.

**calamity,** *n.* — *Syn.* disaster, cataclysm, distress, trial; see **catastrophe, disaster, misfortune** 1, 2, **tragedy** 2.
*See Synonym Study at* DISASTER.

**calculable,** *modif.* — *Syn.* measurable, ascertainable, predictable, foreseeable, accountable, reckonable, discoverable, estimable, computable, countable.

**calculate,** *v.* **1.** [To determine, especially by using mathematics] — *Syn.* compute, reckon, determine, enumerate, count, figure out, figure, ascertain, ascertain mathematically, work out, estimate, forecast, rate, weigh, gauge, assess, number, figure up, account, sum up, total, divide, multiply, subtract, add, cipher, tally, cast, dope out\*, crunch numbers\*; see also **count, estimate** 1, **measure** 1, **reckon.**
**2.** [To determine by reasoning or evaluating] — *Syn.* estimate, judge, gauge, think, think likely; see also **anticipate** 1, **assume** 1, **estimate** 1, 2, **guess** 1.

---

*SYN.* — **calculate** refers to the mathematical determination of a quantity, amount, etc. and usually implies the use of higher mathematics /to *calculate* distances in astronomy/; **compute** suggests simpler mathematics and implies a determinable, hence precise, result /to *compute* the volume of a cylinder/; **estimate** implies the judging, usually in advance, of a quantity, cost, etc. and connotes an approximate result /to *estimate* the cost of building a house/; **reckon,** an informal substitute for **compute,** suggests the use of simple arithmetic such as can be performed mentally /to *reckon* the days before elections/

---

**calculated,** *modif.* **1.** [Figured by mathematical calculation] — *Syn.* computed, reckoned, determined, figured, ascertained, estimated, assessed, tallied.
**2.** [Deliberately planned] — *Syn.* planned, intended, designed, premeditated; see **deliberate** 1.

**calculating,** *modif.* — *Syn.* scheming, crafty, shrewd; see **intelligent** 1, **sly** 1.

**calculation,** *n.* **1.** [The act of calculating] — *Syn.*

computation, estimation, prediction, figuring, reckoning, adding, subtracting, dividing, multiplying, totaling, count; see also **estimate** 1, **guess.**

**2.** [A forecast] — *Syn.* prediction, prognosis, prognostication, estimation; see **divination, forecast.**

**3.** [Prudence] — *Syn.* forethought, consideration, circumspection, scheming; see **discretion** 1, **prudence, thought** 1.

**calculator,** *n.* — *Syn.* adding machine, pocket calculator, computer, calculating machine, abacus, slide rule; see also **computer.**

**calculus,** *n.* — *Syn.* calculation, computation, analysis; see **mathematics.**

**caldron,** *n.* — *Syn.* kettle, boiler, vat; see **container, pan, pot** 1.

**calendar,** *n.* — *Syn.* timetable, schedule, datebook, appointment book, diary, Filofax (trademark), chronology, log, logbook, table, register, almanac, agenda, docket, program, annals, menology, journal, daybook, time, timeline, perpetual calendar, system of reckoning; Gregorian calendar, Julian calendar, Muslim calendar, Jewish calendar, Hebrew calendar, ecclesiastical calendar, church calendar, ordo, Chinese calendar, Hindu calendar, French Revolutionary calendar; see also **list, program** 2, **record** 1.

**calf,** *n.* — *Syn.* young cow, young bull, yearling, freemartin, maverick, dogie*.
Related terms for other young animals include: colt, cub, kitten, filly, lionet, pup, puppy, bunny, fawn, foal, piglet, lamb, lambkin, whelp, kid, joey; see also **animal** 1, 2, **cow.**

**kill the fatted calf**— *Syn.* celebrate, have a feast, have a celebration, welcome; see **celebrate** 1, 3.

**caliber,** *n.* **1.** [A measurement] — *Syn.* diameter, bore, gauge, striking power; see **diameter, length** 1, **measurement** 2, **width.**

**2.** [Character] — *Syn.* quality, worth, nature, ability; see **ability** 1, **character** 2, **characteristic, value** 3.

**California,** *n.* — *Syn.* Golden State, El Dorado, Sunny California, Golden Bear State, Gold Rush State, Golden Poppy State, Bear Flag State, Gold Coast, Cal*, Cali*, Sunkist State*, Sunny Cal*, La La Land*.

**calisthenics,** *n.* — *Syn.* exercises, workout, slimnastics*; see **exercise** 1, **gymnastics.**

**call,** *n.* **1.** [A shout] — *Syn.* yell, cry, whoop, hail; see **alarm** 1, **cry** 1, **yell** 1.

**2.** [Characteristic sound] — *Syn.* cry, song, note, shriek; see **cry** 2.

**3.** [A brief visit] — *Syn.* stop, visiting, a few words, afternoon call; see **visit.**

**4.** [Word of command] — *Syn.* signal, command, summons, calling up, bugle call, trumpet call, bell, cry, battle cry, rallying cry, reveille, taps, last post, Sanctus bell, angelus; see also **alarm** 1, **command** 1, **cry** 1.

**5.** [An invitation] — *Syn.* bidding, solicitation, request, proposal; see **appeal** 1, **invitation** 1, **request.**

**on call**— *Syn.* ready, prepared, alerted, standing by; see **available.**

**within call**— *Syn.* close by, not far away, within earshot; see **near** 1.

**call,** *v.* **1.** [To raise the voice] — *Syn.* shout, call out, cry out, exclaim; see **cry** 3, **greet, yell.**

**2.** [To address or label as] — *Syn.* name, denominate, designate, term; see **describe, name** 1.

**3.** [To bring a body of people together] — *Syn.* collect, convene, assemble, convoke, muster, rally; see also **assemble** 2.

**4.** [To invite] — *Syn.* summon, request, ask, beckon, bid come; see also **invite** 1, **summon** 1.

**5.** [To request or demand] — *Syn.* charge, order, call upon, entreat; see **ask** 1, **command** 1, **invite** 2, **summon** 1.

**6.** [To estimate] — *Syn.* guess, make a rough calculation, say it is; see **estimate** 1, 2.

**7.** [To telephone] — *Syn.* phone, call up, ring; see **telephone.**

**8.** [To arouse] — *Syn.* stir, awaken, shake; see **wake** 1.

**9.** [To declare] — *Syn.* announce, proclaim, pronounce; see **declare** 1.

**10.** [To visit briefly] — *Syn.* make a visit, call on, stop by, drop in; see **visit** 2, 4.

---

*SYN.* — **call,** in this comparison, is the basic word signifying to request the presence of someone at some place [he *called* the waiter over]; **summon,** a more formal term, implies authority or peremptoriness in the request [to *summon* a witness]; **convoke** and **convene** refer to the summoning of a group to assemble, as for deliberation or legislation, but **convoke** implies greater authority or formality [to *convene* a class, to *convoke* a congress]; **invite** suggests a courteous request for someone's presence, esp. as a guest or participant, and usually suggests that the decision to come rests with the invited

---

**call back,** *v.* — *Syn.* recall, summon back, order back, return a call; see **revoke, summon** 1, **telephone.**

**call down,** *v.* **1.** [To entreat] — *Syn.* invoke, supplicate, request; see **appeal** 1, **beg** 1, **summon.**

**2.** [*To scold sharply] — *Syn.* rebuke, chide, admonish; see **censure, scold.**

**called,** *modif.* **1.** [Named] — *Syn.* christened, termed, labeled; see **named** 1.

**2.** [Appointed] — *Syn.* chosen, selected, denominated; see **named** 2.

**caller,** *n.* — *Syn.* visitor, guest, visitant; see **visitor.**
*See Synonym Study at* VISITOR.

**call for,** *v.* **1.** [To ask] — *Syn.* ask for, request, make inquiry about; see **ask** 1, **summon** 1.

**2.** [To need] — *Syn.* require, demand, necessitate, deserve; see **need, require** 2.

**3.** [To come to get] — *Syn.* come for, stop for, collect, fetch; see **obtain** 1, **pick up** 6.

**call in,** *v.* **1.** [To collect] — *Syn.* revoke, remove, receive; see **collect** 4, **withdraw** 2.

**2.** [To invite] — *Syn.* ask for, request, solicit, call upon; see **consult, summon** 1.

**calling,** *n.* — *Syn.* occupation, vocation, mission, métier; see **job** 1, **profession** 1.

**call off,** *v.* — *Syn.* cancel, postpone, discontinue, halt; see **cancel** 2, **stop** 2.

**call on,** *v.* **1.** [To visit briefly] — *Syn.* stop in, have an appointment with, go to see; see **visit** 4.

**2.** [To ask to do something] — *Syn.* request, appeal to, entreat, exhort; see **appeal** 1, **ask** 1, **beg** 1, **urge** 2.

**callous,** *modif.* — *Syn.* unfeeling, insensitive, inured, hardened, unsusceptible, uncaring, unaffected by, hard, insensible, stubborn, stiff, unbending, indurated, obdurate, insentient, insensate, inflexible, cold, coldhearted, hardhearted, unresponsive, unconcerned, impassive, apathetic, heartless, coldblooded, impenitent, unsympathetic, soulless, spiritless, toughened, blind to, deaf to, unimpressionable, tough*, hardboiled*, thick-skinned*, case-hardened*, hard as nails*; see also **cruel** 2, **indifferent** 1. — *Ant.* concerned, compassionate, sensitive.

**callow,** *modif.* — *Syn.* puerile, young, green, immature; see **ignorant** 2, **inexperienced, naive, young** 2.

**call up,** *v.* **1.** [To remember] — *Syn.* recollect, recall, summon up, bring to mind; see **remember** 1, **summon** 1.

**2.** [To summon] — *Syn.* send for, bid, order, recruit; see **invite** 1, **recruit** 1, **summon** 1.

**3.** [To telephone] — *Syn.* phone, call, ring, ring up; see **telephone.**

**calm,** *modif.* **1.** [*Said especially of persons*] — *Syn.* cool, composed, collected, serene, tranquil, sedate, levelheaded, coolheaded, impassive, detached, unmoved, aloof, unconcerned, disinterested, incurious, unaroused, unimpressed, nonchalant, neutral, listless, gentle, amicable, peaceable, peaceful, placid, unanxious, unexcited, unperturbed, unruffled, unshaken, amiable, temperate, inoffensive, civil, moderate, self-reliant, confident, poised, self-possessed, relaxed, dispassionate, imperturbable, unexcitable, unflappable, even-tempered, mild, still, phlegmatic, philosophical, self-controlled, patient, untroubled, cool as a cucumber★, with ice in one's veins★, without a nerve in one's body★, laid-back★; see also sense 2, **dignified, serene, tranquil** 1. — *Ant.* VIOLENT, EXCITED, FURIOUS.

**2.** [*Said often of things*] — *Syn.* quiet, tranquil, serene, undisturbed, unruffled, in order, soothing, at peace, placid, smooth, still, restful, harmonious, bland, peaceful, pacific, balmy, waveless, windless, motionless, reposeful, stormless, halcyon, at a standstill, pastoral, rural, low-key, slow; see also sense 1; **moderate** 4, **motionless** 1, **rural, tranquil** 2. — *Ant.* ROUGH, agitated, aroused.

---

*SYN.* — **calm**, originally applied to the weather, suggests a total absence of, and often a contrast with, agitation or disturbance [*a* calm *sea, a* calm, *answer*]; **tranquil** implies a more intrinsic or permanent peace and quiet than **calm** [*they lead a* tranquil *life*]; **serene** suggests an exalted tranquillity [*he died with a* serene *smile on his lips*]; **placid** implies an undisturbed or unruffled calm and is sometimes used disparagingly to suggest dull equanimity [*she looked on with* placid *unconcern*]; **peaceful** suggests a lack of turbulence or disorder [*a* peaceful *gathering*]

---

**calm,** *n.* **1.** [Peace] — *Syn.* stillness, lull, quiet; see **peace** 2, **rest** 1, 2, **silence** 1.

**2.** [Composure] — *Syn.* serenity, tranquillity, peace of mind; see **composure, patience** 1, **restraint** 1, **tranquillity.**

**calm,** *v.* — *Syn.* tranquilize, soothe, pacify; see **quiet** 1, **soothe.**

**calm down,** *v.* — *Syn.* compose oneself, control oneself, calm oneself, restrain oneself, keep oneself under control, regain one's composure, keep cool, take it easy, get organized, relax, rest, get hold of oneself, get a grip on oneself, cool it★, don't get shook★, cool off★, cool down★, simmer down★, go easy★, keep one's shirt on★, chill out★.

**calmly,** *modif.* — *Syn.* quietly, unexcitedly, tranquilly, unconcernedly, serenely, coolly, confidently, sedately, collectedly, composedly, placidly, smoothly, reposefully, impassively, restfully, motionlessly, uninterruptedly, peacefully, naturally, comfortably, unhurriedly, unconfusedly, imperturbably, without anxiety, without fuss, free from agitation, dully, phlegmatically, stolidly, without further ado, without fuss and feathers★; see also **easily** 1, **evenly** 1. — *Ant.* EXCITEDLY, agitatedly, wildly.

**calmness,** *n.* — *Syn.* quietness, tranquillity, calm; see **composure, patience** 1, **peace** 2, **tranquillity.**

**calumny,** *n.* — *Syn.* slander, defamation, detraction; see **lie** 1.

**camaraderie,** *n.* — *Syn.* intimacy, sociability, comrade-

ship, esprit de corps; see **brotherhood** 1, **fellowship** 1, **friendship** 1, 2.

**camera,** *n.*
Kinds of cameras include: camera obscura, astrograph, camera lucida, camcorder, cinecamera, x-ray machine, image orthicon, photochronograph, photogrammeter, iconoscope, microcamera, photographic telescope, photomicroscope, photopitometer, photospectroscope, phototheodolite, cinematograph, photostat, spectrograph, spectroheliograph, spectrohelioscope; motion-picture, television, TV, minicam, press, movie, autofocus, point-and-shoot, flash, still, aerial reconnaissance, electron-diffraction, box, electric eye, 35-mm, stereo, zoom-lens, photomicrographic, Polaroid (trademark), Instamatic (trademark), Kodak (trademark), single-lens reflex, double-lens reflex, spectroscopic, three-dimensional, 3-D, telescopic camera.

**camouflage,** *n.* **1.** [A misleading cover] — *Syn.* disguise, cover, dissimulation, masquerade, simulation, mask, screen, cloak, shade, shroud, veil, blackout, masking, paint, netting, blind, front, protective coloration, protective coloring, incognito, plain brown wrapper★; see also **coat** 2, 3, **disguise, makeup** 1, **mask** 1, **screen** 1.

**2.** [Anything used to conceal or mislead] — *Syn.* veil, subterfuge, deception, coverup; see **deception** 1, **pretense** 2, **trick** 1.

**camouflage,** *v.* — *Syn.* disguise, cover, conceal, veil; see **deceive, disguise, hide** 1, 2.

**camouflaged,** *modif.* — *Syn.* masked, disguised, covered up, falsified; see **covered** 1, **hidden** 2, **wrapped.**

**camp★,** *modif.* — *Syn.* campy★, mannered, theatrical, stylized, posturing, artificial, exaggerated, extravagant, corny, banal, tacky, dated, pop★, kitschy★; see also **affected** 2, **popular** 4.

**camp,** *n.* **1.** [A temporary living place] — *Syn.* campground, campsite, camping ground, encampment, caravansary, trailer park, RV park, RV site, campfire(s), tents, tent city, wigwams, tepees, wickiups; see also sense 2.

**2.** [Prepared facilities for vacationing] — *Syn.* tent, lean-to, cottage, shack, hut, lodge, cabin, log cabin, bungalow, chalet, shed, log house, summer home, cottages, bungalow colony, resort, summer camp, day camp, sleep-away camp; see also **home** 1.

**3.** [A military establishment] — *Syn.* bivouac, post, fort, encampment, quarters, barracks, casern, grounds, installation, compound, reservation, cantonment, laager (South African); see also **barracks, fortification** 2.

**break camp** — *Syn.* dismantle, depart, pack up; see **dismantle, leave** 1.

**camp,** *v.* — *Syn.* camp out, bivouac, stop over, make camp, encamp, dwell, nest, locate, pitch camp, pitch a tent, tent, quarter, lodge, sleep out, rough it, station, lodge temporarily, put up for the night, make a dry camp, sleep under the stars, go backpacking. — *Ant.* break camp, decamp, depart.

**campaign,** *n.* — *Syn.* operations, crusade, drive, warfare; see **attack** 1, **battle** 2.
*See Synonym Study at* BATTLE.

**campaign,** *v.* **1.** [To solicit votes] — *Syn.* crusade, electioneer, run for, agitate, tour, contend for, stand for (British), contest, canvass, swing through the country, solicit votes, lobby, barnstorm, stump, hit the campaign trail, mend fences★, go to the grass roots★, go baby-kissing★, beat the bushes★, whistle-stop★; see also **compete.**

**2.** [To fight] — *Syn.* battle, wage war, invade; see **fight** 2.

**campus,** *n.* — *Syn.* school grounds, college grounds, quadrangle, quad, seat of learning, college, university, academia, the Yard (Harvard), buildings and grounds, plant, physical plant, faculties, alma mater, the backs, the courts (*both* Cambridge, England); see also **college, school** 1, **university.**

**can,** *n.* **1.** [A container] — *Syn.* tin, tin can, canister, receptacle, package, jar, bottle, bucket, pail, vessel; no. 1 can, no. 2 can, etc.; see also **container.**
**2.** [*Jail] — *Syn.* prison, penitentiary, stir*; see **jail.**
**3.** [*A toilet] — *Syn.* lavatory, restroom, washroom; see **toilet** 2.
**4.** [*The buttocks] — *Syn.* seat, backside, posterior; see **rump.**

**can,** *v.* **1.** [To preserve] — *Syn.* bottle, put up, keep; see **preserve** 3.
**2.** [*To discharge] — *Syn.* fire, expel, let go; see **dismiss** 2.
**3.** [*To stop] — *Syn.* cease, halt, put a stop to; see **stop** 2.
**4.** [To be able] — *Syn.* could, may, be capable of, be able to, know how to, be equal to, be up to, lie in one's power, be within one's area, be within one's control, manage, can do, take care of, make it*, make the grade*, make out*, cut the mustard*, cut it*, hack it*.

**canal,** *n.* — *Syn.* waterway, trench, ditch; see **channel** 1, **water** 2.

**cancel,** *v.* **1.** [To mark out] — *Syn.* erase, eradicate, cross off, cross out, wipe out, rub out, scratch out, scratch off, strike out, strike off, blank out, blot out, sponge out, rule out, wash out, wash off, black out, write off, efface, deface, delete, dele, cut, destroy, undo, expunge, obliterate, omit, drop, render invalid, stamp across, wipe the slate clean*; see also **eliminate** 1, **remove** 1. — *Ant.* MAINTAIN, sanction, renew.
**2.** [To make void] — *Syn.* annul, revoke, call off, recant, vacate, repudiate, nullify, negate, neutralize, ignore, invalidate, suppress, countermand, set aside, render null and void, declare null and void, declare invalid, rule out, refute, rescind, remove, repeal, counteract, recall, retract, reverse, abrogate, discharge, void, render void, put an end to, abort, drop, do away with, discontinue, withdraw, offset, counterpoise, balance out, render inert, deprive of force, overthrow, scratch*, scrap*, scrub*; see also **abolish, discard, revoke.** — *Ant.* SUSTAIN, APPROVE, uphold.

**cancellation,** *n.* — *Syn.* canceling, annulment, nullification, abrogation, dissolution, dissolving, invalidation, invalidating, revocation, revoking, repudiation, repeal, abolition, abolishing, retraction, retracting, reversing, reversal, annulling, voidance, voiding, rescinding, recall, recalling, overruling, undoing, withdrawing, abandonment, abandoning; see also **removal** 1, **retirement** 1.

**cancer,** *n.* — *Syn.* malignancy, tumor, growth, carcinoma, sarcoma, melanoma, metastasis; see also **disease, growth** 3.

**cancerous,** *modif.* — *Syn.* malignant, carcinogenic, virulent, mortal; see **destructive** 2, **harmful, malignant** 1.

**candelabrum,** *n.* — *Syn.* candlestick, menorah, candleholder; see **candlestick, chandelier.**

**candid,** *modif.* **1.** [Frank] — *Syn.* straightforward, sincere, open; see **frank, honest** 1.
**2.** [Fair] — *Syn.* impartial, just, upright; see **fair** 1.
**3.** [Informal] — *Syn.* unposed, impromptu, extemporaneous, unstudied; see **extemporaneous, informal** 1.
*See Synonym Study at* FRANK.

**candidacy,** *n.* — *Syn.* willingness, candidature (British), application, readiness, competition, preparedness, offer,

tender, running for office, candidateship, availability, nomination.

**candidate,** *n.* — *Syn.* aspirant, possible choice, nominee, applicant, suitor, political contestant, office-seeker, hopeful, competitor, bidder, place-hunter, solicitor, petitioner, claimant, job-hunter, front-runner, dark horse, running mate, favorite son, campaigner, stumper*; see also **contestant.**

**candidly,** *modif.* — *Syn.* frankly, sincerely, honestly; see **openly** 1.

**candle,** *n.* — *Syn.* taper, rushlight, torch, bougie, dip; see also **light** 3.
Types of candles include: wax, tallow, beeswax, holiday, Christmas, Hanukkah, Paschal, Sabbath, birthday, sacramental, votive, ceremonial, bayberry, scented, mineral, rush, butane, electric, hurricane lamp.
**burn the candle at both ends** — *Syn.* overdo it, take on too much, squander, lavish; see **overdo** 1, **waste** 2.
**not hold a candle to** — *Syn.* be unequal to, be subordinate, be inferior, not be as good as, not compare, not measure up, not stack up, not be on a par with, not touch, not be in the same class, not be in the same league; see also **poor** 2.

**candlestick,** *n.* — *Syn.* candelabrum, candelabra, pricket, taper holder, flat candlestick, menorah, candleholder, sconce.

**candor,** *n.* **1.** [Frankness] — *Syn.* openness, veracity, forthrightness, candidness; see **honesty** 1, **sincerity.**
**2.** [Fairness] — *Syn.* impartiality, probity, uprightness; see **fairness, honesty** 1.

**candy,** *n.* — *Syn.* confection, confectionery, sweet, sweetmeat, bonbon, confit.
Varieties of candy include — *caramel:* chocolate, maple, coconut, fruit; *taffy:* sugar, orange, molasses, saltwater; *fudge:* chocolate, vanilla, maple; *cream:* orange, lemon, walnut; *drop:* lemon, peppermint, butterscotch, licorice; fondant, fruit glacé, nougat, peanut brittle, praline, panocha, pistachio paste, fruit roll, marshmallow, jelly bean, jawbreaker, sourball, cotton candy, crystallized fruit, cinnamon imperial, chocolate bar, coconut bar, chocolate truffle, Turkish delight, lollipop, halvah, marchpane, marzipan, gum drop, divinity, sea foam, toffee, after-dinner mint, Life Saver (trademark), *marron glacé* (French), *torrone* (Italian); stick, seed, hard, rock, spun-sugar; all-day sucker*; see also **pastry.**

**cane,** *n.* — *Syn.* walking stick, staff, pole; see **stick.**

**canker,** *n.* — *Syn.* ulcer, sore, boil, infection; see **injury** 1, **sore.**

**canned,** *modif.* **1.** [Preserved] — *Syn.* bottled, conserved, kept; see **preserved** 2.
**2.** [*Recorded or prepared in advance] — *Syn.* prerecorded, taped, filmed, packaged; see **recorded.**

**cannibal,** *n.* — *Syn.* man-eater, headhunter, savage, native, primitive, aborigine, eater of one's own kind, ogre, ogress, anthropophagus, anthrophagite, anthropophaginian; see also **savage** 1.

**cannibalistic,** *modif.* — *Syn.* man-eating, anthropophagous, Thyestean; see **cruel** 1, **primitive** 3, **savage** 2, 3.

**cannibalize,** *v.* — *Syn.* salvage, strip for repair, disassemble; see **dismantle.**

**canning,** *n.* — *Syn.* preserving, conserving, tinning, putting up, bottling, keeping, storing.

**cannon,** *n.*
Types of cannon include: self-propelled, muzzle-loading, muzzle-loader, breech-loading, breechloader, demi, whole cannon, cannon of seven, cannon of eight, royal cannon, tank destroyer, turret, mountain, siege, coast defense, field, antiaircraft, railway, stratosphere, antitank, bazooka, knee mortar, bombardelle, serpen-

tine, carronade, pompom, recoilless rifle, Howitzer, Bren, Woolwich, Fraser, Armstrong, Parrot, Quaker, Lyle, lifesaving gun.
Some famous cannons include — *14th century:* Bombard, Ribeaudequin, Basilica; *15th century:* English cannon; *17th century:* Rabinet, Falconet, Culverin Bastard, Cannon Royal; *18th century:* American Revolutionary cannon, Howitzer; *19th century:* Columbiad, Union, Army Mortar, French 75mm; *20th century:* Big Bertha or Krupp cannon, 75 mm and 105mm Howitzer, 155mm Howitzer, 8-inch Howitzer; see also **gun** 1.

**cannonade,** *n.* — *Syn.* barrage, curtain of fire, bombardment; see **attack** 1, **fire** 2.

**canny,** *modif.* **1.** [Prudent] — *Syn.* watchful, wary, cautious; see **careful, discreet.**
**2.** [Clever] — *Syn.* skillful, shrewd, sharp, knowing; see **able** 1, 2, **intelligent** 1, **sly** 1.

**canoe,** *n.* — *Syn.* kayak, dugout, outrigger, piragua, war canoe, pirogue, birch-bark canoe, coracle; see also **boat.**

**canon,** *n.* **1.** [A rule or standard] — *Syn.* rule, principle, criterion, code; see **command** 1, **declaration** 2, **law** 3, **measure** 2.
**2.** [Accepted works] — *Syn.* literary canon, oeuvre, complete works, recognized works; see **bible** 1, 2, **literature** 1.
*See Synonym Study at* LAW.

**canonical,** *modif.* — *Syn.* sanctioned, accepted, authoritative, statutory; see **approved, authoritative** 2, **lawful, legal** 1, **official** 3.

**canonize,** *v.* — *Syn.* saint, sanctify, beatify, glorify, deify, apotheosize, idolize, idolatrize, consecrate, enshrine, sanction, dedicate, make canonical, put on a pedestal*; see also **bless** 3, **love** 1, **worship** 2.

**canopy,** *n.* — *Syn.* covering, sunshade, umbrella; see **awning, cover** 1.

**cant,** *n.* **1.** [Insincere talk] — *Syn.* hypocrisy, sham, humbug, lip service; see **dishonesty, hypocrisy, pretense** 1, 2.
**2.** [Private language] — *Syn.* jargon, argot, slang; see **dialect.**
*See Synonym Study at* DIALECT.

**cantaloupe,** *n.* — *Syn.* muskmelon, winter melon, rock melon; see **fruit** 1, **melon.**

**cantankerous,** *modif.* — *Syn.* peevish, quarrelsome, grouchy; see **critical** 2, **irritable, mean** 3, **obstinate.**

**canteen,** *n.* **1.** [Mobile kitchen] — *Syn.* portable kitchen, snack bar, commissary; see **dining room, kitchen, restaurant.**
**2.** [Water bottle] — *Syn.* flask, flasket, *flacon* (French), bota; see **bottle, container, flask, jug.**

**canter,** *v.* — *Syn.* jog, lope, pace; see **run** 2, **trot.**

**canting,** *modif.* — *Syn.* hypocritical, insincere, two-faced, self-righteous; see **dishonest** 2, **false** 1, **hypocritical, prejudiced.**

**canvas,** *n.* **1.** [A coarse cloth] — *Syn.* tenting, awning cloth, sailcloth, duck, coarse cloth, drill; see also **cloth.**
**2.** [Anything made of canvas] — *Syn.* sail, tent, shade, waterproof, fly, tarpaulin, tarp*, boxing ring, ring; see also **awning, cover** 1, **tent.**
**3.** [A painting on canvas] — *Syn.* oil painting, portrait, still life, oil; see **art** 3, **painting** 1.

**canvass,** *v.* **1.** [To seek votes] — *Syn.* campaign, solicit votes, agitate, apply; see **campaign** 1.
**2.** [To sell from house to house] — *Syn.* call upon, peddle, sell door-to-door, ring doorbells; see **sell** 1.
**3.** [To examine or discuss in detail] — *Syn.* investigate, survey, debate, explore; see **consult, discuss, examine** 1, **interview.**

**canvasser,** *n.* — *Syn.* poll-taker, pollster, representative, peddler; see **agent** 1, **salesman** 2.

**canyon,** *n.* — *Syn.* gulch, gorge, gully; see **ravine, valley.**

**cap,** *n.* **1.** [Hat] — *Syn.* beret, beanie, baseball cap; see **hat.**
**2.** [A cover] — *Syn.* top, lid, stopper; see **cover** 1.
**3.** [*Capsule] — *Syn.* dose, pill, tablet, caplet; see **medicine** 2, **tablet** 3.

**capability,** *n.* — *Syn.* capacity, skill, aptitude; see **ability** 2, **inclination** 1.

**capable,** *modif.* — *Syn.* proficient, competent, fitted; see **able** 1, 2, 3, **intelligent** 1.
*See Synonym Study at* ABLE.

**capable of,** *modif.* — *Syn.* susceptible to, susceptible of, admitting of, open to, able to, ready to, ready for, liable to, inclined to, disposed to, predisposed to; see also **able** 3.

**capacious,** *modif.* — *Syn.* spacious, substantial, roomy; see **extensive** 1, **large** 1.

**capaciousness,** *n.* — *Syn.* spaciousness, roominess, vastness, adequacy; see **extent, immensity, size** 2.

**capacity,** *n.* **1.** [The limit of contents] — *Syn.* contents, limit, retention, space, room, size, volume, holding power, cubic contents, burden, amplitude, extent, compass, magnitude, spread, expanse, scope, latitude, bulk, dimensions, measure, range, quantity, reach, containing power, holding ability, sweep, proportions, mass, sufficiency, maximum amount, maximum number.
**2.** [Ability] — *Syn.* aptitude, capability, faculty, potential; see **ability** 1, 2, **inclination** 1.
**3.** [Function] — *Syn.* position, place, role, see **function** 1, **job** 1.
*See Synonym Study at* FUNCTION.

**cape,** *n.* **1.** [Land jutting into the water] — *Syn.* headland, foreland, point, promontory, peninsula, jetty, jutty, head, tongue, point of land, neck of land, chersonese, naze, ness (now chiefly in place names), mole, finger, arm; see also **land** 1, **peninsula.**
**2.** [An overgarment] — *Syn.* cloak, mantle, wrap, poncho, robe, pelerine, bertha, tippet, fichu, wrapper, mantilla, pelisse, paletot, shawl, cope, gabardine, tabard, mantelet, mantelletta, cardinal, victorine; see also **coat** 1.

**caper,** *n.* — *Syn.* prank, trick, escapade; see **joke** 1.

**caper,** *v.* — *Syn.* frolic, gambol, cavort; see **dance** 2, **play** 1, 2.

**capillary,** *modif.* — *Syn.* fine, hairlike, slender; see **narrow** 1, **thin** 2.

**capital,** *modif.* **1.** [Principal] — *Syn.* chief, main, first, dominant; see **principal.**
**2.** [Excellent] — *Syn.* splendid, choice, first-rate, delightful; see **excellent, superior.**
*See Synonym Study at* PRINCIPAL.

**capital,** *n.* **1.** [A seat of government] — *Syn.* metropolis, principal city, seat of government; see **capitol, center** 2, **city.**
**2.** [Money and property] — *Syn.* assets, resources, principal, venture capital; see **funds, industry** 3, **money** 1, 3, **property** 1, **wealth** 1.
**3.** [A letter usually used initially] — *Syn.* initial, uppercase, majuscule; see **letter** 1.
**make capital of** — *Syn.* exploit, make the most of, get advantage from, profit by; see **use** 1.

**capitalism,** *n.* — *Syn.* capitalistic system, free enterprise, laissez-faire, laissez-faire government, private ownership, private enterprise, competitive system, free market, market economy, self-regulating market, creeping capitalism*; see also **business** 1, **democracy** 2, **economics**.

**capitalist,** *n. — Syn.* entrepreneur, investor, industrialist, plutocrat; see **banker** 1, **businessperson, financier, millionaire**.

**capitalize,** *v. — Syn.* gain, benefit, realize, profit by; see **obtain** 1, **profit** 2.

**capitol,** *n. — Syn.* statehouse, legislative hall, U.S. Congress, Senate, House of Representatives, state legislature, seat of government, Capitol Hill, the political front, the political scene; see also **center** 2.

**capitulate,** *v. — Syn.* yield, surrender, submit, give up; see **yield** 1.

*See Synonym Study at* YIELD.

**capitulation,** *n.* **1.** [Surrender] — *Syn.* yielding, giving up, submission; see **resignation** 2, **surrender**.

**2.** [Summary] — *Syn.* synopsis, outline, abstract; see **abbreviation** 1, **abridgment** 2, **summary**.

**caprice,** *n. — Syn.* whim, vagary, notion, fancy, impulse, eccentricity, crotchet, quirk, freak, whimsy, humor, maggot, megrim, capriciousness, fancifulness, whimsicality, flightiness, fickleness, changeableness; see also **quirk**.

---

*SYN. —* **caprice** refers to a sudden, impulsive, apparently unmotivated turn of mind or emotion /discharged at the *caprice* of a foreman/; **whim** and **whimsy** can both refer to an idle, quaint, or curious notion, but **whim** more often suggests willfulness and **whimsy** fancifulness /pursuing a *whim*, he wrote a poem full of *whimsy*/; **vagary** suggests a highly unusual or extravagant notion /the *vagaries* of fashion in women's clothes/; **crotchet** implies great eccentricity and connotes stubbornness in opposition to prevailing thought, usually on some insignificant point /his *crotchets* concerning diet/

---

**capricious,** *modif. — Syn.* whimsical, inconstant, fickle; see **careless** 1, **changeable** 1, 2.

*See Synonym Study at* INCONSTANT.

**capsize,** *v. — Syn.* upset, overturn, invert, tip over; see **turn** 2, **upset** 1.

*See Synonym Study at* UPSET.

**capsule,** *n.* **1.** [Pharmaceutical preparation] — *Syn.* pill, tablet, caplet, cap*; see **medicine** 2, **tablet** 3.

**2.** [A space vehicle] — *Syn.* satellite, re-entry vehicle, spaceship; see **spacecraft**.

**3.** [Container] — *Syn.* receptacle, can, enclosure, case; see **container**.

**captain,** *n.* **1.** [A leader] — *Syn.* director, commander, authority, chief; see **administrator, guide** 1, **leader** 2.

**2.** [The officer in charge of a company] — *Syn.* company commander, commanding officer, junior officer, staff officer, commander, CO, skipper*; see also **officer** 3.

**3.** [One in command of a ship] — *Syn.* skipper, commander, operator, master, shipmaster, cap*, Old Man*; see also **officer** 3, **pilot** 2.

**caption,** *n. — Syn.* inscription, legend, subtitle, heading; see **heading, title** 1.

**captious,** *modif.* **1.** [Critical] — *Syn.* faultfinding, carping, caviling; see **critical** 2, **sarcastic, severe** 1.

**2.** [Tricky] — *Syn.* wily, subtle, sophistical; see **confusing, sly** 1.

*See Synonym Study at* CRITICAL.

**captivate,** *v. — Syn.* delight, charm, enthrall; see **entertain** 1, **fascinate**.

*See Synonym Study at* ATTRACT.

**captive,** *modif.* **1.** [Confined] — *Syn.* restrained, im-

prisoned, incarcerated, in one's power; see **bound** 1, 2, **confined** 3, **restricted**.

**2.** [Captivated] — *Syn.* enthralled, enraptured, enchanted; see **fascinated**.

**captive,** *n. — Syn.* prisoner, bondman, convict, hostage; see **hostage, prisoner, slave** 1.

**captivity,** *n. — Syn.* imprisonment, confinement, bondage, subjection, servitude, duress, detention, incarceration, interment, limbo, enslavement, slavery, impoundment, entombment, constraint, restraint, durance, committal, the guardhouse, custody, serfdom, thralldom, durance vile; see also **confinement** 1, **imprisonment** 1, **jail, pen** 1, **restraint** 2, **slavery** 1. — *Ant.* liberty, FREEDOM, independence.

**capture,** *n. — Syn.* capturing, seizing, taking, seizure, acquisition, acquirement, obtaining, securing, gaining, winning, occupation, appropriation, ensnaring, abduction, laying hold of, grasping, catching, trapping, commandeering, apprehending, annexation, snatching, confiscation, arrest, taking into custody, taking into captivity, apprehension, fall, corralling, nabbing*, nailing*; see also **arrest** 1, **recovery** 3. — *Ant.* liberation, FREEING, setting free.

**capture,** *v.* **1.** [To take into custody] — *Syn.* seize, take, apprehend; see **arrest** 1, **catch** 1, 2, **seize** 2.

**2.** [To seize with armed force] — *Syn.* occupy, conquer, overwhelm; see **defeat** 2, **seize** 2.

**3.** [To seize figuratively] — *Syn.* captivate, attract, charm; see **entertain** 1, **fascinate**.

**4.** [To win] — *Syn.* gain, carry, achieve; see **obtain** 1, **win** 1.

*See Synonym Study at* CATCH.

**captured,** *modif.* **1.** [Caught] — *Syn.* taken, seized, arrested, apprehended, detained, grasped, overtaken, clutched, grabbed, snatched, kidnapped, abducted, netted, hooked, trapped, ensnared, secured, collared*, nabbed*, bagged*; see also **under arrest, arrest**. — *Ant.* released, unbound, loosed.

**2.** [Occupied] — *Syn.* possessed, overcome, won, gained, seized, preempted, confiscated, usurped, repossessed, taken, taken over, appropriated, annexed, conquered, mastered, in possession of, fallen; see also **beaten** 1, **held**. — *Ant.* liberated, FREE, demilitarized.

**car,** *n.* **1.** [An automobile] — *Syn.* auto, passenger car, motor car, wheels*; see **automobile, vehicle** 1.

**2.** [A railroad vehicle] . Kinds of railroad cars include: Pullman, sleeper, smoker, diner, dining, parlor, coach, boxcar, flatcar, goods wagon, caboose, mail, freight, baggage, coal, ore, lounge, bar, automobile, refrigerated, fruit, piggyback, stock, cattle, horse; see also **train** 2.

**caravan,** *n. — Syn.* troop, band, expedition, camels, procession, cavalcade, train, parade, safari, wagon train, pack train, column, convoy, motorcade; see also **journey**.

**carbohydrate,** *n. — Syn.* starch, sugar, monosaccharide, disaccharide, polysaccharide, saccharide, glucose, sucrose, dextrose, fructose, lactose, galactose, maltose, cellulose, dextrin, glycogen, complex carbohydrate, simple carbohydrate, carbs*; see also **sugar**.

**carbon,** *n. — Syn.* carbon copy, reproduction, duplicate; see **copy**.

**carcass,** *n. — Syn.* body, corpse, cadaver, remains; see **body** 1, 2.

*See Synonym Study at* BODY.

**card,** *n. — Syn.* ticket, sheet, square, postcard, badge, slip, voucher, pass, label, tag, placard, plaque, board, paper, cardboard, pasteboard, Bristol board, fiberboard. Varieties of cards include: poster, window card, show card, ticket, fortune-telling cards, tarot cards, tally, check, billet, calling, business, playing, bridge, poker, pinochle, address, visiting, credit, charge, greeting, registration, filing, recipe, index, check-cashing, automated teller machine, ATM, bank, police, social security, membership, insurance, identification, I.D.\*; see also **paper** 1, 5.

**in the cards**— *Syn.* probable, predicted, fated, impending; see **destined** 1, **likely** 1.

**put** or **lay one's cards on the table**— *Syn.* reveal, tell the truth, be open; see **admit** 2, **reveal** 1, **tell** 1.

**cards,** *n.* — *Syn.* deck of cards, card game, game of cards; see **deck** 2, **entertainment** 2, **game** 1.

**care,** *n.* **1.** [Careful conduct] — *Syn.* heed, concern, caution, close attention, consideration, regard, thoughtfulness, forethought, heedfulness, precaution, wariness, vigilance, watchfulness, watching, attending, solicitude, diligence, meticulousness, fastidiousness, nicety, pains, application, conscientiousness, thought, discrimination, carefulness, scrupulousness, exactness, particularity, prudence, circumspection, oversight, watch, concentration; see also **attention** 2, **prudence.** — *Ant.* CARELESSNESS, neglect, negligence.
**2.** [A troubled state of mind] — *Syn.* concern, worry, solicitude, anxiety, interest, chagrin, distress, bother, perplexity, trouble, disturbance, unhappiness, sorrow, grief, aggravation, fretfulness, stress, tribulation, responsibility, strain, pressure, vexation, perturbation, fear, oppression, uneasiness, exasperation, annoyance, misgiving, anguish, foreboding, apprehension, discomposure, pins and needles\*, stew\*, sweat\*, fret\*. — *Ant.* calm, peace, INDIFFERENCE.
**3.** [Custody] — *Syn.* supervision, guardianship, keeping, charge; see **administration** 1, **custody** 1.
**4.** [A cause of worry or concern] — *Syn.* problem, concern, trial, trouble, worry, bother, tribulation, responsibility, strain, load, onus, burden, encumbrance, nuisance, charge, incubus, hindrance, handicap, impediment; see also sense 2, **affliction, difficulty** 2, **misfortune** 1, 2, **trouble** 2.

**take care** or **have a care**— *Syn.* be careful, be cautious, beware, heed; see **mind** 3, **watch out.**

**take care of**— *Syn.* protect, attend to, be responsible for, look after; see **guard** 2, **manage** 1.

---

**SYN.** — **care** suggests a weighing down of the mind, as by apprehension or great responsibility /worn out by the *cares* of the day/; **concern** suggests mental uneasiness over someone or something in which one has an affectionate interest /I feel *concern* for their welfare/; **solicitude** implies concerned thoughtfulness, often excessive apprehension, for the welfare, safety, or comfort of another /she stroked his head with great *solicitude*/; **worry** suggests an actively troubled state of mind, esp. over some anticipated problem /his chief *worry* was lack of money/; **anxiety** suggests an apprehensive or uneasy feeling with less mental activity than **worry**, often over some indefinite but anticipated evil /she viewed the world situation with *anxiety*/

---

**care,** *v.* **1.** [To be concerned] — *Syn.* be interested, feel concern, trouble, mind, regard, attend, worry, fret, object, disapprove, give a damn, give a hang, give a hoot\*; see also **bother** 1, **consider** 1.
**2.** [To be careful] — *Syn.* be cautious, look out for, be on guard, watch out, be aware of, heed, take precautions; see also **mind** 3.

**care about,** *v.* — *Syn.* cherish, be fond of, hold dear, be concerned about; see **care** 1, **like** 2, **love** 1.

**careen,** *v.* — *Syn.* lean, sway, tilt, lurch; see **bend** 2, **lean** 1, **reel.**

**career,** *n.* — *Syn.* occupation, vocation, work, lifework; see **job** 1, **profession** 1.

**care for,** *v.* **1.** [To look after] — *Syn.* provide for, attend to, nurse; see **guard** 2, **raise** 2, **support** 5.
**2.** [To like] — *Syn.* be fond of, hold dear, prize; see **cherish** 1, **like** 1, 2, **love** 1.
**3.** [To want] — *Syn.* desire, yearn for, wish for, have an inclination for; see **like** 3, **want** 1.

**carefree,** *modif.* — *Syn.* lighthearted, cheerful, blithe, happy-go-lucky; see **calm** 1, **happy** 1, **nonchalant.**

**careful,** *modif.* — *Syn.* meticulous, thorough, painstaking, scrupulous, cautious, wary, circumspect, discreet, solicitous, concerned, deliberate, provident, conservative, prudent, particular, rigorous, fussy, finicky, prim, exacting, sober, vigilant, watchful, suspicious, alert, wide-awake, assiduous, overexact, fastidious, hard to please, discriminating, sure-footed, precise, exact, heedful, on one's guard, on guard, on the alert, conscientious, taking measures, politic, attentive, calculating, sparing, regardful, considerate, mindful, canny, guarded, noncommittal, self-possessed, self-disciplined, solid, cool, calm, farsighted, frugal, thrifty, punctilious, religious, stealthy, observant, chary, apprehensive, judicious, leery\*, choosy\*, picky\*, feeling one's way\*, feeling one's ground\*, seeing how the land lies\*, putting the right foot forward\*, keeping a nose to the wind\*, picking one's steps\*, making haste slowly\*, going to great lengths\*, leaving no margin for error; see also **accurate** 2, **economical** 1, **thoughtful** 2. — *Ant.* heedless, CARELESS, haphazard.

---

**SYN.** — **careful** implies close attention to or great concern for whatever is one's work or responsibility, and usually connotes thoroughness, a guarding against error or injury, etc.; **meticulous** implies extreme, sometimes finicky, carefulness about details; **scrupulous** implies a conscientious adherence to what is considered right, true, accurate, or proper in every detail; **circumspect** implies a careful consideration of all circumstances to avoid error or unfavorable consequences; **cautious** implies a careful guarding against possible dangers or risks; **prudent** implies the exercise of both caution and circumspection, suggesting careful management in economic and practical matters; **discreet** implies the exercise of discernment and judgment in the guidance of one's speech and action and suggests careful restraint; **wary** implies a cautiousness that is prompted by suspicion

---

**carefully,** *modif.* **1.** [Scrupulously] — *Syn.* punctiliously, conscientiously, meticulously, exactly, rigidly, correctly, strictly, precisely, minutely, painstakingly, faithfully, trustily, fastidiously, uprightly, honorably, attentively, rigorously, providently, deliberately, fully, reliably, particularly, solicitously, concernedly, laboriously, thoroughly, dependably, in detail, with completeness, nicely, with care, with every care, in a thoroughgoing manner, to a hair\*; see also **accurately.** — *Ant.* neglectfully, HAPHAZARDLY, indifferently, carelessly.
**2.** [Cautiously] — *Syn.* prudently, discreetly, warily, guardedly, circumspectly, providently, watchfully, vigilantly, sparingly, frugally, thoughtfully, heedfully, regardfully, mindfully, with care, with caution, with difficulty, gingerly, delicately, noncommittally, anxiously, with forethought, with reservations. — *Ant.* imprudently, FOOLISHLY, wastefully.

**careless,** *modif.* **1.** [Inattentive] — *Syn.* loose, lax, re-

miss, unguarded, incautious, forgetful, unthinking, unobservant, uncircumspect, reckless, unheeding, indiscreet, injudicious, inadvertent, unconcerned, improvident, wasteful, regardless, imprudent, unconsidered, unwary, cursory, hasty, inconsiderate, irresponsible, indolent, insouciant, lackadaisical, heedless, mindless, negligent, neglectful, sloppy, slapdash, inaccurate, imprecise, inexact, slipshod, slovenly, thoughtless, unmindful, indifferent, casual, disregardful, oblivious, absent-minded, listless, abstracted, nonchalant, undiscerning, offhand, slack, blundering; see also **rash, unconcerned.** — *Ant.* attentive, THOUGHTFUL, careful, painstaking.
2. [Artless] — *Syn.* unstudied, simple, natural; see **modest** 2, **naive, natural** 3.
3. [Carefree] — *Syn.* untroubled, fun-loving, happy-go-lucky; see **calm** 1, **happy** 1.
**carelessly,** *modif.* — *Syn.* heedlessly, negligently, neglectfully, thoughtlessly, nonchalantly, offhandedly, rashly, hastily, unthinkingly, inattentively, unmindfully, unconcernedly, without counting the cost, at random, happen what may, incautiously, improvidently, irresponsibly, wastefully, without caution, without care, without concern, casually, insouciantly, haphazardly, sloppily, helter-skelter, any old way*; see also **anyhow** 2.
**carelessness,** *n.* — *Syn.* unconcern, nonchalance, heedlessness, rashness, omission, slackness, neglectfulness, delinquency, indolence, procrastination, dereliction, neglect, negligence, disregard, imprudence, haphazardness, inattention, sloppiness, slovenliness; see also **indifference** 1. — *Ant.* CARE, consideration, caution, conscientiousness.
**caress,** *n.* — *Syn.* embrace, stroke, touch, feel*; see **hug, kiss, touch** 2.
**caress,** *v.* — *Syn.* pet, stroke, fondle, cuddle, embrace, dandle, make love to, nuzzle, toy with, handle, graze, snuggle, hug, kiss, nestle, rub, massage, brush, coddle, cosset, treat fondly, chuck under the chin, pat, clasp, paw, make out*, neck*, feel*, feel up*, canoodle*, spoon*, see also **hug, kiss, love** 2, **touch** 1. — *Ant.* AVOID, withdraw, repulse, beat.

---

*SYN.* — **caress** refers to a display of affection by gentle stroking or touching; **fondle** implies a more demonstrative show of love or affection, as by stroking or hugging, or may connote touching or stroking in making sexual advances; **pet,** as applied generally, implies treatment with special affection and indulgence, including gentle patting and stroking, but informally it refers to indulgence, esp. by young couples, in hugging, kissing, and amorous caresses; **cuddle** implies affectionate handling, as of a small child by its mother, by pressing or drawing close within the arms; **dandle** implies the showing of playful affection toward a child by moving him or her up and down lightly on the knee

---

**caretaker,** *n.* 1. [One who takes care of property] — *Syn.* custodian, superintendent, keeper, curator; see **custodian** 2, **guardian** 1, **watchman.**
2. [One who takes care of someone requiring attention] — *Syn.* caregiver, guardian, nurse; see **custodian** 1, **guardian** 1, **nurse** 1, 2.
**care to,** *v.* — *Syn.* prefer, desire, want, wish; see **like** 1, 3, **want** 1.
**careworn,** *modif.* — *Syn.* anxious, worn out, haggard, drawn; see **sad** 1, **tired, troubled** 1.
**cargo,** *n.* — *Syn.* shipload, baggage, freight, lading; see **freight** 1, **load** 1.

**caricature,** *n.* — *Syn.* burlesque, exaggeration, cartoon; see **parody, ridicule.**
*See Synonym Study at* PARODY.
**caricature,** *v.* — *Syn.* distort, satirize, mimic; see **parody, ridicule.**
**carillon,** *n.* — *Syn.* bells, chimes, gong, peal of bells, orchestral bells, tocsin, angelus, glockenspiel, lyra, tintinnabulation; see also **bell** 1, 2.
**carnage,** *n.* — *Syn.* slaughter, massacre, slaying, butchery, wholesale killing, mass murder, mass homicide, butchering, manslaughter, gore, blood, bloodshed, shambles, extermination, havoc, holocaust, hecatomb, warfare, annihilation, rapine, pogrom, slaying, bloodletting, blood bath, effusion of blood, saturnalia of blood, blood and guts*; see also **destruction** 1, **murder.**

---

*SYN.* — **carnage** stresses the result of bloody and widespread killing and suggests the accumulation of the bodies of the slain; **slaughter,** as applied to people, suggests extensive and brutal killing, as in battle or by deliberate acts of wanton cruelty; **massacre** implies the indiscriminate and wholesale slaughter of those who are defenseless or helpless to resist; **butchery** adds implications of extreme cruelty and of such coldblooded heartlessness as one might display in the slaughtering of animals; **pogrom** refers to an organized, often officially sanctioned, massacre of a minority group, particularly of the Jews in eastern Europe

---

**carnal,** *modif.* — *Syn.* fleshly, bodily, sensual, sexual; see **lewd** 1, 2, **sensual** 2, **sexual** 2.
**have carnal knowledge of** — *Syn.* be intimate with, have an affair with, seduce, have intercourse with; see **copulate, love** 2.
*See Synonym Study at* SENSUAL.
**carnality,** *n.* — *Syn.* sensuality, lust, eroticism; see **desire** 3, **lewdness.**
**carnival,** *n.* 1. [A festival] — *Syn.* festivity, revelry, merrymaking, carousal, masquerade, debauch, festival, feasting, fete, street fair, celebration, spree, carousing, bacchanal, frolic, gala, heyday, jamboree, jubilee, Saturnalia, orgy, wassail, rout, Mardi Gras, Oktoberfest, feria; see also **celebration** 2, **feast, holiday** 1.
2. [An outdoor amusement] — *Syn.* fair, sideshow, exposition, amusement park; see **amusement park, circus, fair, show** 2.
**carnivorous,** *modif.* — *Syn.* flesh-eating, meat-eating, predatory, voracious; see **greedy** 2, **hungry, rapacious** 2.
**carol,** *n.* — *Syn.* madrigal, Christmas song, noel, hymn; see **hymn, song.**
**carousal,** *n.* — *Syn.* carousing, spree, frolic; see **carnival** 1, **celebration** 2, **feast, merriment** 2.
**carouse,** *v.* — *Syn.* make merry, imbibe, revel, party*; see **celebrate** 3, **drink** 2, **play** 1.
**carp,** *v.* — *Syn.* find fault, criticize, nag, cavil; see **bother** 2, **censure, complain** 1.
**carpenter,** *n.* — *Syn.* woodworker, cabinetmaker, craftsman, artisan; see **builder** 1, **laborer, worker.**
**carpet,** *n.* — *Syn.* carpeting, rug, floor covering, matting, wall-to-wall carpet, indoor carpeting, outdoor carpeting; see also **rug.**
Varieties of carpets include: Axminster, Brussels, Wilton velvet, velvet, plush, moquette, broadloom, mohair, chenille, rag, hit-and-miss rag, ingrain, fiber, jute, hair, shag, Oriental, Chinese, Persian, Turkish, Armenian, Indo-Persian, Anatolian, Damascus, Turkoman, Chinese-Turkestan, Indian, Moroccan, Spanish, Caucasian, Turkestan, English

handwoven, Polish handwoven, Venetian, tapestry, Savonnerie.

**called on the carpet**— *Syn.* reprimanded, censured, interrogated; see **in trouble** 1 at **trouble.**

**carpet,** *v.* — *Syn.* superimpose, lay over, put on, blanket; see **cover** 1.

**carping,** *modif.* — *Syn.* faultfinding, nagging, caviling; see **critical** 2, **sarcastic, severe** 1, 2.

*See Synonym Study at* CRITICAL.

**carriage,** *n.* 1. [The manner of carrying the body] — *Syn.* bearing, posture, walk, mien, pace, step, attitude, aspect, presence, look, comportment, cast, gait, stance, pose, port, deportment, demeanor, poise, air; see also **behavior** 1, **position** 5.

2. [A horse-drawn passenger vehicle] — *Syn.* buggy, surrey, coach, coach-and-four, buckboard, cart, conveyance, dog-cart, two-wheeler, dearborn, van, trap, gig, sulky, hansom, runabout, rockaway, tilbury, tumbrel, coupe, four-wheeler, stagecoach, chariot, chaise, shay, brougham, cab, equipage, victoria, landau, hack, hackney coach, phaeton, calash, calèche, cabriolet, droshky, troika, barouche, curricle; see also **vehicle** 1, **wagon.**

*See Synonym Study at* BEARING.

**carrier,** *n.* 1. [One who carries or transmits something] — *Syn.* mail carrier, letter carrier, courier, delivery person, bearer, messenger, transporter, shipper, trucker, freighter, common carrier, express, courier service, conveyor, vehicle, transmitter, vector, Typhoid Mary; see also **bearer** 2, **letter carrier, messenger, transport.**

2. [A ship that carries airplanes] — *Syn.* aircraft carrier, escort carrier, flattop*; see **ship, warship.**

**carrion,** *n.* — *Syn.* decaying flesh, remains, corpse; see **body** 2, **decay** 2.

**carry,** *v.* 1. [To take from one place to another] — *Syn.* convey, move, transport, transplant, transfer, ship, cart, truck, import, transmit, freight, remove, conduct, bear, take, bring, fetch, shift, displace, waft, portage, pack, shoulder, haul, ferry, lead, convoy, relocate, relay, lug*, tote*, pack off*, schlep*; see also **send** 1, **ship.**

2. [To transmit] — *Syn.* pass on, transfer, communicate, conduct, bear, transport, convey, relay, give; see also **send** 4.

3. [To support, as weight] — *Syn.* bear, sustain, shoulder; see **strengthen, support** 1, 2, **sustain** 1.

4. [To win] — *Syn.* be victorious, prevail, succeed; see **defeat** 1, 2, **win** 1.

5. [To keep in stock] — *Syn.* offer, stock, deal in, display; see **provide** 1, **sell** 1.

**be** or **get carried away**— *Syn.* overreact, be zealous, get excited, be exuberant; see **excited.**

---

*SYN.* — **carry** means to hold and take something from one place to another and implies a person as the agent or the use of a vehicle or other medium; **bear** emphasizes the support of the weight or the importance of that which is carried /to be *borne* on a sedan chair, to *bear* good tidings/; **convey,** often simply a formal equivalent of **carry,** is preferred where continuous movement is involved /the boxes are *conveyed* on a moving belt/ or where passage by means of a channel or medium is implied /words *convey* ideas/; **transport** is applied to the movement of goods or people from one place to another, esp. over long distances; **transmit** stresses causal agency in the sending or conducting of things /the telegrapher *transmitted* the message/

---

**carry away,** *v.* — *Syn.* enchant, charm, enrapture, transport; see **excite** 1, **fascinate.**

**carry off,** *v.* 1. [To win] — *Syn.* earn, gain, get; see **deserve, obtain** 1.

2. [To abduct] — *Syn.* shanghai, capture, make off with, carry away; see **kidnap, obtain** 1, **seize** 2.

3. [To achieve] — *Syn.* do, triumph, accomplish, handle, take care of, bring off, make good, make it*; see also **achieve** 1, 2, **succeed** 1.

**carry on,** *v.* 1. [To continue] — *Syn.* keep going, proceed, persist, persevere; see **achieve** 1, **continue** 1, 2, **endure** 1.

2. [To manage] — *Syn.* conduct, engage in, administer; see **manage** 1.

3. [*To behave badly] — *Syn.* act up, misbehave, create a disturbance, raise Cain, raise hell*; see also **misbehave, rage** 1.

**carry oneself,** *v.* — *Syn.* appear, conduct oneself, bear oneself, hold oneself; see **act** 2, **behave** 2, **walk** 1.

**carry out,** *v.* — *Syn.* complete, accomplish, fulfill; see **achieve** 1, **complete** 1, **succeed** 1.

**carryover,** *n.* — *Syn.* holdover, vestige, remains; see **remainder.**

**carry over,** *v.* — *Syn.* continue, persist, survive, extend; see **continue** 1, **endure** 1.

**cart,** *n.* — *Syn.* truck, wheelbarrow, handbarrow, barrow, little wagon, wagon, carriage, tip cart, handcart, dolly, hand truck, tumbrel, gig, dray, two-wheeler, pushcart, gocart, gurney, shopping cart, dumpcart, dogcart; see also **carriage** 2, **vehicle** 1, **wagon.**

**put the cart before the horse***— *Syn.* reverse, be illogical, err, turn things around; see **mistake.**

**carte blanche,** *n.* — *Syn.* full authority, unconditional authority, full power, unconditional power, full right, complete right, free hand, license, power of attorney, open sanction, open mandate, prerogative, free rein, blank check*; see also **freedom** 2, **permission, power** 2.

**carton,** *n.* — *Syn.* (cardboard) box, corrugated carton, package; see **case** 7, **container.**

**cartoon,** *n.* 1. [A satirical drawing] — *Syn.* caricature, lampoon, satire, joke; see **parody, ridicule.**

2. [A series of humorous drawings] — *Syn.* comic strip, comic, funnies*, animated cartoon, animation.

3. [A preliminary drawing] — *Syn.* sketch, representation, design; see **picture** 3, **sketch** 1.

**cartoonist,** *n.* — *Syn.* illustrator, caricaturist, social critic; see **artist** 1, **critic** 2.

**carve,** *v.* 1. [To form by cutting] — *Syn.* hew, chisel, sculpt, engrave, etch, sculpture, incise, mold, fashion, rough-hew, cut, shape, model, tool, stipple, grave, block out, scrape, pattern, trim, whittle; see also **create** 2, **engrave** 2, **form** 1.

2. [To cut] — *Syn.* slice, cleave, dissect; see **cut** 1.

**carved,** *modif.* — *Syn.* incised, graven, graved, cut, chiseled, engraved, chased, furrowed, hewn, hewed, etched, sculptured, sculptural, sculpted, modeled, whittled, carven, intaglioed, scarified, scratched, sabered, slashed, diapered, done in relief, scrolled, grooved, sliced, scissored; see also **engraved, formed.**

**cascade,** *n.* — *Syn.* waterfall, watercourse, rapids, cataract; see **water** 2, **waterfall.**

**case,** *n.* 1. [An example] — *Syn.* instance, illustration, sample, case study; see **example** 1.

2. [Circumstance] — *Syn.* incident, occurrence, fact, matter; see **cause** 4, **circumstance** 1, **event** 1, 2, **fact** 2, **state** 2.

3. [A legal action] — *Syn.* suit, litigation, lawsuit, proceeding; see **claim, trial** 2.

4. [An organized argument] — *Syn.* argument, petition, evidence; see **claim, proof** 1.

**5.** [Actual conditions] — *Syn.* situation, status, position; see **circumstance** 1, **fact** 1, 2, **state** 2.

**6.** [Difficulty] — *Syn.* plight, quandary, problem; see **crisis, predicament.**

**7.** [A container or its contents] — *Syn.* carton, canister, crate, compact, crating, box, casing, chest, drawer, holder, tray, receptacle, coffer, crib, chamber, chassis, caisson, bin, bag, grip, cabinet, jacket, wrapper, slipcase, sheath, scabbard, wallet, caddy, safe, basket, casket; see also **bag, container, cover** 1, **trunk** 1.

**8.** [*A difficult or eccentric person] — *Syn.* problem, bother, crank; see **character** 4, **trouble** 2.

*See Synonym Study at* INSTANCE.

**get** or **be on one's case** — *Syn.* nag, bother, meddle, bug*; see **bother** 2, **censure.**

**in any case** — *Syn.* in any event, anyway, regardless, no matter what; see **anyhow** 1.

**in case (of)** — *Syn.* in the event that, in the event of, provided that, supposing, if it should happen that, as a precaution, as a provision against; see also **if.**

**in no case** — *Syn.* by no means, under no circumstances, not at all; see **never.**

**casehardened,** *modif.* — *Syn.* unfeeling, callous, unaffected; see **cruel** 2, **hardened** 3, **indifferent** 1.

**casement,** *n.* — *Syn.* casement window, movable pane, single-hung pane, hinged pane, bay window, picture window, oriel, window frame, sash; see also **frame** 2, **window** 1.

**cash,** *n.* **1.** [Currency] — *Syn.* bills, coins, hard cash, legal tender; see **money** 1.

**2.** [Assets] — *Syn.* money in hand, ready money, ready assets, principal, available means, working assets, funds, payment, capital, finances, fluid assets, pay, remuneration, stock, pecuniary resources, resources, wherewithal, supply, supply in hand, investments, savings, riches, wealth, reserve, treasure, moneys, reimbursement, refund, bail, pledge, security; see also **pay** 2, **wealth** 1, 2.

**cash,** *v.* — *Syn.* realize, cash in, change, exchange, redeem for money, realize in cash, liquidate assets, discharge, draw, honor a bill, acknowledge; see also **pay** 1, **redeem** 1. — *Ant.* stop payment, REFUSE, decline.

**cashier,** *n.* — *Syn.* purser, clerk, receiver; see **clerk** 2, **teller, treasurer.**

**cashier,** *v.* — *Syn.* discharge, displace, remove; see **dismiss** 2.

**cash on delivery,** *modif.* — *Syn.* cash down, money down, collect, C.O.D.; see **paid.**

**casino,** *n.* — *Syn.* club, clubhouse, betting house, bank, the house, gambling establishment, dance hall, poolroom, roadhouse, gambling den, betting parlor, OTB, gambling joint*, Monte Carlo*, dive*, honky-tonk*; see also **bar** 2, **saloon** 3.

**cask,** *n.* — *Syn.* barrel, keg, firkin, butt; see **barrel, container.**

**casket,** *n.* **1.** [A coffin] — *Syn.* box, sarcophagus, funerary box; see **coffin.**

**2.** [A small box] — *Syn.* chest, coffer, jewel case, canister; see **case** 7, **chest** 1, **container.**

**casserole,** *n.* **1.** [Dish] — *Syn.* baking dish, Pyrex (trademark) dish, earthenware dish, earthenware pot, terrine, cocotte, marmite, bean pot, clay pot, Römertopf (trademark) dish, gratin dish, soufflé dish, lasagna pan, paella pan, cazuela, ramekin, timbale; see also **china, dish** 1, **pan, pottery.**

**2.** [Food] — *Syn.* one-dish meal, covered dish, loaf, gratin, hot pot, hotchpotch, cassoulet, timbale, terrine, meat pie, baked beans, lasagna, moussaka, paella,

tagine, tajine (*both* North African); see also **hash** 1, **stew.**

**cassette,** *n.* — *Syn.* cartridge, tape, audio cassette, videocassette, recording, film cartridge, case, microcassette, minicassette; see also **record** 3.

**cast,** *n.* **1.** [A plaster reproduction] — *Syn.* replica, mold, impression, facsimile; see **copy, impression** 1, **mold** 2, **sculpture.**

**2.** [Those in a play] — *Syn.* players, performers, actors, characters, list of characters, roles, parts, dramatis personae, company, troupe, dramatic artists; see also **actor** 1, **actress, staff** 2.

**3.** [Aspect] — *Syn.* complexion, appearance, stamp, looks; see **appearance** 1.

**4.** [A surgical dressing] — *Syn.* plaster-of-Paris dressing, plaster cast, splint, sling; see **dressing** 3.

Kinds of casts include: arm cast, leg cast, full leg cast, half leg cast, knee cast, bent leg cast, walking cast, body cast.

**5.** [The act of throwing] — *Syn.* casting, throwing, hurling, shooting, thrusting, pitching, tossing, flinging, chucking, heaving, lobbing, pelting, slinging, launching.

**6.** [A toss] — *Syn.* throw, pitch, heave, lob, fling, thrust, hurl, sling, launching, projection, expulsion, ejection, propulsion, shot; see also **shot** 1.

**7.** [Arrangement] — *Syn.* disposition, plan, method; see **order** 3.

**8.** [A tinge] — *Syn.* shade, tint, hue, blend; see **color** 1, **shade** 2, **tint, tone** 4.

**cast,** *v.* **1.** [To throw] — *Syn.* pitch, fling, hurl; see **throw** 1.

**2.** [To form in a mold] — *Syn.* shape, mold, roughcast, wetcast; see **form** 1.

**3.** [To compute] — *Syn.* calculate, number, reckon, figure; see **add** 1, **calculate** 1, **count.**

**4.** [To select actors for a play] — *Syn.* appoint, designate, decide upon, determine, pick, give parts, assign roles, detail, name, call, audition, screen-test; see also **assign** 1, **choose** 1, **delegate** 1.

**5.** [To give forth] — *Syn.* emit, disperse, spread, project; see **emit** 1, **scatter** 2.

*See Synonym Study at* THROW.

**cast aside,** *v.* — *Syn.* reject, jettison, throw away; see **abandon** 1, **discard.**

**cast away,** *v.* — *Syn.* dispose of, reject, throw out, shipwreck; see **abandon** 1, 2, **discard.**

**cast down,** *v.* **1.** [To discourage] — *Syn.* dishearten, dispirit, sadden, depress; see **depress** 2, **discourage** 1.

**2.** [To overthrow] — *Syn.* raze, demolish, wipe out; see **defeat** 1, 2, **destroy** 1.

**caste,** *n.* **1.** [Class] — *Syn.* station, cultural level, social stratum; see **class** 2, **rank** 3.

**2.** [Status] — *Syn.* standing, position, station; see **degree** 2, **rank** 2.

**castigate,** *v.* — *Syn.* chastise, reprimand, rebuke; see **censure, punish.**

*See Synonym Study at* PUNISH.

**casting,** *n.* — *Syn.* molding, part, cast, chilled casting, compressed casting, dry cast, fitting; see also **equipment, fixture.**

**castle,** *n.* — *Syn.* stronghold, manor, fortress, château, citadel, seat, villa, keep, donjon, fort, hold, safehold, refuge, fastness, acropolis, alcazar; see also **building** 1, **fortification** 2, **palace.**

**cast off,** *v.* — *Syn.* reject, jettison, throw away, disown; see **abandon** 1, 2, **discard.**

**cast out,** *v.* — *Syn.* evict, ostracize, expel; see **banish** 1, **eject** 1.

**castrate**, *v.* — *Syn.* emasculate, sterilize, asexualize, desex, mutilate, cut, spay, geld, neuter, unman, steer, caponize, effeminize, eunuchize, deprive of virility, deprive of manhood, alter, fix*; see also **maim, weaken** 2.

**castrated**, *modif.* — *Syn.* emasculated, emasculate, desexed, crippled, unmanned, impotent, devitalized, weakened, effeminate, neutered, altered, fixed*; see also **disabled, hurt, mutilated.**

**castration**, *n.* — *Syn.* emasculation, gelding, cutting, orchiectomy, orchidotomy, altering, unmanning, effeminization, sterilization, neutering; see also **injury** 1, **operation** 4.

**casual**, *modif.* **1.** [Accidental] — *Syn.* chance, unexpected, unplanned; see **accidental** 1.
**2.** [Occasional] — *Syn.* erratic, random, infrequent; see **irregular** 1.
**3.** [Offhand] — *Syn.* accidental, purposeless, unplanned; see **aimless, haphazard, random.**
**4.** [Nonchalant] — *Syn.* blasé, apathetic, unconcerned; see **careless** 1, **indifferent** 1.
**5.** [Informal] — *Syn.* relaxed, unceremonious, easygoing; see **informal** 1, 2.
*See Synonym Study at* ACCIDENTAL, RANDOM.

**casually**, *modif.* **1.** [Accidentally] — *Syn.* unintentionally, by chance, inadvertently; see **accidentally, haphazardly.**
**2.** [Nonchalantly] — *Syn.* indifferently, unconcernedly, coolly, unemotionally, impassively, reservedly, offhandedly, carelessly, informally, breezily, unceremoniously, plainly, apathetically, lackadaisically; see also **carelessly, easily** 1.
**3.** [Incidentally] — *Syn.* aimlessly, inconstantly, randomly; see **incidentally, haphazardly.**

**casualty**, *n.* **1.** [A misfortune] — *Syn.* accident, mishap, calamity, fatality; see **catastrophe, disaster, misfortune** 2.
**2.** [A loss in personnel; *often plural*] — *Syn.* killed, wounded, and missing; fatalities, losses, death toll, the injured, dead, victims, missing in action, MIA's.

**casuistry**, *n.* — *Syn.* sophistry, delusion, evasion; see **fallacy** 1, **lie** 1, **trick** 1.

**cat**, *n.* **1.** [A domestic animal] — *Syn.* tomcat, tom, kitten, feline, tabby, kitty*, kit*, puss*, pussy*, pussycat*, grimalkin, mouser.
Varieties of domestic cats include: Abyssinian, Maltese, Persian, Himalayan, Kashmir, Siamese, Korat, Manx, Burmese, Sphynx, Angora, British blue, Russian blue, Maine coon, Scottish fold, Egyptian Mau; alley, tiger, tabby, calico, tortoiseshell, shorthair, longhair, wirehair, bobtail.
**2.** [A member of the cat family] — *Syn.* feline, lion, tiger, leopard, panther, liger, tiglon, puma, wildcat, cheetah, lynx, bobcat, mountain lion, ocelot, serval, bushcat, cougar, mountain cat, painter, catamount, jaguar.
**3.** [*A caterpillar vehicle] — *Syn.* caterpillar, caterpillar tractor, tank, tractor, bulldozer, half-track, mucker*, hush-hush*, kitty*, landship*; see also **tank** 2, **tractor, truck** 1.
**let the cat out of the bag*** — *Syn.* expose, tell a secret, let slip*; see **reveal** 1, **tell** 1.

**cataclysm**, *n.* — *Syn.* upheaval, disturbance, disaster, calamity; see **catastrophe, disaster, misfortune** 2.
*See Synonym Study at* DISASTER.

**catalog**, *n.* — *Syn.* list, register, directory, schedule, inventory, bulletin, brochure, syllabus, file, card file, index, brief, enumeration, slate, table, calendar, docket, archive, gazette, gazetteer, muster, classification, record, draft, specification, prospectus, program, price list,

course list, roll, timetable, table of contents, card catalog, union catalog, on-line catalog, *catalogue raisonné* (French), rent roll, cartulary, Domesday Book; see also **description** 1, **file** 2, **index** 2, **list.**
*See Synonym Study at* LIST.

**catalog**, *v.* — *Syn.* classify, record, index, inventory; see **classify, list** 1.

**catalyst**, *n.* **1.** [A substance that permits or accelerates a chemical reaction] — *Syn.* enzyme, reactant, synergist, catalytic agent, chemical reactor.
**2.** [A person or thing acting as a stimulus] — *Syn.* spur, impetus, instigator; see **agitator, incentive.**

**catapult**, *n.* — *Syn.* sling, slingshot, ballista, trebuchet, arbalest; see also **mortar** 2, **weapon** 1.

**cataract**, *n.* — *Syn.* waterfall, rapids, torrent, deluge; see **flood** 1, **water** 2, **waterfall.**

**catastrophe**, *n.* — *Syn.* disaster, calamity, mishap, mischance, misadventure, failure, fiasco, misery, accident, trouble, casualty, misfortune, infliction, affliction, contretemps, stroke, havoc, ravage, wreck, fatality, grief, crash, devastation, desolation, avalanche, hardship, blow, visitation, ruin, reverse, emergency, scourge, cataclysm, convulsion, debacle, tragedy, adversity, bad luck, upheaval, down*; see also **disaster, misfortune** 1, 2.
— *Ant.* benefit, triumph, good luck.
*See Synonym Study at* DISASTER.

**catcall**, *n.* — *Syn.* hiss, jeer, heckling; see **cry** 1, **insult, ridicule.**

**catch**, *n.* **1.** [Something caught or worth catching] — *Syn.* take, haul, treasure, prize, cache, trophy, booty, prey, quarry, game, bag, bonanza, good thing, plum, find, jewel, pride and joy, discovery, gem, lucky strike; see also **booty.**
**2.** [*A desirable mate] — *Syn.* eligible bachelor, conquest, prize, rich man, rich woman, number*, score*, piece*, hunk*, lady-killer*; see also sense 1, **fiancé, lover** 1.
**3.** [The act of catching] — *Syn.* capture, seizure, grasping, apprehension, taking into captivity, take, snatching, disclosure, uncovering, nab*, cop*, bag*, scoop*, pickup*, grab*, haul*, collar*.
**4.** [A hidden qualification] — *Syn.* drawback, snag, trick, catch question, puzzle, conundrum, trap, hitch, rub, joker, kicker*, puzzler*, curve*, gimmick*, strings*; see also **difficulty** 1, **impediment** 1, **trick** 1.
**5.** [A hook] — *Syn.* latch, clasp, clamp, snap; see **fastener, lock** 1.

**catch**, *v.* **1.** [To seize hold of] — *Syn.* snatch, take, take hold of, seize, snag, grab, pick, pounce on, fasten upon, pluck, hook, entangle, claw, clench, clasp, grasp, clutch, grip, glom*, glom onto*, glove*; see also sense 2, **seize** 1. — *Ant.* free, MISS, drop.
**2.** [To bring into captivity] — *Syn.* capture, trap, apprehend, arrest, seize, snare, net, bag, nab*; see also sense 1, **arrest** 1, **seize** 2.
**3.** [To come to from behind] — *Syn.* overtake, intercept, overhaul, reach, go after, get, come upon, run down, gain on, catch up with, cut off; see also **pass** 1, **reach** 1. — *Ant.* falter, FAIL, lag behind.
**4.** [To contract a disease] — *Syn.* get, contract, come down with, fall ill, develop, become infected, incur, suffer from, become subject to, become liable to, fall victim to, take, succumb to, break out with, break out in. — *Ant.* ward off, ESCAPE, get over.
**5.** [To take unawares] — *Syn.* surprise, detect, find, expose; see **discover, find** 1, **surprise** 2.
**6.** [To trick] — *Syn.* fool, hoax, ensnare, trip up*; see **deceive.**
**7.** [To reach in time to board] — *Syn.* get on, climb

on, board, make, take, hop on, grab\*, jump\*; see also **board** 2.

---

*SYN.* — **catch**, the most general term here, refers to the seizing or taking of a person or thing, whether by skill, cunning, or surprise, and usually implies pursuit; **capture** stresses seizure by force or stratagem /to *capture* an outlaw/; **nab**, an informal word, specifically implies a sudden or quick taking into custody /the police *nabbed* the thief/; **trap** and **snare** both imply the literal or figurative use of a device for catching a person or animal and suggest a situation from which escape is difficult or impossible /to *trap* a bear, *snared* by their false promises/

---

**catching**, *modif.* — *Syn.* contagious, communicable, infectious, epidemic, endemic, pestilential, transmittable, pestiferous, noxious, miasmatic, epizootic, pandemic, virulent; see also **dangerous** 2.

**catch it\***, *v.* — *Syn.* be scolded, be punished, suffer the consequences, get caught; see **get it** 2.

**catch on\***, *v.* **1.** [To understand] — *Syn.* grasp, comprehend, perceive, learn; see **understand** 1.
**2.** [To become popular] — *Syn.* become fashionable, become prevalent, become common, become widespread, become acceptable, become the rage, grow in popularity, find a market, find favor, be a hit, take, go over\*, go over big\*, click\*; see also **prosper.**

**catch up**, *v.* — *Syn.* overtake, equal, bring up to date, keep up; see **approach** 2, **reach** 1.

**catch up with** or **to**, *v.* — *Syn.* overtake, join, outstrip, catch; see **approach** 2, **catch** 3, **reach** 1.

**catchword**, *n.* — *Syn.* slogan, watchword, password, catchphrase, byword, buzzword, shibboleth, pet word, pet phrase, tag; see also **motto.**

**catchy**, *modif.* — *Syn.* memorable, popular, appealing, engaging, infectious, haunting, tuneful, singable, bouncy, snappy\*; see also **charming, musical** 1, **pleasant** 2, **sprightly.**

**catechize**, *v.* **1.** [To instruct systematically] — *Syn.* instruct, train, educate, drill; see **teach** 1, 2.
**2.** [To question] — *Syn.* interrogate, inquire, quiz; see **ask** 1, **question** 1.
*See Synonym Study at* ASK.

**categorical**, *modif.* — *Syn.* unqualified, unconditional, unequivocal, flat; see **absolute** 1, **certain** 3, **definite** 1.

**categorize**, *v.* — *Syn.* classify, characterize, pigeonhole; see **classify, describe.**

**category**, *n.* — *Syn.* class, level, section, classification; see **class** 1, **division** 2, **kind** 2.

**cater**, *v.* — *Syn.* provide food, purvey, provision, victual; see **feed, provide** 1.

**cater to**, *v.* — *Syn.* indulge, coddle, wait on, pander to; see **pamper.**

**caterwaul**, *v.* — *Syn.* screech, scream, bawl, wail; see **cry** 1, **yell.**

**catharsis**, *n.* — *Syn.* purgation, cleansing, release; see **cleaning, purification.**

**cathartic**, *modif.* — *Syn.* purging, cleansing, purifying; see **cleaning.**

**cathedral**, *n.* — *Syn.* principal church, bishop's seat, temple, house of God, house of prayer, Holy place, minster, basilica, duomo; see also **church** 1, **temple.**
Parts of a cathedral include: altar, sanctuary, holy of holies, sacristy, sacrarium, holy table, baptistery, chapel, chancel, apse, choir, nave, aisle, transept, crypt, pew, seat, pulpit, confessional.
Famous cathedrals include: St. Peter's (Rome); St. Paul's (London); Notre Dame (Paris); St. Matthew's,

Washington National (Washington D.C.); St. John the Divine, St. Patrick's (New York).
Famous cathedrals are also at: Rouen, Beauvais, Amiens, Strasbourg, Reims, Milan, Pisa, Florence, Cologne, Canterbury, Lincoln, Wells, Nidaros, Madrid, Seville, Mexico City.

**catholic**, *modif.* **1.** [Concerning all humanity] — *Syn.* worldwide, worldly, cosmopolitan, all-inclusive; see **general** 1, **international, universal** 3.
**2.** [Broad in sympathies, tastes, or understanding] — *Syn.* receptive, open-minded, liberal, wide-ranging; see **cultured, fair** 1, **liberal** 2, **rational** 1, **reasonable** 1, 2.
**3.** [Pertaining to the Catholic Church; *usually capitalized*] — *Syn.* Roman, Romish\*, Romanist\*, popish\*, papist\*, papistical\*, ultramontane; see also **papal.**

**cattle**, *n.* — *Syn.* stock, cows, steers, calves, herd, beef cattle, dairy cattle, beef on the hoof; see also **animal** 2, **bull** 1, **calf, cow.**

**caucus**, *n.* — *Syn.* assembly, meeting, council, conclave; see **gathering.**

**caught**, *modif.* — *Syn.* taken, seized, arrested, entangled; see **captured** 1, **under arrest** at **arrest.**

**caught up (in)**, *modif.* — *Syn.* involved, absorbed, engaged, engrossed; see **involved** 1, **rapt** 2.

**cause**, *n.* **1.** [An underlying principle] — *Syn.* motive, reason, causation, object, purpose, explanation, inducement, incitement, prime mover, motive power, mainspring, ultimate cause, basis, justification, ground, matter, element, stimulation, instigation, foundation, determinant, wherefore, the why and wherefore; see also **basis** 1, **reason** 3. — *Ant.* effect, RESULT, outcome.
**2.** [The origin or source, thought of as the cause] — *Syn.* antecedent, root, beginning; see **origin** 3.
**3.** [The immediate moving force] — *Syn.* antecedent, agent, condition, etiology, prompting, ground, problem, subject of dispute, matter, occasion, case, circumstance, precedent, situation, fault, straw that breaks the camel's back; see also **circumstance** 1, **circumstances** 2, **event** 1.
**4.** [A person who brings about a result] — *Syn.* originator, agent, doer, instigator; see **author** 1, **doer.**
**5.** [A belief] — *Syn.* principles, conviction, creed, movement; see **belief** 1, **faith** 2.
**6.** [Aim] — *Syn.* object, goal, ideal, objective; see **plan** 2, **purpose** 1.

---

*SYN.* — **cause** refers to a situation, event, or agent that produces an effect or result /carelessness is often a *cause* of accidents/; **reason** implies the mental activity of a rational being in explaining or justifying some act or thought /she had a *reason* for laughing/; a **motive** is an impulse, emotion, or desire that leads to action /the *motive* for a crime/; an **antecedent** is an event or thing that is the predecessor of, and is usually to some extent responsible for, a later event or thing /war always has its *antecedents*/; a **determinant** is a cause that helps to determine the character of an effect or result /ambition was a *determinant* in his success/

---

**cause**, *v.* **1.** [To bring about] — *Syn.* produce, effect, make, let; see **begin** 1, **create** 2.
**2.** [To be the cause] — *Syn.* originate, provoke, generate, occasion, kindle, give rise to, induce, precipitate, prompt, bring about, bring on, spell, give occasion to, lie at the root of, be at the bottom of, bring to pass, sow the seeds of, breed; see also **begin** 1.

**causeway**, *n.* — *Syn.* highway, raised road, access road; see **path** 1, **road** 1.

**caustic,** *modif.* **1.** [Corrosive] — *Syn.* burning, strongly alkaline, erosive; see **acid** 2, **alkaline.**
**2.** [Sarcastic] — *Syn.* biting, sharp, stinging, scathing; see **sarcastic.**
*See Synonym Study at* SARCASTIC.
**cauterize,** *v.* — *Syn.* disinfect by burning, sear, singe; see **burn** 2, **clean.**
**caution,** *n.* **1.** [The quality of considering beforehand] — *Syn.* care, wariness, heed, discretion; see **attention** 2, **care** 1, **prudence.**
**2.** [A warning] — *Syn.* forewarning, admonition, caveat; see **hint** 1, **sign** 1, **warning.**
**caution,** *v.* — *Syn.* forewarn, alert, advise; see **advise** 1, **warn.**
*See Synonym Study at* ADVISE.
**cautious,** *modif.* — *Syn.* circumspect, wary, careful, unadventurous; see **careful.**
*See Synonym Study at* CAREFUL.
**cautiously,** *modif.* — *Syn.* tentatively, with due precautions, slowly, guardedly; see **carefully** 2.
**cavalcade,** *n.* — *Syn.* procession, parade, spectacle; see **march** 1, **parade** 1, **review** 4.
**cavalier,** *modif.* — *Syn.* offhand, unceremonious, supercilious, disdainful; see **careless** 1, **indifferent** 1, **nonchalant.**
**cavalier,** *n.* **1.** [Horseman] — *Syn.* cavalryman, rider, man-at-arms; see **knight.**
**2.** [Gentleman] — *Syn.* gallant, escort, man of honor; see **aristocrat, escort, gentleman** 1.
**cavalry,** *n.* — *Syn.* hussars, dragoons, rangers, light cavalry, heavy cavalry, air cavalry, Cossacks, uhlans, lancers, cuirassiers, chasseurs, Parthians, mounted riflemen, motorized cavalry, cavalry division, mounted troops, horse soldiers, squadrons; see also **army** 1, 2, **troops.**
**cave,** *n.* — *Syn.* cavern, hollow, rock shelter, grotto; see **hole** 3.
**caveat,** *n.* — *Syn.* warning, alert, admonition, caution; see **hint** 1, **sign** 1, **warning.**
**cave man,** *n.* — *Syn.* cave dweller, cliff dweller, troglodyte; see **hominid.**
**cavern,** *n.* — *Syn.* cave, hollow, grotto; see **hole** 3.
**cavernous,** *modif.* **1.** [Hollow] — *Syn.* sunken, concave, deep-set, deep-toned; see **hollow** 2, 3.
**2.** [Large] — *Syn.* deep, huge, wide; see **broad** 1, **deep** 2, **large** 1.
**cavil,** *v.* — *Syn.* quibble, find fault, criticize, carp; see **censure, complain** 1.
**cavity,** *n.* **1.** [Sunken area] — *Syn.* hollow, pit, depression, basin; see **hole** 2.
**2.** [Hollow place in a tooth] — *Syn.* dental caries, tooth decay, distal pit, gingival pit; see **decay** 2.
*See Synonym Study at* HOLE.
**cavort,** *v.* — *Syn.* prance, caper, frisk; see **dance** 2, **play** 2.
**cease,** *v.* — *Syn.* desist, terminate, discontinue; see **halt** 2, **stop** 1, 2.
*See Synonym Study at* STOP.
**ceaseless,** *modif.* — *Syn.* continual, endless, unending, incessant; see **constant** 1, **eternal** 1, 2, **perpetual** 1.
**ceiling,** *n.* — *Syn.* roof, dome, baldachin, canopy, topside covering, cover, *plafond, planchement* (*both* French), upper limit.
Types of ceilings include: groined, beamed, timbered, plaster, cove, fan vaulting,
**hit the ceiling\*** — *Syn.* become angry, lose one's temper, fume; see **rage** 1.
**ceiling price,** *n.* — *Syn.* fixed price, top price, maximum price, legal price, price ceiling; see also **price.**

**celebrate,** *v.* **1.** [To recognize an occasion] — *Syn.* keep, observe, commemorate, consecrate, hallow, solemnize, sanctify, dedicate, memorialize, mark, honor, proclaim, ritualize, ceremonialize, signalize, mark with a red letter\*.— *Ant.* FORGET, overlook, neglect.
**2.** [To honor] — *Syn.* praise, laud, glorify, extol; see **admire** 1, **praise** 1.
**3.** [To indulge in celebration] — *Syn.* rejoice, carouse, feast, give a party, kill the fatted calf, revel, jubilate, make merry, go out on the town, go on a spree, party\*, live it up\*, make whoopee\*, blow off steam\*, let off steam\*, have a party\*, have a ball\*, kick up one's heels\*, let loose\*, cut loose\*, whoop it up\*, paint the town red\*, fire a salute\*, beat the drum\*.

*SYN.* — **celebrate** means to mark an occasion or event, esp. a joyous one, with ceremonies or festivities /let's *celebrate* your promotion/; to **commemorate** is to honor the memory of some person or event, as with a ceremony or memorial/to *commemorate* Lincoln's birthday/; to **solemnize** is to use a formal, serious ritual to observe an occasion/to *solemnize* a marriage/; **observe** and **keep** mean to respectfully mark a day or occasion in the prescribed and appropriate manner /to *observe,* or *keep,* a religious holiday/

**celebrated,** *modif.* — *Syn.* famous, well-known, renowned, noted; see **famous, important** 2.
*See Synonym Study at* FAMOUS.
**celebration,** *n.* **1.** [An act or instance of recognizing an occasion] — *Syn.* commemoration, observance, honoring, keeping, glorification, magnification, laudation, recognition, anniversary, jubilee, holiday, remembrance, ceremonial, solemnization, memorialization, solemnity, fete, Mardi Gras, birthday, centennial, centenary, bicentennial, bicentenary, tricentennial, tercentenary, millennium, fiesta, red-letter day; see also **holiday** 1.
**2.** [Activities that accompany a celebration] — *Syn.* ceremony, party, gala, inauguration, installation, coronation, presentation, pageantry, carnival, bacchanal, revelry, conviviality, spree, carousing, jubilation, jollification, festivity, festival, feast, jamboree, ovation, triumph, merrymaking, gaiety, frolic, hilarity, joviality, merriment, mirth, wassail, Saturnalia, bash\*; see also **carnival** 1, **ceremony** 2, **party** 1.— *Ant.* sadness, solemnity, sorrow.
**3.** [The celebration of the Mass] — *Syn.* reading, reciting, singing, conducting, performing, intoning, chanting, praising God; see also **worship** 1.
**celebrity,** *n.* **1.** [The quality of being widely known] — *Syn.* fame, renown, notoriety, stardom; see **fame** 1, **honor** 1.
**2.** [A widely known person] — *Syn.* notable, luminary, star, magnate, dignitary, worthy, figure, personage, personality, famous person, person of note, name, big name, superstar, idol, somebody, VIP, lion, toast, toast of the town, bigwig\*, big shot\*, big gun\*, celeb\*; see also **chief** 1, **hero** 1, **heroine** 1, **personage** 2.
**celestial,** *modif.* — *Syn.* heavenly, divine, ethereal, astral; see **angelic, astronomical** 1, **divine** 1.
**celibacy,** *n.* — *Syn.* virginity, abstinence, continence; see **chastity.**
**celibate,** *modif.* — *Syn.* continent, virginal, unmarried, abstinent; see **chaste** 3, **single** 3.
**cell,** *n.* **1.** [Any small container or space] — *Syn.* compartment, cavity, receptacle; see **container, hole** 2.
**2.** [A unit of a living organism] — *Syn.* corpuscle, cellule, microorganism, spore, organism, egg, protoplasm,

cytoplasm, vacuole, protoplast, embryo, germ, follicle, red blood cell, erythrocyte, white blood cell, leukocyte, hemocyte.

**3.** [A small room] — *Syn.* cubicle, vault, hold, pen, cage, hole, coop, dungeon, keep, chamber, den, recess, retreat, alcove, niche, crypt, crib, nook, burrow, stall, closet, booth, cloister, antechamber, compartment, number, lockup*; see also **room** 2.

**4.** [A unit of an organization] — *Syn.* group, block, claque, cadre; see **faction** 1, **organization** 3.

**cellar,** *n.* — *Syn.* basement, half basement, underground room, vault; see **basement** 1.

**cement,** *n.* — *Syn.* glue, lute, lime, putty, tar, gum, mortar, paste, solder, adhesive, rubber cement, size, birdlime, grout, epoxy, epoxy resin, white cement, waterproof cement, bond, sealant, concrete, pavement; see also **adhesive.**

**cement,** *v.* — *Syn.* bond, mortar, plaster, connect; see **fasten** 1, **join** 1, **paste.**

**cemetery,** *n.* — *Syn.* burial ground, graveyard, memorial park, funerary grounds, churchyard, necropolis, potter's field, catacomb, city of the dead, tomb, ossuary, vault, crypt, charnel house, sepulcher, mortuary, last resting place, God's acre, Golgotha, eternal home, boneyard*; see also **grave** 1.

**censor,** *n.* — *Syn.* inspector, judge, expurgator, guardian of morals; see **examiner.**

**censor,** *v.* — *Syn.* control, restrict, strike out, forbid, suppress, ban, withhold, enforce censorship, control the flow of news, inspect, oversee, abridge, cut, edit, edit out, examine, expurgate, bowdlerize, review, criticize, exert pressure, conceal, refuse transmission, prevent publication, kill, blacklist, throttle the press, debase freedom of speech, bleep, bleep out, blue-pencil, black out, stifle, stifle free expression; see also **restrain** 1.

**censorious,** *modif.* — *Syn.* carping, faultfinding, complaining; see **critical** 2, **severe** 2.

**censorship,** *n.* — *Syn.* censoring, suppression, licensing, restriction, forbidding, controlling the press, governmental control, security blackout, news blackout, thought control, the censor's blue pencil, expurgation, bowdlerization, editing, deletion, bleeping; see also **restraint** 2.

**censurable,** *modif.* — *Syn.* blameworthy, culpable, reprehensible; see **guilty** 2, **wrong** 1.

**censure,** *n.* — *Syn.* criticism, reproof, admonition; see **blame** 1, **objection** 2.

**censure,** *v.* — *Syn.* criticize, blame, condemn, reprehend, denounce, judge, reprove, reprimand, rebuff, rebuke, reproach, upbraid, scold, attack, admonish, denigrate, tear apart, pull apart, pick apart, get after, dress down, snap at, bark at, tell off, animadvert, disapprove, impugn, disparage, deprecate, depreciate, lecture, take to task, berate, discipline, chastise, carp at, incriminate, asperse, cavil, nitpick, remonstrate, fault, find fault with, frown upon, moralize upon, look askance, chide, ostracize, castigate, comment upon, decry, inveigh against, damn, reprobate, exclaim against, fulminate against, cast blame upon, cast a slur upon, bring into discredit, discountenance, contemn, blackball, badmouth*, shoot down*, curse out, cuss out*, call down*, cry down*, slam*, blast*, sit on*, rip into*, light into*, hit out at*, knock*, call on the carpet*, rake over the coals*, haul over the coals*, rap on the knuckles*, chew out*, throw the first stone*, cast the first stone*, throw stones at*, give a good talking to, take a dim view of, not speak well of, not be able to say much for, come down on*, pick holes in*, tell a thing or two*, tear into*, give one hell*, cut up*, jump on*, cut one down to size*, give

a piece of one's mind*, jump down one's throat*, bring to book*, read the riot act*, put down*, rap*, pan*, trash*, bash*; see also **denounce, scold.** — *Ant.* PRAISE, laud, commend.

---

*SYN.* — **censure** implies the expression of severe criticism or disapproval by a person in authority or in a position to pass judgment; **condemn** and **denounce** both imply an emphatic pronouncement of blame, guilt, or reprehensibility, **condemn** suggesting the rendering of a judicial or other final decision, and **denounce**, public accusation against people or acts; **reprehend** suggests sharp or severe disapproval, generally of faults, errors, etc. rather than of people; **blame** stresses the fixing of responsibility for an error, fault, etc.; **criticize**, in this comparison, is the most general term for finding fault with or disapproving of a person or thing

---

**census,** *n.* — *Syn.* statistics, enumeration, count, account, registration, listing, census returns, evaluation, demography, demographics, figures, statement, specification, numeration, numbering, registering, roll, roll call, tabulation, tally, poll, capitation, counting, head count*, nose count*.

**cent,** *n.* — *Syn.* penny, Indian penny, 100th part of a dollar, red cent*; see **money** 1.

**centenary,** *n.* — *Syn.* century, 100th anniversary, centennial (celebration); see **anniversary, celebration** 1, **hundred.**

**center,** *modif.* — *Syn.* mid, middle, central, inmost, inner, midway, medial, deepest, inmost, innermost, internal, interior, at the halfway point, median; see also **central** 1. — *Ant.* outer, OUTSIDE, exterior.

**center,** *n.* **1.** [A central point] — *Syn.* middle, midpoint, focus, nucleus, core, heart, nave, hotbed, hub, omphalos, navel, point of convergence, point of concentration, focal point, midst, middle point, focalization, radiant, centrality, marrow, cynosure, kernel, bull's-eye, pivot, axis, marrow, pith, dead center*. — *Ant.* EDGE, verge, rim.

**2.** [A point that attracts people] — *Syn.* city, town, metropolis, plaza, capital, shopping center, trading center, concourse, station, hub, mart, market, crossroads, mall, social center, meeting place, club, market place, common, town common, square.

**3.** [Essence] — *Syn.* core, gist, kernel; see **essence** 1. *See Synonym Study at* MIDDLE.

**center,** *v.* — *Syn.* concentrate, centralize, focus, intensify, unify, unite, combine, converge upon, concenter, join, meet, focalize, gather, close on, consolidate, bring to a focus, center on, center in, center around, revolve around, gather together, flock together, cluster, collect, draw together, bring together, focus attention, attract. — *Ant.* decentralize, SPREAD, branch off.

**central,** *modif.* **1.** [Situated at the center] — *Syn.* middle, midway, equidistant, medial, focal, nuclear, pivotal, axial, umbilical, midmost, mean, centric, inner, median, inmost, middlemost, centroidal, intermediate, interior, in the center of, accessible; see also **center, convenient** 2, **inside** 4. — *Ant.* peripheral, OUTER, verging on.

**2.** [Fundamental] — *Syn.* prime, basic, primary; see **fundamental** 1, **necessary** 1, **principal.**

**centralization,** *n.* — *Syn.* consolidation, systematization, unification, federalization; see **concentration** 1, **incorporation** 2, **organization** 1, 2.

**centralize,** *v.* — *Syn.* concentrate, incorporate, unify, federalize; see **accumulate** 1, **assemble** 2, **gather** 1, **organize** 1.

**centrally,** *modif.* — *Syn.* in the middle, in the center, in the heart of, midway, halfway; see also **central** 1.

**centrifugal,** *modif.* — *Syn.* eccentric, diverging, radiating, outward, radial, diffusive, divergent, deviating, efferent, deviating from the center; see also **spiral, spreading.**

**century,** *n.* — *Syn.* 100 years, centenary, era; see **age** 3, **hundred, time** 1.

**ceramics,** *n.* — *Syn.* pottery, earthenware, crockery, porcelain; see **pottery, sculpture.**

**cereal,** *n.* — *Syn.* grain, seed, corn, breakfast cereal; see **breakfast food, grain** 1.

**ceremonial,** *modif.* — *Syn.* ritual, formal, solemn, stately; see **conventional** 2.

**ceremonious,** *modif.* — *Syn.* punctilious, formal, dignified, ceremonial; see **conventional** 2, **polite** 1.

**ceremony,** *n.* **1.** [A public event] — *Syn.* function, commemoration, services; see **celebration** 1, 2.
**2.** [A formal act] — *Syn.* ritual, rite, observance, service, solemnity, formality, ceremonial, custom, tradition, liturgy, ordinance, sacrament, liturgical practice, protocol, etiquette, politeness, decorum, propriety, preciseness, strictness, nicety, formalism, ceremoniousness, convention, conventionality, usage, prescription, incantation, mummery.
**stand on ceremony** — *Syn.* follow protocol, follow etiquette, be formal, observe formalities, insist on formality, insist on etiquette, be ceremonious; see also **behave** 2.

---

*SYN.* — **ceremony** refers to a formal, usually solemn, act established as proper to some religious or state occasion /the *ceremony* of launching a ship/; **rite** refers to the prescribed form for a religious ceremony or procedure /burial *rites*/; **ritual** refers to rites or ceremonies collectively, esp. to the rites of a particular religion /the *ritual* of voodooism/, and in extended use is applied to a regularly repeated act or series of acts performed in a set, ceremonial manner /bedtime *rituals*/; **formality** suggests a conventional, often meaningless, act or custom, usually one associated with social activity /the *formalities* of polite conversation/

---

**certain,** *modif.* **1.** [Confident] — *Syn.* assured, sure, positive, questionless, satisfied, self-confident, undoubting, unwavering, believing, secure, untroubled, unconcerned, undisturbed, unperturbed, convinced, assertive, cocksure; see also **calm** 1, **confident** 2.
**2.** [Sure] — *Syn.* destined, determined, predestined; see **inevitable.**
**3.** [Beyond doubt] — *Syn.* indisputable, unquestionable, assured, positive, real, true, genuine, plain, clear, undoubted, indubitable, guaranteed, unmistakable, unassailable, sure, incontrovertible, undeniable, definite, supreme, unqualified, infallible, undisputed, unerring, sound, reliable, trustworthy, evident, conclusive, decisive, unambiguous, authoritative, irrefutable, unconditional, incontestable, unquestioned, absolute, unequivocal, inescapable, in the bag*, on ice*; see also **accurate** 1. — *Ant.* doubtful, uncertain, dubious.
**4.** [Dependable] — *Syn.* trustworthy, safe, sound; see **reliable** 2.
**5.** [Fixed] — *Syn.* settled, concluded, set, agreed upon; see **definite** 1, **determined** 1.
**6.** [Specific but not named] — *Syn.* special, marked, specified, defined, one, some, a few, a couple, several, appreciable, upwards of, regular, particular, singular, especial, precise, specific, express; see also **definite** 1, **individual** 1, **special** 1.

**be certain** — *Syn.* be sure, have confidence, feel sure, be confident, have no doubt, make certain; see also **know** 1.

**for certain** — *Syn.* without doubt, absolutely, certainly; see **surely.**

---

*SYN.* — **certain** usually suggests conviction based on specific grounds or evidence /this letter makes me *certain* of his innocence/; **sure** suggests merely an absence of doubt or hesitancy /I'm *sure* you don't mean it/; **confident** stresses the firmness of one's certainty or sureness, esp. in some expectation /she's *confident* she'll win/; **positive** suggests unshakable confidence, esp. in the correctness of one's opinions or conclusions, sometimes to the point of dogmatism /he's too *positive* in his beliefs/

---

**certainly,** *modif.* **1.** [Without doubt; *used to qualify statements*] — *Syn.* positively, absolutely, unquestionably; see **surely.**
**2.** [Without doubt; *used to express agreement*] — *Syn.* assuredly, of course, without fail; see **yes.**

**certainty,** *n.* **1.** [Firmness of belief] — *Syn.* certitude, assurance, conviction, confidence, sureness, faith, positiveness, definiteness, authoritativeness, firmness, persuasion, surety, self-confidence, self-assurance, cocksureness, indisputability, incontestability, irrefutability, unquestionableness; see also **belief** 1, **faith** 1.
**2.** [Something looked upon as certain] — *Syn.* fact, truth, foregone conclusion, sure thing*; see **fact** 1, **reality** 1, **result, truth** 1.

---

*SYN.* — **certainty** suggests a firm, settled belief or positiveness in the truth of something; **certitude** is sometimes distinguished from the preceding as implying an absence of objective proof, hence suggesting unassailable blind faith; **assurance** suggests confidence, but not necessarily positiveness, usually in something that is yet to happen /feel no *assurance* of his continuing support/; **conviction** suggests a being convinced, as of the truth of a belief, because of satisfactory reasons or proof and sometimes implies earlier doubt

---

**certificate,** *n.* — *Syn.* declaration, document, warrant, voucher, testimonial, credential(s), license, testament, endorsement, diploma, affidavit, certification, coupon, authentication, pass, ticket, warranty, guarantee, testimony, attestation, testification, deed, receipt, affirmation, docket, record; see also **diploma.**

**certify,** *v.* **1.** [To give assurance] — *Syn.* guarantee, accredit, vouch for, endorse; see **approve** 1, **guarantee** 1.
**2.** [To state formally] — *Syn.* attest, verify, swear, confirm; see **declare** 1, **testify** 2.
*See Synonym Study at* APPROVE.

**cessation,** *n.* — *Syn.* stop, discontinuance, suspension, recess; see **end** 2, **pause** 1, 2.

**chafe,** *v.* **1.** [To rub] — *Syn.* abrade, grate, scrape, massage; see **rub** 1.
**2.** [To annoy] — *Syn.* irritate, vex, harass; see **bother** 2, 3, **disturb** 2.

**chaff,** *n.* **1.** [Husks] — *Syn.* hulls, shells, crusts, pods; see **shell** 1.
**2.** [Trash] — *Syn.* refuse, waste, debris; see **trash** 1, 3.

**chagrin,** *n.* — *Syn.* mortification, humiliation, dismay, vexation; see **embarrassment** 1, **shame** 2.

**chain,** *n.* **1.** [A series of links] — *Syn.* cable, string, link(s), train, connection, necklace, bracelet, ring series, leash, shackle, manacle.
**2.** [A sequence] — *Syn.* succession, series, string, concatenation; see **series.**

*See Synonym Study at* SERIES.

**chain,** *v.* **1.** [To fasten] — *Syn.* connect, attach, secure, tether; see **fasten 1, hold 1.**

**2.** [To bind] — *Syn.* shackle, fetter, tie up, confine; see **bind 1, hold 1, restrain 1.**

**chains,** *n.* — *Syn.* fetters, bonds, irons, shackles, ball and chain, manacles, leg irons, handcuffs, gyves; see also **captivity, confinement 1, imprisonment 1.**

**chair,** *n.* **1.** [A single seat] — *Syn.* seat, stool, bench, armchair, place, room, space, throne, cathedra; see also **bench 1, couch, furniture, seat 1.**

Types of chairs include: stool, taboret, throne, faldstool, footstool, rocker, recliner, ottoman, wing chair, armchair, easy chair, wheel chair, highchair, roundabout; curule, bath, occasional, dining-room, desk, office, kitchen, lounge, beach, deck, lawn, period, portable, sedan, reclining, rocking, captain's, swivel, folding, bentwood, cane-seated, split-bottom; Duncan Phyfe, Hepplewhite, Breuer, Cromwell, Windsor, Morris, Queen Anne, X-legged Barcelona, Eames, S-squared Tugend hat, S-curved Brno.

**2.** [A position of authority] — *Syn.* seat, chairmanship, directorship, headship, throne, bench, position, endowed chair, professorship, tutorage, instructorship, readership, professorate, fellowship, tutorship; see also **authority 3.**

**3.** [A person who presides] — *Syn.* chairman, chairwoman, chairperson, president, director, head, presiding officer, presider, administrator, toastmaster, speaker, moderator, prolocutor, monitor, leader, principal, captain, master of ceremonies, MC, emcee*; see also **administrator.**

**4.** [A death sentence; *usually used with* the] — *Syn.* execution, electric chair, electrocution, death chair, hot seat*, hot squat*, a burning*, Sing Sing siesta*; see also **execution 2.**

**take the chair** — *Syn.* chair, preside, act as chair, moderate; see **manage 1.**

**chairman,** *n.* — *Syn.* presiding officer, director, chief executive, moderator; see **chair 3.**

**chalice,** *n.* — *Syn.* grail, goblet, vessel; see **cup.**

**chalk up,** *v.* **1.** [To attribute] — *Syn.* ascribe to, credit, charge; see **attribute.**

**2.** [To score or record] — *Syn.* earn, achieve, register, tally; see **record 1, score 1, 2.**

**chalky,** *modif.* — *Syn.* blanched, milky, pale; see **dull 2, gray 1, pale 2, white 1.**

**challenge,** *n.* **1.** [A demand] — *Syn.* dare, summons, provocation, calling into question; see **call 4, objection 2, request.**

**2.** Something that calls for special effort] — *Syn.* test, trial, hurdle, demanding task; see **difficulty 1.**

**challenge,** *v.* **1.** [To invite to a contest] — *Syn.* dare, defy, summon, confront; see **dare 2, invite 2, summon 1.**

**2.** [To question] — *Syn.* dispute, call into question, examine, impugn; see **ask 1, doubt 1, 2, question 1.**

**3.** [To claim] — *Syn.* make demands on, stimulate, test; see **claim 1, excite 1, 2.**

**chamber,** *n.* **1.** [A room] — *Syn.* bedroom, antechamber, office, hall; see **hall 1, room 2.**

**2.** [A small compartment] — *Syn.* box, cell, chest; see **case 7, container.**

**3.** [An organized group] — *Syn.* council, legislative house, assembly, body; see **committee, government 2, legislature.**

**champion,** *n.* **1.** [A winner] — *Syn.* prizewinner, titleholder, victor, vanquisher; see **hero 1, heroine 1, winner.**

**2.** [A defender] — *Syn.* upholder, guardian, backer; see **protector, supporter.**

**chance,** *modif.* — *Syn.* accidental, unplanned, unintentional, random; see **accidental 1, aimless, haphazard, random.**

*See Synonym Study at* RANDOM.

**chance,** *n.* **1.** [The powers of uncertainty] — *Syn.* fate, fortune, fortuity, hazard, lot, accident, luck, good luck, bad luck, destiny, outcome, cast, lottery, gamble, hap, adventure, contingency, coincidence, serendipity, randomness, blind chance, kismet, happening, future, doom, occurrence, happenstance*, the breaks*, hit*, Lady Luck*, Dame Fortune*, turn of the cards*, the way the cookie crumbles*, hazard of the dice*, luck of the draw*, heads or tails*; see also **accident 2.** — *Ant.* aim, PURPOSE, design.

**2.** [A possibility] — *Syn.* opening, occasion, prospect, turn; see **opportunity 1, possibility 2, timeliness.**

**3.** [An uncertainty] — *Syn.* venture, gamble, speculation; see **bet, risk 2, uncertainty 1.**

**4.** [Probability; *often plural*] — *Syn.* likelihood, possibility, odds, indications; see **probability.**

**by chance** — *Syn.* by accident, as it happens, unexpectedly; see **accidentally.**

**on the (off) chance** — *Syn.* in case, in the event that, supposing; see **if.**

**chance,** *v.* **1.** [To happen] — *Syn.* come to pass, befall, occur; see **happen 2.**

**2.** [To take a chance] — *Syn.* venture, stake, hazard, risk, wager, gamble, try, attempt, jeopardize, speculate, tempt fate, tempt fortune, trust to chance, trust to luck, run the risk, try one's luck, play with fire*, take a shot in the dark*, take a leap in the dark*, buy a pig in a poke*, go out on a limb*, chance one's luck*, chance it*, have a fling at*, take a fling at*, put all one's eggs in one basket*, skate on thin ice*, stick one's neck out*; see also **gamble 1, risk.**

*See Synonym Study at* HAPPEN.

**chandelier,** *n.* — *Syn.* ceiling fixture, candelabrum, gasolier, luster, corona, electrolier, crown, candleholder; see also **light 3.**

**change,** *n.* **1.** [The act or fact of altering] — *Syn.* alteration, variation, vicissitude, substitution, swerving, deviation, diversion, shuffling, difference, reconstruction, aberration, evolution, restyling, innovation, move, interchange, trade, switch, fluctuation, wavering, modulation, alternating, exchange, mutation, transformation, transmutation, modification, transition, metamorphosis, transfiguration, reshaping, adoption, transference, reworking, transmogrification, metamorphism, improvisation, revolution, conversion, regeneration, shifting, warping, remodeling, renovation, veering, transubstantiation, shift, reformation, revision, rearrangement, enlargement, renewal, removal, disguising, reversal, about-face, tampering, qualification, turning, metathesis, inflection, vacillation, resolution, metastasis, reorganization; see also **variety 1.** — *Ant.* CONSTANCY, consistency, permanence.

**2.** [An alteration] — *Syn.* modification, correction, remodeling, switch, reformation, reconstruction, shift, difference, reform, conversion, changeover, transformation, tempering, revolution, rearrangement, adjustment, readjustment, reorganization, reshaping, renovation, realignment, redirection, reprogramming, variation, addition, refinement, advance, modulation, development, diversification, turn, turnover, enlargement, revision, qualification, distortion, compression, contraction, telescoping, widening, narrowing, lengthening, flattening, shortening, fitting, setting, adjusting, rounding, getting out of round, ovalization, squaring, getting out of whack*, ups and downs*; see also sense 1.

**3.** [Substitution] — *Syn.* switch, replacement, swap; see **exchange** 3.

**4.** [Variety] — *Syn.* diversity, novelty, variance; see **difference** 1, **variety** 1.

**5.** [Small coins] — *Syn.* pocket money, spending money, pin money, silver, small change, (small) coins, pennies, nickels, dimes, quarters, half dollars, chicken feed*; see also **money** 1.

**change,** *v.* **1.** [To make different] — *Syn.* vary, alter, modify, transform, convert, diversify, turn, modulate, transmute, transfigure, redo, metamorphose, disguise, restyle, revolutionize, reorganize, make over, do over, remake, recondition, remodel, reconvert, refashion, tailor, reform, renew, renovate, recast, revamp, remold, modernize, reconstruct, moderate, temper, adjust, adapt, accommodate, readjust, fine-tune, naturalize, transpose, invert, switch around, reverse, turn upside down, revise, correct, amend, edit, tamper with, make innovations, innovate, render different, translate, mutate, transmogrify, denature, transubstantiate, reshape, inflect, regenerate, improve, worsen, reduce, commute, increase, diminish, intensify, shape, shift, transfer, give a color to, do something about, bring up to date. — *Ant.* maintain, preserve, set, fix.

**2.** [To put in place of another] — *Syn.* exchange, replace, substitute, alternate, switch, interchange, rotate, displace, supplant, transpose, trade, swap*; see also **exchange** 1, **replace** 1, **substitute** 2.

**3.** [To change clothing] — *Syn.* undress, disrobe, dress, make one's toilet; see **dress** 1.

**4.** [To become different] — *Syn.* alter, vary, fluctuate, vacillate, modify, metamorphose, evolve, be converted, turn into, turn from, resolve into, grow, ripen, mellow, mature, develop, be transformed, reform, moderate, adapt, adjust, mutate, diverge, deviate, shift, veer, swerve, tack, deflect, warp, merge into, shade, cloud, break, graduate, grade, come around, take a new turn, reverse oneself, do an about-face*, flip-flop*, blow hot and cold*; see also sense 1, **become** 1.

---

**SYN.** — **change** denotes making or becoming distinctly different and implies either a radical transmutation of character or replacement with something else /success *changed* her; I'll *change* my shoes/; **alter** implies a more partial change, as in appearance, so that the identity is preserved /to *alter* a garment/; **vary** suggests irregular or intermittent change /to *vary* one's reading/; **modify** implies minor change, often so as to limit or moderate /to *modify* the language of a report/; **transform** implies a change in form and now, usually, in nature or function /to *transform* matter into energy/; **convert** suggests more strongly change to suit a new function /to *convert* a barn into a house/

---

**changeable,** *modif.* **1.** [Said of persons] — *Syn.* inconstant, unstable, fickle, irresolute, flighty, irresponsible, unreliable, purposeless, wayward, unsettled, motiveless, uncertain, spasmodic, fanciful, impulsive, wavering, uneasy, unsteady, changeful, undecided, uneven, vagrant, faddish, fidgety, roving, many-sided, vacillating, mutable, versatile, moody, temperamental, irregular, capricious, indecisive, restless, erratic, uneasy, agitated, whimsical, light, lightheaded, volatile, shifty, skittish, mercurial, fitful, unpredictable. — *Ant.* steady, RELIABLE, constant.

**2.** [Said of conditions] — *Syn.* variable, varying, variant, uncertain, mutable, unsteady, unsettled, doubtful, plas-

tic, kaleidoscopic, convertible, transformable, protean, permutable, commutative, reversible, inconstant, transitional, unstable, revocable, wavering, fluid, fluctuating, movable, mobile, unfixed, alterable, alternating, modifiable, everchanging, transmutable, labile; see also **irregular** 1. — *Ant.* immovable, PERMANENT, fixed.

**changed,** *modif.* **1.** [Exchanged] — *Syn.* substituted, interchanged, replaced, commutated, reciprocated, transposed, transferred, shuffled, inverted, switched, swapped*, replaced, traded, bartered, returned, displaced, supplanted, reversed, reverted, restored, retracted, alternated, rotated, surrogated. — *Ant.* PLACED, stored, kept.

**2.** [Altered] — *Syn.* adjusted, adapted, qualified, reconditioned, modified, limited, reformed, shifted, moved, mutated, permutated, deteriorated, aged, become run-down, restated, rewritten, conditioned, modernized, remodeled, renovated, reprogrammed, rescheduled, reorganized, redone, done over, brought up to date, revised, amended, edited, moderated, modulated, inflected, innovated, deviated, diverted, warped, matured, developed, disguised; see also **altered** 2. — *Ant.* UNCHANGED, unvaried, unmodified.

**3.** [Transformed] — *Syn.* remade, recreated, converted, transfigured, metamorphosed, transmuted, transmogrified, transubstantiated, transmigrated, suffered a sea change. — *Ant.* PERMANENT, stabilized, final.

**changeless,** *modif.* — *Syn.* permanent, unchanging, enduring; see **constant** 1, **perpetual** 1, **regular** 3.

**changing,** *modif.* — *Syn.* changeful, changeable, mobile, dynamic, vibratory, alternating, modifying, unstable, inconstant, uncertain, mutable, fluid, mercurial, declining, deteriorating, unsteady, irresolute, degenerating, wavering, altering, developing; see also **changeable** 1, 2, **growing, uncertain** 2. — *Ant.* stable, FIXED, unchanging.

**channel,** *n.* **1.** [A passageway for liquid] — *Syn.* conduit, tube, canal, duct, course, carrier, gutter, furrow, trough, tunnel, tideway, strait, neck, sound, race, raceway, watercourse, waterway, sluice, sluiceway, sewer, main, artery, vein, runway, ditch, trench, moat, aqueduct, canyon, cesspipe, pipe; see also **way** 2. — *Ant.* RIDGE, crest, dam.

**2.** [The deeper portion of a river] — *Syn.* current, marked channel, buoyed channel, dredged channel, body of the river, flood, deep water; see also **flow, water** 2.

**3.** [A groove] — *Syn.* gouge, gutter, slit; see sense 1, **groove.**

**channel,** *v.* — *Syn.* route, send, direct; see **lead** 1, **send** 1.

**chant,** *n.* — *Syn.* religious song, incantation, plainsong, Gregorian chant, chorus, mantra, singsong; see also **hymn, song.**

**chant,** *v.* — *Syn.* intone, chorus, drone; see **sing.**

**chaos,** *n.* — *Syn.* turmoil, anarchy, confusion, entropy; see **confusion** 2, **disorder** 2.

*See Synonym Study at* CONFUSION.

**chaotic,** *mod* — *Syn.* disorganized, formless, uncontrolled; see **confused** 2, **disordered, turbulent.**

**chap,** *v.* — *Syn.* chafe, crack open, roughen; see **rub** 1.

**chapel,** *n.* — *Syn.* place of worship, oratory, God's house; see **church** 1.

**chaperon,** *n.* — *Syn.* escort, governess, duenna; see **companion** 2.

**chaperon,** *v.* — *Syn.* accompany, escort, supervise; see **accompany** 1.

*See Synonym Study at* ACCOMPANY.

**chaplain,** *n.* — *Syn.* clergyman, pastor, cleric; see **minister** 1, **priest, rabbi.**

**chapter,** *n.* — *Syn.* part, section, episode, local branch; see **branch** 1, **division** 2.

**char,** *v.* — *Syn.* scorch, sear, singe, carbonize; see **burn** 2, 6.

*See Synonym Study at* BURN.

**character,** *n.* **1.** [The dominant quality] — *Syn.* temper, temperament, nature, sense, complex, mystique, mood, streak, attribute, trait, quality, singularity, badge, turn, tone, style, aspect, complexion, specialty, spirit, genius, humor, frame, grain, vein, atmosphere, ambience, climate, air, aura; see also **attitude** 2, **characteristic, temperament.**
**2.** [The sum of a person's characteristics] — *Syn.* personality, disposition, nature, makeup, temperament, constitution, reputation, repute, individuality, estimation, record, caliber, standing, type, shape, quality, habit, appearance; see also **kind** 2.
**3.** [A symbol, especially in writing] — *Syn.* letter, sign, figure, emblem; see **letter** 1, **mark, number** 2.
**4.** [*An odd or striking person] — *Syn.* personality, figure, personage, original, eccentric, oddity, crank*, nut*, case*, odd duck*, queer duck*, oddball*, weirdo*, crackpot*, flake*, kook*, freak*.
**5.** [Moral strength] — *Syn.* integrity, honor, probity, backbone; see **determination** 2, **honesty** 1.
**6.** [A role] — *Syn.* part, persona, member of the cast; see **actor** 1, **cast** 2, **role.**
**in character** — *Syn.* consistent, usual, predictable; see **expected** 2.
**out of character** — *Syn.* inconsistent, unpredictable, unusual; see **unexpected.**

*See Synonym Study at* QUALITY, TEMPERAMENT.

**characteristic,** *modif.* — *Syn.* distinctive, typical, representative, distinguishing, peculiar, individual, idiosyncratic, emblematic, natural, normal, innate, fixed, essential, marked, discriminative, symbolic, individualizing, discriminating, specific, personal, signature, trademark, original, individualistic, differentiating, unique, special, appropriate, particular, symptomatic, private, exclusive, inherent, inborn, inbred, ingrained, native, diagnostic, indicative, diacritical, inseparable, ineradicable, in the blood, true to form; see also **natural** 1, 2, **typical.** — *Ant.* uncharacteristic, aberrant, unexpected, erratic.

---

**SYN.** — **characteristic** suggests the indication of a quality that is typical of or peculiar to, and that helps identify, something or someone [her *characteristic* disdain for convention, the *characteristic* taste of honey]; **individual** and **distinctive** suggest the possession of a quality or qualities that distinguish something from others of its class or kind, **distinctive** often adding the implication of excellence [an *individual*, or *distinctive*, literary style]

---

**characteristic,** *n.* — *Syn.* trait, feature, attribute, quality, property, essential, faculty, peculiarity, idiosyncrasy, individuality, style, aspect, flavor, savor, tone, tinge, distinction, manner, bearing, inclination, nature, personality, temperament, frame, originality, singularity, qualification, virtue, mark, essence, point, turn, caliber, complexion, streak, stripe, particularity, lineament, diagnostic, cast, trick, earmark, mannerism, quirk, trademark, badge, symptom, disposition, specialty, mood, character, endowment, bent, tendency, component, thing*.

**characterize,** *v.* **1.** [To describe] — *Syn.* delineate, designate, portray; see **define** 2, **describe.**

**2.** [To distinguish] — *Syn.* discriminate, mark, identify; see **distinguish** 1.

**charade,** *n.* — *Syn.* pantomime, mimicry, pretense, put-on*; see **deception** 1, **fake, pantomime, pretense** 1.

**charge,** *n.* **1.** [A charged sale] — *Syn.* entry, debit, carrying charge, credit, sale on account; see also **sale** 2.
**2.** [Fee] — *Syn.* cost, price, assessment; see **price.**
**3.** [An attack] — *Syn.* assault, invasion, onslaught, onset; see **attack** 1.
**4.** [Superintendence] — *Syn.* supervision, care, custody, management; see **administration** 1, **command** 2, **custody** 1.
**5.** [A quantity of explosive] — *Syn.* clip, round, blast; see **ammunition, explosive, load** 3.
**6.** [An address to the jury] — *Syn.* admonition, statement, adjuration; see **speech** 3.
**7.** [*Pleasurable excitement] — *Syn.* thrill, kick*, bang*; see **enjoyment** 2, **thrill.**
**in charge (of)** — *Syn.* responsible, controlling, managing, supervising; see **managing, responsible** 1.

**charge,** *v.* **1.** [To ask a price] — *Syn.* require, impose, sell for, fix the price at; see **price.**
**2.** [To enter on a charge account] — *Syn.* debit, put on one's account, charge to one's account, run up a bill, receive credit, take on account, incur a debt, put down, credit, accredit, encumber, buy on credit, sell on credit, buy on the installment plan, buy on time, pay with plastic*, chalk up*, put on the books*, carry*, put on the cuff*, put on one's tab*; see also **credit** 2, **sell** 1. — *Ant.* pay cash down, buy for cash, sell cash and carry.
**3.** [To attack] — *Syn.* assail, assault, rush, storm; see **attack** 1.
**4.** [To accuse] — *Syn.* indict, censure, impute; see **accuse, censure.**
**5.** [To load] — *Syn.* fill, fill up, replenish, energize; see **fill** 1, **load** 1, 3.
**6.** [To command] — *Syn.* instruct, direct, entrust; see **command** 1, **commission.**

*See Synonym Study at* ACCUSE, COMMAND.

**chargeable,** *modif.* — *Syn.* liable, answerable, imputable; see **responsible** 1.

**charged,** *modif.* **1.** [Bought but not paid for] — *Syn.* debited, put on one's account, unpaid, on credit, on account, on time, on the installment plan, on layaway, owing, owed, on the bill, on the cuff*, on the tab*; see also **bought, due.**
**2.** [Loaded] — *Syn.* laden, filled, suffused, fraught, permeated, saturated, pervaded, imbued, intense, emotional, provocative; see also **full** 1.
**3.** [Accused] — *Syn.* taxed, confronted with, arraigned; see **accused.**

**charger,** *n.* — *Syn.* war horse, steed, mount; see **horse** 1.

**charily,** *modif.* — *Syn.* cautiously, frugally, sparingly; see **carefully** 2.

**charisma,** *n.* — *Syn.* allure, charm, magnetism, mystique; see **appeal** 3.

**charitable,** *modif.* — *Syn.* beneficent, liberal, philanthropic, kind; see **generous** 1, **humane** 1, **kind** 1, **philanthropic.**

*See Synonym Study at* PHILANTHROPIC.

**charity,** *n.* **1.** [Kindness] — *Syn.* benevolence, magnanimity, compassion; see **kindness** 1, **mercy** 1, **tolerance** 1.
**2.** [An organization to aid the needy] — *Syn.* charitable institution, philanthropy, foundation, fund, welfare organization, eleemosynary corporation; see also **foundation** 3.
Organized charities include: American Cancer Soci-

ety, American Diabetes Association, American Foundation for AIDS Research, American Foundation for the Blind, American Heart Association, American Lung Association, American Red Cross, Arthritis Foundation, CARE, Catholic Charities, Community Chest, Easter Seal Society, Goodwill, Heart and Lung Foundation, Jewish Welfare Fund, Leukemia Society Inc., Lupus Foundation, March of Dimes, Medico, Multiple Sclerosis Research Foundation Corp., Muscular Dystrophy Association of America Inc., National Association of the Deaf, National Association for Retarded Children, National Mental Health Association, Cystic Fibrosis Foundation, National Epilepsy League, National Foundation for Neuromuscular Diseases, National Hemophilia Foundation, National Kidney Foundation Inc., National Paraplegia Foundation Inc., National Society for the Prevention of Blindness, National Tuberculosis Association, St. Vincent de Paul Society, Salvation Army, United Cerebral Palsy Association Inc., United Fund, United Health Foundation Inc., United Leukemia Fund Inc., United Negro College Fund, United Ostomy Association, United Parkinson Foundation, United Way.
**3.** [Money or help given to those in need] — *Syn.* donation, alms, welfare, handout\*; see **gift** 1.
*See Synonym Study at* MERCY.

**charlatan,** *n.* — *Syn.* quack, pretender, fraud; see **cheat** 1, **impostor, quack.**
*See Synonym Study at* QUACK.

**charm,** *n.* **1.** [The quality of being charming] — *Syn.* grace, attractiveness, attraction, winsomeness; see **appeal** 3, **beauty** 1.
**2.** [An object thought to possess power] — *Syn.* amulet, talisman, fetish, mascot, good-luck piece, lucky piece, rabbit's foot, madstone. — *Ant.* hoodoo, CURSE, bad genius.
**3.** [An incantation] — *Syn.* spell, bewitchery, enchantment, sorcery; see **magic** 1.

**charm,** *v.* **1.** [To bewitch] — *Syn.* enchant, captivate, enthrall, possess, enrapture, transport, entrance, vamp, mesmerize, put a spell on, spellbind, voodoo; see also **attract** 2, **fascinate, hypnotize** 1.
**2.** [To delight] — *Syn.* please, beguile, win over; see **entertain** 1.
*See Synonym Study at* ATTRACT.

**charmed,** *modif.* — *Syn.* enchanted, bewitched, enraptured, entranced, captivated, delighted, beguiled, pleased, soothed, attracted, won over, lured, tempted, enticed, bedazzled, fascinated, hypnotized, mesmerized, under a spell, in a trance, spellbound, moonstruck, witch-charmed, hagridden, possessed, protected, privileged; see also **fascinated, protected.**

**charming,** *modif.* — *Syn.* enchanting, bewitching, entrancing, captivating, cute, fascinating, delightful, lovable, sweet, winning, engaging, irresistible, attractive, amiable, appealing, alluring, charismatic, pleasing, choice, nice, graceful, winsome, magnetizing, seductive, desirable, enticing, tempting, inviting, ravishing, enrapturing, glamorous, elegant, infatuating, dainty, delicate, *charmant* (French), absorbing, tantalizing, engrossing, titillating, enamoring, enthralling, rapturous, electrifying, lovely, intriguing, thrilling, fair, exquisite, catching, likable, transporting, diverting, fetching, beguiling, provocative, delectable, having sex appeal\*, sexy\*, smooth\*, adorable\*; see also **beautiful** 2, **entertaining, handsome** 2, **pleasant** 1. — *Ant.* disgusting, offensive, unpleasant, obnoxious.

**chart,** *n.* — *Syn.* graph, outline, diagram, table; see **map, plan** 1.

**chart,** *v.* — *Syn.* map, outline, draft; see **plan** 2.

**charter,** *n.* **1.** [A written grant] — *Syn.* franchise, license, grant, authorization; see **permission, permit.**
**2.** [The constitution of an organization or city] — *Syn.* code, covenant, compact, contract; see **agreement** 3, **law** 2, **treaty.**

**charter,** *v.* **1.** [To license] — *Syn.* authorize, sanction, franchise, establish; see **allow** 1, **approve** 1, **organize** 2.
**2.** [To hire] — *Syn.* lease, contract, engage; see **borrow** 1, **rent** 2.
*See Synonym Study at* HIRE.

**chary,** *modif.* **1.** [Careful] — *Syn.* cautious, circumspect, wary; see **careful.**
**2.** [Frugal] — *Syn.* sparing, stingy, miserly; see **economical** 1.

**chase,** *n.* — *Syn.* pursuit, hunt, quest; see **hunt** 1, 2.
**give chase** — *Syn.* chase, trail, hunt, go after; see **pursue** 1.

**chase,** *v.* **1.** [To pursue] — *Syn.* follow, run after, trail, track; see **hunt** 1, **pursue** 1.
**2.** [To make run away] — *Syn.* drive away, expel, rout, scatter; see **oust.**

**chasm,** *n.* — *Syn.* abyss, gorge, gap; see **hole** 2, **ravine.**

**chassis,** *n.* — *Syn.* framework, skeleton, undercarriage; see **body** 4, **case** 7, **frame** 1.

**chaste,** *modif.* **1.** [Restrained] — *Syn.* classic, classical, pure, simple, modest, Spartan, academic, severe, prudish, subdued, disciplined, inornate, unadorned; see also **modest** 2. — *Ant.* ORNATE, GAUDY, rococo.
**2.** [Morally pure] — *Syn.* moral, virtuous, modest, decent, proper, pure, innocent, virginal, immaculate, unstained, clean, unblemished, unsullied, undefiled, uncontaminated, spotless, wholesome, decorous, pure as the driven snow; see also **decent** 2, **innocent** 4, **pure** 2, **righteous** 1. — *Ant.* unchaste, coarse, debauched, debased.
**3.** [Sexually abstinent] — *Syn.* virgin, celibate, continent, abstinent, abstemious, platonic, controlled, virtuous, monogamous, frigid, impotent, virginal, unmarried, unwed. — *Ant.* LEWD, lascivious, lecherous.

---

**SYN.** — **chaste** and **virtuous,** in this connection, imply forbearance from acts or thoughts that do not accord with virginity or strict marital fidelity; **pure** implies chastity through innocence and an absence of seductive influences rather than through self-restraint; **modest** and **decent** are both applied to propriety in behavior, dress, bearing, or speech as exhibiting moral purity

---

**chasten,** *v.* **1.** [To punish] — *Syn.* humble, humiliate, subdue, chastise, castigate, afflict, discipline, restrain, reprove, berate, take to task, upbraid, chide, rap on the knuckles, reproach, reprehend, admonish, rebuke, fulminate against, reprimand, tongue-lash, objurgate, scourge, penalize, scold, call down\*, roast\*; see also **censure, punish, scold.** — *Ant.* ENCOURAGE, uplift, benefit.
**2.** [To purify] — *Syn.* refine, correct, clarify; see **improve** 1, **purify.**
*See Synonym Study at* PUNISH.

**chastise,** *v.* — *Syn.* scold, discipline, spank; see **punish.**
*See Synonym Study at* PUNISH.

**chastity,** *n.* — *Syn.* innocence, purity, virtue, abstinence, celibacy, virtuousness, uprightness, honor, monogamy, faithfulness, fidelity, integrity, decency, delicacy, goodness, virginity, maidenhood, bachelorhood, unmarried state, demureness, decorousness, temperance, moderation, morality, chasteness, spinsterhood, abstemiousness, modesty, sinlessness, continence, coldness, restraint, simplicity, immaculateness, immaculacy, spotlessness, stainlessness, seemliness, gentleness; see also **abstinence, purity** 1, **virtue** 1.— *Ant.* adultery, LEWDNESS, licentiousness.

**chat,** *v.* — *Syn.* converse, prattle, chatter; see **talk** 1.

**château,** *n.* — *Syn.* manor house, mansion, castle, country estate; see **building** 1, **castle, home** 1.

**chattel,** *n.* — *Syn.* belongings, goods, assets; see **property** 1, **wealth** 1.

**chatter,** *v.* — *Syn.* prattle, jabber, gossip, chat; see **babble.**

**chatterer,** *n.* — *Syn.* chatterbox, prattler, jabberer, talker; see **gossip** 2.

**chatty,** *modif.* — *Syn.* intimate, spontaneous, familiar, talkative; see **friendly** 1, **informal** 1, **talkative.**

**chauffeur,** *n.* — *Syn.* driver, licensed operator, cabdriver; see **driver, servant.**

**chauvinism,** *n.* 1. [Fanatical patriotism] — *Syn.* jingoism, superpatriotism, ultranationalism, hawkishness; see **aggression** 2, **jingoism, patriotism.**
2. [Unreasoning devotion to one's sex, race, etc.] — *Syn.* male chauvinism, female chauvinism, prejudice, ethnocentricity; see **intolerance** 2, **prejudice.**

**chauvinist,** *n.* — *Syn.* jingo, jingoist, superpatriot, sexist; see **bigot, patriot.**

**cheap,** *modif.* 1. [Low in relative price] — *Syn.* inexpensive, low-priced, reasonable, economical, affordable, moderate, family-size, economy-size, economy, budget, utility (grade), reduced, marked down, discounted, depreciated, slashed, standard, modest, cut-rate, on sale, competitive, thrifty, bargain, bargain-priced, sale-priced, irregular, cut-price, low-cost, at a bargain, half-price, popular-priced, worth the money, rock-bottom, second, dime-a-dozen*, dirt-cheap*, costing peanuts*, for a song*, bargain-basement*; see also **economical** 2. — *Ant.* EXPENSIVE, dear, costly.
2. [Low in quality] — *Syn.* inferior, shoddy, poorly made, sleazy*; see **common** 1, **poor** 2.
3. [Dishonest or base] — *Syn.* dirty, tawdry, low, contemptible; see **dishonest** 2.
4. [Stingy*] — *Syn.* miserly, penurious, tight*; see **stingy.**

SYN. — **cheap** and **inexpensive** both mean low in cost or price, but **inexpensive** simply suggests value comparable to the price, and **cheap**, in this sense, stresses a bargain; **cheap** may also imply inferior quality or value, tawdriness, contemptibility, etc. *[cheap* jewelry, to feel *cheap]*

**cheapen,** *v.* — *Syn.* ruin, spoil, debase, mar, degrade, devalue, undervalue, reduce, diminish, demean, depreciate, render worthless; see also **corrupt** 1, **damage** 1, **depreciate** 2.

**cheaply,** *modif.* — *Syn.* economically, inexpensively, reasonably, advantageously, moderately, at a bargain price, at a good price, at a fair price, on sale, at cost, below cost, discounted, at a discount, from a discount house, reduced, at a reduced price, cheap, at a sacrifice, *bon marché* (French), the economy size, the family size, shoddily, poorly, shabbily, dirt cheap*, given away*, for a song*, for peanuts*.

**cheat,** *n.* 1. [One who cheats] — *Syn.* rogue, cheater, swindler, fraud, quack, charlatan, conniver, confidence man, scammer, chiseler, impostor, masquerader, fake, bluff, deceiver, inveigler, hypocrite, double-dealer, trickster, shyster, mountebank, pettifogger, pretender, knave, cozener, dodger, humbug, crook, defrauder, dissembler, bilk, sharper, shark, wolf in sheep's clothing,

enticer, decoy, beguiler, phony*, diddler*, two-timer*, blackleg*, con artist*, con man*, fourflusher*, shill*, sharp*, cardsharp*, flimflammer*, flimflam man*, bunco artist*, grifter*; see also **criminal, impostor, quack, rascal.**
2. [A trick] — *Syn.* fraud, swindle, deceit; see **fake, trick** 1.

**cheat,** *v.* — *Syn.* defraud, swindle, dupe, trick, deceive, victimize, hoax, con*, bilk, gull, bamboozle, fleece, overcharge, shortchange, gyp*, gouge*, rook, chisel*, cozen, mulct, be dishonest, practice fraud, crib*, plagiarize, copy, be unfaithful, play around, fool around, two-time*, stack the deck, stack the cards, play with marked cards, load the dice, diddle*, rip off*, clip*, stick*, sting*, burn*, beat*; see also **deceive.**

SYN. — **cheat**, the most general term in this comparison, implies dealing dishonestly or deceptively with someone to obtain some advantage or gain; **defraud**, chiefly a legal term, stresses the use of deliberate deception in criminally depriving a person of rights or property; **swindle** stresses the winning of a person's confidence in order to cheat or defraud that person of money; **trick** implies deluding by means of a ruse, stratagem, etc., but does not always suggest fraudulence or a harmful motive; **dupe** stresses credulity in the person who is tricked or fooled; **hoax** implies a trick skillfully carried off simply to demonstrate the gullibility of the victim

**cheated,** *modif.* — *Syn.* defrauded, swindled, tricked, duped, finessed, finessed out of, deprived of, scammed, imposed upon, victimized, beguiled, dealt with dishonestly, taken in, bamboozled, hoodwinked, overcharged, bilked, conned*, taken for a ride*, ripped off*, burned*, stung*, gypped*, stuck*; see also **deceived** 1.

**cheating,** *n.* — *Syn.* lying, defrauding, deceiving; see **deception** 1, **dishonesty.**

**check,** *n.* 1. [An order on a bank] — *Syn.* money order, draft, letter of credit, traveler's check, bank check, teller's check, cashier's check, counter check, note, remittance, deposition; see also **draft** 5, **money** 1.
2. [A restraint] — *Syn.* control, limit, curb, rein; see **restraint** 2.
3. [An examination] — *Syn.* test, inspection, investigation, analysis; see **comparison** 1, **examination** 1, 3, **test.**
4. [The symbol √] — *Syn.* cross, ex, sign, line, stroke, score, dot; see also **mark** 1.
5. [A pattern in squares] — *Syn.* tartan, patchwork, quilt, diaper, checkered design, checkerboard, houndstooth check; see also **plaid.**
6. [A reversal] — *Syn.* rebuff, obstruction, trouble; see **defeat** 3, **impediment** 1.
**in check** — *Syn.* controlled, under control, checked; see **restrained.**

**check,** *v.* 1. [To slacken the pace] — *Syn.* curb, hinder, impede, arrest, moderate, obstruct, reduce, slacken, stay, restrain, choke, bottleneck, cause a bottleneck, deadlock, slow down, block, withhold, weaken, lessen, brake, keep back, cog, anchor, rein in; see also **halt** 2, **hinder.** — *Ant.* speed, HASTEN, urge on.
2. [To bring under control] — *Syn.* bridle, repress, inhibit, control, curb, restrain, checkmate, counteract, discourage, repulse, neutralize, bar, suppress, squelch, rebuff, snub; see also **restrain** 1. — *Ant.* LIBERATE, advance, encourage.
3. [To determine accuracy] — *Syn.* review, monitor, examine, inspect, verify, validate, balance accounts, bal-

ance the books, keep account of, correct, compare, find out, investigate, count, tell, call the roll, take account of, take stock, double-check, go through, go over with a fine-toothed comb*; see also **examine** 1, **verify**.

**4.** [To halt] — *Syn.* hold, terminate, cut short; see **halt** 2, **stop** 1.

**5.** [To mark] — *Syn.* indicate, tick, tick off, stamp; see **mark** 1, 2.

*See Synonym Study at* RESTRAIN.

**checker,** *n.* — *Syn.* checkout person, cashier, examiner, tallier, rechecker, controller, validator, checking department, department of weights and measures, checking staff, inspector, examining officer, tally man.

**checkered,** *modif.* — *Syn.* checked, plaid, patterned, spotted, motley, variegated, diversified, diverse, varied, mutable, uneven; see also **irregular** 1, 4.

**check in,** *v.* — *Syn.* register, appear, sign in, report; see **arrive** 1, **register** 4.

**checkmate,** *v.* — *Syn.* halt, thwart, counter, defeat; see **check** 2, **defeat** 1, **halt** 2.

**check off,** *v.* — *Syn.* mark off, check, verify, notice; see **mark** 2.

**check out,** *v.* **1.** [To leave a hotel, hospital, etc.] — *Syn.* depart, pay one's bill, settle up; see **leave** 1, **pay** 1.

**2.** [To examine] — *Syn.* investigate, inspect, verify, appraise; see **examine** 1.

**3.** [To prove accurate or consistent] — *Syn.* correspond, jibe*, measure up, be verifiable; see **agree**.

**checkroom,** *n.* — *Syn.* parcel room, cloakroom, locker, baggage room, left luggage office (British); see also **closet, room** 2.

**check up on,** *v.* — *Syn.* watch, investigate, control; see **examine** 1.

**cheek,** *n.* **1.** [Either side of the face] — *Syn.* jowl, gill, chop*; see **face** 1.

**2.** [*Insolence*] — *Syn.* impertinence, impudence, disrespect; see **rudeness, temerity**.

*See Synonym Study at* TEMERITY.

**cheep,** *v.* — *Syn.* peep, chirp, tweet; see **chirp, sound** 1.

**cheer,** *n.* **1.** [An agreeable mental state] — *Syn.* delight, mirth, glee; see **happiness** 1, **joy** 2.

**2.** [Something that comforts or gladdens] — *Syn.* encouragement, reassurance, comfort, solace; see **encouragement** 2.

**3.** [An encouraging shout] — *Syn.* roar, applause, hurrah, hurray, bravo, huzzah, cheering, organized cheering, college yell, rah, approval, approbation; see also **cry** 1, **yell** 1.

**cheer,** *v.* **1.** [To hearten] — *Syn.* console, inspirit, brighten, gladden; see **comfort, encourage** 2, **gladden, help** 1.

**2.** [To support with cheers] — *Syn.* applaud, shout, salute; see **praise** 1, **support** 2, **yell**.

**cheerful,** *modif.* **1.** [*Said especially of persons*] — *Syn.* gay, merry, optimistic, in good spirits; see **happy** 1, **hopeful** 1, **lively** 2, **sprightly**.

**2.** [*Said especially of things*] — *Syn.* cheery, bright, sunny, sparkling; see **comfortable** 2, **lively** 2, **pleasant** 2, **sprightly**.

*See Synonym Study at* HAPPY.

**cheerfully,** *modif.* — *Syn.* cheerily, gladly, willingly, readily, happily, merrily, joyfully, lightheartedly, blithely, brightly, vivaciously, airily, buoyantly, genially, jovially, sportively, elatedly, pleasantly, gleefully, gaily, mirthfully, playfully, hopefully, optimistically, breezily, briskly, with good cheer; see also **happily** 2. — *Ant.* unwillingly, grudgingly, gloomily.

**cheerfulness,** *n.* — *Syn.* good humor, gaiety, geniality, hopefulness; see **happiness** 1, **humor** 3, **optimism** 2.

**cheering,** *modif.* — *Syn.* heartening, promising, bright; see **hopeful** 2.

**cheerless,** *modif.* — *Syn.* gloomy, sorrowful, bleak; see **dismal** 1, **sad** 1, 2.

**cheers,** *interj.* — *Syn.* here's to you, to your health, *skoal* (Scandinavian); see **toast** 1.

**cheer up,** *v.* **1.** [To make cheerful] — *Syn.* gladden, comfort, enliven, inspirit; see **comfort, encourage** 2, **gladden**.

**2.** [To become cheerful] — *Syn.* improve in outlook, improve in spirits, improve in mood, perk up, take heart, brighten, brighten up, be comforted; see also **improve** 2.

**cheery,** *modif.* — *Syn.* cheerful, lively, bright; see **happy** 1, **lively** 2, **pleasant** 2, **sprightly**.

**cheese,** *n.*

Varieties of cheese include: mild, American, appetitost, aged cheddar, cheddar, Cheshire, Dutch, Saga Blue, Tamales Bay, Philadelphia cream, creamed cottage, Edam, hand, jack, brick, Roquefort, Brie, Jarlsberg, Bleu d'Auvergne, mozzarella, provolone, asiago, sapsago, Havarti, Fleur de Lait, Gorgonzola, Monterey Jack, Swiss, Camembert, Liederkranz, Neufchâtel, Gruyère, Emmenthaler, Wensleydale, Parmesan, Stilton, Gouda, Gloucester, double Gloucester, Limburger, Leyden, muenster, oka, Pecorino, Port du Salut, pot, mascarpone, ricotta, Romano, Schweizer, smearcase, bel paese, tilsit, feta, goat cheese (chèvre); see also **food**.

**chef,** *n.* — *Syn.* head cook, head of the kitchen, *chef de cuisine* (French); see **cook, servant**.

**chemical,** *modif.* — *Syn.* analytic, synthetic, synthesized, petrochemical, biochemical, psychochemical, actinic, artificial, made in the laboratory, ersatz, alchemical.

**chemical,** *n.* — *Syn.* substance, synthetic, compound; see **drug** 2, **element** 2, **medicine** 2.

**chemistry,** *n.*

Branches of chemistry include: pure, quantitative, qualitative, organic, inorganic, theoretical, analytical, structural, nuclear, atomic, physical, physiological, pathological, metallurgical, mineralogical, geological, applied, agricultural, pharmaceutical, sanitary, industrial, technical, engineering; chemurgy, biochemistry, electrochemistry, zoochemistry, petrochemistry, thermochemistry, stereochemistry, phytochemistry; see also **medicine** 3, **science** 1.

**cherish,** *v.* **1.** [To hold dear] — *Syn.* treasure, value, cling to, esteem, appreciate, honor, admire, prize, guard, hold dear, revere, worship, treasure up, entertain, harbor, enshrine, enshrine in the memory, hold fast to, hang on to, love, like, care for, fancy, caress, pet, coddle, clasp, cosset, embrace, adore, dote on, idolize, fondle, hug; see also **love** 1, 2. — *Ant.* disdain, despise, abandon, ill-treat.

**2.** [To tend solicitously] — *Syn.* nurture, harbor, foster; see **defend** 2.

*See Synonym Study at* APPRECIATE.

**cherry,** *modif.* — *Syn.* ruddy, reddish, rosy, cerise, claret, bright red, light red, blushing, incarnadine, rubescent, rubicund, erubescent, cherry-colored, cherry-red, bright, blooming; see also **red**.

**cherry,** *n.*

Varieties of cherries include: Bing, Lambert, black Tartarian, Napoleon, Windsor, Royal Ann, Queen Anne, Royal Duke, Surinam, Cornelian, Japanese flowering, Montmorency, English Morello, wild, pin, chokecherry, bird, black, yellow, golden, red, brush, sour, marasca, amarelle, sweet, mazzard, maraschino, bigarreau, oxheart, native, Barbados; see also **fruit** 1.

**cherub,** *n.* — *Syn.* angel, seraph, beautiful infant; see **angel** 1, **baby** 1, **child.**

**chest,** *n.* **1.** [A box-like container, or a piece of furniture with drawers] — *Syn.* case, box, coffer, cabinet, commode, strongbox, receptacle, crate, locker, chest of drawers, dresser, bureau, chiffonier, clothespress, highboy, lowboy, jewel box, casket, coffin, treasury, reliquary, caddy, pyxis; see also **container, furniture.**
**2.** [The ribbed portion of the body] — *Syn.* breast, thorax, bosom, rib cage, heart, upper trunk, pulmonary cavity, peritoneum, ribs.

**chew,** *v.* — *Syn.* bite, chomp, champ, munch, crunch, masticate, nibble, nibble at, feast upon, gnaw, gulp, dispatch, grind, chew the cud, rend, gnash, crush, scrunch, ruminate; see also **eat** 1.

**Chicago,** *n.* — *Syn.* the Windy City*, Fort Dearborn*, City of the Lakes and Prairies*, Chi*, Chi-town*, the Loop.

**chicanery,** *n.* — *Syn.* deception, trickery, sophistry, cheating; see **deception** 1, **dishonesty.**
*See Synonym Study at* DECEPTION.

**chicken,** *n.* **1.** [A barnyard fowl] — *Syn.* chick, hen, rooster, pullet, cock, cockerel, capon, chanticleer, biddy, broiler, fryer, roaster, fowl, poulard, squab chicken, free-range chicken; see also **fowl.**
Breeds of chickens include: Black Cochin, Buff Cochin, Partridge Cochin, White Cochin, Game, Indian Game, Houdan, Java, Dorking, Hamburg, Wyandotte, Black Leghorn, White Leghorn, Minorca, Buff Orpington, White Orpington, Rhode Island Red, Barred Plymouth Rock, Barred Rock, Plymouth Rock, White Plymouth Rock, White Rock.
**2.** [Flesh of the chicken]. Parts of the chicken include: breast, back, thigh, leg, wing, neck, giblets, heart, liver, gizzard, dark meat, white meat, light meat, drumstick*, part that goes over the fence last*; see also **meat.**
**3.** [*A coward] — *Syn.* recreant, dastard, craven; see **coward.**

**count one's chickens before they are hatched*** — *Syn.* rely, rely on, depend on, put trust in; see **anticipate** 1.

**chide,** *v.* — *Syn.* rebuke, reprimand, criticize; see **censure, scold.**

**chief,** *modif.* — *Syn.* leading, main, foremost; see **principal.**
*See Synonym Study at* PRINCIPAL.

**chief,** *n.* **1.** [The outstanding person or thing] — *Syn.* leader, head, principal, manager, boss, overseer, governor, president, foreman, proprietor, supervisor, superior, director, chair, chairman, ringleader, general, master, dictator, superintendent, ruler, captain, commander, big shot*, brass hat*, higher-up*, bigwig*, big wheel*, big cheese*; high muck-a-muck*, head honcho*, *número uno** (Spanish), prima donna*, triton among minnows*, the only pebble on the beach*, the biggest frog in the puddle*; see also **administrator, leader** 2.— *Ant.* subordinate, underling, retainer.
**2.** [A chieftain] — *Syn.* ruler, prince, master, sachem, sagamore, emperor, duke, majesty, monarch, overlord, suzerain, lord, potentate, sovereign, chieftain, headman, elder, Maharaja, sahib, Rajah, boyar, effendi, emir, sheik, pasha; see also **king** 1, **ruler** 1.

**chiefly,** *modif.* — *Syn.* mainly, particularly, in the first place; see **principally.**

**child,** *n.* — *Syn.* boy, girl, kid*, baby, newborn, infant, nestling, toddler, tot, preschooler, moppet, preteen, youth, adolescent, teenager, youngster, daughter, son, grandchild, stepchild, foster child, offspring, descend-ant, innocent, stripling, minor, youngling, mite, chick, juvenile, tad, tyke, cub, small fry, little one, cherub, chit, whippersnapper, pubescent, progeny, issue, kiddie*, papoose*, teeny-bopper*, nymphet*, whelp*, brat*, imp*, urchin*, shaver*; see also **baby** 1, **boy, daughter, girl** 1, **son.** — *Ant.* PARENT, adult, elder.

**with child** — *Syn.* pregnant, bearing a child, carrying a child, going to have a baby; see **pregnant** 1.

**childbirth,** *n.* — *Syn.* delivery, childbearing, parturition, childbed, labor, birth, nativity, delivering, accouchement, lying-in, confinement, travail, procreation, reproduction, propagation, giving birth, blessed event*; see also **birth** 1, **pregnancy.**

**childhood,** *n.* — *Syn.* infancy, youth, minority, pupilage, juvenility, juniority, school days, adolescence, nonage, nursery days, babyhood, the cradle, boyhood, girlhood, teens, puberty, immaturity, tender age, early years, growing years, pubescence; see also **youth** 1. — *Ant.* MATURITY, adulthood, declining years.

**childish,** *modif.* **1.** [Having qualities of a child] — *Syn.* childlike, immature, babyish, baby, infantile, juvenile, puerile, youthful, primitive, boyish, girlish, adolescent, sophomoric, simple, green, soft, kiddish*; see also **naive, simple** 1, **young** 2. — *Ant.* adult, MATURE, sophisticated.
**2.** [Silly or stupid] — *Syn.* foolish, puerile, absurd, weak; see **silly, stupid** 1.
**3.** [Childlike because of senility] — *Syn.* senile, in one's dotage, in one's second childhood; see **old** 1.

---

*SYN.* — **childish** and **childlike** are both applied to persons of any age in referring to characteristics or qualities considered typical of a child, **childish** suggesting unfavorable qualities such as immaturity, foolishness, petulance, etc. and **childlike,** the favorable, as innocence, guilelessness, trustfulness, etc.

---

**childlike,** *modif.* — *Syn.* unaffected, innocent, childish, ingenuous; see **naive, natural** 3.
*See Synonym Study at* CHILDISH.

**chill,** *modif.* **1.** [Uncomfortably cool] — *Syn.* brisk, frosty, wintry, chilly; see **cold** 1, **cool** 1.
**2.** [Cold in manner] — *Syn.* formal, distant, aloof, icy; see **aloof, indifferent** 1, **unfriendly** 1.
**3.** [Depressing] — *Syn.* discouraging, unhappy, dispiriting; see **dismal** 1, **sad** 2.

**chill,** *n.* **1.** [Chilliness] — *Syn.* coolness, coldness, rigor, crispness, frigidity, sharpness, iciness, nip, bite; see also **cold** 1.
**2.** [An illness] — *Syn.* virus, head cold, ague; see **cold** 3, **disease.**

**chill,** *v.* **1.** [To reduce temperature] — *Syn.* cool, freeze, refrigerate, ice; see **cool** 2, **freeze** 2.
**2.** [To check] — *Syn.* dispirit, dishearten, dampen; see **depress** 2, **discourage** 1.

**chilly,** *modif.* **1.** [Uncomfortably cool] — *Syn.* brisk, crisp, nippy, chilled; see **cold** 1, 2, **cool** 1.
**2.** [Cold in manner] — *Syn.* unresponsive, hostile, frosty; see **aloof, indifferent** 1, **unfriendly** 1.

**chime,** *v.* — *Syn.* peal, tinkle, clang, toll; see **ring** 3, **sound** 1.

**chimera,** *n.* — *Syn.* figment, delusion, fabrication; see **fancy** 3, **illusion** 1.

**chimney,** *n.* — *Syn.* smokestack, fireplace, furnace, hearth, flue, vent, pipe, funnel, smokeshaft, stack, chimney pot, chimney stack, *cheminée* (French).

**chin,** *n.* — *Syn.* jaw, mandible, jawbone, button*; see **jaw** 1.

**china,** *n.* — *Syn.* chinaware, dishes, earthenware, pottery, crockery, porcelain, stoneware; see also **dish** 1.
Varieties of china include: Bow, bone, fine, Chelsea, Lowestoft, Royal Doulton, Spode, Crown Derby, Worcester, Derby, Plymouth, Swansea, Limoges, Haviland, Chantilly, Sèvres, Meissen, Dresden, Delft, eggshell, Belleek, Imari, Hizen, Rose Medallion, Kouan-Ki Rose, Staffordshire, Wedgwood.

**China,** *n.* — *Syn.* People's Republic of China, mainland China, Red China*, Chung Kwoh, the Celestial Empire, the Celestial Kingdom, the Middle Kingdom, Chung Hwa Kwoh, Central Flowery Country, Chinese Empire, Manchu Empire, Sung Empire, Ming Empire, Han Empire, Country of Taoism, Land of Buddhism, Republic of China, Taiwan; see also **Asia.**

**Chinese,** *modif.* — *Syn.* Sinitic, Han, Sino-, Celestial; see **Asian** 1, 2.

**chip,** *n.* **1.** [A fragment] — *Syn.* thin slice, shard, sliver, shaving; see **bit** 1, **flake, part** 1.
**2.** [A microcircuit] — *Syn.* microchip, integrated circuit, semiconductor, microprocessor, silicon chip, computer on a chip.
**3.** [A place where a piece has chipped off] — *Syn.* nick, scratch, flaw; see **blemish, nick.**
**4.** [A counter used in games] — *Syn.* token, poker chip, counter, marker, disk, piece.
**having a chip on one's shoulder*** — *Syn.* ready to fight, belligerent, truculent, hostile; see **aggressive** 2, **angry.**
**in the chips*** — *Syn.* wealthy, having money, flush*; see **rich** 1.
**when the chips are down** — *Syn.* in a crisis, having trouble, in a difficult position; see **in trouble** 1 at **trouble.**

**chip,** *v.* — *Syn.* nick, scratch, gouge, slash, hew, hack, crumble, snip, fragment, break, crack, flake, incise, shape, shape bit by bit, cut fragments from, whittle, crack off, splinter, gash, snick, notch, sliver, cut, cut off, chop, split, slice, chisel, clip, cut away, fracture, shiver, reduce. — *Ant.* JOIN, unite, mend.

**chip in,** *v.* — *Syn.* contribute, ante up*, pitch in*, kick in*; see **contribute, participate** 1, **pay** 1.

**chipper*,** *modif.* — *Syn.* in good spirits, lively, cheerful, jaunty; see **happy** 1, **lively** 2, **sprightly.**

**chirp,** *v.* — *Syn.* chirrup, cheep, twitter, warble, peep, tweet, chip, quaver, trill, pipe, roll, lilt, purl; see also **sound** 1.

**chisel,** *n.* — *Syn.* gouge, blade, edge; see **knife, tool** 1.

**chisel,** *v.* **1.** [To work with a chisel] — *Syn.* carve, hew, incise, sculpt; see **carve** 1, **cut** 1, **form** 1.
**2.** [*To get by imposition] — *Syn.* impose upon, defraud, swindle, bilk; see **beg** 2, **cheat, deceive.**

**chitchat,** *n.* — *Syn.* informal talk, prattle, small talk; see **conversation, gossip** 1, **talk** 5.

**chivalrous,** *modif.* — *Syn.* courteous, courtly, gentlemanly, honorable, noble, heroic, valiant, courageous, gallant, knightly, generous, spirited, high-minded, valorous, lofty, intrepid, noble-minded, gracious; see also **brave** 1, **noble** 1, 2, **polite** 1. — *Ant.* COWARDLY, boorish, churlish.
*See Synonym Study at* POLITE.

**chivalry,** *n.* — *Syn.* valor, gallantry, honor; see **courage** 1, **courtesy** 1, **dignity** 1, **fairness.**

**chock-full,** *modif.* — *Syn.* packed, crammed, stuffed; see **full** 1.

**choice,** *modif.* — *Syn.* superior, fine, exceptional, select; see **best** 1, **excellent.**

**choice,** *n.* **1.** [The act or power of choosing] — *Syn.* option, selection, alternative, free choice, discretion, deci-

sion, determination, voice, free will, opportunity, choosing, election, vote, volition, co-optation, preference, expression of an opinion, say so*, druthers*; see also **choosing, judgment** 2, **selection** 1.
**2.** [A variety from which to choose] — *Syn.* selection, realm of possibilities, supply, assortment, array, stock, fund, variety.
**3.** [That which is chosen] — *Syn.* selection, preference, alternative, election, substitute, favorite, pick, appointee, chosen one, successful candidate; see also **option** 1.

---

*SYN.* — **choice** implies the chance, right, or power to choose, usually by the free exercise of one's judgment [single by *choice*]; **option** implies a choice of a number of possibilities, and may suggest the privilege of choosing as granted by a person or group in authority [no other *options* open to me, local *option* on liquor sales]; **alternative,** in strict usage, limits a choice to one of two possibilities [the *alternative* of paying a fine or serving 30 days]; **preference** suggests the determining of choice by predisposition or partiality [a *preference* for striped ties]; **selection** implies a wide choice and the exercise of careful discrimination [*selections* from the modern French poets]

---

**choke,** *v.* **1.** [To deprive of air] — *Syn.* asphyxiate, strangle, strangulate, stifle, throttle, garrote, drown, overpower, noose, gibbet, smother, gag, grab by the throat, wring the neck, stop the breath, kill by suffocation, cut off one's air supply, suffocate; see also **gag** 1, **kill** 1.
**2.** [To be deprived of air] — *Syn.* strangle, gag, gasp, suffocate, be out of air, drown, burn out, die out, smother, throttle, die by asphyxiation; see also **die** 1.

**choke up*,** *v.* **1.** [To be overcome with emotion] — *Syn.* give way to one's feelings, weep, break down, become speechless; see **cry** 1.
**2.** [To fail under pressure] — *Syn.* falter, become confused, perform poorly; see **fail** 1.

**choleric,** *modif.* — *Syn.* irritable, quick-tempered, peevish, irascible; see **irritable.**
*See Synonym Study at* IRRITABLE.

**chomp,** *v.* — *Syn.* champ, chew, munch, gnaw; see **bite** 1, **chew.**

**choose,** *v.* **1.** [To select] — *Syn.* decide on, pick, take, pick out, draw lots, cull, prefer, make a choice of, elect, vote for, opt for, accept, weigh, judge, sort, appoint, cast, embrace, will, call for, take up, excerpt, extract, separate, favor, exercise, determine, resolve, discriminate, make a decision, adopt, co-opt, engage, collect, mark out for, cut out, arrange, keep, make one's choice, make one's selection, pick and choose, settle on, use one's discretion, determine upon, fix on, fix upon, place one's trust in, glean, single out, espouse, exercise one's choice, exercise one's option, make up one's mind, set aside, set apart, commit oneself, divide the sheep from the goats, separate the wheat from the tares, separate the wheat from the chaff, incline toward, cast one's lot with, take for better or for worse, burn one's bridges, take to one's bosom, go with*; see also **decide.** — *Ant.* DISCARD, reject, refuse.
**2.** [To like] — *Syn.* wish, prefer, feel disposed to, fancy; see **like** 3, **want** 1.

**choosing,** *n.* — *Syn.* selecting, picking, culling, separating, electing, making a choice, making a selection, selection, election, option, separation, deciding, making up one's mind, exercising judgment, segregating, singling out, eliminating the undesirables, choosing by elimination, natural selection, survival of the fittest; see also **choice** 1.

**choosy★**, *modif.* — *Syn.* selective, particular, fussy; see **careful.**

**chop**, *v.* 1. [To cut with an ax] — *Syn.* fell, hack, hew, whack; see **cut** 1.

2. [To cut into small bits] — *Syn.* mince, dice, cube, cut up; see **chip, cut** 1.

**choppy**, *modif.* — *Syn.* wavy, uneven, ripply, disjointed; see **irregular** 1, **rough** 1.

**chord**, *n.* — *Syn.* harmonizing tones, triad, octave; second, third, fourth, fifth, sixth, seventh, ninth; major, minor, diminished, augmented, inverted, broken, primary, secondary, tertiary, tetrachord, perfect fourth, arpeggio, first inversion, second inversion, common chord; see also **harmony** 1, **music** 1.

**chore**, *n.* — *Syn.* task, routine, errand, burden; see **burden** 2, **duty** 2, **job** 2.

*See Synonym Study at* JOB.

**chortle**, *v.* — *Syn.* chuckle, snort, cackle; see **laugh.**

**chorus**, *n.* 1. [A body of singers] — *Syn.* choir, choristers, voices, glee club, choral group, choral society, singing group, singing society, church singers, male chorus, female chorus, mixed chorus, chorale, Liederkranz; see also **music** 1.

2. [A refrain] — *Syn.* burden, melody, theme, motif, leitmotif, recurrent verse, strain, main section, chorale, tune, bob; see also **music, song.**

**chosen**, *modif.* — *Syn.* picked, selected, preferred; see **named** 2.

**Christ**, *n.* — *Syn.* Jesus, Jesus of Nazareth, Jesus Christ, the Savior, the Anointed, the Redeemer, Messiah, Messias, Immanuel, the Intercessor, the Judge, the Word, the Son, the Son of Man, the Son of God, God the Son, the Son of David, the Son of Mary, the Risen, the King of Glory, the Prince of Peace, the Good Shepherd, the King of the Jews, the Lamb of God, the Only Begotten, King of Kings, Alpha and Omega, Lord of Lords, Christ Our Lord, the Way, the Truth, the Life, the Bread of Life, the Light of the World, the Lord of our Righteousness, the Sun of Righteousness, the Incarnate Word, the Word made Flesh; see also **God** 3.

**christen**, *v.* — *Syn.* baptize, name, dedicate to God; see **baptize** 1, **bless** 3, **name** 1.

**Christian**, *modif.* — *Syn.* gentile, evangelical, orthodox, pious, pietistic, reverent, devoted, charitable, Christlike, faithful, believing, strict, scriptural; see also **humble** 1, **religious** 1, 2.

**Christian**, *n.* — *Syn.* Nazarene, gentile, professor, true believer, witness, one of the faithful, one of the flock, convert, probationer, churchgoer, Christian man, Christian woman, true Christian, Christian soul; Methodist, Unitarian, Baptist, Presbyterian, Protestant, Catholic, etc.; see also **Christianity** 2, **church** 3.

**Christianity**, *n.* 1. [A religion based upon the divinity of Christ] — *Syn.* teachings of Christ, religion of Christ, the Church, Christian faith, divine revelation, the Gospel, the Faith, Christian fundamentalism, Evangelicalism; Catholicism, Roman Catholicism, Orthodox Christianity, Protestantism, Anglicanism; see also **church** 3, **faith** 2, **religion** 2.

2. [The body of Christian people] — *Syn.* Christendom, Christians, body of Christ, followers of Christ, Christian community; see also **church** 3.

3. [An attitude associated with Christianity] — *Syn.* Christlike temper, Christian mercy, Christian spirit, loving spirit, loving-kindness, charity, forgiving disposition, having God in one's heart; see also **kindness** 1, **mercy** 1, **tolerance** 1.

**Christmas**, *n.* — *Syn.* Christmastime, Christmastide, Xmas, Yuletide, Noel, Yule, Christmas night, Christmas Eve, Christmas Day, the Nativity, birth of the Christ Child; see also **holiday** 1, **winter.**

**chronic**, *modif.* — *Syn.* inveterate, confirmed, settled, habitual, hardened, rooted, deep-seated, continuing, persistent, persisting, stubborn, uncured, incurable, lasting, unyielding, tenacious, enduring, lingering, deep-rooted, abiding, perennial, perpetual, constant, fixed, continual, incessant, long-standing, recurring, continuous, of long duration, long-lived, unabating, protracted, ceaseless, sustained, lifelong, prolonged, recurrent, periodic, intermittent, continued, obstinate, incorrigible, unceasing, inborn, inbred, ingrained, ever-present; see also **habitual** 1, **permanent** 2. — *Ant.* acute, TEMPORARY, casual.

*SYN.* — **chronic** suggests long duration or frequent recurrence and is used especially of diseases or habits that resist all efforts to eradicate them [*chronic* sinusitis]; **inveterate** implies firm establishment as a result of continued indulgence over a long period of time [an *inveterate* liar]; **confirmed** suggests fixedness in some condition or practice, often from a deep-seated aversion to change [a *confirmed* bachelor]; **hardened** implies fixed tendencies and a callous indifference to emotional or moral considerations [a *hardened* criminal]

**chronicle**, *n.* — *Syn.* narrative, annals, account; see **history** 2, **record** 1.

**chronicler**, *n.* — *Syn.* reporter, annalist, recorder; see **historian, storyteller.**

**chronological**, *modif.* — *Syn.* temporal, chronologic, historical, in sequence, according to chronology, in the order of time, sequential, successive, serial, archival, chronicled, sequent, consecutive, properly dated, measured in time, horological, chronometric, chronoscopic, chronographic, progressive in time, ordered, in order, in due time, in due course.

**chubby**, *modif.* — *Syn.* plump, round, pudgy; see **fat** 1.

**chuck**, *v.* 1. [To caress] — *Syn.* pat, tap, squeeze; see **caress, touch** 1.

2. [★To get rid of] — *Syn.* throw away, relinquish, eject, reject; see **discard, throw** 1.

**chuckle**, *n.* — *Syn.* chortle, laugh, giggle; see **laugh.**

*See Synonym Study at* LAUGH.

**chuckle**, *v.* — *Syn.* chortle, giggle, smile, snicker; see **laugh.**

**chum★**, *modif.* — *Syn.* friend, companion, playmate, pal★; see **associate, friend** 1.

**chummy★**, *modif.* — *Syn.* intimate, close, sociable, palsy-walsy★; see **friendly** 1.

**chunk**, *n.* — *Syn.* piece, mass, lump; see **hunk, part** 1.

**chunky**, *modif.* — *Syn.* stocky, thickset, stout; see **fat** 1.

**church**, *n.* 1. [A building consecrated to worship] — *Syn.* house of God, Lord's house, cathedral, temple, synagogue, mosque, masjid, oratory, place of worship, house of prayer, meetinghouse, chapel, minster, basilica, tabernacle, bethel, abbey, sanctuary, sacellum, chantry, pantheon, conventicle, collegiate church, mission, shrine, duomo (usu. in Italy), pagoda, kirk (Scottish); see also **cathedral, temple.**

2. [A divine service] — *Syn.* service, church service, public worship, rite, religious rite, ordinance, prayers, liturgy, prayer meeting, Sunday school, divine worship, Mass, Holy Mass, Lord's Supper, sacrament, the holy sacrament, Angelus, matins, vespers, ritual, morning prayer, evening prayer, evensong, camp meeting, congregational worship, fellowship, devotions, office, duty, revival meeting, exercises, liturgics, sermon, communion; see also **ceremony** 2.

**3.** [An organized religious body] — *Syn.* congregation, denomination, Christian denomination, sect, chapter, body, order, communion, faith, religion, religious society, religious order, affiliation, persuasion, belief, faction, doctrine, creed, cult, ism*; see also **Christianity** 1, 2, **gathering.**
Christian churches include: Methodist, Presbyterian, Episcopalian, Baptist, Latter-day Saint, Mormon*, Congregational, Lutheran, Roman Catholic, Eastern Orthodox (Greek, Russian, Serbian, Antiochian, Armenian, Bulgarian, etc.), Orthodox Christianity, Coptic, Pentecostal, Evangelical Reformed, Church of England, Uniat, Melkite, Church of Rome, Church of Christ, Church of the Nazarene, Disciples of Christ, Church of the Brethren, Dunkers*, Dunkards*, United Brethren, Society of Friends, Quakers*.

**churl,** *n.* **1.** [A rustic or ill-bred person] — *Syn.* boor, yokel, bear, curmudgeon; see **boor, peasant.**
**2.** [Miser] — *Syn.* niggard, tightwad, skimper; see **miser** 2.

**churlish,** *modif.* — *Syn.* surly, boorish, ungracious, base; see **rude** 1, 2, **vulgar** 1.

**churlishness,** *n.* — *Syn.* surliness, coarseness, roughness; see **rudeness.**

**churn,** *v.* — *Syn.* stir, beat, agitate, shake, paddle, seethe, ferment; see also **boil** 2, **mix** 1.

**chute,** *n.* — *Syn.* trough, slide, rapid(s), watercourse; see **channel** 1, **waterfall.**

**cigarette,** *n.* — *Syn.* smoke, butt*, fag*, coffin nail*; see **tobacco.**

**cinch*,** *n.* — *Syn.* child's play, snap*, breeze*, piece of cake*, duck soup*, setup*, pushover*, lead-pipe cinch*, foregone conclusion, certainty, sure thing*, shoo-in*; see also **snap** 2.

**cinder,** *n.* — *Syn.* embers, hot coals, soot; see **ashes** 1, **coal** 2.

**cinema,** *n.* **1.** [Motion pictures] — *Syn.* film(s), the movies, the screen, silver screen; see **movie, movies** 2.
**2.** [Motion-picture theater] — *Syn.* movie theater, movie house, multiplex; see **auditorium, theater** 1.

**cipher,** *n.* — *Syn.* naught, blank, goose egg*; see **zero** 1.

**cipher,** *v.* — *Syn.* compute, figure, do arithmetic; see **add** 1, **calculate** 1, **count.**

**circle,** *n.* **1.** [A round closed plane figure] — *Syn.* ring, loop, wheel, sphere, globe, disk, hoop, halo, orb, orbit, round, roundlet, annulus, circlet, crown, corona, zodiac, aureole, circus, bowl, stadium, vortex, cirque, horizon, circumference, perimeter, periphery, full turn, revolution, circuit, meridian, parallel of latitude, equator, ecliptic, great circle, colure, cordon, band, bracelet, belt, collar, wreath; see also **ball** 1, **circuit, curve** 1, **disk.**
**2.** [An endless sequence of events] — *Syn.* cycle, round, course, series, succession, continuation, range, period, epicycle, cause and effect, systole and diastole; see also **progress** 1, **sequence** 1, **series.**
**3.** [A coterie] — *Syn.* set, group, society; see **clique, gathering.**
*See Synonym Study at* CLIQUE.
**come full circle** — *Syn.* go through a cycle, go through a series, come around, come back, revert; see also **return** 1.

**circle,** *v.* — *Syn.* round, encircle, surround, compass, girdle, loop, tour, circumnavigate, orbit, ring, belt, embrace, gird, encompass, wind about, rotate, revolve around, circumscribe, hedge in, curve around, circuit, enclose, ensphere, cincture, spiral, compass about, coil, circulate, detour, wind, roll, wheel, swing past, go around, skirt, evade, circumambulate; see also **surround** 1, **turn** 1. — *Ant.* DIVIDE, bisect, cut across.

**circuit,** *n.* — *Syn.* course, round, tour, loop, orbit, revolution, ambit, circumference, periphery, perimeter, turning, turn, line, circling, circle, wind, compass, detour, winding, twist, circumnavigation, circumscription, circuitry, hookup, path; see also **orbit** 1, **revolution** 1.
*See Synonym Study at* CIRCUMFERENCE.

**circuit,** *v.* — *Syn.* move around, detour, encircle, make a circuit; see **circle.**

**circuitous,** *modif.* — *Syn.* complicated, roundabout, devious, meandering; see **indirect.**

**circuitry,** *n.* — *Syn.* circuits, integrated circuits, microcircuitry, systems, solid-state circuits, connections; see also **chip** 2, **electronics, wiring** 3.

**circular,** *modif.* **1.** [Round] — *Syn.* annular, orbicular, disklike; see **round** 1, 2.
**2.** [Circuitous] — *Syn.* indirect, roundabout, winding; see **indirect.**
*See Synonym Study at* ROUND.

**circular,** *n.* — *Syn.* handbill, broadside, leaflet, flier; see **advertisement** 1, 2, **announcement** 3, **pamphlet.**

**circulate,** *v.* **1.** [To go about] — *Syn.* move around, get around, get about, fly about, move about, travel, wander, flow, course, circle, circuit; see also **flow** 3, **travel** 2, **walk** 1.
**2.** [To send about] — *Syn.* diffuse, report, broadcast, disseminate; see **advertise** 1, **distribute** 1, **scatter** 1, 2.

**circulating,** *modif.* — *Syn.* flowing, moving, current, circulatory, ambient, diffusive, rotating, circling, in circulation, in motion, fluid; see also **moving** 1. — *Ant.* still, MOTIONLESS, stationary.

**circulation,** *n.* **1.** [Motion around] — *Syn.* rotation, current, flowing, passage; see **flow, revolution** 1.
**2.** [Distribution] — *Syn.* transmission, apportionment, dissemination; see **distribution** 1.

**circumference,** *n.* — *Syn.* perimeter, periphery, boundary, outline, ambit, circuit, compass, limit, border, bounds, edge, rim, margin; see also **boundary, circuit.**

---

**SYN.** — **circumference** refers to the line bounding a circle or any approximately circular or elliptical area; **perimeter** extends the meaning to a line bounding any area or figure, as a triangle, square, or polygon; **periphery**, in its literal sense identical with **perimeter**, is more frequently used of the edge of a physical object or in an extended metaphoric sense /the *periphery* of understanding/; **circuit** can also denote a line bounding an area, but now usually refers to a course or journey around a periphery /the moon's *circuit* of the earth/; **compass** refers literally to an area within specific limits but is often used figuratively /the *compass* of the city, the *compass* of freedom/

---

**circumlocution,** *n.* — *Syn.* periphrasis, verbal evasion, redundancy, rambling; see **wordiness.**

**circumscribe,** *v.* **1.** [To trace a line around] — *Syn.* encircle, encompass, girdle; see **circle, surround** 1.
**2.** [To limit] — *Syn.* restrict, bound, confine; see **define** 1, **limit, restrict** 2.
*See Synonym Study at* LIMIT.

**circumspect,** *modif.* — *Syn.* cautious, careful, guarded, prudent; see **careful.**
*See Synonym Study at* CAREFUL.

**circumspection,** *n.* — *Syn.* caution, prudence, wariness, heed; see **care** 1, **prudence.**

**circumstance,** *n.* **1.** [An attendant condition] — *Syn.* situation, condition, contingency, phase, factor, detail, item, fact, case, place, time, cause, state, status, element, particular, feature, point, incident, proviso, article, stipulation, concern, matter, thing, event, adjunct, occurrence, juncture, exigency, intervention, supervention, fortuity, coincidence, concurrent event, chance, happenstance*; see also **state** 2.

**2.** [An occurrence] — *Syn.* event, episode, happening, incident; see **event** 1.

*See Synonym Study at* OCCURRENCE.

**circumstances,** *pl.n.* **1.** [Condition in life] — *Syn.* material welfare, finances, outlook, prospects, chances, means, assets, prosperity, financial status, financial condition, resources, funds, worldly goods, affairs, concerns, status, standing, property, net worth, financial standing, credit rating, terms, estate, way of life, pecuniary standing, vicissitudes of fortune, rank, class, degree, capital, degree of wealth, position, command, financial responsibility, footing, income, sphere, substance, stock in trade, lot, prestige, what one is worth, place on the ladder, niche; see also **state** 2, **wealth** 1, 2.

**2.** [Attendant conditions] — *Syn.* situation, environment, surroundings, facts, particulars, factors, features, matters, motives, controlling factors, qualifying factors, governing factors, the times, occasion, basis, grounds, setting, background, context, frame of reference, needs, requirements, necessities, exigencies, course of events, imposed terms, legal status, provisions, economic requirements, terms imposed, milieu, promptings, life, bearings, vicissitudes, change, fluctuation, phase, case, premise, conditions, governing agents, events, accompanying events, state of affairs, modifying features, surrounding facts, order of the day*, the whole picture, the score*, the scene*, the story*, where it's at*, how the land lies*, the lay of the land*, ins and outs*, ups and downs*.

**under no circumstances** — *Syn.* under no conditions, by no means, absolutely not; see **never**.

**under the circumstances** — *Syn.* conditions being what they are, for this reason, that being the case; see **because, therefore**.

**circumstantial,** *modif.* **1.** [Detailed] — *Syn.* minute, environmental, precise; see **detailed.**

**2.** [Depending upon circumstances] — *Syn.* presumptive, presumed, inferential, indirect, inconclusive, inferred, implied, deduced, incidental, secondary, contingent, dependent, extraneous, hearsay, evidential; see also **hypothetical** 1, **uncertain** 2.

**circumvent,** *v.* **1.** [To go around] — *Syn.* encircle, encompass, entrap; see **surround** 1, 2.

**2.** [To gain an advantage over] — *Syn.* outwit, trick, dupe; see **deceive.**

**3.** [To avoid] — *Syn.* dodge, elude, bypass; see **avoid, evade** 1.

**circus,** *n.* — *Syn.* hippodrome, spectacle, entertainment, big top*, carnival, bazaar, show, fair, festival, kermis, ring, sideshow.

**cistern,** *n.* — *Syn.* reservoir, pond, tank; see **well** 1.

**citadel,** *n.* — *Syn.* fortress, stronghold, bastion; see **castle, fortification** 2.

**citation,** *n.* **1.** [Summons] — *Syn.* subpoena, bidding, charge, writ; see **command** 1, **indictment** 2.

**2.** [Citing] — *Syn.* mention, reference, quote, excerpt; see **quotation** 1, **quoting.**

**3.** [Honorable mention] — *Syn.* award, tribute, commendation; see **praise** 2, **prize.**

**cite,** *v.* **1.** [To summon] — *Syn.* call, arraign, order, subpoena; see **summon** 1.

**2.** [To refer to as authority] — *Syn.* quote, mention, refer to, allude to, appeal to, repeat, point out, point up, enumerate, tell, cite an instance, quote chapter and verse, number, recount, recite, rehearse, illustrate with,

excerpt, indicate, give as example, extract, exemplify, call to witness, evidence, commend; see also **mention, praise** 1, **refer** 2. — *Ant.* ignore, NEGLECT, distrust.

**citizen,** *n.* — *Syn.* inhabitant, denizen, national, subject, native, taxpayer, burgher, burgess, cosmopolite, commoner, civilian, urbanite, member of the community, householder, occupant, settler, aborigine, registered voter, voter, dweller, immigrant, naturalized person, townsman, freeman, the man in the street, villager, member of the body politic, John Q. Public*, Jane Q. Public*, see also **compatriot, resident.**

*SYN.* — **citizen** refers to a member of a state or nation, esp. one with a republican government, who owes it allegiance and is entitled to full civil rights either by birth or naturalization; **subject** is the term used when the government is headed by a monarch or other sovereign; **national** is applied to a person residing away from the country of which he or she is, or once was, a citizen or subject; **native** refers to one who was born in the country under question, and is applied specifically to an original or indigenous inhabitant of the region

**city,** *modif.* — *Syn.* urban, metropolitan, civil, civic; see **municipal, urban** 2.

**city,** *n.* — *Syn.* town, municipality, borough, burg*, capital, megalopolis, metropolis, provincial town, county town, county seat, trading center, inner city, downtown, shopping center, shopping district, business district, financial district, urban place, urban center, incorporated town, metropolitan area, township, port, conurbation, urban sprawl, asphalt jungle*; see also **center** 2.

**civic,** *modif.* — *Syn.* community, public, civil, municipal; see **common** 5, **political, public** 2.

**civil,** *modif.* **1.** [Civic] — *Syn.* local, civic, public, civilian; see **municipal, public** 2.

**2.** [Polite] — *Syn.* courteous, formal, cordial; see **polite** 1.

*See Synonym Study at* POLITE.

**civilian,** *modif.* — *Syn.* nonmilitary, unmilitary, nonmilitant, noncombat, noncombatant, pacificist, not in the armed forces, in civilian life, lay, private, in civvies*, in mufti*.

**civilian,** *n.* — *Syn.* (private) citizen, noncombatant, person not in the armed forces; see **commoner.**

**civilization,** *n.* **1.** [Culture] — *Syn.* cultivation, polish, enlightenment, refinement, civility, illumination, advancement of knowledge, elevation, edification, national culture, state of refinement, level of education, advancement, progress, social well-being, degree of cultivation, material well-being, acculturation, *Kultur* (German), education, breeding; see also **culture** 2, 3, **improvement** 1. — *Ant.* barbarism, savagery, degeneration.

**2.** [The civilized world] — *Syn.* civilized life, the modern world, literate society, creature comforts, amenities, populated area, city.

**civilize,** *v.* — *Syn.* enlighten, cultivate, enrich, reclaim, refine, render civil, acculturate, polish, sophisticate, spiritualize, humanize, socialize, edify, uplift, tame, foster, instruct, ethicize, reclaim from barbarism, promote, help forward, better materially, make gentle, acquaint with culture, indoctrinate, elevate, educate, teach, advance, ennoble; see also **develop** 1, **improve** 1, **teach** 1.

**civilized,** *modif.* — *Syn.* enlightened, refined, advanced; see **cultured, educated** 1, **refined** 2.

**civil rights,** *pl.n.* — *Syn.* civil liberties, equality, minority rights, human rights; see **choice** 1, **equality, freedom** 1, 2.

**clack,** *v.* **1.** [To talk heedlessly] — *Syn.* chatter, clatter, rattle, prate; see **babble.**

**2.** [To make a rattling noise] — *Syn.* clatter, click, rattle, clap; see **sound** 1.

**claim,** *n.* — *Syn.* demand, declaration, pretense, requisition, profession, entreaty, petition, suit, ultimatum, call, request, requirement, application, postulation, protestation, case, pretension, assertion, allegation, plea, counterclaim, right, interest, title, part, stake; see also **appeal** 1, **contention** 2. — *Ant.* disclaimer, RENUNCIATION, repudiation.

**lay claim to** — *Syn.* demand, stake out a claim to, appropriate; see **claim** 1, **require** 2, **seize** 2.

**claim,** *v.* **1.** [To assert a claim to] — *Syn.* demand, lay claim to, stake out a claim, exact, challenge, claim as one's due, demand as a right, command, insist upon, pretend to, assert one's right to, make a stand, call upon one for, petition, ask for, call for, require, deserve, have dibs on*; see also **require** 2. — *Ant.* disclaim, renounce, abandon.

**2.** [To assert] — *Syn.* insist, maintain, allege, profess; see **declare** 1, **pretend** 1.

*See Synonym Study at* REQUIRE.

**claimant,** *n.* — *Syn.* petitioner, applicant, claimer; see **candidate.**

**clairvoyance,** *n.* **1.** [Psychic power] — *Syn.* extrasensory perception, ESP, foreknowledge, precognition; see **forecast, sixth sense, telepathy.**

**2.** [Discernment] — *Syn.* penetration, insight, perception; see **acumen.**

**clairvoyant,** *modif.* **1.** [Psychic] — *Syn.* telepathic, second-sighted, spiritualistic; see **mental** 2, **mysterious** 2, **supernatural.**

**2.** [Discerning] — *Syn.* perceptive, penetrating, clear-sighted; see **judicious.**

**clam,** *n.* — *Syn.* bivalve, mollusk, shellfish; see **shellfish.**

Types of clams include: soft-shell, hard-shell, steamer, quahog, quahaug, cherrystone, littleneck, marine, sea, freshwater, surf, hen, thorny, giant, razor, pismo, geoduck.

**clamber,** *v.* — *Syn.* mount, scale, scramble; see **climb** 2.

**clammy,** *modif.* — *Syn.* moist, damp, sticky, sweaty; see **cold** 2, **wet** 1.

**clamor,** *n.* **1.** [A loud outcry] — *Syn.* din, outcry, uproar, vociferation; see **noise** 2, **uproar.**

**2.** [A protesting] — *Syn.* lament, complaint, remonstrance; see **objection** 2, **protest.**

*See Synonym Study at* NOISE.

**clamorous,** *modif.* — *Syn.* noisy, uproarious, vociferous, importunate; see **loud** 2.

*See Synonym Study at* VOCIFEROUS.

**clamp,** *n.* — *Syn.* vise, clasp, brace, clip; see **fastener, lock** 1.

**clan,** *n.* — *Syn.* group, tribe, house, moiety; see **class** 2, **clique, family** 1, **race** 2, **tribe.**

**clandestine,** *modif.* — *Syn.* furtive, secret, private, surreptitious; see **hidden** 2, **secret** 3.

*See Synonym Study at* SECRET.

**clang,** *n.* — *Syn.* clank, clash, jangle; see **noise** 1.

**clank,** *n.* — *Syn.* clang, chink, clink; see **noise** 1.

**clank,** *v.* — *Syn.* clink, clank, chime; see **ring** 2, 3, **sound** 1.

**clannish,** *modif.* **1.** [Of a clan] — *Syn.* close, associative, akin, lineal; see **alike** 2, **like, related** 2, 3.

**2.** [Unreceptive] — *Syn.* select, insular, cliquish; see **exclusive, prejudiced.**

**clap,** *v.* **1.** [To strike the palms together] — *Syn.* applaud, cheer, acclaim; see **praise** 1.

**2.** [To strike] — *Syn.* bang, slap, slam; see **hit** 1.

**clapper,** *n.* — *Syn.* tongue of a bell, clack, noisemaker; see **tongue** 3.

**claptrap,** *n.* — *Syn.* empty talk, drivel, bombast, bunk; see **nonsense** 1.

**clarification,** *n.* — *Syn.* exposition, elucidation, description, simplification; see **definition** 1, **explanation** 1, 2, **interpretation** 1.

**clarify,** *v.* **1.** [To explain] — *Syn.* interpret, define, elucidate, illuminate; see **explain, simplify.**

**2.** [To purify] — *Syn.* filter, refine, strain; see **filter** 2, **purify.**

**clarion,** *modif.* — *Syn.* clear, sharp, shrill, ringing; see **definite** 2.

**clarity,** *n.* — *Syn.* clearness, lucidity, limpidness, limpidity, purity, brightness, precision, explicitness, exactness, decipherability, intelligibility, simplicity, explicability, perceptibility, penetrability, unmistakability, distinctness, comprehensibility, plainness, lack of ambiguity, plain speech, legibility, openness, directness, perspicuity, evidence, prominence, manifestness, overtness, salience, transparency, pellucidity, translucence, palpability, conspicuousness, certainty; see also **accuracy** 2, **simplicity** 1. — *Ant.* haziness, OBSCURITY, vagueness.

**clash,** *n.* **1.** [Collision] — *Syn.* crash, encounter, impact; see **collision** 1.

**2.** [Disagreement] — *Syn.* opposition, conflict, argument; see **disagreement** 1, **dispute.**

**clash,** *v.* — *Syn.* conflict, jar, mismatch, fail to harmonize, not go with, be incompatible, collide, disagree, argue, battle; see also **contrast** 1, **differ** 1, **fight** 2, **oppose** 1, 2, **quarrel.**

**clashing,** *n.* — *Syn.* dissension, opposition, discord; see **disagreement** 1.

**clasp,** *n.* — *Syn.* buckle, pin, hook, catch; see **fastener.**

**clasp,** *v.* **1.** [To hold tightly] — *Syn.* grasp, grip, embrace; see **catch** 1, **hold** 1, **hug.**

**2.** [To fasten with a clasp] — *Syn.* catch, hook, secure; see **fasten** 1.

**class,** *n.* **1.** [A classification] — *Syn.* category, division, group, kind, sort, degree, order, rank, grade, standing, level, genus, distinction, breed, type, kingdom, subdivision, phylum, subphylum, subclass, superorder, family, cast, mold, sect, quality, rate, collection, denomination, department, species, variety, branch, genre, range, brand, set, estate, hierarchy, section, domain, nature, suit, color, origin, character, humor, frame, temperament, school, designation, temper, sphere, brood, spirit, vein, persuasion, head, province, league, make, grain, feather, source, name, mood, habit, form, selection, stamp, stripe, status, range, streak, property, aspect, disposition, tone; see also **classification** 1, **state** 2.

**2.** [A division of society] — *Syn.* caste, social rank, social stratum, stratum, status, station, socioeconomic level, cultural level, family, breed, sect, layer of society, standing, place, sphere, circle, stock, clan, nobility, high rank, pedigree, society, prestige, income bracket, income group, title, degree, position, connection, precedence, genealogy, power, company, derivation, source, descent, birth, ancestry, influence, hierarchy, state, lineage, condition, strain, tribe, moiety, estate, extraction, origin; see also sense 1, **rank** 3, **tribe.**

**3.** [A group organized for study] — *Syn.* course, section, subject, grade, level, year, form, lecture, recitation, seminar, colloquium, discussion group, round table, meeting for study, period, lesson, assembly, group, session, room, division, course of study.

**4.** [*High quality] — *Syn.* elegance, refinement, distinction, panache; see **elegance** 1.

**in a class by itself** — *Syn.* unique, unusual, different, one of a kind; see **unique** 1.

**class,** *v.* — *Syn.* identify, rank, grade, categorize; see **classify, mark** 2.

**classic,** *modif.* — *Syn.* outstanding, excellent, superior, first-rate, standard, authoritative, established, traditional, time-honored, archetypal, prototypical, exemplary, model, ideal, quintessential, definitive, typical, ageless, timeless, enduring, vintage, canonical, immortal, noteworthy, distinguished, paramount, ranking, well-known; see also **excellent, famous, perfect** 2.

**classic,** *n.* — *Syn.* masterwork, exemplar, standard; see **masterpiece, model** 1.

**classical,** *modif.* **1.** [Of recognized importance] — *Syn.* standard, established, authoritative, traditional, ideal, flawless, serious, prestigious, esthetic, artistic, longhair*; see also **classic.** — *Ant.* MODERN, POPULAR, transitory.

**2.** [Of or resembling the art or culture of ancient Greece or Rome] — *Syn.* classic, humanistic, Attic, Hellenic, Greek, Homeric, Latin, Roman, Ciceronian, Augustan, Virgilian, academic, correct, formal, classicistic, refined, restrained, balanced, well-proportioned, chaste, archaic, ancient, neoclassic, Hellenistic, Alexandrian; see also **ancient** 2, **chaste** 1, **Greek, Roman** 1.

**classicism,** *n.* — *Syn.* aesthetic principles, objectivity, dignity, balance, refinement, formality, simplicity, restraint, pure taste, harmony, elegance, understatement, nobility, formal style, classicalism, reverence for the ancients, observance of classical principles, lucidity, classical taste, the grand style, conventional formality, proportion, propriety, rhythm, symmetry, regularity, majesty, grandeur, polish, finish, clarity, rationalism, eloquence, Atticism, purity, neoclassicism, Ciceronianism, sobriety, high art, sublimity, excellence, severity, established forms, well-turned periods, Hellenism; see also **elegance** 2.

**classification,** *n.* **1.** [The act of putting into classes] — *Syn.* arrangement, assortment, grouping, sorting, ordering, allotment, organization, gradation, coordination, graduation, disposal, disposition, reducing to order, categorizing, categorization, apportionment, tabulating, consignment, orderly arrangement, analysis, division, assignment, designation, taxonomy, typology, collocation, sizing, grading, ranking, cataloging, indexing, filing, labeling, distribution, allocation, systematization, codification; see also **order** 3.

**2.** [A division] — *Syn.* kind, order, group; see **class** 1.

**classified,** *modif.* — *Syn.* assorted, grouped, classed, sorted, indexed, filed, orderly, recorded, listed, registered, detailed, arranged, reduced, regulated, compiled, coordinated, characterized, ranked, distributed, cataloged, separated, allocated, labeled, numbered, systematized, tabulated, alphabetized, typed, on file, rated. — *Ant.* confused, MIXED, jumbled.

**classify,** *v.* — *Syn.* arrange, order, pigeonhole, tabulate, organize, distribute, categorize, systematize, assort, sort, coordinate, correlate, incorporate, codify, collocate, label, alphabetize, place in a category, file, range, form into classes, stratify, divide, docket, allocate, number, rate, ticket, class, dispose, assign, rank, catalog, segregate, distinguish, brand, digest, allot, analyze, regiment, name, group, tag, type, put in order, break down, index, grade, match, size, reduce to order, introduce a system; see also **file** 1, **list** 1. — *Ant.* disorganize, DISORDER, disarrange.

**clatter,** *n.* — *Syn.* clack, rattle, bang; see **noise** 1.

**clatter,** *v.* — *Syn.* rattle, clash, crash; see **sound** 1.

**clause,** *n.* **1.** [A provision] — *Syn.* condition, codicil, ultimatum; see **article** 3, **limitation** 2, **requirement** 1.

**2.** [A grammatical structure] — *Syn.* construction, sentence, phrase, constituent, word group, string, sentence modifier, transform; see also **phrase**
Types of clauses include: independent, dependent, relative, subordinate, substantive, noun, adjective, adjectival, adverb, adverbial.

**clavier,** *n.* — *Syn.* keyboard, harpsichord, clavichord, piano; see **keyboard, musical instrument, piano.**

**claw,** *n.* — *Syn.* talon, hook, nail, pincers, chela, tentacle, spur, fang, paw, grappling iron, grappling hook, forked end, clutching hand, nipper, grapnel, crook, barb, fingernail, dewclaw, cant hook, tack claw, nail claw, manus, ungula, unguis.

**claw,** *v.* — *Syn.* tear, scratch, rip open; see **break** 1, **cut** 2, **hurt** 1, **rip.**

**clay,** *n.* — *Syn.* loess, argil, loam, kaolin, earth, till, wacke, slip, bole, argillaceous earth, marl, potter's clay, clayware, green pottery, terra cotta, green brick, china clay, porcelain clay, adobe, Play-Doh (trademark); see also **mud, pottery.**

**having feet of clay** — *Syn.* flawed, ignoble, overestimated, weak; see **faulty, inadequate** 1.

**clean,** *modif.* **1.** [Not soiled] — *Syn.* spotless, washed, stainless, laundered, immaculate, unsoiled, untarnished, speckless, unstained, neat, tidy, clear, blank, white, dirtless, unblemished, unspotted, newly cleaned, cleaned, fresh, unused, snowy, well-kept, dustless, unsmirched, cleansed, scrubbed, sanitary, antiseptic, unsullied, spick-and-span, clean as a whistle*, squeaky-clean*. — *Ant.* soiled, DIRTY, stained.

**2.** [Not contaminated] — *Syn.* unadulterated, wholesome; see **pure** 2, **sanitary.**

**3.** [Neat] — *Syn.* orderly, tidy, regular; see **neat** 1.

**4.** [Having sharp outlines] — *Syn.* clear-cut, sharp, distinct; see **definite** 2.

**5.** [Legible; having few errors] — *Syn.* clear, plain, distinct, readable, precise, correct; see also **accurate** 1. — *Ant.* ILLEGIBLE, confusing, vague.

**6.** [Sinless] — *Syn.* pure, wholesome, unsullied, virtuous; see **innocent** 1, 4.

**7.** [Thorough] — *Syn.* complete, entire, total; see **absolute** 1.

**8.** [Fair] — *Syn.* reliable, decent, lawful, sportsmanlike; see **decent** 2, **fair** 1, **honest** 1.

**9.** [Well-proportioned] — *Syn.* streamlined, shapely, graceful, spare; see **trim** 2.

**10.** [Not obscene or indecent] — *Syn.* inoffensive, decorous, wholesome, G-rated*; see **chaste** 2, **decent** 2.

**11.** [Free from radioactivity] — *Syn.* decontaminated, not dangerous, checked.

**come clean*** — *Syn.* confess, tell the truth, own up*; see **admit** 2.

**clean,** *v.* — *Syn.* cleanse, clean up, clean out, clear up, clear out, wash, wash up, scrub, scrub off, soak, disinfect, tidy, tidy up, neaten, straighten up, shake out, purify, decontaminate, sanitize, deodorize, purge, expurgate, swab, polish, sterilize, scrape, sweep, scour, launder, dry-clean, vacuum, scald, dust, mop, cauterize, rinse, sponge, brush, dress, comb, dredge, pick, blow, whisk, wipe, wipe up, clarify, elutriate, winnow, rake, clean away, lave, bathe, expunge, soap, hose down, rasp, erase, shampoo, refine, flush, depurate, deterge, blot, hackle, leach, lixiviate, rub off, sandblast, freshen, put in order, bleach, spruce up, do up*, slick up*, clear the

decks\*, police up\*; see also **purify, wash** 1. 2.— *Ant.*
DIRTY, soil, smear, mess up.

---

*SYN.* — **clean**, the broader term, denotes generally the
removal of dirt, impurities, or extraneous matter, as by
washing or brushing; **cleanse** suggests more specifically
the removal of impurities, as by the use of chemicals,
and is often used metaphorically to imply purification /to
*cleanse* one's mind of evil thoughts/

---

**cleaner**, *n.* — *Syn.* detergent, disinfectant, cleaning
agent; see **cleanser, soap.**
**cleaning**, *modif.* — *Syn.* cleansing, purgative, detergent,
disinfecting, disinfectant, washing, delousing, sanitizing,
scouring, soaking, sterilizing, purificatory, lustral,
deodorizing, scalding, purifying, cathartic, depurative,
purging, emetic. — *Ant.* dirtying, CORROSIVE, corrup-
tive.
**cleaning**, *n.* — *Syn.* cleansing, purge, purgation, scrubbing, scouring, purification, ablution, sweeping,
brushing, dusting, antisepsis, prophylaxis, sterilization,
sanitation, washing, shampooing, deodorizing, disinfection, making hygienic, catharsis, tidying, spring-
cleaning, dry-cleaning; see also **sanitation.**
**cleanliness**, *n.* — *Syn.* cleanness, neatness, purity, tidiness, trimness, spruceness, nattiness, immaculateness,
spotlessness, dapperness, fastidiousness, finicality, orderliness, freshness, whiteness, daintiness, disinfection,
sanitation, sterility, asepsis. — *Ant.* FILTH, dirtiness,
griminess.
**cleanly**, *modif.* — *Syn.* neat, tidy, spotless; see **clean** 1,
**neat** 1.
**cleanse**, *v.* 1. [To remove dirt from the surface] — *Syn.*
bathe, clean, wash, scrub; see **clean.**
2. [To remove impurities from within] — *Syn.* refine,
disinfect, purge; see **clean, purify.**
3. [To free from sin or its effects] — *Syn.* absolve,
purge, purify, restore; see **excuse.**
*See Synonym Study at* CLEAN.
**cleanser**, *n.* — *Syn.* cleansing agent, cleaning agent,
soap, detergent, abrasive, lather, solvent, purgative,
deodorant, fumigant, soap flakes, polish, disinfectant,
antiseptic, cathartic, purifier, scouring powder, spray
cleaner, cleaner, soap powder, cleaning fluid, dry
cleaner, shampoo, suds, cleansing cream, cold cream;
see also **soap.**
Cleansers include: water, soap and water, soap, washing powder, laundry detergent, dishwashing detergent,
scouring powder, oven cleaner, naphtha, French chalk,
washing soda, furniture polish, borax, lye, household
ammonia, bleach, solvent, cathartic soap, bluing, carbon tetrachloride, toiletbowl cleanser, chloride of lime,
sal soda, baking soda, washing crystals, chlorine compound, wallpaper cleaner, floor polish, floor wax,
silverpolish, kerosene, gasoline, benzine, vinegar, rug
shampoo.
**clear**, *modif.* 1. [Open to the sight or understanding]
— *Syn.* explicit, plain, manifest; see **obvious** 1, 2.
2. [Offering little impediment to vision] — *Syn.* transparent, crystalline, translucent, lucid, pure, apparent, pellucid, limpid, crystal, thin, crystal clear, unobstructed; see also **open** 1, 2.— *Ant.* OPAQUE, dark,
muddy.
3. [Unclouded] — *Syn.* sunny, cloudless, bright, rainless; see **fair** 3.
4. [Discernible] — *Syn.* distinct, precise, sharp; see
**definite** 2.
5. [Freed from legal charges] — *Syn.* free, guiltless,
cleared, exonerated, blameless, innocent, uncensurable,

sinless, exculpated, dismissed, discharged, absolved.
— *Ant.* accused, CHARGED, blamed.
6. [Audible] — *Syn.* loud enough to be heard, distinct,
definite; see **audible.**
**in the clear**\* — *Syn.* guiltless, not suspected, cleared,
exonerated; see **free** 2, **innocent** 1, **pardoned.**

---

*SYN.* — **clear** suggests freedom from cloudiness, haziness, muddiness, etc., either literally or figuratively
/a *clear* liquid, *clear* logic/; **transparent** suggests such
clearness that objects on the other side (or by extension, meanings, etc.) may be seen distinctly /plate glass
is *transparent*, a *transparent* lie/; **translucent** implies the
admission of light, but so diffused that objects on the
other side cannot be clearly distinguished /stained glass
is *translucent*/; **pellucid** suggests the sparkling clearness
of crystal /a slab of *pellucid* ice, *pellucid* writing/

---

**clear**, *v.* 1. [To free from uncertainty] — *Syn.* clear up,
relieve, clarify; see **explain.**
2. [To free from obstacles] — *Syn.* disentangle, rid, unloose, unblock; see **free** 2, **open** 2, **remove** 1.
3. [To free from contents] — *Syn.* clean, unload, unpack, evacuate; see **empty** 1, 2, **remove** 1.
4. [To free from guilt] — *Syn.* acquit, discharge, get off
the hook\*; see **absolve, excuse, free** 1, **release.**
5. [To profit] — *Syn.* realize, net, make; see **profit** 2,
**receive** 1.
**clearance**, *n.* 1. [Removal] — *Syn.* withdrawal, removing, clearing; see **clearing, removal** 1.
2. [Permission] — *Syn.* approval, consent, leave,
authorization; see **permission.**
3. [Space between objects] — *Syn.* margin, room, allowance, headroom; see **extent, leeway.**
**clear-cut**, *modif.* — *Syn.* precise, plain, evident; see **definite** 1, 2, **obvious** 1, 2.
**cleared**, *modif.* 1. [Emptied] — *Syn.* cleaned, unloaded,
cleared away; see **empty** 1.
2. [Freed of charges] — *Syn.* vindicated, exculpated, set
right; see **discharged** 1, **free** 2, **pardoned.**
3. [Made negotiable] — *Syn.* cashable, validated, certified, passed; see **accepted, approved, endorsed.**
**clearheaded**, *modif.* — *Syn.* lucid, sensible, perceptive,
unconfused; see **composed** 2, **intelligent** 1, **judicious.**
**clearing**, *n.* 1. [The act of clearing] — *Syn.* freeing, riddance, clearance, removal, removing, elimination, eradication, deforestation, defoliation, opening up, freeing
from obstruction, unblocking, unclogging, evacuation,
disposal, voidance, dispersal, sweeping out, clearing
away, mopping up, emptying; see also **acquittal, removal** 1.
2. [A cleared space] — *Syn.* open space, glade, opening,
clearance, defoliated area, field, tract, cultivated land,
cleared land; see also **area** 2, **expanse, yard** 1.
**clearly**, *modif.* 1. [In a manner clear to the eye
or mind] — *Syn.* distinctly, plainly, visibly, manifestly,
unmistakably, perceptibly, in full view, transparently,
discernibly, decidedly, starkly, glaringly, incontestably,
undoubtedly, indubitably, noticeably, admittedly, before one's eyes, prominently, obviously, patently,
openly, overtly, observably, certainly, apparently, recog-
nizably, conspicuously, in plain sight, definitely, markedly, evidently, to all appearances, precisely, lucidly,
coherently, articulately, intelligibly, comprehensibly,
understandably, simply, unambiguously, explicitly, in
plain English, limpidly, pellucidly, translucently, with
clarity, in focus, legibly, readably; see also **apparently.**
— *Ant.* hazily, vaguely, fuzzily.
2. [In a manner easy to hear] — *Syn.* distinctly, sharply,

acutely, ringingly, penetratingly, sonorously, audibly, aloud, out loud, articulately, intelligibly, bell-like, with absolute clarity, with good articulation.— *Ant.* indistinctly, mutteringly, unclearly.
**3.** [Undoubtedly] — *Syn.* unquestionably, obviously, decidedly, without a doubt; see **surely.**

**clearness,** *n.* — *Syn.* brightness, distinctness, lucidity; see **clarity.**

**clear out,** *v.* **1.** [To empty] — *Syn.* clean out, dispose of, get rid of; see **eliminate** 1, **empty** 2, **remove** 1.
**2.** [*To leave] — *Syn.* depart, go, remove oneself; see **leave** 1.

**clear-sighted,** *modif.* — *Syn.* perceiving, understanding, discerning; see **conscious** 1, 2, **judicious, observant** 1.

**clear up,** *v.* **1.** [To become clear; *said especially of weather*] — *Syn.* clear, blow over, stop raining, stop snowing, stop storming, lapse, run its course, pass, pass away, die down, pick up, lift, break, become fair, become sunny, brighten, burn off; see also **improve** 2.
**2.** [To make clear] — *Syn.* explain away, clarify, resolve, settle; see **explain, solve.**

**cleat,** *n.* — *Syn.* wedge, lug, brace; see **brace** 1, **fastener, support** 2.

**cleavage,** *n.* **1.** [A cleaving] — *Syn.* dividing, splitting, separating; see **break** 1, **division** 1, **fracture** 1.
**2.** [A fissure] — *Syn.* split, cleft, rift; see **hole** 1, 2.

**cleave,** *v.* **1.** [To split] — *Syn.* sever, hew, separate; see **cut** 1, **divide** 1.
**2.** [To stick] — *Syn.* cling, adhere, hold fast; see **stick** 1. *See Synonym Study at* STICK.

**cleaver,** *n.* — *Syn.* butcher's knife, chopper, blade; see **ax, knife.**

**cleft,** *modif.* — *Syn.* split, rent, parted; see **separated, torn.**

**clemency,** *n.* **1.** [Mildness of temper] — *Syn.* leniency, mercy, charity, compassion; see **kindness** 1, **mercy** 1.
**2.** [Mildness of weather] — *Syn.* mildness, calm, balminess, temperateness; see **peace** 2.
*See Synonym Study at* MERCY.

**clement,** *modif.* **1.** [Merciful] — *Syn.* lenient, forbearing, compassionate; see **humane** 1, **kind, merciful** 1.
**2.** [Mild; *said of weather*] — *Syn.* warm, clear, peaceful; see **calm** 2, **fair** 3, **mild** 2.

**clench,** *v.* — *Syn.* grip, grasp, double up, tense; see **hold** 1.

**clergy,** *n.* — *Syn.* priesthood, prelacy, pastorate; see **ministry** 2.

**clergyman,** *n.* — *Syn.* cleric, pastor, parson, preacher; see **minister** 1, **priest, rabbi.**

**clerical,** *modif.* **1.** [Concerning clerks] — *Syn.* secretarial, office, filing, typing, stenographic, accounting, bookkeeping, written, scribal, administrative, assistant, on the support staff, white-collar.
**2.** [Concerning the clergy] — *Syn.* ministerial, sacerdotal, priestly, pastoral, apostolic, monastic, theocratic, monkish, hierarchic, rabbinical, churchly, cleric, prelatic, papal, episcopal, canonical, pontifical, ecclesiastic, ordained, of the cloth, sacred, holy, ecclesiastical, parsonic, parsonish, in God's service, doing the Lord's work; see also **divine** 2.— *Ant.* lay, WORLDLY, civilian.

**clerk,** *n.* **1.** [A person engaged in selling] — *Syn.* salesclerk, salesperson, saleswoman, saleslady, shop assistant, salesman, counterman, seller, floorwalker, floor manager, sales manager, sales agent.
**2.** [An office assistant] — *Syn.* office worker, file clerk, secretary, assistant, auditor, bookkeeper, recorder, registrar, stenographer, record keeper, timekeeper, cashier,

teller, scribe, notary, copyist, amanuensis, law clerk, gal Friday, man Friday, pencil pusher*, steno*; see also **accountant, secretary** 2, **typist.**

**clever,** *modif.* **1.** [Mentally quick] — *Syn.* smart, bright, intelligent, quick, shrewd, ingenious, cunning, sharp, keen, astute, witty, quick-witted, sharp-witted, quick-thinking, amusing, scintillating, inventive, resourceful, original, talented, gifted, apt, facile, glib, precocious, brainy*, sharp as a tack*, quick on the uptake*, quick on the trigger*; see also **intelligent** 1, **sly** 1.
**2.** [Apt, particularly with one's hands] — *Syn.* skillful, expert, adroit; see **able** 1, 2.

---

**SYN. — clever,** implies quick-wittedness or adroitness, as in contriving the solution to a problem [*a clever reply*]; **cunning** suggests great skill or ingenuity, but often implies deception or craftiness [*cunning as a fox*]; **ingenious** stresses inventive skill, as in origination or fabrication [*an ingenious device*]; **shrewd** suggests cleverness and acumen accompanied by practicality [*a shrewd judge of character*], sometimes verging on craftiness [*a shrewd politician*] See also Synonym Study at INTELLIGENT.

---

**cleverly,** *modif.* **1.** [In a clever manner] — *Syn.* sensibly, astutely, shrewdly, wittily; see **intelligently, shrewdly.**
**2.** [In a dexterous manner] — *Syn.* adroitly, neatly, skillfully, dexterously, aptly, ingeniously, cunningly, resourcefully, handily, deftly, nimbly, agilely, proficiently, expertly, ably, smoothly, facilely, glibly, quickly, readily, in a practiced manner, in a polished manner, with consummate skill; see also **easily** 1.— *Ant.* awkwardly, clumsily, unskillfully.

**cleverness,** *n.* — *Syn.* aptitude, brilliance, quickness, ingenuity; see **ability** 1, 2, **acumen, wit** 1.

**cliché,** *n.* — *Syn.* commonplace, platitude, truism, bromide, stereotype, proverb, saying, slogan, trite phrase, trite remark, saw, old saw, stereotyped saying, vapid expression, prosaism, triteness, tired phrase, threadbare phrase, banality, triviality, staleness, vapidity, hackneyed phrase, hackneyed expression, chestnut*; see also **motto.**

---

**SYN. — a cliché** is an expression or idea which, though once fresh and forceful, has become hackneyed and weak through much repetition; **a platitude** is a trite remark or idea, esp. one uttered as if it were novel or profound; **a commonplace** is any obvious or conventional remark or idea; **a truism** is a statement whose truth is widely known and whose utterance, therefore, seems superfluous; **bromide** is an informal term for a platitude that is especially dull, tiresome, or banal

---

**click,** *n.* — *Syn.* tick, snap, crack; see **noise** 1.

**click,** *v.* **1.** [To make a clicking sound] — *Syn.* tick, snap, bang; see **sound** 1.
**2.** [*To be successful] — *Syn.* match, go off well, hit it off, meet with approval; see **agree, succeed** 1.

**client,** *n.* — *Syn.* customer, patient, patron, buyer, purchaser, consumer, advisee, client state, dependent.

**clientele,** *n.* — *Syn.* clients, customers, patrons, dependents, purchasers of goods, purchasers of services, trade, buyers, shoppers, constituency, patronage, clientage; see also **following.**

**cliff,** *n.* — *Syn.* bluff, crag, precipice; see **hill, mountain** 1, **rock** 2, **wall** 1.

**cliff dweller,** *n.* — *Syn.* Pueblo, aborigine, cave dweller; see **Indian** 1.

**climacteric,** *n.* — *Syn.* trial, crucial period, crux, menopause; see **crisis, emergency.**

**climate,** *n.* — *Syn.* characteristic weather, latitude, atmospheric condition, meteorologic conditions, altitude, aridity, humidity, weather conditions, microclimate, clime*, atmosphere, milieu, spirit; see also **cold** 1, **environment, heat** 1, **mood** 1, **weather.**

**climax,** *n.* — *Syn.* peak, apex, highest point, culmination, acme, pinnacle, meridian, intensification, crest, zenith, height, summit, apogee, extremity, limit, pitch, ascendancy, utmost extent, highest degree, point of highest development, turning point, crowning point, turning of the tide, decisive moment, defining moment, crisis, orgasm, *ne plus ultra* (Latin); see also **maximum, top** 1. — *Ant.* anticlimax, DEPRESSION, nadir.
*See Synonym Study at* SUMMIT.

**climax,** *v.* — *Syn.* culminate, tower, end, top, top off, cap, cap off, crown, conclude, rise to a crescendo, reach a peak, come to a head, bring to a head, reach the zenith, peak, come to bring to a climax, finish, accomplish, fulfill, consummate; see also **achieve** 1, **complete** 1.

**climb,** *n.* 1. [The act of climbing] — *Syn.* climbing, clamber, mounting, ascent; see **rise** 1.
2. [An ascending place] — *Syn.* slope, incline, rise; see **grade** 1, **hill.**

**climb,** *v.* 1. [To ascend] — *Syn.* go up, soar, escalate, slope; see **rise** 1.
2. [To mount] — *Syn.* scale, work one's way up, ascend gradually, scramble up, clamber up, shin up, swarm up, start up, go up, ascend, go on board, labor up, struggle up, get on, climb on, progress upward, rise, rise hand over hand, creep up, twine up, crawl up, strive up, escalade, surmount, soar up, shinny up, scrabble up, shoot up.

**climb down,** *v.* — *Syn.* step off, come down, dismount; see **descend** 1.

**clinch,** *v.* 1. [To settle conclusively] — *Syn.* secure, close, confirm, sew up*; see **decide.**
2. [To attach] — *Syn.* clamp, secure, grip; see **fasten** 1, **hold** 1.

**cling,** *v.* — *Syn.* adhere, clasp, hold fast; see **stick** 1.
*See Synonym Study at* STICK.

**clinic,** *n.* — *Syn.* infirmary, dispensary, group practice, polyclinic; see **hospital.**

**clink,** *n.* — *Syn.* ring, tinkle, jingle; see **noise** 1.

**clink,** *v.* — *Syn.* tinkle, jingle, clang; see **ring** 3, **sound** 1.

**clip,** *v.* — *Syn.* snip, crop, trim, cut off; see **cut** 1, **decrease** 2.

**clippers,** *n.* — *Syn.* scissors, cutting instruments, barber's tools, pruning shears; see **shears.**

**clipping,** *n.* — *Syn.* excerpt, cutting, piece; see **bit** 1, **part** 1, **quotation** 1.

**clique,** *n.* — *Syn.* coterie, set, circle, group, clan, club, inner circle, ring, band, gang, crew, faction, cabal, junta, network, salon, crowd*, in-group*, bunch*, mob*; see also **faction** 1, **organization** 3.

———————————

**SYN.** — **clique** refers to a small, highly exclusive group, often within a larger one, and implies snobbery, selfishness, or, sometimes, intrigue /high-school *cliques*/; **coterie** is a small, intimate, somewhat select group of people associated for social or other reasons /a literary *coterie*/; **circle** suggests any group of people having in common some particular interest or pursuit /in music *circles*/; **set** refers to a group, usually larger and, hence, less exclusive than a **coterie**, having a common background, interests, social status, etc. /the sporting *set*/

———————————

**cloak,** *n.* 1. [An outer garment] — *Syn.* mantle, wrap, shawl; see **coat** 1.

2. [Something that covers or hides] — *Syn.* pretext, cover, mask; see **camouflage** 1, **coat** 3, **disguise.**

**clock,** *n.* — *Syn.* timepiece, timekeeper, time-marker, timer, time clock, horologe.
Kinds of clocks include: alarm, atomic, cuckoo, electric, digital, wall, grandfather, pendulum; hourglass, mission timer, stopwatch, sundial, wrist watch, clock radio, chronometer, chronograph; see also **watch** 1.

**around the clock** — *Syn.* continuously, continually, night and day, twenty-four hours a day; see **regularly** 2.

**clock,** *v.* — *Syn.* time, measure time, register speed, register distance; see **measure** 1, **time.**

**clockwork,** *n.* — *Syn.* perfect timing, precision, regularity; see **accuracy** 2.

**like clockwork** — *Syn.* precisely, smoothly, consistently; see **accurately, regularly** 1, 2.

**clod,** *n.* 1. [Lump of earth] — *Syn.* clay, soil, gob, mass; see **earth** 2, **hunk.**
2. [Stupid fellow] — *Syn.* dolt, simpleton, oaf; see **boor, bungler, fool** 1.

**clodhopper,** *n.* — *Syn.* rustic, hick, yokel; see **boor, fool** 1.

**clodhoppers,** *pl.n.* — *Syn.* construction boots, work boots, brogues, brogans, combat boots, wafflestompers*, gunboats*; see also **boot** 1, **shoe.**

**clog,** *v.* — *Syn.* stop up, seal, obstruct, jam; see **bar** 1, **close** 2, **hinder, plug.**

**cloister,** *n.* 1. [A place of religious seclusion] — *Syn.* monastery, convent, abbey, priory, nunnery, friary, Charterhouse, hermitage, chapter house, house, order, retreat, cell(s), cenoby, retreat from the world, cloistered walls, religious community, lamasery, ashram; see also **sanctuary** 2.
2. [A covered walk] — *Syn.* ambulatory, arcade, gallery; see **colonnade, court** 1.

———————————

**SYN.** — **cloister,** in this comparison, is the general term for a place of religious seclusion, for either men or women, and emphasizes in connotation retirement from the world; **convent,** once a general term synonymous with **cloister,** is now usually restricted to such a place for women (nuns), formerly called a **nunnery; monastery** usually refers to a cloister for men (monks); an **abbey** is a cloister ruled by an abbot or abbess; a **priory** is a cloister ruled by a prior or prioress and is sometimes a subordinate branch of an abbey

———————————

**cloistered,** *modif.* — *Syn.* secluded, sheltered, sequestered, recluse; see **isolated, withdrawn.**

**close,** *modif.* 1. [Near] — *Syn.* neighboring, nearby, adjacent, around the corner; see **approaching, imminent, near** 1.
2. [Intimate] — *Syn.* familiar, dear, close-knit, confidential; see **friendly** 1, **intimate** 1, **private.**
3. [Compact] — *Syn.* dense, solid, compressed; see **thick** 1.
4. [Stingy] — *Syn.* narrow, parsimonious, niggardly; see **stingy.**
5. [Stifling] — *Syn.* sticky, stuffy, unventilated, heavy, motionless, fusty, uncomfortable, choky, stale-smelling, musty, stagnant, moldy, confined, suffocating, sultry, sweltering, sweltry, tight, stale, oppressive, breathless. — *Ant.* FRESH, refreshing, brisk.
6. [Confining] — *Syn.* confined, cramped, restricted; see **confining, narrow** 1.
7. [Similar] — *Syn.* resembling, having common qualities, much the same; see **alike** 2, **like.**
*See Synonym Study at* FAMILIAR, STINGY, THICK.

**close,** *n.* — *Syn.* termination, adjournment, ending, conclusion; see **end** 2.

**close,** *v.* **1.** [To put a stop to] — *Syn.* conclude, finish, terminate; see **end** 1.

**2.** [To put a stopper into] — *Syn.* shut, stop, stopper, choke off, occlude, stuff, clog, fill, calk, prevent passage, retard flow, shut off, turn off, lock, block, bar, dam, cork, seal, seal off, button; see also **plug.** — *Ant.* open, uncork, unseal.

**3.** [To come or bring together] — *Syn.* meet, unite, coalesce, chain, connect, tie, bind, fuse, join, enclose, put together; see also **join** 1. — *Ant.* disconnect, SEPARATE, untie.

**4.** [To shut] — *Syn.* slam, close down, close up, shut down, shut up, seal, fasten, secure, lock, bolt, clench, bar, shutter, clap, bring to, suspend operations, cease operations, go out of business, fold*.

**5.** [To arrive at an agreement] — *Syn.* settle, complete a deal, consummate, clinch; see **achieve** 1, **agree, decide.**

*See Synonym Study at* END.

**closed,** *modif.* **1.** [Terminated] — *Syn.* ended, concluded, final; see **finished** 1.

**2.** [Not in operation] — *Syn.* shut, shut down, out of order, out of service, bankrupt, out of business, closed down, closed up, padlocked, shuttered, folded up*; see also **broken** 2.

**3.** [Not open] — *Syn.* shut, fastened, sealed; see **covered** 1, **tight** 2.

**4.** [Not public] — *Syn.* restricted, exclusive, closed-door, private; see **exclusive, private.**

**closed shop,** *n.* — *Syn.* union shop, union establishment, unionized business; see **union shop.**

**closefisted,** *modif.* — *Syn.* tight, miserly, stingy, niggardly; see **greedy** 1, **stingy.**

**closefitting,** *modif.* — *Syn.* skintight, snug, hugging; see **tight** 3.

**closely,** *modif.* — *Syn.* approximately, similarly, exactly, nearly, strictly, firmly, intimately, jointly, in conjunction with; see also **almost.** — *Ant.* separately, INDIVIDUALLY, one by one.

**closemouthed,** *modif.* — *Syn.* uncommunicative, silent, reticent; see **quiet** 2, **reserved** 3, **taciturn.**

**closet,** *n.* — *Syn.* wardrobe, cabinet, recess, cupboard, locker, receptacle, safe, vault, cold storage, storeroom, pantry, larder, clothespress, press, armoire, clothes room, walk-in, cloakroom, checkroom, ambry; see also **room** 2.

**closure,** *n.* — *Syn.* conclusion, cessation, finish, closing; see **end** 2.

**clot,** *n.* — *Syn.* lump, glob, clotting, curdling, consolidation, coagulation, mass, clump, thrombus, embolus, grume, coagulum, thickness, coalescence, conglutination, coagulated protein, curd, precipitate.

**clot,** *v.* — *Syn.* coagulate, set, lump; see **thicken** 1.

**cloth,** *n.* — *Syn.* fabric, material, stuff, goods, dry goods, textiles, weave, tissue, twill, yard goods, synthetics, rag. Types of cloth include: canvas, linen, piqué, broadcloth, percale, poplin, lawn, chintz, gingham, muslin, lisle, gabardine, chambray, cambric, calico, drill, cotton, terry, khaki, denim, permanent press denim, dimity, tweed, serge, homespun, cheviot, cashmere, worsted, wool, plaid, flannel, silk, mercerized cotton, taffeta, pongee, satin, crepe de Chine, damask, voile chiffon, alpaca, velvet, corduroy, plush, hopsacking, brocade, vicuña, angora, blanketing, bagging, bunting, carpeting, ramie, sacking, skirting, felt, oilcloth, burlap, tarpaulin, organza. organdy, sharkskin.

Types of synthetic cloth include: nylon, rayon, viscose rayon, acrylic, polyester, olefin, polyethelene, acetate; Dacron, Orlon, Acrilan, Avril, Spandex, Saran, Gore-Tex, Terylene, Vinyon, Naugahyde (*all* trademarks).

**clothe,** *v.* — *Syn.* dress, attire, dress up, costume, outfit, robe, put garments on, apparel, array, muffle up, bundle up, don, wrap, cloak, gown, caparison, mantle, jacket, accouter, vest, invest, garb, deck, bedeck, deck out, drape, equip, disguise, coat, cover, shroud, fit out, turn out, rig out*; see also **dress** 1. — *Ant.* unclothe, UNDRESS, strip.

**clothed,** *modif.* — *Syn.* clad, dressed, attired, invested, costumed, robed, shod, decked, disguised, covered, draped, veiled, habited; see also **dressed up.** — *Ant.* NAKED, exposed, undressed.

**clothes,** *n.* — *Syn.* clothing, apparel, wearing apparel, garments, attire, raiment, dress, garb, wear, vestments, array, habiliments, casual wear, informal wear, evening dress, evening clothes, work clothes, *tout ensemble* (French), suit of clothes, costume, ensemble, outfit, equipment, uniform, outerwear, underwear, wardrobe, accouterments, trappings, caparison, harness, gear, livery, habit, regalia, overclothes, finery; sportswear, swimwear, rainwear, footwear; wearables*, get-up*, rags*, tatters*, rigging*, togs*, duds*, things*, threads*, drag*, glad rags*; see also **finery, underwear.**

Types of clothing include: business suit, jacket and slacks, blazer, trousers, blue jeans, jeans, denims, Levis (trademark), overalls, coveralls, sweat pants, double-breasted suit, shorts, breeches, knickerbockers, knickers*; tuxedo, tux*, tuck*; dress suit, dinner jacket, tail coat, swallow-tailed coat, jungle coat, jungle jacket, uniform, shirt, sweat shirt, sweat suit, T-shirt, turtleneck, tank top, vest, body shirt, hiphugger pants, bell-bottom pants, continental suit, socks; sweater, cardigan, windbreaker, raincoat; robe, underwear, unmentionables*, long underwear, long johns*, red flannels*.

Types of clothing worn mainly by women include: housecoat, negligee, morning dress, evening gown, kimono, wrapper, frock, blouse, jumper, slip, shirtwaist, panties, brassiere, bra, bustier, camisole, garter belt, girdle; nightgown, nightie*, pajamas, P.J.'s*; swimsuit, bathing suit, bikini, noon dress, street dress, pullover, slipover sweater, jerkin, golf dress, house dress, tennis dress, dickey, pantyhose, nylon stockings, nylons, A-line dress, A-line skirt, mini-skirt, maxi-skirt, shift, muumuu, little girl's dress, paper dress, gilet, vestee, guimpe, bolero, smock, skirt, toreador pants, leggings, tights, leotard, petticoat, hat, bonnet.

Clothing of foreign origin includes — *Latin American:* rebozo, mantilla, poncho, serape, huipil; *Eskimo:* parka, mukluks, kapta; *Russian:* sarafan; *southeastern European:* fez, bourka, tunic, babushka, chalwar, jube, fustenella; *Muslim:* burnoose, yashmak, tarboosh, djubbeh, chalwar, chador, caftan, aba, chargat; *southeastern Asian:* sarong, sari, dhoti, burka; *Japanese:* kimono, obi, juban, shitagi, dogi, hakama, haori, shito-juban, ymogi, koshimaki; *western European:* mantilla, bolero, kilt, tartan; *historical:* toga, jupon, kirtle, chlamys, jerkin, brachae; see also **coat, dress, hat, pants** 1, 2.

**clothing,** *n.* — *Syn.* attire, apparel, raiment, garb; see **clothes.**

**cloud,** *n.* **1.** [Fog at a distance from the earth] — *Syn.* haze, mist, rack, fogginess, haziness, film, puff, billow, frost, nebula, nebulosity, vapor, veil, cloud cover, cloudiness, overcast, pall.

Types of clouds include: cirrus, cumulus, stratus, nimbus, cirrocumulus, cirrostratus, altostratus, altocumulus, cumulonimbus, stratocumulus, nimbostratus; woolpack\*, scud\*, meteor\*, curl-cloud\*, mare's tail\*, colt's tail\*, cat's tail\*, mackerel sky\*, thunderhead\*, sheep\*.

**2.** [Any nebulous mass]— *Syn.* smoke, dust, vapor, dimness; see sense 1, **darkness** 1, **fog** 1.

**3.** [Anything ominous]— *Syn.* pall, spot, fault, blemish, dark spot, stain, shadow, flaw, blotch, obscurity, gloom; see also **warning.**

**in the clouds**— *Syn.* fanciful, fantastic, lost in reverie; see **absent-minded, impractical, visionary** 1.

**under a cloud**— *Syn.* **1.** suspect, dubious, under suspicion, in disgrace; see **disgraced, suspicious** 2.

**2.** depressed, worried, sad; see **troubled** 1.

**cloudburst,** *n.* — *Syn.* deluge, rain, downpour, torrent; see **storm** 1.

**cloudless,** *modif.* — *Syn.* clear, bright, sunny; see **fair** 3.

**cloudy,** *modif.* **1.** [Hazy]— *Syn.* overcast, lowering, leaden, threatening; see **dark** 1, **hazy** 1.

**2.** [Not clear]— *Syn.* dense, murky, nontransparent, nontranslucent; see **opaque** 1.

**3.** [Obscure]— *Syn.* vague, indistinct, indefinite, unclear; see **obscure** 1.

**clown,** *n.* — *Syn.* buffoon, fool, mime, jester, mummer, joker, harlequin, merry-andrew, Punch, punchinello, funnyman, humorist, pierrot, wag, antic, comedian, comic, wit, zany, droll, cutup\*; see also **actor** 1.

**clown (around),** *v.* — *Syn.* fool around, kid around, cut up\*; see **joke, play** 2.

**cloy,** *v.* — *Syn.* satiate, surfeit, suffice, pall; see **satisfy** 1, **weary** 1.

*See Synonym Study at* SATIATE.

**club,** *n.* **1.** [A social organization] — *Syn.* association, order, society; see **clique, faction** 1, **organization** 3.

**2.** [A clubhouse] — *Syn.* center, base (of operations), meetinghouse; see **headquarters, room** 2.

**3.** [A heavy stick] — *Syn.* cudgel, stick, bat, bludgeon, baton, nightstick, billy club, billy, truncheon, blackjack, shillelagh, staff, mace, crabstick, warclub, hammer, mallet, cane, hickory, single-stick, quarterstaff, bastinado, swatter\*.

**4.** [A golf club] Types include the following: driver, brassie, cleek, midiron, spoon, mashie, niblick, wedge, putter.

**club,** *v.* — *Syn.* bludgeon, cudgel, batter, pound; see **beat** 1, 2, **hit** 1.

**cluck,** *v.* — *Syn.* clack, chuck, cackle, coo; see **sound** 1.

**clue,** *n.* — *Syn.* evidence, trace, mark, intimation; see **hint** 1, **proof** 1, **sign** 1.

**clue in,** *v.* — *Syn.* inform, enlighten, fill in\*; see **notify** 1.

**clump,** *n.* **1.** [A group]— *Syn.* cluster, bundle, knot, mass; see **bunch** 1.

**2.** [A thump]— *Syn.* bump, tramp, stamp, thud; see **noise** 1.

**clump,** *v.* — *Syn.* thump, clomp, tramp; see **bump** 2, **walk** 1.

**clumsily,** *modif.* — *Syn.* crudely, gawkily, stumblingly, bunglingly; see **awkwardly.**

**clumsiness,** *n.* — *Syn.* maladroitness, ineptitude, ungainliness, heavy-handedness; see **awkwardness** 1.

**clumsy,** *modif.* — *Syn.* ungainly, inept, tactless, cumbersome; see **awkward** 1.

*See Synonym Study at* AWKWARD.

**cluster,** *n.* **1.** [A bunch] — *Syn.* group, batch, clump; see **bunch** 1.

**2.** [A gathering] — *Syn.* assemblage, group, pack; see **crowd** 1.

**cluster,** *v.* — *Syn.* collect, assemble, group; see **center, gather** 1.

**clutch,** *n.* **1.** [A mechanical device]— *Syn.* friction clutch, coupling, connection; see **link, part** 2.

**2.** [Grip]— *Syn.* grasp, clasp, hold; see **grip** 2.

**clutch,** *v.* — *Syn.* grab, grasp, grip; see **hold** 1, **seize** 1.

*See Synonym Study at* SEIZE.

**clutches,** *n.* — *Syn.* control, grasp, hands, keeping; see **power** 2.

**clutter,** *n.* — *Syn.* disarray, jumble, disorder; see **confusion** 2.

**coach,** *n.* **1.** [A carriage]— *Syn.* stagecoach, four-wheeler, chaise, victoria; see **carriage** 2, **vehicle** 1.

**2.** [An instructor]— *Syn.* mentor, drillmaster, physical education instructor; see **teacher** 1, **trainer.**

**coach,** *v.* — *Syn.* train, drill, instruct; see **teach** 1, 2.

**coadjutor,** *n.* — *Syn.* assistant, helper, colleague, co-worker; see **assistant, associate.**

**coagulate,** *v.* — *Syn.* curdle, clot, congeal; see **harden** 2, **thicken** 1.

**coagulation,** *n.* — *Syn.* clotting, curdling, thickening, congealing, congelation, caseation, jellification, gelling, agglomeration, consolidation, gelatinization, condensation, concretion, inspissation; see also **concentration** 1.

**coal,** *n.* **1.** [Mineral fuel]— *Syn.* mineral coal, coke, fossil fuel; see **fuel.**

Types of coal include: hard coal, soft coal, charcoal, brown coal, pit coal, lignite, tasmanite, subbituminous coal, cannel, anthracite, bituminous, coke, carbocoal, turf, peat, semianthracite, semibituminous coal.

Grades of coal include: broken, lump, chunk, egg, stove, nut, pea, rice, buckwheat, briquette, slack, duff, flaxseed, mustard seed.

**2.** [An ember]— *Syn.* spark, live coal, brand, clinker; see **embers.**

**haul** or **rake** or **drag over the coals**\*— *Syn.* reprimand, criticize, castigate; see **censure.**

**coalesce,** *v.* — *Syn.* blend, fuse, combine; see **join** 1, **mix** 1.

*See Synonym Study at* MIX.

**coalition,** *n.* — *Syn.* combination, temporary alliance, confederacy; see **alliance** 3, **faction** 1.

*See Synonym Study at* ALLIANCE.

**coarse,** *modif.* **1.** [Not fine or smooth]— *Syn.* rough, harsh, grainy, granular; see **crude** 1, **rough** 1.

**2.** [Lacking in refinement]— *Syn.* vulgar, crude, unrefined, indelicate, unpolished, rude, rough, uncouth, crass, gross, obscene, ribald, indecent; see also **lewd** 1, **ribald, rude** 1, **vulgar** 1.

**3.** [Of poor quality]— *Syn.* inferior, second-rate, common; see **common** 1, **poor** 2.

---

*SYN.* — **coarse,** in this comparison, implies such a lack of refinement in manners or speech as to be offensive to one's aesthetic or moral sense [*coarse* laughter]; **gross** suggests a crudeness or coarseness that is brutish or repellent [*gross* table manners]; **indelicate** suggests impropriety, immodesty, or tactlessness [an *indelicate* remark]; **vulgar** emphasizes a lack of culture, refinement, or good taste [*vulgar* ostentation], or may imply indecency [*vulgar* language]; **obscene** is used of that which is offensive to decency and implies lewdness [*obscene* gestures]; **ribald** suggests such mild indecency or lewdness as might bring laughter from those who are not too squeamish [*ribald* jokes]

---

**coarsen,** *v.* — *Syn.* roughen, callous, toughen, vulgarize; see **harden** 3.

**coarseness,** *n.* **1.** [Crudeness]— *Syn.* vulgarity, unrefinement, callousness; see **rudeness.**

**2.** [Roughness of texture] — *Syn.* stiffness, harshness, scratchiness, crudity; see **roughness** 1.

**coast,** *n.* — *Syn.* seashore, shoreline, beach, seaboard; see **shore.**

*See Synonym Study at* SHORE.

**coast,** *v.* — *Syn.* glide, float, slide, sled; see **drift, ride** 1, 3, **slide** 1.

**coastal,** *modif.* — *Syn.* seaside, beachfront, waterfront, seaboard, bordering, marginal, riverine, riparian, littoral, tidal; see also **marshy.**

**coat,** *n.* **1.** [An outer garment] — *Syn.* topcoat, overcoat, jacket, cloak, suit coat, suit jacket, tuxedo, dinner jacket, sport(s) coat, sport(s) jacket, blazer, dress coat, tail coat, frock coat, fur coat, mink coat, ski jacket, parka, anorak, cutaway, mackintosh, greatcoat, raincoat, trench coat, slicker, ulster, windbreaker, peacoat, pea jacket, car coat, three-quarter length coat, duffle coat, wrap, leather jacket, surtout, redingote, chesterfield, reefer, bolero, doublet, jerkin, shirtjacket, safari jacket, sou'wester*, mac*, tux*, tails*; see also **cape** 2, **clothes.**

**2.** [A natural covering] — *Syn.* fur, hair, wool, hide, integument, protective covering, pellicle, husk, shell, crust, bark, scales, fleece, fell, epidermis, rind, scarfskin, ectoderm, pelt, membrane; see also **fur, hide** 1, **leather, skin.**

**3.** [An applied covering] — *Syn.* coating, layer, sheet, covering, blanket, film, dusting, wash, glaze, priming, crust, painting, overlay, whitewashing, varnish, lacquer, gloss, tinge, finish, roughcast, prime coat, plaster; see also **cover** 2.

**coat,** *v.* — *Syn.* cover, surface, glaze, smear; see **paint** 2, **spread** 4, **varnish.**

**coating,** *n.* — *Syn.* crust, covering, layer, film; see **coat** 3, **cover** 2, **sheet** 2.

**coat of arms,** *n.* — *Syn.* ensign, crest, escutcheon, pennon; see **arms** 2, **emblem.**

**coax,** *v.* — *Syn.* persuade, cajole, wheedle, blandish, urge, inveigle, beguile, induce, manipulate, sweet-talk*, soft-soap*; see also **influence, tempt, urge** 2.

---

*SYN.* — **coax** suggests repeated attempts to persuade someone to do something and implies the use of soothing words, an ingratiating manner, etc.; **cajole** suggests the use of flattery or other blandishments; **wheedle** implies even more strongly the use of subtle flattery or craftily artful behavior in gaining one's ends

---

**cobbler,** *n.* — *Syn.* shoemaker, bootmaker, shoe repairman, cordwainer; see **shoemaker, worker.**

**cobweb,** *n.* **1.** [A spider's web] — *Syn.* filament, gossamer, extrusive threads; see **fiber** 1, **web** 1.

**2.** [A network] — *Syn.* snare, labyrinth, entanglement; see **net, web** 2.

**cock,** *n.* — *Syn.* rooster, capon, cockerel; see **chicken** 1.

**cockade,** *n.* — *Syn.* rosette, knot, spangle, ribbon; see **decoration** 2.

**cockeyed*,** *modif.* **1.** [Tilted] — *Syn.* crooked, awry, askew, twisted; see **crooked** 1, **oblique** 1.

**2.** [Foolish] — *Syn.* silly, preposterous, crazy; see **absurd, stupid** 1.

**cocktail,** *n.* Types of cocktails include: Manhattan, martini, Gibson, gimlet, old-fashioned, champagne, sidecar, horse's neck, Margarita, Bronx, pink lady, whisky sour, black Russian, white Russian, orange blossom, piña colada, mai tai, mimosa, Rob Roy, Sazerac, blue blazer, old Hickory, Vieux Carré, green opal, jitters, Daiquiri, Bloody Mary, screwdriver, Tom Collins, mint julep, orange blossom, Roffignac, Alexander, wassail, toddy, syllabub; see **drink** 2.

**cocoon,** *n.* — *Syn.* silky case, chrysalis, pupa; see **cover** 1, **envelope.**

**coddle,** *v.* **1.** [To cook gently] — *Syn.* simmer, poach, steam; see **cook.**

**2.** [To pamper] — *Syn.* indulge, cosset, favor, baby; see **pamper.**

**code,** *n.* **1.** [A set of rules] — *Syn.* body of law, regulations, principles, digest; see **law** 2, **system** 2.

**2.** [A set of symbols] — *Syn.* cipher, secret language, cryptogram, Morse code; see **key** 2, **language** 1.

**codicil,** *n.* — *Syn.* addendum, supplement, postscript, rider; see **addition** 2, **appendix.**

**codify,** *v.* — *Syn.* systematize, classify, arrange; see **classify, order** 3.

**coequal,** *modif.* — *Syn.* same, parallel, corresponding; see **alike** 1, 2, **equal, like.**

**coerce,** *v.* **1.** [To force] — *Syn.* impel, compel, constrain, pressure; see **force** 1, **threaten** 1.

**2.** [To restrain] — *Syn.* restrict, constrain, curb, control; see **dominate, hinder, restrain** 1.

*See Synonym Study at* FORCE.

**coercion,** *n.* — *Syn.* compulsion, duress, intimidation, constraint; see **oppression** 1, **pressure** 2, **restraint** 2.

**coeval,** *modif.* — *Syn.* contemporary, of the same age, coincident; see **contemporary** 1, **simultaneous.**

*See Synonym Study at* CONTEMPORARY.

**coexist,** *v.* — *Syn.* exist together, synchronize, exist side-by-side; see **accompany** 3, **coincide.**

**coexistence,** *n.* **1.** [Contemporaneousness] — *Syn.* conjunction, coevality, concurrence; see **coincidence.**

**2.** [Harmony] — *Syn.* peaceful coexistence, accord, détente, rapprochement; see **peace** 1, 2.

**coexistent,** *modif.* — *Syn.* contemporary, concurrent, coexisting; see **contemporary, simultaneous.**

**coffee,** *n.* — *Syn.* beverage, decoction, java*; see **drink** 3. Varieties of coffee include: French roast, dark roast, Arabica, Mocha, Sumatra, Java, Brazilian, Santos, Rio, Guatemalan, decaffeinated, decaf, Maracaibo, Arabian, Costa Rican, Royal Kona (trademark), Bogotá, Medellín, Colombian. Prepared coffee includes: Turkish, Armenian, Irish, drip, percolated, vacuum, freeze-dried, instant, French roast, *demitasse, café noir, café au lait, café crème, café filtre* (all French), *Kaffee Wien, Kaffee mit Schlag* (both German), *caffè latte, cappuccino, espresso* (all Italian), *turska kava* (Slavic), *turetskoe kofe* (Russian), camp coffee*.

**coffee break,** *n.* — *Syn.* respite, break, rest period; see **pause** 1, **recess** 1, **rest** 1.

**coffin,** *n.* — *Syn.* box, casket, sarcophagus, pine box, catafalque, pall, burial urn, funerary urn, funerary vase, funerary box, mummy case, ossuary; see also **grave** 1.

**cog,** *n.* — *Syn.* sprocket, geartooth, tooth, cogwheel, gear, pinion, rack, wheel, ratchet, transmission, differential.

**cogent,** *modif.* **1.** [Persuasive] — *Syn.* convincing, sound, forceful, compelling; see **persuasive.**

**2.** [Relevant] — *Syn.* fitting, apt, apposite, pertinent; see **relevant.**

*See Synonym Study at* VALID.

**cogitate,** *v.* — *Syn.* ponder, meditate, contemplate, consider; see **consider** 3, **think** 1.

*See Synonym Study at* THINK.

**cogitation,** *n.* — *Syn.* reflection, consideration, contemplation; see **reflection** 1, **thought** 1.

**cognate,** *modif.* — *Syn.* related, of common descent, akin, analogous; see **alike** 2, **like, related** 2, 3.

*See Synonym Study at* RELATED.

**cognition,** *n.* — *Syn.* perception, knowing, insight, grasp; see **judgment** 2, **knowledge** 1, **thought** 1, 2.

**cognizance,** *n.* — *Syn.* awareness, perception, notice; see **awareness, knowledge** 1, **thought** 1, 2.

**take cognizance of** — *Syn.* notice, acknowledge, be aware of; see **recognize** 1, **regard** 1, **see** 1.

**cognizant,** *modif.* — *Syn.* informed, aware, mindful; see **conscious** 1.

*See Synonym Study at* CONSCIOUS.

**cognomen,** *n.* — *Syn.* last name, surname, nickname; see **name** 1, 3.

**cohabit,** *v.* — *Syn.* live together, stay together, room together, share an address, take up housekeeping, have relations with someone, live as man and wife, live illegally with, live without benefit of matrimony, live without benefit of clergy, be roommates, shack up with*, play house*, live in sin*; see also **live with.**

**cohere,** *v.* **1.** [To stick together] — *Syn.* cleave, adhere, cling; see **stick** 1.

**2.** [To be logically connected] — *Syn.* follow, harmonize, correspond; see **agree, make sense sense.**

*See Synonym Study at* STICK.

**coherence,** *n.* **1.** [Cohesion] — *Syn.* stickiness, viscosity, tackiness, gluiness, gumminess, cementation, congelation, soldering, adhesiveness, glutinousness, sticking together, agglutination, coagulation, viscidity, glutinosity, adherence, set, amalgamation, fusion, sticking, union, adhesion, attachment, tenacity, conglutination, cohesiveness, consistency, solidarity, inseparability, inseparableness.

**2.** [Closely built relationship] — *Syn.* consistency, congruity, logical connection, connectedness, sense, logic, rationality, intelligibility, clarity, continuity, connection, interconnection, integration, integrity, consonance, agreement, harmony, concord, correspondence, construction, unity. — *Ant.* inconsistency, incoherence, disjunction.

**coherent,** *modif.* **1.** [Closely integrated] — *Syn.* consistent, identified, combined; see **joined, unified.**

**2.** [Understandable] — *Syn.* comprehensible, sound, intelligible; see **logical** 1, **understandable.**

**cohesion,** *n.* — *Syn.* union, attachment, adherence; see **coherence** 1.

**cohort,** *n.* **1.** [Gathering] — *Syn.* band, company, group; see **following, gathering.**

**2.** [An associate] — *Syn.* partner, ally, accomplice, companion; see **assistant, associate, friend** 1.

**coiffure,** *n.* — *Syn.* hairstyle, hairdo, haircut, coif; see **hairstyle.**

**coil,** *n.* — *Syn.* ring(s), turn, winding, spiral, helix, whorl, convolution, twine, twist, twirl, lap, loop, curl, curlicue, bight, corkscrew, roll, tendril, scroll; see also **circle** 1, **curl.**

**coil,** *v.* — *Syn.* scroll, wind, loop, spiral, twist, fold, twine, intertwine, entwine, convolute, snake, intervolve, sinuate, lap, twirl, curl, corkscrew, wreathe; see also **curl, roll** 4. — *Ant.* straighten, unwind, ravel.

**coin,** *n.* — *Syn.* gold piece, silver piece, copper coin, specie; see **money** 1.

**coin,** *v.* **1.** [To mint money] — *Syn.* issue, counterfeit, strike, stamp; see **manufacture, mint** 1.

**2.** [To invent a word, etc.] — *Syn.* create a phrase, make up, mint, neologize; see **invent** 1.

**coinage,** *n.* **1.** [The process of making money] — *Syn.* coining, making coins, minting; see **manufacturing, production** 1.

**2.** [Metal money] — *Syn.* silver, cash, coins; see **change** 5.

**coincide,** *v.* — *Syn.* correspond, agree, concur, co-occur, occur simultaneously, fall together, tally, match, accord, harmonize; see also **agree.**

*See Synonym Study at* AGREE.

**coincidence,** *n.* **1.** [Correspondence] — *Syn.* simultaneity, conjunction, concurrence, co-occurrence, co-existence, accord, accordance, consonance, unison, parallelism, concomitance, contemporaneousness, simultaneousness, synchronism, synchronicity; see also **agreement** 2.

**2.** [An incidental occurrence] — *Syn.* accident, fluke*, eventuality; see **accident** 2, **chance** 1, **event** 1.

**coincident,** *modif.* — *Syn.* coinciding, contemporary, concurring; see **simultaneous.**

**coincidental,** *modif.* **1.** [Occurring simultaneously] — *Syn.* concurrent, concomitant, contemporaneous; see **simultaneous.**

**2.** [Apparently accidental] — *Syn.* chance, casual, unplanned; see **accidental** 1.

**coitus,** *n.* — *Syn.* sexual intercourse, coition, union; see **copulation.**

**cold,** *modif.* **1.** [Said of the weather] — *Syn.* chilly, cool, crisp, icy, freezing, frigid, frosty, rimy, wintry, bleak, nippy, brisk, keen, inclement, penetrating, snowy, frozen, sleety, blasting, cutting, brumal, snappy, algid, gelid, piercing, chill, bitter, numbing, severe, boreal, stinging, glacial, intense, Siberian, sharp, raw, nipping, arctic, polar, below zero, biting; see also **wintry.** — *Ant.* warm, HOT, heated.

**2.** [Said of people, animals, or things] — *Syn.* freezing, frozen, clammy, stiff, chilled, frostbitten, shivering, chilly, cool, coldblooded, hypothermic, ice-cold, refrigerated, in cold storage, blue from cold*, chilled to the bone*. — *Ant.* HOT, perspiring, thawed.

**3.** [Said of temperament] — *Syn.* unresponsive, distant, unconcerned; see **aloof, indifferent** 1, **unfriendly** 2.

**cold,** *n.* **1.** [Absence of warmth] — *Syn.* coldness, frozenness, chilliness, frostiness, frost, nip, bitterness, rawness, crispness, briskness, draft, frostbite, chill, shivers, coolness, shivering, goose flesh, numbness, iciness, frigidity, freeze, glaciation, refrigeration, gelidity, congelation; see also **weather.** — *Ant.* warmth, HEAT, heat wave.

**2.** [The outdoors of a cold season] — *Syn.* frost, wintertime, snow; see **winter.**

**3.** [An aural or respiratory congestion] — *Syn.* head cold, common cold, flu, catarrh, rheum, cough, hack, sore throat, sinus trouble, cold on one's chest, bronchitis, ague, laryngitis, hay fever, grippe, influenza, rose fever, rose cold, asthma, whooping cough, pertussis, streptococcic throat, staphylococcic infection, virus, sinusitis, coryza, strep throat*, strep*, sniffles*, bug*, frog in one's throat*; see also **disease.**

**catch cold** — *Syn.* come down with a cold, become ill, take cold; see **sicken** 1.

**have** or **get cold feet*** — *Syn.* lose one's nerve, back down, have qualms, chicken out*; see **fear** 1, **retreat** 1.

**(out) in the cold*** — *Syn.* forgotten, ignored, rejected; see **neglected.**

**throw cold water on*** — *Syn.* dishearten, squelch, dampen; see **discourage** 1.

**cold-blooded,** *modif.* — *Syn.* relentless, pitiless, unfeeling; see **callous, cruel** 2.

**coliseum,** *n.* — *Syn.* stadium, open-air theater, amphitheater; see **arena, theater** 1.

**collaborate,** *v.* — *Syn.* work together, collude, team up; see **cooperate** 1, **help** 1.

**collaborator,** *n.* — *Syn.* partner, contributor, co-author, collaborationist; see **assistant, associate, traitor.**

**collage,** *n.* — *Syn.* photomontage, abstract composition, found art; see **picture** 3.

**collapse,** n. — Syn. breakdown, downfall, destruction, cave-in; see **failure** 1, **fall** 1, **illness** 1, **wreck** 1.

**collapse,** v. — Syn. drop, deflate, give way, crumple; see **fail** 1, **faint**, **fall** 1, 2, **give** 4.

**collar,** n. — Syn. neckband, neckpiece, ruff, frill, jabot, dickey, button-down collar, shawl collar, Vandyke collar, Eton collar, Peter Pan collar, bertha, clerical collar, torque; see also **clothes.**

**collar★,** v. — Syn. apprehend, capture, arrest, grab; see **arrest** 1, **seize** 2.

**collate,** v. 1. [To compare] — Syn. relate, juxtapose, compare point by point; see **compare** 2, **examine** 1.
2. [To check] — Syn. verify, group, assemble, organize, sort, merge; see also **order.**
See Synonym Study at COMPARE.

**collateral,** modif. 1. [Side by side] — Syn. parallel, lateral, coordinate, corresponding; see **parallel** 1.
2. [Accompanying] — Syn. concomitant, corroborative, supporting, ancillary; see **affirmative, simultaneous, subordinate.**

**collateral,** n. — Syn. security, guarantee, pledge, promise, financial promise, insurance, endorsement, warrant, deposit; see also **insurance, pledge, security** 2.

**collation,** n. — Syn. resemblance, examination, relation; see **comparison** 2, **relationship.**

**colleague,** n. — Syn. associate, co-worker, partner, collaborator; see **associate.**
See Synonym Study at ASSOCIATE.

**collect,** v. 1. [To bring into one place] — Syn. amass, consolidate, convoke, gather; see **accumulate** 1, **assemble** 2, **concentrate** 1.
2. [To come together] — Syn. gather, congregate, assemble, flock; see **gather** 1.
3. [To obtain funds] — Syn. solicit, raise, secure, call for; see **obtain** 1.
4. [To arrange settlement of a debt] — Syn. settle, manage, handle, receive payment, draw upon for, receive; see also **negotiate** 1, **receive** 1.
5. [To obtain specimens] — Syn. accumulate, get, assemble, make a collection; see **accumulate** 1.
See Synonym Study at GATHER.

**collected,** modif. 1. [Composed] — Syn. poised, self-possessed, cool, in control; see **calm** 1.
2. [Assembled] — Syn. accumulated, amassed, compiled; see **gathered.**
See Synonym Study at COOL.

**collection,** n. 1. [The act of collecting] — Syn. gathering, finding, making a collection, completing a collection, collecting, compilation, recovering, bringing together, searching for, assembling, amassing, compiling, acquisition, obtaining, securing, discovering, accumulating, acquiring, roundup; see also **accumulation** 1.
2. [That which has been collected] — Syn. accumulation, assortment, specimens, samples, examples, extracts, citations, models, corpus, agglomeration, pile, stack, group, assemblage, set, compilation, mass, quantity, selection, array, battery, treasury, anthology, omnibus, garland, medley, miscellany, hodgepodge, aggregation, combination, number, symposium, festschrift, ana, chrestomathy, compendium, collectanea, amassment, store, stock, cache, hoard, holdings, digest, arrangement, concentration, discoveries, finds, collation, batch, mess, lot, heap, bunch; see also **gathering, heap.**

**collective,** modif. — Syn. collected, combined, aggregate, group, cumulative, accumulated, gathered, concentrated, consolidated, common, cooperative, composite, concerted, corporate, joint, mutual, collectivist; see also **common** 5, **gathered.**

**collective,** n. — Syn. cooperative, collective unit, communistic project; see **cooperative, organization** 3.

**collectivism,** n. — Syn. communalism, cooperation, communization; see **communism, sharing, socialism.**

**collector,** n. 1. [One who collects accounts] — Syn. representative, collection agent, revenue agent, customs official, tax collector, tax officer, toll collector, bill collector, collection agency, office of internal revenue, revenue office, tax man, dun, exciseman (British), revenuer★; see also **agent** 1, **receiver.**
2. [One who collects specimens] — Syn. connoisseur, hobbyist, antiquarian, antiquary, authority, fancier, serious amateur, informed amateur, gatherer, discoverer, compiler, finder, assembler, amasser, accumulator, hoarder, anthologist, curator, librarian, pack rat★; see also **antiquarian, curator, scientist, specialist.**
Collectors include the following — of books: bibliophile, bibliopole, bibliotaph, bibliolater, bibliomaniac, bookworm★; of coins: coin collector, numismatist, specialist in numismatics; of eggs: oologist, egger, egg collector, specialist in oology, bird's egg fancier, devotee of egging, egg hound★; of human materials: archaeologist, historiographer, biographer, local historian, ethnologist, ethnographer, ethnographic specialist, specialist in ethnography, ethnohistorian, ethnolinguist, folklorist, curator of folkloristic materials, ethnobotanist; of insects: entomologist, entomographist, lepidopterist, entomographer, specialist in entomology, practitioner of entomology, practitioner of entomography, practitioner of lepidoptery, collector of bugs, collector of insects, collector of butterflies; of rocks: geologist, geognosist, mineralogist, geographer, rock hound★; of plants: botanist, herbalist, ecologist, paleobotanist, curator of a herbarium, curator of herbal collections, physiobotanist; of stamps: stamp collector, philatelist, philatelic dealer, philatelic specialist, expert in philately, specialist in philately.

**college,** n. — Syn. institute, professional school, university, community college, liberal arts college, teachers college, junior college, four-year college, state college, privately endowed college, denominational college, alma mater, seminary, conservatory, polytechnic, lyceum, hall; see also **school** 1, **university.**

**collide,** v. 1. [To come into violent contact] — Syn. hit, strike, smash; see **crash** 4.
2. [To come into conflict] — Syn. clash, conflict, disagree; see **oppose** 1.

**collision,** n. 1. [A violent meeting] — Syn. crash, impact, colliding, accident, contact, shock, encounter, bump, percussion, concussion, jar, jolt, sideswipe, strike, hit, slam, blow, thud, thump, knock, smash, foul, butt, rap, head-on collision, one-car accident, two-car accident, crackup, wreck, sideswipe, smashup, pileup★, fender bender★; see also **disaster.**
2. [A conflict] — Syn. clash, interference, discord, contention; see **disagreement** 1, **dispute.**

**collocate,** v. — Syn. arrange, set side by side, dispose; see **order** 3, **place** 1.

**colloquial,** modif. — Syn. conversational, informal, vernacular, everyday, casual, idiomatic, nonliterary, spoken, vulgar, slangy, demotic, koine, vulgate, ordinary, natural, native, relaxed, familiar, dialectal, regional, local, nonstandard, substandard; see also **common** 1.

**colloquialism,** n. — Syn. idiom, expression, informality; see **informality, jargon** 3, **language** 1.

**colloquy,** n. — Syn. debate, dialogue, conference; see **conversation, discussion** 1.

**collude,** *v.* — *Syn.* conspire, connive, intrigue, plot; see **cooperate** 1, **plan** 1.

**collusion,** *n.* — *Syn.* conspiracy, complicity, intrigue, plot; see **cooperation** 1, **intrigue** 1, **trick** 1.

**collusive,** *modif.* — *Syn.* deceitful, conniving, tricky; see **dishonest** 1, **false** 1, 2.

**colonial,** *modif.* **1.** [Concerning a colony] — *Syn.* pioneer, isolated, dependent, planted, transplanted, settled, provincial, frontier, imperial, imperialist, pre-Revolutionary, Pilgrim, emigrant, immigrant, territorial, outland, pioneering, daughter, mandated, early American, overseas, protectoral, Puritan, dominion, Anglo-Indian, subject; see also **distant** 2, **remote** 1.
**2.** [Having qualities suggestive of colonial life] — *Syn.* pioneer, hard, raw, crude, harsh, wild, unsettled, limited, uncultured, new, unsophisticated; see also **primitive** 3, **severe** 2. — *Ant.* old, CULTURED, decadent.

**colonist,** *n.* — *Syn.* settler, pilgrim, homesteader, colonial; see **pioneer** 2.

**colonization,** *n.* — *Syn.* immigration, pioneering, settlement, transplanting, founding, peopling, migration, group migration, clearing, expansion, establishment, forging a new home, conquest, subjugation, colonialism, expansionism, imperialism, hegemony.

**colonize,** *v.* — *Syn.* settle, plant, found, people, migrate, immigrate, transplant, pioneer, open a country, subjugate, conquer; see also **establish** 2, **settle** 7.

**colonnade,** *n.* — *Syn.* columns, portico, corridor, pillars, arcade, mezzanine, peristyle, peripteros, columniation, series, covered way, cloister, veranda, gallery, piazza; see also **column** 1.

**colony,** *n.* **1.** [A colonial area] — *Syn.* settlement, dependency, subject state, colonial state, dominion, offshoot, possession, political possession, mandate, province, new land, clearing, protectorate, territory, daughter country, satellite state, satellite province, community, group, group migration, hive, swarm, home in the wilderness; see also **nation** 1, **territory** 2.
**2.** [A colonial people or culture] — *Syn.* pioneers, colonists, forerunners, forefathers, antecedents, beginnings, early days; see also sense 1.

**color,** *n.* **1.** [The quality of reflected light] — *Syn.* hue, tone, shade, tinge, tint, pigment, chroma, tinct, luminosity, chromaticity, undertone, value, iridescence, intensity, polychromasia, colorimetric quality, coloration, discoloration, pigmentation, coloring, complexion, cast, glow, blush, wash, tincture; see also **tint.** — *Ant.* blackness, blankness, pallor.
Colors include — *colors in the solar spectrum:* red, orange, yellow, green, blue, indigo, violet; *physiological or additive primary colors:* red, green, blue; *psychological primary colors:* red, yellow, green, blue, black, white; *primary colors in painting:* red, blue, yellow; *achromatic colors:* black, white, gray; *secondary colors:* green, orange, violet; see also **black** 1, **blue** 1, **brown, gold** 1, **gray** 1, **green** 1, **orange, pink, purple, red, tan, yellow** 1.
**2.** [Vividness] — *Syn.* brilliance, intensity, piquancy, zest, freshness, liveliness, vitality, force, interest, local color, colorfulness, brightness, richness, glow. — *Ant.* drabness, DULLNESS, dimness.
**3.** [Semblance or pretense] — *Syn.* appearance, pretext, guise; see **appearance** 1, 2, **disguise, pretense** 1.
**call to the colors** — *Syn.* draft, conscript, enlist; see **enlist** 1, **recruit** 1.
**change color** — *Syn.* flush, redden, become red in the face; see **blush.**
**lose color** — *Syn.* become pale, blanch, faint; see **whiten** 1.

**under color of** — *Syn.* under the pretext of, pretending to be, disguised as; see **imitating, pretending.**

---

**SYN.** — **color** is the general term for the property of reflecting light of a particular wavelength, allowing the eye to distinguish red, orange, yellow, blue, etc.; **shade** refers to any of the gradations of a color with reference to its degree of darkness /a light *shade* of green/; **hue**, often equivalent to **color**, may more specifically indicate a modification of a basic color /a reddish *hue*/ ; in technical use, **hue** refers to the distinctive property of a color that enables it to be assigned a position in the spectrum; **tint** refers to a gradation of a color with reference to its degree of whiteness and suggests a paleness or delicacy of color /pastel *tints*/; **tinge** suggests the presence of a small amount of color, usually diffused throughout /white with a *tinge* of blue/

---

**color,** *v.* **1.** [To impart color to] — *Syn.* tint, dye, paint, stain, tinge, gloss, infuse, chalk, daub, gild, fresco, japan, enamel, lacquer, suffuse, stipple, variegate, pigment, distemper, glaze, tone, shade, wash, crayon, chrome, enliven, embellish, give color to, adorn, imbue, emblazon, illuminate, rouge; see also **decorate, paint** 1, 2. — *Ant.* bleach, FADE, deaden.
**2.** [To take on color] — *Syn.* blush, flush, redden, become rosy, turn red, bloom, glow, flame; see also **blush.** — *Ant.* pale, WHITEN, grow ashen.
**3.** [To misrepresent] — *Syn.* distort, pervert, slant; see **corrupt** 2, **influence.**

**color blindness,** *n.* — *Syn.* achromatopsia, achromatism, dichromatism, monochromatism, Daltonism, red-green blindness; see also **blindness** 1.

**colored,** *modif.* **1.** [Treated with color] — *Syn.* hued, tinted, tinged, shaded, flushed, reddened, glowing, stained, painted, dyed, washed, rouged, in color; see also **painted** 2, 3.
**2.** [*Belonging to a dark-skinned race] — *Syn.* brown, black, red, bronze, mulatto, melanistic, melanous; see also **black** 3, **Indian** 1, 2.
**3.** [Falsified] — *Syn.* misrepresented, perverted, tampered with, distorted; see **false** 2, 3.

**colorful,** *modif.* — *Syn.* vivid, picturesque, eventful, eccentric; see **bright** 1, 2, **interesting, multicolored, unusual** 2.

**colorless,** *modif.* — *Syn.* achromic, pale, neutral, characterless; see **dull** 2, 4, **pale** 1, **transparent** 1.

**colors,** *pl.n.* — *Syn.* banner, standard, symbol; see **emblem, flag** 1.

**colossal,** *modif.* — *Syn.* huge, enormous, immense; see **large** 1.
See Synonym Study at ENORMOUS.

**colossus,** *n.* — *Syn.* gigantic statue, Goliath, titan, leviathan; see **giant** 1, 2.

**colt,** *n.* — *Syn.* foal, filly, yearling, two-year-old, young horse; see also **horse** 1.

**coltish,** *modif.* — *Syn.* frisky, playful, lively; see **active** 2, **jaunty, sprightly.**

**column,** *n.* **1.** [A post] — *Syn.* pillar, support, prop, shaft, monument, totem, pylon, obelisk, stele, standard, tower, minaret, cylinder, mast, caryatid, telamon, peristyle, monolith, upright, pedestal, pilaster, pier; see also **post** 1.
Types of architectural columns include: fluted, plain, round, square, Egyptian, Doric, Greek, Corinthian, Ionic, Composite, Roman, Romanesque, Tuscan, Gothic.
**2.** [Journalistic commentary] — *Syn.* comment, feature

article, editorial, syndicated column; see **article** 2, **exposition** 2.

**3.** [A military formation] — *Syn.* single file, string, platoon, company; see **army** 2, **caravan, line** 1.

**columnist,** *n.* — *Syn.* journalist, correspondent, analyst, feature writer; see **reporter, writer.**

**coma,** *n.* — *Syn.* unconsciousness, trance, insensibility, catalepsy; see **stupor.**

**comatose,** *modif.* — *Syn.* insensible, lethargic, torpid, out cold*; see **listless** 1, **unconscious** 1.

**comb,** *n.* Combs include the following — hair comb, ivorycomb, currycomb, flax comb, carding knife, graining instrument; see also **brush** 1.

**comb,** *v.* — *Syn.* untangle, disentangle, brush, smooth, dress, groom, curry, scrape, arrange, rasp, straighten, hackle, hatchel, card, separate, pick, tease, back-comb, scour, ransack; see also **clean, rake** 1, **search.**

**combat,** *n.* — *Syn.* struggle, warfare, conflict, armed fighting; see **battle** 2, **fight** 1. action, duel
*See Synonym Study at* BATTLE. buck.

**combat,** *v.* — *Syn.* battle, oppose, resist, contend; see **fight** 2, **oppose** 2. repel, strife,

**combatant,** *n.* — *Syn.* belligerent, warrior, serviceman, servicewoman; see **fighter** 1, **soldier.**

**combination,** *n.* **1.** [The act of combining] — *Syn.* uniting, joining, unification, blending; see **incorporation** 2, **union** 1.

**2.** [An association] — *Syn.* union, alliance, federation; see **alliance** 3, **organization** 3.

**3.** [Something formed by combining] — *Syn.* compound, aggregate, blend; see **mixture** 1.

**4.** [Symbols used as a key] — *Syn.* order, sequence, succession; see **key** 2.

**combine,** *v.* **1.** [To bring together] — *Syn.* join, connect, couple, link; see **consolidate** 2, **join** 1.

**2.** [To become one] — *Syn.* fuse, merge, blend; see **mix** 1, **unite** 1.

*See Synonym Study at* JOIN.

**combined,** *modif.* — *Syn.* linked, mingled, connected; see **joined, mixed** 1.

**combining,** *modif.* — *Syn.* joining, linking, bringing together; see **connecting.**

**combustible,** *modif.* **1.** [Inflammable] — *Syn.* flammable, burnable, ignitable; see **inflammable.**

**2.** [Easily aroused] — *Syn.* passionate, fiery, volatile; see **excitable, irritable.**

**combustion,** *n.* **1.** [Burning] — *Syn.* flaming, kindling, oxidization; see **fire** 1.

**2.** [Violent disturbance] — *Syn.* tumult, agitation, turmoil; see **disturbance** 2, **excitement.**

**come,** *v.* **1.** [To move toward] — *Syn.* approach, close in, advance, draw near; see **approach** 1.

**2.** [To arrive] — *Syn.* appear, appear at, reach, attain; see **arrive** 1.

**3.** [To be available] — *Syn.* appear, be offered, be at one's disposal, be ready, be obtainable, be produced, show up, turn up, be procurable, appear on the market; see also **appear** 1, 3.

**4.** [To reach] — *Syn.* extend, expand, spread; see **reach** 1, **stretch** 3.

**5.** [To become] — *Syn.* evolve, develop, get, proceed; see **become** 1, **grow** 2.

**6.** [To be derived] — *Syn.* issue, emanate, arise, originate; see **appear** 1, **arise** 3, **begin** 2.

**7.** [To happen] — *Syn.* occur, take place, befall; see **happen** 2.

**8.** [*To have an orgasm] — *Syn.* climax, achieve orgasm, reach sexual fulfillment, ejaculate.

**how come?*** — *Syn.* for what reason? how so? what

is the cause of that* what is the reason for that?; see **why.**

**come about,** *v.* — *Syn.* happen, occur, take place, result; see **happen** 1, 2.

**come across,** *v.* **1.** [To find] — *Syn.* uncover, stumble upon, notice; see **discover, find** 1.

**2.** [*To do] — *Syn.* enact, fulfill, accomplish; see **achieve** 1, **perform** 1.

**3.** [*To give] — *Syn.* deliver, pay, part with, hand over; see **give** 1, **pay** 1.

**come again,** *v.* **1.** [To return] — *Syn.* come back, revisit, go back; see **return** 1.

**2.** [*To repeat; *used as a request*] — *Syn.* say that again, restate that, reiterate that; see **repeat** 3.

**come along,** *v.* **1.** [To accompany] — *Syn.* go with, attend, appear, turn up; see **accompany** 1, **appear** 1.

**2.** [To progress] — *Syn.* proceed, make progress, do well, get on; see **advance** 1, **improve** 2, **prosper.**

**come and get it***, *interj.* — *Syn.* grub's on, eat hearty, eat up, soup's on, chow down, dinner time, *bon appétit* (French).

**come around** or **round,** *v.* **1.** [To recover] — *Syn.* rally, revive, regain consciousness, come to; see **recover** 3, **revive** 2.

**2.** [*To visit] — *Syn.* call on, stop by, drop in on; see **visit** 4.

**3.** [To yield] — *Syn.* concede, accede, acquiesce; see **agree, consent, yield** 3.

**4.** [To turn] — *Syn.* veer, tack, change direction, come about; see **turn** 6.

**come at,** *v.* **1.** [To reach] — *Syn.* arrive at, attain, get at, ascertain; see **achieve** 2, **discover, succeed** 1, **touch** 2.

**2.** [To attack] — *Syn.* charge, assail, rush at, have at; see **attack** 1, 2, **reach** 2.

**comeback***, *n.* **1.** [A regaining of a former position] — *Syn.* recovery, revival, rally, triumph; see **improvement** 1, **recovery** 1, **victory** 1, 2.

**2.** [A witty answer] — *Syn.* retort, rejoinder, riposte; see **answer** 1.

**come back,** *v.* **1.** [To return] — *Syn.* come again, reappear, resurface, come to mind; see **return** 1.

**2.** [*To reply] — *Syn.* retort, rejoin, respond; see **answer** 1.

**3.** [*To recover] — *Syn.* do better, triumph, gain, make a comeback; see **improve** 2, **win** 1.

**comeback trail***, *n.* — *Syn.* revival, progress, betterment; see **improvement** 1, **recovery** 1.

**come between,** *v.* — *Syn.* intervene, interpose, divide, estrange; see **alienate, interrupt** 2, **separate** 2.

**come by,** *v.* **1.** [To pass] — *Syn.* go by, overtake, move past; see **pass** 1.

**2.** [To acquire] — *Syn.* get, win, procure; see **obtain** 1.

**comedian,** *n.* — *Syn.* comic, humorist, entertainer, comedienne; see **actor** 1, **clown.**

**comedown,** *n.* — *Syn.* reversal, blow, defeat; see **failure** 1, **fall** 1.

**come down,** *v.* — *Syn.* worsen, decline, suffer, go downhill; see **decrease** 1, **fail** 1, 4.

**come down on,** *v.* — *Syn.* rebuke, reprimand, land on*; see **censure, scold.**

**come down with,** *v.* — *Syn.* contract, catch, be stricken with; see **catch** 4.

**comedy,** *n.* — *Syn.* comic drama, burlesque, light entertainment; see **drama** 1, 2, **parody.**

Types of comedies include: high comedy, low comedy, satirical comedy, comedy of manners, musical comedy, situation comedy, sitcom, farce, skit, interlude, tragicomedy, play of wit, satire, travesty, burlesque; gag show*, laugh sensation*, slapstick*, funnies*.

**comedy of manners,** *n.* — *Syn.* light social satire, high comedy, play; see **drama** 1, **parody.**

Famous comedies of manners include — Goldsmith: *She Stoops to Conquer;* Sheridan: *School for Scandal, The Rivals;* Vanbrugh: *The Relapse, The Provok'd Wife;* Farquhar: *The Recruiting Officer, The Beaux' Stratagem;* Molière: *Les précieuses ridicules, Le bourgeois gentilhomme, Les femmes savantes;* Congreve: *The Way of the World, Love for Love.*

**come for,** *v.* — *Syn.* call for, accompany, come to get, come to collect; see **pick up** 6.

**come forward,** *v.* — *Syn.* offer oneself, step forward, make a proposal; see **volunteer** 2.

**come in,** *v.* **1.** [To enter] — *Syn.* pass in, set foot (in), intrude; see **enter** 1.

**2.** [To arrive] — *Syn.* reach, get in, land; see **arrive** 1, **land** 1, 3, 4.

**come in for*,** *v.* — *Syn.* get, be eligible for, be subject to; see **receive** 1.

**come into,** *v.* **1.** [To inherit] — *Syn.* fall heir to, succeed to, acquire; see **inherit, obtain** 1, **receive** 1.

**2.** [To join] — *Syn.* enter into, associate with, align; see **join** 2.

**comely,** *modif.* — *Syn.* pretty, pleasing, attractive, handsome; see **beautiful** 2, **handsome** 1.

*See Synonym Study at* BEAUTIFUL.

**come off,** *v.* **1.** [To become separated] — *Syn.* fall off, come apart, be disconnected, be disengaged, be severed, be parted, be disjoined, be detached, come unfastened, get loose, come undone; see also **break** 3, **disintegrate** 1.

**2.** [*To happen] — *Syn.* occur, transpire, come about; see **happen** 2.

**come on,** *v.* **1.** [To meet] — *Syn.* encounter, find, come across, come upon; see **discover, find** 1, **meet** 6.

**2.** [To progress] — *Syn.* proceed, develop, increase, gain; see **advance** 1, **improve** 2.

**3.** [To appear] — *Syn.* enter, begin, be broadcast, make an entrance; see **appear** 1, 3, **begin** 2, **enter** 1.

**come out,** *v.* **1.** [To be made public] — *Syn.* be published, be announced, be issued, be brought out, be promulgated, be reported, be revealed, be divulged, leak out, get out, be disclosed, be exposed, become evident, come out into the open, come out of the closet*; see also **appear** 1.

**2.** [To result] — *Syn.* end, conclude, terminate, turn out; see **achieve** 1, **result.**

**come out for,** *v.* — *Syn.* announce, affirm, endorse; see **declare** 1, **endorse** 2, **support** 2.

**come out with,** *v.* — *Syn.* declare, announce, disclose, bring out; see **admit** 2, **declare** 1, **publish** 1, **tell** 1.

**come over,** *v.* — *Syn.* take possession of, befall, overcome; see **affect** 1, **happen** 2, **seize** 1.

**comestibles,** *pl.n.* — *Syn.* food, edibles, foodstuffs, victuals; see **delicacy** 2, **food.**

**come through,** *v.* **1.** [To be successful] — *Syn.* accomplish, score, triumph; see **achieve** 1, **succeed** 1.

**2.** [To survive] — *Syn.* endure, live through, persist, withstand; see **endure** 2.

**3.** [To do] — *Syn.* accomplish, achieve, carry out; see **perform** 1.

**come to,** *v.* **1.** [To recover] — *Syn.* rally, revive, regain consciousness, come around; see **recover** 3, **revive** 2.

**2.** [To result in] — *Syn.* end in, terminate by, conclude by; see **happen** 2, **result.**

**3.** [To amount to] — *Syn.* add up to, total, equal; see

**amount to, cost** 1, **equal.**

**come up,** *v.* — *Syn.* arise, occur, be brought up, come to attention; see **appear** 1, **arise** 3, **happen** 1.

**come upon,** *v.* — *Syn.* encounter, locate, happen on, light upon; see **discover, find** 1, **meet** 6.

**come up to,** *v.* **1.** [To equal] — *Syn.* match, resemble, rank with; see **equal, rival.**

**2.** [To reach] — *Syn.* extend to, get to, come to, near; see **approach** 1, 2, **arrive** 1, **reach** 1.

**come up with,** *v.* **1.** [To propose] — *Syn.* suggest, recommend, offer; see **propose** 1.

**2.** [To find] — *Syn.* uncover, detect, stumble on; see **discover, find** 1.

**3.** [To produce] — *Syn.* supply, bring forth, originate; see **create** 2, **invent** 1, **produce** 2.

**comfort,** *n.* **1.** [A state of ease] — *Syn.* contentment, ease, well-being, rest, quiet, relaxation, repose, alleviation, relief, assuagement, poise, prosperity, opulence, cheer, snugness, abundance, sufficiency, gratification, luxury, warmth, plenty, creature comforts, amenities, satisfaction, satisfaction of bodily wants, coziness, pleasure, happiness, restfulness, peacefulness, cheerfulness, complacency, bed of roses*; see also **convenience** 2, **ease** 1, **enjoyment** 2, **satisfaction** 2. — *Ant.* discomfort, uneasiness, distress.

**2.** [Consolation] — *Syn.* solace, compassion, sympathy; see **pity** 1, **sympathy** 2.

**3.** [Anything that brings comfort] — *Syn.* help, support, succor; see **aid** 1, **encouragement** 2.

**comfort,** *v.* — *Syn.* console, soothe, solace, condole, commiserate, grieve with, compassionate, sympathize, share with, calm, pacify, compose, tranquilize, reassure, hearten, cheer, gladden, inspirit, revive, reanimate, bolster up, put at ease, make comfortable, relieve, alleviate, assuage, allay, mitigate, quiet one's fears, help one in need, lighten one's burden, grant respite, disburden, succor, sustain, support, uphold, encourage, invigorate, enhearten, give one a lift, renew, refresh, revitalize, revivify, strengthen, salve, warm, ameliorate, lighten, soften, abate, remedy, release, restore, pat on the back, hold one's hand, sit by, put in a good humor; see also **encourage** 2, **pity** 1, **sympathize.** — *Ant.* make uneasy, distress, afflict, discourage.

---

**SYN.** — **comfort** suggests the lessening of misery or grief by cheering, calming, or inspiring with hope; **console** suggests less positive relief but implies a moderation of the sense of loss or disappointment /to *console* someone on the death of a parent/; **solace** suggests the relieving of melancholy, boredom, or loneliness /I *solaced* myself with music/; **soothe** implies the calming or allaying of pain, distress, or agitation /to *soothe* a fretful child/

---

**comfortable,** *modif.* **1.** [In a state of ease] — *Syn.* contented, content, easy, relaxed, at ease, at rest, untroubled, rested, cheerful, happy, enjoying, pleased, satisfied, complacent, placid, tranquil, soothed, relieved, restored, healthy, free from pain, in comfort, at home, in one's element, without care, free from want, well off, well-to-do, affluent, prosperous, cared for, snug as a bug in a rug*; see also **rich** 1, **satisfied.** — *Ant.* uncomfortable, miserable, UNEASY, disturbed.

**2.** [Conducive to comfort or ease] — *Syn.* snug, cozy, restful, satisfactory, commodious, sheltered, convenient, protected, homey, homelike, lived-in, agreeable, pleasant, suitable, useful, roomy, spacious, palatial, fit to live in, well-made, luxurious, rich, satisfying, warm, balmy, soft, cushioned, easy, comfy*, cushy*, fit for

a king*; see also **pleasant** 2.— *Ant.* UNCOMFORTABLE, wretched, cramped, dismal.
**3.** [*Adequate] — *Syn.* sufficient, suitable, satisfactory, ample; see **enough** 1.

*SYN.* — **comfortable** implies the absence of disturbing, painful, or distressing features and, in a positive sense, stresses ease, contentment, or freedom from care [a *comfortable* climate]; **cozy** suggests such comfort as might be derived from shelter against storm or cold [a *cozy* nook by the fire]; **snug** is used of something that is small and compact, but just large enough to provide ease and comfort, and often also carries connotations of coziness [a *snug* apartment]; **restful** is applied to that which promotes relaxation and freedom from stress [*restful* music]

**comfortably,** *modif.* — *Syn.* luxuriously, in comfort, restfully, snugly, cozily, reposefully, pleasantly, agreeably, warmly, conveniently, adequately, amply, easily, with ease; see also **easily** 1.— *Ant.* INADEQUATELY, insufficiently, poorly.
**comforter,** *n.* **1.** [A person or thing that comforts] — *Syn.* consoler, pacifier, sympathizer; see **friend** 1.
**2.** [A quilted bed covering] — *Syn.* quilt, duvet, coverlet; see **bedding, bedspread, quilt.**
**comforting,** *modif.* — *Syn.* cheering, encouraging, consoling, inspiriting, heartening, warming, solacing, consolatory, sustaining, reassuring, refreshing, upholding, succoring, relieving, soothing, assuaging, lightening, mitigating, alleviating, allaying, abating, softening, remedying, analeptic, curing, therapeutic, restoring, releasing, revitalizing, revivifying, tranquilizing, supportive; see also **sympathetic.** — *Ant.* DISTURBING, distressing, upsetting.
**comfortless,** *modif.* — *Syn.* forlorn, desolate, cold; see **dismal** 1.
**comic,** *modif.* — *Syn.* funny, ridiculous, humorous, ironic; see **funny** 1.
*See Synonym Study at* FUNNY.
**comical,** *modif.* — *Syn.* funny, droll, amusing, humorous; see **funny** 1.
*See Synonym Study at* FUNNY.
**coming,** *modif.* **1.** [Approaching] — *Syn.* advancing, drawing near, impending, next, forthcoming, upcoming, near, nearing, in the offing, arriving, oncoming, incoming, progressing, gaining on, closing, in, pursuing, running after, getting near, catching up, near at hand, close at hand, almost on one, converging, immediate, future, in view, imminent, preparing, to come, following, instant, predestined, eventual, fated, written, hereafter, at hand, in store, due, about to happen, looked for, hoped for, deserving, owed, close, in prospect, prospective, anticipated, subsequent, certain, ordained, to be, expected, en route, pending, looming, threatening, foreseen, lying ahead, at one's back*, on the horizon*, in the wind*; see also **approaching, expected** 2, **future, imminent.** — *Ant.* going, DISTANT, past.
**2.** [Having a promising future] — *Syn.* promising, up-and-coming, marked, full of promise, on the way to fame, on the way to success, aspiring, progressing, improving one's position, advancing, in the ascendant, likely, probable, giving grounds for expectations, brilliant, hopeful, auspicious, encouraging, making strides, on the way up; see also **able** 1, 2, **ambitious** 1.— *Ant.* unpromising, HOPELESS, discouraging.
**coming,** *n.* — *Syn.* approach, arrival, advent, reception; see **arrival** 1.
**command,** *n.* **1.** [An order] — *Syn.* injunction, direc-

tion, directive, dictation, demand, decree, ultimatum, prohibition, interdiction, canon, rule, call, summons, imposition, precept, mandate, charge, behest, edict, proclamation, instruction, proscription, ban, adjuration, requirement, dictate, subpoena, commandment, dictum, word of command, writ, citation, imperative, notification, will, regulation, ordinance, law, act, fiat, bidding, word, requisition, request, exaction, enactment, order of the day, caveat, prescript, warrant; see also **law** 3, **request.** — *Ant.* countermand, revocation, retraction.
**2.** [The power to issue orders] — *Syn.* authority, control, leadership, mastery, sway, domination, dominion, sovereignty, rule, coercion, compulsion, constraint, restraint, hold, grasp, grip, charge, direction, management, prerogative, right, headship, warrant, authorization, supremacy, primacy, suzerainty, jurisdiction, absolutism, despotism, tyranny, ascendancy, lead, supervision, predominance, government, rulership, superintendence, directorship, presidency, empire, lordship, royalty; see also **administration** 1, **power** 2.
**3.** [Ability to use] — *Syn.* mastery, expertise, facility, grasp; see **ability** 2, **mastery** 2.
**4.** [An area or group subject to orders] — *Syn.* unit, squad, group, company, battalion, regiment, division, army, air command, post, fort, camp, garrison, brigade, platoon, corps, battery, administrative and tactical unit, sector, field of command, vanguard, rear, center, left flank, right flank, area under a commander, station under a commander; see also **army** 2.
*See Synonym Study at* POWER.
**command,** *v.* **1.** [To issue an order] — *Syn.* order, bid, charge, direct, instruct, authorize, enjoin, dictate, decree, proscribe, prescribe, tell, forbid, demand, restrain, check, prohibit, interdict, inhibit, ban, bar, rule, rule out, debar, call, summon, ordinate, mandate, cite, set, require, impose, exact, appoint, commission, give orders, give directions, proclaim, issue a command, call to order, send for, beckon, send on a mission, force upon, call on, call upon, take charge, take the lead, enact, ordain, order with authority, make a requisition, task, inflict, compel, adjure, subpoena, warrant, call for, state authoritatively, lay down the law*, call the shots*, boss around*, put one's foot down*, say the word*; see also **require** 2.— *Ant.* OBEY, submit, follow.
**2.** [To have control] — *Syn.* direct, rule, govern, dominate, overrule, have sway, determine, override, control, master, conquer, guide, lead, have the ascendancy, compel, conduct, administer, supervise, superintend, run, reign, have authority over, overbear, coach, head, dictate, exact, restrain, check, manage, curb, have at one's bidding, have at one's disposal, hold, hold back, force, wield influence, carry authority, be the head of, boss, predominate, preside over, reign over, oppress, tyrannize, repress, prevail, exercise power over, domineer, lord it, constrain, hinder, subdue, prevail over, push, coerce, be master of, oppress, have superiority over, have dominion over, require, oblige, shepherd, captain, train, limit, hold office, occupy a post, officiate, chair, take possession of, impel, drive, move, regulate, have the deciding voice, take charge of, have charge of, take over, take in hand, keep in hand, take the reins, hold the reins, be the boss of, rule the roost*, crack the whip*, run the show*, be in the saddle, be in the driver's seat*, wrap around one's finger*, have the upper hand*, have the whip hand*, call the shots*; see also **govern, manage** 1.

*SYN.* — **command,** when it refers to a giving of orders, implies the formal exercise of absolute authority, as by a sovereign or military leader; **order** often stresses peremptoriness, sometimes suggesting an arbitrary exercise of authority /I *ordered* them out of the house/; **direct** and **instruct** are both used in connection with supervision, as in business relations, **instruct** perhaps more often stressing explicitness of details in the directions given; **enjoin** suggests a directing with urgent admonition /he *enjoined* us to secrecy/ and sometimes implies a legal prohibition /the company was *enjoined* from using false advertising/; **charge** implies the imposition of a task as a duty, trust, or responsibility

---

**commandeer,** *v.* **1.** [To force into military service] — *Syn.* draft, conscript, activate; see **enlist** 1, **enslave, recruit** 1.
**2.** [To seize for public use] — *Syn.* appropriate, sequester, confiscate; see **seize** 2.
**commander,** *n.* — *Syn.* commandant, commanding officer, head; see **administration** 2, **administrator, chief** 1, **leader** 2, **officer** 3.
**commanding,** *modif.* **1.** [Imposing] — *Syn.* authoritative, dominant, dictatorial, imperious; see **absolute** 3, **autocratic** 1, **masterful, powerful** 1.
**2.** [In command] — *Syn.* in charge, at the helm, at the head, chief; see **administrative, governing, managing, powerful** 1.
**commanding,** *n.* — *Syn.* leading, directing, controlling, steering, guiding, determining, ordering, charging, ruling, enjoining, decreeing, instructing, dictating, forbidding, issuing, dominating, overruling, compelling, managing, checking, curbing, forcing, coercing, requiring, restraining, having dominion over, being in command, being in authority, regulating; see also **command** 2, **government** 1. — *Ant.* obeying, YIELDING, submitting.
**commemorate,** *v.* — *Syn.* solemnize, honor, memorialize; see **admire** 1, **celebrate** 1, **remember** 1.
*See Synonym Study at* CELEBRATE.
**commemoration,** *n.* — *Syn.* recognition, remembrance, observance; see **celebration** 1, **ceremony** 2, **custom** 2.
**commemorative,** *modif.* — *Syn.* dedicatory, commemorating, in honor of, observing; see **memorial.**
**commence,** *v.* — *Syn.* start, enter upon, originate, initiate; see **begin** 1, 2.
*See Synonym Study at* BEGIN.
**commencement,** *n.* **1.** [A beginning] — *Syn.* genesis, start, initiation; see **origin** 1.
**2.** [Graduation ceremony] — *Syn.* convocation, graduation, commencement exercises, services; see **celebration** 1, 2, **ceremony** 2, **graduation.**
**commend,** *v.* **1.** [To praise] — *Syn.* laud, compliment, support, acclaim; see **admire** 1, **approve** 1, 2, **praise** 1.
**2.** [To recommend] — *Syn.* accredit, sanction, advocate; see **approve** 1, **recommend** 1.
**3.** [To present with confidence] — *Syn.* entrust, consign, confer; see **assign** 1, **trust** 3.
**commendable,** *modif.* — *Syn.* praiseworthy, laudable, deserving; see **excellent, worthy.**
**commendation,** *n.* **1.** [Approbation] — *Syn.* tribute, approval, acclamation, approbation; see **honor** 1, **praise** 1, **recommendation** 1, **tribute** 1.
**2.** [A tribute] — *Syn.* citation, honor, award; see **praise** 2, **prize.**
**commendatory,** *modif.* — *Syn.* laudatory, praising, approving, recommending; see **complimentary.**
**commensurate,** *modif.* — *Syn.* comparable, equivalent, proportionate, corresponding; see **alike** 2, **equal.**
**comment,** *n.* **1.** [An explanatory or critical note] — *Syn.*

annotation, footnote, criticism, commentary; see **explanation** 2, **judgment** 3, **remark.**
**2.** [A remark] — *Syn.* observation, judgment, animadversion; see **remark.**
*See Synonym Study at* REMARK.
**comment,** *v.* **1.** [To make a remark] — *Syn.* observe, remark, criticize, note, notice, state, express, pronounce, assert, affirm, mention, interject, say, touch upon, remark upon, discuss, explain, expound, interpose, reflect, disclose, bring out, opine, editorialize, point out, conclude, commentate; see also **say, talk** 1, **utter.**
**2.** [To annotate] — *Syn.* illustrate, elucidate, clarify; see **explain.**
**commentary,** *n.* **1.** [An exposition] — *Syn.* discourse, critique, editorial, analysis; see **explanation** 2, **exposition** 2, **review** 2.
**2.** [A comment] — *Syn.* criticism, explication, annotation, remark; see **explanation** 2, **remark.**
*See Synonym Study at* REMARK.
**commentator,** *n.* — *Syn.* observer, analyst, pundit; see **author** 2, **critic** 2, **reporter, writer.**
**commerce,** *n.* — *Syn.* buying and selling, trade, business, dealing; see **business** 1, **economics.**
*See Synonym Study at* BUSINESS.
**commercial,** *modif.* **1.** [Concerning commerce] — *Syn.* business, trade, financial, economic, mercantile, merchandising, marketing, industrial, pecuniary, fiscal, monetary, market, sales, trading, bartering, exchange, jobbing, supplying, retail, retailing, wholesale, wholesaling, marketable, in the market, for sale, over the counter, Wall Street; see also **industrial.**
**2.** [Intended primarily for financial gain] — *Syn.* monetary, for profit, pecuniary, mercenary, materialistic, investment, marketable, salable, popular, mass-produced, profit-making, money-making; see also **practical, profitable.**
**commercial,** *n.* — *Syn.* message from the sponsor, commercial announcement, plug*; see **advertisement** 2.
**commercialize,** *v.* **1.** [To adapt to business] — *Syn.* make marketable, market, make salable, make pay, make profitable, make bring returns, develop as a business, capitalize, cash in on, popularize; see also **advertise** 2, **profit** 2, **sell** 1.
**2.** [To cheapen] — *Syn.* lessen, degrade, lower the quality; see **cheapen, corrupt** 1.
**commination,** *n.* — *Syn.* ban, curse, malediction, condemnation, imprecation, anathema, execration, diatribe, excommunication, threatening, obloquy, threat of punishment, damaging imputation, proscription, denunciation, denouncing as evil; see also **blame** 1, **curse** 1.
**commingle,** *v.* — *Syn.* blend, unite, mingle, intermix; see **mix** 1.
**commiserate,** *v.* — *Syn.* share sorrow, condole, console, empathize; see **pity** 1, **sympathize.**
**commiseration,** *n.* — *Syn.* consolation, compassion, sympathy; see **pity** 1.
*See Synonym Study at* PITY.
**commissary,** *n.* — *Syn.* deputy, representative, legate; see **agent** 1.
**commission,** *n.* **1.** [The act of committing] — *Syn.* delegation, empowering, charging, sending, deputizing, deputation, authorizing, assignment, entrusting, commitment, committing, perpetration, performance, handing over, making over, authorization, engagement, employment, contracting, nomination, appointment, ordaining, ordination, accrediting, investiture, constitution, inauguration, coronation.

**2.** [An authorization] — *Syn.* order, license, command, charge; see **mandate, permission.**

**3.** [A duty] — *Syn.* work, function, obligation, assignment; see **duty** 2, **job** 2.

**4.** [A committee] — *Syn.* commissioners, representatives, board, council; see **committee.**

**5.** [A payment] — *Syn.* fee, percentage, remuneration, royalty, salary, stipend, share, portion, cut\*, rake-off\*; see also **pay** 2, **payment** 1.

**out of commission** — *Syn.* damaged, not working, out of order, disabled; see **broken** 2.

**commission,** *v.* — *Syn.* authorize, appoint, charge, delegate, deputize, empower, accredit, license, order, contract for, requisition, request, send, depute, constitute, ordain, commit, entrust, give in charge, dispatch, consign, assign, entrust with a mission, charge with an errand, confide to, engage, employ, invest, name, nominate, hire, bespeak, enable, command, elect, select; see also **approve** 1.

*SYN.* — **commission** a person is to authorize as well as instruct to perform a certain duty, as the execution of an artistic work, or to appoint to a certain rank or office; **authorize** implies the giving of power or the right to act, ranging in application from a specific legal power to discretionary powers in dealings of any kind; to **accredit**, in this comparison, implies the sending of a person, duly authorized and with the proper credentials, as an ambassador, delegate, etc.; **license** implies the giving of formal legal permission to do some specified thing and often emphasizes regulation /to *license* hunters/

**commissioner,** *n.* — *Syn.* agent, magistrate, government official, chief of police; see **administrator, agent** 1.

**commit,** *v.* **1.** [To perform] — *Syn.* perpetrate, do, act, carry out; see **perform** 1.

**2.** [To give in charge] — *Syn.* entrust, confide, consign, delegate, relegate, leave to, give to do, turn over, assign, head over, put in the hands of, allot, charge, invest, allocate, apportion, rely upon, depend upon, confer a trust, bind over, make responsible for, pledge, bind, oblige, obligate, constrain, make another's duty, empower, employ, dispatch, send, vest in, authorize, deputize, engage, commission, depute, convey, put in custody, institutionalize, confine, imprison, lock up\*, put away\*; see also **assign** 1, **imprison.**

**commit suicide** — *Syn.* kill oneself, take one's own life, take an overdose (of any dangerous drug), slash one's wrists, shoot oneself, slit one's own throat, do away with oneself, die by one's own hand, commit hara-kiri, commit seppuku, end it all\*, throw in the towel\*, pack it in\*, blow one's brains out\*.

*SYN.* — **commit,** the basic term here, implies the delivery of a person or thing into the charge or keeping of another; **entrust** and **confide** imply committal based on trust and confidence, with, **confide** sometimes also suggesting the private nature of what is entrusted; **consign** suggests formal action in transferring something to another's possession or control; **relegate** implies assigning to a specific class, sphere, place, etc., esp. one of inferiority, and usually suggests the literal or figurative removal of something undesirable

**commitment,** *n.* **1.** [An obligation] — *Syn.* pledge, responsibility, engagement, assurance; see **duty** 1, 2, **promise** 1.

**2.** [Committedness] — *Syn.* dedication, devotion, involvement, engagement; see **devotion, loyalty.**

**3.** [An act of committing] — *Syn.* committal, consignment, institutionalization; see **confinement** 1, **delegation** 1.

**committed,** *modif.* — *Syn.* dedicated, devoted, pledged; see **active** 2, **bound** 2, **enthusiastic** 2, **faithful.**

**committee,** *n.* — *Syn.* board, bureau, council, panel, consultants, investigators, trustees, advisory group, task force, board of inquiry, appointed group, cabinet, representatives, investigative committee, study group, executive committee, standing committee, planning board, commission, ad hoc committee, special committee, jury, grand jury, referees, deliberative body, court, convocation, subcommittee, delegation, chamber, soviet; see also **delegate, jury, organization** 3, **representative** 2.

**in committee** — *Syn.* under consideration, being weighed, being evaluated, not settled; see **considered** 1.

**commode,** *n.* **1.** [A piece of furniture] — *Syn.* chest of drawers, cabinet, washstand, dressing table; see **chest** 1, **furniture, table** 1.

**2.** [Toilet] — *Syn.* chamber pot, water closet, potty chair\*; see **toilet** 2.

**commodious,** *modif.* — *Syn.* ample, spacious, roomy; see **comfortable** 2, **enough** 1, **large** 1.

**commodity,** *n.* [*Often plural*] — *Syn.* goods, article(s), merchandise, wares, materials, products, possessions, property, chattel, assets, belongings, item(s), thing(s), specialty, stock, stock in trade, consumers' goods, staples, line, what one handles.

**common,** *modif.* **1.** [Commonplace] — *Syn.* ordinary, everyday, familiar, usual, general, universal, natural, normal, accepted, characteristic, customary, prevalent, current, prevailing, typical, conventional, routine, prosaic, trite, banal, hackneyed, overused, stock, stale, worn thin, worn-out, homely, colloquial, nonliterary, vernacular, vulgar, popular, of the folk, of the masses, plebeian, humble, lowly, workaday, provincial, unsophisticated, average, passable, undistinguished, informal, conformable, probable, basic, simple, unvaried, trivial, oft-repeated, monotonous, tedious, wearisome, casual, unassuming, bourgeois, Philistine, uneducated, artless, unrefined, untutored, plain, homespun, unadorned, uncultured, slangy, platitudinous, truistic, obvious, quotidian, orthodox, traditional, standard, mediocre, second-rate, insipid, stereotyped, patent, moderate, middling, abiding, indifferent, pedestrian, tolerable, innocuous, unremarkable, nondescript, mere, so-so, not too bad, run-of-the-mill\*, humdrum\*, garden variety\*, household\*, warmed-over\*, fair-to-middling\*, low-level\*, nothing to write home about\*, no great shakes\*, *comme ci, comme ca*\* (French), a dime a dozen\*; see also **colloquial, conventional** 1, **dull** 4, **fair** 2, **popular** 1, 3, **traditional** 2. — *Ant.* unusual, unnatural, UNIQUE, extraordinary.

**2.** [Of frequent occurrence] — *Syn.* customary, constant, usual; see **frequent, habitual** 1, **regular** 3.

**3.** [Generally known] — *Syn.* general, prevalent, well-known; see **familiar** 1, **traditional** 2.

**4.** [Low] — *Syn.* cheap, inferior, mean, vulgar; see **poor** 2, **subordinate, vulgar** 1.

**5.** [Held or enjoyed in common] — *Syn.* shared, joint, mutual, communal, public, community, cooperative, united, belonging equally to, collective, reciprocal, coincident, correspondent, collaborative, consensual, general, socialistic, communistic, in common, commutual; see also **cooperative** 2, **public** 2, **universal** 3. — *Ant.* PRIVATE, individual, personal.

**in common**— *Syn.* shared, communal, mutually held, commonly held; see **common 5**.

---

*SYN.* — **common** refers to that which is met with most frequently or is shared by all or most individuals in a group, body, etc., and may imply prevalence, usualness, or, in a depreciatory sense, inferiority or lack of distinction *[a common* belief, a *common* thief*]*; **general** implies connection with all or nearly all of a kind, class, or group and stresses extensiveness *[general* unrest among the people*]*; **ordinary** implies accordance with the regular or customary pattern; stressing commonplaceness and lack of special distinction *[an ordinary* workday*]*; **familiar** applies to that which is widely known and readily recognized *[a familiar* feeling*]*; **popular** and, in this connection, **vulgar** imply widespread currency or acceptance among the general public or the common people *[popular* tastes, *Vulgar* Latin*]*, with **popular** also used to indicate favor *[a popular* song*]*; **vulgar**, however, is rarely used now in this sense without pejorative connotations *See also Synonym Study at* MUTUAL.

---

**commoner,** *n.* — *Syn.* plebeian, bourgeois, bourgeoise, common man, civilian, citizen, peasant, little man, member of the rank and file; see also **citizen.**
**commonly,** *modif.* — *Syn.* usually, ordinarily, generally; see **regularly 1**.
**commonplace,** *modif.* — *Syn.* usual, hackneyed, trite, mundane; see **common 1, conventional 1, dull 4**.
*See Synonym Study at* TRITE.
**commonplace,** *n.* — *Syn.* truism, triteness, platitude; see **cliché, motto.**
*See Synonym Study at* CLICHÉ.
**commons,** *n.* — *Syn.* dining hall, canteen, mess hall; see **dining room, restaurant.**
**common-sense,** *modif.* — *Syn.* sensible, sound, rational; see **judicious, practical, reasonable 1, 2**.
**common sense,** *n.* — *Syn.* good sense, practicality, horse sense*; see **judgment 1, sense 2, wisdom 2**.
**commonwealth,** *n.* **1.** [The body politic] — *Syn.* the people, commonality, polity; see **nation 1, population.**
**2.** [A republic] — *Syn.* federation, democracy, constitutional government; see **republic.**
**commotion,** *n.* — *Syn.* disturbance, bustle, tumult, uproar; see **confusion 2, disorder 2, disturbance 2, uproar.**
**communal,** *modif.* — *Syn.* shared, public, mutual, collective; see **common 5, cooperative 2**.
**commune,** *n.* — *Syn.* collective, cooperative, community, village, municipality, congregate housing; see also **city, cooperative, neighborhood.**
**communicable,** *modif.* — *Syn.* transmittable, infectious, transferable; see **catching, contagious.**
**communicate,** *v.* **1.** [To impart, as information] — *Syn.* make known, convey, impart, inform, tell, express, advise, notify, acquaint, pass on, pass along, give, hand on, carry, transmit, transfer, write, send word, leave word, bestow, promulgate, broadcast, telecast, announce, state, sign, publish, print, publicize, advertise, divulge, disclose, reveal, enlighten, picture, telephone, phone, call in, telegraph, televise, radio, cable, fax, comment, instill, deliver, enunciate, bring word, get across, put across, emit, dictate, say, assert, apprise, utter, describe, enlighten, articulate, narrate, remark, hint, demonstrate, relate, recite, proclaim, insinuate, mention, give one to understand, call attention to, impress upon the mind, lay before, put into one's head, instruct, point out, blurt out, speak out, pour out, shout,

come out with, observe, allege, pronounce, set forth, put forth, give voice to, drop a hint, signal, wigwag, tip*, let fall*, breathe*; see also **declare 1, notify 1, report 1, teach 1, tell 1**.— *Ant.* conceal, CENSOR, keep secret.
**2.** [To be in communication] — *Syn.* be in touch, talk, correspond, have access to, reach, hear from, be within reach, be in correspondence with, be near, be close to, have the confidence of, associate with, commune with, be congenial with, establish contact with, maintain contact with, be in agreement with, confer, converse, confabulate, chat, convey thoughts, discourse together, speak together, deal with, have dealings with, relate, make contact, make advances, write, telephone, call up, fax, wire, cable, have interchange of thoughts, interact, interface, have a meeting of minds, find a common denominator; see also **agree.**— *Ant.* be out of touch, DIFFER, be removed from.
**communication,** *n.* **1.** [The giving or exchanging of information] — *Syn.* speech, talk, utterance, announcement, revelation, conversation, discussion, dialogue, discourse, conference, contact, connection, communion, rapport, dissemination, conveyance, making known, imparting, informing, advisement, notification, acquainting, disclosing, discovering, telling, submitting, delivery, correspondence, disclosure, speaking, description, exposition, pronouncement, mention, presentation, interaction, interchange, intercourse, dealings, interface, expression, narration, relation, declaration, assertion, articulation, elucidation, transfer, transmission, spreading, telepathy, extrasensory perception, ESP, publication, writing, picturing, signaling, signing, broadcasting, passing on, getting across, translating, interpreting; see also **conversation, speech 2**.— *Ant.* concealment, CENSORSHIP, withholding.
Means of communication include: book, letter, electronic mail, E-mail, voice mail, newspaper, magazine, radio, proclamation, broadcast, dispatch, radio report, telecast, telephone call, telegram, facsimile, fax, cable, radiogram, broadside, circular, notes, memorandum, post card, picture post card, poster, billboard; see also **journal 2, news 2, report 1, 2**.
**2.** [Transmitted information] — *Syn.* message, news, ideas, announcement, statement, disclosure, utterance, speech, language, warning, revelation, prophecy, communiqué, briefing, bulletin, dispatch, excerpt, précis, summary, information, report, account, declaration, publicity, translation, (printed) work, advice, intelligence, tidings, conversation, converse, letter, note, fax.
**communications,** *n.* Means and systems of promoting communication include: post office, telegraph, telex, cable, wireless, mass media, television, communications satellite, COMSAT, Telstar, computer, radar, airmail, telephone, modem, beeper, pager, wireless telephone, cellular telephone, wireless telegraph, Internet, dictaphone, address system, PBX, loudspeaker, teletype, two-way radio; intercom*, ship-to-shore*, shore-to-ship*, walkie-talkie*; see also **mail, radar, telephone, television, radio 1, 2**.
**communicative,** *modif.* — *Syn.* forthcoming, voluble, loquacious, unreserved; see **frank*, informative, talkative.**
**communion,** *n.* **1.** [Association] — *Syn.* fellowship, accord, union, sharing; see **agreement 2, association 1, communication 1, fellowship 2**.
**2.** [A Christian sacrament] — *Syn.* Holy Communion, Lord's Supper, Breaking of Bread, Eucharist; see **sacrament.**

**communiqué,** *n.* — *Syn.* official communication, bulletin, dispatch, report; see **announcement** 2, **communication** 2.

**communism,** *n.* — *Syn.* state socialism, Marxism, Marxism-Leninism, Bolshevism, Stalinism, Leninism, dictatorship of the proletariat, collectivism, state ownership of production, equal distribution of wealth; see also **socialism.**
Terms for communist organizations include: Communist Party, The Party, Comintern, The Third International, Red International, Maoism, Castroism, Titoism.

**communist,** *n.* [*Often capital* C] — *Syn.* card-carrying communist, Party member, comrade, fellow traveler, member of the Communist Party, C.P. member, apparatchik, sympathizer, Marxist, Socialist, Bolshevik, Bolshevist, Trotskyite, Leninist, Stalinist, Maoist, Viet Cong, Castroite, Soviet, revisionist, *comunista* (Spanish), Commie*, Red*, com-symp*, pinko*, Bolshie*; see also **agitator, radical.** — *Ant.* fascist, CONSERVATIVE, capitalist.

**communistic,** *modif.* — *Syn.* communist, Bolshevist, red*; see **radical** 2, **revolutionary** 1.

**community,** *modif.* — *Syn.* joint, group, cooperative; see **common** 5, **public** 1, 2.

**community,** *n.* 1. [Society] — *Syn.* the public, the people, the nation, citizenry, inhabitants, cultural group, ethnic group, occupational group, social unit, fellowship, alliance; see also **association** 1, **population, society** 2.
2. [A locality] — *Syn.* neighborhood, district, locale, center; see **area** 2, **city, neighborhood, town** 1, **village.**
3. [Similarity] — *Syn.* likeness, sameness, identity; see **agreement** 2, **similarity.**

**commutation,** *n.* — *Syn.* substitution, replacement, compensation; see **change** 1, 2, **exchange** 1, 3.

**commute,** *v.* 1. [To change one thing for or into another] — *Syn.* interchange, change, substitute, transform; see **change** 1, **exchange** 1, 2.
2. [To exchange for something less severe] — *Syn.* reduce, alleviate, mitigate; see **decrease** 2.
3. [To travel] — *Syn.* go back and forth, drive, take the subway, shuttle; see **travel** 2.

**commuter,** *n.* — *Syn.* suburbanite, city worker, daily traveler, straphanger*; see **driver, passenger.**

**compact,** *modif.* — *Syn.* compressed, condensed, dense, small; see **short** 2, **snug** 1, **thick** 1, 3.
*See Synonym Study at* THICK.

**compact,** *n.* 1. [A small cosmetic case] — *Syn.* vanity case, vanity, makeup case, powder case, powder and rouge box; see also **case** 7, **container.**
2. [An agreement] — *Syn.* pact, contract, covenant; see **agreement** 3, **treaty.**

**companion,** *n.* 1. [An associate] — *Syn.* friend, partner, mate, comrade; see **associate, friend** 1, **mate** 2.
2. [One who accompanies another] — *Syn.* attendant, escort, chaperon, nurse, practical nurse, home health aide, governess, matron, safeguard, protector, guide, convoy.
*See Synonym Study at* ASSOCIATE.

**companionable,** *modif.* — *Syn.* cordial, sociable, amicable; see **friendly** 1, **social** 2.

**companionship,** *n.* — *Syn.* company, camaraderie, fellowship, rapport; see **association** 1, **brotherhood** 1, **fellowship** 1, **friendship** 1.

**company,** *n.* 1. [Associates] — *Syn.* group, club, troop, fellowship; see **organization** 3.
2. [A group of people] — *Syn.* assembly, throng, band; see **gathering.**

3. [People organized for business] — *Syn.* partnership, firm, corporation; see **business** 4.
4. [Social intercourse] — *Syn.* friendly intercourse, society, companionship; see **association** 1, **fellowship** 1.
5. [A guest or guests] — *Syn.* visitor(s), caller(s), overnight guest(s), unexpected guest(s), boarder(s); see also **guest** 1.
*See Synonym Study at* TROOP.

**keep (a person) company** — *Syn.* stay with, visit, amuse; see **accompany** 1, **entertain** 1, **visit** 2.

**keep company** — *Syn.* go together, go steady, associate with; see **accompany** 1, **associate** 1, **date** 2.

**part company** — *Syn.* separate, part, break with, fall out; see **leave** 1, **oppose** 1.

**comparable,** *modif.* 1. [Worthy of comparison] — *Syn.* as good as, equivalent, tantamount; see **equal.**
2. [Capable of comparison] — *Syn.* similar, akin, analogous, relative; see **alike** 2, **like.**

**comparative,** *modif.* — *Syn.* comparable, relative, correlative, corresponding, connected, metaphorical, allusive, similar, analogous, parallel, contrastive, near, close to, approaching, in proportion, matching, rivaling, vying, not positive, not absolute, with reservations, approximate, contingent, restricted, inconclusive, provisional, qualified; see also **conditional, like, related** 2. — *Ant.* ABSOLUTE, exact, unrelated, dissimilar.

**comparatively,** *modif.* — *Syn.* relatively, similarly, analogously; see **approximately, relatively.**

**compare,** *v.* 1. [To regard as similar] — *Syn.* relate, connect, liken, note the similarities, draw a comparison, make a comparison, associate, link, reduce to a common denominator, equate, match, express by metaphor, analogize, show correspondence, allegorize, correlate, parallel, show to be similar, show to be analogous, identify with, draw a parallel between.
2. [To examine on a comparative basis] — *Syn.* collate, contrast, balance, parallel, bring into comparison, estimate relatively, set over against, set off against, compare notes, exchange observations, weigh one thing against another, set side by side, put alongside, hold up together, correlate, weigh, oppose, measure against, juxtapose, place in juxtaposition, confront, counterpose, note the similarities and differences, compare and contrast, distinguish between, differentiate, analyze, examine; see also **distinguish** 1.
3. [To stand in relationship to another] — *Syn.* match, vie, rival, compete with, correspond, resemble, be comparable, be in the same class, parallel, equal, admit of comparison, measure up, match up, be on a par with, hold a candle to*, come up to*, stack up with, stack up against*; see also **equal, match** 3.

**beyond** or **past** or **without compare** — *Syn.* incomparable, without equal, distinctive; see **unique** 1.

---

*SYN.* — **compare** refers to a literal or figurative putting together in order to note points of resemblance and difference, and implies the weighing of parallel features for relative values [*to compare records and compact discs*]; **contrast** implies a comparison for the purpose of emphasizing differences [*to contrast farm life with city life*]; **collate** implies detailed, critical comparison, esp. of different versions of the same text

---

**compared,** *modif.* — *Syn.* distinguished, set side by side, in comparison, brought into comparison, correlated, as to, by comparison with; see also **related** 2.

**compare favorably to** or **with,** *v.* — *Syn.* be better than, improve on, improve upon, do well in comparison with; see **compare** 3, **exceed.**

**compare with** or **to,** *v.* — *Syn.* put beside, relate to, equate, equal; see **compare** 1, 3.

**comparison,** *n.* **1.** [The act of comparing] — *Syn.* likening, collating, analyzing, relative estimation, comparative relation, testing by a criterion, distinguishing between, analogizing, corresponding, paralleling, drawing parallels, contrasting, balancing, relating, collation, dividing, opposition, separation, segregation, bringing together, identification, matching, equating, measuring, weighing, juxtaposing, observation, correlation, discrimination, estimate of likeness and difference; see also **association** 2, **estimate** 1, **judgment** 2.
**2.** [A prepared comparison, sense 1] — *Syn.* metaphor, simile, resemblance, analogy, correspondence, relation, collation, correlation, parable, allegory, similarity, likeness, likening, identification, equation, measurement, illustration, example, contrast, association, ratio, parallel, connection, comparative estimate, comparative statement; see also **similarity, simile.**

**compartment,** *n.* — *Syn.* section, subdivision, cell, partition, pigeonhole, chamber, slot, cubbyhole, cubicle, nook; see also **cell** 3, **part** 1.

**compass,** *n.* **1.** [Boundary] — *Syn.* circumference, range, extent; see **boundary, expanse, extent, range** 2.
**2.** [Instrument] — *Syn.* magnetic compass, mariner's compass, direction finder, direction guide, surveyor's compass, earth inductor, sun compass, induction compass, gyrocompass, cardinal points, radio compass, needle*; see also **device** 1.
*See Synonym Study at* CIRCUMFERENCE, RANGE.

**compassion,** *n.* — *Syn.* sympathy, empathy, clemency; see **kindness** 1, **pity** 1.
*See Synonym Study at* PITY.

**compassionate,** *modif.* — *Syn.* merciful, humane, sympathetic, tender; see **humane** 1, **kind, merciful** 1.
*See Synonym Study at* TENDER.

**compatibility,** *n.* — *Syn.* harmony, unity, congeniality; see **adaptability, agreement** 2.

**compatible,** *modif.* — *Syn.* agreeable, congenial, congruous, cooperative; see **fit** 1, 2, **harmonious** 2.

**compatriot,** *n.* — *Syn.* fellow countryman, fellow countrywoman, fellow citizen, national, *paesano* (Italian), *paisano* (Spanish), landsman; see also **citizen.**

**compeer,** *n.* **1.** [A comrade] — *Syn.* companion, comrade, consort; see **associate, friend** 1.
**2.** [One of equal rank] — *Syn.* peer, match, colleague; see **equal.**

**compel,** *v.* — *Syn.* force, enforce, constrain, coerce; see **force** 1.
*See Synonym Study at* FORCE.

**compendious,** *modif.* — *Syn.* concise, inclusive, succinct; see **comprehensive, concise, short** 2.

**compendium,** *n.* — *Syn.* abridgment, abstract, essence; see **abridgment** 2, **summary.**

**compensate,** *v.* **1.** [To pay] — *Syn.* recompense, remunerate, requite; see **pay** 1, **repay** 1.
**2.** [To offset] — *Syn.* counterbalance, neutralize, counterpoise, make up for; see **offset.**
*See Synonym Study at* PAY.

**compensating,** *modif.* — *Syn.* refunding, atoning, adjusting, reimbursing, repaying, settling, balancing, in compensation; see also **balanced** 1.

**compensation,** *n.* — *Syn.* remuneration, recompense, payment, indemnity, satisfaction, requital, remittal, return for services, commission, gratuity, tip, reimbursement, allowance, deserts, remittance, salary, pay, stipend, wages, hire, earnings, settlement, honorarium, defrayal, coverage, consideration, counterclaim, damages,

repayment, recoupment, fee, quittance, reckoning, equivalent price, indemnification, bonus, premium, amends, reparation, restitution, reciprocity, reward, advantage, profit, benefit, gain, meed, counterbalance, kickback*; see also **pay** 2, **payment** 1, **return** 3, **tip** 2. — *Ant.* LOSS, deprivation, confiscation.

**compete,** *v.* — *Syn.* contend, vie with, vie for, enter into competition, take part, strive, struggle, cope with, be in the running, become a competitor, enter the rolls, enter the lists, run for, participate in, contend for a prize, race, race with, engage in a contest, oppose, wrestle, be rivals, contest, fight, tussle, joust, battle, seek the same prize, bandy with, spar, fence, collide, tilt, bid, face, clash, encounter, match wits with, match strength with, play, grapple, jockey, rival, emulate, keep up with the Joneses, take on*, take on all comers*, go in for*, lock horns with*, go out for*, throw one's hat into the ring*, give a run for one's money*; see also **contest** 2, **fight** 1, 2.

**competence,** *n.* **1.** [Adequate income] — *Syn.* subsistence, provision, sufficient means; see **income, subsistence** 2, **support** 3.
**2.** [Qualification] — *Syn.* capability, skill, fitness, proficiency; see **ability** 1, 2.

**competent,** *modif.* **1.** [Capable] — *Syn.* fit, qualified, skilled; see **able** 1, 2.
**2.** [Adequate] — *Syn.* sufficient, satisfactory, acceptable; see **enough** 1, **fair** 2.
**3.** [Legally qualified] — *Syn.* responsible, accountable, duly constituted, sane, of sound mind, *compos mentis* (Latin); see also **sane** 1.
*See Synonym Study at* ABLE.

**competently,** *modif.* — *Syn.* capably, skillfully, ably, efficiently, proficiently, expertly, dexterously, adeptly; see also **effectively, well** 2.

**competition,** *n.* **1.** [The act of competing] — *Syn.* rivalry, contention, contest, striving, strife, struggle, emulation, vying, controversy, coping with, opposition, pairing off, meeting, engagement, candidacy, racing, trial, contest for advantage, pitting of strength, pitting of wits, combat, fight, conflict, attempt to outsell, rivalry for patronage, attempt at betterment, clash, counteraction, antagonism, wrestling, tug of war*, one-upmanship*, rat race*. — *Ant.* partnership, ALLIANCE, cooperation.
**2.** [An instance of competition] — *Syn.* race, match, contest, game, meet, matchup, fight, bout, boxing match, game of skill, trial, sport, athletic event, championship, tournament, tilt, joust, debate, encounter, rumpus*, tangle*; see also **game** 1, **sport** 3.
**3.** [Competitor or competitors] — *Syn.* rival(s), opposition, the field; see **contestant, opponent** 1.

---

*SYN.* — **competition** denotes a striving for the same object, position, prize, etc., often in accordance with certain fixed rules; **rivalry** implies keen competition between opponents more or less evenly matched, and, unqualified, it often suggests unfriendliness or even hostility; **emulation** implies endeavor to equal or surpass another, usually one greatly admired, in achievement, character, etc.

---

**competitive,** *modif.* — *Syn.* competing, antagonistic, contentious, dog-eat-dog*; see **aggressive** 1, **ambitious 1, rival.**

**competitor,** *n.* — *Syn.* rival, contender, adversary, emulator; see **contestant, opponent** 1.

**compilation,** *n.* **1.** [The action of compiling] — *Syn.* gathering, gathering together, compiling, incorporating, drawing together, codifying, collocating, collecting, aggregating, methodizing, systematizing, gleaning, accumulating, combining, assembling, organizing, coordinating, amassing, selecting, garnering, ordering, arranging, consolidating, joining, unifying; see also **accumulation** 1, **collection** 1.

2. [Something compiled] — *Syn.* collection, accumulation, anthology, assemblage; see **collection** 2.

**compile,** *v.* — *Syn.* collect, gather, amass, put together, group together, bring together, draw together, arrange, edit, collate, recapitulate, digest, concentrate, consolidate, compose, note down, anthologize, cull, glean, select, accumulate, heap up, garner, assemble, collocate, organize, codify, unite, colligate, muster; see also **accumulate** 1, **edit** 1, 2. — *Ant.* originate, SCATTER, disperse.

**complacency,** *n.* — *Syn.* contentment, smugness, sense of security; see **arrogance, satisfaction** 2.

**complacent,** *modif.* — *Syn.* self-satisfied, contented, self-righteous, unconcerned; see **proud** 2, **satisfied, smug.**

**complain,** *v.* **1.** [To express an objection] — *Syn.* remonstrate, grumble, whine, find fault, disapprove, accuse, deplore, criticize, denounce, dissent, cavil, charge, bring charges, report adversely on, reproach, oppose, contravene, whimper, nag, fret, repine, protest, fuss, moan, growl, grump, murmur, mutter, make a fuss about, take exception to, object to, deprecate, enter a demurrer, demur, expostulate, carp, attack, refute, countercharge, air a grievance, lodge a complaint, howl, grouse*, kick*, bitch*, grouch*, gripe*, grunt*, beef*, bellyache*, crab*, squawk*, tattle*, kick up a fuss*, make noises about*, raise a howl*, raise a fuss*, make a stink*, moan and groan*, kvetch*; see also **accuse, censure, oppose** 1. — *Ant.* sanction, APPROVE, countenance.

2. [To express grief] — *Syn.* grieve, lament, bemoan, bewail; see **cry** 1, **mourn** 1.

**complaining,** *modif.* — *Syn.* objecting, lamenting, murmuring, regretting, repining, bewailing, deploring, weeping, mourning, moaning, protesting, charging, accusing, disapproving, grumbling, fretting, whining, peevish, querulous, resentful, dissenting, discontented, malcontent, registering a protest, filing a complaint, kicking*, grousing*, bellyaching*, crabby*, kvetchy*; see also **critical** 2, **irritable.** — *Ant.* ENJOYING, appreciating, praising.

**complaint,** *n.* **1.** [An objection] — *Syn.* grievance, charge, criticism, reproach; see **accusation** 2, **objection** 1, 2.

2. [An illness] — *Syn.* ailment, malady, infirmity; see **disease, illness** 1.

**complaisance,** *n.* — *Syn.* agreeableness, obligingness, graciousness; see **courtesy** 1, **kindness** 1.

**complaisant,** *modif.* — *Syn.* obliging, amiable, compliant; see **docile, friendly** 1.

**complement,** *n.* **1.** [That which completes] — *Syn.* supplement, correlative, counterpart; see **addition** 2, **equal.**

2. [Full amount] — *Syn.* totality, wholeness, entirety; see **whole.**

3. [That which completes the number of something] — *Syn.* balance, filler, rest; see **remainder.**

**complementary,** *modif.* **1.** [Forming a complement] — *Syn.* integral, equivalent, corresponding, reciprocal, parallel, mutual, correlative, correspondent, interrelated, interconnected, interdependent, companion, completing; see also **equal.**

2. [Matched] — *Syn.* paired, mated, corresponding; see **alike** 2, **matched.**

**complete,** *modif.* **1.** [Not lacking in any part] — *Syn.*

full, whole, entire, total, intact, replete, unimpaired, undivided, unabridged, uncut, unbroken, comprehensive, exhaustive; see also **full** 1, 3, **whole** 1.

2. [Finished] — *Syn.* concluded, terminated, ended; see **finished** 1.

3. [Thorough] — *Syn.* thoroughgoing, absolute, total; see **absolute.**

4. [Perfect] — *Syn.* flawless, consummate, impeccable; see **perfect** 2, **whole** 2.

---

*SYN.* — **complete** implies inclusion of all that is needed for the integrity, perfection, or fulfillment of something /a *complete* set, *complete* control/; **full** implies the inclusion of all that is needed /a *full* dozen/ or all that can be held, achieved, etc. /in *full* bloom/; **total** implies an adding together of everything without exception / the *total* number/ and is, in general applications, equivalent to **complete** /*total* abstinence/; **whole** and **entire** imply unbroken unity, stressing that not a single part, individual, instance, etc. has been omitted or diminished /the *whole* student body, one's *entire* attention/; **intact** is applied to that which remains whole after passing through an experience that might have impaired it /the tornado left the barn *intact*/

---

**complete,** *v.* **1.** [To make entire] — *Syn.* execute, consummate, perfect, accomplish, realize, perform, achieve, fill out, fulfill, supplement, complement, effectuate, equip, actualize, furnish, make, make up, elaborate, make good, bring to fullness, bring to completion, bring to fruition, bring to maturity, make complete, develop, fill in, refine, effect, carry out, carry off, crown, go through with, get through, cap, culminate, round out; see also **build** 1, **create** 2, **form** 1.

2. [To bring to an end] — *Syn.* finish, conclude, close; see **achieve, end** 1, **perform** 1.

*See Synonym Study at* END.

**completed,** *modif.* — *Syn.* achieved, ended, concluded; see **built** 1, **done** 1, **finished** 1.

**completely,** *modif.* — *Syn.* entirely, fully, totally, utterly, wholly, undividedly, perfectly, absolutely, unanimously, thoroughly, en masse, exhaustively, minutely, painstakingly, extensively, conclusively, positively, unconditionally, unqualifiedly, finally, without omission, to the utmost, ultimately, in toto, in entirety, exclusively, simply, effectively, competently, solidly, bodily, determinedly, maturely, radically, altogether, quite, downright, all the way, comprehensively, to the end, from beginning to end, on all counts, in all, in full measure, in the mass, to the limit, to the full, in full, to completion, to the nth degree*, to a frazzle*, through thick and thin*, down to the ground*, through and through*, hook, line, and sinker*, rain or shine*, in one lump*, lock, stock, and barrel*, from A to Z*, root and branch*, from head to foot*, inside out*; see also **finally** 1. — *Ant.* somewhat, PARTLY, partially.

**completion,** *n.* — *Syn.* finish, conclusion, fulfillment; see **achievement** 1, **end** 2.

**complex,** *modif.* **1.** [Composed of several parts] — *Syn.* composite, heterogeneous, compound, conglomerate, multiple, mingled, mixed, motley, mosaic, manifold, multifaceted, multiform, many-sided, many-faceted, complicated, elaborate, aggregate, involved, combined, compact, compounded, amalgamated, miscellaneous, multiplex, multifarious, variegated, interwoven, interlaced; see also **mixed** 1. — *Ant.* SIMPLIFIED, single, homogeneous.

2. [Difficult to understand] — *Syn.* complicated, involved, intricate, entangled, tangled, circuitous, convo-

luted, puzzling, mingled, muddled, jumbled, impenetrable, inscrutable, unfathomable, undecipherable, bewildering, perplexing, confused, difficult, obscure, abstruse, recondite, labyrinthine, enigmatic, hidden, knotted, knotty, meandering, winding, sinuous, tortuous, snarled, irreducible, rambling, paradoxical, excursive, Daedalian, Gordian, twisted, disordered, devious, Byzantine, cryptic, inextricable, mazy, roundabout, crabbed; see also **confused** 2, **difficult** 2, **obscure** 1. — *Ant.* simple, UNDERSTANDABLE, plain, apparent.

---

*SYN.* — **complex** refers to that which is made up of many elaborately interrelated or interconnected parts, so that much study or knowledge is needed to understand or operate it *[a complex mechanism]*; **complicated** is applied to that which is highly complex and hence very difficult to analyze, solve, or understand *[a complicated problem]*; **intricate** specifically suggests a perplexingly elaborate interweaving of parts that is difficult to follow *[an intricate maze]*; **involved**, in this connection, is applied to situations, ideas, etc. whose parts are thought of as intertwining in complicated, often disordered, fashion *[an involved argument]*

---

**complex,** *n.* **1.** [An obsession] — *Syn.* exaggerated reaction syndrome, phobia, mania, fixation, repressed emotions, repressed fears, repressed desires, repressed hates, group of repressed associations, hang-up*; see also **fear** 2, **insanity** 1, **neurosis, obsession.**
Types of psychological complexes include: Cain, castration, Diana, Electra, Oedipus, superiority, inferiority, persecution.
**2.** [A composite] — *Syn.* system, network, conglomerate, syndrome, web, tangle, ecosystem, ecological complex, aggregation, association, group, entanglement, totality; see also **collection** 2, **confusion** 2, **system** 1.
**complexion,** *n.* **1.** [Appearance] — *Syn.* aspect, semblance, character; see **appearance** 1, 2, **character** 1.
**2.** [Skin coloring] — *Syn.* tone, color, coloration, coloring, tinge, cast, glow, flush, skin texture, tint, hue, pigmentation; see also **skin.**
Descriptions of complexions include: blond, fair, pale, pallid, ashen, waxen, white, sallow, sickly, dark, olive, bronze, sandy, rosy, red, ruddy, florid, brown, yellow, black, blue-black, Negroid, Caucasian, Nordic, Aryan, Melanesian, Malaysian, mulatto, Oriental, Semitic, Amerindian, tan, tanned, sun-tanned, yellowish-brown, pinkish, sanguine, redheaded; peroxide blond*, drugstore blond*, strawberry and cream*, peaches and cream*.
**compliance,** *n.* — *Syn.* yielding, acquiescence, assent; see **agreement** 1, **docility.**
**compliant,** *modif.* — *Syn.* obedient, pliant, acquiescent, submissive; see **docile, pliant** 2.
*See Synonym Study at* DOCILE.
**complicate,** *v.* — *Syn.* involve, convolute, confound, make difficult, make complex, make intricate, tangle, twist, snarl up, entangle, embroil, obscure, make multiform, make various, muddle, confuse, mix up, elaborate, embellish, compound, implicate, conceal, impede, perplex, vex, hinder, hamper, encumber, bedevil, darken, obfuscate, mystify, render unintelligible, jumble, knot, tie in knots, clog, ball up*; see also **confuse, entangle.** — *Ant.* SIMPLIFY, clear up, disentangle.
**complicated,** *modif.* — *Syn.* intricate, complex, involved; see **complex** 2, **confused** 2, **difficult** 2.
*See Synonym Study at* COMPLEX.
**complication,** *n.* — *Syn.* complexity, dilemma, development; see **confusion** 2, **difficulty** 1, 2.

**complicity,** *n.* — *Syn.* conspiracy, confederacy, collusion; see **cooperation** 1, **intrigue** 1.
**compliment,** *n.* — *Syn.* praise, commendation, felicitation, tribute, encomium, approval, endorsement, sanction, applause, complimentary remark, flattery, acclaim, acclamation, laudation, panegyric, eulogy, adulation, notice, regards, honor, appreciation, recognition, respects, blessing, accolades, kudos, plaudits, veneration, admiration, congratulation, homage, good word, tradelast*, T.L.*, bouquet*, pat on the back*, stroke*; see also **flattery, praise** 2. — *Ant.* CENSURE, abuse, disapproval.
**compliment,** *v.* **1.** [To flatter] — *Syn.* commend, praise, endorse, sanction, acclaim, pay a compliment to, sing the praises of, speak highly of, exalt, make much of, ingratiate oneself with, soothe, charm, applaud, worship, eulogize, glorify, panegyrize, extol, magnify, cajole, fawn upon, toady to, truckle to, laud, adulate, hail, honor, pay tribute to, butter up*, puff up*, hand it to*, pat on the back*, give a bouquet*, stroke*, lay it on thick*; see also **praise** 1. — *Ant.* DENOUNCE, disapprove of, censure.
**2.** [To congratulate] — *Syn.* felicitate, wish joy to, rejoice with, remember, commemorate, send a remembrance, pay one's respects, greet, honor, cheer, salute, hail, toast, applaud, celebrate, pay tribute to.
**complimentary,** *modif.* **1.** [Paying a compliment] — *Syn.* commendatory, flattering, laudatory, praising, approving, encomiastic, eulogistic, adulatory, celebrating, honoring, admiring, respectful, honeyed, fawning, sycophantic, unctuous, congratulatory, well-wishing, fair-spoken, panegyric, highly favorable, approbatory, approbative, appreciative, abounding in praise, singing the praises of, with highest recommendations, with high praise, gushing; see also **appreciative, polite** 1.
**2.** [Given free] — *Syn.* gratis, on the house, as a comp*; see **free** 4.
**comply with,** *v.* — *Syn.* conform, agree to, acquiesce; see **agree to, follow** 2, **obey** 1, 2.
**component,** *modif.* — *Syn.* constituent, composing, elemental, basic; see **fundamental** 1, **integral.**
**component,** *n.* — *Syn.* element, segment, ingredient; see **element** 1, **part** 1.
*See Synonym Study at* ELEMENT.
**compose,** *v.* **1.** [To be the parts or the ingredients] — *Syn.* constitute, comprise, make up, form, be an adjunct, go into the making of, enter into, merge into, go into, be a component of, be an ingredient of, be an element of, be a portion of, belong to, consist of, be made of, be compounded of; see also **comprise, include** 1.
**2.** [To give form] — *Syn.* make, fashion, put together; see **form** 1.
**3.** [To create] — *Syn.* write, indite, pen, author, draft, devise, produce, arrange, score, orchestrate, fabricate, formulate, prepare, design, conceive, imagine, make up, originate, poeticize, turn out, draw up, put together, concoct, dash off; see also **create** 2, **invent** 1, 2, **produce** 2, **write** 1. — *Ant.* blot out, CANCEL, erase.
**4.** [To prepare for printing] — *Syn.* set up, set type, cast, make up; see **form** 1.
**composed,** *modif.* **1.** [Made] — *Syn.* written, created, authored, made of, made up of, comprising, consisting of, compounded, constituted, formed, fashioned, formulated; see also **formed, written** 1.
**2.** [Calm] — *Syn.* poised, collected, confident, self-assured, self-possessed, clearheaded, sensible, relaxed, untroubled, soothed, quieted, sedate, tranquil, serene, cool; see also **calm** 1, **confident** 2.
*See Synonym Study at* COOL.

**compose oneself,** *v.*— *Syn.* control oneself, calm oneself, collect one's wits, pull oneself together; see **calm down, quiet** 1.

**composer,** *n.*— *Syn.* songwriter, arranger, writer, author, melodist, hymnist, symphonist, songsmith\*, tunesmith\*; see also **author** 2, **musician, poet, writer.**
Major classical and orchestral composers include: Giovanni Palestrina, Claudio Monteverdi, Henry Purcell, Georg Telemann, Antonio Vivaldi, Johann Sebastian Bach, George Frederick Handel, Franz Joseph Haydn, Wolfgang Amadeus Mozart, Ludwig van Beethoven, Franz Schubert, Johannes Brahms, Felix Mendelssohn, Robert Schumann, Frédéric Chopin, Franz Liszt, Georges Bizet, Hector Berlioz, Peter Ilyich Tchaikovsky, Giuseppe Verdi, Richard Wagner, Antonin Dvořák, Gustav Mahler, Richard Strauss, Modest Mussorgsky, Nicolas Rimsky-Korsakov, Giacomo Puccini, Jean Sibelius, Claude Debussy, Arthur S. Sullivan, Maurice Ravel, Camille Saint-Saëns, Béla Bartók, Sergei Prokofiev, Dmitri Shostakovich, Ralph Vaughan Williams, George Gershwin, Igor Stravinsky, Arnold Schoenberg, Paul Hindemith, Aaron Copland, John Cage, Benjamin Britten, Leonard Bernstein.

**composition,** *n.* **1.** [The act of arranging for effect] — *Syn.* combination, distribution, arrangement; see **organization** 1, **synthesis** 1.
**2.** [Arrangement] — *Syn.* configuration, structure, makeup, constitution, layout, conformation, construction, organization, symmetry, proportion, balance, harmony, style, concord, agreement, consonance, form, spacing, placing, rhythm; see also **consistency** 1, **form** 1, **organization** 2.
**3.** [The act of producing creative work] — *Syn.* creation, writing, authoring, fashioning, formation, conception, presentation, forging, shaping, sculpturing, invention, designing, planning, bringing into existence, fabrication; see also **production** 1, **writing** 1, 3.
**4.** [A written work] — *Syn.* work, musical work, piece, essay, paper, theme, article, writing exercise, opus, score, production, story, verse, melody; see also **biography, book** 1, **creation** 3, **exposition** 2, **literature** 2, **music** 1, **piece** 3, **poetry, writing** 2.

**compositor,** *n.*— *Syn.* printer, typesetter, typographer, keyboarder, makeup man, Linotype operator, compo\*; see also **printer.**

**compost,** *n.*— *Syn.* organic fertilizer, soil conditioner, humus, leaf mold; see **fertilizer.**

**composure,** *n.*— *Syn.* calmness, equanimity, serenity, self-possession, calm, collectedness, nonchalance, coolheadedness, control, self-control, sang-froid, aplomb, poise, balance, tranquillity, stability, harmony, concord, assurance, self-assurance, imperturbability, peace of mind, serene state of mind, inexcitability, dispassion, even temper, tranquil mind, coolness, level-headedness, placidity, fortitude, moderation, self-command, gravity, sobriety, a cool head, presence of mind, equilibrium, steadiness, self-restraint, repose, quiescence, imperturbation, ease, evenness, staidness, tolerance, dignity, quiet, quietude, command of one's faculties, equability, stoicism, forbearance, cool\*, unflappability\*, the even tenor of one's ways\*; see also **dignity** 1, **patience** 1, **peace** 3, **restraint** 1.— *Ant.* exuberance, PASSION, wildness.

*SYN.* — **composure** implies the disciplining of one's emotions in a trying situation or habitual self-possession in the face of excitement; **equanimity** implies an inherent evenness of temper or disposition that is not easily disturbed; **serenity** implies a lofty, clear peace of mind that is not easily clouded by ordinary stresses or excitements; **nonchalance** implies a casual indifference to or a cool detachment from situations that might be expected to disturb one emotionally; **sang-froid** implies great coolness and presence of mind in dangerous or trying circumstances

**compound,** *modif.*— *Syn.* mixed, combined, composite, complicated; see **complex** 1.

**compound,** *n.*— *Syn.* composite, union, aggregate, synthesis; see **mixture** 1.

**compound,** *v.* **1.** [To blend] — *Syn.* combine, coalesce, unite; see **join** 1, **mix** 1.
**2.** [To complicate] — *Syn.* make complex, intensify, add to; see **complicate, increase** 1, **intensify.**

**comprehend,** *v.* **1.** [To include] — *Syn.* contain, comprise, embrace; see **include** 1, **involve.**
**2.** [To understand] — *Syn.* grasp, discern, perceive; see **know** 1, **understand** 1.
*See Synonym Study at* INCLUDE, UNDERSTAND.

**comprehensible,** *modif.*— *Syn.* intelligible, plain, coherent; see **understandable.**

**comprehension,** *n.* **1.** [Capacity to understand] — *Syn.* understanding, perception, cognizance, grasp; see **awareness, judgment** 1, **knowledge** 1.
**2.** [An including] — *Syn.* incorporation, circumscription, embodiment; see **inclusion.**

**comprehensive,** *modif.*— *Syn.* inclusive, extensive, exhaustive, broad, wide, compendious, synoptic, sweeping, widespread, far-reaching, comprising, containing, all-embracing, all-inclusive, complete, thorough, discursive, encyclopedic, full, general, expansive, overall, blanket, umbrella; see also **absolute** 1, **general** 1, **large** 1, 2, **whole** 1.

**compress,** *v.*— *Syn.* condense, compact, press together, consolidate, concentrate, squeeze, squeeze together, tighten, cramp, contract, crowd, force into a smaller space, constrict, abbreviate, shrivel, make brief, reduce, dehydrate, pack, shorten, shrink, narrow, abridge, restrict in area, make terse, bind tightly, wrap closely, coagulate, abstract, summarize, epitomize, wedge, press, boil down, ram\*, stuff\*, cram\*; see also **concentrate** 1, **decrease** 2, **press** 1, **tighten** 1.— *Ant.* SPREAD, stretch, expand.
*See Synonym Study at* CONTRACT.

**compression,** *n.*— *Syn.* condensation, squeezing, confining; see **concentration** 1.

**comprise,** *v.*— *Syn.* comprehend, contain, embrace, include, involve, enclose, embody, encircle, encompass, sum up, cover, consist of, consist in, be composed of, be made up of, constitute, incorporate, enfold, span, compass, hold, engross, take into account, take into consideration, subsume, be resolvable into, be contained in, add up to, amount to, take in; see also **compose** 1, **include** 1.— *Ant.* NEED, lack, exclude.
*See Synonym Study at* INCLUDE.

**compromise,** *n.* **1.** [The act of compromising] — *Syn.* give-and-take, bargaining, granting concessions, accommodation; see **agreement** 1.
**2.** [An action involving compromise, sense 1] — *Syn.* settlement, bargain, understanding, trade-off; see **agreement** 3.

**compromise,** *v.* **1.** [To make concessions] — *Syn.* settle, conciliate, find a middle ground; see **agree, arbitrate, negotiate** 1, **yield** 1.
**2.** [To lay open to suspicion or danger] — *Syn.* jeopardize, hazard, imperil, discredit; see **endanger.**

**comptroller,** *n.* — *Syn.* controller, financial officer, business manager; see **accountant, administrator.**

**compulsion,** *n.* **1.** [Pressure] — *Syn.* constraint, coercion, duress; see **pressure** 2, **restraint** 2.

**2.** [Driving force] — *Syn.* drive, necessity, need; see **requirement** 2.

**3.** [An obsession] — *Syn.* irresistible impulse, urge, fixation, preoccupation; see **addiction, obsession.**

**compulsive,** *modif.* **1.** [Compelling] — *Syn.* driving, impelling, besetting, urgent; see **necessary** 1, **urgent** 1.

**2.** [Obsessive] — *Syn.* addicted, driven, obsessive-compulsive, overscrupulous; see **addicted, careful, enthusiastic** 2, **habitual** 1.

**compulsorily,** *modif.* — *Syn.* forcibly, imperatively, by force, with force; see **urgently** 1, 2.

**compulsory,** *modif.* — *Syn.* obligatory, mandatory, required, requisite; see **necessary** 1.

**compunction,** *n.* **1.** [A sense of guilt or remorse] — *Syn.* remorse, contrition, shame; see **regret** 1, **repentance, shame** 2.

**2.** [A twinge of uneasiness or pity] — *Syn.* misgiving, qualm, hesitation; see **qualm** 1, **regret** 1.

*See Synonym Study at* QUALM, REPENTANCE.

**computable,** *modif.* — *Syn.* calculable, estimable, measurable, determinable; see **calculable.**

**computation,** *n.* **1.** [A computing] — *Syn.* calculation, counting, data processing, reckoning; see **calculation** 1, **estimate** 1, **guess.**

**2.** [Result of computing] — *Syn.* total, sum, figure; see **estimate** 1, **guess, number.**

**compute,** *v.* — *Syn.* calculate, reckon, figure, measure; see **calculate** 1, **count, estimate** 1.

*See Synonym Study at* CALCULATE.

**computer,** *n.* — *Syn.* personal computer, PC, microcomputer, minicomputer, mainframe, laptop computer, home computer, workstation, supercomputer, electronic brain, thinking machine, data processor, word processor, calculator, processor, supermini, superminicomputer, supermicro, master control, number cruncher*, machine, cybernetic organism, digital computer, analog computer, network, neural net, neural network.

Various trademarked brands of computers include: IBM, Apple, Macintosh, Mac, Compaq, Cray, Hewlett-Packard, Toshiba, Digital, NEC, Sun, Amiga.

**computerized,** *modif.* — *Syn.* electronic, automated, cybernated, computer-operated, computer-aided, computer-assisted, digital, programmed, electronically planned and/or processed; see also **automated.**

**computer language,** *n.* — *Syn.* machine language, programming language, artificial language, computer-processed instructions, macroinstruction system, high-level language, low-level language, assembly language, job-control language, JCL.

Commonly encountered computer languages include: BASIC, COBOL, FORTRAN, ALGOL, PROLOG, Modula-Z, PL1, C, C++, Smalltalk, assembler compiler, Pascal, RPG II; see also **language** 1.

**comrade,** *n.* — *Syn.* companion, confidant, confidante, intimate; see **associate, friend** 1.

*See Synonym Study at* ASSOCIATE.

**con,** *modif.* — *Syn.* against, conversely, opposed to, in opposition; see **against** 3.

**con*,** *n.* — *Syn.* swindle, confidence, game, fraud, scam*; see also **deception** 1, **dishonesty, trick** 1.

**con*,** *v.* — *Syn.* cheat, dupe, mislead; see **deceive.**

**concatenation,** *n.* **1.** [A linking together in a series] — *Syn.* connecting, uniting, linking; see **link, order** 3, **union** 1.

**2.** [A series of interconnected events] — *Syn.* succession, chain, connection; see **chain, sequence** 1, **series.**

**concave,** *modif.* — *Syn.* curved, sunken, cupped; see **hollow** 2.

**concavity,** *n.* — *Syn.* depression, indentation, impression; see **hole** 2.

**conceal,** *v.* — *Syn.* hide, screen, secrete, cover; see **hide** 1, 2.

*See Synonym Study at* HIDE.

**concealed,** *modif.* — *Syn.* covered, obscured, unseen; see **hidden** 2.

**concealment,** *n.* **1.** [Act or means of concealing] — *Syn.* hiding, covering, camouflage, secretion; see **disguise.**

**2.** [Hiding place] — *Syn.* ambush, haven, shield; see **shelter.**

**concede,** *v.* — *Syn.* yield, grant, acknowledge; see **admit** 2, 3, **allow** 1, **yield** 1.

**conceit,** *n.* — *Syn.* vanity, self-admiration, narcissism; see **arrogance, pride** 1.

*See Synonym Study at* PRIDE.

**conceited,** *modif.* — *Syn.* vain, arrogant, stuck up*; see **egotistic** 2, **proud** 2.

**conceivable,** *modif.* — *Syn.* understandable, credible, believable, thinkable; see **convincing** 2, **imaginable, likely** 1.

**conceive,** *v.* **1.** [To form a concept or image of] — *Syn.* imagine, conceptualize, consider, formulate; see **imagine** 1, **invent** 1, **think** 1.

**2.** [To understand] — *Syn.* grasp, comprehend, perceive; see **understand** 1.

**3.** [To become pregnant] — *Syn.* become with child, be impregnated, superfetate, get in the family way*.

**concentrate,** *v.* **1.** [To bring or come together] — *Syn.* focus, amass, mass, assemble, center, converge, combine, consolidate, compact, condense, gather, collect, cluster, coalesce, centralize, concenter, bring into a small compass, bring toward a central point, embody, localize, strengthen, intensify, distill, bring to bear on one point, direct, direct toward one object, fix, channel, constrict, agglomerate, reduce, aggregate, crowd together, draw together, flock together, contract, muster, bunch, store, heap up, swarm, forgather, conglomerate, congest, focalize, narrow, compress, congregate, huddle, hoard, garner; see also **accumulate** 1, **distill, gather** 1, **unite** 1. — *Ant.* disperse, dilute, dissipate.

**2.** [To employ all one's mental powers] — *Syn.* fix one's attention, focus on, apply oneself, bring the mind to bear, think hard, give exclusive attention to, meditate, meditate upon, ponder, focus attention on, fasten on, direct all one's attention to, muse, muse over, weigh, consider closely, scrutinize, attend closely, regard carefully, contemplate, ruminate, study deeply, peruse carefully, examine closely, brood over, put one's mind to, be engrossed in, think about with absorption, occupy the mind with, occupy the thoughts with, apply the mind, give heed, pay heed, fix one's thoughts, focus one's thoughts, give the mind to, direct the mind to, rivet one's attention, rack one's brains*, get on the beam*, keep one's eye on the ball*, knuckle down*, buckle down*, apply the seat of one's pants to the chair*, zero in on*; see also **analyze** 1, **examine** 1, **think** 1. — *Ant.* be inattentive, DRIFT, ignore.

**concentrated,** *modif.* **1.** [Undiluted] — *Syn.* rich, strong, undiffused, unmixed, unadulterated, real, unmingled, straight; see also **strong** 8, **thick** 1, 3. — *Ant.* WEAK, diffused, diluted.

**2.** [Intense] — *Syn.* intensive, deep, hard; see **intense.**

**concentration,** *n.* **1.** [The act of bringing together]

— *Syn.* assembly, consolidation, convergence, collection, combination, massing, amassing, compression, coalescing, compacting, congregation, gathering, flocking, huddling, clustering, fixing, centering, focusing, intensification; see also **collection** 1.— *Ant.* dispersal, SEPARATION, scattering.

**2.** [Anything brought together] — *Syn.* company, concourse, audience, miscellany, band, party, flock, herd, mass, group, array; see also **army** 2, **collection** 2, **crowd** 1.

**3.** [Attention] — *Syn.* close attention, application, absorption; see **attention** 1, 2, **thought** 1.

**4.** [Density] — *Syn.* solidity, consistency, frequency, strength; see **congestion, density** 1, **intensity** 1.

**concept,** *n.* — *Syn.* idea, theory, notion; see **thought** 2.
*See Synonym Study at* IDEA.

**conception,** *n.* **1.** [The act of conceiving mentally] — *Syn.* apprehension, comprehension, imagining, speculating, conceptualization, originating, devising, formulating, bethinking, dreaming, cogitating, deliberating, fancying, philosophizing, realization, considering, musing, speculation, envisaging, understanding, cognition, perception, mental grasp, apperception, formulation of an idea, formulation of a principle, formulation of a mental image, hatching; see also **thought** 1.

**2.** [The act of conceiving physically] — *Syn.* inception, impregnation, insemination; see **fertilization** 2.

**3.** [A mental image] — *Syn.* representation, impression, idea, notion; see **opinion** 1, **thought** 2.

**4.** [Something that is conceived] — *Syn.* original idea, design, plan, interpretation; see **interpretation** 2, **plan** 2.
*See Synonym Study at* IDEA.

**conceptualize,** *v.* — *Syn.* form a concept of, develop a thought, visualize mentally; see **imagine** 1.

**concern,** *n.* **1.** [Affair] — *Syn.* business, matter, interest; see **affair** 1.

**2.** [Regard] — *Syn.* solicitude, anxiety, attention, interest; see **care** 2.

**3.** [A business] — *Syn.* firm, company, business establishment; see **business** 4.
*See Synonym Study at* CARE.

**concern,** *v.* **1.** [To have reference to] — *Syn.* refer to, pertain to, appertain to, relate to, be related to, be pertinent to, have relation to, have significance for, affect, involve, touch, bear on, bear upon, touch on, touch upon, regard, be concerned with, be connected with, be about, have to do with, be a matter of concern to, be of interest to, be of importance to, have a bearing on, have connections with, be applicable to, depend upon, be dependent upon, be interdependent with, stand in relationship to, deal with, belong to, have implications for, be the business of; see also **affect** 1, **treat** 1, 2.

**2.** [To make uneasy] — *Syn.* trouble, disturb, worry, disquiet; see **bother** 3, **disturb** 2.

**as concerns** — *Syn.* regarding, concerning, with reference to, in reference to; see **about** 2.

**concerning,** *modif.* — *Syn.* respecting, touching, regarding; see **about** 2.

**concern oneself,** *v.* — *Syn.* be concerned, become involved, occupy oneself; see **bother** 1, **care** 1, **worry** 2.

**concert,** *n.* **1.** [Agreement] — *Syn.* harmony, accord, concord; see **agreement** 2, **unity** 3.

**2.** [Musical entertainment] — *Syn.* performance, recital, musical program, musical selections, musicale, jam session, music festival, serenade, sing-along\*, gig\*; see also **performance** 2, **show** 2.

**concerted,** *modif.* — *Syn.* combined, mutual, joint; see **collective, united.**

**concession,** *n.* **1.** [A conceding] — *Syn.* granting, giving in, yielding; see **acknowledgment** 1, **admission** 4.

**2.** [A privilege granted by a government or company] — *Syn.* permit, authorization, grant, franchise; see **permission, permit.**

**conciliate,** *v.* — *Syn.* placate, appease, pacify; see **pacify** 1, **satisfy** 1, 3.
*See Synonym Study at* PACIFY.

**conciliatory,** *modif.* — *Syn.* agreeable, propitiatory, mollifying, placatory; see **friendly** 1, **pacific.**

**concise,** *modif.* — *Syn.* succinct, brief, condensed, terse, pithy, laconic, compact, compressed, condensed, tight, compendious, cogent, pointed, to the point, economical, short and sweet\*; see also **short** 2, **terse.**

---

**SYN.** — **concise** implies the stating of much in few words, by removing all superfluous or expanded details *[a concise summary]*; **terse** may add to this the connotation of polished smoothness and cogency *[a terse style]* or of clipped and abrupt expression *[a terse command]*; **laconic** suggests brevity to the point of curtness, ambiguity, or uncommunicativeness *["You'll see," was his laconic reply]*; **succinct** implies clarity but compactness in the fewest words possible *[she spoke in succinct phrases]*; **pithy** suggests forcefulness and wit resulting from compactness *[pithy axioms]*

---

**conclave,** *n.* — *Syn.* conference, parley, meeting; see **gathering.**

**conclude,** *v.* **1.** [To end] — *Syn.* terminate, close, finish up, come to an end; see **achieve** 1, **end** 1, **stop** 2.

**2.** [To determine] — *Syn.* resolve, arrange, decide, settle; see **decide.**

**3.** [To deduce] — *Syn.* presume, reason, gather; see **assume** 1, **infer** 1.
*See Synonym Study at* DECIDE, END, INFER.

**concluded,** *modif.* — *Syn.* closed, terminated, ended; see **finished** 1.

**conclusion,** *n.* **1.** [An end] — *Syn.* finish, termination, completion, summing-up; see **end** 2.

**2.** [A decision] — *Syn.* determination, inference, outcome, resolution; see **judgment** 3, **result.**

**in conclusion** — *Syn.* lastly, in closing, in the end; see **finally** 2.

**conclusive,** *modif.* — *Syn.* final, decisive, deciding, definitive, unquestionable, unmistakable, convincing, demonstrative, resolving, indisputable, determinative, settling, unconditional, undeniable, unanswerable, irrevocable, absolute, determining, telling, revealing; see also **certain** 3.

**concoct,** *v.* **1.** [To make by combining ingredients] — *Syn.* compound, prepare, formulate; see **compose** 3, **cook.**

**2.** [To make up] — *Syn.* devise, plan, create, scheme; see **invent** 1, **plan** 1.

**concoction,** *n.* — *Syn.* mixture, brew, blend, solution; see **mixture** 1.

**concomitant,** *modif.* — *Syn.* accompanying, attendant, connected, coactive, coordinate, associated with, coupled with, contemporaneous, joint, concurrent, conjoint, fellow, collateral, coefficient, attending, conjoined, corollary, belonging, agreeing, coincident, coterminous, accessory, concordant, synchronous, contemporary, coexistent, synergistic, simultaneous, isochronous, synergetic, isochronal; see also **contemporary** 1, **simultaneous.**

**concord,** *n.* **1.** [Unity of feeling] — *Syn.* harmony, consensus, accord; see **agreement** 2, **friendship** 2, **unity** 2, 3.
**2.** [A treaty] — *Syn.* compact, accord, pact; see **agreement** 3, **treaty**.

**concourse,** *n.* **1.** [A gathering] — *Syn.* assembly, throng, confluence; see **crowd** 1, **gathering**.
**2.** [A thoroughfare] — *Syn.* hall, promenade, boulevard, mall; see **hall** 2, **junction** 2, **road** 1, **walk** 2.

**concrete,** *modif.* **1.** [Specific] — *Syn.* particular, solid, precise, actual; see **accurate** 2, **definite** 1, **detailed**, **real** 2, **tangible**.
**2.** [Made of concrete] — *Syn.* cement, monolithic, poured, solid, strong, precast, concrete and steel, compact, unyielding; see also **firm** 2.

**concrete,** *n.* — *Syn.* ferroconcrete, reinforced concrete, prestressed concrete; see **cement, pavement** 1.

**concretion,** *n.* — *Syn.* crystallization, fusion, consolidation; see **coagulation, concentration** 1, **solidification** 1.

**concubine,** *n.* — *Syn.* harlot, courtesan, kept woman; see **mistress** 2, **prostitute**.

**concupiscence,** *n.* — *Syn.* lust, lechery, prurience; see **desire** 1.

**concupiscent,** *modif.* — *Syn.* desirous, lustful, carnal; see **passionate** 2, **sensual, voluptuous** 2.

**concur,** *v.* — *Syn.* accord, agree, coincide, be in harmony; see **agree, approve** 1, **equal**.
*See Synonym Study at* CONSENT.

**concurrent,** *modif.* **1.** [Occurring at the same time] — *Syn.* simultaneous, parallel, coexisting, side-by-side; see **concomitant, simultaneous**.
**2.** [Meeting at the same point] — *Syn.* converging, coinciding, coterminous, convergent, meeting, uniting, confluent, centrolineal; see also **joined**.
**3.** [Acting together] — *Syn.* cooperating, mutual, concerted, joint; see **collective, cooperative** 2.
**4.** [In agreement] — *Syn.* unified, agreeing, concurring, allied; see **alike** 2, **harmonious** 2, **unanimous**.

**concussion,** *n.* **1.** [A violent shock] — *Syn.* impact, jolt, jarring, agitation; see **bump** 1, **collision** 1.
**2.** [The result of a blow] — *Syn.* shock, head trauma, loss of consciousness, crack; see **injury** 1, **stupor**.

**condemn,** *v.* **1.** [To send to punishment] — *Syn.* convict, doom, sentence, damn, adjudge, proscribe, pass sentence on, find guilty, utter judicial sentence against, seal the doom of, pronounce judgment, prescribe punishment; see also **convict, punish**. — *Ant.* acquit, EXCUSE, exonerate.
**2.** [To blame] — *Syn.* denounce, reprobate, censure, rebuke; see **censure, denounce**.
*See Synonym Study at* CENSURE.

**condemnation,** *n.* — *Syn.* denunciation, censure, disapprobation, reproach; see **blame** 1, **conviction** 2, objection 2, **rebuke**.

**condemnatory,** *modif.* — *Syn.* condemning, disapproving, censorious; see **critical** 2.

**condensation,** *n.* **1.** [The act of condensing] — *Syn.* compression, consolidation, crystallization; see **concentration** 1, **reduction** 1.
**2.** [A condensed state or form] — *Syn.* reduction, contraction, synopsis; see **abbreviation** 1, **abridgment** 2, **essence** 1, **summary**.

**condense,** *v.* **1.** [To compress] — *Syn.* press together, constrict, consolidate; see **compress, contract** 1, 2, **decrease** 1, 2.
**2.** [To abridge] — *Syn.* abbreviate, summarize, digest; see **contract** 2, **decrease** 2.
*See Synonym Study at* CONTRACT.

**condensed,** *modif.* **1.** [Shortened] — *Syn.* concise, brief, succinct; see **concise, short** 2, **terse**.
**2.** [Compressed] — *Syn.* hardened, dense, solidified; see **firm** 2, **thick** 1.
**3.** [Concentrated] — *Syn.* undiluted, rich, evaporated; see **concentrated** 1, **thick** 3.

**condescend,** *v.* — *Syn.* vouchsafe, stoop, deign, lower oneself, humble oneself, demean oneself, degrade oneself, submit with good grace, patronize, assume a patronizing air, assume a superior air, talk down to, lower one's tone, graciously stoop, unbend, accommodate oneself to (one regarded as inferior), descend, waive a privilege, favor, accord, come down off one's high horse★, come down a peg★, sing small★; see also **patronize** 2.

---

*SYN.* — **condescend** implies a voluntary descent by one high in rank, power, etc. to act graciously or affably toward one regarded as his inferior /the general *condescended* to talk with the private/; **stoop** implies a descending in dignity, as by committing some shameful or immoral act /to *stoop* to cheating/; **deign** connotes unwilling or arrogant condescension /the duchess *deigned* to shake my hand/ and, hence, is most frequently used in negative constructions or with such qualifications as *hardly, scarcely, barely* /she didn't *deign* to reply; he would scarcely *deign* to appear in public/

---

**condescending,** *modif.* — *Syn.* patronizing, superior, disdainful, supercilious; see **egotistic** 2, **proud** 2.

**condescension,** *n.* — *Syn.* patronization, deigning, haughtiness, disdain; see **arrogance, patronage** 3.

**condiment,** *n.* — *Syn.* seasoning, relish, spice, sauce; see **flavoring, herb, pickle** 2, **relish** 1, **spice**.

**condition,** *n.* **1.** [A state] — *Syn.* situation, position, status; see **state** 2.
**2.** [A requisite] — *Syn.* stipulation, contingency, provision; see **circumstance** 1, **requirement** 1.
**3.** [A limitation] — *Syn.* restriction, qualification, prohibition; see **limitation** 2, **restraint** 2.
**4.** [State of health] — *Syn.* physical state, fitness, lack of fitness, tone, form, trim, shape★; see also **health** 1, 2.
**5.** [★Illness] — *Syn.* ailment, infirmity, malady; see **disease**.
*See Synonym Study at* STATE.

**condition,** *v.* — *Syn.* adapt, modify, accustom, work out; see **practice** 1, **train** 3, 4.

**conditional,** *modif.* — *Syn.* provisional, provisory, conditioned, subject, modified by conditions, contingent, qualified, tentative, limited, restricted, dependent, relying on, subject to, restrictive, guarded, not absolute, granted on certain terms; see also **dependent** 3.

**conditionally,** *modif.* — *Syn.* provisionally, hypothetically, with the condition that, with the stipulation that, with reservations, with limitations, tentatively, possibly, with strings attached★; see also **temporarily**.

**conditioned,** *modif.* — *Syn.* trained, habituated, modified, learned; see **accustomed to, automatic** 2, **trained**.

**conditions,** *n.* — *Syn.* environment, surrounding(s), setting; see **circumstances** 2.

**condole,** *v.* — *Syn.* sympathize, console, commiserate, soothe; see **comfort, pity** 1.

**condolence,** *n.* — *Syn.* sympathy, comfort, solace; see **pity** 1.
*See Synonym Study at* PITY.

**condominium,** *n.* — *Syn.* commonly owned apartment house, cooperative apartment dwelling, jointly owned dwelling, townhouse complex, condo\*, co-op\*; see also **apartment house, home** 1.

**condone,** *v.* — *Syn.* pardon, excuse, overlook; see **approve** 1, **disregard, excuse.**

**condoning,** *modif.* — *Syn.* approving, tolerating, indulgent; see **humane** 1, **kind, lenient.**

**conducive,** *modif.* — *Syn.* accessory, contributory, favorable, promoting; see **helpful** 1.

**conduct,** *n.* **1.** [Behavior] — *Syn.* deportment, demeanor, manner; see **behavior** 1.
**2.** [Management] — *Syn.* guidance, regulation, government, care, charge, direction, treatment, carrying on, transaction, superintendence, oversight, posture, control, handling, wielding, rule, manipulation, strategy, policy, execution, tactics, supervision, regimen, plan, organization; see also **administration** 1.

**conduct,** *v.* **1.** [To guide] — *Syn.* escort, convoy, attend, show the way; see **accompany** 1, **lead** 1.
**2.** [To manage] — *Syn.* administer, handle, carry on, direct; see **manage** 1.
**3.** [To transmit] — *Syn.* convey, carry, pass on, transfer; see **carry** 1, 2, **send** 1, 2, 4.
*See Synonym Study at* MANAGE.

**conduct (oneself),** *v.* — *Syn.* behave, comport oneself, carry oneself; see **behave** 2.
*See Synonym Study at* BEHAVE.

**conductor,** *n.* **1.** [That which conducts] — *Syn.* conduit, conveyor, transmitter; see **channel** 1, **wire** 1, **wiring** 2, 3.
**2.** [One who conducts] — *Syn.* orchestra leader, director, pilot, head; see **administrator, guide** 1, **leader** 3.
**3.** [One in charge of a car or train] — *Syn.* trainman, railroad man, ticket taker, brakeman, streetcar conductor, motorman, bus driver, guard (British); see also **driver, engineer** 2.

**conduit,** *n.* — *Syn.* pipe, duct, channel, flume, canal, tube, conductor, cable, flow area, culvert, lead-in, lead-out, aqueduct, spout, trough, gully, gutter, sewer, watercourse, main, cloaca, race, drain, natural passage; see also **channel** 1.

**cone,** *n.* **1.** [A conical object] — *Syn.* conoid, cone-shaped area, conoidal area, conoidal surface, funnel, cornet, strobiloid.
Types of cones include: circular, right circular, chief, stepped, supplemental, oblique, retinal, endostylic, pyrometric, crystalline; cone of spread, cone of dispersion.
**2.** [A loudspeaker] — *Syn.* diaphragm, cone speaker, amplifier; see **loudspeaker.**
**3.** [A fruit-bearing cluster] — *Syn.* strobile, strobilus, fruit of the Coniferae, fruit of the Coniferales, raceme, catkin, ament; see also **flower** 1, **seed,** 1, 2.

**confection,** *n.* — *Syn.* sweet, candy, jam, dainty; see **cake** 2, **candy, jam** 1, **pastry.**

**confectionery,** *n.* — *Syn.* candy store, ice-cream parlor, pastry shop, carnival concession; see **bakery, store** 1.

**confederacy,** *n.* — *Syn.* alliance, loose union, confederation, conspiracy; see **alliance** 3, **government** 1, 2.
*See Synonym Study at* ALLIANCE.

**Confederacy,** *n.* — *Syn.* Confederate States of America, the South, secessionists, rebel states, Southern Confederacy, Southern aristocracy, Dixie, Dixieland, the Rebs\*; see also **South.**

**confederate,** *modif.* — *Syn.* federated, combined, confederated, federate, in alliance, incorporated, corporate, united, federal, unionized, syndicated, amalgamated, leagued, allied, associated, organized, in league, in cahoots\*; see also **joined, united.**

**confederate,** *n.* **1.** ally, accomplice, associate, partner; see **associate.**
*See Synonym Study at* ASSOCIATE.

**Confederate,** *modif.* — *Syn.* secessionist, Rebel, Southern, slave, slaveholding, south of the Mason Dixon line.

**Confederate,** *n.* — *Syn.* Southerner, secessionist, one of the Gray, Johnny Reb\*; see **rebel** 1.

**confer,** *v.* **1.** [To grant as a gift] — *Syn.* bestow, give, award, present; see **give** 1.
**2.** [To hold a conference] — *Syn.* converse, deliberate, parley; see **consult, discuss, talk** 1.
*See Synonym Study at* GIVE.

**conference,** *n.* **1.** [A meeting for discussion] — *Syn.* convention, colloquium, parley, interchange; see **gathering.**
**2.** [A consultation] — *Syn.* interview, appointment, audience, conferring; see **conversation, discussion** 1.
**3.** [An association of athletic teams] — *Syn.* league, circuit, ring; see **organization** 3.

**conferring,** *modif.* — *Syn.* holding a conference, consulting, discussing, deliberating, counseling, comparing opinions, conversing, meeting, talking, in conference, in conclave, in consultation.

**confess,** *v.* **1.** [To admit] — *Syn.* acknowledge, own, concede; see **admit** 3.
**2.** [To recount one's evil actions] — *Syn.* admit, divulge, relate, own up\*; see **admit** 2.
**3.** [To participate in the sacrament of confession] — *Syn.* go to confession, be shriven, confess to the priest, receive absolution, humble oneself, stand confessed as, make a confession; see also **admit** 2.
**4.** [To profess] — *Syn.* announce, state, avow; see **declare** 1.
*See Synonym Study at* ADMIT.

**confession,** *n.* **1.** [The act of confessing] — *Syn.* concession, acknowledgment, admission, allowance, owning to, owning up\*, revelation, revealing, disclosure, divulgence, publication, affirmation, assertion, unbosoming, utterance, vent, declaration, telling, relation, avowal, exposure, recitation, narration, exposé, acknowledgment of guilt, avowal of error, admission of guilt, admission of fault, proclamation, making public; see also **acknowledgment** 1. — *Ant.* concealment, DENIAL, disclaimer.
**2.** [That which has been confessed] — *Syn.* statement, disclosure, profession; see **admission** 4, **declaration** 1.
**3.** [A sacrament] — *Syn.* penance, absolution, contrition, repentance; see **penance** 2, **sacrament.**

**confessional,** *n.* — *Syn.* confession booth, confession chair, shriving pew; see **booth.**

**confessor,** *n.* **1.** [A priest who hears confessions] — *Syn.* priest, father confessor, spiritual judge, penitentiary; see **adviser, priest.**
**2.** [One who professes his or her faith in spite of persecution] — *Syn.* martyr, true believer, saint; see **believer, victim** 1.

**confidant,** *n.* — *Syn.* confidante, intimate, trusted friend, repository; see **adviser, friend** 1.

**confide,** *v.* **1.** [To reveal in trust] — *Syn.* disclose, admit, divulge; see **admit** 2, **reveal** 1, **tell** 1.
**2.** [To commit to the charge of] — *Syn.* consign, charge, entrust; see **commit** 2, **trust** 3.
*See Synonym Study at* COMMIT.

**confide in,** *v.* — *Syn.* trust in, rely on, talk freely to, open one's heart to; see **admit** 2, **trust** 1.

**confidence,** *n.* **1.** [Faith] — *Syn.* reliance, trust, belief; see **faith** 1.
**2.** [Self-assurance] — *Syn.* self-confidence, self-reliance, assurance, self-possession, aplomb, poise, morale,

fearlessness, boldness, hardihood, resolution, firmness, stoutheartedness, intrepidity, sureness, certitude, conviction, faith in oneself, self-esteem, tenacity, mettle, fortitude, élan, certainty, resoluteness, determination, daring, spirit, overconfidence, cockiness, arrogance, pluck*, dash*, grit*, cool*, heart*, backbone*, nerve*, spunk*, chutzpah*; see also **courage** 1, **determination** 2.

**3.** [A secret] — *Syn.* private matter, personal matter, privileged communication, confidential information; see **secret.**

---

*SYN.* — **confidence**, in this comparison, implies belief in one's own abilities, or, esp. in the form **self-confidence**, reliance on one's own powers *[he has confidence he will succeed; shy and lacking in self-confidence]*; **assurance**, in this connection, suggests an even stronger belief in one's ability, but in an unfavorable sense, it may connote (as may, occasionally, **confidence**) conceited or arrogant self-sufficiency; **self-possession** suggests that presence of mind which results from the ability to control one's feelings and behavior; **aplomb** refers, usually in a favorable sense, to an evident assurance of manner manifesting self-possession *[she stood her ground with admirable aplomb]* See also Synonym Study at BELIEF.

---

**confidence man,** *n.* — *Syn.* swindler, cheat, fraud, con man*; see **cheat** 1, **rascal.**
**confident,** *modif.* **1.** [Certain] — *Syn.* positive, sure, convinced, having faith in; see **certain** 1, 3, **trusting** 2.
**2.** [Self-assured] — *Syn.* self-confident, self-reliant, assured, having no misgivings, bold, fearless, sure of oneself, self-possessed, poised, dauntless, self-sufficient, presumptuous, overconfident, cocksure, cocky*; see also **certain** 1.
*See Synonym Study at CERTAIN.*
**confidential,** *modif.* — *Syn.* classified, intimate, privy, familiar; see **intimate** 1, **private, secret** 1, 3.
*See Synonym Study at FAMILIAR.*
**confidentially,** *modif.* — *Syn.* privately, personally, in confidence; see **secretly.**
**confidently,** *modif.* — *Syn.* in an assured manner, with conviction, having conviction, assuredly; see **boldly** 1, **positively** 1.
**configuration,** *n.* — *Syn.* form, contour, arrangement, shape; see **form** 1.
*See Synonym Study at FORM.*
**confine,** *v.* **1.** [To keep shut up] — *Syn.* imprison, immure, shut in, shut up, enclose; see also **hinder, imprison, separate** 2.
**2.** [To keep within limits] — *Syn.* limit, restrict, circumscribe, hold back; see **define** 1, **limit, restrain** 1, **restrict** 2.
*See Synonym Study at LIMIT.*
**confined,** *modif.* **1.** [Restricted] — *Syn.* limited, hampered, compassed, cramped; see **bound** 1, 2, **restrained, restricted.**
**2.** [Kept in due to indisposition] — *Syn.* indisposed, keeping to the house, bedridden, bedfast, on one's back, flat on one's back, invalided, ill, laid up, shut in, homebound, in childbed; see also **sick.**
**3.** [In prison] — *Syn.* imprisoned, in jail, behind bars, locked up, in bonds, in irons, in chains, jailed, held in custody, cooped up, immured, incarcerated, detained, under lock and key, on ice*. — *Ant.* FREE, released, at liberty.
**confinement,** *n.* **1.** [The state of being confined]

— *Syn.* restriction, limitation, circumscription, constraint, repression, control, coercion, keeping, safekeeping, custody, quarantine, curb, bounding, bounds, trammels, check, closeness, bonds, detention, imprisonment, incarceration, immuration; see also **captivity, chains, imprisonment** 1, **jail, restraint** 2. — *Ant.* FREEDOM, release, independence.
**2.** [The period that accompanies childbirth] — *Syn.* lying-in, accouchement, childbed, delivery, parturition, childbirth, travail, labor, one's time*; see also **childbirth, delivery** 2.
**confines,** *n.* **1.** [Borders] — *Syn.* bounds, limits, periphery; see **boundary.**
**2.** [Scope] — *Syn.* proportions, range, dimension; see **size** 2.
**3.** [Territory] — *Syn.* region, country, terrain; see **region** 1, **territory** 2.
**confining,** *modif.* — *Syn.* limiting, restricting, bounding, circumscribing, compassing, prescribing, restraining, hampering, repressing, trammeling, checking, enclosing, imprisoning, immuring, incarcerating, detaining, keeping locked up, keeping behind bars. — *Ant.* freeing, INFINITE, boundless.
**confining,** *n.* — *Syn.* restricting, enclosing, restraining, bounding, detaining, imprisoning.
**confirm,** *v.* **1.** [To strengthen] — *Syn.* make firm, reinforce, establish, fortify; see **strengthen.**
**2.** [To ratify] — *Syn.* sanction, affirm, settle; see **approve** 1, **endorse** 2.
**3.** [To prove] — *Syn.* verify, authenticate, validate; see **prove, verify.**
*See Synonym Study at VERIFY.*
**confirmation,** *n.* **1.** [The act of confirming] — *Syn.* ratification, proving, authentication, corroboration, verification, support, endorsement, sanction, sanctioning, authorization, substantiation, affirmation, acknowledgment, acceptance, passage, validation, certification, approval, attestation, assent, accord, avowal, admission, recognition, proof, evidence, witness, visa, nod, consent, testimony, agreement, corroborative statement, documentation, backing, circumstantiation, reinforcement, establishment; see also **agreement** 1, 3, **proof** 1. — *Ant.* annulment, CANCELLATION, disapproval, denial.
**2.** [A sacrament] — *Syn.* rite, consecration, liturgy; see **ceremony** 2, **sacrament** 1.
**confirmatory,** *modif.* — *Syn.* corroborative, agreeing, confirming, substantiating; see **affirmative.**
**confirmed,** *modif.* **1.** [Firmly established] — *Syn.* proved, valid, accepted; see **certain** 3, **established** 3, **guaranteed.**
**2.** [Inveterate] — *Syn.* ingrained, seasoned, regular; see **chronic, habitual** 1.
*See Synonym Study at CHRONIC.*
**confiscate,** *v.* — *Syn.* appropriate, impound, usurp; see **seize** 2, **steal.**
**conflagration,** *n.* — *Syn.* blaze, bonfire, holocaust; see **fire** 1.
**conflict,** *n.* **1.** [A fight] — *Syn.* battle, dispute, struggle; see **battle** 1, 2, **dispute, fight** 1.
**2.** [A state of discord] — *Syn.* opposition, friction, ambivalence, struggle; see **disagreement** 1, **opposition** 1.
*See Synonym Study at FIGHT.*
**conflict,** *v.* — *Syn.* clash, collide, contrast, contend; see **clash, differ** 1, **fight** 2, **oppose** 1, 2.
**conflicting,** *modif.* — *Syn.* clashing, contrary, opposing, contradictory, at odds, differing, discrepant, adverse, unfavorable; see also **different** 1, **incompatible.**

**confluence,** *n.* **1.** [Flowing together] — *Syn.* junction, conflux, convergence; see **meeting** 1.
**2.** [A flocking together] — *Syn.* crowd, concourse, assembly; see **gathering.**

**confluent,** *modif.* — *Syn.* meeting, joining, flowing, mingling, concurrent, coalescent, growing together, coming together, convergent; see also **concurrent** 2, **connecting.**

**conform,** *v.* — *Syn.* comply, follow, acquiesce, submit, fit in, assimilate, accommodate, adapt, adjust, accustom, acclimate, acclimatize, correspond, agree, accord, harmonize, fit, suit, reconcile, do as others do, conventionalize, fit the pattern, fit the mold, be conventional, be regular, settle down, obey, abide by, yield, follow the rules, get in line, get into line, go by, keep to, fall in with, adhere, be guided by, follow the lead of, follow suit, live up to, measure up to, keep up with, be in fashion, keep up with the Joneses*, join the parade*, play the game*, go according to Hoyle*, follow the beaten path*, toe the line, toe the mark*, run with the pack*, swim with the stream*, follow the crowd*, travel in a rut*, do in Rome as the Romans do; see also **agree, follow** 2, **settle** 8.
— *Ant.* conflict, DIFFER, disagree, rebel.
*See Synonym Study at* ADJUST, AGREE.

**conformable,** *modif.* **1.** [Alike] — *Syn.* resembling, similar, comparable; see **alike** 2, **like.**
**2.** [In agreement] — *Syn.* unified, consistent, suitable; see **harmonious** 2.
**3.** [Obedient] — *Syn.* amenable, submissive, agreeable; see **docile, obedient** 1.

**conformation,** *n.* **1.** [Agreement] — *Syn.* compliance, conformity, concord, unison, harmony, affinity, congruity, compatibility, synchronism, adaptation, accordance; see also **agreement** 1, 2.
**2.** [Shape] — *Syn.* structure, formation, symmetrical arrangement; see **form** 1, **symmetry.**

**conforming,** *modif.* — *Syn.* agreeing, in line with, in agreement, in conformity; see **conventional** 2, 3, **harmonious** 2, **obedient** 1.

**conformist,** *modif.* — *Syn.* conforming, conventional, complying, unoriginal; see **conventional** 2, 3, **harmonious** 2, **obedient** 1.

**conformist,** *n.* — *Syn.* conformer, conventionalist, follower, traditionalist, bourgeois, Babbitt, sheep, copycat*, clone*; see also **follower.**

**conformity,** *n.* **1.** [Similarity] — *Syn.* congruity, correspondence, resemblance; see **conformation** 1, **similarity.**
**2.** [Obedience] — *Syn.* compliance, conventionality, conformism, lockstep; see **docility.**

**confound,** *v.* **1.** [To mix] — *Syn.* jumble, commingle, blend, mix up; see **mix** 1, **muddle** 1.
**2.** [To confuse] — *Syn.* puzzle, perplex, bewilder, frustrate; see **confuse.**
*See Synonym Study at* CONFUSE.

**confounded,** *modif.* — *Syn.* confused, bewildered, disconcerted; see **doubtful** 2.

**confront,** *v.* — *Syn.* face, brave, defy, stand up to; see **dare** 2, **face** 1.

**confrontation,** *n.* — *Syn.* meeting, encounter, battle, showdown; see **dispute, fight** 1, **meeting** 1.

**confronting,** *modif.* — *Syn.* facing, face to face, meeting, encountering, in the teeth of, in the face of*; see also **opposing** 1, **rebellious** 1.

**confuse,** *v.* — *Syn.* puzzle, perplex, bewilder, confound, nonplus, disconcert, abash, fluster, discompose, flurry, dumbfound, upset, befuddle, baffle, mislead, misinform, embarrass, daze, astonish, disarrange, disorder, jumble, mix up, garble, scramble, blend, mix, mingle,

cloud, becloud, fog, stir up, agitate, bedevil, worry, trouble, snarl, unsettle, disorient, muddle, clutter, darken, addle, discomfit, fuddle, complicate, involve, rattle, unhinge, derange, frustrate, perturb, dismay, faze, distract, entangle, encumber, befog, obscure, obfuscate, mystify, lead astray, addle the wits, embroil, render uncertain, make a hash of*, make a mess of*, throw off*, throw off the scent*, foul up*, ball up*, cross up*, put at a loss*, stump*, make one's head swim*, flummox*, throw*, discombobulate*; see also **disturb** 2, **hide** 1, **tangle.**
— *Ant.* CLEAR, clarify, untangle.

**SYN.** — **confuse** implies a mixing up mentally to a greater or lesser degree; **confound** implies such confusion as completely frustrates or greatly astonishes one; **puzzle** implies that one has great difficulty in understanding or solving something, as a situation or problem, because of its intricacy or baffling quality; **perplex,** in addition, implies uncertainty or even worry as to what to think, say, or do; **bewilder** implies such utter confusion that the mind is staggered beyond the ability to think clearly; **nonplus** implies such perplexity or confusion that one is utterly incapable of speaking, acting, or thinking further; **dumbfound** specifically implies as its effect a nonplused or confounded state in which one is momentarily struck speechless

**confused,** *modif.* **1.** [Puzzled in mind] — *Syn.* disconcerted, perplexed, disoriented; see **bewildered, doubtful** 2.
**2.** [Not properly distinguished] — *Syn.* mixed up, mistaken, jumbled, snarled, deranged, out of order, embroiled, disarrayed, confounded, chaotic, disordered, disorganized, muddled, scrambled, garbled, miscellaneous, inextricable, slovenly, untidy, messy, addled, misapprehended, unclear, incoherent, involved, miscalculated, misunderstood, blurred, obscure, obscured, tangled, mazy, topsy-turvy*, higgledy-piggledy*, balled up*, fouled up*, screwed up*, in a mess*, haywire*, snafu*, bollixed up*; see also **disordered, disorderly** 1, **obscure** 1, **tangled.** — *Ant.* discriminated, DISTINGUISHED, ordered.

**confusing,** *modif.* — *Syn.* puzzling, bewildering, disconcerting, abashing, confounding, baffling, mystifying, perplexing, discomposing, disturbing, disorienting, unsettling, upsetting, obscuring, blurring, fuddling, befuddling, addling, complicated, involved, complex; see also **confused** 2, **difficult** 2, **obscure** 1. — *Ant.* reassuring, ORDERLY, clear.

**confusion,** *n.* **1.** [The act of confusing] — *Syn.* obscuring, blurring, mixing up, upsetting, disturbing, embarrassing, discomfiting, abashing, agitating, addling, fuddling, miscalculation, miscalculating, befuddling, tangling, mixing, cluttering, disarranging, unsettling, dumbfounding, confounding, perplexing, demoralization, stirring up, snarling, embroiling, misconceiving.
— *Ant.* straightening, ORDER, arranging.
**2.** [A confused state] — *Syn.* disorder, disarray, chaos, jumble, mess, muddle, lack of clearness, lack of distinction, mixup, bewilderment, perplexity, puzzlement, disorientation, bafflement, dislocation, anarchy, complication, intricacy, untidiness, complexity, labyrinth, wilderness, discomfiture, embarrassment, abashment, difficulty, mistake, turmoil, tumult, pandemonium, bedlam, commotion, stir, flurry, ferment, imbroglio, convulsion, bustle, trouble, row, riot, uproar, fracas, agitation, discomposure, emotional upset, daze, fog, haze, blur, ambiguity, obscurity, perturbation, mystification, consternation, befuddlement, distraction, stupefaction,

racket, din, Babel, hubbub, ado, disarrangement, mismanagement, excitement, flutter, dither, hysteria, disharmony, turbulence, dismay, uncertainty, maze, quandary, clutter, entanglement, tangle, disorganization, breakdown, knot, congestion, tie-up, interference, nervousness, melee, Gordian knot, derangement, snarl, snag, farrago, hodgepodge, mare's-nest, jungle*, to-do*, hurly-burly*, shutdown*, bungle*, botch*, foul-up*, screw-up*, rumpus*, scramble*, shuffle*, stew*, muddle-headedness*, discombobulation*, tizzy*, going round and round*, jam*, fix*, pretty mess*, pretty pickle*, snafu*; see also **disorder** 2, **disturbance** 2, **embarrassment** 1. — *Ant.* QUIET, calm, order, comprehension.
**covered with confusion** — *Syn.* confused, embarrassed, bewildered; see **ashamed.**

---

*SYN.* — **confusion** suggests an indiscriminate mixing or putting together of things so that it is difficult to distinguish the individual elements or parts /the hall was a *confusion* of languages/; **disorder** and **disarray** imply a disturbance of the proper order or arrangement of parts /the room was in *disorder*, her clothes were in *disarray*/; **chaos** implies total and apparently irremediable lack of organization /the troops are in a state of *chaos*/; **jumble** suggests a confused mixture of dissimilar things /his drawer was a *jumble* of clothing and books/; **muddle** implies a snarled confusion resulting from mismanagement or incompetence /they've made a *muddle* of the negotiations/

---

**confute,** *v.* — *Syn.* disprove, defeat, overwhelm, overcome, silence, expose, bring to naught, rebut, controvert, parry, negate, vanquish, demolish, invalidate, answer conclusively, overturn, prove to be wrong, set aside, overcome in debate, upset, subvert, quash, oppugn, contradict, argue down, get the better of, clinch an argument, discredit, show up*, shut up*, not leave a leg to stand on*, cut the ground from under one's feet*, put down*; see also **deny, oppose** 1, **refute.** — *Ant.* prove, VERIFY, confirm.
*See Synonym Study at* DISPROVE.
**congeal,** *v.* 1. [To solidify as by freezing or curdling] — *Syn.* set, refrigerate, solidify; see **freeze** 1, **harden** 1, 2.
2. [To clot] — *Syn.* solidify, jell, coagulate; see **harden** 1, 2, **thicken** 1.
**congenial,** *modif.* 1. [Agreeable] — *Syn.* kindred, compatible, suitable, simpatico; see **friendly** 1, **harmonious** 2.
2. [Favorable] — *Syn.* agreeable, delightful, genial; see **pleasant** 1, 2.
**congenital,** *modif.* — *Syn.* inborn, innate, intrinsic; see **fundamental** 1, **inherent, native** 1, **natural** 1.
*See Synonym Study at* INNATE.
**congeries,** *n.* — *Syn.* pile, accumulation, mass; see **bunch** 1, **collection** 2, **heap.**
**congested,** *modif.* — *Syn.* clogged, blocked, overcrowded, stuffed; see **full** 1, **jammed** 1, 2.
**congestion,** *n.* — *Syn.* profusion, crowdedness, crowding, overcrowding, clogging, overpopulation, press, jam, traffic jam, bottleneck, gridlock, overdevelopment, too much, too many, excessive concentration, surfeit, blockage, stoppage, cramming, stuffing, obstruction, engorgement, hyperemia; see also **excess** 1.
**conglomerate,** *modif.* — *Syn.* blended, variegated, heterogeneous; see **complex** 1, **different** 2, **mixed** 1.
**congratulate,** *v.* — *Syn.* felicitate, wish joy to, toast; see **compliment** 2, **praise** 1, **salute** 2.

**congratulation,** *n.* — *Syn.* salute, best wishes, well-wishing; see **compliment, praise** 2.
**congratulations,** *interj.* — *Syn.* best wishes, compliments, felicitations, many happy returns, nice going, good work, good for you, bully for you; hear, hear; bless you, congrats*, way to go*; see also **toast** 1.
**congratulatory,** *modif.* — *Syn.* congratulating, celebratory, flattering, laudatory; see **complimentary** 1.
**congregate,** *v.* — *Syn.* assemble, convene, meet, converge; see **gather** 1.
**congregation,** *n.* — *Syn.* meeting, group, assemblage; see **gathering.**
**congress,** *n.* [*Often capital C*] — *Syn.* parliament, deliberative assembly, legislative body; see **committee, government** 2, **legislature.**
**congruent,** *modif.* — *Syn.* in agreement, harmonious, corresponding; see **harmonious** 2, **like.**
**congruous,** *modif.* — *Syn.* suitable, appropriate, fitting, consonant; see **fit** 1, **harmonious** 2.
**conical,** *modif.* — *Syn.* cone-shaped, funnel-shaped, coned, tapering, tapered, conoid, conoidal, strobiloid, strobilate, pointed, pyramidal; see also **sharp** 2.
**conjectural,** *modif.* — *Syn.* theoretical, assumed, unresolved, speculative; see **hypothetical** 1, **theoretical, uncertain** 2.
**conjecture,** *n.* — *Syn.* inference, theory, guess; see **guess, hypothesis, opinion** 1.
*See Synonym Study at* GUESS.
**conjecture,** *v.* — *Syn.* suppose, speculate, surmise; see **assume** 1, **guess** 1, **think** 1.
**conjugal,** *modif.* — *Syn.* nuptial, marital, connubial; see **matrimonial.**
**conjunction,** *n.* 1. [Act of joining together] — *Syn.* combination, connection, association; see **union** 1.
2. [Concurrence] — *Syn.* congruency, concomitance, parallelism; see **agreement** 2, **coincidence** 1.
3. [A syntactic connecting word] .
Conjunctions include: and, but, if, for, or, nor, so, yet, only, else, than, before, since, then, though, when, where, why, both, either, while, as, neither, although, because, unless, until.
**conjure,** *v.* 1. [To practice magic] — *Syn.* enchant, cast a spell, practice legerdemain; see **charm** 1.
2. [To appeal to] — *Syn.* entreat, implore, adjure; see **beg** 1, **urge** 2.
**conjurer,** *n.* — *Syn.* sorcerer, seer, magician; see **magician** 1, 2, **witch, wizard** 1.
**conjure up,** *v.* 1. [To summon] — *Syn.* call, invoke, materialize; see **summon** 1, **urge** 2.
2. [To recollect] — *Syn.* recall, evoke, call to mind, bring to mind; see **remember** 1.
**con man*,** *n.* — *Syn.* confidence man, con artist, swindler, scamp; see **cheat** 1, **rascal.**
**connect,** *v.* 1. [To join] — *Syn.* combine, unite, attach; see **join** 1.
2. [To associate] — *Syn.* relate, equate, correlate; see **compare** 1.
*See Synonym Study at* JOIN.
**connected,** *modif.* 1. [Joined together] — *Syn.* united, combined, coupled; see **joined.**
2. [Related] — *Syn.* associated, applicable, pertinent; see **related** 2, **relevant.**
3. [Joined in proper order] — *Syn.* coherent, associated, consistent; see **consecutive** 1, **logical** 1.
**connecting,** *modif.* — *Syn.* joining, linking, connective, combining, uniting, associating, relating, tying together, bringing together, knitting together, fusing together, hooking together, clinching, attaching, fastening, mixing, mingling, fusing, welding, intertwining, interlacing,

pairing, coupling, bridging, spanning, concatenating, making complementary, making interdependent; see also **joined.**

**connection,** *n.* **1.** [Relationship] — *Syn.* kinship, association, reciprocity; see **association** 2, **relationship.**
**2.** [A junction] — *Syn.* combination, juncture, consolidation, conjunction; see **union** 1.
**3.** [A link] — *Syn.* attachment, fastening, bond, nexus; see **joint** 1, **link.**
**4.** [\*An agent; *often plural*] — *Syn.* contact, go-between, intermediary; see **agent** 1, **associate, messenger.**
**in connection with** — *Syn.* in conjunction with, associated with, together with; see **about** 1, **with.**

**connoisseur,** *n.* — *Syn.* judge, expert, authority, aesthete, epicure, gourmet, epicurean, specialist, critic, collector, dilettante, gastronome, gourmand, bon vivant, tastemaker, arbiter of taste, *cognoscente* (Italian), man of taste, woman of taste, virtuoso, maven\*, culture vulture\*.

---

*SYN.* — **connoisseur** is one who has expert knowledge or a keen discrimination in matters of art and, by extension, in any matters of taste *[a connoisseur of fine foods]*; **aesthete,** although applied to one highly sensitive to art and beauty, is often used derogatorily to connote effeteness or decadence; **dilettante** originally referred to one who appreciates art as distinguished from one who creates it, but is now chiefly used disparagingly of one who dabbles superficially in the arts

---

**connotation,** *n.* — *Syn.* implication, intention, essence, undertone; see **hint** 1, **meaning.**
**connotative,** *modif.* — *Syn.* connoting, meaning, implying, suggesting, suggestive of, hinting; see also **referring.**
**connote,** *v.* — *Syn.* imply, suggest, indicate; see **hint, mean** 1.
**connubial,** *modif.* — *Syn.* marital, nuptial, conjugal; see **matrimonial.**
**conquer,** *v.* **1.** [To gain control over] — *Syn.* surmount, prevail over, capture, overcome; see **succeed** 1, **win** 1.
**2.** [To defeat] — *Syn.* subdue, overcome, vanquish; see **defeat** 2.

---

*SYN.* — **conquer** implies gaining mastery over someone or something by physical, mental, or moral force *[to conquer bad habits]*; **vanquish** implies a thorough overpowering or frustrating, often in a single conflict or battle *[a vanquished army]*; to **defeat** is to win a victory over or get the better of, often only for the time being *[the defeated troops rallied and counterattacked]*; **overcome** implies the overpowering of an antagonist or the surmounting of difficulties; to **subdue** is to defeat so as to break the spirit of resistance; to **subjugate** is to bring under complete subjection; **overthrow** implies a victory in which a prevailing power is dislodged by force; to **rout** is to defeat so overwhelmingly that the enemy is put to disorderly flight

---

**conquering,** *modif.* — *Syn.* victorious, winning, dominating; see **successful, triumphant.**
**conqueror,** *n.* — *Syn.* vanquisher, victor, champion, conquistador; see **hero** 1, **winner.**
**conquest,** *n.* — *Syn.* subjugation, victory, success, conquering; see **triumph** 1, **victory** 1.
*See Synonym Study at* VICTORY.
**consanguinity,** *n.* **1.** [Any close connection] — *Syn.* affiliation, connection, affinity, association; see **brotherhood** 1, **relationship.**

**2.** [Blood relationship] — *Syn.* kinship, lineage, strain; see **brotherhood** 1, **family** 1, **race** 2.
**conscience,** *n.* — *Syn.* moral sense, inner voice, the still small voice\*; see **duty** 1, **morals, shame** 2.
**have on one's conscience** — *Syn.* be culpable, be blamable for, be responsible for; see **guilty** 2.
**in (all) conscience** — *Syn.* in all fairness, rightly, fairly, properly; see **justly** 1, **surely.**
**conscience-stricken,** *modif.* — *Syn.* remorseful, repentant, chastened, guilt-ridden; see **sorry** 1.
**conscientious,** *modif.* **1.** [Principled] — *Syn.* scrupulous, honest, upright, strict; see **faithful, reliable** 1.
**2.** [Thorough] — *Syn.* fastidious, meticulous, painstaking, complete; see **careful.**
**conscientiousness,** *n.* — *Syn.* scrupulousness, pains, exactitude, punctiliousness, dutifulness, faithfulness, mindfulness, steadfastness, veracity, uprightness, honor, meticulousness, incorruptibility; see also **care** 1, **duty** 1, **honesty** 1, **responsibility** 1. — *Ant.* negligence, INDIFFERENCE, nonchalance.
**conscientious objector,** *n.* — *Syn.* pacifist, war-hater, noncombatant, neutralist, nonviolent person, C.O., conchie\*, draft dodger\*, peacenik\*.
Religious groups that object to warfare on conscientious grounds include: Quakers, Seventh Day Adventists, Jehovah's Witnesses, Plymouth Brethren, Jains.
**conscious,** *modif.* **1.** [Aware] — *Syn.* cognizant, informed, sensible of, apprised, assured, inwardly sensible, discerning, percipient, apperceptive, felt, known, perceived, sensitive to, acquainted, attentive, watchful, mindful, vigilant, understanding, perceiving, noticing, knowing, preoccupied, keen, alert, awake to, alert to, alive to, on the qui vive, hip to\*, hep to\*, on to\*, with it\*, wise to\*, on top of\*; see also **intelligent** 1. — *Ant.* UNAWARE, insensitive, inattentive.
**2.** [In possession of one's senses] — *Syn.* awake, alert, sentient, endowed with consciousness, knowing, seeing, recognizing, able to recognize, in one's right mind, wideawake; see also **alive** 1. — *Ant.* UNCONSCIOUS, insensible, in a faint.
**3.** [Deliberate] — *Syn.* intentional, calculated, purposive, studied; see **deliberate** 1.

---

*SYN.* — **conscious** implies awareness of a sensation, feeling, fact, condition, etc. and may suggest mere recognition or a focusing of attention *[conscious of a draft in the room, acutely conscious of her own limitations]*; **aware** implies having knowledge of something through alertness in observing or in interpreting what one sees, hears, feels, etc. *[to be aware of a fact]*; one is **cognizant** of something when one has certain or special knowledge of it through observation or information *[cognizant of the terms of the will]*; **sensible** implies awareness of something that is not expressed directly or explicitly *[sensible of their solemn grief]*

---

**consciousness,** *n.* — *Syn.* awareness, cognizance, mindfulness, sentience; see **awareness, knowledge** 1.
**conscript,** *n.* — *Syn.* recruit, draftee, inductee, infantryman; see **recruit, soldier.**
**conscript,** *v.* — *Syn.* draft, enroll, induct, call up; see **enlist** 1, **recruit** 1.
**conscription,** *n.* — *Syn.* draft, enrollment, induction, choice; see **draft** 6, **selection** 1.
**consecrate,** *v.* **1.** [To dedicate to God] — *Syn.* hallow, sanctify, anoint; see **bless** 3.
**2.** [To set apart] — *Syn.* dedicate, ordain, devote, apply; see **dedicate** 2.
*See Synonym Study at* DEDICATE.

**consecrated,** *modif.* — *Syn.* blessed, sanctified, hallowed; see **divine** 2.

**consecration,** *n.* — *Syn.* sanctification, exaltation, glorification, dedication, devotion, hallowing, ordination, canonization, immortalization, apotheosis, enthronement, making holy, celebrating, blessing, anointing; see also **celebration** 1.

**consecutive,** *modif.* **1.** [Successive] — *Syn.* continuous, serial, seriatim, in turn, progressive, connected, in order, in sequence, sequential, going on, continuing, following, one after the other, serialized, numerical, back-to-back*; see also **chronological, constant** 1.
**2.** [Characterized by logical sequence] — *Syn.* coherent, logical, connected, following; see **logical** 1, **understandable.**

**consecutively,** *modif.* — *Syn.* following, successively, continuously, serially, progressively, sequentially, in succession, in file, Indian file*; see also **consecutive, gradually.**

**consensus,** *n.* — *Syn.* consent, unison, accord, general agreement; see **agreement** 2.

**consent,** *n.* — *Syn.* assent, approval, acquiescence; see **permission.**
**by common consent** — *Syn.* in agreement, in accord, cooperatively, in unison; see **unanimously.**

**consent,** *v.* — *Syn.* accede, assent, acquiesce, agree to, concur, approve of, sanction, permit, allow, subscribe to, comply, yield, go along with, give in; see also **agree, allow** 1, **approve** 1.

---

**SYN.** — **consent** implies compliance with something proposed or requested, stressing this as an act of the will; to **assent** is to express acceptance of or adherence to an opinion or proposition; **agree** implies accord reached by settling differences of opinion or overcoming resistance; **concur** implies agreement arrived at formally on a specific matter, often with regard to a line of action; to **accede** is to yield one's assent to a proposal; **acquiesce** implies tacit agreement or restraint of opposition in accepting something about which one has reservations

---

**consequence,** *n.* **1.** [Effect] — *Syn.* result, outgrowth, end, outcome; see **result.**
**2.** [Importance] — *Syn.* moment, value, weight; see **importance** 1.
*See Synonym Study at* IMPORTANCE, RESULT.
**in consequence (of)** — *Syn.* consequent on, as a result of, following, consequently; see **because.**
**take the consequences** — *Syn.* accept the results of one's actions, suffer, bear the burden of; see **endure** 2.

**consequent,** *modif.* **1.** [Following] — *Syn.* resulting, sequential, ensuing, indirect; see **following.**
**2.** [Logical] — *Syn.* reasonable, consistent, inferable; see **logical** 1, **understandable.**

**consequential,** *modif.* — *Syn.* significant, eventful, considerable; see **important** 1.

**conservation,** *n.* — *Syn.* preservation, maintenance, protection, conservancy, planned management, sustentation, keeping, conserving, guarding, storage, saving, safekeeping, upkeep, husbandry, economy, keeping in trust, keeping in a safe state, environmentalism; see also **custody** 1. — *Ant.* WASTE, destruction, misuse.

**conservatism,** *n.* — *Syn.* opposition to change, traditionalism, orthodoxy, moderation, inaction, preservation, conservativeness, unprogressiveness, ultraconservatism, reactionaryism, rightism, Toryism, Bourbonism, standpattism*; see also **reaction** 2, **stability** 1.

**conservative,** *modif.* — *Syn.* traditional, reactionary, conventional, moderate, unprogressive, illiberal, rightwing, ultraconservative, conserving, holding to, preserving, unchanging, stable, constant, firm, obstinate, inflexible, opposed to change, cautious, careful, sober, Tory, rightist, right-of-center, taking no chances, timid, not extreme, undaring, disliking novelty, die-hard, oldline, unreconstructed, hidebound, rearguard, in a rut*, in a groove*, standpat*; see also **careful, moderate** 3. — *Ant.* LIBERAL, progressive, risky.

**conservative,** *n.* — *Syn.* reactionary, right-winger, preserver, die-hard, conserver, champion of the status quo, opponent of change, classicist, traditionalist, moderate, Tory, Whig, Federalist, Bourbon, rightist, fundamentalist, standpat, ultraconservative, obstructionist, conventionalist, John Bircher, Reaganite, (old) fogy, mossback*, fossil*, Neanderthal*, stick-in-the-mud*, square*. — *Ant.* RADICAL, progressive, liberal.

**conservatory,** *n.* **1.** [A greenhouse] — *Syn.* glasshouse, hothouse, nursery; see **greenhouse.**
**2.** [A school of music] — *Syn.* college of music, conservatoire, studio; see **academy** 1, **school** 1.

**conserve,** *n.* — *Syn.* jam, fruit butter, marmalade; see **jam** 1, **jelly** 1.

**conserve,** *v.* — *Syn.* keep, preserve, husband, save; see **maintain** 3, **preserve** 9.

**consider,** *v.* **1.** [To take into account] — *Syn.* allow for, provide for, grant, accede, concede, acknowledge, admit, assent to, subscribe to, recognize, regard, respect, think of, make allowance for, take into consideration, keep in mind, bear in mind, heed, factor in, reckon with; see also **admit** 3. — *Ant.* deny, ignore, reject.
**2.** [To regard] — *Syn.* look upon, count, analyze, hold, suppose, deem, judge, take for, view, think of, set down, reckon, rate, estimate; see also **estimate** 2, **reckon.**
**3.** [To ponder] — *Syn.* contemplate, think about, think over, reflect, weigh, study, deliberate, cogitate, examine, take up, deal with, take under consideration, take under advisement, talk over, mull over, toss around*, bat around*, kick around*, chew over*, play around with*, see about*, dream of*, flirt with (an idea)*; see also **examine** 1, **reconsider, think** 1.

---

**SYN.** — **consider,** in this comparison, denotes a directing of the mind to something in order to understand it or to make a decision about it /to *consider* suggestions for improvement/; **study** implies more intense concentration of the mind and methodical attention to details /to *study* the effects of a drug/; **contemplate** implies a deep, continued mental viewing of a thing, sometimes suggesting the use of intuitive powers in envisioning something or dwelling upon it; **weigh** suggests a balancing of contradictory information, conflicting opinions, or possible eventualities in reaching a decision; **reflect,** suggesting a turning of one's thoughts back to something, implies quiet, earnest consideration

---

**considerable,** *modif.* **1.** [Important] — *Syn.* noteworthy, significant, essential; see **important** 1, **much** 1.
**2.** [Much or large] — *Syn.* sizable, ample, substantial, goodly; see **large** 1, **much** 2, **plentiful** 1.

**considerate,** *modif.* — *Syn.* thoughtful, attentive, kind, solicitous; see **kind, polite** 1, **thoughtful** 2.
*See Synonym Study at* THOUGHTFUL.

**consideration,** *n.* **1.** [The act of considering] — *Syn.* reflection, study, deliberation, forethought; see **attention** 1, **reflection** 1, **thought** 1.
**2.** [The state of being considerate] — *Syn.* kindliness, thoughtfulness, attentiveness, concern; see **courtesy** 1, **kindness** 1, **tolerance** 1.

**3.** [Payment] — *Syn.* remuneration, compensation, recompense, fee; see **compensation, payment** 1.

**4.** [Something to be considered] — *Syn.* factor, point, concern, situation, problem, judgment, notion, fancy, perplexity, puzzle, proposal, difficulty, incident, evidence, new development, occurrence, state, estate, pass, occasion, motive, cause, exigency, emergency, idea, thought, minutiae, plan, particulars, items, scope, extent, magnitude; see also **event** 1, **opinion** 1.

**in consideration of** — *Syn.* because of, on account of, in return for; see **considering, for.**

**on no consideration** — *Syn.* not for any reason, on no account, by no means; see **never.**

**take into consideration** — *Syn.* take into account, weigh, keep in mind; see **consider** 1, 3.

**under consideration** — *Syn.* being thought over, being discussed, being evaluated; see **considered** 1.

**considered,** *modif.* **1.** [Thought through] — *Syn.* carefully thought about, treated, gone into, contemplated, weighed, mediated, investigated, examined; see also **determined** 1.

**2.** [Deliberate] — *Syn.* well chosen, given due consideration, advised; see **deliberate** 1.

**considering,** *prep. & conj.* — *Syn.* in light of, in view of, in consideration of, pending, taking into account, everything being equal, inasmuch as, insomuch as, forasmuch as, with something in view, being as how*.

**consign,** *v.* **1.** [To give over or deliver] — *Syn.* convey, dispatch, transfer; see **give** 1, **send** 1, **ship.**

**2.** [To put in the charge of] — *Syn.* commit, entrust, relegate; see **commit** 2.

*See Synonym Study at* COMMIT.

**consignee,** *n.* — *Syn.* representative, factor, proctor, recipient; see **agent** 1, **means** 1, **receiver** 1.

**consignor,** *n.* — *Syn.* sender, shipper, dispatcher, distributor; see **merchant.**

**consistency,** *n.* **1.** [Harmony] — *Syn.* congruity, agreement, union, correspondence, uniformity, accord, appropriateness, unity, cohesion, coherence, compatibility, concurrence, proportion, conformability, steadiness, persistence, sameness; see also **agreement** 2, **constancy** 1, **regularity.** — *Ant.* incongruity, DISAGREEMENT, inconsistency.

**2.** [The degree of firmness or thickness] — *Syn.* hardness, softness, elasticity, pliability, density, firmness, flexibility, suppleness, limberness, plasticity, moldability, bendability, bendableness, viscosity, solidity, viscidity; see also **density** 1, **texture** 1.

**consistent,** *modif.* **1.** [Being in logical agreement] — *Syn.* compatible, in accord, consonant; see **harmonious** 2, **like, logical** 1.

**2.** [Holding to the same principles or practice] — *Syn.* steady, uniform, unvarying, unswerving; see **constant** 1, **faithful, regular** 3.

**consist of,** *v.* — *Syn.* be composed of, embody, contain, involve; see **comprise, include** 1.

**consolation,** *n.* **1.** [Solace] — *Syn.* sympathy, comfort, compassion; see **pity** 1, **sympathy** 2.

**2.** [Something that consoles] — *Syn.* comfort, ease, support; see **encouragement** 2, **relief** 4.

**consolation prize,** *n.* — *Syn.* second-place honor, booby prize, red ribbon; see **prize.**

**console,** *v.* — *Syn.* solace, comfort, soothe, reassure; see **comfort, sympathize.**

*See Synonym Study at* COMFORT.

**consolidate,** *v.* **1.** [To become united] — *Syn.* combine, solidify, condense, merge; see **unite** 1.

**2.** [To cause to unite] — *Syn.* combine, join, unite, mass, amass, bring together, piece together, put together, condense, compact, compress, solidify, make firm, thicken, concentrate, fuse, blend, centralize, connect, mix, conjoin, incorporate, compound, hitch, bind, concatenate, unify, streamline; see also **compress, pack** 2. — *Ant.* sever, CUT, scatter.

**3.** [To develop as a defensible position] — *Syn.* fortify, add to, build up; see **strengthen.**

*See Synonym Study at* JOIN.

**consolidation,** *n.* **1.** [Union] — *Syn.* alliance, merger, federation; see **incorporation** 2, **union** 1.

**2.** [Solidification] — *Syn.* compression, concentration, strengthening, stabilization; see **solidification** 1.

**consonant,** *n.*

Linguistic terms referring to consonant sounds include: voiceless, voiced; labial, bilabial, labiodental, apical, dental, alveolar, retroflex, frontal, alveopalatal, prepalatal, dorsal, palatal, velar, uvular, glottal, pharyngeal, interdental, labiovelar; stop, fricative, spirant, lenis, resonant, sibilant; aspirated, unaspirated, affricated, glottalized, preaspirated, prenasalized, implosive, plosive, nasal; click, glide, continuant, trill, flap.

In spelling, English consonants are: b, c, d, f, g, h, j, k, l, m, n, p, q, r, s, t, v, w, x, y, z; see also **letter** 1, **sound** 2, **vowel.**

**consort,** *n.* — *Syn.* spouse, mate, companion, associate; see **friend** 1, **husband, wife.**

**consort,** *v.* **1.** [To join] — *Syn.* fraternize, associate, keep company; see **accompany** 1, **associate** 1, **join** 2.

**2.** [To be in agreement] — *Syn.* harmonize, concur, coincide; see **agree, conform.**

**conspectus,** *n.* — *Syn.* précis, outline, synopsis, survey; see **summary.**

**conspicuous,** *modif.* **1.** [Attracting attention] — *Syn.* outstanding, striking, eminent, distinguished, celebrated, noted, notable, illustrious, prominent, commanding, well-known, salient, signal, marked, arresting, remarkable, renowned, famed, notorious, flagrant, glaring, gross, rank, important, influential, far-famed, noticeable, the observed of all observers; see also **famous, striking.** — *Ant.* unknown, INCONSPICUOUS, unsung.

**2.** [Obvious] — *Syn.* apparent, evident, distinct; see **noticeable, obvious** 1.

*See Synonym Study at* NOTICEABLE.

**conspiracy,** *n.* — *Syn.* plot, intrigue, collusion, connivance; see **intrigue** 1, **plot** 1, **trick** 1.

*See Synonym Study at* PLOT.

**conspirator,** *n.* — *Syn.* betrayer, schemer, cabalist, confederate; see **associate, traitor.**

**conspire,** *v.* **1.** [To plan secretly] — *Syn.* plot, scheme, contrive, intrigue; see **plan** 1.

**2.** [To act together] — *Syn.* join, collude, combine, concur; see **cooperate** 1, **unite** 1.

**constancy,** *n.* **1.** [Faithfulness] — *Syn.* fidelity, attachment, adherence, fealty, allegiance, devotion, ardor, eagerness, zeal, passion, love, earnestness, steadfastness, permanence, staunchness, principle, integrity, honor, faith, honesty, devotedness, abidingness, endurance, dependability, trustworthiness, trustiness, unchangeableness, consistency, regularity, certainty, unfailingness; see also **loyalty, reliability.** — *Ant.* faithlessness, DISLOYALTY, perfidy.

**2.** [Determination] — *Syn.* resolution, perseverance, doggedness, firmness; see **determination** 2.

**constant,** *modif.* **1.** [Not changing or ceasing] — *Syn.* steady, uniform, unchanging, invariable, continuous, persistent, continual, incessant, ceaseless, perpetual, unceasing, unremitting, uninterrupted, regular, repeated, unvarying, equable, even, fixed, consistent, connected, unbroken, nonstop, relentless, immutable, monotonous, monochrome, monochromatic, standardized, regularized, interminable, endless, unending, never-ending, permanent, eternal, everlasting; see also **perpetual** 1, 2, **regular** 3.

**2.** [Faithful] — *Syn.* steadfast, unswerving, resolute; see **faithful.**

*See Synonym Study at* FAITHFUL, PERPETUAL.

**constantly,** *modif.* — *Syn.* uniformly, steadily, invariably, continually; see **regularly** 2.

**constellation,** *n.* — *Syn.* group of stars, configuration of stars, zodiac, sign of the zodiac, stars, planets. Commonly recognized constellations include: Southern Cross, Orion, Cancer, Taurus, Big Dipper, Ursa Major, Great Bear, Little Dipper, Little Bear, Ursa Minor, Leo, Leo Minor, Draco, Pegasus, Aries, Gemini, Virgo, Aquarius, Libra, Scorpio, Capricorn, Sagittarius, Andromeda, Cassiopeia, Canis Major, Canis Minor, Cygnus, Pictor, Pisces; see also **star** 1, **zodiac.**

**consternation,** *n.* — *Syn.* alarm, dismay, shock, terror; see **confusion** 2, **fear** 1, **wonder** 1.

**constipated,** *modif.* — *Syn.* bound, costive, obstructed; see **sick.**

**constipation,** *n.* — *Syn.* stasis of the lower bowel, alimentary stoppage, costiveness; see **illness** 1.

**constituency,** *n.* — *Syn.* voters, the voters, electorate, body politic, electors, voting public, body of voters, balloters, the nation, the people; the district, the county, the ward; supporters, clients; see also **clientele, voter.**

**constituent,** *modif.* **1.** [Composing] — *Syn.* constituting, forming, component; see **fundamental** 1, **integral.**

**2.** [Voting] — *Syn.* electoral, electing, appointing, overruling; see **electoral, voting.**

**constituent,** *n.* — *Syn.* component, element, ingredient; see **element** 1, **part** 1.

*See Synonym Study at* ELEMENT.

**constitute,** *v.* **1.** [To found] — *Syn.* establish, develop, create, set up; see **organize** 2.

**2.** [To empower] — *Syn.* commission, authorize, appoint; see **commission, delegate** 1, 2.

**3.** [To enact] — *Syn.* order, draft, decree, legislate; see **enact.**

**4.** [To make up] — *Syn.* form, frame, compound, aggregate; see **compose** 1.

**constitution,** *n.* **1.** [Health] — *Syn.* physique, build, physical makeup, vitality; see **health** 2, **physique.**

**2.** [A basic political document] — *Syn.* code, written law, charter, custom; see **law** 2.

**3.** [Makeup] — *Syn.* nature, composition, disposition, structure; see **character** 2, **essence** 1, **organization** 1, 2.

**constitutional,** *modif.* **1.** [Based upon a constitution] — *Syn.* representative, republican, safeguarding liberty; see **democratic.**

**2.** [In accordance with a constitution] — *Syn.* lawful, approved, ensured; see **legal** 1.

**3.** [Physical] — *Syn.* built-in, vital, inborn; see **inherent, natural** 1.

**constrain,** *v.* — *Syn.* necessitate, compel, hold back, stifle; see **force** 1, **restrain** 1.

*See Synonym Study at* FORCE.

**constraint,** *n.* **1.** [The use of force] — *Syn.* coercion, force, compulsion; see **pressure** 2, **restraint** 2.

**2.** [Shyness] — *Syn.* bashfulness, restraint, awkwardness, timidity; see **humility, modesty** 1, **reserve** 2, **restraint** 1.

**3.** [Confinement] — *Syn.* captivity, detention, restriction, limitation; see **arrest** 1, **confinement** 1.

**constrict,** *v.* — *Syn.* contract, cramp, choke up, squeeze; see **compress, tighten** 1.

**constriction,** *n.* **1.** [The act of constricting] — *Syn.* narrowing, compression, reduction; see **contraction** 1.

**2.** [That which constricts] — *Syn.* choking, squeezing, binding; see **stricture** 2.

**construct,** *v.* **1.** [To build a physical structure] — *Syn.* build, assemble, erect; see **build** 1, **create** 2, **form** 1.

**2.** [To erect mentally] — *Syn.* create, compose, envision; see **imagine** 1, **invent** 1.

*See Synonym Study at* MAKE.

**construction,** *n.* **1.** [The act of constructing] — *Syn.* building, assembly, creation, composition, origination, planning, invention, formation, conception, improvisation, making, erection, fabrication, manufacture, foundation, roadwork, elevation, erecting, rearing, raising, putting up, installation; see also **architecture, production** 1.

**2.** [A method of constructing] — *Syn.* structure, arrangement, organization, disposition, system, systematization, plan, development, contour, format, mold, cast, outline, type, shape, build, cut, fabric, formation, turn, framework, figuration, conformation, configuration, frame, steel and concrete, fitted stone, brick and mortar, prefabrication, prefab*; see also **form** 1, **frame** 1.

**constructive,** *modif.* — *Syn.* useful, helpful, valuable, productive; see **effective, helpful** 1.

**construe,** *v.* — *Syn.* explain, define, infer, decipher; see **explain, infer** 1, **interpret** 1.

*See Synonym Study at* EXPLAIN.

**consul,** *n.* — *Syn.* legate, envoy, emissary; see **delegate, diplomat** 1, **representative** 1.

**consulate,** *n.* — *Syn.* government office, consular office, embassy, ministry; see **government** 2, **office** 3.

**consult,** *v.* — *Syn.* take counsel, deliberate, confer, parley, discuss, call in, counsel with, be closeted with, conspire with, compare notes, put heads together, confabulate, negotiate, debate, talk over, consider with, seek the opinion of, ask advice of, turn to, refer to, check with, seek advice, advise with, take up with, huddle*; see also **advise** 1, **ask** 1, **discuss, interview.**

**consultant,** *n.* — *Syn.* adviser, expert, counselor, authority; see **adviser, specialist.**

**consultation,** *n.* — *Syn.* interview, conference, deliberation, meeting; see **discussion** 1.

**consume,** *v.* **1.** [To eat or drink] — *Syn.* eat up, absorb, devour, put away*; see **drink** 1, **eat** 1.

**2.** [To use] — *Syn.* utilize, employ, use up, deplete, exhaust, expend, drain, spend, spend wastefully, squander, waste, dissipate, apply, avail oneself of, make use of, put to use, finish up, finish off, run out of, wear out, fritter away; see also **spend** 1, 2, **use** 1, **waste** 1, 2. — *Ant.* SAVE, conserve, preserve.

**3.** [To destroy] — *Syn.* devastate, ravage, demolish, eat away; see **destroy** 1.

**4.** [To absorb completely] — *Syn.* engross, preoccupy, obsess, overwhelm; see **haunt** 3, **occupy** 3.

**consumer,** *n.* — *Syn.* user, customer, purchaser; see **buyer.**

**consuming,** *modif.* — *Syn.* absorbing, engrossing, immoderate, exhausting; see **harmful, urgent** 1.

**consummate,** *modif.* — *Syn.* perfect, total, utter; see **absolute** 1, **perfect** 2, **whole** 1.

**consummate,** *v.* — *Syn.* complete, perfect, finish, fulfill; see **achieve** 1, **complete** 1.

**consummation,** *n.* — *Syn.* fulfillment, completion, culmination; see **end** 2, **perfection** 1.

**consumption,** *n.* **1.** [The act of consuming] — *Syn.*

using, eating, using up, decay, burning, expenditure, exhaustion, depletion, dissipation, dispersion, misuse, destruction, devastation, diminution, loss, damage, wear and tear, ruin, desolation; see also **destruction** 1, **eating, waste** 1.— *Ant.* saving, CONSERVATION, preservation.

**2.** [Tuberculosis] — *Syn.* phthisis, pulmonary consumption, lung disease; see **disease, tuberculosis.**

**consumptive,** *modif.* — *Syn.* destructive, immoderate, devastating; see **harmful, wasteful.**

**contact,** *n.* — *Syn.* touch, junction, connection, association; see **communication** 1, **meeting** 1.

**contact,** *v.* — *Syn.* speak to, reach, get in touch with; see **communicate** 2, **talk** 1.

**contagion,** *n.* **1.** [Infection] — *Syn.* transmittal, transmission, communication; see **contamination, infection** 1.

**2.** [Communicable disease] — *Syn.* poison, virus, illness; see **disease.**

**contagious,** *modif.* — *Syn.* communicable, catching, infectious, transmittable, spreading, poisonous, epidemic, pestiferous, deadly, epizootic, taking, tending to spread, inoculable, impartible; see also **catching.**

**contain,** *v.* **1.** [To include] — *Syn.* hold, accommodate, comprehend, embrace, be composed of, comprise, enclose, receive, admit, seat, bear, carry, consist of, harbor; see also **include** 1.

**2.** [To restrict] — *Syn.* restrain, hold, keep back, check; see **restrain** 1.

*SYN.* — **contain,** in strict usage, signifies the idea of enclosing within or including as a component, part, or fraction, and **hold,** the capacity for containing /the bottle *contains* two ounces of liquid, but it *holds* a pint/; to **accommodate** is to hold comfortably without crowding /an elevator built to *accommodate* twelve people/

**container,** *n.* — *Syn.* receptacle, repository, holder, vessel, box, carton, can, canister, crate, package, packet, case, chest, basket, bottle, jar, pouch, casket, cask, bag, sack, sac, pot, pan, jug, basin, ewer, dish, cup, glass, bucket, barrel, bunker, canteen, crock, storage space, bin, hamper, pit, magnum, pail, kettle, chamber, capsule, pod, cauldron, alembic, tank, vat, scuttle; see also **bag** 1, **basket** 1, **bin, bowl, can** 1, **case** 7, **dish** 1, **jar** 1, **tub, vase.**

**contaminate,** *v.* — *Syn.* taint, pollute, defile, infect, poison, sully, spoil, corrupt, adulterate, dirty, soil, foul, befoul, vitiate, debase, radioactivate; see also **corrupt** 1, **dirty.**

*SYN.* — **contaminate** means to make impure, unclean, or unfit for use through contact or addition /milk *contaminated* by radioactive fallout/; **taint** emphasizes effect over cause and implies that some measure of decay or corruption has taken place /*tainted* meat/; **pollute** implies complete befoulment through contamination, and now often suggests an impairment of purity that makes something injurious to health; **defile** implies pollution or desecration of that which should be kept pure or sacred

**contamination,** *n.* — *Syn.* impurity, pollution, adulteration, corruption, defilement, foulness, rottenness, spoliation, disease, decay, pestilence, contagion, taint, infection, poisoning; see also **pollution.**

**contemn,** *v.* — *Syn.* despise, scorn, disdain; see **despise, hate** 1.

*See Synonym Study at* DESPISE.

**contemplate,** *v.* **1.** [To look at] — *Syn.* regard, view, scan, inspect, examine, gaze at, notice, witness, pore over, peer, pry, behold, observe thoughtfully, study, scrutinize, survey, observe, look over, audit, probe, penetrate, pierce; see also **examine** 1, **see** 1, **witness.** — *Ant.* neglect, DISREGARD, slight.

**2.** [To consider] — *Syn.* ponder, muse, speculate on, envision; see **consider** 3, **think** 1.

*See Synonym Study at* CONSIDER.

**contemplation,** *n.* **1.** [Meditation] — *Syn.* consideration, reflection, study; see **reflection** 1, **thought** 1.

**2.** [Intention] — *Syn.* design, expectation, ambition; see **anticipation** 1, **plan** 2, **purpose** 1.

**contemplative,** *modif.* — *Syn.* meditative, pensive, attentive; see **pensive, studious, thoughtful** 1.

*See Synonym Study at* PENSIVE.

**contemporary,** *modif.* **1.** [Occurring at the same time] — *Syn.* contemporaneous, synchronous, coeval, simultaneous, coexistent, coincident, concurrent, co-occurring, synchronal, synchronic, coetaneous, coexisting; see also **simultaneous.**

**2.** [Current] — *Syn.* modern, present, up-to-date, à la mode; see **modern** 1, 3.

*SYN.* — **contemporary** and **contemporaneous** both mean existing or happening at the same period of time, **contemporary** (often applied to the present) referring more often to persons or their works, and **contemporaneous,** to events; **coeval** implies extension over the same period of time when a remote time or very long duration is involved; **synchronous** implies exact correspondence in time of occurrence or rate of movement; **simultaneous** implies occurrence at the same brief interval of time

**contemporary,** *n.* — *Syn.* peer, coeval, fellow, counterpart; see **equal.**

**contempt,** *n.* **1.** [A feeling of scorn] — *Syn.* scorn, disdain, derision, slight; see **hatred** 1, **ridicule.**

**2.** [A state of disgrace] — *Syn.* shame, dishonor, stigma; see **disgrace** 1.

**beneath contempt** — *Syn.* contemptible, despicable, worthless; see **offensive** 2.

**contemptible,** *modif.* — *Syn.* despicable, base, worthless, degenerate; see **mean** 1, **wicked** 1.

**contemptuous,** *modif.* — *Syn.* disdainful, derisive, disrespectful; see **scornful** 1.

**contend,** *v.* — *Syn.* contest, battle, dispute; see **fight** 2, **quarrel.**

**content,** *modif.* — *Syn.* appeased, gratified, comfortable; see **happy** 1, **satisfied.**

*See Synonym Study at* SATISFIED.

**contented,** *modif.* — *Syn.* content, pleased, thankful; see **happy** 1, **satisfied.**

*See Synonym Study at* SATISFIED.

**contention,** *n.* **1.** [Conflict] — *Syn.* strife, controversy, dispute, competition; see **battle** 2, **competition** 1, **discord** 1, **dispute, fight** 1.

**2.** [An assertion supported by argument] — *Syn.* stand, ground, assertion, allegation, claim, avowal, asseveration, explanation, predication, profession, deposition, advancement, discussion, charge, plea, demurrer; see also **declaration** 1.

*See Synonym Study at* DISCORD, FIGHT.

**contentious,** *modif.* — *Syn.* quarrelsome, argumentative, controversial, hostile; see **controversial, quarrelsome** 1, **unfriendly** 2.

*See Synonym Study at* BELLIGERENT.

**contentment,** *n.* — *Syn.* peace, pleasure, happiness; see **comfort** 1, **ease** 1, **happiness** 2, **satisfaction** 2.

**contents,** *n.* **1.** [Matter contained] — *Syn.* ingredients, constituents, components, elements, filling, content, gist, essence, meaning, significance, intent, text, subject matter, topics, chapters, substance, sum and substance, details, enclosure(s); see also **ingredients, matter** 1, **subject** 1, **writing** 2.
**2.** [Capacity to contain] — *Syn.* volume, space, cubic contents; see **capacity** 1, **size** 2.

**conterminous,** *modif.* **1.** [Contained within the same limits] — *Syn.* commensurate, coterminous, coincident, coextensive; see **equal, like.**
**2.** [Having a common boundary] — *Syn.* proximal, adjacent, bordering; see **adjacent, contiguous.**

**contest,** *n.* **1.** [A competition] — *Syn.* trial, match, game; see **competition** 1, 2.
**2.** [A conflict] — *Syn.* engagement, controversy, struggle; see **battle** 1, 2, **dispute, fight** 1.
*See Synonym Study at* FIGHT.

**contest,** *v.* **1.** [To oppose] — *Syn.* dispute, challenge, question, stand up for the other side; see **argue** 1, **oppose** 1.
**2.** [To fight] — *Syn.* contend, battle, defend, struggle, wrangle, altercate, conflict, quarrel, brawl, scuffle, feud, attack, strike, tilt, have a run-in with*, take on*, take on all comers*; see also **dare** 2, **fight** 2. — *Ant.* concede, REST, shake hands.

**contestant,** *n.* — *Syn.* competitor, contender, participant, rival, challenger, contester, disputant, antagonist, adversary, opponent, combatant, player, entrant, member of the field, team member, candidate, scrapper*, battler*; see also **opponent** 1, 2, **player** 1.

**context,** *n.* — *Syn.* connection, surrounding text, frame of reference; see **circumstances** 2, **meaning, setting.**

**contiguous,** *modif.* — *Syn.* adjacent, adjoining, meeting, bordering, conterminous, coterminous, abutting, touching, contactual, next to, in contact; see also **adjacent.**
*See Synonym Study at* ADJACENT.

**continence,** *n.* — *Syn.* self-restraint, moderation, celibacy; see **abstinence, chastity, restraint** 1.

**continent,** *n.* — *Syn.* mainland, continental landmass, landmass, major earth division, body of land; see also **Africa, America, Asia, Europe, region** 1.

**contingency,** *n.* **1.** [Possibility] — *Syn.* likelihood, chance, odds; see **chance** 1, **possibility** 2, **probability.**
**2.** [Accident] — *Syn.* predicament, incident, emergency, exigency; see **accident** 2, **emergency.**
*See Synonym Study at* EMERGENCY.

**contingent,** *modif.* **1.** [Accidental] — *Syn.* chance, unforeseen, fortuitous; see **accidental** 1, **uncertain** 2, **unexpected.**
**2.** [Possible] — *Syn.* unpredictable, probable, conditional; see **conditional, likely** 1, **uncertain** 2.

**contingent upon,** *modif.* — *Syn.* dependent upon, conditional on, subject to; see **dependent** 3.

**continual,** *modif.* **1.** [Recurring repeatedly] — *Syn.* recurrent, persistent, frequent; see **frequent, perpetual** 2, **regular** 3.
**2.** [Continuing uninterruptedly] — *Syn.* uninterrupted, ceaseless, nonstop, steady; see **constant** 1, **eternal** 1, **perpetual** 1.
*See Synonym Study at* PERPETUAL.

**continually,** *modif.* — *Syn.* steadily, continuously, constantly; see **frequently, regularly** 2.

**continuance,** *n.* — *Syn.* duration, extension, perpetuation; see **continuation** 1.

**continuation,** *n.* **1.** [The act of being continued] — *Syn.* prolongation, continuance, continuing, persis-

tence, perpetuation, protraction, propagation, succession, line, carrying on, perseverance, extension in time, extension in space, continuity, carry-over, production, increase, augmenting, going on, maintenance, maintaining, endurance, enduring, sustenance, sustaining, self-perpetuation, survival, preservation, furtherance, ratification, sanctioning, follow-through; see also **persistence, sequence** 1. — *Ant.* cessation, END, termination.
**2.** [The act of being resumed] — *Syn.* return, resumption, resuming, renewal, recommencement, reinitiation, recurrence, restoring, reoccurrence, restoration, revival, reappearance, reopening, recapitulation, reorganization, reestablishment, reinstitution, reiteration, repetition, iteration, duplication, reduplication, repeating, reinstatement, recrudescence, new start, fresh start; see also **renewal.** — *Ant.* PAUSE, wait, delay.
**3.** [Whatever serves to continue] — *Syn.* supplement, new chapter, sequel, installment, postscript, epilogue, addition, peroration, wake, postlude, appendix, revision, correction, emendation, complement, succession, new version, extension, augmentation, follow-up, afterthought, spinoff; see also **addition** 2, **increase** 1.

**continue,** *interj.* — *Syn.* keep on, carry on, keep going, keep talking, keep reading; keep it up.

**continue,** *v.* **1.** [To persist] — *Syn.* last, endure, go on, abide, persevere, proceed, maintain, carry on, keep on, run on, push on, live on, keep up, keep at, sustain, uphold, perpetuate, forge ahead, remain, stay, linger, press on, press onward, carry forward, make headway, move ahead, never cease, stretch, extend, drag on, wear on, hold on, hold out, keep going, stick to, stick with, keep the ball rolling*, chip away at*, plug away*, hang in*, hang on*, hang on like grim death*; see also **advance** 1, **endure** 1, **remain** 1. — *Ant.* cease, END, give up.
**2.** [To resume] — *Syn.* begin again, renew, recommence, carry over, return to, proceed, recapitulate, take up again, pick up, begin where one left off, carry on with, be reinstated, be reinstituted, be reestablished, be restored; see also **resume.** — *Ant.* discontinue, HALT, postpone.

---

*SYN.* — **continue** implies going on in a specified course or condition and stresses uninterrupted existence rather than duration; **last** stresses duration, either for the specified time, or if unqualified, for a time beyond that which is usual; **endure** implies continued resistance to destructive influences or forces; **abide** is applied to that which remains stable and steadfast, esp. in contrast to that which is changing and transitory; **persist** implies continued existence beyond the expected or normal time

---

**continuing,** *modif.* — *Syn.* ongoing, persisting, persevering, maintaining, carrying on, pursuing, advancing, progressing, enduring, lasting, sustaining; see also **chronic, permanent** 2, **progressive** 1.

**continuity,** *n.* **1.** [The state of being continuous] — *Syn.* continuousness, connectedness, coherence, perpetuity, prolongation, constancy, continuance, flow, succession, uniting, unity, sequence, continuum, chain, linking, train, progression, dovetailing, connection, smoothness; see also **continuation** 1. — *Ant.* intermittence, DISSIPATION, desultoriness.
**2.** [Transitional matter in a radio or television program] — *Syn.* action, preparation, script, dialogue, cue, announcement, cushion*, drool*, cut*.

**continuous,** *modif.* — *Syn.* endless, unbroken, connected, ceaseless; see **consecutive** 1, **constant** 1, **endless** 1, **eternal** 1, **perpetual** 1.
*See Synonym Study at* PERPETUAL.

**contort,** *v.* — *Syn.* distort, deform, misshape, twist; see **bend** 1, **distort** 3.
*See Synonym Study at* DISTORT.

**contortion,** *n.* **1.** [Something contorted] — *Syn.* deformity, distortion, grimace, *moue* (French), pout, twist, torsion, mutilation, deformation, misproportion, wryness, crookedness, lopsidedness, misshapement, anamorphosis, malformation; see also **knot** 2.
**2.** [The act of distorting] — *Syn.* distortion, deforming, dislocating, twisting, warping, turning, bending, doubling, wrenching.

**contortionist,** *n.* — *Syn.* acrobat, gymnast, tumbler, juggler; see **acrobat.**

**contour,** *n.* — *Syn.* profile, outline, silhouette, shape; see **form** 1, **outline** 4.
*See Synonym Study at* OUTLINE.

**contour,** *v.* — *Syn.* shape, mold, carve; see **form** 1.

**contoured,** *modif.* — *Syn.* shaped, molded, modeled; see **formed.**

**contraband,** *modif.* — *Syn.* forbidden, unauthorized, prohibited from import or export; see **illegal.**

**contraband,** *n.* **1.** [Illegal trafficking] — *Syn.* smuggling, poaching, violation of trade laws, piracy, counterfeiting, bootlegging, moonshining, rumrunning, gunrunning, black marketeering, drug traffic, wetbacking*; see also **crime** 2, **theft.**
**2.** [Illegal goods] — *Syn.* smuggled goods, bootlegged goods, poached goods, seized goods, confiscated goods, goods subject to confiscation, goods subject to seizure, contraband of war, plunder, narcotics, hot goods*, forbidden fruit*; see also **booty.**

**contraceptive,** *modif.* — *Syn.* preventive, controlling conception, preventing birth, preventing impregnation, prophylactic, protective.

**contraceptive,** *n.* — *Syn.* prophylactic, birth-control device, preventative, protection.
Contraceptives include: birth-control pill, the pill*; condom*, rubber*, diaphragm*, intrauterine device*, IUD*, loop*, coil*, spermicidal foam, spermicidal cream, spermicidal jelly, contraceptive sponge, contraceptive suppositories, Norplant (trademark)*.

**contract,** *n.* — *Syn.* agreement, legal agreement, covenant, compact, stipulation, contractual statement, contractual obligation, convention, understanding, promise, pledge, engagement, obligation, guarantee, liability, concordat, *entente cordiale* (French), settlement, arrangement, deal, gentleman's agreement, commitment, cartel, bargain, pact, lease, indenture, mise, the papers*; see also **agreement** 3, **record** 1, **treaty.**

**contract,** *v.* **1.** [To diminish] — *Syn.* shrink, condense, constrict, draw in, draw back, shrivel, weaken, be reduced in compass, become smaller, be drawn together, deflate, decline, fall away, abate, subside, grow less, ebb, wane, wrinkle, knit, lessen, lose, dwindle, consume, recede, fall off, wither, waste, evaporate; see also **decrease** 1. — *Ant.* STRETCH, expand, strengthen.
**2.** [To cause to diminish] — *Syn.* compress, condense, abbreviate, abridge, epitomize, edit, omit, narrow, confine; see also **compress, decrease** 2.
**3.** [To enter into an agreement by contract] — *Syn.* covenant, pact, pledge, promise, undertake, come to terms, adjust, negotiate, negotiate a contract, bargain, strike a bargain, agree, settle, limit, bound, reach an agreement, reach an understanding, settle by covenant, engage, stipulate, consent, enter into a contractual obligation, sign the papers, accept an offer, obligate oneself, work out the details, put something in writing, swear to, sign for, assent, give one's word, initial, close, shake hands on it*, get together*; see also **negotiate** 1, **promise** 1.

**4.** [To catch; *said of diseases*] — *Syn.* get, incur, become infected with; see **catch** 4.
**5.** [To become obligated by; *said especially of debts*] — *Syn.* become indebted, take on, obligate oneself; see **owe.**

---

**SYN.** — **contract** implies a drawing together of surface or parts and a resultant decrease in size, bulk, or extent [cold *contracts* metals]; to **shrink** is to contract so as to be short of the original or normal length, amount, extent, etc. [those shirts have *shrunk; shrinking* profits]; **condense** suggests reduction of something into a more compact or more dense form without loss of essential content [*condensed* milk]; to **compress** is to press or squeeze into a more compact, orderly form [a lifetime's work *compressed* into one volume]; **deflate** implies a reduction in size or bulk by the removal of air, gas, or in extended use, anything insubstantial [to *deflate* a balloon, to *deflate* one's ego]

---

**contract for,** *v.* — *Syn.* acquire, order, purchase; see **buy** 1.

**contraction,** *n.* **1.** [The act of contracting] — *Syn.* dwindling, shrinking, receding, withdrawing, shriveling, lessening, recession, withdrawal, consumption, condensation, condensing, elision, omission, deflation, evaporation, constriction, abbreviation, abbreviating, decrease, shortening, abridging, compression, narrowing, confinement, curtailment, omitting, deflating, evaporating, decreasing, abridgment, reducing, reduction, shrinkage, curtailing, diminishing, cutting down, drawing together, constricting, squeezing, flexing, tensing, consolidating, consolidation, diminution, lowering, lopping, epitomizing, editing; see also **abbreviation** 2, **reduction** 1. — *Ant.* expansion, INCREASE, extension.
**2.** [A contracted form] — *Syn.* colloquialism, shortening, syncope; see **abbreviation** 1.

**contractor,** *n.* — *Syn.* builder, entrepreneur, jobber, constructor; see **architect** 1, **builder** 1.

**contradict,** *v.* **1.** [To oppose] — *Syn.* differ, call in question, confront; see **dare** 2, **oppose** 1.
**2.** [To deny] — *Syn.* disclaim, refuse to accept, repudiate; see **deny.**
*See Synonym Study at* DENY.

**contradiction,** *n.* **1.** [Denial] — *Syn.* dissension, dispute, defiance; see **disagreement** 1.
**2.** [Discrepancy] — *Syn.* incongruity, inconsistency, opposition; see **difference** 1, **inconsistency, opposite.**

**contradictory,** *modif.* — *Syn.* opposite, inconsistent, incongruous; see **conflicting, different** 1, **incongruous** 1.

**contrary,** *modif.* **1.** [Opposed] — *Syn.* antagonistic, hostile, inimical; see **against** 3, **opposed.**
**2.** [Opposite] — *Syn.* antithetical, counter, clashing; see **opposite** 1.
**3.** [Unfavorable] — *Syn.* untimely, adverse, unpropitious; see **unfavorable** 2.
**4.** [Obstinate] — *Syn.* perverse, contradictory, headstrong, stubborn, balky, restive, self-willed, wayward, willful, refractory, pigheaded, oppositional, cantankerous, cross-grained, froward, contrarious*; see also **obstinate.**

---

**SYN.** — **contrary**, in this comparison, implies a habitual willful disinclination to accept orders, advice, etc.; **perverse** implies an unreasonable obstinacy in deviating from what is considered right or acceptable; **restive** is applied to those who are impatient under restraint or discipline and hence are hard to control or keep in order; **balky** implies a stopping short and stubbornly refusing to go on *See also Synonym Study at* OPPOSITE.

**contrary,** *n.* — *Syn.* converse, antithesis, just the opposite; see **contrast** 2, **opposite.**
**on** or **to the contrary**— *Syn.* conversely, contrary to, on the other hand, antithetically, contrariwise, inversely, contrasting, at the opposite pole, on the other side, in disagreement with, as opposed to, in opposition to, counter, in contradiction to; see also **against** 3, **opposed.**

**contrast,** *n.* **1.** [The state of being sharply different] — *Syn.* divergence, incompatibility, disparity, variation, variance, dissimilarity, inequality, distinction, incongruousness, heterogeneity, oppositeness, contradiction, dissimilitude, diversity, unlikeness, disagreement, opposition; see also **difference** 1.— *Ant.* AGREEMENT, similarity, uniformity.
**2.** [A contrasting effect] — *Syn.* contrariety, antithesis, contradiction, inconsistency, foil, reverse, contraposition, inverse, adverse, converse, opposition; see also **difference** 2, **opposite.**— *Ant.* EQUALITY, unity, oneness, sameness.

**contrast,** *v.* **1.** [To provide a contrast] — *Syn.* contradict, disagree, conflict, set off, be contrary to, diverge, depart from, deviate from, differ from, mismatch, vary, show difference, stand out, be dissimilar, be diverse, be variable, be unlike, be a foil to; see also **differ** 1, **oppose** 1.— *Ant.* AGREE, concur, be identical.
**2.** [To indicate a contrast] — *Syn.* oppose, differentiate, set over, set off against; see **compare** 2, **distinguish** 1.
*See Synonym Study at* COMPARE.

**contrasting,** *modif.* — *Syn.* divergent, contradictory, dissimilar; see **conflicting, different** 1.

**contravene,** *v.* — *Syn.* contradict, conflict with, violate; see **deny, hinder, oppose** 1, 2, **violate** 1.

**contravention,** *n.* — *Syn.* contradiction, violation, infringement; see **opposition** 1, **refusal, violation** 1.

**contretemps,** *n.* — *Syn.* awkward, mishap, misfortune, misadventure; see **catastrophe, disaster, embarrassment** 2, **predicament.**

**contribute,** *v.* — *Syn.* give, donate, provide, add, share, endow, supply, furnish, bestow, present, confer, commit, accord, dispense, settle upon, enrich, proffer, grant, afford, assign, give away, subscribe, tender, devote, demise, will, dower, bequeath, subsidize, hand out, sacrifice, ante up\*, chip in\*, kick in\*, do one's bit\*, get in the act\*, go Dutch\*; see also **give** 1, **offer** 1, **participate** 1, **provide** 1.— *Ant.* RECEIVE, accept, withhold.

**contribute to,** *v.* — *Syn.* assist, advance, conduce to, have a hand in\*; see **help** 1, **support** 2.

**contributing,** *modif.* — *Syn.* contributory, aiding, helpful, supporting, sharing, causative, providing a background, forming a part of, not to be overlooked, to be considered, conducive, entering in, auxiliary, ancillary, coming into the picture\*; see also **helpful** 1, **relevant, secondary** 1.

**contribution,** *n.* **1.** [Gift] — *Syn.* donation, present, bestowal, offering; see **gift** 1, **grant.**
**2.** [A significant addition] — *Syn.* augmentation, enrichment, supplement; see **addition** 2, **increase** 1.
**3.** [The act of contributing] — *Syn.* supplying, aiding, benefaction, participation; see **giving.**

**contributor,** *n.* — *Syn.* subscriber, donor, giver, grantor; see **donor, patron** 1.

**contrite,** *modif.* — *Syn.* repentant, regretful, humbled, remorseful; see **ashamed, sorry** 1.

**contrition,** *n.* — *Syn.* penitence, remorse, sorrow; see **penance** 1, 2, **regret** 1, **repentance.**
*See Synonym Study at* REPENTANCE.

**contrivance,** *n.* **1.** [A plan, especially an ingenious plan] — *Syn.* expedient, stratagem, scheme, artifice; see **plan** 2.
**2.** [A mechanical device] — *Syn.* appliance, mechanism, gadget, invention, apparatus, gear, implement, discovery, instrument, tool, machine, engine, convenience, contraption, utensil, harness, material, tackle, equipment, creation, brainchild\*, thingamajig\*, thingamabob\*, doohickey\*, dingus\*; see also **device** 1, **equipment, tool** 1.

**contrive,** *v.* **1.** [To invent] — *Syn.* make, improvise, devise, think up; see **create** 2, **invent** 1, **plan** 1.
**2.** [To succeed with difficulty] — *Syn.* manage, pass, compass, negotiate, afford, engineer, manipulate, shift, make shift, get by, arrange, execute, carry out, effect, bring about, maneuver, swing\*, wrangle\*; see also **achieve** 1, **succeed** 1.

**control,** *n.* **1.** [The power to direct] — *Syn.* command, authority, direction, charge; see **administration** 1, **command** 2, **government** 1, **power** 2.
**2.** [Restraint] — *Syn.* check, curb, limitation, restriction; see **restraint** 1, 2.
**3.** [A device that regulates or controls; *often plural*] — *Syn.* instrument, control mechanism, switch, dial, knob, button, key, lever, handle, toggle switch, regulator, controller, governor, instrument panel, dashboard, keyboard, remote control; see also **dial, regulator.**
*See Synonym Study at* POWER.

**control,** *v.* **1.** [To hold in check] — *Syn.* constrain, master, repress; see **check** 2, **command** 2, **restrain** 1.
**2.** [To direct] — *Syn.* manage, regulate, guide, dominate; see **advise** 1, **command** 2, **manage** 1.
**3.** [To verify] — *Syn.* establish, test, experiment; see **check** 3, **compare** 2, **examine** 1, **measure** 1, **verify.**
*See Synonym Study at* MANAGE.
**out of control**— *Syn.* unmanageable, uncontrolled, uncontrollable, irrational; see **unruly.**

**controlling,** *modif.* — *Syn.* ruling, supervising, regulating; see **autocratic** 1, **governing, predominant** 1.

**controversial,** *modif.* — *Syn.* debatable, contestable, arguable, polemic, polemical, controvertible, open to question, open to discussion, open to doubt, open to debate, dubious, doubtful, dubitable, questionable, moot, subject to controversy, in question, suspect, in dispute, at issue, provocative, disputable, contentious, argumentative; see also **questionable** 1, **uncertain** 2.

**controversialist,** *n.* — *Syn.* debater, disputer, parliamentarian, logomacher, belligerent, dialectician, reasoner, casuist, polemicist, polemist, arguer, disputant, wrangler, discussant, litigant; see also **fighter** 1.

**controversy,** *n.* — *Syn.* contention, debate, disagreement, quarrel; see **discussion** 1, **dispute.**
*See Synonym Study at* DISPUTE.

**controvert,** *v.* **1.** [To argue against] — *Syn.* counter, contradict, refute; see **confute, deny, disprove, oppose** 1.
**2.** [To argue about] — *Syn.* argue, debate, dispute, contest; see **debate, discuss.**
*See Synonym Study at* DISPROVE.

**contumacious,** *modif.* — *Syn.* insubordinate, disobedient, unyielding, intractable; see **obstinate, rebellious** 2, 3.

**contusion,** *n.* — *Syn.* bruise, black-and-blue mark, wound; see **bruise, injury** 1.

**conundrum,** *n.* — *Syn.* enigma, riddle, problem; see **puzzle** 2.

*See Synonym Study at* PUZZLE.

**convalescent,** *modif.* — *Syn.* recovering, recuperating, convalescing, improving, discharged, released, ambulatory, getting well, getting better, out of the hospital, past the crisis, out of emergency care, out of intensive care, getting over something, mending, healing, gaining strength, undergoing rehabilitation, restored, rejuvenated, on the mend*; see also **well** 1.

**convalescent,** *n.* — *Syn.* ambulatory patient, one recovering from a sickness, one recovering from an injury, walking case; see **patient.**

**convene,** *v.* — *Syn.* meet, congregate, collect, convoke; see **assemble** 2, **gather** 1.
*See Synonym Study at* CALL.

**convenience,** *n.* **1.** [The quality of being convenient] — *Syn.* fitness, availability, accessibility, handiness, suitability, suitableness, appropriateness, acceptability, receptiveness, openness, adaptability, approachability, usefulness, utility, serviceability, serviceableness, expediency, practicality, nearness; see also **utility** 1. — *Ant.* unfitness, TROUBLE, unsuitability.
**2.** [An aid to ease or comfort] — *Syn.* ease, comfort, accommodation, advantage, amenity, facility, help, aid, assistance, means, support, luxury, succor, personal service, the comforts of home, creature comfort, relief, satisfaction, service, benefit, avail, accessory, utility, labor saver, time saver, appliance, appurtenance, labor-saving device; see also **advantage** 3, **aid** 1, **appliance, comfort** 1. — *Ant.* discomfort, AWKWARDNESS, hindrance.
**3.** [Time and circumstances that are convenient] — *Syn.* leisure, ease, freedom, liberty, a free hour, a minute at liberty, preference, seasonableness, opportuneness; see also **leisure.**
**at one's convenience** — *Syn.* when convenient, at one's leisure, when one has time, when opportune; see **any time, appropriately.**

**convenient,** *modif.* **1.** [Serving one's convenience] — *Syn.* ready, favorable, suitable, adapted, available, fitted, suited, adaptable, commodious, roomy, well-arranged, well-suited, well-planned, agreeable, acceptable, useful, serviceable, handy, helpful, expedient, assisting, aiding, beneficial, accommodating, advantageous, conducive, comfortable, opportune, timely, seasonable, timesaving, labor-saving; see also **available, fit** 1, 2, **helpful** 1, **timely.** — *Ant.* DISTURBING, unserviceable, disadvantageous.
**2.** [Near] — *Syn.* handy, accessible, nearby, at hand, ready to hand, close, close by, near at hand, central, easy to reach, within reach, readily arrived at, nigh, adjacent, adjoining, next door, around the corner, in the neighborhood, within walking distance, on hand, at one's elbow, at one's fingertips*; see also **available, near** 1. — *Ant.* far, DISTANT, inaccessible.

**convent,** *n.* — *Syn.* religious community, cloister, nunnery; see **cloister** 1, **retreat** 2.
*See Synonym Study at* CLOISTER.

**convention,** *n.* **1.** [An occasion at which members or delegates assemble] — *Syn.* assembly, convocation, meeting, conference; see **gathering.**
**2.** [Those assembled at a convention, sense 1] — *Syn.* delegates, representatives, members, conventioneers; see **committee, organization** 3.
**3.** [Custom] — *Syn.* practice, habit, fashion, protocol; see **custom** 1, 2.
**4.** [An established mode of procedure] — *Syn.* canon, code, precept, rule; see **custom** 2, **law** 2, 3.

**conventional,** *modif.* **1.** [Established by convention] — *Syn.* accustomed, prevailing, accepted, customary, regular, standard, orthodox, traditional, habitual, wonted, normal, typical, expected, usual, routine, general, everyday, commonplace, ordinary, plain, current, popular, prevalent, predominant, expected, well-known, stereotyped, in established usage; see also sense 2, **accepted, common** 1, **familiar** 1, **habitual** 1, **popular** 3, **traditional** 2. — *Ant.* atypical, UNUSUAL, unpopular.
**2.** [In accordance with convention] — *Syn.* established, sanctioned, correct, confirmed, seemly, decorous, proper, decent, fit, fitting, fixed, standard, set, conforming, conformable, fashionable, formal, ritual, ceremonious, right, precise, ceremonial, not taboo, prearranged, undivergent, undeviating, orderly, arranged, stiff, rigid, stylish, modish, *comme il faut* (French), according to Hoyle*; see also sense 1, **fit** 1. — *Ant.* relaxed, unconventional, spontaneous.
**3.** [Devoted to or bound by convention] — *Syn.* formal, stereotyped, unoriginal, orthodox, narrow, narrow-minded, illiberal, dogmatic, conformist, insular, parochial, strict, rigid, puritanical, inflexible, hidebound, conservative, traditional, doctrinal, conforming, literal, believing, unheterodox, not heretical, canonical, scriptural, literal, bigoted, obstinate, straight-laced, stodgy, stuffy*, straight*, square*, button-down*; see also **conservative, polite** 1, **prejudiced.** — *Ant.* LIBERAL, broad-minded, unconventional.
**4.** [Formalized; *said especially of artistic designs*] — *Syn.* conventionalized, stylized, regularized; see **regular** 3.

**converge,** *v.* — *Syn.* meet, unite, focalize, concentrate; see **concentrate** 1, **gather** 1.

**convergence,** *n.* — *Syn.* union, concurrence, merging, confluence; see **concentration** 1, **meeting** 1.

**convergent,** *modif.* — *Syn.* converging, meeting, coming together; see **concurrent** 2, **confluent, connecting.**

**conversant with,** *modif.* — *Syn.* acquainted with, versed in, knowledgeable; see **familiar with, knowledgeable.**

**conversation,** *n.* — *Syn.* talk, chat, discourse, discussion, communion, communication, intercourse, consultation, hearing, conference, interview, gossip, converse, colloquy, parley, dialogue, causerie, expression of views, exchange of views, mutual exchange, tête-à-tête, questions and answers, traffic in ideas, engaging in persiflage, repartee, give-and-take, questioning, oral examination, exchange of confidences, unburdening oneself, talking it out, heart-to-heart talk, small talk, chitchat, palaver, interchange, interlocution, confabulation, confab*, powwow*, bull session*, talkfest*, gabfest*, chinfest*, pillow talk*, rap session*, rap*, tattle*; see also **communication** 1, **discussion** 1.

**converse,** *modif.* — *Syn.* reversed, contrary, opposite; see **different** 1, **opposite** 1.

**converse,** *n.* — *Syn.* inverse, antithesis, reverse; see **opposite.**

**converse,** *v.* — *Syn.* talk, speak, chat, have a talk with; see **discuss, speak** 2, **talk** 1.
*See Synonym Study at* SPEAK.

**conversion,** *n.* **1.** [A converting or being converted] — *Syn.* change, transformation, metamorphosis, changeover, growth, passage, metabolism, turning point, alteration, exchange, translation, resolution, passing, transmigration, transfiguration, transmutation, resolving, progress, flux, transmogrification, reduction; see also **change** 1, 2, **reformation** 1. — *Ant.* ESTABLISHING, settlement, fixation.
**2.** [A basic change in belief; especially, espousal of a religion] — *Syn.* turn, spiritual change, regeneration, rebirth, accepting the true faith, turning to the church, turning to God, turning to Christ, being born again, being baptized, accepting baptism, seeing the light, change

of heart, change in character, new birth; see also **reformation** 2.— *Ant.* reversion, DESERTION, fall from grace.

**convert,** *n.* — *Syn.* proselyte, neophyte, disciple; see **beginner, believer, follower.**

**convert,** *v.* **1.** [To alter the form or use] — *Syn.* turn, transform, change; see **change** 1.

**2.** [To alter convictions] — *Syn.* turn, regenerate, save, bring the light to, show the light to, bring to God, make a convert of, baptize, make a Christian of, change into, bring over, bring around, bring round, make over, assimilate to, lead to believe, gain the confidence of, change the heart of, proselytize, create anew, persuade, win over, switch★; see also **reform** 1.

*See Synonym Study at* CHANGE, TRANSFORM.

**converted,** *modif.* — *Syn.* convinced, indoctrinated, transformed, born-again; see **changed** 2, 3, **reformed** 2.

**convertible,** *modif.* — *Syn.* interchangeable, reciprocal, equivalent; see **changeable** 2, **exchangeable.**

**convex,** *modif.* — *Syn.* curved, arched, raised, bulging; see **bent.**

**convey,** *v.* **1.** [To transport] — *Syn.* carry, bear, dispatch, move; see **carry** 1, **send** 1.

**2.** [To transmit] — *Syn.* pass on, communicate, conduct; see **carry** 2, **communicate** 1, **send** 4.

*See Synonym Study at* CARRY.

**conveyance,** *n.* **1.** [The act of conveying] — *Syn.* transfer, transport, movement, transmission; see **communication** 1, **transportation.**

**2.** [Vehicle] — *Syn.* car, carriage, van; see **automobile, bus, transport, truck** 1, **vehicle** 1, **wagon.**

**convict,** *n.* — *Syn.* prisoner, malefactor, felon, con★; see **criminal, prisoner.**

**convict,** *v.* — *Syn.* find guilty, prove guilty, condemn, sentence, pass sentence on, adjudge, doom, declare guilty, pronounce guilty, bring to justice, seal one's doom, sign one's death warrant, lock up, cook★, send up★, bring home to★; see also **condemn** 1.— *Ant.* acquit, exonerate, find not guilty.

**conviction,** *n.* **1.** [Belief] — *Syn.* persuasion, confidence, view; see **belief** 1, **certainty** 1, **faith** 1, 2, **opinion** 1.

**2.** [The state of finding guilty] — *Syn.* unfavorable verdict, guilty verdict, determining guilt, condemnation, condemning; see also **blame** 1, **punishment, sentence** 1.

*See Synonym Study at* CERTAINTY, OPINION.

**convince,** *v.* — *Syn.* prove, prove to, persuade, induce, establish, satisfy, assure, demonstrate, argue into, change, convert, sway, effect, overcome, turn, bring over, win over, gain over, bring around, put across, bring to one's senses, bring to reason, lead to believe, gain the confidence of, carry conviction, ring true, cram into one's head★, put into one's head★, sell on★, sell a bill of goods★, bring home to★; see also **influence, persuade** 1, **prove.**

**convinced,** *modif.* — *Syn.* converted, indoctrinated, talked into something; see **persuaded.**

**convince oneself,** *v.* — *Syn.* be convinced, be converted, persuade oneself, make up one's mind; see **believe** 1, **prove.**

**convincing,** *modif.* **1.** [Persuasive] — *Syn.* impressive, swaying, moving, cogent; see **persuasive.**

**2.** [Believable] — *Syn.* trustworthy, valid, reliable, credible, acceptable, reasonable, creditable, plausible, probable, likely, presumable, possible, dependable, hopeful, worthy of confidence, to be depended on; see also **reliable** 2.

*See Synonym Study at* VALID.

**convivial,** *modif.* **1.** [Sociable] — *Syn.* genial, jovial, companionable, hearty; see **friendly, pleasant** 1.

**2.** [Festive] — *Syn.* festal, merry, holiday, entertaining; see **pleasant** 2.

**conviviality,** *n.* — *Syn.* festivity, gaiety, sociability; see **entertainment** 1, **merriment** 2.

**convocation,** *n.* — *Syn.* assembly, meeting, conference; see **gathering.**

**convoke,** *v.* — *Syn.* convene, call together, assemble, muster; see **assemble** 2.

*See Synonym Study at* CALL.

**convoy,** *n.* — *Syn.* escort, guard, attendance, protection; see **caravan, companion** 2, **escort.**

**convoy,** *v.* — *Syn.* escort, accompany, attend, conduct; see **accompany** 1, **defend** 1, **lead** 1.

*See Synonym Study at* ACCOMPANY.

**convulse,** *v.* — *Syn.* disturb, agitate, shake, shake up, unsettle, rock, stir, torment, torture, writhe; see also **amuse, bother** 3, **disturb** 2.

**convulsion,** *n.* **1.** [Spasm] — *Syn.* paroxysm, seizure, attack; see **fit** 1.

**2.** [Disturbance] — *Syn.* turbulence, agitation, commotion, upheaval; see **disturbance** 2, **outbreak** 1.

**cook,** *n.* — *Syn.* chef, short-order cook, meat cook, salad chef, mess sergeant, *chef de cuisine* (French), sous-chef, cook-general (British), head cook, culinarian, caterer; see also **baker.**

**cook,** *v.* — *Syn.* prepare, fix, make, heat, reheat, warm, boil, fry, bake, roast, broil, grill, stew, simmer, braise, steam, blanch, poach, toast, sauté, stir-fry, barbecue, microwave, sear, fricassee, pressure-cook, parboil, precook, pan-fry, panbroil, deep-fry, French fry, charbroil, coddle, shirr, griddle, pan, brown, blacken, curry, devil, scallop, melt, scald, parch, scorch, dry, steep, marinate, brew, percolate, mull, decoct, concoct, reduce, boil down, baste, cook over a slow fire, nuke★, broast★; see also **boil** 1, **fry, heat** 1, **toast** 2.

**cookie,** *n.* — *Syn.* small cake, wafer, biscuit (British), *biscotto* (Italian).

Common varieties of cookies include: cream, butter, lemon, Boston, seed, icebox, oatmeal, lace, vanilla, chocolate, sugar, peanut butter, almond, eggless, ginger, molasses, gingersnap, fig bar, raisin bar, chocolate chip, jumble, Scotch shortbread, Scotch cake, macaroon, Mary Ann, tart, fruit bar, brownie, drop, bar, Marguerite, *petit beurre* (French), madeleine, pinwheel, wafer; see also **bread** 1, **cake** 2, **pastry.**

**cooking,** *modif.* **1.** [Being cooked] — *Syn.* simmering, heating, boiling, brewing, stewing, frying, broiling, grilling, browning, roasting, baking, toasting, steaming, steeping, mulling, sizzling; see also **boiling.**

**2.** [★In preparation] — *Syn.* being made, going on, under way, happening; see **begun.**

**cooking,** *n.* — *Syn.* cookery, cuisine, culinary art, dish; see **food.**

**cookout,** *n.* — *Syn.* barbecue, picnic, outdoor meal; see **picnic** 1.

**cook up★,** *v.* — *Syn.* make up, concoct, falsify; see **arrange** 2, **invent** 1, 2, **plan** 1.

**cool,** *modif.* **1.** [Having a low temperature] — *Syn.* cooling, chilly, frosty, somewhat cold, moderately cold, heat-repelling, shivery, chill, chilling, refrigerated, iced, air-conditioned, crisp, fresh, snappy, nippy, nipping, biting, bracing, brisk, refreshing; see also **cold** 1.— *Ant.* tepid, WARM, heated.

**2.** [Calm] — *Syn.* unruffled, imperturbable, composed, collected, calm, levelheaded, nonchalant, unexcited, unflappable, coolheaded, dispassionate, uninvolved,

unemotional, restrained, deliberate, controlled, self-possessed, serene, relaxed, together*; see also **calm** 1.
**3.** [Not cordial] — *Syn.* distant, disapproving, lukewarm; see **aloof, indifferent** 1, **unfriendly** 2.
**4.** [*Excellent] — *Syn.* neat*, great*, with-it*; see **excellent, fashionable, modern** 1.
**play it cool***— *Syn.* hold back, underplay, exercise restraint; see **restrain oneself.**

---

*SYN.* — **cool,** in this comparison, implies freedom from the heat of emotion or excitement, suggesting a calm, dispassionate attitude or a controlled alertness in difficult circumstances [to keep *cool* in an emergency]; **composed** suggests readiness to meet a trying situation through self-possession or the disciplining of one's emotions; **collected** stresses being in full command of one's faculties or emotions in a distracting situation; **unruffled** suggests the maintenance of poise or composure in the face of something that might agitate or embarrass one; **nonchalant** stresses a cool lack of concern or casual indifference

---

**cool,** *v.* **1.** [To become cool] — *Syn.* lose heat, moderate, lessen, freeze, reduce, calm, chill, cool off, become cold, be chilled to the bone, become chilly; see also **freeze** 1. — *Ant.* warm up, THAW, heat.
**2.** [To cause to become cool] — *Syn.* chill, refrigerator, ice, temper, mitigate, moderate, lessen, abate, allay, calm, air-cool, air-condition, precool, frost, reduce the temperature of, freeze, quick-freeze; see also **freeze** 2. — *Ant.* BURN, warm, defrost.
**cool it*,** *v.* — *Syn.* calm down, take it easy, quiet down, be sensible; see **calm down.**
**cooperate,** *v.* **1.** [To work together] — *Syn.* unite, combine, collaborate, concur, conspire, concert, pool, join forces, act in concert, stand together, hold together, stick together, team up, show a willingness, comply with, join in, go along with, make common cause, unite efforts, share in, second, cast in one's lot with, take part, be a party to, collude, connive, act jointly, work in unison, interact, participate, work side by side with, side with, join hands with, fraternize, play along with*, play fair*, throw in with*, fall in with*, be in cahoots*, chip in*, pitch in*, stand shoulder to shoulder*, pull together*, play ball*; see also **agree, join** 2, **unite** 1. — *Ant.* act independently, DIFFER, diverge.
**2.** [To help] — *Syn.* contribute, second, espouse, uphold, befriend, succor, lend oneself to, share, lend a hand, go out of the way for, assist, relieve, reinforce, promote, further, forward, advance, sustain, back up, stand by, side with; see also **encourage** 1, **help** 1, **support** 2. — *Ant.* hamper, HINDER, harm.
**cooperating,** *modif.* — *Syn.* assisting, agreeing, collaborating; see **cooperative** 2, **helping.**
**cooperation,** *n.* **1.** [Mutual assistance] — *Syn.* collaboration, participation, combination, concert, joint effort, teamwork, union, concurrence, confederacy, confederation, conspiracy, alliance, partnership, coalition, fusion, pooling of resources, federation, partisanship, bipartisanship, unanimity, concord, harmony, solidarity, interaction, synergy, coaction, collusion, connivance, complicity, team spirit, esprit de corps; see also **agreement** 2, **association** 1. — *Ant.* discord, DISAGREEMENT, separation.
**2.** [Aid] — *Syn.* help, assistance, service; see **aid** 1.
**cooperative,** *modif.* **1.** [Helpful] — *Syn.* supportive, accommodating, neighborly; see **helpful** 1, **kind.**
**2.** [Involving cooperation] — *Syn.* cooperating, agreeing, joining, combining, collaborating, collaborative,

collegial, coactive, uniting, concurring, participating, symbiotic, coadjutant, collective, in joint operation; see also **common** 5, **united.** — *Ant.* competitive, INDEPENDENT, rival.
**cooperative,** *n.* — *Syn.* marketing cooperative, consumer cooperative, communal society, communal enterprise, kibbutz, commune, collective farm, state farm; *kolkhoz, sovkhoz* (*both* Russian); collective, co-op*; see also **organization** 3.
**coordinate,** *modif.* — *Syn.* coequal, correlative, parallel, correspondent; see **equal, like.**
**coordinate,** *v.* — *Syn.* harmonize, regulate, organize, correlate; see **adjust** 1, **agree, order** 3, **organize** 1.
**coordinates,** *n.* — *Syn.* points of reference, latitude and longitude, specifications of the location of a point, set of variables, set of parameters, Cartesian coordinates, ordinate and abscissa; see also **measure** 1, **position** 1.
**coordinator,** *n.* — *Syn.* director, supervisor, organizer; see **administrator, adviser.**
**cope (with),** *v.* — *Syn.* manage, deal with, handle, carry on; see **endure** 2, **face** 1.
**copied,** *modif.* **1.** [Reproduced] — *Syn.* photocopied, duplicated, transcribed; see **printed, reproduced.**
**2.** [Imitated] — *Syn.* made in facsimile, mimicked, aped; see **imitated.**
**copious,** *modif.* **1.** [Abundant] — *Syn.* lavish, plentiful, profuse, extensive; see **plentiful** 2.
**2.** [Verbose] — *Syn.* profuse, prolix, wordy; see **verbose.**
*See Synonym Study at* PLENTIFUL.
**copiousness,** *n.* — *Syn.* abundance, richness, profusion; see **plenty.**
**copse,** *n.* — *Syn.* thicket, brushwood, scrub, coppice; see **brush** 4, **hedge.**
**copulate,** *v.* — *Syn.* make love, have sex, mate, have relations, unite, couple, cover, serve, lie with, know, sleep with, sleep together, bed, go to bed, have sexual relations, have marital relations, have extramarital relations, be carnal, unite sexually, have sexual intercourse, breed, cohabit, have coition, fornicate, break the seventh commandment, lay*, ball*, fool around*, screw*, make out*, have funny business*, do it*, make it*, get it on*, go all the way*; see also **join** 1. — *Ant.* ABSTAIN, be continent, be celibate.
**copulation,** *n.* — *Syn.* coitus, intercourse, sexual intercourse, sex, sex act, sexual union, sexual congress, coupling, mating, coition, carnal knowledge, act of love, lovemaking, relations, sexual relations, fornication, venereal act, nooky*; see also **fornication, sex** 4.
**copulative,** *modif.* — *Syn.* joining, uniting, linking; see **connecting.**
**copy,** *n.* — *Syn.* facsimile, duplicate, reproduction, replica, photocopy, photostat, likeness, print, simulation, impersonation, reprint, offprint, Xerox (trademark), fax, hard copy, microfiche, imitation, forgery, counterfeit, fake, rubbing, transcript, carbon, carbon copy, mimeograph sheet, mimeograph copy, typescript, transcription, cast, tracing, effigy, counterpart, mirror image, semblance, likeness, portrait, model, image, reflection, representation, replication, study, photograph, microcopy, microfilm, examined copy, certified copy, fair copy, example, specimen, impression, text, proof, ditto, knockoff*; see also **duplicate, imitation** 2, **reproduction** 3.

---

*SYN.* — **copy,** the broadest of these terms, refers to a thing that is made to be like another, whether the resulting correspondence is exact or approximate [a carbon *copy*]; **reproduction** implies a close imitation of an original, often, however, with differences, as of material, size, or quality *[a reproduction of a painting]*; a **facsimile** is an exact reproduction in appearance, sometimes, however, differing in scale *[a facsimile of the original Declaration of Independence]*; a **duplicate** is a double, or counterpart, of something, serving all the purposes of the original *[a duplicate of the contract]*; a **replica** is an exact reproduction of a work of art or other object, sometimes on a smaller scale *[a replica of the Parthenon]*, in strict usage referring to a reproduction of a work of art made by the original artist

---

**copy,** *v.* **1.** [To imitate] — *Syn.* follow the example of, mimic, ape; see **follow** 2, **imitate** 2, **parody.**
**2.** [To reproduce] — *Syn.* represent, duplicate, paraphrase, counterfeit, forge, photocopy, ditto, transcribe, delineate, depict, portray, picture, repeat, reduplicate, replicate, clone, plagiarize, borrow, lift\*, crib\*, knock off\*; see also **draw** 2, **reproduce** 1, 2.
*See Synonym Study at* IMITATE.
**copyist,** *n.* **1.** [One who imitates] — *Syn.* mimic, copier, parrot; see **imitator.**
**2.** [One who makes copies] — *Syn.* clerk, copier, scrivener; see **clerk** 2, **photographer, scribe.**
**coquet,** *v.* — *Syn.* flirt, trifle, tease, wink at; see **flirt** 1.
*See Synonym Study at* TRIFLE.
**coquette,** *n.* — *Syn.* flirt, tease, trifler, vamp; see **flirt.**
**cord,** *n.* **1.** [Twine] — *Syn.* string, cordage, fiber; see **rope.**
**2.** [A tendon] — *Syn.* sinew, ligament, vinculum, thew, umbilical cord, vocal cord, spinal cord, connective tissue, tie; see also **muscle.**
**cordial,** *modif.* **1.** [Friendly and sincere] — *Syn.* genial, warm, welcoming, gracious; see **amiable, friendly** 1, **polite** 1.
**2.** [Hearty] — *Syn.* warm, fervent, sincere; see **hearty** 1.
*See Synonym Study at* AMIABLE.
**cordiality,** *n.* — *Syn.* affability, warmth, friendliness, graciousness; see **courtesy** 1, **friendship** 2.
**cordially,** *modif.* — *Syn.* genially, warmly, hospitably; see **kindly** 2, **sympathetically.**
**core,** *n.* **1.** [Essence] — *Syn.* gist, kernel, heart; see **essence** 1.
**2.** [Center] — *Syn.* hub, nucleus, focus; see **center** 1.
**corespondent,** *n.* — *Syn.* third party, second man, second woman, other man, other woman, one corner of the triangle, joint respondent, joint defendant; see also **defendant, other.**
**cork,** *n.* — *Syn.* stopper, tap, spike, bung; see **plug** 1.
**corn,** *n.* — *Syn.* maize, Indian corn, sweet corn, green corn, field corn, corn on the cob, hominy, popcorn; see also **grain** 1.
**corn,** *v.* — *Syn.* cure, salt, pickle; see **preserve** 3.
**corn bread,** *n.* — *Syn.* hoe cake(s), corndodgers, corncakes, hot bread, johnnycake, journey cakes, hush puppies, corn pone, spoon bread, tortilla; see also **bread** 1.
**corner,** *n.* **1.** [A projecting edge] — *Syn.* ridge, sharp edge, projection, angle; see **edge** 1, **rim.**
**2.** [A recess] — *Syn.* niche, nook, indentation; see **hole** 2, **recess** 2.
**3.** [A sharp turn] — *Syn.* bend, veer, shift; see **curve** 1, **turn** 2.
**4.** [The angle made where ways intersect] — *Syn.* fork, branch, V, Y, intersection, junction, four corners, cloverleaf; see also **crossing** 1, **junction** 2.
**5.** [\*Difficulty] — *Syn.* predicament, impasse, tight spot, hole\*; see **difficulty** 1, 2, **predicament.**

**6.** [A monopoly] — *Syn.* control, edge, monopolization; see **monopoly.**
*See Synonym Study at* MONOPOLY.
**around the corner** — *Syn.* imminent, near, close, impending; see **approaching, coming** 1, **convenient** 2, **imminent, near** 1.
**cut corners** — *Syn.* cut back, cut down, take a shortcut; see **decrease** 2, **economize, neglect** 2.
**the (four) corners of the earth** — *Syn.* all over the world, worldwide, the most distant regions; see **everywhere.**
**turn the corner** — *Syn.* survive, bear up, pull through\*; see **endure** 2, **recover** 3.
**corner,** *v.* — *Syn.* trap, bring to bay, drive into a corner, tree\*; see **ambush, approach** 1, **catch** 1, 2, **hinder.**
**cornerstone,** *n.* — *Syn.* base, foundation stone, memorial stone, starting point; see **foundation** 2.
**cornerwise,** *modif.* — *Syn.* cornerways, diagonally, cater-corner, cater-cornerways, catty-corner, kitty-corner, obliquely, askew, slanting, aslant, from corner to corner, on the bias, angling, diagonalwise, slaunchwise\*, catawampus\*.
**corny\*,** *modif.* — *Syn.* stale, trite, sentimental, unsophisticated; see **dull** 4, **sentimental, stupid** 1.
**corollary,** *n.* **1.** [An inference] — *Syn.* deduction, analogy, result; see **judgment** 3.
**2.** [A natural consequence] — *Syn.* culmination, conclusion, upshot; see **end** 2, **result.**
**coronation,** *n.* — *Syn.* accession, crowning, investiture, inauguration; see **installation** 1.
**coronet,** *n.* — *Syn.* crown, headdress, tiara, diadem; see **crown** 2.
**corporal punishment,** *n.* — *Syn.* flogging, spanking, beating, whipping; see **flogging, punishment.**
**corporation,** *n.* — *Syn.* partnership, enterprise, company, multinational; see **business** 4, **organization** 3.
**corporeal,** *modif.* — *Syn.* human, mortal, material; see **bodily** 1, **physical** 1.
*See Synonym Study at* BODILY, PHYSICAL.
**corps,** *n.* — *Syn.* troops, brigade, regiment, crew; see **army** 2, **organization** 3, **team** 2.
**corpse,** *n.* — *Syn.* carcass, remains, cadaver; see **body** 2.
*See Synonym Study at* BODY.
**corpulence,** *n.* — *Syn.* obesity, stoutness, plumpness; see **fatness.**
**corpulent,** *modif.* — *Syn.* overweight, fleshy, beefy; see **fat** 1.
**correct,** *modif.* **1.** [Accurate] — *Syn.* exact, true, right; see **accurate** 1.
**2.** [Proper] — *Syn.* suitable, becoming, fitting; see **conventional** 2, **fit** 1.
*See Synonym Study at* ACCURATE.
**correct,** *v.* **1.** [To make corrections] — *Syn.* remedy, rectify, better, help, ameliorate, remove the errors, remove the faults of, emend, improve, alter, adjust, retouch, redress, reclaim, accommodate for, make right, mend, amend, right, fix, fix up, repair, do over, reform, remodel, review, reconstruct, reorganize, edit, revise, make corrections, make improvements, set aright, put straight, set straight, make compensation for, reparation for, put in order, doctor, touch up, polish; see also **adjust** 3, **change** 1, **improve** 1, **repair.**
**2.** [To administer correction] — *Syn.* admonish, chide, reprimand; see **punish.**
*See Synonym Study at* PUNISH.
**corrected,** *modif.* — *Syn.* rectified, amended, reformed; see **changed** 2, **revised.**
**correction,** *n.* **1.** [The act of correcting] — *Syn.* revision, revising, improvement, amendment, rectification,

remodeling, editing, righting, redress, indemnification, reparation, amelioration, mending, fixing, amending, emendation, changing, reconstruction, reorganization; see also **repairing, revision.**
**2.** [The result of correcting] — *Syn.* improvement, revision, emendation, corrigenda; see **change** 2, **improvement** 2, **repair.**
**corrective,** *modif.* — *Syn.* remedial, restorative, curative, healing; see **improving, remedial.**
**correctly,** *modif.* — *Syn.* rightly, precisely, perfectly; see **accurately.**
**correctness,** *n.* **1.** [Accuracy] — *Syn.* precision, exactness, exactitude; see **accuracy** 2, **truth** 1.
**2.** [Propriety] — *Syn.* decency, decorum, rightness; see **fitness** 1, **propriety** 1.
**correlate,** *v.* **1.** [To relate] — *Syn.* connect, equate, associate; see **compare** 1, 2.
**2.** [To be mutually related] — *Syn.* correspond, reciprocate, relate, interact; see **agree, alternate** 1, **belong, exchange** 2.
**correlation,** *n.* — *Syn.* interdependence, correspondence, equivalence; see **association** 2, **exchange** 2, **relationship, similarity.**
**correspond,** *v.* **1.** [To be alike] — *Syn.* compare, match, be similar, be identical; see **agree, resemble.**
**2.** [To communicate by letter] — *Syn.* exchange letters, write, write to, hear from, communicate with, send word, send a letter, keep up a correspondence, epistolize, reply, drop a line, keep in touch, have a pen pal; see also **answer** 1, **communicate** 2.
*See Synonym Study at* AGREE.
**correspondence,** *n.* **1.** [The quality of being like] — *Syn.* conformity, equivalence, accord; see **agreement** 2, **similarity.**
**2.** [Communication by letter] — *Syn.* messages, mail, exchange of letters, letter writing; see **communication** 2, **letter** 2.
**correspondent,** *n.* **1.** [One who sends or receives letters] — *Syn.* letter writer, friend, acquaintance, pen pal, addressee.
**2.** [One who writes for journals] — *Syn.* journalist, contributor, stringer; see **reporter, writer.**
**corresponding,** *modif.* — *Syn.* identical, similar, analogous, conterminous; see **alike** 2, **equal, like.**
**correspond to,** *v.* — *Syn.* accord, concur, harmonize; see **agree, resemble.**
**corridor,** *n.* — *Syn.* passage, hallway, passageway; see **hall** 2.
**corroborate,** *v.* — *Syn.* confirm, support, establish, bear out; see **approve** 1, **prove, verify.**
*See Synonym Study at* VERIFY.
**corroborative,** *modif.* — *Syn.* confirmatory, supporting, collateral; see **affirmative.**
**corrode,** *v.* **1.** [To destroy] — *Syn.* erode, gnaw, consume, eat away; see **destroy** 1.
**2.** [To deteriorate] — *Syn.* rust, rot, degenerate, deteriorate; see **decay, rust.**
**corrosive,** *modif.* **1.** [Corroding] — *Syn.* eroding, strongly acid, caustic; see **acid** 2, **destructive** 2.
**2.** [Sarcastic] — *Syn.* caustic, incisive, biting; see **sarcastic.**
**corrugated,** *modif.* — *Syn.* ridged, grooved, furrowed, folded, fluted, roughened, creased, wrinkled, flexed, crinkled, crumpled, puckered; see also **wrinkled.** — *Ant.* FLAT, smooth, even.
**corrugation,** *n.* — *Syn.* groove, crease, channel; see **fold** 2, **groove, ridge** 1.
**corrupt,** *modif.* **1.** [Characterized by graft] — *Syn.* dishonest, crooked, underhanded, venal, mercenary,

fraudulent, unscrupulous, profiteering, extortionate, taking bribes, bribable, unethical, shady*, on the pad*, on the take*, fixed*, bought*, crooked as a dog's hind leg*; see also **dishonest** 1, 2.
**2.** [Depraved] — *Syn.* low, debased, evil, nefarious; see **wicked** 1.
**3.** [Inaccurate] — *Syn.* fallacious, misleading, contaminated, defective; see **unreliable** 2, **wrong** 2.
**corrupt,** *v.* **1.** [To debase] — *Syn.* pervert, vitiate, degrade, bribe, suborn, adulterate, depreciate, deprave, debauch, defile, demoralize, pollute, taint, contaminate, infect, stain, spoil, ruin, alloy, bastardize, blight, blemish, mark against, undermine, subvert, impair, mar, injure, harm, hurt, damage, deface, disfigure, deform, abuse, mistreat, misuse, dishonor, disgrace, despoil, violate, demean, lower, pull down, reduce, weaken, abase, poison, warp, mislead, misguide, cause to degenerate, cause to deteriorate; see also **bribe.** — *Ant.* purify, CLEAN, restore.
**2.** [To render inaccurate] — *Syn.* falsify, misrepresent, misstate, alter, garble, disguise, color, gloss over, varnish, counterfeit, adulterate, contaminate, taint, fabricate, invent, twist, warp, tamper with, doctor, fix*, pad*; see also **disguise, forge** 1.
*See Synonym Study at* DEBASE.
**corrupted,** *modif.* — *Syn.* debased, perverted, depraved; see **wicked** 1.
**corrupter,** *n.* — *Syn.* bad influence, debaucher, sensualist; see **criminal, lecher.**
**corruption,** *n.* **1.** [Vice] — *Syn.* baseness, depravity, degradation; see **crime** 1, **evil** 1.
**2.** [Conduct involving graft] — *Syn.* extortion, bribery, fraud, fraudulence, venality, misrepresentation, dishonesty, profiteering, nepotism, breach of trust, malfeasance, exploitation, crookedness, shady deal, jobbery, shuffle, racket; see also **crime** 2.
**3.** [Decay] — *Syn.* rot, rottenness, debasement; see **decay** 2, **pollution.** — *Ant.* reliability, trustworthiness, truthfulness.
**corset,** *n.* — *Syn.* girdle, corselet, foundation garment, maternity corset, abdominal belt, garter belt, bodice, support, stays, whalebones, panty girdle, stomacher; see also **clothes, underwear.**
**cosmetic,** *modif.* — *Syn.* beautifying, corrective, improving the appearance, surface; see **improving, ornamental** 1, **remedial, superficial.**
**cosmetic,** *n.* — *Syn.* makeup, beautifier, beautifying agent, beautifying application, beauty-care product, cosmetic preparation, war paint*, face*; see also **makeup** 1. Types of cosmetics include: cold cream, night cream, hand cream, eye cream, astringent, after-shave lotion, hand lotion, body lotion, suntan lotion, talcum, tooth powder, bath powder, face powder, eyebrow pencil, mascara, eye shadow, eye liner, rouge, blusher, toner, lip slicker, face slicker, lipstick, lip rouge, lip liner, lip gloss, nail polish, powder base, moisturizer, foundation, loose powder, pressed powder, bronzer, pancake makeup, leg makeup, body paint, solid perfume, liquid sachet, toilet water, cologne, eau de cologne, *friction pour le bain* (French), bath salts, bath oil, bath gel, royal jelly, brilliantine, pomade, hair tonic, hair dye, hair bleach, mouthwash, liquid dentifrice, nail polish remover, moustache wax, facial pack, mud pack, toothpaste, shampoo, conditioner, cream rinse, hair mousse, styling gel, hair spray, shaving soap, shaving cream, shaving foam, depilatory, deodorant, antiperspirant; see also **lotion, perfume, powder, soap.**
**cosmic,** *modif.* — *Syn.* vast, empyrean, grandiose; see **astronomical** 1, **infinite** 1, **universal** 1.

**cosmopolitan,** *modif.* **1.** [Not local or national] — *Syn.* metropolitan, gregarious, catholic; see **international, public** 2, **universal** 3.

**2.** [Sophisticated] — *Syn.* urbane, worldly, well-traveled; see **cultured.**

**cosmopolite,** *n.* — *Syn.* citizen of the world, sophisticate, humanist, internationalist, cosmopolitan, wanderer, globe-trotter, eclectic, jet-setter, man of the world, woman of the world; see also **traveler.**

**cosmos,** *n.* — *Syn.* universe, creation, solar system, galaxy; see **universe.**

**cost,** *n.* **1.** [Price] — *Syn.* payment, value, charge, expense; see **price, value** 1.

**2.** [Damage] — *Syn.* harm, detriment, loss, sacrifice; see **damage** 1, 2, **loss** 1.

**cost,** *v.* **1.** [To require in money] — *Syn.* sell for, be priced at, be asked, be demanded, be paid, be given, be received, be needed, require, take, be marked at, be valued (at), be worth, amount to, come to, be for sale at, command a price of, run, mount up to, bring in, get, fetch, set one back*.

**2.** [To require in sacrifice] — *Syn.* necessitate, obligate, lose; see **require** 2.

**costing,** *modif.* — *Syn.* selling for, priced at, as much as, to the amount of, to the tune of*, estimated at, on sale at, reduced to, a bargain at*, a steal at*.

**costly,** *modif.* — *Syn.* high-priced, expensive, precious; see **expensive, harmful.**

*See Synonym Study at* EXPENSIVE.

**costs,** *n.* — *Syn.* price, outgo, living costs; see **expenses.**

**at all costs** — *Syn.* by any means, in spite of difficulties, without fail; see **regardless** 2.

**costume,** *n.* — *Syn.* dress, attire, garb, outfit, ensemble, uniform, fancy dress, masquerade, get-up*; see also **clothes, disguise.**

**costume,** *v.* — *Syn.* dress up, outfit, fit out; see **clothe.**

**cot,** *n.* — *Syn.* folding bed, portable bed, trundle bed; see **bed** 1, **furniture.**

Types of cots include: army cot, canvas cot, folding cot, iron cot, hospital cot, gurney, *charpoy* (Anglo-Indian).

**coterie,** *n.* — *Syn.* clique, circle, cadre; see **clique, faction** 1.

*See Synonym Study at* CLIQUE.

**cottage,** *n.* — *Syn.* bungalow, cabin, cot, small house; see **home** 1.

**cotton,** *n.* — *Syn. gossypium* (Latin), cloth, cotton shrub, King Cotton*.

Varieties of cotton include: long-staple, short-staple, upland, Sea Island, *Barbadense* (Latin), Nankin, Peruvian, Brazil, Bahia, Egyptian, Pima, kidney.

Varieties of cloth made out of cotton include: lawn, batiste, chintz, organdy, dotted swiss, voile, cambric, calico, chambray, broadcloth, denim, lisle, ticking, net, muslin, crinoline, flannelette, gingham, jersey, piqué, eyelet batiste, monkscloth, poplin, velveteen, gabardine, crepe, twill, canvas, percale, balloon cloth, toweling, terry cloth, sailcloth, cheesecloth, shirting, theatrical gauze; see also **cloth.**

**couch,** *n.* — *Syn.* sofa, davenport, settee, lounge, love seat, divan, studio couch, sofa bed, sectional, daybed, chesterfield, chaise longue*, chaise lounge*, récamier, tête-à-tête, vis-à-vis; see also **bed** 1, **furniture.**

**cough,** *n.* — *Syn.* hem, hack, tussis, frog in one's throat*; see **cold** 3, **disease.**

**cough,** *v.* — *Syn.* choke, hack, convulse, bark*; see **choke** 2.

**council,** *n.* **1.** [A chosen group, usually advisory] — *Syn.* advisory board, cabinet, directorate; see **committee.**

**2.** [A deliberative meeting] — *Syn.* chamber, senate, assembly; see **gathering.**

**counsel,** *n.* **1.** [Advice] — *Syn.* guidance, instruction, direction; see **advice, suggestion** 1.

**2.** [A lawyer] — *Syn.* attorney, legal adviser, barrister, counselor(s); see **adviser, lawyer.**

*See Synonym Study at* LAWYER.

**keep one's own counsel** — *Syn.* be secretive, keep to oneself, keep quiet; see **hide** 2, **quiet** 2.

**take counsel** — *Syn.* listen to advice, confer, consult, deliberate; see **consult, discuss.**

**counsel,** *v.* — *Syn.* advise, recommend, direct, instruct; see **advise** 1, **teach** 1.

*See Synonym Study at* ADVISE.

**counselor,** *n.* **1.** [An adviser] — *Syn.* guide, instructor, mentor, guidance counselor; see **adviser, teacher** 1.

**2.** [An attorney] — *Syn.* counsel, advocate, barrister; see **lawyer.**

*See Synonym Study at* LAWYER.

**count,** *n.* **1.** [Man of rank] — *Syn.* nobleman, peer, grandee, earl; see **aristocrat, lord** 2.

**2.** [Total] — *Syn.* number, sum, tally; see **calculation** 1, **whole.**

**count,** *v.* — *Syn.* compute, reckon, enumerate, number, add up, total, sum, figure, count off, count up, cipher, calculate, include, take account of, foot up, tally, score, count noses*; see also **add** 1, **calculate** 1, **total** 1.

**countdown,** *n.* — *Syn.* final preparations, launch procedure, hold; see **preparation** 1, **program** 2.

**countenance,** *n.* — *Syn.* look, aspect, face, visage; see **appearance** 1, **expression** 4, **face** 1.

*See Synonym Study at* FACE.

**countenance,** *v.* — *Syn.* confirm, sanction, endorse, tolerate; see **allow** 1, **approve** 1.

**counter,** *n.* — *Syn.* board, shelf, ledge, stand, bar, buffet, table, worktable, worktop, butcher block, chopping block, showcase, display case; see also **bench** 2, **table** 1.

**under the counter** — *Syn.* black-market, surreptitious, unofficial; see **illegal, secret** 3, **secretly.**

**counteract,** *v.* — *Syn.* frustrate, neutralize, invalidate; see **check** 2, **halt** 2, **hinder, offset, prevent.**

**counteraction,** *n.* **1.** [Opposition] — *Syn.* resistance, contradiction, contravention; see **opposition** 1.

**2.** [Cancellation] — *Syn.* neutralization, offsetting, undoing, counterbalancing; see **cancellation, prevention.**

**counteractive,** *modif.* — *Syn.* nullifying, checking, countering, interfering, counter to, clashing, counterproductive; see also **opposite** 3.

**counteractive,** *n.* — *Syn.* relief, cure, preventive; see **medicine** 2, **remedy** 2.

**counterbalance,** *v.* — *Syn.* compensate, counteract, equalize; see **balance** 2, **offset.**

**counterfeit,** *modif.* **1.** [Not genuine] — *Syn.* sham, forged, bogus, spurious; see **artificial** 1, **false** 3.

**2.** [Pretended] — *Syn.* assumed, pretentious, put-on; see **affected** 2, **pretended.**

*See Synonym Study at* ARTIFICIAL, FALSE.

**counterfeit,** *v.* **1.** [To defraud by making copies of money, stamps, etc.] — *Syn.* forge, print money, copy money, copy stamps, make counterfeit money, falsify, coin, circulate bad money; see also **forge** 1, **mint** 1.

**2.** [To pretend] — *Syn.* simulate, feign, fake, delude; see **pretend** 1, **simulate.**

**counterfeiter,** *n.* — *Syn.* forger, pretender, plagiarist, paperhanger*; see **criminal, impostor, plagiarist.**

**counterfeiting,** *n.* — *Syn.* copying, simulation, duplication; see **imitation** 1, **pretending, reproduction** 1.

**countermand,** *v.* — *Syn.* rescind, reverse, retract; see **cancel** 2, **revoke.**

**counterpart,** *n.* — *Syn.* analogue, complement, correlative, equivalent; see **equal, match** 2.

**countersign,** *n.* — *Syn.* password, watchword, slogan, catchword; see **motto, password.**

**countess,** *n.* — *Syn.* noblewoman, great lady, wife of a count, wife of an earl; see **aristocrat, lady** 3.

**countless,** *modif.* — *Syn.* innumerable, incalculable, numberless, myriad; see **infinite** 1, **many.**

**count off,** *v.* — *Syn.* number, get numbers for, give numbers to; see **check** 3, **count, total** 1.

**count on,** *v.* — *Syn.* rely on, rely upon, depend on, depend upon, calculate on, figure on, bank on*, build upon, rest upon, expect, anticipate, take on trust, take for granted, be sure of, trust in, place trust in, place reliance on, make oneself easy about, reckon on*, stake on*; see also **trust** 1.
*See Synonym Study at* TRUST.

**count out,** *v.* — *Syn.* exclude, omit, disregard, leave out; see **eliminate** 1, **omit** 1.

**count over,** *v.* — *Syn.* audit, tally, review; see **correct** 1, **examine** 1, **revise.**

**countrified,** *modif.* — *Syn.* provincial, agrarian, rural; see **country** 1, **rural, rustic** 2.

**country,** *modif.* **1.** [Said of people, manners, etc.] — *Syn.* countrified, unsophisticated, rural, rustic, homey, down-home, farm, backwoods, provincial, unpolished, unrefined, uncouth, uncultured, hick*; see also **rude** 1, **rural, rustic** 2.
**2.** [*Said of areas*] — *Syn.* rustic, agrarian, provincial, back-country; see **rural.**

**country,** *n.* **1.** [Rural areas] — *Syn.* countryside, farmland, farming district, rural region, rural area, country district, back country, bush, forests, mountains, woodlands, backwoods, sparsely settled areas, the hinterland, the provinces, frontier, wilderness, wilds, outback (Australian), the sticks*, the boondocks, the boonies*; see also **farm, forest, range** 4. — *Ant.* CITY, urban area, municipality.
**2.** [A nation] — *Syn.* sovereign state, realm, land, people; see **nation** 1.
**3.** [Land and all that is associated with it] — *Syn.* homeland, native land, fatherland, motherland, mother country, *patria* (Latin), all we hold dear, roots, *Vaterland* (German), *la patrie* (French), the flag*, mother and apple pie*.

**countryman,** *n.* **1.** [A compatriot] — *Syn.* fellow citizen, national, kinsman; see **citizen, compatriot.**
**2.** [A man living in the country] — *Syn.* rustic, bucolic, farmer, rancher, agriculturist, farm laborer, rural laborer, farm help, farm hand, country person, farm vote, backwoodsman, provincial, rube*, hayseed*, hick*, yokel*, hillbilly*, redneck*; see also **boor, farmer, peasant.**

**countryside,** *n.* — *Syn.* rural area, rural district, farmland, woods; see **country** 1.

**count up,** *v.* — *Syn.* compute, get a total for, bring together; see **add** 1, **count, total** 1.

**county,** *n.* — *Syn.* province, administrative district, constituency, shire; see **division** 6.

**coup,** *n.* **1.** [Maneuver] — *Syn.* stratagem, move, stroke, masterstroke; see **achievement** 2, **tactics.**
**2.** [Revolution] — *Syn.* upset, overthrow, *coup d'état* (French); see **revolution** 2.

**coup de grâce** (French), *n.* — *Syn.* deathblow, final stroke, quietus; see **blow** 1, **defeat** 2, 3.

**coup d'etat,** *n.* — *Syn.* revolt, rebellion, overthrow; see **revolution** 2.

**couple,** *n.* **1.** [A pair] — *Syn.* duo, twosome, two; see **pair.**
**2.** [*A few*] — *Syn.* some, several, a handful; see **few.**
*See Synonym Study at* PAIR.

**couple,** *v.* — *Syn.* unite, come together, bring together, link; see **copulate, join** 1, **unite** 1.

**coupon,** *n.* — *Syn.* token, order blank, certificate, ticket, check, detachable portion, stub, separate ticket, box top, redeemable part, redemption slip, scrip, premium certificate, ration slip, evidence of purchase; see also **card, ticket** 1.

**courage,** *n.* **1.** [Readiness to dare] — *Syn.* bravery, valor, valorousness, boldness, intrepidity, fearlessness, spirit, audacity, audaciousness, temerity, dauntlessness, pluck, mettle, enterprise, stoutheartedness, firmness, self-reliance, hardihood, heroism, gallantry, manliness, daring, prowess, resolution, resoluteness, heart, élan, doughtiness, adventuresomeness, adventurousness, venturesomeness, bravura, dash, recklessness, derring-do, pugnacity, pluckiness, gameness, rashness, defiance, the courage of one's convictions, spunk*, grit*, backbone*, guts*, what it takes*, nerve*, nerves of steel*, intestinal fortitude*, moxie*, cojones*; see also **strength** 1. — *Ant.* cowardice, FEAR, timidity.
**2.** [Ability to endure] — *Syn.* stamina, coolness, firmness; see **determination** 2, **endurance** 2.

**courageous,** *modif.* — *Syn.* brave, daring, gallant, intrepid; see **brave** 1.
*See Synonym Study at* BRAVE.

**courier,** *n.* — *Syn.* messenger, runner, dispatcher, herald; see **carrier** 1, **messenger.**

**course,** *n.* **1.** [A route] — *Syn.* direction, passage, path, way; see **route** 1, **way** 2.
**2.** [A prepared way, especially for racing] — *Syn.* track, trail, ski trail, racecourse; see **road** 1, **track** 1.
**3.** [A plan of study] — *Syn.* course of study, subject, studies, curriculum, matriculation, program, specialty, major, minor, area, field, discipline; see also **education** 1.
**4.** [A series of lessons] — *Syn.* class, subject, classes, lectures, seminar, sessions, colloquia, required course, requirement, elective, refresher course, crash course, gut course*; see also **class** 3.
**5.** [A way of proceeding] — *Syn.* progression, sequence, course of action, mode of conduct; see **development** 2, **plan** 2, **way** 3.
**as a matter of course** — *Syn.* ordinarily, routinely, naturally, customarily; see **customarily, regularly** 1.
**in due course** — *Syn.* in due time, when proper, eventually, in the natural course of events; see **appropriately, finally** 2, **ultimately.**
**in the course of** — *Syn.* during, in the process of, when; see **during, while** 1.
**of course** — *Syn.* certainly, by all means, indeed; see **surely, yes.**
**off course** — *Syn.* misdirected, erratic, going the wrong way; see **lost** 1, **wrong** 2.
**on course** — *Syn.* on target, correct, going in the right direction; see **accurate** 1.

**court,** *n.* **1.** [An enclosed, roofless area] — *Syn.* square, courtyard, quadrangle, quad*, enclosure, atrium, forum, patio, plaza, piazza, common(s), close, cloister; see also **yard** 1.
**2.** [An instrument for administering justice] — *Syn.* tribunal, forum, bench, bar, session, court of law, law court, judiciary, assizes, chancery, seat of justice; see also **judiciary.**

Types of courts include: the Supreme Court, appellate court, Federal court, court of Chancery, court of equity, district court, county court, municipal court, probate court, traffic court, justice's court, magistrate's court, mayor's court, police court, military court, trial court, court of appeals.

**3.** [The home of a court, sense 2] — *Syn.* courthouse, justice building, court building, hall of justice, courtroom, federal building, county courthouse, municipal building, city hall, town hall.

**4.** [A sovereign and his or her surroundings] — *Syn.* retinue, lords and ladies, ladies in waiting, attendants, suite, royal persons, staff, train, royal residence, palace, castle, hall, royal household, entourage; see also **government** 2, **palace, royalty, ruler** 1.

**5.** [An area for playing certain games] — *Syn.* rink, ring, lists, cockpit, circus, the hardwood*; see also **arena, field** 2.

**pay court to** — *Syn.* woo, court, solicit; see **court** 1.

**court,** *v.* **1.** [To woo] — *Syn.* invite, bid, solicit, address, beseech, entice, attract, allure, entreat, importune, sue for, pursue, follow, seek after, make suit, supplicate, plead, make love to, pay court to, pay attentions to, seek the hand of, pay one's addresses to, flirt with, philander, coquet, make overtures, make advances, go courting, propose, make a proposal, ask in marriage, set one's cap for*, pop the question*, chase*, run after*, make time with*, go steady*, go together*, go with*, make a play for*; see also **accompany** 1, **date** 2, **flirt** 1, **woo** 1.

**2.** [To seek favor] — *Syn.* cultivate, curry favor, attend, flatter; see **grovel, praise** 1, **woo** 2.

**courteous,** *modif.* — *Syn.* polite, gracious, affable, cultivated; see **polite** 1.

*See Synonym Study at* POLITE.

**courteously,** *modif.* — *Syn.* civilly, affably, obligingly; see **politely.**

**courtesan,** *n.* — *Syn.* mistress, concubine, whore; see **mistress** 2, **prostitute.**

**courtesy,** *n.* **1.** [Courteous conduct] — *Syn.* politeness, civility, courteousness, graciousness, good manners, kindness, courtliness, complaisance, affability, gentleness, consideration, thoughtfulness, sympathy, geniality, cordiality, friendliness, solicitude, amiability, tact, good behavior, mannerliness, politesse, amenities, etiquette, comity, culture, refinement, address, cultivation, chivalry, urbanity, gallantry, respect, attention, favor, deference, elegance of manners, polished manners, good breeding, gentle breeding, formality, gentility, suavity, blandness; see also **behavior** 1, **ceremony** 2, **kindness** 1.

**2.** [Courteous act] — *Syn.* attention, service, favor, polite gesture, act of politeness, mark of attention, gift, kindness, compassion, benevolence, accommodation, indulgence, generosity, charity; see also **kindness** 2.

**courtier,** *n.* — *Syn.* retainer, subject, squire, flatterer; see **attendant, servant, sycophant.**

**courtliness,** *n.* — *Syn.* gallantry, refinement, politeness; see **courtesy** 1, **elegance** 1.

**courtly,** *modif.* — *Syn.* elegant, dignified, refined, gallant; see **cultured, polite** 1.

**courtship,** *n.* — *Syn.* courting, dating, wooing, lovemaking; see **love** 1.

**courtyard,** *n.* — *Syn.* court, patio, lawn; see **court** 1, **yard** 1.

**cousin,** *n.* — *Syn.* kin, an aunt's child, an uncle's child, first cousin, second cousin, distant cousin, cousin once removed, cousin twice removed, kinsman, kinswoman, coz*; see also **relative.**

**cove,** *n.* **1.** [Bay] — *Syn.* inlet, sound, lagoon; see **bay.**

**2.** [Recess] — *Syn.* cavern, retreat, nook; see **hole** 3, **recess** 3.

**covenant,** *n.* — *Syn.* compact, bond, solemn agreement; see **agreement** 3, **contract, promise** 1, **treaty.**

**covenant,** *v.* — *Syn.* promise, concur, pledge; see **agree, contract** 3, **promise** 1.

**cover,** *n.* **1.** [A covering object] — *Syn.* covering, top, lid, cap, ceiling, canopy, awning, tent, marquee, umbrella, parasol, roof, thatch, dome, blanket, bedspread, coverlet, stopper, plug, cork, canvas, seal, tarpaulin, book cover, binding, folder, wrapper, wrapping paper, jacket, case, sheath, spread, sheet, slipcover, tarp*; see also **bedspread, blanket** 2, **envelope, folder** 2, **hood** 1, 2, **roof, sheath.**

**2.** [A covering substance] — *Syn.* coat, covering, overlay, binding, slate, paint, shingle, veneer, varnish, polish; see also **coat** 3, **sheet** 2.

**3.** [Shelter] — *Syn.* sanctuary, protection, asylum, refuge; see **retreat** 3, **sanctuary** 2, **shelter.**

**4.** [Concealment] — *Syn.* covert, hiding place, screen, blind; see **camouflage** 1, **defense** 2, **shelter, trick** 1.

**take cover** — *Syn.* conceal oneself, take shelter, go indoors; see **hide** 2.

**under cover** — *Syn.* in secrecy, clandestinely, hiding, concealed; see **hidden** 2, **secretive, secretly.**

**cover,** *v.* **1.** [To place as a covering] — *Syn.* cover up, carpet, blanket, put on, put a cover on, put a lid on, cap, close, overlay, lay over, overspread, surface, board up, superimpose, coat; see also **close** 2, 4, **spread** 4.

**2.** [To wrap] — *Syn.* envelop, enshroud, encase, cloak; see **clothe, wrap** 2.

**3.** [To protect] — *Syn.* shield, screen, house; see **defend** 1, 2, **shelter.**

**4.** [To hide] — *Syn.* screen, camouflage, mask, conceal; see **disguise, hide** 1.

**5.** [To include] — *Syn.* embrace, comprise, incorporate; see **comprise, include** 1, **treat** 2.

**6.** [To suffice] — *Syn.* reach, be enough, meet; see **satisfy** 3.

**7.** [To travel over] — *Syn.* traverse, journey over, cross; see **travel** 2.

**8.** [To send down in plenty] — *Syn.* deluge, pour, rain, inundate, submerge, shower, drench, engulf, overcome, drown out, overflow, overspread, send down like manna from heaven*; see also **flood.**

**9.** [*To report news about] — *Syn.* report on, recount, narrate, relate; see **broadcast** 2, **report** 1.

**covered,** *modif.* **1.** [Provided with a cover] — *Syn.* closed, topped, overlaid, lidded, capped, roofed, hooded, wrapped, enveloped, enclosed, sheathed, veiled, bound, painted, varnished, coated, surfaced, camouflaged, sheltered, shielded, disguised, masked, secreted, protected, concealed; see also **hidden** 2, **tight** 2. — *Ant.* revealed, OPEN, exposed.

**2.** [Plentifully bestrewn] — *Syn.* scattered with, bejeweled, sprinkled over, spattered, spangled, dotted, studded, peppered, strewn with, starred, starry with, flowery, flowered, spotted, sown, dusted over, powdered, spread with, overspread, overgrown, carpeted. — *Ant.* bare, EMPTY, unfurnished.

**3.** [Attended to] — *Syn.* noted, taken note of, accounted for, reported, recorded, written, included, marked, explored, regarded, scrutinized, examined, surveyed, investigated, observed, looked to, cared for; see also **included, reported.** — *Ant.* UNHEEDED, unnoticed, passed over.

**covering,** *n.* — *Syn.* top, shelter, integument, housing; see **cover** 1.

**coverlet,** *n.* — *Syn.* spread, cover, comforter; see **bedspread, quilt.**

**covert,** *modif.* — *Syn.* secret, clandestine, furtive; see **secret** 1, 2.

*See Synonym Study at* SECRET.

**covert,** *n.* **1.** [A thicket] — *Syn.* copse, underwood, bushes; see **brush** 4, **bush** 1.

**2.** [A shelter or hiding place] — *Syn.* shield, asylum, harbor; see **refuge** 1, **retreat** 2, **sanctuary** 2, **shelter.**

**coverup,** *n.* — *Syn.* concealment, suppression, whitewash; see **disguise, screen** 1.

**cover up for,** *v.* — *Syn.* front for, lie for, take the rap for*, be the goat*, be the fall guy*; see also **defend** 1, 2, **shelter.**

**covet,** *v.* — *Syn.* desire, envy, wish for; see **envy, want** 1.

*See Synonym Study at* ENVY.

**covetous,** *modif.* — *Syn.* greedy, avaricious, selfish, rapacious; see **greedy** 1.

*See Synonym Study at* GREEDY.

**covetousness,** *n.* — *Syn.* avarice, cupidity, avariciousness; see **greed.**

**covey,** *n.* — *Syn.* flock, bunch, brood; see **herd** 1.

**cow,** *n.* — *Syn.* heifer, milk cow, dairy cow, bovine, critter*, bossy*; see also **bull** 1, **calf.**

Breeds of cows include: — *beef:* Aberdeen Angus, Hereford, Longhorn, Texas Longhorn, Durham, Sussex, Galloway, Charolais, whiteface*; *dairy:* Ayrshire, Guernsey, Jersey, Holstein-Friesian, Alderney, Brown Swiss, Dexter, Kerry, Simmenthal, Jutland, Red Danish; *dual-purpose:* Red Poll, Shorthorn, Devon, Dutch Belted, French Canadian.

**coward,** *n.* — *Syn.* poltroon, craven, recreant, dastard, cur, wheyface, sneak, faintheart, mollycoddle, milksop, milquetoast, baby*, shirker, deserter, bully, blusterer, weakling, panicmonger, scaramouch, alarmist, caitiff, pessimist, malinger, chicken*, wimp*, sissy*, quitter*, punk*, lily-liver*, scaredy-cat*, chicken-heart*, fraidy-cat*, rabbit*, mouse*, yellow-belly*, jellyfish*, pantywaist*, nervous Nellie*; see also **deserter, quitter.**

**cowardice,** *n.* — *Syn.* pusillanimity, cowardliness, cravenness, timorousness, timidity, faintheartedness, baseness, fear, abject fear, weakness, quailing, shrinking, cowering, fawning, groveling, sniveling, abjectness, bullying, recreancy, dastardy, dastardliness, want of courage, spinelessness, poltroonery, desertion, apprehension, dread, diffidence, apprehensiveness, fearfulness, suspicion, baby act*, white feather*, yellow streak*, yellowness*, lack of guts*, gutlessness*, funk*, cold feet*; see also **fear** 2, **shyness.** — *Ant.* bravery, VALOR, fearlessness.

**cowardly,** *modif.* **1.** [Lacking courage] — *Syn.* timid, timorous, frightened, shrinking, afraid, fearful, shy, diffident, backward, retiring, cowering, apprehensive, nervous, anxious, full of dread, dismayed, fainthearted, panicky, scared, scary*, jittery*, chicken*, chicken-hearted*, chicken-livered*, lily-livered*, rabbit-hearted*, yellow*, yellow-bellied*, afraid of one's own shadow*; see also **afraid** 1, **timid** 1. — *Ant.* fearless, BRAVE, intrepid.

**2.** [Suggestive of a coward] — *Syn.* pusillanimous, poltroonish, craven, dastardly, recreant, poor-spirited, mean-spirited, weak, bullying, base, soft, unmanly, irresolute, spineless, gutless*, wimpy*, wimpish*; see also **weak** 3.

**3.** [In the manner of a coward] — *Syn.* skulking, sneaking, cringing, cowering, trembling, shaken, crouching,

wincing, quailing, shaky, running, quaking, shaking like a leaf, pale with fear, in a funk*, showing the white feather*, shaking in one's boots*.

SYN. — **cowardly,** the general term, suggests a reprehensible lack of courage in the face of danger or pain [a *cowardly* deserter]; **craven** implies abject or fainthearted fear [a *craven* fear for one's life]; **pusillanimous** implies an ignoble, contemptible lack of courage or resolution [*pusillanimous* submission]; **dastardly** connotes a sneaking, malicious cowardice that is manifested in a despicable act [a *dastardly* informer]

**cowboy,** *n.* — *Syn.* cowhand, hand, wrangler, top hand, rider, herder, night herder, *vaquero, gaucho, llanero* (all Spanish), cattle-herder, cattlehand, drover, herdsman, cowpuncher*, cowpoke*, puncher*, broncobuster*, buckaroo*; see also **rancher.**

**cower,** *v.* — *Syn.* cringe, flinch, quail; see **wince.**

**coy,** *modif.* — *Syn.* bashful, shy, demure, coquettish; see **flirtatious, humble** 1.

**cozenage,** *n.* — *Syn.* plot, swindle, treachery; see **deception** 1, **trick** 1.

**cozy,** *modif.* — *Syn.* sheltered, snug, homey, intimate; see **comfortable** 2.

*See Synonym Study at* COMFORTABLE.

**crab,** *n.* **1.** [A short-tailed or soft-tailed crustacean] — *Syn.* podothalmian, *Brachyura, Anomura* (both Latin), seafood; see **shellfish.**

Kinds of crabs include: softshell, hardshell, deep-sea, king, horseshoe, blue, spider, giant spider, Japanese spider, shore, rock, land, fiddler, Dungeness, Jonah, green, pea, box, porcelain, lady, ghost, swimming, paddle, shuttle, hermit, purse.

**2.** [A grouchy person] — *Syn.* complainer, grumbler, grump, bellyacher*; see **grouch.**

**crabbed*,** *modif.* **1.** [Sour-tempered] — *Syn.* grouchy, peevish, perverse; see **irritable.**

**2.** [Difficult to understand] — *Syn.* unreadable, intricate, scribbled; see **illegible, obscure** 1.

**crabby,** *modif.* — *Syn.* peevish, querulous, grumpy; see **complaining, irritable.**

**crack*,** *modif.* — *Syn.* first-rate, first-class, skilled; see **able** 1, 2, **excellent.**

**crack,** *n.* **1.** [An incomplete break] — *Syn.* fracture, split, cut, splintering; see **break** 1, **fracture** 1, 2.

**2.** [A crevice] — *Syn.* chink, cleft, fissure, rift; see **hole** 1, 2.

**3.** [A cracking sound] — *Syn.* snap, clap, burst, report; see **noise** 1.

**4.** [A blow] — *Syn.* hit, thwack, smack; see **blow** 1.

**5.** [*A witty or sharp comment] — *Syn.* return, wisecrack, witticism, jest; see **joke** 2, **remark.**

**crack,** *v.* **1.** [To make or become cracked] — *Syn.* split, fracture, shatter, craze; see **break** 1, 2, 3.

**2.** [To make a noise of something breaking] — *Syn.* snap, crackle, bang, crash; see **sound** 1.

**3.** [To damage] — *Syn.* injure, hurt, impair; see **damage** 1.

**4.** [*To lose mental control] — *Syn.* break down, go to pieces, succumb, go crazy; see **crack up** 2, **weaken** 1, **yield** 1.

**5.** [To solve] — *Syn.* figure out, answer, decipher, decode; see **solve.**

*See Synonym Study at* BREAK.

**get cracking*** — *Syn.* get going, go, start, get a move on*; see **begin** 1, **move** 1.

**crack a book*,** *v.* — *Syn.* scrutinize, peruse, scan; see **examine** 1, **read** 1, **study** 1.

**crack a bottle\***, *v.* — *Syn.* have a drink, tipple, open a bottle; see **drink** 2.

**crack a joke\***, *v.* — *Syn.* joke, jest, quip; see **joke**.

**crack down (on)**, *n.* — *Syn.* become strict, regulate, suppress, clamp down; see **punish, restrain** 1, **suppress**.

**cracked**, *modif.* — *Syn.* fissured, split, fractured, crazed; see **broken** 1.

**cracker**, *n.* — *Syn.* wafer, soda cracker, oyster cracker, biscuit, saltine, water biscuit, cream cracker, hardtack, sea biscuit, *knäckebröd* (Swedish), Melba toast, matzo; see also **bread** 1, **cookie**.

**crack up**, *v.* **1.** [\*To crash a vehicle] — *Syn.* collide, be in an accident, smash up, total\*; see **crash** 4.
**2.** [To fail suddenly in health, mind, or strength] — *Syn.* go to pieces, decline, fail, deteriorate, sicken, collapse, succumb, break down, go crazy, go mad, become insane, have a nervous breakdown, become psychotic, be committed to a hospital, be committed to an institution, fall apart, burn out, crack, flip out\*, flip one's lid\*, freak out\*, go out of one's mind\*, blow one's mind\*, go off one's rocker\*, go off the deep end\*, come apart at the seams\*, lose it\*; see also **derange** 2, **weaken** 1.
**3.** [\*To laugh] — *Syn.* roar, howl, burst out laughing, roll in the aisles\*; see **laugh**.

**cradle**, *n.* **1.** [A baby's bed] — *Syn.* crib, bassinet, trundle bed; see **bed** 1.
**2.** [A place of nurture] — *Syn.* spring, fountain, ultimate source; see **foundation** 2, **origin** 2.

**craft**, *n.* **1.** [Skill] — *Syn.* proficiency, competence, adeptness; see **ability** 2, **art** 1.
**2.** [Guile] — *Syn.* cunning, duplicity, trickery, slyness; see **cunning, dishonesty**.
**3.** [Trade] — *Syn.* occupation, vocation, handicraft, work; see **job** 1, **profession** 1.
**4.** [Vessel] — *Syn.* boat, ship, aircraft; see **boat, plane** 3, **ship, spacecraft**.
*See Synonym Study at* ART.

**craftsman**, *n.* — *Syn.* artisan, craftsperson, handicraftsman, skilled worker, skilled tradesman, skilled workman, master craftsman, journeyman, maker, wright, smith, union member, technician, manufacturer, machinist, mechanic, artificer; see also **artist** 2, **worker**.

**crafty**, *modif.* — *Syn.* sly, wily, cunning, artful; see **sly** 1.
*See Synonym Study at* SLY.

**crag**, *n.* — *Syn.* bluff, jutting rock, peak; see **mountain** 1, **rock** 2.

**craggy**, *modif.* — *Syn.* rough, jagged, rugged, steep; see **abrupt** 1, **rocky**.

**cram**, *v.* **1.** [To stuff] — *Syn.* pack, jam, compact, overfill; see **compress, fill** 1, **pack** 2, **press** 1.
**2.** [\*To eat greedily] — *Syn.* gorge, devour, stuff oneself; see **eat** 1.
**3.** [To study hurriedly] — *Syn.* read, review, bone up\*, burn the midnight oil\*; see **study** 1.

**cramp**, *n.* **1.** [A painful muscle contraction] — *Syn.* spasm, crick, pang, charley horse\*; see **pain** 2.
**2.** [An obstruction] — *Syn.* encumbrance, hindrance, restriction; see **impediment** 1.

**cramp**, *v.* **1.** [To restrain] — *Syn.* restrict, confine, hamper, obstruct; see **hinder, restrain** 1.
**2.** [\*To fasten] — *Syn.* clasp, clamp, grip; see **fasten** 1.

**cramped**, *modif.* — *Syn.* narrow, confined, restricted, crowded; see **narrow** 1, **restricted, uncomfortable** 1.

**cramp one's style\***, *v.* — *Syn.* obstruct, hamper, inhibit, stand in one's way; see **hinder, restrain** 1.

**crane**, *n.* — *Syn.* lift, derrick, davit; see **elevator** 1.

**cranium**, *n.* — *Syn.* skull, brainpan, braincase, peri-

cranium, bony covering, crown, brain box\*; see also **brain** 1, **head** 1.
Bones of the cranium include: occipital, frontal, parietal, temporal, sphenoid, mastoid, ethmoid, lacrimal, nasal, mandibular, superior maxillary, inferior maxillary.

**crank**, *n.* **1.** [A device for revolving a shaft] — *Syn.* arm, lever, handle, brace, bracket, turning device, elbow, bend; see also **arm** 2, **handle** 1.
**2.** [\*A person with an obsession] — *Syn.* eccentric, fanatic, monomaniac, crackpot\*; see **character** 4, **zealot**.
**3.** [\*An ill-natured person] — *Syn.* misanthrope, complainer, curmudgeon; see **grouch**.

**cranky**, *modif.* — *Syn.* cross, testy, crotchety, fretful; see **irritable**.
*See Synonym Study at* IRRITABLE.

**cranny**, *n.* — *Syn.* crevice, crack, break; see **hole** 1, 2.

**crash**, *n.* **1.** [A crashing sound] — *Syn.* clatter, clash, bang; see **noise** 1.
**2.** [A collision] — *Syn.* wreck, accident, crackup; see **collision** 1.

**crash**, *v.* **1.** [To fall with a crash] — *Syn.* overturn, upset, break down, plunge, be hurled, pitch, topple, smash, dive, hurtle, plummet, land violently, lurch, sprawl, tumble, fall headlong, fall flat, drop, slip, collapse, precipitate oneself, come a cropper\*, spin in\*; see also **fall** 1.
**2.** [To break into pieces] — *Syn.* shatter, smash, splinter, dash to pieces; see **break** 2, **smash**.
**3.** [To make a crashing sound] — *Syn.* clatter, bang, smash; see **sound** 1.
**4.** [To have a collision] — *Syn.* collide with, hit, strike, run together, run into, smash into, bump into, bang into, slam into, dash into, jostle, impact, bump, rear-end, sideswipe, butt, knock, punch, jar, jolt, go aground, hurtle into, crack up\*, total\*; see also **hit** 1, 2.
**5.** [To break down] — *Syn.* malfunction, shut down, fail; see **break down** 3.
**6.** [\*To sleep] — *Syn.* go to bed, bed down, stay over, bunk\*; see **dwell, lodge** 2, **sleep**.
**7.** [\*To go uninvited] — *Syn.* invade, intrude, crash the gate\*; see **interrupt** 2, **meddle** 1.
*See Synonym Study at* BREAK.

**crash program**, *n.* — *Syn.* crash project, intensive program, accelerated program, marathon, around-the-clock endeavor, all-out effort, intensification, speed-up\*; see also **emergency**.

**crass**, *modif.* — *Syn.* gross, coarse, unrefined, materialistic; see **coarse** 2, **rude** 1, **vulgar** 1.

**crate**, *n.* — *Syn.* carton, box, cage; see **case** 7, **container, package** 1.

**crate**, *v.* — *Syn.* box, enclose, case; see **pack** 1, 2.

**crater**, *n.* — *Syn.* pit, cavity, abyss; see **hole** 2.

**crave**, *v.* **1.** [To long for] — *Syn.* desire, covet, hunger for; see **need, want** 1.
**2.** [To beg] — *Syn.* entreat, ask, plead; see **beg** 1.
*See Synonym Study at* DESIRE.

**craven**, *modif.* — *Syn.* fearful, fainthearted, pusillanimous, yellow\*; see **cowardly** 1, 2, **timid** 1.
*See Synonym Study at* COWARDLY.

**craving**, *n.* — *Syn.* need, longing, yearning; see **desire** 1.

**craw**, *n.* — *Syn.* gizzard, intestines, stomach, crop; see **abdomen**.

**crawfish**, *n.* — *Syn.* crayfish, crustacean, crawdad\*; see **shellfish**.

**crawl**, *v.* **1.** [To move like an insect] — *Syn.* creep, worm along, wriggle, squirm, slither, move on hands and knees, go on hands and knees, writhe, grovel, snake, go on all fours\*, worm one's way\*, go on one's belly\*; see also **grovel**.

**2.** [To move slowly] — *Syn.* inch, inch along, drag, plod, hang back, poke, go at a snail's pace; see also **lag** 1.

*SYN.* — **crawl** and **creep** are often used interchangeably, but **crawl**, in its strict usage, suggests movement by dragging the prone body along the ground /a snake *crawls*/ and **creep** suggests movement, often furtive, on all fours /the cat *crept* up the stairs/; figuratively, **crawl** connotes slowness, abjectness, or servility and **creep** connotes slow, stealthy, or insinuating progress

**crawling,** *modif.* **1.** [Creeping] — *Syn.* moving slowly, dragging, on hands and knees; see **creeping** 1.
  **2.** [Abounding] — *Syn.* overrun, swarming, teeming; see **jammed** 2, **plentiful.**

**crayon,** *n.* — *Syn.* chalk, pastel, colored wax, crayon pencil, lithographic pencil, drawing medium, conté crayon, wax crayon, Crayola (trademark); see also **pencil** 1.

**craze,** *n.* — *Syn.* fad, rage, fashion; see **fad.**
*See Synonym Study at* FASHION.

**crazily,** *modif.* — *Syn.* furiously, irrationally, hastily, madly, rashly, witlessly, insanely, psychotically, maniacally, as though out of one's mind, ravingly, rabidly; see also **violently** 1, 2, **wildly** 1.

**crazy,** *modif.* — *Syn.* crazed, demented, mad; see **absurd, insane** 1, **stupid** 1.

**crazy about,** *modif.* — *Syn.* enthusiastic about, enamored of, keen on, wild about; see **enthusiastic** 2, **fascinated, loving.**

**creak,** *v.* — *Syn.* squeak, grate, rasp; see **sound** 1.

**cream,** *modif.* — *Syn.* beige, eggshell, ivory; see **tan, white** 1, **yellow** 1.

**cream,** *n.* **1.** [The fatty portion of milk] — *Syn.* rich milk, heavy cream, light cream, half-and-half, *crème* (French), coffee cream, whipping cream, whipped cream, ice cream, *Schlag* (German), butterfat, crème fraîche, clotted cream, top of the bottle\*; see also **milk.**
  **2.** [A creamy substance] — *Syn.* emulsion, emollient, lotion; see **cosmetic, lotion, salve.**
  **3.** [\*The best part] — *Syn.* pick, finest, elite; see **best.**

**creamy,** *modif.* — *Syn.* smooth, rich, oily, buttery, luscious, lush, velvety, fatty, creamed; see also **soft** 2.

**crease,** *n.* — *Syn.* tuck, ridge, pleat; see **fold** 2, **wrinkle.**

**crease,** *v.* — *Syn.* double, rumple, crimp; see **fold** 2, **wrinkle** 1.

**create,** *v.* **1.** [To conceive in the mind] — *Syn.* formulate, devise, conceive; see **imagine** 1.
  **2.** [To make] — *Syn.* produce, originate, actualize, effect, form, occasion, perform, cause to exist, bring into being, call into being, call into existence, rear, erect, build, fashion, invent, engender, beget, generate, construct, found, shape, forge, design, plan, fabricate, author, contrive, cause to be, give birth to, bring to pass, bring about, invest, constitute; see also **compose** 3, **invent** 1, **organize** 2, **produce** 2.

**creation,** *n.* **1.** [The process of creating] — *Syn.* origination, production, formulation; see **conception** 1, **making, origin** 1, **production** 1.
  **2.** [All that has been created] — *Syn.* cosmos, nature, totality, world; see **earth** 1, **universe.**
  **3.** [A work of art] — *Syn.* creative work, imaginative work, work of genius, opus, magnum opus, *chef d'oeuvre* (French), piece, production, invention, brainchild\*; see also **art** 3, **work** 3.

**creative,** *modif.* — *Syn.* inventive, imaginative, formative, productive; see **artistic** 2, **original** 2.

**Creator,** *n.* — *Syn.* First Cause, Deity, Maker; see **god** 2.

**creator,** *n.* — *Syn.* inventor, producer, originator; see **author** 1.

**creature,** *n.* **1.** [A living being] — *Syn.* creation, being, beast, human; see **animal** 1, 2, **person** 1.
  **2.** [An imaginary being] — *Syn.* being, extraterrestrial, android, monster; see **alien, monster** 1.

**credence,** *n.* — *Syn.* confidence, belief, faith, reliance; see **belief** 1, **faith** 1.
*See Synonym Study at* BELIEF.

**credentials,** *pl.n.* — *Syn.* certification, accreditation, testimonials, references; see **certificate, record** 1, 2.

**credibility,** *n.* — *Syn.* plausibility, believability, trustworthiness, likelihood; see **honesty** 1, **probability, reliability.**

**credible,** *modif.* **1.** [Likely] — *Syn.* probable, believable, conceivable; see **convincing** 2, **likely** 1.
  **2.** [Reliable] — *Syn.* trustworthy, dependable, sincere; see **reliable** 1, 2.
*See Synonym Study at* SPECIOUS.

**credit,** *n.* **1.** [Belief] — *Syn.* credence, reliance, confidence, trust; see **faith** 1.
  **2.** [Unencumbered funds] — *Syn.* assets, stocks, bonds, paper credit, account, bank account, balance, mortgages, liens, securities, debentures, capital outlay, surplus cash; see also **balance** 3, **wealth** 1.
  **3.** [Recognition] — *Syn.* acknowledgment, commendation, prestige, repute; see **honor** 1, **praise** 1, **reputation** 1, 2.
  **4.** [Permission to defer payment] — *Syn.* extension, respite, continuance, trust in future payment, accounts carried on the books, borrowing power, line of credit; see also **loan.**
  **do credit to** — *Syn.* bring approval to, do honor to, redound to the honor of, reflect well on; see **promote** 2.
  **give credit to** — *Syn.* believe in, rely on, have confidence in; see **believe** 1, **trust** 1.
  **give one credit for** — *Syn.* commend, acknowledge, recognize; see **admit** 3, **praise** 1.
  **on credit** — *Syn.* on a charge, by deferred payment, on loan; see **charged** 1, **unpaid** 1.
  **to one's credit** — *Syn.* commendable, honorable, beneficial; see **worthwhile.**

**credit,** *v.* **1.** [To believe] — *Syn.* trust, have faith in, rely on; see **believe** 1, **trust** 1.
  **2.** [Accounting term] — *Syn.* put on the books, charge to an account, place to the credit of, accredit to, give credit to, extend credit to, place to one's account, defer payments; see also **charge** 2.
  **3.** [To attribute] — *Syn.* give credit, ascribe, recognize; see **attribute.**
*See Synonym Study at* ATTRIBUTE.

**creditable,** *modif.* — *Syn.* decent, honorable, praiseworthy, estimable; see **excellent, respectable, worthy.**

**credit card,** *n.* — *Syn.* plastic money, charge card, plastic, funny money, smart card, gold card.
Major credit cards include: American Express, Mastercard, Visa, Discover, Diners Club, Carte Blanche.

**creditor,** *n.* — *Syn.* lender, lessor, mortgager; see **banker** 1, **lender.**

**credulous,** *modif.* — *Syn.* gullible, unsuspicious, simple, unsophisticated; see **naive, trusting** 1.

**creed,** *n.* — *Syn.* belief, doctrine, dogma; see **faith** 2.

**creek,** *n.* — *Syn.* stream, spring, brook; see **river** 1.
  **up the creek\*** — *Syn.* in difficulty, desperate, in a bind\*; see **in trouble** 1 at **trouble, troubled** 1, **unfortunate** 2.

**creep,** *v.* — *Syn.* crawl, slither, writhe, worm along, sneak, steal, slink, edge; see also **crawl** 1, **sneak.**
*See Synonym Study at* CRAWL.
   **make one's flesh creep***★* — *Syn.* repel, frighten, terrorize; see **disgust, frighten** 1.
**creeper,** *n.* — *Syn.* runner, climber, clinging plant; see **plant, vine.**
**creeping,** *modif.* **1.** [In the act of creeping] — *Syn.* crawling, worming, squirming, writhing, wriggling, slithering, groveling, crouching, cowering, quailing, slinking, skulking, inching, dragging, lagging, shambling, limping, faltering, shuffling, hobbling, staggering, sneaking, moving slowly, barely moving, going at a snail's pace, poking, on all fours.
   **2.** [Given to creeping] — *Syn.* reptant, reptilian, vermicular, serpentine, prostrate, clinging, dwarf, spreading, trailing, procumbent, stoloniferous, growing along the ground, horizontal, recumbent, vinelike, climbing. — *Ant.* UPRIGHT, standing, vertical.
**creepy,** *modif.* — *Syn.* spooky, eerie, disturbing, disgusting; see **frightful** 1, **offensive** 2.
**crescent,** *n.* — *Syn.* crescent moon, waxing moon, waning moon, sickle, convex figure, concave figure, half-moon, demilune, meniscus, bow, lune, lunula; see also **curve** 1, **moon.**
**crest,** *n.* **1.** [Growth on the head of an animal] — *Syn.* plume, tuft, topknot, comb; see **feather.**
   **2.** [Apex] — *Syn.* peak, pinnacle, culmination; see **climax, top** 1.
**crestfallen,** *modif.* — *Syn.* discouraged, dejected, disheartened, chagrined; see **sad** 1.
**crevasse,** *n.* — *Syn.* precipice, abyss, chasm, fissure; see **gap** 3, **hole** 2.
**crevice,** *n.* — *Syn.* fissure, cleft, slit, crack; see **hole** 1, 2, **division** 3.
**crew,** *n.* **1.** [The personnel of a ship or aircraft] — *Syn.* seafarers, sailors, hands, seamen, able seamen, ship's complement, full complement, ship's company, mariners, sea dogs, *matelots* (French), gobs★, Jacks★, manjacks★, shellbacks★, aircrew, flight crew.
   **2.** [A group of people organized to do a particular job] — *Syn.* company, troupe, squad; see **organization** 3, **team** 2.
**crib,** *n.* **1.** [A baby's bed] — *Syn.* trundle bed, cradle, bassinet, cot (British); see **bed** 1.
   **2.** [A storage space, especially for corn] — *Syn.* manger, stall, silo; see **bin, storehouse.**
**crick,** *n.* — *Syn.* spasm, cramp, kink; see **pain** 2.
**crier,** *n.* — *Syn.* herald, proclaimer, town crier, bellman; see **messenger.**
**crime,** *n.* **1.** [An outrageous act] — *Syn.* offense, transgression, misdemeanor, felony, violation, outrage, wickedness, immorality, misdeed, infringement, wrongdoing, depravity, antisocial behavior, abomination, misconduct, corruption, vice, villainy, iniquity, delinquency, negligence, wrong, trespass, malefaction, malfeasance, tort, dereliction, lawlessness, criminality, crime in the streets, white-collar crime, capital crime, scandal, infraction, atrocity, enormity, crime of passion, cold-blooded crime, war crime, crime against humanity, mortal sin, deed without a name★; see also sense 2, **evil** 1, 2, **sin.**
   **2.** [A serious infraction of the law]
   Crimes include: treason, homicide, murder, voluntary manslaughter, involuntary manslaughter, simple assault, aggravated assault, rape, battery, mayhem, larceny, theft, robbery, burglary, holdup, mugging, kidnapping, swindling, arson, defrauding, embezzlement, smuggling, extortion, bribery, malicious mis-

chief, breach of the peace, libel, breaking prison, perjury, act injurious to the public welfare, aggravated misdemeanor, conspiracy, counterfeiting, treason, inciting to revolt, sedition; see also **arson, corruption** 2, **murder, rape, theft, treason.**
**criminal,** *modif.* — *Syn.* unlawful, felonious, illegal, wrongful; see **illegal, wicked** 1, 2.
**criminal,** *n.* — *Syn.* lawbreaker, convict, malefactor, felon, crook★, hardened criminal, underworld character, evildoer, sinner, culprit, offender, perpetrator, perp★, outlaw, fugitive, public enemy, desperado, hoodlum, gangster, wrongdoer, delinquent, transgressor, miscreant, recidivist, mobster★, scofflaw★.
   Criminals include: traitor, murderer, manslayer, assassin, blackmailer, black marketeer, killer, rapist, molester, thug, gangster, raider, burglar, safecracker, quitting-business promoter, racketeer, swindler, clip artist, griffer, confidence man★, con man★, thief, robber, outlaw, highway man, bandit, sneak thief, cat burglar, second-story man, cattle thief★, rustler★, horse thief, pickpocket, grafter, arsonist, counterfeiter, forger, check artist★, smuggler, buccaneer, extortionist, embezzler, kidnapper, mugger, gunman, trigger man, hit man, torpedo plugger, accomplice★, ringer★, stooge★, briber★, fixer★, absconder, convict, con★, dope peddler, drug dealer, pusher★.
**criminality,** *n.* **1.** [Guilt] — *Syn.* culpability, guiltiness, censurability; see **guilt.**
   **2.** [Misbehavior] — *Syn.* corruption, badness, depravity; see **crime** 1, **evil** 1, 2, **sin.**
**crimp,** *v.* **1.** [To fold] — *Syn.* pleat, crease, corrugate; see **fold** 2, **pinch, wrinkle** 1.
   **2.** [To curl] — *Syn.* set, wave, coil; see **curl** 1, **wave** 5.
**crimson,** *modif.* — *Syn.* blood-red, ruby, carmine, claret; see **color** 1, **red.**
**cringe,** *v.* — *Syn.* flinch, quail, recoil; see **wince.**
**cringing,** *modif.* — *Syn.* servile, crouching, submissive; see **cowardly** 1, 3, **obsequious.**
**crinkle,** *v.* — *Syn.* coil, wind, crease, ripple; see **fold** 2, **wrinkle** 1.
**crinkly,** *modif.* — *Syn.* wavy, sinuous, crimped; see **curly** 1, **wrinkled.**
**cripple,** *v.* — *Syn.* disable, paralyze, lame, injure; see **hurt** 1, **maim.**
*See Synonym Study at* MAIM.
**crippled,** *modif.* **1.** [Physically handicapped] — *Syn.* disabled, lame, maimed; see **deformed, disabled.**
   **2.** [Damaged] — *Syn.* harmed, impaired, weakened, disabled; see **broken** 1, 2, **weakened.**
**crisis,** *n.* — *Syn.* straits, exigency, emergency, turning point, urgency, necessity, dilemma, puzzle, perplexity, pressure, embarrassment, pinch, juncture, pass, change, contingency, plight, imbroglio, impasse, deadlock, entanglement, predicament, corner, decisive turn, decisive moment, critical juncture, critical situation, trauma, quandary, extremity, disaster, trial, crux, climacteric, moment of truth, hour of decision, crossroads, climax, clutch★, pickle★, stew★, fix★, mess★, big trouble★, kettle of fish★, hot water, crunch★. — *Ant.* normality, STABILITY, REGULARITY.
*See Synonym Study at* EMERGENCY.
**crisp,** *modif.* **1.** [Fresh and firm] — *Syn.* crunchy, brittle, firm, crumbly; see **crumbly, fragile, fresh** 1, 6, **ripe** 1.
   **2.** [Brisk] — *Syn.* fresh, invigorating, bracing; see **cool** 1, **stimulating.**
   **3.** [Curt] — *Syn.* brusque, brief, terse; see **abrupt** 2, **short** 2.
*See Synonym Study at* FRAGILE.
**criterion,** *n.* — *Syn.* measure, basis, foundation, test,

standard, rule, gauge, proof, model, exemplar, paradigm, scale, prototype, pattern, example, standard of judgment, point of comparison, yardstick, archetype, norm, original, precedent, touchstone, benchmark, principle, guideline; see also **measure** 2, **model** 1, 2. *See Synonym Study at* STANDARD.

**critic,** *n.* **1.** [One who makes adverse comments] — *Syn.* faultfinder, carper, caviler, censor, censurer, quibbler, nitpicker, pettifogger, blamer, detractor, slanderer, maligner, complainer, doubter, nagger, fretter, scolder, disapprover, defamer, disparager, captious critic, Monday morning quarterback*, mudslinger*, knocker*, panner*, basher*. — *Ant.* praiser, BELIEVER, supporter.
**2.** [One who endeavors to interpret and judge] — *Syn.* commentator, analyst, analyzer, connoisseur, reviewer, cartoonist, caricaturist, expert, judge, authority, pundit, diagnostic, annotator, master, evaluator, editor, blurb writer; see also **connoisseur, examiner, scholar** 2.
**critical,** *modif.* **1.** [Capable of observing and judging] — *Syn.* analytical, discriminating, penetrating, perceptive, trenchant, discerning, judging, evaluative, interpretive; see also **explanatory, judicious, observant** 1.
**2.** [Inclined to adverse criticism] — *Syn.* faultfinding, captious, censorious, hypercritical, inclined to judge with severity, caviling, carping, derogatory, disapproving, judgmental, severe, withering, calumniatory, demanding, satirical, cynical, hairsplitting, quibbling, nitpicking, nagging, scolding, condemning, censuring, reproachful, disparaging, exacting, sharp, cutting, biting, fussy, picky*; see also **sarcastic, severe** 1. — *Ant.* praising, flattering, encouraging.
**3.** [Dangerous] — *Syn.* perilous, risky, hazardous; see **dangerous** 1.
**4.** [Crucial] — *Syn.* decisive, significant, deciding; see **crucial, important** 1.

---

*SYN.* — **critical** may imply an attempt at objective judging so as to determine both merits and faults *[a critical review]*, but it often (and **hypercritical,** always) connotes emphasis on the faults or shortcomings; **faultfinding** implies a habitual or unreasonable emphasis on faults or defects; **captious** suggests a characteristic tendency to find fault with, or argue about, even the pettiest details *[a captious critic]*; **caviling** stresses the raising of quibbling objections on the most trivial points *[a caviling grammarian]*; **carping** suggests peevishness, perversity, or censoriousness in seeking out faults *See also Synonym Study at* ACUTE.

---

**criticism,** *n.* **1.** [A serious estimate or interpretation] — *Syn.* study, analysis, critique; see **judgment** 2, **review** 2.
**2.** [Censure] — *Syn.* caviling, carping, faultfinding, stricture; see **blame** 1, **objection** 2.
**3.** [An example of criticism, sense 1] — *Syn.* critique, review, critical essay, survey; see **exposition** 2, **review** 2.
**criticize,** *v.* **1.** [To make a considered criticism] — *Syn.* study, probe, scrutinize; see **analyze** 1, **examine** 1.
**2.** [To make adverse comments] — *Syn.* censure, find fault with, reprimand; see **censure.**
*See Synonym Study at* CENSURE.
**critique,** *n.* — *Syn.* commentary, analysis, evaluation; see **exposition** 2, **judgment** 2, 3, **review** 2.
**croak,** *v.* **1.** [To make a hoarse sound] — *Syn.* caw, quack, squawk, rasp; see **sound** 1.
**2.** [*To die] — *Syn.* expire, pass away, perish; see **die** 1.
**crock,** *n.* — *Syn.* jar, vessel, pitcher, crockery; see **container, jar** 1, **pot** 1.

**crockery,** *n.* — *Syn.* earthenware, ceramics, porcelain; see **pottery.**
**crone,** *n.* — *Syn.* hag, witch, old woman; see **hag.**
**crony,** *n.* — *Syn.* comrade, buddy*, cohort; see **associate, friend** 1.
**crook,** *n.* **1.** [*Criminal] — *Syn.* swindler, thief, rogue; see **criminal.**
**2.** [A bend] — *Syn.* hook, V, notch; see **angle** 1, **curve** 1.
**crooked,** *modif.* **1.** [Not straight] — *Syn.* curved, curving, hooked, bent, bending, incurving, devious, winding, bowed, spiral, serpentine, zigzag, twisted, meandering, tortuous, anfractuous, sinuous, askew, awry, lopsided, cockeyed*; see also **angular** 1, **bent, oblique** 1. — *Ant.* unbent, STRAIGHT, direct.
**2.** [Dishonest] — *Syn.* corrupt, nefarious, fraudulent; see **dishonest** 1, 2.
**croon,** *v.* — *Syn.* sing sentimentally, warble, purr; see **hum, sing** 1.
**crop,** *n.* — *Syn.* harvest, yield, produce, product, growth, annual production, reaping, agricultural production, hay, fodder, grain(s), gathering, gleaning, vintage, fruits, cash crop; see also **produce, vegetable.**
**cross,** *modif.* **1.** [Ill-tempered] — *Syn.* irritable, jumpy, easily annoyed, pettish; see **angry, critical** 2, **irritable.**
**2.** [Crossbred] — *Syn.* crossed, mixed, alloyed; see **hybrid.**
*See Synonym Study at* IRRITABLE.
**cross,** *n.* **1.** [Religious symbol, especially of Christianity] — *Syn.* crucifix, cruciform, rood, Greek cross, papal cross, Maltese cross, St. Andrew's cross, Celtic cross, Jerusalem cross, patriarchal cross, cross of Lorraine, Latin cross, Calvary cross, swastika.
**2.** [A tribulation] — *Syn.* affliction, trial, misfortune; see **affliction, difficulty** 1, 2.
**3.** [A mixed offspring] — *Syn.* hybrid, mongrel, crossbreed; see **hybrid, mixture** 1.
**cross,** *v.* **1.** [To pass over] — *Syn.* traverse, go across, pass across, pass over, go over, pass, ford, cut across, overpass, span, crisscross, travel over.
**2.** [To lie across] — *Syn.* intersect, lie athwart, rest across, extend across, bisect, converge, meet, join; see also **divide** 1.
**3.** [To mix breeds] — *Syn.* mingle, interbreed, cross-pollinate, hybridize, cross-fertilize, crossbreed, intercross, blend; see also **mix** 1.
**cross-country,** *modif.* — *Syn.* across the fields, through field and wood, off the roads, as the crow flies, directly; see also **across, direct** 1.
**cross-examine,** *v.* — *Syn.* investigate, question closely, interrogate, grill*; see **examine** 2, **question** 1.
**crossing,** *n.* **1.** [A place to cross] — *Syn.* intersection, overpass, underpass, crossway, crosswalk, crossroad(s), interchange, cloverleaf, exchange, passage, traverse, loop; see also **bridge** 1, **junction** 2.
**2.** [A mixing of breeds] — *Syn.* hybridization, interbreeding, crossbreeding, cross-fertilization, cross-pollination; see also **mixture** 1.
**cross off** or **out** *v.* — *Syn.* cancel, strike out, delete; see **cancel** 1.
**crossroad,** *n.* **1.** [An intersecting road] — *Syn.* byroad, side road, secondary road, secondary highway, service road, frontage road, driveway, cross-country road; see also **road** 1.
**2.** [A place of convergence; *usually plural]* — *Syn.* junction, intersection, hub; see **center** 2, **crossing** 1, **junction** 2.
**3.** [A critical juncture; *usually plural]* — *Syn.* turning point, juncture, decisive moment; see **crisis.**

**crosswise,** *modif.* — *Syn.* across, athwart, thwart, cross, contrariwise, perpendicular, transversely, vertically, horizontally, at right angles, awry, over, sideways, crisscross, askew, crossways; see also **across.**

**crotch,** *n.* **1.** [Angle] — *Syn.* fork, corner, elbow; see **angle** 1, **curve** 1.

**2.** [Loins] — *Syn.* pubic area, groin, pelvic girdle; see **groin, lap** 1.

**crotchet,** *n.* — *Syn.* whim, quirk, eccentricity; see **caprice, quirk.**

*See Synonym Study at* CAPRICE.

**crotchety,** *modif.* — *Syn.* eccentric, cantankerous, cranky, odd; see **irritable, obstinate** 1, **unusual** 2.

**crouch,** *v.* **1.** [To stoop] — *Syn.* squat, bend, hunch, hunker down; see **bow** 1.

**2.** [To cower] — *Syn.* cringe, flinch, quail; see **grovel.**

**crow,** *n.* — *Syn.* raven, rook, jackdaw, *Corvus brachyrhynchos* (Latin); see **bird** 1.

**as the crow flies** — *Syn.* straight, in a straight line, by a direct route; see **direct** 1.

**eat crow*** — *Syn.* retract, confess an error, take back; see **admit** 2, **apologize, recant.**

**crow,** *v.* **1.** [To boast] — *Syn.* exult, gloat, brag; see **boast** 1.

**2.** [To make a crowing sound] — *Syn.* squawk, caw, cackle; see **cry** 3, **sound** 1.

*See Synonym Study at* BOAST.

**crowd,** *n.* **1.** [Throng] — *Syn.* multitude, concourse, host, horde, flock, mob, swarm, company, confluence, press, crush, surge, stream, troop, conflux, legion, force, bevy, galaxy, rout, group, body, pack, army, posse, drove, array, party, flood, gaggle, troupe, deluge, meet, muster, congregation, cluster, assembly, crew, jam*, herd*, bunch*, gang*, clutch*, batch*, mob scene*; see also **gathering.**

**2.** [The common people] — *Syn.* rank and file, masses, mob*; see **people** 3.

**3.** [*A clique] — *Syn.* set, circle, coterie; see **clique, faction** 1, **organization** 3.

---

SYN. — **crowd** is applied to an assembly of persons or things in close proximity or densely packed together and may suggest lack of order, loss of personal identity, etc. *[crowds* lined the street*]*; **throng** specifically suggests a moving crowd of people pushing one another *[throngs* of celebrators at Times Square*]*; **multitude** stresses greatness of number in referring to persons or things assembled or considered together *[a multitude* arrayed against him*]*; **swarm** suggests a large, continuously moving group *[a swarm* of sightseers*]*; **mob** implies a disorderly or lawless crowd, and is an abusive term when used to describe the mass of common people; **host** specifically suggests a large organized body marshaled together but may be used generally of any sizable group considered collectively *[she has a host* of friends*]*; **horde** specifically refers to a large predatory band *[a horde* of office seekers*]*

---

**crowd,** *v.* — *Syn.* jam, squeeze, throng; see **gather, pack** 2, **press** 1, **push** 1.

**crowded,** *modif.* — *Syn.* packed, congested, huddled, crushed; see **full** 1, **jammed** 2, **thick** 1.

**crown,** *n.* **1.** [The top] — *Syn.* apex, crest, summit; see **top** 1.

**2.** [The symbol of royalty] — *Syn.* diadem, headdress, tiara, coronet, circlet; see also **wreath.**

**3.** [The possessor of sovereign power; *usually capital C*] — *Syn.* monarch, sovereign, potentate, emperor; see **king** 1, **queen, royalty.**

**4.** [The head] — *Syn.* pate, skull, noggin*; see **cranium, head** 1.

**crown,** *v.* **1.** [To make complete or perfect] — *Syn.* round out, fulfill, consummate; see **climax, complete** 1.

**2.** [To empower with a crown] — *Syn.* commission, authorize, invest, install, endow, enable, sanction, inaugurate, induct, empower, fix, dignify, coronate, enthrone, exalt, raise, set up, ennoble, anoint, establish, honor, reward; see also **delegate** 1, 2. — *Ant.* topple, ABOLISH, overthrow.

**3.** [*To hit] — *Syn.* knock, strike, conk*; see **hit** 1.

**crowning,** *modif.* — *Syn.* supreme, ultimate, paramount; see **best** 1, **principal.**

**crucial,** *modif.* — *Syn.* critical, decisive, pivotal, deciding, determining, climactic, vital, momentous, fateful, important, all-important, significant, essential, central, fundamental, basic, acute, severe, urgent, pressing, imperative, compelling, crying, high-priority, of the essence.

*See Synonym Study at* ACUTE.

**crucible,** *n.* — *Syn.* retort, melting pot, cauldron; see **container, pot** 1.

**crucifix,** *n.* — *Syn.* cross, rood, Christian emblem, Latin cross; see **cross** 1.

**crucifixion,** *n.* **1.** [Death by being nailed to a cross] — *Syn.* torture, suffering, martyrdom; see **execution** 2.

**2.** [The death of Jesus or the artistic representation of His death; *usually capitalized*] — *Syn.* the Passion, the execution of Christ, the Martyrdom, the Sacrifice on the Cross.

**crucify,** *v.* **1.** [To kill by crucifixion] — *Syn.* execute, nail to the cross, hang, torture; see **kill** 1.

**2.** [To torment] — *Syn.* torture, persecute, pillory, bedevil; see **bother** 2, **persecute** 1.

**crude,** *modif.* **1.** [Unrefined] — *Syn.* rude, rough, unpolished, in a raw state, unprocessed, unrefined, homemade, homespun, thick, coarse, harsh, rudimentary, roughhewn, makeshift, unfinished, unfashioned, unformed, undeveloped, in the rough, raw, immature, sketchy; see also **savage** 1, **unfinished** 1. — *Ant.* finished, polished, refined.

**2.** [Lacking address or skill] — *Syn.* ungainly, clumsy, unskillful; see **awkward** 1, **primitive** 1.

**3.** [Lacking manners or taste] — *Syn.* uncouth, vulgar, coarse; see **coarse** 2, **rude** 1, 2, **vulgar** 1.

**crudely,** *modif.* — *Syn.* clumsily, coarsely, roughly; see **awkwardly, rudely.**

**cruel,** *modif.* **1.** [Vicious] — *Syn.* malevolent, brutal, sadistic, inhuman, ruthless, spiteful, depraved, wicked, delighting in torture, vengeful, revengeful, evil, sinful, degenerate, disposed to inflict suffering, brutish, demoniac, outrageous, tyrannical, gross, swinish, evil-minded, rancorous, rough, wild, bestial, ferocious, bloodthirsty, savage, fierce, monstrous, barbarous, barbaric, maleficent, fell, ravening, fiendish, satanic, atrocious, truculent, demoniacal, debased, destructive, harmful, malignant, virulent, evilly disposed, pernicious, mischievous; see also sense 2, **fierce** 1, **ruthless** 2, **savage** 2. — *Ant.* KINDLY, humane, tender.

**2.** [Pitiless] — *Syn.* callous, unnatural, merciless, sadistic, unpitying, unmerciful, unyielding, obdurate, coldblooded, ruthless, remorseless, hardhearted, unfeeling, inflexible, inclement, indifferent to suffering, unrelenting, inexorable, relentless, unsparing, absolute, grim, grim-visaged, inhuman, severe, harsh, heartless, stony, stern, unconcerned, iron-handed, without pity, knowing no mercy, giving no quarter*, turning a deaf

ear\*, hard as nails\*; see also **ruthless** 1. — *Ant.* MERCI-
FUL, touched, compassionate.

*SYN.* — **cruel** implies indifference to the suffering of
others or a disposition to inflict it on others *[cruel* fate*]*;
**brutal** implies ruthless force or savage cruelty that is
altogether unfeeling *[a brutal* prison guard*]*; **inhuman**
stresses the complete absence of those qualities expected
of a civilized human being, such as compassion, mercy,
or benevolence; **pitiless** implies a callous refusal to
be moved or influenced by the suffering of those one has
wronged; **ruthless** implies a cruel and relentless disregard for the rights or welfare of others, while in pursuit
of a goal

**cruelly**, *modif.* — *Syn.* savagely, inhumanly, viciously;
see **brutally**.
**cruelty**, *n.* — *Syn.* brutality, barbarity, sadism, savageness, unkindness, inhumanity, barbarism, mercilessness, barbarousness, unmercifulness, wickedness,
ruthlessness, severity, malignity, malice, rancor, venom,
coldness, unfeelingness, callousness, insensibility, indifference, insensitivity, fierceness, viciousness, bestiality, animality, truculence, ferocity, savagery, brutishness, implacability, grimness, monstrousness, inflexibility, fiendishness, hardness of heart, bloodthirstiness, unnaturalness, heartlessness, relentlessness, torture, persecution, inquisition, despotism, harshness, outrage,
atrocity; see also **evil** 1, **tyranny**. — *Ant.* benevolence,
KINDNESS, humanity.
**cruet**, *n.* — *Syn.* bottle, decanter, cruse, flagon; see **bottle, container, jar** 1.
**cruise**, *n.* — *Syn.* voyage, sail, jaunt; see **journey**.
**cruise**, *v.* — *Syn.* sail, voyage, meander, coast; see **drift,
navigate, sail** 2, 3, **travel** 2.
**cruiser**, *n.* — *Syn.* cabin cruiser, powerboat, warship,
privateer; see **boat, ship, warship**.
Types of cruisers include: battle, light, armored, heavy,
rocket cruiser; dreadnought, man-of-war, battlewagon,
corvette, battleship, capital ship.
**crumb**, *n.* — *Syn.* particle, scrap, morsel; see **bit** 1.
**crumble**, *v.* — *Syn.* fall apart, disintegrate, break up; see
**break** 3, **decay, disintegrate** 1.
**crumbling**, *modif.* — *Syn.* rotting, breaking up, disintegrating, collapsing; see **breaking, decaying**.
**crumbly**, *modif.* — *Syn.* breaking up, breaking down,
falling to pieces, friable, fragile, brittle, crisp, short,
frangible, apt to crumble, frail, crumbling, disintegrating, decayed, deteriorated, deteriorating, soft, corroded, rusted, rotted, oxidized, worn away, breakable, shivery, powdery, eroded, disintegrated, tumbling
down; see also **broken** 1, **decaying, gritty** 1. — *Ant.*
sturdy, FIRM, solid.
**crumple**, *v.* **1.** [To wrinkle] — *Syn.* rumple, crush,
crease; see **fold** 2, **wrinkle** 1, 2.
**2.** [To collapse] — *Syn.* give way, fall down, topple; see
**fall** 1, **give** 4.
**crunch\***, *n.* — *Syn.* test, emergency, tight spot, economic squeeze; see **crisis, difficulty** 1.
**crunch**, *v.* — *Syn.* munch, gnaw, chomp, masticate; see
**bite** 1, **chew**.
**crusade**, *n.* — *Syn.* campaign, march, demonstration,
holy war; see **movement** 2.
**crusader**, *n.* — *Syn.* reformer, campaigner, champion,
progressive; see **agitator, radical, zealot**.
**crush**, *v.* **1.** [To break into small pieces] — *Syn.* smash,
pulverize, pound, grind; see **break** 2, **grind** 1.
**2.** [To press so as to injure or break] — *Syn.* press,
mash, crumple, squash; see **damage** 1, **mash, press** 1.

**3.** [To defeat utterly] — *Syn.* overwhelm, beat down,
force down, annihilate; see **defeat** 1, 2.
*See Synonym Study at* BEAT.
**crust**, *n.* **1.** [A crisp covering] — *Syn.* hull, rind, pie-
crust, pastry shell; see **coat** 2, **shell** 1.
**2.** [A surface layer] — *Syn.* coating, covering, deposit;
see **coat** 3, **outside** 1.
**crustacean**, *n.* — *Syn.* arthropod, shrimp, lobster, crab;
see **shellfish**.
**crusty**, *modif.* — *Syn.* cross, harsh, surly, scornful; see **irritable, rude** 2, **sarcastic**.
**cry**, *n.* **1.** [A loud utterance] — *Syn.* exclamation, shout,
clamor, outcry, call, vociferation, scream, shriek, yell,
whoop, yawp, squall, yammer, groan, moan, bellow,
howl, wail, bawl, holler, uproar, acclamation, roar, battle cry, war cry, halloo, hurrah, hullabaloo, cheer, huzza;
see also sense 2, **noise** 1, 2, **yell** 1. — *Ant.* WHISPER,
murmur, silence.
**2.** [A characteristic call] — *Syn.* howl, hoot, wail, grunt,
screech, mewling, bark, squawk, squeak, squeal, yelp,
meow, whinny, neigh, bray, nicker, moo, bleat, chatter,
bay, cluck, crow, whine, pipe, trill, twitter, tweet, quack,
clack, cackle, caw, bellow, coo, whistle, gobble, hiss,
growl, roar, shriek; see also **yell** 1.
**3.** [A fit of weeping] — *Syn.* lamentation, lament, sobbing, weeping, bewailing, wailing, bawl, shedding tears,
sorrowing, mourning, whimpering, ululation, plaint, the
blues\*; see also **tears**.
**a far cry (from)** — *Syn.* unlike, dissimilar, remote; see
**different** 1.
**cry**, *v.* **1.** [To shed tears] — *Syn.* weep, sob, wail, whimper, snivel, blubber, moan, howl, keen, bawl, squall,
lament, bewail, bemoan, whine, weep over, complain,
deplore, sorrow, grieve, fret, groan, caterwaul, burst
into tears, dissolve in tears, ululate, mewl, pule, sniffle,
break down, choke up\*, cry one's eyes out\*, boohoo\*,
yammer\*, take on\*, give way to tears\*, turn on the
waterworks\*; see also **mourn** 1, **regret**. — *Ant.* rejoice,
LAUGH, exult.
**2.** [To raise the voice] — *Syn.* shout, scream, bellow;
see **yell**.
**3.** [To call; *said of other than human creatures*] — *Syn.*
howl, bark, hoot, scream, screech, squawk, squeak, yelp,
yap, grunt, roar, shriek, meow, whinny, neigh, bray,
nicker, moo, bleat, snarl, chatter, bay, cluck, crow,
whine, squeal, yowl, pipe, trill, coo, whistle, caw, bellow,
quack, clack, gabble, hiss, growl, croak, cackle, twitter,
tweet; see also **sound** 1, **yell**.

*SYN.* — **cry**, in this comparison, implies the expression
of grief, sorrow, pain, or distress by making mournful, convulsive sounds and shedding tears; **weep** more
specifically stresses the shedding of tears; to **sob** is to
weep aloud with a catch in the voice and short, gasping
breaths; **wail** implies the uttering of loud, prolonged,
mournful cries in unsuppressed lamentation; **keen**, specifically an Irish term, signifies a wailing in lamentation
for the dead; to **whimper** is to cry with subdued, whining, broken sounds, as a fretful or frightened child does;
**moan** suggests the expression of sorrow or pain in a low,
prolonged, mournful sound or sounds; **blubber**, a derisive term used chiefly of children, implies a contorting or
swelling of the face with weeping, and broken, inarticulate speech

**crying**, *modif.* **1.** [Weeping] — *Syn.* sobbing, mourning,
sorrowing, tearful; see **weeping**.
**2.** [Demanding attention] — *Syn.* urgent, pressing,
compelling; see **crucial, urgent** 1.

**crying,** *n.* — *Syn.* weeping, blubbering, sorrow, sobbing; see **cry** 3, **tears.**

**for crying out loud\*** — *Syn.* for God's sake, for heaven's sake; oh, no; for the love of Mike\*; see **curse** 1.

**crypt,** *n.* — *Syn.* vault, tomb, sepulcher; see **grave** 1.

**cryptic,** *modif.* — *Syn.* enigmatic, mysterious, mystic, hidden; see **mysterious** 2, **obscure** 1, 3, **secret** 1.

*See Synonym Study at* OBSCURE.

**crystal,** *modif.* — *Syn.* limpid, lucid, pellucid; see **clear** 2, **transparent** 1.

**crystal,** *n.* — *Syn.* quartz, clear quartz, sparkling gem, brilliant, cut glass, symmetrically faceted substance; see also **diamond** 1, **gem** 1, **glass** 1, **jewel** 1.

**crystallize,** *v.* — *Syn.* become settled, become delineated, become definite, take shape, take form, assume a pattern, take on character, be outlined, form into crystals, assume crystalline structure; see also **form** 4.

**cub,** *n.* — *Syn.* young, offspring, whelp, young bear, young fox, young lion, young tiger, young wolf; see also **calf, child.**

**cube,** *n.* — *Syn.* six-sided solid, hexahedron, die; see **solid.**

**cuddle,** *v.* **1.** [To nestle] — *Syn.* snuggle, huddle, curl up; see **nestle.**

**2.** [To embrace] — *Syn.* caress, enfold, fondle; see **caress, hold** 1, **hug, touch** 1.

*See Synonym Study at* CARESS.

**cudgel,** *n.* — *Syn.* stick, bat, bludgeon; see **club** 3.

**cudgel,** *v.* — *Syn.* beat, bludgeon, strike, pummel; see **beat** 2, **hit** 1.

**cue,** *n.* **1.** [Theatrical or musical warning] — *Syn.* prompt, signal, preceding speech, catchword, warning signal, reminder, opening bar(s), sign, nod, tip-off\*; see also **sign** 1.

**2.** [Hint] — *Syn.* lead, innuendo, idea, tip; see **hint** 1, 2, **suggestion** 1.

**cuff,** *n.* **1.** [Edge of a sleeve or pants leg] — *Syn.* French cuff, fold, wristband; see **band** 1, **hem.**

**2.** [A blow] — *Syn.* slap, punch, hit; see **blow** 1.

**off the cuff\*** — *Syn.* extemporaneous, extemporaneously, unofficial, offhand; see **extemporaneous, offhand.**

**on the cuff\*** — *Syn.* on credit, charged, delayed; see **charged** 1, **unpaid** 1.

**cuff,** *v.* — *Syn.* slap, punch, beat; see **beat** 2, **hit** 1.

**cuisine,** *n.* — *Syn.* style of cooking, cookery, table, bill of fare; see **food, menu.**

**cul-de-sac,** *n.* — *Syn.* dead end, dead-end street, blind alley, impasse, blind, mew(s), enclosure; see also **street, trap** 1.

**cull,** *v.* **1.** [To choose] — *Syn.* select, winnow, pick out, pick over; see **choose** 1, **separate** 2.

**2.** [To gather] — *Syn.* collect, glean, amass, round up; see **accumulate** 1, **harvest.**

**culminate,** *v.* — *Syn.* finish, crown, consummate, result in; see **climax, complete** 1, **end** 1.

**culmination,** *n.* **1.** [Acme] — *Syn.* peak, summit, zenith; see **climax, top** 1.

**2.** [Finish] — *Syn.* conclusion, finale, finish; see **end** 2.

**culpability,** *n.* — *Syn.* liability, blame, fault; see **guilt.**

**culpable,** *modif.* — *Syn.* blameworthy, punishable, blamable; see **guilty** 2.

**culprit,** *n.* — *Syn.* offender, guilty person, accused; see **criminal, prisoner.**

**cult,** *n.* **1.** [Sect] — *Syn.* clique, band, school, followers; see **church** 3, **faction** 1, **following, religion** 1, 2.

**2.** [Devotion] — *Syn.* veneration, worship, cultism, hero worship; see **admiration, devotion, worship** 1.

**cultivate,** *v.* **1.** [To plant] — *Syn.* till, plow, work the soil, grow; see **farm, grow** 3, **plant, plow** 1.

**2.** [To educate] — *Syn.* nurture, refine, improve; see **civilize, teach** 1, 2.

**3.** [To encourage] — *Syn.* advance, further, foster, develop; see **develop** 1, **encourage** 1, **promote** 1.

**cultivation,** *n.* **1.** [Farming] — *Syn.* horticulture, agriculture, gardening; see **farming.**

**2.** [Refinement] — *Syn.* culture, taste, advancement, breeding; see **civilization** 1, **culture** 3, **education** 1, **improvement** 1, **refinement** 2, 3.

**cultural,** *modif.* — *Syn.* educational, socializing, refining, refined, constructive, influential, nurturing, disciplining, enlightening, civilizing, advancing, instructive, humanizing, beneficial, learned, educative, edifying, illuminating, polishing, enriching, elevating, uplifting, improving, ennobling, raising, inspirational, regenerative, artistic, aesthetic, adorning, ornamenting, dignifying, glorifying, liberalizing, broadening, expanding, widening, catholicizing, developmental, humanistic, freeing from prejudice, stimulating thought, social, anthropological, sociological; see also **artistic** 1.

**culture,** *n.* **1.** [The act of encouraging growth] — *Syn.* tending, raising, growing; see **farming, production** 1.

**2.** [Civilizing tradition] — *Syn.* civilization, society, folklore, folkways, way of life, customs, mores, ethos, value system, education, conventions, habits, lifestyle, inheritance, learning, arts, sciences, knowledge, letters, scholarship, literature, art, music, lore, ethnology, history, religion, humanism, arts and sciences; see also **civilization** 1, **humanities.** — *Ant.* barbarism, DISORDER, chaos.

**3.** [Refinement and education] — *Syn.* breeding, gentility, cultivation, enlightenment, learning, sophistication, refinement, proficiency, practice, erudition, knowledge, intellectuality, education, training, art, perception, discrimination, discernment, finish, taste, grace, dignity, politeness, savoir-faire, manners, polish, elegance, urbanity, address, finesse, suavity; see also **courtesy** 1, **elegance** 1, **experience** 3, **sophistication.** — *Ant.* IGNORANCE, crudeness, vulgarity.

**cultured,** *modif.* — *Syn.* cultivated, educated, informed, accomplished, enlightened, polished, refined, well-bred, genteel, elegant, courteous, intellectual, sophisticated, sensitive, intelligent, *au courant* (French), able, well-read, well-educated, knowledgeable, up-to-date, well-informed, cosmopolitan, traveled, experienced, tolerant, understanding, appreciative, civilized, aesthetic, enjoying the arts, versed in the humanities, literary, urbane, suave, gracious, mannerly, erudite, learned, lettered, high-brow\*, bluestocking\*, high-class\*; see also **learned** 1, 2, **liberal** 2, **polite** 1, **refined** 2. — *Ant.* narrow, IGNORANT, backward.

**culvert,** *n.* — *Syn.* duct, canals, watercourse; see **channel** 1, **conduit, pipe** 1.

**cumulative,** *modif.* **1.** [Becoming more intense] — *Syn.* heightening, intensifying, additive, snowballing; see **increasing** 2.

**2.** [Accumulated] — *Syn.* gathered, combined, aggregate, total; see **acquired** 1, **collective.**

**cunning,** *modif.* **1.** [Sly] — *Syn.* crafty, tricky, wily; see **sly** 1.

**2.** [Shrewd] — *Syn.* clever, skillful, ingenious; see **clever** 1, **intelligent** 1.

*See Synonym Study at* CLEVER, SLY.

**cunning,** *n.* — *Syn.* craft, art, shrewdness, subtlety, artifice, craftiness, guile, slyness, deceit, intrigue, chicanery, finesse; see also **deception** 1.

**cup,** *n.* — *Syn.* mug, vessel, bowl, goblet, tumbler,

beaker, stein, bumper, taster, standard, jorum, por-ringer, cannikin, grail, chalice, noggin, pannikin, *tasse* (French), *tazza* (Italian), gourd; see also **can** 1, **container.**
Varieties of cups include: tea, coffee, demitasse, soup, bouillon, cream soup, ale, chocolate, measuring, mustache.

**cupboard,** *n.* — *Syn.* closet, cabinet, locker, storeroom, sideboard, press, buffet; see also **chest** 1, **closet, furniture.**

**Cupid,** *n.* — *Syn.* Eros (Greek), Roman god of love, Amor, matchmaker, marriage broker, marriage arranger, matrimonial agent, lonely hearts expert, son of Venus, Hymen; see also **love** 1.

**cupidity,** *n.* — *Syn.* avarice, rapacity, avidity, possessiveness; see **greed.**

**cup of tea,** *n.* — *Syn.* preference, favorite, taste, one's thing*; see **inclination** 1, **preference.**

**cupola,** *n.* — *Syn.* dome, lantern, vault, mosque roof; see **arch, belfry, dome** 1, **roof.**

**cur,** *n.* — *Syn.* mongrel, mutt, hound; see **dog** 1.

**curable,** *modif.* — *Syn.* treatable, improvable, remediable, reparable, corrigible, amenable to cure, susceptible to cure, subject to cure, medicable, not hopeless, correctable, capable of improvement, healable, restorable, mendable, reversible; see also **reparable, temporary.**

**curate,** *n.* — *Syn.* chaplain, clergyman, pastor; see **minister** 1, **priest.**

**curative,** *modif.* — *Syn.* therapeutic, healing, corrective; see **remedial.**

**curator,** *n.* — *Syn.* keeper, custodian, guardian, museum officer, officer in charge of a collection, conservator, museologist, museographer, archivist, caretaker; see also **antiquarian, collector** 2, **librarian, scientist.**

**curb,** *n.* 1. [Restraint] — *Syn.* hindrance, chain, check; see **barrier, restraint** 2.
2. [Edge] — *Syn.* curbstone, ledge, lip; see **edge** 1, **rim.**

**curb,** *v.* — *Syn.* restrain, check, control, subdue; see **hinder, restrain** 1, **restrict** 2.
*See Synonym Study at* RESTRAIN.

**curdle,** *v.* — *Syn.* coagulate, clot, clabber*, turn sour; see **sour, thicken** 1.

**cure,** *n.* — *Syn.* restorative, remedy, healing agent, antidote; see **medicine** 2, **remedy** 2.

**cure,** *v.* 1. [To heal] — *Syn.* make well, make healthy, restore, make whole; see **heal** 1.
2. [To preserve] — *Syn.* keep, salt, smoke, pickle; see **preserve** 3.
3. [To correct] — *Syn.* remedy, rectify, counteract, rid; see **correct** 1, **remedy.**
*See Synonym Study at* HEAL.

**curfew,** *n.* — *Syn.* late hour, limit, time limit, check-in time, evening, midnight, lockout*; see also **limitation** 1.

**curiosity,** *n.* 1. [Desire to know] — *Syn.* interest, concern, regard, inquiring mind, inquiringness, inquisitiveness, mental acquisitiveness, thirst for knowledge, a questing mind, questioning, searching, eagerness to find out, disposition to inquire, inclination to ask questions, interest in learning, scientific interest, healthy curiosity.
2. [A tendency to snoop] — *Syn.* meddlesomeness, intrusiveness, officiousness, meddling, prying, voyeurism, nosiness*, snoopiness*.
3. [An unusual object] — *Syn.* exoticism, rarity, oddity, marvel; see **wonder** 2.

**curious,** *modif.* 1. [Strange] — *Syn.* odd, singular, unique; see **unusual** 2.

2. [Interested] — *Syn.* inquiring, questioning, prying; see **inquisitive, interested** 1, **meddlesome.**
*See Synonym Study at* INQUISITIVE.

**curl,** *n.* — *Syn.* ringlet, coil, spiral, wave, kink, curlicue, lock, tress, lovelock; see also **coil, hair** 1, **lock** 2.

**curl,** *v.* 1. [To twist] — *Syn.* curve, coil, wave, bend, spiral, crinkle, wind, twine, loop, crimp, kink, scallop, lap, fold, roll, indent, contort, wreathe, meander, ripple, buckle, zigzag, entwine, wrinkle, undulate, twirl, swirl, whirl, crisp, frizz, turn; see also **coil, wave** 4. — *Ant.* uncurl, STRAIGHTEN, unbend.
2. [To set hair] — *Syn.* pin up, roll up, crimp, form into ringlets; see **wave** 5.

**curly,** *modif.* 1. [Rolled] — *Syn.* curled, kinky, wavy, waving, convoluted, coiled, crinkling, crinkly, frizzy, frizzly, spiraling, looping, looped, winding, wound, whorled, undulating; see also **rolled** 1.
2. [Naturally or artificially curled; *said of hair*] — *Syn.* kinky, wavy, frizzy, frizzly, given a permanent wave, naturally curly, waved, crimped, crisp, nappy*.

**currant,** *n.*
Varieties include: red, white, black, Missouri, buffalo, wild, flowering; see also **berry** 1.

**currency,** *n.* — *Syn.* coin, bank notes, government notes; see **money** 1.

**current,** *modif.* — *Syn.* prevailing, contemporary, in fashion; see **fashionable, modern** 1, **popular** 3, **prevailing.**
*See Synonym Study at* PREVAILING.

**current,** *n.* — *Syn.* drift, tidal motion, ebb and flow, course; see **flow, tide.**
*See Synonym Study at* TENDENCY.

**curry,** *v.* — *Syn.* groom, smooth, dress, brush; see **comb, groom.**

**curse,** *n.* 1. [Malediction] — *Syn.* oath, imprecation, blasphemy, expletive, profanity, obscenity, vulgarity, sacrilege, profanation, execration, anathema, ban, hex, jinx, evil eye, fulmination, cursing, swearing, profane swearing, blaspheming, denunciation, damning, commination, objurgation, vilification, obloquy, swearword, dirty word*, blue word*, cuss word*, cussing*, naughty word*, bad language*, four-letter word*.
Common exclamations and curses include: plague on it, Lord, oh God, the Devil, bless my soul, bless me, by Jove, gracious, goodness, oh my, oh me, in Heaven's name, great Caesar's ghost, the deuce, did you ever; gee*, gee whillikins*, gadzooks*, mercy*, sakes alive*, drat*, good night*, so what*, dang*, land of Goshen*, darn*, hang it all*, bejesus*, blast*, blimy*, by crickey*, Chrisamighty*, Keerist*, damn it*, damn*, double-damn*, goshdamn*, goshdang*, gosh darn*, by golly*, Chrisake*, damn-it-to-hell*, for cripe's sake*, for crying out loud*, Gawd*, Judas Priest*, Jesus H. Christ*, I swan the Deil*, Lord-a-mercy*, I'll be cow-kicked and hornswoggled*, I'll be a lop-eared gazelle*, I'll be damned*, I'll be a son of a gun*, I'll be a monkey's uncle*, God's teeth*, hell's whiskers*, hell's bells*, ye gods, ye gods and little fishes*, holy mackerel*, cheese and crackers*, holy bilge water*, holy smokes*, geez*, jeepers creepers*, ay caramba*, yikes*, shoot*, *ach, Gott in Himmel, Gottlob, Donnerwetter* (all German)*, *sacré bleu*, *mon Dieu*, *diable*, *cochon* (all French)*, *diablo* (Spanish)*.
2. [Trouble or a cause of trouble] — *Syn.* bane, evil, affliction, scourge; see **affliction.**
*See Synonym Study at* BLASPHEMY.

**curse,** *v.* 1. [To utter curses] — *Syn.* swear, blaspheme, profane, swear profanely, use foul language, be foul-mouthed, be obscene, take the Lord's name in vain, use strong language, use invective, turn the air blue\*, swear like a trooper\*, cuss\*.

**2.** [To swear at] — *Syn.* execrate, imprecate, damn, vituperate, abuse, revile, insult, call down curses on the head of, put a curse on, invoke harm on, call down evil on, anathematize, maledict, wish calamity on, blast, doom, fulminate against, thunder against, blaspheme, denounce, vilify, blight, call names\*, cuss out\*, put a whammy on\*.

**3.** [To pronounce a religious curse] — *Syn.* ban, anathematize, read out of the church; see **damn** 1.

---

**SYN.** — **curse** is the general word for calling down evil or injury on someone or something; **damn** carries the same general meaning but, in strict usage, implies the use of the word "damn" in the curse *[he damned his enemies = he said, "Damn my enemies!"]*; **execrate** suggests cursing prompted by great anger or abhorrence; **imprecate** suggests the calling down of calamity on someone, esp. from a desire for revenge; **anathematize** strictly refers to the formal utterance of solemn condemnation by ecclesiastical authority, but in general use suggests vehement denunciation of a person or thing viewed as detestable

---

**cursed,** *modif.* **1.** [Damned] — *Syn.* blighted, doomed, under a curse; see **damned** 1, **doomed.**

**2.** [Detestable] — *Syn.* hateful, odious, disgusting; see **damned** 2, **offensive** 2.

**be cursed with** — *Syn.* suffer from, be afflicted with, bear; see **endure** 2, **suffer** 1.

**cursory,** *modif.* — *Syn.* superficial, quick, slight, desultory; see **careless** 1, **superficial.**

*See Synonym Study at* SUPERFICIAL.

**curt,** *modif.* — *Syn.* brief, terse, uncivil, snippy\*; see **abrupt** 2, **terse.**

*See Synonym Study at* BLUNT.

**curtail,** *v.* — *Syn.* shorten, diminish, reduce, abridge; see **decrease** 2, **halt** 2.

*See Synonym Study at* SHORTEN.

**curtailment,** *n.* — *Syn.* decrease, condensation, cutback; see **abbreviation** 1, 2, **reduction** 1.

**curtain,** *n.* — *Syn.* drape, drapery, hanging, portiere, screen, shade, window covering, film, decoration, blind, valance, awning, veil.

Kinds of curtains include: fiberglass curtain, jalousie, draw curtain, roller shade, pleated shade, shutter, portiere, arras, valance, lambrequin, *purdah* (East Indian), Venetian blind(s), mini-blind(s), vertical blind(s), Austrian drape(s).

**draw the curtain on** — *Syn.* **1.** finish, stop, bring to a close; see **end** 1.

**2.** conceal, keep secret, suppress; see **hide** 1.

**lift the curtain on** — *Syn.* **1.** start, initiate, commence; see **begin** 1.

**2.** expose, disclose, uncover; see **reveal** 1.

**curtsey,** *n.* — *Syn.* bow, salaam, dip; see **bow** 2.

**curvature,** *n.* — *Syn.* curving, bend, shape, deflection; see **curve** 1.

**curve,** *n.* **1.** [A bend] — *Syn.* sweep, flexure, bow, arch, crescent, horseshoe, circuit, curvature, crook, oxbow, catenary, trajectory, conic section, sinus, camber.

Types of curves include: bell curve, bell-shaped curve, hairpin curve, S-curve, sine curve, extrapolated curve, hyperbolic curve, parabolic curve, normal curve, asymptomatic curve, logarithmic curve, French curve, linear curve, parabola, hyperbola, circle, ellipse, ogee, arc, chord.

**2.** [In baseball, a pitch that curves] — *Syn.* incurve,

outcurve, dropcurve, in\*, out\*, drop\*, outdrop\*, screwball\*, upshoot\*, jumpball\*, straight drop\*, slant\*, slider\*, bender\*, curly one\*, breaker\*, hook\*, snake\*.

**curve,** *v.* — *Syn.* bend, arc, crook, curl; see **bend** 1, 2.

*See Synonym Study at* BEND.

**curved,** *modif.* — *Syn.* bowed, arched, rounded; see **bent.**

**cushion,** *n.* — *Syn.* pad, pillow, mat, seat, rest, bolster, woolsack, buffer, shock absorber; see also **pillow.**

**custodian,** *n.* **1.** [Guardian] — *Syn.* caretaker, keeper, curator, governor, overseer, manager, caregiver, governess, babysitter, guard, warden, escort, bodyguard; see also **curator, guardian** 1.

**2.** [Janitor] — *Syn.* superintendent, porter, cleaner, cleaning man, attendant, cleaning woman, janitress, caretaker, building superintendent, doorkeeper, concierge, super, maintenance, keeper, gatekeeper, night watchman, member of the department of buildings and grounds; see also **watchman.**

**custody,** *n.* **1.** [Protection] — *Syn.* care, guardianship, supervision, keeping, safekeeping, charge, watch, trusteeship, superintendence, tutelage, wardship, auspices, aegis, safeguard, ward; see also **administration** 1.

**2.** [Detention] — *Syn.* jail, keeping, confinement; see **arrest** 1, **imprisonment** 1.

**take into custody** — *Syn.* capture, apprehend, seize; see **arrest** 1.

**custom,** *n.* **1.** [A habitual action] — *Syn.* habit, practice, usage, wont, fashion, routine, precedent, use, habitude, form, consuetude, addiction, rule, procedure, manner, observance, characteristic, second nature, matter of course, beaten path\*, rut\*; see also **method** 2, **system** 2. — *Ant.* irregularity, STRANGENESS, newness.

**2.** [A traditional action] — *Syn.* manner, way, mode, method, system, style, vogue, fashion, convention, habit, rule, practice, precedent, formality, form, mold, established way of doing things, pattern, design, type, taste, character, routine, ritual, rite, ceremony, attitude, immemorial usage, observance, social usage, mores, dictates of society, familiar way, unwritten law, etiquette, conventionality, second nature, conventionalism, matter of course; see also **tradition** 1. — *Ant.* deviation, DEPARTURE, shift.

**3.** [The whole body of tradition] — *Syn.* inheritance, folkways, mores; see **culture** 2.

*See Synonym Study at* HABIT.

**customarily,** *modif.* — *Syn.* usually, commonly, traditionally, conventionally, naturally, generally, habitually, frequently, normally, ordinarily, as a rule; see also **regularly** 1.

**customary,** *modif.* — *Syn.* usual, wonted, habitual; see **common** 1, **conventional** 1, 2.

*See Synonym Study at* USUAL.

**customer,** *n.* — *Syn.* client, patron, consumer, shopper; see **buyer, client.**

**customs,** *pl.n.* — *Syn.* duties, imposts, tariffs; see **tax** 1.

**cut,** *modif.* **1.** [Formed by cutting] — *Syn.* carved, chiseled, sculptured, sliced; see **carved, formed.**

**2.** [Reduced] — *Syn.* lowered, marked down, diluted; see **impure** 1, **reduced** 2, **watered** 2.

**3.** [Severed] — *Syn.* split, divided, sliced through, detached; see **separated.**

**4.** [Slashed] — *Syn.* slit, scored, gashed, scratched; see **carved, hurt, wounded.**

**5.** [Abridged] — *Syn.* shortened, abbreviated, truncated, edited; see **reduced** 1.

**cut,** *n.* **1.** [The using of a sharp instrument] — *Syn.* slash, thrust, dig, prick, gouge, knifing, penetrating, dividing, cleaving, incising, separation, severance, hewing, felling, quarter, intersecting, slitting, hack, slice, carve, chop, stroke; see also **division** 1.

**2.** [The path left by a sharp instrument] — *Syn.* slash, prick, incision, wound, cleavage, penetration, gash, cleft, mark, nick, notch, opening, passage, channel, groove, kerf, furrow, intersection, slit, fissure; see also **hole** 1, **injury** 1.

**3.** [A reduction] — *Syn.* decrease, diminution, lessening; see **reduction** 1.

**4.** [Shape] — *Syn.* fashion, style, construction; see **form** 1.

**5.** [An illustration] — *Syn.* printed picture, engraving, plate; see **illustration** 2, **picture** 3.

**6.** [A section] — *Syn.* segment, slice, portion; see **part** 1, **piece** 1, **share.**

**7.** [A piece of butchered meat] — *Syn.* piece, slice, chunk; see **meat.**

**8.** [*An insult] — *Syn.* offense, affront, snub; see **insult, neglect** 1.

**a cut above*** — *Syn.* somewhat better, superior, higher, more capable; see **better** 1, 2, **superior.**

**cut,** *v.* **1.** [To sever] — *Syn.* separate, slice, slice through, cleave, fell, hew, chop down, mow, prune, reap, scythe, sickle, shear, trim, dice, chop, slit, split, rive, sunder, cut apart, cut asunder, rip, saw through, chisel, cut away, cut through, cut off, lop off, snip, sliver, chip, quarter, clip, truncate, behead, saber, scissor, facet, flitch, bite, shave, pare, skive, divide, bisect, amputate, carve, hack; see also **divide** 1, **trim** 1.

**2.** [To cut into] — *Syn.* gash, incise, slash, slice, carve, notch, nick, indent, score, carve into, mark, scratch, furrow, rake, wound, mar, scotch, gouge, scarify, lacerate; see also **carve** 1, **mangle** 1.

**3.** [To penetrate] — *Syn.* pierce, perforate, puncture; see **penetrate** 1.

**4.** [To cross] — *Syn.* intersect, divide, pass through, move across; see **cross** 1, **divide** 1.

**5.** [To shorten] — *Syn.* curtail, abridge, condense, delete; see **cancel** 1, **decrease** 2.

**6.** [To reduce] — *Syn.* lower, diminish, lessen; see **decrease** 2.

**7.** [To hit sharply] — *Syn.* strike, hew, chop, whack; see **hit** 1.

**8.** [To castrate] — *Syn.* alter, geld, emasculate; see **castrate.**

**9.** [*To ignore deliberately] — *Syn.* snub, slight, disregard; see **neglect** 1.

**10.** [*To absent oneself] — *Syn.* shirk, evade, stay away, play truant, play hooky, be absent without leave, be AWOL, sneak out, skip*, duck*; see also **leave** 1.

**11.** [To record electronically] — *Syn.* make a record, make a recording, tape; see **record** 3.

**12.** [To weaken] — *Syn.* dilute, impair, undermine, dissolve; see **adulterate, weaken** 2.

**13.** [To shape] — *Syn.* fashion, cast, make; see **form** 1.

**cut back,** *v.* — *Syn.* reduce, curtail, shorten, retrench; see **decrease** 2.

**cute*,** *modif.* — *Syn.* adorable, dainty, attractive, cutesy*; see **charming, dainty** 1.

**cuticle,** *n.* — *Syn.* dermis, epidermis, integument; see **skin.**

**cut in,** *v.* **1.** [To interrupt] — *Syn.* butt in*, interfere, move in; see **interrupt** 2.

**2.** [To include, especially in card games] — *Syn.* make

room for, deal in, invite to join; see **include** 2, **invite** 1.

**cut off,** *v.* **1.** [To remove] — *Syn.* sever, separate, tear out, disinherit; see **cut** 1, **disinherit, remove** 1, **separate** 2.

**2.** [To interrupt] — *Syn.* intrude, break in, intervene, disconnect; see **halt** 2, **interrupt** 2.

**cutout,** *n.* — *Syn.* paper doll, sticker, newspaper article, article, pattern.

**cut out,** *v.* **1.** [To remove] — *Syn.* eliminate, extract, excise; see **remove** 1.

**2.** [*To stop] — *Syn.* discontinue, refrain from, quit; see **quit** 1, **stop** 2.

**3.** [*To leave] — *Syn.* go away, depart, leave the scene*; see **leave** 1.

**cut out for*,** *modif.* — *Syn.* suited for, fitted for, suitable, adequate; see **fit** 1, 2.

**cut short,** *v.* **1.** [To terminate] — *Syn.* finish, halt, quit, end abruptly; see **end** 1, **stop** 1, 2.

**2.** [To interrupt] — *Syn.* intercept, check, halt; see **hinder, interrupt** 2.

**3.** [To truncate] — *Syn.* abridge, abbreviate, shorten; see **decrease** 2.

**cutthroat,** *modif.* — *Syn.* ruthless, merciless, unprincipled, dog-eat-dog*; see **cruel** 2, **murderous.**

**cutthroat,** *n.* — *Syn.* assassin, murderer, slayer; see **criminal, killer.**

**cutting,** *modif.* — *Syn.* biting, incisive, caustic; see **sarcastic.**

*See Synonym Study at* INCISIVE.

**cut up,** *v.* **1.** [To chop] — *Syn.* chop up, slice, dice; see **cut** 1, 2.

**2.** [*To clown] — *Syn.* show off, play jokes, fool around*; see **joke, play** 2.

**cybernetics,** *n.* — *Syn.* computer science, comparative study of complex electronic machines, artificial intelligence, AI, system to describe the nature of the brain; see also **computer, science** 1.

**cycle,** *n.* — *Syn.* succession, revolution of time, period, round; see **age** 3, **circle** 2, **sequence** 1, **series.**

**cyclone,** *n.* — *Syn.* destructive wind, typhoon, twister*; see **hurricane, storm** 1, **tornado, wind** 1.

**cylinder,** *n.* **1.** [An automobile part] — *Syn.* compression chamber, expansion chamber, machine part, engine part; see **automobile.**

**2.** [A geometrical form] — *Syn.* circular solid, barrel, volumetric curve; see **solid.**

**cylindrical,** *modif.* — *Syn.* tubular, barrel-shaped, columnar, circular; see **round** 2.

**cynic,** *n.* — *Syn.* misanthrope, misogynist, misogamist, mocker, satirist, scoffer, pessimist, sarcastic person, caviler, sneerer, flouter, carper, critic, unbeliever, egoist, manhater, skeptic, doubter, questioner, detractor, negativist, nihilist, doubting Thomas*; see also **critic** 1. — *Ant.* optimist, BELIEVER, idealist.

**cynical,** *modif.* — *Syn.* sardonic, unbelieving, sneering, skeptical; see **pessimistic** 2, **sarcastic.**

*See Synonym Study at* PESSIMISTIC.

**cynicism,** *n.* — *Syn.* acrimony, misanthropy, pessimism, distrust; see **bitterness** 2, **doubt** 1, **sarcasm.**

**cyst,** *n.* — *Syn.* sac, vesicle, wen; see **blister, growth** 3, **sore.**

**czar,** *n.* — *Syn.* emperor, autocrat, despot; see **king** 1, **leader** 2, **ruler** 1.

# D

**dab,** *n.* — *Syn.* bit, pat, dollop; see **bit** 1.

**dab,** *v.* — *Syn.* tap, peck, pat, daub; see **touch** 1.

**dabble,** *v.* — *Syn.* trifle with, putter, fiddle with, dip into, engage in superficially, amuse oneself with, dally, flirt with, toy with, be an amateur, have a dilettante's interest, idle away time, make slight efforts, do something in a light manner, scratch the surface, have sport with, tinker, putter around, diddle*, fool with*, fool around*. — *Ant.* delve into, work at, become an expert.

**dabbler,** *n.* — *Syn.* dilettante, amateur, tinkerer, novice; see **amateur, trifler.**

**dad*,** *n.* — *Syn.* father, male parent, daddy*, papa*; see **father** 1, **parent.**

**daft,** *modif.* 1. [Silly] — *Syn.* foolish, ridiculous, asinine; see **silly, stupid** 1.

2. [Insane] — *Syn.* crazy, demented, deranged; see **insane** 1.

**dagger,** *n.* — *Syn.* stiletto, dirk, blade; see **knife.**

**look daggers at** — *Syn.* glower, look at with anger, look at with hatred, scowl at; see **dislike, glare** 2.

**daily,** *modif.* — *Syn.* diurnal, quotidian, per diem, everyday, occurring every day, issued every day, issued every weekday, periodic, cyclic, recurring day after day, once daily, by day, once a day, during the day, day by day, from day to day; see also **regular** 3.

**dainty,** *modif.* 1. [Notable for fineness *or* fragility] — *Syn.* delicate, fragile, petite, frail, thin, light, pretty, beautiful, lovely, comely, well-made, attractive, graceful, fine, neat, choice, elegant, exquisite, trim, pleasing, tasteful, precious, tasty, delicious, appetizing, rare, soft, tender, feeble, airy, diaphanous, lacy, nice, darling, cute, sweet; see also **charming, weak** 1, 2. — *Ant.* coarse, ROUGH, gross.

2. [Having taste for dainty things] — *Syn.* refined, nice, fastidious, overnice; see **particular** 3, **refined** 2.

---

*SYN.* — **dainty** and **delicate** are both used to describe things that are pleasing to highly refined tastes or sensibilities, **delicate** implying fragility, subtlety, or fineness, and **dainty** suggesting smallness, fastidiousness, or gracefulness; **exquisite** is applied to something so delicately wrought or subtly refined as to be appreciated by only the most keenly discriminating or fastidious *See also Synonym Study at* PARTICULAR.

---

**dairy,** *n.* — *Syn.* creamery, dairy farm, cow barn, processing plant, ice-cream plant, cheese factory, buttery, milk station, Babcock testing station, pasteurizing plant, co-operative; see also **farm.**

**dairy products,** *n.* — *Syn.* milk products, farm products, produce; see **butter, cheese, cream** 1, **milk.**

**dale,** *n.* — *Syn.* lowland, vale, glen; see **valley.**

**dalliance,** *n.* 1. [Flirting] — *Syn.* toying, petting, seduction, flirtation; see **flirting.**

2. [Idling] — *Syn.* dawdling, loitering, loafing, trifling; see **idleness** 1.

**dally,** *v.* 1. [To flirt] — *Syn.* toy, tease, play, trifle; see **flirt** 1.

2. [To trifle] — *Syn.* dawdle, idle, putter; see **dabble, loiter, trifle** 1.

*See Synonym Study at* LOITER, TRIFLE.

**dam,** *n.* 1. [Structure to impound water] — *Syn.* dike, ditch, wall, bank, embankment, barrier, gate, weir, grade, levee, irrigation dam, diversion dam, cofferdam; see also **barrier.**

Famous dams include — *United States:* Gatun, Fort Peck, Kingsley, Glen Canyon, Grand Coulee, Bonneville, Shasta, Boulder, Hoover, Wilson, Bartlett, Bagnell, Conowingo, Tygart River; *Russia:* Dnepropetrovsk; *France:* Sautet, Chambon, Sarrans; *Egypt:* Aswan; *India:* Metur; *South Africa:* Vaalbank.

2. [Mother, usually of a four-legged animal] — *Syn.* ewe, bitch, mare; see **mother** 1, **parent.**

**dam,** *v.* — *Syn.* hold, hold back, keep back, check, obstruct, bar, slow, retard, restrict, stop, stop up, close, clog, choke, block, block up, impede, confine; see also **bar** 1, **hinder, restrain** 1. — *Ant.* advance, RELEASE, clear.

**damage,** *n.* 1. [Injury] — *Syn.* harm, hurt, impairment, wound, bruise, bane, wrong, infliction, casualty, detriment, deprivation, affliction, accident, catastrophe, adversity, outrage, hardship, disturbance, mutilation, mishap, mischance, evil, blow, devastation, destruction, mischief, stroke, loss, disservice, reverse, weakening, ruination, collapse, disablement, crippling, suffering, illness; see also **disaster, injury** 1, **misfortune** 2. — *Ant.* BLESSING, benefit, boon.

2. [Loss occasioned by injury] — *Syn.* ruin, breakage, ruined goods, wreckage, destruction, cost, loss, waste, spoliation, shrinkage, depreciation, deprivation, dry rot, pollution, corruption, blemish, contamination, ravage, atrophy, adulteration, defacement, scratch, scar, vandalism, vitiation, degeneration, canker, deterioration, disintegration, havoc, erosion, disrepair, debasement, corrosion, discoloration, decay, wear and tear; see also **destruction** 2. — *Ant.* REPAIR, profit, recompense.

**damage,** *v.* 1. [To impair the value *or* usefulness of] — *Syn.* ruin, wreck, hurt, harm, injure, impair, destroy, bleach, fade, water-soak, tarnish, burn, scorch, drench, dirty, rot, smash, batter, discolor, mutilate, scratch, smudge, scuff, crack, chip, bang up, abuse, maltreat, mistreat, mar, maul, deface, disfigure, vandalize, mangle, ravage, scathe, contaminate, crumple, crush, dismantle, cheapen, blight, disintegrate, pollute, hamstring, sap, stain, tear, rip, fray, undermine, weaken, gnaw, corrode, break, split, stab, rend, slash, pierce, puncture, mildew, cripple, disable, rust, warp, maim, lacerate, wound, taint, incapacitate, bruise, spoil, wreak havoc on, wear away, defile, wrong, infect, tamper with, mess up*, gum up*; see also **break** 2, **destroy** 1, **hurt** 1.

2. [To debase] — *Syn.* pervert, vitiate, degrade; see **corrupt** 1.

**3.** [To slander] — *Syn.* malign, calumniate, disparage; see **slander.**

*See Synonym Study at* HURT.

**damaged,** *modif.* **1.** [Injured] — *Syn.* in need of repair, in poor condition, marrred, spoiled; see **broken** 1, 2, **hurt.**

**2.** [Reduced in value because of damage] — *Syn.* on sale, as is, depreciated, dated, faded, secondhand, used, shopworn, out of season, out of style, left over, remaindered, reconditioned, repossessed, water-soaked, weathered, smoked, smoke-damaged, imperfect, flawed, beat-up*; see also **cheap** 1. — *Ant.* UNUSED, perfect, prime.

**damages,** *pl.n.* — *Syn.* reparations, costs, reimbursement; see **compensation, expense** 1, **expenses.**

**dame,** *n.* — *Syn.* baroness, aristocrat, peeress, dowager; see **lady** 2, 3, **matron** 2.

**damn,** *v.* **1.** [To consign to hell] — *Syn.* curse, accurse, confound, ban, doom, anathematize, proscribe, banish, read out of the church, excommunicate, fulminate against, declaim against, excoriate, condemn, sentence, convict, cast into hell, consign to the lower regions, torment, condemn to hell, condemn to eternal punishment, doom to perdition, thunder against, call down curses on the head of; curse with bell, book, and candle*; send to a warm climate*; see also **condemn** 1. — *Ant.* bless, FORGIVE, elevate.

**2.** [To swear at] — *Syn.* curse, revile, imprecate, abuse; see **curse** 2.

**3.** [To disapprove strongly] — *Syn.* object to, complain of, condemn, attack; see **censure, denounce.**

*See Synonym Study at* CURSE.

**not give** (*or* **care**) **a damn***— *Syn.* not care, be indifferent, not be concerned; see **neglect** 1.

**not worth a damn***— *Syn.* useless, unproductive, valueless; see **useless** 1, **worthless** 1.

**damnable,** *modif.* — *Syn.* outrageous, execrable, depraved, detestable; see **offensive** 2, **wicked** 1, 2.

**damnation,** *n.* — *Syn.* damning, condemnation, perdition, sending to hell, consigning to perdition, ban, anathema, excommunication, condemnation to eternal punishment, proscription, denunciation, doom, *damnatio* (Latin), *Verdammung* (German), sending to Old Nick*; see also **blame** 1, **curse** 1.

**damned,** *modif.* **1.** [Consigned to hell] — *Syn.* cursed, condemned, accursed, doomed, unhappy, anathematized, lost, fallen, reprobate, infernal, hell-bound*, gone to blazes*; see also **doomed, unfortunate** 2. — *Ant.* saved, BLESSED, on high.

**2.** [*Disapproved of] — *Syn.* bad, unwelcome, detestable, abominable, loathsome, cursed, damn*, goddamned*, goddamn*, darned*, confounded*, blamed*, blankety-blank*, blithering*, blessed*, blasted*, bloody*, cussed*, danged*, goldarned*, doggone*, dashed*, dratted*, infernal*, deuced*, lousy*; see also **offensive** 2, **undesirable.** — *Ant.* desirable, WELCOMED, favorite.

**do** (*or* **try**) **one's damnedest***— *Syn.* endeavor, do one's best, give one's all, do one's utmost; see **try** 1.

**damning,** *modif.* — *Syn.* damaging, ruinous, fatal; see **incriminating.**

**damn with faint praise,** *v.* — *Syn.* condemn, find fault with, reject; see **rebuff** 1.

**damp,** *modif.* **1.** [Somewhat wet] — *Syn.* moist, sodden, soggy, clammy; see **wet** 1.

**2.** [Rainy] — *Syn.* drizzly, wet, cloudy, humid; see **wet** 2.

*See Synonym Study at* WET.

**dampen,** *v.* **1.** [To wet] — *Syn.* sprinkle, moisten, water; see **moisten.**

**2.** [To discourage] — *Syn.* deaden, dispirit, dismay; see **depress** 2, **discourage** 1, 2.

**damper,** *n.* — *Syn.* hindrance, depressant, chill, wet blanket*; see **restraint** 2.

**damp off,** *v.* — *Syn.* wilt, droop, shrivel; see **die** 1, 3.

**damsel,** *n.* — *Syn.* maiden, maid, nymph; see **girl** 1, **lady** 3, **woman** 1.

**dance,** *n.* **1.** [Rhythmic movement] — *Syn.* dancing, choreography, hop, jig, skip, prance, shuffle, fling, swing, caper, hoedown, hoofing*.

Dances include — *Social:* waltz, fox trot, shimmy, polka, conga, rumba, tango, samba, paso doble, cha-cha, mambo, bolero, disco, hustle, line dance, shag, lambada, merengue, vogue, freak, jerk, frug, jitterbug, one-step, two-step, box-step, Charleston, Peabody, bunny hug, twist, monkey, mashed potato; break dancing, slam dancing; *theatrical:* ballet, adagio, tap dance, soft-shoe, toe dance; *traditional:* cotillion, quadrille, pavane, loure, galliard, branle, sarabande, courante, *bourrée, passepied, contredanse* (all French), mazurka, polonaise, beguine, fandango, round dance, square dance, minuet, gavotte, schottische, rigadoon, shuffle, gallopade, galop; *folk and primitive:* sun dance, ghost dance, sword dance, snake dance, fertility dance, morris dance, Virginia reel, belly dance, Highland fling, flamenco, paso doble, Irish jig, buck and wing, clog, tarantella, hora, hornpipe, czardas, hula; see also **waltz.**

**2.** [A dancing party] — *Syn.* ball, promenade, grand ball, dress ball, masked ball, prom, cotillion, reception, masquerade, masque, tea dance, *thé dansant* (French), hoedown, mixer, hop*, shindig*, brawl*; see also **party** 1.

**dance,** *v.* **1.** [To move rhythmically] — *Syn.* step, trip, tread, glide, whirl, jig, perform the steps of, execute the figures of, shuffle the feet, pirouette, trip the light fantastic, hoof it*, hop*, cut a rug*, rock*, foot it*, boogie*, vogue*; see also **dance** *n.*

**2.** [To move in a gay and sprightly manner] — *Syn.* hop, skip, jump, leap, bob, bobble, scamper, skitter, jiggle, jigger, caper, gambol, bounce, cavort, sway, swirl, sweep, swing, careen, curvet, cut capers; see also **jump** 1, 4, **play** 2. — *Ant.* SIT, perch, stand.

**dance attendance on,** *v.* — *Syn.* wait on hand and foot, cater to, be subservient to, serve abjectly; see **obey** 1, **tend.**

**dancer,** *n.* — *Syn.* terpsichorean, *danseur, danseuse* (both French), ballerina, prima ballerina, *danseur noble, premier danseur, première danseuse* (all French), coryphée, figurant, figurante, chorus girl, chorine*, chorus boy, geisha; ballet, tap, toe, hula, belly, taxi, go-go, folk, square, modern, flamenco, ballroom, etc., dancer; hoofer*, stripper*, rock-and-roller*; see also **actor** 1, **actress.**

**dance to another tune,** *v.* — *Syn.* act differently, change one's mind, sing a different tune; see **change** 4, **differ** 1, **reconsider.**

**dander*,** *n.* — *Syn.* wrath, temper, animosity; see **anger.**

**get one's dander up***— *Syn.* enrage, infuriate, annoy, lose one's temper; see **anger** 1, **rage** 1.

**dandle,** *v.* — *Syn.* fondle, pet, ride on the knee; see **caress, touch** 1.

*See Synonym Study at* CARESS.

**dandy,** *n.* **1.** [Fop] — *Syn.* coxcomb, dude, Beau Brummell; see **fop.**

**2.** [*Something first-rate] — *Syn.* paragon, gem, humdinger*, beaut*; see **gem** 2, **model** 1.

**danger,** *n.* — *Syn.* risk, peril, jeopardy, threat, hazard, insecurity, uncertainty, instability, exposure, venture, destabilizing factor, menace, precariousness, vulnerability, slipperiness, shakiness, treacherousness, endangerment, emergency, crisis, exigency, predicament, precipice, thin ice*.— *Ant.* SAFETY, security, certainty.

*SYN.* — **danger** is the general term for liability to injury or evil, of whatever degree or likelihood of occurrence [the *danger* of falling on icy walks]; **peril** suggests great and imminent danger [in *peril* of death]; **jeopardy** emphasizes exposure to extreme danger [liberty is in *jeopardy* under tyrants]; **hazard** implies a foreseeable but uncontrollable possibility of danger, but stresses the element of chance [the *hazards* of hunting big game]; **risk** implies the voluntary taking of a dangerous chance

**dangerous,** *modif.* **1.** [Not safe]— *Syn.* perilous, unsafe, hazardous, risky, precarious, treacherous, unprotected, unshielded, unsheltered, critical, serious, vulnerable, exposed, involving risk, full of risk, threatening, alarming, portentous, causing danger, insecure, ticklish, delicate, speculative, unstable, touchy, bad, fraught with danger, thorny, jeopardous, breakneck, chancy, uncertain, touch-and-go, shaky, slippery, unsteady, rickety, rocky, hairy*, unhealthy*, hot*, dicey*; see also **endangered, uncertain** 2, **unsafe.**— *Ant.* safe, sure, secure.
**2.** [Involving an active threat] — *Syn.* menacing, threatening, serious, critical, impending, ominous, ugly, nasty, imminent, malignant, formidable, terrible, impregnable, armed, fatal, mortal, deadly, explosive, out of the frying pan and into the fire*, on a collision course*; see also **ominous.**— *Ant.* HELPFUL, innocent, beneficial.
**dangerously,** *modif.* — *Syn.* perilously, desperately, precariously, severely; see **seriously** 1.
**dangle,** *v.* — *Syn.* droop, sway, suspend; see **hang** 1, 2.
**dank,** *modif.* — *Syn.* damp, humid, moist, wet; see **close** 5, **wet** 1, 2.
*See Synonym Study at* WET.
**dapper,** *modif.* — *Syn.* trim, smart, spruce, natty; see **fashionable, neat** 1.
**dare,** *v.* **1.** [To be courageous] — *Syn.* venture, take a chance, hazard, chance, brave, risk, presume, adventure, undertake, stake, attempt, endeavor, try, try one's hand, be not afraid, be bold enough to undertake, make bold, despite danger, have the courage of one's convictions, go through fire and water, take heart, nerve oneself, gather courage, muster courage, put up a bold front, go ahead, take the bull by the horns*, shoot the works*, have the nerve, have the guts*; see also **chance** 2, **risk, try** 1. — *Ant.* AVOID, dread, fear.
**2.** [To defy] — *Syn.* challenge, meet, confront, front, provoke, oppose, disregard, brave, cope, scorn, outdare, insult, resist, threaten, spurn, denounce, bully, mock, laugh at, offer defiance to, assume a fighting attitude, square off, stand up to, face up to, throw down the gauntlet, outbrazen, outbrave, show fight, call one's bluff, look full in the face, double the fist at*, call out*, pluck by the beard*, look big*, kick against*, put one's foot down*, bell the cat*, beard the lion in his den*, face the music*, measure swords with*; see also **face** 1. — *Ant.* AVOID, flee, back down.
**daredevil,** *n.* — *Syn.* stuntman, stuntwoman, madcap, gambler; see **adventurer** 1.
**daring,** *modif.* **1.** [Indifferent to danger] — *Syn.* bold, courageous, fearless; see **brave** 1, **rash.**
**2.** [Lacking in modesty and discretion] — *Syn.* audacious, bold, forward, obtrusive; see **rude** 2.
**dark,** *modif.* **1.** [Lacking brightness] — *Syn.* unlighted,

unlit, dim, dusky, murky, gloomy, shadowy, somber, cloudy, foggy, sunless, lightless, indistinct, dull, faint, vague, misty, darkish, deep, drab, dingy, obscure, nebulous, shady, shaded, clouded, darkened, overcast, lowering, Cimmerian, opaque, crepuscular, Stygian, without light, tenebrous, bereft of light, ill-lighted, inky, pitch-dark, black, darkling*, darksome*, pitchy*; see also **black** 1, **dull** 2, **hazy** 1.— *Ant.* BRIGHT, light, illuminated.
**2.** [Dismal] — *Syn.* gloomy, hopeless, cheerless, sullen; see **dismal** 1, **sullen.**
**3.** [Not known] — *Syn.* cryptic, hidden, mysterious; see **obscure** 3, **secret** 1.
**4.** [Lacking light for the future] — *Syn.* sinister, foreboding, unpropitious; see **ominous.**
**5.** [Dark in complexion] — *Syn.* brunet, brunette, swarthy, tan, black, Negro, Negroid, dusky, sable, dark-skinned, dark-haired, dark-complexioned, nonwhite, colored, Indian, melanous; see also **African** 2, **black** 3.
**6.** [Ignorant] — *Syn.* unenlightened, unread, uncultivated; see **ignorant** 2.
**7.** [Evil] — *Syn.* sinister, iniquitous, immoral, corrupt; see **wicked** 1.

*SYN.* — **dark**, the general word in this comparison, denotes a partial or complete absence of light [a *dark* night]; **dim** implies so little light that objects can be seen only indistinctly [dim shapes in the shadows, the *dim* light of the moon]; **dusky** suggests the grayish, shadowy light of twilight [a *dusky* winter evening]; **murky** now usually suggests the thick, heavy darkness of fog or smoke-filled air [the *murky* ruins of a temple]; **gloomy** suggests a cloudy, cheerless darkness [a *gloomy* forest]

**dark,** *n.* **1.** [Darkness] — *Syn.* gloom, murk, duskiness; see **darkness** 1.
**2.** [Night] — *Syn.* nighttime, nightfall, evening; see **night** 1.
**in the dark** — *Syn.* uninformed, in ignorance, unaware, naive; see **ignorant** 1.
**keep dark** — *Syn.* conceal, keep secret, obscure; see **hide** 1.
**darken,** *v.* **1.** [To grow darker] — *Syn.* cloud up *or* over, deepen, become dark, dim; see **shade** 3.
**2.** [To make darker] — *Syn.* cloud, shadow, blacken, eclipse; see **shade** 2.
**darkness,** *n.* **1.** [Absence of light] — *Syn.* dark, gloom, murk, dusk, murkiness, duskiness, dimness, blackness, shadiness, shade, tenebrosity, shadowiness, smokiness, lightlessness, pitch darkness, night, twilight, crepuscule, eclipse, nightfall, obscurity, cloudiness, opacity, somberness, inkiness, swarthiness, melanism, Stygian darkness, Cimmerian shade, Egyptian blackness, shades of evening, shades of night, palpable darkness; see also **night** 1.
**2.** [Ignorance] — *Syn.* backwardness, benightedness, unenlightenment; see **ignorance** 2.
**3.** [Evil] — *Syn.* wickedness, iniquity, sin, corruption; see **evil** 1.
**4.** [Secrecy] — *Syn.* concealment, obscurity, inscrutability, seclusion; see **mystery** 1, **secrecy.**
**5.** [Gloominess] — *Syn.* somberness, bleakness, grimness, pessimism; see **gloom** 2.
**darling,** *modif.* — *Syn.* dearest, dear, favorite; see **beloved.**
**darling,** *n.* **1.** [A beloved one] — *Syn.* love, dear one, beloved, pet; see sense 2, **favorite, friend** 1, **lover** 1.
**2.** [Term of endearment] — *Syn.* dear, sweetheart, honey, dear one, beloved, my own, dear heart,

heart's desire, dearest, lover, pet, sweet, sweetie, angel, truelove, love, jewel, treasure, pearl, sweetie-pie, sugar, honeybun, honeybunch, precious, cutie, princess, dearie, ducky, baby, babe, sweet mama, sugarplum, honey lamb, hon, lamb, lambie pie, chéri, light of my life, lady love, heartsease, one and only.

**darn,** *v.* **1.** [*Variant of damn*] — *Syn.* curse, confound*, drat*, swear at; see **curse** 2.
**2.** [To repair] — *Syn.* mend, sew, patch; see **mend** 1, **repair.**
*See Synonym Study at* MEND.

**darned,** *modif.* **1.** [Mended with thread] — *Syn.* patched, knitted up, stitched; see **repaired, sewn.**
**2.** [*Variant of damned*] — *Syn.* awful, undesirable, confounded*; see **damned** 2, **offensive** 2.

**dart,** *n.* — *Syn.* missile, barb, flechette; see **arrow, weapon** 1.

**dart,** *v.* **1.** [To move in the manner of a dart] — *Syn.* shoot, shoot up, shoot out, speed, plunge, launch, thrust, hurtle, fling, heave, pitch, cast, dash, bolt, spring, spring up, go like an arrow, spurt, scud, skim, fly, fire off*, scoot*, skitter*; see also **move** 1. — *Ant.* STOP, amble, loiter.
**2.** [To move quickly] — *Syn.* hasten, speed, rush, tear; see **hurry** 1, **race** 1, **run** 2.

**dash,** *n.* **1.** [A sprint] .
Common dashes include: 50-yard, 100-yard, century, 220-yard, 50-meter, 100-meter, 200-meter; see also **race** 3, **sport** 3.
**2.** [A short, swift movement] — *Syn.* spurt, sortie, rush, bolt; see **run** 1.
**3.** [Punctuation marking a break in thought] — *Syn.* em, em dash, em quad, quad, quadrat, en, en quad, en dash, two-em quad, etc., mutton quad*, nut quad*; see also **mark** 1, **punctuation.**
**4.** [A little of something] — *Syn.* little, a few drops, pinch, hint, sprinkle, scattering, sprinkling, seasoning, zest, touch, dab, slight admixture, grain, trace, tinge, suspicion, suggestion, squirt, splash, taste, soupçon, infinitesimal amount, teentsy-weentsy bit*, smidgen*; see also **bit** 1, **part** 1, **trace** 1. — *Ant.* too MUCH, quantity, excess.

**dash,** *v.* **1.** [To strike violently] — *Syn.* smash, crash, buffet, pound; see **beat** 1, 3, **break** 2, **smash.**
**2.** [To discourage] — *Syn.* thwart, dampen, dismay, blast; see **destroy** 1, **discourage** 1.
**3.** [To sprint] — *Syn.* race, speed, tear; see **run** 2.
**4.** [To throw] — *Syn.* hurl, fling, cast; see **throw** 1.
**5.** [To splash] — *Syn.* spatter, splatter, swash; see **splash.**

**dashing,** *modif.* **1.** [Bold and lively] — *Syn.* spirited, dynamic, gallant, daring; see **active** 2, **brave** 1.
**2.** [Stylish] — *Syn.* dapper, jaunty, striking, showy; see **fashionable, jaunty.**
**3.** [Being dashed; *said especially of water*] — *Syn.* striking, splashing, beating, being hurled against, being blown against, shattering, breaking, crushing, flinging, tossing, rolling, storm-tossed, wind-blown.

**dash off,** *v.* — *Syn.* rush, fail to take pains, scribble; see **hasten** 1, 2, **write** 2.

**dastardly,** *modif.* — *Syn.* cowardly, pusillanimous, sneaking, base; see **cowardly** 1, 2, **mean** 1.
*See Synonym Study at* COWARDLY.

**data,** *n.* — *Syn.* facts, figures, information, evidence, reports, details, specifics, notes, documents, records, abstracts, dossier, testimony, matters of direct observation, known facts, available figures, information base, raw materials, input, statistics, measurements, numbers, results, findings, circumstances, experiments, info*,

dope*, score*; see also **declaration** 2, **knowledge** 1, **proof** 1.

**date,** *n.* **1.** [A specified period of time] — *Syn.* day, year, time, point in time, epoch, period, era, generation, age, term, course, spell, semester, quarter, trimester, season, duration, span, moment, while, reign, hour, century; see also **age** 3, **time** 2, **year.**
**2.** [*An appointment*] — *Syn.* tryst, assignation, rendezvous, engagement, interview, call, visit, blind date, double date; see also **appointment** 2.
**3.** [Person with whom one has a date, sense 2] — *Syn.* companion, escort, partner, sweetheart, girlfriend, boyfriend, squire, honey*, sweetie*, blind date*, heavy date*, steady*, pickup*, trick*; see also **escort, friend** 1, **lover** 1.

**out of date** — *Syn.* passé, outmoded, old, obsolete; see **old-fashioned.**
**to date** — *Syn.* until now, as yet, so far, up to now, hereunto; see also **now** 1.
**up to date** — *Syn.* modern, contemporary, current, abreast of; see **fashionable, modern** 1, **up-to-date.**

**date,** *v.* **1.** [To indicate historical time] — *Syn.* appoint, determine, mark the time of, ascertain the time of, assign a time to, assign a time to, measure, mark with a date, date-stamp, fix the date of, affix a date to, carbon-date, silicon-date, potassium-argon-date, tree-ring date, furnish with a date, have its origin, originate in, belong to a period, chronologize, chronicle, isolate, measure, indicate the sequence; see also **begin** 2, **define** 1, **measure** 1, **record** 1.
**2.** [To court or be courted] — *Syn.* escort, accompany, go out with, attend, associate with, keep company, consort with, rendezvous, make a date, keep an engagement with, take out*, go with*, go together*, go steady*, see*, take up with*; see also **accompany** 1.

**daub,** *v.* — *Syn.* smear, plaster, dab; see **paint** 2, **spread** 4, **varnish.**

**daughter,** *n.* — *Syn.* female child, girl, offspring, descendant, stepdaughter, heiress, female dependent, infant, her mother's daughter*, apple of her father's eye*; see also **child, girl** 1.

**daunt,** *v.* — *Syn.* dismay, appall, horrify, frighten; see **dismay, frighten** 1.
*See Synonym Study at* DISMAY.

**dauntless,** *modif.* — *Syn.* bold, daring, fearless, gallant; see **brave** 1.

**davenport,** *n.* — *Syn.* sofa, couch, studio couch, daybed; see **couch.**

**dawdle,** *v.* — *Syn.* loaf, idle, lounge; see **loiter.**
*See Synonym Study at* LOITER.

**dawn,** *n.* **1.** [The coming of day] — *Syn.* dawning, sunrise, daybreak; see **morning** 1.
**2.** [The beginning] — *Syn.* source, start, rise, advent; see **appearance** 3, **origin** 1, 2.

**dawn,** *v.* — *Syn.* start, appear, show itself; see **begin** 2.

**day,** *n.* **1.** [The period of the earth's revolution] — *Syn.* twenty-four hours, mean solar day, sidereal day, time between sunrise and sunset, period from dawn to dark, solar day, nautical day, natural day, civil day, astronomical day, diurnal course, date.
**2.** [The time of light or work] — *Syn.* daylight, daytime, broad daylight, full day, workday, working day, daylight hours, broadcast day, eight-hour day, union day; good, bad, hot, cold, damp, etc., day; sizzler*, scorcher*, good day for the races*.
**3.** [A special day] — *Syn.* holiday, celebration, festival; see **anniversary, holiday** 1.
**4.** [A period of time] — *Syn.* era, time, heyday, prime; see **age** 3.

**call it a day**★— *Syn.* finish, quit, stop work, call it quits★; see **end** 1, **stop** 1, 2.

**from day to day** — *Syn.* without thought for the future, sporadically, irresponsibly, heedlessly; see **carelessly, irregularly.**

**day after day,** *modif.* — *Syn.* continually, day by day, every day, steadily; see **daily, regularly** 2.

**daybreak,** *n.* — *Syn.* dawn, sunrise, dayspring, first light; see **morning** 1.

**day by day,** *modif.* — *Syn.* gradually, monotonously, persistently, each day; see **daily, regularly** 2.

**daydream,** *n.* — *Syn.* reverie, vision, fantasy; see **dream** 1, **fantasy** 1.

**daydream,** *v.* — *Syn.* fantasize, muse, stargaze, go woolgathering; see **dream** 2.

**day in and day out,** *modif.* — *Syn.* consistently, steadily, every day; see **daily, regularly** 2.

**daylight,** *n.* — *Syn.* daytime, daylight hours, sunlight, light of day; see **day** 2, **morning** 1, **sunshine.**

**scare the daylights out of**★**, knock the daylights out of**★— *Syn.* frighten, scare, beat; see **beat** 2, **frighten** 1, **threaten** 1.

**daze,** *n.* — *Syn.* stupor, distraction, bewilderment, trance; see **confusion** 2, **stupor.**

**daze,** *v.* — *Syn.* stupefy, stun, bewilder, amaze; see **confuse, hypnotize, surprise** 1.

**dazed,** *modif.* — *Syn.* confused, disoriented, stunned; see **bewildered, doubtful** 2, **unconscious** 1.

**dazzle,** *v.* — *Syn.* impress, astonish, stupefy, overpower; see **charm** 1, **surprise** 1.

**deacon,** *n.* — *Syn.* elder, vicar, church officer; see **minister** 1.

**dead,** *modif.* **1.** [Without life] — *Syn.* deceased, departed, perished, expired, lifeless, inanimate, brain dead, late, former, defunct, cadaverous, mortified, no longer living, not endowed with life, devoid of life, deprived of life, gone, clinically dead, extinct, in the grave, breathless, still, no more, gone the way of all flesh, gone to one's reward, gone to meet one's Maker, out of one's misery, gone to one's last rest, gone to a better place, gathered to one's fathers, with the saints, beneath the sod, numbered with the dead, bereft of life, at rest, asleep in the Lord, resting in peace, fallen, gone to glory, cut off★, bought the farm★, dead as a doornail★, done for★, gone west★, liquidated★, wasted★, snuffed out★, erased★, gone home in a box★, pushing up daisies★, put to bed with a shovel★, grounded for good★, washed up★, claycold★, stone-cold★; see also **extinct.** — *Ant.* ALIVE, animate, enduring.
**2.** [Without the appearance of life] — *Syn.* inert, still, stagnant, lifeless; see **dead** 2, 4, 6.
**3.** [Numb] — *Syn.* insensible, deadened, anesthetized; see **numb** 1, **paralyzed, unconscious** 1.
**4.** [Extinct] — *Syn.* ended, extinguished, terminated, obsolete; see **extinct.**
**5.** [*Exhausted] — *Syn.* wearied, worn, spent; see **tired.**
**6.** [*Complete] — *Syn.* final, total, unconditional; see **absolute** 1.

*SYN.* — **dead** is the general word for someone or something that was alive but is no longer so; **deceased** and **departed** are both euphemistic, esp. for one who has recently died, but the former is largely a legal, and the latter a religious, usage; **late** precedes the name, relationship, or title of one who has died, especially recently /the *late* Mr. Green/ or of one who preceded the incumbent in some office or function /his *late* employer/; **defunct,** applied to a person, is now somewhat rhetorical

or jocular, but it is also commonly used of something that because of failure no longer exists or functions /a *defunct* government/; **extinct** is applied to a species, race, etc. that has no living member; **inanimate** refers to that which has never had life /*inanimate* rocks/; **lifeless** refers to that which has died or appears dead or to things that exhibit no life or spirit /her *lifeless* body, a *lifeless* painting/

**dead,** *n.* [*Usually used with* the] — *Syn.* the departed, the deceased, decedent, one's fathers; see **ancestor, body** 2.

**deadbeat,** *n.* — *Syn.* bad debtor, parasite, bum; see **beggar** 1, **debtor, tramp** 1.

**deaden,** *v.* **1.** [To reduce life or the evidence of life] — *Syn.* blunt, impair, dull, numb, desensitize, repress, slow, paralyze, anesthetize, drug, chloroform, gas, freeze, narcotize, etherize, put to sleep, make unfit, knock out, daze, benumb, incapacitate, depress, stupefy, stun, smother, stifle, suppress, frustrate, weaken, devitalize, injure, exhaust, tire, retard, knock stiff★, KO★, lay out★, dope★, put out of order★, take the edge off★; see also **drug, weaken** 2. — *Ant.* ANIMATE, revitalize, invigorate.
**2.** [To soften] — *Syn.* tone down, dim, muffle, mute, dull, dampen, cushion; see also **decrease** 2, **soften** 2.

**deadlock,** *n.* — *Syn.* standstill, stalemate, impasse, standoff; see **pause** 2, **tie** 4.

**deadly,** *modif.* **1.** [Causing death] — *Syn.* fatal, lethal, murderous, mortal, deathly, poisonous, toxic, homicidal, bloody, noxious, destructive, venomous, deleterious, baleful, malignant, terminal, virulent, injurious, pestilential, pestiferous, death-dealing, carcinogenic, suicidal, bloodthirsty, cannibalistic, life-threatening, killing, baneful, pernicious, harmful, violent, inevitable; see also **dangerous** 2, **destructive** 2. — *Ant.* HEALTHFUL, reviving, beneficial.
**2.** [Very tiresome] — *Syn.* boring, tedious, tiresome; see **dull** 4.

*SYN.* — **deadly** is applied to a thing that can and probably (but not inevitably) will cause death /a *deadly* poison/; **fatal** implies the inevitability or actual occurrence of death or disaster /a *fatal* disease, a *fatal* mistake/; **mortal** implies that death has occurred or is about to occur and is applied to the immediate cause of death /he has received a *mortal* blow/; **lethal** is applied to that which in its nature or purpose is a cause of death /a *lethal* weapon, a *lethal* dose/

**deaf,** *modif.* **1.** [Not able to hear] — *Syn.* hard of hearing, hearing-impaired, unhearing, stone-deaf, earless, dull of hearing, unable to distinguish sound, unable to hear, deaf-mute, stunned, deafened, tone-deaf, deaf and dumb★, deaf as a post, deaf as a doorknob★, with tin ears★. — *Ant.* hearing, sharp-eared, AUDITORY.
**2.** [Not willing to hear] — *Syn.* unaware, stubborn, blind; see **oblivious, obstinate.**

**deafen,** *v.* — *Syn.* make deaf, cause or induce deafness, stun, split the ears★; see **damage** 1, **hurt** 1.

**deafening,** *modif.* — *Syn.* thunderous, earsplitting, overpowering, piercing; see **loud** 1, 2.

**deal,** *n.* **1.** [An agreement, often secret or underhanded] — *Syn.* understanding, settlement, compromise, arrangement; see **agreement** 3, **bargain** 2, **contract.**
**2.** [A business transaction] — *Syn.* venture, proceeding, dealings, sale; see **transaction.**
**3.** [A hand at cards; *often used figuratively*] — *Syn.* new deal, cut and shuffle, single round, appointment, distri-

bution of cards, honest deal, opportunity, chance, fresh start, square deal.

**4.** [A lot] — *Syn.* plethora, abundance, superabundance; see **plenty.**

**a good (or great) deal** — *Syn.* a lot, quite a bit, a considerable amount; see **much.**

**make a big deal out of\*** — *Syn.* expand, magnify, blow up; see **exaggerate.**

**deal,** *v.* **1.** [To distribute] — *Syn.* apportion, allot, dispense; see **administer 2, distribute 1.**

**2.** [To do business with] — *Syn.* trade, traffic, bargain, barter; see **buy 1, sell 1.**

**dealer,** *n.* **1.** [One engaged in buying or selling] — *Syn.* trader, wholesaler, trafficker; see **businessperson, merchant, seller.**

**2.** [One who deals cards] — *Syn.* banker, card player, croupier, shuffler, dispenser, divider, the house, pit man\*, pit boss\*, mechanic\*; see also **gambler.**

**deal in,** *v.* — *Syn.* handle, trade, specialize in; see **buy 1, sell 1.**

**dealings,** *n.* — *Syn.* business, relations, trade, sale; see **business 1, communication 1, transaction.**

**deal with,** *v.* **1.** [To deal with a person] — *Syn.* handle, manage, have to do with, cope with; see **communicate 2, treat 1.**

**2.** [To deal with a subject] — *Syn.* review, discuss, approach; see **concern 1, consider 3, treat 2.**

**dean,** *n.* **1.** [A distinguished person] — *Syn.* doyen, doyenne, senior member, innovator, authority; see also **leader 2.**

**2.** [A high ecclesiastical official] — *Syn.* churchman, ecclesiastic, dignitary; see **minister 1.**

**3.** [A collegiate or administrative official] — *Syn.* administrator, provost, registrar, official, Dean of Students, Dean of Men, Dean of Women, Dean of the Faculties, Dean of the College of: Liberal Arts, Engineering, Law, Education, Medicine, Pharmacy, Agriculture, etc.; Executive Dean, Junior Dean, Assistant Dean; see also **administrator.**

**dear,** *modif.* **1.** [High in one's affections] — *Syn.* loved, precious, endeared, cherished; see **beloved.**

**2.** [High in price] — *Syn.* costly, prized, high-priced; see **expensive, valuable 1.**

*See Synonym Study at* EXPENSIVE.

**dear,** *n.* — *Syn.* loved one, sweetheart, love; see **darling 2, favorite, lover 1.**

**dearly,** *modif.* **1.** [In an affectionate manner] — *Syn.* fondly, affectionately, devotedly; see **lovingly.**

**2.** [To a great extent] — *Syn.* greatly, extremely, profoundly, ardently; see **sincerely, very.**

**dearth,** *n.* — *Syn.* scarcity, deficiency, scantiness, shortage; see **lack 1, poverty 2.**

**death,** *n.* **1.** [The cessation of life] — *Syn.* decease, dying, demise, passing, expiration, failure of vital functions, loss of life, dissolution, departure, release, parting, quietus, end of life, extinction, oblivion, mortality, euthanasia, passing away, loss, perishing, necrosis, brain death, rigor mortis, the Grim Reaper, Thanatos, Azrael, exit\*, end\*, finish\*, finis\*, roll call\*, the way of all flesh\*, debt to nature\*, the Great Divide\*, crossing the river\*, crossing the bar\*, the great adventure\*, eternal rest\*, last rest\*, the deep end\*, last roundup\*, curtains\*; see also **destruction 1.** — *Ant.* BIRTH, beginning, life.

**2.** [The state after death] — *Syn.* repose, sleep, separation, darkness, afterlife, other world, grave, tomb, future home, heaven, paradise, hell, purgatory, eternal rest\*, Abraham's bosom\*, the big sleep\*; see also **heaven 2, hell 1.** — *Ant.* LIFE, living, existence.

**at death's door** — *Syn.* failing, wasting away, nearly dead; see **dying 1, 2.**

**put to death** — *Syn.* execute, cause to be killed, murder; see **kill 1.**

**to death** — *Syn.* very much, extremely, to the extreme; see **very.**

**to the death** — *Syn.* to the end, to the bitter end, constantly, always; see **forever 1, loyally.**

**deathless,** *modif.* — *Syn.* undying, immortal, everlasting, timeless; see **eternal 1, 2, immortal 1.**

**deathly,** *modif.* — *Syn.* deathlike, cadaverous, ghastly, gaunt; see **dead 1, dull 6, pale 1.**

**debacle,** *n.* — *Syn.* downfall, collapse, fiasco, rout; see **catastrophe, disaster, failure 1.**

**debar,** *v.* **1.** [To exclude] — *Syn.* evict, suspend, shut out; see **bar 1, dismiss 1, eliminate 1.**

**2.** [To prevent] — *Syn.* restrict, prohibit, deny; see **bar 2, hinder, prevent.**

*See Synonym Study at* EXCLUDE.

**debase,** *v.* — *Syn.* corrupt, pervert, deprave, debauch, humble, degrade, cheapen, devalue, demean, lower, abase, vitiate; see also **corrupt 1.**

---

*SYN.* — **debase** implies generally a lowering in quality, value, dignity, etc. *[greed had debased his character]*; **deprave** suggests gross degeneration, esp. with reference to morals *[a mind depraved by crime]*; **corrupt** implies a deterioration or loss of soundness by some destructive or contaminating influence *[a government corrupted by bribery]*; **debauch** implies a loss of moral purity or integrity as through dissipation or intemperate indulgence *[debauched young profligates]*; **pervert** suggests a distorting of or departure from what is considered right, natural, or true *[a perverted sense of humor]* See also *Synonym Study at* HUMBLE.

---

**debased,** *modif.* — *Syn.* depraved, degraded, base; see **wicked 1.**

**debasement,** *n.* — *Syn.* perversion, depravation, corruption; see **evil 1, pollution.**

**debatable,** *modif.* — *Syn.* disputable, unsettled, up for discussion; see **controversial, questionable 1.**

**debate,** *n.* — *Syn.* contest, match, argumentation, disputation, polemics, forensics, dialectic, deliberation; see also **discussion 1, dispute.**

**debate,** *v.* — *Syn.* argue, discuss, confute, refute, controvert, oppose, question, contend, contest, reason, wrangle, answer, ponder, weigh, differ, dispute, engage in oral discussion, argue the pros and cons of, hold a confab\*, jaw\*, chew the fat\*, cross verbal swords\*, moot\*, bandy\*; see also **argue 1, discuss.** — *Ant.* AGREE, concur, concede.

*See Synonym Study at* DISCUSS.

**debauch,** *v.* — *Syn.* debase, deprave, defile; see **corrupt 1, seduce.**

*See Synonym Study at* DEBASE.

**debauched,** *modif.* — *Syn.* corrupted, dissipated, depraved; see **lewd 2, wicked 1.**

**debauchee,** *n.* — *Syn.* sensualist, immoralist, carouser, libertine; see **rake 1, rascal.**

**debaucher,** *n.* — *Syn.* rapist, seducer, ravisher; see **lecher.**

**debauchery,** *n.* **1.** [Dissipation] — *Syn.* intemperance, carousal, revelry, profligacy; see **indulgence 3.**

**2.** [Seduction] — *Syn.* lasciviousness, lechery, libertinism; see **desire 3, lewdness.**

**debilitate,** *v.* — *Syn.* enervate, enfeeble, incapacitate; see **weaken 2.**

*See Synonym Study at* WEAKEN.

**debility,** *n.* — *Syn.* incapacity, feebleness, infirmity, disability; see **frailty 1, weakness 1.**

**debit,** *n.* — *Syn.* entry, deficit, indebtedness, obligation, liability, arrears, account, accounts collectible, bills, amount due, amount payable, charge; see also **debt 1.** — *Ant.* CREDIT, tally, settlement.

**debonair,** *modif.* **1.** [Jaunty] — *Syn.* buoyant, carefree, easy; see **jaunty, nonchalant.**
**2.** [Urbane] — *Syn.* suave, smooth, elegant, dapper; see **pleasant 1, polite 1, refined 2.**

**debrief,** *v.* — *Syn.* quiz, interrogate, declassify; see **question 1.**

**debris,** *n.* — *Syn.* rubble, detritus, ruins, wreckage; see **trash 1, wreck 2.**

**debt,** *n.* **1.** [That which is owed] — *Syn.* liability, obligation, mortgage, debit, score, pecuniary due, duty, arrears, deficit, note, bill, accounts outstanding, accounts collectible, debt of honor, encumbrance, commitment, outstandings, claim, indebtedness, arrearage, deferred payment, national debt, contingent liability, floating debt, funded debt, future debt, account, overdraft, amount due, red ink*, IOU*, chit*; see also **lien, mortgage.** — *Ant.* CREDIT, asset, capital.
**2.** [Capital covered by funded obligations] — *Syn.* outstanding issues, mortgages, bonds, shares, stocks, notes, securities, checks, debentures, indentures; see also **money 1.**
**in debt** — *Syn.* owing, liable, in the red, in arrears; see **indebted.**

**debtor,** *n.* — *Syn.* purchaser, borrower, defaulter, mortgagor, account, bankrupt, risk, deadbeat*, lame duck*, welsher*, fly-by-night*; see also **buyer.** — *Ant.* CREDITOR, lender, mortgagee.

**debunk,** *v.* — *Syn.* expose, deflate, demystify; see **expose 1, ridicule.**

**debut,** *n.* — *Syn.* coming out, presentation, entrance into society, first public appearance, première, first step, introduction, graduation, appearance, maiden speech; see also **introduction 1, 2.**

**decadence,** *n.* — *Syn.* deterioration, decline, degeneration, self-indulgence; see **decay 1, evil 1, indulgence 3.**

**decadent,** *modif.* **1.** [Regressive] — *Syn.* declining, moribund, decaying, on the wane; see **dying 2.**
**2.** [Corrupt] — *Syn.* immoral, dissolute, degenerate, self-indulgent; see **sensual 2, wicked 1.**

**decamp,** *v.* — *Syn.* desert, evacuate, flee, abscond; see **escape 1, leave 1.**

**decant,** *v.* — *Syn.* tap, pour off, pour out, draft; see **empty 2.**

**decapitate,** *v.* — *Syn.* behead, guillotine, execute; see **kill 1.**

**decapitation,** *n.* — *Syn.* capital punishment, beheading, the block, the ax; see **execution 2.**

**decay,** *n.* **1.** [A progressive worsening] — *Syn.* decline, decomposition, collapse, degeneracy, downfall, decadence, depreciation, decrease, consumption, corruption, spoilage, spoiling, rotting, retrogradation, wasting away, retrogression, degeneration, gradual crumbling, disrepair, loss of health, loss of strength, weakening, senescence, deterioration, breakdown, failure, ruination, extinction, progressive decline, dilapidation, dissolution, disintegration, decrepitude, ruin, crumbling, waste, breakup, corrosion, impairment, discoloration, reduction, wear and tear, falling off, failing, pejority; see also **sense 2.** — *Ant.* IMPROVEMENT, increase, preservation.
**2.** [Decomposition] — *Syn.* disintegration, putrefaction, corruption, adulteration, rot, rottenness, breakup, spoilage, carrion, putrescence, putridity, decrepitude,

mold, rust, corrosion, oxidation, dry rot, black rot, caries, spur, atrophy, emaciation, blight, marasmus, gangrene, mildew, biodegredation, deliquescence, ravages of time*, way of all flesh*; see also **sense 1.** — *Ant.* GROWTH, germination, freshness.

**decay,** *v.* — *Syn.* spoil, blight, go to seed, fade, be impaired, rot, wither, molder, crumble, disintegrate, break down, turn, break up, curdle, discolor, mold, mildew, dry-rot, rust, corrupt, corrode, putrefy, putresce, decompose, biodegrade, deliquesce, degenerate, become tainted, become contaminated, collapse, shrivel, atrophy, pejorate, suppurate, decline, depreciate, deteriorate, worsen, sink, go bad, fall off, fall apart, fall into decay, fall away, fall to pieces, slump, fade away, wear away, erode, eat away, get worse, lessen, fail, sicken, weaken, waste away, go from bad to worse, touch bottom, slow down, thin out, go to rack and ruin, fall on evil days, go to the dogs*, hit the skids*, go to pot*, die on the vine*, reach a new low*, reach the depths*, hit rock bottom*; see also **die 1, 2, 3.** — *Ant.* CLEAN, refresh, purify.

---

*SYN.* — **decay** implies gradual, often natural, deterioration from a normal or sound condition /his teeth have begun to *decay*/; **rot** refers to the decay of organic, esp. vegetable, matter, caused by bacteria, fungi, etc. /*rotting* apples/; **putrefy** suggests the offensive, foul-smelling rotting of animal matter /bodies *putrefying* in the fields/; **spoil** is the common informal word for the decay of foods /fish *spoils* quickly in summer/; **molder** suggest a slow, progressive, crumbling decay /old buildings *molder* away/; **disintegrate** implies the breaking up of something into parts or fragments so that the wholeness of the original is destroyed /the sunken ship gradually *disintegrated*/; **decompose** suggests the breaking up or separation of something into its component elements /a *decomposing* chemical compound/: it is also a somewhat euphemistic substitute for **rot** and **putrefy**

---

**decayed,** *modif.* — *Syn.* decomposed, putrid, putrefied; see **rotten 1, 2, spoiled.**

**decaying,** *modif.* — *Syn.* rotting, crumbling, spoiling, decomposing, breaking down, breaking up, wasting away, falling, deteriorating, rusting, oxidizing, eroding, wearing away, disintegrating, worsening, collapsing, tumbling down, falling to pieces; see also **dying 2, rotten 1, 3.**

**decease,** *v.* — *Syn.* die, cease, perish, expire; see **die 1.**
*See Synonym Study at* DIE.

**deceased,** *modif.* — *Syn.* dead, departed, late, defunct; see **dead 1.**
*See Synonym Study at* DEAD.

**deceit,** *n.* **1.** [Deceitfulness] — *Syn.* deception, fraud, trickery, duplicity; see **deception 1, dishonesty.**
**2.** [Deceitful action] — *Syn.* sham, fraud, lie, artifice; see **deception 1, trick 1.**

**deceitful,** *modif.* — *Syn.* dishonest, tricky, cunning, insincere; see **dishonest 1, 2.**
*See Synonym Study at* DISHONEST.

**deceive,** *v.* — *Syn.* mislead, delude, swindle, trick, cheat, outwit, fool, rob, defraud, practice deceit, not play fair, victimize, hoax, betray, beguile, take advantage of, impose upon, entrap, ensnare, hoodwink, play one false, gull, cozen, dupe, lead astray, bamboozle, fleece, beguile out of, humbug, circumvent, get around, lie to, falsify accounts, pass off, con*, put on*, scam*, take for*, get around*, finagle*, palm off*, cross up*, buffalo*, nick*, bilk*, gouge*, clip*, skin*, beat*, fake*, gyp*, beat out of*, put on*, burn*, chisel*, sell out*, double-cross*, hook\*, pull a fast one\*, pull something\*, fake out\*, play for a sucker\*, shake down\*, make a sucker out of\*, snooker\*, hustle\*, take to the cleaners\*, pull a quickie\*, sell a gold brick to\*, screw out of\*, drive to the wall\*, do out of\*, string along\*, take for a ride\*, snow\*, put one over on\*, take in\*, sail under false colors\*, take in\*, rope in\*, lead on\*, jive\*, fast-talk\*, sell\*, pull the wool over one's eyes\*, flimflam\*, murphy\*, give someone the runaround\*, dress up\*, trip up\*, bleed white\*, beguile out of\*, do in\*, pack the deal\*, do up brown\*, hit below the belt\*, come over\*, lead astray\*, higgle the market\*, get around\*, euchre out of\*, butter up\*, let in\*, play upon\*, make a monkey of\*; see also **cheat, lie** 1.

*SYN.* — **deceive** implies the often deliberate misrepresentation of facts by words, actions, etc., frequently to further one's ends *[deceived* into buying fraudulent stocks]; to **mislead** is to cause to follow the wrong course or to err in conduct or action, although not always by deliberate deception *[misled* by the sign into going to the wrong floor]; **beguile** implies the use of wiles and enticing prospects in deceiving or misleading *[beguiled* by promises of a fortune]; to **delude** is to fool someone so completely that what is false is accepted as being true; **betray** implies a breaking of faith while appearing to be loyal

**deceived,** *modif.* **1.** [Led astray] — *Syn.* duped, gulled, fooled, humbugged, hoaxed, trifled with, culled, snared, trapped, lured, decoyed, baited, played, hoodwinked, betrayed, circumvented, thwarted, bamboozled, victimized, sucked in\*, conned\*, hauled for a sucker\*, taken\*, had\*. — *Ant.* TRUSTED, dealt with openly, informed.
**2.** [Led into an erroneous conclusion] — *Syn.* deluded, misled, mistaken, misapprehending; see **mistaken** 1.
**3.** [Cheated] — *Syn.* defrauded, imposed upon, swindled; see **cheated.**
**deceiver,** *n.* — *Syn.* conniver, swindler, impostor; see **cheat** 1.
**December,** *n.* — *Syn.* winter month, Christmas season, the holidays, holiday season, last month of the year; see also **Christmas, month, winter.**
**decency,** *n.* — *Syn.* decorum, propriety, seemliness, respectability; see **behavior** 1, **honesty** 1, **propriety** 1, **virtue** 1.
*See Synonym Study at* DECORUM.
**decent,** *modif.* **1.** [In accordance with common standards] — *Syn.* seemly, suitable, fitting; see **conventional** 2, **fit** 1.
**2.** [In accordance with the moral code] — *Syn.* nice, decorous, honorable, proper, seemly, chaste, modest, continent, pure, ethical, fair, generous, kind, obliging, accommodating, gracious, reserved, free from obscenity, spotless, respectable, prudent, *comme il faut* (French), mannerly, virtuous, delicate, stainless, clean, trustworthy, upright, worthy, untarnished, unblemished, straight; see also **honest** 1, **moral** 1.
**3.** [Moderately good] — *Syn.* satisfactory, adequate, average; see **common** 1, **fair** 2.
*See Synonym Study at* CHASTE.
**deception,** *n.* **1.** [The practice of deceiving] — *Syn.* trickery, double-dealing, deceit, dishonesty, fraud, chicanery, subterfuge, duplicity, mendacity, untruth, duplery, insincerity, indirection, craftiness, circumvention, juggling, defraudation, treachery, treason, betrayal, pretense, disinformation, falsehood, trickiness, trumpery, beguilement, cozenage, humbug, hypocrisy, lying, sophism, deceitfulness, equivocation, prevarication, cunning, artifice, guile, misleading, de-

ceiving, imposture, imposition, bamboozlement, snow job\*, skullduggery\*, flimflam\*, blarney\*, hanky-panky\*; see also **dishonesty, hypocrisy.** — *Ant.* HONESTY, frankness, sincerity.
**2.** [A deceptive act] — *Syn.* hoax, swindle, fraud; see **trick** 1.

*SYN.* — **deception** is applied to anything that deceives, whether by design or illusion; **fraud** suggests deliberate deception in dishonestly depriving a person of property, rights, etc.; **subterfuge** suggests an artifice or stratagem used to hide one's true objective, to evade something, or to gain some end; **trickery** implies the use of tricks or ruses in deceiving others; **chicanery** implies the use of clever but tricky talk or action, esp. in legal actions

**deceptive,** *modif.* **1.** [Misleading] — *Syn.* unreliable, ambiguous, illusory; see **false** 2, 3.
**2.** [Dishonest] — *Syn.* deceitful, tricky, lying; see **dishonest** 1, 2.
**decide,** *v.* — *Syn.* settle, settle upon, fix upon, determine, judge, conclude, resolve, adjudge, adjudicate, mediate, conciliate, arbitrate, compromise, award, choose, elect, rule, vote, poll, form a resolution, settle in one's mind, make a decision, come to a conclusion, form an opinion, form a judgment, make up one's mind, make a selection, select, pick, make one's choice, commit oneself, draw a conclusion, come to an agreement, arrive at a conclusion, cast the die, fix on, have the final word, clinch; see also **resolve** 1. — *Ant.* DELAY, hesitate, hedge.

*SYN.* — **decide** implies the bringing to an end of vacillation, doubt, dispute, etc. by making up one's mind as to an action, course, or judgment; **determine** in addition suggests that the form, character, function, scope, etc. of something are precisely fixed *[the club decided on a lecture series and appointed a committee to determine the speakers, the dates, etc.];* **settle** stresses finality in a decision, often one arrived at by arbitration, and implies the termination of all doubt or controversy; to **conclude** is to decide after careful investigation or reasoning; **resolve** implies either finding a solution to a problem *[to resolve a longing-standing issue]* or a firmness of intention to carry through a decision *[he resolved to lose 10 pounds]*

**decided,** *modif.* **1.** [Determined] — *Syn.* settled, decided upon, arranged for; see **determined** 1.
**2.** [Certain] — *Syn.* emphatic, determined, clear; see **certain** 3, **definite** 1, **emphatic** 1, **resolute** 2.
**decidedly,** *modif.* **1.** [In a decided manner] — *Syn.* strongly, determinedly, emphatically; see **firmly** 2, **vigorously.**
**2.** [Surely] — *Syn.* certainly, definitely, unquestionably; see **surely.**
**deciding,** *modif.* — *Syn.* determining, decisive, crucial, conclusive; see **conclusive, crucial, important** 1.
**decipher,** *v.* — *Syn.* decode, interpret, read, make clear, translate, spell, unravel, reveal, unfold, elucidate, solve, interpret by use of a key, find the key to, disentangle, expound, render, construe, explain, unscramble, decrypt, make out, figure out, make head or tail of\*, break (a code)\*, crack\*, dope out\*; see also **solve, translate** 1. — *Ant.* MISUNDERSTAND, fail to solve, misconstrue.
**decision,** *n.* **1.** [The act of deciding] — *Syn.* determination, arrangement, settlement; see **choice** 1, **judgment** 2.
**2.** [A statement involving a decision, sense 1] — *Syn.*

conclusion, declaration, verdict, ruling; see **judg-ment** 3, **resolution** 2, **verdict.**

3. [Firmness of mind] — *Syn.* decisiveness, firmness, resolution; see **determination** 2.

**decisive,** *modif.* **1.** [Crucial] — *Syn.* final, definitive, determining, absolute; see **certain** 3, **conclusive, crucial.**

2. [Showing determination or firmness] — *Syn.* firm, forceful, unhesitating; see **certain** 1, **emphatic** 1, **resolute** 2.

**deck,** *n.* **1.** [The floor of a ship] — *Syn.* level, flight, story, layer, tier, forecastle, fo'c'sle★, topside; see also **floor** 1, 2.
Specific decks of a ship include: upper, lower, main, promenade, hurricane, top, fore, after, poop, poop royal.
2. [Cards sufficient for a game] — *Syn.* pack, set, pinochle deck, playing cards, tarots, the cards, devil's picture book★, book of four kings★; see also **card.**

**on deck★** — *Syn.* prepared, available, on hand; see **ready** 2.

**deck,** *v.* **1.** [To decorate] — *Syn.* ornament, adorn, trim, garnish; see **decorate.**

2. [★To knock (someone) down] — *Syn.* beat, strike down, punch, floor; see **hit** 1.

**declaim,** *v.* — *Syn.* proclaim, speak, recite, harangue; see **address** 2, **recite** 1.

**declamation,** *n.* **1.** [Discourse] — *Syn.* lecture, address, oration, tirade; see **speech** 3.

2. [Ranting] — *Syn.* haranguing, spouting, oratory, speechmaking, speechifying★; see also **wordiness.**

**declamatory,** *modif.* **1.** [Eloquent] — *Syn.* rhetorical, elocutionary, formal; see **fluent** 2, **oratorical.**

2. [Pompous] — *Syn.* bombastic, windy, stuffy; see **bombastic, oratorical, verbose.**

**declaration,** *n.* **1.** [An assertion] — *Syn.* announcement, avowal, statement, formal assertion, utterance, information, notification, affirmation, presentation, exposition, communication, disclosure, allegation, contention, explanation, revelation, answer, advertisement, saying, report, testimony, oath, expression, profession, admission, confession, enunciation, attestation, promulgation, remark, claim, protestation, acknowledgment; see also **announcement** 1. — *Ant.* DENIAL, negation, equivocation.

2. [A formal statement] — *Syn.* proclamation, profession, affirmation, manifesto, public announcement, pronouncement, pronunciamento, decree, edict, document, bulletin, bill, article, publication, broadcast, confirmation, ultimatum, notice, resolution, affidavit, testimony, charge, indictment, allegation, deposition, declaration of war, code, canon, bill of rights, constitution, plea, demurrer, creed, credo, article of faith, gospel, testament; see also **announcement** 2, **communication** 2. — *Ant.* RETRACTION, repudiation, recantation.

3. [The act of announcing] — *Syn.* notification, expression, proclamation; see **announcement** 1, **communication** 1.

**declaratory,** *modif.* — *Syn.* declarative, enunciatory, demonstrative; see **descriptive, explanatory.**

**declare,** *v.* **1.** [To speak formally or emphatically] — *Syn.* assert, announce, pronounce, proclaim, publish, claim, tell, state, say, affirm, maintain, aver, avow, attest, testify, certify, repeat, insist, contend, advance, allege, argue, demonstrate, propound, promulgate, issue a statement, put forward, set forth, stress, cite, inform, report, be positive, utter with conviction, advocate, bring forward, vouch, avouch, state emphatically, proclaim, broadcast, air, acknowledge, reaffirm, reassert, reassure,

asseverate, enunciate, profess, maintain, protest, disclose, divulge, reveal, give out, impart, assure, swear, submit, hold, warrant★; see also **report** 1, **say.** — *Ant.* HIDE, equivocate, withhold.

2. [To admit to one's possessions] — *Syn.* make a statement, confess, reveal, swear, manifest, disclose, represent, convey, indicate, state, name, notify; see also **list** 1. — *Ant.* DENY, contradict, conceal.

---

*SYN.* — **declare** implies making something known openly by an explicit or clear statement, often one expressed formally /he *declared* his intention to run for office/; to **announce** is to make something of interest known publicly or officially, esp. something of the nature of news /to *announce* a sale/; to **publish** is to make known through a medium that reaches the general public, now esp. the medium of printing; **proclaim** implies official, formal announcement, made with the greatest possible publicity, of something of great moment or significance /"*Proclaim* liberty throughout all the land"/ See also Synonym Study at ASSERT.

---

**declared,** *modif.* — *Syn.* asserted, stated, affirmed; see **announced.**

**declare oneself,** *v.* — *Syn.* make an announcement, make a pronouncement, take a stand, assert oneself; see **advertise** 1, **declare** 1.

**declaring,** *modif.* — *Syn.* noting, remarking, asserting; see **saying.**

**decline,** *n.* — *Syn.* deterioration, dissolution, lessening, slump; see **decay** 1, **drop** 2.

**decline,** *v.* **1.** [To refuse] — *Syn.* reject, turn down, beg to be excused, send regrets; see **refuse.**

2. [To decrease] — *Syn.* diminish, wane, dwindle, fade; see **decrease** 1.

3. [To sink slowly] — *Syn.* descend, dip, droop, settle; see **descend** 1, **lean** 1, **sink** 1.

4. [To deteriorate] — *Syn.* fail, sink, degenerate, backslide; see **decay, weaken** 1.
*See Synonym Study at* REFUSE.

**declivity,** *n.* — *Syn.* slope, declination, descent; see **inclination** 5.

**decompose,** *v.* — *Syn.* decay, rot, crumble, break up; see **decay, disintegrate** 1.
*See Synonym Study at* DECAY.

**decomposition,** *n.* — *Syn.* dissolution, breakdown, disintegration; see **decay** 1, 2.

**decontaminate,** *v.* — *Syn.* disinfect, purify, sterilize; see **clean.**

**decor,** *n.* — *Syn.* decoration, decorative scheme, furnishings; see **decoration** 1, **furniture.**

**decorate,** *v.* — *Syn.* adorn, beautify, ornament, embellish, bedeck, deck, garnish, trim, furnish, paint, color, renovate, redecorate, refurbish, enrich, brighten, gild, burnish, enhance, festoon, illuminate, spangle, dress up, trick out, array, emblazon, elaborate, furbish, enamel, polish, varnish, chase, grace, finish, bejewel, encrust, emboss, embroider, beribbon, bedizen, make more beautiful, add the finishing touches, perfect, put up decorations, fix up, deck out★, pretty up★, spruce up★, gussy up★.

---

*SYN.* — **decorate** implies the addition of something to render attractive what would otherwise be plain or bare /to *decorate* a wall with pictures/; **adorn** is used of that which adds to the beauty of something by gracing it with its own beauty /roses *adorned* her hair/; **ornament** is used with reference to accessories that enhance the appearance /a crown *ornamented* with jewels/; **embellish** suggests the addition of something highly ornamental or ostentatious for effect; to **beautify** is to lend beauty to, or heighten the beauty of /to plant trees to *beautify* the neighborhood/; **bedeck** emphasizes the addition of showy things /*bedecked* with jewelry/

**decorated,** *modif.* — *Syn.* adorned, ornamented, embellished; see **elaborate** 1, **ornate** 1.

**decoration,** *n.* **1.** [The act of decorating] — *Syn.* adornment, ornamentation, embellishment, enrichment, gilding, painting, patterning, embossing, redecoration, interior decoration, interior design, furnishing, decor, refurbishing, beautification, festooning, wreathing, trimming, designing, improvement, bedizenment, bedecking, garnishment, enhancement, decking out, illumination, illustration. — *Ant.* DESTRUCTION, demolition, denuding.
**2.** [Something used for decorating] — *Syn.* ornament, embellishment, trim, trimming, design, adornment, accessory, accent, detail, knickknack, tinsel, embroidery, thread work, lace, ribbon, braid, gilt, paint, color, frippery, frill, ruffle, flounce, furbelow, edging, fringe, curlicue, scroll, appliqué, wreath, festoon, glass, parquetry, flourish, tooling, inlay, figure work, cockade, spangle, sequin, bead, garniture, finery, fretwork, filigree, arabesque, plaque, extravagance, gingerbread; see also **embroidery** 1, **jewelry, knickknack, trimming** 1. — *Ant.* SIMPLICITY, plainness, severity.
**3.** [An insignia of honor] — *Syn.* citation, award, emblem, mention, medal, ribbon, badge, cross, laurels; see also **emblem.**
Decorations include — *United States:* Congressional Medal of Honor, Distinguished Service Medal, Bronze Star, Distinguished Service Cross, Air Force Cross, Navy Cross, Distinguished Flying Cross, Silver Star, Legion of Merit, Order of the Purple Heart, Meritorious Service; *Great Britain:* Military Cross, Distinguished Conduct Medal, Victoria Cross, Distinguished Service Order, Military Medal, Distinguished Flying Cross, Cross of St. George; *France:* Medal of French Recognition, Médaille Militaire, Croix de Guerre; *Belgium:* Croix de Guerre, Military Cross, Medal of King Albert; *Italy:* Medal for Valor, Cross of Merit; *Germany:* Iron Cross; *Russia:* Order of Lenin, Order of Suvarov; *Japan:* Supreme Order of the Chrysanthemum, Order of the Golden Kite, Grand Cordon of the Rising Sun with Paulownia Flowers.

**decorative,** *modif.* — *Syn.* ornamental, embellishing, beautifying, florid; see **beautiful** 1, **ornamental** 1.

**decorous,** *modif.* — *Syn.* correct, becoming, proper, seemly; see **conventional** 2, **polite** 1.

**decorum,** *n.* — *Syn.* etiquette, propriety, dignity, seemliness, correctness, decency, decorousness, deportment, gentility, protocol, good form, good behavior, good taste, mannerliness, respectability; see also **behavior** 1.

**SYN.** — **decorum** implies politeness, formality, or even stiffness in rules of conduct or behavior established as suitable to the circumstances /levity not in keeping with *decorum*/; **decency** implies observance of the requirements of modesty, good taste, etc. /have the *decency* to thank her/; **propriety** suggests conformity with conventional standards of proper or correct behavior, manners, etc. /his offensive language oversteps the bounds of *propriety*/; **dignity** implies conduct in keeping with

one's position or one's self-respect; **etiquette** refers to the forms established by convention or social arbiters for behavior in polite society

**decoy,** *n.* — *Syn.* imitation, bait, lure, fake; see **attraction** 2, **camouflage** 1, **trick** 1.

**decoy,** *v.* — *Syn.* lure, bait, trap; see **deceive, fascinate, seduce, tempt.**
*See Synonym Study at* TEMPT.

**decrease,** *n.* — *Syn.* shrinkage, lessening, abatement; see **contraction** 1, **discount, drop** 2, **reduction** 1.
**on the decrease** — *Syn.* decreasing, declining, waning; see **lessening.**

**decrease,** *v.* **1.** [To grow less] — *Syn.* lessen, diminish, decline, abate, modify, wane, deteriorate, degenerate, dwindle, be consumed, sink, settle, lighten, slacken, ebb, lower, melt away, moderate, subside, shrink, contract, recede, shrivel up, depreciate, soften, quiet, narrow down, droop, waste, fade, fade away, run low, weaken, crumble, let up, dry up, slow down, calm down, burn away, burn down, smooth out, die away, die down, lose its edge, wither away, decay, drop off, taper off, tail off, devaluate, evaporate, fall down, fall away, fall off, slack off, wear off, wear away, wear out, wear down, wind down, rev down★, slump★; see also **contract** 1. — *Ant.* GROW, increase, multiply.
**2.** [To make less] — *Syn.* reduce, lessen, lower, check, curb, restrain, quell, tame, mollify, dampen, compose, hush, still, palliate, sober, pacify, allay, blunt, qualify, tranquilize, curtail, subtract, render less, abridge, abbreviate, downsize, condense, shorten, minimize, diminish, slash, attenuate, dilute, retrench, shave, pare, prune, truncate, deplete, abate, mitigate, modify, make brief, digest, limit, level, deflate, compress, contract, strip, thin, bleed, make smaller, devaluate, devalue, clip, abstract, summarize, epitomize, sum up, lighten, trim, rake off, level off, take from, take off, roll back, hold down, mark down, scale down, boil down, let up, cut off, cut down, cut short, cut back, strike off, deduct, knock off★; see also **compress, contract** 2. — *Ant.* INCREASE, expand, augment.

**SYN.** — **decrease** and **dwindle** suggest a growing gradually smaller in bulk, size, volume, or number, but **dwindle** emphasizes a marked wasting away to the point of disappearance /his hopes *decreased* as his fortune *dwindled* away to nothing/; **lessen** is equivalent to **decrease,** except that it does not imply any particular rate of decline /his influence *lessened* overnight/; **diminish** emphasizes subtraction from the whole by some external agent /disease had *diminished* their ranks/; **reduce** implies a lowering, or bringing down /to *reduce* prices/

**decree,** *n.* — *Syn.* edict, pronouncement, proclamation, order; see **declaration** 2, **judgment** 3.

**decree,** *v.* — *Syn.* proclaim, announce, pronounce, ordain; see **command** 1, **declare** 1.

**decrepit,** *modif.* — *Syn.* infirm, feeble, dilapidated, frail; see **old** 1, 2, **weak** 1, 2.
*See Synonym Study at* WEAK.

**decrepitude,** *n.* — *Syn.* feebleness, infirmity, dilapidation; see **age** 2, **decay** 1, **weakness** 1.

**decry,** *v.* — *Syn.* criticize, depreciate, discredit, denounce; see **censure, depreciate** 2.
*See Synonym Study at* DEPRECIATE.

**dedicate,** *v.* **1.** [To consecrate] — *Syn.* sanctify, hallow, anoint; see **bless** 3.
**2.** [To set apart for special use] — *Syn.* devote, apply, give, appropriate, set aside, surrender, allot, consign,

commit, restrict, apportion, assign, give over to, donate.

---

*SYN.* — **dedicate** is to set apart or assign something, as in a formal rite, to some serious, often sacred, purpose [to *dedicate* a temple, to *dedicate* oneself to painting]; to **devote** is to give up or apply oneself or something with the seriousness or earnestness evoked by a formal vow [to *devote* one's life to a cause]; to **consecrate** is to set apart for some religious or holy use [to *consecrate* ground for a church]; **hallow**, a stronger word, suggests an intrinsic holiness in the thing set apart [to *hallow* the Sabbath]

---

**dedication,** *n.* **1.** [The act of dedicating] — *Syn.* consecration, sanctification, inscription; see **consecration.**
**2.** [Wholehearted devotion] — *Syn.* commitment, devotedness, allegiance; see **devotion.**
**deduce,** *v.* — *Syn.* infer, conclude, reason, gather; see **assume** 1, **infer** 1, **understand** 1.
*See Synonym Study at* INFER.
**deducible,** *modif.* — *Syn.* inferable, consequent, following; see **logical** 1, **provable.**
**deduct,** *v.* — *Syn.* take away, take from, diminish, subtract; see **decrease** 2.
**deduction,** *n.* **1.** [The act of deducing] — *Syn.* inferring, concluding, reasoning; see **thought** 1.
**2.** [A conclusion] — *Syn.* result, answer, inference, corollary; see **judgment** 3, **opinion** 1.
**3.** [A reduction] — *Syn.* subtraction, abatement, decrease, write-off; see **discount, reduction** 1.
**deed,** *n.* **1.** [An action] — *Syn.* act, commission, accomplishment, feat; see **action** 2.
**2.** [Legal title to real property] — *Syn.* document, release, agreement, instrument, charter, title, title deed, record, certificate, voucher, indenture, warranty, lease; see also **record** 1, **security** 2.
**deem,** *v.* — *Syn.* judge, assume, consider, regard; see **believe** 1, **consider** 2, **think** 1.
**deep,** *modif.* **1.** [Situated or extending far down] — *Syn.* low, below, beneath, profound, bottomless, submerged, subterranean, submarine, inmost, deep-seated, rooted, deep-rooted, abysmal, extending far downward, fathomless, sunk, deep-set, subaqueous, immersed, dark, dim, unfathomed, impenetrable, buried, inward, underground, underwater, downreaching, of great depth, depthless, immeasurable, yawning; see also **under** 1. — *Ant.* SHALLOW, near the surface, surface.
**2.** [Extending laterally or vertically] — *Syn.* far, wide, broad, yawning, penetrating, distant, thick, fat, spread out, to the bone*, up to the hilt*; see also **broad** 1, **extensive** 1, **long** 1. — *Ant.* NARROW, thin, shallow.
**3.** [Strongly felt] — *Syn.* intense, heartfelt, sincere, profound; see **intense.**
**4.** [*Difficult to penetrate or understand] — *Syn.* profound, abstruse, mysterious, recondite; see **difficult** 2, **profound** 2.
**5.** [Low in pitch] — *Syn.* bass, deep-toned, sonorous, rumbling; see **bass.**
*See Synonym Study at* BROAD.
**go off the deep end*** — *Syn.* **1.** go to extremes, go too far, lose one's good sense, rant; see **overdo** 1, **rage.**
**2.** have a breakdown, lose control, become irresponsible, become insane; see **crack up** 2.
**in deep water** — *Syn.* in trouble, in difficulty, having trouble, suffering; see **in trouble** 1 at **trouble.**
**deepen,** *v.* **1.** [To strengthen] — *Syn.* intensify,

heighten, expand, extend; see **develop** 1, **increase** 1, **intensify.**
**2.** [To make deeper] — *Syn.* dig out, dig down, scrape out, hollow; see **dig** 1.
**deeply,** *modif.* — *Syn.* profoundly, genuinely, intensely; see **sincerely, strongly, very.**
**deer,** *n.* — *Syn.* doe, buck, fawn, stag, roe, hind, hart, pricket, venison, *cervus* (Latin).
Types of deer include: American elk, wapiti, European elk, Chinese water deer, African water deerlet, moose, moose deer, western moose, caribou, reindeer, musk deer, Japanese deer, sika, roebuck, red, muntjac, fallow, mule, blacktail, Barbary, spotted, Virginia, white-tailed, tufted, swamp, spotted, Pampas, Persian, Pudu, Philippine, axis, hog deer.
**deface,** *v.* — *Syn.* disfigure, scratch, mutilate, efface; see **cancel** 1, **damage** 1, **destroy** 1.
**defacement,** *n.* — *Syn.* mutilation, impairment, disfigurement, vandalism; see **damage** 1, 2.
**de facto,** *modif.* — *Syn.* actual, tangible, existing, in fact; see **real** 2.
**defamation,** *n.* — *Syn.* slander, libel, calumny, vilification; see **lie** 1.
**defamatory,** *modif.* — *Syn.* slanderous, libelous, abusive; see **opprobrious** 1, 2.
**defame,** *v.* — *Syn.* traduce, besmirch, malign; see **slander.**
**default,** *n.* — *Syn.* failure, lack, delinquency, dereliction, omission, error, failure to act, inaction, failure to pay, nonpayment, oversight, neglect, negligence, shortcoming, want, inadequacy, insufficiency, failure to appear, lapse, fault, nonfeasance, nonfulfillment, arrears, arrearage; see also **omission** 1. — *Ant.* discharge, fulfillment, payment.
**in default of** — *Syn.* lacking, insufficient, failing, in the absence of; see **wanting** 1.
**defaulter,** *n.* — *Syn.* delinquent, derelict, defalcator, insolvent; see **debtor, delinquent.**
**defeat,** *n.* **1.** [A state of being worsted] — *Syn.* loss, failure, downfall, disappointment; see sense 2, **disappointment** 2, **failure** 1, **loss** 1.
**2.** [Defeat in war] — *Syn.* repulse, reverse, rebuff, conquest, rout, overthrow, subjugation, subduing, vanquishment, destruction, breakdown, collapse, downfall, extermination, annihilation, crushing, check, trap, ambush, breakthrough, encirclement, withdrawal, pincer movement, setback, stalemate, ruin, blow, loss, fall, slaughter, butchery, massacre, debacle, Waterloo; see also sense 3; **destruction** 1. — *Ant.* TRIUMPH, VICTORY, conquest.
**3.** [Defeat in personal encounters and sport] — *Syn.* beating, whipping, thrashing, fall, count, drubbing, repulse, comedown, upset, frustration, checkmate, shutout, knockout, licking*, battering*, pasting*, trouncing*, walloping*, whaling*, thumping*, scalping*, trimming*, cropper*, black eye*, dud*, shellacking*, clobbering*, creaming*, slaughter*, massacre*, hiding*, whitewashing*, lacing*, KO*, no go*, the old one-two*; see also sense 2. — *Ant.* TRIUMPH, VICTORY, SUCCESS.
**defeat,** *v.* **1.** [To get the better of another] — *Syn.* master, baffle, surmount, best, worst, undo, block, thwart, disconcert, frustrate, balk, spoil, nullify, neutralize, quell, subdue, overpower, crush, break, subjugate, vanquish, get the best of, triumph over, beat down, foil, outwit, puzzle, disappoint, contravene, circumvent, cross, checkmate, outargue, refute, outdo, overturn, rebut, expose, silence, overmatch, nonplus, counterplot, disprove, put an end to, invalidate, cast down, scatter to the

winds, reduce to silence, be too much for, give the *coup de gráce* to, give a setback to, take the wind out of one's sails\*, stump\*, steamroller\*, have by the short hairs\*, lay by the heels\*, cook one's goose\*, put down\*, euchre\*; see also senses 2, 3; **confute, win** 1. — *Ant.* YIELD, give up, concede.

**2.** [To worst in war] — *Syn.* overcome, vanquish, conquer, rout, entrap, subdue, overrun, prevail over, overthrow, subjugate, crush, smash, drive off, discomfit, annihilate, overwhelm, scatter, repulse, halt, reduce, outflank, finish off, encircle, slaughter, butcher, outmaneuver, ambush, repel, demolish, parry, sack, bomb, torpedo, sink, shipwreck, drown, swamp, countermine, put to flight, split up, wipe out, decimate, obliterate, roll back, outgeneral, mop up\*, chew up\*, mow down\*, trample in the dust\*, trample under foot\*, drive to the wall\*; see also senses 1, 3; **destroy** 1, **ravage.** — *Ant.* YIELD, give up, surrender.

**3.** [To worst in sport or in personal combat] — *Syn.* beat, overpower, outplay, win, knock out, throw, floor, pummel, pound, flog, outhit, outrun, outjump, thrash, upset, edge out\*, nose out\*, shade\*, lay low\*, skin\*, drub\*, trim\*, lick\*, wallop\*, trounce\*, shellac\*, whip\*, cream\*, clobber\*, whomp\*, zap\*, clean up on\*, beat up\*, take\*, KO\*, scalp\*, skin alive\*, run roughshod over\*, snooker\*, put down\*, take to the cleaners\*, beat the socks off of\*, beat the pants off of\*, pulverize\*, plow under\*, smear\*, massacre\*, make mincemeat out of\*, mop the floor with\*, goose-egg\*, hang a win on\*, blank\*, shut out\*, skunk\*, snow under\*; see also senses 1, 2; **beat** 2. — *Ant.* SUFFER, be defeated, fail.

**defeated,** *modif.* — *Syn.* beaten, crushed, overcome, conquered; see **beaten** 1.

**defecate,** *v.* — *Syn.* move (one's) bowels, void, excrete, pass; see **excrete.**

**defecation,** *n.* — *Syn.* elimination, excretion, expurgation, passing off; see **excrement, excretion** 1.

**defect,** *n.* **1.** [A lack of something needed] — *Syn.* deficiency, shortage, deficit; see **lack** 1, 2.

**2.** [A faulty part] — *Syn.* imperfection, flaw, blemish, drawback, shortcoming, fault, spot, stain, taint, speck, mark, weak point, break, rift, scratch, unsoundness, frailty, gap, twist, crack, check, discoloration, hole, knot, foible, vice, failing, sin, injury, birthmark, blot, scar, marring, deformity, demerit, blotch, weakness, error, patch, seam, mistake, rough spot, blindness, infirmity, bug\*, glitch\*, blind spot\*; see also **blemish.**

---

*SYN.* — **defect** implies a lack of something essential to completeness or perfection *[a defect* in vision*]*; an **imperfection** is any faulty detail that detracts from perfection *[minor imperfections* of style*]*; a **blemish** is a superficial or surface imperfection that mars the appearance *[skin blemishes,* a *blemish* on his record*]*; a **flaw** is an imperfection in structure or substance, such as a crack or gap, that mars the wholeness or continuity *[a flaw* in a metal bar*]*

---

**defect,** *v.* — *Syn.* fall away from, desert, forsake, change allegiance, change sides; see also **abandon** 2, **desert** 2, **leave** 1.

**defection,** *n.* **1.** [Failure] — *Syn.* failing, lack, deficiency; see **failure** 1, **lack** 1, 2.

**2.** [Desertion] — *Syn.* withdrawal, abandonment, apostasy, going over to the other side; see **desertion, disloyalty.**

**defective,** *modif.* — *Syn.* imperfect, incomplete, inadequate; see **broken** 2, **faulty, poor** 2, **unfinished** 1.

**defend,** *v.* **1.** [To keep off an enemy; *often used figura-*

tively] — *Syn.* protect, shield, guard, shelter, screen, resist, beat off, avert, fight for, withstand, cover, retain, hold, repel danger from, ward off, contend for, keep off, stave off, keep at bay, hold at bay, take evasive action, fend off, hedge, entrench, mine, resist invasion, stand on the defensive, provide air cover for; sustain a mortar attack, aerial attack, machine gun attack, etc.; fortify, garrison, convoy, escort, fence round, give an air umbrella; see also sense 2; **guard** 2. — *Ant.* YIELD, surrender, give up.

**2.** [To provide general protection] — *Syn.* safeguard, secure, maintain, uphold, preserve, espouse, champion, insure, patronize, watch, sustain, apologize for, rally to, support, house, keep, second, provide sanctuary, take in, sustain, bolster, nourish, foster, care for, compass about, cherish, guard against, look after; see also sense 1; **raise** 2, **support** 5. — *Ant.* ABANDON, leave, forsake.

**3.** [To support an accused person or thing] — *Syn.* plead, justify, bear one out, uphold, support, second, exonerate, back, back up, vindicate, advocate, aid, espouse the cause of, befriend, say in defense, be a partisan of, guarantee, endorse, warrant, prove a case, exculpate, maintain, recommend, rationalize, plead one's cause, say a good word for, argue for, speak for, stand up for, plead for, put in a good word for, apologize for, take up, go to bat for\*, cover up for\*, stick up for\*; see also **support** 2. — *Ant.* CONVICT, accuse, charge.

**defendant,** *n.* — *Syn.* the accused, defense, respondent, litigant, appellant, offender, prisoner at the bar, party; see also **prisoner.** — *Ant.* ACCUSER, complainant, plaintiff.

**defended,** *modif.* — *Syn.* protected, guarded, safeguarded; see **protected, safe** 1.

**defender,** *n.* — *Syn.* champion, supporter, protector, sponsor; see **guardian** 1, **protector.**

**defense,** *n.* **1.** [An act or means of defending] — *Syn.* resistance, protection, safeguard, aegis, preservation, security, custody, guard, shield, barrier, bumper, buffer, stand, front, backing, advocacy, support, maintenance, guardianship, the defensive, precaution, antitoxin, inoculation, excusing, apologizing, explaining, justifying, exoneration, explanation; see also **justification.** — *Ant.* OFFENSE, retaliation, aggression.

**2.** [A means or system for defending against an enemy] Means or systems of military defense include: trench, Maginot line, Siegfried line, Hindenburg line, defense in depth, bulwark, palisade, dike, stockade, machine-gun nest, bastille, bastion, fortification, fort, breastworks, chemical and biological warfare, CBW, earthworks, bunker, foxhole, redoubt, barricade, garrison, blockhouse, picket, rampart, fence, wall, embankment, scarp, citadel, fortress, armor, antiaircraft, Antiballistic Missile System, ABM, distant early warning line, DEW, Strategic Defense Initiative, SDI, Star Wars\*, camouflage, gas mask, shield, screen, helmet, barbed wire, stronghold, parapet, buttress, moat, fosse, counterattack, counterblow, rolling defense, tank trap, strong point, defense arc; see also **armor** 1, **fortification** 2, **munitions, trench.** — *Ant.* ATTACK, siege, BLITZKRIEG.

**3.** [In law, the reply of the accused] — *Syn.* denial, plea, pleading, rejoinder, answer, reply, retort, writ of mandamus, right of habeas corpus, alibi, testimony, vindication, surrejoinder, counterclaim, rebuttal, argument, assertion, case; see also **declaration** 2, **proof** 1, **statement** 1.

**4.** [An apology] — *Syn.* excuse, justification, argument; see **explanation** 2, **justification.**

**defenseless,** *modif.* — *Syn.* unprotected, helpless, vulnerable; see **dangerous** 1, **open** 4, **weak** 1, 3, 5.

**defensible,** *modif.* — *Syn.* justifiable, proper, permissible, tenable; see **excusable, fit** 1, 2, **logical** 1.

**defensive,** *modif.* — *Syn.* protective, protecting, defending, shielding, guarding, safeguarding, warding off, watchful, wary, guarded, preventive, averting, forestalling, foiling, balking, arresting, checking, frustrating, thwarting, opposing, resistive, withstanding, armored, on the defensive, in self-defense, in opposition, self-justifying, touchy, prickly, self-protective; see also **armed, irritable, unfriendly** 1. — *Ant.* AGGRESSIVE, offensive, combative.

**defensively,** *modif.* — *Syn.* suspiciously, on the defensive, in self-defense, at bay; see **carefully** 2.

**defer,** *v.* **1.** [To postpone] — *Syn.* put off, delay, shelve; see **delay** 1, **suspend** 2.

**2.** [To yield; *usually used with* to] — *Syn.* submit, obey, accede, acquiesce, concede, comply, give in, bow; see also **admit** 3, **agree to, yield** 1, 3.

*See Synonym Study at* YIELD.

**deference,** *n.* **1.** [Courteous regard] — *Syn.* respect, veneration, homage; see **honor** 1, **reverence** 1, 2.

**2.** [Obedience] — *Syn.* submission, compliance, yielding; see **docility.**

*See Synonym Study at* HONOR.

**deferential,** *modif.* — *Syn.* obeisant, respectful, submissive; see **obedient** 1, **polite** 1.

**deferment,** *n.* — *Syn.* postponement, suspension, putting off, moratorium; see **delay** 1, **pause** 1, 2.

**deferred,** *modif.* **1.** [Put off to a later date] — *Syn.* delayed, postponed, protracted, prolonged, retarded, adjourned, held up, temporized, remanded, staved off, stalled; see also **postponed.**

**2.** [To be paid in installments] — *Syn.* partial, indebted, assessed, funded, negotiated, renegotiated; see also **charged** 1.

**defiance,** *n.* — *Syn.* insubordination, rebellion, resistance, insurgence; see **disobedience.**

**in defiance of** — *Syn.* contemptuous of, notwithstanding, in spite of; see **regardless** 2.

**defiant,** *modif.* — *Syn.* resistant, insubordinate, recalcitrant, challenging; see **rebellious** 2, 3.

**deficiency,** *n.* **1.** [The state of being lacking] — *Syn.* scarcity, insufficiency, paucity; see **lack** 1.

**2.** [A lack] — *Syn.* want, need, loss; see **lack** 2.

**deficient,** *modif.* **1.** [Inadequate] — *Syn.* insufficient, skimpy, meager; see **inadequate** 1.

**2.** [Incomplete] — *Syn.* imperfect, defective, lacking, sketchy; see **unfinished** 1, **wanting** 1.

**deficit,** *n.* — *Syn.* shortage, paucity, deficiency, shortfall; see **debt** 1, **lack** 2.

**defile,** *v.* **1.** [To corrupt] — *Syn.* debase, pollute, besmirch, contaminate; see **contaminate, corrupt** 1, **dirty.**

**2.** [To violate] — *Syn.* dishonor, sully, desecrate, deflower; see **disgrace, profane, rape.**

*See Synonym Study at* CONTAMINATE.

**defilement,** *n.* — *Syn.* degradation, corruption, contamination, debasement; see **evil** 1, **pollution.**

**definable,** *modif.* — *Syn.* determinable, describable, apparent, perceptible; see **definite** 2, **obvious** 1, 2.

**define,** *v.* **1.** [To set limits] — *Syn.* delimit, demarcate, fix, settle, bound, confine, limit, outline, circumscribe, mark, set, determine, distinguish, establish, compass, encompass, delineate, mark the limits of, determine the boundaries of, fix the limits of, curb, edge, border, enclose, set bounds to, fence in, rim, encircle, hedge in, wall in, envelop, girdle, gird, belt, flank, stake out; see also **surround** 1, 2. — *Ant.* CONFUSE, distort, MIX.

**2.** [To provide a name or description] — *Syn.* describe, explain, determine, specify, characterize, entitle, ascertain, name, label, designate, individualize, differentiate, formalize, elucidate, interpret, clarify, illustrate, give the meaning of, gloss, paraphrase, annotate, represent, render precise, individuate, find out, spell out, literalize, construe, denominate, denote, expound, translate, exemplify, assign, prescribe, style, dub; see also **describe, explain, name** 1, 2. — *Ant.* MISUNDERSTAND, misconstrue, obscure.

**definite,** *modif.* **1.** [Determined with exactness] — *Syn.* fixed, exact, precise, positive, accurate, correct, decisive, absolute, clearly defined, well-defined, circumscribed, limited, bounded, strict, explicit, specific, particular, settled, determinate, decided, prescribed, restricted, assigned, unequivocal, rigorous, special, express, conclusive, formal, categorical, unerring, unimpeachable, to the point, substantially correct, beyond doubt, hard and fast; see also **certain** 3, **determined** 1. — *Ant.* OBSCURE, indefinite, inexact.

**2.** [Clear in detail] — *Syn.* sharp, distinct, visible, audible, tangible, clear, vivid, minute, unambiguous, unmistakable in meaning, straightforward, obvious, marked, plain, not vague, well-drawn, clearly defined, well-marked, well-defined, clear-cut, explicit, unmistakable, distinguishable, silhouetted, palpable, well-grounded, indubitable, undistorted, crisp, bold, ringing, severe, graphic, downright, in focus, in relief, undisguised, in plain sight, clear as day, standing out like a sore thumb*. — *Ant.* CONFUSED, vague, hazy.

**3.** [Positive] — *Syn.* certain, sure, beyond doubt, convinced; see **certain** 1, **inevitable.**

*See Synonym Study at* EXPLICIT.

**definitely,** *modif.* — *Syn.* clearly, unmistakably, unquestionably, positively; see **surely.**

**definition,** *n.* **1.** [Expressed meaning of a term] — *Syn.* meaning, explanation, description, signification, denotation, diagnosis, analogue, synonym, exposition, elucidation, rendering, drift, sense, referent, interpretation, formalization, explication, clue, individuation, exemplification, annotation, gloss, cue, key, translation, comment, paraphrase, clarification, rendition, rationale, commentary, formal statement of meaning, dictionary meaning, representation, characterization, recursive definition, expounding; see also **description** 1, **explanation** 1, 2, **meaning.** — *Ant.* NONSENSE, absurdity, error.

**2.** [The process or result of making limits clear] — *Syn.* delineation, determination, demarcation, distinctness, sharpness, clarity, encompassment, circumscription, outline, boundary, outlining, surveying; see also **clarity.** — *Ant.* CONFUSION, muddling, mixing.

**definitive,** *modif.* **1.** [Decisive] — *Syn.* conclusive, final, ultimate, absolute; see **conclusive.**

**2.** [Limiting] — *Syn.* precise, clear-cut, absolute, plain; see **definite** 1.

**3.** [Complete and accurate] — *Syn.* authoritative, reliable, exhaustive, consummate; see **authoritative** 1, 2, **classic, comprehensive.**

**deflate,** *v.* — *Syn.* collapse, let the air out, flatten, discourage; see **contract** 1, **decrease** 1, 2, **discourage** 1, **empty** 1, 2, **humble.**

*See Synonym Study at* CONTRACT.

**deflect,** *v.* — *Syn.* swerve, diverge, divert, parry; see **turn** 3, 6, **veer.**

**deflower,** *v.* — *Syn.* ravish, molest, despoil; see **rape.**

**deform,** *v.* — *Syn.* distort, disfigure, deface, injure; see **damage** 1, **distort** 3.

*See Synonym Study at* DISTORT.

**deformed,** *modif.* — *Syn.* distorted, misshapen, disfigured, crippled, misproportioned, malformed, bowed, cramped, ill-proportioned, disjointed, awry, unseemly, ill-favored, dwarfed, hunchbacked, humpbacked, warped, misconceived, maimed, mangled, knock-kneed, splayfooted, pigeon-toed, bowlegged, bandylegged, crushed, unnatural in form, unshapely, clubfooted, curved, contorted, gnarled, askew, crooked, ill-made, grotesque, lame, irregular, sway-backed, lordotic; see also **disabled, twisted** 1, **ugly** 1.— *Ant.* REGULAR, shapely, well-formed.

**deformity,** *n.* — *Syn.* malformation, deformation, disfigurement, unsightliness; see **contortion** 1, **damage** 1.

**defraud,** *v.* — *Syn.* swindle, dupe, cheat; see **cheat, deceive.**

*See Synonym Study at* CHEAT.

**defray,** *v.* — *Syn.* meet, clear, settle; see **pay** 1.

**deft,** *modif.* — *Syn.* dexterous, skilled, expert, adroit; see **able** 1, 2, **dexterous.**

*See Synonym Study at* DEXTEROUS.

**defunct,** *modif.* — *Syn.* dead, deceased, expired, no longer existing, no longer functioning; see also **dead** 1, **extinct, old-fashioned.**

*See Synonym Study at* DEAD.

**defy,** *v.* — *Syn.* resist, challenge, flout; see **dare** 2, **oppose** 1, 2.

**degeneracy,** *n.* **1.** [Deterioration] — *Syn.* degeneration, decline, decadence; see **decay** 1.

**2.** [Perversion] — *Syn.* depravity, debasement, turpitude; see **evil** 1, **perversion** 2.

**degenerate,** *modif.* — *Syn.* depraved, immoral, corrupt, perverted; see **wicked** 1, 2.

**degenerate,** *v.* — *Syn.* worsen, decline, deteriorate, fall off; see **decay, decrease** 1.

**degradation,** *n.* — *Syn.* debasement, depravity, degeneration, dishonor; see **disgrace** 1, **evil** 1.

**degrade,** *v.* **1.** [To humble] — *Syn.* demote, discredit, diminish; see **humble.**

**2.** [To corrupt] — *Syn.* debase, deprave, degenerate, deteriorate; see **corrupt** 1.

*See Synonym Study at* HUMBLE.

**degraded,** *modif.* — *Syn.* disgraced, debased, depraved; see **disgraced, wicked** 1.

**degrading,** *modif.* — *Syn.* demeaning, debasing, shameful, humiliating, disgraceful, corrupting, lowering; see also **insulting, shameful** 1, 2.

*See Synonym Study at* MEAN.

**degree,** *n.* **1.** [One in a series used for measurement] — *Syn.* measure, grade, step, mark, interval, space, measurement, gradation, size, dimension, shade, point, line, plane, step in a series, stage, level, gauge, rung, notch, term, link, tier, stair, ratio, period, stint; see also **division** 2.

**2.** [An expression of relative excellence, attainment, etc.] — *Syn.* extent, station, rank, order, quality, development, standard, height, expanse, length, potency, range, proportion, compass, quantity, amplitude, magnitude, standing, strength, reach, intensity, seriousness, scope, caliber, pitch, point, stage, sort, status, rate, primacy; see also **rank** 2, 3.

**3.** [Recognition of academic achievement] — *Syn.* distinction, title, testimony, testimonial, honor, qualification, approbation, dignity, eminence, credit, approval, credentials, dignification, baccalaureate, doctorate, honorary degree, hood, sheepskin*; see also **diploma, graduation.**

Academic degrees include: Bachelor of Arts (B.A., A.B.), Bachelor of Science (B.Sc.), Bachelor of Laws (LL.B.), Master of Arts (M.A., A.M.), Master of Science (M.Sc.), Master of Arts in Teaching (M.A.T.), Doctor of Philoso-

phy (Ph.D.), Doctor of Medicine (M.D.), Doctor of Dental Surgery (D.D.S.), Doctor of Laws (LL.D.), Doctor of Divinity (D.D.), Doctor of Education (Ed.D.), Doctor of Jurisprudence (J.D.), Bachelor of Literature (B.Litt.), Doctor of Literature (D.Litt.).

**by degrees** — *Syn.* step by step, slowly but surely, inch by inch; see **gradually.**

**to a degree** — *Syn.* somewhat, partially, to an extent; see **moderately, partly.**

**dehydrate,** *v.* — *Syn.* dry, dessicate, parch, evaporate; see **dry** 1, 2.

**deify,** *v.* — *Syn.* idolize, apotheosize, exalt, consecrate; see **revere, worship** 2.

**deign,** *v.* — *Syn.* condescend, vouchsafe, lower oneself, stoop; see **condescend, patronize** 2.

*See Synonym Study at* CONDESCEND.

**deity,** *n.* — *Syn.* divinity, god, goddess, idol; see **god** 1, 2, 3.

**dejected,** *modif.* — *Syn.* depressed, dispirited, disheartened, cast down; see **sad** 1.

*See Synonym Study at* SAD.

**dejection,** *n.* — *Syn.* despondency, sorrow, melancholy; see **depression** 2, **grief** 1, **sadness.**

**de jure,** *modif.* — *Syn.* by right, rightfully, by law; see **legally** 1.

**delay,** *n.* **1.** [Postponement] — *Syn.* deferment, adjournment, putting off, procrastination, suspension, moratorium, deferral, pause, surcease, reprieve, setback, retardation, lag, remission, prorogation, stay, stop, discontinuation, dawdling, foot-dragging, cooling-off period, holdup, holding pattern; see also **pause** 1, 2, **respite.**

**2.** [Hindrance] — *Syn.* stoppage, obstacle, obstruction; see **impediment** 1.

**delay,** *v.* **1.** [To cause a delay] — *Syn.* postpone, defer, put-off, retard, hold up, deter, hinder, hamper, clog, choke, slacken, keep, hold, protract, keep back, impede, discourage, interfere with, detain, stay, stop, withhold, lay over, arrest, check, prevent, repress, curb, obstruct, gain time, inhibit, restrict, prolong, encumber, confine, remand, prorogue, procrastinate, adjourn, block, bar, filibuster, intermit, suspend, stave off, table, shelve, pigeonhole, put aside, lay aside, lay by, push aside, slow, hang up, hang back, hold back, hold off, hold over, hold everything, be dilatory, bide one's time, arrest temporarily, impede the progress of, slow up, limit, slacken, stand off, stall, restrain, put on ice*, hold one's horses*, drag one's feet*; see also **hinder.** — *Ant.* SPEED, accelerate, encourage.

**2.** [To make a delay] — *Syn.* hesitate, slow down, dawdle, dally; see **linger** 1, **loiter, pause.**

**delayed,** *modif.* — *Syn.* held up, slowed, put off; see **late** 1, **postponed.**

**delectable,** *modif.* — *Syn.* tasty, luscious, enjoyable, delightful; see **delicious** 1, **pleasant** 2.

**delegate,** *n.* — *Syn.* representative, emissary, proxy, deputy, agent, substitute, envoy, regent, viceroy, consul, appointee, plenipotentiary, minister, surrogate, spokesperson, alternate, nominee, commissioner, ambassador, legate, member, duly elected representative, the people's choice*, stand-in*, sub*, pinch hitter*; see also **agent** 1, **representative** 1.

**delegate,** *v.* **1.** [To give authority to another] — *Syn.* authorize, commission, appoint, name, designate, accredit, nominate, select, choose, assign, cast, constitute, license, empower, deputize, depute, swear in, send as a deputy, ordain, invest, place trust in, fix upon, assign power of attorney to, elect, warrant, give one the nod*, give one the green light*, give one the go-ahead*; see also **approve** 1, **commission.** — *Ant.* DISMISS, repudiate, reject.

**2.** [To give duties to another] — *Syn.* entrust, authorize, charge, assign, give to, hold responsible for, parcel out among, send on a mission, send on an errand, transfer, relegate, shunt, devolve, shove off on*, dump on*, pass the buck*; see also **commit** 2.— *Ant.* MAINTAIN, retain, keep.

**delegation,** *n.* **1.** [The act of assigning to another] — *Syn.* assignment, giving over, appointment, nomination, trust, mandate, sending, commissioning, ordination, authorization, charge, deputization, investiture, installation, entrustment, investing with authority, deputation, empowering, referring, apportioning, submitting, transferring, transferal, consignment, conveyance, regulation, devolution; see also **appointment** 1, **installation** 1.— *Ant.* RETRACTION, abrogation, revocation.

**2.** [A group with a specific mission] — *Syn.* deputation, commission, envoys, mission; see **committee, gathering, organization** 3.

**delete,** *v.* — *Syn.* cross out, erase, destroy; see **cancel** 1, **eliminate** 1, **remove** 1.

**deleterious,** *modif.* — *Syn.* injurious, pernicious, unhealthy; see **harmful, pernicious.**

*See Synonym Study at* PERNICIOUS.

**deliberate,** *modif.* **1.** [Characterized by forethought; *said of an action*] — *Syn.* thought out, predetermined, outlined beforehand, conscious, advised, prearranged, fixed, with forethought, well-considered, cautious, studied, intentional, planned in advance, done on purpose, aforethought, willful, considered, thoughtful, purposed, purposive, planned, reasoned, pondered, judged, weighed, calculated, intended, purposeful, premeditated, voluntary, designed, cold-blooded, predeterminate, predesigned, resolved, cut-and-dried; see also **careful.**— *Ant.* INCIDENTAL, unintentional, accidental.

**2.** [Characterized by forethought; *said of persons*] — *Syn.* prudent, circumspect, sober; see **careful, judicious.**

**3.** [Slow in motion] — *Syn.* slow-moving, stolid, leisurely; see **slow** 1.

**deliberate,** *v.* — *Syn.* ponder, judge, weigh; see **consider** 3, **think** 1.

**deliberately,** *modif.* — *Syn.* resolutely, determinedly, emphatically, knowingly, meaningfully, voluntarily, consciously, on purpose, purposively, willfully, premeditatedly, in cold blood, with malice aforethought, advisedly, after mature consideration, freely, independently, without any qualms, by design, premeditatively, designed, wittingly, intentionally, purposely, advisedly, predeterminately, with intent, all things considered, studiously, with a view to, with an eye to, pointedly, to that end, with eyes wide open*; see also **carefully** 2.

**deliberation,** *n.* — *Syn.* reflection, consideration, consultation; see **discussion** 1, **thought** 1.

**delicacy,** *n.* **1.** [Fineness of texture] — *Syn.* daintiness, airiness, etherealness, transparency, fragility, flimsiness, softness, smoothness, translucency, filminess, tenuity, diaphanousness, subtlety, tenderness, exquisiteness, gracefulness; see also **lightness** 2.

**2.** [A choice food] — *Syn.* tidbit, luxury, gourmet dish, treat, dainty, morsel, sweet, savory, rarity, delight, ambrosia, nectar, party dish, sweetmeat, imported food, food out of season, *bonne bouche* (French), specialty, goody*, food for the gods*; see also **food.**

**3.** [Lack of strength, usually to resist disease] — *Syn.* frailty, debility, tenderness; see **weakness** 1.

**delicate,** *modif.* **1.** [Dainty] — *Syn.* fragile, frail, fine; see **dainty** 1.

*See Synonym Study at* DAINTY.

**2.** [Sickly] — *Syn.* susceptible, in delicate health, feeble; see **sick, weak** 1.

**3.** [Needing careful handling] — *Syn.* touchy, ticklish, sensitive, precarious; see **dangerous** 1, **unstable** 2.

**4.** [Having fine sensibilities] — *Syn.* gentle, tactful, sensitive, fastidious; see **careful, refined** 2, **tactful.**

**delicately,** *modif.* — *Syn.* deftly, skillfully, cautiously; see **carefully** 2.

**delicatessen,** *n.* **1.** [Ready-to-serve foods] .

Varieties of delicatessen food include: cold meats, cold cuts, luncheon meats, salads, cheeses, blintzes, pastries, salami, pastrami, lox, smoked salmon, bologna, turkey, ham, corned beef, roast beef, wurst, bratwurst, knockwurst, liverwurst, kielbasa, smoked meats, sausage, frankfurters, olives, sauerkraut, sauerbraten, hassenpfeffer, pickled peppers, olives, pickled fish, pickled pigs' knuckles, dill pickles, sweet pickles, kosher pickles, gherkins, caviar, lox, knishes, pirogi, anchovies, liver paste, pâté de foie gras; see also **bread** 1, **cheese, dessert, fish, fruit** 1, **hors d'oeuvre, meat, sausage, roll** 4, **roast, wine.**

**2.** [A place that sells delicatessen, sense 1] — *Syn.* deli*, grocery, *charcuterie* (French), *salumeria* (Italian); see **market** 1.

**delicious,** *modif.* **1.** [Excellent in taste] — *Syn.* tasty, delectable, luscious, savory, good, appetizing, choice, palatable, flavorful, well-prepared, well-seasoned, well-done, spicy, sweet, rich, succulent, toothsome, nice, exquisite, dainty, delicate, distinctive, ambrosial, heavenly, tempting, enticing, mouth-watering, nectareous, piquant, gourmet, epicurean, scrumptious*, yummy*, fit for a king*. — *Ant.* disgusting, unappetizing, flat.

**2.** [Very pleasant or enjoyable] — *Syn.* delightful, gratifying, pleasing; see **pleasant** 2.

**delight,** *n.* — *Syn.* enjoyment, joy, pleasure; see **happiness** 2, **pleasure** 1.

*See Synonym Study at* PLEASURE.

**delight,** *v.* **1.** [To give pleasure] — *Syn.* please, enchant, amuse, charm; see **entertain** 1, **fascinate, gladden.**

**2.** [To take pleasure; *often used with* in] — *Syn.* relish, enjoy, revel in, luxuriate in; see **like** 1.

**delighted,** *modif.* **1.** [Greatly pleased] — *Syn.* entranced, captivated, thrilled, pleasantly surprised; see **fascinated, happy** 1.

**2.** [An expression of acceptance or pleasure] — *Syn.* thank you, by all means, to be sure, of course, certainly, splendid, excellent, overwhelmed, charmed, so glad.

**delightful,** *modif.* **1.** [*Said of occasions*] — *Syn.* charming, pleasing, refreshing; see **pleasant** 2.

**2.** [*Said of persons*] — *Syn.* charming, engaging, amusing; see **pleasant** 1.

**delineate,** *v.* — *Syn.* picture, portray, outline, describe; see **describe, draw** 2.

**delineation,** *n.* **1.** [Drawing] — *Syn.* sketch, portrait, picture; see **drawing** 1, **picture** 3.

**2.** [A description] — *Syn.* account, depiction, rendition; see **description** 1, **picture** 2, **representation.**

**delinquency,** *n.* — *Syn.* dereliction, wrongdoing, misconduct; see **crime** 1, 2, **default, fault** 2.

**delinquent,** *modif.* **1.** [Lax in duty] — *Syn.* derelict, remiss, negligent, slack, behind hand, tardy, procrastinating, criminal, neglectful, faulty, shabby, guilty of misdeed, failing in duty, blameworthy, blamable, culpable, red-handed, censurable, offending, reprehensible; see also **careless** 1.— *Ant.* PUNCTUAL, punctilious, scrupulous.

**2.** [Not paid on time; *said especially of taxes*]— *Syn.* owed, back, overdue; see **due, unpaid** 1.

**delinquent,** *n.*— *Syn.* defaulter, tax evader, offender, reprobate, dawdler, slacker, bad debtor, poor risk, neglecter of duty, felon, miscreant, malefactor, law-breaker, wrongdoer, sinner, juvenile offender, juvenile delinquent, JD★, punk★, hoodlum, hood★, ganster, hoo-ligan★, troublemaker, outlaw, scamp, black sheep, fallen angel, jailbird★, welsher★, tax dodger★, deadbeat★; see also **criminal.**

**delirious,** *modif.*— *Syn.* wild, incoherent, demented, crazy; see **excited, frantic, insane** 1.

**delirium,** *n.*— *Syn.* madness, fever, hallucination, frenzy; see **excitement, insanity** 1.

*See Synonym Study at* HYSTERIA.

**deliver,** *v.* **1.** [To free]— *Syn.* set free, liberate, save; see **free** 1, **release, rescue** 2.

**2.** [To transfer]— *Syn.* pass, remit, hand over, hand in, surrender; see also **abandon** 1, **give** 1.

**3.** [To speak formally]— *Syn.* present, read, give; see **address** 2, **utter.**

**4.** [To bring to birth]— *Syn.* bring forth, be delivered of, accouche; see **produce** 1.

**5.** [To distribute]— *Syn.* allot, dispense, give out; see **distribute** 1.

**6.** [To throw]— *Syn.* pitch, hurl, fling; see **throw** 1.

**7.** [To carry]— *Syn.* transport, transfer, convey, cart; see **carry** 1.

**8.** [★To do something promised]— *Syn.* come through, produce, fulfill, meet expectations; see **achieve** 1, **per-form** 1.

*See Synonym Study at* RESCUE.

**be delivered of**— *Syn.* give birth to, bear, bring into the world; see **produce** 1.

**deliverance,** *n.*— *Syn.* rescue, release, liberation; see **freeing, rescue** 1, **salvation** 1.

**delivered,** *modif.*— *Syn.* brought, deposited, conveyed, handed over, transported, checked in, forwarded, ex-pressed, hand-delivered, mailed, dispatched, sent by messenger, sent by post, sent by express, sent by cou-rier, at the door, on the siding, in the yards, sent out by truck, trucked, laid down, dumped in one's lap★; see also **mailed, sent, shipped.**

**delivery,** *n.* **1.** [Bringing goods into another's pos-session]— *Syn.* consignment, conveyance, distribution, carting, shipment, transfer, portage, freighting, trans-mission, dispatch, commitment, entrusting, mailing, special delivery, parcel post, express, surrender, relin-quishment, handing over, transferral, cash on delivery, C.O.D., free on board, F.O.B.; see also **transporta-tion.**

**2.** [Delivery of a child]— *Syn.* birth, parturition, con-finement, lying-in, childbirth, labor, travail, giving birth, geniture, midwifery, obstetrics, accouchement, Caesarian, Caesarian section, C-section★; see also **birth** 1, **childbirth.**

**3.** [The manner of a speaker]— *Syn.* articulation, enunciation, accent, utterance, pronunciation, empha-sis, intonation, inflection, tone, diction, elocution, pres-entation; see also **diction, eloquence** 1.

**4.** [The manner in which a baseball pitcher throws] — *Syn.* control, performance, game, ball, arm, rendi-tion, hurling, offering, tossing, elbowing★, twirling★, fl-inging★, heaving★, round-arm delivery★, southpaw deliv-ery★, freak delivery★, buggy-whip delivery★.

**delude,** *v.*— *Syn.* deceive, mislead, trick, fool; see **de-ceive.**

*See Synonym Study at* DECEIVE.

**deluded,** *modif.*— *Syn.* tricked, betrayed, fooled; see **de-ceived** 1, **mistaken** 1.

**delusion,** *n.* **1.** [An illusion]— *Syn.* phantasm, halluci-nation, fancy; see **illusion** 1.

**2.** [A false belief]— *Syn.* misconception, misapprehen-sion, self-deception, fallacy; see **error** 1, **mistake** 2.

*See Synonym Study at* ILLUSION.

**deluxe,** *modif.*— *Syn.* elegant, luxurious, grand; see **ex-pensive, luxurious.**

**delve,** *v.*— *Syn.* investigate, search, probe; see **exam-ine** 1.

**demagogue,** *n.*— *Syn.* agitator, rabble-rouser, fanatic, revolutionary; see **agitator, rebel** 1, **speaker** 1.

**demand,** *n.* **1.** [A peremptory communication]— *Syn.* order, call, charge, request; see **command** 1.

**2.** [Willingness to purchase]— *Syn.* trade, request, sale, bid, need, requirement, interest, vogue, call for, rush, pursuit, search, inquiry, desire to buy, market; see also **desire** 1.— *Ant.* INDIFFERENCE, lack of interest, sales resistance.

**in demand**— *Syn.* sought after, desired, requested; see **popular** 1, **wanted.**

**on demand**— *Syn.* ready, prepared, usable, when requested, when required, when due, payable, collect, C.O.D., on call; see also **available, due.**

**demand,** *v.* **1.** [To ask]— *Syn.* charge, direct, enjoin; see **ask** 1, **command** 1.

**2.** [To require]— *Syn.* call for, oblige, necessitate; see **need, require** 2.

*See Synonym Study at* REQUIRE.

**demanding,** *modif.* **1.** [Difficult]— *Syn.* hard, taxing, troublesome; see **difficult** 1, **onerous.**

**2.** [Querulous]— *Syn.* fussy, imperious, exacting; see **critical** 2, **particular.**

**demarcate,** *v.*— *Syn.* differentiate, detach, mark off, delimit; see **define** 1, **divide** 1, **separate** 2.

**demarcation,** *n.* **1.** [Limit]— *Syn.* boundary, margin, confine, terminus; see **boundary.**

**2.** [Distinction]— *Syn.* split, differentiation, separa-tion; see **definition** 2, **distinction** 1, **division** 1.

**demeanor,** *n.*— *Syn.* behavior, deportment, manner; see **attitude** 2, **bearing** 2, **behavior** 1.

*See Synonym Study at* BEARING.

**demented,** *modif.*— *Syn.* crazy, deranged, bemused, unbalanced; see **insane** 1.

**dementia,** *n.*— *Syn.* mental deterioration, loss of one's faculties, insanity, madness; see **insanity** 1, **senility.**

*See Synonym Study at* INSANITY.

**demerit,** *n.*— *Syn.* fault, mark against one, bad mark, loss of points, loss of credit, loss of distinction; see also **defect** 2, **punishment.**

**demilitarized zone,** *n.*— *Syn.* neutral ground, neutral territory, buffer, buffer zone, no man's land, DMZ.

**demise,** *n.*— *Syn.* dying, decease, passing; see **death** 1.

**demobilize,** *v.*— *Syn.* deactivate, retire, disperse, with-draw; see **disarm** 2, **disband.**

**democracy,** *n.* **1.** [Government through representa-tion]— *Syn.* popular government, republic, common-wealth, representative government, constitutional gov-ernment, direct democracy, government by the people, self-government, majority rule, tyranny of the majority★; see also **government** 2.

**2.** [A way of life providing extensive personal rights] — *Syn.* justice, the greatest good for the greatest num-ber, equality before the law, popular suffrage, equalitari-anism, egalitarianism, republicanism, constitutionalism, parliamentarianism, individual enterprise, laissez faire, rugged individualism, freedom of religion, freedom of speech, freedom of the press, the right to work, emancipation, political equality, democratic spirit, social equality, the Four Freedoms*, the American Way*; see also **capitalism, equality, freedom** 1. — *Ant.* AUTOCRACY, dictatorship, feudalism.

**democrat**, *n.* — *Syn.* republican, Social Democrat, evolutionist, state socialist, advocate of democracy, parliamentarian, constitutionalist, individualist, populist, believer in civil liberties, latitudinarian; see also **liberal**. — *Ant.* DICTATOR, fascist, autocrat.

**Democrat**, *n.* — *Syn.* registered Democrat, Southern Democrat, Jeffersonian Democrat, liberal, progressive, Dixiecrat*, Great Society Democrat*, New Dealer*. — *Ant.* 'EPUBLICAN, Tory, Socialist.

**democratic**, *modif.* — *Syn.* popular, constitutional, orderly, just, representative, republican, egalitarian, populist, Jeffersonian, free, equal, advocating democracy, characterized by principles of political equality, common, bourgeois, individualistic, communal, laissez-faire; see also **free** 1, **liberal** 2, **republican**. — *Ant.* AUTOCRATIC, elitist, oligarchic.

**demolish**, *v.* — *Syn.* destroy, wreck, devastate, obliterate; see **destroy** 1, **raze**.
*See Synonym Study at* DESTROY.

**demolition**, *n.* — *Syn.* razing, leveling, annihilation, wrecking; see **destruction** 1, **explosion** 1.

**demon**, *n.* 1. [Evil spirit] — *Syn.* devil, imp, vampire, incubus; see **devil** 1.
2. [Villain] — *Syn.* fiend, brute, rogue; see **beast** 2, **rascal**.

**demonic**, *modif.* 1. [Devilish] — *Syn.* demoniac, fiendish, diabolical, satanic; see **wicked** 2.
2. [Frenzied] — *Syn.* crazed, mad, possessed; see **insane** 1, **violent** 2.

**demonstrable**, *modif.* — *Syn.* deducible, verifiable, ascertainable, evident; see **conclusive, provable**.

**demonstrate**, *v.* 1. [To prove] — *Syn.* show, make evident, confirm; see **prove**.
2. [To explain] — *Syn.* express, illustrate, make clear; see **describe, explain**.
3. [To present for effect] — *Syn.* exhibit, manifest, parade; see **display** 1.

**demonstration**, *n.* 1. [An exhibition] — *Syn.* showing, presentation, exhibit; see **display** 2, **show** 1.
2. [The presentation of evidence] — *Syn.* illustration, proof, induction; see **explanation** 1, 2, **proof** 1.
3. [A mass rally] — *Syn.* picket line, march, peace march, sit-in; see **protest**.

**demonstrative**, *modif.* 1. [Showing feelings openly] — *Syn.* effusive, unreserved, expansive, affectionate; see **effusive, expressive, loving**.
2. [Conclusive] — *Syn.* decisive, specific, convincing; see **conclusive, definite** 2.
3. [Illustrative] — *Syn.* expressive, descriptive, indicative; see **explanatory, illustrative**.

**demoralization**, *n.* — *Syn.* disheartenment, subdual, intimidation, trepidation; see **confusion** 1, 2, **depression** 2.

**demoralize**, *v.* — *Syn.* dispirit, daunt, unnerve, destroy the morale of; see **discourage** 1, **frighten** 1, **weaken** 2.

**demoralized**, *modif.* — *Syn.* dispirited, unnerved, shaken, weakened; see **beaten** 1, **sad** 1.

**demote**, *v.* — *Syn.* downgrade, reduce, bust*; see **decrease** 2, **dismiss** 2, **humble**.

**demur**, *v.* — *Syn.* disagree, dispute, challenge; see **complain** 1, **object, oppose** 1.
*See Synonym Study at* OBJECT.

**demure**, *modif.* — *Syn.* shy, prim, coy, bashful; see **humble** 1, **prudish, shy**.

*See Synonym Study at* SHY.

**demurrer**, *n.* — *Syn.* challenge, demur, protest; see **objection** 1, 2.

**den**, *n.* 1. [The home of an animal] — *Syn.* cave, lair, hollow, shelter; see **hole** 3.
2. [A private or secluded room] — *Syn.* study, sanctum, hideout, family room; see **retreat** 2, **room** 2.

**denial**, *n.* 1. [Refusal to recognize a situation] — *Syn.* disavowal, forswearing, repudiation, contradiction, disclaiming, disclaimer, abnegation, rejection, refutation, negation, retraction, recantation, dismissal, renunciation, dismissing, disowning, disaffirmation, refusal to recognize, refusal to acknowledge, disbelief. — *Ant.* ACKNOWLEDGMENT, avowal, confession.
2. [Refusal to give consent] — *Syn.* rejection, veto, dissent, disapproval; see **opposition** 2, **refusal**.

**denizen**, *n.* — *Syn.* inhabitant, occupant, native, habitué; see **citizen, frequenter, resident**.

**denominate**, *v.* — *Syn.* designate, title, dub; see **name** 1.

**denomination**, *n.* 1. [A class] — *Syn.* category, classification, group; see **class** 1, **value** 1.
2. [A name] — *Syn.* title, identification, label, designation; see **name** 1.
3. [A religious group] — *Syn.* belief, creed, sect, persuasion; see **church** 3, **faith** 2.

**denotation**, *n.* — *Syn.* explicit meaning, implication, signification; see **definition** 1, **meaning**.

**denote**, *v.* — *Syn.* indicate, signify, express; see **mean** 1.

**denouement**, *n.* — *Syn.* outcome, resolution, conclusion, climax; see **end** 2, **result**.

**denounce**, *v.* — *Syn.* condemn, charge, blame, accuse, decry, censure, criticize, indict, arraign, vituperate, implicate, incriminate, upbraid, impugn, vilify, prosecute, revile, stigmatize, ostracize, reproach, castigate, rail at, brand, boycott, rebuke, dress down, take to task, damn, impeach, scold, reprimand, reprehend, reprove, inveigh against, publicly accuse, condemn openly, charge with, blacklist, expose, inform against, derogate, call to account, knock*, pitch into*, rip into*, give away*, blackball*, show up*, smear*, hang something on*; see also **accuse, censure**. — *Ant.* PRAISE, laud, commend.
*See Synonym Study at* CENSURE.

**de novo** (Latin), *modif.* — *Syn.* once more, repeatedly, from the beginning; see **again, anew**.

**dense**, *modif.* 1. [Close together] — *Syn.* solid, compact, impenetrable; see **thick** 1.
2. [Slow-witted] — *Syn.* stupid, obtuse, thick-skulled; see **dull** 3, **ignorant** 1.
*See Synonym Study at* STUPID, THICK.

**density**, *n.* 1. [The quality of being solid or heavy] — *Syn.* solidity, thickness, compactness, impenetrability, consistency, incompressibility, impermeability, massiveness, quantity, bulk, mass, substantiality, heaviness, occurrence, frequency, body, concretion, denseness, crowdedness; see also **weight** 1. — *Ant.* LIGHTNESS, rarity, thinness.
2. [The measure of an electrical charge] — *Syn.* current density, high frequency, relative frequency, kilowatt, kilocycle, ampere, erg; see also **frequency** 2.
3. [Stupidity] — *Syn.* dullness, obtuseness, ineptitude, stolidity; see **stupidity** 1.

**dent**, *n.* — *Syn.* indentation, depression, impression, dimple, dint, nick, notch, dip, cavity, hollow, dimple, cut, incision, sink, scallop, pit, concavity, trough, furrow, scratch, impress; see also **hole** 1, 2.

**dent**, *v.* — *Syn.* hollow, depress, indent, gouge, sink, dig, press in, imprint, mark, dimple, pit, make concave, notch, scratch, nick, make a dent in, perforate, ridge, furrow, bend. — *Ant.* STRAIGHTEN, bulge, make protrude.

**dentist,** *n.* — *Syn.* D.D.S., dental practitioner, dental specialist, tooth-yanker*, jawsmith*, ivory carpenter*, bridge man*; see also **doctor** 1.
Types of dentists include: dental surgeon, oral surgeon, maxillofacial surgeon, extractionist, dental diagnostician, orthodontist, prosthodontist, periodontist, exodontist, endodontist, pedodontist, radiodontist, general dentist, cosmetic dentist, pediatric dentist.

**denude,** *v.* — *Syn.* strip, divest, defoliate, deforest; see **bare, undress.**
*See Synonym Study at* STRIP.

**denunciation,** *n.* — *Syn.* condemnation, indictment, charge, censure; see **accusation** 2, **blame** 1.

**deny,** *v.* — *Syn.* contradict, dispute, disagree with, disprove, disallow, gainsay, disavow, disclaim, negate, repudiate, contravene, controvert, forswear, revoke, recant, rebut, abnegate, call one a liar, rebuff, withhold, reject, refuse, renounce, discard, not admit, take exception to, disbelieve, spurn, doubt, veto, discredit, dismiss, impugn, confute, nullify, abjure, assert the negative of, say "no" to, declare not to be true, refute, disaffirm, refuse to acknowledge, not buy*, give the lie to*; see also **confute, recant, refuse.** — *Ant.* ADMIT, accept, affirm.

---

*SYN.* — **deny** implies a refusal to accept as true, real, valid, existent, or tenable *[he denied the charge]*; to **gainsay** is to dispute what a person says or to challenge the person saying it *[facts that cannot be gainsaid]*; **contradict** not only implies emphatic denial but, in addition, often suggests belief or evidence that the opposite or contrary is true *[the facts contradict his statement]*; **impugn** implies a direct, forceful attack against that which one calls into question *[she impugned his motives]*

---

**deodorant,** *n.* — *Syn.* antiperspirant, disinfectant, deodorizer, fumigator; see **cleanser, cosmetic.**

**deodorize,** *v.* — *Syn.* disinfect, fumigate, aerate; see **clean, purify.**

**depart,** *v.* **1.** [To go away] — *Syn.* go, quit, withdraw; see **leave** 1.
**2.** [To deviate; *usually used with* from] — *Syn.* diverge, turn aside, stray, digress; see **deviate.**
**3.** [To die] — *Syn.* perish, expire, pass on; see **die** 1.

**departed,** *modif.* **1.** [Dead] — *Syn.* defunct, expired, deceased; see **dead** 1.
**2.** [Gone away] — *Syn.* left, disappeared, quitted, moved; see **gone** 1, 2.
*See Synonym Study at* DEAD.

**department,** *n.* **1.** [The field of one's activity] — *Syn.* jurisdiction, activity, interest, occupation, province, bureau, incumbency, business, capacity, dominion, administration, sphere, appointed sphere, sphere of duty, station, function, office, walk of life, avocation, vocation, specialty, field, duty, assignment, bailiwick, berth, niche, spot*; see also **job** 1.
**2.** [An organized subdivision] — *Syn.* section, office, bureau, division, branch, unit, district, precinct, tract, range, quarter, area, arena, corps, agency, board, commission, administration, circuit, territory, canton, parish, shire, constituency, commune, ward, geographical division, regional authority, district office, force, staff, beat*; see also **authority** 3, **branch** 1, **committee, division** 2, 5.

**department store,** *n.* — *Syn.* variety store, notions store, five-and-ten, five-and-dime, general store, chain store, dry-goods store, ready-to-wear, discount store, outlet store, mail-order house, warehouse, emporium,

bazaar, exchange, bargain store, hypermarket, shopping center, mall; see also **market** 1.

**departure,** *n.* **1.** [Leaving for another place] — *Syn.* going, going away, departing, leaving, withdrawal, separation, embarkation, taking leave, sailing, emigration, hegira, evacuation, passage, setting out, setting forth, parting, leave-taking, farewell, takeoff, starting, congé, removal, retreat, flight, escape, abandonment, retirement, exodus, exit, egress, fade-out*, walkout*, getaway*; see also **retreat** 1. — *Ant.* ARRIVAL, landing, entrance.
**2.** [Difference from a norm] — *Syn.* deviation, divergence, variance; see **difference** 2, **variation** 1.

**depend (on** *or* **upon),** *v.* **1.** [To be undecided] — *Syn.* be pending, be under advisement, be uncertain, be doubtful, hang in suspense, be awaiting the issue, hang in the balance*, hang by a thread*.
**2.** [To be contingent] — *Syn.* be dependent on, be determined by, rest with, rest on, be subordinate to, be based on, be predicted on, be subject to, hinge on, turn on, hang on, be in control of, be in the power of, be conditioned by, be connected with, revolve on, be at the mercy of.
**3.** [To rely upon] — *Syn.* put faith in, confide in, count on; see **count on, trust** 1.
*See Synonym Study at* TRUST.

**dependable,** *modif.* — *Syn.* trustworthy, reliable, steady, sure; see **reliable** 1, 2.
*See Synonym Study at* RELIABLE.

**dependence,** *n.* **1.** [The inability to provide for oneself] — *Syn.* need of, yoke, subordination, subservience, servility, inability to act independently, subjection to control, inability to work, reliance on others, helplessness, tutelage, wardship, dependency, addiction, habituation; see also **addiction, necessity** 3.
**2.** [Contingency] — *Syn.* sequence, connection, interdependence; see **relationship.**
**3.** [Reliance] — *Syn.* trust, belief, confidence, credence; see **faith** 1.

**dependency,** *n.* **1.** [The state of being dependent] — *Syn.* dependence, need of, yoke; see **dependence** 1.
**2.** [A territory or state subject to the dominion of another state] — *Syn.* dominion, province, mandate; see **colony** 1, **territory** 2.

**dependent,** *modif.* **1.** [Subordinate] — *Syn.* subject, subservient, secondary, lesser; see **subordinate.**
**2.** [Needing outside support] — *Syn.* helpless, poor, indigent, minor, immature, clinging, reliant, weak, not able to sustain oneself, addicted; see also **weak** 6.
**3.** [Contingent] — *Syn.* liable to, subject to, incidental to, conditional, conditioned, under the control of (something exterior), sustained by, unable to exist without, subordinate, ancillary, accessory to, provisory, controlled by, regulated by, determined by, on a string*; see also **conditional.**

**dependent,** *n.* — *Syn.* minor, child, charge, ward, retired person, orphan, minor, protegé, retainer, hanger-on; see also **child, ward** 2.

**depending (on),** *modif.* — *Syn.* contingent upon, regulated by, controlled by, determined by, in the event of, on the condition that, subject to, providing, provided, incumbent on, secondary to, springing from, growing from; see also **conditional.**

**depict,** *v.* — *Syn.* picture, portray, delineate; see **describe, draw** 2, **paint** 1, **represent** 2.

**deplete,** *v.* — *Syn.* use up, drain, exhaust; see **consume** 2, **drain** 2, **spend** 1, **waste** 1, 2.

**depleted,** *modif.* — *Syn.* reduced, almost sold out, depreciated, emptied, exhausted, spent, used up, consumed, wasted, dissipated, collapsed, vacant, bare, drained, expended, short of, bereft of, out of, destitute of, devoid of, denuded of, slack, sucked out, bled, worn, in want, without resources, at a low ebb; see also **empty** 1, **sold out.**

**depletion,** *n.* — *Syn.* exhaustion, reduction, deficiency; see **consumption** 1, **emptiness.**

**deplorable,** *modif.* — *Syn.* lamentable, regrettable, disgraceful, wretched; see **faulty, pitiful** 1, **poor** 2, **unsatisfactory.**

**deplore,** *v.* — *Syn.* lament, bemoan, disapprove of, object to; see **censure, complain** 1, **dislike, mourn** 1, **regret** 1.

**deploy,** *v.* — *Syn.* marshal, dispose, extend, expand, array, spread out in battle formation, form an extended front, put out patrols, fan out, take up battle stations, assign to positions, assign to battle stations, station; see also **use** 1.

**depopulate,** *v.* — *Syn.* kill, massacre, slaughter, remove the inhabitants from, resettle, evict, oust, exile, eradicate the population of, deprive of inhabitants, commit genocide, commit mass murder, eliminate, wipe out; see also **banish** 1, **kill** 1.

**deport,** *v.* — *Syn.* exile, banish, extradite, expel from a country; see **banish** 1, **dismiss** 1.
*See Synonym Study at* BANISH.

**deportation,** *n.* — *Syn.* expulsion, eviction, banishment, extradition; see **exile** 1, **removal** 1.

**deportment,** *n.* — *Syn.* conduct, manners, actions, demeanor; see **behavior** 1.
*See Synonym Study at* BEARING.

**deport (oneself),** *v.* — *Syn.* behave, comport (oneself), conduct (oneself), bear (oneself); see **behave** 2.
*See Synonym Study at* BEHAVE.

**depose,** *v.* — *Syn.* remove, oust, dethrone, impeach; see **dismiss** 1, 2, **oust.**

**deposit,** *n.* **1.** [Money given as security] — *Syn.* down payment, security deposit, earnest money, partial payment; see **collateral, security** 2.
**2.** [Sediment] — *Syn.* precipitate, silt, alluvium, film; see **coat** 3, **heap, sediment.**
**on deposit** — *Syn.* hoarded, stored, saved; see **kept** 2, **saved** 2.

**deposit,** *v.* **1.** [To lay down] — *Syn.* set down, put, put down, drop, insert; see also **install, place** 1.
**2.** [To present money for safekeeping] — *Syn.* invest, amass, store, keep, stock up, bank, save, accumulate, hoard, collect, garner, treasure, lay away, put in the bank, entrust, enter in an account, commit, give in trust, transfer, deliver over, commit to custody, put for safekeeping, put aside for a rainy day, plump down★, come down with★, salt away★; see also **accumulate** 1, **save** 3. — *Ant.* SPEND, withdraw, pay out.

**deposition,** *n.* **1.** [Legal attestation] — *Syn.* testimony, statement, affidavit, allegation; see **declaration** 2, **oath** 1.
**2.** [Discharge] — *Syn.* ousting, displacement, dethronement; see **removal** 1.

**depositor,** *n.* — *Syn.* patron, creditor, contributor, donor, payee, investor, account, bank customer; see also **client.** — *Ant.* TREASURER, receiver, bursar.

**depository,** *n.* — *Syn.* repository, safety-deposit box, safe-deposit box, vault, safe, museum, storehouse, place of deposit, treasury, repertory, cache, depot, warehouse, magazine, bunker, place of safety, tomb, art gallery, archives, collection, mint, bank, savings bank; see also **bank** 3, **safe, treasury, vault** 2.

**depot,** *n.* **1.** [A warehouse] — *Syn.* annex, depository, magazine; see **arsenal, storehouse.**

**2.** [A railroad *or* bus station] — *Syn.* station, terminal, base, lot, freight depot, passenger terminal, relay depot, parking depot, way station, railroad yards, switching yards, marshaling yards, loading yards, unloading yards, stockyards, sidetrack, loading track, ticket office, waiting room, loft, junction, stop, central station, station house, haven, *gare* (French), *Bahnhof* (German), terminus, stopping-place, halting-place, destination.

**deprave,** *v.* — *Syn.* pervert, debase, degrade; see **corrupt** 1.
*See Synonym Study at* DEBASE.

**depraved,** *modif.* — *Syn.* perverted, degenerate, corrupt, debauched; see **lewd** 2, **wicked** 1.

**depravity,** *n.* — *Syn.* degradation, degeneracy, baseness, wickedness; see **evil** 1.

**deprecate,** *v.* — *Syn.* deplore, object, expostulate, belittle; see **censure, depreciate** 2, **oppose** 1.

**depreciate,** *v.* **1.** [To decline in value or quantity] — *Syn.* devalue, deteriorate, lessen; see **decay, decrease** 1.
**2.** [To lower in reputation] — *Syn.* belittle, disparage, denigrate, deprecate, lower, run down, decry, discredit, minimize, ridicule, condemn, denounce, dispraise, calumniate, undervalue, underrate, traduce, cast aspersions on, attack, vilify, defame, malign, slander, sneer at, fault, revile, deride, spurn, make slighting reference to, speak ill of, derogate, contemn, slight, detract, slur, hold cheap, scoff at, sneer at, find fault with, make light of, make little of, play down, downplay, downgrade, poohpooh★, knock★, smear★, put down★, take down a peg★, cut down to size★, rap★, slam★, roast★; see also **censure, disgrace, humble, humiliate.** — *Ant.* RAISE, praise, extol.

---

SYN. — **depreciate** is to lessen (something) in value as by implying that it has less worth than is usually attributed to it *[he depreciated her generosity]*; to **disparage** is to attempt to lower in esteem, as by insinuation, invidious comparison, faint praise; **decry** implies vigorous public denunciation, often from the best of motives *[to decry corruption in government]*; **belittle** implies depreciation, but stresses a contemptuous attitude in the speaker or writer; **minimize** suggests an ascription of the least possible value or importance *[don't minimize your own efforts]*

---

**depreciation,** *n.* — *Syn.* devaluation, reduction, shrinkage; see **discount, reduction** 1.

**depredation,** *n.* — *Syn.* pillage, plunder, robbery, laying waste; see **destruction** 1, **theft.**

**depress,** *v.* **1.** [To bring to a lower level or state] — *Syn.* press down, squash, reduce; see **deaden** 1, **dent, flatten, lower, press** 1.
**2.** [To lower in spirits] — *Syn.* dispirit, dampen, dishearten, discourage, dismay, mortify, sadden, weary, darken, desolate, reduce to tears, deject, cow, weigh down, cast down, beat down, chill, dull, daunt, damp, oppress, prostrate, give an inferiority complex, cast gloom upon, cast a pall upon, make despondent, throw cold water on, put a damper on, bring down★, get down★, bum out★; see also **discourage** 1. — *Ant.* encourage, animate, stimulate.

**depressed,** *modif.* — *Syn.* discouraged, pessimistic, cast down; see **sad** 1.
*See Synonym Study at* SAD.

**depressing,** *modif.* — *Syn.* discouraging, disheartening, saddening; see **dismal** 1, **sad** 2.

**depression,** *n.* **1.** [Something lower than its surroundings] — *Syn.* cavity, dip, sink; see **dent, hole** 2.

**2.** [Low spirits] — *Syn.* despair, despondency, sadness, sorrow, unhappiness, gloom, dejection, melancholy, misery, wretchedness, trouble, mortification, worry, discouragement, dispiritedness, hopelessness, pessimism, distress, desperation, desolation, dreariness, heaviness of spirit, dullness, disconsolation, downheartedness, woefulness, lugubriousness, moroseness, cheerlessness, disconsolateness, melancholia, dolor, dolefulness, darkness, bleakness, oppression, low-spiritedness, lowness, gloominess, glumness, disheartenment, hypochondria, vapors, malaise, clinical depression, dysthymia, slough of despond, *Weltschmerz* (German), doldrums, dumps*, mulligrubs*, blues*, blue devils*, horrors*, blue funk*, blahs*; see also **gloom** 2, **grief** 1, **sadness.** — *Ant.* JOY, elation, satisfaction.
**3.** [Period of commercial stress] — *Syn.* economic decline, recession, slump, economic downturn, unemployment, slack times, hard times, bad times, inflation, crisis, overproduction, retrenchment, slowdown, economic dislocation, economic paralysis, economic stagnation, financial storm, business inactivity, panic, crash*, bust*, Black Friday*, stagflation*; see also **bankruptcy.** — *Ant.* PROSPERITY, good times, boom.
**deprivation,** *n.* — *Syn.* withholding, divestment, privation, need; see **loss** 3.
**deprive,** *v.* — *Syn.* strip, withhold, bereave, divest; see **deny, seize** 2.
**depth,** *n.* **1.** [Vertical or lateral distance] — *Syn.* lowness, deepness, extent, drop, measurement downward, declination, pitch, distance backward, distance inward, remoteness, extent down from a given point, downward measure, perpendicular measurement from the surface, sounding; see also **expanse, measurement** 2. — *Ant.* HEIGHT, shallowness, flatness.
**2.** [Deepness] — *Syn.* profundity, intensity, lowness, gravity, abyss, pit, bottom, substratum, underground, base, lower register, bottom of the sea; see also **bottom** 1.
**3.** [Intellectual power] — *Syn.* profundity, weightiness, wisdom; see **acumen.**
**in depth** — *Syn.* extensive, broad, thorough, thoroughly; see **completely, comprehensive, detailed.**
**deputation,** *n.* — *Syn.* delegation, commission, assignment, nomination; see **appointment** 1, **committee, delegation** 1, **installation** 1.
**deputy,** *n.* — *Syn.* lieutenant, appointee, aide; see **agent** 1, **assistant, delegate.**
*See Synonym Study at* AGENT.
**derail,** *v.* — *Syn.* go off the rails, be wrecked, thwart, deflect; see **crash** 1, **hinder, wreck** 1.
**derange,** *v.* **1.** [To disarrange] — *Syn.* disorder, muss up, unsettle; see **confuse, misplace.**
**2.** [To upset] — *Syn.* disconcert, perplex, drive insane, drive crazy, dement, madden, unsettle the reason of, craze, unbalance, unhinge, addle the wits, send over the edge*; see also **confuse, disturb** 2.
**deranged,** *modif.* **1.** [Disordered] — *Syn.* displaced, misplaced, dislocated; see **disordered.**
**2.** [Insane] — *Syn.* demented, crazy, mad; see **insane** 1.
**derangement,** *n.* **1.** [Confusion] — *Syn.* disorder, muddle, jumble; see **confusion** 2.
**2.** [Insanity] — *Syn.* dementia, madness, lunacy; see **insanity** 1.
**derelict,** *modif.* **1.** [Abandoned] — *Syn.* forsaken, deserted, relinquished, neglected; see **abandoned** 1.
**2.** [Careless] — *Syn.* lax, remiss, negligent; see **careless** 1, **delinquent** 1, **remiss.**
*See Synonym Study at* REMISS.

**derelict,** *n.* — *Syn.* social outcast, vagrant, pariah, bum*; see **beggar** 2, **tramp** 1.
**dereliction,** *n.* **1.** [Abandonment] — *Syn.* forsaking, desolation, relinquishment; see **desertion.**
**2.** [Delinquency] — *Syn.* negligence, evasion, nonperformance; see **carelessness, crime** 1, **default.**
**deride,** *v.* — *Syn.* scoff at, jeer, mock; see **ridicule.**
*See Synonym Study at* RIDICULE.
**derision,** *n.* — *Syn.* scorn, mockery, disdain; see **ridicule.**
**derisive,** *modif.* — *Syn.* insulting, mocking, taunting, contemptuous; see **sarcastic, scornful** 1, 2.
**derivable,** *modif.* — *Syn.* obtainable, resultant, determinable; see **available, likely** 1.
**derivation,** *n.* — *Syn.* root, source, beginning, descent; see **etymology, origin** 2.
**derivative,** *modif.* — *Syn.* derived from, caused, evolved, not original, imitative, borrowed, copied, plagiarized, unoriginal, rehashed, warmed-over, secondhand, not fundamental, hereditary, inferential, inferred, coming from, obtained from, transmitted, acquired, derivational; see also **ancestral, secondary** 1.
**derive,** *v.* **1.** [To draw a conclusion] — *Syn.* determine, work out, conclude; see **assume** 1, **infer** 1.
**2.** [To receive] — *Syn.* acquire, obtain, procure; see **reap** 2, **receive** 1.
**3.** [To come from] — *Syn.* originate, arise, stem, descend; see **arise** 3, **begin** 2.
*See Synonym Study at* ARISE.
**derogate,** *v.* — *Syn.* take away, disparage, discredit; see **detract, humiliate, insult, slander.**
**derogatory,** *modif.* — *Syn.* belittling, disparaging, slighting, dishonoring, deprecatory, depreciatory, denigrating, disdainful, critical, faultfinding, uncomplimentary, pejorative, slanderous, censorious, unfavorable, unflattering, injurious, defamatory; see also **critical** 2, **opprobrious** 1, **sarcastic.**
**descant,** *n.* — *Syn.* discourse, comment, criticism; see **discussion** 1, **remark, review** 2.
**descant,** *v.* — *Syn.* remark, discourse, criticize; see **comment** 1, **discuss.**
**descend,** *v.* **1.** [To move lower] — *Syn.* come down, go down, slide, settle, drop, stoop, gravitate, slip, dismount, fall, topple, plunge, dive, plummet, sink, dip, pass downward, pitch, slope, decline, alight, light, disembark, detrain, deplane, tumble, move downward, come down on, slump, trip, stumble, flutter down, submerge, penetrate, step down, climb down, get down, swoop down, step off, climb off, get off, swoop, precipitate, plump*, plop (down)*; see also **dive, drop** 1, **fall.** — *Ant.* CLIMB, ascend, mount.
**2.** [To descend figuratively] — *Syn.* decline, deteriorate, degenerate; see **decrease** 1.
**3.** [To lower oneself] — *Syn.* stoop, sink, humble oneself; see **condescend.**
**descendants,** *n.* — *Syn.* offspring, progeny, children; see **family** 1, **offspring.**
**descendent,** *modif.* — *Syn.* descending, downward, sloping, moving down, moving downward, coming down, falling down, going down, sinking, plunging, toppling, drooping, dipping, dropping, slipping, tumbling, plummeting; see also **down** 1, **falling.**
**descend on,** *v.* **1.** [To approach] — *Syn.* close in, converge upon, advance upon; see **approach** 2, **visit** 4.
**2.** [To attack] — *Syn.* beset, invade, raid, pounce on; see **attack** 1.
**descent,** *n.* **1.** [A downward incline] — *Syn.* declivity, slope, drop; see **grade** 1, **inclination** 5.
**2.** [The act of descending] — *Syn.* drop, fall, falling,

coming down, sinking, degradation, abasement, droop, cadence, debasement, slump, downfall, drop, lapse, slide, subsiding, declination, swoop, plunge, dip, reduction, precipitation, landslide, tumble, decline; see also **fall** 1. — *Ant.* RISE, mounting, growth.
**3.** [Lineal relationship] — *Syn.* extraction, origin, lineage; see **family** 1, **relationship.**
**4.** [An invasion] — *Syn.* advance, incursion, assault; see **attack** 1.
**describe,** *v.* — *Syn.* delineate, characterize, portray, depict, picture, give an account of, illuminate, make clear, make vivid, give the details of, convey a verbal image of, particularize, define, specify, elucidate, epitomize, report, draw, narrate, tell of, chronicle, paint, illustrate, detail, represent in words, make sense of, relate, recount, outline, express, label, name, call, term, catch, write up, pin down, give the dope on*; see also **define** 2, **explain, narrate, represent** 2.
**description,** *n.* **1.** [A picture, usually in words] — *Syn.* representation, narration, story, portrayal, portrait, word picture, account, report, delineation, sketch, specification, characterization, declaration, rehearsal, recitation, information, recital, narrative, informal definition, detailing, record, monograph, brief, summary, summarization, depiction, explanation, writeup; see also **record** 1, **representation.**
**2.** [A sort or group] — *Syn.* order, variety, type, classification; see **kind** 2.
**descriptive,** *modif.* — *Syn.* designating, identifying, definitive, graphic, describing, narrative, expository, interpretive, anecdotal, characterizing, illuminating, illuminative, expressive, clear, true to life, illustrative, lifelike, vivid, portraitive, picturesque, circumstantial, eloquent, detailed, pictorial, photographic, classificatory, representative, indicative, revealing; see also **characteristic, explanatory, graphic** 1, 2. — *Ant.* VAGUE, analytical, expository.
**desecrate,** *v.* — *Syn.* defile, commit sacrilege, dishonor, befoul; see **profane.**
**desecration,** *n.* — *Syn.* sacrilege, profanation, irreverence, defilement; see **blasphemy, profanation.**
*See Synonym Study at* SACRILEGE.
**desert,** *n.* — *Syn.* waste, sand, wastelands, sahara, wilderness, badlands, barren plains, barrens, arid region, deserted region, sand dunes, lava beds, uncultivated expanse, infertile area, infertile region, salt flats, alkali flats, abandoned country, dust bowl; see also **wilderness.**
*See Synonym Study at* WASTE.
Famous deserts include: Sahara, Kalahari, Kara Kum, Great Basin, Sonoran, Painted, Death Valley, Mojave, Atakama, Negev, Arabian, Rub" al Khali, Great Sandy, Dahna, Patagonian, Persian, Samnan, Tarim, Sinkiang, Gobi, Shamo, Great Victoria, Great Australian, Gidi, Libyan.
**desert,** *v.* **1.** [To abandon in time of trouble] — *Syn.* forsake, leave, quit; see **abandon** 1, 2.
**2.** [To leave military service, one's post, etc.] — *Syn.* defect, be absent without leave, abandon one's post, sneak off, make off, abscond, run away from duty, run away from military service, go AWOL*, decamp, violate one's oath, leave unlawfully, go over the hill*, rat*, take French leave*, play truant*; see also **abandon** 2. — *Ant.* OBEY, stay, do one's duty.
*See Synonym Study at* ABANDON.
**deserted,** *modif.* — *Syn.* forsaken, desolate, unfrequented, lonely; see **abandoned** 1, **empty** 1.
**deserter,** *n.* — *Syn.* runaway, fugitive, refugee, escapee, truant, defector, derelict, delinquent, apostate, lawbreaker, betrayer, traitor, renegade, turncoat, back-

slider, recreant, slacker, shirker, rat; see also **traitor.**
**desertion,** *n.* — *Syn.* abandonment, flight, escape, departure, leaving, secession, defection, dereliction, renunciation, disavowing, disavowal, disaffection, apostasy, withdrawal, avoidance, evasion, elusion, truancy, repudiation, relinquishment, retirement, resignation, divorce, willful abandonment, abrogation, backsliding, recreancy, falling away, forsaking, decamping, running out on*, going back on*, going AWOL*; see also **retreat** 1. — *Ant.* LOYALTY, cooperation, constancy.
**deserts,** *pl.n.* **1.** [Appropriate reward] — *Syn.* due, compensation, recompense; see **payment** 1.
**2.** [Appropriate punishment] — *Syn.* penalty, retribution, comeuppance*; see **punishment, revenge** 1.
**deserve,** *v.* — *Syn.* merit, be worthy of, earn, be deserving, earn as due compensation, lay claim to, have the right to, be given one's due, be entitled to, warrant, justify, rate*, have it coming*. — *Ant.* FAIL, be unworthy, usurp.
**deserved,** *modif.* — *Syn.* merited, earned, justified, warranted, meet, appropriate, suitable, equitable, right, rightful, proper, fitting, just, due, well-deserved; see also **fit** 1. — *Ant.* UNDUE, excessive, inordinate.
**deserving,** *modif.* — *Syn.* meriting, meritorious, exemplary; see **worthy.**
**desiccate,** *v.* **1.** [To dry] — *Syn.* dry up, parch, exsiccate, drain; see **dry** 2.
**2.** [To preserve] — *Syn.* dehydrate, anhydrate, evaporate, freeze-dry; see **preserve** 3.
**desideratum,** *n.* — *Syn.* objective, aim, goal, heart's desire; see **hope** 2, **purpose** 1, **requirement** 2.
**design,** *n.* **1.** [Arrangement for artistic or other effect] — *Syn.* pattern, motif, configuration, figure, device, decorative pattern, composition, layout, conception, diagram, drawing, sketch, rough representation, draft, blueprint, prototype, picture, tracing, commercial design, architectural design, outline, depiction, chart, map, plan, tracery, delineation, perspective, treatment, idea, study; see also **composition** 2, **form** 1, **plan** 1. — *Ant.* CONFUSION, jumble, mess.
**2.** [Planned intention or procedure] — *Syn.* object, intention, scheme; see **plan** 2, **purpose** 1.
*See Synonym Study at* PLAN.
**by design** — *Syn.* on purpose, with intent, purposely; see **deliberately.**
**design,** *v.* **1.** [To plan in a preliminary way] — *Syn.* block out, outline, sketch; see **plan** 1, 2.
**2.** [To conceive] — *Syn.* create, originate, make up, devise; see **compose** 3, **create** 2, **invent** 1, **produce** 2.
**3.** [To intend] — *Syn.* mean, set apart, aim at; see **intend** 2.
*See Synonym Study at* INTEND.
**designate,** *v.* **1.** [To specify] — *Syn.* indicate, set apart, point out, mark out, name, characterize, entitle, term, denote, signify, set aside, allocate, earmark, appoint, assign, prefer, favor; see also **choose** 1, **name** 1.
**2.** [To appoint] — *Syn.* select, nominate, name, charge; see **assign** 1, **delegate** 1.
**designation,** *n.* **1.** [The act of designating] — *Syn.* selection, indication, specification; see **appointment** 1, **specification.**
**2.** [A mark that designates] — *Syn.* classification, key word, appellation; see **class** 1, **label, name** 1.
**designedly,** *modif.* — *Syn.* purposely, intentionally, on purpose; see **deliberately.**
**designer,** *n.* — *Syn.* planner, deviser, originator, creator, architect, fashioner, shaper, stylist, fashion designer, *couturier, couturière* (both French), interior decorator,

interior designer, set designer, layout person, draftsman, delineator, sketcher, modeler; see also **architect** 1, **artist** 1, **author** 1.

**designing,** *modif.* — *Syn.* scheming, artful, crafty, calculating; see **sly** 1.

**designing,** *n.* — *Syn.* conception, drafting, creating; see **design** 1, **drawing** 1, **plan** 2.

**desirability,** *n.* — *Syn.* worth, advantage, usefulness; see **value** 3.

**desirable,** *modif.* **1.** [Arousing desire] — *Syn.* seductive, alluring, sought-after, to die for*; see **charming, popular** 1.

**2.** [Generally advantageous] — *Syn.* useful, beneficial, expedient, advisable; see **fit** 1, **helpful** 1, **profitable.**

**3.** [Having many good qualities] — *Syn.* good, welcome, acceptable, pleasing; see **excellent.**

**desire,** *n.* **1.** [The wish to enjoy] — *Syn.* aspiration, longing, yearning, craving, wish, want, motive, will, urge, eagerness, ardor, solicitude, propensity, predilection, fancy, greed, avidity, cupidity, covetousness, obsession, frenzy, craze, mania, urge, appetite, hunger, thirst, passion, attraction, rapaciousness, fondness, liking, inclination, proclivity, ravenousness, ardent impulse, voracity, relish, gras ping, monomania, pining, hankering*, itch*, stomach*, yen*; see also **ambition** 1, **greed.** — *Ant.* INDIFFERENCE, apathy, aversion.

**2.** [Wish] — *Syn.* request, hope, want; see **wish** 2.

**3.** [Erotic wish to possess] — *Syn.* lust, concupiscence, passion, urge, hunger, appetite, fascination, doting, infatuation, fervor, excitement, amorousness, sexual love, carnality, libido, lechery, lasciviousness, sensual appetite, sexual appetite, prurience, priapism, carnal passion, salaciousness, lecherousness, erotism, eroticism, erotomania, satyriasis, nymphomania, biological urge, estrus, the hots*, rut*, heat*, horniness*, lech*; see also **love** 1. — *Ant.* ABSTINENCE, coldness, frigidity.

**desire,** *v.* **1.** [To wish for] — *Syn.* want, long for, crave, covet, fancy, aspire, yearn for, desiderate, set one's heart on, ache for*, die for*, die to*; see also **want** 1, **yearn.**

**2.** [To request] — *Syn.* ask for, seek, solicit; see **beg** 1.

**3.** [To want sexually] — *Syn.* lust after, long for, hunger for, wish for, have the hots for*, be turned on by*, have hot pants for*; see also **want** 1.

---

**SYN.** — **desire,** generally interchangeable with the other words here in the sense of 'to long for," stresses intensity or ardor [to *desire* success]; **wish** is not so strong a term as **desire** and has special application when an unrealizable longing is meant [he *wished* summer were here]; **want,** specifically suggesting a longing for something lacking or needed, generally is a more informal equivalent of **wish** [she *wants,* or *wishes,* to go with us]; **crave** suggests a strong desire to gratify a physical appetite or an urgent need [to *crave* affection]

---

**desiring,** *modif.* — *Syn.* yearning, needing, desirous; see **enthusiastic** 2, **envious** 2.

**desirous,** *modif.* — *Syn.* anxious, wishing, covetous, desiring; see **enthusiastic** 2, **envious** 2.

**desist,** *v.* — *Syn.* stop, cease, halt, discontinue; see **stop** 2.

*See Synonym Study at* STOP.

**desk,** *n.* **1.** [A piece of furniture] — *Syn.* secretary, worktable, writing desk, writing table, drafting table, escritoire, bureau, box, lectern, reading desk, reading stand, counter, frame, case, retable, ledge, pulpit; roll-top, flat-top, drop-front, executive's, secretary's, kneehole, ped-

estal, etc., desk; see also **furniture, table** 1.

**2.** [A department, as of an editorial office] — *Syn.* jurisdiction, bureau, section; see **department** 2.

Newspaper desks include: city, telegraph, cable, state, copy, rewrite, financial, business, editorial, community, political, international, crime, art, sports, society, farm; ring*, slot*, horseshoe*.

**desolate,** *modif.* **1.** [Left unused] — *Syn.* deserted, forsaken, uninhabited, laid waste; see **abandoned** 1, **bleak** 1, **isolated.**

**2.** [Gloomy] — *Syn.* forlorn, downcast, melancholy, dolorous; see **dismal** 1, **sad** 1.

**desolation,** *n.* **1.** [The quality of being uninhabited] — *Syn.* bareness, barrenness, bleakness, devastation, destruction, havoc, ruin, wreck, ravaging, demolition, annihilation, extinction, depopulation, emptiness; see also **desert, waste** 3. — *Ant.* FERTILITY, luxuriance, productivity.

**2.** [The quality of being hopeless] — *Syn.* wretchedness, misery, loneliness, forlornness; see **gloom** 2.

**despair,** *n.* — *Syn.* hopelessness, despondency, discouragement; see **depression** 2, **desperation** 1, **gloom** 2.

**despairing,** *modif.* — *Syn.* hopeless, despondent, miserable; see **hopeless** 1, **sad** 1.

*See Synonym Study at* HOPELESS.

**despair of,** *v.* — *Syn.* lose hope, lose faith, lose heart, lose courage, give up, give up hope, abandon hope, give up all expectation, give way, give in to despair, despond, have no hope, have a heavy heart, lose faith in, abandon oneself to fate; see also **abandon** 1.

**desperado,** *n.* — *Syn.* outlaw, bandit, ruffian; see **criminal.**

**desperate,** *modif.* **1.** [Hopeless] — *Syn.* despairing, despondent, desirous, in extremities; see **hopeless** 2, **sad** 1.

**2.** [Reckless] — *Syn.* incautious, frantic, wild; see **careless** 1, **rash.**

**3.** [Extreme] — *Syn.* great, drastic, acute, dire; see **extreme** 2, **urgent** 1.

*See Synonym Study at* HOPELESS.

**desperately,** *modif.* **1.** [Dangerously] — *Syn.* severely, harmfully, perilously; see **carelessly, seriously** 1.

**2.** [Hopelessly] — *Syn.* despairingly, wildly, frantically; see **hopelessly** 1, **urgently** 2.

**desperation,** *n.* **1.** [Hopelessness] — *Syn.* despair, distress, despondency, depression, discomfort, dejection, distraction, desolation, disconsolateness, anxiety, dread, panic, anguish, agony, melancholy, grief, worry, trouble, pain, torture, pang, heartache, concern, misery, urgency, gravity, desperateness, exigency; see also **fear** 2, **gloom** 2, **necessity** 3. — *Ant.* HOPE, hopefulness, confidence.

**2.** [Rashness] — *Syn.* frenzy, recklessness, foolhardiness; see **carelessness.**

**despicable,** *modif.* — *Syn.* contemptible, abject, base, vile; see **mean** 1, 3, **offensive** 2.

**despise,** *v.* — *Syn.* scorn, disdain, contemn, hate, look down on, look down upon, spurn, sneer at, flout, dislike, loathe, detest, abhor; see also **hate** 1.

---

**SYN.** — **despise** implies a strong emotional response toward that which one looks down upon with contempt or aversion [to *despise* a hypocrite]; to **scorn** is to feel indignation toward or deep contempt for, often with the implication of rejection or refusal [to *scorn* the offer of a bribe]; **disdain** implies a haughty or arrogant contempt for what one considers beneath one's dignity [to *disdain* flattery]; **contemn,** chiefly a literary word, implies a vehement disapproval of a person or thing as base, vile, or despicable *See also Synonym Study at* HATE.

**despite,** *prep.* — *Syn.* in spite of, in defiance of, even with; see **notwithstanding.**

**despoil,** *v.* — *Syn.* plunder, pillage, maraud; see **raid, ravage, rob.**
*See Synonym Study at* RAVAGE.

**despoliation,** *n.* — *Syn.* plunder, depredation, piracy, pillage; see **destruction 1, theft.**

**despondency,** *n.* — *Syn.* dejection, despair, sadness; see **depression 2, desperation 1, gloom 2, grief 1.**

**despondent,** *modif.* — *Syn.* dejected, discouraged, depressed; see **sad 1.**
*See Synonym Study at* HOPELESS.

**despot,** *n.* — *Syn.* oppressor, autocrat, tyrant; see **dictator.**

**despotic,** *modif.* — *Syn.* dictatorial, oppressive, authoritarian; see **absolute 3, autocratic 1, tyrannical.**

**despotism,** *n.* **1.** [Autocracy] — *Syn.* absolutism, dictatorship, imperialism; see **autocracy, government 2.**
**2.** [Tyranny] — *Syn.* repression, coercion, domination; see **oppression 1, tyranny.**

**dessert,** *n.* — *Syn.* sweet, pastry, cake, torte, pie, tart, ice cream, ice, sherbet, sundae, compote, fruit salad, pudding, custard, flan, crème caramel, creme brûlée, soufflé, mousse, crepe, cookie, dumpling, trifle, jello, jelly, cobbler, crumble; see also **cake 2, candy, cheese, delicacy 2, fruit 1, pastry, pie, pudding.**

**destination,** *n.* — *Syn.* objective, goal, aim, end, journey's end, stopping place, terminus, target, landing place, stop, last stop, end of the line; see also **address 3, depot, purpose 1.**

**destine,** *v.* **1.** [To predestine] — *Syn.* fate, decide, doom; see **predetermine.**
**2.** [To intend] — *Syn.* design, reserve, dedicate; see **intend 2.**

**destined,** *modif.* **1.** [Fixed by a higher power] — *Syn.* fated, ordained, foreordained, predestined, predetermined, doomed, menacing, near, forthcoming, imminent, instant, brewing, threatening, in prospect, inevitable, ineluctable, preordained, compelled, condemned, at hand, impending, looming, unborn, inexorable, that is to be, that will be, in store, to come, directed, settled, sealed, closed, predesigned, appointed, decreed, written in the book of fate, in the wind, in the lap of the gods, stated, in the cards; see also **doomed, imminent, inevitable.** — *Ant.* VOLUNTARY, at will, by chance.
**2.** [Intended for a certain destination] — *Syn.* bound for, on the road to, headed for, ordered to, consigned, assigned, specified, directed, delegated, appropriated, prepared, chosen, appointed, intended, designated, determined, entrained, en route, bent on; see also **intended.** — *Ant.* WANDERING, aimless, unconsigned.

**destiny,** *n.* **1.** [Fate as a power] — *Syn.* fate, predetermination, predestination, decree, finality, conclusion, foreordination, decrees of fate, course of events, inevitability, doom, certainty, fatality, condition, divine decree, book of fate, future, the Fates, destined way, ordinance, kismet, fortune, luck, karma, inevitable necessity, God's will, providence, Fortune, serendipity, happenstance, wheel of fortune, the stars, Dame Fortune, will of heaven, Sisters Three, Weird Sisters, Ides of March, Hobson's choice, the lap of the gods; see also **chance 1, Fate.**
**2.** [Fate as a personal future] — *Syn.* fate, fortune, lot, end; see **doom 1.**

*See Synonym Study at* FATE.

**destitute,** *modif.* — *Syn.* impoverished, poverty-stricken, penniless; see **poor 1.**
*See Synonym Study at* POOR.

**destitution,** *n.* — *Syn.* indigence, want, privation; see **poverty 1.**
*See Synonym Study at* POVERTY.

**destroy,** *v.* **1.** [To bring to nothing] — *Syn.* ruin, demolish, exterminate, raze, annihilate, tear down, throw down, plunder, ransack, pillage, eradicate, do away with, overthrow, cause the downfall of, devastate, swallow up, butcher, extirpate, consume, liquidate, break up, dissolve, blot out, cast down, put down, quash, quell, level, abort, stamp out, suppress, squelch, scuttle, undo, ravage, lay waste, spoliate, root up, overturn, annul, impair, damage, ravish, deface, maraud, dilapidate, expunge, efface, sweep over, sweep away, shatter, split up, crush, obliterate, burn to the ground, knock to pieces, break to pieces, destruct, self-destruct, abolish, crash, extinguish, put an end to, desolate, dynamite, put a damper on, wrench apart, tear apart, wreck, dismantle, fell, upset, bomb, stave in, despoil, sack, subvert, mutilate, smash, trample, maim, mar, vitiate, end, counteract, nullify, blast, neutralize, gut, snuff out, erase, sabotage, repeal, pull down, pull to pieces, terminate, conclude, finish, bring to ruin, stop, put a stop to, dissipate, dispel, wipe out, do in*, make away with*, finish off*, make short work of*, total*, scorch*, blitz*, cream*, foul up*, make mincemeat of*, seal the doom of, lay in ruins; see also **defeat 2, ravage.** — *Ant.* BUILD, construct, establish.
**2.** [To kill] — *Syn.* murder, slay, slaughter; see **kill 1.**

*SYN.* — **destroy** implies a tearing down or bringing to an end by wrecking, ruining, killing, eradicating, etc. and is the term of broadest application here */to destroy* a city, one's influence, etc./; **demolish** implies such destructive force as to completely smash to pieces and render useless /the bombs *demolished* the factories, she *demolished* his argument/; **raze** means to level to the ground, either destructively or by systematic wrecking with a salvaging of useful parts; to **annihilate** is to destroy so completely as to blot out of existence /rights that cannot be *annihilated*/

**destroyed,** *modif.* — *Syn.* ruined, wrecked, annihilated, killed, lost, devastated, wasted, done away with, abolished, demolished, overturned, overwhelmed, upset, nullified, annulled, undone, put to an end, mown down, felled, fallen, shattered, smashed, broken, ravaged, engulfed, submerged, overrun, desolated, blighted, blasted, extirpated, extinguished, eradicated, obliterated, devoured, consumed, withered, disintegrated, burned up, burned down, incinerated, torn down, gutted, gone to pieces, razed, in ruins, sacked, reduced to ashes, gone by the board, wiped out, totaled*; see also **broken 1, dead 1, ruined 1.** — *Ant.* SAVED, protected, restored, intact.

**destroyer,** *n.* **1.** [A destructive agent] — *Syn.* annihilator, wrecker, vandal, exterminator, iconoclast, nihilist, assassin, executioner, hangman, strangler, butcher, slayer, gunman, decapitator, guillotiner, slaughterer, cutthroat, lyncher, anarchist, terrorist, firebrand, incendiary, arsonist, pyromaniac, bomber, desperado, scourge, dealer of destruction, demolisher, defacer, ruiner, eradicator, despoiler, ransacker, pillager, looter, savage, plague, pestilence, rust, cancer, acid, bane, canker, wild beast, poison, virus, fungus, hatchet man*, Goth*, Hun*, Nazi*; see also **arsonist, criminal, killer, weapon 1.** — *Ant.* AUTHOR, restorer, creator.

**2.** [A swift armed surface vessel] — *Syn.* battleship, light unit, fighting vessel; see **ship, warship.**

**destroying,** *n.* — *Syn.* ruining, spoiling, wrecking; see **carnage, destruction** 1, **wreck** 1.

**destruction,** *n.* **1.** [The act of destroying] — *Syn.* demolition, demolishing, ruin, ruining, wrecking, tearing down, razing, leveling, annihilation, devastation, holocaust, eradication, obliteration, slaying, slaughter, carnage, liquidation, extirpation, overthrow, subversion, extermination, elimination, ravaging, consumption, abolition, murder, assassination, killing, disruption, bombardment, burning, dynamiting, laying waste, tearing apart, disintegration, extinction, ravagement, wreckage, subjugation, despoiling, depredation, dissolution, butchery, sabotage, subverting, ravaging, pillaging, plundering, despoliation, sacking, vandalism, subjugation, crushing, dissolving, invalidating, extinguishing, overthrowing, collision, crashing, falling, felling, dismantling, gutting, defacing, shattering, smashing, trampling, knocking down, stamping out, wiping out, sack, rack and ruin, crack of doom★; see also **carnage, wreck** 1. — *Ant.* PRODUCTION, formation, erection.

**2.** [The condition after destruction] — *Syn.* ruin, waste, ashes, wreck, annihilation, devastation, havoc, vestiges, desolation, ruins, overthrow, decay, dilapidation, disintegration, loss, bane, blight, remains, remnants, prostration, injury, impairment, ravage, downfall, end, bankruptcy, starvation, plague, shipwreck, dissolution, removal, sacrifice, disorganization, immolation; see also **damage** 2. — *Ant.* RESTORATION, renovation, renewal.

---

**SYN.** — **destruction** implies annihilation or demolition, as by fire, explosion, flood, etc. /the *destruction* of the village in an air raid/; **ruin** implies a state of decay, disintegration, etc. especially through such natural processes as age and weather /the barn is in a state of *ruin*/; **havoc** suggests total destruction or devastation, as following an earthquake or hurricane /the storm wreaked *havoc* along the coast/; **dilapidation** implies a state of ruin or shabbiness resulting from neglect /the *dilapidation* of a deserted house/

---

**destructive,** *modif.* **1.** [Unfavorable] — *Syn.* adverse, negative, not constructive; see **unfavorable** 2.

**2.** [Destroying] — *Syn.* ruinous, noxious, baneful, pestiferous, noisome, cancerous, fatal, deleterious, pestilential, catastrophic, calamitous, disastrous, productive of serious evil, cataclysmal, eradicative, fell, demolitionary, devastating, dire, lethal, extirpative, internecine, mortal, mischievous, detrimental, annihilative, hurtful, harmful, arsonistic, conflagrative, subversive, incendiary, murderous, disruptive, suicidal, evil, injurious, venomous, pernicious, toxic, baleful, disintegrative, corrosive, corroding, erosive, eroding, damaging; see also **deadly** 1, **harmful, poisonous.** — *Ant.* HELPFUL, curative, lifesaving.

**desultory,** *modif.* — *Syn.* erratic, random, miscellaneous, disconnected; see **aimless, irregular** 1, **random.**

*See Synonym Study at* RANDOM.

**detach,** *v.* — *Syn.* separate, withdraw, disengage, disconnect; see **divide** 1, **unhitch.**

**detached,** *modif.* **1.** [Cut off or removed] — *Syn.* loosened, divided, disjoined, unconnected; see **separated.**

**2.** [Disinterested] — *Syn.* uninvolved, unconcerned, indifferent, dispassionate; see **aloof, fair** 1, **indifferent** 1.

*See Synonym Study at* INDIFFERENT.

**detachment,** *n.* **1.** [Indifference] — *Syn.* aloofness, impartiality, coolness, unconcern; see **indifference** 1.

**2.** [A small body of troops] — *Syn.* patrol, task force, squad; see **army** 2, **organization** 3.

**detail,** *n.* **1.** [A part] — *Syn.* item, portion, particular, trait, specialty, feature, minute part, aspect, accessory, article, trifle, peculiarity, minutia, fraction, particularity, specification, technicality, singularity, circumstantiality; see also **circumstance** 1, **part** 1.

*See Synonym Study at* ITEM. — *Ant.* ENTIRETY, whole, synthesis.

**2.** [A small military force having a specific duty] — *Syn.* detachment, squad, force; see **army** 2, **organization** 3.

**in detail** — *Syn.* item by item, with particulars, thoroughly; see **completely, detailed, specifically** 2.

**detail,** *v.* **1.** [To make clear in detail] — *Syn.* itemize, specify, particularize, exhibit, show, report, relate, narrate, tell, designate, catalog, list, recite, delineate, specialize, depict, portray, enumerate, specify the particulars of, mention, reveal, recount, recapitulate, rehearse, analyze, set forth, stipulate, go into the particulars, spell out, get down to cases★, cite chapter and verse★; see also **describe.** — *Ant.* GENERALIZE, summarize, epitomize.

**2.** [To assign to a specific duty] — *Syn.* detach, appoint, allocate; see **assign** 1.

**detailed,** *modif.* — *Syn.* itemized, enumerated, specified, explicit, specific, particularized, individual, individualized, developed, definite, minute, thorough, exhaustive, elaborate, precise, full, narrow, complete, exact, fussy, particular, meticulous, point by point, circumstantial, nice, accurate, elaborated, complicated, involved, intricate, all-inclusive, comprehensive, unabridged, in full, in depth, seriatim, one after another, at length, newsy★, blow-by-blow★; see also **elaborate** 2. — *Ant.* GENERAL, brief, sketchy.

**details,** *n.* — *Syn.* analysis, trivia, minutiae, particulars, specifics, itemized account, minute account, distinct parts, trivialities, fine points, technicalities, trifles, niceties, minor circumstances, enumeration, amplification, prospectus, table, bill; see also **detail** 1.

**detain,** *v.* — *Syn.* hold back, keep, inhibit, confine; see **arrest** 1, **delay** 1, **restrain** 1.

**detect,** *v.* **1.** [To find out] — *Syn.* distinguish, recognize, identify; see **discover.**

**2.** [To identify a criminal] — *Syn.* disclose, expose, catch; see **expose** 1.

**detection,** *n.* — *Syn.* apprehension, exposure, disclosure; see **discovery** 1, **exposure** 1.

**detective,** *n.* — *Syn.* police officer, policeman, agent, plainclothesman, private investigator, private eye★, narcotics agent, police sergeant, FBI agent, Scotland Yard man, sleuth, shadow★, P.I., operative, wiretapper, polygraphist, investigator, criminologist, member of a crime detection squad, analyst, prosecutor, patrolman, eavesdropper, spy, reporter, shamus★, newshound★, minion of the law★, gumshoe★, flatfoot★, dick★, bloodhound★, hawkshaw★, Sherlock★, bull★, G-man★, copper★, cop★, fed★, narc★, slewfoot★, bug artist★, tail★; see also **agent** 1, **police officer.**

**detector,** *n.* — *Syn.* indicator, pointer, revealer, warner, locater, discoverer, director, radar, distant early warning line, DEW line, sonar, detectaphone, lie detector, polygraph, listening device, sound detector, spotter; see also **radar.**

**détente,** *n.* — *Syn.* relaxation of hostilities, peaceful coexistence, rapprochement; see **pause** 1, 2, **peace** 1, 2, **rest** 2.

**detention,** *n.* **1.** [Enforced delay] — *Syn.* retention, hin-

drance, detainment; see **arrest** 2, **delay** 1, **impediment** 1.
**2.** [Restraint] — *Syn.* custody, internment, quarantine; see **arrest** 1, **confinement** 1, **restraint** 2.
**deter,** *v.* — *Syn.* caution, stop, dissuade; see **discourage** 1, 3, **hinder, prevent.**
**detergent,** *modif.* — *Syn.* cleansing, purificatory, disinfectant; see **cleaning.**
**detergent,** *n.* — *Syn.* cleansing agent, soap powder, soap flakes, surfactant; see **cleanser, soap.**
**deteriorate,** *v.* — *Syn.* depreciate, decline, worsen, degenerate; see **decay.**
**deterioration,** *n.* — *Syn.* decline, rotting, degeneration, atrophy; see **decay** 1.
**determinable,** *modif.* — *Syn.* definable, discoverable, judicable, ascertainable, subject to law, amenable to law, measurable, fixable, capable of being determined, that may be accurately found out, admitting of decision, assayable, deductive, inductive, inferential; see also **provable.**
**determination,** *n.* **1.** [The act of determining] — *Syn.* ascertainment, perception, measurement, resolution; see **judgment** 2, 3.
**2.** [Firmness of mind] — *Syn.* resolution, resoluteness, persistence, certainty, dogmatism, stubbornness, obstinacy, resolve, certitude, decision, assurance, conviction, purpose, intrepidity, boldness, fixity of purpose, hardihood, tenacity, courage, independence, self-confidence, purposefulness, coolness, fortitude, constancy, steadfastness, self-assurance, firmness, dauntlessness, self-reliance, nerve, heart, bravery, fearlessness, valor, intransigence, will, willpower, firmness of purpose, single-mindedness, energy, vigor, stamina, perseverance, strength of will, undauntedness, brave front, bold front, stout heart, mettle, firm faith, enterprise, drive, doggedness, backbone, guts*, spunk*, grit*, pluck*, a stiff upper lip*; see also **confidence** 2. — *Ant.* HESITATION, vacillation, irresolution.
**determine,** *v.* **1.** [To define] — *Syn.* limit, circumscribe, delimit; see **define** 1, **restrict** 2.
**2.** [To find out the facts] — *Syn.* ascertain, find out, learn; see **discover, learn** 2.
**3.** [To decide the course of affairs] — *Syn.* devise, invent, plot, fix; see **arrange** 2, **command** 2, **manage** 1, **plan** 1, **prepare** 1.
**4.** [To resolve] — *Syn.* decide, fix upon, settle, conclude; see **decide, resolve** 1.
*See Synonym Study at* DECIDE, LEARN.
**determined,** *modif.* **1.** [Already fixed] — *Syn.* decided, settled, agreed, acted upon, agreed upon, concluded, compounded, contracted, set, determinate, defined, resolved, closed, terminated, consummated, achieved, finished, over, at an end, confirmed, checked, measured, tested, budgeted, passed, given approval, given the green light*, given the go-ahead*, over and done with*, case closed*, set to rest*; see also **approved.** — *Ant.* UNFINISHED, uncertain, suspended.
**2.** [Having a fixed attitude] — *Syn.* firm, stubborn, strong-minded; see **resolute** 2.
**determining,** *modif.* — *Syn.* deciding, decisive, definitive; see **certain** 3, **conclusive.**
**deterrent,** *n.* — *Syn.* hindrance, impediment, obstacle; see **impediment** 1, **restraint** 2.
**deterring,** *modif.* — *Syn.* stopping, hampering, discouraging, deterrent; see **impeding.**
**detest,** *v.* — *Syn.* hate, abhor, loathe, despise; see **hate** 1.
*See Synonym Study at* HATE.
**detestable,** *modif.* — *Syn.* hateful, offensive, execrable, abhorrent; see **offensive** 2.

*See Synonym Study at* OFFENSIVE.
**detestation,** *n.* — *Syn.* loathing, abhorrence, aversion, revulsion; see **hatred** 1.
**dethrone,** *v.* — *Syn.* depose, oust, degrade; see **dismiss** 1, **oust.**
**detonate,** *v.* — *Syn.* touch off, discharge, explode, blast; see **explode** 1, **shoot** 1.
**detonation,** *n.* — *Syn.* explosion, blast, discharge, firing; see **explosion** 1.
**detour,** *n.* — *Syn.* alternate route, temporary route, circuitous route, bypass, byway, bypath, back road, service road, alternate highway, secondary highway, indirect way, circuit, deviation, digression, roundabout way; see also **road** 1. — *Ant.* HIGHWAY, direct route, main road.
**detract,** *v.* — *Syn.* decrease, take away from, divert, subtract from, draw away, diminish, lessen, reduce, withdraw, derogate, depreciate, discredit; see also **decrease** 2, **depreciate** 2, **lower.**
**detraction,** *n.* — *Syn.* discrediting, disparagement, derogation, defamation; see **lie** 1.
**detractor,** *n.* — *Syn.* derogator, defamer, depreciator, censor; see **critic** 1.
**detriment,** *n.* — *Syn.* loss, harm, injury, drawback; see **damage** 1, 2, **disadvantage** 2, **impediment** 1.
**detrimental,** *modif.* — *Syn.* damaging, disturbing, deleterious; see **harmful, pernicious.**
*See Synonym Study at* PERNICIOUS.
**detritus,** *n.* — *Syn.* rubbish, rubble, waste, debris; see **trash** 1.
**Detroit,** *n.* — *Syn.* Motor City, Motown, City of Straits, Automobile City, Motor Capital of the World, Fordtown*, Big D*.
**devalue,** *v.* — *Syn.* revalue, depreciate, mark down, devaluate; see **cheapen, decrease** 2.
**devastate,** *v.* **1.** [To lay waste] — *Syn.* ravage, desolate, waste; see **destroy** 1, **ravage.**
**2.** [To make helpless] — *Syn.* overwhelm, confound, crush; see **confuse, confute, defeat** 1.
*See Synonym Study at* RAVAGE.
**devastating,** *modif.* **1.** [Causing devastation] — *Syn.* calamitous, disastrous, desolating, mortifying; see **destructive** 2, **overwhelming** 1.
**2.** [Trenchant] — *Syn.* incisive, biting, caustic, crushing; see **ironic** 1, **sarcastic, trenchant** 2.
**devastation,** *n.* — *Syn.* destruction, defoliation, ruin, waste; see **desolation** 1, **destruction** 1, 2.
**develop,** *v.* **1.** [To improve] — *Syn.* enlarge, expand, strengthen, extend, promote, advance, improve, exploit, realize, magnify, build up, augment, refine, enrich, cultivate, generate, beautify, elaborate, polish, finish, perfect, deepen, lengthen, heighten, widen, intensify, fix up, shape up*; see also **grow** 1, **improve** 1, **promote** 1, **strengthen.** — *Ant.* DAMAGE, reduce, stifle.
**2.** [To grow] — *Syn.* mature, evolve, advance, progress; see **grow** 2.
**3.** [To reveal slowly] — *Syn.* unfold, disclose, exhibit, unravel, disentangle, uncover, make known, explain, unwind, unroll, explicate, produce, detail, tell, state, recount, unfurl, untwist, uncoil, untwine, account for, give account of, bring out; see also **narrate, reveal** 1. — *Ant.* HIDE, conceal, blurt out.
**4.** [To work out] — *Syn.* enlarge upon, expatiate, elaborate, fill out, fill in, amplify, evolve, explicate, expand upon, go into detail, build on; see also **explain, increase** 1. — *Ant.* DECREASE, summarize, abridge.
**5.** [To come into being] — *Syn.* emerge, originate, occur; see **begin** 2, **happen** 2.
**6.** [To come to have] — *Syn.* acquire, manifest, incur, contract; see **catch** 4, **form** 4, **receive** 1.

**developed,** *modif.* — *Syn.* grown, refined, advanced; see **matured, perfected.**

**development,** *n.* **1.** [Improvement] — *Syn.* gain, rise, advancement; see **improvement** 1, **progress** 1.
**2.** [The process of growth] — *Syn.* growth, unfolding, elaboration, maturing, progress (toward a more perfect state), ripening, maturation, progress to maturity, enlargement, expansion, augmentation, addition, spread, evolution, gradual evolution, evolving, advancement, improvement, reinforcement, growing, increasing, elaborating, spreading, developing, adding to, reinforcing, progressing, perfecting, making progress, advancing; see also **increase** 1. — *Ant.* REDUCTION, decrease, lessening.
**3.** [A real estate development] — *Syn.* subdivision, housing development, community, tract, addition, annex, shopping center, enlargement, extension, expansion, branch, construction.

**deviant,** *modif.* — *Syn.* aberrant, atypical, abnormal, perverted; see **different** 1, **unusual** 2, **wicked** 1, **wrong** 1, 2.

**deviate,** *v.* — *Syn.* deflect, digress, swerve, shy, vary, wander, stray, turn aside, veer, bear off, go out of control, divagate, depart from, break the pattern, go amiss, err, angle away, angle off, diverge, leave the beaten path, not conform, break bounds, get off the subject, edge off, go out of the way, cut back, cut across, fly off on a tangent, go off on a tangent, go haywire, sing a different tune, march to a different drummer, swim against the stream; see also **differ** 1. — *Ant.* CONFORM, keep on, keep in line.

---

**SYN.** — **deviate** suggests a turning aside, often to only a slight degree, from the correct or prescribed course, standard, doctrine, etc. /to *deviate* from the truth/; **swerve** implies a sudden or sharp turning from a path, course, etc. /the car *swerved* to avoid hitting us/; **veer**, originally used of wind and ships, suggests a turning or series of turnings so as to change direction; **diverge** suggests the branching of a single path or course into two courses leading away from each other /stay to the left when the road *diverges*/; **digress** suggests a wandering, often deliberate and temporary, from the main topic in speaking or writing

---

**deviation,** *n.* — *Syn.* departure, divergence, aberration; see **difference** 1, 2, **perversion** 2, **variation.**

**device,** *n.* **1.** [An instrument] — *Syn.* invention, contrivance, mechanism, tool, apparatus, machine, gear, equipment, appliance, medium, contraption, gadget, arrangement, expedient, wherewithal, means, agent, tackle, rigging, harness, material, implement, utensil, construction, outfit, article, accessory, makeshift, auxiliary, stopgap, widget, thingamabob*, thingamajig*, whatnot*, gimmick*, wrinkle*, thing*, doohickey*, whatsit*, whatchamacallit*; see also **contrivance** 2, **machine** 1, **tool** 1.
**2.** [A shrewd method] — *Syn.* artifice, scheme, design, trap, dodge, machination, trick, pattern, proposition, loophole, wile, craft, cunningness, stratagem, ruse, expedient, subterfuge, plan, project, plot, fake, chicanery, racket, game, craftiness, cabal, evasion, finesse, clever move, sucker trap*, catch*, joker*; see also **discovery** 2, **method** 2, **trick** 1.
**3.** [A figure or scroll] — *Syn.* slogan, symbol, sign; see **design** 1, **emblem.**

**devil,** *n.* **1.** [The power opposed to God] — *Syn.* Satan, demon, fiend, archenemy of God, powers of evil, powers of darkness, imp, mischiefmaker, Lucifer, Beelzebub,

Prince of Darkness, the archfiend, fallen angel, trickster, hellhound, incubus, succubus, evil spirit, evil principle, error, sin, god of this world, supreme spirit of evil, Asmodeus, Mammon, Moloch, Diabolus, Azazel, Angra Mainyu, Ahriman, Eblis, Belial, Baal, Samael, Hades, Abaddon, Apollyon, Set, Mephistopheles, Lilith, diabolical force, satanic force, evil genius, jinni, dybbuk, goblin, the Deuce*, the Old Boy*, Harry*, Old Nick*, Old Scratch*, the Tempter, the Old One, the Wicked One, author of evil, the Foul Fiend, the common enemy, shadow of shadows, Evil One, the Adversary; see also **evil** 1, **witch.** — *Ant.* ANGEL, seraph, God.
**2.** [A vicious or mischievous person] — *Syn.* villain, renegade, scamp; see **beast** 2, **rascal.**
**between the devil and the deep blue sea** — *Syn.* desperate, in a quandary, in difficulty, between a rock and a hard place*; see **in trouble** 1 at **trouble, troubled** 1.
**give the devil his due*** — *Syn.* give one credit, give credit where credit is due, recognize; see **acknowledge** 2.
**go to the devil*** — *Syn.* **1.** degenerate, fall into bad habits, go to pot*; see **decay, fail** 1.
**2.** go to hell, damn you, be damned; see **curse.**
**raise the devil*** — *Syn.* cause trouble, riot, be boisterous, be unruly, revel; see also **celebrate** 3, **rage** 1.

**devilish,** *modif.* — *Syn.* fiendish, brutish, diabolic, impish; see **naughty, wicked** 2.

**devil-may-care,** *modif.* — *Syn.* defiant, reckless, flippant; see **careless** 1, **jaunty, nonchalant, rash.**

**deviltry,** *n.* — *Syn.* rascality, roguery, trouble; see **mischief** 3.

**devious,** *modif.* **1.** [Indirect] — *Syn.* circuitous, roundable, tortuous, evasive; see **indirect.**
**2.** [Crafty] — *Syn.* foxy, insidious, shrewd, underhanded; see **dishonest** 1, **sly** 1.

**devoid,** *modif.* — *Syn.* void, destitute of, lacking, without; see **empty** 1, **wanting** 1.

**devote,** *v.* — *Syn.* dedicate, apply, consecrate, give; see **bless** 3, **dedicate** 2.
*See Synonym Study at* DEDICATE.

**devoted,** *modif.* — *Syn.* dutiful, loyal, constant, attached; see **faithful, loving.**

**devotee,** *n.* — *Syn.* zealot, adherent, believer, fan; see **enthusiast** 1, **follower.**

**devotion,** *n.* — *Syn.* allegiance, service, consecration, dedication, commitment, devotedness, adoration, piety, zeal, ardor, earnestness, fealty, faithfulness, fidelity, loyalty, constancy, affection, attachment, love, reverence, deference, sincerity, devoutness, adherence, observance; see also **affection** 1, **loyalty, worship** 1. — *Ant.* INDIFFERENCE, apathy, carelessness.

**devotional,** *modif.* — *Syn.* devout, pious, reverential, holy; see **divine** 2, **religious** 1, 2.

**devotions,** *n.* — *Syn.* prayers, worship, religious observances, rituals; see **church** 2, **worship** 1.

**devour,** *v.* — *Syn.* gulp, swallow, gorge; see **eat** 1.

**devout,** *modif.* — *Syn.* religious, devoted, pious, reverent; see **faithful, holy** 2, **religious** 2.
*See Synonym Study at* RELIGIOUS.

**dexterity,** *n.* — *Syn.* adroitness, facility, skill; see **ability** 2.

**dexterous,** *modif.* — *Syn.* artful, skillful, adroit, deft, handy, nimble, quick, clever, ingenious, sharp; see also **able** 1, 2.

---

**SYN.** — **dexterous** implies an expertness, natural or acquired, demonstrated in the ability to do things with skill and precision /a *dexterous* mechanic/; **adroit** adds to this a connotation of cleverness and resourcefulness and is now generally used of mental facility *[an* adroit *evasion];* **deft** suggests a nimbleness and sureness of touch *[a* deft *seamstress];* **handy** suggests skill, usually without training, at a variety of small tasks *[a* handy *man around the house]*

**diabolic,** *modif.* — *Syn.* diabolical, fiendish, devilish, satanic; see **cruel** 1, **sinister, wicked** 2.

**diagnosis,** *n.* — *Syn.* analysis, determination, investigation; see **examination** 1, 3, **judgment** 2, 3.

**diagnostic,** *modif.* — *Syn.* demonstrative, distinguishing, indicative, symptomatic; see **characteristic.**

**diagonal,** *modif.* — *Syn.* slanting, inclining, askew; see **oblique** 1.

**diagonally,** *modif.* — *Syn.* cornerways, slanting, askew; see **cornerwise.**

**diagram,** *n.* — *Syn.* sketch, layout, picture, chart; see **description** 1, **design** 1, **plan** 1.

**dial,** *n.* — *Syn.* face, front, disk with figures, circle, numbers, control, knob, indicator, gauge, device for showing time, meter, register, measuring device, horologe, compass; see also **control** 3.

**dial,** *v.* 1. [To turn] — *Syn.* rotate, twist, wheel; see **turn** 1.
2. [To telephone] — *Syn.* ring (up), call (up), phone; see **telephone.**

**dialect,** *n.* — *Syn.* idiom, accent, vernacular, patois, slang, jargon, argot, cant, lingo★, pidgin, creole; see also **accent** 3, **language** 1.

Accents and dialects of English include — *United States:* Standard American, stage, Northern, Midland, North Midland, South Midland, Black, Southern, General American, Eastern New England, Inland North, Boston, Down East, Upstate New York, New York City, Bronx, Brooklyn, Chelsea, Virginia Piedmont, Highland Southern, Southern Highlands, Southern Tidewater, Coastal Southern, Gulla, Southern Appalachian, Southern Louisiana, Gulf States, Deep South, Texas, Cajun, Chicago, Western, Southwest, Northwest; *British Isles:* British Standard, Received Standard, BBC, public-school, Northern, Midland, Birmingham, Southern, cockney, Southeastern, Kentish, Gloucestershire, Devonshire, Cornish, Shropshire, Oxford, Lincolnshire, Norfolk, Yorkshire, Lancashire, Liverpool, Northumbrian, Lowland Scots, Glasgow, Highland Scots, Edinburgh, Inverness, Welsh, Irish, Dublin, Ulster, Belfast, Aran Islands, Western Irish; *others:* Australian, New Zealand, South African, Canadian, Maritime, Ontario, Western Canadian.

Accents and dialects of languages other than English include — *French:* langue d'oc, langue d'oïl (*both* French), Parisian, Norman, Anglo-Norman, Breton, Gascon, Provençal, Occitan, French Canadian, Algerian; *Spanish:* Castilian, Catalan, Andalusian, South American, Central American, Mexican, Puerto Rican, Cuban, Philippine; *German:* High German, Bavarian, Franconian, Swabian, Swiss German, Austrian, Rhenish, Yiddish; Low German, Plattdeutsch, Prussian, Berlin, Hamburg, Saxon, Pennsylvania Dutch, Pennsylvania German; *Italian:* Tuscan, Piedmontese, Roman, Venetian, Neopolitan, Sicilian; *Russian:* Muscovite, Little Russian, Belorussian, White Russian, Georgian, Siberian; *Chinese:* Mandarin, Fukien, Peking, Beijing, Cantonese, Manchurian, Shansi.

**SYN.** — **dialect,** in this comparison, refers to a form of a language used within a particular locality or group and differing from the standard language in matters of pro-

nunciation, syntax, etc.; **vernacular** today commonly refers to the informal or colloquial spoken variety of a language as distinguished from the formal or literary variety; **cant** refers to the distinctive stock words, phrases, and clichés used by a particular sect, class, etc. *[clergymen's* cant*]*; **jargon** is used of the special vocabulary and idioms of a particular class, occupational group, etc., esp. by one who is unfamiliar with these; **argot** refers esp. to the secret jargon of thieves and tramps; **lingo** is a humorous or mildly contemptuous term applied to any language, dialect, or jargon by one to whom it is unintelligible; **slang** refers to highly informal speech and particularly to new words, phrases, and extended senses, esp. when restricted in use to an identifiable group *[college* slang*]*

**dialectal,** *modif.* — *Syn.* regional, local, provincial, limited, dialectical, colloquial, vernacular, idiomatic, indigenous, rural, geographically restricted, socially restricted, nonstandard, not generally accepted, not generally in use; see also **colloquial, local** 1.

**dialectical,** *modif.* — *Syn.* argumentative, rationalistic, analytic, persuasive; see **controversial, rational** 1.

**dialectic,** *n.* — *Syn.* argumentation, persuasion, deduction; see **debate, logic.**

**dialogue,** *n.* — *Syn.* conversation, talk, exchange, remarks; see **conversation, discussion** 1.

**diameter,** *n.* — *Syn.* bore, caliber, breadth, measurement across, broadness; see also **width.**

**diametrical,** *modif.* — *Syn.* polar, antipodal, contrary, facing; see **opposite** 1, 3.

**diamond,** *n.* 1. [A crystalline jewel] — *Syn.* (precious) stone, solitaire, engagement ring, brilliant, bort(s), diamond chips *or* flakes, crystal, ring, finger ring, rock★, sparkler★, glass★, ice★; see also **jewel** 1.
Grades, sizes, and forms of diamonds include: green, blue, blue-green, yellow, orange, canary, red, pink, brown, gray, smoky, black, rough, uncut, brilliant, double brilliant, half-brilliant, trap-brilliant, split-brilliant, old-mine, Kimberley, Brazilian, industrial, artificial; table, pear-shaped, marquise, baguette, emerald-cut, table-cut, flat-cut, square-cut, oval-cut; diamond of the first water, diamond of the second water, diamond of the third water; see also **gem** 1, **stone.**
Famous diamonds include: Jubilee, Cullinan, Orlof, Nassak, Pigott, Hope, Great Mogul, Shah of Persia, Florentine, Star of the South, Kohinoor, Mountain of Light, Star of Yakutia, Regent, Pitt, Pascha of Egypt.
2. [An instrument using a diamond] — *Syn.* cutter, glass cutter, diamond point; see **tool** 1.
3. [Shape or figure] — *Syn.* lozenge, rhombus, rhomb, quadrilateral; see **form** 1, **solid.**
4. [A baseball playing field, particularly the infield] — *Syn.* lot, ballpark, sandlot, orchard★, pasture★, inner works★; see also **field** 2, **park** 1.

**diaphanous,** *modif.* — *Syn.* translucent, sheer, filmy, gossamer; see **clear** 2, **thin** 1, **transparent** 1.

**diary,** *n.* — *Syn.* chronicle, record, log; see **journal** 1.

**diatribe,** *n.* — *Syn.* criticism, denunciation, tirade, harangue; see **blame** 1, **objection** 2.

**dice,** *n.* — *Syn.* cubes, counters, pair of dice, misspotted dice, bones★, ivories★, tombstones★, galloping dominoes★, rattling bones★, shakers★, craps, crap game.
**no dice★** — *Syn.* never, nothing doing, no deal; see **no.**

**dicker,** *v.* — *Syn.* trade, barter, bargain, haggle; see **argue** 1, **buy** 1, **negotiate** 1, **sell** 1.

**dictate,** *v.* 1. [To speak for record] — *Syn.* speak, deliver, give forth, interview, compose, formulate, verbalize, record, orate, emit, give an account, draft correspondence, prepare the first draft; see also **talk** 1.

**2.** [To give peremptory orders] — *Syn.* direct, prescribe, decree, ordain; see **command** 1, 2, **manage** 1. — *Ant.* FOLLOW, plead, petition.

**dictation,** *n.* — *Syn.* account, record, correspondence, notes, dictated matter, verbal composition, shorthand, stenography, copy, transcription, typescript, material for transcription, message for transcription; see also **notes, shorthand.**

**dictator,** *n.* — *Syn.* autocrat, despot, tyrant, strongman, absolute ruler, absolute monarch, czar, tsar, usurper, oppressor, authoritarian, absolutist, warlord, terrorist, oligarch, inquisitor, master, leader, fascist, *Führer* (German), *duce* (Italian), *caudillo* (Spanish), caesar, kaiser, ringleader, magnate, tycoon, mogul, shah, rajah, sultan, sheik, emir, khan, lama, lord, commander, chief, adviser, overlord, taskmaster, disciplinarian, headman, caliph, pharaoh, martinet, lord of the ascendant, sachem, wirepuller*, cock of the walk*, person at the wheel*, Nazi*, boss*, robber baron*, slave driver*, Simon Legree*; see also **leader** 2, **ruler** 1.

**dictatorial,** *modif.* **1.** [Overbearing] — *Syn.* imperious, domineering, arrogant, dogmatic; see **egotistic** 2, **masterful, proud** 2.

**2.** [Autocratic] — *Syn.* despotic, authoritarian, arbitrary; see **absolute** 3, **autocratic** 1, **tyrannical.**
*See Synonym Study at* DOGMATIC.

---

***SYN.*** — **dictatorial** implies the domineering, autocratic methods or manner of a dictator *[the dictatorial enunciation of his opinions]*; **arbitrary** suggests the unreasoned, unpredictable use of one's power or authority *[an arbitrary decision]*; **dogmatic** suggests the assertion of certain doctrines as absolute truths not open to dispute *[the scientific method is not dogmatic]*; **doctrinaire** implies a rigid adherence to abstract doctrines or theories, without regard to their practical application

---

**dictatorship,** *n.* — *Syn.* despotism, unlimited rule, totalitarianism, coercion; see **autocracy, fascism, government** 2, **tyranny.**

**diction,** *n.* — *Syn.* style, expression, wording, phrasing, usage, choice of words, command of language, literary artistry, manner of expression, literary power, locution, rhetoric, fluency, oratory, pronunciation, articulation, enunciation, delivery, elocution, vocabulary, phraseology, verbiage, language, *Sprachgefühl* (German), lingo*, gift of gab*; see also **eloquence** 1, **speech** 2, **wording.**

**dictionary,** *n.* — *Syn.* glossary, lexicon, wordbook, word list, vocabulary, thesaurus, concordance, reference work, gazetteer, encyclopedia, cyclopedia, dictionary of synonyms, promptory, *promptorium* (Latin), lexicographical work, unabridged dictionary, desk dictionary, college dictionary, bilingual dictionary; dictionary of religion, dictionary of airplane mechanics, dictionary of law, etc., Webster's*; see also **reference** 3.

**dictum,** *n.* **1.** [Pronouncement] — *Syn.* dictate, assertion, decree; see **announcement** 2, **declaration** 1, 2, **judgment** 3.

**2.** [Proverb] — *Syn.* maxim, adage, precept, saying; see **motto, proverb.**

**didactic,** *modif.* — *Syn.* instructive, expository, academic, preachy*; see **educational** 1, **pedantic.**

**die,** *v.* **1.** [To cease living] — *Syn.* decease, expire, pass away, pass on, depart, perish, succumb, go, commit suicide, suffocate, lose one's life, cease respiration, emit the last breath, relinquish life, suffer death, cease to exist,

come to a violent end, come to naught, drown, hang, fall, meet one's death, be no more, end one's earthly career, be taken, drop dead*, go to glory, go up*, go off*, return to the earth, fall asleep*, be done for*, catch one's death*, fade away, rest in peace, go belly up*, be numbered with the dead, join the choir invisible, pay the supreme sacrifice, go to one's last home, cross the Styx, pass over to the great beyond, give up the ghost, go the way of all flesh, pay the debt of nature, shuffle off this mortal coil, slide into oblivion, become one with nature, awake to immortal life, join the great majority, turn to dust, return to dust, close one's eyes, cash in one's chips*, cash in*, go west*, push up daisies*, buy the farm*, kick the bucket*, shut up shop*, answer the last call*, bite the dust*, lay down one's life*, breathe one's last, croak*, bite the bullet*, kick in*, go to one's reward, be gathered to one's fathers, keel over*, conk out*, go home feet first*, check out*, burn out*, kick off*, end one's days, go by the board*. — *Ant.* LIVE, thrive, exist.

**2.** [To cease existing] — *Syn.* stop, extinguish, dissolve, disappear, die out, go out, recede, vanish, evanesce, burn out, be heard of no more, come to nothing, evaporate, become extinct, die off, be null and void, be no more, leave not a trace behind, discontinue, go blooey*, go *pfft**; see also **disappear, stop** 2. — *Ant.* ENDURE, go on, CONTINUE.

**3.** [To decline as though death were inevitable] — *Syn.* fade, wither, decline, wane, sink, wear away, ebb, droop, lapse, retrograde, lose active qualities, run low, rot, crumble, diminish, deteriorate, molder, rankle, dilapidate, die out, die down, melt away, subside, go bad*, totter to a fall*, go downhill*; see also **decay, weaken** 1. — *Ant.* GROW, increase, IMPROVE.

---

***SYN.*** — **die** is the basic, simple, direct word meaning to stop living or to become dead; **decease, expire,** and **pass away** are all euphemisms; **decease** being also the legal term, **expire** meaning literally to breathe one's last breath, and **pass away** suggesting a transition to another state; **perish** implies death by a violent means or under difficult circumstances

---

**die away,** *v.* — *Syn.* diminish, fade away, become fainter, sink; see **decrease** 1, **disappear, stop** 2.

**die down,** *v.* — *Syn.* decline, subside, abate, recede; see **decrease** 1, **die** 3.

**die-hard,** *modif.* — *Syn.* immovable, intransigent, extremist; see **conservative, obstinate, resolute** 2.

**die-hard,** *n.* — *Syn.* zealot, reactionary, extremist, bitter-ender*; see **conservative, zealot.**

**die off** *or* **out,** *v.* — *Syn.* go, cease to exist, vanish; see **die** 2, **disappear.**

**diet,** *n.* **1.** [What one eats] — *Syn.* fare, intake, daily bread*, nutrition; see **food, menu.**

**2.** [Restricted intake of food] — *Syn.* weight-reduction plan, nutritional therapy, dietary regimen, regime, fast, abstinence from food, starvation diet, bread and water*.

**diet,** *v.* — *Syn.* go on a diet, watch one's weight, count calories, go without, starve oneself, lose weight, slim down, reduce, abstain, tighten one's belt*.

**dieter,** *n.* — *Syn.* reducer, weight-watcher, calorie-counter, faster, abstainer from food, health-food nut*.

**differ,** *v.* **1.** [To be unlike] — *Syn.* vary, contrast, diverge, not conform, digress, turn, reverse, alter, change, bear no resemblance, not look like, divaricate from, jar with, clash with, conflict with, be distinguished from, diversify, lack resemblance, show contrast, stand apart, deviate from, depart from, be unlike, be dissimilar, be at variance, disagree, not accord with, distinct in nature, have nothing in common, sing a different tune, leave the beaten path; see also **contrast** 1, **deviate**.— *Ant.* RESEMBLE, parallel, take after, agree.

**2.** [To oppose] — *Syn.* disagree, object, dissent, take exception; see **oppose** 1.

**difference,** *n.* **1.** [The quality of being different] — *Syn.* dissimilarity, disagreement, divergence, contrast, state of being different, nonconformity, contrariety, contrariness, deviation, opposition, antithesis, inequality, diversity, unlikeness, departure, lack of identity, lack of resemblance, variance, variation, discrepancy, separation, differentiation, distinctness, separateness, heterogeneity, dissimilitude, incongruity, asymmetry; see also **contrast** 1, **variety** 1.— *Ant.* AGREEMENT, similarity, resemblance.

**2.** [That which is unlike in comparable things] — *Syn.* disparity, distinction, variance, deviation, departure, discrepancy, inconsistency, distinguishing characteristic, peculiarity, idiosyncrasy, exception, digression, contrast, unconformity, aberration, irregularity, anomaly, abnormality, contradistinction, deflection, interval; see also **variation** 2.— *Ant.* SIMILARITY, likeness, common ground.

**3.** [Personal dissension] — *Syn.* discord, estrangement, dissent, disagreement; see **dispute**.

**make a difference** — *Syn.* change, have an effect, affect; see **matter** 1.

**split the difference**★ — *Syn.* compromise, meet halfway, come to an agreement, share; see **agree, arbitrate.**

**what's the difference?**★ — *Syn.* what does it matter? what difference does it make? so what?★; see **why.**

**different,** *modif.* **1.** [Unlike in nature] — *Syn.* distinct, separate, not the same, nothing like, dissimilar, unlike, in disagreement, divergent, disparate, contrasted, variant, dissonant, deviating, deviant, incongruous, varying, various, diverse, contradistinct, incompatible, inconsistent, changed, modified, dissimilar, unlike, contrary, contradictory, contrasting, discordant, inharmonious, opposed, disagreeing, varied, clashing, antagonistic, unsuitable, diametric, reverse, converse, unidentical, contrastive, ranging, to be contrasted, not identical, set apart, other than, another, far from, out of line with, a far cry from, at odds.— *Ant.* ALIKE, like, similar.

**2.** [Composed of unlike things] — *Syn.* diverse, disparate, manifold, various, divergent, diversified, inconsistent, incongruous, indiscriminate, dissonant, heterogeneous, sundry, variegated, collected, anthologized, miscellaneous, unselected, unclassified, many, several, jarring, asymmetrical, varicolored, assorted; see also **complex** 1, **mixed** 1, **various.**— *Ant.* HARMONIOUS, identical, uniform.

**3.** [Unusual] — *Syn.* unconventional, distinctive, strange, offbeat★; see **unusual** 1, 2.

---

*SYN.* — **different,** applied to things that are not alike, implies individuality [three *different* doctors] or contrast [the twins wore *different* hats]; **diverse** more emphatically sets apart the things referred to, suggesting a conspicuous difference [*diverse* interests]; **divergent** suggests a branching off in different directions with an ever-widening distance between, and stresses irreconcilability [*divergent* schools of thought]; **distinct,** as applied to two or more things, stresses that each has a different identity and is unmistakably separate from the others, whether or not they are similar in kind, class, etc. [charged with two *distinct* offenses]; **dissimilar** stresses absence of similarity in appearance, properties, or nature [*dissimilar* techniques]; **disparate** implies essential or thoroughgoing difference, often stressing an absence of any relationship between things [*disparate* concepts]; **various** emphasizes the number and diversity of kinds, types, etc. [*various* gifts]

---

**differentiate,** *v.* **1.** [To distinguish] — *Syn.* contrast, set apart, separate, discriminate; see **distinguish** 1.

**2.** [To change] — *Syn.* modify, adapt, alter; see **change** 1.

*See Synonym Study at* DISTINGUISH.

**differently,** *modif.* **1.** [In various ways] — *Syn.* variously, diversely, divergently, individually, distinctively, creatively, uniquely, separately, each in one's own way, severally, disparately, incongruously, heterogeneously, abnormally, not normally, contrastively, contrastingly, in differing ways, uncomfortably, nonconformably, unusually, asymmetrically, in a different manner, with a difference, multiformly, otherwise.— *Ant.* EVENLY, uniformly, invariably.

**2.** [In opposition] — *Syn.* adversely, discordantly, dissimilarly, oppositely, contradictorily, contrarily, conflictingly, antagonistically, incompatibly, hostilely, antithetically, negatively, vice versa, conversely, on the contrary, on the other hand, poles apart, on the other side of the fence★; see also **against** 3.— *Ant.* similarly, UNANIMOUSLY, identically.

**difficult,** *modif.* **1.** [Hard to achieve] — *Syn.* laborious, hard, arduous, strenuous, demanding, exacting, hardwon, stiff, heavy, painful, labored, trying, titanic, bothersome, troublesome, burdensome, backbreaking, not easy, wearisome, onerous, attended by obstacles, rigorous, Herculean, requiring much effort, Gargantuan, uphill, Sisyphean, challenging, taxing, formidable, ambitious, intricate, irksome, vexatious, tedious, immense, exhausting, grueling, stressful, unyielding, tricky, delicate, ticklish, beyond one's ability, tough★, heavy★, mansized★, no picnic★, hairy★, sticky★; see also **onerous, severe** 1.— *Ant.* EASY, manageable, light.

**2.** [Hard to understand] — *Syn.* intricate, involved, perplexing, abstruse, abstract, tricky, hard, obscure, complex, complicated, knotty, thorny, troublesome, obstinate, puzzling, mysterious, mystifying, subtle, confusing, bewildering, dark, confounding, esoteric, unclear, mystical, tangled, hard to explain, hard to solve, entangled, profound, vexing, baffling, enmeshed, rambling, loose, meandering, trackless, inexplicable, pathless, awkward, digressive, turgid, deep, stubborn, labyrinthine, hidden, formidable, enigmatic, occult, paradoxical, incomprehensible, unintelligible, inscrutable, inexplicable, unanswerable, not understandable, unsolvable, unfathomable, concealed, unaccountable, ambiguous, equivocal, metaphysical, inconceivable, recondite, overtechnical, unknown, steep★, tough★, over one's head★, beyond one's depth★, too deep★, beyond one's comprehension, not making sense, Greek to★, past comprehension; see also **obscure** 1, 3.— *Ant.* simple, CLEAR, easy.

**3.** [Hard to deal with or manage] — *Syn.* unmanageable, perverse, unaccommodating, finicky; see **careful, contrary** 4, **irritable, obstinate.**

---

*SYN.* — **hard,** in this comparison, is the simple and general word for whatever demands great physical or mental effort [*hard* work, a *hard* problem]; **difficult** applies especially to that which requires great skill, intelligence, tact, etc. rather than physical labor [a *difficult* situation; a *difficult* book]; **arduous** implies the need for diligent, protracted effort /the *arduous* fight ahead of us/; **laborious** suggests long, wearisome toil /the *laborious* task of picking fruit/

**difficulty,** *n.* **1.** [Something difficult or in one's way] — *Syn.* obstacle, obstruction, impediment, stumbling block, complication, problem, snag, hitch, hardship, rigor, adversity, misfortune, vicissitude, dilemma, hard job, struggle, Herculean task, labyrinth, maze, stone wall, barricade, predicament, plight, impasse, knot, knotty problem, thorny problem, challenge, quandary, frustration, quagmire, pass, quicksand, critical situation, crisis, pinch, trouble, embarrassment, entanglement, imbroglio, setback, cul-de-sac, dead end, blind alley, deadlock, mess, slough, paradox, puzzle, muddle, swamp, straits, financial embarrassment, squeeze, poser, crux, emergency, the matter, standstill, hindrance, bother, inconvenience, disadvantage, rub, perplexity, bar, trial, check, hazard, corner, hole, double bind, touchy situation, embarrassing situation, scrape, peck of troubles*, hot water*, hornet's nest*, can of worms*, pickle*, fix*, jam*, bind*, tight spot*, hard nut to crack*, tough nut to crack*, hard row to hoe*, hump*, crimp*, catch*, joker*, monkey wrench in the works*, deep water*, tough proposition*, horns of a dilemma*, Gordian knot*, the devil to pay*, hang-up*, toughie*; see also **barrier, crisis, impediment** 1, **predicament, trouble** 2. — *Ant.* AID, assistance, help.
**2.** [Something mentally disturbing] — *Syn.* trouble, distress, annoyance, to-do, ado, worry, weight, complication, oppression, depression, aggravation, perplexity, bafflement, anxiety, discouragement, embarrassment, burden, grievance, quandary, straits, exigency, irritation, strife, puzzle, responsibility, frustration, harassment, misery, pressure, stress, strain, care, charge, millstone, struggle, bother, headache*, hang-up*, stew*, where the shoe pinches*, pain*; see also sense 1; **affliction.** — *Ant.* ease, comfort, happiness.
**3.** [The fact of being difficult] — *Syn.* arduousness, hardness, intricacy, complexity, laboriousness, strenuousness, rigor, rigorousness, formidability, onerousness, burdensomeness, painfulness, toughness*, hassle*.
**4.** [Objection] — *Syn.* reluctance, unwillingness, demur, flak*; see **objection** 1, 2.
**with difficulty** — *Syn.* in the face of great odds, having a hard time, having a bad time, under a handicap, in spite of one's best efforts; with embarrassment.

**SYN.** — **difficulty** is applied to anything hard to contend with, without restriction as to nature, intensity, etc. /the *difficulty* of learning to read, a life filled with great *ifficulties*/; **hardship**, stronger in connotation, suggests suffering, privation, or trouble that is extremely hard to bear /the *hardships* of poverty/; **rigor** suggests severe hardship but further connotes that it is imposed by external, impersonal circumstances beyond one's control /the *rigors* of winter/; **vicissitude**, a bookish word, suggests a difficulty that is likely to occur in the changeable course of something, often one inherent in a situation /the *vicissitudes* of political life/

**diffidence,** *n.* — *Syn.* timidity, reserve, constraint; see **restraint** 1, **shyness.**
**diffident,** *modif.* — *Syn.* shy, bashful, timid; see **humble** 1, **reserved** 3.
*See Synonym Study at* SHY.
**diffuse,** *modif.* **1.** [Widely separated] — *Syn.* dispersed, thin, diluted; see **distributed, scattered.**
**2.** [Rambling and dull] — *Syn.* discursive, prolix,

wordy; see **verbose.**
*See Synonym Study at* WORDY.
**diffuse,** *v.* — *Syn.* spread, disperse, distribute; see **scatter** 1, 2.
**diffusion,** *n.* — *Syn.* dissemination, spread, dispersion; see **dissipation** 1, **distribution** 1.
**dig,** *n.* **1.** [Insult] — *Syn.* gibe, taunt, innuendo, cut; see **insult, ridicule.**
**2.** [Excavation] — *Syn.* digging, archaeological expedition, exploration; see **excavation** 1, **expedition** 2, **hole** 2, 3.
**dig,** *v.* **1.** [To stir the earth] — *Syn.* delve, shovel, spade, mine, excavate, fork, elevate, channel, deepen, till, drive (a shaft), clean, undermine, burrow, dig out, dig down, depress, gouge, dredge, drill, bore, scoop out, tunnel, hollow out, clean out, muck*, grub, bulldoze, cat*, put a whirler to work, stope; see also **shovel.** — *Ant.* EMBED, fill, bury.
**2.** [To remove by digging] — *Syn.* dig up, discover, uncover, bring to the surface, empty, exhume, unearth, turn up, produce, bring to light, excavate, quarry, dredge up, investigate, sift; see also **harvest.**
**3.** [*To like] — *Syn.* enjoy, love, groove on*; see **like** 1, 2.
**4.** [*To understand] — *Syn.* comprehend, recognize, follow; see **understand** 1.
**digest,** *n.* — *Syn.* compendium, précis, condensation; see **abridgment** 2, **summary.**
*See Synonym Study at* ABRIDGMENT.
**digest,** *v.* **1.** [To transform food] — *Syn.* assimilate, break down, ingest, chymify; see **absorb** 1, **eat** 1.
**2.** [To understand by deliberation] — *Syn.* consider, analyze, think over; see **think** 1, **understand** 1.
**3.** [To summarize] — *Syn.* condense, abstract, survey, abbreviate; see **decrease** 2.
**digestible,** *modif.* — *Syn.* eatable, absorbable, good to eat; see **edible.**
**digestion,** *n.* — *Syn.* digesting, eupepsia, assimilation, separation, disintegration, conversion, ingestion, absorption, metabolism, chymification.
**dig in,** *v.* **1.** [*To begin, especially to begin eating] — *Syn.* start in, attack, fall to; see **begin** 1, **bite** 1, **eat** 1.
**2.** [To entrench] — *Syn.* fortify, brace oneself, stand firm, dig in one's heels; see **defend** 1, **endure** 2, **resolve** 1.
**dig into*,** *v.* — *Syn.* investigate, research, probe, delve into; see **examine** 1.
**digit,** *n.* **1.** [A finger or toe] — *Syn.* phalange, extremity, thumb; see **finger, toe.**
**2.** [A number] — *Syn.* numeral, figure, symbol, Arabic notation; see **number** 2.
**dignified,** *modif.* — *Syn.* stately, somber, solemn, sober, courtly, reserved, decorous, staid, sedate, elegant, exalted, elevated, formal, ceremonious, classical, classic, quiet, lordly, aristocratic, princely, imperial, majestic, queenly, of consequence, respected, ladylike, gentlemanly, noble, regal, superior, magnificent, grand, eminent, sublime, august, marked by dignity of manner, grave, serious, distinguished, magisterial, imperious, imposing, portly, haughty, stiff, honorable, lofty, proud, distingué, glorious, gravely courteous, classy*, like one who has a ramrod down his back*, sober as a judge*, high-brow*; see also **cultured, refined** 2. — *Ant.* undignified, boorish, silly.
**dignify,** *v.* — *Syn.* exalt, elevate, ennoble, glorify; see **praise** 1, **promote** 2.
**dignity,** *n.* **1.** [A presence that commands respect] — *Syn.* stateliness, nobility, self-respect, pride, hauteur,

nobility of manner, lofty bearing, elevated deportment, sublimity, dignified behavior, decorum, propriety, decency, grand air, loftiness, formality, gravity, solemnity, ceremoniousness, distinction, elevation, reserve, presence, gravitas, worthiness, worth, regard, character, importance, renown, splendor, majesty, consequence, that mysterious something*, stuff*, class*, tone*; see also **honor** 1, **pride** 3.— *Ant.* lowliness, unseemliness, meekness.

**2.** [A station that commands respect]— *Syn.* rank, honor, significance; see **fame** 1, **importance** 1, **rank** 3. *See Synonym Study at* DECORUM.

**digress,** *v.* — *Syn.* stray, diverge, maunder, deviate; see **deviate, ramble** 2. *See Synonym Study at* DEVIATE.

**digression,** *n.* — *Syn.* deviation, diversion, divergence, excursus, departure, tangent, aside, wandering, divagation, rambling, straying, circumlocution, parenthesis, apostrophe, going off on a tangent; see also **variation** 1.

**dig up,** *v.* — *Syn.* find, uncover, excavate; see **dig** 2, **discover.**

**dike,** *n.* — *Syn.* embankment, wall, barrier; see **dam** 1.

**dilapidated,** *modif.* — *Syn.* rundown, neglected, tumbledown, in disrepair; see **crumbly, decaying, old** 2.

**dilapidation,** *n.* — *Syn.* ruin, disintegration, disrepair; see **destruction** 2. *See Synonym Study at* RUIN.

**dilate,** *v.* — *Syn.* stretch, expand, enlarge, widen; see **increase** 1, **stretch** 2. *See Synonym Study at* EXPAND.

**dilation,** *n.* — *Syn.* distention, expansion, extension; see **increase** 1.

**dilatory,** *modif.* — *Syn.* tardy, procrastinating, lazy; see **late** 1, **slow** 2.

**dilemma,** *n.* — *Syn.* quandary, perplexity, predicament, double bind; see **difficulty** 1, **predicament.** *See Synonym Study at* PREDICAMENT.

**dilettante,** *n.* — *Syn.* dabbler, trifler, aesthete, amateur; see **amateur.** *See Synonym Study at* AMATEUR, CONNOISSEUR.

**diligence,** *n.* — *Syn.* assiduity, industry, perseverance, persistence, application, constancy, sedulousness, persistent exertion, assiduousness, industriousness, studiousness, pertinacity, tirelessness, carefulness, care, thoroughness, attentiveness, intentness, keenness, earnestness, steadiness, stick-to-itiveness*; see also **attention** 2, **care** 1.— *Ant.* CARELESSNESS, sloth, laziness.

**diligent,** *modif.* — *Syn.* industrious, hard-working, assiduous, sedulous, studious, pertinacious, persevering, persistent, keen, tireless, unflagging, unremitting, untiring, indefatigable, careful, painstaking, thorough, purposeful, resolute, busy, intent, involved, earnest, steady, constant, dogged; see also **busy** 1, **careful.** — *Ant.* LAZY, dilatory, careless.

---

**SYN.** — **diligent** implies persevering and careful attention, usually to a particular task, and often connotes enjoyment in the task *[a diligent student of music]*; **assiduous** suggests painstaking, persevering preoccupation with some task *[assiduous study]*; **sedulous** implies unremitting devotion to a task until the goal is reached *[a sedulous investigation of the crime]*; **industrious** suggests habitual devotion to one's work or activity *[an industrious salesclerk]*

---

**dillydally,** *v.* — *Syn.* dawdle, dally, vacillate, waver; see

**delay** 1, **hesitate, loiter.**

**dilute,** *v.* — *Syn.* water down, reduce, thin; see **adulterate, weaken** 2.

**dim,** *modif.* — *Syn.* faint, dusky, shadowy; see **dark** 1. *See Synonym Study at* DARK.

**take a dim view of**— *Syn.* suspect, disapprove, be skeptical about; see **doubt** 2, **oppose** 1.

**dime,** *n.* — *Syn.* ten cents, thin dime, ten-cent piece, short bit*, ten-center*, thin one*; see also **money** 1.

**dimensions,** *n.* — *Syn.* size, measurements, extent; see **height** 1, **length** 1, 2, **measurement** 2, **width.**

**diminish,** *v.* **1.** [To grow less]— *Syn.* decrease, wane, abate, decline; see **decrease** 1.

**2.** [To make less]— *Syn.* decrease, lessen, reduce, abbreviate; see **decrease** 2, **depreciate** 2. *See Synonym Study at* DECREASE.

**diminution,** *n.* — *Syn.* lessening, decrease, alleviation; see **reduction** 1.

**diminutive,** *modif.* — *Syn.* small, tiny, mini*; see **little** 1, **minute** 1. *See Synonym Study at* SMALL.

**din,** *n.* — *Syn.* clamor, racket, commotion; see **confusion** 2, **noise** 2, **uproar.** *See Synonym Study at* NOISE.

**dine,** *v.* — *Syn.* sup, feast, lunch; see **eat** 1.

**diner,** *n.* **1.** [One who eats]— *Syn.* patron, customer, luncher, guest, boarder, eater, diner-out, gourmet, gourmand, trencherman, snacker, grazer*, nosher*, chowhound*; see also **glutton.**

**2.** [A restaurant, as on a train]— *Syn.* luncheonette, coffee shop, dining car, greasy spoon*; see **dining room, restaurant.**

**dingy,** *modif.* — *Syn.* grimy, soiled, gloomy, shabby; see **dirty** 1, **dismal** 1.

**dining room,** *n.* Types of dining rooms and places of dining include: dining hall, breakfast nook, dinette, tea room, tea shop, buffet, lunch counter, lunch room, luncheonette, cafeteria, café, ice-cream parlor, drug store, grill, coffee shop, inn, hotel, tavern, soda fountain, steakhouse, chophouse, fish house, sandwich shop, deli, sub shop, fast-food outlet, pizza parlor, diner, mess hall, galley, confectionery, canteen, facility, rotisserie, refectory, cookshop, lunch wagon, eatery, automat, chuck wagon, bistro, rathskeller, *salle à manger* (French), *Speisezimmer* (German), *sala da pranzo* (Italian), *comedor* (Spanish); dine-and-dance joint*, hash house*, dump*, dog wagon*, greasy spoon*, grease joint*, hashery*; see also **restaurant.**

**dinner,** *n.* — *Syn.* supper, feast, banquet, main meal, principal meal of the day, refection, collation, repast, course dinner, table d'hôte, *prix fixe dîner* (French), *pranzo* (Italian), *comida principal* (Spanish), high tea (British); see also **meal** 2.

**diocese,** *n.* — *Syn.* episcopate, see, prelacy, benefice; see **bishopric, jurisdiction, parish.**

**dip,** *n.* **1.** [The action of dipping] — *Syn.* plunge, immersion, soaking, dunking, ducking, bath, douche, drenching, sinking; see also **bath** 1.

**2.** [Material into which something is dipped] — *Syn.* bath, preparation, infusion, solution, suspension, dilution, suffusion, concoction, saturation, mixture, dye; see also **bath** 2, **liquid.**

**3.** [A low place] — *Syn.* depression, hollow, slope, inclination; see **grade** 1, **hole** 2.

**4.** [A drop] — *Syn.* sag, slip, decline; see **drop** 2, **fall** 1.

**5.** [A swim] — *Syn.* plunge, bath, dive; see **swim.**

**6.** [Food to be eaten by dipping] — *Syn.* spread, salsa, canapé, party food; see **appetizer,** *hors d'oeuvre.*

Flavors and varieties of dips include: clam, shrimp,

cheese, Roquefort, blue cheese, cheddar, ham salad, egg salad, onion, chili, guacamole, salsa, dill, spinach, vegetable, pickle, poi, sour cream.

**dip,** *v.* **1.** [To put into a liquid] — *Syn.* plunge, immerse, dunk, lower, wet, slosh, submerge, irrigate, steep, drench, douse, duck, souse, moisten, lower and raise quickly, immerse temporarily, splash, bathe, lave, slop, water, rinse, baptize; see also **immerse 1, soak 1, wash 1.**
**2.** [To transfer by scooping] — *Syn.* shovel, lade, bail, spoon, draft off, take out with a ladle, lift by scooping, decant, handle, dredge, lift, draw, drain, strain, dish, dish up, dish out, serve, offer.
**3.** [To fall] — *Syn.* slope, drop, decline, incline, recede, tilt, swoop, slip, spiral, sink, plunge, bend, verge, veer, slant, settle, slump, slide, set, go down; see also **dive, drop 2, fall 1.**

**dip into,** *v.* — *Syn.* skim, sample, flip through; see **browse, dabble.**

**diploma,** *n.* — *Syn.* graduation certificate, credentials, parchment, honor, award, recognition, commission, charter, warrant, voucher, confirmation, sheepskin*; see also **degree 3, graduation.**

**diplomacy,** *n.* — *Syn.* tact, statesmanship, artfulness, discretion; see **tact.**
*See Synonym Study at* TACT.

**diplomat,** *n.* **1.** [An accredited representative abroad] — *Syn.* ambassador, consul, minister, statesman, diplomatist, plenipotentiary, ambassadorial representative, consular representative, member of the diplomatic corps, legate, nuncio, emissary, envoy, attaché, agent, expert on international affairs, shuttle diplomat, cabinet member, chargé d'affaires, chargé; see also **representative 1, statesman.**
**2.** [A suave or tactful person] — *Syn.* politician, strategist, tactician, statesman, negotiator, intermediary, mediator, peacemaker, conciliator, Machiavelli, Machiavellian, propagandist, bargainer, cosmopolitan, manipulator, artful dodger, apple polisher*, smoothie*; see also **judge 2.** — *Ant.* BUNGLER, fumbler, clod.

**diplomatic,** *modif.* — *Syn.* tactful, suave, politic, discreet, calculating, shrewd, smooth, opportunistic, manipulative, adroit, judicious, conciliatory, conniving, scheming, Machiavellian, sly, artful, wily, subtle, crafty, sharp, cunning, contriving, delicate, sensitive, deft, dexterous, adept, intriguing, strategic, astute, statesmanlike, ambassadorial, consular, savvy*, cagey*; see also **polite 1.** — *Ant.* tactless, artless, bungling.
*See Synonym Study at* SUAVE.

**dipped,** *modif.* — *Syn.* immersed, plunged, bathed, ducked, dunked, thrust, doused, plumped, drenched, soused, steeped, coated, covered, waxed, dyed; see also **soaked, wet 1.**

**dipper,** *n.* — *Syn.* ladle, cup, scoop, spoon, tablespoon, basin, pail, bucket, bail, pan, can, shovel, fork, pot, crock, bowl, glass, spatula, mug, jug, pitcher, skimmer, gourd, calabash, steam shovel, spade, dredge, trowel, long-handled cup, bailer; see also **container, silverware, spoon.**

**dipsomania,** *n.* — *Syn.* alcoholism, problem drinking, insobriety; see **addiction, drunkenness.**

**dipsomaniac,** *n.* — *Syn.* alcoholic, sot, boozer*; see **drunkard.**

**dire,** *modif.* — *Syn.* dreadful, terrible, desperate; see **frightful 1, urgent 1.**

**direct,** *modif.* **1.** [Without divergence] — *Syn.* straight, in a straight line, straight ahead, undeviating, uninterrupted, right, unswerving, linear, straightaway, shortest, nonstop, through, in a bee line, as the crow flies, straight as an arrow, point-blank; see also **straight 1.** — *Ant.* ZIGZAG, roundabout, crooked.
**2.** [Frank] — *Syn.* straightforward, outspoken, candid; see **frank, honest 1.**
**3.** [With nothing or no one intervening] — *Syn.* immediate, firsthand, unmediated, close, personal, primary, verbatim; see also **literal 1.**

**direct,** *v.* **1.** [To show the way] — *Syn.* conduct, show, guide, steer; see **lead 1.**
**2.** [To decide the course of affairs] — *Syn.* regulate, govern, influence; see **command 2, manage 1.**
**3.** [To teach] — *Syn.* inform, instruct, give directions; see **advise 1, teach 1.**
**4.** [To address] — *Syn.* deliver, lecture, read; see **address 2.**
**5.** [To aim] — *Syn.* point, train, level, focus; see **aim 2.**
**6.** [To command] — *Syn.* order, bid, charge; see **command 1.**
**7.** [To direct one's effort] — *Syn.* strive, address oneself, focus; see **apply (oneself), try 1, undertake.**
**8.** [To write directions on a letter or package] — *Syn.* inscribe, label, designate; see **address 1, mark 1, 2.**
*See Synonym Study at* COMMAND, MANAGE.

**directed,** *modif.* — *Syn.* supervised, controlled, conducted, sponsored, under supervision, assisted, counseled, guided, serviced, managed, regulated, organized, orderly, purposeful, focused, functioning, under orders; see also **aimed, organized.** — *Ant.* WANDERING, misdirected, vagrant.

**direction,** *n.* **1.** [A position] — *Syn.* point of the compass, objective, bearing, course, way, orientation, heading, route, path, track, region, area, road, place, spot; see also **route 2, way 2.**
Points of the compass include: north, N, south, S, east, E, west, W, NE, NW, SE, SW, NNE, NNW, SSE, SSW, ENE, ESE, WNW, WSW, E by N, E by S, W by N, W by S, N by E, S by E, N by W, S by W, NE by E, NE by N, NW by N, NW by W, SE by E, SE by S, SW by W, SW by S.
**2.** [Supervision] — *Syn.* management, superintendence, control; see **administration 1, regulation 1.**
**3.** [An order] — *Syn.* charge, regulation, injunction; see **command 1.**
**4.** [A tendency] — *Syn.* bias, bent, proclivity, trend; see **drift 1, inclination 1.**

**directions,** *n.* — *Syn.* instructions, advice, guidelines, notification, specification, indication, guidance, orders, assignment, recommendation, summons, directive, regulation, prescription, sealed orders, plans, briefing, information, word from above*, specs*, dope*, lowdown*.

**directly,** *modif.* **1.** [In a direct way or line] — *Syn.* straight, right, undeviatingly, immediately; see **direct 1.**
**2.** [Right away] — *Syn.* instantly, at once, quickly, shortly; see **immediately, soon 1.**

**director,** *n.* **1.** [An executive officer] — *Syn.* manager, supervisor, executive; see **administrator, leader 2.**
**2.** [Person in charge of a theatrical production] — *Syn.* producer, impresario, stage director, motion-picture director, auteur, filmmaker, *régisseur* (French), television director; see also **leader 3.**

**directory,** *n.* — *Syn.* index, catalog, list, syllabus, register, record, almanac, roster, telephone book, phone book, Yellow Pages, business directory, white pages, city directory, Social Register, blue book, professional directory, office of information, student directory, Who's Who, Domesday Book, gazetteer; see also **catalog, index 2.**

**dirge,** *n.* — *Syn.* lament, elegy, requiem, funeral, march; see also **cry** 3, **hymn, song.**

**dirigible,** *n.* — *Syn.* airship, blimp, lighter-than-air machine, zeppelin; see **balloon, plane** 3.

**dirt,** *n.* **1.** [Earth] — *Syn.* soil, loam, clay; see **earth** 2.
**2.** [Filth] — *Syn.* grime, filthiness, smut; see **dust, filth, trash** 1.
**do one dirt★** — *Syn.* harm, hurt, cheat, slander; see **abuse** 1, **deceive, slander.**

**dirty,** *modif.* **1.** [Containing dirt] — *Syn.* soiled, unclean, filthy, grimy, unsanitary, unhygienic, polluted, foul, nasty, slovenly, dusty, undusted, messy, squalid, sloppy, untidy, lousy, disheveled, uncombed, unsightly, slatternly, bedraggled, disarrayed, straggly, unwashed, unkempt, stained, tarnished, spotted, smudged, fouled, infected, greasy, spattered, smutty, smutted, flyspecked, muddy, mucky, sooty, smoky, smoked, slimy, rusty, murky, dingy, unlaundered, unswept, unsalable, unpolished, crummy★, scrubby★, icky★, grubby★, raunchy★, scuzzy★, yucky★, scummy★. — *Ant.* clean, sanitary, spotless, tidy.
**2.** [Obscene] — *Syn.* pornographic, smutty, lewd; see **lewd** 1, 2, **ribald.**
**3.** [Nasty] — *Syn.* mean, contemptible, disagreeable; see **mean** 1, 3, **ruthless** 1.

---

*SYN.* — **dirty** is applied to that which is covered or filled with any kind of dirt and is the broadest of these terms [a *dirty* face, a *dirty* room]; **soiled** generally suggests the presence of superficial dirt in an amount sufficient to impair cleanness or freshness [a *soiled* shirt]; **grimy** suggests soot or granular dirt deposited on or ingrained in a surface [a miner with a *grimy* face]; **filthy** is applied to that which is disgustingly dirty [*filthy* as a pigpen]; **foul** implies extreme filth that is grossly offensive or loathsome because of its stench, putridity, or corruption [*foul* air]

---

**dirty,** *v.* — *Syn.* soil, sully, stain, defile, pollute, foul, encrust, coat, tarnish, spot, smear, daub, blot, blur, make dusty, blacken, smudge, smutch, smoke, muddy, drabble, draggle, heap dirt upon, botch, begrime, bedaub, spoil, speck, sweat up, blotch, spatter, besmear, befoul, splash, debase, corrupt, taint, contaminate, rot, decay, mold, make impure, muck up★. — *Ant.* CLEAN, cleanse, rinse.

**disability,** *n.* **1.** [The state of lacking a necessary quality] — *Syn.* incapacity, unfitness, feebleness; see **inability, injury** 1, **weakness** 1, 2.
**2.** [A specific lack] — *Syn.* handicap, disqualification, disadvantage; see **impediment** 1, **limitation** 3.

**disable,** *v.* — *Syn.* cripple, incapacitate, impair, put out of action; see **damage** 1, **maim.**
*See Synonym Study at* MAIM.

**disabled,** *modif.* — *Syn.* handicapped, incapacitated, crippled, physically challenged, impaired, injured, maimed, hamstrung, wounded, mangled, lame, mutilated, silenced, run-down, worn-out, useless, wrecked, stalled, bedridden, weakened, helpless; confined to one's bed, confined to one's home, confined to a hospital, confined to a nursing home, etc.; impotent, castrated, halting, limping, hobbling, palsied, superannuated, paralyzed, paraplegic, quadriplegic, brain damaged, senile, decrepit, on one's back★, laid up★, done for★, done in★, cracked up★, banged up★, broken down★, out of action★, counted out★; see also **hurt, useless** 1, **weakened.** — *Ant.* able-bodied, HEALTHY, strong.

**disabuse,** *v.* — *Syn.* undeceive, clarify, inform, set straight; see **correct** 1, **disillusion.**

**disadvantage,** *n.* **1.** [Loss] — *Syn.* damage, harm, deprivation; see **loss** 3.
**2.** [An unfavorable situation or circumstance] — *Syn.* drawback, disadvantageousness, weak point, impediment, inconvenience, stumbling block, detriment, downside, liability, obstacle, bar, handicap, disability, limitation, inexpedience, undesirableness, unsatisfactoriness, hindrance, objection, problem, failing, weakness, difficulty, trouble, snag, lack; harmful circumstance, adverse circumstance, disadvantageous circumstance, unfortunate circumstance, damaging circumstance, etc.; ineffectiveness, fault, defect, deficiency, imperfection, inadequacy, negative; see also **impediment** 1, **restraint** 2, **weakness** 2. — *Ant.* ADVANTAGE, benefit, effectiveness.

**disaffect,** *v.* — *Syn.* estrange, antagonize, repel; see **alienate.**

**disaffected,** *modif.* — *Syn.* alienated, antagonistic, disloyal, estranged; see **indifferent** 1, **unfriendly** 1.

**disaffection,** *n.* — *Syn.* estrangement, aversion, resentment; see **alienation, hatred** 1, 2.

**disagree,** *v.* **1.** [To differ] — *Syn.* dissent, object, oppose; see **differ** 1, **oppose** 1, **quarrel.**
**2.** [To have uncomfortable effect; *usually used with* with] — *Syn.* nauseate, sicken, hurt, injure, make sick, bother, go against the grain, be distasteful, be unsuitable, be hard on one's stomach★; see also **bother** 3.

**disagreeable,** *modif.* **1.** [Having an unpleasant disposition] — *Syn.* difficult, grouchy, obnoxious, offensive; see **irritable, rude** 2.
**2.** [Irritating; *said of things and conditions*] — *Syn.* bothersome, unpleasant, upsetting, distasteful; see **disturbing, offensive** 2.

**disagreeably,** *modif.* — *Syn.* unpleasantly, irritatingly, offensively, objectionably, distastefully, unpalatably, antagonistically, adversely, contrarily, incompatibly, incongruously.

**disagreeing,** *modif.* — *Syn.* differing, dissenting, at odds; see **quarreling.**

**disagreeing,** *n.* — *Syn.* disrupting, quarreling, disputing, disapproving, differing; see also **disagreement** 1, **dispute.**

**disagreement,** *n.* **1.** [Discord] — *Syn.* contention, strife, conflict, difference of opinion, cross-purposes, controversy, wrangle, vendetta, dissension, atmospherics, animosity, ill feeling, ill will, misunderstanding, division, opposition, hostility, breach, discord, disunion, feud, clashing, antagonism, disunity, dissidence, dissent, bickering, squabble, divisiveness, lack of concord, tension, friction, split, quarreling, jarring, falling out, break, rupture, quarrel, clash, opposition, altercation, variance, contest; see also **battle** 2, **competition** 1, **fight** 1.
**2.** [Inconsistency] — *Syn.* discrepancy, dissimilarity, disparity; see **difference** 1.
**3.** [A quarrel] — *Syn.* fight, argument, feud; see **dispute.**

**disallow,** *v.* — *Syn.* reject, ban, censor, repudiate; see **deny, forbid, refuse.**

**disappear,** *v.* — *Syn.* vanish, fade, come to naught, cease, die, drop out of sight, become imperceptible, withdraw, dissolve, evaporate, pass out of sight, recede from view, cease to be seen, undergo eclipse, pass, go, leave no trace, be swallowed up, fade away, pass away, pass out, retire, retire from sight, retreat, vanish from sight, be lost to view, sink, exit, go off the stage, pass on, leave, vacate, abscond, depart, decamp, perish, die out, become extinct, be eradicated, be consumed, fade out, die away, go away, escape, be gone, dissipate, evanesce, be no more, cease to exist, come to an end, end gradually, wane, ebb, disperse, fall away, melt away, vanish into thin air, dematerialize, vamoose*, do a disappearing act*, take French leave*, pass out of the picture*, go *poof**; see also **die** 2, **escape, evaporate** 1. — *Ant.* APPEAR, emerge, materialize.

---

*SYN.* — **disappear** implies either a sudden or gradual passing from sight or existence /customs that have long since *disappeared*/; **vanish** implies a sudden, complete, often mysterious passing from sight or existence /the stain had *vanished* overnight/; **fade** suggests a gradual, complete or partial disappearance, as by losing color or brilliance /the design on this fabric won't *fade*, his reputation has *faded*/

---

**disappearance,** *n.* — *Syn.* vanishing, dissolution, dispersal, fading, departure, ebbing away, recession from view, removal, dissipation, vanishment, evanescence, evaporation, ceasing to appear, desertion, flight, retirement, escape, wane, exodus, vanishing point, going, wearing away, disintegration, exit, withdrawal, decline and fall, eclipse; see also **escape** 1, **evaporation.**

**disappoint,** *v.* — *Syn.* fail, let down, delude, deceive, dissatisfy, disgruntle, disillusion, dishearten, tantalize, embitter, disconcert, chagrin, sadden, put out, fall short, cast down, ruin one's prospects, dash one's hopes, frustrate, torment, tease, miscarry, abort, thwart, foil, baffle, founder, disenchant, balk, bring to naught, bungle, fail to live up to the expectations of, leave unsatisfied, discontent, mislead, come to nothing, come to naught, come to grief, meet with disaster, run aground, fall down on*, knock the props from under*, go up in smoke*, fizzle out*, be a flash in the pan*, fall flat*, stand up*, leave in the lurch*.

**disappointed,** *modif.* **1.** [Displeased] — *Syn.* dissatisfied, discouraged, frustrated, let down, unsatisfied, despondent, depressed, objecting, complaining, distressed, downcast, hopeless, disconcerted, disgruntled, disillusioned, laughing out of the wrong side of one's mouth*, shot down*; see also **dissatisfied, sad** 1. — *Ant.* SATISFIED, pleased, content.

**2.** [Beaten] — *Syn.* balked, thwarted, vanquished; see **beaten** 1.

**disappointing,** *modif.* — *Syn.* unsatisfactory, unsatisfying, ineffective, uninteresting, discouraging, unpleasant, inadequate, inferior, unlooked for, lame, insufficient, failing, falling short, limited, second-rate, mediocre, unexpected, unhappy, depressing, disconcerting, disagreeable, irritating, vexing, disheartening, unlucky, bitter, distasteful, displeasing, deplorable, short of expectations, frustrating, unfulfilling; see also **inadequate** 1, **unsatisfactory.** — *Ant.* PLEASING, encouraging, satisfactory.

**disappointment,** *n.* **1.** [The state of being disappointed] — *Syn.* dissatisfaction, nonfulfillment, unfulfillment, frustration, chagrin, thwarted expectations, miscarriage of plans, defeat, failure, lack of success, despondency, displeasure, distress, hope deferred, discouragement, let down, disillusionment, foiling, nonsuccess, mortification, vain expectation, bafflement, disillusion, setback, discontent, blighted hope, dashed hope, balking; see also **defeat** 3, **regret** 1. — *Ant.* satisfaction, SUCCESS, fulfillment.

**2.** [A person *or* thing that disappoints] — *Syn.* letdown, miscarriage, misfortune, mischance, calamity, blunder, inefficacy, setback, downfall, slip, defeat, impasse, mishap, error, mistake, discouragement, frustration, obstacle, check, balk, abortion, bungle, slip 'twixt the cup and

the lip, faux pas, cold comfort, labor in vain, miscalculation, miss, failure, shipwreck, fiasco, no go*, blind alley*, fizzle*, washout*, lemon*, dud*, flash in the pan*, bust*, frost*, false alarm*, non-starter*; see also **failure** 1, 2. — *Ant.* ACHIEVEMENT, successful venture, success.

**disapproval,** *n.* **1.** [A disapproving attitude] — *Syn.* disapprobation, rejection, dissatisfaction, displeasure; see **objection** 1.

**2.** [An adverse expression] — *Syn.* condemnation, criticism, censure, disparagement; see **blame** 1, **objection** 2.

**disapprove,** *v.* **1.** [To condemn; *often used with* of] — *Syn.* object to, dislike, deplore, decry, reprobate, view with disfavor, frown on, frown upon, look askance at; see also **censure, complain** 1, **dislike, oppose** 1.

**2.** [To reject] — *Syn.* spurn, disallow, set aside, veto; see **oppose** 1, **refuse.**

**disarm,** *v.* **1.** [To deprive of weapons] — *Syn.* disable, unarm, weaken, debilitate, render powerless, disqualify, incapacitate, invalidate, deaden, paralyze, muzzle, deprive of weapons, deprive of means of defense, demilitarize, demobilize, put out of combat, put out of action, pacify, conciliate, subdue, subjugate, occupy, bare, strip, tie the hands*, draw the teeth of*, clip the wings of*, spike one's guns*; see also **defeat** 1, 2, **weaken** 2. — *Ant.* ARM, outfit, equip.

**2.** [To reduce national armaments] — *Syn.* demobilize, disband, demilitarize, deactivate, de-escalate, lay down one's arms, unarm, neutralize, internationalize, remove nuclear competence, prevent nuclear competence; see also **disband.** — *Ant.* ARM, mobilize, prepare.

**3.** [To reconcile] — *Syn.* win over, charm, seduce; see **reconcile** 2, **win** 4.

**disarmament,** *n.* — *Syn.* reduction of armaments, arms reduction, demobilization, disbanding, disablement, disabling, disqualification, disqualifying, crippling, unilateral *or* multilateral disarmament, incapacitating, rendering powerless, paralyzing, pacification, laying down of arms, de-escalation, demilitarization, nuclear freeze, subjugation, occupation, conquest, neutralizing, beating swords into plowshares. — *Ant.* TRAINING, armament, escalation.

**disarming,** *modif.* — *Syn.* convincing, seductive, ingratiating; see **charming, persuasive.**

**disarray,** *n.* — *Syn.* disorder, chaos, upset; see **confusion** 2.

*See Synonym Study at* CONFUSION.

**disassemble,** *v.* — *Syn.* take apart, knock down, strike*; see **dismantle.**

**disaster,** *n.* — *Syn.* catastrophe, accident, calamity, misfortune, mishap, debacle, cataclysm, casualty, mischance, emergency, adversity, harm, misadventure, collapse, slip, fall, collision, crash, hazard, crash landing, setback, defeat, sinking, flood, failure, holocaust, affliction, fell stroke, woe, trouble, scourge, depression, grief, bale, undoing, overthrow, bad luck, ill luck, ruination, bane, fiasco, curse, tragedy, blight, visitation, contretemps, exigency, infliction, extremity, downfall, evil day, rainy day, crushing reverse, great mishap, terrible accident, gathering clouds, sudden misfortune, adverse happening, bankruptcy, upset, blast, blow, comedown, fire, blaze, wreck, cave-in, act of God, crackup, smashup, washout*, flop*, bust*, hard luck*; see also **catastrophe, collision** 1, **misfortune** 1.

---

*SYN.* — **disaster** implies great or sudden misfortune that results in loss of life, property, etc. or that is ruinous to an undertaking; **calamity** suggests a grave misfortune that brings deep distress or sorrow to an individual or to the people at large; **catastrophe** is specifically applied to a disastrous end or outcome; **cataclysm** suggests a great upheaval, esp. a political or social one, that causes sudden and violent change with attending distress, suffering, etc.

---

**disastrous,** *modif.* — *Syn.* calamitous, ruinous, unfortunate; see **destructive** 2, **harmful, unfavorable** 2.

**disavow,** *v.* — *Syn.* disclaim, disown, repudiate; see **deny, recant.**

**disband,** *v.* — *Syn.* scatter, disperse, demobilize, disarm, break up, call off, dismiss, send home, go home, disorganize, muster out; see also **leave** 1.

**disbelief,** *n.* — *Syn.* unbelief, skepticism, mistrust, incredulity; see **doubt** 1, **wonder** 1.
*See Synonym Study at* UNBELIEF.

**disbeliever,** *n.* — *Syn.* doubter, questioner, agnostic; see **critic** 1, **skeptic.**

**disburse,** *v.* — *Syn.* expend, pay out, distribute, dispense; see **distribute** 1, **pay** 1, **spend** 1.

**disbursement,** *n.* — *Syn.* expenditure, spending, outlay; see **expense** 1, **payment** 1.

**disbursements,** *n.* — *Syn.* expenditures, outgoings, operating expenses; see **expense** 1.

**discard,** *v.* — *Syn.* reject, throw away, get rid of, dispose of, throw out, expel, repudiate, abandon, cast aside, cast away, cast out, cast off, throw off, throw aside, throw overboard, lay aside, thrust off, thrust away, thrust aside, put by, give up, shuffle off, slough, renounce, supersede, have done with, make away with, drop all idea of, dismantle, discharge, write off, banish, eject, dismiss, divorce, dispossess, dispense with, toss aside, toss away, toss out, dump, shake off, pass up, rid oneself of, free of, root out, get quit of, deliver oneself from, give away, part with, file off, do away with, shed, dismiss from use, abjure, jettison, relinquish, repeal, dispatch, shovel out, sweep away, cancel, forsake, desert, lay on the shelf, cut\*, have nothing to do with, brush away, brush aside, scotch\*, chuck\*, heave overboard\*, toss overboard\*, drop\*, ditch\*, wash one's hands of\*, junk\*, scrap\*, deep-six\*, eighty-six\*; see also **abandon** 1, 2, **dismiss** 1. — *Ant.* SAVE, retain, preserve.

**discarded,** *modif.* — *Syn.* rejected, repudiated, castoff, castaway, thrown away, thrown out, dismantled, dismissed, useless, damaged, outworn, worn-out, done with, run-down, not worth saving, superannuated, superseded, discontinued, abandoned, obsolete, shelved, neglected, deserted, forsaken, outmoded, out-of-date, out-of-style, old-fashioned, archaic, junked\*, scrapped\*, old hat\*. — *Ant.* KEPT, worthwhile, up-to-date.

**discern,** *v.* 1. [To see] — *Syn.* observe, behold, make out, perceive, notice, espy, descry, recognize, spot; see also **see** 1.
2. [To detect] — *Syn.* discover, distinguish, differentiate, find out, determine, ascertain, judge, apprehend, discriminate; see also **discover.**

---

**SYN.** — **discern** implies a making out or recognizing of something visually or mentally /to *discern* one's motives/; **perceive** implies recognition by means of any of the senses, and, with reference to mental apprehension, often implies keen understanding or insight /to *perceive* a change in attitude/; **distinguish** implies perceiving clearly or distinctly by sight, hearing, etc. /he *distinguished* the voices of men down the hall/; **observe** and **notice** both connote some measure of attentiveness,

though the former may imply a more conscious act of will, and both usually suggest use of the sense of sight /to *observe* an eclipse, to *notice* a sign/

---

**discernible,** *modif.* — *Syn.* perceptible, perceivable, observable; see **appreciable, audible, obvious** 1.

**discerning,** *modif.* — *Syn.* discriminating, perceptive, penetrating; see **intelligent** 1, **judicious.**

**discernment,** *n.* — *Syn.* perception, judgment, insight; see **acumen.**

**discharge,** *n.* 1. [Emission] — *Syn.* exudation, secretion, ooze, outflow; see **emanation** 1, 2, **flow.**
2. [Shooting] — *Syn.* detonation, explosion, firing off, report; see **explosion** 1, **gunfire, shooting** 1.
3. [Dismissal] — *Syn.* release, ouster, demobilization; see **freeing, removal** 1.

**discharge,** *v.* 1. [To unload] — *Syn.* unpack, release, remove cargo; see **empty** 1, 2, **unload.**
2. [To remove] — *Syn.* take off, send, carry *or* take away; see **remove** 1.
3. [To emit] — *Syn.* send forth, give off, exude; see **emit** 1.
4. [To cause to fire] — *Syn.* blast, shoot off, fire; see **shoot** 1.
5. [To dismiss] — *Syn.* let go, replace, relieve; see **dismiss** 2.
6. [To release] — *Syn.* emancipate, liberate, let go; see **free** 1, **release.**
7. [To perform] — *Syn.* fulfill, execute, accomplish; see **achieve** 1, **perform** 1.
8. [To pay a debt] — *Syn.* liquidate, settle, satisfy; see **pay** 1.
*See Synonym Study at* FREE.

**discharged,** *modif.* 1. [Dismissed] — *Syn.* mustered out, sent home, dishonorably discharged, honorably released, recalled, freed, liberated, released, let go, furloughed, sent away, expelled, ejected, laid-off, fired, ousted, cashiered, replaced, canned\*, sacked\*, axed\*, given the gate\*, given the ax\*, given the sack\*, given the boot\*, given the old heave-ho\*; see also **free** 1, 2.
2. [Fulfilled] — *Syn.* achieved, performed, accomplished; see **done** 1, **fulfilled.**

**disciple,** *n.* 1. [A follower] — *Syn.* adherent, pupil, believer; see **follower.**
2. [A follower of Christ; *usually capitalized*] — *Syn.* apostle, witness, chosen witness, revealer, revelator, seer.
*See Synonym Study at* FOLLOWER.
Christ's original disciples mentioned in the New Testament include: Matthew, Bartholomew, Nathaniel, John, Peter, James, Philip, Andrew, Thaddaeus, Thomas, Judas Iscariot, James the son of Alphaeus, Simon the Canaanean. Other disciples include: Paul and Matthias.

**disciplinarian,** *n.* — *Syn.* trainer, martinet, sergeant, drill sergeant, advocate of strict discipline, formalist, taskmaster, bully, stickler, hard master, enforcer of discipline, tyrant, despot, slave driver; see also **dictator, teacher** 1.

**discipline,** *n.* 1. [A state of order or control] — *Syn.* orderliness, order, control, self-control, restraint, self-restraint, moderation, self-discipline, obedience, decorum, subordination to rules of conduct, system, method, methodicalness, rigor, spit and polish\*.
2. [A system of obedience] — *Syn.* training, drill, drilling, regimentation, regulation, limitation, curb, indoctrination, brainwashing, preparation, development, exercise, inculcation, regimen, strictness, tight rein, firm hand, iron hand, chastisement, correction; see also **drill** 3, **punishment, training.**

**discipline**, *v.* **1.** [To regulate] — *Syn.* train, control, drill, keep in line; see **restrain** 1, **teach** 2.
**2.** [To punish] — *Syn.* chastise, correct, limit; see **punish.**
*See Synonym Study at* PUNISH.
**disc jockey**, *n.* — *Syn.* radio announcer, DJ, emcee*; see **announcer, reporter.**
**disclaim**, *v.* **1.** [To deny] — *Syn.* repudiate, disavow, revoke, retract; see **deny, recant.**
**2.** [To disown] — *Syn.* renounce, give up, forswear, reject; see **abandon** 1, **discard.**
**disclose**, *v.* **1.** [To expose] — *Syn.* lay bare, uncover, unveil; see **expose** 1.
**2.** [To divulge] — *Syn.* make known, confess, reveal, publish; see **reveal** 1.
*See Synonym Study at* REVEAL.
**disclosure**, *n.* **1.** [The act or process of disclosing] — *Syn.* revealing, divulgence, enlightenment; see **confession** 1, **exposure** 1.
**2.** [That which is disclosed] — *Syn.* exposé, acknowledgment, confession, revelation; see **admission** 4, **declaration** 1.
**discolor**, *v.* — *Syn.* stain, streak, rust, tarnish; see **color** 1, **dirty, fade.**
**discoloration**, *n.* — *Syn.* stain, blot, blotch, splotch; see **blemish, stain.**
**discomfit**, *v.* **1.** [To defeat the plans of] — *Syn.* thwart, frustrate, foil; see **prevent.**
**2.** [To confuse] — *Syn.* disconcert, embarrass, perplex; see **confuse, embarrass** 1.
*See Synonym Study at* EMBARRASS.
**discomfiture**, *n.* **1.** [Frustration] — *Syn.* disappointment, rout, beating; see **defeat** 3, **disappointment** 1.
**2.** [Embarrassment] — *Syn.* chagrin, confusion, humiliation; see **confusion** 2, **embarrassment** 1.
**discomfort**, *n.* — *Syn.* trouble, uneasiness, chagrin, ache; see **distress** 1, **embarrassment** 1, **pain** 1, 2.
**discommode**, *v.* — *Syn.* inconvenience, annoy, trouble; see **bother** 2, **disturb** 2.
**discompose**, *v.* — *Syn.* perturb, upset, ruffle, disturb; see **bother** 3, **disturb** 2, **embarrass** 1.
*See Synonym Study at* DISTURB.
**discomposure**, *n.* — *Syn.* disturbance, agitation, perturbation, discomfiture; see **confusion** 2.
**disconcert**, *v.* — *Syn.* perturb, unsettle, perplex; see **confuse, disturb** 2, **embarrass** 1.
*See Synonym Study at* EMBARRASS.
**disconnect**, *v.* — *Syn.* separate, detach, disengage; see **cut** 1, **divide** 1, **unhitch.**
**disconnected**, *modif.* **1.** [Incoherent] — *Syn.* disjointed, loose, irregular; see **incoherent** 2, **incongruous** 1, **irregular** 1.
**2.** [Separated] — *Syn.* broken off, detached, unplugged, switched off; see **separated.**
**disconnection**, *n.* **1.** [Separation] — *Syn.* detachment, parting, disunion, cleavage; see **division** 1.
**2.** [Break] — *Syn.* discontinuity, intrusion, disruption, cessation; see **interference** 1, **interruption.**
**disconsolate**, *modif.* **1.** [Dejected] — *Syn.* inconsolable, despondent, hopeless, melancholy; see **sad** 1.
**2.** [Dismal] — *Syn.* cheerless, gloomy, dreary, dark; see **dismal** 1.
**discontent**, *n.* — *Syn.* dissatisfaction, envy, uneasiness, restlessness; see **annoyance** 1, **dissatisfaction** 1.
**discontented**, *modif.* — *Syn.* unhappy, disgruntled, malcontented; see **complaining, dissatisfied, sad** 1.
**discontinue**, *v.* — *Syn.* cease, break off, terminate, interrupt; see **abandon** 1, **end** 1, **stop** 2, **suspend** 2.
*See Synonym Study at* STOP.

**discontinued**, *modif.* — *Syn.* ended, canceled, terminated, given up; see **discarded, interrupted.**
**discontinuous**, *modif.* — *Syn.* spasmodic, broken, disconnected; see **intermittent, irregular** 1.
**discord**, *n.* **1.** [Conflict] — *Syn.* strife, contention, dissension, disunity, division, disagreement, dispute, friction, animosity; see also **disagreement** 1.
**2.** [Noise] — *Syn.* din, racket, dissonance, disharmony; see **noise** 2.

---

*SYN.* — **discord** denotes disagreement or lack of concord and may imply quarreling between persons, clashing qualities in things, dissonance in sound, etc.; **strife** stresses the struggle to win in a conflict or disagreement; **contention** suggests verbal strife as expressed in argument, controversy, dispute, etc.; **dissension** implies difference of opinion, usually suggesting contention between opposing groups in a body

---

**discordant**, *modif.* **1.** [Inharmonious] — *Syn.* grating, dissonant, cacophonous; see **harsh** 1.
**2.** [Disagreeing] — *Syn.* clashing, at odds, incompatible; see **conflicting, different** 1, **incongruous, quarreling.**
**discount**, *n.* — *Syn.* deduction, reduction, allowance, rebate, decrease, markdown, abatement, cut, concession, rollback, percentage, salvage, premium, diminution, subtraction, commission, exemption, modification, drawback, refund, tare, tare and tret, depreciation, cut rate, something off*, rake-off*, kickback*; see also **interest** 3, **reduction** 1. — *Ant.* INCREASE, markup, surcharge.
**at a discount** — *Syn.* discounted, cheap, depreciated, below list price; see **reduced** 2.
**discount**, *v.* **1.** [To deduct] — *Syn.* reduce, mark down, lower, redeem, diminish, depreciate, make allowance for, allow, take off, charge off, strike off, rebate, abate, roll back, cut, cut prices, slash, slash prices, undersell, mark the tare of, rake off*, knock off*; see also **decrease** 2. — *Ant.* RAISE, mark up, advance.
**2.** [To disregard] — *Syn.* question, disbelieve, mistrust, discredit; see **disregard, doubt** 2.
**discountenance**, *v.* — *Syn.* disapprove, frown upon, reject, resist; see **disapprove** 1, **discourage** 1, **oppose** 1.
**discount rate**, *n.* — *Syn.* (advance) interest, deduction, charge; see **interest** 3.
**discourage**, *v.* **1.** [To dishearten] — *Syn.* dispirit, dampen, dismay, daunt, intimidate, demoralize, repress, dampen the spirits, deprive of courage, lessen the self-confidence of, break one's heart, deject, prostrate, unnerve, scare, confuse, overawe, cow, bully, cast down, chill, damp, unman, throw a wet blanket on*, throw cold water on*, beat down, cast gloom upon, dash one's hopes; see also **depress** 2, **frighten** 1. — *Ant.* ENCOURAGE, cheer, inspire.
**2.** [To warn] — *Syn.* dissuade, alarm, disincline, talk out of; see **warn** 1.
**3.** [To restrain] — *Syn.* obstruct, impede, hinder, check, quiet, interfere with, withhold, keep back, inhibit, dissuade, disincline, curb, deter, control, turn aside, hold back, hold off, repress; see also **restrain** 1. — *Ant.* HELP, expedite, facilitate.
**discouraged**, *modif.* — *Syn.* downcast, pessimistic, depressed; see **sad** 1.
**discouragement**, *n.* **1.** [Dejection] — *Syn.* melancholy, despair, the blues*; see **depression** 2, **sadness.**
**2.** [A restriction] — *Syn.* constraint, hindrance, deterrent; see **impediment** 1.
**discouraging**, *modif.* **1.** [Acting to discourage one]

— *Syn.* depressing, disheartening, repressing; see **dismal** 1, **sad** 2.

**2.** [Suggesting an unwelcome future] — *Syn.* inopportune, disadvantageous, dissuading; see **unfavorable** 2.

**discourse,** *n.* — *Syn.* dialogue, talk, lecture, dissertation; see **conversation, discussion** 1, **exposition** 2, **speech** 2, 3.

**discourse,** *v.* — *Syn.* treat, converse, lecture; see **address** 2, **discuss, talk** 1.
*See Synonym Study at* SPEAK.

**discourteous,** *modif.* — *Syn.* impolite, uncivil, inconsiderate; see **rude** 2.
*See Synonym Study at* RUDE.

**discourtesy,** *n.* — *Syn.* impudence, impoliteness, incivility; see **rudeness.**

**discover,** *v.* — *Syn.* find, find out, invent, learn, ascertain, detect, discern, descry, recognize, distinguish, determine, observe, contrive, explore, find out once and for all, hear of, hear about, open one's eyes, awake to, gain knowledge of, become aware of, become conscious of, bring to light, uncover, ferret out, root out, trace, elicit, unearth, look up, come on, happen on, run across, come across, light on, hit upon, stumble upon, strike upon, strike, fall upon, meet with, encounter, think of, come up with, perceive, glimpse, identify, devise, disinter, catch, spot, locate, notice, realize, create, make out, evolve, sense, feel, sight, smell, hear, see, spy, bring out, find a clue, catch a glimpse of, get wise to*, dig out*, dig up*, turn up*, sniff out*, nose out*, get wind of*, get one's hands on*, put one's hands on*, lay one's hands on*, put one's finger on*, run down*, track down*, smoke out*; see also **find** 1, **invent** 1, **learn** 2. — *Ant.* MISS, pass by, overlook.
*See Synonym Study at* LEARN.

**discovered,** *modif.* — *Syn.* found, searched out, happened upon, invented, originated, unearthed, ascertained, descried, unlocked, espied, detected, disinterred, revealed, disclosed, unveiled, observed, sighted, shown, exposed, traced, elicited, made out, met with, stumbled upon, brought to light, recognized, identified, empirical, laid bare, opened, presented, spotted, perceived, learned, explored, well-known; see also **famous, observed** 1, **real** 2. — *Ant.* HIDDEN, unfound, lost.

**discovery,** *n.* **1.** [The act of finding the unknown] — *Syn.* invention, detection, uncovering, exploration, unearthing, identification, discernment, distinguishing, sensing, distinction, determination, calculation, experimentation, empiricism, feeling, hearing, sighting, spying, espial, descrial, spotting, strike, ascertainment, finding, hitting, learning, striking, disinterring, revelation, locating, serendipity; see also **examination** 1.
**2.** [Something discovered] — *Syn.* results, findings, find, invention, contrivance, breakthrough, innovation, development, strike, coup, treasure trove, formula, device, design, contraption, machine, process, data, principle, law; see also **result.**

**discredit,** *n.* — *Syn.* censure, reproach, disrepute; see **blame** 1, **disgrace** 1.

**discredit,** *v.* **1.** [To bring into disrepute] — *Syn.* defame, dishonor, cast doubt on, undermine; see **censure, depreciate** 2, **disprove.**
**2.** [To doubt] — *Syn.* question, disbelieve, distrust; see **doubt** 2.

**discreet,** *modif.* — *Syn.* cautious, prudent, circumspect, careful, guarded, politic, diplomatic, tactful, reserved, reticent, restrained, unostentatious, unobtrusive, modest, discerning, discriminating, observant of decencies, decorous, not rash, safe, wise, judicious, well-judged, strategic, noncommittal, sagacious, heedful, civil, sensible, chary, wary, watchful, attentive, considerate, trustworthy, uncommunicative, secretive, close-mouthed, close-lipped, tight-lipped; see also **careful, judicious, thoughtful** 2. — *Ant.* indiscreet, RASH, ostentatious.
*See Synonym Study at* CAREFUL.

**discrepancy,** *n.* **1.** [Inconsistency] — *Syn.* variance, contrariety, disparity; see **difference** 2, **inconsistency.**
**2.** [An error] — *Syn.* miscalculation, mistake, flaw; see **error** 1.

**discretion,** *n.* **1.** [Cautious or prudent conduct] — *Syn.* caution, prudence, tact, diplomacy, foresight, mature judgment, circumspection, carefulness, guardedness, restraint, reserve, decorum, wariness, sound judgment, thoughtfulness, concern, consideration, watchfulness, precaution, good sense, providence, judiciousness, maturity, discernment, solicitude, forethought, deliberation, responsibility, sagacity, wisdom, presence of mind, uncommunicativeness, secrecy, delicacy; see also **care** 1, **prudence, tact.** — *Ant.* CARELESSNESS, thoughtlessness, rashness.
**2.** [Power to judge or act] — *Syn.* option, inclination, preference, volition; see **choice** 1, **will** 3.
**at one's discretion** — *Syn.* as one wishes, at one's option, whenever appropriate; see **any time, appropriately.**

**discretionary,** *modif.* — *Syn.* optional, left to discretion, discretional; see **changeable** 2, **optional.**

**discriminate,** *v.* **1.** [To differentiate] — *Syn.* distinguish, specify, separate, tell apart; see **distinguish** 1.
*See Synonym Study at* DISTINGUISH.
**2.** [To be prejudiced] — *Syn.* show partiality, prejudge, be biased, be a bigot, set apart, segregate, victimize; see also **favor** 2, **hate** 1, **separate** 2.

**discriminating,** *modif.* **1.** [Discerning] — *Syn.* perspicacious, astute, discriminate; see **judicious.**
**2.** [Differentiating] — *Syn.* distinctive, distinguishing, individualizing; see **characteristic.**
**3.** [Particular] — *Syn.* selective, fastidious, finicky, choosy*; see **careful.**

**discrimination,** *n.* **1.** [The power to make distinctions] — *Syn.* discernment, perception, acuteness, taste; see **acumen, judgment** 1, **taste** 3.
**2.** [The act of drawing a distinction] — *Syn.* separation, differentiation, difference; see **distinction** 1.
**3.** [Partiality] — *Syn.* unfairness, bias, bigotry; see **hatred** 2, **prejudice.**

**discriminatory,** *modif.* — *Syn.* prejudicial, biased, unfair, inequitable; see **prejudiced.**

**discursive,** *modif.* — *Syn.* rambling, desultory, digressive; see **verbose.**

**discus,** *n.* — *Syn.* disk, plate, quoit; see **circle** 1, **disk.**

**discuss,** *v.* — *Syn.* argue, debate, dispute, talk about, talk of, explain, contest, confer, consult, talk with, advise with, reason with, exchange observations, deal with, take up, address, examine, look over, consider, deliberate, talk over, talk out, take up in conference, engage in conversation, go into, think over, write about, telephone about, have a conference on, take into consideration, discourse on, reason, contend, wrangle, argue for and against, canvass, handle, present, review, recite, ventilate, air, examine by argument, plead, treat, speak of, converse, commune, have a talk with, have a word with, present varied opinions, parley, discourse, altercate, ratiocinate, take under advisement, exchange views, compare notes, moot, comment upon, have it out, speak on, hold forth, bandy words, kick around*, toss around*, bat around*, have a bull session*, chew the fat*, chew the rag*, jaw*, confabulate*, confab*, knock around*, go into a huddle*, put heads together*, rap*, hash out\*, hash over\*, thrash out\*; see also **consult, debate, talk** 1.— *Ant.* DELAY, table, postpone.

---

*SYN.* — **discuss** implies a talking about something in a deliberative fashion, with varying opinions offered constructively and usually amicably, so as to settle an issue, decide on a course of action, etc.; **argue** implies the citing of reasons or evidence to support or refute an assertion, belief, proposition, etc.; **debate** implies a formal argument, usually on public questions, in contests between opposing groups; **dispute** implies argument in which there is a contradiction of an assertion, often presented in an angry or heated manner

---

**discussed,** *modif.* — *Syn.* talked over, debated, argued; see **considered** 1.

**discussion,** *n.* **1.** [The act of considering in words] — *Syn.* conversation, exchange, consultation, interview, deliberation, argumentation, contention, confabulation, dialogue, meaningful dialogue, talk, excursus, conference, wrangling, argument, disputation, debate, roundtable debate, panel discussion, forensics, summit meeting, negotiations, dealing with the agenda, consideration, controversy, altercation, review, dialectic, dialogism, critical argumentation, dispute, canvass, discourse, symposium, quarrel, pros and cons, disquisition, powwow\*, gabfest\*, wrangle\*, rap session, bull session\*, confab\*; see also **conversation, debate, dispute.**— *Ant.* AGREEMENT, decision, conclusion.
**2.** [A published consideration] — *Syn.* analysis, criticism, examination, forum, study, investigation, determination, inquiry, dissertation, treatment, proposal; see also **exposition** 2, **writing** 2.

**disdain,** *n.* — *Syn.* scorn, haughtiness, contempt; see **arrogance, hatred** 1.

**disdain,** *v.* — *Syn.* reject, scorn, despise, ignore; see **despise, hate** 1, **refuse.**
*See Synonym Study at* DESPISE.

**disdainful,** *modif.* — *Syn.* scornful, contemptuous, supercilious, dismissive; see **egotistic** 2, **indifferent** 1, **proud** 2, **scornful** 1.
*See Synonym Study at* PROUD.

**disease,** *n.* — *Syn.* sickness, malady, ailment, illness, indisposition, unhealthiness, disorder, condition, complaint, spell, distemper, unsoundness, infirmity, affection, visitation, morbidity, pathological case, psychosomatic illness, epidemic, plague, pestilence, infection, virus, contagion, affliction, complication, syndrome, fever, nervous disorder, functional disorder, pathological condition, attack, seizure, collapse, breakdown, pathology, symptomatology, bug\*, temperature\*; see also **illness** 1.— *Ant.* HEALTH, strength, vigor.
Specific diseases include — *diseases affecting various organs or the body generally:* cancer, ulcer, shock, paresis, paralysis, focal infection, atrophy, psittacosis, chicken pox, cholera, diphtheria, malaria, measles, German measles, mumps, Rocky Mountain spotted fever, Lyme disease, Legionnaires' disease, rabies, scarlet fever, scarlatina, smallpox, toxic-shock syndrome, tularemia, typhoid fever, typhus, leprosy, hepatitis, yellow fever; *venereal or social diseases:* gonorrhea, clap\*, dose\*; herpes, AIDS, chlamydia, genital warts, syphilis, French disease\*, *maladie anglaise\** (French), English disease\*, pox\*; *diseases affecting the brain and nervous system:* encephalitis, sleeping sickness, meningitis, aphasia, stroke, Alzheimer's disease, hemiplegia, Reye's syndrome, brain tumor, poliomyelitis, polio, infantile paralysis, sclerosis, amyotrophic lateral sclerosis, Lou Gehrig's disease, multiple sclerosis, MS, de-

lirium tremens, D.T.'s\*; *diseases affecting the respiratory tract:* bronchitis, rhinitis, common cold, sniffles\*, cough, influenza, flu, Asian flu, Hong Kong flu, laryngitis, pleurisy, viral pneumonia, pulmonary pneumonia, phthisis, tonsillitis, emphysema, strep throat\*, sinusitis, croup, tuberculosis, TB, whooping cough; *diseases affecting the digestive system:* acidosis, ulcer, appendicitis, Bright's disease, colitis, diabetes, diarrhea, constipation, diverticulitis, dysentery, anasarca, dropsy, gravel, jaundice; *diseases affecting the circulatory system:* angina pectoris, high blood pressure, hypertension, cystic fibrosis, hemorrhage, hardening of the arteries, hypertension, heart murmur, palpitations, arteriosclerosis, atherosclerosis, coronary thrombosis; *skin diseases:* athlete's foot, boils, warts, eczema, psoriasis, erysipelas, dermatitis, scabies, ringworm, trench foot, acne; *diseases of the joints and muscles:* arthritis, osteoporosis, bends, cramp, charley horse\*, crick\*; rheumatism, lumbago; *diseases of the eye:* cataracts, glaucoma, conjunctivitis, pink eye, trachoma; *allergies:* hay fever, rose fever, asthma, hives; *diseases of the endocrine glands:* hyperthyroidism, hypothyroidism, progeria, hyperpituitarism, hypopituitarism; *diseases common to animals and birds:* anthrax, black leg, blind staggers, bloat, cholera, colic, distemper, encephalitis, hydrophobia, rabies, heaves, hoof and mouth disease, glanders, milk sickness, pneumonitis, roup, spavin, trichomoniasis; *diseases common to plants:* blight, rot, rust, scale, smut, wilt; see also **complex** 1, **insanity** 1.

---

*SYN.* — **disease** may apply generally to any deviation of the body from its normal or healthy state, or it may refer to a particular disorder with a specific cause and characteristic symptoms; **condition** and **affection** refer to a disorder of a specific organ or part /a heart *condition*, an *affection* of the spleen/; **malady** usually refers to a deepseated chronic disease, frequently one that is ultimately fatal; **ailment** refers to a chronic, annoying disorder of whatever degree of seriousness /the minor *ailments* of the aged/

---

**diseased,** *modif.* — *Syn.* unhealthy, unsound, ailing, infected; see **sick.**

**disembark,** *v.* — *Syn.* arrive, debark, deplane; see **land** 3.

**disembodied,** *modif.* — *Syn.* incorporeal, bodiless, discarnate; see **immaterial** 2.

**disembowel,** *v.* — *Syn.* eviscerate, gut, embowel; see **kill** 1.

**disenchant,** *v.* — *Syn.* disenthrall, embitter, disentrance; see **disillusion.**

**disengage,** *v.* — *Syn.* loose, undo, disentangle; see **free** 1, 2, **release, unhitch.**

**disengaged,** *modif.* — *Syn.* detached, unattached, disjoined, unengaged; see **free** 2, 3, **separated.**

**disengagement,** *n.* **1.** [Rest] — *Syn.* ease, leisure, liberty; see **leisure, rest** 1.
**2.** [Detachment] — *Syn.* severance, withdrawal, disentanglement; see **division** 1, **freeing, separation** 1.

**disentangle,** *v.* — *Syn.* disengage, untangle, untwist; see **free** 1, **unhitch.**

**disfavor,** *n.* **1.** [Dissatisfaction] — *Syn.* displeasure, disapproval, disrespect, disesteem; see **dissatisfaction** 1, **objection** 1.
**2.** [Disgrace] — *Syn.* disrepute, disregard, dishonor; see **disgrace** 1.

**disfigure,** *v.* — *Syn.* deface, mar, mutilate, deform; see **damage** 1, **distort** 3, **hurt** 1.

**disgorge,** *v.* — *Syn.* eject, throw up, spew; see **vomit.**

**disgrace,** *n.* **1.** [A shameful condition] — *Syn.* dishonor, ignominy, shame, humiliation, reproach, discredit, odium, degradation, opprobrium, disrepute, disfavor, notoriety, scorn, derision, abuse, obloquy, abasement, infamy, disrespect, contumely, ill repute, scandal, disesteem, disapproval, disapprobation, humbling, ingloriousness, contempt, disbarment, unfrocking, dishonorable discharge; see also **shame** 2. — *Ant.* HONOR, esteem, dignity.
**2.** [Whatever lowers one in the eyes of one's fellows] — *Syn.* scandal, shame, discredit, stain, slur, slight, stigma, brand, spot, slander, blot, blemish, culpability, dishonor, ignominy, reproach, humiliation, degradation, turpitude, corruption, meanness, venality, taint, tarnish, pollution, black mark, mark of Cain★, scarlet A★, scarlet letter★; see also **insult**. — *Ant.* PRIDE, praise, credit.

**disgrace,** *v.* — *Syn.* debase, shame, degrade, abase, dishonor, discredit, deride, disregard, strip of honors, demote, dismiss from favor, disrespect, mock, humble, humiliate, lower, depress, reduce, put to shame, throw dishonor upon, be unworthy of, tarnish, stain, besmirch, blot, sully, taint, defile, stigmatize, bring into discredit, bring low, bring shame upon, be a discredit to, brand, post, drag through the mud, tar and feather, condemn to the stocks, heap dirt upon, put down★, derogate, take down a peg; see also **humble, humiliate, ridicule.** — *Ant.* PRAISE, honor, exalt.

**disgraced,** *modif.* — *Syn.* discredited, in disgrace, dishonored, degraded, demoted, shamed, overcome, downtrodden, humiliated, in disfavor, in disrepute, discharged, defrocked, exposed, in bad repute, mocked, abject, down and out, shown up★, in Dutch★, fallen from one's high estate, tarred and feathered, put down★, out on one's ear★, in the doghouse★. — *Ant.* HONORED, restored, in favor.

**disgraceful,** *modif.* — *Syn.* dishonorable, disreputable, shocking; see **offensive** 2, **shameful** 1, 2.

**disgruntled,** *modif.* — *Syn.* grumpy, discontented, displeased; see **disappointed** 1, **dissatisfied, irritable.**

**disguise,** *n.* — *Syn.* mask, camouflage, deceptive covering, makeup, faking, front, false front, deception, screen, smoke screen, blind, concealment, coverup, counterfeit, pseudonym, guise, costume, masquerade, veil, cover, façade, pen name, alias, pretense, put-on★; see also **camouflage** 1, **costume.**

**disguise,** *v.* — *Syn.* mask, conceal, dissemble, camouflage, pretend, screen, cloak, shroud, cover, cover up, veil, alter, hide, obscure, feign, dissimulate, counterfeit, falsify, misrepresent, varnish, age, antique, redo, make up, simulate, muffle, alter the appearance of, make unrecognizable, employ plastic surgery, dress up, touch up, doctor, phony up★; see also **change** 1, **deceive, hide** 1, 2. — *Ant.* REVEAL, disclose, expose.

**disguised,** *modif.* — *Syn.* cloaked, masked, camouflaged; see **changed** 2, 3, **covered** 1, **hidden** 2.

**disgust,** *n.* — *Syn.* loathing, repugnance, revulsion; see **hatred** 1, **objection** 1.

**disgust,** *v.* — *Syn.* repel, revolt, offend, displease, nauseate, sicken, make one sick, fill with loathing, cause aversion, offend the morals of, repulse, be repulsive, irk, appall, scandalize, shock, upset, pall, turn one's stomach, stick in one's craw, put off, turn off★, gross out★; see also **bother** 3, **disturb** 2.

**disgusted,** *modif.* — *Syn.* displeased, offended, sickened, nauseated, repelled, unhappy, revolted, appalled, outraged, sick of, tired of, fed up★, sick and tired★, had a bellyful★, had it★, had enough★, up to here★; see also **troubled** 1.

**disgusting,** *modif.* — *Syn.* repugnant, revolting, sickening; see **offensive** 2.

**dish,** *n.* **1.** [Plate] — *Syn.* vessel, bowl, platter, saucer, pottery, ceramic; see also **china, plate** 4.
Kinds of dishes include: dinner plate, luncheon plate, salad plate, dessert plate, bread-and-butter plate, platter, casserole, cake plate, coffee cup, coffee mug, espresso cup, demitasse, teacup, chocolate cup, egg cup, bouillon cup, custard cup, saucer, Tom-and-Jerry mug, beer mug, stein, cereal bowl, soup bowl, gravy boat, vegetable dish, open dish, covered dish, au gratin dish, soufflé dish, tureen, serving dish, chafing dish, olive dish, celery dish, conserve dish, relish tray, teapot, pitcher, sugar bowl, butter dish, salt cellar, pepper mill, *presentoir* (French); see also **bowl, container, cup, pottery.**
**2.** [Food] — *Syn.* course, serving, recipe, preparation, side dish, main dish, entree, specialty, fare; see also **food, helping, meal** 2.
**3.** [★A good-looking woman] — *Syn.* beauty, doll★, cutie★; see **beauty** 4.

**dishearten,** *v.* — *Syn.* dampen, dismay, daunt, get down★; see **depress** 2, **discourage** 1.

**disheveled,** *modif.* — *Syn.* rumpled, tousled, untidy, unkempt; see **dirty** 1, **disordered.**

**dishonest,** *modif.* **1.** [Not honest] — *Syn.* deceiving, lying, untruthful, double-dealing, deceitful, fraudulent, false, counterfeit, cunning, crafty, sneaky, tricky, knavish, wily, crooked, deceptive, misleading, bluffing, evasive, slippery, unctuous, insincere, hypocritical, disingenuous, pettifogging, swindling, cheating, sneaking, recreant, roguish, backbiting, treacherous, falsehearted, traitorous, villainous, sinister, mendacious, duplicitous, perfidious, insidious, devious, Machiavellian, hoodwinking, underhanded, shady★, two-timing★, double, two-faced★, double-crossing★, fork-tongued★; see also **false** 1, **hypocritical, mean** 3. — *Ant.* HONEST, truthful, candid.
**2.** [Lacking integrity] — *Syn.* unprincipled, shifty, unscrupulous, undependable, disreputable, questionable, dishonorable, corrupt, immoral, unethical, untrustworthy, discredited, ignoble, unworthy, degraded, shabby, mean, low, venal, self-serving, contemptible, canting, corruptible, crooked, rotten★, dirty★, fishy★; see also sense 1; **corrupt** 1, **false** 1. — *Ant.* scrupulous, trustworthy, ethical.

---

**SYN.** — **dishonest** implies the act or practice of telling a lie, or of cheating, deceiving, stealing, etc. [a *dishonest* official]; **deceitful** implies an intent to make someone believe what is not true, as by giving a false appearance, using fraud, etc. [a *deceitful* advertisement]; **lying** suggests only the act of telling a falsehood [curb your *lying* tongue]; **untruthful** is used as a somewhat softened substitute for lying, esp. with reference to statements, reports, etc. [an *untruthful* account]

---

**dishonesty,** *n.* — *Syn.* deceit, deception, falsehood, trickery, infidelity, faithlessness, falsity, craft, artifice, duplicity, wiliness, untrustworthiness, insidiousness, cunning, guile, perfidiousness, slyness, perfidy, double-dealing, craftiness, trickiness, treachery, knavishness, knavery, cant, crookedness, corruption, mythomania, lying, cheating, stealing, subtlety, hypocrisy, insincerity, prevarication, swindle, fraud, chicanery, rascality, mendacity, artfulness, subtleness, fraudulence, pettifoggery, embezzlement, counterfeiting, forgery, perjury, treason, false pretenses, shadiness★, flimflam★, hocus-pocus★, hanky-panky★, skulduggery★; see also **deception** 1, **hy-**

pocrisy, lie 1.— *Ant.* HONESTY, truthfulness, integrity.

**dishonor,** *n.* **1.** [Disgrace] — *Syn.* shame, ignominy, infamy, abasement; see **disgrace** 1.

**2.** [Discredit] — *Syn.* insult, indignity, reproach, affront; see **disgrace** 2, **insult.**

**dishonorable,** *modif.* — *Syn.* infamous, disgraceful, ignoble; see **offensive** 2, **shameful** 2.

**dish out,** *v.* — *Syn.* give out, hand out, serve, dispense; see **distribute** 1, **give** 1.

**dish towel,** *n.* — *Syn.* tea towel, kitchen towel, drying towel; see **towel.**

**disillusion,** *v.* — *Syn.* disenchant, disenthrall, shatter one's illusions, free from illusion, disabuse, undeceive, embitter, open one's eyes, let down easy★, pull the ground from under★, burst the bubble★, break the spell★, knock the props from under★, bring down to earth★, bring down★, let the air out of★, send one's air castles tumbling★, show the feet of clay★; see also **disappoint.**

**disinclination,** *n.* — *Syn.* reluctance, unwillingness, dislike; see **aversion, hatred** 1, **objection** 1.

**disinclined,** *modif.* — *Syn.* unwilling, reluctant, balking, hesitant; see **reluctant, unwilling.**

*See Synonym Study at* RELUCTANT.

**disinfect,** *v.* — *Syn.* purify, fumigate, sterilize, sanitize; see **clean.**

**disingenuous,** *modif.* — *Syn.* insincere, uncandid, deceitful, calculating; see **dishonest** 1, **hypocritical, sly** 1.

**disinherit,** *v.* — *Syn.* exclude from inheritance, disown, cut off, exheridate, evict, deprive of one's inheritance, dispossess, divest, disaffiliate, cut off without a penny, oust, dispossess of hereditary right, cast off, strike from one's will; see also **dismiss** 1, **neglect** 2.

**disintegrate,** *v.* **1.** [To break up] — *Syn.* break down, separate, atomize, dissolve, divide, dismantle, break into pieces, disunite, disperse, crumble, disband, fall apart, take apart, disorganize, detach, break apart, come apart, sever, disconnect, wash away, wear away, erode, fall to pieces, turn to dust, fade away, reduce to ashes; see also **destroy** 1, **dissolve** 1.— *Ant.* UNITE, put together, combine.

**2.** [To decay] — *Syn.* decompose, crumble, rot, deteriorate; see **decay.**

*See Synonym Study at* DECAY.

**disinter,** *v.* — *Syn.* exhume, unearth, dig up, disentomb; see **exhume, expose** 1.

**disinterested,** *modif.* — *Syn.* impartial, unbiased, not involved; see **aloof, fair** 1, **indifferent** 1.

*See Synonym Study at* INDIFFERENT.

**disjoin,** *v.* — *Syn.* separate, detach, disunite; see **divide** 1.

**disjointed,** *modif.* **1.** [Incoherent] — *Syn.* disconnected, disorganized, rambling, confused; see **incoherent** 2, **incongruous** 1, **irregular** 1.

**2.** [Separated] — *Syn.* divided, dismembered, dislocated, unattached; see **separated.**

**disk,** *n.* — *Syn.* disc, plate, platter, discoid, discoidal object, dish, saucer, discus, quoit, flan, phonograph record, compact disc, CD, diskette, floppy disk, floppy★, hard disk, wheel, Frisbee (trademark); see also **circle** 1, **record** 3.

**dislike,** *n.* — *Syn.* aversion, antipathy, distaste; see **aversion, blame** 1, **hate, hatred** 1, 2, **objection** 1.

**dislike,** *v.* — *Syn.* detest, hate, condemn, deplore, not like, not care for, have no interest in, have hard feelings toward, not take kindly to, not be able to say much for, not have the stomach for, not speak well of, not want any part of, bear malice toward, carry a grudge, want nothing to do with, look coldly upon, keep one's distance, look askance at, not bear with, care nothing for, resent, not appreciate, not be able to bear, not be able to endure, not think much of, hold cheap, not feel like, be averse to, abhor, antipathize, abominate, disapprove, execrate, loathe, despise, eschew, object to, shun, shrink from, recoil from, mind, shudder at, scorn, avoid, feel repugnance toward, be displeased by, be disinclined, turn up one's nose at, disesteem, contemn, consider obnoxious, find disagreeable, look on with aversion, disrelish, not be able to stomach, regard with displeasure, regard with disfavor, have all one can take of★, make faces★, take a dim view of★, have no use for★, have it in for★, give a dirty look★, not give a hoot for★, not go for★, have no taste for, have no relish for, be down on★, look down one's nose at★, have a bone to pick with★, have a bellyful★, be turned off by★; see also **hate** 1.

**dislocate,** *v.* **1.** [To displace] — *Syn.* disorder, disrupt, upset, disturb; see **confuse, disorganize.**

**2.** [To disconnect] — *Syn.* disjoint, disunite, disengage, put out of joint; see **break** 1, **divide** 1, **separate** 2.

**dislocation,** *n.* **1.** [Displacement] — *Syn.* disorder, disruption, disturbance; see **confusion** 2.

**2.** [Disjointing, especially of a bone] — *Syn.* displacement, discontinuity, luxation; see **break** 1, **division** 1, **fracture** 1.

**dislodge,** *v.* — *Syn.* eject, uproot, displace, knock loose; see **oust, remove** 1.

**disloyal,** *modif.* — *Syn.* perfidious, treacherous, traitorous, faithless; see **false** 1, **unfaithful** 1.

*See Synonym Study at* FAITHLESS.

**disloyalty,** *n.* — *Syn.* infidelity, inconstancy, treachery, unfaithfulness, recreancy, apostasy, betrayal of trust, faithlessness, disaffection, subversion, sedition, treason, deliberate breaking of faith, breach of trust, subversive activity, undutifulness, falseness, lack of fidelity, lack of loyalty, double-dealing, wishing harm to one's country, perfidy, Iscariotism, bad faith, dereliction of allegiance, violation of allegiance; see also **dishonesty, treason.**

**dismal,** *modif.* **1.** [Depressing] — *Syn.* gloomy, dreary, melancholy, dark, cheerless, bleak, desolate, doleful, dispiriting, dolorous, sad, sorrowful, inauspicious, morbid, troubling, horrid, shadowy, tenebrous, dim, overcast, cloudy, gray, unhappy, discouraging, hopeless, black, grim, unfortunate, dreadful, ghastly, horrible, monotonous, tedious, boring, frowning, lowering, mournful, dull, disheartening, afflictive, unwholesome, regrettable, dusky, dingy, sepulchral, joyless, forlorn, funereal, comfortless, murky, wan, somber, woebegone, disagreeable, blue★; see also **dark** 1, **sad** 2.— *Ant.* joyful, cheerful, bright.

**2.** [Sad] — *Syn.* miserable, depressed, sorrowful; see **sad** 1.

**dismantle,** *v.* — *Syn.* take apart, disassemble, strip, break up, break down, take down, tear down, pull down, knock down, undo, dismount, demolish, level, unbuild, ruin, unrig, subvert, raze, take to pieces, fell, strike★; see also **destroy** 1.

*See Synonym Study at* STRIP.

**dismay,** *n.* — *Syn.* alarm, consternation, anxiety, disheartenment; see **confusion** 2, **fear** 2.

**dismay,** *v.* — *Syn.* appall, horrify, daunt, frighten, terrify, petrify, unnerve, abash, disconcert, dishearten; see also **confuse, discourage** 1, **frighten** 1.

---

*SYN.* — **dismay** suggests fear or, esp. in modern usage, discouragement at the prospect of some difficulty or problem which one does not quite know how to resolve *[dismayed* at his lack of understanding*]*; **appall** suggests terror or (now more commonly) consternation at a shocking but apparently unalterable situation *[an appalling death rate]*; **horrify** suggests horror or loathing (or, in a weakened sense, irritation) at that which shocks or offends one *[horrified at the suggestion]*; **daunt** implies a becoming disheartened in the performance of an act that requires some courage *[never daunted by adversity]*

**dismember,** *v.* — *Syn.* dissect, disjoint, amputate; see **cut** 1, **divide** 1, **maim.**

**dismiss,** *v.* **1.** [To send away] — *Syn.* discard, reject, decline, repel, repudiate, dispatch, disband, detach, send off, pack off, cast off, cast out, relinquish, dispense with, disperse, dissolve, adjourn, recess, remove, expel, eject, abolish, relegate, supersede, push aside, shed, slough off, do without, have done with, brush aside, brush away, set aside, disregard, discount, put out of one's mind, dispose of, sweep away, clear, rid, rout, chase, bundle, chase out, run out, drive out, turn out, show out, force out, lock out, shut out, let out, release, excuse, ostracize, exclude, blackball, dispossess, dethrone, boycott, exile, expatriate, banish, outlaw, deport, excommunicate, get rid of, send packing*, drop*, brush off*, kick out*, give the gate*, write off*, pitch overboard*, chuck out*, boot out*, hustle out*, give the air*, read out of*, send abroad*, send to Coventry*; see also **refuse.** — *Ant.* RETAIN, keep, admit.
**2.** [To remove an employee] — *Syn.* discharge, give notice, let go, lay off, fire, displace, terminate, replace, oust, pension off, suspend, remove, disemploy, recall, impeach, unseat, drop, disqualify, cashier, can*, bounce*, sack*, ax*, bust*, boot out*, send packing, give one's walking papers*, give the ax*, give the boot*, give the sack*; see also **oust.** — *Ant.* HIRE, employ, engage.
*See Synonym Study at* EJECT.

**dismissal,** *n.* **1.** [Freedom] — *Syn.* release, liberation, dissolution; see **freeing.**
**2.** [Discharge] — *Syn.* deposition, displacement, expulsion; see **removal** 1.

**dismissed,** *modif.* — *Syn.* sent away, ousted, removed; see **discharged** 1, **free** 1, 2.

**dismount,** *v.* — *Syn.* get off, get down, alight; see **descend** 1.

**disobedience,** *n.* — *Syn.* insubordination, defiance, insurgence, disregard, violation, noncompliance, lack of obedience, rebelliousness, mutiny, revolt, nonobservance, strike, infringement, transgression, waywardness, naughtiness, stubbornness, refractoriness, recalcitrance, infraction, insubmission, intractableness, unruliness, dereliction, sedition, rebellion, sabotage, riot; see also **revolution** 2.

**disobedient,** *modif.* — *Syn.* insubordinate, refractory, defiant; see **naughty, rebellious** 2, 3, **unruly.**

**disobey,** *v.* — *Syn.* defy, resist, rebel, balk, decline, neglect, set aside, desert, be remiss, ignore the commands of, refuse submission to, disagree, oppose, contravene, refuse to support, evade, disregard the authority of, break rules, flout, object, revolt, strike, mutiny, riot, violate, infringe, transgress, shirk, misbehave, not heed, not mind, not listen to, pay no attention to, counteract, take the law into one's own hands, kick over the traces, hurl defiance at, go counter to, worm one's way out of, run riot, fly in the face of, thumb one's nose at, get out of line, answer to no man; see also **dare** 2, **oppose** 1, **rebel** 1. — *Ant.* OBEY, follow, fulfill.

**disoblige,** *v.* **1.** [To insult] — *Syn.* offend, affront, displease; see **insult.**

**2.** [To inconvenience] — *Syn.* annoy, discommode, upset, refuse to oblige; see **bother** 2, **disturb** 2.

**disobliging,** *modif.* — *Syn.* uncivil, unaccommodating, uncooperative, ill-disposed; see **rude** 2.

**disorder,** *n.* **1.** [Physical confusion] — *Syn.* disarray, confusion, jumble, shambles; see **confusion** 2.
**2.** [Social confusion] — *Syn.* disturbance, tumult, uproar, bustle, discord, turbulence, misrule, turmoil, upheaval, complication, chaos, mayhem, terrorism, rioting, mob rule, anarchy, anarchism, lawlessness, disorderliness, rowdiness, imbroglio, entanglement, commotion, agitation, insurrection, revolution, rebellion, strike, disorganization, riot, state of violence, reign of terror, mobocracy, ochlocracy, tangled skein, ruckus*; see also **disturbance** 2, **trouble** 2. — *Ant.* ORDER, peace, tranquility.
**3.** [An illness] — *Syn.* ailment, sickness, malady, dysfunction; see **disease.**
*See Synonym Study at* CONFUSION.

**disorder,** *v.* — *Syn.* disarrange, clutter, scatter; see **confuse, disorganize.**

**disordered,** *modif.* — *Syn.* displaced, misplaced, dislocated, mislaid, out of place, deranged, jumbled, in disorder, out of kilter, out of hand, in confusion, in a mess, all over the place, in a muddle, confused, upset, unsettled, disorganized, disarranged, moved, removed, shifted, meddled with, tampered with, shuffled, tumbled, ruffled, rumpled, disheveled, tousled, riffled, uncombed, molested, jarred, tossed, stirred up, roiled, rolled, jolted, muddled, discombobulated*; see also **confused** 2, **tangled.** — *Ant.* ORDERED, arranged, settled.

**disorderly,** *modif.* **1.** [Lacking orderly arrangement] — *Syn.* indiscriminate, confused, tumultuous, jumbled, undisciplined, unrestrained, heterogeneous, scattered, dislocated, unsystematic, messy, slovenly, untidy, cluttered, unkempt, sloppy, scrambled, badly managed, in confusion, chaotic, disorganized, out of order, in disarray, untrained, out of control, topsy-turvy*, helter-skelter*, higgledy-piggledy*, out of whack*, out of line*, out of step*, all over the place, mixed up, cockeyed*, messed up*; see also **irregular** 1, 4. — *Ant.* NEAT, organized, trim.
**2.** [Creating a disturbance] — *Syn.* rowdy, disruptive, obstreperous, drunk; see **turbulent, unruly.**

**disorganization,** *n.* — *Syn.* disorder, derangement, disunion, dissolution; see **confusion** 2.

**disorganize,** *v.* — *Syn.* put out of order, disarrange, disorder, upset, disrupt, derange, break up, disperse, destroy, scatter, litter, clutter, break down, deprive of organization, dislocate, demobilize, disband, jumble, muddle, mislay, misplace, embroil, unsettle, disturb, perturb, shuffle, toss, throw into disorder, throw into confusion, turn topsy-turvy*, complicate, confound, overthrow, overturn, stampede, agitate, disarray, dishevel, scramble, mix up, mess up*; see also **confuse.** — *Ant.* SYSTEMATIZE, order, arrange.

**disorganized,** *modif.* — *Syn.* chaotic, jumbled, unsystematic, undisciplined; see **confused** 2, **disordered, disorderly** 1, **incongruous** 1.

**disoriented,** *modif.* — *Syn.* confused, lost, at sea; see **bewildered, doubtful** 2.

**disown,** *v.* — *Syn.* repudiate, cast off, deny, retract; see **abandon** 2, **discard, disinherit.**

**disparage,** *v.* — *Syn.* depreciate, deprecate, discredit, defame; see **censure, depreciate** 2.
*See Synonym Study at* DEPRECIATE.

**disparagement,** *n.* **1.** [Detraction] — *Syn.* depreciation, belittlement, backbiting; see **lie** 1.

**2.** [Something that discredits] — *Syn.* aspersion, censure, derision; see **blame** 1, **objection** 2, **ridicule.**

**disparate,** *modif.* — *Syn.* different, dissimilar, diverse; see **different** 1, 2.
*See Synonym Study at* DIFFERENT.

**disparity,** *n.* — *Syn.* inequality, difference, incongruity; see **difference** 2, **variation** 2.

**dispassionate,** *modif.* — *Syn.* impartial, judicial, calm, disinterested; see **calm** 1, **cool** 2, **fair** 1.
*See Synonym Study at* FAIR.

**dispatch,** *v.* **1.** [To send something on its way] — *Syn.* transmit, express, forward; see **send** 1.
**2.** [To kill deliberately] — *Syn.* put to death, murder, finish; see **kill** 1.
**3.** [To make an end] — *Syn.* finish, conclude, perform; see **achieve** 1.
*See Synonym Study at* KILL.

**dispel,** *v.* — *Syn.* scatter, disperse, dissipate, clear away; see **dismiss** 1, **scatter** 2.
*See Synonym Study at* SCATTER.

**dispensable,** *modif.* — *Syn.* superfluous, unnecessary, unimportant, nonessential; see **trivial, unnecessary.**

**dispensation,** *n.* **1.** [Distribution] — *Syn.* allocation, allotment, endowment; see **distribution** 1, 2.
**2.** [Management] — *Syn.* direction, regulation, supervision; see **administration** 1.
**3.** [Release from obligation] — *Syn.* exemption, waiver, indulgence, authorization; see **freedom** 2, **permission.**

**dispense,** *v.* **1.** [To distribute] — *Syn.* apportion, assign, allocate; see **administer** 2, **distribute** 1, **give** 1.
**2.** [To administer] — *Syn.* undertake, enforce, direct; see **command** 2, **manage** 1.
*See Synonym Study at* DISTRIBUTE.

**dispenser,** *n.* **1.** [A distributor] — *Syn.* divider, allocator, dealer; see **businessperson, dealer** 2, **distributor** 1, **merchant.**
**2.** [A device that dispenses something] — *Syn.* vendor, vending machine, spray can, aerosol spray, spray gun, paint gun, soap dispenser, automat, squeeze bottle, tapper, beer keg, gum, candy, cigarette, soda, Coke (trademark), coffee, cold drink, etc., machine; see also **can** 1, **container, faucet.**

**dispense with,** *v.* — *Syn.* forgo, do without, ignore, set aside; see **abandon** 1, **abstain, discard, dismiss** 1, **waive.**

**disperse,** *v.* — *Syn.* scatter, break up, separate, disband; see **scatter** 1, 2.
*See Synonym Study at* SCATTER.

**dispersion,** *n.* — *Syn.* dispersal, scattering, diffusion; see **distribution** 1.

**dispirited,** *modif.* — *Syn.* dejected, depressed, disheartened; see **sad** 1.

**displace,** *v.* **1.** [To remove] — *Syn.* uproot, dislodge, relocate, dismiss; see **dismiss** 2, **remove** 1.
**2.** [To take the place of] — *Syn.* replace, supplant, crowd out; see **replace** 2.
*See Synonym Study at* REPLACE.

**display,** *n.* **1.** [Pretentious show] — *Syn.* affectation, pretension, pedantry; see **ostentation** 2, **vanity** 1.
**2.** [A show] — *Syn.* exhibition, exhibit, presentation, representation, exposition, arrangement, demonstration, performance, revelation, procession, parade, pageant, spectacle, exposure, array, example, appearance, waxworks, fireworks, tinsel, carnival, fair, bravura, frippery, pomp, splendor, unfolding, manifestation, image, turnout, splash*, splurge*, chamber of horrors*; see also **show** 1, 2.

**3.** [Matter presented to encourage sale] — *Syn.* sample, layout, spread; see **advertisement** 2.

**display,** *v.* **1.** [To present for effect] — *Syn.* show off, exhibit, expose, uncover, open up, unfold, spread out, parade, manifest, unmask, present, represent, perform, flaunt, lay out, put out, set out, demonstrate, evidence, air, evince, disclose, visualize, unveil, arrange, lay bare, bring to view, make clear, reveal, impart, make known, promulgate, showcase; see also **expose** 1. — *Ant.* HIDE, conceal, veil.
**2.** [To advertise] — *Syn.* illustrate, promote, publicize; see **advertise** 1, 2.
*See Synonym Study at* SHOW.

**displayed,** *modif.* — *Syn.* presented, laid out, spread out, visible, on display, in the public view; see also **advertised, shown** 1.

**displease,** *v.* — *Syn.* vex, provoke, annoy, offend; see **anger** 1, **bother** 3.

**displeased,** *modif.* — *Syn.* unhappy, vexed, annoyed; see **angry, disappointed** 1, **dissatisfied.**

**displeasure,** *n.* — *Syn.* disapproval, annoyance, resentment; see **anger, objection** 1, **offense** 3.
*See Synonym Study at* OFFENSE.

**disposal,** *n.* **1.** [Getting rid of something] — *Syn.* discarding, riddance, dispatching, disposition, transference, transfer, demolition, dispensation, throwing away, dumping, junking*, scrapping*, transaction, sale, clearance, selling, auctioning, trading, vending, bartering, conveyance, sacrifice, reducing to clear, clearing out, making way for new stock, relinquishment, bestowal; see also **destruction** 1, **distribution** 1. — *Ant.* COLLECTION, accumulation, acquirement.
**2.** [The final treatment of a matter] — *Syn.* arrangements, action, provision, determination, disposition, order, placement, deployment, distribution, conclusion, division, ordering, allocation, settlement, control, direction, effectuation, winding up; see also **administration** 1, **end** 2, **order** 3.
**at one's disposal** — *Syn.* ready, at one's command, on hand, usable; see **available.**

**dispose,** *v.* **1.** [To put in place] — *Syn.* arrange, array, settle, distribute; see **deploy, order** 3, **place** 1.
**2.** [To make willing or liable] — *Syn.* incline, predispose, lead, motivate; see **influence.**

**disposed,** *modif.* — *Syn.* inclined, prone, apt; see **likely** 4.

**dispose of,** *v.* **1.** [To eliminate] — *Syn.* get rid of, relinquish, throw away, part with; see **discard, sell** 1.
**2.** [To kill] — *Syn.* murder, eliminate, slaughter, destroy; see **kill** 1.

**disposition,** *n.* **1.** [Arrangement] — *Syn.* placement, distribution, settlement; see **disposal** 1, 2, **order** 3, **organization** 1.
**2.** [Temperament] — *Syn.* character, nature, temper; see **character** 2, **inclination** 1, **mood** 1, **temperament.**
*See Synonym Study at* TEMPERAMENT.

**SYN. — disposition** refers to the normal or prevailing aspect of one's nature /a genial *disposition*/; **temperament** refers to the balance of traits that are manifested in one's behavior or thinking /an artistic *temperament*/; **temper** refers to one's basic emotional nature, esp. as regards relative quickness to anger /a hot *temper*, an even *temper*/; **character** is applied to the sum of moral qualities associated with an individual /a weak *character*/ and, unqualified, suggests moral strength, self-discipline, etc. /a man of *character*/; **personality** is applied to the sum of physical, mental, and emotional qualities that distinguish one as a person [an abrasive *personality*] and, un-qualified, suggests attractiveness or charm [a girl with *personality*]

**dispossess,** *v.* **1.** [To take away from] — *Syn.* confiscate, divest, strip, steal; see **disinherit, seize** 2.
**2.** [To evict] — *Syn.* dislodge, drive out, expel; see **dismiss** 1, **oust.**
**disproportion,** *n.* — *Syn.* disparity, incongruity, lopsidedness; see **difference** 1, **imbalance, inconsistency.**
**disproportionate,** *modif.* — *Syn.* asymmetrical, unbalanced, incommensurate, excessive; see **irregular** 4, **superfluous.**
**disprove,** *v.* — *Syn.* prove false, discredit, controvert, refute, confute, rebut, throw out, set aside, find unfounded, find fault in, point out the weakness of, invalidate, weaken, negate, overthrow, tear down, confound, expose, puncture, cut the ground from under*, blow up*, poke holes in*; see also **deny, refute.**

**SYN.** — **disprove** implies the presenting of evidence or reasoned arguments that demonstrate an assertion or belief to be false or erroneous; **refute** implies a more thorough assembly of evidence and a more careful development of argument, hence suggests conclusiveness of proof; **confute** suggests the overwhelming or silencing of a person by argument, proof, or rhetorical force; **controvert** implies a disputing or denying of statements, arguments, etc. in an endeavor to refute them; **rebut** stresses formality in refuting an argument, such as is observed in debate, court procedure, etc.

**disputable,** *modif.* — *Syn.* debatable, doubtful, dubious; see **controversial, questionable** 1, **uncertain** 2.
**disputant,** *n.* — *Syn.* contender, arguer, discussant, antagonist, debater, opponent, adversary; see also **critic** 1, **controversialist, enemy** 2, **opponent** 1, 2.
**disputation,** *n.* — *Syn.* dissension, debate, controversy; see **discussion** 1, **dispute.**
**disputatious,** *modif.* — *Syn.* contentious, argumentative, captious; see **quarrelsome** 1.
**dispute,** *n.* — *Syn.* argument, quarrel, debate, row, misunderstanding, verbal contention, disputation, disagreement, controversy, fight, conflict, strife, discussion, polemic, bickering, squabble, wrangle, disturbance, feud, uproar, commotion, tiff, fracas, brouhaha, altercation, dissension, variance, squall, difference of opinion, falling-out, lovers' quarrel, broil, words, war of words, set-to*, spat*, rumpus*, flare-up*, fuss*, fireworks*, slanging match*, hassle*; see also **disagreement** 1.
**beyond dispute** — *Syn.* settled, sure, not open to question; see **certain** 3.
**in dispute** — *Syn.* argued, unsettled, undetermined; see **controversial, uncertain** 2.

**SYN.** — **dispute** refers to a clash of opposing opinions, often involving a matter of a legal or official nature, and implies vehemence or anger in debate [a *dispute* over property boundaries]; **argument** refers to a discussion in which there is disagreement and suggests the use of logic and the bringing forth of facts to support or refute a point; **controversy** connotes a disagreement of lengthy duration over a matter of some weight or importance

**dispute,** *v.* — *Syn.* argue, debate, contradict, quarrel; see **argue** 1, **discuss, oppose** 1.
*See Synonym Study at* DISCUSS.
**disqualification,** *n.* **1.** [Disability] — *Syn.* unfitness,

ineligibility, incapacity, incompetence; see **inability, limitation** 3.
**2.** [Elimination] — *Syn.* debarment, exclusion, rejection; see **elimination** 2, **refusal.**
**disqualify,** *v.* **1.** [To disable] — *Syn.* incapacitate, invalidate, disenable, rule out; see **weaken** 2.
**2.** [To debar] — *Syn.* preclude, disentitle, exclude, disbar; see **bar** 2.
**disquiet,** *n.* — *Syn.* anxiety, restlessness, uneasiness; see **anxiety, care** 2, **fear** 2.
**disquieting,** *modif.* — *Syn.* disturbing, troubling, disconcerting; see **disturbing.**
**disquisition,** *n.* — *Syn.* discourse, treatise, dissertation, commentary; see **exposition** 2, **writing** 2.
**disregard,** *v.* — *Syn.* ignore, overlook, slight, dismiss, despise, pass over, let it go, let it pass, make light of, not heed, make allowances for, have no use for, laugh off, take no account of, brush aside, turn a deaf ear to*, be blind to*, shut one's eyes to*, wink at, blink at; see also **neglect** 1, 2.
*See Synonym Study at* NEGLECT.
**disrepair,** *n.* — *Syn.* decrepitude, deterioration, dilapidation; see **decay** 1.
**disreputable,** *modif.* **1.** [In ill repute] — *Syn.* low, objectionable, discreditable, unsavory; see **dishonest** 2, **offensive** 2, **shameful** 1, 2.
**2.** [Suggestive of ill repute] — *Syn.* seedy, shabby, down at heel; see **dirty** 1, **shabby** 1.
**disrepute,** *n.* — *Syn.* dishonor, disfavor, infamy; see **disgrace** 1.
**disrespect,** *n.* — *Syn.* discourtesy, insolence, irreverence; see **rudeness.**
**disrespectful,** *modif.* — *Syn.* ill-bred, discourteous, impolite; see **rude** 2.
**disrobe,** *v.* — *Syn.* undress, strip, divest, unclothe; see **undress.**
**disrupt,** *v.* **1.** [To break] — *Syn.* interrupt, intrude, obstruct, break up; see **interrupt** 2, **meddle** 1.
**2.** [To confuse] — *Syn.* upset, disturb, disorder, agitate; see **confuse.**
**disruption,** *n.* **1.** [Division] — *Syn.* splitting, severance, separation; see **division** 1, **interruption, separation** 1.
**2.** [Turmoil] — *Syn.* disorder, disturbance, agitation; see **confusion** 2, **disturbance** 2.
**dissatisfaction,** *n.* **1.** [Lack of satisfaction] — *Syn.* discontent, disappointment, discontentment, uneasiness, disquiet, desolation, querulousness, hopelessness, boredom, weariness, malaise, anxiety, trouble, worry, oppression, discouragement; see also **disappointment** 1.
— *Ant.* SATISFACTION, contentment, relief.
**2.** [Active disapproval] — *Syn.* dislike, displeasure, disapproval; see **objection** 1, 2.
**dissatisfied,** *modif.* — *Syn.* displeased, discontented, ungratified, querulous, disgruntled, malcontent, offended, unsatisfied, unhappy, unfulfilled, fed up*, put out*; see also **disappointed** 1.
**dissatisfy,** *v.* — *Syn.* displease, discontent, disappoint, perturb; see **anger** 1, **bother** 3, **disappoint.**
**dissect,** *v.* **1.** [To anatomize] — *Syn.* dismember, quarter, operate, perform an autopsy; see **cut** 1, **divide** 1.
**2.** [To examine] — *Syn.* scrutinize, investigate, inspect; see **analyze** 1, **examine** 1.
**dissection,** *n.* **1.** [Anatomization] — *Syn.* dismemberment, vivisection, autopsy; see **division** 1, **operation** 4.
**2.** [Investigation] — *Syn.* study, inquest, analysis; see **examination** 1, **study** 2.
**dissemble,** *v.* **1.** [To disguise] — *Syn.* mask, cover, camouflage; see **disguise, hide** 1.

2. [To behave hypocritically] — *Syn.* feign, sham, dissimulate, put on an act*; see **lie** 1, **pretend** 1.

**dissembler,** *n.* — *Syn.* hypocrite, charlatan, deceiver; see **hypocrite, impostor.**

**disseminate,** *v.* — *Syn.* sow, propagate, broadcast; see **advertise** 1, **distribute** 1, **scatter** 2, 3.

**dissemination,** *n.* — *Syn.* propagation, promulgation, distribution, diffusion; see **announcement** 1, **dissipation** 1, **distribution** 1.

**dissension,** *n.* — *Syn.* difference, quarrel, trouble, discord; see **disagreement** 1, **dispute.**

*See Synonym Study at* DISCORD.

**dissent,** *n.* — *Syn.* nonconformity, difference, dissidence, heterodoxy; see **disagreement** 1, **heresy, nonconformity, objection** 2.

**dissent,** *v.* — *Syn.* disagree, refuse, contradict; see **differ** 1, **oppose** 1.

**dissenter,** *n.* — *Syn.* dissident, separatist, heretic, objector; see **nonconformist, protester, rebel** 1, **skeptic.**

**dissertation,** *n.* — *Syn.* thesis, discourse, treatise, commentary; see **exposition** 2, **thesis** 2.

**disservice,** *n.* — *Syn.* wrong, injury, outrage; see **damage** 1, **injustice** 2, **insult, wrong** 2.

**dissidence,** *n.* — *Syn.* dissent, discordance, nonconformity; see **disagreement** 1, **nonconformity, protest.**

**dissident,** *n.* — *Syn.* dissenter, protester, rebel; see **agitator, nonconformist, protester, rebel** 1.

**dissimilar,** *modif.* — *Syn.* different, disparate, divergent, unique; see **different** 1.

*See Synonym Study at* DIFFERENT.

**dissimilarity,** *n.* — *Syn.* unlikeness, divergence, separation; see **contrast** 1, **difference** 1, **variation** 2.

**dissimulation,** *n.* — *Syn.* pretense, hypocrisy, dissembling, wile; see **deception** 1, **dishonesty, pretense** 1.

**dissipate,** *v.* 1. [To dispel] — *Syn.* scatter, disperse, diffuse, disseminate; see **scatter** 2.

2. [To squander] — *Syn.* use up, consume, misuse; see **spend** 1, **waste** 1, 2.

3. [To vanish] — *Syn.* evanesce, melt away, run dry; see **disappear, evaporate** 1.

*See Synonym Study at* SCATTER.

**dissipated,** *modif.* 1. [Scattered] — *Syn.* dispersed, strewn, disseminated; see **scattered.**

2. [Wasted] — *Syn.* squandered, destroyed, consumed; see **gone** 2, **spent** 2, **wasted.**

3. [Corrupt] — *Syn.* intemperate, dissolute, self-indulgent; see **sensual** 2, **wicked** 1.

**dissipation,** *n.* 1. [Dispersion] — *Syn.* scattering, dissemination, dispersal, diffusion, spread, radiation, emission, disintegration, dissolution; see also **disappearance, distribution** 1.

2. [Debauchery] — *Syn.* indulgence, intemperance, dissolution; see **indulgence** 3, **waste** 1.

**dissociate,** *v.* — *Syn.* separate, disunite, disengage, distance oneself; see **divide** 1, **scatter** 1, **separate** 2.

**dissociation,** *n.* — *Syn.* severance, disunion, disengagement; see **division** 1, **separation** 1.

**dissoluble,** *modif.* — *Syn.* dissolvable, solvent, dispersible; see **soluble.**

**dissolute,** *modif.* — *Syn.* loose, licentious, debauched, dissipated; see **lewd** 2, **wicked** 1.

**dissolution,** *n.* 1. [Disintegration] — *Syn.* resolution, destruction, decomposition; see **decay** 1, **disappearance.**

2. [Termination] — *Syn.* ending, adjournment, dismissal; see **end** 2.

3. [Death] — *Syn.* release, demise, extinction; see **death** 1.

**dissolve,** *v.* 1. [To pass from a solid to a liquid state] — *Syn.* liquefy, melt, melt away, thaw, soften, run, deliquesce, fluidify, defrost, diffuse, waste away, flux, pass into solution; see also **evaporate** 1, **melt** 1. — *Ant.* HARDEN, freeze, solidify.

2. [To disintegrate] — *Syn.* break up, separate, break into pieces; see **decay, disintegrate** 1.

3. [To destroy] — *Syn.* put an end to, eradicate, do away with, terminate; see **destroy** 1, **end** 1.

4. [To dismiss] — *Syn.* adjourn, postpone, discontinue; see **dismiss** 1, **suspend** 2.

5. [To annul] — *Syn.* repeal, invalidate, render void; see **cancel** 2.

6. [To fade away] — *Syn.* vanish, melt away, fade; see **disappear.**

*See Synonym Study at* MELT, SUSPEND.

**dissonance,** *n.* 1. [Discord] — *Syn.* discordance, jangle, cacophony, disharmony; see **noise** 1, 2.

2. [Disagreement] — *Syn.* conflict, incongruity, discrepancy, disaccord; see **disagreement** 1, **inconsistency.**

**dissonant,** *modif.* 1. [Discordant] — *Syn.* strident, inharmonious, tuneless; see **harsh** 1.

2. [Inconsistent] — *Syn.* incompatible, conflicting, anomalous; see **different** 1, **incongruous** 1.

**dissuade,** *v.* — *Syn.* deter, disincline, persuade not to; see **discourage** 1, 3, **hinder, prevent.**

**dissuasion,** *n.* — *Syn.* discouragement, deterrence, check; see **impediment** 1, **restraint** 2.

**distance,** *n.* 1. [A degree or quantity of space] — *Syn.* interval, gap, reach, span, range, remoteness, mileage, yardage, footage; see also **expanse, extent, length** 1, 2.

2. [A place or places far away] — *Syn.* background, horizon, as far as the eye can see, sky, heavens, outer space, the blue, far lands, outpost, outskirts, foreign countries, new worlds, other worlds, strange places, distant terrain, foreign terrain, unknown terrain, objective, the country, beyond the horizon, ends of the earth, antipodes, jumping-off place, the beyond, the back of beyond, the sticks*. see also **country** 1. — *Ant.* NEIGHBORHOOD, surroundings, neighbors.

3. [A measure of space] — *Syn.* mile, statute mile, English mile, rod, yard, foot, inch, kilometer, meter, centimeter, millimeter, micrometer, league, fathom, ell, span, hand, cubit, furlong, block, way, ways*, a stone's throw*, as the crow flies*, down the road a piece*, spitting distance*, whoop and a holler*, long haul*; see also **inch** 1, **measure** 1, **mile.**

4. [Aloofness] — *Syn.* remoteness, coolness, reserve, restraint; see **indifference** 1, **reserve** 2.

**go the distance** — *Syn.* finish, bring to an end, see through; see **complete** 1.

**keep at a distance** — *Syn.* ignore, reject, shun, keep at arm's length; see **avoid.**

**keep one's distance** — *Syn.* remain aloof, keep out of the way, distance oneself, shun; see **avoid.**

**distant,** *modif.* 1. [Removed in space from the speaker] — *Syn.* far, far-off, far back, remote, afar, abroad, not at home, faraway, outlying, yonder, backwoods, removed, abstracted, inaccessible, unapproachable, indirect, indistinct, out of the way, beyond the horizon, wide of, at arm's length, stretching to, Godforsaken, out of range, out of reach, telescopic, out of earshot, out of sight, in the background, in the distance; see also **remote** 1. — *Ant.* NEAR, adjacent, next.

2. [Separated by space] — *Syn.* separate, wide apart, farther, further, far away, at a distance, abroad,

scattered, far-flung, dispersed, diffuse, different, sparse, sparsely sown, transatlantic, transpacific, transmarine, ultramarine, ultramontane, antipodal, excentric, asunder; see also **separated.**— *Ant.* CLOSE, packed, jammed.

**3.** [Aloof in manner]— *Syn.* aloof, cool, withdrawn, cold; see **aloof, indifferent** 1, **reserved** 3.

*See Synonym Study at* FAR.

**distaste,** *n.*— *Syn.* aversion, dislike, abhorrence, repugnance; see **aversion, hatred** 1, 2, **objection** 1.

**distasteful,** *modif.*— *Syn.* disagreeable, repugnant, undesirable; see **offensive** 2.

**distend,** *v.*— *Syn.* enlarge, widen, inflate, expand; see **increase** 1, **stretch** 1, 2, **swell.**

*See Synonym Study at* EXPAND.

**distention,** *n.*— *Syn.* inflation, expansion, enlargement, bloating; see **bulge, increase** 1.

**distill,** *v.*— *Syn.* vaporize and condense, volatilize, draw out, steam, drip, precipitate, sublimate, extract, infuse, press, purify, refine, derive, abstract, boil down, compress; see also **concentrate** 1, **evaporate** 1.

**distinct,** *modif.* **1.** [Having sharp outlines]— *Syn.* plain, unmistakable, sharp, well-defined; see **clear** 2, **definite** 2.

**2.** [Not connected with another]— *Syn.* discrete, different, separate, dissimilar; see **different** 1, **distinguished** 1, **separated.**

**3.** [Clearly heard]— *Syn.* clear, audible, enunciated; see **audible.**

*See Synonym Study at* DIFFERENT.

**distinction,** *n.* **1.** [The act or quality of noticing differences]— *Syn.* differentiation, separation, discrimination, discretion, sharpness, discreteness, discernment, perception, sensitivity, penetration, acuteness, analysis, clearness, judgment, refinement, estimation, nicety, tact, diagnosis, marking out, demarcation; see also **acumen, definition** 2.— *Ant.* DULLNESS, indifference, obtuseness.

**2.** [A difference used for distinction, sense 1]— *Syn.* distinctive feature, particular, qualification, contrast; see **characteristic, detail** 1, **difference** 2.

**3.** [A mark of personal achievement]— *Syn.* eminence, repute, renown, prominence; see **fame** 1.

**4.** [Excellence]— *Syn.* superiority, note, flair, style; see **perfection** 3.

**distinctive,** *modif.*— *Syn.* peculiar, unique, distinguishing, notable; see **characteristic.**

*See Synonym Study at* CHARACTERISTIC.

**distinctly,** *modif.*— *Syn.* clearly, precisely, sharply, plainly; see **clearly** 1, 2, **surely.**

**distinctness,** *n.* **1.** [Discreteness]— *Syn.* detachment, dissociation, separation, dissimilarity; see **difference** 1, **division** 1, **individuality** 1.

**2.** [Clearness]— *Syn.* sharpness, plainness, lucidity, explicitness; see **clarity.**

**distinguish,** *v.* **1.** [To make distinctions]— *Syn.* discriminate, discriminate between, differentiate, classify, specify, identify, individualize, characterize, separate, tell apart, demarcate, divide, collate, sort out, set apart, mark off, select, see the difference, exercise discrimination, make a distinction, single out, sift, draw the line, tell from, pick and choose, tell which is which, separate the wheat from the chaff\*, separate the sheep from the goats\*; see also **classify, define** 1, 2.

**2.** [To discern]— *Syn.* detect, discriminate, notice; see **discover, recognize** 1, **see** 1.

**3.** [To provide an identification]— *Syn.* identify, label, tag; see **mark** 2, **name** 1, 2.

**4.** [To bestow honor upon]— *Syn.* pay tribute to, signalize, celebrate, ennoble; see **admire** 1, **praise** 1.

*See Synonym Study at* DISCERN.

---

**SYN.**— **distinguish** implies a recognizing or marking apart from others by special features or characteristic qualities [to *distinguish* good from evil]; **discriminate** suggests a distinguishing of minute or subtle differences between similar things [to *discriminate* scents]; **differentiate** suggests the noting or ascertaining of specific differences between things by comparing in detail their distinguishing qualities or features

---

**distinguishable,** *modif.*— *Syn.* separable, distinct, perceptible, discernible; see **appreciable, audible, obvious** 1.

**distinguished,** *modif.* **1.** [Made recognizable]— *Syn.* characterized, labeled, marked, stamped, denoted, signed, signified, identified, made certain, obvious, set apart, singled out, branded, earmarked, separate, unique, differentiated, noted, observed, distinct, conspicuous, having distinguishing *or* unusual characteristics.— *Ant.* TYPICAL, unidentified, indistinct.

**2.** [Notable for excellence]— *Syn.* eminent, illustrious, venerable, renowned, honored, memorable, celebrated, famous, well-known, noted, notable, noteworthy, highly regarded, esteemed, prominent, reputable, respected, remarkable, distingué, peerless, superior, outstanding, exceptional, aristocratic, genteel, noble, brilliant, glorious, extraordinary, singular, great, imposing, special, striking, unforgettable, arresting, shining, salient, foremost, nonpareil, dignified, august, royal, stately, signal, radiant, transcendent, famed, talked of, legendary, first-rate, nonesuch, big-name\*, world-class\*, standout\*, ace\*; see also **dignified, famous, important** 2, **noble** 3.— *Ant.* OBSCURE, insignificant, unimportant.

*See Synonym Study at* FAMOUS.

**distinguishing,** *modif.*— *Syn.* distinctive, differentiating, different; see **characteristic.**

**distort,** *v.* **1.** [To change by pressure]— *Syn.* warp, crush, twist; see **bend** 1.

**2.** [To alter the meaning]— *Syn.* pervert, misrepresent, misconstrue, twist; see **deceive, lie** 1.

**3.** [To change shape]— *Syn.* contort, sag, twist, slump, knot, get out of shape, buckle, writhe, melt, warp, decline, deteriorate, deform, wrench, collapse, become misshapen, misshape, deviate from the standard form, deviate from the normal form; see also **change** 4.

---

**SYN.**— **distort** implies a twisting or wrenching out of the normal or proper shape or form [a mind *distorted* by fear]; **deform** implies a marring of form, appearance, or character, as if by pressure or stress [lengthy descriptions that *deform* the novel]; **contort** suggests an even more violent wrenching out of shape so as to produce a grotesque or unpleasant result [a face *contorted* by pain]; **warp** implies a bending out of shape, as of wood in drying, and, hence, suggests a turning aside from the true or right course [judgment *warped* by prejudice]

---

**distortion,** *n.* **1.** [Contortion]— *Syn.* twist, malformation, deformity; see **contortion** 1, 2.

**2.** [Misrepresentation]— *Syn.* perversion, falsification, misuse; see **lie** 1, **parody.**

**distract,** *v.* **1.** [To divert someone's attention]— *Syn.* divert, divert the mind, divert the thoughts, divert the attention, occupy, amuse, entertain, draw away from, beguile, call away, take one's attention from, draw one's attention from, take the mind off, lead astray, attract from, deflect, sidetrack; see also **entertain** 1, **mislead.**

**2.** [To confuse] — *Syn.* bewilder, puzzle, perplex, rattle; see **confuse.**

**distracted,** *modif.* **1.** [Troubled] — *Syn.* distraught, panicked, frenzied; see **troubled** 1.

**2.** [Absent-minded] — *Syn.* preoccupied, inattentive, abstracted; see **absent-minded.**

**distraction,** *n.* **1.** [Confusion] — *Syn.* perplexity, abstraction, madness; see **confusion** 2, **distress** 1.

**2.** [Something that distracts] — *Syn.* diversion, amusement, pastime, disturbance, intrusion, digression, preoccupation, engrossment; see also **entertainment** 1, 2, **game** 1.

**distraught,** *modif.* — *Syn.* agitated, troubled, distracted, beside oneself\*; see **troubled** 1.

*See Synonym Study at* ABSENT-MINDED.

**distress,** *n.* **1.** [Mental agony] — *Syn.* worry, anxiety, perplexity, misery, sorrow, wretchedness, pain, suffering, agony, anguish, dejection, irritation, vexation, ache, heartache, dolor, ordeal, desolation, mortification, affliction, discomfort, trouble, woe, torment, torture, shame, embarrassment, disappointment, tribulation, pang; see also **anxiety, grief** 1. — *Ant.* JOY, happiness, ease, comfort.

**2.** [Physical agony] — *Syn.* agony, anguish, suffering, ache; see **pain** 1, 2.

**3.** [Misfortune] — *Syn.* straits, danger, trouble, adversity; see **crisis, danger, difficulty** 1, 2, **disaster, poverty** 1.

---

**SYN.** — **distress** implies mental or physical strain imposed by pain, trouble, worry, or the like and usually suggests a state or situation that can be relieved *[distress caused by famine]*; **suffering** emphasizes the actual enduring of pain, distress, or tribulation *[the suffering of the wounded]*; **agony** suggests mental or physical torment so excruciating that the body or mind is convulsed with the force of it *[in mortal agony]*; **anguish** has equal force but is more often applied to acute mental suffering *[the anguish of despair]*

---

**distress,** *v.* — *Syn.* trouble, disturb, upset, grieve; see **bother** 3, **depress** 2, **disturb** 2.

**distribute,** *v.* **1.** [To allot] — *Syn.* dispense, divide, share, deal, dole, bestow, issue, endow, dispose, disperse, circulate, mete out, pass out, parcel out, dole out, hand out, pay out, disburse, administer, give away, assign, allocate, ration, measure out, apportion, consign, prorate, appropriate, dish out\*, divvy up\*, cut the pie\*; see also **give** 1. — *Ant.* HOLD, keep, preserve.

**2.** [To scatter] — *Syn.* spread, sow, disseminate, diffuse; see **scatter** 1, 2.

**3.** [To classify] — *Syn.* categorize, group, file; see **classify, order** 3.

---

**SYN.** — **distribute** implies a dealing out of portions or a spreading about of units among a number of recipients *[to distribute leaflets]*; **dispense** suggests the careful measuring out of that which is distributed *[to dispense drugs]*; **divide** suggests separation of a whole into parts to be shared *[an inheritance divided among five children]*; **dole** implies a measured distribution of money, food, favor, etc. in a charitable or in a sparing or niggardly manner

---

**distributed,** *modif.* — *Syn.* delivered, scattered, shared, dealt, divided, apportioned, assigned, awarded, peddled door to door, sown, dispensed, dispersed, allocated, allotted, appropriated, budgeted, made individually available, spread evenly, diffuse, rationed, given away, handed out, parceled out, doled out, spread out; see also **scattered.**

**distribution,** *n.* **1.** [The act of distributing] — *Syn.* dispersal, dispersion, allotment, allocation, partitioning, partition, division, dividing up, assignment, deal, dealing, circulation, disposal, disposing of, apportionment, prorating, rationing, sharing, allowance, arrangement, scattering, diffusion, dissemination, administration, dissipation, sorting, making generally available, assigning by lot, spreading, dispensation, disbursement, giving out, parceling out, doling out, handing out, peddling, delivery, shipping, merchandising; see also sense 2; **division** 1. — *Ant.* COLLECTION, retention, storage.

**2.** [The result or measure of distributing] — *Syn.* frequency, arrangement, occurrence, disposition, disposal, ordering, grouping, pattern, combination, relationships, appearance, configuration, placement, number, plenty, saturation, population, spread, concentration; see also **division** 2, **order** 3. — *Ant.* CONFUSION, tangle, puzzle.

**distributor,** *n.* **1.** [Dispenser] — *Syn.* seller, seeder, scatterer, sower, publisher; see also **dispenser** 2.

**2.** [One who handles goods] — *Syn.* wholesaler, jobber, merchant; see **businessperson.**

**district,** *modif.* — *Syn.* divisional, immediate, ward, provincial, restricted, limited, community, rural, territorial, inferior, superior, higher, lower, state, federal, county; see also **local** 1.

**district,** *n.* — *Syn.* region, quarter, community, vicinity; see **area** 2, **division** 5, **neighborhood.**

**distrust,** *v.* — *Syn.* mistrust, suspect, disbelieve; see **doubt** 2.

**distrustful,** *modif.* — *Syn.* distrusting, doubting, wary, skeptical; see **suspicious** 1.

**disturb,** *v.* **1.** [To upset physical relationship] — *Syn.* disorder, displace, disrupt; see **confuse.**

**2.** [To upset mental calm] — *Syn.* trouble, worry, upset, agitate, discompose, perturb, bother, interrupt, intrude upon, inconvenience, discommode, startle, shake, give one a turn, unnerve, unsettle, disconcert, perplex, rattle, alarm, excite, arouse, affright, affect one's mind, badger, plague, vex, outrage, grieve, depress, distress, dishearten, irk, ail, provoke, afflict, irritate, pain, make uneasy, concern, disquiet, harass, exasperate, pique, gall, displease, fluster, ruffle, shake up\*, throw\*, put out\*, flip out\*, freak out\*; see also **bother** 2, 3, **confuse.** — *Ant.* QUIET, calm, soothe.

---

**SYN.** — **disturb** implies the unsettling of normal mental calm or powers of concentration as by worry, interruption, or interference *[to disturb one's train of thought]*; **discompose** implies the upsetting of one's self-possession *[her sudden outburst discomposed him]*; to **perturb** is to cause to have a troubled or alarmed feeling *[the bad news perturbed him]*; **agitate** suggests the arousal of intense mental or emotional excitement *[he was so agitated, he could not answer]*

---

**disturbance,** *n.* **1.** [Interpersonal disruption] — *Syn.* quarrel, brawl, fray; see **fight** 1.

**2.** [Physical disruption] — *Syn.* commotion, disorder, turmoil, rampage, tumult, clamor, violence, restlessness, uproar, riot, upheaval, disruption, interruption, interference, agitation, turbulence, change, bother, stir, racket, ferment, furor, unruliness, spasm, convulsion, tremor, shock, explosion, eruption, quake, earthquake, tidal wave, flood, shock wave, storm, whirlwind, tempest, gale, hurricane, tornado, twister, avalanche, whirlpool, blowing, flurry, whirl, hurly-burly, ruckus*, long hot summer*; see also **disorder** 2, **revolution** 2, **trouble** 2.

**3.** [The result of disturbance] — *Syn.* disarrangement, irregularity, perplexity; see **confusion** 2.

**4.** [A state of worry or trouble] — *Syn.* agitation, distress, uneasiness; see **care** 2, **confusion** 2.

**disturbed,** *modif.* **1.** [Disturbed physically] — *Syn.* upset, disorganized, confused; see **disordered.**

**2.** [Disturbed mentally] — *Syn.* agitated, disquieted, upset; see **neurotic, troubled** 1.

**disturbing,** *modif.* — *Syn.* disquieting, upsetting, distressing, troubling, perturbing, bothersome, irksome, unpleasant, provoking, annoying, alarming, unsettling, painful, discomforting, nettling, inauspicious, foreboding, consequential, aggravating, disagreeable, troublesome, onerous, worrisome, burdensome, trying, vexatious, vexing, worrying, frightening, startling, perplexing, threatening, galling, laborious, difficult, severe, hard, toilsome, tiresome, inconvenient, discouraging, pessimistic, gloomy, uncertain, disconcerting, discomposing, dismaying, depressing, irritating, harassing, unpropitious, sinister, creepy, prophetic, impeding, discommoding, embarrassing, ruffling, agitating, wearisome, causing worry, causing anxiety, not propitious, not encouraging; see also **ominous.**

**disunion,** *n.* **1.** [Dissension] — *Syn.* dissidence, discord, alienation, disunity; see **disagreement** 1.

**2.** [Separation] — *Syn.* disconnection, partition, detachment; see **division** 1, **separation** 1.

**disunite,** *v.* — *Syn.* divide, separate, dissociate, estrange; see **alienate, divide** 1.

**disuse,** *n.* **1.** [The stoppage of use] — *Syn.* discontinuance, abolition, desuetude, nonobservance, inaction, discarding, cessation, intermission, interruption, abolishment, abrogation, forbearance, abstinence, relinquishment. — *Ant.* USE, continuance, continuation.

**2.** [The state of being unused] — *Syn.* decay, neglect, abandonment, unemployment, desertedness; see also **idleness** 1, **neglect** 1, **omission** 1. — *Ant.* PRODUCTION, usefulness, employment.

**ditch,** *n.* — *Syn.* trench, canal, moat, furrow; see **channel** 1, **trench.**

**ditch,** *v.* **1.** [To make a ditch] — *Syn.* furrow, trench, drain; see **dig** 1.

**2.** [To run into a ditch] — *Syn.* skid, overturn, derail; see **crash** 1, 4, **wreck** 1.

**3.** [*To get rid of] — *Syn.* desert, forsake, leave, jettison; see **abandon** 2, **discard.**

**ditto,** *modif.* — *Syn.* as above, likewise, same here*; see **alike** 3.

**ditto,** *n.* — *Syn.* do., ditto mark ("), an identical item, *idem* (Latin), the same, the very same, agreement, duplicate, an identity; see also **copy, duplicate.**

**diurnal,** *modif.* — *Syn.* during the day, daytime, once a day, every day; see **daily, regular** 3.

**divan,** *n.* — *Syn.* couch, sofa, settee, ottoman; see **chair** 1, **couch, furniture.**

**dive,** *n.* **1.** [A sudden motion downward] — *Syn.* plunge, leap, spring, nosedive, headlong leap, headlong jump, pitch, ducking, swoop, dip, cannonball, jackknife, swan dive, header*, belly-flop*, belly-whopper*; see also **fall** 1, **jump** 1.

**2.** [*An establishment offering accommodation] — *Syn.* bar, saloon, pub, café, cabaret, hotel, motel, pizza parlor, tavern, inn, club, casino, pool hall, billiard parlor, bowling alley, nightclub, diner, coffeehouse, dancehall, hamburger joint, joint*, dump*, dine and

dance*, flophouse*, fleabag*, hole*, hangout*; see also **bar** 2, **casino, restaurant.**

**dive,** *v.* — *Syn.* plunge, spring, jump, vault, leap, go headfirst, plummet, sink, dip, duck, plumb, submerge, disappear, vanish, nose-dive, break water, take a header*; see also **fall** 1, **jump** 1.

**dive-bomber,** *n.* — *Syn.* fighter-bomber, slip bomber, kamikaze; see **plane** 3.

**diver,** *n.* — *Syn.* high diver, fancy diver, submarine diver, deep-sea diver, aquanaut, pearl diver, sponge diver, skin diver, scuba diver, underwater reconnaissance specialist, frogman, swimmer, athlete, competitor, sky diver, parachute jumper, bungee jumper, tanker*; see also **athlete.**

**diverge,** *v.* **1.** [To move in different directions from the same source] — *Syn.* radiate, separate, swerve, branch off; see **deviate, veer.**

**2.** [To be or become different] — *Syn.* differ, deviate, conflict, part company; see **change** 4, **differ** 1.

*See Synonym Study at* DEVIATE.

**divergence,** *n.* **1.** [Radiation] — *Syn.* deviation, ramification, separation; see **division** 1, **radiation** 1.

**2.** [Difference] — *Syn.* mutation, deviation, alteration; see **change** 1, **difference** 1, 2.

**divergent,** *modif.* — *Syn.* diverging, deviating, conflicting, variant; see **centrifugal, different** 1, 2.

*See Synonym Study at* DIFFERENT.

**diverse,** *modif.* — *Syn.* several, assorted, different, distinct; see **different** 1, 2, **various.**

*See Synonym Study at* DIFFERENT.

**diversify,** *v.* — *Syn.* vary, expand, broaden, branch out; see **change** 4, **increase** 1.

**diversion,** *n.* **1.** [The act of changing a course] — *Syn.* detour, alteration, deviation; see **change** 1, **digression.**

**2.** [Entertainment] — *Syn.* amusement, recreation, play; see **distraction** 2, **entertainment** 1, 2, **sport** 1.

**diversity,** *n.* — *Syn.* variety, multifariousness, heterogeneity, unlikeness; see **difference** 1, **variety** 1.

**divert,** *v.* **1.** [To deflect] — *Syn.* turn aside, redirect, avert; see **turn** 3, **veer.**

**2.** [To amuse] — *Syn.* entertain, engage, distract, beguile; see **amuse, entertain** 1.

**3.** [To distract] — *Syn.* attract the attention of, sidetrack, disturb; see **distract** 1.

*See Synonym Study at* AMUSE.

**diverted,** *modif.* — *Syn.* deflected, turned aside, redirected, averted, sidetracked, amused, entertained, turned into other channels, rechanneled, appropriated to other uses, preempted, taken away, wrested away, adopted, used, made use of, taken over, rebudgeted, reclassified; see also **changed** 2, 3, **entertained** 2.

**divest,** *v.* **1.** [To undress] — *Syn.* strip, disrobe, uncover; see **undress.**

**2.** [To deprive] — *Syn.* dispossess, strip, take from; see **seize** 2.

*See Synonym Study at* STRIP.

**divide,** *v.* **1.** [To separate by parting] — *Syn.* separate, part, cut up, partition, split up, sever, sunder, split, cut, fence off, disunite, disconnect, disjoin, detach, disengage, dissolve, rupture, break, dissever, dismember, unravel, carve, cleave, section, subdivide, intersect, cross, bisect, fork, branch, diverge, divaricate, rend, tear, segment, halve, quarter, dislocate, break down, demarcate, graduate, divorce, dissociate, alienate, estrange, insulate, isolate, loose, unchain, undo, unbind, count off, pull away, disentangle, chop, hew, slash, carve, splinter, split off, cut off, pull to pieces, tear apart, break apart, segregate, classify, sort, arrange, distribute, tear limb from limb*; see also **break** 1, **cut** 1, **separate** 2. — *Ant.* UNITE, combine, connect.

**2.** [To distribute] — *Syn.* share, deal, dole, apportion; see **distribute** 1.

*See Synonym Study at* DISTRIBUTE, SEPARATE.

**dividend,** *n.* — *Syn.* profit, interest, bonus, proceeds, returns, return on investment, share, allotment, payback, payout, earnings, pay, yield, distribution, allowance, coupon, check, remittance, cut\*, split\*, rake-off\*, divvy\*; see also **interest** 3, **profit** 2.

*See Synonym Study at* PREMIUM.

**divination,** *n.* — *Syn.* augury, interpretation of omens, prediction, soothsaying, sorcery, calculation, foretelling, foreshadowing, palmistry, prognostics, prognostication, clairvoyance, prophecy, extrasensory perception, ESP, spirit-rapping, table-tipping, thaumaturgy, horoscopy, penetration, intimation, portent, insight, warning, fortunetelling, phrenology, astrology, graphology, tea-leaf reading, hieromancy, necromancy, hydromancy, ichthyomancy, pyromancy, crystal gazing, crystallomancy, sciomancy, ornithomancy, ophiomancy, dactyliomancy, Bibliomancy, anthropomancy, alectryomancy, catoptromancy, psephomancy, alphitomancy, lithomancy, oneiromancy, chiromancy, aeromancy, rhabdomancy, cleromancy, aleuromancy, axinomancy, belomancy, haruspicy, genethliacs, dowsing, Ouija board (trademark), casting the planchette, I Ching; see also **forecast.**

**divine,** *modif.* **1.** [Having qualities of a god] — *Syn.* godlike, godly, supernal, superhuman, celestial, almighty, unearthly, heavenly, deific, eternal, beatific, deiform, supreme, spiritual, ambrosial, angelic, theistic, deistic, eternal, omnipotent, omniscient, omnipresent, all-powerful, ghostly, superphysical, supernatural, transcendent, hyperphysical, extramundane, transmundane, Elysian, Arcadian, Olympian, Jovian, Christlike, immaculate, paradisiacal, all-loving, beyond praise; see also **perfect** 2. — *Ant.* HUMAN, devilish, worldly.

**2.** [Dedicated to the service of a god] — *Syn.* sacred, holy, hallowed, devotional, spiritual, religious, sacrificial, sacramental, ceremonial, ritualistic, reverent, consecrated, dedicated, devoted, venerable, pious, anointed, sanctified, ordained, sanctioned, set apart, sacrosanct, scriptural, blessed, worshiped, revered, venerated, mystical, worshipful, prayerful, adored, reverenced, solemn, faithful, fervid, ministerial; see also **holy** 2. — *Ant.* secular, profane, blasphemous.

**3.** [Excellent] — *Syn.* supreme, superb, marvelous, sublime; see **excellent, perfect** 2.

---

*SYN.* — **divine** suggests that which is of the nature of, is associated with, or is derived from God or a god /the *divine* right of kings/, and, in extended use, connotes supreme greatness [the *divine* Milton] or, colloquially, great attractiveness /these shoes are absolutely *divine*/; **holy** suggests that which is held in deepest religious reverence or is basically associated with a religion and, in extended use, connotes spiritual purity [the *Holy* Ghost, a *holy* love/; **sacred** refers to that which is set apart as holy or is dedicated to some exalted purpose and, therefore, connotes inviolability /Parnassus was *sacred* to Apollo, a *sacred* trust/; **consecrated** and **hallowed** describe that which has been made sacred or holy, **consecrated** in addition connoting solemn devotion or dedication /a life *consecrated* to art/, and **hallowed** connoting inherent or intrinsic holiness [hallowed ground/

---

**divine,** *n.* — *Syn.* priest, theologian, clergyman; see **minister** 1, **priest, rabbi.**

**divine,** *v.* — *Syn.* predict, prophesy, conjecture, intuit; see **foretell, guess** 1.

**diviner,** *n.* — *Syn.* prophet, seer, sorcerer, witch; see **magician** 1, **prophet.**

**divinity,** *n.* — *Syn.* deity, godhead, higher power, sacredness; see **god** 1, **holiness** 2.

**divisible,** *modif.* — *Syn.* separable, distinguishable, distinct, divided, dividable, partible, detachable, severable, breakable, dissolvable, dissoluble, apportionable; see also **separated.** — *Ant.* INSEPARABLE, indivisible, fast.

**division,** *n.* **1.** [The act or result of dividing] — *Syn.* separation, separating, detachment, apportionment, sharing, partition, parting, partitioning, distribution, severance, divorce, dissociation, cutting, disseverance, carving, subdivision, subdividing, dismemberment, disconnecting, disconnection, distinction, distinguishing, classification, selection, segmenting, segmentation, sectioning, parceling, analysis, diagnosis, dissection, autopsy, reduction, breaking down, breaking up, compartmentalization, districting, rending, scissure, splitting, disuniting, disunion, disassociation, breaking, breakdown, fracture, fissure, branching, divergence, bisection, bipartition, demarcation, disjuncture, contrasting, departmentalizing, schizogenesis, fission, schizogony, mitosis, meiosis. — *Ant.* UNION, joining, gluing.

**2.** [A part produced by dividing] — *Syn.* section, kind, sort, portion, compartment, share, split, member, subdivision, parcel, segment, fragment, sector, department, category, branch, ramification, fraction, dividend, measure, percentage, percentile, degree, piece, slice, lump, wedge, cut, lobe, front, movement, column, book, chapter, decade, verse, canto, phrase, clause, line, paragraph, act, scene, episode, passage, apartment, cell, class, moiety, race, clan, tribe, caste, group, unit; see also **army** 2, **class** 1, 2, 3, **department** 1, 2, **part** 1.

**3.** [Discord or disunion] — *Syn.* dissension, disagreement, breach, schism; see sense 1; **disagreement** 1, **dispute.**

**4.** [Something that divides] — *Syn.* dividing line, partition, boundary, divider; see **barrier, boundary.**

**5.** [An organized area] — *Syn.* province, country, state, dominion, shire, department, district, county, municipality, city, town, canton, village, commune, ward, township, residency, constituency, bishopric, prelacy, parish, range; see also **nation** 1, **territory** 2.

*See Synonym Study at* PART.

**divorce,** *n.* — *Syn.* separation, estrangement, dissociation, breach, divorcement, bill of divorce, annulment, separate maintenance, parting of the ways, legal separation, judicial separation, decree nisi, dissolution, rift, split, partition, split-up, breakup, broken home; see also **cancellation, division** 1. — *Ant.* MARRIAGE, betrothal, wedding.

**divorce,** *v.* — *Syn.* separate, unmarry, annul, release from wedlock, release from matrimony, obtain a divorce, sunder, nullify, put away, part, split up, break up; see also **cancel** 2, **divide** 1.

**divorced,** *modif.* — *Syn.* separated, estranged, dissociated, divided, dissolved, parted, disunited, disjoined, isolated, Reno'd\*, split\*, washed up\*, unhitched\*; see also **separated.** — *Ant.* MARRIED, joined, wed.

**divulge,** *v.* — *Syn.* disclose, impart, confess; see **admit** 2, **reveal** 1.

*See Synonym Study at* REVEAL.

**dizzy,** *modif.* **1.** [Having a whirling or spinning sensation] — *Syn.* confused, lightheaded, giddy, bemused, staggering, reeling, staggered, disturbed, dazzled, dazed, bleary-eyed, groggy, seeing double, troubled with vertigo, unsteady, vertiginous, whirling, spinning, swimming, weak-kneed, weak, wobbly, shaky, woozy\*, tipsy\*, punch-drunk\*, punchy\*; see also **unsteady** 1.

**2.** [Causing dizziness] — *Syn.* steep, lofty, vertiginous; see **abrupt** 1, **unstable** 1, **unsteady** 1.

**3.** [*Lacking good sense] — *Syn.* flighty, silly, featherbrained; see **changeable** 1, **silly**, **stupid** 1.

**DNA,** *n.* — *Syn.* genetic alphabet, genetic codon, double helix, template, hereditary information, chromosome, gene, deoxyribonucleic acid, recombinant DNA; see also **genetic code.**

**do,** *v.* **1.** [To discharge one's responsibilities] — *Syn.* effect, execute, accomplish; see **achieve** 1, **act** 1, **perform** 1, **succeed** 1.

**2.** [To execute commands or instructions] — *Syn.* carry out, complete, fulfill; see **obey** 1, **perform** 1.

**3.** [To bring to a close] — *Syn.* fulfill, finish, conclude; see **achieve** 1, **end** 1.

**4.** [To cause] — *Syn.* bring about, produce, effect; see **begin** 1, **cause** 2, **create** 2, **produce** 2.

**5.** [To suffice] — *Syn.* serve, be sufficient, give satisfaction; see **satisfy** 3.

**6.** [To solve] — *Syn.* figure out, work out, decipher; see **solve.**

**7.** [To fare] — *Syn.* get along, manage, proceed; see **advance** 1.

**8.** [To present a play, etc.] — *Syn.* give, put on, produce; see **perform** 2.

**9.** [To attend to] — *Syn.* make, arrange, deal with; see **arrange** 2, **prepare** 1.

**10.** [To travel] — *Syn.* journey, explore, tour, visit; see **travel** 2.

**11.** [To conduct oneself] — *Syn.* behave, acquit oneself, seem, appear; see **behave** 2.

**12.** [*To use, as a drug] — *Syn.* ingest, take, be on, be addicted to. See syn. stud at **perform.**

**have to do with** — *Syn.* be related to, be connected with, deal with; see **concern** 1, **treat** 1.

**do something about,** *v.* — *Syn.* assist, take care of, correct; see **correct** 1, **help** 1, **improve** 1, **repair.**

**do by,** *v.* — *Syn.* handle, act toward, deal with; see **treat** 1.

**docile,** *modif.* — *Syn.* meek, mild, tractable, compliant, obedient, amenable, pliant, submissive, accommodating, complying, acquiescent, adaptable, resigned, agreeable, willing, obliging, well-behaved, manageable, biddable, malleable, pliable, tame, yielding, teachable, easily influenced, easy, easygoing, soft, governable, manipulable, childlike, gentle, complaisant, unassertive, passive, unresisting; see also **gentle** 3, **humble** 1, **obedient** 1. — *Ant.* rebellious, ungovernable, wild.

---

*SYN.* — **docile** implies a temperament that submits easily to control or that fails to resist domination /a *docile* horse/; **tractable** implies ease of management or control but does not connote the submissiveness of **docile** and applies to things as well as people and animals /silver is a *tractable*, i.e., malleable, metal/; **compliant** suggests a weakness of character that allows one to yield meekly to another's request or demand /army life had made him *compliant*/; **amenable** suggests such amiability or desire to be agreeable as would lead one to submit readily /I found her *amenable* to persuasion/; **obedient** suggests a giving in to the orders or instructions of one in authority or control /an *obedient* child/

---

**docility,** *n.* — *Syn.* tractability, obedience, submissiveness, compliance, meekness, mildness, gentleness, manageability, pliability, pliancy, acquiescence, willingness,

amenability, flexibility, adaptability, malleability, tameness, subservience, passivity; see also **humility.** — *Ant.* DISOBEDIENCE, undutifulness, stubbornness.

**dock,** *n.* **1.** [A landing or mooring place] — *Syn.* pier, landing pier, wharf, quay, lock, boat landing, marina, slip, ferry slip, dry dock, floating dock, repair dock, embarcadero, jetty, moorage, embankment, waterfront; see also **harbor** 2.

**2.** [A weed]. Varieties include the following: sour dock, yellow dock, burdock, curled dock, smooth dock, fiddle dock, candock, hardock, patience dock, golden dock, water dock; see **plant, weed** 1.

**dock,** *v.* **1.** [To clip] — *Syn.* crop, bob, shorten; see **cut** 1.

**2.** [To diminish] — *Syn.* lessen, withhold, deduct; see **decrease** 2.

**3.** [To bring a boat into a dock] — *Syn.* moor, anchor, berth; see **anchor** 1, **arrive** 1, **land** 1.

**doctor,** *n.* **1.** [A medical practitioner] — *Syn.* Doctor of Medicine, M.D., physician, surgeon, family doctor, country doctor, medical attendant, specialist, consultant, intern, resident, house physician, homeopath, primary-care physician, quack*, veterinarian, animal doctor, vet*, doc*, sawbones*, bones*, medico*, croaker*.

Types of doctors include: heart specialist; eye, ear, nose, and throat specialist; respiratory specialist, family doctor, general practitioner, G.P.; anesthetist, anesthesiologist, dentist, podiatrist, internist, pediatrician, neonatologist, oculist, obstetrician, psychiatrist, psychoanalyst, public health physician, surgeon, orthopedist, gynecologist, radiologist, neurologist, cardiologist, gerontologist, pathologist, dermatologist, endocrinologist, ophthalmologist, laryngologist, urologist, neurologist, osteopath, oncologist, gastroenterologist, allergist, proctologist, hematologist, diathermist, radiothermist; orthopedic surgeon, cardiac surgeon, heart surgeon, plastic surgeon; see **dentist, medicine** 3.

Alternates to a doctor include: physician's assistant, midwife, chiropractor, acupuncturist, health-care provider, therapist, Christian Science practitioner, faith healer, witch doctor, shaman, medicine man.

**2.** [A holder of a doctoral degree] — *Syn.* Ph.D., Ed.D., expert, professor, student; see also **degree** 3, **professor**, **scholar** 2, **scientist.**

**doctor,** *v.* **1.** [ [To treat] — *Syn.* attend, minister to, medicate; see **treat** 3.

**2.** [To change deceptively] — *Syn.* tamper with, falsify, adulterate, alter; see **adulterate, corrupt** 2, **disguise.**

**doctrinaire,** *modif.* — *Syn.* dogmatic, opinionated, bigoted, inflexible; see **dogmatic** 2.

*See Synonym Study at* DOGMATIC.

**doctrinaire,** *n.* — *Syn.* visionary, utopist, bigot, ideologue; see **bigot, idealist.**

**doctrine,** *n.* **1.** [A statement of position or belief] — *Syn.* tenet, principle, proposition, precept, article, concept, conviction, dogma, position, opinion, belief, theory, convention, established position, policy, attitude, tradition, unwritten law, universal law, natural law, common law, teachings, accepted belief, article of faith, article of belief, canon, regulation, rule, pronouncement, declaration, bull; see also **law** 2, 4.

**2.** [Several tenets built into a faith] — *Syn.* dogma, creed, gospel; see **faith** 2.

---

*SYN.* — **doctrine** refers to a theory based on carefully worked out principles and taught or advocated by its adherents /scientific or social *doctrines*/; **dogma** refers to a belief or doctrine that is handed down by authority as true and indisputable, and may connote arbitrariness, arrogance, etc. /religious *dogma*/; **tenet** connotes a component belief or principle of a system or theory /the *tenets* of a political party/; **precept** refers to an injunction or dogma intended as a rule of action or conduct /to teach by example rather than by *precept*/

---

**document,** *n.* — *Syn.* certificate, official paper, text, report; see **certificate, paper** 1, **record** 1.

**dodder,** *v.* — *Syn.* tremble, totter, quaver; see **reel, shake** 1, **totter** 1, 2.

**doddering,** *modif.* — *Syn.* tottering, senile, trembling, decrepit; see **old** 1, **shaky** 2, **weak** 1.

**dodge,** *n.* — *Syn.* trick, strategy, scheme; see **method** 2, **plan** 2, **trick** 1.

**dodge,** *v.* — *Syn.* duck, elude, evade; see **avoid, evade** 1.

**doer,** *n.* — *Syn.* actor, performer, agent, instrument, participant, perpetrator, operator, man of action, woman of action, mover, organizer, producer, practitioner, activist, dynamo, go-getter*, ball of fire*; see also **means** 1.

**dog,** *n.* **1.** [A domestic animal] — *Syn.* hound, puppy, canine, mongrel, cur, *canis familiaris* (Latin), bitch, pup, whelp, stray, watchdog, lap dog, guide dog, Seeing Eye dog, pye-dog, pooch*, mutt*, bowwow*, Fido*, fleabag*.
Types and breeds of dogs include: hunting, field, racing, courser, boxer, water, shepherd, bloodhound, wolfhound, greyhound, whippet, St. Bernard, mastiff, Newfoundland, Great Dane, borzoi, Rottweiler, German shepherd, Doberman pinscher, Afghan, Irish wolfhound, Labrador retriever, Golden retriever, Chesapeake Bay retriever, malamute, husky, Samoyed, Akita, collie, Briard, Old English sheep dog, Gordon setter, English setter, Irish setter, pointer, springer, spaniel, cocker spaniel, water spaniel, Brittany spaniel, foxhound, basset hound, beagle, dachshund, Dalmatian, English bulldog, pit bull, spitz, chow, Pomeranian, poodle, toy poodle, standard poodle, barbet, French poodle, Pekingese, Maltese, Chihuahua, Mexican hairless, Airedale, schnauzer, Sealyham, fox terrier, wirehaired terrier, Scottie, Kerry blue, black and tan, Bedlington terrier, Aberdeen, Irish terrier, Jack Russell terrier, Yorkshire terrier, West Highland terrier, Cairn terrier, bull terrier, Boston terrier, Manchester terrier, Welsh corgi, Cardigan, Pembroke.
**2.** [Insulting term] — *Syn.* scamp, swine, blackguard; see **rascal.**

**a dog's life*** — *Syn.* wretched existence, hard life, bad luck, trouble; see **difficulty** 1, **poverty** 1.

**every dog has his day*** — *Syn.* have a chance, recover, do well; see **prosper, succeed** 1.

**go to the dogs*** — *Syn.* deteriorate, degenerate, decline; see **decay.**

**let sleeping dogs lie*** — *Syn.* ignore, leave well enough alone, pass over; see **neglect** 1.

**put on the dog*** — *Syn.* show off, entertain lavishly, put on airs; see **display** 1, **dress up, pretend** 1.

**teach an old dog new tricks*** — *Syn.* influence, convince, change; see **change** 1, **persuade** 1.

**dog-eat-dog,** *modif.* — *Syn.* ruthless, competitive, vicious, brutal; see **cruel** 1, 2, **ruthless** 1, 2.

**dogged,** *modif.* — *Syn.* stubborn, tenacious, persistent, firm; see **diligent, obstinate, resolute** 2.
*See Synonym Study at* STUBBORN.

**dogma,** *n.* — *Syn.* doctrine, creed, authoritative opinion, conviction; see **doctrine** 1, **faith** 2.
*See Synonym Study at* DOCTRINE.

**dogmatic,** *modif.* **1.** [Based on an assumption of absolute truth] — *Syn.* doctrinal, categorical, canonical, unchangeable, inevitable, immovable, unqualified, eternal, positive, authoritative, systematic, orthodox, formal, ex cathedra, pontifical, imperative, peremptory, theoretical, axiomatic, unerring, by fiat, on faith, as a matter of course, by nature, by God's will, by natural law; see also **absolute** 1. — *Ant.* IRRESOLUTE, uncertain, whimsical.
**2.** [Acting as though one possessed absolute truth] — *Syn.* dictatorial, doctrinaire, opinionated, arbitrary, overbearing, arrogant, egotistical, bigoted, fanatical, intolerant, imperious, magisterial, domineering, authoritarian, pontifical, positive, peremptory, oracular, tyrannical, fascistic, despotic, obstinate, confident, downright, unequivocal, definite, stubborn, determined, emphatic, insistent, obdurate, closed-minded, narrowminded, wrongheaded, one-sided, wedded to an opinion, hidebound, high and mighty*, stiff-necked*, hardshell*, pushy*, pigheaded*, bullheaded*; see also **absolute** 3, **autocratic** 1, **obstinate.** — *Ant.* tolerant, dubious, flexible.

**dogmatism,** *n.* — *Syn.* opinionatedness, peremptoriness, positiveness; see **belief** 1, **certainty** 1.

**do in*,** *v.* — *Syn.* eliminate, ruin, slay, murder; see **destroy** 1, **kill** 1.

**doing,** *n.* — *Syn.* performing, accomplishing, achieving; see **action** 2, **performance** 1.

**doings*,** *n.* — *Syn.* activities, conduct, dealings, goings-on*; see **action** 1, **event** 1, **proceeding.**

**dole,** *n.* — *Syn.* charity, relief, allotment; see **aid** 1, **gift** 1, **share** 2, **welfare** 2.

**doleful,** *modif.* — *Syn.* sad, sorrowful, mournful, wretched; see **sad** 1, 2.
*See Synonym Study at* SAD.

**dole out,** *v.* — *Syn.* distribute, mete out, assign, parcel; see **distribute** 1.
*See Synonym Study at* DISTRIBUTE.

**doll,** *n.* — *Syn.* baby, puppet, figure, figurine, manikin, model, effigy, dummy, dolly*, moppet*; see also **toy** 1.
Types of dolls include: puppet, marionette, rag, paper, china, troll, talking, Barbie doll (trademark) Kewpie doll (trademark), Cabbage Patch (trademark); mamma doll*, baby doll*.

**dollar,** *n.* — *Syn.* dollar bill, silver dollar, bank note, Federal Reserve note, bill, silver certificate, single*, one*, buck*, greenback*, folding money*, one-spot*, skin*, shekel*, peso*, oner*, smacker*, smackeroo*, iron man*; see also **money** 1.

**dollop,** *n.* — *Syn.* blob, dab, touch; see **bit** 1, **dash** 4.

**doll up*,** *v.* — *Syn.* dress up, put on one's best clothes, primp, deck out; see **dress up.**

**dolorous,** *modif.* — *Syn.* mournful, sorrowful, distressed, grievous; see **sad** 1, 2.

**dolt,** *n.* — *Syn.* simpleton, nitwit, blockhead; see **fool** 1.

**domain,** *n.* — *Syn.* dominion, realm, field, specialty; see **area** 2, **field** 4, **kingdom, region** 1.

**dome,** *n.* **1.** [A hemispherical roof] — *Syn.* cupola, top, bulge, vault, onion dome, coving, mosque roof, church roof, bubble dome, geodesic dome, rotunda, sports dome, stadium; see also **arch, roof.**
**2.** [*The head] — *Syn.* skull, cranium, noggin*; see **head** 1.

**domestic,** *modif.* **1.** [Relating or devoted to home]

— *Syn.* home, household, familial, family, home-loving, devoted to one's family, homely, homelike, homey, domesticated, fond of home, stay-at-home, devoted to the lares and penates, liking one's own fireside, quiet, sedentary, indoor, tame, settled, residential, private, internal, national, interstate, inland (British); see also **home** 1, **tranquil** 1.— *Ant.* UNRULY, roving, foreign.

2. [Home-grown] — *Syn.* indigenous, native, handcrafted, homemade; see **homemade, native** 2.

**domesticate,** *v.* — *Syn.* tame, train, breed, housebreak, subdue, break, gentle, break in, bust*; see also **breed** 3, **teach** 2, **train** 4.

**domesticated,** *modif.* — *Syn.* tame, tamed, trained, housebroken; see **tame** 1.

**domicile,** *n.* — *Syn.* residence, house, habitation; see **home** 1, 2.

**dominant,** *modif.* **1.** [Having effect or power] — *Syn.* ruling, prevailing, governing, predominant; see **governing, predominant** 1, **principal**.

2. [Inclined to use force] — *Syn.* commanding, imperious, imperative, authoritative, lordly, despotic, domineering, demonstrative, assertive, aggressive, bossy*; see also **aggressive** 1, **autocratic** 1, **powerful** 1.— *Ant.* submissive, retiring, meek.

*See Synonym Study at* PREDOMINANT.

**dominate,** *v.* — *Syn.* rule, manage, control, dictate to, predominate, subject, subjugate, keep down, carry authority, tyrannize, keep subjugated, have one's (own) way, have influence over, domineer, browbeat, bully, push around, carry authority, bend to one's will, command, overshadow, tower above, overlook, eclipse, play first fiddle*, lead by the nose*, boss*, keep under one's thumb*, rule the roost*, wear the pants*, walk all over*; see also **command** 2, **govern, subject**.

**domination,** *n.* — *Syn.* rule, control, mastery; see **command** 2, **power** 2.

**domineering,** *modif.* — *Syn.* overbearing, imperious, oppressive, bossy*; see **autocratic** 1, **egotistic** 2, **masterful, tyrannical**.

*See Synonym Study at* MASTERFUL.

**dominion,** *n.* **1.** [The acknowledged right to govern] — *Syn.* authority, seniority, jurisdiction, control, power, rule, sway, authorization, reign, ascendancy, sovereignty, supremacy, mastership, lordship, prerogative, privilege, regency, commission, empire; see also **administration** 1, **power** 2.— *Ant.* ANARCHY, subjugation, bondage.

2. [Actual control] — *Syn.* management, control, domination; see **administration** 1, **government** 1.

3. [A governed area] — *Syn.* domain, territory, realm, kingdom; see **area** 2, **nation** 1, **territory** 2.

*See Synonym Study at* POWER.

**don,** *v.* — *Syn.* clothe, enrobe, put on; see **dress** 1, **wear** 1.

**donate,** *v.* — *Syn.* give, grant, bestow, bequeath; see **distribute** 1, **give** 1, **provide** 1.

*See Synonym Study at* GIVE.

**donation,** *n.* — *Syn.* contribution, benefaction, gift, endowment; see **gift** 1.

*See Synonym Study at* GIFT.

**done,** *modif.* **1.** [Accomplished] — *Syn.* over, through, finished, completed, realized, consummated, effected, executed, wrought, performed, rendered, compassed, fulfilled, brought to pass, brought about, actualized, perfected, over and out*; see also **finished** 1.— *Ant.* UNFINISHED, unrealized, failed.

2. [Cooked] — *Syn.* ready, prepared, well-done, well-

cooked, hot, baked, stewed, broiled, boiled, crisped, crusted, fried, browned, done to a turn; see also **baked**.
— *Ant.* RAW, burned, uncooked.

3. [Agreed upon] — *Syn.* agreed, settled, socially acceptable; see **approved, determined** 1.

**done for***, *modif.* — *Syn.* defeated, vanquished, ruined; see **beaten** 1, **dead** 1, **destroyed, dying** 1.

**done in***, *modif.* — *Syn.* exhausted, worn out, weary; see **tired**.

**done out of,** *modif.* — *Syn.* defrauded, bilked, taken*; see **cheated, deceived** 1.

**done up***, *modif.* — *Syn.* prepared, packaged, wrapped up, fastened; see **tight** 2, **wrapped**.

**done with,** *modif.* — *Syn.* finished with, through, dispatched, no longer in need of; see **finished** 1.

**Don Juan,** *n.* — *Syn.* libertine, lothario, womanizer*; see **lecher, rake** 1, **wolf** 2.

**donkey,** *n.* — *Syn.* burro, ass, jackass, jennet, beast of burden, Jerusalem pony, back burro, jack, jenny, mule, hinny, Rocky Mountain canary*, Missouri hummingbird*, maud*, donk*, hee-haw*; see also **horse** 1.

**donor,** *n.* — *Syn.* benefactor, contributor, patron, patroness, benefactress, philanthropist, giver, donator, subscriber, grantor, public-spirited individual, altruist, humanitarian, savior, Good Samaritan, angel*, the bank*, fairy godmother*, Lady Bountiful*; see also **patron** 1.

**do-nothing,** *modif.* — *Syn.* idle, indolent, passive; see **indifferent** 1, **lazy** 1.

**do-nothing,** *n.* — *Syn.* idler, sluggard, layabout, slacker; see **loafer**.

**don'ts***, *n.* — *Syn.* objections, vetoes, adverse reaction, prohibitions; see **objection** 2, **refusal**.

**doom,** *n.* **1.** [One's appointed end] — *Syn.* fate, lot, destiny, destination, predestination, foreordination, end, ruin, death, adverse fate, tragic fate, terrible ending, annihilation, destruction, downfall, fortune, kismet, portion, conclusion, the inescapable, death knell, fall of the curtain*; see also **destiny** 1.

2. [A verdict] — *Syn.* condemnation, decision, judgment; see **sentence** 1.

*See Synonym Study at* FATE.

**doomed,** *modif.* — *Syn.* ruined, cursed, sentenced, lost, condemned, damned, accursed, unredeemed, unfortunate, ill-fated, star-crossed, ill-starred, foreordained, predestined, fated, fatal, threatened, menaced, overthrown, undone, cut down, wrecked, ruined, convicted; see also **destined** 1, **destroyed**.

**door,** *n.* **1.** [Entrance] — *Syn.* entry, portal, gate, bar, hatch, hatchway, postern, doorway, gateway, opening, aperture, exit; see also **entrance** 2, **gate**.

Varieties of doors include: cellar, front, back, side, kitchen, closet, garage, storm, screen, barn, revolving, electric eye, automatic, secret, sliding, double, French, Dutch, trap, air.

2. [Approach] — *Syn.* gateway, opening, access; see **entrance** 1, **opportunity** 1.

**lay at the door of** — *Syn.* charge, blame, hold accountable; see **accuse**.

**out of doors** — *Syn.* outside, in the air, out; see **outdoors**.

**show (someone) the door*** — *Syn.* show out, ask to leave, eject; see **dismiss** 1, 2, **oust**.

**doorman,** *n.* — *Syn.* doorkeeper, guard, porter, concierge; see **custodian** 2, **watchman**.

**do out of***, *v.* — *Syn.* cheat, trick, beat out of*; see **cheat, deceive, steal**.

**do over,** *v.* **1.** [To repeat] — *Syn.* redo, do again, rework; see **repeat** 1.

**2.** [*To redecorate] — *Syn.* refurbish, remodel, renew; see **redecorate.**

**dope***, *n.* **1.** [A drug] — *Syn.* narcotic, opiate, controlled substance; see **drug** 2.

**2.** [Pertinent information] — *Syn.* details, developments, lowdown*; see **data, knowledge** 1, **news** 1.

**3.** [A dull-witted person] — *Syn.* idiot, dunce, dolt, simpleton; see **fool** 1.

**dope***, *v.* — *Syn.* drug, anesthetize, sedate, put to sleep; see **deaden** 1, **drug.**

**dope out***, *v.* — *Syn.* figure out, comprehend, grasp; see **solve, understand** 1.

**dormant,** *modif.* **1.** [Sleeping] — *Syn.* torpid, somnolent, quiescent, lethargic; see **asleep.**

**2.** [Inactive] — *Syn.* inoperative, inert, in abeyance; see **latent.**

*See Synonym Study at* LATENT.

**dormitory,** *n.* — *Syn.* sleeping quarters, dorm*, barracks, residence hall, room, apartment, hostel, men's dormitory, women's dormitory, residence; see also **bedroom, hotel, room** 2.

**dos and don'ts***, *n.* — *Syn.* rules, regulations, instruction(s); see **advice, command** 1, **custom** 2, **directions.**

**dose,** *n.* **1.** [The amount administered at one time] — *Syn.* dosage, treatment, measurement, measure, fill, spoonful, portion, lot, draft, application, shot, lethal dose, toxic dose, doctor's orders*; see also **prescription, share.**

**2.** [*Venereal disease] — *Syn.* social disease, gonorrhea, the clap*; see **disease.**

**dot,** *n.* — *Syn.* point, period, spot, speck, mark, decimal point, polka dot, pinpoint, atom, particle, grain, iota, droplet, mite, mote, dab, tittle, jot.

**on the dot*** — *Syn.* precisely, exactly, punctually; see **accurate** 2, **accurately.**

**dotage,** *n.* — *Syn.* feebleness, senility, second childhood; see **senility.**

**dote on,** *v.* — *Syn.* adore, pet, idolize; see **cherish** 1, **love** 1.

**doting,** *modif.* — *Syn.* excessively fond, smitten, indulgent, foolish; see **fascinated, loving.**

**double,** *modif.* — *Syn.* twofold, twice, paired, coupled, twin, binary, binate, geminate, doubled, redoubled, duplex, renewed, dual, repeated, second, as much again, duplicated, ambiguous, double-barreled, duple, twoply, folded; see also **twice, twin.** — *Ant.* SINGLE, alone, apart.

**on the double*** — *Syn.* hastily, rapidly, hurriedly, right away; see **quickly** 1.

**double,** *n.* — *Syn.* duplicate, counterpart, twin, stand-in; see **duplicate, equal, substitute.**

**double,** *v.* **1.** [To make or become double] — *Syn.* make twice as much, duplicate, multiply, fold over; see **fold** 2, **grow** 1, **increase** 1.

**2.** [To replace] — *Syn.* substitute for, stand in, act for; see **substitute** 2.

**double back,** *v.* — *Syn.* backtrack, reverse, circle; see **return** 1, **turn** 2, 6.

**double-cross,** *v.* — *Syn.* cheat, defraud, trick; see **betray** 1, **deceive.**

**double-dealer,** *n.* — *Syn.* deceiver, cheater, rogue; see **cheat** 1, **hypocrite, traitor.**

**double-dealing,** *modif.* — *Syn.* tricky, untrustworthy, deceitful; see **dishonest** 1, 2, **hypocritical.**

**double-dealing,** *n.* — *Syn.* deceit, duplicity, treachery; see **deception** 1, **dishonesty.**

**double-entendre,** *n.* — *Syn.* double meaning, ambiguity, pun; see **double meaning, joke** 2.

**double meaning,** *n.* — *Syn.* double-entendre, ambiguity, play on words, innuendo, pun; see also **joke** 2.

**doublet,** *n.* — *Syn.* duplicate, couple, two; see **pair.**

**double up,** *v.* — *Syn.* combine, join, share; see **join** 1, 2, **unite** 1.

**doubly,** *modif.* — *Syn.* twofold, redoubled, increased; see **again, double, twice.**

**doubt,** *n.* **1.** [Questioning] — *Syn.* distrust, mistrust, disbelief, unbelief, suspicion, misgiving, skepticism, reluctance to believe, apprehension, dubiousness, doubtfulness, dubiety, agnosticism, incredulity, faithlessness, lack of faith, want of faith, lack of confidence, lack of certainty, jealousy, discredit, rejection; see also **uncertainty** 1. — *Ant.* FAITH, trust, credence.

**2.** [Hesitation arising from uncertainty] — *Syn.* uncertainty, skepticism, scruple, misgiving, qualm, reservation, perplexity, indecision, irresolution, incertitude, hesitancy, suspense, lack of confidence *or* certainty, dubiety, undecidedness, faltering, vacillation, ambivalence, lack of conviction, ambiguity, dilemma, reluctance, difficulty, apprehension, wavering, demur, demurral, bewilderment, quandary, dubiousness, unsettled opinion, timidity, insecurity, bashfulness, diffidence, feeling of inferiority, inferiority complex; see also **uncertainty** 2. — *Ant.* BELIEF, conviction, certainty.

*See Synonym Study at* UNCERTAINTY.

**beyond a doubt, without doubt** — *Syn.* doubtless, certainly, unquestionably, beyond the shadow of a doubt; see **certain** 3, **surely.**

**no doubt** — *Syn.* doubtless, in all likelihood, certainly; see **probably, surely.**

**doubt,** *v.* **1.** [To be uncertain] — *Syn.* wonder, question, query, ponder, vacillate, waver, hesitate, be dubious, be undecided, be uncertain, be curious, be puzzled, be doubtful, be in a quandary, demur, hold in doubt, have doubts about, have one's doubts, raise a question, stop to consider, have qualms, have reservations, scruple, call in question, hesitate to accept, hold questionable, greet with skepticism, skepticize, cast doubt upon, have no conception, not know which way to turn, not know what to make of, be of two minds; see also **ask** 1, **question** 1. — *Ant.* believe, TRUST, confide.

**2.** [To entertain doubt] — *Syn.* suspect, mistrust, distrust, lack confidence in, discredit, give no credence to, not believe, refuse to believe, disbelieve, impugn, dispute, be apprehensive of, be skeptical of, scoff, insinuate, misgive, read somewhat differently, challenge, harbor suspicions, not admit, doubt one's word, smell a rat*, not buy*, take a dim view of*, set no store by*, put no stock in*, take no stock in*; see also **deny.** — *Ant.* SUPPORT, prove, demonstrate.

**doubter,** *n.* — *Syn.* questioner, unbeliever, agnostic; see **cynic, skeptic.**

**doubtful,** *modif.* **1.** [Ambiguous] — *Syn.* in doubt, questionable, problematic, vague, indistinct, unclear, indefinite, undetermined, unresolved, open to doubt, in question, equivocal, unsure, indeterminate, under examination, debatable, theoretical, up in the air*, iffy*, yes and no*, out of focus*; see also **obscure** 1, **questionable** 1, **uncertain** 2.

**2.** [Uncertain in mind] — *Syn.* dubious, doubting, questioning, skeptical, undecided, unsure, wavering, hesitating, ambivalent, undetermined, uncertain, unsettled, confused, disturbed, lost, puzzled, disconcerted, perplexed, discomposed, flustered, flurried, baffled, hesitant, distracted, faltering, unresolved, in a quandary, of two minds, unable to make up one's mind, vacillating, indecisive, irresolute, agnostic, like a doubting Thomas, troubled with doubt, of little faith, faithless, distrustful, incredulous, cynical, not knowing what's what, having no idea, in a dilemma, under a spell★, in the clouds★, up a tree★, in a haze★, not able to make head or tail of★, from Missouri★, going around in circles★, out of one's bearings★, up in the air★, wishy-washy★; see also **suspicious** 1.

**3.** [Of questionable character] — *Syn.* dubious, sneaky, disreputable, shady★; see **questionable** 2, **suspicious** 2.

---

*SYN.* — **doubtful** implies strong uncertainty as to the probability, value, honesty, validity, etc. of something *[a doubtful remedy]*; **dubious** is less strong, suggesting merely vague suspicion or hesitancy *[dubious about the future]*; **questionable** strictly suggests only that there is some reason for doubt, but it is often used as a euphemism to imply strong suspicion, almost amounting to certainty, of immorality, dishonesty, etc. *[a questionable reputation]*; **problematic** implies only uncertainty with no suggestion of a moral question *[a problematic success]*

---

**doubting,** *modif.* — *Syn.* questioning, dubious, skeptical; see **doubtful** 2, **suspicious** 1.

**doubtless,** *modif.* — *Syn.* without doubt, certainly, unquestionably; see **surely.**

**dough,** *n.* **1.** [A soft mixture] — *Syn.* batter, paste (especially of flour), pulp; see **batter, mixture** 1.

**2.** [★Money] — *Syn.* dollars, change, silver; see **money** 1, **wealth** 2.

**doughnut,** *n.* — *Syn.* donut, fried cake, cruller, raised doughnut, jelly doughnut, powdered doughnut, chocolate doughnut, etc; bismarck, sinker★, dunker★, gasket★; see also **cake** 2, **pastry.**

**do up★,** *v.* **1.** [To launder] — *Syn.* put through the laundry, wash and iron, finish; see **clean, wash** 2.

**2.** [To wrap up] — *Syn.* enclose, package, tie up, gift-wrap; see **fasten** 1, **wrap** 2.

**dour,** *modif.* — *Syn.* forbidding, gloomy, morose; see **grim** 1, **sullen.**

**douse,** *v.* **1.** [To immerse in water] — *Syn.* submerge, splash, drench; see **immerse** 1, **soak** 1.

**2.** [To put out] — *Syn.* quench, drown out, snuff out, splash; see **extinguish** 1.

**dove,** *n.* **1.** [A member of the Columbidae] — *Syn.* domesticated pigeon, turtledove, mourning dove, squab; see **pigeon.**

**2.** [A promoter of peace] — *Syn.* pacifist, peacemaker, peace lover, activist for peace, pacifier, pacificator, conciliator, United Nations representative, reconciler, appeaser, peacemonger★, peacenik★; see also **pacifist.**

**dovetail,** *v.* — *Syn.* link, interlock, fit together; see **fit** 1, **join** 1.

**dowager,** *n.* — *Syn.* widow, matron, dame; see **lady** 3, **widow** 1, **woman** 1.

**dowdy,** *modif.* — *Syn.* frumpy, unfashionable, drab, untidy, slovenly, frowzy, tacky, shabby, homely, plain, old-fashioned, unkempt, baggy, unstylish, tasteless; see also **dull** 2, **old-fashioned.**

**do well by,** *v.* — *Syn.* aid, favor, treat well; see **help** 1.

**do with,** *v.* — *Syn.* make use of, benefit from, find helpful; see **use** 1.

**do without,** *v.* — *Syn.* manage, get along without, forgo; see **abandon** 1, **abstain, contrive** 2, **need.**

**down,** *prep.* and *modif.* **1.** [Having a downward motion] — *Syn.* forward, headlong, downward, downhill, downstairs, bottomward, downgrade, on a downward course, from higher to lower, to the bottom, downwardly, in a descending direction, to a lower position, declining,

falling, descending, gravitating, slipping, sliding, cascading, sagging, precipitating, slumping, dropping, sinking, earthward, groundward, southward, hellward. — *Ant.* UP, upward, rising.

**2.** [Physically lower] — *Syn.* below, depressed, underneath, prostrate; see **resting** 1, **under** 1.

**3.** [Figuratively lower] — *Syn.* inferior, lowly, below par, in check; see **poor** 1, **restrained, sick, under** 2.

**4.** [Dejected] — *Syn.* downcast, depressed, dispirited; see **sad** 1.

**5.** [Not working] — *Syn.* inoperative, out of order, malfunctioning; see **broken** 2.

**down,** *n.* — *Syn.* feathers, fluff, fur; see **feather, hair** 1.

**down,** *v.* — *Syn.* throw down, pull down, knock down, bring down, throw, fell, subdue, tackle, trip, floor, topple, conquer, overthrow, defeat, vanquish, overpower, upset, overturn, shoot down, trample in the dust, gulp down, knock out, deck★; see also **defeat** 3, **drink** 1, 2, **hit** 1. — *Ant.* RAISE, lift, elevate.

**down and out,** *modif.* — *Syn.* destitute, ruined, defeated, finished; see **beaten, poor** 1.

**downcast,** *modif.* — *Syn.* discouraged, dejected, unhappy; see **sad** 1.

**downfall,** *n.* — *Syn.* destruction, fall, comedown, ruin; see **defeat** 2, **destruction** 2.

**downgrade,** *n.* — *Syn.* descent, decline, slope; see **grade** 1, **hill, inclination** 5.

**downgrade,** *v.* — *Syn.* minimize, deprecate, lower, demote; see **decrease** 2, **depreciate** 2, **humble.**

**downhearted,** *modif.* — *Syn.* dejected, despondent, downcast; see **sad** 1.

**down on★,** *modif.* — *Syn.* against, disillusioned (with), hostile to; see **opposed.**

**downpour,** *n.* — *Syn.* rain, deluge, cloudburst, monsoon; see **flood** 1, **storm** 1.

**downright,** *modif.* **1.** [Thorough] — *Syn.* total, complete, utter, thoroughgoing; see **absolute** 1.

**2.** [Thoroughly] — *Syn.* absolutely, entirely, utterly; see **completely.**

**3.** [Frank] — *Syn.* straightforward, blunt, direct, plain; see **abrupt** 2, **frank.**

**downstairs,** *modif.* — *Syn.* underneath, below decks, on the floor below; see **below** 4, **down** 1, **under** 1.

**downstairs,** *n.* — *Syn.* first floor, ground floor, cellar; see **basement** 1.

**down-to-earth,** *modif.* — *Syn.* sensible, practical, pragmatic, unpretentious; see **practical, rational** 1, **unaffected** 1.

**downtown,** *modif.* — *Syn.* city, central, midtown, uptown, inner-city, main, mid-city, in the business district, on the main street, metropolitan, business, shopping; see also **urban** 2. — *Ant.* SUBURBAN, residential, rural.

**downtown,** *n.* — *Syn.* business district, midtown, hub, city center; see **center** 2, **city.**

**downtrodden,** *modif.* — *Syn.* tyrannized, subjugated, overcome; see **oppressed.**

**downward,** *modif.* — *Syn.* earthward, descending, downwards; see **down** 1.

**downy,** *modif.* — *Syn.* woolly, fleecy, fuzzy, fluffy, covered with soft hair *or* feathers, plumose, feathery, velvety, soft, pubescent, silky; see also **light** 5, **soft** 2. — *Ant.* ROUGH, hard, bald.

**dowry,** *n.* — *Syn.* dower, dot, marriage portion, settlement, bride's share, bridal gift, jointure, tocher (Scottish); see also **endowment** 3, **property** 1.

**doxology,** *n.* — *Syn.* paean, hymn, Gloria, glorification, psalm, hallelujah, hosanna, *Te Deum* (Latin); see also **hymn, song.**

**doze,** *v.* — *Syn.* nap, drowse, slumber; see **sleep.**

**dozen,** *modif.* — *Syn.* twelve, baker's dozen, long dozen, handful, pocketful.

**drab,** *modif.* **1.** [Dull] — *Syn.* dreary, colorless, monotonous, somber; see **dull** 2, 4.

**2.** [Dun-colored] — *Syn.* yellowish brown, dull colored, brownish, brownish yellow, dull brown *or* gray, grayish, yellowish gray, olive-drab, khaki, dun, achromatic, murky, mouse-colored, slate-colored, leadenhued; see also **brown, gray** 1.

**draft,** *n.* **1.** [A preliminary sketch] — *Syn.* plans, blueprint, sketch, outline; see **design** 1, **plan** 1.

**2.** [A drink] — *Syn.* swallow, glass, quaff, dose; see **drink** 1.

**3.** [A breeze] — *Syn.* current of air, gust, puff; see **wind** 1.

**4.** [A contrivance for controlling the flow of air] — *Syn.* damper, check, control, flap, front draft, check draft, smoke draft; see also **valve.**

**5.** [An order for payment] — *Syn.* check, cashier's check, bank draft, money order, receipt, promissory note, warrant, coupon, bond, debenture, letter of credit, IOU*; see also **check** 1.

**6.** [The selection of troops] — *Syn.* conscription, induction, assignment, registration, recruitment, enlistment, lottery, levy, selective service, call of duty, call to the colors, roll call, call-up; see also **enrollment** 1, **selection** 1.

**on draft** — *Syn.* on tap, bulk, unbottled; see **available on tap** at **tap.**

**draft,** *v.* **1.** [To make a rough plan] — *Syn.* outline, delineate, sketch; see **compose** 3, **plan** 1, 2.

**2.** [To select for military service] — *Syn.* select, conscript, induct, call up; see **enlist** 1, **recruit** 1.

**draftsman,** *n.* — *Syn.* sketcher, delineator, drawer; see **architect** 1, **artist** 1, **designer.**

**drag,** *n.* **1.** [Anything that is drawn] — *Syn.* harrow, scraper, bar, dragnet, seine, clog, brake, shoe, anchor, grapnel, dragrope, floater; see also **net.**

**2.** [The influence of air on an airplane] — *Syn.* resistance, curb, pull, suction, friction, suck, tow, vacuum action; see also **resistance** 3.

**3.** [A restraint] — *Syn.* hindrance, burden, encumbrance; see **impediment** 1.

**4.** [*A dull or annoying person, thing, or situation] — *Syn.* bore, bother, annoyance; see **nuisance** 3, **trouble** 2.

**drag,** *v.* **1.** [To go slowly; *said of animate beings*] — *Syn.* lag, straggle, dawdle; see **lag, loiter, pause.**

**2.** [To go slowly; *said of an activity*] — *Syn.* slow down, slacken, encounter difficulties, be delayed, be prolonged, be drawn out, be tedious, wear on, fail to show progress, creep, crawl, stagnate, mark time, suffer delays, suffer from a slowdown, be off-season, be quiet; see also **delay** 1. — *Ant.* IMPROVE, progress, pick up.

**3.** [To pull an object] — *Syn.* pull, haul, move, transport; see **draw** 1.

**4.** [*To race] — *Syn.* compete in speed, drag-race, hotrod*; see **race** 2.

**5.** [*To smoke] — *Syn.* puff, inhale deeply, draw; see **smoke** 2.

*See Synonym Study at* PULL.

**dragging,** *modif.* — *Syn.* monotonous, drawn-out, slow, boring; see **dull** 4.

**dragline,** *n.* — *Syn.* dragrope, towline, cable, rope; see **chain** 1, **drag** 1, **wire** 1.

**dragnet,** *n.* **1.** [A net] — *Syn.* trawl, seine, trammel; see **drag** 1, **net.**

**2.** [A system for apprehending criminals or suspects] — *Syn.* police sweep, network, all-points bulletin,

APB, stakeout, roundup; see also **arrest** 1, **hunt** 2, **trap** 1.

**drag on,** *v.* — *Syn.* go on slowly, keep going, persist, wear on; see **continue** 1, **drag** 2, **endure** 1.

**dragon,** *n.* — *Syn.* mythical beast, winged serpent, hydra; see **monster** 1.

**drag one's feet,** *v.* — *Syn.* lag behind, obstruct, hold back, stall; see **delay** 1, **hesitate, hinder.**

**drain,** *n.* **1.** [A pipe or conduit] — *Syn.* duct, channel, sewer; see **conduit, pipe** 1.

**2.** [A gradual reduction] — *Syn.* exhaustion, depletion, draining, strain; see **consumption** 1, **waste** 1.

**down the drain*** — *Syn.* wasted, ruined, gone; see **lost** 1, **wasted.**

**drain,** *v.* **1.** [To withdraw fluid] — *Syn.* divert, bleed, milk, tap, draw off, drink, remove, evaporate, catheterize; see also **empty** 2.

**2.** [To withdraw strength] — *Syn.* exhaust, empty, consume, weary, tire out, expend, sap, dissipate, waste, tax, deplete, impoverish, get rid of, free from, bleed, debilitate, devitalize, enervate, reduce, filter off, remove, milk*; see also **spend** 1, **tire** 2, **weaken** 2. — *Ant.* REVIVE, refresh, replenish.

**3.** [To seep away] — *Syn.* run out, run off, flow off, flow out, seep off, seep out, exude, trickle out, filter off, ooze, percolate, effuse, find an opening, osmose, decline, diminish, leave dry; see also **flow** 1, 2.

**4.** [To empty] — *Syn.* pour, bail out, dump; see **empty** 2.

**drainage,** *n.* — *Syn.* seepage, waste, bilge, waste water, drain water, sewerage, effluvium, effluent; see also **trash** 1.

**dram,** *n.* — *Syn.* measure, sip, drop; see **dose** 1, **drink** 1.

**drama,** *n.* **1.** [A theatrical composition or production] — *Syn.* play, piece, production, dramatic representation, dramatic work, dramatization, show, stage show, vehicle, skit, sketch, legitimate stage, theater; see also **acting, theater** 2.

Types of drama include: melodrama, tragicomedy, comedy of manners, social document, burlesque, pantomime, mime, opera, operetta, light opera, musical comedy, musical, mystery, murder mystery, farce, problem drama, classical drama, historical drama, expressionism, theater of the absurd, theater of cruelty, mixed media theater, epic, pageant, masque, miracle play, revival, serial, radio play, television play, teleplay; thriller*, highbrow stuff*, whodunit*, agitprop*, melo*; see also **comedy, tragedy** 3.

**2.** [Action having the qualities of drama] — *Syn.* histrionics, melodrama, farce, climax, emotion, tension, suspense, scene, tragedy, comedy, theatrics, dramatics, intensity, sob story*, tear-jerker*, soap opera*; see also **excitement.**

**dramatic,** *modif.* — *Syn.* tense, climactic, moving; see **exciting.**

**dramatis personae,** *n.* — *Syn.* players, actors, performers; see **actor** 1, **actress, cast** 2.

**dramatist,** *n.* — *Syn.* playwright, scriptwriter, scenario writer, scenarist, screenwriter, dramaturge, tragedian, scripter*, play doctor*; see also **author** 2, **writer.**

Major dramatists include — *Great Britain:* Christopher Marlowe, Ben Jonson, William Shakespeare, William Congreve, Richard Brinsley Sheridan, Oliver Goldsmith, James Barrie, Oscar Wilde, George Bernard Shaw, Sean O'Casey, John Millington Synge, Tom Stoppard, Noel Coward, Harold Pinter, John Osborne; *United States:* Thornton Wilder, Eugene O'Neill, Maxwell Anderson, William Inge, Tennessee Williams, Arthur Miller, Edward Albee, Sam Shepard, Neil

Simon; *Greece:* Aeschylus, Sophocles, Euripides, Aristophanes; *France:* Molière, Pierre Corneille, Jean Racine, Edmond Rostand, Jean Anouilh, Jean Giraudoux, Eugène Ionesco, Jean Genêt, Jean Cocteau, Jean-Paul Sartre; *Germany:* Wolfgang von Goethe, Friedrich Schiller, Bertolt Brecht, Gerhardt Hauptmann; *other:* Luigi Pirandello, Maxim Gorky, Anton Chekov, Henrik Ibsen, August Strindberg, Friedrich Dürrenmatt, Calderón, Lope de Vega, Federico Garcia Lorca, Samuel Beckett, Karel Čapek, Monzaemon Chikamatsu.

**dramatize,** *v.* **1.** [To present a performance] — *Syn.* enact, produce, stage; see **perform** 2.
**2.** [To exaggerate] — *Syn.* overstate, overplay, give color to, amplify; see **act** 3, **exaggerate.**

**drape,** *v.* — *Syn.* enclose, envelop, hang, dress, wrap, model, display, line, don, festoon; see also **clothe.**

**drapes,** *n.* — *Syn.* window covering, drapery, hanging; see **curtain.**

**drastic,** *modif.* — *Syn.* radical, extreme, severe, harsh; see **extreme** 2.

**draw,** *v.* **1.** [To move an object] — *Syn.* pull, drag, attract, move, bring, convey, tug, trail, lug, tow, take in tow, carry, jerk, wrench, yank, trawl, unsheathe, withdraw, hook, siphon, haul, wind in, draw out, extract, pick, magnetize, draw in. — *Ant.* REPEL, repulse, reject.
**2.** [To make a likeness by drawing] — *Syn.* sketch, depict, portray, delineate, describe, draft, express, etch, crayon, pencil, outline, trace, make a picture of, represent, illustrate, picture, render, limn, model, form, engrave, caricature, lithograph, profile, silhouette, chart, map, diagram, dash off, doodle; see also **paint** 1.
**3.** [To lure] — *Syn.* allure, induce, entice; see **attract** 2, **fascinate.**
*See Synonym Study at* PULL.

**beat to the draw**★ — *Syn.* be quicker than another, forestall, stop; see **anticipate** 2, **defeat** 1, **prevent.**

**draw away,** *v.* — *Syn.* pull away, gain on, increase a lead; see **advance** 1, **leave** 1, **remove** 1.

**drawback,** *n.* — *Syn.* shortcoming, detriment, hindrance, check; see **disadvantage** 2, **impediment** 1.

**draw back,** *v.* — *Syn.* withdraw, recede, draw in; see **retreat** 1, 2.

**drawing,** *n.* **1.** [The practice or study of drawing] — *Syn.* sketching, design, illustration, representation, rendering, tracing, limning, etching, draftsmanship, commercial art, graphic art; see also **art** 2.
Kinds of drawing include: life, line, figure, architectural, mechanical, isometric, scale, freehand, pen and ink, charcoal, red charcoal, pencil, black and white, chiaroscuro, computer-aided design, CAD; see **picture** 3, **representation.**
**2.** [A work produced by drawing] — *Syn.* sketch, likeness, study; see **design** 1, **picture** 3, **representation.**
**3.** [A raffle] — *Syn.* lottery, sweepstakes, pool; see **raffle.**

**drawing room,** *n.* — *Syn.* reception room, living room, sitting room, stateroom, salon, parlor, front room; see also **parlor, room** 2.

**drawl,** *v.* — *Syn.* lengthen, extend, pronounce slowly, protract in utterance, prolong syllables, speak monotonously, spin out; see also **utter.**

**drawling,** *modif.* — *Syn.* monotonous, languid, droning; see **dull** 4, **slow** 1.

**draw on** *or* upon, *v.* — *Syn.* take from, extract, employ, make use of; see **use** 1.

**draw out,** *v.* **1.** [To induce to talk] — *Syn.* make talk, lead on, elicit; see **discover, motivate, obtain** 1.

**2.** [To pull out] — *Syn.* extract, take out, remove; see **draw** 1, **remove** 1.
**3.** [To lengthen] — *Syn.* extend, prolong, drag out, spin out; see **lengthen** 1.

**draw up,** *v.* — *Syn.* draft, execute, prepare (a document), write up; see **compose** 3, **write** 1.

**dray,** *n.* — *Syn.* hand truck, van, vehicle; see **cart, wagon.**

**dread,** *n.* — *Syn.* fear, terror, awe, trepidation; see **fear** 2.
*See Synonym Study at* FEAR, REVERENCE.

**dreadful,** *modif.* — *Syn.* terrible, appalling, fearful; see **frightful** 1, **offensive** 2, **poor** 2.

**dreadnought,** *n.* — *Syn.* man-of-war, battleship, gunboat; see **ship, warship.**

**dream,** *n.* **1.** [Mental pictures] — *Syn.* nightmare, apparition, hallucination, vision, daydream, fantasy, wraith, specter, incubus, image, illusion, mirage, trance, idea, impression, reverie, romance, dream life, evidence of the unconscious, flight of fancy, castle in the air, castle in Spain, air castle; see also **fantasy** 2, **illusion** 1, **thought** 2, **vision** 3, 4. — *Ant.* REALITY, verity, truth.
**2.** [A fond hope] — *Syn.* aspiration, goal, desire, ideal; see **hope** 2, **purpose** 1.
**3.** [Unattainable idea] — *Syn.* chimera, bubble, will-o'-the-wisp, pipe dream★; see sense 1; **fantasy** 2, **illusion** 1.

**dream,** *v.* **1.** [To have visions, usually during sleep or fever] — *Syn.* be delirious, have nightmares, see in a vision, have flashes, hallucinate, fancy, visualize, envisage; see also **visualize.**
**2.** [To entertain or delude oneself with imagined things] — *Syn.* fancy, fantasize, daydream, indulge in reveries, imagine, conceive, have notions, conjure up, create, picture, visualize, muse, stargaze, moon, idealize, be up in the clouds, be on cloud nine, build castles in the air, build castles in Spain, go woolgathering, be moonstruck, let one's mind wander, talk through one's hat★, pipe-dream★, blow bubbles★, search for the rainbow's end, look for the pot of gold; see also **imagine** 1.
**3.** [To conceive mentally; *usually used in the negative*] — *Syn.* think of, consider, believe, suppose; see **assume** 1, **consider** 3.

**dreamer,** *n.* — *Syn.* visionary, fantasist, utopist, theorizer; see **idealist.**

**dreaming,** *modif.* — *Syn.* musing, daydreaming, in a reverie; see **absent-minded, rapt** 2, **thoughtful** 1.

**dreamland,** *n.* — *Syn.* cloudland, fairyland, slumber; see **sleep.**

**dream up**★, *v.* — *Syn.* devise, contrive, concoct; see **imagine** 1, **invent** 1.

**dreamy,** *modif.* **1.** [Given to dreaming] — *Syn.* visionary, daydreaming, whimsical, fanciful, impractical, given to reverie, abstracted, musing, introspective, in a reverie, introversive, not of this world, otherworldly, idealistic, utopian, romantic, quixotic, starry-eyed; see also **absent-minded, impractical.** — *Ant.* PRACTICAL, active, down-to-earth, realistic.
**2.** [Suggestive of a dream] — *Syn.* illusory, dreamlike, vague, dim, indefinite, indistinct, soothing, restful, soft, misty, intangible, fantastic, visionary, phantasmagoric, surreal, nightmarish; see also **imaginary, impractical, unreal.**

**dreary,** *modif.* — *Syn.* gloomy, cheerless, bleak, drab; see **dark** 1, **dismal** 1, **dull** 4.

**dredge up,** *v.* — *Syn.* dig up, unearth, bring to light; see **dig** 1, 2, **discover.**

**dregs,** *n.* **1.** [Sediment] — *Syn.* lees, grounds, slag; see **residue.**

2. [The most worthless part] — *Syn.* scum, refuse, riff-raff; see **trash** 1, 2.

**drench,** *v.* — *Syn.* soak, wet, saturate, flood; see **immerse** 1, **soak** 1.

*See Synonym Study at* SOAK.

**dress,** *n.* **1.** [Clothing] — *Syn.* attire, apparel, formal dress, toilette; see **clothes.**

**2.** [A woman's outer garment] — *Syn.* frock, basic black dress, gown, jumper, sheath, cocktail dress, evening gown, ball gown, formal\*, wedding gown, suit, skirt, tunic, robe, sun dress, tank dress, shirtwaist dress, shift, sack, sweater dress, strapless, wraparound, sari, muumuu, toga, cheongsam, housedress, smock, sarong, housecoat; see also **clothes.**

**dress,** *v.* **1.** [To put on clothes] — *Syn.* don, put on, wear, garb, clothe, change clothes, robe, attire, apparel, costume, drape, array, cover, wrap up, get into, fit into, try on, slip on, slip into, throw on, fix up, spruce up, dress up, overdress, muffle up, bundle up, deck, deck out, doll up\*, trick out\*, tog up\*, underdress, dress down; see also **clothe, dress up, wear** 1.

**2.** [To provide with clothes] — *Syn.* costume, outfit, fit out; see **clothe, provide** 1.

**3.** [To make ready for show or use] — *Syn.* groom, adorn, ornament, make ready; see **decorate, prepare** 1, **trim** 2.

**4.** [To give medical treatment] — *Syn.* attend, treat, bandage, cleanse, sterilize, cauterize, give first aid, bind, apply a surgical dressing, apply antiseptics, apply medication, plaster, sew up, remove stitches; see also **heal** 1.

**dress down,** *v.* — *Syn.* rebuke, scold, reprimand; see **censure, scold.**

**dressed up,** *modif.* — *Syn.* dressed formally, in full dress, dolled up\*, spruced up\*, gussied up\*, dressed to kill\*, dressed to the nines\*, in one's best bib and tucker\*, in one's glad rags\*; see also **fashionable, formal** 4, **ornate.**

**dresser,** *n.* — *Syn.* dressing table, chest of drawers, bureau; see **chest** 1, **furniture, table** 1.

**dressing,** *n.* **1.** [A food mixture] — *Syn.* stuffing, filling, forcemeat.

Types of dressings include: bread, giblet, oyster, chestnut, potato, prune, plum, apple, duck, turkey, chicken, fish, clam, wild rice.

**2.** [A flavoring sauce]

Salad dressings include: mayonnaise, French, Russian, Thousand Island, green goddess, blue cheese, Roquefort, Italian, Caesar, vinaigrette, boiled, oil and vinegar; see also **relish** 1, **sauce** 1.

**3.** [An external medical application] — *Syn.* bandage, cast, plaster cast, gauze pad, adhesive tape, Band-Aid (trademark), compress, strip, gauze, tourniquet, pack, poultice, wet dressing, plaster, fomentation, application; see also **cast** 4.

**4.** [The act of clothing] — *Syn.* getting dressed, arraying, robing, appareling, changing, making a toilette, adorning, decking.

**5.** [Fertilizer] — *Syn.* manure, humus, compost, leaf mold; see **fertilizer.**

**dressing gown,** *n.* — *Syn.* robe, negligee, gown; see **clothes, nightgown, robe.**

**dressmaker,** *n.* — *Syn.* seamstress, ladies' tailor, modiste, designer, draper, manufacturing tailor, garment worker, sewer, sewing woman, fitter, operator, needle pusher\*, shears\*, snips\*; see also **designer, tailor.**

**dress up,** *v.* — *Syn.* primp, dress for dinner, deck out, spruce up, doll up\*, spiff up\*, dude up\*, fix up, trick out, trick up\*, gussy up\*, put on the dog\*; see also **dress** 1.

**dressy,** *modif.* — *Syn.* formal, elegant, elaborate; see **dressed up, fancy** 2, **fashionable, formal** 4, **ornate** 1.

**dribble,** *v.* — *Syn.* trickle, drip, leak, slaver; see **drool** 1, **drop** 1.

**driblet,** *n.* — *Syn.* mite, morsel, droplet; see **bit** 1, **drop** 1.

**dried,** *modif.* — *Syn.* drained, dehydrated, desiccated; see **dry** 1, **preserved** 2.

**drift,** *n.* **1.** [A tendency in movement] — *Syn.* bent, tenor, trend, tendency, end, effort, inclination, course, impulse, impetus, propulsion, aim, scope, tone, goal, push, bias, set, gravity, leaning, progress, conduct, propensity, disposition, bearing, proneness, line, tack, set, spirit; see also **direction** 1, **route** 1. — *Ant.* INDIFFERENCE, aimlessness, inertia.

**2.** [The measure or character of movement] — *Syn.* deviation, wash, aberration, motion, leeway, flux, flow, current, stream, diversion, digression, swerving, sweep, warp, departure; see also **flow.**

**3.** [General meaning] — *Syn.* tenor, purport, intention, object; see **meaning.**

**4.** [Something blown] — *Syn.* bank, mass, pile, snowdrift; see **heap.**

**5.** [A tunnel following a vein of ore] — *Syn.* adit, underground passage, subway; see **tunnel.**

*See Synonym Study at* TENDENCY.

**drift,** *v.* — *Syn.* float, ride, sail, cruise, coast, waft, wander aimlessly, wander at random, move with the current, gravitate, tend, be carried along, go with the tide, be caught in the current, wanderer, roam, rove, stray, go with the flow\*, bum around\*; see also **flow** 1, **roam.** — *Ant.* STEER, push, pull.

**drifter,** *n.* — *Syn.* vagabond, floater, vagrant, wanderer; see **tramp** 1, **traveler.**

**drill,** *n.* **1.** [Practice] — *Syn.* preparation, repetition, learning by doing; see **exercise** 1, **practice** 3.

**2.** [Exercise, especially in military formation] — *Syn.* training, maneuvers, marching, parade, close-order drill, open-order drill, conditioning, survival training, guerilla training, paratroop training, drop training, footslogging\*, monkey drill\*, push and pull\*; see also **march** 1.

*See Synonym Study at* PRACTICE.

**3.** [A tool for boring holes] — *Syn.* borer, wood bit, gimlet, countersink, steel drill, steam drill, electric drill, diamond drill, pneumatic drill, turbo-corer, cylindrical borer, boring tool, tap-borer, auger, corkscrew, awl, wimble, trepan, trephine, riveter, jackhammer; see also **bit** 5.

**4.** [Device for planting seed in holes] — *Syn.* planter, seeder, drill seeder, dibble; see **tool** 1.

**drill,** *v.* **1.** [To bore] — *Syn.* pierce, sink (in), puncture; see **dig** 1, **penetrate** 1.

**2.** [To train] — *Syn.* practice, rehearse, discipline; see **exercise** 1, **practice** 1, **teach** 2.

*See Synonym Study at* PRACTICE.

**drink,** *n.* **1.** [A liquid for drinking, or a portion of this] — *Syn.* beverage, sip, gulp, potion, potable, libation, drop, bottle, glass, toast, belt, refreshment, thirst quencher, draft, potation, drinkable, liquid, quaff, brew, tonic, tall drink, long drink, shot, jigger, dram, double, bumper, stirrup cup, swig\*, slug\*, nip\*, swill\*, drag\*, spot\*; see also sense 2.

**2.** [An alcoholic beverage] — *Syn.* liquor, alcohol, spirits, cocktail, mixed drink, highball, aperitif, hard liquor, intoxicant, strong drink, ardent spirits, aqua vitae, schnapps, punch, booze\*, the bottle\*, the sauce\*, hard stuff\*, hooch\*, juice\*, rotgut\*, moonshine\*, John

Barleycorn\*, firewater\*, poison\*, bracer\*, chaser\*, short one\*, stiff one\*, snort\*, snifter\*, quickie\*, jolt\*, nightcap\*, one for the road\*, eye-opener\*, pick-me-up\*, hair of the dog\*, three fingers\*, the cup that cheers\*, Mickey Finn\*; see also sense 1.
Alcoholic beverages include: beer, wine, whiskey, Scotch, rye, bourbon, Irish whiskey, gin, vodka, rum, Demon Rum\*, brandy, Cognac, liqueur, cordial, Champagne, bubbly\*, ale, stout, grog, hot toddy, sake, ouzo, arrack, absinthe, Pernod (trademark), tequila, pulque, slivovitz, sangria, Southern Comfort, mead, flip, boilermaker\*; see also **beer, brandy, cocktail, gin, whiskey, wine.**
**3.** [A nonalcoholic beverage]. Nonalcoholic beverages include: water, soda water, soft drink, sarsaparilla, mineral water, carbonated water, sparkling water, seltzer, club soda, cola, Coke (trademark), ginger ale, root beer, pop, soda pop, tonic, quinine, Perrier, Vichy water, coffee, tea, cocoa, hot chocolate, chocolate milk, milkshake, frappe, malted milk, shake, smoothie, frosted, lemonade, orangeade, punch, ice-cream soda, bottled drink, orange juice, tomato juice, grapefruit juice, etc.; mixer, Shirley Temple, chaser; see also **coffee, milk, tea** 1, **water** 1.
**drink,** v. **1.** [To swallow liquid] — Syn. gulp, take, sip, quaff, take a draft, suck, guzzle, swig, swill, slake (one's) thirst, imbibe, swallow, absorb, wash down, lap up, toss off, wet one's whistle\*, moisten the tonsils\*, slurp\*, gargle\*, inhale\*, down\*; see also **swallow.**
**2.** [To consume alcoholic liquor] — Syn. tipple, swill, swig, carouse, dissipate, get drunk, booze\*, take a drop\*, take a nip\*, wet one's whistle\*, belt down\*, down\*, chug-a-lug\*, knock back\*, grease the gills\*, soak\*, liquor up\*, hit the bottle\*, drain the cup\*, tie one on\*, tank up\*, bend the elbow\*, go on a drunk, go on a binge, go on a spree, go on a bender\*, cheer the inner man\*.
**drinker,** n. — Syn. tippler, guzzler, alcoholic, lush\*; see **drunkard.**
**drinking bout,** n. — Syn. debauch, spree, bacchanalia, carousal, bender\*, binge\*, tear\*, drunk\*, jag\*, toot\*; see also **orgy.**
**drink to,** v. — Syn. toast, honor, pledge, salute; see **praise** 1, **toast** 1.
**drip,** v. — Syn. dribble, trickle, plop; see **drop** 1.
**drive,** n. **1.** [A ride in a vehicle] — Syn. ride, trip, outing, ramble, airing, tour, expedition, excursion, jaunt, run, turn, spin, Sunday drive; see also **journey.**
**2.** [In baseball, a low, fast fly] — Syn. line drive, infield drive, home run, bleacher drive\*; see **hit** 3.
**3.** [A driveway] — Syn. approach, avenue, road; see **driveway, road** 1.
**4.** [Impelling force] — Syn. energy, initiative, impulse, urge; see **ambition** 1, **force** 3, **impulse** 1.
**drive,** v. **1.** [To urge on] — Syn. impel, propel, instigate, incite, animate, hasten, urge, egg on, compel, coerce, induce, force, press, stimulate, hurry, actuate, frighten, constrain, provoke, motivate, arouse, make, put up to, inspire, prompt, call up, spirit up, rouse, smoke out, ferret out, operate upon, work on, act upon; see also sense 2; **encourage** 1, **push** 2. — Ant. STOP, hinder, drag.
**2.** [To cause to move; usually said of domestic animals] — Syn. chase, herd, prod, goad, worry, spur, hustle, hound, dog, hunt, kick, beat, rap, push, shove, hurry along, round up, drove, wrangle, hit the trail with\*, ride herd on\*; see also sense 1; **push** 2.
**3.** [To manage a propelled vehicle] — Syn. operate, steer, maneuver, direct, manage, handle, pilot, run, propel, send, spin, wheel, bicycle, bike\*, cycle, pedal, ride,

head for, transport, chauffeur, take for a ride, bus, tour, motor, float, drift, put in motion, give an impetus, start, turn, rattle, set going, speed, accelerate, speed up, roll, slide, coast, get under way, keep going, vehiculate, race, back in, back up, bowl along, barrel along\*, burn up the road\*, go like hell\*, go hellbent for election\*, step on it\*, open her up\*, give it the gun\*, floor it\*, rev\*; see also **ride** 1, **speed.** — Ant. WALK, crawl, stay.
**4.** [To force with blows] — Syn. hit, strike, pound, knock, punch, hammer, ram, whack, maul, butt, shoot, thwack, throw, thump, batter, smite, wham\*, sock\*, soak\*, pop\*, tickle\*, jackhammer\*, give it to\*; see also **beat** 1, **hit** 1.
**5.** [To carry on offensive movement] — Syn. push forward, thrust, counterattack; see **attack** 1.
**drive a bargain,** v. — Syn. deal, close a deal, bargain; see **buy** 1, **negotiate** 1, **sell** 1.
**drive at,** v. **1.** [To intend] — Syn. design, contemplate, propose; see **intend** 1.
**2.** [To imply] — Syn. allude to, indicate, signify; see **mean** 1.
**drive away,** v. — Syn. drive off, disperse, banish; see **scatter** 2.
**drive crazy** or mad, v. — Syn. annoy, infuriate, exasperate, madden; see **bother** 2, **derange** 2.
**drivel** n. — Syn. nonsense, twaddle, blather, foolishness; see **nonsense** 1.
**drivel,** v. **1.** [To drool] — Syn. slobber, drip, slaver; see **drool** 1.
**2.** [To ramble] — Syn. talk foolishly, prate, gabble; see **babble, ramble** 2.
**driven,** modif. — Syn. compelled, motivated, impelled, compulsive, obsessed, possessed, consumed, galvanized, inner-directed, monomaniacal, blown, drifted, herded, pushed, guided, steered, directed, induced, urged on, forced, at the mercy of wind and wave, uptight\*, Type A\*; see also **ambitious** 1, **bound** 2, **urged** 2.
**driver,** n. — Syn. chauffeur, motorist, operator, licensed operator, coachman, whip; bus driver, truck driver, cabdriver, four-in-hand driver, etc.; teamster, trucker, busman, person in the driver's seat, speeder, motorman, wagoner, charioteer, muleteer, autoist\*, cabby\*, hack\*, road hog\*, hit-and-runner\*, joy rider\*, mule skinner\*, jitney jockey\*.
**driveway,** n. — Syn. drive, entrance, street, avenue, roadway, parkway, carriage way, boulevard, approach, lane, track, path, pavement, palms; palm drive, oak drive, etc.; see also **road** 1.
**drizzle,** v. — Syn. spray, shower, sprinkle; see **drop** 1, **rain.**
**droll,** modif. — Syn. funny, comical, laughable, whimsical; see **funny** 1.
See Synonym Study at FUNNY.
**drollery,** n. — Syn. buffoonery, humor, pleasantry; see **joke** 1, 2.
**drone,** n. **1.** [A continuous sound] — Syn. hum, buzz, vibration; see **noise** 1.
**2.** [An idle person] — Syn. idler, loafer, parasite; see **loafer.**
**drone,** v. — Syn. hum, buzz, vibrate, maunder; see **hum, ramble** 2, **sound** 1.
**drool,** v. **1.** [To slobber] — Syn. drivel, drip, slaver, salivate, spit, water at the mouth, dribble, trickle, ooze, run (out); see also **drop** 1.
**2.** [To want] — Syn. drool over, rhapsodize, lick one's chops\*; see **want** 1.
**droop,** v. — Syn. sag, sink, hang down, languish; see **hang** 2, **lean** 1, **weaken** 1.

**drop,** *n.* **1.** [Enough fluid to fall] — *Syn.* drip, trickle, droplet, globule, bead, tear, teardrop, dewdrop, raindrop, dribble.
**2.** [A lowering or falling] — *Syn.* fall, reduction, decrease, slide, descent, slump, lapse, slip, decline, downturn, upset, precipitation, lessening, falling-off, plunge, precipice, declivity, slope, dip; see also **fall** 1.
**3.** [A small quantity] — *Syn.* speck, dash, dab; see **bit** 1.
**at the drop of a hat**\* — *Syn.* without warning, at the slightest provocation, quickly; see **immediately.**
**get the drop on**\* — *Syn.* take advantage of, seize the advantage, defeat; see **succeed** 1, **use** 1.
**drop,** *v.* **1.** [To fall in drops] — *Syn.* drip, fall, dribble, trickle, descend, leak, ooze, percolate, emanate, distill, precipitate (out), seep, drain, filter, sink, bleed, bead, splash, rain, snow, purl, trill down, plash, plump, hail; see also **rain.** — *Ant.* RISE, spurt, squirt.
**2.** [To cause or permit to fall] — *Syn.* let go, let fall, release, give up, shed, relinquish, abandon, discard, loosen, lower, plump, floor, ground, shoot, knock down, fell, unload, deposit, topple; see also **down, dump.** — *Ant.* RAISE, elevate, send up.
**3.** [To tumble] — *Syn.* cave in, plummet, sink, collapse; see **faint, fall** 1.
**4.** [To discontinue] — *Syn.* give up, quit, leave out; see **abandon** 1, **dismiss** 1, 2, **omit** 1.
**5.** [\*To break off an acquaintance] — *Syn.* break with, part from, snub, cut, abandon, cast off, forsake, desert, leave, forget about, divorce, become alienated from, separate, withdraw, repudiate, fling aside, have done with, turn one's back on, lose\*, ditch\*, write off\*, shake\*, throw over\*, brush off\*; see also **abandon** 2. — *Ant.* INVITE, welcome, make friends with.
**6.** [To become lower or less] — *Syn.* decline, diminish, dwindle; see **decrease** 1.
**drop a hint,** *v.* — *Syn.* hint, suggest, intimate, imply; see **hint, propose** 1.
**drop a letter,** *v.* — *Syn.* write to, send a letter, post, communicate with; see **communicate** 2, **correspond** 2, **notify** 1.
**drop a line,** *v.* — *Syn.* write to, send a note, post, get in touch with; see **communicate** 2, **correspond** 2, **notify** 1.
**drop an idea,** *v.* — *Syn.* forgo, give up, abandon; see **discard, forget** 1, 2, **stop** 2.
**drop back,** *v.* — *Syn.* lag, fall back, retire; see **recede** 2, **retreat** 1.
**drop behind,** *v.* — *Syn.* fall behind, fail to keep up, be outpaced, slow down; see **fail** 1, **lag** 1, **lose** 3.
**drop dead**\*, *v.* — *Syn.* expire, collapse, succumb; see **die** 1.
**drop in,** *v.* — *Syn.* call, stop, look in on; see **visit** 4.
**drop off,** *v.* **1.** [To sleep] — *Syn.* fall asleep, doze, drowse; see **sleep.**
**2.** [To deliver] — *Syn.* leave, hand over, present; see **give** 1.
**3.** [To become fewer or less] — *Syn.* decline, decrease, fall off, slip; see **decrease** 1.
**dropout,** *n.* — *Syn.* failing student, truant, quitter, maverick; see **failure** 2, **hippie, nonconformist, quitter.**
**drop out,** *v.* — *Syn.* withdraw, leave, pull out, quit; see **abandon** 1, **resign** 2, **retreat** 1.
**dropped,** *modif.* — *Syn.* discontinued, released, expelled; see **abandoned** 1, **discarded, discharged** 1.
**dross,** *n.* — *Syn.* rubbish, waste, garbage; see **trash** 1.
**drought,** *n.* — *Syn.* dry season, aridity, dryness, desication, dehydration, rainless period, dry spell; see also **dryness.**

**drove,** *n.* — *Syn.* flock, pack, throng; see **crowd** 1, **herd** 1.
**drown,** *v.* **1.** [To cover with liquid] — *Syn.* swamp, inundate, overflow; see **flood.**
**2.** [To lower into a liquid] — *Syn.* dip, plunge, submerge; see **immerse** 1, **sink** 2.
**3.** [To kill *or* die by drowning] — *Syn.* sink, suffocate, asphyxiate, go under; see **die** 1, **kill** 1.
**drowned,** *modif.* — *Syn.* suffocated, immersed, submerged, sunk, foundered, asleep in the deep\*, in a watery grave\*, under hatches\*, in Davy Jones's locker\*; see also **dead** 1, **gone** 2.
**drown out,** *v.* — *Syn.* silence, overwhelm, muffle; see **hush** 1.
**drowse,** *v.* — *Syn.* doze, nap, nod, snooze; see **sleep.**
**drowsy,** *modif.* **1.** [Sleepy] — *Syn.* slumberous, dozing, somnolent; see **tired.**
**2.** [Lethargic] — *Syn.* sluggish, languid, indolent; see **lazy** 1.
*See Synonym Study at* SLEEPY.
**drub,** *v.* — *Syn.* cudgel, thrash, trounce; see **beat** 2, **defeat** 3.
**drudge,** *n.* — *Syn.* hard worker, toiler, drone, slave, menial, lackey, grub, hack, scullion, grind, crammer, plodder, burner of midnight oil\*, dogsbody\*; see also **laborer.**
**drug,** *n.* **1.** [Medicinal substance] — *Syn.* medication, remedy, prescription, pill; see **medicine** 2.
**2.** [Any stimulant or depressant] — *Syn.* narcotic, sedative, tranquilizer, pill, potion, powder, opiate, controlled substance, analgesic, painkiller\*, anodyne, inhalant, fumes, smelling salts, hallucinogen, psychedelic drug, mind-altering drug, mind-expanding drug, mind-blowing drug, psychoactive drug, psychotropic drug, sleeping pill, antidepressant, diet pill, designer drug, tonic, arouser, restorative, stupefacient, hypnotic, soporific, hard drug, soft drug, dope\*, upper\*, downer\*, ups and downs\*.
Commonly abused drugs include: alcohol, amphetamines, barbiturates, nicotine; *hallucinogens:* marijuana, pot\*, grass\*, dope\*, weed\*, killer weed\*, boo\*, maryjane\*, reefer\*, doobie\*, ganja\*, hemp\*; THC, synthetic marijuana, peyote, cactus\*, buttons\*; mescaline, psilocybin, mushrooms\*, magic mushroom\*, dots\*, purple dots\*; D-lysergic acid diethylamide, LSD, acid\*, hawk\*, the chief\*; PCP, angel dust\*; dimethyl triptamine\*, DMT\*, grandaddy\*, STP; *stimulants:* cocaine, coke\*, baby powder\*, snort\*, C\*, corinne\*, happy dust\*, crack\*, ice\*, snow\*, nose candy\*; Benzedrine, bennies\*, pep pills\*; Ibogaine, Harmine, telepathine, JB-318, JB-329, Piperidyl Benzilate Esters; amphetamine, ecstasy, MDMA, Dexedrine, dex\*, mother's little helper\*, dexies\*; methedrine, A\*, meth\*, crank\*, crystal\*, speed\*; amyl nitrate, poppers\*; *depressants:* Nembutal (trademark), yellowjackets\*, Seconal (trademark), redbirds\*, Luminal (trademark), purple hearts\*, red hearts\*, Amytal (trademark), blue heavens\*, Thorazine (trademark), downers\*, Miltown (trademark); *narcotics:* opium; morphine, M\*, Miss Emma\*; heroin, H\*, big H\*, horse\*, lady jane\*, junk\*, smack\*, sugar\*.
**drug,** *v.* — *Syn.* sedate, tranquilize, medicate, anesthetize, stupefy, desensitize, narcotize, numb, benumb, knock out, dose, dope\*, dope up\*; see also **deaden** 1.
**drugged,** *modif.* — *Syn.* comatose, doped, stupefied, stoned\*; see **high** 9, **unconscious** 1.
**druggist,** *n.* — *Syn.* licensed pharmacist, chemist (Bri-

tish), manufacturing pharmacist, drugstore owner, dispenser, pharmacologist.

**drum,** *n.* Types of drums include: bass, kettledrum, timpani, snare, side, native, tabor, water, bongo, steel, barrel, flower, tom-tom, tabla, tambour, tambourine; boiler*, thud-box*, tub*, hot skin*, traps*; see also **musical instrument.**

**beat the drum for*** — *Syn.* promote, publicize, support, further; see **advertise** 2, **promote** 1.

**drum up,** *v.* — *Syn.* attract, solicit, succeed in finding, muster; see **find** 1, **obtain** 1.

**drunk,** *modif.* — *Syn.* intoxicated, inebriated, drunken, tipsy, befuddled, muddled, overcome, under the influence, flushed, maudlin, beery, given to drink, sottish, bibulous, high*, tight*, blotto*, stoned*, feeling no pain*, lit up*, bombed*, smashed*, plastered*, out of it*, seeing double*, having a jag on*, canned*, crocked*, gassed*, plowed*, under the table*, tanked*, wired*, wasted*, out cold*, soused*, sloshed*, looped*, pickled*, stewed*, loaded*, boozed up*, in one's cups*, mellow*, schnockered*, sewed up*, higher than a kite*, three sheets to the wind*, boozy*, ripped*, sozzled*, cockeyed*, polluted*, squiffy*, blind drunk*, drunk as a lord*, drunk as a skunk*; see also **dizzy.** — *Ant.* SOBER, steady, temperate.

---

*SYN.* — **drunk** is the simple, direct word, usually used in the predicate, for one who is overcome by alcoholic liquor *[he is drunk]*; **drunken,** usually used attributively, is equivalent to **drunk** but sometimes implies habitual, intemperate drinking of liquor *[a drunken bum]*; the Latinate-terms **intoxicated** and **inebriated** are somewhat more formal and are often used to connote less offensive degrees of drunkenness; there are many euphemistic and slang terms in English expressing varying degrees of drunkenness: e.g., **tipsy** (slight), **tight** (moderate, but without great loss of muscular coordination), **blind drunk** (great), **blotto** (to the point of unconsciousness)

---

**drunkard,** *n.* — *Syn.* drinker, alcoholic, sot, dipsomaniac, heavy drinker, problem drinker, inebriate, toper, souse, tippler, carouser, reveler, drunken sot, drunk*, soak*, sponge*, boozer*, lush*, wino*, barfly*, hooch-hound*, rum-pot*, rummy*, pub-crawler*, rounder*, alky*; see also **addict.**

**drunken,** *modif.* — *Syn.* drunk, intoxicated, inebriated; see **drunk.**

*See Synonym Study at* DRUNK.

**drunkenness,** *n.* — *Syn.* inebriety, inebriation, intoxication, intemperance, insobriety, alcoholism, dipsomania, tipsiness, crapulence, heavy drinking, boozing*, guzzling*, pickle*, glow*, mellowness*, jag*, head full of bees*; see also **drinking bout.** — *Ant.* ABSTINENCE, sobriety, temperance.

**dry,** *modif.* **1.** [Having little or no moisture] — *Syn.* arid, parched, waterless, dried up, evaporated, desiccated, juiceless, barren, dehydrated, anhydrous, drained, rainless, not irrigated, droughty, bare, thirsty, waterproof, rainproof, baked, hard, shriveled, desiccant, desert, dusty, sapless, unmoistened, sere, depleted, dry as dust, bone-dry*; see also **sterile** 2. — *Ant.* WET, moist, damp.

**2.** [Thirsty] — *Syn.* parched, dehydrated, athirst; see **thirsty.**

**3.** [Lacking in interest] — *Syn.* boring, uninteresting, tedious, flat; see **dull** 4.

**4.** [Possessed of intellectual humor] — *Syn.* satirical, subtle, sarcastic, cynical, sly, salty, ironic, wry, droll, hu-

morous, restrained, sardonic, biting; see also **funny** 1, **witty.** — *Ant.* RAUCOUS, crude, slapstick.

**5.** [Having restrictions on alcoholic liquors] — *Syn.* prohibitionist, prohibited, temperate, abstinent, abstemious, sober, restricted, having local option, bone-dry*, arid*, straight*, teetotal*.

**not dry behind the ears*** — *Syn.* immature, young, naive; see **inexperienced, naive.**

---

*SYN.* — **dry** suggests a lack or insufficiency of moisture, in either a favorable or unfavorable sense, and hence figuratively connotes a lack of life or spirit *[a dry climate, a dry river bed, a dry lecture]*; **arid** implies an abnormal, intense dryness, esp. with reference to a region or climate, and strongly implies barrenness or lifelessness *[an arid waste, arid prose]*

---

**dry,** *v.* **1.** [To become dry] — *Syn.* lose moisture, dehydrate, evaporate, dry up, dry out, shrivel, wither, wilt, undergo evaporation; see also **evaporate** 1, **wither.**

**2.** [To cause to become dry] — *Syn.* wipe, drain, air-dry, dehydrate, freeze-dry, blot, sponge, towel, desiccate, exsiccate, parch, scorch, condense, concentrate, exhaust, torrefy; see also **drain** 1, **empty** 2.

**dry goods,** *n.* — *Syn.* cloth, clothes, yard goods, yardage, bolt goods, furnishings, textiles, fabrics, cloth materials. Dry goods include: woolens, woven goods, knit goods, worsted, rayon, acetate, Orlon (trademark), jersey, nylon, artificial silk, synthetics, synthetic cloth, thread; see also **cotton, linen, silk, wool** 2.

**dryness,** *n.* — *Syn.* aridity, drought, dehydration, lack of moisture, desiccation, exsiccation, parchedness; see also **drought, thirst.**

**dual,** *modif.* — *Syn.* binary, twofold, coupled; see **double, twin.**

**dualism,** *n.* — *Syn.* duality, doubleness, duplexity, twofoldness, biformity, polarity; see also **pair.**

**dub,** *v.* — *Syn.* denominate, entitle, christen, call; see **name** 1.

**dubiety,** *n.* — *Syn.* doubt, doubtfulness, indecision, incertitude; see **doubt** 1, 2, **uncertainty** 1.

*See Synonym Study at* UNCERTAINTY.

**dubious,** *modif.* **1.** [Doubtful] — *Syn.* hesitant, skeptical, indecisive; see **doubtful** 2, **suspicious** 1.

**2.** [Vague] — *Syn.* ambiguous, indefinite, unclear; see **doubtful** 1, **obscure** 1, **questionable** 1.

**3.** [Arousing suspicion] — *Syn.* questionable, suspect, shady*; see **questionable** 2, **suspicious** 2.

*See Synonym Study at* DOUBTFUL.

**dubiously,** *modif.* — *Syn.* doubtfully, doubtingly, indecisively; see **suspiciously.**

**duck,** *n.* Types and breeds of ducks include: freshwater, sea, gadwall, garganey, shoveler, spoonbill, widgeon, baldpate, bufflehead, butterball, whistler, broadbill, ruddy, old, squaw, harlequin, ringneck, black, wood, mandarin, musk, pintail, tufted, spotbill, mottled, masked, yellow-billed, redhead, pochard, canvasback, Peking, eider, fulvous, tree, Mexican, Aylesbury; cinnamon teal, green-winged teal, scoter, surf, coot, scaup, merganser, sheldrake; see also **bird** 1, 2.

**like water off a duck's back*** — *Syn.* ineffective, ineffectual, weak; see **useless** 1.

**duck,** *v.* **1.** [To lower the head or body quickly] — *Syn.* bob, bend, stoop; see **bow** 1.

**2.** [To immerse quickly] — *Syn.* plunge, submerge, dunk; see **dip** 1, **immerse** 1.

**3.** [To avoid] — *Syn.* dodge, evade, elude; see **avoid, evade** 1.

**duct**, *n.* — *Syn.* tube, canal, channel; see **channel** 1, **conduit, pipe** 1.

**ductile**, *modif.* — *Syn.* plastic, pliable, malleable, tensile; see **flexible** 1, **pliable** 1.
*See Synonym Study at* PLIABLE.

**ductility**, *n.* — *Syn.* malleability, elasticity, pliancy; see **flexibility** 1.

**dud**, *n.* — *Syn.* failure, flop, washout\*; see **disappointment** 2, **failure** 1.

**dude**, *n.* **1.** [A fop] — *Syn.* dandy, beau, peacock; see **fop.**
**2.** [\*Any man] — *Syn.* fellow, guy\*, chap; see **man** 2.

**duds**\*, *n.* — *Syn.* garb, garments, gear; see **clothes.**

**due**, *modif.* **1.** [Unpaid] — *Syn.* payable, owed, owing, outstanding, overdue, collectable, unsatisfied, unsettled, not met, matured, receivable, to be paid, chargeable, in arrears; see also **unpaid** 1, 2.
**2.** [Suitable] — *Syn.* fitting, proper, rightful, adequate; see **deserved, enough** 1, **fit** 1.
**3.** [Expected] — *Syn.* scheduled, anticipated, slated, promised; see **expected** 2, **planned.**
**become** (*or* **fall**) **due** — *Syn.* mature, become payable, reach maturity, be owing, accrue.

**duel**, *n.* — *Syn.* combat, engagement, contest, *affair d'honneur* (French); see **fight** 1.

**dues**, *n.* — *Syn.* fee, membership fee, contribution, obligation, toll, duty, levy, charges, subscription, assessment, tax, rates, ante\*, kickback\*, protection\*; see also **pay** 1, **tax** 1.

**due to**, *prep.* — *Syn.* because of, as a result of, resulting from, attributable to; see **because.**

**dugout**, *n.* — *Syn.* cave, cellar, burrow; see **hole** 3.

**dulcet**, *modif.* — *Syn.* melodious, sweet-sounding, euphonious; see **harmonious** 1, **musical** 1.

**dull**, *modif.* **1.** [Without point or edge] — *Syn.* blunt, blunted, dulled, unsharpened, pointless, unpointed, round, square, flat, obtuse, edgeless, turned, nicked, battered, used, broken, toothless, edentate. — *Ant.* SHARP, sharpened, keen.
**2.** [Lacking brightness or color] — *Syn.* gloomy, sober, somber, drab, matte, dismal, bleak, dark, dingy, dim, dusky, dun, colorless, plain, obscure, cloudy, lackluster, tarnished, faded, unglazed, lusterless, opaque, leaden, grave, grimy, pitchy, sooty, inky, dead, black, coal-black, unlit, unlighted, sordid, dirty, muddy, murky, gray, ashen, wan, lifeless, rusty, flat, without snap\*; see also **dark** 1. — *Ant.* BRIGHT, colorful, gleaming.
**3.** [Lacking intelligence or sensitivity; *said usually of living beings*] — *Syn.* stupid, stolid, obtuse, sluggish, heavy, slow, retarded, witless, sleepy, backward, dense, dullwitted, tedious, boring, unintelligent, ignorant, unintellectual, vacuous, doltish, besotted, scatterbrained, feeble-minded, half-witted, addled, addlebrained, thickwitted, slow-witted, thick-skulled, imbecilic, insensate, dim, prosy, prosaic, unimaginative, fatuous, insensitive, unfeeling, unresponsive, numb, wooden, blunted, listless, apathetic, phlegmatic, not bright, torpid, spiritless, brainless, shallow, indolent, unentertaining, non compos mentis, simple-minded, simple, moronic, lumpish, stuffy, stodgy, dumb\*, thick\*, dopey\*, lowbrow\*, stupid as an ox\*, blockheaded\*, muscle-bound\*, nitwitted\*, dimwitted\*, dead from the ears up\*, not all there\*; see also **stupid** 1. — *Ant.* WITTY, quick, smart.
**4.** [Lacking interest; *said usually of writing, speaking, or inanimate things*] — *Syn.* tedious, boring, tiresome, prosy, heavy, leaden, prosaic, trite, hackneyed, monotonous, humdrum, dreary, dismal, dry, arid, barren, colorless, insipid, vapid, flat, bland, uninteresting, deadly, longwinded, prolix, stupid, commonplace, ordinary, common, usual, unenlivened, stuffy, stodgy, old, ancient, stale, moth-eaten, out-of-date, antediluvian, archaic, hoary, worn-out, banal, tired, driveling, senseless, pointless, uninspiring, platitudinous, pedestrian, jejune, tame, routine, familiar, well-known, conventional, unimaginative, depressing, sluggish, plodding, repetitious, unvarying, boresome, abused, repetitive, oft-repeated, well-worn, fatiguing, wearisome, wearing, soporific, producing ennui, lifeless, wooden, characterless, wearying, tiring, unexciting, irksome, stereotyped, stereotypical, stock, the usual thing, the same old thing, slow, draggy, dry as dust, cut and dried, without any kick\*, dead as a doornail\*, blah\*, ho-hum\*. — *Ant.* EXCITING, fascinating, exhilarating.
**5.** [Not loud or distinct] — *Syn.* muffled, muted, low, soft; see **faint** 3.
**6.** [Showing little activity] — *Syn.* slow, placid, languid, lethargic, still, sluggish, listless, lackadaisical, regular, depressed, inactive, lifeless, spiritless, uneventful, unexciting, slothful, without incident, quiet, even, torpid, inert, bovine, cowlike, routine, usual, accustomed, slack, monotonous, unresponsive, stagnant, dead, boring, falling off, apathetic, stolid, flat, lumpish, lumpy, bearish, poky, off\*. — *Ant.* STIMULATING, lively, active.

*SYN.* — **dull** is specifically applied to a point or edge that has lost its previous sharpness [a *dull* knife] and generally connotes a lack of keenness, zest, spirit, intensity, etc. [a *dull* book, a *dull* ache]; **blunt** is often equivalent to **dull**, but specifically refers to a point or edge that is intentionally not sharp [a *blunt* fencing saber]; **obtuse** literally applies to a pointed end whose sides form an angle greater than 90°, and figuratively connotes lack of understanding or sensitivity [too *obtuse* to comprehend] See also Synonym Study at STUPID.

**dullard**, *n.* — *Syn.* nitwit, dolt, idiot; see **fool** 1.

**dullness**, *n.* **1.** [Quality of being boring] — *Syn.* flatness, sameness, routine, uninterestingness, aridity, dryness, depression, dimness, drabness, tediousness, commonplaceness, mediocrity, tedium, monotony, deadliness, dreariness, insipidity, vapidity, staleness, lifelessness, tameness, familiarity; see also **boredom, monotony, slowness** 1. — *Ant.* ACTION, liveliness, interest.
**2.** [Stupidity] — *Syn.* stupidness, insensibility, slow-wittedness; see **stupidity** 1.

**dully**, *modif.* — *Syn.* stupidly, densely, obtusely, slowly, lethargically, sluggishly, listlessly, dimly.

**duly**, *modif.* — *Syn.* rightfully, properly, suitably; see **appropriately, justly** 1.

**dumb**, *modif.* **1.** [Unable to speak] — *Syn.* silent, mute, voiceless, speechless, inarticulate, wordless, quiet, mum, aphonic, deaf and dumb\*; see also **mute** 1, **quiet** 2.
**2.** [Temporarily speechless] — *Syn.* speechless, tongue-tied, dumbstruck, wordless, at a loss for words; see also **surprised.**
**3.** [\*Stupid] — *Syn.* simple-minded, feeble-minded, moronic; see **dull** 3, **stupid** 1.

*SYN.* — **dumb** implies a lack of the power of speech and is now more often applied to brute animals and inanimate objects than to persons with impaired speech organs [a *dumb* beast]; **voiceless** is applied to one who has no voice, either from birth or through deprivation [the throat operation left him *voiceless*]; **speechless** usually implies temporary or momentary deprivation of the ability to speak *[speechless* with horror*]*; **mute** is applied to persons incapable of speech because of congenital deafness and not through absence or impairment of the speech organs

---

**dumbbell**\*, *n.* — *Syn.* blockhead, fool, dunce; see **fool** 1.

**dumbfound**, *v.* — *Syn.* amaze, astonish, puzzle, nonplus; see **confuse, surprise** 1.

*See Synonym Study at* CONFUSE.

**dumbfounded**, *modif.* — *Syn.* amazed, astonished, puzzled; see **bewildered, surprised.**

**dummy**, *modif.* — *Syn.* counterfeit, faked, simulated; see **false** 3.

**dummy**, *n.* **1.** [*A stupid person] — *Syn.* dolt, blockhead, oaf; see **fool** 1.
**2.** [A figure in human form] — *Syn.* mannequin, model, waxwork, effigy; see **doll, model** 3.
**3.** [Imitation] — *Syn.* sham, counterfeit, duplicate; see **copy, imitation** 2.

**duo**, *n.* — *Syn.* couple, twosome, mates; see **pair.**

**dump**, *n.* — *Syn.* garbage dump, city dump, dumping ground, refuse heap, rubbish pile, rubbish heap, ash heap, junk pile, junkyard, sanitary landfill, sump, cesspit, landfill, cesspool, scrapheap, dumpsite, midden, discard pile, toxic waste dump, hovel, hole.

**dump**, *v.* — *Syn.* empty, unload, deposit, unpack, discharge, throw down in a mass, fling down, drop, evacuate, drain, eject, exude, expel, throw out, discard, throw overboard; see also **discard, empty** 2. — *Ant.* LOAD, fill, pack.

**dumps**\*, *n.* — *Syn.* despondency, dejection, despair; see **desperation** 1, **gloom** 2.

**dun**, *modif.* — *Syn.* brownish, sallow, dull; see **brown, drab** 2.

**dunce**, *n.* — *Syn.* dolt, dullard, moron; see **fool** 1.

**dune**, *n.* — *Syn.* rise, knoll, sand ridge; see **hill.**

**dung**, *n.* — *Syn.* offal, excrement, manure, guano, fertilizer, night soil, compost, droppings, excreta, chips, pellets, spoor, evidence, leavings, muck, ordure, feces, filth, garbage, sludge, slop, sewage, cowflop\*, cowpat\*, cowpie\*, pancakes\*, road apples\*, buttons\*; see also **excrement, fertilizer.**

**dungeon**, *n.* — *Syn.* stockade, vault, prison; see **cell** 3, **jail.**

**dupe**, *v.* — *Syn.* fool, trick, victimize, hoodwink; see **cheat, deceive.**

*See Synonym Study at* CHEAT.

**duplicate**, *n.* — *Syn.* double, second, mate, match, twin, copy, facsimile, replica, reproduction, photocopy, carbon, carbon copy, ditto, likeness, counterpart, counterfeit, analogue, second edition, parallel, correlate, repetition, duplication, recurrence, Xerox (trademark), lookalike, chip off the old block\*, ringer\*, dead ringer\*, clone\*; see also **copy, imitation** 2, **reproduction** 2. — *Ant.* ORIGINAL, pattern, prototype.

**in duplicate** — *Syn.* duplicated, doubled, copied; see **reproduced.**

*See Synonym Study at* COPY.

**duplicate**, *v.* **1.** [To copy] — *Syn.* reproduce, counterfeit, make a replica of; see **copy** 2.
**2.** [To double] — *Syn.* make twofold, multiply, make twice as much; see **increase** 1.
**3.** [To repeat] — *Syn.* redo, remake, replicate, equal; see **repeat** 1, **reproduce** 2.

**duplicity**, *n.* — *Syn.* double-dealing, deceit, dishonesty; see **deception** 1, **dishonesty, hypocrisy.**

**durability**, *n.* — *Syn.* durableness, lastingness, sturdiness, persistence; see **endurance** 2, **stability** 1, **strength.**

**durable**, *modif.* — *Syn.* enduring, long-lasting, impervious, tough; see **permanent** 2, **strong** 2.

**duration**, *n.* — *Syn.* span, continuation, continuance; see **term** 2.

**duress**, *n.* — *Syn.* coercion, compulsion, intimidation, constraint; see **pressure** 2, **restraint** 2.

**during**, *modif. & prep.* — *Syn.* as, at the time, at the same time as, the whole time, the time between, in the course of, in the middle of, when, all along, pending, throughout, through, in the meanwhile, in the interim, all the while, for the time being; see also **meanwhile, while** 1.

**dusk**, *n.* — *Syn.* twilight, nightfall, gloom; see **night** 1, **sunset.**

**dusky**, *modif.* **1.** [Shadowy] — *Syn.* gloomy, shady, murky; see **dark** 1, **dull** 2.
**2.** [Dark-colored] — *Syn.* dark, swarthy, tawny, swart, ebony, sable, dark-complexioned.

---

*SYN.* — **dusky** suggests a darkness of color or an absence of light, verging on blackness *[dusky* twilight*]* or, in reference to complexion, a shadowy quality; **swarthy** and **tawny** both refer only to color, **swarthy** suggesting a dark brown verging on black *[a swarthy* complexion*]* and **tawny**, a yellowish brown or tan *[tawny* hair*]* See also Synonym Study at DARK.

---

**dust**, *n.* — *Syn.* dirt, lint, soil, sand, particles, flakes, granules, loess, ashes, cinders, grime, soot, grit, filings, sawdust; devil's snow\*, house moss\*, Mormon rain\*; see also **earth** 2, **filth, powder.**

**bite the dust**\* — *Syn.* be killed, fall in battle, succumb, go under; see **die** 1, **fail** 1.

**lick the dust** — *Syn.* be servile, grovel, placate; see **grovel.**

**make the dust fly** — *Syn.* move swiftly, work hard, be active *or* energetic; see **act** 1, **hurry** 1, **move** 1.

**dust**, *v.* — *Syn.* sprinkle, sift, powder; see **scatter** 2.

**dusty**, *modif.* — *Syn.* undusted, grimy, unused, untouched; see **dirty** 1.

**dutiful**, *modif.* — *Syn.* devoted, respectful, conscientious; see **faithful, obedient** 1.

**duty**, *n.* **1.** [A personal sense of what one should do] — *Syn.* obligation, conscience, liability, charge, responsibility, accountability, faithfulness, pledge, commitment, burden, good faith, devoir, honesty, integrity, sense of duty, call of duty, bounden duty, the hell within, inward monitor, still small voice; see also **responsibility** 1, 2. — *Ant.* DISLOYALTY, pleasure, irresponsibility.
**2.** [Whatever one has to do] — *Syn.* work, office, task, occupation, function, business, province, part, calling, charge, service, mission, obligation, contract, commitment, station, trust, trouble, burden, undertaking, commission, engagement, assignment, routine, chore, pains, responsibility; see also **job** 2. — *Ant.* ENTERTAINMENT, amusement, sport.

*See Synonym Study at* FUNCTION.

**3.** [A levy, especially on goods] — *Syn.* charge, revenue, custom, tariff; see **tax** 1.

**off duty** — *Syn.* at liberty, off work, not engaged, free, off, at leisure, inactive; see also **free** 2, **unemployed.**

**on duty** — *Syn.* employed, engaged, at work; see **busy** 1.

**dwarf**, *modif.* — *Syn.* dwarfed, low, diminutive; see **little** 1.

**dwarf**, *n.* — *Syn.* midget, pygmy, Lilliputian, gnome; see **fairy, midget.**

**dwarf**, *v.* **1.** [To keep small] — *Syn.* stunt, retard, hinder, arrest; see **restrain** 1.
**2.** [To cause to appear small] — *Syn.* minimize, over-

shadow, dominate, predominate over, tower over, detract from, belittle, rise over *or* above, look down upon. — *Ant.* INTENSIFY, magnify, enhance.

**dwarfish,** *modif.* — *Syn.* diminutive, tiny, small, minute; see **little** 1.

**dwell,** *v.* — *Syn.* live, reside, inhabit, stay, lodge, room, abide, sojourn, stop, settle, tarry, remain, live in, live at, continue, go on living, rent, tenant, have a lease on, make one's home at, have one's address at, keep house, be at home, quarter, hang out*, hang up one's hat*, flop*, bunk*, crash*, tent, pitch a tent, have digs at*; see also **reside.**

**dweller,** *n.* — *Syn.* tenant, inhabitant, occupant; see **resident.**

**dwelling,** *n.* — *Syn.* house, residence, abode, lodging; see **home** 1.

**dwell on,** *v.* — *Syn.* linger over, tarry over, ponder, harp on; see **brood** 2, **consider** 3, **emphasize.**

**dwindle,** *v.* — *Syn.* decrease, wane, lessen, diminish; see **decrease** 1.

See Synonym Study at DECREASE.

**dye,** *n.* — *Syn.* colorant, stain, tint; see **color** 1.

**dye,** *v.* — *Syn.* tint, stain, impregnate with color; see **color** 1.

**dying,** *modif.* **1.** [Losing life] — *Syn.* expiring, sinking, moribund, on one's deathbed, passing away, going, perishing, failing, fading, near death, at death's door, *in extremis* (Latin), terminal, withering away, paying the debt of nature, not long for this world, fated, done for*, booked*, giving up the ghost*, cashing in*, on one's last legs*, with one foot in the grave; see also **sick.** — *Ant.* IMMORTAL, living, reviving.

**2.** [Becoming worse or less] — *Syn.* declining, sinking, receding, decreasing, disappearing, diminishing, dwindling, dissolving, disintegrating, vanishing, failing, fading, ebbing, decaying, smoldering, recessive, overripe, decadent, passé, doomed, neglected, superannuated, done for*, fizzling out*, in its death throes. — *Ant.* GROWING, eternal, enduring.

**dynamic,** *modif.* — *Syn.* energetic, vigorous, active, powerful, potent, compelling, forceful, changing, progressive, productive, magnetic, electric, vibrant, effective, influential, charismatic, high-powered, peppy*, hopped up*, hyped up*; see also **active** 2, **powerful** 1. — *Ant.* LISTLESS, quiescent, static.

**dynamite,** *n.* — *Syn.* nitroglycerin, trinitrotoluene, TNT, detonator, blasting powder; see also **explosive.**

**dynamite,** *v.* — *Syn.* blow up, explode, raze; see **destroy** 1.

**dynamo,** *n.* — *Syn.* doer, activist, live wire*, go-getter*; see **doer.**

**dynasty,** *n.* — *Syn.* line, house, regime, sovereignty; see **administration** 3, **family** 1, **government** 1.

**dysentery,** *n.* — *Syn.* diarrhea, looseness, diarrheal infection, amebic dysentery, shigellosis, giardiasis, flux, Montezuma's revenge*, Aztec two-step*, turista*, the trots*, the runs*, Delhi belly*, collywobbles*, African drizzles*, GI's*; see also **disease.**

# E

**each,** *modif.* **1.** [Every] — *Syn.* all, any, one by one, separate, particular, specific, private, several, respective, various, piece by piece, individual, personal, without exception.
**2.** [For each time, person, or the like] — *Syn.* individually, proportionately, respectively, for one, per unit, singly, per capita, apiece, separately, every, without exception, by the, per, a whack\*, a throw\*, a shot\*.
**each,** *pron.* — *Syn.* each one, one, each in his own way, each in her own way, every last one, one another, each other.
**eager,** *modif.* — *Syn.* enthusiastic, ardent, avid, keen, anxious, desirous, hopeful, wishful, spirited, enthused, exhilarated, excited, longing, impatient, fervent, earnest, dying to\*; see also **enthusiastic** 1, 2, 3.

---

*SYN.* — **eager** implies great enthusiasm, zeal, or sometimes impatience, in the desire for a pursuit of something *[eager* to begin work*]*: **avid** suggests an intense, sometimes greedy, desire to enjoy or possess something *[avid* for power*]*; **keen** implies deep interest and a spirited readiness to achieve something *[the team was* keen on winning*]*; **anxious** suggests eagerness, but with some uneasiness over the outcome *[anxious* to excel*]*

---

**eagerly,** *modif.* — *Syn.* anxiously, zealously, intently, sincerely, expectantly, anticipatorily, vigorously, readily, earnestly, willingly, heartily, enthusiastically, energetically, strenuously, fiercely, cordially, readily, promptly, rapidly, breathlessly, speedily, hungrily, thirstily, fervently, ardently, zestfully, actively, spiritedly, cravingly, with enthusiasm, longingly, impatiently, gladly, with zeal, with zest, with gusto, with a will, with a good will, with open arms, keenly, with all one's heart, with heart and soul, from the bottom of one's heart, with delight, with relish, with might and main, full tilt\*. — *Ant.* UNWILLINGLY, listlessly, grudgingly.
**eagerness,** *n.* — *Syn.* zest, anticipation, excitement; see **enthusiasm** 1.
**eagle,** *n.* — *Syn. Aquila* (Latin), hawk, bird of Jove, eaglet, falcon, griffin, erne, bird of prey, raptor.
Kinds of eagles include: American, bald, black, golden, white-tailed, tawny, harpy, imperial, osprey.
**eagle-eyed,** *modif.* — *Syn.* discerning, sharp-eyed, hawk-eyed; see **keen-sighted, observant** 1, **sharp-sighted.**
**ear,** *n.* **1.** [The organ of hearing] — *Syn.* outer ear, middle ear, inner ear, auricle, eardrum, labyrinth, semicircular canal, hammer, anvil, stirrup, cochlea, concha, pinna, acoustic organ, lug (Scottish), auditory apparatus, tympanum, flapper\*, listener\*, cauliflower ear\*.
**2.** [A projection] — *Syn.* lug, prong, projection; see **bulge, handle** 1.
**3.** [Hearing] — *Syn.* discrimination, heed, notice; see **attention** 1, **hearing** 3.
**all ears\*** — *Syn.* attentive, hearing, paying attention; see **listening, observant** 2.

**bend someone's ear\*** — *Syn.* jabber, chatter, be discursive; see **babble, talk** 1.
**fall on deaf ears\*** — *Syn.* be ignored, be disregarded, fail to attract notice, be received with indifference; see **fail** 1.
**give** or **lend an ear** — *Syn.* give attention, heed, attend, take notice; see **listen** 1.
**have** or **keep an ear to the ground\*** — *Syn.* be aware of, be attuned to, observe, keep one's eyes open\*; see **listen** 1, **mind** 3.
**in one ear and out the other\*** — *Syn.* ignored, forgotten, received with indifference; see **forgotten, neglected.**
**play by ear** — *Syn.* improvise, recall, play from memory; see **play** 3, **remember** 1, 2.
**play it by ear\*** — *Syn.* improvise, extemporize, concoct, ad-lib\*; see **invent** 1.
**set on its ear\*** — *Syn.* stir up, agitate, arouse; see **excite** 1, 2.
**turn a deaf ear to\*** — *Syn.* be heedless, ignore, refuse to listen to; see **neglect** 1.
**earache,** *n.* — *Syn.* otalgia, otitis, ear infection; see **pain** 2.
**eared,** *modif.* — *Syn.* aurate, spiked, auriculate, having earlike appendages, spicate.
**earl,** *n.* — *Syn.* nobleman, noble, count; see **lord** 2.
**earlier,** *modif.* — *Syn.* former, previous, prior; see **preceding.**
**early,** *modif.* **1.** [Near the beginning] — *Syn.* initial, first, ancient, prehistoric, primitive, primeval, primal, pioneer, pioneering, trailblazing, beginning, prime, new, fresh, budding, raw; see also **old** 3. — *Ant.* LATE, modern, superannuated.
**2.** [Sooner than might have been expected] — *Syn.* premature(ly), beforehand, in advance, ahead, far ahead, before the time, ahead of time, quick, precocious, preceding, anticipatory, advanced, too soon, untimely, unanticipated, immediate, unexpected, precipitant, speedy, hasty, before the appointed time, in good time, on time, direct, prompt(ly), punctual(ly), briefly, shortly, presently, in the bud, unhatched, immature, unlooked-for, betimes, bright and early\*, with the birds\*, on the dot\*, pronto\*, with time to spare\*. — *Ant.* late, SLOW, tardy.
**3.** [Maturing soon] — *Syn.* dwarf, bush, quick-maturing, early-maturing, early-flowering, hardy, short-stemmed, spring, frostproof, northern.
**earmark,** *n.* — *Syn.* characteristic, attribute, quality, sign; see **characteristic.**
**earmark,** *v.* — *Syn.* reserve, set aside, allocate; see **assign** 1, **designate** 1, **maintain** 3.
**earn,** *v.* **1.** [To deserve as reward] — *Syn.* win, merit, gain; see **deserve.**
**2.** [To receive in payment] — *Syn.* obtain, make, collect, get, receive, procure, realize, obtain a return, make money by, be paid, acquire, profit, net, gross, clear, gain, score, draw, gather, secure, derive, reap, gain as

due return, get as one's due, gain by labor, gain by service, take home, bring home, bring in, turn a penny, be the breadwinner, pick up*, pull down*, bring home the bacon*, make a fast buck*, coin money*, make the pot boil*, scrape together*, pocket*, bag*. — *Ant.* SPEND, consume, exhaust.

**earnest**, *modif.* **1.** [Zealous] — *Syn.* sincere, determined, heartfelt, warm; see **diligent, enthusiastic** 2, 3.
**2.** [Solemn] — *Syn.* serious, grave, sober, weighty; see **solemn** 1.
*See Synonym Study at* SERIOUS.

**earnestly**, *modif.* — *Syn.* solemnly, sincerely, soberly, thoughtfully; see **busily, seriously** 2, **sincerely.**

**earnestness**, *n.* **1.** [Fervor] — *Syn.* ardor, intensity, zeal; see **enthusiasm** 1.
**2.** [Solemnity] — *Syn.* gravity, sobriety, sincerity; see **seriousness** 2.
**3.** [Determination] — *Syn.* resolution, persistence, tenacity; see **determination** 2, **diligence.**

**earnings**, *n.* — *Syn.* wages, profits, net proceeds, receipts; see **income, pay** 2, **profit** 2.

**earring**, *n.* — *Syn.* pendant, hoop, stud, ornament; see **jewelry.**

**earth**, *n.* **1.** [The world] — *Syn.* globe, sphere, planet, universe, *terra* (Latin), mundane world, creation, terrestrial sphere, orb, *monde* (French), cosmos, sublunary world, biosphere, Gaea, mother earth, Spaceship Earth.
**2.** [The earthly crust] — *Syn.* dirt, soil, clean dirt, loam, humus, clay, gravel, sand, ground, terra firma, land, dry land, terrain, mud, muck, topsoil, peat moss, fill, compost, decomposed granite, turf, mold, alluvium, marl, terrane, surface, subsoil, shore, coast, littoral, deposit, glebe.
**come back** or **down to earth** — *Syn.* be practical, be sensible, return to one's senses, quit dreaming; see **awake** 1, **calm down.**
**down to earth** — *Syn.* practical, realistic, mundane, unpretentious; see **practical, rational** 1, **unaffected** 1.
**on earth** — *Syn.* of all things, of everything, in the world; see **whatever.**

---

*SYN.* — **earth** is applied to the globe or planet we live on, but in religious use is opposed to heaven or hell; **universe** refers to the whole system of planets, stars, space, etc. and to everything that exists in it; **world** is equivalent to **earth**, esp. as relates to human activities, but is sometimes a generalized synonym for **universe**

---

**earthborn**, *modif.* — *Syn.* human, temporal, perishable; see **mortal** 2.

**earthen**, *modif.* — *Syn.* clay, stone, mud, dirt, rock, fictile, made of earth, made of baked clay, made of burnt clay.

**earthenware**, *n.* — *Syn.* crockery, stoneware, ceramics, terra cotta; see **pottery.**

**earthly**, *modif.* **1.** [Terrestrial] — *Syn.* human, mortal, sublunary, terrene, terraqueous, tellurian, subastral, telluric, global, alluvial, mundane, worldly, natural, under the sun, in all creation. — *Ant.* unearthly, superhuman, unnatural.
**2.** [Temporal] — *Syn.* worldly, mundane, unspiritual, secular, material, physical; see also **worldly** 1.
**3.** [Imaginable] — *Syn.* conceivable, possible, feasible; see **imaginable, practical.**

---

*SYN.* — **earthly** is applied to that which belongs to the earth or to the present life and is chiefly contrasted with *heavenly [earthly* pleasures*]*; **terrestrial**, having as its opposite *celestial* (both Latin-derived parallels of the

preceding terms), has special application in formal and scientific usage *[terrestrial* magnetism*]*; **worldly** implies reference to the material concerns or pursuits of humankind and is chiefly contrasted with *spiritual [worldly* wisdom*]*; **mundane**, although often used as a close synonym of **worldly**, now esp. stresses the commonplace or practical aspects of life *[*to return to *mundane* matters after a flight of fancy*]*

---

**earthquake**, *n.* — *Syn.* quake, tremor, temblor, tremblor, trembler, earthquake shock, shock, fault, slip, movement of the earth's surface, movement of the earth's crust, earth tremor, microseism, seismic upheaval, aftershock; an earthquake registering one, two, etc., points on the Richter scale; secondary tremor, tertiary tremor, volcanic quake, shake*, wiggler*.

**earthwork**, *n.* — *Syn.* embankment, dugout, fortification; see **barrier, fortification** 2, **trench.**

**earthworm**, *n.* — *Syn.* annelid, angleworm, night crawler, dew worm, wiggler; see also **worm** 1.

**earthy**, *modif.* **1.** [Characteristic of earth] — *Syn.* clayey, sandy, dusty, made of earth, of the nature of soil, terrene, earthlike, cloddy, muddy.
**2.** [Unrefined] — *Syn.* coarse, bawdy, lusty, hearty, robust, natural, down-to-earth; see also **crude** 1, **natural** 3, **ribald.**

**ease**, *n.* **1.** [Freedom from pain or anxiety] — *Syn.* comfort, rest, quietness, peace, relaxed physical state, tranquil rest, relaxation, leisure, repose, easiness, satisfaction, well-being, calm, calmness, restfulness, serenity, security, tranquillity, ataraxia, bed of roses, solace, consolation. — *Ant.* PAIN, discomfort, stress.
**2.** [Freedom from difficulty] — *Syn.* facility, adroitness, expertise, expertness, dispatch, efficiency, knack, readiness, quickness, skillfulness, dexterity, artfulness, cleverness, smoothness, effortlessness, child's play, clear sailing, snap*, breeze*, cinch*; see also **cinch.** — *Ant.* difficulty, trouble, clumsiness.
**3.** [Freedom from stiffness or awkwardness] — *Syn.* naturalness, poise, familiarity; see **composure, informality.**
**4.** [Freedom from poverty] — *Syn.* affluence, prosperity, comfort; see **luxury** 1, **wealth** 2.
**at ease** — *Syn.* relaxed, collected, untroubled, carefree; see **calm** 1, **comfortable** 1.
**take one's ease** — *Syn.* be calm, rest, be comfortable; see **relax** 1.

**ease**, *v.* **1.** [To relieve of pain] — *Syn.* alleviate, allay, relieve, mitigate, lessen, assuage, tranquilize, sedate, drug, administer an opiate, administer a sedative, anesthetize, render less painful, give relief, comfort, give an anesthetic, fit a splint, relieve pressure, cure, attend to, doctor, nurse, ameliorate, restore to health, palliate, soothe, abate, reduce, lighten, poultice, meliorate. — *Ant.* HURT, injure, aggravate.
**2.** [To lessen pressure or tension] — *Syn.* slacken, loosen, relax, prop up, lift, hold up, set at ease, make comfortable, comfort, raise, disburden, unburden, release, soften, give repose to, free from anxiety, relieve, relieve one's mind, lighten, let up on, give rest to, quiet, calm, pacify, soothe, cheer; see also **comfort.** — *Ant.* WEIGHT, tighten, distress.
**3.** [To move carefully] — *Syn.* maneuver, guide, induce, extricate, disentangle, set right, fit, insert, join, facilitate, slide, inch, edge, shift, handle. — *Ant.* force, shove, blunder.
**4.** [To make easier] — *Syn.* facilitate, expedite, smooth the way; see **help** 1, **promote** 1.

**easily**, *modif.* **1.** [Without difficulty] — *Syn.* readily, with ease, effortlessly, facilely, simply, with no effort, with no apparent effort, without trouble, handily, evenly, regularly, steadily, efficiently, smoothly, dexterously, plainly, quickly, comfortably, calmly, coolly, surely, just like that*, hand over fist*, hands down*, with one hand tied behind one's back*, like nothing*, like walking on air*, without even trying*. — *Ant.* laboriously, wearily, arduously.

**2.** [Without a doubt] — *Syn.* by far, undoubtedly, clearly; see **surely.**

**easiness,** *n.* — *Syn.* carelessness, nonchalance, facility; see **ability** 2, **carelessness, ease** 1, 2.

**east,** *modif.* **1.** [Situated to the east] — *Syn.* eastern, eastward, in the east, on the east side of, toward the sunrise, east side, lying toward the east, situated toward the east, easterly, easternmost, eastmost.

**2.** [Going toward the east] — *Syn.* eastbound, eastward, easterly, to the east, toward the east, headed east, in an easterly direction.

**3.** [Coming from the east] — *Syn.* easterly, westbound, headed west, out of the east, westward, westerly, tending to the west, tending toward the west.

**East,** *n.* **1.** [The eastern part of the United States] — *Syn.* the eastern states, the Atlantic seaboard, the Eastern seaboard, East Coast, land east of the Alleghenies, land east of the Appalachians, land east of the Mississippi, the Northeast, the Southeast, older sections of the country, Rust Belt*, Snowbelt*; see also **South.**

Areas in the East include: East Coast, Atlantic Coast, Boston to Washington corridor, Boston to Washington megalopolis, Appalachia, Middle Atlantic States, Maine, New England, down East, the Thirteen Colonies; see also **Boston, New York, Washington.**

**2.** [The eastern part of Eurasia] — *Syn.* Asia, Asia Minor, Far East, Middle East, Mideast, Near East, southeast Asia, Orient, Levant, Indian subcontinent, Arabia, Mesopotamia, Siberia, Mongolia; for countries in the East, see **Asia.**

**Easter,** *n.* — *Syn.* Easter Sunday, Easter week, Eastertide, Pascha, *Pasqua* (Italian), *Pascua* (Spanish), *Pâques* (French), *Ostern* (German), paschal festival.

**eastern,** *modif.* **1.** [Concerning the direction to the east] — *Syn.* easterly, eastward, on the east side of; see **east** 1.

**2.** [Concerning the eastern part of the United States] — *Syn.* East, Atlantic, East Coast, Atlantic Seaboard, Northeastern, Southeastern, Allegheny, Appalachian, New England, Middle Atlantic, South Atlantic, down East.

**3.** [Concerning the Near East or Middle East] — *Syn.* Southwest Asian, Levantine, Egyptian, of the Holy Land, Arabic, Hellenic, Hebraic, Israeli, Palestinian, in Asia Minor; see also **ancient** 2.

**4.** [Concerning the Far East] — *Syn.* Far Eastern, East Asian, Asian; see **Asian** 1, 2.

**easy,** *modif.* **1.** [Free from constraint or care] — *Syn.* at ease, secure, prosperous, comfortable, commodious, well-to-do, leisurely, unembarrassed, unconstrained, unaffected, natural, spontaneous, informal, free and easy, dégagé, loose, forthright, calm, peaceful, tranquil, careless, content(ed), carefree, untroubled, relaxed, equable, hospitable, on easy street, in clover*. — *Ant.* hard, impoverished, strained.

**2.** [Providing no difficulty] — *Syn.* simple, facile, effortless, obvious, apparent, clear, uncomplicated, elementary, yielding, easily done, not burdensome, requiring no effort, presenting few difficulties, smooth, manageable, accessible, wieldy, straightforward, foolproof, slight, mere, light, undemanding, nothing to it*, plain

sailing*, simple as ABC*, easy as pie*, like taking candy from a baby*, like shooting fish in a rain barrel*, a piece of cake*, cushy*, soft*, Mickey Mouse*. — *Ant.* DIFFICULT, complicated, hard.

**3.** [Lax] — *Syn.* indulgent, easygoing, permissive; see **lenient.**

**4.** [*Slowly and carefully] — *Syn.* cautiously, gently, lightly; see **carefully** 2.

**on easy street** — *Syn.* well-to-do, wealthy, prosperous; see **rich** 1.

**take it easy** — *Syn.* relax, rest, slow down; see **calm down.**

---

*SYN.* — **easy** is the broadest term here in its application to that which demands little effort or presents little difficulty [*easy* work]; **facile** means occurring, moving, working, etc. easily and quickly, sometimes unfavorably suggesting a lack of thoroughness or depth [a *facile* style]; **effortless**, in contrast, favorably suggests expert skill or knowledge as responsible for performance that seems to require no effort [ the *effortless* grace of the skater]; **smooth** suggests freedom from or riddance of irregularities, obstacles, or difficulties as bringing ease of movement [a *smooth* path to success]; **simple** suggests freedom from complication, elaboration, or involvement, as making something easy to understand [a *simple* explanation]

---

**easygoing,** *modif.* — *Syn.* relaxed, carefree, eventempered, laid-back*; see **amiable, calm** 1, **nonchalant.**

**eat,** *v.* **1.** [To take as food] — *Syn.* consume, devour, bite, chew, swallow, dine, feed, feed on, have a meal, enjoy a meal, lunch, breakfast, sup, snack, munch, nibble, gobble, gorge, stuff oneself, eat out, dine out, have a bite, feast on, fatten on, do justice to, do oneself proud, dispose of, peck at, pick, eat up, digest, masticate, ruminate, graze, browse, dispatch, feast, banquet, batten, discuss, partake of, fare, bolt, wolf down, gulp, fall to, tuck into, tuck away, break bread, live on, take in, have, ingest, taste, try, savor, gormandize, glut, overeat, cram, pack away*, put away*, polish off*, make short work of*, attack*, dig in*, make a pig of oneself*, eat out of house and home*, entertain the inner man*, feed the inner man*, ply a good knife and fork*, eat like a bird*, nosh*, put on the feed bag*, pig out*, stuff one's face*, feed one's face*, chow down*, scarf down*, inhale*, lick the plate*. — *Ant.* FAST, starve, vomit.

**2.** [To reduce gradually] — *Syn.* eat away, corrode, consume, devour, wear away, erode, gnaw, rust away, destroy, ravage, dissolve, melt, eat up, use up, waste, dissipate, squander, drain, putter away, fool away, run through. — *Ant.* INCREASE, swell, build.

**3.** [*To bother] — *Syn.* worry, vex, disturb; see **bother** 2, 3.

**eatable,** *modif.* — *Syn.* edible, palatable, nutritious, digestible; see **edible.**

**eatables,** *n.* — *Syn.* foodstuff, provender, victuals; see **food.**

**eat humble pie,** *v.* — *Syn.* be humiliated, ask pardon, beg pardon, admit an error; see **apologize, recant.**

**eating,** *n.* — *Syn.* consuming, consumption, devouring, dining, feasting on, gorging on, feeding on, biting, chewing, masticating, breakfasting, lunching, supping, snacking, nibbling, munching, banqueting, eating out, dining out, having a meal, having a bite, having a snack, having a coffee, taking a lunch break, taking tea, partaking of food, breaking bread, enjoying a meal, enjoying a repast, taking refreshment, bolting, swallowing, gulping down, gobbling, stuffing oneself, overeating, gluttony, binging, gourmandise, overindulgence, putting on the feed bag★, doing a meal full justice★, pigging out★, noshing★; see also **digestion.**

**eat one's words,** *v.* — *Syn.* retract a statement, abjure, rescind; see **apologize, recant.**

**eat out of house and home★,** *v.* — *Syn.* devour, be ravenous, have a huge appetite; see **eat** 1.

**eat out of one's hand,** *v.* — *Syn.* be tame, submit, acquiesce; see **yield** 1.

**eats★,** *n.* — *Syn.* food, victuals, meal; see **food.**

**eaves,** *n.* — *Syn.* overhang, rim, soffit; see **roof.**

**eavesdrop,** *v.* — *Syn.* overhear, wiretap, listen, listen in on, try to overhear, listen stealthily, monitor, bend an ear★, bug★, tap★, prick up one's ears★, snoop★.

**eavesdropper,** *n.* — *Syn.* listener, wiretapper, hearer, auditor, sleuth, Peeping Tom, snoop★.

**ebb,** *n.* — *Syn.* recession, decline, outward flow, shrinkage, wane, waste, reflux, reduction, lessening, ebb tide, diminution, abatement, regression, withdrawal, decrease, depreciation, decay, falling-off. — *Ant.* flow, INCREASE, rise.

**ebb,** *v.* — *Syn.* recede, subside, abate, retire, flow back, sink, decline, decrease, drop off, melt, fall away, peter out, wane, languish, fall off, decay, dwindle. — *Ant.* FLOW, rise, increase.

*See Synonym Study at* WANE.

**ebony,** *modif.* — *Syn.* jet, midnight, coal black; see **black** 1.

**ebullience,** *n.* — *Syn.* exhilaration, exuberance, high spirits; see **enthusiasm** 1.

**ebullient,** *modif.* — *Syn.* exuberant, effervescent, vivacious; see **enthusiastic** 1, 3, **lively** 2.

**ebullition,** *n.* **1.** [Bubbling up] — *Syn.* effervescence, seething, decoction, boiling, effervescing, fermentation, ebullience; see also **fermentation.**
**2.** [A sudden display, as of emotion] — *Syn.* outburst, overflowing, effusion; see **outbreak** 1.

**eccentric,** *modif.* — *Syn.* odd, unconventional, idiosyncratic, strange; see **unusual** 2.

**eccentric,** *n.* — *Syn.* individualist, original, oddball★, kook★; see **character** 4, **nonconformist.**

**eccentricity,** *n.* — *Syn.* peculiarity, oddity, idiosyncrasy; see **irregularity** 2.

*See Synonym Study at* IDIOSYNCRASY.

**ecclesiastic,** *n.* — *Syn.* clergyman, churchman, preacher; see **minister** 1.

**ecclesiastical,** *modif.* — *Syn.* ministerial, clerical, churchly; see **clerical** 2, **religious** 1.

**echo,** *n.* — *Syn.* repetition, imitation, reverberation; see **answer** 1.

**echo,** *v.* — *Syn.* repeat, mimic, reverberate, resound; see **imitate** 2, **sound** 1.

**éclat,** *n.* **1.** [Brilliant display or success] — *Syn.* brilliance, dash, splendor, pomp; see **ostentation** 2.
**2.** [Renown] — *Syn.* celebrity, fame, acclaim, distinction; see **fame** 1.

**eclectic,** *modif.* — *Syn.* selective, catholic, diverse; see **complex** 1, **general** 1, **universal** 3, **various.**

**eclipse,** *n.* — *Syn.* solar eclipse, eclipse of the sun, lunar eclipse, eclipse of the moon, total eclipse, partial eclipse, annular eclipse, penumbra, obscuration, dimming, darkening, concealment, shroud, shadow, veil, extinguishment, obliteration.

**eclipse,** *v.* — *Syn.* overshadow, surpass, obscure; see **exceed, shade** 2.

**ecological,** *modif.* — *Syn.* environmental, green, ecofriendly; see **biological.**

**ecologist,** *n.* — *Syn.* environmentalist, conservationist, naturalist, preservationist, environmental engineer, ecological engineer, oceanographer, student of environment, student of ecosystems, antipollutionist, biologist, botanist, specialist in marine biology, specialist in population control, specialist in smog control; ecofreak★, treehugger★; see also **scientist.**

**ecology,** *n.* — *Syn.* environmental science, environmental study, environmental engineering, ecological engineering, human ecology, human environment, antipollution projects, pollution control, survival studies, study of ecosystems, conservation of natural resources, environmental policy, environmental protection, earthly livability; see also **biology, botany, environment, science** 1, **zoology.**

**economic,** *modif.* — *Syn.* industrial, business, financial, budgetary; see **commercial** 1.

**economical,** *modif.* **1.** [Careful of expenditures] — *Syn.* thrifty, frugal, saving, sparing, prudent, careful, economizing, provident, niggardly, meager, miserly, stingy, mean, close, shabby, avaricious, penurious, chary, watchful, circumspect, parsimonious, conservative, tight★, closefisted★, penny-pinching★, cheeseparing★; see also **stingy.** — *Ant.* liberal, GENEROUS, wasteful.
**2.** [Advantageously priced] — *Syn.* reasonable, inexpensive, cheap, sound, low-cost, fair, moderate, marked down, on sale, money-saving; see also **cheap** 1.
**3.** [Making good use of materials] — *Syn.* practical, efficient, cost-effective, thrifty; see **efficient** 2.

---

SYN. — **economical** implies prudent management of one's money or resources so as to avoid any waste in expenditure or use /it is often *economical* to buy in large quantities/; **thrifty** implies industry and clever management of one's money or resources, usually so as to result in some savings /the *thrifty* housewife watched for sales/; **frugal** stresses the idea of saving and suggests spending which excludes any luxury or lavishness and provides only the simplest fare, dress, etc. /the Amish are a *frugal* people/; **sparing** implies such restraint in spending as restricts itself to the bare minimum or involves deprivation /*sparing* to the point of niggardliness/; **provident** implies management with the foresight to provide for future needs /never *provident*, he quickly spent his inheritance/

---

**economics,** *n.* — *Syn.* commerce, finance, business, public economy, political economy, science of wealth, economic theory, development of public wealth, commercial theory, business theory, financial theory; science of the production, distribution, and consumption of goods and services, principles of business, principles of finance, principles of industry, study of industry, theory of trade, financial principles, economic principles, the dismal science★; see also **social science.**

Terms relating to economic theories include: balance of trade, fair trade, free trade, trade deficit, Gresham's Law, bad money drives out good, laissez faire, law of supply and demand, supply and demand, theory of the marginal producer, Ricardian economics, Keynesian economics, Laffer Curve, supply-side economics, trickle-down theory, Reaganomics, doctrine of rents, sound money, cheap money, bimetallism, gold standard, fiat money, protective tariff, production for use, right to work, cost of living index, consumer price index, business cycle, debtor's economy, creditor's economy, economy of scarcity, economy of abundance, guns or butter economics, market economy, free-enterprise economy, controlled economy, collective bargaining, mass production, cooperative buying and marketing, Marxian economics, input-output model, socioeconomics, microeconomics, macroeconomics, corporate state, recession, depression, inflation, stagflation, deflation.

**economist,** *n.* — *Syn.* statistician, business analyst, financial expert, efficiency expert, student of business, specialist in economics, political economist, economic thinker, social planner, economic reformer, economic theorist, banker, professor, political scientist, Keynesian, supply-sider, physiocrat, brain truster*.

**economize,** *v.* — *Syn.* save, conserve, husband, manage, stint, scrimp, retrench, cut back, skimp, be frugal, be prudent, pinch, cut costs, cut corners, meet expenses, keep within one's means, cut down, meet a budget, run a tight ship*, make both ends meet*, tighten one's belt*, save for a rainy day*, pinch pennies*; see also **accumulate** 1, **maintain** 3. — *Ant.* SPEND, waste, splurge.

**economy,** *n.* **1.** [A system of producing, distributing, and consuming wealth] — *Syn.* economic system, marketplace, market, gross national product, GNP, standard of living, cost of living, consumer price index, per capita income, financial resources, earnings, prosperity; see also **administration** 1, **economics.**
**2.** [Thrifty administration] — *Syn.* thriftiness, thrift, retrenchment, austerity, caution, prudence, regulation of finances, conservation, prudent use of resources, political economy, saving, economizing, stinginess, frugality, husbandry, care, providence, parsimony, restraint, miserliness, scrimping, cheeseparing*. — *Ant.* CARELESSNESS, lavishness, waste.
**3.** [An example of economy, sense 2] — *Syn.* curtailment, retrenchment, cutback, rollback, austerity program, business recession, reduction in spending, deduction, saving, abridgment, layoff, payroll shrinkage, reduction of forces, wage decrease, cut in wages, volume ordering, cost-effectiveness, economies of scale, moratorium, good gas mileage, good fuel consumption, excursion fare, lowered materials cost, lowered contract price; belt-tightening*; see also **automation, depression** 3. — *Ant.* INCREASE, outlay, raise.

**ecru,** *modif.* — *Syn.* beige, tan, brownish, tawny, flesh colored, natural, unbleached, fawn, grayish yellow, old ivory, chamois; see also **tan.**

**ecstasy,** *n.* — *Syn.* joy, rapture, delight; see **happiness** 2, **rapture** 1, 2.
*See Synonym Study at* RAPTURE.

**ecstatic,** *modif.* — *Syn.* rapturous, elated, overjoyed, euphoric; see **happy** 1.

**eczema,** *n.* — *Syn.* dermatitis, skin disease, inflammation; see **disease.**

**eddy,** *n.* — *Syn.* whirl, whirlpool, maelstrom, vortex, rapids, swirl, back current, countercurrent, backwash, backwater, gorge.

**edge,** *n.* **1.** [The outer portion] — *Syn.* border, frontier, extremity, portal, threshold, brink, boundary, end, term, limit, edging, molding, brim, rim, margin, ring, frame, side, corner, point, bend, crook, hook, split, peak, tip, turn, crust, verge, bound, ledge, skirt, outskirt(s), lip, limb, hem, welt, seam, selvage, terminator, fringe, frill, flange, flounce, list, listing, trimming, mouth, shore, strand, dike, quay, bank, beach, wharf, dock, mole, curb, crest, deckle, berm, groin, arris, gunwale, periphery, circumference, perimeter; see also **rim.** — *Ant.* surface, CENTER, interior.
**2.** [Anything linear and sharp] — *Syn.* blade, cutting edge, razor edge; see **knife, razor.**

**3.** [*Advantage] — *Syn.* upper hand, handicap, head start; see **advantage** 1, 2.

**on edge** — *Syn.* nervous, tense, uptight*; see **excited, irritable.**

**set one's teeth on edge** — *Syn.* irritate, annoy, provoke; see **bother** 2.

**take the edge off** — *Syn.* weaken, subdue, dull; see **soften** 2.
*See Synonym Study at* RIM.

**edge,** *v.* — *Syn.* trim, border, fringe, bind; see **decorate, trim** 2.

**edge out,** *v.* — *Syn.* defeat narrowly, nose out, slip by, squeeze by; see **defeat** 3.

**edgy,** *modif.* **1.** [Nervous] — *Syn.* irritable, touchy, tense, on edge; see **excitable, excited, irritable.**
**2.** [Sharp-edged] — *Syn.* edgelike, angular, keen; see **sharp** 1.

**edible,** *modif.* — *Syn.* eatable, digestible, comestible, consumable, fit to eat, good to eat, esculent, dietary, nutritious, good, safe, delicious, succulent, palatable, appetizing, tempting, satisfying, tasty, nutritive, culinary, kosher, OK, yummy*; see also **delicious** 1. — *Ant.* inedible, ROTTEN, indigestible.

**edict,** *n.* — *Syn.* decree, proclamation, order; see **command** 1, **declaration** 2.

**edification,** *n.* — *Syn.* improvement, instruction, enlightenment, uplift; see **education** 1, **improvement** 1.

**edifice,** *n.* — *Syn.* structure, architectural monument, pile; see **building** 1.
*See Synonym Study at* BUILDING.

**edify,** *v.* — *Syn.* instruct, improve, educate; see **teach** 1.

**edit,** *v.* **1.** [To prepare for publication] — *Syn.* revise, rewrite, correct, alter, redact, emend, excise, delete, expunge, edit out, make up, arrange materials for publication, prepare for the press, compose, compile, select, adapt, rearrange, set up, censor, expurgate, bowdlerize, amplify, polish, touch up, choose, annotate, condense, abridge, discard, strike out, write, rephrase, revamp, rework, restyle, rehash, prepare copy, correct proof, copyedit, proofread, correct galleys, write headlines, cut, trim, redraft, update, blue-pencil*, boil down*, kill*, bleep out*, massacre*, butcher*, doctor up*, chase commas*.
**2.** [To supervise publication] — *Syn.* direct, publish, see through the press, formulate, dictate, style, draw up, prescribe, regulate, bring out, issue, distribute, disseminate.

**edition,** *n.* — *Syn.* printing, publication, issue of a literary work, published form, version, format, impression, number, imprint, reprint, reissue, release, press run.

**editor,** *n.* — *Syn.* redactor, reviser, copyreader, rewriter, supervisor, director, editor-in-chief, annotator, compiler, proofreader, copyholder, reader, editorial writer, columnist, deskman, newspaperman, newspaperwoman, rewrite man, rewrite woman, lexicographer, desk*, blue-penciler*.
Types of editors include: managing, general, associate, assistant, night, newspaper, magazine, city, telegraph, sports, state, wire, women's, society, feature, Sunday, picture, photo, graphics, art, technical, copy, line; see also **author** 2, **journalist, writer.**

**editorial,** *n.* — *Syn.* essay, column, commentary, Op-Ed piece; see **article** 2, **exposition** 2.

**educate,** *v.* — *Syn.* teach, tutor, instruct, train; see **teach** 1.
*See Synonym Study at* TEACH.

**educated,** *modif.* **1.** [Having a formal education] — *Syn.* learned, trained, accomplished, skilled, literate, well-read, well-taught, informed, knowledgeable,

scientific, scholarly, lettered, literary, intelligent, well-informed, well-versed, well-grounded, erudite, developed, formed, disciplined, shaped, prepared, instructed, civilized, fitted, versed in, informed in, acquainted with, nurtured, corrected, enriched, professional, expert, polished, cultured, finished, initiated, enlightened, tutored, schooled, book-learned, bookish, bluestocking(ed)★, highbrow★, up on★. — *Ant.* illiterate, IGNORANT, UNLETTERED.
2. [Cultured] — *Syn.* cultivated, refined, polished; see **cultured.**
**education,** *n.* **1.** [The process of directing learning] — *Syn.* schooling, study, training, direction, instruction, guidance, teaching, tutoring, coaching, tutelage, learning, reading, enlightenment, edification, inculcation, discipline, tuition, preparation, adult education, book learning, self-instruction, informing, indoctrination, brainwashing, proselytism, propagandism, catechism, cultivation, background, rearing, nurture, apprenticeship; reading, writing, and 'rithmetic★; the three R's★, book larnin'★.
2. [Knowledge acquired through education] — *Syn.* learning, wisdom, scholarship, literacy; see **knowledge** 1.
3. [The teaching profession] — *Syn.* teaching, pedagogy, tutoring, instruction, training, pedagogics, didactics, teaching methods, the field of education, progressive education, lecturing, professing (British).
4. [Refinement] — *Syn.* cultivation, finish, enlightenment; see **culture** 3.
**educational,** *modif.* **1.** [Academic] — *Syn.* scholastic, collegiate, pedagogical, didactic, instructional, institutional, school, tutorial, scholarly.
2. [Instructive] — *Syn.* enlightening, educative, edifying, enriching; see **cultural, informative.**
**educator,** *n.* — *Syn.* pedagogue, instructor, principal, educationist★; see **administrator, professor, teacher** 1, 2.
**educe,** *v.* — *Syn.* evoke, elicit, extract; see **obtain** 1.
*See Synonym Study at* EXTRACT.
**eerie,** *modif.* — *Syn.* uncanny, ghostly, weird, spooky; see **frightful** 1, **uncanny.**
*See Synonym Study at* WEIRD.
**efface,** *v.* — *Syn.* rub out, obliterate, erase; see **cancel** 1, **destroy** 1, **erase** 1.
*See Synonym Study at* ERASE.
**effect,** *n.* **1.** [Result] — *Syn.* conclusion, consequence, outcome; see **result.**
2. [Impact] — *Syn.* influence, impression, force; see **impact** 2.
**give effect to**— *Syn.* practice, employ, activate; see **use** 1.
**in effect**— *Syn.* in fact, as a result, actually, virtually; see **essentially, really** 1.
**take effect**— *Syn.* work, produce results, become operative; see **act** 1.
**to the effect (that)** — *Syn.* as a result, so that, therefore; see **for.**
*See Synonym Study at* RESULT.
**effect,** *v.* **1.** [To bring about] — *Syn.* produce, cause, make; see **begin** 1, **cause** 2.
2. [To achieve] — *Syn.* accomplish, conclude, fulfill; see **achieve** 1, **perform** 1.
*See Synonym Study at* PERFORM.
**effective,** *modif.* — *Syn.* efficient, efficacious, effectual, serviceable, producing the expected result, producing the desired result, useful, operative, active, in force, in effect, sufficient, adequate, productive, capable, competent, yielding, practical, valid, telling, striking, forceful,

powerful, compelling, cogent, trenchant. — *Ant.* inoperative, USELESS, inefficient.

---

*SYN.* — **effective** is applied to that which produces a definite effect or result /an *effective* speaker/; **efficacious** refers to that which is capable of producing the desired effect or result /an *efficacious* remedy/; **effectual** specifically implies the production of the desired effect or result in a decisive manner /an *effectual* reply to his charge/; **efficient** implies skill and economy of energy in producing the desired result and when applied to persons implies competence /an *efficient* machine, an *efficient* worker/

---

**effectively,** *modif.* — *Syn.* efficiently, effectually, completely, finally, expertly, conclusively, definitely, energetically, persuasively, to good effect, to good purpose, with telling effect, tellingly, dramatically, adequately, capably, forcefully, cogently, productively; see also **excellently.**
**effects,** *n.* — *Syn.* personal property, belongings, baggage, possessions; see **property** 1.
**effectual,** *modif.* **1.** [Effective] — *Syn.* adequate, efficient, qualified; see **effective.**
2. [Legally valid] — *Syn.* authoritative, binding, valid; see **legal** 1.
*See Synonym Study at* EFFECTIVE.
**effeminate,** *modif.* — *Syn.* unmanly, womanish, emasculate, epicene; see **feminine** 2.
*See Synonym Study at* FEMALE.
**effervesce,** *v.* — *Syn.* fizz, foam, froth; see **bubble.**
**effervescence,** *n.* **1.** [Foaming] — *Syn.* bubbling, fizzing, foaming; see **ebullition** 1, **froth.**
2. [Vivacity] — *Syn.* liveliness, animation, ebullience; see **action** 1, **enthusiasm** 1.
**effervescent,** *modif.* **1.** [Foaming] — *Syn.* bubbling, fizzing, carbonated; see **frothy** 1.
2. [Lively] — *Syn.* bubbly, vivacious, high-spirited, irrepressible; see **active** 2, **happy** 1.
**effete,** *modif.* **1.** [Lacking vigor] — *Syn.* weakened, decadent, exhausted, spent, soft, overrefined, enervated, debilitated, worn out, played out, bloodless, etiolated; see also **weak** 1.
2. [Incapable of production] — *Syn.* unproductive, sterile, barren; see **sterile** 1, 2.
**efficacious,** *modif.* — *Syn.* effective, effectual, efficient, productive; see **effective.**
*See Synonym Study at* EFFECTIVE.
**efficacy,** *n.* — *Syn.* effectiveness, potency, productiveness; see **ability** 2, **efficiency** 2.
**efficiency,** *n.* **1.** [A high degree of effectiveness] — *Syn.* competence, capability, capableness; see **ability** 2.
2. [The relation of results to expenditure] — *Syn.* productivity, effectiveness, power, potency, performance, suitability, adaptability, thoroughness, energy, effectualness, efficaciousness, adequacy, productiveness, powerfulness, efficacy, competence, proficiency, elasticity, conductivity, response, potential energy, faculty, facility, practical utility, profitability, yield.
**efficient,** *modif.* **1.** [Said of persons] — *Syn.* competent, businesslike, proficient, productive, good at, apt, adequate, fitted, able, capable, qualified, skillful, effective, clever, talented, energetic, skilled, adapted, familiar with, deft, adept, expert, experienced, having the requisite skill, workmanlike, having adequate energy, equal to, drilled, exercised, practiced, practical, accomplished, potent, active, dynamic, decisive, tough, shrewd, highpowered★; see also sense 2; **able** 2. — *Ant.* INCOMPETENT, inefficient, unproductive.
2. [Said of things] — *Syn.* economical, fitting, suitable,

suited, effectual, effective, efficacious, adequate, serviceable, useful, profitable, saving, thrifty, labor-saving, time-saving, valuable, expedient, handy, conducive, well-designed, streamlined, cost-effective, unwasteful, practical, good for.— *Ant.* inefficient, ineffectual, WASTEFUL.

*See Synonym Study at* EFFECTIVE.

**effigy,** *n.* — *Syn.* representation, likeness, dummy, puppet; see **image** 2, **model** 3.

**efflorescence,** *n.* — *Syn.* blooming, flowering, sprouting; see **blossoming, flower** 1.

**effluence,** *n.* — *Syn.* discharge, issue, emanation; see **emanation** 1, **flow.**

**effluent,** *modif.* — *Syn.* emanating, issuing forth, profluent; see **flowing.**

**effluvium,** *n.* — *Syn.* emanation, exhalation, exhaust, odor; see **drainage, emanation** 2, **smell** 2, **vapor.**

**effort,** *n.* **1.** [The act of striving] — *Syn.* exertion, endeavor, industry, labor, pains, trouble, force, toil, work, application, energy, travail, struggle, striving, attempting, stress, pull, stretch, push, strain, tension, tug, sweat, sweat of one's brow, toil and trouble, elbow grease*.— *Ant.* ease, CARELESSNESS, sloth.
**2.** [An instance of effort, sense 1] — *Syn.* attempt, try, bid, endeavor, enterprise, undertaking, struggle, battle, trial, spurt, essay, venture, aim, purpose, resolution, exercise, discipline, drill, training, crack*, stab*, shot*, go*, whirl*, the old college try*.

---

*SYN.* — **effort** implies a conscious attempt to achieve a particular end /make some *effort* to be friendly/; **exertion** implies an energetic, vigorous use of power, strength, etc., often without reference to any particular end /she feels faint after any *exertion*/; **endeavor** suggests an earnest, sustained attempt to accomplish a particular, usually meritorious, end /a life spent in the *endeavor* to do good/; **pains** suggests a laborious, diligent attempt /to take *pains* with one's work/

---

**effortless,** *modif.* — *Syn.* easy, simple, offhand, smooth; see **easy** 2.

*See Synonym Study at* EASY.

**effrontery,** *n.* — *Syn.* impudence, audacity, boldness, presumption; see **rudeness.**

*See Synonym Study at* TEMERITY.

**effulgence,** *n.* — *Syn.* radiance, blaze, luster; see **light** 1.

**effulgent,** *modif.* — *Syn.* luminous, glowing, brilliant; see **bright** 1.

**effusion,** *n.* **1.** [An outflow] — *Syn.* diffusion, stream, emanation; see **emanation** 1, **flow.**
**2.** [Unrestrained expression] — *Syn.* gush, outpouring, volubility; see **outbreak** 1, **wordiness.**

**effusive,** *modif.* — *Syn.* unrestrained, unreserved, demonstrative, overdemonstrative, gushing, gushy, expansive, communicative, talkative, voluble, profuse, fulsome, rhapsodic, slobbering; see also **emotional, verbose.**

**egalitarian,** *modif.* — *Syn.* impartial, equal, just; see **fair** 1.

**egg,** *n.* — *Syn.* ovum, seed, germ, spawn, roe, bud, embryo, nucleus, cell, berry*, hen fruit*.
Eggs commonly used as food include: hen, duck, goose, quail, turtle, fish, ostrich, guinea hen.
Sizes and grades of eggs include: fancy, select, farm, ranch, western, day-old, fresh, cold-storage, large pullet, medium, small, large, jumbo, white, brown; grade AA, A, B.
Prepared eggs include: fried, scrambled, poached, deviled, coddled, hard boiled, hard-cooked, soft boiled,

soft-cooked, creamed, shirred, stuffed, soufflé, raw, buttered, baked, on toast, dropped, goldenrod; egg salad, ham and eggs, bacon and eggs, eggs Benedict, omelet, frittata, egg foo yong, over easy*, sunnyside up*, up*, bull's eye*, two shipwrecked on a raft*.

**lay an egg***— *Syn.* be unsuccessful, fall flat, bomb*; see **fail** 1.

**put** or **have all one's eggs in one basket***— *Syn.* chance, gamble, venture; see **risk.**

**egg on,** *v.* — *Syn.* encourage, goad, incite; see **drive** 1, 2, **urge** 2, 3.

**egg-shaped,** *modif.* — *Syn.* oval, ovate, elliptical, pear-shaped; see **oblong.**

**ego,** *n.* **1.** [The self] — *Syn.* personality, individuality, self, the "I"; see **character** 1, 2.
**2.** [Egotism] — *Syn.* narcissism, conceit, self-esteem, self-image; see **egotism, pride** 1, 3.

**egoism,** *n.* — *Syn.* selfishness, egocentricity, vanity, pride; see **egotism.**

**egoist,** *n.* — *Syn.* self-seeker, egotist, boaster; see **braggart.**

**egoistic,** *modif.* — *Syn.* self-centered, egocentric, self-absorbed, self-seeking; see **egotistic** 1, 2, **selfish** 1.

**egotism,** *n.* — *Syn.* egoism, conceit, vanity, pride, assurance, self-love, narcissism, self-confidence, self-glorification, self-conceit, self-assertion, self-esteem, self-applause, elation, presumption, self-worship, arrogance, insolence, overconfidence, immodesty, self-regard, haughtiness, ostentation, boastfulness, vainglory, misanthropy, self-centeredness, egocentricity, egomania; see also **pride** 1.— *Ant.* humility, MODESTY, meekness.

**egotist,** *n.* — *Syn.* narcissist, boaster, egoist, egomaniac; see **braggart.**

**egotistic,** *modif.* **1.** [Centered in self] — *Syn.* egoistic, self-centered, egocentric, personal, subjective, individualistic, introverted, solipsistic, inner-directed, isolationist, idiosyncratic. — *Ant.* SOCIAL, extrinsic, cosmopolitan.
**2.** [Having offensive concern for self] — *Syn.* narcissistic, boastful, conceited, vain, self-centered, egocentric, self-absorbed, self-obsessed, self-glorifying, vainglorious, egoistic, self-important, pompous, arrogant, insolent, autocratic, swollen, puffed up, affected, self-magnifying, presumptuous, overweening, supercilious, condescending, patronizing, superior, blustering, prideful, bumptious, grandiose, haughty, snobbish, high-handed, lordly, imperious, magisterial, scornful, contemptuous, disdainful, proud, bullying, sneering, pretentious, assuming, ostentatious, consequential, cocky*, brazen, impertinent, selfish, bombastic, bragging, flaunting, flamboyant, presuming, impudent, vaunting, inflated, stiff, overbearing, swaggering, domineering, bold, overconfident, self-satisfied, taking merit to oneself, like God Almighty*, stuck up*, too big for one's breeches*, too big for one's boots*, looking down one's nose*, high-hat*, snooty*, uppity*, wrapped up in oneself*, impressed with oneself*, full of oneself*, pleased with oneself*, stuck on oneself*, swell-headed*, big-headed*, know-it-all*, on an ego trip*; see also **pompous, proud** 2.— *Ant.* HUMBLE, meek, modest.

**egotistically,** *modif.* — *Syn.* vainly, conceitedly, self-importantly, boastfully, arrogantly, haughtily, with a flourish of trumpets, ostentatiously, pretentiously, airily, loftily, selfishly; see also **arrogantly.**

**egregious,** *modif.* — *Syn.* flagrant, glaring, extreme; see **outrageous.**

**egress,** *n.* **1.** [A going out] — *Syn.* departure, emergence, escape; see **departure** 1.

**2.** [A place of exit] — *Syn.* doorway, passage, way out; see **exit** 1.

**either,** *conj.* and *modif.* — *Syn.* on the one hand, whether or not, unless, it could be that, it might be that, one or the other, each, both.

**either,** *pron.* — *Syn.* one, one or the other, this one, either/or, each of two, as soon one as the other, one of two.

**ejaculate,** *v.* — *Syn.* exclaim, vociferate, call; see **exclaim, yell.**

**ejaculation,** *n.* **1.** [A cry] — *Syn.* exclamation, shout, outburst, interjection; see **cry** 1.
**2.** [An orgasm] — *Syn.* climax, secretion, discharge, emission; see **copulation, emanation** 1, 2.

**eject,** *v.* **1.** [To remove physically] — *Syn.* expel, drive out, evict, discharge, throw out, cast out, oust, dislodge, discard, reject, emit, disgorge, kick out, heave out, send out, put out, force out, weed out, spit out, turn out, rout out, run out, blow out, squeeze out, do away with, banish, throw off, pour forth, spout, vomit, expectorate, excrete, evacuate, dump, unloose, throw overboard, get rid of, eradicate, exterminate, send packing*, show the gate to*, bundle off*, boot out*, give the boot*, bounce*.
**2.** [To remove from a social or economic position] — *Syn.* dismiss, expel, discharge, oust, remove, expatriate, ostracize, excommunicate; see also **dismiss** 1, 2.

---

*SYN.* — **eject,** the term of broadest application here, implies generally a throwing or casting out from within *[forcibly ejected from the room]*; **expel** suggests a driving out, as by force, specif. a forcing out of a country, organization, etc., often in disgrace *[expelled from school]*; **evict** refers to the forcing out, as of a tenant, by legal procedure; **dismiss** suggests a rejection of or refusal to consider some matter *[the judge dismissed the case, dismissed such thoughts from my mind]* and often refers to the removal of an employee *[dismissed for incompetence]*; **oust** implies the getting rid of something undesirable, as by force or the action of law *[to oust corrupt officials]*

---

**ejection,** *n.* — *Syn.* eviction, expulsion, dismissal; see **removal** 1.

**eke out,** *v.* — *Syn.* barely exist, live a makeshift existence, just get by*; see **subsist.**

**elaborate,** *modif.* **1.** [Ornamented] — *Syn.* ornate, gaudy, decorated, garnished, showy, ostentatious, imposing, intricate, fussy, dressy, fancy, elegant, embellished, extravagant, refined, beautified, festooned, spangled, flowery, bedecked, flashy, baroque, rococo; see also **ornate** 1. — *Ant.* plain, ordinary, austere.
**2.** [Detailed] — *Syn.* complicated, extensive, laborious, minute, widely developed, intricate, involved, highly organized, many-faceted, complex, convoluted, painstaking, studied, labored; see also **complex** 1, 2, **detailed.** — *Ant.* simple, GENERAL, careless.

**elaborate,** *v.* — *Syn.* work out, develop, refine, embellish; see **develop** 1.

**elaborate on** or **upon,** *v.* — *Syn.* expand, enlarge upon, go into detail, comment upon; see **detail** 1, **develop** 4, **explain.**

**elaboration,** *n.* — *Syn.* illustration, comment, discussion, amplification; see **explanation** 1, 2.

**élan,** *n.* — *Syn.* spirit, verve, dash, ardor; see **enthusiasm** 1.

**elapse,** *v.* — *Syn.* pass away, slip by, transpire, lapse; see **pass** 2.

**elastic,** *modif.* — *Syn.* flexible, pliant, springy, stretchy; see **flexible** 1.
*See Synonym Study at* FLEXIBLE.

**elasticity,** *n.* — *Syn.* resiliency, buoyancy, pliability; see **flexibility** 1.

**elate,** *v.* — *Syn.* inspire, cheer, exhilarate; see **encourage** 2, **gladden.**

**elated,** *modif.* — *Syn.* exhilarated, jubilant, overjoyed, ecstatic; see **happy** 1.

**elation,** *n.* — *Syn.* euphoria, delight, rapture, exhilaration; see **happiness** 1, 2.

**elbow,** *n.* — *Syn.* joint, bend, ulna, turn, half turn, crook, angle, curve, fork, crutch, funny bone*.
**rub elbows with*** — *Syn.* mingle with, hobnob with, join; see **associate** 1.
**up to the elbows (in)*** — *Syn.* engaged, employed, working at; see **busy** 1.

**elbowroom,** *n.* — *Syn.* room, scope, latitude, breathing space; see **extent, leeway.**

**elder,** *modif.* — *Syn.* older, senior, ranking, more mature; see **older, senior.**

**elder,** *n.* **1.** [Old person] — *Syn.* old man, old woman, old lady, senior citizen, veteran, old timer, senior, retiree, one of the old folks, one of the older generation, sexagenarian, septuagenarian, octogenarian, nonagenarian, centenarian, ancestor, golden ager*, older adult, Methuselah*, graybeard, oldster*, old fogey*, little old lady*, granny*, gramps*; see also **ancestor, oldster.**
**2.** [A superior] — *Syn.* patriarch, matriarch, chief, tribal head, dignitary, senator, counselor, presbyter, church dignitary, elder statesman, dean, doyen, doyenne, father, mother.

**elderly,** *modif.* — *Syn.* aging, aged, retired, venerable; see **aging, old** 1.

**elect,** *v.* — *Syn.* choose, name, select; see **choose** 1.

**elected,** *modif.* — *Syn.* chosen, duly elected, voted in, in on a landslide; see **named** 2.

**election,** *n.* **1.** [The act of choosing] — *Syn.* option, choice, preference; see **choice** 1, **selection** 1.
**2.** [The act of choosing by votes] — *Syn.* poll, polls, ballot, balloting, ticket, vote, voting, voice vote, vote-casting, primaries, hustings (British), suffrage, plebiscite, referendum, franchise, elective franchise, constitutional right, yea or nay.

**electioneer,** *v.* — *Syn.* canvass, barnstorm, stump; see **campaign** 1.

**elective,** *modif.* **1.** [Pertaining to the right to choose by vote] — *Syn.* constituent, voting, elected; see **electoral.**
**2.** [Subject to choice] — *Syn.* voluntary, discretionary, not required, not compulsory; see **optional.**

**elector,** *n.* — *Syn.* voter, suffragist, constituent, balloter; see **voter.**

**electoral,** *modif.* — *Syn.* electing, selecting, discretionary, elective, by vote, by popular election, appointing, appointive, constituent.

**electorate,** *n.* — *Syn.* voters, registered voters, those casting ballots, body politic; see **constituency, voter.**

**electric,** *modif.* — *Syn.* electrical, electrified, charged, magnetic, voltaic, galvanic, electronic, power driven, battery-operated, cordless, photoelectric, hydroelectric, telegraphic, instantaneous, surcharged, pulsing, vibrating, dynamic, energetic, electrifying, thrilling, galvanizing; see also **exciting.** — *Ant.* mechanical, manual, steam.

**electric chair,** *n.* — *Syn.* means of execution, instrument of execution, form of capital punishment, the chair, hot seat*, roaster*, toaster*; see also **chair** 4.

**electrician,** *n.* — *Syn.* electrical technician, electronics technician, electrical expert, repairman, lineman, wireman, maintenance man, tester, troubleshooter, Alec*, juicer*.

**electricity,** *n.* **1.** [Electricity as a public utility] — *Syn.* power, current, service, heat, light, ignition, spark, charge, utilities, public utilities, alternating current, A.C., direct current, D.C., voltage, 110 volts, 220 volts, high voltage, high tension, kilowatts, kilowatt hours, kilocycles, megacycles, amperage, live wire, juice*, hot stuff*, megs*, kilos*, amps*.
**2.** [Electricity as a form of matter] — *Syn.* magnetism, electromagnetism, radioactivity, electron, neutron, proton, positron, dynatron, heavy electron.
Kinds of electricity include: static, statical, electrostatic, dynamic, dynamical, current, positive, negative, natural, celestial, induced.

**electrify,** *v.* **1.** [To provide electricity] — *Syn.* wire, charge, power, heat, light, equip, lay wires, lay cables, provide service, magnetize, galvanize, faradize, energize, dynamize, amplify, loop in, plug in, pass an electric current through, give an electric shock to, charge with electricity.
**2.** [To give a shock of excitement to] — *Syn.* thrill, stun, stir, galvanize; see **excite** 1, 2, **surprise** 1.

**electrocardiogram,** *n.* — *Syn.* electrical heart recording, cardiogram, EKG, ECG.

**electrocute,** *v.* — *Syn.* execute, put to death, kill by electric shock, put in the electric chair, send to the hot seat*, give the chair*, fry*, burn*, hot-chair*, give a permanent*, top off*.

**electrode,** *n.* — *Syn.* terminal, plate, wire, inert anode, inert cathode, copper cathode, zinc anode, negative electrode, positive electrode.

**electron,** *n.* — *Syn.* particle, negative particle, negatron, electrically charged element; see **atom** 2.

**electronic,** *modif.* — *Syn.* photoelectric, thermionic, cathodic, anodic, voltaic, photoelectronic, autoelectronic, computerized, automatic, automated; see also **electric.**

**electronics,** *n.* — *Syn.* radionics, electron physics, electron dynamics, electron optics, thermionics, spectrophotometry, radar, transistor physics, infrared spectroscopy, X-ray photometry, photoelectronics, automatics, serioinstrumentation, electrical patterning, cybernetics, computer electronics, microelectronics, semiconductor physics; see also **physics, science.**

**eleemosynary,** *modif.* — *Syn.* charitable, philanthropic, tributary; see **generous** 1, **philanthropic.**

**elegance,** *n.* **1.** [Refinement] — *Syn.* culture, tastefulness, taste, cultivation, polish, style, grace, delicacy, class*, tone, politeness, *politesse* (French), gentility, breeding, splendor, beauty, magnificence, grandeur, courtliness, hauteur, nobility, noblesse, charm, sophistication, propriety, dignity, restraint, nicety, fineness, richness, sumptuousness, luxuriousness, opulence, finery, poshness.
**2.** [Proportion] — *Syn.* symmetry, balance, rhythm, clarity, purity, felicity, grace, gracefulness, daintiness, exquisiteness, delicacy, fineness, comeliness; see also **beauty** 1.

**elegant,** *modif.* **1.** [Said of personal surroundings] — *Syn.* rich, tasteful, classic, restrained, graceful, luxurious, sumptuous, opulent, fine, chic, posh*, classy*, tony*, ritzy*; see also **beautiful** 1, **dignified.**
**2.** [Said of persons] — *Syn.* well-bred, cultured, refined, polished, urbane, sophisticated, aristocratic, dignified, courtly, genteel, graceful, fastidious, smart, chic, well-dressed, soigné, debonair, suave, classy*, chichi*; see also **beautiful** 2, **dignified, refined** 2.
**3.** [Said of writing or speech] — *Syn.* polished, perfected, elaborated, finished, ornate, ornamented, rhythmical, adorned, embellished, chaste, balanced, well-turned, flowing, stylized, Ciceronian, artistic, gran-

diloquent, rhetorical, florid, flowery, fancy, rich, artistic, mellifluous, pure, fluent, neat, concise, incisive, succinct, economical, simple. — *Ant.* DULL, ill-chosen, inarticulate.

**elegiac,** *modif.* — *Syn.* sorrowful, mournful, funereal, plaintive; see **sad** 1, 2.

**elegy,** *n.* — *Syn.* funeral poem, requiem, lament, dirge; see **epitaph, poem, song.**

**element,** *n.* **1.** [A part] — *Syn.* component, constituent, factor, ingredient, portion, particle, detail; see also **part** 1.
**2.** [A form of matter]
Ancient science identified the following basic elements: earth, air, fire, water.
Modern chemistry and physics identify the following elements: actinium (Ac), aluminum (Al), americium (Am), antimony (Sb), argon (Ar), arsenic (As), astatine (At), barium (Ba), berkelium (Bk), beryllium (Be), bismuth (Bi), boron (B), bromine (Br), cadmium (Cd), calcium (Ca), californium (Cf), carbon (C), cerium (Ce), cesium (Cs), chlorine (Cl), chromium (Cr), cobalt (Co), copper (Cu), curium (Cm), dysprosium (Dy), einsteinium (Es), erbium (Er), europium (Eu), fermium (Fm), fluorine (F), francium (Fr), gadolinium (Gd), gallium (Ga), germanium (Ge), gold (Au), hafnium (Hf), hassium (Hs), helium (He), holmium (Ho), hydrogen (H), indium (In), iodine (I), iridium (Ir), iron (Fe), krypton (Kr), lanthanum (La), lawrencium (Lr), lead (Pb), lithium (Li), lutetium (Lu), magnesium (Mg), manganese (Mn), meitnerium (Mt), mendelevium (Md), mercury (Hg), molybdenum (Mo), neodymium (Nd), neon (Ne), neptunium (Np), nickel (Ni), nielsbohrium (Ns), niobium (Nb), nitrogen (N), nobelium (No), osmium (Os), oxygen (O), palladium (Pd), phosphorus (P), platinum (Pt), plutonium (Pu), polonium (Po), potassium (K), praseodymium (Pr), promethium (Pm), protactinium (Pa), radium (Ra), radon (Rn), rhenium (Re), rhodium (Rh), rubidium (Rb), ruthenium (Ru), rutherfordium (Rf), samarium (Sm), scandium (Sc), seaborgium (Sg), selenium (Se), silicon (Si), silver (Ag), sodium (Na), strontium (Sr), sulfur (S), tantalum (Ta), technetium (Tc), tellurium (Te), terbium (Tb), thallium (Tl), thorium (Th), thulium (Tm), tin (Sn), titanium (Ti), tungsten (W), uranium (U), vanadium (V), xenon (Xe), ytterbium (Yb), yttrium (Y), zinc (Zn), zirconium (Zr); see **atomic energy.**

---

*SYN.* — **element,** in its general use, is the broadest term for any of the basic, irreducible parts or principles of anything, concrete or abstract /the *elements* of a science/; **component** and **constituent** both refer to any of the simple or compound parts of some complex thing or concept, but **constituent** also implies that the part is essential to the complex /hemoglobin is a *constituent* of blood/; **ingredient** refers to any of the substances (sometimes nonessential) that are mixed together in preparing a food, medicine, etc. /the *ingredients* of a cocktail/; **factor** applies to any of the component parts that are instrumental in determining the nature of the complex /luck was a *factor* in his success/

---

**elementary,** *modif.* **1.** [Suited to beginners] — *Syn.* primary, introductory, rudimentary, simple; see **easy** 2, **introductory** 1.
**2.** [Fundamental] — *Syn.* foundational, essential, basic; see **fundamental** 1.

**elements,** *n.* — *Syn.* basic material, fundamentals, essentials, grammar, ABC's, initial stage, first principles, basis, beginning, first steps, principles, principia, basic work, rudiments, groundwork, grounding, nut and bolts*, nitty-gritty*, brass tacks*.

**elephantine**, *modif.* **1.** [Immense] — *Syn.* huge, monstrous, enormous; see **large** 1.

**2.** [Clumsy] — *Syn.* ungraceful, ungainly, ponderous; see **awkward** 1.

**elevate**, *v.* **1.** [To lift bodily] — *Syn.* hoist, heave, tilt, levitate; see **raise** 1.

**2.** [To promote] — *Syn.* advance, upgrade, further; see **promote** 1.

**3.** [To exalt] — *Syn.* glorify, extol, dignify; see **praise** 1. *See Synonym Study at* LIFT.

**elevated**, *modif.* **1.** [Raised] — *Syn.* aerial, towering, lofty, tall; see **high** 2, **raised** 1.

**2.** [Noble] — *Syn.* exalted, sublime, dignified, eminent; see **grand** 2, **noble** 1.

**elevation**, *n.* — *Syn.* height, altitude, eminence, rise; see **height** 1, **hill**, **mountain** 1. *See Synonym Study at* HEIGHT.

**elevator**, *n.* **1.** [Machine for lifting] — *Syn.* lift, escalator, conveyor, endless belt, endless chain, buckets, elevator stack, chairlift, aerial tramway, passenger elevator, freight elevator, automatic elevator, hoist, dumbwaiter, chute.

**2.** [A building handling grain] — *Syn.* grain elevator, bin, storage plant, shipping point, granary, cooperative elevator, silo; see also **storehouse.**

**elf**, *n.* — *Syn.* brownie, sprite, leprechaun; see **fairy.**

**elfish**, *modif.* — *Syn.* mischievous, prankish, impish, elfin; see **naughty.**

**elicit**, *v.* — *Syn.* evoke, extort, call forth, draw out; see **excite** 2, **extract** 2, **obtain** 1. *See Synonym Study at* EXTRACT.

**elide**, *v.* — *Syn.* omit, delete, suppress, slur over; see **cancel** 1, **neglect** 2, **omit** 1.

**eligibility**, *n.* — *Syn.* fitness, acceptability, qualification; see **ability** 2, **fitness** 1.

**eligible**, *modif.* — *Syn.* qualified, fit, suitable, suited, acceptable, seemly, equal to, worthy of being chosen, fit to be chosen, capable of, fitted for, satisfactory, trained, employable, usable, becoming, likely, desirable, available, single, marriageable, in the running*, in line for*, up to*. — *Ant.* UNFIT, ineligible, disqualified.

**eliminate**, *v.* **1.** [To remove] — *Syn.* take out, get rid of, leave out, omit, dispose of, dispense with, do away with, wipe out, clean out, throw out, weed out, stamp out, cut out, crop out, phase out, drive out, cast out, root out, winnow out, put aside, set aside, exclude, rule out, remove from consideration, remove from competition, drop from competition, reject, eject, cast off, defeat, disqualify, oust, evict, shut the door on, clear away, cancel, eradicate, erase, expel, discharge, dislodge, put out of doors, reduce, disentitle, forfeit, invalidate, abolish, repeal, abrogate, exterminate, annihilate, kill, murder, waive, throw overboard, be done with, relinquish, relegate, discard, dismiss, drop, blot out, elide, obliterate, discount, exile, banish, deport, expatriate, maroon, blackball, ostracize, fire, dump*, ditch*, scrap*, bounce*, sack*, eighty-six*, clear the decks*. — *Ant.* accept, INCLUDE, welcome.

**2.** [To remove waste matter] — *Syn.* discharge, throw off, pass; see **excrete.** *See Synonym Study at* EXCLUDE.

**elimination**, *n.* **1.** [The act of removing] — *Syn.* dismissal, expulsion, exclusion; see **removal** 1.

**2.** [The act of declining to consider] — *Syn.* rejection, repudiation, denial, disqualification, exclusion, debarment, avoidance, rejecting, eliminating, weeding out, winnowing out.

**elite**, *n.* — *Syn.* upper class, ruling class, power elite, cream; see **aristocracy, best.**

**elixir**, *n.* — *Syn.* balm, compound, tincture, panacea; see **potion.**

**ell**, *n.* — *Syn.* addition, annex, extension; see **wing** 2.

**ellipse**, *n.* — *Syn.* oval, conic section, curve; see **circle** 1, **curve** 1.

**elliptical**, *modif.* **1.** [Having the form of an ellipse] — *Syn.* oval, ovoid, egg-shaped; see **oblong.**

**2.** [Marked by omissions in speech or writing] — *Syn.* terse, cryptic, obscure, incomplete; see **obscure** 1, **short** 2, **terse.**

**elm**, *n.* Varieties of elm trees include: American, white, red, slippery, weeping, wych, dwarf, Dutch, English, Japanese, Siberian, Chinese, Grand Rapids oak*; see also **tree, wood** 2.

**elocution**, *n.* **1.** [Speech training] — *Syn.* voice culture, dramatic reading, declamation, art of oral expression, oratory, rhetoric.

**2.** [Manner of speaking] — *Syn.* delivery, locution, articulation; see **delivery** 3, **speech** 2.

**elongate**, *v.* — *Syn.* prolong, stretch, extend; see **lengthen** 1. *See Synonym Study at* EXTEND.

**elope**, *v.* — *Syn.* run away with, run off, escape with a lover, slip out, fly, flee, abscond, go secretly, skip out*, go to Gretna Green*.

**eloquence**, *n.* **1.** [The quality of effective speech] — *Syn.* fluency, articulateness, expressiveness, persuasiveness, forcefulness, expression, appeal, diction, articulation, delivery, power, force, vigor, mellifluousness, facility, vivacity, wit, style, poise, flow, volubility, grandiloquence, loquacity, command of language, dramatic power, felicitousness, felicity of expression, gift of gab*.

**2.** [Formal and fluent speech] — *Syn.* oration, expression, rhetoric; see **speech** 3.

**eloquent**, *modif.* — *Syn.* persuasive, expressive, articulate, silver-tongued; see **expressive, fluent** 2.

**else**, *modif.* — *Syn.* different, other, in addition, more; see **extra, other.**

**elsewhere**, *modif.* — *Syn.* somewhere else, not here, in another place, in some other place, to some other place, gone, away, absent, abroad, hence, removed, remote, outside, not under consideration, formerly, subsequently. — *Ant.* HERE, at this point, in this spot.

**elucidate**, *v.* — *Syn.* explain, interpret, illustrate, clarify; see **explain.** *See Synonym Study at* EXPLAIN.

**elucidation**, *n.* — *Syn.* illustration, clarification, commentary, definition; see **explanation** 1.

**elude**, *v.* — *Syn.* dodge, shun, escape; see **avoid, escape.** *See Synonym Study at* ESCAPE.

**elusive**, *modif.* **1.** [Evasive] — *Syn.* slippery, tricky, evanescent, fugitive; see **fleeting, sly** 1, **temporary.**

**2.** [Mysterious] — *Syn.* baffling, intangible, imponderable, equivocal; see **difficult** 2, **obscure** 1.

**Elysium**, *n.* — *Syn.* abode of the blessed, heaven, nirvana; see **paradise** 3.

**emaciated**, *modif.* — *Syn.* gaunt, starved, wasted; see **thin** 2.

**emaciation**, *n.* — *Syn.* gauntness, skinniness, thinness, boniness, haggardness, anorexia, malnutrition, starvation, undernourishment, atrophy, wasting, wasting away, withering, attenuation, consumption, marasmus, tabes.

**emanate**, *v.* **1.** [To begin] — *Syn.* issue, arise, spring, originate; see **arise** 3, **begin** 2.

*See Synonym Study at* ARISE.

**2.** [To emit] — *Syn.* exude, radiate, exhale; see **emit** 1.

**emanation,** *n.* **1.** [Emergence] — *Syn.* flowing, arising, issuing, emerging, springing, welling, issuance, escape, outflow, emission, effusion, oozing, gush, outpour, effluence, beginning, origin, origination. — *Ant.* stagnation, stoppage, withholding.

**2.** [Emission] — *Syn.* effluvium, discharge, drainage, exhalation, leakage, effluence, efflux, vapor, steam, radiation, radon, exudation, percolation, ejaculation, aura.

**emancipate,** *v.* — *Syn.* free, release, liberate, deliver; see **free** 1.

*See Synonym Study at* FREE.

**emancipation,** *n.* — *Syn.* liberty, release, liberation; see **freedom** 1, **freeing.**

**emancipator,** *n.* — *Syn.* liberator, deliverer, rescuer, redeemer; see **liberator.**

**emasculate,** *v.* **1.** [To sterilize] — *Syn.* geld, unman, mutilate; see **castrate.**

**2.** [To weaken] — *Syn.* soften, enervate, devitalize, cripple; see **weaken** 2.

**emasculation,** *n.* **1.** [Castration] — *Syn.* sterilization, mutilation, eunuchization; see **castration.**

**2.** [Weakness] — *Syn.* enervation, debilitation, unmanliness; see **weakness** 1.

**embalm,** *v.* — *Syn.* preserve, mummify, process, freeze, fill with formaldehyde, anoint, wrap, preserve from putrefaction, prepare for burial, lay out, perpetuate, keep in memory, immortalize.

**embankment,** *n.* — *Syn.* dike, breakwater, bank, causeway; see **dam** 1, **dock** 1, **hill.**

**embargo,** *n.* — *Syn.* restriction, prohibition, ban, impediment; see **refusal, restraint** 2.

**embark,** *v.* — *Syn.* set out, leave port, set sail, start; see **begin** 1, **board** 2, **leave** 1.

**embarrass,** *v.* **1.** [To upset mentally] — *Syn.* disconcert, fluster, abash, chagrin, discompose, discomfit, confuse, discomfort, upset, rattle, agitate, distress, disturb, faze, bewilder, nonplus, confound, bother, perplex, puzzle, vex, worry, trouble, distract, perturb, flurry, mortify, discountenance, dumbfound, shame, humiliate, make blush, put in a hole★, put on the spot★, put to the blush★, discombobulate★, make a monkey of★, put out of countenance★, put out of face★. — *Ant.* compose, ENCOURAGE, assure.

**2.** [To hinder] — *Syn.* keep back, obstruct, hamper; see **hinder.**

---

**SYN.** — **embarrass** is to cause to feel ill at ease so as to result in a loss of composure *[embarrassed* by their compliments*]*; **abash** implies a sudden loss of self-confidence and a growing feeling of shame or inadequacy *[I stood abashed at his rebukes]*; **discomfit** implies a frustration of plans or expectations and often connotes a resultant feeling of discomposure or humiliation; to **disconcert** is to cause someone to lose self-possession quickly, resulting in confusion or mental disorganization *[his interruptions were disconcerting]*; **rattle** and **faze** are less formal equivalents for **disconcert,** but the former emphasizes emotional agitation, and the latter is most commonly used in negative constructions *[danger does not faze him]*

---

**embarrassed,** *modif.* **1.** [In social difficulties] — *Syn.* abashed, flustered, disconcerted; see **ashamed.**

**2.** [In financial difficulties] — *Syn.* bankrupt, in debt, straitened; see **insolvent, poor** 1.

**embarrassing,** *modif.* — *Syn.* awkward, uncomfortable,

disconcerting, difficult, disturbing, confusing, distracting, bewildering, puzzling, rattling, perplexing, delicate, touchy, distressing, upsetting, discomforting, discomfiting, ticklish, flustering, mortifying, humiliating, shameful, shaming, troubling, troublesome, worrisome, disagreeable, inconvenient, inopportune, helpless, unseemly, impossible, uneasy, equivocal, irksome, ambiguous, unpropitious, unmanageable, sticky★. — *Ant.* COMFORTABLE, easy, agreeable.

**embarrassment,** *n.* **1.** [The condition of being embarrassed] — *Syn.* confusion, chagrin, mortification, discomfiture, shame, humiliation, abashment, discomposure, discomfort, disconcertment, disconcertion, bashfulness, self-consciousness, shyness, timidity, inhibition, awkwardness, perplexity, distress, fluster, flurry, shamefacedness, egg on one's face, discombobulation★, stew★.

**2.** [Anything that embarrasses] — *Syn.* mistake, blunder, faux pas, awkwardness, clumsiness, indebtedness, uncertainty, gaucherie, hindrance, poverty, impecuniosity, destitution, distress, difficulties, involvement, intricacy, obligation, crude action, stupid action, indiscretion, default, debt, awkward situation, predicament, dilemma, puzzle, perplexity, tangle, strait, pinch, quandary, plight, fix★, hot seat★, hot water★, pickle★, skeleton in the closet★.

**embassy,** *n.* **1.** [Ambassadorial residence and offices] — *Syn.* government office, consular office, ministry, consulate; see **government** 2, **office** 3.

**2.** [Ambassadorial legation] — *Syn.* commission, mission, delegation; see **committee, diplomat** 1.

**embattle,** *v.* — *Syn.* marshal, mobilize, array; see **arm** 2.

**embed,** *v.* **1.** [To put in] — *Syn.* imbed, insert, implant, install, fix, deposit, stick in, place in, thrust in, stuff in, set in, drive in, press in, ram in, plunge in, tuck in, hammer in, put into, root, plant, sink, bury, enclose, inlay, lodge, set, pierce.

**2.** [To fix] — *Syn.* plant, implant, secure; see **fasten** 1.

**embellish,** *v.* — *Syn.* adorn, ornament, deck; see **decorate.**

*See Synonym Study at* DECORATE.

**embellishment,** *n.* **1.** [Decoration] — *Syn.* ornament, adornment, frill; see **decoration** 1, 2.

**2.** [Exaggeration] — *Syn.* embroidery, hyperbole, elaboration; see **exaggeration** 1.

**embers,** *n.* — *Syn.* coals, cinders, ash, live coals, slag, smoking remnants, smoldering remains of a fire, clinkers.

**embezzle,** *v.* — *Syn.* thieve, misappropriate, peculate, pilfer; see **rob, steal.**

**embezzlement,** *n.* — *Syn.* fraud, misappropriation, defalcation, stealing; see **theft.**

**embezzler,** *n.* — *Syn.* thief, defrauder, defalcator, white-collar criminal; see **criminal, robber.**

**embitter,** *v.* — *Syn.* sour, envenom, rankle, exacerbate; see **alienate, anger** 1, **bother** 2.

**embittered,** *modif.* — *Syn.* bitter, resentful, acrimonious, soured; see **angry, unfriendly** 2.

**emblazon,** *v.* **1.** [To decorate] — *Syn.* embellish, ornament, illuminate; see **decorate.**

**2.** [To proclaim] — *Syn.* herald, extol, glorify, celebrate; see **advertise** 1, **praise** 1.

**emblem,** *n.* — *Syn.* symbol, figure, image, design, token, sign, badge, attribute, insignia, seal, colors, crest, coat of arms, device, memento, type, representation, effigy, reminder, marker, mark, identification, souvenir, keepsake, medal, regalia, miniature, character, motto, impress, hallmark, logotype, logo, monogram, colophon, flag, pennant, banner, standard, arms, ensign.

**emblematic,** *modif.* — *Syn.* typical, symbolic, indicative; see **symbolic.**

**embodiment,** *n.* **1.** [Incarnation] — *Syn.* personification, manifestation, realization, concrete expression; see **epitome** 1, **expression** 2, **representation.**
**2.** [Incorporation] — *Syn.* comprisal, composition, materialization; see **inclusion.**

**embody,** *v.* **1.** [To actualize] — *Syn.* substantiate, personify, materialize, typify; see **complete** 1, **represent** 3.
**2.** [To organize] — *Syn.* incorporate, integrate, embrace, collect; see **comprise, include** 1, **organize** 2.

**embolden,** *v.* — *Syn.* inspirit, animate, hearten, impel; see **encourage** 2.

**emboss,** *v.* — *Syn.* raise, design, enchase, boss; see **decorate.**

**embossment,** *n.* — *Syn.* relief, bas-relief, molding, tracery; see **decoration** 1, **relief** 5.

**embrace,** *v.* **1.** [To clasp] — *Syn.* hug, enfold, squeeze, grip; see **hug.**
**2.** [To adopt] — *Syn.* espouse, welcome, take advantage of; see **adopt** 2.
**3.** [To include] — *Syn.* contain, comprise, cover, encompass; see **comprise, contain** 1, **include** 1.
*See Synonym Study at* INCLUDE.

**embroider,** *v.* **1.** [To adorn with needlework] — *Syn.* stitch, knit, quilt, braid, weave, pattern, ornament, embellish, enrich, garnish, deck, bedeck, decorate, work, gild, pattern; see also **decorate.**
**2.** [To exaggerate] — *Syn.* embellish, falsify, enlarge; see **exaggerate.**

**embroidery,** *n.* **1.** [Stitchery] — *Syn.* needlepoint, needlework, sampler, arabesque, brocade, tracery, lacery, bargello, edging, decoration, patterning, adornment, fringing.
Kinds of embroidery include: cross-stitch, crewel, crochet, needlepoint, tapestry, appliqué, quilting.
**2.** [Exaggeration] — *Syn.* embellishment, fabrication, hyperbole; see **exaggeration** 1.

**embroil,** *v.* — *Syn.* entangle, enmesh, disorder, derange; see **confuse, entangle.**

**embryo,** *n.* — *Syn.* fetus, incipient organism, nucleus; see **egg, fetus.**

**embryonic,** *modif.* — *Syn.* incipient, immature, undeveloped, rudimentary; see **budding, early** 1, **unfinished** 1.

**emend,** *v.* **1.** [To edit] — *Syn.* improve, redact, revise; see **edit** 1.
**2.** [To correct] — *Syn.* rectify, touch up, better; see **correct** 1.

**emendation,** *n.* **1.** [A revision] — *Syn.* editing, revisal, correction, change; see **improvement** 2, **revision.**
**2.** [Improvement] — *Syn.* amendment, amelioration, betterment; see **correction** 1, **improvement** 1.

**emerald,** *modif.* — *Syn.* bright green, verdigris, malachite; see **green** 1.

**emerald,** *n.* — *Syn.* rare green beryl, valuable gem, precious stone; see **jewel** 1.

**emerge,** *v.* — *Syn.* rise, surface, come out, develop; see **appear** 1, 3, **arise** 3, **begin** 2.

**emergence,** *n.* — *Syn.* rise, issue, evolution, materialization; see **appearance** 3, **development** 2, **emanation** 1.

**emergency,** *n.* — *Syn.* accident, crisis, unforeseen occurrence, strait(s), urgency, exigency, contingency, pressing necessity, pressure, tension, distress, extremity, danger, compulsion, turn of events, juncture, pass, predicament, misadventure, turning point, impasse, dilemma, quandary, plight, pinch, clutch*, pretty pass*, fix*, red alert*; see also **crisis, difficulty** 1, 2.

---

*SYN.* — **emergency** refers to any sudden or unforeseen situation that requires immediate action /the flood had created an *emergency*/; **exigency** refers to such a situation with stress upon the need or urgency of a response to it /the *exigencies* of the moment require drastic action/; **contingency** is used of an emergency regarded as remotely possible in the future /prepare for any *contingency*/; **crisis** refers to an event regarded as a turning point which will decisively determine an outcome /an economic *crisis*/; **strait** (or **straits**) refers to a trying situation from which it is difficult to extricate oneself /the loss left them in dire *straits*/

---

**emergent,** *modif.* **1.** [Emerging] — *Syn.* emanant, outgoing, efflorescent, issuing forth, emanating, rising, developing, new.
**2.** [Urgent] — *Syn.* pressing, sudden, immediate; see **urgent** 1.

**emeritus,** *modif.* — *Syn.* retired, retained on the rolls, revered, respected; see **retired** 1.

**emery,** *n.* — *Syn.* grinder, wheel, sharpener, Carborundum (trademark), corundum, emery paper, emery board, emery cloth, sandpaper, garnet paper.

**emigrant,** *n.* — *Syn.* émigré, exile, expatriate, defector, colonist, migrant, migrator, refugee, displaced person, D.P., traveler, foreigner, pilgrim, fugitive, wayfarer, peregrinator, wanderer, immigrant, alien, outcast, stateless person, man without a country.

**emigrate,** *v.* — *Syn.* migrate, immigrate, quit; see **leave** 1, **migrate.**
*See Synonym Study at* MIGRATE.

**emigration,** *n.* — *Syn.* migration, resettlement, relocation, reestablishment, defection, expatriation, departure, removal, leaving, displacement, moving, moving away, crossing, transplanting, uprooting, exodus, exile, trek, journey, movement, march, travel, voyage, wandering, peregrination, shift, settling, homesteading, colonization, *Volkswanderung* (German), brain drain*.
— *Ant.* IMMIGRATION, arriving, remaining.

**émigré,** *n.* — *Syn.* exile, emigrant, refugee; see **emigrant, refugee.**
*See Synonym Study at* ALIEN.

**eminence,** *n.* **1.** [Importance] — *Syn.* standing, prominence, distinction; see **fame** 1.
**2.** [An elevation] — *Syn.* projection, peak, highland; see **height** 1, **hill.**

**eminent,** *modif.* **1.** [Distinguished] — *Syn.* renowned, celebrated, prominent; see **distinguished** 2, **famous, important** 2.
*See Synonym Study at* FAMOUS.
**2.** [Physically lofty] — *Syn.* tall, elevated, raised; see **high** 1, 2.

**eminently,** *modif.* — *Syn.* notably, exceptionally, highly, suitably; see **very, well** 2.

**emissary,** *n.* — *Syn.* intermediary, ambassador, consul, envoy; see **agent** 1, **delegate, diplomat** 1.

**emission,** *n.* — *Syn.* ejection, effusion, eruption, discharge; see **emanation** 1, 2, **radiation** 1.

**emit,** *v.* **1.** [To send forth] — *Syn.* discharge, give off, give out, let off, let out, send out, cast up, cast out, throw up, throw out, breathe out, spill out, pour out, pour forth, give forth, eject, blow, hurl, gush, secrete, spurt, shoot, erupt, squirt, shed, expel, issue, transmit, beam, broadcast, vent, release, expend, vomit, belch, excrete, perspire, void, evacuate, spew, spit, expectorate, ooze, exude, slop over, exhale, extrude, emanate, jet.

**2.** [To express] — *Syn.* voice, pronounce, speak; see **utter.**

**emolument,** *n.* — *Syn.* payment, compensation, returns; see **pay** 2.

*See Synonym Study at* WAGE.

**emotion,** *n.* — *Syn.* feeling(s), sentiment, passion, sensation, affect, perturbation, agitation, tremor, excitement, disturbance, tumult, turmoil, excitability.

Emotions include: love, passion, infatuation, rapture, ecstasy, fire, warmth, affection, glow, fury, vehemence, fervor, ardor, zeal, thrill, elation, flutter, palpitation, joy, satisfaction, happiness, delight, glee, bliss, elation, inspiration, sympathy, empathy, tenderness, concern, grief, remorse, sorrow, sadness, melancholy, despondency, woe, anguish, misery, despair, depression, trepidation, worry, discomposure, disquiet, uneasiness, dread, fear, apprehension, hate, resentment, malice, contempt, animosity, conflict, jealousy, greed, covetousness, cupidity, anger, rage, ire, shame, pride, prurience, concupiscence, sensuality, lust, desire, lechery, pathos, bathos.

*See Synonym Study at* FEELING.

**emotional,** *modif.* **1.** [Stirring one's emotions] — *Syn.* moving, touching, impassioned, heartfelt; see **moving** 2, **passionate** 2.

**2.** [Given to emotion] — *Syn.* sentimental, sensitive, warm, gushing, hysterical, demonstrative, fiery, zealous, fervent, ardent, soulful, enthusiastic, passionate, fanatic, excitable, impulsive, spontaneous, impetuous, nervous, high-strung, disturbed, agitated, excited, wrought-up, overwrought, worked up, temperamental, irrational, overemotional, histrionic, melodramatic, sentient, oversensitive, hypersensitive, maudlin, overflowing, affectionate, loving, warmhearted, tenderhearted, lachrymose, teary, sloppy\*, gaga\*, drooling\*, icky\*, wearing one's heart on one's sleeve\*, mushy\*, gooey\*, soppy\*; see also **sentimental.** — *Ant.* rational, COLD, hard.

**emotionalism,** *n.* — *Syn.* emotion, hysteria, sentimentality, agitation; see **emotion, excitement, sensationalism, sentimentality.**

**empathize,** *v.* — *Syn.* identify with, sympathize, feel for, relate to, understand, put oneself in another's place, put oneself in another's shoes; see also **sympathize.**

**empathy,** *n.* — *Syn.* vicarious emotion, insight, understanding, compassion; see **pity** 1.

**emperor,** *n.* — *Syn.* monarch, sovereign, dictator; see **ruler** 1.

**emphasis,** *n.* — *Syn.* stress, accent, weight; see **accent** 2, **importance** 1.

**emphasize,** *v.* — *Syn.* stress, accentuate, underline, underscore, highlight, feature, spotlight, dramatize, pronounce, enunciate, articulate, accent, point up, point out, bring out, punctuate, play up, speak up, call attention to, reiterate, repeat, insist, maintain, impress, affirm, enlarge, indicate, italicize, lay stress on, make clear, labor the point, belabor, rub in\*, pound into one's head\*, drum into one's head\*, make much of, make a fuss about\*.

**emphatic,** *modif.* **1.** [Having force and certainty] — *Syn.* forceful, insistent, assured, strong, determined, decided, decisive, forcible, earnest, positive, energetic, cogent, potent, powerful, dynamic, stressed, resounding, vigorous, vehement, trenchant, pointed, flat, confident, definite, definitive, categorical, unequivocal, pronounced, dogmatic, express, explicit. — *Ant.* unemphatic, HESITANT, vacillating.

**2.** [Attracting attention by positive character] — *Syn.* notable, outstanding, spectacular; see **important** 1.

**emphatically,** *modif.* — *Syn.* definitely, certainly, of course, undoubtedly, decidedly, assuredly, with decision, decisively, absolutely, entirely, unequivocally, flatly, distinctly; with no ifs, ands, or buts about it\*. — *Ant.* indecisively, hesitantly, indistinctly.

**empire,** *n.* — *Syn.* domain, realm, union, federation; see **imperialism, nation** 1.

**empirical,** *modif.* — *Syn.* experiential, observational, practical; see **experimental, observed** 1.

**empiricism,** *n.* — *Syn.* induction, experimentation, experientialism; see **philosophy** 1.

**employ,** *v.* **1.** [To make use of] — *Syn.* use, operate, manipulate, apply; see **exercise** 2, **use** 1.

**2.** [To obtain services for pay] — *Syn.* engage, contract, take on; see **hire** 1.

*See Synonym Study at* USE.

**employed,** *modif.* — *Syn.* working, occupied, busy, laboring, gainfully employed, holding down a job, not out of work, not on the unemployed rolls, not on the relief rolls, in collar, in someone's employ, in someone's pay, hard at it, on the job, hired, operating, selected, active, engaged, placed, commissioned, on duty, on the payroll, in harness\*, on the grind\*, plugging\*. — *Ant.* out of work, unemployed, jobless.

**employee,** *n.* — *Syn.* worker, laborer, wage earner, agent, representative, hired hand, staff member, assistant, attendant, apprentice, operator, workingman, workingwoman, jobholder, breadwinner, craftsman, workman, help, hired help, servant, domestic, subordinate, underling, helper, staffer, hireling, drudge, lackey, wage slave\*, flunky\*, cog\*, gofer\*.

**employer,** *n.* — *Syn.* owner, manager, proprietor, patron, management, head, director, executive, boss, superintendent, supervisor, president, chief, capitalist, businessperson, entrepreneur, manufacturer, corporation, company, business, firm, organization, outfit, master, front office\*, old man\*, kingpin\*, big shot\*.

**employment,** *n.* **1.** [The act of employing] — *Syn.* hiring, using, calling, commissioning, contracting, awarding, occupying, engaging, retaining; see also **use** 1.

**2.** [An occupation] — *Syn.* job, profession, vocation; see **job** 1, **profession** 1, **trade** 2, **work** 2.

**empower,** *v.* — *Syn.* grant, authorize, enable, permit; see **allow** 1, **approve** 1, **commission, enable.**

**empress,** *n.* — *Syn.* female sovereign, maharani, czarina; see **ruler** 1.

**emptiness,** *n.* — *Syn.* void, vacuum, vacuity, vacancy, gap, chasm, blankness, blank, depletedness, inanition, exhaustion, hollowness, desolation.

**empty,** *modif.* **1.** [Without content] — *Syn.* vacant, void, vacuous, hollow, bare, clear, blank, unfilled, unfurnished, unoccupied, uninhabited, unfrequented, vacated, void of, devoid, lacking, wanting, barren, emptied, abandoned, exhausted, depleted, deserted, desert, stark, deprived of, *in vacuo* (Latin), despoiled, desolate, dry, destitute, negative, deflated, eviscerated, evacuated, cleaned out. — *Ant.* FULL, filled, occupied.

**2.** [Without meaning or force] — *Syn.* vain, hollow, insincere; see **false** 2, **futile** 1.

**3.** [Without sense] — *Syn.* barren, fruitless, meaningless; see **blank** 2.

---

**SYN.** — **empty** means having nothing in it [an *empty* box, street, stomach, etc.]; **vacant** means lacking that which appropriately or customarily occupies or fills it [a *vacant* apartment, position, etc.]; **void** specifically stresses complete or vast emptiness [*void* of judgment];

**vacuous**, now rare in its physical sense, suggests the emptiness of a vacuum [a vacuous expression on her face] See also Synonym Study at VAIN.

---

**empty**, v. **1.** [To become empty] — Syn. discharge, leave, pour out, flow out, ebb, run out, open into, converge, be discharged, void, purge, release, exhaust, vomit forth, leak, spill, drain off, rush out, escape. — Ant. flow in, ENTER, absorb.
**2.** [To cause to become empty] — Syn. remove, pour out, spill out, dump, dip, ladle, decant, tap, void, let out, deplete, exhaust, deflate, drain, shed, bail, bail out, clean out, clear out, unload, unpack, unburden, evacuate, eject, expel, vacate, draw off, draw out, disgorge, suck dry, clear, drink, consume, use up. — Ant. pack, FILL, stuff.

**empyrean**, n. — Syn. cosmos, firmament, space; see **heaven** 1.

**emulate**, v. — Syn. imitate, copy, follow the example of, rival; see **compete, follow** 2.

**enable**, v. — Syn. authorize, empower, capacitate, make possible, sanction, give power to, give authority to, invest, endow, allow, let, permit, license, qualify, equip, set up, facilitate; see also **approve** 1.

**enact**, v. **1.** [To legislate] — Syn. decree, sanction, ordain, order, dictate, make into law, legislate, pass, establish, ratify, vote in, proclaim, vote favorably, determine, transact, authorize, appoint, institute, railroad through, get the floor, put in force, make laws, put through, constitute, fix, set, formulate.
**2.** [To act] — Syn. perform, portray, impersonate, act out; see **act** 3, **perform** 2.

**enactment**, n. **1.** [Law] — Syn. edict, decree, statute; see **law** 3.
**2.** [Acting] — Syn. performance, personification, impersonation, playing; see **acting**.

**enamel**, n. — Syn. lacquer, coating, finish, polish, gloss, glossy surface, top coat, japan, varnish, shellac, paint, glaze, veneer, lead glaze, cloisonné, plique-à-jour, champlevé.

**enamel**, v. — Syn. lacquer, glaze, gloss, japan, paint, veneer, coat, varnish, shellac, finish, paint, give a finish, spray-paint.

**enamored**, modif. — Syn. captivated, enchanted, in love, infatuated; see **fascinated**.

**encage**, v. — Syn. cage, coop up, confine; see **imprison**.

**encamp**, v. — Syn. billet, quarter, settle; see **camp**.

**encampment**, n. — Syn. camp, campsite, bivouac; see **camp** 1, 3.

**enchain**, v. **1.** [To confine] — Syn. pinion, handcuff, bind, fetter; see **bind** 1.
**2.** [To attract] — Syn. captivate, hypnotize, mesmerize; see **fascinate**.

**enchant**, v. **1.** [To put under a spell] — Syn. charm, bewitch, cast a spell over; see **charm** 1, **hypnotize** 1.
**2.** [To attract strongly] — Syn. captivate, charm, delight, entrance; see **fascinate**.
See Synonym Study at ATTRACT.

**enchanted**, modif. **1.** [Captivated] — Syn. enraptured, entranced, delighted; see **fascinated, happy** 1.
**2.** [Charmed] — Syn. bewitched, ensorcelled, under a spell, magical; see **charmed, magic** 1.

**enchanter**, n. — Syn. wizard, conjurer, witch; see **magician** 1.

**enchantment**, n. **1.** [Magic] — Syn. witchery, sorcery, magic spell, charm; see **magic** 1.
**2.** [Great delight] — Syn. captivation, allurement, fascination; see **attraction** 1, **happiness** 2, **rapture** 1, 2.

**enchantress**, n. — Syn. witch, sorceress, siren; see **magician** 1, **witch**.

**encircle**, v. — Syn. encompass, circle, girdle, enclose; see **circle, surround** 1, 2.

**enclose**, v. **1.** [To shut in all around] — Syn. confine, contain, surround, hem in, encircle, encompass, envelop, close in, shut in, circumscribe, corral, impound, blockade, picket, block off, fence in, fence off, set apart, lock up, imprison, immure, intern, jail, shut up, lock in, cage, drive in, keep in, build in, box in, rail in, wall in, box off, box up, bottle up, freeze over; see also **surround** 1, 2. — Ant. free, liberate, open.
**2.** [To put in an envelope, wrapper, etc.] — Syn. insert, include, wrap up, implant; see **embed** 1, **include** 2.

**enclosed**, modif. **1.** [Placed within] — Syn. inserted, included, contained, injected, stuffed in, locked in, penned in, confined, immured, jailed, enfolded, packed up, wrapped up, shut up, buried, encased, embedded, implanted, interred, imprisoned.
**2.** [Encircled] — Syn. girdled, encompassed, hemmed in; see **surrounded**.

**enclosure**, n. **1.** [A space enclosed] — Syn. pen, sty, yard, jail, garden, corral, cage, asylum, pound, kennel, run, park, fenced-in field, arena, precinct, compound, plot, court, courtyard, quadrangle, close, cloister, patch, walk, aviary, mew(s), coop, cote, hutch, fold, den, cell, dungeon, vault, crawl, kraal, paddock, ring, stockade, warren, concentration camp, detention camp, pale, ghetto, prison, stadium, bowl, coliseum; see also **building** 1, **place** 3, **room** 2.
**2.** [Something inserted] — Syn. information, check, money, circular, copy, questionnaire, forms, documents, printed matter.

**encomium**, n. — Syn. tribute, panegyric, eulogy; see **compliment, praise** 2.
See Synonym Study at TRIBUTE.

**encompass**, v. **1.** [To surround] — Syn. encircle, compass, gird, envelop; see **surround** 1, 2.
**2.** [To include] — Syn. embrace, comprise, incorporate, contain; see **comprise, include** 1.

**encore**, interj. — Syn. again, bravo, brava, bravissimo, bis (French), hurrah, olé, well done, once more; see also **congratulations, hurrah**.

**encore**, n. — Syn. repeat performance, reprise, reappearance, final number; see **performance** 2, **piece** 3, **repetition**.

**encounter**, n. **1.** [A coming together] — Syn. meeting, confrontation, contact, rendezvous; see **appointment** 2, **meeting** 1.
**2.** [Hostile or violent contact] — Syn. conflict, clash, collision, brush; see **battle** 1, **fight** 1.
See Synonym Study at BATTLE.

**encounter**, v. **1.** [To meet unexpectedly] — Syn. meet, come upon, face, confront; see **find** 1, **meet** 6.
**2.** [To meet in conflict] — Syn. battle, contend against, attack, struggle; see **fight** 2, **meet** 6.

**encourage**, v. **1.** [To give support] — Syn. help, aid, foster, sanction, approve, incite, instigate, stimulate, goad, spur, sustain, fortify, advocate, reassure, assist, abet, succor, support, befriend, uphold, reinforce, back, bolster, brace, further, promote, boost, forward, favor, strengthen, second, subscribe to, applaud, praise, smile upon, side with, back up, pull for, lead on, egg on, prompt, urge, sway, extend a helping hand, give a hand up, give a foot up, root for, pat on the back★. — Ant. RESTRAIN, discourage, caution.
**2.** [To raise the spirits] — Syn. inspirit, hearten, embolden, animate, cheer, elate, refresh, enliven, exhilarate, inspire, cheer up, brighten, rally, restore, give new

promise, give new life, revitalize, reassure, give encouragement, gladden, fortify, revivify, promise well, augur well, buoy up, bid fair, boost, buck up\*, give a shot in the arm\*. — *Ant.* DISCOURAGE, depress, dispirit.

**encouraged,** *modif.* — *Syn.* heartened, reassured, inspired, animated, enlivened, renewed, aided, supported, prepared, determined, hopeful, confident, optimistic, enthusiastic, emboldened, fearless, roused, cheered, inspirited, buoyed up; see also **helped, hopeful** 1. — *Ant.* dispirited, discouraged, disheartened.

**encouragement,** *n.* **1.** [The act of encouraging] — *Syn.* urging, prodding, reassuring, reassurance, assuring, heartening, animating, abetment, abetting, backing, support, buoying up, cheering, solacing, motivating, supporting, helping, boosting, building up, rallying, inspiriting, egging on.
**2.** [That which encourages] — *Syn.* aid, help, assistance, support, cheer, confidence, trust, faith, advance, promotion, reward, reassurance, incentive, motivation, stimulus, inducement, backing, animation, optimism, comfort, consolation, hope, fortitude, firmness, boost, pat on the back\*, lift\*, shot in the arm\*, pep talk\*, good omen.

**encouraging,** *modif.* — *Syn.* bright, promising, reassuring, supportive; see **hopeful** 2.

**encroach,** *v.* — *Syn.* infringe, trespass, invade, overstep; see **meddle** 1.
*See Synonym Study at* TRESPASS.

**encroachment,** *n.* — *Syn.* infringement, invasion, trespass, inroad; see **attack** 1, **intrusion.**

**encumber,** *v.* — *Syn.* burden, hamper, obstruct, weigh down; see **burden, hinder.**

**encumbrance,** *n.* — *Syn.* burden, hindrance, impediment; see **burden** 2, **difficulty** 1.

**encyclopedia,** *n.* — *Syn.* book of facts, reference book, book of knowledge, almanac, yearbook, compilation, concordance, general reference work, cyclopedia; see also **reference** 3.

**encyclopedic,** *modif.* — *Syn.* exhaustive, broad, all-encompassing, wide-ranging; see **comprehensive, general** 1.

**end,** *n.* **1.** [Purpose] — *Syn.* aim, object, intention; see **purpose** 1.
**2.** [The close of an action] — *Syn.* expiration, completion, termination, adjournment, final event, ending, close, denouement, finish, conclusion, arrangement, finale, cessation, discontinuation, target date, deadline, retirement, accomplishment, attainment, determination, achievement, fulfillment, payoff, realization, period, consummation, concluding part, culmination, perfection, execution, performance, last line, finis, epilogue, closing piece, closing scene, curtain, terminus, omega, last word, swan song, bottom line\*, wrap-up\*, windup\*, beginning of the end, cutoff, mopping up\*, end of the line\*. — *Ant.* beginning, START, opening.
**3.** [A result] — *Syn.* conclusion, effect, outcome, upshot; see **result.**
**4.** [The extremity] — *Syn.* terminal, termination, terminus, boundary, limit, borderline, border, bound(s), point, stub, stump, tail end, edge, tip, top, head, butt end, nib, pole, remnant, fragment. — *Ant.* CENTER, middle, hub.
**5.** [The close of life] — *Syn.* demise, passing, doom; see **death** 1.
**keep one's end up\*** — *Syn.* do one's share, join, participate; see **help** 1, **participate** 1.
**make (both) ends meet\*** — *Syn.* manage, get along, get by, survive; see **budget** 1, **endure** 2, **survive** 1.

**no end\*** — *Syn.* very much, extremely, greatly; see **much** 2, **very.**
**on end** — *Syn.* **1.** ceaselessly, without interruption, continuously; see **consecutively, regularly** 2.
**2.** straight, vertical, standing up; see **upright** 1.
**put an end to** — *Syn.* stop, finish, discontinue; see **end** 1.
*See Synonym Study at* INTENTION.

**end,** *v.* **1.** [To bring to a halt] — *Syn.* stop, finish, quit, close, halt, terminate, conclude, complete, terminate, settle, shut down, leave off, switch off, bring to an end, make an end of, wind up, get done, break off, adjourn, break up, leave unfinished, relinquish, put an end to, discontinue, cut off, cut short, abort, postpone, play out, interrupt, dispose of, drop, give up, call it a day\*, call it quits\*, pull the plug\*, put the lid on\*, call off\*, choke off\*, ring down the curtain\*, wrap up\*. — *Ant.* BEGIN, initiate, start.
**2.** [To bring to a conclusion] — *Syn.* complete, settle, conclude, terminate; see **achieve** 1.
**3.** [To come to an end] — *Syn.* desist, cease, die, peter out\*; see **stop** 2.
**4.** [To die] — *Syn.* expire, depart, pass away; see **die** 1.

---

**SYN.** — **end** means to stop some process, whether or not it has been satisfactorily completed [let's *end* this argument]; to **close** is to come or bring to a stop, as if by shutting something regarded as previously open [nominations are now *closed*]; to **conclude** is to bring or come to a formal termination, often involving some final arrangement, decision, or action [to *conclude* negotiations]; to **finish** is to bring to a desired end that which one has set out to do, as by adding perfecting touches [to *finish* a painting]; to **complete** is to finish by filling in the missing or defective parts [the award *completed* his happiness]; to **terminate** is to bring or come to an end regarded as a limit or boundary [to *terminate* a privilege]

---

**endanger,** *v.* — *Syn.* imperil, jeopardize, expose to danger, risk, hazard, leave defenseless, leave unprotected, put in danger, put in jeopardy, threaten, subject to loss, make liable to danger, put at risk, expose to hazard, expose to peril, compromise, be careless with, fish in troubled waters\*, lay open\*, put on the spot\*, leave in the middle\*. — *Ant.* SAVE, protect, preserve.

**endangered,** *modif.* — *Syn.* exposed, imperiled, in danger, in jeopardy, threatened, at risk, threatened with extinction, in a dilemma, in a predicament, jeopardized, overdue, fraught with danger, in the cannon's mouth\*, in a bad way\*, on thin ice\*, up the creek without a paddle\*, caught between Scylla and Charybdis\*, hanging by a thread\*, at the last extremity.

**endear,** *v.* — *Syn.* attach, win, charm; see **fascinate.**

**endearing,** *modif.* — *Syn.* appealing, engaging, lovable, likable; see **charming.**

**endearment,** *n.* — *Syn.* attachment, fondness, love; see **affection** 1.

**endeavor,** *n.* — *Syn.* effort, try, attempt; see **effort** 1, 2.
*See Synonym Study at* EFFORT.

**endeavor,** *v.* — *Syn.* attempt, aim, essay, strive; see **try** 1.
*See Synonym Study at* TRY.

**ended,** *modif.* — *Syn.* done, completed, concluded; see **finished** 1.

**ending,** *n.* — *Syn.* finish, closing, conclusion; see **end** 2.

**endless,** *modif.* **1.** [Having no end in space] — *Syn.* infinite, measureless, interminable, indeterminable, untold, countless, without end, continuous, unending, unbounded, unlimited, immeasurable, unmeasured, limitless, unsurpassable, having no bounds, multitudinous, boundless, incalculable, illimitable, unfathomable.— *Ant.* FIXED, finite, bounded.

**2.** [Having no end in time] — *Syn.* perpetual, everlasting, interminable, continual; see **eternal** 1, 2, **unending.**

**endorse,** *v.* **1.** [To inscribe one's name] — *Syn.* sign, put one's signature on, countersign, underwrite, sign one's name on, inscribe one's signature, subscribe, superscribe, authorize, notarize, validate, legalize, initial, pay over, make over, put the seal to, say amen to, sign on the dotted line, autograph a check*, put one's John Hancock on*.

**2.** [To indicate one's active support of] — *Syn.* approve, confirm, sanction, ratify, sponsor, back, guarantee, underwrite, support, lend one's name to, stand up for, stand behind, vouch for, uphold, recommend, commend, praise, defend, champion, give one's word for, OK, back up, get behind*, go to bat for*; see also **approve** 1.— *Ant.* CENSURE, condemn, denounce.
*See Synonym Study at* APPROVE.

**endorsed,** *modif.* — *Syn.* signed, notarized, validated, legalized, ratified, sealed, affirmed, concluded, settled, attested, approved, upheld, supported, commended, recommended, sanctioned, advocated, blessed, sponsored, underwritten, backed, OK'd, boosted*; see also **approved.**— *Ant.* cancelled, disapproved, vetoed.

**endorsement,** *n.* — *Syn.* support, sanction, approval; see **advertisement** 2, **permission, signature.**

**endow,** *v.* **1.** [To give to] — *Syn.* enrich, provide, supply, invest; see **give** 1, **provide** 1.

**2.** [To provide support for all times] — *Syn.* bequeath, found, establish in perpetuity, fund; see **organize** 2, **underwrite** 3.

**endowment,** *n.* **1.** [A gift] — *Syn.* donation, grant, bounty, award; see **gift** 1.

**2.** [A human quality or special capacity] — *Syn.* talent, gift, qualification; see **ability** 1.

**3.** [That which supplies perpetual support] — *Syn.* benefit, provision, bequest, grant, pension, stipend, legacy, inheritance, subsidy, revenue, trust, subvention, dispensation, bestowal, nest egg*.

**4.** [The act of providing perpetual support] — *Syn.* funding, subsidizing, providing an endowment for, setting up, supporting, giving money to, giving money for, establishing, underwriting, granting in perpetuity; see also **establishing** 1, **giving.**

**end up,** *v.* — *Syn.* finish, conclude, wind up, culminate; see **arrive** 1, **end** 1, **stop** 2.

**endurable,** *modif.* — *Syn.* bearable, sustainable, tolerable, supportable; see **bearable.**

**endurance,** *n.* **1.** [An enduring state] — *Syn.* persistence, duration, continuance; see **continuation** 1.

**2.** [The power of enduring] — *Syn.* fortitude, perseverance, stamina, staying power, sufferance, submission, forbearance, long-suffering, capacity to endure, resignation, patience, tolerance, persistence, tenacity, diligence, tirelessness, indefatigability, strength, toughness, durability, longevity, lastingness, coolness, courage, restraint, resistance, will, backbone, pluck, mettle, guts*, spunk*, grit*, stick-to-itiveness*; see also **patience** 1.
— *Ant.* WEAKNESS, feebleness, infirmity.

**3.** [The suffering of troubles] — *Syn.* undergoing, bearing, suffering, continuing, holding up, withstanding, enduring, standing.
*See Synonym Study at* PATIENCE.

**endure,** *v.* **1.** [To continue] — *Syn.* persist, remain, last, continue, be long-lived, exist, be, abide, bide, stay, pre-

vail, wear, be timeless, sustain, survive, outlast, superannuate, be left, carry on, stay on, live on, go on, hold on, hang on, keep on, keep going, persevere, linger, outlive, have no end, hold out, wear on, be solid as a rock*, never say die*, go the distance*; see also **continue** 1.— *Ant.* DIE, cease, end.

**2.** [To sustain adversity] — *Syn.* suffer, tolerate, bear, allow, permit, support, undergo, stand, sit through, brook, take, withstand, bear with, bear up, bear up under, hold up, accustom oneself to, abide, submit to, be subjected to, put up with, countenance, sustain, go through, pass through, feel, experience, know, meet with, encounter, be patient with, resign oneself, weather, brave, face, survive, cope with, handle, carry on, live through, live out, brace oneself, bear the brunt, stand for*, swallow*, stomach*, eat*, pocket one's pride*, never say die*, not flag*, grin and bear it*, ride out*, stick it out*, sweat it out*, hang on*, hang in there*, pull through*, make one's own bed and lie in it*, take one's punishment*, keep one's chin up*, bite the bullet*, tough it out*.— *Ant.* AVOID, resist, collapse, succumb.

---

**SYN.** — **endure** implies a holding up against prolonged pain, distress, etc., and stresses stamina or patience; **bear** implies a putting up with something that distresses, annoys, pains, etc., without suggesting the way in which one sustains the imposition; **suffer** suggests passive acceptance of or resignation to that which is painful or unpleasant; **tolerate** and the more informal **stand** both imply self-imposed restraint of one's opposition to what is offensive or repugnant; **brook,** a literary word, is usually used in the negative, suggesting determined refusal to put up with what is distasteful *[I will brook no interference] See also Synonym Study at* CONTINUE.

---

**enduring,** *modif.* — *Syn.* lasting, abiding, surviving; see **permanent** 2.

**enema,** *n.* — *Syn.* douche, purgative, clyster; see **medicine** 2.

**enemy,** *n.* **1.** [A national or public opponent] — *Syn.* foe, attacker, antagonist, opponent, adversary, public enemy, criminal, opposition, fifth column, enemy within the gates, borer from within, saboteur, spy, foreign agent, assassin, murderer, betrayer, traitor, terrorist, revolutionary, seditionist, rebel, guerrilla(s), invader, the other side, hostile nation, hostile forces, villain, bad guy*.— *Ant.* ally, confederate, SUPPORTER.

**2.** [A personal opponent] — *Syn.* rival, opponent, competitor, foe, antagonist, adversary, assailant, nemesis, archenemy, *bête noire* (French), detractor, prosecutor, inquisitor, informer, calumniator, falsifier, disputant, traducer, asperser, defiler, defamer, slanderer, backbiter, vilifier.— *Ant.* FRIEND, supporter, benefactor.
*See Synonym Study at* OPPONENT.

**energetic,** *modif.* — *Syn.* vigorous, dynamic, industrious, forceful; see **active** 2, **dynamic.**
*See Synonym Study at* ACTIVE.

**energetically,** *modif.* — *Syn.* actively, firmly, strenuously; see **vigorously.**

**energize,** *v.* — *Syn.* fortify, invigorate, stimulate; see **animate** 1, **excite** 2, **strengthen.**

**energy,** *n.* **1.** [One's internal powers] — *Syn.* force, power, vigor, vitality, strength, stamina, dynamism, vim, spirit, pep*, get-up-and-go*, starch*, steam*; see also **enthusiasm** 1, **strength** 1, **vitality.**

**2.** [Vigor in expression or action] — *Syn.* effectiveness, drive, vehemence; see **force** 3.

**3.** [Power developed or released by a device] — *Syn.*

horsepower, reaction, response, power, pressure, thrust, propulsion, potential energy, kinetic energy, atomic energy, solar energy, thermonuclear power, foot-pounds, magnetism, friction, voltage, kilowatts, kilowatt-hours, current, service, dynamism, electricity, hydroelectric power, gravity, heat, conductivity, suction, elasticity, rays, radioactivity, potential, burn, critical burn, power descent, PD, gas mileage, fuel consumption.
*See Synonym Study at* STRENGTH.

**enervate,** *v.* — *Syn.* debilitate, devitalize, enfeeble, exhaust; see **drain** 2, **weaken** 2.
*See Synonym Study at* UNNERVE, WEAKEN.

**enfeeble,** *v.* — *Syn.* weaken, debilitate, enervate, cripple; see **weaken** 2.

**enfold,** *v.* — *Syn.* envelop, wrap up, encase, enclose; see **surround** 1, 2, **wrap** 1, 2.

**enforce,** *v.* **1.** [To add strength] — *Syn.* reinforce, fortify, support; see **strengthen.**
**2.** [To require compliance] — *Syn.* urge, compel, impose, exert, drive, demand, carry out vigorously, put in force, implement, invoke, have executed, expect, dictate, exact, require, pressure, constrain, execute, administer, coerce, oblige, insist upon, emphasize, necessitate, press, impel, make, sanction, wrest, extort, force, stress, spur, hound*, dragoon*, whip*, lash*, put the screws on*, crack down*, clamp down*, get tough*. — *Ant.* ABANDON, neglect, waive.

**enforced,** *modif.* — *Syn.* in force, prescribed, ordained, compelled, established, demanded, exacted, required, constrained, executed, pressed, sanctioned, forced upon, kept, dictated, imposed, invoked, advocated, charged, enjoined, prevalent, carried out, in operation.

**enforcement,** *n.* — *Syn.* requirement, enforcing, carrying out, implementation, prescription, exaction, compulsion, constraint, coercion, pressure, duress, martial law, obligation, compelling necessity, necessitation, execution, compulsory action, impulsion, insistence, fulfilling, translating into action, Hobson's choice*, spur*, whip*, lash*, crackdown*.

**enfranchise,** *v.* **1.** [To liberate] — *Syn.* emancipate, release, manumit; see **free** 1.
**2.** [To empower] — *Syn.* license, authorize, sanction, admit to citizenship; see **allow** 1.

**enfranchisement,** *n.* **1.** [Liberation] — *Syn.* emancipation, release, manumission; see **freeing.**
**2.** [Empowerment] — *Syn.* authorization, license, the franchise; see **permission, right** 1, 2, **vote** 3.

**engage,** *v.* **1.** [To hire] — *Syn.* employ, contract, retain, reserve; see **hire** 1, **rent** 2.
**2.** [To engross] — *Syn.* absorb, captivate, bewitch; see **fascinate.**
**3.** [To occupy] — *Syn.* keep busy, employ, interest, involve; see **occupy** 3.
**4.** [To enter into conflict with] — *Syn.* battle, clash with, assault; see **attack** 1, **fight** 2.
**5.** [To enmesh, especially gears] — *Syn.* interlock, mesh, interlace; see **fasten** 1, **join** 1.

**engaged,** *modif.* **1.** [Promised in marriage] — *Syn.* betrothed, affianced, bound, pledged, plighted, matched, intended, committed, hooked*, ringed*. — *Ant.* FREE, available, unbetrothed.
**2.** [Not at liberty] — *Syn.* busy, occupied, involved, tied up; see **busy** 1, 3, **rapt** 2.
**3.** [In a profession, business, or the like] — *Syn.* employed, practicing, performing, working at, dealing in, doing, interested, absorbed in, pursuing, at work, involved in, engaged with, connected with; see also **employed.** — *Ant.* UNEMPLOYED, out of a job, without connection.

**engage in,** *v.* — *Syn.* take part in, undertake, be involved in; see **apply (oneself), participate** 1, **perform** 1.

**engagement,** *n.* **1.** [A predetermined action] — *Syn.* meeting, rendezvous, obligation, commitment; see **appointment** 2, **duty** 2, **promise** 1.
**2.** [The state of being betrothed] — *Syn.* compact, match, betrothal, espousal, commitment, betrothing, publishing the banns, betrothment, troth.
**3.** [A battle] — *Syn.* action, combat, skirmish; see **battle** 1.
*See Synonym Study at* BATTLE.

**engaging,** *modif.* — *Syn.* pleasant, winning, appealing, likable; see **charming.**

**engender,** *v.* — *Syn.* induce, incite, cause; see **cause** 2, **produce** 1, 2.

**engine,** *n.* **1.** [A machine for transforming power] — *Syn.* motor, power plant, dynamo, generator, turbine, diesel engine, traction engine, plasma engine, ion engine, steam turbine, reciprocating engine, transformer, step-up transformer, source of power, diesel, powerhouse*.
**2.** [A locomotive] — *Syn.* steam engine, motor, traction engine; see **locomotive.**

**engineer,** *n.* **1.** [A specialist in engineering] — *Syn.* surveyor, designer, planner, builder, inventor, technician, bridge monkey*, sights*, techie*.
Types of engineers include: mining, civil, metallurgical, geological, atomic, nuclear, architectural, chemical, construction, stationary, military, naval, flight, pneumatic, hydraulic, marine, electronic, communications, electrical, mechanical, acoustic, design, manufacturing, industrial, research, developmental, systems; see also **electronics, science** 1.
**2.** [The operator of a locomotive] — *Syn.* driver, motorman, brakeman, stoker, fireman, engineman, hoghead*, hogger*, Casey Jones*, lokey man*, engine tamer*.

**engineer,** *v.* — *Syn.* direct, superintend, mastermind; see **manage** 1.

**engineering,** *n.* **1.** [The act of turning material to use] — *Syn.* construction, manufacturing, organization, organizing, building, arranging, constructing, implementing, authorizing, systematizing, systematization, handling; see also **sense** 2.
**2.** [The science of applying power to use] — *Syn.* design, planning, blueprinting, structure(s), surveying, metallurgy, architecture, heavy construction, light construction, industrial construction, shipbuilding, installations, stresses, communications; see also sense 1.
Branches of engineering include: acoustic, aeronautical, agricultural, architectural, chemical, civil, contracting, design, electrical, flight, food, heating, highway, human, industrial, irrigation, marine, mechanical, military, mining, naval, nuclear, petroleum, radio, railroad, sanitary, stationary, steam, systems, traction, transportation.

**England,** *n.* — *Syn.* Britain, Great Britain, British Isles, United Kingdom, the UK, Britannia, member of the Commonwealth, "the tight little isle," Albion, John Bull*.

**English,** *modif.* — *Syn.* British, Britannic, Anglian, Anglican, Anglic, Anglo-, England's, His Majesty's, Her Majesty's, Commonwealth, non-Celtic, Anglicized, insular, English-speaking, Anglo-Saxon, Saxon, Norman, Limey*; see also **Anglo-Saxon.**

**English,** *n.* — *Syn.* British, Englishmen, Anglo-Saxons, islanders, Britons, Britishers, John Bulls*, Limeys*, cockneys*.

**engrave,** *v.* **1.** [To impress deeply] — *Syn.* stamp, fix, imprint; see **embed** 1, **mark** 1.
**2.** [To carve letters, designs, etc. on a surface, as for

printing] — *Syn.* etch, incise, lithograph, cut, scratch, burn, ornament with incised designs, intaglio, chase, enchase, grave, chisel, inscribe, mezzotint, stipple, crosshatch, hatch, diaper, use a burin; see also **carve** 1.

**engraved**, *modif.* — *Syn.* carved, decorated, minted, chased, etched, scratched, bitten into, embossed, furrowed, incised, deepened, marked deeply, lithographed.

**engraver**, *n.* — *Syn.* graver, etcher, sculptor, artist, cutter, carver, lithographer, lapidary.

**engraving**, *n.* 1. [A process of reproduction] — *Syn.* photoengraving, etching, carving; see **reproduction** 1. 2. [A picture reproduced by engraving] — *Syn.* print, incised design, wood engraving, xylograph, etching, aquatint, drypoint, graphotype, photogravure, steelplate, rotogravure, lithograph, chromolithograph, copperplate, mezzotint, cut, woodcut, linocut, intaglio, halftone, illustration, impression, copy, print, pull, proof, positive.

**engross**, *v.* — *Syn.* preoccupy, engage, immerse; see **fascinate, monopolize, occupy** 3.

**engrossing**, *modif.* — *Syn.* absorbing, gripping, consuming, involving; see **interesting**.

**engrossment**, *n.* — *Syn.* intentness, preoccupation, study; see **reflection** 1.

**engulf**, *v.* — *Syn.* swallow up, inundate, submerge, overwhelm; see **cover** 8, **immerse** 1, **sink** 2.

**enhance**, *v.* — *Syn.* intensify, heighten, magnify, flatter; see **become** 2, **improve** 1, **intensify**. *See Synonym Study at* INTENSIFY.

**enhancement**, *n.* — *Syn.* augmentation, intensification, enrichment; see **improvement** 1, 2, **increase** 1.

**enigma**, *n.* 1. [Puzzle] — *Syn.* problem, riddle, parable; see **puzzle** 2, 3. 2. [Anything or anyone inexplicable] — *Syn.* mystery, sphinx, puzzler; see **puzzle** 2, **secret**. *See Synonym Study at* PUZZLE.

**enigmatic**, *modif.* — *Syn.* ambiguous, cryptic, baffling, mysterious; see **obscure** 1, **secret** 1. *See Synonym Study at* OBSCURE.

**enjoin**, *v.* — *Syn.* order, charge, urge, prohibit; see **advise** 1, **command** 1, **forbid**. *See Synonym Study at* COMMAND, FORBID.

**enjoy**, *v.* 1. [To take pleasure in] — *Syn.* relish, savor, delight in, luxuriate in, revel in, appreciate, fancy, be pleased with, bask in, feast on, get a kick out of*, get a charge out of*, eat up*, dig*, get off on*; see also **like** 1. — *Ant.* abhor, suffer, endure. 2. [To have the use of] — *Syn.* command, hold, possess, have, experience, partake of, have the benefit of, exercise; see also **own** 1, **use** 1.

**enjoyable**, *modif.* — *Syn.* pleasant, agreeable, delightful, fun; see **pleasant** 2. *See Synonym Study at* PLEASANT.

**enjoyment**, *n.* 1. [The result of obtaining one's desire] — *Syn.* satisfaction, pleasure, delight, happiness; see **pleasure** 1, **satisfaction** 2. 2. [The act of fulfilling one's desire] — *Syn.* satisfaction, gratification, enjoying, rejoicing, delighting, triumph, appreciation, spending, having, using, occupation, use, possession, benefit, fun, diversion, entertainment, amusement, pleasure, luxury, sensuality, indulgence, self-indulgence, self-gratification, voluptuousness, hedonism. — *Ant.* ABSTINENCE, refusal, rejection. *See Synonym Study at* PLEASURE.

**enjoy oneself**, *v.* — *Syn.* have a good time, take pleasure, celebrate, have fun, have a ball*, have the time of one's life*, live it up*, party*; see also **play** 1.

**enkindle**, *v.* 1. [To ignite] — *Syn.* fire, inflame, kindle; see **ignite**. 2. [To stimulate] — *Syn.* incite, evoke, arouse; see **excite** 2.

**enlarge**, *v.* 1. [To become larger] — *Syn.* expand, spread, swell, increase; see **grow** 1. 2. [To make larger] — *Syn.* extend, augment, expand, increase; see **increase** 1. *See Synonym Study at* INCREASE.

**enlarged**, *modif.* — *Syn.* increased, augmented, expanded, blown up, developed, elaborated, exaggerated, caricatured, extended, amplified, spread, added to, aggrandized, lengthened, broadened, widened, thickened, magnified, filled out, inflated, stretched, dilated, distended, swollen, tumid, turgid, heightened, intensified. — *Ant.* REDUCED, contracted, shrunken.

**enlargement**, *n.* 1. [Growth or extension] — *Syn.* augmentation, amplification, expansion; see **increase** 1. 2. [An enlarged photograph] — *Syn.* blowup, enlarged print, view; see **photograph, picture** 2.

**enlarge on** or **upon**, *v.* — *Syn.* expatiate, elaborate on, develop, amplify; see **detail** 1, **develop** 4.

**enlighten**, *v.* 1. [To provide information or understanding] — *Syn.* inform, acquaint, edify, set straight; see **notify** 1, **teach** 1, **tell** 1. 2. [To bring supposed spiritual truth] — *Syn.* illumine, illuminate, reveal, inculcate, indoctrinate, edify, inspirit, uplift, give faith, preach, save, catechize, convert, persuade, show the light, lead to the light, bring out of the wilderness, raise up, open one's eyes.

**enlightened**, *modif.* — *Syn.* informed, well-informed, aware, broad-minded; see **educated** 1, **knowledgeable, liberal** 2, **rational** 1.

**enlightenment**, *n.* — *Syn.* wisdom, awareness, culture, education, edification, understanding, illumination, satori (Zen Buddhism); see also **civilization** 1, **education** 1, **knowledge** 1.

**enlist**, *v.* 1. [To enroll others] — *Syn.* engage, hire, retain, reserve, call up, sign up, recruit, mobilize, induct, register, list, levy, record, initiate, inscribe, employ, place, admit, press into service, draft, conscript, muster, call to arms, incorporate. — *Ant.* REFUSE, neglect, turn away. 2. [To request or secure assistance] — *Syn.* interest, attract, win, procure, induce, obtain, get, secure, engage, oblige, appoint, assign. — *Ant.* shun, AVOID, discourage. 3. [To enroll oneself] — *Syn.* enter, sign up, volunteer, serve; see **join** 2, **register** 4, **volunteer** 2.

**enlisted**, *modif.* — *Syn.* recruited, enrolled, commissioned, engaged, joined, registered, entered, volunteered, lined up, signed up, drafted, inducted, conscripted.

**enlistment**, *n.* — *Syn.* conscription, levy, recruitment; see **draft** 6, **enrollment** 1.

**enliven**, *v.* — *Syn.* cheer, liven up, vivify, quicken; see **animate** 1, **excite** 1.

**enlivenment**, *n.* — *Syn.* cheerfulness, liveliness, animation; see **action** 1, **happiness** 1.

**en masse**, *modif.* — *Syn.* bodily, ensemble, together, as a group; see **altogether** 2, **jointly**.

**enmesh**, *v.* — *Syn.* trap, entrap, snare; see **entangle**.

**enmity**, *n.* — *Syn.* antagonism, hostility, animosity, malice, rancor, ill will; see also **hatred** 1, 2.

---

**SYN.** — **enmity** denotes a strong, settled feeling of hatred, whether concealed, displayed, or latent; **hostility** usually suggests enmity expressed in active opposition, attacks, etc.; **animosity** suggests bitterness of feeling that tends to break out in open hostility; **antagonism** stresses the mutual hostility or enmity of persons, forces, etc.

---

**ennoble,** *v.* — *Syn.* honor, exalt, dignify; see **praise** 1, **promote** 2.

**ennoblement,** *n.* — *Syn.* exaltation, promotion, dignity; see **fame** 1, **honor** 1.

**ennui,** *n.* — *Syn.* apathy, languor, tedium; see **boredom.**

**enormity,** *n.* **1.** [Vice] — *Syn.* atrocity, outrage, depravity, wickedness; see **atrocity** 2, **crime** 1, **evil** 1.

**2.** [Magnitude] — *Syn.* immensity, enormousness, vastness; see **size** 2.

**enormous,** *modif.* — *Syn.* gigantic, tremendous, monstrous, immense, huge, colossal, mammoth; see also **large** 1.

---

**SYN.** — **enormous** implies an exceeding by far what is normal in size, amount, or degree /an *enormous* nose, *enormous* expenses/; **immense**, basically implying immeasurability, suggests size beyond the regular run of measurements but does not connote abnormality in that which is very large /redwoods are *immense* trees/; **huge** usually suggests great mass or bulk /a *huge* building, *huge* profits/; **gigantic**, **colossal**, and **mammoth** etymologically imply a comparison with specific objects of great size (respectively, a giant, the Colossus of Rhodes, and the huge, extinct elephant) and therefore emphasize the idea of great magnitude, force, importance, etc., now often hyperbolically; **tremendous**, literally suggesting that which inspires awe or amazement because of its great size, is also used loosely as an intensive term

---

**enough,** *modif.* **1.** [As much as necessary or desirable] — *Syn.* sufficient, adequate, ample, plenty, abundant, full, replete, plenteous, acceptable, copious, satisfactory, complete, plentiful, satisfying, bounteous, lavish, unlimited, suitable. — *Ant.* INADEQUATE, deficient, insufficient.

**2.** [Sufficiently] — *Syn.* satisfactorily, amply, abundantly; see **adequately** 1.

**3.** [Fully] — *Syn.* quite, rather, just; see **very.**

**4.** [Just adequately] — *Syn.* tolerably, fairly, barely; see **adequately** 2.

---

**SYN.** — **enough** and **sufficient** agree in describing that which satisfies a requirement exactly and is neither more nor less in amount than is needed /*enough* food for a week, a word to the wise is *sufficient*/; **adequate** suggests the meeting of an acceptable (sometimes barely so) standard of fitness or suitability /the supporting players were *adequate*/

---

**enough,** *n.* — *Syn.* abundance, sufficiency, adequacy; see **plenty.**

**enrage,** *v.* — *Syn.* incense, infuriate, madden; see **anger** 1.

**enrapture,** *v.* — *Syn.* enchant, entrance, allure, delight; see **charm** 1, **fascinate.**

**enrich,** *v.* — *Syn.* enhance, adorn, ameliorate, add to; see **contribute, decorate, improve** 1, **supplement.**

**enriched,** *modif.* — *Syn.* improved, embellished, enhanced, fortified; see **improved** 1, **increased.**

**enrichment,** *n.* — *Syn.* advancement, endowment, enhancement, embellishment; see **decoration** 1, **improvement** 1.

**enroll,** *v.* **1.** [To obtain for service] — *Syn.* recruit, obtain, employ; see **enlist** 1, **hire** 1.·

**2.** [To prepare a roll] — *Syn.* register, record, matriculate, schedule, catalog, inventory, place upon a list, en-

ter, put down, poll, inscribe, mark, affix, enlist, bill, book, slate, file, index. — *Ant.* DISCARD, reject, omit.

**3.** [To register oneself] — *Syn.* enter, sign up, enlist; see **join** 2, **register** 4.

**enrolled,** *modif.* — *Syn.* registered, matriculated, entered, on the rolls, signed up, joined, inducted, installed, subscribed, pledged, enlisted, commissioned, employed, recruited, inscribed, recorded, listed, on record, on the books.

**enrollment,** *n.* **1.** [The act of enrolling] — *Syn.* registration, registering, recording, matriculation, listing, record, enlistment, rallying, inducting, induction, entry, enlisting, joining, mobilizing, recruitment, selecting, installing, admission, sign-up*.

**2.** [The persons enrolled] — *Syn.* group, students, student body, volunteers, number enrolled, response, registration, conscription, entrance, accession, subscription, influx, roll, register, roster.

**en route,** *modif.* — *Syn.* in transit, on the way, along the way, traveling, midway, in passage, on the road, flying, driving, entrained, advancing, pressing on, making headway toward, bound, progressing toward, heading toward, *en voyage* (French). — *Ant.* MOTIONLESS, delayed, stalled.

**ensemble,** *n.* **1.** [Entirety] — *Syn.* group, aggregate, composite, set; see **collection** 2, **gathering, organization** 3, **whole.**

**2.** [Costume] — *Syn.* coordinates, outfit, suit, garb; see **clothes, suit** 3.

**3.** [Group of entertainers] — *Syn.* group, band, troupe, company, chamber musicians, chorus, jazz band, combo*; trio, quartet, quintet, sextet.

**enshrine,** *v.* — *Syn.* consecrate, hallow, sanctify; see **bless** 3, **cherish** 1.

**enshroud,** *v.* — *Syn.* cover, conceal, wrap; see **hide** 1.

**ensign,** *n.* **1.** [A symbolic standard] — *Syn.* flag, banner, insignia, colors, jack, pennant, streamer, pennon, pendant, title, badge; see also **badge** 2, **emblem.**

**2.** [The lowest commissioned naval officer] — *Syn.* subaltern, cadet, standard bearer; see **officer** 3.

**enslave,** *v.* — *Syn.* subjugate, bind, put in irons, oppress, hold under, restrain, restrict, enthrall, indenture, reduce to slavery, make a slave of, hold in bondage, chain, fetter, enchain, control, dominate, coerce, compel, circumscribe, check, subdue, capture, take captive, suppress, disfranchise, hold, imprison, incarcerate, confine, immure, hobble, yoke, tie, tether, secure, shackle, clap in irons, bend to the plow, bend to the yoke.

**enslavement,** *n.* — *Syn.* thralldom, subjection, servitude; see **slavery** 1.

**ensnare,** *v.* — *Syn.* entrap, trap, snare, capture; see **catch** 1, 2, **entangle.**

**ensue,** *v.* — *Syn.* result, follow, eventuate arise; see **happen** 2, **result, succeed** 2.
*See Synonym Study at* FOLLOW.

**ensure,** *v.* — *Syn.* guarantee, secure, assure, warrant; see **guarantee** 1.

**entail,** *v.* — *Syn.* occasion, necessitate, involve; see **cause** 2, **require** 2.

**entangle,** *v.* — *Syn.* ensnare, entrap, trap, snare, involve, complicate, implicate, snarl, corner, enmesh, catch, tangle, ravel, dishevel, unsettle, embroil, mix up, muddle, foul up*. — *Ant.* LIBERATE, disentangle, extricate.

**entanglement,** *n.* — *Syn.* complexity, involvement, complication, snare; see **affair** 2, **confusion** 2, **difficulty** 1, 2.

**entente,** *n.* — *Syn.* understanding, rapprochement, harmony, alliance; see **agreement** 2, 3.

**enter,** *v.* **1.** [To enter physically] — *Syn.* come in, go in, get in, get into, set foot in, invade, penetrate, intrude, break in, pass in, pass into, walk in, step in, drive in, burst in, rush in, charge in, storm in, barge in, crash in, make way into, gain entree, gain admission, be admitted, reenter, make an entrance, access, slip in, sneak in, slink in, steal in, wriggle in, creep in, crawl in, edge in, squeeze in, insinuate oneself, worm oneself into, infiltrate, filter in, insert, pierce, put in, push in, move in, work in, hop in, jump in, crowd in, throng in, pile in, jam in, pour in, fall into, butt in, horn in, breeze in\*, bust in\*, blow in\*, bop in\*. — *Ant.* LEAVE, depart, exit.

**2.** [To enter upon] — *Syn.* start, open, make a beginning; see **begin** 1, 2.

**3.** [To join] — *Syn.* enroll, subscribe, take part in; see **join** 2.

**4.** [To write down] — *Syn.* record, register, inscribe; see **list** 1, **record** 1.

**entered,** *modif.* — *Syn.* filed, listed, posted; see **enrolled, recorded.**

**enter into,** *v.* — *Syn.* engage in, take part in, become part of; see **join** 2, **participate** 1.

**enter on** or **upon,** *v.* — *Syn.* start, take up, make a beginning; see **begin** 1.

**enterprise,** *n.* **1.** [A difficult or important project] — *Syn.* undertaking, venture, work, endeavor, performance, scheme, plan, engagement, adventure, affair, business, business venture, company, operation, campaign, action, activity, project, program, cause, crusade, effort, move, risk, hazard, try, task, attempt, pursuit, purpose, speculation, stake.

**2.** [A venturesome or industrious disposition] — *Syn.* initiative, drive, pluck, industry; see **ambition** 1, **courage** 1, **force** 3.

**enterprising,** *modif.* — *Syn.* venturesome, resourceful, energetic, ambitious; see **active** 2, **ambitious** 1.
*See Synonym Study at* AMBITIOUS.

**entertain,** *v.* **1.** [To keep amused] — *Syn.* amuse, divert, cheer, please, interest, enliven, delight, beguile, regale, engross, occupy, enthrall, charm, captivate, recreate, inspire, inspirit, stimulate, exhilarate, gratify, satisfy, humor, distract, indulge, solace, relax, make merry, disport, comfort, put in good humor, elate, gladden, tickle. — *Ant.* tire, BORE, weary, depress.

**2.** [To act as host or hostess] — *Syn.* receive, invite, treat, regale, recreate, gratify, feed, wine and dine, host, chaperon, give a party, have people over, have company, be at home, keep open house, do the honors, welcome, give a warm reception, make welcome, show hospitality to, receive with open arms, roll out the red carpet, kill the fatted calf, throw a party\*. — *Ant.* neglect, ignore, banish.

**3.** [To consider] — *Syn.* contemplate, have in mind, harbor, cherish; see **consider** 1, 3, **think** 1.
*See Synonym Study at* AMUSE.

**entertained,** *modif.* **1.** [Given hospitality] — *Syn.* welcomed, treated, harbored, sheltered, cherished, regaled, honored, received, feasted, banqueted, wined and dined, feted. — *Ant.* NEGLECTED, ignored, spurned.

**2.** [Diverted] — *Syn.* amused, pleased, beguiled, occupied, charmed, engrossed, enthralled, entranced, exhilarated, cheered, interested, relaxed, delighted, enjoying oneself, happy, in good humor, in good company, transported, having fun, having a good time, tickled, tickled pink\*. — *Ant.* BORED, depressed, irritated.

**entertainer,** *n.* — *Syn.* performer, player, artist; see **actor** 1, **actress, clown, dancer, singer.**

**entertaining,** *modif.* — *Syn.* diverting, amusing, fun, funny, humorous, droll, engaging, delightful, pleasing, enchanting, lively, witty, clever, interesting, charming, enjoyable, pleasurable, pleasant, cheerful, gay, jolly, relaxing, restorative, recreational, edifying, affecting, moving, inspiring, captivating, beguiling, thrilling, entrancing, engrossing, enthralling, stirring, enticing, piquant, impressive, stimulating, absorbing, distracting, striking, exciting, compelling, provocative, fascinating, ravishing, rousing, exhilarating, animating, zestful, delectable, satisfying, gratifying, winning, alluring, seductive, enlivening; see also **funny** 1. — *Ant.* BORING, irritating, dull.

**entertainment,** *n.* **1.** [The act of amusing] — *Syn.* amusement, diversion, recreation, fun, enjoyment, merriment, *divertissement* (French), pleasure, delight, cheer, sport, play, frolic, pastime, revelry, merrymaking, relaxation, distraction, escape, regalement. — *Ant.* tediousness, BOREDOM, ennui.

**2.** [Something intended to entertain] — *Syn.* performance, show, play, production, presentation, stage show, floor show, cabaret, party, fete, feast, banquet, picnic, television, motion picture, movie, the movies, sport, dance, concert, reception, treat, game, surprise, hootenanny, refection, refreshment, spectacle, extravaganza; see also **party** 1, **performance** 2, **show** 2.

**enthrall,** *v.* — *Syn.* captivate, bewitch, enchant, spellbind; see **fascinate.**

**enthrallment,** *n.* — *Syn.* fascination, enchantment, charm; see **attraction** 1.

**enthrone,** *v.* — *Syn.* elevate, exalt, ennoble; see **crown** 2, **praise** 1.

**enthused,** *modif.* — *Syn.* enthusiastic, excited, approving, eager; see **enthusiastic** 1, 2.

**enthusiasm,** *n.* **1.** [Ardent zeal] — *Syn.* fervor, zeal, ardor, interest, passion, vehemence, eagerness, zealousness, earnestness, fanaticism, frenzy, intensity, feeling, zest, keenness, vim, energy, activity, ardency, ecstasy, craze, mania, vivacity, impetuosity, fever, fieriness, élan, excitement, vigor, verve, furor, spirit, flare, rapture, heat, relish, gusto, vitality, animation, *brio* (Italian), alacrity, avidity, transport, joy, emotion, warmth, exhilaration, exuberance, *joie de vivre* (French), glow, rage, devotion, fury, fullness of heart, fire, life, go\*, snap\*, pep\*, zip\*, dash\*. — *Ant.* DULLNESS, weariness, ennui.

**2.** [Something arousing interest or zeal] — *Syn.* craze, fad, passion, interest; see **fad.**

---

**SYN.** — **enthusiasm** implies strongly favorable feelings for an object or cause and usually suggests eagerness in the pursuit of something [her *enthusiasm* for golf]; **zeal** implies intense enthusiasm for an object or cause, usually as displayed in vigorous and untiring activity in its support [a *zeal* for reform]; **passion** usually implies a strong emotion that has an overpowering or compelling effect [his *passions* overcame his reason; a *passion* for music]; **fervor** and **ardor** both imply emotion of burning intensity, **fervor** suggesting a constant glow of feeling [religious *fervor*], and **ardor**, a restless, flamelike emotion [the *ardors* of youth]

---

**enthusiast,** *n.* **1.** [A person full of enthusiasm for something] — *Syn.* devotee, fan, aficionado, fanatic, zealot, fancier, admirer, lover, collector, practitioner, follower, supporter, believer, votary, worshiper, partisan, maniac, addict, monomaniac, energumen, buff\*, nut\*, bug\*, fiend\*, crank\*, freak\*, junkie\*, -aholic\* (*used in combination*), hound\*, groupie\*. — *Ant.* detractor, opponent, CYNIC.

**2.** [An ardent supporter] — *Syn.* partisan, champion, booster; see **follower, supporter.**
*See Synonym Study at* ZEALOT.

**enthusiastic,** *modif.* **1.** [Excited by something] — *Syn.* interested, fascinated, animated, willing, thrilled, fevered, feverish, flushed, concerned, pleased, excited, attracted, titillated, exhilarated, anxious, tantalized, athirst, ablaze, agog, intent, eager, heated, breathless, all hepped up★, keyed up★, charged up★, pumped up★, psyched up★, psyched★, dying to★. — *Ant.* INDIFFERENT, detached, uninterested.
**2.** [Strongly in favor of something] — *Syn.* keen, ardent, zealous, avid, passionate, fervent, enthused, inflamed, tireless, absorbed, rapt, devoted, diligent, resolute, indefatigable, desirous, eager, steadfast, assiduous, sleepless, impassioned, partial, voracious, yearning, longing, desiring, sedulous, burning, glowing, warm, spirited, zestful, fervid, ecstatic, transported, impatient, delighted, rapturous, enraptured, rhapsodic, intent, vehement, effusive, gushing, keen on, keen about, wild about★, crazy about★, mad about★, gone on★, hot on★, all worked up over★, nuts about★, gaga over★, jumping at★, all hopped up over★, ape over★, hot for★, gung-ho★, ready and willing★, champing at the bit★, dying to★, aching for★, aching to★, hyped on★. — *Ant.* OPPOSED, reluctant, apathetic.
**3.** [Inclined to enthusiasm] — *Syn.* excitable, warm, ardent, forward, passionate, earnest, impetuous, impatient, aspiring, spirited, vivacious, effervescent, exuberant, willing, inclined, possessed, inspired, intense, hot, impulsive, fiery, rabid, sanguine, maniacal, ambitious, ebullient, mercurial, apt for, overeager, given to enthusiasm(s), not prudent, not restrained. — *Ant.* DULL, lethargic, sluggish.
**entice,** *v.* — *Syn.* lure, allure, attract; see **fascinate, seduce, tempt.**
*See Synonym Study at* TEMPT.
**enticement,** *n.* **1.** [The act of attracting] — *Syn.* allurement, temptation, seduction; see **attraction** 1.
**2.** [That which attracts] — *Syn.* lure, bait, promise; see **attraction** 2.
**entire,** *modif.* — *Syn.* complete, whole, undivided, intact; see **whole** 1, 2.
*See Synonym Study at* COMPLETE.
**entirely,** *modif.* **1.** [Completely] — *Syn.* totally, fully, wholly; see **completely.**
**2.** [Exclusively] — *Syn.* uniquely, solely, undividedly; see **only** 1.
**entirety,** *n.* **1.** [Wholeness] — *Syn.* completeness, totality, collectivity, collectiveness, intactness, plenitude, fullness, entireness, allness, universality, integrality, ensemble.
**2.** [A whole] — *Syn.* total, aggregate, sum; see **whole.**
**entitle,** *v.* **1.** [To name] — *Syn.* call, designate, label; see **name** 1.
**2.** [To permit] — *Syn.* authorize, empower, qualify; see **allow** 1.
**entity,** *n.* **1.** [Essence] — *Syn.* existence, substance, actuality, being; see **reality** 1.
**2.** [Something real in itself] — *Syn.* thing, object, item, article; see **thing** 1.
**entomb,** *v.* — *Syn.* bury, inter, inurn, inhume; see **bury** 1.
**entombment,** *n.* — *Syn.* burial, interment, inurnment, sepulture; see **funeral** 1.
**entourage,** *n.* **1.** [Companions] — *Syn.* retinue, attendants, followers; see **escort, following.**
**2.** [Environment] — *Syn.* surroundings, milieu, locale; see **environment, neighborhood.**
**entrails,** *n.* — *Syn.* viscera, guts, insides; see **intestines.**
**entrance,** *n.* **1.** [The act of coming in] — *Syn.* arrival, entry, ingress, incoming, ingoing, ingression, access, admission, admittance, entree, appearance, coming, passage, approach, progress, induction, initiation, introduction, inception, baptism, accession, import, importation, penetration, trespass, debut, enrollment, enlistment, registering, invasion, immigration. — *Ant.* ESCAPE, exit, issue.
**2.** [A place for entering] — *Syn.* gate, door, doorway, entry, inlet, gateway, portal, porch, portico, opening, passage, vestibule, lobby, foyer, staircase, hall, hallway, archway, ingress, path, way, entranceway, entryway, passageway, threshold, corridor, approach, stoop, aperture, hole, gape, port, gorge, adit, propylaeum. — *Ant.* EXIT, mouth, outlet.
**entrance,** *v.* **1.** [To enchant] — *Syn.* charm, enrapture, captivate, enthrall; see **fascinate.**
**2.** [To put into a trance] — *Syn.* hypnotize, mesmerize, spellbind; see **hypnotize** 1.
**entrant,** *n.* **1.** [A contestant] — *Syn.* participant, competitor, player, candidate; see **contestant, opponent** 1.
**2.** [A new arrival or member] — *Syn.* recruit, newcomer, novice; see **beginner.**
**entrap,** *v.* **1.** [To catch] — *Syn.* ensnare, capture, trap, decoy; see **ambush, catch** 1, 2, **entangle.**
**2.** [To lure into difficulty] — *Syn.* inveigle, trick, seduce; see **deceive, tempt.**
**entrapment,** *n.* — *Syn.* snare, ambush, inveiglement; see **capture, deception** 1, **trap** 1, **trick** 1.
**entreat,** *v.* — *Syn.* beg, implore, supplicate, plead; see **beg** 1.
*See Synonym Study at* BEG.
**entreaty,** *n.* — *Syn.* petition, supplication, plea; see **appeal** 1, **request.**
**entree,** *n.* **1.** [The right or freedom to enter] — *Syn.* admittance, admission, access, in★; see **entrance** 1, **introduction** 1.
**2.** [The principal course of a meal] — *Syn.* main course, main dish, *pièce de résistance* (French), meat course; see **dish** 2, **food.**
**3.** [A dish served before the main course or between principal courses] — *Syn.* side dish, entremets, savory, salad, vegetable, appetizer, tidbit; see also **appetizer, delicatessen** 1.
**entrench,** *v.* **1.** [To surround] — *Syn.* fortify, dig in, barricade, protect; see **defend** 1, **surround** 2.
**2.** [To trespass] — *Syn.* encroach, infringe, invade; see **meddle** 1.
**entrenched,** *modif.* — *Syn.* established, rooted, fixed; see **established** 1, **firm** 1, **fortified, safe** 1.
*entre nous* (French), *modif.* — *Syn.* confidentially, intimately, privately, between ourselves; see **secretly.**
**entrepreneur,** *n.* — *Syn.* organizer, manager, contractor, enterpriser; see **administrator, businessperson.**
**entrust,** *v.* — *Syn.* deposit with, trust to, leave with, consign; see **commit** 2, **trust** 3.
*See Synonym Study at* COMMIT.
**entry,** *n.* **1.** [Entrance] — *Syn.* admission, approach, hall, lobby, foyer, door, gate; see also **entrance** 1, 2.
**2.** [ [An item recorded] — *Syn.* record, note, listing, insertion; see **note** 2.
**entwine,** *v.* — *Syn.* twine, lace, twist; see **twist, weave** 1.
**enumerate,** *v.* — *Syn.* list, mention, identify; see **count, name** 2, **specify.**
**enumeration,** *n.* — *Syn.* inventory, catalog, register; see **catalog, list.**
**enunciate,** *v.* **1.** [To state formally] — *Syn.* announce, proclaim, affirm; see **declare** 1.
**2.** [To pronounce distinctly] — *Syn.* articulate, pronounce, sound, sound out, voice, modulate, intone, vocalize, deliver, express; see also **utter.**

*See Synonym Study at* UTTER.

**enunciation**, *n.* **1.** [Clear speech] — *Syn.* articulation, pronunciation, delivery; see **diction**.

**2.** [A formal statement] — *Syn.* pronouncement, announcement, proclamation; see **declaration** 1, 2.

**envelop**, *v.* — *Syn.* encompass, wrap up, cover, conceal; see **enclose** 1, **hide** 1, **surround** 2, **wrap** 2.

**envelope**, *n.* — *Syn.* receptacle, pouch, mailer, cover, pocket, bag, container, box, covering, case, hide, wrapper, wrapping, jacket, holder, enclosure, vesicle, sheath, casing.

**envenom**, *v.* **1.** [To poison] — *Syn.* infect, contaminate, pollute; see **poison**.

**2.** [To alienate] — *Syn.* embitter, estrange, anger; see **alienate**, **anger** 1.

**enviable**, *modif.* — *Syn.* desirable, sought-after, advantageous, superior; see **excellent**, **fortunate** 1, **wanted**.

**envious**, *modif.* **1.** [Having a jealous nature] — *Syn.* distrustful, suspicious, watchful; see **jealous**.

**2.** [Desiring a possession of another] — *Syn.* covetous, desirous, resentful, jealous, desiring, wishful, longing for, aspiring, greedy, grasping, craving, hankering, begrudging, grudging, jaundiced, green-eyed★, jaundice-eyed★, green with envy★. — *Ant.* GENEROUS, gracious, charitable.

**environment**, *n.* — *Syn.* conditions, living conditions, circumstances, surroundings, ambience, climate, atmosphere, entourage, scene, environs, external conditions, milieu, background, setting, locale, habitat, ecosystem, situation, context.

**environmentalist**, *n.* — *Syn.* ecologist, conservationist, antipollutionist, Green; see **ecologist**.

**environs**, *n.* — *Syn.* suburbs, vicinity, locality; see **environment**, **neighborhood**.

**envisage**, *v.* — *Syn.* visualize, imagine, conceive, envision; see **imagine** 1.

**envoy**, *n.* — *Syn.* emissary, representative, intermediary, envoy extraordinary; see **agent** 1, **diplomat** 1.

**envy**, *n.* — *Syn.* jealousy, resentment, covetousness, rivalry, ill-will, spite, grudge, malice, enviousness, grudgingness, jealous competition, jaundiced eye, discontent at another's good fortune, backbiting, cupidity, greed, bitterness, invidiousness, maliciousness, lack of Christian charity, one of the seven deadly sins, bad sportsmanship, mean-spiritedness, lusting after another's goods, coveting another's possessions, desiring, hankering, longing, begrudging, *invidia* (Latin), the green-eyed monster★.

**envy**, *v.* — *Syn.* grudge, begrudge, covet, lust after, regard with envy, resent, have hard feelings toward, desire inordinately, crave, be envious of, feel resentful toward, hunger after, thirst after, desire, long for, yearn for, hanker after, be green with envy★.

---

*SYN.* — **envy** another is to feel ill will, jealousy, or discontent at the person's possession of something that one keenly desires to have or achieve oneself; **begrudge** implies an unwillingness that someone should possess or enjoy something that is needed or deserved; to **covet** is to long ardently and wrongfully for something that belongs to another

---

**enwreathe**, *v.* — *Syn.* encircle, garland, entwine, festoon, interweave, interlace, twine, twist, wreathe, plait, braid; see **decorate**.

**enzyme**, *n.* — *Syn.* protein, ferment, barm, yeast, leaven, organic catalyst; see also **catalyst** 1.

**eon**, *n.* — *Syn.* eternity, cycle, age; see **age** 3, 4, **period** 1.

*See Synonym Study at* PERIOD.

**epaulet**, *n.* — *Syn.* badge, shoulder ornament, insignia; see **badge** 2, **decoration** 3.

**ephemeral**, *modif.* — *Syn.* transient, evanescent, fleeting; see **evanescent**, **temporary**.

*See Synonym Study at* TRANSIENT.

**epic**, *modif.* — *Syn.* heroic, classic, grand, grandiose, narrative, Homeric, historic, momentous, significant, tremendous, huge, vast, monumental, major, on a grand scale. — *Ant.* UNIMPORTANT, small, lyric.

**epic**, *n.* — *Syn.* narrative poem, heroic poem, heroic story, saga, legend, chronicle, epos, epopee, national epic; see also **poem**, **story**.

**epicure**, *n.* — *Syn.* gourmet, gastronome, gourmand, glutton, epicurean, connoisseur, bon vivant, oenophile, Brillat-Savarin, Lucullus, foodie★; see also **connoisseur**.

---

*SYN.* — **epicure** is a person who has a highly refined taste for fine foods and drinks and takes great pleasure in indulging it; a **gourmet** is a connoisseur in eating and drinking who appreciates subtle differences in flavor or quality; **gourmand**, occasionally equivalent to **gourmet**, is more often applied to a person who has a hearty liking for good food or one who is inclined to eat to excess; a **gastronome** is an expert in all phases of the art or science of good eating; a **glutton** is a greedy, voracious eater and drinker

---

**epicurean**, *n.* — *Syn.* hedonist, sensualist, sybarite; see **glutton**, **hedonist**.

**epicureanism**, *n.* — *Syn.* hedonism, sensuality, self-indulgence; see **enjoyment** 2, **greed**, **indulgence** 3.

**epidemic**, *n.* — *Syn.* plague, scourge, pestilence, pandemic; see **disease**.

**epidermis**, *n.* — *Syn.* cuticle, dermis, hide; see **skin**.

**epigram**, *n.* — *Syn.* witticism, quip, aphorism, bon mot; see **joke** 2, **motto**, **saying**.

*See Synonym Study at* SAYING.

**epigrammatic**, *modif.* — *Syn.* terse, aphoristic, succinct, pointed; see **concise**, **pithy**, **witty**.

**epilogue**, *n.* — *Syn.* afterword, postscript, conclusion, coda; see **appendix**, **postscript**.

**episcopacy**, *n.* — *Syn.* prelacy, pontificate, canonry; see **bishopric**.

**episcopal**, *modif.* — *Syn.* pontifical, ecclesiastical, apostolic; see **clerical** 2.

**episode**, *n.* — *Syn.* happening, occurrence, incident, event, experience, adventure, interlude, installment, scene, chapter, passage; see also **event** 1, 2.

*See Synonym Study at* OCCURRENCE.

**episodic**, *modif.* — *Syn.* rambling, roundabout, discursive, incidental; see **indirect**, **verbose**.

**epitaph**, *n.* — *Syn.* inscription, commemoration, remembrance, memorial, sentiment, eulogy, elegy, tribute, lines on a gravestone, *hic jacet* (Latin).

**epithet**, *n.* — *Syn.* designation, appellation, sobriquet; see **name** 1, 3.

**epitome**, *n.* **1.** [A typical or extreme example] — *Syn.* embodiment, exemplification, quintessence, essence, perfect example, exemplar, representative, type, typification, personification, incarnation, archetype, model, prototype, pattern, ultimate, last word; see also **model** 1.

**2.** [A brief summary] — *Syn.* abstract, abridgment, précis; see **abridgment** 2, **summary**.

*See Synonym Study at* ABRIDGMENT.

**epitomize**, *v.* — *Syn.* outline, summarize, condense; see **compress**, **decrease** 2, **summarize**.

**epoch,** *n.* — *Syn.* era, period, time, milestone; see **age** 3, **period** 1, **time** 2.
*See Synonym Study at* PERIOD.

**equal,** *modif.* — *Syn.* even, regular, like, same, identical, similar, equivalent, commensurate, comparable, tantamount, uniform, invariable, equable, unvarying, balanced, fair, just, impartial, unbiased, to the same degree, on a footing with, without distinction, in as many as, equitable, selfsame, coordinate, one and the same, of a piece, alike, level, parallel, corresponding, correspondent, according, proportionate, coextensive, congruent, coequal, even-steven*. — *Ant.* unequal, uneven, DIFFERENT.
*See Synonym Study at* SAME.

**equal,** *n.* — *Syn.* parallel, match, counterpart, complement, peer, compeer, fellow, mate, twin, double, likeness, opposite number, alter ego, companion, copy, duplicate, equivalent, rival, competitor.

**equal,** *v.* — *Syn.* match, meet, rank with, be the same as, be equal to, rival, touch, parallel, equate, coordinate, approach, live up to, come up to, amount to, consist of, comprise, be made of, be composed of, measure up to, stack up against, tie, knot the score, check with, even off, break even, be the equivalent of, be as good as, keep pace with, come to, reach, compare, accord with, square with, tally with, agree, correspond, be tantamount to, be identical, be commensurate, rise to, rise to meet.

**equality,** *n.* — *Syn.* balance, parity, uniformity, sameness, likeness, identity, equivalence, correspondence, parallelism, evenness, equalization, equation, equilibrium, symmetry, impartiality, fairness, fair play, justice, equitableness, equity, egalitarianism, brotherhood, civil rights, state of being equal, identical value, lack of distinction, equal opportunity, six of one and half a dozen of the other*, a fair shake*, level playing field*. — *Ant.* inequality, unfairness, disparity.

**equalize,** *v.* — *Syn.* make equal, make even, balance, equate, even up, match, bring to a common level, level, square, adjust, standardize, regularize, make uniform, establish equilibrium, democratize.

**equally,** *modif.* — *Syn.* evenly, uniformly, coequally, symmetrically, proportionately, correspondingly, coordinately, equivalently, identically, on a level, both, either ... or, impartially, justly, fairly, equitably, across the board, on even terms, dispassionately, as well as, without distinction, to the same degree, the same for one as for another, "with malice towards none," fifty-fifty*, even-steven*. — *Ant.* unequally, UNFAIRLY, unevenly.

**equal to,** *modif.* — *Syn.* adequate for, capable of, qualified; see **able** 3.

**equanimity,** *n.* — *Syn.* composure, serenity, poise, patience; see **composure**.
*See Synonym Study at* COMPOSURE.

**equate,** *v.* 1. [To compare] — *Syn.* liken, associate, relate; see **compare** 1.
2. [To make equal] — *Syn.* equalize, average, balance; see **equalize**.

**equation,** *n.* — *Syn.* equating, comparison, equalization, mathematical statement, formal statement of equivalence; see also **comparison** 1, 2.
Kinds of equations include: linear, quadratic, conic, cubic.

**equator,** *n.* — *Syn.* middle, circumference of the earth, great circle; see **tropics**.

**equatorial,** *modif.* — *Syn.* tropical, torrid, central; see **hot** 1, **tropic** 1.

**equilibrium,** *n.* 1. [Balance] — *Syn.* stability, steadiness, center of gravity, equipoise; see **balance** 2, **equality**.

2. [Mental or emotional balance] — *Syn.* equanimity, poise, calm; see **composure**.

**equip,** *v.* 1. [To supply] — *Syn.* furnish, outfit, implement; see **provide** 1.
2. [To array] — *Syn.* adorn, deck, dress; see **clothe, decorate**.
*See Synonym Study at* FURNISH.

**equipage,** *n.* — *Syn.* apparatus, outfit, gear; see **equipment**.

**equipment,** *n.* — *Syn.* material, materiel, tools, machinery, facilities, implements, utensils, supplies, apparatus, gear, outfit, kit, furnishings, equipage, appliances, paraphernalia, belongings, devices, accessories, appurtenances, attachments, extras, conveniences, accouterments, contraptions, articles, tackle, rig, fittings, trappings, contrivances, gadgets, fixtures, movables, accompaniments, provisions, armor, fixings*, stuff*, things*; see also **machine** 1.

**equipped,** *modif.* — *Syn.* outfitted, furnished, supplied, rigged, rigged up, fitted, fitted out, arrayed, dressed, accoutered, assembled, readied, provided, implemented, decked, bedecked, clothed, appareled, appointed, completed, complemented, supplemented, set up, harnessed, armed, invested. — *Ant.* unfurnished, stripped, bare.

**equitable,** *modif.* — *Syn.* fair, impartial, just, evenhanded; see **equal, fair** 1.

**equity,** *n.* 1. [Net value of property] — *Syn.* investment, assets, stake, ownership; see **property** 1.
2. [Fairness] — *Syn.* impartiality, justice, evenhandedness; see **equality, fairness**.

**equivalence,** *n.* — *Syn.* parity, identity, equality, sameness; see **equality**.

**equivalent,** *modif.* — *Syn.* commensurate, comparable, equal, similar; see **equal**.
*See Synonym Study at* SAME.

**equivocal,** *modif.* — *Syn.* ambiguous, dubious, puzzling, misleading; see **obscure** 1.
*See Synonym Study at* OBSCURE.

**equivocate,** *v.* — *Syn.* hedge, dodge, prevaricate; see **lie** 1.
*See Synonym Study at* LIE.

**equivocation,** *n.* — *Syn.* quibbling, evasion, prevarication; see **lie** 1.

**era,** *n.* — *Syn.* epoch, period, time; see **age** 3, **period** 1.
*See Synonym Study at* PERIOD.

**eradicate,** *v.* — *Syn.* extirpate, exterminate, annihilate; see **abolish, destroy** 1.
*See Synonym Study at* EXTERMINATE.

**eradication,** *n.* — *Syn.* extermination, annihilation, elimination; see **destruction** 1.

**erase,** *v.* 1. [To rub or wipe out] — *Syn.* delete, cancel, obliterate, expunge, efface, eradicate; see also **cancel** 1.
2. [*To kill] — *Syn.* murder, slay, dispatch; see **kill** 1.

---

**SYN.** — **erase** implies a scraping or rubbing out of something written or drawn, or figuratively, the removal of an impression; to **expunge** is to remove or wipe out completely; **efface** implies a rubbing out from a surface, and, in extended use, suggests a destroying of the distinguishing marks, or even of the very existence, of something; **obliterate** implies a thorough blotting out of something so that all visible traces of it are removed; **delete** implies the marking of written or printed matter for removal, or the removal of the matter itself

---

**erasure,** *n.* — *Syn.* cancellation, deletion, expunging, obliteration, canceling, rubbing out, blotting out, sponging out, crossing out, scratching out, abrasion, effacing, deleting, eradication, wiping out, striking out.

**erect,** *modif.* — *Syn.* upright, vertical, perpendicular, standing up; see **straight** 1, **upright** 1.

**erect,** *v.* **1.** [To build] — *Syn.* construct, raise, fabricate; see **build** 1.

**2.** [To assemble] — *Syn.* put together, fit together, join, set up; see **assemble** 3.

**3.** [To raise] — *Syn.* lift up, set up, plant, upraise; see **raise** 1.

**4.** [To establish] — *Syn.* found, institute, set up, form; see **establish** 2, **organize** 2.

**erected,** *modif.* **1.** [Stood on end] — *Syn.* implanted, reared, upraised, raised, reared, elevated, lifted, hoisted, set up, standing up, uplifted, upreared, boosted. — *Ant.* lowered, leveled, horizontal.

**2.** [Built] — *Syn.* constructed, completed, raised; see **built** 1.

**erection,** *n.* — *Syn.* building, erecting, constructing; see **construction** 1.

**eremite,** *n.* — *Syn.* solitary, recluse, anchorite; see **hermit.**

*ergo* (Latin), *conj. & modif.* — *Syn.* therefore, hence, consequently, thus; see **therefore.**

**erode,** *v.* — *Syn.* disintegrate, corrode, consume, wear away; see **decay.**

**erosion,** *n.* — *Syn.* wearing away, eating away, washing away, land despoliation, desedimentation, ablation, leaching away, depletion, wear and tear, corrosion, abrasion, attrition, detrition, weathering, washout; see also **decay** 1, 2.

**erotic,** *modif.* — *Syn.* sensual, amatory, suggestive, erogenous; see **lewd** 1, 2, **sensual** 2.

**err,** *v.* — *Syn.* misjudge, blunder, be mistaken; see **fail** 1.

**errand,** *n.* — *Syn.* mission, task, commission, chore; see **duty** 2, **job** 2.

**errand runner,** *n.* — *Syn.* messenger, courier, runner, errand boy, errand girl, assistant, personal assistant, aide, helper, deliveryman, office boy, office girl, copy aide, copy boy, clerk, page, bellhop, porter, redcap, shop assistant, dispatch rider, gofer*, flunky*, lackey*, boots*.

**errant,** *modif.* — *Syn.* itinerant, rambling, shifting, straying; see **erring, wandering** 1.

**erratic,** *modif.* **1.** [Strange] — *Syn.* eccentric, queer, irregular, capricious; see **unusual** 2.

**2.** [Variable] — *Syn.* inconsistent, unpredictable, inconstant; see **aimless, changeable** 1, 2, **random.**

**3.** [Wandering] — *Syn.* shifting, directionless, unfixed, rambling; see **aimless, wandering** 1.

**erratically,** *modif.* — *Syn.* intermittently, eccentrically, capriciously, carelessly; see **unevenly.**

**erratum,** *n.* — *Syn.* misprint, mistake, typo*; see **error** 1.

**erring,** *modif.* — *Syn.* mistaken, blundering, in error, fallible, straying, errant, deviating, sinful, sinning, faulty, delinquent, culpable, criminal; see also **wrong** 1, 2.

**erroneous,** *modif.* — *Syn.* mistaken, incorrect, inaccurate, untrue; see **false** 2, **wrong** 2.

**error,** *n.* **1.** [A specific miscalculation] — *Syn.* mistake, blunder, slip, fault, faux pas, gaffe, oversight, inaccuracy, goof, misjudgment, miscalculation, deviation, wrong, lapse, miss, failure, mismanagement, misdoing, omission, slight, misprint, typographical error, typo*, slip of the tongue, misusage, solecism, malapropism, mispronunciation, misstep, misunderstanding, misbelief, absurdity, misreport, untruth, trip, stumble, bungle, botch, flaw, erratum, corrigendum, howler*, glitch*, boner*, boo-boo*, blooper*, slip-up*, muff*, bad job*,

flub*, clinker*, bobble*, miscue*, fluff*, screw-up*, foul-up*, snafu*.

**2.** [General misconception] — *Syn.* falsity, delusion, misunderstanding, erroneousness; see **fallacy** 1, **misunderstanding** 1.

**3.** [A moral offense] — *Syn.* transgression, wrongdoing, sin; see **sin.**

---

**SYN.** — **error** implies deviation from truth, accuracy, correctness or right and is the broadest term in this comparison [an *error* in judgment, in computation, etc.]; **mistake** suggests an error resulting from carelessness, inattention, misunderstanding, etc. and does not in itself carry a strong implication of criticism [ a *mistake* in reading a blueprint]; **blunder** carries a suggestion of more severe criticism and implies such causes as stupidity, clumsiness, or inefficiency [a tactical *blunder* cost them the war]; a **slip** is a mistake, usually slight, made inadvertently in speaking or writing; a **faux pas** is a social blunder or error in etiquette that causes embarrassment; **boner** and **booboo**, slang terms, are applied to a silly or ridiculous blunder

---

**ersatz,** *modif.* — *Syn.* artificial, synthetic, imitation; see **artificial** 1, **false** 3, **manufactured.**
*See Synonym Study at* ARTIFICIAL.

**erstwhile,** *modif.* — *Syn.* former, past, recent; see **preceding.**

**erudite,** *modif.* — *Syn.* learned, scholarly, well-read; see **educated** 1, **learned** 1, 2.

**erudition,** *n.* — *Syn.* learning, scholarship, education, enlightenment; see **culture** 3, **knowledge** 1.
*See Synonym Study at* INFORMATION.

**erupt,** *v.* — *Syn.* eject, vent, burst forth; see **emit** 1, **explode** 1.

**eruption,** *n.* — *Syn.* burst, outburst, flow; see **explosion** 1.

**escalate,** *v.* — *Syn.* heighten, intensify, step up; see **increase** 1.

**escalation,** *n.* — *Syn.* intensification, growth, acceleration; see **increase** 1, **rise** 2.

**escalator,** *n.* — *Syn.* moving staircase, *escalier* (French), people mover, incline; see **elevator** 1.

**escapade,** *n.* — *Syn.* adventure, prank, caper, lark; see **joke** 1, **venture.**

**escape,** *n.* **1.** [The act of escaping] — *Syn.* flight, getaway, retreat, disappearance, evasion, avoidance, leave, departure, withdrawal, hegira, elopement, desertion, abdication, decampment, liberation, deliverance, rescue, freedom, release, extrication, breakout, jailbreak, break*, French leave*, close call*, close shave*, slip*, AWOL*. — *Ant.* IMPRISONMENT, retention, capture.

**2.** [Place of escape] — *Syn.* exit, outlet, way out, loophole, overflow, outflow, leakage, leak, fire escape, waste pipe, sewer, hatch, porthole, alleyway, floodgate, exhaust, draft, escape valve, vent.

**3.** [Mental release] — *Syn.* distraction, diversion, escapism; see **avoidance, entertainment** 1, **oblivion** 1.

**escape,** *v.* — *Syn.* flee, fly, leave, depart, elude, avoid, evade, dodge, run off, run away, get away, get out, slip away, make one's escape, make off, disappear, vanish, steal off, steal away, get away from, break out, break away, bolt, get free, get clear of, desert, slip out, elope, run out, run out on, leak out, flow out, gush forth, emerge, burst out, avoid danger, go free, go scot-free, decamp, abscond, take flight, take off, free oneself, break loose, gain, liberty, break one's bonds, break jail, get off, find a loophole, wriggle out, worm out of, slip by, get by, lead one a merry chase, duck out\*, cut out\*, make a getaway\*, make a break\*, get away with\*, cut and run\*, show one's heels\*, cut loose\*, clear out\*, make oneself scarce\*, play hooky\*, go AWOL\*, bail out\*, save one's bacon\*, save one's neck\*, scram\*, skidoo\*, take a powder\*, give one the slip\*, shake\*, shake off\*, fly the coop\*, take it on the lam\*, leg it\*, play hide and seek\*, take French leave\*, skip\*, jump\*. — *Ant.* RETURN, come back, remain.

**SYN.** — **escape** implies a getting out of, a keeping away from, or simply a remaining unaffected by an impending or present danger, evil, confinement, etc. */to escape* death, criticism, etc./; to **avoid** is to make a conscious effort to keep clear of something undesirable or harmful */to avoid* crowds during a flu epidemic/; to **evade** is to escape or avoid by artifice, cunning, adroitness, etc. */to evade* pursuit, one's duty, etc./; to **elude** is to escape the grasp of someone or something by artful or slippery dodges or because of a baffling quality */the criminal eluded* the police, the meaning *eluded* him/

**escaped,** *modif.* — *Syn.* out, at liberty, liberated; see **free** 2.
**escapist,** *n.* — *Syn.* dreamer, romanticist, evader; see **idealist.**
**escarpment,** *n.* — *Syn.* slope, cliff, ledge; see **hill, mountain** 1, **rock** 2.
**eschew,** *v.* — *Syn.* shun, keep away from, abstain from; see **abstain, avoid.**
**escort,** *n.* — *Syn.* guide, protection, bodyguard, attendant, henchman, safeguard, guard, date, companion, partner, gentleman friend, cavalier, squire, guard of honor, retinue, entourage, train, convoy, cortege, consort; see also **companion** 2.
**escort,** *v.* — *Syn.* accompany, attend, conduct, take out\*; see **accompany** 1, **date** 2.
*See Synonym Study at* ACCOMPANY.
**escutcheon,** *n.* — *Syn.* shield, coat of arms, crest; see **arms** 2, **badge** 2.
**a blot on one's escutcheon** — *Syn.* stain, stigma, disgrace; see **scandal.**
**esophagus,** *n.* — *Syn.* jugular region, gullet, gorge; see **throat.**
**esoteric,** *modif.* — *Syn.* arcane, private, recondite, abstruse; see **difficult** 2, **obscure** 1, 2, **secret** 1.
**especial,** *modif.* — *Syn.* special, particular, exceptional; see **special** 1, **unusual** 1, 2.
*See Synonym Study at* SPECIAL.
**especially,** *modif.* **1.** [To an unusual degree] — *Syn.* particularly, unusually, exceptionally, abnormally, extraordinarily, uncommonly, peculiarly, preeminently, eminently, supremely, remarkably, wonderfully, oddly, queerly, strangely, curiously, notably, markedly, unaccountably, uniquely, uncustomarily, singularly, unexpectedly, observably, strikingly, conspicuously, signally, to a marked degree, in particular, occasioning comment, above all, above the mark; see also **very.** — *Ant.* USUALLY, commonly, normally.
**2.** [For one more than for others] — *Syn.* chiefly, mainly, primarily; see **principally.**
**espionage,** *n.* — *Syn.* spying, undercover work, reconnaissance, surveillance; see **spying.**
**espousal,** *n.* **1.** [Support] — *Syn.* adoption, advocacy, promotion; see **aid** 1.
**2.** [Marriage] — *Syn.* wedding, betrothal, matrimony; see **marriage** 1.
**espouse,** *v.* **1.** [To support] — *Syn.* advocate, adopt, take up, uphold; see **adopt** 2, **support** 2.

**2.** [To take as a spouse] — *Syn.* marry, wed, betroth; see **marry** 1.
**esprit,** *n.* — *Syn.* quickwittedness, intelligence, acumen; see **acumen, wit** 1.
**esprit de corps,** *n.* — *Syn.* morale, group spirit, camaraderie; see **cooperation** 1, **fellowship** 1.
**essay,** *n.* **1.** [Expository writing] — *Syn.* composition, article, piece, theme; see **exposition** 2.
**2.** [An effort] — *Syn.* trial, attempt, endeavor; see **effort** 1, 2.
**essayist,** *n.* — *Syn.* columnist, commentator, critic, editorial writer; see **author** 2, **writer.**
**essence,** *n.* **1.** [Fundamental nature] — *Syn.* pith, core, kernel, gist, root, nature, basis, being, essential quality, spirit, sum and substance, reality, quintessence, constitution, substance, binder, filler, nucleus, vital part, base, chief constituent, primary element, germ, heart, marrow, backbone, caliber, soul, lifeblood, bottom, life, grain, structure, principle, vein, character, fundamentals; see also **characteristic.**
**2.** [A distilled spirit] — *Syn.* concentrate, extract, elixir, distillation, juice, spirit(s), tincture, liquor, alcohol, ammonia, potion, drug, drops, perfume, fragrance, scent.
**in essence** — *Syn.* fundamentally, basically, at bottom; see **essentially.**
**essential,** *modif.* **1.** [Absolutely necessary] — *Syn.* imperative, required, indispensable, requisite, necessary, vital; see also **crucial, necessary** 1.
**2.** [Rooted in the basis or essence] — *Syn.* basic, primary, quintessential; see **fundamental** 1, **inherent.**

**SYN.** — **essential**, in strict usage, is applicable to that which constitutes the absolute essence or the fundamental nature of a thing and therefore must be present for the thing to exist, function, etc. */food is essential* to life/; an **indispensable** person or thing cannot be done without if the specified or implied purpose is to be achieved */her diagnostic skills proved indispensable* to the clinic/; **requisite** is applied to that which is required by the circumstances or for the purpose and generally suggests a requirement that is imposed externally rather than an inherent need */the requisite* experience for a position/; **necessary** implies a pressing need but does not always connote absolute indispensability

**essentially,** *modif.* — *Syn.* basically, fundamentally, radically, at bottom, at heart, centrally, originally, intimately, chiefly, indispensably, naturally, inherently, permanently, determinately, necessarily, primarily, significantly, importantly, at the heart of, in effect, in essence, *au fond* (French), in the main, all the more, characteristically, intrinsically, substantially, typically, vitally, approximately, quite, actually, truly, really, factually, materially, virtually, more or less so; see also **principally.** — *Ant.* APPARENTLY, superficially, on the surface.
**establish,** *v.* **1.** [To set up in a formal manner] — *Syn.* institute, found, authorize; see **organize** 2.
**2.** [To work or settle in a permanent place] — *Syn.* set up, install, build, erect, build up, entrench, set, plant, root, place, settle, lodge, settle in, lay the foundation, lay the foundation for, make provisions for, domiciliate, practice, live, ground, ensconce, set on its feet, land. — *Ant.* unsettle, uproot, break up.
**3.** [To determine] — *Syn.* ascertain, learn, find out; see **discover.**
**4.** [To prove] — *Syn.* verify, authenticate, confirm; see **prove.**
**5.** [To make secure] — *Syn.* fix, secure, stabilize; see **fasten** 1.

**established,** *modif.* **1.** [In a firm position] — *Syn.* secure, fixed, stable, set, entrenched, settled, well-established, rooted, vested, officially recognized, old-line, deep-rooted, ingrained, unshakable; see also **permanent** 2, **traditional** 2.

**2.** [Set up to endure] — *Syn.* endowed, founded, organized, instituted, set up, realized, originated, chartered, incorporated, settled, inaugurated, codified, systematized, ratified, equipped, brought into existence, conceived, produced, begun, initiated, completed, finished. — *Ant.* TEMPORARY, unsound, insolvent.

**3.** [Conclusively proved] — *Syn.* verified, approved, guaranteed, endorsed, demonstrated, determined, confirmed, substantiated, accepted, assured, concluded, closed, authenticated, corroborated, found out, achieved, upheld, certain, ascertained, valid, validated, identified, proved, undeniable, sure, objectified. — *Ant.* FALSE, invalidated, untrue.

**establishing,** *n.* **1.** [The act of founding] — *Syn.* organizing, starting, setting up, beginning, founding, inaugurating, instituting, originating, constituting, initiating, settling, endowing, chartering, fixing, subsidizing, implementing, stabilizing, building, regulating, setting on foot, laying the cornerstone. — *Ant.* ending, tearing down, dissolving.

**2.** [The act of proving] — *Syn.* verifying, substantiating, demonstrating, authenticating, corroborating, validating, confirming, proving; see also **proof** 1.

**establishment,** *n.* **1.** [The act of setting up] — *Syn.* founding, endowment, institution; see **establishing** 1.

**2.** [A business, organization, or the like] — *Syn.* company, corporation, enterprise; see **business** 4.

**3.** [The act of proving] — *Syn.* verification, substantiation, demonstration; see **establishing** 2, **proof** 1.

**estate,** *n.* **1.** [An extensive residence] — *Syn.* holdings, land, property, manor, grounds, domain, farm, rural seat, country place, country home, plantation, ranch, hacienda, freehold, territory, fields, realty.

**2.** [Possessions left at one's death] — *Syn.* property, bequest, inheritance, fortune, endowment, wealth, legacy, heritage, patrimony, belongings, possessions, chattels, effects, earthly possessions, personal property, private property.

**the fourth estate** — *Syn.* the press, mass media, journalists; see **journalism, press** 2, **radio** 1, **television.**

**esteem,** *n.* — *Syn.* regard, respect, appreciation; see **admiration.**

**esteem,** *v.* **1.** [To attach a high value to] — *Syn.* prize, respect, value, hold in high regard; see admire 1, **appreciate** 2.

**2.** [To consider] — *Syn.* account, judge, deem; see **consider** 2, **regard** 2.

*See Synonym Study at* APPRECIATE, REGARD.

**estimable,** *modif.* **1.** [Worthy] — *Syn.* deserving, admirable, respected; see **respectable, worthy.**

**2.** [Calculable] — *Syn.* appreciable, computable, appraisable; see **calculable.**

**estimate,** *n.* **1.** [An appraisal of the value of something] — *Syn.* evaluation, assessment, appraisal, estimation, valuation, appraisement, calculation, gauging, rating, assay, survey, measure, mensuration, reckoning; see also **judgment** 2.

**2.** [Opinion] — *Syn.* judgment, appraisal, estimation, view; see **judgment** 3.

**3.** [A considered guess] — *Syn.* approximation, estimation, educated guess, guesstimate*; see **guess.**

**estimate,** *v.* **1.** [To make a rough or tentative appraisal] — *Syn.* appraise, approximate, rate, value, evaluate, count, number, reckon, guess, judge, gauge, figure, measure, calculate, figure costs, assess, assay, account, compute, prepare an estimate, furnish an estimate, set a value on, set a figure, budget, prepare a budget, do the cost accounting, get figures for, guesstimate*, give a ballpark figure*; see also **calculate** 1. — *Ant.* check, MEASURE, verify.

**2.** [To form an opinion about] — *Syn.* consider, reckon, figure, evaluate, appraise, suspect, predict, suppose, prophesy, reason, think, expect, regard, judge, deem, view, rate, class, rank, look upon, surmise, conjecture, determine, decide, conclude, size up*.

---

*SYN.* — **estimate,** in this comparison, refers broadly to the forming of a personal opinion or judgment; **appraise** implies the aim of giving an accurate or expert judgment, as of value or worth [to *appraise* a new house]; **evaluate** also connotes an attempt at an exact judgment, but rarely with reference to value in terms of money [let us *evaluate* the evidence]; **rate** implies assignment of comparative value, quality, etc. [he is *rated* the best in his field] See also Synonym Study at CALCULATE.

---

**estimated,** *modif.* — *Syn.* supposed, approximated, predicted, guessed at; see **likely** 1.

**estimating,** *n.* — *Syn.* judging, supposing, reckoning; see **guessing.**

**estimation,** *n.* **1.** [A personal estimate] — *Syn.* opinion, appraisal, evaluation, view; see **judgment** 3.

**2.** [The act of making an estimate] — *Syn.* calculating, estimating, predicting, reckoning; see **calculation** 1, **estimate** 1, **guess.**

**estrange,** *v.* — *Syn.* alienate, disaffect, separate, come between; see **alienate, divide** 1.

**estrangement,** *n.* — *Syn.* disaffection, separation, breach, withdrawal; see **alienation, divorce.**

**estuary,** *n.* — *Syn.* river mouth, inlet, arm of the sea, fiord, drowned river, tidewater, tidal river; see also **arm** 3, **bay** 1, **water** 2.

**et cetera** or **etc.,** *modif.* — *Syn.* and so forth, and so on, and others, et al., and the like, and on and on, and all the rest, *und so weiter* (German), along with others, and all, whatever*, whatnot*.

**etch,** *v.* **1.** [To remove metal with acid] — *Syn.* cut, eat away, corrode, scratch; see **bite** 3, **carve** 1.

**2.** [To use etching as an artistic medium] — *Syn.* engrave, incise, prepare a plate; see **draw** 2, **engrave** 2.

**etching,** *n.* **1.** [A process for producing printing plates] — *Syn.* biting, cutting, engraving, photoengraving, delineating, processing, transferring, treating with acid, preparing a plate, reproduction; see also **drawing** 1, **reproduction** 1.

**2.** [A work of art] — *Syn.* print, black and white, colored print, colored etching, old master, aquatint, mezzotint, *eau-forte* (French); the work of an etcher: Rembrandt, Whistler, Pennell, Goya, etc.; see also **engraving** 2, **picture** 3.

**eternal,** *modif.* **1.** [Without pause] — *Syn.* endless, interminable, continual, unbroken, continuous, continued, unceasing, incessant, ceaseless, constant, unending, enduring, persistent, always, relentless, uninterrupted, unremitting; see also **perpetual** 1. — *Ant.* CHANGEABLE, inconstant, fluctuating.

**2.** [Without end] — *Syn.* everlasting, unending, endless, perpetual, never-ending, termless, infinite, indefinite, permanent, ageless, boundless, timeless, immortal, deathless, undying, forever, interminable, indeterminable, dateless, immeasurable, unfading, indestructible, always, limitless, imperishable, illimitable, indomi-

table, unconquerable, unyielding, eonian, sempiternal, to one's dying day, till doomsday, for ever and a day, for ever and ever; see also **perpetual** 1.— *Ant.* finite, TEMPORARY, ending.
*See Synonym Study at* PERPETUAL.

**eternally,** *modif.*— *Syn.* forever, endlessly, continually, perpetually; see **forever** 1, **regularly** 2.

**eternity,** *n.* **1.** [Time without end]— *Syn.* endlessness, forever, endless duration, infinite duration, timelessness, everlastingness, perpetuity, world without end, *saecula saeculorum* (Latin), the future, infinity, all eternity, forever and a day, eon, age; see also **immortality** 1.— *Ant.* moment, instant, second.
**2.** [Life after death]— *Syn.* other world, everlastingness, afterlife; see **immortality** 2.

**ethereal,** *modif.* **1.** [Delicate]— *Syn.* airy, fragile, insubstantial; see **light** 5.
**2.** [Celestial]— *Syn.* heavenly, supernal, empyreal; see **astronomical** 1, **divine** 1.

**ethical,** *modif.*— *Syn.* humane, moral, upright; see **decent** 2, **moral** 1, **noble** 1, 2.
*See Synonym Study at* MORAL.

**ethics,** *n.*— *Syn.* rules of conduct, morality, mores, morals, moral code, decency, integrity, moral conduct, social values, moral practice, principles, values, standards, code of right and wrong, natural law, honesty, goodness, honor, social laws, categorical imperative, the Golden Rule, *bushido* (Japanese).

**ethnology,** *n.*— *Syn.* cultural anthropology, comparative study of cultures, study of mores, study of customs, ethnography; see also **anthropology.**

**etiquette,** *n.*— *Syn.* manners, decorum, social graces, protocol; see **behavior** 1, **custom** 2, **decorum.**
*See Synonym Study at* DECORUM.

**étude,** *n.*— *Syn.* composition, exercise, piece; see **music** 1, **piece** 3.

**etymology,** *n.*— *Syn.* derivation, word origins, word history, development of vocabulary, historical linguistics, philology, onomastics; see also **language** 2.

**Eucharist,** *n.*— *Syn.* Holy Communion, sacrament, mass, oblation; see **communion** 2.

**eugenics,** *n.*— *Syn.* genetics, race improvement, selective breeding, genetic engineering, genetic counseling; see also **biology, heredity, zoology.**

**eulogist,** *n.*— *Syn.* praiser, commender, encomiast, panegyrist, extoller, lauder, glorifier, apologist, flatterer, booster; see also **supporter, sycophant.**

**eulogize,** *v.*— *Syn.* laud, extol, applaud; see **praise** 1.
*See Synonym Study at* PRAISE.

**eulogy,** *n.*— *Syn.* tribute, panegyric, glorification, commendation; see **praise** 2, **tribute** 1.
*See Synonym Study at* TRIBUTE.

**euphemism,** *n.*— *Syn.* substitution, doublespeak, softened expression, polite term, code word, mock modesty, prudishness, indirection, metaphorical speech, verbal extenuation, word in good taste, overdelicacy of speech, affected refinement, genteelism, nice-Nellyism.

**euphemistic,** *modif.*— *Syn.* polite, extenuative, metaphorical, mild, euphemious, softened, indirect, vague, figurative, affected, inoffensive, delicate; see also **refined** 2.

**euphonious,** *modif.*— *Syn.* mellifluous, musical, melodious, pleasant-sounding; see **harmonious** 1, **melodious.**

**euphony,** *n.*— *Syn.* smoothness, harmoniousness, mellifluousness; see **harmony** 1.

**euphoria,** *n.*— *Syn.* elation, exaltation, well-being, cloud nine*; see **happiness** 2, **rapture** 1, 2.

**euphuism,** *n.*— *Syn.* inflation, grandiloquence,

floridness, ornateness of style, delicacy, purism, Gongorism, affected elegance of language, pomposity, bombast, fustian, rhetoric; see also **wordiness.**

**Europe,** *n.*— *Syn.* the Continent, continental Europe, part of Eurasia, part of the Eurasian landmass, the Old World, the old country.
Terms associated with countries, areas, and political divisions in Europe include: *Mittel-Europa* (German), the Mediterranean world, the Low Countries, Balkan states, Adriatic states, Baltic states, Slavic countries, Scandinavian peninsula, Holy Roman Empire, Hellenic peninsula, Balkan peninsula, Albania, Andorra, Austria, Austria-Hungary, Belgium, Bulgaria, Czechoslovakia, Czech, Slovakia, Denmark, Finland, France, *la belle France* (French), Gaul, Alsace-Lorraine, Alsace, Alsatia, Provence, Normandy, Brittany, Gascony, château country, Côte d'Azur, the Riviera, the Midi, Germany, West Germany, East Germany, the Rhine country, Greece, the Greek Isles, Crete, Cyprus, Hungary, Land of the Magyars, Iceland, Republic of Ireland, Eire, Ulster, the Emerald Isle, Italy, Liechtenstein, Luxembourg, Malta, Monaco, Netherlands, Holland, Norway, Sweden, Spitsbergen, Poland, Portugal, Romania, San Marino, Sardinia, Corsica, Gibraltar, Spain, Iberia, Andalusia, Catalonia, Castile, Navarre, Costa Brava, Costa Smeralda, Galicia, Switzerland, Helvetia, Swiss Confederation, Union of Soviet Socialist Republics, USSR, Russia, Ukraine, White Russia, Lithuania, Estonia, Latvia, Moldova, Belarus, United Kingdom of Great Britain and Northern Ireland, England, Britain, Scotland, Wales, the British Isles, Albion, Vatican City, the Vatican, Rome, the Holy See, the Papacy, Slovenia, Yugoslavia, Serbia, Croatia, Montenegro, Bosnia-Herzegovina; see also **England, France, Germany, Great Britain, Greece, Italy, Paris, Rome, Russia, Spain**

**European,** *modif.*— *Syn.* Continental, Old World, old country, Eurasian, Eurafrican, Caucasian, Eurocentric, Indo-European, Western, Western European, Eastern European.
Terms associated with particular European areas include: Anglo-Saxon, British, English, Irish, Anglo-Irish, Irish Gaelic, Ulster, Scottish, Scots, Scotch, Scottish Gaelic, Welsh, Cornish, Kentish, French, Romanic, Romance, Breton, Norman, Corsican, Monegasque, Gallic, Provençal, Gaulish, Alsatian, German, Germanic, Dutch, Netherlandish, Belgian, Flemish, Low German, High German, Saxon, Bavarian, Prussian, Frank, Frankish, Burgundian, Allemanic, Gothic, Teutonic, Nordic, Scandinavian, Danish, Swedish, Norwegian, Icelandic, Swiss, Alpine, Greek, Hellenic, Athenian, Corinthian, Spartan, Peloponnesian, Mycenean, Cretan, Thracian, Illyrian, Ionian, Slovak, Slovakian, Ruthenian, Romanian, Bulgarian, Slav, Slavic, Macedonian, Aegean, Balkan, Adriatic, Albanian, Yugoslavian, Serbian, Croatian, Serbo-Croat, Bosnian, Austro-Hungarian, Hungarian, Magyar, Czechoslovakian, Czech, Bohemian, Russian, Byelorussian, Polish, Baltic, Estonian, Latvian, Lithuanian, Ukranian, Armenian, Moldovian, Muscovite, Uralic, Finnish, Lap, Lappish, Italian, Italic, Latin, Roman, Venetian, Etruscan, Lombard, Tuscan, Florentine, Neapolitan, Sicilian, Maltese, Sardinian, Tyrolese, Savoyard, Apennine, Spanish, Hispanic, Iberian, Portuguese, Catalan, Basque, Majorcan, Castilian, Navarrese, Andalusian, Galician, Romany, Gypsy; see also **Anglo-Saxon, classical** 2, **English, German, Greek, Irish, Italian, Roman, Russian, Scotsman, Scandinavian, Slavic, Spanish.**

**European,** *n.* — *Syn.* Continental, Eastern European, Western European, person from the old country, member of the EEC, member of the European Economic Community, white, Caucasian, Anglo, Westerner.

Terms associated with Europeans from particular areas include: Englishman, Briton, Brit, Britisher; Scotsman, Scot, Highlander, Lowlander; Welshman; Irishman, Ulsterman, Son of Erin, person from the old sod*; Cornishman, Celt, Anglo-Saxon; Frenchman, Savoyard, Norman, Breton, Basque, Gascon; German, Teuton, Prussian, Bavarian, Saxon; Swiss; Dutchman, Netherlander, Hollander; Belgian, Fleming, Flemish, Walloon; Scandinavian, Norseman, Viking, Norlander, Dane, Norwegian, Swede, Icelander, Finn, Lapp; Italian, Roman, Sicilian, Corsican, Calabrese, Venetian, Florentine; Spaniard, Castilian, Catalan, Andalusian, Portuguese, Iberian; Maltese, Austrian, Hungarian, Czechoslovakian, Czech, Bohemian, Slovak, Slav, Monegasque, Russian, Pole, Lithuanian, Latvian, Estonian, Ukrainian, Belarussian, White Russian, Yugoslav, Serb, Croat, Bulgar, Romanian, Balkan, Greek, Gypsy; see also **European,** *modif.*, **French 1, German 2, Greek 1, Spaniard.**

**euthanasia,** *n.* — *Syn.* mercy killing, killing, painless death, easy death, putting one out of one's misery, putting an animal to sleep, release from suffering; see also **death 1, murder.**

**evacuate,** *v.* **1.** [To empty] — *Syn.* void, clear out, deplete, drain; see **empty 2, remove 1.**
**2.** [To withdraw from] — *Syn.* vacate, desert, leave, relocate; see **abandon 2, leave 1.**

**evacuation,** *n.* **1.** [Removal] — *Syn.* draining, discharge, expulsion; see **clearing 1, removal 1.**
**2.** [Withdrawal] — *Syn.* abandonment, removal, retreat, exodus; see **departure 1.**

**evade,** *v.* **1.** [To use trickery to avoid an issue] — *Syn.* equivocate, prevaricate, dodge, sidestep, put off, shuffle, avoid, elude, trick, baffle, quibble, shift, shirk, dissemble, cloak, conceal, deceive, be evasive, fence, parry, change the subject, pretend, confuse, pettifog, circumvent, skirt, hedge, cavil, subtilize, tergiversate, dodge the issue, duck*, beat around the bush*, give someone the runaround*, beg the question*, waffle*, hem and haw*, pussyfoot*, throw off the scent*, lead one a merry chase*, put off*, get around*, get out of*, cop out*, weasel out of *, lie one's way out of*. — *Ant.* FACE, confront, make clear, elucidate.
**2.** [To avoid a meeting] — *Syn.* escape, elude, slip out, sneak away from; see **escape.**
*See Synonym Study at* ESCAPE.

**evaluate,** *v.* — *Syn.* appraise, judge, assess; see **decide, estimate 1, 2.**
*See Synonym Study at* ESTIMATE.

**evanesce,** *v.* — *Syn.* dissipate, vanish, evaporate; see **disappear.**

**evanescence,** *n.* — *Syn.* dissipation, evaporation, vanishing; see **disappearance.**

**evanescent,** *modif.* — *Syn.* vanishing, transient, disappearing, passing, passing away, fading, shifting, fleeting, transitory, flitting, fugitive, ephemeral, short-lived; see also **temporary.**
*See Synonym Study at* TRANSIENT.

**evangelical,** *modif.* **1.** [Fundamentalist] — *Syn.* apostolic, orthodox, pious, scriptural; see **Christian, divine 2, religious 2.**
**2.** [Characterized by missionary zeal] — *Syn.* evangelistic, proselytizing, zealous, fervent; see **enthusiastic 2, 3, religious 2.**

**evangelist,** *n.* — *Syn.* preacher, missionary, revivalist, televangelist; see **minister 1, missionary.**

**evangelize,** *v.* — *Syn.* preach, proselytize, instruct, convert; see **convert 2, preach.**

**evaporate,** *v.* **1.** [To vaporize] — *Syn.* diffuse, dissipate, gasify, steam, steam away, boil away, fume, volatilize, burn off, distill, turn to steam, rise in a fog, rise in a mist.
**2.** [To dehydrate] — *Syn.* concentrate, desiccate, dry up, parch; see **dry 1, 2.**
**3.** [To disappear] — *Syn.* vanish, fade, dissolve; see **disappear.**

**evaporation,** *n.* — *Syn.* drying, dehydration, desiccation, evanescence, vanishing, vaporescence, steaming away, boiling away, vaporization, gasification, volatilization, distillation, dissipation, disappearance, vanishing into thin air, escape; see also **disappearance.** — *Ant.* SOLIDIFICATION, materialization, liquefaction.

**evasion,** *n.* — *Syn.* dodging, quibble, subterfuge, equivocation; see **avoidance, deception 1, trick 1.**

**evasive,** *modif.* — *Syn.* deceptive, misleading, equivocal, shifty; see **dishonest 1, false 2, obscure 1, sly 1.**

**eve,** *n.* — *Syn.* night before, evening before, vigil, verge, brink, threshold; see also **night 1.**

**even,** *modif.* **1.** [Lying in a smooth plane] — *Syn.* flat, smooth, level, flush; see **flat 1, level 2, smooth 1.**
**2.** [Regular] — *Syn.* uniform, constant, steady, homogeneous; see **constant 1, regular 3.**
**3.** [Equal] — *Syn.* balanced, equivalent, square; see **alike 1, 2, equal.**
**4.** [In addition] — *Syn.* still, yet, also, too, as well, still more, moreover, in spite of, despite, notwithstanding, likewise, indeed, but also.
*See Synonym Study at* LEVEL, STEADY.

**break even** — *Syn.* make nothing, tie, neither win nor lose; see **equal, tie 3.**

**evenhanded,** *modif.* — *Syn.* impartial, equitable, just; see **fair 1.**

**evening,** *n.* — *Syn.* twilight, dusk, nightfall, eventide; see **night 1.**

**evening star,** *n.* — *Syn.* morning star, the planet Venus, Vesper, Hesperus; see **planet.**

**evenly,** *modif.* **1.** [On an even plane] — *Syn.* smoothly, regularly, without bumps, uniformly, unvaryingly, steadily, constantly, placidly, tranquilly, fluently, on an even keel, in a groove, without variation, neither up nor down, levelly, straight. — *Ant.* IRREGULARLY, unevenly, roughly.
**2.** [Equally proportioned or distributed] — *Syn.* exactly, justly, fairly, precisely, equally, impartially, identically, equitably, symmetrically, conformably, commensurably, commensurately, proportionately, synonymously, analogously, equivalently, correspondingly, tied, alike, squarely, fifty-fifty*, even-steven*. — *Ant.* inequitably, unjustly, unfairly.

**evenness,** *n.* — *Syn.* smoothness, uniformity, likeness; see **equality, regularity.**

**evensong,** *n.* — *Syn.* vespers, evening prayer, Angelus; see **hymn, prayer 2.**

**event,** *n.* **1.** [Anything that happens] — *Syn.* occurrence, happening, episode, incident, circumstance, affair, phenomenon, development, function, transaction, experience, appearance, turn, tide, shift, phase, accident, chance, pass, ceremony, juncture, conjuncture, situation, proceeding, advent, story, case, matter, occasion, media event, nonevent*.
**2.** [A notable happening] — *Syn.* accident, catastrophe, mishap, mischance, mistake, experience, milestone, landmark, triumph, coincidence, miracle, adventure, holiday, wonder, marvel, celebration, crisis, pre-

dicament, exigency, misfortune, situation, calamity, disaster, emergency, something to write home about*; see also **disaster, holiday** 1, **wonder** 2.

**3.** [A performance] — *Syn.* final event, main event, preliminary event, attraction, contest, competition, bout, joust, display, performance, happening, spectacle, play, drama, match, game, meet, exhibition, curtain raiser; see also **performance** 2.

**4.** [An outcome] — *Syn.* effect, issue, conclusion; see **result.**

**in any event** — *Syn.* anyhow, anyway, in any case, no matter what happens, at all events, whatever may be the case, come what may, happen what may, regardless, at any rate, whatever happens, no matter what else, at least, be that as it may, however; see also **anyhow** 1.

**in the event of** or **that** — *Syn.* in case of, if it should happen that, if there should happen to be; see **if.**

*See Synonym Study at* OCCURRENCE.

**eventful,** *modif.* — *Syn.* momentous, memorable, signal, full; see **active** 2, **important** 1, **memorable** 1.

**eventual,** *modif.* — *Syn.* final, inevitable, ultimate, consequent; see **future, last** 1.

**eventually,** *modif.* — *Syn.* in the end, at last, ultimately; see **finally** 2.

**eventuate,** *v.* — *Syn.* result, come about, ensue, have issue; see **happen** 2, **result.**

**ever,** *modif.* — *Syn.* eternally, always, at all times, at any time; see **always** 1, **at all** at **all, regularly** 2.

**for ever and a day** — *Syn.* always, for ever and ever, perpetually; see **eternal** 2, **forever** 1.

**evergreen,** *n.* — *Syn.* conifer, fir, broad-leaved evergreen, ornamental shrub; see **hedge, pine, tree.**

**everlasting,** *modif.* — *Syn.* eternal, enduring, unending, perpetual; see **eternal** 1, 2, **permanent** 2, **perpetual** 1, 2.

**evermore,** *modif.* — *Syn.* always, eternally, ever; see **forever** 1.

**every,** *modif.* — *Syn.* each one, all, without exception; see **all** 2, **each** 1, 2.

**everybody,** *pron.* — *Syn.* everyone, every person, each one, every one, each and every one, all, one and all, all and sundry, the public, the whole world, *tout le monde* (French), old and young; men, women, and children; the people, the populace, the voters, society, generality, anybody, all sorts, the masses, the man, in the street, Everyman, Everywoman, every man jack, whoever, you and I*, John Q. Public*, Jane Q. Public*, the devil and all*, the hoi polloi*, every Tom, Dick, and Harry*; see also **all, man** 1. — *Ant.* NOBODY, no one, not a one.

**everyday,** *modif.* — *Syn.* commonplace, normal, usual, ordinary; see **common** 1, **daily.**

**every day,** *modif.* — *Syn.* always, all the time, frequently, habitually; see **daily, regularly** 1, 2.

**every now and then,** *modif.* — *Syn.* from time to time, occasionally, once in a while, every so often*; see **frequently, seldom.**

**everyone,** *pron.* — *Syn.* all, each person, whoever; see **everybody.**

**everything,** *pron.* — *Syn.* all, all things, the universe, the whole complex, the whole, the lot, all that, every little thing*, the whole kit and caboodle*; lock, stock and barrel*; the whole bit*, the whole bunch*, the whole shebang*, the whole schmear*, the whole ball of wax*, the whole shooting match*, the works*, you name it*; see also **all.**

**everywhere,** *modif.* — *Syn.* in every place, here and there, all over, all around, at all points, in all places, wherever, wherever one turns, at each point, without exception, ubiquitously, universally, the world over, at all times and places; here, there and everywhere; in every quarter, in every direction, in all quarters, on all hands, on every side, omnipresent, throughout, all over the world, all over the place, all over the map, from Dan to Beersheba, from pole to pole, to the four winds, in all creation, to hell and back*, inside and out*, in every nook and cranny*, to the four corners of the earth, from beginning to end, high and low, far and wide, far and near.

**evict,** *v.* — *Syn.* remove, expel, oust, eject; see **dismiss** 1, **eject** 1.

*See Synonym Study at* EJECT.

**eviction,** *n.* — *Syn.* ouster, ejection, dispossession; see **removal** 1.

**evidence,** *n.* — *Syn.* testimony, data, confirmation, proof, sign, mark, indication, grounds for belief, ammunition*; see also **confirmation** 1, **proof** 1, **sign** 1.

**in evidence** — *Syn.* evident, visible, manifest; see **obvious** 1, 2.

*See Synonym Study at* PROOF.

**evident,** *modif.* **1.** [Open to view] — *Syn.* obvious, apparent, visible, manifest; see **obvious** 1.

**2.** [Clear to the understanding] — *Syn.* apparent, unambiguous, unmistakable, indisputable; see **obvious** 2.

*See Synonym Study at* OBVIOUS.

**evidently,** *modif.* — *Syn.* seemingly, obviously, so far as one can see; see **apparently.**

**evil,** *modif.* **1.** [Morally bad] — *Syn.* immoral, wicked, sinful, corrupt, diabolical, satanic, sinister, heinous, atrocious, monstrous, loathsome, foul, repugnant, despicable, malevolent, malignant; see also **wicked** 1.

**2.** [Unpropitious] — *Syn.* destructive, calamitous, disastrous; see **harmful, ominous, sinister.**

*See Synonym Study at* WICKED.

**evil,** *n.* **1.** [The quality of being evil] — *Syn.* sin, wickedness, depravity, crime, sinfulness, corruption, vice, immorality, iniquity, knavery, perversity, badness, villainy, vileness, baseness, meanness, infamy, heinousness, enormity, criminality, nefariousness, malignity, impiety, malevolence, viciousness, wrong, degeneracy, debauchery, decadence, looseness, lewdness, licentiousness, dissoluteness, wantonness, grossness, turpitude, wrongdoing, darkness, foulness, degradation, worm in the apple, the devil within one, obscenity, profligacy, devilry, diabolism, fiendishness. — *Ant.* VIRTUE, good, goodness.

**2.** [A harmful or malicious action] — *Syn.* ill, harm, injury, damage, mischief, misfortune, wrong, scandal, calamity, pollution, contamination, catastrophe, blow, disaster, plague, curse, outrage, atrocity, abomination, foul play, ill wind*, crying shame*, machinations of the Devil*.

**evildoer,** *n.* — *Syn.* malefactor, sinner, wrongdoer; see **criminal.**

**evil eye,** *n.* — *Syn.* hex, jinx, hostile stare, whammy*; see **curse** 1, **magic** 1, 2.

**evil-minded,** *modif.* **1.** [Wicked] — *Syn.* malicious, depraved, malevolent; see **wicked** 1.

**2.** [Licentious] — *Syn.* salacious, prurient, lecherous, dirty-minded*; see **lewd** 2.

**evince,** *v.* — *Syn.* manifest, reveal, show; see **display** 1, **prove.**

**eviscerate,** *v.* — *Syn.* disembowel, gut, devitalize; see **kill** 1, **weaken** 2.

**evocation,** *n.* — *Syn.* summoning, conjuration, calling forth, invocation, summons.

**evocative,** *modif.* — *Syn.* suggestive, reminiscent, redolent; see **suggestive.**

**evoke,** *v.* **1.** [To call forth] — *Syn.* summon forth, call up, conjure up, invoke; see **summon** 1.

**2.** [To arouse] — *Syn.* elicit, provoke, draw forth; see **excite** 2, **extract** 2.

*See Synonym Study at* EXTRACT.

**evolution,** *n.* — *Syn.* development, growth, unfolding, evolving, gradual change, metamorphosis, progression, phylogeny, Darwinism, Darwinian theory, natural selection; see also **development** 2.

**evolve,** *v.* — *Syn.* develop, result, unfold, emerge; see **develop** 3, 4, **grow** 2.

**ewer,** *n.* — *Syn.* jar, carafe, decanter; see **flask, pitcher** 1.

**exacerbate,** *v.* **1.** [To aggravate] — *Syn.* worsen, heighten, intensify, add fuel to the flames*; see **increase** 1, **intensify.**

**2.** [To irritate] — *Syn.* exasperate, annoy, provoke; see **bother** 2.

**exacerbation,** *n.* **1.** [Intensification] — *Syn.* heightening, worsening, increasing; see **aggravation** 1.

**2.** [Irritation] — *Syn.* exasperation, annoyance, embitterment; see **annoyance** 1.

**exact,** *modif.* **1.** [Accurate] — *Syn.* precise, correct, specific, selfsame; see **accurate** 1, 2, **definite** 1, 2.

**2.** [Strict] — *Syn.* rigorous, scrupulous, methodical, demanding; see **careful, severe** 1, 2.

*See Synonym Study at* ACCURATE, EXPLICIT.

**exact,** *v.* — *Syn.* demand, require, claim, impose, compel, extort, wrest, insist on, call for; see also **claim** 1, **require** 2.

*See Synonym Study at* REQUIRE.

**exacting,** *modif.* — *Syn.* demanding, rigorous, precise; see **critical** 2, **difficult** 1, **onerous, severe** 1.

*See Synonym Study at* ONEROUS.

**exaction,** *n.* **1.** [Extortion] — *Syn.* demand, levying, expropriation, blackmail; see **command** 1, **theft.**

**2.** [Something exacted] — *Syn.* fee, toll, ransom, levy; see **bribe, tax** 1.

**exactly,** *modif.* — *Syn.* precisely, specifically, correctly; see **accurately.**

**exactness,** *n.* — *Syn.* precision, nicety, scrupulousness; see **accuracy** 2, **truth** 1.

**exaggerate,** *v.* — *Syn.* overdraw, overstate, embellish, embroider, misrepresent, falsify, magnify, inflate, expand, amplify, heighten, intensify, distort, enlarge on, stretch, stretch the truth, overemphasize, hyperbolize, go to extremes, give color to, elaborate, romance, romanticize, color, pretty up, make too much of, build up, blow up, overdo, overreach, overcolor, lie, fabricate, misquote, misreport, caricature, burlesque, overestimate, overcharge, draw the longbow*, paint in glowing colors*, sling the bull*, carry too far*, lay it on*, lay it on thick*, lay it on with a trowel*, make a mountain out of a molehill*, play up*, make a big deal of*, blow up out of all proportion*. — *Ant.* understate, tell the truth, minimize.

**exaggerated,** *modif.* — *Syn.* highly colored, magnified, overwrought, overstated, inflated, extravagant, hyperbolic, overblown, overdone, overdrawn, preposterous, impossible, fabulous, outré, sensational, spectacular, melodramatic, out of proportion, blown-up, fantastic, high-flown, overcharged, excessive, farfetched, false, distorted, embroidered, embellished, fabricated, strained, artificial, glaring, pronounced, stylized, unrealistic, whopping*, a bit thick*, too much*. — *Ant.* understated, ACCURATE, exact.

**exaggeration,** *n.* — *Syn.* overstatement, hyperbole, embellishment, embroidery, overestimation, misrepresentation, extravagance, sensationalism, elaboration, coloring, stretching the truth, overreaching, overkill, flight, flight of fancy, fantasy, stretch of the imagination, fig-

ure of speech, yarn, fabrication, falsification, distortion, magnification, enhancement, aggrandizement, puffery, caricature, travesty, tempest in a teapot*, much ado about nothing*, making a mountain out of a molehill*, tall story*, whopper*, play-up*, hype*, bull*; see also **lie** 1. — *Ant.* TRUTH, accuracy, understatement.

**exalt,** *v.* **1.** [To elevate] — *Syn.* ennoble, promote, magnify; see **promote** 2, **raise** 1.

**2.** [To praise] — *Syn.* commend, glorify, laud; see **praise** 1.

**exaltation,** *n.* **1.** [Elevation] — *Syn.* glory, deification, worship; see **praise** 1, 2.

**2.** [Ecstasy] — *Syn.* rapture, elation, rhapsody; see **happiness** 2.

**exalted,** *modif.* **1.** [Noble] — *Syn.* elevated, lofty, illustrious, imposing; see **grand** 2, **noble** 1, 3.

**2.** [Rapturous] — *Syn.* inspired, rhapsodic, elated; see **happy** 1, **inspired** 2.

**examination,** *n.* **1.** [The act of seeking evidence] — *Syn.* search, research, survey, inspection, investigation, inquiry, scrutiny, observation, inquisition, checking, check, exploration, reconnaissance, scan, analysis, review, audit, study, questioning, testing, overhaul, testing program, quest, inquest, probe, test, perusal, trial, cross-examination, catechism, polygraphy, third degree*, grilling*, the eye*, once-over*.

**2.** [A formal test] — *Syn.* test, exam*, experiment, review, questionnaire, battery, quiz, final, midterm, comprehensive, examination, comps*, makeup*, take-home*, tryout*, blue book*, prelims*, orals*, writtens*; see also **test** 1.

**3.** [A medical examination] — *Syn.* checkup, exam*, physical examination, physical, work-up, testing, exploratory examination, self-examination, autopsy, biopsy, scan, medical*; see also **test** 1.

**examine,** *v.* **1.** [To inspect with care] — *Syn.* inspect, analyze, scrutinize, investigate, inquire into, delve into, go into, scan, probe, study, test, sift, explore, reconnoiter, audit, take stock of, take note of, make an inventory of, consider, canvass, survey, search, ransack, review, assay, check, check out, check up on, reexamine, go back over, concentrate on, give one's attention to, look at, observe, contemplate, look into, see into, look over, peruse, pore over, go through, conduct research on, research, fathom, thresh out, search out, track down, smell out, see about, run checks on, run tests on, put to the test, parse, winnow, sound out, feel out, subject to scrutiny, run the eye over, peer at, peer into, search into, pry into, hold up to the light, finger, turn over, pick over, criticize, look for flaws, sample, monitor, vet, experiment with, case*, give the once-over*, size up*, get the lay of*, play around with*, give a going-over*, poke around*, smell around*, nose around*, look up and down*, go over with a fine-toothed comb*, get the lay of the land*, cast the eyes over, eyeball*, flip through the pages, see how the land lies*, bury oneself in*, go behind, fool around with*, sit on, dig into*, dive into*, go deep into.

**2.** [To test] — *Syn.* question, query, interrogate, catechize, cross-examine, judge, measure, experiment, weigh, check, try, give an exam, try out, quiz.

---

**SYN.** — **examine** suggests close observation or investigation to determine the condition, quality, validity, etc. of something *[examined* thoroughly by a doctor*]*; **scrutinize** implies a looking over carefully and searchingly in order to observe the minutest details *[he slowly scrutinized* the bank note*]*; **inspect** implies close, critical observation, esp. for detecting errors, flaws, etc. *[to inspect* a building for fire hazards/; **scan**, in its earlier, stricter sense, implies close scrutiny, but in current usage, it more frequently connotes a quick, rather superficial survey /to *scan* the headlines/

---

**examined,** *modif.* — *Syn.* checked, tested, inspected; see **investigated, tested.**

**examiner,** *n.* — *Syn.* tester, questioner, inquisitor, inquirer, district attorney, inspector, prosecutor, observer, investigator, quizmaster, scrutinizer, interrogator, explorer, assayer, appraiser, analyst, surveyor, catechist, censor, critic, researcher, prober, auditor, reviewer, accountant, interlocutor, doctor, teacher, proctor, psychoanalyst, D.A.*, quizzer*; see also **checker.**

**example,** *n.* **1.** [A representative] — *Syn.* illustration, case, instance, representative, specimen, part, warning, exemplar, exemplification, sample, citation, case in point, concrete example, pattern, model, object lesson, *exempli gratia* (Latin), prototype, archetype, stereotype, original, copy, symbol, quotation, exponent, for instance*.
**2.** [Something to be imitated] — *Syn.* standard, pattern, model, precedent; see **model** 2.
**set an example** — *Syn.* instruct, behave as a model, set a pattern, lead the way; see **lead** 1, **teach** 1.
**without example** — *Syn.* unprecedented, novel, new and different; see **unique** 1, **unprecedented.**

---

**SYN.** — **example** is applied to something that is cited as typical of the members of its group /his novel is an *example* of romantic literature/; **instance** refers to a person, thing, or event that is adduced to prove or support a general statement /here is an *instance* of his sincerity/; **case** is applied to any happening or condition that demonstrates the general existence or occurrence of something /a *case* of mistaken identity/; **illustration** is used of an instance or example that helps to explain or clarify something /this sentence is an *illustration* of the use of a word/ See also Synonym Study at MODEL.

---

**exasperate,** *v.* — *Syn.* irritate, provoke, madden, try one's patience; see **anger** 1, **bother** 2.
*See Synonym Study at* IRRITATE.

**ex cathedra,** *modif.* — *Syn.* authoritative, formal, magisterial; see **authoritative** 2, **official** 3.

**excavate,** *v.* — *Syn.* dig, hollow out, shovel, unearth; see **dig** 1, 2.

**excavation,** *n.* **1.** [The act of excavating] — *Syn.* digging, unearthing, disinterring, mining, quarrying, exhuming, scooping out, digging out, scouring, shoveling, blasting, removal, digging a basement, digging a foundation, using a back hoe, using a trencher, cut and fill, stoping, burrowing, tunneling, pick and shoveling*, mucking out*.
**2.** [The result of excavating] — *Syn.* hole, cavity, hollow, pit; see **hole** 3.
*See Synonym Study at* HOLE.

**exceed,** *v.* — *Syn.* outdo, surpass, transcend, excel, distance, outdistance, pass, top, cap, overstep, outrun, outpace, beat, go beyond, go by, better, best, surmount, outstrip, outreach, outvie, eclipse, outshine, outclass, outperform, outrival, overshadow, rise above, overpass, pass over, overshoot, overdo, go too far, overtake, leave behind, run circles around*, have the edge on*, get the bulge on*, edge out*, have it on*, have it all over*, get the drop on*, beat to the draw*, break the record, carry all before one, get the better of, put one's nose out of joint*, get the best of, hold aces*, have a card up one's sleeve*, have the jump on*, cut out*, meet one at every turn*, beat the wind out of*, be ahead of the game*, have the advantage, gain the ascendancy, gain the upper hand, rank out*. — *Ant.* LAG, dally, fall short.

**exceedingly,** *modif.* — *Syn.* greatly, extremely, remarkably, in a marked degree; see **very.**

**excel,** *v.* — *Syn.* surpass, transcend, improve upon, exceed, go beyond, outdo, outshine, be superior, stand out, shine, have a flair for, have a bent for, have a good head for, have an eye for, have an ear for; see also **exceed.**

---

**SYN.** — **excel** implies superiority in some quality, skill, achievement, etc. over all or over the one (or ones) specified /to *excel* at chess, *excels* her brothers in math/; **surpass** implies a going beyond (someone or something specified) in degree, amount, or quality /no one *surpasses* him in generosity/; **transcend** suggests a surpassing to an extreme degree, even beyond human capability or standards /a faith that *transcends* all understanding/; **outdo** implies a going beyond someone else or a previous record in performance /he will not be *outdone* in bravery/

---

**excellence,** *n.* — *Syn.* superiority, worth, distinction; see **perfection** 3.

**excellent,** *modif.* — *Syn.* first-class, first-rate, outstanding, exceptional, very good, superb, superior, premium, choice, first, best, top, choicest, prime, select, exquisite, fine, very fine, desirable, admirable, magnificent, wonderful, extraordinary, remarkable, distinctive, attractive, great, highest, world-class, champion, prize, striking, capital, accomplished, supreme, estimable, distinguished, enticing, unique, custom-made, hand-picked, the best obtainable, high-grade, high-quality, finest, superfine, incomparable, transcendent, priceless, rare, peerless, matchless, invaluable, skillful, excelling, superlative, worthy, sterling, refined, well-done, foremost, to be desired, exemplary, praiseworthy, commendable, masterful, masterly, competent, skilled, paramount, notable, above par, terrific*, sensational*, marvelous*, splendid*, divine*, heavenly*, sublime*, smashing*, super*, cool*, all right*, crackerjack*, sharp*, keen*, neat*, groovy*, boss*, bully*, dandy*, jim-dandy*, A-one*, grade A*, A-OK*, ace-high*, classy*, topnotch*, tops*, tiptop*, top-flight*, blue-chip*, crack*, frontline*, out of this world*, out of sight*, a jump ahead*, in a class by itself*, as good as they get*, to die for*, dynamite*, hot*, bad*. — *Ant.* POOR, inferior, imperfect.

**excellently,** *modif.* — *Syn.* very well, perfectly, exquisitely, splendidly, distinctively, magnificently, wonderfully, admirably, incomparably, masterfully, skillfully, ingeniously, supremely, superbly, notably, nobly, remarkably, flawlessly, in an excellent manner, famously*, fine*, swimmingly*, sensationally*, marvelously*, divinely*; see also **well** 2. — *Ant.* POORLY, badly, awkwardly.

**excelling,** *modif.* — *Syn.* bearing the palm, surpassing, exceeding, outshining, prevailing; see also **ahead** 2, **excellent, superior.**

**except,** *prep.* — *Syn.* excepting, excluding, omitting, barring, saving, not counting, save, but, with the exception of, with the exclusion of, other than, if not for, without, outside of, aside from, besides, lacking, leaving out, exempting, minus*, short of*.

**except,** *v.* — *Syn.* exclude, leave out, count out, make an exception of; see **omit** 1.

**exception,** *n.* **1.** [The act of excepting] — *Syn.* exclusion, omission, making an exception of, rejection, barring, reservation, leaving out, ruling out, noninclusion, debarment, segregation, limitation, exemption, elimination, repudiation, excusing. — *Ant.* approval, inclusion, acceptance.

**2.** [That which is excepted] — *Syn.* irregularity, peculiarity, anomaly, special case, difference, allowance, exemption, nonconformity, privilege, dispensation, waiver, deviation, eccentricity, rarity, oddity, quirk. — *Ant.* CUSTOM, rule, norm.

**3.** [An adverse reaction] — *Syn.* objection, demurral, protest, complaint; see **objection** 2.

**take exception (to)** — *Syn.* **1.** object, disagree, demur; see **complain** 1, **object, oppose** 1.

**2.** resent, be offended, take offense; see **dislike.**

**exceptional,** *modif.* — *Syn.* uncommon, extraordinary, rare, outstanding; see **excellent, unusual** 1, 2.

**exceptionally,** *modif.* — *Syn.* unusually, particularly, abnormally; see **especially** 1.

**excerpt,** *n.* — *Syn.* selection, extract, passage, citation; see **quotation** 1.

**excerpt,** *v.* — *Syn.* quote, select, extract; see **cite** 2.

**excess,** *n.* **1.** [More than is needed] — *Syn.* profusion, abundance, plethora, superabundance, overabundance, surplus, glut, superfluity, redundancy, redundance, undue amount, too much, too many, overkill, fulsomeness, exuberance, inundation, overflow, exorbitance, surfeit, waste, wastefulness, luxuriance, lavishness, oversupply, overdose, overload, plenty, *embarras de richesses* (French), snootful*, bellyful*, enough and then some*, drug on the market*, too much of a good thing*. — *Ant.* LACK, dearth, deficiency.

**2.** [Conduct that is not temperate] — *Syn.* prodigality, dissipation, intemperance; see **indulgence** 3.

**3.** [The portion that exceeds a minimum] — *Syn.* oversupply, overload, overweight, overflow, superfluity, overstock, overage, overrun, surplus, extra, margin, overcharge, overvaluation, chargeable part, assessable part.

**4.** [The portion that remains] — *Syn.* balance, remainder, rest, surplus, residue, leavings, refuse, by-product, waste, tailings, tare, leftovers.

**in excess of** — *Syn.* surplus, more than, over and above; see **extra.**

**to excess** — *Syn.* too much, excessively, extravagantly, to extremes; see **extreme** 2, **very.**

**excessive,** *modif.* — *Syn.* immoderate, inordinate, extreme, extravagant, exorbitant, too much, too great, disproportionate, unwarranted, undue, unnecessary, unreasonable, uncalled-for, overmuch, superfluous, redundant, lavish, prodigal, overdone; see also **extreme** 2, **undue.**

---

**SYN.** — **excessive** applies to that which goes beyond what is proper, right, or usual [*excessive* demands]; **exorbitant** suggests unreasonable excess and often connotes a greedy desire for more than is just or due [*exorbitant* prices]; **extravagant** and **immoderate** both imply excessiveness resulting from lack of restraint or of prudence [*extravagant* praise, *immoderate* laughter]; **inordinate** implies a going beyond the orderly limits of convention or the bounds of good taste [his *inordinate* pride]

---

**excessively,** *modif.* — *Syn.* extravagantly, extremely, unreasonably; see **very.**

**exchange,** *n.* **1.** [The act of replacing one thing with another] — *Syn.* transfer, substitution, replacement, change, supplanting, rearrangement, shift, revision, resale, transposition, interchange, trade-off, commuta-

tion, switch, shuffle, shuffling, castling, sleight-of-hand, hocus-pocus.

**2.** [The act of giving and receiving reciprocally] — *Syn.* reciprocity, reciprocation, barter, trade, swap, correspondence, interrelation, interdependence, cross-fire, buying and selling, swapping, negotiation, transaction, commerce, interchange, dialogue, tit for tat*, give and take*.

**3.** [A substitution] — *Syn.* change, shift, swap, trade, interchange, replacing, shuffle, reciprocation, supplanting, replacement, switch, supplantment, commutation, trade-off.

**4.** [A place where exchanges take place] — *Syn.* market, clearinghouse, stock exchange, bourse; see **market** 1.

**exchange,** *v.* **1.** [To replace one thing with another] — *Syn.* substitute, transfer, replace, invert, give in exchange, commute, pass to, give over, reverse, provide a substitute, provide a replacement, transpose, shuffle, shift, switch, swap, revise, rearrange, change, interchange, trade off, cash in, return, transmute, reset, change hands, castle, borrow from Peter to pay Paul*, swap horses in the middle of the stream*.

**2.** [To give and receive reciprocally] — *Syn.* reciprocate, barter, trade, swap, alternate, interact, interchange, bandy, trade off, correspond, buy and sell, transact, return the compliment, make an exchange.

**exchangeable,** *modif.* — *Syn.* interchangeable, transmutable, convertible, returnable, commutable, substitutable, replaceable, fungible, substitutive, reciprocal, mutual, complementary, correlative, equivalent.

**exchanged,** *modif.* — *Syn.* replaced, traded, brought back, sent back; see **changed** 1, **returned.**

**exchequer,** *n.* — *Syn.* treasury, bursary, bank; see **treasury.**

**excise,** *v.* — *Syn.* cut out, delete, extract, resect; see **cancel** 1, **remove** 1.

**excision,** *n.* — *Syn.* extraction, cutting, abscission, extirpation; see **removal** 1.

**excitable,** *modif.* — *Syn.* sensitive, high-strung, neurotic, easily excited, peevish, irritable, edgy, impatient, intolerant, moody, touchy, irascible, fiery, volatile, resentful, vehement, demonstrative, restless, uneasy, unquiet, mercurial, galvanic, fidgety, fussy, hysterical, emotional, hotheaded, enthusiastic, overzealous, turbulent, impressible, tempestuous, stormy, impulsive, impetuous, rash, hasty, quick, passionate, heedless, reckless, violent, quick-tempered, temperamental, hot-tempered, short-tempered, easily angered, hot-blooded, combustible, fierce, wild, volcanic, explosive, prickly, huffy, flighty, nervous, jumpy, on edge, tense, overstrung, ready to explode, likely to go off at half cock*, having a short fuse*, like a bundle of nerves*. — *Ant.* CALM, placid, easygoing.

**excite,** *v.* **1.** [To stir one mentally] — *Syn.* stimulate, inflame, arouse, anger, delight, exhilarate, move, pique, infuriate, madden, stir, stir up, fire, fire up, fire the blood, stir the blood, give one a turn, convulse, electrify, galvanize, work up, goad, tease, worry, provoke, incite, agitate, astound, amaze, fluster, annoy, jar, jolt, chill, thrill, awaken, inspire, enliven, feed the fire, fan the flames, set on fire, light up, carry away, arouse one's enthusiasm, warm, irritate, bother, key up*, turn on*, get going*, work up into a lather*.

**2.** [To activate] — *Syn.* irritate, charge, energize, stimulate, intensify, dilate, bring out, bring about, stir up, animate, move, start, induce, precipitate, trigger, instigate, convulse, elicit, kindle, enkindle, foment, attract, fire, fuse, accelerate, impel, touch off a response.

*See Synonym Study at* PROVOKE.

**excited,** *modif.* — *Syn.* aroused, stimulated, inflamed, agitated, eager, enthusiastic, agog, annoyed, seething, wrought up, frantic, flushed, overwrought, wound up, restless, feverish, stirred, apprehensive, roused, disturbed, perturbed, flustered, upset, angry, disconcerted, discomfited, disquieted, tense, discomposed, tumultuous, hurt, piqued, atingle, angered, distracted, distraught, edgy, furious, beside oneself, delighted, delirious, exhilarated, thrilled, frenzied, manic, troubled, ruffled, moved, avid, hysterical, passionate, glowing, provoked, quickened, inspired, wild, fired, nervous, overheated, hot, animated, uneasy, galvanized, electrified, ill at ease, jumpy, jittery*, on the ragged edge*, keyed up*, red hot*, turned on*, in a tailspin*, all atwitter*, boiling over*, all hot and bothered*, hyped up*, in a dither*, in a quiver*, in a lather*, hopped up*, worked up*, feeling one's oats*, on pins and needles*, in a tizzy*, in a flutter*, haywire*, uptight*, in heaven*, all nerves*, wringing one's hands*, blue in the face*, jumping at*, het up*, on fire*, psyched*, psyched up*, steamed up*. — *Ant.* CALM, apathetic, indifferent.

**excitedly,** *modif.* — *Syn.* agitatedly, heatedly, hysterically, restlessly, frantically, frenziedly, eagerly, breathlessly, feverishly, uncontrolledly, uncontrollably, erratically, tempestuously, passionately, hotly, madly, wildly, furiously, tensely, apprehensively, with heart in mouth, in an excited manner, excitably, lacking calm, lacking poise, without balance, without restraint, under stress of emotion; see also **excited.**

**excitement,** *n.* — *Syn.* agitation, confusion, disturbance, tumult, enthusiasm, eagerness, ferment, trepidation, turmoil, stir, excitation, animation, hurry, perturbation, excitedness, delirium, furor, rage, exhilaration, emotion, stimulation, arousal, drama, melodrama, thrill, activity, commotion, ado, fuss, hullabaloo, bother, dither, hubbub, fluster, flutter, flurry, bustle, todo, tizzy*; see also **thrill.** — *Ant.* PEACE, calm, quiet.

**exciting,** *modif.* — *Syn.* stimulating, moving, animating, provocative, arousing, rousing, arresting, impelling, compelling, stirring, thrilling, exhilarating, invigorating, intoxicating, heady, breathtaking, overwhelming, interesting, new, unknown, mysterious, overpowering, inspiring, impressive, soul-stirring, sensational, astonishing, electrifying, galvanizing, bracing, appealing, seductive, titillating, suspenseful, gripping, cliff-hanging*, blood-curdling*, racy*, hair-raising*, mind-blowing*, heart-stopping*. — *Ant.* DULL, tedious, tranquilizing.

**exclaim,** *v.* — *Syn.* cry out, call out, ejaculate, blurt, blurt out, burst out, assert, emit, shout, yell, holler, bellow, call aloud, say loudly, vociferate, speak vehemently, rend the air; see also **yell.**

**exclamation,** *n.* — *Syn.* ejaculation, outcry, vociferation, interjection; see **cry** 1.

**exclude,** *v.* 1. [To bar] — *Syn.* shut out, keep out, reject, ban, debar, eliminate, except, omit, prohibit, disallow, rule out, lock out, shut the door on; see also **bar** 1, 2.
2. [To expel] — *Syn.* banish, suspend, put out, force out, disbar, eject, throw out; see also **dismiss** 1.

**SYN.** — **exclude** implies a keeping out or prohibiting of that which is not yet in [to *exclude* someone from membership]; **debar** connotes the existence of some barrier, as legal authority or force, which excludes someone from a privilege, right, etc. [to *debar* certain groups from voting]; **disbar** refers only to depriving a lawyer of the right to practice law; **eliminate** implies the removal of that which is already in, usually connoting its undesirability or irrelevance [to *eliminate* waste products, to *eliminate* fraud]; **suspend** refers to the removal, usually tempo-

rary, of someone from some organization, institution, etc., as for the infraction of some rule [to *suspend* a student from school]

**exclusion,** *n.* — *Syn.* keeping out, rejection, ejection, elimination, prohibition, cut, embargo, ban, nonadmission, relegation, omission, segregation, isolation, ostracism, interdiction, preventing admission, erecting barriers, blockade, boycott, repudiation, separation, ousting, eviction, dismissal, banishment, suspension, excommunication, refusal, expulsion, debarring, barring, shutting out, blackballing. — *Ant.* WELCOME, invitation, inclusion.

**exclusive,** *modif.* — *Syn.* restricted, restrictive, fashionable, expensive, elite, aristocratic, socially correct, preferential, privileged, selective, particular, circumscribed, closed, select, private, segregated, prohibitive, exclusionary, cliquish, aloof, clannish, snobbish, snobby, undemocratic, independent, incompatible, sole, tony*, posh*, high-hat*, ritzy*, swanky*, snooty*. — *Ant.* FREE, inclusive, unrestricted.

**exclusively,** *modif.* — *Syn.* particularly, solely, completely; see **only** 1.

**excommunicate,** *v.* — *Syn.* expel, oust, anathematize, unchurch; see **banish** 1, **damn** 1, **dismiss** 1.

**excommunication,** *n.* — *Syn.* expulsion, dismissal, suspension; see **damnation, removal** 1.

**excoriate,** *v.* 1. [To remove strips of skin, bark, etc.] — *Syn.* abrade, chafe, flay; see **skin.**
2. [To denounce] — *Syn.* condemn, criticize, flay; see **censure, denounce.**

**excrement,** *n.* — *Syn.* excretion, ordure, stool, waste matter, feces, fecal matter, offal, droppings, evacuation, discharge, exudation, dung, chips, manure, urine, effluvium, secretion, smegma, sweat, perspiration, egesta, excreta, night soil.

**excrescence,** *n.* — *Syn.* outgrowth, swelling, lump, wart; see **bulge, growth** 3.

**excrete,** *v.* — *Syn.* eliminate, eject, defecate, urinate, discharge, secrete, void, expel, throw off waste matter, go to the bathroom, go to the toilet, relieve oneself, answer a call of nature, evacuate, pass, exude, perspire, sweat, squeeze out, give off.

**excretion,** *n.* 1. [The act of excreting] — *Syn.* elimination, urination, evacuation, discharge, discharging, secretion, defecation, expelling, expulsion, ejecting, ejection, voiding, leaving, passing off, perspiration, sweating, exudation. — *Ant.* accretion, eating, receiving.
2. [The product of excretion] — *Syn.* waste matter, excreta, feces; see **excrement.**

**excruciating,** *modif.* — *Syn.* agonizing, tormenting, intense, unbearable; see **intolerable, painful** 1.

**exculpate,** *v.* — *Syn.* absolve, exonerate, forgive; see **excuse.**

**excursion,** *n.* — *Syn.* jaunt, outing, trip, tour; see **journey.**

**excursionist,** *n.* — *Syn.* visitor, sightseer, tourist; see **traveler.**

**excursive,** *modif.* — *Syn.* discursive, digressive, rambling, desultory; see **indirect, verbose.**

**excursus,** *n.* 1. [A supplemental discussion] — *Syn.* essay, dissertation, summary; see **appendix, discussion** 2, **exposition** 2.
2. [A digression] — *Syn.* wandering, aside, deviation, excursion; see **digression.**

**excusable,** *modif.* — *Syn.* pardonable, forgivable, understandable, justifiable, reasonable, defensible, permissible, trivial, passable, slight, minor, vindicable, vindicatory, exculpatory, warrantable, plausible, allowable, venial, remissible, condonable, expiable, explainable, harmless, innocuous, not excessive, not fatal, not too bad, not inexcusable, not injurious, innocent, fair, within limits, not beyond the pale*. — *Ant.* inexcusable, unforgivable, culpable.

**excuse,** *n.* **1.** [An explanation] — *Syn.* apology, reason, defense; see **explanation** 2, **justification.**
**2.** [A pretended reason] — *Syn.* pretext, subterfuge, trick; see **pretense** 1, 2.
**a poor excuse for** — *Syn.* makeshift, sorry specimen, inferior example, mediocrity; see **substitute.**
**make one's excuses** — *Syn.* send regrets, beg off, apologize, offer an explanation; see **apologize, refuse.**
**excuse,** *v.* — *Syn.* pardon, forgive, justify, discharge, vindicate, apologize for, release, free, set free, overlook, exempt, mitigate, extenuate, palliate, rationalize, acquit, condone, reprieve, remit, absolve, exonerate, exculpate, clear of, shrive, grant absolution, pass over, look the other way, shrug off, give as an excuse, make excuses for, make allowances for, make apologies for, let off, let go, permit to leave, dispense with, grant remission, remit a penalty for, grant amnesty, blot out one's sins, expunge the record of, purge, provide with an alibi, plead ignorance, whitewash*, let off the hook*, let off easy*, let off scot-free*, wink at*, wipe the slate clean*, take the rap for*, alibi*.
**excused,** *modif.* — *Syn.* exonerated, freed, permitted; see **discharged** 1, **free** 2, **pardoned.**
**excuse me,** *interj.* — *Syn.* pardon me, forgive me, I beg your pardon, sorry, I'm sorry, *pardonnez-moi, pardon* (*both* French), *entschuldigen Sie mich* (German), *scusi* (Italian).
**execrable,** *modif.* **1.** [Abominable] — *Syn.* detestable, confounded, vile; see **offensive** 2.
**2.** [Inferior] — *Syn.* bad, defective, wretched; see **poor** 2.
**execrate,** *v.* **1.** [To curse] — *Syn.* revile, accurse, denounce; see **curse** 2.
**2.** [To detest] — *Syn.* loathe, abhor, abominate; see **hate** 1.
*See Synonym Study at* CURSE.
**execration,** *n.* **1.** [Loathing] — *Syn.* detestation, abhorrence, abomination; see **hatred** 1.
**2.** [A denunciation] — *Syn.* malediction, anathema, condemnation; see **curse** 1.
**execute,** *v.* **1.** [To carry out instructions] — *Syn.* perform, administer, do, effect; see **perform** 1.
**2.** [To bring to fruition] — *Syn.* complete, produce, accomplish, fulfill; see **achieve** 1.
**3.** [To put to death] — *Syn.* electrocute, hang, behead; see **electrocute, kill** 1.
*See Synonym Study at* KILL, PERFORM.
**executed,** *modif.* **1.** [Performed] — *Syn.* completed, done, carried out; see **finished** 1.
**2.** [Formally put to death] — *Syn.* killed, hanged, electrocuted, gassed, shot, shot at sunrise, sent before a firing squad, beheaded, guillotined, decapitated, brought to the block, impaled, crucified, drawn and quartered, immured, garroted, gibbeted, burned at the stake, murdered by decree, dispatched, sent to the gas chamber, sent to the chair*, scorched*, stretched*, strung up*, hung up to dry*, fried*, cooked*, sent to the showers*.
**execution,** *n.* **1.** [The carrying out of instructions or plans] — *Syn.* fulfilling, accomplishment, doing; see **achievement** 1, 2, **performance** 1.
**2.** [Death by official order] — *Syn.* capital punishment, killing, electrocution, hanging, gassing, lethal injection, beheading, decapitation, guillotining, strangulation, contract killing, strangling, crucifixion, martyr-

dom, impalement, shooting, burning at the stake, death penalty, ultimate penalty, electric chair, firing squad, the gallows, the rope, the block, the chair*, the ax*.
**executioner,** *n.* — *Syn.* hangman, electrocutioner, strangler, firing squad, death squad, headsman, garroter, killer, lyncher, hit man*, hired gun*; see also **killer.**
**executive,** *modif.* — *Syn.* managing, managerial, governing, supervisory; see **administrative.**
**executive,** *n.* — *Syn.* official, manager, businessperson, exec*; see **administrator.**
**executor,** *n.* — *Syn.* trustee, agent, enforcer, executrix; see **administrator, agent** 1.
**exegesis,** *n.* — *Syn.* interpretation, exposition, analysis; see **explanation** 2, **interpretation** 1, 2.
**exegetical,** *modif.* — *Syn.* expository, interpretive, explicatory, hermeneutic; see **explanatory.**
**exemplar,** *n.* — *Syn.* model, pattern, prototype, copy; see **example** 1, **model** 1, 2.
**exemplary,** *modif.* — *Syn.* commendable, praiseworthy, model, representative; see **excellent, typical, worthy.**
**exemplification,** *n.* — *Syn.* embodiment, illustration, instance; see **example** 1.
**exemplify,** *v.* — *Syn.* illustrate, typify, embody, epitomize; see **explain, represent** 3.
**exempt,** *modif.* — *Syn.* free, clear, privileged, excused, absolved, immune, not subject to, released from, not responsible for, void of, set apart, excluded, excepted, freed, cleared, liberated, spared, not liable, unrestrained, untrammeled, unrestricted, not restricted by, outside, off the hook*, grandfathered*. — *Ant.* RESPONSIBLE, liable, subject.
**exempt,** *v.* — *Syn.* release, spare, grant immunity, let off; see **excuse.**
**exemption,** *n.* — *Syn.* exception, immunity, impunity, privilege, exception, exclusion, release, dispensation; see also **exception** 1, 2, **freedom** 2.

---

*SYN.* — **exemption** implies release from some obligation or legal requirement, esp. where others are not so released [*exemption* from military service]; **immunity** implies freedom from or protection against something disagreeable or menacing to which all or many are liable [granted *immunity* from prosecution]; **impunity** specifically implies escape or freedom from punishment [to commit a crime with *impunity*]

---

**exercise,** *n.* **1.** [Action, undertaken for training] — *Syn.* practice, exertion, drill, activity, workout, training, gymnastics, sports, jogging, running, walking, calisthenics, aerobics, isometrics, yoga, warmup, conditioning, bodybuilding, weight lifting, constitutional, daily dozen*.
**2.** [The means by which training is promoted] — *Syn.* performance, act, action, activity, occupation, operation, study, theme, lesson, task, drill, test, examination.
**3.** [Use] — *Syn.* application, employment, operation; see **use** 1.
*See Synonym Study at* PRACTICE.
**exercise,** *v.* **1.** [To move the body] — *Syn.* train, work out, stretch, bend, pull, hike, jog, run, walk, promote muscle tone, labor, strain, move briskly, exert, discipline, drill, execute, do exercises, perform exercises, practice, warm up, limber up, loosen up, maneuver, lift weights, get in trim*, pump iron*, take a constitutional*, do one's daily dozen*; see also **train** 3.
**2.** [To use] — *Syn.* employ, practice, exert, apply, operate, execute, sharpen, handle, utilize, devote, put in practice; see also **use** 1.

3. [To train] — *Syn.* drill, discipline, give training to; see **teach** 2, **train** 3.

*See Synonym Study at* PRACTICE.

**exercises,** *pl.n.* — *Syn.* services, meeting, convocation, ceremony, graduation, commencement.

**exert,** *v.* — *Syn.* put forth, bring to bear, exercise; see **use** 1.

**exertion,** *n.* — *Syn.* effort, struggle, attempt, endeavor; see **effort** 1.

*See Synonym Study at* EFFORT.

**exert oneself,** *v.* — *Syn.* strive, attempt, endeavor, apply oneself; see **try** 1.

**exfoliate,** *v.* — *Syn.* scale, flake, peel; see **shed.**

**exfoliation,** *n.* — *Syn.* molting, peeling, flaking, depilation; see **shedding.**

**exhalation,** *n.* **1.** [Breathing out] — *Syn.* exhaling, expiration, respiration, breath, emission of vapor, vaporization; see also **breath** 1.

**2.** [That which is exhaled] — *Syn.* emanation, vapor, air; see **breath** 1, **emanation** 2.

**exhale,** *v.* — *Syn.* breathe out, expire, blow, sigh; see **breathe** 1, **emit** 1.

**exhaust,** *v.* **1.** [To consume strength] — *Syn.* debilitate, fatigue, wear out, wear down; see **tire** 2, **weaken** 2, **weary** 1.

**2.** [To use entirely] — *Syn.* use up, take the last of, deplete, drain; see **consume** 2.

**exhausted,** *modif.* **1.** [Tired out] — *Syn.* fatigued, debilitated, wearied, worn; see **tired, weak** 1.

**2.** [Having nothing remaining] — *Syn.* all gone, consumed, used, drained; see **empty** 1.

**exhaustible,** *modif.* — *Syn.* expendable, limited, modest; see **inadequate** 1.

**exhaustion,** *n.* — *Syn.* weariness, fatigue, depletion; see **fatigue, lassitude.**

**exhibit,** *n.* **1.** [A display] — *Syn.* show, exhibition, presentation; see **display** 2, **show** 1.

**2.** [Something produced as evidence] — *Syn.* evidence, proof, documentation; see **proof** 1.

*See Synonym Study at* PROOF.

**exhibit,** *v.* — *Syn.* show, present, manifest; see **display** 1.

*See Synonym Study at* SHOW.

**exhibited,** *modif.* — *Syn.* shown, presented, advertised; see **displayed, shown** 1.

**exhibition,** *n.* **1.** [An act or instance of displaying] — *Syn.* presentation, demonstration, showing, exhibit; see **display** 2.

**2.** [An elaborate public show] — *Syn.* exposition, fair, carnival; see **display** 2, **show** 1.

**exhibitionist,** *n.* — *Syn.* show-off, flaunter, grandstander*, flasher*; see **braggart, extrovert, pervert.**

**exhilarate,** *v.* — *Syn.* stimulate, enliven, invigorate, brace, elate, cheer, gladden, refresh, act as a tonic; see also **animate** 1.

*See Synonym Study at* ANIMATE.

**exhilarating,** *modif.* — *Syn.* stimulating, invigorating, bracing, animating; see **exciting, stimulating.**

**exhilaration,** *n.* — *Syn.* liveliness, animation, stimulation; see **enthusiasm** 1, **happiness** 1.

**exhort,** *v.* — *Syn.* urge, admonish, caution, entreat; see **advise** 1, **urge** 2.

*See Synonym Study at* URGE.

**exhortation,** *n.* — *Syn.* persuasion, instigation, urging; see **advice, appeal** 1.

**exhume,** *v.* — *Syn.* unearth, disclose, reveal, disinter, dig up, disinhume, disentomb, unbury, excavate.

**exigency,** *n.* **1.** [A crisis] — *Syn.* emergency, contingency, distress; see **crisis, difficulty** 1, 2, **emergency.**

**2.** [Demand] — *Syn.* need, want, urgency; see **necessity** 1, 2, 3, **need** 3, **requirement** 2.

*See Synonym Study at* EMERGENCY, NEED.

**exigent,** *modif.* **1.** [Urgent] — *Syn.* pressing, critical, imperative; see **urgent** 1.

**2.** [Demanding] — *Syn.* exacting, severe, oppressive; see **difficult** 1, **severe** 1.

**exiguous,** *modif.* — *Syn.* scanty, meager, petty; see **inadequate** 1, **scanty.**

**exile,** *n.* **1.** [Banishment] — *Syn.* expulsion, deportation, expatriation, ostracism, displacement, transportation, proscription, separation; see also **emigration.**

**2.** [An outcast] — *Syn.* expatriate, stateless person, deportee; see **emigrant, fugitive, refugee.**

**exile,** *v.* — *Syn.* ostracize, banish, expatriate, cast out; see **banish** 1.

*See Synonym Study at* BANISH.

**exist,** *v.* **1.** [To have being] — *Syn.* breathe, live, survive; see **be** 1.

**2.** [To carry on life] — *Syn.* be alive, endure, go on; see **endure** 1, **subsist.**

**existence,** *n.* **1.** [The carrying on of life] — *Syn.* being, living, survival; see **continuation** 1, **life** 1.

**2.** [The state of being] — *Syn.* presence, actuality, occurrence, permanence; see **reality** 1.

**existing,** *modif.* — *Syn.* existent, current, actual, extant; see **alive** 1, **extant, present** 1, **real** 2.

**exit,** *n.* **1.** [A means of egress] — *Syn.* way out, passage out, outlet, egress, door, doorway, passageway, ramp, opening, fire escape; see also **door** 1, **hole** 1.

**2.** [The act of leaving] — *Syn.* going, retreat, farewell, exodus; see **departure** 1.

**exodus,** *n.* — *Syn.* mass migration, emigration, flight; see **departure** 1, **emigration, journey.**

**ex officio,** *modif.* — *Syn.* by virtue of office, sanctioned, authoritatively; see **approved, officially** 1.

**exonerate,** *v.* — *Syn.* absolve, vindicate, justify; see **absolve, excuse.**

*See Synonym Study at* ABSOLVE.

**exoneration,** *n.* **1.** [Vindication] — *Syn.* absolution, exculpation, acquittal; see **acquittal, pardon** 1.

**2.** [Liberation] — *Syn.* exemption, release, reprieve; see **freeing.**

**exorbitance,** *n.* — *Syn.* extravagance, costliness, excess; see **excess** 1, **luxury** 1, 2.

**exorbitant,** *modif.* — *Syn.* excessive, extravagant, inordinate, immoderate; see **excessive, expensive, extreme** 2.

*See Synonym Study at* EXCESSIVE.

**exorcism,** *n.* **1.** [Witchcraft] — *Syn.* sorcery, conjuring, driving out; see **magic** 1, 2, **removal** 1.

**2.** [A spell] — *Syn.* charm, incantation, cabala; see **magic** 1.

**exotic,** *modif.* **1.** [Foreign] — *Syn.* imported, not native, not local, extrinsic; see **foreign** 1.

**2.** [Strikingly different] — *Syn.* strange, fascinating, alien; see **foreign** 1, 2, **unfamiliar** 2, **unusual** 2.

**expand,** *v.* — *Syn.* extend, augment, enlarge, increase, dilate, swell, distend, inflate, grow, develop, elaborate, enlarge upon, spread out, stretch out, open, unfold, unfurl; see also **develop** 1, 4, **grow** 1, **increase** 1.

---

*SYN.* — **expand** implies an increasing in size, bulk, or volume and is the broadest term here, being applicable when the enlarging force operates from either the inside or the outside or when the increase comes about by unfolding, puffing out, spreading, or opening; **swell** implies expansion beyond the normal limits or size; **distend** implies a swelling as a result of pressure from within that forces a bulging outward; **inflate** suggests the use of air or gas, or of something insubstantial, to distend or swell a thing; **dilate** suggests a widening or stretching of something circular

**expanse,** *n.* — *Syn.* breadth, width, length, extent, extension, reach, stretch, distance, area, belt, space, field, territory, span, spread, room, fairness, scope, range, compass, sphere, margin, sweep, remoteness, latitude, radius, wilderness, region, wide extent, continuous area, uninterrupted space, expanded surface, amplitude, immensity.

**expansion,** *n.* — *Syn.* enlargement, augmentation, extension; see **development** 2, **increase** 1.

**expansive,** *modif.* **1.** [Widely extended] — *Syn.* broad, widespread, comprehensive; see **comprehensive, extensive** 1.

**2.** [Unreserved] — *Syn.* demonstrative, open, communicative, gregarious; see **effusive, friendly** 1, **talkative.**

**expatiate,** *v.* — *Syn.* elaborate, enlarge, dilate, expound; see **develop** 4, **ramble** 2.

**expatriate,** *n.* — *Syn.* exile, émigré, outcast; see **emigrant, refugee.**

**expatriate,** *v.* — *Syn.* exile, ostracize, deport; see **banish** 1.

*See Synonym Study at* BANISH.

**expect,** *v.* **1.** [To anticipate] — *Syn.* await, look forward to, hope for, foresee; see **anticipate** 1, **count on.**

**2.** [To require] — *Syn.* demand, insist upon, exact; see **require** 2.

**3.** [*To assume] — *Syn.* presume, suppose, suspect; see **assume** 1.

*See Synonym Study at* ANTICIPATE.

**expectancy,** *n.* — *Syn.* hope, prospect, likelihood; see **anticipation** 1, **outlook** 2.

**expectant,** *modif.* **1.** [Characterized by anticipation] — *Syn.* expecting, hoping, hopeful, waiting, awaiting, anticipating, anticipative, in expectation, watchful, vigilant, eager, ready, looking forward to, prepared, in suspense, gaping, apprehensive, on tenterhooks*, on edge*, itching*, raring*, wild*, with bated breath*. — *Ant.* INDIFFERENT, nonchalant, unprepared.

**2.** [Anticipating birth] — *Syn.* pregnant, expecting, with child; see **pregnant** 1.

**expectation,** *modif.* — *Syn.* hope, belief, prospect; see **anticipation** 1.

**expected,** *modif.* **1.** [Wonted] — *Syn.* normal, familiar, habitual; see **conventional** 1.

**2.** [Anticipated] — *Syn.* looked for, awaited, counted upon, contemplated, looked forward to, hoped for, relied upon, foreseeable, foreseen, envisioned, predicted, predictable, foretold, prophesied, planned for, prepared for, budgeted, scheduled, due, in the works*, in the cards*, coming up*, in the bag*; see also **coming** 1, **likely** 1, **proposed.**

**expecting,** *modif.* — *Syn.* expectant, due, about to become a mother; see **pregnant** 1.

**expectorate,** *v.* — *Syn.* cough up, spit out, hawk, spew; see **spit.**

**expediency,** *n.* **1.** [Appropriateness] — *Syn.* suitability, propriety, desirableness; see **fitness** 1.

**2.** [Usefulness] — *Syn.* advantageousness, efficiency, profitableness, self-interest; see **opportunism, usefulness, utility** 1.

**expedient,** *modif.* **1.** [Appropriate] — *Syn.* desirable, advisable, fitting; see **fit** 1, 2.

**2.** [Advantageous] — *Syn.* profitable, useful, convenient, politic; see **helpful** 1, **practical, profitable.**

**expedient,** *n.* — *Syn.* resource, makeshift, means to an end; see **device** 1, 2, **resort** 1, **resource.**

*See Synonym Study at* RESORT.

**expedite,** *v.* — *Syn.* hurry, assist, promote, facilitate; see **advance** 1, **hasten** 2.

**expedition,** *n.* **1.** [Travel undertaken] — *Syn.* excursion, voyage, campaign; see **journey.**

**2.** [Those who undertake travel] — *Syn.* party, band, company, team, hunters, safari, explorers, pioneers, traders, soldiers, squadron, contingent, scouts, archaeologists, tourists, sightseers, cavalcade, patrol, caravan, posse, astronauts, cosmonauts, space travelers; see also **army** 1, 2, **crowd** 1, **fleet.**

**3.** [Efficient speed] — *Syn.* speed, dispatch, promptness, alacrity; see **haste** 1, **speed.**

*See Synonym Study at* HASTE, TRIP.

**expeditious,** *modif.* — *Syn.* speedy, quick, prompt; see **fast** 1, **punctual.**

**expel,** *v.* **1.** [To eject] — *Syn.* get rid of, cast out, dislodge; see **eject** 1.

**2.** [To dismiss] — *Syn.* suspend, discharge, oust; see **dismiss** 1, 2.

*See Synonym Study at* EJECT.

**expend,** *v.* **1.** [To use] — *Syn.* exhaust, use up, employ; see **consume** 2.

**2.** [To spend] — *Syn.* pay out, disburse, write checks for, lay out; see **spend** 1.

**expenditure,** *n.* — *Syn.* outgo, investment, payment; see **expense** 1.

**expense,** *n.* **1.** [Whatever is paid out] — *Syn.* expenditure, cost, price, outlay, charge, fee, payment, outgo, disbursement, alimony, child support, value, worth, sum, amount, risk, capital, rate, custom, excise, tax, carrying charge, budgeted item, cost of materials, overhead, time, payroll, investment, interest, interest charge, operating expense, surcharge, deductible expense, nondeductible expense, duty, assessment, nut*. — *Ant.* PROFIT, income, receipts.

**2.** [Whatever causes money to be paid out] — *Syn.* responsibility, obligation, loan, mortgage, lien, debt, liability, investment, insurance, upkeep, alimony, loss, enterprise, debit, account. — *Ant.* CREDIT, asset, accounts receivable.

**at the expense of** — *Syn.* at the cost of, at the sacrifice of, to the loss of, to the detriment of, paid by, charged to.

**expenses,** *pl.n.* — *Syn.* expense, cost of living, per diem, reparations, damages, outlay, overhead, expense account, traveling expenses, living expenses, out-of-pocket expenses, costs, lodging, room and board, incidentals, cash-out*, swindle sheet*.

**expensive,** *modif.* — *Syn.* costly, high-priced, dear, precious, valuable, invaluable, rare, prized, choice, rich, priceless, high, too high, overpriced, uneconomical, unreasonable, exorbitant, extortionate, fancy, extravagant, upscale, up-market, deluxe, beyond one's means, at a premium, at great cost, worth a king's ransom*, worth a pretty penny*, sky-high*, steep*, stiff*, big-ticket*, pricey*, out of sight*. — *Ant.* inexpensive, CHEAP, low.

---

*SYN.* — **expensive** implies having a price that is high in relation to others of its kind or that is in excess of the thing's worth or the purchaser's ability to pay /an *expensive* car/; **costly** refers to something high in price and usually implies richness, magnificence, rareness, etc. /*costly* gems/: it is often applied to that which it would cost much in money or effort to correct or replace /a *costly* error/; **dear,** less often used today in the U.S., implies an exorbitant price or one considerably beyond the normal or fair price /meat was very *dear* at the time/; **valuable**, in this connection, implies such great value as to bring a high price /a *valuable* collection/; **invaluable** suggests value so great that it cannot be appraised in monetary terms /*invaluable* aid/

**experience,** *n.* **1.** [The act of living through events] — *Syn.* participation, involvement, undergoing, direct observation, encountering, contact, exposure, practice, strife, struggle, endurance, action, actuality, reality, activity, existence, continuance, school of hard knocks*; see also **life** 1, 2.
**2.** [What one lives through] — *Syn.* occurrence, encounter, happening, adventure; see **event** 1, 2.
**3.** [That which one gains from having lived] — *Syn.* background, skill, knowledge, perspicacity, wisdom, practice, familiarity, acquaintance, conversance, maturity, seasoning, judgment, practical knowledge, sense, savoir-faire, sophistication, worldliness, proficiency, expertise, know-how*.
**experience,** *v.* — *Syn.* undergo, feel, live through, encounter; see **endure** 2, **feel** 2, **undergo.**
**experienced,** *modif.* — *Syn.* skilled, practiced, accomplished, versed, well-versed, qualified, able, skillful, knowing, trained, wise, expert, veteran, matured, seasoned, mature, with a good background, mellowed, mastered, old, rounded, conversant, familiar with, sophisticated, worldly-wise, worldly, to hell and back*, knowing the score*, knowing the ropes*, in the know*, having been around*, having been through the mill*, broken in*; see also **able** 2. — *Ant.* NEW, apprentice, beginning.
**experiment,** *n.* **1.** [An operation to establish a principle or a truth] — *Syn.* trial, test, analysis, essay, examination, clinical trial, investigation, experimentation, inspection, search, organized observation, research, scrutiny, trial and error, speculation, check, proof, demonstration, verification, sifting, dissection, operation, exercise, probe.
**2.** [A trial arrangement] — *Syn.* undertaking, trial, probation, probation trial, agreement, attempt, pilot project, pilot, testing program, dry run, rehearsal, practice, venture, enterprise, measure, try, tryout; see also sense 1.

*SYN.* — **trial** implies the trying of a person or thing in order to establish worth in actual performance /hired on *trial*/; **experiment** implies a showing by trial whether a thing will be effective /the honor system was instituted as an *experiment*/ and, in addition, is used of any action or process undertaken to discover something not yet known or to demonstrate something known /*experiments* in nuclear physics/; **test** implies a putting of a thing to decisive proof by thorough examination or trial under controlled conditions and with fixed standards in mind /a *test* of a new jet plane/

**experiment,** *v.* **1.** [To investigate scientifically] — *Syn.* analyze, investigate, test, try, probe, search, venture, explore, diagnose, prove, conduct an experiment, research, verify, speculate, study, examine, scrutinize, weigh, assay, sample, dissect, make inquiry, follow a clue, put to the test, play around with*, fool with*, cut and try*.
**2.** [To put on trial] — *Syn.* test, rehearse, try out, test out, try tentatively, sample, put on one's honor, hold under probation, put through one's paces, try by ordeal, give an opportunity, practice upon, have a go*.

**experimental,** *modif.* — *Syn.* tentative, trial, test, probationary, experiential, provisional, empirical, preliminary, pilot, preparatory, under probation, on approval, on trial, pending verification, temporary, beginning, unconcluded, unproved, speculative, laboratory, exploratory, probative, innovative, in its first stage, in the model stage. — *Ant.* ESTABLISHED, tried, tested.
**experimentally,** *modif.* — *Syn.* tentatively, temporarily, on trial, provisionally, on probation, analytically, step by step, empirically, by trial and error.
**expert,** *modif.* — *Syn.* skillful, practiced, proficient; see **able** 2.
**expert,** *n.* — *Syn.* authority, master, professional connoisseur; see **specialist.**
**expiate,** *v.* — *Syn.* atone for, make amends, appease, compensate; see **apologize, pay for.**
**expiation,** *n.* **1.** [Atonement] — *Syn.* redemption, satisfaction, compensation; see **reparation** 1.
**2.** [Something done in atonement] — *Syn.* amends, penance, flagellation; see **reparation** 2.
**expiration,** *n.* **1.** [End] — *Syn.* close, closing, termination; see **end** 2.
**2.** [Death] — *Syn.* dying, demise, passing; see **death** 1.
**expire,** *v.* **1.** [To end] — *Syn.* terminate, lapse, come to an end, run out; see **stop** 2.
**2.** [To die] — *Syn.* pass on, depart, perish; see **die** 1.
*See Synonym Study at* DIE.
**explain,** *v.* — *Syn.* interpret, explicate, account for, elucidate, illustrate, clarify, illuminate, make clear, describe, expound, teach, manifest, reveal, disclose, point up, point out, demonstrate, tell, refine, read, translate, paraphrase, render, put in other words, decipher, assign a meaning to, construe, define, disentangle, justify, rationalize, untangle, unravel, make plain, unfold, come to the point, put across, throw light upon, show by example, restate, rephrase, simplify, demystify, annotate, comment on, remark upon, offer an explanation, resolve, clear up, set right, put on the right track, unscramble, spell out, articulate, go into detail, get to the bottom of, figure out, speak out, emphasize, cast light upon, get across, get over, get through, get to, bring out, work out, solve, make sense of, make oneself understood, hammer into one's head*, put in plain English*. — *Ant.* puzzle, CONFUSE, confound.

*SYN.* — **explain** implies making clear or intelligible something that is not known or understood /to *explain* how a machine operates/; **expound** implies a systematic and thorough explanation, often by a person having expert knowledge /to *expound* a theory/; **explicate** implies a scholarly analysis or exposition that is developed in detail /the *explication* of a Biblical passage/; **elucidate** implies a shedding light upon by clear and specific explanation, illustration, etc. /to *elucidate* the country's foreign policy/; to **interpret** is to bring out meanings not immediately apparent, as by translation, searching insight, or special knowledge /how do you *interpret* his behavior?/; **construe** suggests a careful interpretation of something especially where meaning is ambiguous /her silence was *construed* as agreement/

**explainable,** *modif.* — *Syn.* explicable, accountable, intelligible; see **understandable.**
**explained,** *modif.* — *Syn.* made clear, interpreted, elucidated; see **obvious** 2, **related** 1, **told.**
**explanation,** *n.* **1.** [The act of making clear] — *Syn.* elucidation, clarification, interpretation, narration, recital, rendition, showing, display, exposition, explication, elaboration, demonstration, specification, defini-

tion, confession, description, telling, talking, writing, expression.
**2.** [Something intended to make clear] — *Syn.* information, answer, account, reason, statement, illustration, description, comment, justification, rationalization, narrative, story, tale, history, annotation, glossary, footnote, anecdote, example, apology, excuse, alibi, plea, defense, rationale, analysis, criticism, exegesis, résumé, gloss, key, solution, commentary, note, summary, report, brief, the details, breakdown, evidence, the dope*; see also **proof** 1.

**explanatory,** *modif.* — *Syn.* expository, illustrative, explaining, clarifying, informing, informative, allegorical, interpretive, hermeneutic, exegetical, annotative, instructive, guiding, illuminating, declarative, descriptive, explicative, analytical, graphic, discursive, critical, supplementary.

**expletive,** *n.* — *Syn.* exclamation, interjection, oath, swearword; see **curse** 1.

**explicable,** *modif.* — *Syn.* explainable, solvable, intelligible; see **understandable.**

**explicate,** *v.* — *Syn.* clarify, illustrate, interpret; see **explain.**
*See Synonym Study at* EXPLAIN.

**explication,** *n.* — *Syn.* clarification, exegesis, interpretation; see **explanation** 1, 2, **interpretation** 1, 2.

**explicit,** *modif.* — *Syn.* express, exact, definite, precise, specific, clear, unambiguous, plain, graphic; see also **definite** 1, 2, **frank, understandable.**

---

*SYN.* — **explicit** is applied to that which is so clearly stated or distinctly set forth that there should be no doubt as to the meaning; **express** adds to **explicit** the ideas of directness and positiveness; **exact** and **precise**, in this connection, both suggest that which is strictly defined, accurately stated, or made unmistakably clear; **definite** implies precise limitations as to the nature, character, meaning, etc. of something; **specific** implies the pointing up of details or the particularizing of references

---

**explode,** *v.* **1.** [To burst] — *Syn.* blow up, blow out, blast, blow a fuse, break out, erupt, go off, detonate, discharge, backfire, fly apart, fly into pieces, shatter, rupture, fracture, split, convulse, collapse, thunder, blow off, pop, blow to smithereens*; see also **rage** 1.
**2.** [To discredit] — *Syn.* disprove, refute, confute; see **disprove.**

**exploit,** *n.* — *Syn.* deed, venture, escapade; see **achievement** 2.

**exploit,** *v.* **1.** [To make use of] — *Syn.* utilize, capitalize on, turn to account, employ; see **use** 1.
**2.** [To make unfair use of] — *Syn.* take advantage of, impose upon, misuse, overwork; see **abuse** 1.

**exploited,** *modif.* — *Syn.* used, taken advantage of, utilized, put to use, worked, overworked, overburdened, overtaxed, oppressed, milked*; see also **abused, oppressed, used** 1.

**exploration,** *n.* — *Syn.* investigation, research, search; see **examination** 1, **journey, travel** 1.

**explore,** *v.* — *Syn.* search, investigate, traverse, reconnoiter; see **examine** 1, **travel** 2.

**explorer,** *n.* — *Syn.* adventurer, traveler, pioneer, wayfarer, pilgrim, voyager, astronaut, space traveler, investigator, inventor, seafarer, mountaineer, mountain climber, scientist, globe-trotter, navigator, circumnavigator, spelunker, creator, founder, pathfinder, trailblazer, colonist, conquistador.
Famous explorers include: Marco Polo, Christopher Columbus, Amerigo Vespucci, Francisco Pizarro, Magellan, Ponce de Leon, Balboa, Vasco da Gama, Sir Francis Drake, Henry Hudson, John Cabot, De Soto, Hernán Cortés, Father Marquette and Joliet, David Livingstone, Lewis and Clark, Robert E. Peary, Robert Scott, Vilhjalmur Stefanson, Roald Amundsen, Richard E. Byrd, Thor Heyerdahl, Sir Edmund Hillary, Maurice Herzog, Yuri Gagarin, Alan Shephard, John Glenn, Jacques Cousteau, Neil Armstrong.

**explosion,** *n.* **1.** [The act of blowing up] — *Syn.* detonation, blast, burst, discharge, blowout, blowup, concussion, eruption, percussion, combustion, outburst, firing, ignition, backfire, fulmination, pop.
**2.** [A loud noise] — *Syn.* report, blast, crack, bang; see **noise** 1.

**explosive,** *modif.* **1.** [Eruptive] — *Syn.* bursting, detonating, dangerous, convulsive, fulminating, atomic, fulminant, fiery, volcanic, flammable, inflammable, combustible. — *Ant.* HARMLESS, burned out, quenched.
**2.** [Violent; *said of persons or events*] — *Syn.* volatile, stormy, fiery, combustible, inflammable, excitable, touchy, unstable, charged, loaded, dangerous, perilous, volcanic, raging, hot-tempered, short-tempered, tense, sensitive, touch-and-go, critical; see also **dangerous** 1, **excitable.** — *Ant.* GENTLE, mild, uneventful.

**explosive,** *n.* — *Syn.* mine, gunpowder, ammunition, high explosive, detonator, propellant, bomb, missile, grenade, charge, shell, Molotov cocktail*; see also **ammunition, mine** 2, **munitions.**
Common explosives include: dynamite, nitroglycerine, TNT, Trinitrotoluene, saltpeter, hexamine, hexamethylenetetramine, ballistite, gun cotton, nitrate compound, nitro cotton, cellulose nitrate, pyroxylin, melinite, gelignite, cordite, plastique, Semtex, lyddite, nitro*, peter*, soup*, vaseline*, grease*, powder*, sawdust*, bang juice*; see also **atomic energy.**

**exponent,** *n.* **1.** [Explainer] — *Syn.* advocate, interpreter, expounder; see **interpreter, supporter.**
**2.** [Index] — *Syn.* representative, type, specimen; see **example** 1, **index** 1.

**export,** *n.* — *Syn.* exportation, shipping, trading, foreign sale, overseas shipment, transoceanic cargo, commodity, merchant traffic, international trade, foreign trade.

**export,** *v.* — *Syn.* send out, sell abroad, trade abroad, market abroad, ship, ship overseas, transport, convey outside, act as a shipper, transship, consign, find a foreign market, find a foreign outlet, dump*.

**expose,** *v.* **1.** [To uncover] — *Syn.* disclose, show, show up, present, prove, reveal, air, exhibit, unmask, debunk, lay open, lay bare, bring to light, open, unearth, dig up, smoke out, drag before the public, give away, detect, betray, divulge, make known, muckrake, bring into view, bare, unveil, unseal, unroll, unfold, unwrap, untie, drag through the mud*, paint in its true color*, put the finger on*, blow the lid off*, blow wide open*; see also **reveal** 1.
**2.** [To endeavor to attract attention] — *Syn.* exhibit, show off, bare, flash*; see **display** 1.
**3.** [To open to danger] — *Syn.* lay open to, subject to, imperil; see **endanger.**
*See Synonym Study at* SHOW.

**exposé,** *n.* — *Syn.* revelation, disclosure, confession; see **exposure** 1.

**exposed,** *modif.* **1.** [In sight] — *Syn.* visible, apparent, clear; see **obvious** 1.
**2.** [Revealed in the true light] — *Syn.* disclosed, revealed, divulged, unmasked, unveiled, bared, uncovered, unsealed, made public, laid bare, pointed out, ferreted out, dug up, brought to light, brought to the

light of day, brought to justice, solved, resolved, untied, unriddled, discovered, found out, seen through, detected, debunked. — *Ant.* HIDDEN, concealed, disguised.

**exposition,** *n.* **1.** [The process of making clear] — *Syn.* elucidation, delineation, explication; see **explanation** 1.
**2.** [A specific piece of explanation] — *Syn.* dissertation, tract, treatise, paper, composition, disquisition, thesis, theme, article, monograph, editorial, comment, commentary, critique, study, report, text, essay, review, analysis, piece, annotation, position paper, data paper, white paper, enunciation, the details, statement, expository, statement, discourse, discussion, story, tale, review, history.
**3.** [A large public exhibition] — *Syn.* fair, exhibit, trade show, expo*; see **fair, show** 1.

**expositor,** *n.* — *Syn.* explainer, commentator, expounder; see **interpreter, professor, teacher** 1.

**expository,** *modif.* — *Syn.* informative, descriptive, interpretive; see **explanatory.**

**ex post facto,** *modif.* — *Syn.* subsequently, retroactively, retrospectively; see **afterward, finally** 2.

**expostulate,** *v.* — *Syn.* remonstrate, reason with, dissuade; see **object, oppose** 1, **remonstrate.**
*See Synonym Study at* OBJECT.

**expostulation,** *n.* — *Syn.* remonstrance, protest, complaint, disapproval; see **objection** 2.

**exposure,** *n.* **1.** [The act of subjecting to outside influences] — *Syn.* disclosure, betrayal, uncovering, baring, unfolding, display, exhibition, laying open, unmasking, presentation, publication, airing, publicizing, publicity, showing, appearance, expression, revelation, confession, unveiling, acknowledgment, exposé, leak, giveaway, bombshell*, show-up*, outing*. — *Ant.* PROTECTION, concealment, secrecy.
**2.** [The condition or result of exposure, as to the elements] — *Syn.* vulnerability, susceptibility, endangerment, weathering, frostbite, hypothermia, heat prostration, sunstroke, heatstroke; see also **danger, illness** 1.

**expound,** *v.* **1.** [To interpret] — *Syn.* explicate, clarify, elucidate; see **explain.**
**2.** [To set forth in detail] — *Syn.* delineate, present, express; see **describe.**
*See Synonym Study at* EXPLAIN.

**express,** *modif.* **1.** [Explicit] — *Syn.* definite, specific, clearly stated; see **definite** 1, 2.
**2.** [Fast] — *Syn.* nonstop, direct, high-speed; see **direct** 1, **fast** 1.
*See Synonym Study at* EXPLICIT.

**express,** *v.* **1.** [To put into words] — *Syn.* state, utter, declare, verbalize, word, phrase, formulate, couch; see also **communicate** 1, **utter.**
**2.** [To make known] — *Syn.* reveal, show, manifest; see **display** 1, **expose** 1, **prove.**
**3.** [To symbolize] — *Syn.* represent, signify, denote; see **mean** 1, **represent** 1.
**4.** [To send by rapid conveyor] — *Syn.* dispatch, forward, ship; see **send** 1.
*See Synonym Study at* UTTER.

**expression,** *n.* **1.** [Significant appearance] — *Syn.* look, cast, character; see **appearance** 1.
**2.** [Putting into understandable form] — *Syn.* representation, articulation, utterance, verbalization, wording, symbolization, narration, exposition, formulation, interpretation, invention, creation, art product, declaration, materialization, commentary, diagnosis, definition, rendition, elucidation, explanation, illustration; see also **composition** 3, **diction.**

**3.** [A traditional form of speech] — *Syn.* locution, idiom, speech pattern; see **phrase, word** 1.
**4.** [Facial cast] — *Syn.* grimace, smile, smirk, mug, sneer, *moue* (French), pout, simper, grin, facial contortion, wry face; see also **smile.**
**5.** [Expressiveness] — *Syn.* feeling, emotion, affect; see **eloquence** 1, **emotion.**

**expressionless,** *modif.* — *Syn.* wooden, impassive, dull, vacuous; see **blank** 2.

**expressive,** *modif.* — *Syn.* eloquent, demonstrative, revealing, indicative, representative, descriptive, dramatic, stirring, sympathetic, articulate, touching, significant, meaningful, suggestive, pregnant, evocative, poignant, moving, pathetic, spirited, emphatic, strong, forceful, powerful, energetic, lively, tender, emotional, passionate, artistic, warm, masterly, colorful, vivid, striking, telling. — *Ant.* expressionless, impassive, wooden.

**express oneself,** *v.* — *Syn.* communicate one's thoughts, communicate one's feelings, do one's thing*; see **communicate** 1, **express** 1.

**expressway,** *n.* — *Syn.* superhighway, freeway, turnpike; see **road** 1.

**expropriate,** *v.* — *Syn.* confiscate, deprive of property, dispossess; see **seize** 2.

**expropriation,** *n.* — *Syn.* confiscation, seizure, dispossession; see **capture.**

**expulsion,** *n.* — *Syn.* ejection, suspension, purge, banishment; see **exile** 1, **removal** 1.

**expunge,** *v.* — *Syn.* erase, delete, efface; see **cancel** 1.
*See Synonym Study at* ERASE.

**expurgate,** *v.* — *Syn.* purify, cleanse, bowdlerize; see **censor.**

**exquisite,** *modif.* — *Syn.* dainty, delicate, lovely, beautiful, elegant, fine, choice, well-crafted, precise, flawless, impeccable; see also **beautiful** 1, 2, **dainty** 1, **excellent.**
*See Synonym Study at* DAINTY.

**extant,** *modif.* — *Syn.* surviving, living, existent, existing, undestroyed, in existence, not lost, not extinct, in current use.

**extemporaneous,** *modif.* — *Syn.* spontaneous, unpremeditated, improvised, extempore, extemporary, impromptu, unprepared, ad-lib*, ad-libbed*, offhand, unstudied, informal, unrehearsed, ad hoc, by ear, on impulse, on the spot, without preparation, off the cuff*, spur-of-the-moment*. — *Ant.* PREPARED, studied, premeditated.
*See Synonym Study at* IMPROMPTU.

**extemporaneously,** *modif.* — *Syn.* without preparation, spontaneously, on the spur of the moment*, off the top of one's head*; see **freely** 1, 2.

**extempore,** *modif.* — *Syn.* offhand, impromptu, unexpectedly; see **extemporaneous.**
*See Synonym Study at* IMPROMPTU.

**extemporize,** *v.* — *Syn.* improvise, ad-lib*, devise; see **invent** 1.

**extend,** *v.* **1.** [To make larger] — *Syn.* lengthen, elongate, protract, stretch out, draw out, enlarge, prolong; see also **increase** 1.
**2.** [To occupy space to a given point] — *Syn.* continue, go as far as, stretch, spread; see **reach** 1.

---

*SYN.* — **extend** and **lengthen** both imply a making longer in space or time, but **extend**, in addition, may signify an enlarging in area, scope, influence, meaning, etc.; **elongate** is a synonym for **lengthen** in the spatial sense and is more commonly used in technical applications; **prolong** and **protract** both primarily imply an extending in time, **prolong** suggesting continuation beyond the usual or expected time, and **protract** a being drawn out needlessly or wearily

---

**extended,** *modif.* **1.** [Outspread] — *Syn.* spread, widespread, expansive; see **extensive** 1, **outspread.**
**2.** [Very long] — *Syn.* elongated, drawn out, lengthened; see **long** 1.
**extending,** *modif.* — *Syn.* reaching, continuing, continuous, continual, perpetual, radiating, ranging, stretching, approaching, spreading, spanning, going on, running to, drawn out to, lengthening; see also **endless** 1.
**extension,** *n.* **1.** [The action of continuing] — *Syn.* augmentation, enlargement, expansion, prolongation; see **continuation** 1, **increase.**
**2.** [The quality of extending] — *Syn.* distance, width, size; see **length** 2.
**3.** [Something added] — *Syn.* annex, branch, additional telephone, extra time; see **addition** 2, 3, **delay** 1.
**extensive,** *modif.* **1.** [Large in area] — *Syn.* wide, broad, long, great, huge, vast, capacious, extended, protracted, expanded, lengthy; see also **large** 1.
**2.** [Widespread] — *Syn.* general, unrestricted, boundless; see **widespread.**
**3.** [Comprehensive] — *Syn.* inclusive, far-reaching, thorough; see **comprehensive.**
**extensively,** *modif.* — *Syn.* widely, broadly, greatly; see **largely** 2.
**extent,** — *Syn.* degree, limit, span, space, area, measure, size, proportions, bulk, length, breadth, compass, scope, reach, sweep, amplitude, spaciousness, capaciousness, width, range, amount, expanse, magnitude, intensity; see also **breadth** 2.
**extenuate,** *v.* — *Syn.* reduce, lessen, diminish, palliate, mitigate, qualify, apologize for; see also **decrease** 2, **excuse, palliate.**
**extenuating circumstances,** *n.* — *Syn.* extenuation, mitigation, uncontrollable situation, palliation, excuse, justification.
**extenuation,** *n.* **1.** [An excuse] — *Syn.* apology, vindication, justification; see **explanation** 2, **justification.**
**2.** [Reduction] — *Syn.* diminution, abatement, mitigation; see **reduction** 1.
**exterior,** *modif.* — *Syn.* outer, outlying, outermost, surface; see **outer, outside.**
**exterior,** *n.* — *Syn.* surface, covering, visible portion; see **outside** 1.
**exterminate,** *v.* — *Syn.* annihilate, eradicate, abolish, extirpate, destroy, wipe out, slaughter, kill off; see also **destroy** 1, **kill** 1.

---

*SYN.* — **exterminate** implies the complete, wholesale destruction of things or living beings whose existence is considered undesirable; **extirpate** and **eradicate** both suggest the extinction or abolition of something, **extirpate** implying destruction at the very source, often through the loss or removal of conditions necessary for survival, and **eradicate** connoting less violence and, often, the working of natural processes or a methodical plan

---

**external,** *modif.* — *Syn.* outer, surface, visible, open to the air; see **obvious** 1, **outer, outside.**
**externals,** *pl.n.* — *Syn.* visible forms, facade, exterior, superficialities; see **appearance** 1, 2, **outside** 1.
**extinct,** *modif.* — *Syn.* dead, ended, terminated, exterminated, deceased, defunct, perished, lost, without a sur-

vivor, vanished, gone, unknown, no longer known, obsolete.
*See Synonym Study at* DEAD.
**extinction,** *n.* **1.** [Extinguishment] — *Syn.* quenching, drowning, putting out, blotting out, darkening, snuffing, turning out, turning off, smothering, stifling, dousing.
**2.** [Annihilation] — *Syn.* abolition, extermination, extirpation, dying out; see **destruction** 1, **murder.**
**extinguish,** *v.* **1.** [To put out] — *Syn.* smother, choke, quench, douse, snuff out, blow out, stamp out, blot out, drown out, stifle, turn off, switch off, suffocate, put down, stub out.
**2.** [To destroy] — *Syn.* wipe out, annihilate, exterminate; see **destroy** 1.
**extirpate,** *v.* — *Syn.* exterminate, annihilate, abolish, root out; see **destroy** 1.
*See Synonym Study at* EXTERMINATE.
**extirpation,** *n.* — *Syn.* extermination, extinction, annihilation; see **destruction** 1.
**extol,** *v.* — *Syn.* laud, exalt, acclaim, eulogize; see **praise** 1, **worship** 2.
*See Synonym Study at* PRAISE.
**extort,** *v.* — *Syn.* extract, wrench, wrest; see **bleed** 3, **force** 1.
*See Synonym Study at* EXTRACT.
**extortion,** *n.* — *Syn.* exaction, blackmail, coercion, shakedown\*; see **corruption** 2, **theft.**
**extortionate,** *modif.* **1.** [Oppressive] — *Syn.* exacting, avaricious, rapacious, bloodsucking; see **corrupt** 1, **greedy** 1, **severe** 1, 2.
**2.** [Excessive] — *Syn.* exorbitant, extravagant, unreasonable; see **expensive.**
**extortionist,** *n.* — *Syn.* thief, blackmailer, oppressor; see **criminal.**
**extra,** *modif.* — *Syn.* additional, in addition, other, one more, spare, reserve, surplus, supplemental, increased, another, new, fresh, auxiliary, backup, added, besides, also, further, more, beyond, over and above, excess, plus, supplementary, extraordinary, accessory, special, unused. — *Ant.* LESS, short, essential.
**extract,** *n.* **1.** [An excerpt] — *Syn.* passage, citation, selection; see **quotation** 1.
**2.** [Essence] — *Syn.* distillation, infusion, decoction; see **essence** 3.
**extract,** *v.* **1.** [To pry out] — *Syn.* extort, extricate, pull out, pluck; see **remove** 1.
**2.** [To obtain] — *Syn.* elicit, evoke, educe, derive, secure, extort, exact, wrest, deduce; see also **obtain** 1.
**3.** [To cite] — *Syn.* excerpt, quote, select; see **cite** 2.

---

*SYN.* — **extract** implies a drawing out of something, as if by pulling, sucking, etc./to *extract* a promise/; **educe** suggests a drawing out or evolving of something that is latent or undeveloped /laws were *educed* from tribal customs/; **elicit** connotes difficulty or skill in drawing out something hidden or buried /careful questioning elicited a reasonable account of the accident/; **evoke** implies a calling forth or summoning, as of a mental image, by stimulating the emotions /the odor *evoked* a memory of childhood/; **extort** suggests a forcing or wresting of something, as by violence or threats /to *extort* a ransom/

---

**extraction,** *n.* **1.** [One's personal or ethnic origin] — *Syn.* ancestry, parentage, descent; see **family** 1.
**2.** [The pulling of a tooth] — *Syn.* toothdrawing, uprooting, removal, wrenching, taking out.
**extradite,** *v.* **1.** [To deliver by extradition] — *Syn.* surrender, give up, deport; see **abandon** 1, **banish** 1.

**2.** [To acquire by extradition] — *Syn.* obtain, apprehend, bring to justice, bring to trial; see **arrest** 1.

**extraneous,** *modif.* **1.** [Foreign] — *Syn.* extrinsic, external, alien, exotic; see **foreign** 1.

**2.** [Irrelevant] — *Syn.* unessential, inappropriate, incidental; see **irrelevant.**

*See Synonym Study at* FOREIGN.

**extraordinarily,** *modif.* — *Syn.* remarkably, notably, exceptionally, unusually; see **especially** 1, **very.**

**extraordinary,** *modif.* — *Syn.* exceptional, remarkable, curious, amazing; see **excellent, unusual** 1.

**extravagance,** *n.* — *Syn.* lavishness, excessive expenditure, improvidence; see **indulgence** 3, **waste** 1.

**extravagant,** *modif.* **1.** [Excessive] — *Syn.* unrestrained, lavish, immoderate, inordinate, unreasonable, fantastic, absurd, wild, exaggerated, extreme, flamboyant, ornate, showy; see also **extreme** 2, **profuse.**

**2.** [Spending or costing too much] — *Syn.* improvident, prodigal, spendthrift, wasteful, exorbitant, overpriced, expensive; see also **expensive, wasteful.**

*See Synonym Study at* EXCESSIVE, PROFUSE.

**extravaganza,** *n.* — *Syn.* spectacle, spectacular, divertissement, fantasy; see **show** 1, 2.

**extreme,** *modif.* **1.** [The most remote] — *Syn.* utmost, final, ultimate, farthest; see **last** 1.

**2.** [Going beyond moderation and reason] — *Syn.* radical, intemperate, immoderate, imprudent, excessive, inordinate, immeasurable, profuse, extravagant, exorbitant, overkill, flagrant, outrageous, unreasonable, irrational, improper, unconventional, fabulous, preposterous, abysmal, greatest, thorough, far, gross, out of proportion, absolute, ultra, extremist, fanatical, rabid, over-zealous, desperate, severe, intense, strict, drastic, sheer, total, advanced, violent, sharp, acute, beyond control, fantastic, to the extreme, nonsensical, unqualified, absurd, monstrous, unmitigated, hyperbolic, exaggerated, big*, almighty*, super*, stiff*, steep*, gonzo*, out of bounds*, at its height*, beyond the pale*, way-out*, far-out*, to the max*. — *Ant.* cautious, RESTRAINED, moderate.

**extreme,** *n.* — *Syn.* height, apogee, utmost, maximum; see **climax, limit** 2.

**go to extremes** — *Syn.* be excessive, be immoderate, go to great lengths, go overboard*; see **overdo** 1.

**in the extreme** — *Syn.* extremely, to the highest degree, inordinately, to the utmost; see **much** 2, **very.**

**extremely,** *modif.* — *Syn.* greatly, remarkably, notably; see **much** 2, **very.**

**extremist,** *modif.* — *Syn.* extreme, fanatic, ultraist; see **fanatical, radical** 2.

**extremist,** *n.* — *Syn.* zealot, fanatic, die-hard; see **agitator, radical, zealot.**

**extremity,** *n.* **1.** [The end] — *Syn.* limit, outside, utmost point; see **edge** 1, **end** 4, **limit** 2.

**2.** [A remote part of the body] — *Syn.* limb, hand, foot; see **appendage** 2, **finger, foot** 2, **hand** 1, **toe.**

**extricate,** *v.* — *Syn.* disentangle, disengage, deliver, liberate; see **free** 1.

**extrinsic,** *modif.* — *Syn.* extraneous, external, foreign, outward; see **foreign** 1.

*See Synonym Study at* FOREIGN.

**extrovert,** *n.* — *Syn.* outgoing person, gregarious person, socializer, exhibitionist, showoff, other-directed individual, mixer, life of the party*.

**extrude,** *v.* — *Syn.* force out, expel, project; see **eject** 1.

**exuberance,** *n.* **1.** [Plenty] — *Syn.* abundance, affluence, profusion; see **plenty.**

**2.** [High spirits] — *Syn.* vitality, ebullience, eagerness, exhilaration; see **enthusiasm** 1, **joy** 2.

**exuberant,** *modif.* **1.** [Plentiful] — *Syn.* abundant, prolific, profuse; see **plentiful** 1, 2.

**2.** [High-spirited] — *Syn.* vivacious, joyous, effervescent; see **enthusiastic** 3, **happy** 1.

**exude,** *v.* — *Syn.* secrete, discharge, ooze, radiate; see **emit** 1, **excrete.**

**exult,** *n.* — *Syn.* glory, revel, delight, triumph, crow, boast, be jubilant, jubilate, jump for joy*, walk on air*, be on cloud nine*; see also **celebrate** 3.

**exultant,** *modif.* — *Syn.* exulting, elated, jubilant; see **happy** 1, **triumphant.**

**exultation,** *n.* — *Syn.* rejoicing, triumph, elation; see **celebration** 2, **happiness** 2.

**eye,** *n.* **1.** [The organ of sight] — *Syn.* instrument of vision, compound eye, *oculus* (Latin), simple eye, *ocellus* (Latin), naked eye, optic, orb*, peeper*, lamp*.

Parts of the eye include: eyeball, ball, conjunctiva, pupil, retina, iris, cornea, ciliary body, eye muscles, lacrimal glands, optic nerve, aqueous humor, fovea, sclera, vitreous humor, choroid, white, lens, optic nerve.

**2.** [The power of seeing or judging] — *Syn.* perception, taste, discrimination; see **appreciation** 3, **sight** 1, **taste** 3.

**3.** [A center] — *Syn.* focus, core, heart, kernel; see **center** 1.

**all eyes*** — *Syn.* attentive, aware, perceptive; see **observant** 2.

**an eye for an eye** — *Syn.* punishment, retaliation, vengeance; see **revenge** 1.

**catch one's eye** — *Syn.* attract one's attention, cause notice, stand out; see **appear** 1, **fascinate.**

**easy on the eyes*** — *Syn.* attractive, appealing, pleasant to look at; see **beautiful** 1, 2, **handsome** 2.

**feast one's eyes on*** — *Syn.* look at with pleasure, be attracted to, watch with delight, admire; see **like** 1, **watch** 1.

**give someone the eye*** — *Syn.* look at, ogle, invite; see **flirt** 1, **look** 2, **watch** 1.

**have an eye for** — *Syn.* appreciate, be interested in, be discerning about; see **appreciate** 3, **like** 1.

**have an eye to** — *Syn.* watch out for, be mindful of, attend to; see **watch out.**

**have eyes for*** — *Syn.* appreciate, be interested in, desire; see **like** 1, **want** 1.

**in a pig's eye*** — *Syn.* under no circumstances, impossible, no way; see **never.**

**in the public eye** — *Syn.* well-known, renowned, celebrated; see **famous.**

**keep an eye on** — *Syn.* look after, watch over, protect; see **guard** 2.

**keep an eye out for*** — *Syn.* watch for, look for, be watchful, be on the alert; see **watch** 1.

**keep one's eyes open** or **peeled** or **skinned*** — *Syn.* be on the lookout, be watchful, be aware, look out; see **watch** 1.

**lay** or **set** or **clap eyes on*** — *Syn.* look at, see, view, notice; see **see** 1.

**make eyes at** — *Syn.* flirt with, ogle, invite; see **flirt** 1.

**my eye!*** — *Syn.* the hell!*, ridiculous, impossible; see **never, no.**

**open one's eyes** — *Syn.* make aware, inform, apprise; see **enlighten** 2, **notify** 6, **tell** 1.

**run one's eyes over*** — *Syn.* scan, skim, glance at; see **examine** 1, **look** 2, **read** 1.

**see with half an eye*** — *Syn.* comprehend, perceive, see; see **understand** 1.

**shut one's eyes to** — *Syn.* ignore, disregard, refuse to see, refuse to consider; see **disregard, neglect** 1, 2.

**with an eye to**— *Syn.* considering, mindful of, aware of; see **considering.**

**eye doctor,** *n.* — *Syn.* optometrist, oculist, ophthalmologist; see **doctor** 1.

**eyeless,** *modif.* — *Syn.* unseeing, sightless, blinded; see **blind** 1.

**eyelet,** *n.* — *Syn.* opening, aperture, perforation; see **hole** 1.

**eye of a needle,** *n.* — *Syn.* opening, aperture, orifice; see **hole** 1.

**eyesight,** *n.* — *Syn.* vision, sight, visual perception; see **sight** 1.

**eyesore,** *n.* — *Syn.* ugly thing, blot, deformity, horror\*; see **blemish, ugliness.**

**eyewitness,** *n.* — *Syn.* onlooker, passerby, observer, informant; see **witness.**

# F

**fable,** *n.* — *Syn.* allegory, tale, parable; see **story**.

**fabled,** *modif.* — *Syn.* mythical, fanciful, unreal, mythological; see **legendary** 2.

**fabric,** *n.* **1.** [Material] — *Syn.* cloth, textile, stuff; see **cloth**.

**2.** [Basic structure] — *Syn.* framework, substance, foundation, makeup; see **frame** 1, **material** 2.

**fabricate,** *v.* **1.** [To construct] — *Syn.* erect, make, form; see **build** 1, **manufacture** 1.

**2.** [To misrepresent] — *Syn.* make up, contrive, prevaricate; see **invent** 2, **lie** 1.

**3.** [To assemble] — *Syn.* put together, fit together, compose, join; see **assemble** 3.

*See Synonym Study at* LIE, MAKE.

**fabrication,** *n.* — *Syn.* invention, untruth, fib; see **lie** 1.

**fabulous,** *modif.* **1.** [Suggestive of a fable] — *Syn.* fabled, apocryphal, mythical; see **legendary** 2.

**2.** [Unbelievable] — *Syn.* remarkable, amazing, incredible; see **unusual** 1.

**3.** [*Exceptionally good] — *Syn.* wonderful, superb, marvelous*; see **excellent**.

**façade,** *n.* — *Syn.* front, face, veneer, false front; see **appearance** 2, **front** 1, 4.

**face,** *n.* **1.** [The front of the head] — *Syn.* visage, countenance, appearance, features, lineaments, silhouette, profile, physiognomy, front, map*, mug*, pan*, puss*, kisser*.

**2.** [Facial expression] — *Syn.* look, cast, grimace; see **appearance** 1, **expression** 4.

**3.** [Bold or inconsiderate conduct] — *Syn.* effrontery, impudence, impertinence; see **rudeness**.

**4.** [A plane surface] — *Syn.* front, surface, right side, dial; see **front** 1, **plane** 1.

**5.** [Prestige] — *Syn.* status, standing, self-respect; see **dignity** 1, **reputation** 2.

**6.** [Appearance] — *Syn.* light, aspect, presentation; see **appearance** 1.

**fly in the face of** — *Syn.* defy, rebel against, disobey; see **dare** 2, **oppose** 2.

**make a face** — *Syn.* distort one's face, grimace, scowl, mug*; see **frown**.

**on the face of it** — *Syn.* to all appearances, seemingly, according to the evidence; see **apparently**.

**pull** or **wear a long face*** — *Syn.* look sad, scowl, pout; see **frown**.

**set one's face against** — *Syn.* oppose, resist, disapprove of, set oneself against; see **disapprove** 1, **oppose** 1.

**show one's face** — *Syn.* be seen, show up, come; see **appear** 1, 3.

**to one's face** — *Syn.* candidly, openly, frankly, boldly; see **openly** 1.

---

**SYN.** — **face** is the basic, direct word for the front of the head; **countenance** refers to the face as it reflects the emotions or feelings and is, hence, often applied to the facial expression /his happy *countenance*/; **visage** re-

fers to the form, proportions, and expression of the face, especially as indicative of general temperament /a man of stern *visage*/; **physiognomy** refers to the general cast of features, esp. when considered as characteristic of an ethnic group or as supposedly indicative of character /the *physiognomy* of an honest man/

---

**face,** *v.* **1.** [To confront conflict or trouble] — *Syn.* confront, oppose, defy, meet, dare, brave, challenge, withstand, beard, court, encounter, risk, tolerate, endure, sustain, suffer, bear, tell to one's face, show a bold front, make a stand, meet face to face, look in the eye, grapple with, come to grips with, stand up to, cope with, contend with, deal with, handle, front, brook, allow, stand, submit, go up against, square up to, meet head-on, not shrink from, take it*, bell the cat*, take the bull by the horns*, face the music*; see also **endure** 2. — *Ant.* EVADE, avoid, run away from.

**2.** [To put a face on a building] — *Syn.* refinish, front, decorate, surface, dress, smooth the surface of, polish, level, redecorate, remodel, brick over, cover, coat, shingle, side, plaster, stucco, veneer.

**3.** [To put facing on goods] — *Syn.* line, bind, trim, hem, back, pipe, tuck, overlay, fold, bias.

**4.** [To look out on] — *Syn.* front, front on, overlook, border, be turned toward, look toward, view, give on *or* onto.

**faced,** *modif.* — *Syn.* plated, covered, sheathed, filmed; see **covered** 1, **finished** 2.

**face lifting,** *n.* — *Syn.* face lift, plastic surgery, cosmetic surgery, rhytidectomy, renovation, rejuvenation.

**facet,** *n.* — *Syn.* aspect, face, side; see **phase**, **plane** 1.

*See Synonym Study at* PHASE.

**facetious,** *modif.* — *Syn.* jocular, jocose, humorous, funny, flippant, waggish, jesting, joking, jokey, tongue-in-cheek, sportive, sprightly, witty, merry, pleasant, comical, droll, amusing, laughable, clever, ludicrous, farcical, whimsical, fanciful, bantering, pert, light, irreverent, quippish, playful, quizzical, dry, wry, salty, sarcastic, ironic, satirical, trifling, not serious, punning, epigrammatic, capering, indecorous, ridiculous, jolly, jocund, flip*, kidding*, joshing*, wisecracking*, pulling one's leg*, putting one on*; see also **funny** 1.

*See Synonym Study at* WITTY.

**face to face,** *modif.* — *Syn.* confronting, eye to eye, facing, person to person, one-on-one, vis-à-vis, eyeball to eyeball*; see also **confronting**.

**facial,** *n.* — *Syn.* facial massage, facial treatment, beauty treatment, mud pack, oatmeal mask, face mask.

**facile,** *modif.* **1.** [Easy] — *Syn.* simple, effortless, obvious, apparent; see **easy** 2.

**2.** [Skillful] — *Syn.* skilled, practiced, accomplished; see **able** 1, 2, **fluent** 2.

**3.** [Superficial] — *Syn.* glib, simplistic, insincere; see **fluent** 2, **superficial**.

*See Synonym Study at* EASY.

**facilitate,** *v.* — *Syn.* promote, aid, make easy, expedite; see **help** 1, **promote** 1.

**facility,** *n.* **1.** [Easy skillfulness] — *Syn.* dexterity, adroitness, ease, fluency; see **ability** 2, **ease** 2.

**2.** [Material; *usually plural*] — *Syn.* tools, plant, buildings; see **equipment.**

**3.** [Agency; *usually plural*] — *Syn.* department, bureau, means, amenity; see **convenience** 2, **means** 1, **office** 3.

**facing,** *n.* **1.** [An architectural finish] — *Syn.* surface, revetment, covering, front, false front, siding.

Facings include: concrete, stucco, brick, tile, glass, stone, plaster, whitewash, shingle, veneer, shiplap, marble.

**2.** [Finish for dress goods] — *Syn.* lining, appliqué, backing, embroidery, hem, piping, tucks, braid, folds, bias, overlay, trim, binding.

**facsimile,** *n.* — *Syn.* duplicate, reproduction, copy, fax; see **copy.**

*See Synonym Study at* COPY.

**fact,** *n.* **1.** [A reliable generality] — *Syn.* reality, actuality, certainty, truth, substantiality, palpability, experience, matter, state of things, truth of the matter, the case, not an illusion, *fait accompli* (French), what really happened, something concrete, what is the case, matter of fact, hard evidence, hard fact, *nuda veritas* (Latin), verity, naked truth, gospel, certitude, scripture, law, solidity, permanence, basis, physical reality, existence, corporeal existence, state of being, fact of life, what's what*, straight dope*, bottom line*; see also **facts.** — *Ant.* FANCY, fiction, imagination.

**2.** [An individual reality] — *Syn.* circumstance, detail, factor, particular, case, consideration, datum, evidence, point, event, action, deed, happening, occurrence, creation, manifestation, being, entity, experience, affair, act, episode, performance, proceeding, phenomenon, incident, thing done, adventure, transaction, organism, construction, truism, truth, plain fact, accomplishment, accomplished fact, *fait accompli* (French). — *Ant.* ERROR, illusion, untruth.

**as a matter of fact** — *Syn.* in reality, in fact, actually, in point of fact; see **really** 1.

**faction,** *n.* **1.** [An organized group] — *Syn.* bloc, cabal, contingent, division, combine, party, gang, crew, wing, claque, junta, clique, conclave, conspiracy, intrigue, splinter party, splinter group, set, clan, club, lobby, camp, inner circle, sect, coterie, partnership, cell, unit, mob, Mafia, side, camarilla, machine, tong, band, pressure group, team, machine, ring, knot, circle, concern, sector, guild, Black Hand, Camorra, cadre, schism, entente, outfit*, crowd*, in-group*, bunch*.

**2.** [Tendency to break into warring groups] — *Syn.* dissension, quarrelsomeness, disunity, schism; see **disagreement** 1.

**factious,** *modif.* — *Syn.* dissident, seditious, divisive, contentious; see **opposing** 1, **quarrelsome** 1.

**factitious,** *modif.* — *Syn.* unnatural, false, artificial; see **affected** 3, **false** 3.

**factor,** *n.* **1.** [A component part] — *Syn.* portion, constituent, determinant; see **circumstance** 1, **part** 1.

**2.** [An agent] — *Syn.* broker, steward, representative; see **administrator, agent** 1.

*See Synonym Study at* AGENT, ELEMENT.

**factory,** *n.* — *Syn.* plant, manufactory, shop, industry, workshop, machine shop, mill, works, laboratory, assembly plant, manufacturing plant, establishment, branch, foundry, forge, loom, mint, carpenter shop, brewery, sawmill, supply house, warehouse, sweatshop, guild, cooperative, processing plant, workroom, firm, company, packing plant, outfitters, facility, layout*.

**factotum,** *n.* — *Syn.* jack-of-all-trades, handyman, gal *or* man Friday; see **assistant, man-of-all-work.**

**facts,** *n.* — *Syn.* information, data, particulars, details, specifics, intelligence, reality, actuality, the score*, the lowdown*, the dope*, the scoop*, the skinny*; see also **data.**

**factual,** *modif.* — *Syn.* exact, true, actual, descriptive; see **accurate** 1, 2, **genuine** 1.

**faculty,** *n.* **1.** [A special aptitude] — *Syn.* ability, talent, capacity, forte; see **ability** 1.

**2.** [A group of specialists, usually engaged in instruction or research] — *Syn.* staff, faculty members, teachers, personnel, instructors, employees, university, college, institute, department, teaching staff, instructional staff, research staff, research workers, teaching assistants, body of professors, professoriate, clinic, society, body, organization, corps, instructional corps, mentors, professors, assistant professors, associate professors, docents, tutors, functionaries, foundation, pedagogues, lecturers, monitors, advisers, masters, scholars, literati, dons, fellows, profs*, TA's*, ABD's*.

*See Synonym Study at* TALENT.

**fad,** *n.* — *Syn.* craze, fashion, vogue, rage, trend, mania, enthusiasm, affectation, fancy, caprice, whim, style, freak, hobby, cry, novelty, innovation, custom, amusement, humor, vagary, *dernier cri* (French), crotchet, maggot, quirk, kink, eccentricity, passing fashion, popular innovation, prevailing taste, frivolity, whimsy, passing fancy, sensation, furor, the latest word*, all the rage*, the thing*, the latest thing*, in thing*, the last word*, the new look*, in joke*, flash in the pan*, nine days' wonder*. — *Ant.* CUSTOM, convention, tradition.

*See Synonym Study at* FASHION.

**fade,** *v.* **1.** [To lose color or brightness] — *Syn.* bleach, tone down, wash out, decolorize, become colorless, blanch, tarnish, dim, dull, discolor, pale, grow dim, flicker, neutralize, become dull, lose luster, achromatize, etiolate. — *Ant.* color, brighten, glow.

**2.** [To lose freshness or strength] — *Syn.* wither, decline, wilt, wane; see **decay, weaken** 1, **wither.**

**3.** [To diminish in sound] — *Syn.* hush, quiet, sink; see **decrease** 1.

**4.** [To disappear slowly] — *Syn.* evaporate, dissolve, die out; see **disappear.**

*See Synonym Study at* DISAPPEAR.

**faded,** *modif.* — *Syn.* washed-out, used, bleached, shopworn; see **dull** 2, **pale** 2.

**fading,** *modif.* — *Syn.* declining, paling, growing dimmer; see **dying** 1, 2, **evanescent, hazy** 1.

**fail,** *v.* **1.** [To be unsuccessful] — *Syn.* miscarry, fall short, miss, slip, lose, make nothing of, come to naught, come to nothing, falter, flounder, blunder, break down, break, run aground, founder, misfire, come to grief, get into trouble, lose ground, abort, neglect, backslide, not pass, be demoted, lose status, come down, fall flat, fall through, go amiss, go astray, fall down, get left, be found lacking, be found wanting, be deficient, be inadequate, go down, go under, lose one's labor, hit a slump, miss an opportunity, not measure up, not measure up to expectation, not pass muster, lose out, give out, not have it in one, be all over with, come short of, break one's word, not make the grade, not make it, miss the mark, lose control, fall from one's high estate, go wrong, flop*, bomb*, flunk*, fall down on the job*, miss the boat*, bite the dust*, blow the chance*, fizzle out*, go belly up*, hit rock bottom*, crap out*, go down the tubes*, go down swinging*, end in smoke*, go up in smoke*, not get to first base*, touch bottom*, lay an egg*, draw a blank*, not come off*, come a cropper*, not cut the mustard*, conk out\*, peter out\*, flunk out\*, strike out\*, wash out\*, fold up\*, go on the rocks\*, die on the vine\*, go over like a lead balloon\*. — *Ant.* succeed, WIN, triumph.

**2.** [To disappoint] — *Syn.* let down, desert, leave, displease; see **abandon** 2, **disappoint**.

**3.** [To grow less] — *Syn.* decline, lessen, worsen, sink; see **decay**.

**4.** [To become insolvent] — *Syn.* go bankrupt, default, be in arrears, overdraw, go out of business, go into receivership, go under, default on payment, dishonor, repudiate, be ruined, collapse, go broke\*, fold\*, go to the wall\*, throw in the sponge\*, be unable to make ends meet\*, drown in red ink\*, crash\*, go belly up\*, go down the tubes\*, lose one's shirt\*, go on the rocks\*, bust\*. — *Ant.* PROSPER, gain, thrive.

**5.** [To dismiss for failure] — *Syn.* send home, dismiss, suspend, put on probation, flunk\*, send down\*.

**without fail** — *Syn.* certainly, constantly, dependably, reliably; see **regularly** 1, 2, **surely, yes**.

**failing,** *modif.* — *Syn.* declining, feeble, faint; see **aging, dying** 1, 2, **weak** 1.

**failing,** *n.* — *Syn.* fault, foible, weakness, shortcoming; see **defect** 2, **fault** 2.

*See Synonym Study at* FAULT.

**fail-safe,** *modif.* **1.** [Ensuring safety in case of malfunction] — *Syn.* safety, emergency, safeguarding; see **protective**.

**2.** [Unlikely to fail] — *Syn.* foolproof, trouble-free, problem-free, guaranteed; see **reliable** 2.

**failure,** *n.* **1.** [An unsuccessful attempt] — *Syn.* fiasco, misadventure, nonperformance, abortion, bankruptcy, insolvency, nonsuccess, miscarriage, labor in vain, botch, bungle, frustration, misstep, false step, faux pas, breakdown, malfunction, checkmate, stoppage, collapse, rupture, defeat, rout, overthrow, downfall, implosion, breakdown in communication, total loss, crash, stalemate, negligence, omission, dereliction, no go\*, flop\*, turkey\*, clinker\*, loser\*, bust\*, dud\*, washout\*, dog\*, bomb\*, bummer\*, lead balloon\*, lemon\*, flash in the pan\*, slip 'twixt the cup and the lip\*, losing game\*, sinking ship\*, sleeveless errand\*, louse-up\*, mess\*, fizzle\*, non-starter\*. — *Ant.* SUCCESS, accomplishment, triumph.

**2.** [An unsuccessful person] — *Syn.* incompetent, defaulter, nonperformer, underachiever, ne'er-do-well, scapegrace, prodigal, bankrupt, derelict, castaway, beachcomber, ski bum, loser\*, flunker\*, born loser\*, turkey\*, dead duck\*, has-been\*, also-ran\*, lemon\*, flop\*, bum\*, no-account\*, dud\*, schlemiel\*. — *Ant.* SUCCESS, veteran, star.

**faint,** *modif.* **1.** [Having little physical strength] — *Syn.* feeble, faltering, enervated, dizzy; see **dizzy** 1, **weak** 1.

**2.** [Having little brightness or color] — *Syn.* dim, vague, indistinct, hazy; see **dull** 2.

**3.** [Having little volume of sound] — *Syn.* inaudible, indistinct, whispered, breathless, murmuring, low, stifled, dull, dim, muted, hoarse, muttering, soft, soothing, bated, heard in the distance, quiet, low-pitched, low-toned, muffled, hushed, padded, distant, subdued, gentle, softened, feeble, from afar, moderate, grave, deep, deadened, rumbling, heavy, far-off, flat, thin, aside, between the teeth, floating on the air, dulcet, imperceptible, out of earshot. — *Ant.* LOUD, audible, raucous.

**faint,** *n.* — *Syn.* swoon, unconsciousness, blackout, syncope; see **stupor**.

**faint,** *v.* — *Syn.* lose consciousness, pass out, black out, swoon, become unconscious, be overcome, fall, go into a coma, have a stroke, suffer syncope, faint away, faint dead away, drop, collapse, succumb, suffer sunstroke,

go out like a light\*, keel over\*. — *Ant.* revive, awaken, come to.

**fainthearted,** *modif.* — *Syn.* timorous, irresolute, pusillanimous, timid; see **cowardly** 1, 2, **weak** 3.

**fair,** *modif.* **1.** [Free from injustice or bias] — *Syn.* just, impartial, equitable, unbiased, dispassionate, objective, unprejudiced, uncolored, evenhanded, even, balanced, nondiscriminatory, forthright, plain, scrupulous, upright, candid, generous, frank, open, sincere, straightforward, honest, lawful, clean, legitimate, decent, honorable, virtuous, righteous, temperate, ethical, reasonable, civil, courteous, sterling, uncorrupted, disinterested, detached, nonpartisan, square, fair-minded, sportsmanlike, sporting, good, handsome, principled, moderate, benevolent, aboveboard, trustworthy, meet, due, fit, appropriate, regular, right, on the level\*, on the up-and-up\*, fair and square\*, straight\*, leaning over backward\*, giving the devil his due\*. — *Ant.* UNFAIR, unjust, biased.

**2.** [Moderately satisfactory] — *Syn.* average, not bad, ordinary, mediocre, adequate, passable, tolerable, medium, usual, common, all right, commonplace, satisfactory, decent, respectable, pretty good, up to standard, middling, fairish, so-so, OK, only fair, fair to middling\*; see also **common** 1. — *Ant.* excellent, poor, unsatisfactory.

**3.** [Not stormy or likely to storm] — *Syn.* clear, pleasant, sunny, bright, cloudless, unclouded, calm, placid, tranquil, unthreatening, favorable, balmy, mild, smiling. — *Ant.* STORMY, threatening, overcast.

**4.** [Of light complexion] — *Syn.* blond, light-colored, light-complexioned, pallid, pale, sallow, white, bleached, white-skinned, milky, flaxen, fair-haired, snow-white, snowy, chalky, silvery, whitish, pearly, blanched, light, lily-white, ivory-white, albino, peaches-and-cream, blue-eyed, rosy, faded, neutral, colorless, platinum blond, whey-faced, pale-faced, white as a sheet\*, white as the driven snow\*; see also **blond**. — *Ant.* DARK, brunet, black.

**5.** [Personally attractive] — *Syn.* lovely, charming, pretty; see **beautiful** 2.

**fair,** *n.* — *Syn.* exposition, county fair, state fair, world's fair, street fair, carnival, bazaar, exhibition, mart, display, festival, market, bourse, exchange, flea market, crafts fair, spectacle, centennial, celebration, kermis, Donnybrook Fair, expo\*; see also **carnival** 1.

---

*SYN.* — **fair**, the general word, implies the treating of both or all sides alike, without reference to one's own feelings or interests /a *fair* exchange/; **just** implies adherence to a standard of rightness or lawfulness without reference to one's own inclinations /a *just* decision/; **impartial** and **unbiased** both imply freedom from prejudice for or against any side /an *impartial* chairman, an *unbiased* account/; **dispassionate** implies the absence of passion or strong emotion, hence, connotes cool, disinterested judgment /a *dispassionate* critic/; **objective** implies a viewing of persons or things without reference to oneself, one's interests, etc. /an *objective* newspaper/ *See also Synonym Study at* BEAUTIFUL.

---

**fairground,** *n.* — *Syn.* enclosure, coliseum, racetrack, racecourse, exhibition place, fairway, concourse, place, rink, booth, stall, midway, exposition, show ring, amusement park.

**fairly,** *modif.* **1.** [In a just manner] — *Syn.* honestly, reasonably, impartially, equitably; see **justly** 1.

**2.** [A qualifying word] — *Syn.* somewhat, moderately, reasonably; see **moderately**.

**fairness,** *n.* — *Syn.* justice, impartiality, justness, decency, honesty, probity, rectitude, uprightness, truth, integrity, charity, charitableness, veracity, tolerance, right, candor, honor, balance, moderation, civility, consideration, good faith, propriety, courtesy, reasonableness, rationality, humanity, rightness, equity, equitableness, righteousness, goodness, seemliness, full measure, measure for measure, suitability, give and take, evenhandedness, disinterestedness, neutrality, fairmindedness, open-mindedness, just dealing, fair treatment, evenhanded justice, due, scrupulousness, exactitude, merit, detachment, disinterest, dispassion, correctness, punctilio, virtue, benignity, benevolence, duty, seeing justice done, legitimacy, legality, rightfulness, lawfulness, straightforwardness, niceness, plain dealing, right doing, sportsmanship, nondiscrimination, lack of bias, giving the devil his due★, square deal★, fair play, fair shake★, square dealing★, straight shooting★, doing right by, a fair field and no favor★, the handsome thing★. — *Ant.* INJUSTICE, unfairness, partiality.

**fair-spoken,** *modif.* — *Syn.* civil, courteous, well-spoken; see **polite** 1, **refined** 2.

**fairy,** *n.* — *Syn.* spirit, sprite, fay, good fairy, elf, brownie, goblin, hobgoblin, dryad, hamadryad, oread, maenad, nymph, bacchante, naiad, pixie, mermaid, nereid, nixie, kelpie, sylph, siren, bogy, genie, jinni, Puck, imp, enchantress, witch, warlock, banshee, werewolf, ogre, ogress, Ariel, Robin Goodfellow, Queen Mab, Oberon, Titania, demon, daemon, daeva, succubus, devil, vampire, lamia, ghoul, Harpy, Lorelei, Circe, demiurge, familiar, poltergeist, troll, gnome, gremlin, leprechaun, kobold, ouphe, will-o'-the-wisp, visitant, afrit, barghest, peri, satyr, faun, fiend, White Lady, Norn, Fate, Weird Sister; see also **ghost** 1.

**fairyland,** *n.* — *Syn.* land of fay, dreamland, cloudland, happy valley, castles in the air, Utopia, Shangri-La, Atlantis, never-never land, cloud-cuckoo-land, land of make-believe, land of enchantment, daydream, East o' the Sun and West o' the Moon, the valley of the moon, Avalon, elfland, faerie; see also **utopia.**

**fairy tale,** *n.* — *Syn.* folk tale, children's story, Mother Goose story, romance; see **story.**

**faith,** *n.* **1.** [Complete trust] — *Syn.* confidence, trust, credence, belief, credit, assurance, acceptance, expectation, hope, dependence, conviction, sureness, fidelity, loyalty, troth, certainty, surety, allegiance, assent, credulity, certitude, reliance. — *Ant.* DOUBT, skepticism, distrust.
**2.** [A formal system of beliefs] — *Syn.* religion, creed, doctrine, dogma, belief, tenet, revelation, credo, gospel, profession, confession, conviction, persuasion, canon, principle, piety, church, orthodoxy, worship, theism, teaching, theology, doxy, decalogue, denomination, cult, sect. For specific faiths see **church** 3, **religion** 2.
*See Synonym Study at* BELIEF.

**bad faith** — *Syn.* insincerity, duplicity, infidelity; see **dishonesty.**

**break faith** — *Syn.* be disloyal, abandon, fail; see **betray** 1.

**good faith** — *Syn.* sincerity, honor, trustworthiness; see **honesty** 1.

**in faith** — *Syn.* indeed, in fact, in reality; see **really** 1.

**keep faith** — *Syn.* be loyal, adhere, follow; see **support** 2.

**faithful,** *modif.* — *Syn.* loyal, constant, devoted, dedicated, true, staunch, steadfast, reliable, dependable, trusty, dutiful, trustworthy, trusted, genuine, incorruptible, firm in adherence, resolute, straight, honest, upright, honorable, scrupulous, firm, sure, unswerving, conscientious, unwavering, enduring, unchanging, steady, committed, supportive, attached, obedient, allegiant, patriotic, sincere, trusting, confiding, veracious, truehearted, true-blue★, hard-core★, true as steel★, tried and true★, at the feet of★. — *Ant.* FICKLE, FALSE, faithless.

**faithful,** *n.* — *Syn.* adherents of a faith, loyal members, believers, true believers, followers, supporters, congregation, the saved, the believing, the children of God.

*SYN.* — **faithful** implies steadfast adherence to a person or thing to which one is bound as by an oath or obligation [a *faithful* wife]; **loyal** implies undeviating allegiance to a person, cause, institution, etc. which one feels morally bound to support or defend [a *loyal* friend]; **constant** suggests freedom from fickleness in affections or loyalties [a *constant* lover]; **staunch** (or **stanch**) implies such strong allegiance to one's principles or purposes as not to be turned aside by any cause [a *staunch* defender of the truth]; **resolute** stresses unwavering determination, often in adhering to one's personal ends or aims [*resolute* in one's decision]

**faithfully,** *modif.* **1.** [Loyally] — *Syn.* devotedly, conscientiously, truly; see **loyally.**
**2.** [Always] — *Syn.* patiently, constantly, forever; see **regular** 3.

**faithfulness,** *n.* — *Syn.* fidelity, allegiance, trustworthiness, care; see **devotion, loyalty.**

**faithless,** *modif.* **1.** [Not keeping faith] — *Syn.* disloyal, deceitful, false, traitorous, treacherous, perfidious, unreliable, untrustworthy; see also **dishonest** 1, 2, **false** 1.
**2.** [Unbelieving] — *Syn.* agnostic, skeptical, dubious; see **atheistic.**

*SYN.* — **faithless** implies failure to adhere, as to an oath or obligation [a *faithless* wife]; **false,** in this connection more or less synonymous with **faithless,** stresses failure in devotion to someone or something that has a moral claim to one's support [a *false* friend]; **disloyal** implies a breach of allegiance to a person, cause, institution, etc. [*disloyal* to one's family]; **treacherous** strictly implies the commission of treason; **treacherous** suggests an inclination or tendency to betray a trust [his *treacherous* colleagues]; **perfidious** adds to the meaning of **treacherous** a connotation of sordidness or depravity [a *perfidious* informer]

**faithlessness,** *n.* **1.** [Disloyalty] — *Syn.* perfidy, fraud, treachery; see **dishonesty, treason.**
**2.** [Doubt] — *Syn.* skepticism, disbelief, agnosticism; see **doubt** 1.

**fake,** *modif.* — *Syn.* false, pretended, fraudulent, bogus; see **artificial** 1, **false** 3.
*See Synonym Study at* FALSE.

**fake,** *n.* — *Syn.* deception, counterfeit, sham, copy, cheat, imitation, charlatan, quack, impostor, fraud, make-believe, pretense, fabrication, forgery, imposition, humbug, sleight, trick, hoax, swindle, stratagem, dummy, phony★, faker★, gyp★, spoof★, plant★, put-on★, scam★, flimflam★, goldbrick★. — *Ant.* FACT, original, reality.
*See Synonym Study at* QUACK.

**fake,** *v.* — *Syn.* feign, simulate, falsify, counterfeit; see **forge** 1, **pretend** 1, **simulate.**

**fakir,** *n.* — *Syn.* dervish, holy beggar, yogi, mendicant; see **ascetic.**

**fall,** *n.* **1.** [The act of falling] — *Syn.* drop, decline, lapse, collapse, breakdown, tumble, spill, downfall, abasement, diminution, lowering, reduction, defeat, degradation, humiliation, descent, plunge, slump, subsidence, recession, ebb, abatement, sinking, dive, nose dive, slip, flop*; see also **drop** 2.— *Ant.* RISE, elevation, ascent.

**2.** [Capture] — *Syn.* overthrow, capitulation, downfall, ruin; see **defeat** 2, **destruction** 2.

**3.** [A yielding to temptation; *often with* the] — *Syn.* original sin, transgression, error, lapse; see **sin.**

**4.** [That which falls] — *Syn.* rainfall, snowfall, precipitation, snow, rain, hail, sleet, blanket, carpet, covering, one *or* two *or* three, etc., inches of snow *or* rain.

**5.** [The season after summer] — *Syn.* autumn, harvest, harvest time, the sere and yellow leaf, the fall of the year, September, October, November, "when the frost is on the punkin' and the fodder's in the shock."

**6.** [A waterfall] — *Syn.* cascade, cataract, chute; see **waterfall.**

**ride for a fall*** — *Syn.* endanger oneself, take risks, take chances, act indiscreetly; see **risk** 1.

**fall,** *v.* **1.** [To pass quickly downward] — *Syn.* sink, topple, drop, stumble, trip, fall down, plunge, plummet, tumble, descend, go down, lower, totter, break down, cave in, decline, subside, collapse, buckle, crumple, settle, droop, slump, hang, regress, lapse, backslide, drop down, pitch, gravitate, come down suddenly, take a dive, take a nose dive, be precipitated, make a forced landing, fall flat, fall in, fold up, keel over, fall over, tip over, slope, slip, recede, relapse, abate, ebb, diminish, depreciate, decrease, flop*, take a spill*, take a header*. — *Ant.* RISE, ascend, climb.

**2.** [To be overthrown] — *Syn.* submit, yield, surrender, succumb, be destroyed, be taken, pass into enemy hands, bend, defer, lie down, resign, capitulate, back down, topple, go down, go under, break up, get one's come-uppance*, fall to pieces*. — *Ant.* prevail, ENDURE, resist.

**3.** [To die in battle] — *Syn.* go down, slump, drop, bite the dust*; see **die** 1.

**4.** [To occur] — *Syn.* take place, befall, come, come to pass; see **happen** 2.

**fallacious,** *modif.* — *Syn.* erroneous, deceptive, misleading, fraudulent; see **false** 2.

**fallacy,** *n.* **1.** [An error in reasoning] — *Syn.* inconsistency, illogicality, sophism, sophistry, casuistry, quibble, quibbling, evasion, deceit, deception, delusion, equivocation, subterfuge, Jesuitry, misinterpretation, erroneousness, inexactness, error, deviation from truth, perversion, bias, prejudice, preconception, non sequitur, deceptive belief, deceptiveness, aberration, falsity, false notion, misleading appearance, illusion, speciousness, equivoke, artifice, ambiguity, solecism, paradox, miscalculation, quirk, flaw, cavil, irrelevancy, erratum, invalidity, heresy, heterodoxy. — *Ant.* LOGIC, REASON, LAW.

**2.** [A mistaken idea] — *Syn.* misconception, misapprehension, delusion; see **error** 1, **mistake** 2.

**fall apart,** *v.* — *Syn.* disintegrate, collapse, break down, go to pieces; see **break** 3, **crack up** 2, **disintegrate** 1.

**fall asleep,** *v.* — *Syn.* go to sleep, doze, drop off*; see **sleep.**

**fall away,** *v.* — *Syn.* pine, waste away, decline; see **decay, decrease** 1.

**fall back,** *v.* — *Syn.* yield, recede, withdraw, give way; see **retreat** 2.

**fall back on,** *v.* — *Syn.* turn to, have recourse to, rely on; see **resort to, trust** 1.

**fallen,** *modif.* **1.** [Overthrown] — *Syn.* captured, ruined, conquered; see **beaten** 1, **captured** 2, **destroyed.**

**2.** [Degraded] — *Syn.* sinful, immoral, lapsed; see **disgraced, wicked** 1.

**fall for*,** *v.* **1.** [To fall in love with] — *Syn.* become infatuated with, take a fancy to, flip over*; see **fall in love** at **love.**

**2.** [To be deceived by] — *Syn.* be tricked by, be taken in by, swallow*, buy*; see **believe** 1.

**fallibility,** *n.* — *Syn.* imperfection, misjudgment, frailty, liability to error, unreliability, errancy; see also **uncertainty** 2.

**fallible,** *modif.* — *Syn.* liable to err, frail, imperfect, faulty, error-prone, mistaken, uncertain, erring, unpredictable, unreliable, in question, liable to be erroneous, liable to mistake, inaccurate, prone to error, human, mortal, untrustworthy, questionable.

**fall in,** *v.* — *Syn.* get into line, form ranks, take a place; see **line up.**

**falling,** *modif.* — *Syn.* dropping, sinking, descending, plunging, slipping, sliding, declining, lowering, settling, toppling, tumbling, tottering, diminishing, weakening, decreasing, abating, ebbing, subsiding, collapsing, crumbling, perishing, dying. — *Ant.* INCREASING, improving, rising.

**fall off,** *v.* — *Syn.* decline, lessen, wane; see **decrease** 1.

**fall on,** *v.* **1.** [To attack] — *Syn.* assault, battle, descend upon; see **attack** 1, 2.

**2.** [To discover] — *Syn.* meet, find, chance upon; see **discover.**

**fallout,** *n.* — *Syn.* radioactivity, radioactive dust, radioactive debris, radioactive waste, byproduct, incidental effect; see also **result.**

**fall out,** *v.* **1.** [To quarrel] — *Syn.* argue, disagree, fight; see **quarrel.**

**2.** [To happen] — *Syn.* result, befall, occur; see **happen** 2.

**fallow,** *modif.* **1.** [Uncultivated] — *Syn.* untilled, unsowed, neglected, unplowed, unseeded, unplanted, unproductive; see also **unused** 1.

**2.** [Idle] — *Syn.* inert, inactive, dormant; see **idle** 1.

**fall short,** *v.* — *Syn.* fail, be deficient, be lacking; see **fail** 1, **need.**

**fall to,** *v.* — *Syn.* set about, start, undertake; see **begin** 1.

**false,** *modif.* **1.** [Said of persons] — *Syn.* perfidious, faithless, treacherous, unfaithful, disloyal, dishonest, lying, untruthful, base, hypocritical, double-dealing, knavish, roguish, malevolent, rascally, scoundrelly, mean, malicious, venal, deceitful, mendacious, underhanded, corrupt, forsworn, unscrupulous, untrustworthy, falsehearted, dishonorable, villainous, treasonable, traitorous, seditious, canting, insincere, two-faced*; see also senses 2, 3. — *Ant.* FAITHFUL, true, honorable.

**2.** [Said of statements or supposed facts] — *Syn.* untrue, mistaken, spurious, apocryphal, fanciful, mendacious, untruthful, fictitious, deceptive, concocted, fallacious, incorrect, inaccurate, wrong, sophistical, casuistic, Jesuitical, misleading, delusive, imaginary, illusive, erroneous, invalid, deceiving, misrepresentative, fraudulent, trumped-up, contrary to fact, fishy*, cooked-up*; see also senses 1, 3. — *Ant.* ACCURATE, correct, established.

**3.** [Said of things] — *Syn.* sham, counterfeit, fabricated, manufactured, synthetic, factitious, bogus, spurious, make-believe, assumed, unreal, not genuine, copied, forged, pretended, faked, made-up, simulated, imitation, lifeless, pseudo, hollow, mock, feigned, bastard, base, shoddy, alloyed, artificial, contrived, colored, disguised, deceptive, adulterated, plated, so-called, meretricious, fake, ersatz, phony*, gyp*, catchpenny*, bum*, false-colored*, queer*, not what it's cracked up to be*; see also senses 1, 2. — *Ant.* REAL, genuine, authentic.

**play someone false**— *Syn.* cheat, trick, betray; see **betray** 1, **deceive.**

**put in a false position**— *Syn.* misrepresent, embarrass, misquote; see **betray** 1, **mistake.**

---

*SYN.* — **false,** in this comparison, refers to anything that is not in essence that which it purports to be and may or may not connote deliberate deception *[false* hair, *false* eyelashes*]*; **sham** refers to an imitation or simulation of something and usually connotes intent to deceive *[sham* piety*]*; **counterfeit** and the colloquial **bogus** apply to a very careful imitation and always imply intent to deceive or defraud *[counterfeit,* or *bogus,* money*]*; **fake** is a less formal term for any person or thing that is not genuine *[a fake* doctor, chimney, etc.*]* See also Synonym Study at FAITHLESS.

---

**falsehood,** *n.* — *Syn.* prevarication, misrepresentation, story, untruth; see **lie** 1.

**falsely,** *modif.* — *Syn.* traitorously, treacherously, deceitfully, faithlessly, falseheartedly, behind one's back, disloyally, underhandedly, basely, unfaithfully, perfidiously, dishonestly, erroneously, fallaciously, wrongly, incorrectly, unjustly, unscrupulously, roguishly, knavishly, under the garb of, hypocritically, insincerely, dishonorably, crookedly*.* — *Ant.* TRULY, JUSTLY, honorably.

**falsetto,** *n.* — *Syn.* artificially high-pitched voice, countertenor, treble, soprano, *voce di testa* (Italian), unnatural register, head register, shrillness, affectation.

**falsify,** *v.* — *Syn.* distort, adulterate, counterfeit, misrepresent; see **deceive, forge,** **lie** 1.

**falter,** *v.* — *Syn.* waver, vacillate, flounder; see **hesitate, stammer, stumble** 1.

**fame,** *n.* **1.** [Illustrious and widespread reputation] — *Syn.* renown, eminence, celebrity, glory, distinction, honor, esteem, prominence, name, estimation, public esteem, credit, note, greatness, dignity, rank, account, luster, splendor, position, standing, preeminence, stardom, one's hour in the sun, place in the sun, acclaim, éclat, regard, notice, recognition, laurels, elevation, station, place, consequence, prestige, popularity, notability, limelight, one's fifteen minutes, public favor, kudos, rep*.* — *Ant.* OBLIVION, obscurity, ignominy.
**2.** [Reputation] — *Syn.* repute, name, character, estimation, notoriety, *réclame* (French), publicity, hearsay, report, rep*.*

**familiar,** *modif.* **1.** [Commonly known] — *Syn.* everyday, well-known, customary, frequent, homely, humble, usual, intimate, habitual, accustomed, common, ordinary, oft-encountered, informal, unceremonious, plain, simple, matter-of-fact, workaday, prosaic, commonplace, homespun, natural, native, unsophisticated, unvarnished, old hat*,* garden variety*.* — *Ant.* UNUSUAL, exotic, strange, new.
**2.** [Friendly] — *Syn.* close, intimate, confidential, casual, cordial, easy, informal, free-and-easy, unceremonious, presumptuous, presuming, forward, bold, overfamiliar, chummy*;* see also **intimate** 1.
*See Synonym Study at* COMMON.

---

*SYN.* — **familiar** is applied to that which is known through constant association, and, with reference to persons, suggests informality, or even presumption, such as might prevail among members of a family *[remain* on *familiar* terms*]*; **close** is applied to persons or things very near to one in affection, attraction, interests, etc. *[close* friends*]*; **intimate** implies very close association, acquaintance, relationship, etc. *[invited her intimate*

friends*]* or suggests something of a very personal or private nature *[intimate* letters*]*; **confidential** implies a relationship in which there is mutual trust and a sharing of private thoughts, problems, etc. *[a confidential* friendship*]*

---

**familiarity,** *n.* **1.** [Acquaintance with people] — *Syn.* friendliness, acquaintanceship, intimacy; see **friendship** 1, 2.
**2.** [Acquaintance with things] — *Syn.* conversance, experience, knowledge, sense of use, the feel of, being at home with, thorough knowledge, mastery, cognition, comprehension; see also **awareness, experience** 3.
**3.** [Informality] — *Syn.* casualness, ease, presumptuousness, liberties; see **informality, rudeness.**

**familiarize with,** *v.* — *Syn.* acquaint, accustom, habituate, enlighten, become adept in, get acquainted with, awaken to, inure, season, condition, come to know, become aware of, make familiar with, make conversant with, orient, brief, initiate, inform, acclimate; see also **notify** 1.

**familiar with,** *modif.* — *Syn.* acquainted with, conversant with, well-acquainted with, aware of, introduced, informed of, on speaking terms with, cognizant of, attuned to, no stranger to; see also **knowledgeable.** — *Ant.* unacquainted, UNAWARE, ignorant.

**family,** *modif.* — *Syn.* kindred, familial, tribal; see **domestic** 1, **group.**

**family,** *n.* **1.** [Blood relatives] — *Syn.* relations, relatives, kin, tribe, folk, clan, dynasty, house, household, kith and kin, kindred, kinfolk, kinsmen, connections, relationship, blood, blood tie, consanguinity, progeny, offspring, descendants, issue, brood, antecedents, forebears, heirs and assigns, generations, race, ancestry, progenitors, forefathers, pedigree, genealogy, descent, parentage, extraction, patrimony, paternity, inheritance, former generations, kinship, lineage, line, one's own flesh and blood, clansmen, strain, stock, breed, parents, siblings, children, in-laws, nuclear family, extended family, the whole tribe*,* homefolks*,* people*,* folks*,* nearest and dearest*.*
**2.** [Several of one kind] — *Syn.* order, class, genus, species, subdivision, group; see also **class** 1.

**in a family way*** — *Syn.* pregnant, with child, going to have a baby; see **pregnant** 1.

**famine,** *n.* — *Syn.* shortage of food, starvation, want, scarcity; see **hunger, lack** 1.

**famished,** *modif.* — *Syn.* starving, hungering, starved; see **hungry.**

**famous,** *modif.* — *Syn.* renowned, celebrated, well-known, noted, notorious, distinguished, eminent, illustrious, famed, foremost, preeminent, acclaimed, conspicuous, far-famed, prominent, honored, reputable, recognized, notable, important, of note, of mark, prestigious, name, exalted, remarkable, extraordinary, great, brilliant, splendid, august, grand, applauded, universally recognized, popular, peerless, imposing, towering, legendary, storied, influential, leading, noteworthy, talked of, outstanding, memorable, in the limelight, in the spotlight, in the public eye, big-name*,* on everyone's lips*.* — *Ant.* UNKNOWN, obscure, humble.

---

*SYN.* — **famous** is applied to persons or things that have received wide public attention and are generally known and talked about; **renowned** suggests fame or honor achieved through some outstanding quality or accomplishment; **celebrated** is applied to persons or things that have received much public honor or praise;

**noted** implies a being brought to the wide notice of the public for some particular quality; **notorious**, in current usage, suggests a being widely but unfavorably known or talked about; **distinguished** implies a being noted as superior in its class or of its kind; **eminent** more strongly stresses the conspicuous superiority of persons or things; **illustrious** suggests a reputation based on brilliance of achievement or splendidness of character

**fan,** *n.* **1.** [An instrument for creating currents of air] — *Syn.* ventilator, blower, air conditioner, cooler, thermantidote, agitator, palm leaf, forced draft, winnower, vane, flabellum, *punkah* (India), propeller, electric fan, Japanese fan, windmill.
**2.** [Anything having the shape of a fan] — *Syn.* vane, fin, wing, plane, blade, sector, section, face, pyramid, triangle, delta.
**3.** [Enthusiast] — *Syn.* devotee, follower, aficionado, supporter; see **enthusiast** 1.
**fanatic,** *n.* — *Syn.* zealot, devotee, extremist; see **enthusiast** 1, **zealot.**
*See Synonym Study at* ZEALOT.
**fanatical,** *modif.* — *Syn.* fanatic, zealous, obsessed, impassioned, passionate, rabid, extreme, extremist, bigoted, devoted, feverish, prejudiced, biased, radical, militant, immoderate, partisan, obstinate, headstrong, burning, fiery, fervent, fervid, ardent, frenzied, excessively enthusiastic, overzealous, overenthusiastic, raving, of the lunatic fringe, maniacal, mad, wild, partial, stubborn, singleminded, one-ideaed, monomaniacal, infatuated, possessed, opinionated, narrow-minded, dogmatic, arbitrary, positive, tenacious, die-hard, ultraist, hard-line, wild-eyed. — *Ant.* MODERATE, reasonable, impartial.
**fanaticism,** *n.* — *Syn.* zeal, zealotry, extremism, militancy, dogmatism, bigotry, intolerance, obsession, prejudice, superstition, narrow-mindedness, monomania, injustice, obstinacy, stubbornness, bias, unreasonableness, unreasoning zeal, excessive enthusiasm, overenthusiasm, overzealousness, partiality, devotion, warmth, fervor, ardor, partisanship, violence, immoderation, radicalism, ultraism, wild and extravagant notions, singlemindedness, infatuation, dogma, arbitrariness, tenacity, enthusiasm, abandonment, frenzy, passion. — *Ant.* moderation, tolerance, INDIFFERENCE.
**fanciful,** *modif.* **1.** [Characterized by use of the fancy] — *Syn.* fantastical, whimsical, capricious, playful, imaginative, inventive, imaginary, chimerical, visionary, dreamlike, illusory; see also **imaginary, unreal.**
**2.** [Showing fancy in design] — *Syn.* quaint, odd, extravagant; see **fantastic** 1.
**fancy,** *modif.* **1.** [Special] — *Syn.* select, choice, deluxe; see **excellent, superior, unusual** 1, 2.
**2.** [Ornamental] — *Syn.* elaborate, decorated, elegant, ornate, embellished, decorative, rich, adorned, ostentatious, gaudy, showy, florid, intricate, rococo, baroque, gingerbread, resplendent, sumptuous, lavish; see also **elaborate** 1, **ornate** 1.
**fancy,** *n.* **1.** [Artistic creative power] — *Syn.* conception, visualization, creation; see **imagination** 1.
**2.** [The mind at play] — *Syn.* whimsy, fantasy, reverie, daydream, caprice, daydreaming, romancing, flight of fancy, flight of imagination, fancifulness, whimsicality, invention, imagining, make-believe.
**3.** [The product of a playful mind] — *Syn.* caprice, whim, vagary, conceit, chimera, illusion, delusion, figment, fantasy, daydream, freak, freak of humor, notion, quirk, maggot, crotchet, passing fancy, humor,

bubble, hallucination, fantastic notion; see also **fantasy** 2.
**4.** [Inclination] — *Syn.* liking, partiality, wishes, preference; see **desire** 1, **inclination** 1.
**fancy,** *v.* **1.** [To imagine] — *Syn.* envision, conceive, conjecture, suppose; see **assume** 1, **imagine** 1.
**2.** [To have a liking for] — *Syn.* like, be fond of, favor; see **like** 1, 2, 3.
**fanfare,** *n.* — *Syn.* parade, demonstration, hoopla*; see **advertising** 1, **display** 2, **ostentation** 1, 2.
**fang,** *n.* — *Syn.* tusk, tooth, canine tooth, prong; see **tooth** 1.
*See Synonym Study at* TOOTH.
**fantasia,** *n.* — *Syn.* rhapsody, musical fantasy, capriccio, roulade, fantastical air, capricious composition.
**fantastic,** *modif.* **1.** [Based on or suggesting fantasy] — *Syn.* whimsical, capricious, extravagant, freakish, strange, odd, queer, quaint, singular, peculiar, outlandish, bizarre, weird, farfetched, erratic, wonderful, comical, foreign, exotic, fabulous, extreme, ludicrous, ridiculous, preposterous, implausible, unreal, grotesque, chimerical, fanciful, eccentric, absurd, vague, illusive, imaginary, hallucinatory, phantasmagoric, high-flown, affected, mannered, artificial, baroque, out of sight*, far-out*. — *Ant.* conventional, ordinary, real.
**2.** [Seemingly impossible] — *Syn.* incredible, unbelievable, phenomenal; see **excellent, unbelievable** 1.

*SYN.* — **fantastic** implies a lack of restraint in imagination, suggesting that which is extravagantly fanciful or unreal in design, conception, construction, etc. */fantastic notions/*; **bizarre** suggests that which is extraordinarily eccentric or strange because of startling incongruities, extreme contrasts, etc. */music with a bizarre atonality/*; **grotesque** suggests a ludicrously unnatural distortion of the normal or real, or a fantastic combination of elements */the grotesque grimaces of the comedian/*

**fantasy,** *n.* **1.** [Whimsical imagination] — *Syn.* reverie, daydream, flight of fancy, escape; see **fancy** 2.
**2.** [Whimsical or fantastic creation] — *Syn.* vision, phantasm, invention, illusion, air castle, extravaganza, castle in Spain, flight, figment, fiction, romance, conceit, chimera, mirage, apparition, will-o'-the-wisp, *ignis fatuus* (Latin), bugbear, nightmare, hallucination, fantasia, science fiction, utopia, Atlantis, fairyland, daydream, pipe dream*.
**far,** *modif.* **1.** [Not near] — *Syn.* distant, removed, faraway, remote; see **distant** 1.
**2.** [To a considerable degree] — *Syn.* considerably, greatly, incomparably, notably; see **very.**
**as far as** — *Syn.* the extent that, to the degree that, insofar as; see **considering.**
**by far** — *Syn.* very much, considerably, to a great degree; see **very.**
**few and far between** — *Syn.* scarce, sparse, in short supply; see **few, rare** 2.
**(in) so far as** — *Syn.* to the extent that, in spite of, within limits; see **considering.**
**so far** — *Syn.* thus far, until now, up to this point, to date; see **now** 1.
**so far, so good*** — *Syn.* all right, favorable, going well; see **successful.**

*SYN.* — **far** generally suggests that which is an indefinitely long way off in space, time, relation, etc. */far lands/*; **distant,** although also suggesting a considerable interval of separation */a distant sound/*, is the term used when the measure of any interval is specified */desks four feet *distant* from one another*]*; **remote** is applied to that which is far off in space, time, connection, etc. from a place, thing, or person understood as a point of reference *[a remote village, the remote past]*; **removed**, used predicatively, stresses separateness, distinctness, or lack of connection more strongly than **remote**

**farce,** *n.* 1. [Broad comedy] — *Syn.* travesty, burlesque, low comedy, slapstick; see **comedy, parody.**
2. [Something absurd or ridiculous] — *Syn.* mockery, sham, travesty, pretense; see **fake, fun, ridicule.**
**farcical,** *modif.* — *Syn.* absurd, ludicrous, ridiculous, comical; see **absurd, funny** 1, **stupid** 1.
*See Synonym Study at* FUNNY.
**fare,** *n.* 1. [A fee paid, usually for transportation] — *Syn.* ticket, charge, passage, carfare, toll, book, tariff, expense, transportation, slug, check, token, admission.
2. [One who pays a fare] — *Syn.* passenger, rider, patron, occupant; see **buyer, passenger.**
3. [Served food] — *Syn.* menu, rations, meals; see **food.**
*See Synonym Study at* FOOD.
**fare,** *v.* — *Syn.* prosper, get along, get on, manage, do, prove, turn out; see also **happen** 2.
**farewell,** *n.* — *Syn.* adieu, valediction, parting; see **departure** 1, **goodbye.**
**farfetched,** *modif.* — *Syn.* improbable, forced, strained; see **fantastic** 1, **unlikely.**
**farina,** *n.* — *Syn.* starch, cereal, flour; see **flour, meal** 1.
**farinaceous,** *modif.* — *Syn.* granular, starchy, mealy; see **gritty.**
**farm,** *n.* — *Syn.* plantation, ranch, homestead, field, grange, pasture, meadow, grassland, truck farm, estate, farmstead, enclosure, land, claim, holding, improved farm, acres, freehold, leasehold, cropland, soil, acreage, garden, patch, vegetable garden, orchard, nursery, vineyard, demesne, hacienda, kibbutz, collective farm, experiment station, *estancia* (Spanish American), croft (*British*), spread*.
**farm,** *v.* — *Syn.* cultivate land, engage in agronomy, raise crops, cultivate, till, garden, work, plow, hoe, plant, sow, operate, superintend, look after, lease, run, ranch, crop, graze, homestead, run cattle, run sheep; raise cattle, raise pigs, raise chickens, etc.; husband, produce, grow, enclose, pasture, break the soil, till the soil, take up a claim, sharecrop, dress the ground, hop clods*; see also **farming.**
**farmer,** *n.* — *Syn.* planter, grower, breeder, livestock breeder, stockman, agriculturist, agriculturalist, agronomist, rancher, dirt farmer, tenant farmer, tenant, lessee, homesteader, granger, husbandman, producer, tiller of the soil, cultivator, peasant, peon, herdsman, plowman, sharecropper, operator, farmhand, hired hand, hired man, gentleman farmer, squire, cropper, grazer, cattleman, sheepman, harvester, son of the soil, countryman, yeoman, truck gardener, sower, gleaner, gardener, nurseryman, orchardist, horticulturist, hydroponist, pomologist, viticulturist, settler, migrant worker, migrant, help, farm laborer, picker, *campesino* (Spanish), villein, sodbuster*.
**farming,** *n.* — *Syn.* agriculture, tillage, cultivation, husbandry, farm management, ranching, sharecropping, homesteading, plantation, horticulture, business of operating a farm, geoponics, agronomics, soil culture, agronomy, pomology, apiculture, viticulture, grazing, livestock raising, renting, leasing, operating, taking up a claim, hydroponics, tank farming, tray agriculture, tenancy, growing, cropraising.
Farming operations include: dressing the ground, fer-

tilizing, manuring, plowing, tilling, disking, listing, harrowing, seeding, sowing, planting, drilling, cultivating, cultipacking, weeding, hoeing, transplanting, harvesting, reaping, gleaning, threshing, winnowing, haying, raking, tedding, binding, combining, stacking, breaking, shocking, husking, digging, picking, curing, strip farming, rotating crops, irrigating, irrigation, contour farming, milking, breeding, grazing, pasturing, herding, feeding, stocking, fattening, marketing, spraying, disinfecting, picking, selecting, grading, clipping, shearing.
**farm out,** *v.* — *Syn.* lease, rent, allot, subcontract; see **distribute** 1, **rent** 1.
**farmyard,** *n.* — *Syn.* barnyard, yard, enclosure, farmstead, barns, ranchyard, corral, farm buildings, buildings, grange, toft, messuage; see also **farm.**
**far-off,** *modif.* — *Syn.* far, remote, distant, faraway; see **distant** 1.
**farrago,** *n.* — *Syn.* medley, hodgepodge, jumble; see **mixture** 1.
**farsighted,** *modif.* 1. [Seeing better at a distance] — *Syn.* hyperopic, hypermetropic, presbyopic, longsighted, seeing to a great distance.
2. [Sagacious] — *Syn.* farseeing, provident, perceptive, sagacious; see **judicious.**
**farther,** *modif.* — *Syn.* at a greater distance, more distant, beyond, further, more remote, remoter, longer.
**farthest,** *modif.* — *Syn.* remotest, furthermost, ultimate, last; see **furthest.**
**fascia,** *n.* — *Syn.* belt, fillet, sash; see **band** 1.
**fascicle,** *n.* — *Syn.* group, bundle, cluster, installment; see **bunch** 1, **collection** 2.
**fascinate,** *v.* — *Syn.* charm, entrance, captivate, enthrall, intrigue, interest, enchant, bewitch, ravish, enrapture, beguile, delight, overpower, subdue, enslave, please, attract, compel, lure, allure, seduce, entice, tempt, ensnare, draw, attach, invite, engage, absorb, engross, grip, excite, titillate, stimulate, overwhelm, provoke, animate, arouse, intoxicate, thrill, fire, stir, kindle, pique, pique one's interest, tantalize, transport, appeal to, win, influence, gain ascendancy over, hold spellbound, transfix, mesmerize, engage the thoughts, invite attention, capture, coax, tease, make one's mouth water*, lead on*, make a hit*, knock dead*, raise to fever heat*, cast a spell over, catch one's eye, inflame with love, carry away*, bait the hook*, grab*, turn one on*, sweep off one's feet*, knock one's socks off*. — *Ant.* DISGUST, repel, bore, weary.
*See Synonym Study at* ATTRACT.
**fascinated,** *modif.* — *Syn.* enraptured, enchanted, bewitched, dazzled, entranced, captivated, beguiled, intrigued, interested, attracted, seduced, enticed, charmed, enamored, transported, mesmerized, hypnotized, gripped, rapt, delighted, infatuated, excited, aroused, intoxicated, thrilled, enthralled, tantalized, titillated, spellbound, transfixed, riveted, engrossed, absorbed, overpowered, in love with, badly smitten, fond of, taken with, hipped on*, gone on*, sweet on*, stuck on*, crazy about*, nuts about*, wild about*, keen about*. — *Ant.* DISGUSTED, repelled, disenchanted, bored.
**fascinating,** *modif.* — *Syn.* engaging, enthralling, engrossing, captivating; see **charming, interesting.**
**fascination,** *n.* — *Syn.* charm, power, enchantment; see **attraction** 1.
**fascism,** *n.* — *Syn.* dictatorship, one-party rule, autocracy, regimentation, racism, totalitarianism, Nazism, National Socialism, Hitlerism, Third Reich, despotism, absolutism, demagogy, authoritarianism, oppres-

sion; see also **government** 2.— *Ant.* DEMOCRACY, self-government, socialism.

**fascist,** *modif.* — *Syn.* Nazi, dictatorial, authoritarian; see **absolute** 3.

**fascist,** *n.* — *Syn.* reactionary, Nazi, rightist, Black Shirt, Falangist, skinhead\*; see also **agitator, radical.**

**fashion,** *n.* **1.** [Form] — *Syn.* make, shape, manner, mode; see **form** 1, **method** 2.
**2.** [Prevailing mode of dress, behavior, etc.] — *Syn.* style, vogue, mode, trend, look, taste, custom, way, convention, etiquette, tendency, trend, form, formality, formula, procedure, practice, precedent, prevalence, usage, observance, wont, order, usual run of things, prescription, guise, new look, *modus operandi* (Latin), mores, high fashion, *haute couture* (French), stylishness, smartness, chic, *ton, bon ton* (both French).
**3.** [Whatever is temporarily in vogue] — *Syn.* fad, craze, rage, cry; see **fad.**
**after** or **in a fashion** — *Syn.* somewhat, to some extent, in a way; see **moderately.**
**in fashion** — *Syn.* stylish, modish, à la mode; see **fashionable, popular** 1.

**SYN.** — **fashion** is the prevailing custom in dress, manners, speech, etc. of a particular place or time, esp. as established by the dominant section of society or the leaders in the fields of art, literature, design, advertising, etc.; **style,** often a close synonym for **fashion** [the latest *fashion* or *style*], may also suggest a distinctive fashion, esp. the way of dressing or living that distinguishes persons with money and taste [eating in *style*]; **mode,** the French word expressing this idea, suggests the height of fashion in dress, behavior, etc. at any particular time; **vogue** stresses the general acceptance or great popularity of a certain fashion [white gloves are back in *vogue*]; **fad** stresses the impulsive enthusiasm with which a fashion is taken up for a short time; **rage** and **craze** both stress an intense, sometimes irrational enthusiasm for a passing fashion [skiing was all the *rage*, the tulip *craze* of the 17th century]

**fashion,** *v.* **1.** [To mold] — *Syn.* model, shape, form, construct; see **create** 2, **form** 1.
**2.** [To adapt] — *Syn.* adjust, accommodate, fit; see **accommodate** 2.
*See Synonym Study at* MAKE.

**fashionable,** *modif.* — *Syn.* in fashion, stylish, in style, in vogue, chic, popular, being done, favored, à la mode, all the rage, contemporary, current, modish, smart, up-to-date, faddish, dashing, rakish, natty, dapper, elegant, chichi, upscale, high-style, in the latest mode, in the swim, prevalent, trendsetting, vogue, voguish, hot\*, in\*, trendy\*, hip\*, yuppie\*, mod\*, going like wildfire\*, up-to-the-minute\*, with-it\*, the thing\*, the cat's pajamas\*, sharp\*, snazzy\*, cool\*, jamming them in\*, now\*.

**fashioned,** *modif.* — *Syn.* molded, shaped, intended; see **formed.**

**fast,** *modif.* **1.** [Rapid] — *Syn.* swift, fleet, quick, speedy, brisk, flying, expeditious, express, accelerated, hasty, nimble, winged, mercurial, lightninglike, flashing, swift-footed, hypersonic, high-speed, active, electric, agile, ready, dashing, swift as an arrow, quick as lightning, like a flash, quick as thought, racing, fleeting, up-tempo, hurried, precipitate, breakneck, headlong, like a bat out of hell\*, lickety-split\*, like a house afire\*, hellbent\*, on the double\*, at warp speed\*. — *Ant.* SLOW, sluggish, tardy.
**2.** [Firmly fixed] — *Syn.* secure, attached, immovable; see **firm** 1.

**3.** [Promiscuous] — *Syn.* wanton, loose, wild, flirtatious; see **lewd** 2.
**4.** [Permanent in color] — *Syn.* fadeproof, colorfast, durable, lasting, washable, vat-dyed, indelible, waterproof, fade-resistant.
**play fast and loose (with)\*** — *Syn.* behave recklessly, run wild, be careless; see **deceive, misbehave.**

**fast,** *n.* — *Syn.* abstinence, fast day, Lent, Ramadan, Yom Kippur, banyan day, xerophagy, anorexia, hunger strike.

**SYN.** — **fast** and **rapid** are generally interchangeable in expressing the idea of a relatively high rate of movement or action, but **fast** more often refers to the person or thing that moves or acts, and **rapid** to the action [a *fast* typist, *rapid* transcription]; **swift** implies great rapidity, but in addition often connotes smooth, easy movement; **fleet** suggests a nimbleness or lightness in that which moves swiftly; **quick** implies promptness of action, or occurrence in a brief amount of time, rather than velocity [a *quick* reply]; **speedy** intensifies the idea of quickness, but may also connote high velocity [a *speedy* recovery, a *speedy* flight]; **hasty** suggests hurried action and may connote carelessness, rashness, or impatience

**fast,** *v.* — *Syn.* abstain from food, forbear eating, not eat, go hungry, starve, observe a fast, diet.

**fasten,** *v.* **1.** [To make something secure] — *Syn.* attach, lock, fix, tie, bind, lace, close, shut, affix, adhere, batten, tighten, secure, anchor, moor, strengthen, grip, zip, zip up, button, hook, shutter, grapple, hold, screw down, clasp, clamp, clutch, pin, nail, tack, bolt, rivet, screw, clinch, solder, set, weld, cement, glue, bond, wedge, jam, mortise, twist, fix firmly in position, chain, tether, lash, tie down, hold immovable, hold fixed, hold fast, make secure, make fast, entangle, stick, cinch, cement, bed, embed, catch, buckle, strap, knot, hitch, harness, bar, grasp, seal up; see also **bind** 1. — *Ant.* RELEASE, loosen, unfasten.
**2.** [To join two or more things] — *Syn.* couple, combine, connect; see **join** 1.

**SYN.** — **fasten,** the somewhat more general word compared here, implies a joining of one thing to another, as by tying, binding, gluing, nailing, pinning, etc.; **tie** and **bind** are often interchangeable, but in discriminating use, **tie** specif. implies the connection of one thing with another by means of a rope, string, etc. which can be knotted [to *tie* a horse to a hitching post], and **bind** suggests the use of an encircling band which holds two or more things firmly together [to *bind* someone's legs]; **attach** emphasizes the joining of two or more things in order to keep them together as a unit [to *attach* one's references to an application]

**fastened,** *modif.* — *Syn.* locked, fixed, tied; see **tight** 2.
**fastener,** *n.* — *Syn.* fastening, buckle, hook, hasp, lock, clamp, tie, stud, vise, mortise, grip, clip, clasp, snap, bolt, bar, lace, lacing, Velcro (trademark), cinch, wedge, grip, pin, safety pin, nail, rivet, tack, thumbtack, screw, dowel, hook, brake, binder, binding, weld, button, zipper, padlock, catch, bond, band, mooring, rope, cable, guy wire, hawser, anchor, grapnel, grappling iron, chain, harness, strap, thong, girdle, latch, staple, skewer, lug, tag, hook and eye, pawl, latchet, turnbuckle.
**fastening,** *n.* — *Syn.* catch, clasp, hook; see **fastener.**
**fastidious,** *modif.* — *Syn.* squeamish, overnice, meticulous; see **careful, particular** 3, **squeamish.**
*See Synonym Study at* PARTICULAR.

**fastness,** *n.* — *Syn.* swiftness, haste, rapidity; see **speed.**
**fat,** *modif.* **1.** [Having excess flesh] — *Syn.* plump, heavy, overweight, obese, corpulent, portly, stout, fleshy, chubby, potbellied, paunchy, beefy, brawny, solid, plumpish, pleasantly plump, rotund, burly, bulky, unwieldly, husky, stocky, heavyset, thickset, chunky, tubby, pudgy, roly-poly, round, dumpy, flabby, puffy, weighty, hefty, meaty, on the heavy side, well-fed, in need of dieting, pursy, abdominous, adipose, porcine, big, massive, swollen, bloated, hypertrophied, ponderous, lumpish, gross, blowzy, broad in the beam*; see also **large** 1. — *Ant.* THIN, lean, skinny.
**2.** [Having a large cross section] — *Syn.* thick, broad, big; see **broad** 1, **deep** 2.
**3.** [Productive] — *Syn.* rich, fruitful, profitable; see **fertile** 1.
**4.** [Oily] — *Syn.* greasy, fatty, oleaginous; see **fatty, oily** 1.
**chew the fat*** — *Syn.* chat, gossip, confer; see **talk** 1.
**fat,** *n.* — *Syn.* blubber, grease, adipose tissue, hydrogenated vegetable fat, tallow, suet, lard, shortening, oil, lipid, flab*.
Edible fats include: butter, butterfat, oleomargarine, margarine, lard, cottonseed oil, olive oil, corn oil, vegetable oil, canola oil, fish oil, coconut oil, palm oil, sesame oil, sunflower oil, soybean oil, safflower oil, cod-liver oil, peanut oil.
Chemical terms used of edible fats include: saturated, unsaturated, monounsaturated, polyunsaturated, hydrogenated, partially hydrogenated.
**fatal,** *modif.* — *Syn.* deadly, disastrous, mortal, lethal; see **deadly.**
*See Synonym Study at* DEADLY.
**fatalism,** *n.* — *Syn.* resignation, acceptance, predestinarianism, passivity, submission to the inevitable, inexorable necessity, determinism, predestination, necessitarianism.
**fatality,** *n.* **1.** [Mortality] — *Syn.* deadliness, virulence, lethality, poisonousness, destructiveness, inevitability, necrosis; see also **death** 1.
**2.** [A death] — *Syn.* casualty, dying, accident; see **body** 2, **casualty** 2.
**fate,** *n.* **1.** [The predetermined course of events] — *Syn.* destiny, fortune, destination, luck, predetermination, predestination; see also **destiny** 1.
**2.** [A personal destiny] — *Syn.* lot, fortune, portion, doom, destiny, destined lot, end, future, prospect, outcome; see also **doom** 1.

---

**SYN.** — **fate** refers to the inevitability of a course of events as supposedly predetermined by a god or other agency beyond human control; **destiny** also refers to an inevitable succession of events as determined supernaturally or by necessity, but often implies a favorable outcome [it was her *destiny* to become famous]; **portion** and **lot** refer to what is supposedly distributed in the determining of fate, but **portion** implies an equitable apportionment and **lot** implies a random assignment; **doom** always connotes an unfavorable or disastrous fate

---

**Fate,** *n.* — *Syn.* destiny, Nemesis, the Fates, the Weird Sisters, Parcae, the Norns, the three sisters; Clotho, Lachesis, and Atropos.
**fated,** *modif.* — *Syn.* destined, predestined, ordained, condemned; see **destined** 1, **doomed.**
**fateful,** *modif.* **1.** [Momentous] — *Syn.* portentous, critical, decisive; see **crucial, ominous.**
**2.** [Fatal] — *Syn.* destructive, ruinous, lethal; see **deadly** 1, **destructive** 2.

*See Synonym Study at* OMINOUS.
**Fates,** *n.* — *Syn.* the three goddesses, Destinies, Weird Sisters; see **fate.**
**fatheaded*,** *modif.* — *Syn.* dull, asinine, thick-witted; see **stupid** 1.
**father,** *n.* **1.** [A male parent] — *Syn.* sire, paterfamilias, progenitor, procreator, forebear, forefather, begetter, ancestor, male head of the household, dad*, daddy*, papa*, pa*, the old man*, the governor*, pappy*, pater*, pop*, pops*.
**2.** [An originator] — *Syn.* founder, inventor, sponsor, promoter, publisher, introducer, supporter, encourager, promulgator, author, creator; see also **author** 1.
**3.** [A civic or tribal elder] — *Syn.* patriarch, city father, dean, Solon; see **administrator, elder** 2.
**4.** [A priest, especially a Roman Catholic or Anglican priest] — *Syn.* pastor, ecclesiastic, parson, padre*; see **priest.**
**5.** [An important early Christian] — *Syn.* hermit, commentator, Gregory, prophet, martyr, patriarch, Doctor of the Church, apostolic father, anti-Nicene father.
**Father,** *n.* — *Syn.* Supreme Being, Creator, Author; see **god** 2.
**fatherhood,** *n.* — *Syn.* paternity, parenthood, parentage, fathership, progenitorship.
**father-in-law,** *n.* — *Syn.* spouse's father, father, connection by marriage, relative, in-law*, shirttail relation*; see also **relative.**
**fatherland,** *n.* — *Syn.* mother country, homeland, native land; see **country** 3.
**fatherless,** *modif.* — *Syn.* orphan, orphaned, illegitimate; see **abandoned** 1, **bastard** 1, **illegitimate** 2.
**fatherly,** *modif.* — *Syn.* paternal, patriarchal, benevolent, protective, kind, kindly, indulgent, forbearing, caring, wise, parental.
**fathom,** *v.* — *Syn.* interpret, comprehend, penetrate; see **understand** 1.
**fatigue,** *n.* — *Syn.* weariness, lassitude, exhaustion, tiredness, languor, enervation, debilitation, weakness, feebleness, faintness, anoxia, combat fatigue, battle fatigue, nervous exhaustion, prostration, dullness, heaviness, listlessness, lethargy, sluggishness, ennui, burnout; see also **sleepiness.** — *Ant.* VIGOR, briskness, energy.
**fatness,** *n.* — *Syn.* plumpness, obesity, weight, flesh, heaviness, portliness, grossness, corpulence, bulkiness, girth, breadth, largeness, stoutness, rotundity, protuberance, bloatedness, distention, hypertrophy, fleshiness, flabbiness, chubbiness, pudginess, overweight, adiposity, *embonpoint* (French), heftiness*.
**fatten,** *v.* **1.** [To grow fat] — *Syn.* expand, swell, fill out, gain weight; see **grow** 1.
**2.** [To make fat] — *Syn.* feed, stuff, prepare for market, plump, cram, fill, round one out, augment. — *Ant.* STARVE, reduce, constrict.
**fatty,** *modif.* — *Syn.* greasy, blubbery, fat, oleaginous, unctuous, lardaceous, adipose, suety, marbled; see also **oily** 1.
**fatuity,** *n.* — *Syn.* folly, asininity, idiocy; see **stupidity** 1, 2.
**fatuous,** *modif.* — *Syn.* inane, silly, foolish, idiotic; see **silly, stupid** 1.
*See Synonym Study at* SILLY.
**faucet,** *n.* — *Syn.* tap, fixture, spigot, cock, drain, petcock, plumbing, stopcock, hot-water faucet, cold-water faucet, hot*, cold*.
**fault,** *n.* **1.** [An imperfection] — *Syn.* flaw, defect, shortcoming, deficiency; see **blemish, defect** 2.
**2.** [A moral delinquency] — *Syn.* misdemeanor, weakness, failing, foible, vice, offense, wrongdoing, misdeed,

transgression, crime, sin, impropriety, solecism, moral shortcoming, frailty, evil doing, delinquency, trespass, fall from virtue, fall from grace, loss of innocence, misconduct, dereliction, malpractice, malefaction, malfeasance, peccadillo, sins of omission and commission.
**3.** [An error]— *Syn.* blunder, mistake, lapse; see **error** 1.
**4.** [Responsibility]— *Syn.* liability, accountability, blame; see **guilt, responsibility** 2.
**at fault**— *Syn.* culpable, blamable, in the wrong; see **guilty** 2.
**find fault with**— *Syn.* complain about, carp at, criticize; see **censure**.
**to a fault**— *Syn.* too much, excessively, to excess; see **very**.

---

*SYN.* — **fault**, in this comparison, refers to a definite, although not strongly condemnatory, imperfection in character /her only *fault* is stubbornness/; **failing** implies an even less serious shortcoming, usually a common one /tardiness was one of his *failings*/; **weakness** applies to a minor shortcoming that results from a lack of perfect self-control /talking too much is my *weakness*/; **foible** refers to a slight weakness that is regarded more as an amusing idiosyncrasy than an actual defect in character /eating desserts first is one of his *foibles*/; **vice**, although stronger in its implication of moral failure than any of the preceding terms, does not in this connection necessarily suggest actual depravity or wickedness /gambling is his only *vice*/

---

**fault,** *v.* — *Syn.* blame, criticize, charge, accuse; see **censure**.
**faulted,** *modif.* — *Syn.* found at fault, blamed, attacked; see **accused**.
**faultfinding,** *modif.* — *Syn.* censorious, captious, carping; see **critical** 2.
*See Synonym Study at* CRITICAL.
**faultless,** *modif.* — *Syn.* perfect, faultless, impeccable, irreproachable; see **innocent** 1, 4, **perfect** 2.
**faulty,** *modif.* — *Syn.* imperfect, defective, flawed, blemished, deficient, impaired, malformed, distorted, weak, tainted, debased, adulterated, leaky, seamed, damaged, incomplete, awry, amiss, unsound, spotted, cracked, warped, lame, maimed, crazy, sprung, injured, broken, wounded, hurt, worn, battered, frail, crude, botched, insufficient, inadequate, incomplete, found wanting, out of order, below par, incorrect, erroneous, unfit, substandard; see also **unsatisfactory, wrong** 2. — *Ant.* WHOLE, perfect, unimpaired.
**faun,** *n.* — *Syn.* woodland deity, satyr, man and goat; see **fairy**.
**faux pas,** *n.* — *Syn.* error, blunder, gaffe, indiscretion; see **error** 1.
*See Synonym Study at* ERROR.
**favor,** *n.* **1.** [Preference]— *Syn.* good will, support, approval, partiality; see **admiration, inclination** 1.
**2.** [A kindness]— *Syn.* service, courtesy, boon; see **kindness** 2.
**3.** [A token]— *Syn.* compliment, present, memento, souvenir; see **gift** 1.
**find favor**— *Syn.* please, suit, be welcome, win praise; see **satisfy** 1.
**in favor**— *Syn.* favored, liked, esteemed, wanted; see **beloved, favorite**.
**in favor of**— *Syn.* approving, endorsing, condoning; see **supporting**.
**in one's favor**— *Syn.* to one's advantage, to one's credit, on one's side, creditable; see **favorable** 3.

**out of favor**— *Syn.* disliked, not favored, unpopular; see **hated, unpopular**.
**favor,** *v.* **1.** [To have a preference]— *Syn.* prefer, like, approve, sanction, endorse, support, advocate, praise, regard with favor, be in favor of, pick, choose, lean toward, incline toward, opt for, honor, value, prize, esteem, think well of, set great store by, look up to, eulogize, fancy, think the world of*, stick up for*, be sweet on*, have in one's good books*, have in one's good graces*.— *Ant.* DISLIKE, misprize, disesteem.
**2.** [To treat with favoritism]— *Syn.* be partial to, oblige, indulge, grant favors to, further, promote, treat with partiality, deal with gently, play favorites, show consideration for, spare, be indulgent toward, make an exception for, treat as a special character, use one's influence for, pull strings for*; see also **promote** 1.— *Ant.* ABUSE, bear a grudge against, mistreat.
**favorable,** *modif.* **1.** [Winning favor]— *Syn.* pleasing, agreeable, desirable, welcome; see **pleasant** 2.
**2.** [Displaying suitable or promising qualities]— *Syn.* advantageous, propitious, auspicious, convenient, beneficial, helpful, promising, boding well; see also **helpful** 1, **hopeful** 2.
**3.** [Commendatory]— *Syn.* approving, commending, positive, approbative, approbatory, assenting, agreeing, recommendatory, complimentary, acclamatory, well-disposed, in favor of, agreeable, in one's favor, affirmative.

---

*SYN.* — **favorable** applies to that which is distinctly helpful or advantageous in gaining an end /a *favorable* climate for citrus fruits/; **auspicious** refers to something regarded as a good omen of some undertaking /he made an *auspicious* debut/; **propitious** is now usually applied to a circumstance or a time that appears favorable for doing or beginning something /a *propitious* moment/

---

**favorably,** *modif.* **1.** [In an encouraging fashion]— *Syn.* approvingly, agreeably, kindly, helpfully, usefully, fairly, willingly, heartily, cordially, genially, generously, amiably, graciously, courteously, receptively, with favor, with approval, with approbation, encouragingly, enthusiastically, in a cordial manner, positively, affirmatively, well, without prejudice.— *Ant.* UNFAVORABLY, adversely, discouragingly.
**2.** [At a propitious time]— *Syn.* opportunely, conveniently, auspiciously; see **fortunately**.
**favorite,** *modif.* — *Syn.* liked, best-liked, beloved, favored, preferred, especial, personal, intimate, dear to one's heart, especially liked, to one's taste, to one's liking, choice, pet, desired, wished-for, adored, chosen, ideal, popular, fair-haired*; see also **beloved**.— *Ant.* UNPOPULAR, unwanted, unwelcome.
**favorite,** *n.* — *Syn.* darling, pet, idol, ideal, preference, pick, favored one, adored one, beloved one, mistress, love, minion, paramour, pampered darling, favorite son, spoiled child, *enfant gâté* (French), favorite child, one in a favored position, one having the odds in his *or* her favor, fair-haired boy *or* girl*, a favorite two to one *or* three to one, etc., teacher's pet*, odds-on favorite*, apple of one's eye*.
**favoritism,** *n.* — *Syn.* bias, partiality, inequity, preferential treatment, partisanship, nepotism; see also **inclination** 1.
**fawn,** *v.* — *Syn.* cringe, flatter, court, grovel, crouch, bow, stoop, kneel, creep, fall on one's knees, curry favor, toady, truckle, kowtow; see also **grovel**.
**fawner,** *n.* — *Syn.* toady, flatterer, parasite, brown-nose*; see **sycophant**.

**fawning**, *modif.* — *Syn.* sniveling, adulatory, flattering; see **obsequious**.

**fay**, *n.* — *Syn.* elf, brownie, pixie; see **fairy**.

**faze**, *v.* — *Syn.* disturb, disconcert, fluster, daunt; see **disturb** 2, **embarrass** 1.

*See Synonym Study at* EMBARRASS.

**FBI**, *n.* — *Syn.* Federal Bureau of Investigation, federal law enforcement agency, feds*; see **police**.

**fealty**, *n.* — *Syn.* homage, allegiance, fidelity; see **loyalty**.

*See Synonym Study at* LOYALTY.

**fear**, *n.* **1.** [Alarm occasioned by immediate danger] — *Syn.* dread, fright, terror, horror, panic, alarm, consternation, dismay, awe, scare, abhorrence, revulsion, aversion, tremor, bodily fear, mortal terror, funk*, cold feet*, cold sweat*, chills*; see also sense 2. — *Ant.* COURAGE, intrepidity, dash.

**2.** [General apprehension] — *Syn.* anxiety, trepidation, dread, timidity, cowardice, misgiving, trembling, uneasiness, fear and trembling, disquietude, perturbation, phobia, bugbear, irresolution, fearfulness, foreboding, despair, agitation, hesitation, nervousness, jumpiness, worry, concern, suspicion, doubt, qualm, presentiment, faintheartedness, timorousness, abject fear, the creeps*; see also sense 1; **cowardice, nervousness** 1. — *Ant.* COURAGE, bravery, boldness.

**for fear of** — *Syn.* to avoid, lest, in order to prevent.

---

**SYN.** — **fear** is the general term for the anxiety and agitation felt at the presence of danger; **dread** refers to the fear or depression felt in anticipating something dangerous or disagreeable /to live in *dread* of poverty/; **fright** applies to a sudden, shocking, usually momentary fear /the mouse gave her a *fright*/; **alarm** implies the fright felt at the sudden realization of danger /he felt *alarm* at the sight of the pistol/; **terror** applies to an overwhelming, often paralyzing fear /the *terror* of soldiers in combat/; **panic** refers to a frantic, unreasoning fear, often one that spreads quickly and leads to irrational, aimless action /the cry of "fire!" created a *panic*/

---

**fear**, *v.* **1.** [To anticipate immediate danger] — *Syn.* be afraid, be frightened, be alarmed, lose courage, falter, stand in awe of, be scared, stand aghast, live in terror, dare not, have qualms, cower, take fright, quaver, flinch, shrink, quail, quake, cringe, shudder, freeze, turn pale, blanch, start, tremble, shy, lose one's nerve, break out in a sweat*, get cold feet*, chicken out*, wimp out*. — *Ant.* outface, withstand, dare.

**2.** [To be apprehensive] — *Syn.* apprehend, dread, fret; see **worry** 2.

**fearful**, *modif.* **1.** [Inclined to fear] — *Syn.* apprehensive, nervous, afraid, timid; see **afraid** 1, 2, **cowardly** 1.

**2.** [Causing fear] — *Syn.* terrifying, dreadful, shocking; see **frightful** 1.

*See Synonym Study at* AFRAID.

**fearfully**, *modif.* **1.** [In fear] — *Syn.* timorously, apprehensively, shyly, diffidently, timidly, nervously, with fear and trembling, shrinkingly, for fear of, with heart in mouth, in terror, in fright, in trepidation, in alarm.

**2.** [Very much] — *Syn.* awfully, frightfully, excessively; see **very**.

**fearless**, *modif.* — *Syn.* bold, daring, courageous, intrepid; see **brave** 1.

**feasibility**, *n.* — *Syn.* practicability, utility, workability, expediency; see **probability, usefulness**.

**feasible**, *modif.* **1.** [Practicable] — *Syn.* achievable, attainable, workable; see **available, likely** 1, **possible** 2.

**2.** [Suitable] — *Syn.* fit, expedient, worthwhile; see **fit** 1.

**3.** [Likely] — *Syn.* reasonable, likely, probable; see **likely** 1.

*See Synonym Study at* POSSIBLE.

**feast**, *n.* — *Syn.* banquet, entertainment, festivity, festival, treat, repast, refreshment, carousal, wassail, merrymaking, carnival, fiesta, jollification, barbecue, carouse, picnic, spread*; see also **celebration** 2, **meal** 2.

**feat**, *n.* — *Syn.* act, effort, deed, exploit; see **achievement** 2, **action** 2.

**feather**, *n.* — *Syn.* quill, plume, plumage, shaft, down, fin, wing, calamus, tuft, crest, fringe, plumule, spike, pompon.

Types of feathers include: wing, powder-down, dust, pulviplume, tail, rudder, rectrix, covert, tail covert, flight, rowing, remex, half-feather, semi-plume, metallic, metallic scale, down, duck, contour, pinfeather, ungrown, auricular, filoplume.

**in fine** or **high** or **good feather** — *Syn.* well, in good humor, in good health, in good form; see **happy** 1, **healthy** 1, **well** 1.

**feathery**, *modif.* — *Syn.* plumed, fluffy, downy; see **downy, light** 5.

**feature**, *n.* **1.** [Anything calculated to attract interest] — *Syn.* highlight, main attraction, main item, innovation, prominent part, drawing card, specialty, special attraction, featured attraction, high point, peculiarity, focus, main event.

**2.** [Special matter published in a newspaper] — *Syn.* article, comment, story, piece, column, editorial, letters to the editor, Op-Ed piece, humor, cartoon, comics, opinion, feature story, leading article, leader, biography, fiction, serial, background, art, human interest, gossip, pix*.

**3.** [A salient quality] — *Syn.* point, peculiarity, trait, hallmark; see **characteristic**.

**feature**, *v.* — *Syn.* highlight, stress, play up, star; see **emphasize**.

**featured**, *modif.* — *Syn.* promoted, recommended, highlighted, in the public eye; see **advertised, displayed**.

**features**, *n.* — *Syn.* lineaments, countenance, looks, appearance; see **face** 1.

**featuring**, *modif.* — *Syn.* presenting, showing, promoting, recommending, calling attention to, giving prominence to, emphasizing, stressing, making much of, pointing up, playing up, drawing attention to, highlighting, spotlighting, turning the spotlight on, giving the center of the stage to, centering attention on, giving elaborate treatment to, starring, headlining, pushing*.

**febrile**, *modif.* — *Syn.* feverish, fevered, delirious, hysterical; see **feverish, hot** 1.

**February**, *n.* — *Syn.* winter, winter month, second month, shortest month, basketball season, month of leap year; see also **month, winter**.

**feces**, *n.* — *Syn.* excretion, waste, dung; see **excrement**.

**fecund**, *modif.* — *Syn.* fertile, prolific, productive, fruitful; see **fertile** 1, 2, **original** 2.

*See Synonym Study at* FERTILE.

**fecundity**, *n.* — *Syn.* productivity, fruitfulness, abundancy; see **fertility** 1.

**federal**, *modif.* — *Syn.* general, central, governmental; see **national** 1.

**federate**, *v.* — *Syn.* combine, unify, confederate, centralize; see **unite** 1.

**federation**, *n.* — *Syn.* confederacy, alliance, league, federal union; see **alliance** 3, **organization** 3.

**fee,** *n.* — *Syn.* charge, payment, remuneration, compensation; see **expense** 1, **pay** 2, **price.**
*See Synonym Study at* WAGE.

**feeble,** *modif.* **1.** [Lacking strength] — *Syn.* fragile, puny, strengthless, infirm; see **weak** 1, 2.
**2.** [Lacking effectiveness] — *Syn.* impotent, ineffectual, insufficient; see **ineffective.**
*See Synonym Study at* WEAK.

**feeble-minded,** *modif.* — *Syn.* retarded, simple-minded, foolish, senile; see **dull** 3.

**feebleness,** *n.* — *Syn.* infirmity, inability, frailty, debility; see **frailty** 1, **weakness** 1.

**feed,** *n.* — *Syn.* fodder, food for animals, pasture, forage, provender, pasturage, roughage, silage, mash, provisions, supplies.
Common feeds include: grain, small grain, corn, oats, barley, rye, wheat, millet, peanuts, pulse, hay, clover, timothy, alsike, sweet clover, alfalfa, vetch, cowpeas, sorghum, rape, kale, soybeans, beets, ensilage, silage, molasses, oil meal, bean meal, tankage, bone meal, fish meal, straw, bran, maize, Kaffir corn, grass, pasture.

**feed,** *v.* — *Syn.* feast, regale, give food to, satisfy the hunger of, nourish, supply, support, sate, satisfy, fill, stuff, cram, gorge, banquet, dine, nurse, give suck to, maintain, augment, fatten, provide for, provision, victual, cater, stock, furnish, nurture, sustain, foster, keep alive, encourage, pasture, graze, gratify, serve, minister to, wait upon, wine and dine*. — *Ant.* STARVE, deprive, quench.

**feed on,** *v.* — *Syn.* eat, batten on, live off of, sponge, feast upon, prey upon; see also **eat** 1.

**feel,** *n.* — *Syn.* touch, sensation, quality, air; see **character** 1, **feeling** 2, **texture** 1.

**feel,** *v.* **1.** [To examine by touch] — *Syn.* touch, handle, finger, explore, stroke, palm, caress, manipulate, press, squeeze, fondle, tickle, paw, feel for, fumble, grope, grasp, grapple, grip, clutch, clasp, run the fingers over, brush, pinch, poke, probe, prod, palpate, twiddle, contact, fiddle with*.
**2.** [To experience] — *Syn.* sense, perceive, apprehend, be aware of, be conscious of, observe, be moved by, respond, be sensible of, welcome, know, intuit, be affected by, be sensitive to, have the experience of, undergo, go through, taste, take to heart. — *Ant.* IGNORE, be insensitive to, be unaware of.
**3.** [To believe] — *Syn.* consider, hold, sense, think; see **assume** 1, **believe** 1.
**4.** [To give an impression through touch] — *Syn.* appear, exhibit, suggest; see **seem.**

**feeler,** *n.* **1.** [Anything that investigates by touch] — *Syn.* tentacle, antenna, finger, claw, hand, tactile organ, vibrissa, whisker, barbel, palpus, palp, exploratory member.
**2.** [An effort to discover opinion] — *Syn.* hint, probe, essay, tentative proposal, prospectus, intimation, trial balloon, test, sample, overture, advance, approach, straw vote.

**feeling,** *n.* **1.** [The sense of touch] — *Syn.* tactile sense, touch, tactility, digital sensibility, perception, tangibility.
**2.** [State of the body, or of a part of it] — *Syn.* sense, sensation, consciousness, awareness, impression, sensibility, feel, sensitiveness, sensory response, perception, perceptiveness, perceptivity, susceptibility, receptivity, responsiveness, excitability, excitement, motility, activity, impressibility, titillation, enjoyment, sensuality, voluptuousness, reaction, shrinking, motor response, synesthesia, galvanism, reflex, contractibility, innervation, excitation. — *Ant.* numbness, anesthesia, insensibility.

**3.** [A personal reaction] — *Syn.* opinion, sentiment, belief, outlook; see **attitude** 2, **belief** 1.
**4.** [Sensitivity] — *Syn.* emotion, passion, sentiment, affect, tenderness, discrimination, delicacy, discernment, sentimentality, taste, refinement, capacity, faculty, judgment, affection, sympathy, empathy, compassion, pity, sensibility, susceptibility, intuition, keenness, sharpness, spirit, *esprit* (French), soul, heart, pathos, ardor, fervor, warmth, aesthetic sense, appreciation, response; see also **emotion.** — *Ant.* indifference, apathy, coldness, insensitivity.
**5.** [A hunch] — *Syn.* premonition, foreboding, inkling, gut reaction*; see **hunch** 2.
**6.** [A general emotional quality] — *Syn.* air, atmosphere, mood; see **character** 1, **characteristic.**

---

**SYN.** — **feeling,** when unqualified in the context, refers to any of the subjective reactions, pleasant or unpleasant, that one may have to a situation and usually connotes an absence of reasoning [I can't trust my own *feelings*]; **emotion** implies an intense feeling, often with physical as well as mental manifestations [the news aroused conflicting *emotions* in him]; **passion** refers to a strong or overpowering emotion, connoting especially sexual love or intense anger; **sentiment** applies to a feeling, often a tender one, accompanied by some thought or reasoning [what are your *sentiments* in this matter?]

---

**feign,** *v.* — *Syn.* pretend, simulate, invent, fabricate; see **invent** 2, **pretend** 1.
*See Synonym Study at* PRETEND.

**feigned,** *modif.* — *Syn.* simulated, counterfeit, sham, false; see **false** 3, **pretended.**

**feint,** *n.* — *Syn.* pretense, dodge, distraction, maneuver; see **device** 2, **trick** 1.

**felicitate,** *v.* — *Syn.* congratulate, wish one joy, hail, salute; see **compliment** 2.

**felicitation,** *n.* — *Syn.* congratulation, good wishes, salutation; see **compliment, congratulations.**

**felicitous,** *modif.* — *Syn.* appropriate, apt, well-chosen; see **fit** 1, 2.

**feline,** *modif.* — *Syn.* catlike, stealthy, slinky, cunning; see **sly** 1.

**fell,** *modif.* — *Syn.* barbarous, vicious, inhuman; see **cruel** 1.

**fell,** *v.* — *Syn.* chop down, cut down, hew down, mow down, fling down, pull down, blow down, strike down, knock down, dash down, hurl down, bring down, cause to fall, ground, floor, down, knock over, blow over, bowl over, deck*.

**fellow,** *n.* **1.** [A man or boy] — *Syn.* chap, guy*, youth, lad, person, male, gentleman, stripling, cadet, *señor* (Spanish), *Herr* (German), *garçon* (French), adolescent, teenager, pubescent, whippersnapper, master, beau, juvenile, youngster, duffer*, kid*, cat*, codger*, geezer*, bloke* (*British*), squirt*, sprig*.
**2.** [An associate] — *Syn.* peer, colleague, comrade; see **associate, equal, friend** 1.
**3.** [An academic or scholarly appointee] — *Syn.* assistant, associate, graduate, graduate student, scholar, licentiate, academician, tutor, master, gownsman, don, instructor, professor, lecturer, assistant professor, associate professor, docent, teaching assistant, TA*, research assistant, RA*, wrangler, drudge, *agrégé* (French), bachelor, candidate, doctor, holder of a fellowship, member, postdoc*.

**fellow feeling,** *n.* — *Syn.* understanding, compassion, sympathy, empathy; see **fellowship** 1, **pity** 1.

**fellowship,** *n.* **1.** [Congenial social feeling] — *Syn.* comradeship, brotherhood, sisterhood, companionability, conviviality, sociality, sociability, intimacy, acquaintance, friendliness, familiarity, good-fellowship, amity, affability, camaraderie, fraternity, fellow feeling, commonality, collegiality, solidarity, bond, community of interest, togetherness*. — *Ant.* enmity, antagonism, unsociability.

**2.** [Congenial social activity] — *Syn.* society, companionship, comradeship, friendship, association, fraternization, communion, familiar intercourse, alliance, bonding, teamwork. — *Ant.* WITHDRAWAL, retirement, aloofness.

**3.** [An association of people] — *Syn.* society, club, alliance, league; see **organization** 3.

**4.** [Subsistence payment to encourage study] — *Syn.* stipend, grant, scholarship, honorarium, subsidy, endowment, foreign fellowship, teaching fellowship, Rockefeller fellowship, Woodrow Wilson fellowship, Rhodes scholarship, Guggenheim fellowship, assistantship.

**felon,** *n.* — *Syn.* criminal, malefactor, outlaw, convict; see **criminal.**

**felonious,** *modif.* — *Syn.* unlawful, nefarious, criminal; see **illegal, wicked** 1, 2.

**felony,** *n.* — *Syn.* major crime, offense, transgression; see **crime** 1, 2.

**female,** *modif.* **1.** [Feminine] — *Syn.* womanly, womanlike, ladylike; see **feminine** 2.

**2.** [Belonging to the female sex] — *Syn.* oviparous, reproductive, fertile, childbearing, pistillate, pistil-bearing, of the female gender, distaff, "more deadly than the male," she*. — *Ant.* masculine, MALE, staminate.

**female,** *n.* — *Syn.* woman, lady, girl; see **woman**
See Synonym Study at WOMAN.

**feminine,** *modif.* **1.** [Belonging to the feminine sex] — *Syn.* female, distaff, pistillate; see **female** 2.

**2.** [Having qualities stereotypically associated with women] — *Syn.* soft, womanly, delicate, gentle, ladylike, female, matronly, maidenly, sensitive, tender, womanish, graceful, changeable, fair, fluttering, shy, yielding, passive, vixenish, effeminate, unmanly; see also **dainty** 1, **refined** 2, **womanly.** — *Ant.* masculine, mainly, virile.

---

**SYN.** — **feminine** refers to qualities, other than those basically biological, thought to be characteristic of or suitable to women, as delicacy, gentleness, etc.; **female** is the basic term applied to members of the sex that is biologically distinguished from the male sex and is used of animals or plants as well as of human beings; **womanly** suggests the generally desirable qualities one associates with a woman, esp. one who has maturity of character; **womanish,** in contrast, suggests weaknesses and faults that are sometimes regarded as characteristic of women; **effeminate,** used chiefly in reference to a man, implies delicacy, softness, or lack of virility; **ladylike** refers to manners, conduct, etc. such as are expected from a refined or well-bred woman

---

**femininity,** *n.* **1.** [The quality of being feminine] — *Syn.* womanhood, femaleness, feminineness, femineity, muliebrity, womanliness, softness, gentleness, delicacy, feminine principle, yin; see also **gentleness** 2, **kindness** 1.

**2.** [Effeminacy] — *Syn.* womanishness, unmanliness, effeminateness; see **weakness** 1.

**feminism,** *n.* — *Syn.* women's rights, women's movement, women's liberation, sisterhood, womanism, women's lib*.

**fen,** *n.* — *Syn.* bog, morass, marsh; see **swamp.**

**fence,** *n.* **1.** [That which surrounds an enclosure] — *Syn.* barricade, barrier, rail, railing, wall, picket fence, wire fence, board fence, electrified fence, barbed-wire fence, post-and-rail fence, chain-link fence, snake fence, Cyclone fence (trademark), rail fence, chain fence, stone wall, hedge, paling, balustrade, palisade, backstop, net, dike, ha-ha.

**2.** [Material to make an enclosure] — *Syn.* fencing, barbed wire, chicken wire, pickets, woven wire, palings, stakes, grape stakes, posts, rails, boarding.

**3.** [A receiver of stolen goods] — *Syn.* accomplice; front, front man, drop*, dump*, family man*, uncle*, swagman*.

**mend one's fences*** — *Syn.* renew contacts, look after one's political interests, solicit votes, politic; see **campaign** 1.

**on the fence*** — *Syn.* uncertain, uncommitted, undecided, neutral; see **doubtful** 2, **undecided.**

**fence,** *v.* **1.** [To enclose with a fence] — *Syn.* surround, encircle, corral; see **enclose** 1.

**2.** [To avoid giving a direct reply] — *Syn.* hedge, parry, dodge, sidestep; see **evade** 1.

**fencing,** *n.* — *Syn.* foils, foil work, fencing match, swordplay, swordsmanship, épée, saber, duel, contest, fight.

**fend,** *v.* — *Syn.* parry, repel, resist; see **defend** 1, **oppose** 2.

**fender,** *n.* — *Syn.* guard, mudguard, shield, apron, buffer, mask, cover, frame, ward, cushion, protector, splashboard, bumper, cowcatcher, screen, fireguard, curb.

**fend for oneself,** *v.* — *Syn.* take care of oneself, stay alive, get along, shift for oneself; see **live** 4, **subsist, survive** 1.

**fend off,** *v.* — *Syn.* keep off, ward off, repel, deflect; see **defend** 1, **repel** 1.

**feral,** *modif.* **1.** [Not tame] — *Syn.* wild, untamed, not domesticated; see **primitive** 3, **savage** 3.

**2.** [Savage] — *Syn.* fierce, bestial, ferocious, vicious; see **ferocious, savage** 2.

**ferment,** *n.* — *Syn.* stir, excitement, agitation, unrest; see **disturbance** 2.

**ferment,** *v.* — *Syn.* effervesce, sour, turn, foam, froth, bubble, seethe, fizz, sparkle, boil, acidify, work, ripen, dissolve, overflow, evaporate, rise, leaven.

**fermentation,** *n.* — *Syn.* effervescence, ebullition, turbulence, souring, agitation, foaming, frothing, seething, bubbling, leavening, evaporation, volatilization, dissolving, overflowing.

**fern,** *n.* — *Syn.* greenery, bracken, lacy plant, pteridophyte, maidenhair, brake, polypody.

**ferocious,** *modif.* — *Syn.* fierce, savage, wild, feral, barbarous, untamed, fell, brutal, cruel, sanguinary, predatory, ravenous, vehement, violent, unrestrained, bloodthirsty, murderous, brutish, pitiless, merciless, unmerciful, fearsome, frightful. — *Ant.* GENTLE, mild, tame.

**ferocity,** *n.* — *Syn.* fierceness, brutality, barbarity, savagery; see **cruelty.**

**ferret out,** *v.* — *Syn.* unearth, search out, track down; see **discover, hunt** 2.

**ferry,** *n.* — *Syn.* passage boat, barge, packet, ferryboat; see **boat, ship.**

**ferry,** *v.* — *Syn.* carry over, transport, ship, shuttle; see **carry** 1, **cross** 1.

**fertile,** *modif.* **1.** [Said of land] — *Syn.* fruitful, rich, productive, fat, teeming, yielding, plenteous, prolific, black, arable, flowering, bearing, lush, flowing with milk and honey. — *Ant.* STERILE, barren, desert.

**2.** [Said of females] — *Syn.* fecund, prolific, generative,

bearing, bringing forth, breeding, pregnant, gravid, with child. — *Ant.* STERILE, infertile, barren.
**3.** [*Said of the mind, imagination, etc.*] — *Syn.* inventive, resourceful, imaginative; see **original** 2.

***SYN.*** — **fertile** implies a producing, or the power of producing, fruit or offspring, and may be used figuratively of the mind; **fecund** implies the abundant production of offspring or fruit, or, figuratively, of creations of the mind; **fruitful** specifically suggests the bearing of much fruit, but it is also used to imply fertility (of soil or plants) or to that which produces favorable or profitable results, etc.; **prolific**, a close synonym for **fecund**, more often carries connotations of rapid production or reproduction and is often derogatory [a *prolific* species, a *prolific* writer]

**fertility,** *n.* **1.** [Reproductive capacity] — *Syn.* fecundity, richness, fruitfulness, prolificacy, prolificness, potency, virility, pregnancy, gravidity, productiveness, productivity, generative capacity. — *Ant.* BARRENNESS, sterility, infertility.
**2.** [Ingenuity] — *Syn.* resourcefulness, imagination, inventiveness; see **originality.**
**fertilization,** *n.* **1.** [The enrichment of land] — *Syn.* manuring, dressing, preparation, covering, liming, mulching, spreading, enrichment, soil amendment.
**2.** [Impregnation of the ovum] — *Syn.* insemination, impregnation, pollination, implantation, breeding, fecundation, propagation, generation, procreation, conjugation, begetting, artificial insemination, in vitro fertilization, IVF.
**fertilize,** *v.* **1.** [To enrich land] — *Syn.* manure, dress, top-dress, feed, lime, prepare, mulch, cover, treat.
**2.** [To impregnate] — *Syn.* breed, make pregnant, fecundate, generate, germinate, pollinate, inseminate, implant, propagate, procreate, get with child, beget, knock up*.
**fertilizer,** *n.* — *Syn.* manure, top dressing, organic fertilizer, commercial fertilizer, chemical fertilizer, plant food, compost, humus, mulch, soil amendment.
Common fertilizers include: manure, guano, sphagnum, peat moss, phosphorus, phosphate, superphosphate, dung, litter, crushed limestone, bone dust, kelp, seaweed, bone meal, nitrogen, nitric nitrogen, ammonic nitrogen, ammonium sulfate, legumes, potash.
**fervent,** *modif.* — *Syn.* zealous, eager, ardent, fervid; see **enthusiastic** 2, 3, **intense, passionate** 2.
*See Synonym Study at* PASSIONATE.
**fervor,** *n.* — *Syn.* fervency, ardor, zeal, warmth; see **enthusiasm** 1.
*See Synonym Study at* ENTHUSIASM.
**fester,** *v.* **1.** [To ulcerate or decay] — *Syn.* suppurate, ooze, putrefy, rot; see **decay.**
**2.** [To cause bitterness] — *Syn.* rankle, smolder, gall, plague; see **anger** 1, **rankle.**
**festival,** *n.* — *Syn.* festivity, holiday, gala, entertainment; see **carnival** 1, **celebration** 1, 2, **entertainment** 2.
**festive,** *modif.* — *Syn.* merry, joyful, celebratory, gala; see **happy** 1, **pleasant** 2.
**festivity,** *n.* — *Syn.* revelry, merrymaking, gaiety, celebration; see **carnival** 1, **celebration** 2, **entertainment** 1, 2.
**festoon,** *n.* — *Syn.* swag, garland, chaplet; see **decoration** 2, **wreath.**
**festoon,** *v.* — *Syn.* trim, array, hang, wreathe; see **decorate.**
**fetch,** *v.* **1.** [To draw forth] — *Syn.* elicit, go after, call for, summon; see **obtain** 1.

**2.** [To get and bring back] — *Syn.* bring, get, retrieve; see **bring** 1, **carry** 1.
*See Synonym Study at* BRING.
**fetching,** *modif.* — *Syn.* attractive, pleasing, captivating; see **charming.**
**fete,** *n.* — *Syn.* festival, entertainment, gala, ball; see **celebration** 1, 2, **party** 1.
**fete,** *v.* — *Syn.* entertain, honor, regale, wine and dine*; see **entertain** 2, **praise** 1.
**fetid,** *modif.* — *Syn.* rank, foul, stinking; see **offensive** 2, **rank** 2.
**fetish,** *n.* **1.** [Obsession] — *Syn.* fixation, craze, mania; see **obsession.**
**2.** [The object of an obsession] — *Syn.* amulet, talisman, object of superstition; see **charm** 2.
**fetter,** *v.* **1.** [To bind] — *Syn.* shackle, tie up, chain; see **bind** 1.
**2.** [To confine] — *Syn.* hamper, check, repress; see **hinder, restrain** 1.
**fetters,** *n.* — *Syn.* manacles, shackles, bonds; see **chains.**
**fetus,** *n.* — *Syn.* embryo, unborn child, germ, blastular, organism, unborn vertebrate, unhatched vertebrate.
**feud,** *n.* — *Syn.* quarrel, strife, vendetta; see **dispute, fight** 1.
**fever,** *n.* — *Syn.* elevated temperature, pyrexia, temperature, hyperpyrexia, hyperthermia, febrile disease, delirium, frenzy, restlessness, feverishness, heat, flush; see also **excitement, illness** 1.
**feverish,** *modif.* — *Syn.* febrile, hot, burning, above normal, running a temperature, pyretic, flushed, fevered, agitated, frenzied, delirious, hectic; see also **excited, hot** 1.
**few,** *modif.* — *Syn.* not many, scarcely any, hardly any, less, sparse, scant, scanty, thin, scattered, straggling, widely spaced, inconsiderable, negligible, infrequent, sporadic, not too many, a few, a couple of, a small number of, some, any, scarce, rare, seldom, few and far between, in the minority; see also **rare** 2, **several** 1. — *Ant.* MANY, numerous, innumerable.
**few,** *pron.* — *Syn.* not many, a small number, a handful, scarcely any, hardly any, not so many as one might expect, not too many, several, some, a scattering, a number that can be counted on one's fingers, three or four, a couple, a sprinkling, a smattering, a minority. — *Ant.* MANY, a multitude, a great many.
**quite a few** — *Syn.* several, some, many, a large number; see **plenty, several.**
**fey,** *modif.* — *Syn.* eccentric, whimsical, elfin, otherworldly; see **unusual** 2.
**fiancé,** *n.* — *Syn.* fiancée, intended, betrothed, boyfriend, girlfriend, bride-to-be, husband-to-be, engaged person, affianced person; see also **lover** 1.
**fiasco,** *n.* — *Syn.* debacle, miscarriage, blunder, farce; see **disaster, failure** 1.
**fiat,** *n.* — *Syn.* order, authorization, decree, proclamation; see **command** 1, **declaration** 2.
**fib,** *n.* — *Syn.* prevarication, fabrication, misrepresentation, white lie; see **lie** 1.
**fib,** *v.* — *Syn.* prevaricate, fabricate, misrepresent; see **lie** 1.
*See Synonym Study at* LIE.
**fiber,** *n.* **1.** [A threadlike structure] — *Syn.* thread, cord, string, rootlet, strand, staple, pile, tissue, filament, vein, hair, tendril, strip, shred, roughage.
Common types of fibers include: vegetable, animal, natural, synthetic, silk, linen, hemp, cotton, wool, flax, ramie, raffia, jute, rayon, nylon, acrylic, polyester; Fiberglas, Acrilan, Dacron, Ban-Lon, Orlon (all trademarks); acetate.

**2.** [Quality] — *Syn.* grain, tissue, nap, grit, tooth, feel, hand, surface, warp and woof; see also **character** 1, **texture** 1.

**fibrous,** *modif.* — *Syn.* stringy, woody, pulpy, veined, hairy, coarse, stalky, threadlike, ropy, tissued, sinewy, tough, fibroid.

**fickle,** *modif.* **1.** [Not to be relied upon] — *Syn.* capricious, whimsical, mercurial; see **changeable** 1, 2.
**2.** [Unfaithful in love] — *Syn.* faithless, inconstant, coquettish, flirtatious, flighty, untrue; see also **flirtatious.** — *Ant.* FAITHFUL, loving, true.
*See Synonym Study at* INCONSTANT.

**fiction,** *n.* **1.** [Something invented or feigned] — *Syn.* fabrication, untruth, invention; see **fantasy** 2, **lie** 1.
**2.** [Imaginative prose narrative] — *Syn.* novel, tale, romance; see **story.**

**fictitious,** *modif.* — *Syn.* made-up, invented, untrue, counterfeit; see **false** 2, 3, **imaginary, legendary** 2.
*See Synonym Study at* LEGENDARY.

**fiddle\*,** *n.* — *Syn.* violin, stringed instrument, cornstalk fiddle\*; see **musical instrument, violin.**
**fit as a fiddle\*** — *Syn.* healthy, strong, sound; see **healthy** 1, **well** 1.

**fiddle with,** *v.* — *Syn.* tinker with, play with, twiddle; see **adjust** 3, **dabble, tinker.**

**fidelity,** *n.* **1.** [Faithfulness in allegiance] — *Syn.* loyalty, constancy, devotion; see **constancy** 1, **loyalty.**
**2.** [Conformity to a standard] — *Syn.* accuracy, closeness, scrupulousness, faithfulness; see **care** 1, **truth** 1.
*See Synonym Study at* LOYALTY.

**fidget,** *v.* — *Syn.* stir, twitch, squirm, toss, wiggle, wriggle, jiggle, joggle, fret, chafe, worry, have the fidgets, have ants in one's pants\*.

**fidgety,** *modif.* — *Syn.* nervous, uneasy, apprehensive; see **restless** 1.

**fiduciary,** *n.* — *Syn.* trustee, depositary, curator; see **guardian** 1, **trustee.**

**field,** *modif.* — *Syn.* farm, stock, meadow, outdoor, agricultural, rural, land, soil, earth, earthen, agrarian, bucolic, pastoral.

**field,** *n.* **1.** [Open land] — *Syn.* meadow, pasture, clearing, range, acreage, plot, patch, garden, enclosure, land under cultivation, grainfield, hayfield, cornfield, tract of land, cultivated ground, grassland, green, farmland, ranchland, arable land, plowed land, cultivated land, cleared land, moor, moorland, heath, lea, cropland, tract, vineyard, glebe, mead.
**2.** [An area devoted to sport] — *Syn.* diamond, gridiron, playing field, track, rink, court, course, racecourse, golf course, racetrack, circus, arena, lists, stadium, theater, amphitheater, playground, park, turf, green, hippodrome, fairground; see also **arena.**
**3.** [An area devoted to a specialized activity] — *Syn.* airfield, airport, landing field, playing field, terminal, battlefield, battleground, terrain, scene of conflict, theater of war, arena, field of honor, parade ground, range, parking lot; see **airport, battlefield.**
**4.** [An area which can be comprehended in a given way] — *Syn.* field of vision, field of investigation, field of operations, territory, province, domain, bailiwick, purview, sphere, reach, range, area, realm, scope, jurisdiction, field of interest, field of study, discipline, specialty, profession, turf\*; see also **department** 1.
**5.** [Competitors or available candidates] — *Syn.* entries, entrants, participants, contestants, applicants, nominees, possibilities, contenders, players, suitable candidates.
**play the field** — *Syn.* experiment, explore, look elsewhere; see **examine** 1, **try** 1.

**take the field** — *Syn.* initiate, start, go forth; see **begin** 1, **campaign** 1.

**field,** *v.* — *Syn.* handle, cover, answer, respond to, reply to, parry, take care of, catch, retrieve, pick up.

**field day,** *n.* — *Syn.* success, holiday, triumph; see **victory** 2.

**fielder,** *n.* — *Syn.* ball chaser, fly chaser, fly hawk\*, gardener\*, shagger\*.
Fielders include: infielder, outfielder, right fielder, left fielder, center fielder, right gardener\*, center gardener\*, left gardener\*.

**fiend,** *n.* **1.** [A devil] — *Syn.* demon, Satan, evil spirit; see **devil** 1.
**2.** [A wicked or cruel person] — *Syn.* monster, barbarian, brute; see **beast** 2.
**3.** [\*An addict] — *Syn.* fan, aficionado, monomaniac; see **addict, enthusiast** 1.

**fiendish,** *modif.* — *Syn.* diabolical, demoniac, infernal; see **cruel** 1, **wicked** 2.

**fierce,** *modif.* **1.** [*Said especially of people and animals*] — *Syn.* ferocious, wild, savage, furious, enraged, raging, impetuous, untamed, angry, passionate, primitive, uncivilized, brutish, feral, animal, raving, terrible, frightening, fearsome, menacing, awful, venomous, bold, malevolent, malign, brutal, cruel, merciless, ruthless, bloodthirsty, bloody, murderous, sanguinary, truculent, aggressive, hostile, violent, monstrous, rough, grim, vicious, dangerous, frenzied, mad, insane, desperate, ravening, frantic, wrathful, irate, rabid, virulent, fanatical, bestial, tigerish, barbarous, hard\*, tough\*, hard-boiled\*; see also **sense** 2. — *Ant.* GENTLE, tame, PEACEFUL.
**2.** [*Said especially of actions and the weather*] — *Syn.* boisterous, violent, vehement, threatening, severe, stormy, thunderous, howling, inclement, tumultuous, turbulent, uncontrolled, unbridled, unrestrained, raging, storming, blustering, cyclonic, blizzardy, torrential, of hurricane force, frightful, fearful, lowering, destructive, devastating, hellish, rip-roaring\*; see also **sense** 1. — *Ant.* MILD, moderate, calm.
**3.** [Intense] — *Syn.* ardent, fervent, deep, acute; see **intense.**

**fiercely,** *modif.* — *Syn.* ferociously, violently, wildly, savagely, terribly, vehemently, angrily, threateningly, menacingly, frighteningly, awfully, horribly, venomously, mightily, passionately, impetuously, boldly, irresistibly, furiously, riotously, malevolently, maleficently, malignly, brutally, monstrously, cruelly, ruthlessly, forcibly, forcefully, convulsively, severely, roughly, viciously, dangerously, madly, tumultuously, raveningly, insanely, desperately, frantically, wrathfully, irately, virulently, rabidly, relentlessly, grimly, truculently, aggressively, turbulently, overpoweringly, strongly, fanatically, with rage, in a frenzy, tooth and nail\*. — *Ant.* MILDLY, reasonably, peacefully.

**fiery,** *modif.* **1.** [Burning] — *Syn.* blazing, flaming, glowing, red-hot; see **burning** 1, **hot** 1.
**2.** [Passionate] — *Syn.* ardent, spirited, impetuous, hotheaded; see **enthusiastic** 3, **excitable, passionate** 2.

**fiesta,** *n.* — *Syn.* festival, holiday, feast; see **celebration** 1, 2, **holiday** 1.

**fifth columnist,** *n.* — *Syn.* quisling, saboteur, secret agent; see **traitor.**

**fight,** *n.* **1.** [A violent struggle] — *Syn.* strife, conflict, contention, feud, quarrel, contest, struggle, encounter, row, dispute, disagreement, battle, battle royal, confrontation, controversy, brawl, affray, affair, fray, bout, match, fisticuffs, boxing match, round, broil, fracas, dif-

ficulty, altercation, bickering, wrangling, riot, argument, dissension, debate, competition, sparring match, a coming to blows, rivalry, skirmish, scrimmage, clash, scuffle, collision, brush, action, engagement, melee, passage of arms, sortie, pitched battle, tilt, joust, combat, duel, exchange of blows, wrestling match, squabble, game, discord, estrangement, hostilities, imbroglio, disturbance, *recontre* (French), tiff, difference of opinion, falling-out, fuss*, mix-up*, tussle*, scrap*, free-for-all*, ruckus*, run-in*, showdown*, flare-up*, go*, rumpus*, donnybrook*, set-to*, rhubarb*, hassle*; see also **dispute**.
2. [Willingness or eagerness to fight] — *Syn.* belligerence, pugnacity, mettle, hardihood; see **aggression** 2, **courage** 1.

---

*SYN.* — **fight**, a rather general word for any contest, struggle, or quarrel, stresses physical or hand-to-hand combat; **conflict**, which may apply to anything from armed fighting to mental struggle, refers to a sharp disagreement or clash, as between opposing groups, interests, or ideas, and emphasizes difficulty of resolution *[the conflict over slavery]*; **struggle** implies great effort or violent exertion, physical or otherwise *[the struggle for existence]*; **contention** most frequently applies to heated verbal strife, or dispute *[religious contention]*; **contest** refers to a struggle, either friendly or hostile, for supremacy in some matter *[athletic contests, a contest of wits]*

---

**fight**, *v.* 1. [To struggle for an end] — *Syn.* carry on, strive, struggle, persevere, persist, push forward, support, uphold, lobby for, labor, work, exert oneself, travail, hammer away, toil on, take pains, spare no effort, fight one's way, put up a fight. — *Ant.* STOP, give up, quit.
2. [To engage in an encounter] — *Syn.* battle, contend, clash, strive, war, struggle, combat, contest, oppose, resist, protest, challenge, confront, meet, attack, argue, quarrel, feud, engage in hostilities, go to war, wage war, take up arms, withstand, do battle, give battle, cross swords, exchange shots, exchange blows, come to blows, engage in fisticuffs, brawl, scuffle, encounter, bear arms against, tussle, grapple, brush with, have a brush with, collide, engage with, close with, wrestle, box, spar, measure swords with, skirmish, wrangle, bicker, squabble, dispute, row, bandy with, have it out, duel, joust, tilt, compete, vie, join issue, assert oneself, enter the lists, take up the gauntlet, set to, fight the good fight, fight to the last ditch, tangle*, pitch into*, tear into*, take on all comers*, pick a bone with*, take the field*, scrap*, mix it up with*, hassle*, lock horns*, go to the mat*, make the fur fly*, go at it tooth and nail*, duke it out*. — *Ant.* RETREAT, submit, yield.
**fight back**, *v.* — *Syn.* defend oneself, resist, retaliate; see **oppose** 2, **resist** 1.
**fighter**, *n.* 1. [One who fights] — *Syn.* contestant, disputant, contender, party to a quarrel, warrior, soldier, combatant, belligerent, assailant, aggressor, antagonist, rival, opponent, champion, swashbuckler, swordsman, duelist, bully, gladiator, janissary, feudist, competitor, wrestler, controversialist, quarrelsome person, fireeater, brawler, scrapper*.
2. [A professional pugilist] — *Syn.* boxer, prizefighter, battler*, pug*, palooka*, chump*, bruiser*, slugger*.
3. [An airplane built to fight] — *Syn.* combat plane, interceptor, pursuit plane; see **plane** 3.
**fighting**, *modif.* — *Syn.* combative, battling, warring, brawling, determined, resolute, striving, contentious,

disputatious, under arms, argumentative, angry, ferocious, quarrelsome, ready to fight, ripe for a fight, bellicose, belligerent, militant, boxing, wrestling, sparring, fencing, jousting, skirmishing, tilting, pugnacious, warlike, contending, at war, in the thick of the fray, like cats and dogs*, at the point of the bayonet*, in the cannon's mouth*, up in arms*, at swords' points*. — *Ant.* PEACEFUL, peaceable, meek.
**fighting**, *n.* — *Syn.* combat, struggle, strife; see **fight** 1.
**fight off**, *v.* — *Syn.* fend off, hold back, resist, repulse; see **defend** 1, **repel** 1.
**figment**, *n.* — *Syn.* illusion, invention, fabrication, coinage of the brain; see **fancy** 2, **fantasy** 2, **lie** 1.
**figurative**, *modif.* — *Syn.* metaphorical, allegorical, not literal, symbolic; see **illustrative, metaphorical**.
**figure**, *n.* 1. [A form] — *Syn.* shape, mass, structure; see **form** 1.
2. [The human torso] — *Syn.* body, frame, torso, shape, form, development, configuration, build, physique, appearance, outline, posture, attitude, pose, carriage, chassis*, bod*.
3. [An arrangement of lines, masses, and the like] — *Syn.* illustration, sketch, composition, pattern; see **design** 1, **picture** 3, **statue**.
4. [A representation of quantity] — *Syn.* numeral, sum, total, symbol; see **number** 2, **symbol**.
5. [Price] — *Syn.* value, amount, sum, terms; see **price**.
6. [A person] — *Syn.* character, personage, personality; see **person** 1, **personage** 2.
*See Synonym Study at* FORM.
**figure**, *v.* 1. [To compute] — *Syn.* calculate, reckon, number, count; see **calculate** 1.
2. [To estimate] — *Syn.* set a figure, appraise, guess, fix a price; see **estimate** 1.
3. [*To come to a conclusion] — *Syn.* conclude, suppose, think, opine; see **decide, estimate** 2, **infer** 1.
4. [To figure out] — *Syn.* comprehend, master, reason out; see **solve, understand** 1.
**figured**, *modif.* — *Syn.* patterned, scrolled, flowered, geometric; see **ornate** 1.
**figurehead**, *n.* — *Syn.* titular head, nonentity, cipher; see **nobody** 2.
**figure of speech**, *n.* Figures of speech include: image, comparison, metaphor, simile, alliteration, onomatopoeia, metonymy, synecdoche, trope, epic simile, Homeric simile, personification, apostrophe, oxymoron, malapropism, hysteron proteron, litotes, hyperbole, repetition, allegory, parable, allusion, euphemism, euphuism, analogue, adumbration, parallel, irony, satire, sarcasm, understatement, paradox.
**figurine**, *n.* — *Syn.* puppet, manikin, statuette, small figure, ornamental model, doll, small-scale sculpture, marionette, knickknack.
**filament**, *n.* — *Syn.* wire, tendril, thread; see **fiber** 1.
**filch**, *n.* — *Syn.* rob, pilfer, purloin; see **steal**.
**file**, *n.* 1. [A receptacle for keeping papers in order] — *Syn.* folder, filing cabinet, letter file, card file, letter case, pigeonhole, repository, organizer, drawer; see also **folder** 2.
2. [An orderly collection of papers] — *Syn.* card index, card file, portfolio, record, data, classified index, list, ready reference list, register, dossier, notebook, docket, census; see also **catalog**.
3. [Steel abrasive] — *Syn.* rasp, steel, sharpener, emery board.
Types of files include: flat, round, rat-tail, triangular, saw, fingernail, wood, 10-inch, 12-inch, etc.
4. [A line] — *Syn.* rank, row, column; see **line** 1.

**on file**— *Syn.* filed, cataloged, registered; see **recorded.**

**file,** *v.* 1. [To arrange in order]— *Syn.* classify, index, deposit, categorize, catalog, record, register, list, arrange, interfile, pigeonhole, docket; see also **classify.**
2. [To use an abrasive]— *Syn.* abrade, rasp, scrape, smooth, rub down, level off, finish, sharpen, hone, grind.

**file clerk,** *n.*— *Syn.* secretary, assistant, office worker; see **clerk** 2.

**filial,** *modif.*— *Syn.* dutiful, affectionate, respectful; see **obedient** 1.

**filibuster,** *n.*— *Syn.* delaying tactic, hindrance, postponement, interference, opposition, procrastination, delay, obstruction to congressional action, obstructionism, stonewalling, holding the floor, peroration, long-windedness.

**filiform,** *modif.*— *Syn.* threadlike, filamentous, stringy; see **fibrous.**

**filigree,** *n.*— *Syn.* fretwork, scrollwork, lacework, tracery, wirework; see also **decoration** 2.

**fill,** *n.*— *Syn.* enough, capacity, satiety; see **plenty.**

**fill,** *v.* 1. [To put as much as possible into]— *Syn.* pack, stuff, load, lade, replenish, furnish, supply, satisfy, fulfill, sate, satiate, gorge, blow up, fill up, pump up, puff up, inflate, fuel, fill to capacity, fill to overflowing, swell, charge, cram in, ram, crowd, jam, top off*.— *Ant.* empty, exhaust, DRAIN.
2. [To occupy available space]— *Syn.* take up, pervade, overflow, stretch, bulge out, curve out, distend, brim over, overspread, stretch, swell, blow up, belly, run over at the top, permeate, saturate, congest, take over; see also sense 1.
3. [To supply with an occupant]— *Syn.* elect, name, appoint; see **choose** 1.

**fill an order,** *v.*— *Syn.* supply, put up, dispatch, pack; see **distribute** 1, **satisfy** 3, **send** 1.

**fill a prescription,** *v.*— *Syn.* compound, fix, blend; see **mix** 1.

**filled,** *modif.*— *Syn.* suffused, permeated, replete, brimming; see **full** 1.

**filler,** *n.* 1. [Waste material]— *Syn.* padding, packing, calking, fill; see **stuffing** 1.
2. [A replaceable portion]— *Syn.* refill, cartridge, pad, pack, cylinder, liner, bushing, shim.
3. [In journalism, matter used to fill a column]— *Syn.* features, squib, time copy*, locals*, shorts*, wire shorts*.

**fill in,** *v.* 1. [To insert]— *Syn.* write in, answer, complete; see **complete** 1, **fill out** 2.
2. [To substitute]— *Syn.* replace, act for, represent; see **substitute** 2.
3. [To inform]— *Syn.* apprise, acquaint, bring up to date, clue in*; see **notify** 1.

**filling,** *n.*— *Syn.* stuffing, dressing, custard, contents, mixture, center, layer, filler, fill, sauce, insides, lining, wadding, padding, bushing, cement, innards*, guts*.

**fillip,** *n.* 1. [A snap of a finger against the thumb]— *Syn.* tap, rap, stroke; see **blow** 1.
2. [A stimulus]— *Syn.* incentive, goad, spur; see **incentive.**

**fill out,** *v.* 1. [To enlarge]— *Syn.* swell out, expand, round out, gain weight; see **grow** 1.
2. [To insert]— *Syn.* complete, write in, fill in, make out, sign, supply information, answer, apply, put one's signature on, fill in the blanks.

**fill up,** *v.*— *Syn.* saturate, pack, stuff; see **fill** 1.

**filly,** *n.*— *Syn.* young mare, foal, female horse; see **colt, horse** 1.

**film,** *n.* 1. [Thin, membranous matter]— *Syn.* gauze, tissue, fabric, sheet, membrane, integument, layer, veneer, foil, skin, onionskin, coat, coating, scum, slick, oil slick, pellicle, veil, cobweb, web, mist, cloud, nebula, haze, obscuration.
2. [A preparation containing a light-sensitive emulsion]— *Syn.* negative, positive, Kodachrome (trademark), microfilm, panchromatic film, color film, black-and-white film, cellulose, plate, transparency, videotape.
3. [A movie]— *Syn.* motion picture, cinema, flick*; see **movie.**

**film,** *v.*— *Syn.* record, take, tape, shoot*; see **photograph.**

**filmy,** *modif.* 1. [Composed of or like film]— *Syn.* gauzy, flimsy, diaphanous, gossamer; see **sheer** 2.
2. [Covered with a film]— *Syn.* misty, cloudy, dim, coated; see **hazy** 1.

**filter,** *v.* 1. [To soak slowly]— *Syn.* seep, osmose, soak through, penetrate, permeate, distill, percolate, leach, exude, ooze, drain, metastasize, infiltrate, trickle.
2. [To clean by filtering]— *Syn.* purify, sift, sieve, strain, refine, filtrate, clarify, clean, separate.

**filth,** *n.*— *Syn.* dirt, muck, sewage, garbage, ordure, dung, feces, contamination, corruption, pollution, uncleanness, foul matter, excreta, coprolite, guano, manure, slop, squalor, trash, grime, mud, smudge, silt, mire, offal, carrion, slush, slime, sludge, foulness, nastiness, filthiness, excrement, pus, dregs, lees, sediment, scum, putridity, putrescence, putrefaction, rottenness, impurity, obscenity, smut, pornography, crud*, grunge*, scuzz*.— *Ant.* CLEANLINESS, purity, spotlessness.

**filthy,** *modif.*— *Syn.* dirty, foul, squalid, nasty; see **dirty** 1.
*See Synonym Study at* DIRTY.

**fin,** *n.*— *Syn.* membrane, paddle, propeller, balance, guide, blade, ridge, airfoil, organ, spine, pectoral fin, ventral fin, pelvic fin, dorsal fin, caudal fin, anal fin, flipper, fishtail.

**final,** *modif.* 1. [Last]— *Syn.* terminal, concluding, closing, ultimate; see **last** 1.
2. [Conclusive]— *Syn.* decisive, definitive, irrevocable; see **conclusive.**

**finale,** *n.*— *Syn.* close, denouement, finish; see **end** 2.

**finality,** *n.*— *Syn.* decisiveness, conclusiveness, totality, completeness, intactness, entirety, wholeness, integrity, perfection, final character, terminality, definiteness, definitiveness, irrevocableness, finish.

**finalize,** *v.*— *Syn.* conclude, settle, clinch, wrap up*; see **achieve** 1, **end** 1.

**finalized,** *modif.*— *Syn.* concluded, decided, completed; see **finished** 1.

**finally,** *modif.* 1. [As though a matter were settled]— *Syn.* conclusively, decisively, with finality, with conviction, in a final manner, certainly, irrevocably, definitely, beyond recall, past regret, permanently, for all time, determinately, enduringly, assuredly, once and for all, for good, beyond the shadow of a doubt, in fine.— *Ant.* TEMPORARILY, momentarily, for the time being.
2. [After a long period]— *Syn.* at last, in the end, at the end, at length, eventually, ultimately, subsequently, in conclusion, lastly, after all, after a time, after a while, as a sequel, despite delay, at long last, at the final point, at the last moment, tardily, belatedly, when all is said and done, in the long run, late in the day*, as the world goes*, as things go*, at the eleventh hour*, in the crunch*, in spite of all, as it may be.

**finance,** *n.*— *Syn.* investment, money management, banking, financial affairs; see **economics.**

**finance,** *v.* — *Syn.* fund, pay for, back, bankroll\*; see **support** 5, **underwrite** 3.

**finances,** *n.* — *Syn.* revenue, capital, funds, monetary resources; see **funds, wealth** 1.

**financial,** *modif.* — *Syn.* commercial, economic, business, monetary, fiscal, pecuniary, budgetary; see also **commercial** 1.

---

*SYN.* — **financial** implies reference to money matters, esp. where large sums are involved *[a financial success]*; **fiscal** is used with reference to government revenues and expenditures or the administering of the financial affairs of an organization or corporation *[a fiscal year]*; **monetary** refers directly to money itself and is used in connection with coinage, circulation, standards, relative values, etc. *[the monetary unit of a country]*; **pecuniary** is applied to money matters of a practical or personal nature *[pecuniary motives]*

---

**financier,** *n.* — *Syn.* capitalist, moneylender, banker, investor, merchant, broker, operator, manipulator, speculator, backer, money-changer, entrepreneur, stockbroker, Wall Streeter, usurer, Shylock\*, moneybags\*, angel\*; see also **banker** 1, **businessperson.**

**financing,** *n.* — *Syn.* funding, backing, grant, matching funds; see **aid** 1, **investment.**

**find,** *n.* — *Syn.* fortunate discovery, acquisition, bonanza, windfall; see **catch** 1, **discovery** 2.

**find,** *v.* **1.** [To happen upon] — *Syn.* discover, come upon, happen on, spot, descry, espy, detect, notice, observe, perceive, discern, hit upon, chance on, chance upon, encounter, uncover, locate, recover, expose, come across, run across, meet with, stumble on, run into, light upon, strike upon, catch sight of, bring to light, dig up\*, turn up\*, scare up\*, smell out\*, make out\*, trip up on\*, trip over\*, meet up with\*, lay one's finger on\*, lay one's hand on\*, bump into\*; see also **see** 1. — *Ant.* LOSE, mislay, miss.

**2.** [To achieve] — *Syn.* attain, win, get, gain; see **obtain** 1.

**3.** [To discover by search or effort] — *Syn.* ascertain, unearth, locate, track down\*; see **discover.**

**4.** [To reach a legal decision] — *Syn.* pronounce, determine, affirm; see **decide.**

**finder,** *n.* **1.** [One who discovers a thing] — *Syn.* discoverer, spotter, acquirer, appropriator, claimant, lucky searcher, search party. — *Ant.* LOSER, owner, stray.

**2.** [A locating device] — *Syn.* sight, telescopic sight, bombsight, gunsight, electronic finder, homing device, synchronic radar detector, radar reflector, viewfinder, rangefinder, periscope, glass, radar, sonar.

**finding,** *n.* — *Syn.* verdict, decision, conclusion; see **judgment** 3, **verdict.**

**findings,** *n.* — *Syn.* data, discoveries, conclusions; see **data, summary.**

**find out,** *v.* — *Syn.* ascertain, learn, identify; see **discover.**

**fine,** *modif.* **1.** [Not coarse or thick] — *Syn.* light, powdery, granular, slender; see **little** 1, **minute** 1, **narrow** 1.

**2.** [Of superior quality] — *Syn.* choice, exceptional, select, well-made; see **excellent.**

**3.** [Refined] — *Syn.* delicate, elegant, exquisite, expensive; see **dainty** 1, **elegant** 1.

**4.** [Exact] — *Syn.* subtle, precise, distinct, strict; see **accurate** 2, **definite** 2, **nice** 3.

**fine,** *n.* — *Syn.* penalty, damages, forfeit; see **punishment.**

**fine,** *v.* — *Syn.* penalize, mulct, exact, amerce, tax, con-

fiscate, levy, sequestrate, seize, extort, make pay; see also **punish.**

**finery,** *n.* — *Syn.* frippery, regalia, dress clothes, trappings, trimmings, glad rags\*, best bib and tucker\*, Sunday best\*, Sunday-go-to-meeting clothes\*; see also **clothes.**

**finespun,** *modif.* — *Syn.* refined, slight, subtle, hairsplitting; see **dainty** 1, **nice** 3, **trivial.**

**finesse,** *n.* — *Syn.* adroitness, diplomacy, delicacy, artfulness; see **ability** 2, **art** 1, **tact.**

**finger,** *n.* — *Syn.* digit, organ of touch, tactile member, forefinger, thumb, index finger, ring finger, pinkie, extremity, pointer, feeler, antenna, tentacle, claw.

**have a finger in the pie\*** — *Syn.* participate, join, be a part of; see **participate** 1, **share** 2.

**keep one's fingers crossed\*** — *Syn.* wish, hope for the best, pray for; see **hope.**

**lift a finger** — *Syn.* make an effort, endeavor, exert oneself, help out; see **help** 1, **try** 1.

**put one's finger on\*** — *Syn.* indicate, ascertain, identify, pinpoint; see **discover.**

**put the finger on\*** — *Syn.* inform on, turn in, spy on; see **betray** 1, **inform** 2.

**finger,** *v.* **1.** [To feel] — *Syn.* handle, touch, manipulate; see **feel** 1.

**2.** [\*To specify or inform against] — *Syn.* point out, name, put the finger on\*; see **designate** 1, **inform** 2.

**fingernail,** *n.* — *Syn.* nail, claw, talon, matrix, hook\*.

**finial,** *n.* — *Syn.* pinnacle, peak, terminal, knob, épi, pineapple; see also **decoration** 2.

**finis,** *n.* — *Syn.* close, finale, conclusion; see **end** 2.

**finish,** *n.* **1.** [The end] — *Syn.* close, termination, ending; see **end** 2.

**2.** [An applied surface] — *Syn.* shine, polish, burnish, glaze, surface, coating.

Finishes include: shellac, shellack, oil, turpentine, lacquer, size, stain, varnish, polish, wall paper, wash, whitewash, alabastine, calcimine, paint, casein paint, flat paint, cold-water paint, Bakelite enamel (trademark), tung-oil, enamel, gold leaf, aluminum paint, anticorrosion paint, wax, veneer, japan, cement, stucco, megilp, luster.

**finish,** *v.* **1.** [To bring to an end] — *Syn.* complete, conclude, end, perfect; see **achieve** 1, **end** 1.

**2.** [To develop a surface] — *Syn.* polish, wax, stain; see **decorate, spread** 4, **varnish.**

**3.** [\*To cause the defeat or death of] — *Syn.* annihilate, worst, finish off, destroy; see **defeat** 2, 3, **destroy** 1, **kill** 1.

**4.** [To come to an end] — *Syn.* cease, close, end, terminate; see **stop** 2.

**5.** [To consume entirely] — *Syn.* use up, dispatch, polish off\*; see **consume** 2, **drink** 1, **eat** 1.

*See Synonym Study at* END.

**finished,** *modif.* **1.** [Completed] — *Syn.* done, accomplished, perfected, achieved, ended, concluded, performed, executed, dispatched, complete, through, fulfilled, closed, over, decided, consummated, effected, effectuated, brought about, ceased, stopped, lapsed, terminated, resolved, settled, compassed, elaborated, made, worked out, polished, rounded out, discharged, satisfied, disposed of, consumed, used up, gone, no more, broken up, realized, finalized, put into effect, all over with, attained, turned off, shut off, done with, at an end, come to an end, made an end of, brought to a conclusion, brought to a close, said and done\*, sewed up\*, wound up\*, wrapped up\*, all over but the shooting\*. — *Ant.* UNFINISHED, imperfect, incomplete.

**2.** [Given a finish] — *Syn.* polished, rubbed, sanded,

planed, beaten, burnished, etched, smoothed, coated, washed, dusted, brushed, buffed, lacquered, shellacked, varnished, painted, waxed, oiled, sized, stained, enameled, glazed, japanned, surfaced.

**3.** [Ruined or dying] — *Syn.* defeated, doomed, done for*; see **beaten** 1, **destroyed, dying** 1.

**finite,** *modif.* — *Syn.* limited, measurable, terminable, restricted; see **calculable, restricted.**

**fiord,** *n.* — *Syn.* inlet, gulf, cove; see **bay, water** 2.

**fire,** *n.* **1.** [Visible oxidation] — *Syn.* flame, conflagration, burning, blaze, campfire, pyre, bonfire, brush fire, signal fire, incandescence, devouring element, sparks, heat, glow, warmth, luminosity, combustion, flare, flareup, inferno, holocaust, wildfire, blazing fire, hearth, ignition, scintillation, phlogiston.

**2.** [The discharge of ordnance] — *Syn.* gunfire, shooting, firing, bombardment, volley, barrage, artillery attack, cannonade, cannonading, bombarding, rounds, explosion, shot, report, bombing, fusillade, sniping, mortar attack, salvo, shelling, blast, burst, shellburst, spray, discharge, detonation, drumfire, creeping barrage, artillery support, cross-fire, enfilade, broadside, curtain, curtain of fire, air support, air strike, firepower, antiaircraft fire, flak, ack-ack*; see also **attack** 1.

**3.** [Fiery temperament] — *Syn.* dash, sparkle, verve, ardor; see **enthusiasm** 1.

**catch (on) fire** — *Syn.* begin burning, ignite, flare up, burst into flame; see **burn** 1.

**go through fire and water** — *Syn.* brave danger, endure hardship, survive, suffer; see **dare** 1, **endure** 2.

**light (or build) a fire under** — *Syn.* spur, goad, inspire, motivate; see **drive** 1, **motivate.**

**on fire, 1.** [Burning] — *Syn.* flaming, blazing, fiery; see **burning** 1.

**2.** [Excited] — *Syn.* full of ardor, enthusiastic, zealous; see **enthusiastic** 1, **excited.**

**open fire** — *Syn.* start shooting, shoot at, attack, start; see **begin** 1, **shoot** 1.

**play with fire*** — *Syn.* gamble, court danger, tempt fate; see **chance** 2, **risk.**

**set fire to** — *Syn.* ignite, set on fire, make burn, torch; see **burn** 2, **ignite.**

**set the world on fire*** — *Syn.* achieve, become famous, excel; see **succeed** 1.

**under fire** — *Syn.* criticized, censured, under attack, embattled; see **accused, questionable** 1, 2.

**fire,** *v.* **1.** [To set on fire] — *Syn.* ignite, light, put a match to, set burning; see **burn** 2, **ignite.**

**2.** [To shoot] — *Syn.* discharge, shoot off, set off, hurl; see **shoot** 1.

**3.** [To dismiss] — *Syn.* discharge, let go, oust, give the ax*; see **dismiss** 2.

**4.** [To animate] — *Syn.* inspirit, inspire, arouse, inflame; see **excite** 1, 2.

**firearm,** *n.* — *Syn.* gun, sidearm, pistol, revolver; see **gun** 2.

**firebrand,** *n.* **1.** [A burning stick] — *Syn.* torch, brand, burning ember, spill; see **embers.**

**2.** [An inflammatory person] — *Syn.* incendiary, mischiefmaker, rabble-rouser; see **agitator.**

**firecracker,** *n.* — *Syn.* cherry bomb, cannon cracker, cracker*; see **fireworks.**

**fired,** *modif.* **1.** [Subjected to fire] — *Syn.* set on fire, burned, baked, ablaze, afire, on fire, aflame, burning, incandescent, scorched, glowing, kindled, enkindled, kindling, alight, smoking, smoldering, unquenched, heated; see also **baked.**

**2.** [Discharged] — *Syn.* dismissed, let go, given one's walking papers*; see **discharged** 1.

**fire escape,** *n.* — *Syn.* ladder, chute, rope ladder, net, stair, fire exit, fire door, emergency exit.

**fireman,** *n.* **1.** [One who extinguishes fires] — *Syn.* firefighter, engineman, ladderman, fire chief, fire warden, smoke jumper.

**2.** [One who fuels engines or furnaces] — *Syn.* stoker, engineer's helper, trainman, attendant, oil feeder, cinder monkey*, hell-holer*, bakehead*.

**fireplace,** *n.* — *Syn.* hearth, chimney, ingle, inglenook, ingleside, hob, settle, fireside, hearthside, stove, furnace, fire, blaze, grate.

**fireproof,** *modif.* — *Syn.* flameproof, noninflammable, noncombustible, nonflammable, fire-resistant, fire-retardant, flame-retardant, incombustible, noncandescent, concrete and steel, asbestos. — *Ant.* flammable, combustible, incandescent, inflammable.

**fireside,** *n.* — *Syn.* hearth, hearthside, home; see **fireplace.**

**firewood,** *n.* — *Syn.* cordwood, kindling, stove-lengths, woodpile; see **fuel.**

**fireworks,** *pl.n.* — *Syn.* pyrotechnics, rockets, Roman candles, sparklers, Catherine wheels, pinwheels, skyrockets, girandoles, squibs, firecrackers, cherry bombs, illuminations, *feux d'artifice* (French).

**firm,** *modif.* **1.** [Stable] — *Syn.* fixed, solid, rooted, immovable, fastened, motionless, secured, steady, substantial, durable, rigid, bolted, welded, riveted, soldered, embedded, nailed, tightened, screwed, spiked, anchored, moored, fast, secure, sound, immobile, unmovable, mounted, unmoving, stationary, set, petrified, settled. — *Ant.* LOOSE, movable, mobile.

**2.** [Firm in texture] — *Syn.* solid, dense, compact, hard, stiff, impenetrable, close-grained, fine-grained, impervious, rigid, inelastic, hardened, inflexible, congealed, unyielding, thick, compressed, substantial, heavy, nonporous, close, condensed, thickset, impermeable, refractory. — *Ant.* SOFT, porous, flabby.

**3.** [Settled in purpose] — *Syn.* determined, steadfast, constant, unwavering; see **resolute** 2.

**4.** [Definite] — *Syn.* specific, explicit, fixed, confirmed; see **definite** 1, **determined** 1.

**5.** [Indicating firmness] — *Syn.* strong, vigorous, steady, determined, adamant, hard, cold, sound, stout, sturdy, staunch. — *Ant.* WEAK, irresolute, unsteady.

**stand (or hold) firm** — *Syn.* be steadfast, hold one's ground, maintain one's resolution; see **resist** 1, **resolve** 1.

---

**SYN. — firm**, in referring to material consistency, suggests a compactness that does not yield easily to, or is very resilient under, pressure /a *firm* mattress/; **hard** is applied to that which is so firm that it is not easily penetrated, cut, or crushed /*hard* as rock/; **solid** suggests a dense consistency throughout a mass or substance that is firm or hard and often connotes heaviness or substantiality /*solid* brick/; **stiff** implies resistance to bending or stretching /a *stiff* collar/

---

**firmament,** *n.* — *Syn.* sky, heaven, vault of heaven, atmosphere; see **heaven** 1, **sky.**

**firmly,** *modif.* **1.** [Not easily moved] — *Syn.* immovably, solidly, rigidly, stably, fast, tight, tightly, fixedly, durably, enduringly, substantially, securely, heavily, sturdily, stiffly, inflexibly, unshakably, soundly, strongly, steadily, solid as a rock*, like the Rock of Gibraltar*, there for all time*. — *Ant.* loosely, tenuously, insecurely.

**2.** [Showing determination] — *Syn.* resolutely, steadfastly, doggedly, stolidly, tenaciously, determinedly, staunchly, adamantly, constantly, intently, purposefully, obdurately, persistently, obstinately, stubbornly, perseveringly, pertinaciously, unwaveringly, unswervingly, unchangeably, indefeasibly, with a heavy hand, through thick and thin*. — *Ant.* TEMPORARILY, weakly, feebly.

**firmness,** *n.* **1.** [Firmness of position] — *Syn.* solidity, steadiness, durability, substantiality; see **stability** 1.
**2.** [Firmness of material] — *Syn.* stiffness, impliability, hardness, toughness, solidity, density, impenetrability, durability, imperviousness, temper, impermeability, tensile strength, inflexibility, rigidity. — *Ant.* penetrability, FLEXIBILITY, fluidity.
**3.** [Firmness of mind] — *Syn.* resolution, steadfastness, staunchness, strictness; see **determination** 2.

**first,** *modif.* **1.** [Foremost in order] — *Syn.* beginning, original, earliest, primary, prime, primal, antecedent, anterior, initial, virgin, maiden, opening, introductory, inceptive, incipient, inaugural, premier, primeval, aboriginal, leading, in the beginning, front, head, rudimentary, fundamental. — *Ant.* LAST, ultimate, final.
**2.** [Foremost in importance] — *Syn.* chief, greatest, prime, preeminent; see **principal.**

**in the first place** — *Syn.* firstly, initially, to begin with; see **at first** under **first.**

**first,** *n.* — *Syn.* beginning, outset, start, the word "go"*; see **origin** 1.

**at first** — *Syn.* in the beginning, initially, firstly, in the first place, at the outset, at the start, at the beginning, at the commencement, originally, to begin win, first off*, for openers*.

**first aid,** *n.* — *Syn.* emergency medical aid, Red Cross, emergency treatment, relief, roadside treatment, field dressing.

**first-class,** *modif.* — *Syn.* superior, supreme, choice; see **excellent.**

**first-rate,** *modif.* — *Syn.* prime, very good, choice; see **excellent.**

**fiscal,** *modif.* — *Syn.* monetary, economic, financial; see **commercial** 1.

*See Synonym Study at* FINANCIAL.

**fish,** *n.* — *Syn. piscis* (Latin), seafood, panfish, denizen of the deep, finny prey, one of the finny tribe.
Types of fish include: catfish, pickerel, pike, perch, trout, flounder, sucker, sunfish, bass, crappy, bream, sole, turbot, mackerel, cod, horse mackerel, salmon, carp, minnow, porgy, eel, bullhead, hogfish, blenny, blindfish, herring, shad, barracuda, monkfish, bluefish, shark, tilefish, swordfish, goldfish, gar, bowfin, flatfish, devilfish, dogfish, goby, flying fish, blackfish, whitefish, tuna, marlin, red snapper, grouper, mahi-mahi, roughy, grampus, pompano, haddock, hake, halibut, mullet, loach, muskellunge, bluefish, sardine, anchovy, smelt; see also **bass, clam, lobster, oyster, shrimp, trout, turtle, whale** 1.

**drink like a fish*** — *Syn.* drink heavily, imbibe, get drunk; see **drink** 2.

**like a fish out of water*** — *Syn.* out of place, out of one's element, alien, displaced; see **improper** 1, **unfamiliar** 2.

**neither fish, flesh, nor fowl** — *Syn.* unrecognizable, indefinite, unknown, amorphous; see **uncertain** 2, **vague** 2.

**fish,** *v.* — *Syn.* go fishing, angle, troll, seine, net, trawl, fly-cast, bob, shrimp, clam, cast one's hook, bait the hook, whale, cast one's net, bait up*.

**fisherman,** *n.* — *Syn.* angler, fisher, fly fisherman, Waltonian, piscator, harpooner, sailor, seaman, trawler, caster, whaler, seiner, drift netter.

**fishery,** *n.* — *Syn.* fish hatchery, spawning place, fishing banks, fishtrap, weir, fish cannery, aquarium, tank, piscary, processing plant.

**fish for,** *v.* — *Syn.* hint at, elicit, try to evoke; see **angle for.**

**fishing,** *n.* — *Syn.* angling, casting, fly fishing, trawling, seining, netting, spearing, harpooning, the piscatorial sport.

**fishing rod,** *n.* — *Syn.* fishpole, bamboo, casting rod, jointed rod, pole.

**fish market,** *n.* — *Syn.* dock, seafood market, embarcadero, Fisherman's Wharf, fish mart.

**fishy*,** *modif.* — *Syn.* improbable, dubious, implausible, suspect; see **questionable** 1, **suspicious** 2, **unlikely.**

**fission,** *n.* — *Syn.* splitting, cleavage, parting; see **division** 1.

**fissure,** *n.* — *Syn.* gap, cleft, crevice; see **hole** 1.

**fist,** *n.* — *Syn.* clenched hand, clenched fist, hand, clutch, clasp, grasp, grip, hold, vise, mitt*, duke*, paw*.

**fisticuffs,** *n.* — *Syn.* fistfight, boxing, encounter; see **boxing, fight** 1.

**fit,** *modif.* **1.** [Appropriate by nature] — *Syn.* suitable, proper, fitting, appropriate, likely, expedient, apt, adapted, apposite, meet, convenient, timely, opportune, feasible, practicable, wise, advantageous, favorable, preferable, beneficial, desirable, *comme il faut* (French), adequate, conformable, seemly, comely, tasteful, becoming, correspondent, agreeable, seasonable, befitting, due, rightful, equitable, legitimate, decent, decorous, congruous, harmonious, pertinent, concordant, according, accordant, consonant, relevant, in keeping, consistent, congenial, applicable, apropos, compatible, admissible, concurrent, pat, felicitous, to the point, to the purpose, answerable to, agreeable to, suited, right, auspicious, happy, lucky, cut out for*. — *Ant.* UNFIT, unseemly, inappropriate.
**2.** [Appropriate by adaption] — *Syn.* fitted, adapted, suited, well-contrived, calculated, prepared, qualified, competent, matched, ready-made, accommodated, adjusted, tailor-made, worthy, eligible; see also sense 1. — *Ant.* unsuited, ill-contrived, mismatched.
**3.** [In good physical condition] — *Syn.* trim, hale, sound, robust; see **hardy** 2, **healthy** 1, **strong** 1.

---

**SYN.** — **fit,** the broadest term here, means having the qualities or qualifications to meet some condition, circumstance, purpose, or demand *[fit* for a king]; **suitable** is applied to that which accords with the requirements or needs of the occasion or circumstances /shoes *suitable* for hiking/; **proper** implies reference to that which naturally or rightfully belongs to something or suggests a fitness or suitability dictated by good judgment [*proper* respect for one's elders/; **appropriate** implies that something is especially or distinctively fit or suitable /books *appropriate* for young children/; **fitting** is applied to that which accords harmoniously with the character, spirit, or tone of something /a *fitting* end to a fine day/; **apt** is used of that which is exactly suited to the purpose /an *apt* phrase/

---

**fit,** *n.* **1.** [A sudden attack of disease] — *Syn.* attack, seizure, paroxysm, spasm, throes, convulsion, epileptic attack, epilepsy, stroke, apoplectic attack, apoplexy, attack of Saint Vitus' dance *or* chorea, episode, crisis, bout, ictus, spell*, the jumps*, staggers*; see also **illness** 1.
**2.** [A transitory spell of action or feeling] — *Syn.* burst, outburst, outbreak, rush, torrent, spate, tantrum, explosion, eruption, convulsion, paroxysm, spasm, access,

rage, frenzy, fury, caprice, mood, transitory mood, passing humor, huff, miff, snit, period, spurt, seizure, flare-up, spell*, conniption*, conniption fit*, blowup*.

**by fits and starts**— *Syn.* intermittently, episodically, fitfully, unevenly; see **irregularly.**

**have (*or* throw) a fit***— *Syn.* lose one's temper, become angry, get excited, blow one's top*; see **rage** 1, 3.

**fit,** *v.* **1.** [To be suitable in character] — *Syn.* agree, suit, accord, harmonize, apply, belong, conform, fit in, fit right in, be in keeping, be in accord, be consonant, be apposite, parallel, relate, concur, match, tally, correspond, dovetail, be apt, be adapted, befit, respond, have its place, answer the purpose, meet, chime, go, comport with, consist, click*, jibe*. — *Ant.* disagree, OPPOSE, clash.

**2.** [To be suitable in size and shape] — *Syn.* be comfortable, be becoming, suit, become, conform to the body, hang, drape, give support, permit free movement.

**3.** [To make suitable] — *Syn.* arrange, alter, adapt, tailor; see **adjust** 1, 3.

**4.** [To equip] — *Syn.* outfit, furnish, implement, fit out; see **provide** 1.

**fitful,** *modif.* — *Syn.* erratic, intermittent, spasmodic, restless; see **changeable** 1, **irregular** 1, **restless** 1.

**fitfully,** *modif.* — *Syn.* intermittently, erratically, restlessly, off and on; see **irregularly.**

**fitness,** *n.* **1.** [Appropriateness] — *Syn.* suitability, aptness, propriety, expediency, aptitude, convenience, adequacy, seemliness, correspondence, agreeableness, seasonableness, decency, decorum, congruousness, harmony, pertinence, accordance, consonance, relevance, keeping, consistency, congeniality, applicability, compatibility, admissibility, concurrence, patness, rightness, timeliness, auspiciousness, adaptation, qualification, accommodation, assimilation, competence, eligibility. — *Ant.* inappropriateness, unfitness, ineptitude.

**2.** [Health] — *Syn.* physical fitness, robustness, shape, good shape; see **health** 1, 2.

**fit out,** *v.* — *Syn.* supply, equip, outfit; see **provide** 1.

**fitted,** *modif.* **1.** [Appropriate] — *Syn.* suited, proper, adapted; see **fit** 1, 2.

**2.** [Having proper equipment] — *Syn.* furnished, outfitted, implemented; see **equipped.**

**fitting,** *modif.* — *Syn.* suitable, appropriate, apt, due; see **fit** 1.

*See Synonym Study at* FIT.

**fitting,** *n.* — *Syn.* connection, instrument, attachment, part; see **fixture.**

**fix*,** *n.* — *Syn.* predicament, dilemma, jam*; see **difficulty** 1, **predicament.**

*See Synonym Study at* PREDICAMENT.

**fix,** *v.* **1.** [To make firm] — *Syn.* plant, implant, secure, attach; see **fasten** 1.

**2.** [To prepare a meal] — *Syn.* cook, make, heat, get ready; see **cook.**

**3.** [To put in order] — *Syn.* correct, mend, adjust; see **adjust** 3, **repair.**

**4.** [*To prearrange] — *Syn.* precontrive, predesign, preorder, preplan, influence, stack the deck*, frame*, set up*, put up*, rig*, pull wires*; see also **bribe.**

**5.** [*To get even with] — *Syn.* punish, retaliate, pay back, get*; see **revenge.**

**6.** [To decide] — *Syn.* determine, settle, conclude, establish; see **arrange** 2, **decide** 1.

**7.** [To harden] — *Syn.* solidify, set, thicken; see **harden** 2.

**fixation,** *n.* — *Syn.* preoccupation, mania, fetish; see **obsession.**

**fixed,** *modif.* **1.** [Firm] — *Syn.* solid, rigid, immovable, settled; see **established** 1, **firm** 1.

**2.** [Repaired] — *Syn.* mended, in order, in working order; see **repaired.**

**3.** [*Prearranged] — *Syn.* arranged, planned, precontrived, predesigned, preordered, rigged*, packed*, put-up*, set-up*, in the bag*, framed*. — *Ant.* UNEXPECTED, surprising, unplanned.

**fixing,** *n.* — *Syn.* repairing, mending, adjusting, ordering, arranging, adapting, fixing up*; see also **adjustment** 1, **repairing.**

**fixings,** *pl.n.* — *Syn.* components, constituents, accompaniments, trimmings; see **accessories, ingredients.**

**fixity,** *n.* — *Syn.* permanence, persistence, steadiness, endurance; see **stability** 1, 2.

**fixture,** *n.* — *Syn.* attachment, fitting, apparatus, light fixture, electric fixture, gas fixture, plumbing fixture, castings, faucet, bibcock, outlet, switch, connection, plug, tap, head, plumbing, appliance, convenience, accessory, equipment, installation.

**fix up*,** *v.* — *Syn.* fix, mend, refurbish; see **redecorate, repair.**

**fizz,** *n.* **1.** [A hissing sound] — *Syn.* hissing, sputtering, bubbling; see **noise** 1.

**2.** [A drink] — *Syn.* soda, soda water, cocktail, pop; see **drink** 2, 3, **soda.**

**fizz,** *v.* — *Syn.* effervesce, bubble up, hiss, sputter; see **bubble.**

**fizzle*,** *n.* — *Syn.* disappointment, fiasco, defeat; see **failure** 1.

**flabbergast,** *v.* — *Syn.* confound, amaze, astound; see **surprise** 1.

*See Synonym Study at* SURPRISE.

**flabbiness,** *n.* — *Syn.* softness, obesity, roundness; see **fatness.**

**flabby,** *modif.* — *Syn.* flaccid, soft, slack, out of shape*; see **fat** 1, **limp** 1.

**flaccid,** *modif.* — *Syn.* soft, flabby, weak; see **limp** 1.

**flaccidity,** *n.* — *Syn.* limpness, flabbiness, softness; see **fatness.**

**flag,** *n.* **1.** [A symbol, especially of a nation, usually on cloth] — *Syn.* banner, standard, pennant, pennon, streamer, colors, ensign, emblem, bunting, gonfalon, oriflamme, jack, Stars and Stripes, Old Glory, Union Jack, tricolor, Jolly Roger.

**2.** [Iris] — *Syn.* blue flag, fleur-de-lis, sweet flag; see **iris.**

**strike the flag**— *Syn.* surrender, quit, give up; see **yield** 1.

**flag,** *v.* **1.** [To signal] — *Syn.* wave, hail, give a sign to; see **signal.**

**2.** [To lose strength] — *Syn.* languish, dwindle, wane; see **decrease** 1, **weaken** 1.

**flagellate,** *v.* — *Syn.* whip, flog, lash; see **beat** 2.

**flagon,** *n.* — *Syn.* canteen, jug, decanter; see **bottle, flask.**

**flagrant,** *modif.* — *Syn.* glaring, egregious, blatant, notorious; see **obvious** 1, **outrageous.**

*See Synonym Study at* OUTRAGEOUS.

**flagstone,** *n.* — *Syn.* stone, paving stone, flag; see **pavement** 1.

**flail,** *v.* — *Syn.* thrash, beat, swing; see **beat** 2, **swing** 2.

**flair,** *n.* — *Syn.* talent, aptitude, gift; see **ability** 1, 2.

**flak,** *n.* **1.** [Antiaircraft fire] — *Syn.* shells, shrapnel, ack-ack*; see **fire** 1.

**2.** [*Criticism] — *Syn.* censure, opposition, hostility; see **blame** 1, **objection** 2.

**flake,** *n.* — *Syn.* scale, cell, sheet, wafer, peel, skin, slice, chip, sliver, membrane, lamina, layer, sheet, leaf, shaving, pellicle, foil, plate, lamella, drop, section, scab.

**flake,** *v.* — *Syn.* scale, peel, sliver, shed, drop, chip, exfoliate, scab, slice, pare, trim, wear away, desquamate.

**flamboyant,** *modif.* **1.** [Showy] — *Syn.* colorful, ostentatious, florid, flashy; see **extravagant** 1, **ornate** 1.
**2.** [Brilliant in color] — *Syn.* flaming, flashy, resplendent; see **bright** 2.

**flame,** *n.* **1.** [Fire] — *Syn.* blaze, flare, spark, flash, glare, glow, gleam, flicker; see also **fire** 1.
**2.** Sweetheart] — *Syn.* boyfriend, girlfriend, heartthrob, beau; see **lover** 1.

**SYN.** — **flame** generally refers to a single, shimmering, tonguelike emanation of burning gas [the *flame* of a candle]; **blaze** suggests a hot, intensely bright, relatively large and steady fire [a roaring *blaze* in the hearth]; **flicker** suggests an unsteady, fluttering flame, esp. one that is dying out [the last *flicker* of his oil lamp]; **flare** implies a sudden, bright, unsteady light shooting up into darkness [the *flare* of a torch]; **glow** suggests a steady, warm, subdued light without flame or blaze [the *glow* of burning embers]; **glare** implies a steady, unpleasantly bright light [the *glare* of a bare light bulb]

**flame,** *v.* — *Syn.* blaze, oxidize, flare up; see **burn** 1.
**flaming,** *modif.* **1.** [In flames] — *Syn.* blazing, ablaze, fiery; see **burning** 1.
**2.** [Flamelike] — *Syn.* brilliant, scintillating, vivid; see **bright** 1, 2.
**flammable,** *modif.* — *Syn.* inflammable, combustible, ignitable; see **inflammable.**
**flange,** *n.* — *Syn.* rib, spine, collar; see **rim.**
**flank,** *n.* — *Syn.* loin, thigh, haunch, side, quarter, pleuron.
**flannel,** *n.* — *Syn.* woolen cloth, cotton flannel, flannelette; see **cloth.**
**flap,** *n.* — *Syn.* fold, ply, tab, lapel, fly, cover, adjunct, overlap, hanging, pendant, drop, tippet, tail, lobe, lappet, appendage, tag, accessory, apron, skirt, strip, queue, wing, pendulosity.
**flap,** *v.* — *Syn.* flutter, beat, swing; see **wave** 1.
**flapjack,** *n.* — *Syn.* griddlecake, johnnycake, hotcake; see **pancake.**
**flare,** *n.* — *Syn.* glare, brief blaze, flash, beacon; see **beacon, flash** 1.
*See Synonym Study at* FLAME.
**flare,** *v.* **1.** [To flash] — *Syn.* blaze, glow, burn; see **burn** 1, **flash** 1.
**2.** [To spread outward] — *Syn.* widen, spread out, splay; see **swell, widen** 1, 2.
**flare up,** *v.* **1.** [To burst out in anger] — *Syn.* lose one's temper, seethe, flare out, blow up; see **rage** 1.
**2.** [To burst into flame] — *Syn.* flame, blaze, glow; see **burn** 1, **flash** 1.
**3.** [To burst out in violence] — *Syn.* erupt, break out, intensify; see **explode** 1, **rage** 2.
**flash,** *n.* **1.** [Sudden, brief light] — *Syn.* glimmer, sparkle, glitter, glisten, scintillation, gleam, glance, beam, coruscation, blaze, flicker, flare, flame, glare, burst, impulse, vision, imprint, display, dazzle, shimmer, shine, glow, twinkle, twinkling, phosphorescence, reflection, bedazzlement, radiation, ray, luster, spark, streak, pencil, stream, illumination, incandescence.
**2.** [Brief, important news] — *Syn.* bulletin, dispatch, report; see **news** 1, 2.

**SYN.** — **flash** implies a sudden, brief, brilliant light; **glance** refers to a darting light, esp. one that is reflected

from a surface at an angle; **gleam** suggests a steady, narrow ray of light shining through a background of relative darkness; **sparkle** implies a number of brief, bright, intermittent flashes; **glitter** implies the reflection of such bright, intermittent flashes; **glisten** suggests the reflection of a lustrous light, as from a wet surface; **shimmer** refers to a soft, tremulous reflection, as from a slightly disturbed body of water

**flash,** *v.* **1.** [To give forth a light by flashing] — *Syn.* glimmer, sparkle, glitter, glisten, scintillate, gleam, beam, coruscate, blaze, flame, flare, glare, dazzle, shimmer, shine, glow, twinkle, blink, phosphoresce, reflect, bedazzle, radiate, shoot out beams, shed luster, flicker, glance; see also **shine** 1, 2.
**2.** [To move with the speed of a flash] — *Syn.* speed, flit, shoot, fly; see **run** 2, **speed.**
**flash in the pan,** *n.* — *Syn.* fiasco, disappointment, dud★, nine days' wonder★; see **fad, failure** 1, 2.
**flashlight,** *n.* — *Syn.* pocket flash, electric lantern, electric lamp, flash lamp, spotlight, torch.
**flashy,** *modif.* — *Syn.* gaudy, showy, ostentatious; see **ornate** 1.
**flask,** *n.* — *Syn.* bottle, decanter, flagon, demijohn, container, jar, jug, crystal, glass, ewer, cruse, carafe, crock, canteen, leather bottle, bota bag, flasket, noggin, vial, phial, cruet, caster, gourd, urn, chalice, tumbler, goblet, beaker, horn, alembic, retort, fiasco, hip flask, pocket flask.
**flat,** *modif.* **1.** [Lying in a smooth plane] — *Syn.* level, even, smooth, plane, spread out, extended, stretched out, prostrate, horizontal, low, low-lying, on a level, fallen, flattened, collapsed, deflated, punctured, prone, supine, recumbent, lying down, reclining, two-dimensional, flat as a billiard table★, flat as a pancake★; see also **level** 2, **smooth** 1. — *Ant.* ROUGH, raised, uneven.
**2.** [Lacking savor] — *Syn.* unseasoned, insipid, flavorless; see **dull** 4, **tasteless** 1.
*See Synonym Study at* INSIPID, LEVEL.
**flatboat,** *n.* — *Syn.* barge, ferry, clam boat; see **boat.**
**flat-footed,** *modif.* **1.** [Standing solidly] — *Syn.* uncompromising, forthright, unwavering, firm; see **resolute** 2.
**2.** [★Awkward] — *Syn.* clumsy, maladroit, plodding, tedious; see **awkward** 1, **dull** 4.
**catch flat-footed★** — *Syn.* take by surprise, catch off-guard, catch in the act; see **surprise** 2.
**flatiron,** *n.* — *Syn.* iron, sadiron, electric iron; see **iron** 3.
**flatten,** *v.* — *Syn.* level, level off, level out, even out, even, smooth, smooth out, spread out, depress, squash, smash, crush, raze, bulldoze, steamroller, debase, prostrate, knock down, wear down, beat down, fell, floor, ground, abrade, roll out, straighten, grade, plane, deflate, plaster down; see also **fell.** — *Ant.* RAISE, elevate, inflate.
**flattened,** *modif.* — *Syn.* leveled, depressed, planed, smoothed; see **flat** 1.
**flatter,** *v.* **1.** [To praise unduly] — *Syn.* overpraise, adulate, laud, glorify; see **compliment** 1, **praise** 1.
**2.** [To fawn upon] — *Syn.* kowtow to, toady to, butter up★; see **compliment** 1, **grovel.**
**3.** [To be becoming to a wearer] — *Syn.* become, enhance, suit, beautify, grace, embellish, enrich, adorn, go with; see also **become** 2.
**flattered,** *modif.* — *Syn.* praised, lauded, complimented, exalted, deceived, lulled, soothed.
**flatterer,** *n.* — *Syn.* toady, truckler, courtier, brown-noser★; see **sycophant.**

**flattering,** *modif.* — *Syn.* laudatory, favorable, unduly favorable; see **complimentary**.

**flattery,** *n.* — *Syn.* adulation, blandishment, compliments, flattering remarks, gallantry, honeyed words, unctuousness, sycophancy, praise, fulsome praise, excessive compliment, plaudits, applause, eulogy, accolade, insincere commendation, false praise, commendation, tribute, encomium, puffery, cajolery, palaver, gratification, pretty speeches, soft words, fawning, toadying, wheedling, sweet talk, blarney, applesauce★, apple polishing★, banana oil★, soft soap★, eyewash★, hokum★, oil★, lip salve★, stroking★, strokes★, brown-nosing★, bootlicking★, ego massage★. — *Ant.* CRITICISM, censure, derision.

**flatulence,** *n.* — *Syn.* pomposity, bombast, empty talk, boasting, twaddle, babble, idle words, mere words, fustian, claptrap, turgidity, windiness, hot air★.

**flatulent,** *modif.* — *Syn.* pretentious, bombastic, pompous; see **bombastic, oratorical**.

**flaunt,** *v.* — *Syn.* vaunt, display, parade, show off; see **boast** 1.
*See Synonym Study at* SHOW.

**flaunting,** *modif.* — *Syn.* gaudy, ostentatious, pretentious; see **ornate** 1.

**flavor,** *n.* **1.** [That which pleases the palate] — *Syn.* taste, savor, tang, relish, smack, sapidity, gusto, piquancy, flavoring, aftertaste, zest, wallop★, zing★.
Descriptive terms for flavors include: tartness, sweetness, acidity, saltiness, spiciness, pungency, piquancy, astringency, bitterness, sourness, pepperiness, hotness, gaminess, greasiness, fishy taste.
**2.** [Essential nature] — *Syn.* character, quality, feeling; see **character** 1, **characteristic, essence** 1.

**flavor,** *v.* — *Syn.* season, spice, salt, pepper, spice up, give a tang to, accent, bring out a flavor in, put in flavoring, imbue, lace, pep up★, give a zing to★.

**flavorful,** *modif.* — *Syn.* tasty, savory, flavorsome; see **delicious** 1.

**flavoring,** *n.* — *Syn.* essence, extract, seasoning, spice, herb, flavor, distillation, quintessence, additive, condiment, sauce, dressing, relish, marinade, pepper-upper★.
Commonly used flavorings include: vanilla, lemon, lime, chocolate, butterscotch, peppermint, anise, ginger, clove, cinnamon, almond, pistachio, nutmeg, raspberry, strawberry, banana, licorice, caramel, burnt sugar, cherry, orange, peach, sarsaparilla, coconut, rum.
Common herbs and spices used as flavorings include: salt, pepper, onion, garlic, clove, pimento, turmeric, purslane, parsley, celery, marjoram, rosemary, basil, tarragon, oregano, dill, bay leaf, chili powder, saffron, thyme, cumin, cilantro, sage, summer savory, saffron, rose; see also **herb, relish** 1, **spice**.

**flavorless,** *modif.* — *Syn.* insipid, flat, bland, vapid; see **tasteless** 1.

**flaw,** *n.* — *Syn.* defect, imperfection, blemish, stain; see **blemish, defect** 2.
*See Synonym Study at* DEFECT.

**flawless,** *modif.* — *Syn.* faultless, sound, impeccable; see **perfect** 2.

**flaxen,** *modif.* — *Syn.* straw-colored, golden, yellowish; see **blond, yellow** 1.

**flay,** *v.* **1.** [To remove skin, bark, hide, etc.] — *Syn.* peel, scalp, excoriate; see **skin**.
**2.** [To criticize] — *Syn.* reprove, castigate, rebuke; see **censure**.

**flea,** *n.* — *Syn.* hopper, skipper, jumper, dog flea, sand flea, leaper, flea louse, fleahopper, flea beetle, chigoe; see also **insect**.

**fleck,** *n.* **1.** [A tiny bit] — *Syn.* mite, speck, particle; see **bit** 1.
**2.** [A spot] — *Syn.* streak, patch, speckle; see **dot**.

**flecked,** *modif.* — *Syn.* streaked, spotted, mottled; see **multicolored**.

**flee,** *v.* — *Syn.* run away, escape, decamp, bolt; see **escape, leave** 1, **retreat** 2.

**fleece,** *n.* — *Syn.* wool, fell, hide, pelt; see **coat** 2, **fur, wool** 1.

**fleecy,** *modif.* — *Syn.* fuzzy, fluffy, woolly; see **downy**.

**fleer,** *v.* — *Syn.* deride, mock, scoff; see **ridicule, sneer**.

**fleet,** *modif.* — *Syn.* swift, rapid, speedy; see **fast** 1.
*See Synonym Study at* FAST.

**fleet,** *n.* — *Syn.* armada, flotilla, naval force, argosy, invasion force, task force, squadron, formation, line; see also **navy**.

**fleeting,** *modif.* — *Syn.* transient, transitory, brief, ephemeral, evanescent, short, flitting, flying, fugitive, passing, swift, meteoric, sudden, cursory, short-lived, fading, temporary, vanishing, momentary; see also **temporary**. — *Ant.* enduring, CONSTANT, lasting.
*See Synonym Study at* TRANSIENT.

**fleetness,** *n.* — *Syn.* quickness, velocity, rapidity; see **speed**.

**flesh,** *modif.* — *Syn.* flesh-colored, beige, cream, creamy; see **tan**.

**flesh,** *n.* **1.** [Soft parts of an animal] — *Syn.* meat, fat, muscle, brawn, tissue, cells, flesh and blood, protoplasm, plasm, body, corporeality, physicality.
**2.** [Soft parts of a fruit, root, or the like] — *Syn.* meat, tissue, cortex, edible portion, pulp, bulb, heart, insides★.

**one's (own) flesh and blood** — *Syn.* family, kindred, kin, relatives; see **family** 1.

**fleshiness,** *n.* — *Syn.* corpulence, obesity, plumpness; see **fatness**.

**fleshly,** *modif.* **1.** [Pertaining to the body] — *Syn.* human, corporeal, physical, mundane; see **bodily** 1.
**2.** [Sensual] — *Syn.* carnal, erotic, sensuous, lascivious; see **lewd** 2, **sensual** 2.
*See Synonym Study at* SENSUAL.

**fleshy,** *modif.* — *Syn.* plump, corpulent, chubby, beefy; see **fat** 1.

**flexibility,** *n.* **1.** [Pliability] — *Syn.* pliancy, plasticity, flexibleness, pliableness, suppleness, elasticity, flaccidity, extensibility, limberness, litheness.
**2.** [Tractability] — *Syn.* compliance, affability, complaisance, versatility; see **adaptability, docility**.

**flexible,** *modif.* **1.** [Pliant] — *Syn.* limber, lithe, supple, willowy, plastic, elastic, bending, springy, malleable, ductile, pliable, soft, extensile, extensible, spongy, tractable, moldable, yielding, tractile, flexile, formable, bendable, impressionable, like putty, like wax, adaptable, adjustable, modifiable, stretchable, stretchy, resilient, rubbery, loose-limbed, double-jointed. — *Ant.* STIFF, hard, rigid.
**2.** [Tractable] — *Syn.* compliant, manageable, amenable; see **docile**.

---

**SYN.** — **flexible** refers to anything that can be bent without breaking, whether or not it returns to its original form [a *flexible* wire]; **elastic** implies ability to return without permanent injury to the original size or shape after being stretched, expanded, etc. [an *elastic* garter]; **resilient** implies ability to spring back into shape after being deformed, esp. by compression [*resilient* skin], and in figurative use suggests an ease in returning to good health or spirits [a *resilient* attitude towards life]; **sup-**

**ple** is applied to that which is easily bent, twisted, or folded without breaking, cracking, etc. /kidskin is *supple*/

---

**flicker,** *n.* — *Syn.* twinkle, glimmer, gleam, glint; see **flash** 1.
*See Synonym Study at* FLAME.

**flicker,** *v.* **1.** [To shine] — *Syn.* sparkle, twinkle, glitter; see **flash** 1, **shine** 1.
**2.** [To quiver] — *Syn.* flutter, waver, vibrate; see **wave** 1, 3.

**flier,** *n.* **1.** [One who flies] — *Syn.* aviator, navigator, airman; see **pilot** 1.
**2.** [\*A venture, especially in stocks] — *Syn.* gamble, speculation, investment, plunge\*; see **bet, venture.**
**3.** [A handbill] — *Syn.* circular, leaflet, notice; see **advertisement** 2, **announcement** 3, **folder** 1.

**flight,** *n.* **1.** [Act of remaining aloft] — *Syn.* flying, soaring, winging, gliding, volitation, hovering, cruising.
**2.** [Travel by air] — *Syn.* aviation, aerial navigation, aeronautics, flying, space flight, air transport, stratospheric travel, space probe, ballooning, hang gliding, sailplaning, trip by air, hop\*, hedgehopping\*.
**3.** [Flight conceived figuratively] — *Syn.* effort, inspiration, sublime conception; see **fancy** 2, **imagination** 1.
**4.** [Act of fleeing] — *Syn.* fleeing, running away, retreating; see **escape** 1, **retreat** 1.
**5.** [Stairs] — *Syn.* steps, staircase, ascent; see **stairs.**
**put to flight** — *Syn.* chase away, rout, scatter, scare off; see **defeat** 1, 2, **rout.**
**take (to) flight** — *Syn.* flee, run away, fly, decamp; see **escape, leave** 1, **retreat** 1.

**flightiness,** *n.* — *Syn.* giddiness, fickleness, inconstancy, changeability, volatility, mercurialness, frivolity, levity, capriciousness, whimsicality, eccentricity, variability, irresponsibility, instability, lightheadedness, dizziness\*.

**flighty,** *modif.* — *Syn.* capricious, fickle, giddy; see **changeable** 1, **irresponsible, silly.**

**flimflam,** *n.* **1.** [Nonsense] — *Syn.* trifling, drivel, foolishness; see **nonsense** 1.
**2.** [Deception] — *Syn.* trickery, deception, craft; see **deception** 1, **trick** 1.

**flimsy,** *modif.* **1.** [Said of physical things] — *Syn.* slight, frail, weak, gauzy, sleazy, sheer, shoddy, unsubstantial, defective, shaky, wobbly, rickety, fragile, wispy, makeshift, decrepit, infirm; see also **poor** 2. — *Ant.* sturdy, heavy, strong.
**2.** [Said of arguments, reasons, and the like] — *Syn.* feeble, weak, inadequate, unconvincing, lame, trifling, inept, superficial, inane, implausible, ill-conceived, puerile, fallacious, false, assailable, controvertible, contemptible, wishful; see also sense 1, **illogical.** — *Ant.* cogent, LOGICAL, unanswerable.

**flinch,** *v.* — *Syn.* start, shrink back, blench, recoil; see **wince.**

**fling,** *n.* — *Syn.* indulgence, party, binge, spree; see **celebration** 2.

**fling,** *v.* — *Syn.* toss, sling, throw, dump; see **throw** 1.
*See Synonym Study at* THROW.

**flint,** *n.* — *Syn.* quartz, adamant, silica; see **mineral, rock** 1, **stone.**

**flinty,** *modif.* — *Syn.* hard, unmerciful, obdurate; see **callous, cruel** 2.

**flippancy,** *n.* — *Syn.* impertinence, impudence, sauciness, levity; see **frivolity, rudeness.**

**flippant,** *modif.* — *Syn.* impudent, saucy, smart; see **facetious, rude** 2.

**flirt,** *n.* — *Syn.* coquette, tease, heartbreaker, siren, trifler, philanderer, inconstant, seducer, seductress, temptress, vamp, vixen, wanton, flibbertigibbet\*, gold digger\*, wolf\*, masher\*, lady-killer\*.

**flirt,** *v.* **1.** [To pay amorous attentions to] — *Syn.* coquet, ogle, wink at, play with, toy with, sport with, trifle with, dally with, banter with, make advances, philander, tease, display one's charms, make eyes at, look sweetly upon, cast sheep's eyes at\*, give a come-hither look\*, make goo-goo eyes at\*, come on to\*, make a play for\*, lead on\*.
**2.** [To play with] — *Syn.* toy with, expose oneself carelessly to, monkey with\*; see **trifle** 1.
*See Synonym Study at* TRIFLE.

**flirtation,** *n.* — *Syn.* dalliance, coquetry, courting; see **flirting.**

**flirtatious,** *modif.* — *Syn.* flirty, coquettish, seductive, provocative, coy, teasing, philandering, dallying, amorous, wolfish, libidinous, nymphomaniac, wanton, come-hither\*.

**flirting,** *n.* — *Syn.* coquetry, flirtation, trifling, dalliance, amorous pursuit, toying, banter, sport, ogling, seduction, wooing, blandishment, beguilement, philandering, wantonness, come-on\*.

**flit,** *v.* — *Syn.* flutter, flash, dart; see **dance** 2, **fly** 1, **race** 1.

**flitting,** *modif.* — *Syn.* transitory, ephemeral, evanescent; see **fleeting, temporary.**

**float,** *n.* **1.** [A watertight vessel used for buoyancy] — *Syn.* buoy, air cell, air cushion, lifesaver, pontoon, outrigger, cell, bobber, cork, quill, raft, diving platform, life preserver.
**2.** [A vehicle used for display] — *Syn.* exhibit, display, entry, car, chariot, platform.

**float,** *v.* — *Syn.* waft, stay afloat, bob, hover; see **drift, glide** 2, **swim.**

**floating,** *modif.* — *Syn.* buoyant, hollow, unsinkable, nonsubmersible, lighter-than-water, light, swimming, inflated, sailing, soaring, wafting, volatile, loose, free, unsubstantial, hovering, unattached, vagrant. — *Ant.* HEAVY, submerged, SUNK.

**flocculent,** *modif.* — *Syn.* hairy, woolly, fluffy; see **downy, woolly.**

**flock,** *n.* **1.** [Herd] — *Syn.* drove, pack, flight; see **herd** 1.
**2.** [Gathering] — *Syn.* assembly, throng, congregation; see **crowd** 1, **gathering.**

**flock,** *v.* — *Syn.* throng, congregate, crowd; see **gather** 1.

**floe,** *n.* — *Syn.* berg, ice floe, icefield; see **iceberg.**

**flog,** *v.* — *Syn.* beat, thrash, whip, lash; see **beat** 2.
*See Synonym Study at* BEAT.

**flogging,** *n.* — *Syn.* lashing, beating, whipping, thrashing, caning, corporal punishment, giving lashes, horsewhipping, flagellation, flailing, stripes, using the cat o' nine tails; see also **punishment.**

**flood,** *n.* **1.** [A great flow of water] — *Syn.* deluge, surge, tide, high tide, freshet, overflow, torrent, flash flood, inundation, alluvion, wave, bore, flood tide, eagre, tidal flood, tidal flow.
**2.** [An overwhelming quantity] — *Syn.* outpouring, spate, abundance, superabundance; see sense 1, **plenty.**

**flood,** *v.* — *Syn.* inundate, swamp, overflow, deluge, submerge, drown, engulf, immerse, brim over, rush upon, overwhelm.

**floodgate,** *n.* — *Syn.* sluice gate, sluice, spout, conduit; see **gate.**

**floor,** *n.* **1.** [The lower limit of a room] — *Syn.* floorboards, deck, flagstones, tiles, planking, parterre, ground, carpet, rug, linoleum, subfloor, platform.
**2.** [The space in a building between two floors] — *Syn.* story, stage, landing, level, flat, basement, cellar, ground

floor, lower story, first floor, mezzanine, upper story, downstairs, upstairs, loft, attic, garret, penthouse.

**floor,** *v.* **1.** [To knock down] — *Syn.* fell, bring down, bowl over; see **fell.**

**2.** [*To confound] — *Syn.* flabbergast, astound, dumbfound, nonplus; see **confuse, surprise** 1.

**flooring,** *n.* — *Syn.* floor covering, floors, woodwork, oak flooring, hardwood flooring, parquet, tile, tiling, flagstones, boards, earthen floor, cement, carpeting, rug, linoleum, inlaid linoleum, planks, mosaic, tesselation, terrazzo; see also **carpet, tile.**

**flop,** *v.* **1.** [To move with little control] — *Syn.* wobble, teeter, totter, tumble, flounder, flap, wave, flutter, shake, bounce, turn topsy-turvy, flip-flop.

**2.** [To fall without restraint] — *Syn.* slump, drop, plump down, plop; see **fall** 1.

**3.** [To be limp] — *Syn.* flap, droop, dangle; see **hang** 2.

**4.** [*To be a complete failure] — *Syn.* miscarry, founder, fall flat, bomb*; see **fail** 1.

**flora,** *n.* — *Syn.* vegetable life, verdure, plants; see **vegetation.**

**floral,** *modif.* — *Syn.* flowery, flowering, flowered, botanical, horticultural, garden, sylvan, blossoming, herbaceous, blooming, efflorescent, verdant, decorative, floriated.

**florescence,** *n.* — *Syn.* flowering, blossoming, flourishing, prosperity; see **development** 2, **success** 1, 2.

**floriculture,** *n.* — *Syn.* horticulture, arboriculture, cultivation; see **gardening.**

**florid,** *modif.* — *Syn.* ornate, flowery, flamboyant, grandiloquent; see **bombastic, flowery, ornate** 1.

**florist,** *n.* — *Syn.* floriculturist, flower dealer, professional gardener, nurseryman.

**flotsam,** *n.* — *Syn.* debris, floating wreckage, refuse, flotsam and jetsam; see **trash** 1, **wreckage.**

**flounce,** *n.* — *Syn.* frill, ruffle, furbelow, trimming; see **decoration** 2, **fringe** 2.

**flounce,** *v.* — *Syn.* fling, jerk, toss, twist, bounce, flop, prance, storm, march, sashay.

**flounder,** *v.* — *Syn.* struggle, wallow, blunder, fumble; see **hesitate, toss** 2.

**flour,** *n.* — *Syn.* meal, pulp, powder, grit, bran, farina, breadstuff, gluten, starch, bleached flour, unbleached flour, wheat germ, semolina, patent flour, middlings, shorts, white flour, wheat flour, whole wheat flour, rye flour, graham flour, buckwheat flour, potato flour, barley meal, cornmeal, oatmeal, rolled oats, cake flour, pancake flour, soybean flour, soy flour.

**flourish,** *n.* — *Syn.* embellishment, fanfare, wave; see **decoration** 2, **ostentation** 1, 2.

**flourish,** *v.* **1.** [To wave triumphantly] — *Syn.* brandish, twirl, shake, flaunt, gesture, wave, swing, wield.

**2.** [To prosper] — *Syn.* thrive, increase, wax; see **grow** 1, **prosper.**

**flourishing,** *modif.* — *Syn.* thriving, prosperous, booming, luxuriant; see **growing, rich** 1, **successful.**

**flout,** *v.* — *Syn.* mock, scoff at, spurn; see **ridicule, scorn** 2, **sneer.**

**flow,** *n.* — *Syn.* current, movement, progress, stream, tide, run, river, flood, ebb, gush, spurt, surge, spout, leakage, dribble, oozing, flux, outpouring, overflow, emanation, issue, discharge, effusion, outflow, drift, course, draft, downdraft, up-current, draw, wind, breeze, indraft, slipstream, race.

**flow,** *v.* **1.** [To move in one direction] — *Syn.* stream, course, slide, slip, glide, move, progress, proceed, run, pass, float, sweep, rush, whirl, surge, roll, tumble, march, continue, swell, ebb.

**2.** [To issue forth] — *Syn.* pour out, spurt, squirt, flood, jet, spout, rush, gush, emerge, spring, well out, drop, drip, seep, emanate, trickle, overflow, spill, run, sputter, spew, stream, brim, cascade, teem, swell, gurgle, surge, leak, exudate, run out, ooze, regurgitate, splash, distill, dribble, percolate, exude, pour forth, bubble.

**3.** [To keep up a circular motion] — *Syn.* swirl, eddy, ripple, circle, circulate, percolate, whirl, purl, slosh.

*See Synonym Study at* ARISE.

**flower,** *n.* **1.** [A bloom] — *Syn.* blossom, bud, floret, posy, pompon, efflorescence, spike, spray, cluster, head, panicle, raceme, floweret, shoot, inflorescence, cone, petals.

**2.** [A plant valued for its bloom] — *Syn.* flowering plant, wildflower, herb, vine, annual, perennial, biennial, flowering shrub, potted plant, houseplant, bulb.

Common flowers include: daisy, violet, African violet, cowslip, jack-in-the-pulpit, goldenrod, orchid, primrose, bluebell, salvia, geranium, begonia, pansy, calendula, forsythia, daffodil, jonquil, crocus, dahlia, cosmos, zinnia, tulip, iris, lily, petunia, gladiolus, aster, carnation, baby's breath, gardenia, narcissus, rose, peony, nasturtium, cyclamen, chrysanthemum, four-o'clock, sunflower, snapdragon, hibiscus, periwinkle, gaillardia, poppy, morning-glory, lily-of-the-valley, clematis, buttercup, bougainvillea, dandelion, fuchsia, lilac, stock, sweet William, marigold, yarrow, Queen Anne's lace, bachelor's button, bleeding heart, phlox, poinsettia; see also **fruit** 1.

**flower,** *v.* — *Syn.* open, blossom, blow; see **bloom.**

**flowerpot,** *n.* — *Syn.* jardiniere, vase, stand, plant stand, window box, tub, pot, vessel, receptacle.

**flowery,** *modif.* — *Syn.* florid, ornate, elaborate, ornamented, fancy, fussy, rhetorical, overblown, euphuistic, affected, artificial, precious, purple*; see also **bombastic, elegant** 3, **ornate** 1.

*See Synonym Study at* BOMBASTIC.

**flowing,** *modif.* — *Syn.* sweeping, sinuous, spouting, running, streaming, gushing, pouring out, issuing, circulating, rippling, smooth, fluent, easy, fluid, tidal, liquid.

**fluctuate,** *v.* **1.** [To be continually changing] — *Syn.* vacillate, waver, shift, vary; see **alternate** 2, **hesitate.**

**2.** [To oscillate] — *Syn.* undulate, vibrate, flutter; see **swing** 1, **wave** 3.

*See Synonym Study at* SWING.

**fluctuation,** *n.* — *Syn.* vacillation, variation, inconstancy; see **change** 1.

**flue,** *n.* — *Syn.* pipe, vent, exhaust; see **chimney.**

**fluency,** *n.* — *Syn.* facility, volubility, ease of expression; see **eloquence** 1.

**fluent,** *modif.* **1.** [Flowing] — *Syn.* fluid, easy, graceful; see **flowing.**

**2.** [Capable of speaking easily] — *Syn.* eloquent, articulate, voluble, loquacious, glib, facile, wordy, smooth, copious, talkative, mellifluent, mellifluous, able to speak readily, smooth-spoken, well-spoken, ready in speech, garrulous, effusive, declamatory, verbose, chatty, disputatious, argumentative, vocal, clamorous, cogent, persuasive, silver-tongued, honeyed, blarneying*, blabbery*, having the gift of gab*, fast-talking*. — *Ant.* inarticulate, tongue-tied, stammering.

**fluff,** *n.* — *Syn.* down, fuzz, lint; see **dust, fur.**

**fluffy,** *modif.* — *Syn.* fleecy, fuzzy, feathery; see **downy.**

**fluid,** *modif.* **1.** [Capable of flowing] — *Syn.* liquid, fluent, flowing, running, aqueous, watery, molten, liquefied, juicy, serous, lymphatic, uncongealed, in solution. — *Ant.* STIFF, solid, frozen.

**2.** [Not settled or fixed] — *Syn.* shifting, changeable, mutable; see **changeable** 2.

**fluid,** *n.* — *Syn.* liquor, vapor, solution; see **liquid.**

**flunk*,** *v.* — *Syn.* fail, miss, drop out, have to repeat; see **fail** 1.

**flush,** *modif.* **1.** [Flat] — *Syn.* even, level, abutting; see **contiguous, flat** 1, **level** 2.
**2.** [Well-supplied, esp. with money] — *Syn.* prosperous, affluent, in the chips*; see **plentiful** 1, **rich** 1.

**flush,** *n.* — *Syn.* blush, glow, reddening, redness, rosiness, bloom, rubescence, warmth, heat, feverishness, radiance.

**flush,** *v.* **1.** [To clean with a sudden flow of water] — *Syn.* rinse, rinse out, wash, wash out, sluice, irrigate, flood, spray, douse, empty out; see also **clean, wash** 1.
**2.** [To redden] — *Syn.* blush, color, crimson; see **blush.**

**fluster,** *v.* — *Syn.* discompose, rattle, agitate; see **confuse, disturb** 2, **embarrass** 1.

**flute,** *n.* — *Syn.* pipe, piccolo, whistle, woodwind, wind instrument, fife, tube, panpipe, recorder, fipple flute, *Blockflöte* (German), flageolet, transverse flute, direct flute, *flûte-à-bec* (French), German flute; see also **musical instrument.**

**flutter,** *v.* — *Syn.* flap, ripple, tremble; see **shake** 1, **wave** 1, 3.

**fly,** *n.* **1.** [An insect] — *Syn.* housefly, bluebottle, bug, winged insect, gnat, horsefly, fruit fly, tsetse fly.
**2.** [A ball batted into the air] — *Syn.* fly ball, infield fly, high fly, pop fly, sacrifice fly, Texas Leaguer, fungo, aerial*, boost*, hoist*, pop-up*.
**3.** [A hook baited artificially] — *Syn.* lure, weed, fish lure, dry fly, wet fly, spinner, trout fly, bass fly, minnow.

**fly,** *v.* **1.** [To pass through the air] — *Syn.* wing, soar, float, glide, remain aloft, take to the air, take flight, fly aloft, float in the air, take wing, hover, sail, swoop, dart, flit, plummet, drift, flutter, flap, circle.
**2.** [To move swiftly] — *Syn.* rush, dart, tear; see **race** 1, **speed.**
**3.** [To flee from danger] — *Syn.* retreat, run away, take flight; see **escape, retreat** 2.
**4.** [To manage a plane in the air] — *Syn.* pilot, navigate, control, aviate, jet, take off, become airborne, operate, glide, cruise, climb, dive, manipulate, maneuver, zoom.
**5.** [To pass over by flying] — *Syn.* cross, circumnavigate, shuttle, hop*; see **travel** 2.

**fly at,** *v.* — *Syn.* assail, assault, rush at; see **attack** 1, 2.

**fly-by-night,** *modif.* — *Syn.* undependable, untrustworthy, transient, shaky; see **temporary, unreliable** 1.

**flying,** *modif.* — *Syn.* soaring, floating, airborne, in flight, gliding, winging, swooping, darting, flitting, plummeting, zooming, cruising, drifting, fluttering, hovering, blowing, on the wing, volant, volitant, winged, avian, rising, fleeting, swift, jet-propelled, in mid-air, airminded, Icarian. — *Ant.* earthbound, sinking, crawling.

**flyleaf,** *n.* — *Syn.* endpaper, blank page, title page, end sheet, frontispiece.

**foal,** *n.* — *Syn.* filly, colt, young horse; see **colt, horse** 1.

**foam,** *n.* — *Syn.* bubbles, lather, spume; see **froth.**

**foamy,** *modif.* — *Syn.* bubbly, creamy, lathery; see **frothy** 1.

**focus,** *n.* — *Syn.* focal point, locus, point of convergence, center of attention; see **center** 1.
**in focus** — *Syn.* distinct, clear, sharply defined; see **definite** 2.
**out of focus** — *Syn.* indistinct, unclear, blurred; see **obscure** 1.

**focus,** *v.* **1.** [To draw toward a center] — *Syn.* converge, direct, fix on, zero in on; see **center, concentrate** 1, 2.
**2.** [To make an image clear] — *Syn.* adjust, bring into focus, bring out, get detail; see **sharpen** 2.

**fodder,** *n.* — *Syn.* food, hay, grain; see **feed.**

**foe,** *n.* — *Syn.* enemy, opponent, antagonist, adversary; see **enemy** 1, 2.
*See Synonym Study at* OPPONENT.

**fog,** *n.* **1.** [Vapor near the earth] — *Syn.* mist, haze, smog, exhalation, murk, cloud, nebula, film, steam, wisp, effluvium, brume, smoke, vapor, London fog, soup*, pea soup*; see also **haze, mist.**
**2.** [Mental obscurity] — *Syn.* stupor, daze, befuddlement; see **confusion** 2.
*See Synonym Study at* MIST.

**foggy,** *modif.* — *Syn.* misty, murky, gray; see **hazy** 1.

**foible,** *n.* — *Syn.* weakness, failing, quirk, oddity; see **characteristic, defect** 2.
*See Synonym Study at* FAULT.

**foil,** *n.* **1.** [Leaf metal] — *Syn.* aluminum foil, lead foil, gold foil, tin foil, film, flake, leaf, sheet.
**2.** [A person or thing that sets off another] — *Syn.* complement, antithesis, counterpart; see **contrast** 2, **opposite.**

**foil,** *v.* — *Syn.* thwart, frustrate, impede; see **defeat** 1, **hinder, prevent.**
*See Synonym Study at* FRUSTRATE.

**fold,** *n.* **1.** [Folded material] — *Syn.* lap, pleat, plait, lapel, tuck, overlap, folded portion, part turned over, part turned back, shirring, smocking, gathers, gatherings, doubled material.
**2.** [The line at which material is folded] — *Syn.* crease, turn, folded edge, crimp, wrinkle, knife-edge, pleat, plait, corrugation.
**3.** [Animal pen] — *Syn.* cage, corral, coop; see **enclosure** 1.

**fold,** *v.* **1.** [To enclose] — *Syn.* envelop, wrap up, do up; see **wrap** 1, 2.
**2.** [To place or lay in folds] — *Syn.* double, pleat, plait, crease, curl, crimp, wrinkle, crinkle, crumple, laminate, ruffle, corrugate, pucker, gather, double over, telescope, lap, overlap, dogear. — *Ant.* UNFOLD, straighten, expand.
**3.** [*To fail] — *Syn.* go out of business, close, collapse; see **fail** 4, **give** 4.

**folder,** *n.* **1.** [A folded sheet of printed matter] — *Syn.* circular, pamphlet, paper, circular letter, broadsheet, broadside, bulletin, advertisement, enclosure, stuffer, brochure, throwaway*.
**2.** [A light, flexible case] — *Syn.* envelope, binder, portfolio, wrapper, wrapping, sheath, pocket, manila folder.

**folk,** *n.* **1.** [A people] — *Syn.* nation, race, community, tribe, society, body politic, nationality, population, state, group, settlement, culture group, ethnic group, clan, confederation.
**2.** [The common people] — *Syn.* populace, the masses, proletariat; see **people** 3.

**folklore,** *n.* — *Syn.* traditions, lore, folk tales, oral tradition, folk wisdom, oral literature, ballad lore, customs, superstitions, legends, fables, folkways, folk wisdom, traditional lore; see also **myth.**

**folks*,** *n.* — *Syn.* relatives, parents, relations, kin; see **family** 1.

**follow,** *v.* **1.** [To come after] — *Syn.* succeed, come next, ensue, replace, supplant, postdate, go behind, bring up the rear, tailgate, tag along*; see also **succeed** 2.
**2.** [To regulate one's action] — *Syn.* conform, observe, imitate, copy, take after, match, follow in the footsteps of, walk in the shoes of, mirror, reflect, follow the example of, do as, mimic, hold fast, follow suit, do like*, emulate, obey, abide by, adhere to, heed, string along, comply, be in keeping, harmonize, be consistent with,

attend to, accord; see also **conform.** — *Ant.* disregard, NEGLECT, depart from.

**3.** [To be a follower] — *Syn.* serve, support, attend; see **accompany** 1, **obey** 2.

**4.** [To go in pursuit of] — *Syn.* chase, trail, track, stalk; see **pursue** 1.

**5.** [To observe] — *Syn.* heed, regard, keep an eye on, keep up with; see **watch** 1.

**6.** [To understand] — *Syn.* comprehend, catch, grasp; see **understand** 1.

**7.** [To result] — *Syn.* result, ensue, proceed from, spring from, come from, happen, develop, arise; see also **result.**

---

**SYN.** — **follow** is the general word meaning to come or occur after, but it does not necessarily imply a causal relationship with what goes before /sunshine *followed* by rain/; **ensue** implies that what follows comes as a logical consequence of what preceded /clouds appeared and rain *ensued*/; **succeed** implies that what follows takes the place of what preceded /who *succeeded* Polk to the presidency?/; **result** stresses a definite relationship of cause and effect between what follows and what preceded /crime that *results* from poverty/

---

**follower,** *n.* — *Syn.* adherent, disciple, supporter, fan, partisan, attendant, henchman, hanger-on, companion, vassal, lackey, helper, acolyte, recruit, pupil, protégé, imitator, worshiper, satellite, votary, apostle, proselyte, zealot, backer, participant, sponsor, evangelist, witness, devotee, believer, advocate, member, admirer, aficionado, patron, promoter, true believer, auxiliary, coadjutor, sectary, seconder, upholder, stooge\*, copycat\*, yes man\*, groupie\*. — *Ant.* OPPONENT, deserter, apostate.

---

**SYN.** — **follower** is the general term for one who follows or believes in the teachings or theories of someone /a *follower* of Freud/; **supporter** applies to one who upholds or defends opinions or theories that are disputed or under attack /a *supporter* of technocracy/; **adherent** refers to a close, active follower of some theory, cause, etc. /the *adherents* of a political party/; **disciple** implies a personal, devoted relationship to the teacher of some doctrine or leader of some movement /Plato was a *disciple* of Socrates/; **partisan** refers to an unswerving, often blindly devoted, adherent of some person or cause

---

**following,** *modif.* — *Syn.* succeeding, next, ensuing, subsequent, coming, later, after a while, by and by, later on, a while later, then, henceforth, afterwards, presently, afterward, coming after, directly after, successive, in the wake of, pursuing, in pursuit of, in search of, on the scent, in full cry, resulting, consequent, latter, posterior, rear, hinder, back. — *Ant.* PRECEDING, former, earlier.

**following,** *n.* — *Syn.* coterie, discipleship, clientele, public, audience, retinue, entourage, train, backing, followers, adherents, supporters, admirers, fans, devotees, hangers-on, patrons, dependents, retainers.

**folly,** *n.* — *Syn.* absurdity, foolishness, imprudence, silliness; see **indiscretion** 1, **stupidity** 2, 3.

**foment,** *v.* — *Syn.* incite, instigate, stir up, foster; see **incite, promote** 1.

*See Synonym Study at* INCITE.

**fond,** *modif.* — *Syn.* enamored, attached, affectionate, partial to; see **loving.**

**fondle,** *v.* — *Syn.* caress, stroke, pet; see **caress.**

*See Synonym Study at* CARESS.

**fondness,** *n.* — *Syn.* partiality, attachment, tenderness, liking; see **affection** 1, **inclination** 1.

**food,** *n.* — *Syn.* nourishment, sustenance, victuals, diet, fare, foodstuffs, nutriment, refreshment, edibles, comestibles, viands, provisions, stores, rations, ration, cuisine, cooking, menu, meat and drink, meat, bread, table, subsistence, mess, board, meals, aliment, cookery, haute cuisine, fast food, junk food, health food, soul food, comfort food, larder, pabulum, grub\*, vittles\*, eats\*, chow\*; see also **feed, meal** 2. For food in the menu, see also **bread, butter, cake** 2, **candy, cheese, delicatessen** 1, **dessert, drink** 2, 3, **egg, entree** 2, **fish, flavoring, fowl, fruit** 1, **hors d'oeuvre, jam** 1, **jelly, milk, meat, nut** 1, **oil, pastry, pudding, salad, sauce** 1, 2, **soup, spice, stew, vegetable.**

Food as diet includes: cellulose, carbohydrates, fats, fibers, iron, minerals, oils, protein, proteids, salts, starches, sugars, vitamins.

---

**SYN.** — **food** is the general term for all matter that is taken into the body for nourishment; **fare** refers to the range of foods eaten by a particular organism or available at a particular time and place /the *fare* of horses, a bill of *fare*/; **victuals** is now largely a dialectal or colloquial word for human fare or diet; **provisions** refers to a stock of food assembled in advance /*provisions* for the hike/; **ration** refers to a fixed allowance or allotment of food /the weekly *ration*/ and in the plural (**rations**) to food in general /how are the *rations* in this outfit?/

---

**food for thought,** *n.* — *Syn.* meditations, reflections, point to ponder, something to think about, stimulation, stimulus.

**fool,** *n.* **1.** [A silly or stupid person] — *Syn.* nitwit, simpleton, dunce, ninny, cretin, nincompoop, dolt, idiot, jackass, ass, buffoon, blockhead, numskull, oaf, booby, boob, clod, dunderhead, goose, ignoramus, imbecile, moron, clown, tomfool, wiseacre, donkey, looby, noddy, noodle, innocent, loon, dullard, fathead, halfwit, mooncalf, lightweight, dotard, babbler, driveler, Simple Simon, silly, scatterbrain, bonehead\*, simp\*, dope\*, nerd\*, turkey\*, dumbdumb\*, meathead\*, sap\*, birdbrain\*, lamebrain\*, noodlehead\*, \*airhead\*, bubblehead\*, ditz\*, dumb ox\*, lunkhead\*, knucklehead\*, dimwit\*, dumbbell\*, jerk\*, chump\*, twit\*, dumb bunny\*. — *Ant.* PHILOSOPHER, sage, scholar.

**2.** [One made to seem foolish] — *Syn.* butt, laughingstock, victim, clown, poor fish, schlemiel, dupe, gull, gudgeon, cully, stooge, fair game, goat\*, pigeon\*, sucker\*, patsy\*, fall guy\*, pushover\*, setup\*, mark\*, easy mark\*, chump\*.

**no** or **nobody's fool** — *Syn.* shrewd, calculating, capable; see **able** 1, 2, **intelligent** 1.

**play the fool** — *Syn.* be silly, show off, clown; see **joke.**

**fool,** *v.* — *Syn.* trick, dupe, mislead; see **deceive.**

**fool around,** *v.* — *Syn.* waste time, putter, idle, dawdle; see **dabble, play** 1, 2, **trifle** 1.

**fooled,** *modif.* — *Syn.* tricked, duped, deluded; see **deceived** 1.

**foolery,** *n.* — *Syn.* foolishness, folly, shenanigans\*; see **joke** 1, **nonsense** 1, 2.

**foolhardy,** *modif.* — *Syn.* impetuous, reckless, precipitate, headlong; see **rash.**

**fooling,** *modif.* — *Syn.* joking, jesting, pretending, feigning, humorous, deceitful, waggish, roguish, impish, teasing, bantering, trifling, jovial, frivolous, flippant, droll, insincere, misleading, prankish, light, frolicking, facetious, tongue-in-cheek, jocular, playful, merry, sportive, kidding\*, joshing\*, jollying\*, jiving\*, smart\*, putting one on\*, pulling one's leg\*. — *Ant.* SERIOUS, grave, earnest.

**foolish,** *modif.* — *Syn.* silly, senseless, unwise, absurd; see **silly, stupid** 1.
*See Synonym Study at* ABSURD.

**foolishly,** *modif.* — *Syn.* stupidly, irrationally, idiotically, senselessly, witlessly, fatuously, inanely, injudiciously, imprudently, unwisely, weakmindedly, unintelligently, uncomprehendingly, mistakenly, illogically, ill-advisedly, insanely, crazily, thoughtlessly, carelessly, irresponsibly, regrettably, absurdly, preposterously, ridiculously, with bad judgment, without good sense, boneheadedly\*, dumbly\*, like a jackass\*. — *Ant.* INTELLIGENTLY, wisely, advisedly.

**foolishness,** *n.* **1.** [The quality of lacking good sense] — *Syn.* folly, weakness, silliness; see **stupidity** 1, 2.
**2.** [Conduct or acts lacking good sense] — *Syn.* nonsense, imprudence, indiscretion; see **stupidity** 2, 3.

**foolproof,** *modif.* — *Syn.* dependable, infallible, fail-safe, sure-fire\*; see **reliable** 2.

**foot,** *n.* **1.** [A unit of measurement] — *Syn.* twelve inches, running foot, front foot, board foot, square foot, cubic foot.
**2.** [End of the leg] — *Syn.* extremity, pedal extremity, *pes* (Latin), hoof, paw, pad, heel, sole, arch, instep, toes, dog\*, tootsie\*, kicker\*, trotter\*.
**3.** [A foundation] — *Syn.* footing, base, bottom, pier; see **foundation** 2.
**4.** [A metrical unit in verse] — *Syn.* measure, accent, interval, meter, duple meter, triple meter.
Metrical feet include: iamb, dactyl, spondee, trochee, anapest, dipod, amphibrach.
**on foot** — *Syn.* walking, running, hiking, marching; see **walking.**
**on one's feet** — *Syn.* **1.** standing, erect, vertical; see **upright** 1.
**2.** sound, settled, secure; see **established** 1.
**on the wrong foot** — *Syn.* unfavorably, ineptly, incapably, inauspiciously; see **awkwardly, wrongly** 2.
**put one's best foot forward\*** — *Syn.* do one's best, appear at one's best, try hard; see **display** 1, **try** 1.
**put one's foot down\*** — *Syn.* be firm, act decisively, take a firm stand; see **resolve** 1.
**put one's foot in it** or **in one's mouth\*** — *Syn.* embarrass oneself and others, blunder, be indiscreet; see **botch.**
**under foot** — *Syn.* on the ground, on the floor, at one's feet, in the way; see **disturbing, under** 1.

**football,** *n.* **1.** [A sport] — *Syn.* American football, Association football, rugby, soccer, the pigskin sport\*, grid game\*, gridiron pastime\*.
**2.** [The ball used in football] — *Syn.* regulation football, pigskin\*, oval\*, inflated oval\*, apple\*, bacon\*, hide\*, porkhide\*, leather oval\*, peanut\*, pineapple\*, porker\*, moleskin\*, sphere\*, watermelon\*.
The teams of the National Football League include —
*National Conference:* Arizona Cardinals, Atlanta Falcons, Carolina Panthers, Chicago Bears, Dallas Cowboys, Detroit Lions, Green Bay Packers, Minnesota Vikings, New Orleans Saints, New York Giants, Philadelphia Eagles, San Francisco 49ers, St. Louis Rams, Tampa Bay Buccaneers, Washington Redskins; *American Conference:* Baltimore Ravens, Buffalo Bills, Cincinnati Bengals, Cleveland Browns, Denver Broncos, Houston Oilers, Indianapolis Colts, Jacksonville Jaguars, Kansas City Chiefs, Miami Dolphins, New England Patriots,

New York Jets, Oakland Raiders, Pittsburgh Steelers, San Diego Chargers, Seattle Seahawks.

**football player,** *n.* — *Syn.* footballer, pigskin player\*, gridder\*, booter\*.
In the United States, positions in football include: end, tackle, guard, center, quarterback, halfback, tailback, running back, fullback; safety, linebacker, tight end, split end, receiver, cornerback, flanker, nose guard, kicker.

**footfall,** *n.* — *Syn.* tread, step, footstep; see **gait** 1, **step** 1.

**foothold,** *n.* — *Syn.* ledge, crevice, footing, purchase, hold, toehold, space, niche, perch.

**footing,** *n.* **1.** [Foothold] — *Syn.* purchase, hold, stability, steadiness; see **foothold, stability** 1.
**2.** [A position or base] — *Syn.* basis, foundation, standing, status; see **foundation** 2, **rank** 3.

**footman,** *n.* — *Syn.* man in waiting, liveryman, lackey; see **servant.**

**footnote,** *n.* — *Syn.* note, endnote, commentary, gloss; see **note** 1.

**footpath,** *n.* — *Syn.* pathway, trail, track, walkway; see **path** 1.

**footprint,** *n.* — *Syn.* trace, trail, footstep; see **step** 3, **track** 2.

**foot soldier,** *n.* — *Syn.* infantryman, trooper, regular; see **soldier.**

**footstep,** *n.* — *Syn.* footfall, tread, footprint; see **gait** 1, **step** 1, 3, **track** 2.
**follow in someone's footsteps** — *Syn.* emulate, succeed, resemble a predecessor; see **follow** 2, **imitate** 2.

**footstool,** *n.* — *Syn.* footrest, ottoman, hassock; see **stool.**

**fop,** *n.* — *Syn.* dandy, dude, fashion plate, clotheshorse, coxcomb, buck, peacock, exquisite, macaroni, blade, man about town, fine gentleman, Beau Brummell, blood, swell\*, sport\*.

**foppery,** *n.* — *Syn.* coxcombry, showiness, dandyism; see **ostentation** 1, **vanity** 1.

**foppish,** *modif.* — *Syn.* dapper, natty, vain; see **egotistic** 2, **fashionable.**

**for,** *conj.* — *Syn.* as, since, in consequence of the fact that; see **because.**

**for,** *prep.* — *Syn.* toward, to, in favor of, to be given to, in order to get, under the authority of, in the interest of, during, in order to, in the direction of, to go to, to the amount of, to the extent of, in place of, instead of, in exchange for, as, in spite of, supposing, to counterbalance, concerning, with respect to, with regard to, conducive to, beneficial to, notwithstanding, with a view to, for the sake of, in contemplation of, in consideration of, in furtherance of, in honor of, on behalf of, in the name of, on the part of, in pursuance of.

**forage,** *v.* — *Syn.* search, scavenge, scrounge, rummage; see **hunt** 2, **search, seek** 1.

**forasmuch as,** *conj.* — *Syn.* since, inasmuch as, whereas; see **because, since** 1.

**foray,** *n.* — *Syn.* raid, invasion, incursion, venture; see **attack** 1, **venture.**

**forbear,** *v.* — *Syn.* cease, refrain, pause; see **abstain.**
*See Synonym Study at* ABSTAIN.

**forbearance,** *n.* — *Syn.* restraint, self-control, tolerance; see **abstinence, patience** 1.
*See Synonym Study at* PATIENCE.

**forbid,** *v.* — *Syn.* prohibit, ban, debar, interdict, enjoin, outlaw, restrain, inhibit, preclude, proscribe, disallow, oppose, cancel, hinder, obstruct, bar, prevent, censor, declare illegal, withhold, restrict, deny, refuse, block, check, exclude, embargo, taboo, veto, say "no" to, put under the ban, put under an injunction; see also **halt** 2. — *Ant.* APPROVE, permit, authorize.

**SYN.** — **forbid** is the basic, direct word meaning to command a person to refrain from some action; **prohibit** implies a forbidding by law or official decree; **interdict** implies legal or ecclesiastical prohibition, usually for a limited time, as an exemplary punishment or to forestall unfavorable developments; **enjoin** implies a legal order from a court prohibiting (or ordering) a given action, under penalty; **ban** implies legal or ecclesiastical prohibition with an added connotation of strong condemnation or censure

**forbidden,** *modif.* — *Syn.* prohibited, denied, taboo; see **illegal, refused.**

**forbidding,** *modif.* **1.** [Having an unfriendly appearance] — *Syn.* unapproachable, hostile, stern, inhospitable; see **grim** 1, **severe** 1.
**2.** [Having an ominous look] — *Syn.* sinister, threatening, frightening, dangerous; see **dangerous** 1, 2, **ominous.**

**force,** *n.* **1.** [Physical power] — *Syn.* strength, energy, might; see **strength** 1.
**2.** [Physical power exerted against a person or thing] — *Syn.* coercion, violence, compulsion, duress; see **oppression** 1, **restraint** 2.
**3.** [The power to act effectively] — *Syn.* forcefulness, vitality, energy, vigor, assertiveness, dominance, competence, persistence, willpower, drive, determination, effectiveness, efficiency, efficacy, authority, strength, impressiveness, intensity, vehemence, dynamism, capability, potency, power, puissance, punch\*, push\*, gumption\*, oomph\*, pizazz\*. — *Ant.* weakness, impotence, incompetence.
**4.** [A group organized for joint action] — *Syn.* band, crew, detachment, team, troop, cell, division, unit, contingent; see also **army** 2, **organization** 3.
**in force** — *Syn.* **1.** in full strength, totally, all together; see **all** 2.
**2.** operative, valid, in effect; see **working.**
*See Synonym Study at* STRENGTH.
**force,** *v.* **1.** [To use force] — *Syn.* compel, coerce, press, drive, make, impel, constrain, oblige, urge, push, thrust, propel, urge forward, obligate, necessitate, require, enforce, demand, order, decree, command, inflict, burden, impose, fix, apply, insist, exact, draft, dragoon, blackmail, extort, bind, put under obligation, contract, charge, restrict, limit, pin down, choke out, bring pressure to bear upon, pressure, bear hard upon, bear down upon, obtrude on, break through, bludgeon, steamroller, ram down one's throat\*, put the squeeze on\*, high-pressure\*, strong-arm\*, put the screws on\*, twist one's arm\*, smoke out\*.
**2.** [To break open] — *Syn.* burst, pry open, prize open, break into, extort, wrest, undo, use a bar on, assault, jimmy, crack\*, crack open\*, bust\*, bust open\*.
**3.** [To rape] — *Syn.* violate, attack, assault; see **rape.**
**4.** [To capture by assault] — *Syn.* take, win, overcome, overpower; see **seize** 2.

**SYN.** — **force** implies the exertion of power in causing a person or thing to act, move, or comply against his or its resistance and may refer to physical strength or to any impelling motive [forced the protestors into the van, circumstances forced him to lie]; **compel** implies a driving irresistibly to some action, condition, etc. [hunger compelled him to look for work] to **coerce** is to compel submission or obedience by the use of superior power,

intimidation, threats, etc. [troops coerced the crowd to disperse]; **constrain** implies the operation of a restricting force and therefore suggests a strained, repressed, or unnatural quality in that which results [a constrained laugh]

**forced,** *modif.* — *Syn.* compelled, coerced, constrained; see **bound** 2.
**forceful,** *modif.* — *Syn.* commanding, vigorous, effective, electric; see **dynamic, persuasive, powerful** 1.
**forcefully,** *modif.* — *Syn.* forcibly, energetically, strenuously, emphatically; see **vigorously.**
**forcible,** *modif.* — *Syn.* coercive, vigorous, cogent; see **persuasive, violent** 1.
**forcibly,** *modif.* — *Syn.* coercively, compulsorily, against one's will, effectively; see **vigorously, violently** 1.
**ford,** *n.* — *Syn.* portage, passage, shallow; see **crossing** 1.
**fore,** *modif.* — *Syn.* forward, near, nearest; see **front.**
**forebear,** *n.* — *Syn.* ancestor, forefather, forerunner, progenitor; see **ancestor.**
**forebode,** *v.* — *Syn.* forewarn, portend, augur; see **foretell.**
**foreboding,** *n.* **1.** [A feeling of impending evil] — *Syn.* premonition, dread, presentiment; see **anticipation** 2, **hunch** 2.
**2.** [An omen] — *Syn.* prediction, portent, prophecy; see **sign** 1, **warning.**
**forecast,** *n.* — *Syn.* prediction, prognostication, prognosis, projection, outlook, guess, estimate, budget, divination, foretoken, conjecture, prophecy, foretelling, calculation, vaticination, augury. — *Ant.* REMINISCENCE, retrospect, retrospection.
**forecast,** *v.* **1.** [To foresee] — *Syn.* divine, augur, prophesy; see **anticipate** 1.
**2.** [To predict] — *Syn.* prognosticate, prophesy, project, gauge, calculate, determine, predetermine, presage, portend, infer, reason, guess, figure out, dope out\*, call\*; see also **foretell.**
**foreclose,** *v.* **1.** [To exclude] — *Syn.* shut out, exclude, preclude, deprive; see **bar** 1, 2.
**2.** [To take away the right to redeem a mortgage] — *Syn.* dispossess, expropriate, confiscate, impound; see **seize** 2.
**forefather,** *n.* — *Syn.* ancestor, progenitor, forebear; see **ancestor.**
**forefinger,** *n.* — *Syn.* index finger, pointer, digit; see **finger.**
**forefront,** *n.* — *Syn.* fore, lead, front line, cutting edge; see **vanguard.**
**foregoing,** *modif.* — *Syn.* prior, former, previous; see **former, preceding.**
*See Synonym Study at* PREVIOUS.
**foregone,** *modif.* — *Syn.* predestined, certain, predictable, inescapable; see **destined** 1, **inevitable.**
**foreground,** *n.* — *Syn.* front, fore, forefront, prominence, immediate prospect, nearer view, anteriority, proximity, propinquity, nearness, contiguity, adjacency, purview, immediate survey, view. — *Ant.* BACKGROUND, distance, perspective.
**forehanded,** *modif.* **1.** [Wealthy] — *Syn.* well-to-do, well-off, prosperous; see **rich** 1.
**2.** [Prudent] — *Syn.* sparing, thrifty, frugal, provident; see **careful, economical** 1.
**forehead,** *n.* — *Syn.* brow, front, aspect, visage, countenance, temples.
**foreign,** *modif.* **1.** [Concerning a country, idea, or way of life not one's own] — *Syn.* remote, exotic, strange, alien, far, distant, inaccessible, unaccustomed, different, un-

known, unfamiliar, extrinsic, extraneous, external, outside, expatriate, exiled, from abroad, not native, not domestic, international, nonnative, nonresident, alienated, estranged, antipodal, faraway, far-off, hyperborean, beyond the rainbow, unexplored, transoceanic, transmarine, ultramontane, at the far corners of the earth, at the uttermost end of the earth, extralocal, beyond the pale, outlandish, picturesque, colorful.— *Ant.* LOCAL, national, indigenous.

**2.** [Coming from a country not one's own] — *Syn.* alien, imported, borrowed, nonnative, immigrant, barbarian, barbaric, adopted, coming from another land, not domestic; see also sense 1.— *Ant.* NATIVE, domestic, aboriginal.

**3.** [Organically or essentially different] — *Syn.* heterogeneous, unassimilable, unrelated, extraneous; see **irrelevant, unsuitable.**

---

*SYN.* — **foreign** implies that the external object is organically so different that it cannot become assimilated *[a foreign substance in the blood];* **alien** emphasizes the incompatibility of the external object with the subject in question *[such anger seems alien to his nature];* **extrinsic** refers to that which, coming from outside a thing, is not inherent in its real nature *[the souvenir had great extrinsic value for him];* **extraneous,** often synonymous with **extrinsic,** may connote the possibility of integration of the external object into the thing to which it is added *[extraneous grace notes]*

---

**foreigner,** *n.* — *Syn.* stranger, immigrant, newcomer, nonnative; see **alien.**
See Synonym Study at ALIEN.

**foreignism,** *n.* — *Syn.* exoticism, borrowing, loan word; see **language** 1.

**foreknowledge,** *n.* — *Syn.* foresight, prescience, premonition; see **anticipation 2, hunch** 2.

**foreman,** *n.* — *Syn.* overseer, manager, supervisor, boss, superintendent, taskmaster, head, headman, shop foreman, gang foreman, straw boss★, bossman★, slavedriver★.

**foremost,** *modif.* — *Syn.* first, chief, principal, leading; see **first** 1, **principal.**
See Synonym Study at PRINCIPAL.

**forenoon,** *n.* — *Syn.* morn, early part of the day, cool of the day; see **morning** 2.

**forensic,** *modif.* **1.** [Judicial] — *Syn.* juridical, legal, criminological; see **judicial, legal** 2.

**2.** [Of or suitable for debate] — *Syn.* disputative, rhetorical, polemic; see **controversial.**

**foreordain,** *v.* — *Syn.* predestine, destine, fate; see **predetermine.**

**forerunner,** *n.* — *Syn.* precursor, predecessor, herald, harbinger, antecedent, ancestor, prototype, foregoer, forebear, vanguard, trailblazer, pioneer, presager, foreshadower, foretoken, sign, portent, prognostic; see also **ancestor, messenger.**

**foresee,** *v.* — *Syn.* predict, envision, divine; see **anticipate** 1, **foretell.**

**foreseen,** *modif.* — *Syn.* anticipated, predictable, prepared for; see **expected** 2, **likely** 1.

**foreshadow,** *v.* — *Syn.* prefigure, presage, portend, imply; see **foretell.**

**foresight,** *n.* **1.** [Power to imagine the future] — *Syn.* prescience, prevision, foreknowledge, vision; see **acumen, anticipation** 2.

**2.** [Provision for the future] — *Syn.* forethought, prudence, forehandedness, preparedness; see **prudence.**

**forest,** *n.* — *Syn.* woods, wood, timberland, woodland,

jungle, timber, growth, stand of trees, grove, virgin forest, the forest primeval, backwoods, park, greenwood, cover, covert, clump, thicket, brushwood, brush, area below timberline, shelter, chase, brake, copse, coppice, bosk, wold, weald, spinney, boscage, dell, dingle, tall timber, second growth, scrub; see also **timber** 1.

**forestall,** *v.* **1.** [To hinder] — *Syn.* thwart, prevent, avert; see **hinder, prevent.**

**2.** [To anticipate] — *Syn.* provide against, be ready for, get ahead of; see **anticipate** 2.
See Synonym Study at PREVENT.

**forest fire,** *n.* — *Syn.* brush fire, blaze, conflagration; see **fire** 1.

**forestry,** *n.* — *Syn.* forest management, forest ranging, ranger service, arboriculture, dendrology, woodcraft, afforestation, silviculture, forestation, reclamation, tree-planting, woodsmanship, conservation.

**foretaste,** *n.* — *Syn.* preliminary experience, presentiment, forerunner; see **anticipation** 2.

**foretell,** *v.* — *Syn.* predict, prophesy, prognosticate, divine, foresee, announce in advance, forecast, soothsay, tell fortunes, cast a horoscope, vaticinate, foreknow, forebode, augur, betoken, portend, foreshadow, adumbrate, foretoken, presage, prefigure, foreshow.— *Ant.* RECORD, confirm, recount.

**forethought,** *n.* — *Syn.* provision, planning, foresight; see **prudence.**

**forever,** *modif.* **1.** [For all time] — *Syn.* everlastingly, permanently, always, eternally, immortally, until the end of time, until Doomsday, until the Day of Judgment, on and on, ever, perpetually, always, evermore, in perpetuity, world without end, *saecula saeculorum* (Latin), lastingly, interminably, enduringly, unchangingly, durably, ever and again, indestructibly, endlessly, infinitely, forevermore, aye, for good, for good and all, till hell freezes over★, for keeps★, from the cradle to the grave, for life, for always, for eternity, without cease, now and forever, in all ages, till death do us part. — *Ant.* TEMPORARILY, for a time, at present.

**2.** [Continuously] — *Syn.* perpetually, unendingly, ceaselessly; see **regularly** 2.

**forewarn,** *v.* — *Syn.* caution, alert, admonish; see **warn.**

**foreword,** *n.* — *Syn.* introduction, preface, prologue, preamble; see **introduction** 4.
See Synonym Study at INTRODUCTION.

**for example,** *modif.* — *Syn.* for instance, as an example, to illustrate, e.g., to cite an instance, as a model, by way of illustration, to give an example, as a case in point, as, such as, like★.

**forfeit,** *v.* — *Syn.* sacrifice, give up, give over, relinquish; see **abandon** 1.

**forfeiture,** *n.* — *Syn.* abandonment, giving up, relinquishment, fine; see **loss** 1, **punishment.**

**forgather,** *v.* — *Syn.* congregate, convene, assemble; see **gather** 1.

**forge,** *v.* **1.** [To imitate fraudulently] — *Syn.* falsify, counterfeit, fake, trump up, coin, invent, frame, fabricate, feign, imitate, copy, transcribe, duplicate, reproduce, simulate, trace.

**2.** [To form] — *Syn.* shape, produce, fashion, hammer out; see **form** 1, **manufacture** 1.

**3.** [To move ahead; *often used with "ahead"*] — *Syn.* progress, press onward, make strides; see **advance** 1.

**forger,** *n.* — *Syn.* falsifier, counterfeiter, coiner; see **criminal, impostor, plagiarist.**

**forgery,** *n.* — *Syn.* imitation, copy, imposture, cheat, counterfeit, fake, fabrication, sham, imposition, fraud, hoax, falsification, reproduction, phony★.— *Ant.* ORIGINAL, real thing, authentic work.

**forget,** v. 1. [To lose memory] — Syn. be unable to recall, have no recollection of, fail to remember, lose consciousness of, put out of one's head, let slip one's mind, misremember, let bygones be bygones, be forgetful, have a short memory, consign to oblivion, think no more of, dismiss from the mind, close one's eyes to, not give another thought, disremember★, clean forget★, draw a blank★. — Ant. REMEMBER, recall, recollect.
2. [To neglect intentionally or unintentionally] — Syn. overlook, ignore, omit, neglect, slight, disregard, pass over, lose sight of, skip, drop it★; see also **neglect** 1, 2.
See Synonym Study at NEGLECT.
**forgetful,** modif. 1. [Absent-minded] — Syn. preoccupied, dreamy, distracted; see **absent-minded.**
2. [Careless] — Syn. inattentive, neglectful, heedless; see **careless** 1.
**forgetfulness,** n. — Syn. negligence, heedlessness, inattention; see **carelessness, oblivion** 1.
**forget oneself,** v. — Syn. act badly, offend, trespass, daydream; see **misbehave.**
**forgivable,** modif. — Syn. excusable, venial, trivial, pardonable; see **excusable.**
**forgive,** v. 1. [To cease to resent] — Syn. pardon, overlook, dismiss from the mind, efface from the memory, pocket the affront, forgive and forget, let pass, palliate, excuse, condone, remit, forget, relent, bear no malice, exonerate, exculpate, let bygones be bygones, laugh it off, let it go, kiss and make up, bury the hatchet, turn the other cheek, charge to experience, make allowance, let up on★, write off★, charge off★; see also **forget** 1. — Ant. blame, resent, retaliate.
2. [To absolve] — Syn. acquit, pardon, release; see **absolve, excuse.**
See Synonym Study at ABSOLVE.
**forgiven,** modif. — Syn. excused, reinstated, taken back, welcomed home; see **pardoned.**
**forgiveness,** n. — Syn. absolution, pardon, acquittal, exoneration, remission, dispensation, exculpation, extenuation, reprieve, quittance, justification, amnesty, respite, indulgence, mercy, clemency.
**forgiving,** modif. — Syn. sparing, magnanimous, lenient, accepting; see **humane** 1, **kind, merciful** 1.
**forgo,** v. — Syn. do without, relinquish, waive, sacrifice; see **abandon** 1, **abstain, waive.**
See Synonym Study at WAIVE.
**forgotten,** modif. — Syn. not remembered, not recalled, not recollected, unremembered, unrecalled, unrecollected, unretained, obliterated, lost, lapsed, out of one's mind, clear out of one's mind, clean out of one's mind, gone out of one's head, erased from one's mind, having slipped one's mind, erased from one's consciousness, beyond recall, past recollection, past recall, consigned to oblivion, sunk in oblivion, overlooked, ignored, lost sight of, not recoverable, blotted out, blanked out; see also **abandoned, neglected.**
**fork,** n. 1. [A furcated implement] — Syn. table fork, hay fork, pitchfork, manure fork, trident, prong, spear, scepter.
2. [A branch of a road or river] — Syn. bend, turn, crossroad, crotch, tributary, byway, junction, confluence, branch, stream, creek.
**forked,** modif. — Syn. angled, zigzag, pronged, branching, bifurcate, bifurcated, furcate, furcated, tridentate, trident, branched.
**forlorn,** modif. — Syn. forsaken, desolate, forgotten, miserable; see **abandoned** 1.
**form,** n. 1. [Shape] — Syn. figure, appearance, plan, arrangement, design, outline, conformation, configuration, formation, structure, style, stance, construction,

fashion, mode, scheme, framework, Gestalt (German), contour, profile, silhouette, skeleton, anatomy, articulation.
2. [The human form] — Syn. body, frame, torso; see **figure** 2.
3. [The approved procedure] — Syn. manner, mode, custom; see **method** 2.
4. [Anything intended to give form] — Syn. pattern, model, die; see **mold** 1.
5. [A standard document] — Syn. application, questionnaire, blank, data sheet, information, blank, form letter, duplicate, routine letter, pattern, chart, card, report, reference form, order form; see also **copy.**
6. [A rite] — Syn. ritual, formality, custom; see **ceremony** 2.
7. [Type] — Syn. make, sort, class; see **class** 1, **kind** 2.
8. [Arrangement] — Syn. organization, placement, scheme; see **order** 3.
9. [Convention] — Syn. habit, practice, usage; see **custom** 1, 2.

---

SYN. — **form** denotes the arrangement of the parts of a thing that gives it its distinctive appearance and is the broadest term here, applying also to abstract concepts; **figure** is applied to physical form as determined by the bounding lines or surfaces; **outline** is used of the lines bounding the limits of an object and, in an extended sense, suggests a general plan without detail; **shape,** although also stressing outline, is usually applied to something that has mass or bulk and may refer to nonphysical concepts /her story began to take shape/; **configuration** stresses the relative disposition of parts or elements /an irregular configuration of streets, the configuration of the landscape/

---

**form,** v. 1. [To give shape to a thing] — Syn. mold, shape, pattern, model, arrange, make, block out, block, fashion, construct, devise, plan, design, contrive, produce, invent, frame, scheme, plot, compose, erect, build, cast, cut, carve, chisel, hammer out, forge, put together, plane, whittle, assemble, conceive, create, outline, trace, develop, cultivate, work, complete, finish, consummate, perfect, fix, regulate, knock together, establish, sculpture, sculpt, pat, bend, twist, knead, set, determine, arrive at, reach, settle, articulate. — Ant. DESTROY, demolish, shatter.
2. [To give character to a person] — Syn. instruct, rear, breed, mold; see **teach** 1, 2, **train** 4.
3. [To comprise] — Syn. constitute, make up, figure in, act as; see **compose** 1.
4. [To take form] — Syn. accumulate, condense, harden, set, settle, rise, appear, take shape, grow, develop, unfold, mature, materialize, eventuate, become a reality, take on character, crystallize, assume definite characteristics, become visible, be finalized, fall into place, shape up★, get into shape★. — Ant. DISAPPEAR, dissolve, waste away.
See Synonym Study at MAKE.
**formal,** modif. 1. [Notable for arrangement] — Syn. orderly, precise, set, symmetrical; see **regular** 3.
2. [Concerned with etiquette and behavior] — Syn. reserved, distant, stiff, ceremonious; see **conventional** 2, 3, **polite** 1.
3. [Official] — Syn. prescribed, confirmed, directed, lawful; see **approved, legal** 1.
4. [In or requiring evening clothes] — Syn. full-dress, black tie, white tie, dressy, dressed up, ceremonious, social, in tails and top hat, in one's glad rags★, in a soup and fish★.

**formality,** *n.* **1.** [Propriety] — *Syn.* decorum, etiquette, correctness; see **behavior** 1, **decorum.**

**2.** [Custom] — *Syn.* rule, convention, conventionality; see **ceremony** 2, **custom** 2.

*See Synonym Study at* CEREMONY.

**format,** *n.* — *Syn.* makeup, arrangement, construction, setup; see **composition** 2, **form** 1.

**formation,** *n.* **1.** [The process of forming] — *Syn.* development, establishment, arrangement, crystallization, deposit, accumulation, production, composition, fabrication, generation, creation, genesis, induction, embodiment, synthesis, compilation, constitution, organization. — *Ant.* DESTRUCTION, dissolution, annihilation.

**2.** [An arrangement] — *Syn.* configuration, disposition, structure, phalanx; see **form** 1, **order** 3.

**formative,** *modif.* — *Syn.* developmental, impressionable, moldable; see **impressionable, juvenile** 1, **pliable** 2.

**formed,** *modif.* — *Syn.* shaped, molded, patterned, modeled, carved, outlined, developed, cultivated, completed, finished, built, fashioned, constructed, created, invented, forged, concocted, designed, accomplished, manufactured, produced, made, composed, born, authored, consummated, perfected, fixed, established, solidified, hardened, set, determined, arrived at, reached, settled, articulated, structured. — *Ant.* SHAPELESS, formless, nebulous.

**former,** *modif.* — *Syn.* earlier, previous, prior, foregoing, preceding, above-mentioned, above, onetime, once, ex, late, recent, retired, erstwhile, then, quondam, past, bygone, ancient, long ago, olden; see also **preceding.**

*See Synonym Study at* PREVIOUS.

**formerly,** *modif.* — *Syn.* before now, some time ago, once, in the past, once upon a time, already, in former times, previously, earlier, time out of mind, in the early days, centuries ago, eons ago, anciently, in the old days, in olden times, used to be, long ago, before this, in time past, in days gone by, in days of yore, heretofore, a while back\*, way back when\*, in Grandfather's time\*, in Grandmother's time\*. — *Ant.* NOW, subsequently, immediately.

**formidable,** *modif.* **1.** [Inspiring fear or apprehension] — *Syn.* fearful, forbidding, intimidating, impregnable; see **dangerous** 1, 2, **terrible** 1.

**2.** [Hard to deal with or overcome] — *Syn.* challenging, arduous, onerous, overwhelming; see **difficult** 1.

**3.** [Inspiring awe or admiration] — *Syn.* impressive, imposing, awesome, redoubtable; see **grand** 2, **impressive** 1.

**formless,** *modif.* — *Syn.* chaotic, vague, indeterminate; see **shapeless** 1.

**formula,** *n.* **1.** [A prescription] — *Syn.* direction, specifications, description, formulary, recipe; see also **method** 2.

**2.** [A set speech or form] — *Syn.* rote, creed, credo, ritual, established mode, rubric, code, formal statement; see also **custom** 1, 2.

**3.** [A statement of a supposed truth] — *Syn.* ratio, logarithm, equation, recipe, prescription, theorem.

For formulas of the elements; see **element** 2.

**formulary,** *n.* — *Syn.* formula, model, form; see **method** 2.

**formulate,** *v.* — *Syn.* express, give form to, set down; see **express** 1, **form** 1.

**fornication,** *n.* — *Syn.* adultery, illicit intercourse, unlicensed intercourse, promiscuousness, extramarital sex, premarital sex, incontinence, carnality, lechery, unchastity, lewdness, lubricity, libidinousness, licentiousness, venery, unfaithfulness, whoredom, harlotry,

prostitution, concubinage, concupiscence, coitus, debauchery, libertinism; see also **copulation.**

**forsake,** *v.* **1.** [To abandon] — *Syn.* desert, leave, quit; see **abandon** 2.

**2.** [To relinquish] — *Syn.* renounce, give up, surrender; see **abandon** 1.

*See Synonym Study at* ABANDON.

**forsaken,** *modif.* — *Syn.* abandoned, deserted, forlorn, desolate; see **abandoned** 1.

**forswear,** *v.* — *Syn.* abjure, renounce, repudiate, retract; see **abandon** 1, **deny.**

**forswear oneself,** *v.* — *Syn.* perjure oneself, swear falsely, bear false witness; see **lie** 1.

**fort,** *n.* — *Syn.* fortress, citadel, post, garrison; see **fortification** 2.

**forte,** *n.* — *Syn.* gift, strong point, talent, specialty, strength, bent, métier, long suit, thing\*; see also **talent** 1.

**forth,** *modif.* — *Syn.* onward, out, ahead, hence; see **forward** 1.

**and so forth** — *Syn.* and so on, similarly, and others; see **et cetera.**

**forthcoming,** *modif.* — *Syn.* expected, inevitable, anticipated, future, resulting, impending, pending, awaited, destined, fated, predestined, approaching, in store, at hand, inescapable, imminent, in prospect, prospective, in the wind, in preparation, in the cards\*.

**forthright,** *modif.* — *Syn.* straightforward, direct, candid, blunt; see **frank.**

**forthwith,** *modif.* — *Syn.* at once, instantly, directly, straightaway; see **immediately.**

**fortification,** *n.* **1.** [The process of fortification] — *Syn.* trench digging, consolidating, strengthening, reinforcement, defensive preparation, entrenchment, arming, defending, trenching, fortifying, buttressing, preparing bases, digging in.

**2.** [Work prepared for defense] — *Syn.* fort, fortress, breastwork, defense, dugout, bunker, trench, entrenchment, gun emplacement, barricade, battlement, blockhouse, stockade, outpost, citadel, bastion, bulwark, support, outwork, wall, barrier, groin, buffer, block, barbican, earthwork, rampart, barbette, parapet, castle, stronghold, acropolis, garrison, redoubt, pillbox, riflepit, defense in depth, hedgehog defense, Maginot line.

**fortified,** *modif.* — *Syn.* defended, guarded, safeguarded, protected, manned, garrisoned, barricaded, armed, barbed, electrified, entrenched, secured, strong, covered, strengthened, reinforced, buttressed, supported, surrounded, fortressed, walled, enclosed, stockaded, bulwarked, bastioned, armored, dug in, deeply entrenched, hidden, camouflaged, revetted, bristling with guns, supplied with antiaircraft guns, equipped with air bases, equipped with an antimissile system, equipped with an early warning system. — *Ant.* OPEN, unprotected, unguarded.

**fortify,** *v.* **1.** [To strengthen against attack] — *Syn.* barricade, entrench, buttress; see **defend** 1.

**2.** [To strengthen physically or emotionally] — *Syn.* hearten, cheer, sustain, brace, encourage, invigorate, embolden, reinforce; see also **strengthen, support** 1.

**3.** [To add ingredients to] — *Syn.* enrich, supplement, boost; see **supplement.**

**fortitude,** *n.* — *Syn.* firmness, courage, mettle, fearlessness, grit, backbone, determination, pluck, strength, stoicism, guts\*; see also **determination** 2, **endurance** 2.

---

**SYN.** — **fortitude** refers to the strength or courage that permits one to endure patiently misfortune, pain, etc.

/to face a calamity with *fortitude]*; **grit** applies to an obstinate sort of courage that refuses to succumb under any circumstances; **backbone** refers to the strength of character and resoluteness that permits one to face opposition unflinchingly; **pluck**, like **guts** referred originally to visceral organs, hence **pluck** implies courage or a strong heart in the face of danger or difficulty and **guts**, a colloquial word, suggests the sort of stamina that permits one to "stomach" a disagreeable or frightening experience *See also Synonym Study at* PATIENCE.

**fortress**, *n.* — *Syn.* stronghold, fort, citadel; see **fortification** 2.

**fortuitous**, *modif.* — *Syn.* accidental, chance, serendipitous; see **accidental**.
*See Synonym Study at* ACCIDENTAL.

**fortunate**, *modif.* **1.** [*Said of persons*] — *Syn.* lucky, blessed, prosperous, successful, having a charmed life, in luck, favored, well-to-do, happy, triumphant, victorious, overcoming, winning, gaining, affluent, thriving, flourishing, healthy, wealthy, in good estate, well-fixed*, well-heeled*, in the gravy*, born with a silver spoon in one's mouth*, born on the sunny side*, born under a lucky star*. — *Ant.* UNFORTUNATE, unlucky, cursed.
**2.** [*Said of things*] — *Syn.* auspicious, fortuitous, advantageous; see **helpful** 1, **hopeful** 2.

**fortunately**, *modif.* — *Syn.* luckily, happily, by a happy chance, as luck would have it, providentially, fortuitously, opportunely, seasonably, in good time, in good season, auspiciously, propitiously, favorably, prosperously, in the nick of time*. — *Ant.* UNFORTUNATELY, by an evil chance, unhappily.

**fortune**, *n.* **1.** [Chance] — *Syn.* luck, fate, lot; see **chance** 1, **destiny** 1.
**2.** [Great riches] — *Syn.* wealth, prosperity, possessions, estate; see **wealth** 2.
**3.** [A large sum of money] — *Syn.* a small fortune, tidy sum, mint, pretty penny*, bundle*, pile*, wad*, big bucks*, megabucks*, king's ransom*, packet*, heap*, loads*.
**tell one's fortune** — *Syn.* predict, prognosticate, foretell; see **forecast** 2, **foretell**.

**fortuneteller**, *n.* — *Syn.* spiritualist, medium, seer, crystal gazer, clairvoyant, psychic, soothsayer, augur, oracle, prophet, sibyl, astrologer, stargazer, palmist, palm-reader, chiromancer, tea-leaf reader, tarot reader, phrenologist, Cassandra, mind-reader.

**forum**, *n.* — *Syn.* conference, mass meeting, panel, tribunal; see **discussion** 1, **gathering**, **hearing** 1.

**forward**, *modif.* **1.** [Going forward] — *Syn.* advancing, progressing, leading on, ahead, progressive, onward, forth, propulsive, in advance. — *Ant.* BACKWARD, retreating, regressive.
**2.** [At a forward position] — *Syn.* front, first, foremost; see **ahead** 2.
**3.** [Bold] — *Syn.* presumptuous, impertinent, fresh*; see **rude** 2.

**forward**, *v.* **1.** [To help advance] — *Syn.* advance, assist, further, promote; see **promote** 1.
**2.** [To send on] — *Syn.* deliver, transmit, reroute; see **send** 1.
*See Synonym Study at* PROMOTE.

**forwarded**, *modif.* — *Syn.* shipped, expressed, dispatched; see **delivered**.

**forwardness**, *n.* — *Syn.* boldness, presumptuousness, impertinence; see **rudeness**.

**fossil**, *n.* — *Syn.* remains, organic remains, reconstruc-

tion, specimen, skeleton, relic, impression, imprint, trace, petrified deposit, petrifaction.

**foster**, *v.* **1.** [To support] — *Syn.* cherish, nurse, nourish, rear; see **raise** 2.
**2.** [To harbor] — *Syn.* encourage, nurture, cultivate, further; see **promote** 1.

**foul**, *modif.* **1.** [Soiled] — *Syn.* dirty, unclean, filthy, impure; see **dirty** 1.
**2.** [Disgusting] — *Syn.* loathsome, fetid, odious; see **offensive** 2, **rank** 2.
**3.** [Obscene or abusive] — *Syn.* nasty, vulgar, coarse; see **lewd** 1, **opprobrious** 1, **ribald**.
**4.** [Unfair] — *Syn.* inequitable, unjust, dishonorable, vicious; see **dishonest** 2.
**run** or **fall foul of** — *Syn.* get into trouble with, encounter, come into conflict with; see **fight** 2, **meet** 6, **oppose** 1.
*See Synonym Study at* DIRTY.

**foul**, *v.* **1.** [To make dirty] — *Syn.* defile, pollute, sully, soil; see **dirty**.
**2.** [To become dirty or entangled] — *Syn.* soil, spot, discolor, stain, clog, jam, snarl, catch, be clogged, be choked, be tangled, be coated, be encrusted, be blocked, be filled.

**foulmouthed**, *modif.* — *Syn.* coarse, obscene, indecent, abusive; see **lewd** 1, **ribald**, **rude** 2.

**foul play**, *n.* — *Syn.* unfairness, treachery, violence, violation; see **crime** 1, **dishonesty**, **injustice** 2.

**foul up***, *v.* — *Syn.* make a mess of, bungle, spoil, entangle; see **botch**, **confuse**.

**found**, *modif.* **1.** [Discovered] — *Syn.* unearthed, located, detected; see **discovered**.
**2.** [Occurring customarily] — *Syn.* common, native to, characteristic of; see **conventional** 1.

**found**, *v.* — *Syn.* establish, endow, set up; see **organize** 2.

**foundation**, *n.* **1.** [An intellectual basis] — *Syn.* reason, justification, grounds; see **basis** 1.
**2.** [A physical basis] — *Syn.* base, footing, foot, basement, pier, groundwork, bed, ground, resting place, bottom, substructure, wall, understructure, underpinning, solid rock, rest, roadbed, support, substratum, prop, stand, bolster, stay, skid, shore, pediment, post, pillar, infrastructure, skeleton, column, shaft, pedestal, buttress, abutment, framework, scaffold, beam, chassis, skewback, pile.
**3.** [That which has been founded] — *Syn.* institution, organization, endowment, institute, society, establishment, company, guild, trusteeship, corporation, association, charity, fund.
**4.** [The act of founding] — *Syn.* establishment, origination, institution; see **establishing** 1.
*See Synonym Study at* BASE.

**founded**, *modif.* — *Syn.* organized, endowed, set up; see **established** 2.

**founder**, *n.* — *Syn.* originator, patron, prime mover; see **ancestor**, **author** 1.

**founder**, *v.* — *Syn.* sink, collapse, bog down, miscarry; see **break down** 3, **fail** 1, **sink** 1.

**founding**, *modif.* — *Syn.* establishing, endowing, instituting, originating, setting up, planting, colonizing, authorizing.

**founding**, *n.* — *Syn.* originating, setting up, starting; see **establishing** 1.

**foundling**, *n.* — *Syn.* orphan, waif, castaway; see **orphan**.

**foundry**, *n.* — *Syn.* plant, shop, forge; see **factory**.

**fountain**, *n.* **1.** [A source] — *Syn.* origin, well, spring, font; see **origin** 2.

**2.** [A jet of water] — *Syn.* spray, jet, stream, spring, gush, bubbler, drinking fountain, water fountain, water cooler, basin, spout, geyser, pump, spurt, play.

**3.** [A soda-water dispensary] — *Syn.* soda fountain, bar, soda bar, ice-cream parlor, drugstore fountain.

**fountainhead,** *n.* — *Syn.* source, rise, cause; see **origin** 2, 3.

**fourflusher\*,** *n.* — *Syn.* fake, cheat, pretender, bluffer; see **cheat** 1, **impostor.**

**fourfold,** *modif.* — *Syn.* four-part, four-way, four-ply, four times as many; see **quadruple.**

**four-handed,** *modif.* — *Syn.* quadrumanous, for two players, involving four hands, rendering a duet.

**four hundred,** *n.* [*Used with* "*the*"] — *Syn.* jet set, high society, elite; see **aristocracy.**

**foursome,** *n.* — *Syn.* quartet, two couples, team, party, ensemble, group, four-handed game, quadruplet, quaternion, tetrad.

**foursquare,** *modif.* **1.** [Square] — *Syn.* quadrangular, rectangular, geometrical; see **square** 1.

**2.** [Firm] — *Syn.* stable, solid, steady; see **firm** 1.

**3.** [Frank] — *Syn.* direct, honest, forthright; see **frank.**

**fowl,** *n.* — *Syn.* barnyard fowl, wild fowl, game, poultry, stewing chicken; see also **bird** 1, **chicken** 1, **pigeon.**
Types of fowl include: chicken, duck, goose, turkey, guinea hen, peafowl, capon, squab, cock, hen, Cornish hen, pheasant, partridge, quail, pigeon, dove, prairie chicken, woodcock, grouse, ptarmigan, moorfowl, swan.

**fox,** *n.* **1.** [A clever person] — *Syn.* Reynard, Volpone, artful dodger, cheat, trickster, slick operator, slyboots, sly dog\*, con artist\*; see also **cheat** 1, **rascal.**

**2.** [An animal] — *Syn.* canine, red fox, gray fox, silver fox, arctic fox, Reynard.

**fox trot,** *n.* — *Syn.* one-step, two-step, slow dance; see **dance** 1.

**foxy,** *modif.* **1.** [Shrewd] — *Syn.* subtle, experienced, knowing; see **intelligent** 1.

**2.** [Cunning] — *Syn.* sly, wily, crafty, artful; see **sly** 1.

**3.** [\*Physically attractive] — *Syn.* good-looking, desirable, sexy\*; see **beautiful** 2, **charming, handsome** 2.
*See Synonym Study at* SLY.

**foyer,** *n.* — *Syn.* anteroom, hall, lobby; see **entrance** 2.

**fracas,** *n.* — *Syn.* dispute, uproar, tumult, brawl; see **fight** 1.

**fraction,** *n.* — *Syn.* section, portion, part; see **division** 2, **part** 1.
*See Synonym Study at* PART.

**fractional,** *modif.* — *Syn.* partial, constituent, sectional, fragmentary, incomplete, divided, segmented, compartmented, parceled, apportioned, dismembered, dispersed, by fractions, piecemeal, fractionary. — *Ant.* WHOLE, total, complete.

**fractious,** *modif.* **1.** [Irritable] — *Syn.* peevish, perverse, touchy, cross; see **irritable.**

**2.** [Hard to manage] — *Syn.* unruly, refractory, troublesome; see **contrary** 4, **rebellious** 2.

**fracture,** *n.* **1.** [The act of breaking] — *Syn.* rupture, breakage, disjunction, cleaving, cleavage, disseverment, riving, displacement, dislocation, severing, separating, dismemberment.

**2.** [The result of being broken] — *Syn.* break, wound, cleft, mutilation, crack, shattering, breach, split, rupture, fragmentation, fissure, fault; see also sense 1; hole 1.

**3.** [A break in the skeletal system] — *Syn.* broken bone, broken limb, simple fracture, closed fracture, compound fracture, greenstick fracture, ruptured cartilage; see also senses 1 and 2.

**fracture,** *v.* — *Syn.* break, crack, split, shatter; see **break** 1.
*See Synonym Study at* BREAK.

**fragile,** *modif.* — *Syn.* frail, delicate, breakable, frangible, friable, brittle, dainty, weak, flimsy; see also **dainty** 1, **weak** 1, 2.

**SYN.** — **fragile** implies such delicacy of structure as to be easily broken [a *fragile* china teacup]; **frangible** connotes a liability to being broken because of the use to which the thing is put [the bridge was constructed with *frangible* stone]; **brittle** implies such inelasticity as to be easily broken or shattered by pressure or a blow [the bones of the body become *brittle* with age]; **crisp** suggests a desirable sort of brittleness, as of fresh celery or crackers; **friable** is applied to something that is easily crumbled or crushed into powder [*friable* rock]

**fragility,** *n.* — *Syn.* frangibleness, frailty, brittleness; see **delicacy** 1, **frailty** 1.

**fragment,** *n.* — *Syn.* piece, scrap, remnant, particle; see **bit** 1, **part** 1.
*See Synonym Study at* PART.

**fragmentary,** *modif.* — *Syn.* broken, incomplete, disconnected, sketchy; see **broken** 1, **fractional.**

**fragrance,** *n.* — *Syn.* perfume, aroma, scent, redolence; see **smell** 1.
*See Synonym Study at* PERFUME.

**fragrant,** *modif.* — *Syn.* aromatic, redolent, perfumed; see **odorous** 2.

**frail,** *modif.* — *Syn.* fragile, delicate, infirm, slight; see **dainty** 1, **fragile, sick, weak** 1.
*See Synonym Study at* WEAK.

**frailty,** *n.* **1.** [Quality of being weak] — *Syn.* fragility, weakness, debility, delicacy, infirmity, feebleness, decrepitude, daintiness, puniness, slightness, frangibility, susceptibility, brittleness, softness, flaccidity, unsubstantiality, flimsiness, limpness, shakiness, wobbliness, rustiness. — *Ant.* STRENGTH, indestructibility, firmness.

**2.** [A moral or social weakness] — *Syn.* failing, foible, imperfection; see **defect** 2, **fault** 2.

**frame,** *n.* **1.** [The structural portion] — *Syn.* skeleton, structure, scaffold, truss, framework, shell, scaffolding, casing, framing, support, stage, groundwork, organization, anatomy, build, carcass, gantry, fabric, warp, architecture.

**2.** [An open structure] — *Syn.* case, enclosure, support, shutter, girdle, span, clasp, jamb, mold, block, stay, window frame, doorjamb.

**3.** [A border intended as an ornament] — *Syn.* border, edging, margin, verge, fringe, hem, valance, flounce, trim, trimming, wreath, outline, mounting, mat, matting, molding, frieze.

**frame,** *v.* **1.** [To make] — *Syn.* construct, erect, raise; see **build** 1.

**2.** [To formulate] — *Syn.* draft, draw up, devise, contrive; see **compose** 3, **express** 1, **write** 1.

**3.** [To enclose in a frame] — *Syn.* mount, border, enclose, encase, back, mat.

**4.** [To act as a frame] — *Syn.* encircle, set off, edge, fringe, envelop, outline, block out, limit, confine, enshrine, enclose, wreathe, wrap, clasp, girdle, compass.

**5.** [\*To cause a miscarriage of justice] — *Syn.* falsely incriminate, conspire against, entrap, double-cross\*, set up\*, shop (British)\*, plant\*, put up a job on\*, fix\*.

**framed,** *modif.* **1.** [Surrounded by a frame] — *Syn.* mounted, encased, bordered, matted, encircled, fringed,

enveloped, outlined, confined, enclosed, wreathed, wrapped, clasped, girdled, compassed.
**2.** [*Arranged beforehand] — *Syn.* faked, fixed*, planted*, cooked up*, set up*, trumped up*.
**3.** [Made of wood] — *Syn.* timbered, beamed, raftered, girdered, scaffolded, trussed, constructed, carpentered.
**frame of mind,** *n.* — *Syn.* temper, attitude, outlook, humor; see **mood** 1.
**framer,** *n.* — *Syn.* originator, organizer, creator, composer; see **author** 1.
**frame-up\*,** *n.* — *Syn.* hoax, dodge, trumped-up charge*; see **trick** 1.
**framework,** *n.* — *Syn.* skeleton, structure, core; see **frame** 1.
**France,** *n.* — *Syn.* French nation, French people, French Republic, Fifth Republic, French Community, Gaul, *la Patrie, La France, La belle France,* (all French).
**franchise,** *n.* **1.** [A right, especially the right to vote] — *Syn.* privilege, freedom, suffrage, enfranchisement; see **right** 1, **vote** 3.
**2.** [The right to market a product or service] — *Syn.* concession, license, charter, distributorship; see **permission, permit.**
**frank,** *modif.* — *Syn.* candid, straightforward, sincere, open, forthright, outspoken, direct, honest, artless, free, easy, familiar, free in speaking, unreserved, undissembling, uninhibited, unguarded, downright, aboveboard, ingenuous, unsophisticated, unaffected, plain, apparent, open-faced, saying what one thinks, straight, plain-spoken, free-spoken, natural, guileless, blunt, bold, openhearted, matter-of-fact, explicit, straight from the shoulder*, flat-out*, straightout*, calling a spade a spade*, upfront*. — *Ant.* SECRETIVE, dishonest, insincere.

---

*SYN.* — **frank** applies to a person, remark, etc. that is free or blunt in expressing the truth or an opinion, unhampered by conventional reticence */a frank criticism/*; **candid** implies a basic honesty that makes deceit or evasion impossible, sometimes to the embarrassment of the listener */a candid opinion/*; **open** implies a lack of concealment and often connotes an ingenuous quality */the open candor of a child/*; **outspoken** suggests a lack of restraint or reserve in speech, esp. when reticence might be preferable

---

**frankfurter,** *n.* — *Syn.* hot dog, wiener, wiener sausage, frank*, weenie*, chili dog*, dog*, link*.
**frankincense,** *n.* — *Syn.* perfume, resin, olibanum; see **incense.**
**frankly,** *modif.* — *Syn.* freely, honestly, candidly; see **openly** 1.
**frankness,** *n.* — *Syn.* openness, sincerity, ingenuousness; see **honesty** 1.
**frantic,** *modif.* — *Syn.* frenzied, agitated, overwrought, distraught, distracted, beside oneself, wild, hysterical, desperate, frenetic, upset, excited, overexcited, worked up, in a state, delirious, out of one's mind, mad, berserk, wild-eyed, furious, raging, unhinged, unstrung, unglued*, at the end of one's rope*; see also **excited.** — *Ant.* calm, composed, subdued.
**fraternal,** *modif.* — *Syn.* brotherly, friendly, intimate, congenial; see **brotherly.**
**fraternity,** *n.* — *Syn.* brotherhood, Greek letter society, fellowship; see **organization** 3.
**fraternize,** *v.* — *Syn.* consort, associate, socialize, hobnob; see **associate** 1, **join** 2.
**fraud,** *n.* **1.** [Deceit] — *Syn.* trickery, duplicity, cheating, sharp practice; see **deception** 1.

**2.** [An act of deception or trickery] — *Syn.* swindle, hoax, scam*; see **trick** 1.
**3.** [An impostor] — *Syn.* pretender, sham, charlatan, quack; see **cheat** 1, **impostor.**
*See Synonym Study at* DECEPTION.
**fraudulent,** *modif.* — *Syn.* deceitful, crooked, swindling; see **dishonest** 1, 2, **false** 2.
**fraught,** *modif.* — *Syn.* abounding, filled, laden; see **full** 1.
**fray,** *n.* — *Syn.* conflict, quarrel, brawl; see **fight** 1.
**fray,** *v.* — *Syn.* shred, tatter, wear away; see **ravel.**
**frazzle\*,** *n.* — *Syn.* nervous exhaustion, enervation, prostration, collapse; see **fatigue, lassitude.**
**freak,** *n.* **1.** [A caprice] — *Syn.* vagary, whim, crotchet; see **fancy** 3, **impulse** 2.
**2.** [An abnormal or odd person or thing] — *Syn.* monstrosity, monster, aberration, oddity, abnormality, rarity, anomaly, malformation, mutation, mutant, *lusus naturae* (Latin), grotesquerie, abortion, freak of nature, curiosity, *rara avis* (Latin), misfit, queer fish, black swan, sport, hybrid, mooncalf, changeling.
**freakish,** *modif.* — *Syn.* abnormal, odd, strange; see **unusual** 2.
**freckle,** *n.* — *Syn.* pigmentation, macula, lentigo, mole, patch, blemish, blotch.
**free,** *modif.* **1.** [Not restricted politically] — *Syn.* sovereign, independent, liberated, autonomous, freed, released, delivered, emancipated, freeborn, enjoying democracy, enjoying political independence, democratic, self-governing, self-directing, autarkic, not subject to regulation, released from bondage, self-ruling, enfranchised, unenslaved, unregimented, unregulated, deregulated, decontrolled. — *Ant.* enslaved, subject, bound.
**2.** [Not restricted in space; *said of persons*] — *Syn.* unconfined, unconstrained, at large, loose, cast loose, clear of, escaped, let out, let off, unshackled, unfettered, scot-free, free as air, free as a bird, free to come and go, unoccupied, at liberty, at leisure, unengaged, disengaged, available, not tied down, footloose and fancy-free*, on the loose*. — *Ant.* CONFINED, imprisoned, restrained.
**3.** [Not restricted in space; *said of things*] — *Syn.* unimpeded, unobstructed, unhampered, unrestricted, unattached, loose, not held fast, unfastened, clear, open, unentangled, unengaged, disengaged, unoccupied, vacant, available, extricated, untrammeled, clear of, devoid of. — *Ant.* FIXED, fastened, rooted.
**4.** [Given without charge] — *Syn.* gratis, gratuitous, free of charge, without charge, for nothing, free of cost, complimentary, on the house, for free*, for love*, as a comp*, as a freebie*, for a thank-you*, free for nothing*. — *Ant.* PAID, charged, costly.
**5.** [Not restricted in speech or conduct] — *Syn.* candid, lax, loose, freewheeling*; see **easy** 1, **frank.**
**6.** [Generous] — *Syn.* liberal, lavish, openhanded; see **generous** 1.
**for free\*** — *Syn.* without cost, gratis, for nothing; see **free** 4.
**give a free hand\*** — *Syn.* permit, give permission, encourage; see **allow** 1.
**make free with\*** — *Syn.* exploit, utilize, appropriate, take liberties with; see **use** 1.
**set free** — *Syn.* release, liberate, discharge, emancipate; see **free** 1, **release.**
**with a free hand** — *Syn.* generously, lavishly, liberally, freely; see **generously** 1.
**free,** *v.* **1.** [To set loose] — *Syn.* liberate, release, discharge, deliver, save, emancipate, rescue, extricate, loose, loosen, unfix, unbind, disengage, undo, set free,

set at liberty, let out, let go, let loose, bail out, turn loose, cut loose, relieve, reprieve, restore, absolve, acquit, dismiss, pardon, clear, exonerate, enfranchise, affranchise, ransom, redeem, unfetter, unbind, unshackle, manumit, unchain, disentangle, disenthrall, disimprison, demobilize, untie, unlock, unhand, unbar, let out of prison, parole, open the cage, spring*. — *Ant.* SEIZE, capture, incarcerate.

**2.** [To clear of obstruction or entanglement] — *Syn.* disengage, clear, disentangle, unfasten, extricate, untangle, disburden, disencumber, free up, relieve, discharge, unload, cast off, put off, empty, unburden, disembarrass, decontaminate.

---

**SYN. — free** is the general term meaning to set loose from any sort of restraint, entanglement, burden, etc. *[to free a convict, one's conscience, etc.]*; **release**, more or less interchangeable with **free**, stresses a setting loose from confinement, literally or figuratively *[release me from my promise]*; **liberate** emphasizes the state of liberty into which the freed person or thing is brought *[to liberate prisoners of war]*; **emancipate** refers to a freeing from the bondage of slavery or of social institutions or conventions regarded as equivalent to slavery *[emancipated from medieval superstition]*; **discharge** implies a being permitted to leave that which confines or restrains *[discharged at last from the army]*

---

**freebooter,** *n.* — *Syn.* pirate, buccaneer, plunderer, marauder; see **pirate.**

**freed,** *modif.* — *Syn.* liberated, released, discharged; see **free** 1, 2, 3.

**freedom,** *n.* **1.** [Political liberty] — *Syn.* liberty, independence, sovereignty, autonomy, democracy, self-government, self-rule, emancipation, liberation, enfranchisement, franchise, citizenship, right, civil liberty, autarky, self-determination; see also **liberty** 4. — *Ant.* SLAVERY, bondage, repression.

**2.** [Exemption from necessity] — *Syn.* privilege, immunity, liberty, license, prerogative, right, carte blanche, indulgence, unrestraint, leisure, facility, range, latitude, scope, bent, play, own accord, free rein, full play, laissez faire, leeway, run, plenty of rope*. — *Ant.* RESTRAINT, constraint, hindrance.

**3.** [Natural ease and facility] — *Syn.* readiness, forthrightness, spontaneity; see **ease** 2, **informality.**

**4.** [Liberty of action] — *Syn.* right to decide, freedom of choice, option, license; see **choice** 1.

---

**SYN. — freedom,** the broadest in scope of these words, implies the absence of hindrance, restraint, confinement, or repression *[freedom of speech]*; **liberty,** often interchangeable with **freedom,** strictly connotes past or potential restriction, repression, etc. *[civil liberties]*; **license** implies freedom that consists in violating the usual rules, laws, or practices, either by consent *[poetic license]* or as an abuse of liberty *[slander is license of the tongue]*

---

**free-for-all*,** *n.* — *Syn.* riot, brawl, melee, knock-down, drag-out fight; see also **fight** 1.

**free hand,** *n.* — *Syn.* scope, latitude, facility, opportunity, complete liberty, discretion, authority, carte blanche; see also **freedom** 2.

**freehanded,** *modif.* — *Syn.* charitable, liberal, openhanded; see **generous** 1.

**freeing,** *n.* — *Syn.* emancipation, liberation, releasing, deliverance, manumission, delivery, saving, rescuing, salvation, restoration, ransoming, extrication, loosing,

unfettering, unlocking, unchaining, unbinding, reprieve, discharging, loosening, pardoning, clearing, granting freedom, letting loose, setting free, disentangling, removing fetters, setting at liberty, giving to the open air, releasing from prison, demobilizing, untying.

**free-lance,** *modif.* — *Syn.* self-employed, not under contract, unattached, independent, itinerant, amateur.

**freely,** *modif.* **1.** [Without physical restriction] — *Syn.* loosely, easily, smoothly, without encumbrance, unobstructedly, without restraint, as one pleases, without let or hindrance. — *Ant.* with difficulty, under obstacles, under restraint.

**2.** [Without mental restriction] — *Syn.* voluntarily, willingly, of one's own accord, at will, at pleasure, at discretion, of one's own free will, of one's own volition, purposely, deliberately, intentionally, advisedly, designedly, without urging, generously, liberally, without stint, with abandon, spontaneously, frankly, openly, unreservedly, candidly, without constraint. — *Ant.* UNWILLINGLY, under compulsion, hesitantly.

**free on board,** *modif.* — *Syn.* plus shipping costs, net, F.O.B.

**free-spoken,** *modif.* — *Syn.* candid, outspoken, blunt; see **frank.**

**freethinker,** *n.* — *Syn.* latitudinarian, skeptic, agnostic; see **radical, skeptic.**

See Synonym Study at ATHEIST.

**freeway,** *n.* — *Syn.* turnpike, expressway, superhighway, skyway; see **highway, road** 1.

**free will,** *n.* — *Syn.* volition, choice, free choice, power of choice, willingness, intention, purpose, voluntary decision, unrestrained will, will and pleasure, velleity, freedom, pleasure, discretion, inclination, desire, wish, intent, full intent and purpose, option, determination, mind, consent. — *Ant.* determinism, compulsion, unwillingness.

**freeze,** *v.* **1.** [To change to a solid state] — *Syn.* congeal, harden, solidify, ice, stiffen, glaciate, ice up. — *Ant.* MELT, thaw, liquefy.

**2.** [To make cold] — *Syn.* chill, refrigerate, ice, quick-freeze, deep-freeze, flash-freeze, nip, bite, cool, pierce, chill to the marrow, make one's teeth chatter, numb, anesthetize, benumb. — *Ant.* heat, warm, cook.

**3.** [To halt] — *Syn.* fix, arrest, suspend, become immobilized; see **halt** 2, **stop** 1.

**4.** [To discourage] — *Syn.* dishearten, depress, dampen; see **discourage** 1.

**freezing,** *modif.* — *Syn.* frosty, wintry, frigid; see **cold** 1.

**freight,** *modif.* — *Syn.* rail, railway, railroad, shipping, delivery, transportation, carrying, handling, moving, storage, express, baggage.

**freight,** *n.* **1.** [That which is carried] — *Syn.* cargo, shipment, goods, lading, burden, load, contents, weight, bulk, encumbrance, ballast, consignment, freightage, tonnage, bales, packages, baggage, wares.

**2.** [Charges for transportation] — *Syn.* freightage, shipping costs, transportation costs, carrying charges, handling charges, transfer charges, storage charges, rates, bill, rail charges.

**3.** [The transportation of goods] — *Syn.* shipping, conveyance, delivery, freightage; see **transportation.**

**freighter,** *n.* — *Syn.* tanker, tramp, cargo ship; see **ship.**

**French,** *modif.* **1.** [Referring to the culture or people of France] — *Syn.* Gallic, Latin, Frenchified, Parisian.

**2.** [Referring to the French language] — *Syn.* Romance, Romanic, Provençal, Parisian, Gallic.

**French,** *n.* **1.** [The French people] — *Syn.* Gallic nation, Latins, Auvergnats, Basques, Bretons, Burgundians, Gascons, Gauls, Normans, Picards,

Provençals, Savoyards, French Canadians, Quebecois, Quebecers, overseas French, French provincials.
**2.** [The French tongue] — *Syn.* Romance language, modern French, Middle French, Old French, Norman, Anglo-Norman, Parisian French, provincial French, Canadian French, *langue d'oc, langue d'oïl* (*both* French).
**frenetic,** *modif.* — *Syn.* frenzied, frantic, hectic, hyper\*; see **excited, frantic.**
**frenzy,** *n.* — *Syn.* rage, craze, furor; see **excitement, insanity** 1.
*See Synonym Study at* HYSTERIA.
**frequency,** *n.* **1.** [The state or quality of being frequent] — *Syn.* recurrence, number, reiteration, repetition; see **incidence, regularity.**
**2.** [The number of occurrences in a unit of time] — *Syn.* beat, pulse, cycle, wavelength, radio wave, periodicity, pulsation, oscillation, rhythm, meter, round, rotation, rate.
**frequent,** *modif.* — *Syn.* recurrent, repeated, recurring, many, numerous, common, habitual, usual, regular, continual, constant, incessant, perpetual, persistent, customary, prevalent, ubiquitous, familiar, commonplace, ordinary, expected, routine, normal, everyday, daily, periodic, oft-repeated, reiterated, reiterative, monotonous, redundant, successive, thick, numberless, various, a good many; see also **regular** 3. — *Ant.* RARE, infrequent, occasional.
**frequent,** *v.* — *Syn.* visit often, go to, resort to, visit repeatedly, haunt, patronize, be seen at daily, visit and revisit, attend regularly, be at home in, be often in, be habitually in, hang around\*, hang out\*; see also **visit** 2.
**frequenter,** *n.* — *Syn.* haunter, habitué, denizen, customer, patron, regular attender, frequent visitor, fan, daily customer.
**frequently,** *modif.* — *Syn.* often, regularly, usually, commonly, habitually, generally, customarily, ordinarily, many times, in many instances, repeatedly, again and again, over and over, time after time, time and again, recurrently, many a time, continually, constantly, not infrequently, often enough, more often than not, chronically, perpetually, persistently, successively, periodically, every now and then, intermittently, spasmodically, at times, oftentimes, oft, a lot, every time one turns around\*, more times than you can shake a stick at\*; see also **regularly** 1, 2. — *Ant.* SELDOM, infrequently, rarely.
**fresh,** *modif.* **1.** [Newly produced] — *Syn.* new, green, crisp, raw, recent, current, late, this season's, factory-fresh, garden-fresh, farm-fresh, new-crop, newly born, brand-new, newborn, immature, young, beginning, newfound, just out, newfangled, hot off the press\*. — *Ant.* OLD, stale, musty.
**2.** [Novel] — *Syn.* unconventional, original, radical, different; see **original** 2, 3, **unusual** 1, 2.
**3.** [Additional] — *Syn.* further, increased, supplementary, new; see **extra.**
**4.** [Not preserved] — *Syn.* unsalted, uncured, unpickled, undried, unsmoked, uncanned; see also sense 1.
**5.** [Unspoiled] — *Syn.* uncontaminated, not stale, good, unwilted, undecayed, well-preserved, odor-free, in good condition, unwithered, unblemished, unspotted, preserved, faultless, new, pure, pristine, virgin, unimpaired, wholesome. — *Ant.* DECAYED, spoiled, contaminated.
**6.** [Not faded, worn, or soiled] — *Syn.* vivid, unworn, unsullied, sharp; see **bright** 2, **clean, definite** 2.
**7.** [Not salt; *said of water*] — *Syn.* potable, drinkable,

cool, clear, pure, clean, sweet, fit to drink, safe. — *Ant.* DIRTY, brackish, briny.
**8.** [Brisk; *said of air or wind*] — *Syn.* cool, refreshing, bracing, invigorating, quickening, spanking, refreshing, steady, stimulating, crisp, clear, unpolluted, clean, pure, stiff.
**9.** [Energetic] — *Syn.* vigorous, spry, sprightly, alert; see **active** 2.
**10.** [Refreshed] — *Syn.* rested, restored, rehabilitated, like new, like a new man, like a new woman, renewed, relaxed, stimulated, freshened, invigorated, revived, recharged, energized, bright-eyed and bushy-tailed\*. — *Ant.* TIRED, exhausted, worn-out.
**11.** [Inexperienced] — *Syn.* untrained, untried, unskilled, green; see **inexperienced.**
**12.** [\*Impudent] — *Syn.* saucy, disrespectful, impertinent; see **rude** 2.
*See Synonym Study at* NEW.
**freshen,** *v.* **1.** [To sweeten] — *Syn.* desalinate, cleanse, purify, spruce up; see **clean.**
**2.** [To revive] — *Syn.* invigorate, rouse, refresh; see **renew** 1, **revive** 1, 2.
**freshet,** *n.* — *Syn.* overflow, deluge, surge; see **flood** 1.
**freshman,** *n.* — *Syn.* beginner, first-year student, novice, recruit, lowerclassman, tenderfoot, greenhorn, learner, apprentice, tyro, neophyte, probationer, frosh\*, freshie\*, plebe\*, yearling\*, rookie\*; see also **beginner.**
**fret,** *v.* **1.** [To cause annoyance] — *Syn.* disturb, agitate, vex, irritate; see **bother** 2, 3.
**2.** [To suffer annoyance] — *Syn.* anguish, chafe, fuss; see **brood** 2, **worry** 2.
**3.** [To rub painfully] — *Syn.* chafe, gall, gnaw, corrode; see **rub** 1.
**fretful,** *modif.* — *Syn.* peevish, petulant, cross, captious; see **irritable.**
**friable,** *modif.* — *Syn.* brittle, fragile, breakable; see **crumbly, fragile.**
*See Synonym Study at* FRAGILE.
**friar,** *n.* — *Syn.* brother, monk, mendicant, begging friar, abbot, father, padre, abbé, curé, prior, pilgrim, penitent, holy man, palmer, Dominican, Franciscan, Carmelite, Augustinian; see also **monk.**
**friction,** *n.* **1.** [The rubbing of two bodies] — *Syn.* abrasion, attrition, wearing away, erosion, rasping, filing, grinding, grating, scraping, massage, chafing, irritation.
**2.** [Trouble between individuals or groups] — *Syn.* conflict, discord, dissension, animosity; see **disagreement** 1, **dispute.**
**3.** [Resistance] — *Syn.* impedance, counteraction, interference; see **resistance** 3.
**fried,** *modif.* — *Syn.* deep-fried, French-fried, sautéed, pan-fried, stir-fried, browned, frizzled, grilled, cooked, rendered; see also **done** 2.
**friend,** *n.* **1.** [A person with whom one has mutual attachment] — *Syn.* companion, intimate, confidant, comrade, familiar, schoolmate, playmate, best friend, close friend, roommate, bedfellow, fellow, fast friend, bosom friend, boon companion, mate, alter ego, other self, soul mate, crony\*, buddy\*, sidekick\*, bosom buddy\*, homeboy\*, homegirl\*. — *Ant.* foe, ENEMY, stranger.
**2.** [An ally] — *Syn.* compatriot, confrere, colleague; see **associate.**
**3.** [A patron] — *Syn.* supporter, backer, advocate, sympathizer; see **patron** 1.
**make friends with** — *Syn.* befriend, strike up a friendship with, buddy up to\*; see **associate** 1.

**friendless,** *modif.* — *Syn.* forsaken, lonely, outcast, forlorn; see **abandoned** 1, **alone** 1.

**friendliness,** *n.* — *Syn.* cordiality, kindness, amiability, geniality; see **friendship** 2.

**friendly,** *modif.* **1.** [Well-intentioned] — *Syn.* amiable, amicable, sociable, affable, cordial, congenial, approachable, kind, kindly, helpful, sympathetic, well-disposed, neighborly, civil, peaceful, warm, loving, affectionate, fond, warm-hearted, attentive, agreeable, genial, benevolent, accommodating, obliging, acquiescent, unoffensive, nonbelligerent, hearty, convivial, solicitous, pleasant, companionable, likable, welcoming, hospitable, with open arms, familiar, intimate, confiding, on intimate terms, on good terms, on borrowing terms, in with, close, devoted, dear, attached, inseparable, loyal, faithful, steadfast, true, staunch, in favor, trusted, fast, brotherly, fraternal, sisterly, courteous, respectful, on visiting terms, cheerful, benign, good-humored, good-natured, generous, gracious, cooperative, simpatico, big-hearted\*, folksy\*, chummy\*, solid\*, thick\*, palsy-walsy\*, buddy-buddy\*, arm in arm\*. — *Ant.* UNFRIENDLY, antagonistic, hostile.
**2.** [Helpful] — *Syn.* favorable, beneficial, helping; see **helpful** 1.

**friendship,** *n.* **1.** [The state of being friends] — *Syn.* association, companionship, alliance, confraternity, amity, concord, harmony, camaraderie, fellowship, comradeship, fraternization, attachment, bond, closeness, brotherhood, sisterhood, fraternity, comity, mutual regard, affinity, accord, league, pact, *rapprochement* (French), sympathy, rapport, understanding, agreement, compatibility, fellow feeling, intercourse, intimacy, familiarity, bonding. — *Ant.* HATRED, hostility, enmity.
**2.** [Friendly feeling] — *Syn.* friendliness, good will, favor, devotion, regard, brotherly love, affection, fondness, consideration, esteem, good intentions, kindness, kindliness, amiability, amicability, neighborliness, sociability, loving-kindness, respect, attention, attentiveness, appreciation, tenderness, geniality, congeniality, heartiness, conviviality, affability, companionability, cordiality, good faith, confidence, attachment, loyalty, steadfastness, staunchness, responsiveness, understanding, warmth, sympathy, good humor, good nature, graciousness, benevolence, sincerity, generosity, chumminess\*, clubbability\*. — *Ant.* HATRED, animosity, disfavor.

**fright,** *n.* **1.** [Alarm] — *Syn.* panic, terror, fear, horror; see **fear** 1.
**2.** [\*A person or thing of unattractive or startling appearance] — *Syn.* eyesore, monstrosity, pitiable object, frump, horror\*, sight\*; see also **ugliness.**
*See Synonym Study at* FEAR.

**frighten,** *v.* **1.** [To strike with fear] — *Syn.* scare, alarm, terrify, daunt, dismay, cow, terrorize, shock, startle, dishearten, abash, dispirit, throw into a fright, raise apprehension, intimidate, deter, threaten, prey on the mind, badger, petrify, panic, demoralize, give cause for alarm, put in fear, give one a fright, horrify, appall, awe, perturb, disturb, disquiet, faze, discomfort, unnerve, harrow, unman, confound with dread, strike terror into, affright, spook\*, frighten out of one's wits\*, take one's breath away\*, chill to the bone\*, make one's hair stand on end\*, make one's blood run cold\*, make one's flesh creep\*, put one's heart in one's mouth\*, give one a turn\*, scare one stiff\*, freeze the blood\*, curdle the blood\*, scare the daylights out of\*. — *Ant.* ENCOURAGE, hearten, reassure.
**2.** [To drive off, because of alarm] — *Syn.* scare off,

scare away, intimidate, discourage, repel, stave off, frighten away, stampede, put to flight, deter, browbeat, bulldoze\*. — *Ant.* FASCINATE, inveigle, entice.

---

*SYN.* — **frighten** is the broadest of these terms and implies, usually, a sudden, temporary feeling of fear [*frightened* by a mouse] but sometimes, a state of continued dread [she's *frightened* when she's alone]; **scare**, often equivalent to **frighten**, often implies a fear that causes one to flee or to stop doing something [I *scared* him from the room]; **alarm** suggests a sudden fear or apprehension at the realization of an approaching danger [*alarmed* by his warning]; to **terrify** is to cause to feel an overwhelming, often paralyzing fear [*terrified* at the thought of war]; **terrorize** implies deliberate intention to terrify by threat or intimidation [the gangsters *terrorized* the city]

---

**frightened,** *modif.* — *Syn.* scared, terrified, afraid, startled; see **afraid** 1, 2.
*See Synonym Study at* AFRAID.

**frightening,** *modif.* — *Syn.* scary, terrifying, hair-raising; see **frightful** 1.

**frightful,** *modif.* **1.** [Causing fright] — *Syn.* fearful, awful, dreadful, horrifying, frightening, terrifying, alarming, scary, horrible, terrible, awesome, awe-inspiring, direful, gruesome, traumatic, ghastly, grisly, macabre, lurid, petrifying, unnerving, hair-raising, bloodcurdling, nightmarish, shocking, repellent, harrowing, appalling, horrific, atrocious, unspeakable, inconceivable, ominous, portentous, fearsome, dismaying, demoralizing, disturbing, disquieting, eerie, weird, uncanny, spooky\*, creepy\*. — *Ant.* CHARMING, reassuring, alluring.
**2.** [Very bad or unpleasant] — *Syn.* calamitous, shocking, terrible, horrendous; see **offensive** 2.

**frigid,** *modif.* **1.** [Thermally cold] — *Syn.* freezing, frosty, icy; see **cold** 1.
**2.** [Unresponsive] — *Syn.* undersexed, inhibited, chilly, distant; see **aloof, indifferent** 1.

**frigidity,** *n.* — *Syn.* impassivity, coldness, aloofness, stiffness; see **indifference** 1.

**frill,** *n.* **1.** [Anything thought to be unnecessary] — *Syn.* embellishment, luxury, affection, ornament, superfluity, frippery, gewgaw, gimcrack, furbelow, foppery, flourish, doodad\*, bells and whistles\*.
**2.** [A lacy decoration] — *Syn.* ruffle, flounce, trimming; see **decoration** 2, **fringe** 2.

**fringe,** *n.* **1.** [The extreme edge] — *Syn.* border, borderline, margin, periphery; see **edge** 1.
**2.** [A raveled or decorative edge] — *Syn.* flounce, hem, trimming, rickrack, edging, frill, ruffle, lace, knitting, tatting, crochet, needlepoint, border, binding, tape, bias, pinking.

**fringed,** *modif.* — *Syn.* edged, befringed, bordered; see **ornate** 1.

**frippery,** *n.* — *Syn.* finery, trifles, gewgaws, trumpery; see **finery, frill** 1.

**frisk,** *v.* **1.** [To caper] — *Syn.* romp, skip, leap; see **play** 2.
**2.** [\*To search] — *Syn.* inspect, do a body search, shake down\*; see **examine** 1, **search.**

**frisky,** *modif.* — *Syn.* spirited, lively, playful, frolicsome; see **active** 2, **jaunty.**

**fritter,** *n.* — *Syn.* friedcake, beignet, batter cake; see **pancake.**

**frivolity,** *n.* — *Syn.* flightiness, triviality, silliness, levity, flippancy, lightness, puerility, trifling, folly, frippery, flummery, giddiness.

**frivolous,** *modif.* **1.** [Trivial] — *Syn.* superficial, petty, trifling; see **trivial.**
**2.** [Silly] — *Syn.* idle, foolish, flighty, light-minded; see **silly, stupid** 1.

**frizzle,** *v.* — *Syn.* sizzle, crisp, fry; see **cook, fry.**

**frizzy,** *modif.* — *Syn.* curly, kinky, crimped, frizzly; see **curly** 1, 2.

**frock,** *n.* — *Syn.* dress, gown, habit, robe; see **clothes, dress** 2.

**frog,** *n.* **1.** [An amphibian] — *Syn.* batrachian, bullfrog, tree frog, flying frog, leopard frog, pickerel frog, spring peeper, ranid, tadpole, polliwog, toad, croaker.
**2.** [*Hoarseness] — *Syn.* catch, obstruction, irritation; see **cold** 3.
**3.** [An ornamental fastening] — *Syn.* loop, eye, clasp, buttonhole, braid, twist, curlicue.

**frolic,** *n.* **1.** [Gaiety] — *Syn.* joviality, fun, play; see **merriment** 2.
**2.** [Playful action] — *Syn.* prank, lark, trick, antic; see **joke** 1.

**frolic,** *v.* — *Syn.* caper, gambol, frisk; see **play** 1, 2.

**frolicsome,** *modif.* — *Syn.* playful, merry, sportive; see **jaunty.**

**from,** *prep.* — *Syn.* starting from, beginning with, out of, in distinction to; see **of.**

**front,** *modif.* — *Syn.* fore, forward, frontal, foremost, head, headmost, leading, first, anterior, in the foreground. — *Ant.* REAR, back, hindmost.

**front,** *n.* **1.** [The forward part or surface] — *Syn.* frontage, exterior, forepart, anterior, obverse, façade, bow, foreground, face, head, breast, frontal area, beginning. — *Ant.* posterior, back, rear.
**2.** [The fighting line] — *Syn.* front line, van, no man's land, advance position, line of battle, vanguard, outpost, advance guard, firing line.
**3.** [The appearance one presents before others] — *Syn.* mien, carriage, bearing, port, demeanor, aspect, countenance, face, presence, expression, figure, exterior.
**4.** [*Something assumed for show] — *Syn.* façade, false front, mask, pretense, exterior, display, window dressing*; see also **appearance** 2, **pose.**
**5.** [A person or group used to obscure activities] — *Syn.* blind, cover, camouflage; see **camouflage** 1, **disguise.**
**in front of** — *Syn.* before, preceding, leading; see **ahead** 2.

**front,** *v.* — *Syn.* border, look out on, overlook; see **face** 4.

**frontier,** *n.* **1.** [Boundary] — *Syn.* edge, verge, limit; see **boundary.**
**2.** [Backwoods] — *Syn.* hinterland, remote districts, outskirts; see **country** 1.

**frontispiece,** *n.* — *Syn.* illustration, flyleaf, endpaper; see **flyleaf, illustration** 2.

**frost,** *n.* **1.** [Temperature that causes freezing] — *Syn.* freeze, drop, killing frost; see **cold** 1.
**2.** [Frozen dew or vapor] — *Syn.* blight, hoarfrost, black frost, white frost, rime.

**frosting,** *n.* — *Syn.* icing, coating, filling, glaze; see **icing.**

**frosty,** *modif.* — *Syn.* frigid, freezing, chilly; see **cold** 1.

**froth,** *n.* — *Syn.* bubbles, scum, fizz, effervescence, foam, ferment, head, fume, lather, suds, scud, spume, spray, spindrift, barm, ebullition, meerschaum, carbonation.

**frothy,** *modif.* **1.** [Fizzing] — *Syn.* bubbling, foaming, soapy, sudsy, bubbly, fizzy, foamy, with a head on.
**2.** [Trivial] — *Syn.* unsubstantial, light, shallow, frivolous; see **trivial.**

**froward,** *modif.* — *Syn.* disobedient, intractable, naughty; see **contrary** 4, **obstinate** 1.

**frown,** *n.* — *Syn.* scowl, grimace, glower, glare, pout, wry face, gloomy countenance, forbidding aspect, stern visage, dirty look*.

**frown,** *v.* — *Syn.* scowl, grimace, lower, make a wry face, pout, glare, look black, knit the brow, sulk, glower, gloom, look stern, look daggers*. — *Ant.* SMILE, laugh, grin.

**frowning,** *modif.* — *Syn.* scowling, glowering, sulky; see **grim** 1, **irritable.**

**frowzy,** *modif.* — *Syn.* slovenly, untidy, unkempt, slatternly; see **dirty** 1.

**frozen,** *modif.* — *Syn.* chilled, frosted, iced; see **cold** 1, 2.

**fructify,** *v.* — *Syn.* fertilize, impregnate, fecundate, pollinate; see **fertilize** 2.

**frugal,** *modif.* **1.** [Not wasteful] — *Syn.* thrifty, saving, prudent, parsimonious; see **careful, economical** 1.
**2.** [Not costly or luxurious] — *Syn.* meager, skimpy, Spartan; see **moderate** 5, **scanty.**
*See Synonym Study at* THRIFTY.

**frugality,** *n.* — *Syn.* economy, thrift, carefulness, conservation, husbandry, management, prudence, saving, parsimony, parsimoniousness, miserliness, scrimping, stinginess, niggardliness, penuriousness, sparingness, penny-pinching, cheapness*, tightness*; see also **economy** 2. — *Ant.* WASTE, lavishness, prodigality.

**fruit,** *n.* **1.** [The edible growth of a plant] — *Syn.* fruitage, berry, drupe, grain, nut, root, tuber, pome. Common fruits include: apple, pear, peach, nectarine, plum, orange, tangerine, tangelo, grapefruit, banana, pineapple, coconut, carambola, star fruit, watermelon, cantaloupe, honeydew melon, casaba, papaya, mango, kiwi, guava, passion fruit, grape, lime, lemon, persimmon, pomegranate, raspberry, blackberry, loganberry, strawberry, cranberry, blueberry, olive, date, fig, apricot, cherry, raisin, avocado, huckleberry, gooseberry, quince, kumquat, durian; see also **apple** 1, **cherry, melon, orange** 2, **peach, pear.**
**2.** [The ripened ovary of a seed plant] — *Syn.* seed pod, envelope, capsule, follicle, grain, nut, schizocarp, legume, silique.
**3.** [The reward of labor; *often plural*] — *Syn.* profits, products, consequences, outcome; see **pay** 1, **result.**

**fruitful,** *modif.* **1.** [Fertile in a literal sense] — *Syn.* prolific, productive, fecund; see **fertile** 1, 2.
**2.** [Producing results, or likely to produce results] — *Syn.* productive, conducive, useful; see **profitable.**
*See Synonym Study at* FERTILE.

**fruition,** *n.* — *Syn.* achievement, attainment, fulfillment, realization; see **achievement** 1, **success** 1, 2.

**fruitless,** *modif.* — *Syn.* futile, vain, unprofitable, empty; see **futile** 1.
*See Synonym Study at* FUTILE.

**frump,** *n.* — *Syn.* slob, slattern, drab woman, dowdy person, slovenly person, schlump*, old bag*.

**frustrate,** *v.* — *Syn.* prevent, thwart, defeat, foil, balk, baffle, nullify, stymie, disappoint, discourage; see also **disappoint, hinder, prevent.**

---

**SYN.** — **frustrate** means to deprive of effect or render worthless an effort directed to some end; **thwart** and **balk** both mean to frustrate by blocking someone or something moving toward some objective; **foil** means to throw off course so as to discourage further effort or make it of no avail [*our plans were foiled by bad weather*]; to **baffle** is to defeat the efforts of by bewildering or confusing [*the crime baffled the police*]

---

**frustration,** *n.* — *Syn.* disappointment, impediment, failure; see **defeat** 3, **difficulty** 1, 2, **disappointment** 1, 2.

**fry,** *v.* — *Syn.* sauté, brown, pan-fry, deep-fry, French fry, stir-fry, sear, singe, grill, fricassee, frizzle, sizzle; see also **cook.**

**small fry**— *Syn.* children, infants, toddlers; see **baby** 1, **child.**

**frying pan,** *n.* — *Syn.* skillet, spider, griddle, wok; see **pan.**

**out of the frying pan and into the fire**— *Syn.* from bad to worse, worse off, in a bind*; see **endangered, in trouble** 1 at **trouble.**

**fuddle,** *v.* — *Syn.* befuddle, confuse, muddle, puzzle, intoxicate, inebriate, stupefy, make drunk, confound; see also **confuse.**

**fuddled,** *modif.* — *Syn.* intoxicated, muddled, confused; see **bewildered, doubtful** 2, **drunk.**

**fudge,** *n.* — *Syn.* penuche, chocolate fudge, divinity fudge; see **candy.**

**fuel,** *n.* — *Syn.* liquid propellant, solid propellant, combustible, firing material, fossil fuel, energy source, ammunition.

Types of fuel include: coal, coke, charcoal, anthracite, bituminous coal, peat, slack, stoker coal, stove coal, lump coal, lignite, brown coal, carbon, briquette, turf, cordwood, firewood, log, faggot, kindling, slabs, blocks, waste products, furze, timber, touchwood, crude oil, fuel oil, gas, natural gas, artificial gas, gasoline, petroleum, diesel fuel, gasohol, ethanol, propane, kerosene, paraffin, alcohol, petrol (British); see also **wood** 2.

**fuel,** *v.* — *Syn.* supply with fuel, stoke, feed, service, fill up, fire, kindle, gas*, tank up*, gas up*, fuel up*.

**fugitive,** *n.* — *Syn.* outlaw, refugee, runaway, truant, exile, deserter, escapee, vagabond, waif, stray, derelict, outcast, Ishmael, hunted person, absconder, bolter, fly-by-night*.

**fugitive,** *modif.* — *Syn.* runaway, escaped, outlaw, criminal, wandering, fleeting, evanescent, elusive, fleeing, running away, evading, avoiding, on the run, on the lam*; see also **fleeting, wandering** 1.

**fulcrum,** *n.* — *Syn.* block, prop, support of a lever; see **support** 2.

**fulfill,** *v.* 1. [To carry out] — *Syn.* accomplish, effect, live up to; see **achieve** 1, **perform** 1.

2. [To satisfy] — *Syn.* meet, answer, fill; see **satisfy** 3.
*See Synonym Study at* PERFORM.

**fulfilled,** *modif.* — *Syn.* accomplished, completed, achieved, realized, satisfied, effectuated, effected, finished, obtained, perfected, attained, reached, actualized, consummated, executed, dispatched, concluded, compassed, brought about, performed, carried out, put into effect, made good, brought to a close, crowned, matured. — *Ant.* DISAPPOINTED, unfulfilled, unrealized.

**fulfillment,** *n.* — *Syn.* attainment, accomplishment, realization; see **achievement** 1, 2, **satisfaction** 1, 2.

**full,** *modif.* 1. [Filled] — *Syn.* sated, replete, brimful, overflowing, running over, bursting, abundant, burdened, depressed, weighted, freighted, borne down, satisfied, saturated, suffused, charged, crammed, packed, stuffed, jammed, jam full, glutted, cloyed, gorged, surfeited, abounding, loaded, fraught, laden, chock-full, stocked, satiated, crowded, plethoric, full as a tick*, stuffed to the gills*, jampacked*, crawling with*, up to the brim*, packed like sardines*, fit to burst*, fit to bust*, bursting at the seams*. — *Ant.* EMPTY, exhausted, void.

2. [Occupied] — *Syn.* assigned, reserved, in use; see **taken** 2.

3. [Well supplied] — *Syn.* abundant, complete, copious, ample, bounteous, plentiful, plenteous, sufficient,

adequate, competent, lavish, extravagant, profuse. — *Ant.* INADEQUATE, scanty, insufficient.

4. [Not limited] — *Syn.* complete, thorough, broad, extensive; see **absolute** 1, **complete** 1, **comprehensive, whole** 1.

5. [Loose] — *Syn.* flapping, baggy, flowing; see **loose** 1.

6. [Mature] — *Syn.* grown, entire, complete; see **mature** 1.

7. [Deep] — *Syn.* resonant, rounded, throaty; see **loud** 1.

**in full**— *Syn.* for the entire amount, fully, thoroughly; see **completely.**

**to the full**— *Syn.* entirely, thoroughly, fully; see **completely.**

*See Synonym Study at* COMPLETE.

**fullback,** *n.* — *Syn.* backfield man, safety man, blocking back, running back; see **football player.**

**full-dress,** *modif.* — *Syn.* formal, dressy, black tie; see **formal** 4.

**full-grown,** *modif.* — *Syn.* adult, developed, grown-up; see **mature** 1.

**fullness,** *n.* — *Syn.* abundance, saturation, completion; see **plenty, saturation.**

**fully,** *modif.* 1. [Completely] — *Syn.* entirely, thoroughly, wholly; see **completely.**

2. [Adequately] — *Syn.* sufficiently, amply, enough; see **adequately** 1.

**fulminate,** *v.* 1. [To explode] — *Syn.* blow up, discharge, detonate; see **explode** 1.

2. [To intimidate] — *Syn.* menace, bluster, upbraid; see **threaten** 1.

3. [To denounce] — *Syn.* swear at, condemn, rail; see **censure, curse** 1, 2, **denounce.**

**fulmination,** *n.* 1. [Detonation] — *Syn.* discharge, blast, outburst; see **explosion** 1.

2. [Denunciation] — *Syn.* condemnation, censure, thundering against; see **blame** 1, **curse** 1, **objection** 2.

**fulsome,** *modif.* — *Syn.* disgusting, offensive, excessive, insincere; see **effusive, excessive, offensive** 2.

**fumble,** *n.* — *Syn.* mistake, blunder, dropped ball; see **error** 1.

**fumble,** *v.* — *Syn.* mishandle, bungle, mismanage; see **botch.**

**fume,** *v.* — *Syn.* seethe, boil, sputter, simmer, smolder, stew, sizzle, quiver with rage, chafe, fret, bristle, get mad, rage, rant, steam*, see red*, get hot under the collar*, do a slow burn*; see also **rage** 1.

**fumes,** *pl.n.* — *Syn.* vapor, gas, exhaust, effluvium; see **smell** 2, **smoke, vapor.**

**fumigate,** *v.* — *Syn.* cleanse thoroughly, treat, disinfect; see **purify.**

**fun*,** *modif.* — *Syn.* merry, enjoyable, amusing; see **entertaining, happy** 1, **pleasant** 2.

**fun,** *n.* — *Syn.* play, game, sport, jest, amusement, relaxation, pastime, diversion, frolic, mirth, entertainment, recreation, solace, merriment, jollity, jollification, pleasure, good time, drollery, buffoonery, foolery, fooling, romping, joke, absurdity, playfulness, laughter, frolicsomeness, festivity, carnival, tomfoolery, escapade, antic, romp, gambol, prank, lark, comedy, banter, teasing, raillery, high jinks, celebration, holiday, rejoicing, good humor, joking, jocularity, enjoyment, gladness, good cheer, delight, glee, high glee, treat, hilarity, blitheness, joy, jocundity, joviality, time of one's life*, blast*, whoopee*, picnic*, riot*. — *Ant.* UNHAPPINESS, tedium, sorrow.

**for** or **in fun**— *Syn.* for amusement, not seriously, playfully, for no reason, for the fun of it, as a joke, for laughs, for kicks*; see also **happily** 2.

**make fun of**— *Syn.* mock, satirize, poke fun at; see **ridicule**.

**function,** *n.* 1. [Use] — *Syn.* employment, capacity, office, duty, faculty, role, purpose; see also **use** 2.

2. [A social gathering] — *Syn.* celebration, reception, get-together; see **gathering, party** 1.

---

*SYN.* — **function** is the broad, general term for the natural, required, or expected activity of a person or thing /the *function* of the liver, of education, etc./; **office**, in this connection, refers to the function of a person, as determined by his position, profession, or employment /the *office* of a priest/; **duty** is applied to a task necessary in or appropriate to one's occupation, rank, status, etc. and carries a strong connotation of obligation /the *duties* of a vicar/; **capacity** refers to a specific function or status, not necessarily the usual or customary one /the judge spoke to him in the *capacity* of a friend/

---

**function,** *v.* — *Syn.* perform, run, work; see **operate** 2.

**functional,** *modif.* — *Syn.* operative, useful, utilitarian, working; see **practical**.

**functionary,** *n.* — *Syn.* deputy, representative, official; see **agent** 1.

**fund,** *n.* — *Syn.* endowment, trust fund, capital, supply, stock, store, reserve, repository; see also **reserve** 1.

**fund,** *v.* — *Syn.* finance, back, endow, subsidize; see **support** 5, **underwrite** 3.

**fundamental,** *modif.* 1. [Providing the foundation] — *Syn.* basic, underlying, basal, radical, primary, first, underived, rudimentary, elementary, substrative, supporting, axiomatic, key, crucial, vital, major, principal, grass-roots, requisite, elemental, primal, cardinal, organic, axiological, theoretical, structural, sustaining, central, original, integral. — *Ant.* SUPERFICIAL, incidental, consequent.

2. [Essential] — *Syn.* primary, requisite, significant; see **necessary** 1.

**fundamentally,** *modif.* — *Syn.* basically, radically, centrally, at heart; see **essentially**.

**fundamentals,** *n.* — *Syn.* essentials, basics, foundation; see **basics, basis** 1.

**funds,** *pl.n.* — *Syn.* capital, cash, collateral, money, assets, corporate assets, currency, savings, pecuniary resources, revenue, substance, wherewithal, *de quoi* (French), proceeds, hard cash, fluid assets, specie, stocks and bonds, money on hand, money in the bank, letters of credit, accounts receivable, accounts collectible, property, means, affluence, belongings, wealth, resources, finances, securities, stakes, earnings, winnings, possessions, profits, treasure, stocks, stores, pelf*, nest egg*, jack*, scratch*, green stuff*, lucre*, filthy lucre*.

**funeral,** *n.* 1. [Rites for the dead] — *Syn.* burial, interment, last rites, obsequies, memorial service, burial ceremony, sepulture, entombment, mortuary rites, requiem, inhumation, cremation, funeral solemnities, funeral service.

2. [Those attending a dead body] — *Syn.* cortege, mourners, pall bearers, funeral procession, funeral train.

**be one's funeral**— *Syn.* harm oneself, hurt, damage; see **destroy** 1, **ruin** 2.

**funereal,** *modif.* — *Syn.* melancholy, gloomy, mournful; see **dismal, sad** 1, 2.

**fungus,** *n.* — *Syn.* mushroom, toadstool, parasite, puffball, saprophyte, lichen, mold, rust, mildew, rot, truffle.

**funk*,** *n.* 1. [Fear] — *Syn.* fright, alarm, panic; see **fear** 1.

2. [Depression] — *Syn.* gloom, despondency, dejection, blue funk*; see **depression** 2.

**funky,** *modif.* — *Syn.* offbeat, unconventional, earthy, hip*; see **fashionable, unusual** 2.

**funnel,** *n.* — *Syn.* duct, shaft, conduit; see **pipe** 1, **tube** 1.

**funny,** *modif.* 1. [Stirring to laughter] — *Syn.* laughable, comic, droll, amusing, comical, whimsical, entertaining, diverting, humorous, witty, farcical, hilarious, jocular, jocose, jocund, waggish, facetious, clever, mirthful, laugh-provoking, hysterical, uproarious, ludicrous, absurd, ridiculous, risible, joking, jesting, sportive, playful, merry, gay, antic, jolly, good-humored, glad, gleeful, blithe, jovial, ironic, sly, rich*, side-splitting*, a laugh*, too funny for words*, killing*, priceless*; see also **facetious**. — *Ant.* SAD, serious, melancholy.

2. [*Likely to arouse suspicion] — *Syn.* curious, unusual, odd; see **suspicious** 2.

---

*SYN.* — **funny** is the simple, general term for anything that excites laughter or mirth; **laughable** applies to that which is fit to be laughed at and may connote contempt or scorn; that is **amusing** which provokes smiles, laughter, or pleasure by its pleasant, entertaining quality; that is **droll** which amuses one because of its quaintness or strangeness, or its wry or waggish humor; **comic** is applied to that which contains the elements of comedy (in a dramatic or literary sense) and amuses one in a thoughtful way; **comical** suggests that which evokes laughter of a more spontaneous, unrestrained kind; **farcical** suggests a broad comical quality based on nonsense, extravagantly boisterous humor, etc.

---

**funny*,** *n.* — *Syn.* joke, witticism, jest; see **joke** 2.

**fur,** *n.* — *Syn.* pelt, hide, hair, coat, brush, fluff, wool, fleece, fuzz.

Types of fur include: sable, mink, chinchilla, Persian lamb, astrakhan, karakul, Alaska seal, Hudson seal, muskrat, silver muskrat, ermine, American broadtail, monkey, beaver, skunk, otter, marten, stone marten, weasel, Chinese weasel, Chinese mink, American mink, kolinsky, fitch, squirrel, leopard, leopard cat, raccoon, wolverine, Russian pony, fox, white fox, blue fox, cross fox, red fox, silver fox, gray fox, Manchurian dog, sheepskin, bearskin, calfskin, kidskin, mouton, lamb, rabbit, cony.

**make the fur fly*,** 1. fight, bicker, stir up trouble; see **excite** 2, **fight** 2.

2. hasten, act hastily, rush through; see **hurry** 1.

**furbish,** *v.* 1. [To restore] — *Syn.* refurbish, improve, renovate; see **renew** 1.

2. [To burnish] — *Syn.* polish, clean, brighten; see **shine** 3.

**furious,** *modif.* 1. [Very angry] — *Syn.* enraged, raging, infuriated; see **angry**.

2. [Intense] — *Syn.* extreme, excessive, intensified; see **intense**.

3. [Turbulent] — *Syn.* violent, agitated, tumultuous; see **turbulent**.

**furl,** *v.* — *Syn.* wrap up, curl, roll; see **fold** 2.

**furlough,** *n.* — *Syn.* leave of absence, leave, rest and recuperation, R&R; see **vacation**.

**furnace,** *n.* — *Syn.* heater, heating system, boiler, hot-air furnace, steam furnace, hot-water furnace, oil burner, gas furnace, electric furnace, annealing furnace, kiln, reduction furnace, blast furnace, open-hearth furnace, BOF, basic oxygen furnace, stove, forge, smithy.

**furnish,** *v.* 1. [To supply necessities] — *Syn.* supply, provide, outfit, fit out, equip, stock, appoint, arm; see also **provide** 1.

**2.** [To equip with furniture] — *Syn.* appoint, decorate, fit, make habitable, do interior decorating.

---

*SYN.* — **furnish** implies the provision of all the things requisite for a particular service, action, etc. *[to furnish* a house*]*; to **equip** is to furnish with what is requisite for efficient action *[a car equipped* with overdrive*]*; to **outfit** is to equip completely with the articles needed for a specific undertaking, occupation, etc. *[to outfit* a hunting expedition*]*; **appoint**, a formal word now generally used in the past participle, implies the provision of all the requisites and accessories for proper service *[a well-appointed* studio*]*; **arm** literally implies equipping with weapons and materiel for war but, in extended use, connotes provision with what is necessary to meet any circumstance *[armed* with enough evidence to convict the defendant*]*

---

**furnished,** *modif.* — *Syn.* supplied, provided, fitted out; see **equipped.**

**furnishings,** *pl.n.* — *Syn.* household goods, decorations, fittings; see **furniture.**

**furniture,** *n.* — *Syn.* movables, household goods, home furnishings, appointments, fittings, chattels, household effects.

Types of furniture include — *home:* kitchen table, sofa table, end table, coffee table, chair, sofa, davenport, couch, settee, cabinet, breakfront, picture, chest, bureau, highboy, buffet, cupboard, bed, dresser, vanity, mirror, chiffonier, tapestry, footstool, secretary, press, sideboard, clock, bookcase; *office:* desk, drafting table, printer stand, bookcase, filing cabinet, stool, chair.

Styles of furniture include: modern, contemporary, tubular, Scandinavian modern, early American, Shaker, Pennsylvania Dutch, colonial, Italian Renaissance, French Renaissance, Tudor, Jacobean, Gothic, Rococo, Georgian, Queen Anne, Victorian, Louis XIV, Louis Quatorze, Louis XV, Louis Quinze, Chinese, Ming, Japanese, Oriental, Moorish, Adam, Hepplewhite, Sheraton, Chippendale, Duncan Phyfe, Empire, French colonial, French provincial, Spanish colonial, mission, Biedermeier, Mediterranean, Monterey, neoclassical.

**furor,** *n.* **1.** [Commotion] — *Syn.* tumult, excitement, stir; see **disturbance** 2.

**2.** [Frenzy] — *Syn.* rage, madness, fury; see **excitement.**

**furrier,** *n.* — *Syn.* fur dealer, tailor, modiste.

**furrow,** *n.* — *Syn.* rut, channel, corrugation, ditch; see **groove, trench** 1, **wrinkle.**

**furrowed,** *modif.* — *Syn.* grooved, ribbed, channeled; see **corrugated.**

**further,** *modif.* **1.** [To a greater distance] — *Syn.* farther, more remote, at a greater distance; see **distant** 2, **farther.**

**2.** [In addition] — *Syn.* additional, more, moreover; see **besides, extra.**

**further,** *v.* — *Syn.* advance, promote, assist, facilitate; see **promote** 1.

*See Synonym Study at* PROMOTE.

**furtherance,** *n.* — *Syn.* advancement, promotion, progression; see **improvement** 1, **progress** 1.

**furthermore,** *modif.* — *Syn.* moreover, too, in addition; see **besides.**

**furthest,** *modif.* — *Syn.* farthest, furthermost, most remote, most distant, remotest, uttermost, outermost, ultimate, extreme, outmost.

**furtive,** *modif.* **1.** [Clandestine] — *Syn.* secret, hidden, surreptitious, stealthy; see **secret** 3.

**2.** [Evasive] — *Syn.* sneaky, shifty, elusive; see **sly** 1.

*See Synonym Study at* SECRET.

**fury,** *n.* — *Syn.* wrath, rage, violence, fierceness; see **anger.**

*See Synonym Study at* ANGER.

**fuse,** *n.* — *Syn.* circuit breaker, plug fuse, wick, detonator, igniter.

**blow a fuse★** — *Syn.* become angry, lose one's temper, rant; see **rage** 1.

**fuse,** *v.* — *Syn.* blend, combine, melt together, weld; see **join** 1, **mix** 1.

*See Synonym Study at* MIX.

**fusillade,** *n.* — *Syn.* volley, crossfire, firing; see **fire** 2.

**fusion,** *n.* **1.** [A melting] — *Syn.* liquefaction, liquefying, melting, heating, smelting.

**2.** [Unification] — *Syn.* amalgamation, blending, merging, coalition; see **union** 1.

**fuss,** *n.* — *Syn.* bustle, ado, bother, complaint; see **confusion** 2, **excitement, uproar.**

**fuss,** *v.* — *Syn.* whine, whimper, object; see **complain** 1.

**fussy,** *modif.* — *Syn.* fastidious, particular, meticulous; see **careful** 1.

**fustian,** *n.* — *Syn.* bombast, ranting, pomposity; see **euphuism, wordiness.**

**futile,** *modif.* **1.** [To no purpose] — *Syn.* vain, unavailing, useless, in vain, fruitless, hopeless, impractical, worthless, impracticable, unprofitable, to no effect, not successful, abortive, profitless, valueless, unneeded, resultless, unsatisfactory, unsatisfying, ineffective, ineffectual, bootless, unproductive, to no avail, idle, empty, nugatory, hollow, barren, exhausted, unreal, delusive, unsubstantial, visionary. — *Ant.* effective, fruitful, effectual.

**2.** [Frivolous] — *Syn.* trifling, petty, unimportant, small; see **trivial.**

---

*SYN.* — **futile** is applied to that which fails completely of the desired end or is incapable of producing any result; **vain** also implies failure but does not have as strong a connotation of intrinsic inefficacy as **futile**; **fruitless** stresses the idea of great and prolonged effort that is profitless or fails to yield results; that is **abortive** which fails to succeed or miscarries at an early stage of its development; that is **useless** which has proved to be ineffectual in practice or is theoretically considered to be of no avail

---

**futility,** *n.* — *Syn.* uselessness, ineffectiveness, fruitlessness, falseness, hollowness, triviality, frivolity, idleness, vanity, emptiness, hopelessness, worthlessness, labor in vain, lost trouble, unprofitableness, purposelessness, pointlessness, meaninglessness, insubstantiality, vainness, bootlessness, falsity, illusion, folly, want of substance, unimportance, carrying water in a sieve, wild-goose chase, sowing the sand, labor of Sisyphus, running around in circles, beating the air, spinning one's wheels, carrying coals to Newcastle. — *Ant.* IMPORTANCE, fruitfulness, significance.

**future,** *modif.* — *Syn.* coming, impending, imminent, forthcoming, destined, fated, prospective, to come, to be, in the course of time, expected, anticipated, inevitable, approaching, unfolding, eventual, ultimate, later, planned, scheduled, projected, on the schedule, budgeted, in the planning stage, booked, in the plans for the future, not ruled out, looked toward, in the natural course of events, likely, coming up, in the cards★, in the offing★, down the road★, a gleam in someone's eye★; see also **coming** 1. — *Ant.* PAST, previous, completed.

**future,** *n.* **1.** [All time that is to come] — *Syn.* futurity, aftertime, infinity, eternity, world to come, subsequent time, coming time, events to come, prospect, eventuality, tomorrow, the morrow, *mañana* (Spanish), the hereafter, by and by, the sweet by and by*. — *Ant.* PAST, historic ages, recorded time.
**2.** [One's personal time to come] — *Syn.* destiny, fate, expectation; see **doom** 1, **fate** 2.

**fuzz,** *n.* **1.** [Down] — *Syn.* nap, fluff, fur; see **fur, hair** 1.
**2.** [*Police] — *Syn.* police officers, cops*, policemen; see **police.**
**fuzzy,** *modif.* **1.** [Like or covered with fuzz] — *Syn.* hairy, woolly, furry; see **downy.**
**2.** [Not clear] — *Syn.* blurred, indistinct, indefinite, out of focus, shadowy, dim, misty, hazy, foggy; see also **hazy** 1, **obscure** 1.

# G

**gab,** *n.* — *Syn.* gossip, idle talk, chatter; see **gossip** 1, **nonsense** 1.

**gift of (the) gab★** — *Syn.* loquacity, volubility, verbal ability; see **eloquence** 1.

**gab,** *v.* — *Syn.* gossip, jabber, chatter, chat; see **babble.**

**gabble,** *v.* — *Syn.* jabber, chatter, rattle; see **babble.**

**gable,** *n.* — *Syn.* peak, end wall, roof, housetop, ridge, corbel gable, step gable.

**gad,** *v.* — *Syn.* ramble, wander, stray; see **roam, walk** 1.

**gadabout,** *n.* — *Syn.* rambler, rover, gallivanter; see **loafer, traveler.**

**gadget,** *n.* — *Syn.* device, contrivance, contraption, gizmo★; see **device** 1.

**gaffe,** *n.* — *Syn.* blunder, faux pas, indiscretion; see **error** 1.

**gag,** *v.* **1.** [To stop the mouth] — *Syn.* choke, muzzle, muffle, obstruct, stifle, smother, throttle, strangle, garrote, silence by violence, tape up, suffocate.
**2.** [To forbid expression to] — *Syn.* silence, constrain, suppress, repress, hush; see also **quiet** 2.
**3.** [To retch] — *Syn.* be nauseated, sicken, choke; see **vomit.**

**gaiety,** *n.* — *Syn.* jollity, mirth, exhilaration; see **happiness** 1.

**gaily,** *modif.* **1.** [Cheerfully] — *Syn.* merrily, laughingly, vivaciously; see **happily** 2.
**2.** [Brightly] — *Syn.* showily, vivaciously, spiritedly, brilliantly, splendidly, gaudily, expensively, colorfully, extravagantly, flamboyantly, flashily, garishly, sparklingly, scintillatingly, glowingly, in a sprightly manner, with spirit, with élan, in holiday attire, with spirit and force, *con brio, con spirito* (*both* Italian). — *Ant.* QUIETLY, modestly, drably.

**gain,** *n.* **1.** [The act of increasing] — *Syn.* addition, accrual, accumulation, accretion; see **accumulation** 1, **increase** 1.
**2.** [Excess of returns over expenditures] — *Syn.* receipts, earnings, winnings; see **addition** 2, **profit** 2.

**gain,** *v.* **1.** [To increase] — *Syn.* augment, expand, enlarge; see **grow** 1, **increase** 1.
**2.** [To advance] — *Syn.* progress, overtake, move forward; see **advance** 1.
**3.** [To win] — *Syn.* get, cash in on, obtain, earn; see **obtain** 1, **win** 1.
**4.** [To achieve] — *Syn.* attain, realize, reach; see **achieve** 2, **succeed** 1.
*See Synonym Study at* ACHIEVE, OBTAIN.

**gainful,** *modif.* — *Syn.* profitable, lucrative, remunerative, productive; see **profitable.**

**gainfully,** *modif.* — *Syn.* productively, profitably, for money; see **profitably.**

**gainsay,** *v.* **1.** [To deny] — *Syn.* disclaim, refute, repudiate; see **deny.**
**2.** [To contradict] — *Syn.* disagree, dispute, controvert; see **oppose** 1.
*See Synonym Study at* DENY.

**gait,** *n.* **1.** [Manner of moving on foot] — *Syn.* walk, run,

motion, step, tread, stride, pace, tramp, march, carriage, movements.
**2.** [Style of foot movement; *said of horses*] — *Syn.* walk, single-foot, rack, amble, canter, pace, trot, run, gallop.

**gala,** *modif.* — *Syn.* festive, celebratory, joyous, grand; see **elaborate** 1, **happy** 1, 2, **pleasant** 2.

**gala,** *n.* — *Syn.* affair, function, fete; see **celebration** 2, **party** 1.

**galaxy,** *n.* **1.** [A large system of stars] — *Syn.* cosmic system, star cluster, nebula, Milky Way; see **constellation, universe.**
**2.** [Any brilliant group, as of persons] — *Syn.* assemblage of celebrities, brilliant company, elite, pleiad; see **gathering.**

**gale,** *n.* — *Syn.* hurricane, windstorm, blow, typhoon; see **storm** 1, **wind** 1.
*See Synonym Study at* WIND.

**gall,** *n.* **1.** [Spite] — *Syn.* cynicism, rancor, bitterness; see **bitterness** 2, **malice.**
**2.** [★Impudence] — *Syn.* effrontery, insolence, temerity, impertinence; see **rudeness.**
*See Synonym Study at* TEMERITY.

**gall,** *v.* — *Syn.* annoy, irk, irritate; see **bother** 2, **rankle.**

**gallant,** *modif.* — *Syn.* courageous, spirited, noble, chivalrous; see **brave** 1, **chivalrous.**
*See Synonym Study at* POLITE.

**gallantry,** *n.* — *Syn.* heroism, valor, chivalry; see **courage** 1, **courtesy** 1.

**galleon,** *n.* — *Syn.* man-of-war, argosy, sailing vessel; see **ship.**

**gallery,** *n.* **1.** [An elevated section of seats] — *Syn.* arcade, upstairs, loggia; see **balcony.**
**2.** [Onlookers, especially from the gallery] — *Syn.* spectators, audience, public; see **attendance** 2, **audience** 1.
**3.** [A room for showing works of art] — *Syn.* salon, museum, exhibition room, studio, hall, exhibit, showroom, wing.

**play to the gallery★** — *Syn.* show off, ham★, pander; see **act** 3, **satisfy** 1.

**galley,** *n.* **1.** [A ship] — *Syn.* galleon, quarter galley, galleass, galiot, bireme, trireme, dinghy, rowboat, tender; see also **boat, ship.**
**2.** [A kitchen] — *Syn.* caboose, scullery, cookroom; see **kitchen.**

**galling,** *modif.* — *Syn.* annoying, irritating, bothersome, rankling; see **disturbing.**

**gallivant,** *v.* — *Syn.* gad about, wander, traipse; see **roam, walk** 1.

**gallon,** *n.* — *Syn.* 231 cubic inches, 3.7853 liters, tun, measure of capacity, liquid measure, four quarts, eight pints, imperial gallon.

**gallop,** *v.* — *Syn.* run, speed, tear, sprint, spring, leap, jump, ride at full speed, go at a gallop, bound, hurdle, swing, stride, lope, canter, trot, pace, rack, single-foot; see also **race** 1.

**gallows,** *n.* — *Syn.* gibbet, scaffold, yardarm, hangman's tree, Tyburn Tree, tree, noose, halter, drop★.

**galore,** *modif.* — *Syn.* in abundance, in quantity, in profusion, aplenty*; see **plentiful** 1, 2.

**galoshes,** *pl.n.* — *Syn.* overshoes, rubbers, arctics, boots; see **boot** 1.

**galvanize,** *v.* **1.** [To stimulate into activity] — *Syn.* excite, arouse, stir, electrify; see **animate** 1, **excite** 1, 2, **incite.**
**2.** [To coat with zinc] — *Syn.* plate, protect, electroplate; see **cover** 1, **plate.**

**gamble,** *n.* — *Syn.* chance, risk, crapshoot*; see **bet, uncertainty** 3, **venture.**

**gamble,** *v.* **1.** [To play for money] — *Syn.* game, wager, bet, play, plunge, play at dice, shoot craps, cut the cards, play at hazard, cast lots, speculate, stake, back, lay money on, try one's luck, take a flier*, go for broke*, flip a coin*, leap into the dark*, shoot the moon*, buy a pig in a poke*, buck the tiger*, double the blind*, get in on the action*; see also **bet.**
**2.** [To take chances] — *Syn.* hazard, venture, risk; see **chance** 2.

**gambler,** *n.* — *Syn.* gamester, player, speculator, bettor, plunger, backer, layer, sharper, cardsharp*, player for stakes, dicer, crapshooter, hazarder, adventurer, risk-taker, operator, bookmaker, croupier, banker, numbers runner, sport*, highroller*, stabber*, tinhorn*, black-leg*, shark*, shell-worker*, knight of the elbow*, shill*, bookie*.

**gambling,** *n.* — *Syn.* betting, staking, gaming, playing, wagering, playing at hazard, venturing, plunging, backing, laying money on, speculation, action*, taking a flier*, taking a shot*, laying odds*.
Types of gambling include: dicing, sports betting, lottery, lotto, matching, casino, baccarat, *chemin de fer* (French), roulette, bingo, keno, faro, poker, gin rummy, stud poker, draw poker, strip poker, straight poker, fan-tan, newmarket, nap, blackjack, twenty-one, seven-up, Napoleon, Wellington, chuck-farthing, playing slot machines, craps*, crap-shooting*, shooting crap*, rolling bones*, playing the ponies*, spit in the ocean*, backing the cards*, working the machines*, penny-ante*.

**gambol,** *v.* — *Syn.* frolic, caper, romp; see **play** 2.

**game,** *modif.* **1.** [Plucky] — *Syn.* spirited, adventuresome, ready and willing*; see **brave** 1.
**2.** [*Lame] — *Syn.* bad, injured, weak; see **disabled.**

**game,** *n.* **1.** [Entertainment] — *Syn.* pastime, amusement, diversion, recreation, sport, play; see also **entertainment** 1, 2, **sport** 1.
Card games include: poker, whist, bridgewhist, bridge, contract bridge, duplicate bridge, honeymoon bridge, auction bridge, rummy, gin rummy, five hundred, casino, war, euchre, taroc, tarok, railroad euchre, seven-up, cribbage, patience, solitaire, pedro, cinch, hearts, canasta, pitch, old maid, nap, Napoleon, Wellington, bezique, twenty-one, blackjack, baccarat, chemin de fer, Pan (trademark), Uno (trademark).
Children's games include: hide-and-go-seek, tag, tap on the icebox, hopscotch, jump rope, hen-and-chickens, andy over, ante over, pretty girl station, prisoner's base, dare base, jacks, marbles, tiddlywinks, mumble-the-peg, mumbletypeg, ball, one old cat, fox and geese, red Rover, king of the hill, crack the whip, leapfrog, statues, London Bridge, ring around the roses, drop the handkerchief; clap in, clap out; puss in the corner, blindman's bluff, shinny, tin-tin-come-in, follow the leader, Simon says, giant step, catch, pom-pom-pullaway, post office, favors, Jerusalem, musical chairs, streets and alleys, run the gauntlet, cops and robbers, soldier, Indian, Marco Polo, duck-on-a-rock, mother-may-I; red light, green light.

Party games include: charades, ha-ha, spin-the-bottle, post office, stagecoach, concentration, Twister (trademark), buzz, pin-the-tail-on-the-donkey.
Word games include: Scrabble (trademark), crossword puzzles, anagrams, ghost.
Board games include: chess, checkers, Chinese checkers, cribbage, backgammon, go; Monopoly, Sorry, Clue, Pictionary, Trivial Pursuit, Parcheesi, Ouija, Mah-Jongg (*all* trademarks).
Guessing games include: twenty questions, Botticelli, geography, charades.
**2.** [Competition] — *Syn.* sport, contest, match, tournament; see **competition** 2, **sport** 3.
**3.** [*A trick] — *Syn.* prank, practical joke, hoax; see **joke** 1.
**4.** [Wild meat, fish, or fowl] — *Syn.* quarry, prey, ravin; see **fish, fowl, meat.**
**ahead of the game*** — *Syn.* winning, doing well, thriving; see **successful.**
**off one's game*** — *Syn.* performing poorly, doing badly, failing; see **losing** 1.
**play games** — *Syn.* be evasive, dissemble, put on an act; see **deceive, evade** 1, **pretend** 1.
**play the game*** — *Syn.* behave properly, follow the rules, do what is expected; see **behave** 2, **conform.**

**game plan,** *n.* — *Syn.* strategy, tactics, course of action; see **plan** 2.

**gamin,** *n.* — *Syn.* waif, urchin, minx; see **child, orphan.**

**gamut,** *n.* — *Syn.* compass, range, sweep, scale; see **extent, range** 2.
*See Synonym Study at* RANGE.

**gamy,** *modif.* — *Syn.* strong-tasting, tangy, tainted, high; see **rotten** 1, **strong** 8.

**gander,** *n.* — *Syn.* male goose, drake, brant; see **fowl, goose** 1.

**gang,** *n.* — *Syn.* group, band, pack, crowd; see **clique, organization** 3.

**gangling,** *modif.* — *Syn.* spindly, lanky, rangy, gangly; see **thin** 2.

**gangplank,** *n.* — *Syn.* plank, bridge, gangway, ladder, approach, ramp.

**gangrene,** *n.* — *Syn.* necrosis, decay, infection; see **decay** 2, **disease.**

**gangster,** *n.* — *Syn.* racketeer, mobster, hoodlum, gunman; see **criminal.**

**gang up on*,** *v.* — *Syn.* combine against, join forces against, overwhelm; see **attack** 2, **unite** 1.

**gangway,** *n.* — *Syn.* passage, passageway, corridor, walkway; see **hall** 2.

**gap,** *n.* **1.** [A breach] — *Syn.* cleft, break, rift; see **hole** 1, 2.
**2.** [A break in continuity] — *Syn.* hiatus, recess, lull; see **pause** 1, 2.
**3.** [A mountain pass] — *Syn.* way, chasm, hollow, cleft, passage, ravine, gorge, arroyo, canyon, defile, passageway, notch, couloir, *barranca* (Spanish), gully, gulch.

**gape,** *v.* **1.** [To stare] — *Syn.* goggle, gawk, peer; see **look** 2.
**2.** [To split] — *Syn.* yawn, part, crack, open wide; see **break** 1, **yawn** 2.

**garage,** *n.* **1.** [Housing for cars] — *Syn.* parking garage, parking, parking space, parking lot, carport, self-parking*.
**2.** [Commercial establishment] — *Syn.* repair shop, service station, service garage; chop shop*.

**garb,** *n.* **1.** [Clothes] — *Syn.* clothing, outfit, attire; see **clothes.**

**2.** [Outward appearance] — *Syn.* guise, form, semblance; see **appearance** 1.

**garbage,** *n.* — *Syn.* refuse, waste, rubbish, litter; see **trash** 1, 3.

**garble,** *v.* — *Syn.* jumble, misquote, falsify, distort; see **confuse, mislead.**

**garden,** *n.* — *Syn.* vegetable patch, plot, bed, border, cultivated area, enclosure, field, truck garden, herb garden, rock garden, rose garden, Victory garden, formal garden, kitchen garden, hotbed, cold frame, greenhouse, patio, terrace, backyard, conservatory, nursery, flower garden, water garden, hanging garden, floating garden, cactus garden, desert garden, cottage garden, English garden, Japanese garden, botanical garden, arboretum, garden spot, oasis.

**gardener,** *n.* — *Syn.* vegetable grower, truck farmer, nurseryman, grower, seedsman, caretaker, landscaper, greenskeeper, landscape gardener, landscape architect, horticulturist.

**gardening,** *n.* — *Syn.* horticulture, cultivation, growing, planting, truck farming, vegetable raising, tillage, landscaping, landscape gardening, landscape architecture, flower gardening, floriculture, groundskeeping.

**gargantuan,** *modif.* — *Syn.* enormous, huge, immense; see **large** 1.

**gargle,** *v.* — *Syn.* swish, rinse, trill, rinse the mouth, irrigate the throat, use a mouthwash.

**gargoyle,** *n.* — *Syn.* spout, grotesque figure, drain, waterspout, rainspout, gutter; see also **sculpture.**

**garish,** *modif.* — *Syn.* showy, gaudy, loud, ostentatious; see **ornate** 1, **vulgar** 1.

**garland,** *n.* **1.** [Wreath] — *Syn.* crown, festoon, laurel; see **wreath.**

**2.** [Collection] — *Syn.* excerpts, miscellany, anthology; see **collection** 2.

**garments,** *pl.n.* — *Syn.* dress, attire, apparel; see **clothes.**

**garner,** *v.* — *Syn.* store, reap, collect, amass; see **accumulate** 1, **earn** 1, **harvest.**

**garnish,** *n.* — *Syn.* trimming, embellishment, topping; see **decoration** 2.

**garnish,** *v.* — *Syn.* embellish, trim, beautify, deck; see **decorate.**

**garret,** *n.* — *Syn.* attic, upper story, loft, cupola, penthouse, tower, lookout, dormer, clerestory, top story, belfry.

**garrison,** *n.* **1.** [Militia] — *Syn.* militia, defenders, occupation troops; see **army** 1, 2.

**2.** [A fortress] — *Syn.* post, stronghold, blockhouse; see **fortification** 2.

**garrison,** *v.* — *Syn.* fortify, protect, guard; see **defend** 1, 2.

**garrote,** *v.* — *Syn.* throttle, strangle, suffocate; see **choke** 1.

**garrulity,** *n.* — *Syn.* loquacity, wordiness, verbosity, glibness, grandiloquence, talkativeness, chattiness, garrulousness, volubility, loquaciousness, effusion, verboseness, prolixity, long-windedness, logorrhea.

**garrulous,** *modif.* — *Syn.* talkative, loquacious, chattering; see **talkative, verbose.**

*See Synonym Study at* TALKATIVE.

**garter,** *n.* — *Syn.* band, strap, tie; see **band** 1, **fastener.**

**gas,** *n.* **1.** [A state of matter] — *Syn.* vapor, volatile substance, fumes, aeriform fluid, gaseous mixture.

**2.** [*Gasoline] — *Syn.* propellant, petrol (British), motor fuel; see **gasoline.**

**3.** [Poisonous gas]

Poisonous gases include: vesicant, incendiary gas, Lew-

isite, mustard gas, chloral gas, chlorine, carbon monoxide, methyl isocyanate, bromide, bromoacetone, phosgene, chloropicrin, Agent Orange, hydrocyanic acid, arsine, stibine, chloracetophenone, brombenzylcyanide, Adamsite, asphyxiating gas, vesicatory gas, moldy hay*.

**4.** [An anesthetic] — *Syn.* ether, general anesthetic, chloroform, nitrous oxide, laughing gas*.

**step on the gas*** — *Syn.* rush, move fast, speed up, step on it*; see **hurry** 1, **speed.**

**gaseous,** *modif.* — *Syn.* vaporous, effervescent, aeriform; see **volatile** 1.

**gash,** *n.* — *Syn.* slash, slice, wound; see **cut** 2.

**gasoline,** *n.* — *Syn.* petrol (British), motor fuel, propellant, combustible material, diesel fuel, gas*, juice*.

Types of gasoline include: low octane, high octane, ethanol, ethyl, gasohol, unleaded, super unleaded, regular, airplane, high test*, low test*, high grade*, mid grade*, low grade*, white gas*, soup*, gasso*.

**gasp,** *v.* — *Syn.* labor for breath, breathe convulsively, gulp, have difficulty in breathing, pant, puff, wheeze, heave, blow, sniffle, snort, catch one's breath, struggle for breath.

**at the last gasp*** — *Syn.* at the last moment, just in time, penultimately; see **finally** 2.

**gassy*,** *modif.* — *Syn.* bombastic, boastful, pompous, windy; see **bombastic, verbose.**

**gastronome,** *n.* — *Syn.* epicure, gourmet, gourmand; see **epicure.**

*See Synonym Study at* EPICURE.

**gate,** *n.* — *Syn.* gateway, entrance, portal, ingress, passage, way, port, turnstile, revolving door, means of access, issue, wicket, portcullis, lich gate (British), barrier, bar, weir; see also **door** 1, **entrance** 2.

**get the gate*** — *Syn.* be dismissed, be rejected, be asked to leave, be thrown out, be fired, get the boot*; see also **get it** 2.

**give (someone) the gate*** — *Syn.* dismiss, reject, force out; see **dismiss** 1, 2, **oust.**

**gate-crasher,** *n.* — *Syn.* interloper, trespasser, uninvited, guest, crasher*; see also **intruder.**

**gatekeeper,** *n.* — *Syn.* sentry, guard, doorkeeper; see **watchman.**

**gather,** *v.* **1.** [To come together] — *Syn.* assemble, meet, gather around, congregate, rally, crowd, throng, convene, collect, muster, unite, get together, flock together, hang around, flock in, pour in, associate, hold a reunion, reunite, forgather, resort, swarm, huddle, go into a huddle, rally around, group, converge, accumulate, cluster, concentrate, close, gang up*. — *Ant.* SCATTER, disperse, part.

**2.** [To bring together] — *Syn.* collect, assemble, rally, accumulate, aggregate, amass, muster, marshal, mobilize, round up, draw in, pick up, rake up, fish up, swoop up, scoop up, pile up; see also **accumulate** 1, **assemble** 2.

**3.** [To conclude] — *Syn.* infer, deduce, find; see **assume** 1.

**4.** [To harvest] — *Syn.* garner, reap, glean, take in; see **harvest.**

**5.** [To choose] — *Syn.* pick, cull, select; see **choose** 1.

---

*SYN.* — **gather** is the general term for a bringing or coming together [to *gather* scattered objects, people *gathered* at the corners]; **collect** usually implies careful choice in gathering from various sources, a bringing into an orderly arrangement, etc. [he *collects* coins]; **assemble** applies especially to the gathering together of persons for some special purpose [*assemble* the students in the auditorium/; **muster** applies to a formal assembling, especially of troops for inspection, roll call, etc.*See also Synonym Study at* INFER.

---

**gathered,** *modif.* — *Syn.* assembled, met, forgathered, congregated, joined, rallied, crowded together, thronged, collected, united, associated, swarmed, huddled, grouped, massed, amassed, accumulated, aggregated, picked, garnered, harvested, stored, gleaned, hoarded, culled, mustered, combined, brought together, convened, convoked, summoned, reunited, compiled, collated, mobilized, lumped together, amalgamated, incorporated, collocated, raked up, rounded up, marshaled, concentrated, heaped, stacked, piled, stowed away. — *Ant.* SCATTERED, dispersed, separated.
**be gathered to one's fathers** — *Syn.* die, pass away, expire; see **die** 1.
**gathering,** *n.* — *Syn.* assembly, meeting, conclave, caucus, parley, council, conference, convention, band, congregation, junction, company, rally, crowd, throng, bunch, collection, union, association, society, committee, legislature, house, senate, parliament, diet, swarm, huddle, group, body, mass, aggregation, herd, turnout, forgathering, flock, muster, levy, combination, caravan, mobilization, collocation, assemblage, panel, forum, discussion, concourse, interchange, reunion, meet, congress, conflux, gathering of the clans, coven, eisteddfod, synod, reception, conventicle, vestry, posse, attendance, multitude, ingathering, audience, press, rout, horde, mob, queue, crush, party, entertainment, social gathering, function, get-together, crew, gang, school, array, galaxy, bevy, troop, drove, concentration, convocation, council meeting, council of war, gemote, folkmoot, moot, witenagemot, confab*, huddle*, bull session*.
**gauche,** *modif.* — *Syn.* uncouth, clumsy, inept, tactless; see **awkward** 1.
**gaucherie,** *n.* — *Syn.* clumsiness, boorishness, blunder; see **awkwardness** 1, **error** 1.
**gaudy,** *modif.* — *Syn.* showy, flashy, tawdry; see **ornate** 1, **vulgar** 1.
**gauge,** *n.* — *Syn.* measure, mark, check, scale, criterion, guideline, yardstick, standard, norm; see also **criterion.**
*See Synonym Study at* STANDARD.
**gauge,** *v.* — *Syn.* weigh, assess, calibrate, calculate; see **estimate** 1, **measure** 1.
**gaunt,** *modif.* — *Syn.* emaciated, scraggy, skinny; see **thin** 2.
**gauze,** *n.* — *Syn.* film, veil, cheesecloth, mosquito netting, bandage, sterile cloth, sterile dressing, dressing.
**gauzy,** *modif.* — *Syn.* filmy, light, transparent, diaphanous; see **sheer** 2.
**gavel,** *n.* — *Syn.* mallet, maul, symbol of office; see **hammer.**
**gawk,** *v.* — *Syn.* stare, ogle, gape, rubberneck*; see **look** 2.
**gawky,** *modif.* — *Syn.* clumsy, ungainly, rustic, uncouth; see **awkward** 1, **rude** 1.
**gay,** *modif.* 1. [Happy] — *Syn.* lighthearted, merry, vivacious; see **happy** 1, **lively** 2, **sprightly.**
2. [Bright] — *Syn.* brilliant, intense, vivid, showy; see **bright** 1, 2.
3. [Homosexual] — *Syn.* homophile, homoerotic, lesbian; see **homosexual.**
*See Synonym Study at* LIVELY.
**gaze,** *v.* — *Syn.* stare, eye, contemplate, gape; see **look** 2.
**gazette,** *n.* — *Syn.* journal, publication, periodical; see **newspaper.**
**gear,** *n.* 1. [Equipment] — *Syn.* material, tackle, apparatus, paraphernalia; see **equipment.**

2. [A geared wheel] — *Syn.* cog, cogwheel, pinion, toothed wheel, spurwheel, sprocket, ragwheel, lanternwheel.
Types of gears include: spur, bevel, crown, worm, internal, inside, drive, driving, transmission, differential, timing, conical, Hooke's, spiral, stepped, angular, beveled, elliptical, hooked, idling, overhead, hypoid, nylon, plastic, first, low, second, intermediate, third, high, fourth, reverse, overdrive, multiplying, quick-return.
3. [Clothes or other personal belongings] — *Syn.* clothing, apparel, effects, things; see **baggage, clothes, property** 1.
**high gear*** — *Syn.* high speed, productivity, efficiency, activity; see **action** 1, **speed.**
**in gear*** — *Syn.* usable, efficient, productive, in working order; see **working.**
**low gear*** — *Syn.* low speed, slowness, inactivity, inefficiency; see **idleness** 1.
**out of gear*** — *Syn.* inefficient, not working, inoperative; see **broken** 2, **useless** 1.
**shift gears*** — *Syn.* alter one's approach, proceed along a different course, readjust; see **change** 1.
**gear,** *v.* 1. [To prepare] — *Syn.* organize, harness, ready, equip; see **prepare** 1, **provide** 1.
2. [To regulate] — *Syn.* adjust, match, blend; see **adjust** 1, **regulate** 2.
**gelatinous,** *modif.* — *Syn.* jellied, coagulated, viscous; see **thick** 3.
**gem,** *n.* 1. [A jewel] — *Syn.* precious stone, gemstone, bauble, ornament; see **jewel** 1.
Types of gems include: diamond, emerald, ruby, pearl, brilliant, aquamarine, amethyst, topaz, turquoise, jade, opal, sapphire, garnet, carnelian, jacinth, beryl, cat's eye, chrysoprase, chalcedony, agate, bloodstone, moonstone, onyx, sard, lapis lazuli, chrysolite, carbuncle, coral, zircon, tourmaline, peridot.
2. [A highly valued thing or person] — *Syn.* jewel, prize, treasure, pearl, pearl beyond price, flower, paragon, acme of perfection, masterpiece, trump, ace, nonpareil, beau ideal.
**geminate,** *modif.* — *Syn.* coupled, doubled, paired; see **matched, twin.**
**gender,** *n.* — *Syn.* sex, sexuality, grammatical class; see **kind** 2, **sex** 3.
**genealogy,** *n.* — *Syn.* derivation, pedigree, parentage, generation, descent, history, family tree, lineage, extraction, begats*; see also **family** 1.
**general,** *modif.* 1. [Having wide application] — *Syn.* comprehensive, widespread, universal, overall, sweeping, extensive, ecumenical, all-embracing, ubiquitous, unconfined, broad, generic, generalized, across-the-board, taken as a whole, not partial, not particular, not specific, blanket, inclusive, all-inclusive, catholic, wide, worldwide, endless, far-reaching, global, ample. — *Ant.* PARTICULAR, special, limited.
2. [Of common occurrence] — *Syn.* common, usual, customary, prevailing; see **common** 1.
3. [Not specific or precise] — *Syn.* indefinite, inexact, imprecise; see **obscure** 1, **vague** 2.
**in general** — *Syn.* generally, usually, in the main, as a whole; see **customarily, frequently, regularly** 1.
*See Synonym Study at* COMMON, UNIVERSAL.
**general,** *n.* — *Syn.* commanding officer, general officer, brigadier general, major general, lieutenant general, general of the army, general of the air force; see also **officer** 3.
**generality,** *n.* — *Syn.* abstraction, generalization, indefinite statement, general statement, vague statement, sweeping statement, loose statement, half-truth, simplistic

statement, observation, universality, principle; see also **cliché, law** 4.

**generalize,** *v.* 1. [To make generally applicable] — *Syn.* theorize, hypothesize, conclude, induce, infer, derive a law, establish a criterion, observe similarities, discover order in apparent disorder, establish rules of probability, discern affinities, globalize, stereotype. — *Ant.* SEPARATE, particularize, DEDUCE.

2. [To speak in general terms] — *Syn.* vapor, theorize, speculate, postulate, be metaphysical, discuss in the abstract, speak in generalities, deal in abstractions, speak in terms of the ideal, philosophize, stay up in the clouds*. — *Ant.* SPECIFY, apply, particularize.

**generally,** *modif.* — *Syn.* usually, commonly, ordinarily; see **customarily, frequently, regularly** 1.

**generalship,** *n.* — *Syn.* strategics, logistics, leadership; see **administration** 1, **tactics.**

**generate,** *v.* — *Syn.* form, make, beget, create; see **cause** 2, **create** 2, **produce** 1, 2.

**generation,** *n.* 1. [The act of producing] — *Syn.* engendering, formation, creation; see **production** 1.

2. [The act of producing offspring] — *Syn.* procreation, propagation, reproduction, breeding, bearing, spawning, bringing forth, multiplying, fructifying. — *Ant.* perishing, dying out, becoming extinct.

3. [One cycle in the succession of parents and children] — *Syn.* age, crop, rank, contemporaries, peers, coevals, peer group, age group.

4. [The time required for a generation, sense 3] — *Syn.* span, 20 to 30 years, period; see **age** 3.

**generator,** *n.* — *Syn.* source of power, dynamo, dynamo-electric machine.
Varieties include: AC, DC, shunt-wound, shunt, series-wound, series, compound.

**generic,** *modif.* — *Syn.* universal, general, nonexclusive, nonproprietary; see **general** 1, **universal** 3.
*See Synonym Study at* UNIVERSAL.

**generosity,** *n.* 1. [Unselfish giving] — *Syn.* liberality, bounty, munificence, largess, readiness in giving, free giving, hospitality, charitableness, benevolence, charity, bounteousness, profusion, hospitality, beneficence, almsgiving, philanthropy, openhandedness, altruism, unselfishness, playing Lady Bountiful*. — *Ant.* GREED, miserliness, stinginess.

2. [Humane largeness of sympathy] — *Syn.* magnanimity, charity, humanity; see **kindness** 1.

**generous,** *modif.* 1. [Open-handed] — *Syn.* bountiful, liberal, munificent, unselfish, charitable, altruistic, free-handed, beneficent, hospitable, philanthropic, prodigal, free, unsparing, unstinting, lavish, profuse. — *Ant.* STINGY, close, tightfisted.

2. [Considerate or favorable; *said of conditions, terms, etc.*] — *Syn.* liberal, magnanimous, unselfish, easy, fair, moderate, reasonable, handsome, princely, ungrudging, acceptable, just, equitable. — *Ant.* UNFAIR, unreasonable, restrictive.

3. [Noble] — *Syn.* honorable, chivalrous, magnanimous, bighearted; see **noble** 1, 2.

4. [Abundant] — *Syn.* ample, overflowing, large, bountiful; see **plentiful** 1, 2.

**generously,** *modif.* 1. [With a free hand] — *Syn.* bountifully, liberally, lavishly, unsparingly, unstintingly, in full measure, handsomely, freely, openhandedly, profusely, with open hands, without stint, abundantly, amply, munificently, charitably, prodigally, copiously. — *Ant.* stingily, grudgingly, sparingly.

2. [With an open heart] — *Syn.* charitably, liberally, magnanimously, wholeheartedly, unreservedly, ungrudgingly, nobly, majestically, genially, graciously, candidly, enthusiastically, unselfishly, altruistically, disinterestedly, chivalrously, benevolently, warmly, bigheartedly; see also **politely.** — *Ant.* SELFISHLY, coldly, heartlessly.

**genetic,** *modif.* — *Syn.* hereditary, transmitted, generative, sporogenous, xenogenetic, matriclinous, patrimonial, oögenetic, phytogenetic, digenetic, biogenetic, abiogenetic, dysmerogenetic; see also **ancestral.**

**genetic code,** *n.* — *Syn.* genetic alphabet, ribonucleic acid, RNA, language of heredity, adenine, thymine, guanine, cytosine, base pairing; see also **DNA.**

**genetics,** *n.* — *Syn.* heredity, genetic engineering, eugenics; see **heredity.**

**genial,** *modif.* 1. [Friendly] — *Syn.* cordial, affable, cheerful, warmhearted; see **amiable, friendly** 1.

2. [Pleasant or favorable; *said of the weather, surroundings, etc.*] — *Syn.* warm, agreeable, cheering, cheerful; see **fair** 3, **mild** 2, **pleasant** 2.
*See Synonym Study at* AMIABLE.

**geniality,** *n.* — *Syn.* kindliness, cheerfulness, friendliness; see **friendship** 2, **happiness** 1.

**genitals,** *n.* — *Syn.* organs, sexual organs, genitalia, organs of generation, private parts, reproductive organs, organs of excretion, pudenda, gonads, testicles, testes, vulva, stones*, nuts*, privates*.

**genius,** *n.* 1. [The highest degree of intellectual capacity] — *Syn.* ability, talent, intellect, brains, intelligence, brilliance, endowment, precocity, inspiration, imagination, gift, aptitude, faculty, propensity, wisdom, astuteness, penetration, grasp, discernment, acumen, acuteness, percipience, power, capacity, capability, accomplishment, sagacity, subtlety, perspicacity, understanding, reach, sympathy, daemon, afflatus, enthusiasm, creative gift, knack, bent, turn, flair.

2. [One having genius, sense 1] — *Syn.* gifted person, prodigy, adept, virtuoso, master, maestro, mastermind, intellectual, Einstein, mental giant, *Wunderkind* (German), brain*, intellect*, rocket scientist*, whiz*, wizard*; see also **artist** 2, **author** 1, **master** 3.

3. [Character or characteristics] — *Syn.* nature, taste, disposition; see **character** 1, 2.
*See Synonym Study at* TALENT.

**genre,** *n.* — *Syn.* sort, style, kind; see **class** 1.

**genteel,** *modif.* 1. [Polite] — *Syn.* courteous, mannerly, well-behaved; see **polite** 1.

2. [Elegant] — *Syn.* polished, cultured, well-bred; see **refined** 2.

3. [Refined, but mannered and pompous] — *Syn.* affected, pretentious, formal, prim, mannered, mincing, artificial, hollow, conventional, imitative, la-di-da*. — *Ant.* HONEST, genuine, cultured.

**gentile,** *n.* — *Syn.* heathen, non-Jew, non-Mormon; see **Christian.**
*See Synonym Study at* PAGAN.

**gentility,** *n.* — *Syn.* decorum, propriety, refinement; see **behavior** 1, **decorum, refinement** 3.

**gentle,** *modif.* 1. [Soft] — *Syn.* mild, moderate, tender, soothing; see **faint** 3, **mild** 2, **soft** 2, 3.

2. [Kind] — *Syn.* tender, considerate, benign, sensitive; see **kind** 1.

3. [Tamed] — *Syn.* domesticated, tame, docile, broken, housebroken, disciplined, educated, trained, cowed, civilized, tractable, pliable, taught, cultivated, obedient to the rein. — *Ant.* WILD, savage, untamed.

4. [Well-born] — *Syn.* highbred, blue-blooded, aristocratic; see **noble** 3, **refined** 2.
*See Synonym Study at* SOFT.

**gentlefolk,** *n.* — *Syn.* lords and ladies, upper class, nobility; see **aristocracy.**

**gentleman,** *n.* **1.** [A courteous and honorable man] — *Syn.* man of honor, refined man, man of his word, polished man, perfect gentleman, cavalier, sir, don, Sir Galahad, gentleman and a scholar\*, brick\*, trump\*. — *Ant.* BOOR, sneak, cad.

**2.** [A well-born person] — *Syn.* nobleman, patrician, man of breeding; see **aristocrat, lord** 2.

**gentlemanly,** *modif.* — *Syn.* polite, polished, gallant; see **polite** 1, **refined** 2.

**gentleness,** *n.* **1.** [Intentional mildness] — *Syn.* tenderness, carefulness, caution; see **kindness** 1.

**2.** [Physical sensitivity] — *Syn.* tenderness, mildness, softness, pliability, delicacy, smoothness, fragility, pliancy, sweetness. — *Ant.* ROUGHNESS, hardness, imperviousness.

**3.** [Docility] — *Syn.* meekness, obedience, tameness; see **docility.**

**gentlewoman,** *n.* — *Syn.* dame, noblewoman, woman of breeding; see **lady** 2, 3.

**gently,** *modif.* **1.** [Quietly and softly] — *Syn.* mildly, blandly, smoothly; see **lightly** 1, **mildly.**

**2.** [Kindly] — *Syn.* considerately, tenderly, benevolently; see **kindly** 2.

**gentrification,** *n.* — *Syn.* renovation, urban renewal, upscaling; see **renewal, restoration** 1.

**gentry,** *n.* — *Syn.* nobility, high society, upper class; see **aristocracy.**

**genuflect,** *v.* — *Syn.* kneel, bend the knee, curtsy, stoop; see **bow** 1, **kneel.**

**genuine,** *modif.* **1.** [Real; *said of things*] — *Syn.* authentic, true, actual, bona fide, original, veritable, unadulterated, pure, unmixed, undisguised, unerring, official, certified, verified, confirmed, whole, accurate, proved, tested, ascertained, good, natural, unimpeachable, unquestionable, authenticated, substantial, unalloyed, factual, demonstrable, palpable, exact, precise, indisputable, absolute, positive, valid, literal, sound, plain, unvarnished, certain, legitimate, sterling, simon-pure, pukka, legit\*, for real\*, 18-karat\*, the real thing\*, honest-to-goodness\*, sure-enough\*, real live\*, in the flesh\*, the real McCoy\*. — *Ant.* counterfeit, spurious, sham.

**2.** [Sincere] — *Syn.* real, actual, unaffected, unfeigned, honest, forthright, straightforward, veritable, unquestionable, certain, unimpeachable, definite, uncontradictable, incontrovertible, well-established, known, manifest, reliable, bona fide, staunch, trustworthy, free from pretense, without artificiality, natural, frank, candid, heartfelt, not dissimulated, without hypocrisy, ingenuous. — *Ant.* HYPOCRITICAL, affected, simulated.

---

**SYN.** — **genuine** is applied to that which really is what it is represented to be, emphasizing freedom from admixture, adulteration, sham, etc. *[genuine* silk; *genuine* grief*]*; **authentic** implies reliability and trustworthiness, stressing that the thing considered is in agreement with fact or actuality *[an authentic* report*]* or proceeds from the alleged source *[an authentic* medieval manuscript*]*; **bona fide** is properly used when a question of good faith is involved *[a bona fide* offer to negotiate*]*; **veritable** implies correspondence with the truth and connotes absolute affirmation *[a veritable* feast*]*

---

**genus,** *n.* — *Syn.* sort, variety, species, family; see **class** 1.

**geographical,** *modif.* — *Syn.* terrestrial, geographic, earthly, geological, topographical, cartographic, geo-physical, physiographic, of the earth, concerning the earth, mundane.

**geography,** *n.* — *Syn.* earth science, geology, topography, physical geography, economic geography, political geography, geopolitics, physiography, cartography.

**geology,** *n.*
Divisions of geology include: dynamic geology, structural geology, volcanology, tectonics, seismology, selenology, applied geology, mineralogy, mining geology, historical geology, paleontology, physiography, petrology, oil geology, geochemistry, geophysics, hydrology.

**geometrical,** *modif.* — *Syn.* rectilinear, curvilinear, regular, square, many-sided, multilateral, bilateral, triangular, polyhedral, polyhedrous, dihedral, trilateral, tetrahedral, quadrilateral.

**geopolitics,** *modif.* — *Syn.* world politics, political geography, economic geography; see **geography, political science.**

**germ,** *n.* **1.** [Origin] — *Syn.* inception, source, root, basis; see **origin** 3.

**2.** [Embryo] — *Syn.* seed, bud, sprig; see **egg, fetus.**

**3.** [Bacillus] — *Syn.* microbe, bacteria, disease germ, microorganism, virus, bacterium, pathogen, parasite, bug\*.

**German,** *modif.* — *Syn.* Germanic, *Deutsch, Hochdeutsch* (*both* German), Teutonic, Prussian, Saxon, Bavarian, Rhenish, Thuringian, Hanoverian, Swabian, Franconian, thorough, systematic, *gemütlich* (German).

**German,** *n.* **1.** [The German language] — *Syn.* Teutonic language, Proto-Germanic, West Germanic, High German, Low German, Old High German, Middle High German, Modern German, New High German, *Plattdeutsch* (German), High Dutch, *Deutsch* (German), Dutch\*; see also **language** 2.
Languages grouped with German as belonging to the Germanic family are — *East Germanic:* Gothic, Vandalic; *North Germanic:* Old Norse, Icelandic, Faroese, Norwegian, Danish, Swedish; *West Germanic:* English, Yiddish, Dutch, Afrikaans, Flemish, Frisian.

**2.** [A German person] — *Syn.* East German, West German, Teuton, Berliner, East Berliner, West Berliner, Bavarian, Hanoverian, Prussian, Franconian, Rhinelander, Saxon, Swabian.

**germane,** *modif.* — *Syn.* apropos, pertinent, fitting; see **relevant.**

*See Synonym Study at* RELEVANT.

**Germany,** *n.* — *Syn.* German nation, *Deutschland, Deutsches Reich* (*both* German), *Allemagne* (French), German Reich, German people, West Germany, *Bundesrepublik Deutschland, BRD* (*both* German), East Germany, *Deutsche Demokratische Republik, DDR* (*both* German), Axis power, Third Reich, German Empire, Nazi state, Weimar Republic.

**germicide,** *n.* — *Syn.* disinfectant, bactericide, microbicide, fumigant; see **antiseptic.**

**germinate,** *v.* — *Syn.* sprout, develop, shoot up, pullulate; see **grow** 1, **sprout.**

**gestation,** *n.* **1.** [Development] — *Syn.* incubation, maturation, growth; see **development** 2.

**2.** [Pregnancy] — *Syn.* reproduction, gravidity, fecundation; see **pregnancy.**

**gesticulate,** *v.* — *Syn.* pantomime, motion, signal; see **gesture.**

**gesture,** *n.* **1.** [A deliberately significant motion] — *Syn.* gesticulation, indication, signal, movement; see **sign** 1.

**2.** [A formality or pretense] — *Syn.* display, pose, posture; see **appearance** 2.

**gesture,** *v.* — *Syn.* make a sign, motion, signal, gesticulate, pantomime, act out, use sign language, sign, use one's hands, indicate, saw the air*; see also **signal.**

**get,** *v.* **1.** [To obtain] — *Syn.* gain, procure, acquire; see **obtain** 1.

**2.** [To become] — *Syn.* grow, develop into, go; see **become** 1.

**3.** [To receive] — *Syn.* be given, take, accept; see **receive** 1.

**4.** [To induce] — *Syn.* persuade, talk into, compel; see **urge** 2.

**5.** [To catch] — *Syn.* capture, take, occupy; see **seize** 2.

**6.** [*To hit] — *Syn.* sock, strike, touch; see **hit** 1.

**7.** [*To overcome] — *Syn.* beat, vanquish, overpower; see **defeat** 1, 2, 3.

**8.** [To prepare] — *Syn.* make, arrange, dress; see **prepare** 1.

**9.** [To adjust] — *Syn.* order, straighten, dispose; see **adjust** 1, 3.

**10.** [To beget; *used of animals*] — *Syn.* produce, generate, procreate; see **propagate** 1.

**11.** [To contract; *said of bodily disorders*] — *Syn.* fall victim to, succumb to, get sick; see **catch** 4.

**12.** [To remove] — *Syn.* carry away, take away, displace, cart off; see **remove** 1.

**13.** [To learn] — *Syn.* acquire, gain, receive; see **learn** 1.

**14.** [*To understand] — *Syn.* comprehend, perceive, know; see **understand** 1.

**15.** [*To puzzle] — *Syn.* upset, bewilder, confound; see **confuse.**

**16.** [*To please] — *Syn.* gratify, satisfy, amuse; see **entertain** 1.

**17.** [*To irritate] — *Syn.* annoy, provoke, vex; see **bother** 2.

**18.** [*To excite] — *Syn.* arouse, stir up, stimulate; see **excite** 2.

**19.** [*To observe] — *Syn.* look at, perceive, notice; see **see** 1.

**20.** [*To arrive] — *Syn.* come to, reach, land; see **arrive** 1.

**21.** [To come] — *Syn.* converge, advance, draw near; see **approach** 2, 3.

*See Synonym Study at* OBTAIN.

**get across*,** *v.* — *Syn.* impart, convey, pass on; see **communicate** 1.

**get ahead,** *v.* — *Syn.* climb, prosper, thrive; see **succeed** 1.

**get along,** *v.* **1.** [To be successful] — *Syn.* thrive, prosper, flourish, make ends meet; see **succeed** 1.

**2.** [To proceed] — *Syn.* progress, move on, push ahead; see **advance** 1.

**3.** [To grow old] — *Syn.* wane, decline, decay, advance in years; see **age** 1.

**4.** [To be on friendly terms] — *Syn.* be compatible, agree, concur; see **agree.**

**get angry,** *v.* — *Syn.* become enraged, become infuriated, become furious, lose one's temper, lose one's self-control, lose one's sense of balance, get mad*, get sore*, blow up*, blow one's cool*, lose one's cool*, get hot under the collar*, get steamed up*, fly off the handle*, blow a fuse*.

**get at,** *v.* **1.** [To arrive at] — *Syn.* achieve, reach, ascertain; see **arrive** 1.

**2.** [To intend] — *Syn.* mean, aim, purpose; see **intend** 1.

**get away (from),** *v.* — *Syn.* flee, run away, elude; see **escape.**

**get away with,** *v.* — *Syn.* escape notice, get off cheap*, fall on deaf ears*; see **achieve** 1, **satisfy** 3.

**get back,** *v.* **1.** [To return] — *Syn.* reappear, turn back, revisit; see **return** 1.

**2.** [To regain] — *Syn.* retrieve, reclaim, salvage; see **recover** 1.

**get back at,** *v.* — *Syn.* get even with, pay back, retaliate; see **revenge.**

**get behind,** *v.* — *Syn.* loiter, fall behind, hesitate; see **lag** 1.

**get by*,** *v.* — *Syn.* manage, get along, do well enough, make ends meet; see **contrive** 2.

**get down,** *v.* — *Syn.* dismount, come down, alight; see **descend** 1.

**get even with,** *v.* — *Syn.* settle a score, avenge, pay back; see **revenge.**

**get going,** *v.* — *Syn.* start, progress, move; see **begin** 1, 2.

**get in,** *v.* **1.** [To arrive] — *Syn.* come, land, reach, **arrive** 1.

**2.** [To enter] — *Syn.* get inside, find a way in, gain ingress; see **enter** 1.

**get it*,** *v.* **1.** [To understand] — *Syn.* comprehend, perceive, know; see **understand** 1.

**2.** [To be punished] — *Syn.* suffer, get what is coming to one, get one's just deserts, be scolded, be reprimanded, be admonished, be rebuked, be upbraided, suffer for, suffer the consequences, pay the penalty, catch it*, get in trouble*, get it in the neck*, get one's comeuppance*.

**get mad*,** *v.* — *Syn.* lose one's temper, become angry; see **get angry, rage** 1.

**get off,** *v.* **1.** [To go away] — *Syn.* depart, escape, go, embark; see **leave** 1.

**2.** [To dismount] — *Syn.* alight, light, disembark; see **descend** 1.

**get on,** *v.* **1.** [To put on] — *Syn.* dress, attire, don; see **wear** 1.

**2.** [To mount] — *Syn.* go up, ascend, scale; see **climb** 2.

**3.** [To succeed] — *Syn.* manage, do well enough, get along; see **succeed** 1.

**4.** [To age] — *Syn.* grow old, advance in years, approach retirement; see **age** 1.

**5.** [To be on friendly terms] — *Syn.* be compatible, be congenial, get along; see **agree.**

**get out,** *interj.* — *Syn.* no!, no kidding?, honestly?; see **really.**

**get out,** *v.* **1.** [To leave] — *Syn.* go, depart, take one's leave, be off, begone, scram*, split*, take a powder*, skedaddle*, beat it*, get the hell out*; see also **leave** 1.

**2.** [To escape] — *Syn.* break out, run away, flee; see **escape.**

**get out of,** *v.* **1.** [To obtain] — *Syn.* get from, secure, gain; see **obtain** 1.

**2.** [To escape] — *Syn.* flee, fly, run away; see **escape.**

**3.** [To evade] — *Syn.* dodge, shun, avoid; see **evade** 1.

**4.** [To leave] — *Syn.* depart, go away, withdraw; see **leave** 1.

**5.** [To find out from] — *Syn.* elicit, extract, force out of; see **obtain** 1.

**get over,** *v.* — *Syn.* overcome, recuperate, survive; see **recover** 3.

**get past,** *v.* — *Syn.* progress, proceed, get on; see **advance** 1.

**get ready,** *v.* — *Syn.* make preparations, arrange, plan; see **prepare** 1.

**get rid of,** *v.* — *Syn.* eject, expel, remove; see **eliminate** 1.

**get set,** *v.* — *Syn.* be on the alert, be ready, consolidate one's position; see **prepare** 1.

**get sick,** *v.* — *Syn.* become sick or ill, contract a disease, take sick; see **sicken.**

**get through,** *v.* **1.** [To complete] — *Syn.* discharge, enact, finish; see **achieve** 1.

**2.** [To endure] — *Syn.* live through, come through, survive, subsist; see **endure** 1, 2.

**get through to★,** *v.* — *Syn.* make understand, make listen, reach, come to an agreement with; see **influence.**

**getting,** *n.* **1.** [The act of procuring] — *Syn.* taking, obtaining, gaining, grasping, catching, earning, winning, seizing, clutching, pursuing, securing, capturing, mastering, possessing oneself of, confiscating, appropriating, assimilating, seeking out, snatching. — *Ant.* LOSING, giving up, abandoning.

**2.** [The act of changing] — *Syn.* succumbing, growing, becoming, altering, accepting, submitting to, being subjected to. — *Ant.* REFUSAL, rejecting, throwing off.

**get to,** *v.* **1.** [To arrive] — *Syn.* reach, approach, land at; see **arrive** 1.

**2.** [★To make listen or understand] — *Syn.* reach, talk to, approach; see **influence.**

**3.** [To irritate] — *Syn.* get, annoy, vex; see **bother** 2, 3.

**get together,** *v.* **1.** [To gather] — *Syn.* collect, accumulate, congregate; see **assemble** 2.

**2.** [To reach an agreement] — *Syn.* come to terms, settle, make a bargain; see **agree on.**

**get up,** *v.* **1.** [To climb] — *Syn.* ascend, mount, go up; see **climb** 2.

**2.** [To arise] — *Syn.* get out of bed, rise, turn out; see **arise** 1.

**get wind of,** *v.* — *Syn.* hear about, find out, learn; see **discover, hear** 2.

**get wise (to)★,** *v.* — *Syn.* find out, understand, learn; see **discover.**

**geyser,** *n.* — *Syn.* hot springs, water spout, jet; see **fountain** 2.

**ghastly,** *modif.* **1.** [Like a ghost] — *Syn.* spectral, wan, wraithlike, pallid, ashen, grim, deathlike, corpselike, funereal, cadaverous, ghostly, unearthly, weird, unnatural, supernatural, uncanny, grisly, gruesome, macabre. — *Ant.* natural, real, substantial.

**2.** [Terrifying] — *Syn.* hideous, horrible, frightening; see **frightful** 1.

**3.** [★Unpleasant] — *Syn.* repulsive, disgusting, abhorrent; see **offensive** 2.

**ghost,** *n.* **1.** [An unsubstantial being] — *Syn.* vision, specter, wraith, apparition, spirit, daemon, demon, shade, phantom, appearance, incorporeal being, ethereal being, etheric being, spook, supernatural visitant, phantasm, kelpie, zombie; see also **devil** 1.

**2.** [A disembodied human soul] — *Syn.* spirit, manes, revenant, shade, soul.

**give up the ghost** — *Syn.* succumb, perish, expire; see **die** 1.

**ghostly,** *modif.* **1.** [Concerning a ghost] — *Syn.* ghostlike, pale, wan; see **frightful** 1.

**2.** [Concerning the soul] — *Syn.* spiritual, holy, religious; see **divine** 1, 2.

**ghoul,** *n.* — *Syn.* fiend, demon, vampire; see **devil** 1.

**giant,** *modif.* — *Syn.* monstrous, colossal, enormous; see **large** 1.

**giant,** *n.* **1.** [A gigantic humanlike being] — *Syn.* ogre, Cyclops, Titan, Olympian, colossus, Gargantuan creature, Goliath, Antaeus, Brobdingnagian, man-mountain, Hercules, Atlas; see also **monster.** — *Ant.* DWARF, pigmy, mannikin.

**2.** [Anything very large] — *Syn.* mammoth, behemoth,

colossus, monster, whale, elephant, jumbo, leviathan, mountain, hulk, lump, bulk, whopper★, super-duper★. — *Ant.* DWARF, mite, midget.

**gibberish,** *n.* — *Syn.* jargon, chatter, claptrap; see **nonsense** 1.

**gibbet,** *n.* — *Syn.* yardarm, scaffold, lynching tree; see **gallows.**

**gibe,** *v.* — *Syn.* scoff, sneer, flout; see **ridicule.**

**giddy,** *modif.* **1.** [Fickle] — *Syn.* unsettled, capricious, inconstant; see **changeable** 1.

**2.** [Dizzy] — *Syn.* vertiginous, reeling, unsteady; see **dizzy** 1.

**3.** [Promoting dizziness] — *Syn.* steep, towering, awful, precipitate, lofty, confusing, whirling, stupendous, flashing, unaccustomed, tremendous, overpowering. — *Ant.* regular, steadying, balancing.

**gift,** *n.* **1.** [Something given] — *Syn.* present, donation, presentation, gratuity, benefaction, largesse, grant, tip, boon, alms, endowment, bequest, bounty, charity, provision, favor, lagniappe, legacy, bestowal, award, reward, dispensation, philanthropy, offering, souvenir, keepsake, premium, token, pittance, remembrance, courtesy, bonus, subsidy, tribute, honorarium, subvention, contribution, subscription, donative, dole, relief, ration, benefit, offertory, Peter's pence, *Trinkgeld* (German), *pourboire* (French), baksheesh, allowance, handsel, remittance, giveaway, handout★, hand-me-down★, freebie★.

**2.** [An aptitude] — *Syn.* faculty, capacity, capability; see **ability** 1, 2.

**look a gift horse in the mouth★** — *Syn.* carp, criticize, be ungrateful; see **censure.**

*See Synonym Study at* TALENT.

---

*SYN.* — **gift** and **present** both refer to something given as an expression of friendship, affection, esteem, etc., but **gift**, in current use, more often suggests formal bestowal /Christmas *presents*, the painting was a *gift* to the museum/; **donation** applies to a gift of money, etc. for a philanthropic, charitable, or religious purpose, esp. as solicited in a public drive for funds /a *donation* to the orchestra fund/; **gratuity** applies to a gift of money for services rendered, such as a tip to a waiter

---

**gifted,** *modif.* — *Syn.* smart, skilled, talented; see **able** 1, 2.

**gigantic,** *modif.* — *Syn.* enormous, massive, huge, immense; see **large** 1, **enormous.**

*See Synonym Study at* ENORMOUS.

**giggle,** *n. & v.* — *Syn.* titter, chuckle, snicker; see **laugh.**

*See Synonym Study at* LAUGH *n.*

**gigolo,** *n.* — *Syn.* paid companion, escort, playboy, paramour; see **lover** 1, **pimp.**

**gild,** *v.* **1.** [To give the appearance of gold] — *Syn.* wash, plate, overlay, tinsel, electroplate, overlay with gold, coat with gold leaf.

**2.** [To adorn] — *Syn.* varnish, overlay, lay on color, give glitter to, impart a specious appearance, whitewash, paint in rosy colors.

**gilt,** *modif.* — *Syn.* gilded, golden, plated, gold-washed, tinseled, glittering, showy, gaudy, specious, meretricious, painted, varnished, shiny, sparkling, gleaming, lustrous, gold-filled, alloyed, overlaid, gold-edged, tinsel, trumpery, tawdry, cheap, brummagem★. — *Ant.* GENUINE, solid gold, 18-carat.

**gimcrack,** *n.* — *Syn.* trifle, bauble, knick-knack; see **trinket.**

**gimmick★,** *n.* **1.** [Gadget] — *Syn.* apparatus, fixture, contrivance; see **device** 1.

2. [Means] — *Syn.* catch, secret device, method; see **trick** 1.

**gin,** *n.* Types of gin include: dry, sloe, cordial, unflavored, Old Tom, English, Dutch, Holland, London, Geneva, Schiedam; see **drink** 2.

**gingerly,** *modif.* — *Syn.* cautiously, warily, suspiciously; see **carefully** 2.

**gipsy,** *n.* — *Syn.* wanderer, rover, vagabond; see **gypsy** 1, **tramp** 1, **traveler.**

**gird,** *v.* 1. [To encircle] — *Syn.* girdle, secure, bind; see **fasten** 1, **surround** 1, 2.

2. [To support] — *Syn.* brace, fortify, strengthen; see **support** 1.

**girder,** *n.* — *Syn.* truss, rafter, mainstay; see **beam** 1.

**girdle,** *n.* 1. [A corset] — *Syn.* foundation garment, panty girdle, stays; see **corset.**

2. [A belt] — *Syn.* sash, obi, cummerbund, cinch; see **band** 1.

**girdle,** *v.* — *Syn.* encircle, enclose, clasp; see **surround** 1, 2.

**girl,** *n.* 1. [A young female] — *Syn.* young woman, schoolgirl, miss, lass, coed, lassie, damsel, damosel, maid, maiden, tomboy, teenager, colleen, mademoiselle, señorita, senhorita, young thing, filly★, subdeb★, junior miss★, nymph★, nymphet★, bobby soxer★, chick★, bird★, pigeon★, kitten★, minx★, broad★, deb★, skirt★, dame★, babe★.

2. [A female domestic] — *Syn.* maid, help, waitress; see **servant.**

3. [★A female beloved] — *Syn.* sweetheart, girlfriend, fiancée; see **girlfriend, lover** 1.

**girlfriend,** *n.* — *Syn.* sweetheart, lover, lady friend, steady, date, young lady, inamorata, paramour, truelove, old lady★; see also **lover** 1.

**girlish,** *modif.* — *Syn.* juvenile, naive, mincing, boycrazy, unsophisticated, fresh, affected, unaffected, hoydenish, teenage; see also **young** 1. — *Ant.* MATURE, matronly, sophisticated.

**girth,** *n.* 1. [Measurement around the waist] — *Syn.* circumference, distance around, bigness, compass, waist measure, expansion, size.

2. [A band] — *Syn.* strap, cinch, surcingle; see **band** 1.

**gist,** *n.* — *Syn.* substance, essence, significance; see **basis** 1, **summary.**

**give,** *v.* 1. [To transfer] — *Syn.* grant, bestow, confer, impart, present, endow, bequeath, award, dispense, subsidize, contribute, parcel out, hand out, dole out, give out, pass in, hand in, throw in, hand down, hand over, deliver, let have, tip, remit, pass down, convey, deed, sell, will, give over, make over, put into the hands of, contribute to, lavish upon, consign, negotiate, relinquish, cede, lease, accord, invest, dispose of, part with, fob off, lay upon, turn over, heap upon, transmit, settle, take delivery on, come through with, come across with, shell out, dish out, deal out, fork over, untie the purse strings, kick in, palm off. — *Ant.* MAINTAIN, withhold, take.

2. [To provide] — *Syn.* furnish, proffer, supply; see **provide** 1.

3. [To produce] — *Syn.* yield, furnish, return; see **produce** 1.

4. [To yield under pressure] — *Syn.* give way, retreat, collapse, fall, contract, offer no resistance, shrink, recede, open, relax, sag, bend, flex, crumble, crumple, yield, bow to. — *Ant.* RESIST, remain rigid, stand firm.

5. [To allot] — *Syn.* assign, dispense, deal; see **distribute** 1.

6. [To inflict] — *Syn.* strike, deliver, mete out; see **inflict** 1.

7. [To pass on] — *Syn.* communicate, transmit, transfer; see **carry** 2.

8. [To give a speech] — *Syn.* deliver, present, read; see **address** 2.

9. [To give a play] — *Syn.* put on, present, produce; see **perform** 2.

10. [To administer] — *Syn.* minister, provide with, dispense; see **administer** 2.

**what gives★** — *Syn.* what happened? what is going on? tell me the facts; see **what** 2.

---

**SYN.** — **give** is the general word meaning to transfer from one's own possession to that of another; **grant** implies that there has been a request or an expressed desire for the thing given [to *grant* a favor]; **present** implies a certain formality in the giving and often connotes considerable value in the gift [he *presented* the school with a library]; **donate** is used especially of a giving to some philanthropic or religious cause; **bestow** stresses that the thing is given gratuitously and may imply condescension in the giver [to *bestow* charity upon the poor]; **confer** implies that the giver is a superior and that the thing given is an honor, privilege, etc. [to *confer* a title, a college degree, etc.]

---

**give away,** *v.* 1. [★To reveal] — *Syn.* betray, divulge, disclose; see **reveal** 1.

2. [To give] — *Syn.* bestow, award, present; see **give** 1.

**give back,** *v.* — *Syn.* return, refund, reimburse; see **repay** 1.

**give forth,** *v.* — *Syn.* expel, discharge, send forth; see **emit** 1.

**give in,** *v.* — *Syn.* capitulate, submit, surrender; see **admit** 2, 3, **yield** 1.

**given,** *modif.* — *Syn.* granted, supplied, donated, conferred, bestowed, presented, imparted, awarded, bequeathed, dispensed, doled out, handed out, contributed, subscribed, remitted, transferred, conveyed, consigned, disposed of, communicated, furnished, allowed, expended, lavished, released, yielded, offered, ceded. — *Ant.* KEPT, taken, withheld.

**give notice,** *v.* — *Syn.* inform, advise, warn; see **notify** 1.

**given to,** *v.* — *Syn.* inured, habituated, obsessed with; see **addicted (to).**

**give off,** *v.* — *Syn.* smell of, effuse, emanate; see **emit** 1, **smell** 1.

**give (one) a black eye★,** *v.* — *Syn.* discredit, blame, vilify; see **damage** 1, **slander.**

**give out,** *v.* 1. [To emit] — *Syn.* emanate, expend, exude; see **emit** 1, **smell** 1.

2. [To deliver] — *Syn.* deal, dole, hand out, pass out; see **distribute** 1.

3. [To publish] — *Syn.* proclaim, make known, announce; see **advertise** 1, **declare** 1.

4. [To weaken] — *Syn.* faint, fail, break down; see **tire** 1, **weaken** 1.

**give over,** *v.* 1. [To hand over] — *Syn.* give up, deliver, relinquish; see **give** 1.

2. [To cease] — *Syn.* desist, finish, end; see **stop** 2.

**give place,** *v.* — *Syn.* retire, withdraw, be succeeded; see **retreat** 1, 2.

**giver,** *n.* — *Syn.* provider, supplier, donator; see **donor.**

**give rise to,** *v.* — *Syn.* originate, institute, cause; see **begin** 1.

**give up,** *v.* 1. [To surrender] — *Syn.* stop fighting, cede, hand over; see **yield** 1.

**2.** [To stop] — *Syn.* quit, halt, cease, renounce, forswear, abjure; see also **abandon** 1, **end** 1.

**3.** [To despair] — *Syn.* lose heart, lose courage, give in, abandon hope; see **despair of.**

**give way,** *v.* **1.** [To collapse] — *Syn.* sag, fall, crumble, crumple; see **give** 4.

**2.** [To draw back] — *Syn.* recede, withdraw, retire; see **retreat** 1.

**3.** [To concede] — *Syn.* yield, accede, grant; see **admit** 2, 3.

**giving,** *n.* — *Syn.* bestowing, donating, granting, conferring, imparting, supplying, awarding, presenting, bequeathing, dispensing, doling out, passing out, handing out, contributing, distributing, remitting, transferring, conveying, consigning, communicating, yielding, giving up, furnishing, allowing, expending, lavishing, offering, ceding, permitting, tipping, parting with, endowing, producing, disgorging, pouring forth, discharging, emitting. — *Ant.* GETTING, taking, appropriating.

**giving up,** *n.* — *Syn.* quitting, losing, giving in; see **stopping.**

**glacial,** *modif.* **1.** [Cold] — *Syn.* icy, frozen, polar; see **cold** 1.

**2.** [Indifferent] — *Syn.* cool, unfriendly, antagonistic; see **cold** 2, **indifferent** 1.

**glacier,** *n.* — *Syn.* ice floe, floe, ice sheet, iceberg, berg, glacial mass, snow slide, icecap, ice field, ice stream, ice torrent, glacial table, névé, firn, sérac, *mer de glace* (French).

**glad,** *modif.* **1.** [Happy] — *Syn.* happy, exhilarated, animated, jovial; see **happy** 1.

*See Synonym Study at* HAPPY.

**2.** [Encouraging] — *Syn.* cheering, exhilarating, pleasing; see **hopeful** 2.

**gladden,** *v.* — *Syn.* delight, please, hearten, encourage, elate, amuse, transport, titillate, cheer, make happy, warm; see also **entertain** 1.

**glade,** *n.* — *Syn.* dell, dale, meadow; see **valley.**

**gladiator,** *n.* — *Syn.* prize fighter, combatant, swordsman; see **fighter** 1.

**gladly,** *modif.* — *Syn.* joyously, happily, gaily, blithely, cheerfully, ecstatically, blissfully, contentedly, readily, gratefully, enthusiastically, merrily, heartily, jocundly, willingly, zealously, pleasantly, pleasurably, pleasingly, zestfully, complacently, delightfully, gleefully, cheerily, felicitously, enchantedly, paradisiacally, beatifically, warmly, rapturously, passionately, transportedly, ardently, delightedly, gloatingly, lovingly, cordially, genially, sweetly, joyfully, acquiescently, seraphically, with pleasure, with relish, with deep satisfaction, with active support, with full agreement, with full approval, with delight. — *Ant.* UNWILLINGLY, sadly, gloomily.

**gladness,** *n.* — *Syn.* cheer, mirth, delight; see **happiness** 1.

**glamorous,** *modif.* — *Syn.* fascinating, alluring, captivating, bewitching, exciting, charismatic, magnetic, dazzling; see also **charming.**

**glamour,** *n.* — *Syn.* allurement, charm, attraction; see **beauty** 1.

**glance,** *n.* — *Syn.* glimpse, sight, flash, fleeting impression; see **look** 3.

*See Synonym Study at* FLASH.

**glance,** *v.* **1.** [To look] — *Syn.* see, peep, glimpse; see **look** 2.

**2.** [To ricochet] — *Syn.* skip, slide, carom, rebound, careen, brush, skim, touch, graze, dart, bounce; see also **hit** 3.

**gland,** *n.* — *Syn.* organ, endocrine organ, glandule, pancreas, kidney, liver, testicle, spleen, epithelial cells.

Kinds of glands include: simple, compound, tubular, saccular, racemose, ductless, adrenal, carotid, endocrine, lymphatic, parathyroid, parotid, pineal, pituitary, thyroid, thymus, sebaceous, sudoriparous, tear, sweat, lacrimal, serous, muciparous, salivary, piloric, mammary, seminal, prostrate, urethral, vaginal.

**glandular,** *modif.* — *Syn.* glandulous, epithelial, secretory, glanduliferous.

**glare,** *n.* **1.** [Harsh light] — *Syn.* dazzle, brightness, flash; see **light** 1.

**2.** [An angry stare] — *Syn.* scowl, glower, withering look; see **frown.**

*See Synonym Study at* FLAME.

**glare,** *v.* **1.** [To shine brightly] — *Syn.* beam, glow, radiate; see **shine** 1, 2.

**2.** [To stare fiercely] — *Syn.* fix with a look, pierce, gaze, glower, scowl, lower, goggle, menace, stare icily, fix, wither, look daggers*; see also **frown, look** 2.

**glaring,** *modif.* **1.** [Shining] — *Syn.* blinding, dazzling, blazing; see **bright** 1.

**2.** [Staring] — *Syn.* gazing, piercing, fixing, searching, intent, penetrating, sharp, burning, withering.

**3.** [Obvious] — *Syn.* evident, conspicuous, obtrusive; see **obvious** 2.

**glass,** *n.* **1.** Types of glass include: silica, potash-lime, safety, tempered, bulletproof, sodium, crown, smalt, basalt, lead, flint, plate, cut, pressed, stained, tinted, frosted, etched, crystal, Pyrex (trademark).

Objects referred to as *glass* include: tumbler, goblet, beaker, chalice, cup, jigger, shot glass, looking glass, mirror, barometer, thermometer, altiscope, hourglass, windowpane, watch crystal, monocle, telescope, microscope, spyglass, binocular, burning glass, eyeglass, lens, magnifying glass, prism, speculum, optical glass.

**2.** [The contents of a tumbler] — *Syn.* glassful, half-pint, libation; see **drink** 1.

**glasses,** *pl.n.* — *Syn.* spectacles, eyeglasses, bifocals, trifocals, goggles, field glasses, opera glasses, contact lenses, contacts, sunglasses, steel-rimmed glasses, rimless glasses, silver-rimmed glasses, horn-rimmed glasses, tortoise-shell glasses, nose glasses, pince nez, binoculars, cheaters*, windows*, specs*, shades*, blinkers*.

**glassware,** *n.* — *Syn.* vitreous ware, crystal, glasswork, glass.

Types of common glassware include: tumbler, mug, jug, decanter, bottle, jar, tableware, glass ovenware, vase, lamp base, flower bowl, goblet, sherbet glass, wine glass, liqueur glass, champagne glass, tulip glass, cocktail glass, highball glass, old-fashioned glass, margarita glass, water glass, cordial glass, brandy snifter, pony, shot glass, jigger, Pilsener glass, beer shell, stein, cake tray, parfait glass, beer mug, aleyard.

**glassy,** *modif.* — *Syn.* vitreous, lustrous, polished; see **smooth** 1.

**glaze,** *n.* — *Syn.* enamel, polish, varnish; see **finish** 2.

**glaze,** *v.* — *Syn.* glass, incrust, coat, make vitreous, overlay, cover, enamel, glass over, make lustrous, polish, burnish, vitrify; see also **shine** 3.

**glazed,** *modif.* — *Syn.* glassy, translucent, transparent, enameled, varnished, vitreous, filmed over, shiny, incrusted, burnished, lustrous, smooth; see also **finished** 2. — *Ant.* fresh, ROUGH, unglazed.

**gleam,** *n.* — *Syn.* glow, beam, shimmer; see **light** 1, 3.

**gleam,** *v.* — *Syn.* shimmer, glimmer, sparkle, flash; see **shine** 1, 2.

*See Synonym Study at* FLASH.

**glean,** *v.* **1.** [To collect]— *Syn.* harvest, cull, reap, gather; see **harvest, reap** 1.
**2.** [To find out]— *Syn.* learn, discover, gather, ferret out, get wind of; see also **discover.**

**glee,** *n.* — *Syn.* joviality, merriment, mirth; see **happiness** 1.

**gleeful,** *modif.* — *Syn.* joyous, jolly, merry; see **happy** 1.

**glen,** *n.* — *Syn.* dale, dell, glade; see **valley.**

**glib,** *modif.* — *Syn.* smooth, offhand, smooth-talking, suave, unctuous, loquacious; see also **fluent** 2.

**glide,** *n.* **1.** [A gradual downward motion]— *Syn.* sinking, descent, loss of altitude, downward spiral, landing operation, volplaning, slide— *Ant.* plunge, debacle, crash.
**2.** [A smooth motion]— *Syn.* floating, continuous motion, smooth movement, flowing, slide, drift, swoop, wafting, skimming, flight, soaring, slither, zoom★. — *Ant.* shuffle, trot, jerk.

**glide,** *v.* **1.** [To move downward gradually]— *Syn.* descend, slip, decline, slide, stream, spiral, lose altitude.
**2.** [To move gently]— *Syn.* float, slide, drift, waft, skim, skip, trip, fly, coast, flit, wing, soar, coast along, drift along.— *Ant.* hit, rattle, lurch.

**glider,** *n.* — *Syn.* lighter-than-air craft, sailplane, engineless airplane; see **plane** 3.

**glimmer,** *n.* — *Syn.* gleam, flash, flicker; see **light** 1.

**glimmer,** *v.* — *Syn.* gleam, fade, shimmer; see **shine** 1.

**glimpse,** *n.* — *Syn.* flash, impression, sight; see **look** 3.

**glint,** *n.* — *Syn.* glimmer, gleam, shimmer; see **light** 1.

**glisten,** *v.* — *Syn.* shine, sparkle, shimmer, flicker, flash; see also **shine** 1.
*See Synonym Study at* FLASH.

**glitter,** *n.* — *Syn.* sparkle, shimmer, gleam; see **light** 1.

**glitter,** *v.* — *Syn.* glare, shimmer, sparkle, flash; see **shine** 1.
*See Synonym Study at* FLASH.

**gloaming,** *n.* — *Syn.* dusk, evening, twilight; see **night** 1.

**gloat,** *v.* — *Syn.* rejoice, revel, exult; see **celebrate** 3.

**globe,** *n.* **1.** [A sphere]— *Syn.* balloon, orb, spheroid; see **ball** 1.
**2.** [The earth; *usually with* "the"]— *Syn.* terrestrial globe, celestial globe, Copernican sphere; see **earth** 1.

**globe-trotter,** *n.* — *Syn.* jet-setter, voyager, world traveler, tourist; see **traveler.**

**gloom,** *n.* **1.** [Heavy shade]— *Syn.* shadow, murk, dimness, dark; see **darkness** 1.
**2.** [Heavy spirits]— *Syn.* woe, sadness, depression, dejection, melancholy, melancholia, dullness, despondency, misery, sorrow, morbidity, pensiveness, hypochondriasis, catatonia, dolor, malaise, vexation, pessimism, foreboding, low spirits, cheerlessness, heaviness of mind, weariness, apprehension, misgiving, distress, affliction, despair, oppression, anguish, grief, horror, mourning, bitterness, mortification, chagrin, discouragement, disconsolateness, the blues★, the dumps★, the doldrums★, blue funk★.— *Ant.* HAPPINESS, optimism, gaiety.

**gloomy,** *modif.* **1.** [Dark]— *Syn.* dim, clouded, unlit; see **dark** 1.
**2.** [Melancholy]— *Syn.* downhearted, depressed, morose; see **sad** 1.
**3.** [Encouraging melancholy]— *Syn.* dreary, depressing, discouraging; see **dismal** 1.
*See Synonym Study at* DARK.

**glorify,** *v.* **1.** [To praise]— *Syn.* laud, commend, extol, acclaim; see **praise** 1.
**2.** [To worship]— *Syn.* exalt, honor, venerate; see **worship** 2.

**glorious,** *modif.* **1.** [Characterized by glory]— *Syn.* famous, renowned, far-famed, famed, well-known, distinguished, splendid, excellent, noble, venerable, exalted, grand, illustrious, notable, celebrated, esteemed, honored, eminent, preeminent, supreme, remarkable, brilliant, great, heroic, memorable, immortal, deathless, never-to-be-forgotten, immortalized, time-honored, admirable, praiseworthy, remarkable; see also **famous.** — *Ant.* UNIMPORTANT, inglorious, ignominious.
**2.** [Characterized by splendor]— *Syn.* splendid, magnificent, marvelous, grand; see **beautiful** 1.
**3.** [★Delightful]— *Syn.* gratifying, festive, enchanting, agreeable; see **pleasant** 1, 2.

**glory,** *n.* **1.** [Renown]— *Syn.* honor, distinction, reputation; see **fame** 1.
**2.** [Splendor]— *Syn.* gorgeousness, brightness, grandeur, radiance, effulgence, majesty, brilliance, sumptuousness, richness, preciousness, beauty, fineness. — *Ant.* tawdriness, meanness, baseness.
**gone to glory★** — *Syn.* late, passed on, deceased; see **dead** 1.
**in one's glory★** — *Syn.* at one's best, successful, in one's prime; see **happy** 1.
**1.** [Heaven]— *Syn.* beatitude, bliss, eternal life; see **heaven** 2.

**gloss,** *n.* **1.** [Shine]— *Syn.* gleam, shimmer, polish; see **finish** 2.
**2.** [Explanatory note]— *Syn.* translation, commentary, footnote, annotation; see **note** 1.

**glossary,** *n.* — *Syn.* gloss, lexicon, compendium; see **dictionary.**

**glossy,** *modif.* — *Syn.* shining, reflecting, lustrous; see **bright** 1.

**glove,** *n.* — *Syn.* gauntlet, mitten, gage, mitt, finger mitten.

**glow,** *n.* — *Syn.* luminosity, radiance, brightness, flush; see **light** 1.
*See Synonym Study at* FLAME.

**glow,** *v.* — *Syn.* gleam, redden, radiate; see **burn** 1, **shine** 1.

**glower,** *v.* — *Syn.* glare, scowl, sulk; see **frown.**

**glowing,** *modif.* **1.** [Radiating heat and light]— *Syn.* gleaming, lustrous, phosphorescent; see **bright** 1.
**2.** [Radiating enthusiasm]— *Syn.* ardent, zealous, fervent; see **enthusiastic** 1, 2.

**gloze,** *v.* — *Syn.* gloss over, cover up, extenuate; see **palliate.**

**glue,** *n.* — *Syn.* paste, mucilage, cement; see **adhesive.**

**glue,** *v.* — *Syn.* paste, gum, cement, fix, stick, adhere; see also **repair** 1.

**gluey,** *modif.* — *Syn.* glutinous, viscid, sticky; see **adhesive.**

**glum,** *modif.* — *Syn.* moody, morose, sullen; see **sad** 1.

**glut,** *n.* — *Syn.* oversupply, overabundance, excess; see **excess** 1.

**glut,** *v.* **1.** [To oversupply]— *Syn.* flood, overwhelm, overstock, fill, load, congest, inundate, overload, surcharge, burden, deluge, saturate, clog, choke, cloy, gorge.— *Ant.* SAVE, scant, undersupply.
**2.** [To eat to satiety]— *Syn.* satiate, surfeit, stuff, cram, gorge, overeat, hog, eat one's fill, gobble up, eat out of house and home, fill, cloy, feast, raven, wolf, bolt, devour, eat like a horse★.
*See Synonym Study at* SATIATE. — *Ant.* STARVE, DIET.

**glutton,** *n.* — *Syn.* gourmand, greedy person, epicure, overeater, sensualist, hog, pig, garbage hound★.

*See Synonym Study at* EPICURE.

**gluttonous,** *modif.* — *Syn.* ravenous, voracious, cormorant, omnivorous, avaricious; see also **greedy** 2.

**gluttony,** *n.* — *Syn.* voracity, edacity, intemperance, insatiability; see **greed.**

**gnarled,** *modif.* — *Syn.* knotted, twisted, contorted; see **bent.**

**gnash,** *v.* — *Syn.* grind, snap, rotate the teeth; see **bite** 1, **chew.**

**gnaw,** *v.* — *Syn.* crunch, champ, masticate; see **bite** 1, **chew.**

**gnome,** *n.* — *Syn.* dwarf, troll, elf; see **fairy** 1.

**go,** *v.* **1.** [To depart] — *Syn.* quit, withdraw, run away; see **leave** 1.
**2.** [To proceed] — *Syn.* travel, progress, proceed; see **advance** 1, **move** 1.
**3.** [To function] — *Syn.* work, run, perform; see **operate** 2.
**4.** [To fit or suit] — *Syn.* conform, accord, harmonize; see **agree, agree with** 2, **fit** 1.
**5.** [To extend] — *Syn.* stretch, cover, spread; see **reach** 1.
**6.** [To belong] — *Syn.* mesh, fit in, be designed for, be adapted for; see **belong** 1, 2, **fit** 1.
**7.** [To elapse] — *Syn.* be spent, waste away, transpire; see **pass** 2.
**8.** [To fail] — *Syn.* decline, weaken, worsen; see **fail** 1.
**9.** [To continue] — *Syn.* maintain, carry on, persist; see **continue** 1.
**10.** [To appeal] — *Syn.* apply for a retrial, contest, reopen; see **appeal** 2.
**11.** [To die] — *Syn.* pass on, depart, succumb; see **die** 1.
**12.** [To end] — *Syn.* terminate, finish, conclude; see **stop** 2.
**13.** [To endure] — *Syn.* persevere, go on, persist; see **endure** 1.
**14.** [*To bet] — *Syn.* wager, gamble, hazard; see **bet.**
**15.** [*To tolerate] — *Syn.* let, permit, consent to; see **allow** 1.

**as people (or things) go** — *Syn.* in comparison with other people, in comparison with other things, by general standards, according to certain criteria; see **compared.**

**from the word "go"*** — *Syn.* from the outset, at the start, beginning with; see **at first** at **first.**

**go (a person) one better*** — *Syn.* outdo, surpass, do better than; see **exceed.**

**have a go at*** — *Syn.* attempt, endeavor, try one's hand at; see **try** 1.

**let oneself go** — *Syn.* be unrestrained, be uninhibited, free oneself, have fun; see **relax** 1.

**no go*** — *Syn.* impossible, worthless, without value; see **useless** 1.

**on the go*** — *Syn.* in constant motion, moving, busy; see **active** 2.

**what goes?*** — *Syn.* what's is happening?, what's up?, what is going on?; see **what** 2.

**go about,** *v.* **1.** [To be occupied] — *Syn.* engage in, busy oneself with, be employed; see **work** 1, 2.
**2.** [To circulate] — *Syn.* move about, pass around, wander; see **circulate** 1, **travel** 2.

**goad,** *v.* — *Syn.* prod, urge, prick, prompt, spur, drive, rowel, whip, press, push, impel, force, stimulate, provoke, tease, excite, needle, instigate, inspirit, arouse, animate, encourage, bully, coerce, propel, thrust. — *Ant.* RESTRAIN, curb, rein in.

**go after,** *v.* **1.** [To chase] — *Syn.* seek, run after, hunt; see **pursue** 1.

**2.** [To follow in time] — *Syn.* come after, supersede, supplant; see **succeed** 2.

**go against,** *v.* — *Syn.* be opposed to, contradict, counteract; see **oppose** 1, 2.

**go ahead,** *v.* — *Syn.* move on, proceed, progress; see **advance** 1.

**goal,** *n.* — *Syn.* object, aim, intent, intention; see **end** 2, **purpose** 1.
*See Synonym Study at* INTENTION.

**go all out*,** *v.* — *Syn.* attempt, make a great effort, strive; see **try** 1.

**go all the way,** *v.* **1.** [To yield] — *Syn.* agree completely, give in, capitulate; see **agree, yield** 1.
**2.** [*To engage in sexual intercourse] — *Syn.* sleep with, fornicate, make love; see **copulate.**

**go along,** *v.* — *Syn.* carry on, keep up, go; see **continue** 1.

**go along with,** *v.* **1.** [To agree with] — *Syn.* concur, conspire, collaborate; see **agree to.**
**2.** [To cooperate] — *Syn.* work together, act jointly, share in; see **cooperate** 1.
**3.** [To accompany] — *Syn.* escort, squire, go with; see **accompany** 1.

**goat,** *n.* — *Syn. Capra* (Latin), nanny goat, billy goat, buck, kid, he-goat, she-goat, billy*.
Types of goats include: ibex, markhor, bezoar, dzeren, Rocky Mountain, Angora, Cashmere, dwarf, Guinean, Egyptian, Granada, Nubian, Maltese, Nepal, Syrian, Alpine, Toggenburg, Saanen, African pygmy; see also **animal** 2.

**get one's goat*** — *Syn.* annoy, irritate, bother, vex; see **anger** 1.

**go at,** *v.* — *Syn.* blame, impugn, criticize; see **censure.**

**go back on,** *v.* **1.** [To fail to keep] — *Syn.* renege, back out of, default; see **abandon** 1.
**2.** [*To betray] — *Syn.* desert, be unfaithful, leave in the lurch; see **abandon** 2, **betray** 1.

**go bad,** *v.* — *Syn.* degenerate, deteriorate, rot; see **decay.**

**gobble,** *v.* **1.** [To make a sound like a turkey] — *Syn.* gaggle, gurgle, cackle; see **sound** 1.
**2.** [*To eat rapidly] — *Syn.* bolt, cram, stuff; see **eat** 1.

**go behind,** *v.* — *Syn.* look into, pry into, probe, investigate; see **examine** 1.

**go better with,** *v.* — *Syn.* progress, enhance, meliorate; see **improve** 2, **intensify.**

**go-between,** *n.* — *Syn.* intermediary, middleman, referee, mediator; see **agent** 1, **messenger.**

**go between,** *v.* — *Syn.* intervene, mediate, arbitrate; see **meddle** 1, **reconcile** 2.

**go beyond,** *v.* — *Syn.* overdo, distance, surpass; see **exceed.**

**goblet,** *n.* — *Syn.* tumbler, beaker, grail; see **cup.**

**goblin,** *n.* — *Syn.* troll, hobgoblin, sprite; see **fairy** 1.

**go by,** *v.* **1.** [To pass] — *Syn.* move onward, make one's way, proceed, go past; see **pass** 1.
**2.** [To conform to] — *Syn.* fall in with, comply, adjust to; see **agree, cooperate** 1.

**go crazy,** *v.* — *Syn.* become insane, lose one's wits, get angry; see **rage** 3.

**god,** *n.* **1.** [A supernatural being] — *Syn.* deity, male deity, divinity, divine being, superhuman being, spirit, numen, power, tutelary, Olympian, Valhallan, demigod, demiurge, oversoul, prime mover, godhead, omnipotence, world spirit, world soul, universal life force, infinite spirit, totem, idol, demon, daimon, daemon.
Greek gods and their Roman counterparts include: Zeus, Jupiter, Jove; Phoebus, Phoebus Apollo, Apollo;

Ares, Mars; Hermes, Mercury; Poseidon, Neptune; Hephaestus, Vulcan; Dionysus, Bacchus; Hades, Pluto; Kronos, Saturn; Eros, Cupid.

Norse gods, known as the Aesir and Vanir, include: Aegir, Bragi, Balder, Frey, Freyr, Heimdall, Höder, Hoenir, Loki, Odin, Woden, Wotan, Thor, Donar, Tyr, Tiu, Ull, Ullr, Vali, Vidar, Ymir.

Hindu and Brahmanic gods include: Agni, Dyaus, Ganesa, Ganpati, Hanuman, Indra, Marut, Savitar, Soma, Surya, Varuna, Vayu, Yama.

The avatars of Vishnu include: Buddha, Kalki, Karma, Krishna, Matsya, Narsinh, Parshuram, Rama, Vaman, Varah, Jagannath.

● Egyptian gods include: Anubis, Bast, Horus; Isis, Khem, Min, Neph, Nephthys, Nut, Osiris, Ptah, Ra, Amun, Amen-Ra, Set, Shu, Thoth.

● Other gods include: Baal, Moloch, Shamash (*all* Semitic); Dagon (Philistine); Astarte, Ashtoreth (*both* Phoenician); Anu, Bel, Ea (*all* Babylonian); Quetzalcoatl (Mexican). For specific female deities see also **goddess.**

**2.** [*Capitalized*, the Jewish-Christian-Islamic deity] — *Syn.* Lord, Jehovah, Yahweh, YHWH, Jhvh, Adonai, Allah, the Almighty, the King of Kings, the Omnipotent, the Compassionate, the Merciful, Lord of Mercies, the Godhead, the Creator, the Maker, the Supreme Being, the Ruler of Heaven, the All-holy, the Everlasting, the Divine Author, Our Father in Heaven, Almighty God, God Almighty, the Preserver, the Deity, the Divinity, the Omniscient, Providence, the All-knowing, the Infinite Spirit, the Absolute, the Infinite, the Eternal, I Am, the All-father, the Author of All Things, the First Cause, the Lord of Lords, the Supreme Soul, the All-wise, the All-merciful, the All-powerful.

**3.** [*Capitalized*, the Christian deity] — *Syn.* the Trinity, the Holy Trinity, the Triune God, Threefold Unity, Three in One and One in Three; Father, Son, and Holy Ghost; Holy Spirit, Paraclete; God the Son, Jesus Christ, Christ, Jesus, Jesus of Nazareth, the Nazarene, the Galilean, the Man of Sorrows, the Messiah, the Savior, the Redeemer, the Advocate, the Son of God, the Son of Man, the Son of Mary, the Only Begotten, the Lamb, the Lamb of God, Immanuel, Emmanuel, the King of Glory, the King of the Jews, the Prince of Peace, the Good Shepherd, the Way, the Truth, the Life, the Light, the Christ Child.

**4.** [*Capitalized*, the supreme deity of other religions] — *Syn.* Brahman, the Supreme Soul, Atman, the Universal Self, Brahma, the Creator, Vishnu, the Preserver, Shiva, the Destroyer (*all* Hinduism); Adibuddha, the Primordial Buddha (Buddhism); Ahura Mazda, Ormazd (Zoroastrianism).

**goddess,** *n.* — *Syn.* female deity, demigoddess, dryad, fury, muse; see also **god.**

Greek goddesses and their Roman counterparts include: Hera, Juno; Demeter, Ceres; Persephone, Proserpina; Artemis, Diana; Athena, Minerva; Aphrodite, Venus; Hestia, Vesta; Cybele, Rhea; Gaea, Ge.

Norse goddesses include: Freya, Freyja, Frigg, Frigga, Hel, Nanna, Ithunn, Idun, Sif, Sigyn, Vor, Ran, Nerthus.

Hindu and Brahmanic goddesses include: Chandi, Devi, Durga, Gauri, Kali, Lakshmi, Parvati, Sarasvati, Uma, Ushas.

**godfather,** *n.* — *Syn.* sponsor, elder, patron, adoptive parent.

**godhead,** *n.* — *Syn.* divinity, deity, holiness; see **god** 1.

**godless,** *modif.* — *Syn.* agnostic, heathen, pagan, atheistic; see **impious.**

**godlike,** *modif.* — *Syn.* divine, celestial, supernatural; see **holy** 1, 3.

**godliness,** *n.* — *Syn.* holiness, piety, sanctity; see **virtue** 1.

**godly,** *modif.* — *Syn.* righteous, devout, pious; see **holy** 2.

**godmother,** *n.* — *Syn.* female sponsor, elder, patroness, adoptive parent, gossip.

**go down,** *v.* **1.** [To sink] — *Syn.* descend, decline, submerge; see **sink** 1.

**2.** [To lose] — *Syn.* be defeated, submit, succumb; see **fail** 1, **lose** 3.

**3.** [To decrease] — *Syn.* reduce, make less, lessen; see **decrease** 1.

**godsend,** *n.* — *Syn.* benefit, gift, boon; see **blessing** 2.

**go easy,** *v.* — *Syn.* skimp, be sparing, be careful, reprieve; see **pity** 2, **save** 3.

**go far,** *v.* **1.** [To contribute to] — *Syn.* assist, support, back up; see **contribute, help** 1.

**2.** [To extend] — *Syn.* reach, buy, reinforce; see **increase** 1.

**3.** [To succeed] — *Syn.* rise, achieve, go up in the world★; see **succeed** 1.

**go for,** *v.* **1.** [To reach for] — *Syn.* stretch out for, outreach, clutch at; see **reach** 2.

**2.** [★To attack] — *Syn.* rush upon, run at, spring; see **attack** 1, 2, 4.

**3.** [★To like] — *Syn.* be fond of, fancy, care for; see **like** 2.

**go in for★,** *v.* **1.** [To advocate] — *Syn.* endorse, favor, back; see **promote** 1.

**2.** [To like] — *Syn.* care for, be fond of, fancy; see **like** 1.

**going★,** *modif.* — *Syn.* flourishing, thriving, profitable; see **successful.**

**be going to** — *Syn.* shall, be intending to, be prepared to; see **will** 1, 3.

**get one going★** — *Syn.* annoy, excite, enrage; see **anger** 1.

**have (something) going for one★** — *Syn.* have an advantage, be successful, be able, be talented, have opportunity; see also **succeed** 1.

**goings on★,** *n.* — *Syn.* events, deportment, conduct; see **behavior** 1.

**going strong★,** *modif.* — *Syn.* flourishing, surviving, thriving; see **successful.**

**go into,** *v.* **1.** [To investigate] — *Syn.* analyze, probe, look into; see **examine** 1.

**2.** [To take up an occupation, hobby, etc.] — *Syn.* develop, undertake, enter into, participate in, take upon oneself, engage in, take up, take on, get involved with, be absorbed in.

**go in with,** *v.* — *Syn.* form a partnership, join forces, consolidate; see **unite** 1.

**gold,** *modif.* **1.** [Made of gold, or plated with gold] — *Syn.* golden, aurous, gilded, gilt, beaten gold, carat metal, 24-carat, 18-carat.

**2.** [Of the color of gold] — *Syn.* yellow, aureate, gold-colored, red-gold, greenish gold, ochroid, flaxen, wheat-colored, deep tan, tawny.

**gold,** *n.* **1.** [A color] — *Syn.* deep yellow, ochroid, tawny; see **color** 1, **gold,** *modif.*, sense 2.

**2.** [A precious metal] — *Syn.* aurum (AU), green gold, white gold, red gold, gold foil, gold leaf, gold plate, filled gold, commercial gold, gold alloy, cloth of gold, gold cloth, gold thread, gold wire, gold lace, gold tooling, rolled gold, mosaic gold, Mannheim gold, German gold, dead gold, Etruscan gold, Roman gold, colored gold; see also **metal.**

**as good as gold★** — *Syn.* very good, well behaved, reliable, obedient; see **excellent.**

**goldsmith,** *n.* — *Syn.* artisan, craftsman, lapidary; see **jeweler.**

**golf,** *n.* — *Syn.* match play, medal play, nine holes, eighteen holes, game, pasture pool★, heather marbles★, divot digging★.

**golf course,** *n.* — *Syn.* links, course, green, fairway, front nine, back nine.

**gone,** *modif.* **1.** [Having left] — *Syn.* gone out, gone away, moved, removed, traveling, traveled, journeyed, transferred, displaced, shifted, withdrawn, retired, left, taken leave, departed, deserted, abandoned, quit, disappeared, not here, no more, flown, run off, decamped, AWOL★, taken French leave★, upped stakes★, flown the coop★, split★, taken a powder★. — *Ant.* COME, returned, remained.

**2.** [Being no longer in existence] — *Syn.* dead, vanished, passed, dissipated, disappeared, nonextant, dissolved, burned up, disintegrated, decayed, rotted away, turned to dust.

**far gone★** — *Syn.* **1.** advanced, deeply involved, absorbed; see **interested** 2.

**2.** crazy, mad, eccentric; see **insane** 1.

**gong,** *n.* — *Syn.* tocsin, cymbal, bell, alarum, drum, kettledrum, signal, carillon, tympanum, sounding board, fire alarm, dinner gong, doorbell, Chinese gong, tamtam.

**gonorrhea,** *n.* — *Syn.* venereal disease, social disease, sexual disease, clap★; see **disease.**

**good,** *modif.* **1.** [Moral] — *Syn.* upright, honorable, charitable; see **moral** 1, **righteous** 1.

**2.** [Kind] — *Syn.* considerate, tolerant, generous; see **kind** 1.

**3.** [Proper] — *Syn.* suitable, becoming, desirable; see **fit** 1, 2.

**4.** [Reliable] — *Syn.* trustworthy, dependable, loyal; see **reliable** 2.

**5.** [Sound] — *Syn.* safe, solid, stable; see **reliable** 1, 2.

**6.** [Pleasant] — *Syn.* agreeable, satisfying, enjoyable; see **pleasant** 1, 2.

**7.** [Honorable] — *Syn.* worthy, reputable, respectable; see **noble** 1, 2.

**8.** [Helpful] — *Syn.* beneficial, salutary, useful; see **helpful** 1.

**9.** [Qualified] — *Syn.* suited, competent, suitable; see **able** 1, 2.

**10.** [Skillful] — *Syn.* skilled, expert, qualified; see **able** 2.

**11.** [Of approved quality] — *Syn.* choice, select, high-grade; see **excellent.**

**12.** [Healthy] — *Syn.* sound, normal, vigorous; see **healthy** 1.

**13.** [Obedient] — *Syn.* dutiful, tractable, well-behaved; see **obedient** 1.

**14.** [Genuine] — *Syn.* valid, real, sound; see **genuine** 1.

**15.** [Thorough] — *Syn.* fussy, meticulous, painstaking; see **careful.**

**16.** [Orthodox] — *Syn.* conforming, regular, strict; see **conventional** 2, 3.

**17.** [Fresh] — *Syn.* unspoiled, uncontaminated, undecayed; see **fresh** 5.

**18.** [Considerable] — *Syn.* great, big, immeasurable; see **large** 1, **much** 2.

**19.** [Favorable] — *Syn.* approving, commendatory, commending; see **favorable** 3.

**20.** [Adequate] — *Syn.* sufficient, ample, satisfying; see **enough** 1.

**21.** [Sound, as an asset] — *Syn.* valid, cashable, backed, not void, not counterfeit, worth it, safe, guaranteed, warranted, cleared, not debased, certified, not outlawed.

**as good as** — *Syn.* in effect, virtually, nearly; see **almost.**

**good and★** — *Syn.* very, altogether, thoroughly; see **very.**

**make good** — *Syn.* fulfill, satisfy the requirement(s), accomplish; see **satisfy** 3.

**no good** — *Syn.* useless, valueless, unserviceable; see **worthless** 1.

**good,** *n.* **1.** [A benefit] — *Syn.* welfare, gain, asset; see **advantage** 3.

**2.** [That which is morally approved] — *Syn.* ethic, merit, ideal; see **virtue** 1.

**3.** [Good people] — *Syn.* the virtuous, the pious, children of light, the elect, men of good will, philanthropists, God-fearing people, law-abiding citizens, enemies of darkness, just men.

**come to no good** — *Syn.* come to a bad end, get into trouble, have difficulty; see **fail** 1.

**for good and all★** — *Syn.* forever, always, permanently; see **finally** 1.

**to the good** — *Syn.* favorable, advantageous, beneficial; see **profitable.** — *Ant.* RASCAL, the wicked, the sinful.

**good breeding,** *n.* — *Syn.* civility, refinement, manners, propriety; see **culture** 3.

**goodbye,** *interj.* — *Syn.* farewell, Godspeed, fare you well, God bless you and keep you, God be with you, adieu, *adios* (Spanish), *au revoir* (French), *auf Wiedersehen* (German), *a rivederci* (Italian), so long★, be good★, bye-bye★, *ciao*★ (Italian), see you later★, toodle-oo★, cheerio★, don't take any wooden nickels★, take it easy★, don't work too hard★; see you later, alligator★; have a nice day★.

**good fellowship,** *n.* — *Syn.* companionship, brotherhood, fraternity; see **friendship** 1.

**good for,** *modif.* **1.** [Helpful] — *Syn.* useful, beneficial, salubrious; see **helpful** 1.

**2.** [Financially sound] — *Syn.* safe, competent, worth it; see **good** 21, **valid** 2.

**good-for-nothing,** *n.* — *Syn.* loafer, layabout, bum; see **tramp** 1.

**good fortune,** *n.* — *Syn.* good luck, affluence, prosperity; see **success** 2.

**Good Friday,** *n.* — *Syn.* Crucifixion Day, Holy Friday, fast day, solemn fast day, Friday before Easter, Friday in Ember Week; see also **Easter, holiday.**

**good graces,** *n.* — *Syn.* affection, good will, favor; see **friendship** 2.

**good-hearted,** *modif.* — *Syn.* charitable, gracious, benevolent; see **kind** 1.

**good humor,** *n.* — *Syn.* amiability, levity, geniality; see **happiness** 1.

**good-humored,** *modif.* — *Syn.* cheerful, merry, amiable; see **happy** 1.

**good-looking,** *modif.* — *Syn.* attractive, beautiful, handsome, nice-looking; see **beautiful** 1, 2, **handsome** 1, 2. *See Synonym Study at* BEAUTIFUL.

**good luck,** *interj.* — *Syn.* cheers, skoal, *skaal* (Scandinavian), best wishes, Godspeed, *shalom* (Hebrew), *salaam* (Arabic), God bless you, peace be with you, *pax vobiscum* (Latin), *Gesundheit* (German), *bonne chance* (French), *salut* (French).

**good luck,** *n.* — *Syn.* prosperity, fortune, affluence; see **success** 2.

**good morning,** *interj.* — *Syn.* good day, good morrow, greetings, *bonjour* (French), *guten Morgen* (German), *buenos días* (Spanish), top o' the mornin' to you★.

**good nature,** *n.* — *Syn.* tolerance, consideration, benevolence; see **kindness** 1.

**good-natured,** *modif.* — *Syn.* agreeable, easygoing, kindly, amiable; see **amiable, friendly** 1.
*See Synonym Study at* AMIABLE.

**goodness,** *n.* — *Syn.* decency, morality, honesty; see **virtue** 1, 2.

**good night,** *interj.* — *Syn.* bon nuit, à demain (*both* French), gute Nacht (German), buenas noches (Spanish), nighty-night★.

**goods,** *pl.n.* **1.** [Commodities] — *Syn.* merchandise, materials, wares; see **commodity.**

**2.** [Effects] — *Syn.* equipment, personal property, possessions; see **property** 1.

**deliver the goods★** — *Syn.* fulfill, accomplish, succeed, produce; see **satisfy** 3.

**get** (or **have**) **the goods on★** — *Syn.* uncover, obtain evidence on, prove the guilt of; see **expose** 1.

**good will,** *n.* — *Syn.* benevolence, charity, kindness, cordiality, sympathy, tolerance, helpfulness, favorable disposition, altruism. — *Ant.* HATRED, malevolence, animosity.

**goody★,** *n.* — *Syn.* good thing, tidbit, reward; see **prize.**

**goody-goody,** *n.* — *Syn.* prude, moralist, prig, good-two-shoes; see **prude.**

**goof★,** *v.* — *Syn.* err, make a mistake, flub★; see **fail** 1.

**go off,** *v.* **1.** [To leave] — *Syn.* quit, depart, part; see **leave** 1.

**2.** [To explode] — *Syn.* blow up, detonate, discharge; see **explode** 1.

**3.** [★To occur] — *Syn.* take place, pass, befall; see **happen** 2.

**go on,** *v.* **1.** [To act] — *Syn.* execute, behave, conduct; see **act** 1, 2.

**2.** [To happen] — *Syn.* occur, come about, take place; see **happen** 2.

**3.** [To persevere] — *Syn.* persist, continue, bear; see **endure** 1.

**4.** [To approach] — *Syn.* creep *or* loom up, near, advance; see **approach** 2.

**5.** [★To talk] — *Syn.* chatter, converse, speak; see **talk** 1.

**goose,** *n.* **1.** Types of geese include: gray, graylag, bean, pink-footed, white-fronted, snow, emperor, kelp, upland, black, barnacle, brant, Canada, Chinese, Egyptian, Orinoco.

**2.** [A stupid person] — *Syn.* loony, dope, silly; see **fool** 1.

**cook one's goose★** — *Syn.* ruin, spoil, defeat; see **destroy** 1.

**goose flesh,** *n.* — *Syn.* goose pimples, goose bumps, goose skin, the creeps, the shivers, horripilation.

**go out,** *v.* **1.** [To be extinguished] — *Syn.* cease, die, darken, flicker out, flash out, become dark, become black, burn out, stop shining; see also **shade** 3.

**2.** [To strike] — *Syn.* go on strike, walk out, picket; see **strike** 2.

**go out of one's head,** *v.* — *Syn.* go crazy, go mad, become insane, flip★; see **rage** 1.

**go over,** *v.* **1.** [To rehearse] — *Syn.* repeat, say something repeatedly, practice; see **rehearse** 3.

**2.** [To examine] — *Syn.* look at, investigate, analyze; see **examine** 1, **study** 1.

**3.** [★To succeed] — *Syn.* be successful, not fail, be impressive; see **succeed** 1.

**gore,** *n.* — *Syn.* blood, slaughter, massacre; see **carnage.**

**gorge,** *n.* — *Syn.* chasm, canyon, abyss, crevasse; see **ravine.**

**gorge,** *v.* — *Syn.* glut, surfeit, stuff oneself; see **eat** 1, **fill** 1.

**gorgeous,** *modif.* — *Syn.* superb, sumptuous, impressive; see **beautiful** 1, **grand** 2.

**gory,** *modif.* — *Syn.* blood-soaked, bloodstained, bloody; see **offensive** 2.

**gosh★,** *interj.* — *Syn.* imagine, gee, golly, dear me, Lord, goodness gracious; see also **curse.**

**gospel,** *n.* **1.** [A record of Christ] — *Syn.* New Testament, Christian Scripture, Christian revelation; see **Bible** 2.

**2.** [A text] — *Syn.* authority, testament, scripture; see **Bible** 1.

**3.** [Belief or statement supposedly infallible] — *Syn.* creed, certainty, dogma; see **doctrine** 1, **faith** 2, **truth** 1.

**gossamer,** *n.* **1.** [Cobweb] — *Syn.* spiderweb, filament, tendril; see **fiber** 1, **thread.**

**2.** [Thin cloth] — *Syn.* gauze, tissue, chiffon, sheer silk, sheer nylon.

**gossip,** *n.* **1.** [Local, petty talk] — *Syn.* babble, chatter, meddling, small talk, malicious talk, whispering gallery, hearsay, rumor, scandal, news, slander, calumny, defamation, injury, blackening, grapevine★, grapevine telegraph★.

**2.** [One who indulges in petty talk] — *Syn.* snoop, meddler, tattler, newsmonger, gossipmonger, scandalmonger, scandal-bearer, backbiter, magpie, chatterbox, talkative person, babbler, bigmouth, blatherskite, parrot★, long-nose★, sticky-beak★, blabbermouth★, telltale★, old hen★, fuss-budget★, Mrs. Grundy★, gabbler★.

**gossip,** *v.* — *Syn.* tattle, prattle, tell tales, talk idly, chat, chatter, rumor, report, tell secrets, blab, babble, repeat, prate, spread a story all over town, dish the dirt★.

**go straight,** *v.* — *Syn.* lead a moral life, live within the law, improve; see **behave** 2, **reform** 2, 3.

**go the rounds,** *v.* — *Syn.* inspect, investigate, check; see **examine** 1, **guard** 2.

**gothic,** *modif.* — *Syn.* medieval, barbaric, barbarous, rude, eerie, grotesque, mysterious; see also **old** 3.

**go through,** *v.* **1.** [To inspect] — *Syn.* search, audit, investigate; see **examine** 1.

**2.** [To undergo] — *Syn.* withstand, survive, suffer; see **endure** 2.

**3.** [To spend] — *Syn.* consume, deplete, pay, expend; see **spend** 1.

**go through with,** *v.* — *Syn.* fulfill, finish, follow through with; see **achieve** 1, **complete** 1.

**go together,** *v.* **1.** [To harmonize] — *Syn.* be suitable, match, fit; see **agree.**

**2.** [To keep company] — *Syn.* go steady, escort, go with; see **date** 2.

**go to law★,** *v.* — *Syn.* bring court action, file suit, take to court; see **accuse.**

**gouge,** *v.* **1.** [To hollow out] — *Syn.* scoop, chisel, channel; see **dig** 1.

**2.** [★To obtain illegally or immorally] — *Syn.* blackmail, take advantage, extort; see **steal.**

**go under,** *v.* **1.** [Drown] — *Syn.* sink, drown; suffocate; see **die** 1.

**2.** [To become bankrupt] — *Syn.* default, go broke, go bankrupt; see **fail** 4.

**go up,** *v.* — *Syn.* increase, rise, double; see **grow** 1.

**gourd,** *n.* **1.** [A melon] — *Syn.* squash, calabash, pumpkin; see **melon.**

**2.** [A cup] — *Syn.* bottle, dipper, flask; see **cup.**

**gourmand,** *n.* — *Syn.* epicure, gourmet, glutton; see **epicure.**
*See Synonym Study at* EPICURE.

**gourmet,** *n.* — *Syn.* gastronome, epicure, *bon vivant* (French); see **connoisseur, epicure.**

*See Synonym Study at* EPICURE.

**govern,** *v.* — *Syn.* rule, command, administer, reign, legislate, oversee, hold dominion, hold sway, occupy the throne, assume command, hold office, serve the people, administer the laws, exercise authority, be in power, supervise, superintend, direct, dictate, lay down the law, tyrannize, wield the scepter★, wear the crown★, hold the reins of empire★.

---

**SYN.** — **govern** implies the exercise of authority in controlling the actions of the members of a body politic and directing the affairs of state, and generally connotes as its purpose the maintenance of public order and the promotion of the common welfare; **rule** now usually signifies the exercise of arbitrary or autocratic power; **administer** implies the orderly management of governmental or institutional affairs by executive officials

---

**governable,** *modif.* — *Syn.* manageable, submissive, controllable; see **docile.**

**governed,** *modif.* **1.** [Ruled] — *Syn.* commanded, administered, under authority, supervised, superintended, directed, overseen, tyrannized over, dictated to, conducted, guided, piloted, mastered, led, driven, subjugated, subordinate. — *Ant.* FREE, autonomous, archaic. **2.** [Controlled] — *Syn.* determined, guided, influenced, swayed, inclined, regulated, directed, ordered, dependent, consequent, obedient, under one's jurisdiction. — *Ant.* UNRULY, self-determined, capricious.

**governess,** *n.* — *Syn.* tutor, nanny, tutoress★, mistress, duenna; see also **guardian** 1, 2, **teacher** 1.

**governing,** *modif.* — *Syn.* commanding, administrative, executive, authoritative, supervisory, regulatory, controlling, directing, restraining, superintending, surveillant, overseeing, tyrannizing, dictatorial, arbitrary, conducting, guiding, mastering, potent, dominating, dominant, magisterial, determining, ascendant, in the ascendant, ordering, compulsive, supreme, influential, gubernatorial, presidential, regal, absolute, ruling, checking, curbing, inhibiting, limiting, confining. — *Ant.* subordinate, powerless, tributary.

**government,** *n.* **1.** [The process of governing] — *Syn.* rule, control, command, regulation, administration, bureaucracy, direction, equity, dominion, sway, authority, jurisdiction, hegemony, suzerainty, sovereignty, prerogative, polity, direction, power, management, authorization, patronage, mastery, predominance, superiority, supervision, superintendence, magistracy, supremacy, domination, preponderance, ascendancy, influence, presidency, politics, regimentation, state, statecraft, political practice, caretaker government, governmental procedure; see also **administration.** **2.** [The instrument of governing] — *Syn.* administration, assembly, legislature, congress, cabinet, executive power, regime, supreme authority, ministry, party, chamber, council, parliament, senate, department of justice, soviet, diet, synod, convocation, convention, court, directory, house.

Types of government include: absolute monarchy, dictatorship, empire, tyranny, fascism, imperialism, colonialism, despotism, limited monarchy, constitutional monarchy, hereditary kingship, oligarchy, aristocracy, democracy, popular government, representative government, democratic socialism, communism, socialism, party government.

Divisions of government include: state, province, kingdom, territory, colony, dominion, commonwealth, soviet, republic, shire, city, county, canton, town, village, hamlet, township, municipality, principality, precinct, borough, commune, ward, district, suburb, department, *arrondissement, département* (*both* French), nome, nomarchy, parish.

**governmental,** *modif.* — *Syn.* political, administrative, executive, legislative, regulatory, bureaucratic, legal, magisterial, supervisory, sovereign, presidential, official, gubernatorial, national.

**governor,** *n.* **1.** [An administrator] — *Syn.* director, presiding officer, ruler; see **administrator.** **2.** [Chief executive of a major political division] — *Syn.* executive head of a state, provincial magistrate, territorial executive, local executive, representative of the crown, gubernatorial leader, *gubernator* (Latin), governor of the state. **3.** [A regulating mechanism] — *Syn.* automatic control, fuel control, heat control, thermocouple, thermostat, on-off thermostat, alarm, rheostat, butterfly valve; see also **valve.**

**go well with,** *v.* — *Syn.* match, correspond, harmonize; see **go with** 2.

**go with,** *v.* **1.** [★To keep company with] — *Syn.* escort, attend, be with; see **accompany** 1, **date** 2. **2.** [To be appropriate to] — *Syn.* match, suit, correspond, not clash, go well with, harmonize, complement, fit; see also **agree.**

**go without,** *v.* — *Syn.* lack, fall short, want; see **need.**

**gown,** *n.* — *Syn.* dress, frock, evening gown, garment, vestment; see also **clothes, dress** 2.

**go wrong,** *v.* — *Syn.* slip, break down, go amiss; see **fail** 1.

**grab,** *n.* — *Syn.* grasp, clutch, snatch; see **grip** 2.

**up for grabs★** — *Syn.* offered, obtainable, for the taking; see **available, free** 4.

**grab,** *v.* — *Syn.* clutch, grasp, take; see **seize** 1, 2.

*See Synonym Study at* SEIZE.

**grace,** *n.* **1.** [The quality of being graceful] — *Syn.* suppleness, lithesomeness, lissomeness, ease of movement, nimbleness, agility, pliancy, smoothness, form, address, poise, dexterity, adroitness, symmetry, balance, style, elegance, harmony. — *Ant.* AWKWARDNESS, stiffness, maladroitness. **2.** [Mercy] — *Syn.* forgiveness, love, charity; see **mercy** 1. **3.** [Charm] — *Syn.* allure, attractiveness, comeliness, refinement, decorum, finesse; see also **beauty** 1. **4.** [A prayer at table] — *Syn.* invocation, thanks, thanksgiving, blessing, benediction, petition.

**fall from grace** — *Syn.* do wrong, misbehave, err; see **sin.**

**have the grace** — *Syn.* be proper or gracious, accept conditions, resign oneself; see **agree, obey** 1, 2.

**in the bad graces of** — *Syn.* in disfavor, rejected, disapproved; see **hated.**

**in the good graces of** — *Syn.* favored, accepted, admired; see **approved.**

**with bad grace** — *Syn.* sullenly, gracelessly, unwillingly; see **reluctantly.**

**with good grace** — *Syn.* graciously, willingly, generously; see **gracefully.**

**graceful,** *modif.* **1.** [Said of movement] — *Syn.* lissome, supple, limber, agile, lithe, pliant, nimble, elastic, springy, easy, dexterous, adroit, smooth, controlled, balletic, sylphlike, light-footed, willowy, poised, practiced, skilled, rhythmic, sprightly, elegant. — *Ant.* AWKWARD, fumbling, stiff. **2.** [Said of objects or persons] — *Syn.* elegant, neat, well-proportioned, trim, balanced, well-turned, symmetrical, dainty, pretty, harmonious, beautiful, comely, seemly, handsome, fair, delicate, tasteful, slender, decorative, artistic, exquisite, statuesque. — *Ant.* UGLY, shapeless, cumbersome.

**3.** [*Said of conduct*] — *Syn.* cultured, seemly, becoming; see **polite** 1.

**gracefully,** *modif.* — *Syn.* lithely, agilely, harmoniously, daintily, nimbly, elegantly, trimly, symmetrically, beautifully, felicitously, delicately, tastefully, artistically, pliantly, easily, dexterously, smoothly, skillfully, fairly, adroitly, handsomely, rhythmically, exquisitely, neatly, sprucely, delightfully, charmingly, imaginatively, becomingly, suitably, fitly, sweetly, pleasingly, congruously, appropriately, happily, decoratively, prettily. — *Ant.* awkwardly, insipidly, grotesquely.

**graceless,** *modif.* **1.** [Rude] — *Syn.* corrupt, shameless, uncouth; see **rude** 1, 2.

**2.** [Awkward] — *Syn.* clumsy, inept, inelegant; see **awkward** 1.

**gracious,** *modif.* **1.** [Genial] — *Syn.* amiable, courteous, condescending; see **polite** 1.

**2.** [Merciful] — *Syn.* tender, loving, charitable; see **kind** 1.

**gradation,** *n.* — *Syn.* step, stage, scale; see **degree** 1.

**grade,** *n.* **1.** [An incline] — *Syn.* hill, slope, inclined plane, gradient, slant, inclination, pitch, ascent, descent, obliquity, tangent, ramp, upgrade, acclivity, declivity, downgrade, climb, elevation, height; see also **hill.**

**2.** [An embankment] — *Syn.* fill, causeway, dike; see **dam** 1.

**3.** [Rank or degree] — *Syn.* class, category, classification; see **degree** 2.

**4.** [A division of a school] — *Syn.* class, standard, form, rank; see **class** 3.

**5.** [*A hybrid] — *Syn.* mixture, mongrel, ordinary specimen; see **hybrid.**

**make the grade★** — *Syn.* win, prosper, achieve; see **succeed** 1.

**grade,** *v.* — *Syn.* rate, give a grade to, assort; see **rank** 2.

**graded,** *modif.* — *Syn.* sorted, ranked, grouped; see **classified.**

**gradient,** *n.* — *Syn.* angle, slope, pitch; see **grade** 1, **inclination** 5.

**gradual,** *modif.* — *Syn.* creeping, regular, continuous; see **progressive** 1.

**gradually,** *modif.* — *Syn.* step by step, by degrees, steadily, increasingly, slowly, regularly, a little at a time, little by little, stone by stone, bit by bit, inch by inch, grade by grade, by installments, in small doses, continuously, in due succession, through all gradations, by regular stages, progressively, successively, sequentially, serially, constantly, unceasingly, perceptibly, imperceptibly, insinuatingly, deliberately. — *Ant.* QUICKLY, haphazardly, by leaps and bounds.

**graduate,** *n.* — *Syn.* recipient of a degree, recipient of a certificate, alumnus, alumna, former student, holder of a degree, holder of a certificate, baccalaureate, bachelor, licentiate, diplomate, product, grad★, alum★.

**graduate,** *v.* **1.** [To give a degree] — *Syn.* grant a degree to, grant a diploma to, grant a certificate to, confer a degree on, confer a diploma on, confer a certificate on, send out, certify, give a sheepskin to★.

**2.** [To receive a degree] — *Syn.* receive a degree, be awarded a degree, win a degree, earn a degree, take a degree, receive a diploma, be awarded a diploma, win a diploma, earn a diploma, receive a certificate, be awarded a certificate, earn a certificate, become an alumna, become an alumnus, get out, finish, finish up, become qualified, be certificated, be commissioned, get

a B.A., get an M.A., get a Ph.D., get an M.D., get a sheepskin★.

**3.** [To mark gradations] — *Syn.* calibrate, grade, measure, regulate; see **measure** 1.

**graduated,** *modif.* **1.** [Granted a degree] — *Syn.* certified, ordained, accredited, passed, invested, promoted.

**2.** [Arranged or marked according to a scale] — *Syn.* serialized, graded, tapered, sequential, measured, progressive, registered.

**graduation,** *n.* — *Syn.* commencement, convocation, conferring of degrees, granting of diplomas, promotion, bestowal of honors, commissioning.

**graffito,** *n.* — *Syn.* scribbling, tag, writing on walls, inscription, aphorism; see also **writing** 2.

**graft,** *n.* **1.** [A jointure for growth] — *Syn.* scion, shoot, union, slip, hybridization, graff, grafting.

**2.** [Dishonest gain] — *Syn.* fraud, peculation, thievery; see **corruption** 2.

**graft,** *v.* **1.** [To join for growth] — *Syn.* engraft, unite, propagate, splice.

**2.** [★To gain dishonestly] — *Syn.* thieve, cheat, swindle; see **steal.**

**grail,** *n.* — *Syn.* sacred vessel, holy dish, chalice; see **cup.**

**grain,** *n.* **1.** [Seeds of domesticated grasses] — *Syn.* cereal, cereals, corn (British), small grain, seed, maize. Varieties of grain include: rice, wheat, oats, barley, corn, rye, millet.

**2.** [A particle] — *Syn.* speck, pellet, fragment; see **bit** 1.

**3.** [Character imparted by fiber] — *Syn.* texture, warp and woof, striation, tendency, fabric, staple, tissue, weft, current, direction, tooth, nap.

**against the grain★** — *Syn.* disturbing, irritating, bothersome, contrary; see **offensive** 2.

**grammar,** *n.* — *Syn.* syntax, accidence, morphology, structure, morphophonemics, syntactic structure, sentence structure, language pattern, sentence pattern, linguistic science, rationalized language, stratificational grammar, transformational grammar, universal grammar, tagmemics, tagmemic grammar, phrase structure grammar, PS, incorporating grammar, synthetic grammar, inflectional grammar, analytic grammar, distributive grammar, isolating grammar, traditional grammar, the new grammar★.

Terms in grammar include: tense, mood, person, gender, voice, number, aspect, case, sandhi, modification, inflection, concord, agreement, sentence, phrase, clause, predicate, nexus, coordination, subordination, deep structure, surface structure, part of speech, punctuation, phoneme, phonemics, morpheme, morphemics, sememe, semiotics, tagmeme; see also **language** 2.

**grammarian,** *n.* — *Syn.* linguist, philologist, grammatist, rhetorician; see **linguist** 1.

**grammatical,** *modif.* **1.** [Having to do with grammar] — *Syn.* linguistic, syntactic, morphophonemic, sememic, morphological, logical, philological, analytic, analytical.

**2.** [Conforming to rules of grammar] — *Syn.* grammatically correct, conventional, accepted. — *Ant.* ungrammatical, solecistic, irregular.

**grammatical construction,** *n.* — *Syn.* structure, locution, sequence; see **clause** 2, **phrase, sentence** 2, **transformation** 2.

**granary,** *n.* — *Syn.* bin, crib, barn; see **storehouse.**

**grand,** *modif.* **1.** [Sumptuous] — *Syn.* rich, splendid, magnificent; see **sumptuous.**

**2.** [Exalted] — *Syn.* majestic, lofty, stately, dignified, elevated, high, regal, awful, noble, illustrious, sublime, great, ambitious, august, solemn, grave, preeminent,

extraordinary, monumental, stupendous, huge, chief, soaring, vaulting, aspiring, transcendent, commanding, towering, overwhelming, impressive, imposing, foremost, awe-inspiring, mighty, empyrean, sensational*, the cat's whiskers*, terrif*, great*, swell*. — *Ant.* poor, low, mediocre.
**3.** [Strongly approved of] — *Syn.* first-class, good, superb; see **excellent.**

*SYN.* — **grand** is applied to that which makes a strong impression because of its greatness (in size or some favorable quality), dignity, and splendor /the *Grand* Canyon, a *grand* parade/; **magnificent** suggests a surpassing beauty, richness, or splendor, or an exalted or glorious quality /a *magnificent* voice/; **imposing** suggests that which strikingly impresses one by its size, dignity, or excellence of character /an *imposing* array of facts/; **stately** suggests that which is imposing in dignified grace and may imply a greatness of size /a *stately* mansion/; **majestic** adds to stately the idea of lofty grandeur /the *majestic* Rockies/; **august** suggests an exalted dignity or impressiveness such as inspires awe /an *august* personage/; **grandiose** is often used disparagingly of a grandeur that is affected or exaggerated /a *grandiose* manner/

**grandeur,** *n.* — *Syn.* splendor, superbity, magnificence, pomp, circumstance, impressiveness, eminence, distinction, fame, glory, brilliancy, opulence, richness, sumptuousness, luxuriousness, stateliness, beauty, handsomeness, ceremony, importance, exalted rank, celebrity, solemnity, fineness, majesty, sublimity, nobility, scope, dignity, loftiness, elevation, preeminence, height, greatness, transcendency, might, breadth, expansiveness, immensity, amplitude, vastness, sway, inclusiveness. — *Ant.* meanness, commonness, baseness.
**grandfather,** *n.* — *Syn.* grandsire, paternal forebear, elder, forefather, ancestor, patriarch, grandpa*, granddaddy*, grandpappy*, grandad*, pap*, gramps*.
**grandiloquent,** *modif.* — *Syn.* pompous, histrionic, bombastic; see **bombastic, oratorical.**
*See Synonym Study at* BOMBASTIC.
**grandiose,** *modif.* — *Syn.* grand, pompous, flamboyant, theatrical; see **egotistic** 2.
*See Synonym Study at* GRAND.
**grandly,** *modif.* — *Syn.* royally, regally, sumptuously; see **wonderfully.**
**grandmother,** *n.* — *Syn.* grandam, matriarch, dowager, ancestor, maternal forebear, *Grossmutter* (German), *babushka* (Russian), grandma*, gram*, granny*.
**grandstand,** *n.* — *Syn.* amphitheater, stadium, stands, stand, stalls, field house, coliseum, field, benches, boxes, bleachers, pit; see also **field** 2, **theater** 1.
**grange,** *n.* **1.** [Manor] — *Syn.* plantation, farm, hacienda; see **ranch.**
**2.** [Farmer's organization] — *Syn.* society, secret society, farmer's union, farmer's guild, agricultural party, farm vote, grass-roots movement.
**granite,** *modif.* — *Syn.* stone, igneous, durable; see **firm** 2.
**grant,** *n.* — *Syn.* gift, boon, reward, award, honorarium, present, allowance, stipend, donation, matching grant, benefaction, gratuity, endowment, concession, bequest, privilege, federal grant. — *Ant.* deprivation, deduction, detriment.
**grant,** *v.* **1.** [To permit] — *Syn.* allow, yield, cede, impart; see **allow** 1.
**2.** [To accept as true] — *Syn.* concede, accede, acqui-

esce; see **admit** 3.
**3.** [To bestow] — *Syn.* give, confer, award, invest; see **give** 1.
*See Synonym Study at* GIVE.
**granted,** *modif.* **1.** [Awarded] — *Syn.* conferred, bestowed, awarded; see **given.**
**2.** [Allowed] — *Syn.* accepted, admitted, acknowledged; see **assumed** 1.
**take for granted** — *Syn.* accept, presume, consider true, consider settled; see **assume** 1.
**granulate,** *v.* — *Syn.* grate, pulverize, powder; see **grind** 1.
**grape,** *n.* Types of grapes include: wine, raisin, seedless, white, red, lambrusca, Concord, scuppernong, summer, plum, chicken, frost, winter, fox, bush, sand, muscadine, Catawba, Delaware, Hartford, Iona, Adirondack, Rogers, Old World, Mission, Vinifera, Euvitis, Niagara, bullace, viparia, rotundifolia, Malaga, Muscat, Thompson, Pinot, Riesling, Chardonnay, Cabernet Sauvignon, Merlot, Sauvignon Blanc, black Hamberg, Isabella.
**grapevine,** *n.* **1.** [Vine] — *Syn.* climber, creeper, trailer; see **vine.**
**2.** [Gossip, used with "the"] — *Syn.* rumor, the grapevine telegraph, hearsay; see **gossip** 1.
**graph,** *n.* — *Syn.* diagram, chart, linear representation; see **design** 1, **plan** 1.
**graphic,** *modif.* **1.** [Pictorial] — *Syn.* visible, illustrated, descriptive, blow-by-blow, naturalistic, realistic, lifelike, photographic, visual, depicted, seen, drawn, portrayed, traced, sketched, outlined, pictured, painted, limned, marked out, blocked out, in full color, engraved, etched, graven, chiseled, hewn, in bold relief, stenciled, penciled, printed. — *Ant.* UNREAL, imagined, chimerical.
**2.** [Vivid] — *Syn.* forcible, telling, picturesque, intelligible, comprehensible, clear, explicit, striking, definite, lucid, distinct, precise, expressive, eloquent, moving, stirring, unequivocal, concrete, energetic, colorful, strong, figurative, poetic. — *Ant.* OBSCURE, ambiguous, abstract.
**grapple,** *v.* **1.** [Fasten] — *Syn.* hook, catch, close; see **fasten** 1, **join** 1.
**2.** [Fight hand to hand] — *Syn.* engage, close, wrestle; see **fight** 2.
**grasp,** *v.* **1.** [To clutch] — *Syn.* seize, take, grip, clasp; see **seize** 1, 2.
**2.** [To comprehend] — *Syn.* perceive, apprehend, follow; see **understand** 1.
*See Synonym Study at* SEIZE.
**grasp,** *n.* — *Syn.* hold, clutch, cinch; see **grip** 2.
**grasping,** *modif.* — *Syn.* niggardly, rapacious, penurious; see **greedy** 1.
*See Synonym Study at* GREEDY.
**grasping,** *n.* — *Syn.* hold, taking, grabbing; see **catch** 3.
**grass,** *n.* **1.** Wild grasses include: Johnson grass, salt grass, blue grass, beach grass, bent grass, foxtail, sedge, rush, reed, buffalo grass, bulrush, sand-bur, couch grass, carpet grass, crab grass, crowfoot, deer grass, bunch grass, meadow grass, fescue, heath grass, joint grass, orchard grass, pampas grass, June grass, redtop, river grass, slough grass, ribbon grass, stink grass, sweet grass, tickle grass, brome, canary grass, cattail, bamboo, wild rice.
Cultivated grasses include: cane, millet, oats, wheat, barley, maize, rye, broomcorn, timothy, kaffir corn, Milo maize, bent grass, Bermuda grass, fescue, Kentucky blue grass, rice, sesame, sorghum.
**2.** [Grassed area] — *Syn.* grassland, meadow, lawn, garden (British), turf, green, fairway, sward, green-

sward, pasture, prairie, bottom, bottomland, hayfield; see also **field** 1, **yard** 1.

**3.** [*A drug] — *Syn.* marijuana, *Nicotanea glauca* (Latin), hemp, cannabis, pot*, weed*, maryjane*, boo*; see also **drug** 2.

**let the grass grow under one's feet*** — *Syn.* waste time, be lazy, fail; see **neglect** 1.

**grasshopper,** *n.*
Insects commonly called grasshoppers include: katydid, locust, cricket, green grasshopper, short-horned grasshopper, long-horned grasshopper, red-legged grasshopper, Rocky Mountain grasshopper, Mormon cricket, hateful grasshopper; *Acristida, Locusta, Gryllus* (all Latin); hopper*, hoppergrass*.

**grassland,** *n.* — *Syn.* plains, meadow, prairie, pampas; see **field** 1.

**grassy,** *modif.* — *Syn.* grass-grown, verdant, green, sedgy, reedy, lush, matted, tangled, carpeted, lawnlike, turfy, sodded, sowed, luxurious, deep.

**grate,** *n.* **1.** [Fireholder] — *Syn.* firebox, bed, furnace, stove, grill, barbecue, gridiron, andiron, firepot.
**2.** [Grid] — *Syn.* grating, lattice, grille, screen.

**grate,** *v.* — *Syn.* rasp, grind, abrade; see **rub** 1.

**grateful,** *modif.* **1.** [Thankful] — *Syn.* appreciative, beholden, obliged; see **thankful.**
**2.** [Welcome] — *Syn.* agreeable, delectable, pleasing; see **pleasant** 2.

**gratefully,** *modif.* — *Syn.* appreciatively, thankfully, with a sense of obligation, delightedly, responsively, admiringly. — *Ant.* RUDELY, ungratefully, thanklessly.

**gratification,** *n.* **1.** [Satisfaction] — *Syn.* enjoyment, pleasure, delight; see **satisfaction** 2.
**2.** [A source of satisfaction] — *Syn.* delight, regalement, luxury; see **satisfaction** 2, 3.

**gratify,** *v.* — *Syn.* indulge, humor, delight; see **satisfy** 1.

**gratifying,** *modif.* — *Syn.* satisfying, delightful, pleasing; see **pleasant** 2.
*See Synonym Study at* PLEASANT.

**grating,** *modif.* — *Syn.* offensive, strident, harsh; see **shrill.**

**gratis,** *modif.* — *Syn.* free, without charge, complimentary, as a gift; see **free** 4.

**gratitude,** *n.* — *Syn.* thankfulness, appreciation, gratefulness, acknowledgment, response, sense of obligation, sense of indebtedness, feeling of obligation, responsiveness, thanks, praise, guerdon, requital, recognition, honor, thanksgiving, grace. — *Ant.* ingratitude, INDIFFERENCE, thanklessness.

**gratuitous,** *modif.* **1.** [Voluntary] — *Syn.* for nothing, gratis, complimentary; see **free** 4.
**2.** [Uncalled-for] — *Syn.* needless, unwarranted, unessential; see **unnecessary.**

**gratuity,** *n.* — *Syn.* tip, lagniappe, reward, *pourboire* (French); see **gift** 1, **tip** 2.
*See Synonym Study at* GIFT.

**grave,** *modif.* **1.** [Important] — *Syn.* momentous, weighty, consequential; see **important** 1.
**2.** [Dangerous] — *Syn.* critical, serious, ominous; see **dangerous** 1.
**3.** [Solemn] — *Syn.* serious, sober, earnest; see **solemn** 1.
*See Synonym Study at* SERIOUS.

**grave,** *n.* **1.** [A burial place] — *Syn.* vault, sepulcher, tomb, pit, crypt, mausoleum, catacomb, long home, burial chamber, burial pit, burial place, six feet of earth, last resting place, narrow house, place of interment, mound, barrow, cromlech, clay, cairn, tumulus, dolmen, cold mud*, pine*, wooden shroud*, pit for the dead*, charnel house*, last home*, permanent address*.

**2.** [Death] — *Syn.* dissolution, decay, last sleep; see **death** 2.

**make one turn (over) in one's grave*** — *Syn.* do something shocking, do something disrespectful, sin, err; see **misbehave.**

**have one foot in the grave*** — *Syn.* be near death, be very ill, be very old, be infirm; see **dying** 2.

**gravel,** *n.* — *Syn.* pebbles, rocks, shale, pea gravel, marl, macadam, screenings, crushed rock, sand, washings, alluvium, tailing.

**graven,** *modif.* — *Syn.* engraved, etched, sculptured, cut; see **engraved.**

**graveyard,** *n.* — *Syn.* burial ground, churchyard, memorial park, necropolis, God's acre; see also **cemetery.**

**gravitate,** *v.* — *Syn.* drift, be attracted to, incline toward; see **approach** 2.

**gravitation,** *n.* — *Syn.* mutual attraction, agitation, settling together, planetary motion, earthward motion, gravity, resistless tendency.

**gravity,** *n.* **1.** [Weight] — *Syn.* heaviness, pressure, force; see **gravitation.**
**2.** [Importance] — *Syn.* seriousness, concern, significance; see **importance** 1.

**gravy,** *n.* — *Syn.* sauce, dressing, brown gravy, white gravy, milk gravy, pan gravy, meat gravy, juice, white sauce, butter sauce.

**gray,** *modif.* **1.** [Between black and white] — *Syn.* neutral, dusky, silvery, livid, dingy, somber, sere, shaded, drab, pale, colorless, leaden, grayish, ashen, grizzly, grizzled.
Hues of gray include: Oxford gray, blue-gray, silver-gray, smoke-gray, slate, bat, mouse-colored, iron-gray, lead, charcoal, ash-gray, pepper and salt, grizzled, powder, dusty, smoky, pearl, taupe, heather, battleship gray.
**2.** [Aged] — *Syn.* grizzled, hoary, decrepit; see **old** 1, 2.

**gray,** *n.* — *Syn.* shade, drabness, dusk.

**graze,** *v.* **1.** [To touch or score lightly] — *Syn.* brush, scrape, rub; see **touch** 1, 2.
**2.** [To pasture] — *Syn.* browse, feed, batten, crop, gnaw, nibble, bite, uproot, pull grass, forage, eat, champ, munch, crunch, masticate, ruminate.

**grazing,** *modif.* **1.** [Browsing] — *Syn.* battening, cropping, feeding, gnawing, nibbling, biting, uprooting, pasturing, pulling grass, foraging, eating, champing, munching, crunching, masticating, ruminating.
**2.** [Keeping livestock on the range] — *Syn.* herding, pasturing, feeding, ranging, running cattle, running stock, stocking, fattening.

**grease,** *n.* — *Syn.* oil, wax, fat, lubricant, salve, Vaseline (trademark), unguent, goose grease, chicken fat, olive oil, cottonseed oil, peanut oil; see also **fat.**
Lubricating greases include: axle grease, hard oil, graphite, lithium grease, petroleum jelly, hypoid lubricant.

**grease,** *v.* — *Syn.* oil, lubricate, smear, salve, coat with oil, rub with oil, cream, daub, inunct, pomade, grease the wheels, anoint, swab, give a grease job*, lube*.

**grease job,** *n.* — *Syn.* lubricating, lubrication service, lube*, lube job*; see **lubrication.**

**greasy,** *modif.* — *Syn.* creamy, fat, oleaginous, fatty; see **oily** 1.

**great,** *modif.* **1.** [Eminent] — *Syn.* noble, grand, august, majestic, dignified, exalted, commanding, puissant, famous, renowned, widely acclaimed, Olympic, famed, celebrated, distinguished, noted, illustrious, highly regarded, conspicuous, elevated, prominent, high, stately, honorable, lordly, princely, magnificent, glorious, regal, royal, kingly, imposing, peerless, preeminent, unrivaled, fabulous, fabled, storied. — *Ant.* OBSCURE, retired, anonymous.

**2.** [Large] — *Syn.* numerous, big, vast; see **large** 1.

**3.** [*Excellent] — *Syn.* exceptional, surpassing, transcendant; see **excellent.**

**4.** [Extensive] — *Syn.* inclusive, all-embracing, sweeping; see **comprehensive.**

*See Synonym Study at* LARGE.

**Great Britain,** *n.* — *Syn.* Britain, British Isles, United Kingdom, England, Wales, Scotland and Northern Ireland; see also **England.**

**greatly,** *modif.* — *Syn.* exceedingly, considerably, hugely; see **very.**

**greatness,** *n.* **1.** [Eminence] — *Syn.* prominence, renown, importance; see **fame** 1.

**2.** [Size] — *Syn.* bulk, extent, largeness; see **size** 2.

**3.** [Character] — *Syn.* magnanimity, merit, morality; see **virtue** 1.

**Greece,** *n.* — *Syn.* Hellas, Graecia, Achaia, Argos, Greek peninsula, Hellenic peoples, the Peloponnesus, the Peloponnese.

**greed,** *n.* — *Syn.* greediness, avidity, selfishness, eagerness, avarice, voracity, excess, rapacity, gluttony, piggishness, indulgence, hoggishness, gourmandism, ravenousness, avariciousness, voraciousness, niggardliness, acquisitiveness, intemperance, cupidity, graspingness, covetousness, desire, grabbiness*, an itching palm*, taking ways*. — *Ant.* GENEROSITY, liberality, munificence.

**greedy,** *modif.* **1.** [Avaricious] — *Syn.* avid, grasping, rapacious, selfish, miserly, parsimonious, close, close-fisted, tight, tight-fisted, niggardly, exploitative, grudging, sordid, mercenary, illiberal, stingy, covetous, penurious, acquisitive, pennypinching*. — *Ant.* GENEROUS, munificent, bountiful.

**2.** [Gluttonous] — *Syn.* rapacious, swinish, voracious, devouring, hoggish, ravening, ravenous, omnivorous, carnivorous, insatiate, gorging, belly-worshiping, surfeiting, crapulous, intemperate, gormandizing, guzzling, gobbling, gulping, selfish, indulging one's appetites. — *Ant.* ASCETIC, fasting, abstemious.

---

*SYN.* — **greedy** implies an insatiable desire to possess or acquire something to an amount inordinately beyond what one needs or deserves and is the broadest of the terms compared here; **avaricious** stresses greed for money or riches and often connotes miserliness; **grasping** suggests an unscrupulous eagerness for gain that manifests itself in a seizing upon every opportunity to get what one desires; **acquisitive** stresses the exertion of effort in acquiring or accumulating wealth or material possessions to an excessive amount; **covetous** implies greed for something that another person rightfully possesses

---

**Greek,** *modif.* — *Syn.* Hellenic, Hellenistic, Helladic, Minoan, Dorian, Attic, Boeotian, Athenian, Spartan, Peloponnesian, Ionian, Corinthian, Thessalonian, ancient, classic, Homeric; see also **classical** 2.

**Greek,** *n.* **1.** [A citizen of Greece] — *Syn.* Hellene, Athenian, Spartan, Achaean, Dorian, Ionian, Corinthian, Thessalonian, Arcadian, Boeotian, Argolid, Laconian, Messenian, Attican, Peloponnesian.

**2.** [The Greek language] — *Syn.* Hellenic, Ionic, New Ionic, Attic, Æolic, Doric, Modern Greek, Romaic, Neo-Hellenic, language of Homer, koine, demotic Greek, hieratic Greek.

**Greeks,** *n.* — *Syn.* Greek culture, Hellenes, the Ancients, Hellenism, classical times, Athens, the glory that was Greece.

**green,** *modif.* **1.** [Of the color green] — *Syn.* greenish, virid, virescent.

Hues of green include: emerald, sage, vert, verdant, verdigris, malachite, beryl, aquamarine, chartreuse, lime, kelly, glaucous, olive drab, Mittler's green, Prussian green, bronze-green, Lincoln green, yellow-green, blue-green, bottle-green, pea-green, sea-green, apple-green, grass-green, forest-green, spinach-green, moss-green, pine-green, Nile green, olive-green, jade, Oriental emerald, Oriental aquamarine, viridian, turquoise, Veronese green.

**2.** [Verdant] — *Syn.* foliate, growing, leafy, bosky, sprouting, visculent, pullulating, grassy, grass-grown, burgeoning, flourishing, lush. — *Ant.* WITHERED, sere, yellow.

**3.** [Immature] — *Syn.* young, growing, unripe, maturing, developing, half-formed, half-baked, fresh, sappy. — *Ant.* MATURE, ripe, gone to seed.

**4.** [Inexperienced] — *Syn.* youthful, callow, raw; see **inexperienced.**

**5.** [Pale, usually from illness, envy, or jealousy] — *Syn.* pallid, peaked, wan; see **pale** 1.

**green,** *n.* **1.** [A color] — *Syn.* greenness, verdure, virescence, emerald, chlorophyll, verdantness, greenhood, viridity.

**2.** [A grass plot] — *Syn.* lawn, field, park; see **grass** 3.

**long green*, folding green*** — *Syn.* bills, paper money, greenbacks; see **money** 1.

**greenhorn,** *n.* **1.** [Beginner] — *Syn.* apprentice, new hand, novice; see **amateur.**

**2.** [A boor] — *Syn.* yokel, crude fellow, rustic; see **boor.**

**greenhouse,** *n.* — *Syn.* hothouse, conservatory, glass-house, arboretum, coolhouse, planthouse, potting shed, nursery, warmhouse (British).

**greensward,** *n.* — *Syn.* lawn, turf, verdancy, verdure, greenery, viridity, virescence, viridescence.

**greet,** *v.* — *Syn.* welcome, accost, speak to, salute, address, hail, recognize, embrace, shake hands, nod, bow, curtsy, receive, call to, stop, acknowledge, bow to, approach, give one's love, hold out the hand, extend the right of friendship, herald, bid good day, bid hello, bid welcome, make welcome, exchange greetings, move to, usher in, attend, pay one's respects. — *Ant.* IGNORE, snub, slight.

**greeting,** *n.* **1.** [A salutation] — *Syn.* welcome, address, notice, reception, attention, accosting, speaking to, heralding, ushering in, acknowledgement, salutation, one's compliments, regards.

Common greetings include: hello, how do you do? how are you? aloha (Hawaiian); *hola, qué tal?* (*both* Spanish); shalom (Hebrew); *wie geht's?* (German); *comment allez-vous?, comment ça va?* (*both* French); good morning, good day, good afternoon, good evening, good morrow; *bonjour, bon soir, bonne nuit* (*all* French); *guten Morgen, guten Abend* (*both* German); *buenos días, buenas tardes, buenas noches* (*all* Spanish); *ciao, buon giorno, buona notte* (*all* Italian); hi*, hey*, howdy*, yo*, you*, say*, I say*, what's new?*, how's it going?* what's up?* what do you know?* how's tricks?* how goes it?* what's happening?* what's going on?*

**2.** [A message of courtesy] — *Syn.* testimonial, note, card; see **letter** 2.

**gremlin,** *n.* — *Syn.* imp, demon, sprite, pixie; see **fairy** 1.

**grenade,** *n.* — *Syn.* hand grenade, shell, projectile, missile; see **weapon** 1.

**grey,** *modif.* — *Syn.* dun, drab, grayish; see **gray** 1.

**grid,** *n.* **1.** [Gridiron] — *Syn.* framework, grill, grille, network, lattice; see also **grate** 1, 2.

**2.** [Conducting plate] — *Syn.* plate, terminal, layer; see **electrode.**

**griddle,** *n.* — *Syn.* grill, gridiron, broiler, broiler pan, frying pan, spider, skillet.

**gridiron,** *n.* **1.** [*A football field] — *Syn.* turf, playing field, griddle*; see **field** 2.

**2.** [A broiler] — *Syn.* griddle, roaster, barbecue rack; see **broiler.**

**grief,** *n.* **1.** [Mental distress] — *Syn.* sorrow, sadness, regret, melancholy, vexation, mourning, misery, trouble, anguish, bereavement, painful regret, distress over loss, depression, despondency, pain, worry, harassment, anxiety, woe, heartache, repining, lamentation, dole, dolor, malaise, disquiet, discomfort, smart, mortification, affliction, gloom, unhappiness, wretchedness, infelicity, desolation, despair, agony, torture, purgatory. — *Ant.* HAPPINESS, exhilaration, pleasure.

**2.** [The cause of distress] — *Syn.* affliction, tribulation, vexation; see **difficulty** 2.

**come to grief**— *Syn.* be ruined, be unsuccessful, be harmed, have trouble, suffer; see also **fail** 1.

**grievance,** *n.* — *Syn.* complaint, injury, case; see **objection** 1, 2.

**grieve,** *v.* — *Syn.* lament, bewail, regret, sorrow for; see **mourn** 1.

**grievous,** *modif.* **1.** [Distressing] — *Syn.* disquieting, upsetting, troublesome; see **disturbing.**

**2.** [Mournful] — *Syn.* dismal, tragic, pathetic; see **sad** 1, 2.

**3.** [Painful] — *Syn.* severe, hurtful, sharp; see **painful** 1.

**4.** [Atrocious] — *Syn.* villainous, flagrant, heinous; see **outrageous.**

**grill,** *n.* **1.** [A broiler] — *Syn.* grid, griddle, rack; see **broiler.**

**2.** [A restaurant, especially one that grills food] — *Syn.* barbecue, lunchroom, cafeteria, diner, short order restaurant, café; see also **restaurant.**

**grill,** *v.* **1.** [To broil] — *Syn.* roast, sauté, barbecue; see **cook.**

**2.** [To question closely] — *Syn.* cross-examine, interrogate, catechise; see **question** 1.

**grim,** *modif.* **1.** [Sullen] — *Syn.* crabbed, sour, repellent, crusty, gloomy, intractable, sulky, morose, somber, sullen, splenetic, churlish, forbidding, glum, grumpy, scowling, grouchy, dour, glowering, dogged, stubborn, cantankerous. — *Ant.* HAPPY, cheerful, gay.

**2.** [Stern] — *Syn.* austere, strict, harsh; see **severe** 1.

**3.** [Relentless] — *Syn.* unrelenting, implacable, inexorable; see **severe** 2, **wicked** 2.

**grimace,** *n.* — *Syn.* smirk, smile, sneer; see **expression** 4.

**grime,** *n.* — *Syn.* soil, smudge, dirt; see **filth.**

**grimy,** *modif.* — *Syn.* dirty, begrimed, dingy, soiled; see **dirty** 1.

*See Synonym Study at* DIRTY.

**grin,** *n.* — *Syn.* smirk, simper, wry face; see **smile.**

**grin,** *v.* — *Syn.* smirk, simper, beam; see **smile.**

**grind,** *n.* **1.** [A difficult or tedious job] — *Syn.* drudgery, toil, labor; see **work** 2.

**2.** [A drudge] — *Syn.* hard worker, toiler, crammer; see **drudge.**

**grind,** *v.* **1.** [To pulverize] — *Syn.* crush, powder, mill, grate, reduce to powder, attenuate, granulate, disintegrate, comminute, triturate, rasp, scrape, reduce to fine particles, levigate, file, abrade, pound, pestle, bray, beat into particles, crunch, crumple, roll out, pound out, shiver, atomize, chop up, crumble. — *Ant.* ORGANIZE, mold, solidify.

**2.** [To sharpen] — *Syn.* whet, rub, give an edge to; see **sharpen** 1.

**3.** [Oppress] — *Syn.* persecute, harass, annoy; see **oppress.**

**grinder,** *n.* **1.** [A chopper or pulverizer] — *Syn.* food chopper, food processor, blender, mill, meat grinder, sausage stuffer, coffee grinder.

**2.** [An abrasive] — *Syn.* grindstone, whetstone, stone; see **abrasive.**

**grinding,** *modif.* — *Syn.* abrasive, crushing, pulverizing, grating, fricative, rasping, rubbing, milling, powdering, granulating, disintegrating, cracking, reducing to dust, comminutive, triturative, bone-crushing, crunching, splintering, shivering, smashing, crumbling, scraping, chopping, wearing away, eroding.

**grind out*,** *v.* — *Syn.* create, manufacture, compose; see **produce** 2.

**grindstone,** *n.* — *Syn.* stone, emery wheel, wheel; see **abrasive.**

**grip,** *n.* **1.** [The power of gripping] — *Syn.* grasp, hold, manual strength, digital strength, ligature, musculature, purchase, government, governance.

**2.** [Application of the power to grip] — *Syn.* hold, grasp, clutch, gripe, purchase, clasp, catch, cinch, vise, clench, clinch, embrace, handclasp, handhold, fist, handgrip, handshake, snatch, grapple, anchor, squeeze, wrench, grab, cincture, enclosing, enclosure, fixing, fastening, crushing, clamp, clamping, iron grip, hoops of steel, vicelike grip, jaws, snag*, glom*, nip*.

**3.** [Something suited to grasping] — *Syn.* knocker, knob, ear; see **handle** 1.

**4.** [*A traveling bag] — *Syn.* valise, suitcase, satchel; see **bag.**

**grip,** *v.* — *Syn.* clutch, grasp, clasp; see **seize** 1.

**come to grips**— *Syn.* engage, encounter, cope with; see **fight** 1, 2, **try** 1.

**gripe*,** *n.* **1.** [An objection] — *Syn.* complaint, grievance, beef*; see **objection** 2.

**2.** [Illness] — *Syn.* infirmity, indisposition, disorder; see **illness** 1.

**gripe,** *v.* **1.** [*To disturb] — *Syn.* annoy, vex, irritate; see **bother** 2, 3.

**2.** [*To complain] — *Syn.* grumble, mutter, fuss; see **complain** 1.

**grippe,** *n.* — *Syn.* influenza, epidemic catarrh, flu; see **disease.**

**grisly,** *modif.* — *Syn.* horrible, terrible, disgusting; see **frightful** 1, **offensive** 2.

**grist,** *n.* — *Syn.* seed, meal, milling; see **grain** 1.

**gristle,** *n.* — *Syn.* ossein, cartilage, osseous matter; see **bone.**

**grit,** *n.* **1.** [Fine particles] — *Syn.* gravel, sand, abrasive powder, dust, lumps, bits of foreign matter, crushed rock.

**2.** [Courage] — *Syn.* pluck, resolution, daring, fortitude; see **courage** 1.

*See Synonym Study at* FORTITUDE.

**gritty,** *modif.* **1.** [Containing grit] — *Syn.* rough, abrasive, sandy, rasping, lumpy, calculous, gravelly, muddy, dusty, powdery, pulverent, granular, friable, branny, floury, crumbly, permeable, porous, sabulous, arenose, loose, raspy, scratchy.

**2.** [Brave] — *Syn.* plucky, determined, resolute; see **brave** 1.

**grizzled,** *modif.* — *Syn.* silvery, grizzly, leaden; see **gray** 1, **old** 1, 2.

**grizzly,** *modif.* — *Syn.* grizzled, graying, hoary; see **gray** 1.

**groan,** *n.* — *Syn.* moan, sob, grunt; see **cry** 1.

**groan,** *v.* — *Syn.* moan, murmur, keen; see **cry** 1.

**grocer,** *n.* — *Syn.* greengrocer, food merchant, operator of a market, chain store manager, prune ped-dler*.

**groceries,** *n.* — *Syn.* food, edibles, produce, comes-tibles, foodstuffs, perishables, vegetables, viands, sta-ples, green groceries, produce, fruits, dairy products, processed foods, frozen foods, freeze-dried foods, dried foods, desiccated foods, instant foods, packaged foods, canned foods.

**grocery,** *n.* — *Syn.* grocery store, supermarket, food store, vegetable market, corner store; see also **market** 1.

**groggy,** *modif.* — *Syn.* drunken, dizzy, reeling; see **tired.**

**groin,** *n.* — *Syn.* crotch, *inguen, inguina* (*both* Latin), intersection of thighs and abdomen, genitals, privates*, private parts*.

**groom,** *n.* **1.** [A male servant] — *Syn.* hostler, stable boy, equerry; see **servant.**
**2.** [A man being married] — *Syn.* bridegroom, hus-band, spouse, benedict, married man, successful suitor; see also **husband.**

**groom,** *v.* — *Syn.* make presentable, make attractive, make acceptable, rub down, remove crudity, refine, get into being, comb, brush, ready, tidy, refresh, curry, spruce up*, pretty up*, slick up*; see also **prepare** 1.

**groove,** *n.* — *Syn.* channel, trench, gouge, depression, score, scratch, canal, valley, notch, furrow, crimp, rut, incision, slit, scallop, chamfer, gutter, fluting, corruga-tion, corduroy, pucker, ditch, crease, crimp, vallecula.
**in the groove*** — *Syn.* efficient, skillful, operative; see **working.**

**grope,** *v.* — *Syn.* fumble, touch, feel blindly; see **feel** 1.

**gross,** *modif.* **1.** [Fat] — *Syn.* corpulent, obese, porcine; see **fat** 1.
**2.** [Obscene] — *Syn.* foul, offensive, indecent; see **lewd** 1, 2.
**3.** [Coarse] — *Syn.* crude, unrefined, crass; see **coarse** 2, **rude** 1, **vulgar** 1.
**4.** [Without deduction] — *Syn.* in sum, total, entire; see **whole** 1.
**5.** [Flagrant] — *Syn.* obvious, out-and-out, patent; see **obvious** 1.
**6.** [Disgusting] — *Syn.* repugnant, revolting, sickening; see **offensive** 2.
*See Synonym Study at* COARSE.

**gross,** *n.* — *Syn.* total, aggregate, sum total, total amount; see **whole.**

**gross,** *v.* — *Syn.* earn, bring in, take in; see **earn** 2.

**grotesque,** *modif.* **1.** [Ludicrously incongruous] — *Syn.* odd, abnormal, bizarre, queer; see **unusual** 2.
**2.** [Incongruous in form] — *Syn.* malformed, ugly, dis-torted; see **deformed.**
**3.** [Deliberately incongruous for artistic purposes] — *Syn.* fantastic, surrealistic, dadaist; see **art** 2.
*See Synonym Study at* FANTASTIC.

**grotto,** *n.* — *Syn.* cavern, cave, hollow; see **hole** 3.

**grouch*,** *n.* — *Syn.* complainer, grumbler, grump, mal-content, growler, bear*, sourpuss*, sorehead*, crab*, crank*, griper*, bellyacher*, grouser*, kicker*.

**grouch*,** *v.* — *Syn.* mutter, grumble, gripe*; see **com-plain** 1.

**grouchy,** *modif.* — *Syn.* surly, ill-tempered, crusty; see **irritable.**

**ground,** *n.* **1.** [Soil] — *Syn.* sand, dirt, soil; see **earth** 2.
**2.** [An area] — *Syn.* spot, terrain, territory; see **area** 2.
**break ground** — *Syn.* start, initiate, commence; see **be-gin** 1.
**cover ground** — *Syn.* move, go on, progress; see **ad-vance** 1.
**cut the ground from under one** or **one's feet*** — *Syn.* deprive, prove wrong, talk down; see **defeat** 1.

**from the ground up** — *Syn.* thoroughly, wholly, en-tirely; see **completely.**

**gain ground** — *Syn.* move, go on, progress; see **ad-vance** 1.

**get off the ground*** — *Syn.* start, commence, come into being; see **begin** 2.

**give ground** — *Syn.* withdraw, yield, retire; see **re-treat** 1.

**hold** or **stand one's ground** — *Syn.* maintain one's position, defend, sustain, dig in one's heels; see **en-dure** 2.

**lose ground** — *Syn.* withdraw, fall behind, drop back; see **lag** 1.

**on delicate ground** — *Syn.* in a sensitive position, unsteady, insecure; see **weak** 3, 6.

**on firm ground** — *Syn.* reliable, secure, supported; see **safe** 1.

**on one's own ground*** — *Syn.* comfortable in, capable, proficient; see **able** 1, 2.

**on shaky ground*** — *Syn.* uncertain, unreliable, weak; see **inadequate** 1.

**run into the ground*** — *Syn.* exaggerate, do too much, press; see **overdo** 1.

**suit (right) down to the ground*** — *Syn.* suit, be suit-able for, be appropriate for, fulfill; see **fit** 1, 2.

**ground,** *v.* **1.** [To bring to the ground] — *Syn.* floor, bring down, prostrate; see **fell.**
**2.** [To restrict] — *Syn.* cause to remain on the ground, bar from flying, take wings away, prevent from driving*, confine to one's home; see also **restrict** 2.
**3.** [To instruct in essentials] — *Syn.* train, indoctrinate, educate; see **teach** 1.

**groundhog,** *n.* — *Syn.* woodchuck, chuck, rockchuck, marmot, rodent, aardvark, whistle pig, woodshock*.

**groundless,** *modif.* — *Syn.* causeless, baseless, un-founded.; see **illogical.**

**grounds,** *n.* **1.** [Real estate] — *Syn.* estate, lot, environs, territory; see **property** 2.
**2.** [Basis] — *Syn.* reasons, arguments, proof; see **ba-sis** 1.
**3.** [Sediment] — *Syn.* dregs, lees, leavings; see **resi-due.**

**groundwork,** *n.* — *Syn.* foundation, basis, preparation, preliminaries; see **basis** 1, **foundation** 2.
*See Synonym Study at* BASE.

**group,** *modif.* — *Syn.* family, kindred, tribal, communal, racial; see also **common** 5.

**group,** *n.* **1.** [A gathering of persons] — *Syn.* assembly, assemblage, crowd; see **gathering.**
**2.** [Collected things] — *Syn.* accumulation, assort-ment, combination; see **collection** 2.
**3.** [An organized body of people] — *Syn.* association, club, society; see **organization** 3.

**group,** *v.* — *Syn.* file, assort, arrange; see **classify.**

**grove,** *n.* — *Syn.* woods, stand, spinney, copse; see **for-est.**

**grovel,** *v.* — *Syn.* crawl, cringe, fawn, fawn upon, beg, sneak, stoop, kneel, crouch before, truckle, kowtow, im-plore, toady, sponge, cower, snivel, beseech, wheedle, blandish, flatter, cater to, humor, pamper, curry favor with, make much of, court, act up to, play up to*, beg for mercy, prostrate, reverence, eat humble pie*, soft-soap*, butter up*, make up to*, kiss one's feet*, lick the dust*, dance attendance on*, lick another's boots*, knuckle under*, polish the apple*, eat dirt*, brown-nose*, suck up to*, shine up to*, kiss up to*. — *Ant.* HATE, spurn, scorn.

**groveling,** *modif.* — *Syn.* servile, cringing, fawning; see **docile, humble** 1.

**grow,** *v.* **1.** [To become larger] — *Syn.* increase, expand, swell, wax, pullulate, thrive, gain, enlarge, swell in substance, augment, advance, dilate, stretch, mount, build, burst forth, spread, burgeon, amplify, germinate, multiply, develop, abound, accumulate, mature, jump up, flourish, luxuriate, grow up, rise, sprout, shoot up, start up, spring up, spread like wildfire*, pop up*, jump up*, branch out*, fill out*, puff out. — *Ant.* LESSEN, shrink, wither.

**2.** [To change slowly] — *Syn.* become, develop, alter, tend, pass, evolve, flower, shift, flow, progress, advance, get, wax, turn into, work up, turn, improve, mellow, age, better, ripen, ripen into, blossom, assume the form of, open out, resolve itself into, mature. — *Ant.* CONTINUE, regress, preserve.

**3.** [To cultivate] — *Syn.* raise, nurture, tend, nurse, foster, produce, plant, breed, market. — *Ant.* HARM, impede, neglect.

**4.** [To begin] — *Syn.* originate, start, arise; see **begin** 2.

**5.** [To become] — *Syn.* develop into, grow to be, change to; see **become** 1.

**grower,** *n.* — *Syn.* raiser, producer, breeder; see **farmer.**

**growing,** *modif.* — *Syn.* increasing, ever-widening, crescive, crescent, expanding, budding, germinating, maturing, burgeoning, fructifying, waxing, enlarging, amplifying, swelling, developing, mushrooming, spreading, thriving, flourishing, pullulating, dilating, augmenting, stretching, living, sprouting, cloning, viable, organic, animate, spreading like wildfire*. — *Ant.* lessening, withering, shrinking.

**growl,** *n.* **1.** [A low, beastlike sound] — *Syn.* snarl, gnarl, gnar*, moan, bark, bellow, rumble, roar, howl, grumble, grunt.

**2.** [Speech resembling a growl, sense 1] — *Syn.* grumble, rumble, mumble; see **noise** 1.

**growl,** *v.* **1.** [To make a low, deep sound] — *Syn.* snarl, gnarl, gnar*; see **grumble** 2.

**2.** [To speak as if growling] — *Syn.* snarl, grumble, upbraid; see **complain** 1, **scold.**

**grown,** *modif.* — *Syn.* of age, adult, grown up; see **mature** 1.

**grown-up,** *n.* — *Syn.* adult, grown man, grown woman, grown person; see **adult.**

**growth,** *n.* **1.** [The process of growing] — *Syn.* extension, organic development, germination; see **increase** 1.

**2.** [The result of growing] — *Syn.* completion, adulthood, fullness; see **majority** 2, **maturity** 3.

**3.** [An organic excrescence] — *Syn.* tumor, cancer, swelling, mass, lump, mole, fungus, parasite, outgrowth, button, thickening, fibrousness, fribrous tissue, cancroid, X-ray shadow; see also **bulge.**

**grub,** *n.* **1.** [A larva] — *Syn.* entozoon, caterpillar, maggot; see **worm** 1.

**2.** [*Food] — *Syn.* victuals, comestibles, eats*, chow*; see **food.**

**grub,** *v.* **1.** [To dig] — *Syn.* delve, burrow, excavate; see **dig** 1.

**2.** [To clear land] — *Syn.* uproot stumps, prepare for the plow, break; see **clean.**

**3.** [*To work laboriously] — *Syn.* moil, toil, drudge; see **work** 1.

**grubby,** *modif.* — *Syn.* dirty, sloppy, grimy; see **dirty** 1.

**grudge,** *n.* — *Syn.* spite, rancor, animosity; see **hatred** 1, 2, **malice.**

**grudge,** *v.* — *Syn.* begrudge, covet, be reluctant; see **envy.**

**grueling,** *modif.* — *Syn.* exhausting, tiring, fatiguing; see **difficult** 1, 2.

**gruesome,** *modif.* — *Syn.* grim, grisly, fearful; see **frightful** 1, **offensive** 2.

**gruff,** *modif.* **1.** [Brusque] — *Syn.* blunt, rough, crusty, surly; see **abrupt** 2, **blunt** 2, **irritable, rude** 1, 2.

**2.** [Hoarse] — *Syn.* harsh, grating, rough; see **hoarse.** *See Synonym Study at* BLUNT.

**grumble,** *v.* **1.** [To complain] — *Syn.* whine, protest, fuss; see **complain** 1.

**2.** [To growl] — *Syn.* snarl, gnarl, gnarr*, snap, bark, grunt, mutter, rumble, croak, roar, splutter, snuffle, whine.

**3.** [To mutter] — *Syn.* murmur, mumble, whine; see **mutter** 2.

**grumbling,** *modif.* — *Syn.* discontented, sour, grouchy; see **irritable.**

**grumpy,** *modif.* — *Syn.* sullen, grouchy, cantankerous; see **irritable.**

**grunt,** *v.* — *Syn.* snort, squawk, squeak; see **cry** 3.

**guarantee,** *v.* **1.** [To certify] — *Syn.* attest, testify, aver, vouch for, declare, assure, ensure, answer for, be responsible for, stand behind, become surety for, evince, evidence, endorse, secure, make sure, make certain, warrant, insure, witness, prove, reassure, support, affirm, confirm.

**2.** [To give security] — *Syn.* pledge, give bond, go bail, wager, stake, give a guarantee, stand good for, mortgage, pawn, back, sign for.

**3.** [To promise] — *Syn.* swear, assure, insure, cross one's heart*; see **promise** 1.

**guaranteed,** *modif.* — *Syn.* warranted, certified, bonded, secured, endorsed, insured, pledged, vouched for, plighted, confirmed, assured, ascertained, approved, attested, sealed, certificated, protected, on ice, affirmed, sure-fire*. — *Ant.* unsupported, ANONYMOUS, unendorsed.

**guarantor,** *n.* — *Syn.* bondsman, bondswoman, underwriter, patron; see **sponsor.**

**guaranty,** *n.* **1.** [Assurance] — *Syn.* pledge, attestation, certification; see **promise** 1.

**2.** [A document giving assurance] — *Syn.* warrant, warranty, bond, contract, recognizance, certificate, charter, testament, security.

**guard,** *n.* — *Syn.* sentry, sentinel, protector, curator, watchman, night watchman, security officer, security guard, lookout, caretaker, custodian, keeper, police officer, patrolman, defender, warder, jailer, turnkey, watchdog, screw*; see also **guardian** 1, **police officer.**
**off one's guard** — *Syn.* unaware, unprotected, defenseless; see **unprepared.**
**on one's guard** — *Syn.* alert, mindful, vigilant; see **watchful.**

**guard,** *v.* **1.** [To protect] — *Syn.* secure, shield, safeguard; see **defend** 1, 2.

**2.** [To watch over] — *Syn.* watch, observe, superintend, stand sentinel, patrol, picket, police, look out, look after, see after, supervise, tend, keep in view, keep an eye on, keep under surveillance, attend, overlook, keep a prisoner, hold in custody, stand over, babysit, care for, keep vigil, look to, see to, chaperone, shepherd, oversee, keep a weather eye*, ride herd on*, keep tabs on*, be a father to*. — *Ant.* disregard, NEGLECT, forsake.

**guarded,** *modif.* **1.** [Protected] — *Syn.* safeguarded, secured, defended; see **safe** 1.

**2.** [Cautious] — *Syn.* circumspect, attentive, overcautious; see **careful.**

**guardian,** *n.* **1.** [One who regulates or protects] — *Syn.* overseer, safeguard, curator, guard, vigilante, protector, conservator, preserver, trustee, custodian, keeper, patrol, warden, defender, paladin, member of a vigilance

committee, supervisor, babysitter, sponsor, superinten-dent, sentinel, member of the Watch and Ward★.
**2.** [A foster parent] — *Syn.* adoptive parent, foster mother, foster father, nurse, protector, custodian.
**guardsman,** *n.* — *Syn.* guard, sentry, patrol; see **guard.**
**guerrilla,** *modif.* — *Syn.* auxiliary, independent, irregu-lar, underground, predatory; see also **fighting.**
**guerrilla,** *n.* — *Syn.* partisan, underground soldier, ir-regular, resistance fighter, member of the underground, member of the resistance, irregular soldier, saboteur, independent; see also **soldier.**
**guess,** *n.* — *Syn.* conjecture, surmise, supposition, theory, hypothesis, presupposition, presumption, opin-ion, postulate, estimate, divination, association of ideas, surmisal, suspicion, thesis, guesswork, view, belief, as-sumption, speculation, supposal, postulation, fancy, inference, conclusion, deduction, induction, guessti-mate★, shot in the dark★.

*SYN.* — **guess** implies the forming of a judgment or estimate (often a correct one) without sufficient knowl-edge for certainty /he *guessed* the number of beans in the jar/; to **conjecture** is to infer or predict from incomplete or uncertain evidence /I cannot *conjecture* what his plans are/; **surmise** implies a conjecturing through mere in-tuition or imagination /she *surmised* the truth/

**guess,** *v.* **1.** [To attempt an answer on inadequate evidence] — *Syn.* conjecture, presume, infer, suspect, speculate, imagine, surmise, theorize, opine, hypoth-esize, predicate, hazard a supposition *or* conjecture, sug-gest, figure, incline to a view, divine, reckon, calcu-late.
**2.** [To make a choice, almost at hazard] — *Syn.* chance, take a leap in the dark, light on, venture, suppose, pre-sume, imagine, think likely, jump at a conclusion, guess maybe★, make a stab at★, lump it★, have a shot at★, haz-ard a guess★.
**3.** [To choose rightly on little or no evidence] — *Syn.* pick, select, happen upon; see **choose** 1.
**guess at,** *v.* — *Syn.* reckon, calculate, survey; see **esti-mate** 1, 2.
**guessing,** *n.* — *Syn.* guesswork, supposition, imagina-tion, fancy, inference, deduction, presumption, predis-position, reckoning, surmise, theorizing, taking for gran-ted, positing, postulating, assuming, presuming, opin-ion, going by dead reckoning, leaping to conclusions★, going by guess and by God★.
**guest,** *n.* **1.** [One to whom hospitality is extended] — *Syn.* visitor, caller, house guest, dinner guest, visi-tant, company, partaker of hospitality, sharer, recipient of one's bounty, inmate, confidant, confidante, fellow, messmate, boon companion, bedfellow.
**2.** [One who is received for pay] — *Syn.* tenant, boarder, patron, customer, paying guest, roomer, habitué, sojourner, frequenter, lodger, renter.
*See Synonym Study at* VISITOR.
**guffaw,** *n.* — *Syn.* roar, cachinnation, horselaugh, belly laugh; see **laugh.**
*See Synonym Study at* LAUGH.
**guidance,** *n.* — *Syn.* direction, leadership, supervision; see **administration** 1.
**guide,** *n.* **1.** [One who guides others] — *Syn.* pilot, cap-tain, pathfinder, scout, escort, cicerone, convoy, cou-rier, director, exhibitor, vanguard, discoverer, explorer, lead, modernist, guru, conductor, usher, docent, pio-neer, leader, superintendent, chaperone.
**2.** [A model] — *Syn.* pattern, design, example; see **model** 2.

**guide,** *v.* **1.** [Direct] — *Syn.* supervise, oversee, control; see **manage** 1.
**2.** [To lead] — *Syn.* conduct, escort, show the way; see **lead** 1.
**guidebook,** *n.* — *Syn.* guide, chart, manual, Baedeker; see **handbook.**
**guild,** *n.* — *Syn.* profession, society, trade; see **organiza-tion** 3.
**guile,** *n.* — *Syn.* craft, cunning, cleverness, duplicity; see **cunning, dishonesty.**
**guileless,** *modif.* — *Syn.* honest, frank, sincere; see **na-ive.**
**guilt,** *n.* — *Syn.* culpability, blame, error, fault, lapse, slip, crime, sin, offense, answerability, liability, misstep, solecism, criminality, blameworthiness, sinfulness, mis-conduct, dereliction, misbehavior, malpractice, pecca-bility, frailty, delinquency, transgression, dereliction, in-discretion, weakness, failing, malefaction, malfeasance, felonious conduct. — *Ant.* INNOCENCE, freedom from fault, blamelessness.
**guiltless,** *modif.* — *Syn.* harmless, above suspicion, free; see **innocent** 1.
**guilty,** *modif.* **1.** [Convicted] — *Syn.* found guilty, guilty as charged, condemned, sentenced, criminal, censured, impeached, incriminated, indicted, liable, condemned, proscribed, having violated law, weighed and found wanting, judged, damned, doomed, cast into outer dark-ness. — *Ant.* cleared, vindicated, absolved.
**2.** [Culpable] — *Syn.* at fault, sinful, on one's head, to blame, in the wrong, in error, accusable, censurable, wrong, blameworthy, blamable, reproachable, derelict, chargeable, indictable, convictable, looking like the cat that swallowed the canary★, caught red-handed★, caught with one's pants down★, caught with one's hand in the cookie jar★. — *Ant.* blameless, INNOCENT, right.
**3.** [Wicked] — *Syn.* evil, depraved, licentious; see **wicked** 1.
**guise,** *n.* — *Syn.* semblance, pretense, form; see **appear-ance** 1, 2.
*See Synonym Study at* APPEARANCE.
**gulch,** *n.* — *Syn.* gully, ditch, gorge; see **ravine.**
**gulf,** *n.* **1.** [Chasm] — *Syn.* abyss, abysm, depth; see **ra-vine.**
**2.** [An arm of the sea] — *Syn.* inlet, sound, cove; see **bay.**
**3.** [A vast interval] — *Syn.* distance, hiatus, inter-regnum; see **expanse.**
**gull,** *n.* — *Syn.* sucker, dope, dupe, sap, puppet; see also **fool** 2.
**gullet,** *n.* — *Syn.* neck, gorge, craw, maw; see **throat.**
**gullible,** *modif.* — *Syn.* innocent, trustful, simple; see **na-ive.**
**gully,** *n.* — *Syn.* ditch, chasm, crevasse; see **ravine.**
**gulp,** *v.* — *Syn.* pour, swill, bolt, take in one draught, swig, choke down, toss off, toss down; see also **swal-low.**
**gum,** *n.* — *Syn.* resin, glue, pitch, tar, pine tar, cohesive substance, rosin, amber, wax.
Commercial gums include: chewing gum, sealing wax, rosin, mucilage, eucalyptus, caoutchouc, crude rub-ber, chicle, latex, gum arabic, gum acacia, wattle gum, Kordofan, British gum, cherry-gum, Sonora gum, gutta-percha, sweet gum, guar gum, mesquite gum, gum mag-uey, gum ledon.
Varieties and flavors of chewing gum include: cinnamon, bubble gum, spearmint, peppermint, sugar-free, winter-green, teaberry, licorice, fruit, pepsin.
**gummy,** *modif.* — *Syn.* sticky, cohesive, viscid; see **adhe-sive.**

**gumption***, *n.* — *Syn.* shrewdness, sagacity, initiative; see **acumen, industry** 1.

**gun,** *n.* **1.** [A cannon] — *Syn.* piece, ordnance, heavy ordnance, rifle.

Types of large guns include: long gun, siege gun, howitzer, mortar, antitank gun, culverin, field piece, bazooka, pom-pom, antiaircraft gun, ack ack*; see **artillery** 1, **cannon, rocket.**

**2.** [A portable firearm]. Types of hand-held guns include: rifle, automatic rifle, semiautomatic rifle, repeating rifle, repeater, recoilless rifle, air rifle, BB gun, air gun, shotgun, sawed-off shotgun, double-barreled shotgun, magazine shotgun, pump-action gun, fowling piece, musket, flintlock, wheel lock, hand gun, muzzleloader, breech-loader, squirrel gun, needle gun, blunderbuss, carbine, machine gun, submachine gun, Uzi, AK-47, M-1, M-14, M-16, machine pistol, long rifle, laser gun, matchlock, revolver, pistol, automatic, semiautomatic, 9-mm., derringer, horse pistol, gat*, persuader*, rod*, piece*, heater*, burp gun*, Saturday night special*, zip gun*; see also **machine gun, pistol.**

**3.** [A device suggestive of a gun] — *Syn.* spray gun, air brush, grease gun, atomizer, syringe, tranquilizer gun.

**give it the gun***— *Syn.* quicken, stimulate, speed up, accelerate; see **hasten** 2.

**go great guns***— *Syn.* do well, succeed, triumph; see **prosper.**

**jump the gun***— *Syn.* start too soon, act inappropriately, give oneself away; see **begin** 1, **hurry** 1.

**stick to one's guns**— *Syn.* maintain one's position, be firm, sustain; see **endure** 2.

**gunfire,** *n.* — *Syn.* shot, shots, shooting, cannonading, bombardment, fire to pin down someone, artillery support, air support, air strike, mortar fire, heavy arms attack, explosion, report, artillery, shellburst, volley, discharge, enfilade, detonation, blast, firing, burst, thunder, crackle, barrage, creeping barrage, curtain, curtain of fire, cannonade, box of fire, salvo.

**gunman,** *n.* — *Syn.* killer, thug, gangster; see **criminal.**

**gunner,** *n.* — *Syn.* machine gunner, mortar man, mortar specialist, rocket man, rocketeer, missile man, missile launcher, bazooka carrier, bazooka launcher, sniper, sharpshooter, BAR man, rifleman, aerial gunner, artilleryman, cannoneer, body snatcher*, Archie*.

**gunpowder,** *n.* — *Syn.* black powder, high explosive, smokeless powder; see **explosive.**

**gurgle,** *v.* — *Syn.* ripple, murmur, purl; see **flow** 1.

**gush,** *n.* — *Syn.* jet, spray, spout; see **fountain** 2.

**gush,** *v.* **1.** [To spout] — *Syn.* pour, well, spew; see **flow** 2.

**2.** [To emit copiously] — *Syn.* pour fourth, flood, surge; see **flow** 1.

**3.** [*To act or speak effusively] — *Syn.* prate, prattle, gloze; see **babble.**

**gushing,** *modif.* **1.** [Flowing] — *Syn.* spouting, pouring out, emitting; see **flowing.**

**2.** [*Sentimental] — *Syn.* enthusiastic, blubbery, mushy*; see **effusive, sentimental.**

**gust,** *n.* — *Syn.* blast, wind, blow, breeze; see **wind** 1.
*See Synonym Study at* WIND.

**gusto,** *n.* — *Syn.* zeal, fervor, ardor; see **enthusiasm** 1.

**gusty,** *modif.* — *Syn.* breezy, hearty, robust; see **windy** 1.

**gut,** *n.* — *Syn.* small intestine, large intestine, duodenum, stomach; see **abdomen.**

**guts,** *n.* **1.** [*Bowels] — *Syn.* viscera, insides, belly; see **abdomen.**

**2.** [*Fortitude] — *Syn.* pluck, hardihood, effrontery; see **courage** 1.

**hate someone's guts***— *Syn.* detest, dislike, despise; see **hate** 1.

**gutter,** *n.* **1.** [A ditch] — *Syn.* canal, runnel, gully, sewer, watercourse, channel, dike, drain, moat, fosse, trough; see also **trench** 1.

**2.** [A drain for a roof] — *Syn.* eaves trough, rainspout, rain pipe, eavespout, gargoyle, eaves, conduit, cistern pipe, funnel.

**guttural,** *modif.* — *Syn.* throaty, hoarse, gruff, rough, grating, harsh, rasping, glottal, deep, sepulchral, growling, thick, inarticulate. — *Ant.* high-pitched, shrill, nasal.

**guy,** *n.* **1.** [Lateral tensile support] — *Syn.* cable, truss, sling, hawser, guy wire, guy rope, tent rope, tackle, cinch, bond, line, stay, painter, chain, tie, thong, bowline, strap, lanyard, brace, tendon, vinculum, copula.

**2.** [*Fellow] — *Syn.* chap, lad, person; see **fellow** 1.

**guzzle,** *v.* — *Syn.* swill, quaff, swig; see **drink** 1.

**gymnasium,** *n.* — *Syn.* health *or* recreation center, playing floor, exercise room, sports center, athletic department, *Turnverein* (German), field house, court, athletic club, arena, coliseum, theater, circus, stadium, ring, rink, pit, amphitheater, course, platform, floor, hippodrome, canvas, alley, garden, gallery, gym*.

**gymnast,** *n.* — *Syn.* acrobat, tumbler, jumper; see **athlete.**

**gymnastics,** *n.* — *Syn.* trapeze performance, health exercises, acrobatics, aerobatics, aerobics, therapeutics, body-building exercises, tumbling, vaulting, free exercise, floor exercise, dancercise, Jazzercise (trademark), work on the rings, bars, balance beam, horizontal bars, horse; slimnastics*.

**gyp,** *n.* — *Syn.* cheat, fraud, trick; see **fake, trick** 1.

**gyp,** *v.* — *Syn.* cheat, defraud, swindle; see **deceive.**

**gypsy,** *n.* **1.** [One of nomadic Caucasoid people] — *Syn.* Egyptian, Caucasian, *Rom* (Romany), *Bohémien* (French), *Zingaro* (Italian), *gitano* (Spanish).

**2.** [One who lives a roving life] — *Syn.* tramp, Bohemian, vagrant; see **traveler.**

**gyrate,** *v.* — *Syn.* spin, rotate, revolve; see **whirl.**

**gyro,** *n.* — *Syn.* gyrator, whirligig, spinner, gyroscope, gyroscopic control, gyrostat, gyroscopic governor.

# H

**habit,** *n.* **1.** [Tendency to repeated action] — *Syn.* disposition, way, fashion, manner, propensity, bent, turn, gravitation, proclivity, inclination, addiction, impulsion, predisposition, susceptibility, weakness, bias, proneness, fixed attitude, persuasion, second nature, penchant; see also **attitude** 2, **inclination** 1.
**2.** [A customary action] — *Syn.* custom, usage, wont, mode, practice, rule; see also **custom** 1.
**3.** [An obsession] — *Syn.* addiction, fixation, hang-up★; see **obsession.**
**4.** [Dress] — *Syn.* vestments, costume, riding costume, habiliment; see **clothes.**

---

*SYN.* — **habit** refers to an act repeated so often by an individual that it has become automatic with him /his *habit* of tugging at his ear in perplexity/; **practice** also implies the regular repetition of an act but does not suggest that it is automatic /the *practice* of reading in bed/; **custom** applies to any act or procedure carried on by tradition and often enforced by social disapproval of any violation /the *custom* of dressing for dinner/; **usage** refers to custom or practice that has become sanctioned through being long established /the meanings of words are established by *usage*/; **wont** is a literary or somewhat archaic equivalent for **practice** /it was his *wont* to rise early/

---

**habitable,** *modif.* — *Syn.* inhabitable, fit for habitation, livable; see **comfortable** 2.
**habitat,** *n.* — *Syn.* locality, territory, natural surroundings; see **environment, home** 1, **position** 1.
**habitation,** *n.* — *Syn.* abode, dwelling, occupancy; see **home** 1.
**habitual,** *modif.* **1.** [Of the nature of a habit] — *Syn.* ingrained, confirmed, frequent, periodic, continual, routine, mechanical, automatic, perfunctory, seasoned, iterated, permanent, perpetual, on-going, consuetudinary, consuetudinal, fixed, rooted, inveterate, systematic, recurrent, periodical, methodical, repeated, iterative, reiterative, disciplined, practiced, accustomed, established, set, repetitious, cyclic, reiterated, settled, trite, stereotyped, formal, addicted, acting by force of habit, being such by habit, in a groove, in a rut; see also **chronic, constant** 1, **regular** 3. — *Ant.* DIFFERENT, exceptional, departing.
**2.** [Usual] — *Syn.* customary, accustomed, normal; see **common** 1, **conventional** 1.
*See Synonym Study at* USUAL.
**habitué,** *n.* — *Syn.* devotee, customer, patron; see **client, frequenter.**
**hack,** *n.* **1.** [A literary drudge] — *Syn.* scribbler, pulp-story writer, ghost writer, propaganda writer, inferior writer, writer of potboilers, free-lance writer, commercial writer, popular novelist, ghost★, free lance★, tenth rater★, penny-a-liner★; see also **writer.** — *Ant.* ARTIST, literary master, literary genius.
**2.** [A coach for hire] — *Syn.* cab, taxicab, taxi, hackney;

see **carriage** 2, **vehicle** 1.
**3.** [A cut] — *Syn.* notch, nick, cleavage; see **cut** 2.
**4.** [A horse for hire] — *Syn.* nag, hackney, crowbait★; see **horse** 1.
**5.** [★Commercial driver, especially of a taxicab] — *Syn.* taxi driver, cab driver, chauffeur, cabbie; see **driver.**
**hack,** *v.* — *Syn.* chop, whack, mangle; see **cut** 1.
**hackle,** *n.* — *Syn.* plumage, mantle, feathers; see **feather.**
**hackles,** *n.* — *Syn.* temper, dander, passion; see **anger.**
**hackneyed,** *modif.* — *Syn.* worn-out, old, trite; see **common** 1, **dull** 4.
*See Synonym Study at* TRITE.
**hag,** *n.* — *Syn.* old woman, crone, witch, virago, vixen, withered old woman, shrew, ogress, hellhag, hellcat, grandmother, fishwife, gorgon, harridan, old witch, Xanthippe, Medusa, battle-ax★, old cat★; see also **witch, woman** 1.
**haggard,** *modif.* — *Syn.* gaunt, careworn, fretted; see **thin** 2, **weak** 1.
**haggle,** *v.* **1.** [To bargain] — *Syn.* deal, wrangle, argue; see **buy** 1, **sell** 1.
**2.** [To mangle] — *Syn.* whack, hack, chop; see **cut** 1.
**hail,** *n.* — *Syn.* hailstorm, sleet, hailstone, graupel, soft hail, ice; see also **rain** 1, **storm.**
**hail,** *v.* **1.** [To salute] — *Syn.* cheer, welcome, honor; see **greet.**
**2.** [To call to] — *Syn.* signal, address, speak to; see **summon** 1.
**3.** [To praise] — *Syn.* applaud, recognize, acclaim; see **praise** 1.
**hail from★,** *v.* — *Syn.* come from, be born in, be a native of, claim origin in, claim as one's birthplace, originate; see also **begin** 2.
**hair,** *n.* **1.** [Threadlike growth] — *Syn.* locks, tresses, wig, moustache, whiskers, eyebrow, eyelash, thatch, sideburn, down, tress, wool, shock, mane, filament, fluff; see also **beard, fur.**
**2.** [One threadlike growth] — *Syn.* whisker, cilium, bristle, vibrissa, striga, villus; see also **fiber** 1, **thread.**
**3.** [Anything suggesting the thickness of a hair] — *Syn.* filament, strand, thread, fiber, a hairbreadth, a narrow margin, whisker, nose, hair trigger, hairspring, splinter, shaving, sliver; see also **bit** 3.
**get in one's hair★** — *Syn.* irritate, annoy, disturb; see **bother** 2.
**have by the short hairs★** — *Syn.* have at one's mercy, victimize, have over a barrel★; see **defeat** 1.
**let one's hair down★** — *Syn.* relax, be informal, have fun, let oneself go; see **relax** 1.
**make one's hair stand on end** — *Syn.* terrify, scare, horrify; see **frighten** 1.
**split hairs** — *Syn.* quibble, cavil, nag; see **fight** 1.
**to a hair** — *Syn.* precisely, perfectly, right in every detail; see **exactly.**
**hairbreadth,** *modif.* — *Syn.* hazardous, narrow, close; see **dangerous** 1, **unsafe.**

**hairbreadth,** *n.* — *Syn.* small margin, fraction, jot; see **bit** 3, **hair** 3.

**haircut,** *n.* — *Syn.* trim, trimming, shingling, bob, crew cut, page boy, pompadour, feather cut, bangs, buzz cut, convict cut, GI haircut, butch, mohawk, D.A.*, D.T.*; see also **hairstyle.**

**hairdo,** *n.* — *Syn.* coiffure, hairdressing, do*; see **haircut, hairstyle.**

**hairdresser,** *n.* — *Syn.* hairstylist, beauty culturist, beautician, beauty specialist; see **barber.**

**hairiness,** *n.* — *Syn.* shagginess, downiness, pubescence, pilosity, hispidity, crinosity, bristliness, hirsuteness, furriness, fluffiness.

**hairless,** *n.* — *Syn.* glabrescent, glabrous, shorn, tonsured, whiskerless, clean-shaven, beardless, shaven, smooth-faced; see also **bald** 1, **smooth** 3. — *Ant.* HAIRY, shaggy, bearded.

**hairpin,** *n.* — *Syn.* hair fastener, pin, bobby pin, clasp, hair clip, barrette; see also **fastener.**

**hairsplitting,** *modif.* — *Syn.* unimportant, minute, subtle; see **trivial, irrelevant, unimportant.**

**hairstyle,** *n.* — *Syn.* hairdo, coiffure, haircut, bob, headdress; see also **haircut.**
Types of hairstyles include: crew cut, butch, buzz, flat-top, DA, ducktail, pompadour, Beatle, Prince Valiant, Yul Brynner, bubble, page boy, bob, shag, bouffant, beehive, flip, pigtails, French roll, bun, ponytail, braid, French braid, chignon, Afro, dreadlocks, rat's tail, Mohican, Mohawk.

**hairy,** *modif.* **1.** [Bushy] — *Syn.* bristly, shaggy, woolly, unshorn, downy, fleecy, whiskered, pileous, pubescent, setaceous, tufted, unshaven, bearded, bewhiskered, furry, fuzzy, hirsute, pilose, flocculent, nappy, lanate, tufted, piliferous, ulotrichous, comose, strigose, fluffy, villous, crinite. — *Ant.* HAIRLESS, bald, smooth.
**2.** [*Dangerous] — *Syn.* hazardous, difficult, perilous, frightening; see **dangerous** 1, **uncertain** 2.

**hale,** *modif.* — *Syn.* sound, robust, vigorous; see **healthy** 1, **strong** 1.

**half,** *modif.* — *Syn.* partly, partial, divided by two, divided in two, equally distributed in halves, mixed, divided, halved, bisected, half-and-half, fifty-fifty; see also **halfway, two.** — *Ant.* all, FULL, filled.
**by half** — *Syn.* considerably, many, very much; see **much** 1, 2.
**in half** — *Syn.* into halves, split, divided; see **half.**
**not the half of it** — *Syn.* not all of it, partial, incomplete; see **unfinished** 1.

**half,** *n.* — *Syn.* share, equal share, moiety, fifty percent.
**go halves** or **halvsies*** — *Syn.* share expenses, pay one's own way, go Dutch; see **share** 4.

**halfback,** *n.* — *Syn.* right halfback, left halfback, back; see **football player.**

**half-baked,** *modif.* — *Syn.* senseless, brainless, foolish, shallow, superficial; see also **stupid** 1.

**half-breed,** *modif.* — *Syn.* half-blooded, crossed, half-caste, mestizo, crossbreed, creole; see also **hybrid, outcast.**

**half brother,** *n.* — *Syn.* sibling, kin, stepbrother, brother by one parent; see **brother** 1, **relative.**

**half dollar,** *n.* — *Syn.* fifty cents, fifty-cent piece, silver half, four bits, turkey, fifty-center; see also **money** 1.

**halfhearted,** *modif.* — *Syn.* lukewarm, impassive, irresolute; see **indifferent** 1.

**half sister,** *n.* — *Syn.* sibling, kin, stepsister, sister by one parent; see **sister, relative.**

**halfway,** *modif.* — *Syn.* midway, half the distance, in the middle, to the middle, incomplete, unsatisfactory, compromising, conciliatory, partially, fairly, medially,

in the midst, imperfectly, in part, partly, nearly, pretty, insufficiently, to a degree, to some extent, restrictedly, comparatively, rather with divided effort, moderately, mediumly, at half the distance, in some measure, within the mean, middling*; see also **half.** — *Ant.* wholly, COMPLETELY, entirely.

**halfway house,** *n.* **1.** [A midway inn] — *Syn.* midpoint, country place, stopping place, intermediate point; see **hotel, restaurant.**
**2.** [Resettlement lodging] — *Syn.* shelter, nursing home, retreat, asylum.

**half-wit,** *n.* — *Syn.* imbecile, simpleton, idiot; see **fool** 1.

**half-witted,** *modif.* — *Syn.* moronic, imbecilic, mentally deficient; see **ignorant** 2, **stupid** 1.

**half-yearly,** *modif.* — *Syn.* semestral, semiannual, twice a year; see **biannual.**

**hall,** *n.* **1.** [A large public or semipublic building or room] — *Syn.* legislative chamber, assembly room, assembly, meeting place, banquet hall, town hall, concert hall, dance hall, music hall, arena, ballroom, clubroom, church, lyceum, exchange, drawing room, salon, refectory, lounge, bourse, chamber, mart, stateroom, gymnasium, dining hall, armory, amphitheater, *sala* (Spanish), rotunda, council chamber, reception room, waiting room, lecture room, gallery, casino, gym*, mess hall*; see also **auditorium, building** 1, **room** 2, **theater** 1.
**2.** [An entrance way] — *Syn.* vestibule, passage, lobby, foyer, gallery, anteroom, propylaeum, corridor, hallway, pass, entry; see also **entrance** 2, **room** 2.
**3.** [Rural seat of a titled person] — *Syn.* manor, manor house, country estate; see **castle, estate** 1.

**hallelujah,** *interj.* — *Syn.* praise God, praise the Lord, *Deo gratias* (Latin), praise ye the Lord, hosanna, alleluia, praise ye Jehovah, glory be, praise be, huzza, lift up your hearts, heaven be praised, thanks be to God, thank God, glory be to God in the highest, bless the Lord, thank heaven, hurray*.

**hallmark,** *n.* — *Syn.* certification, mark of excellence, mark of genuineness, mark of quality, device, endorsement, symbol, sign, sigil, authentication, signet, seal of approval, stamp showing conformity to standards, plate mark, mark of acceptance, ratification; see also **emblem, trademark.**

**hallow,** *v.* — *Syn.* consecrate, sanctify, beatify, dedicate; see **bless** 3, **praise** 1, **dedicate.**
*See Synonym Study at* DEDICATE.

**hallowed,** *modif.* — *Syn.* sacred, sacrosanct, consecrated; see **divine** 2.
*See Synonym Study at* DIVINE.

**hallucinate,** *v.* — *Syn.* fantasize, have visions, visualize; see **dream.**

**hallucination,** *n.* — *Syn.* illusion, phantasm, mirage, delusion; see **dream, illusion** 1.
*See Synonym Study at* ILLUSION.

**hallucinogen,** *n.* — *Syn.* psychedelic drug, mind-expanding drug, stimulant; see **drug** 2.

**hallway,** *n.* — *Syn.* foyer, entrance way, corridor; see **entrance, hall** 2.

**halo,** *n.* — *Syn.* corona, aurora, crown of light, radiance, nimbus; see also **light** 1.

**halt,** *n.* — *Syn.* stop, cessation, standstill; see **end** 2, **pause** 1, 2.
**call a halt to** — *Syn.* suspend, check, stop; see **halt** *v.* 2.

**halt,** *v.* **1.** [To cease] — *Syn.* stand still, pause, rest; see **stop** 1.
**2.** [To cause to cease] — *Syn.* pull up, check, terminate, suspend, put an end to, interrupt, intermit, break into, punctuate, block, cut short, bar someone's way, cut into, adjourn, hold off, cease fire, keep at arm's length, hold

at bay, stop an advance, cause to halt, stem, balk, deter, stay, bring to a stand, bring to a standstill, stall, bring to an end, curb, stop, restrict, arrest, hold in check, foil, defeat, thwart, hamper, frustrate, suppress, clog, abate, intercept, extinguish, blockade, obstruct, repress, inhibit, hinder, barricade, impede, undermine, constrain, preclude, overthrow, vanquish, disconcert, override, dam, forbid the banns, upset, stand in the way of, baffle, discountenance, confound, debar, contravene, overturn, reduce, counteract, worst, quell, outwit, prohibit, rout, outdo, put down, quash, subdue, discomfit, finish, forbid, oppose, crush, disallow, spike one's guns*, scotch*, choke off*, nip in the bud*, lay by the heels*, shut down on*, break up*, freeze*, put on the brakes*, hang fire*, ring down on*, hold on*, steal one's thunder*, throw a wet blanket on*, throw a monkey wrench in the works*, throw a spanner in the works* (British), clip one's wings*, tie one's hands*, faze*, dash the cup from one's lips*, cut the ground from under one*, scotch the wheel*, take the wind out of one's sails*, squelch*; see also **end** 1, **prevent, restrain** 1. — *Ant.* BEGIN, start, instigate.

**halter,** *n.* **1.** [Harness] — *Syn.* noose, tie, strap, holder, leash, bridle, headstall, hackamore, rein; see also **bit** 4, **rope.**
**2.** [Noose] — *Syn.* hangman's noose, gallows, scaffold; see **gallows.**
**3.** [Garment] — *Syn.* halter top, top, tank top, bikini top; see **clothes.**

**halting,** *modif.* — *Syn.* hesitant, uncertain, indecisive; see **doubtful** 2, **slow** 2.

**halve,** *v.* — *Syn.* split, bisect, cut in two; see **divide** 1.

**ham,** *n.* **1.** [Smoked pork thigh] — *Syn.* gammon, sugarcured ham, whole ham, half ham, butt, shank, York ham, Brandenburg ham, Virginia ham, Smithfield ham, Canadian bacon, peach-fed ham, picnic ham, rump; see also **bacon, meat, pork.**
**2.** [The thigh of an animal] — *Syn.* buttocks, hind part, hind leg, rear, back part, hind quarter; see also **thigh.**
**3.** [One who overacts] — *Syn.* exhibitionist, melodramatic actor, grandstander, showoff, hot dog*, hotshot*.

**ham,** *v.* — *Syn.* overact, overdramatize, milk a scene, ham it up*, out-herod Herod, mug*; see also **exaggerate.**

**hamburger,** *n.* — *Syn.* chopped beefsteak, minute steak, Salisbury steak, ground round, ground chuck, ground beef, mince (British), burger*; see also **beef** 1, **meat.**

**hamlet,** *n.* — *Syn.* villa, settlement, pueblo; see **village.**

**hammer,** *n.* — *Syn.* maul, mallet, mace, club, gavel, sledge, peen, rammer, ram, flatter, nailer*, slug*, knocker*; see also **stick.**
Types of hammers include: claw, boilermaker's, bricklayer's, blacksmith's, machinist's, riveting, stone, spalling, prospecting, pneumatic, cross-peen, ballpeen, Exeter, joiner's, Canterbury claw, sealing, raising, welding, rawhide-laced, veneering, blocking, die, Nasmyth, set, double, dental, tilt hammer, steam hammer, sledgehammer, triphammer, jackhammer.

**hammer,** *v.* — *Syn.* strike, whack, bang, bear down upon, pound, pound away at; see also **beat** 2, **hit** 1.

**hammer and tongs,** *modif.* — *Syn.* hard, as hard as possible, mightily; see **fiercely.**

**hammer away,** *v.* — *Syn.* try hard, try repeatedly, continue, endeavor; see **hit** 1, **try** 1.

**hammer out,** *v.* — *Syn.* work out, fight through, get settled; see **decide.**

**hammock,** *n.* — *Syn.* swing, swinging couch, hanging

bed, bunk, sailor's bed; see also **bed** 1.

**hamper,** *n.* — *Syn.* creel, pannier, laundry box; see **basket** 1.

**hamper,** *v.* — *Syn.* impede, thwart, embarrass; see **hinder.**

**hamstring,** *v.* — *Syn.* cripple, disable, injure; see **hurt** 1, **weaken** 2.

**hand,** *n.* **1.** [The termination of the arm] — *Syn.* fingers, palm, grip, grasp, hold, phalanges, metacarpus, knuckles, paw*, duke*, hook*, shaker*, fin*, grappler*, forklift*; see also **fist.**
**2.** [*A workman] — *Syn.* helper, worker, hired hand; see **laborer.**
**3.** [Handwriting] — *Syn.* chirography, script, penmanship; see **handwriting.**
**4.** [Aid] — *Syn.* help, guidance, instruction; see **aid** 1, **support** 3.
**5.** [Ability] — *Syn.* control, knack, skill; see **ability** 2.
**6.** [*Applause] — *Syn.* ovation, round of applause, thunderous reception, handclapping; see **praise** 2.
**7.** [Round of cards] — *Syn.* cards, deal, round; see **game** 1.

**at first hand** — *Syn.* from the original source, directly, originally; see **original** 1.

**at hand** — *Syn.* **1.** near, close by, accessible, convenient; see **available, near** 1.
**2.** imminent, approaching, coming, impending; see **approaching, imminent.**

**at second hand** — *Syn.* by the way, on hearsay, by rumor; see **indirectly.**

**at the hand of** — *Syn.* done by, responsible for, in charge of; see **by** 2.

**by hand** — *Syn.* handcrafted, home-made, manual; see **handmade.**

**change hands** — *Syn.* transfer, pass on, shift, be sold, be under new management, change ownership, be conveyed; see also **give** 1.

**eat out of one's hand** — *Syn.* be tame, submit, acquiesce; see **obey** 1, **yield** 1.

**force one's hand** — *Syn.* drive, force, pressure; see **press** 1.

**from hand to hand** — *Syn.* shifted, given over, changed; see **transferred.**

**from hand to mouth** — *Syn.* from day to day, from paycheck to paycheck, by necessity, in poverty, precariously, meagerly; see **poor** 1.

**in hand** — *Syn.* under control, in order, all right; see **managed.**

**join hands** — *Syn.* unite, associate, agree; see **join** 1.

**keep one's hand in** — *Syn.* carry on, continue, make a practice of; see **practice** 1.

**lay hands on** — *Syn.* find, take, arrest, apprehend; see **seize** 1, 2.

**not lift a hand** — *Syn.* do nothing, be lazy, not try; see **neglect** 1, 2.

**off one's hands** — *Syn.* out of one's responsibility, no longer one's concern, not accountable for; see **irresponsible.**

**on every hand** — *Syn.* on all sides, at all times, all over; see **everywhere.**

**on hand** — *Syn.* ready, close by, usable; see **available.**

**on one's hands** — *Syn.* in one's care or responsibility, chargeable to one, accountable to; see **responsible** 1.

**on the other hand** — *Syn.* otherwise, conversely, however, from the opposite position; see **opposing** 2.

**out of hand** — *Syn.* out of control, wild, unmanageable; see **unruly.**

**show** or **tip one's hand** — *Syn.* disclose, divulge, confess; see **reveal** 1.

**take in hand**— *Syn.* take control of, take responsibility for, take over, handle; see **try** 1.

**throw up one's hands**— *Syn.* give up, resign, quit; see **yield** 1.

**to hand**— *Syn.* close by, at hand, immediate; see **near** 1.

**turn one's hand to**— *Syn.* attempt, endeavor, try one's hand at; see **try** 2.

**wash one's hands of**— *Syn.* deny, reject, refuse; see **denounce**.

**with a heavy hand**— *Syn.* oppressive, harsh, coercive; see **cruel** 2, **severe** 2.

**with a high hand**— *Syn.* arbitrarily, tyrannically, oppressively, highhandedly; see **arrogantly**.

**with clean hands**— *Syn.* guiltless, blameless, inculpable; see **innocent** 1.

**hand,** *v.*— *Syn.* deliver, give to, return; see **give** 1.

**hand and foot,** *modif.*— *Syn.* entirely, fully, absolutely; see **completely**.

**hand around,** *v.*— *Syn.* hand out, pass out, pass around, allot; see **distribute** 1, **give** 1.

**handbag,** *n.*— *Syn.* pocketbook, bag, clutch purse, valise, carry-on; see also **purse**.

**handbill,** *n.*— *Syn.* leaflet, flyer, throwaway, circular; see **announcement** 2, **pamphlet**.

**handbook,** *n.*— *Syn.* manual, textbook, directory, guidebook, Baedeker, basic text, instruction book, book of fundamentals, enchiridion; see also **book** 1, **manual**, **text** 1.

**handcart,** *n.*— *Syn.* wheelbarrow, pushcart, tumbrel; see **cart**, **vehicle** 1, **wagon**.

**handcuffs,** *n.*— *Syn.* manacles, fetters, shackles, iron rings, bracelets*, wristlets*, cuffs*, clamps*, braces*, snaps*; see also **chains**.

**hand down,** *v.*— *Syn.* pass on, bequeath, grant; see **give** 1.

**handed,** *modif.*— *Syn.* given to, conveyed, bestowed; see **given**.

**handful,** *n.*— *Syn.* a small quantity, some, a little, a sprinkling; see **few**.

**handicap,** *n.* **1.** [A disadvantage] — *Syn.* hindrance, obstacle, block; see **impediment** 1.
**2.** [A physical injury] — *Syn.* disability, impairment, affliction, chronic disorder; see **impediment** 2, **injury** 1.
**3.** [Advantage] — *Syn.* favor, upper hand, additional points; see **advantage** 1.

**handicapped,** *modif.*— *Syn.* thwarted, crippled, disabled, physically challenged, impeded, burdened, hampered, obstructed, encumbered, foiled, balked, put at a disadvantage, deterred, under handicap, disadvantaged, checked, blocked, limited, restrained, wounded, curbed, put behind, queered*, stymied*, behind the eight ball*; see also **restricted**.— *Ant.* aided, HELPED, supported.

**handicraft,** *n.*— *Syn.* creation, embroidery, craftsmanship; see **handiwork, workmanship**.

**handily,** *modif.*— *Syn.* skillfully, intelligently, smoothly; see **cleverly** 2, **easily** 1.

**hand in,** *v.*— *Syn.* deliver, submit, return; see **give** 1, **offer** 1.

**hand in glove,** *modif.*— *Syn.* allied, working together, closely associated; see **together** 2, **united** 1.

**hand in hand,** *modif.*— *Syn.* closely associated, working together, related; see **together** 2, **united** 1.

**handiwork,** *n.*— *Syn.* personal work, handicraft, creation, doing, invention, design, manual effort, handwork, needlework, embroidery; see also **workmanship**.

**handkerchief,** *n.*— *Syn.* kerchief, napkin, neckerchief, headband, tissue, paper handkerchief, rag*, hanky*; see also **towel**.

**handle,** *n.* **1.** [A holder]— *Syn.* handhold, hilt, ear, grasp, tiller, crank, knocker, haft, bail, knob, stem, grip, arm; see also **holder** 1.
**2.** [*A title]— *Syn.* nickname, designation, moniker*; see **name** 1, **title** 3.
**fly off the handle***— *Syn.* become angry, lose one's temper, blow off steam*; see **rage** 1.

**handle,** *v.* **1.** [To deal in]— *Syn.* retail, market, offer for sale; see **sell** 1.
**2.** [To touch]— *Syn.* finger, check, examine; see **feel** 2, **touch** 1.
**3.** [To direct]— *Syn.* supervise, control, manage; see **advise** 1, **command** 2.
**4.** [To operate]— *Syn.* manipulate, work, wield, ply; see also **manage** 1.

---

*SYN.* — **handle** implies the possession of sufficient (or a specified degree of) skill in managing or operating with or as with the hands [to *handle* a tool or a problem]; **manipulate** suggests skill, dexterity, or craftiness in handling [to *manipulate* a machine or an account]; **wield** implies skill and control in handling effectively [to *wield* an ax, to *wield* influence]; **ply** suggests great diligence in operating [to *ply* an oar, to *ply* one's trade]

---

**handled,** *modif.*— *Syn.* controlled, organized, taken care of; see **directed, managed**.

**handling,** *n.*— *Syn.* treatment, approach, styling; see **administration** 1.

**handmade,** *modif.*— *Syn.* made by hand, handicraft, handsewn, hand-carved, hand-knit, improvised, hand-tailored, handcrafted; see also **homemade**.— *Ant.* factory-made, MANUFACTURED, machine-made.

**hand-me-down,** *modif.*— *Syn.* used, inherited, handed down; see **old** 2, **secondhand, worn** 2.

**hand-me-down,** *n.*— *Syn.* secondhand article, discard, old clothes, old utensils, etc.; see **rummage**.

**hand on,** *v.*— *Syn.* pass on, bequeath, hand down; see **give** 1.

**handout*,** *n.*— *Syn.* contribution, donation, free meal; see **gift** 1, **grant** 1.

**hand out,** *v.*— *Syn.* give to, deliver, disseminate; see **distribute** 1, **give** 1, **provide** 1.

**hand over,** *v.*— *Syn.* deliver, surrender, give up; see **give** 1, **yield** 1.

**hands down*,** *modif.*— *Syn.* handily, with no trouble, completely; see **easily** 1, **surely** 1.

**hands-off,** *modif.*— *Syn.* tolerant, indulgent, permissive, accommodating; see **lenient**.

**hands off,** *interj.*— *Syn.* keep off, don't touch, leave alone, don't, keep away, leave me alone, stay back, keep your distance; see also **avoid**.

**handsome,** *modif.* **1.** [Beautiful or elegant]— *Syn.* fine, attractive, good-looking, beautiful, elegant, stately, well-proportioned, impressive, imposing, aristocratic, comely; see also **beautiful** 1, 2, **dignified, stately** 2.
**2.** [Having good masculine appearance]— *Syn.* good-looking, attractive, dapper, spruce, clean-cut, virile, well-built, athletic, personable, strong, muscular, smooth*, sharp*, sexy*, easy on the eyes*, tall, dark and handsome*, cute*, hunky*; see also sense 1; **manly**.
— *Ant.* homely, UGLY, unattractive.
**3.** [Large or extensive]— *Syn.* full, ample, considerable; see **extensive** 1, **large** 1.
**4.** [Noble]— *Syn.* gracious, princely, magnanimous; see **noble** 2, **worthy**.
*See Synonym Study at* BEAUTIFUL.

**handsomely,** *modif.*— *Syn.* nobly, liberally, magnanimously; see **abundantly, generously** 1.

**hand-to-hand,** *modif.* — *Syn.* at close quarters, face-to-face, facing, close; see **near** 1.

**handwriting,** *n.* — *Syn.* penmanship, hand, writing, script, longhand, chirography, scrawl, scribble, manuscript, style of penmanship, autography, holographic writing, scription, calligraphy, scrivening, penscript, pencraft, scrivenery, griffonage, hieroglyphics*, pothooks*, scratching*, chicken tracks*, fist*; see also **autograph, signature.**

**handwritten,** *modif.* — *Syn.* in manuscript, in writing, transcribed, not typed; see **reproduced, written** 2.

**handy,** *modif.* **1.** [Near] — *Syn.* nearby, at hand, close by; see **convenient** 2, **near** 1.
**2.** [Useful] — *Syn.* beneficial, advantageous, gainful; see **helpful** 1, **profitable, usable.**
**3.** [Dexterous] — *Syn.* dexterous, apt, skillful, ingenious; see **able** 1, 2, **fit** 1, 2, **dexterous.**
*See Synonym Study at* DEXTEROUS.

**come in handy** — *Syn.* prove useful, be of service, have a use, aid; see **help** 1.

**handyman,** *n.* — *Syn.* jack-of-all-trades, helper, hired man; see **laborer, man-of-all-work, servant.**

**hang,** *v.* **1.** [To suspend] — *Syn.* dangle, attach, drape, hook up, put in a sling, hang up, nail on the wall, put on a clothesline, fix, pin up, tack up, drape on the wall, fasten up; see also **fasten** 1. — *Ant.* DROP, throw down, let fall.
**2.** [To be suspended] — *Syn.* overhang, be held aloft, wave, flap, be loose, be pendent, droop, flop, be in mid air, swing, dangle, jut, be fastened, impend, hover, stay up. — *Ant.* FALL, come down, drop.
**3.** [To kill by hanging] — *Syn.* execute, lynch, hang by the neck until dead, garrote, string up*, stretch*; see also **kill** 1.
**4.** [To depend] — *Syn.* cling, turn on, be determined by; see **depend** 1, 2.

**get** or **have the hang of** — *Syn.* have the knack of, grasp, comprehend, learn; see **understand** 1.

**not care** or **give a hang about** — *Syn.* be indifferent toward, not care about, ignore; see **neglect** 2.

**hang about,** *v.* — *Syn.* hang around, haunt, roam; see **frequent, loiter, wait** 1.

**hangar,** *n.* — *Syn.* shed, aircraft shelter, stall, nest; see also **airport, garage** 1.

**hang around,** *v.* **1.** [To spend time with] — *Syn.* associate with, get along with, have relations with, hang out with, hang with*; see also **associate** 1.
**2.** [*To wait] — *Syn.* linger, loiter, dawdle, hang about; see **loiter, wait** 1.

**hang back,** *v.* — *Syn.* hesitate, pull away, recoil; see **avoid.**

**hanged,** *modif.* — *Syn.* lynched, strung up, brought to the gallows; see **executed** 2.

**hanger,** *n.* — *Syn.* coat hook, hook, nail, peg, coat hanger, clothes hanger, holder, clothes rod, wire hanger, collapsible hanger; see also **rack** 1, **rod** 1.

**hanger-on,** *n.* — *Syn.* leech, nuisance, parasite; see **dependent, sycophant.**

**hang fire,** *v.* — *Syn.* drag on, remain unsettled, remain unfinished, recommence; see **continue** 2, **resume.**

**hanging,** *modif.* — *Syn.* dangling, swaying, swinging, jutting, overhanging, beetling, projecting, pendent, suspended, fastened to, pendulous, drooping.

**hangman,** *n.* — *Syn.* garroter, lyncher, public executioner; see **executioner, killer.**

**hang on,** *v.* — *Syn.* persist, remain, continue; see **endure** 1, 2.

**hangout*,** *n.* — *Syn.* bar*, joint*, hole*; see **dive** 2.

**hang out,** *v.* **1.** [To project] — *Syn.* overhang, hang over, lean out, jut; see **project** 1.
**2.** [*To be exposed] — *Syn.* stick out, be conspicuous, display; see **display** 1.
**3.** [To frequent] — *Syn.* idle, loiter, spend time, haunt; see **frequent, wait** 1.

**hangover,** *n.* — *Syn.* aftereffects, crapulence, headache, morning after; see **drunkenness, illness** 1.

**hang together,** *v.* — *Syn.* work together, comply with, assist one another; see **cooperate** 1.

**hang-up*,** *n.* — *Syn.* problem, predicament, disturbance, fixation, psychological block; see also **difficulty** 1, 2.

**hang up,** *v.* — *Syn.* cease speaking, replace the receiver, finish a telephone call, ring off, hang up the phone, put off, buzz off*.

**hank,** *n.* — *Syn.* knot, portion, length; see **part** 1, **piece** 1.

**hanker,** *v.* — *Syn.* crave, desire, wish for; see **want** 1.

**hankering,** *n.* — *Syn.* craving, longing, wish; see **desire** 1.

**haphazard,** *modif.* — *Syn.* aimless, accidental, casual, random, chance, offhand, careless, slipshod, incidental, unexpected, unthinking, unconscious, uncoordinated, slovenly, reckless, unconcerned, unpremeditated, loose, indiscriminate, unsystematic, unrestricted, unselected, irregular, motley, multifarious, blind, purposeless, unplanned, chaotic, hit-or-miss, devil-may-care*, willy-nilly*, what-the-hell*; see also **aimless, random.** — *Ant.* careful, studied, planned.
*See Synonym Study at* RANDOM.

**haphazardly,** *modif.* — *Syn.* unexpectedly, casually, randomly, aimlessly, inconstantly, every now and then, every once in a while; see also **accidentally, carelessly.**

**happen,** *v.* **1.** [To be by chance] — *Syn.* come up, come about, turn up, crop up, chance, stumble upon, light upon, occur unexpectedly, come face to face with, befall, hit one like a ton of bricks*, be one's luck*, fall to one's lot*, smack right up against*.
**2.** [To occur] — *Syn.* occur, take place, pass, come to pass, arrive, ensue, befall, eventuate, come after, arise, take effect, come into existence, recur, come into being, spring, proceed, issue, follow, come about, fall, repeat, appear, go on, become a fact, turn out, become known, supervene, be found, come to mind, come and go, come around, come round, come forth, transpire*, come off*; see also **result.**

---

*SYN.* — **happen** is the general word meaning to take place or come to pass and may suggest either direct cause or apparent accident; **chance,** more or less equivalent to **happen,** always implies apparent lack of cause or purpose in the event; **occur** often suggests a specific event that appears in actuality or in the mind /the accident *occurred* last week, the idea of quitting never *occurred* to her/; **transpire,** in the sense of to take place, is now frequently used as a more formal or even pretentious equivalent for **happen** or **occur** /what *transpired* at the conference/, a development from the sense of to become known, or leak out /it *transpired* that he had cheated/

---

**happening,** *n.* — *Syn.* incident, affair, accident; see **event** 1.

**happenstance*,** *n.* — *Syn.* chance, fate, incident; see **event** 2, **luck** 1.

**happily,** *modif.* **1.** [Fortunately] — *Syn.* gracefully, successfully, felicitously; see **fortunately.**
**2.** [In a happy mood] — *Syn.* contentedly, joyously, exultantly, gladly, joyfully, cheerily, blithely, gaily, laugh-

ingly, smilingly, jovially, merrily, brightly, vivaciously, hilariously, sportively, chucklingly, mockingly, exhilaratingly, jauntily, with pleasure, delightedly, peacefully, blissfully, cheerfully, gleefully, playfully, heartily, lightheartedly, lightly, to one's delight, optimistically, with all one's heart, delightfully, with relish, with good will, buoyantly, in a happy manner, *de bonne volonté, de bonne grace* (*both* French), with zeal, with good grace, zestfully, of one's own accord, with open arms, sincerely, willingly, with willingness, heart and soul, in happy circumstances, with right good will, freely, graciously, *con amore* (Italian), tactfully, lovingly, without demur, without reluctance, devotedly, elatedly, agreeably, *ex animo* (Latin).— *Ant.* morosely, SADLY, dejectedly.

**happiness,** *n.* **1.** [Good humor]— *Syn.* mirth, merrymaking, cheer, merriment, joyousness, vivacity, laughter, delight, gladness, good spirits, hilarity, playfulness, exuberance, gaiety, cheerfulness, buoyancy, good will, rejoicing, joviality, exhilaration, felicity, jollity, jocularity, glee, geniality, good cheer, lightheartedness, joy; see also **humor** 3.— *Ant.* SADNESS, sorrow, unhappiness.
**2.** [Inner satisfaction]— *Syn.* exhilaration, contentment, bliss, blissfulness, joyfulness, beatitude, blessedness, enchantment, sanctity, ecstasy, rapture, transport, exultation, entrancement, peace, felicity, euphoria, peace of mind, tranquillity, inner joy, freedom from care, pleasure, elation, delirium, optimism, self-satisfaction, benignity, hopefulness, serenity, comfort, blitheness, complacency, gratification, paradise\*, seventh heaven\*; see also **comfort** 1, **ease** 1, **satisfaction** 2.— *Ant.* melancholy, DEPRESSION, dejection.

**happy,** *modif.* **1.** [In good humor]— *Syn.* joyous, joyful, merry, mirthful, glad, gleeful, delighted, cheerful, gay, captivated, blest, laughing, contented, genial, convivial, satisfied, rapturous, enraptured, relieved, congenial, cheery, blithe, jolly, hilarious, sparkling, enchanted, unalloyed, transported, rejoicing, blissful, jovial, jocund, delightful, delirious, exhilarated, cloudless, rhapsodic, rapt, enrapt, gladsome, pleased, gratified, peaceful, comfortable, beatific, intoxicated, debonair, light, bright, buoyant, ecstatic, charmed, bonny, pleasant, exultant, hearty, overjoyed, well, lighthearted, lightsome, radiant, vivacious, sunny, smiling, content, sprightful, zesty, animated, zestful, lively, spirited, exuberant, good-humored, elated, frisky, frolicsome, expressing happiness, jubilant, sportive, rollicking, playful, thrilled, dashing, fun-loving, gladdened, Elysian, jaunty, breezy, carefree, at peace, in good spirits, in high spirits, happy as a lark, happy as the day is long, of good cheer, in ecstasies, flushed with excitement, flushed with pleasure, chipper\*, perky\*, peppy\*, fit\*, beside oneself\*, full of beans\*, bubbling over\*, tickled\*, happy-go-lucky\*, in seventh heaven\*.— *Ant.* sorrowful, SAD, melancholy.
**2.** [Expressive of good humor]— *Syn.* laughing, smiling, shouting, cheering, cavorting, sparkling, giggling, chuckling, jesting, amusing, backslapping, joking, roaring, applauding, guffawing, celebrating, carousing, reveling, festive, making whoopee\*, kicking up one's heels\*, having a hot time\*, raising hell\*.— *Ant.* crying, WEEPING, mourning.
**3.** [Fortunate or apt]— *Syn.* nice, felicitous, right; see **fortunate** 1.

**SYN.** — **happy** generally suggests a feeling of great pleasure, contentment, etc. /a *happy* marriage/; **glad** implies more strongly an exultant feeling of joy /your letter made her so *glad*/ , but both **glad** and **happy** are commonly used in merely polite formulas expressing gratification /I'm *glad*, or *happy*, to have met you/; **cheerful**

implies a steady display of bright spirits, optimism, etc. /he's always *cheerful* in the morning/; **joyful** and **joyous** both imply great elation and rejoicing, the former generally because of a particular event, and the latter as a matter of usual temperament /the *joyful* throngs, a *joyous* family/

**happy-go-lucky,** *modif.*— *Syn.* cheerful, easygoing, unconcerned; see **happy** 1.
**harangue,** *n.*— *Syn.* lecture, discourse, sermon; see **discussion** 1, **speech** 3.
**harass,** *v.* **1.** [To annoy an individual]— *Syn.* tease, vex, irritate; see **bother** 2.
**2.** [To make small, persistent attacks]— *Syn.* despoil, harry, raid; see **attack** 1.
**harbinger,** *n.*— *Syn.* forerunner, herald, indication, sign, signal; see also **messenger, signal.**
**harbor,** *n.* **1.** [A place of refuge]— *Syn.* refuge, retreat, sanctuary; see **shelter.**
**2.** [A port]— *Syn.* anchorage, haven, roadstead, pier, breakwater, landing place, navigable bay, arm of the sea, harborage, inlet, jetty, embankment, wharf, mole; see also **dock** 1.
**harbor,** *v.* **1.** [To protect]— *Syn.* shelter, provide refuge, secure; see **defend** 2.
**2.** [To consider]— *Syn.* entertain, cherish, regard; see **consider** 1.
**3.** [To keep hidden]— *Syn.* suppress, withhold, hold back; see **hide** 1.
**hard,** *modif.* **1.** [Compact]— *Syn.* solid, unyielding, dense; see **firm** 2, **thick** 3.
**2.** [Difficult]— *Syn.* arduous, troublesome, laborious; see **difficult** 1, 2.
**3.** [Cruel]— *Syn.* perverse, unrelenting, vengeful; see **cruel** 1, 2.
**4.** [Persistent or energetic]— *Syn.* obdurate, stubborn, tough; see **active** 2, **obstinate** 1.
**5.** [Severe]— *Syn.* harsh, exacting, grim; see **severe** 1, 2.
**6.** [Alcoholic]— *Syn.* intoxicating, inebriating, stimulating; see **strong** 8.
**7.** [With difficulty]— *Syn.* strenuously, laboriously, with great effort; see **carefully** 1, **vigorously.**
*See Synonym Study at* DIFFICULT, FIRM.
**be hard on**— *Syn.* treat severely, be harsh toward, be painful to; see **abuse** 1.
**go hard with**— *Syn.* be difficult, hinder, plague; see **oppress.**
**hard and fast\*,** *modif.*— *Syn.* rigid, unchangeable, unalterable; see **firm** 5, **resolute** 2.
**hard-core,** *modif.* **1.** [Devoted]— *Syn.* dedicated, steadfast, unwavering; see **faithful.**
**2.** [Unyielding]— *Syn.* determined, intransigent, uncompromising; see **obstinate** 1, **resolute** 2.
**3.** [Absolute]— *Syn.* unqualified, hard-line, uncompromising, relentless.
**harden,** *v.* **1.** [To make less pervious]— *Syn.* steel, temper, anneal, solidify, mineralize, vitrify, precipitate, hornify, cornify, crystallize, freeze, amalgamate, coagulate, clot, granulate, make callous, make firm, make compact, make tight, make hard, convert to stone, congeal, ossify, petrify, starch, cure, bake, dry, flatten, cement, compact, consolidate, concentrate, sun, fire, fossilize, desiccate, braze, vulcanize, Harveyize, callous, incrassate, indurate, deposit, candy, toughen, fix, concrete, inspissate, encrust, lapidify; see also **compress, press** 1, **stiffen** 2, **thicken** 2.— *Ant.* SOFTEN, unloose, melt.
**2.** [To become less penetrable]— *Syn.* solidify, con-

geal, jell, become dense, fix, settle, become fast, petrify, ossify, freeze over, fossilize, clot, cake, set, firm, curdle, coagulate, close, contract; see also **freeze** 1, **stiffen** 1, **thicken** 1. — *Ant.* liquefy, THAW, thin.

**3.** [To toughen] — *Syn.* acclimate, acclimatize, indurate, habituate, inure, season, make callous, make unfeeling, make obdurate, discipline, accustom, train, coarsen, roughen, sear, embitter, develop, strengthen, brutalize, render insensitive, render insensible, render unimpressible, blunt, dull, envenom, numb, stupefy, benumb, stun, paralyze, steel; see also **deaden** 1, **stiffen** 2, **teach** 2. — *Ant.* WEAKEN, debilitate, soften.

**hardened,** *modif.* **1.** [Made hard] — *Syn.* compacted, stiffened, stiff; see **firm** 2.

**2.** [Inured to labor or hardship] — *Syn.* disciplined, trained, accustomed, habituated, inured, resistant, steeled, toughened, seasoned. — *Ant.* unaccustomed, inexperienced, raw.

**3.** [Confirmed, especially in error or vice] — *Syn.* callous, inveterate, obdurate, impenitent, unrepenting, impenetrable, unyielding, bad, shameless, irreclaimable, lost, incorrigible, irreligious, profane, abandoned, irredeemable, unfeeling, depraved, degenerate, tough, reprobate, insensible, chronic, hard, deadened, benumbed, habituated, unashamed, uncaring, hardhearted, inaccessible, untouched, uncontrite, sacrilegious, unsubmissive, implacable, disdainful, habitual, seared, cold, blasphemous, irreverent, impious, unrelenting, contemptuous, indurated, indurate, unbending, hard as nails*, hard-boiled*; see also **callous, chronic, cruel** 2.

*See Synonym Study at* CHRONIC.

**hardening,** *modif.* — *Syn.* stiffening, solidifying, strengthening, settling, freezing, fixing, fossilizing, coagulating.

**hardening,** *n.* — *Syn.* thickening, crystallization, setting; see **solidification** 1.

**hard-featured,** *modif.* — *Syn.* rough-featured, hard-favored, severe, austere; see **ugly.**

**hard-fisted,** *modif.* — *Syn.* selfish, miserly, niggardly, tight-fisted; see **stingy.**

**hard going,** *modif.* — *Syn.* tough, laborious, tight; see **difficult** 1, 2.

**hardheaded,** *modif.* **1.** [Obstinate] — *Syn.* willful, stubborn, headstrong; see **obstinate** 1.

**2.** [Practical] — *Syn.* sensible, rational, shrewd; see **practical.**

**hardhearted,** *modif.* — *Syn.* brutish, unfeeling, heartless; see **cruel** 1.

**hardihood,** *n.* **1.** [Courage] — *Syn.* fearlessness, resolution; see **confidence** 2, **courage** 1.

**2.** [Presumption] — *Syn.* effrontery, impudence, impertinence; see **rudeness.**

**hardly,** *modif.* — *Syn.* scarcely, barely, just, merely, detectably, infinitesimally, perceptibly, imperceptibly, noticeably, not noticeably, gradually, measurably, not measurably, not markedly, not notably, no more than, not likely, not a bit, almost not, only just, with difficulty, with trouble, by a narrow margin, not by a great deal, only in spite of difficulties, with much ado, seldom, sporadically, almost not at all, but just, in no manner, by no means, little, infrequently, somewhat, not quite, here and there, simply, not much, rarely, faintly, comparatively, scantly, almost inconceivably, miserably, uncommonly, slightly, sparsely, not often, rather, with little likelihood, once in a blue moon, once in a coon's age, within two whoops and a holler, by the skin of one's teeth, just enough to swear by; see also **moderately, only** 1. — *Ant.* EASILY, without difficulty, readily.

**hard-nosed,** *modif.* — *Syn.* stubborn, unyielding, hardheaded; see **obstinate** 1, **resolute** 2.

**hard of hearing,** *modif.* — *Syn.* hearing impaired, almost deaf, having a hearing problem, in need of a hearing device; see **deaf** 1.

**hard on,** *modif.* — *Syn.* unjust to, unkind to, cruel to, brutal, inclined to blame; see also **cruel** 2, **harmful.**

**hardship,** *n.* **1.** [Injury] — *Syn.* misfortune, calamity, accident; see **catastrophe, disaster.**

**2.** [Burden] — *Syn.* trial, sorrow, worry, difficulty; see **difficulty** 2, **grief** 1.

*See Synonym Study at* DIFFICULTY.

**hard up,** *modif.* — *Syn.* in trouble, poverty-stricken, in the lower income brackets; see **poor** 1.

**hardware,** *n.* — *Syn.* domestic appliances, fixtures, metal manufactures, hollowware, castings, plumbing, metalware, implements, tools, housewares, fittings, fasteners, nails, brads, screws, bolts, nuts, aluminum ware, cutlery, house furnishings, kitchenware, household utensils, appointments, accouterments; see also **appliance, device** 1, **tool** 1.

**hardware store,** *n.* — *Syn.* metalware store, household utensil store, kitchenware store, ironmonger's (British), tool shop; see also **store** 1.

**hardwood,** *n.* — *Syn.* oak, beech, elm, ash, mahogany, chestnut, walnut, maple, teak, sycamore, greenheart, rosewood; see also **tree, wood** 2.

**hardy,** *modif.* **1.** [Strong] — *Syn.* vigorous, firm, tough; see **strong** 2.

**2.** [Suited to rigorous climates] — *Syn.* inured, tough, toughened, in good shape, in good condition, hardened, resistant, solid, staunch, seasoned, capable of endurance, able-bodied, physically fit, tenacious, well-equipped, acclimatized, Herculean, Atlantean, rugged, lusty, mighty, well, fit, robust, hearty, rigorous, wiry, stout, sound, sinewy, fresh, hale, brawny, able, vigorous, enduring, burly, powerful, firm, sturdy, leathery, virile, stalwart, solid, muscular, substantial, hefty*; see also **healthy** 1, **strong** 1. — *Ant.* WEAK, unaccustomed, unhabituated.

**3.** [Brave] — *Syn.* resolute, dauntless, bold; see **brave** 1.

**hare,** *n.* — *Syn.* jack rabbit, cottontail, coney, bunny; see **animal** 1, **rabbit.**

**harebrained,** *modif.* — *Syn.* foolish, flighty, irresponsible; see **changeable** 1, 2, **stupid** 1.

**harem,** *n.* — *Syn.* seraglio, concubines, purdah, zenana, gynaeceum, oda, stable*.

**hark,** *v.* — *Syn.* harken, pay attention, give heed; see **listen** 1.

**harlot,** *n.* — *Syn.* whore, strumpet, call girl; see **prostitute.**

**harm,** *n.* **1.** [Injury] — *Syn.* hurt, infliction, impairment; see **injury** 1.

**2.** [Evil] — *Syn.* wickedness, outrage, foul play; see **abuse** 3, **evil** 2, **wrong** 2.

**harm,** *v.* — *Syn.* injure, hurt, wreck, cripple; see **hurt** 1.

*See Synonym Study at* HURT.

**harmed,** *modif.* — *Syn.* damaged, injured, wounded; see **hurt.**

**harmful,** *modif.* — *Syn.* injurious, detrimental, hurtful, noxious, evil, mischievous, ruinous, malefic, demolitionary, internecine, adverse, inimical, harassing, sinister, subversive, incendiary, virulent, calamitous, cataclysmic, corroding, toxic, baleful, nocuous, consumptive, painful, wounding, crippling, bad, malicious, malignant, sinful, pernicious, baneful, unwholesome, pestilential, pestiferous, deleterious, annihilative, corrupting, menacing, ill-omened, dire, morbific, de-

*(harmful)* vouring, prejudicial, damaging, corrupt, vicious, insidious, treacherous, devastating, catastrophic, disastrous, wild, murderous, undetermining, sapping, destructive, unhealthy, stunting, habit-forming, killing, fatal, mortal, serious, costly, fraught with harm, doing harm, fraught with evil, painful, sore, extirpative, afflicting, distressing, fell, diabolic, brutal, unhealthful, satanic, demoniac, ill, grievous, mortal, lethal, malevolent, mephitic, venomous, cruel, unfortunate, disadvantageous, felonious, aching, pricking, objectionable, fiendish, maleficent, unpropitious, unlucky, malign, sinistrous, noisome, devilish, corrosive; see also **dangerous** 1, 2. **deadly, ominous, poisonous, wicked.** — *Ant.* pure, HEALTHFUL, good.

**harmless,** *modif.* **1.** [*Usually said of persons*] — *Syn.* inoffensive, naive, simple; see **kind** 1.
**2.** [*Usually said of things*] — *Syn.* pure, undefiled, spotless, unblemished, innocent, painless, unoffending, innoxious, navigable, powerless, controllable, manageable, safe, innocuous, not habit-forming, sure, nonirritating, reliable, noninjurious, trustworthy, sanitary, germproof, sound, not hurtful, out of operation, out of gear, inoffensive, sterile, without power, without tendency to harm, inoperative, disarmed; see also **gentle** 3, **kind** 1, **weak** 5, 6. — *Ant.* injurious, HARMFUL, poisonous.

**harmonic,** *modif.* — *Syn.* consonant, tuneful, symphonious; see **harmonious.**

**harmonica,** *n.* — *Syn.* mouth organ, harmonicon, blues harp, French harp, harp, mouth harp, mouth Steinway; see also **musical instrument.**

**harmonious,** *modif.* **1.** [Harmonic] — *Syn.* melodious, tuneful, musical, rhythmical, dulcet, sweet-sounding, melodic, symphonic, sonorous, in tune, in chorus, silvery, in unison, tuny*, earful*. — *Ant.* SHRILL, jangling, dissonant.
**2.** [Congruous] — *Syn.* agreeable to, accordant, concordant, consonant, corresponding, suitable, adapted, similar, like, peaceful, in accord, amicable, cooperative, congenial, on borrowing terms, in step, in accordance with, in concord with, in favor with, in harmony with, on a footing with, friendly, of one accord, in concert, conforming, well-matched, evenly balanced, symmetrical, congruent; see also **fit** 1, 2. — *Ant.* incongruous, incompatible, OPPOSED.

**harmonize,** *v.* **1.** [To render harmonic] — *Syn.* blend, arrange, put to harmony, adapt, set, orchestrate, symphonize, tune, sing a duet, play in harmony with, sing in harmony with, make contrapuntal.
**2.** [To accord with one another] — *Syn.* correspond, be in harmony with, fit in with, accord, put on an even keel; see **agree.**
*See Synonym Study at* AGREE.

**harmony,** *n.* **1.** [Musical concord] — *Syn.* chord, consonance, triad, diapason, accord, euphony, tunefulness, symphony, harmonics, counterpoint, concert, concordance, music, chorus, organum, sympathy, blending, unity, accordance, attunement, symphoniousness, chime, polyphony, unison, richness, overtone, musical pattern, musical concurrence, musical blend, concinnity.
**2.** [Social concord] — *Syn.* compatibility, equanimity, unanimity; see **agreement** 1, **peace** 2.
**3.** [Logical concord] — *Syn.* form, symmetry, accord, balance; see **agreement** 2, **consistency** 1, **regularity, symmetry.**
**4.** [Musical composition] — *Syn.* melody, piece, arrangement; see **composition** 2, **music** 1, **tune.**
*See Synonym Study at* SYMMETRY.

**harness,** *n.* — *Syn.* tackle, gear, yoke, apparatus, bridle, accoutrements, rigging, fittings.
Parts of a horse's harness include: bellyband, terret, breeching, breeching strap, crupper, front, blind, crownpiece, overcheck, facepiece, cheekpiece, breast collar, breastband, throatlatch, bit, martingale, blinker, browband, noseband, neck strap, checkhook, overcheck rein, hipstrap, trace, tug, collar, collar pad, hame, surcingle; see also **bit** 4, **halter** 1, **saddle.**
**in harness** — *Syn.* at work, occupied, working; see **busy** 1.
**in harness with** — *Syn.* in cooperation with, associated with, joined to; see **together** 2.

**harness,** *v.* — *Syn.* fetter, saddle, yoke, equip, outfit, bridle, hold in, leash, hitch up, control, limit, govern, fit out for work, cinch, tame, strap, domesticate, accouter, tackle, gear, collar, put in harness, rig up, rig out, furnish, enchain, tie, secure, rein in, curb, check, constrain, fit for electric power; see also **bind** 1, **fasten** 1, **muzzle** 1, 2, **provide** 1, **restrain** 1.

**harp,** *n.* — *Syn.* concert harp, pedal harp, triple harp, Welsh harp, folk harp, Irish harp, Celtic harp, clarsach, Aeolian harp, lyre, psaltery, zither, Autoharp (trademark); see also **harmonica, musical instrument.**

**harp on,** *v.* — *Syn.* repeat, pester, nag; see **bother** 2, **disturb** 2.

**harpoon,** *n.* — *Syn.* spear, missile, lance, javelin; see **spear, weapon** 1.

**harpy,** *n.* **1.** [A shrewish woman] — *Syn.* shrew, virago, nag, Xanthippe; see **hag, woman** 1.
**2.** [A greedy person] — *Syn.* swindler, shark, loan shark, Shylock.

**harrow,** *n.* — *Syn.* disk, cultivator, drag; see **plow, shovel, tractor.**
Types of harrows include: disk harrow, Scotch harrow, cultipacker, double-action harrow, cutaway harrow, spading harrow.

**harrow,** *v.* **1.** [To use a harrow on land] — *Syn.* drag, dig, cultivate; see **plow, shovel.**
**2.** [To torment] — *Syn.* tormenting, trying, nerve-racking; see also **disturbing.**

**harrowing,** *modif.* — *Syn.* frightening, tormenting, trying, nerve-racking; see also **disturbing.**

**harry,** *v.* **1.** [To raid] — *Syn.* pillage, sack, spoil, despoil, lay waste; see also **attack** 1, **raid, ravage, steal.**
**2.** [To harass] — *Syn.* annoy, pester, torment; see **bother** 2, **disturb** 2.

**harsh,** *modif.* **1.** [Inharmonious] — *Syn.* discordant, jangling, cacophonous, grating, rusty, dissonant, absonant, inconsonant, strident, creaking, clashing, sharp, jarring, jangled, clamorous, cracked, hoarse, out of tune, unmelodious, rasping, screeching, earsplitting, caterwauling, stridulous, disturbing, off balance, noisy, flat, sour, out of key, tuneless, unmusical, off key, disagreeing, uncongenial, unsympathetic, uncomforting, incompatible; see also **loud** 1, 2, **raucous** 1, **shrill.**
**2.** [Discourteous] — *Syn.* gruff, ungracious, uncivil; see **rude** 1, 2, **ungrateful.**
**3.** [Severe] — *Syn.* rigid, unrelenting, hard; see **firm** 1, **resolute** 1, **severe** 2.

**harshly,** *modif.* — *Syn.* sternly, powerfully, grimly; see **brutally, firmly** 2, **loudly, seriously** 1, 2.

**harshness,** *n.* — *Syn.* crudity, brutality, acerbity; see **anger, cruelty, tyranny.**

**harum-scarum,** *modif.* — *Syn.* reckless, harebrained, disconnected; see **careless** 1, **irresponsible, loose** 1, **thoughtless** 1, 2.

**Harvard,** *n.* — *Syn.* Harvard University, Harvard College, the Yard★, the Crimson★; see also **college, university**.

**harvest,** *n.* **1.** [Crop] — *Syn.* reaping, yield, yielding, fruitage; see **crop, fruit 1, grain 1, produce, vegetable**.

**2.** [Product] — *Syn.* intake, results, return, yield; see **product 2, result**.

**3.** [A season] — *Syn.* harvest time, summer, fall; see **autumn, month, season**.

**harvest,** *v.* — *Syn.* gather in, accumulate, pile up, collect, garner, crop, cut, pluck, pick, cull, take in, draw in, glean, amass, gather the harvest, hoard, mow, take the yield, take the crop, take the second crop, strip the fields, put in barns, gather the first fruits; see also **reap 1, store 2.** — *Ant.* sow, plant, seed.

**harvester,** *n.* **1.** [A harvesting machine] — *Syn.* binder, reaper, header, combine, harvesting machinery; see also **cat 3, equipment, tractor**.

**2.** [A man] — *Syn.* farm hand, worker, helper; see **farmer, laborer, workman**.

**harvesting,** *n.* — *Syn.* gathering, collecting, reaping; see **accumulation, collection 1**.

**hash,** *n.* **1.** [A dish of meat and vegetables] — *Syn.* ground meat and vegetables, baked ground meat, meat loaf, gallimaufry, leftovers, *fricandeau* (French), mash, chowchow, ragout, stew, hashed meat, olla-podrida, casserole, salmagundi, olio, minced meat, *réchauffé* (French), insult to a square meal★, great unknown★; see also **meat, stew**.

**2.** [A mixture] — *Syn.* mess, jumble, hodgepodge; see **confusion 2, mixture 1**.

**hash out★,** *v.* — *Syn.* settle, conclude, negotiate, get a decision on; see **decide**.

**hash over★,** *v.* — *Syn.* debate, argue about, review; see **discuss**.

**hasp,** *n.* — *Syn.* hook, catch, clasp; see **fastener**.

**hassle★,** *n.* **1.** [An argument] — *Syn.* quarrel, squabble, row; see **dispute**.

**2.** [A troublesome situation] — *Syn.* bother, nuisance, annoyance; see **trouble 2**.

**hassle★,** *v.* — *Syn.* bother, annoy, harass; see **bother 2**.

**hassock,** *n.* — *Syn.* footrest, ottoman, footstool, cushion, stool; see also **furniture, seat 1**.

**haste,** *n.* **1.** [Rapidity] — *Syn.* speed, rapidity, expedition, dispatch, rapidness, hurry, swiftness; see also **speed**.

**2.** [Undue rapidity] — *Syn.* scramble, bustle, scurry, precipitation, flurry, hurly-burly, impetuosity, rashness, scuttle, impetuousness, foolhardiness, want of caution, untimeliness, hurriedness, scamper, hustling, undue celerity, press, recklessness, rush, hastiness, incautiousness, carelessness, irrationality, rashness, expedience, giddiness, precipitancy, impatience, heedlessness, plunge, unrestraint, vehemence, testiness, rapidity, excitation, fretfulness, outburst, abruptness, anticipation, intempestivity, prematureness, leap in the dark★, speed-up★, speedomania★, smoke★. — *Ant.* PRUDENCE, caution, attention.

**3.** [Urgency] — *Syn.* promptness, promptitude, dispatch; see **importance 2**.

**in haste** — *Syn.* hastening, in a hurry, moving fast; see **hurrying**.

**make haste** — *Syn.* hurry, move quickly, act quickly, speed up; see **hasten 1**.

---

**SYN.** — **haste** implies quick or precipitate movement or action, as from the pressure of circumstances or intense eagerness; **hurry**, often interchangeable with **haste**, specifically suggests excitement, bustle, or confusion /the *hurry* of city life/; **speed** implies rapidity of movement, operation, etc., of persons or things, suggesting effectiveness and the absence of excitement or confusion /to increase the *speed* of an assembly line/; **expedition** adds to **speed** the implication of efficiency and stresses the facilitation of an action or procedure; **dispatch** comes close to **expedition** in meaning but more strongly stresses promptness in finishing something /completed the report with *dispatch*/

---

**hasten,** *v.* **1.** [To make haste] — *Syn.* rush, sprint, spurt, scurry, move quickly, bestir oneself, dash off, plunge, bustle, waste no time, lose no time, fly, be in a hurry, cover ground, not lose a moment, hurry, hurry up, press, press on, express, haste, flee, be on the run, skip, tear, post, scamper, pace, move speedily, push on, hie, hustle, bolt, scuttle, careen, make haste, make time, dart, trip, be quick, ride hard, leap, clip, bound, zoom, skim, brush, spring, make forced marches, whip off, whip away, jump, speed up, work under pressure, make the best of one's time, make short work of, go at full blast, go at full tilt, run like mad, march in double time, put on more speed, carry sail, take wing, make strides, go all out, trot, run wide open, pack off, pack away, gallop, make a dash for★, step on it★, shake a leg★, beat the devil around a stump★, go like sixty★, work against time★, put on steam★, hie on★, break one's neck★, fall all over oneself★, make up for lost time★, hop to it★, hop on it★, scoot★, spin★, whiz★, beat a retreat★, sweep★, bundle★, get cracking★, skedaddle★, outstrip the wind★, fly on the wings of the wind★, shoot★, bowl along★, cut along★, clap spurs to one's horse★, swoop★, wing one's way★, crowd sail★, rip★, go on the double★, stir one's stumps★, go like (greased) lightning★, go like a shot★, whisk★, go hell-bent★, burn up the road★, zip★, go like a bat out of hell★, flit★, step lively, step on the gas★, give her the gas★; see also **race 1, run 2, speed.** — *Ant.* creep, CRAWL, plod.

**2.** [To expedite] — *Syn.* accelerate, dispatch, speed up, fillip, advance, move up, quicken, stimulate, hurry up, push, make short work of, urge, goad, press, whip on, agitate, push forward, push ahead, put into action, get started, give a start, drive on, set in motion, take in hand, take over, put on wheels★, blast off★, railroad through★, gear up★, cut the red tape★; see also **speed.** — *Ant.* defer, DELAY, put off.

**hastily,** *modif.* **1.** [Rapidly] — *Syn.* hurriedly, speedily, nimbly; see **quickly 1**.

**2.** [Carelessly] — *Syn.* thoughtlessly, recklessly, rashly; see **carelessly**.

**hasty,** *modif.* **1.** [Hurried] — *Syn.* fast, quick, speedy, swift; see **fast 1**.

**2.** [Careless] — *Syn.* ill-advised, precipitate, foolhardy; see **careless 1, rash**.

*See Synonym Study at FAST.*

**hat,** *n.* — *Syn.* headgear, cap, millinery, headpiece, helmet, chapeau, bonnet, lid★, roof★, bean pod★; see also **helmet**.

Types of hats and hatlike coverings include: *for men*: cap, service cap, forage cap, baseball cap, visor, beanie, skullcap, yarmulke, kipa, overseas cap, derby, straw hat, Panama hat, felt hat, sombrero, cowboy's hat, Stetson, southwestern, ten-gallon hat, top hat, opera hat, crush hat, stovepipe, tall silk hat, collapsible, topper, miter, bowler, leghorn, tam-o'-shanter, beret, cocked hat, tricornered hat, sailor hat, boater, digger, bycocket, fez, turban, shako, kepi, bearskin, coonskin, tarboosh, toque, busby, sun helmet, pith helmet, mortarboard, soft-brimmed hat, fedora, homburg, deerstalker, domino; *for women*: hood, wimple, snood, cowl, kerchief, picture hat, mantilla, turban, veil, cloche, calot, straw, skimmer, beret, bandanna, toque, mobcap, Talbot, bonnet, poke bonnet, Louise Bourbon, Princesse Eugénie, Descat, pillbox, Gainsborough, scarf, chapel cap, whimsey, babushka.

**pass the hat** — *Syn.* take up a collection, gather funds, collect; see **accumulate** 1,

**take one's hat off to** — *Syn.* salute, cheer, congratulate; see **praise** 1.

**talk through one's hat★** — *Syn.* chatter, talk nonsense, make foolish statements; see **babble.**

**throw one's hat into the ring** — *Syn.* enter a contest, run for office, enter politics; see **campaign** 1.

**under one's hat★** — *Syn.* confidential, private, hidden; see **secret** 1.

**hatch,** *v.* 1. [To bring forth] — *Syn.* bear, lay eggs, give birth; see **produce** 1.

2. [To plan] — *Syn.* prepare, scheme, plot; see **invent** 1, **plan** 1.

**hatched,** *modif.* — *Syn.* contrived, concluded, devised; see **planned.**

**hatchery,** *n.* — *Syn.* brooder, incubator, breeding place, fish hatchery.

**hatchet,** *n.* — *Syn.* ax, machete, bill, billhook, tomahawk; see also **ax.**

Types of hatches include: bench hatchet, lathing hatchet, roofer's hatchet, claw hatchet, broad hatchet, tomahawk, pipe-tomahawk, battleax.

**bury the hatchet** — *Syn.* make peace, stop fighting, settle one's differences, come to terms, smoke a peace pipe.

**hatchway,** *n.* — *Syn.* trap door, scuttle, hatch; see **door** 1, **entrance** 2, **gate.**

**hate,** *n.* — *Syn.* ill will, venom, disgust, antipathy, aversion, detestation, hostility, rancor, malevolence, rankling, revenge, malignity, loathing, abomination, abhorrence, animosity, enmity, frost★, scunner★, dog-eye★, nasty look★, no love lost★; see also **hatred** 1, 2, **malice, resentment.** — *Ant.* LOVE, favor, desire.

**hate,** *v.* 1. [To detest] — *Syn.* detest, abhor, execrate, abominate, loathe, scorn, despise, have an aversion toward, look at with loathing, spit upon, anathematize, curse, contemn, swear eternal enmity, dislike intensely, shudder at, not care for, sicken at, have enough of, be repelled by, feel repulsion for, have no use for, object to, bear malice, have ill feelings toward, bear a grudge against, spurn, shrink from, recoil from, disparage, shun, nauseate, denounce, resent, esteem slightly, curse, be sick of, be tired of, reject, revolt against, hold cheap, deride, have no taste for, have no stomach for, disfavor, look down upon, feel malice toward, hold aloof from, mislike, be malevolent, hold in contempt, have no use for, be disgusted with, view with horror, owe a grudge to, be down on★, look daggers at★, have it in for★, hate like poison★; see also **dislike.** — *Ant.* LOVE, adore, worship.

2. [★To dislike; *often used with infinitive or participle*] — *Syn.* object to, rebel, recoil from, shrink from, shudder at, think nothing of, not like, have no liking for, find abhorrent, be set against, find obnoxious, not relish the idea, shun, avoid, mind, have no taste for, have no stomach for, be disinclined, disapprove of, wish to avoid, struggle against, shun, pull back from, demur, feel sick at, put off, hesitate, eschew, not have the heart to, wish to abstain from, keep clear of, steer clear of, quail from, turn from, wince from, blench from, be reluctant, shy away★, turn up one's nose at★, look coldly upon★, look down upon★, speak ill of★, look down one's nose★, get on one's high horse★,

hold cheap★, be cold about★. — *Ant.* LIKE, favor, approve.

---

*SYN.* — **hate** implies a feeling of great dislike or aversion, and, with persons as the object, connotes the bearing of malice; **detest** implies vehement dislike or antipathy; **despise** suggests a looking down with great contempt upon the person or thing one hates; **abhor** implies a feeling of great repugnance or disgust; **loathe** implies utter abhorrence See also Synonym Study at DESPISE.

---

**hated,** *modif.* — *Syn.* despised, loathed, abhorred, abominated, detested, disliked, execrated, cursed, anathematized, unpopular, avoided, shunned, out of favor, condemned; see also **offensive** 2, **undesirable.**

**hateful,** *modif.* — *Syn.* offensive, odious, detestable, repugnant; see **offensive** 2, **undesirable.**

*See Synonym Study at* OFFENSIVE.

**hater,** *n.* — *Syn.* enemy, despiser, execrator, ill-wisher, racist, abominator, calumniator, militant, antagonist, advocate of race hatred, jingoist; see also **bigot, enemy** 1, 2.

**hatred,** *n.* 1. [Strong aversion] — *Syn.* abhorrence, loathing, rancor, detestation, revulsion, malignance, antipathy, repugnance, repulsion, disgust, contempt, dislike, intense dislike, execration, scorn, abomination, distaste, disapproval, horror, hard feelings, displeasure; see also sense 2; see also **hate, malice, resentment.** — *Ant.* liking, AFFECTION, attraction.

2. [Personal enmity] — *Syn.* ill will, antipathy, bitterness, antagonism, animosity, acrimony, pique, grudge, malice, malevolence, animus, revulsion, repugnance, militancy, disfavor, ignominy, prejudice, invidiousness, spite, revenge, hate, venom, envy, spleen, coldness, distaste, pitilessness, contempt, asperity, derision, race prejudice, malignity, hostility, odium, alienation, disaffection, bad blood★, chip on one's shoulder★, grudge★; see also sense 1; see also **anger, opposition** 2, **resentment.** — *Ant.* friendship, DEVOTION, affection.

**haughtiness,** *n.* — *Syn.* insolence, aloofness, snobbishness; see **arrogance.**

**haughty,** *modif.* — *Syn.* arrogant, disdainful, proud; see **egotistic** 2, **proud** 2.

*See Synonym Study at* PROUD.

**haul,** *n.* 1. [A pull] — *Syn.* tug, lift, wrench; see **pull** 1.

2. [The distance something is hauled] — *Syn.* trip, voyage, yards; see **distance** 3.

3. [★Something obtained, especially loot] — *Syn.* find, spoils, take; see **booty, catch** 1.

**in** or **over the long haul** — *Syn.* over a long period of time, for a long time, in the end; see **for a time** at **time.**

**haul,** *v.* — *Syn.* pull, drag, bring; see **draw** 1.

*See Synonym Study at* PULL.

**haul off,** *v.* — *Syn.* take, cart off, truck off, drag off, appropriate; see **remove** 1.

**haunch,** *n.* — *Syn.* backside, side, hindquarter; see **hip, rump.**

**haunt,** *n.* 1. [A retreat] — *Syn.* den, resort, headquarters, lair, meeting place, rendezvous, trysting place; see also **bar** 2, **refuge** 1, **retreat** 2.

2. [A spirit] — *Syn.* poltergeist, spook, phantom; see **ghost** 1, 2.

**haunt,** *v.* 1. [To frequent persistently] — *Syn.* habituate, visit often, resort to; see **frequent.**

2. [To frequent as a spirit] — *Syn.* come as a ghost, appear as a phantom, permeate, pervade, rise, float, before the eyes, dwell in, walk, be disclosed, inhabit, hover about, return from the dead, manifest itself, materialize,

reappear frequently to after death, visit habitually after death, spook★, ha'nt★.

**3.** [To prey upon] — *Syn.* recur in one's mind, obsess, torment, beset, possess, trouble, weigh on one's mind, touch one's conscience, craze, madden, hound, terrify, bedevil, plague, dwell heavily upon, intrude upon continually, vex, harass, weigh on, prey on, infest, pester, be ever present, besiege, worry, tease, terrorize, disquiet, recur to persistently, frighten, annoy, possess one's mind, cause regret, cause sorrow, molest, harrow, appall, agitate, rack, overrun, sting, nettle, hang over one's head, agonize, unman, drive one nuts★; see also **bother** 2, **disturb** 2.

**haunted,** *modif.* — *Syn.* frequented, visited by, preyed upon; see **obsessed.**

**haunting,** *modif.* — *Syn.* eerie, unforgettable, seductive; see **frightful** 1, **remembered.**

**have,** *v.* **1.** [To be in possession of] — *Syn.* possess, take unto oneself, hold; see **own** 1.

**2.** [To bear] — *Syn.* beget, give birth to, bring forth; see **produce** 1.

**3.** [To be obliged; *used with infinitive*] — *Syn.* be compelled, be forced to, should, ought, be one's duty to, rest with, become, fall on, devolve upon, be up to★, have got to★; see also **must.**

**4.** [To have sexual intercourse with] — *Syn.* seduce, sleep with, deflower; see **copulate.**

**have at,** *v.* — *Syn.* thrust, strike, attack; see **hit** 1.

**have done,** *v.* — *Syn.* leave, quit, outgrow, stop, get through, finish; see also **achieve** 1, **stop** 2.

**have had it★,** *v.* **1.** [To have reached a limit] — *Syn.* be exhausted, be defeated, be disgusted, be bored, be ready to quit, be fed up; see also **depleted.**

**2.** [To have come to an end] — *Syn.* be no longer popular, be no longer accepted, be worn out, be broken, be useless.

**have it good★,** *v.* — *Syn.* do well, thrive, have it easy★; see **prosper.**

**haven,** *n.* — *Syn.* port, harbor, roadstead; see **refuge** 1, **shelter.**

**have on,** *v.* — *Syn.* be clothed in, be wearing, try on; see **wear** 1.

**haversack,** *n.* — *Syn.* saddlebag, knapsack, satchel; see **bag.**

**have something on one,** *v.* — *Syn.* be able to expose, have special knowledge of, be able to control; see **convict, know** 1.

**having,** *modif.* — *Syn.* owning, possessing, enjoying, commanding, holding, controlling; see also **retaining.**

**havoc,** *n.* — *Syn.* destruction, devastation, plunder, ruin; see **destruction** 2.

*See Synonym Study at* DESTRUCTION.

**hawk,** *n.* **1.** [A member of the Accipitridae] — *Syn.* bird of prey, one of the Falconiformes, falcon; see **bird** 1.

Types of hawks include: red-tailed, zone-tailed, white tailed, short-tailed, broad-winged, short-winged, common black, American sparrow hawk, English sparrow hawk, bush, roadside, duck hawk, hen, fish hawk, prairie, marsh, gray, blue, Cooper's, Harlan's, Swainson's, Harris', noble, ignoble, ferruginous, sharp-shinned, broad-winged, rough-legged, goshawk, windhover, night-hawk, English hobby, hobby, merlin, jack merlin, peregrine, tiercel, osprey, harrier, kite, kestrel, caracara, lugar, lanner, saker, eyas, haggard, gyrefalcon.

**2.** [A warlike person] — *Syn.* militarist, chauvinist, jingoist, belligerent, warmonger, chauvin, jingo, hothead; see also **conservative, radical.**

**hawker★,** *n.* — *Syn.* vendor, seller, peddler; see **businessperson, merchant, salesman** 2.

**hay,** *n.* — *Syn.* provender, fodder, roughage, forage, feed; see also **grass** 1.

Types of hay include: red clover, wild hay, timothy, sweetgrass, alsike, sweet clover, soybeans, swamp hay, alfalfa, oat hay, millet.

**hit the hay★** — *Syn.* go to bed, rest, recline; see **sleep.**

**make hay out of** — *Syn.* profit by, utilize, turn to one's advantage; see **use** 1.

**make hay while the sun shines** — *Syn.* opportunize, take advantage, make the most of an opportunity; see **use** 1.

**haycock,** *n.* — *Syn.* sheaf, stack, rick; see **haystack.**

**hayfield,** *n.* — *Syn.* pasture, mead, grassland; see **field** 1, **meadow.**

**hayloft,** *n.* — *Syn.* barn, silo, storage space; see **storehouse.**

**haymow,** *n.* — *Syn.* hayloft, storage space, barn; see **storehouse.**

**hayseed,** *n.* **1.** [Chaff and bits of hay] — *Syn.* grass, chaff, hay; see **grain** 1, **seed** 2.

**2.** [★An unsophisticated person] — *Syn.* hick, country bumpkin, bumpkin, yokel, rustic; see **boor.**

**haystack,** *n.* — *Syn.* sheaf, stack, rick, hay, haycock, hayrick, pile.

**hazard,** *n.* **1.** [Danger] — *Syn.* risk, peril, jeopardy; see **danger.**

**2.** [Luck] — *Syn.* chance, possibility, accident; see **risk** 2, **uncertainty** 3, **venture.**

*See Synonym Study at* DANGER.

**hazard,** *v.* — *Syn.* stake, try, guess; see **chance** 2, **gamble** 1, **risk, venture.**

**hazardous,** *modif.* — *Syn.* perilous, uncertain, precarious; see **dangerous** 1.

**haze,** *n.* — *Syn.* mist, smokiness, indistinctness, fume, fog, smog, steam, cloudiness, miasma, film, haziness; see also **fog** 1, **mist.**

*See Synonym Study at* MIST.

**hazel,** *modif.* — *Syn.* brownish-gray, hazel-gray, bluish-green, greenish-brown, yellowish-green; see also **brown, mellow.**

**hazy,** *modif.* **1.** [Obscured to the sight] — *Syn.* cloudy, foggy, smoggy, murky, misty, unclear, overcast, steaming, screened, fuliginous, fumy, rimy, filmy, gauzy, vaporous, smoky, dim, dull, indistinct, nebulous, spraylike, shadowy, dusky, obscure, wavering, thick, opaque, bleared, obfuscated, frosty, lowering, veiled, blurred, glimmering, semitransparent, blurry, crepuscular, faint, bleary; see also **dark** 1. — *Ant.* bright, CLEAR, cloudless.

**2.** [Obscured to the understanding] — *Syn.* unclear, vague, unsound, unintelligible; see **obscure** 1.

**he,** *pron.* — *Syn.* this one, this boy, this man, that boy, that man, this male animal, that male animal; see also **boy, man** 2, 3.

**head,** *n.* **1.** [The skull] — *Syn.* brainpan, scalp, brain box, pate, crown, headpiece, pow (Scotch), poll, bean★, noggin★, coconut★, noodle★, nut★, nob★, loaf (British); see also **cranium.**

**2.** [A leader or supervisor] — *Syn.* commander, commanding officer, ruler; see **administrator, leader** 2.

**3.** [The top] — *Syn.* summit, peak, crest; see **top** 1.

**4.** [The beginning] — *Syn.* front, start, source; see **origin** 2.

**5.** [A climax] — *Syn.* acme, turning point, end; see **climax, crisis.**

**6.** [Stored power] — *Syn.* latent force, static energy, potential energy; see **energy** 3.

**7.** [An attachment] — *Syn.* cap, bottle top, cork; see **cover** 1, **fixture**.

**8.** [*Intelligence] — *Syn.* brains, foresight, ingenuity; see **judgment** 1.

**9.** [A headline] — *Syn.* leader, caption, title; see **headline**.

**10.** [*A drug user] — *Syn.* hippie, acidhead*, pothead*; see **addict**.

**come to a head** — *Syn.* culminate, reach a crisis, come to a climax; see **climax**.

**get it through one's head** — *Syn.* learn, comprehend, see; see **understand** 1.

**give one his head** — *Syn.* permit, condone, approve; see **allow** 1.

**go to one's head** — *Syn.* stir mentally, stimulate, intoxicate, make one arrogant; see **excite** 1.

**hang** or **hide one's head** — *Syn.* repent, be sorry, be ashamed, grieve; see **regret**.

**keep one's head** — *Syn.* remain calm, keep one's self-control, hold one's emotions in check; see **restrain** 1.

**lose one's head** — *Syn.* become excited, get angry, go mad, rave; see **rage** 1.

**make head** — *Syn.* make headway, progress, go forward, proceed; see **advance** 1.

**make head or tail of** — *Syn.* comprehend, apprehend, see; see **understand** 1.

**one's head off** — *Syn.* greatly, extremely, considerably; see **much** 1.

**on** or **upon one's head** — *Syn.* burdensome, taxing, strenuous; see **difficult** 1.

**out of** or **off one's head*** — *Syn.* crazy, delirious, raving; see **insane** 1.

**over one's head** — *Syn.* incomprehensible, not understandable, hard; see **difficult** 2.

**put** or **lay heads together** — *Syn.* consult, talk over, confer; see **discuss**.

**take it into one's head** — *Syn.* conceive, concoct, devise; see **invent** 2.

**head,** *v.* **1.** [To lead] — *Syn.* direct, oversee, supervise; see **command** 2, **manage** 1.

**2.** [To travel] — *Syn.* go, set out, head for; see **travel** 2.

**headache,** *n.* **1.** [A pain in the head] — *Syn.* migraine, sick headache, bilious headache, neuralgia, organic headache, megrim, cephalalgia, hemialgia, hemicrania, reflex headache, head-on*, big head*; see also **pain** 2.

**2.** [*A source of vexation and difficulty] — *Syn.* problem, jumble, mess; see **difficulty** 1, 2, **trouble** 2.

**headdress,** *n.* — *Syn.* bonnet, helmet, hood; see **crown** 2, **hat**.

**headed,** *modif.* — *Syn.* in transit, in motion, en route, going, directed, started, aimed, slated for, on the way to, pointed toward, in process of reaching, on the road to; see also **moving** 1. — *Ant.* STOPPING, landed, disembarked.

**headfirst,** *modif.* — *Syn.* recklessly, hastily, rashly; see **carelessly**.

**head for,** *v.* — *Syn.* go for, set out for, make a dash for, break for, start toward, hit for*; see **travel** 2.

**heading,** *n.* — *Syn.* headline, subtitle, inscription, address, caption, legend, head, subject, overline, docket, section head, frontispiece, capital, superscription, ticket, headnote, display line, preface, imprint, prologue, preamble, topic, title page, designation, specification, indication of contents; see also **headline, label, title** 1.

**headland,** *n.* — *Syn.* bluff, cliff, cape; see **hill, cape**.

**headless,** *modif.* **1.** [Unthinking] — *Syn.* witless, fatuous, brainless; see **dull** 3, **stupid** 1.

**2.** [Without a head] — *Syn.* decapitated, lifeless, truncated; see **dead** 1.

**headlight,** *n.* — *Syn.* searchlight, automobile light, front light, beacon, fog lamp, spotlight; see also **light** 3.

**headline,** *n.* — *Syn.* head, heading, caption, title, leader, header, screamer*, scarehead*.

Types and parts of headlines include: deck, bank, line, streamer, banner, pyramid, inverted pyramid, read-out, two-line head, three-line head, subhead, ribbon, drop head.

**headlong,** *modif.* — *Syn.* reckless, precipitate, impetuous; see **rash**.

**headmaster,** *n.* — *Syn.* dean, director, superintendent; see **administrator, principal**.

**headmost,** *modif.* — *Syn.* initial, outstanding, main; see **principal**.

**head off*,** *v.* — *Syn.* block off, interfere with, intervene; see **stop** 1.

**head on,** *modif.* — *Syn.* headfirst, with full force, body to body; see **opposed**.

**head over heels*,** *modif.* — *Syn.* entirely, precipitately, unreservedly; see **completely**.

**headquarters,** *n.* — *Syn.* main office, home office, chief office, central station, central place, distributing center, police station, office of the commanding officer, meeting place, meeting house, haunt, manager's office, quarters, base, military station, club, post, cantonment, center of operations, base of operations, H.Q.; see also **office** 3.

**headship,** *n.* — *Syn.* primacy, authority, control; see **administration** 1, **command** 2, **leadership** 1, **power** 2.

**headsman,** *n.* — *Syn.* hangman, beheader, public executioner; see **killer**.

**headstone,** *n.* — *Syn.* gravestone, marker, stone; see **grave** 1, **tombstone**.

**headstrong,** *modif.* — *Syn.* determined, strong-minded, stubborn; see **obstinate** 1.

**headway,** *n.* — *Syn.* advance, increase, forward motion, promotion; see **progress** 1.

**heady,** *modif.* — *Syn.* overwhelming, intoxicating, powerful; see **exciting, strong** 8.

**heal,** *v.* **1.** [To make well or sound] — *Syn.* cure, remedy, restore, rehabilitate, renew, treat, attend, minister to, restore to health, renovate, fix, repair, mend, make whole, reconstruct, regenerate, bring around, relieve, alleviate, ease, meliorate, set, purify, rejuvenate, medicate, recall to life, reinvigorate, dress a wound, rebuild, revive, revitalize, revivify, purge, reanimate, work a cure, cause to heal up, resuscitate, salve, help to get well, make better, nurse, care for, take care of, physic, ameliorate, patch up, reconcile, conciliate, set right, snatch from the jaws of death*, doctor*, set up*, fix up*, put one on one's feet again*, breathe new life into*, give a new lease on life*; see also **improve** 1, **nurse**. — *Ant.* make ill, harm, sicken, infect.

**2.** [To recover] — *Syn.* get well, knit, mend, recuperate, set, close up, scab over, cicatrize, improve, pull through; see also **improve** 2, **recover** 3.

*SYN.* — **heal** and **cure** both imply a restoring to health or soundness, with **heal** usually applied to the making or becoming whole of a wound, sore, etc. or, figuratively, the mending of a breach, and **cure** specifically suggesting the elimination of disease, distress, evil, etc.; **remedy** stresses the use of medication or a specific corrective treatment in relieving disease, injury, distress, etc.

**healing,** *modif.* — *Syn.* restorative, invigorating, medicinal; see **remedial**.

**health,** *n.* **1.** [Physical or mental well-being] — *Syn.* vigor, haleness, wholeness, good condition, healthfulness, good health, fitness, robustness, bloom, sound-

ness of body, freedom from disease, freedom from ailment, lustiness, tone, hardiness, hardihood, well-being, wellness, stamina, salubriousness, energy, euphoria, full bloom, eupepsia, salubrity, rosy cheeks*, fine feather*, fine fettle*, good form*, top shape*, clean bill of health*; see also **sanity** 1, **strength** 1, **vitality**.
**2.** [Condition of body or mind] — *Syn.* fitness, physical state, mental state, form, shape, tone, constitution, well-being, circumstance, fettle, complexion, state of health, tendency.

**healthful**, *modif.* — *Syn.* nutritious, restorative, body-building, sanative, sanitary, hygienic, salutary, invigorating, tonic, stimulating, bracing, salubrious, wholesome, beneficial, health-giving, nutritive, nourishing, energy-giving, fresh, pure, clean, corrective, compensatory, cathartic, sedative, conducive to health, sustentative, regenerative, digestible, restoring, substantial, sustaining, promoting health, benign, good for one, aseptic, sanatory, desirable, clean, harmless, innocuous, healing, preventive, untainted, disease-free, unpolluted, unadulterated, uninjurious, favorable, advantageous, innoxious; see also **healthy, remedial**. — *Ant.* sickly, UNWHOLESOME, noxious.

**healthy**, *modif.* **1.** [In good health] — *Syn.* sound, trim, all right, normal, robust, hale, vigorous, well, hearty, husky, athletic, stout, lusty, rosy-cheeked, potent, hardy, able-bodied, virile, muscular, blooming, sturdy, safe and sound, in good condition, in sound condition, combat-ready, in full possession of one's faculties, in good health, enjoying good health, possessing good health, full of pep, never feeling better, as well as can be expected, bursting with health, fresh, of a sound constitution, whole, healthful, firm, stout, unimpaired, buxom, lively, undecayed, flourishing, good, ruddy, cured, fit, clear-eyed, plump, full of life and vigor, spirited, in fine fettle, burly, restored, tough, youthful, sound of wind and limb, free from disease, free from infirmity, in fine whack*, fine*, bobbish*, at the peak of good health*, fine and dandy*, hunky-dory*, chipper*, in good shape*, sound as a bell*, in fine feather*, in the pink*, rugged*, fit as a fiddle*, sound as a dollar*, looking like a million*, fit and fine*, full of beans*, feeling one's oats*, hard as nails*; see also **sane** 1, **strong** 1. — *Ant.* UNHEALTHY, ill, diseased.
**2.** [Healthful] — *Syn.* salubrious, salutary, wholesome; see **healthful**.

**heap**, *n.* — *Syn.* pile, accumulation, mass, agglomeration, stack, load, collection, aggregation, stock, store, hoard, mountain, mound, abundance, profusion, bulk, fullness, volume, plenty, lump, total, sum, whole, huddle, mow, barrow, cartload, swell, harvest, hillock, deposit, carload, cargo, cock, wagonload, block, pyre, packet, jumble, pyramid, hill, cluster, confused mass, drift, bale, clump, shock, batch, bundle, bunch, gathering, amassment, acervation, concentration, haul*, junk pile*, full house*, lots*; see also **quantity**. — *Ant.* handful, BIT, a few specks.

**heap**, *v.* **1.** [To place in a heap] — *Syn.* pile, add, swell, bunch, lump, stack, rank, order, cord, bank, fill up, arrange, pile high, dike, hill, barricade, fill to overflowing, throw together, rake together, batch together, bunch together, draw together, fill up, pile up, heap up, mass, barrow, ruck, gather, dump, concentrate, mound, coacervate, deposit, dredge, group, throw in a heap, cast in a heap, gather in a heap, shock; see also **load** 1, **pack** 2. — *Ant.* SCATTER, flatten, level.
**2.** [To amass] — *Syn.* gather, pile up, lay up, store; see **accumulate** 1.

**heaped**, *modif.* — *Syn.* amassed, collected, stored; see **gathered**.

**heaping**, *modif.* — *Syn.* sated, running over, abundant; see **full** 1, **large** 1.

**hear**, *v.* **1.** [To perceive by ear] — *Syn.* listen to, hearken, hark, give attention, attend to, make out, auscultate, become aware of, catch, descry, apprehend, take in, eavesdrop, detect, perceive by the ear, overhear, take cognizance of, listen with both ears, keep one's ears open, have the sense of hearing, give ear to*, read loud and clear*, strain one's ears*, listen in*, devour someone's words*, get an earful*; see also **listen** 1.
**2.** [To receive information aurally] — *Syn.* overhear, eavesdrop, be advised, find out, catch, learn, have it on good authority, learn by general report, have an account, ascertain, descry, receive information, discover, gather, apperceive, be told, understand, hear of, be led to believe, be made aware of, be informed, learn by ear, hear say*, hear tell of*, get wise to*, get an earful*, get wind of*, get the signal*, sit in on*, tune in*; see also **listen** 2.
**3.** [To hold a hearing] — *Syn.* preside over, put on trial, summon to court; see **try** 3.
**not hear of** — *Syn.* not allow, refuse to consider, reject; see **forbid**.

**heard**, *modif.* — *Syn.* perceived, listened to, witnessed, caught, made out, understood, heeded, noted, made clear.

**hearer**, *n.* — *Syn.* listener, witness, bystander; see **auditor** 1.

**hear from**, *v.* — *Syn.* get word from, receive communication from, be informed, learn through; see **hear** 2, **receive** 1.

**hearing**, *modif.* — *Syn.* heeding, auditive, hearkening; see **auditory, listening, sensory** 1.

**hearing**, *n.* **1.** [An opportunity to be heard] — *Syn.* audition, interview, trial, inquest, test, fair hearing, tryout, attendance, congress, conference, audit, notice, performance, admittance, consultation, council, reception, presentation, audience, attention; see also **discussion** 1, **gathering, trial** 2.
**2.** [The act of hearing] — *Syn.* detecting, recording, distinguishing; see **listening**.
**3.** [The faculty for hearing] — *Syn.* ear, auditory faculty, aural apparatus, perception, listening ear, sense of hearing, audition, act of perceiving sound, acoustic sensation.
**4.** [Range of hearing] — *Syn.* earshot, hearing distance, reach, sound, carrying distance, range, earreach, acoustical effect, auditory range; see also **extent**.

**hearing aid**, *n.* — *Syn.* listening device, ear trumpet, otophone, sonifer, amplifier, sound intensifier, headphone.

**hearken**, *v.* — *Syn.* notice, attend, observe; see **hear** 1, **listen** 1.

**hear of**, *v.* — *Syn.* hear about, know about, be aware of, become aware of, discover; see **know** 1, 3.

**hear out**, *v.* — *Syn.* listen to, yield to, yield the floor to, remain silent; see **listen** 2.

**hearsay**, *n.* — *Syn.* noise, scandal, report; see **gossip** 1, **rumor** 1, 2.

**hearse**, *n.* — *Syn.* funeral van, funeral coach, conveyance for a coffin, undertaker's limousine, meat wagon*, dead wagon*; see also **automobile, vehicle** 1.

**heart**, *n.* **1.** [The pump in the circulatory system] — *Syn.* vital organ, vascular organ, blood pump, cardiac organ, artificial heart, pacemaker, ticker*, clock*; see also **organ** 2.
**2.** [Feeling] — *Syn.* pity, response, sympathy, sensitivity; see **emotion, feeling, pity** 1.

**3.** [The center] — *Syn.* core, middle, pith; see **center** 1.

**4.** [The most important portion] — *Syn.* core, gist, quintessence, root; see **essence** 1, **soul** 2.

**5.** [Courage] — *Syn.* fortitude, gallantry, spirit; see **courage** 1, **mind** 1, **soul** 4.

**6.** [The breast] — *Syn.* bosom, marrow, soul; see **breast** 3.

**after one's own heart** — *Syn.* suitable, pleasing, lovable; see **pleasant** 2.

**at heart** — *Syn.* basically, fundamentally, privately; see **essentially, secretly.**

**break one's heart** — *Syn.* grieve, disappoint, pain; see **hurt** 1.

**by heart** — *Syn.* from memory, memorized, learned; see **remembered.**

**change of heart** — *Syn.* change of mind, reversal, alteration; see **change** 2.

**do one's heart good** — *Syn.* please, make content, delight; see **satisfy** 1.

**eat one's heart out** — *Syn.* worry, regret, nurse one's troubles, fret, pine, grieve; see also **brood** 2, **worry** 2.

**from the bottom of one's heart** — *Syn.* deeply, honestly, frankly; see **sincerely.**

**have a heart** — *Syn.* be kind, empathize, take pity; see **sympathize.**

**have one's heart in one's mouth** — *Syn.* be frightened, have anxiety, become nervous; see **fear** 1.

**have one's heart in the right place** — *Syn.* be well-intentioned, be well-meaning, be kind; see **generous** *modif.* 2.

**in one's heart of hearts** — *Syn.* fundamentally, basically, privately; see **secretly.**

**lay to heart** — *Syn.* take into account, take to heart, believe; see **consider** 1.

**lose one's heart to** — *Syn.* love, cherish, adore; see **fall in love** at **love.**

**near one's heart** — *Syn.* important, dear, cherished; see **beloved.**

**set one's heart at rest** — *Syn.* calm, placate, soothe; see **comfort.**

**set one's heart on** — *Syn.* long for, need, desire; see **want** 1.

**take heart** — *Syn.* cheer up, be comforted, take courage; see **encourage** 2.

**take to heart,**

**1.** [To consider seriously] — *Syn.* take seriously, lay to heart, take into account, believe; see **consider** 1, 3.

**2.** [To take offense] — *Syn.* take personally, be insulted, take the wrong way, take umbrage.

**to one's heart's content** — *Syn.* as much as one likes, as long as one pleases, until satisfied, sufficiently; see **enough** 1.

**1.** [To concern oneself with] — *Syn.* be affected by, feel deeply, trouble oneself, empathize, sympathize; see also **feel** 2, **understand** 1.

**wear one's heart on one's sleeve** — *Syn.* show one's affections, reveal one's emotions, be open.

**with all one's heart** — *Syn.* honestly, deeply, frankly; see **sincerely.**

**with half a heart** — *Syn.* half-heartedly, apathetically, listlessly; see **indifferent** 1.

**heartache,** *n.* — *Syn.* sorrow, despair, anguish; see **grief** 1, **regret.**

**heart and soul,** *modif.* — *Syn.* entirely, devotedly, absolutely; see **completely.**

**heartbeat,** *n.* — *Syn.* pulsation, throb of the heart, cardiovascular activity, instant, moment; see also **beat** 2, **pulse.**

**heartbreaking,** *modif.* — *Syn.* cheerless, deplorable, unbearable; see **pitiful** 1, **sad** 2, **tragic.**

**heartbroken,** *modif.* — *Syn.* melancholy, sorrowful, doleful; see **sad** 1.

**heartburn,** *n.* — *Syn.* pyrosis, dyspepsia, indigestion, cardialgia, ulceritis, stomach upset, water qualm; see also **disease.**

**heart disease,** *n.* — *Syn.* heart failure, coronary illness, thrombosis; see **disease.**

**hearten,** *v.* — *Syn.* rouse, cheer, inspirit; see **encourage** 2.

**heartfelt,** *modif.* — *Syn.* sincere, deep, ardent; see **genuine** 2, **honest** 1.

**hearth,** *n.* **1.** [A fireplace] — *Syn.* grate, fireside, hearthstone; see **fireplace.**

**2.** [Home] — *Syn.* dwelling, abode, residence; see **home** 1.

**heartily,** *modif.* **1.** [Sincerely] — *Syn.* enthusiastically, earnestly, cordially; see **seriously** 2, **sincerely.**

**2.** [Vigorously] — *Syn.* zealously, enthusiastically, energetically; see **vigorously.**

**3.** [Completely] — *Syn.* totally, thoroughly, wholly; see **completely.**

**heartless,** *modif.* — *Syn.* cruel, unkind, unthinking, insensitive; see **cruel** 1, 2, **ruthless** 1, 2, **savage** 2.

**heart-rending,** *modif.* — *Syn.* moving, piteous, grievous, mournful; see **pitiful** 1, **sad** 2.

**hearty,** *modif.* **1.** [Cordial] — *Syn.* warm, zealous, sincere, cheery, cheerful, jovial, wholehearted, neighborly, well-meant, vivacious, gay, animated, jolly, ardent, genial, fervid, zestful, glowing, enthusiastic, genuine, avid, deepest, passionate, frank, glad, deep, intense, exuberant, profuse, eager, unalloyed, effusive, gushing, devout, deep-felt, unfeigned, unrestrained, fervent, warmhearted, authentic, amicable, heartwarming, impassioned, heartfelt, brotherly, responsive; see also **friendly** 1, **happy** 1, 2. — *Ant.* FALSE, mock, sham.

**2.** [Healthy] — *Syn.* good, lively, full; see **healthful.**

**heat,** *n.* **1.** [Warmth] — *Syn.* hotness, warmth, warmness, calefaction, calidity, torridity, high temperature, hot wind, heat wave, fever, hot weather, temperature, incandescence, tepidity, incalescence, sultriness, red heat, white heat, torridness, tropical heat, dog days*; see also **warmth, weather.** — *Ant.* COLD, frost, frigidity.

**2.** [Fervor] — *Syn.* ardor, passion, excitement; see **desire** 2, **enthusiasm** 1.

**3.** [Anger] — *Syn.* agitation, fury, ferocity; see **anger, rage** 2.

**4.** [A section of a race] — *Syn.* run, course, trial, qualifier; see **race** 3.

**5.** [Sources of heat] — *Syn.* flame, fire, radiation, radioactivity, atomic energy, solar energy; see also **energy** 3, **fire** 1.

**heat,** *v.* **1.** [To make hot] — *Syn.* cook, warm, fire, heat up, burn, enflame, inflame, kindle, enkindle, calcine, calefy, tepefy, subject to heat, put on the fire, make hot, make warm, calorify, smelt, scald, flush, carbonize, thaw, mull, boil, char, superheat, roast, chafe, seethe, oxidate, toast, oxidize, set fire to, melt, cauterize, sun, reheat, steam, incinerate, sear, singe, scorch, fuse, raise the temperature of, liquefy, gasify, fry, frizzle, use a blowtorch on, turn on the heat; see also **burn** 2, **cook, ignite.** — *Ant.* COOL, freeze, reduce the temperature.

**2.** [To become hot] — *Syn.* glow, warm up, rise in temperature, become fevered, become feverish, grow hot, incandesce, blaze, flame, flush, seethe, burst into flame, kindle, ignite, liquefy, gasify, thaw, swelter, perspire, reek, begin to pant, record a higher temperature, reach a higher thermal register; see also **boil** 1, **burn** 1, **sweat** 1.

**heated,** *modif.* **1.** [Warmed] — *Syn.* toasted, fired, cooked, broiled, fried, burnt, parched, scorched; see also **baked, burned** 1.— *Ant.* COOL, frozen, iced.
**2.** [Fervent] — *Syn.* fiery, ardent, avid; see **excited, passionate** 2.

**heater,** *n.* — *Syn.* radiator, auto heater, oil heater, gas heater, electric heater; see **furnace.**

**heathen,** *modif.* — *Syn.* idolatrous, pagan, unchristian, non-Jewish, non-Muslim, uncivilized, uncircumcised, unconverted, barbaric, amoral, godless, ungodly, atheistic, agnostic, irreligious, paganish, gentile, sunworshiping, ethnic, idolistic, henotheistic, polytheistic, demonolatrous, paynim, infidel, fetishistic, infidelic; see also **impious, primitive** 3.— *Ant.* CHRISTIAN, religious, moral.

**heathen,** *n.* — *Syn.* pagan, infidel, idolater, barbarian; see **barbarian** 1, **pagan, skeptic.**
*See Synonym Study at* PAGAN.

**heating,** *n.* — *Syn.* calefaction, steaming, boiling, scalding, roasting, broiling, melting, baking, warming, cooking, grilling; see also **heat** 1.— *Ant.* REFRIGERATION, freezing, cooling.

**heave,** *n.* — *Syn.* throw, hurl, fling, cast, wing, toss; see also **pitch** 2.

**heave,** *v.* **1.** [To raise laboriously] — *Syn.* lift, hoist, boost; see **raise** 1.
**2.** [To rise and fall] — *Syn.* rock, bob, pitch, go up and down, lurch, roll, reel, sway, swell, pant, palpitate, dilate, expand, billow, swirl, throb, waft, ebb and flow, wax and wane, undulate, puff, slosh, wash; see also **flow** 3, **toss** 2, **wave** 3, 4.— *Ant.* REST, lie still, quiet.
**3.** [To throw] — *Syn.* hurl, fling, cast; see **throw** 1.

**heaven,** *n.* **1.** [The sky; *often plural*] — *Syn.* welkin, empyrean, firmament, stratosphere, heights, atmosphere, azure, beyond, heavenly spheres, ether, the blue★, the wild blue yonder★; see also **air** 1, **sky.**
**2.** [The abode of the blessed] — *Syn.* Paradise, Elysian fields, Elysium, Great Beyond, Abode of the Dead, Olympus, Arcadia, Home of the Gods, Heavenly Home, God's Kingdom, Valhalla, Asgard, bliss, abodes of bliss, Zion, Holy City, Nirvana, welkin, inheritance of the saints, City Celestial, throne of God, Land of Beulah, Garden of Eden, Happy Isles, the New Jerusalem, afterworld, the divine abode, heavenly city, the city of God, abode of God and angels, our eternal home, the abode of saints, Kingdom of Heaven, next world, world to come, our Father's house, life beyond the grave, islands of the blessed, abode of spirits of the righteous after death, Fortunate Isles, happy hunting grounds★, the eternal rest★, Kingdom Come★, Abraham's bosom★, sweet by-and-by★, the hereafter★, the house not built with hands★; see also **paradise** 3.— *Ant.* HELL, underworld, inferno.
**3.** [A state of great comfort] — *Syn.* bliss, felicity, harmony; see **happiness** 2.
**4.** [Supernatural power; *capital* H] — *Syn.* God Almighty, Providence, Divine Love; see **god.**
**move heaven and earth** — *Syn.* do all one can do, exert the most influence, do one's best; see **try** 1.

**heavenly,** *modif.* **1.** [Concerning heaven] — *Syn.* paradisiacal, celestial, supernal; see **angelic, divine** 1, **holy** 1.
**2.** [★Much approved of or liked] — *Syn.* blissful, sweet, enjoyable; see **excellent, pleasant** 1, 2.

**heavily,** *modif.* — *Syn.* laboriously, tediously, weightily, massively, ponderously, dully, gloomily, with difficulty, wearily, dejectedly, profoundly, densely; see also **gradually, slowly.** — *Ant.* LIGHTLY, gently, easily.

**heaviness,** *n.* — *Syn.* burden, denseness, ballast; see **density** 1, **mass** 1, **weight** 1.

**heavy,** *modif.* **1.** [Weighty] — *Syn.* weighty, bulky, massive, cumbersome, unwieldy, ponderous, huge, overweight, top-heavy, of great weight, burdensome, portly, weighty, cumbrous, stout, big, hard to lift, hard to carry, dense, elephantine, fat, substantial, ample, corpulent, abundant, beefy★, hefty★, chunky★; see also **large** 1. — *Ant.* LIGHT, buoyant, feather-light.
**2.** [Viscous] — *Syn.* dense, viscid, syrupy; see **thick** 3.
**3.** [Burdensome] — *Syn.* troublesome, oppressive, vexatious; see **difficult** 1, **disturbing, onerous** 1.
**4.** [Dull] — *Syn.* listless, slow, apathetic; see **dull** 6, **indifferent** 1.
**5.** [Gloomy] — *Syn.* dejected, cloudy, overcast; see **dark** 1, **dismal** 1, **sad** 2.
**6.** [Difficult] — *Syn.* complicated, troublesome, knotty; see **complex** 2, **confused** 2, **difficult** 2, **obscure** 1.
**7.** [Soggy] — *Syn.* inedible, damp, sodden; see **indigestible, wet** 1.
**hang heavy** — *Syn.* pass tediously, go slowly, be tedious; see **drag** 2.

**SYN.** — **heavy** implies relatively great density, quantity, intensity, etc. and figuratively connotes a pressing down on the mind, spirits, or senses [*heavy* water, *heavy*-hearted]; **weighty** suggests heaviness as an absolute rather than a relative quality and figuratively connotes great importance or influence [a *weighty* problem]; **ponderous** applies to something that is very heavy because of size or bulk and figuratively connotes a labored or dull quality [a *ponderous* dissertation]; **massive** stresses largeness and solidity rather than heaviness and connotes an impressiveness due to great size [*massive* structures]; **cumbersome** implies a heaviness and bulkiness that makes for awkward handling and, in extended use, connotes unwieldiness [*cumbersome* formalities]

**heavy-handed,** *modif.* **1.** [Strict] — *Syn.* oppressive, harsh, coercive; see **cruel** 2, **severe** 2.
**2.** [Awkward] — *Syn.* clumsy, inept, unskillful; see **awkward** 1.

**heavy-hearted,** *modif.* — *Syn.* forlorn, cheerless, melancholy; see **sad** 1, **sorrowful.**

**heckle,** *v.* — *Syn.* bait, badger, taunt, harass; see **bait** 2, **bother** 2, **ridicule.**
*See Synonym Study at* BAIT.

**hectic,** *modif.* — *Syn.* frenetic, excited, rambunctious, tumultuous, boisterous, restless; see also **confused** 2, **disordered.**

**hector,** *v.* — *Syn.* browbeat, bully, nag; see **bait** 2, **bother** 2.
*See Synonym Study at* BAIT.

**hedge,** *n.* — *Syn.* fence, hedgerow, thornbush, shrubbery, enclosure, boundary, bushes, thicket, hurdle, obstacle, windbreak, quickset (British); see also **bush** 1, **plant.**
Shrubs and plants used for hedges include: boxwood, box, holly, Russian privet, Japanese privet, California privet, mock privet, jasmine box, hawthorn, hedge thorn, Osage orange, honey locust, Russian olive, rose, honeysuckle, white willow, hedge laurel, myrtle, dogrose, juniper, Glastonbury thorn, wait-a-bit thorn, Washington thorn, furze, broom, gorse, yucca, prickly pear cactus, ocatilla cactus, organ-pipe cactus, forsythia, lilac, azalea, camellia, hibiscus, oleander, rhododendron, spirea, hydrangea, barberry.

**hedonism,** *n.* — *Syn.* sensualism, gratification, debauchery, epicureanism; see **enjoyment** 2, **indulgence** 3.

**hedonist,** *n.* — *Syn.* sensualist, libertine, profligate, pleasure-lover, thrill-seeker, Sybarite, voluptuary, eudaemonist, epicurean, epicure, gourmand, roué, rake, debauchee, Sardanapalus, Lucullus; see also **glutton, lecher.**

**heed,** *v.* — *Syn.* pay attention to, notice, be aware; see **regard** 1, **see** 3.

**heedful,** *modif.* — *Syn.* attentive, discreet, conscientious; see **careful, observant** 2.

**heedless,** *modif.* — *Syn.* thoughtless, negligent, inconsiderate; see **careless** 1, **rash.**

**heel,** *n.* **1.** [Hind part of the foot] — *Syn.* hock, spur, hind toe, Achilles' tendon; see also **foot** 2.
**2.** [The portion of the shoe under the heel, sense 1] — *Syn.* lift, heelpiece, wedgie.
Varieties of heels include: French, military, Cuban, low, high, spike, sensible, rubber, leather, plastic, wooden, stacked, spring, wedge; see also **bottom** 1, **foundation** 2.
**3.** [An object resembling a heel] — *Syn.* crust, spur, base, after-end, cyma reversa; see also **bottom** 1, **end** 4.
**4.** [*A worthless individual] — *Syn.* scamp, skunk, trickster; see **rascal.**
**at heel** — *Syn.* close behind, in back of, behind; see **following.**
**cool one's heels★** — *Syn.* be kept waiting, loiter, linger; see **wait** 1.
**down at the heel(s)** — *Syn.* shabby, seedy, rundown; see **worn** 2.
**kick up one's heels** — *Syn.* be lively, have fun, enjoy oneself; see **play** 1, 2.
**on the heels of** — *Syn.* close behind, in back of, behind; see **following.**
**out at the heel(s)** — *Syn.* shabby, seedy, rundown; see **worn** 2.
**show one's heels** — *Syn.* run away, flee, take flight; see **escape.**
**take to one's heels,** — *Ant.* run away, flee, take flight; see **escape.**
**turn on one's heel** — *Syn.* turn around, reverse, shift; see **turn** 1, 2.

**heel,** *v.* — *Syn.* follow, stay by one's heel, attend; see **obey** 1.

**hefty,** *modif.* — *Syn.* strong, husky, sturdy, stout, heavy, beefy, strapping, bulky, muscular, hearty, substantial, massive; see also **strong** 1.

**hegemony,** *n.* — *Syn.* dominion, authority, leadership; see **administration** 1, **command** 2, **power** 2.

**hegira,** *n.* — *Syn.* flight, fleeing, exodus; see **departure** 1, **escape** 1, **journey, retreat** 1.

**heifer,** *n.* **1.** [A young cow] — *Syn.* yearling, springer, stirk (British); see **animal** 1, **calf, cow.**
**2.** [*A girl] — *Syn.* maid, lass, young thing★, filly★; see **girl** 1.

**height,** *n.* **1.** [Altitude] — *Syn.* altitude, elevation, extent upward, pitch, prominence, loftiness, highness, perpendicular distance, angular measurement, upright distance, tallness, stature; see also **expanse, extent, length** 2. — *Ant.* depth, BREADTH, width.
**2.** [Climax] — *Syn.* crowning point, end, crisis; see **climax, maximum, top** 1.
**3.** [An eminence] — *Syn.* rise, slope, alp; see **hill, mountain** 1.

---

*SYN.* — **height** refers to distance from bottom to top /a figurine four inches in *height*/ or to distance above a given level /he dropped it from a *height* of ten feet/; **altitude** and **elevation** refer especially to distance above a given level (usually the surface of the earth) and generally connote great distance /the *altitude* of an airplane,

the *elevation* of a mountain/; **stature** refers especially to the height of a human being standing erect /he was short in *stature*/

---

**heighten,** *v.* **1.** [Increase] — *Syn.* sharpen, redouble, emphasize; see **increase** 1, **intensify, strengthen.**
**2.** [Raise] — *Syn.* uplift, elevate, lift; see **raise** 1.
*See Synonym Study at* INTENSIFY.

**heinous,** *modif.* — *Syn.* atrocious, horrendous, monstrous; see **cruel** 1, **frightful** 1, **outrageous, wicked** 2.
*See Synonym Study at* OUTRAGEOUS.

**heir,** *n.* — *Syn.* scion, inheritor, heir presumptive, future possessor, legal heir, heir apparent, successor, descendent, one who inherits, heiress, beneficiary, heir expectant, heir general, heir at law, coheir, inheritor, grantee, devisee, crown prince. — *Ant.* predecessor, incumbent, parent.

**heiress,** *n.* — *Syn.* female inheritor, crown princess, inheritress, inheritrix, wealthy girl, debutante; see also **heir.**

**heirloom,** *n.* — *Syn.* inheritance, legacy, heritage, patrimony, family treasure, antique, bequest, birthright, reversion; see also **gift** 1.

**held,** *modif.* — *Syn.* grasped, controlled, occupied, guarded, taken, gripped, clutched, defended, adhered, stuck, detained, sustained, believed; see also **retained** 1. — *Ant.* released, FREED, lost.

**held over,** *v.* — *Syn.* returned, presented again, continued, retold; see **repeated** 1.

**held up,** *modif.* **1.** [Robbed] — *Syn.* assaulted, shot at, beaten; see **attacked.**
**2.** [Postponed] — *Syn.* withheld, put off, delayed; see **postponed.**

**hell,** *n.* **1.** [Place of the dead, especially of the wicked dead; *often capital H*] — *Syn.* underworld, inferno, place of departed spirits, the lower world, the grave, infernal regions, Sheol, Hades, Tartarus, Gehenna, abyss, realm of Pluto, Tophet, Styx, Acheron, Dis, Cocytus, Avernus, Abaddon, Satan's Kingdom, abode of the damned, abode of the dead, everlasting fire, perdition, purgatory, limbo, Erebus, nether world, Pandemonium, Avichi, hell-fire, Malebolge, bottomless pit, perdition, hellfire, lake of fire and brimstone, place of the lost, place of torment, habitation of fallen angels, blue blazes★, Halifax★, Hoboken★, hot place★, you-know-where★, the hereafter★. — *Ant.* HEAVEN, earth, paradise.
**2.** [A condition of torment] — *Syn.* trial, hellfire, ordeal; see **crisis, difficulty** 1, 2, **emergency.**
**be hell on★** — *Syn.* be painful for, be difficult to, be harsh with; see **abuse** 1.
**catch** or **get hell★** — *Syn.* get into trouble, be scolded, receive punishment; see **get it** 2.
**for the hell of it★** — *Syn.* for no reason, for the fun of it, playfully; see **lightly** 1.

**Hellenic,** *modif.* **1.** [Greek] — *Syn.* Grecian, Athenian, Attic, pan-Hellenic, Ionian, Doric, Spartan.
**2.** [Refined] — *Syn.* cultured, balanced, well-proportioned; see **ancient** 2, **classical** 2.

**Hellenist,** *n.* — *Syn.* Greek scholar, classicist, philosopher; see **professor, scholar** 2.

**hellish,** *modif.* **1.** [Concerning hell] — *Syn.* Stygian, Tartarean, Hadean, chthonian, devilish, fiery; see also **infernal** 1. — *Ant.* DIVINE, heavenly, blessed.
**2.** [Extremely bad or unpleasant] — *Syn.* diabolical, fiendish, destructive; see **wicked** 2.

**hello,** *interj.* — *Syn.* how do you do, greetings, welcome, how are you, good morning, good day, *ciao* (Italian), *bonjour* (French), *buenos días, buenas tardes, buenas noches* (all Spanish), *shalom* (Hebrew), hey, hi, howdy★, howdy-do★, hi-ya★, yo★, what's up★, what's happening★; put it there, how goes it; see also **greeting** 1. — *Ant.* GOODBYE, *au revoir* (French), *adiós* (Spanish).

**hell of a★**, *modif.* — *Syn.* helluva★, bad, awful, very; see **faulty, poor** 2.

**hell on★**, *modif.* — *Syn.* hard on, severe on, prejudiced against, strict with, exacting with, firm with; see **cruel** 1, 2, **firm** 5, **harmful.**

**helm,** *n.* — *Syn.* tiller, steering wheel, rudder, steerage, steering apparatus; see also **wheel** 1.

**helmet,** *n.* — *Syn.* headgear, hat, headpiece, mask, protective headgear.
Kinds of helmets include: crest, casque, sallet, burgonet, morion, armet, beaume, Roman, stephane, Greek, basinet, football, sun, pith, diver's, hard hat, trench, motorcycle, bicycle, fencing, batter's, batting, tin hat★, battle bowler★, chamber pot★, jerry★, steel derby★; see also **hat.**

**help,** *n.* **1.** [Assistance] — *Syn.* advice, cooperation, guidance; see **aid** 1.
**2.** [Employees] — *Syn.* aides, representatives, hired help; see **assistant, staff** 2.
**3.** [Physical relief] — *Syn.* maintenance, sustenance, nourishment; see **relief** 4, **remedy** 2.

**help,** *v.* **1.** [To aid] — *Syn.* aid, assist, abet, succor, uphold, advise, encourage, stand by, cooperate, intercede for, patronize, befriend, accommodate, work for, back up, maintain, sustain, prop, benefit, bolster, lend a hand, do a service, see through, do one's part, cheer, give a hand, be of use, come to the aid of, bail out, be of some help, help along, do a favor, promote, endorse, sanction, back, advocate, abet, stimulate, uphold, second, further, work for, stick up for★, take under one's wing★, go to bat for★, side with★, give a lift★, boost★, take in tow★, pitch in★, set to★; see also **support** 2. — *Ant.* OPPOSE, rival, combat.
**2.** [To assist in recovery] — *Syn.* attend, nourish, doctor★; see **heal** 1, **nurse, revive** 2, **treat** 3.
**3.** [To serve at table] — *Syn.* wait on, accommodate, tend to; see **serve** 4.
**4.** [To improve] — *Syn.* better, correct, ease; see **improve** 1.

**cannot help but** — *Syn.* be compelled to, be obliged to, cannot fail to, have to; see **must.**

**cannot help oneself** — *Syn.* be compelled to, have a need to, be the victim of circumstance, be the victim of habit; see **must.**

**so help me God** — *Syn.* as God is my witness, by God, I swear; see **oath** 1.

---

**SYN.** — **help** is the simplest and strongest of these words meaning to supply another with whatever is necessary to accomplish his or her ends or relieve his or her wants; **aid** and **assist** are somewhat more formal and weaker, **assist** esp. implying a subordinate role in the helper and less need for help /she *assisted* him in his experiments/; **succor** suggests timely help to one in distress /to *succor* a besieged city/

---

**helped,** *modif.* — *Syn.* aided, maintained, supported, advised, abetted, befriended, relieved, sustained, nursed, patronized, encouraged, assisted, accompanied, taken care of, subsidized, bolstered, upheld; see also **backed** 1. — *Ant.* impeded, hindered, HARMED.

**helper,** *n.* — *Syn.* apprentice, aide, secretary; see **assistant, supporter.**

**helpful,** *modif.* **1.** [Useful] — *Syn.* valuable, important, significant, crucial, essential, cooperative, symbiotic, serviceable, invaluable, profitable, advantageous, favor-

able, convenient, suitable, practical, pragmatic, operative, effectual, efficacious, of use, usable, accessible, applicable, conducive, utilitarian, improving, bettering, of service, serendipitous, all-purpose, desirable, instrumental, contributive, good for, to one's advantage, at one's command; see also **effective, necessary** 1. — *Ant.* USELESS, ineffective, impractical.
**2.** [Curative] — *Syn.* healthy, salutary, restorative; see **healthful, remedial.**
**3.** [Obliging] — *Syn.* accommodating, considerate, neighborly; see **kind** 1.

**helpfully,** *modif.* — *Syn.* usefully, beneficially, constructively, kindly, profitably, to the good, advantageously; see also **effectively, excellently.**

**helpfulness,** *n.* — *Syn.* assistance, convenience, help; see **aid** 1, **use** 2, **usefulness.**

**helping,** *modif.* — *Syn.* aiding, assisting, cooperating, collaborating, synergistic, working with, cooperating with, collaborating with, being assistant to, being consultant to, in cooperation with, in collaboration with, in combination with, contributing, accessory to, going along with, acceding to, in cahoots with, hand in glove with, thick as thieves, in the same boat with, up to one's ears in; see **helpful** 1, **practical.**

**helping,** *n.* — *Syn.* share, serving, plateful, order, course, portion, ration, piece, allowance; see also **food, meal** 2, **share.**

**helpless,** *modif.* **1.** [Dependent] — *Syn.* feeble, unable, invalid; see **dependent** 2, **disabled, weak** 1, 6.
**2.** [Incompetent] — *Syn.* incapable, unfit, inexpert; see **incompetent.**

**helplessness,** *n.* **1.** [Disability] — *Syn.* poor health, disorder, convalescence; see **illness** 1, **weakness** 1, 2.
**2.** [Incompetence] — *Syn.* incapacity, weakness, failure; see **inability.**

**helpmate,** *n.* — *Syn.* spouse, companion, aide; see **assistant, husband, mate** 3, **wife.**

**help oneself to,** *v.* — *Syn.* take, grab, pick, pick up; see **appropriate, seize** 1, 2, **steal.**

**helter-skelter,** *modif.* **1.** [Carelessly] — *Syn.* incautiously, unmindfully, rashly; see **carelessly.**
**2.** [Confused] — *Syn.* tumultuous, jumbled, cluttered, harum-scarum, higgeldy-piggeldy, pell-mell; see also **disorderly** 1, **irregular** 1, 4.

**hem,** *n.* — *Syn.* border, skirting, edging, piping, selvage; see also **edge** 1, **fringe** 2, **rim, trimming.**

**hem and haw,** *v.* — *Syn.* stutter, hesitate in speech, prevaricate, falter; see **hesitate, pause, stammer.**

**hemisphere,** *n.* — *Syn.* half of the globe, Western Hemisphere, Eastern Hemisphere, Northern Hemisphere, Southern Hemisphere, region, realm, territory; see also **earth** 1.

**hemorrhage,** *n.* — *Syn.* discharge, bleeding, issue, emission of blood, hemorrhea, bloody flux, effusion; see also **illness** 1, **injury** 1.

**hemp,** *n.* — *Syn.* burlap, sacking, jute; see **cloth.**

**hen,** *n.* — *Syn.* female chicken, pullet, brooder, setting hen; see **bird** 1, **chicken** 1, **fowl.**

**hence,** *modif.* **1.** [Therefore] — *Syn.* consequently, for that reason, on that account; see **so** 2, **therefore.**
**2.** [From now] — *Syn.* henceforth, henceforward, from here; see **hereafter.**
**3.** [Away] — *Syn.* forward, onward, out; see **away** 1, **from.**

**henceforth,** *n.* — *Syn.* from now on, hence, in the future; see **hereafter.**

**henchman,** *n.* — *Syn.* partner, advocate, aid, sidekick; see **associate, follower.**

**henna,** *modif.* — *Syn.* reddish-orange, reddish-brown, dyed with henna; see **brown, red.**

**henpeck,** *v.* — *Syn.* bully, suppress, intimidate, nag; see **bother** 2, **threaten** 1.

**henpecked,** *modif.* — *Syn.* dominated by one's wife, in fear of one's wife, subjected to nagging, browbeaten, intimidated, passive, constrained, compliant, in bondage, yielding, without freedom or independence, acquiescent, in subjection, subject, obedient, resigned, submissive, wife-ridden, docile, meek, cringing, unresisting, unassertive, led by the nose*, under one's thumb*, at one's beck and call*, tied to one's apron strings*, nagged*, in harness*; see also **dependent** 2, **subordinate, timid** 1, 2.

**herald,** *n.* — *Syn.* envoy, bearer, prophet, adviser; see **messenger, reporter, runner** 1.

**herald,** *v.* — *Syn.* proclaim, publicize, announce; see **advertise** 1, **declare** 1.

**heraldry,** *n.* — *Syn.* genealogy, scutcheon, heraldic device, coat of arms, ceremony, pomp; see also **ceremony** 2, **ostentation** 1.

**herb,** *n.*
Varieties of herbs include: *those used mainly in medicine*: foxglove, digitalis, belladonna, verbena, lemon verbena, vervain, coltsfoot, madder, baneberry, betony, herb-of-grace, herb-robert, leopard's-bane, thoroughwort, hyssop, hedge-hyssop, musk root, cinchona, chamomile, Solomon's seal, boneset, horehound, wormwood, valerian; *those used mainly in cookery*: ginger, peppermint, spearmint, thyme, summer savory, sage, garlic, winter savory, mustard, chicory, chives, chervil, sweet chervil, needle chervil, cardamom, coriander, cilantro, dill, bay leaf, cumin, marjoram, sweet basil, borage, peppergrass, parsley, anise, sweet cicely, cumin, fennel, caraway, rosemary, tarragon, oregano, wintergreen, Oswego tea, bergamot; see also **flavoring, pickle** 2, **plant, spice.**

**herbal,** *modif.* — *Syn.* herbaceous, verdant, grassy, vegetal, vegetative; see also **green** 2.

**herbalist,** *n.* — *Syn.* planter, botanist, greenskeeper, cultivator; see **gardener, scientist.**

**herbarium,** *n.* — *Syn.* garden, hothouse, nursery, botanical garden; see **greenhouse.**

**herculean,** *modif.* **1.** [Laborious] — *Syn.* strenuous, heavy, arduous; see **difficult** 1.
**2.** [Gigantic] — *Syn.* titanic, colossal, enormous; see **large** 1.

**herd,** *n.* **1.** [A number of animals] — *Syn.* flock, drove, pack, brood, swarm, lot, bevy, covey, gaggle, nest, brood, flight, school, clan; see also **gathering.**
**2.** [Disparaging term for common people] — *Syn.* rabble, mob, multitude, the masses, hoi polloi; see also **crowd** 1, **people** 3.

**herdsman,** *n.* — *Syn.* shepherd, herder, sheepherder, cowherd, goatherd, ranch hand, cattleman, range rider, buckaroo, vaquero, gaucho, cowhand*, cowpuncher*, saddle stiff*, wrangler*; see also **cowboy** 1, **rancher.**

**here,** *modif.* — *Syn.* in this place, hereabouts, in this direction, hither, on this spot, over here, up here, down here, right here, on hand, on board, on deck, in the face of, within reach or call.

**hereafter,** *modif.* — *Syn.* hence, henceforth, henceforward, from now on, after this, in the future, hereupon, in the course of time.

**hereafter,** *n.* — *Syn.* underworld, abode of the dead, the great beyond*; see **heaven** 2, **hell** 1.

**here and there,** *modif.* — *Syn.* scatteringly, patchily, sometimes; see **everywhere, scattered.**

**hereby,** *modif.* — *Syn.* at this moment, with these means, with this, thus, herewith.

**hereditable,** *modif.* — *Syn.* congenital, genetic, intrinsic; see **ancestral, inherent.**

**hereditary,** *modif.* — *Syn.* inherited, genetic, innate, paternal; see **ancestral.**
*See Synonym Study at* INNATE.

**heredity,** *n.* — *Syn.* inheritance, ancestry, hereditary transmission, hereditary succession, genetic makeup, Mendelism, Mendelianism, genetics, eugenics.

**herein,** *modif.* — *Syn.* included, in this place, here; see **within.**

**hereof,** *modif.* — *Syn.* concerning this, in this regard, on this subject; see **about** 2.

**heresy,** *n.* — *Syn.* nonconformity, dissidence, revisionism, protestantism, dissent, heterodoxy, sectarianism, doctrinal divergence, apostasy, agnosticism, schism, unorthodoxy, secularism; see also **blasphemy, paganism, sin.**

**heretic,** *n.* — *Syn.* schismatic, apostate, sectarian; see **cynic, pagan, skeptic.**

**heretical,** *modif.* — *Syn.* skeptical, unorthodox, apostate; see **atheistic.**

**heretofore,** *modif.* — *Syn.* since, until now, up to this time; see **before** 1, **formerly.**

**hereupon,** *modif.* — *Syn.* subsequently, hence, next; see **hereafter.**

**heritage,** *n.* **1.** [Inheritance] — *Syn.* inheritance, patrimony, legacy, birthright, heirship, ancestry, lot, right, dowry; see also **division** 2, **heredity, share.**
**2.** [Tradition] — *Syn.* convention, endowment, cultural inheritance; see **culture** 2, **custom** 2, **fashion** 2, **method** 2, **system** 2.

---

**SYN.** — **heritage,** the most general of these words, applies either to property passed on to an heir, or to a tradition, culture, etc. passed on to a later generation /our *heritage* of freedom/; **inheritance** applies to property, a characteristic, etc. passed on to an heir; **patrimony** strictly refers to an estate inherited from one's father, but it is also used of anything passed on from an ancestor; **birthright** applies to the rights one has because of being born in a certain family, nation, etc.

**hermaphrodite,** *n.* — *Syn.* bisexual, intersex, androgyne, epicene, transsexual, gynandroid.

**hermaphroditic,** *modif.* — *Syn.* hermaphrodite, androgynous, intersexual, transsexual.

**hermetic,** *modif.* **1.** [Closed] — *Syn.* sealed, shut, airtight; see **tight** 2.
**2.** [Magical] — *Syn.* alchemical, mystical, occult; see **magic, mysterious** 2, **secret** 1.

**hermit,** *n.* — *Syn.* holy man, ascetic, anchorite, cenobite, solitary, recluse, eremite, santon, Hieronymite, stylite, hermitress, Marabout, solitarian, pillarist, anchoress, pillar saint; see also **ascetic, misanthrope, skeptic.**

**hermitage,** *n.* **1.** [Isolation] — *Syn.* seclusion, withdrawal, self-exile; see **isolation, privacy.**
**2.** [A retreat] — *Syn.* shelter, asylum, monastery; see **retreat** 2.

**hero,** *n.* **1.** [One distinguished for action] — *Syn.* brave man, model, conqueror, victorious general, god, martyr, champion, paladin, ace, exemplar, prize athlete, master, man of distinguished valor, brave, warrior, demigod, saint, man of courage, man of mettle, lion, star, combatant, worthy, popular figure, great man, knight-errant, a man among men, man of the hour, man of the day, intrepid warrior, fearless soldier, dauntless flier, tin god*; see also **celebrity** 2, **idol** 2, **victor.**
**2.** [Principal male character in a literary composition] — *Syn.* protagonist, male lead, gallant, main actor, tra-

gedian, leading man, chief character, principal male character, antihero, matinee idol, heavy*, heavy lead*, Sir Galahad*, Romeo*; see also **actor** 1, **cast** 2, **star** 3.

**heroic,** *modif.* — *Syn.* valiant, valorous, fearless; see **brave** 1, **noble** 1, 2.

**heroine,** *n.* **1.** [A female hero] — *Syn.* courageous woman, champion, goddess, ideal, intrepid woman, demigoddess, woman of heroic character, woman of the hour, woman of the day; see also **celebrity** 2, **hero** 1, **idol** 2.
**2.** [Leading female character in a literary composition] — *Syn.* feminine lead, protagonist, leading lady, diva, prima donna, principal female character, female star, female lead, romantic interest, heart interest, girl; see also **actress, cast** 2, **star** 3.

**heroism,** *n.* — *Syn.* rare fortitude, valor, bravery; see **courage** 1, **strength** 1, **valor.**

**hesitancy,** *n.* **1.** [Doubt] — *Syn.* indecision, skepticism, irresolution; see **doubt** 2, **uncertainty** 1.
**2.** [Delay] — *Syn.* wavering, delaying, procrastination; see **delay** 1, **hesitation** 2, **pause** 1, 2.

**hesitant,** *modif.* **1.** [Doubtful] — *Syn.* vacillating, wavering, irresolute, indecisive; see **doubtful** 2, **reluctant.**
**2.** [Slow] — *Syn.* delaying, faltering, reluctant, disinclined; see **reluctant, slow** 2, **unwilling.**
*See Synonym Study at* RELUCTANT.

**hesitantly,** *modif.* — *Syn.* dubiously, falteringly, shyly; see **carefully** 2.

**hesitate,** *v.* — *Syn.* falter, stutter, fluctuate, vacillate, pause, stop, hold off, hold back, be dubious, be uncertain, flounder, alternate, straddle, hover, scruple, balk, ponder, think about, defer, stay one's hand, delay, wait, think it over, change one's mind, trim, recoil, shy at, demur, dally, seesaw back and forth, not know what to do, be irresolute, pull back, catch one's breath, weigh and consider, oscillate, hang back, swerve, tergiversate, debate, shift, shrink, wait, deliberate, linger, balance, equivocate, think twice*, drag one's feet*, hang off*, shilly-shally*, hem and haw*, blow hot and cold*, dillydally*, straddle the fence*, leave up in the air*, make bones about*, hang in the air*, do figure eights*; see also **stammer, waver.** — *Ant.* decide, RESOLVE, conclude.

**hesitating,** *modif.* **1.** [Doubtful] — *Syn.* skeptical, unsure, irresolute; see **doubtful** 2, **uncertain** 2.
**2.** [Slow] — *Syn.* delaying, wavering, dawdling; see **slow** 2.

**hesitation,** *n.* **1.** [Doubt] — *Syn.* equivocation, skepticism, irresolution; see **doubt** 2, **uncertainty** 2.
**2.** [Delay] — *Syn.* wavering, delaying, procrastination, dawdling, vacillation, fluctuation, oscillation, faltering; see also **delay** 1, **pause** 1, 2.

**heterodox,** *modif.* — *Syn.* heretical, skeptical, iconoclastic; see **atheistic, doubtful** 2.

**heterogeneous,** *modif.* — *Syn.* miscellaneous, variant, varied, nonhomogeneous, mingled, discordant, dissimilar, conglomerate, confused, inharmonious, eclectic, unrelated, variegated, amalgamate, diversified, multiplex, unallied, motley, unmatched, independent, mosaic, mongrel, incompatible, composite, jumbled, assorted, odd, job-lot*, mixy*; see also **complex** 1, **different** 1, 2, **mixed** 1, **unlike, various.**

**heterosexual,** *modif.* — *Syn.* attracted to the opposite sex, sexually normal, straight*, hetero*; see **female** 2, **male.**

**heterosexual,** *n.* — *Syn.* sexually normal male, sexually normal female, one attracted to the opposite sex, hetero*, straight*; see **man** 2, **woman** 1.

**hew,** *v.* — *Syn.* slit, slash, fell; see **cut** 1.

**hey***, *interj.* — *Syn.* you there, say, hey there, I say, hold on*, hold up*; see also **halt** 2, **hello, stop.**

**heyday,** *n.* — *Syn.* adolescence, bloom, prime of life; see **youth** 1.

**hiatus,** *n.* — *Syn.* interval, gap, break; see **blank** 1, **pause** 1, 2.

**hibernate,** *v.* — *Syn.* sleep through the winter, winter, vegetate, seclude oneself, immure oneself, keep out of society, lie dormant, lie torpid for the winter, hole up*; see also **sleep.**

**hidden,** *modif.* **1.** [Secret] — *Syn.* esoteric, clandestine, surreptitious; see **secret** 3, **obscure** 3, **unknown** 1.
**2.** [Concealed from view] — *Syn.* secreted, secluded, out of sight, private, covert, concealed, undercover, occult, arcane, in the dark, in a haze, in a fog, in darkness, masked, screened, veiled, cloaked, obscured, disguised, socked in, invisible, clouded, sealed, unobserved, blotted, in eclipse, impenetrable, unseen, eclipsed, unexposed, camouflaged, enshrouded, undetected, shrouded, shadowy, unknown, indiscernible, latent, buried, opaque, deep, unsuspected, inscrutable, unapparent, inexplicable, illegible, unintelligible, imperceptible, puzzling, unobserved, out of view, dim, recondite, overlaid, clandestine, subterranean, cloistered, suppressed, secured, hermetic, dark, inward, underground, unrevealed, undisclosed, imperceivable, inert, withheld, surreptitious, sequestered, underhand, unsearchable, kept in the dark*, under wraps*, kept dark*; see also **covered** 1, **isolated, obscure** 1, **withdrawn.** — *Ant.* OBVIOUS, open, apparent.
**3.** [Mysterious] — *Syn.* symbolical, abstruse, cryptic; see **magic** 1, **mysterious** 2, **secret** 1.

**hide,** *n.* **1.** [Skin of an animal] — *Syn.* pelt, fell, rawhide, pigskin, chamois, shammy, bearskin, goatskin, jacket, integument, sheepskin, sealskin, snakeskin, alligator skin, calfskin; see also **coat** 2, **fur, leather, skin.**
**2.** [*Human skin] — *Syn.* integument, epidermis, pellicle; see **skin.**
*See Synonym Study at* SKIN.

**neither hide nor hair** — *Syn.* nothing whatsoever, no indication, not at all; see **nothing.**

**hide,** *v.* **1.** [To conceal] — *Syn.* conceal, shroud, curtain, veil, camouflage, cover, mask, cloak, keep in ignorance, not give away, ensconce, screen, adumbrate, blot out, reserve, bury, suppress, withhold, keep underground, stifle, tuck away, keep secret, hush up, shield, shade, eclipse, not tell, lock up, confuse, put out of sight, put out of the way, hold back, keep from, secrete, dissemble, smuggle, cache, harbor, overlay, shadow, conceal from sight, keep out of sight, entomb, stow away, protect, couch, block out, obstruct the view of, hoard, store, seclude, closet, inter, put in concealment, hush, darken, obscure, render invisible, wrap, shelter, envelop, throw a veil over, keep in the dark*, keep under one's hat*, seal one's lips*, put the lid on*, plant*, put in lavender*, sink*, salt away*, drop*, dump*; see also **censor, disguise.** — *Ant.* EXPOSE, lay bare, uncover.
**2.** [To keep oneself concealed] — *Syn.* disguise oneself, change one's identity, cover one's traces, travel incognito, keep out of sight, go underground, lie in ambush, sneak, prowl, hermitize, burrow, skulk, avoid notice, lie in wait, hibernate, be concealed, stand aloof, hold oneself aloof, take refuge in a hiding place, lie low, conceal oneself, lie snug, lie close, rusticate, lie in ambush, lurk, shut oneself up, seclude oneself, lie hidden, keep out of the way, stay in hiding, retire from sight, hide out*, cover up*, duck*, keep shady*, lie hid*,

keep in the background*; see also **deceive, disappear, sneak.**

---

*SYN.* — **hide**, the general word, refers to the putting of something in a place where it will not easily be seen or found /the view is *hidden* by the billboard/; **conceal**, a somewhat formal equivalent for **hide**, more often connotes intent /to *conceal* one's face, motives, etc.;/ **secrete** and **cache** suggest a careful hiding in a secret place /they *secreted*, or *cached*, the loot in the cellar/, but **cache** now often refers merely to a storing for safekeeping /let's *cache* our supplies in the cave/; **bury** implies a covering for, or as if for, concealment /to *bury* treasure, they were *buried* in paperwork/

---

**hidebound**, *modif.* — *Syn.* unchangeable, traditional, stubborn; see **conservative, dogmatic** 2, **obstinate** 1, **prejudiced.**

**hide one's head**, *modif.* — *Syn.* be ashamed, hang one's head, be embarrassed about, crawl; see **apologize, regret.**

**hideous**, *modif.* **1.** [Extremely ugly] — *Syn.* ghastly, grisly, frightful; see **ugly** 1.
**2.** [Shocking] — *Syn.* repulsive, hateful, revolting; see **frightful** 1, **offensive** 2.

**hideout**, *n.* — *Syn.* lair, den, hermitage; see **refuge** 1, **retreat** 2, **sanctuary** 2, **shelter.**

**hiding**, *modif.* — *Syn.* concealing, masking, screening, covering, going underground, veiling, suppressing, cloaking, in ambush, in concealment, out of sight. — *Ant.* OBVIOUS, in plain view, in evidence.

**hierarchy**, *n.* — *Syn.* ministry, regime, theocracy, chain of command, pecking order; see also **authority** 3, **bureaucracy** 1, **government** 1, 2.

**hieroglyph**, *n.* — *Syn.* pictograph, code, cryptograph; see **symbol.**

**high**, *modif.* **1.** [Tall] — *Syn.* towering, gigantic, big, colossal, tremendous, great, giant, huge, formidable, immense, lank, lanky, long, sky-scraping, steep*, sky-high*; see also **large** 1. — *Ant.* SHORT, diminutive, undersized.
**2.** [Elevated] — *Syn.* lofty, uplifted, upraised, soaring, aerial, high-reaching, flying, hovering, overtopping, beetling, jutting, cloud-swept*; see also **above** 1, **raised** 1. — *Ant.* LOW, depressed, underground.
**3.** [Exalted] — *Syn.* eminent, leading, powerful; see **distinguished** 2, **important** 2, **noble** 1, 2.
**4.** [Important] — *Syn.* essential, chief, crucial; see **important** 1, **necessary** 1.
**5.** [Expensive] — *Syn.* high-priced, costly, precious; see **expensive.**
**6.** [To an unusual degree] — *Syn.* great, extraordinary, special; see **unusual** 1, 2.
**7.** [Shrill] — *Syn.* piercing, sharp, penetrating; see **loud** 1, **shrill.**
**8.** [*Drunk] — *Syn.* intoxicated, tipsy, inebriated; see **drunk.**
**9.** [*Under the influence of drugs] — *Syn.* drugged, stoned*, hopped-up*, freaked-out*, wasted*, spaced out*, tuned-in*, turned-on*, potted*, on a trip*, tripping*, tripped-out*, hyped-up*, psyched*.
**on high** — *Syn.* high in position, up in space, in heaven; see **above** 1.

**high and dry***, *modif.* — *Syn.* marooned, stranded, left helpless; see also **abandoned, dry** 1.

**high and low**, *modif.* — *Syn.* in every nook and cranny, in all possible places, exhaustively; see **completely, everywhere.**

**high and mighty**, *modif.* — *Syn.* pompous, vain, conceited; see **egotistic** 2.

**highball**, *n.* — *Syn.* cocktail, beverage, alcoholic drink, long drink; see **cocktail, drink** 2.

**highborn**, *modif.* — *Syn.* patrician, aristocratic, lordly; see **noble** 1, 2, 3.

**higher**, *modif.* — *Syn.* taller, more advanced, superior to, over, larger than, ahead, surpassing, more towering, bigger, greater; see also **above** 1, **beyond.** — *Ant.* smaller, SHORTER, inferior.

**highest**, *modif.* — *Syn.* topmost, superlative, supreme, maximal, most, top-notch, top, overmost, apical, maximum, head, preeminent, capital, chief, paramount, tiptop, zenithal, crown; see also **best** 1, **principal.**

**high-flown**, *modif.* — *Syn.* extravagant, pretentious, haughty, high-sounding, grandiloquent; see also **egotistic** 2.

**high-handed**, *modif.* — *Syn.* oppressive, arbitrary, overbearing; see **autocratic** 1, **severe** 2.

**highland**, *n.* — *Syn.* uplands, plateau, high country; see **mountain** 1, **ridge** 2.

**highly**, *modif.* — *Syn.* extremely, profoundly, deeply; see **very.**

**high-minded**, *modif.* — *Syn.* honorable, conscientious, ethical; see **decent** 2, **honest** 1, **noble** 1, 2.

**highness**, *n.* **1.** [Quality of being high] — *Syn.* length, tallness, loftiness; see **height** 1.
**2.** [Term of respect, usually to royalty; *often capital*] — *Syn.* majesty, lordship, ladyship, excellency, honor, sire, grace, reverence, worship; see also **royalty.**

**high on the hog***, *modif.* — *Syn.* extravagantly, expensively, beyond one's means; see **wastefully.**

**high-pressure**, *modif.* — *Syn.* forceful, potent, compelling; see **powerful** 1.

**high-pressure***, *v.* — *Syn.* plead, adjure, ask; see **urge** 2.

**high-priced**, *modif.* — *Syn.* costly, precious, extravagant; see **expensive**

**high school**, *n.* — *Syn.* public school, secondary school, preparatory school, *lycée* (French), *Gymnasium, Realschule* (both German), Latin school, private academy, military school, upper grades, trade school, seminary, middle school, junior high school, intermediate school, vocational school, high*, junior high*, prep school*; see also **academy** 1, **school** 1.

**high-sounding**, *modif.* — *Syn.* artificial, pompous, ostentatious; see **egotistic** 2.

**high-speed**, *modif.* — *Syn.* swift, rapid, quick; see **fast** 1.

**high-spirited**, *modif.* — *Syn.* daring, dauntless, reckless; see **brave** 1, **valiant** 1.

**high-strung**, *modif.* — *Syn.* nervous, tense, impatient; see **excitable, restless** 1.

**high-toned**, *modif.* **1.** [High-pitched] — *Syn.* raucous, sharp, piercing; see **loud** 1, **shrill.**
**2.** [*Dignified] — *Syn.* grand, noble, righteous, upper-class; see **cultured, dignified, refined** 2.

**highway**, *n.* — *Syn.* roadway, parkway, superhighway, freeway, turnpike, thruway, expressway, interstate, interstate highway, motorway (British), dual carriageway (British), limited access highway, toll road, skyway, post road, state highway, national highway, *Autobahn* (German); two-lane highway, four-lane highway, six-lane highway, etc.; see also **road** 1.

**highwayman**, *n.* — *Syn.* bandit, outlaw, thief; see **criminal, robber.**

**high, wide, and handsome***, *modif.* — *Syn.* extravagantly, expansively, without restraint; see **widely** 1.

**hijack**, *v.* — *Syn.* highjack, skyjack, commandeer, privateer, capture; see **seize** 2.

**hijacker,** *n.* — *Syn.* pirate, skyjacker, carjacker, terrorist, kidnapper.

**hike,** *n.* — *Syn.* tramp, trip, backpack, tour, trek, excursion, ramble; see also **journey, walk** 3.

**hike,** *v.* **1.** [To tramp] — *Syn.* take a hike, tour, explore; see **travel** 2, **walk** 1.
**2.** [*To raise] — *Syn.* lift, advance, pull up; see **increase** 1.

**hiking,** *modif.* — *Syn.* tramping, hitchhiking, backpacking, rambling, wandering, exploring; see also **marching, walking.**

**hilarious,** *modif.* — *Syn.* amusing, lively, witty; see **entertaining, funny** 1.

**hilarity,** *n.* — *Syn.* play, amusement, excitement; see **entertainment** 1, **fun, laugh.**

**hill,** *n.* — *Syn.* mound, knoll, hillock, butte, mesa, bluff, promontory, precipice, cliff, range, rising ground, headland, monadnock, upland, hummock, mount, downgrade, inclination, descent, ascent, slant, grade, incline, eminence, height, dune, highland, rise, helicline, *kopje* (South African), *tope* (Hindu), foothill, chine, spine, barrow, steep, down, fell, tumulus, climb, elevation, protuberance, ridge, heap, acclivity, hillside, talus, upgrade, hilltop, tor, vantage point, pitch, swell, declivity, knap, gradient, Acropolis, hold, summit, esker, kop; see also **mountain** 1.

**hillside,** *n.* — *Syn.* grade, gradient, acclivity; see **hill.**

**hilltop,** *n.* — *Syn.* peak, acme, elevation; see **height** 1, **hill, top** 1.

**hilly,** *modif.* — *Syn.* bumpy, uneven, undulating, rolling, rangy, steep, sloping, craggy, rocky, broken, rugged, precipitous; see also **abrupt** 1, **irregular** 4, **mountainous, rough** 1. — *Ant.* LEVEL, even, regular.

**hilt,** *n.* — *Syn.* hold, handhold, grip; see **handle** 1.

**hind,** *modif.* — *Syn.* rear, hindmost, after; see **back.**

**hinder,** *v.* — *Syn.* impede, obstruct, interfere with, check, retard, fetter, block, thwart, bar, clog, encumber, burden, cripple, handicap, cramp, preclude, inhibit, debar, shackle, interrupt, arrest, contravene, curb, resist, oppose, baffle, muzzle, balk, deter, hamper, stand in the way of, frustrate, nullify, checkmate, outwit, foil, entangle, stop, counteract, offset, neutralize, derange, tie up, hold up, repress, obviate, embarrass, delay, defer, postpone, keep back, set back, dam, close, box in, end, terminate, shut out, stay, choke, intercept, overreach, bottleneck, entrap, defeat, interpose, trammel, trap, antagonize, control, conflict with, deadlock, hold from, hold back, repulse, clash with, circumscribe, be an obstacle to, be an impediment to, repel, cross, exclude, limit, keep in bounds, shorten, hamstring, filibuster, go against, prohibit, withhold, forestall, hedge, stem, slow down, stall, bring to a standstill, forbid, cause to delay, pinion, disallow, smother, stanch, disappoint, spoil, throttle, countervail, gag, bind hand and foot, annul, silence, invalidate, vitiate, cancel out, hobble, constrict, cage, corner, detain, deprive, stalemate, taboo, suspend, render difficult, set against, pit against, put back, clip one's wings*, fly in the face of*, tie one's hands*, set one's face against*, get in the way of*, hold up*, jam*, throw a monkey wrench into the works*, snafu*, scotch*, spike one's guns*, hang fire*, bog down*, stymie*, put the lid on*, hang up*, knock the bottom out of*, knock the props from under*; see also **prevent, restrain** 1. — *Ant.* HELP, assist, aid.

---

*SYN.* — **hinder** implies a holding back of something about to begin and connotes a thwarting of progress [*hindered* by a lack of education]; **obstruct** implies a retarding of passage or progress by placing obstacles in the way [to *obstruct* the passage of a bill by a filibuster]; **block** implies the complete, but not necessarily permanent, obstruction of a passage or progress [the road was *blocked* by a landslide]; **impede** suggests a slowing up of movement or progress by interfering with the normal action [a tourniquet *impedes* the circulation of the blood]; **bar** implies an obstructing as if by means of a barrier [he was *barred* from the club]

---

**hindmost,** *modif.* — *Syn.* final, terminal, concluding; see **last** 1.

**hindrance,** *n.* — *Syn.* obstacle, impediment, restraint; see **barrier, impediment** 1, **interference** 1.
*See Synonym Study at* IMPEDIMENT.

**Hindu,** *modif.* — *Syn.* Rajput, Sanskrit, Brahminic, East Indian.

**Hindu,** *n.* — *Syn.* Asian, Buddhist, Brahmin; see **Indian** 2.

**hinge,** *n.* — *Syn.* hook, pivot, juncture, articulation, link, elbow, ball-and-socket, knee, butt, lifting butt, strap, cross garnet, articulated joint, flap; see also **joint** 1.
Hinges include: gate, blind, T, flap, strap, loose-pin, backflap, hook-and-eye, skew, H, turnover, spring, fastjoint, rising, sliding.

**hinge,** *v.* — *Syn.* connect, add, couple; see **join** 1.

**hinged,** *modif.* — *Syn.* linked, coupled, put together; see **joined.**

**hint,** *n.* **1.** [An intimation] — *Syn.* allusion, inkling, insinuation, implication, reference, advice, observation, adumbration, reminder, communication, notice, information, announcement, inside information, tip, clue, implied warning, token, idea, omen, scent, cue, trace, whiff, iota, suspicion, notion, whisper, taste, evidence, reminder, memorandum, innuendo, prompter, signification, symptom, connotation, smattering, sign, wink, bare suggestion, glimmering, impression, denotation, supposition, tinge, vague knowledge, inference, prefigurement, premonition, broad hint, gentle hint, word to the wise, memorandum, mnemonic device, manifestation, foretoken, indirection, indication, slight knowledge, tip-off*, pointer*, dope*; see also **suggestion** 1.
**2.** [A guarded remark] — *Syn.* innuendo, whisper, reflection, aside, insinuation, admonition, sign, suggestion, mention; see also sense 1, **allusion, warning.**

**hint,** *v.* — *Syn.* touch on, refer to, allude to, intimate, apprise, inform, hint at, imply, infer, acquaint, remind, impart, bring up, recall, cue, prompt, insinuate, indicate, wink, broach, signify, foreshadow, advise, adumbrate, cause to remember, inform by indirection, make an allusion to, jog the memory, give a hint of, make indirect suggestion, suggest, give indirect information, make mention of, remark in passing, drop a hint, whisper, give an inkling of*, tip off*, put a bug in one's ear*, tip the wink*, slip the dope*; see also **mention, propose** 1, **refer** 2, **warn** 1. — *Ant.* HIDE, conceal, cover.
*See Synonym Study at* SUGGEST.

**hinted at,** *modif.* — *Syn.* signified, intimated, referred to; see **implied, suggested.**

**hip*,** *modif.* — *Syn.* aware, in the know, informed, unsquare, enlightened, *au courant* (French), groovy*, with it*, out of sight*, with the beat*, in the groove*, boss*, bad*, hep*, cool*, in*, too much*, fresh*, dope*; see also **modern** 1, **observant** 1.

**hip,** *n.* — *Syn.* haunch, side, hipbone, pelvis, beam*, hench*, ham*; see also **bone.**

**hipped*,** *modif.* — *Syn.* crazy about, doting on, foolish about; see **insane** 1, **stupid** 1.

**hippie\***, *modif.* — *Syn.* unorthodox, psychedelic, mod\*; see **radical** 2, **unconventional, unusual** 2.

**hippie,** *n.* — *Syn.* Bohemian, radical, dropout, protestor, demonstrator, nonconformist, dissenter, flower child\*, yippie\*, peacenik\*, hipster\*, longhair\*; see also **beatnik, radical.**

**hire,** *v.* **1.** [To employ] — *Syn.* engage, sign up, draft, obtain, secure, take into one's employ, enlist, give a job to, take on, give work to, give employment to, put to work, set to work, bring in, occupy, use, fill a position, appoint, delegate, authorize, retain, commission, promise, empower, book, utilize, select, pick, pledge, bespeak, contract, procure, fill an opening, find help, find a place for, exploit, make use of, use another's services, add to the payroll, carry\*, give someone a break\*; see also **approve** 1, **choose** 1. — *Ant.* discharge, DISMISS, fire.

**2.** [To let] — *Syn.* let, rent, lease, charter, contract for; see also **borrow** 1, **let** 2, **rent** 1.

---

*SYN.* — **hire**, in strict usage, means to get, and **let** means to give the use of something in return for payment, although **hire**, which is also applied to persons or their services, may be used in either sense *[to hire a hall, a worker, etc., rooms to let]*; **lease** implies the letting or the hiring of property (usually real property) by written contract; **rent** implies payment of a specific amount, often at fixed intervals, for hiring or letting a house, land, equipment, a vehicle, etc.; **charter** implies the hiring or leasing of a ship, bus, etc.

---

**hired,** *modif.* — *Syn.* contracted, signed up, given work; see **busy** 1, **employed, engaged** 3, **working.**

**hireling,** *n.* — *Syn.* hack, worker, aide; see **employee, laborer, worker.**

**hiring,** *n.* — *Syn.* chartering, leasing, letting, engaging, booking, contracting, employing.

**hiring hall,** *n.* — *Syn.* union hall, union employment office, employment office, labor office, labor temple.

**hirsute,** *modif.* — *Syn.* hairy, woolly, bearded, furry; see **hairy** 1, **shaggy.**

**hiss,** *n.* — *Syn.* buzz, sibilance, hissing, whisper; see **noise** 1.

**hiss,** *v.* **1.** [To make a hissing sound] — *Syn.* sibilate, fizz, seethe; see **buzz, sound** 1.

**2.** [To condemn] — *Syn.* boo, disapprove, shout down; see **censure, ridicule.**

**historian,** *n.* — *Syn.* history professor, recorder, annalist, archivist, chronicler, historiographer, writer of history, biographer; see **antiquarian, archaeologist.**

**historic,** *modif.* — *Syn.* well-known, celebrated, memorable; see **famous, important** 1.

**historical,** *modif.* — *Syn.* actual, authentic, factual, true, important in history, constituting history, archival, traditional, commemorated, chronicled; see **ancient** 2, **classical** 2, **old** 3, **past** 1.

**history,** *n.* **1.** [A narrative] — *Syn.* account, memoir, tale; see **story.**

**2.** [The systematic, documented account of the past] — *Syn.* annals, records, archives, recorded history, chronicle, historical knowledge, historical writings, historical evidence, historical development.

Specific divisions of the study of history include: local, state, national, American, United States, world, European, Asian, African, modern, medieval, classical, ancient, Roman, Greek, literary, cultural, intellectual; narrative, folk, ethnic, oral, genealogy; see also **record** 1, 2, **social science.**

**3.** [Past events] — *Syn.* antiquity, the past, the old days, ancient times, the good old days\*, ancient history\*; see also **antiquity** 3, **past** 1.

**make history** — *Syn.* accomplish, do something important, achieve, go down in history; see **succeed** 1.

**histrionic,** *modif.* — *Syn.* dramatic, melodramatic, artificial, theatrical; see **affected** 2.

**histrionics,** *n.* **1.** [Acting] — *Syn.* dramatics, showmanship, performing; see **acting, drama** 1, 2, **performance** 2.

**2.** [Affectation] — *Syn.* deceit, pretension, put-on\*; see **deception** 1, **pretense** 1.

**hit,** *modif.* — *Syn.* shot, struck, slugged, cuffed, slapped, smacked, pummeled, clouted, punched, boxed, slammed, knocked, beat, beaten, pounded, thrashed, spanked, banged, smashed, cudgeled, basted, slogged, smitten, tapped, rapped, whacked, thwacked, thumped, kicked, swatted\*, mugged\*, pasted\*, plastered\*, biffed\*, binged\*, poked\*, rocked\*, knocked out\*; see also **hurt.** — *Ant.* UNHURT, unscathed, untouched.

**hit,** *n.* **1.** [A blow] — *Syn.* slap, rap, punch; see **blow** 1.

**2.** [A popular success] — *Syn.* favorite, achievement, masterstroke, bestseller, sleeper, platinum record, gold record, succés fou (French), sellout, smash\*, knockout\*; see also **success** 2.

**3.** [In baseball, a batted ball that cannot be fielded] — *Syn.* base hit, single, two-base hit, double, three-base hit, triple, home run, wallop\*, bagger\*, wham\*; see also **run** 3, **score** 1.

**hit,** *v.* **1.** [To strike] — *Syn.* knock, beat, sock, slap, punch, punish, smite, thump, bump, hammer, strike down, bang, whack, thwack, jab, clap, tap, pat, dab, smack, kick at, pelt, flail, thrash, cuff, kick, rap, cudgel, clout, club, buffet, bat around, kick around, lay low, lash out at, not hold one's punches, hit at, hit out at, make a dent in, let have it, give a black eye, swing at, take a swing at, crack, squail, mug\*, pop\*, biff\*, hook\*, bash\*, bob\*, slug\*, nail\*, conk\*, paste\*, whomp\*, nail one on\*, let fly at\*, box off\*, ride roughshod over\*, box the ears\*, whang\*, hang a mouse on\*; see also **knock out.**

**2.** [To bump against] — *Syn.* jostle, butt, knock against, scrape, bump, run against, thump, collide with, bump into, meet head-on; see also **crash** 4.

**3.** [To fire in time; *said of an internal combustion motor*] — *Syn.* catch, respond, go, run, connect, function, hit on all fours\*; see also **operate** 2.

**4.** [In baseball, to hit safely] — *Syn.* make a hit, single, double, triple, hit safe\*, get on\*, rip a single\*, rip a double\*, rip a triple\*, blast one\*, make a homer\*; see also **score** 1.

**hit-and-run,** *modif.* — *Syn.* leaving illegally, leaving without offering assistance, fugitive, illegally departed; see **illegal, wicked** 2.

**hitch,** *n.* **1.** [A knot] — *Syn.* loop, noose, yoke; see **knot** 1, **tie** 1.

**2.** [A difficulty] — *Syn.* block, obstacle, tangle, glitch; see **catch** 4, **difficulty** 1, **impediment** 1.

**hitch,** *v.* **1.** [To harness] — *Syn.* yoke, tie up, strap, couple, lash, moor, chain, hook; see also **fasten** 1, **join** 1.

**2.** [To move with a jerk] — *Syn.* hobble, waggle, hop; see **limp, reel, totter** 2, **wobble.**

**hitchhike,** *v.* — *Syn.* take a lift, hitch, bum a ride, thumb a ride, thumb\*; see **ride** 1, **travel** 2.

**hither,** *modif.* — *Syn.* to, next, forward; see **near** 1, **toward.**

**hitherto,** *modif.* — *Syn.* until now, previously, heretofore; see **before** 1, **formerly.**

**hit it off\*,** *v.* — *Syn.* get on well, get along well, become friends, become friendly; see **agree, like** 1, 2.

**hit on** *or* **upon,** *v. — Syn.* realize, come upon, stumble on; see **discover, find** 1, **recognize** 1.

**hit or miss,** *modif. — Syn.* at random, uncertainly, scatteringly; see **irregularly, scattered, unevenly.**

**hit the hay\*,** *v. — Syn.* go to bed, go to sleep, retire, get some sleep; see **sleep.**

**hit the jackpot\*,** *v. — Syn.* win, be lucky, be well paid, strike it rich\*, hit paydirt\*, strike oil\*; see also **win** 1.

**hitting,** *modif.* **1.** [Striking] — *Syn.* slapping, beating, punishing, whipping, slamming, thumping, whacking, smacking, cuffing, clubbing, clouting.
**2.** [Firing smoothly; *said of an internal combustion engine*] — *Syn.* functioning, operating, going; see **running** 2, **working.**

**hit town\*,** *v. — Syn.* enter, approach, land; see **arrive** 1.

**hive,** *n. — Syn.* apiary, swarm, colony; see **beehive.**

**hoard,** *n. — Syn.* riches, treasure, cache; see **wealth** 1.

**hoard,** *v. — Syn.* store up, acquire, keep; see **accumulate** 1, **save** 3.

**hoarse,** *modif. — Syn.* grating, rough, uneven, harsh, raucous, discordant, gruff, strident, husky, throaty, thick, growling, croaking, cracked, ragged, guttural, gravelly, dry, piercing, whispering, blatant, breathy, scratching, absonant, indistinct, squawking, unmusical, jarring, rasping; see also **loud** 1, **shrill.** — *Ant.* sweet, PURE, mellifluous.

**hoary,** *modif. — Syn.* ancient, aged, antique; see **old** 1, 3.

**hoax,** *n. — Syn.* falsification, fabrication, deceit; see **deception** 2, **lie** 2, **trick** 1, 2.

**hobble,** *v.* **1.** [To restrict] — *Syn.* clog, fetter, shackle; see **hinder, restrain** 1.
**2.** [To move as though hobbled] — *Syn.* totter, dodder, halt; see **limp, stumble** 1.

**hobby,** *n. — Syn.* avocation, pastime, diversion, sideline, side interest, leisure-time activity, personal obsession, specialty, whim, fad, unremunerative occupation, favorite occupation, favorite pursuit, pet topic, fancy, caprice, relaxation, whimsy, labor of love, play, craze, *divertissement* (French), sport, amusement, quest, craft, fun, art, game, vagary; see also **distraction** 2, **entertainment** 2.

**hobgoblin,** *n. — Syn.* imp, ghost, ogre; see **bugbear, fairy** 1.

**hobnob,** *v. — Syn.* fraternize, consort with, associate with; see **associate** 1, **join** 2.

**hobo,** *n. — Syn.* tramp, vagrant, vagabond, wanderer; see **beggar** 1, **tramp** 1.
*See Synonym Study at* TRAMP.

**hock\*,** *v. — Syn.* pawn, sell temporarily, pledge, deposit; see **pawn, sell** 1.

**hockey,** *n. — Syn.* ice hockey, field hockey, hockey game, shinny\*, block-and-bunt\*; see also **game** 1, **sport** 3.

**hocus-pocus,** *n.* **1.** [Charm] — *Syn.* incantation, spell, chant; see **magic** 1.
**2.** [A trick] — *Syn.* fraud, hoax, flimflam\*; see **deception** 1, **trick** 1.

**hod,** *n. — Syn.* trough, tray, pail, scuttle; see **bucket, container.**

**hodgepodge,** *n. — Syn.* jumble, combination, mess; see **mixture** 1.

**hoe,** *n. — Syn.* digger, scraper, scuffle hoe, warren hoe, garden hoe, grub hoe, weeding hoe, wheel hoe, cultivator; see also **tool** 1.

**hog,** *n.* **1.** [A pig] — *Syn.* swine, sow, boar, shoat, razorback, wild boar, wart hog, babirusa, truffle pig, peccary, collared peccary, white-lipped peccary, porker\*, piggy\*, pork\*, cob-roller\*, scrub\*, runt\*; see also **animal** 1.
Breeds of hogs include: Duroc, Duroc-Jersey, Hampshire, Berkshire, Gloucester Old Spot, Landrace, Chester White, Poland China, Tamworth, Lincolnshire, Cumberland, Essex, Wessex Saddleback, large white, Large Yorkshire, miniature pig, Vietnamese potbellied pig.
**2.** [A person whose habits resemble a pig's] — *Syn.* pig, selfish person, filthy person; see **glutton, slob.**

**go (the) whole hog\*** — *Syn.* go all the way, do something fully, complete something; see **achieve** 1.

**high on the hog\*** — *Syn.* luxurious, extravagant, rich; see **expensive.**

**hoggish,** *modif.* **1.** [Squalid] — *Syn.* smelly, foul, unclean; see **dirty** 1, **squalid.**
**2.** [Greedy] — *Syn.* grasping, rapacious, gluttonous; see **greedy** 2.

**hogtie,** *v. — Syn.* fetter, shackle, tie up; see **bind** 1.

**hogwash,** *n.* **1.** [Garbage] — *Syn.* scum, debris, swill, refuse; see **trash** 1, 3.
**2.** [Nonsense] — *Syn.* foolishness, absurdity, ridiculousness; see **nonsense** 1.

**hog-wild\*,** *modif. — Syn.* extravagant, outlandish, unrestrained; see **extreme** 2, **unruly, wild** 1.

**hoi polloi** (Greek), *n. — Syn.* the masses, proletariat, crowd; see **people** 3.

**hoist,** *n. — Syn.* crane, lift, derrick; see **elevator** 1.

**hoist,** *v. — Syn.* lift, raise, pull up, winch; see **raise** 1.
*See Synonym Study at* LIFT.

**hold,** *n. — Syn.* grasp, clutch, clasp; see **grip** 1, 2.

**catch hold of** — *Syn.* take, grasp, catch; see **seize** 1.

**get hold of** — *Syn.* **1.** take, grasp, catch; see **seize** 1.
**2.** get, acquire, receive; see **obtain** 1.

**lay** *or* **take hold of** — *Syn.* take, grasp, get; see **seize** 1.

**no holds barred\*** — *Syn.* without rules, unrestricted, unrestrained; see **unlimited.**

**hold,** *v.* **1.** [To have in one's grasp] — *Syn.* grasp, grip, clutch, carry, embrace, clench, cling to, detain, enclose, restrain, confine, check, take hold of, contain, hold down, hold onto, not let go, never let go, hang on, have a firm hold of, squeeze, press, secure, hug, handle, fondle, have in hand, keep in hand, keep fast, retain, keep, keep a grasp on, maintain a grasp on, clasp, hold fast, hold tight, keep a firm hold on, tie, keep close, unite, palm, take, catch, clinch, fasten upon, cradle, have an iron grip on\*, hang on to\*; see also **seize** 1. — *Ant.* let fall, RELEASE, let go.
**2.** [To have in one's possession] — *Syn.* keep, retain, possess; see **maintain** 3, **own** 1.
**3.** [To remain firm] — *Syn.* resist, persevere, keep staunch; see **continue** 1, **endure** 2.
**4.** [To adhere] — *Syn.* attach, cling, take hold; see **adhere, fasten** 1, **stick** 1.
**5.** [To be valid] — *Syn.* exist, continue, remain true, have bearing, be the case, endure, be in effect, operate, be in force; see also **be** 1. — *Ant.* STOP, expire, be out-of-date.
**6.** [To believe] — *Syn.* regard, aver, judge; see **believe** 1, **think** 1.
**7.** [To contain] — *Syn.* have the capacity for, accommodate, be equipped for; see **contain** 1, **include** 1.
**8.** [To support; *often used with up*] — *Syn.* sustain, brace, buttress, prop, lock, stay, shoulder, underpin, uphold, underprop, shore up, bear up, bolster up; see also **support** 1.
*See Synonym Study at* CONTAIN.

**hold back,** *v.* **1.** [To restrain] — *Syn.* inhibit, control, curb; see **check** 2, **prevent, restrain** 1.
**2.** [To refrain] — *Syn.* desist, hesitate, forbear; see **abstain, avoid.**

**hold down,** *v. — Syn.* fix, pin down, control; see **prevent, restrain** 1.

**holder,** *n.* **1.** [An instrument used for holding] — *Syn.* sheath, container, folder, holster, bag, sack, fastener, clip, handle, rack, arm, crank, knob, stem; see also **container, fastener.**

**2.** [An owner or occupant] — *Syn.* leaseholder, renter, dweller; see **owner, possessor, resident, tenant.**

**hold fast,** *v.* — *Syn.* clasp, lock, clamp; see **adhere, fasten** 1, **stick** 1.

**hold firm,** *v.* — *Syn.* retain, keep, preserve; see **maintain** 3.

**hold forth,** *v.* — *Syn.* speak, soliloquize, declaim, harangue; see **address** 2, **lecture.**

**hold high,** *v.* — *Syn.* exalt, observe, celebrate; see **admire** 1, **praise** 1.

**holding,** *modif.* — *Syn.* impeding, stopping, closing; see **block.**

**holdings,** *n.* — *Syn.* lands, possessions, security; see **estate** 2, **property** 1.

**hold off,** *v.* — *Syn.* be above, keep aloof, stave off; see **avoid, prevent.**

**hold office,** *v.* — *Syn.* be in office, direct, rule; see **command** 2, **govern, manage** 1.

**hold on,** *v.* — *Syn.* hang on, attach oneself to, cling to; see **seize** 1.

**hold oneself,** *v.* — *Syn.* stand up, carry oneself, walk; see **behave** 2, **stand** 1.

**hold one's horses\*,** *v.* — *Syn.* wait, be calm, keep one's head\*, restrain oneself; see **stop** 2, **wait** 1.

**hold one's own,** *v.* — *Syn.* keep one's advantage, stand one's ground, do well, keep up; see also **succeed** 1.

**hold one's tongue** *or* **one's peace,** *v.* — *Syn.* be silent, conceal, keep secret, not say a word; see also **hide** 1.

**holdout,** *n.* — *Syn.* obstructionist, adversary, die-hard, resister, objector, damper, killjoy, wet blanket\*, spoilsport\*; see also **resister.**

**hold out,** *v.* **1.** [To offer] — *Syn.* proffer, tempt with, grant; see **give** 1, **offer** 1.

**2.** [To endure] — *Syn.* suffer, hold on, withstand, stick to one's guns\*; see **continue** 1, **endure** 2.

**hold out for,** *v.* — *Syn.* persist, go on supporting, stand firmly for; see **continue** 1.

**holdover,** *n.* — *Syn.* remnant, relic, surplus; see **remainder.**

**hold over,** *v.* — *Syn.* do again, do over, show again, play over; see **redo, repeat** 1.

**hold the line,** *v.* — *Syn.* wait, be patient, be quiet; see **quiet down.**

**hold the road,** *v.* — *Syn.* track, cling to the road, hug the road, ride well, corner well; see **ride** 5, **travel** 2.

**hold together,** *v.* — *Syn.* attach, clip, cling; see **adhere, fasten** 1, **stick** 1.

**holdup,** *n.* — *Syn.* robbery, burglary, stick-up\*; see **crime** 2, **theft.**

**hold up,** *v.* **1.** [To show] — *Syn.* exhibit, raise high, elevate; see **display** 1.

**2.** [To delay] — *Syn.* stop, pause, interfere with; see **delay** 1, **hinder, interrupt** 2.

**3.** [To rob forcibly] — *Syn.* waylay, burglarize, steal from, mug; see **rob.**

**4.** [To support] — *Syn.* brace, prop, shoulder; see **hold** 8, **support** 1.

**hole,** *n.* **1.** [A perforation] — *Syn.* notch, puncture, slot, eyelet, keyhole, porthole, buttonhole, peephole, loophole, embrasure, crenel, air hole, stop, mousehole, window, crack, rent, split, tear, cleft, opening, fissure, gap, gash, rift, rupture, fracture, break, leak, nostril, *oeil-de-boeuf* (French), aperture, space, chasm, breach, slit, nick, cut, chink, scission, vent, incision, orifice, scissure,

spiracle, leak, interstice, vent hole, scupper, foramen, eye, rime, acupuncture; see also **sense** 2.

**2.** [A cavity] — *Syn.* crater, mouth, gorge, throat, gullet, orifice, aperture, cranny, foramen, manhole, dent, opening, depression, indentation, impression, corner, shell hole, pockmark, swimming hole, pocket, dimple, dip, void, lacuna, vacuum, drop, gulf, depth, pit, abyss, hollow, basin, chasm, vent, crevasse, trench, foxhole, mine, concavity, shaft, chamber, defile, scoop, valley, ravine, burrow, rift, fossa, cell, cistern, niche, alveolus, spider hole\*; see also **sense** 1.

**3.** [A cave] — *Syn.* burrow, den, lair, grotto, cavern, cove, tunnel, excavation, mound, passage, refuge, retreat, furrow, dugout, honeycomb, warren, covert, shelter; see also **sense** 2.

**4.** [\*Serious difficulty] — *Syn.* impasse, tangle, mess; see **crisis, difficulty** 1, **emergency.**

**5.** [In golf, a depression made for the ball] — *Syn.* drop, cup, pocket, first to 18th hole, pot\*, mocking cup\*.

**burn a hole in one's pocket** — *Syn.* entice, lure, attract; see **tempt.**

**in the hole\*** — *Syn.* broke, without money, in debt; see **poor** 1.

**make a hole in** — *Syn.* use up, consume, expend; see **spend** 1.

**pick holes in** — *Syn.* criticize, disprove, pick out errors in; see **censure.**

---

**SYN.** — **hole** is the general word for an open space in a thing and may suggest a depression in a surface or an opening from surface to surface [*a hole* in the ground, a *hole* in a sock]; **hollow** basically suggests an empty space within a solid body, whether or not it extends to the surface, but it may also be applied to a depressed place in a surface [*a wooded hollow*]; **cavity** is generally equivalent to **hole** or **hollow** and also has special application in formal and scientific usage [*the thoracic cavity*]; an **excavation** is a hollow made in or through ground by digging [*the excavations* at Pompeii]

---

**hole up\*,** *v.* — *Syn.* take cover, go into hiding, withdraw; see **hide** 2.

**holiday,** *n.* **1.** [A memorial day] — *Syn.* feast day, fiesta, saint's day, legal holiday, holy day, festival, fete, centennial, bicentennial, tercentenary, carnival, gala day, jubilee, red-letter day, fast day; see also **anniversary, celebration** 1, 2.

Common holidays in the United States include: New Year's Day, Martin Luther King's Birthday, Lincoln's Birthday, Valentine's Day, Washington's Birthday, Presidents' Day, St. Patrick's Day, Memorial Day, Independence Day, Fourth of July, Labor Day, Columbus Day, Halloween, Veterans Day, Armistice Day, Thanksgiving Day, Christmas Day.

Christian holidays include: Epiphany, Shrove Tuesday, Ash Wednesday, Palm Sunday, Maundy, Thursday, Passion Sunday, Good Friday, Easter, Ascension, Pentecost, Whitsunday, All Saint's Day, Christmas, Feast of the Nativity.

Jewish holidays include: Purim, Feast of Lots, Passover, Shavuot, Hebrew Pentecost, Feast of Weeks, Rosh Hashana, Jewish New Year, Yom Kippur, Day of Atonement, Sukkot, Feast of Tabernacles, Simhat Torah, Rejoicing of the Law, Hanukkah, Festival of Lights.

**2.** [A vacation] — *Syn.* weekend, time off, leave, day off; see **vacation.**

**holiness,** *n.* **1.** [Piety] — *Syn.* devoutness, humility, asceticism, saintliness, righteousness, godliness, beatitude, religiosity, blessedness, grace, reverence, faith, religiousness; see also **devotion, worship** 1.— *Ant.* EVIL, impiety, wickedness.

**2.** [Sanctity] — *Syn.* sanctification, venerableness, sacredness, unction, inviolability, divine protection; see also **consecration.** — *Ant.* SIN, blasphemy, profaneness.

**Holiness,** *n.* — *Syn.* head of the Roman Catholic church, Vicar of Christ, bishop of Rome; see **Pope.**

**hollow,** *modif.* **1.** [Empty] — *Syn.* vacant, unfilled, void, vain; see **empty** 1.

**2.** [Concave] — *Syn.* rounded inward, curving inward, bellshaped, curved, carved out, sunken, depressed, arched, vaulted, cup-shaped, excavated, infundibular, hollowed out, indented, incurved, cupped, cyathiform, incurving, incurvate, troughlike; see also **bent, round** 3. — *Ant.* convex, RAISED, elevated.

**3.** [Sounding as though from a cave] — *Syn.* cavernous, echoing, deep, resonant, ghostly, deep-toned, blooming, roaring, rumbling, reverberating, muffled, nonresonant, plangent, dull, resounding, vibrant, muffled, sepulchral, vibrating, low, booming, ringing, clangorous, deep, mute, deep-mouthed, deep-toned, muted, thunderous; see also **loud** 1.— *Ant.* DEAD, mute, silent.

**4.** [False] — *Syn.* flimsy, artificial, unsound; see **false** 2.

**5.** [*Hungry] — *Syn.* unsatisfied, ravenous, starved; see **hungry.**

*See Synonym Study at* VAIN.

**beat all hollow★** — *Syn.* outdo, beat, overcome; see **surpass.**

**hollow,** *n.* **1.** [A cavity] — *Syn.* depression, dip, pit; see **hole** 2.

**2.** [*A valley] — *Syn.* dale, bowl, basin; see **valley.**

*See Synonym Study at* HOLE.

**hollow (out),** *v.* — *Syn.* excavate, indent, remove earth; see **dig** 1, **shovel.**

**Hollywood,** *n.* — *Syn.* Movie Capital of America, Screenland, Home of the Stars, Filmdom★, the great intellectual desert★, Sin City★.

**holocaust,** *n.* — *Syn.* ruin, fire, ravage; see **catastrophe, destruction** 1, **disaster.**

**holy,** *modif.* **1.** [Divine] — *Syn.* sacred, divine, consecrated; see **divine** 2.

**2.** [Sinless] — *Syn.* devout, pious, blessed, righteous, moral, just, good, angelic, godly, venerable, immaculate, pure, spotless, clean, blameless, humble, saintly, guileless, innocent, godlike, saintlike, perfect, faultless, uncorrupt, undefiled, untainted, chaste, upright, virtuous, incorrupt, revered, dedicated to the service of God, sainted, heaven-sent, believing, heavenly minded, profoundly good, sanctified, inviolable, devotional, reverent, pietistic, spiritual, unstained, unworldly, pure in heart, zealous, seraphic, dedicated, rightminded, unspotted; see also **faithful, religious** 2. — *Ant.* evil, WICKED, sinful.

**3.** [Associated with a deity, especially with Christ; *often capitalized*] — *Syn.* Apostolic, Almighty, Omnipotent, True, Good, Eternal, Infinite, Blessed, Merciful.

*See Synonym Study at* DIVINE.

**Holy Ghost,** *n.* — *Syn.* Holy Spirit, the Dove, third person of the Holy Trinity; see **god** 2, **trinity** 2.

**Holy Writ,** *n.* — *Syn.* Scriptures, the Gospel, the Canon; see **Bible** 2.

**homage,** *n.* — *Syn.* respect, honor, tribute, allegiance; see **devotion, loyalty, praise** 1, **reverence** 2.

*See Synonym Study at* HONOR, LOYALTY.

**home,** *modif.* **1.** [At home] — *Syn.* in one's home, in one's house, at ease, in the family, at rest, about home, homely, domestic, familiar, being oneself, before one's own fireside, homey, in the bosom of one's

family, down home, in one's element; see also **comfortable** 1.

**2.** [Toward home] — *Syn.* to one's home, back, homeward bound; see **homeward.**

**home,** *n.* **1.** [A dwelling place] — *Syn.* house, dwelling, residence, habitation, habitat, tenement, abode, lodging, quarters, homestead, hospice, hostel, domicile, dormitory, seat, berth, apartment, condominium, flat, living quarters, messuage (British), palace, shelter, asylum, *pied à terre* (French), hut, haunt, resort, cabin, bungalow, cottage, chalet, mansion, castle, summer home, rooming house, country home, place, address, diggings, shanty, wigwam, igloo, topek, hovel, cave, *isba* (Russian), lodge, villa, hotel, inn, manor, tepee, farmhouse, tavern, resthouse, barrack, tent, pad★, hideout★, dump★, hang-out★, headquarters★, parking place★, digs★, nest★, condo★, where one hangs one's hat★; see also **apartment, trailer.**

**2.** [The whole complex associated with domestic life] — *Syn.* homestead, hearth, fireside, birthplace, hometown, haven, rest, roof, the farm, the ancestral halls, the hills, the land, neck of the woods★, camping ground★, home-sweet-home★; see also sense 1.

**3.** [An asylum] — *Syn.* orphanage, orphan asylum, rest home, home for the aged, soldiers' home, shelter, sanatorium, insane asylum, mental hospital, poorhouse, poor farm, almshouse★, booby hatch★, bathouse★; see also **hospital, sanitarium.**

**4.** [In baseball, the base at which the batter stands] — *Syn.* home plate, the plate, batter's box, head of the diamond, the rubber★, the platter★; see also **base** 5.

**at home** — *Syn.* relaxed, at ease, familiar; see **comfortable** 1, **home** 1.

**bring (something) home to** — *Syn.* impress upon, make apparent, make clear to, convince; see **emphasize, persuade** 1.

**come home** — *Syn.* come back, go back, return home, regress; see **return** 1.

**homecoming,** *n.* — *Syn.* homecoming celebration, entry, revisitation; see **arrival** 1, **return** 1.

**homeland,** *n.* — *Syn.* fatherland, motherland, home, the old country★; see **country** 3.

**homeless,** *modif.* — *Syn.* desolate, outcast, destitute, vagrant, wandering, uncared-for, itinerant, friendless, banished, estranged, derelict, without a country, exiled, having no home, vagabond, forsaken, displaced, unplaced, unhoused, friendless, unsettled, houseless, unwelcome, dispossessed, disinherited, unestablished, left to shift for oneself★, beyond the pale★, outside the gates★, without a roof over one's head★; see also **abandoned** 1, **poor** 1.— *Ant.* at home, ESTABLISHED, settled.

**homelike,** *modif.* — *Syn.* cozy, cheerful, informal; see **comfortable** 2.

**homely,** *modif.* **1.** [Unpretentious] — *Syn.* snug, simple, cozy; see **modest** 2.

**2.** [Ill-favored] — *Syn.* plain, unattractive, uncomely; see **ugly** 1.

**homemade,** *modif.* — *Syn.* homespun, domestic, do-it-yourself, indigenous, home-loomed, self-made, home-wrought, home-worked, made at home, of domestic manufacture, home, not foreign; see **handmade, manufactured, native** 1.

**home rule,** *n.* — *Syn.* independence, sovereignty, autonomy; see **freedom** 1.

**home run,** *n.* — *Syn.* four-base hit, run, homer★, circuit clout★, four-bagger★, grand tour★, grand slam★, round trip★, looper★.

**homesick,** *modif.* — *Syn.* nostalgic, pining, yearning for home, ill with longing, unhappy, unoriented, alienated, estranged, rootless; see also **lonely** 1.

**homesickness,** *n.* — *Syn.* nostalgia, rootlessness, longing, alienation, isolation, unhappiness, yearning for home; see also **loneliness.**

**homespun,** *modif.* **1.** [Made at home] — *Syn.* handicrafted, domestic, handspun; see **handmade, homemade.**

**2.** [Plain] — *Syn.* simple, unsophisticated, unassuming, homey; see **rustic** 3.

**homestead,** *n.* — *Syn.* house, residence, home place, farm, ranch, home grounds, place of settlement, home and grounds, grange, manor, farmstead, country house, country seat, messuage, plantation, estate, demesne, hacienda; see also **home** 1, **property** 2.

**homeward,** *modif.* — *Syn.* toward home, back home, on the way home, homewards, homewardly, home, homeward bound, to one's family, to one's native land.

**homework,** *n.* — *Syn.* outside assignment, library assignment, home study, preparation; see **study** 2. — *Ant.* classwork, EXAMINATION, recitation.

**homey,** *modif.* **1.** [Having the qualities of a home] — *Syn.* enjoyable, livable, familiar; see **comfortable** 2, **pleasant** 2.

**2.** [Genial] — *Syn.* warm-hearted, homespun, unassuming; see **friendly** 1.

**homicidal,** *modif.* — *Syn.* murderous, maniacal, lethal, destructive; see **murderous, violent** 4.

**homicide,** *n.* — *Syn.* murder, killing, manslaughter, death; see **crime** 2, **murder.**

**homiletic,** *modif.* — *Syn.* persuasive, moralizing, sermonizing, instructive, sermonic, preaching, edifying, expository, disciplinary, instructional, disquisitional, doctrinal, teaching, admonitory, didactic, relating to sermons, propagative, of the nature of a homily, of sermons; see **educational** 1.

**homiletics,** *n.* — *Syn.* moralizing, theology, rhetoric; see **preaching.**

**homily,** *n.* — *Syn.* lesson, doctrine, lecture; see **sermon.**

**hominid,** *n.* — *Syn.* human, early human, prehistoric human, cave dweller, caveman, cliff dweller, troglodyte, aborigine, savage, Stone-Age man, Paleolithic man, early man, ape man, dawn man, primitive man, *Homo sapiens fossilis* (Latin); see **man** 2.

Terms for early human or humanlike creatures include: Acheulean, Aurignacian, Australopithecus afarensis, Azilian, Chellean, Combe-Capelle, Creopithecus, Cro-Magnon, Eolithic, *Homo habilis,* Kenyapithecus, Magdalenian, Mousterian, Neanderthal man, Stone Age man, neolithic man, Paleolithic man, Peking man, *Homo erectus,* Heidelberg man, Pithecanthropus, Java man, Prechellean, Proconsul africanus, Rhodesian, Solutrean, Steinheim man, Swanscombe man, Trinil, Zinjanthropus.

**homogeneity,** *n.* — *Syn.* uniformity, sameness, oneness, similitude, identity, congruity, analogy, correlation; see also **agreement** 2.

**homogeneous,** *modif.* — *Syn.* uniform, unvaried, comparable, similar, analogous, of a piece, much of a muchness*; see also **alike** 2, **like.**

**homosexual,** *modif.*—*Syn.* gay, same-sex, camp, homoerotic, homophile, lesbian, Sapphic, androgynous, epicene, gynandrous, inverted, Uranian*.

**homosexual,** *n.*—*Syn.* gay, lesbian, Sapphist, gynandroid, daughter of Bilitis, daughter of Sappho, Ganymede, androgyne, hermaphrodite, invert, Uranian*, jocker*, pathic*, tribade*.

**hone,** *v.* — *Syn.* point, smooth, set; see **sharpen** 1.

**honest,** *modif.* **1.** [Truthful] — *Syn.* true, trustworthy, correct, exact, verifiable, undisguised, respectable, factual, sound, veritable, unimpeachable, legitimate, unquestionable, realistic, true-to-life, reasonable, aboveboard, unvarnished, naked, irrefutable, literal, plain, intrinsic, precise, straight*, square*, honest as the day is long*, on the level*, on the legit*, on the up and up*, kosher*, fair and square*; see also **accurate** 1, 2. — *Ant.* deceptive, FALSE, misleading.

honest

**2.** [Honorable] — *Syn.* upright, respectable, worthy; see **noble** 1, 2, **reliable** 1.

**3.** [Frank] — *Syn.* candid, straightforward, aboveboard; see sense 1; see **frank.**

**4.** [Fair] — *Syn.* just, equitable, impartial; see **fair** 1.

**honestly,** *modif.* **1.** [In an honest manner] — *Syn.* uprightly, fairly, genuinely; see **justly** 1, 2, **sincerely.**

**2.** [Really] — *Syn.* indeed, truly, naturally; see **really** 1.

**honesty,** *n.* **1.** [Integrity] — *Syn.* probity, honor, uprightness, veridicality, fidelity, scrupulousness, self-respect, straight-forwardness, forthrightness, directness, trustworthiness, confidence, soundness, veracity, rectitude, right, principle, truthfulness, candor, frankness, openness, incorruptibility, morality, goodness, responsibility, loyalty, faithfulness, good faith, constancy, courage, quality of being honest, moral strength, virtue, reliability, character, veraciousness, conscience, worth, impeccability, conscientiousness, trustiness, faith, freedom from fraud, justice, respectability, honorableness; see also **sincerity.** — *Ant.* DISHONESTY, deception, deceit.

**2.** [Fair dealing] — *Syn.* probity, justice, rectitude; see **fairness.**

**honey,** *n.* — *Syn.* nectar, syrup, molasses, treacle (British), sugar.

Types of honey include: comb, extracted, strained, creamed, wild, mountain, desert, select, grated; linn, basswood, white clover, sweet clover, buckwheat, goldenrod, alfalfa, orange blossom, tupelo, locust, sage, currant, cleome, cotton, eucalyptus, sycamore, teasel, thyme, barberry, heather, hawthorn; see also **food, syrup.**

**honeycomb,** *n.* — *Syn.* comb, maze, labyrinth, sieve, pattern, filter; see also **maze, screen.**

**honeycombed,** *modif.* — *Syn.* riddled, perforated, patterned; see **porous.**

**honeyed,** *modif.* — *Syn.* sugary, candied, enticing; see **persuasive, sweet** 1.

**honeymoon,** *n.* — *Syn.* post-nuptial vacation, married couple's first holiday, wedding trip, first month after marriage; see also **vacation.**

**honk,** *n.* — *Syn.* croak, quack, blare; see **noise** 1.

**honk,** *v.* — *Syn.* blow a horn, blare, quack, croak, signal, make a noise like a goose, trumpet, bellow; see also **sound** 1.

**honor,** *n.* **1.** [Respect] — *Syn.* reverence, esteem, worship, adoration, veneration, high reward, trust, faith, confidence, recognition, praise, attention, deference, notice, consideration, renown, reputation, repute, homage, account, laurel, elevation, approbation, wreath, credit, eulogium, adulation, laud, tribute, celebration, exaltation, good report, apotheosis, lionization, immortalization, fealty, mark of approval, deification, dignification, glorification, canonization, aggrandizement, righteousness; see also **admiration.** — *Ant.* opprobrium, DISGRACE, disrepute.

**2.** [Glory] — *Syn.* exaltation, greatness, renown; see **fame** 1.

**3.** [Integrity] — *Syn.* courage, character, truthfulness; see **honesty** 1.

**do honor to** — *Syn.* show respect for, please, bring honor to; see **honor** *v.*

**do the honors**— *Syn.* act as host or hostess, present, host; see **serve** 1.

**on one's honor**— *Syn.* by one's faith, on one's word, staking one's good name; see **sincerely.**

---

*SYN.* — **honor** implies popular acknowledgment of a person's right to great respect as well as any expression of such respect /in *honor* of the martyred dead/; **homage** suggests great esteem shown in praise, tributes, or obeisance /to pay *homage* to the genius of Bach/; **reverence** implies deep respect together with love /he held her memory in *reverence*/; **deference** suggests a display of courteous regard for a superior, or for one to whom respect is due, by yielding to the person's status, claims, or wishes /in *deference* to his age/

---

**honor,** *v.* 1. [To treat with respect] — *Syn.* worship, sanctify, venerate; see **praise** 1.

**2.** [To recognize worth] — *Syn.* esteem, value, look up to; see **admire** 1.

**3.** [To recognize as valid] — *Syn.* clear, pass, accept; see **acknowledge** 2.

**Honor,** *n.* — *Syn.* Excellency, Lordship, Majesty, Honorable Sir, Reverence, Justice, Governor; see also **judge** 1.

**honorable,** *modif.* — *Syn.* proud, reputable, creditable; see **distinguished, important** 2, **noble** 2, 3, **upright** 2.

**honorably,** *modif.* — *Syn.* nobly, fairly, virtuously; see **justly** 1.

**honorarium,** *n.* — *Syn.* complimentary fee, gratuity, reward; see **compensation, pay** 2, **payment** 1, **return** 3, **tip** 2.

**honorary,** *modif.* — *Syn.* titular, ex officio, gratuitous, honorific, *honoris causa* (Latin), nominal, favored, privileged; see also **complimentary.**

**honored,** *modif.* — *Syn.* respected, reversed, decorated, privileged, celebrated, reputable, well-known, esteemed, eminent, distinguished, dignified, noble, recognized, highly regarded, venerated; see also **famous, important** 2.— *Ant.* dishonored, DISGRACED, shamed.

**honors,** *n.* 1. [Courtesies] — *Syn.* ceremony, privilege, duties.

**2.** [Distinction] — *Syn.* high honors, award, prize, medal, laurels, wreath, garland, favor, kudos, feather in one's cap*.

**hood,** *n.* 1. [Covering worn over the head] — *Syn.* cowl, shawl, bonnet, protector, coif, capuche, veil, wimple, capuchin, kerchief, mantle, mantilla, babushka, yashmak, purdah; see also **hat.**

**2.** [A covering for vehicles and the like] — *Syn.* canopy, awning, bonnet, shade, carriage top, auto top, calash, chimney top, convertible top; see also **cover** 1.

**3.** [*A criminal] — *Syn.* gangster, hoodlum, crook; see **criminal.**

**hoodlum,** *n.* — *Syn.* outlaw, gangster, crook; see **criminal.**

**hoodwink,** *v.* — *Syn.* blind, cheat, outwit; see **deceive.**

**hoof,** *n.* — *Syn.* foot, unguis, ungula, cloven foot, animal foot, paw, coffin bone, trotter; see also **foot** 2.

**hook,** *n.* 1. [An implement for snagging] — *Syn.* lock, catch, clasp, latch; see **fastener.**

**2.** [A curved implement for cutting] — *Syn.* sickle, bill, billhook, machete, adze, scythe; see also **tool** 1.

**hook,** *v.* 1. [To curve in the shape of a hook] — *Syn.* angle, crook, curve; see **arch** 1.

**2.** [To catch on a hook] — *Syn.* pin, catch, secure; see **fasten** 1.

**3.** [*To attain one's end by trickery] — *Syn.* cheat, defraud, dupe; see **deceive.**

**hooked,** *modif.* 1. [Bent] — *Syn.* curved, angled, arched; see **bent, crooked** 1.

**2.** [Addicted] — *Syn.* dependant, using, anywhere*, on*.

**hooked in,** *modif.* — *Syn.* fastened, attached, connected; see **joined, wired.**

**hooked up,** *modif.* — *Syn.* connected, circuited, attached; see **joined, wired.**

**hook, line, and sinker*,** *modif.* — *Syn.* whole, entire, entirely, gullibly; see **completely.**

**hookup,** *n.* — *Syn.* attachment, connection, plug, jack, outlet, consolidation; see also **junction** 2, **link, union** 1.

**hook up,** *v.* — *Syn.* combine, connect, attach; see **join** 1, **unite** 1.

**hoop,** *n.* 1. [Ring] — *Syn.* loop, band, circlet; see **circle** 1.

**2.** [Basketball goal] — *Syn.* basket, net, rim; see **basket** 3.

**hoot,** *n.* — *Syn.* howl, whoo, boo; see **cry** 2.

**hoot,** *v.* — *Syn.* cry out against, boo, howl down; see **cry** 3.

**hop,** *n.* 1. [A quick jump] — *Syn.* spring, bounce, leap; see **jump** 1.

**2.** [*A short flight] — *Syn.* commuter flight, trip, jaunt; see **flight** 2, **journey.**

**hop,** *v.* — *Syn.* leap, skip, jump on one leg; see **bounce** 1, **jump** 1.

*See Synonym Study at* SKIP.

**hope,** *n.* 1. [Reliance upon the future] — *Syn.* faith, expectation, confidence; see **anticipation** 1, **optimism** 2.

**2.** [The object of hope] — *Syn.* wish, concern, aspiration, goal, promise, dream, utopia, promised land, fortune, reward, gain, achievement; see also **desire** 1, **end** 2, **purpose** 1.

**3.** [A reason for hope] — *Syn.* support, prop, mainstay, strength, bet, investment, faith, endurance; see also **belief** 1.

**hope,** *v.* — *Syn.* be hopeful, lean on, wish, expect, desire, live in hope, rely on, depend on, count on, aspire to, doubt not, keep one's fingers crossed, be of good cheer, pray, cherish the hope, look forward to, await, contemplate, dream, presume, watch for, bank on, reckon on, calculate on, foresee, think to, promise oneself, suppose, deem likely, believe, suspect, surmise, hold, be assured, be confident, anticipate, be prepared for, make plans for, rest on the hope, hold in prospect, aspire, assume, have faith, entertain hope, feel confident, be sure of, take as a certainty, be reassured, take heart, knock on wood*, catch at a straw*, look on the bright side*, look on the sunny side*; see also **expect, trust** 1.

*See Synonym Study at* EXPECT.

**hopeful,** *modif.* 1. [Optimistic] — *Syn.* expectant, assured, sanguine, buoyant, enthusiastic, trustful, reassured, emboldened, full of hope, faithful, cheerful, anticipative, anticipating, trusting, inspirited, expecting, anticipatory, at ease, in hopes of, forward-looking, lighthearted, serene, calm, poised, comfortable, blithe, eager, elated, Pollyannaish*, beamish*, looking through rose-colored glasses*; see also **confident** 3, **trusting** 2.

**2.** [Encouraging] — *Syn.* promising, reassuring, assuring, favorable, bright, cheering, flattering, gracious, opportune, timely, fortunate, propitious, auspicious, well-timed, fit, suitable, convenient, beneficial, reasonable, fair, uplifting, heartening, inspiring, exciting, pleasing, fine, inspiriting, fortifying, rousing, arousing, enlivening, lucky, stirring, making glad, gladdening, elating, provi-

*hopeful* ↙

dential, helpful, rose-colored, rosy, animating, attractive, satisfactory, refreshing, probable, good, conducive, advantageous, of good omen, pleasant, consoling, of promise, happy, cheerful, comforting, calming, proper, expeditious, enlivening.— *Ant.* discouraging, UNFORTUNATE, unfavorable.

**hopefully,** *modif.* **1.** [Optimistically] — *Syn.* confidently, expectantly, sanguinely, with confidence, with hope, trustingly, naively, with some reassurance, trustfully; see also **boldly** 1, **positively** 1, **surely.**— *Ant.* doubtfully, HOPELESSLY, gloomily.
**2.** [Probably] — *Syn.* expectedly, conceivably, feasibly; see **probably.**

**hopeless,** *modif.* **1.** [Despairing] — *Syn.* despondent, despairing, desperate, forlorn, disconsolate, depressed, dejected, melancholy, pessimistic, cynical; see also **sad** 1.
**2.** [Discouraging] — *Syn.* futile, unfortunate, threatening, bad, sinister, unyielding, irrevocable, irredeemable, incurable, beyond recall, past hope, past cure, irretrievable, vain, unmitigable, irreversible, irreparable, irreclaimable, irrecoverable, cureless, without hope, with no hope, impracticable, ill-fated, disastrous, menacing, foreboding, unfavorable, dying, worsening, past recall, tragic, fatal, desperate, helpless, unavailing, lost, unreclaimable, to no avail, forlorn, remediless, relapsing, abandoned, gone, empty, idle, recidivous, valueless, incorrigible, useless, unserviceable, pointless, worthless, insurmountable; see **futile** 1, **impossible** 1.— *Ant.* FAVORABLE, heartening, cheering.

---

*SYN.* — **hopeless** means having no expectation of, or showing no sign of, a favorable outcome [a *hopeless* situation]; **despondent** implies a being in very low spirits because of a loss of hope and a sense of futility about continuing one's efforts [her rejection of his proposal left him *despondent*]; **despairing** implies utter loss of hope and may suggest the extreme dejection that results [the *despairing* lover spoke of suicide]; **desperate** implies such despair as makes one resort to extreme measures [hunger makes men *desperate*]

---

**hopelessly,** *modif.* **1.** [Without hope] — *Syn.* cynically, pessimistically, despondently, despairingly, dejectedly, disconsolately, desperately, mechanically, automatically, emptily, spiritlessly, darkly, gloomily, dismally, desolately, down in the mouth*, under the weather*, fit to be tied*; see also **sadly.**— *Ant.* confidently, HOPEFULLY, expectantly.
**2.** [Giving small ground for hope] — *Syn.* impossibly, incurably, desperately, fatally, unavailingly, unfortunately, badly, without a chance in the world*, with all odds against*.
**hoping,** *modif.* — *Syn.* believing, expecting, wishing, assuming, anticipating, looking forward; see also **trusting** 2.
**hopper,** *n.* — *Syn.* receptacle, storage place, tank, freight car, hopper car; see also **storehouse.**
**horde,** *n.* — *Syn.* pack, throng, swarm; see **crowd** 1, **gathering.**
*See Synonym Study at* CROWD.
**horizon,** *n.* — *Syn.* skyline, azimuth, compass, range, border, limit; see also **boundary, extent.**
**on the horizon** — *Syn.* in the near future, upcoming, coming soon, in the cards.
**horizontal,** *modif.* **1.** [Level] — *Syn.* plane, aligned, parallel; see **flat** 1, **level** 3, **straight** 1.
**2.** [Even] — *Syn.* flush, uniform, regular; see **flat** 1, **smooth** 1.

**horn,** *n.* **1.** [A wind instrument] — *Syn.* woodwind, brass instrument, trumpet, air horn, electric horn.
Types of horns include: bugle, trumpet, trombone, cornet, fluegelhorn, French horn, baritone, tuba, sax-tuba, saxophone, sousaphone, brass tuba, bombardon, serpent, alpenhorn, hunting horn, bass horn, conch, lure, ram's horn, shofar; see also **musical instrument.**
**2.** [Hard growth on the head of certain animals] — *Syn.* tusk, antler, rack, outgrowth, pronghorn, hornbill, frontal bone, epiphysis, apophysis, quill, corniculum, spine, spike, corniplume, point, cornu, cornicle, cornule; see also **bone, tooth** 1.
**3.** [The material comprising horns, sense 2] — *Syn.* keratin, elastin, epidermal tissue, corneous matter, corneate matter.
**blow one's own horn***— *Syn.* praise oneself, gloat, brag; see **boast** 1.
**lock horns** — *Syn.* disagree, conflict, defy; see **oppose** 1.
**on the horns of a dilemma** — *Syn.* torn between two alternatives, having to make a difficult decision, between the devil and the deep blue sea*, between a rock and a hard place; see **in trouble** at **trouble.**
**pull** or **draw** or **haul in one's horns** — *Syn.* withdraw, recant, hold oneself back; see **restrain** 1.
**horn in (on)***, *v.* — *Syn.* intrude, impose, impose upon, get in on*; see **enter** 1, **meddle** 1.
**horny,** *modif.* **1.** [Callous] — *Syn.* hard, firm, tough; see **bony** 1.
**2.** [*Sexually excited] — *Syn.* sensual, aroused, lecherous, lascivious, on the make*; see also **excited, lewd** 2.
**horrendous,** *modif.* — *Syn.* horrible, frightful, terrifying; see **poor** 2, **terrible** 1.
**horrible,** *modif.* **1.** [Offensive] — *Syn.* repulsive, dreadful, disgusting; see **offensive** 2.
**2.** [Frightful] — *Syn.* shameful, shocking, awful; see **frightful** 1, **terrible** 1.
**horrid,** *modif.* — *Syn.* hideous, disturbing, shameful; see **offensive** 2, **pitiful** 1.
**horrified,** *modif.* — *Syn.* frightened, repelled, aghast; see **afraid** 2, **shocked, troubled.**
**horrify,** *v.* — *Syn.* terrify, appall, petrify, dismay; see **frighten** 1.
*See Synonym Study at* DISMAY.
**horror,** *n.* **1.** [Dread] — *Syn.* awe, terror, fright; see **fear** 2.
**2.** [Abhorrence] — *Syn.* aversion, dislike, loathing; see **hate, hatred** 1.
**horror-stricken,** *modif.* — *Syn.* petrified, paralyzed, shocked, overcome with fear, overcome with horror, aghast, scared to death, horrified, freaked*; see also **afraid** 2.
**hors d'oeuvre,** *n.* — *Syn.* appetizers, canapés, relishes, antipasto, *zakuska* (Russian), smörgasbord, crudités, *tapas* (Spanish), *meze* (Greek); see also **appetizer, delicatessen** 1.
**horse,** *n.* **1.** [A domestic animal] — *Syn.* nag, draft animal, plow horse, racer, saddlehorse, steed, mount, charger, stallion, gelding, hack, mare, dobbin, roadster, palfrey, pad, thoroughbred, pacer, trotter, cob, hunter, courser, posthorse, piebald, calico pony, equine, quadruped, *Pferd* (German), *cheval* (French), *caballo* (Spanish); see also **animal, pony.**
Breeds and types of horses include: Clydesdale, Shire, Belgian, Galloway, Shetland, Lipizzaner, Waler, Percheron, Appaloosa, French coach, Morgan, Suffolk, Hackney, Ardennes, Hanoverian, Flemish, Arabian, Thoroughbred, quarter horse, Barbary, barb, mustang, bronco, pinto, palomino, Hambletonian.

**2.** [An upright structure] — *Syn.* trestle, support, bench, stage, scaffold, easel, tripod, bolster, clotheshorse, sawhorse, vaulting block.

**back the wrong horse** — *Syn.* support the losing side, pick the loser, misjudge; see **lose** 3.

**beat** or **flog a dead horse*** — *Syn.* argue an issue that is already settled, nag, harp on; see **overdo** 1.

**from the horse's mouth*** — *Syn.* originally, from an authority, according to the source of the information; see **officially** 1.

**hold one's horses*** — *Syn.* curb one's impatience, slow down, relax; see **restrain** 1.

**on one's high horse*** — *Syn.* arrogant, haughty, disdainful; see **egotistic** 2.

**horse around***, *v.* — *Syn.* fool around*, cavort, cause trouble; see **misbehave, play** 2.

**horseback**, *modif.* — *Syn.* by horse, on a horse, in the saddle, bareback, equestrian, mounted; see also **moving** 1.

**horseman**, *n.* — *Syn.* rider, equestrian, equerry, roughrider, cavalryman, horse guard, dragoon, horse driver, horse trainer, keeper of horses, gaucho, pricker, buckaroo, postilion, broncobuster*, saddle sitter*, live weight*, monkey*, gypsy*; see also **cowboy** 1, **jockey, rider** 1.

**horsemanship**, *n.* — *Syn.* riding skill, management of horses, equestrian skill, *manège* (French).

**horseplay**, *n.* — *Syn.* clowning, play, fooling around; see **fun, joke** 1.

**horsepower**, *n.* — *Syn.* strength, pull, power; see **energy** 3.

**horticulture**, *n.* — *Syn.* cultivation of gardens, agriculture, floriculture; see **farming, gardening.**

**hose**, *n.* **1.** [Stocking] — *Syn.* sock, tights, pantyhose; see **hosiery.**

**2.** [A flexible conduit] — *Syn.* garden hose, fire hose, line, tubing; see also **conduit, pipe** 1, **tube** 1.

**hosiery**, *n.* — *Syn.* stockings, nylons, full-fashioned hose, seamless hose, trunk hose, half hose, socks, anklets, tights, pantyhose, leotards, knee stocks, ankle socks, bobby socks, bobby sox, body stocking.

**hospitable**, *modif.* — *Syn.* cordial, courteous, neighborly, congenial; see **friendly** 1.

**hospital**, *n.* — *Syn.* clinic, infirmary, sanatorium, sanitarium, dispensary, Red Cross hospital, VA hospital, mental hospital, army hospital, city hospital, public hospital, ship's hospital, veteran's hospital, institution for the physically sick, hospital for the mentally sick, medical center, treatment center, rehabilitation center, valetudinarium, lying-in hospital, health service, outpatient ward, sick bay, detox*, sick house*, repair shop*, croaker joint*.

Medical terms and abbreviations commonly used by hospitals include: acute respiratory disease (ARD), barium enema (BE), basal body temperature (BBT), basal metabolic rate (BMR), blood pressure (BP), cancer (Ca), cardiac care unit, CCU, central nervous system (CNS), cerebrospinal fluid (CSF), CT scan, CAT scan, computerized axial tomography, coronary artery bypass surgery (CABS), dilation and curettage, D & C, dose*, dead on arrival, DOA, electrocardiogram, EKG, electroencephalogram, EEG, emergency medical service, EMS, emergency room, ER, fever of undetermined origin (FUO), gastrointestinal (GI), genitourinary (GU), gunshot wound (GSW), hemoglobin (Hb), ideal body weight (IBW), stat ("immediately"), intramuscular (IM), intensive care unit, ICU, intravenous, IV, last menstrual period (LMP), magnetic resonance imaging, MRI, myocardial infarction (MI), normal (n),

normal temperature and pressure (NTP), obstetrics and gynecology, OB-GYN, operating room, OR, outpatient department (OPD), PET scan, positron emission tomography, pharmacy, Rx, pharm, physical examination (PE), pulse (P), respiration (R), red blood cell (rbc), shortness of breath (SOB), temperature (T), venereal disease (VD), weight (wt), white blood cell (wbc), x-ray.

**hospitality**, *n.* **1.** [Entertainment] — *Syn.* accommodation, good cheer, warm welcome, warm reception, conviviality, companionship, good fellowship, comradeship, one's best; see also **entertainment** 1, **welcome.**

**2.** [Generosity in offering entertainment] — *Syn.* bountifulness, liberality, graciousness, geniality, solicitousness, heartiness, obligingness, affability, consideration, amiability, cordiality; see also **courtesy** 1, **generosity** 1.

**host**, *n.* **1.** [One who entertains] — *Syn.* entertainer, toastmaster, master, mistress, hostess, talk-show moderator, master of ceremonies, mistress of ceremonies, M.C., emcee; see also **hostess** 1, 3.

**2.** [One who operates a place of public hospitality] — *Syn.* innkeeper, hotel keeper, tavern keeper, saloon keeper, barkeeper, barkeep, bartender, restaurant owner, restaurateur, manager, maitre d', night club owner, proprietor; see also **hostess** 2, **owner.**

**3.** [A large group] — *Syn.* throng, multitude, army; see **crowd** 1, **gathering.**

**4.** [Organism on which a parasite subsists] — *Syn.* host mother, host body, animal; see **organism.**

**5.** [Sacramental bread; *capitalized*] — *Syn.* Bread of the Last Supper, wafer, Communion loaf, altar bread, Eucharist; see also **communion** 2, **sacrament.**

*See Synonym Study at* CROWD.

**host**, *v.* — *Syn.* receive, treat, wine and dine; see **entertain** 2.

**hostage**, *n.* — *Syn.* security, guaranty, captive, prisoner, pawn, scapegoat, victim of a kidnapping, sacrificial victim; see also **pledge.**

*See Synonym Study at* PLEDGE.

**hostel**, *n.* — *Syn.* lodging, youth hotel, accommodations for bicyclists, inn; see **hotel.**

**hostel**, *v.* — *Syn.* travel by bicycle, hitchhike, make a tour; see **travel** 2.

**hostess**, *n.* **1.** [A woman who entertains] — *Syn.* society lady, socialite, clubwoman, social leader, social climber, entertainer, lion hunter*, queen bee*; see also **host** 1.

**2.** [A woman in charge of public hospitality] — *Syn.* proprietress, innkeeper, concierge, madame, owner, airline hostess, receptionist; see also **administrator, host** 2.

**3.** [A woman who hosts visitors] — *Syn.* lady of the house, mistress of the household, toastmistress, mistress of ceremonies, M.C., emcee; see also **host** 1.

**hostile**, *modif.* — *Syn.* antagonistic, hateful, opposed; see **unfriendly** 1.

**hostility**, *n.* — *Syn.* enmity, hatred, abhorrence, aversion; see **hatred** 1, **malice, resentment.**

*See Synonym Study at* ENMITY.

**hot**, *modif.* **1.** [Having a high temperature] — *Syn.* torrid, burning, fiery, flaming, blazing, very warm, feverish, baking, roasting, smoking, scorching, blistering, searing, sizzling, tropical, warm, calescent, broiling, igneous, red-hot, grilling, piping-hot, white-hot, scalding, parching, sultry, on fire, at high temperature, incandescent, ovenlike, smoldering, thermal, calid, toasting, simmering, thermogenic, recalescent, decalescent, blazing hot*, boiling hot*, like an oven*, hotter than blazes*; see also **boiling, cooking** 1, **heated** 1, **molten.** — *Ant.* COLD, frigid, chilly.

**2.** [Close] — *Syn.* sultry, humid, stuffy; see **close** 5.

**3.** [Eager]— *Syn.* ardent, passionate, distracted; see **enthusiastic** 2, 3, **excited.**

**4.** [Aroused]— *Syn.* furious, ill-tempered, indignant; see **angry.**

**5.** [*Erotic]— *Syn.* spicy, salacious, horny, carnal; see **lascivious** 2, **lewd** 1, 2, **sensual.**

**get hot***— *Syn.* become excited or enthusiastic, burn with fervor, burn with anger, rave; see **rage** 1.

**make it hot for***— *Syn.* create discomfort for, cause trouble for, vex; see **disturb** 1.

**hot and bothered***, *modif.* — *Syn.* upset, excited, disturbed; see **troubled.**

**hotel,** *n.* — *Syn.* inn, motel, lodging house, halfway house, boarding house, hostel, hospice, health resort, watering place, tavern, house, spa, rooming house, khan, caravansary, flophouse*, bughouse*, dump*, boatel*; see also **lodge, motel, resort** 2.

**hotheaded,** *modif.* **1.** [Impetuous]— *Syn.* unmanageable, wild, reckless; see **rash, unruly.**

**2.** [Irritable] — *Syn.* quick-tempered, crabby, touchy; see **irritable.**

**hothouse,** *n.* — *Syn.* glasshouse, conservatoire, nursery; see **greenhouse.**

**hot plate,** *n.* — *Syn.* electric burner, warmer, portable stove; see **stove.**

**hot rod,** *n.* — *Syn.* dragster, speedster, stock car; see **automobile, racer** 2, **vehicle** 1.

**hot under the collar***, *modif.* — *Syn.* furious, mad, resentful; see **angry.**

**hound,** *n.* **1.** [A dog]— *Syn.* hunting dog, bird dog, hound dog, coon dog.
Types of hounds include: greyhound, bloodhound, foxhound, staghound, deerhound, wolfhound, otterhound, harrier, basset, beagle, dachshund; see also **animal** 1, **dog** 1.

**2.** [A fan] — *Syn.* devotee, fanatic, groupie; see **enthusiast** 1, **follower.**

**hound,** *v.* — *Syn.* badger, harass, pursue; see **bait** 2, **bother** 2, **pursue** 1.

*See Synonym Study at* BAIT.

**hour,** *n.* **1.** [A period of time] — *Syn.* time unit, sixty minutes, man-hour, ampere-hour, planetary hour, horsepower hour, recitation hour, lecture hour, class hour, supper hour, study hour, rush hour; see also **time** 1.

**2.** [An appointed time]— *Syn.* moment, minute, term; see **appointment** 2.

**of the hour**— *Syn.* most important, significant, relevant; see **important** 1.

**one's hour**— *Syn.* the time of one's death, one's dying, one's time*; see **death** 1.

**the small** or **wee hours**— *Syn.* midnight, middle of the night, early morning; see **morning** 1, **night** 1.

**hour after hour,** *modif.* — *Syn.* continually, steadily, on and on; see **continuing, regularly** 2.

**hourly,** *modif.* — *Syn.* hour by hour, each hour, every hour, every sixty minutes, continually, at the striking of the hour, every hour on the hour; see also **frequently, regularly** 2.

**house,** *n.* **1.** [A habitation]— *Syn.* home, dwelling, apartment house, residence; see **apartment, home** 1.

**2.** [A large business establishment] — *Syn.* corporation, partnership, stock company; see **business** 4, **organization** 3.

**3.** [A family] — *Syn.* line, family tradition, ancestry; see **family** 1.

**4.** [A legislative body] — *Syn.* congress, council, parliament; see **legislature.**

**bring down the house***— *Syn.* receive applause, create enthusiasm, please; see **excite** 2.

**clean house**— *Syn.* arrange, put in order, tidy up; see **clean.**

**keep house**— *Syn.* manage a home, run a house, be a housekeeper; see **manage** 1.

**like a house on fire**— *Syn.* actively, vigorously, energetically; see **quickly** 1.

**on the house**— *Syn.* without expense, gratis, for nothing; see **free** 4.

**play house**— *Syn.* make-believe, play games, play at keeping a home; see **pretend** 1.

**set** or **put one's house in order**— *Syn.* order one's affairs, arrange, put in order, manage; see **order** 3.

**housebreaker,** *n.* — *Syn.* thief, lock-picker, burglar; see **criminal, robber.**

**household,** *n.* — *Syn.* family unit, house, domestic establishment; see **family** 1, **home.**

**householder,** *n.* — *Syn.* proprietor, landlord, mortgagee; see **owner.**

**housekeeper,** *n.* — *Syn.* wife and mother, caretaker, serving woman, help*; see **housewife, servant.**

**housekeeping,** *n.* — *Syn.* household management, domestic science, home economy, housewifery, stewardship, husbandry, hotel administration; see also **housework.**

**housetop,** *n.* — *Syn.* roof, shingles, gables, chimney; see **gable, roof.**

**housewife,** *n.* — *Syn.* wife, mistress of the house, lady of the house, housekeeper, mother to one's children, *Hausfrau* (German), *mater familias* (Latin), home economist, home engineer, homemaker, mistress of a family, family manager, wife and mother, chief cook and bottlewasher*; see also **wife.**

**housework,** *n.* — *Syn.* cleaning, housewifery, housecleaning, spring cleaning, window-washing, sweeping, cooking, baking, dusting, mopping, washing, laundering, bed-making, sewing, ironing, mending; see also **housekeeping, job** 2.

**housing,** *n.* — *Syn.* habitation, home construction, problem of providing houses, house-building program, sheltering, installation, covering, protection, shelter, abode, domicile, cantonment, house, accommodations, lodgment, quarters, roof, dwelling, lodging, residence, headquarters, stopping place, digs; see also **home, shelter.**

**hovel,** *n.* — *Syn.* cottage, shed, cabin; see **hut, shack.**

**hover,** *v.* — *Syn.* float, flutter, waver; see **fly** 1, **hang** 2.

**hovering,** *modif.* **1.** [Floating] — *Syn.* gliding, swaying, airborne; see **flying, hanging.**

**2.** [Attending carefully] — *Syn.* considerate, attentive, shielding; see **protective, thoughtful** 2.

**how,** *conj. & modif.* — *Syn.* in what way, to what degree, by what method, in what manner, after what precedent, according to what specifications, from what source, by whose help, whence, wherewith, by virtue of what, whereby, through what medium, by what means.

**however,** *conj. & modif.* **1.** [But]— *Syn.* still, though, nevertheless; see **but** 1, **yet** 1.

**2.** [In spite of] — *Syn.* despite, without regard to, nonetheless; see **notwithstanding.**

**howl,** *n.* — *Syn.* moan, wail, lament; see **cry** 2, **yell** 1.

**howl,** *v.* — *Syn.* bawl, wail, lament; see **cry** 3, **yell.**

**one's night to howl**— *Syn.* time for fun, relaxation, recreation; see **leisure.**

**howling,** *modif.* — *Syn.* noisy, crying, moaning; see **loud** 2, **yelling.**

**hub,** *n.* — *Syn.* core, heart, middle; see **center** 1.

**hubbub,** *n.* — *Syn.* din, tumult, uproar, commotion; see **confusion** 2, **noise, uproar.**

*See Synonym Study at* NOISE.

**huckster,** *n.* — *Syn.* hawker, vendor, peddler, hustler; see **businessperson, salesman.**

**huddle,** *n.* — *Syn.* group, assemblage, cluster; see **bunch** 1, **crowd** 1, **gathering.**

**huddle,** *v.* — *Syn.* crouch, press close, crowd, bunch, draw together, mass, cluster, throng, nestle, cuddle, hug, curl up, snuggle; see also **gather** 1, **press** 1.

**hue,** *n.* **1.** [A shade of color] — *Syn.* value, tone, shade, tint; see **color** 1, **tint.**
**2.** [A color] — *Syn.* color, chroma, tone; see **color** 1.
*See Synonym Study at* COLOR.

**hue and cry\*,** *n.* — *Syn.* clamor, shout, pursuit; see **cry** 1, **hunt** 2.

**huff,** *n.* — *Syn.* annoyance, offense, perturbation, temper; see **anger, rage** 2.

**huffy,** *modif.* — *Syn.* offended, piqued, huffish; see **angry, insulted, irritable.**

**hug,** *n.* — *Syn.* embrace, squeeze, tight grip, caress, demonstration of affection, clinch\*, bunny hug\*, bear hug\*; see also **touch** 2.

**hug,** *v.* — *Syn.* embrace, squeeze, clasp, press close, hold to one's heart, love, keep close to, catch hold of, be near to, clasp tightly in one's arms, cling, fold in the arms, clutch, seize, envelop, press, grasp, enfold, embosom, nestle, welcome, cuddle, lock, press to the bosom, snuggle, lie close, cling together, receive warmly, fold to the breast, take to the heart, go into a clinch\*, clinch\*; see also **caress, hold** 1, **touch** 1.

**huge,** *modif.* — *Syn.* tremendous, enormous, immense; see **enormous, large** 1.
*See Synonym Study at* ENORMOUS.

**hug the road,** *v.* — *Syn.* track, cling to the road, drive well; see **ride** 5, **travel** 2.

**hulk,** *n.* **1.** [A large, unshapely object] — *Syn.* bulk, blob, hunk, chunk, lump, clump, clod, slather\*; see also **mass** 1, **part** 1.
**2.** [A wreck] — *Syn.* shell, remains, ruins, shambles, skeleton, frame, hull, dismasted ship, derelict, body; see also **wreck** 2.

**hulking,** *modif.* — *Syn.* bulky, cumbersome, clumsy; see **awkward** 1.

**hull,** *n.* **1.** [The body of a vessel] — *Syn.* framework, skeleton, main structure, wetted surface, underbody, water lines, decks, cladding, casing, covering, cast, mold, sides; see also **frame** 1.
**2.** [A shell] — *Syn.* peeling, husk, shuck; see **peel, shell** 1.

**hull,** *v.* — *Syn.* husk, shuck, peel; see **skin.**

**hullabaloo,** *n.* — *Syn.* tumult, chaos, clamor; see **confusion** 2, **noise, uproar.**

**hum,** *v.* — *Syn.* buzz, drone, murmur, sing low, hum a tune, croon, sing in an undertone, whisper, sing without articulation, zoom, moan, make a buzzing sound, bombinate, thrum, bum, whir, vibrate, bombilate, purr; see also **sound** 1.

**human,** *modif.* — *Syn.* anthropoid, animal, biped, civilized, man-made, anthropomorphic, anthropocentric, anthropological, humanlike, manlike, of man, belonging to humans, humanistic, individual, man's, hominid, proper to man, personal, hominal; see also **mortal** 2, **rational** 1, **social** 1. — *Ant.* DIVINE, bestial, nonhuman.

**human,** *n.* — *Syn.* man, woman, human being, individual, member of the human race, living soul; see also **man** 1, 2, 3, **person** 1, **woman** 1.

**human being,** *n.* — *Syn.* being, mortal, individual; see **man** 1, 2, 3, **person** 1, **woman** 1.

**humane,** *modif.* **1.** [Kindly] — *Syn.* benevolent, sympathetic, understanding, pitying, compassionate, kindhearted, human, tenderhearted, forgiving, gracious, charitable, benignant, gentle, tender, clement, benign, obliging, friendly, indulgent, generous, lenient, tolerant, democratic, accommodating, good-natured, liberal, humanitarian, righteous, open-minded, broad-minded, altruistic, philanthropic, helpful, magnanimous, amiable, genial, cordial, unselfish, warmhearted, large-hearted, big-hearted, beneficent, soft-hearted, sympathizing, freehearted, liberal, pitying, good, soft\*, easy\*; see also **kind** 1, **merciful** 1. — *Ant.* CRUEL, barbaric, inhuman.
**2.** [Cultural] — *Syn.* civilized, advanced, cultured; see **educated** 1, **refined** 2.

**humanist,** *n.* — *Syn.* classicist, altruist, scholastic; see **philanthropist, philosopher, scholar** 2.

**humanitarian,** *modif.* — *Syn.* compassionate, philanthropic, public-spirited, altruistic; see **generous** 1, **humane** 1, **kind, philanthropic.**
*See Synonym Study at* PHILANTHROPIC.

**humanitarian,** *n.* — *Syn.* altruist, helper, benefactor, good Samaritan; see **patron** 1, **philanthropist.**

**humanities,** *n.* — *Syn.* liberal arts, letters, belles-lettres, arts, the fine arts, languages, the classics; see also **art** 4, **history** 2, **language** 2, **literature** 1, **philosophy** 1.

**humanity,** *n.* **1.** [The human race] — *Syn.* man, mankind, men; see **man** 1.
**2.** [An ideal of human behavior] — *Syn.* tolerance, sympathy, understanding; see **kindness** 1, **virtue** 1, 2.

**humanize,** *v.* — *Syn.* acculturate, cultivate, refine, tame, temper; see also **civilize, teach** 1, 2.

**humanizing,** *modif.* — *Syn.* civilizing, refining, uplifting; see **cultural.**

**humble,** *modif.* **1.** [Meek] — *Syn.* lowly, submissive, gentle, quiet, unassuming, diffident, simple, retiring, bashful, shy, timid, reserved, docile, deferential, backward, self-conscious, soft-spoken, coy, demure, blushing, sheepish, standoffish, mild, timorous, withdrawn, unpretentious, unobtrusive, hesitant, apprehensive, fearful, tentative, self-belittling, poor in spirit, tractable, sedate, unpretending, supplicatory, small, biddable, unpresuming, self-effacing, little, slavish, broken, ductile, obsequious, reverential, manageable, subservient, ordinary, unambitious, commonplace, free from pride, peaceful, placid, without arrogance, peaceable, obedient, passive, broken in spirit, tame, clement, restrained, enduring, stoic, yielding, stoical, acquiescent, unostentatious, unimportant, of little importance, of small importance, gentle as a lamb, meek-spirited, meek-hearted, low, unresisting, resigned, subdued, tolerant, content, compliant, underdogmatic\*, mealy-mouthed\*, Micawberish\*, eating humble pie\*; see also **modest** 2. — *Ant.* PROUD, haughty, conceited.
**2.** [Lowly] — *Syn.* unpretentious, unassuming, modest, seemly, becoming, homespun, natural, plebeian, low, cringing, out-of-the-way, proletarian, servile, undistinguished, pitiful, sordid, shabby, underprivileged, meager, beggarly, log-cabin, commonplace, menial, unimportant, insignificant, small, poor, untouched, unvarnished, unaffected, rough, hard, severe, unpretending, earthborn, base, meek, little, of low birth, obscure, inferior, baseborn, mean, inglorious, low-ranking, plain, common, homely, ignoble, low in rank, of low rank, simple, lowbred, uncouth, ignominious, of mean parentage, measly, contemptible, miserable, scrubby, ordinary, inferior, puny, humdrum, poorish, trivial, ill-bred, petty, underbred, paltry, unequal, vulgar, unrefined, wretched, unfit. — *Ant.* upper-class, NOBLE, privileged.

**humble,** *v.* — *Syn.* shame, mortify, chasten, demean (oneself), demote, lower, crush, abash, hide one's face, bring low, put to shame, silence, reduce, humiliate, de-

*humble*

grade, overcome, strike dumb, take down, put down, pull down, bring down, override, snub, confuse, discredit, deflate, upset, abase, make ashamed, put out of countenance, confound, deny, discomfit, take down a peg*, pull one off one's high horse*, put down*, squelch*, squash*, hide one's light under a bushel*, kiss the rod*; see also **disgrace, embarrass** 1. — *Ant.* exalt, PRAISE, glorify.

---

*SYN.* — **humble** is to lower the pride or increase the humility of oneself or another, and, unqualified, suggests that such lowering is deserved *[humbled* by the frightening experience]*; to **humiliate** is to humble or shame another painfully and in public *[humiliated* by their laughter]*; **degrade** literally means to lower in grade or rank, but it commonly implies a lowering or corrupting of moral character and self-respect; **abase** suggests a loss, often merely temporary and self-imposed, of dignity and respect *[he* abased *himself before his employer]*; **debase** implies a decline in value, quality, or character *[a* debased *mind]*

---

**humbly,** *modif.* — *Syn.* meekly, submissively, abjectly, simply, poorly, ingloriously, obscurely, on bended knee, apologetically. — *Ant.* haughtily, PROUDLY, boastfully.

**humbug,** *n.* **1.** [Deception] — *Syn.* lie, fraud, hoax, sham; see **deception** 1, **fake, nonsense.**

**2.** [An impostor] — *Syn.* charlatan, imposter, fake, faker, phony*, quack*.

**humdrum,** *modif.* — *Syn.* monotonous, common, uninteresting; see **dull** 4.

**humid,** *modif.* — *Syn.* stuffy, sticky, muggy, wet; see **close** 5, **wet** 1.

*See Synonym Study at* WET.

**humidity,** *n.* — *Syn.* moisture, wetness, dampness, mugginess, dankness, heaviness, sogginess, thickness, fogginess, wet, sultriness, steaminess, steam, vaporization, dankness, evaporation, sweatiness, humectation, dewiness, humidification, liquidity, stickiness, moistness, swelter, oppressiveness; see also **rain** 1. — *Ant.* DRYNESS, aridity, drought.

**humiliate,** *v.* — *Syn.* debase, chasten, mortify, make a fool of, put to shame, humble, degrade, denigrate, crush, shame, discomfit, abash, make lowly, deny, confuse, snub, confound, lower, dishonor, depress, fill with shame, chagrin, break, demean, bring low, base, conquer, make ashamed, vanquish, pout out of countenance, cast down, take down, put down, bring down, pull down, take down a peg*, put one's nose out of joint*; see also **disgrace, embarrass** 1, **humble.**

*See Synonym Study at* HUMBLE.

**humiliated,** *modif.* — *Syn.* humbled, abashed, disgraced, mortified; see **ashamed.**

*See Synonym Study at* ASHAMED.

**humiliating,** *modif.* — *Syn.* mortifying, humbling, disgracing; see **embarrassing, opprobrious** 1.

**humiliation,** *n.* — *Syn.* chagrin, mortification, mental pain; see **disgrace** 1, **embarrassment** 1, **shame** 2.

**humility,** *n.* — *Syn.* meekness, timidity, self-abasement, self-abnegation, submissiveness, servility, obsequiousness, mortification, reserve, lowliness, demureness, unobtrusiveness, subservience, subjection, humbleness, submission, abasement, diffidence, self-effacement, fawning, obedience, passiveness, nonresistance, resignation, bashfulness, shyness, timorousness, inferiority complex; see also **docility, modesty** 1. — *Ant.* PRIDE, vainglory, conceit.

**hummock,** *n.* — *Syn.* bump, knob, hump; see **bulge, hill, lump.**

**humor,** *n.* **1.** [Comedy] — *Syn.* amusement, jesting, raillery, joking, merriment, buffoonery, tomfoolery, badinage, clowning, jocularity, jocoseness, farce, drollery, facetiousness, black humor, salt, whimsicality, comedy stuff*, laugh business*; see also **entertainment** 1, **fun.**

**2.** [An example of humor] — *Syn.* witticism, pleasantry, banter; see **joke** 1, 2.

**3.** [The ability to appreciate comedy] — *Syn.* good humor, sense of humor, wittiness, high spirits, merry disposition, joviality, jolliness, jocularity, jocundity, gaiety, joyfulness, playfulness, happy frame of mind, jauntiness; see also **happiness** 1.

**4.** [Mood] — *Syn.* disposition, frame of mind, temper; see **mood** 1.

*See Synonym Study at* MOOD, WIT.

**out of humor** — *Syn.* cross, disagreeable, grouchy; see **irritable.**

**humor,** *v.* — *Syn.* indulge, pamper, baby, play up to, gratify, please, pet, coddle, tickle, gladden, mollycoddle, spoil, oblige, comply with, appease, placate, soften, be playful with; see also **comfort, entertain** 1, **satisfy** 1. — *Ant.* provoke, anger, enrage.

---

*SYN.* — **humor** suggests compliance with the mood or whim of another *[they* humored *the dying man]*; **indulge** implies a yielding to the wishes or desires of oneself or another, as because of a weak will or an amiable nature; **pamper** implies overindulgence or excessive gratification; **spoil** emphasizes the harm done to the personality or character by overindulgence or excessive attention *[grandparents often* spoil *children]*; **baby** suggests the sort of pampering and devoted care lavished on infants and connotes a potential loss of self-reliance *[because he was sickly, his mother continued to* baby *him]*

---

**humorous,** *modif.* — *Syn.* comical, comic, witty, entertaining; see **funny** 1, **witty.**

*See Synonym Study at* WITTY.

**humorously,** *modif.* — *Syn.* comically, ridiculously, playfully, absurdly, ludicrously, amusingly, jokingly, mirthfully, ironically, satirically, facetiously, merrily, genially, jovially, jocosely, jocundly, not seriously, not solemnly, screamingly, archly, in a comical manner, in an amusing manner, just for fun*.

**hump,** *n.* — *Syn.* protuberance, mound, bump, swelling, camel hump, humpback, hunchback, hummock, protrusion, elevation, convexity, knob, knap, convexedness, excrescence, prominence, knurl, monticle, eminence, boss, projection, swell, hunch, barrow, gibbosity, lump, dune, tumescence, kopje; see also **bulge, hill.**

**hump*,** *v.* — *Syn.* rush, work hard, speed up; see **hurry** 1.

**humpback,** *n.* — *Syn.* cripple, deformed person, Quasimodo; see **hunchback.**

**humpbacked,** *modif.* — *Syn.* stooped, malformed, distorted; see **deformed, disabled.**

**hunch,** *n.* **1.** [Hump] — *Syn.* protuberance, bump, swelling; see **bulge, hump, hill, lump.**

**2.** [*Intuition] — *Syn.* idea, notion, feeling, premonition, presage, forecast, presentiment, instinct, expectation, anticipation, foreknowledge, preconceived notion, forewisdom, omination, precognition, preapprehension, prescience, forewarning, clue, presagement, foreboding, boding, prenotice, prenotation, augury, auguration, hint, portent, apprehension, misgiving, qualm, suspicion, inkling, glimmer; see also **thought** 2.

**hunch,** *v.* — *Syn.* arch, draw together, cower, bunch; see **bow** 1, **lean** 1.

**hunchback,** *n.* — *Syn.* humpback, cripple, crookbacked, humpbacked person, Quasimodo.

**hundred,** *n.* — *Syn.* ten tens, five score, century; see **number** 1.

**hung,** *modif.* — *Syn.* suspended, swaying, dangling; see **hanging.**

**hunger,** *n.* — *Syn.* craving, longing, yearning, mania, ravenousness, voracity, lust, desire for food, famine, starvation, appetite, gluttony, hungriness, panting, drought, appetition, glut, appetence, want, polydipsia, appetency, vacancy, void, greed, greediness, bottomless pit*, peckishness*, the munchies*, a stomach for*, sweet tooth*, aching void*; see also **appetite** 1, **desire** 1, **starvation.** — *Ant.* SATISFACTION, satiety, glut.

**hungry,** *modif.* — *Syn.* starved, famished, craving, ravenous, desirous, hankering, unsatisfied, unfilled, starving, edacious, insatiate, voracious, of keen appetite, famishing, half-starved, hungered, ravening, omnivorous, carnivorous, supperless, greedy as a hog, dinnerless, piggish, hoggish, peckish, half-famished, on an empty stomach*, hungry as a wolf*, empty*; see also **greedy** 2. — *Ant.* satisfied, FULL, fed.

**hung up*, 1.** [Troubled] — *Syn.* disturbed, psychotic, psychopathic; see **neurotic, troubled** 2.

**2.** [Intent] — *Syn.* absorbed, engrossed, preoccupied, obsessed; see **enthusiastic** 2, **rapt** 2, **thoughtful** 1.

**hunk,** *n.* — *Syn.* lump, large piece, good-sized bit, portion, a fair quantity, a good bit, chunk, bunch, mass, clod, a pile, thick slice, morsel, a lot, slice, gob, hank, loaf, nugget, block, loads, bulk, batch, wad*; see also **part** 1, **piece** 1.

**hunt,** *n.* **1.** [The pursuit of game] — *Syn.* chase, sporting, shooting, coursing; lion hunt, tiger hunt, fox hunt, deer hunt, duck hunt, etc.; tracking, hawking, steeplechase, venery, *battue* (French), course, race, angling, fishing, game, gunning, pursuit, field sport, riding to hounds, piscation, beagling, piscatology; see also **hunting, sport** 3.

**2.** [A search] — *Syn.* investigation, probe, inquiry, raid, quest, pursuit, exploration, research, sifting, seeking, pursuance, hounding, prosecution, trailing, inquisition, scrutiny, inquest, study, interrogation, prying, meddling, tracing, snooping, research, rummage, following, pursuing, reconnaissance, look-see*, frisking*; see also **examination** 1.

**hunt,** *v.* **1.** [To pursue with intent to kill] — *Syn.* follow, chase, give chase, stalk, hound, trail, dog, seek, capture, kill, shoot, press on, track, heel, shadow, chase after, hunt out, ride to hounds, snare, look for, fish, run, ride, drive, fish for, hawk, poach, grouse, ferret, drag, course, start game, beagle*, gun for*, go gunning for*; see also **pursue** 1.

**2.** [To try to find] — *Syn.* investigate, seek for, sift, winnow, drag, probe, fish out, fish for, look for, be on the lookout for, go after, trail, cast about, ransack, trace, ferret out, spoor, inquire, hunt for, hunt out, search for, search out, grope in the dark, leave no stone unturned, delve for, scour, prowl after, examine, interrogate, question, catechise, nose around*, rummage*; see also **seek** 1.

**hunted,** *modif.* — *Syn.* pursued, followed, tracked, sought for, trailed, chased, stalked, hounded, tracked, dogged, tailed, harried, outcast, outlawed, wanted, driven out, searched for.

**hunted down,** *modif.* — *Syn.* found, brought to bay, run to earth, taken; see **captured** 1.

**hunter,** *n.* **1.** [A person who hunts] — *Syn.* huntsman, stalker, chaser, sportsman, pursuer, ferreter, big-game hunter, hawker, falconer, beater, gunner, poacher, nimrod, pigsticker, horsewoman, huntress, horseman, archer, deerstalker, pursuant, equestrian, fisher, angler, equestrienne, piscator, fisherman, piscatorian, piscatorialist, toxophile, Waltonian, toxophilite, toxophilist, bowman, shooter; see also **trapper.**

**2.** [A dog or horse bred for hunting] — *Syn.* hunting dog, gun dog, hound, hound dog, courser, foxhound, rabbit hound, chaser, steed, equine, stalking horse, hunting horse, mount; see also **animal** 1, **dog** 1, **horse** 1.

Hunting dogs include: pointer, setter, boarhound, Great Dane, retriever, spaniel, bloodhound, whippet, borzoi, saluki, terrier, foxhound, wolfhound, Rhodesian ridgeback, beagle.

**hunting,** *modif.* — *Syn.* looking for, looking around, seeking, in search of; see **searching** 2.

**hunting,** *n.* — *Syn.* the chase, the hunt, sporting, shooting, coursing, venery, stalking, falconry, trapping, big-game hunting, deer hunting, boar hunting, fox hunting, pheasant shooting, fowling, field, chevy (British), chivy (British), angling, pursuit, falconry, fishing, hawking, still hunt, venatics, fishery, steeplechase, fox hunting, riding to hounds, piscation, gunning, halieutics, beagling*; see also **hunt, sport** 3.

**hurdle,** *n.* **1.** [A physical barrier] — *Syn.* barricade, earthwork, blockade; see **barrier.**

**2.** [Something in one's way] — *Syn.* complication, obstacle, obstruction; see **difficulty** 1, **impediment** 1, **interference** 1.

**hurdle,** *v.* — *Syn.* jump over, jump across, scale, vault, surmount, leap over, overcome, hop the sticks*; see also **jump** 1.

**hurl,** *v.* — *Syn.* throw, cast, fling, heave; see **throw** 1.

*See Synonym Study at* THROW.

**hurly-burly,** *n.* — *Syn.* restlessness, turmoil, turbulence; see **confusion** 2, **uproar.**

**hurrah,** *interj.* — *Syn.* yeah, yay, three cheers, hurray, rah-rah, huzza, yippee, whoopee; hear, hear; hip-hip; see also **cheer** 3, **cry** 1, **encouragement** 2, **yell** 1.

**hurricane,** *n.* — *Syn.* whirlwind, tropical storm, line storm, typhoon, tempest, monsoon, blow*; see also **storm.**

**hurried,** *modif.* — *Syn.* quick, speedy, in a hurry; see **fast** 1.

**hurriedly,** *modif.* — *Syn.* rapidly, speedily, fast; see **quickly** 1.

**hurry,** *interj.* — *Syn.* run, hasten, speed, move, step on it*, step on the gas*, get on it, hustle, gain time, look alive, get a move on, shake a leg*, bear down on it*, on the double*, hump it*; see also **hurry** *v.*

**hurry,** *n.* **1.** [The press of time] — *Syn.* rush, drive, scurry, dash, push, precipitateness, hustle*.

**2.** [Confusion] — *Syn.* bustle, flurry, fluster; see **confusion** 2.

**3.** [Haste] — *Syn.* dispatch, expedition, rush; see **speed.**

*See Synonym Study at* HASTE.

**hurry,** *v.* **1.** [To act hastily] — *Syn.* hasten, be quick, make haste, bestir oneself, bustle, rush, make short work of, scoot, work at high speed, dash on, hurry about, bundle on, run off, sally, work under pressure, hurry up, lose no time, make time, speed, act on a moment's notice, turn on the steam*, step on the gas*, get cracking*, don't spare the horses*, step on it*, fly about*, put on a burst of speed*, dig out*, dart to and fro*, race one's motor*, floor it*, shake a leg*. — *Ant.* DELAY, lose time, procrastinate.

**2.** [To move rapidly] — *Syn.* fly, bustle, dash off; see **race** 1, **run** 2.

**3.** [To urge others] — *Syn.* push, spur, goad on; see **drive** 1, **goad, urge** 2.

**hurrying,** *modif.* — *Syn.* bustling, scurrying, darting, hastening, speeding, in a hurry, running, rushing, dashing, flying, expediting, propelling, racing, racing against time. — *Ant.* CREEPING, crawling, inching along.

**hurt,** *modif.* — *Syn.* wounded, injured, damaged, harmed, marred, impaired, shot, warped, struck, contused, bruised, stricken, battered, buffeted, mauled, hit, stabbed, mutilated, lacerated, disfigured, blemished, pained, in pain, disturbed, suffering, distressed, tortured, agonized, in a serious state, unhappy, slightly wounded, grazed, scratched, severely wounded, sorely hurt, nicked*, winged*; see also **wounded.** — *Ant.* aided, helped, assisted.

**hurt,** *n.* **1.** [A wound] — *Syn.* blow, gash, ache; see **injury** 1, **pain** 1.

**2.** [Damage] — *Syn.* ill-treatment, harm, persecution; see **damage** 1, **disaster, misfortune** 1.

**hurt,** *v.* **1.** [To cause pain] — *Syn.* cramp, squeeze, cut, bruise, tear, pain, torment, try, afflict, kick, puncture, do violence, slap, abuse, administer punishment, flog, whip, whack, torture, gnaw, stab, pierce, maul, cut up, harm, damage, injure, wound, lacerate, harrow, convulse, prick, sting, do evil, chafe, bite, flail, give pain, grate, martyr, inflict pain, rasp, excruciate, burn, grind, rack, wring, nip, fret, crucify, martyrize, tweak, gripe, agonize, thrash, punch, prolong the agony, pinch, gall, spank, chastise, punish, pummel, lace, flail, buffet, drub, smite, trounce, scourge, flagellate, lambaste, baste, lash, cudgel, bastinado, belabor, birch, cane, switch, sandbag, cause pain, anguish, distress, displease, discommode, discompose, incommode, put out, give someone the works*, give no quarter*, barb the dart*, work over*, lay up*, wrack up*, wallop*, blackjack*, belt*, slug*; see also **beat** 2. — *Ant.* COMFORT, ease, soothe.

**2.** [To harm] — *Syn.* damage, maltreat, injure, spoil; see **damage** 1, **destroy** 1.

**3.** [To distress] — *Syn.* worry, outrage, trouble; see **bother** 2, 3, **disturb** 2.

**4.** [To give a feeling of pain] — *Syn.* be sore, ache, throb, pain, be tender, be bruised, sting, bother, burn, irritate.

---

*SYN.* — **hurt** implies a wounding physically or emotionally or a causing of any kind of harm or damage /the rumors *hurt* his business/; **injure** implies the marring of the appearance, health, soundness, etc. of a person or thing /*injured* pride/; **harm** more strongly suggests the pain or distress caused /he wouldn't *harm* a fly/; **damage** stresses the loss, as in value, usefulness, etc., resulting from an injury /*damaged* goods/; to **impair** something is to cause it to deteriorate in quality or to lessen in value, strength, etc. /*impaired* hearing/; **spoil** implies such serious impairment of a thing as to destroy its value, usefulness, etc. /rain *spoiled* the party, the canned food was *spoiled*/

---

**hurtful,** *modif.* — *Syn.* harmful, aching, injurious, bad; see **dangerous** 1, 2, **deadly, harmful, ominous, poisonous.**

**hurtle,** *v.* **1.** [To dash against] — *Syn.* collide, bump, push; see **crash** 4.

**2.** [To move swiftly and forcefully] — *Syn.* rush, rush headlong, plunge, tear; see **race** 1, **speed.**

**husband,** *n.* — *Syn.* spouse, married man, mate, bedmate, benedict, helpmate, consort, bridegroom, groom, breadwinner, provider, man, polygynist, polygamist, cuckold, goodman, monogamist, monogynist,

bigamist, commonlaw husband, hubby*, lord*, head of the house*, the man of the house*, lord and master*, meal ticket*, old man*; see also **man** 2.

**husband,** *v.* — *Syn.* conserve, manage, preserve; see **save** 3, 4, 5.

**husbandman,** *n.* — *Syn.* planter, agriculturalist, forester; see **farmer.**

**husbandry,** *n.* **1.** [Farming] — *Syn.* agriculture, tillage, land management; see **farming.**

**2.** [Management of one's private affairs] — *Syn.* home management, personal transactions, budgeting, housekeeping, domestic arrangement, business dealings, management, managership, stewardship, retrenchment; see also **administration** 1.

**3.** [Thrift] — *Syn.* providence, wise administration, thriftiness; see **economy** 2, **frugality.**

**hush,** *interj.* — *Syn.* quiet, be quiet, stop talking, soft, less noise, pipe down*, sign off*, hush up*; see also **shut up.**

**hush,** *n.* — *Syn.* peace, stillness, quiet; see **silence** 1.

**hush,** *v.* — *Syn.* silence, still, muffle, gag, stop, stifle, force into silence; see also **quiet** 2.

**hush money,** *n.* — *Syn.* bribe, graft, blackmail, extortion, payola; see **bribe, theft.**

**hush (up),** *v.* — *Syn.* cover, conceal, suppress; see **hide** 1.

**husk,** *n.* — *Syn.* shuck, hull, covering, outside; see **cover** 1, **shell** 1.

**husky,** *modif.* **1.** [Hoarse] — *Syn.* throaty, growling, gruff; see **hoarse, loud** 1.

**2.** [Strong] — *Syn.* muscular, sinewy, strapping, heavyset; see **strong** 1.

**hussar,** *n.* — *Syn.* cavalryman, trooper, horse soldier; see **cavalry, soldier.**

**hussy,** *n.* — *Syn.* seductress, loose woman, vamp, temptress, slut; see also **prostitute.**

**hustle*,** *v.* **1.** [To hurry] — *Syn.* act quickly, rush, push; see **hasten** 1, **hurry** 1, **race** 1, **run** 2, **speed.**

**2.** [To work zealously] — *Syn.* do a thriving business, be conscientious, make many sales, apply oneself, do a good job, press one's business, give all one's energy to, at it all the time*, keep humming*, get on the ball*; see also **work** 1.

**3.** [To cheat] — *Syn.* con, swindle, flimflam; see **deceive, trick.**

**hustler*,** *n.* **1.** [A professional gambler] — *Syn.* gamester, bookmaker, plunger; see **gambler.**

**2.** [A prostitute] — *Syn.* whore, harlot, call girl, working girl; see **prostitute.**

**3.** [A fast worker] — *Syn.* person with initiative, man of action, fanatic, cohort, busy bee, enthusiast, human dynamo, worker, pusher, workaholic, devotee, bug*, nut*, freak*, live wire*, go-getter*, Johnny-on-the-spot*, speed-up man*; see also **zealot.**

**hustling,** *modif.* — *Syn.* fast-moving, bustling, occupied; see **active** 2, **busy** 1.

**hut,** *n.* — *Syn.* shack, shanty, lean-to, crib, bungalow, bunkhouse, refuge, lodge, hutch, igloo, dugout, hovel, cottage, cabin, A-frame, hogan, tepee, tupek, cot, log cabin, log house, cote, wigwam, wickiup, mean dwelling, poor cottage, pigeonhole*, dump*, rathole*; see also **home** 1, **shack, shelter** 1, **shed.**

**hutch,** *n.* **1.** [A pen] — *Syn.* cage, coop, corral; see **pen** 1.

**2.** [A cupboard] — *Syn.* sideboard, buffet, cabinet; see **cupboard, furniture.**

**hybrid,** *modif.* — *Syn.* crossed, alloyed, crossbred, cross, variegated, mongrel, amphibious, half-blooded, half-breed, half-caste, heterogeneous, commingled, impure, mutated, intermingled, interbred, composite, half-and-half; see also **bred.**

**hybrid,** *n.* — *Syn.* crossbreed, cross, mixture, composite, half-breed, half-blood, half-caste, mongrel, combination, mestizo, quadroon, Eurasian, outcross, Ladino, mustee, octoroon; see also **mixture** 1.

**hydrant,** *n.* — *Syn.* fire hydrant, water plug, fireplug, outdoor faucet, spigot, tap, water outlet, stop valve, discharge pipe, cock; see also **faucet.**

**hydraulic,** *modif.* — *Syn.* water-pumping, using water, pressure-driven, water-powered.

**hydraulics,** *n.* — *Syn.* laws of the motion of water, science of the movement of liquids, science of liquids in motion, hydrodynamics, hydrostatics, hydrokinetics, hydromechanics, hydrography, hydrology, fluviology, hydrometry, pegology; see also **science** 1.

**hydropathy,** *n.* — *Syn.* physiotherapy, water treatment, cure; see **therapy, treatment** 2.

**hygiene,** *n.* — *Syn.* cleanliness, hygienics, hygiology, regimen, preventive medicine, hygienization, healthful living, public health, hygiantics, sanitary measures, sanitary provisions; see also **health** 1, **sanitation.**

**hygienic,** *modif.* — *Syn.* healthful, sanitary, clean; see **pure** 2, **sterile** 3.

**hymn,** *n.* — *Syn.* religious song, song of worship, ode, chant, psalm, paean, carol, anthem, evensong, litany, hosanna, motet, canticle, oratorio; see also **song.**

**hyperbole,** *n.* — *Syn.* overstatement, metaphor, distortion; see **exaggeration.**

**hypercritical,** *modif.* — *Syn.* overcritical, hard to please, faultfinding; see **critical** 2, **sarcastic, severe** 1.

*See Synonym Study at* CRITICAL.

**hypersensitive,** *modif.* — *Syn.* high-strung, fastidious, jumpy; see **emotional** 2, **neurotic.**

**hypertrophy,** *n.* — *Syn.* profusion, excess, exaggeration, overgrowth, overexpansion, enlargement of an organ, excessive growth, superfluity, amplitude, redundance, surfeit, oversupply, prolixity, overflow, profusion, exuberance, superabundance, affluence, prodigality, surplus, copiousness, overdevelopment; see also **growth** 3.

**hypnosis,** *n.* — *Syn.* trance, anesthesia, lethargy; see **stupor.**

**hypnotic,** *modif.* — *Syn.* soporose, sleep-inducing, mesmeric, opiate, narcotic, anesthetic, anodyne, lenitive, pertaining to hypnosis, soporific, sleep-producing, soothing, somniferous, somnolent, calmative, somnific, somnifacient, soporiferous, trance-inducing.

**hypnotism,** *n.* — *Syn.* bewitchment, suggestion, mesmerism, hypnotherapy, deep sleep, spell-casting, self-hypnosis, hypnoanalysis, autohypnosis, hypnotic suggestion, induction of hypnosis, sleep production, fascination, psychokinesis.

**hypnotize,** *v.* **1.** [To put in a trance] — *Syn.* mesmerize, put to sleep, lull to sleep, dull the will, hold under a spell, entrance, bring under one's control, induce hypnosis, place in a trance, stupefy, drug, narcotize, soothe, psychologize, anesthetize, subject to suggestion, place under control, make drowsy or sleepy.

**2.** [To charm] — *Syn.* magnetize, captivate, entrance; see **charm** 1, **fascinate.**

**hypnotized,** *modif.* — *Syn.* entranced, mesmerized, enchanted; see **charmed.**

**hypochondria,** *n.* — *Syn.* depression, anxiety, melancholia, imagined ill-health, melancholy, despondency, doldrums, low spirits, dejection, anxiety neurosis; see also **neurosis, pretense** 1.

**hypochondriac,** *n.* — *Syn.* malingerer, melancholic, masochist, hypochondriast, mope, dispirited person, self-tormenter; see also **impostor, neurotic.**

**hypocrisy,** *n.* — *Syn.* quackery, casuistry, pharisaism, sanctimoniousness, affectation, pietism, false guise, bad faith, hollowness, display, charlatanry, lip service, bigotry, dissimulation, sham, fraud, pretense of virtue, false goodness, lip homage, formalism, false piety, assumed piety, empty ceremony, tartuffism, solemn mockery, tartuffery, lip reverence, sanctimony, false profession, cant, bunkum\*, bunk\*; see also **deception** 1, **dishonesty, lie** 1, **pretense** 1. — *Ant.* VIRTUE, devotion, piety.

**hypocrite,** *n.* — *Syn.* pretender, fraud, faker, dissembler, deceiver, casuist, charlatan, poseur, poser, pharisee, bigot, quack, tartuffe, backslider, whited sepulcher, sham, actor, cheat, informer, trickster, one given to hypocrisy, sophist, mountebank, adventurer, sharper, confidence man, malingerer, humbug, swindler, informer, knave, rascal, traitor, Judas, Uriah Heep, decoy, wolf in sheep's clothing, Pecksniff, actor, masquerader, dissimulator, attitudinizer, ass in lion's skin, bluenose\*, four-flusher\*, two-timer\*, two-face\*, God on wheels\*, Holy Joe\*, goody-goody\*, Holy Willie\*, bunko steerer\*, crook\*, spieler\*, stool pigeon\*, faker\*; see also **impostor.**

**hypocritical,** *modif.* — *Syn.* deceiving, deceptive, deluding, double-dealing, shamming, sanctimonious, dissembling, pious, unctuous, unreliable, mealy-mouthed, canting, insincere, double-faced, smooth-tongued, affected, false, caviling, dissimulating, lying, artificial, two-faced, smooth-spoken, spurious, captious, feigning, deceitful, assuming, unnatural, faithless, plausible, pretentious, mannered, Janus-faced, phoney; see also **dishonest** 1, 2. — *Ant.* upright, HONEST, sincere.

**hypodermic,** *n.* — *Syn.* syringe, injector, shot; see **needle.**

**hypothesis,** *n.* — *Syn.* theory, supposition, surmise, speculation, scheme, system, conjecture, prediction, assumption, presumption, condition, suggestion, thesis, proposal, working hypothesis, preliminary layout, tentative plans, basis for discussion, apriority, law, inference, antecedent, reason, position, assignment, starting point, basis, derivation, philosopheme, ground, term, scheme, belief, foundation, postulate, axiom, presupposition, premise, data, attribution, interpretation, deduction, demonstration, tentative law, principle, lemma, explanation, theorem, rationale, philosophy, shot in the dark\*, guess-so\*, clotheshorse\*; see also **guess, opinion** 1, **theory** 1.

*See Synonym Study at* THEORY.

**hypothetical,** *modif.* **1.** [Supposed] — *Syn.* presupposed, suppositious, suppositional, conditional, conjectural, imagined, indeterminate, speculative, indefinite, questionable, unconfirmed, equivocal, doubtful, conjecturable, concocted, suspect, stochastic, stochastical, assumed by hypothesis, possible, uncertain, debatable, imaginary, of the nature of hypothesis, vague, theoretical, pretending, open, provisory, casual, disputable, refutable, postulational, contestable, presumptive, hypothesized, assumptive, contingent, theoretic, postulated, based on incomplete knowledge; see also **assumed** 1, **likely** 1. — *Ant.* PROVED, demonstrated, confirmed.

**2.** [Characterized by hypothesis] — *Syn.* postulated, academic, philosophical; see **theoretical.**

**hysteria,** *n.* — *Syn.* delirium, frenzy, agitation, feverishness, mania, rage, hysterics, madness, insanity, craze, excitement, uproar, convulsion, fit, paroxysm, laughing jag*, crying jag*; see also **confusion** 2, **excitement, nervousness** 1.

*SYN.* — **hysteria** is applied in psychiatry to certain psychogenic disorders characterized by excitability, anxiety, sensory and motor disturbances, or the involuntary simulation of blindness, deafness, etc.; **mania** in its basic sense of a mental disorder characterized by excitability, exaggerated feelings of well-being, excessive activity, etc. describes the phase of manic-depressive psychosis that is distinguished from *depression;* **delirium** denotes a temporary state of extreme mental disturbance (marked by restlessness, incoherence, and hallucinations) that occurs during fevers, in alcoholic psychosis, etc.; **frenzy,** not used technically in psychiatry, implies extreme emotional agitation in which self-control is lost; in extended use, **hysteria** suggests an outburst of wild, uncontrolled feeling *[* laughed and cried in a fit of *hysteria] ,* **mania,** a craze for something *[a mania* for surfing*],* and **delirium,** rapturous excitement *[a delirium of joy]*

**hysterical,** *modif. — Syn.* convulsed, uncontrolled, raving, delirious, wildly emotional, psychoneurotic, unnerved, neurotic, resembling hysteria, spasmodic, emotional, rabid, emotionally disordered, distracted, morbidly excited, overexcited, fuming, distraught, unrestrained, possessed, wrought-up, fanatical, irrepressible, harrowed, convulsive, carried away, frothing, seething, beside oneself, rampant, out of one's wits, turbulent, mad, affected with hysteria, suffering from hysteria, uncontrollable, agitated, raging, frenzied, uproarious, incensed, confused, tempestuous, maddened, blazing, crazy, impetuous, crazed, furious, violent, boiling, impassioned, panic-stricken, nervous, vehement, overwrought, fiery, passionate, cracked wide open*, in a frazzle*, in a fit*, jittery*, amuck*, tempest-tossed*, wild-eyed*, on a laughing jag*, on a crying jag*; see also **angry, excited, frantic, troubled** 1.

# I

**I,** *pron.* — *Syn.* myself, ego, self, yours truly*, number one*; see also **character** 2, **id.**

**iambic,** *n.* **1.** [Verse] — *Syn.* iambic pentameter, rhyme, versification; see **poetry, verse** 1.

**2.** [A poetic meter] — *Syn.* metrical foot, iambus, iamb; see **foot** 4, **meter.**

***ibidem*** (Latin), *modif.* — *Syn.* *ibid.* (Latin), in the same place, in the work, in the same book, on the same page, in the same chapter.

**ICBM,** *n.* — *Syn.* Intercontinental Ballistic Missile, guided missile, strategic deterrent; see **missile, rocket, weapon** 1.

**ice,** *n.* — *Syn.* frost, crystal, hail, icicle, glacier, floe, ice cube, dry ice, black ice, white ice, chunk ice, crushed ice, iceberg, permafrost; see also **frost** 2, **iceberg.**

**break the ice** — *Syn.* make a start, initiate, commence; see **approach** 1, **begin** 1.

**cut no ice*** — *Syn.* have no influence, have no effect, not matter, be unimportant; see **fail** 1.

**on ice*** — *Syn.* in reserve, in readiness, held, in abeyance; see **reserved** 2, **saved** 2.

**on thin ice*** — *Syn.* in a dangerous situation, imperiled, insecure; see **endangered.**

**ice,** *v.* **1.** [To become covered with ice] — *Syn.* frost, coat, mist, rime; see **freeze** 1.

**2.** [To cover with icing] — *Syn.* frost, coat, glaze, trim; see **decorate.**

**iceberg,** *n.* — *Syn.* ice sheet, ice field, floe, berg, snowberg, icecap, ice shelf, ice pack, ice mass, growler*; see also **ice.**

**icebox,** *n.* — *Syn.* cooler, freezer, fridge*; see **refrigerator.**

**ice cream,** *n.* — *Syn.* mousse, *gelato* (Italian), *glace* (French), sherbet, sorbet, ice milk, frozen yogurt, tofutti, ice, sundae, parfait, frozen custard, frozen dessert, spumoni, tortoni, cassata; see also **dessert.**

**icing,** *n.* — *Syn.* frosting, coating, glaze, sugar coating, topping, fudge, filling.

**icky*,** *modif.* — *Syn.* distasteful, cloying, gooey*; see **adhesive, offensive** 2, **sentimental.**

**icon,** *n.* — *Syn.* image, likeness, representation, figure; see **picture** 2, **representation, symbol.**

**iconoclast,** *n.* **1.** [A destroyer of religious images] — *Syn.* dissenter, vandal, heathen, antichrist; see **atheist, pagan, skeptic.**

**2.** [A nonconformist] — *Syn.* individualist, renegade, dissenter; see **nonconformist, radical, rebel** 1.

**iconoclastic,** *modif.* **1.** [Skeptical] — *Syn.* individualistic, nonconforming, dissident, irreverent; see **radical** 2.

**2.** [Irreligious] — *Syn.* heretical, fanatical, heathenish; see **atheistic, heathen, impious.**

**icy,** *modif.* **1.** [Covered with ice] — *Syn.* frozen over, iced, glaring, freezing, glacial, frostbound, glassy, sleeted, frosted, frosty, smooth as glass; see also **slippery.**

**2.** [Cold] — *Syn.* freezing, glacial, polar; see **cold** 1.

**id,** *n.* — *Syn.* self, source of ego and libido, generative force, instinctive force, inner nature, *Es* (German), psyche; see also **character** 2.

**idea,** *n.* **1.** [Something one thinks or knows] — *Syn.* concept, conception, thought, notion, impression, inkling, construct; see also **opinion** 1, **thought** 2.

**2.** [A conviction] — *Syn.* opinion, view, doctrine, conception; see **belief** 1, **faith** 2.

**3.** [A plan] — *Syn.* intention, design, scheme, approach; see **plan** 2, **purpose** 1.

**4.** [Fancy] — *Syn.* whimsy, whim, fantasy; see **fancy** 3.

**5.** [Meaning] — *Syn.* sense, import, purport; see **meaning.**

---

*SYN.* — **idea,** the most general of these terms, may be applied to anything existing in the mind as an object of knowledge or thought; **concept** refers to a generalized idea of a class of objects, based on knowledge of particular instances of the class /his *concept* of a republic/; **conception,** often equivalent to **concept,** specifically refers to something conceived in the mind, or imagined /my *conception* of how the role should be played/; **thought** is used of any idea, whether or not expressed, that occurs to the mind in reasoning or contemplation /she rarely speaks her *thoughts*/; **notion** suggests a vague thought or one not fully considered /I had a *notion* to go/; **impression** also implies vagueness of an idea provoked by some external stimulus /I have the *impression* that she's unhappy/

---

**ideal,** *modif.* **1.** [Typical] — *Syn.* prototypical, model, archetypical; see **typical.**

**2.** [Perfect] — *Syn.* supreme, consummate, fitting, exemplary; see **absolute** 1, **excellent, perfect** 2.

**3.** [Characterizing the unattainable] — *Syn.* utopian, imaginary, visionary, fanciful, unreal, abstract, quixotic, Panglossian, high-flown, impractical, impracticable, chimerical, extravagant, theoretical, in the clouds, mercurial, out of reach, dreamlike, fictitious, unearthly; see also **impractical, romantic** 1, **visionary** 1. — *Ant.* PRACTICAL, practicable, down-to-earth.

**ideal,** *n.* — *Syn.* paragon, goal, prototype, standard of perfection; see **model** 1.

**idealism,** *n.* **1.** [Devotion to high principles] — *Syn.* perfectionism, high-mindedness, aspiration, sense of duty, humanitarianism, meliorism, utopianism, romanticism, quixotism, knight-errantry, impracticality, idealization, principle, virtue, conscience, philosophy.

**2.** [The conception of the universe as idea] — *Syn.* Platonism, metaphysical idealism, epistemological idealism, metaphysics, immaterialism, immateriality, subjective idealism, Hegelianism, Transcendentalism, Fichteism.

**idealist,** *n.* — *Syn.* visionary, romanticist, romantic, escapist, optimist, enthusiast, utopist, perfectionist, dreamer, stargazer, theorizer, Platonist, reformer.

**idealistic,** *modif.* — *Syn.* lofty, exalted, utopian, unrealistic; see **impractical, visionary** 1.

**idealization,** *n.* — *Syn.* glorification, ennoblement, magnification; see **honor** 1.

**idealize,** *v.* — *Syn.* romanticize, glorify, rhapsodize, put on a pedestal*; see **admire** 1, **dream** 2.

**ideals,** *n.* — *Syn.* standards, principles, goals; see **ethics, morals, purpose** 1.

**idea man,** *n.* — *Syn.* thinker, consultant, originator; see **adviser, author** 1.

*idem* (Latin), *modif.* — *Syn.* likewise, ditto, the same, as before, self-same, the same as given above; see also **alike** 3.

**identical,** *modif.* — *Syn.* like, same, twin, indistinguishable; see **alike** 1, **equal**
See Synonym Study at SAME.

**identification,** *n.* **1.** [The act of identifying] — *Syn.* classifying, naming, cataloging, connecting; see **association** 2, **classification** 1, **description** 1.
**2.** [Means of identifying] — *Syn.* ID, ID card, badge, papers, license, passport, credentials, letter of introduction, testimony, letter of credit; see also **passport**.

**identify,** *v.* — *Syn.* classify, catalog, recognize; see **classify, distinguish** 1, **know** 2, **name** 1, 2.

**identify with,** *v.* — *Syn.* associate with, connect with, equate with, relate to; see **compare** 1, **empathize**.

**identity,** *n.* **1.** [Distinctive character] — *Syn.* individuality, uniqueness, integrity, personality; see **character** 2.
**2.** [The state of fulfilling a description] — *Syn.* sameness, oneness, correspondence, indistinguishability, identification, antecedents, true circumstances, parentage, status, citizenship, nationality, connections; see also **name** 1, **sameness**.

**ideology,** *n.* — *Syn.* beliefs, ideas, philosophy; see **doctrine** 1, **faith** 2.

**idiocy,** *n.* **1.** [Folly] — *Syn.* foolishness, madness, inanity; see **stupidity** 1, 2.
**2.** [Feeble-mindedness] — *Syn.* imbecility, cretinism, retardation; see **insanity** 1.

**idiom,** *n.* — *Syn.* expression, colloquialism, language, vernacular; see **dialect, jargon** 2, 3, **language** 1, **phrase**.

**idiomatic,** *modif.* — *Syn.* informal, natural, vernacular, local; see **colloquial, dialectal**.

**idiosyncrasy,** *n.* — *Syn.* eccentricity, characteristic, peculiarity, quirk, affectation, mannerism, habit, trait; see also **quirk**.

---

**SYN.** — **idiosyncrasy** refers to any personal mannerism or peculiarity and connotes strong individuality /the *idiosyncrasies* of a writer's style/; **eccentricity** implies considerable deviation from what is normal or customary and connotes whimsicality or even mental aberration /his *eccentricity* of wearing overshoes in the summer/

---

**idiosyncratic,** *modif.* — *Syn.* peculiar, distinctive, personal, quirky; see **characteristic**.

**idiot,** *n.* — *Syn.* simpleton, nincompoop, booby; see **fool** 1.

**idiotic,** *modif.* **1.** [Having the mind of an idiot] — *Syn.* thick-witted, dull, moronic; see **stupid** 1.
**2.** [Characterized by bad judgment] — *Syn.* fatuous, asinine, dumb*; see **silly, stupid** 1.

**idle,** *modif.* **1.** [Unused or inactive] — *Syn.* unoccupied, unemployed, jobless, workless, laid-off, uncultivated, untilled, fallow, vacant, deserted, not in use, not in operation, waste, barren, void, empty, abandoned, still, quiet, motionless, resting, stagnant, dormant, inert, passive, dead, untouched, rusty, gathering dust, dusty, down, out of action, at loose ends, out of a job, out of harness*, on the bum*; see also **unemployed, unused** 1.— *Ant.* ACTIVE, busy, engaged.
**2.** [Empty] — *Syn.* pointless, baseless, rambling, vain; see **futile** 1, **shallow** 2, **trivial**.
**3.** [Lazy] — *Syn.* indolent, shiftless, slothful; see **lazy** 1.
See Synonym Study at VAIN.

**idle,** *v.* — *Syn.* slack, shirk, while away time, loaf; see **loaf** 1, **loiter**.
See Synonym Study at LOITER.

**idleness,** *n.* **1.** [State of being inactive] — *Syn.* loafing, loitering, lounging, idling, time-killing, dawdling, inertia, inactivity, indolence, sluggishness, unemployment, joblessness, torpor, otiosity, dormancy, lethargy, stupor, puttering, trifling, truancy, droning, vegetation, dallying, dalliance, shilly-shallying, dilly-dallying, fooling around*, goofing off*, lollygagging*, goldbricking*; see also **leisure**.— *Ant.* industry, ACTION, occupation.
**2.** [Disinclination to activity] — *Syn.* slowness, indolence, slothfulness; see **laziness**.

**idler,** *n.* — *Syn.* lounger, slacker, drone, couch potato*; see **loafer**.

**idling,** *modif.* — *Syn.* lounging, drifting, lolling; see **loafing** 2, **resting** 1.

**idol,** *n.* **1.** [A deified image] — *Syn.* icon, graven image, effigy, god, false god, Baal, figurine, fetish, totem, joss, golden calf, avatar, simulacrum, pagan deity, mumbo-jumbo*; see also **image** 2, **statue**.
**2.** [A venerated object or person] — *Syn.* hero, heroine, god, goddess, desire, true-love, beloved, darling, favorite, ideal, role model, inamorata.

**idolater,** *n.* — *Syn.* fetishist, heathen, votary; see **enthusiast** 1, **pagan**.

**idolatrous,** *modif.* — *Syn.* fetishistic, pagan, idol-worshiping; see **heathen**.

**idolatry,** *n.* **1.** [The worship of idols] — *Syn.* idolism, adoration, burnt offering; see **worship** 1.
**2.** [Extreme devotion] — *Syn.* infatuation, fervor, adulation, hero worship; see **admiration, enthusiasm** 1.

**idolize,** *v.* — *Syn.* glorify, adore, revere, canonize; see **admire** 1, **worship** 2.

**I don't know,** *interj.* — *Syn.* Beats me!, Who knows?, The Lord knows!, How should I know?, You've got me!, Ask me another!, Search me!, *Quién sabe?* (Spanish).

**idyllic,** *modif.* — *Syn.* pastoral, bucolic, unspoiled; see **comfortable** 2, **pleasant** 2, **rural**.

**if,** *conj.* — *Syn.* provided that, with the condition that, supposing that, conceding that, on the assumption that, granted that, assuming that, on the occasion that, whenever, wherever.
**as if** — *Syn.* as though, as the situation would be, in a way like; see **apparently, as if** 1.

**iffy,** *modif.* — *Syn.* unsettled, doubtful, uncertain; see **doubtful** 1, **uncertain** 2.

**igneous,** *modif.* — *Syn.* formed by heat, volcanic, fiery; see **hot** 1, **molten**.

**ignite,** *v.* — *Syn.* kindle, enkindle, light, set on fire, strike a light, start up, burst into flames, touch off, touch a match to, set off, inflame; see also **burn** 1, 2.

**ignition,** *n.* **1.** [Igniting] — *Syn.* combustion, bursting into flame, kindling; see **fire** 1.
**2.** [A system for igniting] — *Syn.* timing system, timer, distributor, sparking system, firing system, wiring system, spark*.
Types of ignition include: impulse ignition, electronic ignition, make-and-break ignition, magneto ignition, spark ignition, sparkplug ignition; see also **engine, machine** 1, **motor**.

**ignoble,** *modif.* **1.** [Shameful] — *Syn.* disgraceful, mean, dishonorable; see **corrupt** 1, **mean** 1, **shameful** 1, 2, **wicked** 1.
**2.** [Lowly] — *Syn.* mean, base, abject; see **humble** 2.
*See Synonym Study at* MEAN.
**ignominious,** *modif.* **1.** [Humiliating] — *Syn.* shameful, dishonorable, disgraceful, inglorious; see **embarrassing, mean** 2.
**2.** [Offensive] — *Syn.* contemptible, despicable, vile, nasty; see **mean** 3, **offensive** 2, **rotten** 3.
**ignominy,** *n.* **1.** [Offensive behavior] — *Syn.* lowness, baseness, sordidness; see **disgrace** 2, **evil** 1, **meanness** 1.
**2.** [Shame] — *Syn.* mortification, dishonor, humiliation, disrepute; see **disgrace** 1.
**ignoramus,** *n.* — *Syn.* simpleton, imbecile, idiot, know-nothing; see **fool** 1, **moron.**
**ignorance,** *n.* **1.** [Lack of specific knowledge] — *Syn.* unawareness, unconsciousness, unfamiliarity, incomprehension, bewilderment, incapacity, inexperience, simplicity, disregard, obliviousness, insensitivity, sciolism, nescience, shallowness, superficiality, confusion, fog, vagueness, half-knowledge, a little learning, no more than a tyro's background, greenness; see also sense 2, **confusion** 2. — *Ant.* ABILITY, learning, erudition.
**2.** [Lack of general knowledge] — *Syn.* illiteracy, unenlightenment, mental incapacity, denseness, dumbness, empty-headedness, crudeness, barbarism, philistinism, vulgarity, obtuseness, unfamiliarity, unintelligence, rawness, benightedness, superstition, darkness, blindness, simplicity, innocence, stolidity, unscholarliness, functional illiteracy, know-nothingism, lack of learning, lack of education, lack of erudition, lack of information; see also sense 1, **stupidity** 1. — *Ant.* KNOWLEDGE, acquaintance, understanding.
**ignorant,** *modif.* **1.** [Unaware] — *Syn.* unconscious, uninformed, unknowing, uninitiated, inexperienced, unwitting, unmindful, disregarding, misinformed, unsuspecting, oblivious, insensible, mindless, witless, unconversant with, unintelligent, obtuse, thick, dense, moronic, imbecilic, shallow-brained, cretinous, unbookish, inept at learning, not gifted in learning, unscholarly, unscientific, half-learned, bird-brained*, sappy*, in the dark*, out of it*; see also sense 2, **dull** 3, **shallow** 2, **stupid** 1, **unaware.** — *Ant.* alert, aware, cognizant.
**2.** [Untrained] — *Syn.* illiterate, uneducated, unlettered, unlearned, untaught, uninstructed, uncultivated, unenlightened, untutored, unread, unschooled, inexperienced, uninformed, nescient, benighted, superstitious, shallow, superficial, coarse, vulgar, crude, gross, gauche, callow, green, naive, simple, ingenuous, inerudite, know-nothing, destitute of knowledge, misinformed, misguided, just beginning, undergoing apprenticeship, apprenticed, unbriefed, lowbrow*; see also **inexperienced, naive.** — *Ant.* LEARNED, educated, knowledgeable.

---

*SYN.* — **ignorant** implies a lack of knowledge, either generally /an *ignorant* man/ or on some particular subject /*ignorant* of the reason for their quarrel/; **illiterate** implies a failure to conform to some standard of knowledge, esp. an inability to read or write; **unlettered,** sometimes a milder term for **illiterate,** often implies unfamiliarity with fine literature /although a graduate engineer, he is relatively *unlettered*/; **uneducated** and **untutored** imply a lack of formal or systematic education, as of that acquired in schools /his brilliant, though un-

*educated* mind/; **unlearned** suggests a lack of learning, either generally or in some specific subject /*unlearned* in science/

---

**ignore,** *v.* — *Syn.* disregard, overlook, pass over, snub; see **disregard, neglect** 1, **ostracize, scorn** 2.
*See Synonym Study at* NEGLECT.
**ill,** *modif.* **1.** [Bad] — *Syn.* evil, harmful, injurious, noxious, hostile, unkind, unfavorable, unpropitious, unfortunate, adverse; see also **wicked** 1.
**2.** [Sick] — *Syn.* unwell, unhealthy, ailing; see **sick.**
*See Synonym Study at* SICK, WICKED.
**go ill with** — *Syn.* be unfortunate for, be unfavorable to, hurt; see **disturb** 2.
**take ill, 1.** become sick, become unwell, fall ill; see **sicken** 1, **weaken** 1.
**2.** take offense, resent, be annoyed at, be offended by; see **dislike.**
**ill,** *n.* **1.** [Anything causing pain, distress, etc.] — *Syn.* harm, misfortune, mischief, trouble; see **evil** 2, **insult, wrong** 1, 2.
**2.** [Sickness] — *Syn.* ailment, malady, affliction; see **disease.**
**ill-advised,** *modif.* — *Syn.* foolish, unwise, imprudent, ill-considered; see **rash, stupid** 1, **wrong** 3.
**ill at ease,** *modif.* — *Syn.* anxious, uneasy, uncomfortable, awkward; see **restless** 1, **suspicious** 1, **uneasy** 1.
**ill-bred,** *modif.* — *Syn.* uncouth, vulgar, uncivil; see **rude** 1, 2.
**illegal,** *modif.* — *Syn.* illicit, unlawful, prohibited, contraband, banned, unconstitutional, outside the law, extralegal, outlawed, not legal, unauthorized, unlicensed, lawless, actionable, *verboten* (German), *sub rosa* (Latin), illegitimate, taboo, forbidden, interdicted, proscribed, misbegotten, irregular, criminal, felonious, against the law, after-hours, not approved, uncertified, unwarranted, unwarrantable, smuggled, black-market, bootlegged, hot*; see also **stolen.** — *Ant.* lawful, LEGAL, authorized.
**illegible,** *modif.* — *Syn.* unreadable, indecipherable, unintelligible, faint, obscured, difficult to read, scribbled, scrawled, crabbed, hieroglyphic; see also **confused** 2, **obscure** 1.
**illegibly,** *modif.* — *Syn.* faintly, unintelligibly, indistinctly; see **obscurely.**
**illegitimacy,** *n.* — *Syn.* illegitimateness, bastardy, bastardism, illegitimation.
**illegitimate,** *modif.* **1.** [Unlawful] — *Syn.* contraband, wrong, illicit, irregular; see **illegal, wicked** 1.
**2.** [Born of unmarried parents] — *Syn.* born out of wedlock, natural, fatherless, bastard, misbegotten, unlawfully begotten, of illicit union, baseborn, unfathered, byblown, born on the wrong side of the sheet*.
**3.** [Illogical] — *Syn.* twisted, unsound, incorrect, unacceptable; see **illogical, wrong** 2.
**ill-fated,** *modif.* — *Syn.* ill-starred, catastrophic, disastrous; see **destructive** 2, **doomed, unfortunate** 2.
**ill-favored,** *modif.* — *Syn.* horrible, unattractive, homely, unpleasant; see **disturbing, offensive** 2, **ugly** 1.
**ill humor,** *n.* — *Syn.* moodiness, testiness, irritability; see **anger, annoyance** 1, **gloom** 2.
**ill-humored,** *modif.* — *Syn.* touchy, crabby, cross; see **bothered, irritable, sullen.**
**illiberal,** *modif.* **1.** [Prejudiced] — *Syn.* biased, intolerant, bigoted, narrow-minded; see **prejudiced, selfish** 1.
**2.** [Miserly] — *Syn.* selfish, niggardly, miserly; see **greedy** 1, **stingy.**

**illicit,** *modif.* — *Syn.* unlawful, prohibited, unauthorized, improper; see **adulterous, illegal, wrong** 1.

**illiteracy,** *n.* — *Syn.* lack of education, ignorance, stupidity; see **ignorance** 2.

**illiterate,** *modif.* — *Syn.* ignorant, uneducated, unenlightened, unlettered; see **ignorant** 2.

*See Synonym Study at* IGNORANT.

**ill-mannered,** *modif.* — *Syn.* impolite, discourteous, ill-bred, uncouth; see **rude** 1, 2.

*See Synonym Study at* RUDE.

**ill-natured,** *modif.* — *Syn.* cross, disagreeable, surly, spiteful; see **irritable, sullen.**

**illness,** *n.* **1.** [The state of being sick] — *Syn.* sickness, poor health, failing health, ailing, ill health, infirmity, queasiness, vomiting, indisposition, malaise, disorder, relapse, attack, fit, seizure, convalescence, complaint, delicate health, sickliness, unhealthiness, invalidism, decrepitude, collapse, breakdown, confinement, prostration, disability, disturbance, hypochondria, valetudinarianism; see also **weakness** 1.
**2.** [A particular disease] — *Syn.* sickness, ailment, malady; see **disease, insanity** 1.

**illogical,** *modif.* — *Syn.* irrational, unreasonable, absurd, specious, fallacious, sophistical, inconsequent, unsubstantial, incorrect, inconsistent, false, flawed, casuistic, unscientific, paralogistic, contradictory, untenable, unsound, preposterous, invalid, self-contradictory, Kafkaesque, unproved, groundless, baseless, implausible, hollow, irrelevant, inconclusive, fatuous, senseless, incongruous, prejudiced, biased, unconnected, without foundation, not following, out of bounds, without basis, without rhyme or reason*, nutty*, screwy*, not ringing true*, wacky*, far out*, dopey*, having the cart before the horse*, Jesuitical*; see also **fallible, wrong** 2. — *Ant.* sound, reasonable, LOGICAL.

**ill-proportioned,** *modif.* — *Syn.* distorted, grotesque, misshapen; see **deformed.**

**ill-smelling,** *modif.* — *Syn.* malodorous, rancid, putrefied, stale; see **decaying, odorous** 1, **rank** 2, **rotten** 1, 3.

**ill-sounding,** *modif.* — *Syn.* cacophonous, jangling, dissonant; see **harsh** 1, **loud** 1, 2, **raucous** 1, **shrill.**

**ill-starred,** *modif.* — *Syn.* luckless, unhappy, ill-fated, futile; see **doomed, unfortunate** 2.

**ill-suited,** *modif.* — *Syn.* inappropriate, unsuitable, mismatched; see **unsuitable.**

**ill temper,** *n.* — *Syn.* petulance, animosity, indignation; see **anger, hatred** 2, **resentment.**

**ill-tempered,** *modif.* — *Syn.* cross, touchy, querulous; see **irritable, quarrelsome** 2, **sullen.**

**ill-timed,** *modif.* — *Syn.* inopportune, awkward, inappropriate; see **unfavorable** 2, **untimely.**

**ill-treat,** *v.* — *Syn.* abuse, mistreat, persecute, victimize; see **abuse** 1, **hurt** 1.

**illuminate,** *v.* **1.** [To make light] — *Syn.* lighten, irradiate, illumine, brighten; see **brighten** 1, **light** 1.
**2.** [To explain] — *Syn.* interpret, elucidate, clarify; see **explain.**
**3.** [To decorate] — *Syn.* illustrate, ornament, trim; see **decorate.**

**illuminated,** *modif.* — *Syn.* lighted, lit up, having adequate illumination; see **bright** 1.

**illumination,** *n.* **1.** [A light] — *Syn.* gleam, flame, brilliance, lighting; see **flash** 1, **light** 1, 3.
**2.** [Instruction] — *Syn.* teaching, education, information; see **knowledge** 1.
**3.** [Decoration] — *Syn.* flourish, ornament, embellishment; see **decoration** 1, 2.

**illumine,** *v.* **1.** [To light up] — *Syn.* light up, irradiate, brighten; see **light** 1.
**2.** [To explain] — *Syn.* interpret, clarify, elucidate; see **explain.**

**illusion,** *n.* **1.** [Unreal appearance] — *Syn.* fancy, hallucination, mirage, apparition, ghost, chimera, delusion, deception, fantasy, figment of the imagination, dream, vision, phantasm, image, trick of vision, optical illusion, myth, make-believe, *déjà vu* (French), paramnesia, castle in Spain, will-o'-the-wisp, *ignis fatuus* (Latin); see also **dream** 1, **fantasy** 2, **vision** 3, 4.
**2.** [Misconception] — *Syn.* delusion, confusion, false impression; see **mistake** 2, **misunderstanding** 1.

*SYN.* — **illusion** suggests the false perception or interpretation of something that has objective existence /perspective in drawing gives the *illusion* of depth/; **delusion** implies belief in something that is contrary to fact or reality, resulting from deception, a misconception, or a mental disorder /to have *delusions* of grandeur/; **hallucination** implies the apparent perception, in nervous or mental disorder, of something external that is actually not present; **mirage** refers to an optical illusion caused by atmospheric conditions, and, in figurative use, implies an unrealizable hope or aspiration

**illusory,** *modif.* — *Syn.* deceptive, unreal, illusive, fancied; see **false** 2, 3, **imaginary, unreal.**

**illustrate,** *v.* **1.** [To make clear by illustration] — *Syn.* exemplify, demonstrate, explain, elucidate, illuminate, picture, represent, delineate, portray, depict, give an example, instance, give evidence, give particulars, cite a case in point, allegorize, attest, show, evidence, give a for-instance*; see also **draw** 2, **explain, paint** 1.
**2.** [To adorn with illustrations] — *Syn.* embellish, adorn, illuminate; see **decorate.**

**illustrated,** *modif.* — *Syn.* pictorial, pictured, adorned, engraved, illuminated, embellished, decorated, delineated, portrayed, depicted, wrought, garlanded, embossed, exemplified, graphic, containing illustrations; see also **graphic** 1.

**illustration,** *n.* **1.** [An example] — *Syn.* instance, case, model, sample; see **example** 1.
**2.** [An illustrative picture] — *Syn.* drawing, painting, engraving, etching, line drawing, diagram, figure, sketch, frontispiece, tailpiece, cartoon, vignette, halftone, inset picture, newsphoto; see also **design** 1, **picture** 3, **representation.**

*See Synonym Study at* INSTANCE.

**illustrative,** *modif.* — *Syn.* exemplifying, explanatory, corroborative, clarifying, specifying, explicatory, interpretive, explicative, illuminative, symbolic, emblematic, representative, sample, imitative, indicative, pictorial, graphic, imagistic, comparative, metaphoric, figurative, allegorical, expository, revealing; see also **descriptive, explanatory, graphic** 1, 2.

**illustrator,** *n.* — *Syn.* commercial artist, painter, draftsman, cartoonist; see **artist** 1.

**illustrious,** *modif.* — *Syn.* distinguished, celebrated, renowned, eminent; see **distinguished** 2, **famous, glorious** 1, **important** 2.

*See Synonym Study at* FAMOUS.

**ill will,** *n.* — *Syn.* malevolence, dislike, hostility; see **hate, hatred** 1, 2, **malice, resentment.**

**image,** *n.* **1.** [Mental impression] — *Syn.* concept, conception, perception, vision; see **memory** 2, **thought** 2.
**2.** [Representation] — *Syn.* idol, effigy, picture, icon, form, drawing, model, illustration, portrait, photograph, reproduction, reflection, copy, likeness, fac-

simile, counterpart, replica, statue, carved figure, spittin' image\*, dead ringer\*, chip off the old block\*; see also **painting** 1, **picture** 3, **representation, statue.**

**imagery,** *n.* — *Syn.* metaphors, representation, symbolism, mental images; see **comparison** 2, **description** 1, **figure of speech.**

**imaginable,** *modif.* — *Syn.* conceivable, thinkable, comprehensible, apprehensible, credible, sensible, possible, plausible, believable, conjecturable, supposable, reasonable, calculable; see also **convincing, likely** 1.— *Ant.* unimaginable, UNBELIEVABLE, inconceivable.

**imaginary,** *modif.* — *Syn.* fancied, illusory, fanciful, unreal, invented, visionary, shadowy, chimerical, dreamy, dreamlike, hypothetical, theoretical, delusive, deceptive, imagined, hallucinatory, ideal, notional, whimsical, fabulous, unsubstantial, nonexistent, apocryphal, fantastic, mythological, legendary, fictitious, make-believe, imaginative; see also **fanciful** 1, **unreal.** — *Ant.* REAL, factual, existing.

**imagination,** *n.* **1.** [Power to visualize] — *Syn.* inventiveness, creativity, fancy, mind's eye, ingenuity, artistry, imaginativeness, invention, originality, vision, resourcefulness, intelligence, thoughtfulness, impressionableness, acuteness, mental agility, sensitivity, mental receptivity, suggestibility, visualization, fictionalization, dramatization, pictorialization, insight, mental adaptability, creative ability, right brain; see also **mind** 1.
**2.** [A product of the power to visualize] — *Syn.* creation, invention, fabrication; see **fancy** 2, **thought** 2.

**imaginative,** *modif.* — *Syn.* creative, inventive, ingenious, resourceful; see **artistic** 2, **original** 2.

**imagine,** *v.* **1.** [To visualize mentally] — *Syn.* conceive, picture, conjure up, envisage, envision, see in one's mind, invent, fabricate, formulate, devise, think of, make up, conceptualize, dream, nurture, harbor, perceive, fancy, dramatize, pictorialize, image, figure to oneself, create, build castles in the air\*; see also **visualize.**
**2.** [To suppose] — *Syn.* think, guess, presume, believe; see **assume** 1.

**imagined,** *modif.* — *Syn.* not real, insubstantial, fancied, thought up; see **false** 2, 3, **imaginary.**

**imbalance,** *n.* — *Syn.* lack of balance, unevenness, inequality, shortcoming, disproportion, lopsidedness, asymmetry; see also **irregularity** 1.

**imbecile,** *n.* — *Syn.* dolt, bungler, idiot; see **fool** 1, **moron.**

**imbecilic,** *modif.* — *Syn.* imbecile, feeble-minded, idiotic, asinine; see **silly, stupid** 1.

**imbecility,** *n.* **1.** [Folly] — *Syn.* foolishness, idiocy, silliness, absurdity; see **stupidity** 1, 2.
**2.** [Feeble-mindedness] — *Syn.* moronity, retardation, cretinism; see **insanity** 1.

**imbibe,** *v.* **1.** [To drink] — *Syn.* quaff, guzzle, ingest; see **drink** 1, 2, **swallow.**
**2.** [To absorb] — *Syn.* take in, assimilate, soak up, drink in; see **absorb** 1.

**imbue,** *v.* — *Syn.* inspire, permeate, tinge, inculcate; see **instill, teach** 1.

**imitate,** *v.* **1.** [To follow the example of] — *Syn.* emulate, follow suit, do likewise, take as a model; see **follow** 2.
**2.** [To act like] — *Syn.* mimic, impersonate, mirror, copy, mime, ape, parrot, parody, mock, simulate, duplicate, assume, repeat, echo, reecho, reflect, pretend, play a part, personate, do like\*, make like\*, take off\*, put on\*; see also **parody.**
**3.** [To copy] — *Syn.* duplicate, counterfeit, fake; see **copy** 2, **reproduce** 1.

**4.** [To resemble] — *Syn.* look like, be like, simulate, parallel; see **resemble.**

---

**SYN.** — **imitate** implies the following of something as an example or model but does not necessarily connote exact correspondence with the original /the child *imitates* her father's mannerisms/; **copy** implies as nearly exact imitation or reproduction as is possible /to *copy* a painting/; **mimic** suggests close imitation, often in fun or ridicule /to *mimic* the speech peculiarities of another/; **mock** implies imitation with the intent to deride or affront /he *mocked* the teacher's gesture of rebuke/; **ape** implies close imitation either in mimicry or in servile emulation /she *aped* the fashions of the court ladies/

---

**imitated,** *modif.* — *Syn.* copied, duplicated, reproduced, mimicked, mocked, aped, parroted, counterfeited, caricatured, parodied, burlesqued, made similar, made to resemble, done in facsimile, plagiarized; see also **printed, reproduced.**

**imitating,** *modif.* — *Syn.* copying, following, reflecting, emulating, echoing, matching, paralleling, in imitation of.

**imitation,** *modif.* — *Syn.* copied, feigned, simulated, bogus; see **artificial** 1, **false** 3.

**imitation,** *n.* **1.** [The act of imitating] — *Syn.* simulation, counterfeiting, copying, duplication, reproduction, emulation, patterning after, picturing, representing, mimicry, aping, impersonation, impression, parody, paraphrasing, parroting, echoing, matching, mirroring, paralleling; see also **parody, reproduction** 1.
**2.** [An object made by imitating] — *Syn.* counterfeit, copy, simulacrum, sham, fake, picture, replica, facsimile, echo, reflection, match, parallel, opposite number, animation, resemblance, transcription, image, mockery, takeoff, substitution, forgery, artist's copy, ersatz, knockoff\*; see also **copy, duplicate, reproduction** 2.— *Ant.* original, NOVELTY, pattern.

**imitative,** *modif.* **1.** [Copying] — *Syn.* mimicking, copying, reflecting, echoic; see **mimetic.**
**2.** [Counterfeit] — *Syn.* forged, sham, deceptive; see **false** 2, 3.

**imitator,** *n.* — *Syn.* copyist, follower, copier, impersonator, mime, mimic, parrot, ape, echo, pretender, counterfeiter, forger, plagiarist, copycat\*.

**immaculate,** *modif.* **1.** [Clean] — *Syn.* unsullied, spotless, stainless; see **bright** 1, **clean** 1.
**2.** [Morally pure] — *Syn.* undefiled, sinless, unsullied; see **chaste** 2, **innocent** 4.

**immanent,** *modif.* — *Syn.* native, intrinsic, inborn, indwelling; see **inherent.**

**immaterial,** *modif.* **1.** [Inconsequential] — *Syn.* insignificant, irrelevant, meaningless, unimportant; see **irrelevant, trivial, unnecessary.**
**2.** [Insubstantial] — *Syn.* incorporeal, spiritual, bodiless, disembodied, without substance, intangible, ethereal, aerial, shadowy, ghostly, metaphysical, impalpable. — *Ant.* real, PHYSICAL, substantial.

**immature,** *modif.* — *Syn.* youthful, sophomoric, half-grown; see **childish** 1, **juvenile** 1, **naive, young** 1, 2.

**immaturity,** *n.* **1.** [Childhood] — *Syn.* youthfulness, adolescence, infancy; see **childhood, youth** 1.
**2.** [Inexperience] — *Syn.* childishness, puerility, ignorance, callowness, babyishness, rawness, greenness, imperfection, incompleteness, childish behavior, infantilism; see also **instability.**

**immeasurable,** *modif.* — *Syn.* limitless, vast, extensive; see **endless** 1, **large** 1.

**immediate,** *modif.* **1.** [Without delay] — *Syn.* at once, instantaneous, instant, on the instant, live, now, at this moment, at the present time, next, prompt, quick; see also **direct** 3, **fast** 1. — *Ant.* SOMEDAY, later, any time.

**2.** [Primary] — *Syn.* pressing, critical, paramount; see **important** 1, **urgent** 1.

**immediately,** *modif.* — *Syn.* at once, without delay, instantly, directly, right away, instanter, at the first opportunity, forthwith, straightaway, in a trice, in that instant, at short notice, now, this instant, speedily, quickly, promptly, on the spot, on the dot, rapidly, summarily, instantaneously, unhesitatingly, shortly, *tout de suite* (French), before you could say Jack Robinson*, on the double*, now or never*, in a jiffy*, straight off*, right off the bat*, pronto*, PDQ*; see also **quickly** 1, 2. — *Ant.* in the future, LATER, in a while.

**immemorial,** *modif.* — *Syn.* olden, primeval, ancient; see **old** 3, **traditional** 2.

**immense,** *modif.* **1.** [Huge] — *Syn.* gigantic, tremendous, enormous; see **extensive** 1, **large** 1.

**2.** [Boundless] — *Syn.* eternal, limitless, endless; see **infinite** 1.

*See Synonym Study at* ENORMOUS.

**immensity,** *n.* — *Syn.* infinity, vastness, greatness, massiveness, hugeness, enormousness, immeasurableness, boundlessness, bulkiness, sizableness, immenseness, bigness, largeness, gigantism, tremendousness, stupendousness, monstrousness, enormity, magnitude; see also **extent.** — *Ant.* tininess, minuteness, insignificance.

**immerse,** *v.* **1.** [To put under water] — *Syn.* submerge, dip, douse, plunge, bury, duck, cover with water, drown, sink, bathe, steep, soak, drench, dunk, souse, slop*, put in the drink*; see also **baptize** 1, **cover** 8, **sink** 2. — *Ant.* raise up, UNCOVER, draw out.

**2.** [Engross] — *Syn.* interest, engage, involve, absorb; see **fascinate, occupy** 3.

**immersed,** *modif.* **1.** [Sunk] — *Syn.* drowned, plunged, bathed; see **dipped, soaked, wet** 1.

**2.** [Engrossed] — *Syn.* absorbed, preoccupied, buried; see **rapt** 2.

**immersible,** *modif.* — *Syn.* sinkable, submersible, waterproof; see **waterproof.**

**immigrant,** *n.* — *Syn.* foreigner, newcomer, settler, nonnative, outlander, naturalized citizen, adoptive citizen, resident alien, hyphenated American*; see also **alien, emigrant.**

*See Synonym Study at* ALIEN.

**immigrate,** *v.* — *Syn.* migrate, colonize, resettle; see **leave** 1, **migrate** 1.

*See Synonym Study at* MIGRATE.

**immigration,** *n.* — *Syn.* colonization, settlement, migration, crossing the border, change of allegiance; see also **emigration, entrance** 1. — *Ant.* EMIGRATION, exile, defection.

**imminent,** *modif.* — *Syn.* approaching, impending, coming, in store, at hand, brewing, about to happen, near, immediate, next, following, on its way, looming, to come, in view, in the offing, forthcoming, expected, threatening, in the wind*, on the horizon*, on the verge*, in the cards*, around the corner*, staring one in the face*; see also **coming** 1, **destined** 1. — *Ant.* remote, POSSIBLE, future.

**immobile,** *modif.* **1.** [Stable] — *Syn.* fixed, stationary, still; see **firm** 1.

**2.** [Not moving or changing] — *Syn.* inexpressive, paralyzed, imperturbable, inscrutable; see **impassive, motionless** 1.

**immobility,** *n.* **1.** [Stability] — *Syn.* stabilization, constancy, fixity; see **stability** 1.

**2.** [Inflexibility] — *Syn.* rigidity, stolidity, stiffness; see **inflexibility** 1, **stability** 2.

**immoderate,** *modif.* — *Syn.* unbalanced, extravagant, excessive; see **extreme** 2.

*See Synonym Study at* EXCESSIVE.

**immodest,** *modif.* — *Syn.* forward, brazen, shameless, indecent; see **egotistic** 2, **improper** 2, **rude** 2.

**immodesty,** *n.* — *Syn.* boldness, forwardness, conceit, indecency; see **indecency** 2, **pride** 1, **rudeness.**

**immoral,** *modif.* — *Syn.* unethical, sinful, corrupt, shameless; see **dishonest** 2, **wicked** 1, **wrong** 1.

**immorality,** *n.* — *Syn.* vice, depravity, dissoluteness; see **evil** 1, **lewdness, sin.**

**immorally,** *modif.* — *Syn.* sinfully, wickedly, unrighteously, unethically; see **wrongly** 1.

**immortal,** *modif.* **1.** [Deathless] — *Syn.* undying, eternal, permanent, phoenixlike, imperishable, endless, timeless, everlasting, sempiternal, interminable, death-defying, unfading, evergreen, amaranthine, never-ending, perennial, constant, ceaseless, never-ceasing, undecaying, indestructible, indissoluble, incorruptible, unchanging, ever-living, never-dying, enduring, godlike; see also **eternal** 2, **perpetual** 1. — *Ant.* MORTAL, perishable, corrupt.

**2.** [Illustrious] — *Syn.* celebrated, eminent, glorious; see **famous.**

**immortality,** *n.* **1.** [Eternal life] — *Syn.* deathlessness, permanence, endlessness, timelessness, everlastingness, eternity, divinity, unceasingness, indestructibility, everlasting life, unending life, continuity, perpetuation, sempiternity, imperishability, endless life, athanasy, everness, unlimited existence, eternal continuance, perpetuity; see also **eternity** 1. — *Ant.* mortality, DEATH, decease.

**2.** [Life after death] — *Syn.* hereafter, afterlife, resurrection, eternal life, beatitude, other world, heaven, eternal bliss, redemption; see also **heaven** 2, **hell** 1, **salvation** 3.

**3.** [Enduring fame] — *Syn.* glory, eminence, renown; see **fame** 1.

**immortalize,** *v.* — *Syn.* memorialize, ennoble, canonize, deify; see **celebrate** 1, **praise** 1.

**immortalized,** *modif.* — *Syn.* made famous, canonized, deathless; see **famous.**

**immovable,** *modif.* — *Syn.* solid, stable, fixed; see **firm** 1.

**immune,** *modif.* — *Syn.* free, exempt, unaffected by, resistant, invulnerable, protected, immunized, inoculated, hardened to, unsusceptible, privileged, not liable, excused, unanswerable, licensed, favored, let off*; see also **exempt, safe** 1.

**immunity,** *n.* **1.** [Exemption] — *Syn.* freedom, privilege, license; see **freedom** 2.

**2.** [Freedom from disease] — *Syn.* resistance, immunization, protection, active immunity, passive immunity; see also **safety** 1, **vaccination** 2.

*See Synonym Study at* EXEMPTION.

**immutable,** *modif.* — *Syn.* stable, changeless, perpetual; see **permanent** 2.

**imp,** *n.* — *Syn.* demon, pixie, rascal; see **brat, devil** 1.

**impact,** *n.* **1.** [Collision] — *Syn.* shock, impression, contact; see **collision** 1.

**2.** [Effect] — *Syn.* influence, bearing, force, consequence, repercussions, reverberations, impinging, impression; see also **meaning, result.**

**impact,** *v.* **1.** [To hit with force] — *Syn.* strike, collide with, smash into; see **crash** 4, **hit** 2.

**2.** [*To affect] — *Syn.* impinge on, bear on, reshape; see **affect** 1, **change** 1, **influence.**

**impair,** *v.* 1. [To damage] — *Syn.* spoil, injure, hurt; see **break** 2, **damage** 1, **destroy** 1.

2. [To weaken] — *Syn.* diminish, undermine, reduce; see **weaken** 2.

*See Synonym Study at* HURT.

**impaired,** *modif.* — *Syn.* injured, weakened, spoiled, harmed; see **damaged** 2, **disabled, hurt.**

**impale,** *v.* — *Syn.* spear, spike, pierce; see **kill** 1, **stab.**

**impalpable,** *modif.* — *Syn.* imperceptible, intangible, indistinct; see **immaterial** 2, **vague** 2.

**impart,** *v.* 1. [To give] — *Syn.* bestow, grant, present, confer; see **allow** 1, **give** 1.

2. [To inform] — *Syn.* tell, announce, divulge; see **admit** 2, **expose** 1, **reveal** 1.

**impartial,** *modif.* — *Syn.* unbiased, unprejudiced, disinterested; see **equal, fair** 1.

*See Synonym Study at* FAIR.

**impartiality,** *n.* — *Syn.* evenhandedness, neutrality, probity, justice; see **equality, fairness.**

**impassable,** *modif.* — *Syn.* closed, blockaded, not fit for travel, obstructed, pathless, trackless, untrodden, impenetrable, forbidden, insurmountable; see also **difficult** 1. — *Ant.* OPEN, passable, traveled.

**impasse,** *n.* 1. [Stalemate] — *Syn.* deadlock, standstill, cessation; see **pause** 2, **rest** 2.

2. [A cul-de-sac] — *Syn.* dead end, obstacle, blind alley; see **cul-de-sac, trap** 1.

**impassible,** *modif.* 1. [Unfeeling] — *Syn.* unconcerned, passionless, insensible, impassive; see **callous, indifferent** 1, **nonchalant** 1.

2. [Invulnerable] — *Syn.* strong, invincible, secure; see **protected, safe** 1, **strong** 2.

**impassioned,** *modif.* — *Syn.* moving, fervid, ardent; see **intense, passionate** 2.

*See Synonym Study at* PASSIONATE.

**impassive,** *modif.* — *Syn.* indifferent, apathetic, stoic, stolid, phlegmatic, callous, sedate, insensitive, emotionless; see also **blank** 2, indifferent 1.

SYN. — **impassive** means not having or showing any feeling or emotion, although it does not necessarily connote an incapability of being affected /his *impassive* face did not betray his anguish/; **apathetic** stresses an indifference or listlessness from which one cannot easily be stirred to feeling /an *apathetic* electorate/; **stoic** implies an austere indifference to pleasure or pain and specifically suggests the ability to endure suffering without flinching /he received the bad news with *stoic* calm/; **stolid** suggests dullness, obtuseness, or stupidity in one who is not easily moved or excited; **phlegmatic** is applied to one who by temperament is not easily disconcerted or aroused

**impatience,** *n.* 1. [Irritability] — *Syn.* fretfulness, hastiness, quick temper; see **anger, annoyance** 1.

2. [Restlessness] — *Syn.* eagerness, agitation, disquietude, anxiety; see **care** 2, **excitement, nervousness** 1, 2.

**impatient,** *modif.* 1. [Irritable] — *Syn.* excitable, quick-tempered, fretful; see **bothered, excitable, irritable, troubled** 1.

2. [Restless] — *Syn.* anxious, eager, feverish; see **eager, excitable, restless** 1.

**impeach,** *v.* — *Syn.* criticize, charge, accuse, arraign, impugn, challenge, denounce, indict, discredit, reprehend, reprimand, accuse of misconduct in office, reprobate, arraign for malfeasance, call to account, blame, incriminate, try, bring charges against, question, hold at

fault; see also **accuse, censure.** — *Ant.* support, acquit, absolve.

*See Synonym Study at* ACCUSE.

**impeccable,** *modif.* — *Syn.* faultless, pure, flawless, irreproachable; see **excellent, perfect** 2.

**impecunious,** *modif.* — *Syn.* insolvent, destitute, broke★; see **poor** 1.

*See Synonym Study at* POOR.

**impede,** *v.* — *Syn.* hinder, thwart, block, deter; see **bar** 1, 2, **hinder, prevent.**

*See Synonym Study at* HINDER.

**impediment,** *n.* 1. [Something that impedes] — *Syn.* hindrance, obstacle, obstruction, barrier, block, bar, clog, stop, encumbrance, difficulty, check, retardation, stoppage, restriction, stricture, restraint, blockage, prohibition, inhibition, hurdle, wall, barricade, trammel, shackle, handicap, disability, disadvantage, deterrent, detriment, delay, traffic hazard, traffic jam, manacle, chain, tie, hitch, snag, setback, drag, burden, load, dead weight, drawback, stumbling block, fault, flaw, rub, roadblock★, holdup★, catch-22★, catch★, cramp★, bottleneck★, gridlock★, millstone around one's neck★, red tape★, monkey wrench in the machinery★, crimp★, joker★; see also **barrier.** — *Ant.* HELP, aid, assistance.

2. [An obstruction in speech] — *Syn.* speech impediment, speech defect, speech disorder, difficulty, block, stutter, stuttering, stammer, stammering, lisp, lisping, lallation, lambdacism, halting, hairlip, cleft palate, aphasia, dysphasia.

SYN. — **impediment** applies to anything that delays or retards progress by interfering with normal action /a speech *impediment*/; **obstruction** refers to anything that blocks progress or some activity as if by stopping up a passage /your interference is an *obstruction* of justice/; **hindrance** applies to anything that thwarts progress by holding back or delaying /lack of supplies is the greatest *hindrance* to my experiment/; **obstacle** is used of anything that literally or figuratively stands in the way of one's progress /her father's opposition remained their only *obstacle*/; **barrier** applies to any apparently insurmountable obstacle that prevents progress or access or keeps separate and apart /cultural differences are often a *barrier* to understanding/

**impedimenta,** *n.* — *Syn.* paraphernalia, gear, encumbrances, junk★; see **baggage, equipment.**

**impeding,** *modif.* — *Syn.* obstructing, encumbering, holding, blocking, hampering, hindering, deterring, deterrent, frustrating, delaying, checking, stopping, barring, inhibiting, obstructive, counterproductive.

**impel,** *v.* 1. [To urge or force] — *Syn.* induce, instigate, animate, compel; see **drive** 1, **force** 1, **motivate, urge** 2.

2. [To press] — *Syn.* move, push, actuate, prod, start, set in motion, propel, activate, thrust forward, drive, jog, shove, poke, boost, boom, give someone a start, nudge, lend one's weight to.

**impend,** *v.* — *Syn.* be imminent, loom, menace, hover; see **approach** 3, **threaten** 2.

**impending,** *modif.* — *Syn.* approaching, in the offing, threatening, menacing; see **coming** 1, **imminent.**

**impenetrable,** *modif.* 1. [Dense] — *Syn.* impervious, impermeable, solid, compact; see **firm** 2, **impassable, thick** 1.

2. [Incomprehensible] — *Syn.* unintelligible, inscrutable, unfathomable; see **obscure** 1.

**impenitent,** *modif.* — *Syn.* unrepentant, uncontrite, obdurate; see **hardened** 3, **remorseless** 1.

**imperative,** *modif.* **1.** [Necessary] — *Syn.* inescapable, immediate, crucial, compelling; see **crucial, important** 1, **necessary** 1, **urgent** 1.
**2.** [Authoritative] — *Syn.* masterful, commanding, dominant; see **autocratic** 1, **dominant** 2, **powerful** 1.
**imperceptible,** *modif.* — *Syn.* subtle, slight, gradual, faint, indistinct, indiscernible, undetectable, invisible, intangible, subliminal; see also **faint** 3, **hidden** 2, **invisible** 1, **obscure** 1.
**imperceptibly,** *modif.* — *Syn.* slowly, just barely, scarcely; see **gradually, hardly.**
**imperfect,** *modif.* — *Syn.* flawed, defective, incomplete, deficient; see **damaged** 2, **faulty.**
**imperfection,** *n.* — *Syn.* defect, fault, flaw, shortcoming; see **blemish, defect** 2.
*See Synonym Study at* DEFECT.
**imperial,** *modif.* **1.** [Concerning an emperor or empress] — *Syn.* sovereign, supreme, hegemonic, imperatorial, august; see also **royal** 1.
**2.** [Suited to the dignity of an emperor] — *Syn.* regal, majestic, august, magnificent; see **royal** 2.
**imperialism,** *n.* — *Syn.* empire, hegemony, sway, colonialism, neocolonialism, international domination, expansionism, power politics, white man's burden*; see also **dominion** 1, **power** 2.
**imperil,** *v.* — *Syn.* jeopardize, expose, hazard; see **endanger, risk.**
**imperious,** *modif.* **1.** [Domineering] — *Syn.* overbearing, commanding, haughty; see **autocratic** 1, **masterful, powerful** 1.
**2.** [Urgent] — *Syn.* pressing, critical, imperative; see **crucial, important** 1, **urgent** 1.
*See Synonym Study at* MASTERFUL.
**imperishable,** *modif.* — *Syn.* enduring, immortal, perpetual; see **immortal** 1, **permanent** 2.
**impersonal,** *modif.* — *Syn.* detached, disinterested, cold; see **aloof, indifferent** 1.
**impersonate,** *v.* — *Syn.* mimic, portray, mime, act out, pose as, pass for, double for, assume the character of, put on an act, pretend to be, act the part of, act a part, dress as, represent; see also **imitate** 2.
**impersonation,** *n.* — *Syn.* imitation, role, enactment, pose; see **acting, imitation** 1.
**impertinence,** *n.* **1.** [Disrespectfulness] — *Syn.* impudence, insolence, disrespectfulness; see **rudeness.**
**2.** [Lack of pertinence] — *Syn.* irrelevance, immateriality, unsuitability, inappropriateness; see **inconsistency, irrelevance.**
**impertinent,** *modif.* **1.** [Disrespectful] — *Syn.* saucy, insolent, impudent, pert, fresh, rude, audacious, cheeky*, sassy*; see also **rude** 2.
**2.** [Not to the point] — *Syn.* irrelevant, inapplicable, inappropriate; see **irrelevant.**

---

*SYN.* — **impertinent** implies a forwardness of speech or action that is disrespectful and oversteps the bounds of propriety or courtesy; **impudent** implies a shameless or brazen impertinence; **insolent** implies defiant disrespect as displayed in openly insulting and contemptuous speech or behavior; **saucy** implies a flippancy and provocative levity toward one to whom respect should be shown

---

**imperturbable,** *modif.* — *Syn.* composed, sedate, immovable, unflappable*; see **calm** 1.
**impervious,** *modif.* **1.** [Unreceptive] — *Syn.* inaccessible, invulnerable, unmoved, impassive; see **callous, indifferent** 1.

**2.** [Impermeable] — *Syn.* impenetrable, watertight, hermetic; see **tight** 2.
**impetuosity,** *n.* — *Syn.* rashness, recklessness, hastiness; see **carelessness, nonsense** 2.
**impetuous,** *modif.* — *Syn.* impulsive, hasty, precipitate, sudden; see **careless** 1, **changeable** 1, **rash.**
*See Synonym Study at* SUDDEN.
**impetuously,** *modif.* — *Syn.* hastily, thoughtlessly, heedlessly; see **carelessly, foolishly, rashly.**
**impetus,** *n.* — *Syn.* force, impulsion, spur, stimulus; see **incentive, purpose** 1, **reason** 3.
**impiety,** *n.* **1.** [Ungodliness] — *Syn.* irreverence, profanity, godlessness; see **blasphemy, heresy, hypocrisy.**
**2.** [An impious act] — *Syn.* error, iniquity, sacrilege; see **injustice** 2, **sin, wrong** 1.
**impinge,** *v.* **1.** [To infringe upon] — *Syn.* encroach, intrude, invade; see **meddle** 1.
**2.** [To hit] — *Syn.* strike, ricochet, crash against; see **crash** 4, **hit** 2.
**3.** [To have an effect; *usually used with "on"*] — *Syn.* affect, touch, make an impression; see **affect** 1, **influence.**
**impious,** *modif.* — *Syn.* irreligious, godless, sinful, profane, blasphemous, sacrilegious, unholy, sanctimonious, hypocritical, canting, desecrating, defiling, disrespectful, irreverent, undutiful, deceitful, disobedient, unethical, immoral, apostate, pietistical, unctuous, hardened, perverted, recusant, lacking reverence for God, unsanctified, unhallowed, desecrative, iniquitous, unrighteous, atheistic, agnostic, unregenerate, reprobate, ungodly, satanic, diabolic; see also **atheistic, wicked** 1. — *Ant.* PIOUS, virtuous, devout.
**impish,** *modif.* — *Syn.* mischievous, elfish, devilish; see **jaunty, naughty, rude** 2.
**implacability,** *n.* — *Syn.* mercilessness, inexorability, rancor, revengefulness; see **cruelty, malice.**
**implacable,** *modif.* — *Syn.* inexorable, unyielding, inflexible, remorseless; see **cruel** 2, **ruthless** 1, 2, **vindictive.**
*See Synonym Study at* INFLEXIBLE.
**implant,** *v.* — *Syn.* insert, root, fix, inculcate; see **embed** 1, **instill.**
**implausible,** *modif.* — *Syn.* inconceivable, improbable, unreasonable; see **impossible** 1, **unbelievable, unlikely.**
**implement,** *n.* — *Syn.* tool, utensil, device, instrument; see **device** 1, **tool** 1.
*See Synonym Study at* TOOL.
**implement,** *v.* — *Syn.* carry out, realize, execute, fulfill; see **achieve** 1, **complete** 1, **perform** 1.
**implicate,** *v.* — *Syn.* involve, connect, cite, impute, associate, tie up with, charge, incriminate, inculpate, stigmatize, link, catch up in, draw in, relate, compromise, ensnare, embroil, mire, entangle, entail; see also **accuse, involve.**
**implicated,** *modif.* — *Syn.* under suspicion, suspected, known to have been associated with; see **guilty** 2, **involved** 1, **suspicious** 2.
**implication,** *n.* **1.** [Assumption] — *Syn.* indication, inference, suggestion, connotation; see **assumption** 1, **guess, hint** 1, **meaning.**
**2.** [A link] — *Syn.* association, connection, involvement, entanglement; see **relationship, union** 1.
**implicit,** *modif.* **1.** [Implied] — *Syn.* tacit, understood, inferable, inherent; see **implied.**
**2.** [Without reservation or doubt] — *Syn.* unquestioning, certain, absolute; see **absolute** 1, **certain** 3, **inevitable.**

**implicitly,** *modif.* — *Syn.* inevitably, inherently, unreservedly, unquestioningly; see **completely, essentially.**

**implied,** *modif.* — *Syn.* implicit, indicated, suggested, tacit, hinted at, understood, unexpressed, unspoken, unstated, undeclared, intimated, insinuated, alluded to, meant, connoted, intended, involved, latent, hidden, occult, lurking, indirectly meant, inferred, inferable, allusive, potential, foreshadowed, adumbrated, tacitly assumed, inferential, indirect, between the lines*.

**implore,** *v.* — *Syn.* supplicate, beseech, entreat; see **beg** 1, **urge** 2.
*See Synonym Study at* BEG.

**imply,** *v.* **1.** [To indicate] — *Syn.* intimate, hint at, suggest; see **hint, mention, refer** 2.
**2.** [To mean] — *Syn.* import, indicate, signify; see **designate** 1, **intend** 2, **mean** 1.
**3.** [To assume] — *Syn.* infer, presuppose, presume; see **assume** 1, **intend** 1, **propose** 1.
*See Synonym Study at* SUGGEST.

**impolite,** *modif.* — *Syn.* discourteous, ill-mannered, indelicate; see **rude** 2.
*See Synonym Study at* RUDE.

**impolitic,** *modif.* — *Syn.* unwise, indiscreet, injudicious; see **careless** 1, **rash, stupid** 1.

**imponderable,** *modif.* — *Syn.* inestimable, incalculable, indeterminable; see **endless** 1, **impossible** 1, **obscure** 1.

**import,** *v.* **1.** [To bring in] — *Syn.* introduce, ship in, carry in, transport in, ferry in, truck in, freight in, buy abroad; see also **carry** 1, **send** 1, **ship.** — *Ant.* EXPORT, ship out, sell abroad.
**2.** [To signify] — *Syn.* denote, imply, convey; see **mean** 1.

**importance,** *n.* **1.** [The quality of being important] — *Syn.* significance, consequence, import, weight, moment, signification, drift, force, sense, tenor, purport, bearing, denotation, gist, effect, distinction, influence, usefulness, weightiness, momentousness, magnitude, value, materialness, emphasis, standing, caliber, stress, accent, concern, attention, interest, seriousness, gravity, point, substance, relevance, notable feature, sum and substance, cardinal point, essence; see also **meaning, value** 3, 4. — *Ant.* INSIGNIFICANCE, triviality, emptiness.
**2.** [Prominence] — *Syn.* greatness, eminence, consequence, moment; see **fame** 1, **quality** 3, **rank** 2, 3.

---

**SYN.** — **importance,** the broadest of these terms, implies greatness of worth, meaning, influence, etc. /news of *importance*/; **consequence,** often interchangeable with the preceding, more specifically suggests importance with regard to outcome or result /a disagreement of no *consequence*/ or resulting from social position /a woman of consequence/; **moment** expresses this same idea of importance in effect with somewhat stronger force /affairs of great *moment*/; **weight** implies an estimation of the relative importance of something /his word carries great *weight* with us/; **significance** implies an importance or momentousness because of a special meaning that may or may not be immediately apparent /an event of *significance*/

---

**important,** *modif.* **1.** [Weighty; *said usually of things*] — *Syn.* significant, considerable, momentous, essential, great, decisive, critical, determining, chief, paramount, primary, foremost, principal, major, big, consequential, influential, marked, salient, imperative, exigent, of great consequence, mattering much, of moment, earth-shaking, portentous, ponderous, of importance, never

to be forgotten, of note, valuable, crucial, substantial, material, meaningful, vital, serious, grave, relevant, pressing, far-reaching, extensive, conspicuous, heavy*, front-page*, standout*, smash*; see also **necessary** 1, **urgent** 1. — *Ant.* TRIVIAL, inconsequential, unimportant.
**2.** [Eminent; *said usually of persons*] — *Syn.* illustrious, influential, prominent, leading, great, notable, well-recognized, well-known, imposing, distinguished, prestigious, extraordinary, remarkable, powerful, noteworthy, signal, grand, outstanding, noted, noble, aristocratic, high-ranking, high-level, honored, esteemed, talented, distinctive, first-class, superior, foremost, big, major, big-league*, big-name*, top-notch*, solid*, four-star*, high-up*, high-powered*; see also **dignified, distinguished** 2, **famous.** — *Ant.* OBSCURE, unknown, unrecognized.
**3.** [Relevant] — *Syn.* material, significant, mattering, of concern; see **related** 2, **relevant.**

**importation,** *n.* — *Syn.* import, borrowing, shipping in, bringing in, admission, entrance, acceptance, reception, introduction, purchase abroad, adoption; see also **transportation.**

**imported,** *modif.* — *Syn.* foreign-made, shipped in, produced abroad, exotic; see **foreign** 2.

**importer,** *n.* — *Syn.* shipper, international merchant, foreign buyer, importing wholesaler, import-export jobber; see also **merchant, salesman** 2.

**importunate,** *modif.* — *Syn.* insistent, pressing, harassing, clamorous; see **disturbing, urgent** 2.

**importune,** *v.* — *Syn.* plead, implore, press, urge; see **beg** 1, **urge** 2.
*See Synonym Study at* BEG, URGE.

**importunity,** *n.* — *Syn.* insistence, persistence, solicitation, petition; see **appeal** 1, **request, urging.**

**impose,** *v.* — *Syn.* force upon, inflict, foist, exact; see **command** 2, **force** 1, **require** 2, **tax** 1.

**impose on** or **upon,** *v.* **1.** [To disturb] — *Syn.* intrude, interrupt, presume, inconvenience; see **bother** 2, **disturb** 2, **meddle** 1.
**2.** [To deceive] — *Syn.* trick, cheat, delude, defraud; see **cheat, deceive.**

**imposing,** *modif.* — *Syn.* impressive, grand, majestic, monumental; see **dignified, grand** 2, **impressive** 1.
*See Synonym Study at* GRAND.

**imposition,** *n.* **1.** [A constraint] — *Syn.* demand, encumbrance, obtrusion; see **command** 1, **intrusion, pressure** 2.
**2.** [Deception] — *Syn.* craftiness, trickery, fraud; see **deception** 1, **hypocrisy, trick** 1.

**impossibility,** *n.* — *Syn.* hopelessness, unattainability, unreasonableness, contrariety, impracticality, unfeasibility, impracticability, difficulty, unlikelihood, failure, unworkability; see also **futility.** — *Ant.* PROBABILITY, feasibility, practicality.

**impossible,** *modif.* **1.** [Incapable of being considered] — *Syn.* inconceivable, unthinkable, vain, hopeless, infeasible, unachievable, unattainable, out of the question, insurmountable, useless, impassable, inaccessible, unworkable, preposterous, absurd, illogical, incredible, untenable, implausible, unimaginable, unobtainable, not to be thought of, hardly possible, beyond the bounds of possibility, like finding a needle in a haystack*, a hundred to one*; see also **futile** 1, **hopeless** 2. — *Ant.* POSSIBLE, likely, reasonable.
**2.** [Having little likelihood of accomplishment] — *Syn.* improbable, unlikely, impracticable, too much for; see **difficult** 1, 2.
**3.** [Undesirable; *said of things*] — *Syn.* unacceptable,

improper, objectionable, incongruous; see **offensive** 2, **undesirable, unsuitable.**

**4.** [Disagreeable; *said of persons*] — *Syn.* difficult, unmanageable, hard to deal with; see **irritable, obstinate, undesirable.**

**impostor,** *n.* — *Syn.* pretender, charlatan, quack, fraud, impersonator, masquerader, mountebank, deceiver, dissembler, sham, hypocrite, fake*, faker*, phony*, sharper*, con artist*; see also **cheat** 1, **hypocrite.**
*See Synonym Study at* QUACK.

**imposture,** *n.* — *Syn.* deceit, deception, hoax; see **deception** 1, **trick** 1.

**impotence,** *n.* **1.** [Sterility] — *Syn.* infertility, unproductiveness, infecundity; see **barrenness.**

**2.** [Weakness] — *Syn.* powerlessness, helplessness, feebleness, infirmity; see **inability, weakness** 1.

**impotent,** *modif.* **1.** [Weak] — *Syn.* powerless, ineffective, inept, infirm; see **unable, weak** 1.

**2.** [Sterile] — *Syn.* barren, frigid, unproductive; see **sterile** 1.
*See Synonym Study at* STERILE.

**impound,** *v.* **1.** [To imprison] — *Syn.* encage, incarcerate, confine; see **enclose** 1, **imprison.**

**2.** [To seize] — *Syn.* appropriate, take, confiscate; see **seize** 2.

**impounded,** *modif.* — *Syn.* kept, seized, confiscated; see **captured** 2, **held.**

**impoverish,** *v.* — *Syn.* make poor, bankrupt, exhaust; see **ruin** 2.

**impoverished,** *modif.* — *Syn.* poverty-stricken, bankrupt, broke*; see **insolvent, poor** 1, **ruined** 4.
*See Synonym Study at* POOR.

**impracticability,** *n.* — *Syn.* hopelessness, infeasibility, uselessness, emptiness; see **futility, impossibility.**

**impracticable,** *modif.* — *Syn.* infeasible, unworkable, unachievable; see **impossible** 1.

**impractical,** *modif.* — *Syn.* unrealistic, unworkable, unreal, improbable, illogical, unreasonable, impracticable, inefficacious, ineffective, speculative, absurd, wild, quixotic, chimerical, abstract, theoretical, impossible, idealistic, infeasible, unfeasible, unwise, out of the question, useless; see also **visionary** 1. — *Ant.* PRACTICAL, useful, reasonable.

**impracticality,** *n.* — *Syn.* inefficiency, unworkability, uselessness, inapplicability; see **idealism** 1, **impossibility, worthlessness.**

**imprecation,** *n.* — *Syn.* blasphemy, malediction, swearing; see **curse** 1.

**impregnable,** *modif.* — *Syn.* immovable, invulnerable, unconquerable, secure; see **safe** 1, **strong** 2.

**impregnate,** *v.* **1.** [To imbue] — *Syn.* catechize, indoctrinate, implant; see **instill, teach** 1.

**2.** [To permeate] — *Syn.* fill up, pervade, saturate, infuse; see **fill** 2, **soak** 1.

**3.** [To beget] — *Syn.* inseminate, procreate, conceive; see **fertilize** 2, **produce** 1, **propagate** 1.
*See Synonym Study at* SOAK.

**impregnated,** *modif.* **1.** [Full] — *Syn.* saturated, shot through and through, permeated; see **full** 1.

**2.** [Pregnant] — *Syn.* bred, *enceinte* (French), with child; see **pregnant** 1.

**impresario,** *n.* — *Syn.* producer, stage director, manager; see **director** 2, **leader** 3.

**impress,** *v.* **1.** [To affect strongly or deeply] — *Syn.* influence, affect, make an impact, make an impression, stand out, be conspicuous, cause a stir, move, stir, touch, sway, strike, excite, disturb, excite notice, engage the thoughts, engage attention, leave one's mark, find favor with, arouse comment, get to*, grab*, make a hit*,

make a splash*, wow*, cut a figure*; see also **influence.**

**2.** [To command respect] — *Syn.* awe, dazzle, overawe, overwhelm; see **fascinate, surprise** 1.

**3.** [To make an impression] — *Syn.* indent, emboss, imprint; see **dent, mark** 1, **print** 2.
*See Synonym Study at* AFFECT.

**impressed,** *modif.* — *Syn.* aroused, dazzled, snowed*; see **affected** 1, **fascinated.**

**impressibility,** *n.* — *Syn.* susceptibility, impressionability, sentimentality, flexibility, pliancy, plasticity, affectability, tenderness, perceptivity, emotionality, sensitivity, sensitiveness, susceptibleness, sensibility; see also **feeling** 4, **sensitivity** 2.

**impressible,** *modif.* — *Syn.* penetrable, susceptible, responsive, yielding; see **affected** 1, **impressionable, responsive, sensitive** 3.

**impression,** *n.* **1.** [An imprint] — *Syn.* print, footprint, fingerprint, dent, mold, indentation, depression, impress, mark, cast, form, track, spoor, pattern, matrix; see also **mark** 1.

**2.** [An effect] — *Syn.* response, consequence, reaction; see **impact** 2, **result.**

**3.** [A notion based on scanty evidence] — *Syn.* theory, conjecture, supposition, idea; see **guess, hypothesis, opinion** 1.
*See Synonym Study at* IDEA.

**impressionable,** *modif.* — *Syn.* susceptible, impressible, receptive, easily affected, sensitive, responsive, suggestible, penetrable, flexible, pliable, pliant, tender, emotional, sensible, sentient, perceptive, sympathetic, amenable, persuadable, persuasible, empathetic; see also **affected** 1, **responsive, sensitive** 3.

**impressive,** *modif.* **1.** [Striking] — *Syn.* stirring, moving, inspiring, effective, affecting, telling, eloquent, thrilling, exciting, intense, rousing, well-done, well-organized, dramatic, absorbing, deep, profound, penetrating, convincing, persuasive, powerful, memorable, remarkable, consequential, extraordinary, notable, admirable, awe-inspiring, soul-stirring, awesome, resounding, high-sounding, important, imposing, formidable, momentous, vital, big-time*; see also **striking.** — *Ant.* DULL, uninteresting, common.

**2.** [Grand] — *Syn.* majestic, noble, stately; see **grand** 2.

**impress on** or **upon,** *v.* — *Syn.* urge, stress, implant in the mind, drive home*; see **emphasize, instill.**

**imprimatur,** *n.* — *Syn.* approval, sanction, charter, permit; see **permission.**

**imprint,** *n.* **1.** [A printed identification] — *Syn.* publisher's name, banner, trademark, sponsorship, direction, heading, colophon, logo; see also **emblem, signature.**

**2.** [An impression] — *Syn.* dent, indentation, print; see **mark** 1.

**imprint,** *v.* — *Syn.* print, stamp, designate; see **dent, mark** 1, 2.

**imprinted,** *modif.* — *Syn.* branded, printed, impressed; see **marked** 1, **stamped.**

**imprison,** *v.* — *Syn.* jail, confine, incarcerate, lock up, coop up, immure, impound, detain, keep in, hold, intern, circumscribe, shut in, bottle up, lock in, bolt in, rail in, box in, fence in, cage, send to prison, throw in jail, keep as captive, hold as hostage, enclose, keep in custody, hold captive, put behind bars, commit, remand, remit, commit to an institution, institutionalize, put away*, slap in the can*, dress in steel*, lay in lavender*, clap under hatches*, send up*, send up the river*; see also **enclose** 1. — *Ant.* FREE, liberate, release.

**imprisoned,** *modif.* — *Syn.* arrested, jailed, incarcerated; see **confined** 3.

**imprisonment,** *n.* **1.** [Forcible detention] — *Syn.* incarceration, custody, confinement, captivity, isolation, duress, durance, bondage, thralldom, quarantine, limbo, immuration, remand; see also **arrest** 1, **confinement** 1, **restraint** 2. — *Ant.* FREEDOM, liberty, enlargement.
**2.** [Placing in forcible detention] — *Syn.* confining, jailing, imprisoning, capturing, incarcerating, locking up, subjecting, enthralling, quarantining, immuring, detaining. — *Ant.* RELEASE, liberating, discharge.

**improbability,** *n.* — *Syn.* unlikelihood, implausibility, doubtfulness, rarity; see **impossibility, uncertainty** 2.

**improbable,** *modif.* — *Syn.* not likely, doubtful, remote, not to be expected; see **unlikely.**

**impromptu,** *modif.* — *Syn.* extemporaneous, extemporary, extempore, improvised, unprepared, offhand; see also **extemporaneous.**

---

*SYN.* — **impromptu** is applied to that which is spoken, made, or done on the spur of the moment to suit the occasion and stresses spontaneity; **extemporaneous, extempore** (more commonly used as an adverb), and **extemporary** may express the same idea but are now more often used of a speech that has received some preparation, but has not been written out or memorized; **improvised** applies to something composed or devised without any preparation and, with reference to things other than music, suggests the ingenious use of whatever is at hand to fill an unforeseen and immediate need

---

**improper,** *modif.* **1.** [Unsuitable] — *Syn.* unseemly, unbecoming, at odds, ill-advised, unsuited, indecorous, incongruous, out of place, ludicrous, incorrect, preposterous, unwarranted, undue, imprudent, unadapted, abnormal, irregular, inexpedient, unseasonable, inadvisable, untimely, inopportune, unfit, malapropos, unfitting, inappropriate, unapt, unbefitting, untoward, unmeet, ill-timed, awkward, inharmonious, discordant, discrepant, inapplicable, ill-assorted, odd; see also **unsuitable.**
**2.** [Immoral] — *Syn.* indecent, indelicate, immodest, lewd, naughty, suggestive, smutty; see also **lewd** 1.

---

*SYN.* — **improper,** the word of broadest application in this list, refers to anything that is not proper or suitable, esp. to that which does not conform to conventional standards; **unseemly** applies to that which is improper or inappropriate to the particular situation /her *unseemly* laughter at the funeral/; **unbecoming** applies to that which is inappropriate to a certain kind of person, his character, etc. /his rigid views are most *unbecoming* in a teacher/; **indecorous** refers to that which violates propriety or good taste in behavior, speech, etc. /his *indecorous* interruption of their chat/; **indelicate** implies a lack of propriety or tact and connotes immodesty or coarseness /an *indelicate* anecdote/; **indecent** is used of that which is regarded as highly offensive to morals or modesty /*indecent* exposure/

---

**improperly,** *modif.* — *Syn.* poorly, inappropriately, clumsily; see **awkwardly, badly** 1, **inadequately.**

**impropriety,** *n.* — *Syn.* unseemliness, incongruity, indecency, blunder; see **error** 1, **indecency** 2, **rudeness.**

**improve,** *v.* **1.** [To make better] — *Syn.* better, ameliorate, mend, amend, enhance, enrich, cultivate, revise, update, upgrade, elevate, polish, refine, purify, enlarge, touch up, edit, emend, civilize, educate, meliorate, landscape, develop, revamp, renew, give color to, set right, reorganize, promote, reform, raise, lift, rectify, correct, rehabilitate, renovate, spruce up, gentrify, refashion, regenerate, retread, overhaul, fix, straighten out, distill, change for the better, fix up*, doctor up*, give a good going over*, be the making of*; see also **adjust** 3, **change** 1, **correct** 1, **repair.** — *Ant.* DESTROY, impair, downgrade.
**2.** [To become better] — *Syn.* get better, advance, progress, make progress, show improvement, make strides, make headway, gain ground, ameliorate, regenerate, renew, recover, gain strength, develop, grow better, grow, rally, mend, gain, come around, profit, augment, widen, increase, mellow, mature, come along, come on, get on, get along, take a new lease on life*, look up*, shape up*, pick up*, perk up*, snap out of it*; see also **recover** 2, 3. — *Ant.* WEAKEN, worsen, deteriorate.

---

*SYN.* — **improve** and **better** both imply a correcting or advancing of something that is not in itself necessarily bad, the former by supplying a lack or want /to *improve* a method/ and the latter by seeking something more satisfying /he's left his job to *better* himself/; **ameliorate** implies improving to some degree a condition that is bad, oppressive, or intolerable to begin with /to *ameliorate* the lot of the poor/

---

**improved,** *modif.* **1.** [Made better] — *Syn.* enhanced, augmented, corrected, ameliorated, bettered, amended, mended, reformed, elaborated, enriched, refined, processed, upgraded, modernized, brought up-to-date, repaired, bolstered up, rectified, rehabilitated, remodeled, renovated, reorganized, made over, better for, fixed up*, doctored up*, polished up*; see also **changed** 2, **revised.** — *Ant.* DAMAGED, injured, worsened.
**2.** [In better health] — *Syn.* recovered, convalescent, making a rapid recovery; see **convalescent, well** 1.

**improvement,** *n.* **1.** [The process of making or becoming better] — *Syn.* betterment, amelioration, melioration, rectification, change, amendment, alteration, reformation, progression, advance, advancement, development, refinement, growth, rise, reclamation, civilization, gain, cultivation, progressiveness, increase, enrichment, promotion, recovery, recuperation, healing, regeneration, furtherance, renovation, modernization, remodeling, refurbishment, repair, reorganization, reform, emendation, revision, elaboration, enhancement, elevation, preferment, ennoblement, shaking down*, getting the bugs out*; see also **revision.** — *Ant.* DECAY, deterioration, retrogression.
**2.** [That which has been improved] — *Syn.* addition, supplement, repair, extra, attachment, correction, reform, remodeling, modernization, betterment, refinement, luxury, advance, advancement, step forward, enhancement, new model, deluxe model, latest thing*, last word*; see also **change** 2.

**improve on** or **upon,** *v.* — *Syn.* make better, develop, refine; see **adjust** 3, **change** 1, **correct** 1, **improve** 1.

**improvidence,** *n.* — *Syn.* extravagance, wastefulness, shortsightedness; see **carelessness, neglect** 1, **waste** 1.

**improvident,** *modif.* — *Syn.* spendthrift, extravagant, imprudent; see **rash, wasteful.**

**improvidently,** *modif.* — *Syn.* impulsively, unwisely, thoughtlessly; see **foolishly, rashly.**

**improving,** *modif.* — *Syn.* reconstructing, repairing, elaborating, bettering, correcting, developing, fixing, remodeling, on the mend*; see also **convalescent.**

**improvisation,** *n.* — *Syn.* improvising, extemporization, ad-libbing*, ad-lib*, impromptu creation, spontaneous creation, makeshift device, stopgap, making do, playing it by ear*, jamming*, lick*; see also **discovery** 2, **resort** 1.

**improvise,** *v.* — *Syn.* ad-lib*, coin, devise, extemporize; see **invent** 1.

**imprudence,** *n.* — *Syn.* indiscretion, foolishness, recklessness; see **carelessness, indiscretion** 1, **neglect** 1.

**imprudent,** *modif.* — *Syn.* incautious, impulsive, ill-advised, indiscreet; see **rash.**

**imprudently,** *modif.* — *Syn.* unwisely, inadvisedly, indiscreetly; see **foolishly, rashly.**

**impudence,** *n.* — *Syn.* insolence, impertinence, effrontery; see **rudeness.**

**impudent,** *modif.* — *Syn.* forward, insolent, impertinent, saucy; see **rude** 2.

*See Synonym Study at* IMPERTINENT.

**impudently,** *modif.* — *Syn.* saucily, brashly, insolently, presumptuously; see **rudely.**

**impugn,** *v.* — *Syn.* question, attack, challenge, call in question, contradict, gainsay, deny, assail, knock*; see also **deny, doubt** 1, 2.

*See Synonym Study at* DENY.

**impulse,** *n.* **1.** [An impelling force] — *Syn.* push, thrust, surge, impetus, throb, vibration, pulse, pulsation, pressure, augmentation, rush, motivation, actuation, stimulus, incentive, impulsion, propulsion, stroke, momentum, shove, shock, bump, movement; see also **beat** 2, **incentive.**
**2.** [A sudden urge] — *Syn.* fancy, whim, caprice, motive, spontaneity, drive, appeal, notion, inclination, disposition, bent, vagary, freak, wish, whimsy, inspiration, hunch, flash, thought, extemporization; see also **desire** 1, **inclination** 1.

**impulsive,** *modif.* **1.** [Spontaneous] — *Syn.* offhand, unpremeditated, extemporaneous, spur-of-the-moment*; see **automatic** 2, **extemporaneous, spontaneous.**
**2.** [Impetuous] — *Syn.* sudden, hasty, unpredictable; see **careless** 1, **changeable** 1, **rash.**

*See Synonym Study at* SPONTANEOUS.

**impulsively,** *modif.* — *Syn.* imprudently, hastily, impetuously; see **carelessly, foolishly, rashly.**

**impunity,** *n.* — *Syn.* exemption, dispensation, privilege; see **exception** 1, **exemption.**

*See Synonym Study at* EXEMPTION.

**impure,** *modif.* **1.** [Not pure] — *Syn.* adulterated, diluted, debased, contaminated, mixed, watered, watered down, polluted, dirty, sullied, corrupted, vitiated, tainted, raw, unrefined, sugared, cut, dilute, loaded, weighted, salted, doctored*, tampered with*; see also **dirty** 1, **unclean.**
**2.** [Not chaste] — *Syn.* unclean, unchaste, improper, corrupt; see **lewd** 2, **wicked** 1.

**impurity,** *n.* **1.** [Contamination] — *Syn.* adulteration, pollution, defilement, infection; see **contamination, pollution.**
**2.** [An impure element] — *Syn.* dirt, contaminant, pollutant; see **filth, germ** 3.
**3.** [Lewdness] — *Syn.* indecency, immorality, pornography; see **lewdness.**

**imputation,** *n.* — *Syn.* ascription, allegation, insinuation, incrimination; see **accusation** 2.

**impute,** *v.* **1.** [To attribute] — *Syn.* ascribe, assign, credit; see **attribute.**
**2.** [To charge with] — *Syn.* brand, blame, implicate; see **accuse.**

*See Synonym Study at* ATTRIBUTE.

**imputed,** *modif.* — *Syn.* supposed, claimed, charged; see **accused, likely** 1.

**in,** *prep. & modif.* **1.** [Within] — *Syn.* inside, surrounded by, in the midst of, within the boundaries of, in the area of, within the time of, concerning the subject of, as a part of, inside of, enclosed in, protected by; see also **within.**
**2.** [Into] — *Syn.* to the center of, into the midst of, in the direction of, within the extent of, under, near, against; see also **into, toward.**
**3.** [While engaged in] — *Syn.* in the act of, during the process of, while occupied with; see **during, meanwhile, while** 1.
**4.** [*In favor] — *Syn.* stylish, popular, in vogue; see **fashionable, favorite.**
**have it in for*** — *Syn.* hold a grudge against, wish to harm, be out to destroy, detest; see **hate** 1.

**inability,** *n.* — *Syn.* incapacity, incompetence, inadequacy, shortcoming, disability, handicap, incapability, insufficiency, impotence, powerlessness, failure, ineptitude, ineptness, inefficacy, inutility, unfitness, inefficiency, incapacitation, frailty; see also **failure** 1, **weakness** 1, 2. — *Ant.* ABILITY, capability, capacity.

**inaccessible,** *modif.* — *Syn.* unobtainable, remote, far, unachievable, unattainable, insurmountable, impracticable, aloof, unapproachable, unfeasible, unworkable, unavailable, unrealizable, insoluble, impassable, impervious, impenetrable, unavailable, not at hand, out of reach, inconvenient, elusive, unreachable; see also **difficult** 2, **distant** 1, **rare** 2, **remote** 1, **tight** 2.

**inaccuracy,** *n.* — *Syn.* exaggeration, mistake, imprecision; see **error** 1.

**inaccurate,** *modif.* — *Syn.* fallacious, in error, incorrect, inexact; see **mistaken** 1, **wrong** 2.

**inaccurately,** *modif.* — *Syn.* inexactly, clumsily, crudely; see **badly** 1, **inadequately.**

**inactive,** *modif.* **1.** [Inert] — *Syn.* dormant, stable, still; see **idle** 1, **latent, motionless** 1.
**2.** [Indolent] — *Syn.* idle, sedentary, sluggish, lethargic; see **dull** 6, **lazy** 1.

**inadequacy,** *n.* **1.** [Inferiority] — *Syn.* ineptitude, incompetence, insufficiency; see **inability, lack** 1.
**2.** [A defect] — *Syn.* flaw, drawback, shortcoming, deficiency; see **defect** 2, **lack** 2.

**inadequate,** *modif.* **1.** [Insufficient] — *Syn.* lacking, deficient, scanty, short, meager, failing, found wanting, unequal, not enough, sparing, stinted, stunted, feeble, sparse, too little, falling short, small, thin, incomplete, inappreciable, inconsiderable, spare, bare, parsimonious, niggardly, miserly, scarce, unsubstantial, barren, depleted, low, weak, flaccid, impotent, unproductive, dry, sterile, jejune, imperfect, defective, lame, sorry, pathetic, pitiful, exiguous, skimpy*, shy*, at low-water mark*; see also **faulty, poor** 2, **unsatisfactory, wanting** 1. — *Ant.* ENOUGH, adequate, sufficient.
**2.** [Incompetent] — *Syn.* unequal, inept, ineffectual; see **incompetent.**

**inadequately,** *modif.* — *Syn.* insufficiently, not enough, partly, partially, incompletely, scantily, deficiently, perfunctorily, ineffectively, inefficiently, ineptly, ineffectually, incompetently, not up to standards, not up to specifications, not fulfilling requirements, meagerly, not in sufficient quantity, not of sufficient quality, in a limited manner, to a limited degree, not up to snuff*; see also **badly** 1.

**inadmissible,** *modif.* — *Syn.* not allowed, unacceptable, prohibited, objectionable; see **refused, unsuitable.**

**inadvertence,** *n.* — *Syn.* neglect, indifference, oversight; see **neglect** 1, **omission** 1.

**inadvertent,** *modif.* **1.** [Careless] — *Syn.* inattentive, heedless, negligent; see **careless** 1.
**2.** [Unintentional] — *Syn.* accidental, unpremeditated, unthinking; see **accidental** 1.
**inadvertently,** *modif.* **1.** [Carelessly] — *Syn.* heedlessly, negligently, recklessly; see **carelessly, rashly.**
**2.** [Unintentionally] — *Syn.* unwittingly, involuntarily, not by design; see **accidentally.**
**inadvisable,** *modif.* — *Syn.* unwise, imprudent, impolitic, ill-advised; see **improper** 1, **rash, stupid** 1.
**inadvisedly,** *modif.* — *Syn.* impulsively, regrettably, unwisely; see **foolishly, rashly.**
**inalienable,** *modif.* — *Syn.* inviolable, unassailable, basic, natural; see **absolute** 1, **inherent.**
**inamorata,** *n.* — *Syn.* paramour, mistress, sweetheart; see **lover** 1.
**in and about** or **around,** *modif.* — *Syn.* close to, nearby, there, around; see **around** 1, **near** 1.
**inane,** *modif.* — *Syn.* pointless, foolish, fatuous, asinine; see **illogical, silly, stupid** 1.
**inanimate,** *modif.* **1.** [Inorganic] — *Syn.* lifeless, dead, mineral, nonanimal, nonvegetable, azoic; see also **inorganic.**
**2.** [Inactive] — *Syn.* dull, inert, dormant, spiritless; see **dull** 6, **idle** 1, **motionless** 1.
*See Synonym Study at* DEAD.
**inanition,** *n.* — *Syn.* starvation, exhaustion, malnutrition, collapse; see **fatigue, starvation.**
**inanity,** *n.* — *Syn.* silliness, asininity, foolishness; see **stupidity** 1, 2.
**inapplicable,** *modif.* — *Syn.* inappropriate, unsuited, inconsistent; see **irrelevant, unsuitable.**
**inappropriate,** *modif.* — *Syn.* improper, inapt, unseemly, inapplicable; see **improper** 1, **unsuitable.**
**inaptitude,** *n.* — *Syn.* unfitness, inexperience, unskillfulness, incompetence; see **inability.**
**inarticulate,** *modif.* **1.** [Mute] — *Syn.* reticent, wordless, mute, tongue-tied; see **dumb** 1, 2.
**2.** [Indistinct] — *Syn.* unintelligible, incoherent, garbled, vague; see **incoherent** 2, **obscure** 1.
**inasmuch as,** *conj.* — *Syn.* in view of the fact that, making allowance for, seeing that, while; see **because, since** 1.
**inattention,** *n.* — *Syn.* heedlessness, negligence, distraction; see **carelessness, indifference, neglect** 1.
**inattentive,** *modif.* — *Syn.* heedless, unmindful, negligent, distracted; see **absent-minded, careless** 1.
*See Synonym Study at* ABSENT-MINDED.
**inaudible,** *modif.* — *Syn.* low, indistinct, imperceptible, muffled; see **faint** 3.
**inaudibly,** *modif.* — *Syn.* unintelligibly, indistinctly, softly; see **obscurely, silently.**
**inaugurate,** *v.* — *Syn.* introduce, initiate, originate; see **begin** 1.
*See Synonym Study at* BEGIN.
**inaugurated,** *modif.* — *Syn.* originated, started, installed, introduced; see **begun, initiated** 1, 3.
**inauguration,** *n.* — *Syn.* initiation, commencement, installment, dedication; see **installation** 1, **introduction** 1.
**inauspicious,** *modif.* — *Syn.* foreboding, unlucky, unpropitious, ill-omened; see **ominous, unfavorable** 2.
**inborn,** *modif.* — *Syn.* essential, intrinsic, innate, inbred; see **inherent, native** 1.
*See Synonym Study at* INNATE.
**inbred,** *modif.* — *Syn.* innate, inborn, ingrained; see **inherent, native** 1.
*See Synonym Study at* INNATE.

**incalculable,** *modif.* **1.** [Immense] — *Syn.* inestimable, limitless, boundless; see **endless** 1, **infinite** 1.
**2.** [Unpredictable] — *Syn.* unforeseeable, unforeseen, unfixed, undeterminable; see **uncertain** 2.
**incandescence,** *n.* — *Syn.* radiance, luster, brilliance; see **light** 1.
**incandescent,** *modif.* — *Syn.* radiant, glowing, brilliant, intense; see **bright** 1.
**incantation,** *n.* **1.** [Invocation] — *Syn.* charm, chant, spell, mantra; see **chant, magic** 2.
**2.** [Witchcraft] — *Syn.* sorcery, black magic, enchantment; see **magic** 1, **witchcraft.**
**incapability,** *n.* — *Syn.* incapacity, incompetence, impotence; see **inability.**
**incapable,** *modif.* — *Syn.* unsuited, inept, ineffective, inadequate; see **incompetent.**
**incapable of,** *modif.* **1.** [Unable] — *Syn.* unequipped, unqualified, powerless; see **incompetent, unable.**
**2.** [Not admitting] — *Syn.* not allowing, not open to, insusceptible, not disposed to, not liable to, resistant.
**incapacitate,** *v.* — *Syn.* disable, hinder, undermine; see **damage** 1, **hurt** 1, **weaken** 2.
**incapacity,** *n.* — *Syn.* inadequacy, insufficiency, disqualification; see **inability.**
**incarcerate,** *v.* — *Syn.* jail, detain, confine; see **enclose** 1, **imprison.**
**incarceration,** *n.* — *Syn.* imprisonment, captivity, restraint; see **confinement** 1, **imprisonment** 1.
**incarnate,** *modif.* — *Syn.* embodied, personified, tangible; see **physical** 1, **real** 2.
**incarnation,** *n.* **1.** [Personification] — *Syn.* manifestation, embodiment, incorporation; see **epitome** 1.
**2.** [Matter] — *Syn.* substance, body, flesh-and-blood; see **matter** 1.
**incautious,** *modif.* — *Syn.* hasty, reckless, impetuous; see **rash.**
**incautiously,** *modif.* — *Syn.* brashly, thoughtlessly, heedlessly; see **carelessly, rashly.**
**incendiary,** *modif.* **1.** [Combustible] — *Syn.* ignitable, burnable, flammable; see **burning** 1, **inflammable.**
**2.** [Stirring up strife or rebellion] — *Syn.* inflammatory, provocative, subversive; see **dangerous** 1, **inflammatory, rebellious** 2, **treacherous** 2.
**incendiary,** *n.* **1.** [Arsonist] — *Syn.* pyromaniac, firebug*, *petroleur* (French); see **arsonist, criminal.**
**2.** [An agitator] — *Syn.* insurgent, instigator, *provocateur* (French); see **agitator, rebel** 1.
**incense,** *n.* — *Syn.* scent, fragrance, fuel, punk, joss stick, flame, odor, frankincense, essence, burnt offering, aroma, redolence, sandalwood, myrrh; see also **perfume.**
**incense,** *v.* — *Syn.* enrage, infuriate, exasperate, provoke; see **anger** 1, **bother** 2.
**incensed,** *modif.* — *Syn.* irate, indignant, furious; see **angry.**
**incentive,** *n.* — *Syn.* spur, inducement, motivation, motive, stimulus, stimulation, spring, impetus, catalyst, ground, provocation, enticement, temptation, bait, consideration, determinant, excuse, rationale, goad, prod, whip, urge, impulse, influence, lure, come-on*, allurement, persuasion, inspiration, exhortation, encouragement, instigation, incitement, reason why, carrot*; see also **impulse** 1, **purpose** 1, **reason** 3.
**inception,** *n.* — *Syn.* initiation, beginning, commencement, conception; see **origin** 1.
*See Synonym Study at* ORIGIN.
**incertitude,** *n.* — *Syn.* hesitation, perplexity, misgiving; see **doubt** 2, **uncertainty** 1, 2.

**incessant,** *modif.* — *Syn.* ceaseless, continuous, unending, unremitting; see **constant** 1, **perpetual** 1, 2.
*See Synonym Study at* PERPETUAL.

**incessantly,** *modif.* — *Syn.* steadily, monotonously, perpetually; see **regularly** 2.

**incest,** *n.* — *Syn.* inbreeding, interbreeding, Oedipal love, Electral love, mother-son relationship, father-daughter relationship, brother-sister relationship, sexual abuse; see also **abuse** 3, **lewdness.**

**incestuous,** *modif.* — *Syn.* abusive, depraved, interbred, carnal; see **lewd** 2.

**inch,** *n.* **1.** [Twelfth of a foot] — *Syn.* fingerbreadth, 2.54 centimeters, measurement, 1/36 yard, length; see also **measure** 1.
**2.** [Small degree] — *Syn.* jot, tittle, iota; see **bit** 3.
**by inches** — *Syn.* slowly, by degrees, inch by inch, step by step; see **gradually.**
**every inch** — *Syn.* in all respects, thoroughly, entirely; see **completely, in all respects** at **respect.**
**within an inch of** — *Syn.* very close to, near to, nearly; see **almost.**

**inch,** *v.* — *Syn.* creep, barely move, worm along; see **crawl** 2.

**inchoate,** *modif.* — *Syn.* incipient, rudimentary, preliminary, beginning, just begun, not fully formed; see also **unfinished** 1.

**incidence,** *n.* — *Syn.* occurrence, frequency, rate, degree, number, extent, range of occurrence, percentage, proportion, measure, scope, commonness, prevalence, tendency, trend, drift.

**incident,** *n.* — *Syn.* episode, occurrence, conflict, disturbance; see **event** 1.
*See Synonym Study at* OCCURRENCE.

**incidental,** *modif.* — *Syn.* subsidiary, as an incident of, concomitant, accidental; see **accidental, related** 2, **trivial.**
*See Synonym Study at* ACCIDENTAL.

**incidentally,** *modif.* — *Syn.* by the way, parenthetically, by the by, in passing, *en passant* (French), apropos of, speaking of, by chance, subordinately, in an incidental manner, concomitant to, as a side effect, as a by-product, accidentally, unexpectedly; see also **accidentally.**

**incidentals,** *n.* — *Syn.* miscellaneous items, minor needs, odds and ends, incidental expenses; see **expenses, necessity** 2.

**incinerate,** *v.* — *Syn.* cremate, parch, burn up; see **burn** 2.

**incipient,** *modif.* — *Syn.* beginning, developing, embryonic, nascent; see **budding, early** 1, **inchoate.**

**incise,** *v.* — *Syn.* cut into, engrave, chisel, etch; see **carve** 1, **cut** 2, **engrave** 2.

**incised,** *modif.* — *Syn.* etched, engraved, cut; see **carved, engraved.**

**incision,** *n.* — *Syn.* gash, slash, surgery; see **cut** 2, **hole** 1.

**incisive,** *modif.* **1.** [Sarcastic] — *Syn.* penetrating, cutting, biting, sharp, severe; see also **sarcastic.**
**2.** [Intelligent] — *Syn.* trenchant, penetrating, perceptive, clever, bright, profound; see also **intelligent** 1.

**SYN.** — **incisive** is applied to speech or writing that seems to penetrate directly to the heart of the matter, resulting in a clear and unambiguous statement /an *incisive* criticism/; **trenchant** implies clean-cut expression that results in sharply defined categories, differences, etc. /a *trenchant* analysis/; **cutting** implies incisive qualities but also connotes such harshness or sarcasm as to hurt the feelings /his *cutting* allusion to her inefficiency/; **biting**

implies a caustic or stinging quality that makes a deep impression on the mind /his *biting* satire/

**incisor,** *n.* — *Syn.* tusk, eyetooth, canine tooth; see **tooth** 1.

**incite,** *v.* — *Syn.* arouse, rouse, instigate, impel, stimulate, provoke, foment, excite, spur, goad, sic, exhort, persuade, influence, induce, prick, prod, push, taunt, actuate, activate, animate, inspirit, coax, stir up, fire up, inflame, whip up, motivate, prompt, drive, urge, urge on, egg on, inspire, abet, work up, lash into a fury, talk into, whip on, hold sway over, blow the coals, fan the flame; see also **drive** 1, **encourage** 1, **push** 2, **urge** 2.
— *Ant.* DISCOURAGE, dissuade, check.

**SYN.** — **incite** implies an urging or stimulating to action, either in a favorable or unfavorable sense /incited to achievement by rivalry/; **instigate** always implies responsibility for initiating an action and usually connotes a bad or evil purpose /who *instigated* the riot?/; **foment** suggests continued incitement over an extended period of time /the unjust taxes *fomented* rebellion/

**incited,** *modif.* — *Syn.* driven, pushed, motivated; see **urged** 2.

**incitement,** *n.* — *Syn.* motive, stimulus, instigation, provocation; see **incentive.**

**inclemency,** *n.* **1.** [Bitterness; *said of weather*] — *Syn.* raininess, storminess, coldness, rawness, harshness, weather, severity, wintriness, arctic conditions, low temperature; see also **rain** 1, **snow** 2, **storm** 1, **wind** 1.
**2.** [Strictness] — *Syn.* harshness, barbarity, unkindness; see **cruelty, severity.**

**inclement,** *modif.* **1.** [Bitter; *said of weather*] — *Syn.* wintry, severe, raw, nasty; see **cold** 1, **stormy** 1.
**2.** [Ruthless] — *Syn.* unkind, harsh, unmerciful; see **cruel** 2, **ruthless** 1, **severe** 1, 2.

**inclination,** *n.* **1.** [A tendency] — *Syn.* bent, bias, propensity, predilection, partiality, penchant, proclivity, leaning, predisposition, attachment, capability, capacity, proneness, aptness, fondness, disposition, liking, preference, movement, susceptibility, weakness, drift, trend, turn, slant, impulse, attraction, affection, affinity, desire, temperament, whim, idiosyncrasy, urge, persuasion.
**2.** [A bow] — *Syn.* bend, bending, bowing; see **bow** 2.
**3.** [A slope] — *Syn.* grade, downgrade, incline; see **hill.**
**4.** [A trend] — *Syn.* slant, direction, bent; see **drift** 1.
**5.** [A slant] — *Syn.* pitch, slope, incline, angle, ramp, declivity, bevel, acclivity, bank, lean, list, tilt; see also **grade** 1.

**SYN.** — **inclination** refers to a more or less vague mental disposition toward some action, practice, or thing /he had an *inclination* to refuse/; **leaning** suggests a general inclination toward something but implies only the direction of attraction and not the final choice /Dr. Green had always had a *leaning* toward the study of law/; **bent** and **propensity** imply a natural or inherent inclination coupled with a skill or ability, the latter also connoting an almost uncontrollable attraction /she has a *bent* for art, he has a *propensity* for getting into trouble/; **proclivity** usually suggests strong inclination as a result of habitual indulgence, usually toward something bad or wrong /a *proclivity* to falsehood/

**incline,** *n.* — *Syn.* slope, slant, inclined plane, approach; see **grade** 1, **inclination** 5.

**incline,** *v.* **1.** [To deviate from the horizontal or verti-

cal] — *Syn.* tilt, twist, slope, slant; see **bend** 1, **turn** 6, **veer.**
**2.** [To lean] — *Syn.* bow, bend, nod, cock; see **bow** 1, **lean** 1.
**3.** [To tend toward] — *Syn.* prefer, be disposed, be predisposed; see **favor** 1, **tend** 2.
**inclined,** *modif.* **1.** [Disposed] — *Syn.* prone, willing, tending; see **likely** 4.
**2.** [Diagonal] — *Syn.* tilted, slanted, tipped, sloping; see **oblique** 1.
**include,** *v.* **1.** [To contain] — *Syn.* hold, admit, cover, embrace, involve, consist of, take in, entail, encompass, incorporate, constitute, accommodate, comprise, compose, be comprised of, be composed of, comprehend, embody, implicate, be made up of, number among, carry, bear; see also **compose** 1, **comprise.** — *Ant.* OMIT, be outside of, exclude.
**2.** [To place into or among] — *Syn.* enter, add, append, introduce, take in, incorporate, subsume, make room for, build in, work in, inject, interject, add on, interpolate, insert, combine, make a part of, make allowance for, give consideration to, count in*; see also **add** 2. — *Ant.* DISCARD, exclude, reject.

---

**SYN.** — **include** implies a containing as part of a whole; **comprise** means to consist of and takes as its object the various parts that make up the whole /his library *comprises* 2,000 volumes and *includes* many first editions/ and it is often used to mean to make up or constitute /the techniques which *comprise* the scientific method; an audience *comprised* entirely of students/; **comprehend** suggests that the object is contained within the total scope or range of the subject, sometimes by implication /the word "beauty" *comprehends* various concepts/; **embrace** stresses the variety of objects comprehended /he had *embraced* a number of hobbies/; **involve** implies inclusion of an object because of its connection with the subject as a consequence or antecedent /acceptance of the office *involves* responsibilities/

---

**included,** *modif.* — *Syn.* contained, enclosed, counted, numbered, admitted, covered, involved, comprehended, encompassed, constituted, embodied, given a place among, inserted, built in, entered, incorporated, combined, comprised, subsumed, part of. — *Ant.* excluded, left out, rejected.
**including,** *modif.* — *Syn.* together with, along with, coupled with, as well as, inclusive of, in conjunction with, not to mention, to say nothing of, among other things, with the addition of, in addition to, counting, numbering, comprising, embracing, containing, covering, incorporating, made up of. — *Ant.* BESIDES, not counting, aside from.
**inclusion,** *n.* — *Syn.* admittance, incorporation, embodiment, comprisal, formation, composition; see also **addition** 1, **insertion.** — *Ant.* EXCLUSION, elimination, exception.
**inclusive,** *modif.* — *Syn.* including, all together, from beginning to end, in toto; see **comprehensive, general** 1, **including, whole** 1.
**incognito,** *modif.* — *Syn.* camouflaged, disguised, under cover, under an assumed name; see **hidden** 2, **secret** 3. *See Synonym Study at* ALIAS.
**incoherence,** *n.* — *Syn.* disjointedness, rambling, unintelligibility, incongruity; see **inconsistency, nonsense** 1, **uncertainty** 2.
**incoherent,** *modif.* **1.** [Not hanging together] — *Syn.* loose, uneven, uncoordinated, inconsistent; see **incongruous** 1, **irregular** 1.

**2.** [Inarticulate] — *Syn.* disjointed, rambling, confused, muddled, unintelligible, broken, disconnected, disorganized, illogical, garbled, mumbling, stammering, maundering, speechless, uncommunicative, unclear, puzzling, indistinct, faltering, stuttering, muttered, mumbled, jumbled, gasping, breathless, tongue-tied, muffled, indistinguishable, incomprehensible; see also **dumb** 1, 2, **obscure** 1. — *Ant.* CLEAR, eloquent, distinct.
**incoherently,** *modif.* — *Syn.* inarticulately, brokenly, confusedly, frantically, frenziedly, wildly, drunkenly, discontinuously, disjointedly, disconnectedly, spasmodically, chaotically, randomly, ineptly, unsystematically, aimlessly, sloppily, ambiguously, unintelligibly, illegibly, incomprehensibly, unrecognizably, uncertainly, indistinctly, unclearly, illogically, by fits and starts*, in snatches*; see also **irregularly, wildly** 1.
**incombustible,** *modif.* — *Syn.* nonflammable, noncombustible, unburnable; see **fireproof.**
**income,** *n.* — *Syn.* earnings, salary, wages, pay, livelihood, returns, profit, dividends, interest, assets, proceeds, benefits, receipts, gains, revenue, commission, drawings, rent, royalty, honorarium, annuity, pension, income after taxes, net income, gross income, taxable income, bottom line*, pickings*, take*; see also **pay** 2, **revenue** 1, 2. — *Ant.* EXPENSE, expenditures, outgo.
**incommensurate,** *modif.* — *Syn.* not proportional, unequal, disproportionate; see **unfair** 1.
**incommode,** *v.* — *Syn.* discommode, inconvenience, annoy; see **bother** 2, **disturb** 2.
**incommodious,** *modif.* — *Syn.* uncomfortable, troublesome, inconvenient, cramped; see **awkward** 2, **disturbing.**
**incommunicable,** *modif.* — *Syn.* not contagious, not catching, retained, kept in, inexpressible, unutterable.
**incommunicado,** *modif.* — *Syn.* sequestered, in retreat, secluded, silenced; see **hidden** 2, **isolated, silenced.**
**incommunicative,** *modif.* — *Syn.* quiet, secretive, silent, uncommunicative; see **reserved** 3, **taciturn.**
**incomparable,** *modif.* — *Syn.* unequaled, exceptional, superior; see **excellent, perfect** 2, **unique** 1.
**incomparably,** *modif.* — *Syn.* exceptionally, eminently, superlatively; see **especially** 1.
**incompatibility,** *n.* — *Syn.* variance, conflict, discordance, animosity; see **disagreement** 1, **opposition** 2.
**incompatible,** *modif.* — *Syn.* inconsistent, contrary, clashing, conflicting, inappropriate, unsuited, mismatched, contradictory, disagreeing, antagonistic, antipathetic, factious, unadapted, opposite, jarring, discordant, inharmonious, irreconcilable, incoherent, inadmissible; see also **opposed, unsuitable.**
**incompetence,** *n.* — *Syn.* inadequacy, inexperience, ineptitude; see **inability.**
**incompetent,** *modif.* — *Syn.* incapable, inefficient, inept, unskillful, inadequate, unfit, unskilled, unqualified, disqualified, bungling, inexpert, floundering, ineffectual, unsuitable, untrained, maladroit, unhandy, clumsy, awkward, uninitiated, raw, inexperienced, unequipped, unadapted, not equal to, amateurish; see also **unable.** — *Ant.* ABLE, fit, qualified.
**incompetently,** *modif.* — *Syn.* poorly, ineptly, clumsily; see **awkwardly, badly** 1.
**incomplete,** *modif.* **1.** [Unfinished] — *Syn.* rough, half-done, under construction; see **unfinished** 1.
**2.** [Partial] — *Syn.* sketchy, meager, deficient, fragmentary; see **inadequate** 1.
**incompletely,** *modif.* — *Syn.* imperfectly, not entirely, not completely, faultily; see **inadequately.**

**incomprehensible,** *modif.* — *Syn.* unintelligible, unclear, impenetrable; see **difficult** 2, **obscure** 1.

**incompressible,** *modif.* — *Syn.* dense, impenetrable, compact; see **thick** 1, 3.

**inconceivable,** *modif.* — *Syn.* fantastic, unimaginable, incredible; see **impossible** 1, **unbelievable, unimaginable.**

**inconclusive,** *modif.* — *Syn.* indecisive, unresolved, unsettled, indefinite; see **uncertain** 2.

**incongruity,** *n.* — *Syn.* discrepancy, inappropriateness, mismatch, anachronism; see **difference** 1, **inconsistency.**

**incongruous,** *modif.* **1.** [Inconsistent] — *Syn.* contradictory, conflicting, incompatible, mismatched, irreconcilable, uncoordinated, unconnected, twisted, incoherent, distorted, unrelated, divergent, discrepant, irregular, unpredictable, shifting, loose, lopsided, disparate, discordant, inharmonious, inconsonant, jumbled, unbalanced, incongruent, bizarre, out of keeping, out of step, at odds; see also **illogical, unsuitable.** — *Ant.* like, coordinated, harmonious.
**2.** [Unsuitable] — *Syn.* inappropriate, unseemly, out of place; see **improper** 1.

**inconsequential,** *modif.* — *Syn.* unimportant, immaterial, insignificant; see **irrelevant, trivial, unnecessary.**

**inconsiderable,** *modif.* — *Syn.* negligible, unimportant, insignificant; see **trivial, unimportant.**

**inconsiderate,** *modif.* — *Syn.* thoughtless, insensitive, boorish; see **rude** 2, **thoughtless** 2.

**inconsistency,** *n.* — *Syn.* discrepancy, disagreement, dissimilarity, disparity, variance, contrariety, incongruity, inequality, unlikeness, divergence, deviation, inconsonance, dissonance, disproportion, disproportionateness, paradox; see also **difference** 1. — *Ant.* CONSISTENCY, congruity, similarity.

**inconsistent,** *modif.* **1.** [Incompatible] — *Syn.* contradictory, discrepant, at variance; see **incompatible, incongruous** 1.
**2.** [Changeable] — *Syn.* self-contradictory, erratic, variable; see **changeable** 1, 2, **irregular** 1.

**inconsistently,** *modif.* — *Syn.* unpredictably, illogically, eccentrically; see **differently** 1.

**inconsolable,** *modif.* — *Syn.* heartbroken, forlorn, discouraged; see **sad** 1.

**inconspicuous,** *modif.* — *Syn.* unnoticeable, unobtrusive, concealed, indistinct; see **hidden** 2, **modest** 2, **obscure** 3.

**inconspicuously,** *modif.* — *Syn.* unobtrusively, surreptitiously, not openly; see **modestly** 1, **secretly.**

**inconstant,** *modif.* — *Syn.* changeable, fickle, variable, capricious, unstable; see also **changeable** 1, 2.

---

**SYN.** — **inconstant** implies an inherent tendency to change or a lack of steadfastness *[an inconstant lover]*; **fickle** suggests an even greater instability or readiness to change, especially in affection *[spurned by a fickle public]*; **capricious** implies an instability or irregularity that seems to be the product of whim, chance, or erratic impulse *[a capricious climate]*; **unstable** implies a liability to change, and in reference to persons applies to one who is emotionally unsettled or variable *[an unstable person laughs and cries easily]*

---

**incontinence,** *n.* — *Syn.* debauchery, lechery, unrestraint, lack of self-control; see **desire** 3, **indulgence** 3, **lewdness.**

**incontinent,** *modif.* — *Syn.* lustful, licentious, unrestrained, lacking control; see **lewd** 2, **uncontrolled.**

**incontrovertible,** *modif.* — *Syn.* established, undeniable, indisputable, authentic; see **accurate** 1, **certain** 3.

**inconvenience,** *n.* — *Syn.* bother, nuisance, difficulty, awkward detail; see **trouble** 2.

**inconvenient,** *modif.* — *Syn.* awkward, badly arranged, unhandy, inopportune; see **disturbing, embarrassing, inaccessible, untimely.**

**inconveniently,** *modif.* — *Syn.* inaccessibly, awkwardly, inappropriately, in an inconvenient manner; see **badly** 1.

**incorporate,** *v.* **1.** [To include] — *Syn.* add to, combine, fuse; see **consolidate** 2, **include** 2, **join** 1.
**2.** [To organize] — *Syn.* form a company, charter, start a business, consolidate; see **organize** 2, **unite** 1.

**incorporated,** *modif.* **1.** [Included] — *Syn.* assimilated, integrated, fused; see **included, joined.**
**2.** [Organized] — *Syn.* united, consolidated, coordinated, corporate; see **organized, united.**

**incorporation,** *n.* **1.** [Inclusion] — *Syn.* embodiment, adding, fusion; see **inclusion.**
**2.** [The act of becoming a corporate body] — *Syn.* chartering, consolidation, amalgamation, federation, establishment, confederation, affiliation, merger, unification, alliance, fraternization, unionization; see also **association** 1, **business** 4. — *Ant.* DIVISION, dissolution, disbanding.

**incorporeal,** *modif.* **1.** [Insubstantial] — *Syn.* spiritual, bodiless, ethereal; see **immaterial** 2.
**2.** [Divine] — *Syn.* celestial, angelic, deistic; see **divine** 1, **eternal** 2.

**incorrect,** *modif.* — *Syn.* inaccurate, not trustworthy, false; see **mistaken** 1, **unreliable** 2, **wrong** 2.

**incorrectly,** *modif.* — *Syn.* mistakenly, inaccurately, clumsily; see **badly** 1, **wrongly** 2.

**incorrectness,** *n.* — *Syn.* fault, blunder, inaccuracy; see **error** 1, **mistake** 2.

**incorrigible,** *modif.* — *Syn.* incurable, uncorrectable, intractable; see **hopeless** 2, **irreparable, unruly.**

**incorruptibility,** *n.* **1.** [Honesty] — *Syn.* integrity, honor, loyalty; see **honesty** 1, **reliability.**
**2.** [Persistence] — *Syn.* immortality, continuance, perpetuity; see **continuation** 1, **immortality** 1, **persistence.**

**incorruptible,** *modif.* — *Syn.* honest, honorable, scrupulous, ethical; see **moral** 1, **reliable** 1, **upright** 2.

**increase,** *n.* **1.** [Growth] — *Syn.* development, spread, enlargement, expansion, escalation, elaboration, optimization, burgeoning, swelling, addition, accession, incorporation, merger, inflation, appreciation, heightening, extension, dilation, multiplication, augmentation, rise, broadening, advance, gain, intensification, deepening, swell, amplification, progression, buildup, uptick, improvement, boost*, hike*, jump*, boom*; see also **progress** 1. — *Ant.* REDUCTION, decline, decrease.
**2.** [An addition] — *Syn.* increment, accession, accretion, raise; see **addition** 2.
**on the increase** — *Syn.* growing, developing, spreading; see **increasing** 1.

**increase,** *v.* **1.** [To add to] — *Syn.* extend, enlarge, augment, expand, dilate, broaden, widen, thicken, deepen, heighten, build, lengthen, magnify, add on, multiply, escalate, let out, open out, further, mark up, sharpen, build up, raise, enhance, amplify, reinforce, supplement, annex, distend, swell, double, triple, stretch, intensify, exaggerate, blow up, aggravate, protract, prolong, aggrandize, redouble, boost*, raise the ante*, step up*, rev up*, jack up*; see also **develop** 1, **improve** 1, **strengthen.** — *Ant.* DECREASE, reduce, abridge.

**2.** [To grow] — *Syn.* rise, progress, develop; see **grow** 1.

*SYN.* — **increase**, the general word in this list, means to make or become greater in size, amount, degree, etc. *[to increase one's weight, one's power, debts, etc.]*; **enlarge** specifically implies a making or becoming greater in size, volume, extent, etc. *[to enlarge a house, a business, etc.]*; **augment**, a more formal word, generally implies increase by addition, often of something that is already of a considerable size, amount, etc. *[to augment one's income]*; **multiply** suggests increase in number, specif. by procreation *[rabbits multiply rapidly]*

**increased,** *modif.* — *Syn.* raised, marked up, heightened, elevated, expanded, added on, doubled; see also **enlarged.**

**increasing,** *modif.* **1.** [Becoming larger] — *Syn.* growing, developing, maturing, multiplying, proliferating, broadening, widening, augmenting, waxing, sprouting, flourishing, rising, ever-widening, expanding, branching out, enlarging, accumulating, piling up, doubling, crescent, shooting up, getting big, swelling, spiraling, snowballing, on the rise, on the increase, on the upgrade, booming; see also **growing.**
**2.** [Becoming more intense] — *Syn.* intensifying, heightening, escalating, growing, dominant, advancing, getting louder, sharpening, accentuating, aggravating, emphasizing, accelerating, deepening, building, building up, revving up*.

**increasingly,** *modif.* — *Syn.* more and more, more frequently, with continual acceleration, with steady increase, with steady buildup; see also **frequently, more** 1, 2.

**incredible,** *modif.* — *Syn.* unbelievable, improbable, ridiculous; see **impossible** 1, **unbelievable, unimaginable.**

**incredibly,** *modif.* — *Syn.* amazingly, astonishingly, uncommonly; see **especially** 1, **strangely.**

**incredulity,** *n.* — *Syn.* disbelief, skepticism, amazement, unbelief; see **doubt** 1, **wonder** 1.
*See Synonym Study at UNBELIEF.*

**incredulous,** *modif.* — *Syn.* skeptical, unbelieving, dubious; see **doubtful** 2, **suspicious** 1.

**increment,** *n.* — *Syn.* accretion, supplement, gain; see **addition** 2, **increase** 1, **profit** 2.

**incriminate,** *v.* — *Syn.* implicate, blame, charge; see **accuse, implicate.**

**incriminating,** *modif.* — *Syn.* inculpating, damning, damaging, convicting, condemnatory, accusatory, compromising.

**incubate,** *v.* — *Syn.* hatch, brood, breed, nurture; see **nurse, produce** 1.

**inculcate,** *v.* — *Syn.* instill, implant, impress; see **instill, teach** 1.

**incumbent,** *modif.* — *Syn.* obligatory, binding, compelling; see **necessary** 1, **urgent** 1.

**incumbent,** *n.* — *Syn.* officeholder, official, occupant, in*; see **administrator, authority** 3.

**incur,** *v.* — *Syn.* bring upon oneself, provoke, contract, acquire; see **catch** 4, **incite.**

**incurable,** *modif.* — *Syn.* fatal, serious, hopeless; see **deadly** 1, **hopeless** 2.

**incurious,** *modif.* — *Syn.* apathetic, indifferent, uninterested; see **dull** 3, **indifferent** 1.
*See Synonym Study at INDIFFERENT.*

**incursion,** *n.* — *Syn.* intrusion, aggression, invasion, raid; see **attack** 1.

**indebted,** *modif.* — *Syn.* obligated, in debt, beholden,

obliged, under obligation, owing, grateful, appreciative, liable, answerable for, chargeable, accountable, bound, in arrears, in the red, in the hole*; see also **responsible** 1, **thankful.**

**indebtedness,** *n.* — *Syn.* deficit, responsibility, obligation; see **debit, debt** 1, **liability** 1.

**indecency,** *n.* **1.** [The quality of being indecent] — *Syn.* coarseness, grossness, bawdiness, vulgarity; see **lewdness.**
**2.** [An instance of indecency] — *Syn.* impurity, immodesty, offense, incivility, impropriety, indecorum, ribaldry, indelicacy, obscenity, vulgarity, raciness, four-letter word, lewdness, drunkenness, quadriliteral, pornography, smut, foulness. — *Ant.* propriety, purity, delicacy.

**indecent,** *modif.* — *Syn.* immoral, shocking, shameless, improper; see **coarse** 2, **lewd** 1, **shameful** 1.
*See Synonym Study at IMPROPER.*

**indecipherable,** *modif.* — *Syn.* mysterious, unreadable, vague; see **illegible, obscure** 1.

**indecision,** *n.* — *Syn.* hesitation, vacillation, irresolution; see **doubt** 2, **uncertainty** 1.

**indecisive,** *modif.* — *Syn.* irresolute, ambivalent, wishy-washy*; see **changeable** 1, **doubtful** 2.

**indecorous,** *modif.* — *Syn.* coarse, vulgar, uncouth, improper; see **improper** 1, **rude** 1, 2.
*See Synonym Study at IMPROPER.*

**indecorum,** *n.* — *Syn.* impropriety, indiscretion, vulgarity; see **indecency** 2, **rudeness.**

**indeed,** *interj.* — *Syn.* Really?, Honestly?, For sure?; see **really.**

**indeed,** *modif.* — *Syn.* in fact, in reality, admittedly, certainly; see **really** 1, **surely.**

**indefatigable,** *modif.* — *Syn.* inexhaustible, unwearied, tireless; see **active** 2, **tireless.**

**indefensible,** *modif.* **1.** [Vulnerable] — *Syn.* yielding, vincible, defenseless, unprotected; see **open** 4, **weak** 1, 3, 5.
**2.** [Inexcusable] — *Syn.* unjustifiable, inexpiable, unpardonable; see **unforgivable.**

**indefinite,** *modif.* **1.** [Vague] — *Syn.* imprecise, indistinct, unsure, unsettled; see **doubtful** 1, **uncertain** 2, **vague** 2.
**2.** [Unlimited] — *Syn.* indeterminate, unspecified, innumerable; see **infinite** 1, **unlimited.**

**indefinitely,** *modif.* **1.** [Vaguely] — *Syn.* loosely, unclearly, vaguely, ambiguously, indistinctly, incoherently, obscurely, indecisively, incompletely, lightly, briefly, momentarily, equivocally, inexactly, amorphously, generally, irresolutely, undecidedly; see also **vaguely.** — *Ant.* POSITIVELY, clearly, exactly.
**2.** [Without stated limit] — *Syn.* endlessly, continually, considerably; see **frequently, regularly** 2.

**indelible,** *modif.* — *Syn.* ingrained, enduring, lasting, unforgettable; see **permanent** 2.

**indelicacy,** *n.* — *Syn.* impertinence, immodesty, impropriety; see **indecency** 2, **rudeness.**

**indelicate,** *modif.* — *Syn.* improper, coarse, tactless; see **coarse** 2, **lewd** 1, **tactless.**
*See Synonym Study at COARSE, IMPROPER.*

**indemnify,** *v.* **1.** [To repay] — *Syn.* return, remit, reimburse; see **pay** 1, **repay** 1.
**2.** [To answer for] — *Syn.* register, assure, insure; see **guarantee** 1, 2.
*See Synonym Study at PAY.*

**indemnity,** *n.* — *Syn.* reimbursement, repayment, restitution; see **compensation, pay** 2, **payment** 1.

**indent,** *v.* — *Syn.* make a margin, range, set in, set back; see **order** 3, **paragraph.**

**indentation,** *n.* **1.** [Gouge] — *Syn.* imprint, impression, depression; see **dent.**
**2.** [Division] — *Syn.* indention, arrangement, section; see **paragraph.**
**indented,** *modif.* — *Syn.* depressed, set in, sectioned, paragraphed; see **organized.**
**indenture,** *n.* — *Syn.* agreement, compact, arrangement; see **contract.**
**indentured,** *modif.* — *Syn.* obligated, contracted, articled, enslaved; see **bound** 2.
**independence,** *n.* **1.** [Liberty] — *Syn.* sovereignty, autonomy, liberation, license; see **freedom** 1, 2.
**2.** [Self-reliance] — *Syn.* self-sufficiency, self-confidence, self-containment; see **confidence** 2.
**3.** [Neutrality] — *Syn.* nonpartisanship, nonalignment, detachment, objectivity; see **fairness, noninterference.**
**independent,** *modif.* **1.** [Free] — *Syn.* self-governing, autonomous, sovereign; see **free** 1, 2.
**2.** [Self-reliant] — *Syn.* self-sufficient, self-supporting, individualistic, inner-directed; see **confident** 2, **unconventional.**
**3.** [Neutral] — *Syn.* objective, detached, nonpartisan; see **fair** 1, **nonpartisan.**
**independently,** *modif.* — *Syn.* alone, unrestrictedly, autonomously, without support, without assistance, separately, exclusive of, without regard to, of one's own volition, by oneself, on one's own, all by one's lonesome*; see also **freely** 2, **individually.**
**indescribable,** *modif.* — *Syn.* indefinable, unutterable, incredible; see **impossible** 1.
**indestructible,** *modif.* — *Syn.* durable, unchangeable, immortal; see **permanent** 2, **strong** 2.
**indeterminate,** *modif.* — *Syn.* vague, general, indefinite; see **doubtful** 1, **uncertain** 2.
**index,** *n.* **1.** [An indicator] — *Syn.* pointer, token, basis for judgment, formula, ratio, rule, average, average rate, average price, sign, symbol, indication, indicant, guide; see also **criterion.**
**2.** [An alphabetic arrangement] — *Syn.* tabular matter, contents, book index, guide to publications, bibliography, bibliographical work, catalog, card file, book list, appendix, end list, directory, dictionary; see also **catalog, file** 2, **list, record** 1, **table** 2.
**index,** *v.* — *Syn.* alphabetize, arrange, tabulate; see **classify, file** 1, **list** 1, **record** 1.
**indexed,** *modif.* — *Syn.* alphabetized, tabulated, filed; see **recorded.**
**India,** *n.* — *Syn.* Indian Empire, Mogul Empire, *Bharat* (Hindi), South Asia, The Orient, The East, The Fabulous East, Country of the Indus, British India, Jewel in the Crown, Mother India, Hindustan; see also **Asia.**
**India ink,** *n.* — *Syn.* drawing ink, black pigment, lampblack, tusche; see **ink.**
**Indian,** *modif.* — *Syn.* Native American, American Indian, West Indian, Antillean, aboriginal American, pre-Columbian, Amerindian, prehistoric American.
**Indian,** *n.* **1.** [American native] — *Syn.* Native American, American Indian, Amerindian, Homo Americanus, American aborigine, red man*.
Terms for specific Indian groups include — *United States and Canada: Arctic Indians:* Inuit, Eskimo, Aleut, Sitka, Yupik; *eastern* or *Woods Indians:* Iroquois *or* Six Nations, Mohawk, Oneida, Seneca, Onandaga, Cayuga, Ottawa, Huron *or* Wyandot, Algonquin *or* Algonkin, Pequot, Micmac, Narragansett, Mohican, Delaware, Penobscot, Conestoga, Tuscarora, Ojibway *or* Chippewa, Menominee, Sauk, Fox, Pottawattamie, Seminole, Cherokee, Choctaw, Chickasaw, Creek *or*

Muskogee, Natchez, Biloxi, Winnebago; *Plains Indians:* Sioux, Missouri, Oglala, Mandan, Iowa, Omaha, Comanche, Dakota *or* Lakota, Crow, Kaw, Osage, Ponca, Apache, Kiowa, Arapahoe, Cheyenne, Pawnee, Caddo; *Great Basin Indians:* Blackfoot, Ute, Paiute, Shoshone, Bannock, Modoc, Digger, Pueblo, Hopi, Navaho, Pima, Cree, Anasazi, Moqui, Papago, Zuni, Folsom; *west coast Indians:* Athabascan, Salish, Costanoa, Chinook, Coos, Nez Percé, Maidu, Tlingit, Flathead, Pend d'Oreille, Coeur d'Alene, Kwakiutl, Bella Coola, Thompson, Miwok, Yuma, Klamath, Shasta, Luiseño, Pomo, Nutka, Haida; *Mexico and Central America:* Maya, Aztec, Toltec, Mixtec, Nahuat *or* Nahuatl, Pepil, Tabasco, Zacateca, Huasteco, Serrano, Seri, Macateco, Quiche; *South America:* Inca, Quechua, Carib, Aymara, Otuke, Bravo, Campa, Ande, Chiquito, Fuega, Patagonia, Tupi, Arawak, Calchaquia, Tocomona, Charrua, Mataguaya, Chango; for terms arranged by language; see **language** 2.
**2.** [A native of India] — *Syn.* South Asian, Hindu, Hindustani, Bengali, Punjabi, Maratha, Rajput, Dravidian, Indo-Aryan, Brahmin, Kshatriya, Sudra.
**indicate,** *v.* **1.** [To signify] — *Syn.* symbolize, betoken, intimate; see **mean** 1.
**2.** [To designate] — *Syn.* show, point out, point to, register; see **designate** 1.
**indicated,** *modif.* — *Syn.* pointed out, designated, determined, registered; see **marked** 2, **recorded.**
**indication,** *n.* — *Syn.* evidence, sign, implication; see **hint** 1, **suggestion** 1.
**indicative,** *modif.* — *Syn.* characteristic, significatory, connotative, suggestive; see **characteristic, symbolic.**
**indicator,** *n.* — *Syn.* notice, pointer, symbol; see **sign** 1.
**indict,** *v.* — *Syn.* charge, face with charges, arraign; see **accuse, censure.**
*See Synonym Study at* ACCUSE.
**indictable,** *modif.* **1.** [Guilty] — *Syn.* chargeable, blamable, accountable; see **guilty** 2.
**2.** [Indefensible] — *Syn.* criminal, illicit, felonious; see **illegal.**
**indictment,** *n.* **1.** [The act of indicting] — *Syn.* arraignment, censure, incrimination; see **blame** 1.
**2.** [A legal document] — *Syn.* bill, true bill, summons, statement, citation, ticket, replevin; see also **warrant, writ.**
**3.** [An accusation supported by evidence] — *Syn.* charge, presentment, findings; see **accusation** 2.
**indifference,** *n.* **1.** [Apathy] — *Syn.* unconcern, nonchalance, aloofness, impassiveness, impassivity, impassibility, coldness, coolness, insensitivity, insensibility, callousness, alienation, disregard, disinterest, insouciance, noninterference, inertia, neutrality, isolationism, insusceptibility, immunity, phlegm, heedlessness, detachment, dullness, sluggishness, listlessness, torpor, stupor, cold-bloodedness, disdain, stoicism, cool*.
**2.** [Insignificance] — *Syn.* unimportance, irrelevance, triviality; see **insignificance.**
**indifferent,** *modif.* **1.** [Lacking interest] — *Syn.* apathetic, unconcerned, uninterested, disinterested, detached, unaroused, listless, cold, cool, unemotional, unsympathetic, emotionless, passionless, heartless, unresponsive, incurious, lymphatic, unfeeling, uncommunicative, nonchalant, impassive, impervious, callous, supine, stony, icy, chill, glacial, reticent, remote, reserved, distant, unsocial, diffident, scornful, supercilious, blasé, phlegmatic, stoical, stolid, unimpressed, heedless, unmoved, not inclined toward, neutral, impartial, uncaring, aloof, silent, disdainful, haughty,

superior, condescending, snobbish, standoffish, not caring, lukewarm; see also **unconcerned.** — *Ant.* EX-CITED, aroused, enthusiastic.

**2.** [Ordinary] — *Syn.* average, routine, mediocre, undistinguished; see **common** 1, **dull** 4, **fair** 2.

---

*SYN.* — **indifferent** implies either apathy or neutrality, esp. with reference to choice /to remain *indifferent* in a dispute/; **unconcerned** implies a lack of concern, solicitude, or anxiety, as because of callousness, ingenuousness, etc. /to remain *unconcerned* in a time of danger/; **incurious** suggests a lack of interest or curiosity /*incurious* about the details/; **detached** implies an impartiality or aloofness resulting from a lack of emotional involvement in a situation /he viewed the struggle with *detached* interest/; **disinterested** strictly implies a commendable impartiality resulting from a lack of selfish motive or desire for personal gain /a *disinterested* journalist/, but it is often used to mean not interested, or indifferent

---

**indifferently,** *modif.* **1.** [Rather badly] — *Syn.* poorly, not very well, in a mediocre manner; see **badly** 1, **inadequately.**

**2.** [In an indifferent manner] — *Syn.* nonchalantly, coolly, in a detached manner; see **calmly, casually** 2.

**indigence,** *n.* — *Syn.* want, need, destitution; see **poverty** 1.

*See Synonym Study at* POVERTY.

**indigenous,** *modif.* **1.** [Native] — *Syn.* domestic, autochthonous, original; see **native** 2.

**2.** [Inborn] — *Syn.* natural, congenital, innate; see **inherent.**

*See Synonym Study at* NATIVE.

**indigent,** *modif.* — *Syn.* needy, impoverished, poverty-stricken; see **poor** 1.

*See Synonym Study at* POOR.

**indigestible,** *modif.* — *Syn.* inedible, rough, hard, unripe, green, unpalatable, tasteless, disagreeing, unhealthy, undercooked, raw, poisonous, toxic, moldy, badsmelling, malodorous, rotten, putrid, uneatable, heavy, hard on the stomach★; see also **inedible, unwholesome.**

**indigestion,** *n.* — *Syn.* dyspepsia, upset stomach, gas, heartburn, nausea, acid indigestion, acidosis, reflux, stomach ache, gastralgia; see also **illness** 1, **pain** 2.

**indignant,** *modif.* — *Syn.* incensed, displeased, piqued; see **angry.**

**indignation,** *n.* — *Syn.* pique, resentment, ire; see **anger.**

*See Synonym Study at* ANGER.

**indignity,** *n.* — *Syn.* affront, outrage, offense, injury; see **insult.**

**indirect,** *modif.* — *Syn.* roundabout, circuitous, out-of-the-way, tortuous, twisting, long, complicated, devious, aberrant, erratic, sidelong, zigzag, crooked, backhanded, obscure, discursive, rambling, long-winded, secondary, incidental, subsidiary, auxiliary, implied, oblique. — *Ant.* DIRECT, straight, immediate.

**indirectly,** *modif.* — *Syn.* obliquely, by implication, by indirection, in a roundabout way, from a secondary source, secondhand, not immediately, diffusely, circumlocutorily, periphrastically, discursively, lengthily. — *Ant.* IMMEDIATELY, directly, primarily.

**indiscernible,** *modif.* — *Syn.* imperceptible, indistinct, vague; see **imperceptible, obscure** 1.

**indiscreet,** *modif.* — *Syn.* impolitic, incautious, inopportune, misguided; see **careless** 1, **rash, tactless.**

**indiscreetly,** *modif.* — *Syn.* incautiously, inadvisedly, naively; see **carelessly, foolishly, rashly.**

**indiscretion,** *n.* **1.** [The quality of lacking prudence and judgment] — *Syn.* recklessness, imprudence, heedlessness, indiscreetness, tactlessness, rashness, misjudgment, thoughtlessness, unseemliness, impropriety, crudeness, hot-headedness, bullheadedness, excitability, foolishness, stupidity, naiveté, ingenuousness, simple-mindedness, injudiciousness, insensitivity; see also **carelessness.** — *Ant.* PRUDENCE, caution, discretion, tact.

**2.** [An example of indiscretion] — *Syn.* blunder, slip, gaffe, faux pas; see **error** 1.

**indiscriminate,** *modif.* — *Syn.* random, confused, chaotic; see **aimless, confused** 2.

**indispensable,** *modif.* — *Syn.* essential, vital, requisite, needed; see **necessary** 1.

*See Synonym Study at* ESSENTIAL.

**indispose,** *v.* **1.** [To disqualify] — *Syn.* disallow, disable, incapacitate; see **bar** 2.

**2.** [To discourage] — *Syn.* dissuade, dishearten, disincline; see **depress** 2, **discourage** 1, 3.

**indisposed,** *modif.* **1.** [Sick] — *Syn.* ill, ailing, infirm; see **sick.**

**2.** [Unwilling] — *Syn.* disinclined, averse, hesitant; see **reluctant, unwilling.**

*See Synonym Study at* SICK.

**indisposition,** *n.* **1.** [Illness] — *Syn.* ailment, sickness, infirmity; see **illness** 1.

**2.** [Aversion] — *Syn.* hesitancy, disinclination, unwillingness; see **aversion, hatred** 1, **objection** 1.

**indisputable,** *modif.* — *Syn.* undeniable, undoubted, unquestionable; see **accurate** 1, **certain** 3.

**indissoluble,** *modif.* **1.** [Stable] — *Syn.* infusible, lasting, firm, insoluble, infrangible, irrefrangible; see also **constant** 1, **firm** 1, **whole** 1.

**2.** [Binding] — *Syn.* durable, unchangeable, enduring; see **permanent** 2, **perpetual** 1, **regular** 3.

**indistinct,** *modif.* — *Syn.* vague, confused, indefinite; see **faint** 3, **imperceptible, obscure** 1.

**indistinguishable,** *modif.* **1.** [Identical] — *Syn.* alike, same, twin, interchangeable; see **alike** 1, **equal.**

**2.** [Indistinct] — *Syn.* vague, invisible, imperceptible; see **imperceptible, obscure** 1.

**individual,** *modif.* **1.** [Separate] — *Syn.* specific, personal, private, proper, own, particular, singular, special, especial, definite, lone, alone, solitary, secluded, original, distinct, distinctive, characteristic, personalized, individualized, exclusive, select, single, only, indivisible, reserved, sole; see also **private, special** 1. — *Ant.* COLLECTIVE, public, social.

**2.** [Unusual] — *Syn.* uncommon, singular, peculiar; see **different** 1, **unique** 1, **unusual** 2.

*See Synonym Study at* CHARACTERISTIC.

**individual,** *n.* — *Syn.* human being, person, self, somebody; see **child, man** 2, **person** 1, **woman** 1.

**individualist,** *n.* — *Syn.* nonconformist, independent, maverick, lone wolf; see **character** 4, **nonconformist.**

**individuality,** *n.* **1.** [The quality of being individual] — *Syn.* distinctiveness, distinction, peculiarity, particularity, separateness, dissimilarity, singularity, uniqueness, originality, idiosyncrasy, eccentricity, oddity, rarity, special way of doing things; see also **difference** 1, **originality.**

**2.** [Character] — *Syn.* identity, personality, uniqueness, selfhood; see **attitude** 2, **behavior** 1, **character** 2.

**individually,** *modif.* — *Syn.* separately, singly, severally, one by one, one at a time, personally, restrictedly, exclusively, by oneself, alone, independently, without help,

distinctively, apart; see also **only** 1, **singly.** — *Ant.* TO-
GETHER, collectively, cooperatively.

**indivisible,** *modif.* — *Syn.* indissoluble, unified, inseparable, impenetrable; see **inseparable** 1, **joined, permanent** 2, **unbreakable.**

**indoctrinate,** *v.* — *Syn.* inculcate, imbue, brainwash,
propagandize; see **convince, influence, teach** 1, 2.

**indoctrinated,** *modif.* — *Syn.* convinced, programmed,
brainwashed; see **educated** 1, **persuaded, trained.**

**indoctrination,** *n.* — *Syn.* propagandism, instruction,
brainwashing; see **education** 1, **persuasion** 1, **training.**

**indolence,** *n.* — *Syn.* sloth, disinclination, procrastination; see **idleness** 1, **laziness.**

**indolent,** *modif.* — *Syn.* slow, inactive, lethargic, sluggish; see **idle** 1, **lazy** 1, **listless** 1.

**indomitable,** *modif.* — *Syn.* unyielding, unconquerable,
unstoppable, dauntless; see **brave** 1, **resolute** 2.

**indoors,** *modif.* — *Syn.* inside, in the house, at home, under a roof; see **inside** 2.

**induce,** *v.* **1.** [To prevail on] — *Syn.* persuade, convince, coax; see **influence, urge** 2.
**2.** [To cause] — *Syn.* produce, effect, provoke, bring
about; see **begin** 1, **cause** 2.

**induced,** *modif.* **1.** [Persuaded] — *Syn.* convinced, ca-
joled, lured; see **persuaded.**
**2.** [Brought about] — *Syn.* effected, achieved, caused;
see **done** 1, **finished** 1.
**3.** [Inferred] — *Syn.* thought, concluded, reasoned, rationalized, ratiocinated, explained, argued, debated, discussed, analyzed, posited, postulated, hypothesized; see
also **assumed** 1, **considered** 1, **determined** 1.

**inducement,** *n.* — *Syn.* bait, lure, stimulus; see **attraction** 2, **incentive, temptation.**

**induct,** *v.* — *Syn.* conscript, initiate, draft; see **enlist** 1,
**recruit** 1.

**inducted,** *modif.* — *Syn.* conscripted, called up, drafted;
see **initiated** 3.

**induction,** *n.* **1.** [Logical reasoning] — *Syn.* inference,
rationalization, generalization, conclusion, ratiocination, judgment, conjecture; see also **reason** 2.
**2.** [The process of electrical attraction] — *Syn.* electric
induction, magnetic induction, electromagnetic action,
electrostatic induction; see **electricity** 2.
**3.** [The process of being initiated] — *Syn.* initiation,
installation, introduction, ordination, consecration, instatement, investiture, conscription, entrance into service; see also **draft** 6, **installation** 1, **selection** 1.

**indulge,** *v.* **1.** [To humor] — *Syn.* pamper, spoil, coddle; see **humor, pamper.**
**2.** [To give way to] — *Syn.* yield to, gratify, revel, luxuriate; see **entertain** 1, **satisfy** 1.
*See Synonym Study at* HUMOR.

**indulgence,** *n.* **1.** [Humoring] — *Syn.* coddling, pampering, petting, overweening attention, fondling, baby-
ing, spoiling, placating, pleasing, toadying, favoring,
kowtowing, gratifying, catering to.
**2.** [Forbearance] — *Syn.* allowance, lenience, toleration; see **mercy** 1, **patience** 1, **tolerance** 1.
**3.** [Revelry] — *Syn.* prodigality, dissipation, intemperance, drunkenness, overindulgence, luxury, waste, self-
indulgence, hedonism, self-gratification, decadence,
high living, *la dolce vita* (Italian), sybaritism, overdoing
it*; see also **greed, waste** 1.

**indulgent,** *modif.* — *Syn.* permissive, tolerant, easygoing, fond; see **kind, lenient.**

**industrial,** *modif.* — *Syn.* manufacturing, manufactured, mechanized, automated, industrialized, factory-
made, machine-made, modern, streamlined, in industry, technical, metropolitan, smokestack; see also **mechanical** 1. — *Ant.* HANDMADE, domestic, handcrafted.

**industrialist,** *n.* — *Syn.* tycoon, owner, manager, captain of industry; see **businessperson, financier,
manufacturer.**

**industrious,** *modif.* — *Syn.* assiduous, hard-working,
diligent, enterprising; see **active** 2, **busy** 1, **diligent.**
*See Synonym Study at* DILIGENT.

**industriously,** *modif.* — *Syn.* diligently, steadily, assiduously, laboriously, energetically, actively, busily; see also
**carefully** 1, **vigorously.**

**industry,** *n.* **1.** [Attention to work] — *Syn.* diligence,
activity, assiduity, persistence, application, patience, intentness, perseverance, enterprise, hard work, zeal, energy, dynamism, pains, inventiveness; see also **attention** 2, **care** 1, **diligence.** — *Ant.* LAZINESS, sloth, idleness.
**2.** [Commercial enterprise] — *Syn.* manufacturing,
business, commerce, trade, enterprise, production, mass
production, assembly-line production; see also **business** 1.
**3.** [Business as a division of society] — *Syn.* big business, management, corporation officers, manufacturers,
shareholders, high finance, entrepreneurs, capital, private enterprise, monied interests, stockholders.
*See Synonym Study at* BUSINESS.

**inebriate,** *v.* — *Syn.* intoxicate, exhilarate, stimulate,
make drunk; see **intoxicate** 1.

**inebriated,** *modif.* — *Syn.* drunk, intoxicated, tipsy,
plastered*; see **drunk.**
*See Synonym Study at* DRUNK.

**inebriety,** *n.* — *Syn.* alcoholism, intoxication, insobriety; see **drunkenness.**

**inedible,** *modif.* — *Syn.* unpalatable, uneatable, tasteless,
unsavory, unappetizing, not fit to eat, bad, spoiled, rotten, rancid, turned, tainted, sour, bitter, sickening, disagreeable, nauseating, unpleasant-tasting, foul-tasting,
indigestible, unwholesome, harmful, poisonous, contaminated, not fit for human consumption, yukky*; see
also **indigestible, offensive** 2, **rotten** 1. — *Ant.* edible,
appetizing, delicious.

**ineffable,** *modif.* — *Syn.* inexpressible, unutterable,
unspeakable, indescribable; see **impossible** 1, **mysterious** 2.

**ineffaceable,** *modif.* — *Syn.* ingrained, ineradicable, indelible; see **permanent** 2.

**ineffective,** *modif.* — *Syn.* not effective, ineffectual, incompetent, inefficient, incapable, bungling, weak, impotent, feeble, unproductive, unfruitful, futile, vain,
worthless, neutralized; see also **incompetent, useless** 1.

**ineffectively,** *modif.* — *Syn.* inefficiently, weakly,
poorly; see **badly** 1, **inadequately.**

**ineffectual,** *modif.* — *Syn.* ineffective, impotent, unavailing, useless; see **incompetent, ineffective, useless** 1.

**inefficiency,** *n.* — *Syn.* incompetence, incapability, disorganization, wastefulness; see **carelessness, inability.**

**inefficient,** *modif.* **1.** [Wasteful] — *Syn.* extravagant,
improvident, slack, disorganized; see **careless, wasteful.**
**2.** [Lacking competence] — *Syn.* incapable, unproductive, unfit; see **incompetent, ineffective.**

**inefficiently,** *modif.* — *Syn.* ineffectively, wastefully, un-
productively; see **badly** 1, **carelessly, inadequately.**

**inelastic,** *modif.* — *Syn.* rigid, unyielding, stable; see
**stiff** 1.

**inelegant,** *modif.* — *Syn.* coarse, crude, unrefined; see
**rude** 2, **vulgar** 1.

**ineligible,** *modif.* — *Syn.* inappropriate, unavailable, unsuitable; see **incompetent, unfit** 1, 2, **unsuitable.**

**ineluctable,** *modif.* — *Syn.* certain, inevitable, unavoidable; see **inevitable.**

**inept,** *modif.* 1. [Unsuitable] — *Syn.* not adapted, inappropriate, out of place; see **unfit** 2, **unsuitable.**
2. [Awkward] — *Syn.* clumsy, gauche, bungling, incompetent; see **awkward** 1, **incompetent.**
*See Synonym Study at* AWKWARD.

**ineptitude,** *n.* — *Syn.* incapacity, incompetence, clumsiness, ungracefulness; see **awkwardness** 1, **inability.**

**inequality,** *n.* — *Syn.* disparity, dissimilarity, irregularity, bias; see **contrast** 1, **difference** 1, **favoritism, imbalance, variation** 2.

**inequitable,** *modif.* — *Syn.* unjust, biased, discriminatory; see **unfair** 1.

**inert,** *modif.* — *Syn.* still, dormant, inactive; see **idle** 1.

**inertia,** *n.* — *Syn.* passivity, indolence, inactivity; see **laziness.**

**in escrow,** *modif.* — *Syn.* held, bonded, deposited; see **in trust** at **trust, retained** 1.

**inestimable,** *modif.* — *Syn.* priceless, invaluable, precious; see **valuable** 1.

**inevitable,** *modif.* — *Syn.* fated, certain, sure, unavoidable, impending, imminent, inescapable, necessary, ineluctable, unpreventable, irresistible, prescribed, destined, assured, ineludible, compulsory, obligatory, binding, irrevocable, inexorable, without fail, undeniable, fateful, doomed, determined, predetermined, decreed, fixed, ordained, foreordained, decided, unalterable, sure as shooting★, sure as blazes★, as sure as your name is ... ★, in the cards★, come rain or shine★; see also **certain** 3, **destined** 1. — *Ant.* DOUBTFUL, contingent, avoidable.

**inevitably,** *modif.* — *Syn.* unavoidably, inescapably, surely; see **necessarily.**

**inexact,** *modif.* — *Syn.* inaccurate, ambiguous, imprecise; see **obscure** 1, **vague** 2, **wrong** 2.

**inexcusable,** *modif.* — *Syn.* unpardonable, reprehensible, indefensible; see **unforgivable, wrong** 1.

**inexcusably,** *modif.* — *Syn.* unforgivably, unpardonably, crudely; see **badly** 1, **wrongly** 1.

**inexhaustible,** *modif.* 1. [Tireless] — *Syn.* indefatigable, unwearied, unflagging, unsleeping; see **active** 2, **tireless.**
2. [Unlimited] — *Syn.* limitless, unbounded, boundless, never-ending; see **endless** 1, **infinite** 1, **unlimited.**

**inexorable,** *modif.* 1. [Implacable] — *Syn.* unyielding, inflexible, obdurate; see **cruel** 2, **obstinate.**
2. [Necessary] — *Syn.* relentless, compulsory, unalterable; see **inevitable, necessary** 1.

**inexorably,** *modif.* — *Syn.* relentlessly, irresistibly, inevitably; see **necessarily.**

**inexpedient,** *modif.* — *Syn.* injudicious, unwise, inadvisable, impolitic; see **careless** 1, **rash, wasteful.**

**inexpensive,** *modif.* — *Syn.* low-priced, reasonable, cheap, modest; see **cheap** 1, **economical** 2.
*See Synonym Study at* CHEAP.

**inexpensively,** *modif.* — *Syn.* economically, advantageously, reasonably; see **cheaply.**

**inexperience,** *n.* — *Syn.* naiveté, ignorance, incompetence, greenness; see **ignorance** 1, **inability.**

**inexperienced,** *modif.* — *Syn.* unused, unaccustomed, unhabituated, unadapted, unskilled, untrained, unlicensed, untried, undeveloped, naive, unsophisticated, amateur, untutored, unschooled, unpracticed, inexpert, inefficient, fresh, unversed, ignorant, innocent, uninformed, callow, unacquainted, undisciplined, new, immature, unripe, tender, unseasoned, green, raw, ver-

dant, youthful, beardless, chaste, virgin, wet behind the ears★, tenderfoot★, soft★; see also **incompetent, young** 2. — *Ant.* EXPERIENCED, seasoned, hardened.

**inexpert,** *modif.* — *Syn.* incompetent, unskillful, inept; see **awkward** 1, **incompetent, inexperienced.**

**inexplicable,** *modif.* — *Syn.* unexplainable, incomprehensible, puzzling, unaccountable; see **difficult** 2, **obscure** 1.

**inexpressible,** *modif.* — *Syn.* unspeakable, indefinable, indescribable, unutterable; see **impossible** 1.

**inexpressive,** *modif.* — *Syn.* vacant, impassive, expressionless; see **blank** 2, **dull** 3.

**inextinguishable,** *modif.* — *Syn.* irrepressible, insatiable, unquenchable, eternal, ever-burning, indestructible, irreducible, imperishable, undying, fiery, burning, raging, rampant, violent.

*in extremis* (Latin), *modif.* — *Syn.* moribund, near death, at one's end, on one's deathbed; see **dying** 1.

**inextricable,** *modif.* — *Syn.* complicated, involved, intricate, tangled; see **complex** 2.

**inextricably,** *modif.* — *Syn.* inseparably, totally, indistinguishably, inevitably; see **completely.**

**infallibility,** *n.* 1. [Reliability] — *Syn.* dependability, faithfulness, safety; see **reliability.**
2. [Perfection] — *Syn.* supremacy, impeccability, faultlessness; see **perfection** 3.

**infallible,** *modif.* — *Syn.* unerring, exact, perfect, unfailing, faultless, sure, reliable, dependable, trustworthy, unquestionable, true, authoritative, positive, irrefutable, apodictic, incontrovertible, fail-safe, sure-fire★; see also **accurate** 1, 2, **certain** 3. — *Ant.* FALSE, fallible, unreliable.

**infamous,** *modif.* 1. [Bad] — *Syn.* odious, nefarious, base, vile; see **wicked** 1, 2.
2. [Scandalous] — *Syn.* notorious, ill-famed, shocking, disgraceful; see **offensive** 2, **shameful** 2.

**infamy,** *n.* 1. [Scandal] — *Syn.* notoriety, disapprobation, ignominy; see **disgrace** 1, **scandal, shame** 2.
2. [Infamous conduct] — *Syn.* wickedness, immorality, perfidy; see **evil** 1, 2.

**infancy,** *n.* 1. [The time of life's beginning] — *Syn.* cradle, babyhood, early childhood; see **childhood.**
2. [Any period of beginning] — *Syn.* outset, start, opening, early stages; see **origin** 1.

**infant,** *n.* — *Syn.* baby, newborn, tot, little one; see **baby** 1, **child.**

**infanticide,** *n.* — *Syn.* child-murder, puericide, abortion; see **murder.**

**infantile,** *modif.* — *Syn.* babyish, childlike, juvenile; see **childish** 1, **naive.**

**infantry,** *n.* — *Syn.* foot soldiers, infantrymen, rifles, riflemen, dogfaces★, grunts★, doughboys★, combat troops, shock troops; see also **army** 1, **soldier.**
Infantrymen include: hoplite, arquebusier, crossbowman, pikeman, spearman, longbowman, archer, arbalester, *soldad* (Spanish), *fantassin* (French), swordsman, fusilier, skirmisher, scout, grenadier, *sepoy* (Hindu), Zouave, uhlan, sniper-scout, intelligence and reconnaissance (I&R), sharpshooter, air-borne infantry, paratrooper.

**infatuate,** *v.* — *Syn.* beguile, captivate, charm; see **charm** 1, **fascinate.**

**infatuated,** *modif.* — *Syn.* enamored, smitten, bewitched, captivated, taken, besotted, beguiled, spellbound, intoxicated, obsessed, crazy about★, wild about★, nuts about★, gone on★, hung up on★, head over heels in love★; see also **charmed, fascinated.**

**infatuation,** *n.* — *Syn.* captivation, passion, fascination, crush★; see **desire** 3, **love** 1, **obsession.**

*See Synonym Study at* LOVE.

**infect,** *v.* — *Syn.* defile, taint, spoil; see **affect** 1, **contaminate, poison.**

**infection,** *n.* **1.** [The spread of a disease] — *Syn.* contagiousness, contagion, communicability, epidemic, poisoning, contamination; see also **contamination, pollution.**
**2.** [Disease] — *Syn.* virus, plague, germs; see **disease, germ** 3.

**infectious,** *modif.* — *Syn.* catching, communicable, transmissible, irresistible; see **catching, contagious, dangerous** 2.

**infelicitous,** *modif.* — *Syn.* inappropriate, unfortunate, awkward, malapropos; see **embarrassing, improper** 1, **unsuitable.**

**infer,** *v.* **1.** [To reach a conclusion] — *Syn.* conclude, deduce, gather, judge, come to the conclusion that, draw the inference that, induce, conjecture, arrive at, reason, construe, understand, assume, reckon, read between the lines; see also **assume** 1, **reason** 2, **understand** 1.
**2.** [To assume] — *Syn.* suppose, presume, presuppose; see **assume** 1.
**3.** [To imply] — *Syn.* insinuate, suggest, indicate, mean to say*; see **hint** 1.

---

**SYN.** — **infer** suggests the arriving at a decision or opinion by reasoning from known facts or evidence /from your smile, I *infer* that you're pleased/; **deduce,** in strict discrimination, implies inference from a general principle by logical reasoning /the method was *deduced* from earlier experiments/; **conclude** strictly implies an inference that is the final logical result in a process of reasoning /I must, therefore, *conclude* that you are wrong/; **judge** stresses the careful checking and weighing of premises, etc. in arriving at a conclusion; **gather** is an informal substitute for **infer** or **conclude** /I *gather* that you don't care/

---

**inference,** *n.* **1.** [A judgment] — *Syn.* deduction, conclusion, summation, answer; see **judgment** 3, **result.**
**2.** [A concluding] — *Syn.* reasoning, inferring, deducing; see **thought** 1.
**3.** [A supposition] — *Syn.* presumption, conjecture, surmise; see **assumption** 1, **opinion** 1, **thought** 2.

**inferential,** *modif.* — *Syn.* probable, presumed, to be inferred, to be expected; see **likely** 1.

**inferior,** *modif.* **1.** [Low in rank] — *Syn.* secondary, lower, minor, junior; see **subordinate, under** 2.
**2.** [Low in quality] — *Syn.* mediocre, second-rate, substandard; see **poor** 2.

**inferior,** *n.* — *Syn.* subordinate, junior, underling, subaltern; see **assistant.**

**inferiority,** *n.* — *Syn.* deficiency, mediocrity, inadequacy; see **inability, lack** 1, 2, **weakness** 2.

**infernal,** *modif.* **1.** [Pertaining to hell] — *Syn.* underworld, nether, Stygian, subterranean, chthonian, Hadean, Tartarean, Plutonian. — *Ant.* ETHEREAL, divine, supernal.
**2.** [Hellish] — *Syn.* damned, devilish, diabolical, fiendish; see **damned** 1, 2, **wicked** 1, 2.

**infernally,** *modif.* — *Syn.* hellishly, unbelievably, horribly; see **badly** 1, **wrongly** 1.

**infertile,** *modif.* — *Syn.* sterile, barren, impotent, fruitless; see **sterile** 1, 2.
*See Synonym Study at* STERILE.

**infertility,** *n.* — *Syn.* unproductiveness, impotence, sterility; see **barrenness.**

**infest,** *v.* — *Syn.* overrun, swarm, crowd, press, harass, beset, plague, parasitize, jam, pack, teem, abound, per-

vade, overwhelm, assail, fill, flood, throng, flock, crawl with, be thick as flies*; see also **swarm, teem.**

**infested,** *modif.* **1.** [Overrun] — *Syn.* beset, crowded, overwhelmed; see **full** 1, **jammed** 2.
**2.** [Diseased] — *Syn.* ravaged, wormy, lousy, pediculous, pedicular, ratty, grubby; see also **sick.**

**infidel,** *n.* — *Syn.* heathen, unbeliever, atheist; see **atheist, skeptic.**
*See Synonym Study at* ATHEIST.

**infidelity,** *n.* **1.** [Disloyalty] — *Syn.* faithlessness, treachery, betrayal; see **disloyalty.**
**2.** [Marital disloyalty] — *Syn.* unfaithfulness, adultery, cheating, cuckoldry; see **fornication.**

**infield,** *n.* — *Syn.* diamond, right infield, center infield, left infield, short field, pasture*, inner works*; see also **field** 2.

**infielder,** *n.* — *Syn.* first baseman, first sacker*, first*, second baseman, second*, keystone man*, third baseman, third*, hot-corner man*, shortstop, shortfielder*.

**infiltrate,** *n.* — *Syn.* permeate, pervade, penetrate, invade; see **filter** 1, **insinuate** 2, **join** 2.

**infinite,** *modif.* **1.** [Unlimited] — *Syn.* unbounded, boundless, endless, illimitable, unconfined, countless, incalculable, interminable, measureless, untold, inexhaustible, bottomless, unfathomable, without number, without end, without limit, limitless, tremendous, immense, having no limit, having no end, never-ending, immeasurable; see also **endless** 1, **unlimited.** — *Ant.* limited, BOUNDED, restricted, finite.
**2.** [Endless] — *Syn.* without end, unending, incessant; see **constant** 1, **eternal** 2, **perpetual** 1.
**3.** [Absolute] — *Syn.* supreme, perpetual, enduring; see **absolute** 1, **immortal** 1.

**infinite,** *n.* — *Syn.* boundlessness, infinity, the unknown; see **eternity** 1, **space** 1.

**infinitely,** *modif.* — *Syn.* extremely, very much, unbelievably; see **very.**

**infinitesimal,** *modif.* — *Syn.* tiny, microscopic, minuscule, negligible; see **little** 1, **minute** 1.

**infinitesimally,** *modif.* — *Syn.* imperceptibly, barely, minutely; see **hardly.**

**infinitude,** *n.* — *Syn.* endlessness, vastness, boundlessness; see **extent, immensity, infinity.**

**infinity,** *n.* — *Syn.* boundlessness, endlessness, the beyond, infinitude, limitlessness, expanse, extent, continuum, eternity, continuity, infinite space, ubiquity; see also **eternity** 1, **space** 1.

**infirm,** *modif.* **1.** [Sick] — *Syn.* decrepit, ill, anemic; see **sick.**
**2.** [Weak] — *Syn.* delicate, faint, decrepit, feeble; see **weak** 1, 2.
*See Synonym Study at* WEAK.

**infirmary,** *n.* — *Syn.* clinic, sickroom, sick bay; see **hospital.**

**infirmity,** *n.* **1.** [Weakness] — *Syn.* frailty, deficiency, debility, feebleness; see **frailty** 1, **weakness** 1.
**2.** [Illness] — *Syn.* sickness, ailment, ailing, confinement; see **illness** 1.

**inflame,** *v.* **1.** [To irritate] — *Syn.* incense, aggravate, disturb, madden; see **anger** 1, **bother** 2.
**2.** [To arouse emotions] — *Syn.* incite, impassion, kindle, stir up; see **excite** 1, **incite.**
**3.** [To cause physical soreness] — *Syn.* irritate, redden, chafe, congest, erupt, break into a rash, infect, swell, raise the temperature; see also **hurt** 4, **irritate** 2.
**4.** [To burn] — *Syn.* kindle, set on fire, torch; see **burn** 2, **ignite.**

**inflamed,** *modif.* **1.** [Stirred to anger] — *Syn.* aroused, incited, angered; see **angry**.

**2.** [Congested] — *Syn.* sore, fevered, chafed, irritated, festered, festering, infected, raw, blistered, burnt, scalded, swollen, bloodshot, red, tender, septic; see also **hurt, painful** 1, **sore** 1.

**inflammability,** *n.* — *Syn.* flammability, ignitability, combustibility; see **danger**.

**inflammable,** *modif.* — *Syn.* flammable, combustible, ignitable, burnable, liable to burn, risky, hazardous, dangerous, unsafe, explosive, volatile; see also **excitable**. — *Ant.* SAFE, FIREPROOF, nonflammable.

**inflammation,** *n.* — *Syn.* soreness, infection, redness; see **pain** 2, **sore, swelling**.

**inflammatory,** *modif.* — *Syn.* incendiary, provocative, fiery, instigative, rabble-rousing; see also **passionate** 2, **rebellious** 2.

**inflate,** *v.* **1.** [To fill with air or gas] — *Syn.* blow up, pump up, puff up, puff out, expand, bloat, distend, swell, swell up, dilate, spread out, widen, balloon, cram, surcharge; see also **fill** 1, **stretch** 2, **swell**.

**2.** [To increase or raise abnormally] — *Syn.* exaggerate, magnify, stretch, overstate, aggrandize, exalt, blow up, build up, boost, raise, maximize, overestimate, escalate, mount, skyrocket, expand, balloon, swell, augment, enlarge; see also **exaggerate, increase** 1. — *Ant.* UNDERESTIMATE, deflate, minimize.

*See Synonym Study at* EXPAND.

**inflated,** *modif.* — *Syn.* distended, swollen, puffed, puffed up, extended, filled, grown, stretched, dilated, spread, enlarged, amplified, augmented, pumped up, overblown, blown up, exaggerated, exalted, bloated, full, crammed, aggrandized, elevated, magnified, overestimated, surcharged, turgid, tumid, bombastic, flatulent, pretentious, pompous, high-flown, fustian, euphuistic, verbose; see also **enlarged, increased**. — *Ant.* REDUCED, deflated, minimized.

**inflation,** *n.* **1.** [Increase] — *Syn.* expansion, extension, buildup; see **increase** 1.

**2.** [General rise in price levels] — *Syn.* inflationary trend, inflationary cycle, inflationary spiral, rising prices, spiraling prices, move toward higher price levels, reflation, expanding economy, boom, financial crisis; see also **rise** 2.

**inflect,** *v.* — *Syn.* turn, curve, crook; see **arch, bend** 1.

**inflection,** *n.* — *Syn.* modulation, intonation, pitch variation, pronunciation, enunciation, voice change, change of grammatical form, articulation, stress, emphasis, expression, tone of voice, delivery; see also **accent** 2, 3, **sound** 2.

**inflexibility,** *n.* **1.** [Solidity] — *Syn.* rigidity, stiffness, stability, toughness, inflexibleness, temper, induration, ossification, petrifaction, fossilization, glaciation, crystallization, vitrification; see also **firmness** 2.

**2.** [Stubbornness] — *Syn.* obduracy, tenacity, obstinacy; see **determination** 2, **stubbornness**.

**inflexible,** *modif.* **1.** [Stiff] — *Syn.* rigid, hardened, unbendable, taut; see **firm** 2, **stiff** 1.

**2.** [Firm of purpose] — *Syn.* implacable, resolute, obdurate, adamant, stubborn, unyielding, unshakable, immovable, determined, unrelenting, unalterable, fixed, ironclad; see also **obstinate, resolute** 2.

*SYN.* — **inflexible** implies an unyielding or unshakable firmness in mind or purpose, sometimes connoting stubbornness /his *inflexible* attitude/; **adamant** implies a firm or unbreakable resolve that remains unaffected by temptation or pleading /*adamant* to her entreaties/; **implacable** suggests the impossibility of pacifying or appeasing /*implacable* in his hatred/; **obdurate** im-

plies a hardheartedness that is not easily moved to pity, sympathy, or forgiveness /her *obdurate* refusal to help/

**inflexibly,** *modif.* — *Syn.* rigidly, unalterably, unchangeably; see **firmly** 1, 2, **obstinately**.

**inflict,** *v.* **1.** [To deal] — *Syn.* deliver, mete out, deal out, strike, do to, perpetrate, dispense, give out, wreak, bring down upon, lay on, administer; see also **cause** 2.

**2.** [To impose] — *Syn.* force upon, apply, exact, visit; see **force** 1, **require** 2.

**infliction,** *n.* — *Syn.* curse, visitation, castigation; see **pain** 1, **punishment**.

**influence,** *n.* **1.** [Attraction] — *Syn.* sway, spell, magnetism; see **attraction** 1.

**2.** [Power to influence others] — *Syn.* control, weight, authority, supremacy, command, domination, leadership, power, leverage, prerogative, esteem, monopoly, rule, sway, hold, fame, prominence, prestige, character, reputation, force, impact, importance, significance, connections, power behind the throne*, clout*, juice*, pull*; see also **impact** 2, **leadership** 1, **power** 2.

*SYN.* — **influence** implies the power of persons or things (whether or not exerted consciously or overtly) to affect others /used his *influence* to get elected/; **authority** implies the power to command acceptance, belief, obedience, etc., based on strength of character, expertness of knowledge, etc. /a statement made on good *authority*/; **prestige** implies the power to command esteem or admiration, based on brilliance of achievement or outstanding superiority; **weight** implies influence that is more or less preponderant in its effect /his viewpoint had great *weight* with his colleagues/

**influence,** *v.* — *Syn.* affect, sway, impress, incline, move, dispose, carry weight, count, be influential, determine, make oneself felt, have influence over, lead, touch, lead to believe, get into favor, bring pressure to bear, bribe, seduce, talk into, alter, change, modify, act upon, act on, brainwash, direct, control, regulate, rule, guide, compel, urge, incite, bias, prejudice, turn, train, channel, mold, form, shape, argue into, exercise influence, exert influence, have a part in, bear upon, impact, impact on, gain the confidence of, gain a hold upon, be recognized, make one's voice heard, manipulate, bend to one's will, induce, cajole, convince, persuade, inveigle, motivate, inspire, actuate, prevail over, get at*, have an in*, pull strings*, fix*, wear the pants*, have pull*, have clout*, twist around one's little finger*, have a finger in the pie*, lead by the nose*, have one's ear*, lobby through*, have the inside track*, have in one's pocket*.

*See Synonym Study at* AFFECT.

**influenced,** *modif.* — *Syn.* affected, changed, swayed, turned, altered, persuaded, inveigled, shaped, formed, determined, moved, motivated; see also **affected** 1.

**influential,** *modif.* — *Syn.* prominent, substantial, powerful, instrumental; see **famous, important** 2.

**influenza,** *n.* — *Syn.* grippe, flu, severe cold; see **disease**.

**influx,** *n.* — *Syn.* introduction, penetration, coming in, inrush; see **entrance** 1.

**inform,** *v.* **1.** [To give information] — *Syn.* apprise, notify, acquaint, familiarize; see **notify** 1, **tell** 1.

**2.** [To give incriminating information; *often used with* "on"] — *Syn.* denounce, betray, implicate, report on, tattle, name names, tell tales, tell on*, snitch*, squeal*, rat*, talk*, blab*, sell out*, sell down the river*, blow the whistle*, put the finger on*, finger*, spill the beans*,

sing\*, squawk\*, fink\*, stool\*, drop a dime\*.
*See Synonym Study at* NOTIFY.

**informal,** *modif.* **1.** [Without formality] — *Syn.* casual, natural, relaxed, intimate, unceremonious, unstudied, frank, open, straightforward, free, extempore, spontaneous, congenial, easygoing, easy, unconstrained, unrestrained, unconventional, without ceremony, simple, unpretentious, homey; see also **colloquial, friendly** 1. — *Ant.* RESTRAINED, ceremonial, ritualistic.
**2.** [Not requiring formal dress] — *Syn.* casual, ordinary, everyday, unofficial, habitual, motley, mixed, democratic, shirt-sleeve, sporty\*; see also **common** 1. — *Ant.* formal, dressy, exclusive.

**informality,** *n.* — *Syn.* casualness, familiarity, naturalness, affability, comfort, relaxation, warmth, friendliness, ease, lack of constraint, simplicity; see also **comfort** 1.

**informant,** *n.* — *Syn.* source, witness, informer, subject, interviewee, native speaker, local resident, native, qualified person, adviser, tipster\*; see also **source** 2.

**information,** *n.* **1.** [Derived knowledge] — *Syn.* acquired facts, learning, erudition; see **data, knowledge** 1.
**2.** [News] — *Syn.* report, notice, message; see **news** 1, 2.
*See Synonym Study at* KNOWLEDGE.

**informative,** *modif.* — *Syn.* instructive, enlightening, communicative, informing, free-spoken, advisory, informational, educational, edifying, illuminating, educative.

**informed,** *modif.* — *Syn.* versed, knowledgeable, well-read; see **educated** 1, **knowledgeable, learned** 1.

**informer,** *n.* — *Syn.* squealer, tattletale, whistle-blower, snitch\*, ratfink\*, stool pigeon\*, stoolie\*, fink\*, canary\*.

**infraction,** *n.* — *Syn.* violation, infringement, breach; see **violation** 1.

**infrastructure,** *n.* — *Syn.* foundation, basic structure, base, support; see **foundation** 2.

**infrequency,** *n.* — *Syn.* rarity, unpredictability, scarcity, uncommonness; see **irregularity** 2, **lack** 1, 2.

**infrequent,** *modif.* — *Syn.* sparse, occasional, scarce, uncommon; see **rare** 2.

**infrequently,** *modif.* — *Syn.* seldom, scarcely, not habitually, not regularly, occasionally, uncommonly, sparingly, now and then, sporadically, intermittently, rarely, unusually, hardly ever; see also **seldom.**

**infringe,** *v.* — *Syn.* transgress, violate, trespass, encroach; see **meddle** 1, **transgress.**
*See Synonym Study at* TRESPASS.

**infringement,** *n.* — *Syn.* breach, infraction, invasion, transgression; see **violation** 1.

**infuriate,** *v.* — *Syn.* enrage, incense, madden, provoke; see **anger.**

**infuriated,** *modif.* — *Syn.* furious, enraged, incensed; see **angry.**

**infuse,** *v.* **1.** [To instill] — *Syn.* inspire, introduce, implant, imbue; see **instill.**
**2.** [To soak] — *Syn.* steep, brew, saturate; see **cook, soak** 1, 2.

**infusion,** *n.* — *Syn.* immersion, strain, admixture; see **liquid, mixture** 1.

**ingenious,** *modif.* — *Syn.* clever, inventive, original, resourceful; see **artistic** 2, **clever** 1, **intelligent** 1, **original** 2.
*See Synonym Study at* CLEVER.

**ingenuity,** *n.* — *Syn.* inventiveness, imagination, resourcefulness; see **ability** 1, 2, **originality.**

**ingenuous,** *modif.* **1.** [Frank] — *Syn.* open, candid, straightforward, undisguised; see **frank.**
**2.** [Simple] — *Syn.* unsophisticated, artless, plain; see **naive.**

*See Synonym Study at* NAIVE.

**ingenuously,** *modif.* — *Syn.* frankly, naively, freely; see **openly** 1.

**ingenuousness,** *n.* — *Syn.* frankness, openness, guilelessness, simplicity; see **innocence** 2, **sincerity.**

**inglorious,** *modif.* — *Syn.* ignoble, ignominious, disgraceful, undignified; see **offensive** 2, **shameful** 2.

**ingot,** *n.* — *Syn.* bullion, nugget, casting; see **bar** 1, **metal.**

**ingrain,** *v.* — *Syn.* imbue, fix, implant, instill; see **instill, teach** 1.

**ingrained,** *modif.* — *Syn.* congenital, inborn, indelible, fixed; see **established** 1, **inherent.**

**ingrate,** *n.* — *Syn.* thankless person, ungrateful person, self-seeker, bounder\*; see **opportunist.**

**ingratiate oneself,** *v.* — *Syn.* court, insinuate oneself, curry favor, get in with\*; see **compliment** 1, **grovel, insinuate** 2.

**ingratiating,** *modif.* **1.** [Charming] — *Syn.* disarming, pleasing, appealing, winning; see **charming, pleasant** 1.
**2.** [Deliberately trying to gain favor] — *Syn.* unctuous, sycophantic, fawning, flattering; see **obsequious.**

**ingratitude,** *n.* — *Syn.* thanklessness, ungratefulness, callousness, boorishness, disloyalty, lack of appreciation, inconsiderateness, thoughtlessness; see also **rudeness.** — *Ant.* GRATITUDE, appreciation, consideration.

**ingredient,** *n.* — *Syn.* constituent, component, element; see **element** 1, **part** 1.
*See Synonym Study at* ELEMENT.

**ingredients,** *pl.n.* — *Syn.* parts, elements, constituents, pieces, components, additives, factors, contents, makings, fixings\*, innards\*.

**ingress,** *n.* **1.** [The act or right of entering] — *Syn.* entrance, admission, access; see **entrance** 1, **intrusion.**
**2.** [Opening] — *Syn.* doorway, entry, portal; see **door** 1, **entrance** 2, **gate.**

**inhabit,** *v.* — *Syn.* occupy, live in, dwell in, populate; see **dwell, reside.**

**inhabitant,** *n.* — *Syn.* occupant, resident, dweller, denizen, settler, lodger, permanent resident, tenant, incumbent, roomer, boarder, renter, lessee, occupier, indweller, householder, addressee, inmate, squatter, settler, colonist, citizen, native; see also **citizen, resident.** — *Ant.* ALIEN, transient, nonresident.

**inhabited,** *modif.* — *Syn.* occupied, lived in, populated, peopled, settled, colonized, possessed, owned, dwelt in, sustaining human life, rented, tenanted, developed, pioneered, filled with people, populous.

**inhalation,** *n.* — *Syn.* gasp, inhaling, puff, drag\*; see **breath** 1.

**inhale,** *v.* — *Syn.* breathe in, gasp, smell, sniff; see **breathe** 1.

**inharmonious,** *modif.* — *Syn.* discordant, tuneless, dissonant; see **harsh** 1, **incompatible, loud** 1, 2, **shrill.**

**inharmoniously,** *modif.* — *Syn.* incompatibly, dissonantly, jarringly, inconsistently; see **differently** 2.

**inherent,** *modif.* — *Syn.* innate, inborn, inbred, indigenous to, intrinsic, internal, original, native, deep-rooted, built-in, latent, implicit, ingrained, immanent, congenital, connate, fixed, indwelling, inseparable, inalienable, subjective, indispensable, essential, basic, hereditary, constitutional, natural, integral, integrated, in one's blood, bred in the bone, running in the family, in the grain, part and parcel of; see also **native** 1, **natural** 1. — *Ant.* INCIDENTAL, extrinsic, superficial.

**inherently,** *modif.* — *Syn.* innately, congenitally, inseparably, naturally, intrinsically, constitutionally, natively, immanently, genetically, by birth; see also **essentially.**

**inherit,** *v.* — *Syn.* succeed to, acquire, receive, get one's inheritance, fall heir to, be bequeathed, be willed, be granted a legacy, come into, derive, take into possession, take over, receive an endowment, come in for*; see also **obtain** 1. — *Ant.* LOSE, be disowned, miss.

**inheritance,** *n.* — *Syn.* legacy, bequest, patrimony, heritage; see **estate** 2, **gift** 1.

*See Synonym Study at* HERITAGE.

**inheritor,** *n.* — *Syn.* recipient, successor, grantee; see **beneficiary, heir, heiress.**

**inhibit,** *v.* — *Syn.* repress, frustrate, hold back; see **hinder, restrain** 1.

*See Synonym Study at* RESTRAIN.

**inhibition,** *n.* — *Syn.* restraint, hindrance, repression, hang-up*; see **impediment** 1, **interference** 1, **reserve** 2, **restraint** 1.

**inhospitable,** *modif.* **1.** [Unfriendly] — *Syn.* unwelcoming, cold, brusque, ungracious; see **aloof, rude** 2, **unfriendly** 2.
**2.** [Not offering protection or shelter] — *Syn.* forbidding, barren, desolate, uninhabitable; see **bleak** 1, **sterile** 2.

**inhospitality,** *n.* — *Syn.* unfriendliness, coldness, ungraciousness, unsociability; see **rudeness.**

**inhuman,** *modif.* — *Syn.* mean, heartless, cold-blooded; see **cruel** 1, 2, **fierce** 1, **ruthless** 1, 2, **savage** 2.

*See Synonym Study at* CRUEL.

**inhumanity,** *n.* — *Syn.* savagery, barbarity, brutality; see **cruelty, evil** 1, **tyranny.**

**inhumanly,** *modif.* — *Syn.* cruelly, viciously, immorally; see **brutally.**

**inimical,** *modif.* — *Syn.* antagonistic, hostile, contrary, adverse; see **opposing** 2, **unfriendly** 1.

**inimitable,** *modif.* — *Syn.* matchless, supreme, incomparable; see **perfect** 2, **unique** 1.

**inimitably,** *modif.* — *Syn.* uniquely, distinctively, characteristically; see **excellently.**

**iniquitous,** *modif.* — *Syn.* unjust, vicious, evil, sinful; see **unfair** 1, **wicked** 1, 2.

**iniquity,** *n.* — *Syn.* unfairness, immorality, evildoing; see **evil** 1, **injustice** 2, **sin, wrong** 1.

**initial,** *modif.* — *Syn.* beginning, opening, original, primary; see **first** 1, **fundamental** 1, **introductory** 1.

**initially,** *modif.* — *Syn.* at first, at the beginning, originally; see **at first** at **first.**

**initiate,** *v.* **1.** [To begin] — *Syn.* open, start, inaugurate, launch; see **begin** 1.
**2.** [To introduce] — *Syn.* instate, induct, admit; see **receive** 4.

*See Synonym Study at* BEGIN.

**initiated,** *modif.* **1.** [Introduced into] — *Syn.* proposed, sponsored, originated, entered, brought into, admitted, inserted, put into, instituted; see also **proposed.**
**2.** [Begun] — *Syn.* inaugurated, established, started; see **begun.**
**3.** [Having undergone initiation] — *Syn.* installed, inducted, instated, instructed, grounded, coached, tutored, passed, admitted, made part of, made a member of, received, acknowledged, accepted, introduced, conscripted, drafted, called up, levied, confirmed, approved, volunteered*, hazed*.

**initiation,** *n.* **1.** [Initial experiences] — *Syn.* first trials, early adventures, grounding, process of learning, elementary steps, start, beginning, preliminaries; see also **introduction** 3.
**2.** [Formal introduction] — *Syn.* investment, induction, indoctrination, hazing; see **admission** 2, **introduction** 1.

**initiative,** *n.* **1.** [Ability to start things] — *Syn.* enter-

prise, drive, energy, inventiveness; see **ambition** 1, **force** 3.
**2.** [The starting of things] — *Syn.* action, lead, first step; see **action** 1, **leadership** 1.

**inject,** *v.* **1.** [To introduce with a syringe] — *Syn.* inoculate, vaccinate, shoot, jab, shoot up*, mainline*, skin-pop*; see also **vaccinate.**
**2.** [To include] — *Syn.* insert, interject, force into, introduce, place into, impregnate, implant, imbue, instill, interpolate, infuse, stick in, throw in, add; see also **include** 2.

**injection,** *n.* — *Syn.* dose, shot, hypodermic, vaccination, inoculation, jab*, hypo*, needle*; see also **medicine** 2, **vaccination** 1.

**injudicious,** *modif.* — *Syn.* imprudent, foolish, impulsive; see **rash.**

**injunction,** *n.* — *Syn.* order, directive, restraining order; see **command** 1, **sanction** 2, **writ.**

**injure,** *v.* — *Syn.* hurt, harm, damage, wound; see **damage** 1, **hurt** 1.

*See Synonym Study at* HURT.

**injured,** *modif.* — *Syn.* spoiled, damaged, harmed; see **hurt, wounded.**

**injurious,** *modif.* **1.** [Harmful] — *Syn.* detrimental, damaging, deleterious; see **dangerous** 1, 2, **deadly** 1, **harmful, poisonous.**
**2.** [Slanderous] — *Syn.* abusive, insulting, libelous, defamatory; see **insulting, opprobrious** 1.

**injuriously,** *modif.* — *Syn.* harmfully, seriously, ruinously; see **badly** 1, **seriously** 1.

**injury,** *n.* **1.** [A physical hurt] — *Syn.* harm, wound, damage, impairment, trauma, cut, sprain, gash, scratch, stab, lesion, bite, fracture, hemorrhage, sting, bruise, contusion, sore, puncture, cramp, twinge, abrasion, burn, swelling, scar, distress, laceration, affliction, mutilation, deformation, blemish, boo-boo*; see also **bruise, damage** 1, **pain** 1.
**2.** [A moral hurt] — *Syn.* wrong, injustice, offense, disservice; see **damage** 1, **injustice** 2, **insult, wrong** 2.

**injustice,** *n.* **1.** [Unfairness] — *Syn.* favoritism, inequality, inequity, partisanship; see **favoritism, prejudice.**
**2.** [An unfair act] — *Syn.* wrong, injury, miscarriage, unfairness, partiality, wrongdoing, malpractice, malfeasance, misfeasance, offense, crime, villainy, iniquity, encroachment, infringement, violation, maltreatment, abuse, outrage, criminal negligence, transgression, tort, grievance, breach, damage, infraction, miscarriage of justice, rotten deal*, a crying shame*, bum rap*; see also **evil** 1, **wrong** 2. — *Ant.* RIGHT, fairness, just decision.

**ink,** *n.* — *Syn.* tusche, paint, watercolor.
Kinds of ink include: printing, printer's, drawing, indelible, India, sympathetic, copying, marking, logwood, Chinese, tannin, aniline, soy-based, permanent, safety, lithographic, invisible, disappearing, erasable, rotogravure, engraver's, soluble, waterproof.

**inkling,** *n.* — *Syn.* intimation, indication, notion, suspicion; see **hint** 1, **suggestion** 1.

**inky,** *modif.* — *Syn.* sooty, murky, pitch-black; see **black** 1, **dark** 1.

**inlaid,** *modif.* — *Syn.* checkered, parqueted, mosaic, enameled; see **ornate** 1.

**inland,** *modif.* — *Syn.* interior, back-country, backland, hinterland, midland, provincial, boondock*, domestic, inward, upcountry, heartland, intranational, intrastate; see also **central** 1. — *Ant.* coastal, border, frontier.

**inlay,** *v.* — *Syn.* parquet, inset, tessellate, veneer; see **decorate, trim** 2.

**inlet,** *n.* — *Syn.* delta, gulf, channel; see **bay** 1.

**inmate,** *n.* — *Syn.* patient, convict, internee; see **patient, prisoner.**

**inmost,** *modif.* **1.** [Deep] — *Syn.* deepest, innermost, interior, intestinal; see **deep** 1, **inner.**
**2.** [Intimate] — *Syn.* innermost, private, personal, secret; see **inner, intimate** 1, **private.**

**inn,** *n.* — *Syn.* hotel, hostelry, bed-and-breakfast, tavern; see **bar** 2, **hotel, lodge, motel, resort** 2.

**innate,** *modif.* — *Syn.* inherent, natural, native, intrinsic, inborn, inbred, congenital, hereditary; see also **inherent, native** 1, **natural** 1.

*SYN.* — **innate** and **inborn** are often interchangeable, but **innate** has more extensive connotations, describing that which belongs to something as part of its nature or constitution, and **inborn,** the simpler term, more specifically suggesting qualities so much a part of one's nature as to seem to have been born in or with one *[inborn* modesty*]*; **inbred** refers to qualities that are deeply ingrained by breeding *[an inbred* love of learning*]*; **congenital** implies existence at or from one's birth *[congenital* blindness*]*; **hereditary** implies acquirement of characteristics by transmission genetically from parents or ancestors *[hereditary* blondness*]*

**inner,** *modif.* — *Syn.* interior, inward, internal, inside, central, intrinsic, essential, fundamental, private, personal, intimate, secret, hidden, innermost, inmost, mental, emotional, spiritual, psychic, deep-seated, deep-rooted, subconscious, intuitive, visceral, gut*; see also **fundamental, inherent, private.** — *Ant.* OUTER, surface, external.

**innermost,** *modif.* — *Syn.* inmost, personal, deepest; see **deep** 1, **inner, intimate** 1, **private.**

**inning,** *n.* — *Syn.* chance to bat, turn, period, stanza*, session*, heat*; see also **opportunity** 1.

**innkeeper,** *n.* — *Syn.* hotelier, host, landlord, proprietor; see **host** 2, **owner, possessor.**

**innocence,** *n.* **1.** [Freedom from guilt] — *Syn.* guiltlessness, blamelessness, integrity, probity, impeccability, inculpability, clear conscience, faultlessness, clean hands*; see also **honesty** 1. — *Ant.* GUILT, culpability, dishonesty.
**2.** [Freedom from guile] — *Syn.* guilelessness, artlessness, naiveté, frankness, candor, candidness, simplicity, unaffectedness, plainness, forthrightness, ingenuousness, trustfulness, credulity, harmlessness, inoffensiveness; see also **simplicity** 2, **sincerity.** — *Ant.* TRICKERY, shrewdness, wariness.
**3.** [Lack of experience] — *Syn.* purity, virginity, naiveté; see **chastity, ignorance** 1.

**innocent,** *modif.* **1.** [Not guilty] — *Syn.* guiltless, blameless, inculpable, impeccable, faultless, unoffending, free of, uninvolved, honest, above suspicion, clean*, in the clear*; see also **reliable** 1, **upright** 2. — *Ant.* GUILTY, culpable, blameworthy.
**2.** [Without guile] — *Syn.* open, ingenuous, fresh, guileless; see **childish** 1, **frank, naive, natural** 3.
**3.** [Inexperienced] — *Syn.* youthful, raw, green*; see **inexperienced, young** 2.
**4.** [Morally pure] — *Syn.* sinless, unblemished, pure, unsullied, undefiled, spotless, wholesome, upright, unimpeachable, clean, virtuous, chaste, virginal, immaculate, impeccable, righteous, uncorrupted, irreproachable, unstained, stainless, unspotted, incorrupt, moral, angelic, squeaky-clean*; see also **chaste** 2, 3, **perfect** 2. — *Ant.* sinful, corrupt, dissolute.
**5.** [Harmless] — *Syn.* innocuous, inoffensive, safe, benign; see **harmless** 2.

**innocently,** *modif.* — *Syn.* without guilt, with the best of intentions, ignorantly; see **kindly** 2, **politely.**

**innocuous,** *modif.* — *Syn.* harmless, inoffensive, bland, weak; see **dull** 4, **harmless** 2, **kind.**

**innocuously,** *modif.* — *Syn.* harmlessly, innocently, without harm, without damage; see **kindly** 2, **politely.**

**innovation,** *n.* — *Syn.* change, alteration, novelty, newness, newfangled idea, deviation, shift, variation, modification, modernization, reform, addition, novel contribution, new wrinkle*; see also **change** 2, **discovery** 2.

**innuendo,** *n.* — *Syn.* insinuation, intimation, imputation, aside; see **allusion, hint** 1, **suggestion** 1.

**innumerable,** *modif.* — *Syn.* numberless, countless, multitudinous; see **frequent, many.**

**inoculate,** *v.* — *Syn.* immunize, vaccinate, protect; see **inject** 1, **treat** 3, **vaccinate.**

**inoculation,** *n.* — *Syn.* immunization, vaccination, shot*; see **injection, medicine** 2, **vaccination** 1, 2.

**inoffensive,** *modif.* — *Syn.* innocuous, unoffending, peaceable; see **friendly** 1, **harmless** 2, **kind.**

**inoperative,** *modif.* — *Syn.* ineffectual, unworkable, defective; see **broken** 2, **faulty, void** 1, **weak** 2, 5.

**inopportune,** *modif.* — *Syn.* inconvenient, ill-timed, troublesome, unsuitable; see **unfavorable** 2, **untimely.**

**inordinate,** *modif.* — *Syn.* immoderate, excessive, overmuch, undue; see **excessive, extreme** 2, **wasteful.**
*See Synonym Study at* EXCESSIVE.

**inorganic,** *modif.* — *Syn.* mineral, inanimate, azoic, lithoidal, nonliving, without life, artificial, chemical. — *Ant.* ORGANIC, vegetable, animal.

**input,** *n.* — *Syn.* raw data, information, facts, figures; see **data.**

**input,** *v.* — *Syn.* enter, keyboard, key in, feed in, insert, code; see also **include** 2, **record** 1.

**inquest,** *n.* — *Syn.* investigation, hearing, inquiry; see **examination** 1, **trial** 2.

**inquietude,** *n.* — *Syn.* anxiety, disquiet, restlessness, uneasiness; see **anxiety, care** 2, **uneasiness.**

**inquire,** *v.* **1.** [To ask about] — *Syn.* make an inquiry, probe, interrogate, query; see **ask** 1, **question** 1.
**2.** [To seek into] — *Syn.* investigate, analyze, study; see **examine** 1.
*See Synonym Study at* ASK.

**inquiring,** *modif.* — *Syn.* questioning, analytical, curious, examining, probing, Socratic, investigatory, fact-finding, maieutic, heuristic, speculative, searching; see also **inquisitive, interested** 1.

**inquiry,** *n.* **1.** [An act or instance of questioning] — *Syn.* query, request, interrogation, questioning; see **question** 1.
**2.** [An investigation] — *Syn.* probe, analysis, hearing; see **examination** 1.

**inquisition,** *n.* — *Syn.* official inquiry, cross-examination, interrogation, third degree*; see **examination, trial** 2.

**inquisitive,** *modif.* — *Syn.* curious, inquiring, prying, speculative, questioning, interested, intrusive, meddling, meddlesome, searching, challenging, analytical, poking, sifting, scrutinizing, investigative, querying, inquisitorial, forward, presumptuous, impertinent, snoopy*, nosy*, long-nosed*, rubbernecking*, big-eyed*, consumed with curiosity*; see also **interested** 1, **meddlesome.** — *Ant.* INDIFFERENT, unconcerned, aloof.

*SYN.* — **inquisitive** implies a habitual tendency to be curious, esp. about matters that do not concern one, and an attempt to gain information by persistent questioning; **curious** implies eagerness or anxiousness to find out things and may suggest a wholesome desire to be informed; **meddlesome** suggests unwelcome intrusion into the affairs of others; **prying** suggests an officious inquisitiveness and meddlesomeness that persists against resistance

---

**inroad,** *n.* — *Syn.* encroachment, invasion, incursion; see **intrusion.**

**insane,** *modif.* **1.** [Deranged] — *Syn.* crazy, crazed, mad, wild, raging, frenzied, lunatic, schizophrenic, psychotic, psychopathic, psychoneurotic, paranoid, *non compos mentis* (Latin), maniacal, raving, demented, rabid, berserk, unbalanced, unhinged, act of one's mind, out of one's head, moonstruck, unsettled, mentally unsound, mentally diseased, sick, suffering from hallucinations, bereft of reason, daft, deluded, possessed, stark mad, having a devil, obsessed, disordered, touched, addlebrained, addlepated, addleheaded, nutty*, loony*, nuts*, schizo*, schizzy*, tetched*, balmy*, screwy*, loco*, off the wall*, wacko*, cuckoo*, bughouse*, crazy as a coot*, mad as a March hare*, gone*, derailed*, half-cocked*, haywire*, bats*, batty*, off the beam*, having bats in the belfry*, round the bend*, bonkers*, unglued*, nutty as a fruitcake*, off one's nut*, off one's rocker*, out of one's gourd*, dotty*, pixilated*, cracked*, having a few buttons missing*, one can short of a six-pack*, frothing at the mouth*, bananas*, not playing with a full deck*, out to lunch*, not all there*, wigged out*, off the deep end*; see also **sick, violent** 2, 4. — *Ant.* SANE, rational, sensible.
**2.** [Utterly foolish] — *Syn.* madcap, daft, idiotic; see **stupid** 1.

**insanely,** *modif.* **1.** [Crazily] — *Syn.* madly, furiously, psychopathically, fiercely; see **crazily, violently** 1, 2, **wildly** 1.
**2.** [Stupidly] — *Syn.* idiotically, senselessly, irrationally; see **foolishly.**

**insanity,** *n.* **1.** [Mental derangement] — *Syn.* mental illness, mental disorder, derangement, psychopathy, madness, dementia, amentia, lunacy, psychosis, alienation, neurosis, psychoneurosis, phobia, mania, craziness, aberration; see also **complex** 1, **disease.**
Mental illnesses and disorders include: schizophrenia, dementia praecox, catatonia, paranoia, hysteria, catalepsy, manic-depressive disorder, bipolar disorder, depression, melancholia, cyclothymia, delusion, hallucination, delirium, amnesia, split personality, multiple personality, autism, mental retardation, senile dementia, obsession, fixation, compulsion, obsessive-compulsive disorder, mania, phobia; nervous breakdown*.
Disorders usually accompanied by impaired mental functioning include: Down syndrome, Mongolism*, cretinism, microcephaly, hydrocephaly, Alzheimer's disease. — *Ant.* SANITY, reason, normality.
**2.** [Utter folly] — *Syn.* senselessness, foolishness, foolhardiness; see **stupidity** 2.

---

*SYN.* — **insanity,** current in popular and legal language but not used technically in medicine, implies mental derangement in one who formerly had mental health; **lunacy** specifically suggests periodic spells of insanity, but is now most commonly used in its extended sense of extreme folly; **dementia** is the general term for an acquired mental disorder, now generally one of organic origin, as distinguished from *amentia* (congenital mental deficiency); **psychosis** is the psychiatric term for any

of various specialized mental disorders, functional or organic, in which the personality is seriously disorganized

---

**insatiable,** *modif.* — *Syn.* voracious, unsatisfied, unappeasable, unquenchable; see **greedy** 1, 2.

**inscribe,** *v.* — *Syn.* list, engrave, impress; see **engrave** 2, **record** 1, **write** 1, 2.

**inscription,** *n.* — *Syn.* engraving, saying, legend, dedication; see **epitaph, heading, writing** 2.

**inscrutable,** *modif.* — *Syn.* incomprehensible, mysterious, impenetrable; see **blank** 2, **difficult** 2, **mysterious** 1, 2, **secret** 1.
*See Synonym Study at* MYSTERIOUS.

**insect,** *n.* — *Syn.* bug, beetle, arthropod, scarab, mite, vermin, cootie*; see also **pest** 1.
Kinds of insects include: ant, bristletail, louse, flea, gnat, springtail, earwig, stone fly, May fly, dragonfly, darning needle, termite, thrips, plant bug, cicada, aphid, scale insect, leaf insect, alder fly, lacewing, mealy wing, mantis, ant lion, beetle, Japanese beetle, scorpion fly, caddis fly, butterfly, moth, true fly, sawfly, ichneumon fly, seventeen-year locust, bedbug, caterpillar, centipede, millipede, grasshopper, cricket, walking stick, katydid, daddy-longlegs, wasp, bumblebee, honeybee, yellow jacket, hornet, cockroach, silverfish, potato bug, corn borer, boll weevil, stinkbug, firefly; see also **ant, bee** 1, **flea, fly** 1, **mosquito.**

**insecticide,** *n.* — *Syn.* pesticide, DDT, bug spray*, pyrethrin, rotenone, neem, sabadilla; see also **poison.**

**insecure,** *modif.* **1.** [Apprehensive] — *Syn.* anxious, hesitant, unsure of oneself, lacking confidence; see **timid, troubled** 1, **uneasy** 1.
**2.** [Not safe] — *Syn.* vulnerable, unstable, precarious; see **unsafe, weak** 2.

**insecurity,** *n.* **1.** [Anxiety] — *Syn.* vacillation, self-doubt, hesitancy, indecision; see **doubt** 2, **uncertainty** 1.
**2.** [Danger] — *Syn.* precariousness, instability, hazard, vulnerability; see **chance** 1, **danger.**

**insensate,** *modif.* **1.** [Indifferent] — *Syn.* impassive, apathetic, cold, unfeeling; see **callous, indifferent** 1, **unmoved** 2.
**2.** [Stupid] — *Syn.* senseless, irrational, foolish, dumb*; see **stupid** 1.

**insensibility,** *n.* — *Syn.* apathy, unconsciousness, unresponsiveness; see **indifference** 1.

**insensible,** *modif.* **1.** [Unconscious] — *Syn.* swooning, torpid, numb, unaware; see **unaware, unconscious** 1.
**2.** [Indifferent] — *Syn.* impassive, apathetic, unappreciative, impervious; see **callous, indifferent** 1, **unmoved** 2.

**insensitive,** *modif.* — *Syn.* unfeeling, uncaring, tactless, inconsiderate; see **callous, indifferent** 1, **tactless.**

**inseparable,** *modif.* **1.** [Not separable] — *Syn.* indivisible, as one, joined, tied up, molded together, intertwined, interwoven, entwined, integrated, integral, whole, connected, attached, conjoined, united; see also **joined, unified.** — *Ant.* separable, DIVISIBLE, apart.
**2.** [Very congenial] — *Syn.* loving, close, attached, intimate; see **friendly** 1.

**insert,** *n.* — *Syn.* enclosure, supplement, new material; see **addition** 2, **advertisement** 2, **insertion.**

**insert,** *v.* **1.** [To put in] — *Syn.* implant, stick in, slip in, place in; see **embed** 1.
**2.** [To introduce] — *Syn.* enter, interpolate, inject; see **include** 2.

**inserted,** *modif.* — *Syn.* introduced, added, interpolated, placed with, infused, stuck in, enclosed; see also **en-**

closed 1, **included.**

**insertion,** *n.* — *Syn.* insert, interpolation, injection, interjection, infusion, introduction, inclusion; see also **addition** 2.

**inside,** *modif.* **1.** [Within] — *Syn.* within the boundaries of, within the circumference of, bounded, surrounded by; see **in** 1, 2, **under** 1, 3, **within.** — *Ant.* after, BEYOND, outside.
**2.** [Within doors] — *Syn.* indoors, under a roof, in a house, out of the open, behind closed doors, under a shelter, in, in under, in the interior. — *Ant.* OUTSIDE, out-of-doors, in the open.
**3.** [*Known only to insiders] — *Syn.* private, privileged, confidential, exclusive; see **private, secret** 1.
**4.** [Toward the center] — *Syn.* inner, inward, internal, interior, close up; see also **central** 1.

**inside,** *n.* — *Syn.* interior, center, core, middle, inner surface, lining, inner recesses; see also **center** 1, **lining.**

**inside out,** *modif.* **1.** [With the inside where the outside should be] — *Syn.* reversed, backwards, everted, wrong side out; see **reversed.**
**2.** [*Completely] — *Syn.* thoroughly, entirely, backwards and forwards*; see **completely.**

**insides,** *pl.n.* — *Syn.* interior, inner parts, internal organs, bowels, entrails, viscera, recesses, middle, center, belly, womb, heart, soul, breast, contents, components, workings, guts*, innards*; see also **abdomen, center** 1, **contents** 1.

**insidious,** *modif.* — *Syn.* deceptive, ensnaring, treacherous, stealthy; see **dishonest** 1, **false** 1, **secret** 3, **sly** 1.

**insight,** *n.* — *Syn.* penetration, perspicacity, shrewdness; see **acumen.**

**insignia,** *n.* — *Syn.* badge, ensign, coat of arms, symbol; see **badge** 2, **decoration** 3, **emblem.**

**insignificance,** *n.* — *Syn.* unimportance, worthlessness, indifference, triviality, negligibility, nothingness, smallness, meanness, pettiness, paltriness, immateriality, inconsequence, inconsequentiality, matter of no consequence, trifling matter, nothing to speak of, nothing particular, drop in the bucket*, molehill*, drop in the ocean*.

**insignificant,** *modif.* — *Syn.* irrelevant, petty, trifling; see **trivial, unimportant.**

**insincere,** *modif.* — *Syn.* deceitful, artificial, shifty, two-faced*; see **affected** 2, **dishonest** 1, **hypocritical, sly** 1.

**insincerity,** *n.* — *Syn.* distortion, falsity, pretense, lies; see **deception** 1, **dishonesty, hypocrisy.**

**insinuate,** *v.* **1.** [To make an indirect hint] — *Syn.* imply, suggest, intimate; see **hint, mention, propose** 1, **refer** 2.
**2.** [To introduce slowly or artfully] — *Syn.* infuse, instill, ingratiate, slip in, sneak in, worm in, work in, edge in, ease in, insert gradually, infiltrate, inject, maneuver, foist oneself, horn in*, muscle in*; see also **instill.** — *Ant.* PUSH, dash, crowd.
*See Synonym Study at* SUGGEST.

**insinuation,** — *Syn.* implication, veiled remark, innuendo; see **hint** 1, 2, **suggestion** 1.

**insipid,** *modif.* **1.** [Tasteless] — *Syn.* flat, stale, vapid; see **tasteless** 1.
**2.** [Uninteresting] — *Syn.* vapid, flat, banal, weak, lifeless, characterless; see also **dull** 4.

---

*SYN.* — **insipid** implies a lack of taste or flavor and is, hence, figuratively applied to anything that is lifeless, dull, etc. *[insipid table talk]*; **vapid** and **flat** apply to that which once had, but has since lost, freshness, sharpness, tang, zest, etc. *[the vapid, or flat, epigrams that had once*

so delighted him*]*; **banal** is used of that which is so trite or hackneyed as to seem highly vapid or flat *[her banal compliments]*

---

**insist,** *v.* **1.** [To declare firmly or persistently] — *Syn.* maintain, contend, assert, dwell on; see **declare** 1, **emphasize.**
**2.** [To demand] — *Syn.* request, order, exhort; see **ask** 1, **command** 1, **require** 2.

**insistence,** *n.* — *Syn.* demand, perseverance, importunity, emphasis; see **persistence, urging.**

**insistent,** *modif.* — *Syn.* persistent, reiterative, continuous; see **emphatic** 1, **obstinate, resolute** 2.

**insobriety,** *n.* — *Syn.* alcoholism, inebriety, intoxication; see **drunkenness.**

**insolence,** *n.* — *Syn.* effrontery, impertinence, presumption, audacity; see **rudeness.**

**insolent,** *modif.* — *Syn.* impertinent, impudent, offensive, arrogant; see **proud** 2, **rude** 2.
*See Synonym Study at* IMPERTINENT, PROUD.

**insolently,** *modif.* — *Syn.* insultingly, presumptuously, brazenly, impertinently; see **boldly** 1, **rudely.**

**insoluble,** *modif.* — *Syn.* insolvable, unsolvable, unconcluded, unresolved, unsolved, inexplicable, mysterious, baffling; see also **difficult** 1.

**insolvency,** *n.* — *Syn.* distress, destitution, liquidation; see **bankruptcy, poverty** 1.

**insolvent,** *modif.* — *Syn.* bankrupt, indebted, foreclosed, failed, unbalanced, out of credit, out of funds, out of money, broken, ruined, in default, in the hands of receivers, in receivership, in chapter XI, broke*, on the rocks*, flat*, busted*, wiped out*, done for*, gone to the wall*, in the red*, in a hole*, sent to the cleaners*; see also **poor** 1, **ruined** 4. — *Ant.* SOLVENT, prosperous, in good condition.

**insomnia,** *n.* — *Syn.* wakefulness, sleeplessness, restlessness, insomnolence, fitfulness, tossing and turning, inability to sleep.

**insomniac,** *n.* — *Syn.* victim of insomnia, light sleeper, broken sleeper; see **patient.**

**insouciant,** *modif.* — *Syn.* carefree, nonchalant, breezy, careless; see **jaunty, unconcerned.**

**inspect,** *v.* — *Syn.* scrutinize, probe, investigate; see **examine** 1.
*See Synonym Study at* SCRUTINIZE.

**inspected,** *modif.* — *Syn.* examined, tried, checked, authorized; see **approved, investigated, tested.**

**inspection,** *n.* **1.** [An examination] — *Syn.* inventory, investigation, inquiry; see **examination** 1.
**2.** [A military review] — *Syn.* maneuvers, pageant, dress parade; see **drill** 3, **parade** 1, **review** 4.

**inspector,** *n.* — *Syn.* examiner, checker, overseer, monitor, controller, auditor, reviewer, police inspector, chief detective, investigating officer, railroad inspector, customs officer, immigration inspector, government inspector, quality-control inspector; see also **detective, examiner, investigator, policeman.**

**inspiration,** *n.* **1.** [An idea] — *Syn.* notion, hunch, flash, revelation; see **impulse** 2, **thought** 2.
**2.** [A stimulant to creative activity] — *Syn.* stimulus, spur, motivation, influence; see **incentive.**

**inspire,** *v.* **1.** [To encourage] — *Syn.* inspirit, invigorate, spur, animate; see **encourage** 2, **incite.**
**2.** [To stimulate to creative activity] — *Syn.* fire, spark, stimulate, rouse, kindle, quicken, be the cause of, start off, put one in the mood, set aglow, give one the idea for, motivate, touch the imagination, give an impetus; see also **cause** 2, **excite** 1, **urge** 2.

**inspired,** *modif.* **1.** [Stimulated] — *Syn.* roused, animated, inspirited, energized, motivated, stirred, excited, exhilarated, influenced, set going, started, activated, galvanized, moved; see also **encouraged.**

2. [Seemingly moved by supernatural powers] — *Syn.* possessed, ecstatic, transported, carried away, fired, exalted, uplifted, caught on fire, in a frenzy, held, guided, touched.

**inspiring,** *modif.* — *Syn.* rousing, encouraging, inspirational, inspiriting, heartening, enlivening, animating, refreshing, exhilarating, uplifting, moving, stirring, stimulating, motivating; see also **exciting, moving** 2, **stimulating.**

**inspirit,** *v.* — *Syn.* arouse, stimulate, animate; see **encourage** 2, **excite** 1, **incite.**

**instability,** *n.* — *Syn.* inconstancy, changeability, immaturity, mutability, variability, unstableness, nonuniformity, inconsistency, irregularity, imbalance, disequilibrium, unsteadiness, shakiness, precariousness, vulnerability, pliancy, fluidity, restlessness, inquietude, disquiet, anxiety, fluctuation, alternation, oscillation, fitfulness, impermanence, transience, vacillation, hesitation, flightiness, capriciousness, wavering, irresolution, uncertainty, fickleness, volatility; see also **change** 1, **mobility, weakness** 1, 2.

**install,** *v.* — *Syn.* set up, establish, induct, put in, build in, place, situate, instate, invest, introduce, inaugurate, furnish with, put up, connect, fit, emplace, fix, ensconce.

**installation,** *n.* 1. [The act of installing] — *Syn.* placing, induction, investiture, ordination, inauguration, launching, accession, investment, coronation, instatement, establishment, furnishing, fitting, connection.

2. [That which has been installed] — *Syn.* machinery, apparatus, wiring, lighting, insulation, power, power plant, heating system, furnishings, fittings, foundation, base.

3. [Naval and military installations] — *Syn.* fort, bunker, ammo dump*; see **arsenal, fortification** 2, **harbor** 2.

**installed,** *modif.* — *Syn.* set up, put up, inaugurated, connected; see **equipped, established** 2, **initiated** 3.

**installment,** *n.* — *Syn.* partial payment, periodic payment, downpayment, contract payment, section, chapter, episode, portion; see also **episode, part** 1, **payment** 1.

**instance,** *n.* — *Syn.* example, case, situation, occurrence; see **example** 1.
*See Synonym Study at* EXAMPLE.

**instance,** *v.* — *Syn.* exemplify, show, cite examples; see **cite** 2, **mention, refer** 2.

**for instance** — *Syn.* as an example, by way of illustration, to cite an instance; see **for example** at **example.**

**instant,** *modif.* — *Syn.* immediate, prompt, instantaneous, on-the-spot, ready-to-use, ready-to-eat, ready-to-serve, premixed, precooked; see also **immediate** 1, **prepared** 2, 3.

**instant,** *n.* — *Syn.* moment, second, short while, flash, trice, split second, twinkling, wink of an eye, jiffy*, shake*, two shakes of a lamb's tail*, jiff*, sec*; see also **moment** 1.

**on the instant** — *Syn.* instantly, without delay, simultaneously; see **immediately.**

**instantaneous,** *modif.* — *Syn.* immediate, instant, prompt, unhesitating; see **immediate** 1.

**instantaneously,** *modif.* — *Syn.* promptly, directly, at once; see **immediately, spontaneously.**

**instantly,** *modif.* — *Syn.* directly, at once, without delay; see **immediately, spontaneously.**

**instead,** *modif.* — *Syn.* in its place, in its stead, as a

substitute, as an alternative, alternatively, alternately, rather, in preference, preferably, on second thought; see also **rather** 2.

**instead of,** *prep.* — *Syn.* rather than, in place of, in lieu of, as a substitute for, as an alternative for, as a proxy for, in behalf of.

**instigate,** *v.* — *Syn.* prompt, stimulate, induce, incite; see **incite, urge** 2.
*See Synonym Study at* INCITE.

**instigation,** *n.* — *Syn.* prompting, influence, stimulation; see **encouragement** 1, **incentive, urging.**

**instill,** *v.* — *Syn.* infuse, suffuse, transfuse, intermix, imbue, inject, infiltrate, interject, inoculate, impregnate, implant, impress into the mind, ingrain, impart, impart gradually, disseminate, inspire, diffuse, impress, propagandize, catechize, brainwash, introduce, teach, inculcate, insinuate, indoctrinate, insert, impenetrate, inseminate, force in, put into someone's head*; see also **teach** 1. — *Ant.* REMOVE, draw out, extract.

**instinct,** *n.* — *Syn.* sense, feel, impulse, intuition, automatic response, aptitude, proclivity, bent, knack, gift, natural tendency, drive; see also **ability** 1, **hunch** 2, **inclination** 1.

**instinctive,** *modif.* 1. [Automatic] — *Syn.* mechanical, intuitive, reflex, unlearned; see **automatic** 2, **habitual** 1, **inherent.**

2. [Natural] — *Syn.* spontaneous, accustomed, normal; see **natural** 1, 2, **spontaneous.**
*See Synonym Study at* SPONTANEOUS.

**instinctively,** *modif.* — *Syn.* inherently, intuitively, by instinct; see **naturally** 2.

**institute,** *v.* 1. [To organize] — *Syn.* found, establish, launch; see **organize** 2.

2. [To begin] — *Syn.* initiate, start, open; see **begin** 1.

**institution,** *n.* 1. [The act of setting up] — *Syn.* establishment, foundation, organization; see **establishing, organization** 1.

2. [An organization, corporation, etc.] — *Syn.* company, system, institute, asylum; see **business** 4, **hospital, organization** 3, **school** 1, **university.**

3. [An established custom, practice, etc.] — *Syn.* convention, tradition, fixture; see **custom** 2.

**institutionalize,** *v.* — *Syn.* standardize, incorporate into a system, make official; see **order** 3, **regulate** 2, **systematize.**

**institutionalized,** *modif.* — *Syn.* standardized, regularized, incorporated into a system; see **regulated, traditional** 2.

**instruct,** *v.* 1. [To teach] — *Syn.* educate, give lessons, guide; see **teach** 1.

2. [To order] — *Syn.* tell, direct, bid; see **command** 1.

3. [To inform] — *Syn.* reveal, disclose, apprise; see **notify** 1, **tell** 1.
*See Synonym Study at* COMMAND, TEACH.

**instructed,** *modif.* — *Syn.* trained, advised, informed, briefed; see **educated** 1, **knowledgeable, learned** 1.

**instruction,** *n.* — *Syn.* guidance, preparation, direction; see **education** 1.

**instructions,** *pl.n.* — *Syn.* orders, guidelines, plans, directive; see **advice, directions.**

**instructive,** *modif.* — *Syn.* illuminating, enlightening, informative; see **informative.**

**instructor,** *n.* — *Syn.* professor, tutor, lecturer; see **teacher** 1, 2.

**instrument,** *n.* — *Syn.* tool, means, apparatus, implement; see **device** 1, **machine** 1, **tool** 1.
*See Synonym Study at* TOOL.

**instrumental,** *modif.* — *Syn.* partly responsible for, contributory, conducive, of service; see **effective, helpful** 1, **necessary** 1.

**instrumentality,** *n.* — *Syn.* contribution, help, assistance, agency; see **aid** 1, **means** 1.

**insubordinate,** *modif.* — *Syn.* disobedient, mutinous, defiant; see **rebellious** 2, 3.

**insubordination,** *n.* — *Syn.* defiance, rebelliousness, mutiny, rebellion; see **disobedience, revolution** 2.

**insubstantial,** *modif.* **1.** [Imaginary] — *Syn.* ephemeral, illusory, intangible; see **fanciful** 1, **imaginary, unreal.**

**2.** [Flimsy] — *Syn.* petty, slight, frail, tenuous; see **flimsy** 1, **poor** 2, **weak** 2.

**insufferable,** *modif.* — *Syn.* unbearable, intolerable, unendurable; see **intolerable, painful** 1.

**insufficient,** *modif.* — *Syn.* deficient, lacking, skimpy, meager; see **faulty, inadequate** 1, **unfinished** 1, **wanting** 1.

**insufficiently,** *modif.* — *Syn.* barely, incompletely, partly; see **inadequately.**

**insular,** *modif.* **1.** [Isolated] — *Syn.* detached, alone, separate; see **isolated, separated.**

**2.** [Biased] — *Syn.* narrow-minded, bigoted, illiberal, provincial; see **prejudiced.**

**insulate,** *v.* — *Syn.* protect, cork, cushion, coat, cover, line, wrap, encase, shield, separate, segregate, isolate, treat, apply insulation, tape up, glass in; see also **line** 1.

**insulation,** *n.* **1.** [The act of insulating] — *Syn.* taping, covering, caulking, lining, cushioning, furring, protecting, padding, packing, surrounding, isolating, defending, neutralizing, cording.

**2.** [An insulator] — *Syn.* nonconductor, protector, resistant material.

Types of insulation and insulating materials include: knob, standoff, split-knob, double-cup, shackle, covering, pad, padding, sleeve, tape, air space, tube, tubing; rock wool, wool bat, asbestos, conduit, pack, packing, rubber, tarred felt, silk, furring, oiled silk, vacuum hair, lead, polarized layer, fiberglass, foam, cork.

**insulator,** *n.* — *Syn.* nonconductor, nonconveyor, nontransmitter; see **insulation** 2.

**insult,** *n.* — *Syn.* indignity, offense, affront, abuse, contumely, ill treatment, scurrility, opprobrium, outrage, vilification, incivility, impudence, insolence, blasphemy, mockery, derision, impertinence, discourtesy, invective, slight, snub, ignominy, disrespect, slander, libel, name-calling, taunt, gibe, slap in the face★, put-down★, dig★, black eye★; see also **curse** 1, **rudeness.** — *Ant.* PRAISE, tribute, homage.

**insult,** *v.* — *Syn.* affront, revile, vilify, libel, offend, outrage, abuse, humiliate, mock, vex, tease, call names, irritate, annoy, aggravate, provoke, deride, taunt, laugh down, ridicule, gibe at, jeer, slight, demean, underestimate, take a slap at★, step on one's toes★, rank out★; see also **offend, slander.**

Insulting remarks include: nuts, nerts, says you, go jump in the lake, in my eye, don't make me laugh, shut your face, shut up, so's your old man, you're crazy, baloney, bull, nuts to you, in a pig's eye, up yours, horse manure, tell it to the marines, my foot, my eye, does your mother know you're out?, another country heard from, drop dead, stuff it, stick it, read my lips, go suck eggs, go to hell, go pound salt, go pound sand, stick it where the sun don't shine, stick it in your ear, you know where you can stick it. — *Ant.* PRAISE, extol, glorify.

*See Synonym Study at* OFFEND.

**insulted,** *modif.* — *Syn.* offended, affronted, slighted,

slandered, libeled, vilified, reviled, cursed, defamed, dishonored, mocked, ridiculed, jeered at, humiliated, mistreated, maltreated, aggrieved, hurt, outraged, shamed, underestimated, cut to the quick; see also **disgraced.** — *Ant.* flattered, complimented, PRAISED.

**insulting,** *modif.* — *Syn.* abusive, offensive, disparaging, derogatory, hurtful, debasing, degrading, affronting, outrageous, humiliating, scoffing, derisive, contemptuous, disrespectful, insolent, scurrilous, nasty, dyslogistic; see also **opprobrious** 1, **rude** 2. — *Ant.* RESPECTFUL, complimentary, honoring.

**insuperable,** *modif.* — *Syn.* impassable, insuperable, overwhelming; see **impossible** 1.

**insupportable,** *modif.* — *Syn.* insufferable, dreadful, intolerable; see **intolerable, painful** 1.

**insurance,** *n.* — *Syn.* indemnity, assurance, warrant, guarantee, protection, backing, allowance, safeguard, security, support, coverage, something to fall back on; see also **protection** 2, **security** 2.

**insure,** *v.* — *Syn.* register, warrant, protect, underwrite; see **guarantee** 1.

**insured,** *modif.* — *Syn.* safeguarded, protected, covered, warranteed; see **guaranteed, protected.**

**insurgent,** *modif.* — *Syn.* insurrectionary, mutinous, insubordinate, anarchical; see **rebellious** 1, 2.

**insurgent,** *n.* — *Syn.* rebel, revolutionary, guerrilla; see **agitator, radical, rebel** 1.

**insurmountable,** *modif.* — *Syn.* insuperable, unconquerable, unbeatable; see **impossible** 1.

**insurrection,** *n.* — *Syn.* insurgence, revolt, rebellion; see **disorder** 2, **revolution** 2.

**insurrectionary,** *modif.* — *Syn.* mutinous, insurgent, riotous; see **rebellious** 1, 2.

**insusceptible,** *modif.* — *Syn.* impassive, unfeeling, unresponsive; see **callous, immune, indifferent** 1.

**intact,** *modif.* — *Syn.* unimpaired, sound, entire, uninjured; see **whole** 2.

*See Synonym Study at* COMPLETE.

**intake,** *n.* — *Syn.* consumption, taking in, input, admission; see **absorption** 1, **admission** 2, **consumption** 1, **eating, profit** 2.

**intangible,** *modif.* **1.** [Uncertain] — *Syn.* indefinite, unsure, elusive, hypothetical; see **uncertain** 2, **vague** 2.

**2.** [Ethereal] — *Syn.* impalpable, airy, ephemeral; see **immaterial** 2.

**intangibly,** *modif.* — *Syn.* barely, slightly, undetectably; see **hardly, indefinitely** 1, **vaguely.**

**integer,** *n.* — *Syn.* integral, whole number, individual, entity; see **number** 1, **whole.**

**integral,** *modif.* **1.** [Necessary for completeness] — *Syn.* essential, indispensable, constituent, component, requisite, necessary, basic, elemental; see also **fundamental** 1.

**2.** [Made up of parts forming a whole] — *Syn.* complete, entire, indivisible, aggregate, undivided, unbroken; see also **whole** 1.

**integrate,** *v.* **1.** [To unify] — *Syn.* mix, blend, combine; see **mix** 1, **unite** 1.

**2.** [To abolish racial segregation] — *Syn.* desegregate, remove racial barriers, provide equal access, abolish segregation, make available to all, bus.

**integrated,** *modif.* **1.** [Joined] — *Syn.* combined, interspersed, mingled; see **joined, mixed** 1, **unified.**

**2.** [Open to all races] — *Syn.* nonsegregated, desegregated, multiracial, multicultural, interracial, nonracial, nonsectarian; without restriction as to race, creed, or color; making no distinctions, racially mixed, combined; see also **open** 3.

**integration,** *n.* — *Syn.* unification, combination, amalgamation, assimilation; see **alliance** 1, **mixture** 1, **synthesis** 1, **union** 1.

**integrity,** *n.* — *Syn.* uprightness, honor, probity; see **honesty** 1, **sincerity**.

**intellect,** *n.* **1.** [The power to reason] — *Syn.* understanding, comprehension, ability; see **acumen, judgment** 1.

**2.** [The mind] — *Syn.* intelligence, brain, mentality; see **mind** 1.

**intellectual,** *modif.* — *Syn.* mental, cerebral, intelligent, bookish; see **intelligent** 1, **learned** 1, **rational** 1, **studious**.

*See Synonym Study at* INTELLIGENT.

**intellectual,** *n.* — *Syn.* scholar, pundit, genius, philosopher, thinker, academic, academician, bookworm, highbrow, member of the intelligentsia, egghead*, brain*, Einstein*, longhair*, bluestocking*, braintruster*; see also **genius** 2, **scholar** 2.

**intelligence,** *n.* **1.** [Understanding] — *Syn.* perspicacity, discernment, comprehension; see **acumen, judgment** 1.

**2.** [Ability] — *Syn.* capacity, skill, aptitude; see **ability** 1, 2.

**3.** [Secret information] — *Syn.* report, news, statistics, facts, inside information, account, knowledge, info*, the dope*, the lowdown*; see also **data, knowledge** 1, **news** 1, **secret**.

**4.** [The mind] — *Syn.* intellect, brain, mentality; see **mind** 1.

**intelligent,** *modif.* **1.** [*Said of persons or beings*] — *Syn.* clever, bright, astute, acute, smart, brilliant, perceptive, well-informed, resourceful, profound, penetrating, original, exceptional, perspicacious, keen, imaginative, inventive, reasonable, capable, able, precocious, gifted, ingenious, knowledgeable, creative, alive, responsible, understanding, alert, quick-witted, keen-witted, clearheaded, quick, sharp, witty, ready, calculating, rational, thoughtful, comprehending, listening to reason, discerning, having one's wits about one, having it in one, discriminating, knowing, intellectual, on the qui vive, sagacious, studious, contemplative, having a head on one's shoulders, talented, apt, deep, sage, wise, shrewd, brainy*, smart as a whip*, all there*, on the ball*, on the beam*, not born yesterday*, nobody's fool*, crazy like a fox*; see also **clever** 1, **judicious**. — *Ant.* DULL, slow-witted, stupid.

**2.** [*Said of conduct*] — *Syn.* sensible, farsighted, rational; see sense 1; **judicious**.

---

*SYN.* — **intelligent** implies the ability to learn or understand from experience or to respond successfully to a new experience; **clever** implies quickness in learning or understanding, but sometimes connotes a lack of thoroughness or depth; **alert** emphasizes quickness in sizing up a situation; **bright** and **smart** are somewhat informal, less precise equivalents for any of the preceding; **brilliant** implies an unusually high degree of intelligence; **intellectual** suggests keen intelligence coupled with interest and ability in the more advanced fields of knowledge

---

**intelligently,** *modif.* — *Syn.* cleverly, skillfully, reasonably, rationally, logically, judiciously, capably, sharply, shrewdly, sagaciously, wisely, astutely, discerningly, perspicaciously, comprehendingly, knowingly, knowledgeably, farsightedly, sensibly, prudently, alertly, keenly, resourcefully, aptly, well, admirably, brilliantly, discriminatingly; see also **effectively, shrewdly**. — *Ant.* BADLY, foolishly, stupidly.

**intelligentsia,** *pl.n.* — *Syn.* the learned, intellectuals, literati, eggheads*; see **intellectual**.

**intelligibility,** *n.* — *Syn.* readability, understandability, lucidity; see **clarity, coherence** 2.

**intelligible,** *modif.* — *Syn.* plain, clear, comprehensible; see **understandable**.

**intemperance,** *n.* — *Syn.* insobriety, immoderation, alcoholism; see **drunkenness**.

**intemperate,** *modif.* **1.** [Drunken] — *Syn.* inebriated, dissipated, alcoholic; see **drunk**.

**2.** [Excessive] — *Syn.* immoderate, inordinate, unrestrained; see **excessive, extreme** 2.

**intend,** *v.* **1.** [To have in mind as a purpose] — *Syn.* propose, plan, purpose, aim, expect, mean, be resolved to, be determined to, aspire to, have in view, hope to, contemplate, think, aim at, take into one's head; see also **resolve** 1.

**2.** [To destine for] — *Syn.* design, mean, devote to, reserve, appoint, purpose, set apart, aim at, aim for, have in view; see also **assign** 1, **dedicate** 2, **designate** 1.

**3.** [To mean] — *Syn.* indicate, signify, denote; see **mean** 1.

---

*SYN.* — **intend** implies a having in mind of something to be done, said, etc. /I *intended* to write you/; **mean,** a more general word, does not connote so clearly a specific, deliberate purpose /he always *means* well/; **design** suggests careful planning in order to bring about a particular result /their delay was *designed* to forestall suspicion/; **propose** implies a clear declaration, openly or to oneself, of one's intention /I *propose* to speak for an hour/; **purpose** adds to **propose** a connotation of strong determination to effect one's intention /he *purposes* to become a doctor/

---

**intended,** *modif.* — *Syn.* planned, proposed, designed, contemplated, meditated, expected, predetermined, calculated, prearranged, predestined, meant, deliberate, intentional; see also **deliberate** 1, **planned, proposed**.

**intense,** *modif.* — *Syn.* intensified, strong, deep, profound, extraordinary, exceptional, heightened, strained, marked, vivid, ardent, extreme, undue, powerful, passionate, impassioned, emotional, high-strung, serious, diligent, hard, full, great, supreme, exaggerated, violent, excessive, acute, keen, piercing, cutting, bitter, severe, concentrated, intensive, forceful, all-consuming, sharp, biting, stinging, shrill, high-pitched, fervid, strenuous, fervent, earnest, zealous, vehement, harsh, strong, pungent, bright, brilliant; see also **emotional** 2, **extreme** 2.

**intensely,** *modif.* — *Syn.* deeply, profoundly, strongly; see **very**.

**intensify,** *v.* — *Syn.* strengthen, heighten, sharpen, emphasize, deepen, escalate, increase, aggravate, exacerbate, enhance, raise, point, step up, set off, tone up, brighten, lighten, darken, concentrate, redouble, augment, reinforce, magnify, amplify, add to, quicken, hop up*, jazz up*; see also **increase** 1, **strengthen**. — *Ant.* DECREASE, diminish, relax.

---

*SYN.* — **intensify** implies an increasing in the degree of force, vehemence, vividness, etc. /his absence only *intensified* her longing/; **aggravate** implies a making more serious, unbearable, etc. and connotes something that is unpleasant or troublesome in itself /your insolence only *aggravates* the offense/; to **heighten** is to make greater, stronger, more vivid, etc. so as to raise above the ordinary or commonplace /music served to *heighten* the effect/; **enhance** implies the addition of something so as to make more attractive or desirable /she used cosmetics to *enhance* her beauty/

---

**intensity,** *n.* **1.** [A high degree of anything] — *Syn.* strain, force, concentration, power, energy, vehemence, violence, ferocity, fury, fervor, heat, warmth, ferment, extremity, severity, acuteness, depth, deepness, weightiness, forcefulness, high pitch, sharpness, emphasis, magnitude, strength, vigor; see also **force** 3.
**2.** [Depth of feeling] — *Syn.* passion, fervor, ardor, warmth; see **emotion, enthusiasm** 1, **excitement, nervousness** 2.
**intensive,** *modif.* — *Syn.* concentrated, exhaustive, all-out, accelerated; see **absolute** 1, **fast** 1, **intense.**
**intensive care unit,** *n.* — *Syn.* ICU, hospital room, emergency unit, critical room; see **hospital.**
**intent,** *modif.* **1.** [Absorbed] — *Syn.* engrossed, attentive, concentrating; see **enthusiastic** 1, **rapt** 2.
**2.** [Resolved; *used with "on"*] — *Syn.* determined, set, bent, committed; see **resolute** 2.
**intent,** *n.* — *Syn.* purpose, intention, plan; see **purpose** 1.
**to all intents and purposes** — *Syn.* in almost every respect, practically, virtually; see **almost.**
*See Synonym Study at* PURPOSE.
**intention,** *n.* — *Syn.* aim, end, plan; see **purpose** 1.
*See Synonym Study at* PURPOSE.
**intentional,** *modif.* — *Syn.* intended, voluntary, meditated, prearranged; see **deliberate** 1.
*See Synonym Study at* VOLUNTARY.
**intentionally,** *modif.* — *Syn.* purposely, designedly, willfully, in cold blood; see **deliberately.**
**intently,** *modif.* — *Syn.* closely, hard, with concentration; see **eagerly, keenly.**
**inter,** *v.* — *Syn.* tomb, entomb, inhume; see **bury** 1.
**interact,** *v.* — *Syn.* coact, interreact, combine, socialize; see **associate** 1, **communicate** 2, **cooperate** 1, **mix** 1.
**interaction,** *n.* — *Syn.* interplay, intercommunication, reciprocal action, synergy; see **communication** 1, **cooperation** 1.
**intercede,** *v.* — *Syn.* intervene, arbitrate, mediate; see **arbitrate, negotiate** 1, **reconcile** 2.
**intercept,** *v.* — *Syn.* cut off, head off, stop, ambush, block, catch, seize midway, take away, interpose, appropriate, interlope, make off with, hijack; see also **hinder, prevent.**
**interception,** *n.* — *Syn.* blocking, interfering with, interposing; see **capture, interference** 1, **stopping.**
**intercession,** *n.* — *Syn.* mediation, petition, prayer; see **appeal** 1, **intervention** 1, **request.**
**intercessor,** *n.* — *Syn.* mediator, negotiator, arbitrator; see **judge** 2.
**interchange,** *n.* **1.** [The act of giving and receiving reciprocally] — *Syn.* barter, trade, reciprocation; see **exchange** 2.
**2.** [Alternation] — *Syn.* variation, varying, altering, exchange, transposition, shift, change of places, alternating; see also **exchange** 1, 3.
**3.** [A highway intersection] — *Syn.* cloverleaf, intersection, off-ramp; see **crossing** 1, **junction** 2, **road** 1.
**interchangeably,** *modif.* — *Syn.* correspondingly, reciprocally, conversely; see **mutually, vice versa.**
**intercommunication,** *n.* — *Syn.* interaction, interchange, intercourse, intercommunion; see **communication** 1.
**intercom system,** *n.* — *Syn.* two-way radio, public address system, walkie-talkie; see **communications,**

**radio** 2.
**intercourse,** *n.* **1.** [Communication] — *Syn.* association, dealings, interchange; see **communication** 1.
**2.** [Sex act] — *Syn.* coitus, coition, sexual relations; see **copulation, fornication, sex** 4.
**interdependence,** *n.* — *Syn.* reliance, mutuality, dependence, confidence; see **necessity** 1, **relationship.**
**interdict,** *v.* — *Syn.* forbid, hinder, prohibit, stop; see **forbid, halt** 2, **prevent.**
*See Synonym Study at* FORBID.
**interest,** *n.* **1.** [Concern] — *Syn.* attention, curiosity, engagement, excitement; see **attention** 1, 2, **care** 2, **curiosity** 1, **enthusiasm** 1.
**2.** [Advantage] — *Syn.* profit, benefit, gain; see **advantage** 3.
**3.** [Premium] — *Syn.* credit, due, discount, percentage, gain, bonus, earnings, accrual, dividend, yield; see also **addition** 2, **profit** 2.
**4.** [Share] — *Syn.* stake, piece, title, investment; see **credit** 2, **share.**
**5.** [Affair] — *Syn.* concern, matter, business, case; see **affair** 1.
**6.** [Importance] — *Syn.* consequence, concern, moment; see **importance** 1.
**7.** [Something that engages the attention] — *Syn.* pursuit, preoccupation, pastime; see **hobby.**
**8.** [Persons with a common trade or purpose; *often plural*] — *Syn.* class, powers, business interests; see **industry** 3.
**in the interest(s) of** — *Syn.* for the sake of, on behalf of, in order to promote; see **for.**
**interest,** *v.* — *Syn.* intrigue, amuse, please; see **entertain** 1, **fascinate.**
**interested,** *modif.* **1.** [Having one's interest aroused] — *Syn.* stimulated, sympathetic, attentive, engaged, attracted, enticed, lured, curious, intrigued, fascinated, drawn, touched, moved, affected, excited, inspired, inspirited, responsive, struck, impressed, roused, awakened, stirred, keen on*, all for*; see also **charmed, enthusiastic** 1, **excited, fascinated.** — *Ant.* BORED, tired, apathetic.
**2.** [Concerned with or engaged in] — *Syn.* occupied, engrossed, partial, prejudiced, biased, taken, obsessed with, fired, absorbed in, personally interested in, having investments in, owning stock in, likely to profit from, all wrapped up in*; see also **busy** 1, **involved** 1. — *Ant.* INDIFFERENT, impartial, disinterested.
**interesting,** *modif.* — *Syn.* absorbing, intriguing, fascinating, stimulating, gripping, riveting, compelling, arresting, entrancing, engaging, entertaining, exciting, engrossing, provocative, thought-provoking, pleasing, pleasurable, enjoyable, satisfying, readable, stirring, enthralling, spellbinding, affecting, alluring, exotic, unusual, exceptional, impressive, striking, attractive, appealing, captivating, enchanting, inviting, winning, magnetic, prepossessing, delightful, amusing, refreshing; see also **charming, exciting, stimulating.** — *Ant.* DULL, tedious, boring.
**interfere,** *v.* **1.** [To meddle] — *Syn.* intervene, interpose, interlope; see **meddle** 1.
**2.** [To prevent] — *Syn.* impede, stop, oppose, conflict; see **hinder, prevent.**
**interference,** *n.* **1.** [The act of obstructing] — *Syn.* intervention, resistance, retardation, impedance, checking, blocking, barring, hampering, clashing, collision, tackling, interception, hindrance, restraint, inhibition, shutting off, clogging, choking, arrest, barricading, thrusting between, interposition; see also **opposition** 1, **restraint** 2. — *Ant.* REMOVAL, clearance, releasing.

**2.** [Taking forcible part in the affairs of others] — *Syn.* meddling, interposition, interruption, prying, trespassing, tampering, intermeddling, advising, kibitzing*, butting in*, horning in*, barging in*, backseat driving*; see also **intrusion.**

**3.** [That which obstructs] — *Syn.* obstruction, check, obstacle; see **barrier, impediment 1, restraint 2.**

**interim,** *n.* — *Syn.* interval, the meantime, interlude; see **pause 1.**

**interior,** *modif.* — *Syn.* inner, internal, inward; see **central 1, inland, inner, inside 2.**

**interior,** *n.* **1.** [Inside] — *Syn.* inner part, depths, lining, heart; see **center 1, inside, insides.**
**2.** [The inside of a building] — *Syn.* rooms, halls, hall, stairway, hearth, vestibule, cloister, nave, lobby, transept, chapel, choir, gallery, basement.

**interject,** *v.* — *Syn.* introduce, interpose, insert, interrupt with, interpolate, parenthesize, infiltrate, intersperse, inject, infuse, splice, import, insinuate, implant, throw in, force in; see also **add 3, include 2, inject.**

**interjection,** *n.* **1.** [Insertion] — *Syn.* interpolation, insinuation, inclusion, parenthesis; see **insertion.**
**2.** [Exclamation] — *Syn.* utterance, ejaculation, cry; see **cry 1.**

**interlace,** *v.* **1.** [To weave] — *Syn.* intertwine, braid, entangle; see **twist, weave 1.**
**2.** [To mingle] — *Syn.* blend, combine, connect; see **join 1, merge, mix 1.**

**interline,** *v.* **1.** [To write between the lines] — *Syn.* interpolate, interscribe, annotate; see **explain.**
**2.** [To put in an interlining] — *Syn.* pack, fill, back, line, face, stuff, pad, quilt, bush, insulate, upholster, cushion; see also **line 1.**

**interlocutor,** *n.* — *Syn.* conversationalist, dialogist, interviewer, questioner; see **examiner, speaker 2, talker.**

**interloper,** *n.* — *Syn.* meddler, trespasser, encroacher, alien; see **intruder.**

**interlude,** *n.* **1.** [A recess] — *Syn.* interval, intermission, hiatus, interruption; see **delay 1, pause 1, recess 1.**
**2.** [A short play or musical piece performed during an interlude, sense 1] — *Syn.* entr'acte, intermezzo, *divertissement* (French), farce, masquerade; see also **comedy, drama 1, music 1.**

**intermediary,** *n.* — *Syn.* emissary, mediator, go-between; see **agent 1, delegate.**

**intermediate,** *modif.* — *Syn.* middle, halfway, midway, mid, between, in-between, intermediary, transitional, intervening, mean, medium, compromising, neutral, standard, median, moderate, average, about the fiftieth percentile; see also **central 1, common 1, middle.**

**interment,** *n.* — *Syn.* entombment, burial, inhumation; see **funeral 1.**

**intermezzo,** *n.* — *Syn.* musical interlude, intermission, divertimento; see **music 1.**

**interminable,** *modif.* — *Syn.* unending, overlong, wearisome, dragging on and on; see **dull 4, eternal 1, 2.**

**interminably,** *modif.* — *Syn.* endlessly, continually, going on and on, persistently; see **forever 1, frequently, regularly 2.**

**intermingle,** *v.* — *Syn.* mingle, fuse, combine, blend; see **join 1, merge, mix 1.**

**intermission,** *n.* — *Syn.* break, interlude, interim, respite; see **pause 1, recess 1.**

**intermit,** *v.* — *Syn.* suspend, cease, discontinue, interrupt; see **halt 2, pause.**

**intermittent,** *modif.* — *Syn.* periodic, alternate, shifting, coming and going, recurrent, sporadic, irregular, broken, seasonal, rhythmic, serial, epochal, cyclical, cyclic, discontinuous, interrupted, every other, spasmodic, on and off, fitful, occasional, now and then, by snatches*, here and there*, on-again off-again*; see also **irregular 1.** — *Ant.* CONSTANT, lasting, incessant.

*SYN.* — **intermittent** and **recurrent** both apply to something that stops and starts, or disappears and reappears, from time to time, but the former usually stresses the breaks or pauses, and the latter, the repetition or return [an *intermittent* fever, *recurrent* attacks of the hives]; **periodic** refers to something that recurs at more or less regular intervals [*periodic* economic crises]; **alternate** is usually used of two recurrent things that succeed each other in turns [*alternate* stripes of blue and white, a life of *alternate* sorrow and joy]

**intern,** *n.* — *Syn.* apprentice doctor, assistant resident, medical graduate; see **doctor 1.**

**internal,** *modif.* **1.** [Within] — *Syn.* inside, inner, inward, interior, private, intrinsic, innate, inherent, under the surface, intimate, subjective, enclosed, circumscribed; see also **inner.** — *Ant.* external, OUTER, outward.
**2.** [Within the body] — *Syn.* intestinal, constitutional, physiological, physical, bodily, organic, neurological, abdominal, ventral, visceral; see also **bodily 1, organic.** — *Ant.* FOREIGN, external, superficial.
**3.** [Within a group or area] — *Syn.* domestic, intrastate, civil, in-house; see **domestic 1, national 2, native 2, regional.**

**internally,** *modif.* — *Syn.* inside, within the body, beneath the surface, below the surface, inwardly, deep down, spiritually, mentally, privately, invisibly, orally, by injection, within the limits, within the termini, out of sight; see also **inside 1, within.**

**international,** *modif.* — *Syn.* worldwide, universal, global, worldly, world, intercontinental, transcontinental, between nations, supranational, all over the world, all-embracing, foreign, cosmopolitan, multicultural; see also **general 1, universal 3.** — *Ant.* DOMESTIC, national, internal.

**internationalize,** *v.* — *Syn.* universalize, globalize, generalize, hold between nations, establish on an international basis, make worldwide, make universal, broaden, expand, include everybody, bring under international control, demilitarize; see also **increase 1, unite 1.** — *Ant.* DIVIDE, localize, limit.

**internationally,** *modif.* — *Syn.* globally, universally, all over the world, the world over, interculturally, interracially, multiculturally, cooperatively, in the spirit of the United Nations, interreliantly, not provincially; see also **abroad, everywhere, universally 2.**

**internecine,** *modif.* **1.** [Involving conflict within a group] — *Syn.* internal, civil, fratricidal; see **domestic 1.**
**2.** [Mutually harmful] — *Syn.* exterminatory, mutually destructive, murderous; see **dangerous 1, 2, deadly 1.**

**interplay,** *n.* — *Syn.* interaction, transaction, reciprocation; see **exchange 1, 2.**

**interpolate,** *v.* — *Syn.* insert, inject, introduce, add; see **include 2, interject.**

**interpolation,** *n.* — *Syn.* insert, interjection, incorporation; see **addition 2, insertion.**

**interpose,** *v.* **1.** [To break into] — *Syn.* intrude, intervene, interfere, intercede; see **arbitrate, interrupt 2.**
**2.** [To insert] — *Syn.* introduce, interject, inject; see **include 2, interject.**

**interposing,** *modif.* — *Syn.* interceding, interfering, mediating; see **advisory, judicial, meddlesome.**

**interposition,** *n.* — *Syn.* insertion, intrusion, intercession; see **intervention** 1.

**interpret,** *v.* **1.** [To convey the meaning of; *said especially of a work of art*] — *Syn.* give one's impression of, render, represent, play, perform, depict, delineate, enact, portray, make sense of, construe, understand, evaluate, read, read into, improvise on, reenact, mimic, gather from, view as, give one an idea about, make of*; see also **define** 2, **describe, represent** 2.
**2.** [To explain] — *Syn.* translate, paraphrase, render; see **decipher, explain.**
*See Synonym Study at* EXPLAIN.

**interpretation,** *n.* **1.** [An explanation] — *Syn.* account, rendition, exposition, paraphrase, statement, diagnosis, description, representation, definition, elucidation, presentation, argument, paraphrase, translation, gloss, answer, solution; see also **explanation** 1, **translation.**
**2.** [A conception] — *Syn.* version, reading, construction, understanding, deduction, point of view, commentary, annotation, idea, analysis, recreation, criticism, dissertation, essay, discussion, appreciation, theme, critique, examination, study, take*, spin*; see also **exposition** 2, **review** 2.

**interpreted,** *modif.* — *Syn.* elucidated, explained, made clear; see **obvious** 2, **understood** 1.

**interpreter,** *n.* — *Syn.* translator, commentator, paraphraser, critic, reviewer, annotator, expositor, analyst, explicator, exegete, exponent, writer, artist, editor, biographer, scholar, spokesman, spokesperson, delegate, speaker, demonstrator, philosopher, professor, glossographer, simultaneous interpreter, linguist, language expert, decoder, guide, preacher; see also **critic** 2.

**interregnum,** *n.* — *Syn.* interval, suspension, interruption; see **pause** 1, 2, **respite.**

**interrogate,** *v.* — *Syn.* cross-examine, ask, grill*, give the third degree*; see **examine** 2, **question** 1.
*See Synonym Study at* ASK.

**interrogation,** *n.* — *Syn.* questioning, cross-examination, inquiry, investigation; see **examination** 1.

**interrogative,** *modif.* — *Syn.* quizzical, curious, questioning; see **inquisitive.**

**interrupt,** *v.* **1.** [To make a break in the continuity of] — *Syn.* obstruct, discontinue, break off, get in the way of; see **hinder, prevent, suspend** 2.
**2.** [To break in on] — *Syn.* intrude, intervene, cut in on, break in, interfere, infringe, obtrude, chime in, cut off, break someone's train of thought, disrupt, come between, work in, crowd in, edge in, insinuate in, inject in, interpose, put in, talk out of turn, chip in*, break the thread*, worm in*, muscle in*, butt in*, horn in*, barge in*, bust in*, crash*; see also **meddle** 1.

**interrupted,** *modif.* — *Syn.* stopped, checked, held up, obstructed, delayed, disrupted, broken, broken off, discontinuous, irregular, interfered with, meddled with, hindered, suspended, discontinued, cut short; see also **intermittent, postponed.**

**interruption,** *n.* — *Syn.* check, break, hiatus, gap, lacuna, cessation, suspension, delay, halt, pause, intermission, parenthesis, intrusion, obstruction, holding over; see also **arrest** 2, **delay** 1, **interference** 2, **pause** 1.

**intersect,** *v.* **1.** [To divide] — *Syn.* cut across, bisect, intercross; see **divide** 1.
**2.** [To come together] — *Syn.* meet, converge, touch; see **cross** 2, **join** 1.

**intersection,** *n.* — *Syn.* traffic circle, cloverleaf, fourway stop; see **crossing** 1, **junction** 2.

**intersperse,** *v.* — *Syn.* sprinkle, distribute, interlard; see **scatter** 1, 2.

**interstate,** *modif.* — *Syn.* interterritorial, between states, internal, interior, domestic; see also **regional.**

**interstice,** *n.* — *Syn.* interval, crack, space, crevice; see **hole** 1.

**intertwine,** *v.* — *Syn.* twist, braid, tangle; see **twist, weave** 1.

**interval,** *n.* — *Syn.* period, interlude, interim; see **pause** 1, 2, **period** 1.

**intervene,** *v.* **1.** [To settle] — *Syn.* step in, intercede, mediate; see **arbitrate, negotiate** 1, **reconcile** 2.
**2.** [To happen] — *Syn.* take place, occur, be between; see **happen** 2.
**3.** [To meddle] — *Syn.* come between, interpose, intrude; see **interrupt** 2, **meddle** 1.

**intervening,** *modif.* — *Syn.* intermediary, interceding, sandwiched; see **intermediate, middle.**

**intervention,** *n.* **1.** [The act of intervening] — *Syn.* interposition, mediation, arbitration, intercession, interruption, interference, breaking in, stepping in, entrance of a third party; see also **interference** 2, **intrusion.**
**2.** [Armed interference] — *Syn.* invasion, military occupation, armed intrusion; see **attack** 1.

**interview,** *n.* **1.** [A relatively formal conversation] — *Syn.* meeting, audience, conference, press conference, question and answer session, Q and A*; see also **conversation, discussion** 1.
**2.** [The record of a conversation] — *Syn.* transcript, account, case history; see **record** 1.

**interview,** *v.* — *Syn.* question, examine, interrogate, converse with, hold a colloquy with, get one's opinion, sound out, consult with, survey, poll, hold an inquiry, get something for the record; see also **examine** 2, **question** 1, **talk** 1.

**interweave,** *v.* — *Syn.* entwine, twist, braid, intermingle; see **knit** 1, **mix** 1, **weave** 1.

**interwoven,** *modif.* — *Syn.* knit, mingled, intermixed; see **knitted, mixed** 1, **woven.**

**intestinal,** *modif.* — *Syn.* inner, visceral, colonic, rectal, ventral, duodenal, celiac; see also **abdominal, internal** 2.

**intestine,** *n.* — *Syn.* alimentary canal, large intestine, small intestine, bowels, food passage, gut*, pipe*, spaghetti*; see also **intestines, organ** 2.

**intestines,** *pl.n.* — *Syn.* entrails, bowels, viscera, vitals, digestive organs, visceral parts, splanchnic parts, guts, innards*; see also **abdomen, insides.**
Parts of the human intestine include: large intestine, colon, cecum, small intestine, duodenum, jejunum, ileum, rectum, anus.

**in the meantime,** *modif.* — *Syn.* meanwhile, in the interim, until then, for the nonce; see **during, meanwhile.**

**in the offing,** *modif.* — *Syn.* forthcoming, projected, in the foreseeable future; see **coming** 1, **future, imminent.**

**intimacy,** *n.* — *Syn.* closeness, familiarity, confidence; see **affection** 1, **familiarity** 2, **friendship** 1.

**intimate,** *modif.* **1.** [Personal] — *Syn.* close, guarded, private, secret, near, familiar, trusted, confidential, inmost, innermost; see also **informal** 1, **private, secret** 1, **special** 1. — *Ant.* PUBLIC, open, unguarded.
**2.** [Close] — *Syn.* devoted, fond, fast; see **faithful, friendly** 1.
*See Synonym Study at* FAMILIAR.

**intimate,** *n.* — *Syn.* associate, constant companion, close friend, confidant; see **friend** 1.

**intimate,** *v.* — *Syn.* suggest, imply, infer; see **hint** 1.
*See Synonym Study at* SUGGEST.

**intimately,** *modif.* — *Syn.* closely, personally, informally, familiarly, confidentially, without reserve, privately, secretly, in detail, off the record; see also **lovingly, secretly.** — *Ant.* OPENLY, reservedly, publicly.

**intimation,** *n.* — *Syn.* implication, innuendo, tip; see **allusion, hint** 1, **suggestion** 1.

**intimidate,** *v.* — *Syn.* scare, overawe, cow, browbeat; see **frighten** 1, 2, **threaten** 1.

**intimidated,** *modif.* — *Syn.* frightened, terrified, cowed, daunted, browbeaten, bullied; see also **afraid** 1, 2, **horror-stricken.**

**intimidation,** *n.* — *Syn.* bullying, browbeating, coercion, threatening, cowing, daunting, frightening, terrorizing, demoralizing, awing, one-upmanship, scare tactics*.

**into,** *prep.* — *Syn.* inside, in the direction of, through to, to the middle of; see **in** 1, 2, **toward, within.**

**intolerable,** *modif.* — *Syn.* insufferable, insupportable, unendurable, unbearable, enough to drive one mad, extreme, excessive, past bearing, past enduring, too much for; see also **offensive** 2, **painful** 1.

**intolerance,** *n.* **1.** [Lack of willingness to tolerate] — *Syn.* bigotry, dogmatism, narrow-mindedness; see **fanaticism, prejudice.**

**2.** [An example of intolerance, sense 1] — *Syn.* racism, chauvinism, superpatriotism, religious fanaticism, provincialism, class prejudice, sexism, ageism, classism, sectionalism, regionalism, nationalism, fascism, imperialism, xenophobia; see also **jingoism, prejudice.**

**intolerant,** *modif.* — *Syn.* dogmatic, narrow, bigoted; see **prejudiced.**

**intonation,** *n.* — *Syn.* inflection, pitch pattern, tone, accent; see **accent** 2, 3, **inflection, sound** 2.

**intone,** *v.* — *Syn.* articulate, chant, recite; see **hum, sing** 1, **utter.**

*in toto* (Latin), *modif.* — *Syn.* fully, totally, entirely, in all; see **completely.**

**intoxicant,** *n.* **1.** [Alcohol] — *Syn.* alcoholic drink, liquor, booze*; see **alcohol, drink** 2.

**2.** [Drug] — *Syn.* narcotic, hallucinogen, dope*; see **drug** 2, **marijuana.**

**intoxicate,** *v.* **1.** [To make drunk] — *Syn.* inebriate, befuddle, muddle, drug, dope up, make tipsy, go to one's head*; see also **confuse, drug.**

**2.** [To excite] — *Syn.* exhilarate, stimulate, elate, turn on*; see **excite** 1, **exhilarate.**

**intoxicated,** *modif.* **1.** [Drunk] — *Syn.* inebriated, tipsy, plastered*; see **dizzy** 1, **drunk.**

**2.** [Unduly elated] — *Syn.* stimulated, exhilarated, enthralled, overwhelmed; see **excited, rapt.**

**intoxication,** *n.* — *Syn.* exhilaration, inebriation, intemperance; see **drunkenness.**

**intractability,** *n.* — *Syn.* mulishness, tenacity, obstinacy; see **determination, stubbornness.**

**intractable,** *modif.* — *Syn.* unmanageable, contrary, stubborn, recalcitrant; see **contrary** 4, **obstinate, unruly.**

**intransigent,** *modif.* — *Syn.* uncompromising, tenacious, stubborn; see **obstinate, resolute** 2.

**intransigently,** *modif.* — *Syn.* stubbornly, obdurately, uncompromisingly; see **firmly** 1, 2, **obstinately.**

**intrepid,** *modif.* — *Syn.* fearless, courageous, bold, dauntless; see **brave** 1.

*See Synonym Study at* BRAVE.

**intrepidity,** *n.* — *Syn.* bravery, assurance, boldness; see **courage** 1, **determination** 2, **endurance** 2.

**intricacy,** *n.* — *Syn.* complication, elaborateness, complexity; see **confusion** 2, **difficulty** 1, 2.

**intricate,** *modif.* — *Syn.* involved, elaborate, tricky, tangled; see **complex** 2, **difficult** 1, 2, **obscure** 1.

*See Synonym Study at* COMPLEX.

**intrigue,** *n.* **1.** [Plot] — *Syn.* scheme, conspiracy, cabal, machination, plan, secret arrangement, complication, ruse, artifice, design, dodge, contrivance, collusion, maneuver, maneuvering, manipulation, double-dealing, secret plot, wire-pulling*, deal*, game*; see also **plot** 1, **trick** 1.

**2.** [Love affair] — *Syn.* liaison, amour, affair, interlude, entanglement, attachment, intimacy, infatuation, flirtation, romance, hush-hush affair*; see also **affair** 2.

*See Synonym Study at* PLOT.

**intrigue,** *v.* **1.** [To fascinate] — *Syn.* interest, pique, attract, beguile; see **attract** 2, **charm** 1, **entertain** 1, **fascinate.**

**2.** [To plot] — *Syn.* scheme, conspire, connive; see **maneuver, plan** 1.

**intrigued,** *modif.* — *Syn.* attracted, absorbed, captivated; see **charmed, entertained** 2, **fascinated, interested** 1.

**intriguing,** *modif.* **1.** [Fascinating] — *Syn.* engaging, attractive, delightful, absorbing; see **charming, entertaining, interesting.**

**2.** [Sly] — *Syn.* crafty, clever, tricky; see **sly** 1.

**intrinsic,** *modif.* — *Syn.* essential, central, natural; see **fundamental** 1, **inherent.**

**introduce,** *v.* **1.** [To bring in] — *Syn.* import, carry in, transport; see **carry, import** 1.

**2.** [To present] — *Syn.* set forth, submit, advance; see **offer** 1, **propose** 1.

**3.** [To make strangers acquainted] — *Syn.* present, acquaint, give an introduction, make known, hold a debut for, put on speaking terms, do the honors*, give a knockdown*, break the ice*.

**4.** [To institute] — *Syn.* launch, found, originate, inaugurate; see **begin** 1, **organize** 2.

**5.** [To insert] — *Syn.* put in, add, enter; see **include** 2, **inject** 2, **interject.**

**6.** [To begin] — *Syn.* start, open, preface; see **begin** 1, **precede.**

**introduced,** *modif.* **1.** [Brought in] — *Syn.* made current, made known, imported, popularized; see **foreign** 2, **received.**

**2.** [Made acquainted] — *Syn.* acquainted with, on speaking terms, not unknown to each other; see **familiar with.**

**introduction,** *n.* **1.** [The act of bringing in] — *Syn.* admittance, initiation, inception, installation, influx, ingress, institution, induction, inauguration, launching, debut; see also **entrance** 1.

**2.** [The act of making strangers acquainted] — *Syn.* presentation, debut, meeting, formal acquaintance, preliminary encounter.

**3.** [Introductory knowledge] — *Syn.* initiation, first acquaintance, elementary statement, first contact, start, awakening, enlightenment, first taste, baptism, preliminary training, basic principles; see also **initiation** 1.

**4.** [An introductory explanation] — *Syn.* preface, foreword, preamble, prologue, prefatory note, prelude, overture, intro*, opening, proem, prolegomena, dedication.

**5.** [A work supplying introductory knowledge] — *Syn.* primer, basic text, beginner's book, elements, foundation, manual, handbook, first book, grammar, survey, essentials; see also **book** 1, **text** 1.

---

**SYN.** — **introduction,** in strict usage, refers to the preliminary section of a book, etc. that explains and leads into the subject proper; **preface** refers to a statement preliminary to a book, written by the author or editor and explaining the purpose, plan, or preparation of the work; the preface may also include acknowledgments for help or for permissions granted for use of previously published material; **foreword** is a brief preface written by someone other than the author; **preamble** refers to a formal, but usually brief, introduction to a constitution, treaty, etc.; **prologue** applies to the preliminary section as of a play or poem, serving as an introduction and, in the play, frequently spoken by one of the characters

---

**introductory,** *modif.* **1.** [Preliminary] — *Syn.* prefatory, initial, incipient, initiatory, opening, early, prior, starting, beginning, precursory, preparatory, primary, original, anterior, provisional, explanatory, background; see also **first** 1. — *Ant.* PRINCIPAL, substantial, secondary.
**2.** [Elementary] — *Syn.* rudimentary, basic, beginning; see sense 1; **fundamental** 1.
**introspection,** *n.* — *Syn.* self-examination, self-analysis, rumination, brooding, meditation, contemplation, soul-searching, self-questioning, introversion; see also **thought** 1.
**introspective,** *modif.* — *Syn.* contemplative, reflective, subjective, inner-directed; see **thoughtful** 1.
**introversion,** *n.* — *Syn.* inner-directedness, preoccupation with self, withdrawal; see **egotism, introspection, reserve** 2, **retirement** 2.
**introvert,** *n.* — *Syn.* shy person, brooder, self-observer, egoist, egotist, narcissist, autist, solitary, loner*, lone wolf*, wallflower*.
**introverted,** *modif.* — *Syn.* withdrawn, indrawn, introspective, shy; see **egotistic** 1, **humble** 1.
**intrude,** *v.* — *Syn.* meddle, interfere, interrupt, obtrude, interlope, impose, trespass, encroach, interpose, butt in*; see also **interrupt** 2, **meddle** 1.

---

*SYN.* — **intrude** implies the forcing of oneself or something upon another without invitation, permission, or welcome /to *intrude* upon another's privacy/; **obtrude** connotes even more strongly the distractive nature or the undesirability of the invasion /side issues keep *obtruding* into the discussion/; **interlope** implies an intrusion upon the rights or privileges of another to the disadvantage or harm of the latter /the *interloping* merchants have ruined our trade/; **butt in or into** is a slang term implying intrusion in a meddling or officious way /stop *butting into* my business/ See also Synonym Study at TRESPASS.

---

**intruder,** *n.* — *Syn.* trespasser, prowler, thief, unwelcome guest, meddler, interloper, invader, encroacher, unwanted person, crasher*, gate-crasher*, interferer, interrupter, disrupting element, busybody, snoop; see also **busybody, robber, trouble** 2.
**intrusion,** *n.* — *Syn.* interruption, forced entrance, trespass, intervention, interposition, meddling, obtrusion, encroachment, invasion, incursion, inroad, infraction, overrunning, unwelcome suggestion, overstepping, impingement, imposition, transgression, nose-in*, horn-in*, muscle-in*; see also **interference** 2.
**intrusive,** *modif.* — *Syn.* interfering, untimely, impertinent, nosy*; see **meddlesome, rude** 2.
**intuition,** *n.* — *Syn.* presentiment, foreknowledge, inspiration, sixth sense; see **feeling** 4, **hunch** 2.
**intuitive,** *modif.* — *Syn.* instantaneously apprehended, untaught, instinctive; see **automatic** 2, **habitual** 1, **inherent, natural** 1, **spontaneous**.

**inundate,** *v.* — *Syn.* submerge, engulf, deluge, overwhelm; see **flood, immerse** 1.
**inundation,** *n.* — *Syn.* deluge, torrent, tide; see **flood** 1.
**inure,** *v.* — *Syn.* accustom, habituate, toughen; see **familiarize with, harden** 3, **strengthen, teach** 1.
**invade,** *v.* **1.** [To enter with armed force] — *Syn.* force a landing, penetrate, overrun; see **attack** 1.
**2.** [To encroach upon] — *Syn.* infringe on, trespass, interfere with; see **meddle** 1.
*See Synonym Study at* TRESPASS.
**invader,** *n.* — *Syn.* trespasser, alien, attacking force; see **attacker, enemy** 1, **intruder.**
**invalid,** *modif.* — *Syn.* fallacious, unreasonable, indefensible, null and void; see **illogical, void** 1, **wrong** 2.
**invalid,** *n.* — *Syn.* disabled person, handicapped person, sickly person, patient, convalescent, valetudinarian, paralytic, cripple, weakling, sufferer, shut-in, incurable, consumptive, tubercular, neurasthenic, bedridden person, bed case*; see also **patient.**
**invalidate,** *v.* — *Syn.* annul, refute, nullify; see **cancel** 2, **revoke.**
**invalidism,** *n.* — *Syn.* feebleness, infirmity, sickness; see **illness** 1, **weakness** 1.
**invalidity,** *n.* — *Syn.* falsity, inconsistency, unsoundness; see **fallacy** 1.
**invaluable,** *modif.* — *Syn.* priceless, valuable, precious; see **valuable** 1.
*See Synonym Study at* EXPENSIVE.
**invariable,** *modif.* — *Syn.* unchanging, uniform, static; see **constant** 1, **perpetual** 1, **regular** 3.
**invariability,** *n.* — *Syn.* constancy, uniformity, consistency, unchangingness; see **regularity, stability** 1.
**invariably,** *modif.* — *Syn.* perpetually, constantly, unfailingly, habitually; see **always** 1, **customarily, regularly** 1, 2.
**invasion,** *n.* — *Syn.* forced entrance, intrusion, incursion, aggression; see **attack** 1.
**invective,** *n.* — *Syn.* denunciation, vituperation, condemnation; see **accusation** 2, **blame** 1, **insult.**
**inveigh,** *v.* — *Syn.* rail, protest, reproach, admonish; see **censure, denounce.**
**inveigle,** *v.* — *Syn.* entice, cajole, ensnare, trick; see **coax, influence, tempt, urge** 2.
*See Synonym Study at* TEMPT.
**invent,** *v.* **1.** [To create] — *Syn.* originate, devise, fashion, form, project, design, develop, discover, coin, improvise, contrive, execute, carry into execution, conceive, author, plan, formulate, think up, make up, bring into being, bear, turn out, forge, make, ad-lib*, hatch*, wing it*, dream up*, cook up*; see also **compose** 3, **create** 2, **discover, produce** 2.
**2.** [To fabricate] — *Syn.* misrepresent, create out of thin air, simulate, fake, feign, make believe, trump up, equivocate, falsify, make up, conjure up, think up, misstate, concoct, cook up*; see also **lie** 1.
**invention,** *n.* **1.** [Ingenuity] — *Syn.* inventiveness, imagination, creativity; see **originality.**
**2.** [An original device] — *Syn.* contrivance, contraption, design; see **contrivance** 2, **device** 1, **discovery** 2.
**inventive,** *modif.* — *Syn.* creative, imaginative, resourceful, innovative; see **artistic** 2, **clever** 1, **original** 2.
**inventor,** *n.* — *Syn.* author, originator, creator; see **architect** 1, **author** 1, **designer.**
**inventory,** *n.* **1.** [A list] — *Syn.* stock book, itemization, register; see **catalog, file** 2, **index** 2, **list, record** 1, **table** 2.
**take inventory** — *Syn.* take stock, examine the books, look over; see **examine** 1, **inventory** *v.*

**1.** [The act of taking stock] — *Syn.* inspection, review, examination, tabulation, checking, counting, accounting, investigation; see also **summary**.

**2.** [Store of goods] — *Syn.* stock, merchandise, wares; see **commodity**.

*See Synonym Study at* LIST.

**inventory,** *v.* — *Syn.* take stock of, look over, go over, account for, count, tabulate, itemize, check, investigate, review, examine, inspect, list, catalog, audit, tally; see also **file** 1, **list** 1, **record** 1.

**inverse,** *modif.* — *Syn.* inverted, converse, transposed; see **opposite** 1, **reversed**.

**inversion,** *n.* — *Syn.* transposition, reversal, contradiction; see **conversion** 1, **opposite**.

**invert,** *v.* **1.** [To upset] — *Syn.* overturn, turn upside-down, tip; see **upset** 1.

**2.** [To reverse] — *Syn.* change, rearrange, transpose; see **exchange** 1.

**3.** [To change] — *Syn.* alter, modify, convert; see **change** 1.

**invertebrate,** *modif.* — *Syn.* cowardly, spineless, weak, indecisive; see **cowardly** 2, **irresolute**.

**invertebrate,** *n.* — *Syn.* nonskeletal creature, spineless animal, protozoan, arthropod; see **clam, crab, insect, jellyfish, lobster, shellfish, worm** 1.

**invest,** *v.* — *Syn.* put money into, lay out, spend, lend on security, advance, entrust, give money over, buy stocks, make an investment, loan, lend, sink money into, finance, fund, endow, reinvest, roll over, buy into*, salt away*, put up the dough*; see also **buy** 1.

**investigate,** *v.* — *Syn.* inquire into, look into, review; see **examine** 1, **study** 1.

**investigated,** *modif.* — *Syn.* examined, tried, tested, inspected, searched, questioned, probed, explored, considered, measured, checked, studied, researched, reviewed, made the subject of an investigation, given a hearing, subjected to scrutiny, worked on, thought out, thought through, scrutinized, put to the test, gone over, gone into, inquired into, cross-examined; see also **reviewed**.

**investigating,** *modif.* — *Syn.* fact-finding, investigative, inspecting; see **research**.

**investigation,** *n.* — *Syn.* inquiry, search, research, probe; see **examination** 1, **study** 2.

**investigator,** *n.* — *Syn.* inquirer, researcher, detective, tester, inspector, reviewer, analyst, auditor, reviewing board member, prosecutor; see also **examiner**.

Investigators include: sleuth, detective, spy, counter-spy, plainclothesman, police inspector, district attorney, prosecuting attorney, government agent, Federal agent, fed*, census taker, insurance investigator, Treasury agent, T-man, FBI agent, CIA agent, Gestapo agent, double agent, narcotics agent, narc*, ombudsman, plain-clothes man, secret police, secret agent, informer, G-man*, snooper*, dick*, operative*, undercover man*, flatfoot*, private eye*, spotter*; see also **detective, policeman, spy**.

**investiture,** *n.* — *Syn.* induction, inauguration, instatement, admission; see **installation** 1.

**investment,** *n.* — *Syn.* endowment, grant, loan, expenditure, expense, backing, speculation, venture, disintermediation, financing, finance, purchase, advance, bail, plunge*, grease*, stake*, nut*; see also **property** 1.

Types of investment include: stocks, bonds, securities, treasury bills, mutual funds, money market funds, certificate of deposit, CD, individual retirement account, IRA, annuities, real estate, capital goods, insurance liens, debentures, futures.

**inveterate,** *modif.* — *Syn.* ingrained, confirmed, deep-rooted; see **chronic, habitual** 1, **permanent** 2.

*See Synonym Study at* CHRONIC.

**invidious,** *modif.* — *Syn.* injurious, discriminatory, repugnant, odious; see **harmful, offensive** 2, **unfair** 1.

**invigorate,** *v.* — *Syn.* energize, stimulate, refresh, exhilarate; see **animate** 1, **excite** 1.

*See Synonym Study at* ANIMATE.

**invigorating,** *modif.* — *Syn.* refreshing, exhilarating, bracing; see **stimulating**.

**invincible,** *modif.* — *Syn.* unconquerable, invulnerable, insuperable, impregnable; see **powerful** 1, **strong** 1, 2.

**inviolability,** *n.* — *Syn.* indestructibility, purity, sanctity; see **consecration, holiness** 2, **stability** 1.

**inviolable,** *modif.* **1.** [Divine] — *Syn.* holy, sacred, sacrosanct; see **divine** 2.

**2.** [Indestructible] — *Syn.* durable, unbreakable, stable, unassailable; see **permanent** 2.

**inviolate,** *modif.* — *Syn.* unbroken, intact, untouched; see **perfect** 2, **whole** 2.

**invisibility,** *n.* — *Syn.* obscurity, concealment, camouflage, indistinctness, imperceptibility, invisibleness, indefiniteness, seclusion, latency, cloudiness, haziness, fogginess, mistiness, duskiness, nebulousness, darkness, gloominess, gloom, insubstantiality, incorporeality, immateriality, intangibility, disappearance, vagueness, indefiniteness, indiscernibility, indistinguishability, unnoticeability.

**invisible,** *modif.* **1.** [Beyond unaided vision] — *Syn.* imperceptible, undetectable, indiscernible, indistinguishable, intangible, ungraspable, out of sight, indistinct, infinitesimal, microscopic, not visible, beyond the visual range, unseeable, unviewable, supernatural, ghostly, wraithlike, unseen, undisclosed, covert, occult, airy, impalpable, ethereal, ideal, unreal, vaporous, gaseous, supersensory; see also **dark** 1, **transparent** 1. — *Ant.* REAL, visible, material.

**2.** [Not apparent] — *Syn.* veiled, shrouded, inconspicuous; see **hidden** 2, **obscure** 1, **vague** 2.

**invisibly,** *modif.* — *Syn.* imperceptibly, undetectably, out of sight, not visibly, uncertainly, obscurely, inconspicuously, indistinctly, in a hidden manner, secretly, in an unknown manner; see also **vaguely**.

**invitation,** *n.* **1.** [The act of inviting] — *Syn.* summons, solicitation, request, bidding, call, compliments, bid*, invite*; see also **request**.

**2.** [That which invites] — *Syn.* note, card, message, call, encouragement, overture, offer, proposition, proposal, petition, enticement, temptation, attraction, allurement, lure, open door, prompting, urge, pressure, reason, motive, ground, come-on*; see also **appeal** 1, **letter** 2, **suggestion** 1.

**invite,** *v.* **1.** [To request the presence of] — *Syn.* ask, have over, have in, ask out, bid come, extend an invitation to, send an invitation to, request, summon, beckon, call, request the pleasure of one's company, include in the guest list, request an R.S.V.P.

**2.** [To ask politely or offer an inducement to] — *Syn.* bid, request, induce, beg, suggest, encourage, welcome, entice, tempt, solicit, entreat, pray, supplicate, petition, persuade, prevail on, insist, ask insistently, press, ply, propose, lure, allure, attract, draw, call forth, court, beseech, importune, crave, appeal to, implore, call upon, sue, beg leave; see also **urge** 2. — *Ant.* DISCOURAGE, repulse, rebuff.

*See Synonym Study at* CALL.

**inviting,** *modif.* — *Syn.* appealing, alluring, cordial, tempting, attractive, winning, winsome, captivating, agreeable, engaging, open, encouraging, delightful, pleasing, enticing, persuasive, magnetic, fascinating, intriguing, provocative, bewitching; see also **charming**. — *Ant.* repellent, repulsive, forbidding.

**invoice**, *n.* — *Syn.* bill, statement, bill of goods, bill of lading, bill of shipment, receipt, manifest, itemized account, checklist, inventory, reckoning, request for payment, statement of account, tab★; see also **statement** 3.

**invoke**, *v.* **1.** [To call upon] — *Syn.* request, entreat, appeal to; see **beg** 1.
**2.** [To summon] — *Syn.* send for, bid, conjure up; see **summon** 1.

**involuntary**, *modif.* — *Syn.* unintentional, uncontrolled, instinctive, spontaneous; see **automatic** 2, **habitual** 1, **spontaneous**.
*See Synonym Study at* SPONTANEOUS.

**involution**, *n.* — *Syn.* intricacy, complication, complexity; see **difficulty** 1, 2.

**involve**, *v.* — *Syn.* include, draw into, compromise, implicate, entangle, entail, link, connect, incriminate, associate, affect, concern, relate to, catch up, wrap up in, denote, argue, suggest, prove, comprise, point to, commit, mix up, bring up; see also **include** 1, **mean** 1, **occupy** 3, **require** 2.
*See Synonym Study at* INCLUDE.

**involved**, *modif.* **1.** [Interested] — *Syn.* implicated, affected, concerned, entangled, incriminated, embroiled, caught up, wrapped up, immersed, absorbed, preoccupied, engrossed, committed, engaged, dedicated, associated, connected, mixed up in★, mixed up with★, into★, in on★; see also **interested** 2.
**2.** [Complicated] — *Syn.* intricate, complex, tangled; see **complex** 2, **confused** 2, **difficult** 2.
*See Synonym Study at* COMPLEX.

**involvement**, *n.* **1.** [Difficulty] — *Syn.* entanglement, quandary, crisis, embarrassment; see **difficulty** 1, 2.
**2.** [Connection] — *Syn.* engagement, embroilment, association, responsibility; see **relationship**.
**3.** [Engrossment] — *Syn.* intentness, study, preoccupation; see **reflection** 1.

**invulnerability**, *n.* — *Syn.* assurance, impenetrability, strength; see **protection** 2, **safety** 1, **security** 1.

**invulnerable**, *modif.* — *Syn.* strong, invincible, unassailable, secure; see **immune**, **safe** 1, **strong** 2.

**inward**, *modif.* **1.** [Moving into] — *Syn.* penetrating, ingoing, through, incoming, entering, inbound, inpouring, infiltrating, inflowing; see also **penetrating** 1.
**2.** [Placed within] — *Syn.* inside, internal, interior; see **in** 1, **within**.
**3.** [Private] — *Syn.* spiritual, intellectual, intimate; see **inner**, **internal** 1, **private**.

**inwardly**, *modif.* — *Syn.* by nature, within, inside, deep down, internally, privately, at heart, fundamentally, basically, not outwardly, not visibly, below the surface, secretly; see also **internally**, **naturally** 2.

**ion**, *n.* — *Syn.* cation, anion, electrically charged particle; see **atom** 2.

**iota**, *n.* — *Syn.* grain, particle, speck; see **bit** 1.

**irascibility**, *n.* — *Syn.* wrath, irritability, quick temper, testiness; see **anger**, **annoyance** 1.

**irascible**, *modif.* — *Syn.* peevish, cranky, irritable; see **angry**, **irritable**.
*See Synonym Study at* IRRITABLE.

**irate**, *modif.* — *Syn.* enraged, furious, incensed; see **angry**.

**ire**, *n.* — *Syn.* anger, wrath, fury, rage; see **anger**.
*See Synonym Study at* ANGER.

**iridescence**, *n.* — *Syn.* luminosity, phosphorescence, radiance, opalescence; see **color** 1, **light** 1.

**iridescent**, *modif.* — *Syn.* pearly, nacreous, shimmering, prismatic, rainbow-colored, multicolored, polychromatic, opalescent, lustrous; see also **bright** 1, 2.

**iris**, *n.* — *Syn.* flag, blue flag, yellow flag, fleur-de-lis, bearded iris, Siberian iris, Japanese iris, Dutch iris, orrisroot, gladdon, *Iris germanica* (Latin); see also **flower** 2, **plant**.

**Irish**, *modif.* — *Syn.* Celtic, Hibernian, Gaelic, Irish Gaelic, Goidelic, Old Irish, Middle Irish, from the old sod★.

**irk**, *v.* — *Syn.* irritate, annoy, exasperate; see **bother** 2, 3.
*See Synonym Study at* BOTHER.

**irksome**, *modif.* — *Syn.* tiresome, tedious, troublesome; see **disturbing**.

**iron**, *modif.* **1.** [Made of iron] — *Syn.* ferrous, ferruginous, ironclad, ironcased, ironshod.
**2.** [Having the qualities of iron] — *Syn.* hard, robust, strong, firm, indomitable, unyielding, dense, insensible, inflexible, adamant, cruel, stubborn, implacable, heavy; see also **firm** 2.

**iron**, *n.* **1.** [A metallic element] — *Syn.* pig iron, cast iron, wrought iron, sheet iron, coke, *Fe* (chemical symbol); see also **alloy**, **metal**.
**2.** [An implement or apparatus made, or originally made, of iron]
Items referred to as irons include: flatiron, branding iron, golf club, midiron, heavy iron, driving iron, light iron, shackles, manacles, handcuffs, iron pan, sadiron, electric iron, press, mangle, hardware, curling iron.
**3.** [An appliance for pressing clothes] — *Syn.* presser, steam iron, Teflon iron, travel iron, electric iron, press, mangle; see also **appliance**.
**having many irons in the fire** — *Syn.* engaged, active, occupied; see **busy** 1.

**iron**, *v.* — *Syn.* press, mangle, roll, finish, smooth, smooth out, steam, give a *coup de fer* (French); see also **flatten**, **smooth** 1.

**ironed**, *modif.* — *Syn.* pressed, flat, flattened; see **smooth** 1.

**ironic**, *modif.* **1.** [Said of events, works, statements, and the like] — *Syn.* ironical, paradoxical, contradictory, incongruous, satiric, satirical, wry, sardonic, sarcastic, mocking, humorous, facetious, tongue-in-cheek, ambiguous, double-edged, equivocal, nonliteral, subtle, dry, unexpected, implausible, ridiculous, exaggerated, twisted, critical, cynical, sneering, chaffing, derisive, caustic, biting, cutting, trenchant, incisive, mordant, scathing, pungent, bitter, spicy, acrid, jibing, disparaging, uncomplimentary, backbiting; see also sense 2, **facetious**, **sarcastic**.
**2.** [Said especially of people] — *Syn.* sarcastic, sardonic, satirical, quick-witted, witty, clever, sharp, keen, quipmaking, cynical, contemptuous, scornful, irreverent; see also sense 1, **facetious**, **witty**.
*See Synonym Study at* SARCASTIC.

**ironing**, *n.* — *Syn.* pressing, steam-pressing, mangling, smoothing, doing flatwork, flattening.

**iron out**, *v.* — *Syn.* compromise, resolve, settle differences, reach an agreement about; see **agree**, **arbitrate**, **negotiate** 1, **settle** 9.

**irons**, *pl.n.* — *Syn.* shackles, manacles, fetters; see **chains**, **handcuffs**.
**in irons** — *Syn.* shackled, fettered, tied, imprisoned; see **bound** 1, **confined** 3.

**ironworks**, *n.* — *Syn.* furnace, hearth, forge; see **factory**.

**irony**, *n.* — *Syn.* sarcasm, wit, humor, paradox, incon-

gruity, double meaning, twist, absurdity, ridicule, raillery, mockery, burlesque, parody, quip, banter, derision, jibe, taunt, cynicism, black humor, gallows humor, repartee, contradiction, ambiguity, equivocation, innuendo, backhanded compliment*; see also **sarcasm.**
See Synonym Study at WIT.
**irradiate,** v. — Syn. illuminate, lighten, brighten; see **light** 1.
**irradiation,** n. — Syn. reflection, radiation, radiance; see **light** 1.
**irrational,** modif. 1. [Illogical] — Syn. unreasonable, specious, fallacious, untenable; see **illogical, wrong** 2.
2. [Stupid] — Syn. senseless, silly, ridiculous, absurd; see **stupid** 1.

---

**SYN.** — **irrational** implies mental unsoundness or may be used to stress the utterly illogical nature of that which is directly contrary to reason [an irrational belief that everybody was his enemy]; **unreasonable** implies bad judgment, willfulness, prejudice, etc. as responsible for that which is not justified by reason [unreasonable demands]

---

**irrationality,** n. 1. [Irrationality] — Syn. absurdity, illogicality, invalidity; see **inconsistency.**
2. [Senselessness] — Syn. unreasonableness, insanity, idiocy; see **nonsense** 1, 2, **stupidity** 1, 2.
**irrationally,** modif. — Syn. illogically, unreasonably, stupidly; see **foolishly.**
**irreclaimable,** modif. — Syn. irreparable, incorrigible, beyond hope; see **hopeless** 2, **irreparable.**
**irreconcilable,** modif. — Syn. hostile, conflicting, unresolvable, opposed; see **incompatible, unfriendly** 1.
**irrecoverable,** modif. — Syn. irretrievable, unrectifiable, unremediable; see **gone** 2, **hopeless** 2, **lost** 1.
**irredeemable,** modif. — Syn. irreparable, incurable, beyond redemption; see **hopeless** 2, **irreparable.**
**irreducible,** modif. — Syn. immutable, irrevocable, unchangeable, intransmutable, incapable of being diminished, indelible, indestructible, imperishable, indissoluble, inextinguishable, basic, fundamental; see also **firm** 1, **permanent** 2.
**irrefutable,** modif. — Syn. evident, final, proven, undeniable; see **accurate** 1, **certain** 3, **conclusive, obvious** 2.
**irregular,** modif. 1. [Not even] — Syn. uneven, spasmodic, fitful, uncertain, erratic, variable, aberrant, random, unsettled, inconstant, unsteady, fragmentary, unsystematic, occasional, infrequent, fluctuating, faltering, wavering, recurrent, intermittent, discontinuous, sporadic, changeable, capricious, casual, shifting, unmethodical, unreliable, unpredictable, jerky, up and down*; see also **changing, unsteady** 2. — Ant. REGULAR, even, punctual.
2. [Not customary] — Syn. unique, extraordinary, unconventional, unorthodox, anomalous, unnatural, abnormal, peculiar; see also **different** 1, **unusual** 2.
3. [Questionable] — Syn. strange, improper, dubious; see **questionable** 2, **suspicious** 2.
4. [Not regular in form or outline] — Syn. not uniform, crooked, devious, unsymmetrical, asymmetrical, nonsymmetrical, uneven, unequal, craggy, hilly, broken, jagged, aberrant, notched, serrate, eccentric, elliptic, elliptical, bumpy, meandering, zigzagged, bent, unaligned, amorphous, variable, wobbly, lumpy, off balance, off center, protuberant, lopsided, pockmarked, scarred, crinkled, bristling, bumpy, sprawling, out of

proportion, flawed, damaged, imperfect, cockeyed*, gallywampus*; see also **bent, crooked** 1.

---

**SYN.** — **irregular** implies deviation from the customary or established rule, procedure, etc. [irregular conduct]; **abnormal** and **anomalous** imply deviation from the normal condition or from the ordinary type, **abnormal** stressing atypical form or character [a man of abnormal height], and **anomalous,** stressing an exceptional condition or circumstance [in the anomalous position of a leader without followers]; **unnatural** applies to that which is contrary to the order of nature or to natural laws [an unnatural appetite for chalk]

---

**irregularity,** n. 1. [Unevenness] — Syn. roughness, bumpiness, jaggedness, stop, break, uncertainty, aberration, shift, change, twist, bump, hump, flaw, imperfection, dent, hole, variation, variability, spasm, deviation, inconsistency, distortion, asymmetry; see also **roughness** 1, **variation** 1, 2.
2. [Something that is irregular] — Syn. peculiarity, singularity, anomaly, abnormality, strangeness, uniqueness, exception, excess, unorthodoxy, malfunction, malformation, deviation, dispensation, allowance, exemption, privilege, nonconformity, unconformity, innovation, oddity, eccentricity, rarity, looseness, laxity; see also **characteristic, quirk.** — Ant. CUSTOM, regularity, rule.
3. [A suspicious or illegal occurrence] — Syn. breach, infringement, violation; see **crime** 1, **sin, violation** 1.
**irregularly,** modif. — Syn. erratically, intermittently, periodically, episodically, sporadically, at intervals, at irregular intervals, by fits and starts, fitfully, unevenly, spasmodically, by snatches, by jerks, by turns, off and on, hit or miss*; see also **unevenly.**
**irrelevance,** modif. — Syn. irrelevancy, immateriality, inapplicability, impertinence, lack of connection, remoteness, unrelatedness, inappositeness, inappropriateness, incongruity, inconsistency, insignificance, triviality; see also **inconsistency.**
**irrelevant,** modif. — Syn. inapplicable, unrelated, extraneous, impertinent, off the topic, inappropriate, inconsequent, inconsequential, immaterial, unconnected, inapropos, not germane, beside the point, off the point, foreign, beside the question, out of order, out of place, not to the purpose, pointless, trivial, not connected with, not pertaining to, without reference to, out of the way, remote, tangential, neither here nor there*; see also **trivial, unnecessary.**
**irreligion,** n. — Syn. atheism, disbelief, skepticism; see **atheism, doubt** 1.
**irreligious,** modif. — Syn. unbelieving, ungodly, profane, sacrilegious; see **atheistic, impious.**
**irremediable,** modif. — Syn. irreparable, incurable, dire; see **deadly** 1, **hopeless** 2, **irreparable.**
**irremovable,** modif. — Syn. stable, unchangeable, fixed; see **established** 1, **firm** 1, **permanent** 2.
**irreparable,** modif. — Syn. incurable, hopeless, irreversible, irremediable, irretrievable, irredeemable, irreclaimable, ruined, unsalvageable, incorrigible; see also **broken** 1, **destroyed, hopeless** 2, **ruined** 1.
**irreplaceable,** modif. — Syn. unique, one of a kind, nonrenewable, invaluable; see **unique** 1, **valuable** 1.
**irrepressible,** modif. — Syn. insuppressible, unconstrained, uncontrollable, uninhibited, unrestrained, uncontainable, effervescent, bubbling over; see also **lively** 2, **unruly.**
**irreproachable,** modif. — Syn. faultless, blameless, impeccable; see **innocent** 4, **perfect** 2.

**irresistible,** *modif.* **1.** [Overwhelming] — *Syn.* compelling, overpowering, invincible; see **overwhelming** 1, **persuasive, powerful** 1.
**2.** [Fascinating] — *Syn.* lovable, alluring, enchanting; see **charming, tempting.**
**irresolute,** *modif.* — *Syn.* indecisive, undecided, wavering, faltering, vacillating, uncertain, fluctuating, unsettled, hesitant, hesitating, doubting, ambivalent, unstable, inconstant, fickle, fearful, timid, undetermined, wobbly, halfhearted, weak-willed, shilly-shallying, pussyfooting*, wishy-washy*; see also **changeable** 1, **shaky** 1, **undecided.** — *Ant.* RESOLUTE, firm, determined.
**irrespective of,** *modif.* — *Syn.* regardless of, independent of, discounting, apart from; see **notwithstanding, regardless** 2.
**irresponsible,** *modif.* — *Syn.* untrustworthy, unreliable, capricious, flighty, fickle, giddy, thoughtless, rash, reckless, undependable, unstable, loose, lax, immoral, shiftless, careless, negligent, unpredictable, wild, devil-may-care; see also **careless** 1, **changeable** 1, **unreliable** 1. — *Ant.* RESPONSIBLE, trustworthy, dependable.
**irresponsive,** *modif.* — *Syn.* taciturn, unmoved, unresponsive; see **indifferent** 1, **unconcerned.**
**irretrievable,** *modif.* — *Syn.* unrecoverable, irrecoverable, irreparable, irrevocable; see **gone** 2, **lost** 1, **irreparable.**
**irreverence,** *n.* **1.** [Blasphemy] — *Syn.* sacrilege, sinfulness, profanity, impiety; see **blasphemy, heresy.**
**2.** [Indignity] — *Syn.* disrespect, ridicule, discourtesy; see **insult, rudeness.**
**irreverent,** *modif.* — *Syn.* profane, sacrilegious, disrespectful; see **impious, rude** 2.
**irreversible,** *modif.* — *Syn.* unchangeable, invariable, immutable; see **constant** 1, **resolute** 2.
**irrevocable,** *modif.* — *Syn.* permanent, unalterable, irreversible, indelible; see **certain** 3, **conclusive, inevitable.**
**irrigate,** *v.* — *Syn.* water, spray, sprinkle, pass water through, install an artificial watering system, divert water to, soak, inundate; see also **flood.**
**irrigation,** *n.* — *Syn.* watering, sprinkling, spraying, flooding, inundation, soaking, fertilization, making productive.
**irritability,** *n.* — *Syn.* irascibility, peevishness, impatience; see **anger, annoyance** 1, **irritation** 1.
**irritable,** *modif.* — *Syn.* sensitive, irascible, touchy, testy, ill-tempered, huffy, peevish, petulant, fractious, tense, high-strung, contentious, disputatious, resentful, fretting, carping, crabbed, hypercritical, out of humor, bearish, quick-tempered, short-tempered, easily offended, choleric, splenetic, glum, complaining, brooding, dissatisfied, plaintive, snarling, grumbling, surly, gloomy, ill-natured, morose, moody, fidgety, snappish, waspish, cantankerous, crotchety, curmudgeonly, captious, fretful, querulous, hypersensitive, ill-humored, annoyed, cross, cranky, churlish, grouchy, gruff, short, shrewish, sulky, sullen, crusty*, snappy*, having a short fuse*, thin-skinned*, pickle-pussed*, grumpy*, sour-bellied*; see also **critical** 2, **excitable, quarrelsome** 2. — *Ant.* PLEASANT, agreeable, good-natured.

*SYN.* — **irritable** implies quick excitability to annoyance or anger, usually resulting from emotional tension, restlessness, physical indisposition, etc.; **irascible** and **choleric** are applied to persons who are hot-tempered and can be roused to a fit of anger at the slightest irritation; **splenetic** suggests a peevish moroseness in one quick to vent his malice or spite; **touchy** applies to one

who is acutely irritable or sensitive and is too easily offended; **cranky** and **cross** suggest moods in which one cannot be easily pleased or satisfied, **cranky** because of stubborn notions or whims, and **cross** because of ill humor

**irritant,** *n.* — *Syn.* annoyance, bother, burden, nuisance; see **trouble** 2.
**irritate,** *v.* **1.** [To bother] — *Syn.* provoke, annoy, exasperate, pester, peeve, nettle; see also **bother** 2, 3, **disturb** 2.
**2.** [To inflame] — *Syn.* redden, chafe, swell, erupt, pain, sting, burn, aggravate; see also **hurt** 4, **itch** 1.

*SYN.* — **irritate,** the broadest in scope of these terms, may suggest temporary superficial impatience, or constant annoyance in, or an outburst of anger from, the person stirred to feeling /their smugness *irritated* him/; to **provoke** is to arouse strong annoyance or resentment, or, sometimes, vindictive anger [*provoked* by an insult]; **nettle** implies irritation that stings or piques rather than infuriates /sly, *nettling* remarks/; **exasperate** implies intense irritation such as exhausts one's patience or makes one lose one's self-control [*exasperating* impudence]; **peeve,** an informal word, means to cause to be annoyed, cross, or fretful /he seems *peeved* about something/

**irritated,** *modif.* — *Syn.* annoyed, irked, disturbed, bothered; see **angry, troubled** 1.
**irritating,** *modif.* — *Syn.* vexatious, bothersome, trying; see **disturbing.**
**irritation,** *n.* **1.** [Sensitivity] — *Syn.* soreness, susceptibility, tenderness, inflammation, excitability, rawness, tenseness, irritability, oversensitiveness, hypersensitivity, oversensitivity, extreme sensibility, susceptibleness; see also **sensitivity** 2.
**2.** [A disturbed mental state] — *Syn.* vexation, exasperation, upset, provocation; see **anger, annoyance** 1, **stress** 3.
**irruption,** *n.* — *Syn.* aggression, incursion, invasion; see **attack** 1.
**is,** *v.* — *Syn.* lives, breathes, subsists, transpires, happens, amounts to, equals, comprises, signifies, means.
**Islam,** *n.* — *Syn.* Moslemism, Mohammedanism, Islamism; see **church** 3, **religion** 2.
**island,** *n.* **1.** [Land surrounded by water] — *Syn.* isle, islet, bar, key, cay, atoll, holm, *isla* (Spanish), *île* (French), *jima* (Japanese), archipelago; see also **land** 1, **reef.**
**2.** [An isolated spot] — *Syn.* haven, retreat, refuge, sanctuary; see **refuge** 1, **shelter.**
**ism,** *n.* — *Syn.* dogma, belief, theory; see **doctrine** 1.
**isolate,** *v.* — *Syn.* confine, detach, seclude; see **divide** 1, **quarantine, separate** 2.
**isolated,** *modif.* — *Syn.* secluded, apart, alone, solitary, insular, segregated, confined, sequestered, quarantined, screened, withdrawn, rustic, backwoods, separate, lonely, forsaken, hidden, remote, out-of-the-way, unfrequented, lonesome, in a backwater, God-forsaken; see also **alone** 1, **private, solitary.**
**isolation,** *n.* — *Syn.* detachment, solitude, loneliness, seclusion, segregation, confinement, quarantine, separation, self-sufficiency, obscurity, remoteness, withdrawal, retreat, retirement, privacy, insulation; see also **retirement** 2, **withdrawal.**
*See Synonym Study at* SOLITUDE.
**isolationism,** *n.* — *Syn.* nonintervention, neutrality, insularity; see **noninterference.**
**isolationist,** *n.* — *Syn.* nationalist, xenophobe, high-

tariff advocate, neutralist, conservative, America-firster*. — *Ant.* LIBERAL, internationalist, free trader.

**Israel,** *n.* **1.** [The land of Israel] — *Syn.* Palestine, Judea, Canaan, the State of Israel, Jerusalem, Zion, the land of milk and honey, the Promised Land, the Homeland; see also **Asia.**
**2.** [The Jewish people] — *Syn.* Hebrews, the children of God, the children of Abraham, Israelites; see **Jew.**

**Israelite,** *n.* — *Syn.* Hebrew, sabra, Israeli; see **Jew.**

**issue,** *n.* **1.** [Question] — *Syn.* point, matter, problem, concern, point in question, matter of contention, bone of contention, argument, point of departure; see also **puzzle** 2, **subject** 1.
**2.** [Result] — *Syn.* upshot, culmination, effect; see **result.**
**3.** [Edition] — *Syn.* number, copy, impression; see **edition.**
**4.** [Release] — *Syn.* issuance, circulation, delivery; see **distribution** 1.
**5.** [That which has been released on the market] — *Syn.* stocks, issue of stock, bond issue; see **investment.**
**at issue** — *Syn.* in dispute, unsettled, controversial, undecided; see **controversial, uncertain** 2.
**take issue** — *Syn.* differ, disagree, take a stand against; see **oppose** 1.
*See Synonym Study at* RESULT.

**issue,** *v.* **1.** [To emerge] — *Syn.* flow out, emanate, proceed, come forth; see **appear** 1, **arise** 3.
**2.** [To be a result of] — *Syn.* arise from, spring, originate; see **arise** 3, **begin** 2, **result.**
**3.** [To release] — *Syn.* circulate, send out, announce; see **advertise** 1, **declare** 1, **publish** 1.
**4.** [To distribute] — *Syn.* allot, dispense, assign; see **distribute** 1.
**5.** [To emit] — *Syn.* exude, give off, send forth; see **emit** 1.
*See Synonym Study at* ARISE.

**issued,** *modif.* — *Syn.* circulated, broadcast, televised, made public, announced, disseminated, published, sent out, promulgated, expressed, spread; see also **delivered, distributed, published.**

**isthmus,** *n.* — *Syn.* land passage, land bridge, neck of land, portage; see **land** 1.

**it,** *pron.* — *Syn.* such a thing, that which, the object, this thing, the subject; see also **that, this.**

**with it*** — *Syn.* alert, aware, up-to-date; see **conscious** 1, **hip, modern** 1.

**Italian,** *modif.* — *Syn.* Italic, Roman, Latin, Etruscan, Umbrian, Ligurian, Tuscan, Florentine, Milanese, Venetian, Neapolitan, Sicilian, Calabrian, Adriatic.

**Italicism,** *n.* — *Syn.* Italianism, Latinism, Italian idiom, Romanism.

**italicize,** *v.* — *Syn.* stress, underline, print in italic type, draw attention to; see **distinguish** 1, **emphasize.**

**Italy,** *n.* — *Syn. Italia* (Latin and Italian), country of the Latins, Italian peninsula, Italian people, Italian Republic, Rome, Italian boot*.

**itch,** *n.* **1.** [An uncomfortable sensation in the skin] — *Syn.* itchiness, tingling, prickling, crawling, creeping sensation, tickle, rawness, scabbiness, pruritus, psoriasis, psora; see also **irritation** 1.
**2.** [A strong desire] — *Syn.* hankering, yearning, craving; see **desire** 1.

**itch,** *v.* **1.** [To have a tingling sensation] — *Syn.* creep,

prickle, prick, tingle, be irritated, crawl, tickle; see also **tingle.**
**2.** [To have a strong desire] — *Syn.* yearn, crave, long for; see **want** 1.

**itchy,** *modif.* — *Syn.* itching, having an itch, tingling, prickling, crawly, crawling, tickling; see also **tender** 6.

**item,** *n.* — *Syn.* detail, particular, piece, article, matter, object; see also **article** 2, 3, **detail** 1, **part** 1, **thing** 1.

---

**SYN.** — **item** applies to each separate article or thing entered or included in a list, inventory, record, etc.; **detail** applies to any single thing or small section that is part of a whole structure, design, etc. /an architectural *detail,* the *details* of a plot/; **particular** stresses the distinctness of a thing as an individual unit in a whole /to go into *particulars*/

---

**itemize,** *v.* — *Syn.* inventory, enumerate, number; see **count, detail** 1, **list** 1.

**itemized,** *modif.* — *Syn.* counted, particularized, enumerated; see **detailed.**

**iterate,** *v.* — *Syn.* say again, go over, emphasize; see **repeat** 3.
*See Synonym Study at* REPEAT.

**iteration,** *n.* — *Syn.* redundancy, monotony, emphasis; see **repetition.**

**itinerant,** *modif.* — *Syn.* wandering, roving, nomadic, vagrant, migratory, peripatetic; see also **vagrant** 2, **wandering** 1.

---

**SYN.** — **itinerant** applies to persons whose work or profession requires them to travel from place to place /*itinerant* laborers, an *itinerant* preacher/; **ambulatory** specifically implies ability to walk about /an *ambulatory* patient/; **peripatetic** implies a walking or moving about in carrying on some activity and is applied humorously to persons who are always on the go; **nomadic** is applied to tribes or groups of people who have no permanent home, but move about constantly in search of food for themselves, pasture for the animals they herd, etc.; **vagrant** is applied to individuals who wander about without a fixed home, and implies shiftlessness, disorderliness, etc.

---

**itinerant,** *n.* — *Syn.* nomad, wanderer, vagabond; see **tramp** 1, **traveler.**

**itinerary,** *n.* — *Syn.* course, travel plans, route, agenda; see **plan** 2, **program** 2, **route** 1, 2.

**ivory,** *modif.* — *Syn.* creamy, cream-colored, tawny, fulvous; see **tan, white** 1.

**ivory,** *n.* — *Syn.* animal tusk, whalebone, boar tooth, horn, hippo ivory, walrus ivory, hard ivory, soft ivory, live ivory, dead ivory; see also **bone.**
Objects called ivory include: piano key, die, billiard ball, chessman, statuette, false tooth, ivory carving, cameo.

**ivy,** *n.* — *Syn.* climber, creeper, *hedera* (Latin); see **vine.**
Varieties of ivy include: American, German, English, true, wild, ground, Boston, European, African, Asiatic, Irish, Dutch, Swedish, Indian, poison, black, five-leaf; woodbine, Virginia creeper.

**Ivy League*,** *modif.* — *Syn.* exclusive, elite, mannerly, posh*; see **exclusive.**

# J

**jab,** *n.* — *Syn.* poke, punch, hit, dig; see **blow** 1.

**jabber,** *v.* — *Syn.* gibber, chatter, rattle; see **babble, cry** 3, **sound** 1, **talk** 1.

**jack,** *n.* **1.** [An instrument for elevating] — *Syn.* jackscrew, ratchet, jack, automobile jack, pneumatic jack, hydraulic jack; see also **device** 1, **tool** 1.
**2.** [The male of certain animals] — *Syn.* buck, stud, stag; see **animal** 2, **bull** 1.
**every man jack** — *Syn.* every man, everyone, all; see **everybody.**

**jackanapes,** *n.* — *Syn.* wiseacre, whippersnapper, coxcomb, scamp; see **rascal.**

**jackass,** *n.* **1.** [A male donkey] — *Syn.* he-ass, burro, Rocky Mountain canary*; see **animal** 2, **donkey.**
**2.** [*A stupid or foolish person] — *Syn.* dolt, blockhead, nitwit; see **fool** 1.

**jacket,** *n.* — *Syn.* blazer, parka, windbreaker, tunic; see **clothes, coat** 1.

**jackknife,** *n.* — *Syn.* pocketknife, clasp knife, case knife, Barlow knife; see **knife.**

**jackknife,** *v.* — *Syn.* double up, double over, fold, fold up, twist, crash, be wrecked, skid into a jackknife; see also **bend** 1, 2, **crash** 4.

**jack-of-all-trades,** *n.* — *Syn.* handyman, factotum, versatile person; see **laborer, man-of-all-work, worker.**

**jackpot,** *n.* — *Syn.* bonanza, find, winnings, highest prize, reward, stakes, pot, pool, kitty; see also **luck** 1, **prize, success** 2.
**hit the jackpot*** — *Syn.* succeed, achieve, score; see **succeed** 1, **win** 1.

**jack up*,** *v.* — *Syn.* lift, raise, add to, accelerate; see **increase** 1, **raise** 1.

**jade,** *modif.* — *Syn.* jade-green, yellow-green, pale green; see **green** 1.

**jade,** *n.* — *Syn.* jadeite, true jade, nephrite, pyroxene.

**jaded,** *modif.* **1.** [Exhausted] — *Syn.* spent, fatigued, worn-out, wearied; see **bored, tired.**
**2.** [Satiated] — *Syn.* dulled, blunted, surfeited; see **full** 1.

**jag*,** *n.* **1.** [An intoxicated condition] — *Syn.* inebriety, intoxication, buzz*, glow*; see **drunkenness.**
**2.** [A spree] — *Syn.* binge, bout, bender*; see **indulgence** 3, **orgy.**

**jagged,** *modif.* — *Syn.* serrated, ragged, notched; see **irregular** 4, **rough** 1.

**jail,** *n.* — *Syn.* prison, penitentiary, house of correction, penal institution, correctional facility, goal, cell, carcel, cage, guardhouse, guardroom, brig, pound, reformatory, stockade, detention camp, concentration camp, penal settlement, penal colony, house of detention, dungeon, bastille, oubliette, bridewell, debtor's prison, sponging house, slammer*, cooler*, lockup*, stir*, pen*, clink*, jug*, can*, big house*, black hole*, tank*, hulks*, limbo*, death house*, pokey*, calaboose*, coop*, hoosegow*.
Some well-known jails and prison camps include: Sing

Sing, Devils' Island, Attica, San Quentin, Leavenworth, Alcatraz *or* the Rock*, Dartmoor *or* the Moor*, Newgate, Bridewell, Tower of London, Fleet, Marshalsea, Wormwood Scrubs, Holloway, Dannemora, Broadmoor, the Bastille, Belsen, Botany Bay, Andaman Islands.

**jail,** *v.* — *Syn.* confine, imprison, lock up, incarcerate, sentence, throw into the dungeon, impound, detain, put behind bars, jug*, put in the clink*, throw in stir*, throw away the keys*, send up the river*; see also **imprison.** — *Ant.* LIBERATE, discharge, let out.

**jailbird*,** *n.* — *Syn.* convict, felon, inmate; see **criminal, prisoner.**

**jailbreak,** *n.* — *Syn.* breakout, break, forcible escape, planned escape; see **escape** 1.

**jailed,** *modif.* — *Syn.* arrested, incarcerated, in jail; see **confined** 3, **under arrest** at **arrest.**

**jailer,** *n.* — *Syn.* prison guard, corrections officer, turnkey, keeper, gaoler, warden, captor, screw*; see also **warden, watchman.**

**jam,** *n.* **1.** [Preserves] — *Syn.* jelly, conserve, fruit butter, spread, marmalade, sweet, sugarplums, candied fruit; see also **jelly** 1.
**2.** [*A troublesome situation] — *Syn.* dilemma, trouble, bind*, fix*; see **difficulty** 1, **predicament.**

**jam,** *v.* **1.** [To force one's way] — *Syn.* jostle, squeeze, crowd, throng, wedge, press, elbow, thrust, pack; see also **press** 1, **push** 1.
**2.** [To pack full] — *Syn.* fill, block, cram, squeeze; see **bar** 1, **compress, pack** 2.
**3.** [To interfere with radio signals] — *Syn.* drown out, garble, scramble, muddle; see **confuse.**

**jamb,** *n.* — *Syn.* pillar, support, lintel; see **frame** 2, **post** 1.

**jamboree,** *n.* — *Syn.* festival, gathering, jubilee; see **celebration** 1, 2.

**jammed,** *modif.* **1.** [Stuck fast] — *Syn.* out of order, malfunctioning, obstructed, blocked, barred, clogged, trammeled, wedged, sandwiched, caught, lodged, warped, swollen, stiff, immovable, fast, fastened, fixed, frozen, unworkable; see also **tight** 2. — *Ant.* LOOSE, operating, clear.
**2.** [Thronged] — *Syn.* crowded, overcrowded, populous, busy, humming, full, filled, overflowing, lively, deluged, teeming, flooded, swarming, multitudinous, congested, packed, crammed, jampacked, mobbed, loaded; see also **full** 1. — *Ant.* EMPTY, vacant, silent.

**jampacked,** *modif.* — *Syn.* stuffed, overcrowded, loaded down; see **full** 1, **jammed** 2.

**jangle,** *v.* — *Syn.* jingle, clink, clatter; see **ring** 3, **sound** 1.

**janitor,** *n.* — *Syn.* caretaker, maintenance person, porter, handyman; see **custodian** 2.

**January,** *n.* — *Syn.* New Year's, the new year, first month of the year, post-holiday season, time of sales, inventory time; see also **month, winter.**

**Japan,** *n.* — *Syn.* Japanese Empire, the Island Kingdom,

Zipangu, Yamato, Nihon, Dai Nihon, Great Nihon, Nippon, the Land of the Rising Sun, the Flowery Kingdom, the Land of Cherry Blossoms.

**Japanese,** *modif.* — *Syn.* Ainu, Nipponese, East Asian; see **Asian** 1, 2.

**Japanese,** *n.* — *Syn.* Ainus, Nipponese, Nisei, Issei, East Asians.

**jar,** *n.* **1.** [A glass or earthen container] — *Syn.* crock, pot, fruit jar, Mason jar, can, vessel, basin, beaker, jug, cruet, vat, canister, decanter, pitcher, ewer, bottle, carafe, flagon, flask, cruse, burette, phial, gallipot, vase, amphora, ampulla, chalice, mug, Toby jug, urn, canopic jar, olla, *pithos* (Greek), *dolium* (Latin); see also **bottle, container.**
**2.** [The contents of a jar] — *Syn.* pot, quart, pint, jarful, jugful, can, tin; see also **contents** 1.
**3.** [A jolt] — *Syn.* jounce, thud, shock; see **bump** 1.

**jar,** *v.* **1.** [To cause to tremble] — *Syn.* shake, shake up, agitate, jolt, bounce, jounce, jiggle, bump, thump, bang, wiggle, rock, jerk, slam, rattle, wobble, vibrate; see also **crash** 4, **hit** 1, 2.
**2.** [To create discordant sounds] — *Syn.* grate, clash, jangle, bang; see **sound** 1.
**3.** [To disconcert] — *Syn.* rattle, shock, jolt; see **disturb** 2.

**jargon,** *n.* **1.** [Unintelligible, trite, or pretentious speech] — *Syn.* gibberish, mumbo jumbo, bombast, gobbledygook*; see **cliché, nonsense** 1.
**2.** [Hybrid language] — *Syn.* patois, dialect, idiom, pidgin English, broken English, creole, vernacular, koine, lingua franca, Chinook jargon, calque, lingo*; see also **dialect, language** 1.
**3.** [Specialized vocabulary] — *Syn.* argot, shoptalk, slang, colloquialism, neologism, coined word, coinage, cant, buzzword, officialese, legalese, bureaucratese, journalese, computerese, novelese, academese, medicalese, businessspeak, newspeak, pig Latin, dog Latin, patter, localism, rhyming slang, doubletalk, doublespeak, double Dutch, thieves' Latin, peddler's French, lingo*, gobbledygook*, slanguage*, psychobabble*, technobabble*; see also **dialect, slang.**
*See Synonym Study at* DIALECT.

**jarring,** *modif.* **1.** [Discordant] — *Syn.* unharmonious, grating, rasping, clashing; see **harsh** 1, **loud** 1, 2, **shrill.**
**2.** [Jolting] — *Syn.* bumpy, rough, shaking, unsettling, agitating, disconcerting, uneven, bouncy, jouncy, jumpy, wobbly, crushing, smashing, jerky, rocky, staggering, jiggly, wiggly, slam-bang*. — *Ant.* FIRM, smooth, steady.

**jaundice,** *n.* — *Syn.* icterus, biliousness, hepatitis, leptospirosis; see **disease.**

**jaundiced,** *modif.* — *Syn.* envious, hostile, embittered, cynical; see **envious** 2, **jealous, prejudiced, unfriendly** 1, 2.

**jaunt,** *n.* — *Syn.* excursion, sally, trip, saunter, stroll, safari, tour, round, run, gallop, canter, expedition, circuit, peregrination, trek, amble, tramp, hike, promenade, constitutional, turn, airing, outing, ride, drive, spin, march, picnic, voyage, jog, ramble, prowl, course, patrol, beat, frolic, adventure; see also **journey, walk** 3.
*See Synonym Study at* TRIP.

**jauntily,** *modif.* — *Syn.* buoyantly, gaily, briskly; see **briskly, cheerfully, happily** 2.

**jaunty,** *modif.* — *Syn.* debonair, airy, free, free and easy, easy, buoyant, sprightly, carefree, lighthearted, light, sportive, sporty, dapper, natty, breezy, blithe, nonchalant, insouciant, devil-may-care, rakish, raffish, dashing, high-spirited, animated, spirited, lively, gay, jovial,

jolly, joking, frisky, perky, chipper, bouncy, confident, swaggering, cocky, bold, reckless, careless, swashbuckling, venturesome, provocative, hoydenish, frolicsome, jocose, rollicking, gamesome, vivacious, prankish, playful, cocksure, impish, devilish, brash, forward, exhilarated, impetuous, assured, presumptuous, sporting, facetious, scampish, merry, waggish, irreverent, roistering, conceited, strutting, flippant, flip, audacious, bumptious, impertinent, saucy, cheeky, pert, brazen, cavalier; see **happy** 1, **nonchalant.** — *Ant.* RESERVED, staid, sedate.

**javelin,** *n.* — *Syn.* lance, shaft, harpoon; see **spear.**

**jaw,** *n.* **1.** [The bones of the mouth] — *Syn.* jawbone, muzzle, jowl, mandible, maxilla, chops; see also **bone.**
**2.** [A jawlike object] — *Syn.* clamp, grip, vise, wrench, monkey wrench, clasp, clutch; see also **vise.**

**jaw*,** *v.* — *Syn.* jabber, chatter, gab; see **babble, talk** 1.

**jay,** *n.* — *Syn.* bluejay, jaybird, scrub jay, gray jay; see **bird** 1.

**jazz,** *n.* — *Syn.* Dixieland, ragtime, modern jazz, progressive jazz, swing, big band music, bop, bebop, boogie-woogie, blues, syncopated music, improvisation, fusion, third-stream, hot music*, cool jazz*, straight jazz*, le jazz hot*, jive*; see also **music** 1.

**jazz up*,** *v.* — *Syn.* enliven, embellish, speed up; see **animate** 1, **decorate, excite** 1, **hasten** 2.

**jazzy*,** *modif.* — *Syn.* lively, animated, flashy, snazzy*; see **elaborate** 1, **exciting.**

**jealous,** *modif.* — *Syn.* possessive, envious, resentful, demanding, monopolizing, protective, watchful, covetous, begrudging, mistrustful, suspicious, skeptical, doubting, jaundiced, insecure, apprehensive, green-eyed*; see also **envious** 2, **suspicious** 1. — *Ant.* TRUSTING, confiding, forgiving.

**jealousy,** *n.* — *Syn.* resentment, possessiveness, suspicion; see **doubt** 1, **envy.**

**jeans,** *pl.n.* — *Syn.* blue jeans, dungarees, Levi's (trademark), denims; see **clothes, pants** 1.

**jeep,** *n.* — *Syn.* four-wheel drive vehicle, general purpose vehicle, G.P. vehicle, army car; see **automobile, vehicle** 1.
Jeeplike vehicles include: Wagoneer, Jeepster, Scout, Land Rover, Land Cruiser, Bronco, Explorer, Range Rover, Blazer, Cherokee, Trooper (all trademarks).

**jeeplike,** *modif.* — *Syn.* four-wheel drive, reconnaissance, rough-country, back-country, general purpose, multipurpose.

**jeer,** *v.* — *Syn.* scoff, gibe, mock; see **ridicule.**

**jeering,** *modif.* — *Syn.* mocking, raucous, taunting; see **rude** 2, **scornful** 2, **yelling.**

**jeering,** *n.* — *Syn.* taunting, shouting, mocking; see **cry** 1, **ridicule.**

**jell,** *v.* — *Syn.* set, crystallize, condense; see **freeze** 1, **harden** 2, **stiffen** 1, **thicken** 1.

**jelly,** *n.* **1.** [Jam] — *Syn.* jell, extract, preserve, gelatin, pulp, mass, pectin; see also **jam** 1.
**2.** [Cream] — *Syn.* ointment, unction, balm; see **salve.**

**jellyfish,** *n.* — *Syn.* medusa, coelenterate, ctenophore, hydrozoan, scyphozoan; see also **fish.**

**jeopardize,** *v.* — *Syn.* imperil, expose, venture; see **endanger, risk.**

**jeopardy,** *n.* — *Syn.* risk, peril, exposure; see **danger.**
*See Synonym Study at* DANGER.

**jerk,** *n.* **1.** [A spasmodic movement] — *Syn.* twitch, tic, shrug, wiggle, shake, quiver, flick, snap, yank, tug, wrench, lurch, jolt, jump, jounce, jiggle; see also **bump** 1.
**2.** [*A contemptible person] — *Syn.* brute, rat*, fool, chump*; see **fool** 1, **rascal.**

**jerk,** *v.* **1.** [To undergo a spasm] — *Syn.* twitch, shrug, have a convulsion, wriggle, shake, quake, quiver, shiver, wiggle, jiggle, dance; see also **shake** 1, **twitch** 2.
**2.** [To move an object with a quick tug] — *Syn.* snatch, grab, tug, yank, whisk, pluck, snag, hook, flip, bounce, fling, hurtle, flick, wrench, twist, pull.

**jerry-built,** *modif.* — *Syn.* flimsy, shoddy, rickety, cheap; see **faulty, flimsy** 1, **unfinished** 1.

**jersey,** *n.* — *Syn.* pullover, T-shirt, Rugby shirt, turtleneck; see **clothes, sweater.**

**jest,** *n.* — *Syn.* witticism, prank, quip; see **joke** 2.
**in jest** — *Syn.* jokingly, facetiously, in fun; see **for fun** at **fun, humorously.**

**jester,** *n.* — *Syn.* fool, comedian, buffoon, joker; see **actor** 1, **clown.**

**jesting,** *n.* — *Syn.* buffoonery, joking, clowning; see **humor** 1, **wit** 1.

**Jesus,** *n.* — *Syn.* Jesus Christ, Jesus of Nazareth, Saviour, the Son of God; see **Christ, god** 2.

**jet,** *modif.* — *Syn.* ebony, raven, obsidian; see **black** 1, **dark** 1.

**jet,** *n.* **1.** [A stream of liquid or gas] — *Syn.* spray, stream, spurt; see **fountain** 2.
**2.** [A jet-propelled airplane] — *Syn.* jet plane, twin jet, supersonic jet, supersonic transport (SST), jetliner, jumbo jet, turbojet; see also **plane** 3.

**jet,** *v.* **1.** [To gush out in a stream] — *Syn.* spout, spurt, squirt; see **flow** 2.
**2.** [To travel by jet airplane] — *Syn.* take a jet, go by jet, fly, zoom; see **fly** 4, **travel** 2.

**jet set,** *n.* — *Syn.* élite, international set, beautiful people\*, glitterati\*; see **society** 3.

**jettison,** *v.* — *Syn.* eject, cast off, throw away; see **discard.**

**jetty,** *n.* — *Syn.* breakwater, sea wall, pier, wharf; see **dock** 1, **harbor** 2.

**Jew,** *n.* — *Syn.* Hebrew, Israelite, Judaist, Semite, Orthodox Jew, Conservative Jew, Reform Jew, Hasid, Israeli, Ashkenazi, Sephardi, sabra, descendant of Abraham, wandering Jew, Jewess, son of Israel.

**jewel,** *n.* **1.** [A precious stone] — *Syn.* gem, gemstone, bauble, brilliant, bijou, trinket, ornament, rock\*, sparkler\*; see also **gem** 1.
Jewels, gems, and precious stones include: diamond, pearl, opal, emerald, amethyst, sapphire, jade, aquamarine, moonstone, agate, beryl, ruby, turquoise, topaz, garnet, carbuncle, cornelian, jasper, coral, peridot, chrysoprase, lapis lazuli, bloodstone, onyx, brilliant, tourmaline, zircon; see also **diamond** 1, **opal, pearl** 1.
**2.** [An excellent person or thing] — *Syn.* treasure, find, prize, phenomenon; see **gem** 2.

**jeweler,** *n.* — *Syn.* goldsmith, silversmith, diamond setter, gem dealer, gemologist, watchmaker, horologist, lapidary; see also **artist** 2, **craftsman.**

**jewelry,** *n.* — *Syn.* gems, precious stones, jewels, gold, silver, baubles, trinkets, adornments, frippery, bijoux, bijouterie, ornaments, costume jewelry, bangles, gewgaws, gimcrackery, junk jewelry\*; see also **jewel** 1.
Types of jewelry include: diadem, coronet, tiara, cross, locket, brooch, lavalliere, watch chain, pendant, armlet, anklet, bracelet, necklace, ring, pin, choker, earrings, cameo, chain, beads, charm; see also **bracelet, crown** 2, **necklace, pin** 2, **ring** 2.

**Jewish,** *modif.* — *Syn.* Judaic, Hebrew, Hebraic, Mosaic, Semitic, Ashkenazic, Sephardic, Israeli, Yiddish, Israelitish, Zionist, Hasidic.

**jibe\*,** *v.* — *Syn.* agree, correspond, match, accord; see **agree, resemble.**

**jig,** *n.* — *Syn.* song and dance, contredanse, hop; see **dance** 1, **music** 1.

**jiggle,** *v.* — *Syn.* shake, twitch, wiggle; see **jar** 1, **jerk** 1.

**jilt,** *v.* — *Syn.* reject, forsake, desert; see **abandon** 2.

**jilted,** *modif.* — *Syn.* left, neglected, forsaken, thrown over; see **abandoned** 1.

**jingle,** *n.* **1.** [A light ringing sound] — *Syn.* tinkle, jangle, clank; see **noise** 1.
**2.** [A catchy verse or tune] — *Syn.* ditty, chant, rhyme, doggerel; see **song, verse** 1.

**jingle,** *v.* — *Syn.* tinkle, clink, rattle; see **ring** 3, **sound** 1.

**jingoism,** *n.* — *Syn.* chauvinism, superpatriotism, overpatriotism, flag-waving, ultranationalism, xenophobia, warmongering, hawkishness; see also **patriotism.**

**jinx,** *n.* — *Syn.* evil eye, hex, spell; see **curse** 1.

**jitters\*,** *pl.n.* — *Syn.* nervousness, anxiety, fidgets, butterflies; see **fear** 1, 2, **nervousness** 1.

**jittery\*,** *modif.* — *Syn.* nervous, tense, panicky, jumpy; see **afraid** 1, **excited.**

**job,** *n.* **1.** [Gainful employment] — *Syn.* situation, post, position, appointment, office, work, occupation, employment, business, profession, trade, line, calling, field, vocation, career, craft, paying job, place, berth, pursuit, function, role, capacity, faculty, means of livelihood, métier, gig\*; see also **business** 1, **profession** 1, **trade** 2, **work** 2.
**2.** [Something to be done] — *Syn.* task, assignment, chore, stint, duty, responsibility, business, burden, action, act, mission, affair, concern, obligation, enterprise, undertaking, project, errand, care, matter, matter in hand, commission, function, charge, province, deed, office, tour of duty, operation, transaction, work, labor, toil, drudgery, grind, lookout\*, scutwork\*; see also **duty** 2.
**3.** [The amount of work done] — *Syn.* assignment, day's work, output, input, throughput, block of work, responsibility; see also sense 2; **duty** 2.
*See Synonym Study at* TASK.

**odd jobs** — *Syn.* miscellaneous duties, chores, occasional labor; see **job** 2.

**on the job** — *Syn.* busy, engaged, occupied; see **working.**

---

**SYN.** — **job,** the common, comprehensive equivalent for any of the following terms, refers to any work done by agreement for pay; **position** may apply to any specific employment for salary or wages, but often connotes white-collar or professional employment; **situation** now usually refers to a position that is open or that is desired [*situation* wanted as instructor]; **office** refers to a position of authority or trust, esp. in government or a corporation; **post** implies a position or office that carries heavy responsibilities, esp. one to which a person is appointed

---

**jobber,** *n.* — *Syn.* middleman, wholesaler, business agent; see **businessperson, merchant.**

**job lot,** *modif.* — *Syn.* by lot price, reduced, at a cut rate; see **cheap** 1.

**jockey,** *n.* — *Syn.* rider, racer, steeplechaser, saddlesitter\*, monkey\*, jock\*, jocker\*, live weight\*; see also **horseman, rider** 1.

**jockey,** *v.* — *Syn.* maneuver, slip into, manage, angle\*; see **insinuate** 2, **maneuver.**

**jocose,** *modif.* — *Syn.* joking, playful, humorous, merry; see **facetious, funny** 1.
*See Synonym Study at* WITTY.

**jocular,** *modif.* — *Syn.* joking, waggish, tongue-in-cheek, jokey; see **facetious, funny** 1.

*See Synonym Study at* WITTY.

**jog,** *n.* **1.** [A slow run] — *Syn.* trot, lope, dogtrot, pace; see **run** 1.

**2.** [A bump] — *Syn.* jiggle, shake, nudge; see **bump** 1, **push.**

**jog,** *v.* — *Syn.* trot, lope, take one's exercise, do laps; see **run** 2.

**joggle,** *v.* — *Syn.* wiggle, jiggle, shake; see **fidget, jar** 1.

**jog (someone's) memory,** *v.* — *Syn.* bring up, recall, suggest; see **remind** 2.

**John Bull★,** *n.* — *Syn.* England, Englishman, Briton; see **England, English.**

**John Doe,** *n.* — *Syn.* the average citizen, John Q. Public, Jane Doe, Mr. and Mrs. America, Joe Doakes, Mr. Taxpayer, man in the street, anyone, stock legal personage, unknown person, anonymous person; see also **everybody.**

**John Hancock★,** *n.* — *Syn.* autograph, mark, initials; see **signature.**

**join,** *v.* **1.** [To put or bring together] — *Syn.* unite, connect, link, piece together, blend, combine, merge, consolidate, amalgamate, juxtapose, bring in contact, touch, connect up, couple, conjoin, affix, mix, assemble, stick together, bind together, lump together, fasten, append, attach, secure, tie, annex, agglutinate, bracket, span, intermix, cross with, pair with, leash, yoke, marry, wed, melt into one, copulate, cement, weld, splice, clasp, fuse, lock, grapple, clamp, clip, interlace, entwine, subjoin, involve together, associate; see also **unite** 1. — *Ant.* SEPARATE, sunder, sever.

**2.** [To enter the company of] — *Syn.* enlist, enroll, enter, become a member, associate with, go to, meet, accompany, mingle with, seek, join forces, go to the aid of, follow, rejoin, register, team up with, take up with, tie up with, line up with, be in, sign on, sign up, go in with, fall in with, align, consort, fraternize, throw in with, pair with, affiliate, side with, align with, ally oneself, make one of, take part in, participate, seek a place among, advance toward, go to meet; see also **associate** 1, **unite** 1. — *Ant.* LEAVE, desert, quit.

**3.** [To adjoin] — *Syn.* lie next to, be contiguous to, neighbor, border, fringe, butt, trench on, verge upon, be adjacent to, open into, be close to, bound, lie beside, lie near, be at hand, abut, touch, skirt, flank, parallel, rim, hem, abound and abut upon.

---

**SYN.** — **join** is the general term implying a bringing or coming together of two or more things and may suggest direct contact, affiliation, etc.; **combine** implies a mingling together of things, often with a loss of distinction of elements that completely merge with one another [to *combine* milk and water]; **unite** implies a joining or combining of things to form a single whole [the United States]; **connect** implies attachment by some fastening or relationship [roads *connected* by a bridge, the duties *connected* with a job]; **link** stresses firmness of a connection [*linked* together in a common cause]; **associate** implies a joining with another or others as a companion, partner, etc. and, in extended use, suggests a connection made in the mind [to *associate* Freud's name with psychoanalysis]; **consolidate** implies a merger of distinct and separate units into a single whole for resulting compactness, strength, efficiency, etc. [to *consolidate* one's debts]

---

**join battle,** *v.* — *Syn.* engage with, fight against, open combat, join issue; see **attack** 1, 2, **fight** 2.

**joined,** *modif.* — *Syn.* linked, yoked, coupled, conjoined, allied, akin, cognate, interallied, intertwined, entwined,

blended, connected, united, federated, amalgamated, banded, paired, wedded, married, interfused, merged, mixed, put together, tied together, interdependent, combined, touching, interclasped, clasped together, cemented, welded, fused, locked, grappled, interlaced, clipped together, conjugated, accompanying, associated, confederated, mingled, intermixed, clutched, hitched, spliced, engrafted, affixed, reciprocally attached, joint, conjoint, assimilated, mortised, interlaid, corporate, incorporated, involved, inseparable, bracketed, affiliated, related, pieced together, fastened together, stuck together, coupled with, bound up with, bound up in; see also **unified.** — *Ant.* SEPARATED, disparate, apart.

**joint,** *modif.* — *Syn.* common, shared, mutual; see **collective, common** 5.

**joint,** *n.* **1.** [A juncture] — *Syn.* union, crux, nexus, articulation, coupling, hinge, tie, swivel, link, connection, interconnection, junction, point of union, bond, splice, vinculum, bend, copula, hyphen, bracket, tangency, bridge, conjuncture, impingement, confluence, joining structure, linking device, combining process, association; see also **link.**

**2.** [A section] — *Syn.* piece, member, unit, digit, portion, division, block, step, chink, sector, fragment, segment, limb, bone, lobe, cell, offshoot, constituent, slab, chunk; see also **part** 1, **piece** 1.

**3.** [★An establishment, particularly one providing entertainment] — *Syn.* hangout★, dump★, hole in the wall★; see **dive** 2.

**4.** [★A marijuana cigarette] — *Syn.* reefer★, stick★, roach★; see **marijuana.**

**out of joint** — *Syn.* dislocated, disorganized, disjointed, wrong; see **disordered.**

**jointly,** *modif.* — *Syn.* conjointly, mutually, together, combined, in common, in federation, in unison, in conjunction, in partnership, in concert, in alliance, in association, in league, in combination, connectedly, unitedly, federally, co-operatively, corporately, harmoniously, reciprocally, inseparably, with mutual reliance, concomitantly, companionably, hand in hand, hand in glove, collectively, in a body, with one accord, with one assent, in company with, arm in arm, side by side, en masse, in a group, in ensemble, as one, with one another, agreeably, simultaneously, coincidentally, synchronically, concurrently, inextricably, contemporaneously, cheek by jowl★, in cahoots★. — *Ant.* SINGLY, separately, severally.

**join up,** *v.* — *Syn.* enlist, sign up, enter the armed forces, respond to the call of duty; see **join** 2, **volunteer** 2.

**joist,** *n.* — *Syn.* girder, scantling, strip; see **beam** 1, **post** 1, **support** 2.

**joke,** *n.* **1.** [An action intended to be funny] — *Syn.* prank, buffoonery, game, sport, frolic, practical joke, gag, trick, hoax, revel, clowning, caper, caprice, mischief, escapade, stunt, fooling, foolery, tomfoolery, horseplay, pleasantry, fun, play, gambol, antic, lark, drollery, waggery, farce, mummery, monkeyshine★, shenanigan★, put-on★; see also sense 2; **trick** 1.

**2.** [Words intended to be funny] — *Syn.* jest, witticism, pun, play on words, quip, bon mot, one-liner, gag, anecdote, pleasantry, banter, drollery, jocularity, riposte, retort, conceit, repartee, give-and-take, rejoinder, sally, persiflage, mot, *jeu d'esprit* (French), chestnut, epigram, badinage, raillery, smart answer, punch line, jape, crack★, wisecrack★, funny★, shaggy dog story★, zinger★, rib-tickler★; see also sense 1.

**3.** [A ridiculous person or thing] — *Syn.* laughingstock, butt, mockery, figure of fun, farce, laugh, sham; see also **fake, fool** 2.

**joke,** *v.* — *Syn.* jest, quip, banter, tell jokes, raise laughter, play, sport, frolic, revel, play tricks, pun, poke fun, twit, trick, fool, fool around, clown around, make merry, play the fool, play the clown, be facetious, be waggish, kid\*, josh\*, crack jokes\*, wisecrack\*, pull someone's leg\*, put someone on\*, jive\*, fun\*; see also **deceive, trifle** 1.

**joker,** *n.* **1.** [Comedian] — *Syn.* jester, comic, fool; see **actor** 1, **clown.**
**2.** [A hidden, unsuspected clause or difficulty] — *Syn.* rider, proviso, snag, kicker\*; see **article** 3, **catch** 4, **impediment** 1.

**joking,** *modif.* — *Syn.* humorous, facetious, not serious; see **funny** 1.

**jokingly,** *modif.* — *Syn.* facetiously, in jest, jocularly; see **humorously.**

**jollity,** *n.* — *Syn.* vivacity, merriment, sport; see **fun, happiness** 1.

**jolly,** *modif.* **1.** [Cheerful] — *Syn.* jovial, merry, joyful; see **happy** 1, 2.
**2.** [Festive] — *Syn.* convivial, enjoyable, holidayish\*; see **entertaining, pleasant** 2.

**jolt,** *n.* **1.** [A bump] — *Syn.* jar, lurch, punch, bounce; see **blow** 1, **bump** 1, **jerk** 1.
**2.** [A surprise] — *Syn.* shock, start, jar; see **surprise** 2, **wonder** 1.

**jostle,** *v.* — *Syn.* nudge, elbow, shoulder; see **press** 1, **push** 1.

**jot,** *v.* — *Syn.* scribble down, note, indicate, list; see **record** 1, **write** 1, 2.

**jotting,** *n.* — *Syn.* note, item, entry, scribbling; see **note** 2, **record** 1.

**jounce,** *v.* — *Syn.* jerk, jolt, bump; see **bounce** 1, **jar** 1, **jump** 3.

**journal,** *n.* **1.** [A daily record] — *Syn.* diary, account, record, memoir, jottings, reminiscence, contemporary account, almanac, annual, chronology, log, daybook, commonplace book, chronicle, yearbook, annals, register, calendar, datebook, notes, minutes, transactions, observations, album, scrapbook, notebook, memento, reminder; see also **record** 1.
**2.** [A periodical] — *Syn.* publication, magazine, review, organ, weekly, monthly, quarterly, annual, daily; see also **magazine** 2, **newspaper.**

**journalese,** *n.* — *Syn.* newspaper idiom, editorial style, newspeak; see **dialect, jargon** 3, **language** 1.

**journalism,** *n.* — *Syn.* newspaper writing, newspaper publishing, reporting, reportage, news coverage, broadcasting, newscasting, media, the press, the fourth estate; see also **press** 2, **writing** 3.

**journalist,** *n.* — *Syn.* reporter, commentator, columnist, member of the fourth estate; see **announcer, reporter, writer.**

**journalistic,** *modif.* **1.** [Concerning newspapers] — *Syn.* periodical, publishing, editorial, reportorial, commentative.
**2.** [Having the qualities of hasty writing] — *Syn.* ephemeral, sensational, current, timely, dated, prosy, slangy, facile, stereotyped.

**journey,** *n.* — *Syn.* transit, passage, trip, tour, excursion, wayfaring, jaunt, pilgrimage, saunter, voyage, junket, package tour, crossing, expedition, odyssey, range, patrol, beat, sally, venture, adventure, itinerary, course, route, circuit, Grand Tour, peregrination, ramble, wandering, *Wanderjahr* (German), traverse, traversal, visit, sojourn, traveling, travels, campaign, trek, hegira, migration, caravan, transmigration, roaming, quest, sa-

fari, exploration, vagabondage, vagrancy, round, stroll, run, tramp, hike, promenade, constitutional, turn, airing, outing, drive, march, picnic, jog, prowl, look, survey, setting forth, crusade, perambulation, cruise, flight, sail, navigation, circumnavigation of the globe, nonstop flight, mission, ride; see also **travel** 1, **walk** 3.
*See Synonym Study at* TRIP.

**journey,** *v.* — *Syn.* travel, tour, jaunt, take a trip; see **travel** 2.

**journeyman,** *n.* — *Syn.* apprentice, artisan, tradesman; see **artist** 2, **craftsman, specialist, worker.**

**Jove,** *n.* — *Syn.* Jupiter, Zeus, Odin, Wotan, Dyaus, Ammon, Amen-Ra, Min, the Father of the Gods, the Lord of Olympus; see also **god** 1.

**jovial,** *modif.* — *Syn.* convivial, good-humored, jollly, affable; see **happy** 1, **jaunty.**

**joviality,** *n.* — *Syn.* joy, geniality, good humor; see **happiness** 1, **joy** 2.

**jowl,** *n.* — *Syn.* mandible, dewlap, cheek; see **jaw** 1.

**joy,** *n.* **1.** [A very glad feeling] — *Syn.* happiness, delight, gladness, rapture; see **happiness** 1, 2, **pleasure** 1, **satisfaction** 2.
**2.** [The exhibition of joy] — *Syn.* gaiety, jubilation, rejoicing, cheerfulness, merriment, glee, gleefulness, mirth, mirthfulness, revelry, hilarity, hilariousness, blitheness, frolic, playfulness, heartiness, geniality, good humor, sprightliness, merrymaking, joviality, sportiveness, jocularity, jollity, jocundity, levity, exulting, joyfulness, joyousness, elation, friskiness, animation, liveliness, high spirits, good spirits, transport, vivacity, sunniness, jocosity, celebration; see also **laughter.** — *Ant.* WEEPING, mourning, complaining.
**3.** [The cause of joy] — *Syn.* delight, solace, treasure, pride and joy, pleasure, gratification, comfort, blessing, treat, regalement, diversion, sport, refreshment, enjoyment, dainty, indulgence, luxury. — *Ant.* thorn in the flesh, CARE, burden.
*See Synonym Study at* PLEASURE.

**joyful,** *modif.* — *Syn.* joyous, cheery, glad; see **happy** 1.
*See Synonym Study at* HAPPY.

**joyless,** *modif.* — *Syn.* doleful, heavy, dreary; see **dismal** 1, **sad** 2.

**joyous,** *modif.* — *Syn.* blithe, glad, joyful; see **happy** 1.
*See Synonym Study at* HAPPY.

**joy ride\*,** *n.* — *Syn.* reckless drive, pleasure trip, spin; see **drive** 1, **race** 3.

**joy rider\*,** *n.* — *Syn.* fast driver, reckless driver, speeder, drag racer; see **driver.**

**jubilant,** *modif.* — *Syn.* rejoicing, exultant, elated, celebrating; see **happy** 1, 2, **triumphant.**

**jubilation,** *n.* — *Syn.* celebration, exultation, triumph, gladness; see **celebration** 2, **happiness** 1, **joy** 2.

**Judaic,** *modif.* — *Syn.* Jewish, Semitic, Hebrew; see **Jewish.**

**Judaism,** *n.* — *Syn.* Jewish religion, Hebraism, Orthodox Judaism, Conservative Judaism, Reform Judaism, Reconstructionism, Hasidism, Zionism; see also **religion** 2.

**Judaist,** *n.* — *Syn.* Jew, Hebrew, Israelite; see **Jew.**

**Judas,** *n.* — *Syn.* betrayer, fraud, informer; see **hypocrite, traitor.**

**judge,** *n.* **1.** [A legal official] — *Syn.* justice, magistrate, chancellor, justice of the peace (JP), chief justice, associate justice, circuit judge, county judge, judge of the district court, appeals judge, surrogate, jurist, master of assize, marshal of assize, chancery judge, tribune, bencher, hanging judge\*; see also **judiciary.**
**2.** [A moderator] — *Syn.* referee, umpire, arbitrator, arbiter, adjudicator, mediator, ombudsman, interpreter,

inspector, negotiator, intercessor, final authority, go-between, assessor, ump*.
**3.** [A connoisseur] — *Syn.* expert, authority, professional; see **connoisseur, critic** 2, **specialist.**

---

*SYN.* — **judge** is applied to one who, by the authority vested in him or her by expertness of knowledge, is qualified to settle a controversy or decide on the relative merit of things [a *judge* of a beauty contest]; **arbiter** emphasizes the authoritativeness of decision of one whose judgment in a particular matter is considered indisputable [an *arbiter* of the social graces]; **referee** and **umpire** both apply to a person to whom anything is referred for decision or settlement [a *referee* in bankruptcy] and, in sports, to officials charged with the regulation of a contest, ruling on the plays in a game, etc. [a *referee* in boxing, basketball, etc., an *umpire* in baseball, cricket, etc.]

---

**judge,** *v.* **1.** [To pass judgment] — *Syn.* adjudge, adjudicate, try, hear, sit in judgment, doom, sentence, act on, find, rule, give a hearing to, hold the scales, arbitrate, referee.
**2.** [To form an opinion] — *Syn.* conclude, infer, suppose, assess; see **decide, estimate** 1, 2, **resolve** 2.
*See Synonym Study at* INFER.
**judged,** *modif.* — *Syn.* found guilty, found innocent, tried, settled; see **determined** 1, **guilty** 1.
**judging,** *n.* — *Syn.* determining, deciding, reaching a decision, arriving at a decision; see **judgment** 2.
**judgment,** *n.* **1.** [The ability to judge] — *Syn.* discernment, discrimination, taste, penetration, shrewdness, sapience, sagacity, understanding, knowledge, sense, good sense, wit, keenness, sharpness, critical faculty, reason, reasoning power, rationality, rational faculty, acumen, intuition, acuteness, perception, incisiveness, intelligence, awareness, sophistication, ingenuity, experience, profundity, depth, brilliance, mentality, subtlety, intellectual power, critical spirit, capacity, comprehension, sanity, lucidity, levelheadedness, clearheadedness, mother wit, quickness, readiness, grasp, apprehension, perspicacity, perspicuousness, soundness, genius, reach, range, breadth, astuteness, prudence, discretion, wisdom, *sagesse* (French), savvy*, gray matter*, brains*, a good head*, horse sense*; see also **acumen.** — *Ant.* STUPIDITY, simplicity, naiveté.
**2.** [The act of judging] — *Syn.* decision, consideration, appraisal, examination, judging, weighing, sifting, assaying, determination, inspection, assessment, estimation, diagnosis, probing, appreciation, evaluation, interpretation, study, review, contemplation, analysis, inquiry, inquisition, inquest, search, quest, pursuit, scrutiny, exploration, reconnaissance, close study, observation, exhaustive inquiry, regard; see also **study** 2.
**3.** [A pronouncement] — *Syn.* conclusion, decision, ruling, sentence, verdict, appraisal, estimate, opinion, report, view, summary, belief, idea, conviction, inference, resolution, deduction, induction, moral, critique, determination, dictum, decree, best opinion, supposition, comment, commentary, finding, recommendation, diagnosis; see also **sentence** 1, **verdict.**
**4.** [An act of God] — *Syn.* retribution, visitation, misfortune, manifestation, chastisement, correction, castigation, mortification, affliction, infliction, Nemesis; see also **punishment.**
**Judgment Day,** *n.* — *Syn.* doomsday, day of judgment, day of the Apocalypse, end of the world, last day, day of reckoning, Last Judgment, Final Judgment, private judgment, general judgment day.

**judicial,** *modif.* — *Syn.* legal, legalistic, juristic, judiciary, pontifical, authoritative, judgelike, equitable, fair, impartial, principled, jurisdictional, administrative, constitutional, statutory; see also **legal** 1.
**judiciary,** *n.* — *Syn.* judges, justices, bench, courts, assizes, tribunal, bar, judicature, courts of justice, criminal justice system, legal profession, members of the bar, judicial branch, interpreters of the law; see also **court** 2, **jury.**
**judicious,** *modif.* — *Syn.* well-advised, prudent, sensible, wise, discreet, reasonable, rational, seasonable, timely, sagacious, sound, proper, thoughtful, thorough, efficacious, perceptive, acute, shrewd, discriminating, judicial, keen, astute, sage, discerning, sharp, careful, wary, worldly-wise, farsighted, clearsighted, sophisticated, calculating, profound, perspicacious, accurate, penetrating, informed, sane, practical, seemly, decorous, cautious, politic, diplomatic, circumspect, prudential, precautionary, expedient, capable, ready, tactful, cool, calm, considered, deliberated, well-considered, well-judged, prescient, knowing, sapient, well-timed, moderate, temperate, sober; see also **discreet, intelligent** 1, **rational** 1, **reasonable** 1, 2. — *Ant.* RASH, ill-advised, hasty.
**judo,** *n.* — *Syn.* jujitsu, martial art, self-defense, wrestling; see **fight** 1.
**jug,** *n.* — *Syn.* crock, pot, canteen, bottle, flagon, demijohn, cruet, flask, stone jar, pitcher, ewer, cruse; see also **container, jar** 1.
**juggle,** *v.* **1.** [To keep in the air by tossing] — *Syn.* toss, poise, balance, keep in motion, perform sleight of hand; see also **balance** 2.
**2.** [To alter, usually to deceive] — *Syn.* shuffle, manipulate, falsify; see **deceive, disguise.**
**juggler,** *n.* **1.** [A performer of juggling feats] — *Syn.* balancer, magician, prestidigitator, entertainer; see **acrobat.**
**2.** [A person who practices trickery] — *Syn.* trickster, con artist, charlatan; see **cheat** 1, **swindler.**
**juice,** *n.* — *Syn.* sap, extract, liquid, fluid, nectar, water, oil, latex, syrup, sauce, milk, spirit; see also **liquid.**
**juicy,** *modif.* **1.** [Full of juice] — *Syn.* succulent, moist, wet, watery, humid, lush, dewy, sappy, viscid, dank, slushy, slippery, oozy, dripping, sodden, soaked, saturated, liquid, oily, syrupy, sauced; see also **delicious** 1. — *Ant.* DRY, dehydrated, bone-dry.
**2.** [*Full of interest] — *Syn.* spicy, piquant, intriguing, racy, risqué, tantalizing, fascinating, sensational, exciting, colorful, provocative, suggestive, titillating, scandalous.
**3.** [*Profitable] — *Syn.* lucrative, rewarding, favorable, substantive; see **profitable.**
**July,** *n.* — *Syn.* summer month, midsummer, baseball season, seventh month, vacation time, dog days, silly season*; see also **month, summer.**
**jumble,** *n.* — *Syn.* clutter, mess, hodgepodge; see **confusion** 2, **mixture** 1.
*See Synonym Study at* CONFUSION.
**jumbo,** *modif.* — *Syn.* immense, mammoth, gigantic, king-sized; see **large** 1.
**jump,** *n.* **1.** [A leap up or across] — *Syn.* skip, hop, leap, hopping, rise, upsurge, rising, pounce, lunge, leaping, jumping, skipping, running jump, broad jump, high jump, vault, bounce, hurdle, spring, bound, saltation, buckjump, leapfrogging, caper, dance, gambol.
**2.** [A leap down] — *Syn.* precipitation, plunge, dive, diving, nosedive, plummet, headlong fall, descent, drop,

fall, parachute jump, bungee jump, sky diving; see also **dive** 1, **drop** 2.

**3.** [An obstacle] — *Syn.* hurdle, bar, fence; see **barrier.**

**4.** [Distance jumped] — *Syn.* leap, stretch, vault; see **height** 1, **length** 1.

**5.** [A sudden nervous movement] — *Syn.* start, jerk, twitch, jolt; see **jerk** 1.

**6.** [A sudden rise] — *Syn.* ascent, spurt, inflation, hike*; see **increase** 1, **rise** 2.

**get** (*or* **have**) **the jump on*** — *Syn.* get an advantage over, get a head start, have the upper hand, beat; see **exceed, surpass.**

**jump,** *v.* **1.** [To leap across or up] — *Syn.* vault, leap, leap over, spring, surge, lurch, lunge, pounce, pop up, pop out, bound, hop, skip, high-jump, broad-jump, take, hurdle, top, cavort, gambol, bounce.

**2.** [To leap down] — *Syn.* drop, plummet, plunge, skydive, parachute, bail out; see also **dive, fall** 1.

**3.** [To pass over] — *Syn.* skip, bypass, cover, cross, traverse, flit, shift, leave out, omit, miss.

**4.** [To jerk] — *Syn.* start, twitch, jiggle, jounce, rattle, quiver, shake, rebound, recoil, flinch, wince, dance, skip, ricochet, bounce; see also **bounce** 1.

**5.** [*To leave suddenly] — *Syn.* skip, abandon, clear out; see **escape, leave** 1.

**6.** [To board] — *Syn.* mount, climb on, hop on, spring upon; see sense 1; **board** 2, **catch** 7.

**7.** [*To accost belligerently] — *Syn.* ambush, hold up, pounce on, mug*; see **ambush, attack** 2.

**jump a claim,** *v.* — *Syn.* preempt, stake out, attach; see **seize** 2, **steal.**

**jump at,** *v.* — *Syn.* embrace, snatch at, agree to; see **seize** 1.

**jump bail,** *v.* — *Syn.* abscond, run off, leave town; see **escape, leave** 1.

**jumping,** *modif.* — *Syn.* vaulting, hopping, skipping, bounding, leaping, hurdling, springing, bouncing, buoyant, active, lively, animated, beating, vibrant, irregular, dynamic, pulsating, shaking, quivering, quaking, trembling, unsteady, throbbing, hammering, thudding, agitated, tripping.

**jump in with both feet*,** *v.* — *Syn.* plunge in, throw oneself into, rush in, be impetuous; see **begin** 1, **hurry** 1.

**jump on*,** *v.* — *Syn.* blame, charge, berate, jump all over*; see **accuse, censure.**

**jump ship,** *v.* — *Syn.* run off, depart, take French leave; see **escape, leave** 1.

**jump the track,** *v.* — *Syn.* leave the rails, be wrecked, be derailed; see **crash** 4.

**jumpy,** *modif.* — *Syn.* nervous, apprehensive, restless, jittery*; see **afraid** 1, **excitable, excited.**

**junction,** *n.* **1.** [A meeting] — *Syn.* joining, coupling, linkage; see **joint** 1, **union** 1.

**2.** [A place of meeting, especially of roads] — *Syn.* crossroads, confluence, terminal, collocation, crossing, four corners, intersection, interchange, traffic circle, rotary, roundabout (British); see also **crossing** 1.

**juncture,** *n.* — *Syn.* point in time, crossroads, turning point, meeting point; see **circumstance** 1, **crisis, meeting** 1, **position** 1, **time** 2.

**June,** *n.* — *Syn.* spring month, summer month, sixth month, summer solstice, month of weddings, graduation month, month of roses, baseball season, beginning of summer; see also **month, spring** 2, **summer.**

**jungle,** *n.* — *Syn.* rain forest, tropical rain forest, bush, wilderness, undergrowth, primeval forest, wood, bos-

cage, trackless waste; see also **forest.** — *Ant.* CLEARING, cultivation, settlement.

**junior,** *modif.* — *Syn.* subordinate, younger, lesser, lower; see **subordinate.**

**junk,** *n.* **1.** [Rubbish] — *Syn.* waste, garbage, refuse; see **trash** 1.

**2.** [Salvage] — *Syn.* scraps, odds and ends, miscellany, stuff; see **rummage, trash** 3.

**junk*,** *v.* — *Syn.* scrap, dump, sell for scrap, throw away; see **discard.**

**junk dealer,** *n.* — *Syn.* junkman, salvage man, ragpicker, garbage man, beachcomber, trashman, scavenger.

**junket,** *n.* **1.** [Pudding] — *Syn.* custard, milk dessert, rennet; see **dessert, pudding.**

**2.** [A trip] — *Syn.* excursion, outing, political tour, pleasure trip; see **journey.**

**junk food,** *n.* — *Syn.* snack food, fast food, junk; see **food.**

**junkie*,** *n.* — *Syn.* drug addict, drug abuser, addict, freak*; see **addict, enthusiast** 1.

**junta,** *n.* **1.** [Administrative body] — *Syn.* council, assembly, meeting; see **committee, gathering.**

**2.** [Political faction] — *Syn.* cabal, party, insurrectionary force; see **faction** 1.

**jurisdiction,** *n.* — *Syn.* authority, purview, range, supervision, control, legal direction, legal power, discretion, judicature, bailiwick, province, sphere, magistracy, commission, scope, arbitration, prerogative, right, rule, sway, reign, domain, extent, empire, hegemony, sovereignty; see also **administration** 1, **command** 2, **field** 4, **power** 2.

*See Synonym Study at* POWER.

**jurisprudence,** *n.* — *Syn.* law, legal science, statute, constitution; see **law** 5.

**jurist,** *n.* — *Syn.* attorney, judge, legal scholar, legal adviser; see **judge** 1, **lawyer.**

**juror,** *n.* — *Syn.* juryman, jurywoman, peer, hearer, foreman, foreperson, member of the jury, good man and true*; see also **witness.**

**jury,** *n.* — *Syn.* tribunal, judges, peers, panel, board, grand jury, petit jury, coroner's jury.

**just,** *modif.* **1.** [Precisely] — *Syn.* exactly, correctly, perfectly; see **accurately.**

**2.** [Hardly] — *Syn.* barely, scarcely, by very little; see **hardly.**

**3.** [Only] — *Syn.* merely, simply, plainly; see **only** 2.

**4.** [At the present] — *Syn.* right now, just now, at this moment, presently; see **now** 1.

**5.** [Recently] — *Syn.* just a while ago, lately, a moment ago; see **just now, recently.**

**6.** [*Very] — *Syn.* really, simply, quite; see **very.**

**7.** [Fair] — *Syn.* impartial, equitable, righteous; see **fair** 1.

*See Synonym Study at* FAIR.

**justice,** *n.* **1.** [Fairness] — *Syn.* right, truth, equity; see **fairness.**

**2.** [Lawfulness] — *Syn.* legality, equity, rightfulness, prescriptive right, statutory right, established right, legitimacy, validity, sanction, legalization, constitutionality, authority, code, charter, creed, credo, decree, legitimization, rule, regularity, legal process, authorization; see also **legality.** — *Ant.* illegality, ILLEGITIMACY, inequity.

**3.** [The administration of law] — *Syn.* judicature, adjudication, equity, settlement, arbitration, hearing, legal process, the forms of the law, due process, judicial procedure, jury trial, trial by law, trial by jury, regulation, decision, pronouncement, review, appeal, sentence, consideration, rehearsing, pleading, taking evidence, litigation, prosecution, presentment; see also **judgment** 2, **law** 1, 2, **trial** 2.— *Ant.* lawlessness, DISORDER, despotism.

**4.** [A judge] — *Syn.* magistrate, justice of the peace, chancellor; see **judge** 1.

**bring to justice**— *Syn.* capture, try, exact punishment from; see **arrest** 1, **punish.**

**do justice to**— *Syn.* treat fairly, do right by, appreciate, esteem; see **admire** 1, **respect** 2, **treat** 1.

**do oneself justice**— *Syn.* be fair to oneself, give oneself credit, acquit oneself well; see **justify** 2, **succeed** 1.

**justifiable,** *modif.* — *Syn.* defensible, warrantable, legitimate, proper; see **excusable, fit** 1, **logical** 1.

**justification,** *n.* — *Syn.* excuse, defense, pretext, reason, argument, palliation, extenuation, vindication, redemption, approval, validation, warrant, response, exoneration, exculpation, mitigation, explanation, rationalization, rationale, reply, palliative, apology, apologia, acquittal, salvation, answer, raison d'être, grounds, advocacy, plea, support, confirmation, sanctification, rebuttal, whitewashing; see also **appeal** 1, **explanation** 2. — *Ant.* BLAME, conviction, incrimination.

**justify,** *v.* **1.** [To vindicate] — *Syn.* absolve, acquit, clear; see **excuse.**

**2.** [To give reasons for] — *Syn.* plead, argue for, defend, support, apologize for, palliate, excuse, explain, sustain, maintain, advocate, brief, answer for, be answerable for, put in a plea for, stand up for, make allowances, rationalize, exculpate, speak in favor of, favor, champion, make a plea, acquit oneself of, show sufficient grounds for, countenance, do justice to, condone, pardon, make good, confirm, rebut, show cause; see also **defend** 3, **explain.** — *Ant.* CONVICT, condemn, implicate.

**3.** [To prove by the event] — *Syn.* warrant, verify, bear out; see **prove.**

**justly,** *modif.* **1.** [Honorably] — *Syn.* impartially, honestly, rightly, fairly, straightforwardly, uprightly, reasonably, moderately, temperately, evenhandedly, righteously, piously, equitably, equably, tolerantly, charitably, virtuously, ethically, beneficently, respectably, benevolently, dutifully, duteously, lawfully, legally, legitimately, rightfully, properly, duly, deservedly, in justice, as deserved, as merited, as it ought to be; see also **morally** 1.

**2.** [Exactly] — *Syn.* judiciously, fittingly, properly, well, closely, particularly, discriminatingly, distinctly, clearly, precisely, lucidly, realistically, rationally, credibly, nicely, delicately, correctly, scrupulously, meticulously, sedulously, strictly, faithfully, punctiliously, unerringly, unimpeachably, rigorously, severely, religiously, sharply, critically, shrewdly, painstakingly, factually, objectively, detachedly, pictorially, in detail, verbatim, with mathematical exactitude; see also **accurately.**

**just now,** *modif.* — *Syn.* very recently, quite recently, a moment ago, a minute ago, a little while ago, a short time ago, not long ago, a little while back, a little earlier; see also **recently.**

**just the same,** *modif.* — *Syn.* nevertheless, all the same, nonetheless, in spite of that; see **but** 1, **notwithstanding.**

**jut,** *v.* — *Syn.* extend, bulge, stick out; see **project** 1.

**juvenile,** *modif.* **1.** [Young] — *Syn.* youthful, adolescent, pubescent, tender, immature, infantile, growing, undeveloped, babyish, beardless, boyish, girlish, formative, budding, unfledged, teenage, junior, younger, developing, fresh, milk-fed, blooming, unweaned, unformed, plastic, green★, sappy★, kiddish★; see also **young** 1.— *Ant.* OLD, elder, elderly.

**2.** [Suited to youth] — *Syn.* immature, callow, puerile, childish; see **childish** 1, **naive, young** 2.

*See Synonym Study at* YOUNG.

**juxtapose,** *v.* — *Syn.* place next to, put side by side, compare, oppose; see **compare** 2, **place** 1.

# K

**kaleidoscopic,** *modif.* **1.** [Brightly colored] — *Syn.* colorful, multicolored, vivid; see **bright** 2, **multicolored.**
**2.** [Ever changing] — *Syn.* protean, plastic, fluid; see **changeable** 2, **changing.**
**kaput,** *modif.* — *Syn.* ruined, defunct, out of order, done for\*; see **beaten** 1, **broken** 2, **dead** 1, **destroyed.**
**karate,** *n.* — *Syn.* martial art, self-defense, kung fu, tae kwon do; see **fight** 1.
**keel,** *n.* — *Syn.* board, bottom timber, keelson; see **base** 3, **bottom** 1, **hull** 1.
   **on an even keel** — *Syn.* steady, level, stable; see **balanced** 1.
**keel over,** *v.* — *Syn.* overturn, capsize, pitch; see **upset** 1.
**keen,** *modif.* **1.** [Sharp] — *Syn.* pointed, edged, well-honed, acute; see **sharp** 1, 2.
**2.** [Astute] — *Syn.* bright, clever, shrewd; see **clever** 1, **intelligent** 1, **judicious.**
**3.** [Intense] — *Syn.* cutting, piercing, biting, strong; see **extreme** 2, **intense.**
**4.** [Eager] — *Syn.* ardent, interested, intent; see **enthusiastic** 1, 2.
**5.** [Sensitive] — *Syn.* perceptive, penetrating, sharp; see **observant** 1.
*See Synonym Study at* EAGER, SHARP.
**keenly,** *modif.* — *Syn.* acutely, sharply, perceptively, astutely, cleverly, penetratingly, piercingly, precisely, alertly, distinctly, eagerly, avidly, intently, vividly, intensely, with acumen, with perception, with precision, on the ball\*; see also **eagerly, very, vigorously.**
**keenness,** *n.* — *Syn.* insight, sharpness, shrewdness; see **acumen, judgment** 1.
**keen-sighted,** *modif.* — *Syn.* keen-eyed, clearsighted, sharp-eyed, sharp-sighted, eagle-eyed, hawk-eyed, farsighted, telescopic, Argus-eyed, cat-eyed; see also **observant** 1.
**keep,** *v.* **1.** [To hold] — *Syn.* retain, grip, grasp, have; see **hold** 1.
**2.** [To maintain] — *Syn.* preserve, conserve, care for; see **maintain** 3, **preserve** 3.
**3.** [To continue] — *Syn.* keep going, carry on, persist, sustain; see **continue** 1, **endure** 1.
**4.** [To operate] — *Syn.* administer, run, direct; see **command** 2, **manage** 1.
**5.** [To tend] — *Syn.* care for, minister to, attend; see **tend** 1.
**6.** [To remain] — *Syn.* stay, continue, last, abide; see **continue** 1, **endure** 1, **remain** 1.
**7.** [To store] — *Syn.* deposit, cache, put; see **save** 3, **store.**
**8.** [To prevent; *used with from*] — *Syn.* stop, block, avert; see **hinder, prevent, restrain** 1.
**9.** [To observe] — *Syn.* adhere to, fulfill, celebrate; see **celebrate** 1, **follow** 2, **obey** 2.
*See Synonym Study at* CELEBRATE.
   **for keeps\*** — *Syn.* permanently, finally, for always, for good; see **finally** 1, **forever** 1.

**keep after,** *v.* **1.** [To pursue] — *Syn.* track, trail, follow; see **pursue** 1.
**2.** [To nag] — *Syn.* push, remind, pester; see **bother** 2, **remind** 2.
**keep an appointment,** *v.* — *Syn.* show up, be on time, be there; see **arrive** 1.
**keep at,** *v.* — *Syn.* persist in, persevere, carry on, plug away\*; see **continue** 1, **endure** 1.
**keep away,** *v.* **1.** [To keep one's distance] — *Syn.* stay away, keep clear, give a wide berth; see **avoid.**
**2.** [To restrain] — *Syn.* keep off, hold back, defend one from; see **hinder, prevent, restrict** 2.
**keep back,** *v.* **1.** [To delay] — *Syn.* check, hold back, impede, hold up; see **delay** 1, **hinder.**
**2.** [To restrict] — *Syn.* restrain, inhibit, hold in check; see **forbid, hinder, restrict** 2.
**3.** [To refuse to reveal] — *Syn.* withhold, reserve, keep to oneself; see **hide** 1.
**keep calm,** *v.* — *Syn.* take one's time, keep cool, be patient; see **calm down, relax** 1.
**keep down,** *v.* **1.** [To keep under control] — *Syn.* reduce, deaden, muffle; see **decrease** 2, **quiet** 2.
**2.** [To subdue] — *Syn.* oppress, keep under, hold down, subjugate; see **command** 2, **restrain** 1, **subject.**
**keeper,** *n.* **1.** [Operator] — *Syn.* manager, owner, entrepreneur; see **administrator, owner.**
**2.** [Watchman] — *Syn.* guard, official, attendant; see **guardian** 1, **warden, watchman.**
**keep from,** *v.* **1.** [To abstain] — *Syn.* desist, refrain, avoid; see **abstain.**
**2.** [To prevent] — *Syn.* prohibit, forestall, impede; see **hinder, prevent, restrain** 1.
**keep going,** *v.* — *Syn.* progress, proceed, persevere, keep on; see **advance** 1, **continue** 1, **endure** 1.
**keeping,** *n.* **1.** [Custody] — *Syn.* care, charge, protection, safekeeping; see **custody** 1, **preservation.**
**2.** [Consistency] — *Syn.* uniformity, conformity, balance, harmony; see **agreement** 2, **consistency** 1.
   **in keeping with** — *Syn.* similar to, much the same as, in accord with, in conformity with; see **alike** 2, 3.
**keep off,** *v.* — *Syn.* fend off, stave off, hold off, avert; see **defend** 1, **prevent, repel** 1.
**keep off** *or* **out,** *interj.* — *Syn.* Hands off! Stay away! Stop! Keep off the grass! No trespassing! No hunting or fishing! Private property!
**keep on,** *v.* — *Syn.* continue, persist, repeat, pursue; see **continue** 1, **endure** 1.
**keep out,** *v.* — *Syn.* exclude, bar, shut out; see **bar** 2.
**keep safe,** *v.* — *Syn.* care for, safeguard, protect; see **defend** 2, **guard** 2.
**keepsake,** *n.* — *Syn.* memento, token, remembrance; see **souvenir.**
**keep to,** *v.* — *Syn.* adhere to, be devoted to, restrict oneself to, confine oneself to; see **follow** 2, **obey** 2.
**keep to oneself,** *v.* — *Syn.* cultivate solitude, avoid human companionship, remain aloof, be a recluse, be a hermit, be a lone wolf, stay away, not mingle, not mix,

hold oneself aloof, keep oneself to oneself, keep one's own counsel, keep secret, keep confidential, not breathe a word, hold one's tongue, keep under one's hat\*.

**keep under,** *v.* — *Syn.* suppress, prevent, subdue; see **check** 2, **restrain** 1, **subject.**

**keep up,** *v.* **1.** [To keep in repair] — *Syn.* maintain, sustain, care for, safeguard; see **maintain** 3.

**2.** [To continue] — *Syn.* persist, persevere, carry on; see **continue** 1.

**3.** [To maintain the pace] — *Syn.* keep pace, keep step, keep abreast, keep up-to-date; see **compete, equal, rival.**

**keep up with the Joneses,** *v.* — *Syn.* climb socially, emulate, scramble for position; see **compete, conform.**

**keg,** *n.* — *Syn.* cask, drum, vat; see **barrel, container.**

**kennel,** *n.* — *Syn.* doghouse, den, pound, run; see **enclosure** 1.

**kept,** *modif.* **1.** [Preserved] — *Syn.* put up, stored, conserved; see **preserved** 2.

**2.** [Retained] — *Syn.* maintained, withheld, held, clutched, guarded, watched over, reserved, saved, on file, at hand, kept in reserve; see also **retained** 1, **saved** 2.

**3.** [Observed] — *Syn.* obeyed, honored, solemnized, commemorated, celebrated, followed, continued, regarded, discharged, maintained, carried on, held inviolate; see also **fulfilled.** — *Ant.* ABANDONED, dishonored, forgotten.

**kept woman,** *n.* — *Syn.* mistress, concubine, paramour; see **mistress** 2.

**kerchief,** *n.* — *Syn.* scarf, bandanna, babushka, shawl; see **handkerchief, scarf.**

**kernel,** *n.* **1.** [Grain] — *Syn.* nut, core, heart, germ, fruit, seed; see also **grain** 1, **seed** 1.

**2.** [Essential portion] — *Syn.* heart, center, root; see **essence** 1.

**3.** [A small piece] — *Syn.* piece, atom, morsel; see **bit** 1, **division** 2, **part** 1.

**kerosene,** *v.* — *Syn.* fuel, petroleum distillate, coal oil, lighting oil, lamp oil, paraffin (British); see also **fuel, oil** 2.

**ketchup,** *n.* — *Syn.* tomato sauce, tomato purée, condiment, salsa; see **relish** 1.

**kettle,** *n.* — *Syn.* teakettle, cauldron, saucepan, stewpot; see **pot** 1.

**kettledrum,** *n.* — *Syn.* timpano, tabla, tambour; see **drum, musical instrument.**

**key,** *modif.* — *Syn.* essential, important, chief, pivotal; see **fundamental** 1, **principal.**

**key,** *n.* **1.** [Instrument to open a lock] — *Syn.* latchkey, opener, master key, passkey, skeleton key, *passe-partout* (French).

**2.** [A means of solution] — *Syn.* answer, explanation, solution, clue, index, pointer, pivot, hinge, crux, fulcrum, lever, nexus, core, root, taproot, nucleus, earmark, marker, symptom, sign, brand, cipher, code, indicator, blueprint, signboard, tip-off\*; see also **answer** 2.

**keyboard,** *n.* — *Syn.* row of keys, clavier, console, claviature, manual, blacks and whites\*, the eighty-eight\*, ivories\*; see also **piano.**

**keyed up\*,** *modif.* — *Syn.* stimulated, tense, nervous, hyped up\*; see **excited.**

**keynote,** *modif.* — *Syn.* main, leading, official, opening; see **important** 1, **principal.**

**keynote,** *n.* — *Syn.* basic idea, ruling principle, theme; see **criterion, essence** 1.

**keystone,** *n.* — *Syn.* buttress, prop, mainstay, cornerstone; see **brace** 1, **foundation** 2, **support** 2.

**kick,** *n.* **1.** [A blow with the foot] — *Syn.* boot, swift kick, jolt, jar, thrust, fillip; see also **blow** 1.

**2.** [In sports, a kicked ball] — *Syn.* punt, drop kick, place kick, free kick, boot\*.

**3.** [\*An objection] — *Syn.* complaint, reproof, animadversion, beef\*; see **objection** 2.

**4.** [\*Pleasurable reaction; *often plural*] — *Syn.* excitement, amusement, charge\*; see **enjoyment** 2, **thrill.**

**5.** [\*A stimulating quality] — *Syn.* vitality, potency, punch\*, wallop\*; see **flavor** 1, **force** 3.

**kick,** *v.* **1.** [To give a blow with the foot] — *Syn.* boot, jolt, thrust, propel, punt, drop-kick, place-kick, kick off; see also **beat** 2, **hit** 1.

**2.** [\*To object] — *Syn.* complain, criticize, carp; see **complain** 1, **oppose** 1.

**kick around\*,** *v.* — *Syn.* mistreat, treat badly, treat roughly, misuse; see **abuse** 1.

**kickback\*,** *n.* — *Syn.* payment, percentage, payola\*; see **bribe, refund.**

**kick back\*,** *v.* — *Syn.* pay in, repay, return; see **pay** 1, **refund** 1.

**kick in\*,** *v.* — *Syn.* contribute, donate, pay, chip in\*; see **contribute, give** 1.

**kickoff,** *modif.* — *Syn.* opening, starting, initial; see **first** 1.

**kickoff,** *n.* — *Syn.* opening, beginning, launching; see **origin** 1.

**kick off,** *v.* — *Syn.* start, open, get under way; see **begin** 1.

**kick out\*,** *v.* — *Syn.* reject, throw out, eject; see **dismiss** 1, **oust, remove** 1.

**kid,** *n.* **1.** [The young of certain animals] — *Syn.* billikin, nannikin, lamb, lambkin, fawn, calf, weanling; see also **animal** 2, **goat, leather.**

**2.** [\*A child or young person] — *Syn.* youngster, teenager, tot; see **boy, child, girl** 1, **youth** 3.

**kid\*,** *v.* — *Syn.* tease, pretend, fool, rib\*; see **joke, ridicule.**

**kiddish\*,** *modif.* — *Syn.* juvenile, immature, babyish; see **childish** 1, **naive, young** 2.

**kidnap,** *v.* — *Syn.* abduct, seize, take hostage, carry off, carry away, hold for ransom, ravish, capture, steal, rape, waylay, shanghai, make off with, make away with, grab, remove, lay hands on, put under duress, impress, spirit away, snatch\*, pirate\*, bundle off\*; see also **seize** 2. — *Ant.* ransom, RESCUE, release.

**kidnapped,** *modif.* — *Syn.* abducted, held for ransom, taken hostage, seized, captured, made off with, transported, ravished, stolen, raped, carried away, carried off, shanghaied, waylaid, manhandled, kept under duress, held in durance vile, impressed, spirited away, held under illegal restraint, snatched\*; see also **captured** 1. — *Ant.* FREE, rescued, released.

**kidnapper,** *n.* — *Syn.* abductor, felon, shanghaier, carjacker\*; see **criminal.**

**kidnapping,** *n.* — *Syn.* abduction, seizure, taking hostage, baby-snatching\*; see **crime** 2.

**kidney,** *n.* — *Syn.* excretory organ, urinary organ, abdominal gland; see **organ** 2.

**kill,** *v.* **1.** [To deprive of life] — *Syn.* slay, slaughter, murder, assassinate, massacre, butcher, execute, put to death, dispatch, hang, lynch, electrocute, knife, immolate, sacrifice, shoot, strangle, garrote, stifle, poison, choke, smother, suffocate, asphyxiate, drown, behead, hack, guillotine, crucify, dismember, decapitate, disembowel, quarter, tear limb from limb, destroy, give the death blow, give the *coup de grâce*, take someone's life, put an end to, victimize, martyr, exterminate, purge, stab, cut the throat, shoot down, put to the sword, mangle, cut down, bring down, mow down, machine-gun, decimate, carry off, pick off, liquidate, eliminate, remove, put one out of one's misery, put to sleep, put away, euthanize, starve, bludgeon, make away with, do away with, commit murder, spill blood, bump off*, rub out*, wipe out*, hit*, erase*, waste*, grease*, take for a ride*, do in*, knock off*, heave overboard*, finish off*, get rid of*, blow one's brains out*, send to glory*, brain*, zap*, ice*, off*, blow away*. — *Ant.* RESCUE, resuscitate, animate.

**2.** [To deprive of existence] — *Syn.* exterminate, ruin, annihilate; see **abolish, destroy** 1.

**3.** [To cancel] — *Syn.* annul, nullify, counteract; see **cancel** 2, **recant, revoke.**

**4.** [To turn off] — *Syn.* halt, shut off, stop; see **halt** 2, **turn off** 1.

**5.** [To veto] — *Syn.* cancel, prohibit, refuse; see **forbid, refuse.**

*SYN.* — **kill** is the general word in this list, meaning to cause the death of in any way, and may be applied to persons, animals, or plants; **slay**, now largely a literary word, implies deliberate and violent killing; **murder** applies to an unlawful and malicious or premeditated killing; **assassinate** implies specifically the sudden killing of a politically important person, often by someone hired or delegated to do this; **execute** denotes a killing in accordance with a legally imposed sentence; **dispatch** suggests a killing by direct action, such as shooting, and emphasizes speed or promptness

**killer,** *n.* — *Syn.* murderer, assassin, slayer, gunman, gangster, shooter, strangler, poisoner, butcher, executioner, hangman, assassinator, hit man*, manslayer, serial murderer, sniper, electrocutioner, headsman, axman, cutthroat, ruffian, garroter, lyncher, exterminator, homicide, patricide, matricide, parricide, fratricide, regicide, suicide, hired gun*, hatchet man*; see also **criminal, destroyer** 1, **executioner.**

**killing,** *modif.* **1.** [Destructive] — *Syn.* mortal, lethal, fatal; see **deadly** 1, **destructive** 2.

**2.** [*Funny] — *Syn.* ludicrous, overpowering, irresistible; see **funny** 1.

**killing,** *n.* **1.** [Murder] — *Syn.* slaying, assassination, slaughter; see **crime** 2, **murder.**

**2.** [*A sudden great profit] — *Syn.* windfall, bonanza, coup; see **profit** 2, **success** 2.

**kiln,** *n.* — *Syn.* hearth, pottery oven, reduction furnace; see **furnace, oven.**

**kin,** *n.* — *Syn.* blood relatives, family, kindred, kinfolk; see **family** 1, **relative.**

**kind,** *modif.* — *Syn.* tender, well-meaning, considerate, compassionate, benevolent, kindly, benign, generous, charitable, humane, merciful, loving, pleasant, amiable, soft, softhearted, kindhearted, sympathetic, understanding, solicitous, sweet, gentle, compliant, helpful, obliging, neighborly, accommodating, gracious, indulgent, noble-minded, motherly, fatherly, delicate, tactful, tenderhearted, warmhearted, good-natured, good-hearted, inoffensive, altruistic, other-directed, complaisant, lenient, acquiescent, easy-going, patient, tolerant, mellow, genial, sensitive, courteous, agreeable, thoughtful, assisting, well-disposed, willing, mollifying, benignant, good, doing good unto others; see also **humane** 1, **merciful** 1. — *Ant.* cruel, brutal, unfeeling.

*SYN.* — **kind** implies the possession of sympathetic or generous qualities, either habitually or specifically, or is

applied to actions manifesting these [he is *kind* only to his mother, your *kind* remarks]; **kindly** usually implies a characteristic nature or general disposition marked by such qualities [his *kindly* old uncle]; **benign** suggests a mild or kindly nature and is applied especially to a gracious superior [a *benign* employer]; **benevolent** implies a charitable or altruistic inclination to do good [his *benevolent* interest in orphans]

**kind,** *n.* **1.** [Class] — *Syn.* classification, species, genus; see **class** 1.

**2.** [Type] — *Syn.* sort, variety, description, fiber, stamp, ilk, character, complexion, tendency, gender, habit, breed, feather, set, tribe, denomination, persuasion, manner, connection, designation, brand.

**in kind** — *Syn.* in the same way, with something like that received, in a similar fashion; see **similarly.**

**of a kind** — *Syn.* similar, same, like; see **alike** 1.

**kindhearted,** *modif.* — *Syn.* compassionate, generous, sympathetic; see **humane** 1, **kind, merciful** 1.

**kindheartedness,** *n.* — *Syn.* generosity, benevolence, goodness; see **kindness** 1.

**kindle,** *v.* **1.** [To start a fire] — *Syn.* light, ignite, set on fire; see **burn** 1, 2, **ignite.**

**2.** [To excite] — *Syn.* arouse, inspire, animate; see **excite** 1, 2.

**kindliness,** *n.* — *Syn.* generosity, charity, benevolence; see **kindness** 1.

**kindling,** *n.* **1.** [Material for starting a fire] — *Syn.* firewood, tinder, coals, twigs; see **fuel, wood** 2.

**2.** [Combustion] — *Syn.* ignition, burning, lighting; see **fire** 1.

**kindly,** *modif.* **1.** [Kind] — *Syn.* generous, helpful, benevolent; see **humane** 1, **kind, merciful** 1.

**2.** [In a kind manner] — *Syn.* cordially, considerately, benevolently, genially, graciously, warmly, affectionately, tenderly, solicitously, good-naturedly, humanely, helpfully, sympathetically, courteously, politely, thoughtfully, compassionately, benignly, understandingly, charitably, tolerantly, delicately; see also **generously** 2.

*See Synonym Study at* KIND.

**kindness,** *n.* **1.** [The quality of being kind] — *Syn.* tenderness, good intentions, consideration, sympathy, sweetness, benevolence, generosity, helpfulness, kindheartedness, indulgence, delicacy, tact, benignity, mildness, courtesy, thoughtfulness, humanity, courteousness, understanding, solicitude, solicitousness, compassion, unselfishness, altruism, agreeableness, amicableness, commiseration, warmheartedness, softheartedness, politeness, kindliness, clemency, goodness, beneficence, philanthropy, charity, friendliness, good disposition, good nature, mercy, affection, loving-kindness, cordiality, amiability, forbearance, tolerance, graciousness, virtue; see also **generosity** 1, **tolerance** 1. — *Ant.* brutality, cruelty, selfishness.

**2.** [A kindly act] — *Syn.* favor, service, good deed, good turn, benefit, act of kindness, relief, succor, charity, benevolence, philanthropy, boon, blessing, courtesy, kind office, bounty, benefaction, self-sacrifice, mercy, lift*, boost*, good lick*, break*; see also **aid** 1. — *Ant.* transgression, INJURY, wrong.

**kind of*,** *modif.* — *Syn.* somewhat, rather, sort of*; see **moderately.**

**kindred,** *modif.* — *Syn.* similar, like, akin; see **alike** 2, **related** 2, 3.

*See Synonym Study at* RELATED.

**kindred,** *n.* — *Syn.* kin, relations, relatives; see **family** 1, **relative.**

**kinetic,** *modif.* — *Syn.* motor, dynamic, motive; see **active** 1, **moving** 1.

**kinfolk,** *n.* — *Syn.* relatives, kin, kindred; see **family** 1, **relative.**

**king,** *n.* 1. [A male sovereign] — *Syn.* monarch, ruler, majesty, despot, tyrant, potentate, prince, crowned head, emperor, autocrat, czar, tsar, caesar, kaiser, *rex* (Latin), suzerain, overlord, imperator, regal personage, liege, lord temporal, sultan, caliph, shah, pasha, Dalai Lama, mogul, rajah, maharajah, khan, mikado; see also **dictator, ruler** 1. — *Ant.* subject, servant, slave.
2. [A man who is preeminent] — *Syn.* lord, chief, head, commander, boss, mogul, tycoon, magnate, master, authority, power, senior, dean, patriarch, star, luminary, leading light, high muck-a-muck*, big shot*, bigwig*, noise*, head honcho*; see also **administrator, chief** 1, **leader** 2, **personage** 2. — *Ant.* underling, menial, flunky.

**kingdom,** *n.* — *Syn.* realm, domain, country, empire, lands, possessions, principality, state, dominions, monarchy, suzerainty, duchy, sway, rule, scepter, crown, throne, subject territory; see also **area** 2, **nation** 1, **territory** 2.

**kingdom come,** *n.* — *Syn.* afterlife, the hereafter, abode of the blessed; see **heaven** 2.

**kingly,** *modif.* — *Syn.* majestic, regal, aristocratic; see **noble** 3, **royal** 1, 2.

**kingship,** *n.* — *Syn.* supremacy, sovereignty, monarchy, majesty; see **power** 2, **royalty.**

**king-size,** *modif.* — *Syn.* extra-large, large-size, giant; see **broad** 1, **large** 1.

**kink,** *n.* 1. [A twist] — *Syn.* curl, tangle, crimp, crinkle; see **curl, curve** 1.
2. [A muscle spasm] — *Syn.* cramp, knot, twinge, crick; see **pain** 2.
3. [An eccentricity] — *Syn.* notion, whim, peculiarity; see **quirk.**
4. [A difficulty] — *Syn.* hitch, defect, complication; see **difficulty** 1, **impediment** 1.

**kinky,** *modif.* 1. [Full of kinks] — *Syn.* curly, frizzy, knotted, frizzled; see **curly** 1, 2, **knotted.**
2. [*Bizarre] — *Syn.* weird, odd, deviant, sick*; see **unusual** 2.

**kinship,** *n.* — *Syn.* family relationship, affiliation, connection, alliance; see **family** 1, **relationship.**

**kinsman,** *n.* — *Syn.* relative, sibling, parent, kin; see **family** 1, **relative.**

**kiosk,** *n.* — *Syn.* pavilion, newsstand, stall; see **booth.**

**kipper,** *v.* — *Syn.* curl, dry, smoke, smoke-cure; see **preserve** 3.

**kismet,** *n.* — *Syn.* karma, fortune, fate, destiny; see **chance** 1, **destiny** 1, **doom** 1.

**kiss,** *n.* — *Syn.* salutation, embrace, salute, endearment, osculation, touch of the lips, butterfly kiss, caress, French kiss, soul kiss, buss*, smack*, smooch*, peck*; see also **touch** 2.

**kiss,** *v.* — *Syn.* salute, osculate, *baiser* (French), caress, French-kiss, soul-kiss, blow a kiss, smack*, smooch*, pet*, buss*, neck*, make out*, play post office*; see also **caress, love** 2, **touch** 1.

**kiss goodbye*,** *v.* — *Syn.* give up, suffer the loss of, sign away, forfeit; see **abandon** 1, **lose** 2.

**kissing,** *n.* — *Syn.* osculation, exchange of kisses, embracing, fondling, love-making, spooning*, necking*, petting*, making out*, smooching*, bussing*, parking*.

**kit,** *n.* 1. [A set] — *Syn.* assortment, selection, stock; see **collection** 2.
2. [Equipment] — *Syn.* material, tools, outfit; see **equipment.**

3. [A pack] — *Syn.* case, knapsack, satchel; see **bag** 1, **case** 7, **container.**

**the whole kit and caboodle*** — *Syn.* lot, collection, all; see **everything.**

**kitchen,** *n.* — *Syn.* kitchenette, scullery, galley, cuisine, canteen, cook's room, cookhouse, pantry, larder, mess*.

**kite,** *n.* — *Syn.* box kite, Hargrave kite, Chinese kite, cellular kite, Eddy kite, tailless kite, tetrahedral kite.

**kith and kin,** *n.* — *Syn.* friends and relatives, family, relations; see **family** 1, **relative.**

**kitten,** *n.* — *Syn.* pussy, kitty, puss, pussycat, kittycat, kit, tabbykin, young cat; see also **cat** 1.

**kittenish,** *modif.* — *Syn.* playful, mischievous, frisky, coy; see **flirtatious, jaunty.**

**kleptomania,** *n.* — *Syn.* compulsion to steal, thievishness, light-fingeredness; see **neurosis, theft.**

**kleptomaniac,** *n.* — *Syn.* thief, pilferer, compulsive stealer; see **neurotic, robber.**

**klutz*,** *n.* — *Syn.* clod, fumbler, dolt, oaf; see **bungler, fool** 1.

**knack,** *n.* — *Syn.* trick, skill, talent, faculty; see **ability** 1, 2, **talent** 1.
*See Synonym Study at* TALENT.

**knapsack,** *n.* — *Syn.* backpack, pack, kit, rucksack; see **bag** 1.

**knave,** *n.* — *Syn.* scamp, fraud, villain; see **rascal.**

**knavery,** *n.* — *Syn.* thievery, rascality, fraud; see **deception** 1, **dishonesty, evil** 1.

**knavish,** *modif.* — *Syn.* felonious, fraudulent, conniving, untrustworthy; see **dishonest** 1, 2.

**knead,** *v.* — *Syn.* work, mix, ply, massage, squeeze, manipulate, shape, alter, twist, fold, aerate, blend, press, rub.

**knee,** *n.* — *Syn.* joint, knee joint, kneecap, patella, crook, bend, hinge, ginglymus joint, articulation of the femur and the tibia; see also **bone.**

**bring to one's knees** — *Syn.* beat, force to submit, coerce; see **defeat** 1, 2.

**kneel,** *v.* — *Syn.* bend the knee, rest on the knees, do obeisance, genuflect, bend, stoop, bow down, curtsey; see also **bow** 1.

**knell,** *n.* — *Syn.* ring, toll, signal, death bell; see **bell** 2, **noise** 1.

**knell,** *v.* — *Syn.* peal, toll, chime; see **ring** 3, **sound** 1.

**knickers,** *pl.n.* — *Syn.* knickerbockers, knee breeches, trousers, shorts; see **clothes, pants** 1.

**knickknack,** *n.* — *Syn.* ornament, curio, gewgaw, gimcrack, *objet d'art* (French), conversation piece, bric-a-brac, curiosity, bibelot, bauble, trinket, gadget, trifle, toy, plaything, frill, furbelow, showpiece, eye-catcher, decoration, embellishment, trapping, collectible, kickshaw, gingerbread, whimsy, tchotchke*; see also **decoration** 2, **device** 1, **thing** 1.

**knife,** *n.* — *Syn.* blade, cutter, sword, bayonet, cutting edge, dagger, stiletto, lance, lancet, bit, cutlass, machete, kris, whittle, poniard, scalpel, edge, dirk, sickle, scythe, sabre, scimitar, claymore, broadsword, bodkin, snickersnee, point, skiver, skewer, spit, guillotine, skean, misericord, pigsticker*, toad-stabber*, tickler*, shiv*; see also **razor, sword.**
Kinds of knives include: carving, chef's, paring, chopping, table, dinner, breakfast, dessert, grapefruit, fish, pocket, clasp, hunting, Bowie, corn, cane, butcher, skinning, surgical, paper, pruning, oyster, putty, palette, ferrule, bread, butter, cake, wood carver's, molding, paper hanger's, miter, excelsior, stiletto, jackknife, switchblade, Boy Scout, Swiss Army, Buck.

**knife,** *v.* 1. [To stab] — *Syn.* cut, slash, pierce, lance; see **cut** 2, **hurt** 1, **stab.**

**2.** [*To injure in an underhanded way] — *Syn.* trick, betray, give a coward's blow, strike below the belt; see **betray** 1, **deceive.**

**knife through,** *v.* — *Syn.* dash, plunge through, slip through, pierce; see **dart** 1, **slide** 1.

**knight,** *n.* — *Syn.* cavalier, *caballero* (Spanish), gentleman, champion, knight-errant, thane, bachelor, man-at-arms, paladin, Templar, Hospitaler; see also **aristocrat, Sir** 1.

**knight-errantry,** *n.* **1.** [Bravery] — *Syn.* boldness, gallantry, chivalry; see **courage** 1, **strength** 1.

**2.** [Recklessness] — *Syn.* craziness, quixotism, impetuosity, idealism; see **carelessness, idealism** 1, **indiscretion** 1.

**knighthood,** *n.* — *Syn.* chivalry, gallantry, courtliness; see **courage** 1, **courtesy** 1.

**knightly,** *modif.* — *Syn.* gallant, courteous, *gentil* (French); see **brave** 1, **chivalrous, noble** 1, 2.

**knit,** *v.* **1.** [To form by knitting] — *Syn.* weave, crochet, purl, cable, spin, web, net, loop; see also **sew, weave** 1.

**2.** [To combine or join closely] — *Syn.* intermingle, connect, affiliate; see **join** 1.

**3.** [To grow together] — *Syn.* heal, mend, repair; see **improve** 2, **recover** 3, **unite** 1.

**knitted,** *modif.* — *Syn.* knit, purled, crocheted, woven, stitched, spun, meshed, webbed, wefted; see also **sewn, woven.**

**knob,** *n.* **1.** [A projection] — *Syn.* lump, bump, protuberance, boss; see **bulge.**

**2.** [A handle] — *Syn.* doorknob, latch, control; see **dial, handle** 1.

**knobby,** *modif.* — *Syn.* knobbed, lumpy, bumpy; see **bent, crooked** 1, **irregular** 4.

**knock,** *n.* — *Syn.* rap, thump, whack; see **beat** 1, **blow** 1, **injury** 1.

**knock,** *v.* — *Syn.* tap, rap, thump; see **beat** 1, 2, **hit** 1, **hurt** 1.

**knock about*,** *v.* — *Syn.* rove, drift, wander; see **drift, roam, walk** 1.

**knock down,** *v.* **1.** [To ruin] — *Syn.* devastate, damage, trample; see **destroy** 1, **ravage.**

**2.** [To hit] — *Syn.* thrash, drub, kayo*; see **beat** 2, **hit** 1, **knock out** 2.

**knock off*,** *v.* **1.** [To kill] — *Syn.* murder, assassinate, shoot; see **kill** 1.

**2.** [To accomplish] — *Syn.* complete, finish, dispose of; see **achieve** 1.

**3.** [To stop work] — *Syn.* quit, leave off, call it a day*; see **quit** 2, **stop** 2.

**knock oneself out*,** *v.* — *Syn.* slave, labor, do one's utmost, exhaust oneself; see **tire** 1, 2, **work** 1.

**knockout,** *n.* **1.** [A blow that knocks unconscious] — *Syn.* knockout blow, finishing blow, final blow, technical knockout, TKO, *coup de grâce* (French), KO*, kayo*, blackout*, cold pack*, hearts and flowers*, the count*; see also **blow** 1.

**2.** [*A striking person or thing] — *Syn.* sensation, smash, stunner*; see **beauty** 4, **gem** 3, **success** 3.

**knock out,** *v.* **1.** [To make unconscious or exhausted] — *Syn.* put to sleep, stupefy, anesthetize, exhaust; see **deaden** 1, **drug, tire** 2.

**2.** [To strike down] — *Syn.* strike senseless, render unconscious, knock one out of one's senses, knock down for the count*, knock cold*, kayo*, KO*, knock for a loop*, put a silencer on*, put out like a light*, flatten*, lay out*; see also **beat** 2, **defeat** 3, **hit** 1.

**knock together*,** *v.* — *Syn.* make, throw together, construct; see **build** 1, **create** 2.

**knock up*,** *v.* — *Syn.* impregnate, make pregnant, inseminate; see **fertilize** 2, **propagate** 1.

**knoll,** *n.* — *Syn.* rise, mound, hillock; see **hill, mountain** 1.

**knot,** *n.* **1.** [An arrangement of strands] — *Syn.* tie, hitch, splice, ligature, bond, bow.
Types of knots include: anchor, sheet bend, timber hitch, bowknot, clove hitch, carrick bend, half crown, diamond hitch, figure-of-eight, fisherman's bend, flat, Windsor, square, granny, half hitch, inside clinch, thief, outside clinch, lanyard, loop, mesh, midshipman's hitch, open hand, overhand, rolling hitch, round seizing, bowline on a bight, running bowline, sheepshank, shroud, running, slide, single, slip, stopper, surgeon's, trefoil, weaver's hitch, stevedore's, harness hitch, reef, cat's-paw, Blackwall hitch, magnus hitch, halyard bend.

**2.** [A hard or twisted portion] — *Syn.* snarl, tangle, gnarl, snag, bunch, contortion, coil, spiral, warp, screw, helix, perplexity, entanglement, twist, twirl, whirl, whorl.

**3.** [A group] — *Syn.* cluster, clump, assortment, gathering; see **bunch** 1, **collection** 2.

**tie the knot*** — *Syn.* wed, get married, get hitched*; see **marry** 1.

**knot,** *v.* — *Syn.* bind, tie, hitch, snarl; see **entangle, fasten** 1, **tie** 2.

**knotted,** *modif.* — *Syn.* tied, twisted, tangled, snarled, entangled, bunched, clustered, clumped, snagged, whirled, engaged, perplexed, looped, coiled, hitched, spliced, fastened, bent, warped, lashed, clinched, meshed, seized, banded, lassoed, braided, intertwined, linked, involved; see also **tight** 2. — *Ant.* FREE, loose, separate.

**knotty,** *modif.* — *Syn.* troublesome, tricky, complicated; see **complex** 2, **difficult** 2.

**know,** *v.* **1.** [To possess information] — *Syn.* be aware of, be cognizant of, be acquainted with, be informed, be in possession of the facts, have knowledge of, be schooled in, be read in, be learned in, be versed in, be conversant with, be familiar with, appreciate, prize, ken, recognize, be sensible of, know full well, be sure of, have at one's fingertips, be master of, have a grasp of, know by heart, know inside and out, know by rote, remember, be instructed, be awake to, keep up on, have information about, know what's what, know all the answers, have someone's number*, have the jump on*, have down cold*, have the goods on*, be hep to*, know one's stuff*, know the score*, know the ropes*. — *Ant.* be oblivious of, be ignorant of, misunderstand.

**2.** [To understand] — *Syn.* comprehend, apprehend, grasp, see into; see **understand** 1.

**3.** [To recognize] — *Syn.* perceive, discern, distinguish, identify, be familiar with, have the friendship of, acknowledge, be accustomed to, associate with, be acquainted with; see also **associate** 1.

**in the know*** — *Syn.* informed, knowing, aware, privy; see **conscious** 1, **educated** 1, **knowledgeable.**

**knowable,** *modif.* — *Syn.* distinct, visible, plain, comprehensible; see **obvious** 1, 2, **understandable.**

**know-how*,** *n.* — *Syn.* skill, background, competence, expertise; see **ability** 1, **experience** 3, **knowledge** 1.

**know how,** *v.* — *Syn.* be able, have the necessary background, be trained in, be skilled in; see **understand** 1.

**knowing,** *modif.* **1.** [Shrewd] — *Syn.* sharp, clever, acute; see **intelligent** 1, **judicious, reasonable** 1.

**2.** [Implying possession of private information] — *Syn.* significant, meaningful, conspiratorial; see **expressive.**

**knowingly,** *modif.* — *Syn.* intentionally, purposely, consciously; see **carefully** 2, **deliberately.**

**knowledge,** *n.* **1.** [That which is known] — *Syn.* information, learning, lore, erudition, wisdom, scholarship, facts, data, instruction, book-learning, cognizance, understanding, comprehension, enlightenment, expertise, intelligence, light, doctrine, dogma, theory, science, principles, data base, philosophy, awareness, insight, proficiency, attainments, accomplishments, education, culture, substance, observation, experience, store of learning, know-how\*, the scoop\*, the goods\*, the know\*; see also **culture** 3, **data, experience** 3. — *Ant.* emptiness, IGNORANCE, pretension.
**2.** [Awareness] — *Syn.* acquaintance, familiarity, conversance, consciousness; see **awareness, familiarity** 2.

*SYN.* — **knowledge** applies to any body of facts gathered by study, observation, etc., and to the ideas inferred from these facts, and connotes an understanding of what is known [man's *knowledge* of the universe]; **information** applies to data that are gathered in any way, as by reading, observation, hearsay, etc. and does not necessarily connote validity [inaccurate *information*]; **learning** is knowledge acquired by study, especially in languages, literature, philosophy, etc.; **erudition** implies profound or abstruse learning beyond the comprehension of most people; **wisdom** implies superior judgment and understanding based on broad knowledge and experience

**knowledgeable,** *modif.* — *Syn.* informed, well-informed, aware, conversant, well-versed, versed, educated, erudite, learned, well-read, proficient, expert, knowing, up-to-date, abreast of, *au courant* (French), familiar with, cognizant, schooled, trained, instructed, well-grounded, competent, practiced, wise, sage, enlightened, *au fait* (French), literate, up on\*, in the know\*; see also **conscious** 1, **cultured, educated** 1, **learned** 1.

**known,** *modif.* **1.** [Open] — *Syn.* discovered, disclosed, revealed; see **observed** 1, **obvious** 1, **public** 1.
**2.** [Established] — *Syn.* well-known, published, recognized, notorious, received, accepted, noted, proverbial, hackneyed, certified, down pat\*; see also **established** 3, **familiar** 1.

**know-nothing,** *n.* — *Syn.* ignoramus, imbecile, clod, illiterate; see **fool** 1, **moron**.

**knuckle down,** *v.* — *Syn.* apply oneself, try hard, labor, set to work; see **apply (oneself), concentrate** 2, **work** 1.

**knuckle under,** *v.* — *Syn.* give in, give up, acquiesce, submit; see **retreat** 1, **yield** 1.

**kook\*,** *n.* — *Syn.* eccentric, crackpot\*, oddball\*, loony\*, cuckoo\*, ding-a-ling\*, nut\*, screwball\*, crazy\*, weirdo\*, wacko\*, flake\*, fruitcake\*, nutcase\*, dingbat\*, harebrain\*, lamebrain\*; see also **character** 4.

**kosher\*,** *modif.* — *Syn.* proper, legitimate, genuine, on the up and up\*; see **conventional** 2, **fit** 1, **official** 3, **reliable** 1.

**kowtow to\*,** *v.* — *Syn.* stoop, fawn, prostrate oneself; see **grovel**.

**kudos,** *n.* — *Syn.* praise, credit, glory, honor; see **honor** 1, **praise** 2.

**Ku Klux Klan,** *n.* — *Syn.* secret racist society, white supremacy group, hate group, KKK, the Klan, cloaked avengers\*, bedsheet nightriders\*.

# L

**label,** *n.* — *Syn.* tag, marker, ticket, mark, stamp, hallmark, insignia, design, number, identification, description, classification, copyright label, characterization, epithet, sticker, bumper sticker, price mark; see also **emblem, name** 1, **trademark.**

**label,** *v.* — *Syn.* specify, mark, identify; see **designate** 1, **name** 1, 2.

**labor,** *n.* 1. [The act of doing work] — *Syn.* activity, toil, operation; see **work** 2.

2. [Work to be done] — *Syn.* task, employment, undertaking; see **job** 2.

3. [Exertion required in work] — *Syn.* effort, exertion, energy, industry, diligence, strain, stress, pull, push, drudgery, travail; see also **effort** 1, **exercise** 1.

4. [The body of workers] — *Syn.* laborers, employees, wage earners, workers, workingmen, operatives, proletariat, blue-collar workers, work force, labor force, working people, employee(s); see also **labor union, worker.** — *Ant.* EMPLOYER, capitalist, businessperson.

5. [Childbirth] — *Syn.* parturition, giving birth, contractions, labor pains; see **birth** 1.

**labor,** *v.* — *Syn.* work, toil, strive; see **work** 1.

**laboratory,** *n.* — *Syn.* proving ground, testing ground, research facility, workroom, experiment room, research room, testing room, experiment laboratory, lab*, kitchen*.

**labored,** *modif.* — *Syn.* forced, strained, heavy; see **difficult** 1.

**laborer,** *n.* — *Syn.* worker, day laborer, unskilled worker, toiler, blue-collar worker, manual laborer; carpenter's helper, bricklayer's helper, etc.; ranch hand, farm hand, construction hand, etc.; apprentice, learner, hired man, hand, transient worker, seasonal laborer, ditchdigger, pick-and-shovel man, roust-about, stevedore, miner, street cleaner, thrall, helot, serf, villein, galley slave, wage slave, chattel, instrument, stooge*, robot*, automaton*, peon*, mercenary*, flunky*, lackey, hireling*, hack*, beast of burden*; see also **worker.**

**laborious,** *modif.* 1. [Difficult] — *Syn.* arduous, hard, stiff; see **difficult** 1.

2. [Industrious] — *Syn.* assiduous, indefatigable, diligent; see **active** 2.

*See Synonym Study at* DIFFICULT.

**laboriously,** *modif.* 1. [Strenuously] — *Syn.* hard, energetically, painfully, with difficulty, resolutely, tiresomely; see also **vigorously.**

2. [Diligently] — *Syn.* earnestly, eagerly, steadily; see **carefully** 1, **industriously.**

**labor union,** *n.* — *Syn.* organized labor, independent union, craft union, guild, industrial union, local, labor party; see also **labor** 4, **organization** 3.
American labor unions include: American Federation of Labor and Congress of Industrial Organizations (AFL-CIO), International Ladies' Garment Workers' Union (ILGWU), United Automobile Workers of America (UAW), International Union of Electrical, Radio, and Machine Workers (IUE), United Steelworkers of America (USW), American Federation of Teachers (AFT), American Federation of Television and Radio Artists (AFTRA), American Federation of State, County, and Municipal Employees (AFSCME), International Longshoremen's and Warehousemen's Union (ILWU), United Mine Workers of America (UMW), United Farm Workers of America (UFWA), International Brotherhood of Teamsters, Chauffeurs, Warehousemen, and Helpers of America, Teamsters' Union.

**labyrinth,** *n.* — *Syn.* maze, problem, complication, complexity; see **maze, puzzle** 2.

**labyrinthine,** *modif.* — *Syn.* circuitous, Byzantine, tangled, twisted, complicated, gnarled; see also **confused** 2, **difficult** 2.

**lace,** *n.* 1. [Ornamental threadwork] — *Syn.* edging, trimming, banding, border, tatting, needlework, insertion, ornament, mesh, tissue, net; see also **decoration** 2.
Types of lace include: needle-point, Valenciennes, tulle, bobbin, pillow, Venetian, flat, Venetian point, Alençon, Alostlace, bone, cutwork, *merletti a piombini* (Italian), reticella, point d'esprit, torchon, macramé, blond, d'Angleterre, Mechlin, Brussels, point de Gaze, Duchesse, point appliqué, Bruges, Binche, filet, plat appliqué, English, Irish crochet, Limerick, Carrickmacross, passementerie, guipure.

2. [Material for binding through openings] — *Syn.* thong, cord, band, shoelace; see **rope, thread.**

**lace,** *v.* — *Syn.* strap, bind, close; see **fasten** 1, **tie** 2.

**lacerate,** *v.* 1. [To tear] — *Syn.* slash, rip (open), stab; see **break** 1, **cut** 2.

2. [To injure] — *Syn.* wound, harm, maim; see **hurt** 1.

**laceration,** *n.* — *Syn.* tear, gash, incision; see **cut** 2, **injury** 1.

**lachrymose,** *modif.* — *Syn.* weeping, tearful, crying; see **sad** 1, 2.

**lacing,** *n.* — *Syn.* bond, hitch, tie; see **fastener, knot** 1.

**lack,** *n.* 1. [The state of being lacking] — *Syn.* destitution, absence, need, dearth, shortage, paucity, deprivation, deficiency, deficit, scarcity, exiguity, exigency, insufficiency, inadequacy, privation, poverty, distress, scantiness. — *Ant.* PLENTY, sufficiency, abundance.

2. [That which is lacking] — *Syn.* need, decrease, want, loss, depletion, shrinkage, shortage, shortness, short fall, shortcoming, abridgment, defect, meagerness, scantiness, slightness, inferiority, paucity, stint, curtailment, retrenchment, reduction; see also **necessity** 2. — *Ant.* WEALTH, overflow, satisfaction.

**lack,** *v.* — *Syn.* need, want, require, have need (of); see **need.**

---

**SYN.** — **lack** implies an absence or insufficiency of something essential or desired [she *lacks* experience]; **want** (in this sense, chiefly British) and **need** stress the urgency of supplying what is lacking [this matter *needs*, or *wants*, immediate attention]; **require** emphasizes even more strongly imperative need, connoting that what is needed is indispensable /his work *requires* great powers of concentration/

**lackadaisical,** *modif.* — *Syn.* idle, inattentive, lazy; see **dull** 6, **listless** 1.

**lackey,** *n.* — *Syn.* attendant, manservant, footman, flunky; see **servant.**

**lacking,** *modif.* — *Syn.* needed, deprived of, missing; see **wanting.**

**lackluster,** *modif.* — *Syn.* dim, colorless, obscure; see **dark** 1, **dull** 2.

**laconic,** *modif.* — *Syn.* concise, brief, uncommunicative; see **concise, short** 2, **taciturn, terse.**
*See Synonym Study at* CONCISE.

**lacquer,** *n.* — *Syn.* shellac, veneer, finish; see **coat** 3, **cover** 2, **varnish.**

**lacuna,** *n.* — *Syn.* gap, hiatus, space; see **blank** 1, **emptiness.**

**lacy,** *modif.* **1.** [Transparent] — *Syn.* sheer, thin, gauzy; see **transparent** 1.
**2.** [Fancy] — *Syn.* frilly, patterned, elegant; see **fancy** 2, **ornate** 1.

**lad,** *n.* — *Syn.* boy, fellow, youth, stripling; see **boy, child.**

**ladder,** *n.* — *Syn.* stairway, step-stool, steps, scale; see **stairs.**
Ladders include: stepladder, rope ladder, ship's ladder, stern ladder, accommodation ladder, fireman's scaling ladder, extension ladder, companionway, collapsing ladder, folding ladder, fire ladder, hook ladder, Jacob's ladder, gangway, fire escape, standing ladder.

**lade,** *v.* **1.** [To fill] — *Syn.* replenish, stuff, pack; see **fill** 1.
**2.** [To dip] — *Syn.* scoop, bail, spoon; see **dip** 2.

**laden,** *modif.* — *Syn.* weighted, loaded, burdened; see **full** 1.

**lading,** *n.* — *Syn.* cargo, shipment, shipping; see **freight** 1.

**ladle,** *n.* — *Syn.* skimmer, scoop, vessel; see **dipper, silverware, spoon.**

**lady,** *n.* **1.** [A woman] — *Syn.* female, adult, matron; see **woman** 1.
**2.** [A ladylike woman] — *Syn.* well-bred woman, dame, woman of good taste, woman of breeding, woman of quality, woman of education, cultured woman.
**3.** [A woman of gentle breeding] — *Syn.* gentlewoman, high-born lady, mistress of a manor, noblewoman, titled lady.
Titles of nobility for ladies include: queen, princess, empress, czarina, duchess, archduchess, grand duchess, marchioness, viscountess, countess, contessa, baroness, margravine, maharani, sultana.
*See Synonym Study at* WOMAN.

**ladylike,** *modif.* — *Syn.* womanly, cultured, genteel; see **polite** 1, **refined** 2.
*See Synonym Study at* FEMALE.

**ladylove,** *n.* — *Syn.* sweetheart, girl friend, darling; see **lover** 1.

**lag,** *n.* — *Syn.* slack, retardation, slowness, belatedness, tardiness, falling behind, interval, pulling back, delay, slowdown, drag, sluggishness, backwardness. — *Ant.* PROGRESS, progression, advance.

**lag,** *v.* **1.** [To move slowly] — *Syn.* dawdle, linger, fall back, hold back, loiter, tarry, straggle, saunter, be retarded, inch along, inch, get behind, slacken, slow up, fall behind, lag behind, procrastinate, have lead in one's rear*, get no place fast*; see also **delay** 1. — *Ant.* hasten, HURRY, keep pace with.

**2.** [To move without spirit] — *Syn.* plod, trudge, toddle, slouch, lounge, shuffle, falter, flag, stagger, hobble, limp, shamble. — *Ant.* DANCE, scamper, bound.

**laggard,** *n.* — *Syn.* loiterer, straggler, slowpoke, dawdler, loafer, slouch.

**lagoon,** *n.* — *Syn.* inlet, sound, pool; see **bay, lake.**

**lair,** *n.* **1.** [Burrow] — *Syn.* den, nest, covert; see **hole** 3.
**2.** [Hideout] — *Syn.* den, refuge, sanctuary; see **retreat** 2.

**laissez faire,** *n.* — *Syn.* isolationism, neutrality, indifference; see **noninterference.**

**laity,** *n.* — *Syn.* believers, congregation, parish; see **laymen.**

**lake,** *n.* — *Syn.* pond, creek, mouth, tarn, loch, lough, lagoon, mere, pool, inland sea; see also **sea.**
Famous lakes include: Titicaca, Yellowstone, Geneva, Leman, Lucerne, Constance, Ladoga, Great Salt, Superior, Huron, Michigan, Erie, Ontario, Finger Lakes, Champlain, Tahoe, Great Bear, Great Slave, Millac, Victoria, Nyanza, Tanganyika, Nyasa, Como, Maggiore, Windermere, Coniston Water, Derwentwater, Crummock Water, Wastwater, Haweswater, Ennerdale Water, Lake of the Woods, Buttermere, Bassenthwaite Water, Baikal, Lyn Cawlyd, Loch Ness, Loch Tay, Loch Lomond, Lough Neagh, Lough Erne.

**lamb,** *n.* — *Syn.* young sheep, young one, yeanling; see **sheep.**

**lambaste*,** *v.* — *Syn.* punish, thrash, whip; see **beat** 2, **hit** 1.

**lame,** *modif.* **1.** [Forced to limp] — *Syn.* crippled, defective, limping; see **deformed, disabled.**
**2.** [Sore] — *Syn.* bruised, stiff, raw; see **painful** 1.
**3.** [Weak; *usually used figuratively*] — *Syn.* inefficient, ineffective, faltering; see **faulty, inadequate** 1, **poor** 2, **unfinished** 1, **unsatisfactory, wanting.**

**lame duck,** *n.* — *Syn.* incompetent, nonperformer, pensioner; see **failure** 2.

**lament,** *v.* **1.** [To express sorrow] — *Syn.* regret, grieve, sorrow; see **mourn** 1.
**2.** [To weep] — *Syn.* sob, bawl, wail; see **cry** 1.
**3.** [To regret] — *Syn.* deplore, rue, repine; see **regret.**

**lamentable,** *modif.* — *Syn.* unfortunate, deplorable, regrettable; see **sad** 1, **unfavorable** 2.

**lamentation,** *n.* **1.** [Mourning] — *Syn.* weeping, complaining, sobbing; see **mourning** 1.
**2.** [A cry] — *Syn.* lament, wail, sob; see **cry** 3, **tears.**

**lamenting,** *modif.* — *Syn.* sobbing, regretting, mournful; see **sad** 1.

**laminate,** *v.* — *Syn.* stratify, overlay, layer; see **cover** 1, **plate.**

**laminated,** *modif.* — *Syn.* flaky, scaly, layered; see **covered** 1, **stratified.**

**lamp,** *n.* — *Syn.* light, lantern, torch, light bulb; see **light** 3.
Types and forms of lamps include: wick, oil, gas, electric, sun, hanging, bracket, portable, table, standing, floor, torchiere, halogen, bridge, safety, miner's, street, arc, incandescent, vapor, gasoline, temple, domestic, terra cotta, clay, pottery, vase, bronze, brass, iron, glass, night, gooseneck, chandelier, gaselier, lantern, torch.

**lampoon,** *n.* — *Syn.* satire, parody, squib; see **parody.**
*See Synonym Study at* PARODY.

**lampoon,** *v.* — *Syn.* satirize, caricature, parody; see **ridicule.**

**lance,** *n.* — *Syn.* lancet, pike, dart; see **spear, weapon** 1.

**lance-shaped,** *modif.* — *Syn.* spearlike, hastate, lanceolate, spear-shaped, pointed, lanciform, lancelike; see also **sharp** 2.

**land,** *n.* **1.** [The solid surface of the earth] — *Syn.*

ground, soil, dirt, earth, clay, loam, leaf mold, glebe, marl, gravel, subsoil, clod, sand, rock, mineral, metal, pebble, stone, dry land, terra firma, valley, desert, table-land, hill, bank, seaboard, seaside, shore, beach, strand, crag, cliff, boulder, ledge, peninsula, delta, promontory, neck, tongue; see also **earth** 2, **mountain** 1, **plain**. — *Ant.* SEA, stream, ocean.

**2.** [Land as property] — *Syn.* estate, tract, real estate; see **area** 2, **property** 2.

**3.** [Land as an agent of production] — *Syn.* ranch, quarry, field; see **farm**.

**4.** [A country] — *Syn.* homeland, realm, state; see **country** 3, **home** 2, **nation** 1.

**land,** *v.* **1.** [To bring a boat to shore] — *Syn.* dock, set on shore, set down, bring in, come to land, beach, pilot, steer, bring into her slip, drop anchor, cast anchor, put in, make land. — *Ant.* board, weigh anchor, cast off.

**2.** [To come into port] — *Syn.* dock, berth, come to berth; see **arrive** 1.

**3.** [To go ashore] — *Syn.* disembark, debark, come ashore, invade, arrive, alight, leave the boat, light on, leave the ship, go down the gangplank, hit the beach★, lift anchor and pack gear★; see also **descend** 1. — *Ant.* LEAVE, go on shipboard, embark.

**4.** [To bring an airplane to earth] — *Syn.* touch down, get down, ground, take down, arrive, alight, get into the field, come in, bring in the ship, settle, land into the wind, level off, flatten out, come down, descend upon, make a forced landing, set it on the deck★, balloon in★, bounce in★, crash-land★, up-wind★, fishtail down★, nose over★, overshoot★, splash down★, check in★, under-shoot★, pancake★; see also **arrive** 1.

**landed,** *modif.* — *Syn.* property-holding, secure, wealthy; see **rich** 1.

**landing,** *n.* **1.** [The act of reaching shore] — *Syn.* arriv-ing, docking, berthing, wharfing, piloting, making port, steering, casting anchor, anchoring, dropping anchor, disembarkation; see also **arrival** 1.

**2.** [The place where landing, sense 1, is possible] — *Syn.* marina, pier, wharf; see **dock** 1, **harbor** 2.

**3.** [The act of reaching the earth] — *Syn.* setting down, grounding, getting in, arriving, deplaning, reaching an airport, touchdown, splashdown, completing a mission, vertical landing, settling, alighting, ballooning in★.

**landing field,** *n.* — *Syn.* airfield, flying field, airstrip; see **airport**.

**landlady,** *n.* — *Syn.* proprietress, concierge, innkeeper; see **owner**.

**landlord,** *n.* — *Syn.* landowner, lessor, proprietor, inn-keeper; see **owner**.

**landmark,** *n.* **1.** [A notable relic] — *Syn.* survival, rem-nant, historic structure, memorial; see **monument** 1, **relic** 1, **ruins**.

**2.** [A crisis] — *Syn.* milestone, turning point, stage; see **crisis, event** 1.

**3.** [A point from which a course may be taken] — *Syn.* vantage point, mark, benchmark, blaze, guide, marker, stone, tree, hill, mountain, bend, promontory, duck on a rock★; see also **position** 1.

**landscape,** *n.* **1.** [Natural scenery] — *Syn.* scene, scen-ery, panorama, aspect; see **view** 1, 2.

**2.** [Scenic art] — *Syn.* mural, photograph, scene; see **painting** 1, **sketch** 1.

**landscape,** *v.* — *Syn.* provide the landscaping, finish off, put in the lawn and shrubbery; see **decorate, trim** 2.

**landscaping,** *n.* — *Syn.* lawn, shrubbery, garden, (the) grounds, beautification program, setting, background; see also **decoration** 2.

**landslide★,** *modif.* — *Syn.* conclusive, lopsided, decisive; see **large** 1, **many, overwhelming** 2.

**landslide,** *n.* — *Syn.* avalanche, slide, slip, *Lawine* (Ger-man), snow slide, rock slide, mud slide; see also **de-scent** 2.

**lane,** *n.* — *Syn.* way, alley, passage; see **path** 1, **road** 1.

**language,** *n.* **1.** [A means of communication] — *Syn.* speech, dialect, voice, utterance, expression, vocaliza-tion, phonation, native tongue, mother tongue, articula-tion, meta-language, object language, sense-datum lan-guage, thing-language, physical language; language of diplomacy, language of chemistry, language of flowers, etc.; accent, word, sign, signal, pantomime, gesture, fa-cial gesture, vocabulary, diction, idiom, local speech, broken English, pidgin English, lingo, brogue, poly-glot, patois, vernacular, lingua franca, trade language, jargon, gibberish, debased speech, inscription, picture writing, hieroglyphics, cuneiform, printing, writing, po-etry, prose, song, style, phraseology, lingo★; see also **communication** 1, **conversation, speech** 2.

**2.** [The study of language, sense 1] — *Syn.* morphology, phonology, phonemics, morphemics, morphophonemics, phonics, phonetics, semantics, se-masiology, criticism, letters, linguistic studies, his-tory of language, etymology, dialectology, linguistic geography, anthropological linguistics, sociolinguistics, lexicostatistics, glottochronology, structural linguistics, descriptive linguistics, taxonomic linguistics, histori-cal linguistics, diachronic linguistics, comparative lin-guistics, synchronic linguistics, contrastive grammar, descriptive grammar, prescriptive grammar, phrase-structure grammar, PS grammar, generative grammar, immediate-constituent grammar, IC grammar, trans-formational grammar, tagmemics, stratificational gram-mar, glossematics, Prague school of linguistics, London school of linguistics, Firthian school of linguistics; see also **anthropology, etymology, grammar, linguis-tics, literature** 1.

Types of languages include: synthetic, inflectional, ana-lytic, isolating, distributive, incorporating, symbolic, fusional, polytonic, agglutinative, computer, artificial, polysynthetic.

Families of language include: Indo-European, Finno-Ugric, Altaic, Caucasian, Afro-Asiatic, Nilo-Saharan, Niger-Congo, Khoisan, Malayo-Polynesian, Dravidian, Austro-Asiatic, Sino-Tibetan, Kadai, Eskimo-Aleut, Athabaskan, Algonquian, Mosan, Iroquoian, Natchez-Muskogean, Siouan, Penutian, Hokan, Uto-Aztecan, Mayan.

Indo-European languages include — *Greek:* Mod-ern Greek; *Celtic:* Breton, Welsh, Scottish Gaelic, Irish Gaelic; *Italic:* Latin, Romanian, Italian, Rhaeto-Romanic, French, Provençal, Spanish, Catalan, Por-tuguese; *Germanic:* Swedish, Danish, Norwegian, Icelandic, Modern High German, Yiddish, Afri-kaans, Dutch, Flemish, Modern Low German, Frisian, English; *Slavic:* Polish, Czech, Slovak, Bulgarian, Slovenian, Serbo-Croatian, Ukrainian, Russian; *Bal-tic:* Latvian, Lithuanian; *Iranian:* Persian, Pashto; *Indo-Aryan:* Bengali, Punjabi, Hindi, Urdu, Marathi, Gujarati, Romany, Dard.

Other Eurasian languages include — *Uralic:* Finnish, Estonian, Hungarian, Samoyed; *Altaic:* Turkish, Mon-golian; Georgian; Abkhasian, Kabardian, Chechen; Basque; Etruscan.

African and Asian languages include — *Afro-Asiatic* or *Hamito-Semitic:* Akkadian, Assyro-Babylonian, Aramaic, Syriac, Phoenician, Talmudic, Hebrew, Arabic, Amharic, Egyptian, Coptic, Tuareg, Somali, Hausa; *Sumerian; Niger-Congo:* Wolof, Mande, Ewe, Yoruba, Ibo, Efik, Tiv, Swahili, Kikuyu, Rwanda, Zulu, Xhosa, Swazi, Venda; *Nilo-Saharan:* Songhai, Kanuri, Nilotic, Dinka, Nuer, Masai; *Khoisan:* Sandawe, Hatsa, Bushman-Hottentot.

Asian and Malayo-Polynesian languages —: Japanese, Ryukyu; Korean; *Sino-Tibetan:* Burmese, Tibetan, Mandarin, Cantonese; *Kadai:* Thai, Siamese, Laotian, Lao; Miao-Yao; *Malayo-Polynesian:* Malay, Indonesian, Javanese, Balinese, Tagalog, Filipino, Malagasy, Micronesian, Hawaiian, Tahitian, Samoan, Maori, Fijian; Papuan, Australian; *Tasmanian; Dravidian:* Telegu, Tamil, Kanerese, Kannada, Malayalam; *Austro-Asiatic:* Santali, Palaung, Mon-Khmer, Vietnamese.

North, Central, and South American languages include — *Algonquian:* Massachusetts, Delaware, Mohegan, Penobscot, Pasamaquoddy, Fox-Sauk-Kickapoo, Cree, Menomini, Shawnee, Blackfoot, Arapaho, Cheyenne; Wiyot, Yurok; Kutenai; *Salishan:* Tillamook, Lillooet; *Wakashan:* Nootka, Kwakiutl; *Muskogean:* Creek, Choctaw-Chickasaw, Seminole; Natchez, Chitimacha; *Iroquoian:* Cherokee, Huron, Wayondot, Erie, Oneida, Mohawk, Seneca, Cayuga, Susquehanna, Conestoga; *Siouan:* Biloxi, Dakota, Mandan, Winnebago, Hidatsa, Crow; *Caddoan:* Caddo, Wichita, Pawnee; Yuchi; Aleut, Eskimo; *Penutian:* Tsimshian, Maidu, Miwok, Klamath-Modoc; Zuni; *Hokan:* Karok, Shasta, Washo, Pomo; Subtiaba-Tlapanec, Tequistlatec, Jicaque; Comecrudo, Tonkawa; *Mayan:* Kekchi, Quiche, Tseltal-Tsotzil, Tojolabal, Yucatec; Totonac; Mixe, Zoque, Vera Cruz; Huave; Zapotec, Chatino; Mixtec; Pueblo, Popoluca; Otomi, Pame; Tarascan; *Uto-Aztecan:* Tubatulabal, Luiseño, Tepehuan, Pima-Papago, Hopi, Huichol, Nahuatl, Aztec, Northern Paiute, Paviotso, Mono, Shoshoni-Comanche, Southern Paiute-Ute, Chemehuevi; Kiowa-Tanoan; Keresan; *Na-Dené:* Haida, Tlingit, Athabaskan, Chipewyan, Apachean, Navaho, Hupa; Yukian; Quechua; Aymara; Araucanian.

**speak the same language**— *Syn.* understand one another, communicate, get along; see **agree.**

**languid,** *modif.* **1.** [Weak] — *Syn.* feeble, weary, infirm; see **weak** 1, 3.
**2.** [Dull] — *Syn.* sluggish, heavy, lethargic; see **dull** 6.
**3.** [Listless] — *Syn.* dull, inattentive, spiritless; see **indifferent** 1, **listless** 1, **unconcerned.**

**languidly,** *modif.* — *Syn.* nonchalantly, indifferently, gently; see **calmly, easily** 1, **slowly.**

**languidness,** *n.* **1.** [Dullness] — *Syn.* listlessness, sluggishness, apathy; see **indifference** 1, **slowness** 1.
**2.** [Weakness] — *Syn.* feebleness, impotence, prostration; see **weakness** 1.

**languish,** *v.* **1.** [To weaken] — *Syn.* fade, fail, droop; see **weaken** 1.
**2.** [To want] — *Syn.* hunger, pine, desire; see **need, want** 1.

**languishing,** *modif.* **1.** [Weak] — *Syn.* droopy, dull, sluggish; see **slow** 1, 2, **weak** 1.
**2.** [Pensive] — *Syn.* pining, melancholy, longing; see **sad** 1.

**languor,** *n.* — *Syn.* lethargy, listlessness, lassitude; see **indifference** 1, **laziness.**

**lank,** *modif.* — *Syn.* lean, slender, meager; see **thin** 2.

**lanky,** *modif.* — *Syn.* lean, bony, rangy; see **thin** 2.

**lantern,** *n.* — *Syn.* torch, lamp, lighting device; see **light** 3.

Varieties of lanterns include: lighthouse, magic, cupola, tower, barn, searchlight, police, dark, bull's eye, railroad, flashlight, oil, gas, electric, horn, glass, paper,

architectural, hand, hanging, Chinese, Japanese, ship's, poop, optical, lantern of the dead.

**lanyard,** *n.* — *Syn.* cord, line, string; see **rope.**

**lap,** *n.* **1.** [The body from the waist to the knees when sitting] — *Syn.* knees, legs, thighs, front, seat.
**2.** [The portion that overlaps] — *Syn.* extension, overlap, fold; see **flap, overhang.**
**3.** [Part of a race] — *Syn.* circuit, round, loop; see **distance** 3, **race** 3.

**drop into someone's lap**— *Syn.* transfer responsibility, shift blame, pass the buck*; see **give** 1.

**in the lap of luxury**— *Syn.* surrounded by luxury, living elegantly, prospering; see **rich** 1.

**in the lap of the gods**— *Syn.* superhuman, extraordinary, beyond human control, beyond human understanding; see **supernatural.**

**lapse,** *n.* — *Syn.* slip, mistake, failure; see **error** 1.

**lapse,** *v.* **1.** [To fail slowly] — *Syn.* slip, deteriorate, decline; see **weaken** 1.
**2.** [To become void] — *Syn.* end, cease, terminate; see **stop** 2.

**lapsed,** *modif.* — *Syn.* past, expired, extinct, dead; see **finished** 1.

**larceny,** *n.* — *Syn.* burglary, thievery, robbery; see **crime** 2, **theft.**
*See Synonym Study at* THEFT.

**lard,** *n.* — *Syn.* fat, tallow, suet, leaf lard; see **fat, grease.**

**larder,** *n.* — *Syn.* pantry, storeroom, scullery; see **pantry, room** 2, **storehouse.**

**lardy,** *modif.* — *Syn.* fat, fatty, buttery, greasy; see **oily** 1.

**large,** *modif.* **1.** [Of great size] — *Syn.* big, great, huge, wide, grand, considerable, substantial, vast, massive, immense, spacious, bulky, sizable, broad, capacious, colossal, gigantic, mammoth, mountainous, immeasurable, extensive, boundless, plentiful, copious, populous, ample, abundant, goodly, liberal, comprehensive, lavish, hefty, stout, burly, husky, heavyset, fat, swollen, bloated, corpulent, obese, herculean, titanic, monstrous, towering, tall, lofty, mighty, magnificent, commodious, enormous, cyclopean, giant, jumbo, Brobdingnagian, tremendous, prodigious, monumental, stupendous, enlarged, voluminous, overgrown, cumbersome, ponderous, Gargantuan, Antaean, heroic, epic, immoderate, extravagant, astronomical, prodigal, king-size, queen-size, outsize, oversized, elephantine, gigantesque, monster, super*, booming*, healthy*, bumper*, whopping*, thumping*, thundering*, walloping*, humongous*, larger-than-life*; see also **broad** 1, **deep** 2, **enlarged, extensive** 1, **fat** 1, **high** 1, **long** 1.
— *Ant.* LITTLE, small, tiny.
**2.** [Involving great plans] — *Syn.* extensive, extended, considerable; see **comprehensive, general** 1.
**3.** [Magnanimous] — *Syn.* open, noble, big-hearted; see **generous** 1, **kind.**

---

**SYN. — large, big,** and **great** are often interchangeable in meaning of more than usual size, extent, etc. *[a large, big,* or *great oak]*, but **large** is typically used with reference to dimensions or amount *[a large studio, a large sum]*, **big,** to bulk, weight, or extent *[a big baby, big business]*, and **great,** which is less often used of physical things, to size or extent that is impressive, imposing, surprising, etc. *[a great river, a great success]*

---

**largely,** *modif.* **1.** [In large measure] — *Syn.* mostly, mainly, chiefly; see **principally.**
**2.** [In a large way] — *Syn.* extensively, abundantly, comprehensively, on a large scale, broadly, magnificently, grandly, lavishly, liberally, prodigiously, volumi-

nously, generously, expansively, imposingly, considerably, copiously, commodiously, extravagantly, immoderately, prodigally, in a big way, in the grand manner, open-handedly; see also **widely**.

**largeness,** *n.* — *Syn.* magnitude, proportion, breath; see **measure** 1, **measurement** 2, **quantity, size** 2.

**largess,** *n.* **1.** [Gift] — *Syn.* present, donation, contribution; see **gift** 1.
**2.** [Generosity] — *Syn.* bounty, charity, open-handedness; see **generosity** 1.

**lariat,** *n.* — *Syn.* lasso, tether, riata, reata; see **rope.**

**lark,** *n.* — *Syn.* songbird, warbler, philomel; see **bird** 1. Larks include: skylark, horned, shore, Sprague's, pipit, wagtail, titlark, meadowlark.

**larva,** *n.* — *Syn.* maggot, grub, caterpillar; see **invertebrate, worm** 1.

**lascivious,** *modif.* **1.** [Filled with lust] — *Syn.* lecherous, lustful, libidinous; see **lewd** 1, 2, **sensual.**
**2.** [Suggestive of intercourse] — *Syn.* fleshly, carnal, orgiastic, bodily, earthly, animal, natural, voluptuous, obscene; see also **sensual.** — *Ant.* ascetic, SPIRITUAL, abstemious.

**lasciviousness,** *n.* — *Syn.* lechery, wantonness, lust, lustfulness; see **desire** 3, **lewdness.**

**lash,** *n.* — *Syn.* cane, thong, rod; see **beat** 2.

**lash,** *v.* **1.** [To whip] — *Syn.* cane, scourge, strap; see **beat** 2.
**2.** [To tie up] — *Syn.* bind, fasten, truss; see **bind** 1.

**lashing,** *modif.* — *Syn.* thrashing, beating, floundering; see **hitting** 1, **punishment.**

**lash (out),** *v.* — *Syn.* strike, thrash, scourge; see **beat** 2, **hit** 1.

**lass,** *n.* — *Syn.* young woman, young lady, damsel, maiden; see **girl** 1, **woman** 1.

**lassitude,** *n.* — *Syn.* languor, faintness, weariness, tiredness, fatigue, heaviness, stupor, dullness, drowsiness, yawning, exhaustion, burnout, prostration, drooping, torpor, torpidity, lethargy, apathy, ennui, stupefaction, inappetence, phlegm, hebetude, supineness, inertia, fag*, the dumps*, spring fever*; see also **indifference** 1. — *Ant.* ACTION, vivaciousness, sprightliness.

**lasso,** *n.* — *Syn.* tether, lariat, noose; see **rope.**

**last,** *modif.* **1.** [Final] — *Syn.* ultimate, utmost, lowest, meanest, least, latest, latter, end, extreme, remotest, furthest, outermost, farthest, uttermost, conclusive, concluding, hindmost, far, far-off, aftermost, hindermost, determinative, determinate, ulterior, once and for all, definitive, after all others, ending, at the end, terminal, eventual, antipodal, terminative, terminating, directing, settling, resolving, decisive, crowning, climactic, closing, ending, finishing, unanswerable, irrefutable. — *Ant.* FIRST, foremost, beginning.
**2.** [Most recent] — *Syn.* latest, newest, current, freshest, immediate, most fashionable, in the fashion, modish, the last word*; see also **fashionable, modern** 1. — *Ant.* OLD, stale, outmoded.

**last,** *n.* **1.** [The end] — *Syn.* tail end, last one, terminal one, final one, ending; see also **end** 4.
**2.** [A shoemaker's mold] — *Syn.* form, cast, shape; see **mold** 1, 2.
**at (long) last** — *Syn.* after a long time, in the end, ultimately; see **finally** 2.
**see the last of** — *Syn.* see for the last time, never see again, dispose of, get rid of; see **end** 1.

**last,** *v.* **1.** [To endure] — *Syn.* continue, remain, persist, go on; see **continue** 1, **endure** 1, 2.
**2.** [To be sufficient] — *Syn.* hold out, be adequate, be enough, be ample, be satisfactory, serve, do, accomplish the purpose, answer; see also **satisfy** 3.

See Synonym Study at CONTINUE.

**lasting,** *modif.* — *Syn.* enduring, abiding, constant; see **permanent** 2, **perpetual** 1.

**lastly,** *modif.* — *Syn.* in conclusion, at last, ultimately; see **finally** 2.

**latch,** *n.* — *Syn.* catch, hook, bar; see **fastener, lock** 1.

**latch,** *v.* — *Syn.* lock, cinch, close up; see **close** 4, **fasten** 1.

**latch onto***, *v.* — *Syn.* grab, take, steal; see **seize** 1, 2.

**late,** *modif.* **1.** [Tardy] — *Syn.* too late, held up, overdue, stayed, postponed, put off, not on time, belated, behind time, lagging, delayed, remiss, behindhand, backward, not in time, in the lurch*, later than you think*, at the eleventh hour*; see also **slow** 2, 3. — *Ant.* EARLY, punctual, on time.
**2.** [Recently dead] — *Syn.* dead, defunct, deceased, departed; see **dead** 1.
**3.** [Recent] — *Syn.* new, just out, recently published; see **fresh** 1.
**4.** [Far into the night] — *Syn.* nocturnal, night-loving, after hours, advanced, tardy, toward morning, after midnight.
**5.** [At an advanced cultural stage] — *Syn.* developed, cultured, advanced; see **modern** 1, 3.
See Synonym Study at DEAD.
**of late** — *Syn.* lately, in recent times, a short time ago; see **recently.**

**lately,** *modif.* — *Syn.* a short time ago, in recent times, of late; see **recently.**

**lateness,** *n.* — *Syn.* belatedness, tardiness, retardation, protraction, prolongation, slowness, backwardness, advanced hour, late date; see also **delay** 1. — *Ant.* ANTICIPATION, earliness, promptness.

**latent,** *modif.* — *Syn.* potential, dormant, quiescent, implied, inherent, undeveloped, unrealized, underdeveloped, torpid, suspended, in abeyance, abeyant, inactive, in the making, possible, intrinsic, sleeping, slumbering, inert, lurking, unexposed, covert, inoperative, suppressed, passive, underlying, contained, unexpressed, tacit, inferred, escaping notice, hidden, unconscious, inferential, between the lines*; see also **hidden** 2. — *Ant.* ACTIVE, developed, operative.

---

**SYN.** — **latent** applies to that which exists but is as yet concealed or unrevealed [*latent* abilities]; **potential** applies to that which exists in an undeveloped state but which can be brought to development in the normal course of events [a *potential* concert pianist]; **dormant** suggests a lack of visible activity, as of something asleep [a *dormant* volcano]; **quiescent** implies a stopping of activity, usually only temporarily [the raging sea had become *quiescent*]

---

**later,** *modif.* — *Syn.* succeeding, next, more recent; see **following.**

**lateral,** *modif.* — *Syn.* oblique, sidelong, side by side; see **parallel** 1, **side.**

**laterally,** *modif.* — *Syn.* alongside, next to, sideways; see **parallel** 1.

**latest,** *modif.* — *Syn.* most recent, immediately prior (to), just done, just finished, just completed; see also **last** 1, 2.

**lath,** *n.* — *Syn.* strip, slat, batten, mesh, groundwork. Kinds of laths include: wooden, metal, sheet metal, perforated metal, wire mesh, chicken wire, single, double, thinnest, 1/4 inch, 1/2 inch.

**lathe,** *n.* — *Syn.* turret lathe, turning lathe, cutter; see **machine** 1.

**lather,** *n.* — *Syn.* suds, foam, bubbles; see **froth.**

**lather,** *v.* — *Syn.* foam, scrub, soap; see **wash** 2.

**lathery,** *modif.* — *Syn.* sudsy, foamy, bubbly; see **frothy** 1.

**Latin,** *modif.* **1.** [Pertaining to ancient Rome or to its language] — *Syn.* Roman, Romanic, Latinic; see **classical** 2.

**2.** [Pertaining to southwestern Europe] — *Syn.* Latinate, Roman, Gallic, Mediterranean, Italian, Spanish, French, Portuguese.

**Latin,** *n.* — *Syn.* Roman language, Romance language, language of Latium; see **language** 2.

Divisions of Latin include: classical, Golden Age, Silver Age, provincial, Late, medieval, Vulgar, monks', made Latin, church, New, Modern.

Languages descended from Latin include: Portuguese, Spanish, Catalan, Provençal, Rhaeto-Romanic, Italian, Romanian, French.

**latitude,** *n.* **1.** [Freedom within limits] — *Syn.* range, scope, independence; see **extent, freedom** 2.

**2.** [A point in its relationship to the equator] — *Syn.* meridional distance, degree, measure, degrees of latitude; see **measure** 1.

**latitudinarian,** *modif.* — *Syn.* tolerant, libertine, accepting; see **lenient, liberal** 2.

**latrine,** *n.* — *Syn.* privy, outhouse, lavatory, restroom; see **bath** 3, **toilet** 2.

**latter,** *modif.* — *Syn.* late, last, recent; see **following, last** 1.

**latter,** *n.* — *Syn.* the second of the two, the last mentioned, the last named; see **end** 4.

**latterly,** *modif.* — *Syn.* lately, hitherto, of late; see **recently.**

**lattice,** *n.* — *Syn.* screen, web, mesh, structure, framework, fretwork, trellis, grate, grating; see also **frame** 1, **net.**

**laud,** *v.* — *Syn.* praise, eulogize, flatter, commend; see **admire** 1, **praise** 1, **compliment** 1, 2.
*See Synonym Study at* PRAISE.

**laudable,** *modif.* — *Syn.* praiseworthy, commendable, of note; see **excellent, worthy.**

**laudatory,** *modif.* — *Syn.* flattering, approving, eulogistic; see **complimentary.**

**laugh,** *n.* — *Syn.* chuckle, giggle, titter, snicker, snigger, guffaw, chortle, cackle, fit of laughter, peal of laughter, horse laugh, belly laugh, roar, snort, crow, shout of laughter, shriek, howl, sound of merriment, mirth, amusement, convulsion, cachinnation, ha-ha★, haw-haw★, hee-haw★, ho-ho★, tee-hee★, yuk★; see also **laughter, smile.** — *Ant.* sob, CRY, whimper.

**have the last laugh** — *Syn.* defeat (finally), beat in the end, overcome all obstacles; see **win** 1.

**no laughing matter** — *Syn.* serious, grave, significant, no joke★; see **important** 1.

---

*SYN.* — **laugh** is the general word for the sounds or exhalation made in expressing mirth, amusement, etc.; **chuckle** implies soft laughter in low tones, expressive of mild amusement or inward satisfaction; **giggle** and **titter** both refer to a laugh consisting of a series of rapid, high-pitched sounds, suggesting embarrassment, nervousness, or silliness, but **giggle** often implies an uncontrollable fit of such laughter and **titter** implies a half-suppressed laugh, as a laugh of mild amusement suppressed in affected politeness; **snicker** is used of a sly, half-suppressed laugh, as at another's discomfiture or a bawdy story; **guffaw** refers to loud, coarse laughter

---

**laugh,** *v.* — *Syn.* chuckle, chortle, guffaw, laugh off, smile away, snicker, snigger, titter, giggle, burst out (laughing), be convulsed, shriek, roar, howl, cachin-

nate, beam, grin, smile, smirk, roar, shout, crow, have a hemorrhage★, die laughing★, break up★, haw-haw★, split one's sides★, bust up★, roll in the aisles★, tee-hee★, snort★, be in stitches★; see also **smile.** — *Ant.* CRY, sob, weep.

**laugh out of court** — *Syn.* mock, deride, laugh at; see **ridicule.**

**laugh out the other side of one's mouth** — *Syn.* be disappointed, be sorry, have qualms about; see **regret.**

**laughable,** *modif.* **1.** [Exciting humor] — *Syn.* funny, ludicrous, comic, comical; see **funny** 1.

**2.** [Exciting humor and some contempt] — *Syn.* eccentric, bizarre, fantastic; see **unusual** 2.
*See Synonym Study at* FUNNY.

**laugh at,** *v.* — *Syn.* deride, taunt, make fun of; see **ridicule.**

**laughing,** *modif.* — *Syn.* chortling, giggling, chuckling; see **happy** 2.

**laughingstock,** *n.* — *Syn.* target, butt, victim; see **fool** 2.

**laugh off,** *v.* — *Syn.* deride, dismiss, ignore, shrug off; see **scorn** 2.

**laughter,** *n.* — *Syn.* chortling, chuckling, guffawing, tittering, giggling, shouting, roaring, crowing, merriment, hilarity, howling★, haw-hawing★, snorting★; see also **laugh.** — *Ant.* CRY, weeping, wailing.

**launch,** *n.* — *Syn.* motorboat, cabin cruiser, ship's launch; see **boat, ship.**

**launch,** *v.* **1.** [To initiate] — *Syn.* originate, start, set going; see **begin** 1.

**2.** [To send off] — *Syn.* set in motion, propel, drive, lance, thrust, fire off, send forth, eject; see also **drive** 1, 3.

**launched,** *modif.* — *Syn.* started, sent, set in motion, floated, begun, aloft, afloat, lofted, put into orbit, sent into orbit, lofted into orbit, made airborne, put in motion, put on the water, put to sea, put in the air; see also **begun, driven, sent.**

**launder,** *v.* — *Syn.* cleanse, do the wash, wash and iron; see **clean, wash** 2.

**laundress,** *n.* — *Syn.* washerwoman, cleaning lady, domestic; see **servant.**

**laundry,** *n.* — *Syn.* ironing, washing, clothes; see **wash** 1.

**laurel,** *n.* **1.** [An evergreen tree] — *Syn.* bay, mountain laurel, evergreen tree, shrub; see **tree.**

**2.** [A crown] — *Syn.* crown, honor, garland; see **wreath.**

**rest on one's laurels** — *Syn.* be satisfied, retire, stop trying to achieve, give up, give in; see also **stop** 2.

**lava,** *n.* — *Syn.* basalt, pumice, volcanic rock, igneous rock; see **rock** 1.

**lavatory,** *n.* — *Syn.* washroom, bathroom, privy; see **bath** 3, **toilet** 2.

**lavender,** *modif. & n.* — *Syn.* lilac, lilac-purple, bluish-red; see **color** 1, **purple.**

**lavish,** *modif.* — *Syn.* profuse, generous, unstinted, unsparing, plentiful, prodigal, extravagant, opulent, rich, sumptuous, inordinate, excessive, wasteful; see also **plentiful** 1, 2, **profuse, rich** 2, **wasteful.**
*See Synonym Study at* PROFUSE.

**lavish,** *v.* — *Syn.* bestow, scatter freely, give generously, squander; see **spend** 1, **waste** 2.

**lavishly,** *modif.* — *Syn.* profusely, richly, extravagantly; see **carelessly, foolishly, wastefully.**

**lavishness,** *n.* **1.** [Extravagance] — *Syn.* wastefulness, dissipation, squandering; see **waste** 1.

**2.** [Plenty] — *Syn.* profuseness, plenitude, abundance; see **excess** 1, **plenty.**

**3.** [Generosity] — *Syn.* largess, munificence, openhandedness; see **generosity** 1.

**law,** *n.* **1.** [The judicial system] — *Syn.* judicial procedure, judicature, legal process, the authorities, the legal authorities, the police, writ, writ of habeas corpus, due process, precept, summons, notice, warrant, bench warrant, search warrant, warrant of arrest, subpoena, garnishment, They*; see also **authority** 3, **government** 1, 2, **legality.**

**2.** [Bodies of the law] — *Syn.* code, constitution, organic act, criminal law, statute law, civil law, law of the press, maritime law, martial law, military law, private law, public law, commercial law, probate law, substantive law, statutory law, chancery, statutes, civil code, ordinances, precepts, equity, cases, archives, common law, canon law, decisions, unwritten law, natural law.

**3.** [An enactment] — *Syn.* statute, ordinance, regulation, rule, edict, decree, order, judicial decision, ruling, injunction, summons, act, charge, prescription, canon, caveat, enactment, requirement, demand, divestiture, rescript, commandment, mandate, dictate, precept, instruction, behest, bidding, legislation, bill, bylaw; see also **command** 1, **indictment** 2, **warrant, writ.**

**4.** [A principle] — *Syn.* foundation, fundamental, origin, source, ultimate cause, truth, truism, axiom, maxim, tenet, doctrine, ground, base, reason, rule, rule of action, theorem, guide, precept, usage, postulate, proposition, generalization, proposal, assumption, hard and fast rule; see also **basis** 1.

**5.** [The study of law, sense 1] — *Syn.* jurisprudence, legal precedent, legal science, equity, legal practice.

**6.** [Officers appointed to enforce the law] — *Syn.* district attorney, prosecuting attorney, sheriff, constable, state police, city police, lawman, the man*, cops*, pigs*; see also **judge** 1, **lawyer, police, policeman.**

**7.** [The Bible] — *Syn.* Word, Old and New Testaments, the Book, Gospel, Scripture, Revelation; see also **Bible** 2.

*See Synonym Study at* THEORY.

**go to law*** — *Syn.* take legal action, take to court, prosecute; see **sue.**

**lay down the law*** — *Syn.* establish rules, order, prohibit; see **command** 1.

**read law** — *Syn.* prepare for a career as lawyer, study law, practice law, attend law school.

***SYN.*** — **law,** in its specific application, implies prescription and enforcement by a ruling authority /the *law* of the land/; a **rule** may not be authoritatively enforced, but it is generally observed in the interests of order, uniformity, etc. /the *rules* of golf/; **regulation** refers to a rule of a group or organization, enforced by authority /military *regulations*/; a **statute** is a law enacted by a legislative body; an **ordinance** is a local, generally municipal, law; a **canon** is, in its original meaning, a law of a church, but the term is also used of any established rule or principle regarded as true or as a standard to judge by usage /the *canons* of good taste/

**lawbreaker,** *n.* — *Syn.* felon, offender, violator; see **criminal.**

**lawbreaking,** *n.* — *Syn.* felony, violation, offense; see **crime** 1, 2.

**lawful,** *modif.* — *Syn.* legitimate, legal, legalized, rightful, just, right, valid, statutory, passed, decreed, judged, commanded, ruled, enjoined, ordained, ordered, mandated, authorized, according to edict, constitutional, adjudged, legislated, enacted, official, according to fiat, enforced, protected, licit, vested, within the law, in conformity to the law, conformable with the law, legitimatized, canonical, established; see also **legal** 1, **permitted.** — *Ant.* ILLEGAL, unlawful, illegitimate.

*See Synonym Study at* LEGAL.

**lawfully,** *modif.* — *Syn.* licitly, in accordance with the law, by law; see **legally** 1.

**lawfulness,** *n.* — *Syn.* authenticity, validity, legitimacy; see **legality.**

**lawless,** *modif.* **1.** [Without law] — *Syn.* wild, untamed, uncivilized, savage, native, uncultivated, barbarous, fierce, violent, turbulent, unpeaceful, tempestuous, disordered, agitated, disturbed, warlike; see also **uncontrolled.** — *Ant.* CULTURED, cultivated, controlled.

**2.** [Not restrained by law] — *Syn.* insurgent, mutinous, riotous, ungovernable, nihilistic, nonconformist, unorthodox, seditious, in defiance of the law, traitorous, recusant, contumacious, seditious, revolutionary, insubordinate, disobedient, piratical, terrorizing, tyrannous, anarchic, anarchistic, anarchical, heterodox, despotic, bad, criminal, evil, infringing, noncompliant, defiant, rude, recalcitrant, refractory, transgressive; see also **mobbish, rebellious** 2, **unruly.**

**lawlessness,** *n.* — *Syn.* anarchy, irresponsibility, terrorism, chaos; see **disorder** 2, **disturbance** 2.

**lawmaker,** *n.* — *Syn.* lawgiver, congressman, councilman; see **administrator, legislator.**

**lawn,** *n.* — *Syn.* garden, park, green, grassplot, grassland; see also **grass** 3, **yard** 1.

**lawsuit,** *n.* — *Syn.* action, prosecution, suit; see **claim, trial** 2.

**lawyer,** *n.* — *Syn.* attorney, counsel, counselor, counselor-at-law, attorney-at-law, solicitor, barrister, legal adviser, legal practitioner, member of the bar, jurist, defender, attorney for the defense, prosecuting attorney, prosecutor, legist, sergeant, advocate, professor of law, deputy, agent, public defender, assigned counsel, attorney general, solicitor general, proctor, procurator, district attorney, D.A., friend of the court, amicus curiae, jurisconsult, jurisprudent, Philadelphia lawyer*, shyster*, ambulance chaser*, mouthpiece*, legal eagle*, pettifogger*.

***SYN.*** — **lawyer** is the general term for a person trained in the law and authorized to advise or represent others in legal matters; **counselor** and its British equivalent, **barrister,** refer to a lawyer who conducts cases in court; **attorney,** usually, and its British equivalent, **solicitor,** always, refer to a lawyer legally empowered to act for a client, as in drawing up a contract or will, settling property, etc.; **counsel,** often equivalent to **counselor,** is frequently used collectively for a group of counselors

**lax,** *modif.* — *Syn.* slack, remiss, soft; see **careless** 1, **remiss, unconcerned.**

*See Synonym Study at* REMISS.

**laxative,** *modif.* — *Syn.* relaxing, loosening, opening, freeing, unbinding, purgative, purging, diarrheic, diarrheal, diuretic, unconstipative, physicking, cathartic. — *Ant.* binding, CONFINING, restricting.

**laxative,** *n.* — *Syn.* physic, aperient, purgative, diuretic, cathartic, purge, medicament, remedy, cure, specific, dose, drench; see also **medicine** 2.
Common laxatives include: castor oil, mineral oil, agaragar, cascara sagrada, flaxseed, milk of magnesia, croton oil, epsom salts, phenolphthalein, cascarin compound, psyllium seeds, Ex-Lax (trademark), Metamucil (trademark).

**laxity,** *n.* — *Syn.* indulgence, indecision, leniency; see **carelessness, indifference** 1.

**lay,** *n.* — *Syn.* order, arrangement, situation; see **position** 1.

**lay,** *v.* **1.** [To knock down] — *Syn.* trounce, defeat, club; see **beat** 2, **hit** 1.

**2.** [To place] — *Syn.* put, deposit, set; see **place** 1.

**3.** [To put in order] — *Syn.* arrange, organize, systematize; see **order** 3.

**4.** [To bring forth] — *Syn.* generate, deposit, yield; see **produce** 1.

**5.** [To smooth out] — *Syn.* steam, lay flat, iron out; see **iron, press** 2, **smooth** 1.

**6.** [To bet] — *Syn.* game, wager, lay odds; see **bet, gamble** 1.

**7.** [To work out] — *Syn.* devise, concoct, design; see **plan** 1, 2.

**lay about one,** *v.* **1.** [To act] — *Syn.* move, do, operate; see **act** 1, **perform** 1.

**2.** [To attack] — *Syn.* hurt, punch, thrash; see **attack** 2, **beat** 2, **hit** 1.

**lay a course,** *v.* — *Syn.* chart, outline, project; see **plan** 1, 2.

**lay aside,** *v.* **1.** [To set aside] — *Syn.* put aside, put to one side, dismiss, abandon, reject, drop, put off; see also **abandon.**

**2.** [To save] — *Syn.* lay away, collect, keep; see **save** 3, **store** 2.

**lay away,** *v.* **1.** [To save] — *Syn.* lay aside, keep, collect; see **save** 3, **store** 2.

**2.** [To bury] — *Syn.* entomb, inter, inhume; see **bury** 1.

**lay bare,** *v.* — *Syn.* reveal, show, disclose; see **expose** 1, **undress.**

**lay by,** *v.* — *Syn.* hoard, put aside, build up savings; see **save** 3, **store** 2.

**lay by the heels,** *v.* — *Syn.* thrash, overcome, overpower; see **beat** 2, **defeat** 1, 2, 3, **win** 1.

**lay down,** *v.* **1.** [To declare] — *Syn.* assert, state, affirm; see **declare** 1, **report** 1, **say.**

**2.** [To bet] — *Syn.* game, put up, wager; see **bet, gamble** 1.

**lay down one's life (for),** *v.* — *Syn.* die for, sacrifice, perish; see **die** 1.

**layer,** *n.* — *Syn.* stratum, bed, thickness, fold, band, cover, covering, sheet, coat, coating, overlay, lap, overlap, ply, seam, coping, course, substratum, floor, story, tier, zone, stripe, girdle, lamination, lamella, lamina, delamination, film, slab, flap, panel.

**lay eyes on,** *v.* — *Syn.* stare, view, notice; see **see** 1.

**lay figure,** *n.* — *Syn.* nonentity, puppet, zero, nonperson; see **nobody** 2.

**lay for,** *v.* — *Syn.* await, waylay, wait; see **ambush, attack** 1.

**lay hands on,** *v.* — *Syn.* get, acquire, grasp; see **obtain** 1, **seize** 1, 2.

**lay hold of,** *v.* — *Syn.* get, grasp, grab; see **seize** 1, 2.

**lay in,** *v.* — *Syn.* collect, gather, amass; see **accumulate** 1, **store** 2.

**laying,** *n.* — *Syn.* arranging, setting, putting; see **placing.**

**lay into,** *v.* — *Syn.* battle, invade, fire at; see **attack** 1, **fight** 2.

**lay it on★,** *v.* — *Syn.* flatter, commend, glorify; see **compliment** 1, 2, **encourage** 2, **praise** 1.

**lay low★,** *v.* **1.** [Hide] — *Syn.* go underground, disappear, hide out; see **hide** 2, **sneak.**

**2.** [Knock down] — *Syn.* prostrate, trounce, knockout, KO★; see **beat** 2, **hit** 1.

**layman,** *n.* **1.** [One who does not make religion a profession] — *Syn.* secular, one of the laity, laic, catechumen, neophyte, proselyte, convert, parishioner, communicant, believer, one of the people, one of the flock, congregation; see also **follower, member** 1. — *Ant.* PRIEST, ecclesiastic, cleric.

**2.** [One who is not versed in a subject] — *Syn.* nonprofessional, novice, dilettante; see **amateur, recruit.**

**laymen,** *n.* — *Syn.* laity, converts, congregation, neophytes, parish, parishioners, the faithful, communicants, members, believers, the uninitiated; see also **following.**

**lay off,** *v.* **1.** [To discharge employees, usually temporarily] — *Syn.* fire, discharge, let go; see **dismiss** 2, **oust.**

**2.** [★To stop] — *Syn.* cease, halt, desist; see **end** 1, **stop** 2.

**lay on,** *v.* — *Syn.* invade, besiege, beat; see **attack** 1, **fight** 2.

**lay open,** *v.* — *Syn.* incise, knife, slice; see **cut** 2, **expose** 1.

**layout,** *n.* — *Syn.* arrangement, design, draft; see **organization** 2, **plan** 3, **purpose** 1.

**lay out,** *v.* **1.** [To spend] — *Syn.* lend, put out (at interest), put up; see **invest, spend** 1.

**2.** [To spread out] — *Syn.* arrange, display, exhibit, set out; see **display** 1.

**layover,** *n.* — *Syn.* break, hiatus, rest; see **delay** 1, **pause** 1, 2, **respite.**

**lay over,** *v.* — *Syn.* delay, stay over, break a journey; see **rest** 2, **stop** 1.

**lay plans (for),** *v.* — *Syn.* draft, design, think out; see **form** 1, **intend** 1, **plan** 2.

**lay the foundation for,** *v.* — *Syn.* construct, put up, fabricate; see **build** 1, **create** 2, **form** 1.

**lay to,** *v.* — *Syn.* (give) credit, ascribe, pin on★; see **assign** 1, **attribute.**

**lay to rest,** *v.* — *Syn.* inter, give burial (to), lay in the grave; see **bury** 1.

**lay up,** *v.* **1.** [To save] — *Syn.* conserve, preserve, hoard; see **save** 3, **store** 2.

**2.** [★To disable] — *Syn.* injure, harm, beat up; see **hurt** 1.

**lay waste,** *v.* — *Syn.* ravage, devastate, ruin; see **destroy** 1.

**lazily,** *modif.* — *Syn.* indolently, nonchalantly, slackly; see **gradually, slowly.**

**laziness,** *n.* — *Syn.* indolence, slothfulness, sloth, lethargy, inactivity, slackness, sluggishness, dullness, lackadaisicalness, torpidness, heaviness, inertia, inertness, drowsiness, supineness, passivity, languor, languidness, languorousness, laggardliness, listlessness, otiosity, otioseness, laxness, negligence, sleepiness, neglectfulness, remissness, dullness, stupidity, dormancy, torpescence, leadenness, dreaminess, weariness, apathy, stolidity, somnolence, somnolency, somnolescence, indifference, unconcern, laggardness, dilatoriness, tardiness, shiftlessness, deliberateness, leisureliness, procrastination; see also **idleness** 1. — *Ant.* ACTION, promptitude, agility.

**lazy,** *modif.* **1.** [Indolent] — *Syn.* indolent, slothful, idle, slack, remiss, laggard, sluggish, heavy-footed, lagging, apathetic, loafing, dallying, languid, passive, asleep on the job, procrastinating, neglectful, unconcerned, indifferent, dilatory, tardy, inattentive, careless, unready, unpersevering, lethargic, lifeless, flagging, logy★, weary, tired, supine, lackadaisical; see also **listless** 1. — *Ant.* ACTIVE, businesslike, indefatigable.

**2.** [Slow] — *Syn.* slothful, inactive, lethargic; see **dull** 6, **slow** 1, 2.

**leach,** *v.* — *Syn.* strain, drain, purge, percolate; see **filter** 1, 2.

**lead,** *modif.* — *Syn.* leading, head, foremost; see **best** 1, **first** 1, **principal.**

**lead,** *n.* **1.** [The position at the front] — *Syn.* head, advance, first place, contact, point, edge, fore part, van, advanced guard, façade, front rank, first line, line of battle, scout, outpost, scouting party, patrol, sniper scouts, advance position, cutting edge, forerunner; see also **front** 2, **vanguard.** — *Ant.* END, rear, last place.
**2.** [Leadership] — *Syn.* direction, guidance, headship; see **administration** 1, **leadership** 1, 2.
**3.** [A clue] — *Syn.* evidence, trace, hint; see **proof** 1, **sign** 1.
**4.** [A leading performer] — *Syn.* diva, prima donna, star; see **actor** 1, **actress.**
**5.** [A leading role] — *Syn.* principal part, important role, chief character, heavy★, fat lines★, lead spot★, standout role★, top bracket★, top spot★; see also **role.**

**lead,** *n.* — *Syn.* metallic lead, galena, blue lead; see **element** 2, **metal.**

**lead,** *v.* **1.** [To conduct] — *Syn.* guide, head, precede, steer, pilot, attend, direct, channel, orient, show the way, point, point the way, show in, show to, show around, convoy, point out, squire, escort, chaperone, accompany, protect, guard, safeguard, watch over, convey, go along with, drive, shepherd, feel out the path, discover the way, find a way through, be responsible for; see also **manage** 1. — *Ant.* FOLLOW, be conveyed, be piloted.
**2.** [To exercise leadership] — *Syn.* direct, manage, supervise; see **command** 2, **manage** 1.
**3.** [To influence] — *Syn.* prevail on, affect, spur (on); see **influence, motivate.**
**4.** [To play a first card] — *Syn.* start, commence, play first, take the initiative, make the start; see also **begin** 1.
**5.** [To extend] — *Syn.* traverse, pass along, span; see **reach** 1.

**leaden,** *modif.* **1.** [Made of lead] — *Syn.* lead, plumbous, plumbic, plumbean, plumbiferous, pewter, galena; see also **metallic** 1.
**2.** [Heavy] — *Syn.* burdensome, ponderous, oppressive, weighty; see **heavy** 1, **onerous** 1.
**3.** [Lead-colored] — *Syn.* dull, ashen, pale, pewter, blue-gray; see also **gray.**

**leader,** *n.* **1.** [A guide] — *Syn.* conductor, lead, pilot; see **guide** 1.
**2.** [One who provides leadership] — *Syn.* general, commander, pacesetter, director, floor leader, manager, head, officer, captain, master, chieftain, headman, governor, ruler, *Führer* (German), *duce* (Italian), *caudillo* (Spanish), *vozhd* (Russian), executor, boss, boss man★, brains★; see also **administration** 2, **administrator, chief** 1.
**3.** [One who directs a musical group] — *Syn.* conductor, director, choir leader, bandleader, impresario, Kappelmeister, orchestra leader, maestro, manager, baton★, stick waver★; see also **musician.**
**4.** [An article sold to attract trade] — *Syn.* special, bargain, introduction, novelty; see **commodity.**

**leadership,** *n.* **1.** [The quality notable in leaders] — *Syn.* authority, control, executiveness, administration, effectiveness, activity, primacy, superiority, supremacy, skillfulness, skill, initiative, foresight, energy, capacity; see also **influence** 2, **power** 2.
**2.** [The action of leading] — *Syn.* direction, guidance, management; see **administration** 1.

**leading,** *modif.* **1.** [Principal] — *Syn.* foremost, chief, preeminent; see **best** 1, **principal.**
**2.** [First] — *Syn.* front, head, advance; see **first** 1.

**lead off,** *v.* — *Syn.* start, open, initiate; see **begin** 1, 2.
**lead on,** *v.* — *Syn.* lure, entice, mislead; see **deceive.**

**lead one's life,** *v.* — *Syn.* persist, endure, press on, live on; see **be** 1.
**lead up to,** *v.* — *Syn.* prepare, introduce, make preparations for; see **begin** 2, **propose** 1.
**lead with one's chin★,** *v.* — *Syn.* blunder into, be indiscreet, be rash, act foolishly; see **dare** 1, 2, **risk.**

**leaf,** *n.* **1.** [The leafy organ of a plant] — *Syn.* leaflet, needle, bract, petiole, blade, frond, stalk, stipule, scale, protective leaf, floral leaf, leaf stalk, seed leaf, calyx leaf, bracteole, sepal, lithophyl, caulis, perianth, petal.
**2.** [Matter in thin, smooth form] — *Syn.* skin, coat, sheath; see **sheet** 2.

**in leaf** — *Syn.* foliated, in foliage, fully leaved out; see **green** 2.

**take a leaf from someone's book** — *Syn.* follow someone's example, take after, copy; see **imitate** 2.

**turn over a new leaf** — *Syn.* make a new start, redo, begin again; see **change** 4.

**leaflet,** *n.* — *Syn.* handbill, flyer, circular, broadside; see **pamphlet.**

**leafy,** *modif.* — *Syn.* leaf-covered, leafed out, in foliage, in leaf, verdant, abounding, abundant, springlike, summery, covered, hidden, secluded, shady, shaded, umbrageous; see also **green** 2. — *Ant.* BARE, leafless, austere.

**league,** *n.* — *Syn.* association, alliance, group, class; see **alliance** 3, **organization** 3.
*See Synonym Study at* ALLIANCE.

**leagued,** *modif.* — *Syn.* in league with, related, allied, joined; see **united** 2.

**leak,** *n.* **1.** [Loss through leakage] — *Syn.* leakage, loss, flow, seepage, drop, escape, outgoing, incoming, detriment, short circuit, falling off, destruction, expenditure, decrease; see also **waste** 1.
**2.** [An aperture through which a leak may take place] — *Syn.* puncture, chink, crevice; see **hole** 1.
**3.** [Surreptitious news] — *Syn.* news leak, exposure, slip; see **advertisement** 1, **news** 1.

**leak,** *v.* **1.** [To escape by leaking] — *Syn.* drip, ooze, drool; see **flow** 2.
**2.** [To permit leakage] — *Syn.* be cracked, be broken, be split, have a fissure, have a hole, be out of order, be in disrepair, permit wastage, have a slow leak.

**leakproof,** *modif.* — *Syn.* watertight, impervious, waterproof; see **tight** 2, **waterproof.**

**leaky,** *modif.* — *Syn.* punctured, cracked, split; see **broken** 1.

**lean,** *modif.* **1.** [Thin] — *Syn.* lank, meager, slim; see **thin** 2.
**2.** [Containing little fat] — *Syn.* fibrous, muscular, sinewy, meaty, free from fat, all-meat, protein-rich; see also **strong** 1.

**lean,** *v.* **1.** [To incline] — *Syn.* slope, slant, sag, sink, decline, list, tip, bow, nod, twist, cock, place, careen, roll, veer, droop, drift, dip, pitch, cant, bend, heel, be not perpendicular, be slanting, be slanted, be off; see also **bend** 2, **tilt** 1.
**2.** [To tend] — *Syn.* favor, be disposed, incline; see **tend** 2.

**leaning,** *n.* — *Syn.* inclination, bent, propensity; see **inclination.**
*See Synonym Study at* INCLINATION.

**lean on** *or* **upon,** *v.* **1.** [To be supported by] — *Syn.* rest on, be upheld by, bear on, put one's weight on, hang on, hang upon, fasten on; see also **lean** 1.
**2.** [To rely upon] — *Syn.* believe in, count on, put faith in; see **depend (on), trust** 1.

**lean-to,** *n.* — *Syn.* shelter, shanty, cabin; see **hut, shack, shed.**

**leap,** *v.* — *Syn.* spring, vault, bound; see **bounce** 2, **jump** 1.

**learn,** *v.* **1.** [To acquire mentally] — *Syn.* acquire, receive, imbibe, get, absorb, assimilate, digest, take in, drink in, pick up, read, master, ground oneself in, peruse, con, pore over, study, gain information, learn by heart, memorize, be taught a lesson, become well-versed in, soak in, collect one's knowledge, improve one's mind, build one's background, get up on*, get the signal*; see also **study** 1.
**2.** [To find out] — *Syn.* discover, ascertain, discern, uncover, unearth, find out, determine, hear, see, read, detect, come to know, come upon, chance on, chance upon, stumble upon, get wind of*, get wise to*; see also **discover**.

---

**SYN.** — **learn**, as considered here, implies a finding out of something, often without conscious effort *[I learned of their marriage from a friend]*; **ascertain** implies a finding out with certainty, as by careful inquiry, experimentation, or research *[I ascertained the firm's credit rating]*; **determine** stresses intention to establish the facts exactly, often so as to settle something in doubt *[to determine the exact denotation of a word]*; **discover** implies a finding out, either by chance or by exploration or study, of something already existing or known to others *[to discover a star, to discover a plot]*; **unearth**, in its figurative sense, implies a bringing to light, as by diligent search, of something that has been concealed, lost, or forgotten *[to unearth old documents, to unearth a secret]*

---

**learned,** *modif.* **1.** [Having great learning; *said of people*] — *Syn.* scholarly, erudite, scholastic, academic, accomplished, conversant with, lettered, instructed, collegiate, well-read, well-informed, bookish, pansophic, omniscient, polymathic, pedantic, professorial; see also **cultured, educated** 1. — *Ant.* IGNORANT, incapable, illiterate.
**2.** [Showing evidence of learning; *said of productions*] — *Syn.* scholarly, scientific, deep, solid, sound, sage, philosophic, philosophical, literary, erudite, grave, solemn, sober, judicious, studied, studious, sapient, abstract, recondite, esoteric, arcane, far out*; see also **profound** 2. — *Ant.* SUPERFICIAL, unscholarly, shallow.

**learner,** *n.* — *Syn.* pupil, apprentice, scholar; see **student**.

**learning,** *n.* — *Syn.* knowledge, lore, scholarship, training; see **education** 1, **knowledge** 1.
*See Synonym Study at* KNOWLEDGE.

**lease,** *n.* — *Syn.* rental agreement, permission to rent, charter; see **contract, record** 1.
**new lease on life** — *Syn.* another chance, new perspective, new outlook, opportunity; see **change** 2.

**lease,** *v.* — *Syn.* let, charter, hire, rent out; see **rent** 1.
*See Synonym Study at* HIRE.

**leash,** *n.* — *Syn.* cord, chain, strap; see **rope**.
**hold in leash** — *Syn.* check, curb, control; see **restrain** 1.
**strain at the leash** — *Syn.* be impatient, act hastily, get excited; see **hurry** 1.

**least,** *modif.* **1.** [Smallest] — *Syn.* tiniest, minutest, infinitesimal, molecular, microcosmic, microscopic, atomic; see also **minute** 1.
**2.** [Least important] — *Syn.* slightest, most trivial, niggling, piddling, finical, next to nothing; see also **trivial, unimportant.**
**3.** [In the lowest degree] — *Syn.* minimal, at the nadir, most inferior, bottom; see **lowest, minimum.** — *Ant.* MAXIMUM, highest, at the zenith.

**at (the) least** — *Syn.* in any event, with no less than, at any rate; see **anyhow** 1.
**not in the least** — *Syn.* not at all, in no way, not in the slightest degree; see **never**.

**leather,** *n.* — *Syn.* tanned hide, parchment, vellum, kangaroo hide, calfskin, horsehide, buckskin, deerskin, elk hide, goatskin, sheepskin, scarfskin, capeskin, rawhide, cowhide, buffalo hide, buffalo robe, snakeskin, sharkskin, lizard, shoe leather, glove leather, chamois, sole leather, alligator hide; see also **hide** 1, **skin.**
Leathers include: pebble grain, cordovan, kid, natural, split, Scotch grain, suede, patent, Morocco, shagreen, tooled, embossed.

**leathery,** *modif.* — *Syn.* rugged, coriaceous, durable; see **strong** 2, **tough** 2.

**leave,** *n.* **1.** [Permission] — *Syn.* consent, dispensation, allowance; see **permission.**
**2.** [Authorized absence] — *Syn.* leave of absence, holiday, furlough, sabbatical; see **vacation.**
**beg leave** — *Syn.* ask permission, request, inquire; see **ask** 1.
**by your leave** — *Syn.* with your permission, if your permission is granted, if you please; see **please.**
**on leave** — *Syn.* away, gone, on vacation; see **absent** 1.
**take leave of** — *Syn.* say good-by (to), bid farewell, leave alone; see **leave** (*v.*) 1.
**take one's leave** — *Syn.* go away, depart, remove oneself; see **leave** (*v.*) 1.

**leave,** *v.* **1.** [To go away] — *Syn.* go, depart, take leave, withdraw, move, set out, come away, go forth, take off, start, remove oneself, step down, quit (a place), part, part company, defect, vanish, elope, retire, walk out, walk off, get out, get off, get away, slip away, break away, break out, ride off, go off, go away, move out, move away, vacate, issue, decamp, abscond, flee, get out, flit, migrate, fly, run along, embark, emplane, sally forth, say good-by, entrain, emigrate, clear out, pull out, cut out*, push off*, cast off, scram*, split*, blow*, head out*, ditch*, give the slip*, vamoose*, sign out*, check out*, beat it*, take a powder*, take to the tall timber*, get rolling*, fade away*, pull up stakes*, get along*, make oneself scarce*, break squares with*, bid a long farewell*; see also **disappear, resign** 2, **retreat** 1, 2. — *Ant.* ARRIVE, get to, reach.
**2.** [To abandon] — *Syn.* back out, forsake, desert; see **abandon** 2.
**3.** [To allow to remain] — *Syn.* let be, let stay, leave behind, let continue, let go, drop, lay down, omit, forget; see also **neglect** 1, 2. — *Ant.* SEIZE, take away, keep.
**4.** [To allow to fall to another] — *Syn.* bequeath, will, devise, leave behind, bequest, hand down, transmit; see also **give** 1.

**leaven,** *v.* **1.** [To ferment] — *Syn.* raise, pepsinate, lighten; see **ferment.**
**2.** [To influence] — *Syn.* change, cause, affect; see **influence.**

**leave off,** *v.* — *Syn.* cease, end, halt; see **stop** 2.

**leave out,** *v.* — *Syn.* cast aside, reject, dispose of; see **discard, eliminate** 1.

**leave-taking,** *n.* — *Syn.* farewell, parting, departing; see **departure** 1.

**leave to,** *v.* — *Syn.* bequeath, hand down, pass on; see **give** 1.

**leave word,** *v.* — *Syn.* inform, let know, report; see **notify** 1, **tell** 1.

**leavings,** *n.* — *Syn.* remains, residue, garbage; see **trash** 1, 3.

**lecher,** *n.* — *Syn.* debauchee, debaucher, reprobate, libertine, adulterer, philanderer, rake, Don Juan,

Casanova, playboy, swinger, fornicator, womanizer, lady-killer★, gigolo, dirty old man★, lech★, roué.

**lecherous,** *modif.* — *Syn.* carnal, lustful, corrupt; see **lewd** 2, **sensual.**

**lechery,** *n.* — *Syn.* lust, debauchery, sensuality; see **desire** 3.

**lectern,** *n.* — *Syn.* platform, podium, rostrum, pulpit, stand, desk.

**lecture,** *n.* **1.** [A speech] — *Syn.* discourse, address, talk; see **speech** 3.
**2.** [A reprimand] — *Syn.* rebuke, talking-to, dressing-down; see **rebuke.**
*See Synonym Study at* SPEECH.

**lecture,** *v.* **1.** [To give a speech] — *Syn.* talk, speak, expound; see **address** 2, **teach** 1.
**2.** [To rebuke] — *Syn.* scold, reprimand, admonish, chide, take to task★, upbraid, chew out★, give a good talking to★; give a going-over★, give a piece of one's mind★; see also **censure, scold.**

**lecturer,** *n.* — *Syn.* preacher, orator, instructor; see **speaker** 2, **teacher** 1, 2.

**led,** *modif.* — *Syn.* taken, escorted, guided.

**ledge,** *n.* — *Syn.* shelf, mantle, jut, strip, bar, setback, offset, step, ridge, reef, rim, bench, berm, edge, path, route, way, walk, track, trail; see also **projection.**

**ledger,** *n.* — *Syn.* entries, books, account book; see **record** 1.

**lee,** *n.* — *Syn.* protection, harbor, shield; see **refuge** 1, **shelter.**

**leech,** *n.* **1.** [A parasite] — *Syn.* tapeworm, hookworm, bloodsucker; see **parasite** 1.
**2.** [★Dependent] — *Syn.* parasite, hanger-on, sponger★; see **sycophant.**

**leer,** *n.* — *Syn.* smirk, squint, evil grin, stare, ogle; see also **sneer.**

**leery,** *modif.* — *Syn.* cautious, doubting, uncertain; see **suspicious** 1, 2.

**lees,** *n.* — *Syn.* remains, deposit, dregs; see **residue, sediment.**

**leeward,** *modif.* — *Syn.* lee, sheltered, leeside, quiet, peaceful, still, secure, undisturbed, serene, smooth, shielded, protected, screened, safe; see also **calm** 2. — *Ant.* windward, STORMY, windy.

**leeway,** *n.* — *Syn.* space, margin, latitude, room, play, scope, allowance, elbowroom, breathing room, breathing space, slack, freedom, headroom, room to swing a cat★.

**left,** *modif.* **1.** [Opposite to right] — *Syn.* leftward, lefthand, near, sinister, sinistral, sinistrous, larboard, port, portside, nigh side★. — *Ant.* RIGHT, right-hand, starboard.
**2.** [Remaining] — *Syn.* staying, continuing, over; see **extra, remaining** 2.
**3.** [Radical] — *Syn.* left-wing, liberal, progressive; see **liberal** 2, **radical** 2, **revolutionary** 1.
**4.** [Departed] — *Syn.* gone out, taken a powder★, split★; see **gone** 1.
*See Synonym Study at* LIBERAL.

**left,** *n.* — *Syn.* left hand, left side, port, larboard, sinister, portside, verso.

**left-handed,** *modif.* — *Syn.* clumsy, careless, gauche; see **awkward** 1.

**leftist,** *n.* — *Syn.* socialist, anarchist, communist; see **agitator, liberal, radical.**

**left out,** *modif.* — *Syn.* lost, neglected, removed; see **omitted.**

**leftover,** *modif.* — *Syn.* remaining, unwanted, unused, residual, uneaten, unconsumed, untouched, perfectly good; see also **extra, remaining** 2.

**leftovers,** *n.* — *Syn.* leavings, scraps, debris; see **food, remainder, trash** 1, 3.

**left-wing,** *modif.* — *Syn.* leftist, not conservative, reform; see **liberal** 2, **radical** 2.

**leg,** *n.* **1.** [The limb of a creature] — *Syn.* part, member, lower appendage, hind leg, foreleg, back leg, front leg, left leg, right leg, shank, shank's mare★, underpinning★, gam★, stem★, pin★, bender★, landing gear★; see also **limb** 2.
**2.** [A relatively long, narrow support] — *Syn.* post, column, stake; see **brace** 1, **support** 2.

**get up on one's hind legs★** — *Syn.* assert oneself, be aggressive, take a stand; see **declare** 1.

**give a leg up★** — *Syn.* aid, support, assist; see **help** 1.

**not have a leg to stand on★** — *Syn.* be illogical, be unreasonable, make rash statements, have no defense, have no excuse, have no justification; see also **mistake.**

**on one's last legs★** — *Syn.* decaying, failing, collapsing, on the verge of collapse, near death, fading fast★; see also **dying** 2, **worn** 2.

**pull someone's leg★** — *Syn.* make fun of, fool, tease, play a trick on; see **deceive.**

**shake a leg★** — *Syn.* hasten, act hastily, get moving; see **hurry** 1.

**stretch one's legs★** — *Syn.* exercise, go for a walk, move about; see **walk** 1.

**take to one's legs★** — *Syn.* walk away, run away, depart, take flight; see **leave** 1.

**legal,** *modif.* **1.** [In accordance with the law] — *Syn.* lawful, licit, legitimate, constitutional, statutory, permissible, admissible, allowable, allowed, proper, legalized, sanctioned, right, just, justifiable, justified, fair, prescribed, authorized, hereditary, accustomed, due, rightful, precedented, warranted, licensed, admitted, sound, conceded, granted, mandated, acknowledged, ordained, condign, equitable, according to equity, within the law, protected, enforced, enforceable, judged, adjudicated, adjudged, enjoined, decreed, contracted, contractual, from time out of mind, customary, chartered, de jure, clean★, legit★, straight★, on the up and up★; see also **lawful, permitted.** — *Ant.* ILLEGAL, unlawful, prohibited.
**2.** [Concerning the law] — *Syn.* statutory, juridical, constitutional, judicial, forensic, jurisprudent, jurisprudential, jural, nomothetic; see also **judicial.**

**SYN.** — **legal** implies literal connection or conformity with statute or common law or its administration *[legal rights]*; **lawful** refers to that which is permitted, recognized, or established by civil, religious, or moral law and may suggest conformity to the principle rather than, or in addition to, the letter of the law *[a lawful marriage, the lawful owner]*; **legitimate** implies legality of a claim to a title or right *[a legitimate heir]* or accordance with what is sanctioned or accepted as lawful, reasonable, etc. *[a legitimate argument]*; **licit** implies strict conformity to the law, especially in trade, commerce, or personal relations *[the licit sale of drugs]*

**legality,** *n.* — *Syn.* legitimacy, lawfulness, authority, permissibility, validity, justice, defendability, status de jure, status before the law, status in court; see also **right** 1, 2.

**legalize,** *v.* — *Syn.* authorize, formulate, sanction; see **approve** 1.

**legally,** *modif.* **1.** [In accordance with the law] — *Syn.* lawfully, legitimately, permissibly, authorized, conceded, warranted, licitly, allowably, admittedly, enforcibly, juridically, constitutionally, with due process of law, by statute, by law, as developed by the courts, in the eyes of the law, in accordance with the law, in accordance with the constitution, in accordance with the ordinance; see also **rightfully.**— *Ant.* ILLEGAL, unauthorized, illicitly.

**2.** [In a manner suggestive of the law] — *Syn.* legislatively, judicially, constitutionally, juridically, in legal terminology, with legal phrasing, professionally.

**legatee,** *n.* — *Syn.* heir, heiress, inheritor, receiver; see **beneficiary, heir.**

**legation,** *n.* — *Syn.* committee, deputation, assignment; see **commission** 1, **delegation** 1, **installation** 1.

**legend,** *n.* **1.** [An improbable, traditional story] — *Syn.* folk tale, saga, fable; see **myth, story.**

**2.** [A brief piece of written matter] — *Syn.* caption, motto, inscription, title, key; see also **writing** 2.

**legendary,** *modif.* **1.** [Traditional] — *Syn.* handed-down, customary, related; see **told, traditional** 1.

**2.** [Probably fictitious] — *Syn.* fabulous, fabled, fictitious, mythical, mythological, fabricated, fanciful, imaginative, created, invented, allegorical, apocryphal, improbable, imaginary, dubious, doubtful, romantic, unhistoric, unhistorical, figmental, storied, unverifiable; see also **false** 2.— *Ant.* HISTORICAL, historic, actual.

---

*SYN.* — **legendary** refers to something that may have a historical basis in fact but, in popular tradition, has undergone great elaboration and exaggeration /the *legendary* deeds of Robin Hood/; **fictitious** refers to that which is invented by the imagination and is therefore not real, true, or actually existent /Gulliver is a *fictitious* character/; **fabulous** suggests that which is incredible or astounding, but does not necessarily connote nonexistence /the man's wealth is *fabulous*/; **mythical** basically applies to the highly imaginary explanation of natural or historical phenomena by a people and, therefore, connotes that what it qualifies is a product of the imagination; **apocryphal** suggests that which is of doubtful authenticity or authorship

---

**legerdemain,** *n.* — *Syn.* deceit, trickery, deception, sleight of hand; see **deception** 1, **trick** 1.

**leggings,** *n.* — *Syn.* gaiters, stockings, chaps, puttees, half-boots, buskins, cothurnus, putts*, chaps*, leggins*; see also **clothes.**

**legibility,** *n.* — *Syn.* readability, decipherability, lucidity, intelligibility; see **clarity.**

**legible,** *modif.* — *Syn.* readable, decipherable, distinct, plain; see **clear** 2.

**legion,** *n.* **1.** [An army] — *Syn.* division, phalanx, brigade; see **army** 2, **troops.**

**2.** [A crowd] — *Syn.* multitude, body, group; see **crowd** 1, **gathering.**

**legislate,** *v.* — *Syn.* make laws, enforce laws, pass, constitute; see **enact.**

**legislation,** *n.* — *Syn.* bill, enactment, act; see **law** 3.

**legislative,** *modif.* — *Syn.* lawmaking, enacting, decreeing, ordaining, lawgiving, legislational, legislatorial, congressional, juridical, jurisdictive, parliamentarian, nomothetic, senatorial, synodical, parliamentary, aldermanic, statute-making, from the legislature, by the legislature; see also **authoritative** 2.

**legislator,** *n.* — *Syn.* lawmaker, lawgiver, assemblyman, congressman, congresswoman, representative, senator, member of Congress, member of parliament, M.P., floor leader, deputy, councilman, alderman; see also **administrator.**

**legislature,** *n.* — *Syn.* lawmakers, congress, parliament, chamber, assembly, senate, house, house of representatives, council, soviet, plenum, law-making body, diet,

voice of the people, duly constituted legislative body, bicameral legislature; see also **authority** 3, **bureaucracy** 1, **government** 1, 2.

Important legislatures include: Congress of the United States, Parliament of Great Britain, National Assembly of France, Supreme Soviet and Congress of People's Deputies of the Russian Federation, United Nations Assembly, Riksdag of Sweden, Congresso Nacional of Brazil, National People's Congress of the People's Republic of China, Parliament of Canada, Federal Parliament of Australia, Parliament of the Union of South Africa, Oireachtas of Ireland, Knesset of Israel, Grand National Assembly of Turkey, Congreso Nacional of Argentina, Eduskunta of Finland, Congreso of Mexico, Nationalrat of Switzerland, House of Representatives of New Zealand, Congreso Nacional de Chile, National Assembly of Cuba, Diet of Japan, Supreme People's Assembly of North Korea.

**legitimate,** *modif.* **1.** [In accordance with legal provisions] — *Syn.* licit, legal, rightful, authorized; see **lawful, legal** 1.

**2.** [Logical] — *Syn.* reasonable, probable, consistent; see **logical** 1, **understandable.**

**3.** [Authentic] — *Syn.* verifiable, valid, reliable; see **genuine** 1, 2.

**4.** [Born of wedded parents] — *Syn.* accredited, received, accepted, authentic, genuine, certain, sure, true, recognized, sired in wedlock.— *Ant.* ILLEGITIMATE, bastard, unrecognized.

*See Synonym Study at* LEGAL.

**legume,** *n.* — *Syn.* pea, fruit, pod; see **bean** 1, **plant, vegetable.**

Legumes include: pea, bean, lentil, chick pea, garbanzo, peanut, clover, alfalfa, lucerne, soybean, vetch, pulse.

**leisure,** *n.* — *Syn.* freedom, free time, spare time, free moments, vacant hour, relaxation, recreation, repose, ease, intermission, recess, holiday, leave of absence, scope, range, convenience, idle hours, opportunity; see also **rest** 1, **vacation.**— *Ant.* WORK, toil, travail.

**at leisure**— *Syn.* idle, resting, not busy; see **unoccupied** 2.

**at one's leisure**— *Syn.* when one has time, at one's convenience, at an early opportunity; see **whenever.**

**leisurely,** *modif.* **1.** [Enjoying leisure] — *Syn.* lax, slow, free; see **comfortable** 1, **lazy** 1.

**2.** [In a manner suggestive of leisure] — *Syn.* slowly, unhurriedly, lazily, deliberately, laggardly, dilatorily, with delay, calmly, composedly, lingeringly, tardily, inactively, taking one's time, gradually, languidly, langorously, sluggishly, lethargically, indolently, listlessly. — *Ant.* QUICKLY, rapidly, hastily.

**leitmotiv,** *n.* — *Syn.* recurrent musical phrase, suggestive melody, motif; see **theme** 2.

**lemon,** *n.* **1.** [Citrus fruit] — *Syn.* juicy fruit, citron, food; see **fruit** 1.

**2.** [*An inadequate object or person] — *Syn.* bad one, dud*, clunker*, piece of junk*, hunk of junk*, turkey*, worthless person, worthless thing; see also **failure** 1, 2.

**lend,** *v.* **1.** [To make a loan] — *Syn.* advance, provide with, let out, furnish, permit to borrow, allow, trust with, lend on security, extend credit, entrust, place at interest, loan*, accommodate. — *Ant.* BORROW, repay, pay back.

**2.** [To impart] — *Syn.* confer, grant, present; see **give** 1.

**3.** [To adapt oneself] — *Syn.* suit oneself, adjust, comply; see **accommodate** 2, **conform.**

**lend a hand,** *v.* — *Syn.* assist, aid, succor; see **help** 1.

**lender,** *n.* — *Syn.* bestower, granter, usurer, moneylender, bank, pawnbroker, pawnshop, loan company, loan shark\*, moneymonger\*, angel\*, stakeman\*, Shylock\*; see also **banker** 1, **donor**.

**lend itself to,** *v.* — *Syn.* be adaptable to, fit in, suit; see **fit** 1, 2.

**lend oneself to,** *v.* — *Syn.* agree to, consent, give support to; see **agree**.

**length,** *n.* **1.** [Linear distance] — *Syn.* distance, space, measure, span, reach, range, longitude, remoteness, stride, magnitude, compass, portion, dimension, unit, radius, diameter, linearity, longness, mileage, stretch; see also **extent**.

**2.** [Extent in space] — *Syn.* extensiveness, spaciousness, ranginess, endlessness, continuance, tallness, height, loftiness, lengthiness, expansion; see also **breadth** 2, **expanse, width.** — *Ant.* shortness, NEARNESS, closeness.

**3.** [Duration] — *Syn.* period, interval, season, year, month, week, day, minute, continuance, limit, lastingness; see also **term** 2, **time** 1.

**at full length** — *Syn.* extended, stretched out, lengthwise; see **long** 1.

**at length, 1.** — *Syn.* after a long time, eventually, in the end; see **finally** 2.

**2.** — *Syn.* extensively, in full, wholly, without omission; see **completely**.

**go to any length** *or* **go to great lengths** — *Syn.* do anything, stop at nothing, achieve by any means; see **try** 1.

**lengthen,** *v.* **1.** [To make longer] — *Syn.* extend, stretch, reach, elongate, protract, prolongate, prolong, distend, dilate, amplify, draw out, expand, augment, proceed, continue, string out\*, let out\*; see also **increase** 1. — *Ant.* DECREASE, contract, draw in.

**2.** [To grow longer] — *Syn.* produce, increase, expand; see **grow** 1.

*See Synonym Study at* EXTEND.

**lengthwise,** *modif.* — *Syn.* longitudinally, the long way, along, endlong, from end to end, from stem to stern, overall, fore and aft, from head to foot, from top to toe, from top to bottom; see also **alongside.** — *Ant.* crosswise, across, from side to side.

**lengthy,** *modif.* — *Syn.* prolix, not brief, long; see **dull** 4.

**leniency,** *n.* — *Syn.* forbearance, tolerance, charity; see **kindness** 1, **mercy** 1.

**lenient,** *modif.* — *Syn.* loving, soft, soft-hearted, easygoing, permissive, favoring, mild, tender, yielding, complaint, pampering, clement, indulgent, humoring, tolerant, forbearing, pardoning, letting, permitting, allowing, gratifying, sympathetic, assuaging, assuasive, emollient; see also **kind.** — *Ant.* SEVERE, firm, austere.

**lens,** *n.* — *Syn.* optical instrument, microscope, camera, eyeglass, spectacles, eyepiece.

Types of lenses include: spherical, planoconcave, double concave, biconcave, plano-convex, double convex, biconvex, diverging concavo-convex, converging concavo-convex, diverging, converging, diverging meniscus, converging meniscus, achromatic, anastigmatic, photographic, simple.

**lent,** *modif.* — *Syn.* loaned, out at interest, borrowed; see **given**.

**leonine,** *modif.* — *Syn.* like a lion, lionlike, powerful, kingly; see **brave** 1, **strong** 1.

**leopard,** *n.* — *Syn.* panther, hunting leopard, jaguar; see **animal** 2, **cat** 2.

**leper,** *n.* — *Syn.* pariah, untouchable, outcast, leprosy case; see **invalid, patient**.

**leprechaun,** *n.* — *Syn.* goblin, brownie, gnome, one of the little people; see **fairy** 1.

**leprosy,** *n.* — *Syn.* leprous infection, leprous inflamma-

tion, nerve paralysis, lepra; see **disease**.

Terms for leprous diseases include: elephantiasis, joint-evil, black leprosy, dry leprosy, nontuberculated lepra, *lepra cutanea, lepra nervosum* (*both* Latin).

**leprous,** *modif.* — *Syn.* unclean, infected, diseased; see **sick**.

**lesbian,** *n.* — *Syn.* gay woman, gay\*, sapphist, homosexual; see **homosexual**.

**lèse-majesté,** *n.* — *Syn.* mutiny, betrayal, revolt; see **dishonesty, treason**.

**lesion,** *n.* — *Syn.* wound, tumor, sore; see **injury**.

**less,** *modif.* — *Syn.* smaller, lower, not so much as, not as much, lesser, minor, fewer, reduced, declined, not as great, not so significant, in decline, depressed, inferior, secondary, subordinate, beneath, minus, deficient, diminished, shortened, circumscribed, limited; see also **shorter.** — *Ant.* MORE, more than, longer.

**less and less,** *modif.* — *Syn.* declining, decreasing, shrinking; see **lessening**.

**lessee,** *n.* — *Syn.* boarder, resident, rentee; see **renter**.

**lessen,** *v.* **1.** [To grow less] — *Syn.* decrease, diminish, dwindle, decline; see **decrease** 1.

**2.** [To make less] — *Syn.* decrease, reduce, diminish, slack up; see **decrease** 2.

*See Synonym Study at* DECREASE.

**lessening,** *modif.* — *Syn.* decreasing, declining, waning, ebbing, dropping, diminishing, abating, slowing, dwindling, sinking, sagging, subsiding, moderating, slackening, ebbing, lowering, shrinking, drying up, shriveling up, depreciating, softening, quieting, lightening, weakening, decaying, narrowing, drooping, wasting, running low, running down, dying away, dying down, withering away, fading away, wearing off, wearing out, wearing away, wearing down, falling away, falling off, slacking off, growing less and less, losing momentum, losing spirit, slumping, in a slump, plunging, plummeting, going down, going back, in reverse, getting worse, getting lower, getting slower.

**lessening,** *n.* — *Syn.* decrease, decline, shrinkage; see **discount, reducing, reduction** 1.

**lesser,** *modif.* — *Syn.* inferior, minor, secondary; see **subordinate**.

**lesson,** *n.* **1.** [An instructive assignment] — *Syn.* recitation, drill, reading; see **exercise** 2.

**2.** [Instruction] — *Syn.* teaching, tutoring, schooling; see **education** 1.

**3.** [Anything instructive] — *Syn.* helpful word, good example, noble action; see **model** 2.

**lessor,** *n.* — *Syn.* landlady, landlord, property owner; see **owner**.

**lest,** *conj.* — *Syn.* for fear that, so that, in order to avoid, to prevent; see **or**.

**let,** *v.* **1.** [To permit] — *Syn.* allow, permit, suffer, cause to; see **allow** 1.

**2.** [To award; *said especially of contracts*] — *Syn.* make, sign, grant, assign, engage, let out, hire out; see also **give** 1. — *Ant.* CANCEL, repudiate, break.

**3.** [To rent] — *Syn.* lease, hire, sublet; see **rent** 1.

*See Synonym Study at* ALLOW, HIRE.

**letdown,** *n.* — *Syn.* frustration, setback, disillusionment; see **disappointment** 1.

**let down,** *v.* — *Syn.* disappoint, disillusion, not support; see **abandon** 2, **fail** 1.

**let go,** *v.* — *Syn.* relinquish, dismiss, release, part with; see **abandon** 1.

**lethal,** *modif.* — *Syn.* deadly, fatal, mortal, malignant; see **deadly** 1, **harmful, poisonous**.

*See Synonym Study at* DEADLY.

**lethargic,** *modif.* — *Syn.* inert, sluggish, indifferent; see **lazy** 1, **listless** 1.

**lethargy,** *n.* — *Syn.* inactivity, apathy, sloth; see **laziness.**

**let in,** *v.* — *Syn.* admit, allow to enter, give admission to; see **allow** 1.

**let off,** *v.* — *Syn.* leave, excuse, let go, remove; see **abandon** 1, **drop** 1.

**let on\*,** *v.* — *Syn.* imply, indicate, suggest; see **hint.**

**let out,** *v.* — *Syn.* liberate, let go, eject; see **free** 1.

**letter,** *n.* 1. [A unit of the alphabet] — *Syn.* character, digraph, diphthong, capital, cap\*, upper case, lower case, LC\*, l.c.\*, small letter, majuscule, minuscule, rune, uncial, alphabet, logotype, ligature; see also **consonant, vowel.**

The Greek letters are: alpha, beta, gamma, delta, epsilon, zeta, eta, theta, iota, kappa, lambda, mu, nu, xi, omicron, pi, rho, sigma, tau, upsilon, phi, chi, psi, omega.

2. [A written communication] — *Syn.* note, epistle, missive, message, billet\*, memorandum, report, line\*; see also **word** 3.

Types of letters include: business, form, circular, drop, open, chain, cover, fan, love, personal; letter of credit, letter of resignation, billet-doux, postcard, postal, direct mail advertising, junk mail\*.

**to the letter** — *Syn.* just as written, just as directed, perfectly, precisely; see **exactly.**

**letter carrier,** *n.* — *Syn.* mail carrier, mailman, mail clerk, postman, mail handler, courier, postal clerk, postal worker, postmaster, postmistress; see also **messenger.**

**lettered,** *modif.* — *Syn.* literate, erudite, scholarly; see **educated** 1, **learned** 1.

**letup,** *n.* — *Syn.* interval, recess, respite; see **pause** 1, 2.

**let up,** *v.* — *Syn.* cease, release, slow down; see **slow** 1, **stop** 2.

**levee,** *n.* — *Syn.* embankment, dike, ridge, obstruction, block; see also **dam** 1.

**level,** *modif.* 1. [Smooth] — *Syn.* smooth, polished, rolled, planed; see **flat** 1, **smooth** 1.

2. [Of an even height] — *Syn.* even, flat, plane, regular, equal, uniform, flush, of the same height, in the same plane, common, same, constant, straight, true, parallel, equable, balanced, steady, unfluctuating, stable, trim, trimmed, precise, exact, matching, matched, on a line, lined up, aligned, uninterrupted, continuous; see also **parallel** 1, **smooth** 1. — *Ant.* IRREGULAR, uneven, crooked.

3. [Horizontal] — *Syn.* horizontal, plane, flat, leveled, true, flattened, tabular, recumbent, supine, lying prone; see also **flat** 1. — *Ant.* UPRIGHT, vertical, perpendicular.

**find one's** (*or* **its**) **level** — *Syn.* develop, find the proper place, find the proper station, suit; see **fit** 1, 2.

**one's level best\*,** one's best, the best one can do, all one's effort; see **best.**

**on the level\*** — *Syn.* fair, sincere, truthful; see **honest** 1.

---

*SYN.* — **level** describes a surface that has no part higher than any other, and is applied to a surface that is parallel to the plane of the horizon or that is the same height as, or in the same plane with, another; **flat** implies the absence to any marked degree of depressions or elevations in a surface, in whatever direction it lies; **plane** describes a real or imaginary surface that is absolutely flat and wholly contains every straight line joining any two points lying in it; **even** is applied to a surface that is uniformly level or flat, or to a surface that is in the same plane with,

or in a plane parallel to, another; a **smooth** surface has no roughness or projections, often as a result of wear, planing, polishing, etc.

---

**level,** *v.* 1. [To straighten] — *Syn.* surface, bulldoze, equalize; see **smooth** 1, **straighten.**

2. [To demolish] — *Syn.* ruin, waste, wreck; see **destroy** 1.

3. [\*To be honest with] — *Syn.* be frank with, be level with, be straight with, come to terms, be open and aboveboard.

**level-headed,** *modif.* — *Syn.* wise, practical, prudent; see **discreet, judicious, rational** 1, **reasonable** 1.

**level off,** *v.* — *Syn.* level out, find a level, reach an equilibrium; see **decrease** 1, **straighten.**

**lever,** *n.* — *Syn.* lifter, pry, leverage, prise, bar, pry bar, prying bar, pinch bar, crowbar, crow, handspike, arm, advantage; see also **machine** 1, **tool** 1.

**leverage,** *n.* — *Syn.* purchase, lift, hold, advantage, force, backing; see also **support** 2.

**levied,** *modif.* — *Syn.* exacted, taken, collected, raised, assessed, imposed, conscripted, mustered, drafted, required, demanded, called out, tasked, made liable for; see also **taxed** 1.

**levity,** *n.* — *Syn.* flippancy, high spirits, giddiness; see **frivolity, happiness** 1.

**levy,** *n.* — *Syn.* toll, duty, custom; see **tax** 1.

**lewd,** *modif.* 1. [Suggestive of lewdness] — *Syn.* ribald, smutty, risqué, dirty, indecent, loose, foul-mouthed, obscene, vulgar, bawdy, raunchy, naughty, off-color, questionable, taboo, unconventional, immoral, racy, impure, immodest, unclean, suggestive, indelicate, scandalous, scurrilous, coarse, rakish, vile, ungentlemanly, unladylike, unvirtuous, salacious, pornographic, gross, shameless, erotic, in bad taste, unfit for the young; see also sense 2, **sensual.** — *Ant.* DECENT, refined, clean.

2. [Inclined to lewdness] — *Syn.* lustful, wanton, lascivious, libidinous, licentious, lecherous, libertine, lubricious, profligate, dissolute, voluptuous, reprobate, carnal, orgiastic, sensual, debauched, corrupt, unchaste, depraved, unbridled, Rabelaisian, unregenerate, polluted, ruttish, nymphomaniacal, satyric, prurient, concupiscent, incontinent, masochistic, sadistic, incestuous, fornicative, unbridled, beastly, goatish, hircine, caprine, horny\*, hot\*, hot for\*, hot to trot\*. — *Ant.* chaste, PURE, modest.

**lewdly,** *modif.* — *Syn.* wantonly, shockingly, indecently, lasciviously, lecherously, libidinously, unchastely, carnally, dissolutely, immodestly, voluptuously, sensually, profligately, depravedly, orgiastically, incontinently, indelicately, like a wanton woman, like a loose woman, in a lewd manner, with lewd gestures, in a suggestive manner, with phallic implications, suggesting the libido, unbecoming polite society.

**lewdness,** *n.* — *Syn.* indecency, unchastity, incontinence, fleshliness, vulgarity, lechery, wantonness, lubricity, lasciviousness, aphrodisia, bodily appetite, libidinousness, sensuality, licentiousness, voluptuousness, lecherousness, profligacy, dissoluteness, obscenity, salacity, scurrility, coarseness, carnal passion, grossness, boorishness, sensuous desire, vileness, salaciousness, pornography, fleshly lust, depravity, brutishness, lustfulness, carnality, ruttishness, pederasty, nymphomania, pruriency, prurience, incontinency, corruptness, satyriasis, corruption, raunchiness, unnatural desires, dirtiness, ribaldry, incest, indelicacy, incestuousness, concupiscence, eroticism, sadism, erotism, smut, smuttiness, evil, evilness, evil-mindedness, impurity, debauchery; see also **evil** 1. — *Ant.* MODESTY, decency, continency.

**lexicographer,** *n.* — *Syn.* dictionary writer, definer, etymologist, philologist, polyglot, dictionary maker, dictionarist, lexicologist, lexicographist, glossarian, glossarist, glossologist, glossographer, glottologist, philologer, vocabulist, phonologist, philologian, phonetician, phoneticist, wordsmith*; see also **linguist** 1.

**lexicography,** *n.* — *Syn.* dictionary making, philology, derivation, etymology, origin, genesis, glossography, terminology, orismology, glottogony, glossology, lexicology, phonology; see also **grammar, language** 2.

**lexicon,** *n.* — *Syn.* glossary, thesaurus, vocabulary; see **dictionary, vocabulary.**

**liability,** *n.* **1.** [The state of being liable] — *Syn.* obligation, indebtedness, owing, susceptibility, subjection to, amenability, answerability, accountability, accountableness, exposedness, compulsion, amenableness, being made accountable; see also **responsibility** 2. — *Ant.* FREEDOM, exemption, immunity.
**2.** [A source of liability, sense 1] — *Syn.* balance, burden, arrearage, arrears, account, debit, remainder, pledge, accident, chance, involvement, responsibility, encumbrance, exposed position, contingency, indebtment, possibility, misfortune, onus, contract, lease, mortgage; see also **debt** 1.

**liable,** *modif.* **1.** [Responsible] — *Syn.* answerable, subject, accountable; see **responsible** 1.
**2.** [Likely] — *Syn.* likely, subject, apt, inclined; see **likely** 4.
*See Synonym Study at* LIKELY.

**liaison,** *n.* **1.** [Love affair] — *Syn.* love affair, romance, amour; see **affair** 2.
**2.** [Affiliation] — *Syn.* contact, connection, link, alliance; see **relationship.**

**liar,** *n.* — *Syn.* prevaricator, false witness, deceiver, dissimulator, romancer, maligner, deluder, trickster, cheat, misleader, falsifier, story-teller, equivocator, fibber, one who lies, fabricator, pseudologue, perjurer, fabulist, pseudologist; see also **cheat** 1.

**libation,** *n.* — *Syn.* oblation, gift, offering; see **drink** 1, **sacrifice** 1.

**libel,** *n.* — *Syn.* calumny, slander, lying; see **lie** 1.

**libelous,** *modif.* — *Syn.* derogatory, slanderous, sarcastic; see **opprobrious** 1.

**liberal,** *modif.* **1.** [Openhanded] — *Syn.* unselfish, bountiful, benevolent; see **generous** 1, **kind.**
**2.** [Open-minded or progressive] — *Syn.* tolerant, open-minded, receptive, progressive, libertarian, reformist, advanced, left, radical, broadminded, understanding, permissive, lax, indulgent, unprejudiced, impartial, disinterested, reasonable, enlightened, unbigoted, undogmatic, unbiased, dispassionate, unorthodox, unconventional, avant-garde, broad-gauge, left-wing, left-of-center, freethinking, latitudinarian, magnanimous, fair, free, flexible, idealistic, highminded, bleeding-heart*; see also **lenient.** — *Ant.* PREJUDICED, narrow-minded, conservative.
**3.** [Plentiful] — *Syn.* abundant, profuse, bountiful; see **plentiful** 1.

**SYN.** — **liberal** implies tolerance of others' views as well as open-mindedness to ideas that challenge tradition, established institutions, etc.; **progressive**, a relative term opposed to *reactionary* or *conservative*, is applied to persons favoring progress and reform in politics, education, etc. and connotes an inclination to more direct action than **liberal**; **advanced** specifically implies being ahead of the times, as in science, the arts, or philosophy; **radical** implies a favoring of fundamental or extreme change, specifically of the social structure; **left**, origi-

nally referring to the position in legislatures of the seats occupied by parties holding such views, implies political liberalism or radicalism

**liberal,** *n.* — *Syn.* reformer, progressive, libertarian, insurgent, rebel, revolutionary, anarchist, socialist, communist, humanist, independent, individualist, extremist, eccentric, freethinker, leftist, left-winger; see also **agitator.**

**liberalism,** *n.* — *Syn.* broad-mindedness, liberality, free-thinking, freedom, radicalism, humanitarianism, humanism, free thought, progressivism, universality, forward view, breadth of mind, latitudinarianism.

**liberality,** *n.* **1.** [Generosity] — *Syn.* benevolence, charity, giving; see **generosity** 1.
**2.** [Broad-mindedness] — *Syn.*
free thought, progressivism, universality; see **liberalism.**

**liberalize,** *v.* — *Syn.* expand, increase, grow; see **change** 1, **grow** 1, **improve** 1.

**liberate,** *v.* **1.** [To free from bondage] — *Syn.* set free, loose, release; see **free** 1.
**2.** [To free from chemical or physical restraint] — *Syn.* disengage, render gaseous, extract, separate, aerify, etherify, set free from combination, drive off, purify, gasify, make volatile, sublimate, analyze, catalyze, subject to catalysis, induce catalysis; see also **release.**
*See Synonym Study at* FREE.

**liberation,** *n.* **1.** [Emancipation] — *Syn.* rescue, freedom, deliverance; see **freeing.**
**2.** [Release; *said of chemicals*] — *Syn.* freeing, separation, displacement, hydrolysis, diffusion, sublimation, distillation, breaking ionic bonding, breaking covalent bonding, evaporation, osmosis, breakdown of organic compounds, breakdown of inorganic compounds, splitting of molecular structure, dividing of molecular structure.

**liberator,** *n.* — *Syn.* preserver, emancipator, deliverer, rescuer, freer, manumitter, redeemer; see also **savior** 1.

**liberty,** *n.* **1.** [Freedom from bondage] — *Syn.* deliverance, emancipation, enfranchisement; see **freedom** 1.
**2.** [Freedom from occupation] — *Syn.* rest, leave, relaxation; see **freedom** 2, **leisure, recreation.**
**3.** [Freedom to choose] — *Syn.* permission, alternative, decision; see **choice** 1, **selection** 1.
**4.** [The rights supposedly natural to man] — *Syn.* freedom, free speech, suffrage, autonomy, sovereignty, franchise, independence, enfranchisement, freedom from arbitrary government, freedom from despotic government, power of choice, right of habeas corpus, affranchisement, opportunity, right, immunity, privilege, exemption, birthright, self-government, education, enlightenment, bail, life, self-development, self-determination, autarchy; see also **democracy** 2.
*See Synonym Study at* FREEDOM.

**at liberty** — *Syn.* unrestricted, unlimited, not confined; see **free** 1, 2.

**take liberties** — *Syn.* be too familiar, be too impertinent, act too freely, use carelessly; see **abuse** 1.

**libidinous,** *modif.* — *Syn.* lustful, licentious, salacious; see **lewd** 2, **sensual.**

**libido,** *n.* — *Syn.* urge, impulse, psychic energy; see **desire** 3.

**librarian,** *n.* — *Syn.* custodian, keeper, caretaker, curator, bibliosoph, bibliothecary, cataloger, officer in charge of the library, bibliognost; see also **administrator.**
Types of librarians include: reference, children's,

county, state, college, university, museum, departmental.

**library,** *n.* — *Syn.* books, book collection, manuscripts, manuscript collection, institution, public library, ambry, bookery, athenaeum, private library, book room, lending library, collection of manuscripts, circulating library, reference library, reference collection, archives, museum, treasury, thesaurus, muniments, memorabilia, rare books, incunabula, incunables, reading room; see also **building** 1.

Great libraries of the world include: Bibliothéque Nationale, Paris; British Library, London; Bodleian Library, Oxford; Cambridge University Library; Biblioteca Vaticana, Biblioteca Nazionale Centrale Vittorio Emanuele, Rome; Biblioteca Laurentiana, Biblioteca Nazionale Centrale, Florence; Biblioteca Ambrosiana, Milan; Biblioteca Marciana, Venice; Bibliothèque Royale, Brussels; Biblioteca Nacional, Madrid; Biblioteca Nacional, Lisbon; Koninklijke Bibliotheek, The Hague; Kongelige Bibliothek, Copenhagen; Gosudarstvennaya Publichnaya Biblioteka, Leningrad; Staatsbibliothek, Berlin; National Library, Athens; Metropolitan Library, Beijing, Library of the Imperial Cabinet, Tokyo; Biblioteca Nacional, Mexico City; Biblioteca Nacional, Rio de Janeiro; Library of Congress, Folger Shakespeare Library, Washington, D.C.; Widener Library, Harvard University; Columbia University Library, New York Public Library, Morgan Library, New York; Boston Public Library; Cleveland Public Library; Harper Library, University of Chicago; Huntington Library, Pasadena, Calif.; Sterling Library, Yale University; University of California Libraries; Hoover War Library, Stanford University.

**librettist,** *n.* — *Syn.* writer, poet, lyricist; see **author** 2.

**libretto,** *n.* — *Syn.* song book, lyrics, lines, words, book, opera; see also **writing** 2.

**license,** *n.* **1.** [Unbridled use of freedom] — *Syn.* looseness, excess, laxity, slackness, relaxedness, effrontery, arrogance, sauciness, immoderation, debauchery, sensuality, gluttony, audacity, forwardness, temerity, boldness, complacency, wantonness, prodigality, epicureanism, wild living, lawlessness, indulgence, presumptuousness, unrestraint, licentiousness, self-indulgence, profligacy, unruliness, refractoriness, gall*, brass*, crust*.

**2.** [A formal permission] — *Syn.* permit, consent, grant; see **permission.**

*See Synonym Study at* FREEDOM.

**license,** *v.* — *Syn.* permit, authorize, privilege, accredit; see **allow** 1, **commission.**

*See Synonym Study at* COMMISSION.

**licensed,** *modif.* — *Syn.* authorized, permitted, allowed; see **approved.**

**licentious,** *modif.* — *Syn.* lascivious, sensuous, desirous; see **lewd** 2, **sensual.**

**lichen,** *n.* — *Syn.* fungus growth, fungus-alga, thallophyte, epiphyte, symbiont; see also **plant.**

Types of lichen include: foliaceous, crustaceous, fruticose, gelatinous, Iceland moss, reindeer moss, reindeer lichen, *Rocella tinctoria, Rocella fuciformis* (both Latin).

**lick,** *v.* **1.** [To pass the tongue over] — *Syn.* kiss, lap, tongue, lap up, stroke, rub, touch, pass over, pass across, move over, gloss over, caress, wash, play, graze, brush, glance, sweep, tongue, ripple, fondle, soothe, tranquilize, calm, quiet.

**2.** [To play over; *said of flames*] — *Syn.* run over, shoot, rise and fall, advance, fluctuate, flutter, vibrate, fly to and fro, leap, waver, vacillate, quiver, tremble, palpitate, blaze; see also **burn** 1, **dart** 1, **wave** 3.

**3.** [*To beat*] — *Syn.* whip, trim, thrash; see **beat** 2.

**4.** [*To defeat*] — *Syn.* overcome, vanquish, frustrate; see **defeat** 1.

**licking*,** *n.* — *Syn.* whipping, beating, thrashing; see **defeat** 3, **mauling.**

**lid,** *n.* — *Syn.* cap, top, roof; see **cover** 1, **hood** 2.

**lie,** *n.* **1.** [An intentional misstatement] — *Syn.* falsehood, untruth, fib, fiction, hyperbole, fraudulence, inaccuracy, misstatement, myth, fable, deceptiveness, disinformation, barefaced lie, dirty lie, misrepresentation, inoperative statement, lying, untruthfulness, prevarication, mendacity, falsification, falseness, falsifying, subterfuge, defamation, detraction, tale, story, tall story, cock-and-bull story, calumny, fabrication, deception, slander, backbiting, calumniation, aspersion, revilement, untruism, vilification, reviling, false swearing, perjury, libel, forgery, distortion, obloquy, garbled version, guile, white lie, corker*, fish story*, lollapalooza*, whopper*, cock and bull*, crock*, moonshine*, hogwash*; see also **dishonesty.** — *Ant.* TRUTH, veracity, truthfulness.

**2.** [Anything calculated to mislead another] — *Syn.* falsification, evasion, deceit; see **deception** 1, **trick** 1.

**give the lie to** — *Syn.* dispute, belie, prove false; see **disprove.**

**lie,** *v.* **1.** [To utter an untruth] — *Syn.* falsify, prevaricate, fib, tell a lie, equivocate, fabricate, deceive, mislead, misinform, misrepresent, exaggerate, distort, misstate, misspeak, concoct, tell a falsehood, be untruthful, forswear, be a liar, dupe, pervert, slant, twist, overstate, embellish, embroider, overdraw, bear false witness, say one thing and mean another, dissimulate, dissemble, perjure oneself, delude, malign, invent, manufacture, make up, trump up, palter, beguile, tell a white lie, stretch the truth, spin a long yarn*, bull*, make out of whole cloth*.

**2.** [To be situated] — *Syn.* extend, be on, be beside, be located, be fixed, be established, be placed, be seated, be set, be level, be smooth, be even, be plane, exist in space, prevail, endure, stretch along, reach along, spread along; see also **occupy** 2.

**3.** [To be prostrate] — *Syn.* be recumbent, be helpless, be supine, be exhausted, be flat, be prone, sprawl, loll, laze, be stretched out, be powerless, be thrown down; see also sense 4, **rest** 2. — *Ant.* STAND, be upright, sit.

**4.** [To assume a prostrate position] — *Syn.* lie down, recline, repose, stretch out, couch, go to bed, turn in, retire, take a nap, take a siesta, hit the hay*; see also **rest** 1, **sleep.** — *Ant.* RISE, get up, arise.

**take lying down** — *Syn.* submit, surrender, be passive; see **yield** 1.

---

**SYN.** — **lie** is the simple direct word meaning to make a deliberately false statement; **prevaricate** strictly means to quibble or confuse the issue in order to evade the truth, but it is loosely used as a formal or affected substitute for **lie**; **equivocate** implies the deliberate use of ambiguity in order to deceive or mislead; **fabricate** suggests the invention of a false story, excuse, etc. intended to deceive but may be somewhat softer in connotation than **lie**; **fib** implies the telling of a falsehood about something unimportant and is sometimes a euphemism for **lie**

---

**lie down on the job*,** *v.* — *Syn.* dawdle, slack off, fool around; see **loiter.**

**liege,** *n.* — *Syn.* master, lord, sovereign; see **owner.**

**lie low,** *v.* — *Syn.* keep out of sight, conceal oneself, go underground; see **hide** 2, **sneak.**

**lien,** *n.* — *Syn.* right to dispose of property, hold on property, charge, security on property, real security; see also **claim.**

**lie over,** *v.* — *Syn.* stay over, break a journey, stop off; see **halt** 2, **pause, stop** 1.

**lieutenant,** *n.* — *Syn.* officer, army officer, navy officer, marine officer, military man, soldier, platoon leader, fighter, commissioned officer, leader, looie★, 90-day wonder★, shavetail★; see also **officer** 3.
Lieutenants include: first, second, junior grade, sublieutenant.

**life,** *n.* **1.** [The fact or act of living] — *Syn.* being, entity, growth, animation, animate existence, endurance, survival, presence, living, consciousness, subsistence, symbiosis, breath, continuance, flesh and blood, animateness, viability, substantiality, mortal being, reproduction, metabolism, vitality, vital spark; see also **experience** 1. — *Ant.* DEATH, discontinuance, nonexistence.
**2.** [The sum of one's experiences] — *Syn.* life experience, conduct, behavior, way of life, reaction, response, participation, tide of events, circumstances, unhappiness, realization, knowledge, enlightenment, attainment, development, growth, personality; see also **world** 1.
**3.** [A biography] — *Syn.* life story, memoir, memorial; see **biography, journal** 1, **story.**
**4.** [Duration] — *Syn.* lifetime, one's natural life, longevity, actuarial expectancy, period of existence, duration of life, endurance, continuance, span, history, career, course, era, epoch, century, decade, days, generation, time, day, period, life span, season, cycle, record, one's born days★; see also **extent, length** 3.
**5.** [One who promotes gaiety] — *Syn.* life-giver, spirit, animator, entertainer, invigorator, life of the party★, master of ceremonies★; see also **host** 1, **hostess** 1, 3.
**6.** [Vital spirit] — *Syn.* vital force, vital principle, life-blood, *élan vital* (French); see **enthusiasm** 1, **excitement.**

**as large** (*or* **big**) **as life** — *Syn.* actually, truly, in fact; see **accurately.**

**bring to life** — *Syn.* inspirit, activate, liven, enliven; see **animate** 1, **excite** 2.

**come to life** — *Syn.* revive, awaken, show signs of life; see **recover** 3, **revive** 2.

**for dear life★** — *Syn.* intensely, desperately, for all one is worth; see **strongly.**

**for life** — *Syn.* for the duration of one's life, for a long time, as long as one lives; see **forever** 1.

**for the life of me★** — *Syn.* by any means, as if one's life were at stake, whatever happens; see **anyhow** 1.

**from life** — *Syn.* from a living model, descriptive, representational; see **genuine** 1.

**matter of life and death** — *Syn.* crisis, grave concern, something vitally important; see **importance** 1.

**not on your life★** — *Syn.* by no means, certainly not, never; see **no.**

**see life** — *Syn.* experience, do, act; see **live** 2.

**take a life** — *Syn.* deprive of life, murder, destroy; see **kill** 1.

**take one's own life** — *Syn.* kill oneself, die by one's own hand, murder; see **commit suicide.**

**true to life** — *Syn.* true to reality, realistic, representational; see **genuine** 1.

**lifeboat,** *n.* — *Syn.* quarter boat, rowboat, ship's boat, liferaft; see **boat, raft.**

**life expectancy,** *n.* — *Syn.* probable future, statistical probability, chances; see **future** 1.

**life-giving,** *modif.* **1.** [Fertile] — *Syn.* prolific, generative, productive; see **fertile** 1, 2.
**2.** [Inspiring] — *Syn.* invigorating, animating, revealing; see **inspiring, stimulating.**

**lifeless,** *modif.* **1.** [Without life] — *Syn.* dead, inert, inanimate, departed; see **dead** 1.
**2.** [Lacking spirit] — *Syn.* lackluster, listless, heavy; see **dull** 3, 4, **slow** 2.
*See Synonym Study at* DEAD.

**lifelike,** *modif.* — *Syn.* simulated, exact, imitative; see **graphic** 1, 2.

**lifeline,** *n.* — *Syn.* help, salvation, line; see **aid** 1, **rope.**

**lifelong,** *modif.* — *Syn.* lifetime, enduring, livelong; see **permanent** 2.

**life of Riley★,** *n.* — *Syn.* contentment, prosperity, luxury; see **comfort** 1, **ease** 1, **satisfaction** 2.

**life or death,** *modif.* — *Syn.* decisive, crucial, necessary, critical; see **important** 1.

**life story,** *n.* — *Syn.* autobiography, memoir, profile; see **biography, journal** 1, **record** 1.

**lifetime,** *modif.* — *Syn.* lifelong, continuing, enduring; see **permanent** 2.

**lifetime,** *n.* — *Syn.* life, existence, endurance, continuance; see **life** 3, 4, **record** 2.

**lifework,** *n.* — *Syn.* occupation, career, vocation; see **business** 1, **profession** 1, **purpose** 1.

**lift,** *n.* **1.** [The work of lifting] — *Syn.* pull, lifting, upthrow, ascension, raising, weight, foot-pounds, elevation, sub-elevation, escalation, ascent, mounting.
**2.** [★A ride] — *Syn.* transportation, drive, passage; see **journey.**
**3.** [★Aid] — *Syn.* help, assistance, support; see **aid** 1.

**lift,** *v.* — *Syn.* raise, hoist, elevate, boost, rear, heave, pick up, hold up, uplift, exalt, heft★; see also **raise** 1.

---

*SYN.* — **lift,** in its general literal sense, implies the use of some effort in bringing something up to a higher position /help me *lift* the table/; **raise,** often interchangeable with **lift,** may specifically imply bringing into an upright position by lifting one end /to *raise* a flagpole/; **elevate** is now a less frequent synonym for **lift** or **raise** /the balloon had been *elevated* 500 feet/; **rear** is a literary equivalent of **raise** /the giant trees *reared* their branches to the sky/; **hoist** implies the lifting of something heavy, usually by some mechanical means, as a block and tackle or a crane /to *hoist* bales of cotton into a ship/; **boost** is a colloquial term and implies lifting by or as if by a push from behind or below /*boost* me into the tree/. All these terms are used figuratively to imply bringing into a higher or better state /to *lift,* or *hoist,* one's spirits, to *raise* one's hopes, to *elevate* one's mind, to *rear* children, to *boost* sales/

---

**lifter,** *n.* — *Syn.* jackscrew, pry, lift; see **jack** 1, **lever.**

**ligature,** *n.* — *Syn.* link, bond, connection; see **band** 2, **rope.**

**light,** *modif.* **1.** [Having illumination] — *Syn.* illuminated, radiant, luminous; see **bright** 1.
**2.** [Having color] — *Syn.* vivid, rich, clear; see **bright** 2.
**3.** [Having little content] — *Syn.* superficial, slight, frivolous; see **trivial, unimportant.**
**4.** [Having gaiety and spirit] — *Syn.* lively, merry, animated; see **jaunty.**
**5.** [Having little weight] — *Syn.* airy, fluffy, feathery, imponderable, slender, downy, floating, lighter than air, light as air, floatable, gossamery, light as a feather, frothy, buoyant, easy, dainty, filmy, veil-like, tissuelike,

thin, sheer, gaseous, effervescent, unsubstantial, insubstantial, ethereal, graceful, charming, weightless, atmospheric; see also **volatile** 1. — *Ant.* HEAVY, ponderous, weighty.

**6.** [Digestible] — *Syn.* slight, edible, moderate; see **edible.**

**7.** [Small in quantity or number] — *Syn.* wee, small, tiny, minute, thin, inadequate, minuscule, insufficient, hardly enough, not much, hardly any, not many, slender, scanty, slight, moderate, puny, sparse, fragmentary, fractional, shredlike; see also **dainty** 1, **few.** — *Ant.* LARGE, great, immense.

**8.** [Wanton] — *Syn.* carnal, immodest, indecent; see **lewd** 2, **sensual.**

**make light of** — *Syn.* make fun of, mock, belittle; see **neglect** 1, **ridicule.**

**light,** *n.* **1.** [The condition opposed to darkness] — *Syn.* radiance, luminous energy, luminosity, brilliance, splendor, irradiation, glare, brightness, clearness, lightness, brilliancy, coruscation, incandescence, scintillation, shine, fulgor, refulgence, emanation, lucency, luster, sheen, sparkle, glitter, glow, glimmer, glister, effulgence, resplendence, flood of light, blare, radiation, gleam. — *Ant.* DARKNESS, blackness, blankness.

**2.** [Emanations from a source of light] — *Syn.* radiation, stream, blaze; see **beam** 2, **flash** 1, **ray.**

**3.** [A source of light] — *Syn.* lamp, lantern, match, wick, sun, planet, star, moon, lightning, torch, flashlight, chandelier, spotlight, halo, nimbus, northern lights, aurora borealis, aureole, corona; see also **bulb, candle, lamp.**

**4.** [Day] — *Syn.* daylight, daytime, sun, sunrise; see **day** 2.

**5.** [Aspect] — *Syn.* point of view, condition, standing; see **circumstances** 2.

**6.** [Basis for understanding] — *Syn.* enlightenment, information, education; see **data, knowledge** 1.

**in light of** — *Syn.* with knowledge of, because of, in view of, in consideration of; see **considering.**

**see the light (of day)** — *Syn.* **1.** come into being, exist, begin; see **be.**

**2.** comprehend, realize, be aware; see **understand** 1.

**stand in one's own light** — *Syn.* harm oneself, act carelessly, act thoughtlessly, err; see **fail** 1.

**strike a light** — *Syn.* inflame, cause to burn, kindle; see **burn** 2, **ignite.**

**light,** *v.* **1.** [To provide light] — *Syn.* illuminate, illumine, illume, lighten, give light to, shine upon, furnish with light, light up, turn on the electricity, make a light, make visible, provide adequate illumination, provide adequate candlepower, turn on a light, switch on a light, floodlight, throw light upon, make bright, flood with light, animate, fill with light, irradiate; see also **brighten** 1. — *Ant.* SHADE, put out, darken.

**2.** [To cause to ignite] — *Syn.* inflame, spark, kindle; see **burn** 2, **ignite.**

**3.** [To become ignited] — *Syn.* take fire, become inflamed, flame; see **burn** 1, **ignite.**

**4.** [To come to rest from flight or travel] — *Syn.* perch, roost, rest, alight, fly down, come down, disembark, settle on, stop, drop, sit down, debus, come to rest, get down, detrain, unhorse, settle down; see also **arrive** 1. — *Ant.* FLY, soar off, take off.

**lighted,** *modif.* **1.** [Illuminated] — *Syn.* brilliant, alight, glowing; see **bright** 1.

**2.** [Burning] — *Syn.* blazing, flaming, aflame; see **afire, burning** 1.

**lighten,** *v.* **1.** [To make lighter] — *Syn.* unburden, disburden, make lighter, reduce the load of, lessen the

weight of, uplift, buoy up, mitigate, levitate, alleviate, make less burdensome, disencumber, take off a load, remove, take from, pour out, throw overboard, jettison, reduce, cut down, put off, facilitate, upraise, make buoyant, take off weight, eradicate, shift, change; see also **decrease** 1, **empty** 2, **unload.** — *Ant.* LOAD, burden, overload.

**2.** [To ease] — *Syn.* ease, comfort, cheer, gladden; see **comfort, relieve** 2.

*See Synonym Study at* RELIEVE.

**lighter,** *n.* **1.** [Boat] — *Syn.* craft, barge, keel; see **boat.**

**2.** [Mechanical igniter] — *Syn.* cigarette lighter, cigar lighter, pipe lighter, igniter, flame; see also **light** 3, **match** 1.

**light-fingered,** *modif.* — *Syn.* thievish, stealthy, pilfering, filching, stealing, dishonest.

**light-footed,** *modif.* — *Syn.* swift, buoyant, adroit; see **agile, graceful** 1.

**lightheaded,** *modif.* **1.** [Giddy] — *Syn.* inane, fickle, frivolous; see **changeable** 1, **silly** 1.

**2.** [Faint] — *Syn.* tired, delirious, dizzy; see **weak** 1.

**lighthearted,** *modif.* — *Syn.* gay, joyous, cheerful; see **happy** 1.

**lighthouse,** *n.* — *Syn.* guide, lightship, beam; see **beacon, tower.**

**lighting,** *n.* **1.** [Illumination] — *Syn.* brilliance, flame, brightness; see **flash** 1, **illumination** 1, **light** 1, 3.

**2.** [Ignition] — *Syn.* kindling, setting aflame, burning; see **fire** 1.

**light in the head,** *modif.* — *Syn.* foolish, senseless, incompetent; see **silly, stupid** 1.

**light into,** *v.* — *Syn.* rebuke, blame, assault; see **censure, scold.**

**lightless,** *modif.* — *Syn.* unilluminated, dusky, without light; see **black** 1, **dark** 1.

**lightly,** *modif.* **1.** [With lightness] — *Syn.* delicately, airily, buoyantly, daintily, readily, gently, subtly, exquisitely, ethereally, mildly, softly, tenderly, carefully, leniently, tenuously, unsubstantially, effortlessly, nimbly, agilely, smoothly, blandly, sweetly, comfortably, restfully, peacefully, quietly, ripplingly, soaringly; see also **easily** 1, **gracefully.** — *Ant.* HEAVILY, ponderously, roughly.

**2.** [With indifference] — *Syn.* slightingly, carelessly, indifferently; see **casually** 2.

**light-minded,** *modif.* — *Syn.* capricious, flighty, frivolous; see **changeable** 1.

**lightness,** *n.* **1.** [Illumination] — *Syn.* brightness, glow, sparkle, blaze, shine; see also **flash, light** 1, 3.

**2.** [The state of being light] — *Syn.* airiness, volatileness, etherealness, downiness, thinness, sheerness, fluffiness, featheriness; see also **buoyancy** 1, **delicacy** 1.

**3.** [Agility] — *Syn.* balance, deftness, nimbleness; see **agility, grace** 1.

**lightning,** *n.* — *Syn.* electrical discharge, fulmination, streak of lightning, lightning flash, thunderball, thunderstroke, firebolt, thunderlight, thunderbolt, bolt, bolt from the blue; see also **electricity** 2.

Types of lightning include: ball, globular, chain, forked, heat, summer, sheet.

**light out,** *v.* — *Syn.* run, abscond, depart; see **leave** 1.

**lightweight\*,** *n.* — *Syn.* incompetent, bungler, stupid person, nebbish\*; see **failure** 2, **fool** 1.

**likable,** *modif.* — *Syn.* agreeable, amiable, attractive; see **friendly** 1.

**like,** *modif.* — *Syn.* similar, same, near, resembling, close, not far from, according to, conforming with, matching, equaling, jibing, allying, not unlike, akin, related, analogous, twin, corresponding, allied to, much the same, of the same form, comparable, identical, congeneric, congenerous, approximative, in the manner of, parallel, homologous, to the effect that, consistent, of a piece, approximating; see also **alike** 1, 2.— *Ant.* DIFFERENT, far, unrelated.

**like,** *prep.* — *Syn.* similar, same, near to; see **alike** 2, **like** (*modif.*).

**like,** *n.* — *Syn.* counterpart, match, equal, peer, equivalent, resemblance, parallelism; see also **similarity.**

**and the like**— *Syn.* and so forth, etcetera, etc., similar kinds; see **others, same.**

**more like it***— *Syn.* acceptable, good, improved; see **better** 2.

**nothing like**— *Syn.* dissimilar, contrasting, opposed; see **different** 1, 2.

**something like**— *Syn.* similar, resembling, akin; see **like** (*modif.*).

**like,** *v.* **1.** [To enjoy] — *Syn.* take delight in, relish, take pleasure in, derive pleasure from, be pleased by, revel in, indulge in, rejoice in, find agreeable, find congenial, find appealing, be gratified by, take satisfaction in, be keen on, exclaim over, savor, fancy, dote on, take an interest in, develop interest for, delight in, bask in, luxuriate in, regard with favor, have a liking for, love, have a taste for, care to, feast on, get a kick out of*, feast one's eyes on*, be tickled by*, eat up*, go in for*, lick one's lips over*. — *Ant.* ENDURE, detest, dislike.

**2.** [To be fond of] — *Syn.* have a fondness for, admire, hold in regard, take a fancy to, feel warmly toward, feel affectionately toward, prize, esteem, hold dear, dote on, care about, care for, approve, be pleased with, take to*, have a soft spot in one's heart for*, go for in a big way*, hunger and thirst after*, hanker for*, have a yen for*, become attached to*, be sweet on*, cotton to*, have eyes for*; see also **cherish** 1, **love** 1. — *Ant.* HATE, disapprove, dislike.

**3.** [To be inclined] — *Syn.* choose, feel disposed, wish, desire, have a preference for, prefer, fancy, feel like, incline toward; see also **want** 1.

**like anything** *or* **blazes** *or* **crazy** etc.*, *modif.* — *Syn.* very much, exceedingly, greatly; see **much** 1, **very.**

**liked,** *modif.* — *Syn.* popular, loved, admired, well-liked; see **beloved, honored.**

**like father, like son,** *modif.* — *Syn.* similar, resembling each other, showing a family resemblance; see **alike** 1, 2, 3.

**likelihood,** *n.* — *Syn.* plausibility, reasonableness, possibility; see **probability.**

**likely,** *modif.* **1.** [Probable] — *Syn.* apparent, probable, seeming, credible, possible, feasible, presumable, conceivable, reasonable, conjecturable, practicable, workable, attainable, achievable, ostensible, surmisable, inferable, believable, rational, thinkable, imaginable, plausible, to be supposed, supposable, to be guessed, anticipated, expected, imminent, destined, assumable, grantable, persuasive, warrantable, as like as not.— *Ant.* IMPOSSIBLE, doubtful, questionable.

**2.** [Promising] — *Syn.* suitable, apt, assuring; see **fit** 1, 2, **hopeful** 2.

**3.** [Believable] — *Syn.* plausible, true, acceptable; see **convincing** 2.

**4.** [Apt] — *Syn.* inclined, tending, disposed, predisposed, apt, prone, liable, subject to, on the verge of, in the habit of, given to, in favor of, having a weakness for.

**SYN.** — **likely** suggests probability or an eventuality that can reasonably be expected /he's not *likely* to win/; **liable** and **apt** are loosely or informally used equiva-

lents of **likely,** but in strict discrimination, **liable** implies exposure or susceptibility to something undesirable /you're *liable* to hurt yourself playing with that knife/ and **apt** suggests a natural or habitual inclination or tendency /such people are *apt* to be fearful/; **prone** suggests a propensity or predisposition to something that seems almost inevitable /she's *prone* to have accidents/

**like-minded,** *modif.* — *Syn.* compatible, unanimous, agreeable; see **fit** 1, **harmonious** 2.

**liken,** *v.* — *Syn.* parallel, set beside, equate; see **compare** 1.

**likeness,** *n.* **1.** [Similarity] — *Syn.* resemblance, correspondence, similarity, analogy, parallelism, affinity, similitude, congruence, concordance, sameness; see also **similarity.**

**2.** [A representation] — *Syn.* image, effigy, portrait; see **copy, picture** 3, **representation.**

**SYN.** — **likeness** implies close correspondence in appearance, qualities, nature, etc. /her remarkable *likeness* to her sister/; **similarity** suggests only partial correspondence /a certain *similarity* between your problem and mine/; **resemblance** usually implies correspondence in appearance or in superficial aspects /the *resemblance* between a diamond and a zircon/; **analogy** refers to a correspondence between attributes or circumstances of things that are basically unlike /the *analogy* between a computer and the human brain/

**likewise,** *modif.* — *Syn.* in like manner, furthermore, moreover; see **besides.**

**liking,** *n.* — *Syn.* desire, fondness, devotion; see **affection** 1, **love** 1.

**Lilliputian,** *modif.* — *Syn.* diminutive, dwarfed, small; see **little** 1.

**lily,** *n.* — *Syn.* bulb, *Lilium* (Latin), fleur-de-lis; see **flower** 1, **plant.**

Varieties of lilies include: wood, meadow, Easter, Bermuda, Canada, canadense, superbum, golden-banded, tiger, regal, Madonna, Annunciation, coral, Turk's-cap, common white, Jacob's, orange.

Flowers resembling or related to lilies include: sego, lily of the valley, fleur-de-lis, iris, amaryllis, belladonna lily, daffodil, narcissus, spider lily, Guernsey lily, star grass, agapanthus, day lily, mariposa lily, cape lily, water lily, calla lily.

**gild the lily**— *Syn.* overdo, exaggerate, try to improve something already perfect; see **improve** 1.

**limb,** *n.* **1.** [A branch] — *Syn.* arm, bough, offshoot; see **branch** 2.

**2.** [A bodily appendage] — *Syn.* arm, leg, appendage, part, wing, pinion, fin, flipper, lobe; see also **member** 3.

**limber,** *modif.* **1.** [Agile] — *Syn.* nimble, spry, deft; see **agile, graceful** 1.

**2.** [Pliant] — *Syn.* supple, lithe, plastic; see **flexible** 1.

**limbo,** *n.* **1.** [Abode of the (righteous) dead] — *Syn.* nothingness, purgatory, nether regions; see **hell** 1, **oblivion** 2.

**2.** [Confinement] — *Syn.* imprisonment, internment, captivity; see **confinement** 1.

**3.** [Exclusion] — *Syn.* exile, isolation, banishment; see **exclusion.**

**in limbo**— *Syn.* up in the air, on hold, pending, in abeyance.

**limelight,** *n.* — *Syn.* publicity, spotlight, recognition; see **attention** 1, 2, **fame** 1.

**limit,** *n.* **1.** [The boundary] — *Syn.* end, frontier, border; see **boundary.**
**2.** [The ultimate] — *Syn.* utmost, bourne, ultimate, farthest point, farthest reach, destination, goal, conclusion, extremity, eventuality, termination, absolute, ultima Thule, the bitter end*, deadline*, cut-off point*, the nines*; see also **end** 4, **finality, purpose** 1. — *Ant.* ORIGIN, incipience, start.
**3.** [The breaking point] — *Syn.* the last straw, breaking point, boiling point, *coup de grâce* (French).
**limit,** *v.* — *Syn.* restrict, bound, confine, circumscribe, curb, restrain, delimit, define, narrow, straiten, check, keep within bounds, hold in check, hem in, draw the line*; see also **define** 1, **restrict** 2.

---

**SYN.** — **limit** implies the prescribing of a point in space, time, or extent, beyond which it is impossible or forbidden to go *[limit your slogan to 25 words]*; **bound** implies an enclosing in boundaries or borders *[a meadow bounded by hills]*; **restrict** implies a boundary that completely encloses and connotes a restraining within these bounds, or a restriction of action within narrow limits *[the soldier was restricted to the camp area]*; **circumscribe** emphasizes more strongly the cutting off or isolation of that which is within the bounds, or a restriction of action within narrow limits *[he leads the circumscribed life of a monk]*; **confine** stresses the restraint or hampering of enclosing limits *[confined in jail]*

---

**limitation,** *n.* **1.** [The act of limiting] — *Syn.* restriction, obstruction, deprivation, hindrance, restraint, constraint, deterrence, control, determent, prohibition, repression, suppression, discouragement, interdiction, cutoff, interception, stoppage; see also **arrest** 2, **interference** 1, **interruption, prevention.** — *Ant.* INCREASE, permission, toleration.
**2.** [That which limits] — *Syn.* condition, definition, qualification, reservation, control, curb, check, injunction, bar, obstruction, stricture, constraint, taboo, circumspection, inhibition, modification; see also **arrest** 1, **barrier, boundary, impediment** 1, **refusal, restraint** 2. — *Ant.* FREEDOM, latitude, LIBERTY.
**3.** [A shortcoming] — *Syn.* inadequacy, insufficiency, deficiency, shortcoming, weakness, want, imperfection, weak spot, failing, fault, frailty, flaw, incompleteness; see also **blemish, defect** 2, **lack** 2. — *Ant.* STRENGTH, PERFECTION, ABILITY.
**limited,** *modif.* **1.** [Restricted] — *Syn.* confined, checked, curbed; see **bound** 2, **bounded, restrained, restricted.**
**2.** [Having only moderate capacity] — *Syn.* cramped, insufficient, short; see **faulty, inadequate** 1, **poor** 2, **unsatisfactory.**
**limitless,** *modif.* — *Syn.* unending, boundless, immeasurable; see **endless** 1, **infinite** 1, **unlimited.**
**limp,** *modif.* **1.** [Without stiffness] — *Syn.* pliant, soft, flaccid, flabby, formative, supple, pliable, limber, relaxed, bending readily, ductile, plastic, impressible, yielding, lax, slack, droopy, loose, flimsy, unsubstantial; see also **flexible** 1. — *Ant.* STIFF, rigid, wooden.
**2.** [Weak] — *Syn.* feeble, infirm, debilitated; see **weak** 2.
**limp,** *n.* — *Syn.* halt, lameness, hobble, falter, hitch, shamble, shuffle, gimp.
**limp,** *v.* — *Syn.* halt, walk lamely, proceed slowly, flag, shuffle, teeter, lag, stagger, claudicate, totter, dodder, hobble, hitch, falter; see also **stumble** 1.
**limpid,** *modif.* **1.** [Transparent] — *Syn.* pellucid, filmy,

thin; see **clear** 2, **pure** 1, **transparent** 1.
**2.** [Intelligible] — *Syn.* clear, distinct, lucid; see **definite** 2, **obvious** 1.
**line,** *n.* **1.** [A row] — *Syn.* length, list, rank, file, catalogue, array, order, group, arrangement, furrow, ridge, range, seam, band, border, block, series, sequence, succession, chain, train, string, column, procession, formation, division, queue, magazine, concatenation, trench, channel, groove, drain, mark, scar, thread, fissure, crack, straight line; see also **seam, series.**
**2.** [A mark] — *Syn.* outline, tracing, stroke; see **mark** 1.
**3.** [A rope] — *Syn.* cord, filament, steel tape; see **rope, wire** 1.
**4.** [Lineal descent] — *Syn.* descent, pedigree, genealogy, lineage; see **family** 1, **heredity.**
**5.** [A border line] — *Syn.* border, mark, limit; see **boundary, edge** 1.
**6.** [A course] — *Syn.* street, lane, path; see **road** 1, **route** 1.
**7.** [Policy] — *Syn.* belief, principle, course; see **plan** 2, **policy, route** 2.
**8.** [Matter printed in a row of type] — *Syn.* row, words, letters; see **copy.**
**9.** [A military front] — *Syn.* front line, disposition, formation, position; see **front** 2.
**10.** [A railroad] — *Syn.* trunk line, sideline, mainline; see **railroad, track** 1.
**11.** [An organization supplying transportation] — *Syn.* steamship line, airline, bus company; see **transportation.**
**12.** [*The kind or materials of trade] — *Syn.* materials, trade, involvement; see **business** 1, **industry** 3.
**13.** [*Goods handled by a given house] — *Syn.* wares, merchandise, produce; see **commodity, material** 2.
**14.** [*Talk intended to influence another] — *Syn.* prepared speech, patter, persuasion; see **conversation, speech** 3.
**all along the line** — *Syn.* at every turn, completely, constantly; see **everywhere.**
**bring into line** — *Syn.* align, make uniform, regulate; see **order** 3.
**down the line, 1.** [Completely] — *Syn.* entirely, thoroughly, wholly; see **completely.**
**2.** [Later] — *Syn.* after a while, presently, by and by; see **following.**
**draw the** (*or* **a**) **line** — *Syn.* set a limit, prohibit, restrain; see **restrict** 2.
**get a line on*** — *Syn.* find out about, investigate, expose; see **discover.**
**in line** — *Syn.* agreeing, conforming, uniform; see **regular** 3.
**in line for** — *Syn.* being considered for, ready, thought about; see **considered** 1.
**in line of duty** — *Syn.* authorized, prescribed, required; see **approved, legal** 1.
**lay** (*or* **put**) **it on the line*** — *Syn.* elucidate, define, clarify; see **explain.**
**on a line** — *Syn.* linear, lined, level; see **direct** 1, **straight** 1.
**out of line** — *Syn.* misdirected, not uniform, not even; see **irregular** 1, 2.
**read between the lines** — *Syn.* read meaning into, discover a hidden meaning, expose; see **understand** 1.
**line,** *v.* **1.** [To provide a lining] — *Syn.* interline, encrust, stuff, wad, panel, incrust, reinforce the back of, pad, quilt, fill, overlay, bush, sheath, wainscot; see also **face** 3.
**2.** [To provide lines] — *Syn.* trace, delineate, outline; see **draw** 2, **mark** 1.

**3.** [To be in a line] — *Syn.* border, edge, outline, rank, rim, bound, skirt, fall in, fall into line, fringe, follow; see also **succeed** 2.

**4.** [To arrange in a line] — *Syn.* align, queue, marshal, dress, face in, arrange, range, array, group, set out, bring into a line with others, fix, place, list space, line right, line left, rank, draw up; see also **file** 1, **line up, order** 3. — *Ant.* disarrange, disperse, scatter.

**lineage,** *n.* — *Syn.* forefathers, ancestors, genealogy, progenitors; see **family** 1, **heredity.**

**lineal,** *modif.* **1.** [Having to do with a line] — *Syn.* longitudinal, on a line, marking; see **linear.**
**2.** [Hereditary] — *Syn.* inherited, transmitted, descended; see **ancestral, inherent.**

**lineament,** *n.* — *Syn.* feature, configuration, contour; see **characteristic, feature** 1.

**linear,** *modif.* — *Syn.* lineal, lined, long, extended in a line, elongated, resembling a thread, continuing, unintermitting, looking like a line, rectilinear, successive, in the direction of a line, undeviating, narrow, threadlike, outstretched, extended; see also **direct** 1, **straight** 1.

**lined,** *modif.* — *Syn.* interlined, stuffed, encrusted, coated, wadded, faced, brushed, sheathed, wainscoted, ceiled.

**linen,** *n.* — *Syn.* cloth, material, flaxen fabric, sheeting, linen cloth.
Types of linen include: damask, single damask, five-leaf damask, eight-leaf damask, linen duck, linen huckaback, linen crash, dowlas, osnaburg, low sheeting, low brown linen, plain bleached linen, twilled linen, linen drilling, diaper linen, cambric linen, lawn, toile, linsey-woolsey, handkerchief linen, printed linen, hand-blocked linen, dyed linen; see also **bedding, cloth, sheet** 1, **towel.**
Articles called linens include: handkerchiefs, towels, bedding, sheets, pillowcases, comforters, bedspreads, blankets, quilts, underwear, shirts, dishtowels, tablecloths, napkins, doilies.

**liner,** *n.* — *Syn.* ocean liner, airliner, cruiser; see **plane** 3, **ship.**

**linesman,** *n.* — *Syn.* umpire, referee, arbiter; see **judge** 2, **official** 2.

**lineup,** *n.* — *Syn.* starters, entrants, first string; see **list, register** 1.

**line up,** *v.* — *Syn.* fall in, form in a line, form into a line, take one's proper place in line, queue up, form ranks, form a column by two's, four's, etc., get in line, get in formation; see also **march.**

**linger,** *v.* **1.** [To go reluctantly] — *Syn.* tarry, stay, wait, saunter, lag, trail, hesitate, delay, plod, trudge, traipse, falter, totter, stagger, dawdle, lumber, procrastinate, slouch, shuffle, trifle, potter, fritter away time, shilly-shally, dillydally, idle, crawl, loll, vacillate, take one's time, wait, putter, hobble, be dilatory, be tardy, be long, sit around★, hang around★, hang back★, let the grass grow under one's feet★; see also **loiter.** — *Ant.* hasten, HURRY, speed.
**2.** [To go slowly] — *Syn.* hang on, remain, be moribund; see **delay** 1, **hinder.**
*See Synonym Study at* WAIT.

**lingerie,** *n.* — *Syn.* women's underwear; dainties★, unmentionables★; see **clothes, underwear.**

**lingo,** *n.* — *Syn.* dialect, idiom, jargon; see **dialect, language** 1.
*See Synonym Study at* DIALECT.

**linguist,** *n.* **1.** [Student of language] — *Syn.* etymologist, philologist, philologer, structuralist, structural linguist, usagist, transformationalist, transformational grammarian, phonologist, dialectician,

vocabulist, glossographer, glossologist, phoneticist, phonetician, phonemist, grammatist, grammarian, lexiconist, lexicographer, philologue, linguistician, stratificationalist, stratificational grammarian, tagmemist, glottochronologist, comparativist, comparative (Indo-European) grammarian, reconstructionist, linguistic geographer, semanticist.
**2.** [Speaker of many languages] — *Syn.* polyglot, translator, polyglottist, savant, conversant, Pangloss; see also **scholar** 2.

**linguistic,** *modif.* — *Syn.* semantic, dialectal, philological, etymological, phonological, morphological, lingual, phonetic, phonemic, grammatical, syntactical, usagistic, glottal, scientific, exact, oral, lexical, lexemic.

**linguistics,** *pl.n.* — *Syn.* grammar, semantics, phonology, morphology, syntax, philology; see also **etymology, grammar, language** 2.
Branches of the study of linguistics include: historical, diachronic, descriptive, comparative, synchronic, geographical, anthropological, psycholinguistics, sociolinguistics, symbolic logic, glottochronology.

**liniment,** *n.* — *Syn.* ointment, cream, lotion; see **balm** 2, **medicine** 2, **salve.**

**lining,** *modif.* — *Syn.* edging, skirting, fringing, outlining, rimming, insulating; see also **bordering.**

**lining,** *n.* — *Syn.* interlining, inner coating, inner layer, inner surface, filling, quilting, stuffing, wadding, padding, bushing, sheathing, wainscot, wainscoting, covering, wall, reinforcement, in layer, brattice, partition, doublure, paneling; see also **facing** 2, **insulation** 2.

**link,** *n.* — *Syn.* ring, loop, coupling, coupler, section, seam, weld, ligation, connective, hitch, intersection, nexus, copula, connection, fastening, splice, interconnection, junction, joining, ligature, vinculum, articulation; see also **bond** 2, **fastener, joint** 1, **knot** 1, **tie** 1.

**link,** *v.* — *Syn.* join, connect, associate, combine; see **join** 1.
*See Synonym Study at* JOIN.

**linked,** *modif.* — *Syn.* connected, combined, associated; see **joined.**

**linking,** *modif.* — *Syn.* combining, joining, associating; see **connecting.**

**links,** *n.* — *Syn.* golf course, greens, fairways, club course, public course, golf links, country club, cow pasture★, spinach plot★, divot garden★.

**linoleum,** *n.* — *Syn.* linoxyn, floor covering, lino★, cork composition, Congoleum, Linowall (*both* trademarks); see also **floor** 1, **flooring, tile.**

**lint,** *n.* — *Syn.* raveling, fluff, fiber; see **dust.**

**lion,** *n.* **1.** [Celebrity] — *Syn.* favorite, wonder, prodigy; see **celebrity** 2.
**2.** [A leonine carnivore] — *Syn.* leo, *Felis leo* (Latin), king of beasts, king of the jungle, African cat, Asian cat, lioness; see also **animal** 2, **cat** 2.
Kinds of lions include: Arabian, Persian, Barbary, Bengal, Cape, Gambian, Senegal, lion of Gujerat.

**lionhearted,** *modif.* — *Syn.* strong, noble, courageous; see **brave** 1.

**lionize,** *v.* — *Syn.* dignify, celebrate, honor; see **praise** 1.

**lip,** *n.* **1.** [A fleshy portion of the mouth] — *Syn.* speech organ, fold of flesh, edge of the mouth, liplike part, labium, labrum; see also **mouth** 1.
**2.** [An edge] — *Syn.* spout, margin, brim, flange, portal, nozzle, overlap, projection, flare; see also **edge** 1, **rim.**
**bite one's lips** — *Syn.* show restraint, keep back one's anger, hold one's temper in check; see **restrain oneself.**
**hang on the lips of** — *Syn.* attend to, heed, hang on one's every word; see **listen** 2.

**keep a stiff upper lip★**— *Syn.* take heart, be encouraged, remain strong; see **suffer** 3.

**smack one's lips**— *Syn.* express satisfaction, enjoy, be delighted; see **appreciate** 1.

**liquefy,** *v.*— *Syn.* melt, deliquesce, condense, flux; see **dissolve** 1, **melt** 1.

*See Synonym Study at* MELT.

**liqueur,** *n.*— *Syn.* cordial, brandy, after-dinner drink; see **cocktail, drink** 2.

**liquid,** *modif.* **1.** [In a state neither solid nor gaseous] — *Syn.* fluid, watery, liquescent, fluidic, liquiform, molten, damp, moist, aqueous, liquefied, dissolved, deliquescent, melted, thawed; see also **fluid, wet** 1. — *Ant.* SOLID, solidified, frozen.

**2.** [Having qualities suggestive of fluids] — *Syn.* flowing, running, splashing, sappy, thin, ichorous, solvent, moving, viscous, diluting; see also **fluid, juicy** 1. — *Ant.* dense, imporous, impenetrable.

**3.** [Readily available in cash] — *Syn.* ready, free, realizable, marketable, quick, fluid; see also **usable.** — *Ant.* tied up, permanent, fixed.

**liquid,** *n.*— *Syn.* liquor, fluid, flux, inelastic fluid, juice, sap, extract, secretion, flow, matter in a liquid state, matter in a fluid state; see also **water** 1.

**liquidate,** *v.* **1.** [To pay] — *Syn.* settle, repay, reimburse; see **pay** 1.

**2.** [To change into money] — *Syn.* sell, convert, change; see **cash, exchange** 2.

**3.** [To abolish] — *Syn.* annul, cancel, destroy; see **abolish, eliminate** 1.

**4.** [★To kill] — *Syn.* annihilate, murder, do in★; see **kill** 1.

**liquor,** *n.* **1.** [Matter in liquid form] — *Syn.* water, drink, extract, potable, fluid, decoction, infusion, dissolvent, solvent; see also **liquid.**

**2.** [Strong alcoholic drink] — *Syn.* whiskey, booze★, alcohol★; see **cocktail, drink** 2.

**lisp,** *v.*— *Syn.* falter, mispronounce, sputter, stutter, clip one's words, drawl; see also **utter.**

**lissome,** *modif.*— *Syn.* lithe, supple, flexible; see **agile, flexible** 1.

**list,** *n.*— *Syn.* roll, record, catalog, register, inventory, schedule, listing, program, agenda, arrangement, enrollment, gazette, slate, archive, enumeration, itemization, draft, panel, brief, invoice, memorandum, account, outline, syllabus, tally, manifest, prospectus, bulletin, directory, roster, subscribers, census, muster, poll, ballot, table, table of contents, index, bibliography, menu, bill of fare, dictionary, glossary, lexicon, vocabulary, bill of lading, docket, shortlist, backlist, lineup, laundry list★; see also **catalog, file** 2, **index** 2, **table** 2.

---

**SYN.** — **list**, the broadest in scope of these terms, applies to a series of items of any kind, no matter what the arrangement or purpose; **catalog** implies an extensive list that is methodically arranged and often contains descriptive information */a mail-order catalog, the card catalog in a library/*; an **inventory** is an itemized list of goods or property, esp. a list made periodically of the stock of a business; a **register** is a book, etc. in which names, events, or other items are formally or officially recorded */a register of voters/*; a **roll** is an official list of the members of a group, esp. as used for checking attendance

---

**list,** *v.* **1.** [To enter in a list] — *Syn.* set down, arrange, bill, catalogue, schedule, enter, note, place, chronicle, post, insert, classify, file, enroll, register, manifest, in-

scribe, tally, inventory, enumerate, record, index, calendar, tabulate, book, invoice, census, draft, poll, impanel, slate, docket, keep count of, run down, call the roll; see also **file** 1, **record** 1.— *Ant.* REMOVE, wipe out, obliterate.

**2.** [To cultivate with a lister] — *Syn.* cultivate, seed, prepare; see **plow** 1.

**3.** [To lean] — *Syn.* pitch, slant, incline; see **lean** 1.

**listed,** *modif.*— *Syn.* filed, catalogued, indexed; see **recorded.**

**listen,** *v.* **1.** [To endeavor to hear] — *Syn.* attend, keep one's ears open, be attentive, listen in, pick up, overhear, give attention to, give a hearing to, give ear, hearken, hark, listen to, pay attention, give attention, hear, monitor, tune in★, give ear to★, incline an ear to★, not miss a trick★, lend an ear★, strain one's ears★, prick up one's ears, cock one's ears★.— *Ant.* be deaf to, turn a deaf ear to, ignore.

**2.** [To receive advice cordially] — *Syn.* heed, receive, take advice, take under advisement, welcome, accept, entertain, admit, take into consideration, adopt, hear out★.— *Ant.* DISCARD, scorn, refuse.

**listener,** *n.*— *Syn.* hearer, audience, heeder, witness; see **auditor** 1.

**listening,** *modif.*— *Syn.* hearing, paying attention, heeding, attending, overhearing, hearkening, giving ear, straining to hear, receiving, accepting, lending an ear★, pricking up one's ears★; see also **interested** 1, **involved** 1.— *Ant.* INDIFFERENT, giving no attention, inattentive.

**listless,** *modif.* **1.** [Lacking spirit or desire] — *Syn.* dull, stupid, spiritless, inattentive, drowsy, sleepy, languid, dreamy, thoughtless, indolent, heedless, lifeless, abstracted, absent, laggard, faint, lacking zest, slack, mopish, supine, inanimate, phlegmatic, dormant, insouciant, lukewarm, nonchalant, careless, torpid, sluggish, leaden, heavy, lethargic, bored, uninterested, languorous, neutral, lackadaisical, enervated, apathetic, easy-going; see also **indifferent** 1, **unconcerned.** — *Ant.* ACTIVE, vivacious, vigorous.

**2.** [Lacking action] — *Syn.* passive, sluggish, indolent; see **slow** 2.

**listlessness,** *n.*— *Syn.* idleness, lethargy, inactivity; see **indifference** 1, **laziness.**

**lit,** *modif.*— *Syn.* illuminated, lighted, resplendent; see **afire, bright** 1, **burning** 1.

**litany,** *n.*— *Syn.* petition, invocation, act of devotion; see **prayer** 2.

**literacy,** *n.*— *Syn.* refinement, scholarship, knowledgeability; see **education** 1, **knowledge** 1.

**literal,** *modif.* **1.** [Word for word] — *Syn.* verbatim, *literatim* (Latin), verbal, written, natural, usual, ordinary, apparent, real, not figurative, not metaphorical, not allegorical, strict, following the exact words, unerring, veracious, scrupulous, veritable, accurate, critical, authentic, undeviating; to the letter.— *Ant.* FREE, interpretive, figurative.

**2.** [Exact] — *Syn.* true, veritable, methodical; see **accurate** 1.

**literally,** *modif.*— *Syn.* really, actually, precisely, exactly, completely, undeviatingly, unerringly, indisputably, undisputably, correctly, strictly, to the letter, faithfully, rigorously, straight, unmistakably, veritably, truly, not metaphorically, not figuratively, rightly, word for word, verbatim, unimaginatively, letter by letter; see also **accurately** 1.— *Ant.* FREELY, figuratively, fancifully.

**literary,** *modif.*— *Syn.* arcane, bookish, belletristic; see **learned** 2.

**literate,** *modif.* — *Syn.* informed, scholarly, erudite; see **educated** 1, **intelligent** 1, **learned** 1.

**literature,** *n.* **1.** [Artistic production in language] — *Syn.* letters, lore, belles-lettres, literary works, literary productions, writing, the humanities, classics, books, polite literature, polite letters, republic of letters, writings; see also **biography, drama** 1, **exposition** 2, **history** 2, **novel, poetry, record** 1, 2, **story, writing** 2. Great bodies of literature include: Greek, Latin, Egyptian, Sanskrit, Icelandic, Hebraic, Arabic, Coptic, Chinese, Japanese, Persian, Hindu, French, Italian, Spanish, German, Russian, English, Danish, Swedish, Norwegian, Provençal, Slavic. Periods in western literature include: classical, heroic, medieval, neoclassical, renaissance, Georgian, pseudoclassical, Augustan, Romantic, Victorian, contemporary, modern, recent, twentieth-century, postmodern. **2.** [Written matter treating a given subject] — *Syn.* discourse, composition, treatise, dissertation, thesis, tract, paper, theme, treatment, disquisition, essay, discussion, research, observation, comment, findings, abstract, précis, report, critique, summary; see also **article** 3, **exposition** 2.

**lithe,** *modif.* — *Syn.* supple, pliant, pliable; see **agile, flexible** 1.

**litigant,** *n.* — *Syn.* litigator, claimant, disputant, contestant; see **defendant, prosecution** 2.

**litigate,** *v.* — *Syn.* dispute, contest, prosecute; see **sue.**

**litigation,** *n.* — *Syn.* case, prosecution, lawsuit, action; see **trial** 2.

**litigious,** *modif.* — *Syn.* belligerent, hostile, argumentative; see **quarrelsome** 1.

**litter,** *n.* **1.** [A mess] — *Syn.* scattering, jumble, hodgepodge; see **rash** 1, 3. **2.** [The young of certain animals] — *Syn.* cubs, pigs, piglets, puppies, kittens; see also **offspring.**

**litter,** *v.* — *Syn.* scatter, confuse, jumble; see **dirty.**

**litterbug\*,** *n.* — *Syn.* litterer, polluter, delinquent, slob\*; see **malefactor.**

**little,** *modif.* **1.** [Small in size] — *Syn.* diminutive, dwarfish, small, tiny, shrunk, atomic, wee, undersized, not big, not large, stunted, limited, cramped, wizened, scraggy, imperceptible, light, slight, microscopic, short, Lilliputian, runty, embryonic, elfin, invisible, shriveled, amoebic, microzoic, animalcular, pugged, vestigial, stubby, truncated, snub, molecular, microbic, toy, miniature, scrubby, cramped, puny, pygmy, dwarfed, inappreciable, bantam, half-pint\*, pocket-sized\*, pint-sized\*; see also **minute** 1. — *Ant.* LARGE, big, huge. **2.** [Small in quantity] — *Syn.* inappreciable, inconsiderable, insufficient; see **inadequate** 1. **3.** [Few in number] — *Syn.* scarce, not many, hardly any; see **few.** **4.** [Brief] — *Syn.* concise, succinct, abrupt; see **short** 2. **5.** [Small in importance] — *Syn.* trifling, insignificant, inconsiderable; see **trivial, unimportant.** **6.** [Small in character] — *Syn.* base, mean, petty; see **mean** 1, **wicked** 1. **7.** [Weak] — *Syn.* stunted, runty, undersized; see **weak** 1. *See Synonym Study at* SMALL. **make little of—** *Syn.* make fun of, mock, abuse; see **ridicule.**

**little,** *n.* — *Syn.* trifle, modicum, whit; see **bit** 1.

**littleness,** *n.* — *Syn.* small size, petiteness, insignificance; see **smallness.**

**liturgical,** *modif.* — *Syn.* ceremonial, solemn, ritual; see **conventional** 2, **divine** 2.

**liturgy,** *n.* — *Syn.* rite, formula, ritual; see **ceremony** 2, **sacrament.**

**livable,** *modif.* — *Syn.* habitable, tenantable, inhabitable; see **bearable, comfortable** 2.

**live,** *modif.* **1.** [Active] — *Syn.* energetic, vital, vivid; see **active** 2. **2.** [Not dead] — *Syn.* aware, conscious, existing; see **alive** 1. **3.** [Not taped or filmed] — *Syn.* broadcast direct, unrehearsed, in the flesh\*; see **real** 2.

**live,** *v.* **1.** [To have life] — *Syn.* exist, breathe, be alive; see **be** 1. **2.** [To enjoy life] — *Syn.* relish, savor, experience, love, delight in, live richly, make every moment count, have rich experiences, experience life to the full, live abundantly, make the most of life, take the earth's bounty, have a meaningful existence, take pleasure in, get a great deal from life, live it up\*. — *Ant.* SUFFER, endure pain, be discouraged. **3.** [To dwell] — *Syn.* live in, inhabit, abide; see **dwell, reside.** **4.** [To gain subsistence] — *Syn.* remain, continue, earn a living, support oneself, acquire a livelihood, earn money, get ahead, provide for one's needs, make ends meet, maintain oneself; see also **earn** 2, **profit** 2, **subsist.** **5.** [To persist in human memory] — *Syn.* prevail, remain, survive, last, be remembered, be unforgotten, live on in men's minds; see also **endure** 1. **where one lives\*** — *Syn.* personally, in a sensitive area, in a vulnerable area, at one's heart; see **painfully** 2.

**live and let live,** *v.* — *Syn.* be tolerant *or* broadminded, accept, ignore; see **allow** 1, **tolerate** 1.

**live at,** *v.* — *Syn.* inhabit, tenant, occupy; see **dwell, reside.**

**live by,** *v.* — *Syn.* survive, maintain life, acquire a livelihood; see **live** 4, **subsist.**

**live down,** *v.* — *Syn.* overcome, survive, outgrow; see **endure** 2.

**live it up\*,** *v.* — *Syn.* have fun, enjoy, paint the town red\*; see **celebrate** 3.

**livelihood,** *n.* **1.** [The supporting of life] — *Syn.* living, sustenance, maintenance; see **subsistence** 1. **2.** [The means of supporting life] — *Syn.* means, circumstances, resources; see **subsistence** 2.

**liveliness,** *n.* — *Syn.* animation, energy, spiritedness, briskness; see **action** 1.

**livelong,** *modif.* — *Syn.* everlasting, entire, complete; see **whole** 1.

**lively,** *modif.* **1.** [Energetic] — *Syn.* active, vigorous, energetic, brisk, industrious, vital, full of life, quick, nimble, spry, snappy\*, peppy\*, zippy\*; see also **active** 1, 2. **2.** [Spirited] — *Syn.* animated, spirited, vivacious, sprightly, gay, cheerful, perky, jaunty, high-spirited, in high spirits, bubbly, effervescent, bouncy, buoyant, frisky, cheery, exuberant, ebullient, sparkling, zestful, chipper\*, chirpy\*, zingy\*; see also **happy** 1, **sprightly.** **3.** [Stimulating] — *Syn.* rousing, provocative, invigorating, stimulating; see **exciting, stimulating.**

---

*SYN.* — **lively** implies being full of life and energy and suggests an active or vigorous quality *[a lively* dance, a *lively* talk*]*; **animated** is applied to that which is made alive or bright and suggests a spirited quality *[an animated* face, an *animated* discussion*]*; **vivacious** and **sprightly** imply buoyancy of spirit or sparkling brightness, **vivacious** also suggesting liveliness *[a viva-*

*cious* manner*]*, and **sprightly**, cheerfulness or vigor *[a sprightly* tune*]*; *gay* suggests lightheartedness and unrestrained good spirits *[in gay* spirits*]*

---

**live on**, *v.* — *Syn.* be supported, earn, augment; see **live** 4, **subsist.**

**liver**, *n.* — *Syn.* innard, glandular organ, vital part; see **organ** 2.

**livery**, *n.* — *Syn.* uniform, attire, costume, clothing; see **clothes.**

**livestock**, *n.* — *Syn.* cows, sheep, domestic animals; see **cattle, herd** 1.

**live up to**, *v.* — *Syn.* meet expectations, do well, give satisfaction; see **satisfy** 3.

**live with**, *v.* — *Syn.* dwell with, reside with, commit adultery, live in sin, cohabit, dwell as man and wife, play house*; see also **misbehave.**

**livid**, *modif.* **1.** [Discolored] — *Syn.* purplish, gray, lead-colored, black and blue; see **pale** 1, **purple.**
**2.** [Angry] — *Syn.* outraged, offended, black*; see **angry.**
*See Synonym Study at* PALE.

**living**, *modif.* **1.** [Alive] — *Syn.* alive, existing, breathing, having being; see **alive** 1.
**2.** [Vigorous] — *Syn.* awake, brisk, alert; see **active** 2.
*See Synonym Study at* ALIVE.

**living**, *n.* **1.** [A means of survival] — *Syn.* existence, sustenance, maintenance; see **subsistence** 2.
**2.** [Those not dead; *usually used with* the] — *Syn.* the quick, real people, flesh and blood*.

**living room**, *n.* — *Syn.* lounge, family room, front room, den; see **parlor, room** 2.

**lizard**, *n.* — *Syn.* reptile, saurian.
Types of lizards include: iguana, gecko, gila monster, European green, ringed, night, tree, bearded, chameleon, anole, basilisk, dragon, Komodo dragon, monitor, chuckwalla, racerunner, whiptail, skink, galliwasp.
Lizardlike creatures include: alligator, crocodile, horned toad, salamander, water dog, mud puppy, hellbender, newt, triton, dinosaur; see also **reptile.**

**load**, *n.* **1.** [A physical burden] — *Syn.* weight, encumbrance, carload, wagonload, hindrance, shipload, parcel, pressure, cargo, haul, incubus, lading, charge, pack, mass, payload, shipment, bale, contents, capacity, bundle, fardel, base load, peak load, heft*; see also **freight** 1, **shipment.** — *Ant.* LIGHTNESS, buoyancy, weightlessness.
**2.** [Responsibility] — *Syn.* charge, obligation, trust; see **duty** 1.
**3.** [A charge; *said especially of firearms*] — *Syn.* powder, shot, clip, round, shell, projectile, powder and shot; see also **ammunition.**
**4.** [A measure] — *Syn.* shot, amount, part; see **measurement** 2, **quantity.**
**get a load of**\* — *Syn.* be aware of, take a look at, listen, attend; see **hear** 2, **look** 2, **see** 1.
**have a load on**\* — *Syn.* intoxicated, tipsy, inebriated; see **drunk.**

**load**, *v.* **1.** [To place a load] — *Syn.* place, arrange, stow away, store, lumber, burden, stuff, put goods in, put goods on, containerize, freight, weight, pile, heap, fill, fill up, cram, mass, ballast, lade, heap on, put aboard, stack, pour in, take on cargo, take on ballast; see also **pack** 1. — *Ant.* unload, UNPACK, take off cargo.
**2.** [To overload] — *Syn.* encumber, saddle, weigh down; see **burden, oppress.**
**3.** [to charge; *said especially of firearms*] — *Syn.* prime, ready, make ready to fire, prepare for shooting, insert a clip.

**loaded**, *modif.* **1.** [Supplied with a load] — *Syn.* laden, burdened, weighted; see **full** 1.
**2.** [Ready to discharge; *said of firearms*] — *Syn.* charged, primed, ready to shoot, ready, readied, ready to fire. — *Ant.* uncharged, UNLOADED, unprimed.
**3.** [*Intoxicated] — *Syn.* wired*, tanked*, gassed*; see **drunk.**
**4.** [*Tricky] — *Syn.* deceitful, leading, touchy; see **mean** 3, **tricky** 3.

**loading**, *n.* — *Syn.* stowing, storing, arranging cargo, putting on cargo, taking on freight, taking on passengers, filling, lading, weighing down, ballasting, cramming, burdening, encumbering, charging, priming, readying, cumbering, containerization, putting on a load, filling the hold, receiving a consignment; see also **packing** 1.

**loaf**, *n.* — *Syn.* dough, roll, twist, bun, pastry, mass, lump, cube; see also **bread** 1, **cake** 2.

**loaf**, *v.* **1.** [To do nothing useful] — *Syn.* idle, trifle, lounge, kill time, be inactive, be unoccupied, be slothful, be indolent, vegetate, dally, take it easy, laze, twiddle the thumbs, not lift a finger, be lazy, loll, malinger, potter, drift, relax, slack, shirk, waste time, slow down, evade, dillydally, sit around, stand around, slack off, fritter time away, dream, let down, goof off*, bum*, goldbrick*, stall*, lollygag*, hand out*, hold up a corner*, piddle*; see also **relax** 1, **rest** 1.
**2.** [To travel at an easy pace] — *Syn.* loiter, stroll, saunter; see **walk** 1.

**loafer**, *n.* — *Syn.* idler, lounger, lazy person, ne'er-do-well, good-for-nothing, lazybones, sluggard, malingerer, waster, wastrel, slacker, shirker, beachcomber, wanderer, sundowner, ski bum, bum*, lizard*, goldbrick*, lollygagger*, deadbeat*.

**loafing**, *modif.* **1.** [Doing nothing useful] — *Syn.* rambling, worthless, futile; see **lazy** 1.
**2.** [Ostensibly employed, but wasting time] — *Syn.* slacking, shirking, evading, letting up, slowing down, slowing up, putting in time, apathetic, indifferent, uninterested, careless, pretending, sojering*, whipping the cat*; see also **resting** 1. — *Ant.* ACTIVE, toiling, energetic.

**loam**, *n.* — *Syn.* topsoil, dirt, wood's earth; see **earth** 2.

**loan**, *n.* — *Syn.* accommodation, trust, advance, permission to borrow, investment, giving credit, mortgage, advancing, time payment, touch*, bite*, coins*; see also **allowance** 2, **credit** 4. — *Ant.* PROMISE, borrowing, pledge.

**loan**, *v.* — *Syn.* provide with, advance, let out; see **lend** 1.

**loaned**, *modif.* — *Syn.* lent, advanced, on trust, on security, on credit, invested, granted, furnished, bestowed, afforded, ventured, intrusted, put out at interest, let, risked, leased; see also **given.**

**loath**, *modif.* — *Syn.* averse, indisposed, disinclined; see **opposed, reluctant, unwilling.**
*See Synonym Study at* RELUCTANT.

**loathe**, *v.* — *Syn.* hate, abhor, detest, abominate; see **dislike, hate** 1.
*See Synonym Study at* HATE.

**loathing**, *n.* — *Syn.* hatred, abhorrence, aversion, disgust; see **aversion, hate, hatred** 1, 2, **malice.**
*See Synonym Study at* AVERSION.

**loathsome**, *modif.* — *Syn.* obnoxious, deplorable, disgusting; see **offensive** 2.

**lob**, *v.* — *Syn.* toss, heave, launch; see **throw** 2.

**lobate**, *modif.* — *Syn.* divided, lobular, globular; see **round** 1.

**lobby**, *n.* — *Syn.* vestibule, entryway, antechamber; see **hall** 2, **room** 2.

**lobby**, *v.* — *Syn.* procure, sway, persuade, change, alter, advance, solicit votes, exercise influence, further, induce, bring pressure to bear, put pressure on, jawbone, press, pressure, affect, modify, promote, request, urge, carry by solicitation, pull strings, pull wires*, wirepull*, politick*; see also **influence.**

**lobe,** *n.* — *Syn.* flap, fold, section, projection, portion, lap, convexity, protuberance, node, wattle, excurvation; see also **bulge, ear** 1.

**lobster,** *n.* — *Syn.* crustacean, invertebrate, crawfish; see **shellfish.**

Types of lobsters include: American, Maine, European, Norway, Spanish, spiny, black, grasshopper, rock, mud.

**local,** *modif.* **1.** [Associated with a locality] — *Syn.* sectional, insular, divisional, territorial, situal, district, provincial, neighborhood, town, civic, topographical, geographical, descriptive, historical, geologic, geodetic, botanical, small-town, parochial, zoological, social, economic; see also **political, regional.**

**2.** [Restricted to a locality] — *Syn.* limited, confined, bounded; see **restricted.**

**locale,** *n.* — *Syn.* vicinity, territory, district; see **area** 2, **region** 1.

**localism,** *n.* — *Syn.* idiom, patois, idiosyncrasy, provincialism; see **custom** 2, **dialect.**

**locality,** *n.* **1.** [Area] — *Syn.* district, section, sector; see **area** 2, **region** 1.

**2.** [Position] — *Syn.* spot, location, site; see **position** 1.

**3.** [Neighborhood] — *Syn.* block, vicinity, district; see **neighborhood.**

**localize,** *v.* — *Syn.* surround, confine, limit; see **restrict** 2.

**locally,** *modif.* — *Syn.* regionally, sectionally, provincially, in the neighborhood, in the town, nearby, restrictedly, in a limited manner, narrowly. — *Ant.* distantly, nationally, widespread.

**locate,** *v.* **1.** [To determine a location] — *Syn.* discover, search out, find, come on, come across, meet with, position, ferret out, stumble on, discover the location of, get at, hit upon, light upon, come upon, happen upon, fix upon, lay one's hands on, track down, establish, determine, station, place, unearth; see also **designate** 1, **discover.**

**2.** [To take up residence] — *Syn.* settle down, establish oneself, inhabit; see **dwell, reside, settle** 7.

**located,** *modif.* **1.** [Determined in space] — *Syn.* traced, found, happened on; see **discovered.**

**2.** [Situated] — *Syn.* positioned, seated, fixed; see **placed, resting** 2.

**locating,** *n.* — *Syn.* location, finding, discovering, unearthing, searching out, tracing out, digging up, coming on, stumbling on, happening upon, lighting upon, unclosing, placing, spotting, settling upon, establishing.

**location,** *n.* **1.** [The act of locating] — *Syn.* finding, discovering, searching out; see **locating.**

**2.** [A position] — *Syn.* place, spot, section; see **position** 1.

**3.** [A site] — *Syn.* situation, place, scene; see **area** 2, **neighborhood** 1.

**lock,** *n.* **1.** [A device for locking] — *Syn.* hook, catch, latch, bolt, bar, staple, hasp, clinch, bond, fastening, padlock, safety catch, clamp, holdfast, clasp, link, junction, connection, barrier, canal gate, device, fixture, grip, grapple; see also **fastener.**

Types of locks include: deadbolt, double-cylinder, single-cylinder, tumbler, pin-tumbler cylinder, sash ward, fine ward, solid ward, lever, safety lever, keyless, combination, cabinet, duplex key, action, rim, mortise, padlock, timelock.

**2.** [A tuft or ringlet of hair] — *Syn.* tuft, tress, ringlet,

bunch, twist, portion of hair, snip, braid, plait; see also **curl, hair** 1.

**under lock and key** — *Syn.* locked up, imprisoned, in jail; see **confined** 3.

**lock,** *v.* — *Syn.* bolt, bar, clasp, secure; see **fasten** 1.

**locked,** *modif.* — *Syn.* secured, padlocked, cinched; see **tight** 2.

**locker,** *n.* — *Syn.* cabinet, wardrobe, cupboard; see **closet, furniture.**

**locket,** *n.* — *Syn.* miniature case, memento case, pendant; see **bracelet, jewelry, necklace.**

**lockup,** *n.* — *Syn.* prison, jail, penitentiary; see **jail.**

**lock up,** *v.* — *Syn.* confine, put behind bars, shut up; see **imprison.**

**locomotion,** *n.* — *Syn.* velocity, headway, travel; see **movement** 1.

**locomotive,** *n.* — *Syn.* steam engine, electric locomotive, diesel locomotive, wood-burner, coal-burner, passenger locomotive, freight locomotive; see also **engine** 1, **train** 2.

**locust,** *n.* — *Syn.* dog-day cicada, short-horned grasshopper, migratory grasshopper, beetle; see **grasshopper, insect.**

Locusts include: Rocky Mountain, western cricket, stone-cricket, Mormon cricket, seventeen-year, migratory, clumsy, bald, green-striped.

**lode,** *n.* — *Syn.* ore deposit, vein, strike*; see **mine** 1.

**lodestone,** *n.* — *Syn.* magnetic ore, magnetic stone, loadstone, magnetite; see **magnet.**

**lodge,** *n.* — *Syn.* abode, dwelling place, home, stopover, inn, ski lodge, dormitory, hostel, youth hostel, chalet; see also **hotel, motel, resort** 2.

**lodge,** *v.* **1.** [To become fixed] — *Syn.* catch, stick, abide; see **remain** 1, **stay** 1.

**2.** [To take (temporary) residence] — *Syn.* room, stay over, stop over, abide, hostel, board, dorm*; see also **dwell, reside.**

**lodger,** *n.* — *Syn.* guest, roomer, resident; see **boarder, tenant.**

**lodging,** *n.* **1.** [Personal accommodation] — *Syn.* harbor, asylum, *pied-à-terre* (French), port, protection, cover, roof over one's head; see also **refuge** 1, **shelter.**

**2.** [A temporary living place; *usually plural*] — *Syn.* inn, tourist camp, lodging place, lodgment, address, chambers, domicile, residence, habitation, apartment, home, room, tourist court; see also **hotel, lodge, motel, resort** 2.

**loft,** *n.* — *Syn.* attic, garret, hayloft, storage area; see **attic.**

**lofty,** *modif.* **1.** [High] — *Syn.* tall, elevated, towering; see **high** 2, **raised** 1.

**2.** [Idealistic] — *Syn.* exalted, enhanced, heightened; see **grand** 2.

**log,** *n.* **1.** [The main stem of a fallen or cut tree] — *Syn.* bole, timber, stick, length; see **trunk** 3, **wood** 2.

**2.** [The record of a voyage] — *Syn.* account, chart, diary; see **journal** 1, **record** 1.

**loge,** *n.* — *Syn.* stall, gallery, box; see **balcony.**

**logger,** *n.* — *Syn.* rafter, bucker, cutter; see **lumberjack.**

**logging,** *n.* — *Syn.* felling trees, woodcutting, woodchopping, lumberjacking, cutting off; see also **lumbering.**

**logic,** *n.* — *Syn.* reasoning, dialectic, deduction, syllogism, induction, inference, course of argument, course of thought; thesis, antithesis and synthesis, chain of reasoning; see also **philosophy** 1, **thought** 1.

Branches of logic include: traditional, Aristotelian, Ramist, Ramistic, modern, epistemological, pragmatic, formal, instrumental, experimental, psychological, symbolic, mathematical, deductive, inductive, Baconian.

**logical,** *modif.* 1. [Being in logical agreement] — *Syn.* deducible, coherent, consistent, inferential, probable, sound, extensional, cogent, pertinent, germane, legitimate, relevant, congruent with, consistent with, as it ought to be; see also **valid** 1.
2. [Rational] — *Syn.* perceptive, sensible, discerning; see **judicious, rational** 1, **reasonable** 1.
**logically,** *modif.* — *Syn.* rationally, by logic, by reason, inevitably; see **reasonably** 1, 2.
**logician,** *n.* — *Syn.* rationalist, syllogist, sophist; see **philosopher, scholar** 2.
**logrolling\*,** *n.* — *Syn.* promotion, help, back scratching, chicanery; see **aid** 1, **improvement** 1, **influence** 2.
**logy\*,** *modif.* — *Syn.* dull, sluggish, drowsy; see **lazy** 1.
**loiter,** *v.* — *Syn.* linger, linger idly, dawdle, dally, idle, lag, saunter, stroll, delay, shuffle, waste time, putter, procrastinate, traipse, shamble, pass time in idleness, loaf, lounge, tarry, fritter away time, loll, wait, hover, pause, dillydally, hang back, shilly-shally, amble, slacken, trail, drag, flag, ramble, laze along, hang around\*, hang out\*, let the grass grow under one's feet\*; see also **loaf** 1. — *Ant.* HURRY, hasten, stride along.

---

*SYN.* — **loiter** implies aimlessness or slowness of movement and may suggest a wasting of time in lingering or lagging [to *loiter* around street corners]; **dawdle** implies a wasting of time over trifles or a frittering away of time that makes for slow progress [to *dawdle* over a cup of tea]; **dally** suggests spending time in trifling or frivolous pursuits or in indecision; **idle** suggests habitual avoidance of work, or inactivity, indolence, etc. [to *idle* away the hours]

---

**loll,** *v.* — *Syn.* lounge, lean, recline, loaf; see **rest** 1.
**lollipop,** *n.* — *Syn.* sucker, sweet, confection; see **candy.**
**lone,** *modif.* — *Syn.* solitary, lonesome, deserted; see **alone** 1.
*See Synonym Study at* ALONE.
**loneliness,** *n.* — *Syn.* lonesomeness, solitude, detachment, separation, desolation, aloneness, solitariness, desertedness, forlornness; see also **homesickness, isolation.**
**lonely,** *modif.* 1. [Without company] — *Syn.* forlorn, lonesome, solitary, lone, alone, abandoned, comfortless, forsaken, friendless, deserted, desolate, homeless, bereft, companionless, withdrawn, secluded, unattended, by oneself, empty, apart, unsocial, reclusive, anchoritic, troglodytic, single, lorn, rejected, unaccompanied, unbefriended, disconsolate, uncherished, unwanted, outcast, alienated, lonely-hearts; see also **homesick.** — *Ant.* accompanied, associated, social.
2. [Inaccessible or unfrequented] — *Syn.* remote, desolate, unfrequented, uninhabited; see **isolated.**
*See Synonym Study at* ALONE.
**loner,** *n.* — *Syn.* independent, recluse, lone wolf; see **hermit, misanthrope.**
**lonesome,** *modif.* — *Syn.* lonely, solitary, forlorn, alone; see **homesick, lonely** 1, 2.
*See Synonym Study at* ALONE.
**long,** *modif.* 1. [Extended in space] — *Syn.* lengthy, extended, outstretched, elongated, interminable, boundless, unending, limitless, stretching, great, high, deep, drawn out, enlarged, expanded, spread, tall, lofty, towering, continued, lengthened, stringy, long-limbed, rangy, lanky, gangling, far-reaching, far-seeing, distant, running, faraway, far-off, remote; see also **endless** 1, **large** 1. — *Ant.* SHORT, small, stubby.

2. [Extended in time] — *Syn.* protracted, prolonged, enduring, unending, meandering, long-winded, spun out, lengthy, for ages, without end, forever and a day, day after day, hour after hour, lasting, prospective, continued, long-lived, sustained, tardy, dilatory, delayed, lingering; see also **eternal** 1, **perpetual** 1. — *Ant.* SHORT, brief, uncontinued.
3. [Tedious] — *Syn.* hard, longspun, long-drawn; see **dull** 4.
4. [Having (a certain commodity) in excess] — *Syn.* rich, profuse, abundant; see **plentiful** 1.
**as** (*or* **so**) **long as** — *Syn.* seeing that, inasmuch as, since; see **because, since** 1. — *Syn.* provided that, if, on condition that; see **if.**
**before long** — *Syn.* in the near future, immediately, shortly; see **soon** 1.
**long,** *v.* — *Syn.* desire, yearn for, wish; see **want** 1.
**long and short of it\*,** *n.* — *Syn.* conclusion, totality, upshot, bottom line; see **result, whole.**
**longevity,** *n.* 1. [Life span] — *Syn.* survival, perpetuity, durability, persistence, long life, endurance, continuance; see also **continuation** 1.
2. [Length of service] — *Syn.* seniority, tenure, ranking; see **advantage** 1.
**longing,** *modif.* — *Syn.* wanting, desirous, ravenous; see **enthusiastic** 2.
**longing,** *n.* — *Syn.* yearning, pining, hunger; see **desire** 1, **wish** 1.
**longitude,** *n.* — *Syn.* longitude in arc, longitude in time, celestial longitude; see **distance** 3, **measure** 1.
**long-lived,** *modif.* — *Syn.* long-lasting, macrobiotic, enduring; see **permanent** 2, **perpetual** 1.
**long-suffering,** *modif.* — *Syn.* tolerant, uncomplaining, forgiving, easygoing, clement, forbearing, resigned, lax, lenient, indulgent; see also **patient** 1.
**long-winded,** *modif.* — *Syn.* redundant, wordy, prolix; see **verbose.**
**look,** *n.* 1. [Appearance] — *Syn.* appearance, aspect, looks, expression; see **appearance** 1, **expression** 4.
2. [An effort to see] — *Syn.* gaze, stare, scrutiny, inspection, contemplation, visual search, reconnaissance, introspection, speculation, attending, noticing, regarding, marking, observation, keeping watch, once-over\*, look see\*, gander; see also **attention** 1, **examination** 1.
3. [A quick use of the eyes] — *Syn.* glance, quick cast of the eyes, survey, squint, glimpse, peek, peep, twinkle of an eye, *coup d'oeil* (French), leer, flash, peekaboo\*, the eye\*.
*See Synonym Study at* APPEARANCE.
**look,** *v.* 1. [To appear] — *Syn.* seem to be, look like, resemble; see **seem.**
2. [To endeavor to see] — *Syn.* view, gaze, glance, scan, stare, behold, contemplate, watch, survey, scrutinize, regard, inspect, discern, spy, observe, attend, examine, mark, gape, turn the eyes upon, give attention, peer, ogle, have an eye on, study, peep, look on, look at, look upon, look through, cock the eye\*, take a gander at\*, get a load of\*; see also **see** 1.
**it looks like** — *Syn.* probably, it seems that there will be, it seems as if; see **seem.**
**look after,** *v.* — *Syn.* look out for, support, watch; see **guard** 2.
**look for,** *v.* — *Syn.* research, pry, follow; see **hunt** 2, **search, seek** 1.
**looking glass,** *n.* — *Syn.* hand glass, pier, full-length mirror; see **mirror.**
**look into,** *v.* — *Syn.* investigate, study, probe; see **examine** 1, 2.
**lookout,** *n.* 1. [A place of vantage] — *Syn.* outlook, view,

prospect, panorama, post, scene, beacon, cupola, crow's nest, watchtower, observation tower, observatory, belvedere, observation post, signal station, patrol station, sentry box, captain's lookout\*, widow's walk\*, seawidow's roost\*; see also **tower.**

**2.** [One stationed at a lookout, sense 1] — *Syn.* watcher, sentinel, scout; see **watchman.**

**look out,** *interj.* — *Syn.* be careful, pay attention, hearken, listen, notice, have a care, heads up\*; see also **watch out.**

**look up,** *v.* **1.** [\*To improve] — *Syn.* get better, advance, progress; see **improve** 2.

**2.** [To find by search] — *Syn.* come upon, research, find; see **discover, search, seek** 1.

**look up to,** *v.* — *Syn.* respect, adulate, honor; see **admire** 1.

**loom,** *n.* — *Syn.* weaver, knitting machine, table loom; see **machine** 1.

Types of looms include: hand, draw, Jacquard, bar, power, dobby, small ware, double pile, single pile, terry, lappet, horizontal, vertical, Navajo.

**loom,** *v.* **1.** [To appear] — *Syn.* come into view, come on the scene, rise; see **appear** 1.

**2.** [To appear large or imposing] — *Syn.* menace, emerge, overshadow, shadow, bulk, figure, show, tower, hulk, be seen in shadow, issue, emanate, top, overtop, impress, hang over, rise gradually, seem large, seem huge, be coming, be near, be imminent, hover, approach, impend, come forth, break through the clouds; see also **threaten** 2.

**looming,** *modif.* — *Syn.* rising, appearing, emerging; see **imminent.**

**loop,** *n.* — *Syn.* ring, eye, circuit; see **circle** 1.

**knock** (*or* **throw**) **for a loop\*** — *Syn.* confuse, disturb, startle; see **shock** 2.

**loop,** *v.* **1.** [To form a loop] — *Syn.* curve, connect, tie together; see **bend** 1.

**2.** [To be in the form of a loop] — *Syn.* fold, coil, ring; see **circle.**

**loophole,** *n.* **1.** [An evasion] — *Syn.* avoidance, means of escape, escape clause, deception; see **lie** 1, **trick** 1.

**2.** [An opening] — *Syn.* slot, knothole, aperture; see **hole** 1.

**loose,** *modif.* **1.** [Unbound] — *Syn.* unfastened, undone, unsewed, untied, unpinned, insecure, unsecure, unsecured, unshackled, relaxed, unhasped, unattached, unconnected, disconnected, untethered, unfettered, uncaged, liberated, unbuttoned, unclasped, unhooked, slack, loosened, baggy, unconfined, unlatched, unlocked, unbolted, unscrewed, unhinged, worked free; see also **free** 3. — *Ant.* TIGHT, confined, bound.

**2.** [Movable] — *Syn.* unattached, free, wobbly; see **movable.**

**3.** [Vague] — *Syn.* disconnected, detached, random; see **obscure** 1, **vague** 2.

**4.** [Wanton] — *Syn.* unrestrained, dissolute, disreputable; see **lewd** 2.

**break loose** — *Syn.* free oneself, shake off restraint, flee; see **escape.**

**cast loose** — *Syn.* set free, untie, release; see **free** 1.

**let loose** (**with**)\* — *Syn.* give out, come out with, issue; see **release.**

**on the loose\*** — *Syn.* unconfined, unrestrained, wild; see **free** 2, 3.

**set** (*or* **turn**) **loose** — *Syn.* set free, release, untie; see **free** 1.

**loosen,** *v.* **1.** [To make loose] — *Syn.* extricate, release, unfix; see **free** 1.

**2.** [To become loose] — *Syn.* relax, slacken, work loose,

work free, go slack, break up, let go, become unfastened, become undone, become unstuck\*. — *Ant.* TIGHTEN, tighten up, become rigid.

**loot,** *n.* — *Syn.* booty, spoils, plunder, take\*; see **booty.**
See Synonym Study at BOOTY.

**loot,** *v.* — *Syn.* plunder, thieve, rifle; see **rob, steal.**

**lop,** *v.* **1.** [To hang] — *Syn.* slump, flop, droop; see **hang** 2.

**2.** [To cut off; *said especially of branches*] — *Syn.* crop, prune, chop; see **cut** 1, **trim** 1.

**lopsided,** *modif.* — *Syn.* uneven, unbalanced, crooked; see **irregular** 4.

**loquacious,** *modif.* — *Syn.* talkative, voluble, chattering, fluent; see **talkative, verbose.**
See Synonym Study at TALKATIVE.

**loquacity,** *n.* — *Syn.* talkativeness, verboseness, prolixity; see **conversation, discussion** 1.

**Lord,** *n.* — *Syn.* Divinity, the Supreme Being, Jehovah; see **God** 2, 3, 4.

**lord,** *n.* **1.** [A master] — *Syn.* ruler, governor, prince; see **master** 1.

**2.** [A member of the nobility] — *Syn.* peer, nobleman, count, don, patrician, hidalgo, grandee, seigneur, magnate, titled person; see also **aristocrat, royalty.**
Titles of nobility called lords include: duke, grand duke, archduke, marquis, marquess, earl, count, viscount, baron, baronet, bishop, Scottish Lord of Session, margrave.

**lord it over\*,** *v.* — *Syn.* boss, order around, dictate to; see **abuse** 1, **command** 2.

**lordly,** *modif.* **1.** [Noble] — *Syn.* grand, dignified, honorable; see **noble** 1, 2, 3.

**2.** [Pompous] — *Syn.* overbearing, imperious, haughty; see **egotistic** 1, 2.

**lore,** *n.* — *Syn.* enlightenment, wisdom, learning, folklore; see **knowledge** 1.

**lose,** *v.* **1.** [To bring about a loss] — *Syn.* mislay, forget, be careless with; see **misplace.**

**2.** [To incur loss] — *Syn.* suffer, miss, be deprived of, fail to keep, suffer loss, be reduced by, be impoverished from, become poorer by, be at a disadvantage because of, let slip through the fingers\*, come out of the small end of the horn\*; see also **waste** 1. — *Ant.* PROFIT, gain, improve.

**3.** [To fail to win] — *Syn.* be defeated, suffer defeat, be worsted, be left behind, be outdistanced, go down in defeat, succumb, fall, be the loser, miss, have the worst of it, be humbled, take defeat at the hands of, drop\*, go down for the count\*, get it in the neck\*, come out on the short end of the score\*, be sunk\*; see also **fail** 1. — *Ant.* WIN, triumph, be victorious.

**4.** [To suffer financially] — *Syn.* squander, expend, dissipate; see **spend** 1, **waste** 2.

**loser,** *n.* — *Syn.* sufferer, defeated, vanquished, runner-up, deprived, worsted, bereaved, forfeiter, incurrer, dispossessed, destroyed, ruined, wrecked, undone, overthrown, underdog, disadvantaged, underprivileged, fallen, bereft, denuded, unredeemed; see also **failure** 2. — *Ant.* WINNER, gainer, conqueror.

**losing,** *modif.* **1.** [Said of one who loses] — *Syn.* failing, falling, undone, defeated, worsted, ruined, doomed, being wrecked, being destroyed, being shorn of, being denuded, being deprived of, being bereft of, having the worst of it, coming to grief, quit of\*, on the way out\*; see also **sad** 2.

**2.** [Said of an activity in which one must lose] — *Syn.* futile, desperate, lost; see **hopeless** 2.

**loss,** *n.* **1.** [The act or fact of losing] — *Syn.* ruin, destruction, perdition, mishap, misfortune, forfeiture, giving up, bereavement, ill fortune, misadventure, ill luck, accident, calamity, trouble, disaster, death, sacrifice, catastrophe, cataclysm, trial, failure, misplacing, mislaying.

**2.** [Damage suffered by loss, sense 1] — *Syn.* hurt, injury, wound; see **damage** 1, 2.

**3.** [The result of unprofitable activity] — *Syn.* privation, want, bereavement, deprivation, need, destitution, being without, lack, waste, deterioration, impairment, degeneration, retrogression, retardation, decline, disadvantage, wreck, wreckage, extermination, eradication, extinction, undoing, dissolution, annihilation, extirpation, perdition, bane, end, undoing, disorganization, breaking up, immolation, suppression, relapse; see also **bankruptcy.** — *Ant.* ADVANTAGE, advancement, supply.

**at a loss** — *Syn.* confused, puzzled, unsure, at sea; see **undecided, doubtful** 2.

**losses,** *n.* — *Syn.* casualties, death toll, deaths; see **casualty** 2.

**lost,** *modif.* **1.** [Not to be found] — *Syn.* misplaced, mislaid, invisible, cast away, missing, hidden, obscured, gone astray, nowhere to be found, strayed, lacking, wandered off, forfeited, vanished, wandering, minus, without, gone out of one's possession; see also **absent, gone** 2. — *Ant.* FOUND, come back, returned.

**2.** [Ignorant of the way] — *Syn.* disoriented, perplexed, bewildered, ignorant; see **doubtful** 2.

**3.** [Destroyed] — *Syn.* demolished, devastated, wasted; see **destroyed, ruined** 1.

**4.** [No longer to be gained] — *Syn.* gone, passed, costly; see **destroyed, ruined** 1, **unprofitable** 1.

**5.** [Helpless] — *Syn.* feeble, sickly, disabled; see **weak** 1, 3.

**get lost\*** — *Syn.* go away, leave, begone; see **get out.**

**lot,** *n.* **1.** [A small parcel of land] — *Syn.* parcel, part, division, patch, clearing, piece of ground, plat, plot, field, tract, block, portion, allotment, apportionment, parking lot, piece, plottage, acreage; see also **area** 2, **property** 2.

**2.** [A number of individual items, usually alike] — *Syn.* number, quantity, group, batch, set, order, consignment, requisition; see also **shipment.**

**3.** [Destiny] — *Syn.* doom, portion, fate; see **chance** 1, **destiny** 1, **doom** 1.

*See Synonym Study at* FATE.

**4.** [\*A great quantity] — *Syn.* large amount, abundance, amplitude, considerable amount, plenitude, great numbers, bundle, bunch, cluster, group, pack, batch, large numbers, much, many, ever so much, quantities, enough and to spare, quite a lot, quite a bit, quite a sum, a good deal, oodles and gobs\*, a whole bunch\*, loads\*, heaps\*, zillion\*, gobs\*, oodles\*; see also **plenty.**

**cast** (*or* **throw**) **in one's lot with** — *Syn.* associate with, share, unite; see **join** 1, 2.

**draw** (*or* **cast**) **lots** — *Syn.* choose, pick, elect; see **decide.**

**lotion,** *n.* — *Syn.* liniment, hand lotion, cream, moisturizer, cold cream, after shave, solution, embrocation, liquid preparation, wash, lenitive, abirritant, unguent, palliative, demulcent; see also **balm** 2, **cosmetic, medicine** 2, **salve.**

**loud,** *modif.* **1.** [Having volume of sound] — *Syn.* deafening, ringing, ear-rending, ear-piercing, ear-splitting, booming, fulminating, intense, resounding, piercing, high-sounding, trumpet-toned, blaring, sonorous, resonant, crashing, deep, full, powerful, emphatic, vehement, thundering, heavy, big, deep-toned, full-tongued,

roaring, strident, enough to wake the dead\*; see also **shrill.** — *Ant.* SOFT, faint, feeble.

**2.** [Producing loud sounds] — *Syn.* clamorous, noisy, uproarious, blatant, vociferous, stentorian, bombastic, turbulent, tumultuous, blustering, clarion-voiced, lusty, loud-voiced, boisterous, obstreperous, rambunctious, cacophonous, raucous, loud-tongued; see also **harsh** 1. — *Ant.* QUIET, soft-voiced, calm.

**3.** [\*Lacking manners and refinement] — *Syn.* loud-mouthed, brash, offensive; see **rude** 2, **vulgar** 1.

**4.** [\*Flashy, *used of colors or taste in color*] — *Syn.* garish, flashy, gaudy; see **ornate** 1.

**loudly,** *modif.* — *Syn.* audibly, vociferously, ringingly, fully, powerfully, crashingly, shrilly, deafeningly, piercingly, resonantly, emphatically, vehemently, thunderingly, ear-splittingly, in a full-toned voice, full-sounding, articulately, with full tongue, in full cry, clamorously, noisily, uproariously, plainly, blatantly, lustily, in a loud-mouthed manner, vulgarly, rudely, obstreperously, ostentatiously, boorishly, garishly, flashily, tawdrily, gaudily, conspicuously, cheaply, tastelessly, obtrusively, showily, theatrically, in full cry, aloud, resoundingly, at the top of one's lungs\*.

**loudspeaker,** *n.* — *Syn.* speaker, amplifier, public address system, PA system, speaker cone, diaphragm, electrodynamic speaker, high-fidelity speaker, full-frequency speaker, high-frequency speaker, low-frequency speaker, woofer, tweeter, sound truck, megaphone, bullhorn, hog caller\*.

**lounge,** *n.* **1.** [A bedlike seat] — *Syn.* couch, settee, divan; see **couch, furniture.**

**2.** [A social room] — *Syn.* reception room, parlor, mezzanine, club room, cocktail lounge, bar, public room, hotel lobby; see also **bar** 2, **room** 2.

**lounge,** *v.* — *Syn.* idle, repose, kill time\*; see **loaf** 1, **rest** 1.

**louse,** *n.* — *Syn. Hemiptera* (Latin), pediculus, mite; see **insect.**

Types of lice include: human, body, head, crab, chewing, sucking, rodent, elephant, plant, bird, bee, book, cootie\*, livestock\*.

**lousy,** *modif.* **1.** [Infested with lice] — *Syn.* lice-ridden, lice-infested, pediculous, pediculate, pedicular, hemipteroid, with lice; see also **infested** 2.

**2.** [\*Bad] — *Syn.* horrible, miserable, disliked, unwelcome; see **faulty, harmful, poor** 2, **unpopular.**

**lout,** *n.* — *Syn.* oaf, dolt, hick, rustic; see **boor.**

**loutish,** *modif.* — *Syn.* bungling, rustic, clumsy; see **awkward** 1, **rude** 2, **vulgar** 1.

**lovable,** *modif.* — *Syn.* adorable, winning, winsome, lovely; see **friendly** 1.

**love,** *n.* **1.** [Passionate and tender devotion] — *Syn.* affection, attachment, devotion, infatuation, passion, tenderness, tender passion, fondness, adoration, yearning, flame, rapture, enchantment, ardor, emotion, sentiment, amorousness, free love, enjoyment, cherishing, devotedness, worship, desire, fancy, weakness, amativeness, Eros, Cupid, Amor, Venus, Aphrodite, Kama, crush\*, puppy love\*, calf love\*; see also **affection** 1, **desire** 3. — *Ant.* HATE, aversion, antipathy.

**2.** [Affection based on esteem] — *Syn.* respect, regard, appreciation; see **admiration.**

**3.** [A lively and enduring interest] — *Syn.* relish, predilection, penchant, passion; see **affection** 1, **inclination** 1, **zest** 1.

**4.** [A beloved] — *Syn.* dear one, loved one, cherished one; see **lover** 1.

**fall in love** (**with**) — *Syn.* begin to feel love, adore, be infatuated.

**for love**— *Syn.* as a favor, voluntarily, without payment; see **freely** 2.

**for the love of**— *Syn.* for the sake of, with fond concern for, because of; see **for.**

**in love**— *Syn.* enamored, infatuated, smitten, besotted; see **loving.**

**make love**— *Syn.* fondle, embrace, caress; see **love** (*v.*) 2.

**not for love or money**— *Syn.* under no conditions, by no means, no; see **never.**

**with no love lost between**— *Syn.* unkindly, vengefully, full of dislike; see **angrily.**

---

**SYN.** — **love** implies intense fondness or deep devotion and may apply to various relationships or objects [sexual *love*, brotherly *love*, *love* of one's work]; **affection** suggests warm, tender feelings, usually not as powerful or deep as those implied by **love** [he has no *affection* for children]; **attachment** implies connection by ties of affection, attraction, devotion, etc. and may be felt for inanimate things as well as for people [an *attachment* to an old hat]; **infatuation** implies a foolish or unreasoning passion or affection, often a transient one [an elderly man's *infatuation* for a young girl]

---

**love,** *v.* **1.** [To be passionately devoted]— *Syn.* adore, be in love with, care for, delight in, hold dear, choose, fancy, venerate, be enchanted by, be passionately attached to, have affection for, be enamored of, dote on, glorify, exalt, idolize, prize, put on a pedestal, hold in affection, deify, be fascinated by, hold high, canonize, think the world of, treasure, prefer, yearn for, esteem, be captivated by, be enraptured by, lose one's heart to, be fond of, admire, long for, be oneself with, thrive with, flip over*, fall for*, be nuts about*, be crazy about*, go for*, have it bad*, cotton to*; see also **cherish** 1, **like** 2. — *Ant.* HATE, detest, loathe.

**2.** [To express love by caresses] — *Syn.* cherish, fondle, make love, make much of, feast one's eyes on, embrace, cling to, clasp, hug, take into one's arms, hold, pet, soothe, stroke, encircle with one's arms, press to the heart, draw close, remain near to, bring to one's side, look tenderly at, look deeply into one's eyes, chase after*, make a play for*, shine up to*, neck*, make out*, love up*, make it*; see also **caress, copulate, kiss.** — *Ant.* exclude, spurn, refuse.

**3.** [To possess a deep and abiding interest] — *Syn.* enjoy, delight in, relish; see **admire** 1, **like** 1.

**loved,** *modif.* — *Syn.* desired, cherished, well beloved; see **beloved.**

**loveless,** *modif.* **1.** [Rejected] — *Syn.* disliked, forsaken, unloved; see **refused.**

**2.** [Heartless] — *Syn.* cold, hard, insensitive; see **cruel** 2, **ruthless** 1.

**loveliness,** *n.* — *Syn.* appeal, charm, fairness; see **beauty** 1.

**lovely,** *modif.* **1.** [Beautiful] — *Syn.* attractive, beautiful, pretty, graceful; see **beautiful** 1, 2.

**2.** [Charming] — *Syn.* engaging, enchanting, captivating; see **charming.**

**3.** [*Very pleasing] — *Syn.* nice, splendid, delightful; see **pleasant** 1, 2.

*See Synonym Study at* BEAUTIFUL.

**lover,** *n.* **1.** [A suitor] — *Syn.* wooer, sweetheart, darling, dear, girlfriend, boyfriend, beau, mate, significant other, partner, dearest, beloved, admirer, courter, escort, infatuate, paramour, fiancé, fiancée, swain, inamorato, petitioner, suppliant, applicant, solicitor, entreater, gentleman friend*, lady friend*, flame*, steady*.

**2.** [A willing student or practitioner; *used only in phrases*] — *Syn.* dilettante, amateur, practitioner, fan, hobbyist, fanatic, neophyte; see also **enthusiast** 1, **zealot.**

**3.** [An epithet for a beloved] — *Syn.* beloved, sweetheart, dear; see **darling** 2.

**loving,** *modif.* — *Syn.* admiring, respecting, valuing, liking, fond, tender, kind, enamored, in love, attached, devoted, appreciative, having a good will toward, attentive, thoughtful, ardent, solicitous, doting, amiable, warm, amorous, smitten, warm-hearted, affectionate, zealous for, anxious, concerned, sentimental, amatory, benign, earnest, benevolent, cordial, caring, considerate, loyal, generous; see also **friendly** 1, **passionate** 2.

**lovingly,** *modif.* — *Syn.* tenderly, devotedly, adoringly, warmly, ardently, fervently, zealously, earnestly, loyally, generously, kindly, considerately, thoughtfully, dotingly, fondly, affectionately, passionately, impassionedly, yearningly, longingly, endearingly, enrapturedly, rapturously, admiringly, respectfully, appreciatively, reverently, with friendship toward, with love, attentively.

**low,** *modif.* **1.** [Close to the earth] — *Syn.* squat, flat, level, low-lying, profound, decumbent, prostrate, crouched, below, ankle-high, not far above the horizon, low-hanging, lowering, knee-high, beneath, under, depressed, sunken, nether, inferior, unelevated, lying under; see also **deep** 1. — *Ant.* HIGH, lofty, elevated.

**2.** [Quiet] — *Syn.* muffled, hushed, quiet; see **faint** 3.

**3.** [Low in spirits] — *Syn.* dejected, moody, blue; see **sad** 1.

**4.** [Base] — *Syn.* base, mean, coarse, despicable; see **mean** 1, **vulgar** 1.

**5.** [Faint] — *Syn.* ill, dizzy, feeble; see **sick, weak** 1.

**6.** [Simple] — *Syn.* economical, moderate, inexpensive; see **cheap** 1.

*See Synonym Study at* MEAN.

**lay low**— *Syn.* bring to ruin, overcome, kill; see **destroy** 1.

**lie low**— *Syn.* wait, conceal oneself, take cover; see **hide** 2.

**lower,** *v.* — *Syn.* reduce, diminish, lessen, scale down, demote, de-escalate, push down, bring low, set down, let down, cast down, ground, depress; see also **decrease** 1, 2, **drop** 2.

**lowering,** *modif.* — *Syn.* threatening, overhanging, menacing; see **ominous.**

**lowest,** *modif.* — *Syn.* shortest, littlest, smallest, slightest, bottom, rock-bottom, ground, base, undermost, nethermost; see also **least** 1, 2, 3, **minimum.**

**low-grade,** *modif.* — *Syn.* inferior, bad, second-rate; see **poor** 2.

**low-key,** *modif.* — *Syn.* subdued, restrained, understated, subtle, toned-down, relaxed, easygoing, laid-back*, loose*, soft-sell*.

**lowland,** *n.* — *Syn.* bog, bottom land, marsh; see **swamp, valley.**

**lowly,** *modif.* — *Syn.* unpretentious, cast down, meek; see **humble** 1, 2.

**loyal,** *modif.* — *Syn.* faithful, true, dependable, firm; see **faithful.**

*See Synonym Study at* FAITHFUL.

**loyalist,** *n.* — *Syn.* supporter, follower, chauvinist, Tory; see **patriot.**

**loyally,** *modif.* — *Syn.* faithfully, conscientiously, trustworthily, devotedly, constantly, sincerely, obediently, resolutely, staunchly, earnestly, submissively, steadfastly, with fidelity, with fealty, with allegiance, with constancy, in good faith; see also **truly** 2.

**loyalty,** *n.* — *Syn.* allegiance, faithfulness, fidelity, devotion, constancy, fealty, homage, trustworthiness, integrity, attachment, trueness, sincerity, steadfastness, adherence, staunchness, stalwartness, dependability, devotedness, support, dedication, commitment, steadiness, single-heartedness, singleness of heart, bond, tie, group feeling, probity, uprightness, honor, reliability, good faith, faith, incorruptibility, scrupulousness, conscientiousness, singlemindedness, inviolability, firmness, zeal, ardor, earnestness, resolution, obedience, duty, esprit de corps, solidarity. — *Ant.* DISLOYALTY, perfidy, faithlessness.

*SYN.* — **loyalty** suggests a steadfast devotion of an unquestioning kind that one may feel for one's family, friends, or country; **allegiance** refers to the duty of a citizen to the government or a similarly felt obligation to support a cause or leader; **fidelity** implies strict adherence to an obligation or trust; **fealty**, now chiefly a literary word, suggests faithfulness that one has sworn to uphold; **homage** implies respect or honor rendered to a person because of rank or achievement, often accompanied by a sense of allegiance

**lozenge,** *n.* — *Syn.* troche, capsule, pill; see **medicine** 2, **tablet** 3.

**lubber,** *n.* — *Syn.* rustic, clod, fool, loafer; see **boor, peasant.**

**lubberly,** *modif.* — *Syn.* clumsy, rough, crude; see **awkward** 1, **rude** 1, 2.

**lubricant,** *n.* — *Syn.* cream, ointment, oil; see **grease.**

**lubricate,** *v.* — *Syn.* oil, anoint, smear; see **grease.**

**lubrication,** *n.* — *Syn.* lubricating, greasing, oiling, oiling and greasing up, lubing\*, lube, lube job\*, grease job\*.

**lucid,** *modif.* **1.** [Clear to the sight] — *Syn.* pellucid, transparent, diaphanous; see **clear** 2, **obvious** 1.
**2.** [Clear to the understanding] — *Syn.* plain, evident, explicit; see **obvious** 2.
**3.** [Bright] — *Syn.* shining, resplendent, luminous; see **bright** 1.

**lucidity,** *n.* — *Syn.* clearness, purity, transparency; see **clarity.**

**luck,** *n.* **1.** [Good fortune] — *Syn.* good luck, prosperity, weal, wealth, favorable issue, fluke, master stroke, run of luck, piece of luck, streak of luck, windfall, advantage, profit, triumph, victory, kismet, karma, win, health, friends, happiness, blessings, godsend, opportunity, low probability, lucky break, occasion, turn of the wheel of fortune, break\*, walkover\*, the breaks\*, smiles of fortune\*; see also **success** 2. — *Ant.* FAILURE, ill-fortune, bad luck.
**2.** [Chance] — *Syn.* unforeseen occurrence, fluke, fate; see **accident** 2, **chance** 1.
**crowd** (*or* **push**) **one's luck**\* — *Syn.* gamble, take risks, chance; see **risk.**
**down on one's luck**\* — *Syn.* in misfortune, unlucky, discouraged; see **unfortunate** 2.
**in luck** — *Syn.* lucky, successful, prosperous; see **fortunate** 1.
**out of luck** — *Syn.* unlucky, in misfortune, in trouble; see **unfortunate** 2.
**try one's luck** — *Syn.* attempt, risk, endeavor; see **try** 1.
**worse luck** — *Syn.* unhappily, unluckily, unfavorably; see **unfortunately** 1.

**luckily,** *modif.* — *Syn.* opportunely, happily, favorably; see **fortunately.**

**luckless,** *modif.* — *Syn.* cursed, hopeless, stricken; see **unfortunate** 2.

**lucky,** *modif.* **1.** [Enjoying good luck] — *Syn.* blessed, successful, prosperous; see **fortunate** 1.
**2.** [Characterized by good luck] — *Syn.* favorable, advantageous, serendipitous; see **hopeful** 2.
**3.** [Supposed to bring good luck] — *Syn.* providential, propitious, auspicious; see **magic** 1.

**lucrative,** *modif.* — *Syn.* fruitful, productive, gainful; see **profitable.**

**lucre,** *n.* — *Syn.* gain, spoils, profit; see **wealth** 2.

**ludicrous,** *modif.* — *Syn.* laughable, farcical, ridiculous, outlandish; see **absurd, funny** 1.
*See Synonym Study at* ABSURD.

**lug,** *v.* — *Syn.* carry, tug, lift, haul; see **draw** 1.

**luggage,** *n.* — *Syn.* trunks, bags, valises; see **baggage.**

**lugubrious,** *modif.* — *Syn.* dismal, mournful, pensive; see **sad** 2.

**lukewarm,** *modif.* — *Syn.* cool, tepid, chilly; see **warm** 1.

**lull,** *n.* **1.** [A cessation of sound] — *Syn.* quiet, stillness, hush; see **silence** 1.
**2.** [A cessation of activity] — *Syn.* hiatus, calm, quiet; see **pause** 2.

**lull,** *v.* — *Syn.* calm, quiet down, pacify; see **quiet** 1, 2.

**lullaby,** *n.* — *Syn.* good-night song, bedtime song, cradlesong; see **song.**

**lumber,** *n.* — *Syn.* cut timber, logs, sawed timber, forest products, boards, hardwood, softwood, lumbering products; see also **timber** 1, **tree, wood** 2.
Lumber includes: flooring, tongue and groove, siding, sheeting, shingle, trim, beam, post, plank, finish, lath, clapboard, walk board, timbers, tie, molding, plywood, particleboard, fiberboard, pressure-treated wood, welded wood, pressed wood, shake, scantling; two-by-four, two-by-six, two-by-eight, two-by-twelve, four-by-four, six-by-eight, one-by-four, one-by-six, one-by-twelve; see also **beam** 1.
Uses of lumber include: joist, rafter, plate, stringer, frame, ridge, planking, clapboarding, roofing, flooring, siding, paneling, decking, molding, cabinetwork, studding, door, door jamb, tread.
Grades of lumber include: select, choice, clear, first and second clear, FAS, common, FAS common, cull.

**lumbering,** *modif.* — *Syn.* clumsy, blundering, overgrown; see **awkward** 1, **crude** 1, **heavy** 1.

**lumbering,** *n.* — *Syn.* timbering, felling trees, cutting logs, getting out lumber, cutting off, cutting over, lumberjacking, milling, tree farming, sawing, logging, ground-hogging\*, donkey-setting\*, river-driving\*.

**lumberjack,** *n.* — *Syn.* lumberer, logger, lumberman, lumber cutter, feller, trimmer, cruiser, scaler, skid man, rafter, topper, birler, choker, rigger, bucker, bellman, whistle punk\*, brush rat\*, bush-whacker\*; see also **laborer, woodsman, worker.**

**lumberman,** *n.* — *Syn.* logger, woodman, forester; see **laborer, lumberjack, woodsman, worker.**

**luminary,** *n.* **1.** [A light] — *Syn.* star, lamp, radiance; see **light** 3.
**2.** [A philosopher] — *Syn.* teacher, prophet, notable; see **intellectual, personage** 2.

**luminescence,** *n.* — *Syn.* fluorescence, fire, radiance; see **light** 1.

**luminescent,** *modif.* — *Syn.* glowing, luminous, radiant, luminescent; see **bright** 1.

**luminosity,** *n.* — *Syn.* radiance, fluorescence, glow; see **light** 1.

**luminous,** *modif.* — *Syn.* lighted, glowing, radiant, luminescent; see **bright** 1.
*See Synonym Study at* BRIGHT.

**lump,** *n.* — *Syn.* handful, protuberance, bunch, bump,

agglomeration, block, bulk, chunk, piece, portion, section; see also **mass** 1, **part** 1.

**get** (*or* **take**) **one's lumps**★ — *Syn.* be punished, undergo, receive punishment; see **suffer** 1.

**in the lump** — *Syn.* amassed, aggregated, collected; see **gathered.**

**lumpish,** *modif.* — *Syn.* heavy, clumsy, bungling; see **awkward** 1, **stupid** 1.

**lumpy,** *modif.* — *Syn.* knotty, bumpy, uneven; see **irregular** 4, **thick** 1, 3.

**lunacy,** *n.* — *Syn.* insanity, madness, dementia, mania; see **insanity** 1.

*See Synonym Study at* INSANITY.

**lunate,** *modif.* — *Syn.* semicircular, crescent-shaped, horned, crescent; see **round** 1.

**lunatic,** *modif.* **1.** [Insane] — *Syn.* demented, deranged, psychotic; see **insane** 1.

**2.** [Foolish] — *Syn.* irrational, idiotic, daft; see **stupid** 1.

**lunatic,** *n.* — *Syn.* maniac, demoniac, insane person; see **madman, neurotic.**

**lunch,** *n.* — *Syn.* meal, light repast, luncheon, refreshment, sandwich, snack, tea, high tea.

**lunch,** *v.* — *Syn.* dine, have lunch, take a lunch break, do lunch; see **eat** 1.

**lunge,** *n.* — *Syn.* plunge, jab, thrust; see **jump** 1, 2.

**lunge,** *v.* — *Syn.* surge, lurch, bound; see **jump** 1.

**lurch,** *v.* — *Syn.* stagger, weave, sway; see **reel.**

**leave in the lurch** — *Syn.* leave, forsake, desert; see **abandon** 2.

**lure,** *n.* — *Syn.* bait, decoy, fake; see **camouflage** 1, **trick** 1.

**lure,** *v.* — *Syn.* attract, tempt, entice, allure; see **fascinate, seduce, tempt.**

*See Synonym Study at* TEMPT.

**lurid,** *modif.* **1.** [Shocking] — *Syn.* startling, offensive, sensational; see **unusual** 2, **violent** 4.

**2.** [Vivid] — *Syn.* distinct, extreme, deep; see **bright** 2, **intense.**

**lurk,** *v.* — *Syn.* slink, prowl, steal, conceal oneself; see **hide** 2, **sneak.**

**lurking,** *modif.* — *Syn.* hiding out, sneaking, hidden; see **hiding.**

**luscious,** *modif.* — *Syn.* sweet, tasty, toothsome, palatable; see **delicious** 1.

**lush,** *modif.* **1.** [Green] — *Syn.* luxuriant, verdant, dense, grassy; see **green** 2, **rich** 3, **rank** 1.

**2.** [Delicious] — *Syn.* rich, juicy, succulent; see **delicious** 1.

**3.** [Elaborate] — *Syn.* opulent, luxurious, ornamental; see **elaborate** 1, **lavish, ornate** 1.

*See Synonym Study at* PROFUSE.

**lust,** *n.* — *Syn.* appetite, passion, concupiscence; see **desire** 3.

**lust (after),** *v.* — *Syn.* long for, desire, hunger for, wish for; see **want** 1.

**luster,** *n.* **1.** [Brightness] — *Syn.* glow, brilliance, radiance; see **light** 1.

**2.** [Fame] — *Syn.* glory, respect, renown; see **fame** 1, **honor** 1.

**lusterless,** *modif.* — *Syn.* pale, colorless, drab; see **dull** 2.

**lustful,** *modif.* — *Syn.* lecherous, wanton, lascivious; see **lewd** 2, **sensual.**

**lustrous,** *modif.* — *Syn.* shiny, radiant, glistening, glossy; see **bright** 1.

*See Synonym Study at* BRIGHT.

**lusty,** *modif.* — *Syn.* hearty, robust, vigorous; see **healthy** 1.

**luxuriant,** *modif.* — *Syn.* lush, dense, abundant, florid; see **green** 2, **ornate** 1, **profuse, rank** 1, **rich** 3.

*See Synonym Study at* PROFUSE.

**luxuriate,** *v.* **1.** [To indulge] — *Syn.* overdo, indulge in, live extravagantly; see **prosper.**

**2.** [To flourish] — *Syn.* abound, increase, thrive; see **grow** 1.

**luxurious,** *modif.* — *Syn.* self-indulgent, voluptuous, comfortable, pleasurable, costly, rich, extravagant, sumptuous, posh, gratifying, sybaritic, hedonistic, epicurean, sensuous, deluxe, sumptuous, self-pampering, languorous, languishing, easy, affluent, inordinate, immoderate, opulent, fit for a king, deeply comfortable, in the lap of luxury★; see also **expensive, rich** 2, **sensual.** — *Ant.* POOR, ascetic, self-denying.

*See Synonym Study at* SENSUAL.

**luxury,** *n.* **1.** [Indulgence of the senses, regardless of the cost] — *Syn.* gratification, costliness, expensiveness, richness, idleness, leisure, luxuriousness, high-living, prodigality, epicureanism, sybaritism, hedonism, lavishness; see also **enjoyment** 2, **indulgence** 3. — *Ant.* POVERTY, poorness, lack.

**2.** [An indulgence beyond one's means] — *Syn.* expensive rarity, extravagance, intemperance, immoderation, unrestraint, exorbitance, wastefulness, spree★, splurging★; see also **excess** 1, **waste** 1.

**lyceum,** *n.* **1.** [School] — *Syn.* secondary school, institute, private school; see **academy** 1, **school** 1.

**2.** [Hall] — *Syn.* gallery, hall, lecture room, saloon; see **auditorium, hall** 1.

**lying,** *modif.* **1.** [In the act of lying] — *Syn.* untruthful, falsifying, prevaricating, swearing falsely, committing perjury, fibbing, misstating, misrepresenting, inventing, dissimulating, equivocating, malingering. — *Ant.* FRANK, truthful, veracious.

**2.** [Given to lying] — *Syn.* dishonest, deceitful, unreliable, double-dealing; see **dishonest** 1, 2.

**3.** [Not reliable] — *Syn.* unsound, tricky, treacherous; see **false** 2, **unreliable** 2.

**4.** [Prostrate] — *Syn.* supine, reclining, jacent, resting, horizontal, procumbent, resupine, reposing, recumbent, flat, fallen, prone, crashed, dropped, tumbled, powerless.

*See Synonym Study at* DISHONEST.

**lying down,** *modif.* — *Syn.* reclining, reposing, sleeping; see **asleep, resting** 1.

**lymphatic,** *modif.* — *Syn.* lethargic, indecisive, listless, dull; see **indifferent** 1, **unconcerned.**

**lynch,** *v.* — *Syn.* hang, mob, murder; see **kill** 1.

**lynx-eyed,** *modif.* — *Syn.* observant, attentive, aware; see **sharp-sighted.**

**lyric,** *n.* **1.** [A libretto] — *Syn.* opera text, words of the opera, story of the opera, words of a choral; see **libretto.**

**2.** [Verses set to music] — *Syn.* the words, the poem, the verse; see **poem.**

**3.** [A short, songlike poem] — *Syn.* lyrical poem, ode, sonnet, hymn, roundel; see also **poetry, song, verse** 1.

**lyrical,** *modif.* — *Syn.* emotional, expressive, songful, melodious, sweet, rhythmical; see also **musical** 1, **poetic.**

# M

**ma\***, *n.* — *Syn.* mama, *mater* (Latin), mom; see **mother.**

**macabre**, *modif.* — *Syn.* grotesque, horrible, ghastly, grim; see **offensive** 2.

**mace**, *n.* **1.** [A weapon or symbol of authority] — *Syn.* staff, baton, scepter, verge; see **club** 3, **stick.**
**2.** [A compound] — *Syn.* Chemical Mace (trademark), fear gas, nerve gas; see **gas** 3, **weapon** 1.

**machete**, *n.* — *Syn.* sickle, cleaver, steel, blade; see **knife, sword.**

**Machiavellian**, *modif.* — *Syn.* cunning, crafty, ambitious; see **sly** 1.

**machination**, *n.* — *Syn.* scheme, plot, ruse, maneuver; see **intrigue** 1, **plot** 1, **trick** 1.
*See Synonym Study at* PLOT.

**machine**, *n.* **1.** [A mechanical contrivance] — *Syn.* instrument, implement, mechanism, apparatus; see **computer, device** 1, **engine** 1, **motor, press** 3, **tool** 1.
Types of machine tools include: drill press, belt-driven press, hydraulic press, pillar press, pendulum press, punch press, steam hammer, drop hammer, radial drill, gang drill, die sinker, rough grinder, precision grinder, lathe-tool grinder, planer-tool grinder, jig borer, rip saw, crosscut saw, jigsaw, band saw, table saw, speed lathe, lathe-planer, engine lathe, turret lathe, automatic lathe, electric lathe, vertical lathe, crank planer, plate planer, shaper, slotter, broacher, milling machine, gear-cutting machine, die-threading machine, pipe-threading machine.
**2.** [A political organization] — *Syn.* movement, party, gang\*, ring\*, line-up\*; see also **organization** 3.
**3.** [A person who resembles a machine] — *Syn.* automaton, grind, robot; see **drudge, laborer.**

**machine**, *v.* — *Syn.* tool, shape, plane, turn, drill, weld, die, grind, thread, bore, lathe; see also **manufacture** 1.

**machine gun**, *n.* — *Syn.* automatic rifle, assault rifle, semi-automatic rifle, automatic arms, light arms, light ordnance, Tommy gun\*, burp gun\*; see also **gun** 1, 2, **weapon** 1.
Types of machine guns include: pom-pom, mitrailleuse, Garand, AK-47, M-14, M-16, M-60, Gatling gun, Maxim gun, Bren gun, Sten gun, Thompson, tommy gun, Uzi, submachine gun, light 30-caliber machine gun, heavy 30-caliber machine gun, 50-caliber machine gun.
Makes of machine guns include: Bofors, Lewis, Chauchat, Thompson, Browning, BAR, Browning Automatic Rifle, Maxim, Hotchkiss, Sten, Bren, Kalashnikov, Vickers, Spandau, Johnson, Nambu.

**machinery**, *n.* **1.** [Mechanical equipment] — *Syn.* appliances, implements, tools; see **appliance, device** 1, **engine, machine** 1, **motor.**
**2.** [Devices] — *Syn.* contrivances, machinations, plans, artifices; see **device** 2, **means, method** 2.

**machinist**, *n.* — *Syn.* machine operator, engineer, skilled worker; see **mechanic, worker.**

**macrocosm**, *n.* — *Syn.* cosmos, nature, totality; see **universe, whole.**

**macroscopic**, *modif.* — *Syn.* visible, apparent to the naked eye, perceptible; see **obvious** 1.

**mad**, *modif.* **1.** [Insane] — *Syn.* crazy, demented, deranged, psychotic; see **insane** 1.
**2.** [Angry] — *Syn.* irate, enraged, exasperated; see **angry.**
**3.** [Distraught] — *Syn.* distracted, frenetic, badly upset; see **frantic.**
**4.** [Afflicted with rabies] — *Syn.* frenzied, raging, foaming at the mouth; see **rabid** 3.

**madam**, *n.* **1.** [A title of address] — *Syn.* Mrs., madame, dame, *Frau* (German), madonna, *signora* (Italian), *señora* (Spanish), ma'am, marm\*.
**2.** [A woman in charge of an establishment] — *Syn.* matron, housekeeper, housemother, manageress; see **administrator, hostess** 2.
**3.** [The mistress of a brothel] — *Syn.* procuress, bawd, whore; see **prostitute.**

**madcap**, *modif.* — *Syn.* frivolous, foolish, wild, impulsive, impetuous, daring, adventurous; see also **rash, stupid** 1.

**madcap**, *n.* — *Syn.* daredevil, hothead, prankster, adventuress; see **adventurer** 1.

**madden**, *v.* — *Syn.* craze, infuriate, enrage; see **anger** 1.

**maddening**, *modif.* — *Syn.* annoying, infuriating, offensive; see **disturbing.**

**made**, *modif.* — *Syn.* fashioned, shaped, finished; see **built** 1, **formed, manufactured.**

**have (got) it made\***, — *Syn.* confident, secure, prosperous; see **successful.**

**made easy**, *modif.* — *Syn.* reduced, made plain, uncomplicated; see **easy** 2, **simplified.**

**made over**, *modif.* — *Syn.* remade, rebuilt, redecorated; see **improved** 1, **remodeled, repaired.**

**made-up**, *modif.* **1.** [False] — *Syn.* invented, concocted, fabricated, fictitious; see **false** 2, 3, **unreal.**
**2.** [Marked by the use of make-up] — *Syn.* painted, rouged, powdered, colored, freshened, reddened, cosmeticized.

**made work**, *n.* — *Syn.* work, employment, welfare; see **job** 1.

**madhouse**, *n.* — *Syn.* mental hospital, state hospital, asylum, insane asylum, lunatic asylum\*, looney bin\*, bedlam\*; see also **hospital, sanitarium.**

**madly**, *modif.* **1.** [Insanely] — *Syn.* psychopathically, psychotically, irrationally; see **crazily, violently** 2.
**2.** [Wildly] — *Syn.* rashly, crazily, hastily; see **violently** 1, **wildly** 1.

**madman**, *n.* — *Syn.* lunatic, one who is mentally ill, maniac, raver, bedlamite, insane man, deranged person, psychiatric patient, Tom o'Bedlam\*, nut\*, looney\*, cuckoo\*, psychotic\*, crazyman\*, screwball\*, oddball\*, psycho\*, stir-nut\*; see also **fool** 1, **psychopath.**

**madness**, *n.* — *Syn.* mental illness, derangement, aberration, delusion; see **insanity** 1.

**maelstrom**, *n.* **1.** [Whirlpool] — *Syn.* vortex, undertow, eddy; see **storm** 1, **whirlpool.**

2. [Disturbance] — *Syn.* commotion, turmoil, fury; see **confusion** 2, **storm** 2.

**magazine,** *n.* 1. [A storage chamber] — *Syn.* armory, ammunition storehouse, ammunition dump, cache, ammunition clip; see also **arsenal, storehouse.**

2. [A periodical] — *Syn.* publication, broadside, pamphlet, booklet, manual, circular, brochure; see also **journal** 2, **review** 2.

Types of magazines include: critical review, literary review; daily, weekly, monthly, bimonthly, quarterly, annual; supplement, digest, art, pictorial, theatrical, movie, entertainment, travel, poetry, news, science fiction, home; scholarly journal, scientific journal, professional journal, trade journal; computer, women's, men's, fashion, food, health and fitness, house organ, mystery, magazine of reprints, college, humorous, fanzine, fan, radio; mag*, rag*, sheet*, pulp*, slick*.

Well-known magazines include — *United States:* Reader's Digest, Ebony, Time, Newsweek, U.S. News & World Report, Playboy, Saturday Review, Vogue, Cosmopolitan, Ladies Home Journal, Better Homes and Gardens, Good Housekeeping, McCall's, Forbes, Fortune, Harper's Bazaar, Harper's, Atlantic Monthly, New Republic, Nation, National Review, People, New York Times Magazine, The New Yorker, Sports Illustrated, National Geographic, TV Guide, Rolling Stone, Field and Stream; *Britain:* New Statesman, Spectator, Economist, New Society, Nature, Encounter, Times Literary Supplement, Punch; *France:* Paris Match, La Revue, Réalités; *Germany:* Der Stern, Der Spiegel, Bunte, Illustrierte, Quick; *U.S.S.R. and Russian Federation:* Kulturali Zhizn, Mezhnunarodnaia Zhizn, Novoe Vremia, Sovetskii Soyuz, Krokodil.

**magenta,** *n.* — *Syn.* maroon, fuchsia, vermilion; see **color** 1.

**maggot,** *n.* — *Syn.* grub, slug, larva; see **worm** 1.

**maggoty,** *modif.* — *Syn.* wormy, gone bad, tainted; see **infested, rancid** 1, **rotten** 1, 2.

**magic,** *modif.* 1. [Occult] — *Syn.* enchanted, enchanting, fascinating, charmed, magical, mystical, mystic, mythical, mythic, otherworldly, fairylike, spooky, ghostly, haunted, weird, uncanny, eerie, supernatural, sorcerous, wizardly, witchlike, Circean, Chaldean, thaumaturgic, theurgic, diabolic, Satanic, theurgical, necromantic, fiendish, demoniac, malevolent, shamanist, voodooistic, runic, conjuring, witching, spellbinding, cabalistic, cryptic, transcendental, alchemistic, necromantic, eldritch, numinous, spectral, apparitional, wraithlike, disembodied, discarnate, immaterial, ectoplasmic, astral, spiritualistic, mediumistic, psychic, phenomenological, amuletic, talismanic, phylacteric, tutelary, ensorcelled, tranced, entranced, fay, spellbound, under a spell, under a charm, under the evil eye, under a curse, cursed, mantological, prophetic, telepathic, clairvoyant, clairaudient, thought-reading, telekinetic, spirit-rapping, paranormal, parapsychological, metapsychological, hyperpsychological, hyperphysical; see also **mysterious** 2.

2. [Mysterious] — *Syn.* wonderful, miraculous, fantastical; see **imaginary, unusual** 2.

**magic,** *n.* 1. [The controlling of supernatural powers] — *Syn.* sorcery, occultism, witchcraft, wizardry, necromancy, legerdemain, thaumaturgy, incantation, spell, alchemy, bewitchery, superstition, enchantment, conjury, sortilege, shamanism, prestidigitation, sleight of hand, hocus-pocus, prophecy, divination, diabolism, vaticination, augury, astrology, horoscopy, taboo, astromancy, black magic, black art, voodoo, voodooism,

hoodoo, *obeah* (West Indian), *pishogue* (Irish); see also **witchcraft.**

2. [An example of magic] — *Syn.* spell, incantation, prediction, soothsaying, fortunetelling, presage, evil eye, presaging, foreboding, exorcism, ghost dance; see also **charm** 2, **divination, forecast.**

---

*SYN.* — **magic** is the general term for any of the supposed arts of producing marvelous effects by supernatural or occult power and is figuratively applied to any extraordinary, seemingly inexplicable power; **sorcery** implies magic in which spells are cast or charms are used, usually for a harmful or sinister purpose; **witchcraft** (of women) and **wizardry** (of men) imply the possession of supernatural power by compact with evil spirits, **witchcraft** figuratively suggesting the use of wiles, and **wizardry**, remarkable skill, cleverness

---

**magical,** *modif.* — *Syn.* occult, enchanting, mystic; see **magic** 1, **mysterious** 2.

**magician,** *n.* 1. [Wizard] — *Syn.* enchanter, necromancer, conjurer, seer, soothsayer, diviner, evocator, sorcerer, warlock, medicine man, talismanic, powwow, voodoo, Magian, Shaman, exorcist; see also **prophet, witch.**

2. [Illusionist] — *Syn.* conjurer, sleight-of-hand performer, escape artist, prestidigitator, Houdini.

**magic lantern,** *n.* — *Syn.* slide projector, tachistoscope, optical projector.

**magisterial,** *modif.* — *Syn.* authoritative, imperious, masterful, pompous; see **egotistic** 2, **masterful.**
*See Synonym Study at* MASTERFUL.

**magistrate,** *n.* — *Syn.* justice, officer, police judge; see **judge** 1.

**magnanimity,** *n.* — *Syn.* benevolence, unselfishness, altruism; see **generosity** 2, **kindness** 1, 2.

**magnanimous,** *modif.* — *Syn.* high-minded, unselfish, great-hearted; see **generous** 2, **kind** 1, **noble** 1, 2.

**magnate,** *n.* 1. [An important person in business] — *Syn.* industrialist, capitalist, tycoon; see **businessperson, financier.**

2. [A person of rank] — *Syn.* nobleman, notable, peer; see **aristocrat.**

**magnet,** *n.* — *Syn.* lodestone, magnetite, magnetic iron ore, bar magnet, electromagnet, horseshoe magnet; see also **attraction** 2.

**magnetic,** *modif.* — *Syn.* irresistible, captivating, fascinating; see **inviting.**

**magnetism,** *n.* — *Syn.* lure, influence, charm; see **attraction** 1.

**magnetize,** *v.* — *Syn.* lure, charm, attract; see **draw** 1, **fascinate.**

**magnificence,** *n.* — *Syn.* grandeur, sublimity, exaltedness, majesty, stateliness, nobleness, impressiveness, glory, radiance, show, ostentation, grace, beauty, pulchritude, style, flourish, luxuriousness, glitter, nobility, greatness, loftiness, lavishness, brilliance, sumptuousness, splendor, ostentatiousness, richness, pomp, resplendency, spectacularity, swank*, posh*; see also **elegance** 1, **plenty.** — *Ant.* DULLNESS, simplicity, unostentatiousness.

**magnificent,** *modif.* 1. [Grand] — *Syn.* exalted, great, majestic; see **grand** 2.

2. [Gorgeous] — *Syn.* brilliant, radiant, glittering; see **beautiful** 1, 2, **luxurious, sumptuous.**

3. [Noble] — *Syn.* chivalric, magnanimous, highminded; see **noble.**
*See Synonym Study at* GRAND.

**magnificently,** *modif.* — *Syn.* very well, superbly, gorgeously; see **splendidly.**

**magnify,** *v.* **1.** [To enlarge] — *Syn.* amplify, blow up, expand; see **increase** 1.

**2.** [To exaggerate] — *Syn.* overstate, intensify, embroider; see **exaggerate.**

**magniloquence,** *n.* — *Syn.* pomposity, bombast, grandiloquence; see **eloquence** 1, **nonsense** 1, **speech** 2.

**magnitude,** *n.* **1.** [Size] — *Syn.* extent, breadth, dimension; see **measure** 1, **measurement** 2, **quantity, size** 2.

**2.** [Importance] — *Syn.* greatness, consequence, significance; see **degree** 2, **importance** 1.

**magpie,** *n.* **1.** [Gossip] — *Syn.* chatterer, windbag, idle talker; see **gossip** 2.

**2.** [Black and white bird] — *Syn.* jackdaw, jay, crow, raven; see **bird** 1.

**maid,** *n.* **1.** [A female servant] — *Syn.* maidservant, nursemaid, housemaid, domestic, cleaning woman, chambermaid, barmaid, charwoman, *bonne* (French), *au pair* (French); see also **servant.**

**2.** [A girl] — *Syn.* child, virgin, maiden, kid*; see **girl** 1, **woman** 1.

**maiden,** *modif.* — *Syn.* earliest, beginning, virgin; see **first** 1, **virgin** 2.

**maidenhood,** *n.* — *Syn.* virginity, maidenhead, maidhood, purity; see **chastity, innocence** 3.

**maidenly,** *modif.* — *Syn.* girlish, gentle, reserved, virginal; see **chaste** 2, **feminine** 2.

**maiden name,** *n.* — *Syn.* family name, inherited name, surname, cognomen; see **name** 1.

**maidservant,** *n.* — *Syn.* waitress, domestic, housemaid; see **maid** 1, **servant.**

**mail,** *n.* — *Syn.* letter, post, correspondence, communication, air-mail letter, postal, junk mail, post card, printed matter; see also **letter** 2.

**mail,** *v.* — *Syn.* post, send by post, send by mail, drop into a letter box; see **send** 1.

**mailed,** *modif.* — *Syn.* posted, sent by post, transmitted by post, in the mail, shipped, consigned, dispatched, sent by mail, dropped in the post office; see also **delivered, sent.**

**mailing,** *n.* — *Syn.* posting, airmailing, expressing, getting the mail out, addressing, stamping, stuffing; see also **transportation.**

**mailing list,** *n.* — *Syn.* address list, recipients, prospects, subscribers; see **list.**

**mailman,** *n.* — *Syn.* postman, carrier, mail carrier; see **letter carrier.**

**maim,** *v.* — *Syn.* mutilate, mangle, cripple, incapacitate, disable, disfigure, injure, hack, truncate, impair, disqualify, damage, hurt, castrate, spoil, mar, blemish, deface, warp, dismember, hamstring; see also **damage** 1, **hurt** 1, **mangle** 1.

---

*SYN.* — **maim** implies a severe injury that deprives a person of some bodily member or its use *[maimed* in an auto accident*]*; to **cripple** is to cause to be legless, armless, or lame in any member *[crippled* by rheumatism*]*; to **mutilate** is to remove or severely damage a part essential to the completeness of a person or thing, and suggests disfigurement *[*a speech *mutilated* by censors*]*; **mangle** implies injury or disfigurement by or as if by repeated tearing, hacking, or crushing *[*his arm was *mangled* in the press*]*; to **disable** is to make incapable of normal physical activity, as by crippling *[disabled* war veterans*]*

---

**maimed,** *modif.* — *Syn.* injured, damaged, wounded; see **hurt.**

**main,** *modif.* — *Syn.* principal, chief, foremost, central; see **principal.**

*See Synonym Study at* PRINCIPAL.

**main,** *n.* — *Syn.* trunk, channel, trough; see **pipe** 1.

**mainland,** *n.* — *Syn.* shore, beach, dry land; see **continent, land** 1, **region** 1.

**mainly,** *modif.* — *Syn.* chiefly, largely, essentially; see **principally.**

**mainspring,** *n.* — *Syn.* heart, root, power; see **origin** 3.

**mainstay,** *n.* — *Syn.* pillar, backbone, strength; see **aid** 1.

**maintain,** *v.* **1.** [To uphold] — *Syn.* support, hold up, advance, keep; see **support** 2, **sustain** 1.

**2.** [To assert] — *Syn.* state, affirm, attest; see **declare** 1, **report** 1, **say.**

**3.** [To keep ready for use] — *Syn.* preserve, keep, conserve, repair, withhold, renew, cache, reserve, defer, hold back, have in store, keep on, care for, save, put away, set aside, store up, husband, keep for, keep prepared, lay aside, lay away, set by, keep on hand, keep in reserve, set apart, keep in condition, keep in readiness, keep up, keep aside, control, hold over, manage, direct, have, own, sustain, secure, stick to, stand by; see also **prepare** 1. — *Ant.* WASTE, neglect, consume.

**4.** [To continue] — *Syn.* carry on, persevere, keep up, keep on; see **continue** 1.

**5.** [To support] — *Syn.* provide for, care for, take care of, keep; see **support** 5, **sustain** 2.

*See Synonym Study at* SUPPORT.

**maintenance,** *n.* **1.** [The act of maintaining] — *Syn.* keeping, sustaining, continuance, upholding, carrying; see also **preservation, support** 3, **subsistence** 1.

**2.** [The means of maintaining] — *Syn.* sustenance, livelihood, resources; see **pay** 1, 2, **subsistence** 2.

**majestic,** *modif.* — *Syn.* grand, dignified, sumptuous, exalted; see **grand** 2, **noble** 1, 3.

*See Synonym Study at* GRAND.

**majestically,** *modif.* — *Syn.* grandly, royally, regally; see **wonderfully.**

**majesty,** *n.* **1.** [Grandeur] — *Syn.* nobility, illustriousness, greatness; see **grandeur.**

**2.** [The power of a ruler] — *Syn.* sovereignty, divine right, supremacy; see **power** 2.

**3.** [A form of address; *usually capital*] — *Syn.* Lord, King, Emperor, Prince, Royal Highness, Highness, Sire, Eminence, Queen; see also **title** 3.

**major,** *modif.* **1.** [Greater] — *Syn.* higher, larger, dominant, primary, upper, exceeding, extreme, ultra, over, above; see also **better** 2, **superior.**

**2.** [Important] — *Syn.* significant, main, influential; see **important** 1, 2, **principal.**

**major,** *n.* — *Syn.* field of study, subject, field, program, area; see also **field** 4.

**major-domo,** *n.* — *Syn.* butler, steward, retainer; see **servant.**

**majority,** *n.* **1.** [The larger part] — *Syn.* more than half, preponderance, greater number; see **bulk** 2.

**2.** [Legal maturity] — *Syn.* adulthood, manhood, womanhood, coming of age, prime of life, middle age, voting age, drinking age.

**make,** *v.* **1.** [To produce] — *Syn.* construct, fabricate, produce, manufacture, form, shape, fashion, mold, build, assemble, set up; see also **build** 1, **form** 1, **manufacture** 1.

**2.** [To total] — *Syn.* add up to, come to, equal; see **amount to.**

**3.** [To create] — *Syn.* originate, cause, conceive; see **compose** 3, **create** 2, **invent** 1, **produce** 2.

**4.** [To acquire] — *Syn.* gain, get, secure, earn; see **obtain** 1.

**5.** [To force] — *Syn.* constrain, compel, coerce; see **force** 1.

**6.** [To reach] — *Syn.* progress, reach, arrive at; see **arrive** 1.

**7.** [To cause] — *Syn.* start, effect, initiate; see **begin** 1, **cause** 2.

**8.** [To appoint] — *Syn.* name, select, constitute; see **assign** 1, **delegate** 1, 2.

**9.** [To offer] — *Syn.* proffer, tender, advance; see **offer** 1.

**10.** [To wage] — *Syn.* carry on, conduct, engage in; see **wage**.

**11.** [To enact] — *Syn.* decree, legislate, establish; see **declare** 1, **enact**.

**12.** [To prepare] — *Syn.* get ready, arrange, adjust; see **cook**, **prepare** 1.

**13.** [To perform] — *Syn.* do, carry through, execute; see **perform** 1.

**14.** [To move] — *Syn.* proceed, advance, go; see **move** 1.

**15.** [To utter] — *Syn.* deliver, give, present; see **address** 2.

**on the make★** — *Syn.* belligerent, desirous, lustful; see **aggressive** 2.

---

**SYN.** — **make** is the general term meaning to bring into being and may imply the producing of something physically or mentally; **form** suggests a definite contour, structure, or design in the thing made; **shape** suggests the imparting of a specific form, as by molding, cutting, hammering, etc.; **fashion** implies inventiveness, cleverness of design, the use of skill, etc.; **construct** implies the putting of parts together systematically according to some design; **manufacture** implies production from raw materials, now esp. by machinery and on a large scale, and, in extended use, may suggest a mechanical or uninspired quality; **fabricate** implies building or manufacturing, often by assembling standardized parts, and, in extended use, connotes fictitious invention

---

**make a clean sweep,** *v.* — *Syn.* triumph, succeed, win everything; see **win** 1.

**make after,** *v.* — *Syn.* trail, follow, chase; see **pursue** 1.

**make a joke of,** *v.* — *Syn.* jest, make light of, josh; see **joke.**

**make amends,** *v.* — *Syn.* atone, make up for, compensate; see **reconcile** 2, **repay** 1, **settle** 9.

**make as if** *or* **as though,** *v.* — *Syn.* make believe, simulate, affect; see **pretend** 1.

**make a trip,** *v.* — *Syn.* tour, journey, trek; see **travel** 2.

**make away with,** *v.* — *Syn.* rape, carry off, abduct; see **steal.**

**make-believe,** *modif.* — *Syn.* pretended, fraudulent, acted; see **false** 3, **fantastic** 1, **unreal.**

**make-believe,** *n.* — *Syn.* sham, unreality, fairy tale; see **fancy** 2, **fantasy** 2, **pretense** 2.

**make believe,** *v.* — *Syn.* feign, simulate, counterfeit; see **dream** 2, **pretend** 1.

**make certain (of),** *v.* — *Syn.* make sure of, check into, find out, investigate; see **examine** 1, **guarantee** 1.

**make do,** *v.* — *Syn.* get by, get along, manage, accept; see **endure** 2, **survive** 1, **use** 1.

**make ends meet,** *v.* — *Syn.* survive, subsist, get along; see **budget** 1, **estimate** 3, **manage** 1.

**make eyes at,** *v.* — *Syn.* wink at, flirt with, tease; see **flirt** 1.

**make for,** *v.* — *Syn.* aim for, travel to, go toward, head toward; see **advance** 1, **approach** 2.

**make fun of,** *v.* — *Syn.* tease, embarrass, mimic; see **bother** 2, **ridicule.**

**make good,** *v.* **1.** [To repay] — *Syn.* compensate, adjust, reimburse; see **pay** 1, **repay** 1.

**2.** [To justify] — *Syn.* maintain, support, uphold; see **justify** 2.

**3.** [To complete] — *Syn.* succeed, finish, accomplish; see **achieve** 1, **end** 1.

**4.** [To succeed] — *Syn.* arrive, pay off, prove oneself; see **pay** 2, **succeed** 1.

**make headway,** *v.* — *Syn.* progress, achieve, become better; see **advance** 1, **improve** 2.

**make into,** *v.* — *Syn.* transform, reform, alter; see **change** 1, **convert** 2, **revise.**

**make it★,** *v.* — *Syn.* achieve, triumph, accomplish; see **succeed** 1.

**make known,** *v.* — *Syn.* tell, advise, announce; see **advertise** 1, **declare** 1, 2.

**make like★,** *v.* — *Syn.* fake, feign, simulate; see **pretend** 1.

**make love,** *v.* — *Syn.* sleep with, unite sexually, have intercourse, have sexual relations; see **copulate, join** 1, **love** 2.

**make merry,** *v.* — *Syn.* frolic, revel, enjoy; see **enjoy oneself, play** 1.

**make much of,** *v.* **1.** [To enlarge] — *Syn.* magnify, overstate, blow up★; see **exaggerate.**

**2.** [To favor] — *Syn.* advance, tout, praise; see **encourage** 2, **favor** 1, 2, **promote** 1.

**make of,** *v.* — *Syn.* interpret, translate, understand; see **think** 1.

**make off,** *v.* — *Syn.* depart, run, go; see **leave** 1.

**make off with,** *v.* — *Syn.* abduct, rob, kidnap; see **steal.**

**make out,** *v.* **1.** [To understand] — *Syn.* perceive, recognize, see; see **understand** 1.

**2.** [To succeed] — *Syn.* accomplish, achieve, prosper; see **succeed** 1.

**3.** [★To kiss] — *Syn.* neck, fondle, pet; see **kiss.**

**4.** [To see] — *Syn.* discern, perceive, detect; see **discover, see** 1.

**5.** [To do moderately well] — *Syn.* manage, do well enough, get along; see **contrive** 2, **endure** 2.

**make over,** *v.* **1.** [To improve] — *Syn.* amend, correct, renovate, refashion, refurbish, restore; see also **improve** 1, **redecorate, remodel, repair.**

**2.** [To transfer] — *Syn.* deliver, convey, pass; see **give** 1.

**make overtures,** *v.* — *Syn.* woo, attend, pursue; see **court** 1.

**make peace,** *v.* — *Syn.* propitiate, negotiate, make up; see **reconcile** 2.

**make progress,** *v.* — *Syn.* go forward, progress, proceed; see **advance** 1, **improve** 2.

**maker,** *n.* — *Syn.* creator, producer, inventor; see **author** 1.

**make ready,** *v.* — *Syn.* arrange, get ready, prearrange; see **cook, prepare** 1.

**make sense,** *v.* — *Syn.* be reasonable, be plausible, be probable, be intelligible, be clear, be lucid, be understandable, be logical, be coherent, articulate, scan, add up, follow, infer, deduce, induct, hang together★, hold water★, put two and two together★, straighten up, straighten out★, stand to reason★; see also **reason** 2, **think** 1.

**makeshift,** *modif.* — *Syn.* substitute, alternative, stopgap; see **temporary.**

**makeshift,** *n.* — *Syn.* stopgap, substitute, replacement; see **device 1, resort 1.**

*See Synonym Study at* RESORT.

**make sport of,** *v.* — *Syn.* tease, deride, mock; see **ridicule.**

**make sure of,** *v.* — *Syn.* ensure, determine, review; see **check 3, discover.**

**make the most of,** *v.* — *Syn.* take advantage of, employ, promote; see **improve 1, use 1.**

**make the rounds,** *v.* — *Syn.* inspect, scrutinize, check up on; see **examine 1, visit 4.**

**make time,** *v.* — *Syn.* gain, speed up, rush; see **hurry 1, speed 1, travel.**

**make uneasy,** *v.* — *Syn.* disturb, upset, trouble; see **frighten 1.**

**makeup,** *n.* **1.** [Cosmetics] — *Syn.* mascara, eyeliner, liner, eye shadow, blush, rouge, greasepaint, lipstick, lip gloss, pancake, face powder, powder, pomade, pomatum; see also **cosmetic.**
**2.** [*Anything offered to make good a shortage] — *Syn.* atonement, compensation, conciliation; see **payment 2, reparation 2.**
**3.** [Composition] — *Syn.* scheme, structure, arrangement; see **composition 2, design 1, formation 1.**
**4.** [The arrangement of printed matter] — *Syn.* layout, dummy, spread; see **order 3, plan 1.**

**make up,** *v.* **1.** [To compose] — *Syn.* compound, combine, mingle; see **join 1, mix 1.**
**2.** [To constitute] — *Syn.* comprise, include, consist of; see **compose 1.**
**3.** [To invent] — *Syn.* fabricate, devise, fashion; see **compose 3, create 2, invent 1, 2.**
**4.** [To provide] — *Syn.* furnish, fill, supply; see **provide 1.**
**5.** [To reconcile] — *Syn.* conciliate, pacify, accommodate; see **reconcile 2.**
**6.** [To apply cosmetics] — *Syn.* powder, rouge, beautify, do up*.

**make up for,** *v.* — *Syn.* compensate, balance, counterbalance; see **offset.**

**make up (one's) mind,** *v.* — *Syn.* choose, pick, elect; see **decide, resolve 1.**

**make up to*,** *v.* — *Syn.* flatter, cater to, humor; see **grovel, praise 1.**

**make use of,** *v.* — *Syn.* use, employ, utilize; see **use 1.**

**make war,** *v.* — *Syn.* battle, combat, encounter; see **fight 2.**

**make way,** *v.* — *Syn.* progress, proceed, break ground, break trail*; see **advance 1.**

**make with*,** *v.* **1.** [To give] — *Syn.* hand over, deliver, part with; see **give 1.**
**2.** [To do] — *Syn.* put on, act, carry out; see **perform 1.**
**3.** [To display] — *Syn.* present, exhibit, show; see **display 1.**

**making,** *modif.* **1.** [Preparing] — *Syn.* forming, fashioning, manufacturing, producing, fabricating, constructing, forging, turning out, executing, effecting, shaping, building, creating, accomplishing, generating, originating, composing.
**2.** [Totaling] — *Syn.* computing, constituting, reckoning, concluding, consisting of, aggregating, summing, adding up to, producing, arriving at, completing.

**making,** *n.* — *Syn.* imagination, conception, formulation, devising, fancying, producing, constituting, occasioning, causation, performing, fashioning,

building, origination, shaping, forging, designing, planning, fabrication, composition, authoring, contriving; see also **construction 1, production 1.**

**maladministration,** *n.* — *Syn.* mismanagement, misrule, incompetency; see **disorder 2.**

**maladroit,** *modif.* — *Syn.* clumsy, gauche, inept; see **awkward 1.**

*See Synonym Study at* AWKWARD.

**malady,** *n.* — *Syn.* disease, ailment, sickness, illness; see **disease.**

*See Synonym Study at* DISEASE.

**malaise,** *n.* — *Syn.* uneasiness, discomfort, despair, disquietude; see **depression 2, pain 1.**

**malapert,** *modif.* — *Syn.* saucy, pert, bold, impudent, presumptuous; see also **rude 2.**

**malapropos,** *modif.* — *Syn.* inopportune, inappropriate, out of place, inexpedient, irrelevant; see also **unfit 2, untimely.**

**malaria,** *n.* — *Syn.* malarial fever, sickness, jungle fever*; see **disease.**

**malarious,** *modif.* — *Syn.* fetid, unwholesome, noxious; see **harmful, poisonous.**

**malcontent,** *modif.* — *Syn.* disobedient, restless, discontented; see **rebellious 2, 3, unruly.**

**malcontent,** *n.* **1.** [Complainer] — *Syn.* faultfinder, grumbler, griper, grouch, killjoy, kvetch*, sourpuss*, sorehead*, bellyacher*; see also **grouch.**
**2.** [Rebel] — *Syn.* maverick, troublemaker, reactionary, nonconformist; see **agitator, radical, rebel 1, 2.**

**male,** *modif.* — *Syn.* masculine, manly, manlike, manful, virile, macho, vigorous, potent, staminate, he*; see also **manly, masculine 2.**

---

**SYN.** — **male** is the basic term applied to members of the sex that is biologically distinguished from the female sex and is used of animals and plants as well as of human beings; **masculine** is applied to qualities, such as strength and vigor, traditionally ascribed to men, or to things thought to be characteristic of or appropriate to men; **manly** suggests the generally desirable qualities, such as courage and independence, that a culture ideally associates with a man who has maturity of character; **mannish,** used chiefly of women, is most often used derogatorily and implies the possession or adoption of traits and manners thought to be more appropriate to a man; **virile** stresses qualities such as robustness, vigor, and, specif., sexual potency, that belong to a physically mature man

---

**male,** *n.* — *Syn.* man, fellow, guy*, male sex, man-child, he; see also **boy, father, man 2.**

**malediction,** *n.* — *Syn.* imprecation, denunciation, damnation; see **curse 1.**

**malefactor,** *n.* — *Syn.* criminal, evildoer, wrongdoer, transgressor, convict, villain, rascal, scoundrel, hellhound, wretch, jailbird, culprit, delinquent, outlaw, felon, murderer, scamp, scapegrace, outcast, vagabond, varlet, rapscallion, rogue, ruffian, black sheep, hoodlum, sinner, *larrikin* (Australian), tough*, rough*, rowdy*, rounder*, bad egg*, holy terror*, thug*, bum*, gorilla*; see also **criminal.**

**malevolence,** *n.* — *Syn.* ill will, enmity, indignity; see **evil 1, hate, hatred 1, 2, malice, resentment.**

**malevolent,** *modif.* — *Syn.* spiteful, malicious, evil; see **wicked 1, 2.**

**malfeasance,** *n.* — *Syn.* wrongdoing, misbehavior, impropriety; see **mischief 3.**

**malformation,** *n.* — *Syn.* distortion, abnormality, deformity; see **contortion 1.**

**malformed,** *modif.* — *Syn.* distorted, grotesque, abnormal; see **deformed, twisted** 1.

**malfunction,** *n.* — *Syn.* breakdown, defect, fault, flaw, bug*, glitch*; see also **failure** 1.

**malfunction,** *v.* — *Syn.* break down, fail, get out of order; see **break down** 3.

**malice,** *n.* — *Syn.* spite, rancor, animosity, maliciousness, hate, ill-feeling, hostility, grudge, implacability, bitterness, antipathy, umbrage, repugnance, dislike, resentment, venom, acerbity, mordacity, malignance, malignity, bad blood, viciousness, pure cussedness*, dirt*, cat bite*; see also **evil** 1, **hatred** 1, 2. — *Ant.* KINDNESS, benevolence, goodness.

**malicious,** *modif.* — *Syn.* ill-disposed, spiteful, hateful; see **wicked** 1, 2.

**malign,** *v.* — *Syn.* accuse, misrepresent, scandalize; see **censure, curse** 2, **insult, slander**.

**malignancy,** *n.* — *Syn.* fatality, virulence, hatred; see **malice**.

**malignant,** *modif.* **1.** [Diseased] — *Syn.* cancerous, fatal, lethal, deadly, poisonous, destructive, internecine, mortal, pestilential; see also **deadly, poisonous**.
**2.** [Harmful] — *Syn.* deleterious, corrupt, sapping; see **dangerous** 1, 2, **harmful**.

**maligned,** *modif.* — *Syn.* reviled, scorned, rejected; see **abused**.

**malignity,** *n.* **1.** [Fatality] — *Syn.* deadliness, virulence, noxiousness; see **fatality**.
**2.** [Hostility] — *Syn.* hostility, envy, spite; see **hate, hatred** 1, 2, **malice, resentment**.

**mall,** *n.* **1.** [Pedestrian area] — *Syn.* court, walk, lane; see **lawn, park** 1, **road** 1.
**2.** [Shopping center] — *Syn.* shopping plaza, plaza, shopping arcade, shopping complex, market, marketplace, mart.

**malleable,** *modif.* — *Syn.* pliant, tractable, plastic, moldable; see **flexible** 1, **pliable** 1, 2.
*See Synonym Study at* PLIABLE.

**mallet,** *n.* — *Syn.* maul, mall, club; see **hammer**.

**malnutrition,** *n.* — *Syn.* scurvy, consumption, rickets; see **hunger, illness** 1, **starvation**.

**malodorous,** *modif.* — *Syn.* infested, stinking, rancid; see **rank** 2, **rotten** 1.

**malpractice,** *n.* — *Syn.* negligence, misbehavior, neglect; see **carelessness, violation** 1.

**malt,** *n.* — *Syn.* slops, malt liquor, ale; see **beer**.

**maltreat,** *v.* — *Syn.* injure, damage, ill-treat; see **abuse** 1, **hurt** 1.

**maltreatment,** *n.* — *Syn.* punishment, injury, injustice; see **abuse** 3, **violation** 2.

**mama,** *n.* — *Syn.* female progenitor, mamma, parent; see **mother** 1.

**mammal,** *n.* — *Syn.* vertebrate, creature, beast; see **animal** 1.

**mammoth,** *modif.* — *Syn.* gigantic, immense, enormous; see **high** 1, **large** 1, **enormous**.
*See Synonym Study at* ENORMOUS.

**mammy,** *n.* **1.** [*A black nursemaid] — *Syn.* nanny, nursemaid, aunty*, wet nurse; see **nurse** 2, 3.
**2.** [*Mother] — *Syn.* mom, mama, mommy; see **mother** 1.

**man,** *n.* **1.** [The human race] — *Syn.* men and women, mankind, humankind, human beings, human race, humanity, human species, human nature, persons, mortals, populace, individuals, earthlings, civilized society, *Homo faber* (Latin), creatures, fellow creatures, people, folk, society, *Homo sapiens* (Latin); see also **hominid**.
**2.** [An adult male] — *Syn.* he, gentleman, Sir, Mr.,

esquire, swain, fellow, blade, yeoman, mister, master, beau, chap*, guy*, buck*; see also **boy**.
**3.** [Anyone] — *Syn.* human being, an individual, fellow creature; see **person** 1.
**4.** [*Husband] — *Syn.* married man, spouse, partner; see **husband**.
**as a man** — *Syn.* in unison, united, all together; see **unanimously**.
**be one's own man** — *Syn.* be independent, stand alone, be free; see **endure** 1.
**man and boy*** — *Syn.* all of a man's life, a lifetime, a long time; see **boy, man** 2.
**to a man** — *Syn.* all, everyone, with no exception; see **everybody**.

**man,** *v.* — *Syn.* garrison, protect, fortify; see **defend** 1, **guard** 2.

**manacle,** *n.* — *Syn.* handcuffs, irons, fetters; see **band** 2, **chains**.

**manage,** *v.* **1.** [To direct] — *Syn.* lead, oversee, direct, administer, conduct, supervise, control, mastermind, engineer, carry on, execute, handle, watch, guide, engage in, officiate, pilot, steer, minister, regulate, manipulate, maneuver, dominate, officiate, superintend, preside, head, run, operate, administrate, quarterback, be at the head of, be responsible for, deal with, maintain, care for, take over, take care of, watch over, have in one's charge, look after, see to, train, instruct, disburse, distribute, husband, arrange, command, govern, steward, boss, occupy the chair, run the show*, call the shots, call the tune*, be at the helm*, take the helm*, run a tight ship*, be in the driver's seat*; see also **command** 2. — *Ant.* OBEY, follow, take orders.
**2.** [To contrive] — *Syn.* accomplish, bring about, effect; see **achieve** 1, **contrive** 2, **succeed** 1.
**3.** [To get along] — *Syn.* bear up, survive, scrape by*, get by*; see **endure** 2.

---

*SYN.* — **manage** implies supervision that involves the personal handling of all details [to *manage* a department]; **control** implies firm direction by regulation or restraint and often connotes complete domination [the school board *controls* the system]; **conduct** implies supervising by using one's executive skill, knowledge, and wisdom [to *conduct* a sales campaign]; **direct** implies less supervision of actual details, but stresses the issuance of general orders or instructions [to *direct* the construction of a dam]

---

**manageable,** *modif.* — *Syn.* controllable, docile, compliant, pliant, governable, teachable, tractable, willing, obedient, submissive, yielding, adaptable, flexible, dutiful, humble, meek, easy, soft, malleable; see also **gentle** 3, **obedient** 1, **willing** 2. — *Ant.* REBELLIOUS, ungovernable, unruly.

**managed,** *modif.* **1.** [Trained] — *Syn.* handled, guided, persuaded, influenced, driven, counseled, urged, taught, instructed, coached, groomed*, primed*, shined up*, tuned up*, trained fine*, given a workout*; see also **educated** 1, **trained**. — *Ant.* WILD, undisciplined, uneducated.
**2.** [Governed] — *Syn.* ruled, controlled, dominated, commanded, directed, swayed, mastered, run, regulated, ordered, compelled, supervised, piloted, cared for, taken care of; see also **governed** 1, 2. — *Ant.* ungoverned, FREE, unsupervised.

**management,** *modif.* — *Syn.* business, governmental, supervisory; see **administrative, official** 1, 3.

**management,** *n.* **1.** [Direction] — *Syn.* supervision, superintendence, control; see **administration** 1, **command** 2.

**2.** [Those who undertake management] — *Syn.* directors, administrators, executives; see **administration** 2, **authority** 3.

**manager,** *n.* — *Syn.* director, handler, superintendent, supervisor; see **administrator.**

**managing,** *modif.* — *Syn.* directing, supervising, superintending, advising, admonishing, overseeing, controlling, guiding, operating, taking charge of, caring for, husbanding, administering, executing, organizing, regulating, inspecting, leading, piloting, steering, handling, charging, manipulating; see also **governing.**

**mandate,** *n.* — *Syn.* command, decree, behest, order, commission, fiat, charge; see also **command** 1.

**mandated,** *modif.* — *Syn.* administered, assigned, ordered, commanded, decreed, charged, dictated, proclaimed, summoned, requisitioned, bid.

**mandatory,** *modif.* — *Syn.* compulsory, forced, obligatory; see **necessary** 1.

**mandible,** *n.* — *Syn.* mouth, lower jaw, jawbone; see **bone, jaw** 1.

**mane,** *n.* — *Syn.* brush, ruff, fringe; see **fur, hair** 1.

**man-eater,** *n.* — *Syn.* vampire, anthropophage, carnivore; see **cannibal, savage** 1.

**man-eating,** *modif.* — *Syn.* cannibal, carnivorous, creophagous; see **deadly, ferocious, murderous, savage** 2.

**maneuver,** *n.* **1.** [A movement, usually military] — *Syn.* stratagem, movement, procedure; see **plan** 2, **tactics.**

**2.** [A trick] — *Syn.* trick, subterfuge, finesse, ruse; see **trick** 1.

**3.** [Extensive practice in arms; *plural*] — *Syn.* sham battle, imitation war, exercises, war games, summer maneuvers; see also **drill** 3, **exercise** 1, **parade** 1.

*See Synonym Study at* TRICK.

**maneuver,** *v.* — *Syn.* plot, scheme, machinate, intrigue, move, finesse, manage, contrive, design, devise, trick, cheat, conspire, shift, sham, proceed, angle for\*, wangle into\*; see also **plan** 1.

**maneuverer,** *n.* — *Syn.* operator, manager, wheeler-dealer\*, planner, tactician, strategist; see also **agent** 1, **diplomat** 2, **politician** 1, 3.

**mange,** *n.* — *Syn.* rash, scales, eruption, psoriasis, eczema, skin disease, scabies, scab, scurvy, sores; see also **disease.**

**manger,** *n.* **1.** [A feed rack] — *Syn.* rack, trough, receptacle, feed box, crib; see also **bin, storehouse.**

**2.** [The birthplace of Christ] — *Syn.* Bethlehem, crèche, stable, cradle, Holy Cradle, the lowly cattle shed, the oxen's stall.

**mangle,** *n.* — *Syn.* press, iron, electric ironer; see **iron** 3.

**mangle,** *v.* **1.** [To mutilate] — *Syn.* tear, lacerate, crush, wound, injure, cripple, maim, rend, disfigure, cut, hack, flay, slit, hash, butcher, slash, slice, carve, bruise, mutilate, mar, botch, spoil, deform, maul, batter; see also **damage** 1, **destroy** 1, **maim.**

*See Synonym Study at* MAIM.

**2.** [To iron with a power roller] — *Syn.* steam press, smooth, iron; see **press** 2.

**mangy,** *modif.* **1.** [Scabby] — *Syn.* psoriatic, rashy, scabby; see **dirty** 1, **sick.**

**2.** [Poverty-stricken] — *Syn.* impoverished, shabby, indigent; see **poor** 2, **squalid.**

**manhandle,** *v.* — *Syn.* damage, maul, mistreat; see **abuse** 1, **beat** 2.

**man-hater,** *n.* — *Syn.* misanthropist, solitary, eremite; see **hermit, misanthrope.**

**manhole,** *n.* — *Syn.* vent, scuttle, hatch; see **hole** 2, **sewer.**

**manhood,** *n.* **1.** [Male maturity] — *Syn.* post-pubescence, coming of age, adulthood; see **majority** 2.

**2.** [Manly qualities] — *Syn.* virility, valor, resoluteness, honor, gallantry, nobility, forcefulness, machismo, daring, chivalry, boldness, tenacity, potency, sturdiness, self-reliance, tenderness, gentleness; see also **courage** 1, **strength** 1.

**mania,** *n.* — *Syn.* craze, obsession, madness, manic disorder; see **desire** 1, **insanity** 1, **obsession.**

*See Synonym Study at* HYSTERIA.

**maniac,** *n.* — *Syn.* lunatic, insane person, crazy person; see **madman, psychopath.**

**maniacal,** *modif.* — *Syn.* raving, mad, hysterical, deranged; see **insane** 1.

**manicure,** *v.* — *Syn.* trim, beautify, cut, polish, color, shape; see also **trim** 1.

**manifest,** *modif.* — *Syn.* clear, evident, visible, unmistakable; see **obvious** 1, 2.

*See Synonym Study at* EVIDENT.

**manifest,** *v.* **1.** [To display] — *Syn.* show, exhibit, disclose; see **display** 1, **expose** 1, **reveal** 1.

**2.** [To evidence] — *Syn.* confirm, declare, demonstrate, substantiate; see **prove.**

**manifestation,** *n.* — *Syn.* display, exhibition, demonstration, indication; see **sign** 1.

**manifesto,** *n.* — *Syn.* pronouncement, declaration, decree, proclamation; see **announcement** 1.

**manifold,** *modif.* — *Syn.* various, numerous, diverse; see **complex** 1, **different** 2.

**manikin,** *n.* — *Syn.* puppet, marionette, figure; see **doll, model** 3, 4.

**manipulate,** *v.* — *Syn.* handle, shape, mold; see **form** 1, **manage** 1, **plan** 1.

*See Synonym Study at* HANDLE.

**manipulation,** *n.* — *Syn.* guidance, use, direction; see **administration** 1.

**manipulator,** *n.* — *Syn.* handler, agent, operator, conductor, controller, schemer, conspirator.

**mankind,** *n.* — *Syn.* humanity, human race, society; see **man** 1.

**manlike,** *modif.* **1.** [Humanlike] — *Syn.* anthropoid, simian, anthropomorphic; see **human.**

**2.** [Male] — *Syn.* masculine, manly, virile; see **male, manly.**

**manliness,** *n.* — *Syn.* masculinity, manlikeness, virility; see **courage** 1, **manhood** 2, **strength** 1.

**manly,** *modif.* — *Syn.* masculine, virile, strong, brave, courageous, undaunted, fearless, firm, staunch, dignified, noble, honorable, valiant, valorous, high-spirited, plucky, lionhearted, intrepid, gallant, resolute, bold, macho, stouthearted, confident, self-reliant, manful; see also **masculine** 2. — *Ant.* COWARDLY, timid, effeminate.

*See Synonym Study at* MALE.

**man-made,** *modif.* — *Syn.* manufactured, artificial, unnatural, counterfeit, not genuine; see also **false** 3, **synthetic** 2.

**manna,** *n.* — *Syn.* nourishment, sustenance, maintenance; see **bread** 1, 2, **food, subsistence** 1.

**manner,** *n.* **1.** [Personal conduct] — *Syn.* mien, deportment, demeanor; see **bearing** 2, **behavior** 1.

*See Synonym Study at* BEARING.

**2.** [Customary action] — *Syn.* use, way, practice; see **custom** 1, 2, **habit** 1.

**3.** [Method] — *Syn.* mode, fashion, style; see **method** 2.

**by all manner of means** — *Syn.* certainly, of course, without doubt; see **surely.**

**by any manner of means**— *Syn.* in any way, at all, however; see **anyhow** 2.

**by no manner of means**— *Syn.* in no way, not at all, definitely not; see **never.**

**in a manner of speaking**— *Syn.* in a way, so to speak, so to say; see **rather.**

**to the manner born**— *Syn.* naturally fit, suited, accustomed from birth; see **able** 1.

**mannered,** *modif.* — *Syn.* artificial, self-conscious, posed; see **affected** 2.

**mannerism,** *n.* — *Syn.* idiosyncrasy, pretension, peculiarity; see **characteristic, pose, quirk.**
*See Synonym Study at* POSE.

**mannerly,** *modif.* — *Syn.* courteous, well-behaved, polished, considerate, charming; see also **polite** 1.

**manners,** *n.* **1.** [Personal behavior] — *Syn.* conduct, deportment, bearing; see **behavior** 1.
**2.** [Polite behavior] — *Syn.* etiquette, decorum, refinement, good manners; see **courtesy** 1, **culture** 3, **elegance** 1.
*See Synonym Study at* BEARING.

**mannish,** *modif.* — *Syn.* manlike, masculine, unfeminine, unwomanly, mannified, tomboyish, hoydenish, butch*; see also **male, masculine** 2.
*See Synonym Study at* MALE.

**man-of-all-work,** *n.* — *Syn.* jack-of-all-trades, handyman, servant, factotum, caretaker, servant, majordomo*, do-all*, dogsbody*; see also **laborer, worker.**

**man of means,** *n.* — *Syn.* wealthy man, rich man, man of substance, capitalist, tycoon; see also **financier, millionaire.**

**man-of-war,** *n.* — *Syn.* battleship, destroyer, naval vessel, ship of the line; see **ship, warship.**

**manor,** *n.* — *Syn.* manor house, demesne, mansion, hotel; see **estate** 1.

**manor house,** *n.* — *Syn.* lodge, villa, mansion; see **home** 1.

**manpower,** *n.* — *Syn.* laborers, work force, labor force, workers, men of military age, males; see also **labor** 4.

**manse,** *n.* — *Syn.* rectory, vicarage, minister's residence; see **parsonage.**

**manservant,** *n.* — *Syn.* valet, steward, attendant, man; see **servant.**

**mansion,** *n.* — *Syn.* villa, house, hall, palace, stately home; see also **estate** 1, **home** 1.

**manslaughter,** *n.* — *Syn.* killing, homicide, assassination; see **crime** 2, **murder.**

**manslayer,** *n.* — *Syn.* assassin, murderer, gangster; see **criminal, killer.**

**mantel,** *n.* — *Syn.* fireplace, mantelpiece, chimney piece; see **shelf.**

**mantilla,** *n.* — *Syn.* kerchief, scarf, lace covering; see **veil.**

**mantle,** *n.* — *Syn.* cloak, cape, covering, veil, blanket, screen, curtain.

**manual,** *modif.* — *Syn.* by hand, hand-operated, not automatic, standard; see **old-fashioned.**

**manual,** *n.* — *Syn.* guidebook, reference book, textbook, exercise book, manual of arms; see also **handbook, text** 1.

**manufacture,** *n.* — *Syn.* fashioning, forming, assembling; see **production** 1.

**manufacture,** *v.* **1.** [To make a product] — *Syn.* make, construct, fabricate, produce, mass-produce, form, fashion, carve, mold, cast, frame, put together, forge, turn out, stamp out, print out, cut out, have in production, have on the assembly line, print, erect, shape, execute, accomplish, complete, tool, machine, mill, make

up; see also **assemble** 3, **build** 1. — *Ant.* DESTROY, demolish, tear down.
**2.** [To devise from almost nothing] — *Syn.* make up, fabricate, contrive; see **create** 2, **invent** 1, **produce** 2.
*See Synonym Study at* MAKE.

**manufactured,** *modif.* — *Syn.* made, produced, mass-produced, constructed, fabricated, erected, fashioned, shaped, forged, turned out, tooled, machined, executed, done, assembled, ready for the market, in shape, complete, completed; see also **built** 1, **formed.**

**manufacturer,** *n.* — *Syn.* maker, producer, fabricator, constructor, builder, operator, smith, forger, artificer, craftsman, corporation, entrepreneur, company; see also **business** 4.

**manufacturing,** *modif.* — *Syn.* producing, industrial, fabricative; see **making** 1.

**manufacturing,** *n.* — *Syn.* production, fabrication, building, construction, assembling, casting, tooling, preparing for market, putting in production, mass production, forging, formation, erection, composition, composing, accomplishment, completion, finishing, doing, turning out; see also **making, production** 1.
— *Ant.* destruction, WRECK, DEMOLITION.

**manumit,** *v.* — *Syn.* liberate, emancipate, release; see **free** 1.

**manure,** *n.* — *Syn.* guano, plant-food, compost; see **dung, fertilizer.**

**manuscript,** *n.* — *Syn.* composition, papyrus, parchment, vellum, tablet, stone, paper, document, original, copy, typescript, scroll, letterpress, autograph, translation, facsimile, palimpsest, book, piece of music, typewritten copy, script; see also **writing** 2.
Famous manuscripts include: Bankes Homer, Harris Homer, Codex Argentus of Ulfilas, the Vatican Virgils, Codex Vaticanus, Codex Sinaiticus, Codex Alexandrinus, Dead Sea Scrolls, Laurentian Herodotus, Gospels of Vercelli, Charter of King Edgar, Iliad of the Ambrosian, Lindisfarne Gospels, the Book of Deir, the Book of Kells, the Book of the Dun Cow, Gospel Book of Charlemagne, Paris Psalter, Oxford Euclid, Oxford Plato, Cotton Vitellius A-15, Beowulf, Ellesmere Manuscript, Canterbury Tales, Finnsburg Fragment, the Book of the Dead, Rosetta Stone.

**many,** *modif.* — *Syn.* numerous, multiplied, manifold, multifold, multitudinous, multifarious, multiplex, diverse, divers, sundry, profuse, innumerable, not a few, numberless, a world of, countless, uncounted, untold, alive with, teeming, in heaps, several, of every description, prevalent, no end of, no end to, everywhere, thick with, crowded, common, usual, plentiful, abundant, galore*, lousy with*, bursting out all over*; see also **multiple** 1, **various.** — *Ant.* FEW, meager, scanty.

**many,** *n.* — *Syn.* a great number, abundance, thousands*; see **plenty.**

**a good (or great) many**— *Syn.* a great number, abundance, thousands; see **plenty.**

**as many (as)**— *Syn.* as much, an equal number, a similar amount; see **same.**

**be one too many for**— *Syn.* overwhelm, overcome, beat down; see **defeat** 1, 2.

**many-colored,** *modif.* — *Syn.* varicolored, kaleidoscopic, prismatic; see **bright** 2, **multicolored.**

**many-sided,** *modif.* **1.** [Multilateral] — *Syn.* polyhedral, geometric, bilateral, polyhedrous, dihedral, trilateral, quadrilateral, tetrahedral; see also **geometrical.**
**2.** [Gifted] — *Syn.* endowed, talented, adaptable; see **able** 1, 2, **versatile.**

**map,** *n.* — *Syn.* chart, graph, plat, sketch, diagram, pro-

**map** 487 **mark**

jection, delineation, drawing, picture, portrayal, draft, tracing, outline, ground plan, atlas, gazetteer; see also **plan** 1.

Types of maps include: conical projection, Mercator projection, topographical, relief, model, political, isothermic, isothermal, isobaric, contour, gravity, industrial, military, geodetic, marine, weather, road, street, railroad, cartogramic, surface, air, aerial; globe.

**put on the map**★— *Syn.* make famous, bring fame to, glorify; see **establish** 2.

**wipe off the map**★— *Syn.* eliminate, put out of existence, ruin; see **destroy** 1.

**map,** *v.* — *Syn.* map out, outline, draft, chart; see **plan** 2.

**mar,** *v.* **1.** [To damage slightly] — *Syn.* harm, bruise, scratch; see **break** 2, **damage** 1.

**2.** [To impair] — *Syn.* deform, deface, warp; see **destroy** 1.

**maraud,** *v.* — *Syn.* plunder, rape, pillage; see **attack** 1, **raid, ravage.**

**marauder,** *n.* — *Syn.* raider, privateer, thief; see **pirate, robber.**

**marauding,** *modif.* — *Syn.* thieving, ravaging, extortionate; see **rapacious** 2.

**marble,** *modif.* **1.** [Composed of marble] — *Syn.* marmoreal, adamant, flinty, vitreous, horny, corneus, bony, osseous, petrified, granitelike, unyielding, indurated; see also **stone.**

**2.** [Giving the effect of marble] — *Syn.* marbled, mottled, marmoreal, veined, flecked, striated, barred, striped, watered, pied, variegated, mosaic, diapered.

**marble,** *n.* **1.** [Metamorphic limestone] — *Syn.* limestone, chalcedony, quartz, alabaster.

Varieties of marble include: Parian, Pentelic, Carrara, Carrian, Serpentine, Algerian, Italian, Tecali, onyx marbles, Siena, Tuscan, Gibraltar, Vermont, Georgia, fire, black, rance, cipolin, giallo antico, brocatello, verdantique, ophicalcite; see **stone.**

**2.** [A piece of carved marble] — *Syn.* carving, figurine, figure; see **art** 2, **sculpture, statue.**

**3.** [A ball used in marbles] — *Syn.* nib, ivory, mig, shooter, ante, bait, taw, aggie, cat's eye, glassy; see also **toy** 1.

**marbles,** *n.* — *Syn.* marbs★, nibs★, funs★, keepsies★, keeps★, taw★, date up★, ante up★; see also **game** 1.

**March,** *n.* — *Syn.* spring month, beginning of spring, Lent, windy month, month that comes in like a lion and goes out like a lamb; see also **month, spring** 2.

**march,** *n.* **1.** [The act of marching] — *Syn.* walk, parade, pace, hike, trudge, progression, movement, advancing, advancement, double march, countermarch, goose step, military parade, quick step, double time, quick march, route march; see also **step** 1, **walk** 3.

**2.** [The distance or route marched] — *Syn.* walk, trek, hike; see **journey, route** 2.

**3.** [Music for marching] — *Syn.* martial music, wedding march, processional; see **music.**

**march,** *v.* — *Syn.* move, advance, step out, go on, proceed, space, step, tread, tramp, journey, stroll, saunter, patrol, prowl, walk, promenade, parade, goose-step, file, mount a patrol, range, strut, maintain contact, proceed, progress, go ahead, file off, do the lock step, forge ahead; see also **travel** 2, **walk** 1. — *Ant.* PAUSE, halt, retreat.

**on the march**— *Syn.* proceeding, advancing, tramping; see **marching.**

**steal a march on**★— *Syn.* outdo, gain an advantage over, overcome; see **surpass.**

**marching,** *modif.* — *Syn.* advancing, parading, filing, proceeding, tramping, hiking, pacing, stepping, double-marching, patrolling, policing, checking, in motion, be-

ing brought up, en route, retreating, quick-marching, route-marching; see also **moving** 1, **traveling** 2, **walking.**

**Mardi Gras,** *n.* — *Syn.* Shrove Tuesday, fat Tuesday, last day of carnival, last day of Folly, last day before Lent, carnival, festival in New Orleans; see also **Easter, holiday, spring** 2.

**mare,** *n.* — *Syn.* female horse, brood mare, dam, breeding stock, filly, jenny; see also **animal** 2, **horse.**

**mare's-nest,** *n.* **1.** [Delusion] — *Syn.* deception, hoax, lie; see **trick** 1.

**2.** [Confusion] — *Syn.* mess, disorder, jumble, chaos, mix-up.

**margin,** *n.* — *Syn.* border, edge, perimeter; see **boundary, edge** 1. **rim.**

*See Synonym Study at* RIM.

**marginal,** *modif.* **1.** [Borderline] — *Syn.* peripheral, nonessential, negligible, limited; see **bordering.**

**2.** [Barely adequate] — *Syn.* minimal, tolerable, passable, so-so, indifferent.

**marijuana,** *n.* — *Syn.* cannabis, *cannabis sativa, cannabis indica* (*both* Latin), hemp, bhang, ganja, hashish, charas, majoon, cannabin, cannabidiol, THC, dope★, grass★, pot★, weed★, boo★, maryjane★, sensimilla★, queen mary★, hash★, acapulco gold★, gold★, California brown★, brown; see also **drug** 2.

**marine,** *modif.* — *Syn.* aquatic, seagoing, oceangoing, seafaring, maritime, of the sea, oceanic; see also **maritime** 2, **nautical.**

**mariner,** *n.* — *Syn.* seaman, tar, navigator; see **sailor.**

**marines,** *n.* — *Syn.* United States Marines, Royal Marines, landing party, amphibious forces, sea soldiers, devil dogs★, grunts★, Seabees★, leathernecks★; see also **troops.**

**marionette,** *n.* — *Syn.* mannikin, model, puppet, dummy; see **doll, toy** 1.

**marital,** *modif.* — *Syn.* conjugal, connubial, nuptial; see **matrimonial.**

**maritime,** *modif.* **1.** [Bordering on the sea] — *Syn.* seaside, seashore, shore, oceanic. — *Ant.* INLAND, hinterland, continental.

**2.** [Concerned with the sea] — *Syn.* naval, marine, oceanic, seagoing, hydrographic, seafaring, aquatic, natatorial, pelagic, Neptunian; see also **nautical.**

**Mark,** *n.* — *Syn.* "John whose name was Mark," John Mark, apostle, the second Gospel; see **disciple, saint** 2.

**mark,** *n.* **1.** [The physical result of marking] — *Syn.* brand, stamp, blaze, imprint, impression, line, trace, check, stroke, streak, dot, point, nick, underlining.

**2.** [A target] — *Syn.* butt, prey, bull's eye; see **target.**

**3.** [A record] — *Syn.* register, record, trademark, impression, price tag, price mark, ticket, label, score, representation.

**4.** [Effect] — *Syn.* manifestation, consequence, value; see **result.**

**5.** [A symbol] — *Syn.* sign, image, badge; see **emblem.**

**6.** [An evidence of character] — *Syn.* idiosyncrasy, particularity, indication; see **characteristic, trait.**

**7.** [The point at which a race begins] — *Syn.* starting line, start, holes, gun.

**beside the mark**— *Syn.* beside the point, extraneous, immaterial; see **irrelevant.**

**hit the mark**★— *Syn.* achieve, accomplish, do right, do well; see **succeed** 1.

**make one's mark**— *Syn.* accomplish, prosper, become famous; see **succeed** 1.

**miss the mark**— *Syn.* be unsuccessful, err, mistake, misunderstand; see **fail** 1.

**wide of the mark** — *Syn.* erring, mistaken, inaccurate; see **wrong** 2.

**mark,** *v.* **1.** [To make a mark] — *Syn.* brand, stamp, imprint, blaze, print, emboss, check, chalk, label, sign, impress, identify, check off, trace, stroke, streak, dot, point, nick, underline, score, inscribe, seal.
**2.** [To designate] — *Syn.* earmark, point out, stake out, indicate, signal, signalize, check off, mark off, signify, remark, denote; see also **designate** 1.
**3.** [To distinguish] — *Syn.* characterize, signalize, qualify; see **distinguish** 1.
**4.** [To note carefully] — *Syn.* chronicle, register, write down; see **list** 1, **record** 1.
**5.** [To observe] — *Syn.* note, head, take notice of, pay attention to, bear in mind, consider; see also **regard** 1.
**6.** [To give a grade to] — *Syn.* grade, rate, evaluate; see **rank** 2.
**7.** [To put prices upon] — *Syn.* ticket, label, tag; see **price.**

**mark down,** *v.* — *Syn.* reduce, put on sale, discount, cut the price of; see **lower, price.**

**marked,** *modif.* **1.** [Carrying a mark] — *Syn.* branded, signed, sealed, stamped, blazed, imprinted, impressed, inscribed, characterized by, distinguished by, recognized by, identified by.
**2.** [Priced] — *Syn.* labeled, trademarked, price-marked, marked down, marked up, ticketed, priced, tagged; see also **costing.**

**marked down,** *modif.* — *Syn.* lowered, priced lower, discounted; see **reduced** 2.

**markedly,** *modif.* — *Syn.* notably, particularly, considerably, appreciably; see **especially** 1.

**marked up,** *modif.* — *Syn.* added on, more expensive, raised; see **increased.**

**marker,** *n.* **1.** [A sign] — *Syn.* ticket, price mark, trademark, seal, brand, stamp, boundary mark, tombstone, inscription; see also **label, tag** 2.
**2.** [A writing instrument] — *Syn.* felt tip pen, laundry marker, Magic Marker (trademark), colored pen, broad tip pen; see also **pen** 3.

**market,** *n.* **1.** [A place devoted to sale] — *Syn.* store, grocery store, trading post, mart, shopping mall, shopper's square, emporium, exchange, city market, public market, farmer's market, supermarket, green-grocer's, meat market, fish market, curb market, open-air market, flea market, fair, dime store, drug store, department store, variety store, general store, bazaar, stall, booth, warehouse, business, delicatessen; see also **shop, store** 1.
**2.** [Stock market] — *Syn.* stock exchange, exchange, bourse, Bourse, commodities exchange, Dow-Jones, the Dow, Nikkei, syndicate.
**3.** [The state of trade] — *Syn.* supply and demand, sale, run; see **business** 1, 5, **demand** 2.
**be in the market (for)** — *Syn.* want to buy, be willing to purchase, need; see **want** 1.
**on the market** — *Syn.* salable, ready for purchase, available; see **for sale** at **sale.**

**market,** *v.* — *Syn.* vend, exchange, barter; see **sell** 1.

**marketable,** *modif.* — *Syn.* for the consumer, wholesale, for sale; see **commercial** 1, **retail.**

**marketing,** *n.* — *Syn.* shopping, retailing, purchasing; see **buying, selling** 1.

**market place,** *n.* — *Syn.* selling place, department store, curb market; see **market** 1, **shop, store** 1.

**marking,** *modif. & n.* **1.** [Designating] — *Syn.* pointing out, characterizing, noticing, recognizing, distinguishing, showing, specifying, indicating, naming, terming, calling, denominating; see also **sense** 2.

**2.** [Making a mark upon] — *Syn.* imprinting, scoring, blazing, stamping, tagging, branding, ticketing, labeling, notching, lettering, initialing, inscribing, impressing, earmarking, signing; see also **sense** 1.

**mark off,** *v.* — *Syn.* segregate, separate, indicate; see **designate** 1, **mark** 2.

**marksman,** *n.* — *Syn.* sharpshooter, sniper, shooter; see **rifleman.**

**mark time,** *v.* — *Syn.* put off, postpone, sit idle, kill time*; see **delay** 1, **wait** 1.

**markup,** *n.* — *Syn.* raise, margin, gross profit; see **increase** 1, **profit** 2.

**mark up,** *v.* — *Syn.* raise the price, adjust, add to; see **increase** 1.

**marmalade,** *n.* — *Syn.* preserves, conserve, apple butter; see **jam** 1, **jelly** 1.

**maroon,** *v.* — *Syn.* desert, isolate, forsake; see **abandon** 2.

**marriage,** *n.* **1.** [The act of marrying] — *Syn.* wedding, espousal, spousal, nuptials, pledging, mating; see also **ceremony** 2, **sacrament.** — *Ant.* DIVORCE, separation, annulment.
**2.** [The state following marriage] — *Syn.* matrimony, conjugality, nuptial tie, nuptial knot, union, match, connubiality, wedlock, wedded state, wedded bliss, holy matrimony. — *Ant.* CHASTITY, bachelorhood, spinsterhood.
**3.** [A close union] — *Syn.* intimacy, compatibility, comradeship, alliance; see **friendship** 1.

**marriageable,** *modif.* — *Syn.* nubile, grown-up, of age, adult; see **mature** 1.

**married,** *modif.* — *Syn.* wedded, mated, espoused, united, given in marriage, joined in holy matrimony, living in the married state, in the state of matrimony; see also **joined.** — *Ant.* SINGLE, unwedded, unmarried.

**marrow,** *n.* — *Syn.* nucleus, kernel, heart; see **essence** 1.

**marry,** *v.* **1.** [To take a spouse] — *Syn.* wed, espouse, enter the matrimonial state, contract matrimony, promise in marriage, pledge in marriage, mate, take a helpmate, lead to the altar, bestow one's hand upon, take the vows, plight one's troth, become one, tie the knot, double up, get hooked, get hitched. — *Ant.* DIVORCE, put away, reject.
**2.** [To join in wedlock] — *Syn.* unite, give, join in matrimony, pronounce man and wife, mate, pair up with, couple, partner; see also **join** 1. — *Ant.* DIVORCE, annul, separate.

**marry off\*,** *v.* — *Syn.* give in marriage, bestow, make a match, find a mate for; see **give** 1.

**marsh,** *n.* — *Syn.* morass, bog, quagmire; see **swamp.**

**marshal,** *n.* **1.** [A high military officer] — *Syn.* provost marshal, field marshal, air marshal; see **officer** 1.
**2.** [A local policeman] — *Syn.* constable, patrolman, deputy; see **officer** 2, **policeman, sheriff.**

**marshal,** *v.* — *Syn.* order, dispose, direct; see **lead** 1.

**marshy,** *modif.* — *Syn.* swampy, boggy, low, wet, spongy, sopping, swamplike, fenny, mucky, low-lying, wetland, moory, plashy, soft, squashy, damp, sloppy, poachy; see also **muddy** 1, 2.

**mart,** *n.* — *Syn.* emporium, mall, bazaar; see **market** 1, **shop, store** 1.

**martial,** *modif.* — *Syn.* military, warlike, soldierly, combative; see **military.**
*See Synonym Study at* MILITARY.

**martinet,** *n.* — *Syn.* taskmaster, disciplinarian, overseer; see **dictator, master** 1.

**martyr,** *n.* — *Syn.* sufferer, offering, scapegoat; see **saint** 2, **victim** 1.

**martyrdom,** *n.* — *Syn.* torment, agony, pain, distress, ordeal, affliction, suffering, devotion, eternal glory, life everlasting; see also **sacrifice** 1, **torture.** — *Ant.* self-gratification, INDULGENCE, worldliness.

**marvel,** *n.* — *Syn.* miracle, phenomenon, curiosity; see **wonder** 2.

**marvel,** *v.* — *Syn.* stare, stand in awe, stare with open mouth; see **wonder** 1.

**marvelous,** *modif.* **1.** [Wonderful] — *Syn.* fabulous, astonishing, spectacular; see **unusual** 1.
**2.** [So unusual as to suggest the supernatural] — *Syn.* miraculous, phenomenal, supernatural; see **unusual** 2.

**marvelously,** *modif.* **1.** [Strangely] — *Syn.* wondrously, magically, unusually; see **strangely.**
**2.** [Excellently] — *Syn.* very well, superbly, admirably; see **excellently.**

**mascot,** *n.* — *Syn.* luck piece, talisman, amulet; see **charm** 2.

**masculine,** *modif.* **1.** [Male] — *Syn.* male, virile, generative, potent; see **male.**
**2.** [Having qualities stereotypically associated with men] — *Syn.* virile, manly, mannish, gentlemanly, strong, vigorous, brawny, muscular, broad-shouldered, powerful, forceful, macho, red-blooded*, two-fisted*; see also **manly.** — *Ant.* feminine, effeminate, unmanly.
*See Synonym Study at* MALE.

**masculinity,** *n.* — *Syn.* virility, power, manliness; see **manhood** 2, **strength** 1.

**mash,** *n.* — *Syn.* mix, brew, bran mash, chicken feed, pulp, paste, dough, batter, pap, emulsion, poultice, sponge, jam, infusion, decoction, *masa* (Mexican); see also **feed, mixture** 1.

**mash,** *v.* — *Syn.* crush, hash, bruise, squash, chew, masticate, macerate, smash, pound, reduce, squeeze, batter in, brew, infuse, decoct, steep, pulverize; see also **grind** 1, **press** 1.

**mashed,** *modif.* — *Syn.* crushed, pressed, brewed, mixed, pulped, pulpy, battered, pounded, smashed, squashed, softened, reduced, spongy, pasty, doughy, hashed, steeped, infused, decocted, pulverized, masticated, chewed, macerated, bruised; see also **limp** 1, **soft** 2. — *Ant.* WHOLE, hard, uncrushed.

**mask,** *n.* **1.** [A disguise] — *Syn.* cover, false face, veil, domino, hood, costume, theater device; see also **camouflage** 1, **disguise.**
**2.** [A protection] — *Syn.* safety mask, safety goggles, safety glasses, gas mask, catcher's mask, fencing mask, fireman's mask, welder's mask, respirator; see also **protection** 2.
**3.** [A masquerade] — *Syn.* revel, party, carnival; see **masquerade.**

**mask,** *v.* — *Syn.* cloak, conceal, veil; see **disguise, hide** 1.

**Mason,** *n.* — *Syn.* Freemason, a member of the Masonic order, Shriner.
Degrees of Masons include: Blue Lodge: First, Entered Apprentice, Second, Fellowcraft, Third, Master Mason, Fifth, Past Master, Twelfth, Knight Templar; *Scottish Rite:* Fourth, Secret Master, Fifth, Perfect Master, Twelfth, Master Architect; Thirty-third Degree.

**mason,** *n.* — *Syn.* bricklayer, brickmason, stonemason, tiler; see **worker.**

**masonry,** *n.* — *Syn.* stone wall, brick wall, mason work, handiwork, artifact; see also **workmanship.**

**masquerade,** *n.* — *Syn.* revel, circus, mask, festivity, mummery, Mardi Gras, masked ball, mask-ball, masking, pretense, imposture; see also **carnival** 1, **dance** 1, **entertainment** 2, **party** 1.

**masquerade,** *v.* — *Syn.* mask, revel, frolic; see **disguise, pretend** 2.

**masquerader,** *n.* — *Syn.* mimic, impostor, pretender, imitator, sham, performer, mummer, domino, poseur; see also **actor** 1, **dancer.**

**mass,** *n.* **1.** [A body of matter] — *Syn.* lump, bulk, piece, portion, section, batch, block, hunk, chunk, wad, gob, body, core, clot, coagulation, tumor, concretion; see also **hunk.**
**2.** [A considerable quantity] — *Syn.* heap, volume, crowd; see **quantity, size** 2.
**3.** [The greater portion] — *Syn.* majority, plurality; see **bulk** 2.
**4.** [Size] — *Syn.* magnitude, bulk, expanse, massiveness; see **bulk** 1, **extent, size** 2.
*See Synonym Study at* BULK.
**in the mass** — *Syn.* en masse, as a whole, collectively; see **gathered.**

**Mass,** *n.* — *Syn.* Eucharist, Lord's Supper, Holy Communion, Eucharistic rite, Liturgy, observance, form; see also **celebration** 3, **worship** 1.
Types of Masses include — High, Low, Solemn High, Requiem, Mass for the Dead, Nuptial, Votive.
Parts of the Mass include: *Gathering Rites:* Greeting, Penitential Rite, Gloria, Opening Prayer; *Liturgy of the Word:* First Reading, Responsorial Psalm, Second Reading, Alleluia, Gospel, Homily, Profession of Faith, Creed, Prayers of the Faithful, Petitions; *Liturgy of the Eucharist:* Preparation and Offering of the Gifts, Prayer Over the Gifts, Consecration, Eucharistic Prayer, Memorial, Acclamation, Lord's Prayer, Sign of Peace, Breaking of the Bread, Communion, Prayer after Communion; *Concluding Rites:* Blessing, Dismissal.

**massacre,** *n.* — *Syn.* butchering, killing, slaughter; see **carnage, murder.**
*See Synonym Study at* SLAUGHTER.

**massacre,** *v.* — *Syn.* exterminate, decimate, annihilate; see **depopulate, kill** 1.

**massage,** *v.* — *Syn.* rub down, caress, stroke, press; see **knead, rub** 1.

**massed,** *modif.* — *Syn.* collected, assembled, brought together; see **jammed** 2, **gathered.**

**masses,** *n.* — *Syn.* proletariat, the rank and file, common folk, *hoi polloi* (Greek); see **people** 3.

**massive,** *modif.* — *Syn.* huge, heavy, bulky, cumbersome; see **extensive, large** 1.
*See Synonym Study at* HEAVY.

**mass media,** *n.* — *Syn.* news media, audio-visual media, press and radio; see **broadcasting, magazine** 2, **newspaper, radio** 1, 2, **television.**

**mass meeting,** *n.* — *Syn.* public meeting, open meeting, assemblage, group; see **gathering.**

**mass production,** *n.* — *Syn.* mass producing, assembly-line methods, automation, automated production; see **manufacturing, production** 1.

**mast,** *n.* — *Syn.* spar, pole, post, timber, trunk, Maypole, flagstaff; see also **column** 1.
Masts include: mainmast, foremast, mizzen, mizzenmast, topmast, topgallant mast, lower mast, jurymast, jigger.

**master,** *modif.* — *Syn.* leading, supreme, main; see **excellent, major** 1, **principal.**

**master,** *n.* **1.** [One who directs others] — *Syn.* chief, leader, governor, ruler, director, lord, overseer, supervisor, superintendent, boss, lord and master*, honcho, sachem, judge, patriarch, chieftain, commander, commandant; see also **administrator.** — *Ant.* SERVANT, underling, subject.

**2.** [A teacher] — *Syn.* instructor, preceptor, mentor; see **teacher** 1.

**3.** [One who possesses great skill] — *Syn.* genius, maestro, savant, sage, scientist, past master, champion, prima donna, virtuoso, protagonist, connoisseur, academician, pundit, fellow, doctor, boss*; see also **artist** 1, 2, **scholar** 2. — *Ant.* DISCIPLE, beginner, novice.

**4.** [A supreme being, especially Christ] — *Syn.* supreme being, Christ, Messiah; see **god** 1, 2, 3.

**5.** [The source of copies] — *Syn.* original, control, file copy; see **copy.**

**master,** *v.* **1.** [To conquer] — *Syn.* subdue, rule, vanquish; see **defeat** 1.

**2.** [To become proficient in] — *Syn.* gain mastery in, understand, comprehend; see **learn** 1, **study** 1.

**masterful,** *modif.* — *Syn.* commanding, imperious, domineering, magisterial, forceful, dominating, dictatorial, high-handed, self-willed, strong-willed, powerful, authoritative, authoritarian, bossy*; see also **autocratic** 1, **tyrannical.**

---

**SYN.** — **masterful** implies such strength of personality as enables one to impose one's will on others *[a masterful orchestral conductor]*; **domineering** implies the overbearing, tyrannical manner of one who openly tries to dominate another *[a domineering spouse]*; **imperious** suggests the arbitrary ruling of an emperor, and connotes more haughtiness than **domineering** *[the imperious old dean of the college]*; **magisterial,** while not suggesting an assumption of arbitrary powers, implies an excessive use or display of such inherent powers as a magistrate might have *[he dismissed me with a magisterial air]*

---

**masterly,** *modif.* — *Syn.* superior, skillful, superb; see **excellent.**

**mastermind,** *n.* — *Syn.* leader, expert, genius, originator; see **artist** 1, 2, **author** 1, **doctor, philosopher.**

**mastermind,** *v.* — *Syn.* direct, supervise, engineer; see **manage** 1.

**master of ceremonies,** *n.* — *Syn.* chairman, presiding officer, emcee; see **speaker** 3.

**masterpiece,** *n.* — *Syn.* masterwork, *magnum opus* (Latin), *chef d'oeuvre, coup de maître, pièce de résistance* (*all* French), classic, work of art, prize, gem, jewel, showpiece, treasure.

**mastership,** *n.* — *Syn.* control, command, authority; see **leadership** 1, **power** 2.

**master stroke,** *n.* — *Syn.* conquest, advantage, achievement; see **triumph** 1, **victory** 1, 2.

**mastery,** *n.* **1.** [Control] — *Syn.* dominance, sovereignty, government, hegemony; see **command** 2, **power** 2.

**2.** [Ability to use to the full] — *Syn.* power, influence, force, backing, skill, cunning, adroitness, capacity, knowledge, expertness, proficiency, genius, adeptness; see also **ability** 2, **education** 1.

**masticate,** *v.* — *Syn.* gnaw, nibble, chew up; see **bite** 1, **chew, eat** 1.

**mastication,** *n.* — *Syn.* rumination, chewing, deglutition, Fletcherizing, Fletcherism; see also **bite** 1, **digestion.**

**mat,** *n.* — *Syn.* covering, floor covering, doormat, table runner, doily, place mat, landing mat, boat fender, network, table mat, place setting, intertexture, web, mesh, wattle, woven fabric, cloth, straw mat; see also **cover** 1, **rug, tablecloth.**

**mat,** *v.* — *Syn.* plait, twine, felt, entwine, braid, tangle, snarl, entangle, dishevel; see also **twist, weave** 1.

**matador,** *n.* — *Syn.* bullfighter, toreador, torero, picador, tauromachist, killer of bulls; see also **contestant, fighter** 1.

**match,** *n.* **1.** [An instrument to produce fire] — *Syn.* safety match, sulphur match, matchstick, fuse, lucifer, locofoco*; see also **light** 3.

**2.** [An article that is like another] — *Syn.* peer, equivalent, mate, analogue, counterpart, approximation; see also **equal.**

**3.** [A formal contest] — *Syn.* race, event, rivalry; see **competition** 2, **sport** 3.

**4.** [A marriage or engagement] — *Syn.* mating, union, espousal; see **marriage** 2.

**match,** *v.* **1.** [To find or make equals] — *Syn.* equalize, liken, equate, make equal, pair, coordinate, level, even, match up, balance, mate, marry, unite; see also **equal.**

**2.** [To be alike] — *Syn.* harmonize, suit, be twins, be counterparts, be doubles, match with, check with, go together, go with, rhyme with, take after; see also **agree, resemble.** — *Ant.* DIFFER, be unlike, clash.

**3.** [To meet in contest] — *Syn.* equal, keep pace with, run side by side, come up with, be on a level with, cope with, meet, compete with; see also **rival.**

**matched,** *modif.* — *Syn.* doubled, similar, equated, evened, coordinated, harmonized, paired, mated; see also **alike** 1, **balanced** 1. — *Ant.* UNLIKE, unequal, DIFFERENT.

**matching,** *modif.* — *Syn.* comparable, analogous, parallel; see **equal.**

**matchless,** *modif.* — *Syn.* incomparable, unparalleled, unequaled; see **excellent, perfect** 2, **superior.**

**matchmaker,** *n.* — *Syn.* arranger, go-between, agent; see **Cupid.**

**mate,** *n.* **1.** [One of a pair] — *Syn.* complement, analog, counterpart; see **match** 2.

**2.** [A companion] — *Syn.* partner, comrade, schoolfellow, stable companion, helpmate, playmate, classmate, buddy*, pal*, chum*, roomie*; see also **friend** 1.

**3.** [A marriage partner] — *Syn.* spouse, bride, groom, bedmate, the old man*, the old lady*; see also **husband, wife.**

**4.** [A naval officer] — *Syn.* warrant officer, skipper, petty officer, next in command to a captain, first mate, second mate, third mate, boatswain's mate; see also **officer** 3.

**material,** *modif.* **1.** [Composed of matter] — *Syn.* physical, tangible, palpable, corporeal; see **physical** 1, **real** 2, **tangible.**

**2.** [Large in quantity] — *Syn.* considerable, substantial, notable; see **appreciable, much** 2.

*See Synonym Study at* PHYSICAL.

**material,** *n.* **1.** [Matter] — *Syn.* body, corporeality, substance; see **element** 2, **matter** 1.

**2.** [Unfinished matter; *often plural*] — *Syn.* raw material, stuff, stock, staple, ore, stockpile, crop, supply, accumulation; see also **alloy, cloth, cotton, element, linen, metal, mineral, plastic, rock** 1, **rubber, wool** 1, 2.

**materialist,** *n.* — *Syn.* realist, self-seeker, capitalist; see **opportunist.**

**materialistic,** *modif.* — *Syn.* mundane, carnal, earthly-minded, object-oriented, possessive, acquisitive, capitalistic, unspiritual, secular, earthy, material; see also **greedy** 1, **worldly** 1. — *Ant.* IMPRACTICAL, spiritual, ascetic.

**materialize,** *v.* **1.** [To become matter] — *Syn.* be realized, form, take on form, take form, become real, actualize, reify, become embodied, be incarnate, coalesce, become concrete, metamorphose, reintegrate;

see also **form** 4.— *Ant.* DISSOLVE, DISINTEGRATE, disperse.

**2.** [To develop] — *Syn.* unfold, emerge, evolve; see **develop** 3, **grow** 2.

**materially,** *modif.* **1.** [Concerning matter] — *Syn.* physically, corporeally, bodily, really, objectively, substantially, sensibly, actually, tangibly, palpably, ponderably, mundanely; see also **physically.** — *Ant.* unsubstantially, slightly, immaterially.

**2.** [To a considerable degree] — *Syn.* markedly, notably, substantially; see **very.**

**materiel,** *n.* — *Syn.* machinery, implements, war equipment; see **equipment.**

**maternal,** *modif.* — *Syn.* parental, sympathetic, protective; see **motherly.**

**maternity,** *n.* — *Syn.* parenthood, mothership, motherliness; see **motherhood.**

**mathematical,** *modif.* **1.** [Concerning mathematics] — *Syn.* arithmetical, numerical, computative, measurable, geometrical, scientific; see also **analytical** 2.

**2.** [Exact] — *Syn.* precise, verified, substantiated; see **accurate** 2.

**mathematics,** *n.* — *Syn.* science of numbers, language of numbers, computation, reckoning, calculation, correlation and deduction of numbers, new math, math; see also **arithmetic, science** 1.

Branches of mathematics include: arithmetic, algebra, geometry, trigonometry, trig\*, calculus, calc\*, statistics, topology, geodesy, Fourier analysis, game theory, set theory, number theory, systems analysis, quadratics.

Commonly used mathematical terms include: number, fraction, symbol, equation, function, variable, constant, average, mean, median, mode, locus, graph, formula, square, square root, volume, cube, curve, circle, sector, segment, derivative, cube root, sine, cosine, secant, cosecant, tangent, cotangent, progression, parabola, hyperbola, ellipse, theorem, hypothesis, algorithm, logarithm, log, vector, dividend, quotient, sum, difference, product.

**matinee,** *n.* — *Syn.* afternoon performance, early show, play, show; see **entertainment** 2, **movie.**

**matriarch,** *n.* — *Syn.* female ruler, dowager, matron, materfamilias, head of the family, ancestress; see also **ancestor, queen.**

**matriculate,** *v.* — *Syn.* sign up for, enroll, enter; see **join** 2, **register** 4.

**matriculation,** *n.* **1.** [Registration] — *Syn.* entry, registering, enlisting; see **enrollment** 1, **registration** 1.

**2.** [Instruction] — *Syn.* practice, drill, preparation; see **education** 3, **training.**

**matrimonial,** *modif.* — *Syn.* conjugal, connubial, hymeneal, wedded, spousal, engaged, espoused, bridal, betrothed, nuptial, marital.

**matrimony,** *n.* — *Syn.* conjugality, wedlock, union; see **marriage** 2.

**matrix,** *n.* — *Syn.* form, cast, pattern; see **model** 2, **mold** 1.

**matron,** *n.* **1.** [A woman in a supervisory position] — *Syn.* housekeeper, superintendent, housemother; see **administrator.**

**2.** [An older married woman] — *Syn.* dame, lady, dowager, wife, mother, matriarch; see also **woman** 1.

**matronly,** *modif.* — *Syn.* middle-aged, wifely, grave, sedate, womanly, ladylike; see also **mature** 1, **motherly.** — *Ant.* INEXPERIENCED, immature, girlish.

**matted,** *modif.* — *Syn.* snarled, rumpled, disordered; see **tangled, twisted** 1.

**matter,** *n.* **1.** [Substance] — *Syn.* body, material, substantiality, corporeality, corporeity, protoplasm, con-

stituents, stuff, materialness, object, thing, physical world; see also **element** 2.— *Ant.* NOTHING, nihility, immateriality.

**2.** [Difficulty] — *Syn.* trouble, distress, perplexity; see **difficulty** 2.

**3.** [Subject] — *Syn.* interest, focus, resolution; see **subject** 1, **theme** 1, **topic.**

**4.** [An affair] — *Syn.* undertaking, circumstance, concern; see **affair** 1.

**5.** [Pus] — *Syn.* suppuration, maturation, discharge, purulence, ulceration, infection; see also **sore.**

**as a matter of fact**— *Syn.* in fact, in actuality, truly; see **really** 1.

**for that matter**— *Syn.* in regard to that, as far as that is concerned, concerning that; see **and.**

**no matter**— *Syn.* it doesn't matter, it is of no concern, regardless of; see **regardless** 2.

**matter,** *v.* **1.** [To be of importance] — *Syn.* value, carry weight, weigh, signify, be substantive, be important, have influence, import, imply, denote, express, be of consequence, involve, be worthy of notice; see also **mean** 1.

**2.** [To form or discharge pus] — *Syn.* suppurate, come to a head, fester; see **decay.**

**matter-of-course,** *modif.* — *Syn.* routine, usual, ordinary; see **natural** 1, 2, **regular** 3.

**matter of course,** *n.* — *Syn.* expected result, anticipated result, routine event, routine happening, the usual thing; see also **event** 1, **result.**

**matter-of-fact,** *modif.* — *Syn.* objective, prosaic, feasible; see **practical.**

**Matthew,** *n.* — *Syn.* Levi the tax-gatherer, apostle, first Gospel; see **disciple, saint** 2.

**matting,** *n.* — *Syn.* floor covering, door mat, drugget, table covering, tatami, fiber mat; see also **cover** 1, **mat, rug.**

**mattock,** *n.* — *Syn.* pick, hoe, hatchet; see **ax, tool** 1.

**mattress,** *n.* — *Syn.* pallet, innerspring, springs, box spring, bedding, cushion, futon; see also **bed** 1.

**mature,** *modif.* **1.** [Adult] — *Syn.* adult, full-grown, middle-aged, prime, grown, grown-up, of age, in full bloom, full-fledged, in one's prime, womanly, manly, matronly, older, developed, prepared, settled, sedate, experienced, seasoned, knowledgeable, sophisticated; see also **experienced, matured, ripe** 2.— *Ant.* juvenile, YOUNG, immature.

**2.** [Ripe] — *Syn.* ready, seasoned, perfected; see **mellow** 1, **ripe** 1, 2.

**3.** [Considered] — *Syn.* thought about, reasoned, seasoned; see **considered** 1, **thoughtful** 1.

*See Synonym Study at* RIPE.

**mature,** *v.* **1.** [To come to maturity] — *Syn.* grow up, become a man, become a woman, come of age, reach adulthood, become experienced, settle down, become full-blown, ripen into, ripen, reach perfection, become prime, attain majority, culminate, become wise, become perfected, grow skilled, fill out; see also **age** 1, **develop** 1.

**2.** [To grow] — *Syn.* ripen, mellow, evolve; see **grow** 2.

**matured,** *modif.* — *Syn.* ripened, grown, full-grown, mellowed, aged, middle-aged, developed, prime, advanced, full-blown, perfected, prepared, consummated, evolved, reasoned, considered, complete, cured, culminated, cultivated, cultured, at a high peak, brought to perfection, reached its goal, manly, womanly, sophisticated, experienced; see also **finished.** — *Ant.* YOUNG, CHILDISH, adolescent.

**maturing,** *modif.* — *Syn.* ripening, growing, sweetening, mellowing, developing, near prime, growing up, approaching middle age, nearing the meridian, moving, stirring, advancing, preparing, evolving, perfecting, consummating; see also **increasing** 1.— *Ant.* DYING, fading, declining.

**maturity,** *n.* **1.** [Mental competence]— *Syn.* development, sophistication, cultivation, culture, civilization, advancement, mental power, mentality, capability; see also **ability** 1, 2.— *Ant.* immaturity, childishness, adolescence.
**2.** [Physical development]— *Syn.* prime of life, post-pubescence, adulthood; see **majority** 2.
**3.** [Ripeness]— *Syn.* readiness, mellowness, fitness, full growth, sweetness; see also **development** 2.

**maudlin,** *modif.*— *Syn.* mawkish, romantic, mushy*, teary*, weepy*, weak, insipid, gushing; see also **emotional** 2, **sentimental.**

**maul,** *n.*— *Syn.* mallet, club, sledge; see **hammer, tool** 1.

**maul,** *v.*— *Syn.* mangle, manhandle, batter, rough up; see **beat** 2, **hurt** 1, **paw** 3.
*See Synonym Study at* BEAT.

**mauling,** *n.*— *Syn.* clubbing, whipping, beating, manhandling, drubbing, thrashing, threshing, pummeling, thumping, pounding, strapping, ill-treatment, flogging, licking, trouncing, chastisement, caning, rawhiding; see also **defeat** 3.

**maunder,** *v.* **1.** [To digress]— *Syn.* drift, stray, wander; see **deviate, ramble** 2.
**2.** [To mumble]— *Syn.* mutter, mouth, drivel; see **mumble.**

**mausoleum,** *n.*— *Syn.* crypt, catacomb, tomb, sepulcher; see **grave** 1, **memorial, monument** 1.

**mauve,** *modif.*— *Syn.* violet, lavender, lilac; see **purple.**

**maverick,** *modif.*— *Syn.* in opposition, in revolt, contentious, aberrant, nonconformist; see also **quarrelsome** 1, **radical** 2, **unusual** 2.

**maverick,** *n.* **1.** [Calf]— *Syn.* unbranded calf, yearling, renegade calf; see **animal** 2, **calf.**
**2.** [Nonconformist]— *Syn.* dissenter, malcontent, extremist; see **nonconformist, radical.**

**maw,** *n.*— *Syn.* gorge, craw, gullet, jaws, mouth; see also **throat.**

**mawkish,** *modif.*— *Syn.* tasteless, nauseating, garish; see **emotional** 2, **sentimental.**

**maxim,** *n.*— *Syn.* aphorism, adage, saying, epithet; see **proverb, saying.**
*See Synonym Study at* SAYING.

**maximum,** *modif.*— *Syn.* supreme, highest, most, greatest; see **best** 1.

**maximum,** *n.*— *Syn.* supremacy, height, pinnacle, preeminence, culmination, matchlessness, preponderance, apex, acme, zenith, peak, greatest number, highest degree, summit, nonpareil; see also **climax.**— *Ant.* MINIMUM, foot, bottom.

**May,** *n.*— *Syn.* spring month, opening of the fishing season, garden month, fifth month; see **month, spring** 2.

**may,** *v.* **1.** [Grant permission]— *Syn.* be permitted, be allowed, can, be privileged to, be authorized, be at liberty to.
**2.** [Concede possibility]— *Syn.* will, shall, be going to, should, be conceivable, be possible, be credible, be practicable, be within reach, be obtainable; see also **will** 3.

**Mayan,** *modif.*— *Syn.* Maya, pre-Columbian, Yucatan; see **Indian** 1.

**maybe,** *modif.*— *Syn.* perhaps, possibly, can be, might be, could be, maybe so, mayhap, as it may be, conceivable, credible, feasible, obtainable, wind and weather permitting, in the cards*, God willing.— *Ant.* HARDLY, scarcely, probably not.

**mayflower,** *n.*— *Syn.* hawthorn, marsh marigold, hepatica, anemone, spring beauty, trailing arbutus, May apple, greater stitchwort, cuckooflower; see also **flower** 1, **plant.**

**mayhem,** *n.*— *Syn.* maiming, mutilating, dismembering, dismemberment, injury, great bodily injury, disfiguring, crippling, *immedicable vulnus* (Latin), deforming, deformation, violence, destruction; see also **crime** 2.

**mayor,** *n.*— *Syn.* magistrate, Lord Mayor, borough president, prefect, burgomaster, chairman of a city council, president of a city council, civil administrator, civil judge, *maire* (French), *Burgermeister* (German), city father*; see also **administrator.**

**maze,** *n.*— *Syn.* tangle, entanglement, twist, labyrinth, winding, convolution, intricacy, confusion, meandering, torsion, puzzle; see also **network** 1.— *Ant.* ORDER, disentanglement, simplicity.

**meadow,** *n.*— *Syn.* grass, pasture, mead, lea, mountain meadow, upland pasture, alp, meadow land, bottom land, bottoms, grassland, pasturage, salt marsh, polder, veldt, high veldt, sweet veldt, sour veldt, bush-veldt, steppe, *Heide* (German), heath, *champ* (French), pampas, llano, savanna; see also **field** 1, **plain.**

**meager,** *modif.* **1.** [Thin]— *Syn.* lank, lanky, gaunt, starved, emaciated, lean, bony, slender, slim, spare, little, sparing, bare, scant, stinted, lacking, wanting, niggard, scraggy, scrawny, withered, wandlike, willowlike, willowy, lithe, narrow, tenuous, slightly-made, skinny, weedy*, peaked; see also **thin** 2, 4.— *Ant.* FAT, plump, stout.
**2.** [Scanty]— *Syn.* scanty, short, deficient, insufficient; see **inadequate** 1, **scanty, wanting.**
*See Synonym Study at* SCANTY.

**meagerly,** *modif.*— *Syn.* scantily, skimpily, not much; see **inadequately.**

**meagerness,** *n.* **1.** [Lack]— *Syn.* scarcity, aridity, need; see **lack** 1, **poverty** 2.
**2.** [Dullness]— *Syn.* flatness, tedium, sameness; see **boredom, dullness** 1, **monotony** 1, **slowness** 1.

**meal,** *n.* **1.** [Ground feed]— *Syn.* bran, farina, grits, groats, fodder, provender, forage; see also **feed, flour, grain** 1.
Types of meal include: cornmeal, grits, corn grits, hominy grits, corn starch, corn gluten, barley meal, oatmeal, wheat meal, linseed meal, soybean meal, soybean flour, cottonseed meal, bonemeal, tankage, alum meal.
**2.** [The quantity of food taken at one time]— *Syn.* repast, feast, refreshment, refection, collation, mess*, feed bag*, feed, eats*, grub*, bag*, chow*, spread*, stand-up*, square meal*, munchies*, carry-out*, snack*, blowout*, grubfest*.
Meals include: banquet, brunch, snack, tea, high tea, picnic, luncheon, dessert, supper; see also **breakfast, dinner, lunch.**

**mealy,** *modif.*— *Syn.* powdery, friable, crumbly; see **gritty.**

**mealy-mouthed,** *modif.*— *Syn.* pretentious, insincere, equivocal, disingenuous; see **affected** 2, **euphemistic, hypocritical.**

**mean,** *modif.* **1.** [Small-minded]— *Syn.* base, ignoble, low, small-minded, petty, contemptible, degrading, sordid, mean-spirited, dishonorable, discreditable, unworthy, selfish, debased, degraded, ignominious, shabby, scurvy, crummy*, lowdown*.
**2.** [Of low estate]— *Syn.* abject, pitiful, shabby; see **humble** 2.
**3.** [Vicious]— *Syn.* spiteful, vicious, malicious, cruel, unkind, nasty, offensive, vile, shameless, dishonorable, malign, evil, infamous, treacherous, sneaking, crooked,

fraudulent, unscrupulous, deceitful, villainous, black-guard, faithless, ill-tempered, bad-tempered, cantanker-ous, ornery*, disagreeable, unaccommodating, despicable, odious, scurrilous, perfidious, knavish, rotten*, hard as nails*.

**4.** [Stingy] — *Syn.* miserly, niggardly, rapacious; see **greedy** 1, **stingy.**

**5.** [Average] — *Syn.* mediocre, middling, halfway; see **common** 1, **conventional** 1, **popular** 3, **traditional** 2.

---

*SYN.* — **mean** suggests a contemptible pettiness or un-kindness of character or conduct /his *mean* attempts to slander her/; **base** implies a dishonorable putting of one's own interests ahead of one's obligations, as because of greed or cowardice /*base* motives/; **ignoble** suggests a lack of high moral or intellectual qualities /to work for an *ignoble* end/; **abject** implies debasement and a contemptible lack of self-respect /an *abject* coward/; **sordid** connotes the depressing drabness of that which is mean or base /the *sordid* details of their affair/; **vile** suggests disgusting foulness or depravity /*vile* epithets/; **low** suggests rather generally coarseness, vulgarity, de-pravity, etc., specif. in reference to taking grossly unfair advantage /so *low* as to steal from one's own mother/; **degrading** suggests a lowering or corruption of moral standards or a lowering of self-respect or dignity /the *degrading* aspects of prison life/

---

**mean,** *n.* — *Syn.* average, middle, median, midpoint; see **average, center** 1.
*See Synonym Study at* AVERAGE.

**mean,** *v.* **1.** [To have as meaning] — *Syn.* indicate, spell, denote, signify, betoken, import, add up, determine, symbolize, imply, involve, allude, speak of, touch on, stand for, drive at, point to, connote, suggest, express, designate, intimate, tell the meaning of, purport.

**2.** [To have in mind] — *Syn.* anticipate, propose, ex-pect; see **intend** 1.

**3.** [To design for] — *Syn.* destine for, aim at, set apart; see **intend** 2.
*See Synonym Study at* INTEND.

**meander,** *v.* **1.** [To turn] — *Syn.* recoil, change, twine; see **turn** 2, **wind** 3.

**2.** [To wander] — *Syn.* twist and turn, roam, drift; see **ramble** 3, **walk** 1.

**meandering,** *modif.* — *Syn.* rambling, nomadic, circu-lar; see **travelling** 2, **wandering** 1.

**meanie*,** *n.* — *Syn.* brute, bully, tyrant, mean person, cruel person, nasty person; see also **beast** 2, **rascal.**

**meaning,** *n.* — *Syn.* sense, denotation, import, purport, purpose, definition, object, implication, application, in-tent, suggestion, connotation, symbolization, aim, drift, significance, essence, worth, intrinsic value, interest. — *Ant.* NONSENSE, aimlessness, absurdity.

**meaningful,** *modif.* — *Syn.* significant, exact, essential; see **important** 1.

**meaningless,** *modif.* — *Syn.* vague, absurd, insignifi-cant; see **trivial, unimportant.**

**meanly,** *modif.* — *Syn.* niggardly, meagerly, miserly; see **selfishly.**

**meanness,** *n.* **1.** [The quality of being mean] — *Syn.* smallmindedness, baseness, lowness, pettiness, wicked-ness, debasement, degradation, abjection, shameless-ness, infamy, degeneracy, blackguardism, knavishness, unscrupulousness, stinginess, closeness, niggardliness, frugality, churlishness, corruptness, cupidity, sordid-ness, contemptibleness, disrepute, rapacity, malice, in-iquity, malignity, unworthiness, ill-temper, unkindness,

covetousness, avarice, miserliness, parsimony; see also **greed.** — *Ant.* GENEROSITY, nobility, worthiness.

**2.** [A mean action] — *Syn.* belittling, defaming, groveling, cheating, sneaking, quarreling, scolding, ta-king advantage of, deceiving, coveting, grudging, grasp-ing, dishonoring, defrauding, perjuring, shaming, de-grading, beggaring, stealing.

**means,** *n.* **1.** [An instrumentality or instrumentalities] — *Syn.* machinery, mechanism, agency, organ, channel, medium, factor, agent, auspices, power, organization; see also **method** 2, **system** 2.

**2.** [Wealth] — *Syn.* resources, substance, property; see **wealth** 2.

**by all means** — *Syn.* of course, certainly, yes indeed; see **surely, yes.**

**by any means** — *Syn.* in any way, at all, somehow; see **anyhow** 2.

**by means of** — *Syn.* with the aid of, somehow, through; see **by** 2.

**by no (manner of) means** — *Syn.* in no way, not pos-sible, not, definitely not; see **never, no.**

**mean-spirited,** *modif.* — *Syn.* base, timid, servile; see **cowardly, mean** 1, **weak** 3.

**meanwhile,** *modif.* — *Syn.* meantime, during the inter-val, in the interim, ad interim, for the time being, un-til, till, up to, in the meantime, when; see also **during, while** 1.

**measurable,** *modif.* **1.** [Estimable] — *Syn.* weighable, fathomable, assessable; see **calculable.**

**2.** [Limited] — *Syn.* moderate, proscribed, measured; see **restricted.**

**measure,** *n.* **1.** [A unit of measurement] — *Syn.* dimen-sion, capacity, weight, volume, distance, degree, quan-tity, area, mass, frequency, density, viscosity, intensity, rapidity, speed, caliber, bulk, sum, duration, magni-tude, amplitude, size, pitch, ratio, depth, scope, height, strength, breadth, amplification.
Commonly used units of measure include— *linear:* inch, foot, yard, rod, mile (U.S. Customary system); millimeter, centimeter, decimeter, meter, kilometer (metric system); *volume:* fluid dram, fluid ounce, gill, pint, quart, gallon (U.S. Customary system); milliliter, centiliter, deciliter, liter, kiloliter (metric system); *weight:* dram, ounce, pound (U.S. Customary system); milligram, centigram, decigram, gram, kilogram (metric system).
Units of measure and their abbreviations commonly used in medicine include: Celsius (C), cubic centimeter (cc), dram (dr), drop (gt), drops (gtt), Fahrenheit (F), fluid dram (fl dr), fluid ounce (fl oz), foot (ft), gram (gm), grain (gr), hour (hr), kilogram (kg), microgram (mcg), milligram (mg), milliliter (ml), millimeter (mm), minute (min), ounce (oz), pint (O), pound (lb), unit (U).

**2.** [Anything used as a standard] — *Syn.* rule, test, trial, example, standard, gauge, benchmark, touchstone, yardstick, norm, canon, pattern, type, model; see also **criterion.**

**3.** [A beat] — *Syn.* rhythm, tempo, time, step, throb, stroke, accent, meter, cadence, tune, melody, stress, vi-bration, division; see also **beat** 3.

**4.** [A bill] — *Syn.* project, proposition, proposal; see **bill** 3.

**5.** [A preventive or counteractive action] — *Syn.* agency, device, stratagem; see **action** 2, **means** 1.

**beyond** (*or* **above**) **measure** — *Syn.* immeasurably, exceedingly, extremely; see **much** 1, 2.

**for good measure** — *Syn.* added, as a bonus, addition-ally; see **extra.**

**in a measure**— *Syn.* to some extent, somewhat, in a way; see **rather**.

**made to measure**— *Syn.* suited, custom-made, made to order; see **tailored**.

**take measures**— *Syn.* take action, do things to accomplish a purpose, employ; see **act** 1.

**take someone's measure***— *Syn.* measure, judge, weigh; see **estimate** 1, 2.

**measure,** *v.* **1.** [To apply a standard of measurement] — *Syn.* rule, weigh, mark, lay off, lay out, grade, graduate, gauge, sound, pitch, beat, stroke, time, mete, mark off, pace off, plumb, scale, rank, even, level, gradate, shade, blend, rhyme, line, align, line out, regulate, portion, set a criterion, set a standard, average, equate, encircle, square, calibrate, block in, survey, telemeter, map; see also **estimate** 1, 2.

**2.** [To contain by measurement]— *Syn.* hold, cover, contain; see **include** 1.

**measured,** *modif.* **1.** [Steady] — *Syn.* steady, systematic, deliberate; see **regular** 3.

**2.** [Moderate] — *Syn.* limited, restrained, confined; see **restricted**.

**3.** [Determined] — *Syn.* checked, evaluated, calculated; see **determined** 1.

**measure for measure,** *n.* — *Syn.* retaliation, vengeance, repayment; see **revenge** 1.

**measureless,** *modif.* — *Syn.* bottomless, immense, indefinite; see **endless** 1, **infinite** 1, **unlimited**.

**measurement,** *n.* **1.** [The act of measuring] — *Syn.* estimation, determination, analysis, computation; see **judgment** 2.

**2.** [The result of measuring] — *Syn.* distance, dimension, weight, degree, pitch, time, height, width, depth, density, volume, area, length, measure, thickness, quantity, magnitude, extent, range, altitude, scope, reach, amount, capacity, frequency, viscosity, intensity, pressure, speed, acceleration, rapidity, caliber, hardness, grade, span, step, calibration, strength, mass; see also **size** 2.

**3.** [A set of measures] — *Syn.* inch, foot, yard; see **measure** 1.

**measure off,** *v.* — *Syn.* mark out, limit, determine boundaries, set up boundaries; see **divide** 1, **mark** 1.

**measure out,** *v.* — *Syn.* allot, deal, apportion; see **distribute** 1.

**measuring,** *n.* — *Syn.* weighing, grading, gauging, graduating, scaling, calibrating, rhyming, aligning, blending, leveling, mapping, squaring, surveying, shading, averaging, spanning, stepping off, cruising, checking, calculating.

**meat,** *n.* **1.** [Animal flesh] — *Syn.* food, flesh, veal, mutton, lamb, chicken, turkey, goose, duck, rabbit, venison, goat's meat, horsemeat; see also **beef** 1, **pork**.

Cuts and types of meat include: roast, cutlet, steak, filet, leg, shoulder, loin, sirloin, tenderloin, rib, short rib, round, rump, chuck, brisket, plate, skirt, shank, flank, chop; liver, brains, kidneys, heart, bacon, ham, tripe, oxtail, sausage, frankfurter, hamburger; ground, chipped, dried, jerked, salt, pickled.

Grades of meats include: prime, choice, select, standard, commercial, utility.

**2.** [Substance] — *Syn.* gist, heart of the matter, import, meaning, crux, content.

**meaty,** *modif.* **1.** [Full of substance] — *Syn.* fat, tough, sinewy; see **lean** 2.

**2.** [Full of content] — *Syn.* significant, factual, weighty; see **important** 1.

**mechanic,** *n.* — *Syn.* machinist, skilled workman, technician, repairman, grease monkey*; see also **worker**.

Kinds of mechanics include: auto mechanic, fender and body man, metalworker, aircraft mechanic, welder, machinist, tool-and-die cutter, bolt-cutter, lathe operator.

**mechanical,** *modif.* **1.** [Concerning machinery] — *Syn.* engineering, production, manufacturing, tooling, tuning, implementing, fabricating, fabrication, forging, machining, building, construction, constructing.

**2.** [Like a machine] — *Syn.* habitual, routine, automatic, unthinking, made to a pattern, machinelike, stereotyped, standardized, without variation, fixed, unchanging, monotonous. — *Ant.* ORIGINAL, varied, CHANGING.

**3.** [Operated by the use of machinery] — *Syn.* power-driven, involuntary, programmed; see **automated, automatic**.

**mechanically,** *modif.* — *Syn.* automatically, unreasoningly, unchangeably; see **regularly** 1.

**mechanics,** *n.* **1.** [Theory of motion and work] — *Syn.* kinetics, aeromechanics, pure mechanics, rational mechanics, machine technology, technical details; see also **physics, science** 1.

**2.** [Mechanical details] — *Syn.* logistics, workings, procedures, nitty-gritty*, nuts and bolts*.

**mechanism,** *n.* — *Syn.* working parts, mechanical action, system of parts; see **device** 1, **tool** 1.

**mechanistic,** *modif.* — *Syn.* monotonous, Godless, inhuman; see **arbitrary** 2, **automatic** 2, **mechanical** 2, **ruthless** 1, 2.

**mechanization,** *n.* — *Syn.* automation, industrialization, trade; see **business** 4.

**mechanize,** *v.* — *Syn.* equip, computerize, industrialize, motorize, automate, put on the assembly line, make mechanical, introduce machinery into.

**medal,** *n.* — *Syn.* reward, commemoration, badge; see **decoration** 3.

**medallion,** *n.* — *Syn.* ornament, emblem, necklace; see **jewelry**.

**meddle,** *v.* **1.** [To interfere in others' affairs] — *Syn.* intermeddle, interpose, interfere, obtrude, interlope, intervene, pry, snoop, impose oneself, infringe, break in upon, advance upon, make it one's business, abuse one's rights, push in, chime in, force an entrance, encroach, intrude, be officious, obstruct, impede, hinder, encumber, busy oneself with, come uninvited, tamper with, inquire, be curious, stick one's nose in*, crash the gates*, monkey with*, bust in*, muscle in*, barge in*, worm in*, have a finger in*, fool with*, butt in*, horn in*; see also **interrupt** 2.— *Ant.* NEGLECT, ignore, let alone.

**2.** [To handle others' things] — *Syn.* tamper, molest, pry, fool with, trespass, snoop, nose, dabble in, use improperly, monkey with*.

**meddlesome,** *modif.* — *Syn.* intrusive, prying, obtrusive, interfering, officious, meddling, impertinent, interposing, interrupting, obstructive, impeding, hindering, encumbering, curious, tampering, snooping, troublesome, busy, snoopy*, nosy*, kibitzing*, chiseling in*, butting in*, sticking one's nose in*; see also **inquisitive**.

*See Synonym Study at* INQUISITIVE.

**meddling,** *n.* — *Syn.* interfering, interrupting, snooping; see **interference** 2, **rudeness**.

**medial,** *modif.* — *Syn.* median, average, mean, between, intermediate, innermost; see also **center, central** 1, **middle**.

**median,** *modif.* — *Syn.* medial, middle, halfway; see **center** 1, **central** 1.

**median,** *n.* — *Syn.* mean, midpoint, norm; see **average, center** 1.

*See Synonym Study at* AVERAGE.

**mediate,** *v.* — *Syn.* arbitrate, propitiate, interfere, intercede; see **negotiate** 1, **reconcile** 2.

**mediation,** *n.* — *Syn.* interposition, arbitration, negotiation, reconciliation; see **agreement** 1, **intervention** 1.

**mediator,** *n.* — *Syn.* intercessor, medium, negotiator, arbitrator, peacemaker; see also **judge** 2.

**medic,** *n.* — *Syn.* physician, practitioner, surgeon, corpsman; see **doctor** 1.

**medical,** *modif.* — *Syn.* healing, medicinal, curative, therapeutic, restorative, prophylactic, preventive, alleviating, medicating, pharmaceutical, salutary, sedative, narcotic, tonic, disinfectant, corrective, pathological, cathartic, health-bringing, peptic, corroborant, lenitive, demulcent, balsamic, depuritory, emollient; see also **remedial.** — *Ant.* DESTRUCTIVE, disease-giving, HARMFUL. Commonly used medical terms and their abbreviations include: acute respiratory disease (ARD), anterior (A), barium enema (BE), basal body temperature (BBT), basal metabolic rate (BMR), blood pressure (BP), cancer (Ca), Celsius (C), central nervous system (CNS), cerebrospinal fluid (CSF), coronary artery bypass surgery (CABS), cubic centimeter (cc), dilation and curettage (D & C), dose*, ear, nose, and throat (ENT), electrocardiogram (EKG), electroconvulsive therapy (ECT), electroencephalogram (EEG), Fahrenheit (F), fever of undetermined origin (FUO), gastrointestinal (GI), genitourinary (GU), gram (gm), hemoglobin (Hb), ideal body weight (IBW), immediately (stat), intramuscular (IM), intravenous (IV), milliliter (ml), multiple sclerosis (MS), myocardial infarction (MI), normal (n), obstetrics (OB), physical examination (PE), pulse (P), respiration (R), red blood cell (rbc), shortness of breath (SOB), staphylococcus (staph), streptococcus (strep), temperature (T), unit (U), venereal disease (VD), weight (wt), white blood cell (wbc).

**medicament,** *n.* — *Syn.* antidote, remedy, panacea, drug; see **medicine** 2.

**Medicare,** *n.* — *Syn.* health care, socialized medicine, social security, old-age insurance, hospitalization insurance, public health; see also **insurance, security** 2.

**medication,** *n.* — *Syn.* remedy, pill, vaccination; see **medicine** 2, **prescription.**

**medicinal,** *modif.* — *Syn.* curative, healing, therapeutic; see **remedial.**

**medicine,** *n.* 1. [The healing profession] — *Syn.* medical men, healers, practitioners, doctors, physicians, surgeons, osteopaths, chiropractors, the profession, American Medical Association, A.M.A.

2. [A medical preparation] — *Syn.* medication, drug, dose, potion, prescription, pill, tablet, capsule, draft, curative preparation, patent medicine, remedy, cure, antivenin, anti-poison, antibiotic, medicament, vaccination, inoculation, injection, draught, simple, herb, specific, nostrum, elixir, tonic, balm, alterant, salve, lotion, ointment, emetic, pharmacopoeia, shot. Types of medicines include: antibiotic, antiseptic, antitoxin, antidote, antifungal, vaccine; analgesic, pain reliever, pain killer, anti-inflammatory, muscle relaxer, anesthetic, antispasmodic, antipyretic, febrifuge, steroid; sedative, tranquilizer, anticonvulsant, antidepressant; demulcent, antipruritic, astringent, counterirritant; laxative, cathartic, purgative, antacid, emetic, vermifuge; cough suppressant, expectorant, decongestant, antihistamine; antineoplastic, chemotherapeutic, chemo, immunosuppressive drug; anticoagulant, vasodilator, vasoconstrictor, beta blocker.

3. [The study and practice of medicine] — *Syn.* medical science, physic, healing art, medical profession, doctoring*, bed-panology*. Branches of medicine include: general practice, family practice, internal medicine, surgery, sports medicine, orthopedics, cardiology, hematology, respiratory medicine, otorhinolaryngology, (ear, nose, and throat), audiology, ophthalmology, allergology, immunology, rheumatology, anesthesiology, endocrinology, dermatology, gastroenterology, nephrology, urology, gynecology, obstetrics, neonatology, pediatrics, neurology, neurosurgery, psychiatry, geriatrics, oncology, radiology, pathology, toxicology, public health, epidemiology, tropical medicine, occupational medicine, industrial medicine. The following are not always recognized as branches of medicine: osteopathy, homeopathy, chiropractic.

**medieval,** *modif.* — *Syn.* pertaining to the Middle Ages, feudal, antiquated, ancient; see **old** 3.

**mediocre,** *modif.* — *Syn.* average, ordinary, standard; see **common** 1, **dull** 4, **fair** 2.

**mediocrity,** *n.* 1. [Ordinariness] — *Syn.* commonplaceness, commonness; see **normality** 1.

2. [A mediocre person] — *Syn.* upstart, cipher, nonentity; Tom, Dick, and Harry; see **citizen, commoner, nobody** 2.

**meditate,** *v.* 1. [To muse] — *Syn.* ponder, study, contemplate, ruminate, muse, revolve, say to oneself, reflect, view, brood over, cogitate, be in an abstraction, cherish the idea, entertain the idea, dream, mull over, be in a brown study*, chew the cud*; see also **consider** 3.

2. [To think over] — *Syn.* weigh, consider, speculate; see **think** 1.

**meditation,** *n.* — *Syn.* examination, contemplation, speculation; see **reflection** 1, **study** 2, **thought** 1.

**meditative,** *modif.* — *Syn.* reflective, pensive, absorbed; see **pensive, studious, thoughtful** 1.
*See Synonym Study at* PENSIVE.

**Mediterranean,** *modif.* — *Syn.* south European, Latinate, Italianate; see **classical** 2, **European, Latin** 2.

**medium,** *modif.* — *Syn.* commonplace, mediocre, ordinary, average; see **common** 1.

**medium,** *n.* 1. [A means] — *Syn.* mechanism, tool, factor; see **means** 1.

2. [A means of expression] — *Syn.* symbol, sign, token, interpretation, exponent, manifestation, revelation, evidence, mark, statement, delineation; see also **communication** 1, **communications, speech** 2. Common modes of expression include: speech, facial expression, gesture, signs, pantomime, music, drama, writing, painting, sculpture, radio, television.

3. [A supposed channel of supernatural knowledge] — *Syn.* oracle, seer, spiritualist; see **fortuneteller, prophet.**

**medley,** *n.* 1. [A mixture] — *Syn.* mingling, melee, conglomeration; see **mixture** 1, **variety** 1.

2. [A musical piece made up of various tunes] — *Syn.* assortment, potpourri, miscellany, *pasticcio* (Italian), pastiche; see also **composition** 4, **music** 1.

**meed,** *n.* — *Syn.* pay, award, reward; see **honors** 2, **pay** 2, **prize.**

**meek,** *modif.* 1. [Humble] — *Syn.* unassuming, plain, mild; see **humble** 1, **modest** 2.

2. [Long-suffering] — *Syn.* passive, resigned, serene; see **patient** 1.

3. [Lacking spirit] — *Syn.* submissive, compliant, subdued; see **docile, resigned.**

**meekness,** *n.* — *Syn.* submission, mildness, timidity; see **docility, humility.**

**meet,** *modif.* — *Syn.* fitting, apt, expedient; see **fair** 1, **fit** 1, 2, **timely.**

**meet,** *n.* — *Syn.* match, athletic event, tournament; see **competition** 2, **event** 3.

**meet,** *v.* **1.** [To come together] — *Syn.* converge, get together, enter in; see **gather** 1.

**2.** [To go to a place of meeting] — *Syn.* resort, be present at, gather together, foregather, convene, congregate, muster, appear; see also **assemble** 2, **attend** 2. — *Ant.* LEAVE, disperse, scatter.

**3.** [To touch] — *Syn.* reach, coincide, adhere; see **join** 1.

**4.** [To become acquainted] — *Syn.* make the acquaintance of, be presented to, be introduced, present oneself, make oneself known, get next to*, get to know; see also **familiarize with.**

**5.** [To fulfill] — *Syn.* answer, fit, suffice; see **satisfy** 3.

**6.** [To encounter] — *Syn.* fall in with, come on, come upon, meet by accident, come across, run into, meet with, meet up with, meet face to face, face up to, bump into, touch shoulders with, meet at every turn, engage, join issue with, battle, grapple with, match, jostle, push, brush against, shove; see also **face** 1, **fight** 2. — *Ant.* ABANDON, turn one's back on, leave.

**meeting,** *n.* **1.** [The act of coming together] — *Syn.* encounter, juxtaposition, juxtaposing, joining, confluence, juncture, apposition, unifying, unification, adherence, rencounter, convergence, confrontation, abutment, contacting, connection, recontact possibility, conflict, contention, accord, agreement, compromising, reception, harmonizing. — *Ant.* DEPARTURE, separation, dispersal.

**2.** [A gathering, usually of people] — *Syn.* conference, assemblage, rally; see **gathering.**

**meetinghouse,** *n.* — *Syn.* church, hall, auditorium; see **church** 1, **headquarters, room** 2.

**meeting of minds,** *n.* — *Syn.* approval, assent, negotiation; see **agreement** 3.

**meet one's responsibilities,** *v.* — *Syn.* accomplish, transact, complete, carry out; see **achieve** 1, **perform** 1.

**meet up with,** *v.* — *Syn.* encounter, become acquainted with, be introduced; see **meet** 4.

**meet with,** *v.* — *Syn.* observe, experience, encounter; see **find** 1, **meet** 4.

**megalith,** *n.* — *Syn.* stone monument, cromlech, standing stone, boulder, monolith; see also **rock** 1, **stone.**

**megalomania,** *n.* — *Syn.* lust for power, compulsion, instability, mental disorder; see **insanity** 1, **neurosis, obsession.**

**megalopolis,** *n.* — *Syn.* municipality, group of cities, metropolis; see **city** 1.

**megaphone,** *n.* — *Syn.* bull horn, sound device, microphone; see **amplifier.**

**melancholia,** *n.* — *Syn.* despondency, melancholy, despair; see **depression** 2, **sadness.**

**melancholy,** *modif.* **1.** [Sad; *said of persons*] — *Syn.* depressed, unhappy, dispirited; see **sad** 1.

**2.** [Depressing; *said of information or events*] — *Syn.* dreary, unfortunate, saddening; see **sad** 2.

*See Synonym Study at* SAD.

**melancholy,** *n.* — *Syn.* wistfulness, despair, unhappiness; see **depression** 2, **grief** 1, **sadness.**

*mélange* (French), *n.* — *Syn.* medley, combination, jumble; see **mixture** 1.

**meld,** *v.* — *Syn.* blend, merge, unite; see **mix** 1, **unite** 1.

**melee,** *n.* — *Syn.* scuffle, rumpus, skirmish; see **fight** 1.

**meliorate,** *v.* — *Syn.* amend, advance, correct; see **improve** 1.

**mellifluous,** *modif.* — *Syn.* resonant, smooth, liquid; see **harmonious** 1, **melodious, musical** 1.

**mellow,** *modif.* **1.** [Ripe] — *Syn.* sweet, soft, ripe, mature, perfected, full-flavored, seasoned, aged, cured, tender, well-matured; see also **matured, ripe** 1. — *Ant.* GREEN, hard, unripe.

**2.** [Culturally mature] — *Syn.* gracious, cultured, cordial; see **matured.**

**3.** [Easygoing] — *Syn.* calm, genial, softened; see **calm** 1, 2, **friendly** 1, **pleasant** 1.

*See Synonym Study at* RIPE.

**mellowed,** *modif.* — *Syn.* mature, ripened, softened; see **matured, ripe** 1, 2, **soft** 2, 3.

**melodeon,** *n.* — *Syn.* harmonium, wind instrument, accordion; see **musical instrument, organ** 3.

**melodious,** *modif.* — *Syn.* agreeable, pleasing, euphonic, sweet, tuneful, dulcet, accordant, assonant, mellifluous, resonant, mellow, in tune, well tuned, harmonic, symphonic, symphonious, unisonant, soft, clear, silvery, silver-toned, euphonious; see also **harmonious** 1, **musical** 1. — *Ant.* HARSH, grating, discordant.

**melodrama,** *n.* — *Syn.* play, opera, theater; see **drama** 1.

**melodramatic,** *modif.* — *Syn.* artificial, spectacular, sensational; see **exaggerated.**

**melody,** *n.* **1.** [The quality of being melodious] — *Syn.* consonance, assonance, concord, unison, euphony, resonance, inflection, chime; see also **harmony** 1. — *Ant.* NOISE, discord, disharmony.

**2.** [A melodious arrangement] — *Syn.* tune, air, song, strain, theme, line, descant; see also **music** 1, **song, tune.**

***SYN.*** — **melody** refers to a rhythmic arrangement of tones in sequence expressing a musical idea; **air,** in strict application, refers to the principal, or leading, melody of a harmonized composition, but it is sometimes used as an equivalent of **tune,** which is the popular term for any easily remembered melody that identifies a song, dance, etc.

**melon,** *n.* — *Syn.* pepo, *Cucurbitaceae* (Latin), gourd; see **food, fruit** 1.

Types of melons include: watermelon, muskmelon, cantaloupe, Rocky Ford, gourd melon, winter melon, Casaba, Crenshaw, Persian, Spanish, honeydew.

**melt,** *v.* **1.** [To liquefy] — *Syn.* dissolve, liquefy, thaw, deliquesce, render, fuse, blend, merge, soften, flow, run, disintegrate, waste away; see also **dissolve** 1. — *Ant.* FREEZE, harden, solidify.

**2.** [To relent] — *Syn.* forgive, show mercy, become lenient; see **yield** 1.

**3.** [To decrease] — *Syn.* vanish, pass away, go; see **decrease** 1.

***SYN.*** — **melt** implies the bringing of a substance from its solid to its liquid state, usually by heat [*to melt butter*]; **dissolve** refers specifically to the reduction of a solid to a liquid by placing it in another liquid so that its particles are evenly distributed among those of the solvent [*to dissolve sugar in water*]; **liquefy** is the general term meaning to change to a liquid state and may be applied to gases as well as solids; **thaw** implies the reducing of a frozen substance to its normal state, usually to a liquid or a semiliquid, by raising its temperature [*the ice has thawed*]

**melted,** *modif.* — *Syn.* softened, thawed, molten, liquefied, dwindled, deliquesced, run away, rendered, fused, blended, merged, wasted away, disintegrated, vanished, decreased, diminished, tempered, abated, mitigated, mollified, relaxed.

**melting,** *modif.* — *Syn.* softening, liquefying, reducing; see **soft** 2.

**melting pot,** *n.* — *Syn.* mingling, common ground, international meeting place; see **mixture** 1.

**member,** *n.* **1.** [A person or group] — *Syn.* constituent, charter member, active member, member in good standing, honorary member, affiliate, affiliate member, brother, sister, comrade, *tovarish* (Russian), chapter, post, branch, lodge.
**2.** [A part] — *Syn.* portion, segment, fragment; see **division** 2, **part** 1.
**3.** [A part of the body] — *Syn.* organ, feature, segment, arm, leg; see also **limb** 2.

**membership,** *n.* — *Syn.* club, society, association, body of members, fellowship, company, group, brotherhood, sisterhood, fraternity, sorority.

**membrane,** *n.* — *Syn.* layer, sheath, lamina; see **film** 1.

**memento,** *n.* — *Syn.* token, relic, keepsake; see **souvenir.**

**memo,** *n.* — *Syn.* memorandum, notice, record; see **note** 2, 3, **reminder.**

**memoir,** *n.* — *Syn.* life story, diary, autobiography; see **biography, journal** 1.

**memorable,** *modif.* **1.** [Historic] — *Syn.* momentous, critical, unforgettable, surpassing, crucial, famous, illustrious, distinguished, great, notable, significant, decisive, enduring, lasting, monumental, eventful, interesting; see also **important** 1.
**2.** [Unusual] — *Syn.* remarkable, exceptional, extraordinary, singular; see sense 1, **unusual** 1.

**memorandum,** *n.* — *Syn.* notice, record, jotting; see **note** 2, 3, **reminder.**

**memorial,** *modif.* — *Syn.* dedicatory, commemorative, remembering, consecrating, canonizing, enshrining, memorializing, deifying, in tribute.

**memorial,** *n.* — *Syn.* remembrance, testimonial, tablet, slab, pillar, tombstone, headstone, column, shaft, obelisk, monolith, mausoleum, record, inscription, memento, statue, *hic jacet, requiescat in pace* (both Latin), R.I.P., slat*; see also **celebration** 1, **ceremony** 2, **monument** 1, **souvenir.**

**Memorial Day,** *n.* — *Syn.* Decoration Day, Confederate Memorial Day, May 10, May 30, April 26, June 3; see also **holiday** 1, **spring** 2.

**memorize,** *v.* — *Syn.* commit to memory, learn by heart, fix in the memory, make memorable, record, commemorate, memorialize, retain, imprint in one's mind, bear in mind, treasure up, enshrine, learn by rote, use mnemonics, give word for word, get down pat, have in one's head, have at one's fingertips, bottle up; see also **learn** 1, **remember** 2. — *Ant.* NEGLECT, forget, fail to remember.

**memory,** *n.* **1.** [The power to call up the past] — *Syn.* recollection, recall, retention, retrospection, reminiscence, thought, mindfulness, consciousness, subconsciousness, unconscious memory, retentive memory, *déjà vu* (French), ready memory, photographic memory, visual memory, auditory memory; see also **mind** 1, **remembrance** 1.
**2.** [That which can be recalled] — *Syn.* remembrance, recollection, mental image, picture, vision, sound image, representation, fantasy, concept; see also **thought** 2.

**menace,** *n.* **1.** [A threat] — *Syn.* caution, intimidation, foretelling; see **warning.**

**2.** [An imminent danger] — *Syn.* hazard, peril, threat; see **danger.**

**menace,** *v.* — *Syn.* threaten, intimidate, portend, loom; see **threaten** 2.
*See Synonym Study at* THREATEN.

**menacing,** *modif.* — *Syn.* approaching, impending, threatening; see **imminent, ominous.**

**menagerie,** *n.* — *Syn.* zoological garden, terrarium, vivarium; see **zoo.**

**mend,** *v.* **1.** [To repair] — *Syn.* repair, patch, patch up, darn, sew, fix, restore, reconstruct, retouch, put in shape, heal, put back together, cobble, doctor*; see also **reconstruct, repair, restore** 3.
**2.** [To improve] — *Syn.* aid, remedy, cure; see **correct** 1, **improve** 1.
**3.** [Reform] — *Syn.* regenerate, behave, mend one's manners, mend one's ways; see **improve** 2, **reform** 3.
**4.** [To get well] — *Syn.* recover, respond to medication, knit; see **heal** 1, **recover** 3.
**on the mend** — *Syn.* getting better, recuperating, recovering; see **improving.**

---

**SYN.** — **mend** is the general word implying the making whole again of something that has been broken, torn, etc. [to *mend* a toy, to *mend* a dress]; **repair,** often equivalent to **mend,** is preferred when the object is a relatively complex one that has become damaged or decayed through use, age, exhaustion, etc. [to *repair* an automobile, to *repair* a radio]; **patch** and **darn** imply the mending of a hole, tear, etc., the former by inserting or applying a piece of similar material [to *patch* a coat, to *patch* a tire], the latter by sewing a network of stitches across the gap [to *darn* a sock]

---

**mendacious,** *modif.* — *Syn.* lying, untrue, spurious; see **false** 2.

**mendacity,** *n.* — *Syn.* lying, prevarication, falsification; see **deception** 1, **lie** 1.

**mended,** *modif.* — *Syn.* restored, put in shape, patched up, renovated, refreshed, renewed, corrected, helped, bettered, abated, lessened, ameliorated, remedied, cured, relieved, rectified, rejuvenated, refurbished, emended, enhanced, remodeled, altered, changed, fixed, regulated, rebuilt, regenerated, reorganized, revived, touched up, cobbled*, tinkered*, gone over*, doctored*; see also **improved** 1, **repaired.**

**mendicant,** *n.* — *Syn.* panhandler, vagabond, pauper; see **beggar** 1, 2, **tramp** 1.

**mending,** *n.* — *Syn.* restoring, renovating, repairing, renewing, putting into shape, patching up, refreshing, freshening, helping, bettering, ameliorating, relieving, remedying, curing, rectifying, correcting, enhancing, emending, changing, altering, rebuilding, remodeling, renovation, repair, restoration, reviving, tinkering, going over*; see also **correction** 1, **fixing** 1.

**menial,** *modif.* — *Syn.* common, servile, abject; see **humble** 1, 2.

**menial,** *n.* — *Syn.* domestic, maid, lackey; see **servant.**

**menstruation,** *n.* — *Syn.* period, menses, bleeding, discharge, the curse*, monthlies*.

**mensurable,** *modif.* — *Syn.* assayable, estimable, measurable; see **calculable, determinable.**

**mensuration,** *n.* — *Syn.* survey, measure, evaluation; see **estimate** 1, **judgment** 2.

**mental,** *modif.* **1.** [Concerning the mind] — *Syn.* reasoning, cerebral, thinking; see **rational** 1, **thoughtful** 1.
**2.** [Existing only in the mind] — *Syn.* subjective, subliminal, subconscious, telepathic, psychic, clairvoyant,

unreal, imaginative; see also **mysterious** 2. — *Ant.* OB-JECTIVE, BODILY, SENSUAL.

**mental health,** *n.* — *Syn.* normality, mental balance, mental stability, freedom from mental illness; see **sanity** 1.

**mentality,** *n.* — *Syn.* intellect, comprehension, reasoning; see **brain** 1, **mind** 1.

**mentally,** *modif.* — *Syn.* rationally, thoughtfully, theoretically, psychically, intellectually, inwardly, pensively, psychologically, introspectively, subjectively.

**mention,** *n.* — *Syn.* notice, naming, specifying; see **allusion, remark**.

**make mention of** — *Syn.* notice, consider, cite; see **mention** (*v.*)

**mention,** *v.* — *Syn.* notice, specify, cite, adduce, introduce, state, declare, quote, refer to, discuss, touch on, instance, acquaint with, infer, intimate, notify, communicate, suggest, make known, point out, point to, point at, speak of, throw out\*; see also **consider** 2, **designate** 1, **name** 2. — *Ant.* OVERLOOK, take no notice of, disregard.

**not to mention** — *Syn.* in addition, too, besides; see **also.**

**mentioned,** *modif.* — *Syn.* noticed, cited, specified, named, quoted, introduced, referred to, discussed, declared, intimated, revealed, brought to one's attention, brought up, considered, communicated, made known, spoken of; see also **suggested, told.**

**mentioning,** *modif.* — *Syn.* remarking, noting, observing; see **saying.**

**mentioning,** *n.* — *Syn.* speaking of, taking note of, referring to, introduction, inferring, intimating, making known, specifying, citing; see also **naming, suggesting.**

**mentor,** *n.* — *Syn.* instructor, guide, coach; see **teacher** 1, **trainer.**

**menu,** *n.* — *Syn.* bill of fare, carte, cuisine, table, cover, spread, card, food\*; see also **list.**

**mercantile,** *modif.* — *Syn.* trading, business, marketing; see **commercial** 1, **industrial.**

**mercenary,** *modif.* — *Syn.* acquisitive, selfish, miserly; see **greedy** 1, **stingy.**

**mercenary,** *n.* — *Syn.* legionnaire, professional soldier, soldier of fortune; see **soldier.**

**merchandise,** *n.* — *Syn.* wares, commodities, stock; see **commodity.**

**merchandise,** *v.* — *Syn.* market, distribute, promote; see **sell** 1.

**merchant,** *n.* — *Syn.* trader, storekeeper, retailer, shopkeeper, wholesaler, salesman, handler, sender, consignor, exporter, shipper, dealer, local representative, jobber, tradesman; see also **businessperson.**

**merchantable,** *modif.* — *Syn.* in demand, marketable, salable; see **commercial** 1, **be in the market** at **market.**

**merchantman,** *n.* — *Syn.* galleon, steamship, freighter, commercial vessel; see **boat, ship.**

**merciful,** *modif.* **1.** [Giving evidence of mercy] — *Syn.* lenient, clement, feeling, compassionate, pitiful, softhearted, mild, sparing, tolerant, kindly, indulgent, benign, benignant; see also **humane** 1, **kind.** — *Ant.* CRUEL, pitiless, unsparing.
**2.** [Having mercy as a character trait] — *Syn.* gentle, tender, gracious; see **kind, thoughtful** 2.

**merciless,** *modif.* — *Syn.* pitiless, unsparing, relentless; see **cruel** 2, **fierce** 1, **ruthless** 1.

**mercurial,** *modif.* — *Syn.* variable, fluctuating, inconstant; see **changeable** 1, 2, **irregular** 1.

**mercy,** *n.* **1.** [Willingness to spare others] — *Syn.* le-

niency, lenience, clemency, softheartedness, mildness, tenderness, lenity, charity, charitableness, compassion, gentleness, benevolence, benignancy, forbearance, toleration, forgiveness, kindness, quarter, humaneness, humanity, indulgence; see also **kindness** 1, **tolerance** 1. — *Ant.* intolerance, INDIFFERENCE, cruelty.
**2.** [Compassionate assistance to those in distress] — *Syn.* compassion, commiseration, sympathy; see **aid** 1, **pity** 1.

**at the mercy of** — *Syn.* in the power of, vulnerable to, controlled by; see **subject** 1.

---

*SYN.* — **mercy** implies compassion or forbearance, as in punishing offenders, in excess of what may be demanded by fairness, or it may connote kindness and sympathy to those in distress; **clemency** suggests a tendency toward mercy or leniency in one whose duty it is to punish offenders; **lenity** usually implies excessive mercy or mildness toward offenders where greater strictness might be preferable; **charity**, in this connection, implies a kindly understanding and tolerance in judging others

---

**mere,** *modif.* — *Syn.* small, minor, insignificant; see **little** 1, **poor** 2.

**merely,** *modif.* — *Syn.* slightly, solely, simply; see **hardly, only** 2.

**meretricious,** *modif.* — *Syn.* gaudy, flashy, loud, pretentious; see **ornate** 1, **specious.**

**merge,** *v.* — *Syn.* fuse, join, mix, unite, synthesize, amalgamate, blend, marry, absorb, consolidate, coalesce, conglomerate, centralize, impregnate, assimilate, melt into one; see also **mix** 1, **unite** 1.
*See Synonym Study at* MIX.

**merger,** *n.* — *Syn.* amalgamation, consolidation, alliance; see **incorporation** 2, **organization** 1.

**meridian,** *n.* **1.** [Noon] — *Syn.* noontime, midday, noonday; see **noon, time** 1, 2.
**2.** [Summit] — *Syn.* apex, extremity, peak; see **climax.**

**meridional,** *modif.* **1.** [Noon] — *Syn.* midday, noontime, sunny, resplendent, blazing, radiant; see also **bright** 1.
**2.** [Southern] — *Syn.* austral, southerly, to the south; see **southeast, southern, southwest.**

**merit,** *n.* **1.** [Worth] — *Syn.* credit, benefit, advantage; see **quality** 3, **value** 3.
**2.** [A creditable quality] — *Syn.* worthiness, excellence, honor; see **character** 2, **virtue** 1.

**merit,** *v.* — *Syn.* be worth, warrant, justify; see **deserve.**

**merited,** *modif.* — *Syn.* earned, proper, fitting; see **deserved, fit** 1, **warranted.**

**meritorious,** *modif.* — *Syn.* praiseworthy, exemplary, commendable, honorable; see **noble** 1, 2, **worthy.**

**merrily,** *modif.* — *Syn.* joyfully, gleefully, genially; see **cheerfully, happily** 2.

**merriment,** *n.* **1.** [A merry feeling] — *Syn.* joy, cheerfulness, gaiety; see **happiness** 1, **humor** 3.
**2.** [A merry occasion] — *Syn.* fun, enjoyment, carousal, sport, frolic, festivity, good time, recreation, tomfoolery, buffoonery, mummery, merry-making; see also **fun, party** 1. — *Ant.* FUNERAL, wake, work.

**merry,** *modif.* **1.** [Happy] — *Syn.* cheerful, joyous, mirthful; see **happy** 1.
**2.** [Festive] — *Syn.* enjoyable, amusing, lively; see **entertaining, pleasant** 2.

**merry-go-round,** *n.* — *Syn.* carousel, revolving platform, amusement device, whirligig, roundabout (British).

**merrymaking,** *n.* — *Syn.* frolic, amusement, revelry; see **entertainment** 1, **fun, merriment** 2.

**mesa,** *n.* — *Syn.* plateau, table, tableland, butte, table mountain; see also **hill, mountain** 1.

**mesh,** *n.* — *Syn.* snare, trap, screen; see **net, web** 1, 2.

**mesh,** *v.* — *Syn.* coincide, suit, interlock, coordinate, be in gear; see also **agree, fit** 1.

**mesmerism,** *n.* — *Syn.* hypnosis, catalepsy, trance, spell, entrancing, hypnotism; see also **numbness, stupor.**

**mesmerize,** *v.* — *Syn.* render unconscious, control, stupefy; see **deaden** 1, **drug, hypnotize.**

**mess,** *n.* **1.** [A mixture] — *Syn.* combination, compound, blend; see **mash, mixture** 1.
**2.** [A confusion] — *Syn.* jumble, mayhem, hodgepodge*; see **confusion** 2, **disorder** 2.
**3.** [Military term for meals] — *Syn.* rations, chow*, grub*; see **meal** 2.

**message,** *n.* **1.** [Communicated information] — *Syn.* tidings, information, intelligence; see **advice, broadcast, communication** 2, **directions.**
**2.** [A communication] — *Syn.* note, word, paper; see **communications, letter** 2, **news** 1, 2, **report** 1.
**get the message*** — *Syn.* get the hint, comprehend, perceive; see **understand** 1.

**mess around** *or* **about (with)*,** *v.* — *Syn.* dawdle, fool around, play the fool; see **loiter, play** 1, 2.

**messenger,** *n.* — *Syn.* bearer, minister, angel, prophet, dispatcher, herald, carrier, courier, runner, crier, errand boy, intermediary, envoy, emissary, internuncio, go-between, ambassador, commissionaire, flag-bearer, gofer*, boy*; see also **agent** 1.

**Messiah,** *n.* — *Syn.* Saviour, Redeemer, Jesus Christ; see **Christ, god** 2.

**messmate,** *n.* — *Syn.* comrade, buddy, shipmate; see **friend** 1, **mate** 2.

**mess up,** *v.* — *Syn.* spoil, ruin, foul up, damage; see **botch, destroy** 1.

**messy,** *modif.* — *Syn.* rumpled, untidy, slovenly; see **dirty** 1, **disordered.**

**metal,** *n.* — *Syn.* element, native rock, ore, metalliferous ore, ore deposit, free metal, refined ore, smelted ore; see also **alloy, mineral.**
Elementary metals and varieties of metal include: gold, silver, copper, iron, steel, aluminum, manganese, nickel, lead, cobalt, platinum, zinc, tin, barium, cadmium, chromium, tungsten, mercury, iridium, molybdenum, antimony, vanadium, alunite, corundum, lithium, sodium, potassium, ribidium, caesium, casium, strontium, radium, beryllium, magnesium, gallium, indium, thallium, cerium, calcium, celtium, anthanium, americium, terbium, holmium, titanium, germanium, arsenic, bismuth, uranium, dysprosium, erbium, rhodium, ruthenium, palladium, osmium, indium, lanthanum, entecium, neodymium, niobium, praseodymion, samarium, tantalum, thorium, thulium, ytterbium, zirconium.

**metallic,** *modif.* **1.** [Made of metal] — *Syn.* hard, rocklike, fusible, ory, iron, leaden, silvery, golden, tinny, stannic, metallurgic, mineral, geologic.
**2.** [Suggestive of metal; *said especially of sound*] — *Syn.* ringing, resounding, resonant, trumpet-tongued, bell-like, clanging, clangorous; see also **loud** 1, 2.

**metamorphic,** *modif.* — *Syn.* variable, unstable, mobile, versatile; see **changeable** 2, **growing.**

**metamorphose,** *v.* — *Syn.* alter, diverge, transform; see **change** 4, **vary** 1.
*See Synonym Study at* TRANSFORM.

**metamorphosis,** *n.* — *Syn.* transformation, evolution, modification; see **change** 1, 2, **variety** 1.

**metaphor,** *n.* — *Syn.* trope, simile, implied comparison, figure of speech; see **comparison** 2.

**mix metaphors** — *Syn.* be inconsistent, garble, talk illogically; see **confuse.**

**metaphoric** *or* **metaphorical,** *modif.* — *Syn.* symbolic, symbolical, allegorical, figurative, referential, allusive, comparative, mystical, anagogic, metonymic, poetic, anagogical, contrastive, exegetical, symbolistic, involved, imaginative, mythic, antonomastic, catachrestic; see also **descriptive, graphic** 1, 2, **illustrative, symbolic.**

**metaphysical,** *modif.* — *Syn.* mystical, abstract, spiritual; see **difficult** 2, **transcendental.**

**metaphysics,** *n.* — *Syn.* epistemology, ontology, cosmology, mysticism, transcendentalism; see also **philosophy, religion** 1.

**mete,** *v.* — *Syn.* allot, measure out, dispense, administer; see **distribute** 1, **give** 1.

**metempsychosis,** *n.* — *Syn.* rebirth, transmigration, reincarnation, incarnation, reanimation; see also **renewal, spiritualism** 1.

**meteor,** *n.* — *Syn.* falling star, shooting star, meteorite, fireball, bolide, meteroid; see also **satellite** 1, **star** 1.

**meteoric,** *modif.* — *Syn.* brilliant, swift, transient, sudden; see **bright** 1, **fleeting.**

**meteoroid,** *n.* — *Syn.* meteorite, shooting star, falling stone; see **meteor, star** 1.

**meteorology,** *n.* — *Syn.* climate science, atmospheric science, climatology, aerology, climatography, aerography; see also **science** 1, **weather.**

**meter,** *n.* — *Syn.* measure, rhythm, verse, metrical feet, quantitative feet, syllabic groups, metrical structure, metrical pattern, common meter, long meter, ballad meter, tetrameter, pentameter, hendecasyllable, heptameter, sprung rhythm, dipodic rhythm; see also **beat** 3, **music** 1, **poetry.**

**method,** *n.* **1.** [Order] — *Syn.* classification, organization, arrangement; see **order** 3, **system** 1.
**2.** [A procedure] — *Syn.* mode, style, standard procedure, fashion, way, means, program, tenor, process, proceeding, adjustment, disposition, disposal, practice, routine, technic, technique, approach, method of attack, mode of operation, manner of working, ways and means, habit, custom, *modus operandi* (Latin), manner, formula, process, course, rule; see also **system** 2.
**3.** [Plan] — *Syn.* design, outline, scheme; see **opinion** 1, **plan** 2, **purpose** 1.

**methodical,** *modif.* — *Syn.* well-regulated, systematic, exact; see **regular** 3, **orderly** 2.

**Methodist,** *n.* — *Syn.* Trinitarian, Protestant, Southern Methodist, Methodist-Episcopal; see **Christian, Christianity** 2, **church** 3.

**meticulous,** *modif.* — *Syn.* scrupulous, fastidious, precise, careful; see **accurate** 1, 2, **careful.**
*See Synonym Study at* CAREFUL.

**métier,** *n.* — *Syn.* trade, profession, occupation, skill, forte; see also **job** 1, **profession** 1, **specialty** 1, **trade** 2.

**metropolis,** *n.* — *Syn.* capital, megalopolis, conurbation, municipality; see **center** 2, **city.**

**metropolitan,** *modif.* — *Syn.* city, municipal, cosmopolitan; see **modern** 2, **urban** 2.

**mettle,** *n.* **1.** [Spirit] — *Syn.* animation, energy, spunk; see **force** 3, **life** 1, **vitality.**
**2.** [Hardihood] — *Syn.* stamina, bravery, pluck; see **courage** 1, **strength** 1.

**mettlesome,** *modif.* **1.** [High-spirited] — *Syn.* spirited, vigorous, spunky; see **active** 2.

**2.** [Gallant] — *Syn.* plucky, valiant, dauntless; see **brave** 1.

**Mexican,** *modif.* — *Syn.* Latin American, Hispanic, Chicano, Chicana, TexMex; see also **American** 1.

**Mexico,** *n.* — *Syn. Mejico, El Pais* (*both* Spanish), the other side of the Rio Grande, land south of the border, a sister republic, the republic to the south; see also **America** 1.

**mezzanine,** *n.* — *Syn.* second floor, balcony, intermediate floor; see **attic, floor** 2.

**mezzo,** *modif.* — *Syn.* medium, medial, mean; see **central** 1.

**mezzotint,** *n.* — *Syn.* half tone, line engraving, black and white; see **engraving** 2, **plate** 3.

**miasma,** *n.* — *Syn.* vapor, steam, fume, reek, stench; see also **gas** 1, **haze.**

**miasmatic,** *modif.* — *Syn.* miasmal, dangerous, contagious, lethal; see **deadly, poisonous.**

**mickey mouse★,** *modif.* — *Syn.* trite, platitudinous, simplistic; see **dull** 4, **easy** 2, **naive, simple** 2.

**microbe,** *n.* — *Syn.* microorganism, bacterium, bacillus; see **germ** 3.

**microphone,** *n.* — *Syn.* sound transmitter, receiver, pickup instrument, mike, loudspeaker, bug, mike boom, walkie-talkie; see also **amplifier.**

**microscope,** *n.* — *Syn.* lens, magnifying glass, optical instrument, scope★, mike★; see also **lens.**
Microscopes include: high-powered, compound, photographic, electron, electronic.

**microscopic,** *modif.* — *Syn.* diminutive, tiny, infinitesimal; see **little** 1, **minute** 1.

**mid,** *modif.* — *Syn.* intervening, medial, median; see **halfway, intermediate, middle.**

**middle,** *modif.* — *Syn.* between, mean, midway, medial, average, mezzo, equidistant; see also **central** 1, **halfway, intermediate.**

**middle,** *n.* — *Syn.* center, midpoint, midst, nucleus, core, heart, mean, median, midriff, waist, midsection, halfway point, thick, thick of things; see also **center** 1.

---

*SYN.* — **middle** refers to the point or part equally distant from either or all sides or extremities and may apply to space, time, or a sequence /the *middle* of the stage, the *middle* of the day/; **center** more precisely stresses the point equidistant from the bounding lines or surfaces of a plane or solid figure /the *center* of a circle, the *center* of the globe/ and is often used figuratively /the *center* of town, a trade *center*/; **midst,** used in prepositional phrases, denotes a middle part that is surrounded by persons or things or a middle point in some action /in the *midst* of a crowd, in the *midst* of one's work/

---

**middle age,** *n.* — *Syn.* adulthood, prime, maturity, wrong side of forty★; see **majority** 2.

**middle-aged,** *modif.* — *Syn.* adult, in one's prime, matronly, mid-life; see **mature** 1, **matured.**

**middle-class,** *modif.* — *Syn.* white-collar, bourgeois, substantial; see **common** 1, **popular** 1, 3.

**middle class,** *n.* — *Syn.* white-collar class, the rank and file, bourgeoisie, common people; see **people** 3.

**middleman,** *n.* — *Syn.* representative, broker, salesman; see **agent** 1.

**middle-sized,** *modif.* — *Syn.* fair-sized, mid-sized, moderate-sized, average, normal, ordinary, so-so, indifferent, in-between, fair to middling★; see also **common** 1.

**Middle Western,** *modif.* — *Syn.* Midwestern, Midwest, midland, prairie, prairie-state, Middle American; see also **western** 1, 3.

**middling,** *modif.* — *Syn.* mediocre, ordinary, average, fair-to-middling; see **common** 1, **conventional** 1, 3, **traditional** 2. — *Syn.* moderately good, ordinary, average; see **fair** 2.

**midget,** *n.* — *Syn.* dwarf, pygmy, small person, mannikin, shrimp★, squirt★, Tom Thumb★, pipsqueak★, half-pint★, Lilliputian, shorty★.

**midnight,** *n.* — *Syn.* dead of night, stroke of midnight, 12:00 P.M., noon of night, witching hour; see also **night** 1.

**burn the midnight oil**— *Syn.* stay up late, work late, study late, keep late hours; see **study** 1, **work** 1.

**midshipman,** *n.* — *Syn.* seaman, mariner, navigator; see **sailor.**

**midst,** *n.* — *Syn.* midpoint, nucleus, middle; see **center** 1, **middle.**
*See Synonym Study at* MIDDLE.

**in our** (*or* **your** *or* **their**) **midst**— *Syn.* between us, with, accompanying; see **among.**

**in the midst of**— *Syn.* in the course of, engaged in, in the middle of; see **central** 1.

**midsummer,** *n.* — *Syn.* solstice, June 22, longest day of the year; see **summer.**

**midway,** *modif.* — *Syn.* in the thick of, between, in the middle; see **central** 1, **halfway, intermediate, middle.**

**midwife,** *n.* — *Syn.* accoucheuse, attendant, practitioner, assistant, obstetrician, one who delivers, *sage-femme* (French).

**mien,** *n.* — *Syn.* aspect, manner, air, demeanor; see **appearance** 1, **bearing** 2.
*See Synonym Study at* BEARING.

**miff,** *n.* — *Syn.* huff, tantrum, fit; see **anger, rage** 2.

**miff,** *v.* **1.** [To annoy] — *Syn.* provoke, pester, offend; see **bother** 2.

**2.** [To frown] — *Syn.* scowl, frown, seethe; see **rage** 1.

**might,** *n.* — *Syn.* strength, force, sway; see **strength** 1.
*See Synonym Study at* STRENGTH.

**mightily,** *modif.* — *Syn.* energetically, strongly, forcibly; see **powerfully, vigorously.**

**mighty,** *modif.* **1.** [Strong] — *Syn.* powerful, stalwart, muscular; see **strong** 1.

**2.** [Powerful through influence] — *Syn.* great, all-powerful, omnipotent; see **powerful** 1.

**3.** [Imposing] — *Syn.* great, remarkably large, extensive, impressive, gigantic, magnificent, majestic, towering, dynamic, irresistible, notable, extraordinary, grand, considerable, monumental, titanic, tremendous, high and mighty; see also **large** 1. — *Ant.* PLAIN, unimpressive, ordinary.

**4.** [★Very] — *Syn.* great, exceedingly, extremely; see **very.**

**migrant,** *n.* **1.** [Traveler] — *Syn.* wanderer, wayfarer, journeyer, globe-trotter, vagabond, hobo, vagrant, transient.

**2.** [Temporary laborer] — *Syn.* migrant worker, day laborer, itinerant worker, migratory worker.

**migrate,** *v.* — *Syn.* move, emigrate, immigrate, resettle, relocate, transfer, transmigrate, in-migrate, out-migrate, expatriate, trek, run (*said of fish*); see also **leave** 1, **move** 6.

---

*SYN.* — **migrate** denotes a moving from one region or country to another and may imply, of people, intention to settle in a new land, or, of animals, a periodic movement influenced by climate, food supply, etc.; **emigrate** and **immigrate** are used only of people, **emigrate** specifically denoting the leaving of a country to settle in another, and **immigrate**, the coming into the new country to settle

**migration,** *n.* — *Syn.* emigration, immigration, voyage; see **departure** 1, **journey, movement** 2.

**migratory,** *modif.* **1.** [Having fixed habits of migration; *said especially of birds*] — *Syn.* seasonal, transient, impermanent, emigrating, immigrating, passing over, like birds of passage, here for the winter, arrived for the summer, in a flyway. — *Ant.* LOCAL, hibernating, nonmigratory.
**2.** [Given to moving; *said especially of transient labor*] — *Syn.* shifting, changing, unsettled, casual, roving, wandering, nomadic, tramp, vagrant, on the move; see also **temporary.** — *Ant.* PERMANENT, steady, settled.

**mild,** *modif.* **1.** [Gentle; *said especially of persons*] — *Syn.* meek, easygoing, patient; see **kind.**
**2.** [Temperate; *said especially of weather*] — *Syn.* bland, untroubled, tropical, peaceful, pacific, calm, summery, tepid, medium, cool, balmy, breezy, gentle, soft, lukewarm, clement, clear, moderate, genial, mellow, fine, uncloudy, sunny, warm; see also **calm** 2, **fair** 3. — *Ant.* ROUGH, COLD, STORMY.
**3.** [Easy; *said especially of burdens or punishment*] — *Syn.* soft, light, tempered; see **moderate** 4.
**4.** [Not irritating] — *Syn.* bland, soothing, soft, smooth, gentle, moderate, easy, mollifying, mellow, delicate, temperate.
*See Synonym Study at* SOFT.

**mildew,** *n.* — *Syn.* smut, fungus, rust; see **decay** 2, **mold** 3.

**mildew,** *v.* — *Syn.* mold, spoil, must; see **decay.**

**mildly,** *modif.* — *Syn.* gently, meekly, blandly, calmly, genially, tranquilly, tepidly, softly, lightly, moderately, tenderly, compassionately, tolerantly, patiently, imperturbably, temperately, indifferently, quietly, soothingly, indulgently, mollifyingly; see also **kindly** 2. — *Ant.* VIOLENTLY, harshly, roughly.

**mildness,** *n.* — *Syn.* tolerance, tenderness, gentleness; see **kindness** 1.

**mile,** *n.* — *Syn.* 5,280 feet, statute mile, geographical mile, nautical mile, Admiralty mile; see also **distance** 3, **measure** 1.

**mileage,** *n.* — *Syn.* rate, space, measure; see **distance** 3, **length** 1.

**milestone,** *n.* **1.** [Sign] — *Syn.* post, pillar, stone; see **sign** 1.
**2.** [Event] — *Syn.* discovery, breakthrough, anniversary; see **event** 1, 2.

**militant,** *modif.* — *Syn.* combative, aggressive, belligerent, activist; see **aggressive** 1, 2, **militaristic.**
*See Synonym Study at* AGGRESSIVE.

**militant,** *n.* — *Syn.* rioter, violent objector, demonstrator; see **protester.**

**militarism,** *n.* — *Syn.* martial policy, regimentation, militancy; see **power** 2, **war.**

**militarist,** *n.* — *Syn.* warlord, warmonger, combatant; see **soldier.**

**militaristic,** *modif.* — *Syn.* warmongering, jingoistic, chauvinistic, warlike, antagonistic, belligerent; see also **aggressive** 2.

**military,** *modif.* — *Syn.* armed, martial, militant, fighting, combatant, soldierly, warlike, combative, army, service, naval, noncivil, for war; see also **aggressive** 2, **army, militaristic.**

**military,** *n.* — *Syn.* armed forces, military establishment, soldiery, the Pentagon; see **army** 1.

**SYN.** — **military** applies to anything having to do with armies or soldiers [*military* uniforms, *military* police]; **martial** refers to something connected with or characteristic of war or armies, often specif. connoting pomp and display or discipline [*martial* music, *martial* law]; **warlike** stresses the bellicose or aggressive nature or temperament that leads to war or results from preparations for war [a *warlike* nation]

**militia,** *n.* — *Syn.* military force, civilian army, National Guard; see **army** 1.

**milk,** *n.* — *Syn.* fluid, juice, whey, sap; see **liquid.**
Types of milk include: whole, low-fat, skim, raw, pasteurized, homogenized, certified; loose, acidophilous, condensed, sweetened-condensed, dried, evaporated, powdered, goat's, cow's, ewe's, mare's, mother's; cream, half-and-half, baby formula, buttermilk, koumiss, kefir.

**cry over spilt milk** — *Syn.* mourn, lament, sulk; see **regret.**

**milk,** *v.* — *Syn.* drain, extract, squeeze out, bleed, suck dry; see also **drain** 1, 2.

**milking,** *n.* — *Syn.* drawing from, pumping, draining, suction, sapping, emptying, suckling, sucking; see also **extraction** 2.

**milksop,** *n.* — *Syn.* pantywaist, milquetoast, sissy; see **coward.**

**milky,** *modif.* — *Syn.* opaque, pearly, cloudy; see **white** 1.

**Milky Way,** *n.* — *Syn.* galaxy, galactic circle, zodiac, universe, *Via Lactea* (Latin); see also **constellation.**

**mill,** *n.* **1.** [A factory] — *Syn.* manufactory, plant, millhouse; see **factory.**
**2.** [A machine for grinding, crushing, pressing, etc.] — *Syn.* grinder, grater, quern, windmill, waterwheel.
Types of mills include: flour, coffee, bone, cotton, weaving, spinning, powder, rolling, cider, cane, lapidary; sawmill, gristmill, *arrastra* (Spanish), coin press, diesinking machine.

**in the mill** — *Syn.* in production, developing, in the works*; see **growing.**

**through the mill** * — *Syn.* tested, completed, produced; see **finished** 1.

**millennium,** *n.* — *Syn.* a thousand years, millenary, the Second Coming, happiness, golden age, golden dream, kingdom come, heaven on earth, thousand years of peace; see also **utopia.**

**miller,** *n.* — *Syn.* mill operator, meal grinder, mill owner; see **worker.**

**milliner,** *n.* — *Syn.* modiste, haberdasher, hat salesman, hatter, hat maker.

**millinery,** *n.* — *Syn.* bonnet, cap, headgear; see **hat.**

**millionaire,** *n.* — *Syn.* man of wealth, man of means, capitalist, tycoon, rich man, moneyed man, man of substance, plutocrat, Croesus, nabob, Midas, Dives, man of millions, moneybags*, tippybob*, doughbag*, butter-and-egg man*, big-money man*, money baron*, robber baron*, bankroll*; see also **financier.** — *Ant.* BEGGAR, poor man, pauper.

**millions** *, *n.* **1.** [Said of people] — *Syn.* the masses, population, populace; see **people** 3.
**2.** [Said of money] — *Syn.* a fortune, great wealth, profits; see **wealth** 1, 2.

**millstone,** *n.* **1.** [A grinder] — *Syn.* stone, chopper, mill; see **grinder** 1, **tool** 1.

**2.** [A burden] — *Syn.* impediment, load, albatross, responsibility; see **difficulty** 2.

**mime,** *n.* **1.** [An imitator] — *Syn.* mimic, impersonator, comedian; see **actor** 1, **imitator.**

**2.** [An imitation] — *Syn.* mockery, caricature, mimicry; see **imitation** 2, **parody.**

**mime,** *v.* — *Syn.* impersonate, mimic, pretend; see **act** 1, **imitate** 2, **parody.**

**mimetic,** *modif.* — *Syn.* imitative, reflective, mocking, mimicking, copying, make-believe, echoic.

**mimic,** *n.* — *Syn.* mime, impersonator, comedian; see **actor** 1, **imitator.**

**mimic,** *v.* **1.** [To imitate] — *Syn.* copy, simulate, impersonate; see **imitate** 2.

**2.** [To mock] — *Syn.* make fun of, burlesque, caricature; see **parody, ridicule.**

See Synonym Study at IMITATE.

**mimicry,** *n.* — *Syn.* mime, pretense, mockery; see **imitation** 2, **parody.**

**minaret,** *n.* — *Syn.* steeple, spire, belfry; see **tower.**

**mince,** *v.* **1.** [To chop] — *Syn.* dice, hash, divide; see **chip.**

**2.** [To minimize] — *Syn.* mitigate, alleviate, lessen; see **decrease** 2.

**mincing,** *modif.* — *Syn.* insincere, unnatural, artificial; see **affected** 2.

**mind,** *n.* **1.** [Intellectual potentiality] — *Syn.* soul, spirit, intellect, brain, consciousness, thought, mentality, intuition, perception, conception, intelligence, intellectuality, apperception, percipience, psyche, conscious, subconscious, ego, capacity, judgment, understanding, wisdom, genius, talent, reasoning, instinct, ratiocination, thinking principle, wit, mental faculties, intellectual faculties, creativity, ingenuity, intellectual powers, intellectual processes, gray matter\*, brainstuff\*, brainpower\*, milk in the coconut\*, what it takes\*.

**2.** [Purpose] — *Syn.* intention, inclination, determination; see **purpose** 1.

**3.** [Memory] — *Syn.* subconscious, remembrance, cognizance; see **memory** 1.

**bear** (*or* **keep**) **in mind**— *Syn.* heed, recollect, recall; see **remember** 1.

**be in one's right mind**— *Syn.* be mentally well, be rational, be sane; see **reason** 2.

**be of one mind**— *Syn.* have the same opinion, concur, be in accord; see **agree.**

**be of two minds**— *Syn.* be undecided, be irresolute, vacillate, ride the fence, sit on the fence; see also **waver.**

**call to mind**— *Syn.* recall, recollect, bring to mind; see **remember** 1.

**change one's mind**— *Syn.* alter one's opinion, change one's views, decide against, recant, alter one's convictions, modify one's ideas, have second thoughts, have a change of heart, think better of something; see also **change** 1.

**give someone a piece of one's mind**— *Syn.* rebuke, confute, criticize; see **censure.**

**have** (**a good** *or* **great** *or* **half a**) **mind to**— *Syn.* be inclined to, propose, tend to; see **intend** 1.

**have in mind**— *Syn.* **1.** recall, recollect, think of; see **remember** 1.

**2.** purpose, propose, be inclined to; see **intend** 1.

**know one's own mind**— *Syn.* know oneself, be deliberate, have a plan; see **know** 1.

**make up one's mind**— *Syn.* form a definite opinion, choose, finalize; see **decide** 1.

**meeting of the minds**— *Syn.* concurrence, unity, harmony; see **agreement** 2.

**on one's mind**— *Syn.* occupying one's thoughts, causing concern, worrying one; see **important** 1.

**out of one's mind**— *Syn.* mentally ill, raving, mad, crazy; see **insane** 1.

**put in mind**— *Syn.* recall, inform, call attention to; see **remind** 2.

**set one's mind on**— *Syn.* determine, intend, plan; see **decide** 1, **intend** 1.

**take one's mind off**— *Syn.* turn one's attention from, divert, change; see **distract** 1.

**to one's mind**— *Syn.* in one's opinion, as one sees it, according to one; see **personally** 2.

**mind,** *v.* **1.** [To obey] — *Syn.* be under the authority of, heed, do as told; see **behave** 2, **obey** 1.

**2.** [To give one's attention] — *Syn.* heed, attend, be attentive to; see **regard** 1.

**3.** [To be careful] — *Syn.* tend, watch out for, have oversight of, take care, trouble, be wary, be concerned for, be solicitous, dislike, object, mind one's *p*'s and *q*'s\*, have a care\*, sleep with one eye open\*, keep one's chin in\*; see also **care** 2. — *Ant.* NEGLECT, ignore, be careless.

**4.** [To remember] — *Syn.* recollect, recall, bring to mind; see **remember** 1.

**5.** [To object to] — *Syn.* complain, deplore, be opposed to; see **dislike, object** 1.

**minded,** *modif.* — *Syn.* disposed, inclined, liking, turned toward, leaning toward, desirous, intending, purposing, planning, contemplating, convinced, determined, resolved, decided, settled on, fixed on, harboring a design, proposing to oneself, aspiring to, aiming at, driving for, thinking of, having a good mind to; see also **willing** 2. — *Ant.* UNWILLING, disinclined, undetermined.

**mindful,** *modif.* — *Syn.* attentive, heedful, watchful; see **careful.**

**mindless,** *modif.* **1.** [Careless] — *Syn.* inattentive, oblivious, neglectful; see **careless** 1, **indifferent** 1, **rash.**

**2.** [Stupid] — *Syn.* foolish, senseless, unintelligent; see **stupid** 1.

**mind one's p's and q's,** *v.* — *Syn.* act properly, conform, mind; see **behave** 2, **mind** 3.

**mind's eye\*,** *n.* — *Syn.* imagination, fantasy, vision; see **thought** 2.

**mine,** *modif.* — *Syn.* my own, belonging to me, possessed by me, mine by right, owned by me, left to me, from me, by me; see also **our.**

**mine,** *n.* **1.** [A source of natural wealth] — *Syn.* pit, well, shaft, diggings, excavation, adit, workings, works, quarry, deposit, vein, lode, dike, ore bed, placer, matrix, pay dirt\*, pay streak\*, bonanza\*; see also **tunnel.**

Types of mines, sense 1, include: placer, surface, open pit, dredging, open cut, strip; quartz, coal, iron, copper, silver, gold, diamond, underhand stope, bottom stope, overhand stope, top stope, rill stope, opencast stope, shrinkage stope.

**2.** [An explosive charge] — *Syn.* landmine, ambush, trap; see **bomb, explosive, weapon** 1.

Types of mines, sense 2, include: smart, floating, anchor, ratchet, magnetic, aerial, antipersonnel, castrator\*, Bouncing Betty\*, Leaping Lena\*; S-mine, *Teller* (German), claymore, countermine, delayed action mine, time bomb, booby trap.

**mine,** *v.* **1.** [To dig for minerals] — *Syn.* excavate, burrow, pan, stope, drill, work, quarry, wash for gold; see also **dig** 1.

**2.** [To lay mines] — *Syn.* sow with mines, prepare mine fields, set booby traps; see **defend** 1.

**miner,** *n.* — *Syn.* excavator, digger, driller, dredger, mineworker, prospector, desert rat\*, sourdough\*, forty-niner\*; see also **laborer, worker.**

Types of miners include: gold, silver, coal, diamond, amber, quarry, placer; collier, tarrier, driller, blaster, dredger, prospector, hard-rock geologist, caisson worker, gold panner, geologist, geological engineer, mining engineer, mine superintendent; mucker\*, donkey engineer\*, muckman\*, powderman\*, high-grader\*, rusher\*, pocket hunter\*, hardrocker\*.

**mineral,** *modif.* — *Syn.* geologic, rock, metallurgic; see **metallic** 1.

**mineral,** *n.* — *Syn.* inorganic material, earth's crust, geologic formation, geologic rock, rock deposit, country rock, ore deposit, gangue, igneous rock, metamorphic rock, morphologic rock, magma, petroleums, crystal; see also **metal, ore.**

Common minerals include: quartz, feldspar, mica, hornblende, pyroxene, olivine, calcite, dolomite, pyrite, chalcopyrite, barite, garnet, diopside, gypsum, staurolite, tourmaline, obsidian, malachite, azurite, limonite, galena, aragonite, magnetite, ilmenite, serpentine, epidote, fluorite, cinnabar, talc, bauxite, corundum, cryolite, spinel, sheelite, wolframite, graphite, diatomite, pitchblende.

**mingle,** *v.* — *Syn.* combine, blend, admix; see **mix** 1.
*See Synonym Study at* MIX.

**mingling,** *n.* — *Syn.* compound, composite, blend; see **mixture** 1.

**miniature,** *modif.* — *Syn.* diminutive, small, tiny; see **little** 1, **minute** 1.
*See Synonym Study at* SMALL.

**minimal,** *modif.* — *Syn.* insignificant, smallest, minimum; see **least** 1.

**minimize,** *v.* — *Syn.* lessen, depreciate, reduce; see **decrease** 2, **depreciate.**
*See Synonym Study at* DEPRECIATE.

**minimum,** *modif.* — *Syn.* smallest, tiniest, merest; see **least** 1.

**minimum,** *n.* — *Syn.* least amount, lowest amount, smallest, least, lowest, narrowest, modicum, atom, molecule, particle, dot, jot, iota, point, spark, shadow, whit, tittle, soupçon, scintilla, trifle, gleam, grain, scruple.

**mining,** *n.* — *Syn.* excavating, quarrying, hollowing, opening, digging, scooping, tapping, boring, drilling, pitting, undermining, delving, burrowing, tunneling, staving in, honeycombing, placer mining, stoping, hard-rock mining, prospecting.

**minion,** *n.* — *Syn.* creature, slave, dependent, servant; see **follower.**

**minister,** *n.* **1.** [One authorized to conduct Christian worship] — *Syn.* pastor, parson, preacher, clergyman, rector, monk, abbot, prelate, curate, vicar, deacon, chaplain, pulpiteer, servant of God, shepherd, churchman, cleric, padre, ecclesiastic, bishop, archbishop, suffragan, confessor, reverend, dean, archdeacon, abbé, curé, prebendary, canon, diocesan, primate, metropolitan, reverence, reader, lecturer, divine, shepherd, Bible-reader, missionary, Bible thumper\*, evangelist, sky pilot\*, black coat\*, psalm singer\*; see also **priest.** — *Ant.* LAYMAN, church member, parishioner.
**2.** [A high servant of the state] — *Syn.* cabinet member, ambassador, consul, liaison officer; see **diplomat** 1, **representative, statesman.**

**minister,** *v.* — *Syn.* administer to, tend, wait on; see **help** 1.

**ministerial,** *modif.* **1.** [Priestly] — *Syn.* pastoral, ecclesiastical, canonical; see **clerical** 2, **religious** 1.
**2.** [Official] — *Syn.* valid, consular, diplomatic; see **official** 3.

**ministration,** *n.* — *Syn.* assistance, help, support; see **aid** 1.

**ministry,** *n.* **1.** [The functions of the clergy] — *Syn.* pastoral care, preaching, exhortation, administration of the sacraments, prayer, spiritual leadership, service.
**2.** [The clergy] — *Syn.* the cloth, clergymen, ecclesiastics, clerics, the clerical order, priesthood, the pulpit, clericals, prelacy, vicarage, the desk, clergy.
**3.** [A department of state] — *Syn.* bureau, administrative agency, executive branch; see **department** 2.

**minor,** *modif.* — *Syn.* secondary, lesser, insignificant; see **trivial, unimportant.**

**minor,** *n.* — *Syn.* person under eighteen, person under twenty-one, underage person, boy, girl, child, infant, little one, lad, slip, spring, schoolboy, schoolgirl, lassie, miss, maid; see also **youth** 3.

**minority,** *n.* **1.** [An outnumbered group] — *Syn.* opposition, less than half, the outvoted, the few, the outnumbered, the losing side, splinter group\*, the outs\*.
**2.** [The time before one is of legal age] — *Syn.* childhood, immaturity, adolescence; see **youth** 1.

**minor-league,** *modif.* — *Syn.* second-rate, minor, small-time; see **unimportant, trivial.**

**minstrel,** *n.* — *Syn.* ballad singer, balladeer, bard, minnesinger, troubadour, jongleur, street singer, songsmith, *trovatore* (Italian), *trouvère* (French), *Meistersinger* (German); see also **musician, poet.**

**minstrelsy,** *n.* — *Syn.* balladry, folk music, *Lieder* (German); see **song.**

**mint,** *v.* **1.** [To print or press money] — *Syn.* strike, mold, punch, coin, cast, forge, stamp, issue, provide legal tender; see also **print** 2.
**2.** [To invent a word, etc.] — *Syn.* coin, devise, create; see **invent** 1.

**minus,** *modif.* — *Syn.* diminished, short of, deficient; see **less.**

**minute,** *modif.* **1.** [Extremely small] — *Syn.* microscopic, diminutive, wee, tiny, atomic, miniature, puny, infinitesimal, inframicroscopic, microbic, molecular, exact, precise, pulverized, fine, exiguous, inconsiderable, teeny\*, weeny\*, teensy\*, peewee\*, itsy\*, itsy-bitsy\*, invisible\*; see also **little** 1. — *Ant.* LARGE, huge, immense.
**2.** [Trivial] — *Syn.* immaterial, nonessential, paltry; see **trivial, unimportant.**
**3.** [Exact] — *Syn.* particular, circumstantial, specialized; see **detailed, elaborate** 2.
*See Synonym Study at* SMALL.

**minute,** *n.* **1.** [The sixtieth part of an hour] — *Syn.* sixty seconds, unit of time, measure of time, space of time; see **time** 1.
**2.** [A brief time] — *Syn.* short time, second, trice, flash, twinkling, breath, jiffy\*, bat of an eye\*, shake of a lamb's tail\*, couple of humps\*, tick\*, twink\*; see also **instant, moment** 1, **time** 2. — *Ant.* ETERNITY, long time, FOREVER.

**up to the minute\*** — *Syn.* **1.** modern, contemporary, in the latest style, up to date; see **fashionable.**
**2.** current, prompt, recent; see **modern** 1.

**(the) minute that,** *conj.* — *Syn.* as soon as, the second that, at the time that; see **when** 1, 2, **whenever.**

**minutiae,** *n.* — *Syn.* trivia, particulars, items; see **details.**

**minx,** *n.* — *Syn.* wench, malapert, saucy young woman, hussy; see **girl** 1.

**miracle,** *n.* — *Syn.* marvel, revelation, supernatural occurrence; see **wonder** 2.

**miraculous,** *modif.* **1.** [Caused by divine intervention]

— *Syn.* supernatural, preternatural, marvelous, super-human, beyond understanding, phenomenal, anoma-lous, unimaginable, stupendous, stupefying, awesome, monstrous; see also **mysterious** 2, **unknown** 1.— *Ant.* NATURAL, FAMILIAR, imaginable.

**2.** [So unusual as to suggest a miracle] — *Syn.* extra-ordinary, freakish, wondrous; see **unusual** 1, 2.

**mirage,** *n.* — *Syn.* illusion, phantasm, delusion, halluci-nation; see **fantasy** 2, **illusion** 1.
*See Synonym Study at* ILLUSION.

**mire,** *n.* — *Syn.* marsh, bog, ooze; see **mud, swamp.**

**mirror,** *n.* — *Syn.* looking glass, speculum, reflector, polished metal, imager, hand glass, cheval glass, pier glass, mirroring surface, camera finder, hand mirror, full-length mirror; see also **glass** 2.

**mirror,** *v.* — *Syn.* reflect, echo, imitate, copy; see **fol-low** 2, **reflect** 2, 3.

**mirth,** *n.* — *Syn.* frolic, jollity, entertainment; see **fun, merriment** 2.

**miry,** *modif.* — *Syn.* slimy, swampy, grimy; see **dirty** 1, **marshy, muddy** 1.

**misadventure,** *n.* — *Syn.* adversity, ill luck, catastro-phe; see **misfortune** 1.

**misanthrope,** *n.* — *Syn.* misanthropist, misogynist, doubter, man-hater, woman-hater, recluse, isolate, loner\*; see also **cynic, pessimist, skeptic.**

**misanthropic,** *modif.* — *Syn.* cynical, egotistical, selfish, people-hating, man-hating, woman-hating, misogynistic, antisocial, unsocial, unsociable, un-friendly, reclusive, hostile, inhumane; see also **pessi-mistic** 2, **sarcastic.**
*See Synonym Study at* PESSIMISTIC.

**misanthropy,** *n.* — *Syn.* cynicism, selfishness, egoism; see **egotism, pride** 1.

**misapply,** *v.* — *Syn.* misdirect, waste, distort; see **mis-understand.**

**misapprehend,** *v.* — *Syn.* err, blunder, confuse; see **mistake, misunderstand.**

**misapprehension,** *n.* — *Syn.* misconception, fallacy, delusion; see **mistake** 2, **misunderstanding** 1.

**misappropriate,** *v.* — *Syn.* plunder, appropriate, abuse; see **rob, steal.**

**misbegotten,** *modif.* — *Syn.* baseborn, unlawful, bas-tard, natural; see **illegal, illegitimate** 2, **poor** 2.

**misbehave,** *v.* — *Syn.* do wrong, do evil, sin, fail, trip, blunder, work iniquity, offend, trespass, act up, carry on, behave badly, misdo, err, lapse, be delinquent, be at fault, be culpable, be blameworthy, be guilty, be censurable, be reprehensible, be bad, misdemean one-self, forget oneself, misconduct oneself, be immoral, be dissolute, be disreputable, be indecorous, carry on, be naughty, go astray, take a wrong course, deviate from the path of virtue, sow one's wild oats\*, cut up\*, screw up\*; see also **transgress.** — *Ant.* BEHAVE, be good, do well.

**misbehaved,** *modif.* — *Syn.* uncivil, discourteous, ill-mannered; see **naughty, rude** 2.

**misbehavior,** *n.* — *Syn.* transgression, misconduct, fault; see **mischief** 3.

**misbelief,** *n.* — *Syn.* heresy, scepticism, heterodoxy, superstition; see **doubt** 1, **heresy.**

**misbelieve,** *v.* — *Syn.* err, have doubts, be unorthodox; see **doubt** 1.

**misbeliever,** *n.* — *Syn.* doubter, pessimist, heretic; see **cynic, skeptic.**

**miscalculate,** *v.* — *Syn.* blunder, miscount, err; see **mistake.**

**miscall,** *v.* — *Syn.* call by a wrong name, misterm, mis-title, misname; see **mistake.**

**miscarriage,** *n.* **1.** [Failure] — *Syn.* malfunction, de-feat, mistake; see **failure** 1.
**2.** [A too premature delivery] — *Syn.* unnatural birth, untimely delivery, birth interruption; see **abortion** 1.

**miscarry,** *v.* — *Syn.* abort, lose, go wrong; see **fail** 1.

**miscellaneous,** *modif.* **1.** [Lacking unity] — *Syn.* di-verse, disparate, eclectic, unmatched; see **different** 2.
**2.** [Lacking order] — *Syn.* mixed, muddled, scattered; see **confused** 2, **disordered.**

**miscellany,** *n.* **1.** [Medley] — *Syn.* jumble, collection, hodgepodge; see **mixture** 1.
**2.** [Anthology] — *Syn.* collectanea, extracts, compen-dium, symposium, compilation, excerpta, miscellanea; see also **collection** 2.

**mischance,** *n.* — *Syn.* casualty, accident, emergency; see **catastrophe, disaster, misfortune** 1.

**mischief,** *n.* **1.** [Damage] — *Syn.* hurt, injury, trouble, harm; see **damage** 1.
**2.** [Evil] — *Syn.* atrocity, ill, catastrophe; see **evil** 2, **wrong** 2.
**3.** [Prankishness] — *Syn.* troublesomeness, harmful-ness, impishness, waggishness, sportiveness, ro-guishness, rascality, misbehavior, misconduct, fault, transgression, wrongdoing, misdoing, playfulness, frolicsomeness, naughtiness, mischief-making, devil-ment, friskiness, shenanigans\*, funny business\*.— *Ant.* DIGNITY, demureness, sedateness.

**mischief-maker,** *n.* — *Syn.* scoundrel, troublemaker, rogue; see **rascal.**

**mischievous,** *modif.* — *Syn.* playful, roguish, prankish; see **naughty, rude** 2.

**misconceive,** *v.* — *Syn.* misconstrue, miscalculate, mis-interpret, err; see **mistake, misunderstand.**

**misconception,** *n.* — *Syn.* misinterpretation, delusion, blunder, fault; see **error** 1, **mistake** 2, **misunder-standing** 1.

**misconduct,** *n.* — *Syn.* misbehavior, offense, wrong-doing; see **evil** 2, **mischief** 3.

**misconduct,** *v.* **1.** [Mismanage] — *Syn.* misapply, mis-handle, misdirect; see **confuse, mismanage.**
**2.** [Misbehave oneself] — *Syn.* err, transgress, do wrong; see **misbehave.**

**misconstruction,** *n.* — *Syn.* distortion, misunderstand-ing, fallacy; see **error** 1, **mistake** 2.

**misconstrue,** *v.* — *Syn.* exaggerate, distort, pervert; see **mistake, misunderstand.**

**miscount,** *n.* — *Syn.* miscalculation, wrong total, incor-rect sum; see **error** 1, **mistake** 2.

**miscount,** *v.* — *Syn.* misestimate, err, miscalculate; see **mistake.**

**miscreant,** *n.* — *Syn.* wretch, villain, knave, rogue, ruf-fian, rapscallion, scamp, caitiff, sneak, scoundrel, cul-prit, reprobate, delinquent, bully, malefactor, felon, criminal, convict, outlaw, jailbird, drunkard, bootlegger, blackguard, outcast, scapegrace, scallawag, racketeer, hoodlum, pickpocket, loafer, rounder, rowdy, rough; see also **criminal, rascal.**— *Ant.* GENTLEMAN, LADY, good man.

**misdate,** *v.* — *Syn.* date wrongly, predate, antedate, postdate; see **mistake.**

**misdeed,** *n.* — *Syn.* fault, transgression, offense; see **crime** 1.

**misdemeanor,** *n.* — *Syn.* misconduct, misbehavior, misdeed; see **crime** 2.

**misdirect,** *v.* — *Syn.* lead astray, misinform, instruct badly; see **deceive, mislead.**

**misdoer,** *n.* — *Syn.* malefactor, offender, evildoer; see **criminal, miscreant.**

**misdoing,** *n.* — *Syn.* fault, betrayal, transgression; see **error** 1, **mistake** 2.

**misemploy,** *v.* — *Syn.* misuse, waste, mistreat; see **abuse** 1.

**miser,** *n.* **1.** [A hoarder of gold] — *Syn.* extortioner, usurer, skinflint, Scrooge, money-grubber, hoarder\*, harpy\*, lickpenny\*, screw\*, hunks\*, scrimp\*, rakerenter\*. — *Ant.* BEGGAR, spendthrift, waster.
**2.** [A niggardly person] — *Syn.* churl, misanthropist, niggard, skinflint, piker\*, cheapskate\*, pinchpenny\*, cheeseparer\*, penny pincher\*, tightwad\*, muckworm\*; see also **misanthrope.** — *Ant.* PATRON, philanthropist, benefactor.

**miserable,** *modif.* **1.** [In misery] — *Syn.* distressed, afflicted, sickly, ill, wretched, sick, ailing, unfortunate, pitiable, uncomfortable, suffering, hurt, wounded, tormented, tortured, in pain, strained, racked, injured, anguished, agonized, fevered, burning, convulsed; see also **troubled** 1, 2. — *Ant.* HELPED, aided, COMFORTABLE.
**2.** [Unhappy] — *Syn.* pained, discontented, sorrowful; see **sad** 1.
**3.** [Of very low standard] — *Syn.* sorry, worthless, inferior; see **poor** 2.

**miserably,** *modif.* — *Syn.* poorly, unsatisfactorily, imperfectly; see **badly** 1, **inadequately.**

**miserly,** *modif.* — *Syn.* stingy, covetous, parsimonious, close-fisted; see **stingy.**
*See Synonym Study at* STINGY.

**misery,** *n.* **1.** [Pain] — *Syn.* distress, suffering, agony; see **pain** 2.
**2.** [Dejection] — *Syn.* worry, despair, desolation; see **depression** 2, **grief** 1, **sadness.**
**3.** [Trouble] — *Syn.* grief, anxiety, problem; see **difficulty** 2.

**misfire,** *v.* — *Syn.* fail to fire, miss, fizzle out\*; see **explode** 1, **fail** 1.

**misfit,** *n.* — *Syn.* maverick, loner, dropout, nonconformist, oddball, psychotic, sociopath; see also **neurotic.**

**misfortune,** *n.* **1.** [Bad luck] — *Syn.* back luck, ill fortune, ill luck, adversity, affliction, adverse fortune, trouble, hardship, disadvantage, mischance, disappointment, reversal, setback, hard luck\*, vexatiousness, discomfort, distress, loss, hard times, unpleasantness, untowardness, worry, anxiety, hard knocks. — *Ant.* good fortune, luck, advantage.
**2.** [An unlucky accident] — *Syn.* mishap, calamity, accident, misadventure, unlucky accident, disaster, reversal, disappointment, setback, mischance, blow, contretemps, comedown, tough break\*; see also **disaster.**
*See Synonym Study at* AFFLICTION.

**misgiving,** *n.* — *Syn.* doubt, apprehension, qualm, hesitation; see **doubt** 2, **qualm** 1.
*See Synonym Study at* QUALM.

**misguided,** *modif.* — *Syn.* misled, deceived, confused; see **mistaken** 1.

**mishandle,** *v.* — *Syn.* mistreat, harm, misemploy; see **abuse** 1.

**mishap,** *n.* — *Syn.* accident, mischance, misadventure; see **catastrophe, disaster, misfortune** 1.

**mishmash\*,** *n.* — *Syn.* hodgepodge, combination, jumble; see **mixture** 1.

**misinform,** *v.* — *Syn.* mislead, report inaccurately, misstate; see **deceive, lie** 1.

**misinterpret,** *v.* — *Syn.* misconstrue, garble, misrepresent, falsify, distort, miscalculate; see also **mistake, misunderstand.**

**misinterpretation,** *n.* — *Syn.* distortion, misreckoning, delusion; see **error** 1, **mistake** 2, **misunderstanding** 1.

**misjudge,** *v.* **1.** [To make a wrong judgment, usually of a person] — *Syn.* presume, prejudge, suppose, presuppose, misapprehend, be partial, be overcritical, be unfair, be one-sided, be misled, come to a hasty conclusion; see also **misunderstand.** — *Ant.* UNDERSTAND, discern, detect.
**2.** [To make an inaccurate estimate] — *Syn.* miss, miscalculate, misconceive, misthink, misconstrue, overestimate, underestimate, dogmatize, bark up the wrong tree\*; see also **mistake.** — *Ant.* ESTIMATE, predict, calculate.

**misjudgment,** *n.* **1.** [Mistake] — *Syn.* distortion, misinterpretation, misconception; see **error** 1, **mistake** 2.
**2.** [Prejudice] — *Syn.* unfairness, bias, partiality; see **prejudice.**

**mislaid,** *modif.* — *Syn.* gone, misplaced, disarranged; see **lost** 1.

**mislay,** *v.* — *Syn.* disorder, displace, disarrange; see **misplace.**

**mislead,** *v.* — *Syn.* delude, cheat, deceive, defraud, cozen, bilk, take in, overreach, outwit, ensnare, trick, enmesh, entangle, victimize, lure, beguile, inveigle, hoax, dupe, gull, bait, misrepresent, bluff, give a bum steer\*, throw off the scent\*, lead one on a merry chase\*, bamboozle\*, gull\*, dupe\*, scam\*, humbug\*, hoodwink\*, put someone on\*; see also **deceive, lie** 1.
*See Synonym Study at* DECEIVE.

**misled,** *modif.* — *Syn.* misguided, deluded, wronged; see **deceived** 1, **mistaken** 1.

**mislike,** *v.* — *Syn.* condemn, disdain, not care for; see **dislike.**

**mismanage,** *v.* — *Syn.* bungle, blunder, overlook, confound, misconduct, fumble, mess up\*, foul up\*, kill the goose that lays the golden eggs\*, bark up the wrong tree\*; see also **fail** 1.

**mismatched,** *modif.* — *Syn.* incompatible, discordant, inconsistent; see **incongruous** 1, **unsuitable.**

**misname,** *v.* — *Syn.* label incorrectly, miscall, mistitle, misterm, mislabel, misidentify, misdenominate, misstyle, misconstrue; see also **mistake.**

**misogynist,** *n.* — *Syn.* sexist, male chauvinist, celibate, misanthrope, woman-hater, bachelor, agamist, misogamist, encratite; see also **cynic, skeptic.**

**misplace,** *v.* — *Syn.* mislay, displace, shuffle, disarrange, remove, disturb, take out of its place, disorder, tumble, dishevel, confuse, mix, scatter, unsettle, muss, disorganize; see also **lose** 2. — *Ant.* FIND, LOCATE, PLACE.

**misplaced,** *modif.* — *Syn.* displaced, mislaid, out of place; see **lost** 1.

**misprint,** *n.* — *Syn.* typing error, fault, typo; see **error** 1, **mistake** 2.

**misprision,** *n.* — *Syn.* indiscretion, offense, misdemeanor; see **crime** 2.

**misprize,** *v.* — *Syn.* ridicule, miscalculate, disregard; see **underestimate.**

**mispronounce,** *v.* — *Syn.* falter, misspeak, murder the Queen's English, murder the King's English\*; see **hesitate, stammer.**

**mispronunciation,** *n.* — *Syn.* misaccentuation, cacology, cacoepy; see **error** 1, **mistake** 2.

**misquote,** *v.* — *Syn.* distort, overstate, misrepresent; see **exaggerate.**

**misreport,** *v.* — *Syn.* distort, falsify, misquote; see **exaggerate.**

**misrepresent,** *v.* — *Syn.* misstate, embroider, distort, falsify, understate; see also **deceive, lie** 1, **mislead.**

**misrepresentation,** *n.* — *Syn.* counterfeit, untruth, mask, cloak, mendacity, deceit, dissembling, disguise, simulation, feigning, misstatement, distortion, falsification, understatement, overdrawing, exaggeration, caricature, travesty, burlesque, parody, extravaganza, imitation, bad likeness, misapprehension, misconception, misunderstanding, misapplication, misinterpretation, misconstruction, misguidance, misdirection, perversion, sophistry, phoney\*, lollapalooza\*, barnumism\*; see also **deception** 1, **lie** 1. — *Ant.* TRUTH, HONESTY, candor.

**misrule,** *n.* — *Syn.* mismanagement, chaos, anarchy, mobacracy; see **disorder** 2.

**miss,** *n.* **1.** [A failure] — *Syn.* slip, blunder, mishap; see **error** 1, **mistake** 2.
**2.** [A young woman] — *Syn.* lass, lassie, female; see **girl** 1.
**3.** [Title for a woman] — *Syn.* Ms., mistress\*, *mademoiselle* (French), *señorita* (Spanish).
**a miss is as good as a mile** — *Syn.* err, miscalculate, misjudge; see **mistake.**

**miss,** *v.* **1.** [To feel a want] — *Syn.* desire, crave, yearn; see **need, want** 1.
**2.** [To fail to catch] — *Syn.* snatch at, drop, fumble, bungle, muff\*, goof\*, butter a catch\*, foozle\*, blow\*, have butterfingers\*, juggle\*, louse\*, boot\*. — *Ant.* CATCH, grab, HOLD.
**3.** [To fail to hit] — *Syn.* miss one's aim, miss the mark, be wide of the mark, overshoot, undershoot, go above, go below, go to the side, carve the breeze\*, fan the air\*. — *Ant.* HIT, shoot, get.
**4.** [To fail to use] — *Syn.* avoid, refrain, give up; see **abstain.**

**missal,** *n.* — *Syn.* service book, Mass book, psalter; see **prayer book.**

**missed,** *modif.* **1.** [Not found or noticed] — *Syn.* gone, misplaced, mislaid, forgotten, unrecalled, unnoticed, not in sight, put away, in hiding, hidden, strayed, wandered off, moved, removed, borrowed, unseen; see also **lost** 1. — *Ant.* REMEMBERED, found, located.
**2.** [Longed for] — *Syn.* needed, desired, wished for, pined for, wanted, yearned for, clung to, craved, hungered for, thirsted for. — *Ant.* HATED, disliked, unwanted.

**misshapen,** *modif.* — *Syn.* distorted, disfigured, twisted; see **deformed.**

**missile,** *n.* — *Syn.* cartridge, projectile, ammunition, rocket, guided missile; see also **bullet, shot** 2, **weapon** 1.
Types of missiles include: Polaris, Poseidon, Submarine-Launched Ballistic Missile (SLBM), Titan, Pershing, cruise, MX, Minuteman, Intercontinental Ballistic Missile (ICBM), Intermediate Range Ballistic Missile (IRBM), Anti-Ballistic Missile (ABM), Fractional Orbital Bombardment System (FOBS), Multiple Independently Targetable Re-entry Vehicle (MIRV), Air to Surface Missile (ASM), Air to Air Missile (ATA), Surface to Air Missile (ASM), Surface to Surface Missile (SSM), Viking, Lance, Patriot, Hawk, Stinger, M-109, ton, Trident, Tomahawk, cruise, Sidewinder, Scud, Frog, Silkworm, Exocet.

**missing,** *modif.* — *Syn.* disappeared, lacking, removed; see **absent, lost** 1.

**missing link,** *n.* — *Syn.* connection, needed part, necessary part, pertinent evidence; see **link, hominid.**

**mission,** *n.* **1.** [Purpose] — *Syn.* charge, sortie, commission; see **purpose** 1.
**2.** [Vocation] — *Syn.* calling, occupation, profession, mission in life; see **profession** 1.

**3.** [A delegation] — *Syn.* legation, deputation, embassy, commission.

**missionary,** *n.* — *Syn.* apostle, evangelist, revivalist, preacher, teacher, pastor, herald, padre; see also **messenger, minister** 1.

**missish,** *modif.* — *Syn.* prudish, formal, priggish; see **prim.**

**Mississippi River,** *n.* — *Syn.* Great Water, Father of Waters, *Missi sepe* (Algonquin), Old Man River\*, the Big Drink\*; see also **river** 1.

**missive,** *n.* — *Syn.* word, note, message; see **letter** 2.

**misspend,** *v.* — *Syn.* squander, exhaust, lavish; see **waste** 2.

**misspent,** *modif.* — *Syn.* wasted, squandered, thrown away; see **wasted.**

**misstate,** *v.* — *Syn.* deceive, misrepresent, misquote; see **exaggerate.**

**misstatement,** *n.* — *Syn.* exaggeration, distortion, falsity; see **error** 1, **mistake** 2.

**misstep,** *n.* — *Syn.* slip, miss, trip, bungle, stumble; see also **failure** 1.

**mist,** *n.* — *Syn.* drizzle, spray, haze, fog, smog, vapor, cloud, film, gauze, fine rain, mizzle\*; see also **fog** 1, **haze.**

---

**SYN.** — **mist** applies to a visible atmospheric vapor of rather fine density that blurs the vision; **haze** suggests a thin dispersion of smoke, dust, moisture, etc. that makes objects indistinct; **fog** suggests a greater density of moisture particles than **mist,** sometimes suggesting a thickness impenetrable by the vision; **smog** is applied to a low-lying, perceptible layer of polluted air or to a mixture of fog and smoke sometimes appearing in industrial centers: the first three terms are also used figuratively *[lost in the mists of the past, a troublesome haze of confusion, in a fog of doubt]*

---

**mist,** *v.* — *Syn.* shower, drizzle, fog; see **mizzle, rain.**

**mistake,** *n.* **1.** [A blunder] — *Syn.* error, false step, blunder, slip; see **error** 1.
**2.** [A misunderstanding] — *Syn.* misapprehension, confusion, misconception, misconstruction, delusion, illusion, overestimation, underestimation, impression, aberration, muddle, bemuddling, confounding, disregarding, misinterpretation, misapplication, misdoubt, misstatement, perversion, perplexity, bewilderment, misjudgment; see also **exaggeration** 1, **misunderstanding** 1. — *Ant.* KNOWLEDGE, certainty, interpretation.
*See Synonym Study at* ERROR.

**mistake,** *v.* — *Syn.* err, blunder, slip, lapse, miss, overlook, omit, underestimate, overestimate, fail to know, fail to recognize, substitute, misjudge, misapprehend, misconceive, misunderstand, confound, misinterpret, misconstrue, confuse, botch, bungle, be at cross purposes, have the wrong impression, tangle, snarl, slip up, mix, make a mess of\*, come a cropper\*, miss the boat\*, slip a cog\*, put one's foot in one's mouth\*. — *Ant.* SUCCEED, be accurate, explain.

**mistaken,** *modif.* **1.** [In error] — *Syn.* inaccurate, inexact, misinformed, deceived, confounded, confused, misinterpreting the facts, misconceiving the meaning, misunderstanding the situation, misapprehending the situation, misjudging the facts, having the wrong impression, deluded, misinformed, misguided, at fault, off the track, having been too credulous; see also **wrong** 2.
**2.** [Ill-advised] — *Syn.* unadvised, duped, fooled, misled, tricked, unwarranted; see also **deceived** 1.
**3.** [Taken for another] — *Syn.* improperly identified,

wrongly identified, unrecognized, confused with, taken for, in a case of mistaken identity, misnamed, miscataloged, misconstrued.

**mistakenly,** *modif.* — *Syn.* badly, falsely, inadvisedly; see **wrongly** 1, 2.

**mister,** *n.* — *Syn.* Mr., sir, Esquire, Esq., man, *monsieur* (French), *Herr* (German), *signor* (Italian), *señor* (Spanish), *gospodin, grazhdanin, tovarishch* (all Russian).

**misterm,** *v.* — *Syn.* mislabel, miscall, mistitle; see **misname.**

**mistimed,** *modif.* — *Syn.* untimely, unfavorable, inappropriate; see **unsuitable.**

**mistiness,** *n.* — *Syn.* cloudiness, dimness, fogginess; see **fog** 1.

**mistranslate,** *v.* — *Syn.* misinterpret, distort, falsify; see **mistake, misunderstand.**

**mistreat,** *v.* — *Syn.* harm, injure, wrong; see **abuse** 1.

**mistreatment,** *n.* — *Syn.* injury, harm, violation; see **abuse** 3.

**mistress,** *n.* 1. [A woman in authority] — *Syn.* housekeeper, schoolmistress, caretaker, chaperone, housemother, manager, wife, mother, consort; see also **lady** 2, **matron** 2.
2. [An illegitimate consort] — *Syn.* courtesan, paramour, sweetheart, ladylove, voluptuary, woman of easy virtue, concubine, kept woman, the other woman*; see also **prostitute.**

**mistrial,** *n.* — *Syn.* malfeasance, miscarriage of justice, legal slip, blunder; see **error** 1, **failure** 1, **mistake** 2.

**mistrust,** *n.* — *Syn.* distrust, wariness, skepticism, suspicion; see **doubt** 1.

**mistrust,** *v.* — *Syn.* suspect, distrust, scruple; see **doubt** 2.

**mistrustful,** *modif.* — *Syn.* skeptical, dubious, unsure; see **doubtful** 2, **suspicious** 1.

**misty,** *modif.* — *Syn.* dim, foggy, hazy, murky, shrouded, obscure, enveloped in mist, enveloped in spray; see also **dark** 1.

**misunderstand,** *v.* — *Syn.* err, misconceive, misinterpret, miscomprehend, misjudge, miscalculate, misreckon, misapply, misconstrue, be at crosspurposes, be perplexed, be bewildered, confuse, confound, have the wrong impression, fail to understand, misapprehend, overestimate, underestimate, be misled, be unfamiliar with, be unconversant with, have the wrong slant on*, not understand all one knows*, not register*; see also **mistake.** — *Ant.* UNDERSTAND, grasp, apprehend.

**misunderstanding,** *n.* 1. [Misapprehension] — *Syn.* delusion, misreckoning, miscalculation, confusion, misinterpretation, confounding; see also **error** 1, **mistake** 2. — *Ant.* CONCEPTION, understanding, apprehension.
2. [Disagreement] — *Syn.* debate, dissension, difference, quarrel; see **disagreement** 1, **dispute.**

**misunderstood,** *modif.* — *Syn.* misinterpreted, falsely interpreted, misconceived; see **mistaken** 1, **wrong** 2.

**misusage,** *n.* — *Syn.* malapropism, mispronunciation, spoonerism, cacology, antiphrasis, solecism, catachresis, ungrammaticalness, barbarism, improper use of words; see also **error** 1, **mistake** 2.

**misuse,** *n.* — *Syn.* ill-usage, misapplication, perversion; see **abuse** 1.

**misuse,** *v.* — *Syn.* maltreat, mistreat, ill-treat; see **abuse** 1.

**mite,** *n.* — *Syn.* parasite, bug, tick; see **insect, vermin.**
Types of mites include: clover, dust, flour, follicle, house, itch, cheese, blister, chicken.

**mitigate,** *v.* — *Syn.* alleviate, lessen, moderate; see **decrease** 1, **relieve** 2.

*See Synonym Study at* RELIEVE.

**mitigation,** *n.* — *Syn.* alleviation, reduction, remission; see **moderation** 2, **relief** 1.

**mitt,** *n.* — *Syn.* glove, baseball glove, catcher's mitt, first baseman's mitt; see **glove.**

**mitten,** *n.* — *Syn.* glove, mitt, gauntlet, boxing glove; see **glove.**

**mix,** *v.* 1. [To blend] — *Syn.* blend, fuse, merge, coalesce, mingle, unite, combine, meld, cross, hybridize, interbreed, immix, admix, commix, intermix, amalgamate, incorporate, alloy, compound, agitate, commingle, intermingle, homogenize, weave, throw together, interweave, adulterate, infiltrate, intertwine, knead, stir, beat, fold in, whip, whisk, process, brew, suffuse, instill, transfuse, synthesize, infuse, saturate, tincture, shuffle, marry; see also **join** 1.
2. [To confuse] — *Syn.* mix up, jumble, tangle; see **confuse.**
3. [To associate] — *Syn.* fraternize, get along, consort with; see **associate** 1.

---

**SYN.** — **mix** implies a combining of things so that the resulting substance is uniform in composition, whether or not the separate elements can be distinguished /to *mix* paints/; **mingle** usually implies that the separate elements can be distinguished /*mingled* feelings of joy and sorrow/; **blend** implies a mixing of different varieties to produce a desired quality /a *blended* tea, whiskey, etc./ or the mingling of different elements to form an inseparable or harmonious whole /a novel *blending* fact and fiction/; **merge** stresses the loss of distinction of elements by combination or may suggest the total absorption of one thing in another /the companies *merged* to form a large corporation/; **coalesce** implies a union or growing together of things into a single body or mass /the factions *coalesced* into a party of opposition/; **fuse** means to unite by melting together and stresses the indissoluble nature of the union

---

**mixed,** *modif.* 1. [Commingled] — *Syn.* admixed, blended, fused, mingled, commixed, compounded, combined, amalgamated, united, brewed, tied, merged, embodied, infused, transfused, crossed, hybridized, assimilated, married, woven, kneaded, incorporated; see also **joined.** — *Ant.* SEPARATED, severed, raveled.
2. [Various] — *Syn.* miscellaneous, unselected, diverse; see **different** 2, **various.**
3. [Confused] — *Syn.* mixed up, jumbled, disordered; see **confused** 2.

**mixed-up,** *modif.* — *Syn.* confused, muddled, confounded, mistaken, disoriented, discombobulated*.

**mixer,** *n.* 1. [An instrument used to mix materials] — *Syn.* blender, Osterizer (Trademark), food processor, juicer, egg beater, cake mixer, food mixer, cocktail shaker, converter, carburetor, concrete mixer, cement mixer, paint mixer, turbine beater; see also **appliance, machine** 1.
2. [A substance used in a mixture] — *Syn.* ingredient, component, combining element; see **part** 1.
3. [Liquids used in prepared drinks] — *Syn.* carbonated water, soda water, tonic, quinine water, tap water, distilled water, seltzer, mineral water, ginger ale; see also **drink** 3, **soda, water** 1.
4. [*A party] — *Syn.* tea, social gathering, cocktail party; see **party** 1.

**mixture,** *n.* 1. [A combination] — *Syn.* blend, compound, composite, amalgam, miscellany, intermixture, admixture, mingling, medley, mix, potpourri, salmagundi, alloy, fusion, jumble, mishmash*, mash, brew,

merger, adulteration, hybridization, hybrid, crossing, infiltration, magma, transfusion, infusion, mélange, interweavement, saturation, assimilation, incorporation, olio, olla podrida, broth, stew, dough, batter, hodgepodge*.
2. [A mess] — *Syn.* mix-up, muddle, disorder; see **confusion** 2.

**mix-up,** *n.* — *Syn.* turmoil, chaos, commotion; see **confusion** 2, **disorder** 2.

**mizzle,** *v.* — *Syn.* mist, drizzle, sprinkle, shower, trickle, ooze, dribble, rain in small drops; see also **rain.**

**mnemonic,** *modif.* — *Syn.* of the memory, reminiscential, intended to assist the memory, mnemotechnic; see **helpful** 1.

**moan,** *n.* — *Syn.* plaint, groan, wail; see **cry** 1.
**moan,** *v.* — *Syn.* groan, wail, whine; see **cry** 1.
*See Synonym Study at* CRY.

**moat,** *n.* — *Syn.* ditch, fosse, canal, furrow; see **channel** 1, **trench** 1.

**mob,** *n.* **1.** [A disorderly crowd of people] — *Syn.* swarm, rabble, throng, press, multitude, horde, rout, riot, host, lawless element; see also **crowd** 1, **gathering.**
**2.** [The common people] — *Syn.* masses, populace, plebeians, proletariat; see **people** 3.
*See Synonym Study at* CROWD.

**mob,** *v.* — *Syn.* hustle, crowd, swarm; see **attack** 1, **rebel** 1, **riot.**

**mobbish,** *modif.* — *Syn.* vulgar, disorderly, ignoble, mean, vile, base, beggarly, proletarian, sorry, lowbred, unpolished, plebeian, uncivilized, unwashed, boorish, churlish, boisterous, rude, barbarous, savage, frenzied, hysteric, wild, impetuous, explosive, fierce; see also **unruly.**

**mobile,** *modif.* **1.** [Movable] — *Syn.* portable, transportable, loose, free; see **movable.**
**2.** [Capable of rapid motion] — *Syn.* motile, motor-activated; see **motorized.**
Types of mobile units of the armed forces include: motorized, tank, paratroop, air, naval, torpedoboat, patrolboat, task-force, search-and-destroy, patrol.

**mobility,** *n.* — *Syn.* changeability, versatility, flow, flux, plasticity, fluidity, changefulness, mutability; see also **movement** 1.

**mobilize,** *v.* — *Syn.* assemble, prepare, gather; see **enlist** 1.

**mob law,** *n.* — *Syn.* mob rule, anarchy, lawlessness; see **disorder** 2.

**mobocracy,** *n.* — *Syn.* anarchy, lawlessness, mob rule; see **disorder** 2.

**moccasin,** *n.* — *Syn.* slipper, sandal, heelless shoe, wedgie, play-shoe, *huarache* (Spanish); see also **shoe.**

**mock,** *modif.* — *Syn.* counterfeit, sham, pretended; see **false** 3, **unreal.**

**mock,** *v.* **1.** [To ridicule] — *Syn.* deride, make fun of, taunt; see **ridicule.**
**2.** [To mimic] — *Syn.* mimic, burlesque, caricature; see **imitate** 2, **parody.**
**3.** [To dare] — *Syn.* brave, defy, challenge; see **dare** 2.
*See Synonym Study at* IMITATE, RIDICULE.

**mocker,** *n.* — *Syn.* charlatan, scorner, pretender; see **cheat** 1, **impostor.**

**mockery,** *n.* **1.** [Derision] — *Syn.* teasing, jeering, badinage; see **ridicule.**
**2.** [Mimicry] — *Syn.* imitation, spoof, burlesque, lampoon; see **parody.**
**3.** [Something preposterous] — *Syn.* absurdity, inanity, laugh; see **joke** 1.

**mocking,** *modif.* — *Syn.* uncivil, insulting, unkind; see **rude** 2.

**mode,** *n.* **1.** [Manner] — *Syn.* tone, form, style; see **method** 2.
**2.** [The prevailing fashion] — *Syn.* fashion, style, convention, vogue; see **fashion** 2.
*See Synonym Study at* FASHION.

**model,** *n.* **1.** [A person or thing worthy of imitation] — *Syn.* paragon, archetype, prototype, exemplar, pattern, paradigm, ideal, role model, beau ideal, good example, shining example, hero, heroine, idol, demigod, saint, epitome, mirror; see also **paragon.**
**2.** [Anything that is copied] — *Syn.* original, example, pattern, standard, precedent, archetype, prototype, type, paradigm, text, guide, design, mold, criterion, rule, touchstone, gauge, ideal, shape, form, specimen, exemplar, principle, basis, sketch, antetype; see also **criterion.**
**3.** [A duplicate on a small scale] — *Syn.* miniature, image, illustration, representation, reduction, statue, statuette, figure, figurine, effigy, idol, mock-up, skeleton, portrait, photograph, relief, print, engraving; see also **copy, duplicate.**
**4.** [One who poses professionally] — *Syn.* poser, sitter, manikin, mannequin; see **nude.**
Kinds of models include: portrait, artist's, fashion, sculptor's, photographic.

**SYN.** — **model** refers to a representation made to be copied or, more generally, to any person or thing to be followed or imitated because of excellence, worth, etc.; **example** suggests that which is presented as a sample, or that which sets a precedent for imitation, whether good or bad; a **pattern** is a model, guide, plan, etc. to be strictly followed; **paradigm** can refer to an example that serves as a model, but is uncommon now except in its grammatical sense of an example of a declension or conjugation giving all the inflectional forms of a word; **archetype** applies to the original pattern serving as the model for all later things of the same kind or to a typical or perfect example of a type; **standard** refers to something established for use as a rule or a basis of comparison in judging quality, value, etc.

**model,** *v.* **1.** [To form] — *Syn.* shape, mold, fashion; see **create** 2, **form** 1.
**2.** [To imitate a model] — *Syn.* copy, trace, duplicate, sketch, reduce, represent, print, die, counterfeit, caricature, parody, burlesque, steal one's stuff*, register*; see also **illustrate** 1, **paint** 1.
**3.** [To serve as a model] — *Syn.* sit, act as model, set an example; see **pose** 2.
**4.** [To demonstrate] — *Syn.* show, show off, wear, parade, pose in; see also **display** 1.

**modeled,** *modif.* — *Syn.* designed, shaped, cast; see **formed.**

**moderate,** *modif.* **1.** [Not expensive] — *Syn.* inexpensive, low-priced, medium-priced, reasonable, within reason, modest, inexorbitant, not excessive, not dear, average, nominal, at par, usual, inconsiderable, marked down, at a bargain, half-price, reduced, worth the money, relatively low, of small yield; see also **cheap** 1, **economical** 2. — *Ant.* EXPENSIVE, dear, exorbitant.
**2.** [Not extreme] — *Syn.* temperate, measured, judicious, unexcessive, restrained, considered, reasonable, unextreme, balanced, equable, easy, average, steady, even, deliberate, calm, cool, mild, clement, gentle, unimpassioned, low-key, dispassionate, cautious, sober, prudent, sound, controlled, regulated, modest, con-

servative, medium, midway, within compass, within limits, striking the golden mean; see also **calm** 1, **conservative, mild** 2. — *Ant.* immoderate, intemperate, extreme, excessive.

**3.** [Not radical] — *Syn.* centrist, middle-of-the-road, tolerant, nonpartisan, unopinionated, undogmatic, not given to extremes, nonviolent, neutral, impartial, respectable, middle-class, preserving the middle course, compromising. — *Ant.* radical, extremist, fanatic.

**4.** [Average] — *Syn.* middling, modest, fair, mediocre; see **common** 1.

**5.** [Not indulgent] — *Syn.* temperate, restrained, sober, sparing, abstemious, frugal, self-denying, abstinent, unindulgent, self-controlled, disciplined, careful, teetotaling, on the wagon★, straight★, sworn off★; see also **restrained, sober** 3. — *Ant.* self-indulgent, intemperate, wasteful.

---

**SYN.** — **moderate** and **temperate** are often interchangeable in denoting a staying within reasonable limits, but in strict discrimination, **moderate** implies merely the absence of excesses or extremes, while **temperate** suggests deliberate self-restraint [*moderate* demands, a *temperate* reply]

---

**moderate,** *v.* **1.** [To become less] — *Syn.* abate, modify, lessen, decline; see **decrease** 1.

**2.** [To make less] — *Syn.* check, curb, reduce; see **decrease** 2.

**3.** [To preside over] — *Syn.* lead, direct, supervise, govern; see **manage** 1.

**moderately,** *modif.* — *Syn.* tolerantly, tolerably, temperately, somewhat, to a degree, enough, to some extent, to a certain extent, a little, to some degree, fairly, more than not, not exactly, quite a bit, in moderation, within reason, within reasonable limits, as far as could be expected, within the bounds of reason, in reason, in a tempered manner, pretty★, tolerable★; see also **reasonably** 2, **slightly.** — *Ant.* MUCH, extremely, remarkably.

**moderation,** *n.* **1.** [Restraint] — *Syn.* toleration, steadiness, sobriety, coolness, the golden mean, temperateness, quiet, temperance, lenity, patience, sedation, fairness, justice, constraint, forbearance, reasonableness, dispassionateness, poise, balance; see also **restraint** 1.

**2.** [The act of moderating] — *Syn.* mediation, settlement, governance, regulation, restriction, limitation, reduction, controlling, assuagement, alleviation, composing, soothing, quieting, placating, sobering, tempering; see also **restraint** 2. — *Ant.* INCREASE, license, misgovernance.

**moderator,** *n.* — *Syn.* chairman, arbitrator, mediator; see **judge** 2.

**modern,** *modif.* **1.** [Up to date] — *Syn.* current, new, up-to-date, latest, up-to-the-minute, stylish, modish, chic, smart, conforming, swank, late, recent, of the present, prevailing, prevalent, faddish, avant-garde, present-day, advanced, modernistic, streamlined, breaking with tradition, untraditional, new-fashioned, having the new look, contemporary, in vogue, in use, in the air, common, just out, state-of-the-art, space-age, ahead of its time, postmodern, with it★, in the swim★, newfangled★, sharp★, smooth★, mod★, cool★, now★, trendy★; see also **fashionable, fresh** 1. — *Ant.* OLD-FASHIONED, out-of-date, out-of-style.

**2.** [Having the comforts of modern life] — *Syn.* modernistic, modernized, renovated, functional, with modern conveniences, done over, having modern improvements, strictly modern; see also **convenient** 1, **improved** 1. — *Ant.* VICTORIAN, dilapidated, run down.

**3.** [Concerning recent times] — *Syn.* contemporary, contemporaneous, recent, concurrent, present-day, coincident, synchronous, twentieth-century, latter-day, mechanical, of the Machine Age, automated, of modern times, modernist; see also **now** 1, **present** 1. — *Ant.* OLD, medieval, primordial.

*See Synonym Study at* NEW.

**modernism,** *n.* — *Syn.* innovation, fashion, newness; see **fad, novelty** 1.

**modernist,** *n.* — *Syn.* innovator, futurist, pioneer; see **guide** 1, **leader** 2.

**modernistic,** *modif.* — *Syn.* modern, surrealistic, futuristic, high-style; see **fashionable, modern** 1.

*See Synonym Study at* NEW.

**modernize,** *v.* — *Syn.* regenerate, refurbish, bring up to date; see **improve** 1, **renew** 1, **revive** 1.

**modest,** *modif.* **1.** [Humble] — *Syn.* unassuming, meek, diffident, shy; see **humble** 1, **resigned.**

**2.** [Not showy] — *Syn.* unpretentious, unostentatious, unobtrusive, demure, quiet, seemly, proper, decorous, unstudied, plain, simple, natural, unassuming, humble, unornamented, tasteful, unadorned, unembellished, unvarnished, unaffected, homely, taking a back seat★, hiding one's face★; see also **dignified, reserved** 3. — *Ant.* IMMODEST, ostentatious, pretentious.

**3.** [Moderate] — *Syn.* reasonable, inexpensive, average; see **cheap** 1, **economical** 2, **moderate** 1.

**4.** [Proper] — *Syn.* decent, proper, chaste, seemly; see **decent** 2, **innocent** 4, **prudish.**

**5.** [Lowly] — *Syn.* plain, simple, unaffected; see **humble** 2.

*See Synonym Study at* CHASTE, SHY.

**modestly,** *modif.* **1.** [In a modest manner] — *Syn.* humbly, unobtrusively, retiringly, quietly, simply, unpretentiously, unpresumptuously, diffidently, bashfully, unassumingly, chastely, virtuously, purely, shyly, demurely, shrinkingly. — *Ant.* BOLDLY, boastfully, pretentiously.

**2.** [Within reasonable limits] — *Syn.* reasonably, coolly, sensibly; see **cheaply, moderately.**

**modesty,** *n.* **1.** [The state of being modest] — *Syn.* humility, unpretentiousness, unassumingness, delicacy, unostentatiousness, reticence, reserve, constraint, unobtrusiveness, self-effacement, meekness; see also **courtesy** 1, **dignity** 1, **restraint** 1. — *Ant.* VANITY, conceit, EGOTISM.

**2.** [Shyness] — *Syn.* inhibition, timidity, diffidence; see **shyness.**

**3.** [Chastity] — *Syn.* decency, innocence, seemliness, celibacy; see **chastity, purity** 1, **virtue** 1.

**modicum,** *n.* — *Syn.* trifle, fraction, particle; see **bit** 1.

**modification,** *n.* — *Syn.* qualification, alteration, correction; see **adjustment** 1, **change** 2.

**modified,** *modif.* **1.** [Changed] — *Syn.* varied, mutated, adjusted; see **changed** 2.

**2.** [Reduced] — *Syn.* qualified, limited, diminished; see **reduced** 1.

**modifier,** *n.* — *Syn.* limiter, conditioner, alterant, alterer, transformer.

Types of grammatical modifiers include: adjective, adjectival, adverb, adverbial, pronominal adjective, pronominal, phrasal modifier, verbal adjective, adjectival clause, adverbial clause; see also **word** 1.

**modify,** *v.* **1.** [To change] — *Syn.* alter, revise, adjust, change, remodel, refashion, transform, mutate; see also **change** 1, 4, **revise.**

**2.** [To moderate] — *Syn.* mitigate, qualify, restrain, curb; see **decrease** 2, **restrict** 2.

*See Synonym Study at* CHANGE.

**modish,** *modif.* — *Syn.* stylish, smart, mod*; see **fashionable, modern** 1.

**modiste,** *n.* — *Syn.* clothier, seamstress, designer; see **dressmaker, tailor.**

**modulate,** *v.* — *Syn.* inflect, accentuate, temper, vibrate; see **change** 1, **sound** 1.

**modulation,** *n.* — *Syn.* timbre, intonation, inflection; see **pitch** 3, **sound** 2.

***modus operandi*** (Latin), *n.* — *Syn.* M.O., operation, organization, procedure; see **method** 2, **system** 2.

**mogul,** *n.* — *Syn.* personage, magnate, czar, notable; see **lord** 2, **royalty.**

**Mohammedan,** *modif.* — *Syn.* Muslim, Islamic, Sulmanic; see **Moslem.**

**moiety,** *n.* **1.** [Part] — *Syn.* half, section, fraction; see **division** 2, **part** 1.
**2.** [Clan] — *Syn.* affiliation, kinship, group; see **family** 1.

**moist,** *modif.* **1.** [Damp] — *Syn.* humid, dank, moistened; see **wet** 1.
**2.** [Rainy] — *Syn.* drizzly, muggy, clammy; see **wet** 2.
*See Synonym Study at* WET.

**moisten,** *v.* — *Syn.* wet, sprinkle, dampen, saturate, drench, moisturize, waterlog, steep, sog, sop, dip, rinse, wash, wash over, wet down, humidify, water, water down, squirt, shower, rain on, splash, splatter, bathe, steam, bedew, spray, mist, sponge; see also **soak** 1.

**moisture,** *n.* — *Syn.* precipitation, mist, drizzle, condensation, dampness, damp; see also **fog** 1, **rain** 1.

**mold,** *n.* **1.** [A form] — *Syn.* form, matrix, womb, cavity, shape, frame, pattern, design, die, cast, dish, fossil cavity, depression, cup, image, mold-board, core; see also **form** 1, **model** 2.
**2.** [The body shaped in a mold, sense 1] — *Syn.* cast, kind, molding, casting, image, reproduction, form, pottery, shell, core; see also **impression** 1.
**3.** [A parasitic growth] — *Syn.* rust, smut, mildew, blue mold, mould, black mold, parasite, pennicillium, fungus, lichen; see also **decay** 2.

**mold,** *v.* **1.** [To give physical shape to] — *Syn.* make, round into, fashion; see **form** 1.
**2.** [To determine a course of action or an opinion] — *Syn.* devise, plot, scheme; see **plant** 1.
**3.** [To decay through the action of mold] — *Syn.* molder, mildew, rust; see **decay.**

**molder,** *v.* — *Syn.* decay, crumble, disintegrate; see **decay.**
*See Synonym Study at* DECAY.

**molding,** *n.* **1.** [A molded or carved strip] — *Syn.* architectural ornament, embellishment, decoration, frieze, picture frame, cornice, wainscoting; see also **frame** 2.
Types of molding include: fillet and fascia, sunk fillet, quarter round, torus, billet, crown, bead, reed, ovolo, ogee, cavetto, scotia, conge, cyma recta, cyma reversa, beak, splay.
**2.** [Forming as in a mold] — *Syn.* shaping, creating, casting; see **making.**

**moldy,** *modif.* — *Syn.* musty, mildewed, dank; see **rotten** 1.

**mole,** *n.* **1.** [Dike] — *Syn.* hill, mound, breakwater; see **dam** 1.
**2.** [Blemish] — *Syn.* flaw, birthmark, blotch; see **blemish.**

**molecular,** *modif.* — *Syn.* microscopic, atomic, subatomic, infinitesimal; see **little** 1, **minute** 1.

**molecule,** *n.* **1.** [Unit] — *Syn.* particle, fragment, unit; see **bit** 1.
**2.** [Atom] — *Syn.* electron, ion, particle; see **atom** 2.

**molest,** *v.* **1.** [To disturb objects] — *Syn.* displace, meddle, disorganize; see **disturb** 2.
**2.** [To disturb people] — *Syn.* interrupt, accost, break in upon, intrude, obtrude oneself, encroach upon, annoy, worry, disquiet, irritate, discommode, discompose, plague, badger, abuse sexually, bait, pester, hinder, tease, irk, vex, trouble, confuse, perturb, frighten, terrify, scare, misuse, maltreat; see also **bother** 2.

**mollify,** *v.* **1.** [To quiet one who is angry] — *Syn.* soothe, appease, calm; see **pacify** 1, **quiet** 1.
**2.** [To lessen] — *Syn.* ameliorate, alleviate, diminish; see **decrease** 2.
*See Synonym Study at* PACIFY.

**mollycoddle,** *n.* — *Syn.* recreant, craven, milquetoast, weakling; see **coward.**

**mollycoddle,** *v.* — *Syn.* pamper, coddle, spoil, baby; see **pamper, baby.**

**molt,** *v.* — *Syn.* lose, cast off, remove skin; see **shed.**

**molten,** *modif.* — *Syn.* heated, melted, fused, liquefied, running, fluid, seething; see also **hot** 1. — *Ant.* COLD, COOL, solid.

**moment,** *n.* **1.** [A brief time] — *Syn.* minute, instant, millisecond, trice, second, bit, while, flash, twinkling, jiff*, jiffy*, three winks*; see also **time** 2.
**2.** [Importance] — *Syn.* significance, note, consequence; see **importance** 2.
*See Synonym Study at* IMPORTANCE.

**momentarily,** *modif.* — *Syn.* immediately, right now, instantly; see **now** 1.

**momentary,** *modif.* — *Syn.* fleeting, flying, quick, summary, passing, flitting, flashing, transient, evanescent, fugitive, impermanent, shifting, spasmodic, ephemeral, vanishing, cursory, temporary, fugacious, like lightning, like a summer shower, bubblelike, dreamlike, gone in a flash*, in the bat of an eye*, in the wink of an eye*, quicker than one can say Jack Robinson*. — *Ant.* ETERNAL, continual, ceaseless.
*See Synonym Study at* TRANSIENT.

**momentous,** *modif.* — *Syn.* far-reaching, serious, consequential; see **important** 1.

**momentum,** *n.* — *Syn.* impulse, force, drive; see **energy** 3.

**mommy*,** *n.* — *Syn.* mom, female parent, mama; see **mother** 1, **parent.**

**monarch,** *n.* — *Syn.* ruler, despot, sovereign, autocrat; see **king** 1.

**monarchal,** *modif.* — *Syn.* regal, autocratic, eminent; see **noble** 3, **royal** 2.

**monarchy,** *n.* — *Syn.* kingship, sovereignty, command; see **government** 2, **power** 2.

**monastery,** *n.* — *Syn.* abbey, priory, religious community; see **cloister** 1.
*See Synonym Study at* CLOISTER.

**monastic,** *modif.* — *Syn.* humble, pious, devout, ascetic; see **religious** 2.

**monasticism,** *n.* — *Syn.* priesthood, cloistered life, celibacy; see **ministry** 2.

**monetary,** *modif.* — *Syn.* pecuniary, financial, fiscal; see **commercial** 1.
*See Synonym Study at* FINANCIAL.

**money,** *n.* **1.** [A medium of exchange] — *Syn.* gold, silver, cash, currency, check, bills, coin, coin of the realm, notes, coinage, specie, legal tender, Almighty Dollar*, beans*, gravy*, wampum*, shekels*, dough*, roll*, long green*, coins*, lucre*, folding money*, jack*, wad*, bucks*, ducats*, pesos*, dineros*, cabbage*, hard cash*, mazuma*, bread*.
Types of money in various countries include— *United States:* dollar, cent; *United Kingdom:* pound, penny;

*Russian Federation:* ruble, kopeck; *Brazil:* cruzado, centavo; *Mexico:* peso, centavo; *France:* franc, centime; *Italy:* lira, centismo; *Spain:* peseta, centimo; *Germany:* mark, pfennig; *Austria:* schilling, groschen; *Greece:* drachma, lepton; *Saudi Arabia:* riyal, halala; *Iran:* rial, dinar; *Libya:* dinat, dirham; *Turkey:* lira, kurus; *India:* rupee, paisa; *South Africa:* rand, cent; *Nigeria:* naira, kobo; *China:* yuan, fen; *Japan:* yen, sen; *Indonesia:* rupiah, sen; *Australia:* dollar, cent.
**2.** [Wealth] — *Syn.* funds, capital, property; see **wealth** 1, 2.
**3.** [Merged interests] — *Syn.* financiers, corporate interests, capitalists, capital, financial structure, vested interests, moneyed group; see also **banking, business** 4.
**4.** [Pay] — *Syn.* payment, salary, wages; see **pay** 2.
**for one's money★** — *Syn.* for one's choice, in one's opinion, to one's mind; see **personally** 2.
**in the money★** — *Syn.* wealthy, flush★, loaded★; see **rich** 1.
**make money** — *Syn.* gain profits, become wealthy, earn; see **profit** 2.
**one's money's worth** — *Syn.* full value, gain, benefit; see **value** 1, 3.
**place** (*or* **put**) **money on** — *Syn.* risk, bet, wager; see **gamble** 1.
**put money into** — *Syn.* invest in, support, underwrite; see **invest.**
**moneybags★,** *n.* — *Syn.* tycoon, capitalist, banker; see **financier, millionaire.**
**moneyed,** *modif.* — *Syn.* wealthy, well-to-do, affluent; see **rich** 1.
**moneyless,** *modif.* — *Syn.* bankrupt, destitute, indigent; see **poor** 1, **ruined** 4.
**(one's) money's worth,** *n.* — *Syn.* return, payment, reimbursement; see **pay** 1, **value** 1.
**mongrel,** *modif.* — *Syn.* crossbred, halfbred, hybrid; see **confused** 2, **mixed** 1.
**mongrel,** *n.* — *Syn.* mutt, cur, crossbreed, cross.
**monitor,** *n.* — *Syn.* counselor, informant, director, proctor; see **adviser.**
**monitor,** *v.* — *Syn.* watch, observe, control; see **advise** 1.
**monitory,** *modif.* — *Syn.* sinister, warning, portentous; see **ominous.**
**monk,** *n.* — *Syn.* hermit, eremite, cenobite, religious, anchorite, ascetic, solitary, recluse, abbot, prior; see also **friar, priest.**
Orders of monks include: Benedictine, Cistercian, Carthusian, Trappist, Franciscan, Capuchin, Dominican, Vincentian, Carmelite, Augustinian, Jesuit, Templar, Bernardine.
**monkey★,** *n.* — *Syn.* primate, lemur, anthropoid ape; see **animal** 2.
Types of monkeys include: marmoset, tamarin; capuchin, squirrel, howler, spider, woolly, macaque, baboon, mandrill, drill, mangabey, guenon, vervet, redtail, blue, colobus, leaf, proboscis.
Primates resembling monkeys include: gibbon, chimpanzee, orangutan, gorilla.
**a monkey on one's back** — *Syn.* addiction, compulsion, need; see **obsession.**
**monkey,** *v.* — *Syn.* pry, fool around, tamper with; see **meddle** 2.
**monkey business★,** *n.* — *Syn.* deceit, conniving, misconduct; see **deception** 1, **lie** 1.
**monkeyshines★,** *n.* — *Syn.* jokes, amusement, antics, mischief; see **joke** 1.
**monody,** *n.* — *Syn.* dirge, chant, lament; see **cry** 3, **song.**

**monolithic,** *modif.* — *Syn.* solid, unified, of one sort, inflexible, unyielding, consistent; see also **firm** 2, **uniform, united.**
**monologue,** *n.* — *Syn.* talk, speech, discourse, soliloquy; see **address** 2.
**monomania,** *n.* — *Syn.* fanaticism, furor, compulsion; see **neurosis, obsession.**
**monoplane,** *n.* — *Syn.* airplane, single-seater, aircraft; see **plane** 3.
**monopolize,** *v.* — *Syn.* engross, acquire, exclude, own exclusively, absorb, consume, manage, have, hold, corner, cartelize, syndicate, restrain, patent, copyright, corner the market★. — *Ant.* INCLUDE, give, invite.
**monopoly,** *n.* — *Syn.* trust, corner, syndicate, cartel, merger, oligopoly, pool, copyright, patent, restraint of trade. — *Ant.* open market, free trade.

***

*SYN.* — **monopoly** applies to the exclusive control of a commodity or service in a given market, or control that makes possible the fixing of prices and the virtual elimination of competition; **trust** is a combination of corporations, organized for the purpose of gaining a monopoly, in which stock is turned over to trustees who issue stock certificates to the stockholders: trusts are now illegal in the U.S.; **cartel,** the European term for a trust, now usually implies an international trust; a **syndicate** is now usually a group of bankers, corporations, etc. organized to buy large blocks of securities, afterward selling them in small parcels to the public at a profit; a **corner** is a temporary speculative monopoly of some stock or commodity for the purpose of raising the price

***

**monotonous,** *modif.* **1.** [Tiresome] — *Syn.* tedious, wearisome, wearying; see **dull** 4.
**2.** [Having but one tone] — *Syn.* monotonic, monotonical, unvarying, lacking variety, in one key, unchanged, reiterated, recurrent, single, uniform. — *Ant.* VARYING, VARIOUS, multiple.
**monotony,** *n.* — *Syn.* invariability, likeness, sameness, tediousness, similarity, continuity, continuance, oneness, identicalness, evenness, levelness, flatness, dreariness, unchangeableness, equability, boredom; jog trot★, even tenor★, the same old thing★; see also **boredom, dullness** 1. — *Ant.* DIFFERENCE, variability, VARIETY.
**monsoon,** *n.* — *Syn.* typhoon, hurricane, tempest; see **storm** 1.
**monster,** *n.* **1.** [A great beast] — *Syn.* beast, beastlike creature, basilisk, imaginary monster, centaur, monstrosity, Gorgon, sphinx, Minotaur, Hydra, kraken, Python, salamander, chimera, lamia, unicorn, echidna, dragon, griffin, cyclops, cockatrice, hippocampus, phoenix, mermaid, hippogriff, gyascutus, androsphinx, dipsas, sagittary, sea serpent, hippocentaur, manticore, hippocert, whangdoodle, roe, bucentaur, rhinoceros, elephant, lycanthrope, werewolf, uturuncu.
**2.** [An unnatural creation] — *Syn.* abnormality, abnormity, monstrosity; see **freak** 2.
**monstrous,** *modif.* **1.** [Huge] — *Syn.* stupendous, prodigious, enormous; see **large** 1.
**2.** [Unnatural] — *Syn.* abnormal, preposterous, uncanny; see **unnatural** 1, **unusual** 2.
**3.** [Shocking] — *Syn.* horrible, terrible, atrocious; see **frightful** 1, **outrageous, terrible** 1.
*See Synonym Study at* OUTRAGEOUS.
**monstrously,** *modif.* — *Syn.* horribly, cruelly, outrageously; see **badly** 1, **brutally.**
**month,** *n.* — *Syn.* measure of time, thirty days, one-twelfth of a year, four weeks, moon, period.

Types of months include: calendar, lunar, synodical, anomalistic, nodical, tropical, sidereal, solar.

**monthly,** *modif.* — *Syn.* once a month, every month, menstrual, mensal, phaseal, phasic, punctually, steadily, recurrent, cyclic, cyclical, repeated, rhythmic, methodically, periodically, from month to month, in its turn; see also **regularly** 2.

**monument,** *n.* **1.** [Anything erected to preserve a memory] — *Syn.* tomb, tombstone, marker, shaft, column, pillar, headstone, gravestone, cenotaph, mausoleum, obelisk, shrine, statue, building, erection, pile, tower, monolith, tablet, slab, stone; see also **memorial**. **2.** [A landmark in the history of creative work] — *Syn.* work of art, magnum opus, exemplar, permanent contribution; see **achievement** 2, **masterpiece**.

**monumental,** *modif.* — *Syn.* lofty, impressive, majestic; see **grand** 2, **great** 1.

**mood,** *n.* **1.** [A state of mind] — *Syn.* frame of mind, state, condition, temper, humor, temperament, spirits, disposition, inclination, caprice, whim, fancy, vein, spirit, feeling, climate, pleasure, vagary, crotchet, freak, wish, desire, attitude, mind-set, bent, propensity, tendency; see also **attitude** 2. **2.** [Grammatical mode] — *Syn.* aspect, inflection, mode.
Moods in English grammar include: indicative, subjunctive, imperative, interrogative, conditional, potential.

---

*SYN.* — **mood** is the broadest of these terms referring to a temporary state of mind and emphasizes the constraining or pervading quality of the feeling /she's in a merry *mood*/; **humor** emphasizes the variability or capriciousness of the mood /he wept and laughed as his *humor* moved him/; **temper,** in this comparison, applies to a mood characterized by a single, strong emotion, esp. that of anger /my, you're in a nasty *temper!*/; **vein** suggests a transient mood, often one manifested in speech, writing, action, etc. /if I may speak in a serious *vein* for a moment/

---

**moody,** *modif.* — *Syn.* pensive, unhappy, low-spirited; see **sad** 1.

**moon,** *n.* — *Syn.* satellite, celestial body, heavenly body, planet, secondary planet, planetoid, crescent, new moon, halfmoon, full moon, old moon, orb of night★, Diana★, Luna★, Phoebe★, Cynthia★, moon goddess★, dry moon★, wet moon★, sailor's friend★; see also **satellite** 1.

**moonbeam,** *n.* — *Syn.* light, stream, gleam, streak, glint, spark, glitter, sparkle, scintillation, lambency, play of moonlight, pearl blue★; see also **beam** 2, **flash** 1, **ray.**

**mooncalf,** *n.* — *Syn.* idiot, simpleton, incompetent; see **fool.**

**moonlight,** *n.* — *Syn.* moonshine, effulgence, radiance, luminescence; see **light** 3.

**moon-shaped,** *modif.* — *Syn.* lunar, sickle-shaped, crescent; see **bent.**

**moonshine,** *n.* **1.** [Moonlight] — *Syn.* effulgence, radiance, luminosity; see **light** 3. **2.** [Whisky distilled illicitly] — *Syn.* mountain dew★, swamp root★, donk★, jackass★, mule★, white lightning★, white mule★; see also **whiskey.**

**moonshiner★,** *n.* — *Syn.* illegal distiller, illegal dealer, racketeer, bootlegger, legger★, shiner★, moonlighter★, mountain moonlighter★, hootcher★, boozelegger★; see also **criminal.**

**moonstruck,** *modif.* — *Syn.* infatuated, lovesick, foolish; see **insane** 1.

**moor,** *n.* — *Syn.* moorland, downs, wasteland, upland; see **field** 1.

**Moorish,** *modif.* — *Syn.* Arab, Mohammedan, Moresque; see **Arabian, Moslem.**

**moory,** *modif.* — *Syn.* muddy, spongy, swampy; see **marshy.**

**moot,** *modif.* — *Syn.* unsettled, debatable, disputable; see **controversial, questionable** 1, **uncertain** 2.

**mop,** *n.* — *Syn.* swab, duster, sweeper; see **broom.**
Types of mops include: oil, floor, dust, dish, rag, wet, dry, soldering, metalworker's polishing, surgical; gun swab, miner's swab stick.

**mop,** *v.* — *Syn.* swab, wipe, rub, scrub, dab, pat, polish, wash, dust, wipe up; see also **clean.**

**mope,** *v.* — *Syn.* be low-spirited, fret, pine away, grieve, despond, droop, sink, lose heart, brood, pine, yearn, repine, despair, grumble, chafe, lament, regret, look glum, sulk, be in a funk★, give way★, look blue★, croak★, be sunk in the doldrums★, pull a long face★; see also **mourn** 1. — *Ant.* REVIVE, CELEBRATE, cheer up.

**mopped,** *modif.* — *Syn.* swabbed, washed, polished; see **clean** 1.

**mop the floor** *or* **the earth (with)★** *v.* — *Syn.* beat, thrash, trounce; see **defeat** 1, 2.

**mop up★,** *v.* — *Syn.* finish off, dispatch, clean up; see **achieve** 1, **defeat** 1, 2, **eliminate** 1.

**moral,** *modif.* **1.** [Good or right in conduct or character] — *Syn.* ethical, principled, virtuous, righteous, good, right, upright, honorable, trustworthy, conscientious, scrupulous, respectable, proper, truthful, decent, just, honest, right-minded, high-minded, saintly, pure, exemplary, laudable, worthy, correct, praiseworthy, showing integrity, incorruptible, noble, upstanding, seemly, aboveboard, dutiful, godly; see also **noble** 1, 2, **reliable** 1, **righteous** 1, **upright** 2. — *Ant.* immoral, unscrupulous, DISHONEST. **2.** [Conforming to approved standards of sexual conduct] — *Syn.* virtuous, chaste, pure, decent; see **chaste** 2, **innocent** 4. **3.** [Moralizing] — *Syn.* didactic, moralizing, moralistic, preachy, sermonizing, monitory, sanctimonious, holier-than-thou.

---

*SYN.* — **moral** implies conformity with generally accepted standards of goodness or rightness in conduct or character, sometimes, specif., in sexual conduct /a *moral* person/; **ethical** implies conformity with an elaborated, ideal code of moral principles, sometimes, specif., with the code of a particular profession /an *ethical* lawyer/; **virtuous** implies a morally excellent character, connoting integrity, self-discipline, or often, specif., chastity; **righteous** implies being morally blameless or justifiable /*righteous* anger/

---

**morale,** *n.* — *Syn.* assurance, resolve, spirit; see **confidence** 2.

**morality,** *n.* **1.** [Virtue] — *Syn.* righteousness, uprightness, honesty; see **virtue** 1. **2.** [Adherence to approved standards of sexual conduct] — *Syn.* purity, gentleness, decency; see **chastity.**

**moralize,** *v.* — *Syn.* sermonize, admonish, exhort, pontificate; see **lecture, scold.**

**morally,** *modif.* **1.** [In accordance with accepted standards of conduct] — *Syn.* conscientiously, truthfully, honestly, honorably, appropriately, laudably, respectably, courteously, scrupulously, uprightly, righteously, trustworthily, decently, properly, in a manner approved by society; see also **justly** 1, 2, **sincerely.** — *Ant.* WRONGLY, worthlessly, dishonorably.

**2.** [In a chaste manner] — *Syn.* chastely, virtuously, purely; see **modestly** 1.

**3.** [Practically] — *Syn.* potentially, implicitly, substantially; see **probably**.

**morals,** *n.* — *Syn.* ideals, customs, standards, mores, policies, beliefs, dogmas, social standards, principles; see also **ethics**.

**morass,** *n.* — *Syn.* marsh, bog, quagmire, slough; see **swamp**.

**moratorium,** *n.* — *Syn.* halt, cessation, interim; see **end** 2.

**morbid,** *modif.* **1.** [Diseased] — *Syn.* sickly, unhealthy, ailing; see **sick**.

**2.** [Pathological] — *Syn.* abnormal, unsound, gruesome, gloomy, sorrowful, sad, melancholic, irascible, suspecting, depressed, morose, sullen, hypochondriac, despondent, ill-natured, ill-balanced, aberrant, eccentric, unnatural, unusual, unsound, psychotic, paranoid, deranged, demented; see also **insane** 1, **sad** 1. — *Ant.* SANE, normal, usual.

**morbidly,** *modif.* — *Syn.* unnaturally, insanely, weirdly; see **crazily, sick**.

**mordacity,** *n.* — *Syn.* sharpness, acerbity, acridity; see **bitterness** 1, 2.

**mordant,** *modif.* — *Syn.* stringent, bitter, sharp; see **severe** 2.

**more,** *modif.* **1.** [Additional] — *Syn.* also, likewise, and, over and above, more than that, further, in addition, beside, besides, added; see also **extra**. — *Ant.* less than, less, subtracted from.

**2.** [Greater in quantity, amount, degree, or quality] — *Syn.* expanded, increased, major, augmented, extended, further, expanded, enhanced, aggrandized, added to, larger, higher, wider, deeper, heavier, longer, solider, stronger, amassed, massed, over the mark, above the mark. — *Ant.* lessened, weaker, decreased.

**3.** [Greater in numbers] — *Syn.* exceeding, too many for, numerous, innumerable, bounteous, extra; see also **infinite** 1, **plentiful** 2. — *Ant.* too few, scanty, scarce.

**more and more,** *modif.* — *Syn.* increasingly, more frequently, increasing in weight, increasing in size, increasing in number; see also **frequently, increasing** 2.

**more or less,** *modif.* — *Syn.* about, somewhat, in general; see **approximate, approximately, moderately**.

**moreover,** *modif.* — *Syn.* further, by the same token, furthermore; see **besides**.

**Moresque,** *modif.* — *Syn.* Arabic, Mohammedan, Moorish; see **Arabian, Moslem**.

**morgue,** *n.* **1.** [A place where the dead are received] — *Syn.* funeral home, funeral parlor, the undertaker's, mortuary, deadhouse, charnel house.

**2.** [The library of a newspaper] — *Syn.* archives, reference room, photographic collection, file; see **library, museum**.

**moribund,** *modif.* — *Syn.* incurable, on one's deathbed, sinking; see **dying** 1.

**Mormon,** *modif.* — *Syn.* concerning the Church of Jesus Christ of Latter-day Saints, concerning the State of Desert, saintly, churchly; see **religious** 1, **Protestant**.

**morning,** *n.* **1.** [Dawn] — *Syn.* aurora, Eos, the East, morn, daybreak, dayspring, break of day, first blush of morning, first flush of morning, daylight, cockcrow, sun-up, the small hours, the wee small hours*, crack of dawn*, milk-wagon time*; see also **day** 2, **time** 1.

**2.** [The time before noon] — *Syn.* forenoon, morningtide, prime, after midnight, before noon, breakfast time, before lunch; see also **A.M., day** 2.

**mornings,** *modif.* — *Syn.* in the mornings, every morning, before noon, in the A.M., early, in good season; see also **daily, regularly** 1, 2.

**morning star,** *n.* — *Syn.* Venus, evening star, eastern star; see **planet, star** 1.

**moron,** *n.* — *Syn.* feeble-minded person, mentally handicapped person, retardate, imbecile, idiot*, simpleton, natural, goose*, addlepate*, dullard, dunce, gawk*, blockhead*, mental defective, cretin*, tomfool, dunce, dunderhead*, lunkhead*, muttonhead*, numskull*, dimwit*, retard*, halfwit*, boob*, dingbat*, saphead*, mutt*, loony*; see also **fool** 1. — *Ant.* PHILOSOPHER, sage, scientist.

**moronic,** *modif.* — *Syn.* foolish, mentally retarded, dumb*; see **stupid** 1.

**morose,** *modif.* **1.** [Gloomy] — *Syn.* depressed, dolorous, melancholy; see **sad** 1, **troubled** 1.

**2.** [Ill-humored] — *Syn.* sullen, severe, glum, sour, splenetic, acrimonious, ill-natured, gruff, perversive, ill-tempered, sulky, gloomy, crusty, grouchy, surly, saturnine, churlish, mumpish, cantankerous, crabbed, cross, snappish, frowning, cross-grained, harsh; see also **irritable, sullen**.

**morsel,** *n.* — *Syn.* bite, chunk, piece; see **bit** 1, **part** 1.

**mortal,** *modif.* **1.** [Causing death] — *Syn.* malignant, fatal, lethal; see **deadly, poisonous**.

**2.** [Subject to death] — *Syn.* human, transient, temporal, passing, frail, impermanent, evanescent, fugacious, perishable, precarious, fading, passing away, ephemeral, momentary; see also **temporary**. — *Ant.* ETERNAL, PERPETUAL, everlasting.

**3.** [*Very great] — *Syn.* extreme, deadly, last, ending; see **grand** 2.

*See Synonym Study at* FATAL.

**mortal,** *n.* — *Syn.* creature, being, human; see **animal** 1, **man** 1.

**mortality,** *n.* **1.** [Destruction] — *Syn.* dying, extinction, fatality; see **death** 1, **destruction** 1.

**2.** [Humanity] — *Syn.* being, mankind, human race; see **man** 1.

**mortar,** *n.* **1.** [A receptacle used with a pestle] — *Syn.* basin, pot, caldron; see **bowl**.

**2.** [A short-barreled cannon] — *Syn.* field gun, cannon, siege gun, howitzer, trench mortar, knee mortar, training mortar, stovepipe*; see also **cannon, weapon** 1.

**mortgage,** *n.* — *Syn.* lease, title, debt; see **contract**. Types of mortgages include: construction, installment, leasehold, anticipating, trust, chattel, first, second.

**mortgaged,** *modif.* — *Syn.* tied, bound, pledged, obligated, held under mortgage, liable, under lien; see also **guaranteed, promised**.

**mortification,** *n.* **1.** [Humiliation] — *Syn.* regret, remorse, chagrin; see **disgrace** 1, **embarrassment** 1, **shame** 2.

**2.** [Penance] — *Syn.* purgation, flagellation, discipline; see **penance** 1.

**mortify,** *v.* — *Syn.* shame, embarrass, discipline, belittle; see **disgrace, humiliate, ridicule**.

**mortuary,** *n.* — *Syn.* charnel house, funeral parlor, funeral home; see **morgue** 1.

**mosaic,** *modif.* — *Syn.* diapered, varied, inlaid; see **ornate** 1.

**mosaic,** *n.* **1.** [Inlaid work] — *Syn.* parquetry, parquet, marquetry, inlay.

**2.** [Collection] — *Syn.* miscellany, potpourri, pastiche; see **collection** 1.

**Moslem,** *modif.* — *Syn.* Muslim, Mohammedan, Islamic, Musselmanic, worshiping Allah, believing in Mohammed, looking toward Mecca, following the Koran; see also **Arabian**.

**mosquito,** *n.* Types of mosquitoes include: anopheles, culex, aedes, stegomyia, trichopronsoon, corethra, psorophora, mansonia; see also **insect, pest** 1.

**moss,** *n.* Types of mosses include: musci, bryophyta, sphagnum, peat moss, mosslike lichen, Iceland, rock, club; see also **plant.**

**mossback\*,** *n.* — *Syn.* right-winger, reactionary, diehard; see **conservative.**

**mossy,** *modif.* — *Syn.* tufted, velvety, plushy, downy, mosslike, smooth, fresh, damp, moist, cushiony, resilient, soft, covered, overgrown; see also **green** 2. — *Ant.* DRY, bare, prickly.

**most,** *modif.* — *Syn.* maximum, greatest, largest, utmost, nearly all, all but, well-nigh all, not quite all, close upon all, in the majority.

**at the most**— *Syn.* in toto, not more than, at the outside\*.

**make the most of**— *Syn.* exploit, utilize, take advantage of; see **use** 1.

**mostly,** *modif.* **1.** [Frequently] — *Syn.* often, many times, in many instances; see **frequently, regularly** 1.
**2.** [Largely] — *Syn.* chiefly, essentially, for the most part; see **principally.**

**mot,** *n.* — *Syn.* bon mot, quip, witticism, remark, adage, maxim; see also **proverb, saying.**

**mote,** *n.* — *Syn.* speck, scrap, crumb; see **bit** 1.

**motel,** *n.* — *Syn.* motor hotel, motor inn, cabins, stopping place, road house, court, motor court; see also **hotel, lodge, resort** 2.

**moth,** *n.* — *Syn.* miller, tineid, *Heterocera* (Latin); see **insect.**
Mothlike creatures include: carpet beetle, dermestid beetle, silkworm, gypsy, clothes, honeycomb, death's head, buffalo, lappet, luna, emperor, harlequin, deltoid, cabbage, tiger, lackey, ermine, plume.

**mother,** *n.* **1.** [A female parent] — *Syn.* parent, ancestress, matriarch, mamma, dam, materfamilias, mater, mama\*, mammy\*, motherkin\*, mum\*, mummy\*, ma\*, mom\*, mommy\*, muzzer\*, maw\*; see also **parent, relative.**
**2.** [A matron] — *Syn.* superintendent, mother superior, housemother; see **administrator.**
**3.** [The source] — *Syn.* fountainhead, font, beginning; see **origin** 2.

**mother country,** *n.* — *Syn.* motherland, native land, native country, homeland, old country; see also **country** 3, **nation** 1.

**motherhood,** *n.* — *Syn.* maternity, mothership, parenthood.

**mother-in-law,** *n.* — *Syn.* husband's mother, wife's mother, mother by marriage, mater-in-law\*; see **relative.**

**motherly,** *modif.* — *Syn.* maternal, devoted, careful, watchful, kind, warm, gentle, tender, comprehending, sympathetic, caretaking, supporting, protective, protecting; see also **loving.**

**mother tongue,** *n.* — *Syn.* native speech, native language, native tongue, dialect, ideolect, local idiom; see also **language** 1.

**mother wit,** *n.* — *Syn.* common sense, perception, reason; see **wisdom** 2.

**motif,** *n.* — *Syn.* subject, main feature, topic, leitmotif; see **theme** 1, 2.

**motion,** *n.* **1.** [A movement] — *Syn.* change, act, action; see **movement** 2.
**2.** [The state of moving] — *Syn.* passage, translating, changing; see **movement** 1.
**3.** [An act formally proposed] — *Syn.* proposal, suggestion, consideration, proposition; see **plan** 2.

**motionless,** *modif.* **1.** [Not moving] — *Syn.* still, unmoving, dead, deathly still, inert, stock-still, stagnant, becalmed, quiet, quiescent, at a dead calm, at a full stop, in a deadlock, lying at anchor. — *Ant.* MOVING, shifting, CHANGING.
**2.** [Firm] — *Syn.* unmovable, fixed, stationary; see **firm** 1.

**motion picture,** *n.* — *Syn.* moving picture, cinema, film, the silver screen; see **movie.**

**motivate,** *v.* — *Syn.* impel, inspire hope, stimulate, incite, propel, spur, goad, move, induce, prompt, arouse, whet, instigate, fire, provoke, actuate, cause, touch off\*, egg on\*, trigger\*; see also **drive** 1, **excite** 1, **urge** 2.

**motivation,** *n.* — *Syn.* impulse, driving force, urge; see **motive.**

**motive,** *n.* — *Syn.* incentive, cause, purpose, object, inducement, aim, goal, motivation, incitement, stimulus, rationale, basis, ground, occasion, consideration, idea, impulse, lure, spur, goad, what makes one tick\*, angle\*; see also **cause** 1, **incentive, reason** 3.
*See Synonym Study at* CAUSE.

**motley,** *modif.* **1.** [Varied] — *Syn.* multiform, mixed, heterogeneous, ragged; see **various.**
**2.** [Varicolored] — *Syn.* prismatic, mottled, kaleidoscopic; see **bright** 2, **multicolored.**

**motor,** *n.* — *Syn.* machine, device, instrument; see **engine** 1.
Types of motors include: internal combustion, Wankel, diesel, spark diesel, compound, steam, turbine, gas turbine, electric, auxiliary, jet, rotary, radial, in line, airplane, automobile, truck, A.C. electric, D.C. electric, V-type, T-head, L-head, high compression, low compression.

**motor,** *v.* — *Syn.* tour, drive, ride; see **travel** 2.

**motorboat,** *n.* — *Syn.* speedboat, powerboat, racer, putt-putt\*, hop-up\*, bronco\*, skip-jack\*; see also **boat.**
Types of motorboats include: open, outboard, inboard, cruiser, cabin cruiser, runabout, launch, ski boat, cigarette boat, whaleboat, yawl, auxiliary yacht, sea sled.

**motorcycle,** *n.* — *Syn.* motorbike, bike, cycle, pig\*, hog\*, chopper\*, sickle\*; see also **racer** 2, **vehicle** 1.
Makes of motorcycles include: Harley-Davidson, Kawasaki, Honda, BMW, Yamaha, Suzuki, Polaris, BSA, Triumph, Bultaco, Greeves, Cimatti, Vespa, Ducati, Garelli, Lambretta, Matchless, Norton, Indian, Volocette, Jawa, Royal Enfield, Bridgestone, Maico, Hodaka.

**motorist,** *n.* — *Syn.* driver, traveler, tourist, automobile operator, autoist\*, gear grinder\*; see also **driver.**

**motorized,** *modif.* — *Syn.* motor-driven, motor-powered, engine-driven, engine-powered, electric-driven, gasoline-driven, oil-driven, motor-equipped, motor-operated; see also **mobile** 2.

**motorman,** *n.* — *Syn.* operator, engineer, pilot; see **driver.**

**motto,** *n.* — *Syn.* maxim, adage, saying, saw, epigram, aphorism, apothegm, pretty sentiment, slogan, catchword, watchword, byword, catch phrase, axiom, sententious phrase; see also **proverb, saying.**
*See Synonym Study at* SAYING.
Familiar mottoes include: in God we trust; one from many, *e pluribus unum* (Latin); time flies, *tempus fugit* (Latin); seize the day, *carpe diem* (Latin); art for art's sake, *ars pro arte* (Latin); art is long and time is fleeting, *ars longa, vita brevis* (Latin); hail and farewell, *ave atque vale* (Latin); rest in peace, *requiescat in pace* (Latin), R.I.P.; peace be with you, *pax vobiscum* (Latin); love

conquers all, labor conquers all, *amor omnia vincit, labor omnia vincit* (Latin); one for all and all for one; I came, I saw, I conquered, *veni, vidi, vici* (Latin); home sweet home, God bless our home, don't tread on me, thus be it always with tyrants, *sic semper tyrannis* (Latin); liberty, equality, fraternity, *liberté, égalité, fraternité* (French); God and my right, *Dieu et mon droit* (French), *honi soit qui mal y pense* (French), shamed be anyone who thinks evil of it; all is lost save honor, *tout est perdu fors l'honneur* (French); don't give up the ship; remember the Alamo; Our Country, right or wrong; abandon hope, all ye who enter here; knowledge is power; winning isn't everything, it's the only thing.

**mound,** *n.* — *Syn.* pile, heap, knoll, hillock; see **hill.**

**mount,** *v.* **1.** [To rise] — *Syn.* ascend, arise, uprise; see **rise** 1.

**2.** [To climb] — *Syn.* ascend, scale, clamber; see **climb** 2.

**3.** [To install] — *Syn.* set up, attach, position, fix; see **install.**

**mountain,** *modif.* — *Syn.* towering, weighty, steep, isolated, lofty, elevated, plateau, broken, ski-country, snow-capped, above the timber line, above the snow line; see also **mountainous.** — *Ant.* LEVEL, FLAT, hollow.

**mountain,** *n.* **1.** [A lofty land mass] — *Syn.* mount, elevation, peak, sierra, butte, hill, alp, range, ridge, pike, bluff, headland, land mass, knap, steeps, palisade, volcano, crater, lava cap, lava plug, tableland, mesa, plateau, height, crag, tor, precipice, cliff, massif, earth mass. — *Ant.* VALLEY, ravine, flatland.

Famous chains of mountains include: Alps, Himalayas, Caucasus, Urals, Pyrenees, Ruwenzori, Andes, Rockies, Canadian Rockies, Appalachians, Great Smoky, Blue Ridge, Ozarks, Cascades, Adirondacks, White Mountains, Sierra Nevada, Sierra Madre, Tetons, Cordillera, Apennine, Sentinel Range, Grampian Mountains.

Famous mountain peaks include: Mont Blanc, Mt. Etna, Vesuvius, the Matterhorn, Olympus, Pike's Peak, Mt. Whitney, Mt. Shasta, Mt. Washington, Mt. Mitchell, Mt. Rushmore, Mt. Saint Helens, Mt. Rainier, the Jungfrau, Wetterhorn, Dent du Midi, the Grand Teton, Mt. McKinley, Mt. St. Elias, Mt. Logan, Mt. Robson, Krakatoa, Pelee, Citlaltepetl, Cotopaxi, Chimborazo, Popocatepetl, Iztaccihuatl, Mt. Cook, Mt. Everest, Annapurna, Mt. Dhaulagiri, Nanga Parbat, Lhotse, Nupseg, K2, Godwin Austen, Mt. Ushba, Mount of Olives, Mt. Sinai, Fujiyama, Mt. Kenya, Mt. Kilimanjaro.

**2.** [A pile] — *Syn.* mass, mound, glob*; see **heap.**

**mountaineer,** *n.* — *Syn.* mountain man, mountain dweller, hillman, highlander, uplander, native of mountains, mountain climber, rock climber, mountain guide, mountain scaler, hillbilly*.

**mountainous,** *modif.* — *Syn.* mountainlike, mountain, with mountains, difficult, barbarous, wild, untamed, strange, remote, uncivilized, rude, crude, unpopulated, solitary, unfamiliar, hard to penetrate, isolated, steep, lofty, hilly, alpine, upland, aerial, elevated, volcanic, towering, ridged, craggy, cliffy, rugged; see also **high** 2, **rocky.** — *Ant.* LOW, small, FLAT.

**mountebank,** *n.* — *Syn.* pretender, charlatan, huckster; see **cheat** 1, **impostor, quack.**

*See Synonym Study at* QUACK.

**mounted,** *modif.* **1.** [On horseback] — *Syn.* seated, riding, in the saddle, cavalry, provided with a horse, horsed*, up*. — *Ant.* AFOOT, unhorsed, dismounted.

**2.** [Firmly fixed] — *Syn.* supported, set, attached; see **firm** 1.

**3.** [Backed] — *Syn.* pasted on, set off, strengthened; see **reinforced.**

**mourn,** *v.* **1.** [To lament] — *Syn.* deplore, grieve, fret, sorrow, rue, regret, bemoan, sigh, long for, miss, droop, languish, yearn, ache, pine, anguish, complain, agonize, repine, weep over, weep, bewail, suffer, wring one's hands, be brokenhearted, be in distress, be sad, beat one's breast, take on*. — *Ant.* CELEBRATE, rejoice, be happy.

**2.** [To cry] — *Syn.* sob, wail, moan; see **cry.**

**mourner,** *n.* — *Syn.* lamenter, bereaved person, griever, keener, weeper, wailer, repiner, sorrower, willowwearer, pallbearer, commiserator, bemoaner, condoler, friend of the deceased, member of the family.

**mournful,** *modif.* **1.** [Afflicted with sorrow] — *Syn.* sorrowful, mourning, forlorn, unhappy; see **sad** 1.

**2.** [Suggestive of sorrow] — *Syn.* distressing, pitiable, pathetic; see **sad** 2.

**mournfully,** *modif.* — *Syn.* sorrowfully, regretfully, with sorrow, forlornly; see **sadly.**

**mourning,** *n.* **1.** [The act of expressing grief] — *Syn.* sorrowing, grieving, yearning, aching, sorrow, lamentation, lamenting, pining, repining, sighing, regretting, deploring, weeping over, drooping, languishing, wailing, crying, moaning, murmuring, complaining, bemoaning, sobbing, keening; see also **depression** 1, **grief** 1, **sadness.** — *Ant.* CELEBRATION, rejoicing, being glad.

**2.** [Symbols of mourning] — *Syn.* black, mourning coach, mourning ring, mourning cloak, arm band, mourning veil, mourning garb, widow's weeds, black suit, black tie, sackcloth and ashes, rent garment.

**mouse,** *n.* — *Syn.* rodent, vermin, rat.

Types of mice include: white-footed, meadow, field, house, deer, wood, pygmy, harvest, pocket, kangaroo, jumping; see also **animal** 2, **pest** 1.

**mouth,** *n.* **1.** [Oral cavity] — *Syn.* maw, jaws, stoma, muzzle, lips, kisser*, yap*, trap*, chops*, bazoo*, mandible, cake hole (British).

Parts of the mouth include: lips, orifice, roof, floor, tongue, jaws, gums, teeth, pharynx, soft palate, alveolar ridge, hard palate, alveoli, uvula.

**2.** [Any opening resembling a mouth] — *Syn.* orifice, entrance, aperture; see **opening** 1.

**3.** [The end of a river] — *Syn.* estuary, firth, delta, confluence, portal, harbor, roads, sound, tidewater.

**down in** (*or* **at**) **the mouth**\* — *Syn.* depressed, discouraged, unhappy; see **sad** 1.

**give mouth to** — *Syn.* express, tell, reveal; see **say.**

**have a big mouth**\* — *Syn.* talk loudly, exaggerate, brag; see **talk** 1.

**mouthful,** *n.* — *Syn.* portion, piece, morsel; see **bite** 1.

**mouthpiece**\*, *n.* — *Syn.* spokesman, adviser, lawyer, counselor; see **adviser.**

**mouthy**\*, *modif.* — *Syn.* bombastic, loud-mouthed, pompous; see **oratorical.**

**movable,** *modif.* — *Syn.* not fastened, portable, adjustable, adaptable, not fixed, unstationary, mobile, transportable, motile, liftable, conveyable, demountable, detachable, turnable, removable, separable, drawable, deployable, pullable, derangeable, transferable, shiftable, ambulatory, unfixate, loose, unfastened, free, unattached, in parts, in sections, knocked down, on wheels. — *Ant.* FIXED, fastened, stationary.

**movables,** *n.* — *Syn.* household equipment, wares, goods; see **furniture.**

**move,** *n.* — *Syn.* motility, transit, progress; see **movement** 1, 2.

**get a move on**\* — *Syn.* go faster, start moving, get cracking*; see **hurry** 1.

**on the move**— *Syn.* moving, busy, acting; see **active** 2.

**move,** *v.* **1.** [To be in motion] — *Syn.* go, walk, run, glide, travel, drift, budge, stir, shift, pass, cross, roll, metastasize, flow, march, travel, progress, proceed, traverse, drive, off-load, ride, fly, hurry, head for, bustle, climb, crawl, jump, leap, shove along*, jump to it*, get a move on*, get a wiggle on*, take off*, get going; see also **advance** 1.— *Ant.* STOP, remain stationary, stay quiet.

**2.** [To set in motion] — *Syn.* impel, actuate, propel; see **push** 2.

**3.** [To arouse the emotions of] — *Syn.* affect, stir, touch, influence, impress, arouse, rouse, upset, excite, trouble, shake up, disturb, agitate, work on, touch a chord, strike a sympathetic chord, touch to the quick, soften, melt, tug at the heartstrings, choke up*.— *Ant.* soothe, lull, pacify.

**4.** [To propose an action formally] — *Syn.* suggest, introduce, submit; see **propose** 1.

**5.** [To prompt to action] — *Syn.* prompt, provoke, induce, spur, influence, instigate, stimulate, sway, play on, quicken, excite, incite, rouse, inspirit, prevail upon, work on, work upon, lead; see also **incite, influence.** *See Synonym Study at* AFFECT.

**6.** [Change one's place of residence] — *Syn.* relocate, remove, transfer, vacate, depart, leave, emigrate, migrate.

**moved,** *modif.* **1.** [Transported] — *Syn.* conveyed, carried, sent, taken, shifted, transferred, reassigned, reallocated, changed, flown, driven, drawn, pushed, lifted, elevated, lowered, let down, displaced, withdrawn, replaced, sent abroad, put abroad, trucked, hauled, dragged, lugged, kicked upstairs*, snaked*, toted*; see also **transported.**

**2.** [Gone to a different residence] — *Syn.* transferred, relocated, emigrated, migrated, vacated, removed, at a new address, at a different address, departed, gone away, changed residences, left, gone for good*; see also **gone** 1.— *Ant.* RESIDENT, remaining, still there, still here.

**3.** [Proposed] — *Syn.* recommended, submitted, introduced; see **proposed.**

**movement,** *n.* **1.** [The state of moving] — *Syn.* move, transit, passage, progress, journey, advance, velocity, motility, mobility, change, movableness, shift, translation, translating, alteration, ascension, descension, propulsion, flow, flux, action, flight, declination, wandering, journeying, voyaging, migration, emigration, transplanting, evolving, shifting, changing, locomotion, drive, evolution, undertaking, regression.— *Ant.* immobility, quiet, fixity.

**2.** [An example of movement] — *Syn.* immigration, migration, march, demonstration, crusade, patrol, sweep, emigration, evolution, unrest, transition, change, transfer, displacement, withdrawal, ascension, descension, progression, regression, transportation, removal, departure, trip, day's trip, shift, flight, slip, slide, step, footfall, stride, gesture, act, action, vacating, campaign, mobilization, pilgrimage, expedition, procession, locomotion, cavalcade; see also **journey.**

**3.** [A trend] — *Syn.* drift, tendency, bent; see **inclination** 1.

**movie,** *modif.* — *Syn.* screen, cinematic, filmic, motion, sound, picture, photographic.

**movie,** *n.* — *Syn.* motion picture, moving picture, photoplay, cinema, film, show, screenplay, video, talking picture, silent picture, photodrama, cinematograph, cartoon, animated cartoon, serial, comedy, foreign film, travelogue, short, documentary, videotape, talkie*, flick*, flicker*; see also **drama, entertainment** 2.

**move in,** *v.* — *Syn.* take up residence, take occupancy, occupy, get a home; see **arrive** 1, **establish** 2.

**movies,** *n.* **1.** [*A showing of a moving picture] — *Syn.* motion picture, film, photoplay; see **movie.**

**2.** [The motion picture industry] — *Syn.* moving pictures, screen pictures, cinema, the cinematic industry, cinematography, Hollywood, the screen world, the silver screen*, the industry*, pictures*, the flicks*, celluloids*; see also **theater** 2.

**move off,** *v.* — *Syn.* depart, be in motion, go; see **leave** 1.

**move on,** *v.* — *Syn.* keep moving, keep going, continue, go; see **travel** 2, **walk** 1.

**move up,** *v.* — *Syn.* go forward, do well, go ahead, get ahead; see **advance** 1, **prosper, rise** 1.

**moving,** *modif.* **1.** [In motion] — *Syn.* going, changing, progressing, advancing, shifting, evolving, withdrawing, rising, going down, descending, ascending, getting up, traveling, on the track, journeying, on the march, moving up, starting, proceeding, traversing, flying, climbing, up-tempo*, on the jump*, on the wing*, under sail*, going great guns*.— *Ant.* unchanging, unmoving, let be.

**2.** [Arousing the emotions] — *Syn.* touching, affecting, poignant, stirring, rousing, arousing, inspiring, heart-rending, pathetic, heartbreaking, pitiful, emotional, emotive, telling, eloquent, persuasive, effective, impressive, inspirational, impelling, motivating, soul-stirring, heart-swelling, thrilling; see also **passionate** 2, **pitiful** 1.

---

*SYN.* — **moving** implies a general arousing or stirring of the emotions or feelings, sometimes, specif., of pathos [her *moving* plea for help]; **poignant** is applied to that which is sharply painful to the feelings [the *poignant* cry of a lost child]; **affecting** applies to that which stirs the emotions, as to tears [the *affecting* scene of their reunion]; **touching** is used of that which arouses tender feelings, as of sympathy, gratitude, etc. [a *touching* little gift]; **pathetic** applies to that which arouses pity, compassion, or sympathetic sorrow, or pity mingled with contempt [the *pathetic* sight of homeless children, a *pathetic* attempt at wit]

---

**mow,** *n.* — *Syn.* loft, hayloft, haymow, hay barn; see **attic.**

**mow,** *v.* — *Syn.* scythe, reap, lay in swaths; see **harvest.**

**much,** *modif.* **1.** [To a great degree or extent] — *Syn.* important, weighty, notable, signal, considerable, prominent, memorable, salient, momentous, stirring, eventful, serious, urgent, pressing, critical, paramount, principal, leading, significant, telling, trenchant, first-rate*, high-flying*, in the front rank*.— *Ant.* LITTLE, inconsiderable, trivial.

**2.** [In great quantity] — *Syn.* full, many, very many, abundant, satisfying, enough, sufficient, adequate, considerable, substantial, ample, everywhere, copious, voluminous, plentiful, profuse, complete, lavish, generous, immeasurable, endless, countless, fabulous, extravagant, preposterous, overwrought, overcharged, hell of a lot*, all over the place*, no end*.— *Ant.* INADEQUATE, insufficient, limited.

**3.** [Very] — *Syn.* greatly, enormously, extremely; see **very.**

**much,** *n.* — *Syn.* a great quantity, abundance, quantities, a great deal, sufficiency, riches, wealth, amplitude, plethora, volume, very much, breadth, copiousness, plentifulness, fullness, profuseness, exuberance, completeness, fruitfulness, lavishness, generousness, lot*, great lot*, quite a bit*, gobs*, thousands*, tons*, oodles*; see also **plenty**. — *Ant.* PENURY, scarcity, little.

**as much as** — *Syn.* practically, virtually, in effect; see **almost, equal.**

**make much of** — *Syn.* treat with importance, expand, exaggerate; see **overdo** 1.

**not much of a** — *Syn.* inferior, mediocre, unsatisfactory; see **poor** 2.

**mucilage,** *n.* — *Syn.* paste, cement, glue; see **adhesive.**

**mucilaginous,** *modif.* — *Syn.* viscid, gummy, sticky; see **adhesive.**

**muck,** *n.* — *Syn.* refuse, dung, waste; see **trash** 1, 3

**muckraker,** *n.* — *Syn.* exposer, scandalbearer, meddler; see **gossip** 2.

**mucky,** *modif.* — *Syn.* foul, filthy, unclean; see **dirty.**

**mucus,** *n.* — *Syn.* snot, phlegm, excretion, slime.

**mud,** *n.* — *Syn.* dirt, muck, clay, alluvia, mire, slush, silt, muddiness, turbidity, stickiness, ooze, clayeyness, bog, marsh, swamp, hardpan, percolation, viscidity, soup*, axle grease*; see also **filth.**

**muddle,** *n.* **1.** [Confusion] — *Syn.* confusion, mess, jumble; see **confusion** 2.

**2.** [Difficulty] — *Syn.* perplexity, quandary, predicament, pother, dilemma, complication, intricacy, complexity, awkwardness, involvement, emergency, struggle, unmanageableness, encumbrance, jam*, pickle*; see also **difficulty** 2, **puzzle.**

*See Synonym Study at* CONFUSION.

**muddle,** *v.* **1.** [To confuse; *said of affairs*] — *Syn.* stir up, misarrange, disarrange, entangle, foul, mix, jumble, bungle, derange, shake up, mess, botch, potter, clutter, snarl, pi, complicate, disorder; see also **confuse.**

**2.** [To confuse; *said usually of people*] — *Syn.* disturb, perturb, ruffle; see **confuse.**

**muddled,** *modif.* **1.** [Drunk] — *Syn.* tipsy, inebriated, intoxicated; see **drunk.**

**2.** [Confused] — *Syn.* uncertain, addled, stupid; see **confused** 2.

**muddle through,** *v.* — *Syn.* manage, get by, make it, hang in there*; see **succeed** 1, **survive** 1.

**muddy,** *modif.* **1.** [Containing sediment] — *Syn.* stirred, turbid, roiled, roily, dull, dark, cloudy, murky, indistinct, confused, obscure, opaque, reddened; see also **dirty** 1. — *Ant.* CLEAR, translucent, pellucid.

**2.** [Deep with mud] — *Syn.* sloppy, mucky, swampy, soggy, sodden, slushy, watery, miry, fenny, boggy, soaked; see also **marshy.** — *Ant.* DRY, barren, parched.

**muff,** *v.* — *Syn.* miscarry, fumble, blunder; see **fail** 1.

**muffin,** *n.* — *Syn.* quick bread, biscuit, bun; see **bread.**

**muffle,** *v.* — *Syn.* deaden, mute, stifle; see **decrease** 2, **soften** 2.

**muffled,** *modif.* — *Syn.* suppressed, stifled, indistinct; see **obscure** 1.

**muffler,** *n.* — *Syn.* scarf, chest protector, tippet, neckpiece, babushka, neckerchief, kerchief, neckband, neck cloth, wimple, Ascot, fur piece, choker, mantle, stole, boa, fichu, veil, fascinator*; see also **scarf.**

**mug,** *n.* — *Syn.* vessel, stein, flagon; see **cup.**

**muggy,** *modif.* — *Syn.* damp, humid, moist; see **wet** 1.

**mulct,** *v.* **1.** [To cheat someone] — *Syn.* defraud, trick, swindle; see **deceive, lie** 1.

**2.** [Punish] — *Syn.* penalize, fine, reprove; see **punish.**

**mule,** *n.* — *Syn.* jackass, donkey, ass, burro, jenny, hinney, army mule, Missouri mule; see also **animal** 2.

**mulish,** *modif.* — *Syn.* opinionated, headstrong, stubborn; see **obstinate** 1.

**mull,** *v.* — *Syn.* reflect, meditate, ponder; see **think** 1.

**multicolored,** *modif.* — *Syn.* colorful, brilliant, prismatic, mottled, varicolored, kaleidoscopic, dappled,

motley, spotted, polychrome, marbled, speckled, checkered, piebald, flecked, veined, streaked, pied; see also **bright** 2.

**multifarious,** *modif.* — *Syn.* heterogeneous, manifold, mixed, diverse; see **different** 2, **various.**

**multiform,** *modif.* — *Syn.* various, many-shaped, manifold; see **multiple** 1.

**multiple,** *modif.* **1.** [Various] — *Syn.* complicated, more than one, many, manifold, compound, having many uses, multifold, multiplex, multitudinous, aggregated, many-sided, multifarious, versatile, increased, varied, compound, added; see also **various.** — *Ant.* SIMPLE, UNITED, centralized.

**2.** [Repeated] — *Syn.* reoccurring, recurring, repetitious, duplicated; see **multiplied.**

**multiplication,** *n.* — *Syn.* duplication, reproduction, addition, increase, repetition, compounding, recurrence, amplification, augmentation, manifolding, reduplication, making more, reduplification, reproducing, repeating, augmenting; see also **arithmetic.** — *Ant.* REDUCTION, subtraction, decrease.

**multiplied,** *modif.* — *Syn.* manifolded, compounded, aggregated, added, reproduced, amplified, repeated, augmented, duplicated, reduplicated, made many; see also **increased.** — *Ant.* REDUCED, divided, decreased.

**multiply,** *v.* **1.** [To increase] — *Syn.* add, augment, double; see **increase** 1.

**2.** [To bring forth young] — *Syn.* generate, produce, populate; see **propagate** 1, **reproduce** 3.

**3.** [To employ multiplication as an arithmetical process] — *Syn.* repeat, compound, aggregate, manifold, raise, square, cube, raise to a higher power, employ a function, calculate; see also **increase** 1. — *Ant.* divide, DECREASE, subtract.

*See Synonym Study at* INCREASE.

**multitude,** *n.* **1.** [The state of being numerous] — *Syn.* aggregation, plenitude, abundance; see **number** 1.

**2.** [A great crowd] — *Syn.* throng, drove, mob; see **crowd** 1, **gathering, people** 3.

*See Synonym Study at* CROWD.

**mum,** *modif.* — *Syn.* hushed, soundless, without a word; see **quiet** 2.

**mumble,** *v.* — *Syn.* mutter, murmur, utter, whine, whimper, rumble, grumble, maunder, ramble on, whisper, speak indistinctly, speak inarticulately, swallow one's words*, hem and haw, slur one's speech, speak with mush in one's mouth*; see also **mutter** 1, **stammer.** — *Ant.* shout, articulate, enunciate.

---

**SYN.** — **mumble** is to utter almost inaudible or inarticulate sounds in low tones, with the mouth nearly closed *[an old woman mumbling to herself]*; **murmur** implies a continuous flow of words or sounds in a low, indistinct voice and may apply to utterances of satisfaction or dissatisfaction *[to murmur a prayer]*; **mutter** usually suggests angry or discontented words or sounds of this kind *[to mutter curses]*

---

**mumbo jumbo,** *n.* **1.** [Nonsense] — *Syn.* jabber, gibberish, hocus-pocus, double talk, drivel, gobbledegook, psychobabble, doublespeak, wish-wash*, jazz*, guff*; see also **nonsense** 1.

**2.** [Red tape] — *Syn.* smoke screen, run-around, officialism; see **bureaucracy** 1, 2, **details.**

**mummer,** *n.* — *Syn.* masquerade, quizzer, masker, harlequin; see **actor** 1, **clown.**

**mummery,** *n.* — *Syn.* revel, amusement, performance; see **masquerade.**

**mummify,** *v.* — *Syn.* embalm, dry up, mortify; see **preserve** 3.

**mummy,** *n.* — *Syn.* remains, cadaver, corpse; see **body** 2.

**mumpish,** *modif.* — *Syn.* sulky, morose, dull; see **irritable.**

**munch,** *v.* — *Syn.* crunch, bite, grind, masticate, ruminate, crush, mash, smash, reduce, soften, press, break up; see also **chew, eat** 1.

**mundane,** *modif.* — *Syn.* worldly, earthly, normal, ordinary; see **worldly** 1.

*See Synonym Study at* EARTHLY.

**municipal,** *modif.* — *Syn.* self-governing, metropolitan, city, town, community, local, civil, borough, incorporated, corporate; see also **public.** — *Ant.* national, state, world-wide.

**municipality,** *n.* — *Syn.* district, village, borough; see **city, town** 1.

**munificence,** *n.* — *Syn.* generosity, consideration, benevolence; see **kindness** 1.

**munificent,** *modif.* — *Syn.* open-handed, charitable, benevolent; see **generous** 1, **kind.**

**muniment,** *n.* — *Syn.* deed, warrant, document; see **certificate, record** 1.

**munitions,** *n.* — *Syn.* materiel, weapons, war material, preparations for defense, offensive material, equipment, military provisions, military stores, arms, armament, ordnance; see also **ammunition, shell** 2, **weapon** 2.

Common types of munitions include: artillery, cannon, rocket, explosive, automatic rifle, machine gun, antiaircraft gun, rifle, cartridge, shell, bayonet, hand grenade, mortar, grenade launcher, bomb, guided missile, ballistic missile, aerial bomb, depth charge, torpedo, mine, flame thrower, nuclear warhead, biological weapons, chemical weapons.

**mural,** *n.* — *Syn.* wall painting, decoration, representation; see **painting** 1.

**murder,** *n.* — *Syn.* killing, homicide, unlawful homicide, death, destruction, annihilation, carnage, putting an end to, slaying, shooting, knifing, assassination, terrorism, dispatching, lynching, crime, felony, killing with malice aforethought, murder in the first degree, first degree murder, contract killing, murder in the second degree, murder in the third degree, manslaughter, massacre, genocide, butchery, mayhem, patricide, matricide, infanticide, fratricide, genocide, the Holocaust, suicide, foul play, ride*, dust-off*, bump-off*, the works*, the business*, one-way ticket*, dowser*; see also **crime** 2.

**get away with murder*,** escape punishment, take flight, avoid prosecution, avoid punishment; see **evade** 1.

**murder,** *v.* 1. [To kill unlawfully] — *Syn.* slay, assassinate, butcher; see **kill** 1.

2. [*To ruin, especially by incompetence] — *Syn.* spoil, mar, misuse; see **botch, destroy** 1, **fail** 1.

*See Synonym Study at* KILL.

**murdered,** *modif.* — *Syn.* killed, assassinated, massacred; see **dead** 1.

**murderer,** *n.* — *Syn.* slayer, assassin, butcher; see **criminal, killer.**

**murderous,** *modif.* — *Syn.* destroying, killing, felonious, lethal, law-breaking, fell, sanguinary, cruel, bloodthirsty, savage, criminal; see also **deadly, destructive** 2.

**murderously,** *modif.* — *Syn.* cruelly, viciously, wickedly; see **brutally.**

**murky,** *modif.* 1. [Dark] — *Syn.* dim, dusky, dingy; see **dark** 1, **dirty** 1.

2. [Gloomy] — *Syn.* cheerless, dismal, somber; see **sad** 1.

3. [Having the natural light obscured] — *Syn.* overcast, darkened, misty; see **stormy** 1.

*See Synonym Study at* DARK.

**murmur,** *v.* 1. [To make a low, continuous sound] — *Syn.* purl, ripple, moan, trickle, burble, babble, tinkle, gurgle, ooze, drip, meander, flow gently; see also **hum, whisper.** — *Ant.* NOISE, peal, clang.

2. [To mutter] — *Syn.* breathe, whisper, mumble, grumble; see **mumble, mutter** 1, **whisper.**

*See Synonym Study at* MUMBLE.

**murmurer,** *n.* — *Syn.* grumbler, complainer, malcontent; see **agitator, radical.**

**murmurous,** *modif.* — *Syn.* indistinct, muffled, low; see **faint** 3.

**murrain,** *n.* — *Syn.* anthrax, hoof-and-mouth disease, cattle disease, epizootic disease, murr, Texas fever, plague, pox, pestilence, cattle plague; see also **disease.**

**muscle,** *n.* — *Syn.* fiber, flesh, protoplasm, meat, brawn, beef, beefcake, horseflesh; see also **tissue** 3.

Types of muscle include: smooth, striated, skeletal, cardiac, voluntary, involuntary.

Muscles of the human body include: frontal, temporal, zygomatic, masseter, trapezius, pectoral, deltoid, latissimus dorsi, biceps, brachial, triceps, abdominal, intercostal, serratus, oblique, gluteus maximus, sartorius, quadriceps, hamstring, gastrocnemius, soleus.

**muscular,** *modif.* — *Syn.* brawny, powerful, husky; see **strong** 1.

**muse,** *v.* — *Syn.* ponder, meditate, reflect; see **think** 1.

**muse,** *n.* — *Syn.* inspiration, stimulus, creative impulse, creative spirit, genius, poetic genius, talent.

**Muses,** *pl.n.* — *Syn.* goddesses, sacred Nine, the tuneful Nine, Nine goddesses, the Graces, the arts, classical deities.

Names of the classical Muses include: Calliope, Clio, Erato, Euterpe, Melpomene, Polyhymnia, Terpsichore, Thalia, Urania.

**museum,** *n.* — *Syn.* institution, gallery, hall, place of exhibition, foundation, art gallery, library, picture gallery, archives, treasury, storehouse, depository, vault, repository, aquarium, menagerie, zoological garden, zoological park, zoo, botanical garden, herbarium, arboretum.

Famous museums include: Museum of the Archaeological Society, National Museum of Antiquities, Athens; Archaeological Museum, Cairo; Louvre, Orsay, Army, Paris; British Museum, National Gallery, Victoria and Albert Museum, London; Museo Nazionale, Naples; Vatican Gallery, Museo Nazionale, Rome; Museo del Prado, Madrid; Kaiser Friedrich Museum, Berlin; Rumiantsov Museum, Moscow; Hermitage, Imperial Academy of Science, Leningrad; Museo Nacional, Mexico City; Museum of Fine Arts, Boston; National Air and Space Museum, National Gallery of Art Museum, Library of Congress, Smithsonian Institution, Washington; Field Museum, Art Institute, Chicago; Cleveland Museum of Art; Metropolitan Museum of Art, Guggenheim Museum, Museum of Modern Art, American Museum of Natural History, Museum of the American Indian, New York; Huntington Library, Pasadena, California.

**mush,** *n.* 1. [Boiled meal] — *Syn.* Indian meal, hasty pudding, supawn, samp, hominy, cereal, grain, spoon*, victual*; see also **food.**

2. [Any soft mass] — *Syn.* pulp, slush, dough; see **mash.**

3. [*Sentimentality] — *Syn.* sentimentalism, excessive sentiment, mawkishness, affectation, superficiality,

superficial sentiment, exaggerated sentiment, romanticism, maudlinism, a sentiment about sentiment, puppy love*, gush*, flap-doodle*, hearts and flowers*, sob stuff*; see also **love.**

**mushroom,** *n.* — *Syn.* toadstool, fungus, *champignon* (French), truffle.

Edible mushrooms include: morel, chanterelle, cremini, enoki, shiitake, portobello, porcini, puffball, earth star, honey, agaric, button, cèpe, meadow, Caesar's, fairy ring, shaggy mane, inky cap, oyster, parasol, golden clavaria, bear's head, hedgehog, angel trumpet, soft-skinned crepidotus, green russula, tan-colored russula, Mary russula, sheathed amanitopsis, large-sheathed amanitopsis, smooth lepiota, American lepiota.

Poisonous mushrooms or toadstools include: jack-my-lantern, fetid russula, fly agaric, death angel, death cup, amanita.

**mushroom,** *v.* — *Syn.* augment, spread, sprout; see **grow 1, increase** 1.

**mushy,** *modif.* **1.** [Soft] — *Syn.* pulpy, mashy, muddy; see **soft** 2.

**2.** [*Sentimental] — *Syn.* romantic, maudlin, effusive; see **emotional** 2, **sentimental.**

**music,** *n.* **1.** [A combination of tone and rhythm] — *Syn.* harmony, melody, tune, air, strain, harmonics, song, minstrelsy, euphony, measure, refrain, phrasing, modulation cadence, the Nine*.

Terms used in music include: scale, chromatic scale, tempered scale, clef, note, tone, pitch, sharp, flat, accidental, major, minor, key, mode, orchestral coloring, orchestration, instrumentation, transposition, variation, improvisation, rhythm, melody, harmony, tempo, accent, beat, down-beat, up-beat, off-beat, syncopation, chord, dominant chord, subdominant chord, tonic chord, counterpoint, interval, timbre, volume, resonance.

Musical forms for the voice include: opera, oratorio, hymn, art song, folk song, aria; see **song.**

Musical forms for instruments include: symphony (the conventional four movements of a symphony are sonata, andante, scherzo, finale), concerto, concerto grosso, suite, partita; trio, quartet, quintet, overture, prelude, sonata, sonatina, Mass, scherzo, rondo, nocturne, caprice, invention, concertino, toccata, chaconne, passacaglia, fugue, étude, exercise, tone poem, symphonic poem, symphonic fantasy, fantasia, variations, rhapsody, ballet music, serenade, ballad, march, canzonetta, rondino, pastorale, dance.

Musical dance forms include: ballet, waltz, tango, polka; see **dance** 1.

General styles of music include: classical, long-hair*, serious, medieval, modern, folk, primitive, popular, national, sacred, secular, impressionistic, neoteric, baroque, neoclassical, neo-Bachian, modernistic, formal, romantic, a cappella, program, pure, jazz; rhythm and blues, R and B, blues, jive, ragtime, boogiewoogie, light rock, hard rock, folk rock, acid rock, heavy metal, new wave, punk rock, funk, technopop, rock-and-roll, bebop, bop, soul, New Age, rap, grunge, reggae, zydeco, fusion, ragtime, swing, barrelhouse, big band, bluegrass, country and western, country.

Styles of music according to its technical form include: melodic, polyphonic, contrapuntal, homophonic, Gregorian, strict, free, harmonic, lyric, epic, dramatic, pastoral, figured, atonal, whole toned, diatonic, pentatonic, twelve-tone, aleatoric, modal, syncopated.

Styles of music according to its method of performance include: vocal, instrumental, solo, choral, orchestral.

Styles of music according to its use include: operatic, symphonic, chamber, dance, concert, motion picture, theatrical, ecclesiastical, church, military, concert, ballet.

**2.** [The study or writing of music] — *Syn.* musicology, ethnomusicology, musicography, hymnology, hymnography.

**3.** [Responsiveness to music] — *Syn.* musical appreciation, sensitivity, aesthetic sense; see **appreciation** 3, **feeling** 4.

**face the music*** — *Syn.* accept the consequences of one's actions, suffer, undergo; see **endure** 2.

**set to music** — *Syn.* compose music for, write a song around, provide a musical setting; see **compose** 3.

**musical,** *modif.* **1.** [Having the qualities of music] — *Syn.* harmonious, tuneful, dulcet, sweet, pleasing, agreeable, euphonious, melic, symphonious, symphonic, lyric, mellow, vocal, choral, silvery, canorous, assonant, unisonant, unisonous, homophonous, consonant, rhythmical; see also **harmonious** 1, **melodious.** — *Ant.* tuneless, discordant, harsh.

**2.** [Having aptitude for music] — *Syn.* gifted, talented, musically inclined; see **artistic** 2.

**musical,** *n.* — *Syn.* musicale, choral service, songfest, musical comedy, Broadway show, song-and-dance, minstrel show, oratorio, burlesque; see also **opera, performance** 2, **show** 1.

**musical instrument,** *n.* Types of musical instruments include: lyre, bell, tubular bells, chimes, pipes of Pan, flute, piccolo, flageolet, oboe, clarinet, licorice stick*, alto clarinet, bass clarinet, A clarinet, E-flat clarinet, B-flat clarinet, bassoon, contrabassoon, fife, bagpipe, ocarina, sweet potato*, trombone, bazooka, French horn, English horn, basset horn, tuba, baritone, sousaphone, helicon, cornet, trumpet, flugelhorn, alpenhorn, saxophone, virginal, dulcimer, spinet, harpsichord, harmonica, *Hammer Klavier* (German), piano, clavichord, organ, pipe organ, reed organ, mouth organ, jew's harp, harp, vina, calabash, tambourine, ukelele, Hawaiian guitar, guitar, electric guitar, flamenco guitar, bass guitar, sitar, steel guitar, banjo, mandolin, lute, theorbo, viola, violin, fiddle*, violoncello, cello, bass viol, xylophone, marimba, *Glockenspiel* (German), vibraharp, vibraphone, vibes*, cymbal, drum, accordian, concertina, zamar, tom-tom, magoudhi, balalaika, kokiri, samisen, cheng, siao, kin, che, koto, crowd, recorder, grand piano, concert piano, baby grand piano, upright piano, spinet, player piano, tuning fork, calliope, synthesizer, drums, cymbals, tambourine. See also **drum, flute, horn** 1, **organ, piano.**

**musician,** *n.* — *Syn.* player, performer, composer; see **artist** 1, **genius** 2.

Musicians include: singer, vocalist, director, conductor, teacher, instrumentalist, soloist, soprano, first soprano, second soprano, alto, contralto, tenor, baritone, bass, basso, basso profundo, coloratura soprano, mezzosoprano, folk singer; guitarist, guitar player, bassist, bass player, keyboardist, percussionist, organist, drummer, pianist, flautist, flutist, violinist, cellist; jazzman, blues man, rocker, torch singer.

**musing,** *modif.* — *Syn.* pensive, introspective, absorbed; see **thoughtful** 1.

**musing,** *n.* — *Syn.* absorption, meditation, deliberation; see **reflection** 1, **thought** 1.

**musket,** *n.* — *Syn.* flintlock, carbine, matchlock; see **gun** 2, **rifle, weapon** 1.

**musketeer,** *n.* — *Syn.* enlisted man, rifleman, hussar, grenadier; see **fighter** 1, **soldier.**

**muskrat,** *n.* — *Syn.* musk shrew, Pyrenean desman,

Muscovitic desman, civet cat, musquash, musk cat*, muskbox*; see also **animal** 2.

**muss***, *n.* — *Syn.* mess, chaos, disarrangement, turmoil; see **confusion** 2, **disorder** 2.

**muss**, *v.* — *Syn.* rumble, tousle, dishevel, ruffle, crumple, jumble, disarrange, disturb, mess up; see also **tangle**.

**mussy**, *modif.* — *Syn.* messy, chaotic, rumpled; see **tangled.**

**must***, *n.* — *Syn.* requirement, need, obligation; see **necessity** 2.

**must**, *v.* — *Syn.* ought, should, have to, have got to, be compelled, be necessitated, be obliged, be required, be doomed, be destined, be ordered, be directed, be made, be driven, must needs*, have no choice*, be pushed to the wall*, be one's fate*; see also **need.**

**mustache**, *n.* — *Syn.* moustachio, handlebars*, soup-strainer*; see **beard, whiskers.**

**mustang**, *n.* — *Syn.* bronco, colt, wild stallion; see **horse** 1.

**muster**, *v.* — *Syn.* gather, call together, marshal, summon; see **assemble** 2, **gather** 1.

*See Synonym Study at* GATHER.

**musty**, *modif.* **1.** [Spoiled] — *Syn.* moldy, putrid, rank; see **rotten** 1, **spoiled.**
**2.** [Stale with age] — *Syn.* fusty, dusty, moth-eaten, crumbling, dry, dried-out, antediluvian, mummyish, decrepit; see also **wasted, withered.** — *Ant.* NEW, well-cared-for, in good condition.
**3.** [Trite] — *Syn.* worn, worn out, commonplace, hackneyed; see **common** 1, **dull** 4.

**mutability**, *n.* — *Syn.* instability, indecision, inconstancy, variableness, changeability, changeableness, volatility, versatility, fickleness, vacillation, indecision, irresolution, changefulness; see also **uncertainty** 2, 3.

**mutable**, *modif.* — *Syn.* fickle, uncertain, doubtful; see **changeable** 2, **unreliable** 2.

**mutation**, *n.* — *Syn.* modification, deviation, variation; see **change** 1, 2, **variety** 1, 2.

**mute**, *modif.* **1.** [Without power of speech] — *Syn.* tongueless, aphonic, aphasic, deaf and dumb, inarticulate, voiceless, tonguetied; see also **dumb** 1, **quiet** 2. — *Ant.* VOCAL, noisy, unimpaired.
**2.** [Suddenly deprived of speech] — *Syn.* speechless, wordless, silent; see **bewildered, surprised.**

*See Synonym Study at* DUMB.

**mute**, *v.* — *Syn.* silence, reduce, benumb; see **soften** 2.

**mutilate**, *v.* **1.** [To maim] — *Syn.* disfigure, dismember, mangle, cut off, cut up; see also **maim, mangle** 1.
**2.** [To damage] — *Syn.* mar, deface, slash; see **damage** 1, **hurt** 1, **mangle** 1.

*See Synonym Study at* MAIM.

**mutilated**, *modif.* — *Syn.* garbled, disfigured, distorted, castrated, maimed, mangled, dismembered, truncated, amputated, butchered, excised, defaced, dislimbed; see also **deformed, twisted** 1, **weakened.**

**mutineer**, *n.* — *Syn.* rebel, insurgent, revolutionary, subversive; see **radical, rebel** 1.

**mutinous**, *modif.* — *Syn.* insubordinate, riotous, anarchistic; see **lawless** 1, 2, **radical** 2, **rebellious** 1, 2, 3.

**mutiny**, *n.* — *Syn.* insurrection, revolt, resistance; see **revolution** 2.

**mutter**, *v.* **1.** [To speak as if to oneself] — *Syn.* mumble, murmur, grunt, grumble, sputter, whisper, speak *sotto voce* (Italian), speak in an undertone, say to oneself, speak under one's breath, swallow one's words; see also **mumble, utter.**
**2.** [To complain] — *Syn.* grumble, moan, groan, grouse*; see **complain** 1.

*See Synonym Study at* MUMBLE.

**mutton**, *n.* — *Syn.* lamb, sheep flesh, *mouton* (French); see **meat, sheep.**
Cuts of mutton include: shoulder, leg, spigot (Scotch), rib chop, loin chop, lamb chop, rack of lamb, crown roast, shank, leg of lamb, brisket.

**mutual**, *modif.* **1.** [Reciprocal] — *Syn.* reciprocal, interchangeable, correlative, complementary, done reciprocally, acting reciprocally, convertible, interchanged, responded to, reciprocated, requited, respective, two-sided, bilateral, give-and-take, interactive; see also **exchangeable.** — *Ant.* unreciprocated, one-sided, noninterchangeable.
**2.** [Common] — *Syn.* joint, shared, belonging equally to; see **common** 5.

---

**SYN.** — **mutual** may imply an interchange of feeling between two persons */mutual* admiration, *mutual* enemies*/*, or a sharing jointly with others */the mutual* efforts of a group*/*; **reciprocal** implies a return in kind or degree by each of two sides of what is given or demonstrated by the other */a reciprocal* trade agreement*/* or may refer to any inversely corresponding relationship */the reciprocal* functions of two machine parts*/*; **common** simply implies being shared by others or by all the members of a group */our common* interests*/*

---

**mutual fund**, *n.* — *Syn.* trust fund, investment corporation, cushioned stock list; see **bank** 3, **funds.**

**mutuality**, *n.* — *Syn.* reciprocity, correlation, alternation; see **exchange** 2, **sale** 1, 2, **transaction.**

**mutually**, *modif.* — *Syn.* commonly, co-operatively, respectively, reciprocally, in cooperation, in collaboration, in combination, by common consent, by agreement, by contract, in conjunction with, to the common profit, for the common advantage, each to each, to one another, all at once, en masse, as a group, as a company, as an organization; see also **jointly, together** 2. — *Ant.* INDIVIDUALLY, independently, separately.

**muzzle**, *v.* **1.** [To fasten a muzzle upon] — *Syn.* cage, sheathe, cover, wrap, muffle, envelop, deaden; see also **bind** 1, **gag** 1. — *Ant.* RELEASE, unfasten, unbind.
**2.** [To silence] — *Syn.* gag, restrain, trammel, stifle, restrict, repress, suppress, check, stop, stop one's mouth, hush, still, shush*; see also **prevent, quiet** 2.

**muzzled**, *modif.* — *Syn.* silenced, gagged, quieted; see **abused, trapped.**

**myopia**, *n.* **1.** [Poor vision at a distance] — *Syn.* nearsightedness, shortsightedness, astigmatism, strabismus, blindness; see also **sight** 1, **vision** 1.
**2.** [Narrow-mindedness] — *Syn.* intolerance, bigotry, parochialism, narrowness, bias; see also **prejudice.**

**myopic**, *modif.* **1.** [Nearsighted] — *Syn.* nearsighted, shortsighted, astigmatic, bleary-eyed, shortsighted, halfsighted, dimsighted, presbyopic, moon-eyed*, mole-eyed*, goggle-eyed*, blind*.
**2.** [Narrow-minded] — *Syn.* close-minded, intolerant, bigoted, parochial; see **prejudiced.**

**myriad**, *modif.* — *Syn.* variable, infinite, innumerable; see **endless** 1, **multiple** 1.

**myself**, *pron.* — *Syn.* me, personally, in my proper person, I personally, me personally, the speaker, the author, the writer, on my own authority, on my own responsibility, yours truly*, your humble servant*, me myself*, my own sweet self*; me, myself, and I*.

**mysterious**, *modif.* **1.** [Puzzling] — *Syn.* puzzling, en-

igmatic, perplexing, strange, baffling, inexplicable, insoluble, unaccountable, inscrutable, confounding, shrouded in mystery; see also **difficult** 2, **unnatural** 1.
**2.** [Concerning powers beyond those supposedly natural] — *Syn.* mystic, mystical, occult, mystifying, inscrutable, arcane, transcendental, cabalistic, spiritual, magical, abstruse, dark, veiled, strange, alchemistic, supernormal, necromantic, astrological, unknowable, unfathomable, ineffable, esoteric, numinous, cryptic, oracular, unrevealed; see also **magic** 1, **secret** 1.
**3.** [Not generally known] — *Syn.* obscure, hidden, ambiguous; see **obscure** 1, **secret** 1.

---

*SYN.* — **mysterious** is applied to that which excites curiosity, wonder, etc. but is impossible or difficult to explain or solve *[a mysterious murder]*; what is **inscrutable** is completely mysterious and altogether incapable of being searched out, interpreted, or understood *[the inscrutable ways of God]*; **mystical** or **mystic** applies to that which is beyond ordinary human understanding or perception in connection with religious rites or spiritual experience

---

**mystery,** *n.* **1.** [The quality of being mysterious] — *Syn.* inscrutability, inscrutableness, unfathomableness, unfathomability, undiscoverability, unanswerableness, unexplainableness, inexplicableness, abstruseness, equivocality, esoterism, occultism, cabalism; see also **irregularity** 2, **magic** 1, 2, **strangeness.** — *Ant.* CLARITY, discoverability, scrutability.
**2.** [Something difficult to know] — *Syn.* riddle, conundrum, enigma, secret; see **puzzle** 2, **secret.**
**3.** [A trick] — *Syn.* sleight-of-hand, trick of magic, juggle; see **trick** 1.
**4.** [\*A mystery story] — *Syn.* detective story, mystery play, mystery movie; see **story.**
*See Synonym Study at* PUZZLE.

**mystic,** *modif.* — *Syn.* mystical, occult, transcendental, spiritual; see **mysterious** 2, **secret** 1.
*See Synonym Study at* MYSTERIOUS.

**mysticism,** *n.* — *Syn.* occultism, pietism, ontologism, cabala, cabalism, quietism, orphism, divine afflatus, enthusiasm; see also **spiritualism** 1.

**mystification,** *n.* — *Syn.* bewilderment, uncertainty, complexity; see **confusion** 2, **wonder** 1.

**mystify,** *v.* — *Syn.* perplex, trick, hoodwink; see **deceive, lie** 1.

**mystique,** *n.* — *Syn.* attitude, complex, nature; see **character** 1, **temperament.**

**myth,** *n.* — *Syn.* fable, folk tale, legend, religion, lore, saga, folk ballad, *mythos* (Greek), allegory, parable, tale; see also **story.**

**mythical,** *modif.* — *Syn.* mythological, fabricated, fictitious; see **false** 3, **unreal.**
*See Synonym Study at* FICTITIOUS.

**mythological,** *modif.* — *Syn.* whimsical, fictitious, chimerical; see **fanciful** 1, **fantastic** 1, **imaginary.**

**mythology,** *n.* — *Syn.* belief, conviction, mythicism; see **faith** 2, **religion** 1.
Systems of mythology include: Chaldean, Roman, Semitic, Bantu, Sumerian, Greek, Egyptian, Norse, Germanic, Celtic, Hindu, American Indian.

# N

**nab\***, *v.* **1.** [\*To arrest]— *Syn.* apprehend, capture, arrest, catch; see **arrest** 1, **catch** 2.
**2.** [To seize]— *Syn.* grab, take, snatch, seize; see **catch** 1, **seize** 1, 2.
*See Synonym Study at* CATCH.

**nadir**, *n.* — *Syn.* depth(s), lowest point, foot; see **bottom** 1, **opposite** 3.

**nag**, *n.* — *Syn.* plug, mount, hack; see **animal** 2, **horse** 1.

**nag**, *v.* — *Syn.* vex, annoy, pester; see **bother** 2, 3.

**naiad**, *n.* — *Syn.* nymph, sprite, undine; see **fairy**.

**nail**, *n.* — *Syn.* brad, pin, peg, hob, stud; see also **spike** 1.
Types and sizes of nails include: common, copper, cement coated, masonry, dry wall, galvanized, finishing, flooring, shingle, roofing, doublehead scaffold, spiral siding, staging, boat, hinge, chair, horseshoe, brad, cut, upholsterer's, clout, box, shoe, headless, hobnail; twopenny, fourpenny, sixpenny, eightpenny, tenpenny, twelvepenny.

**nail**, *v.* **1.** [To hammer]— *Syn.* drive, pound, spike; see **beat** 2, **hammer, hit** 1.
**2.** [To fasten with nails]— *Syn.* secure, hold, bind; see **fasten** 1.
**3.** [\*To arrest]— *Syn.* capture, detain, apprehend; see **arrest** 1, **seize** 2.

**hard as nails**— *Syn.* callous, unfeeling, remorseless; see **cruel** 2.

**hit the nail on the head\***— *Syn.* say what is exactly right, be accurate, come to the point; see **define** 2.

**naive**, *modif.* — *Syn.* ingenuous, artless, unsophisticated, unaffected, innocent, simple, inexperienced, untrained, countrified, callow, jejune, *naïf* (French), natural, unschooled, ignorant, untaught, provincial, unworldly, guileless, spontaneous, instinctive, impulsive, simple-minded, innocuous, unsuspecting, harmless, confiding, childlike, gullible, credulous, trusting, fresh, unjaded, original, rustic, boorish, unpolished, primitive, sincere, unfeigned, open, candid, forthright, aboveboard, romantic, fanciful, unpretentious, transparent, unsuspicious, straightforward, uncomplicated, easily imposed upon, green\*; see also **childish** 1, **frank, inexperienced, simple** 1.— *Ant.* EXPERIENCED, sophisticated, artful.

**SYN.** — **naive** implies a genuine, innocent simplicity or lack of artificiality, but sometimes connotes an almost foolish lack of worldly wisdom /his *naive* belief in the kindness of others/; **ingenuous** implies a frankness or straightforwardness that suggests the simplicity of a child /her *ingenuous* confession of her real motives/; **artless** suggests a lack of artificiality or guile that derives from indifference to the effect one has upon others /*artless* beauty/; **unsophisticated**, like **naive**, implies a lack of worldly wisdom but connotes that this is the result merely of a lack of experience /simple, *unsophisticated* tastes/

**naively**, *modif.* — *Syn.* childishly, ingenuously, stupidly; see **foolishly, openly** 1.

**naiveté**, *n.* — *Syn.* ingenuousness, childishness, inexperience; see **innocence** 2, **simplicity** 2, 3.

**naked**, *modif.* **1.** [Nude]— *Syn.* unclothed, undressed, nude, stripped, unclad, disrobed, unrobed, divested, leafless, hairless, bare, undraped, exposed, ungarmented, having nothing on, in dishabille, unappareled, denuded, unveiled, uncovered, uncloaked, stark naked, bald, bareheaded, barren, dismantled, *au naturel* (French), mother-naked, buck naked\*, in the altogether\*, in one's birthday suit\*, in the buff\*, peeled\*, without a stitch\*, in the raw\*, topless, bottomless, not decent\*, in a state of nature\*, starkers\*.— *Ant.* CLOTHED, clad, dressed.
**2.** [Without covering]— *Syn.* exposed, bared, unconcealed, unprotected; see **exposed** 2, **open** 4.
**3.** [Unadorned]— *Syn.* plain, stark, simple, artless; see **abrupt** 2, **modest** 2, **natural** 3.

**SYN.** — **naked** implies the absence of clothing, either entirely or from some part, and connotes a revealing of the body /a *naked* bosom/; in extended use, **naked** often connotes lack of concealment or embellishment /*naked* ambition /; **nude**, which is somewhat euphemistic for **naked**, is commonly applied to the undraped human figure in art; **bare**, in this comparison, implies the absence of the conventional or appropriate covering /*bare* legs, *bare* floors/; **bald** suggests a lack of natural covering, as of hair on the head, and in extended use may suggest plainness or bluntness /the *bald* facts/; **barren** implies a lack of natural covering, esp. vegetation, and connotes destitution and fruitlessness /*barren* lands/

**nakedness**, *n.* — *Syn.* nudity, bareness, nature in the raw, undress, baldness, exposure, state of nature\*, the raw\*.

**namby-pamby**, *modif.* — *Syn.* insipid, wishy-washy, simpering; see **cowardly** 1, 2, **irresolute, sentimental**.

**name**, *n.* **1.** [A title]— *Syn.* proper name, Christian name, given name, cognomen, appellation, designation, first name, family name, compellation, title, prenomen, denomination, surname, agnomen, agname, style, sign, patronymic, matronymic, eponym\*, moniker\*, handle\*; see also **signature**.
**2.** [Reputation]— *Syn.* renown, honor, repute; see **fame** 1.
**3.** [An epithet]— *Syn.* nickname, pen name, pseudonym, sobriquet, stage name, *nom de plume, nom de guerre* (both French), pet name, fictitious name; see also **alias**.
Insulting names include: devil, imbecile, idiot, blackguard, rat, skunk, dog, pig, fool, moron, punk, brute, *cochon, canaille* (both French), *ladrón, galopin* (both Spanish), *Schweinhund, Schweinigel, Lausejunge, Lausehund* (all German); bum\*, boob\*, oaf\*, goon\*, sourpuss\*, dumb Dora\*, specks\*, four-eyes\*, skinny\*, fatty\*, wind-

bag\*, buttinski\*, meshugana\*, nerd\*, dork\*, doofus\*, jerk\*, louse\*, schmuck\*, sap\*, sleaze\*, creep\*, wimp\*, weenie\*, wuss\*, dweeb\*, geek\*, turkey\*, bimbo\*, pinhead\*, dingbat\*, ditz\*, airhead\*, nitwit\*, klutz\*, bonehead\*, musclehead\*; see also **curse** 1, **insult**.

**4.** [A famous person]— *Syn.* star, hero, lion, person of renown, celeb\*, headline attraction\*, blue-booker\*, headliner\*; see also **celebrity** 2, **personage** 2.

**call names**— *Syn.* swear at, castigate, slander, defame, attack; see also **curse** 2, **insult**.

**in the name of**— *Syn.* by authority of, in reference to, as representative of; see **for**.

**know only by name**— *Syn.* be acquainted with, not know personally, have heard of; see **know** 3.

**to one's name**— *Syn.* belonging to one, in one's possession, possessed by; see **owned**.

**name**, *v.* **1.** [To give a name]— *Syn.* call, christen, baptize, style, term, label, identify, provide with nomenclature, classify, denominate, designate, title, entitle, nickname, characterize, label, ticket, dub\*, pin a moniker on\*, put the tag on\*, give a handle\*; see also **describe, define**.

**2.** [To indicate by name]— *Syn.* refer to, specify, signify, denote, single out, mark, suggest, connote, point to, note, remark, index, list, cite; see also **mention, refer** 2.

**3.** [To appoint]— *Syn.* elect, nominate, select; see **delegate** 1.

**name calling**, *n.*— *Syn.* insulting, abusing, derogating; see **insult**.

**named**, *modif.* **1.** [Having as a name]— *Syn.* called, designated, entitled, titled, termed, specified, styled, appellated, denominated, christened, baptized, nicknamed, labeled, tagged\*, dubbed\*.

**2.** [Chosen]— *Syn.* appointed, commissioned, delegated, deputed, authorized, nominated, returned, elected, invested, vested, assigned, ordained, entrusted, picked, selected, chosen, decided upon, fixed upon, determined on, settled on, picked out, preferred, favored, supported, approved, certified, called, anointed, consecrated, sanctioned, drafted, opted, declared, announced, singled out.

**name-dropper**, *n.*— *Syn.* snob, poseur, showoff; see **braggart**.

**name-dropping**, *n.*— *Syn.* posing, showing off, assuming a pose; see **boast**.

**nameless**, *modif.* **1.** [Anonymous]— *Syn.* unacknowledged, unknown, unnamed; see **anonymous**.

**2.** [Unrenowned]— *Syn.* inconspicuous, undistinguished, obscure; see **unknown** 2.

**3.** [Unspeakable]— *Syn.* unmentionable, disreputable, despicable; see **offensive** 2.

**namely**, *modif.*— *Syn.* to wit, that is to say, particularly, by way of explanation, strictly speaking, as much as to say, viz., in other words, in plain English, i.e., *id est, videlicet scilicet* (all Latin); see also **specifically** 1.

**naming**, *n.*— *Syn.* identifying, pinning down, giving a name to, finding a name for, providing an identification for; see also **classification** 1, **description** 1.

**nanny**, *n.*— *Syn.* nursemaid, *au pair* (French), babysitter; see **nurse** 3.

**nap**, *n.* **1.** [A short sleep]— *Syn.* siesta, cat nap, snooze, doze; see **rest** 1, **sleep**.

**2.** [The finish of certain goods, especially fabric]— *Syn.* pile, shag, surface, feel, grit, ingrain, tooth, fiber, woof, wale, warp and weft, roughness, smoothness; see also **grain** 3, **outside** 1, **texture** 1.

**nape**, *n.*— *Syn.* the back of the neck, cervix, cervical area, scruff, scruff of the neck, poll, occiput; see also **neck** 1.

**napkin**, *n.*— *Syn.* serviette, paper napkin, (table) linen; see **towel**.

**narcotic**, *modif.*— *Syn.* opiate, soporific, anodyne, calming, deadening, numbing, dulling, analgesic, anesthetic, stupefying.

**narcotic**, *n.*— *Syn.* stupefacient, anodyne, opiate; see **drug** 2.

**narrate**, *v.*— *Syn.* tell, recite, make known, rehearse, detail, enumerate, describe, recount, set forth, hold forth, depict, characterize, delineate, portray, picture, proclaim, unfold, paint, disclose, reveal, chronicle, repeat, relate, relate the particulars, give an account of, tell a story, spin a yarn\*, unfold a tale\*, hand a lingo\*, spin a windy\*; see also **report** 1, **tell** 1.

**narration**, *n.*— *Syn.* description, narrative, account; see **report** 1, **story**.

**narrative**, *modif.*— *Syn.* storylike, fictional, retold, recounted, narrated, sequential, reported; see also **chronological, historical**.

**narrative**, *n.*— *Syn.* story, tale, anecdote, account; see **story**.

*See Synonym Study at* STORY.

**narrator**, *n.*— *Syn.* teller of tales, reciter, raconteur; see **storyteller**.

**narrow**, *modif.* **1.** [Lacking breadth]— *Syn.* close, cramped, tight, confined, shrunken, compressed, slender, thin, fine, linear, threadlike, tapering, tapered, slim, spare, scant, scanty, incapacious, attenuated, strait, coarctate, lanky, spindling, small, meager; see also **restricted**.— *Ant.* broad, wide, extensive.

**2.** [Lacking tolerance]— *Syn.* dogmatic, narrowminded, parochial; see **conservative, conventional** 3, **prejudiced**.

**3.** [Lacking understanding]— *Syn.* ill-advised, imprudent, irrational; see **stupid** 1.

**4.** [Lacking a comfortable margin]— *Syn.* close, near, precarious; see **dangerous** 1, **endangered, unsafe**.

**narrowing**, *n.*— *Syn.* shortening, restricting, lessening; see **abbreviation** 2, **contraction** 1, **reduction** 1.

**narrowly**, *modif.*— *Syn.* nearly, close(ly), by a (narrow) margin; see **almost**.

**narrow-minded**, *modif.*— *Syn.* bigoted, biased, provincial; see **conservative, conventional** 3, **prejudiced**.

**narrow-mindedness**, *n.*— *Syn.* intolerance, bigotry, provincialism; see **prejudice**.

**narrowness**, *n.* **1.** [A physical restriction]— *Syn.* confinement, slimness, thinness, restriction; see **barrier, impediment** 1, **interference** 1.

**2.** [A mental restriction]— *Syn.* insularity, intolerance, bigotry, bias; see **prejudice, stubbornness**.

**narrows**, *n.*— *Syn.* strait, neck, canal; see **channel** 1.

**nasty**, *modif.* **1.** [Offensive to the senses]— *Syn.* dirty, foul, gross, revolting; see **offensive** 2, **vulgar** 1.

**2.** [Indecent]— *Syn.* immoral, immodest, smutty; see **lewd** 1, 2, **shameful** 1, **wicked** 1.

**3.** [Likely to be harmful]— *Syn.* injurious, damaging, noxious; see **dangerous** 1, **fierce** 2, **harmful, poisonous**.

**4.** [Unkind]— *Syn.* sarcastic, critical, mean; see **cruel** 1, **fierce** 1, **ruthless** 1.

**nation**, *n.* **1.** [An organized state]— *Syn.* realm, country, commonwealth, republic, democracy, state, monarchy, dominion, body politic, land, domain, empire, kingdom, principality, sovereignty, colony; see also **government** 1.

**2.** [A people having some unity]— *Syn.* nationality, populace, community, public; see **population, race** 2, **society** 2.

**national**, *modif.* **1.** [Concerning a nation]— *Syn.* federal, political, sovereign, state, social, societal, politic, civic, civil, communal, royal, imperial, ethnic; see also **governmental, public** 2.

**2.** [Operative throughout a nation] — *Syn.* nationwide, inland, internal, country-wide, interstate, social, widespread, sweeping; see also **general** 1.

**national,** *n.* — *Syn.* citizen, subject, inhabitant, native.

**nationalism,** *n.* — *Syn.* provincialism, chauvinism, jingoism; see **loyalty, patriotism.**

**nationality,** *n.* **1.** [Citizenship] — *Syn.* native land, allegiance, adopted country, political home; see **country** 3, **origin** 2.

**2.** [A national group] — *Syn.* body politic, society, community; see **citizen, population, race** 2.

**nationally,** *modif.* **1.** [Concerning a nation] — *Syn.* politically, governmentally, as a state, as a country, publicly, of the people, throughout the country, transcending state boundaries, for the general welfare.

**2.** [Everywhere] — *Syn.* nationwide, generally, commonly, entirely; see **everywhere, universally** 2, 3.

**nationwide,** *modif.* — *Syn.* general, federal, universal; see **national** 2, **regional, public** 1, 2.

**native,** *modif.* **1.** [Natural] — *Syn.* innate, inherent, inborn, implanted, inbred, ingrained, inwrought, congenital, fundamental, hereditary, inherited, essential, constitutional; see also **natural** 1. — *Ant.* UNNATURAL, foreign, alien.

**2.** [Originating in or characteristic of a region] — *Syn.* aboriginal, indigenous, endemic, original, native-born, belonging, coming from, autochthonous, autochthonal, primary, primeval, primitive, vernacular, domestic, local, found locally, regional, homegrown, natal, mother, by birth; see also **regional.** — *Ant.* IMPORTED, brought in, transplanted, foreign.

**go native** — *Syn.* adopt a different way of life, live simply, vegetate; see **change** 4.

---

**SYN.** — **native** applies to a person born, or thing originating, in a certain place or country [a *native* New Yorker, *native* fruits]; **indigenous,** which also suggests natural origin in a particular region, is applied to races or species rather than to individuals [the potato is *indigenous* to South America]; **aboriginal** applies to the earliest known inhabitants (or, rarely, animals or plants) of a region [the Indians are the *aboriginal* Americans]; **endemic,** applied esp. to plants and diseases, implies prevalence in or restriction to a particular region [typhus is *endemic* in some tropical areas]

---

**native,** *n.* **1.** [Aborigine] — *Syn.* aboriginal, autochthon, primitive, ancient, original inhabitant, indigenous inhabitant, tribesman, savage*.

**2.** [Citizen] — *Syn.* citizen, inhabitant, indigene, local*; see **citizen, resident.**

*See Synonym Study at* CITIZEN.

**native son,** *n.* — *Syn.* local candidate, favorite son, home boy*, local boy*; see **candidate, favorite, resident.**

**Nativity,** *n.* — *Syn.* the birth of Christ, Holy Night, coming of the Christ-child; see **Christmas.**

**natty,** *modif.* — *Syn.* smart, chic, well-dressed; see **clean** 1, **fashionable, neat** 1.

**natural,** *modif.* **1.** [Rooted in nature] — *Syn.* intrinsic, original, essential, true, fundamental, inborn, ingrained, inherent, instinctive, implanted, innate, inbred, subjective, inherited, congenital, genetic, incarnate, bred in the bone; see also **native** 1. — *Ant.* FOREIGN, alien, acquired.

**2.** [To be expected] — *Syn.* normal, typical, characteristic, usual, customary, habitual, accustomed, involuntary, spontaneous, uncontrolled, uncontrollable,

wonted, familiar, expected, routine, regular, common, universal, prevailing, prevalent, general, uniform, constant, consistent, probable, predictable, ordinary, logical, reasonable, anticipated, looked for, hoped for, counted on, relied on, generally occurring, in the natural course of events, matter-of-course; see also **regular** 3. — *Ant.* UNUSUAL, unexpected, unheard of.

**3.** [Not affected] — *Syn.* ingenuous, simple, artless, innocent, spontaneous, impulsive, childlike, unfeigned, unaffected, open, frank, candid, unsophisticated, homey, unpretentious, forthright, sincere, unstudied, straightforward, undesigning, being oneself, unsuspecting, credulous, trusting, plain, unassumed, direct, unpolished, rustic; see also **naive.** — *Ant.* ORNATE, pretentious, affected.

**4.** [Concerning the physical universe] — *Syn.* actual, tangible, according to nature; see **physical** 1, **real.**

*See Synonym Study at* NORMAL.

**natural child,** *n.* — *Syn.* love child, illegitimate offspring, *nullius filius* (Latin); see **baby** 1, **child, illegitimate** 2.

**naturalist,** *n.* — *Syn.* botanist, zoologist, biologist; see **scientist.**

**naturalization,** *n.* — *Syn.* adoption, acclimatization, acculturation, adapting, conditioning, habituation, accustoming, inurement, making new allegiances, rooting, grounding; see also **adjustment** 2.

**naturalize,** *v.* — *Syn.* confer citizenship upon, adapt, acclimate, accustom; see **adopt** 2, **change** 1, **conform.**

**naturally,** *interj.* — *Syn.* certainly, absolutely, of course; see **surely, yes.**

**naturally,** *modif.* **1.** [In an unaffected manner] — *Syn.* artlessly, spontaneously, innocently, candidly, openly, impulsively, freely, readily, easily, without restraint, unceremoniously, unconstrainedly, directly; see also **simply** 1, **sincerely.** — *Ant.* AWKWARDLY, restrainedly, clumsily.

**2.** [As a matter of course] — *Syn.* casually, according to expectation, as anticipated, characteristically, typically, normally, commonly, usually, ordinarily, habitually, instinctively, intuitively, by nature, by birth, uniformly, generally, consistently; see also **customarily.** — *Ant.* STRANGELY, astonishingly, amazingly.

**natural science,** *n.* — *Syn.* popular science, organic and inorganic science, life science, physical science, science of nature; see also **science** 1.

**nature,** *n.* **1.** [The external universe] — *Syn.* cosmos, creation, macrocosm, world; see **universe, earth** 1.

**2.** [The complex of essential qualities] — *Syn.* characteristics, quality, constitution; see **character** 1, **essence** 1.

**3.** [Natural surroundings] — *Syn.* outside world, out-of-doors, scenery, rural setting, natural setting, view, seascape, landscape, the outdoors, external nature, natural scenery, God's hand, recreational facilities, forest primeval, the great outdoors*, the birds and the bees*; see also **environment, reality** 1.

**4.** [Natural forces] — *Syn.* natural law, natural order, the forces of nature, underlying cause, cosmic process, physical energy, kinetic energy, potential energy, water power, fission, fusion, hydrogen atom, heavy water, atomic power, the sun, radiation, rays; beta rays, gamma rays; see also **energy** 3, **physics.**

**5.** [Vital forces in an organism] — *Syn.* creation, generation, regeneration, restoration, vivification, animation, energy, quickening, reproductiveness, life force, the nature of the beast*; see also **life** 1, 2, **strength** 1.

**6.** [Kind] — *Syn.* species, sort, type; see **kind** 2, **variety** 1, 2.

**by nature**— *Syn.* inherently, by birth, as a matter of course; see **naturally** 2.

**in a state of nature**— *Syn.* uncultivated, not tamed, primitive; see **wild** 3.

**of** or **in the nature of**— *Syn.* similar to, having the essential character of, as compared to; see **like.**

**naught,** *n.* — *Syn.* nought, zero, not anything; see **nothing.**

**naughty,** *modif.* — *Syn.* wayward, disobedient, mischievous, impish, fiendish, badly behaved, roguish, bad, unmanageable, ungovernable, refractory, recalcitrant, wanton, froward, insubordinate; see also **unruly.**
See Synonym Study at WICKED.

**nausea,** *n.* **1.** [Sickness] — *Syn.* motion sickness, queasiness, vomiting; see **illness** 1.
**2.** [Disgust] — *Syn.* offense, revulsion, aversion; see **hatred** 1.

**nauseate,** *v.* — *Syn.* sicken, offend, repulse; see **bother** 3, **disgust, disturb** 2.

**nauseated,** *modif.* **1.** [Sick] — *Syn.* squeamish, ill, queasy, nauseous; see **sick.**
**2.** [Disgusted] — *Syn.* revolted, sickened, offended; see **disgusted, insulted, shocked.**

**nauseating,** *modif.* — *Syn.* sickening, repulsive, disgusting; see **offensive** 2.

**nauseous,** *modif.* **1.** [Sick] — *Syn.* queasy, ill, squeamish, nauseated; see **sick.**
**2.** [Disgusting] — *Syn.* revolting, loathsome, nauseating, sickening; see **offensive** 2.

**nautical,** *modif.* — *Syn.* maritime, ocean-going, marine, naval, oceanic, deep-sea, aquatic, sailing, seafaring, seaworthy, sea-going, boating, rowing, oceanographic, sea-loving, navy-trained, yachting, whaling, cruising, navigating, salty, pelagic, thalassic, abyssal; see also **maritime** 2.

**naval,** *modif.* — *Syn.* seagoing, marine, aquatic; see **maritime** 2, **nautical.**

**nave,** *n.* — *Syn.* hub, core, middle; see **center** 1.

**navel,** *n.* — *Syn.* omphalos, depression, umbilicus, belly-button; see **abdomen, center** 1.

**navigable,** *modif.* — *Syn.* traversable, off-soundings, passable, open; see **safe** 1.

**navigate,** *v.* — *Syn.* pilot, steer, lie to, head out for, ride out, lay the course, operate, cruise, sail, travel; see also **drive** 3.

**navigation,** *n.* — *Syn.* navigating, seamanship, piloting, pilotage, aeronautics, flying, sailing, seafaring, ocean travel, exploration, voyaging, shipping, cruising, steerage, plotting a course, aquatics, boating, yachting, transoceanic travel, transatlantic travel, transpacific travel, arctic travel, coasting, island-hopping, plane sailing, traverse sailing, sailing against the wind, middle sailing, parallel sailing, latitude sailing, mercator sailing, great-circle sailing, spherical navigation; see also **travel** 1.

**navigator,** *n.* — *Syn.* seaman, explorer, mariner; see **pilot** 1, **sailor.**

**navy,** *n.* — *Syn.* fleet, naval forces, squadron, flotilla, armada, task force, scouting force, submarine force, amphibious force, marine air arm, coast guard, first line of defense.

**nazi,** *modif.* — *Syn.* fascist, totalitarian, right-wing; see **absolute** 3, **autocratic** 1, **tyrannical.**

**Nazi,** *n.* — *Syn.* National Socialist, fascist, reactionary, right winger; see **agitator, radical.**

**near,** *modif.* **1.** [Not distant in space] — *Syn.* nigh, adjacent, adjoining, proximal, neighboring, not remote, close at hand, proximate, contiguous, handy, near by, hard by, next door to, at close quarters, beside, side by side, in close proximity; see also **bordering.** — *Ant.* DISTANT, removed, far off.
**2.** [Not distant in relationship] — *Syn.* touching, affecting, akin; see **friendly** 1, **related** 3.
**3.** [Not distant in time] — *Syn.* at hand, approaching, next; see **coming** 1, **expected** 2, **imminent.**

**nearing,** *modif.* — *Syn.* coming, impending, threatening; see **approaching, imminent.**

**nearly,** *modif.* — *Syn.* within a little, all but, just about, approximately; see **almost.**

**nearness,** *n.* **1.** [Nearness in time or space] — *Syn.* closeness, contiguity, adjacency, proximity, propinquity, vicinity, vicinage, approximation, approach, intimacy, resemblance, likeness, handiness, close quarters, imminence, immediacy, loom, threat, menace, prospectiveness; see also **neighborhood, similarity.** — *Ant.* DISTANCE, remoteness, difference.
**2.** [Nearness in feeling] — *Syn.* familiarity, dearness, intimacy; see **admiration, affection** 1, **friendship** 2.

**nearsighted,** *modif.* — *Syn.* shortsighted, astigmatic, mope-eyed; see **myopic.**

**nearsightedness,** *n.* — *Syn.* shortsightedness, blindness, astigmatism; see **myopia.**

**neat,** *modif.* **1.** [Clean and orderly] — *Syn.* clean, tidy, trim, prim, spruce, natty, dapper, smart, correct, shipshape, methodical, regular, orderly, systematic, spotless, finical, nice, dainty, elegant, well kept, spick-and-span, immaculate, meticulous, trig, chic, well-groomed, exact, precise, proper, neat as a pin, in good order, spruced up, put to right; see also **clean** 1. — *Ant.* unkempt, DISORDERED, slovenly.
**2.** [Clever; *said of something done*] — *Syn.* dexterous, deft, skillful, expert, proficient, handy, apt, ready, quick, artful, nimble, agile, adept, speedy, finished, practiced, easy, effortless; see also **able** 2. — *Ant.* AWKWARD, clumsy, fumbling.
**3.** [Pure] — *Syn.* unadulterated, unmixed, unalloyed; see **clear** 2, **pure** 1.
**4.** [*Nice] — *Syn.* pleasing, fine, great; see **excellent.**

**neatly,** *modif.* **1.** [Arranged so as to present a neat appearance] — *Syn.* tidily, orderly, systematically, methodically, immaculately, correctly, exactly, trimly, primly, uniformly, levelly, flatly, smoothly, regularly, precisely; see also **evenly** 1, **organized.** — *Ant.* UNEVENLY, untidily, unsystematically.
**2.** [In an adroit manner] — *Syn.* skillfully, deftly, agilely; see **cleverly** 2, **easily** 1.

**neatness,** *n.* **1.** [Neatness in persons] — *Syn.* cleanness, tidiness, orderliness; see **cleanliness.**
**2.** [Neatness in things] — *Syn.* cleanness, clearness, correctness; see **order** 3, **system** 1.

**nebula,** *n.* — *Syn.* galaxy, galactic vapor, cloud cluster, nimbus, rarified gas, interstellar dust, luminous vapor. Kinds of nebulae include: spiral, planetary, diffuse, galactic, gaseous, whirlpool, ring; Crab nebula, nebula of Lyra, nebula of Orion, dark; see also **constellation.**

**nebulous,** *modif.* — *Syn.* indistinct, dim, vague; see **dark** 1, **hazy** 1, **obscure** 1, 3.

**necessarily,** *modif.* — *Syn.* vitally, cardinally, fundamentally, importantly, indispensably, momentously, unavoidably, undeniably, certainly, as a matter of course, inexorably, inescapably, ineluctably, inevasively, unpreventably, irresistibly, inevitably, assuredly, exigently, pressingly, significantly, undoubtedly, indubitably, positively, unquestionably, no doubt, without fail, of necessity, of course, by force, come what may, willy-nilly, without recourse, beyond one's control, by its own nature, from within, by definition; see also **surely.**

**necessary,** *modif.* **1.** [Essential] — *Syn.* essential, requisite, expedient, needful, indispensable, needed, required, urgent, wanted, imperative, prerequisite, exigent, pressing, vital, cardinal, fundamental, significant, momentous, compulsory, mandatory, basic, paramount, obligatory, essential, compelling, incumbent on, incumbent upon, all-important, nuts-and-bolts, binding, specified, unavoidable, decisive, crucial, elementary, quintessential, chief, principal, prime, intrinsic, fixed, constant, permanent, determinate, inherent, ingrained, innate, without choice, without appeal; see also **important** 1.— *Ant.* UNIMPORTANT, unessential, insignificant.

**2.** [Inevitable] — *Syn.* unavoidable, undeniable, assured; see **certain** 2, **imminent, inevitable.**

**necessitate,** *v.* — *Syn.* compel, constrain, oblige; see **command** 1, **force** 1, **require** 2.

**necessity,** *n.* **1.** [The state of being required] — *Syn.* need, compulsion, constraint, pressure, obligation, needfulness, essentiality, indispensability, undeniability, requisiteness, prerequisiteness; see also **need** 3, **requirement** 2.

**2.** [That which is needed] — *Syn.* need, want, requisite, vital part, essential, demand, imperative, fundamental, claim, exaction, desideratum, must*; see also **lack** 2, **need** 3, **requirement** 2.

**3.** [The state of being forced by circumstances] — *Syn.* exigency, pinch, stress, urgency, extremity, destitution, privation, obligation, inexorableness, inescapableness, case of life or death; see also **emergency, poverty** 1, 2. *See Synonym Study at* NEED.

**of necessity** — *Syn.* inevitably, importantly, surely; see **necessarily.**

**neck,** *n.* **1.** [The juncture of the head and the trunk] — *Syn.* cervix, cervical vertebrae, nape, scruff; see **throat.**

**2.** [The part of a dress at the neck] — *Syn.* neckband, neckline, collar line; see **collar.**

**get it in the neck*** — *Syn.* be punished, be discharged, undergo; see **suffer** 1.

**risk one's neck** — *Syn.* endanger oneself, gamble, take a chance; see **risk.**

**stick one's neck out*** — *Syn.* endanger oneself, take a chance, gamble; see **risk.**

**by a neck** — *Syn.* by a close margin, barely, by a hair, by a nose.

**neck*,** *v.* — *Syn.* kiss, make out*, pet, smooch*, make love.

**necklace,** *n.* — *Syn.* ornament, accessory, (string of) beads, jewels, chain, neckband, necklet, lavaliere, pearls, diamonds, choker; see also **jewelry.**

**neck of the woods*,** *n.* — *Syn.* locality, area, section; see **place** 3.

**necktie,** *n.* — *Syn.* neckwear, knot, ascot; see **tie** 2. Neckties include: cravat, flowing tie, bow tie, stock, four-in-hand tie, string tie, bolo tie, white tie, black tie, Windsor tie, scarf.

**necromancer,** *n.* — *Syn.* sorcerer, warlock, conjuror; see **magician** 1, **wizard** 1.

**necromancy,** *n.* — *Syn.* wizardry, thaumaturgy, sorcery; see **magic** 1, **witchcraft.**

**necrosis,** *n.* — *Syn.* corruption, rot, putrefaction; see **decay** 2, **disease.**

**need,** *n.* **1.** [Poverty] — *Syn.* indigence, penury, pennilessness; see **poverty** 1.

**2.** [Lack] — *Syn.* insufficiency, shortage, inadequacy; see **lack** 1, 2.

**3.** [A requirement] — *Syn.* necessity, requirement, requisite, obligation, compulsion, exigency, demand, call, want, essential, necessary, urgency, matter of life

and death, desideratum, *sine qua non* (Latin), must*; see also **necessity** 1, 2, 3, **requirement** 2.

**have need to** — *Syn.* be compelled to, require, want; see **must.**

**if need be** — *Syn.* if it is required, if the occasion demands, if necessary; see **if.**

SYN. — **need** refers to a pressing requirement of something essential or desirable that is lacking; **necessity,** a more formal word, suggests an imperative need for something indispensable but lacks the emotional connotations of **need** /they are in *need* of food, food is a *necessity* for all living things/; **exigency** refers to a necessity created by some emergency, crisis, or compelling circumstances /the *exigencies* created by the flood/; **requisite** applies to something that is indispensable to a particular end or purpose /a sense of rhythm is a *requisite* in a dancer/

**need,** *v.* — *Syn.* lack, require, feel the necessity for, be in need, suffer privation, be in want, be destitute, be short, be inadequate, have occasion for, feel a dearth, have use for, have need for, miss, be without, do without, be needy, be poor, be bereft, be deprived of, be deficient in, go hungry, not approach, live from hand to mouth, feel the pinch*, be down and out*, be hard up*, be up against it*, do with*; see also **want** 1.— *Ant.* OWN, have, hold. **1.** [Require] — *Syn.* demand, necessitate, oblige; see **must, need to.** *See Synonym Study at* LACK.

**needed,** *modif.* — *Syn.* wanted, required, desired; see **necessary** 1.

**needle,** *n.* **1.** [Sewing instrument] — *Syn.* awl, spike, skewer, pin, darner. Varieties and sizes of needles include: sewing, sewing-machine, straight, tacking, darning, upholsterer's, shoemaker's, sail-maker's, surgical, knitting, crochet, straw, long-eyed sharp, sharp, ground-down, between, blunt, embroidery, crewel.

**2.** [Sharp, pointed wirelike instrument] — *Syn.* hypodermic, hypodermic needle, syringe, phonograph needle, stylus, electric needle, electrolytic needle, probe.

**3.** [A pointing instrument] — *Syn.* gauge, indicator, director; see **pointer** 1.

**needle,** *v.* — *Syn.* quiz, question, nag; see **bother** 2, 3, **examine** 1, 2.

**needless,** *modif.* — *Syn.* unwanted, excessive, groundless; see **unnecessary, useless** 1.

**needlework,** *n.* — *Syn.* fancywork, tailoring, stitchery; see **embroidery** 1, **sewing.**

**need to,** *v.* — *Syn.* have to, be obligated to, have reason to; see **must, need** 1, 2.

**needy,** *modif.* — *Syn.* destitute, indigent, penniless; see **poor** 1.

**ne'er-do-well,** *n.* — *Syn.* good-for-nothing, idler, layabout; see **loafer.**

**nefarious,** *modif.* — *Syn.* bad, treacherous, evil; see **wicked** 1.

**negate,** *v.* **1.** [To nullify] — *Syn.* repeal, retract, neutralize; see **cancel** 2.

**2.** [To contradict] — *Syn.* belie, oppose, refute; see **deny.**

**negation,** *n.* **1.** [Opposite] — *Syn.* contradiction, converse, contrary; see **opposite.**

**2.** [Denial] — *Syn.* opposition, contradiction, repudiation; see **denial** 1, **refusal.**

**negative,** *modif.* **1.** [Involving a refusal] — *Syn.* denying, negatory, dissentient, disavowing, contradictory, contrary, adverse, adversarial, repugnant, recusant, gainsaying, impugning, contravening, rejecting, naysaying, disallowing, nullifying, negating. — *Ant.* ADMISSIBLE, assenting, accepting.

**2.** [Lacking positive qualities] — *Syn.* unaffirmative, absent, removed, privative, neutralizing, counteractive, annulling, abrogating, invalidating. — *Ant.* EMPHATIC, positive, affirmative.

**3.** [Pessimistic] — *Syn.* cynical, unenthusiastic, uninterested, glum, morose, cool*, cold*.

**negative,** *n.* **1.** [A refusal] — *Syn.* contradiction, disavowal, refutation; see **denial** 1, **refusal.**

**2.** [A negative image] — *Syn.* film, plate, developed film; see **image** 2, **picture** 2.

**neglect,** *n.* **1.** [The act of showing indifference to a person] — *Syn.* slight, disregard, thoughtlessness, disrespect, carelessness, scorn, oversight, inadvertence, heedlessness, inattention, unconcern, inconsideration, disdain, coolness; see also **indifference** 1.

**2.** [The act of neglecting duties or charges] — *Syn.* negligence, dereliction, neglectfulness; see **carelessness.**

**3.** [The result of neglecting] — *Syn.* chaos, default, lapse; see **delay** 1, **failure** 1.

**neglect,** *v.* **1.** [To treat with indifference] — *Syn.* overlook, slight, disregard, ignore, forget, disdain, scorn, rebuff, affront, dismiss, depreciate, spurn, underestimate, undervalue, shake off, make light of, laugh off, keep one's distance, pass over, pass up, pass by, have nothing to do with, let alone, keep aloof, keep aloof from, let go, not care for, pay no attention to, leave alone, take no notice of, be inattentive to, take for granted, not give a hoot, not give a darn, not give a damn, pay no heed, pay no mind, turn one's back on, set at nought, contemn, let well enough alone, leave well enough alone, let it ride*, keep at arm's length*, leave out in the cold*, give the cold shoulder*; see also **disregard.** — *Ant.* CONSIDER, appreciate, value.

**2.** [To fail to attend to responsibilities] — *Syn.* omit, leave undone, forget, pass over, defer, procrastinate, let slide, let pass, let slip, miss, skip, gloss over, let things go, ignore, be remiss, be negligent, be derelict, trifle, slur, skimp, shirk, slack, postpone, lose sight of, look the other way, dismiss from the mind, not trouble oneself with, not take care of, be slack, evade, pretermit, be careless, be irresponsible, let the grass grow under one's feet*, lie down on the job*. — *Ant.* take care of, attend to, TEND.

*SYN.* — **neglect** implies a failure to carry out some expected or required action, either through carelessness or by intention [I *neglected* to set the alarm]; **omit,** in this connection, implies a neglecting through oversight, absorption, etc. [I *omitted* to give him directions to the house]; **overlook** suggests a failure to see or to take action, either inadvertently or indulgently [I'll *overlook* your error this time]; **disregard** implies inattention or neglect, usually intentional [to *disregard* someone's wishes]; **ignore** suggests a deliberate disregarding, sometimes through stubborn refusal to face the facts [but you *ignore* the necessity for action]; **slight** implies a disregarding or neglecting in an indifferent or disdainful way [a critic who seems to *slight* younger writers]; **forget,** in this connection, implies an intentional disregarding or omitting [let's *forget* our differences]

**neglected,** *modif.* — *Syn.* slighted, disregarded, scorned, disdained, despised, affronted, overlooked, ignored, spurned, contemned, undervalued, deferred, dismissed, passed over, postponed, evaded, deteriorated, underestimated, declined, decayed, unheeded, lapsed, uncared for, unwatched, depreciated, unconsidered, unthought

of, shaken off, unused, unwanted, tossed aside, abandoned, forgotten, out in the cold*, in the cold*, hid under a bushel*, hid under a basket*, dropped*, put on the shelf*; see also **omitted.** — *Ant.* CONSIDERED, cared for, heeded.

**neglectful,** *modif.* — *Syn.* heedless, negligent, negligent of, inattentive; see **careless** 1, **lazy** 1, **remiss.**
*See Synonym Study at* REMISS.

**neglecting,** *modif.* — *Syn.* disregarding, ignoring, slighting; see **omitting, overlooking** 2.

**negligee,** *n.* — *Syn.* kimono, nightdress, pajamas; see **clothes, nightgown, robe.**

**negligence,** *n.* — *Syn.* remissness, oversight, heedlessness; see **carelessness, indifference** 1, **neglect** 1.

**negligent,** *modif.* — *Syn.* inattentive, neglectful, careless, offhand; see **careless** 1, **remiss, unconcerned.**
*See Synonym Study at* REMISS.

**negligently,** *modif.* — *Syn.* heedlessly, indifferently, sloppily; see **carelessly.**

**negotiable,** *modif.* — *Syn.* variable, transactional, debatable; see **transferable.**

**negotiate,** *v.* **1.** [To make arrangements for] — *Syn.* arrange, bargain, confer, consult, parley, transact, mediate, make peace, contract, settle, adjust, conciliate, concert, accommodate, bring to terms, make terms, make the best of, treat with, moderate, umpire, referee, work out, dicker*, haggle*, bury the hatchet*; see also **arbitrate.**

**2.** [To transfer] — *Syn.* barter, allocate, transmit; see **assign** 1, **sell** 1.

**negotiating,** *n.* — *Syn.* transacting, trading, bargaining, conferring.

**negotiation,** *n.* **1.** [Arbitration] — *Syn.* compromise, intervention, mediation; see **agreement** 1.

**2.** [A conference] — *Syn.* meeting, consultation, colloquy; see **discussion** 1.

**negotiator,** *n.* — *Syn.* mediator, moderator, arbitrator; see **judge** 2.

**Negro,** *n.* — *Syn.* Black, African, African-American, Afro-American, person of color, colored person, mulatto, Ethiopian*, colored*, spade*, brother*, sister*, nigger*.

**neigh,** *v.* — *Syn.* nicker, whinny, call; see **sound** 1.

**neighbor,** *n.* — *Syn.* acquaintance, bystander, next-door-neighbor, nearby resident; see **friend** 1.

**neighborhood,** *n.* — *Syn.* environs, block, vicinity, vicinage, locality, proximity, purlieus, district, adjacency, quarter, parish, closeness, nearness, precinct, ward, propinquity, community, contiguity, region, area, zone, section, suburb, part, tract; see also **area** 2.

**in the neighborhood of*** — *Syn.* about, approximately, close to; see **near** 1.

**neighboring,** *modif.* — *Syn.* adjacent, adjoining, nearby; see **adjacent, bordering, near** 1.
*See Synonym Study at* ADJACENT.

**neighborly,** *modif.* — *Syn.* sociable, hospitable, helpful; see **friendly** 1.

**neither,** *conj. & modif.* — *Syn.* nor yet, also not, not either, not, not at all.

**neither,** *pron.* — *Syn.* not one or the other, neither one, not either, not either one, not this one, none of two, nor this nor that, no one of two, not the one, not any one; see also **none** 1, **nothing.**

**neologism,** *n.* — *Syn.* coinage, neology, new word, new phrase, nonce word, synthetic word, vogue word; see also **phrase, word** 1.

**neophyte,** *n.* — *Syn.* novice, student, beginner; see **amateur, beginner.**
*See Synonym Study at* AMATEUR.

**nephew,** *n.* — *Syn.* brother's son, sister's son, grand-nephew, son of a brother-in-law, son of a sister-in-law, nephew by marriage; see also **niece, relative.**

**Neptune,** *n.* — *Syn.* god of the sea, Poseidon, Oceanus; see **god** 1.

**nerve,** *n.* **1.** [The path of nervous impulses] — *Syn.* nerve fiber, nerve tissue, nerve filament, nerve cord, nervure, venation; see also **tissue** 3.

Types of nerves include: motor, sensory, afferent, efferent, mixed, excitatory, inhibitory, vasomotor, somatic. The twelve cranial nerves of the human body are: olfactory, optic, oculomotor, trochlear, trigeminal, abducent, facial, vestibulocochlear, glossopharyngeal, vagus, accessory, hypoglossal.

**2.** [Courage] — *Syn.* resolution, spirit, mettle; see **courage** 1.

**3.** [Impudence] — *Syn.* temerity, audacity, effrontery; see **rudeness.**

*See Synonym Study at* TEMERITY.

**nerveless,** *modif.* **1.** [Weak] — *Syn.* spineless, nervous, feeble; see **afraid** 1, **cowardly** 1, **weak** 3.

**2.** [Calm] — *Syn.* controlled, intrepid, impassive; see **calm** 1, **patient** 2, **tranquil** 2.

**nerve oneself,** *v.* — *Syn.* take courage, pluck up one's courage, prepare, get ready; see **fight** 2, **oppose** 2, **prepare** 1, **resist** 1.

**nerve-racking,** *modif.* — *Syn.* exhausting, horrible, wearisome; see **difficult** 1, **painful** 1.

**nerves,** *n.* **1.** [Stamina] — *Syn.* fortitude, firmness, pluck; see **endurance** 2.

**2.** [\*A nervous excitement] — *Syn.* strain, tension, hysteria, emotional stress, sleeplessness, neurasthenia; see also **nervousness** 1.

**get on one's nerves\*** — *Syn.* exasperate, irritate, annoy; see **bother** 2, 3.

**nervous,** *modif.* **1.** [Excitable] — *Syn.* sensitive, high-strung, neurotic; see **excitable.**

**2.** [Excited] — *Syn.* agitated, bothered, annoyed; see **excited.**

**3.** [Timid] — *Syn.* apprehensive, shy, worried; see **afraid** 1, **timid** 2.

**nervously,** *modif.* — *Syn.* tensely, apprehensively, restlessly; see **excitedly.**

**nervousness,** *n.* **1.** [The state of being temporarily nervous] — *Syn.* stimulation, agitation, perturbation, inspiration, animation, intoxication, disquietude, delirium, discomfiture, elation, feverishness, anger, the jerks\*, stage fright\*, butterflies in the stomach\*, the jitters\*, the shakes\*; see also **embarrassment** 1, **excitement.** — *Ant.* REST, calm, relaxation.

**2.** [The quality of being nervous in temperament] — *Syn.* sensitivity, sensitiveness, mettlesomeness, demonstrativeness, excitability, irascibility, impulsiveness, impetuosity, uncontrollability, turbulence, moodiness, hastiness, vehemence, hypersensitivity, neuroticism, impatience, neurasthenia; see also **sensitivity.** — *Ant.* COMPOSURE, poise, steadiness.

**nervy\*,** *modif.* — *Syn.* crass, pushy, inconsiderate; see **crude** 1, **rude** 1, 2.

**nescience,** *n.* — *Syn.* naïveté, inexperience, unawareness; see **ignorance** 2.

**nest,** *n.* — *Syn.* den, lair, haunt, cradle, aerie, womb, incubator; see also **retreat** 2.

**nest egg\*,** *n.* — *Syn.* savings, personal savings, accumulated savings, personal property, something for a rainy day\*; see also **money** 1, **property** 1, **savings** 1.

**nestle,** *v.* — *Syn.* cuddle, snuggle, nuzzle, settle down, take shelter, lie close, make oneself snug, huddle, move close to, lie against, curl up.

**nestling,** *n.* — *Syn.* fledgling, chick, suckling, infant; see **baby** 1, **bird** 1.

**net,** *modif.* — *Syn.* clear, pure, remaining, exclusive, excluding, after deductions, take-home, after taxes, irreducible, undeductible.

**net,** *n.* **1.** [Web] — *Syn.* screen, mesh, lace; see **web** 1. Varieties of nets include: hair, mosquito, tennis, badminton, ping-pong, volleyball, hockey, basketball, soccer, lacrosse, goal, bird, butterfly, fish, gill, dip, beating, draw, drag, fishing, seine, drift, drop, hand, landing, set, stake, scoop, bag, purse, bull, casting, clues.

**2.** [Earnings] — *Syn.* return(s), profit, loss, take, gain.

**net,** *v.* — *Syn.* make, clear, gain above expenses; see **profit** 2.

**nether,** *modif.* — *Syn.* beneath, below, lower; see **under** 1.

**netlike,** *modif.* — *Syn.* spun, meshlike, webbed; see **woven.**

**netted,** *modif.* **1.** [Webbed] — *Syn.* spun, interwoven, mesh; see **woven.**

**2.** [\*Caught] — *Syn.* caught, enmeshed, apprehended, seized; see **captured** 1, **under arrest.**

**netting,** *n.* — *Syn.* mesh, trellis, screen; see **cloth, material** 2, **web** 2.

**nettle,** *v.* — *Syn.* annoy, pester, irritate; see **bother** 3, **disturb** 2, **insult.**

*See Synonym Study at* IRRITATE.

**nettled,** *modif.* — *Syn.* vexed, irritated, disturbed; see **angry.**

**network,** *n.* **1.** [System of channels] — *Syn.* tracks, circuitry, channels, interface, system, labyrinth, reticule, artery, arrangement, jungle\*; see also **chain** 1, **wiring** 2, 3.

**2.** [Netting] — *Syn.* fabric, fiber, weave, knitting, mesh, plexus, grillwork, wattle, screening; see also **cloth, material** 2, **web** 2.

**neurosis,** *n.* — *Syn.* psychoneurosis, compulsion, deviation, instability, mental disorder, mental illness, emotional disturbance, neurotic condition, aberration; see also **insanity** 1, **obsession.**

**neurotic,** *modif.* — *Syn.* disoriented, disturbed, unstable, mentally ill, erratic, psychoneurotic, aberrant, deranged, obsessive, compulsive, upset, sick; see also **insane** 1, **troubled** 1.

**neurotic,** *n.* — *Syn.* paranoid, psychoneurotic, sick person, psychotic, hypochondriac, neuropath, kleptomaniac.

**neuter,** *modif.* — *Syn.* barren, infertile, sexless, asexual, unfertile, impotent, frigid, fallow; see also **sterile** 1.

**neutral,** *modif.* **1.** [Not fighting] — *Syn.* noncombatant, noncombative, nonpartisan, on the side lines, nonparticipating, inactive, disengaged, uninvolved, bystanding, standing by, inert, on the fence\*. — *Ant.* ENGAGED, involved, ACTIVE.

**2.** [Without opinion] — *Syn.* unbiased, open-minded, disinterested, impartial; see **indifferent** 1, **unconcerned.**

**3.** [Without distinctive color] — *Syn.* drab, indeterminate, vague; see **dull** 2.

**neutrality,** *n.* — *Syn.* impartiality, nonpartisanship, disinterest; see **noninterference.**

**neutralize,** *v.* — *Syn.* counterbalance, counterpoise, compensate; see **offset.**

**neutrally,** *modif.* — *Syn.* impartially, without taking sides, equally; see **objectively.**

**never,** *modif.* — *Syn.* not ever, at no time, not at any time, not in the least, not in any way, in no way, not at all, not under any condition, absolutely not, under no circumstances, nevermore, never again, no way*, when hell freezes over*.

**never-ceasing,**  *modif.* — *Syn.*  persistent, steady, neverending; see **constant** 1, **perpetual** 1, 2, **regular** 3.

**never-dying,** *modif.* — *Syn.* sempiternal, endless, undying; see **eternal** 2, **immortal** 1, **perpetual** 1.

**never-ending,** *modif.* — *Syn.* timeless, endless, persistent; see **constant** 1, **eternal** 2, **perpetual** 1, 2, **regular** 3.

**never mind,** *interj.* — *Syn.* forget it, it doesn't matter, ignore it, nothing, don't bother, let it go, *macht nichts* (German), drop it*; see also **stop** 2.

**nevertheless,** *modif.* — *Syn.* not the less, nonetheless, notwithstanding; see **although, but** 1.

**never-tiring,** *modif.* — *Syn.* diligent, tenacious, persevering; see **busy** 1, **resolute** 2.

**new,** *modif.* **1.** [Recent] — *Syn.* current, late, just out, brand-new; see **fresh** 1.
**2.** [Modern] — *Syn.* modish, modern, latest, *au courant* (French); see **fashionable, modern** 1.
**3.** [Novel] — *Syn.* unique, novel, original, innovative; see **original** 2, 3, **unusual** 1, 2.
**4.** [Different] — *Syn.* unlike, dissimilar, distinct; see **different** 1, 2.
**5.** [Additional] — *Syn.* further, increased, supplementary; see **extra.**
**6.** [Inexperienced] — *Syn.* unseasoned, unskilled, untrained; see **incompetent, inexperienced.**
**7.** [Fresh] — *Syn.* unspoiled, uncontaminated, undecayed; see **fresh** 5.
**8.** [Recently] — *Syn.* newly, freshly, lately; see **recently.**

---

*SYN.* — **new** is applied to that which has never existed before or which has only just come into being, possession, use, etc. *[new words, a new coat]*; **fresh** implies such newness that the original appearance, quality, vigor, etc. have not been affected by time or use *[fresh eggs, a fresh start]*; **novel** implies a newness that is strikingly unusual or strange *[a novel suggestion, a novel combination]*; **modern** and **modernistic** apply to that which is of the present time, as distinguished from earlier periods, and connote up-to-dateness, the latter word, sometimes, with derogatory implications; **original** emphasizes that a thing is the first of its kind *[an original idea, an original melody]*

---

**new blood*,** *n.* — *Syn.* replacements, younger personnel, another generation, fresh ideas; see **recruit, youth** 2.

**newborn,** *modif.* — *Syn.* infant, recent, new; see **fresh** 1, **young** 1.

**newcomer,** *n.* — *Syn.* new arrival, immigrant, outsider, foreigner, novice, neophyte, tenderfoot*, rookie*, maverick*, Johnny-come-lately*, youngtimer*, blow-in*; see also **alien, stranger.**

**newfangled,** *modif.* — *Syn.* novel, unique, contemporary; see **fashionable, modern** 1.

**new-fashioned,** *modif.* — *Syn.* current, avant-garde, stylish; see **fashionable, modern** 1.

**newly,** *modif.* — *Syn.* lately, anew, afresh; see **recently.**

**newlywed,** *n.* — *Syn.* blushing bride, bridegroom, honeymooner; see **bride, groom** 2, **husband, wife.**

**newness,** *n.* — *Syn.* originality, uniqueness, modernity, innovation, recentness; see also **novelty** 1.

**news,** *n.* **1.** [Information] — *Syn.* intelligence, tidings, advice, discovery, enlightenment, recognition, cognizance, the scoop*, the goods*, headlines*, front-

page news*; see also **data, knowledge** 1, **revelation** 1.
**2.** [A specific report] — *Syn.* report, telling, narration, recital, account, description, specification, particularization, itemization, message, copy, communication, release, communiqué, telegram, cable, radiogram, broadcast, telecast, bulletin, dispatch, story, news story*, scoop*, big news*, eye-opener*; see also **announcement** 2, **report** 1.

**make news** — *Syn.* become famous, become notorious, accomplish, create events; see **expose** 1, **reveal** 1.

**newsboy,** *n.* — *Syn.* paperboy, papergirl, paper carrier, newsy*.

**newscast,** *n.* — *Syn.* news broadcasting, telecast, newscasting; see **announcement** 2, **broadcast, news** 2, **report** 1.

**newscaster,** *n.* — *Syn.* news analyst, commentator, broadcaster, anchor, anchorman, anchorwoman; see also **reporter, writer.**

**newsmonger,** *n.* — *Syn.* gossip, gossipmonger, scandalmonger, busybody; see **gossip** 2.

**newspaper,** *n.* — *Syn.* publication, paper, daily paper, press, fourth estate, public press, sheet, tabloid, gazette; see also **journal** 1, **record** 1.
Varieties of newspapers include: daily, weekly, bi-weekly, metropolitan, rural, national, business, tabloid, trade, provincial, community.
Parts of newspapers include: front page, editorial page, local news, domestic news, international news, magazine, business, society, sports, entertainment section, amusement section, rotogravure, comics, comic page, classified, advertising, syndicated section*, boiler plate*.
Editions of newspapers include: morning, afternoon, evening, home, extra, special, suburban, city, metro, final, mail, Sunday.
Famous newspapers include: England: *The Times, Financial Times, Daily Mail, Daily Express, Daily Mirror, Guardian, Sun, News of the World;* France: *Le Temps, Le Figaro, Le Monde;* Russia: *Pravda, Izvestiya, Trud;* Germany: *Die Welt, Frankfurter Allgemeine;* U.S.: *USA Today, Washington Post, New York Times, Boston Globe, Chicago Sun-Times, Christian Science Monitor, Wall Street Journal,* Baltimore *Sun, Miami Herald, Chicago Tribune, Milwaukee Journal,* San Francisco *Chronicle, Los Angeles Times.*

**newspaperman,** *n.* — *Syn.* reporter, journalist, editor, publisher, newspaperwoman, newsman, newswoman; see also **author** 2, **editor, reporter, writer.**

**newsy,** *modif.* — *Syn.* significant, informative, instructive; see **detailed, elaborate** 2.

**New York,** *n.* — *Syn.* Manhattan, Greater New York, Metropolitan New York, the City, the Big City*, Town*, the Big Apple*, Gotham*, the Garment Capital*, Metropolis of America*, Wall Street*, Financial Capital of the World*; see also **city.**
The boroughs of New York City are: Manhattan, Bronx, Queens, Brooklyn, Staten Island.
Sections of New York City include: Harlem, Soho, East Side, West Side, Midtown, Little Italy, Tribeca, Greenwich Village, East Village, Bowery, Chinatown, the Battery, Washington Heights, Morningside Heights, Wall Street, Times Square, Broadway, Theater District, Long Island City, Jamaica, Flushing, Far Rockaway.

**next,** *modif.* **1.** [Following in order] — *Syn.* succeeding, subsequent, ensuing, attendant; see **following.**
**2.** [Adjacent] — *Syn.* next to, beside, close, alongside, on one side, on the side, adjoining, neighboring, meeting, hard by, touching, cheek by jowl, side by side, coterminous, attached, abutting, next-door, back to back,

to the left, to the right; see also **bordering, contiguous, near** 1.

**get next to★** — *Syn.* become friendly with, befriend, join the company of; see **associate** 1.

**next-door (to),** *modif.* — *Syn.* adjacent to, neighboring, adjoining; see **beside, near** 1, **next** 2.

**nib,** *n.* — *Syn.* neb, tip, pen, penpoint; see **point** 2.

**nibble,** *n.* — *Syn.* morsel, peck, cautious bite; see **bit** 1, **bite** 1.

**nibble,** *v.* — *Syn.* nip, gnaw, snack; see **bite** 1, **eat** 1.

**nice,** *modif.* **1.** [Approved] — *Syn.* likable, superior, admirable; see **excellent.**

**2.** [Behaving in a becoming manner] — *Syn.* pleasing, friendly, agreeable, winning, winsome, prepossessing, refined, cultured, amiable, delightful, charming, inviting, pleasant, cordial, courteous, ingratiating, considerate, kind, kindly, helpful, gracious, obliging, genial, gentle, *simpático* (Spanish), seemly, decorous, becoming, unassuming, unpresumptuous, modest, demure; see also **friendly** 1. — *Ant.* RUDE, indecorous, crude.

**3.** [Involving a careful distinction] — *Syn.* delicate, minute, exacting, fastidious, finicky, finical, finicking, discerning, discriminating, fine, subtle, careful, precise, critical, distinguishing, trivial, hairsplitting; see also **careful, detailed, particular** 3. — *Ant.* CARELESS, broad, sweeping.

**4.** [Accurate] — *Syn.* correct, exact, right; see **accurate** 1.

*See Synonym Study at* PARTICULAR.

**nice and★** — *Syn.* exceptionally, unusually, agreeably; see **very.**

**nicely,** *modif.* **1.** [In a welcome manner] — *Syn.* pleasantly, pleasingly, amiably, winningly, creditably, acceptably, excellently, distinctively, happily, felicitously, triumphantly, admirably, desirably, pleasurably, attractively, likably, enjoyably, beautifully, graciously, charmingly, finely; see also **agreeably, perfectly** 1. — *Ant.* BADLY, unfortunately, unsuccessfully.

**2.** [In a becoming manner] — *Syn.* winsomely, invitingly, charmingly; see **modestly** 1, **politely.**

**3.** [Carefully] — *Syn.* rightly, correctly, conscientiously; see **accurately, carefully** 1.

**niceness,** *n.* **1.** [Accuracy] — *Syn.* exactitude, surety, precision; see **accuracy** 2.

**2.** [Kindness] — *Syn.* discernment, taste, refinement; see **care** 1, **discretion** 1, **kindness, prudence, tact.**

**nice to,** *modif.* — *Syn.* helpful to, kindly to, thoughtful of, generous; see **kind.**

**nicety,** *n.* — *Syn.* fine point, detail, nuance, distinction, refinement, amenity, creature comfort; see also **culture** 3, **refinement** 3.

**niche,** *n.* — *Syn.* recess, cranny, corner, cubbyhole; see **recess** 2, 3.

**nick,** *n.* — *Syn.* scratch, indent, indentation, notch, slit, knock, dint, impression; see also **cut** 2, **dent.**

**nick,** *v.* — *Syn.* indent, notch, slit; see **cut** 2, **dent.**

**nickel,** *n.* **1.** [A mineral] — *Syn.* Ni, metallic element, chemical element, plating material; see **element** 2, **metal, mineral.**

**2.** [A coin made of nickel] — *Syn.* five-cent piece, coin, five cents; see **money** 1.

**niece,** *n.* — *Syn.* sister's daughter, brother's daughter, niece by marriage, grandniece, daughter of a brother-in-law, daughter of a sister-in-law; see also **nephew, relative.**

**niggard,** *n.* — *Syn.* tightwad, Scrooge, skinflint; see **miser** 2.

**niggardliness,** *n.* — *Syn.* thrift, frugality, stinginess; see **greed.**

**niggardly,** *modif.* — *Syn.* miserly, parsimonious, stingy; see **greedy** 1.

*See Synonym Study at* STINGY.

**niggling,** *modif.* — *Syn.* trifling, petty, piddling; see **trivial, unimportant.**

**nigh,** *modif.* — *Syn.* near, approaching, imminent, close at hand; see **near, close.**

**night,** *n.* **1.** [The diurnal dark period] — *Syn.* evening, from dusk to dawn, nightfall, twilight, eventide, nighttime, bedtime, midnight, before dawn, the dark hours, obscurity, witching hour, dead of night.

**2.** [The dark] — *Syn.* blackness, duskiness, gloom; see **darkness** 1.

**make a night of it★** — *Syn.* enjoy, have fun, party; see **celebrate** 3.

**night clothes,** *n.* — *Syn.* negligee, nightshirt, nightwear; see **clothes, nightgown, pajamas, robe.**

**nightclub,** *n.* — *Syn.* casino, discotheque, cabaret, tavern, café, roadhouse, floor show, night spot, nitery★; see also **restaurant, saloon** 3, **theater** 1.

**nightfall,** *n.* — *Syn.* dusk, twilight, evening; see **night** 1.

**nightgown,** *n.* — *Syn.* nightdress, pajamas, nightrobe, negligee, bedgown, lingerie, night gear, nightshirt, shift, muu-muu, sleeping clothes, lounging pajamas, nightwear, sleeper★, nightie★, PJ's★, 'jamas★; see also **clothes, pajamas, robe.**

**nightingale,** *n.* — *Syn.* songbird, warbler, wood thrush, philomel; see **bird** 1.

**nightly,** *modif.* — *Syn.* nocturnal, night inhabiting, in the hours of night, every twenty-four hours, during the hours of darkness, at night, each night, every night, by night; see also **regularly** 1. — *Ant.* DAILY, by day, diurnal.

**nightmare,** *n.* **1.** [A dream] — *Syn.* bad dream, horror, incubus; see **dream** 1, **fantasy** 2, **illusion** 1, **vision** 3, 4.

**2.** [An unpleasant experience] — *Syn.* ordeal, torture, trial, bummer★, bad trip★.

**night school,** *n.* — *Syn.* night classes, university extension, college extension, community college; see **school** 1, **university.**

**nighttime,** *n.* — *Syn.* darkness, bedtime, midnight; see **night** 1.

**nihilism,** *n.* **1.** [Rejection] — *Syn.* repudiation, atheism, renunciation; see **denial** 1, **refusal.**

**2.** [Anarchy] — *Syn.* misrule, terrorism, lawlessness, mob rule; see **disorder** 2.

**nihilist,** *n.* — *Syn.* skeptic, cynic, revolutionary, insurgent, anarchist; see also **agitator, rebel** 1, **skeptic.**

**nihilistic,** *modif.* — *Syn.* insurgent, unruly, anarchic; see **lawless** 2, **rebellious** 2.

**nil,** *n.* — *Syn.* zero, naught, nihil; see **nothing.**

**nimble,** *modif.* **1.** [Agile] — *Syn.* agile, quick, spry, deft; see **agile, graceful** 1.

**2.** [Alert] — *Syn.* quick-witted, bright, clever; see **intelligent** 1, **judicious.**

*See Synonym Study at* AGILE.

**nimble-fingered,** *modif.* — *Syn.* proficient, skillful, capable; see **agile, graceful** 1.

**nimble-footed,** *modif.* — *Syn.* swift, active, adept; see **agile, graceful** 1.

**nimbleness,** *n.* — *Syn.* grace, vivacity, skill; see **agility.**

**nimble-witted,** *modif.* — *Syn.* shrewd, clever, alert; see **intelligent** 1, **judicious.**

**nimbly,** *modif.* — *Syn.* swiftly, rapidly, agilely; see **gracefully.**

**nimbus,** *n.* — *Syn.* aura, radiance, glow, halo, circle of light, aureole, nebula, aurora, cloud, nebulous light, effulgence, emanation; see also **halo, light** 1.

**nincompoop,** *n.* — *Syn.* imbecile, simpleton, dope★; see **fool** 1.

**ninefold,** *modif.* — *Syn.* novenary, nonary, three times three, ninth, nonahedral, nonuple, enneahedral.

**ninth,** *modif.* — *Syn.* three times three, nonary, novenary; see **ninefold.**

**nip,** *n.* — *Syn.* nibble, morsel, catch; see **bite** 1, **pinch.**

**nip,** *v.* — *Syn.* nibble, snap, munch; see **bite** 1, **pinch.**

**nipple,** *n.* — *Syn.* mammilla, papilla, areola, mammary, mammary gland, dug, teat, tit, teatlike object, breast, udder, pacifier.

**nitty-gritty★,** *n.* — *Syn.* essentials, reality, low-down★; see **facts.**

**nitwit,** *n.* — *Syn.* blockhead, dummy, dimwit; see **fool** 1.

**no,** *modif. & interj.* — *Syn.* not, absolutely not, not at all, by no means, the answer is in the negative, not by any means, *nyet* (Russian), *nein* (German), negative★, nix★, no way★; see also **negative** 2, **neither, never, none.**

**nobility,** *n.* **1.** [Magnificence] — *Syn.* grandeur, majesty, greatness; see **dignity** 1, **magnificence.**
**2.** [Aristocracy; *usually used with* the] — *Syn.* ruling class, gentry, peerage; see **aristocracy, royalty, society** 3.

**noble,** *modif.* **1.** [Possessing an exalted mind and character] — *Syn.* generous, princely, magnanimous, magnificent, courtly, lofty, elevated, splendid, excellent, august, reputable, supreme, eminent, preeminent, lordly, dignified, sublime, great, good, superior, chivalric, chivalrous, great-hearted, high-minded, honorable, distinguished, liberal, tolerant, gracious, benign, beneficient, humane, benevolent, charitable, sympathetic, bounteous, brilliant, extraordinary, remarkable, self-denying, devoted, self-forgetful, heroic, resolute, lionhearted, mettlesome, valorous; see also **worthy.** — *Ant.* COR-RUPT, low, ignoble.
**2.** [Possessing excellent qualities or properties] — *Syn.* meritorious, virtuous, worthy, valuable, useful, incorrupt, first-rate, refined, cultivated, chivalrous, trustworthy, candid, liberal, gracious, princely, munificent, magnanimous, generous, distinctive, sincere, truthful, constant, faithful, upright, honest, honorable, warmhearted, true, veracious, distinctive, reputable, respectable, admirable, good, above-board, fair, manly, just, estimable; see also **excellent, perfect** 2. — *Ant.* POOR, inferior, second-rate.
**3.** [Belonging to the nobility] — *Syn.* royal, titled, aristocratic, patrician, highborn, wellborn, blue-blooded, of high rank, of good family, highborn, gentle, of gentle birth, of gentle blood, imperial, lordly, highbred, princely, of good breed, kingly, to the manner born, born to the purple★; see also **royal** 2. — *Ant.* COMMON, plebeian, lowborn.
**4.** [Grand] — *Syn.* stately, impressive, imposing; see **grand** 2.

**nobleman,** *n.* — *Syn.* peer, noble, aristocrat, member of the nobility; see **lord** 2, **royalty.**

**noble-minded,** *modif.* — *Syn.* just, principled, generous; see **fair** 1, **kind.**

**noblesse,** *n.* — *Syn.* nobility, gentility, gentry; see **aristocracy, royalty, society** 3.

**noblewoman,** *n.* — *Syn.* gentlewoman, aristocrat, countess, empress; see **lady** 2, 3, **royalty.**

**nobly,** *modif.* **1.** [Majestically] — *Syn.* regally, magnificently, magnanimously; see **generously** 2, **politely.**
**2.** [Honorably] — *Syn.* fairly, respectably, honestly; see **justly** 1.

**nobody,** *modif.* **1.** [No one at all] — *Syn.* no one, not anybody, not a soul; see **none** 1.
**2.** [A person of little importance] — *Syn.* upstart, ci-

pher, nonentity, nullity, jackstraw, parvenu, whippersnapper, no great shakes★, man of straw★, punk★, a nothing★, nix★, zero★, schlepp★, nebbish★; see also **sycophant.**

**nocturnal,** *modif.* — *Syn.* at night, night-loving, nighttime; see **late** 4, **nightly.**

**nocturne,** *n.* — *Syn.* lullaby, evening song, serenade; see **song.**

**nocuous,** *modif.* — *Syn.* noxious, malignant, injurious; see **dangerous** 1, 2, **deadly, harmful, poisonous.**

**nod,** *n.* **1.** [A slight bow] — *Syn.* dip, inclination, greeting; see **bow** 2.
**2.** [★Approval; *usually used with* the] — *Syn.* acceptance, affirmative answer, yes; see **permission.**

**nod,** *v.* **1.** [To make a nodding movement] — *Syn.* assent, agree, sign, signal, greet, salaam, bend, curtsy, incline the head, acquiesce, consent, respond, fall in with, concur, acknowledge, recognize; see also **agree, approve** 1, **bow** 1. — *Ant.* DENY, dissent, disagree.
**2.** [To become sleepy or inattentive] — *Syn.* drowse, nap, drift, drift off; see **sleep.**

**node,** *n.* **1.** [Protuberance] — *Syn.* bump, swelling, clot; see **bulge, lump.**
**2.** [Juncture] — *Syn.* joint, junction, connection, link.

**nodule,** *n.* — *Syn.* bud, protuberance, knob; see **bulge.**

**noise,** *n.* **1.** [A sound] — *Syn.* sound, sonance, something heard, something audible, impact of sound waves. Kinds of noises include — *brief, loud noises:* bang, boom, crash, thud, blast, blast off, roar, bellow, howl, shriek, growl, bark, blat, shout, peal, cry, yelp, squawk, yawp, hee-haw, blare, clang, ring, shot, sonic boom, jangle, eruption, explosion, detonation; blow-up★, zowie★, whang★, cachunk★, splat★; *brief, faint noises:* peep, squeak, squawk, cackle, cluck, tweet, clink, tinkle, pop, click, tick, rustle, gurgle, whisper, stage whisper, sigh, splash, swish, note, sough, sob, whine, whimper, plink, plunk, plop, plump, pad, pat, pitter-patter, ping, rustle, murmur, beat, stir, purr, twitter; *continuing noises:* reverberation, ringing, tone, tune, clangor, clanging, tinkling, sonorousness, resonance, rock, rattle, rattling, whistle, whistling, piping, twittering, shouting, roaring, howling, growling, barking, caterwauling, bellowing, rumble, rumbling, grunting, murmuring, drone, droning, thunder, thundering, firing, tramp, tramping, whine, whining, screech, screeching, scream, screaming, banging, clanging, hum, humming, buzz, buzzing, hiss, hissing, laugh, laughing, chuckle, chuckling, whir, whirring, purr, purring, swishing, rustling, ripple, rippling, strumming, thrumming, beating, drumming, patter, pattering, clatter, clattering, tintinnabulation, ululation, trill, trilling, whinney, whinneying, neigh, neighing, caw, cawing, clucking, cackling, quaver, semiquaver.
**2.** [Clamor] — *Syn.* din, racket, uproar, clamor, hubbub, tumult, commotion, hullabaloo, fanfare, cry, outcry, shouting, yelling, fracas, pandemonium, bedlam, turbulence, uproariousness, boisterousness, clamorousness, babel, shivaree, charivari, cacophony, dissonance, discord, static, stridency, blatancy; see also sense 1, **cry** 1, **uproar.** — *Ant.* SILENCE, lull, quietness.

---

**SYN.** — **noise** is the general word for any loud, unmusical, or disagreeable sound; **din** refers to a loud, prolonged, deafening sound, painful to the ears /the *din* of the steeple bells/; **uproar** applies to a loud, confused sound, as of shouting, laughing, etc., and connotes commotion or disturbance /her remarks threw the audience into an *uproar*/; **clamor** suggests loud, continued, excited shouting, as in protest or demand /the *clamor* of the crowd for his arrest*]*; **hubbub** implies the confused mingling of many voices *[*tried to make myself heard above the *hubbub* in the cafeteria*]*; **racket** refers to a loud, clattering combination of noises regarded as annoyingly excessive *[*he couldn't work because of the *racket* next door*]*

---

**noised about\***, *modif.* — *Syn.* generally known, commonly known, well known, recognized, revealed; see also **advertised, discovered, rumored.**

**noiseless,** *modif.* **1.** [Containing no noise] — *Syn.* silent, still, soundless; see **quiet** 2.

**2.** [Making no noise] — *Syn.* voiceless, speechless, wordless, silent; see **dumb** 1, **mute** 1.

**noiselessly,** *modif.* — *Syn.* inaudibly, quietly, without a sound; see **silently.**

**noisome,** *modif.* **1.** [Harmful] — *Syn.* baneful, pernicious, unwholesome; see **dangerous** 1, 2, **deadly.**

**2.** [Evil-smelling] — *Syn.* putrid, malodorous, mephitic; see **rank** 2, **rotten** 1.

**noisy,** *modif.* — *Syn.* clamorous, vociferous, boisterous; see **loud** 1, 2.

**nomad,** *n.* — *Syn.* wanderer, migrant, vagabond; see **traveler.**

**nomadic,** *modif.* — *Syn.* roaming, drifting, roving, itinerant; see **traveling** 2, **wandering.**
*See Synonym Study at* ITINERANT.

**nom de plume,** *n.* — *Syn.* alias, pen name, pseudonym; see **alias.**
*See Synonym Study at* ALIAS.

**nomenclature,** *n.* — *Syn.* terminology, taxonomy, locution, vocabulary; see **classification** 1.

**nominal,** *modif.* **1.** [In name only] — *Syn.* titular, stated, mentioned, suggested, formal, simple, ostensible, professed, purported, supposed, theoretical, pretended, so-called, in effect only; see also **given, named** 1. — *Ant.* REAL, obvious, GENUINE.

**2.** [Insignificant] — *Syn.* meaningless, trifling, low; see **trivial, unnecessary.**

**nominate,** *v.* — *Syn.* propose as a candidate, designate for election, call, specify, put up, draft\*; see also **choose** 1, **decide.**

**nominated,** *modif.* — *Syn.* designated, called, proposed, suggested; see **approved, named** 2.

**nomination,** *n.* — *Syn.* naming, designation, proposal, submission; see **appointment** 1.

**nominee,** *n.* — *Syn.* aspirant, appointee, selectee, office seeker; see **candidate, contestant.**

**nonacceptance,** *n.* — *Syn.* renunciation, disapproval, rejection; see **refusal.**

**nonage,** *n.* — *Syn.* immaturity, childhood, minority, adolescence; see **youth** 1.

**nonaligned,** *modif.* — *Syn.* uncommitted, undecided, not committed; see **neutral** 1.

**nonappearance,** *n.* — *Syn.* avoidance, truancy, failure to appear; see **absence** 1.

**nonchalance,** *n.* — *Syn.* apathy, disregard, insouciance, composure; see **indifference** 1, **composure.**
*See Synonym Study at* COMPOSURE.

**nonchalant,** *modif.* — *Syn.* unconcerned, casual, indifferent, insouciant, untroubled, cool, imperturbable, easygoing, lackadaisical, apathetic, lukewarm, unruffled, unexcited, composed, collected, aloof, detached, offhand, unexcitable, unflappable, calm, serene, placid, incurious, disinterested, easy, effortless, relaxed, light, smooth, neutral, unimpressible, blasé, devil-may-care, heedless, regardless, careless, laid-back\*; see also **calm** 1, **careless** 1, **unconcerned.** — *Ant.* WARM, ardent, enthusiastic.

*See Synonym Study at* COOL.

**nonchalantly,** *modif.* — *Syn.* coolly, indifferently, casually; see **calmly.**

**noncommittal,** *modif.* — *Syn.* reserved, wary, cautious; see **careful, judicious, tactful.**

**noncompletion,** *n.* — *Syn.* nonfulfillment, unfulfillment, incompleteness, deficiency; see **defect** 1, **lack** 1, 2.

**noncompliance,** *n.* — *Syn.* nonconformity, refusal, dissent; see **disagreement** 1, **objection** 2, **protest.**

**noncompliant,** *modif.* — *Syn.* negative, divergent, irregular, refusing, declinatory, refractory, impatient, contumacious; see also **rebellious** 2.

**non compos mentis,** *modif.* — *Syn.* not of sound mind, crazy, deranged, lunatic; see **insane** 1, **sick, violent** 2, 4.

**nonconformist,** *n.* — *Syn.* rebel, eccentric, maverick, iconoclast, loner, malcontent, dissenter, dissentient, demonstrator, hippie, protester, protestant, dissident, Bohemian, weirdo\*, oddball\*; see also **beatnik, liberal, radical.**

**nonconformity,** *n.* — *Syn.* dissent, opposition, contumaciousness, lawlessness, transgressiveness, heresy, heterodoxy, recusance, violation, breach of custom, denial, unorthodoxy, iconoclasm, uniqueness, strangeness, disobedience, unruliness, mutinousness, insubordination, recalcitrance, noncompliance, unconventionality, originality, Bohemianism, disagreement, recusancy, contumacy, obstinacy, refusal, refusing, nonagreement, disaffection, discordance, disapproval, nonconsent, rejection, nonacceptance, negation, disapprobation, opposition, objection, exception, veto, nonobservance; see also **individuality** 1.

**nondescript,** *modif.* — *Syn.* uninteresting, empty, indescribable; see **common** 1, **dull** 4.

**none,** *pron.* **1.** [No person] — *Syn.* no one, not one, not anyone, no one at all, not a person, not a soul, neither one (nor the other); see also **neither.** — *Ant.* MANY, some, a few.

**2.** [No thing] — *Syn.* not a thing, not anything, not any; see **nothing.**

**nonentity,** *n.* — *Syn.* nullity, upstart, no-account\*; see **nobody** 2, **sycophant.**

**nonessential,** *modif.* — *Syn.* superfluous, insignificant, petty; see **trivial, unimportant.**

**nonesuch,** *n.* — *Syn.* quintessence, select, nonpareil; see **paragon.**

**nonetheless,** *modif.* — *Syn.* nevertheless, in spite of that, anyway; see **although, but** 1.

**nonexistence,** *n.* — *Syn.* nonbeing, negation, nothingness; see **oblivion** 2.

**nonexistent,** *modif.* — *Syn.* missing, unsubstantial, fictitious; see **hypothetical** 1, **imaginary, unreal.**

**nonfulfillment,** *n.* — *Syn.* incompletion, miscarriage, disappointment; see **failure** 1.

**nonhero,** *n.* — *Syn.* antihero, protagonist, untraditional hero, nontraditional hero; see **hero** 2.

**noninterference,** *n.* — *Syn.* nonintervention, neutrality, laissez faire, isolationism, nonresistance, refraining, refusal to become involved, failure to intervene, nonpartisanship, adherence to the Monroe Doctrine.

**nonintervention,** *n.* — *Syn.* apathy, dormancy, neutrality; see **noninterference.**

**nonjuror,** *n.* — *Syn.* dissenter, heretic, eccentric; see **nonconformist, radical.**

**nonlegal,** *modif.* — *Syn.* unlawful, prohibited, forbidden; see **illegal.**

**nonobjective,** *modif.* — *Syn.* subjective, free-form, abstract, nonrepresentational, not traditional, unconventional, revolutionary; see also **free** 2, **irregular** 2, **unusual** 2.

**nonobservance,** *n.* — *Syn.* infidelity, inattention, failure; see **carelessness, indifference** 1, **neglect** 1.

**no-nonsense,** *modif.* — *Syn.* matter-of-fact, practical, serious, earnest, purposeful, serious-minded, solemn, dedicated, resolute; see also **practical, resolute** 2.

**nonpareil,** *n.* — *Syn.* quintessence, the best, nonesuch; see **paragon.**

**nonpartisan,** *modif.* — *Syn.* unprejudiced, just, nonaligned, unbiased, independent, uninfluenced, unaffected, uninvolved, unimplicated, unbigoted, objective; see also **neutral** 1.

**nonpayment,** *n.* — *Syn.* failure, delinquency, bankruptcy; see **default.**

**nonplus,** *v.* — *Syn.* baffle, bewilder, confound; see **confuse.**

*See Synonym Study at* CONFUSE.

**nonplussed,** *modif.* — *Syn.* baffled, confused, at a loss (for words); see **bewildered, doubtful** 2.

**nonproductive,** *modif.* — *Syn.* profitless, unproductive, unprofitable, not producing, ineffectual, ineffective, vain, futile, worthless; see also **useless** 1, 2.

**nonprofit,** *modif.* — *Syn.* charitable, altruistic, humane, public-service; see **generous** 1, **philanthropic.**

**nonproliferation,** *n.* — *Syn.* restriction, limiting, holding down, holding back; see **restraint** 2.

**nonresident,** *modif.* — *Syn.* absentee, out-of-state, living abroad; see **foreign** 1.

**nonresistance,** *n.* — *Syn.* passivity, pacifism, nonviolence, tolerance, submission, conformity; see also **docility.**

**nonresistant,** *modif.* — *Syn.* passive, nonviolent, yielding, tolerant, submissive; see also **docile, obedient** 1.

**nonsense,** *n.* **1.** [Matter that has no meaning] — *Syn.* balderdash, rubbish, twaddle, trash, gobbledygook, drivel, scribble, scrawl, inanity, senselessness, babble, palaver, buncombe, idle chatter, pretense, prattle, blather, nonsensicalness, rant, bombast, claptrap, bull\*, baloney\*, trash\*, gas\*, tripe\*, hooey\*, soft soap\*, bunk\*, rant\*, poppycock\*, mumbo jumbo\*, gab\*, twaddle\*, garbage\*, rubbish\*, hogwash\*, rot\*, hot air\*. **2.** [Frivolous behavior] — *Syn.* unsteadiness, flightiness, thoughtlessness, fickleness, foolishness, fatuousness, giddiness, rashness, infatuation, extravagance, imprudence, irrationality, madness, senselessness, inconsistency, shallowness; see also **stupidity** 2. — *Ant.* CONSIDERATION, steadiness, thoughtfulness. **3.** [Pure fun] — *Syn.* antics, absurdity, jest, joke, monkeybusiness; see also **fun.**

**nonsensical,** *modif.* — *Syn.* absurd, silly, senseless; see **stupid** 1.

**nonsentient,** *modif.* — *Syn.* insensible, apathetic, impervious, senseless; see **indifferent** 1, **paralyzed.**

**non sequitur,** *n.* — *Syn.* illogical conclusion, fallacy, conclusion that does not follow, non seq.\*; see **nonsense** 1, **stupidity** 2.

**nonspiritual,** *modif.* — *Syn.* substantial, tangible, material; see **real** 2.

**nonstop,** *modif.* — *Syn.* uninterrupted, unbroken, continuous, round-the-clock; see **constant** 1.

**nonsubjective,** *modif.* — *Syn.* impersonal, scientific, detached; see **objective** 1.

**nonviolent,** *modif.* — *Syn.* passive, passively resistant, pacifist, without violence; see **peaceful** 2, **quiet** 4.

**nook,** *n.* — *Syn.* niche, cubbyhole, cranny; see **hole** 2, **recess** 2, 3.

**noon,** *n.* — *Syn.* noontime, noontide, noonday, midday,

twelve noon, high noon, meridian, noon hour; see also **time** 1, 2.

**noonday,** *n.* — *Syn.* twelve o'clock, noontide, meridian; see **noon, time** 1.

**no one,** *pron.* — *Syn.* no person, not one, nobody, not anybody; see **neither, none** 1.

**noose,** *n.* — *Syn.* hitch, running knot, loop, lasso; see **knot** 1, **rope.**

**nor,** *conj.* — *Syn.* and not, not any, not either, not one, nor yet; see also **neither.**

**norm,** *n.* — *Syn.* average, standard, model, pattern; see **average** 1, **criterion, measure** 2, **model** 2.

*See Synonym Study at* AVERAGE.

**normal,** *modif.* **1.** [Usual] — *Syn.* ordinary, usual, standard, regular, typical, natural, average, common, run-of-the-mill; see also **common** 1, **conventional** 1, **natural** 2, **traditional** 2. **2.** [Regular] — *Syn.* routine, orderly, methodical; see **regular** 3. **3.** [Sane] — *Syn.* lucid, wholesome, right-minded; see **rational, reasonable, sane** 1. **4.** [Showing no abnormal bodily condition] — *Syn.* in good health, whole, sound; see **healthy** 1.

---

*SYN.* — **normal** implies conformity with the established norm or standard for its kind *[normal* intelligence*];* **regular** implies conformity with the prescribed rule or accepted pattern for its kind *[the regular* working day*];* **typical** applies to that which has the representative characteristics of its type or class *[a typical* Southern town*];* **natural** implies behavior, operation, etc. that conforms with the nature or inherent character of the person, thing, or circumstances *[natural* fears, a *natural* outcome*];* **usual** applies to that which conforms to the common or ordinary use or occurrence *[the usual* price*];* **average,** in this connection, implies conformity with what is regarded as normal or ordinary *[the average* man*]*

---

**normality,** *n.* **1.** [Mediocrity] — *Syn.* regularity, ordinariness, commonplaceness, uniformity, standardness, averageness, commonness, commonality, unremarkableness; see also **regularity.** **2.** [Sanity] — *Syn.* normalcy, mental balance, reason; see **sanity** 1.

**normally,** *modif.* — *Syn.* usually, commonly, ordinarily; see **frequently, regularly** 1, 2.

**normative,** *modif.* — *Syn.* normalizing, regulating, regularizing; see **standardizing.**

**north,** *modif.* **1.** [Situated to the north] — *Syn.* northward, northern, in the north, on the north side of, northerly, northmost, northernmost. **2.** [Moving toward the north] — *Syn.* northerly, northbound, northward, to the north, headed north, toward the North Pole, in a northerly direction; see also **south** 4. **3.** [Coming from the north] — *Syn.* northerly, southbound, headed south, out of the north, moving toward the equator, moving toward the South Pole; see also **south** 3. **4.** [Associated with the north] — *Syn.* northern, polar, hyperborean, boreal; see **arctic, cold** 1.

**North,** *n.* — *Syn.* Union, Federals, Northerners, Yankees, Yanks, the men in blue, carpetbaggers, damyankees\*; see also **confederacy, south, union** 2.

**north,** *n.* — *Syn.* the Barrens, tundra, northern section, northland, Northern Hemisphere, the north country, the north woods, Arctic regions, polar regions, the frozen north, land of ice and snow; see also **direction** 1.

**northeast,** *modif.* — *Syn.* NE, nor'east, northeastern, northeasterly, northeastward, north-north-east, NNE, northeast by east, NEbE, northeast by north, NEbN; see also **direction** 1.

**northeaster**, *n.* — *Syn.* nor'easter, northeast wind, storm, tempest; see **storm** 1.

**northerly**, *modif.* — *Syn.* boreal, northern, polar; see **arctic, north** 1, 2, 3.

**northern**, *modif.* — *Syn.* northerly, boreal, polar; see **arctic, north** 1.

**North Pole**, *n.* — *Syn.* arctic, Arctic Circle, North Terrestrial Pole, north magnetic pole; see **north**.

**North Star**, *n.* — *Syn.* Pole Star, polestar, lodestar, Polaris; see **star** 1.

**northward(s)**, *modif.* — *Syn.* to the north, toward the north, northerly, up; see **north** 2.

**northwest**, *modif.* — *Syn.* NW, nor'west, northwestern, northwesterly, northwestward, north-north-west, NNW, northwest by west, NWbW, northwest by north, NWbN; see also **direction** 1.

**nose**, *n.* **1.** [The organ of smell] — *Syn.* nasal organ, nasal cavity, nares, nasal passages, nostrils, olfactory nerves, snoot*, proboscis*, beak*, bill*, trunk*; see also **organ** 2.

**2.** [A projection] — *Syn.* snout, nozzle, muzzle; see **projection**.

**by a nose** — *Syn.* by a very small margin, too close for comfort, barely; see **almost**.

**count noses** — *Syn.* take attendance, add, total, sum up; see **count**.

**cut off one's nose to spite one's face** — *Syn.* injure one's own interests, hurt oneself, be self-destructive; see **hurt** 1.

**follow one's nose** — *Syn.* go straight forward, continue blindly, keep going; see **advance** 1, **continue** 1.

**look down one's nose at** — *Syn.* disdain, snub, be disgusted by; see **scorn** 1.

**on the nose** — *Syn.* precisely, to the point, correctly; see **exactly**.

**pay through the nose** — *Syn.* pay an unreasonable price, pay heavily, get taken*; see **pay** 1.

**put one's nose out of joint** — *Syn.* harm, irritate, hurt; see **anger** 1.

**turn up one's nose at** — *Syn.* sneer at, refuse, disdain; see **scorn** 1.

**under one's (very) nose** — *Syn.* in plain sight, visible, at one's fingertips; see **obvious** 1.

**nose**, *v.* — *Syn.* search, inspect, pry; see **examine** 1.

**nose dive**, *n.* — *Syn.* plunge, drop, decline, crash, turn for the worse; see also **fall** 1.

**nose for news***, *n.* — *Syn.* news sense, an eye for the unusual, interest; see **curiosity** 1.

**nose out***, *v.* — *Syn.* beat, win from, better; see **defeat** 1.

**nostalgia**, *n.* — *Syn.* remorse, wistfulness, sentimentality; see **homesickness, loneliness.**

**nostalgic**, *modif.* — *Syn.* lonesome, regretful, sentimental; see **homesick, lonely** 1.

**nostril**, *n.* — *Syn.* nasal passage, nasal opening, snout; see **nose** 1.

**nostrum**, *n.* — *Syn.* formula, patent medicine, panacea; see **medicine** 2, **remedy** 2.

**nosy**, *modif.* — *Syn.* meddlesome, snooping, curious; see **inquisitive, interested** 2.

**not**, *modif.* — *Syn.* no, non-, un-, in-; see **negative** 2.

**notability**, *n.* — *Syn.* precedence, notoriety, esteem; see **fame** 1.

**notable**, *modif.* **1.** [Remarkable] — *Syn.* distinguished, important, striking; see **unusual** 1.

**2.** [Famous] — *Syn.* well-known, celebrated, renowned; see **famous.**

**notable**, *n.* — *Syn.* luminary, personage, celebrity, big shot*, V.I.P.*; see also **celebrity** 2, **personality** 3.

**notably**, *modif.* — *Syn.* reputably, prominently, distinctly; see **very.**

**not a little**, *modif.* — *Syn.* great, large, copious; see **many, much** 1, 2.

**not a little**, *n.* — *Syn.* not a few, profusion, abundance; see **lot** 4, **much, plenty.**

**not always**, *modif.* — *Syn.* not usually, sometimes, occasionally; see **seldom.**

**notarize**, *v.* — *Syn.* sign legally, attach a legal signature, affix a legal signature, make legal; see **approve** 1.

**notary**, *n.* — *Syn.* public accountant, attorney, official; see **accountant, clerk** 2, **lawyer.**

**not at all**, *modif.* — *Syn.* by no means, not by any means, not in any way, no way*; see **no.**

**notation**, *n.* **1.** [Arithmetic] — *Syn.* mathematical system, algebra, math*; see **arithmetic, mathematics.**

**2.** [Symbols] — *Syn.* signs, figures, characters; see **notes, representation, symbol, system** 1.

**notch**, *n.* — *Syn.* nock, nick, indent; see **cut** 2, **dent, groove.**

**notch**, *v.* — *Syn.* indent, nick, chisel; see **cut** 1, **dent.**

**notched**, *modif.* — *Syn.* nicked, jagged, saw-toothed; see **irregular** 4, **rough** 1.

**not completely**, *modif.* — *Syn.* incompletely, partially, not fully, not thoroughly; see **halfway, unfinished** 1.

**note**, *n.* **1.** [A representation] — *Syn.* sign, figure, mark; see **representation, symbol.**

**2.** [A brief record] — *Syn.* notation, jotting, scribble, reminder, scrawl, annotation, agenda, datum, minute, entry, memorandum, journal, inscription, calendar, diary; see also **mark** 3, **notes, record** 1, **summary.**

**3.** [A brief communication] — *Syn.* dispatch, epistle, announcement; see **letter** 2, **word** 3.

**4.** [A musical tone, or its symbol] — *Syn.* tone, key, scale, shape note, interval, degree, step, sharp, flat, natural; see also **pitch** 3.

Musical notes include: whole note, semibreve, double whole note, breve, half note, minim, quarter note, crotchet, eighth note, quaver, sixteenth note, semiquaver, thirty-second note, demisemiquaver, sixty-fourth note, hemidemisemiquaver, triplet, grace note, appoggiatura.

**5.** [Paper money] — *Syn.* bill, currency, banknote, folding money*, greenback*; see also **money** 1.

**note**, *v.* **1.** [To notice] — *Syn.* remark, heed, perceive; see **regard** 1, **see** 1.

**2.** [To record] — *Syn.* write down, enter, transcribe; see **record** 1, **write.**

**notebook**, *n.* — *Syn.* note pad, memorandum book, record book, diary; see **journal** 1, **record** 1.

**noted**, *modif.* — *Syn.* famous, well-known, celebrated, notorious; see **famous.**

*See Synonym Study at* FAMOUS.

**not entirely**, *modif.* — *Syn.* incompletely, partially, not perfectly, not thoroughly; see **halfway, unfinished** 1.

**notes**, *n.* — *Syn.* commentary, interpretation, explanation, findings, recordings, field notes, observations; see also **data, records.**

**compare notes** — *Syn.* exchange views, confer, go over; see **discuss.**

**strike the right note** — *Syn.* be correct, do what is expected, do what is pleasing, respond correctly; see **succeed** 1.

**take notes** — *Syn.* write down, keep a record, enter; see **record** 1.

**not especially**, *modif.* — *Syn.* somewhat, to a degree, within limits; see **moderately.**

**noteworthy,** *modif.* — *Syn.* outstanding, remarkable, exceptional; see **unique** 1, **unusual** 1.

**nothing,** *n.* — *Syn.* not anything, no thing, trifle, triviality, bagatelle, nothingness, nonexistence, inexistence, nonbeing, nullity, zero, nihility, extinction, oblivion, obliteration, annihilation, nonentity, neither hide nor hair, goose egg★, zip★, zilch★; see also **blank** 1, **emptiness.**

**for nothing** — *Syn.* **1.** gratis, without cost, unencumbered; see **free** 4.

**2.** in vain, for naught, emptily; see **unnecessary.**

**in nothing flat★** — *Syn.* in almost no time at all, speedily, rapidly; see **quickly** 1.

**make nothing of** — *Syn.* minimize, underplay, play down; see **neglect** 1.

**think nothing of** — *Syn.* minimize, underplay, disregard; see **neglect** 1.

**nothing but,** *modif. & prep.* — *Syn.* only that, nothing else, without exception; see **only** 1, 2, 3.

**nothing doing★,** *interj.* — *Syn.* certainly not, by no means, the reply is in the negative; see **no.**

**nothing for it★,** *modif.* — *Syn.* no alternative, certainly, of necessity; see **necessarily, surely.**

**nothing less than,** *modif. & prep.* — *Syn.* no less than, the same as, a minimum of, simply, merely, nothing but.

**nothingness,** *n.* **1.** [Void] — *Syn.* vacuum, blank, hollowness; see **emptiness, nothing, oblivion** 2.

**2.** [Worthlessness] — *Syn.* pettiness, unimportance, smallness; see **insignificance.**

**nothing to it★,** *modif.* — *Syn.* facile, easily done, like taking candy from a baby★; see **easy** 2, **simple** 3.

**notice,** *n.* **1.** [A warning] — *Syn.* note, notification, intimation; see **sign** 1, **warning.**

**2.** [An announcement] — *Syn.* comments, remark, enlightenment; see **announcement** 2, **declaration** 2, **report** 1.

**serve notice** — *Syn.* give warning, declare, announce; see **notify** 1, 2.

**take notice** — *Syn.* become aware, pay attention, observe; see **regard** 1, **see** 1.

**notice,** *v.* **1.** [To observe] — *Syn.* mark, remark, discern, look at; see **regard** 1, **see** 1, **discern.**

*See Synonym Study at* DISCERN.

**2.** [To publish a notice] — *Syn.* mention, comment on, notify; see **publish** 1.

**noticeable,** *modif.* — *Syn.* observable, appreciable, discernible, perceptible, detectable, conspicuous, prominent, striking, notable, remarkable, outstanding, noteworthy, salient, pronounced; see also **obvious** 1.

---

*SYN.* — **noticeable** is applied to that which is readily noticed *[a noticeable coolness in his manner]*; **remarkable** applies to that which is noticeable because it is unusual or exceptional *[remarkable beauty]*; **prominent** refers to that which literally or figuratively stands out from its background *[a prominent nose, a prominent author]*; an **outstanding** person or thing stands out from others of its kind, usually because of superiority *[an outstanding sculptor]*; **conspicuous** applies to that which is so obvious or manifest as to be immediately perceptible *[conspicuous gallantry]*; **striking** is used of something so out of the ordinary that it leaves a sharp impression on the mind *[a striking epigram]*

---

**noticed,** *modif.* — *Syn.* seen, remarked, recorded; see **observed** 1.

**noticing,** *modif.* — *Syn.* perceiving, regarding, heeding; see **observant** 2, **saying, seeing.**

**notification,** *n.* — *Syn.* information, advice, intelli-

gence; see **announcement** 2, **publicity** 3, **warning.**

**notify,** *v.* **1.** [To provide with information] — *Syn.* inform, tell, acquaint, apprise, declare, announce, enlighten, give notice, make known, publish, express, mention, advise, state, proclaim, convey, circulate, disseminate, report, communicate, reveal, divulge, disclose, instruct, teach, brief, air, vent, assert, let know, leave word, send word, keep posted, let in on, promulgate, telephone, write, speak to, fax, radio, cable, wire, broadcast, spread abroad, herald, blazon, tip off★, clue in★, cue in★, fill in★, give a good steer★, wise up★, hip★; see also **advertise** 1, **communicate** 1, **tell** 1.

**2.** [To warn] — *Syn.* caution, apprise, suggest; see **hint.**

---

*SYN.* — **notify** implies the sending of a formal notice imparting required or pertinent information *[ to notify members that the meeting has been postponed]*; **inform** implies making aware of something by giving knowledge of it *[he informed me of your decision to join us]*; **acquaint** suggests making familiar with something hitherto unknown to one *[she acquainted me with the problem]*; **apprise** implies notifying someone of something that has particular interest for the person *[to be apprised of the risks involved]*

---

**noting,** *modif.* — *Syn.* noticing, seeing, perceiving; see **observant** 2, **saying, seeing.**

**notion,** *n.* **1.** [Opinion] — *Syn.* idea, assumption, sentiment; see **opinion** 1, **thought** 2.

**2.** [Conception] — *Syn.* concept, understanding, inkling, intimation, conceit, whim, fancy, imagination, perception, impression, insight, consciousness, mental apprehension, inclination, indication, intuition, comprehension, penetration, discernment; see also **awareness, knowledge** 1.

*See Synonym Study at* IDEA.

**not less than,** *modif. & prep.* — *Syn.* more, more than, at least, at a minimum; see **more** 1, 2, 3.

**notoriety,** *n.* — *Syn.* repute, renown, name; see **fame** 1, **reputation** 1, 2.

**notorious,** *modif.* — *Syn.* ill-famed, infamous, disreputable, famous; see **famous, wicked** 1, 2.

*See Synonym Study at* FAMOUS.

**notoriously,** *modif.* — *Syn.* particularly, notably, spectacularly; see **especially** 1.

**not particularly,** *modif.* — *Syn.* not expressly, not exclusively, barely, scarcely; see **hardly.**

**not really,** *modif.* — *Syn.* not entirely, doubtful, uncertain; see **questionable** 1.

**not usually,** *modif.* — *Syn.* sometimes, occasionally, now and then; see **seldom.**

**not with it★,** *modif.* — *Syn.* uninformed, lacking understanding, uncomprehending, out of it; see **ignorant** 1, **stupid** 1, **unaware.**

**notwithstanding,** *modif. & conj.* — *Syn.* despite, in spite of, in any case, in any event, regardless of, for all that, on the other hand, after all, however, at any rate, at all events, to the contrary, nevertheless, nonetheless, though, howbeit, yet; see also **although, but** 1.

**nought,** *n.* — *Syn.* naught, not anything, cipher; see **nothing.**

**noun,** *n.* — *Syn.* substantive, term, part of speech, nominal, common noun, proper noun; see also **label, language** 2, **name** 1.

**nourish,** *v.* — *Syn.* feed, supply, sustain; see **feed, provide** 1, **support** 5.

**nourishing,** *modif.* — *Syn.* wholesome, healthy, nutritious; see **healthful.**

**nourishment,** *n.* — *Syn.* nurture, nutriment, provender; see **food.**

**nouveau riche,** *n.* — *Syn.* parvenu, newly-rich, status-seeker, yuppie*; see **upstart.**

**novel,** *modif.* — *Syn.* new, odd, innovative, different; see **original** 2, 3, **unique** 1, **unusual** 1, 2.
*See Synonym Study at* NEW.

**novel,** *n.* — *Syn.* paperback, best-seller, fiction; see **book** 1, **story.**
Types of novels include: romance, historical romance, autobiographical, epistolary, detective, love, *Bildungsroman* (German), *roman fleuve, roman à clef* (*both* French), novella, adventure, ghost, mystery, western, science fiction, sci-fi, SF, science fantasy, novel of the soil; historical, regional, naturalistic, Gothic, problem, biographical, psychological, political, pornographic, satirical, picaresque, social, adventure, supernatural; thriller*, chiller*, shocker*, bodice-ripper*, techno-thriller*, potboiler*, pulp*, porn*.

**novelist,** *n.* — *Syn.* fiction writer, prose writer, fictionist, story-teller, narrative writer, writer of novels; see also **author** 2, **writer.**

**novelty*,** *modif.* — *Syn.* curious, odd, fashionable; see **unusual** 2.

**novelty,** *n.* **1.** [The quality of being novel] — *Syn.* originality, recentness, modernity, freshness; see **newness.**
**2.** [Something popular because it is new] — *Syn.* innovation, origination, creation; see **fad.**
**3.** [A striking article, usually one that is cheap and garish] — *Syn.* oddity, curiosity, gimcrack; see **knick-knack.**

**November,** *n.* — *Syn.* month, fall, autumn month, Thanksgiving season, football season, hunting season; see also **month, autumn.**

**novice,** *n.* — *Syn.* beginner, learner, neophyte, postulant; see **amateur, beginner.**
*See Synonym Study at* AMATEUR.

**novitiate,** *n.* **1.** [Apprenticeship] — *Syn.* internship, tutelage, trial period; see **origin** 1.
**2.** [Novice] — *Syn.* intern, beginner, apprentice; see **amateur.**

**now,** *modif.* **1.** [At the present] — *Syn.* at this time, right now, at this moment, at the moment, just now, momentarily, this day, these days, here and now, for the nonce.
**2.** [In the immediate future] — *Syn.* promptly, in a moment, presently, in a minute; see **soon** 1.
**3.** [Immediately] — *Syn.* at once, forthwith, instantly; see **immediately.**

**nowadays,** *modif.* — *Syn.* in these days, these days, in this age, in the present age; see **now** 1.

**now and then,** *modif.* — *Syn.* sometimes, infrequently, occasionally; see **seldom.**

**noway,** *modif.* — *Syn.* in no manner, not at all, on no account, by no means, nowise, not a jot, not a bit of it, nowhere(s) near, in no case, in no respect.

**no way*,** *interj.* — *Syn.* no, by no means, not at all; see **no.**

**nowhere,** *modif.* — *Syn.* not anywhere, not in any place, not at any place, nowhere at all, in no place, to no place.

**noxious,** *modif.* **1.** [Harmful] — *Syn.* baneful, pernicious, deleterious; see **harmful, pernicious.**
**2.** [Foul] — *Syn.* noisome, foul, putrid; see **offensive** 2, **rotten** 1.
**3.** [Poisonous] — *Syn.* toxic, virulent, venomous; see **deadly, harmful, poisonous.**
*See Synonym Study at* PERNICIOUS.

**nozzle,** *n.* — *Syn.* spout, nose, mouthpiece, beak, outlet, vent, hose end; see also **end** 4.

**nuance,** *n.* — *Syn.* subtlety, refinement, distinction; see **difference** 1.

**nub*,** *n.* — *Syn.* essence, crux, core, nitty-gritty*; see **essence** 1.

**nuclear,** *modif.* **1.** [Concerning a nucleus] — *Syn.* endoplastic, endoplasmic, nucleate, nucleal, chromosomal.
**2.** [Concerning atomic energy] — *Syn.* atomic, thermonuclear, fissionable; see **atomic** 2.

**nuclear bomb,** *n.* — *Syn.* nuclear armament, nuclear warhead, nuclear device, hydrogen bomb, H-bomb, atomic bomb, A-bomb, neutron bomb, cobalt bomb, C-bomb, atomic weapon, nuclear weapon, thermonuclear device, thermonuclear weapon; see also **arms** 1.

**nuclear fission,** *n.* — *Syn.* fusion, atomic power, splitting the atom; see **energy** 3, **power** 2.

**nucleus,** *n.* **1.** [Essence] — *Syn.* core, gist, kernel; see **essence** 1, **matter.**
**2.** [Basis] — *Syn.* foundation, premise, crux; see **basis** 1.
**3.** [Center] — *Syn.* hub, focus, pivot; see **center** 1.

**nude,** *modif.* — *Syn.* naked, stripped, unclothed, bare; see **naked** 1.
*See Synonym Study at* NAKED.

**nude,** *n.* — *Syn.* naked person, naked body, naked man, naked woman, nudist, gymnosophist, pin-up, ecdysiast, model, stripper*, peeler*.
**in the nude** — *Syn.* naked, in the buff*, in the raw*, in one's birthday suit*, in a state of undress.

**nudge,** *n.* — *Syn.* tap, poke, shove; see **bump** 1, **push, touch** 2.

**nudge,** *v.* — *Syn.* poke, bump, tap; see **push** 1, **touch** 1.

**nudity,** *n.* — *Syn.* bareness, nudeness, undress; see **nakedness.**

**nugatory,** *modif.* — *Syn.* worthless, trifling, inadequate, piddling; see **useless** 1, **worthless** 1.

**nugget,** *n.* — *Syn.* lump, ingot, chunk; see **gold** 2, **lump, mass** 1, **rock** 1.

**nuisance,** *n.* **1.** [A bother] — *Syn.* annoyance, vexation, bore; see **trouble** 2.
**2.** [An offense against the public] — *Syn.* breach, infraction, affront; see **crime** 1.
**3.** [*An unpleasant or unwelcome person] — *Syn.* pest, bore, annoyance, problem, problem child, frump, bother, holy terror*, prune*, bad egg*, foul ball*, insect*, human mistake*, louse*, pain in the neck*, nudnik*, poor excuse*, bum*; see also **trouble** 2.

**null,** *modif.* **1.** [Void] — *Syn.* invalid, vain, unsanctioned; see **void** 1.
**2.** [Nonexistent] — *Syn.* absent, nothing, negative; see **imaginary, unreal.**
**3.** [Useless] — *Syn.* ineffective, valueless, barren; see **useless** 1, **worthless** 1.

**nullification,** *n.* — *Syn.* neutralization, repeal, revocation; see **cancellation, withdrawal.**

**nullify,** *v.* — *Syn.* annul, repeal, invalidate, quash; see **cancel** 2, **revoke.**

**numb,** *modif.* **1.** [Insensible] — *Syn.* deadened, dead, unfeeling, insensate, insentient, benumbed, numbed, asleep, senseless, anesthetized, stupefied, comatose; see also **paralyzed.**
**2.** [Insensitive] — *Syn.* apathetic, callous, inured, thickskinned; see **callous, indifferent** 1, **listless** 1.

**numb,** *v.* — *Syn.* paralyze, drug, anesthetize, dull; see **deaden** 1.

**number,** *n.* **1.** [A quantity] — *Syn.* amount, sum total, totality, aggregate, whole, whole number, product,

measurable quantity, recorded total, estimate, the lot, conglomeration, plenty, manifoldness, plenitude, abundance; see also **quantity.**
**2.** [A representation of quantity] — *Syn.* numeral, digit, figure, cipher, integer, fraction, cardinal number, ordinal number, Roman numeral, Arabic numeral, character, sign, emblem; see also **representation, symbol.**
**beyond number** — *Syn.* too many to count, too much to count, innumerable, countless; see **many.**
**get** or **have one's number\*** — *Syn.* discover one's true character, find out about, know; see **understand** 1.
**one's number is up\*** — *Syn.* one's time to die has arrived, one's time has come, one's destiny is fulfilled; see **doomed.**
**without number** — *Syn.* too numerous to be counted, innumerable, countless; see **many.**
**number,** *v.* — *Syn.* calculate, enumerate, estimate, amount to; see **add** 1, **count, total** 1.
**numbered,** *modif.* **1.** [Given numbers] — *Syn.* designated, told, enumerated, checked, specified, indicated; see also **marked** 1.
**2.** [Approaching an end] — *Syn.* fixed, limited, fated; see **doomed.**
**numbering,** *modif.* — *Syn.* totaling, adding up to, reaching; see **making** 2.
**numbering,** *n.* — *Syn.* count, tally, valuation; see **estimate** 1.
**numberless,** *modif.* — *Syn.* countless, limitless, numerous; see **infinite** 1, **many.**
**number one\*,** *n.* — *Syn.* numero uno\*, I, me, yourself, myself, himself, herself; see also **myself.**
**numbness,** *n.* — *Syn.* deadness, anesthesia, stupefaction, dullness, insensitivity, insensibility, paralysis, loss of motion, loss of sensation.
**numeral,** *n.* — *Syn.* number, cipher, digit; see **number** 2.
**numerate,** *v.* — *Syn.* number, measure, enumerate; see **add** 1, **count, total** 1.
**numerical,** *modif.* — *Syn.* arithmetical, mathematical, fractional, exponential, logarithmic, differential, integral, digital, binary; see also **statistical.**
**numerous,** *modif.* — *Syn.* copious, various, diverse; see **infinite** 1, **many.**
**numskull,** *n.* — *Syn.* simpleton, jackass, nitwit; see **fool** 1.
**numskulled,** *modif.* — *Syn.* brainless, inane, dumb; see **dull** 3, **stupid** 1.
**nun,** *n.* — *Syn.* religious, abbess, postulant, novice, novitiate, sister, religious woman, anchorite, prioress, mother superior, canoness.
**nunnery,** *n.* — *Syn.* convent, priory, abbey; see **cloister** 1, **retreat** 2.
*See Synonym Study at* CLOISTER.
**nuptial,** *modif.* — *Syn.* conjugal, connubial, marital; see **matrimonial.**
**nuptials,** *n.* — *Syn.* wedding, matrimony, marriage ceremony; see **marriage** 2.
**nurse,** *n.* **1.** [One who cares for the sick] — *Syn.* attendant, male nurse, practical nurse, licensed practical nurse, L.P.N., private nurse, registered nurse, R.N., floor nurse, night nurse, day nurse, orderly, health care provider, doctor's assistant, student nurse, nurse's aide, therapist, Red Cross nurse, Lady in Gray\*, Florence Nightingale\*.
Nursing specialties include: pediatric, geriatric, cardiac, surgical, obstetric, psychiatric, occupational health, public health, nurse practitioner.
**2.** [One who cares for the young] — *Syn.* servant,

nursemaid, caretaker, attendant, babysitter, child care provider, nanny\*, minder\*, nurserymam\*.
**3.** [One who suckles the young] — *Syn.* wet nurse, *amah* (India), foster mother, mammy.
**nurse,** *v.* **1.** [To provide medical care] — *Syn.* attend to, minister to, aid, medicate, irradiate, X-ray, immunize, inoculate, vaccinate, care for, take
**2.** [To care for (an infant)] — *Syn.* cherish, nurture, foster, mother, father, be a mother to, be a father to, suckle, cradle, dry-nurse, wet-nurse, feed; see also **sustain** 2.
**nursery,** *n.* **1.** [A place for children] — *Syn.* child's room, playroom, nursery school, preschool, day care center, day nursery, crèche, kindergarten; see also **school** 1.
**2.** [A place for plants] — *Syn.* hothouse, hotbed, plantation; see **greenhouse.** care of, take charge of, look after, look to, see to; see also **heal** 1, **tend** 1, **treat** 3.
**nursing,** *modif.* **1.** [Acting as a nurse] — *Syn.* fostering, cherishing, watching over, caring for, attending, devoting oneself to, bringing up; see also **tending** 2.
**2.** [Gaining nourishment by suckling] — *Syn.* taking nourishment, sucking, milking, feeding, suckling.
**nursing,** *n.* — *Syn.* nurse's training, profession of a nurse, duties of a nurse, health care, healing, treating.
**nurture,** *n.* **1.** [Nourishment] — *Syn.* pabulum, nutriment, sustenance; see **food, subsistence** 1.
**2.** [Training] — *Syn.* upbringing, breeding, care; see **education** 1, **training.**
**nurture,** *v.* — *Syn.* nourish, care for, provide (for); see **feed, sustain** 2, **train** 4.
**nurturing,** *n.* — *Syn.* maintenance, development, sustenance; see **subsistence** 2.
**nut,** *n.* **1.** [A dry fruit] — *Syn.* seed, kernel, stone, achene, caryopsis, utricle; see also **fruit** 1.
Common nuts include: peanut, acorn, beechnut, hazelnut, black walnut, English walnut, almond, nutmeg, pecan, filbert, coconut, pistachio, cashew, hognut, chestnut, water chestnut, butternut, kola; hickory, swamp hickory, pine, Brazil, macadamia, groundnut, ginkgo, quandong, betel nut.
**2.** [A threaded metal block] — *Syn.* bur, lock nut, cap, ratchet nut, bolt nut, screw nut, jam nut; see also **bolt** 1.
**3.** [\*An eccentric or insane person] — *Syn.* eccentric, fanatic, maniac; see **zealot.**
**4.** [\*The head] — *Syn.* crown, skull, brain; see **cranium, head** 1.
**hard** (*or* **tough**) **nut to crack** — *Syn.* problem, responsibility, burden; see **difficulty** 1, 2.
**off one's nut\*** — *Syn.* silly, crazy, eccentric; see **insane** 1.
**nutbrown,** *modif.* — *Syn.* roan, chestnut, brownish; see **brown.**
**nutriment,** *n.* — *Syn.* nourishment, provisions, sustenance; see **food, subsistence** 1.
**nutrition,** *n.* — *Syn.* diet, nourishment, victuals; see **food, menu, subsistence** 1.
**nutritive,** *modif.* — *Syn.* edible, wholesome, nutritious; see **healthful.**
**nuts\*,** *modif.* — *Syn.* crazy, deranged, ridiculous; see **insane** 1, **unusual.**
**nutty\*,** *modif.* — *Syn.* deranged, eccentric, irrational; see **insane** 1.
**nuzzle,** *v.* — *Syn.* caress, cuddle, snuggle, nudge; see **nestle.**
**nylon,** *n.* — *Syn.* synthetic(s), polyamide product; synthetic fiber, synthetic cloth, synthetic plastic; see **cloth, fiber** 1, **plastic.**
**nymph,** *n.* — *Syn.* nature goddess, sprite, mermaid; see **fairy** 1.

# O

**oaf,** *n.* — *Syn.* blockhead, goon, lout; see **fool** 1, **moron.**

**oak,** *n.* **1.** [An oak tree] — *Syn. Quercus, Lithocarpus* (*both* Latin), casuarina; see **tree.**
Varieties of oaks include: white, red, scarlet, Spanish, black, live, bur, British, pin, post, blackjack, tulip, cork, jack, scrub, valley, swamp white, willow, laurel, California blue.
**2.** [Oak woods] — *Syn.* hardwood, oaken wood, oak paneling; see **wood** 2.

**oar,** *n.* — *Syn.* pole, sweep, scull; see **paddle.**

**oarsman,** *n.* — *Syn.* gondolier, oar, ferryman, boatman, rower, boatswain, bosun*, bo's'n*; see also **sailor.**

**oasis,** *n.* — *Syn.* green area, fertile area, irrigated land, watered tract, garden spot, desert garden, spring, water hole, watering place, desert resting place, haven; see also **refuge** 1, **retreat** 2, **sanctuary** 2.

**oath,** *n.* **1.** [An attestation of the truth] — *Syn.* affirmation, affidavit, vow, sworn statement, testimony, word, deposition, sworn declaration, contract, adjuration, avowal, pledge; see also **declaration** 1, **promise** 1. — *Ant.* DENIAL, disavowal, lie.
**2.** [Curse] — *Syn.* malediction, swearword, blasphemy; see **curse** 1.

**oatmeal,** *n.* — *Syn.* rolled oats, porridge, cereal; see **breakfast food, grain** 1.

**obdurate,** *modif.* — *Syn.* stubborn, inflexible, unyielding; see **callous, obstinate** 1.
*See Synonym Study at* INFLEXIBLE.

**obedience,** *n.* — *Syn.* willingness, submission, compliance; see **docility.**

**obedient,** *modif.* **1.** [Dutiful] — *Syn.* amenable, loyal, law-abiding, governable, tractable, resigned, devoted, respectful, complaisant, controllable, attentive, obliging, willing, deferential, under the control of, at one's command, obeisant, faithful, honoring, reverential, venerating, at one's beck and call*, on a string*, wrapped around one's finger*; see also **faithful.** — *Ant.* UNRULY, disobedient, undutiful.
**2.** [Docile] — *Syn.* pliant, acquiescent, compliant; see **docile.**
*See Synonym Study at* DOCILE.

**obediently,** *modif.* — *Syn.* dutifully, submissively, devotedly, loyally, faithfully, compliantly, at one's orders; see also **willingly.**

**obeisance,** *n.* — *Syn.* courtesy, homage, deference; see **praise** 1, **reverence** 2.

**obelisk,** *n.* — *Syn.* pillar, needle, shaft, monolith; see **column** 1, **tower.**

**obese,** *modif.* — *Syn.* corpulent, overweight, stout; see **fat** 1.

**obey,** *v.* **1.** [To act in accordance with orders] — *Syn.* submit, answer to, respond, act, act on, bow to, surrender, yield, perform, do, carry out, attend to orders, do what one is told, accept, accord, consent, do what is expected of one, do one's duty, redeem one's pledge, do as one says, come at call, serve, concur, accede, assent, conform, acquiesce, mind, take orders, do the will of, do

one's bidding, comply, fulfill, play second fiddle*; see also **agree.** — *Ant.* REBEL, disobey, mutiny.
**2.** [To act in accordance with a recognized principle] — *Syn.* live by, set one's course by, accept, agree, give allegiance to, be loyal to, reconcile, adjust, accommodate to, adopt, own, make one's own, abide by, hold fast, embrace, practice, adhere to, conform to, be devoted to, be attached to, serve, exercise; see also **behave** 2, **conform, follow** 2. — *Ant.* OPPOSE, refuse, cast off.

**obfuscate,** *v.* — *Syn.* obscure, muddle, confuse; see **muddle** 1, **confuse.**

**obituary,** *n.* — *Syn.* death notice, mortuary tribute, eulogy, necrology, obit*; see also **announcement** 2.

**object,** *n.* **1.** [A corporeal body] — *Syn.* article, something, gadget; see **thing** 1.
**2.** [A purpose] — *Syn.* objective, aim, intention, wish; see **purpose** 1.
**3.** [One who receives] — *Syn.* recipient, target, victim; see **receiver.**
*See Synonym Study at* INTENTION.

**object,** *v.* — *Syn.* oppose, protest, demur, dispute, remonstrate, expostulate, raise objections, take exception to, disapprove, dissent, take a stand against, cry out against, put up a fight, kick*; see also **complain** 1, **oppose** 1.

---

**SYN.** — **object** implies opposition to something, whether openly expressed or not, because of strong dislike or disapproval [I *object* to their meddling]; **protest** implies the making of strong, often formal, spoken or written objection to something [they *protested* the new tax increases]; **remonstrate** implies protest and argument in demonstrating to another that he or she is wrong or blameworthy [he *remonstrated* against her hostile attitude]; **expostulate** suggests strong, earnest pleading or argument to change another's views or actions [his father *expostulated* with him about his impulsiveness]; **demur** implies the raising of objections or the taking of exception so as to delay action [I *demurred* at her proposal to keep the store open late]

---

**objectify,** *v.* — *Syn.* actualize, substantiate, make objective; see **materialize** 1.

**objection,** *n.* **1.** [The reason for disapproval] — *Syn.* disapproval, scruple, hesitation, question, demurring, reluctance, disinclination, declination, unwillingness, rejection, dislike, dissatisfaction, discontent, displeasure, repugnance, disesteem, disapprobation, shrinking, boggling, shunning, revulsion, repudiation, low opinion, abhorrence, hesitancy, unacceptance, discarding, dubiousness; see also **doubt** 1, 2. — *Ant.* PERMISSION, acceptance, desire.
**2.** [The statement or instance of an objection, sense 1] — *Syn.* protestation, criticism, complaint, charge, accusation, remonstrance, expostulation, gainsaying, reprimand, exception, execration, admonition, disapproval, reproach, dispute, opposition, adverse comment, re-

jection, ban, countercharge, grievance, contradiction, contravention, invective, censure, abuse, scolding, denunciation, lecture, disagreement, vituperation, difference, disdain, reprehension, plaint, upbraiding, chiding, insistence, condemnation, depreciation, animadversion, grumbling, caviling, clamor, faultfinding, tonguelashing, vilification, carping, reproof, depreciation, revilement, dissent, indictment, imputation, demurrer, insinuation, complaining, frown, blame, sarcasm, odium, whining, croaking, gravamen, moaning, wail, groan, murmur, lament, regret, lamentation, aspersion, beef\*, problem\*, gripe\*, kick\*, crack\*, dressing-down\*, knock\*; see also **rebuke**.— *Ant.* PRAISE, commendation, recommendation.

**objectionable**, *modif.* **1.** [Revolting] — *Syn.* gross, repugnant, abhorrent; see **offensive** 2.
**2.** [Undesirable] — *Syn.* unacceptable, unsatisfactory, inexpedient; see **undesirable.**

**objective**, *modif.* **1.** [Existing independently of the mind] — *Syn.* actual, external, material, scientific, sure, extrinsic, nonsubjective, measurable, extraneous, unintrospective, reified, tactile, corporeal, bodily, palpable, physical, phenomenal, sensible, outward, outside, determinable, invariable; see also **real** 2.— *Ant.* MENTAL, subjective, introspective.
**2.** [Free from personal bias] — *Syn.* fair, detached, impersonal, unbiased; see **accurate** 2, **fair** 1.
*See Synonym Study at* FAIR.

**objective**, *n.* — *Syn.* goal, aim, intention, aspiration; see **purpose** 1.
*See Synonym Study at* INTENTION.

**objectively**, *modif.* — *Syn.* impartially, indifferently, neutrally, open-mindedly, dispassionately, justly, equitably, detachedly, soberly, accurately, candidly, considerately, not subjectively, with objectivity, with impartiality, with due consideration, with judgment, without prejudice, without bias, without partiality, without passion, squarely\*, on the square\*, like a square shooter\*, on the up and up\*.

**object to**, *v.* — *Syn.* disapprove, doubt, question; see **oppose** 1.

**obligate**, *v.* — *Syn.* bind, restrict, commit; see **force** 1, **restrain** 1.

**obligation**, *n.* — *Syn.* necessity, commitment, burden, debt; see **duty** 1, **responsibility** 2.

**obligatory**, *modif.* — *Syn.* required, essential, binding; see **necessary** 1.

**oblige**, *v.* **1.** [To accommodate] — *Syn.* assist, aid, contribute; see **accommodate** 1, **help** 1, **serve** 1.
**2.** [To require] — *Syn.* compel, coerce, bind; see **command** 1, **force** 1, **require** 2.

**obliged**, *modif.* — *Syn.* compelled, obligated, required; see **bound** 2.

**obliging**, *modif.* — *Syn.* amiable, accommodating, helpful, complaisant; see **amiable, kind.**
*See Synonym Study at* AMIABLE.

**obligingly**, *modif.* — *Syn.* helpfully, agreeably, thoughtfully; see **kindly** 2.

**oblique**, *modif.* **1.** [Slanting] — *Syn.* inclined, inclining, diverging, leaning, sloping, angled, diagonal, catercornered, kitty-cornered, unperpendicular, unvertical, skew, askew, asymmetrical, turned, twisted, awry, strained, askance, distorted, unhorizontal, off level, sideways, slanted, tipping, tipped, aslant, athwart, at an angle, skewwise, on the bias, skewy\*, slaunchwise\*, geewhacky\*, northeast by southwest\*; see also **askew, awry, bent, crooked** 1.— *Ant.* VERTICAL, perpendicular, straight.

**2.** [Indirect] — *Syn.* obscure, circuitous, roundabout; see **indirect, vague** 2.

**obliquely**, *modif.* — *Syn.* cornerways, diagonally, catercorner; see **cornerwise.**

**obliterate**, *v.* **1.** [To destroy] — *Syn.* liquidate, annihilate, level; see **defeat** 2, **destroy** 1, **ravage.**
**2.** [To erase] — *Syn.* erase, delete, wipe out, mark out, rub off; see also **cancel** 1, **eliminate** 1.
*See Synonym Study at* ERASE.

**obliterated**, *modif.* — *Syn.* eliminated, wiped out, removed; see **destroyed.**

**oblivion**, *n.* **1.** [Blankness] — *Syn.* forgetfulness, unmindfulness, obliviousness, Lethe, insensibleness, waters of oblivion, amnesia; see also **carelessness, indifference** 1.— *Ant.* MEMORY, remembrance, recollection.
**2.** [Nothingness] — *Syn.* nonexistence, Nirvana, obscurity, nullity, nihility, void, limbo; see also **emptiness, nothing.**— *Ant.* EXISTENCE, fullness, being.

**oblivious**, *modif.* — *Syn.* abstracted, preoccupied, inattentive, absent-minded, absorbed, absent, heedless, distracted, forgetful, unmindful, forgetting, unrecognizing, unnoticing, blundering, unobservant, unconscious, unaware, overlooking, stargazing, woolgathering, spaced out\*, spacey\*; see also **absent-minded, dreamy** 1. — *Ant.* OBSERVANT, attentive, mindful.

**obliviously**, *modif.* — *Syn.* thoughtlessly, heedlessly, ignorantly; see **carelessly.**

**oblong**, *modif.* — *Syn.* elongated, rectangular, eggshaped, ovate, ovaliform, ovated, oval, elliptical, ellipsoidal, ovaloid, elongate, ovopyriform.— *Ant.* SQUARE, circle, circular.

**obloquy**, *n.* **1.** [Disgrace] — *Syn.* infamy, ill repute, dishonor; see **disgrace** 1, **shame** 2.
**2.** [Slanderous matter] — *Syn.* slander, backbiting, defamation; see **accusation** 2, **blame** 1, **insult, objection** 2.

**obnoxious**, *modif.* — *Syn.* offensive, annoying, disagreeable, displeasing; see **offensive** 2.
*See Synonym Study at* OFFENSIVE.

**obnoxiously**, *modif.* — *Syn.* cruelly, indecently, unwelcomely; see **badly** 1, **brutally.**

**obscene**, *modif.* **1.** [Lewd] — *Syn.* indecent, lewd, pornographic, smutty; see **lewd** 1, 2, **ribald.**
**2.** [Foul] — *Syn.* unwholesome, filthy, unclean; see **offensive** 2.
*See Synonym Study at* COARSE.

**obscenely**, *modif.* — *Syn.* indecently, viciously, suggestively; see **lewdly.**

**obscenity**, *n.* **1.** [The state or quality of being obscene] — *Syn.* salacity, vulgarity, scurrility; see **lewdness.**
**2.** [That which is obscene] — *Syn.* vulgarity, impropriety, smut; see **curse** 1, **indecency** 2, **pornography.**

**obscure**, *modif.* **1.** [Vague] — *Syn.* indistinct, vague, ambiguous, indeterminate, indefinite, enigmatic, cryptic, equivocal, unintelligible, impenetrable, inscrutable, unfathomable, unclear, insoluble, involved, uncertain, indecisive, undefined, intricate, illegible, incomprehensible, hazy, dark, dim, abstruse, unaccountable, inexplicable, inconceivable, complicated, illogical, imprecise, unreasoned, mixed up, doubtful, questionable, dubious, inexact, unreasoned, loose, ill-defined, unidentified, invisible, undisclosed, perplexing, escaping notice, mystical, veiled, secret, concealed, mysterious, recondite, esoteric, puzzling, confusing, confused, difficult, complex, lacking clarity, unreadable, contradictory, wanting precision, in need of clarifying, out of focus, in need of translation, murky, clear as mud\*, too much for\*, over one's head\*, deep\*, far out\*; see also **complex** 2, **con-**

fused 2, **confusing, difficult** 2, **uncertain** 2, **vague** 2. — *Ant.* CLEAR, definite, distinct.

**2.** [Dark] — *Syn.* cloudy, dense, hazy; see **dark** 1.

**3.** [Little known] — *Syn.* unknown, rare, hidden, covered, remote, removed, retired, reticent, secretive, seldom seen, unseen, inconspicuous, humble, invisible, abstruse, mysterious, deep, cryptic, oracular, enigmatic, esoteric, arcane, undisclosed, cabalistic, inexpressible, unapprehended, dark; see also **distant** 1, **irrelevant**, **profound** 2, **secret** 1.

---

*SYN.* — **obscure** applies to that which is perceived with difficulty either because it is concealed or veiled or because of obtuseness in the perceiver [their reasons remain *obscure*]; **vague** implies such a lack of precision or exactness as to be indistinct or unclear [a *vague* foreboding]; **enigmatic** and **cryptic** are used of that which baffles or perplexes, the latter word implying deliberate intention to puzzle [an *enigmatic* smile, a *cryptic* warning]; **ambiguous** applies to that which puzzles because it allows of more than one interpretation [an *ambiguous* title]; **equivocal** is used of something ambiguous that is deliberately used to mislead or confuse [an *equivocal* answer]

---

**obscure**, *v.* **1.** [To dim] — *Syn.* shadow, cloud, screen; see **shade** 2.

**2.** [To conceal] — *Syn.* cover, veil, wrap; see **disguise**, **hide** 1.

**obscurely**, *modif.* — *Syn.* dimly, darkly, thickly, duskily, nebulously, dingily, tenebrously, generally, dully, indistinctly, gloomily, hazily, unintelligibly, indefinitely, indefinably, indecisively, unobtrusively; see also **vaguely**.

**obscurity**, *n.* — *Syn.* vagueness, dimness, fuzziness; see **uncertainty** 1, 2, 3.

**obsequious**, *modif.* — *Syn.* docile, submissive, cringing, slavish, sycophantic, deferential, servile, subject, enslaved, subordinate, parasitical, stipendiary, toadyish, toadying, fawning, truckling, groveling, spineless, crouching, cringing, mealy-mouthed, subservient, abject, beggarly, sniveling, prostrate, sneaking, oily, bootlicking*, brown-nosing*, kowtowing*, apple-polishing*, flunkyish*, toad-eating*; see also **docile**, **obedient** 1. — *Ant.* INSULTING, proud, haughty.

**obsequiously**, *modif.* — *Syn.* servilely, slavishly, subserviently, sycophantically, ingratiatingly, fawningly, abjectly, grovelingly, on one's knees.

**observable**, *modif.* — *Syn.* perceptible, visible, noticeable, discernible; see **obvious** 1.

**observably**, *modif.* — *Syn.* noticeably, obviously, notably; see **clearly** 1.

**observance**, *n.* **1.** [A custom] — *Syn.* ritual, practice, devotion; see **custom** 2.

**2.** [Attention] — *Syn.* awareness, observation, notice; see **attention** 1.

**observant**, *modif.* **1.** [Given to observing] — *Syn.* keen, alert, penetrating, wide-awake, discerning, perceptive, sharp, eager, interested, discovering, detecting, discriminating, searching, understanding, questioning, deducing, surveying, alive, contemplating, regardful, considering, sensitive, clear-sighted, comprehending, bright, intelligent, on the ball*, on the beam*, on one's toes*; see also **intelligent** 1, **judicious**. — *Ant.* THOUGHTLESS, unobservant, insensitive.

**2.** [Engaged in observing] — *Syn.* watchful, gazing, attentive, alert, awake, wide-awake, sleepless, wakeful, noticing, viewing, vigilant, reconnoitering, guarding, mindful, on guard, regardful, listening, heedful, on the watch, on the lookout, on the qui vive, looking out,

intent on, alive to, careful, undistracted, intent, open-eyed, sharp-eyed, circumspect, cautious, wary, prudent, marking, inspecting, scrutinizing, examining, surveying, all ears*, all eyes*; see also **watching**. — *Ant.* CARELESS, heedless, inattentive.

**observation**, *n.* **1.** [The power of observing] — *Syn.* noticing, recognizing, view, regard, overlook, mark, consideration, heed, heedfulness, note, perception, measurement, estimation, conclusion, inspection, scrutiny, investigation, research, search, probe, check, detection, ascertainment, once-over*; see also **acumen, sight** 1. — *Ant.* INDIFFERENCE, obstruction, blindness.

**2.** [A remark] — *Syn.* comment, note, remark, pronouncement; see **remark**.

*See Synonym Study at* REMARK.

**observatory**, *n.* — *Syn.* watchtower, observation post, beacon; see **lookout** 1, **tower**.

**observe**, *v.* **1.** [To notice] — *Syn.* look at, perceive, recognize, discern; see **discern, see** 1, **witness**.

*See Synonym Study at* DISCERN.

**2.** [To watch] — *Syn.* scrutinize, inspect, examine; see **watch** 1.

**3.** [To comment] — *Syn.* note, remark, mention; see **comment** 1.

**4.** [To commemorate] — *Syn.* celebrate, commemorate, keep; see **celebrate** 1.

*See Synonym Study at* CELEBRATE.

**5.** [To abide by] — *Syn.* conform to, comply, adopt; see **follow** 2, **obey** 2.

**observed**, *modif.* **1.** [Noticed] — *Syn.* seen, noted, marked, attended, detected, perceived, viewed, espied, regarded, looked at, looked over, found, overlooked, heeded, ascertained, pointed out, minded, watched, noticed, inspected, discerned, discovered, surveyed, descried, beheld, contemplated, scrutinized, revealed, realized, examined, listened to, heard, checked, checked off; see also **recognized**. — *Ant.* UNNOTICED, unseen, unperceived.

**2.** [Commemorated] — *Syn.* recalled, memorialized, preserved, respected, freshened, kept, celebrated, solemnized, esteemed, reverenced, honored, venerated, sanctified, regarded, worshiped, kept in mind, minded, consecrated; see also **remembered**. — *Ant.* ABANDONED, forgotten, desecrated.

**observer**, *n.* **1.** [One who watches] — *Syn.* watcher, watchman, sentinel, lookout, sentry, guard, detective, policeman, reconnoiterer, spectator, eyewitness, beholder, onlooker, bystander, passer-by, meddler, peeper, voyeur, prying person, peeping Tom*, rubberneck*; see also **spy, witness**.

**2.** [One who offers original comment] — *Syn.* commentator, novelist, columnist, armchair quarterback*, drugstore cowboy*; see also **author** 2, **historian**, **writer**.

**observing**, *modif.* **1.** [Observant] — *Syn.* alert, keen, penetrating; see **intelligent** 1, **observant** 1.

**2.** [Engaged in observing] — *Syn.* attentive, watchful, looking on; see **observant** 2, **watching**.

**obsess**, *v.* — *Syn.* dominate, possess, hound; see **haunt** 3.

**obsessed**, *modif.* — *Syn.* haunted, beset, controlled, preoccupied, overpowered, captivated, perplexed, seized, bedeviled, plagued, fixated, hung up*; see also **troubled** 1, 2.

**obsession**, *n.* — *Syn.* fixation, fascination, passion, fancy, phantom, craze, delusion, mania, infatuation, fixed idea, *idée fixe* (French), compulsion, fetish, bee in one's bonnet*, hang-up*; see also **attraction** 1, **neurosis**.

**obsolescent,** *modif.* — *Syn.* becoming obsolete, growing old, out of fashion, senescent; see **aging.**

**obsolete,** *modif.* — *Syn.* antiquated, archaic, out-of-date; see **old** 2, 3, **old-fashioned.**
*See Synonym Study at* OLD.

**obstacle,** *n.* — *Syn.* barrier, restriction, obstruction, hindrance; see **barrier, impediment** 1.
*See Synonym Study at* IMPEDIMENT.

**obstetrics,** *n.* — *Syn.* tocology, midwifery, O.B.\*; see **medicine** 3.

**obstinacy,** *n.* — *Syn.* stubbornness, tenacity, reluctance; see **determination** 2, **purpose** 1.

**obstinate,** *modif.* — *Syn.* stubborn, firm, headstrong, dogged, pertinacious, opinionated, strong-minded, contumacious, opinionative, contradictory, inflexible, positive, perverse, contrary, cantankerous, unimpressible, determined, convinced, resolved, indomitable, adamant, intractable, crotchety, obdurate, self-willed, refractory, unamenable, unalterable, unconquerable, restive, unflinching, unyielding, unbending, immovable, tenacious, decided, heady, unmanageable, bull-headed, mulish, pigheaded, plucky, sulky, case-hardened, fixed, stiff-necked, callous, hard, hardened, relentless, recalcitrant, unrelenting, resistant, repulsive, willful, unwavering, prejudiced, biased, bigoted, dogmatic, unreasonable, unreasoning, hellbent\*, die-hard\*, set in one's ways\*; see also **resolute** 2. — *Ant.* DOCILE, submissive, amenable.

*SYN.* — **obstinate** applies to one who adheres persistently, and often unreasonably, to a purpose, course, etc., against argument or persuasion /a panel hung by an *obstinate* juror/; **stubborn** implies a strong, even innate, resistance to change or manipulation of purpose, course, condition, etc. /a *stubborn* child, a *stubborn* belief in astrology/; **dogged** implies thoroughgoing determination or, sometimes, sullen obstinacy /the *dogged* pursuit of a goal/; **pertinacious** implies a strong tenacity of purpose that is regarded unfavorably by others /a *pertinacious* critic/

**obstinately,** *modif.* — *Syn.* doggedly, stubbornly, tenaciously, pertinaciously, mulishly, stiff-neckedly, pigheadedly, bullheadedly, like a bull, persistently, unwaveringly, determinedly, unyieldingly, fixedly, resolutely, unreasonably, unreasoningly, perversely, stolidly, resistantly, intractably, inflexibly, headstrongly, willfully, recalcitrantly, obdurately, steadfastly, staunchly, unflinchingly, resolvedly, opinionatedly, immovably, unimpressibly, unconquerably, contumaciously, indomitably, unrelentingly, unamenably, stubbornly as a mule, like a jackass; see also **firmly** 2. — *Ant.* OBEDIENTLY, docilely, graciously.

**obstreperous,** *modif.* — *Syn.* boisterous, noisy, vociferous, raucous; see **loud** 2.
*See Synonym Study at* VOCIFEROUS.

**obstruct,** *v.* **1.** [To impede with an obstruction] — *Syn.* hinder, stop, interfere, terminate; see **hinder, prevent, restrain** 1.
**2.** [To place an obstruction] — *Syn.* block, clog, barricade; see **bar** 1.
*See Synonym Study at* HINDER.

**obstruction,** *n.* **1.** [The act of obstructing] — *Syn.* circumvention, blocking, checkmate; see **interference** 1, **restraint** 2.
**2.** [That which obstructs] — *Syn.* obstacle, hindrance, difficulty, roadblock; see **barrier, impediment** 1.
*See Synonym Study at* IMPEDIMENT.

**obtain,** *v.* **1.** [To gain possession] — *Syn.* occupy, reach,

invade, capture, recover, take, grab, accomplish, acquire, procure, get, force from, make use of, fetch and carry, bring out, bring back, bring forth, attain, gain, win, secure, achieve, glean, reap, retrieve, recover, collect, gather, earn, pick up, purchase, effect, receive, inherit, salvage, pocket, compass, realize, save, hoard, lay up, corral\*, drum up\*, scrape up, scrape together\*, come by\*, score\*, nab\*, gobble up\*, get at\*, get hold of\*; beg, borrow, or steal; see also **seize** 2. — *Ant.* GIVE, donate, present.
**2.** [Pertain] — *Syn.* be pertinent to, appertain to, bear upon; see **concern** 1.

*SYN.* — **obtain** implies that there is effort or desire in the getting /he has *obtained* aid/; **get** is the word of broadest application meaning to come into possession of, with or without effort or volition /to *get* a job, an idea, a headache, etc./; **procure** suggests active effort or contrivance in getting or bringing to pass /to *procure* a settlement of the dispute/; **secure** implies difficulty in obtaining something and perhaps in retaining it /to *secure* a lasting peace/; **acquire** implies a lengthy process in the getting and connotes collection or accretion /he *acquired* a fine education/; **gain** always implies effort in the getting of something advantageous or profitable /to *gain* fame/

**obtainable,** *modif.* — *Syn.* ready, attainable, achievable; see **available.**

**obtrusive,** *modif.* **1.** [Protruding] — *Syn.* jutting, bulging, projecting; see **prominent** 1.
**2.** [Presumptuous] — *Syn.* forward, intrusive, impertinent; see **rude** 2.

**obtrusively,** *modif.* — *Syn.* obviously, crassly, bluntly; see **clearly** 1, 2.

**obtuse,** *modif.* **1.** [Stupid] — *Syn.* dull, dense, stolid, insensible; see **dull** 3.
**2.** [Not sharp] — *Syn.* dull, round, blunt, greater than 90°; see **dull** 1.
*See Synonym Study at* DULL.

**obtusely,** *modif.* — *Syn.* stupidly, dully, unintelligently; see **foolishly.**

**obverse,** *n.* — *Syn.* face, opposite side, main surface; see **front** 1.

**obviate,** *v.* — *Syn.* preclude, forestall, block; see **hinder, prevent, restrain** 1.
*See Synonym Study at* PREVENT.

**obvious,** *modif.* **1.** [Clearly apparent to the eye] — *Syn.* clear, visible, apparent, public, transparent, observable, perceptible, exposed, undisguised, noticeable, plain, conspicuous, overt, glaring, blatant, prominent, standing out, light, bright, open, unmistakable, evident, recognizable, discernible, in evidence, exoteric, in view, in sight, perceivable, discoverable, distinguishable, accessible, precise, patent, manifest, palpable, distinct, clear as a bell\*, clear as day\*, sticking out a mile\*, sticking out like a sore thumb\*, plain as the nose on one's face\*, hitting one in the face\*, leaping to the eye\*; see also **definite** 2. — *Ant.* OBSCURE, hidden, indistinct.
**2.** [Clearly apparent to the mind] — *Syn.* lucid, apparent, conclusive, explicit, understood, intelligible, comprehensible, self-evident, patent, indisputable, unquestionable, undeniable, blatant, axiomatic, proverbial, aphoristic, reasonable, broad, unequivocal, unambiguous, on the surface, unmysterious, as plain as the nose on one's face\*, going without saying\*, staring one in the face\*, open and shut\*; see also **definite** 1, **understandable.** — *Ant.* PROFOUND, ambiguous, equivocal.

**3.** [Naive] — *Syn.* simple, innocent, unsophisticated; see **inexperienced, naive, young** 2.

*SYN.* — **obvious** refers to that which is so noticeable or obtrusive that no one can fail to perceive it; **evident** and **apparent** apply to that which can be readily perceived or easily inferred, but **evident** implies the existence of external signs *[his evident disappointment]* and **apparent** suggests the use of deductive reasoning *[it's apparent he'll win]*; **manifest** applies to that which is immediately, often intuitively, clear to the understanding; **palpable** applies esp. to that which can be perceived through some sense other than that of sight, most particularly touch *[palpable signs of fever, an almost palpable sense of dread]*; **clear** implies that there is no confusion or obscurity to hinder understanding *[clear proof]*; **plain** implies such simplicity or lack of complexity as to be easily perceptible *[the plain facts are these]*

**obviously,** *interj.* — *Syn.* of course, yes, evidently; see **surely.**

**obviously,** *modif.* — *Syn.* without doubt, unmistakably, certainly; see **clearly** 1, 2.

**occasion,** *n.* **1.** [An event] — *Syn.* occurrence, incident, happening; see **event** 1, 2.

**2.** [An opportunity] — *Syn.* chance, excuse, opening; see **opportunity** 1, **possibility** 2.

**3.** [A time] — *Syn.* moment, instant, season; see **time** 2.

**4.** [An (immediate) cause] — *Syn.* prompting, incident, antecedent; see **cause** 1, 3, **circumstance** 1.

**on occasion** — *Syn.* once in a while, sometimes, occasionally, at certain times; see **hardly, seldom.**

**on the occasion of** — *Syn.* at the time when, because of, since; see **at** 1, **because, on** 1.

**rise to the occasion** — *Syn.* do what is necessary, meet an emergency, carry on; see **succeed** 1.

**take the occasion** — *Syn.* seize the opportunity, use the opportunity, do something, bring about; see **act** 1, **use** 1.

**occasion,** *v.* — *Syn.* bring about, introduce, do; see **cause.**

**occasional,** *modif.* **1.** [Irregular] — *Syn.* sporadic, random, infrequent; see **irregular** 1, **rare** 2.

**2.** [Associated with a special occasion] — *Syn.* uncommon, not habitual, exceptional; see **unusual** 1, 2.

**3.** [Intended for special use] — *Syn.* especial, particular, specific; see **exclusive, special** 1.

**occasionally,** *modif.* — *Syn.* infrequently, at random, irregularly; see **hardly, seldom.**

**occlude,** *v.* — *Syn.* block, curb, impede; see **close** 2, **prevent.**

**occult,** *modif.* **1.** [Hidden] — *Syn.* unrevealed, esoteric, obscure; see **hidden** 2, **secret** 1, 3.

**2.** [Concerning supernatural powers] — *Syn.* mystical, magical, supernatural; see **mysterious** 2, **secret** 1.

**occult,** *n.* — *Syn.* mysticism, the supernatural, hermetics; see **mysticism, spiritualism** 1.

**occupancy,** *n.* — *Syn.* possession, occupation, inhabitance; see **deed** 2, **ownership, title** 2.

**occupant,** *n.* — *Syn.* lessee, inhabitant, renter; see **resident, tenant.**

**occupation,** *n.* **1.** [The act of occupying] — *Syn.* seizure, entering, invasion; see **attack** 1, **capture.**

**2.** [A vocation] — *Syn.* calling, affair, chosen work; see **job** 1, **profession** 1, **trade** 2.

**3.** [The state of being in possession] — *Syn.* control, use, rule; see **ownership, title** 2.

**occupational,** *modif.* — *Syn.* professional, career, technical, functional, workaday, official, industrial.

**occupied,** *modif.* **1.** [Busy] — *Syn.* engaged, working, engrossed, entertained; see **busy** 1.

**2.** [Full] — *Syn.* in use, leased, utilized; see **busy** 3, **rented, taken** 2.

**occupy,** *v.* **1.** [To take possession] — *Syn.* conquer, take over, invade; see **obtain** 1, **seize** 2.

**2.** [To fill space] — *Syn.* remain, tenant, reside, live in, hold, take up, pervade, keep, own, be in command, extend, control, fill an office, maintain, involve, permeate; see also **fill** 2, **sit** 2. — *Ant.* EMPTY, remove, move.

**3.** [To absorb attention] — *Syn.* engage, employ, engross, attend, monopolize, fill, interest, immerse, arrest, absorb, take up, utilize, involve, employ one's time in, keep busy, busy, be active with, be concerned with; see also **fascinate.**

**occupying,** *modif.* **1.** [Filling a place] — *Syn.* holding, obtaining, remaining, situated, posted, assigned to, tenanting, residing, living in, taking up, possessing, permeating, pervading, covering, settled on, controlling, maintaining, commanding, sitting, staying, established in, established at, owning, set up*, running*; see also **placed, resting** 2. — *Ant.* GONE, leaving, removing.

**2.** [Engaging attention] — *Syn.* absorbing, concentrated upon, utilizing, engrossing, attending upon, concerned with, embarking upon, monopolizing, engaging, arresting, working at, attracting, focusing, drawing, exacting, requiring; see also **exciting, interesting.**

**occur,** *v.* — *Syn.* happen, take place, transpire, befall; see **happen** 1, 2.

*See Synonym Study at* HAPPEN.

**occurrence,** *n.* — *Syn.* event, happening, incident, episode, circumstance, occasion, experience, phenomenon, existence, appearance, occurring; see also **event** 1, 2.

*SYN.* — **occurrence** is the general word for anything that happens or takes place *[an unforeseen occurrence]*; **event** implies an occurrence of relative significance, often one growing out of earlier happenings or conditions *[the events that followed the surrender]*; **incident** usually suggests an occurrence of relatively minor significance, often one connected with a more important event *[the award was just another incident in her career]*, though it can also imply conflict or disturbance *[the demonstration continued without further incident]*; an **episode** is a distinct event that is complete in itself but forms part of a larger event or is one of a series of events *[an episode of his childhood]*; a **circumstance** is an event that is either incidental to, or a determining factor of, another event *[the circumstances surrounding my decision]*

**occur to,** *v.* — *Syn.* come to, come to mind, present itself, suggest itself, spring, issue, rise, appear, catch one's attention, arrest the thoughts, pass through one's mind, impress one, enter one's mind, cross one's mind, crop up, strike one.

**occur with,** *v.* — *Syn.* happen with, coexist, appear with; see **accompany** 3.

**ocean,** *n.* — *Syn.* sea, great sea, high seas, salt water, seashore, seaside, beach, shores, Oceanus, Neptune, the mighty deep, the main, the great waters, the Seven Seas, mare, big pond*, puddle*, briny deep*, Davy Jones' locker*, the cradle of the deep*; see also **sea.**
Oceans of the world include: Atlantic, Pacific, Arctic, Antarctic, Indian, North Atlantic, South Atlantic, North Pacific, South Pacific.

**ocean floor,** *n.* — *Syn.* sea bed, bottom of the sea, offshore lands; see **sea bottom.**

**ocean-going,** *modif.* — *Syn.* seagoing, seafaring, marine; see **maritime** 2, **nautical.**

**oceanic,** *modif.* — *Syn.* marine, aquatic, pelagic; see **maritime** 2, **nautical.**

**October,** *n.* — *Syn.* fall month, autumn month, harvest month, football season, "October's bright blue weather," Indian summer, hunting season; see also **autumn, month.**

**ocular,** *modif.* — *Syn.* visual, viewed, perceived visually, beheld; see **visual.**

**oculist,** *n.* — *Syn.* ophthalmologist, eye specialist, eye doctor, optometrist; see **doctor** 1.

**odd,** *modif.* 1. [Unusual] — *Syn.* queer, unique, strange; see **unusual** 2.
   2. [Indefinite] — *Syn.* doubtful, insecure, inexplicit; see **obscure** 1, **uncertain** 2, **vague** 2.
   3. [Miscellaneous] — *Syn.* fragmentary, odd-lot, varied, occasional; see **different** 2, **various.**
   4. [Single] — *Syn.* sole, unpaired, unmatched; see **alone** 1, **single** 1.
   5. [Not even] — *Syn.* uneven, remaining, over and above, additional, exceeding, spare, leftover; see also **irregular** 1, 4. — *Ant.* even, REGULAR, even-numbered.
   *See Synonym Study at* STRANGE.

**oddity,** *n.* — *Syn.* eccentricity, idiosyncrasy, abnormality, peculiarity; see **characteristic, irregularity** 2, **quirk.**

**oddly,** *modif.* — *Syn.* curiously, ridiculously, inexplicably; see **foolishly, strangely.**

**oddment,** *n.* — *Syn.* scrap, shred, fragment; see **bit** 1.

**odds,** *n.* 1. [An advantage] — *Syn.* allowance, edge, benefit, difference, superiority, overlay*, square odds*, place money*, show money*; see also **advantage** 1.
   2. [A probability] — *Syn.* likelihood, favor, superiority, chances; see **probability.**
   **at odds** — *Syn.* disagreeing, at variance, discordant; see **quarreling.**

**odds and ends,** *n.* — *Syn.* miscellany, scraps, particles; see **remnants, rummage.**

**ode,** *n.* — *Syn.* poem, Pindaric ode, lyric, *canzone* (Italian); see **poetry.**

**odious,** *modif.* — *Syn.* offensive, repellent, repulsive, disgusting; see **offensive** 2.
   *See Synonym Study at* OFFENSIVE.

**odium,** *n.* 1. [Hostility] — *Syn.* enmity, malice, aversion; see **hatred** 2, **resentment.**
   2. [Disgrace] — *Syn.* dishonor, opprobrium, disfavor; see **disgrace** 1, **shame** 2.

**odor,** *n.* — *Syn.* smell, perfume, fragrance, bouquet; see **smell** 1, 2.
   *See Synonym Study at* SMELL.

**odorless,** *modif.* — *Syn.* flat, scentless, unaromatic, unperfumed, unsmelling, unscented, without odor, odor-free, unfragrant, lacking fragrance. — *Ant.* ODOROUS, fragrant, perfumed.

**odorous,** *modif.* 1. [Having an offensive odor] — *Syn.* smelly, stinking, fetid, musty, putrid, foul, redolent, odoriferous, odoriferant, emitting an odor, strong, malodorous, mephitic, tumaceous, stench-laden, nauseous, cloying, cloacal, unsavory, effluvious, moldy, stale, dank, miasmic, stinky*, skunky*, pewy*; see also **offensive** 2, **rotten** 1.
   2. [Having a pleasant odor] — *Syn.* sweet, spicy, pungent, sweet-scented, sweet-smelling, savory, fragrant, aromatic, perfumed, scented, scent-laden, redolent, odoriferous, odoriferant, olent, spice-laden, honeyed, perfumy, perfumatory, balmy, savorous, flower-scented, nectar-scented, rose-scented. — *Ant.* ODORLESS, stinking, smelly.

**of,** *prep.* — *Syn.* from, out of, out from, away from, proceeding from, coming from, going from, about, concerning, as concerns, pertaining to, appertaining to, peculiar to, attributed to, characterized by, regarding, as regards, in regard to, referring to, in reference to, appropriate to, like, belonging to, related to, having relation to, native to, consequent to, based on, akin to, consanguineous to, connected with; see also **about** 2.

**off,** *modif. & prep.* 1. [Situated at a distance] — *Syn.* ahead, behind, up front, to one side, divergent, beside, aside, below, beneath, above, far, afar, absent, not here, removed, apart, in the distance, at a distance, gone, away; see also **distant** 1. — *Ant.* HERE, at hand, present.
   2. [Moving away] — *Syn.* into the distance, away from, farther away, disappearing, vanishing, removing, sheering off, turning aside; see also **away** 1. — *Ant.* RETURNING, coming, approaching.
   3. [Started] — *Syn.* initiated, commenced, originated; see **begun.**
   4. [Mistaken] — *Syn.* erring, in error, confused; see **mistaken** 1, **wrong** 2.
   5. [*Crazy] — *Syn.* odd, peculiar, queer; see **insane** 1.
   6. [*Not employed] — *Syn.* not on duty, on vacation, gone; see **unemployed.**
   7. [Not up to standard] — *Syn.* substandard, abnormal, subnormal, unproductive; see **poor** 2.
   **get off on*** — *Syn. vb* enjoy, appreciate, take pleasure in; see **like** 1.

**offal,** *n.* — *Syn.* garbage, refuse, waste; see **trash** 1, 3.

**off and on,** *modif.* — *Syn.* now and again, now and then, sometimes, occasionally; see **seldom.**

**offbeat*,** *modif.* — *Syn.* strange, unique, idiosyncratic; see **unusual** 2.

**off-Broadway,** *modif.* — *Syn.* noncommercial, not commercialized, avant-garde, experimental, off-off-Broadway, unconventional, low-cost; see also **art** 2, **artistic** 2.

**off-center,** *modif.* — *Syn.* off-centered, not centered, off balance, eccentric; see **irregular** 1, 4, **unsteady** 1.

**off-color,** *modif.* — *Syn.* racy, spicy, indelicate; see **risqué.**

**offend,** *v.* — *Syn.* affront, insult, outrage, annoy, hurt, hurt one's feelings, wound, cut, nettle, pique, anger, irritate, provoke, displease, aggrieve, chagrin, give offense, repel, disgust, sicken, revolt, shock, transgress, trespass, step on one's toes, tread on one's toes*; see also **anger** 1, **disgust.**

---

*SYN.* — **offend** implies the causing of displeasure or resentment in another, intentionally or unintentionally, by wounding the person's feelings or by a breach of the person's sense of propriety /she will be *offended* if she is not invited/; **affront** implies open and deliberate disrespect or offense /to *affront* someone's pride/; **insult** implies an affront so insolent or contemptuously rude as to cause humiliation and resentment /a book that *insults* the reader's intelligence/; **outrage** implies an extreme offense against someone's sense of right, justice, propriety, etc. /he was *outraged* by the offer of a bribe/

---

**offended,** *modif.* — *Syn.* vexed, provoked, exasperated; see **angry, insulted.**

**offense,** *n.* 1. [A misdeed] — *Syn.* misdemeanor, malfeasance, transgression; see **crime** 1, 2, **sin.**
   2. [An attack] — *Syn.* assault, aggression, battery; see **attack** 1.
   Styles of offense in football include: running attack*, shotgun offense*, T-formation*, wishbone*, passing attack*, straight football*, power plays*, cross-bucks

and spinners★, flying wedge★, razzle-dazzle★, the aerial route★, the bust-em philosophy★.

Styles of offense in basketball include: five-man attack★, four-man offense★, center fan★, cartwheel★, slow-breaking attack★, fast-breaking attack★.

**3.** [Resentment] — *Syn.* umbrage, resentment, pique, indignation, displeasure, hurt, huff, disgust, high dudgeon; see also **anger, resentment.**

---

*SYN.* — **offense**, in this connection, implies displeased or hurt feelings as the result of a slight, insult, etc. /don't take *offense* at my criticism/; **resentment** adds implications of indignation, a brooding over an injury, and ill will toward the offender /a *resentment* cherished for days/; **umbrage** implies offense or resentment at being slighted or having one's pride hurt /he took *umbrage* at the tone of her letter/; **pique** suggests a passing feeling of ruffled pride, usually over a trifle; **displeasure** may describe a feeling varying from dissatisfaction or disapproval to anger and indignation

---

**offensive,** *modif.* **1.** [Concerned with an attack] — *Syn.* assaulting, attacking, invading; see **aggressive** 2.
**2.** [Revolting] — *Syn.* obnoxious, odious, opprobrious, disagreeable, displeasing, abhorrent, reprehensible, detestable, repulsive, repugnant, shocking, horrible, horrid, hideous, repellent, nauseating, invidious, nauseous, revolting, distasteful, impious, blasphemous, unspeakable, accursed, unutterable, dreadful, terrible, grisly, ghastly, bloody, gory, infamous, hateful, low, foul, corrupt, bad, indecent, nasty, dirty, unclean, filthy, sickening, malignant, rancid, disgusting, feculent, lousy, verminous, macabre, putrid, vile, impure, beastly, monstrous, coarse, ribald, noxious, loathsome, abominable, stinking, reeking, execrable, purulent, obscene, saprogenous, pernicious, smutty, damnable, distressing, irritating, uncongenial, unpleasant, uninviting, contaminated, unsympathetic, frightful, malodorous, unattractive, forbidding, disagreeing, adverse, inimical, repelling, incompatible, unsavory, intolerable, unpalatable, dissatisfactory, unpleasing, inharmonious, unsuited, objectionable, annoying, antipathetic, in disfavor, to one's disgust, beneath contempt, bad vibes★, cussed★, blankety★, helluva★, gosh-awful★, hell-fired★, icky★, jerkwater★, lousy★, mangy★, rummy★, snide★, two-bit★, pewy★; see also **rotten** 1, 3, **shameful** 1, 2, **ugly** 1, 2, **vulgar** 1, **wicked** 1, 2.— *Ant.* PLEASANT, agreeable, likable.
**3.** [Insolent] — *Syn.* impertinent, impudent, insulting; see **rude** 2.

---

*SYN.* — **hateful** is applied to that which provokes extreme dislike or aversion; **odious** stresses a disagreeable or offensive quality in that which is hateful; **detestable** refers to that which arouses vehement dislike or antipathy; **obnoxious** is applied to that which is very objectionable to one and causes great annoyance or discomfort by its presence; that is **repugnant** which is so distasteful or offensive that one offers strong resistance to it; that is **abhorrent** which is regarded with extreme repugnance or disgust; **abominable** is applied to that which is execrably offensive or loathsome

---

**offensive,** *n.* — *Syn.* attack, position of attack, invasion, assault; see **attack** 1.
**offer,** *n.* — *Syn.* proposal, presentation, proposition; see **suggestion** 1.
**offer,** *v.* **1.** [To present] — *Syn.* proffer, tender, administer, donate, put forth, advance, extend, submit, hold

out, grant, allow, award, volunteer, accord, place at one's disposal, lay at one's feet★, put up★; see also **contribute, give** 1.— *Ant.* REFUSE, withhold, keep.
**2.** [To propose] — *Syn.* suggest, submit, advise; see **propose** 1.
**3.** [To try] — *Syn.* attempt, endeavor, strive; see **try** 1.
**4.** [To occur] — *Syn.* happen, present itself, appear; see **occur to.**
**offering,** *n.* **1.** [Something contributed] — *Syn.* contribution, donation, present; see **gift** 1.
**2.** [Something offered to a deity] — *Syn.* oblation, libation, expiation, atonement; see **sacrifice** 1.
**offer up,** *v.* — *Syn.* present, proffer, immolate; see **sacrifice** 1.
**off for,** *modif.* — *Syn.* going, departing, leaving; see **traveling** 2.
**offhand,** *modif.* — *Syn.* at the moment, unprepared, impromptu, informal, extemporary, unpremeditated, ad-lib, off-the-cuff, off-the-record, spontaneous, off the top of one's head★, unstudied, unrehearsed, improvised, by ear; see also **extemporaneous.**
**offhandedly,** *modif.* — *Syn.* nonchalantly, heedlessly, thoughtlessly; see **carelessly, indifferently.**
**office,** *n.* **1.** [A position involving responsibility] — *Syn.* position, appointment, post, occupation; see **job** 1, **profession** 1, **trade** 2.
**2.** [A function] — *Syn.* performance, province, service; see **duty** 2.
**3.** [A place in which office work is done] — *Syn.* room, office building, factory, bureau, agency, warehouse, facility, school building, suite; see also **building** 1, **department** 2.
Types of offices include: consular, customs, foreign, ambassadorial, ministerial, governmental, business, principal's, counseling, professional, home, secretarial, stenographic, filing, typing, insurance, accountant, data processing, real estate, brokerage, bookkeeping, journalistic, recording, sheriff, police, credit union, law, bank, doctor's, dentist's, psychiatrist's, advertising agency, theater; booking office, box office.
See Synonym Study at FUNCTION, JOB.
**officer,** *n.* **1.** [An executive] — *Syn.* manager, director, president; see **administrator, leader** 2.
**2.** [One who enforces civil law] — *Syn.* police officer, magistrate, military police, deputy; see **police, police officer, sheriff.**
**3.** [One holding a responsible post in the armed forces] American officers include— *Army and Marine Corps commissioned officers, and Army special officers:* Commander in Chief, General of the Army, Lieutenant General, Major General, Brigadier General, Colonel, Lieutenant Colonel, Major, Captain, First Lieutenant, Second Lieutenant, Adjutant General, Aide-de-Camp, Chief of Staff, Assistant Chief of Staff, Chaplain, Inspector General, Judge Advocate General, Provost Marshal General, Quartermaster General, Surgeon General; *Navy commissioned officers:* Admiral of the Fleet, Fleet Admiral, Admiral, Rear Admiral, Vice Admiral, Commodore, Captain, Commander, Lieutenant Commander, Lieutenant, Lieutenant, junior grade; Ensign, *Army and Marine Corps noncommissioned officers:* Sergeant Major, Command Sergeant Major, Master Sergeant, First Sergeant, Staff Sergeant, Sergeant, Mate, Corporal, Lance Corporal, Private First Class, PFC, Private, *Navy noncommissioned officers:* Master Chief Petty Officer, Senior Chief, Chief, Seaman; *temporary officers:* Officer Commanding, Commanding Officer *or* CO★, officer of the day.
**official,** *modif.* **1.** [Having to do with one's office]

— *Syn.* formal, fitting, suitable, befitting, precise, established, ceremonious, according to precedent, according to protocol, proper, correct, accepted, recognized, customary; see also **conventional** 1, 2, 3, **fit** 1, 2. — *Ant.* INFORMAL, unceremonious, ill-fitting.

**2.** [Authorized] — *Syn.* ordered, endorsed, sanctioned; see **approved.**

**3.** [Reliable] — *Syn.* authoritative, authentic, trustworthy, true, unquestionable, indubitable, veritable, real, sure, absolute, canonical, positive, clear, unequivocal, unmistakable, decisive, conclusive, unimpeachable, valid, authenticated, credible, bona fide, accurate, faithful, standard, irrefutable, incontestable, verified, proven, indisputable, not to be questioned, definite, assured, decided, to be depended on, to be trusted, worthy of confidence, undeniable, guaranteed, insured; see also **certain** 3, **genuine** 1, **reliable** 2. — *Ant.* UNRELIABLE, unauthentic, unverified.

**official,** *n.* **1.** [Administrator] — *Syn.* comptroller, director, executive; see **administrator, leader** 2.

**2.** [A sports official] — *Syn.* referee, umpire, judge, linesman, adjudicator, ref*, ump*, chain gang*; see also **judge** 2.

**officially,** *modif.* **1.** [In an official manner] — *Syn.* regularly, formally, orderly, befittingly, fittingly, suitably, according to form, ceremoniously, in set form, precisely, according to precedent, conventionally, in an established manner, as prescribed, according to protocol, all in order, according to etiquette, correctly, properly, customarily. — *Ant.* CASUALLY, informally, unceremoniously.

**2.** [With official approval] — *Syn.* authoritatively, authorized, sanctioned; see **approved, authoritative** 2.

**officiate,** *v.* — *Syn.* govern, umpire, direct; see **command** 2, **manage** 1.

**officious,** *modif.* — *Syn.* interfering, self-important, impertinent; see **meddlesome, rude** 2.

**offprint,** *n.* — *Syn.* reprint, impression, photocopy; see **copy.**

**offscouring,** *n.* — *Syn.* refuse, rubbish, waste; see **trash** 1, 3.

**offset,** *v.* — *Syn.* balance, counterbalance, compensate, equalize, set off, requite, recompense, be equivalent, make amends, allow for, charge against, place against, equipoise, counterpoise, neutralize, counteract, countervail, equal, counterpose, negate, account, rob Peter to pay Paul*. — *Ant.* BURDEN, overbalance, overload.

**offshoot,** *n.* — *Syn.* offspring, by-product, limb; see **branch** 1, 2.

**offshore,** *modif.* — *Syn.* oceanic, in the sea, marine, foreign; see **foreign** 1, 2, **maritime** 2, **nautical.**

**offside*,** *modif.* — *Syn.* foul, faulty, not in line, not on the line; see **illegal, wrong** 1, 2, 3.

**offspring,** *n.* — *Syn.* child, children, progeny, issue, descendant, sibling, lineage, 'scion, generation, posterity, brood, seed, family, heirs, offshoot, heredity, succession, successor, next generation, chip off the old block*; see also **baby** 1, **child.**

**off to,** *modif.* — *Syn.* going, departing, leaving; see **traveling** 2.

**often,** *modif.* — *Syn.* usually, many times, oftentimes; see **frequently, regularly** 1.

**ogle,** *v.* — *Syn.* gaze, gape, stare, leer; see **look** 2.

**ogre,** *n.* — *Syn.* fiend, demon, monstrosity; see **freak** 2, **monster** 1.

**oh,** *interj.* — *Syn.* indeed! oh-oh! oh, no! oh, yes! oops*; see **no, yes.**

**oil,** *n.* **1.** [Liquid, greasy substance] — *Syn.* melted fat, unction, lubricant; see **fat, grease.**
Common oils include: vegetable, animal, mineral, fixed, fatty, volatile, essential, machine, crude, lubricating, cottonseed, olive, canola, coconut, sunflower, peanut, safflower, castor, palm, corn, whale, sperm, linseed, drying, semidrying, nondrying, polyunsaturated, monounsaturated, wormwood, candlenut, poppy-seed, soybean, sesame, cinnamon-bark, tung, cassia, vetiver, bergamot, wintergreen, cameline, palmarosa, chenopodium, ilang-ilang, cod-liver, halibut-liver, hake, fish; petroleum, kerosene, lard, tallow, oleo, oil of amber, oil of spike lavender, lanolin, turpentine.

**2.** [Liquid substance used for power or illumination] — *Syn.* petroleum, kerosene, coal oil, crude oil, liquid coal, rock oil, fossil fuel, fossil oil, cerate, liquid gold*; see also **fuel, petroleum.**

**oil,** *v.* — *Syn.* lubricate, smear, coat with oil, lube*; see **grease.**

**oilcloth,** *n.* — *Syn.* tablecloth, oilskin, waterproof, shower cloth, oil silk, linoleum, rubberized cloth, tarpaulin; see also **cloth.**

**oily,** *modif.* **1.** [Rich with oil] — *Syn.* oleaginous, fatty, greasy, buttery, oil-soaked, rich, adipose, pinguid, lardy, bland, soapy, soothing, creamy, oil-bearing, oil-rich, saponaceous, petroliferous. — *Ant.* DRY, dried, gritty.

**2.** [Having a surface suggestive of oil] — *Syn.* oiled, waxy, sleek, slippery, smooth, polished, lustrous, bright, brilliant, gleaming, glistening, shining, smeary; see also **smooth.** — *Ant.* ROUGH, dull, unpolished.

**3.** [Unctuous] — *Syn.* fulsome, supple, suave, compliant, insinuating, flattering, cajoling, coaxing, ingratiating, glib, smooth-tongued, smooth, gushing, smarmy*; see also **affected** 2. — *Ant.* FRANK, candid, brusque.

**ointment,** *n.* — *Syn.* unguent, lotion, cream; see **balm** 2, **medicine** 2, **salve.**

**O.K.,** *interj.* — *Syn.* all right, correct, surely; see **yes.**

**O.K.,** *n.* — *Syn.* approval, endorsement, affirmation; see **permission.**

**O.K.,** *v.* — *Syn.* confirm, condone, notarize; see **approve** 1, **endorse** 2.

**old,** *modif.* **1.** [No longer vigorous] — *Syn.* aged, elderly, patriarchal, superannuated, gray, grizzled, venerable, hoary, not young, of long life, past one's prime, far advanced in years, matured, having lived long, full of years, seasoned, debilitated, infirm, inactive, deficient, enfeebled, decrepit, exhausted, tired, impaired, anemic, broken down, wasted, doddering, senile, on the shelf*, ancient*, gone to seed*, with one foot in the grave*. — *Ant.* YOUNG, fresh, youthful.

**2.** [Worn] — *Syn.* time-worn, worn-out, thin, patched, ragged, faded, used, in holes, rubbed off, mended, broken-down, fallen to pieces, tumbled down, fallen in, given way, long used, out of use, rusted, crumbled, past usefulness, dilapidated, weather-beaten, ramshackle, battered, shattered, shabby, castoff, decayed, antiquated, decaying, stale, useless, tattered, in rags, torn, moth-eaten; see also sense 1, **worn** 2. — *Ant.* FRESH, new, unused.

**3.** [Ancient] — *Syn.* ancient, archaic, antique, time-honored, prehistoric, bygone, early, forgotten, age-old, immemorial, antediluvian, olden, remote, past, distant, former, of old, of yore, gone by, long ago, classical, medieval, out of the dim past, primordial, primeval, pristine, belonging to antiquity, timeless, dateless, unrecorded, handed down, long-standing, venerable, hoary, old-time, of earliest time, of the old order, ancestral, traditional, primitive, atavistic, time out of mind, trogloditic, before the Flood, Noachian, pre-Adamite, old as time, old as the hills*; see also senses 1, 2, **old-fashioned.** — *Ant.* MODERN, recent, late.

**4.** [Cherished] — *Syn.* good, dear, adored; see **beloved.**

**5.** [*Wonderful] — *Syn.* great, magnificent, superb; see **excellent.**

**6.** [Grown up] — *Syn.* adult, of age, of legal age, grown; see **experienced, mature** 1.

**7.** [Out-of-date] — *Syn.* antiquated, obsolete, outmoded; see **old-fashioned.**

---

*SYN.* — **old** implies having been in existence or use for a relatively long time [an *old* civilization, *old* shoes]; **ancient** implies reference to the remote past, often specif. the time of the early history of the world before the end of the Roman Empire (A.D. 476) [*ancient* history]; **antique** is applied to that which dates from ancient times, or, more commonly, from a former period [*antique* furniture]; **antiquated** is used to describe that which has become old-fashioned or outdated [*antiquated* notions of decorum]; **archaic** applies to something marked by the characteristics of an earlier period [*thou* is an *archaic* form of *you*]; **obsolete** is applied to that which has fallen into disuse, is out-of-date, or has been superseded [*obsolete* weapons]

---

**old age,** *n.* — *Syn.* seniority, dotage, infirmity; see **age** 2, **senility.**

**Old English,** *modif.* — *Syn.* Anglo-Saxon, early English, Anglian, Alfredian; see **Anglo-Saxon.**

**older,** *modif.* — *Syn.* elder, senior, sooner, former, preceding, of the greater age, prior, more aged, less young, not so new, earlier, first, first-born, having come before, more antique, more antiquated, more ancient, lower, of an earlier time, of an earlier vintage, of a former period; see also **old** 3. — *Ant.* YOUNG, newer, of a later vintage.

**oldest,** *modif.* — *Syn.* most aged, initial, earliest, primeval; see **first** 1, **original** 1.

**old-fashioned,** *modif.* — *Syn.* antiquated, out-of-date, dated, obsolete, obsolescent, outmoded, demoded, unfashionable, traditional, unstylish, passé, démodé (French), Victorian, not modern, old-time, unaccepted, disapproved, time-honored, not current, antique, ancient, no longer prevailing, bygone, disused, archaic, grown old, superannuated, antediluvian, Neanderthal, primitive, quaint, amusing, odd, neglected, outworn, dowdy, musty, unused, of great age, of the old times, past, oldfangled, behind the times, exploded, gone by, of the old school, extinct, out, gone out, out of it, Model-T*, out of the swim*, back number*, old hat*, mossbacked*, moss-grown*, mossy*, fossilized*, olden*; see also **old** 3. — *Ant.* MODERN, fashionable, stylish.

**old hand,** *n.* — *Syn.* old-timer, master, one of the old guard*; see **veteran** 1.

**old lady*,** *n.* — *Syn.* wife, female parent, female spouse, woman, girlfriend, lover, female member of the family; see also **mother** 1, **parent, wife.**

**old man*,** *n.* **1.** [Father *or* husband] — *Syn.* head of the house, male parent, male spouse, boyfriend, lover, man; see also **father** 1, **husband, parent.**

**2.** [An affectionate address] — *Syn.* my friend, old boy, old chap, old fellow, old bean, buddy; see also **friend** 1.

**Old Nick,** *n.* — *Syn.* Satan, Prince of Darkness, Evil One; see **devil** 1.

**oldster*,** *n.* — *Syn.* senior citizen, old man, old woman, old lady, veteran, patriarch, dowager, golden-ager, senior adult, retired man, retired woman, old duffer*, old codger*, geezer*, old coot*, old goat*, old bag*, no spring chicken*; see also **grandfather, grandmother.**

**Old Testament,** *n.* — *Syn.* the Covenant, Hebrew Scripture, Jewish Law, Mosaic Law, Pentateuch, the Five Books, Hexateuch, Heptateuch, the Law, the Torah, the Prophets, Neviim, Hagiographa, Ketubim, Apocrypha; see also **Bible** 2.

Books of the Old Testament include: Genesis, Exodus, Leviticus, Numbers, Deuteronomy; Joshua, Judges, Samuel I, Samuel II, Kings I, Kings II, Isaiah, Jeremiah, Ezekiel, Hosea, Joel, Amos, Obadiah, Jonah, Micah, Nahum, Habakkuk, Zephaniah, Haggai, Zechariah, Malachi, Psalms, Proverbs, Job, Song of Songs, Song of Solomon, Ruth, Lamentations, Ecclesiastes, Esther, Daniel, Ezra, Nehemiah, Chronicles I, Chronicles II, Tobit, Judith, Maccabees I, Maccabees II, Sirach, Ecclesiasticus.

**old-time,** *modif.* — *Syn.* outmoded, ancient, obsolete; see **old-fashioned.**

**old-world,** *modif.* — *Syn.* Hellenic, archaic, traditional, European; see **ancient** 2, **classical** 2.

**Old World,** *n.* — *Syn.* Europe; Eastern Hemisphere; Europe, Asia, and Africa; Eurasia, the cradle of civilization, the Hither-East, the Fertile Crescent; see also **East** 2, **Europe.**

**oleaginous,** *modif.* — *Syn.* suety, greasy, adipose; see **fatty, oily** 1.

**oligarchy,** *n.* — *Syn.* theocracy, thearchy, diarchy, triarchy, duarchy, duumvirate, triumvirate, regency, gerontocracy, aristocracy; see also **government** 2.

**olive,** *modif.* — *Syn.* greenish yellow, blackish green, yellowish green, olive-drab, khaki; see also **drab** 2, **green,** *n.*

**olive,** *n.* — *Syn.* stuffed olive, pitted olive, ripe olive, black olive, green olive; see also **fruit** 1.

**Olympics,** *n.* — *Syn.* Olympic Games, world championships, international amateur athletic competition; see **competition** 2, **sport** 3.

Modern winter Olympic competitions include— *alpine skiing:* downhill, slalom, giant slalom, super giant slalom, combined; *freestyle skiing:* moguls, aerials; Nordic skiing; Nordic combined; ski jumping, biathlon; bobsledding; luge; figure skating; ice dancing; speed skating; short-track speed skating; ice hockey.

Modern summer Olympic competitions include: track, marathon, hurdles, steeplechase, walk, relay, high jump, long jump, triple jump, pole vault, shot put, discus throw, javelin throw, hammer throw, heptathlon (women), decathlon (men); modern pentathlon; swimming, freestyle, backstroke, breaststroke, butterfly, individual medley, freestyle relay, medley relay; springboard diving, platform diving; synchronized swimming; gymnastics, rhythmic gymnastics; boxing; freestyle wrestling, Greco-Roman wrestling; judo; fencing; weightlifting; shooting, archery; tennis, table tennis; badminton; basketball; baseball, soccer, field hockey; volleyball; team handball; water polo; canoe/kayak, kayak; rowing; yachting; equestrian; cycling.

**Olympus,** *n.* — *Syn.* Mount Olympus, abode of the gods, home of the Olympians; see **heaven** 2.

**omelet,** *n.* — *Syn.* omelette, fried egg, scrambled egg, soufflé; see **egg, food.**

Kinds of omelet include: plain, jelly, ham, cheese, spinach, parsley, mushroom, vegetable, Spanish, Denver, chicken-liver, western, frittata.

**omen,** *n.* — *Syn.* portent, augury, indication; see **sign** 1.

**ominous,** *modif.* — *Syn.* foreboding, portentous, threatening, forbidding, fateful, baleful, menacing, sinister, dark, black, lowering, suggestive, ever-threatening, premonitory, dire, direful, ill-omened, grim, gloomy, haunting, perilous, ill-starred, ill-fated, impending, looming, fearful, clouded, unpropitious, inauspicious, unlucky, forewarning, foreshadowing, presaging, prophetic, of evil portent, apocalyptic; see also **dangerous** 2, **dismal** 1, **doomed, frightful** 1, **oracular** 2, **sinister.** — *Ant.* FAVORABLE, encouraging, auspicious.

---

*SYN.* — **ominous** implies a threatening character but does not necessarily connote a disastrous outcome /the request was met by an *ominous* silence/; **portentous** may imply a foreshadowing, esp. of evil, but is now more often used of that which arouses awe or amazement because of its prodigious or marvelous character /a *portentous* event/; **fateful** may imply a fatal character or control by fate, but is now usually applied to that which is of momentous or decisive significance /a *fateful* decision/; **foreboding** implies a portent or presentiment of something evil or harmful /a *foreboding* anxiety/

---

**omission,** *n.* 1. [The act of omitting] — *Syn.* exclusion, overlooking, missing, leaving out, withholding, disregard, oversight, ignoring, failing to mention, neglect, not inserting, not naming, preclusion, prohibition, elision, breach, cancellation, repudiation, elimination, cutting out, excluding, passing over, slighting; see also **carelessness, exclusion, neglect** 1. — *Ant.* INCLUSION, mentioning, inserting.
2. [Something omitted] — *Syn.* need, want, imperfection; see **lack** 2.
**omit,** *v.* 1. [To fail to include] — *Syn.* leave out, except, reject, preclude, repudiate, prohibit, exclude, pass over, pass by, count out, cast aside, delete, drop, cut out, cancel, void, withhold; see also **bar** 2, **discard, dismiss** 1, **eliminate** 1. — *Ant.* INCLUDE, accept, put in.
2. [To neglect] — *Syn.* ignore, slight, overlook; see **disregard, neglect** 2.
*See Synonym Study at* NEGLECT.
**omitted,** *modif.* — *Syn.* left out, overlooked, neglected, missing, wanting, slighted, unmentioned, unnamed, not included, uninserted, absent, not present, unnoted, unnoticed, voided, lacking, ignored, withheld, excluded, disregarded, passed over, passed by, counted out, excepted, repudiated, barred, rejected, canceled, cut out, excised, deleted, dropped, precluded, prohibited, kept out; see also **missed** 1, **neglected.** — *Ant.* INCLUDED, present, mentioned.
**omitting,** *modif.* — *Syn.* leaving out, missing, failing to mention, not naming, not including, not inserting, discarding, withholding, ignoring, neglecting, repudiating, passing over, passing by, excluding, slighting, disregarding, excepting, canceling, casting aside, prohibiting, precluding; see also **overlooking** 2. — *Ant.* INCLUDING, mentioning, inserting.
**omitting,** *n.* — *Syn.* neglecting, ignoring, excluding; see **omission** 1.
**omnibus,** *n.* 1. [Anthology] — *Syn.* miscellany, treasury, compilation, selection; see **collection** 2.
2. [Vehicle] — *Syn.* bus, motorcoach, tram, streetcar; see **bus.**
**omnipotence,** *n.* — *Syn.* supremacy, mastery, authority, control; see **dominion** 1, **power** 2.
**omnipotent,** *modif.* — *Syn.* all-powerful, unlimited in power, godlike; see **almighty** 2.
**omnipresent,** *modif.* — *Syn.* infinite, everywhere, ubiquitous; see **almighty** 2.
**omniscient,** *modif.* — *Syn.* infinite, pre-eminent, all-knowing; see **almighty** 2.
**omnivorous,** *modif.* — *Syn.* rapacious, voracious,

gluttonous; see **greedy** 1, 2.
**on,** *modif.* and *prep.* 1. [Upon] — *Syn.* above, in contact with, touching, supported by, situated upon, resting upon, on top of, about, held by, moving across, moving over, covering; see also **upon** 1. — *Ant.* UNDER, underneath, below.
2. [Against] — *Syn.* in contact with, close to, leaning on; see **against** 2, **next** 2.
3. [Toward] — *Syn.* proceeding, at, moving; see **approaching, toward.**
4. [Forward] — *Syn.* onward, ahead, advancing; see **forward** 1.
5. [Near] — *Syn.* beside, close to, adjacent to; see **bordering, near** 1.
**and so on** — *Syn.* and so forth, also, in addition; see **et cetera.**
**have something on someone★** — *Syn.* know something, have proof, be able to discredit; see **expose** 1.
**on again, off again★,** *modif.* — *Syn.* intermittent, intermittently, sometimes, occasionally; see **varying.**
**on and off,** *modif.* — *Syn.* now and then, intermittently, sometimes, infrequently; see **seldom.**
**once,** *modif.* 1. [One time] — *Syn.* this time, but once, once only, one time before, already, one, just this once, for the nonce, not more than once, never again, a single time, one time previously, on one occasion, only one time. — *Ant.* TWICE, many times, frequently.
2. [Formerly] — *Syn.* long ago, previously, earlier; see **formerly.**
**at once,** 1. [Immediately] — *Syn.* now, quickly, this moment; see **immediately.**
2. [Simultaneously] — *Syn.* all at once, at the same time, concurrently; see **together** 2.
**for once** — *Syn.* for at least one time, once only, uniquely; see **once** 1.
**once and for all★,** *modif.* — *Syn.* with finality, permanently, unalterably; see **finally** 1.
**once in a while,** *modif.* — *Syn.* sometimes, occasionally, on occasion; see **seldom.**
**once more,** *modif.* — *Syn.* again, once again, another time, over; see **again.**
**once or twice,** *modif.* — *Syn.* a few times, infrequently, not much; see **seldom.**
**once-over★,** *n.* — *Syn.* look, inspection, checkup; see **examination** 1.
**once over lightly★,** *modif.* — *Syn.* hastily, sketchily, with a lick and a promise★; see **lightly** 1, **quickly** 1.
**once upon a time,** *modif.* — *Syn.* formerly, in the olden days, long ago, in ancient times; see **formerly.**
**oncoming,** *modif.* — *Syn.* impending, expected, imminent; see **approaching.**
**one,** *modif.* 1. [Single] — *Syn.* individual, peculiar, especial, specific, separate, single, lone, singular, odd, one and only, solitary, singular, precise, definite, sole, uncommon; see also **different** 1, 2, **special** 1, **unique** 1, **unusual** 2.
2. [Unified] — *Syn.* united, bound, entire, complete; see **unified, united, whole** 1, 2. — *Ant.* COMMON, several, imprecise.
**one,** *n.* 1. [A single item] — *Syn.* unit, 1, whole, person, thing, identity, ace, integer, item, example, digit, singleness, individual, individuality, individuation. — *Ant.* plural, MANY, several.
2. [The quality of being united] — *Syn.* unitedness, totality, entirety; see **unity** 1.
**all one** — *Syn.* making no difference, insignificant, of no importance; see **unimportant.**
**at one** — *Syn.* in accord, agreeing, of the same opinion; see **united.**

**one another,** *pron.* — *Syn.* each other, reciprocally, each to the other; see **each.**

**one-horse\*,** *modif.* — *Syn.* small, inadequate, junky\*; see **little** 1, **poor** 2.

**one-man,** *modif.* — *Syn.* small, limited, restricted; see **little** 1, **single** 5.

**one man, one vote,** *modif.* — *Syn.* by direct representation, constitutional, representative; see **democratic.**

**oneness,** *n.* — *Syn.* integrity, harmony, indivisibility; see **unity** 1.

**onerous,** *modif.* — *Syn.* oppressive, burdensome, heavy, serious, exacting, demanding, galling, troublesome, formidable, grinding, laborious, strenuous, tedious, tiresome, hard, embittering, arduous, plodding, backbreaking, grueling, toilsome, cumbersome, weighty, ponderous, responsible, rigorous, severe, vexatious, harsh, painful, overpowering, crushing, excessive, merciless, overtaxing, taxing, fatiguing, pressing, tiring, exhausting, intolerable, austere, causing care, irksome, distressing, grievous, heartbreaking, afflictive; see also **difficult** 1, 2. — *Ant.* EASY, light, trifling.

---

*SYN.* — **onerous** applies to that which is laborious or troublesome, often because of its annoying or tedious character */the onerous task of taking inventory/;* **burdensome** applies to that which is wearisome or oppressive to the mind or spirit as well as to the body *[burdensome responsibilities];* **oppressive** suggests a hardship that weighs heavily on the mind, spirits, or senses, or stresses the overbearing cruelty of the person or thing that inflicts the hardship *[oppressive weather, an oppressive king];* **exacting** suggests the making of great demands on the attention, skill, care, etc. *[an exacting supervisor, exacting work]*

---

**one-shot\*,** *modif.* — *Syn.* singular, unique, not repeatable; see **once** 1, **single** 5.

**one-sided,** *modif.* 1. [Unilateral] — *Syn.* single, uneven, partial; see **irregular** 4, **unilateral.**

2. [Prejudiced] — *Syn.* biased, partial, narrow-minded; see **prejudiced, unfair** 1.

**onetime,** *modif.* — *Syn.* prior, former, previous; see **former, past** 1.

**one-to-one,** *modif.* — *Syn.* made even, in accord, coordinated; see **balanced** 1.

**one-way,** *modif.* — *Syn.* directional, one-sided, unilateral, restricted; see **directed, narrow** 1.

**one with,** *modif.* — *Syn.* like, similar to, in accord with, following; see **alike** 1, 2.

**ongoing,** *modif.* — *Syn.* open-ended, continuous, in process; see **continuing.**

**onlooker,** *n.* — *Syn.* eyewitness, sightseer, spectator; see **observer** 1.

**only,** *modif.* 1. [Solely] — *Syn.* exclusively, uniquely, wholly, entirely, severally, particularly, alone, and no other, and no more, and nothing else, undividedly, nothing but, totally, utterly, first and last, one and only; see also **individually, singly.**

2. [Merely] — *Syn.* just, simply, plainly, barely, solely; see also **hardly.**

3. [Sole] — *Syn.* single, without another, companionless, by oneself, isolated, apart, unaccompanied, exclusive, unique, unclassified; see also **alone** 1, **solitary.**

**onomatopoeia,** *n.* — *Syn.* imitation of sounds, echo, mimesis; see **figure of speech.**

**on or about,** *prep.* — *Syn.* at about, approximately, in the vicinity of; see **at** 1.

**on or before,** *prep.* — *Syn.* at about the time of, prior to, in anticipation of; see **before.**

**onrush,** *n.* — *Syn.* rush, assault, surge; see **attack** 1.

**onset,** *n.* 1. [An attack] — *Syn.* rush, assault, encounter; see **attack** 1.

2. [A beginning] — *Syn.* start, incipience, opening, start; see **origin** 1.

**onshore,** *modif.* — *Syn.* coastal, aground, inland, toward shore; see **ashore**

**onslaught,** *n.* — *Syn.* assault, invasion, onrush, barrage; see **attack** 1.

**onto,** *modif. & prep.* 1. [To] — *Syn.* toward, in contact with, adjacent; see **against** 1.

2. [Upon] — *Syn.* on, over, out upon, above; see **upon** 1.

**ontology,** *n.* — *Syn.* philosophy of existence, the nature of being, cosmology; see **metaphysics, philosophy.**

**onward,** *modif.* — *Syn.* onwards, on ahead, beyond, in front of; see **forward** 1, **moving** 1.

**onward and upward\*,** *modif.* — *Syn.* getting better, profiting, going ahead; see **improving** 1, **rising.**

**oodles\*,** *n.* — *Syn.* mass, heap, abundance, lots\*; see **much.**

**oops\*,** *interj.* — *Syn.* sorry, I beg your pardon, excuse me; see **exclamation.**

**ooze,** *n.* — *Syn.* slime, fluid, mire; see **mud.**

**ooze,** *v.* — *Syn.* seep, exude, leak, leach; see **flow** 2.

**oozy,** *modif.* — *Syn.* muddy, sloppy, slimy; see **wet** 1.

**opacity,** *n.* — *Syn.* cloudiness, obscurity, murkiness; see **darkness** 1.

**opal,** *n.* — *Syn.* silica, semiprecious stone, opaline; see **gem** 1, **jewel** 1.

Types of opals include: fire, precious, noble, harlequin, black, common, resin, pitch, wood, cacholong, girasol, hyalite, geyserite, menilite.

**opalescent,** *modif.* — *Syn.* prismatic, rainbow-colored, pearly, polychromatic; see **bright** 1, 2, **iridescent.**

**opaque,** *modif.* 1. [Impervious to light] — *Syn.* nontransparent, dim, dusky, darkened, darkling, murky, gloomy, lusterless, smoky, thick, misty, cloudy, clouded, shady, turbid, muddy, dull, blurred, frosty, filmy, foggy, sooty, dirty, dusty, fuliginous, nubilous, nontranslucent, absorbing light, coated over, covered; see also **dark** 1, **hazy** 1. — *Ant.* CLEAR, transparent, translucent.

2. [Relatively impervious to understanding] — *Syn.* concealed, enigmatic, perplexing; see **obscure** 1, **vague** 2.

**op art,** *n.* — *Syn.* optical illusion, abstraction, distortion; see **art** 2, **painting** 1, **sculpture.**

**open,** *modif.* 1. [Not closed] — *Syn.* unclosed, accessible, clear, open to view, uncovered, disclosed, divulged, introduced, initiated, inaugurated, begun, full-blown, unfurled, susceptible, ajar, agape, gaping, yawning, wide, rent, torn, spacious, broad gauge, unshut, expansive, extensive, spread out, vistaed, revealed, unenclosed; see also senses 2, 4. — *Ant.* TIGHT, closed, shut.

2. [Not obstructed] — *Syn.* unlocked, unbarred, unbolted, unlatched, unblocked, unfastened, cleared, removed, made passable, unsealed, unobstructed, unoccupied, vacated, unburdened, emptied; see also sense 1. — *Ant.* TAKEN, barred, blocked.

3. [Not forbidden] — *Syn.* free, unrestricted, permitted, allowable, free of access, public, welcoming, not posted; see also **admissible, permitted.** — *Ant.* REFUSED, restricted, forbidden.

4. [Not protected] — *Syn.* unguarded, unsecluded, liable, exposed, out in the weather, uncovered, apart, fallen open, unshut, unroofed, insecure, unsafe, conspicuous, unhidden, unconcealed, subject, sensitive; see also sense 1, **unsafe.** — *Ant.* SAFE, secluded, secure.

**5.** [Not decided] — *Syn.* in question, up for discussion, debatable; see **controversial, questionable** 1, **uncertain** 2.

**6.** [Not solid] — *Syn.* airy, fretted, fretworked, openworked, intersticed, filigree; see also **penetrable.** — *Ant.* FIRM, solid, impenetrable.

**7.** [Frank] — *Syn.* plain, candid, straightforward; see **frank.**

**8.** [Obvious] — *Syn.* apparent, well-known, clear; see **obvious** 1.

*See Synonym Study at* FRANK.

**open,** *v.* **1.** [To begin] — *Syn.* start, inaugurate, initiate; see **begin** 1, 2.

**2.** [To move aside a prepared obstruction] — *Syn.* unbar, unlock, unclose, clear, admit, turn back, reopen, open the lock, lift the latch, free, loosen, disengage, throw open, lay open, swing wide, unfasten, undo, unbolt, throw back the bolt, turn the key, turn the knob. — *Ant.* CLOSE, shut, lock.

**3.** [To make an opening] — *Syn.* force an entrance, breach, make an aperture, cut in, tear down, push in, shatter, destroy, burst in, break open, cave in, burst out from, penetrate, cleave, pierce, force one's way into, smash, prick, punch a hole into, slit, puncture, crack, muscle in*, jimmy*; see also **force** 2, **remove** 1. — *Ant.* REPAIR, seal, mend.

**4.** [To make available] — *Syn.* make accessible, put on sale, put on view, open to the public, make public, put forward, free, make obtainable, make usable, prepare, present, make convenient, make ready. — *Ant.* REMOVE, put away, lock up.

**5.** [To begin business] — *Syn.* open for business, hang out one's shingle, receive business, go into business, set up shop, get to work.

**6.** [To expose to fuller view] — *Syn.* unroll, unfold, uncover; see **expose** 1, **reveal** 1.

**open-air,** *modif.* — *Syn.* spacious, outside, outdoor, outdoors; see **airy** 1.

**open-door,** *modif.* — *Syn.* unrestricted, unlimited, hospitable; see **free** 1, 2, 3.

**opened,** *modif.* — *Syn.* unlocked, made open, thrown open, not closed; see **free** 3, **open** 2.

**open-ended,** *modif.* — *Syn.* going on, without specified limits, optional, indefinite, indeterminate; see also **continuing.**

**open-eyed,** *modif.* **1.** [Amazed] — *Syn.* wide-eyed, intrigued, astounded, startled; see **surprised.**

**2.** [Watchful] — *Syn.* gazing, aware, perceptive; see **observant** 2, **watching.**

**open fire,** *v.* — *Syn.* start, blast, explode; see **begin, shoot** 1.

**openhanded,** *modif.* — *Syn.* benevolent, charitable, altruistic; see **generous** 1, **kind.**

**openhandedly,** *modif.* — *Syn.* freely, unstintingly, lavishly; see **generously** 1.

**openhearted,** *modif.* — *Syn.* true, good, candid, kindhearted, benevolent; see also **frank, honest** 1, **kind.**

**open house,** *n.* **1.** [Party] — *Syn.* reception, informal gathering, entertainment, big party, celebration; see also **party** 1.

**2.** [Inspection] — *Syn.* viewing, observation, walk-in inspection, tour; see **examination** 1.

**open housing,** *n.* — *Syn.* selling without regard to race, creed, or color; unrestricted rentals, fair housing, integrated neighborhood, integration, housing available to anyone, civil rights; see also **choice** 1, **freedom** 1, **liberty** 4, **union** 1.

**opening,** *modif.* — *Syn.* initial, beginning, primary; see **first** 1.

**opening,** *n.* **1.** [A hole] — *Syn.* break, crack, tear; see **hole** 1, 2.

**2.** [An opportunity] — *Syn.* chance, availability, occasion; see **opportunity** 1, **possibility** 2.

**openly,** *modif.* **1.** [Frankly] — *Syn.* naturally, simply, artlessly, naively, ingenuously, unsophisticatedly, out in the open, candidly, aboveboard, forthrightly, straightforwardly, honestly, unreservedly, fully, readily, willingly, without restraint, plainly, undisguisedly, unabashedly, unhesitatingly, without reserve, to one's face, in public, straight from the shoulder*, face to face*, in the marketplace*; see also **sincerely.** — *Ant.* SECRETLY, furtively, surreptitiously.

**2.** [Shamelessly] — *Syn.* immodestly, unblushingly, brazenly, not caring, regardlessly, insensibly, unconcernedly, crassly, arrantly, brassily, insolvently, flagrantly, wantonly, notoriously, without pretense, in defiance of the law; see also **carelessly, lewdly.** — *Ant.* CAREFULLY, prudently, discreetly.

**open-minded,** *modif.* — *Syn.* tolerant, fair-minded, receptive, just; see **fair** 1, **liberal** 2.

**open-mouthed,** *modif.* — *Syn.* astonished, amazed, aghast; see **surprised.**

**open out,** *v.* — *Syn.* fan out, diverge, enlarge; see **grow** 1, **spread** 2.

**open sea,** *n.* — *Syn.* high seas, the briny deep, the deep, the waves; see **ocean.**

**open season*,** *n.* — *Syn.* license to kill, unrestricted hostility, freedom to criticize, freedom to denounce; see **objection** 1.

**open sesame*,** *n.* — *Syn.* means of admission, code, sign; see **key** 2, **password.**

**open shop,** *n.* — *Syn.* non-union labor, non-union employment, anti-union business, free business; see **labor** 4.

**open up,** *v.* — *Syn.* reveal, unfold, start; see **begin** 2, **grow** 1, **spread** 2.

**opera,** *n.* — *Syn.* musical drama, opera score, libretto, opera performance; see **performance** 2, **show** 1.

Kinds of operas include: grand, light, comic; *opéra bouffe, opéra comique* (*both* French), *opera buffa* (Italian), operetta.

**operate,** *v.* **1.** [To keep in operation] — *Syn.* manipulate, conduct, administer; see **command** 2, **manage** 1.

**2.** [To be in operation] — *Syn.* function, work, serve, carry on, run, revolve, act, behave, fulfill, turn, roll, spin, pump, lift, spark, explode, burn, move, progress, advance, proceed, go, contact, hit, engage, transport, convey, contain, exert, click*, tick*, percolate*; see also **perform** 1. — *Ant.* STOP, stall, break down.

**3.** [To produce an effect] — *Syn.* react, act on, influence, bring about, determine, turn, bend, contrive, work, accomplish, fulfill, finish, complete, benefit, compel, promote, concern, enforce, take effect, have effect, work on, succeed, get results*, get across*, turn the trick*; see also **achieve** 1, **produce** 1.

**4.** [To carry out a surgical procedure] — *Syn.* excise, cut, remove diseased tissue, amputate, transplant an organ, set a bone, explore, carve up*; see also **treat** 3.

**operated,** *modif.* — *Syn.* conducted, handled, run, carried on, regulated, ordered, maintained, supervised, superintended, governed, administered, wielded, transacted, performed, conveyed, transported, moved, determined, achieved, contrived, accomplished, fulfilled, promoted, enforced, worked, served, guided, executed, sustained, used, practiced, put into effect, revolved, turned, spun, finished, driven, brought about, bent, manipulated, negotiated; see also **directed, managed** 2.

**operating,** *modif.* **1.** [Causing to function] — *Syn.* managing, conducting, directing, executing, manipulating, administering, ordering, regulating, supervising, running, wielding, transacting, guiding, putting into effect, sustaining, maintaining, performing, practicing, revolving, promoting, determining, moving, turning, spinning, driving, contriving, fulfilling, accomplishing, finishing, effecting, bringing about, serving, enforcing, in operation, at work; see also **using.**
**2.** [Functioning] — *Syn.* acting, producing, going; see **running** 2, **working.**

**operating,** *n.* — *Syn.* management, direction, control; see **managing, operation** 1.

**operation,** *n.* **1.** [The act of causing to function] — *Syn.* execution, guidance, superintendence, carrying out, ordering, order, maintenance, handling, manipulating, manipulation, supervision, control, conduct, agency, compelling, promoting, enforcing, enforcement, advancement, controlling, administering, regulating, running, supervising, directing, transacting, transaction, conducting; see also **administration** 1, **regulation** 1.
**2.** [An action] — *Syn.* performance, act, employment, labor, service, carrying on, transaction, deed, doing, proceeding, handiwork, workmanship, exploitation, enterprise, movement, progression, progress, development, engagement, transference, conveyance, undertaking; see also **action** 1, **work** 2.
**3.** [A method] — *Syn.* process, formula, procedure; see **method** 2, **plan** 2.
**4.** [Surgical treatment] — *Syn.* surgery, biopsy, emergency operation, acupuncture, exploratory operation, clinical trial, section, excision, removal, vivisection, dissection, the knife*; see also **medicine** 3, **surgery, transplant.**
Common surgical operations include: appendectomy, cystectomy, hysterectomy, mastectomy, tonsillectomy, gastrectomy, hemorrhoidectomy, colostomy, lobotomy, caesarian section, plastic surgery, facelift*, dermoplasty, rhinoplasty, amputation, coronary bypass, thyroidectomy, prostatectomy, laparotomy, keratotomy, keratoplasty, tracheotomy, spinal fusion, thoracotomy.

**operative,** *modif.* — *Syn.* influential, adequate, efficient; see **effective.**

**operator,** *n.* **1.** [One who operates a machine] — *Syn.* engineer, driver, operative, operant, skilled employee, trained employee; see also **laborer, worker.**
Kinds of operators include: telephone, switchboard, PBX, long-distance, international, elevator, heavy equipment.
**2.** [One who operates workable property] — *Syn.* executive, supervisor, director; see **administrator.**
**3.** [*Manipulator] — *Syn.* speculator, scoundrel, fraud; see **rascal.**

**ophthalmologist,** *n.* — *Syn.* eye doctor, eye specialist, optic surgeon, oculist; see **doctor** 1.

**opiate,** *n.* **1.** [Anything that pacifies] — *Syn.* pacifier, sedative, anodyne; see **tranquilizer** 2.
**2.** [A pacifying drug] — *Syn.* morphine, codeine, opium derivative; see **drug** 2, **medicine** 2, **opium.**

**opinion,** *n.* **1.** [A belief] — *Syn.* belief, notion, view, viewpoint, sentiment, conviction, persuasion, conception, idea, surmise, impression, inference, conjecture, inclination, feeling, fancy, imagining, supposition, suspicion, notion, assumption, guess, theory, thesis, theorem, postulate, hypothesis, point of view, presumption, presupposition, mind; see also **belief** 1, **viewpoint.**

**2.** [A considered judgment] — *Syn.* estimation, appraisal, evaluation, conclusion; see **judgment** 3, **verdict.**

**SYN.** — **opinion** applies to a conclusion or judgment which, while it remains open to dispute, seems true or probable to one's own mind /it's my *opinion* that he'll agree/; **belief** refers to the mental acceptance of an idea or conclusion, often a doctrine or dogma proposed to one for acceptance /religious *beliefs*/; **view** suggests an opinion affected by one's personal manner of looking at things /she gave us her *views* on life/; a **conviction** is a strong belief about whose truth one has no doubts /I have a *conviction* of your innocence/; **sentiment** (often in the plural) suggests an opinion that is the result of deliberation but is colored with emotion; **persuasion** refers to a strong belief that is unshakable because one wishes to believe in its truth

**opinionated,** *modif.* — *Syn.* bigoted, stubborn, unyielding; see **obstinate, prejudiced.**

**opium,** *n.* — *Syn.* opiate, soporific, dope*; see **drug** 2.
Derivatives of opium include: morphine, heroin, laudanum, codeine, narcotine, narceine, papaverine, thebaine, paregoric, metopon, hydromorphone, paramorphine, diamorphine, laudanidine, diacetylmorphine, cryptopine, oxydimorphine, rheadine, oxynarcotine, gnoscopine, lanthopine, laudanine, deuteropine, laudanosine, protopine, hydrocotarnine, chandu.

**opponent,** *n.* **1.** [A rival] — *Syn.* competitor, claimant, emulator, striver, contender, challenger, candidate, equal, entrant, the opposition, oppositionist, aspirant, bidder; see also **contestant.** — *Ant.* SUPPORTER, defender, abettor.
**2.** [An opposing contestant] — *Syn.* antagonist, disputant, contestant, filibusterer, litigant, learned colleague*; see also **player** 1. — *Ant.* ASSOCIATE, partner, colleague.
**3.** [An enemy] — *Syn.* enemy, foe, adversary, antagonist, combatant, assailant; see also **enemy** 1, 2.

**SYN.** — **opponent,** an unemotional word, refers to anyone who is opposed to one, as in a fight, game, contest, or debate; **antagonist** implies more active opposition, esp. in a struggle for control or power; **adversary** usually suggests actual hostility in the conflict; **enemy** may imply actual hatred in the opponent and a desire to injure, or it may simply refer to any member of the opposing group, nation, etc. in a conflict, whether or not there is personal animosity or hostility involved; **foe,** now a somewhat literary synonym for **enemy,** connotes more active hostility

**opportune,** *modif.* — *Syn.* timely, fitting, suitable, fortuitous; see **convenient** 1, **helpful** 1, **timely.**
See Synonym Study at TIMELY.

**opportunism,** *n.* — *Syn.* expediency, timeliness, exploitation, making hay while the sun shines*, striking while the iron is hot*, getting while the getting is good*; see also **advantage** 3.

**opportunist,** *n.* — *Syn.* vacillator, carpetbagger, timeserver, trimmer, ingrate, bounder, self-seeker, go-getter; see also **businessperson, politician** 3, **rascal.**

**opportunity,** *n.* **1.** [Favorable circumstances] — *Syn.* chance, occasion, suitable circumstance, juncture, opening, excuse, happening, contingency, event, befalling, probability, fitness, fortuity, good fortune, luck, hap*, fair go*, break*, even break*, shot*; see also **possibility** 2.

**2.** [A suitable time] — *Syn.* occasion, moment, time and tide; see **timeliness.**

**oppose,** *v.* **1.** [To hold a contrary opinion] — *Syn.* object, expose, disapprove, debate, dispute, contradict, argue, search out, deny, run counter to, protest, defy, cross, taunt, controvert, cope, speak against, gainsay, confront, thwart, neutralize, reverse, turn the tables, not countenance, be opposed to, oppose change, not have any part of, face down, militate against, interfere with, disapprove of, cry out against, disagree with, not conform, run against, run counter to, come in conflict with, not abide, go contrary to, part company with, frown at, not be good for, not accept, call in question, be at cross purposes, contrast with, conflict with, grapple with, doubt, be reluctant, be against, be unwilling, reject, dislike, demur, deprecate, take exception, repudiate, repugn, question, probe, resist, confound, confute, refute, stand up for the other side, cry out against★, buck★, turn thumbs down★, cry down★, swim against the stream★, have a brush with★; see also sense 2, **dare** 2, **face** 1. — *Ant.* AGREE, approve, accept.

**2.** [To fight] — *Syn.* resist, battle, encounter, confront, bombard, assault, attack, assail, storm, protest, clash, meet, skirmish, engage, contest, face, restrain, go against, match against, turn against, count against, mark against, uphold, defend, rebel, revolt, secede, mutiny, strike back, combat, run counter to, defy, snub, infringe, strive against, run against, grapple with, fight off, withstand, repel, guard, safeguard, act, shield, counterattack, struggle, outflank, antagonize, retaliate, impede, overpower, take on all comers★, scrap★, lock horns with★, go to the mat★, fly in the face of★; see also **fight** 2.

**opposed,** *modif.* — *Syn.* antagonistic to, averse, opposite, against, contrary, restrictive, hostile to, at odds, disputed, counter to, at cross-purposes, up against★, against the grain★, at the other end of the spectrum★; see also **reluctant, unwilling.**

**opposing,** *modif.* **1.** [In the act of opposition] — *Syn.* conflicting, clashing, combating, fending, objecting, disagreeing, exposing, disputing, denying, protesting, controverting, crossing, gainsaying, battling, confronting, reversing, neutralizing, facing, stemming, meeting, breasting, withstanding, repelling, defending, resisting, counteracting, outflanking, in defiance of, at variance, at cross-purposes, in disagreement with, in opposition to, at loggerheads★, at odds★, on the outs★, with daggers drawn★. — *Ant.* HELPING, agreeing, defending.

**2.** [Belonging to the opposition or constituting the opposition] — *Syn.* inimical, antonymous, hostile, adverse, antithetical, antithetic, obstructive, recalcitrant, antagonistic, conflicting, calumniating, competitive, rival, aspiring, contesting, defensive, resistive, resistant, challenging, disputative, litigative, defying, unfavorable, sinister, contradictory; see also **unfriendly.** — *Ant.* FRIENDLY, favorable, allied.

**3.** [Situated opposite] — *Syn.* contrary, facing, fronting; see **opposite** 3.

**opposing,** *n.* — *Syn.* opposition, denial, contest; see **fight** 1, **opposition** 1.

**opposite,** *modif.* **1.** [Radically different] — *Syn.* contrary, antithetical, antithetic, reverse, inverse, converse, diametric, diametrical, antonymous, contrasting, contradictory, counter, conflicting, opposed, opposing, polar, poles apart, antipodal, antipodean, incompatible, irreconcilable; see also **different** 1. — *Ant.* same, synonymous, alike.

**2.** [In conflict] — *Syn.* adverse, inimical, hostile; see **opposed, opposing** 2.

**3.** [So situated as to seem to oppose] — *Syn.* facing, fronting, in front of, across from, on different sides, on opposite sides, in opposition to, on the other side, confronting, looking out on, against, front to front, back to back, nose to nose, on the farther side, retrograde, opposing, opposed, diametrical, vis-à-vis, *en face* (French), eyeball to eyeball★. — *Ant.* MATCHED, on the same side, side by side.

**opposite,** *n.* — *Syn.* contradiction, contrary, converse, direct opposite, opposition, foil, vice versa, antithesis, antipodes, antistrophe, antonym, counter term, counterpart, inverse, reverse, adverse, the opposite pole, the other side, the other side, the opposite term, the opposite force, the opposite idea; see also **contrast** 2. — *Ant.* ALIKE, same, a related thing, a similar thing.

---

*SYN.* — **opposite** is applied to things that are symmetrically opposed in position, direction, character, etc. /they sat at *opposite* ends of the table; the *opposite* sex/; **contrary** adds to this connotations of conflict or antagonism /they hold *contrary* views/; **antithetical** implies diametrical opposition so that the contrasted things are as far apart or as different as is possible /our interests are completely *antithetical*/; **reverse** applies to that which moves or faces in the opposite direction /the *reverse* side of a fabric/; **antonymous** is used specifically of words that are so opposed in meaning that each contradicts, reverses, or negates the other /good and bad are *antonymous* terms/

---

**oppositely,** *modif.* — *Syn.* contrarily, reversely, counter, opposed, in the negative, any rather; see also **otherwise** 1.

**opposition,** *n.* **1.** [The act of opposing] — *Syn.* conflict, clash, strife, combat, contention, competition, facing, confronting, coping with, breasting, meeting, stemming, belying, struggle, encounter, buffeting, resisting, resistance, defense, counterattack, outflanking, neutralizing, hostilities, war, warfare, skirmish, brush, fray, engagement, action, withstanding, repelling, duel, trial by battle, collision, contest, overpowering, running counter to, race, handicap, check, counteraction, contradiction, debate, countervail, vying with, obstruction, thwart; see also **battle** 2, **fight** 1. — *Ant.* PEACE, cessation, surrender.

**2.** [The attitude suggestive of opposition] — *Syn.* dislike, repugnance, hostility, antagonism, defiance, objectionableness, antipathy, abhorrence, detestation, aversion, constraint, restriction, restraint, hindrance, tyranny, misrule, discord, want of harmony, incompatibility, distaste, disfavor, dissatisfaction, discontent, displeasure, irritation, offense, chagrin, humiliation, mortification, disagreement, anger, loathing, disapproval, complaint, discontentment, inconvenience; see also **hate, hatred** 1, 2, **malice, resentment.** — *Ant.* SUPPORT, enthusiasm, accord.

**3.** [The individual or group that opposes] — *Syn.* antagonist, disputant, adversary; see **enemy** 1, 2, **opponent** 1, 2.

**oppress,** *v.* — *Syn.* trouble, plague, suppress, trample, harass, wrong, worry, crush, annoy, maltreat, hinder, vex, handicap, overload, hamper, strain, encumber, press down, beat down, saddle, smother, hound, ride roughshod over, burden with, depress, dispirit, dishearten, bear hard upon, go ill with, lie on, keep under, keep down, take liberties with, put upon; see also **abuse** 1, **bother** 2.

*See Synonym Study at* WRONG.

**oppressed,** *modif.* — *Syn.* misused, downtrodden, browbeaten, enslaved, henpecked, mistreated, maltreated, burdened, taxed, hampered, like dirt, like dirt under one's feet; see also **abused.**

**oppression,** *n.* **1.** [Organized cruelty] — *Syn.* tyranny, hardness, domination, coercion, dictatorship, fascism, persecution, severity, harshness, subjugation, abusiveness, abuse, subduing, conquering, overthrowing, compulsion, force, forcibleness, torment, military control, martial law; see also **cruelty.** — *Ant.* FREEDOM, liberalism, voluntary control.
**2.** [Low spirits] — *Syn.* melancholy, weariness, worry; see **depression** 2, **grief** 1.

**oppressive,** *modif.* **1.** [Difficult to bear] — *Syn.* burdensome, onerous, harsh, tyrannical; see **autocratic** 1, **difficult** 1, **onerous, severe** 2.
**2.** [Weighing on the senses or spirits] — *Syn.* suffocating, stifling, confining, depressing; see **close** 5, **dismal** 1.
*See Synonym Study at* ONEROUS.

**oppressively,** *modif.* — *Syn.* severely, hard, restrictively; see **brutally.**

**opprobrious,** *modif.* **1.** [Expressing slander] — *Syn.* scurrilous, slanderous, abusive, insulting, libeling, defamatory, defaming, shaming, reproaching, offending, dishonoring, disgracing, pejorative, abasing, humiliating, calumniating, damaging, injuring, injurious, hurting, causing disrepute, maligning, detractive, derogative, disparaging, depreciative, debasing, denigrating, vituperative, spiteful, contumelious, reviling, malevolent, malignant, malign, despiteful; see also **embarrassing, insulting.** — *Ant.* APPRECIATIVE, praising, eulogizing.
**2.** [Involving slander] — *Syn.* hateful, infamous, disgraceful, scandalous, vulgar, vile, abusive, ignoble, contemptuous, ignominious, dishonorable, base, libelous, defamatory, odious, atrocious, detestable, malicious, abominable, nefarious, ill-willed, heinous, outrageous, shocking, flagrant, execrable; see also **offensive** 2, **shameful** 1, 2. — *Ant.* FRIENDLY, honorable, commendable.

**opprobrium,** *n.* — *Syn.* disrepute, ignominy, stigma; see **disgrace** 2, **insult** 1.

**opt (for),** *v.* — *Syn.* choose, decide, pick; see **choose** 1, **decide.**

**optic,** *modif.* — *Syn.* ocular, of the vision, optical; see **visual.**

**optical,** *modif.* — *Syn.* ocular, seeing, visible; see **visual.**

**optimism,** *n.* **1.** [Belief in the essential goodness of the universe] — *Syn.* idealism, mysticism, logical realism, philosophy of progress, belief in progress, Leibnitz's doctrine; see also **faith, idealism** 2. — *Ant.* SADNESS, pessimism, cynicism.
**2.** [An inclination to expect or to hope for the best] — *Syn.* cheerfulness, hopefulness, confidence, assurance, sanguineness, encouragement, happiness, brightness, enthusiasm, good cheer, exhilaration, buoyancy, trust, looking on the bright side, seeing through rose-colored glasses, calmness, elation, expectancy, expectation, anticipation, easiness, sureness, Pollyannaism, certainty. — *Ant.* GLOOM, despair, melancholy.

**optimist,** *n.* — *Syn.* Pollyanna, dreamer, positivist; see **idealist.**

**optimistic,** *modif.* **1.** [Inclined to hope for the best, or to expect it] — *Syn.* positive, cheerful, sanguine, assured; see **confident** 3, **hopeful** 1, **trusting** 2.
**2.** [Predicting improvement] — *Syn.* promising, cheering, encouraging; see **hopeful** 2.

**optimistically,** *modif.* — *Syn.* expectantly, encouragingly, with good hopes, with high expectations; see **favorably** 1, **hopefully** 1.

**optimum,** *modif.* — *Syn.* select, choice, maximum; see **best** 1, **excellent.**

**option,** *n.* **1.** [Something that can be chosen] — *Syn.* choice, alternative, possibility, opportunity, prospect, substitute, special feature, added feature, elective, recourse, way out, loophole.
**2.** [A privilege to purchase] — *Syn.* right, prerogative, grant, claim, lien, license, lease, franchise, advantage, security, immunity, benefit, title, prior claim, dibs*.
**3.** [The power or act of choosing] — *Syn.* choice, selection, decision; see **choice** 1, **choosing.**
*See Synonym Study at* CHOICE.

**optional,** *modif.* — *Syn.* discretionary, elective, nonobligatory, noncompulsory, free, unrestricted, arbitrary, unforced, volitional, not required, according to one's will, with no strings attached*, take it or leave it*; see also **voluntary.** — *Ant.* NECESSARY, compulsory, enforced.

**opt out,** — *Syn.* drop out, quit, reject; see **leave** 1.

**opulent,** *modif.* **1.** [Rich] — *Syn.* affluent, prosperous, wealthy, sumptuous; see **rich** 1, 2.
**2.** [Plentiful] — *Syn.* profuse, abundant, luxuriant; see **plentiful** 1, 2.
*See Synonym Study at* RICH.

**opulently,** *modif.* — *Syn.* richly, wealthily, luxuriously; see **largely** 2, **well** 2, 3.

**opus,** *n.* — *Syn.* piece, creation, product; see **literature** 2, **music** 1, **work** 3.

**or,** *conj.* **1.** [A suggestion of choice] — *Syn.* or only, or but, as an alternative, as a choice, as a substitute, on the other hand, in turn, conversely, in other words, or else, in preference to, preferentially; see also **either.** — *Ant.* NEITHER, nor, without choice.
**2.** [A suggestion of correction] — *Syn.* or not, or not exactly, in reverse, reversing it, on the contrary, contrary to, oppositely, or rather, instead of, correctly speaking; see also **instead, rather** 2.
**3.** [A suggestion of approximation] — *Syn.* roughly, about, practically; see **approximately.**

**oracle,** *n.* **1.** [A revelation] — *Syn.* commandment, edict, canon; see **law** 3.
**2.** [A prophet] — *Syn.* soothsayer, Cassandra, fortuneteller; see **prophet.**

**oracular,** *modif.* **1.** [Vague or obscure] — *Syn.* ambiguous, mysterious, cryptic; see **obscure** 1, 3, **vague** 2.
**2.** [Prophetic] — *Syn.* prescient, soothsaying, foretelling, prophesying, forecasting, predicting, presaging, foreboding, auguring, augural, precursory, portending, prognosticating, discovering, divining, foreknowing, foreseeing, clairvoyant, divulging, anticipating, apprehending, declaring, proclaiming, fatidic, occult, sibylline, vaticinal, vatic, interpretive; see also **mysterious** 2. — *Ant.* OBJECTIVE, scientific, realistic.
**3.** [Authoritative] — *Syn.* dogmatic, peremptory, imperious; see **authoritative** 2.

**oral,** *modif.* — *Syn.* spoken, vocal, verbal, uttered, voiced, lingual, unwritten, phonetic, phonic, articulated, pronounced, phonated, sounded, from the lips, from the mouth, in the mouth, not written, nuncupative, word-of-mouth, *viva voce* (Latin); see also **spoken.** — *Ant.* WRITTEN, unspoken, printed.

---

**SYN.** — **oral** refers to that which is spoken, as distinguished from that which is written or otherwise communicated [*an oral report, oral traditions*]; **verbal,** though sometimes synonymous with **oral,** in strict discrimination refers to anything using words, either written or oral, to communicate an idea or feeling [a *verbal* image, *verbal* skills]

**orally**, *modif.* — *Syn.* verbally, not written, by word of mouth; see **literally, personally** 2, **spoken.**

**orange**, *modif.* — *Syn.* reddish, ocherous, glowing; see **orange**, *n.* 1.

**orange**, *n.* 1. [Color] — *Syn.* red-yellow, apricot, tangerine, burnt orange, peach, coral, salmon; see also **red, yellow.**

2. [Fruit] — *Syn.* citrus fruit, tropical fruit, sour orange; see **food, fruit** 1.

Classes and varieties of oranges include: navel, Valencia, Temple, blood, wild, China, bitter, Seville, bergamot, mandarin, tangerine, clementine, tangelo, Ugli, Bahia, St. Michael's, egg, Bittencourt, Dom Louise, Maltese, Excelsior, Osage, Brown's white, silver, Plata, Jaffa, king, Satsuma, Florida, California.

**oration**, *n.* — *Syn.* speech, discourse, sermon, address; see **speech** 3.

*See Synonym Study at* SPEECH.

**orator**, *n.* — *Syn.* speaker, lecturer, declaimer, pleader; see **speaker** 2.

**oratorical**, *modif.* — *Syn.* rhetorical, eloquent, declamatory, bombastic, loud, noisy, stentorian, pompous, theatrical, stylistic, expressive, forceful, persuasive, fervid, vivid, elocutionary, intoning, senatorial, gesturing, gesticulative, elaborate, impassioned, lofty, noble, high-sounding, inflated, orotund, tumid, grandiloquent, dramatic, histrionic, artificial, important, stagy, imposing, ostentatious, in the grand style, Periclean; see also **fluent** 2, **verbose.** — *Ant.* NATURAL, undramatic, simple.

**oratorically**, *modif.* — *Syn.* wordily, bombastically, rhetorically; see **loudly, spoken, verbosely.**

**oratory**, *n.* — *Syn.* speech, rhetoric, eloquence, elocution; see **speech** 3.

**orb**, *n.* — *Syn.* sphere, globe, ball; see **circle** 1.

**orbit**, *n.* 1. [Path described by one body revolving around another] — *Syn.* revolution, ellipse, circle, ring, circuit, path, apogee, course, perigee, lap, round, cycle, curve, parabolic orbit, synchronous orbit, hold pattern, transfer orbit, flight path; see also **revolution** 1.

2. [Range of activity or influence] — *Syn.* sphere, arena, range, field, boundary, limit, circumference, compass, circle, bounds, department, domain, dominion, jurisdiction, precinct, province, realm; see also **area** 2.

**orbit**, *v.* 1. [To revolve around another body] — *Syn.* circle, encircle, compass, encompass, ring, move in a circuit, go around, revolve; see also **circle.**

2. [To put into orbit] — *Syn.* fire, blast off, lift off, project; see **launch** 2.

**orbited**, *modif.* — *Syn.* put into orbit, placed into orbit, lofted into orbit, sent into orbit, put up, sent up, rocketed; see also **driven, launched, sent.**

**orbiting**, *modif.* — *Syn.* circling, encircling, going around; see **revolving** 1.

**orchard**, *n.* — *Syn.* fruit trees, nut trees, fruit plantation, fruit farm, apple orchard, peach orchard; see also **farm.**

**orchestra**, *n.* — *Syn.* musical ensemble, symphony, *Kapelle* (German); see **band** 4.

Types of orchestras include: concert, symphony, philharmonic, chamber, string, dance, jazz, radio, television, studio, theater, swing, sinfonietta, jazz band.

**orchestral**, *modif.* — *Syn.* symphonic, operatic, instrumental, concert, philharmonic, scored for orchestra; see also **musical** 1.

**orchestrate**, *v.* 1. [To arrange for orchestra] — *Syn.* harmonize, score, arrange; see **arrange** 3, **compose** 3.

2. [Coordinate] — *Syn.* arrange, organize, choreograph; see **organize** 1.

**ordain**, *v.* 1. [To establish] — *Syn.* install, institute, appoint; see **enact.**

2. [To destine] — *Syn.* determine, foreordain, intend; see **predetermine.**

3. [To invest with priestly functions] — *Syn.* install, confer holy orders upon, consecrate, anoint, frock, delegate, invest; see also **bless** 3.

**ordained**, *modif.* 1. [Ordered] — *Syn.* commanded, determined, established by law, established by declaration; see **established** 2, **ordered** 2.

2. [Invested into the ministry] — *Syn.* consecrated, anointed, received into the ministry; see **graduated** 1, **named** 2.

**ordeal**, *n.* — *Syn.* tribulation, distress, calamity; see **difficulty** 1, 2, **trial** 3.

**order**, *n.* 1. [A command] — *Syn.* direction, mandate, injunction; see **command** 1, **law** 3.

2. [Sequence] — *Syn.* progression, succession, procession; see **line** 1, **sequence** 1, **series.**

3. [Orderly arrangement] — *Syn.* regulation, plan, disposition, management, establishment, method, distribution, placement, scale, rule, computation, adjustment, adaptation, ordering, ranging, standardizing, marshaling, aligning, lining up, trimming, grouping, composition, cast, assortment, disposal, scheme, form, routine, array, procedure, method, index, cosmos, regularity, uniformity, symmetry, harmony, placement, layout, line-up, setup; see also **classification** 1, **system** 1. — *Ant.* CONFUSION, disarray, displacement.

4. [Organization] — *Syn.* society, sect, company; see **organization** 3.

5. [A formal agreement to purchase] — *Syn.* engagement, reserve, application, requisition, request, stipulation, booking, arrangement; see also **buying, reservation** 1.

6. [The amount purchased in an order, sense 5] — *Syn.* amount, purchase, bulk; see **quantity, shipment.**

7. [Peace] — *Syn.* calm, quiet, peacefulness; see **peace** 1, 2.

8. [Kind] — *Syn.* hierarchy, rank, degree; see **class** 1, **classification** 1.

9. [Customary method] — *Syn.* ritual, rite, plan; see **custom** 2, **tradition** 1.

10. [Social rank] — *Syn.* station, status, position; see **rank** 3.

**by order of**— *Syn.* according to, by the authority of, under the command of; see **for.**

**call to order**— *Syn.* ask to be quiet, start a meeting, congregate; see **assemble** 1.

**in order**— *Syn.* working, efficient, operative; see **effective.**

**in order that**— *Syn.* so that, to the end that, for; see **because.**

**in order to**— *Syn.* for the purpose of, as a means to, so that; see **to** 6.

**in short order**— *Syn.* rapidly, without delay, soon; see **quickly** 1.

**on order**— *Syn.* requested, on the way, sent for; see **ordered** 1.

**on the order of**— *Syn.* approximately, roughly, similar to; see **like.**

**tall order**\*— *Syn.* a difficult task, problem, responsibility; see **difficulty** 2.

**order**, *v.* 1. [To give a command] — *Syn.* direct, command, dictate, decree; see **command** 1, **require** 2.

**2.** [To authorize a purchase] — *Syn.* secure, reserve, request, ask for, requisition; see also **buy** 1, **obtain** 1.

**3.** [To put in order] — *Syn.* arrange, furnish, regulate, establish, dispose, manage, systematize, space, methodize, file, put away, classify, codify, distribute, alphabetize, regularize, normalize, get information, pattern, formalize, settle, fix, locate, dress up, get things into proportion, sort out, index, put to rights, establish guidelines for, adjust, adapt, set in order, assign, place, regiment, trim, range, align, standardize, marshal, plan, group; see also **line** 4, **organize** 1. — *Ant.* CONFUSE, disarrange, disarray.

*See Synonym Study at* COMMAND.

**ordered,** *modif.* **1.** [On order] — *Syn.* requested, requisitioned, applied for, sent for, bespoken, spoken for, engaged, booked, arranged for, stipulated, retained, written for, telephoned for; see also **requested** 2, **reserved** 1.

**2.** [Commanded] — *Syn.* directed, ordained, charged, dictated, regulated, decreed, ruled, enjoined, bidden, imposed, authorized, proclaimed, exacted, forbidden, interdicted, required, proscribed, prescribed, announced, by order, by command, as ordered, under one's jurisdiction; see also **approved, requested** 1. — *Ant.* OMITTED, revoked, optional.

**3.** [Put in order] — *Syn.* arranged, regulated, placed; see **classified, organized.**

**ordering,** *n.* — *Syn.* regulation, organization, systemization; see **order** 3, **system** 1.

**orderly,** *modif.* **1.** [Ordered; *said of objects and places*] — *Syn.* neat, tidy, arranged; see **clean** 1, **neat** 1.

**2.** [Methodical; *said of persons*] — *Syn.* systematic, correct, formal, businesslike, systematical, exact, tidy, neat, uncluttered, shipshape, thorough, precise; see also **careful, regular** 3. — *Ant.* IRREGULAR, inaccurate, unmethodical.

**3.** [Peaceful] — *Syn.* quiet, law-abiding, well-mannered, well-behaved, restrained, nonviolent, submissive; see also **calm** 1, 2, **tranquil** 1.

**orderly,** *n.* — *Syn.* aide, steward, valet; see **attendant.**

**ordinance,** *n.* — *Syn.* law, statute, directive, mandate; see **command** 1, **law** 3.

*See Synonym Study at* LAW.

**ordinarily,** *modif.* — *Syn.* usually, generally, habitually; see **customarily, frequently, regularly** 1.

**ordinary,** *modif.* **1.** [In accordance with a regular or customary pattern] — *Syn.* customary, normal, usual, everyday; see **common** 1, **conventional** 1, **frequent, habitual** 1, **regular** 3.

**2.** [Lacking distinction] — *Syn.* average, mediocre, undistinguished; see **common** 1, **dull** 4, **fair** 2.

*See Synonym Study at* COMMON.

**out of the ordinary** — *Syn.* extraordinary, uncommon, special; see **unusual** 2.

**ordination,** *n.* **1.** [An installation] — *Syn.* consecration, coronation, investiture; see **installation** 1.

**2.** [A system] — *Syn.* plan, classification, organization; see **order** 3, **system** 1.

**ordnance,** *n.* — *Syn.* arms, military weapons, cannon, artillery; see **ammunition.**

**ore,** *n.* — *Syn.* mineral, metal, metalliferous earth, unrefined earth, unrefined rock, ore bed, parent rock, native mineral, matrix; see also **mineral.**

**organ,** *n.* **1.** [An instrument] — *Syn.* medium, means, way; see **device** 1, **tool** 1.

**2.** [A part of an organism having a specialized use] — *Syn.* vital part, vital structure, functional division, process; see **gland.**

Human organs include: brain, heart, eye, ear, nose, tongue, lung, kidney, stomach, intestine, spleen, pancreas, gallbladder, liver, testis, uterus, ovary, fallopian tube, bladder, penis.

**3.** [A musical instrument] — *Syn.* wind instrument, keyboard instrument, harmonium, melodeon, calliope, hurdy-gurdy, accordion; see also **musical instrument.** Types of organs include: great, swell, choir, orchestral, solo, pipe, echo, pedal, altar, chancel, antiphonal, gallery, floating, barrel, reed, electric, electronic, hand, grind, street.

**4.** [A periodical] — *Syn.* journal, newsletter, newspaper, publication, rag*; see also **journal** 2.

**organic,** *modif.* **1.** [Living] — *Syn.* animate, alive, live, biotic, plasmic, protoplasmic, cellular, nuclear, amoebic, amoeboid, vacuolated, vacuolar; see also **alive** 1.

**2.** [Structural] — *Syn.* constitutional, anatomical, fundamental, vital, radical, necessary, essential, inherent, elemental, basic, primary, basal, important, original, initial, principal, prime, primitive; see also **fundamental** 1, **important** 2, **structural.**

**3.** [Organized] — *Syn.* systematic, systemic, coordinated; see **organized, regular** 3.

**4.** [Naturally grown] — *Syn.* natural, nonchemical, without additives, unadulterated; see **pure** 1.

**organically,** *modif.* — *Syn.* by nature, inevitably, wholly; see **essentially, naturally** 2.

**organism,** *n.* — *Syn.* person, organic structure, bion, morphon, physiological individual, morphological individual; see **animal** 1, **body** 1, **plant.**

**organist,** *n.* — *Syn.* instrumentalist, keyboardist, organ-player; see **musician.**

**organization,** *n.* **1.** [The process of organizing] — *Syn.* establishment, formulation, schematization, plan, planning, disposition, ordering, creation, molding, grouping, projection, design, provision, working out, assembling, construction, deliberation, institution, foundation, preparation, rehearsal, direction, structure, situation, formation, association; see also **classification** 1. — *Ant.* CONFUSION, confounding, disintegration.

**2.** [The manner of organizing] — *Syn.* regulation, systematization, system, method, methodizing, coordination, adjustment, harmony, unity, correlation, standard, standardization, settlement, arrangement, disposition, classification, alignment, group, symmetry, uniformity; see also **order** 3. — *Ant.* CONFUSION, bedlam, chance.

**3.** [An organized body] — *Syn.* aggregation, association, federation, combine, corporation, union, institute, trust, cartel, confederation, monopoly, combination, machine, business, industry, company, society, league, club, fraternity, house, order, alliance, party, cooperative, guild, profession, trade, coalition, syndicate, fellowship, lodge, brotherhood, concord, confederacy, affiliation, body, band, sodality, sorority, team, squad, crew, clique, circle, set, coterie, troupe, group.

**organize,** *v.* **1.** [To put in order] — *Syn.* arrange, compose, combine, systematize, methodize, coordinate, adjust, synthesize, dispose, put in order, line up, regulate, harmonize, range, adapt, settle, fit, straighten, reorganize, correlate, standardize, whip into shape*, fall into*, keep in line*; see also **classify, order** 3. — *Ant.* UPSET, disarrange, disturb.

**2.** [To form an organization] — *Syn.* establish, constitute, prepare, scheme, formulate, lay out, form, create, mold, fashion, project, design, build, found, authorize, raise, appoint, fix, secure, instate, erect, assemble, make, direct, construct, institute; see also **plan** 2. — *Ant.* DESTROY, eradicate, break down.

**organized,** *modif.* — *Syn.* established, methodized, coordinated, systematized, systematic, constituted, directed, adjusted, assigned, distributed, grouped, fixed up, standardized, in place, in order, in turn, in succession, in good form, placed, put away, orderly, in series, in sequence, arranged, prepared, made ready, regimented, constructed, synthesized, settled, composed, marshaled, framed, planned, schematized, ranked, put in order, ordered, regulated, ranged, disposed, formulated, formed, fashioned, shaped, made, projected, designed, harmonized, related, interrelated, correlated, oriented, founded, associated; see also **classified.** — *Ant.* SHAPELESS, unplanned, formless.

**organizing,** *n.* — *Syn.* coordination, systemization, formation; see **organization** 1.

**orgy,** *n.* — *Syn.* revelry, debauch, revel, spree, feast, bout, debauchery, bacchanal, bacchanalia, saturnalia, carousal, dissipation, group grope★, fling★, nude-in★, be-in★, bash★, bust★, jag★, binge★, bender, hellbender★; see also **celebration** 2, **indulgence** 3.

**orient,** *v.* **1.** [To direct] — *Syn.* determine, turn, locate; see **lead** 1.
**2.** [To adjust] — *Syn.* orientate, get one's bearings, familiarize, adapt; see **conform.**
**3.** [To turn around] — *Syn.* face, turn, situate, line up, square, true, true up.

**Orient,** *n.* **1.** [Eastern Asia] — *Syn.* Far East, Asia, China, Hong Kong, Macao, India, Japan, Vietnam, Siam, Thailand, Laos, Indo-China, Cambodia, Korea, Philippines, Borneo, Java, Burma, Myanmar, the mysterious East, Celestial Kingdom, land of the rising sun, land of Confucianism; see also **east** 2. — *Ant.* ᵉUROPE, Occident, Western World.
**2.** [Southwestern Asia] — *Syn.* Near East, Middle East, Levant, Egypt, Turkey, Syria, Lebanon, Israel, Jordan, Iraq, Iran, Persia, Muslim world, Arabia, Golden Crescent, Fertile Crescent, the cradle of mankind; see also **east** 2.

**Oriental,** *modif.* — *Syn.* Eastern, Far Eastern, Near Eastern, Asian; see **Asian** 1, 2.

**orientation,** *n.* — *Syn.* familiarization, bearings, introduction; see **adjustment** 1, **introduction** 3, 4.

**orifice,** *n.* — *Syn.* opening, cleft, crack; see **hole** 1, 2.

**origin,** *n.* **1.** [The act of beginning] — *Syn.* rise, start, starting, genesis, alpha, commencement, outset, incipience, inception, initiation, nativity, dawn, introduction, embarkation, forging, entrance, ingress, entry, outbreak, onset, first move, first step, foundation, origination, authoring, ascent, first appearance, creation, induction, launching, inauguration, forming, fashioning, molding, devising, invention; see also **birth** 1. — *Ant.* END, close, termination.
**2.** [The place or time of beginning] — *Syn.* source, root, beginning, inception, spring, issue, fountain, inlet, derivation, etymology, provenance, provenience, stem, shoot, twig, sapling, portal, door, gate, gateway, fountainhead, wellspring, springhead, font, fount, well, *fons et origo* (Latin), birthplace, square one★, omphalos, cradle, nest, womb, hotbed, reservoir, forge, dawn, infancy, babyhood, childhood, youth. — *Ant.* RESULT, outcome, issue.
**3.** [Cause] — *Syn.* seed, germ, stock, parentage, ancestry, parent, ancestor, genesis, *raison d'être* (French), egg, sperm, embryo, principle, element, nucleus, first cause, First Great Cause, author, creator, heart, prime mover, *primum mobile* (Latin), begetter, progenitor, producer, determinant, agent, leaven, mainspring, causality, causation, impulse, source, influence, prime motive, generator, ultimate cause, remote cause, occasion, root, first

act, spring, antecedent, motive, inducement, activation, inspiration. — *Ant.* RESULT, consequence, conclusion.

---

**SYN.** — **origin** is applied to that from which a person or thing has its very beginning [the *origin* of a word]; **source** is applied to the point or place from which something arises, comes, or develops [the sun is our *source* of energy]; **beginning** is the basic general term for a starting point or place [the *beginning* of a quarrel]; **inception** is specifically applied to the beginning of an undertaking, organization, etc. [Smith headed the business from its *inception*]; **root** suggests an origin so deep and basic as to be the ultimate cause from which something stems [to get to the *root* of the matter]

---

**original,** *modif.* **1.** [Pertaining to the source] — *Syn.* primary, primeval, primordial, rudimentary, rudimental, aboriginal, elementary, inceptive, in embryo, fundamental, protogenic, primitive, initial, beginning, commencing, starting, opening, dawning, incipient; see also **first** 1. — *Ant.* LATE, recent, developed.
**2.** [Creative] — *Syn.* originative, productive, causal, causative, generative, imaginative, inventive, innovative, ingenious, unconventional, constitutive, formative, demiurgic, resourceful, ready, quick, seminal, envisioning, sensitive, archetypal, inspiring, devising, conceiving, fertile, fictive, fashioning, molding. — *Ant.* STUPID, imitative, unproductive.
**3.** [Not copied] — *Syn.* first, new, fresh, novel, earliest, initial, primary, principal, genuine, firsthand, uncopied, underived, unused, independent, one, sole, lone, single, solitary, neoteric, authentic, pure, new-fashioned, untranslated, nonimitative, unexampled, elemental, real, absolute; see also **unique** 1, **unusual** 1, 2. — *Ant.* IMITATED, copied, repeated.
*See Synonym Study at* NEW.

**originality,** *n.* — *Syn.* creativity, creativeness, inventiveness, innovation, invention, ingenuity, ingeniousness, conception, realization, authenticity, novelty, freshness, nonconformity, newness, modernity, individuality, brilliance, intellectual independence, a creative spirit, a creative mind; see also **imagination** 1. — *Ant.* IMITATION, dependency, imitativeness.

**originally,** *modif.* **1.** [In an original manner] — *Syn.* imaginatively, creatively, ingeniously, inventively, novelly, freshly, startlingly, modernly, in a new fashion, in the first instance, in the first place, in a new manner, independently, originatively, artistically, with genius.
**2.** [In the beginning] — *Syn.* first, incipiently, basically; see **formerly.**

**originate,** *v.* **1.** [To have a beginning] — *Syn.* start, arise, dawn; see **arise** 3, **begin** 2.
**2.** [To bring about a beginning] — *Syn.* start, introduce, found; see **begin** 1.
*See Synonym Study at* ARISE.

**originated,** *modif.* — *Syn.* introduced, started, commenced; see **begun.**

**originating,** *modif.* — *Syn.* rising, starting, beginning, commencing, issuing, springing from, emanating, arising, deriving, flowing from, dawning, given birth, generated, induced, produced, determined, caused, activated, motivated, begot, given source, leavened, inspired, descending, formed, fashioned, made, incepted, created, authored, cradled, forged.

**ornament,** *n.* — *Syn.* embellishment, adornment, beautification; see **decoration** 2, **embroidery** 1, **trimming** 1.

**ornament,** *v.* — *Syn.* decorate, embellish, adorn, trim; see **decorate.**

*See Synonym Study at* DECORATE.

**ornamental,** *modif.* **1.** [Providing ornament] — *Syn.* embellishing, adorning, decorative, decorating, making pleasing, rendering attractive, decking, setting off, gracing, garnishing, enhancing, heightening, furbishing, ornamentive, dressy, accessory, florid. — *Ant.* UGLY, detractive, plain.

**2.** [Intended for ornament] — *Syn.* fancy, luxurious, showy; see **elaborate** 1, **ornate** 1.

**3.** [Beautiful] — *Syn.* delicate, exquisite, spiritual; see **beautiful** 1.

**ornamentation,** *n.* — *Syn.* adornment, embellishment, elaboration; see **decoration** 1.

**ornate,** *modif.* **1.** [Highly decorated] — *Syn.* showy, flamboyant, bedight*, superficial, curved, flowery, resplendent, sumptuous, lavish, bespangled, many-colored, brilliant, parti-colored, bright, colored, tinseled, jeweled, embroidered, begilt, glossy, tessellated, burnished, polished, gorgeous, pompous, stylish, magnificent, adorned, festooned, trimmed, gilded, embellished, furbished, encrusted, striped, waved, scrolled, inlaid, illuminated, garnished, decked, bedecked, flowered, glowing, vivid, variegated, radiant, fine, gay, alluring, dazzling, sparkling, scintillating, shining, flashing, glistening, glamorous, glittering, grotesque, ornamented, artificial, ostentatious, pretentious, flaunting, baroque, rococo, gaudy, glitzy, tawdry, flashy, meretricious; see also **elaborate** 1.

**2.** [Referring to writing or speech] — *Syn.* adorned, ornamented, embellished, euphuistic; see **elegant** 3.

**orphan,** *n.* — *Syn.* parentless child, orphaned child, waif, stray, foundling, ragamuffin; see also **child.**

**orphanage,** *n.* — *Syn.* orphans' home, shelter, children's home, halfway house, asylum for orphaned children, institution, foundling home; see also **school** 1.

**orthodox,** *modif.* — *Syn.* standard, customary, doctrinal; see **conservative, conventional** 3.

**orthodoxy,** *n.* — *Syn.* dogma, belief, tradition, doctrine; see **faith** 2, **religion** 2.

**oscillate,** *v.* **1.** [To swing] — *Syn.* palpitate, vibrate, sway; see **swing** 1, **wave** 3, **waver.**

**2.** [To fluctuate] — *Syn.* be unsteady, waver, vacillate; see **change** 4.

*See Synonym Study at* SWING.

**oscillation,** *n.* **1.** [Swinging] — *Syn.* waving, swaying, quivering; see **vibration.**

**2.** [Fluctuation] — *Syn.* hesitancy, misgiving, faltering; see **doubt** 2, **uncertainty** 2.

**osculate,** *v.* — *Syn.* kiss, touch lips, buss*, smack*, make out*; see also **kiss.**

**osculation,** *n.* — *Syn.* kiss, peck, smooch*, endearment, embrace, caress; see also **kiss, touch** 2.

**osseous,** *modif.* — *Syn.* bony, rigid, stiff, calcified, ossified, skeletal, callous, inflexible, unyielding; see also **firm** 2, **thick** 3.

**ossification,** *n.* — *Syn.* fossilization, induration, hardening, bone formation, ostosis, calcification.

**ossify,** *v.* — *Syn.* congeal, fossilize, turn to bone; see **harden** 2, **stiffen** 1, **thicken** 1.

**ostensible,** *modif.* — *Syn.* manifest, demonstrative, notable; see **likely** 1.

**ostensibly,** *modif.* — *Syn.* superficially, purportedly, to all intents and purposes, for show; see **apparently.**

**ostentation,** *n.* **1.** [The quality of being ostentatious] — *Syn.* exhibitionism, showiness, pomp, pompousness, pomposity, parading, bravado, vaunting, magnificence, pageant, pageantry, splendor, spectacle, flourish, flamboyance, garishness, array, demonstration, pretending, boasting, bragging, swaggering, vainglory, braggartism;

see also **pretense** 1. — *Ant.* RESERVE, diffidence, timidity.

**2.** [Ostentatious conduct] — *Syn.* show, display, brag, boast, vaunt, swagger, flourish, parade, fuss, exhibition, braggadocio, pretension; see also **display** 2, **vanity** 1. — *Ant.* RESERVE, modest behavior, quiet.

**ostentatious,** *modif.* — *Syn.* pretentious, showy, pompous; see **egotistic** 2.

**ostentatiously,** *modif.* — *Syn.* blatantly, showily, proudly; see **egotistically, pompously.**

**ostracism,** *n.* — *Syn.* banishment, segregation, elimination, eviction; see **exclusion, exile** 1, **removal** 1.

**ostracize,** *v.* — *Syn.* exclude, banish, cast out, shun, blackball, boycott, blacklist, excommunicate, exile, expel, isolate, segregate, snub, reject, cut*, cut dead*, give the cold shoulder*; see also **banish** 1, **bar** 1.

*See Synonym Study at* BANISH.

**ostracized,** *modif.* — *Syn.* banished, treated like a pariah, ignored, blackballed; see **punished.**

**other,** *modif.* — *Syn.* one of two, the remaining one, another, one beside, some beside, additional, different, separate, distinct, opposite, across from, lately, recently, not long ago, other than; see also **extra.**

**other,** *pron.* — *Syn.* the one remaining, the part remaining, the alternate, the alternative; see **another.** — *Ant.* THIS, that, the first choice.

**of all others** — *Syn.* above all others, superior to, highest, supreme; see **best** 1.

**the other day (***or* **night)** — *Syn.* recently, not long ago, a while back, a while ago, yesterday or the day before; see also **recently.**

**others,** *n.* — *Syn.* unnamed persons, the remainder, some, a few, any others, a number, a handful, a small number, not many, hardly any, two or three, more than one, many, a great number, a great many, they*, folks*, the rest*; see also **everybody.** — *Ant.* no ONE, none, not any.

**otherwise,** *modif.* **1.** [In another way] — *Syn.* differently, in a different way, contrarily, in an opposed way, under other conditions, in different circumstances, on the other hand, in other respects, in other ways; see also **oppositely.** — *Ant.* LIKE, so, in like manner.

**2.** [Introducing an alternative threat] — *Syn.* unless you do, with this exception, except on these conditions, barring this, in any other circumstances, except that, without this, unless … then, other than; see also **unless.**

**otherworldly,** *modif.* — *Syn.* spectral, abstract, metaphysical; see **mysterious** 2, **supernatural.**

**otiose,** *modif.* **1.** [Lazy] — *Syn.* indolent, slothful, idle; see **lazy** 1, **listless** 1.

**2.** [Futile] — *Syn.* vain, useless, hopeless; see **futile** 1.

*See Synonym Study at* VAIN.

**ottoman,** *n.* — *Syn.* footstool, footrest, hassock; see **furniture, stool.**

**ouch,** *interj.* — *Syn.* oh, oh dear*, ooh*, gosh*, ach*, darn*, damnation*, damn*, gee*, geez*, great Scot*, dash it all*, shoot*, oops*, oy*, hooee*, goldarn*, good land*, gracious*, great Caesar*, great guns*, oh Lordy*, blazes*, the deuce*, hell*.

**ought (to),** *v.* — *Syn.* should, have to, is necessary, is fitting, is becoming, is expedient, behooves, is reasonable, is logical, is natural, requires, is in need of, is responsible for; see also **must.**

**ounce,** *n.* — *Syn.* uncia, measure, troy ounce, avoirdupois ounce, fluid ounce, one sixteenth of a pound (avoirdupois), one sixteenth of a pint, one twelfth of a pound (troy); see also **measure** 1.

**our,** *modif.* — *Syn.* ours, our own, belonging to us, owned by us, used by us, due to us, inherent in us, a part of us, of interest to us, done by us, accomplished by us, in our employ, with us, near us, of us.

**ourselves,** *pron.* — *Syn.* us, our own selves, the speakers, individually, personally, privately, without help, our very own selves*; see also **we.**

**oust,** *v.* — *Syn.* eject, discharge, dispossess, evict, dislodge, remove, deprive, expel, drive out, force out, show the door, chase out, cast out, depose, dethrone, distrain, disinherit, banish, boot out*, bundle off*, send packing*, bounce*, buck off*, wash out*, give the gate*, sack*, pack off*, send to Coventry*; see also **dismiss** 1, 2.
*See Synonym Study at* EJECT. — *Ant.* RESTORE, reinstate, commission.

**ousted,** *modif.* — *Syn.* removed, fired, defeated; see **beaten** 1.

**out,** *modif. & prep.* **1.** [In motion from within] — *Syn.* out of, away from, from, from within, out from, out toward, outward, on the way. — *Ant.* in from, in, into.
**2.** [Not situated within] — *Syn.* outside, on the outer side, on the surface, external, extrinsic, extraneous, outer, outdoors, out-of-doors, unconcealed, open, exposed, in the open; see also **outside** 1, **without.** — *Ant.* WITHIN, inside, on the inner side.
**3.** [Beyond] — *Syn.* distant, removed, removed from; see **away** 1, **beyond.**
**4.** [Continued to the limit or near it] — *Syn.* ended, accomplished, fulfilled, over, passed; see also **done** 1, **finished** 1. — *Ant.* UNFINISHED, unaccomplished, unfulfilled.
**5.** [Not at home or at one's office] — *Syn.* not in, away, busy, on vacation, at lunch, gone, left; see also **absent.** — *Ant.* IN, receiving, not busy.
**6.** [No longer at bat; *in sport*] — *Syn.* retired, put out, in the field, struck out, away*, down*, fanned*.
**7.** [*Unconscious] — *Syn.* insensible, out cold*, blotto*; see **unconscious** 1.
**8.** [Wanting] — *Syn.* lacking, missing, without; see **wanting.**
**9.** [Completely] — *Syn.* out and out, utterly, totally; see **completely.**
**10.** [*Not acceptable] — *Syn.* out-of-date, outmoded, unfashionable; see **old-fashioned, unpopular.**
**all out*** — *Syn.* wholeheartedly, with great effort, entirely; see **completely.**
**on the outs*** — *Syn.* on unfriendly terms, disagreeing, fighting, estranged; see **opposing** 1.

**out*,** *n.* — *Syn.* means of escape, way out, excuse; see **escape** 1, 2, **explanation** 2.

**outage,** *n.* — *Syn.* interruption of service, blackout, dimout, brownout; failure of electrical service, electrical failure, failure of gas, interruption of utilities; see also **interruption.**

**out-and-out,** *modif.* — *Syn.* complete, entire, total; see **absolute** 1, **completely.**

**out back,** *modif.* — *Syn.* behind, in back of, to the rear; see **back.**

**outbalance,** *v.* — *Syn.* outweigh, transcend, outdo; see **exceed.**

**outbid,** *v.* — *Syn.* bid higher, bid more, raise the price, bid something up; see **bid** 1, **pay** 1.

**outboard motor,** *n.* — *Syn.* marine motor, two-cycle motor, detachable motor, boat motor, boating equipment; see also **motor.**

**outbreak,** *n.* **1.** [A sudden violent appearance] — *Syn.* eruption, irruption, ebullition, explosion, outburst, disruption, burst, bursting, bursting forth, detonation, thunder, commotion, rending, break, breaking out, breaking forth, gush, gushing forth, outpouring, pouring

forth, breaking bonds, tumult, spurt, sundering, snapping apart, discharge, volley, blast, blowup, crash, roar, earthquake, temblor, squall, paroxysm, spasm, convulsion, fit, ictus, effervescence, boiling, flash, flare, crack. — *Ant.* PEACE, tranquility, quiet.
**2.** [Sudden violence] — *Syn.* fury, mutiny, brawl; see **disorder** 2, **revolution** 2.

**outbuilding,** *n.* — *Syn.* outhouse, stable, barn, backhouse, outside building, storehouse; see also **building** 1, **shed.**

**outburst,** *n.* — *Syn.* discharge, upheaval, eruption; see **disturbance** 2, **outbreak** 1.

**outcast,** *modif.* — *Syn.* vagabond, proscribed, driven out, hounded, untouchable, rejected, ostracized, thrown aside, pushed out, hunted, Ishmaellike, not accepted by society, cast out, degraded, expelled, outlawed, cast away, exiled, expatriated, made a vagabond, serving a life sentence, having a price on one's head; see also **disgraced.**

**outcast,** *n.* **1.** [One who has been cast out] — *Syn.* fugitive, pariah, untouchable; see **refugee.**
**2.** [A vagabond] — *Syn.* wanderer, itinerant, vagrant; see **rascal, tramp** 1.

**outclass,** *v.* — *Syn.* outdo, excel, surpass; see **exceed.**

**outcome,** *n.* — *Syn.* result, end, issue, upshot, consequence; see also **end** 2, **result.**
*See Synonym Study at* RESULT.

**outcrop,** *n.* — *Syn.* bared rock, bared soil, exposed surface, projecting land mass; see **earth** 2, **land** 1.

**outcry,** *n.* — *Syn.* complaint, clamor, scream; see **objection** 2.

**outdated,** *modif.* — *Syn.* outmoded, out of fashion, antiquated; see **old** 3.

**outdistance,** *v.* — *Syn.* exceed, better, beat; see **defeat** 3.

**outdo,** *v.* — *Syn.* surpass, excel, overdo, beat; see **defeat** 1, **exceed.**
*See Synonym Study at* EXCEL.

**outdone,** *modif.* — *Syn.* surpassed, defeated, bettered, improved upon; see **beaten** 1.

**outdoor,** *modif.* — *Syn.* outside, out-of-doors, open-air, alfresco, picnic, out of the house, out in the open, free, unrestricted, rustic, informal, free and easy, healthful, invigorating, nature-loving, given to outdoor sports; see also **airy** 1. — *Ant.* INTERIOR, indoor, in the house.

**outdoors,** *modif.* — *Syn.* out-of-doors, outdoor, without, out of the house, outside, on the outside, in the yard, in the open, in the garden, on the patio, into the street.

**outdoors,** *n.* — *Syn.* the out-of-doors, natural scenery, fresh air, garden, patio, woods, hills, mountains, streams, Mother Nature, the great outdoors, God's great outdoors, countryside, the country; see also **environment, nature** 3. — *Ant.* INSIDE, domestic matters, household concerns.

**outer,** *modif.* — *Syn.* outward, without, external, exterior, outside, extrinsic to, extraneous to, foreign to, alien to, beyond, exposed. — *Ant.* INNER, inward, inside.

**outermost,** *modif.* — *Syn.* surface, peripheral, external; see **outside** 1.

**outer space,** *n.* — *Syn.* infinity, the heavens, the universe; see **space** 1.

**outface,** *v.* — *Syn.* confront, oppose, defy; see **dare** 2, **face** 1.

**outfield,** *n.* — *Syn.* field, pasture*, garden*, outer works*, playpen*; see also **baseball, field** 2.

**outfielder,** *n.* — *Syn.* fielder, pasture police*, gardener*, fly hawk*, flypaper*, fly chaser*; see also **fielder, player** 1.

In baseball, outfielders include: left fielder, center fielder, right fielder.

**outfight,** *v.* — *Syn.* excel, beat, whip; see **defeat** 1, **exceed.**

**outfit,** *n.* — *Syn.* trappings, outlay, gear; see **equipment.**

**outfit,** *v.* — *Syn.* equip, fit out, furnish, supply; see **provide** 1.

*See Synonym Study at* FURNISH.

**outfitted,** *modif.* — *Syn.* ready, provided with, provided for, suited up; see **equipped.**

**outfitter,** *n.* — *Syn.* supplier, clothier, seamstress, costumer; see **tailor.**

**outflank,** *v.* — *Syn.* bypass, surround, outmaneuver; see **defeat** 1, 2, **pass** 1.

**outflow,** *n.* — *Syn.* effluence, flow, outpouring, discharge, current, drainage, movement of tide; see also **ebb, flow.**

**outfly,** *v.* — *Syn.* fly past, exceed in speed, outdistance; see **defeat** 3, **leave** 1, **pass** 1.

**out front,** *modif.* — *Syn.* ahead, winning, victorious; see **triumphant.**

**outgo,** *n.* — *Syn.* costs, losses, outflow; see **expenses, loss, reduction** 1.

**outgoing,** *modif.* — *Syn.* sociable, civil, kind; see **friendly** 1.

**outgrow,** *v.* — *Syn.* grow beyond, leave behind, relinquish, discontinue, give up; see also **abandon** 1, **discard.**

**outgrowth,** *n.* 1. [A product] — *Syn.* end result, outcome, effect; see **end** 2, **result.**

2. [A projection] — *Syn.* offshoot, prominence, jut, protuberance; see **bulge, projection.**

**outguess,** *v.* — *Syn.* predict, predict successfully, outmaneuver, think faster; see **defeat** 1, **think** 1.

**outhouse,** *n.* — *Syn.* latrine, privy, backhouse, shed; see **outbuilding, toilet** 2.

**outing,** *n.* — *Syn.* excursion, trip, airing, drive; see **vacation.**

**out in left field\*,** *modif.* — *Syn.* unlikely, crazy, wild; see **impractical, insane** 1.

**outlander,** *n.* — *Syn.* foreigner, intruder, settler, migrant, émigré, immigrant; see also **alien, stranger.**

**outlandish,** *modif.* 1. [Uncouth] — *Syn.* gauche, boorish, clumsy; see **awkward** 1, **rude** 1, 2.

2. [Ridiculous] — *Syn.* odd, queer, strange, bizarre; see **unusual** 2.

*See Synonym Study at* STRANGE.

**outlandishly,** *modif.* — *Syn.* ridiculously, insanely, crazily; see **foolishly.**

**outlast,** *v.* — *Syn.* outlive, outwear, remain; see **endure** 1, **survive** 1.

**outlaw,** *n.* — *Syn.* fugitive, bandit, badman; see **criminal.**

**outlaw,** *v.* — *Syn.* make illegal, stop, ban; see **banish, condemn** 1, **prevent.**

**outlawed,** *modif.* — *Syn.* stopped, banned, illegitimate, made illegal; see **illegal.**

**outlay,** *n.* — *Syn.* expenditure, cost, charge; see **expense** 1.

**outlet,** *n.* 1. [An opening] — *Syn.* exit, way out, vent, break, crack, tear; see also **hole** 1, 2.

2. [An electric terminal] — *Syn.* socket, terminal, electrical device, plug, wallplug; see also **socket.**

**outline,** *n.* 1. [A skeletonized plan] — *Syn.* frame, skeleton, framework; see **plan** 1, **sketch** 1.

2. [A preliminary plan] — *Syn.* sketch, drawing, draft; see **plan** 2.

3. [The line surrounding an object; *often plural*] — *Syn.* contour, edge, side, boundary; see **edge** 1, **frame** 3.

4. [A shape seen in outline] — *Syn.* silhouette, profile, contour, form, configuration, shape, figure, formation, lineament, aspect, appearance, representation, footprint; see also **form** 1.

*See Synonym Study at* FORM.

**SYN.** — **outline** is used of the line bounding the limits of an object and showing its shape /the sketch shows only the *outline* of the skyscrapers/; **contour**, specifically applied to the configuration of a land mass, in general use stresses the shape of an object or mass as determined by its outline /the irregular *contours* of the building/; **profile** is used of the outline or contour of the face in a side view or of the outline of any object as it is seen against a background /the *profile* of the trees against the sky/; **silhouette** applies to a profile portrait, esp. of the head and usually in solid black, or it may be used of any dark shape seen against a light background /the *silhouette* of a house against the moonlight/

**outline,** *v.* 1. [To draw] — *Syn.* sketch, paint, describe; see **draw** 2.

2. [To plan] — *Syn.* rough out, block out, draft, sketch; see **plan** 2.

**outlined,** *modif.* 1. [Marked in outline] — *Syn.* bounded, delineated, edged, bordered, circumscribed, marked, zoned, girdled, banded, configurated, delimited.

2. [Given in summary] — *Syn.* epitomized, profiled, roughed out, generalized, charted, diagramed, mapped, graphed; see also **summarized.**

**outlining,** *modif.* — *Syn.* edging, bounding, marking, zoning, circumscribing, girdling, banding, configurating, delimiting; see also **bordering.**

**outlining,** *n.* — *Syn.* sketching, planning, delineating, tracing, diagraming, drafting, plotting, circumscribing, delineating, blocking out, charting, mapping, bounding, girdling, banding, delimiting, depicting, aligning, drawing up, designing, projecting; see also **drawing.**

**outlive,** *v.* — *Syn.* live longer than, outlast, last; see **endure** 1, **survive.**

**outlook,** *n.* 1. [Point of view] — *Syn.* scope, vision, standpoint; see **viewpoint.**

2. [Apparent future] — *Syn.* probability, prospect, likelihood, possibility, expectation, chances, opportunity, promise, appearances, probable future, openings, normal course of events, probabilities, risk, mathematical chances, law of averages; see also **forecast.**

**out loud,** *modif.* — *Syn.* aloud, above a whisper, audible; see **aloud, loud** 1, **loudly.**

**outlying,** *modif.* — *Syn.* afar, far-off, external, out-of-the-way, peripheral; see also **distant** 1, **remote** 1.

**outmaneuver,** *v.* — *Syn.* outwit, outdo, excel; see **defeat** 1, **exceed.**

**outmoded,** *modif.* — *Syn.* out-of-date, old-fashioned, superannuated; see **old** 1, 2, 3.

**outnumbered,** *modif.* — *Syn.* exceeded, bested, overcome; see **beaten** 1.

**out of,** *modif.* 1. [Having none in stock] — *Syn.* all out of stock, not in stock, gone; see **depleted, sold out.**

2. [From] — *Syn.* out from, away from, from within; see **from.**

3. [Beyond] — *Syn.* outside of, on the border of, in the outskirts; see **beyond.**

**out-of-date,** *modif.* — *Syn.* obsolete, passé, antiquated; see **old-fashioned.**

**out-of-doors,** *modif.* — *Syn.* in the open, outside, open-air; see **out** 2, 5, **outdoor, outdoors.**

**out of it★,** *modif.* — *Syn.* uninformed, behind the times, square★, unaware; see **ignorant** 1, **old-fashioned.**

**out of one's mind** or **head,** *modif.* — *Syn.* crazy, deranged, irresponsible; see **insane** 1.

**out of order,** *modif.* — *Syn.* broken down, defective, ineffective; see **broken** 2, **faulty.**

**out-of-the-way,** *modif.* **1.** [Remote] — *Syn.* far-off, secluded, isolated; see **distant** 1, **remote** 1.

**2.** [Strange] — *Syn.* bizarre, odd, weird; see **unusual** 2.

**outperform,** *v.* — *Syn.* beat, better, exceed; see **defeat** 1, 3.

**outplay,** *v.* — *Syn.* overcome, surpass, beat; see **defeat** 1, **exceed.**

**outpost,** *n.* — *Syn.* forward position, outstation, forward line, vanguard, listening post, point of attack; see also **boundary, position** 1.

**outpouring,** *n.* — *Syn.* overflow, emission, drainage; see **ebb, flow.**

**output,** *n.* **1.** [Production] — *Syn.* producing, making, manufacturing; see **production** 1.

**2.** [Product] — *Syn.* yield, amount, crop; see **product** 2.

**outrage,** *n.* — *Syn.* indignity, abuse, affront; see **insult.**

**outrage,** *v.* — *Syn.* offend, wrong, affront; see **abuse** 1, **insult, offend.**

*See Synonym Study at* OFFEND.

**outrageous,** *modif.* — *Syn.* offensive, shocking, flagrant, monstrous, atrocious, heinous, intolerable, appalling, extreme, excessive, inordinate, immoderate, intemperate, extravagant, fantastic, wild, unconventional, unrestrained, unreasonable, unspeakable, unconscionable, exorbitant, wanton, shameful, opprobrious, notorious, shameless, disgraceful, brazen, barefaced, gross, scandalous, insulting, abusive, oppressive, dishonorable, reprehensible, injurious, glaring, egregious, rank, despicable, ignoble, contumelious, scurrilous, odious, flagitious, nefarious, iniquitous, barbarous, wicked, violent, villainous, horrendous, infamous, corrupt, degenerate, criminal, abandoned, vile, horrifying, abominable, execrable, bizarre, outlandish, outré, overmuch; see also **offensive** 2, **shameful** 1, 2. — *Ant.* acceptable, honorable, moderate.

---

**SYN.** — **outrageous** applies to that which so exceeds all bounds of right, morality, decency, or reasonableness, as to be intolerable /an *outrageous* insult, *outrageous* prices/; **flagrant** implies a glaringly bad or openly evil character in people or their acts /a *flagrant* sinner, a *flagrant* violation/; **monstrous** and **atrocious** are applied to that which is shockingly evil, wrong, or cruel /a *monstrous* lie, *atrocious* cruelty/; or, in a weakened sense, extremely bad /*atrocious* manners /; **heinous** implies such extreme wickedness as to arouse the strongest hatred and revulsion /a *heinous* crime/

---

**outrageously,** *modif.* — *Syn.* horribly, shamefully, awfully; see **badly** 1, **brutally, foolishly.**

**outrank,** *v.* — *Syn.* rank above, excel, rival; see **exceed.**

**outreach,** *v.* — *Syn.* excel, predominate, surpass; see **exceed.**

**outrider,** *n.* — *Syn.* guardian, attendant, guide, scout; see **escort.**

**outright,** *modif.* — *Syn.* downright, out-and-out, unmitigated, arrant; see **completely, obvious** 1, **unconditional.**

**outrun,** *v.* — *Syn.* beat, win, forge ahead; see **defeat** 1, **exceed.**

**outsell,** *v.* — *Syn.* excel, surpass, sell more than; see **exceed.**

**outset,** *n.* — *Syn.* starting, source, rise; see **origin** 1.

**outshine,** *v.* **1.** [To obscure] — *Syn.* cloud, dim, eclipse; see **shade** 2.

**2.** [To outdo] — *Syn.* transcend, surpass, excel; see **defeat** 1, **exceed.**

**outside,** *modif.* **1.** [Outermost] — *Syn.* extreme, farthest, apart from, external, away from, farther; see also **furthest.**

**2.** [Exterior] — *Syn.* outdoor, external, outward; see **outer.** — *Ant.* inner, inside, interior.

**outside,** *n.* **1.** [An outer surface] — *Syn.* exterior, outer side, surface, integument, covering, sheath, shell, façade, topside, upper side, front side, face, appearance, outer aspect, seeming; see also **body** 4, **cover** 1, 2, **skin.** — *Ant.* interior, INSIDE, inner side.

**2.** [The limit] — *Syn.* outline, border, bounds; see **boundary, edge** 1, **end** 4.

**at the outside** — *Syn.* at the most, at the absolute limit, no more than, not more than; see **most.**

**outsider,** *n.* — *Syn.* foreigner, stranger, refugee, carpetbagger; see **alien.**

**outskirts,** *n.* — *Syn.* border, suburbs, limits; see **boundary, edge** 1.

**outsmart,** *v.* — *Syn.* outguess, outdo, get the better of; see **deceive, defeat** 1, **trick.**

**outspoken,** *modif.* — *Syn.* frank, blunt, candid, artless; see **abrupt** 2, **frank.**

*See Synonym Study at* FRANK.

**outspread,** *modif.* — *Syn.* spread, spread out, spread wide, spread far, expanded, extensive, expansive, extended, unlimited, beyond limits, unbounded, beyond boundaries, unheld, unrestrained, unrestricted, unconfined, unenclosed, uncircumscribed, free; see also **extensive** 1, **widespread.** — *Ant.* NARROW, contracted, bounded.

**outstanding,** *modif.* — *Syn.* prominent, exceptional, leading, notable; see **conspicuous, distinguished** 2, **excellent, unusual** 1.

*See Synonym Study at* NOTICEABLE.

**outstandingly,** *modif.* — *Syn.* superbly, notably, supremely; see **excellently, well** 2, 3.

**outstay,** *v.* — *Syn.* outwait, stay longer than, hang on, hang in there★; see **endure** 1, **wait** 1.

**outstrip,** *v.* — *Syn.* surpass, outdo, excel; see **exceed.**

**outthink,** *v.* — *Syn.* outguess, outplan, outsmart, outmaneuver, think better than; see also **defeat** 1.

**outvote,** *v.* — *Syn.* overwhelm, out-ballot, snow under★; see **defeat** 1.

**outward,** *modif.* **1.** [In an outwardly direction] — *Syn.* out, toward the edge, from within; see **outer, outside** 1.

**2.** [To outward appearance] — *Syn.* on the surface, visible, to the eye; see **obvious** 1, **open** 1.

**outward bound,** *modif.* — *Syn.* going, leaving, departed; see **afloat, gone** 1, **traveling** 1, 2.

**outwardly,** *modif.* — *Syn.* superficially, in appearance, on the surface; see **apparently.**

**outwear,** *v.* **1.** [To survive] — *Syn.* sustain, last longer than, outlast; see **continue** 1, **endure** 1, **survive** 1.

**2.** [To exhaust] — *Syn.* spend, wear out, deplete; see **tire** 1, 2, **weary** 1, 2.

**outweigh,** *v.* **1.** [To exceed in weight] — *Syn.* overbalance, overweigh, weigh more than, go beyond; see **burden.**

**2.** [To exceed in importance] — *Syn.* excel, surpass, outrun; see **exceed.**

**outwit,** *v.* — *Syn.* baffle, trick, bewilder; see **confuse, deceive.**

**outwitted,** *modif.* — *Syn.* tricked, outsmarted, taken in; see **deceived** 1.

**outwork,** *v.* — *Syn.* work harder than, work better than, outperform, improve upon; see **defeat** 1, **work** 1.

**outworn,** *modif.* **1.** [Obsolete] — *Syn.* out of use, archaic, extinct; see **old** 2, **old-fashioned.**
**2.** [Exhausted] — *Syn.* consumed, run-down, weary; see **spent** 2, **tired.**

**oval,** *modif.* — *Syn.* egg-shaped, elliptical, ellipsoidal; see **oblong.**

**oval,** *n.* — *Syn.* ellipse, oblong, ovoid, egg-shape.

**ovation,** *n.* — *Syn.* laudation, acclaim, applause; see **praise** 2.

**oven,** *n.* — *Syn.* stove, toaster oven, rotisserie, hot-air chamber, oil burner, broiler; see also **furnace, stove.**
Types of ovens include: baking, coke, annealing, pottery, metallurgical, Aladdin's, charcoal, electric, gas, Egyptian, firing, bush, Dutch, beehive, drying; kiln, leer, hot-air sterilizer.

**over,** *modif. & prep.* **1.** [Situated above] — *Syn.* above, aloft, overhead, overtop, up beyond, covering, roofing, protecting, higher than, farther up, upstairs, in the sky, at the zenith, straight up, high up, up there, in the clouds, among the stars, in heaven, just over, up from, outer, on top of, atop; see also **above** 1, **up** 1, **upper.** — *Ant.* UNDER, below, beneath.
**2.** [Passing above] — *Syn.* overhead, aloft, up high; see **across.**
**3.** [Again] — *Syn.* once more, afresh, another time; see **again.**
**4.** [Beyond] — *Syn.* past, farther on, out of sight; see **beyond.**
**5.** [Done] — *Syn.* accomplished, ended, completed; see **done** 2, **finished** 1.
**6.** [*In addition] — *Syn.* over and above, extra, additionally; see **besides.**
**7.** [Having authority] — *Syn.* superior to, in authority, above; see **higher, superior.**

**overabundance,** *n.* — *Syn.* surplus, profusion, superfluity; see **excess** 1.

**overact,** *v.* — *Syn.* affect, overdo, act, ham, ham up*; see also **exceed, exaggerate.**

**over-all,** *modif.* — *Syn.* complete, thorough, comprehensive; see **general** 1.

**overalls,** *n.* — *Syn.* an over-all garment, jump suit, coveralls; see **clothes, pants** 1.

**overbalance,** *v.* **1.** [To exceed] — *Syn.* pass over, surpass, transcend; see **exceed.**
**2.** [To upset] — *Syn.* subvert, capsize, overturn; see **upset** 1.

**overbearing,** *modif.* **1.** [Haughty] — *Syn.* arrogant, proud, insolent; see **egotistic** 2, **proud** 2.
**2.** [Autocratic] — *Syn.* despotic, oppressive, dictatorial; see **absolute** 3, **autocratic** 1, **tyrannical.**
*See Synonym Study at* PROUD.

**overblown,** *modif.* — *Syn.* superfluous, excessive, profuse, flowery; see **oratorical, verbose.**

**overboard,** *modif.* — *Syn.* over the side, from on board, off the ship, out of the boat, into the water.
**go overboard** — *Syn.* go to extremes, get carried away, get overenthusiastic, go off the deep end; see **overdo.**

**overbuilt,** *modif.* — *Syn.* overly promoted, overgrown, built up too much, built excessively; see **exaggerated.**

**overcast,** *modif.* — *Syn.* cloudy, clouded, not clear, not fair; see **dark** 1.

**overcharge,** *v.* — *Syn.* overtax, cheat, charge to excess, overburden, strain, lay it on*, rip off*, diddle*; see also **deceive.**

**overcoat,** *n.* — *Syn.* topcoat, greatcoat, raincoat; see **clothes, coat** 1.

**overcome,** *modif.* **1.** [Beaten] — *Syn.* conquered, overwhelmed, overthrown; see **beaten** 1.
**2.** [Seized] — *Syn.* apprehended, appropriated, preempted; see **captured** 1, **held.**

**overcome,** *v.* — *Syn.* overwhelm, subdue, master, surmount; see **defeat** 1, 2, **succeed** 1, **win** 1.
*See Synonym Study at* DEFEAT.

**overcompensate,** *v.* — *Syn.* overreact, overdo a good thing, blunder, lean over too far backward*; see **correct** 1, **destroy** 1, **overdo** 1.

**overconfident,** *modif.* — *Syn.* reckless, impudent, heedless; see **careless** 1, **rash.**

**overcritical,** *modif.* — *Syn.* domineering, harsh, hypercritical, finicky, picky, niggling; see also **severe** 1, 2.

**overcrowd,** *v.* — *Syn.* crowd, stuff, fill; see **pack** 2, **press** 1.

**overcrowded,** *modif.* — *Syn.* congested, overbuilt, overpopulated; see **full** 1.

**overcrowding,** *n.* — *Syn.* overpopulation, overbuilding, population explosion; see **congestion.**

**overdeveloped,** *modif.* — *Syn.* congested, pushed too much, promoted too much, overbuilt; see **growing.**

**overdevelopment,** *n.* — *Syn.* overbuilding, overexpansion, crowding, overoptimistic handling, overoptimistic treatment; see also **congestion.**

**overdo,** *v.* **1.** [To do too much] — *Syn.* magnify, pile up, pile on, amplify, overestimate, overreach, stretch, overvalue, go too far, carry too far, overplay, overrate, exaggerate, hyperbolize, go to extremes, overstate, enlarge, enhance, exalt, bite off more than one can chew*, run into the ground*, do to death*, go overboard*, butter one's bread on both sides*, carry coals to Newcastle*, burn the candle at both ends*, lay it on*, have too many irons in the fire*, have one's cake and eat it too*; see also **exceed.** — *Ant.* NEGLECT, underdo, slack.
**2.** [To overtax oneself physically] — *Syn.* overlabor, overwork, overload, overlade, overdrive, strain, overstrain, fatigue, exhaust, overtire, wear down, collapse; see also **tire** 1, **weary** 2. — *Ant.* LOAF, take it easy, dawdle.

**overdone,** *modif.* **1.** [Overcooked] — *Syn.* burned, burned to a crisp, scorched, charred.
**2.** [Excessive] — *Syn.* exaggerated, extravagant, too much; see **exaggerated.**

**overdose,** *n.* — *Syn.* excessive dose, heavy dose, excessive dosage, too much, overtreatment; see also **excess** 1, 3, **treatment** 2.

**overdrawn,** *modif.* — *Syn.* exhausted, depleted, all paid out, in arrears; see **gone** 2.

**overdue,** *modif.* — *Syn.* delayed, belated, tardy; see **late** 1.

**overeager,** *modif.* — *Syn.* overzealous, vigorous, overenthusiastic; see **enthusiastic** 1, 2, 3.

**overeat,** *v.* — *Syn.* overindulge, stuff, gorge; see **eat** 1.

**overemphasize,** *v.* — *Syn.* stress, exaggerate, make a big thing of*, make something out of nothing*; see **emphasize, exceed.**

**overestimate,** *v.* — *Syn.* overvalue, overprice, overrate; see **exaggerate, exceed.**

**overexcite,** *v.* — *Syn.* overstimulate, quicken, provoke, arouse; see **excite** 1.

**overexcited,** *modif.* — *Syn.* aroused, overstimulated, incited; see **excited.**

**overexert,** *v.* — *Syn.* fatigue, strain, exhaust, overdo; see **tire** 2.

**overexpand,** *v.* — *Syn.* grow too much, develop too much, grow too fast, develop too fast, overdevelop, overextend; see also **grow** 1.

**overextended,** *modif.* — *Syn.* overexpanded, spread too thin, spread out; see **enlarged.**

**overfeed,** *v.* — *Syn.* overfill, satiate, stuff; see **eat** 1.

**overfill,** *v.* — *Syn.* cram, overload, stuff; see **compress, pack** 2, **press** 1.

**overflight,** *n.* — *Syn.* flyover, survey, reconnaissance flight, spy mission; see **flight** 2, **spying.**

**overflow,** *n.* **1.** [The act of overflowing] — *Syn.* inundation, exuberance, overproduction, congestion, deluge, spillover, overabundance, engorgement, flooding, spilling over, submergence, submersion, overspreading, superabounding, overcrowding, redundancy, push, propulsion, encroachment, advance, infringement, overtopping, overwhelming, overbrimming; see also **flood** 1. — *Ant.* LACK, deficiency, scarcity.
**2.** [That which overflows] — *Syn.* superfluity, surplus, surplusage; see **excess** 1.
**3.** [The vent through which overflow occurs] — *Syn.* outlet, passage, exit; see **hole** 1, 2.

**overflow,** *v.* **1.** [To flow over the top, or out at a vent] — *Syn.* spill over, fall, run out, run over, pour out, pour over, waste, shed, cascade, spout, spout forth, jet, spurt, drain, leak, squirt, spray, shower, gush, shoot, issue, rush, irrupt, wave, surge, overtop, overbrim, brim over, lap over, bubble over, flow over; see also **flow** 2, **spill.**
**2.** [To flow out upon] — *Syn.* inundate, water, wet; see **flood.**

**overflowing,** *modif.* — *Syn.* abundant, in God's plenty, plenteous, bountiful; see **plentiful** 2.

**overfly,** *v.* — *Syn.* survey, fly across, fly over, inspect; see **fly** 1, 4.

**overgrown,** *modif.* **1.** [Grown to an unnatural size] — *Syn.* disproportionate, excessive, huge; see **large** 1.
**2.** [Grown without being tended] — *Syn.* thick, crowded, disordered; see **green** 2, **wild** 3.

**overgrowth,** *n.* — *Syn.* growth, abundance, luxuriance; see **excess** 1.

**overhang,** *n.* — *Syn.* protrusion, obtrusion, overlap, overlie, droop, suspension, imbrication, beetling, jutting, extension; see also **projection.**

**overhang,** *v.* **1.** [To hang over] — *Syn.* jut, be suspended, beetle, impend, command, overtop, swing over, dangle over, droop over, flap over; see also **project** 1, **protrude.**
**2.** [To threaten] — *Syn.* be imminent, endanger, menace; see **threaten** 2.

**overhaul,** *v.* — *Syn.* modernize, fix, renew; see **improve** 1, **reconstruct, repair** 1, **restore** 3.

**overhead,** *modif.* — *Syn.* above, aloft, hanging; see **over** 1.

**overhead,** *n.* — *Syn.* expenses, cost, rent, insurance, depreciation, current expense, factory cost, burden; see also **expenses.**

**overhear,** *v.* — *Syn.* hear intentionally, listen in on, catch; see **eavesdrop, hear** 1, 2, **listen** 1.

**overheard,** *modif.* — *Syn.* listened to, recorded, discovered; see **heard.**

**overheat,** *v.* — *Syn.* heat too much, heat up too much, bake, blister; see **heat** 2.

**overindulgence,** *n.* — *Syn.* gluttony, overeating, overdrinking, eating too much, drinking too much; see also **drunkenness, eating, greed.**

**overjoyed,** *modif.* — *Syn.* enraptured, transported, charmed; see **happy** 1, **thrilled.**

**overkill,** *n.* — *Syn.* excessive force, slaughter, needless slaughter, extermination, genocide; see also **carnage, destruction** 1, 2.

**overland,** *modif.* — *Syn.* transcontinental, coast-to-coast, fast, west-coast, east-coast, plane, train, stage, bus, air, Pullman, through*; see also **cross-country.**

**overlap,** *n.* — *Syn.* extension, overlay, addition; see **flap, overhang, projection.**

**overlap,** *v.* — *Syn.* overlie, overhang, imbricate, lap over, fold over, extend alongside, flap, extend over, project over, overlay; see also **project** 1, **protrude.**

**overlapping,** *modif.* — *Syn.* coinciding, coincidental, overlying, super-imposed, extending, protruding, projecting.

**overlay,** *v.* **1.** [To burden] — *Syn.* overload, cram, encumber; see **burden** 1, **load** 1.
**2.** [To overlap] — *Syn.* extend, superimpose, cover; see **overlap.**

**overleap,** *v.* **1.** [To jump over] — *Syn.* spring, leap over, pass; see **jump** 1.
**2.** [To omit] — *Syn.* reject, overlook, miss; see **omit** 1.

**overload,** *v.* — *Syn.* oppress, weigh down, encumber; see **burden, load** 1.

**overlook,** *v.* **1.** [To occupy a commanding height] — *Syn.* look over, top, survey, inspect, watch over, look out, view, give upon, give on, front on, command, tower over, have a prospect of, surmount, mount over; see also **face** 4.
**2.** [To ignore deliberately] — *Syn.* disregard, ignore, excuse, look the other way; see **disregard, excuse, neglect** 1.
**3.** [To fail to see] — *Syn.* miss, leave out, neglect; see **neglect** 1, **omit** 1.
*See Synonym Study at* NEGLECT.

**overlooked,** *modif.* — *Syn.* missed, left out, forgotten; see **neglected, omitted.**

**overlooking,** *modif.* **1.** [Providing a view] — *Syn.* viewing, topping, surmounting, looking over, giving on, looking out on, giving a survey of, giving a vantage point, lofty, commanding.
**2.** [Disregarding] — *Syn.* missing, neglecting, forgetting, passing over, disdaining, scorning, snubbing, cutting, slighting, being inattentive to, being unobservant, making light of, passing; see also **omitting.**

**overnight,** *modif.* — *Syn.* one night, lasting one night, during the night; see **late** 4.

**overpass,** *n.* — *Syn.* bridge, viaduct, walkway, skyway, span, footbridge, gangplank; see also **bridge** 1.

**overpay,** *v.* — *Syn.* pay too much, pay excessively, overcompensate, overrecompense, over-reward, over-remunerate, overreimburse, overyield, overexceed, oversettle, pay the Devil*. — *Ant.* DECEIVE, deprive, cheat.

**overpayment,** *n.* — *Syn.* overcharge, too much, excessive payment; see **money** 1, **payment** 1.

**overplay,** *v.* — *Syn.* overdo, labor, belabor, show off; see **promote** 1, **work** 1.

**overpower,** *v.* — *Syn.* overwhelm, master, subjugate; see **defeat** 2, 3.

**overpowering,** *modif.* — *Syn.* irresistible, uncontrollable, overwhelming; see **intense.**

**overproduction,** *n.* — *Syn.* excess, excessive production, overstock; see **production** 1, 2.

**overrate,** *v.* — *Syn.* overvalue, build up, magnify, overestimate; see **exaggerate, exceed.**

**overrated,** *modif.* — *Syn.* overestimated, not good, overblown, not satisfactory; see **poor** 2, **unsatisfactory.**

**overreach,** *v.* **1.** [To exceed] — *Syn.* overact, outreach, overdo, overextend; see **exceed.**
**2.** [To outwit] — *Syn.* outsmart, cheat, fool; see **deceive.**
**3.** [To spread over] — *Syn.* overlay, encroach on, encroach upon, overlap; see **cover** 1, **spread** 4.

**overreact,** v. — Syn. make too much of, blow out of proportion, make a mountain out of a molehill; see **exaggerate.**

**overridden,** modif. — Syn. defeated, rejected, voted down; see **refused.**

**override,** v. 1. [To dismiss] — Syn. pass over, not heed, take no account of; see **disregard, neglect** 1.
2. [To thwart] — Syn. make void, reverse, annul, vote down; see **cancel** 2, **revoke.**

**overriding,** modif. — Syn. dominant, prevailing, main, determining; see **major** 1.

**overripe,** modif. — Syn. rotting, decayed, decaying, overmature; see **rotten** 1.

**overrule,** v. 1. [To nullify] — Syn. invalidate, rule against, override; see **cancel** 2, **revoke.**
2. [To rule] — Syn. direct, control, manage; see **govern** 1.

**overrun,** v. 1. [To defeat] — Syn. overwhelm, invade, occupy; see **defeat** 2.
2. [To infest] — Syn. ravage, invade, overwhelm; see **infest, swarm.**

**overseas,** modif. — Syn. away, across, in foreign countries; see **abroad.**

**oversee,** v. — Syn. superintend, supervise, look after; see **command** 2, **manage** 1.

**overseer,** n. — Syn. supervisor, manager, superintendent; see **foreman.**

**oversell,** v. — Syn. glut the market with, overpromote, promote too hard, promote too much; see **sell** 1.

**overshadow,** v. 1. [To dominate] — Syn. manage, tower above, rule; see **command** 2, **dominate, govern.**
2. [To shade] — Syn. shadow, dim, cloud; see **shade** 2.

**overshoes,** n. — Syn. galoshes, rubbers, rubber boots, waterproof boots, wellingtons, arctics; see also **shoe.**

**overshoot,** v. — Syn. overreach, overdo, overact; see **exceed.**

**oversight,** n. — Syn. failure, overlooking, mistake; see **error** 1, **omission** 1.

**oversimplification,** n. — Syn. reduction, too great a reduction, excessive simplification, simplism; see **simplicity.**

**oversimplified,** modif. — Syn. simplistic, distorted, simple, made easy; see **simplified.**

**oversimplify,** v. — Syn. reduce, over reduce, reduce to an absurdity, make too simple, make too simplistic, restrict; see also **simplify.**

**oversleep,** v. — Syn. sleep late, sleep in, miss the alarm, stay in bed; see **sleep.**

**overspecialize,** v. — Syn. limit oneself, specialize too much, be a specialist; see **restrain** 1, **restrict** 2.

**overspread,** v. — Syn. envelop, sheathe, coat; see **cover** 1.

**overstaffed,** modif. — Syn. having too many workers, having too many employees, having excess labor, having excess help, having no openings; see also **full** 1, 3.

**overstate,** v. — Syn. overstress, expand upon, amplify, emphasize; see **exaggerate, exceed.**

**overstay,** v. — Syn. stay too long, stop, outstay one's welcome; see **remain** 1.

**overstep,** v. — Syn. exceed, violate, encroach, trespass; see **exceed, meddle** 1.

**overstock,** v. — Syn. oversupply, overfill, cram, overload; see **burden, load** 1.

**overstress,** v. — Syn. overemphasize, stress too much, promote out of proportion; see **emphasize.**

**overstrung,** modif. — Syn. highstrung, tense, excitable, distraught, hypersensitive, nervous; see also **excited, frantic, hysterical, troubled** 1.

**oversubscribed,** modif. — Syn. contributed to, overpurchased, put over the top*; see **bought, given.**

**oversubscription,** n. — Syn. oversubscribing, lively market, generous contributions; see **gift** 1, **sale** 1, 2.

**overt,** modif. — Syn. apparent, clear, open, plain; see **definite** 2, **obvious** 1.

**overtake,** v. — Syn. overhaul, catch up with, get to, pass; see **catch** 3, **reach** 1.

**overtaken,** modif. — Syn. caught up with, caught up to, reached, apprehended; see **beaten** 1, **captured** 1.

**overtax,** v. — Syn. exhaust, strain, trouble; see **oppress, tire** 2, **weary** 1.

**over the hill*,** modif. — Syn. old, past, removed, departed; see **dead** 1, **gone** 1, 2, **old** 1, 2.

**overthrow,** v. — Syn. overcome, depose, bring down, topple; see **abolish, defeat** 2, **oust.**
See Synonym Study at DEFEAT.

**overthrown,** modif. — Syn. ousted, overcome, overwhelmed, vanquished; see **beaten** 1.

**overtime,** modif. — Syn. additional, added, supplementary; see **extra, late** 4.

**overtime,** n. — Syn. extra pay, additional pay, late hours, larger check; see **pay** 2.

**overtone,** n. — Syn. tone, inference, hint, connotation; see **meaning, suggestion** 1.

**overtop,** v. — Syn. dominate, command, surpass; see **exceed.**

**overture,** n. 1. [Preliminary negotiations; sometimes plural] — Syn. approach, advance, tender, offer; see **suggestion** 1.
2. [A musical introduction] — Syn. prelude, prologue, Vorspiel (German), voluntary, proem, preface; see also **introduction** 1.

**overturn,** v. — Syn. upset, reverse, upturn, overthrow; see **upset** 1.
See Synonym Study at UPSET.

**overuse,** v. — Syn. use too much, use too frequently, wear out, misuse; see **abuse** 1, **use** 1.

**overvalue,** v. — Syn. overrate, magnify, overestimate, overemphasize; see **exaggerate, exceed, overdo** 1.

**overview,** n. — Syn. survey, sketch, general outlook; see **summary.**

**overweening,** modif. — Syn. presumptuous, haughty, insolent, arrogant; see **egotistic** 2.

**overweigh,** v. — Syn. weigh down, overload, strain; see **burden, outweigh.**

**overwhelm,** v. 1. [To defeat] — Syn. overcome, overthrow, conquer, destroy; see **confute, defeat** 1, **win** 1.
2. [To drown] — Syn. submerge, inundate, waste; see **flood, sink** 1.
3. [To astonish] — Syn. puzzle, bewilder, confound; see **confuse, surprise** 1.

**overwhelmed,** modif. — Syn. beaten, worsted, overpowered, vanquished, devastated, repulsed, engulfed, submerged; see also **beaten** 2, **drowned.**

**overwhelming,** modif. 1. [In the act of destroying] — Syn. conquering, subjugating, defeating, subduing, overpowering, overthrowing, crushing, routing, ruining, smashing, wiping out, extinguishing, invading, occupying, ravaging, devastating, breaking, reducing, overturning, overriding, overrunning, upsetting; see also **triumphant.** — Ant. PROTECTIVE, saving, defending.
2. [In the act of submerging] — Syn. wasting, inundating, drowning, deluging, surging, overspreading, desolating, obliterating, dissolving, blotting out, wrecking, erasing, effacing, expunging, burying, immersing, engulfing, engrossing, covering. — Ant. FLOATING, reclaiming, raising.

**3.** [Astonishing] — *Syn.* amazing, terrifying, awful; see **frightful** 1, **might** 3, **powerful** 1, **strong** 1, 2, 8.
**4.** [Unbelievable] — *Syn.* remarkable, strange, baffling; see **unbelievable, unusual** 1, 2.

**overwork,** *n.* — *Syn.* extra work, overtime, exploitation, overburdening, overloading, exhaustion, going too far, overdoing it; see also **abuse** 3.

**overwork,** *v.* — *Syn.* overdo, exhaust, wear out; see **burden, tire** 1, 2, **weary** 1.

**overworked,** *modif.* — *Syn.* too busy, overburdened, worked too hard; see **tired.**

**overwrought,** *modif.* **1.** [Weary from exhaustion] — *Syn.* affected, worn, weary; see **spent** 2, **tired.**
**2.** [Excitable from exhaustion] — *Syn.* worked-up, high-strung, emotional, nervous, neurotic; see also **excitable.**

**overzealous,** *modif.* — *Syn.* overeager, carrying a good thing too far, bossy; see **enthusiastic** 1, 2, 3.

**owe,** *v.* — *Syn.* be under obligation, be indebted to, be obligated to, have an obligation, ought to, be bound, become beholden, get on credit, feel bound, be bound to pay, be contracted to, be subject to draft for, be in debt for, have signed a note for, have borrowed, have lost, bind out★.

**owed,** *modif.* — *Syn.* owing, becoming due, indebted; see **due, unpaid** 1.

**owing,** *modif.* — *Syn.* owed, attributable, in debt, outstanding; see **due.**

**owing to** — *Syn.* as a result of, because of, due to; see **because.**

**owl,** *n.* — *Syn.* owlet, bird of prey, night bird, nocturnal bird, owl pigeon, satinette, turbit, Bubo, Strix; see also **bird** 1.
Kinds of owls include: hoot, barn, burrowing, great horned, great gray, screech, spotted, snow, snowy, tawny, barred, long-eared, short-eared, pigmy, boobook, saw-whet, hissing, African, Chinese; hawk owl, Richardson's owl.

**own,** *modif.* — *Syn.* mine, yours, his, hers, its, theirs, personal, individual, owned, very own★; see also **private.**

**come into one's own** — *Syn.* receive what one deserves, gain proper credit, gain proper recognition, thrive; see **prosper.**

**of one's own** — *Syn.* personal, private, belonging to one; see **owned.**

**on one's own** — *Syn.* by oneself, acted independently, singly; see **independently.**

**own,** *v.* **1.** [To possess] — *Syn.* hold, have, enjoy, have inherited, fallen heir to, have title to, have rights to, be master of, occupy, control, dominate, have claim upon, boast, reserve, retain, keep, have in hand, have a deed for; see also **maintain** 3. — *Ant.* LACK, want, need.
**2.** [To acknowledge] — *Syn.* admit, assent to, grant, recognize; see **admit** 2, 3, **declare** 2.
*See Synonym Study at* ADMIT.

**owned,** *modif.* — *Syn.* possessed, had, bought, purchased, kept, inherited, enjoyed, fallen into the possession of, seized by, in the seizin of, in hand, on hand, bound over, descended upon, dowered upon, in the possession of, among the possessions of, the property of; see also **held, retained** 1.

**owner,** *n.* — *Syn.* proprietor, possessor, keeper, buyer, purchaser, heir, heiress, coinheritor, joint heir, heritor, legatee, proprietress, landlord, landlady, sharer, partner, titleholder, master, heir-apparent; see also **possessor.**

**ownership,** *n.* — *Syn.* possession, having, holding, claim, deed, title, control, buying, purchasing, purchase, falling heir to, heirship, possessorship, proprietorship, occupancy, tenure, use, residence, tenancy, dominion, seizin.

**own up★,** *v.* — *Syn.* be honest, admit error, confess; see **admit** 2.

**ox,** *n.* — *Syn.* castrated bull, bullock, steer, *Bos taurus* (Latin); see **animal** 1, **bull** 1, **cow.**
Types of oxen include: wild, musk, Indian, Galla, gayal, gaur, kouprey.

**oxford,** *n.* — *Syn.* low shoe, walking shoe, tie shoe, wingtip, blucher, brogue, comfort shoe, nurse's shoe; see also **shoe.**

**oyster,** *n.* — *Syn.* bivalve, mollusk, sea food; see **clam, fish, shellfish.**
Types of oysters include: blue point, rock, pearl, saddle, Olympia, Wellfleet, American-Canadian, Portuguese, Japanese, Gigantic, Chinese, European, British Columbian, Australian mud, flat, saddlerock, cove, box, wild, tonged, dredged.

# P

**pa★**, *n.* — *Syn.* father, sire, papa, dad; see **father** 1, **parent.**

**pabulum,** *n.* — *Syn.* sustenance, nutrition, diet; see **food.**

**pace,** *n.* — *Syn.* step, velocity, movement; see **speed.**

  **change of pace** — *Syn.* variation, alteration, diversity; see **change** 2.

  **go through one's paces** — *Syn.* show one's abilities, perform, exhibit; see **display** 1.

  **keep pace (with)** — *Syn.* go at the same speed, maintain the same rate of progress, keep up with; see **equal.**

  **off the pace** — *Syn.* out of first place, behind the leader, trailing after; see **behind** 3.

  **put through one's paces** — *Syn.* challenge, put to the test, run through a routine; see **test** 1.

  **set the pace** — *Syn.* begin, initiate, establish criteria; see **lead** 1.

**pace,** *v.* **1.** [To stride] — *Syn.* walk, tread, traverse, travel, walk the floor, pace back and forth; see also **walk** 1.

**2.** [To measure by pacing] — *Syn.* determine, pace off, step off; see **measure** 1.

**pacer,** *n.* **1.** [A horse] — *Syn.* pony, mount, steed; see **animal** 2, **horse** 1.

**2.** [A criterion] — *Syn.* standard, example, pacemaker; see **criterion, measure** 2.

**pacifiable,** *modif.* — *Syn.* forgiving, peaceable, appeasable, placable, conciliable, propitiable, pacificatory, propitiatory.

**Pacific,** *n.* — *Syn.* North Pacific, South Pacific, Central Pacific, South Seas; see **ocean.**

**pacific,** *modif.* — *Syn.* peaceable, peaceful, tranquil, untroubled, smooth, gentle, quiet, still, composed, restful, unruffled, halcyon, appeasing, conciliatory, mild, kindly, placid, serene, easygoing; see also **calm** 1, 2. — *Ant.* QUARRELSOME, turbulent, rough.

**pacification,** *n.* — *Syn.* appeasement, accommodation, settlement, adjustment; see **agreement** 3.

**pacifist,** *n.* — *Syn.* peace-lover, peacemonger★, passive resister, conscientious objector, Satyagrahist, noncooperator, civil disobedience campaigner, peacenik★, conchie★, sit-downer★, flower child★, dove★; see also **radical, conscientious objector, resister.**

**pacify,** *v.* **1.** [To mollify] — *Syn.* conciliate, appease, placate, mollify, propitiate, assuage, soothe, smooth over, calm, tranquilize, subdue, pour oil on troubled waters; see also **quiet** 1.

**2.** [To quiet] — *Syn.* soothe, silence, lull; see **quiet** 2.

*SYN.* — **pacify** implies the making quiet, calm, and peaceful of someone or something that has become agitated, angry, or disorderly /to *pacify* a crying child/; **appease** suggests a pacifying by gratifying or giving in to the demands of /to *appease* one's hunger/; **mollify** suggests a soothing of wounded feelings or an allaying of indignation /his compliments failed to *mollify* her/; **placate** implies the changing of a hostile or angry attitude to a friendly or favorable one /to *placate* an offended colleague/; **propitiate** implies an allaying or forestalling of hostile feeling by winning the good will of /sacrifices made to *propitiate* a deity/; **conciliate** implies the use of arbitration, concession, persuasion, etc. in an attempt to win over

---

**pack,** *n.* **1.** [A package] — *Syn.* package, box, packet; see **package** 1.

**2.** [Kit] — *Syn.* bundle, backpack, knapsack, duffel bag, bag, baggage, kit, gear, outfit, load, burden; see also **bag** 1, **equipment.**

**3.** [A group] — *Syn.* number, gang, mob; see **crowd** 1.

**4.** [A medical dressing] — *Syn.* application, hot pack, ice pack, cold pack, plaster, pledget, pad, sponge, tampon, compress, bandage, wet dressing; see also **dressing** 3.

**5.** [A set of cards] — *Syn.* deck, canasta deck, poker deck, rummy deck, bridge deck, pinochle deck, set, assortment; see also **deck** 2.

*See Synonym Study at* PACKAGE.

**pack,** *v.* **1.** [To prepare for transportation] — *Syn.* prepare, gather, collect, (make) ready, get ready, put in (order), stow away, dispose, cinch, sock up, tie with a diamond hitch, tie, bind, brace, fasten. — *Ant.* UNDO, untie, take out.

**2.** [To stow compactly] — *Syn.* stuff, squeeze, bind, compress, condense, arrange, ram, cram, jam, insert, press, contract, put away, pack in, thrust in, drive in, run in. — *Ant.* SCATTER, loosen, fluff up.

**3.** [To fill by entering; *often used with "in" or "out"*] — *Syn.* crowd, throng, mob; see **press** 1, **push** 1.

**4.** [To transport by using pack animals; *often used with "in" or "out"*] — *Syn.* carry, freight, journey, trek, backpack, haul around, go by muleback, take a pack train; see also **carry** 1.

**package,** *n.* **1.** [A bundle] — *Syn.* parcel, packet, bundle, pack, burden, load, kit, bunch, sheaf, bale, batch, roll, bag, box, case, carton, crate, container, can, tin, sack, bottle, packaging, wrapping, packing, shrink-wrap; see also **bag** 1, **container.**

**2.** [A set of things offered as a unit] — *Syn.* unit, package deal, set, lot, combination, aggregate, grouping, ensemble, assortment.

---

*SYN.* — **package** and **parcel** are applied to something wrapped or boxed for transportation, sale, etc. and imply moderateness of size and a compact or orderly arrangement; **bundle** refers to a number of things bound together for convenience in carrying, storing, etc. and does not in itself carry connotations as to size or compactness /a *bundle* of discarded clothing/; **bale** implies a standardized or uniform quantity of goods, as raw cotton or hay, compressed into a rectangular mass and tightly bound; **pack** is applied to a package of a standard amount /a *pack* of cigarettes*/* or to a compact bundle carried on the back of a person or animal

---

**packed,** *modif.* **1.** [Ready for storage or shipment] — *Syn.* arranged, prepared, bundled, wrapped, consigned; see also **ready** 2.
**2.** [Pressed together] — *Syn.* compact, compressed, pressed down; see **full** 1, **jammed** 2.

**packet,** *n.* **1.** [A small bundle or container] — *Syn.* pack, receptacle, parcel; see **container, package** 1.
**2.** [A ship with a regular schedule] — *Syn.* mail ship, mail steamer, steamboat, ferry; see **ship.**

**packhorse,** *n.* — *Syn.* nag, pack animal, workhorse, transportation; see **animal** 2, **horse** 1.

**packing,** *n.* **1.** [The preparation of goods for shipment or storage] — *Syn.* preparation, arrangement, compression, consignment, disposal, disposition, sorting, grading, laying away.
**2.** [Material used to fill space] — *Syn.* stuffing, wadding, waste, styrofoam, peanuts*; see also **filling.**

**packing house,** *n.* — *Syn.* packing plant, processing plant, meat packers, butchery; see **butcher, factory.**

**packrat,** *n.* — *Syn.* hoarder, collector, accumulator, gatherer; see **collector** 2.

**packsaddle,** *n.* — *Syn.* mule chair, seat, cushion; see **saddle.**

**pack train,** *n.* — *Syn.* caravan, safari, supply train; see **equipment.**

**pact,** *n.* — *Syn.* settlement, compact, bargain; see **agreement** 3, **treaty.**

**pad,** *n.* **1.** [Material for writing] — *Syn.* note paper, note pad, memorandum, block, foolscap, parchment, *tabula rasa* (Latin); see also **paper** 5, **tablet** 2.
**2.** [Cushion] — *Syn.* mat, pillow, bolster, mattress, pallet, padding, stuffing; see also **bed** 1, **filling.**
**3.** [*A residence] — *Syn.* room, apartment, living quarters; see **home** 1, 2.

**pad,** *v.* **1.** [To thicken] — *Syn.* stuff, fill out, pad out; see **fill** 1.
**2.** [To increase] — *Syn.* lengthen, expand, augment, amplify, inflate, spread, stretch, enlarge; see also **increase** 1.

**padded,** *modif.* — *Syn.* stuffed, filled, quilted; see **full** 1, **jammed** 2.

**padding,** *n.* **1.** [Filling] — *Syn.* stuffing, wadding, waste; see **filling.**
**2.** [Verbosity] — *Syn.* diffuseness, redundancy, triteness; see **wordiness.**

**paddle,** *n.* — *Syn.* oar, pole, scull, sweep, paddle wheel; see also **propeller.**

**paddle,** *v.* **1.** [To propel by paddling] — *Syn.* row, scull, boat, cruise, drift, navigate, cut water, run rapids; see also **drive** 3, **propel.**
**2.** [To beat, usually rather lightly] — *Syn.* spank, thrash, rap; see **beat** 2, **punish.**

**paddled,** *modif.* — *Syn.* beaten, spanked, pounded; see **hit, punished.**

**paddle one's own canoe**★**,** *v.* — *Syn.* do without assistance, go alone, ask no favors, manage, rely upon oneself.

**paddock,** *n.* — *Syn.* enclosure, corral, pen, stockyard; see **barnyard, enclosure** 1.

**padlock,** *n.* — *Syn.* latch, fastener, catch; see **lock** 1.

**padre,** *n.* — *Syn.* priest, clergyman, pastor, monk; see **minister** 1, **priest.**

**padrone,** *n.* — *Syn.* master, lord, patron, boss, chief; see also **master** 1.

**paean,** *n.* — *Syn.* hymn, ovation, oratorio, anthem; see **hymn, song.**

**pagan,** *modif.* — *Syn.* unchristian, gentile, idolatrous, heathenish; see **atheistic, heathen, impious.**

**pagan,** *n.* — *Syn.* heathen, idolater, gentile, pantheist, Pyrrhonist, skeptic, doubter, scoffer, heretic, unbeliever, nonbeliever, infidel, paynim, Philistine, Zoroastrian, animist, polytheist, freethinker, atheist, agnostic; see also **atheist, skeptic.** — *Ant.* CHRISTIAN, Jew, Muslim.

---

**SYN.** — **pagan** and **heathen** are both applied to polytheistic peoples, but **pagan** often refers specifically to ancient peoples, esp. the Greeks and Romans, and **heathen** is applied to peoples regarded as uncivilized or primitive idolaters; **gentile** (often **Gentile**) is applied to one who is not a Jew, or, among Mormons, to one who is not a Mormon

---

**paganism,** *n.* — *Syn.* heathenism, agnosticism, idolatry, pagandom, mythology, mysticism, henotheism, ditheism, dualism, pantheism, animism, cosmotheism, nonbelief, infidelity, doubt, heresy, demonism, demon worship, devil worship, sun worship, heliolatry, pyrolatry, fetishism, heathenry; see also **atheism.**

**page,** *n.* **1.** [One side of a sheet] — *Syn.* leaf, sheet, folio, side, surface, recto, verso.
**2.** [A youth] — *Syn.* attendant, errand boy, errand girl, boy; see **servant.**

**page,** *v.* **1.** [To call] — *Syn.* hunt for, seek for, call the name of; see **summon** 1.
**2.** [To mark the pages] — *Syn.* number, check, paginate, foliate; see **count.**

**pageant,** *n.* — *Syn.* show, exhibition, celebration, pomp; see **parade** 1.

**pageantry,** *n.* — *Syn.* pomp, show, spectacle; see **display** 2, **parade** 1.

**paged,** *modif.* — *Syn.* summoned, called for, asked for, sought; see **requested** 1.

**paid,** *modif.* — *Syn.* rewarded, paid off, reimbursed, compensated, indemnified, remunerated, solvent, unindebted, unowed, recompensed, salaried, hired, out of debt, refunded; see also **repaid.**

**paid for,** *modif.* — *Syn.* purchased, bought and paid for, owned; see **bought.**

**paid off,** *modif.* — *Syn.* out of debt, solvent, (in the) clear; see **bought.**

**pail,** *n.* — *Syn.* bucket, pot, receptacle, jug; see **bucket, container.**

**pain,** *n.* **1.** [Suffering, physical or mental] — *Syn.* hurt, anguish, distress, discomfort, disorder, agony, misery, crucifixion, martyrdom, wretchedness, shock, torture, torment, passion; see also **injury** 1. — *Ant.* HEALTH, well-being, ease.
**2.** [Suffering, usually physical] — *Syn.* ache, twinge, catch, throb, throe, spasm, cramp, gripe, stitch, torture, malady, sickness, rack, laceration, paroxysm, soreness, fever, burning, prick, torment, distress, agony, affliction, discomfort, hurt, pang, wound, strain, sting, burn, crick; see also **illness** 1, **injury** 1.
Specific kinds of pains (including aches) include: housemaid's knee, tennis elbow, shin splint, arthritis, arthritic pain, rheumatism, inflammatory rheumatism, gout, peritonitis, bursitis, earache, headache, stomachache, bellyache, toothache, backache.
**3.** [Suffering, usually mental] — *Syn.* despondency, worry, anxiety; see **depression** 2, **grief** 1, **sadness.**
**4.** [Effort; *used in plural*] — *Syn.* effort, endeavor, care; see **effort.**
*See Synonym Study at* EFFORT.

**feeling no pain**★ — *Syn.* intoxicated, inebriated, stoned*; see **drunk.**

**upon** or **under pain of**— *Syn.* at the risk of, in danger of, risking; see **gambling.**

**pain,** *v.* — *Syn.* distress, grieve, trouble; see **hurt** 1.

**pained,** *modif.* — *Syn.* upset, worried, distressed; see **hurt, troubled** 1.

**painful,** *modif.* **1.** [Referring to physical anguish] — *Syn.* sore, raw, aching, throbbing, burning, torturing, hurtful, biting, piercing, sharp, severe, caustic, tormenting, smarting, extreme, grievous, griping, stinging, lacerating, bruised, sensitive, tender, irritated, irritable, vexatious, distressing, agonizing, excruciating, torturous, grievous, inflamed, burned, unpleasant, ulcerated, abscessed, uncomfortable; see also **sore.** — *Ant.* HEALTHY, comfortable, well.
**2.** [Referring to mental anguish] — *Syn.* unpleasant, distasteful, grievous, worrying, depressing, saddening; see also **disturbing.**

**painfully,** *modif.* **1.** [With pain] — *Syn.* in pain, achingly, in suffering, racked by pain, sorely, with difficulty.
**2.** [With extreme care] — *Syn.* painstakingly, slowly, tortuously; see **carefully** 1, 2.

**painstaking,** *modif.* — *Syn.* scrupulous, exacting, meticulous; see **careful.**

**paint,** *n.* **1.** [Pigment] — *Syn.* coloring material, chroma, chlorophyll; see **color** 1.
Paints and colorings include — *artist's materials:* oil, acrylic, pastel, gouache, crayon, charcoal, watercolor, ink, pencil, showcard color, tempera; *architectural finishes:* polyurethane, latex, alkyd, enamel, varnish, calcimine, casein paint, stain, wood stain, waterproofing stain, oil, wax, whitewash, tempera, fresco, encaustic, anticorrosion paint, antifouling paint, metallic paint, fireproof paint, cellulose paint, luminous paint, house paint, barn paint, inside paint, outside paint, wall paint, floor paint, ceiling paint, trim paint, flat paint, white lead, linseed oil paint.
**2.** [*Makeup] — *Syn.* cosmetics, tint, rouge; see **cosmetic, makeup** 1.
**3.** [Covering] — *Syn.* overlay, varnish, veneer; see **cover** 2.

**paint,** *v.* **1.** [To represent by painting] — *Syn.* draw, portray, paint in oils, sketch, outline, picture, depict, delineate, draft, catch a likeness, limn, design, shade, tint, compose, apply pigment, fresco, wash; see also **draw** 2.
**2.** [To protect, or decorate by painting] — *Syn.* coat, decorate, apply, brush, tint, touch up, stipple, ornament, gloss over, swab, daub, slap on, (use an) airbrush; see also **cover** 1, **spread** 4.
**3.** [*To apply cosmetics] — *Syn.* cosmeticize, rouge, powder; see **make up** 6.

**paintable,** *modif.* — *Syn.* scenic, pictorial, graphic; see **picturesque** 1.

**painted,** *modif.* **1.** [Portrayed] — *Syn.* outlined, pictured, drawn, sketched, composed, designed, depicted, delineated, frescoed, limned, washed on; see also **colored** 1.
**2.** [Finished] — *Syn.* coated, covered, enameled, decorated, ornamented, brushed over, tinted, washed, daubed, touched up, smeared; see also **ornate** 1.
**3.** [*Made-up] — *Syn.* rouged, reddened, colored, powdered, freshened, daubed; see also **made-up** 2.

**painter,** *n.* **1.** [A house painter] — *Syn.* interior decorator, calciminer, dauber*, paint-slinger*; see **worker.**
**2.** [An artist] — *Syn.* craftsman, artisan, illustrator, landscapist, portrait painter, miniaturist, draftsman, etcher, sketcher, cartoonist, artificer, animator, dauber; see also **artist** 1.
Major painters include: Cimabue, Giotto, Sandro Botticelli, Andrea del Sarto, Veronese, Jan van Eyck, Albrecht Dürer, Lucas Cranach, Hieronymus Bosch, Pieter Bruegel (the elder and the younger), Hans Holbein (the elder and the younger), Frans Hals, Leonardo da Vinci, Michelangelo Buonarroti, Raphael, Titian, Tintoretto, El Greco, Correggio, Caravaggio, Canaletto, Tiepolo, Peter Paul Rubens, Anthony Van Dyck, Rembrandt van Rijn, Jan Vermeer, Nicolas Poussin, Antoine Watteau, Sir Joshua Reynolds, Thomas Gainsborough, John Constable, J.M.W. Turner, J.S. Copley, William Hogarth, Diego Velázquez, Francisco Goya, Eugène Delacroix, Auguste Renoir, Edgar Degas, James Whistler, Winslow Homer, Édouard Manet, Claude Monet, Walter Sickert, Paul Cézanne, Vincent van Gogh, Paul Gauguin, Henri de Toulouse-Lautrec, Pablo Picasso, Henri ("le Douanier") Rousseau, Amedeo Modigliani, Marc Chagall, Georges Braque, Henri Matisse, Piet Mondrian, Paul Klee, Salvador Dali, Max Ernst, Georgia O'Keefe, Jackson Pollock, Andy Warhol, Roy Lichtenstein.

**painting,** *n.* **1.** [A work of art] — *Syn.* oil painting, water color, abstract design, landscape, cityscape, seascape, composition, sketch, portrait, portrayal, picture, likeness, representation, art work, canvas, mural, depiction, delineation; see also **art** 3.
Schools of painting include: primitive, Romanesque, Medieval, Florentine, Sienese, Flemish, Venetian, Mannerist, Dutch, Spanish, French, *tableau de genre* (French), pre-Raphaelite, Impressionism, Postimpressionism, Neoimpressionism, *plein air* (French), Realism, Fauvism, primitivism, Naturalism, Expressionism, Cubism, Futurism, Symbolism, Dadaism, Surrealism, Abstract Expressionism, pop, op.
**2.** [The act of applying paint] — *Syn.* enameling, covering, coating, varnishing, decorating, calcimining, daubing, splashing, brushing, airbrushing, the brush*; see also **art** 2.

**pair,** *n.* — *Syn.* couple, mates, two, two of a kind, duo, twosome, combination, combo*, set, twins, brace, yoke, span, tandem, dyad, doublet, deuce, partners, duality; see also **both.**

*SYN.* — **pair** is used of two similar or corresponding things that are associated together or are necessary in twos for proper use *[a pair of socks]* or of a single thing made up of two corresponding parts *[a pair of scissors]*; **couple** applies to any two things of the same sort that are somehow associated *[a couple of dollars]*, or is used colloquially to mean several or a few *[I have to buy a couple of things]*; a **brace,** meaning two of a kind, applies esp. to certain animals or game birds *[a brace of pheasants, hounds, etc.]*; **yoke** applies to a pair of animals harnessed together for pulling *[a yoke of oxen]*; **span** is used esp. of a pair of horses harnessed together

**pair,** *v.* — *Syn.* combine (with), match, balance (off); see **join** 1, 2.

**pajamas,** *n.* — *Syn.* nightwear, lounging pajamas, lounging robe, slacks*, PJ's*, 'jamas*, nightie*.

**pal\*,** *n.* — *Syn.* companion, bosom friend, buddy; see **friend** 1.

**palace,** *n.* — *Syn.* royal residence, official residence, hall, manor, mansion, dwelling; see also **castle.**

**palatable,** *modif.* — *Syn.* tasty, appetizing, savory; see **delicious** 1.

**palate,** *n.* **1.** [Roof of the mouth] — *Syn.* velum, hard palate, soft palate; see **mouth** 1.
**2.** [Sense of taste] — *Syn.* taste, appetite, tongue; see **taste** 1.

**palatial,** *modif.* — *Syn.* regal, illustrious, magnificent; see **grand** 2, **stately** 2.

**palatinate,** *n.* — *Syn.* country, province, mandate; see **area** 2, **territory** 2.

**palatine,** *n.* — *Syn.* minister, chamberlain, official, vassal lord; see **lord** 2, **royalty.**

**palaver,** *n.* — *Syn.* speech, babble, conversation; see **nonsense** 1, **talk** 5.

**pale,** *modif.* **1.** [Wan] — *Syn.* pallid, wan, ashen, ashy, pasty, waxen, sickly, anemic, colorless, bloodless, livid, ghastly, cadaverous, haggard, deathlike, ghostly, spectral, white, gray, sallow, etiolated, blanched, whey-faced, drained, peaked, washed-out*, white as a sheet*, green around the gills*.
**2.** [Lacking color or intensity] — *Syn.* bleached, light, pastel, soft, soft-hued, creamy, whitish, dim, faint, faded, feeble, chalky, washed-out.

*SYN.* — **pale,** in this comparison the least connotative of these words, implies merely an unnatural whiteness or colorlessness, often temporary, of the complexion; **pallid** suggests a paleness resulting from exhaustion, faintness, emotional strain, etc.; **wan** suggests the paleness resulting from an emaciating illness; **ashen** implies the grayish paleness of the skin as in death; **livid** refers to a grayish-blue complexion, as of one in great rage or fear, but is also sometimes used now of a white or red complexion

**pale,** *v.* — *Syn.* grow pale, lose color, blanch; see **faint, whiten** 1.

**paleness,** *n.* **1.** [Pallor] — *Syn.* sickness, whiteness, anemia, pallidness, colorlessness.
**2.** [Dimness] — *Syn.* translucency, dullness, obscurity; see **darkness** 1.

**paleontology,** *n.* — *Syn.* paleology, archaism, prehistory; see **archaeology, science** 1.

**palimpsest,** *n.* — *Syn.* re-inscription, overwritten, document, writing; see **manuscript.**

**palindrome,** *n.* — *Syn.* wordplay, play on words, witticism; see **pun.**

**paling,** *n.* — *Syn.* enclosure, hedge, picket; see **fence** 1.

**palisade,** *n.* — *Syn.* stockade, defense, bank; see **barrier, fortification** 2, **wall** 1.

**palisades,** *n.* — *Syn.* cliff, face, slope; see **mountain** 1, **wall** 2.

**pall,** *n.* — *Syn.* cloak, cloth, covering; see **cover** 1.

**pall,** *v.* — *Syn.* satiate, surfeit, glut, bore; see **disgust, weary** 1.

**pallet,** *n.* — *Syn.* cot, stretcher, couch; see **bed** 1.

**palliate,** *v.* — *Syn.* apologize for, make light of, screen, hide, conceal, cover, veil, gloss over, cloak, mitigate, assuage, varnish, veneer, whitewash, soften, soft-pedal, subdue, moderate, gloze, bolster up, exculpate, vindicate, justify, alleviate; see also **excuse, extenuate.**

**pallid,** *modif.* — *Syn.* gray, colorless, wan; see **pale** 1.
*See Synonym Study at* PALE.

**pallor,** *n.* — *Syn.* wanness, whiteness, lack of color; see **paleness** 1.

**palm,** *n.* Types of palm trees include: feather, fan, date, Washington, doom, wax, cabbage, curly, fern, coconut, sea-coconut, rattan, oil, para, walkstick, wine, betel, palmyra, Bourbon, raphia, royal, umbrella, palmetto, piasava, assai, West African, Brazilian; see also **tree.**

**palmate,** *modif.* — *Syn.* hand-like, radial, jagged, scalloped, toothed, dentate, lobed, nicked, serrated, escalloped, digitate; see also **irregular** 4, **notched.**

**palmist,** *n.* — *Syn.* spiritualist, clairvoyant, prophet; see **fortuneteller.**

**palmistry,** *n.* — *Syn.* chiromancy, fortunetelling, prediction, prophecy; see **divination, forecast.**

**palmy,** *modif.* — *Syn.* prosperous, glorious, delightful; see **rich** 1, **successful, triumphant.**

**palpable,** *modif.* — *Syn.* tangible, plain, manifest, evident, unmistakable; see also **obvious** 1, **tangible.**
*See Synonym Study at* TANGIBLE, EVIDENT.

**palpitate,** *v.* — *Syn.* pulse, throb, vibrate; see **beat** 3.

**palpitation,** *n.* — *Syn.* throbbing, tremble, pulsation; see **beat** 2.

**palsied,** *modif.* — *Syn.* disabled, paralyzed, paralytic, neurasthenic, weak, debilitated, atonic, helpless, tremorous, trembling, tremulous, shaking, diseased; see also **sick.**

**palsy,** *n.* — *Syn.* paralysis, cerebral palsy, Parkinson's disease; see **disease.**

**paltriness,** *n.* — *Syn.* pettiness, irrelevance, triviality; see **insignificance.**

**paltry,** *modif.* — *Syn.* small, insignificant, trifling, piddling; see **trivial, unimportant.**

**pampas,** *n.* — *Syn.* prairie, tundra, plains; see **plain.**

**pamper,** *v.* — *Syn.* spoil, indulge, baby, pet, cater to, humor, gratify, yield to, coddle, overindulge, dote on, please, cosset; see also **satisfy** 1.
*See Synonym Study at* INDULGE.

**pamphlet,** *n.* — *Syn.* booklet, brochure, pocketbook, chapbook, leaflet, bulletin, compilation, circular, broadside, throwaway, handbill; see also **announcement** 3.

**pamphleteer,** *n.* — *Syn.* carper, commentator, essayist; see **critic** 1.

**pan,** *n.* — *Syn.* pot, vessel, kettle, container, pail, bucket, baking pan, gold pan; see also **container, utensil** 1.
Kitchen pans include: kettle, stew pan, saucepan, saucepot, stockpot, dutch oven, double boiler, roaster, casserole, cake pan, bread pan, pie pan, muffin tin, springform pan, tart pan, cookie sheet, frying pan *or* skillet *or* spider, dishpan, vegetable steamer, wok.

**pan,** *v.* **1.** [To obtain gold] — *Syn.* wash, shake, agitate, separate, placer, mine, secure, obtain.
**2.** [*To disparage] — *Syn.* criticize, review unfavorably, jeer at; see **censure.**
**3.** [To swing; *said of a camera*] — *Syn.* sweep, pan to *or* toward, follow; see **move** 1.

**panacea,** *n.* — *Syn.* relief, elixir, cure; see **remedy** 2.

**pancake,** *n.* — *Syn.* flapjack, hot cake, batter cake, griddlecake, cake, fried bread, fried mush, sourdough, *latke, blintz* (*both* Yiddish), *tortilla* (Spanish), *blini* (Russian), *crêpe, crêpes suzette* (*both* French), *chapati* (Hindi); see also **food.**

**pandemonium,** *n.* **1.** [Confusion] — *Syn.* uproar, anarchy, riot; see **confusion** 2.
**2.** [Hell] — *Syn.* underworld, inferno, abyss; see **hell** 1.

**pander,** *n.* — *Syn.* procurer, pimp, white slaver, whoremonger; see **pimp.**

**pane,** *n.* — *Syn.* window glass, stained glass, mirror; see **glass** 2.

**panegyric,** *modif.* — *Syn.* laudatory, acclamatory, flattering; see **complimentary.**

**panegyric,** *n.* — *Syn.* compliment, honor, eulogy, tribute; see **praise** 2.
*See Synonym Study at* TRIBUTE.

**panel,** *n.* **1.** [Rectangular section of a surface] — *Syn.* ornament, tablet, inset, wainscoting, plyboard, hanging, tapestry, arras; see also **decoration** 5.
**2.** [Group of persons] — *Syn.* jury, committee, board, council, tribunal; see also **jury.**

**pang,** *n.* — *Syn.* throb, sting, bite; see **pain** 1.

**panhandle*,** *v.* — *Syn.* solicit, ask alms, bum*; see **beg** 2.

**panhandler,** *n.* — *Syn.* vagrant, bum, mendicant; see **beggar** 1, **tramp** 1.

**panic,** *n.* 1. [Overpowering fright] — *Syn.* fear, dread, alarm, fright; see **fear** 1.

2. [Mob action, impelled by panic, sense 1] — *Syn.* mob hysteria, group hysteria, frenzy, crush, rush, jam; see also **confusion** 2.

3. [A wave of financial hysteria] — *Syn.* run on the bank, crash, economic decline; see **depression** 3.
*See Synonym Study at* FEAR.

**push the panic button\*** — *Syn.* panic, become afraid, dread; see **fear** 1.

**panic-stricken,** *modif.* — *Syn.* terrified, hysterical, fearful; see **afraid** 2.

**panoply,** *n.* — *Syn.* covering, shield, protection, garb, array, display, show; see also **armor** 1.

**panorama,** *n.* — *Syn.* spectacle, scene, scenery, prospect; see **view** 2.

**panoramic,** *modif.* — *Syn.* pictorial, general, scenic; see **picturesque** 1.

**pan out\*,** *v.* — *Syn.* yield, net, come *or* work out; see **result.**

**pansy,** *n.* — *Syn.* viola, *Viola tricolor hortensis* (Latin), *pensée* (French), heartsease; see **flower** 2, **plant.**

**pant,** *v.* — *Syn.* gasp, wheeze, throb, palpitate; see **breathe** 1, **gasp.**

**pantaloons,** *n.* — *Syn.* pants, trousers, breeches, knickers; see **clothes, pants** 1.

**pantheism,** *n.* — *Syn.* heathenism, polytheism, animism; see **paganism.**

**panther,** *n.* — *Syn.* jaguar, puma, wildcat; see **animal** 2, **cat** 2.

**panties\*,** *n.* — *Syn.* underpants, briefs, undies\*; see **pants** 2, **underwear.**

**panting,** *n.* 1. [Breathing] — *Syn.* respiring, gasping, heaving; see **breathing.**

2. [A desire] — *Syn.* passion, lust, hunger; see **desire** 3.

**pantomime,** *n.* — *Syn.* sign, sign language, dumb show, mimicry, play without words, acting without speech, charade, mime; see also **parody.**

**pantry,** *n.* — *Syn.* storeroom, scullery, larder, cupboard, cooler, buttery; see also **closet, room** 2.

**pants,** *n.* 1. [Trousers] — *Syn.* breeches, slacks, jeans, bluejeans, denims, dungarees, Levi's (trademark) overalls, cords, shorts, Bermuda shorts, corduroys, pantaloons, jodhpurs, bell-bottoms, toreador pants, hiphuggers, riding breeches, chaps, short pants, knee britches, clam diggers, knee pants, knickerbockers, knickers, bloomers, rompers, sun suit; see also **clothes.**

2. [\*Underclothing, especially women's] — *Syn.* underpants, shorts, drawers, briefs, panties, bikinis, scanties, *cache-sexe* (French), knickers (British); see also **clothes, underwear.**

**papa,** *n.* — *Syn.* father, dad, daddy, male parent; see **father** 1, **parent.**

**papacy,** *n.* — *Syn.* the Vatican, the Holy See, the See of Rome, Pontificate, popedom, the shoes of the fisherman\*.

**papal,** *modif.* — *Syn.* pontifical, emanating from the Pope *or* the Vatican, papist\*, papistic\*, papistical\*, popish\*, Romanistic\*, Romish\*.

**paper,** *modif.* — *Syn.* unsubstantial, flimsy, cardboard; see **thin** 1.

**paper,** *n.* 1. [A piece of legal or official writing] — *Syn.* document, official document, legal paper; see **record** 1.
Papers, sense 1, include: abstract, affidavit, warranty, bill, certificate, citation, contract, instrument, credentials, data, deed, diploma, indictment, grant, orders, passport, visa, plea, records, safe-conduct, subpoena,

summons, testimony, writ, decree, true bill, voucher, warrant, will.

2. [A newspaper] — *Syn.* journal, daily, daily journal; see **newspaper.**

3. [A piece of writing] — *Syn.* essay, article, theme; see **exposition** 2, **writing** 2.

4. [Means of commercial exchange] — *Syn.* paper money, bills, bank notes; see **money** 1.

5. [A manufactured product]
Paper, sense 5, includes — *writing material:* typing, typewriter, stationery, bond paper, letterhead, personal stationery, ruled, rag, handmade, handtorn, deckle-edge, laid, crown, post paper, correspondence card, foolscap, second sheet, onion skin, manifold, carbon paper, note pad, note paper, note card, filing card; *printing paper:* newsprint, enameled, glazed, enameled book, coated stock, free sheet, machine-finished book, publication book, poster, computer, copier, xerographic, linen finish, ripple finish, vellum, eggshell, parchment, India, wove, four-ply blank, six-ply blank, writing; Bristol board, strawboard; *miscellaneous:* art, rice, Chinese rice, Japanese rice, Japanese tea oatmeal, crêpe, butcher's, wrapping, Kraft, tissue, brown, tar, roofing, building, tracing, graph, Whatman, transfer, scrap, blotting, filter, toilet, wax, photographic, sensitive, sensitized; wallpaper, Cellophane, Pliofilm (trademarks), paper towel, cleansing tissue.

**on paper** — *Syn.* 1. recorded, signed, official; see **written** 2.

2. in theory, assumed to be feasible, not yet in practice; see **theoretical.**

**paper,** *v.* — *Syn.* hang, paste up, plaster; see **cover** 1.

**paperback,** *n.* — *Syn.* softcover, pocket book, reprint; see **book** 1.

**papered,** *modif.* — *Syn.* hung, decorated, ornamented, papercovered, plastered over, placarded; see also **covered** 1.

**paper money,** *n.* — *Syn.* currency, folding money\*; bill, silver certificate, Federal Reserve note, greenback, legal tender; see also **money** 1.

**papers,** *n.* 1. [Evidence of identity or authorization] — *Syn.* naturalization papers, identification card, ID\*; see **identification** 2, **passport.**

2. [Documentary materials] — *Syn.* writings, documents, effects; see **record** 1.

**paper work,** *n.* — *Syn.* office work, desk work, inside work, keeping up with correspondence, handling the correspondence, keeping one's desk clear, doing the office chores, keeping records, filing, preparing reports, getting up reports, taking dictation, typing, keeping books; see also **administration** 1, **letter** 2.

**papery,** *modif.* — *Syn.* flimsy, insubstantial, slight; see **poor** 2, **thin** 1.

**papism\*,** *n.* — *Syn.* Romanism, Catholicity, Catholicism, Roman Catholicism, popery, popism.

**papist\*,** *n.* — *Syn.* Roman Catholic, Romanist, Christian; see **catholic** 3.

**papistry\*,** *n.* — *Syn.* the Roman Catholic Church, Roman Catholicism, Catholicism; see **papism.**

**papoose,** *n.* — *Syn.* infant, child, nursling; see **baby** 1, **Indian** 1.

**pappy\*,** *n.* — *Syn.* father, papa, daddy, pa; see **father** 1, **parent.**

**par,** *n.* — *Syn.* standard, level, norm; see **criterion, model** 2.

**above par** — *Syn.* superior, above average, first-rate; see **excellent.**

**below par** — *Syn.* inferior, below average, substandard; see **poor** 2.

**parable,** *n.* — *Syn.* fable, moral story, tale; see **story.**

**parabolic,** *modif.* **1.** [Figurative] — *Syn.* figurative, metaphorical, allegorical; see **descriptive, explanatory, illustrative.**
**2.** [Curved] — *Syn.* elliptical, hyperbolic, intersected; see **bent.**

**parachute,** *n.* — *Syn.* chute, seat pack parachute, lap pack parachute, harness and pack, umbrella\*, brolly\*, bailer\*, silk\*.

**parachute,** *v.* — *Syn.* make a lift-off jump, make a free fall, side-slip, glide down, fall, plummet, hurtle, bail out, hit the silk\*; see also **jump** 1.

**parade,** *n.* **1.** [A procession] — *Syn.* march, spectacle, ceremony, cavalcade, motorcade, demonstration, review, line of floats, line of march, pageant, ritual; see also **march** 1.
**2.** [An ostentatious show] — *Syn.* display, show, ostentation, ceremony; see **display** 2.

**parade,** *v.* **1.** [To participate in a parade] — *Syn.* file past, march past, march in review, demonstrate, display, exhibit; see also **march.**
**2.** [To make an ostentatious show] — *Syn.* show off, exhibit, flaunt; see **display** 1.

**paradigm,** *n.* — *Syn.* chart, sample, standard, model; see **criterion, model** 2.
*See Synonym Study at* MODEL.

**paradise,** *n.* **1.** [The other world] — *Syn.* heaven, Kingdom Come, Celestial Home, By-and-By; see **heaven** 2.
**2.** [The home of Adam and Eve] — *Syn.* Garden of Eden, Eden, the Garden.
**3.** [An idyllic land] — *Syn.* Arcadia, Cockaigne, Carcassonne, El Dorado, Elysium, the Elysian Fields, Erewhon, Eden, Valhalla, Xanadu, Beulah Land, Shangrila, Arcady, Arcadia; see also **utopia.**

**paradox,** *n.* **1.** [A seeming contradiction] — *Syn.* mystery, enigma, ambiguity; see **puzzle** 2.
**2.** [An actual contradiction] — *Syn.* absurdity, inconsistency, oxymoron, nonsense; see **error** 1, **mistake** 2.

**paradoxical,** *modif.* — *Syn.* contradictory, incomprehensible, ambiguous; see **obscure** 1.

**paragon,** *n.* — *Syn.* ideal, perfection, sublimation, paradigm, best, nonpareil, nonesuch; see also **model** 1.

**paragraph,** *n.* — *Syn.* passage, section, division of thought, topic, statement, verse, article, item, notice.

**paragraph,** *v.* — *Syn.* group, section, divide, arrange, break.

**parallel,** *modif.* **1.** [Equidistant at all points] — *Syn.* side by side, never meeting, running parallel, co-ordinate, coextending, lateral, laterally, in the same direction, extending equally.
**2.** [Similar in kind, position, or the like] — *Syn.* identical, equal, conforming; see **alike** 1, 2.

**parallel,** *n.* — *Syn.* resemblance, likeness, correspondence; see **similarity.**

**parallel,** *v.* — *Syn.* match, correspond, correlate; see **equal.**

**parallelism,** *n.* — *Syn.* affinity, correspondence, likeness; see **similarity.**

**paralysis,** *n.* — *Syn.* insensibility, loss of motion, loss of sensation; see **disease.**

**paralytic,** *modif.* — *Syn.* powerless, immobile, inactive, paralyzed, crippled, insensible, physically disabled, palsied, siderated, paraplegic, diplegic, palsified; see also **disabled, sick.**

**paralytic,** *n.* — *Syn.* paralysis victim, paretic, cripple, paralyzed person, palsy victim; see also **patient.**

**paralyze,** *v.* — *Syn.* strike with paralysis, make inert, render nerveless; see **deaden** 1.

**paralyzed,** *modif.* — *Syn.* insensible, nerveless,

benumbed, stupefied, inert, inactive, unmoving, helpless, torpid; see also **disabled, paralytic.**

**paramount,** *modif.* — *Syn.* predominant, supreme, eminent, pre-eminent; see **predominant** 1.
*See Synonym Study at* PREDOMINANT.

**paramour,** *n.* — *Syn.* concubine, courtesan, lover; see **mistress** 2.

**paranoia,** *n.* — *Syn.* mental disorder, fright, fear; see **complex** 1, **insanity** 1.

**paranoiac,** *n.* — *Syn.* psychopath, maniac, neuropath; see **neurotic.**

**paranoid,** *modif.* — *Syn.* affected by paranoia, unreasonably distrustful, overly suspicious, having a persecution complex; see **neurotic.**

**parapet,** *n.* — *Syn.* rampart, obstruction, hindrance; see **barrier, wall** 1.

**paraphernalia,** *n.* — *Syn.* gear, material, apparatus; see **equipment.**

**paraphrase,** *n.* — *Syn.* digest, restatement, explanation, translation; see **interpretation** 1, **summary.**
*See Synonym Study at* TRANSLATION.

**paraphrase,** *v.* — *Syn.* restate, reword, rephrase, summarize, quote, cite, recapitulate.

**paraphrastic,** *modif.* — *Syn.* expository, translatory, interpretive; see **explanatory.**

**parasite,** *n.* **1.** [A plant or animal living on another] — *Syn.* bacteria, parasitoid, saprophyte, epiphyte; see **fungus.**
**2.** [A hanger-on] — *Syn.* dependent, slave, sponge, freeloader, hanger-on, sponger; see also **sycophant.**

**parasitical,** *modif.* — *Syn.* ravenous, parasitic, ravening, wolfish, predacious; see also **predatory.**

**parasitism,** *n.* — *Syn.* bloodsucking, sponging, dependency, predatoriness, predaciousness, ravenousness; see also **dependence** 1.

**parasol,** *n.* — *Syn.* sunshade, shade, canopy; see **umbrella.**

**paratrooper,** *n.* — *Syn.* commando, parachute jumper, shock trooper; see **soldier.**

**parboil,** *v.* — *Syn.* simmer, steam, blanch; see **boil** 1, **cook.**

**parcel,** *n.* — *Syn.* bundle, package, box, carton; see **package** 1.
*See Synonym Study at* PACKAGE.

**parceling,** *n.* — *Syn.* division, allotment, distribution; see **share.**

**parcel out,** *v.* — *Syn.* allot, allocate, measure (out); see **distribute** 1, **give** 1, **share** 1.

**parcel post,** *n.* — *Syn.* post, postal service, express, C.O.D.; see **mail.**

**parch,** *v.* — *Syn.* dessicate, dehydrate, dry up; see **dry** 1.

**parched,** *modif.* — *Syn.* burned, withered, dried; see **dry** 1.

**parching,** *modif.* — *Syn.* burning, drying, withering; see **dry** 1.

**parchment,** *n.* — *Syn.* vellum, Parthian leather, goatskin, sheepskin, diploma; see also **paper** 5.

**pardon,** *n.* **1.** [The reduction or removal of punishment] — *Syn.* absolution, grace, remission, amnesty, leniency, clemency, exoneration, discharge, exculpation; see also **acquittal, mercy** 1. — *Ant.* PUNISHMENT, condemnation, conviction.
**2.** [Forgiveness] — *Syn.* excuse, forbearance, conciliation; see **forgiveness, kindness** 1.
**3.** [A statement granting pardon, sense 1] — *Syn.* reprieve, acquittal, exoneration, indulgence, amnesty, release, discharge; see also **acquittal, freeing.**

**pardon,** *v.* **1.** [To reduce punishment] — *Syn.* exonerate, exculpate, clear, absolve, remit, reprieve, acquit, set free, liberate, discharge, spring\*, justify, suspend charges, put on probation, grant amnesty to; see also **absolve, free** 1, **release.** — *Ant.* PUNISH, penalize, sentence.

**2.** [To forgive] — *Syn.* excuse, condone, overlook, exculpate; see **excuse, forgive** 1.

*See Synonym Study at* ABSOLVE.

**pardonable,** *modif.* — *Syn.* passable, forgivable, venial, justifiable; see **excusable.**

**pardoned,** *modif.* — *Syn.* forgiven, freed, excused, released, granted amnesty, given a pardon, reprieved, exonerated, granted a reprieve, acquitted, manumitted, let off\*, whitewashed\*, outside the wall\*, sprung\*, back in circulation\*; see also **discharged** 1, **free** 1. — *Ant.* ACCUSED, convicted, condemned.

**pare,** *v.* **1.** [To peel] — *Syn.* skin, scalp, strip, flay; see **cut** 1, **shave** 1, **skin.**

**2.** [To trim] — *Syn.* prune, clip, crop, trim off; see **carve** 1, **cut** 1, **trim** 1.

**parent,** *n.* — *Syn.* father, mother, foster parent, foster father, foster mother, stepparent, stepfather, stepmother, immediate forebear, procreator, progenitor, sire, the one from whom one has one's being; see also **father** 1, **mother** 1, **origin** 3.

**parent,** *v.* — *Syn.* raise, rear, foster, bring up; see **raise** 2.

**parentage,** *n.* — *Syn.* ancestry, origin, paternity; see **family** 1, **heredity.**

**parental,** *modif.* — *Syn.* paternal, maternal, fatherly, motherly, familial, patrimonial, phylogenetic, phyletic, hereditary; see also **ancestral.**

**parenthesis,** *n.* — *Syn.* brackets, braces, enclosure, punctuation marks, crotchets; see also **punctuation.**

**parenthetical,** *modif.* — *Syn.* parenthetic, episodic, intermediate, incidental; see **related** 2, **subordinate.**

**par excellence,** *modif.* — *Syn.* superior, pre-eminent, the very finest; see **excellent, supreme.**

**pariah,** *n.* — *Syn.* outcast, leper, nonperson, scapegoat, one in disgrace, untouchable; see also **refugee.**

**Paris,** *n.* — *Syn.* capital of France, city on the Seine, city of love, fashion capital, gay Paree\*; see also **France.**

**parish,** *n.* — *Syn.* ecclesiastical unit, charge, archdiocese, congregation, demesne, cure, parochial unit, territory, county (in Louisiana), diocese; see also **area** 2, **church** 3.

**parity,** *n.* — *Syn.* equality, congruity, correspondence, equivalence, similarity; see also **equality.**

**park,** *n.* **1.** [A place designated for outdoor recreation] — *Syn.* square, plaza, place, lawn, green, village green, common, commons, esplanade, promenade, boulevard, tract, recreational area, pleasure ground, national park, national forest, national monument, enclosure, market place, woodland, parkland, parkway, meadow; see also **grass** 3, **lot** 1, **playground.**

**2.** [A place designed for outdoor storage] — *Syn.* parking lot, car park, parking space, lot; see **garage** 1, **parking lot.**

**park,** *v.* — *Syn.* mass, collect, order, place in order, station, place in rows, leave, store, impound, deposit; see also **line up, place** 1.

**parked,** *modif.* — *Syn.* stationed, standing, left, put, ranked, lined up, in rows, by the curb, in the parking lot, stored, halted, unmoving; see also **placed.**

**parking lot,** *n.* — *Syn.* lot, parking area, parking garage, garage, off-street parking, parking space.

**parking orbit,** *n.* — *Syn.* temporary orbit, temporary maneuver, interim stage, interim phase, orbital holding pattern; see also **orbit** 1.

**parking space,** *n.* — *Syn.* space, car space, pigeonhole\*; see **parking lot.**

**parkway,** *n.* — *Syn.* thruway, expressway, turnpike; see **highway, road** 1.

**parlance,** *n.* — *Syn.* speech, manner of speech, tongue; see **language** 1.

**parley,** *n.* — *Syn.* meeting, council, conference; see **conversation, discussion** 1.

**parley,** *v.* — *Syn.* speak, negotiate, confer; see **discuss, talk** 1.

**parliament,** *n.* **1.** [National legislative body of Great Britain; *usually capitalized*] — *Syn.* House of Commons, House of Lords, British Legislature; see **authority** 3. **committee, government** 2, **legislature.**

**2.** [Meeting] — *Syn.* convention, convocation, congress; see **gathering.**

**parliamentary,** *modif.* — *Syn.* congressional, administrative, lawmaking; see **authoritative** 2, **governmental, legislative, political.**

**parlor,** *n.* — *Syn.* living room, sitting room, drawing room, front room, reception room, salon, waiting room, guest room; see also **room** 2.

**parlous,** *modif.* — *Syn.* risky, perilous, hazardous; see **dangerous** 1, **deadly, unsafe.**

**parochial,** *modif.* **1.** [Regional] — *Syn.* provincial, insular, sectional; see **local** 1, **regional.**

**2.** [Narrow-minded] — *Syn.* biased, provincial, shallow; see **conservative, conventional** 3, **prejudiced.**

**parodist,** *n.* — *Syn.* cartoonist, humorist, satirist, author, caricaturist, poetaster, ridiculer; see also **critic** 2.

**parody,** *n.* — *Syn.* travesty, caricature, burlesque, satire, lampoon, spoof, farce, imitation, mimicry, takeoff, pastiche, copy, cartoon, exaggeration, distortion, misrepresentation, feeble imitation, roast, mock-heroic, pasquinade, extravaganza, mockery, derision, mime, irony, jest, raillery; see also **imitation** 1, 2, **joke** 1, **ridicule.** — *Ant.* TRUTH, accuracy, exactness.

---

*SYN.* — **parody** ridicules a written work or writer by imitating the style closely, esp. so as to point up peculiarities or affectations, and usually also by distorting the content nonsensically or changing it to something absurdly incongruous; **travesty**, in contrast, implies that the subject matter is retained, but that the style and language are changed so as to give a grotesquely absurd effect; **satire** refers to a literary work in which follies, vices, stupidities, and abuses in life are held up to ridicule or contempt, esp. through the use of irony, sarcasm, and wit; **lampoon** refers to a piece of strongly satirical writing that uses broad humor in attacking and ridiculing the faults and weaknesses of an individual or institution; **caricature** refers to a representation of a person or thing, in writing, performance, or esp. drawing, that ludicrously exaggerates its distinguishing features; **burlesque**, in this comparison, refers to a broadly comic or satirical imitation, and implies the handling of a serious subject lightly or flippantly, or of a trifling subject with mock seriousness

---

**parody,** *v.* — *Syn.* mimic, satirize, copy, burlesque, travesty, exaggerate, deride, mime, caricature, jest, distort, mock, laugh at, jeer, lampoon, roast, disparage; see also **imitate** 2, **impersonate, joke, ridicule.**

**parole,** *v.* — *Syn.* discharge, pardon, liberate; see **free** 1, **release.**

**paronomasia,** *n.* — *Syn.* wordplay, ambiguity, phrase; see **pun, word** 1.

**paroxysm,** *n.* **1.** [Outburst] — *Syn.* passion, hysterics, outbreak, frenzy, furor, fury, violence, agitation, explosion, frothing, fuming, (berserk) fit; see also **anger, ex-**

citement, rage 2. — *Ant.* PEACE, tranquillity, equanimity.

**2.** [A fit] — *Syn.* attack, spasm, convulsion, seizure; see **outbreak** 1.

**parquet,** *n.* — *Syn.* tiling, inlay, mosaic; see **flooring, tile.**

**parricide,** *n.* — *Syn.* patricide, matricide, killing, killer; see **crime** 2, **killer, murder.**

**parrot,** *n.* **1.** [A bird] — *Syn.* parakeet, lovebird, cockatoo, macaw, quetzal, trogon, lory, lorikeet, psittaciformes; see also **bird** 1.

**2.** [One who copies others] — *Syn.* plagiarist, mimic, mimicker, ape, disciple, impersonator, impostor, mocker, copycat*; see also **imitator.**

**parry,** *v.* **1.** [To ward off] — *Syn.* rebuke, rebuff, hold one's own; see **repel** 1, **resist** 1.

**2.** [To avoid] — *Syn.* shun, elude, dodge; see **avoid, evade** 1.

**parsimonious,** *modif.* — *Syn.* stingy, selfish, tight, frugal; see **greedy** 1, **stingy.**

*See Synonym Study at* STINGY.

**parsimony,** *n.* — *Syn.* stinginess, selfishness, providence; see **frugality, greed.**

**parson,** *n.* — *Syn.* minister, clergyman, cleric, preacher; see **minister** 1.

**parsonage,** *n.* — *Syn.* rectory, pastor's dwelling, minister's residence, manse, parsonage house, presbytery, deanery, vicarage, mansion.

**part,** *n.* **1.** [A portion] — *Syn.* piece, portion, fragment, fraction, section, segment, division, share, sector, member, allotment, apportionment, ingredient, element, subsystem, slab, subdivision, partition, particle, installment, component, constituent, bit, slice, rasher, scrap, chip, chunk, lump, sliver, splinter, shaving, shard, molecule, atom, electron, proton, neutron; see also **share.** — *Ant.* WHOLE, total, aggregate.

**2.** [A machine part] — *Syn.* molding, casting, fitting, lever, shaft, cam, spring, band, belt, chain, pulley, clutch, spare part, replacement; see also **bolt** 1, **brace** 1, **frame** 1, 2, **gear** 2, **machine** 1, **nut** 2, **rod** 1, **wheel** 1.

**3.** [A character in a drama] — *Syn.* hero, heroine, character; see **role.**

**for one's part** — *Syn.* privately, so far as one is concerned, in one's opinion; see **personally** 2.

**for the most part** — *Syn.* mainly, mostly, to the greatest part *or* extent; see **largely.**

**in good part** — *Syn.* good-naturedly, without offense, cordially; see **agreeably.**

**in part** — *Syn.* to a certain extent, somewhat, slightly; see **partly.**

**on one's part** — *Syn.* privately, as far as one is concerned, coming from one; see **personally** 2.

**on the part of** — *Syn.* for, in support of, to help, in the interest of; see **for.**

**play a part, 1.** — *Syn.* behave unnaturally, put on, disguise; see **deceive.**

**2.** — *Syn.* share, join, take part; see **participate** 1.

**take someone's part** — *Syn.* act in behalf of someone, aid, help; see **support** 2.

---

SYN. — **part** is the general word for any of the components of a whole [a *part* of one's life]; a **portion** is specifically a part allotted to someone [her *portion* of the inheritance]; a **piece** is either a part separated from the whole [a *piece* of pie] or a single standardized unit of a collection [a *piece* of statuary]; a **division** is a part formed by cutting, partitioning, classifying, etc. [the fine-arts *division* of a library]; **section** is equivalent to **division** but usually connotes a smaller part [a *section* of a bookcase];

**segment** implies a part separated along natural lines of division [a *segment* of a tangerine]; a **fraction** is strictly a part contained by the whole an integral number of times, but generally connotes an insignificant part [he received only a *fraction* of the benefits]; a **fragment** is a relatively small part separated by or as if by breaking off [a *fragment* of rock, a *fragment* of a song]

---

**part,** *v.* **1.** [To put apart] — *Syn.* separate, break, sever; see **divide** 1.

**2.** [To depart] — *Syn.* withdraw, take leave, part company; see **leave** 1.

*See Synonym Study at* SEPARATE.

**partake,** *v.* — *Syn.* participate, share, divide, take; see **share** 2.

*See Synonym Study at* SHARE.

**partaking,** *n.* — *Syn.* communion, collectivism, partition; see **sharing.**

**parted,** *modif.* — *Syn.* divided, severed, sundered; see **separated.**

**parterre,** *n.* — *Syn.* seats, orchestra circle, orchestra pit, pit, parquet circle.

**part from,** *v.* — *Syn.* separate, part, break up with; see **leave** 1.

**parthenogenesis,** *n.* — *Syn.* parthenogeny, reproduction, birth, virgin birth; see **reproduction** 1.

**partial,** *modif.* **1.** [Not complete] — *Syn.* unperformed, incomplete, half done; see **unfinished** 1.

**2.** [Showing favoritism] — *Syn.* unfair, influenced, biased; see **prejudiced.**

**be partial to** — *Syn.* be fond of, be attracted to, have a taste for; see **like** 1, 2, 3.

**partiality,** *n.* **1.** [Bias] — *Syn.* favoritism, unfairness, intolerance; see **inclination** 1, **prejudice.**

**2.** [Liking] — *Syn.* fondness, inclination, preference; see **affection** 1, **inclination** 1.

*See Synonym Study at* PREJUDICE.

**partially,** *modif.* — *Syn.* partly, somewhat, in part; see **partly.**

**participant,** *n.* — *Syn.* participator, partaker, cooperator, partner, sharer, copartner, shareholder, member, a party to; see also **associate.**

**participate,** *v.* **1.** [To take part in] — *Syn.* share, partake, aid, cooperate, join in, come in, associate with, be a party to, bear a hand, have a hand in, concur, take an interest in, take part in, answer the call of duty, enter into, have to do with, get in the act, go into, chip in*; see also **associate** 1, **join** 2. — *Ant.* RETIRE, withdraw, refuse.

**2.** [To engage in a contest] — *Syn.* play, strive, engage; see **compete.**

*See Synonym Study at* SHARE.

**participation,** *n.* — *Syn.* partnership, joining in, sharing, support, aid, assistance, help, encouragement, concurrence, seconding, standing by, taking part; see also **cooperation** 1.

**participator,** *n.* — *Syn.* sharer, cooperator, partaker; see **associate, participant.**

**particle,** *n.* — *Syn.* jot, scrap, shred; see **bit** 1.

**particle accelerator,** *n.* — *Syn.* atom smasher, linear accelerator, cyclotron; see **accelerator.**

**parti-colored,** *modif.* — *Syn.* kaleidoscopic, colorful, prismatic; see **bright** 2, **multicolored.**

**particular,** *modif.* **1.** [Specific] — *Syn.* special, distinct, singular, appropriate; see **special** 1.

**2.** [Exact] — *Syn.* precise, minute, circumstantial; see **accurate** 1, 2.

**3.** [Fastidious] — *Syn.* discriminating, fastidious, finicky, hard to please, fussy, dainty, nice, squeamish, selective, exacting, demanding, critical, careful, meticulous, finicking, finical, picky*, choosy*, persnickety*; see also **careful, squeamish.**

**4.** [Notable] — *Syn.* remarkable, singular, odd; see **unusual** 1.

*See Synonym Study at* SPECIAL.

**in particular** — *Syn.* expressly, particularly, individually; see **especially** 1.

---

**SYN.** — **particular** implies dissatisfaction with anything that fails to conform in detail with one's standards *[particular* in one's choice of friends*]*; **fastidious** implies adherence to such high standards as to be disdainfully critical of even minor nonconformities *[a fastidious* taste in literature*]*; **dainty,** in this comparison, suggests delicate taste and implies a tendency to reject that which does not fully accord with one's refined sensibilities *[a dainty* appetite*]*; **nice** suggests fine or subtle discriminative powers, esp. in intellectual matters *[a nice* distinction in definition*]*; **squeamish** suggests such extreme sensitiveness to what is unpleasant, or such prudishness, as to result in disgust or nausea *[not too squeamish* in his business dealings*]*

---

**particular,** *n.* — *Syn.* fact, specification, item; see **detail** 1.

*See Synonym Study at* ITEM.

**particularize,** *v.* — *Syn.* itemize, enumerate, specify; see **file** 1, **list** 1, **record** 1.

**particularly,** *modif.* — *Syn.* unusually, expressly, individually; see **especially.**

**parting,** *n.* **1.** [The act of separating] — *Syn.* leavetaking, good-bye, farewell; see **departure.**

**2.** [The time or place of separating] — *Syn.* split, crossroads, Y break, divergence, hour of parting, parting of the ways, where the path divides, where the brook and river meet*.

**3.** [The act of dividing] — *Syn.* bisection, severance, separation; see **division** 1.

**partisan,** *modif.* — *Syn.* factional, biased, sympathetic, blind, devoted, fanatic, warped, zealous, overzealous, unreasoning, cliquish, cliquey, conspiratorial, exclusive, accessory, adhering, leagued together, unjust, unconsidered, ganged-up*.

**partisan,** *n.* — *Syn.* adherent, supporter, sympathizer, follower, disciple, satellite, sycophant, devotee, zealot, accessory, backer; see also **follower.**

*See Synonym Study at* FOLLOWER.

**partition,** *n.* **1.** [Division] — *Syn.* apportionment, separation, severance; see **distribution** 1.

**2.** [That which divides or separates] — *Syn.* bar, obstruction, hindrance; see **barrier, wall** 1.

**partly,** *modif.* — *Syn.* in part, partially, to a degree, in some degree, in some measure, measurably, somewhat, noticeably, notably, in some part, incompletely, insufficiently, inadequately, up to a certain point, so far as possible, insofar as was then possible, not wholly, not entirely, as much as could be expected, to some extent, to a certain extent, within limits, slightly, to a slight degree, in a portion only, in some ways, in certain particulars, only in details, in a general way, not strictly speaking, not in accordance with the letter of the law, in bits and pieces, by fits and starts, carelessly, with large omissions, short of the end, at best, at worst, at most, at least, at the outside. — *Ant.* COMPLETELY, wholly, entirely.

**partner,** *n.* **1.** [Associate] — *Syn.* co-worker, ally, comrade; see **associate.**

**2.** [Lover] — *Syn.* spouse, companion, significant other.

**partnership,** *n.* — *Syn.* alliance, union, marriage, cooperation, company, combination, corporation, cartel, connection, brotherhood, society, lodge, club, fellowship, fraternity, confederation, band, body, crew, coterie, clique, gang, ring, faction, party, community, conjunction, joining, companionship, friendship, help, assistance, chumminess*; see also **business** 4, **organization** 3.

**part of,** *pron.* — *Syn.* portion, section, division; see **some.**

**part of speech,** *n.* — *Syn.* grammatical form, word class, function word, lexeme; see **adjective, adverb, conjunction, grammar, noun, preposition, pronoun, verb, word.**

**partway,** *modif.* — *Syn.* started, toward the middle, partially, somewhat; see **begun, partly, some.**

**part with,** *v.* — *Syn.* let go (of), suffer loss, give up; see **lose** 2.

**party,** *n.* **1.** [A social affair] — *Syn.* at-home, tea, luncheon, dinner party, dinner, cocktail hour, surprise party, house party, social, bee, reception, banquet, feast, affair, gathering, soirée, function, gala, fete, ball, recreation, fun, jollification, cheer, beguilement, accommodation, amusement, entertainment, festive occasion, carousal, diversion, performance, high tea, kaffee-klatsch, binge*, spree*, toot*, riot*, splurge*, tear*, shindig*, blowout*, bash*.

**2.** [A group of people] — *Syn.* multitude, mob, company; see **crowd** 1, **gathering.**

**3.** [A political organization] — *Syn.* organized group, body, electorate, combine, combination, bloc, ring, junta, partisans, cabal; see also **faction** 1.

Well-known political parties include — *historical:* Guelph, Ghibelline, Jacobin, Girondist, Yorkist, Lancastrian, Puritan, Roundhead, Politique, Tory, Whig, Know-Nothing, Grangers, Greenback, People's, Mugwump, Prohibition, Bull Moose, Farmer-Labor, Progressive, Populist; *twentieth-century:* Republican, GOP*, Democratic, Libertarian, Liberal, Conservative, Labour, Popular Front, National Socialist, Nazi, Fascist, Falangist, Congress Party, Kuomintang, Comintern, Third International, Socialist, Communist, Cooperative Commonwealth Federation, Independent, Peace and Freedom, Black Panther, American Independent, Townsendite, Epic.

**4.** [An individual or group involved in legal proceedings] — *Syn.* litigant, participant, contractor, agent, plotter, confederate, cojuror, compurgator; see also **defendant.**

Types of parties, sense 4, include: plaintiff, complainant, defendant, purchaser, buyer, seller, lessor, lessee, employer, employee, licenser, licensee.

**5.** [*A specified but unnamed individual] — *Syn.* party of the first part, party of the second part, etc.; someone, individual; see **person** 1, **somebody.**

**party line,** *n.* — *Syn.* principles, dogma, official stand, orders; see **policy, propaganda.**

**parvenu,** *modif.* — *Syn.* nouveau riche (French), upstart, pretentious, arrogant, snobbish; see also **egotistic** 2.

**parvenu,** *n.* — *Syn.* status-seeker, snob, nouveau riche; see **upstart.**

**pass,** *n.* **1.** [An opening through mountains] — *Syn.* defile, gorge, ravine, crossing, track, way, path, passageway, water gap, col (French); see also **route** 1.

**2.** [A document assuring permission to pass] — *Syn.* permit, ticket, passport, visa, order, admission, furlough, permission, right, license; see also **permit.**

**3.** [In sports, the passing of the ball from one player

to another] — *Syn.* toss, throw, hurl, fling, flip; see also **pitch** 2.

Types of passes, sense 3, include: forward, lateral, line, bounce, touchdown pass\*, bullet\*, shovel\*, spot\*, flat\*, passback\*, snapback\*.

**4.** [\*An advance] — *Syn.* approach, sexual overture, proposition, move; see **suggestion** 1.

**pass,** *v.* **1.** [To move past] — *Syn.* go by, go past, run by, run past, flit by, come by, shoot ahead of, catch, come to the front, go beyond, roll on, fly past, reach, roll by, cross, flow past, glide by, go in opposite directions, blow over\*; see also **move** 1.

**2.** [To elapse] — *Syn.* transpire, slip away, slip by, pass away, pass by, fly, fly by, linger, glide by, run out, drag, crawl.

**3.** [To complete a course successfully] — *Syn.* matriculate, be graduated, pass with honors, qualify; see **succeed** 1.

**4.** [To hand to others] — *Syn.* transfer, relinquish, hand over; see **give** 1.

**5.** [To enact] — *Syn.* legislate, establish, vote in; see **enact**.

**6.** [To become enacted] — *Syn.* carry, become law, become valid, be ratified, be established, be ordained, be sanctioned.

**7.** [To refuse to act] — *Syn.* decline, ignore, omit, skip a turn; see **disregard, neglect** 1, **refuse**.

**8.** [To exceed] — *Syn.* excel, transcend, go beyond; see **exceed, surpass.**

**9.** [To spend time] — *Syn.* fill, occupy oneself, while away\*; see **spend** 2.

**10.** [To pronounce formally] — *Syn.* announce, claim, state; see **declare** 1.

**11.** [To proceed] — *Syn.* progress, get ahead, move on, go on; see **advance** 1.

**12.** [To emit] — *Syn.* give off, send forth, exude; see **emit** 1.

**bring to pass** — *Syn.* bring about, initiate, start; see **cause** 1.

**come to pass** — *Syn.* occur, develop, come about; see **happen** 2.

**passable,** *modif.* **1.** [Capable of being crossed or traveled] — *Syn.* open, fair, penetrable, navigable, traversable, beaten, accessible, traveled, easy, broad, graded, travelable; see also **available.** — *Ant.* IMPASSABLE, impossible, inaccessible.

**2.** [Admissible] — *Syn.* adequate, all right, mediocre, tolerable; see **common** 1, **fair** 2.

**passage,** *n.* **1.** [A journey] — *Syn.* voyage, crossing, trek; see **journey.**

**2.** [A passageway] — *Syn.* way, exit, entrance, corridor, tunnel; see also **hall** 2.

**3.** [A reading] — *Syn.* section, portion, paragraph; see **reading** 3.

**passageway,** *n.* — *Syn.* gate, door, way; see **hall** 2.

**pass away,** *v.* — *Syn.* die, depart, expire, pass on; see **die** 1.

**pass by,** *v.* **1.** [To go past] — *Syn.* travel, move past, depart from; see **leave** 1, **pass** 1.

**2.** [To neglect] — *Syn.* pass over, not choose, omit; see **abandon** 1, **neglect** 1.

**passé,** *modif.* — *Syn.* old-fashioned, out-of-date, outmoded; see **old-fashioned.**

**passenger,** *n.* — *Syn.* wayfarer, voyager, fellow traveler, fellow passenger, rider, customer, patron, fare, commuter, tourist, excursionist, pilgrim, wanderer, straphanger\*; see also **traveler.**

**passer-by,** *n.* — *Syn.* witness, traveler, bystander; see **observer** 1.

**passing,** *modif.* **1.** [In the act of going past] — *Syn.* departing, crossing, going by, gliding by, flashing by, speeding by, going in opposite directions, passing in the night; see also **moving** 1.

**2.** [Of brief duration] — *Syn.* fleeting, transitory, transient; see **temporary.**

**passion,** *n.* **1.** [Sexual desire] — *Syn.* lust, craving, appetite, amorousness, concupiscence, sexual excitement; see also **desire** 3.

**2.** [Strong emotion] — *Syn.* emotion, feeling, ardor, outburst, intensity; see also **anger, emotion, enthusiasm** 1, **love** 1.

*See Synonym Study at* ENTHUSIASM, FEELING.

**passionate,** *modif.* **1.** [Excitable] — *Syn.* vehement, hotheaded, tempestuous; see **excitable.**

**2.** [Ardent] — *Syn.* intense, impassioned, ardent, loving, fervent, fervid, emotional, moving, inspiring, dramatic, melodramatic, romantic, amorous, erotic, lustful, concupiscent, poignant, swelling, enthusiastic, eager, zealous, excited, stimulating, wistful, stirring, thrilling, warm, burning, glowing, blazing, vehement, deep, affecting, eloquent, spirited, fiery, expressive, forceful, heated, hot, flaming, feverish, sultry, high-powered\*, steamed-up\*, horny\*, steamy\*, hot-blooded\*; see also **enthusiastic** 2, 3, **excited, exciting, stimulating.**

**3.** [Intense] — *Syn.* strong, vehement, violent; see **intense.**

---

SYN. — **passionate** implies strong or violent emotion, often of an impetuous kind /a *passionate* rage/; **impassioned** suggests an expression of emotion that is deeply and sincerely felt /an *impassioned* plea for tolerance/; **ardent** and **fervent** suggest a fiery or glowing feeling of eagerness, enthusiasm, devotion, etc. /an *ardent* admirer, a *fervent* prayer/; **fervid** differs from **fervent** in often suggesting an outburst of intense feeling that is at a fever pitch /a vengeful, *fervid* hatred/

---

**passionately,** *modif.* — *Syn.* deeply, dearly, devotedly, intensely; see **angrily, excitedly, lovingly.**

**passionless,** *modif.* — *Syn.* uncaring, apathetic, cold, frigid; see **indifferent** 1, **unconcerned.**

**passive,** *modif.* **1.** [Being acted upon] — *Syn.* receptive, stirred, influenced; see **affected** 1.

**2.** [Not active] — *Syn.* inactive, inert, lifeless; see **idle** 1, **latent, motionless** 1.

**3.** [Patient] — *Syn.* submissive, yielding, enduring, forbearing, quiet; see also **patient** 1, **resigned.**

**passively,** *modif.* — *Syn.* indifferently, without resistance, quietly; see **calmly.**

**passiveness,** *n.* — *Syn.* apathy, resignation, unconcern; see **indifference** 1.

**pass judgment,** *v.* — *Syn.* sentence, decide, consider; see **condemn** 1, **judge** 1.

**pass off,** *v.* **1.** [To pretend] — *Syn.* pass for, make a pretense of, palm off\*; see **pretend** 1.

**2.** [To disappear] — *Syn.* cease, vanish, fade out, fall away; see **disappear.**

**pass on,** *v.* **1.** [To decide] — *Syn.* determine, conclude, make a judgment; see **decide, judge** 1.

**2.** [To die] — *Syn.* expire, depart, succumb; see **die** 1.

**pass out,** *v.* **1.** [To faint] — *Syn.* swoon, lose consciousness, black out\*; see **faint.**

**2.** [To distribute] — *Syn.* hand out, circulate, deal out; see **distribute** 1, **give** 1.

**pass over,** *v.* **1.** [To traverse] — *Syn.* travel through, go over, move over, go across; see **cross** 1.

**2.** [To ignore] — *Syn.* dismiss, overlook, neglect; see **disregard.**

**passport,** *n.* — *Syn.* identification, pass, license, permit, safe-conduct, visa, travel permit, authorization, warrant, papers, credentials; see also **identification** 2.

**pass up\*,** *v.* — *Syn.* refuse, let go by, forgo, dismiss, send away, reject; see also **deny** 1, **refuse.**

**password,** *n.* — *Syn.* countersign, signal, phrase, secret word, watchword, parole, identification, key word, open sesame\*; see also **key** 2.

**past,** *modif.* **1.** [Having occurred previously] — *Syn.* former, preceding, gone by, foregoing, elapsed, anterior, antecedent, prior.

**2.** [No longer serving] — *Syn.* ex-, retired, earlier; see **preceding.**

**not put it past someone** — *Syn.* suspect, accuse, expect; see **anticipate** 1, **fear** 1, **guess** 2.

**past,** *n.* **1.** [Past time] — *Syn.* antiquity, long ago, past times, old times, years ago, good old days, good old times, ancient times, former times, days gone by, auld lang syne, yore, days of old, days of yore, yesterday. — *Ant.* FUTURE, the present, tomorrow.

**2.** [Past events] — *Syn.* knowledge, happenings, events; see **history.**

**3.** [Concealed experiences] — *Syn.* secret affair, love affair, amour, hidden past, bronzed past, scarlet past, scarlet letter, scarlet A.

**past,** *prep.* — *Syn.* through, farther than, behind; see **beyond.**

**paste,** *n.* — *Syn.* cement, glue, mucilage; see **adhesive.**

**paste,** *v.* — *Syn.* glue, fix, affix, repair, patch; see also **stick** 1.

**pasteboard,** *n.* — *Syn.* paper board, bristol board, cardboard, tagboard, oak tag, corrugated paper, carton material, backing; see also **paper** 5.

**pastel,** *n.* **1.** [A sketch] — *Syn.* portrait, depiction, design; see **drawing** 1, **picture** 3, **representation, sketch** 1.

**2.** [A pale color] — *Syn.* tint, tinge, hue, tone, delicate color; see also **color** 1.

**pasteurize,** *v.* — *Syn.* render germ-free, sterilize, purify, make safe for human consumption; see **clean, heat** 2.

**pastime,** *n.* — *Syn.* diversion, recreation, amusement, sport; see **distraction** 2, **entertainment** 1, 2, **game** 1, **hobby.**

**pastor,** *n.* — *Syn.* priest, rector, clergyman; see **minister** 1.

**pastoral,** *modif.* — *Syn.* rural, rustic, agrarian, simple; see **rural.**

*See Synonym Study at* RURAL.

**pastoral,** *n.* — *Syn.* verse, play, idyll; see **poem.**

**pastorate,** *n.* — *Syn.* pastorship, clergy, priesthood; see **ministry** 2.

**pastry,** *n.* — *Syn.* baked goods, dainty, delicacy, patisserie, bread; see also **cake** 2, **doughnut.**

Types of pastries include: French, Danish; tart, pie, turnover, phyllo, oatcake, shortbread, rusk, pudding, brioche, *frangipane* (Italian), petit four (French), puff, *croissant* (French), eclair, cream puff, Napoleon, profiterole, trifle, baklava, panettone, *Strudel* (German), cakes, sweet roll.

**pasturage,** *n.* — *Syn.* grassland, grazing land, pasture; see **field** 1, **meadow, plain.**

**pasture,** *n.* — *Syn.* grazing land, pasturage, hayfield; see **field** 1, **meadow, plain.**

**pasty,** *modif.* **1.** [Like paste] — *Syn.* gluey, gelatinous, gooey, doughy; see **sticky, adhesive.**

**2.** [Pale] — *Syn.* wan, pallid, sickly, ashen, sallow, anemic, bloodless; see also **pale** 1, **dull** 2.

**pat,** *v.* **1.** [To strike lightly] — *Syn.* tap, beat, punch; see **hit** 1.

**2.** [To strike lightly and affectionately] — *Syn.* stroke, pet, rub; see **caress.**

**patch,** *n.* — *Syn.* piece, mend, bit, scrap, spot, application, appliqué.

**patch,** *v.* — *Syn.* mend, cover, reinforce; see **mend** 1, **repair.**

*See Synonym Study at* MEND.

**patch up,** *v.* — *Syn.* appease, adjust, compensate; see **settle** 9.

**patchwork,** *n.* — *Syn.* jumble, hodgepodge, pastiche, potpourri, grab bag, muddle; see also **confusion** 2, **disorder** 2.

**patchy,** *modif.* — *Syn.* sketchy, uneven, inconsistent, varying; see **irregular.**

**patent,** *modif.* **1.** [Concerning a product for which a patent has been obtained] — *Syn.* controlled, monopolized, patented, licensed, limited, copyrighted, protected, exclusive. — *Ant.* FREE, unpatented, uncontrolled.

**2.** [Obvious] — *Syn.* evident, open, clear; see **obvious** 1.

**patent,** *n.* — *Syn.* patent right, letters patent, protection, concession, control, limitation, license, copyright, privilege, grant, charter, franchise; see also **monopoly.**

**patent,** *v.* — *Syn.* license, secure, control, limit, monopolize, safeguard, exclude, copyright, register, trademark.

**patented,** *modif.* — *Syn.* copyright(ed), patent applied for, trademarked, under patent, under copyright, patent pending; see also **restricted.**

**patent medicine,** *n.* — *Syn.* trademarked medicine, prepared medicine, over-the-counter medicine, packaged medicine, drugs, nostrum, panacea, cure-all, patented medicine; see also **medicine** 2.

**paternal,** *modif.* — *Syn.* patrimonial, patrilineal, fatherly, protective; see **parental.**

**paternalism,** *n.* — *Syn.* collectivism, totalitarianism, socialism, benevolent despotism, jurisdiction, Fourierism.

**paternity,** *n.* **1.** [Fatherhood] — *Syn.* progenitorship, paternal parentage, fathership; see **fatherhood.**

**2.** [Authorship] — *Syn.* creation, derivation, origin; see **authorship.**

**path,** *n.* **1.** [A trodden way] — *Syn.* pathway, trail, way, track, short cut, footpath, bridle path, crosscut, footway, roadway, walkway, cinder track, trod (British), byway; see also **route** 1.

**2.** [A course] — *Syn.* route, beat, beaten path; see **way** 2.

**pathetic,** *modif.* **1.** [Affecting] — *Syn.* touching, affecting, moving; see **moving** 2, **pitiful** 1.

**2.** [Pitifully inadequate] — *Syn.* pitiful, feeble, sorry, wretched; see **inadequate** 1, **sorry** 2.

*See Synonym Study at* MOVING.

**pathfinder,** *n.* — *Syn.* explorer, searcher, discoverer; see **scout** 1.

**pathless,** *modif.* — *Syn.* unpenetrated, impassable, untrodden, impervious; see **unused** 1.

**pathological,** *modif.* — *Syn.* unhealthy, disordered, diseased, morbid; see **neurotic, sick.**

**pathology,** *n.* — *Syn.* diagnostics, bacteriology, pathogeny; see **medicine** 3.

**pathos,** *n.* — *Syn.* poignancy, bathos, sentiment, desolation, woe, sadness, tenderness, sympathy, compassion, pity, sympathetic chord; see also **emotion, feeling** 4.

*SYN.* — **pathos** names that quality, in a real situation or in a literary or artistic work, which evokes sympathy and a sense of sorrow or pity; **bathos** applies to a false or overdone pathos that is absurd in its effect; **poignancy** implies an emotional quality, as sadness or pity, that is keenly felt, often to the point of being sharply painful

**patience,** *n.* **1.** [Willingness to endure] — *Syn.* forbearance, fortitude, composure, submission, endurance, stoicism, tolerance, impeturbability, nonresistance, longanimity, self-control, passiveness, bearing, serenity, calmness, even temper, equanimity, yielding, poise, sufferance, long-suffering, moderation, leniency, indulgence; see also **resignation** 1. — *Ant.* impatience, hastiness, restlessness.
**2.** [Ability to continue] — *Syn.* perseverance, persistence, steadiness; see **endurance** 2.

**SYN.** — **patience** implies the bearing of suffering, provocation, delay, tediousness, etc. with calmness and self-control /her *patience* with children/; **endurance** stresses the capacity to bear suffering, hardship, or prolonged strain /Job's *endurance* of his afflictions/; **fortitude** suggests the resolute endurance that results from firm, sustained courage /the *fortitude* of the pioneers/; **forbearance** implies restraint under provocation or a refraining from retaliation for a wrong /he acted with *forbearance* toward the hecklers/; **stoicism** suggests such endurance of suffering without flinching as to indicate an almost austere indifference to pain or pleasure

**patient,** *modif.* **1.** [Enduring without complaint] — *Syn.* forbearing, mild-tempered, composed, tranquil, serene, long-suffering, unruffled, imperturbable, passive, submissive, weak, cold-blooded, easy-going, philosophic, tolerant, gentle, unresentful; see also **resigned.** — *Ant.* IRRITABLE, violent, resentful.
**2.** [Quietly persistent in an activity] — *Syn.* pertinacious, assiduous, steady, dependable, calm, reliable, placid, stable, composed, unwavering, imperturbable, quiet, serene, unimpassioned, dispassionate, enduring; see also **regular** 3. — *Ant.* RESTLESS, irrepressible, feverish.

**patient,** *n.* — *Syn.* case, inmate, victim, sufferer, sick individual, ill individual, one seeking help, one seeking cure, one seeking relief, outpatient, inpatient, bed patient, emergency ward patient, convalescent, one recovering from an illness, one recovering from an injury, hospital case, hospitalized person, subject, victim.

**patiently,** *modif.* **1.** [Suffering without complaint] — *Syn.* calmly, quietly, enduringly, bravely, impassively, resignedly, numbly, forbearingly, imperturbably, dispassionately, tolerantly, submissively, meekly; see also **calmly.**
**2.** [Continuing without impatience] — *Syn.* steadily, firmly, unabatingly; see **regularly** 2.

**patio,** *n.* — *Syn.* porch, piazza, courtyard, terrace, court, square, open porch; see also **yard** 1.

**patriarch,** *n.* — *Syn.* master, head of family, ancestor; see **ancestor, chief** 2, **elder** 2, **ruler** 1.

**patrician,** *modif.* — *Syn.* highborn, grand, aristocratic; see **noble** 3, **royal** 1.

**patrician,** *n.* — *Syn.* nobleman, gentleman, noble; see **aristocrat, lord** 2.

**patriciate,** *n.* — *Syn.* nobility, gentry, peerage; see **aristocracy, royalty.**

**patricide,** *n.* — *Syn.* parricide, father killing, homicide, killing; see **crime** 2, **murder.**

**patrimony,** *n.* — *Syn.* inheritance, birthright, dowry, heritage; see **gift** 1.
*See Synonym Study at* HERITAGE.

**patriot,** *n.* — *Syn.* lover of his country, good citizen, statesman, nationalist, volunteer, loyalist, jingoist, chauvinist.

**patriotic,** *modif.* — *Syn.* devoted, zealous, public-spirited, consecrated, dedicated, fervid, statesmanlike, nationalistic, jingoistic, chauvinistic. — *Ant.* TRAITOROUS, antisocial, misanthropic.

**patriotism,** *n.* — *Syn.* allegiance, love of country, public spirit, *amor patriae* (Latin), good citizenship, civism, nationality, nationalism; see also **loyalty.**

**patrol,** *n.* **1.** [A unit engaged in patrolling] — *Syn.* guard, watch, protection; see **army** 2.
**2.** [The action of patrolling] — *Syn.* guarding, watching, safeguarding, protecting, defending, escorting, convoying, scouting.

**patrol,** *v.* — *Syn.* watch, walk, walk a beat, make inspection; see **guard** 2.

**patrolman,** *n.* — *Syn.* police, police officer, constable; see **police officer.**

**patron,** *n.* **1.** [One who provides support] — *Syn.* philanthropist, sponsor, benefactor, benefactress, Maecenas, helper, protector, encourager, supporter, champion, backer, financer, funder, patronizer, advocate, defender, guide, leader, friend, ally, sympathizer, well-wisher, partisan, employer, buyer, angel*, sugar daddy*, booster*, philanthropoid*; see also **supporter.** — *Ant.* ENEMY, obstructionist, adversary.
**2.** [One who uses facilities] — *Syn.* client, habitué, purchaser; see **buyer.**
*See Synonym Study at* SPONSOR.

**patronage,** *n.* **1.** [The support provided by a patron] — *Syn.* assistance, grant, financing, special privileges, protection, aegis, support, benefaction, aid, sponsorship, commercial backing, recommendation, guardianship, encouragement, help; see also **subsidy.**
**2.** [Trade] — *Syn.* commerce, trading, shopping; see **business** 1.
**3.** [Condescension] — *Syn.* deference, civility, condescendence, patronization, toleration, insolence, sufferance, brazenness, condescending favor.

**patronize,** *v.* **1.** [To trade with] — *Syn.* habituate, buy from, purchase from, shop with; see **buy** 1, **sell** 1.
**2.** [To assume a condescending attitude] — *Syn.* talk down to, be overbearing, stoop, be gracious to, indulge, favor, pat on the back, play the snob, snub, lord it over; see also **condescend.**

**patronizing,** *modif.* — *Syn.* condescending, gracious, stooping; see **polite** 1.

**patronymic,** *n.* — *Syn.* surname, family name, cognomen, father's name; see **name** 1.

**patter,** *n.* — *Syn.* tapping, patting, sound; see **noise** 2.

**patter,** *v.* — *Syn.* tap, chatter, rattle; see **sound** 1.

**pattern,** *n.* **1.** [A model] — *Syn.* original, guide, model, exemplar; see **model** 1, 2.
**2.** [Markings] — *Syn.* decoration, trim, ornament; see **design** 1.
*See Synonym Study at* MODEL.

**paucity,** *n.* — *Syn.* insufficiency, scarcity, absence; see **lack** 1.

**Paul,** *n.* — *Syn.* Saul, Saul of Tarsus, the Apostle Paul, Jew of Tarsus, writer of the Pauline epistles; see also **disciple.**

**paunch,** *n.* — *Syn.* stomach, epigastrium, belly, gut*, breadbasket*, bay window*; see also **abdomen.**

**pauper,** *n.* — *Syn.* dependent, indigent, destitute person, have-not, poverty-stricken person, suppliant; see also **beggar** 1, 2.

**pause,** *n.* **1.** [A break] — *Syn.* intermission, suspension, discontinuance, breathing space, breather*, hitch, hesitancy, interlude, hiatus, abeyance, interim, lapse, cessation, stopover, interval, rest period, gap, stoppage; see also **recess** 1.— *Ant.* CONTINUATION, prolongation, progression.

**2.** [Temporary inaction] — *Syn.* lull, rest, stop, halt, truce, suspension of active hostilities, stay, respite, interregnum, standstill, stand, deadlock, stillness. — *Ant.* PERSISTENCE, steadiness, ceaselessness.

**give one pause**— *Syn.* make one stop and think, cause doubt, create suspicion, create uncertainty; see **confuse.**

**pause,** *v.* — *Syn.* delay, halt, rest, catch one's breath, cease, hold back, reflect, deliberate, suspend, think twice, discontinue, interrupt, rest one's oars*; see also **hesitate.**

**pave,** *v.* — *Syn.* flag, lay concrete, lay asphalt, asphalt, gravel, macadamize, floor, tile; see also **cover** 1.

**paved,** *modif.* — *Syn.* hard-surfaced, flagged, cobblestone, asphalt, concrete, brick, bricked, corduroy, surfaced with wood blocks; see also **covered** 1.

**pavement,** *n.* **1.** [A hard surface for traffic] — *Syn.* hard surface, paving, paving stone, paving tile, flagging, pave; see also **asphalt.**
Road surfaces include: concrete, asphalt, Bitulithic (trademark), stone, brick, tile, macadam, gravel, cobblestone, wood blocks, flagstone.

**2.** [A paved road or area] — *Syn.* highway, thoroughfare, street; see **road** 1, **sidewalk.**

**pave the way (for),** *v.* — *Syn.* prepare, prepare for, make ready, facilitate; see **prepare** 1.

**pavilion,** *n.* **1.** [Tent] — *Syn.* canopy, covering, awning; see **cover** 1, **tent.**

**2.** [Shelter] — *Syn.* gazebo, shed, pergola, bandstand, summerhouse, arcade; see also **building** 1.

**paving,** *n.* — *Syn.* hard surface, concrete, paved highway; see **asphalt, pavement** 1.

**paw,** *n.* — *Syn.* forefoot, talon, hand; see **claw.**

**paw,** *v.* **1.** [To strike wildly] — *Syn.* clutch, grasp, smite; see **hit** 1.

**2.** [To scrape with the front foot] — *Syn.* scratch, rake, rub, claw, search, rasp, grate; see also **dig** 1.

**3.** [To handle clumsily] — *Syn.* fondle, handle, stroke, pat, clap, slap, maul; see also **botch.**

**pawn,** *n.* **1.** [A person used for another's purposes] — *Syn.* cat's-paw, dupe, fool; see **tool** 2, **victim** 2.

**2.** [Something given as security] — *Syn.* pledge, collateral, security; see **pledge.**
*See Synonym Study at* PLEDGE.

**pawn,** *v.* — *Syn.* deposit, pledge, give in earnest, hock*, hang up*, leave with uncle*, lay in lavender*, soak*, pop*; see also **sell** 1.

**pawnbroker,** *n.* — *Syn.* moneylender, broker, usurer, moneymonger, lumberer*, loan shark, Shylock; see also **lender.**

**pawned,** *modif.* — *Syn.* deposited, pledged, hocked, borrowed on, given security, on deposit, in hock; see also **sold.**

**pawnshop,** *n.* — *Syn.* pawnbrokery, the pawnbroker's, my uncle's*, hock shop*, pop shop*; see also **shop, store.**

**pay,** *n.* **1.** [Monetary return] — *Syn.* profit, proceeds, interest, return, recompense, indemnity, reparation, rake-off, reward, perquisite, consideration, defrayment. — *Ant.* EXPENSE, disbursement, outlay.

**2.** [Wages] — *Syn.* wage, compensation, salary, payment, hire, remuneration, commission, redress, fee, stipend, indemnity, earnings, settlement, consideration, reimbursement, recompensation, reckoning, satisfaction, honorarium, meed, reward, requital, emolu-

ment, time*, time and a half*, double time*, overtime*.
*See Synonym Study at* WAGE.

**in the pay of**— *Syn.* working for, engaged by, in the service of, in the employ of; see **employed.**

**pay,** *v.* **1.** [To give payment] — *Syn.* compensate, recompense, make payment, reward, remunerate, reimburse, repay, indemnify, discharge, recoup, refund, requite, settle, reckon with, put down, lay down, remit, make restitution, make reparation, hand over, liquidate, handle, take care of, give, confer, bequeath, defray, meet, prepay, advance, expend, disburse, clear, adjust, satisfy, bear the cost, bear the expense, finance, fund, shell out*, kick in*, dig up*, plank down*, plunk down*, put up*, stake*, foot the bill*, get square with the world*, sweeten the kitty*, pick up the tab*, pick up the check*, put one's money on the line*, fork out*, fork over*, come across*, come through with*, chip in*, square*, ante up*, cough up*; see also **spend** 1.— *Ant.* RECEIVE, owe, withhold, swindle.

**2.** [To produce a profit] — *Syn.* return, pay off, pay out, show profit, yield profit, yield excess, show gain, pay dividends, sweeten*, kick back*, weigh out*.— *Ant.* FAIL, lose, become bankrupt.

**3.** [To retaliate] — *Syn.* repay, punish, requite; see **revenge.**

---

*SYN.* — **pay** is the simple, direct word meaning to give money, etc. due for services rendered, goods received, etc.; **compensate** implies a return, whether monetary or not, thought of as equivalent to the service given, the effort expended, or the loss sustained /one could never be *compensated* for the loss of a child/; **remunerate** stresses the idea of payment for a service rendered, but it often also carries an implication of reward /a bumper crop *remunerated* the farmer for past labors/; to **reimburse** is to pay back what has been expended /to *reimburse* employees for traveling expenses/; to **indemnify** is to pay for what has been lost or damaged /they were *indemnified* for the war destruction/; **repay** implies a paying back of money given to one or may refer to a doing or giving of anything in requital /how can I *repay* you for your kindness?/; **recompense** stresses the idea of compensation or requital /they felt adequately *recompensed* for their efforts/

---

**payable,** *modif.* — *Syn.* owed, owing, obligatory; see **due.**

**pay back,** *v.* — *Syn.* discharge a responsibility, even up, compound for; see **return** 2.

**pay down on,** *v.* — *Syn.* make a payment on, pay in on, start the purchase of; see **pay** 1.

**payee,** *n.* — *Syn.* recipient, receiver, wage-earner, laborer, worker, seller.

**pay for,** *v.* — *Syn.* atone for, make amends for, do penance for, compensate for, make up for, make satisfaction for, expiate, make reparation for, give satisfaction for, pay the penalty for, make compensation for, suffer for, regret, be punished for.

**paying,** *modif.* — *Syn.* productive, good, sound; see **profitable.**

**paymaster,** *n.* — *Syn.* purser, bursar, cashier; see **accountant, clerk** 2, **treasurer.**

**payment,** *n.* **1.** [The act of paying or being paid] — *Syn.* recompense, reimbursement, restitution, subsidy, return, redress, refund, remittance, reparation, disbursement, down, amends, cash, salary, wage, fee, sum, payoff, repayment, indemnification, requital, defrayment, retaliation; see also **pay** 1.

**2.** [An installment] — *Syn.* portion part, amount; see **adjustment** 2, **debt** 1, **installment, mortgage.**

**pay-off,** *n.* — *Syn.* settlement, conclusion, reward, result; see **adjustment** 2, **pay** 1, **payment** 1.

**pay off,** *v.* — *Syn.* discharge, let go, drop from the payroll; see **dismiss** 2.

**payroll,** *n.* **1.** [Those receiving pay] — *Syn.* employees, workers, pay list; see **faculty** 2, **staff.**
**2.** [Wages for a period] — *Syn.* salary, receipts, payment; see **pay** 2.

**pea,** *n.* — *Syn.*
Types and varieties of peas include: garden, early June, dwarf, everbearing, field, sweet, snow, black-eyed, sugar snap, split, chick-pea, cowpea; see also **flower** 1, **plant, vegetable.**
**as like as two peas in a pod\*** — *Syn.* identical, the same, similar; see **alike** 1.

**peace,** *n.* **1.** [The state of being without war] — *Syn.* armistice, pacification, conciliation, order, concord, amity, union, unity, reconciliation, fraternalism, fraternization, brotherhood, love, unanimity, standdown\*; see also **agreement** 2, **friendship** 1, 2. — *Ant.* WAR, warfare, battle.
**2.** [State of being without disturbance] — *Syn.* calm, repose, quiet, tranquillity, harmony, lull, hush, congeniality, equanimity, silence, stillness; see also **rest** 1. — *Ant.* FIGHT, noisiness, quarrel.
**3.** [Mental or emotional calm] — *Syn.* calmness, repose, harmony, concord, contentment, sympathy; see also **composure, reserve** 2, **tranquillity.** — *Ant.* DISTRESS, disturbance, agitation.
**at peace** — *Syn.* peaceful, quiet, tranquil; see **calm** 1, 2.
**hold** or **keep one's peace** — *Syn.* be silent, keep quiet, not speak; see **shut up.**
**keep the peace** — *Syn.* avoid violating the law, keep order, obey the law; see **obey** 1, 2.
**make one's peace with** — *Syn.* conciliate, submit to, appease; see **quiet** 1.
**make peace** — *Syn.* end hostilities, settle, reconcile; see **quiet** 1.

**peaceable,** *modif.* **1.** [At peace] — *Syn.* serene, quiet, balmy; see **calm** 1, 2, **tranquil** 1, 2.
**2.** [Inclined to peace] — *Syn.* conciliatory, pacific, peaceful; see **friendly** 1.

**peaceful,** *modif.* **1.** [At peace] — *Syn.* quiet, tranquil, serene; see **calm** 1, 2, **tranquil** 1, 2.
**2.** [Inclined to peace] — *Syn.* well-disposed, amicable, nonviolent, peaceabale; see **friendly** 1, **pacific.**
*See Synonym Study at* CALM.

**peacefully,** *modif.* **1.** [Calmly] — *Syn.* tranquilly, quietly, composedly; see **calmly, resting** 1.
**2.** [Without making trouble] — *Syn.* pacifically, conciliatingly, harmoniously, fraternally, placatingly, inoffensively, temperately, civilly; see also **modestly** 1. — *Ant.* ANGRILY, belligerently, hostile.

**peacekeeper,** *n.* — *Syn.* soldier, observer, neutral party; see **diplomat** 1, 2.

**peacemaker,** *n.* — *Syn.* arbitrator, negotiator, mediator; see **diplomat** 1, 2, **statesman.**

**peace offering,** *n.* — *Syn.* placation, sacrifice, overture; see **appeasement, gift** 1.

**peace officer,** *n.* — *Syn.* policeman, police officer, constable; see **police officer.**

**peach,** *n.* Varieties of peaches include: North China, South China, Peen-to, Indian, Persian, cling, clingstone, freestone, white-fleshed, yellow-fleshed, Elberta, Hale, Golden Jubilee, Redhaven, Fairhaven, Desert Gold, Sunhaven, Halehaven, South Haven, Red Bird Cling, Heath Cling, Orange Cling, May Flower, Champion,

Alexander, Rochester, Belle of Georgia, Early Crawford, Crawford's Late Red-Elberta, nectarine; see also **fruit** 1.

**peak,** *n.* **1.** [A mountain] — *Syn.* summit, top, crown; see **hill, mountain** 1.
**2.** [The maximum] — *Syn.* zenith, highest point, greatest quantity; see **height** 1, **tip** 1, **top** 1.
*See Synonym Study at* SUMMIT.

**peak,** *v.* — *Syn.* top, top out, climax, rise, tower, crest; see also **climax.**

**peaked,** *modif.* **1.** [Sharp] — *Syn.* pointed, topped, triangle-topped; see **sharp** 1.
**2.** [\*Appearing ill] — *Syn.* sickly, ailing, poorly, drawn, wan, sallow, haggard, pallid; see also **pale** 1, **sick.**

**peal,** *n.* **1.** [Ringing sound] — *Syn.* ring, ringing, clang, clash, rumble; see also **noise** 1, **sound** 2.
**2.** [Set of bells] — *Syn.* chimes, carillon, glockenspiel.

**peal,** *v.* — *Syn.* chime, ring out, resound; see **ring** 3, **sound** 1.

**peanut,** *n.* — *Syn.* goober, groundpea, groundnut, Bambara, goober pea.

**pear,** *n.*
Varieties of pears include: Bartlett, Max Red, Bartlett, Winter Bartlett, Gorham, Royal Riviera, Clapp's Favorite, Keiffer's Hybrid, Parrish Favorite, Seckel, Winter Nellis, D'Anjou, Anjou, Bosc, Comice, Forelle; see also **fruit** 1, **tree.**

**pearl,** *modif.* — *Syn.* blue-gray, silver-white, nacreous, mother-of-pearly, pearly, lustrous, gray-white; see also **iridescent, silver** 1.

**pearl,** *n.* **1.** [A concretion in a mollusk shell] — *Syn.* nacre, margarite, cultured pearl; see **gem** 1, **jewel** 1.
**2.** [A droplet] — *Syn.* dewdrop, raindrop, globule; see **drop** 1.
**cast pearls before swine** — *Syn.* throw something away, give something away, be unappreciated, be misunderstood; see **confuse, waste.**

**pearly,** *modif.* — *Syn.* opaline, opalescent, nacreous; see **iridescent, pearl, silver** 1.

**peasant,** *n.* — *Syn.* small farmer, rustic, provincial, tenant farmer, farm-laborer, farm worker, kulak, sharecropper; see also **farmer, laborer, rancher, worker.**

**peasantry,** *n.* **1.** [The masses] — *Syn.* rank and file, commonality, commonalty, proletariat; see **people** 3.
**2.** [Vulgarity] — *Syn.* crudity, impropriety, indelicacy; see **meanness** 1, **rudeness.**

**pea soup\*,** *n.* — *Syn.* fog, smog, traffic hazard, peasouper\*; see **fog.**

**pebble,** *n.* — *Syn.* stone, gravel, cobblestone, cobble; see **rock** 1, **stone.**

**peccadillo,** *n.* — *Syn.* mistake, violation, error; see **fault** 2, **sin.**

**peck,** *n.* **1.** [A slight, sharp blow] — *Syn.* pinch, tap, rap; see **blow** 1.
**2.** [The impression made by a peck, sense 1] — *Syn.* depression, blemish, mark; see **hole** 1, **scar.**
**3.** [One fourth of a bushel] — *Syn.* eight quarts, quarter-bushel, large amount; see **measure** 1, **quantity.**

**peck,** *v.* — *Syn.* nip, pick, hit, tap, rap; see also **bite** 1, **pinch.**

**pectoral,** *modif.* — *Syn.* intimate, inner, subjective; see **emotional** 2.

**peculiar,** *modif.* **1.** [Unusual] — *Syn.* strange, wonderful, singular, outlandish; see **strange** 1, 2, **unusual** 1.
**2.** [Characteristic of only one] — *Syn.* strange, uncommon, eccentric; see **characteristic, unique** 1.
*See Synonym Study at* STRANGE.

**peculiarity,** *n.* — *Syn.* distinctiveness, unusualness, singularity; see **characteristic.**

**peculiarly,** *modif.* — *Syn.* oddly, queerly, unusually; see **especially** 1, **strangely.**

**pecuniary,** *modif.* — *Syn.* financial, fiscal, monetary; see **commercial** 1.

*See Synonym Study at* FINANCIAL.

**pedagogic,** *modif.* — *Syn.* professorial, academic, scholastic; see **educational** 1, **learned** 1, **profound** 2.

**pedagogue,** *n.* **1.** [Instructor] — *Syn.* schoolmaster, educator, lecturer; see **teacher** 1, 2.

**2.** [Dogmatist] — *Syn.* pedant, sophist, know-it-all; see **bigot, pedant.**

**pedagogy,** *n.* — *Syn.* instruction, guidance, teaching; see **education** 1, 3.

**pedal,** *n.* — *Syn.* treadle, foot lever, pedal keyboard, clutch, brake, foot feed, gas feed, accelerator; see also **lever.**

**pedal,** *v.* — *Syn.* treadle, operate, control, accelerate, clutch, brake, work; see also **drive** 3, **propel.**

**pedant,** *n.* — *Syn.* formalist, doctrinaire, dogmatist, methodologist, precisian, bluestocking, bookworm, pedagogue, egghead*, walking encyclopedia*.

**pedantic,** *modif.* — *Syn.* formal, precise, pompous, ostentatious of learning, pedagogic, punctilious, bookish, didactic, doctrinaire, academic, scholastic, hypercritical, finicky; see also **egotistic** 2.

**pedantry,** *n.* — *Syn.* sophistry, meticulousness, precision, display of knowledge, bookishness, exactness, pretension, dogmatism, pedagogery, finicalness; see also **egotism.**

**peddle,** *v.* — *Syn.* hawk, vend, trade; see **sell** 1.

**peddler,** *n.* — *Syn.* hawker, vender, seller; see **businessperson, salesman** 2.

**pedestal,** *n.* — *Syn.* stand, foundation, footstall, plinth; see **column** 1, **support** 2.

**pedestrian,** *n.* — *Syn.* walker, foot-traveler, stroller, hiker; see **walker.**

**pedigree,** *n.* — *Syn.* lineage, clan, ancestry, genealogy; see **family** 1, **heredity.**

**peek,** *n.* — *Syn.* sight, glimpse, glance; see **look** 3.

**peek,** *v.* — *Syn.* glance, peep, glimpse; see **look** 2, **see** 1.

**peel,** *n.* — *Syn.* skin, peeling, husk, bark, shuck, shell; see also **cover** 2, **skin.**

*See Synonym Study at* SKIN.

**peel,** *v.* — *Syn.* pare, strip, tear off, pull off, flay, uncover, decorticate; see also **skin.**

**peeling,** *n.* — *Syn.* paring, strip, sliver; see **skin.**

**peep,** *n.* **1.** [A peek] — *Syn.* glimpse, glance, sight; see **look** 3.

**2.** [A peeping sound] — *Syn.* cheep, chirp, hoot; see **cry** 2.

**peep,** *v.* **1.** [To look cautiously] — *Syn.* peek, glimpse, glance; see **look** 2, **see** 1.

**2.** [To make a peeping sound] — *Syn.* cheep, chirp, squeak; see **cry** 3.

**peephole,** *n.* — *Syn.* aperture, slit, crevice, slot; see **hole** 1.

**peer,** *n.* **1.** [An equal] — *Syn.* match, rival, companion; see **equal.**

**2.** [A lord] — *Syn.* nobleman, titled person, count; see **lord** 2.

**peer,** *v.* — *Syn.* gaze, inspect, scrutinize; see **see** 1.

**peerage,** *n.* — *Syn.* gentry, nobility, ruling class; see **aristocracy, royalty.**

**peer group,** *n.* — *Syn.* equals, age group, social group, one's peers; see **associate, fellowship** 2, **equal.**

**peerless,** *modif.* **1.** [Not equaled] — *Syn.* unequaled, supreme, best; see **excellent.**

**2.** [Faultless] — *Syn.* unique, superior, consummate; see **perfect** 2.

**peeve,** *v.* — *Syn.* irritate, annoy, anger; see **bother** 2.

*See Synonym Study at* IRRITATE.

**peeved*,** *modif.* — *Syn.* sullen, irritated, upset; see **angry.**

**peevish,** *modif.* **1.** [Having a sour disposition] — *Syn.* perverse, pertinacious, morose; see **obstinate.**

**2.** [Inclined to complain] — *Syn.* querulous, complaining, growling; see **irritable.**

**3.** [In bad humor] — *Syn.* cross, fretful, fretting; see **angry.**

**peg,** *n.* — *Syn.* pin, holder, marker, tack, screw, fastener, plug, bolt, dowel, treenail, linchpin; see **nail.**

**round peg in a square hole** *or* **square peg in a round hole** — *Syn.* misfit, sorry figure, odd ball*.

**take down a peg*** — *Syn.* humiliate, criticize, diminish; see **humble.**

**peg,** *v.* — *Syn.* clinch, tighten, secure; see **fasten** 1.

**peignoir,** *n.* — *Syn.* gown, dressing gown, negligee; see **clothes, nightgown, robe.**

**pejorative,** *modif.* — *Syn.* disparaging, derogatory, deprecatory, derisive; see **rude** 2.

**pelf,** *n.* — *Syn.* profit, gain, spoils, booty, mammon; see also **money** 1, **wealth** 2.

**pellet,** *n.* — *Syn.* pill, globule, bullet, bead, pebble, grain, orblet, spherule; see also **rock** 2, **stone.**

**pell-mell,** *modif.* — *Syn.* impetuously, hurriedly, indiscreetly; see **foolishly, rashly.**

**pellucid,** *modif.* **1.** [Transparent] — *Syn.* clear, crystalline, transparent, translucent; see **clear** 2, **transparent** 1.

**2.** [Explicit] — *Syn.* simple, clear, plain; see **understandable.**

*See Synonym Study at* CLEAR.

**pelt,** *n.* — *Syn.* hide, skin, fell, hair, wool; see also **hide** 1.

*See Synonym Study at* SKIN.

**pelt,** *v.* — *Syn.* swat, wham, knock; see **beat** 2, **hit** 1.

**pen,** *n.* **1.** [An enclosed place] — *Syn.* coop, cage, pound, fold, corral, sty, close, concentration camp, penitentiary; see also **enclosure** 1.

**2.** [The means of enclosure] — *Syn.* wire fence, hedge, wall; see **fence** 1.

**3.** [A writing instrument]

Types of pens and pen points include: fountain, ink, common, desk, drawing, ruling, marker, artist's, calligraphic, reed, quill, steel, ball point, felt tip, roller ball, highlighter, biro (British); nib, stub, fine, coarse, Spencerian; Speedball, Sharpie, Osmiroid (*all* trademarks).

**pen,** *v.* **1.** [To enclose] — *Syn.* close in, fence in, confine, corral, coop up*; see also **enclose** 1.

**2.** [To write] — *Syn.* compose, indite, commit to writing; see **write** 1, 2.

**penal,** *modif.* — *Syn.* punitive, causing suffering, retributive, chastening, reformatory, corrective, correctional, punishing, punitory.

**penalize,** *v.* — *Syn.* scold, chasten, castigate; see **punish.**

**penalty,** *n.* — *Syn.* fine, sentence, discipline; see **punishment.**

**penance,** *n.* **1.** [Voluntary punishment] — *Syn.* mortification, purgation, repentance, retribution, compensation, self-imposed atonement, self-flagellation, fasting, suffering, expiation, *paenitentia* (Latin), *Beichte* (German), sackcloth and ashes, hair shirt, inward penance, outward penance, reparation; see also **punishment.**

**2.** [A sacrament] — *Syn.* repentance, penitence, confession, absolution, sorrow for sin, contrition, remorse, forgiveness for sin; see also **repentance, sacrament.**

**penchant,** *n.* — *Syn.* inclination, propensity, affinity; see **affection** 1.

**pencil,** *n.* **1.** [A graphic instrument]
Types of pencils include: lead, mechanical, colored, drawing, slate, indelible, charcoal, eyebrow, cosmetic, drafting; chalk, crayon, stylus.
**2.** [Anything suggestive of a pencil] — *Syn.* shaft, gleam, streak, line, pointer, indicator.

**pendant,** *n.* **1.** [Ornament] — *Syn.* earring, locket, lavalière; see **decoration** 2, **jewelry.**
**2.** [Correlative] — *Syn.* parallel, one of a pair, equal; see **match** 2, **mate** 1.

**pendent,** *modif.* — *Syn.* pendant, dependent, suspended; see **hanging.**

**pending,** *modif.* — *Syn.* continuing, indeterminate, unfinished, up-in-the-air, in abeyance; see also **imminent, ominous.**

**pendulous,** *modif.* — *Syn.* swaying, dangling, swinging; see **hanging.**

**pendulum,** *n.* — *Syn.* swing, pendant, oscillator, suspended body; see **device** 1, **machine** 1.

**penetrable,** *modif.* — *Syn.* permeable, susceptible, receptive, pervious, open, passable, accessible; see also **porous.**

**penetrate,** *v.* **1.** [To pierce] — *Syn.* bore, perforate, enter, insert, go through, make an entrance, stick into, jab, thrust, stab, force a way, make a hole, run into, seep in, filter in, run through, punch, puncture, drive into, stick, drill, ream, eat through, spear, impale, wound, gore, sting, prick, transfix, sink into, knife, bayonet, go through, pass through. — *Ant.* LEAVE, withdraw, turn aside.
**2.** [To permeate] — *Syn.* enter, infiltrate, seep; see **filter** 1.
**3.** [To understand] — *Syn.* discern, perceive, grasp, comprehend, fathom; see also **understand** 1.

**penetrating,** *modif.* **1.** [Entering] — *Syn.* piercing, boring, going through, puncturing, sticking into, permeating, infiltrating, forcing, passing through, punching into.
**2.** [Sharp] — *Syn.* pointed, edged, keen-edged; see **sharp** 1, 2.
**3.** [Mentally keen] — *Syn.* astute, shrewd, sharp; see **intelligent** 1.

**penetration,** *n.* **1.** [Act of entering] — *Syn.* insertion, invasion, boring into, perforation, thrusting, stabbing, punching, forcing, infiltration, seepage, ingress, diffusion, sticking into, driving into, osmosis, piercing; see also **entrance** 1. — *Ant.* DEPARTURE, evacuation, egress.
**2.** [Mental acuteness] — *Syn.* discernment, perception, keen-sightedness; see **acumen.**

**peninsula,** *n.* — *Syn.* point, foreland, promontory, cape, headland, neck, spit, chersonese; see also **land** 1.

**penitence,** *n.* — *Syn.* remorse, repentance, contrition; see **penance** 1, 2, **regret** 1, **repentance.**
*See Synonym Study at* REPENTANCE.

**penitent,** *modif.* — *Syn.* repentant, sorrowful, contrite; see **sorry** 1.

**penitentiary,** *modif.* — *Syn.* punitive, disciplinary, refractory; see **penal.**

**penitentiary,** *n.* — *Syn.* prison, reformatory, penal institution, pen*; see **jail, prison.**

**penknife,** *n.* — *Syn.* pocketknife, jackknife, Boy Scout knife, Barlow knife; see **knife.**

**penman,** *n.* **1.** [Scribe] — *Syn.* clerk, recorder, copyist; see **scribe** 1, **secretary** 2.
**2.** [Writer] — *Syn.* journalist, essayist, novelist; see **author** 2, **writer.**

**penmanship,** *n.* — *Syn.* script, longhand, chirography; see **handwriting.**

**pen name,** *n.* — *Syn.* nom de plume, anonym, pseudonym; see **alias.**
*See Synonym Study at* ALIAS.

**pennant,** *n.* — *Syn.* flag, streamer, decoration, emblem; see **flag** 1.

**penniless,** *modif.* — *Syn.* poverty-stricken, lacking means, indigent, broke*; see **poor** 1.

**pennon,** *n.* — *Syn.* banner, pennant, streamer; see **flag** 1.

**penny,** *n.* — *Syn.* cent, copper, red cent*; see **money** 1.
**a pretty penny*** — *Syn.* a large sum of money, fortune, riches; see **wealth.**
**turn an honest penny** — *Syn.* profit, earn money honestly, gain; see **earn** 2.

**penny ante*,** *modif.* — *Syn.* trifling, insignificant, petty; see **trivial, unimportant.**

**pension,** *n.* — *Syn.* annuity, premium, payment, grant, social security, gift, reward, subvention, old age benefits, fixed income; see also **allowance** 2, **subsidy.**

**pensioner,** *n.* — *Syn.* retired person, dependent, grantee, accipient; see **beneficiary.**

**pensive,** *modif.* — *Syn.* ruminating, meditative, contemplative, reflective, thoughtful, ruminative, serious, musing, dreamy, wistful, melancholy, abstracted, preoccupied, lost in thought, wrapped in thought; see also **thoughtful** 1.

*SYN.* — **pensive** suggests a dreamy, often somewhat sad or melancholy concentration of thought /the *pensive* look in her eye/; **contemplative** implies intent concentration of thought, as on some abstract matter, often connoting this as a habitual practice /a *contemplative* scholar/; **reflective** suggests an orderly, often analytical turning over in the mind, as of past events, usually with the aim of reaching some definite understanding /after a *reflective* pause he answered/; **meditative** implies a quiet and sustained musing, without necessarily having a definite intention of understanding or reaching a conclusion /a *meditative* walk in the cloister/

**Pentecost,** *n.* — *Syn.* seventh Sunday after Easter, Whitsunday, festival, the descent of the Holy Spirit on the Apostles.

**pent-up,** *modif.* — *Syn.* held in check, repressed, restrained; see **restrained, restricted.**

**penurious,** *modif.* — *Syn.* stingy, mean, frugal, niggardly; see **stingy.**
*See Synonym Study at* STINGY.

**penury,** *n.* — *Syn.* need, bankruptcy, destitution; see **poverty** 1.
*See Synonym Study at* POVERTY.

**people,** *n.* **1.** [Humankind] — *Syn.* humanity, mankind, the human race; see **man** 1.
**2.** [A body of persons having racial or social ties] — *Syn.* nationality, tribe, community; see **race** 2.
**3.** [The humbler portions of society] — *Syn.* mass, folk, proletariat, rabble, masses, plebeians, the multitude, the majority, democracy, crowd, submerged tenth, common people, common herd, rank and file, the underprivileged, underdogs, the public, the man in the street, commons, commonalty, *hoi polloi* (Greek), *bourgeoisie* (French), *los de abajo* (Spanish), riffraff*; rag, tag and bobtail*; the mob*, the herd*, the horde*, the many*, the great unwashed*, John Q. Public*, Jane Q. Public*.
**4.** [Family] — *Syn.* close relatives, kinsmen, siblings; see **family** 1.

**5.** [Society in general] — *Syn.* they, anybody, the public; see **everybody**.

**peopled,** *modif.* — *Syn.* lived in, dwelt in, sustaining human life; see **inhabited**.

**pep\*,** *n.* — *Syn.* energy, vigor, liveliness; see **vigor** 1, 3, **action** 1.

**pepper,** *n.*
Common peppers include: red, sweet, hot, black, purple, yellow, cayenne, green, pimiento, jalapeño, banana, chili, habanero, paprika, bonnet; see also **spice**.
Varieties of peppers include: California Wonder, Chinese Giant, Ruby King, Perfection, King of the North, Yellow Giant, Sweet Mango, Hungarian Wax, Banana, Tuscan, Pepperoncini, Sante Fe Grande, Ancho chili, Poblano, Red Cherry, Anaheim, Serrano.

**peppery,** *modif.* **1.** [Seasoned] — *Syn.* hot, piquant, pungent; see **spicy** 1.
**2.** [Incisive; *said of speech*] — *Syn.* acute, keen, sharp; see **sarcastic**.

**peppy\*,** *modif.* — *Syn.* lively, vigorous, sprightly; see **active** 1, 2.

**per,** *prep.* — *Syn.* to each, for each, contained in each, according to, through, by, by means of.

**perambulate,** *v.* **1.** [To ramble] — *Syn.* walk, wander, stroll, hike; see **walk** 1.
**2.** [To inspect] — *Syn.* study, scan, patrol; see **examine** 1.

**perceivable,** *modif.* — *Syn.* open, observable, visible; see **obvious** 1.

**perceive,** *v.* **1.** [See] — *Syn.* observe, note, notice, discern; see **discern, look** 2, **regard** 1, **see** 1.
**2.** [Understand] — *Syn.* comprehend, sense, grasp; see **distinguish** 1, **learn** 1, **recognize** 1, **understand** 1.
*See Synonym Study at* DISCERN.

**perceived,** *modif.* — *Syn.* seen, felt, touched, reacted to, witnessed, made out, heeded, observed, noted, sensed, grasped, noticed, anticipated, overheard, picked up; see also **heard, recognized, understood** 1.

**perceiving,** *modif.* — *Syn.* alert, aware, cognizant; see **discreet, judicious, rational** 1, **sensitive** 3.

**per cent,** *modif.* — *Syn.* by the hundred, reckoned on the basis of a hundred, percentaged, in a hundred, percentile; see also **fractional**.

**percentage,** *n.* — *Syn.* per cent, rate, rate per cent, portion, section, allotment, duty, discount, commission, winnings, washout rate, cut, rake-off, holdout, corner, pay-off, slice, split, shake, squeeze; see also **division** 2, **interest** 1.

**perceptible,** *modif.* — *Syn.* perceivable, discernible, cognizable; see **appreciable, audible, obvious** 1, **tangible**.
*See Synonym Study at* TANGIBLE.

**perception,** *n.* **1.** [The act of perceiving] — *Syn.* comprehension, understanding, apprehending; see **attention** 2, **judgment** 2, **study** 2, **thought** 1.
**2.** [The result of perceiving] — *Syn.* insight, knowledge, observation; see **attitude** 2, **opinion** 1, **plan** 2, **thought** 2, **viewpoint**.
**3.** [The power to perceive] — *Syn.* discernment, perspicacity, sagacity; see **acumen, judgment** 1.

**perceptive,** *modif.* **1.** [Aware] — *Syn.* alert, incisive, keen; see **conscious** 1, **observant** 1.
**2.** [Discerning] — *Syn.* perspicacious, sharp, sagacious; see **discreet, judicious, rational** 1.

**perch,** *n.* — *Syn.* seat, pole, landing place; see **roost**.

**perch,** *v.* — *Syn.* roost, settle down, land; see **rest** 1, **sit** 1, 2.

**percolate,** *v.* — *Syn.* pass through, pervade, permeate, penetrate, bubble, leach; see also **filter** 1.

**percussion,** *n.* — *Syn.* shock, blow, impact; see **collision** 1, **crash** 4.

**per diem,** *n.* — *Syn.* costs, daily expense(s), routine expense(s), outlay; see **expense** 1.

**perdition,** *n.* — *Syn.* condemnation, destruction, doom, hell; see **blame** 1, **damnation**.

**perdurable,** *modif.* — *Syn.* lasting, stable, enduring; see **permanent** 2, **perpetual** 1.

**peregrinate,** *v.* — *Syn.* wander, ramble, rove; see **roam, travel** 2.

**peremptory,** *modif.* **1.** [Not subject to revision] — *Syn.* fixed, authoritative, uncompromising; see **absolute** 1, **comprehensive, finished** 1, **firm** 1.
**2.** [Harsh] — *Syn.* rigorous, firm, stringent; see **cruel** 2, **sarcastic, severe** 2.
**3.** [Dictatorial] — *Syn.* overbearing, decisive, assertive; see **absolute** 3, **autocratic** 1, **tyrannical**.

**perennial,** *modif.* — *Syn.* enduring, sustained, continuing; see **permanent** 2, **perpetual** 1.

**perfect,** *modif.* **1.** [Having all necessary qualities] — *Syn.* complete, sound, entire; see **absolute** 1, **comprehensive, whole** 1, 2.
**2.** [Without defect] — *Syn.* excelling, faultless, flawless, impeccable, immaculate, unblemished, defectless, foolproof, untainted, unspotted, consummate, absolute, matchless, unequaled, impeccable, peerless, taintless, classic, stainless, spotless, crowning, culminating, exemplary, supreme, pure, ideal, sublime, beyond all praise, beyond compare; see also **excellent, pure** 2, **whole** 2. — *Ant.* RUINED, damaged, faulty.
**3.** [Exact] — *Syn.* precise, sharp, distinct; see **accurate** 1, 2, **certain** 3, **definite** 1, 2.
**4.** [\*Excessive] — *Syn.* very great, flagrant, gross; see **extreme** 2, **superfluous**.

**perfect,** *v.* **1.** [Finish] — *Syn.* fulfill, realize, develop; see **achieve** 1, **complete** 1.
**2.** [Make faultless] — *Syn.* rectify, improve, make perfect, amend; see **correct** 1, **improve** 1.

**perfected,** *modif.* — *Syn.* completed, consummate, developed, mature, conclusive, full, elaborate, thorough; see also **finished** 1, **fulfilled, ripe** 3.

**perfection,** *n.* **1.** [The act of perfecting] — *Syn.* completion, fulfillment, finishing, consummation, ending, realization, touching up; see also **achievement** 2. — *Ant.* RUIN, DESTRUCTION, NEGLECT.
**2.** [The state of being complete] — *Syn.* ripeness, completeness, completion; see **end** 2, **maturity** 3, **result**.
**3.** [A high degree of excellence] — *Syn.* consummation, supremacy, impeccability, crown, ideal, paragon, phoenix, faultlessness.

**perfectly,** *modif.* **1.** [In a perfect manner] — *Syn.* excellently, fitly, correctly, flawlessly, faultlessly, supremely, ideally. — *Ant.* BADLY, poorly, incorrectly.
**2.** [To a sufficient degree] — *Syn.* quite, utterly, absolutely; see **well** 2, 3.

**perfervid,** *modif.* — *Syn.* fervid, ardent, zealous, intense; see **enthusiastic** 2, 3.

**perfidious,** *modif.* — *Syn.* treacherous, mean, corrupt, faithless; see **dishonest** 2.
*See Synonym Study at* FAITHLESS.

**perfidy,** *n.* — *Syn.* deceit, falseness, disloyalty; see **dishonesty**.

**perforate,** *v.* — *Syn.* drill, slit, stab; see **penetrate** 1.

**perforation,** *n.* — *Syn.* break, aperture, slit; see **hole** 1.

**perform,** *v.* **1.** [To accomplish an action] — *Syn.* do, make, achieve, accomplish, fulfill, execute, transact, carry out, carry off, carry through, discharge, effect, enforce, administer, complete, consummate, carry on, conduct, act, operate, function, work, finish, realize,

implement, go about, go through with, discharge the duties of, put through, work out, devote oneself to, come through with, be engaged in, see to, bring off, bring about, engage in, concern oneself with, have effect, fall to, do justice to, do one's part, give oneself up to, make a move, put in motion, put in force, follow through, apply oneself to, put across, deal with, carry into execution, take care of, look to, take measures, acquit oneself, act on, make it one's business, dispose of, bring to pass, do what is expected of one, put into effect, occupy oneself with, take action, address oneself to, put in action, deliver, do one's stuff★, lift a finger★, keep one's hand in★, muddle through★, have free play★, go in for★, make short work of★, pull off; see also **achieve** 1, **act** 1, **operate** 2. — *Ant.* FAIL, neglect, ignore.
**2.** [To present a performance] — *Syn.* give, present, enact, play, offer, impersonate, show, exhibit, display, act out, dramatize, execute, put on the stage, produce, rehearse, act the part of, tread the boards, put on an act, act one's part, go through one's repertoire, go through tricks; see also **act** 3.
**3.** [★To behave in a ludicrous manner] — *Syn.* clown, play the fool, show off; see **joke, misbehave.**

**SYN.** — **perform**, sometimes a mere formal equivalent for **do**, is usually used of an involved, demanding, or established process /to *perform* an experiment, to *perform* a marriage ceremony/; **execute** implies the putting into effect or completing of something that has been planned or ordered /to *execute* a law/; **accomplish** implies success in carrying out a plan or purpose and may suggest effort and perseverance /to *accomplish* a mission/; **achieve** implies the overcoming of obstacles in accomplishing something of worth or importance /to *achieve* a lasting peace/; **effect** also suggests the conquering of difficulties but emphasizes what has been done to bring about the result /his cure was *effected* by the use of a combination of drugs/; **fulfill** implies the full realization of what is expected or demanded /to *fulfill* a promise/

---

**performance,** *n.* **1.** [The fulfilling of a function] — *Syn.* completion, fulfillment, attainment, doing, achievement, accomplishment, execution, carrying out, administration, enforcement, consummation, realization, fruition. — *Ant.* FAILURE, unfulfillment, frustration.
**2.** [A public presentation] — *Syn.* production, appearance, rehearsal, exhibition, offering, representation, pageant, burlesque, spectacle, review, revue, opera, masque, play, drama, dance recital, concert, exhibit, display, special★; see also **act** 4, **drama** 1, **show** 1.
**performer,** *n.* — *Syn.* entertainer, actor, actress, player, trouper, thespian, comedian, comedienne, comic, musician, singer, mime, magician, clown, ham.
**performing,** *modif.* **1.** [Fulfilling a function] — *Syn.* doing, acting, operating, carrying out, in the act of, fulfilling, achieving, effecting.
**2.** [Taking part in a presentation] — *Syn.* playing, displaying, exhibiting, going through one's paces, doing a routine.
**performing,** *n.* — *Syn.* making, acting, accomplishing; see **doing.**
**perfume,** *n.* — *Syn.* scent, fragrance, aroma, odor, sweetness, bouquet, redolence, sachet, incense; see also **smell** 1.
Perfumes include: attar of roses, sandalwood, balm, bergamot, essential oil, bay oil, bay, rosemary, bay rum, frankincense, myrrh, civet, eau de cologne, musk, rose water, eau de toilette, toilet water, orange-flowers,

potpourri, muscadine, spice, sachet, lavender, jasmine, patchouli, rose geranium.

**SYN.** — **perfume** suggests a relatively strong, but usually pleasant, smell, either natural or manufactured /the rich *perfume* of gardenias/; **scent**, in this comparison, implies a relatively faint but pervasive smell, esp. one characteristic of a particular thing /the *scent* of apple blossoms/; **fragrance** implies an agreeable, sweet smell, esp. of growing things /the *fragrance* of a freshly mowed field/; **bouquet** is specifically applied to the fragrance of a wine or brandy; **redolence** implies a rich, pleasant combination of smells /the *redolence* of a grocery/

---

**perfumed,** *modif.* — *Syn.* aromatic, scented, fragrant; see **odorous** 2.
**perfunctory,** *modif.* — *Syn.* cursory, superficial, shallow, hurried, apathetic, mechanical, routine; see also **careless** 1, **indifferent** 1.
**pergola,** *n.* — *Syn.* trellis, kiosk, arbor; see **lattice.**
**perhaps,** *modif.* — *Syn.* conceivably, possibly, reasonably; see **maybe.**
**peril,** *n.* — *Syn.* danger, hazard, jeopardy, risk; see **danger.**
*See Synonym Study at* DANGER.
**perilous,** *modif.* — *Syn.* precarious, unsafe, uncertain; see **dangerous** 1.
**perimeter,** *n.* — *Syn.* margin, outline, border; see **boundary, edge** 1.
*See Synonym Study at* CIRCUMFERENCE.
**period,** *n.* **1.** [A measure of time] — *Syn.* epoch, time, era, age, eon, interval, duration, term, span, time span, stretch, spell, space, stage, years, days, season, phase, session, while; see also **age** 3.
**2.** [An end] — *Syn.* limit, conclusion, close; see **end** 2.
**3.** [A mark of punctuation] — *Syn.* point, full stop, full pause, dot, ending-pitch; see also **punctuation.**

**SYN.** — **period** is the general term for any portion of time; **epoch** and **era** are often used interchangeably to refer to a period marked by radical change, noteworthy developments, etc. /an *era*, or *epoch*, of great discoveries/, but **epoch** may specifically apply to the beginning of such a new period /the steam engine marked an *epoch* in transportation/, while **era** applies only to the entire period; **age** is applied to a period identified with some dominant personality or distinctive characteristic /the Stone *Age*/; **eon** refers to an indefinitely long period /it all happened *eons* ago/

---

**periodic,** *modif.* — *Syn.* intermittent, periodical, recurrent, cyclic; see **intermittent.**
*See Synonym Study at* INTERMITTENT.
**periodical,** *modif.* — *Syn.* periodic, rhythmic, regular, cyclic, cyclical, fluctuating, orbital, pendulumlike, recurrent, recurring, intermittent, alternate, serial, hourly, daily, weekly, monthly, yearly, at various times, at regular intervals, at fixed intervals, on certain occasions, at predetermined times, at regular times, annual, perennial, centennial; see also **regular** 3.
**periodical,** *n.* — *Syn.* review, number, publication; see **magazine** 2, **newspaper.**
**periodically,** *modif.* — *Syn.* rhythmically, systematically, annually; see **regularly** 2.
**peripatetic,** *modif.* — *Syn.* roaming, itinerant, roving; see **wandering** 1.
*See Synonym Study at* ITINERANT.
**peripheral,** *modif.* — *Syn.* external, outer, surface; see **outside.**

**periphery,** *n.* — *Syn.* outskirts, fringe, perimeter, border; see **boundary, edge** 1, **outside** 1.
*See Synonym Study at* CIRCUMFERENCE.

**periphrasis,** *n.* — *Syn.* circumlocution, ambiguity, evasion; see **wordiness.**

**periphrastic,** *modif.* — *Syn.* equivocal, roundabout, circumlocutory; see **obscure** 1.

**perish,** *v.* — *Syn.* die, pass away, be lost, depart; see **die** 1.
*See Synonym Study at* DIE.

**perjure,** *v.* — *Syn.* prevaricate, swear falsely, falsify; see **lie** 1.

**perjurer,** *n.* — *Syn.* prevaricator, falsifier, deceiver; see **liar.**

**perjury,** *n.* — *Syn.* false statement, violation of an oath, willful falsehood; see **lie** 1.

**perk (up),** *v.* **1.** [Be refreshed] — *Syn.* revive, recuperate, liven up; see **recover** 3.
**2.** [Cheer or refresh] — *Syn.* invigorate, shake, enliven; see **renew** 1, **revive** 1.

**perky,** *modif.* **1.** [Proud] — *Syn.* dignified, haughty, jaunty; see **proud** 1.
**2.** [Alert] — *Syn.* aware, brisk, lively; see **active** 2.

**permanence,** *n.* — *Syn.* continuity, dependability, durability, immutability; see **stability** 1.

**permanent,** *modif.* **1.** [Perpetual] — *Syn.* unchanging, continual, changeless; see **perpetual** 1.
**2.** [Intended to last for a considerable time] — *Syn.* durable, enduring, abiding, uninterrupted, stable, continuing, unremitting, unremittent, lasting, perdurable, firm, hard, tough, strong, rocklike, hardy, robust, sound, sturdy, steadfast, imperishable, surviving, living, long-lived, long-standing, invariable, persisting, tenacious, persevering, unyielding, resisting, resistant, impenetrable, recurring, wearing, constant, changeless, holding, persistent, perennial.

**permanently,** *modif.* — *Syn.* for all time, enduringly, lastingly; see **forever** 1.

**permeable,** *modif.* — *Syn.* pervious, penetrable, perforable; see **porous.**

**permeate,** *v.* — *Syn.* pervade, saturate, penetrate, fill; see **filter** 1.

**permeation,** *n.* — *Syn.* diffusion, saturation, osmosis, seepage; see **penetration** 1.

**permissible,** *modif.* — *Syn.* allowable, sanctioned, lawful, permitted; see **admissible.**

**permissibly,** *modif.* — *Syn.* fittingly, allowably, lawfully, legitimately, properly, by one's leave; see also **legally** 1.

**permission,** *n.* — *Syn.* leave, liberty, consent, assent, acquiescence, acceptance, letting, approbation, agreement, license, permit, allowance, authority, tolerance, toleration, authorization, imprimatur, approval, acknowledgment, admission, verification, recognition, concurrence, promise, avowal, support, corroboration, guarantee, guaranty, warrant, visa, advocacy, carte blanche, commendation, encouragement, ratification, grace, authority, sanction, dispensation, confirmation, endorsement, affirmation, concordance, assurance, empowering, legalization, grant, indulgence, trust, connivance, concession, adjustment, settlement, accord, subscription, nod*, O.K.*, rubber stamp*, the go-ahead*, high-sign*, green light*. — *Ant.* DENIAL, injunction, interdiction.

**permissive,** *modif.* **1.** [Permitting] — *Syn.* authorizing, allowing, agreeable, lax; see **lenient, permitting.**
**2.** [Authorized] — *Syn.* allowed, licensed, permitted; see **approved.**

**permit,** *n.* — *Syn.* license, grant, consent, favor, toleration, authorization, empowering, charter, sanction, legalization, concession, indulgence, privilege; see also **permission.** — *Ant.* DENIAL, veto, prohibition.

**permit,** *v.* — *Syn.* allow, authorize, sanction, consent to; see **allow** 1.
*See Synonym Study at* ALLOW.

**permitted,** *modif.* — *Syn.* granted, allowed, licensed, authorized, legalized, tolerated, empowered, sanctioned, conceded, consented, favored, suffered, chartered, accorded, vouchsafed, let, indulged, privileged; see also **approved.** — *Ant.* REFUSED, denied, prohibited.

**permitting,** *modif.* — *Syn.* consenting, allowing, tolerating, authorizing, empowering, chartering, sanctioning, granting, suffering, licensing, letting, vouchsafing; see also **lenient.**

**permutation,** *n.* — *Syn.* alteration, transformation, shift; see **change** 2.

**pernicious,** *modif.* — *Syn.* harmful, deleterious, detrimental, noxious, baneful, damaging, prejudicial, ruinous, destructive, insidious, hurtful, malignant, sinister, virulent, deadly, fatal, lethal, poisonous, venomous, unwholesome; see also **deadly** 1, **harmful, poisonous.**

**SYN.** — **pernicious** applies to that which does great harm by insidiously undermining or weakening *[pernicious* anemia, a *pernicious* dogma]; **baneful** implies a harming by or as if by poisoning *[a baneful* superstition]; **noxious** refers to something that is injurious to physical or mental health *[noxious* fumes]; **deleterious** implies slower, less irreparable injury to the health *[the deleterious* effects of an unbalanced diet]; **detrimental** implies a causing of damage, loss, or disadvantage to something specified *[the speech was detrimental* to our cause]

**perorate,** *v.* **1.** [To harangue] — *Syn.* speak, lecture, expatiate; see **address** 2.
**2.** [To summarize] — *Syn.* epitomize, conclude, sum up; see **decrease** 2, **summarize.**

**peroration,** *n.* **1.** [A speech] — *Syn.* discourse, talk, lecture; see **speech** 3.
**2.** [A conclusion] — *Syn.* restatement, outline, end; see **summary.**

**peroxide\*,** *modif.* — *Syn.* bleached, fair, light, flaxen; see **blond.**

**perpendicular,** *modif.* — *Syn.* vertical, plumb, straight, at 90 degrees; see **upright** 1.

**perpetrate,** *v.* — *Syn.* commit, execute, pull off*; see **perform** 1.

**perpetual,** *modif.* **1.** [Never stopping] — *Syn.* continuous, unceasing, constant, ceaseless, never-ceasing, incessant, permanent, lasting, perennial, uninterrupted, eternal, endless, everlasting, interminable, unremitting, enduring, continued, without end, imperishable, undying, immortal, sempiternal; see also **eternal** 2. — *Ant.* SHORT, transitory, fleeting.
**2.** [Continually repeating] — *Syn.* incessant, repetitious, continual, recurring, repeating, recurrent, intermittent, going on and on, persistent, returning, annual; see also **constant** 1, **regular** 3.

**SYN.** — **perpetual** applies to that which lasts or persists for an indefinitely long time *[a perpetual* nuisance]; **continual** applies to that which recurs repeatedly or goes on unceasingly over a long period of time *[continual* arguments, *continual* rain]; **continuous** applies to that which extends without interruption in either space or time *[a continuous* expanse, a *continuous* flow of traffic]; **constant** stresses uniformity, steadiness, or regularity in occurrence or recurrence *[the constant* beat of the heart];

**incessant** implies unceasing or uninterrupted activity *[incessant* chatter*]*; **eternal** stresses endlessness or timelessness *[*the *eternal* verities*]*

**perpetually,** *modif.* — *Syn.* enduringly, unceasingly, permanently; see **forever** 1, 2.

**perpetuate,** *v.* — *Syn.* keep alive, preserve, keep in existence, immortalize; see **continue** 1.

**perpetuation,** *n.* — *Syn.* maintenance, permanence, propagation; see **continuation** 1.

**perpetuity,** *n.* 1. [State of being perpetual] — *Syn.* constancy, endurance, continuance; see **continuity** 1.
2. [Unlimited time] — *Syn.* eternity, forever, all time, life; see **eternity** 1.

**perplex,** *v.* — *Syn.* puzzle, confound, bewilder; see **confuse.**
*See Synonym Study at* CONFUSE.

**perplexed,** *modif.* 1. [Confused] — *Syn.* troubled, uncertain, bewildered; see **doubtful** 2.
2. [Involved] — *Syn.* intricate, bewildering, confusing; see **complex** 2, **difficult** 2.

**perplexing,** *modif.* — *Syn.* bewildering, confusing, mystifying; see **difficult** 2.

**perplexity,** *n.* 1. [Uncertainty based on doubt] — *Syn.* bewilderment, confusion, quandary; see **doubt** 2, **uncertainty** 2.
2. [Difficulty causing uncertainty] — *Syn.* complication, crisis, emergency; see **difficulty** 2.

**perquisite,** *n.* — *Syn.* income, proceeds, gain, perk*; see **profit** 2, **tip** 2.

**per se,** *modif.* — *Syn.* as such, intrinsically, alone, singularly, fundamentally, in essence, in itself, by itself, virtually; see also **essentially.**

**persecute,** *v.* 1. [To oppress, especially for religious reasons] — *Syn.* afflict, harass, hector, bait, victimize, tyrannize, outrage, ill-treat, oppress, wrong, imprison, torment, torture, rack, flog, strike, beat, scourge, kill, crucify, maltreat, banish, expel, exile; see also **abuse** 1. — *Ant.* ENCOURAGE, endorse, patronize.
2. [To torment persistently] — *Syn.* annoy, worry, tease; see **bother** 2.
*See Synonym Study at* WRONG.

**persecution,** *n.* — *Syn.* affliction, infliction, torture, ill-treatment, maltreatment, torment, killing, murder, massacre, banishment, expulsion, exile, imprisonment, mistreatment, annoyance, teasing, galling, provoking, pestering; see also **abuse** 3, **oppression** 1, **torture.** — *Ant.* HELP, succor, stimulation.

**perseverance,** *n.* 1. [The act of perseverance] — *Syn.* continuance, prolonging, pursuance; see **continuation** 1.
2. [The attitude of mind] — *Syn.* resolve, pertinacity, resolution, pluck; see **determination** 2.

**persevere,** *v.* 1. [To continue] — *Syn.* persist, remain, pursue; see **continue** 1, **endure** 1.
2. [To be steadfast] — *Syn.* stand firm, insist, be obstinate, stick to one's guns, not take "no" for an answer, hold one's ground.

**persist,** *v.* — *Syn.* persevere, continue, keep on, insist; see **continue** 1, **endure** 1.
*See Synonym Study at* CONTINUE.

**persistence,** *n.* — *Syn.* steadfastness, tenacity, constancy, indefatigability, resolution, grit, stamina, pluck; see also **endurance** 2. — *Ant.* INDIFFERENCE, indolence, idleness.

**persistent,** *modif.* — *Syn.* tenacious, steadfast, determined; see **resolute** 2.

**persnickety***, *modif.* — *Syn.* fussy, fastidious, particular; see **careful.**

**person,** *n.* 1. [An individual] — *Syn.* human being, child, somebody, self, oneself, I, me, soul, spirit, mortal, character, individuality, personage, personality, personal identity; see also **man** 2, **woman** 1.
2. [An individual enjoying distinction] — *Syn.* distinguished person, personality, success; see **character** 4, **personage** 2.
3. [Bodily form] — *Syn.* physique, frame, form; see **body** 1.
**in person**— *Syn.* personally, in the flesh, present; see **near, there.**

**personable,** *modif.* — *Syn.* agreeable, pleasant, attractive; see **charming.**

**personage,** *n.* 1. [An individual]— *Syn.* human being, someone, individual; see **man** 3, **person** 1, **woman** 1.
2. [A notable] — *Syn.* personality, individual, distinguished person, dignitary, well-known person, person in the limelight, celebrity, cynosure, star, somebody*, big man*, big boss*, bigwig*, brass*, chief*, prince*, nabob*, very important person*, VIP*, big man on campus*, BMOC*; see also **success** 3.

**personal,** *modif.* 1. [Private] — *Syn.* secluded, secret, retired, intimate; see **private.**
2. [Individual] — *Syn.* own, peculiar, particular; see **individual** 1, **special** 1.
3. [Pertaining to one's person] — *Syn.* fleshly, corporeal, corporal; see **bodily** 1.

**personality,** *n.* 1. [The total of one's nature] — *Syn.* self, oneself, being; see **character** 2.
2. [Individual characteristics] — *Syn.* disposition, nature, temper, temperament; see **character** 1, **temperament.**
3. [A notable person] — *Syn.* celebrity, star, cynosure; see **character** 4, **personage** 2.
*See Synonym Study at* TEMPERAMENT.

**personally,** *modif.* 1. [Viewed in a personal manner] — *Syn.* individually, privately, especially, in person, by oneself, in the flesh.— *Ant.* PUBLICLY, generally, broadly.
2. [From the point of view of the speaker] — *Syn.* for me, myself, by myself, for myself, for my part, as I see it, according to my opinion; see also **individually, mentally, subjectively.** — *Ant.* CERTAINLY, objectively, scientifically.

***persona non grata*** (Latin), *n.* — *Syn.* trespasser, antagonist, undesirable; see **enemy.**

**personification,** *n.* — *Syn.* metaphor, anthropomorphism, imagery; see **representation.**

**personify,** *v.* 1. [To impersonate] — *Syn.* represent, live as, act out; see **imitate** 2, **impersonate.**
2. [To embody] — *Syn.* substantiate, contain, materialize; see **complete** 1.
3. [To represent] — *Syn.* copy, symbolize, exemplify; see **represent** 3.

**personnel,** *n.* — *Syn.* workers, employees, staff, work force, help, faculty, corps, cadre, organization, group, troop; see also **staff** 2.

**perspective,** *n.* 1. [Viewpoint] — *Syn.* aspect, attitude, outlook; see **viewpoint.**
2. [Vista] — *Syn.* view, scene, prospect, panorama; see **view** 1, 2.

**perspicacious,** *modif.* — *Syn.* observant, perceptive, alert, shrewd; see **judicious.**
*See Synonym Study at* SHREWD.

**perspicacity,** *n.* — *Syn.* insight, discrimination, penetration; see **acumen.**

**perspicuity,** *n.* — *Syn.* lucidity, plainness, clearness; see **clarity.**

**perspicuous,** *modif.* — *Syn.* lucid, distinct, intelligible; see **clear** 2, **obvious** 1.

**perspiration,** *n.* — *Syn.* water, exudation, beads of moisture; see **sweat.**

**perspire,** *v.* — *Syn.* secrete, exude, lather; see **sweat** 1.

**persuade,** *v.* **1.** [To influence] — *Syn.* convince, move, induce, satisfy, inveigle, assure, cajole, incline, talk someone into something, win over, bring around, bring over, lead to believe, gain the confidence of, prevail on, prevail upon, overcome another's resistance, wear down, bring to one's senses, win an argument, make one's point, gain the confidence of, make someone see the light★, cram down one's throat★, sell★, sell a bill of goods★, sell on★, turn someone on to★; see also **influence.** — *Ant.* DISSUADE, neglect, dampen.

**2.** [To urge] — *Syn.* exhort, coax, prompt; see **urge** 1, 2.

**persuaded,** *modif.* — *Syn.* convinced, won over, moved to, led, influenced, motivated, lured, allured, attracted to, prevailed upon, decoyed, seduced, wheedled, inveigled, impelled, having succumbed to pressure, brought to see the light★, turned on to★.

**persuasion,** *n.* **1.** [The act of persuading] — *Syn.* inducing, suasion, influencing, enticing, enticement, exhorting, exhortation, seducing, seduction, inveigling, inveiglement, alluring, wheedling, cajoling, cajolery, winning over, talking over, bringing someone around, making someone see the light★, bringing to heel★, talking someone into something★, turning someone on to something★. — *Ant.* PREVENTION, dissuasion, confusion.

**2.** [A belief] — *Syn.* creed, tenet, religion, conviction; see **belief** 1, **faith** 1, 2, **opinion** 1.

*See Synonym Study at* OPINION.

**persuasive,** *modif.* — *Syn.* convincing, alluring, plausible, luring, seductive, wheedling, influential, winning, enticing, impelling, moving, actuating, inspiriting, efficient, efficacious, effectual, compelling, touching, forceful, potent, powerful, swaying, cogent, pointed, strong, energetic, forcible, inveigling; see also **effective, stimulating.**

**persuasiveness,** *n.* — *Syn.* control, forcefulness, strength; see **influence** 2, **power** 2.

**pert,** *modif.* — *Syn.* bold, daring, saucy; see **rude** 2.

**pertain,** *v.* — *Syn.* relate to, belong to, refer to; see **concern** 1.

**pertaining,** *modif.* — *Syn.* belonging to, appropriate to, connected with; see **referring.**

**pertinacious,** *modif.* **1.** [Resolute] — *Syn.* determined, attentive, tenacious; see **resolute** 2.

**2.** [Obstinate] — *Syn.* stubborn, insistent, perverse, persistent; see **obstinate.**

*See Synonym Study at* OBSTINATE.

**pertinence,** *n.* — *Syn.* consistency, congruity, relevance; see **importance** 1.

**pertinent,** *modif.* — *Syn.* relevant, appropriate, related; see **relevant.**

*See Synonym Study at* RELEVANT.

**pertness,** *n.* — *Syn.* insolence, arrogance, audacity; see **rudeness.**

**perturb,** *v.* **1.** [To annoy] — *Syn.* pester, worry, irritate, disturb; see **bother** 2.

**2.** [To confuse] — *Syn.* perplex, confound, bewilder; see **confuse.**

*See Synonym Study at* DISTURB.

**perturbation,** *n.* — *Syn.* distress, disturbance, anxiety; see **confusion** 1, 2, **disorder** 2.

**perturbed,** *modif.* **1.** [Troubled] — *Syn.* uneasy, anxious, restless; see **troubled** 1.

**2.** [Angry] — *Syn.* annoyed, irritated, vexed; see **angry.**

**perusal,** *n.* — *Syn.* scrutiny, inspection, research; see **examination** 1.

**peruse,** *v.* **1.** [To inspect] — *Syn.* study, scrutinize, analyze; see **examine** 1.

**2.** [To read] — *Syn.* glance over, scan, skim; see **read** 1.

**pervade,** *v.* — *Syn.* saturate, diffuse, permeate, spread through; see **penetrate** 1.

**perverse,** *modif.* **1.** [Obstinate] — *Syn.* headstrong, obdurate, self-willed, wrongheaded; see **contrary** 4, **obstinate** 1.

**2.** [Inclined to opposition and bad temper] — *Syn.* cranky, contrary, unreasonable; see **contrary** 4, **irritable.**

**3.** [Erring] — *Syn.* wayward, delinquent, malicious, capricious; see **wicked** 1.

*See Synonym Study at* CONTRARY.

**perversion,** *n.* **1.** [A distortion] — *Syn.* involution, regression, abuse; see **contortion** 1.

**2.** [Deviation] — *Syn.* aberration, abnormality, corruption, debasement, depravity, wickedness, depredation, degeneration, degeneracy, vitiation, degradation, impairment, self-defilement, vice, bestiality.

**pervert,** *v.* — *Syn.* ruin, vitiate, debase, divert; see **corrupt** 1.

*See Synonym Study at* DEBASE.

**perverted,** *modif.* — *Syn.* distorted, deviating, corrupt; see **wicked** 1.

**pervious,** *modif.* — *Syn.* permeable, penetrable, open, passable; see **porous.**

**pesky,** *modif.* — *Syn.* troublesome, provoking, annoying; see **disturbing.**

**peso,** *n.* — *Syn.* cash, legal tender, coin; see **money** 1.

**pessimism,** *n.* — *Syn.* doubt, cynicism, hopelessness, nihilism, unhappiness, gloom, low spirits, despondency, melancholy, blighted hope, lack of expectation; see also **depression** 2, **grief** 1, **sadness.**

**pessimist,** *n.* — *Syn.* cynic, misanthrope, realist, worrier, melancholic, depreciator, complainer, croaker★, Cassandra★, crepehanger★, worrywart★, gloomy Gus★.

**pessimistic,** *modif.* **1.** [Discouraging] — *Syn.* bleak, dismal, worrisome, downbeat★; see **dismal** 1.

**2.** [Inclined to a discouraging view] — *Syn.* hopeless, gloomy, cynical, misanthropic, negative, negativistic, defeatist, melancholy, depressed, sullen, morose, morbid, despondent, downhearted, despairing, distrustful, sullen, sneering; see also **sad** 1. — *Ant.* CONFIDENT, optimistic, sanguine.

**3.** [Believing in philosophic pessimism] — *Syn.* fatalistic, deterministic, mechanistic, rationalistic, realistic.

---

**SYN.** — **pessimistic** implies an attitude, often habitual, of seeing the dark side of things or expecting the worst to happen [*pessimistic* about the prospects for peace]; **cynical** implies a contemptuous disbelief in human goodness and sincerity [*cynical* about recovering a lost watch]; **misanthropic** suggests a deep-seated hatred or distrust of people in general [a *misanthropic* hermit]

---

**pest,** *n.* **1.** [Anything destructive] — *Syn.* virus, germ, insect pest, bug, harmful bird, bird of prey, destructive animal; see also **disease, insect.**

Common pests include: house fly, mosquito, flea, louse, mite, chigger, bedbug, ant, silverfish, earwig, mealybug, cricket, grub, cockroach, termite, carpenter ant, fire ant, centipede, millipede, tick, botfly, screw-worm fly, leaf hopper, aphid, codling moth, peachtree borer, Japanese beetle, Colorado beetle, grain beetle, corn borer, boll weevil, San Jose scale, oyster shell scale, squash bug, peach moth, gypsy moth, hawk moth, wasp, wireworm, cutworm, tent caterpillar, plum curculio, pear slug, tomato slug, mouse, rat, gopher, prairie dog, woodchuck, groundhog, rabbit, mole, weasel, coyote, hawk.

**2.** [A nuisance] — *Syn.* bother, vexation, thorn in the side, annoyance; see **trouble** 2.

**pester,** *v.* — *Syn.* annoy, harass, provoke; see **bother** 2.

**pestiferous,** *modif.* — *Syn.* virulent, toxic, unhealthy; see **harmful, deadly, poisonous.**

**pestilence,** *n.* — *Syn.* epidemic, plague, endemic, sickness; see **disease.**

**pestilential,** *modif.* **1.** [Deadly] — *Syn.* infectious, pestiferous, malignant; see **dangerous** 1, 2, **deadly.**

**2.** [Harmful] — *Syn.* destructive, troublesome, contaminating; see **harmful.**

**pestle,** *n.* — *Syn.* grinder, pulverizer, pounder, brayer, muller, masher.

**pet,** *modif.* — *Syn.* beloved, dear, preferred; see **favorite.**

**pet,** *n.* **1.** [A term of endearment] — *Syn.* lover, dear, love; see **darling** 2.

**2.** [Favorite] — *Syn.* darling, idol, adored one; see **favorite.**

**3.** [A creature kept as an object of affection]
Animals commonly kept as pets include: dog, cat, bird, snake, iguana, salamander, pony, horse, goldfish, guppies, angel fish, rabbit, guinea pig, hamster, gerbil, lamb, mouse, white rat, chicken, pigeon, canary, parakeet, parrot; see also **animal** 1, **bird** 1, **cat** 1, **dog.**

**pet,** *v.* **1.** [To caress] — *Syn.* stroke, caress, pat, fondle; see **touch** 1.

**2.** [To make love] — *Syn.* neck*, make out*, embrace, hug; see **caress, kiss, love** 2.

*See Synonym Study at* CARESS.

**petal,** *n.* — *Syn.* floral leaf, corolla, floral envelope, perianth, leaf, bract, scale.

**petard,** *n.* — *Syn.* firecracker, explosive, squib; see **fireworks.**

**hoist with one's own petard** — *Syn.* caught in one's own trap, too smart for one's own good, tangled in one's own web.

**peter out*,** *v.* — *Syn.* stop, dwindle, miscarry; see **fail** 1.

**1.** petite, *modif.* — *Syn.* small, dainty, delicate, slight; see **small.**

*See Synonym Study at* SMALL.

**petition,** *n.* — *Syn.* prayer, request, supplication; see **appeal** 1.

**petition,** *v.* — *Syn.* request, present a petition, appeal; see **appeal** 1, **ask** 1.

*See Synonym Study at* APPEAL.

**petitioner,** *n.* — *Syn.* applicant, solicitor, claimant, suitor; see **candidate.**

**petrifaction,** *n.* — *Syn.* fossilization, solidification, hardening, toughening, firmness, compactness, ossification, calcification.

**petrified,** *modif.* **1.** [Hardened] — *Syn.* stone, hardened, calcified, silicified, ossified, infiltrated, mineralized; see also **firm** 2.

**2.** [Frightened] — *Syn.* terrified, startled, scared; see **afraid** 2.

**petrify,** *v.* **1.** [To harden] — *Syn.* mineralize, clarify, solidify; see **harden** 2.

**2.** [To frighten] — *Syn.* startle, alarm, astonish; see **frighten** 1.

**petroleum,** *n.* — *Syn.* crude oil, paraffin-base oil, asphalt-base oil, naphthene-base oil, coal oil; see also **oil.**

**petticoat,** *n.* — *Syn.* skirt, underskirt, slip, half-slip, shift, crinoline; see also **clothes, underwear.**

**pettifogger,** *n.* — *Syn.* inferior lawyer, trickster, shyster, mouthpiece*; see **cheat** 1, **lawyer, rascal.**

**pettifoggery,** *n.* — *Syn.* treachery, fraud, deceit; see **deception** 1, **dishonesty, lie** 1.

**pettifogging,** *modif.* — *Syn.* shifty, evasive, deceitful; see **dishonest** 1, 2, **sly** 1.

**petty,** *modif.* **1.** [Trivial] — *Syn.* small, insignificant, frivolous; see **trivial, unimportant.**

**2.** [Mean] — *Syn.* small-minded, close-minded, narrow, narrow-minded, insular, parochial; see also **mean** 3.

**3.** [Inferior] — *Syn.* puny, weak, undersized; see **poor** 2.

**petulance,** *n.* — *Syn.* peevishness, ill-humor, cynicism; see **bitterness** 2.

**petulant,** *modif.* — *Syn.* grouchy, testy, cross; see **irritable.**

**pew,** *n.* — *Syn.* bench, slip, place, stall; see **bench** 1, **seat** 1.

**phantasm,** *n.* — *Syn.* apparition, vision, illusion; see also **ghost** 1.

**phantasmal,** *modif.* — *Syn.* fancied, fanciful, unreal; see **imaginary.**

**phantom,** *n.* — *Syn.* apparition, specter, shade, illusion, delusion; see also **ghost** 1.

**pharisaic,** *modif.* — *Syn.* sanctimonious, insincere, deceiving, holier-than-thou; see **hypocritical.**

**pharisee,** *n.* — *Syn.* fraud, faker, dissembler; see **bigot, hypocrite.**

**pharmacist,** *n.* — *Syn.* druggist, pharmacologist, chemist (British), apothecary, pharmaceutist; see also **druggist.**

**pharmacy,** *n.* **1.** [Pharmacology] — *Syn.* medicine, drug manufacturing, chemistry; see **science.**

**2.** [A drugstore] — *Syn.* drugstore, medical distributor, variety store; see **store** 1.

**phase,** *n.* — *Syn.* condition, state, stage, aspect, facet, angle, side, form, appearance, point, period, juncture; see also **state** 2, **viewpoint.**

---

**SYN.** — **phase** applies to any of the ways in which something may be observed, considered, or presented, and often refers to a stage in development or in a cycle of changes /the *phases* of the moon/; **aspect** emphasizes the appearance of a thing as seen or considered from a particular point of view /to consider a problem from all *aspects*/; **facet** literally or figuratively applies to any of the faces of a many-sided thing /the *facets* of a diamond, another *facet* of her personality/; **angle** suggests a specific aspect seen from a point of view sharply limited in scope, or, sometimes, an aspect seen only by a sharply acute observer /he knows all the *angles*/

---

**phase out,** *v.* — *Syn.* slowly get rid of, gradually dispose of, weed out*; see **eliminate** 1.

**pheasant,** *n.*
Types of pheasants include: Reeves, silver, golden, Lady Amherst's, peacock, Chinese ring-necked, argus, great crested argus, kallege, Mongolian, tragopan, Indian horned, monal, Impeyan; see also **bird** 1, **fowl.**

**phenomenal,** *modif.* — *Syn.* extraordinary, unique, remarkable; see **unusual** 1.

**phenomenon,** *n.* **1.** [Event] — *Syn.* aspect, appearance, happening; see **event** 1.

**2.** [Something amazing] — *Syn.* marvel, wonder, miracle, sensation, phenom*; see also **wonder** 2.

**phial,** *n.* — *Syn.* cruet, test tube, vial; see **bottle, container, flask.**

**philander,** *v.* — *Syn.* sue for, coquet, flirt; see **court** 1, **love** 1.

**philanderer,** *n.* — *Syn.* flirt, adulterer, debaucher; see **lecher, pimp.**

**philanthropic,** *modif.* — *Syn.* charitable, humanitarian, altruistic, benevolent, public-spirited, liberal, bountiful, magnanimous, generous, munificent, beneficent, helpful, humane, kindly, kindhearted, unselfish, giving, civic-minded, openhanded, eleemosynary, nonprofit, patriotic; see also **generous** 1, **humane** 1, **kind.** — *Ant.* misanthropic, hardhearted, selfish.

---

*SYN.* — **philanthropic** implies interest in the general human welfare, esp. as shown in large-scale gifts to charities or the endowment of institutions for human advancement; **humanitarian** implies more direct concern with promoting the welfare of humanity, esp. through reducing pain and suffering; **charitable** usually implies the giving of money or other help to those in need; **altruistic** implies a putting of the welfare of others before one's own interests and therefore stresses freedom from selfishness

---

**philanthropist,** *n.* — *Syn.* benefactor, sympathizer, donor, humanitarian, altruist, giver, contributor, donor, benefactor, friend to man; see also **patron** 1.

**philanthropy,** *n.* — *Syn.* benevolence, humanitarianism, beneficence; see **generosity** 1, **patronage** 1.

**philippic,** *n.* — *Syn.* tirade, diatribe, reproach, exchange; see **discussion** 1, **speech** 3.

**philistine,** *n.* — *Syn.* conformist, conventionalist, pedant; see **follower, sycophant.**

**philistinism,** *n.* — *Syn.* pedantry, conventionalism, conformity; see **docility.**

**philologist,** *n.* — *Syn.* historical linguist, etymologist, lexicographer, grammarian; see **linguist** 1, **scholar** 2.

**philology,** *n.* — *Syn.* etymology, lexicography, linguistics; see **grammar, language** 2.

**philosopher,** *n.* — *Syn.* logician, wise man, sage, savant, sophist, Solon; see also **scholar** 2.
Major philosophers include: Confucius, Thales, Parmenides, Epicurus, Socrates, Plato, Aristotle, Democritus, Marcus Aurelius, St. Augustine, St. Thomas Aquinas, Boethius, Baruch Spinoza, Francis Bacon, Voltaire, René Descartes, Edmund Burke, Thomas Hobbes, John Locke, Immanuel Kant, John Stuart Mill, George Berkeley, Friedrich Schiller, Jean Jacques Rousseau, Arthur Schopenhauer, G.W.F. Hegel, Søren Kierkegaard, Friedrich Nietzsche, William James, Martin Heidegger, Karl Marx, Ernst Cassirer, Jean-Paul Sartre, Martin Buber, Bertrand Russell, Ludwig Wittgenstein.

**philosophic,** *modif.* — *Syn.* pensive, profound, sapient; see **learned** 2, **thoughtful** 1.

**philosophical,** *modif.* 1. [Given to thought] — *Syn.* reflective, cogitative, rational; see **judicious, thoughtful** 1.
2. [Embodying deep thought] — *Syn.* erudite, thoughtful, deep; see **learned** 2, **profound** 2.
3. [Calm] — *Syn.* composed, cool, unmoved, resigned; see **calm** 1, **patient** 2.

**philosophize,** *v.* — *Syn.* ponder, weigh, deliberate (upon); see **think** 1.

**philosophy,** *n.* 1. [The study of knowledge] — *Syn.* theory, reasoned doctrine, explanation of phenomena, logical concept, systematic view, theory of knowledge, early science, natural philosophy; see also **knowledge** 1.
Fields of philosophy include: aesthetics, logic, ethics, ontology, cosmology, metaphysics, epistemology, psychology, axiology.
Schools of philosophy include: Egyptian, Confucianism, Ionian, Milesian, Pythagorean, Eleatic, Sophist, Cyrenaic, Cynic, Megarian, Platonic, Aristotelian, Epicurean, Stoic, Skeptic, Gnostic, Neo-Platonic, Eclectic, Patristic, Arabian, Jewish, Cabalist, Scholastic, Modern, Marxist.
Philosophic attitudes include: idealism, realism, stoicism, deism, existentialism, nihilism, mechanism, naturalism, determinism, natural realism, intuitionism, utilitarianism, teleology, nominalism, conceptualism, pragmatism, monism, dualism, egoism, pluralism, pejorism, Kantianism, Hegelianism, logical empiricism, absolutism, transcendentalism, logical positivism.
2. [A fundamental principle] — *Syn.* truth, axiom, conception; see **basis** 1, **law** 4, **theory** 1.
3. [A personal attitude or belief] — *Syn.* outlook, view, worldview, *Weltanschauung* (German); see **belief** 1, **opinion** 1, **viewpoint.**

**phlebotomy,** *n.* — *Syn.* bloodletting, bleeding, lancing, leeching, sanguisage, drainage, draining; see also **blood** 1, **transfusion.**

**phlegm,** *n.* 1. [Apathy] — *Syn.* nonchalance, unconcern, stoicism; see **indifference** 1.
2. [Sputum] — *Syn.* mucus, spittle, discharge, slime, viscous matter, morbid matter, spit*; see also **mucus, saliva.**

**phlegmatic,** *modif.* — *Syn.* apathetic, impassive, tiresome, cold; see **dull** 4, **indifferent** 1.
*See Synonym Study at* IMPASSIVE.

**phobia,** *n.* 1. [Neurosis] — *Syn.* fear, dread, unreasoned fear, *Angst* (German); see **fear** 2, **neurosis.**
2. [Dislike] — *Syn.* disgust, avoidance, aversion; see **hatred** 1, 2, **resentment.**

**Phoebus,** *n.* — *Syn.* deity, Apollo, god of the sun; see **god** 3.

**phoenix,** *n.* — *Syn.* bird, symbol of immortality, mythical monster; see **idol** 1, **statue.**

**phone,** *n.* — *Syn.* telephone, receiver, radiophone; see **telephone.**

**phoneme,** *n.* — *Syn.* meaningful unit of sound, ceneme, minimal distinctive unit of sound; see **grammar.**

**phonemics,** *n.* — *Syn.* linguistic analysis, study of phonemes, linguistics; see **language** 2.

**phonetics,** *n.* — *Syn.* study of sounds, phonetic system, science of language speaking; see **language** 2.

**phonics,** *n.* — *Syn.* sounds, sound system, pronunciation; see **diction.**

**phonograph,** *n.* — *Syn.* stereo, hi-fi, gramophone, juke box; see **record player.**

**phonology,** *n.* — *Syn.* phonics, acoustics, linguistics; see **language** 2.

**phony,** *modif.* — *Syn.* affected, imitation, artificial; see **false** 3.

**phony,** *n.* — *Syn.* fake, forgery, fraud, quack, charlatan; see also **fake, impostor.**

**phosphorescence,** *n.* — *Syn.* brightness, luminescence, glowing; see **light** 1.

**phosphorescent,** *modif.* — *Syn.* radiant, glowing, luminous; see **bright** 1.

**photo finish*,** *n.* — *Syn.* close race, close finish, almost a tie, a close one*; see **end** 2, **race** 3.

**photograph,** *n.* — *Syn.* photo, print, portrait, image, likeness, Kodachrome (trademark), snapshot, Kodak (trademark), photogram, microcopy, microfilm, bibliofilm, tactical photograph, photomicrogram, photomicrograph, radiograph, photomontage, photomural, snap★, shot★, pic★, close-up★, candid photo★; see also **picture** 2, 3.

**photograph,** *v.* — *Syn.* take a picture, get a likeness, film, copy, reproduce, illustrate, make an exposure, make a picture, catch a likeness, get a film, make a moving picture of, microfilm, photogram, snap★, shoot★, get a close-up★; see also **record** 3.

**photographer,** *n.* — *Syn.* picture-taker, photographist, cameraman, cinematographer, daguerreotypist, *paparazzo* (Italian), shutterbug★; see also **artist** 1, 2.
Kinds of photographers include: aerial, portrait, news, professional, amateur; X-ray technician, radiographer, photojournalist, videographer, photogrammetrist.

**photographic,** *modif.* — *Syn.* accurate, detailed, exact; see **graphic** 1.

**photography,** *n.* — *Syn.* picture-taking, portrait photography, view photography, aerial photography, tactical photography, photogrammetry, candid camera photography, snapshooting★; see also **reproduction** 1.

**phrase,** *n.* — *Syn.* group of words, idiom, expression, slogan, catchword, maxim, wordgroup.
Grammatical phrases include: prepositional, gerund, gerundive, participial, infinitive, noun, adjective, adjectival, adverbial, conjunctive, absolute, attributive, headed, nonheaded, exocentric, endocentric, subordinate, restrictive, nonrestrictive.

**phraseology,** *n.* — *Syn.* style, manner, idiom; see **diction.**

**phrenetic,** *modif.* — *Syn.* delirious, maniacal, deranged; see **insane** 1.

**phrenology,** *n.* — *Syn.* craniology, craniometry, metoposcopy, physiognomy, cranioscopy, physiognomics, craniognomy.

**phylum,** *n.* — *Syn.* variety, species, kind; see **class** 1.

**physic,** *n.* — *Syn.* cathartic, purge, purgative; see **laxative.**

**physical,** *modif.* **1.** [Concerning matter] — *Syn.* material, corporeal, visible, tangible, sensible, environmental, palpable, substantial, natural, real, solid, concrete, ponderable, materialistic; see also **real** 2.
**2.** [Concerning the body] — *Syn.* bodily, corporal, corporeal, fleshly; see **bodily** 1.
**3.** [Concerning physics] — *Syn.* mechanical, motive, electrical, sonic, vibratory, vibrational, thermal, radioactive, radiational, atomic, relating to matter, relating to motive forces, dynamic.

---

*SYN.* — **physical** applies either to material things as they are perceivable by the senses or to forces that are scientifically measurable /the *physical* world, the *physical* properties of sound/; **material** is applied to anything that is formed of matter and has substance [material objects, *material* possessions/; **corporeal** applies only to such material objects as have bodily form and are tangible [corporeal property/; **sensible,** in this connection, is applied to that which can be known through the senses rather than through the intellect /a *sensible* phenomenon/
*See also Synonym Study at* BODILY.

---

**physical,** *n.* — *Syn.* medical checkup, health examination, exam★; see **examination** 3.

**physically,** *modif.* — *Syn.* corporally, really, actually; see **bodily** 1, **materially** 1.

**physician,** *n.* — *Syn.* practitioner, doctor of medicine, M.D., surgeon; see **doctor** 1.

**physicist,** *n.* — *Syn.* physical scientist, natural philosopher, aerophysicist, astrophysicist, biophysicist, geophysicist, nuclear physicist, theoretical physicist, plasma physicist, physiochemist, radiation physicist; see also **scientist.**

**physics,** *n.* — *Syn.* natural philosophy, science of the material world, science of matter and motion; see **science** 1.
Branches of physics include: electronics, mechanics, acoustics, thermodynamics, optics, geophysics, dynamics, kinetics, spectroscopy, hydraulics, pneumatics, aerophysics, astrophysics, chaos theory, theoretical physics, nuclear physics.

**physiognomy,** *n.* — *Syn.* countenance, face, features, look; see **appearance** 1.
*See Synonym Study at* FACE.

**physiology,** *n.* — *Syn.* study of living organisms, study of organic functions, biology; see **anatomy** 1, **biology, science** 1.
Branches of physiology include: endocrinology, kinesiology, enzymology, nutrition, immunology, cytology, hemodynamics, neurophysiology.

**physique,** *n.* — *Syn.* build, structure, constitution, configuration, frame, strength, power, physical nature, bodily character; see also **anatomy** 2.

**pi,** *v.* — *Syn.* jumble, disarrange, mix up; see **disorganize.**

**pianist,** *n.* — *Syn.* piano player, *pianiste* (French), performer, artist, virtuoso, keyboard artist★, ivory tickler★, ivory pounder★, piano tinkler★, piano thumper★; see also **musician.**

**piano,** *n.* — *Syn.* pianoforte, grand, baby grand, upright, square, concert grand, apartment grand, boudoir, cabinet, cottage piano, spinet, clavichord, pianette, *bibi* (French), pianino, oblique pianoforte, sostinente pianoforte, electric piano, keyboard, player piano, digitorium, dumb piano; see also **musical instrument.**

**piazza,** *n.* — *Syn.* veranda, yard, patio, porch; see **court** 1.

**picaresque,** *modif.* — *Syn.* roguish, bold, adventurous; see **brave** 1.

**picayune,** *modif.* — *Syn.* trivial, petty, small; see **trivial, unimportant.**

**piccolo,** *n.* — *Syn.* woodwind, pipe, flute; see **musical instrument.**

**pick,** *n.* **1.** [An implement for picking] — *Syn.* pickax, mattock, rock hammer; see **tool** 1.
**2.** [A blow with a pointed instrument] — *Syn.* peck, nip, dent; see **blow** 1.
**3.** [★A choice selection] — *Syn.* best, elect, select, cream, upper per cent, top, topnotchers★, aces★; see also **best.**

**pick,** *v.* **1.** [To choose] — *Syn.* select, pick out, separate; see **choose** 1.
**2.** [To gather] — *Syn.* pluck, pull, choose; see **accumulate** 1.
**3.** [To deprive, especially by pecking or plucking] — *Syn.* pluck, strip, defeather, pinfeather, pull off.
**4.** [To use a pointed instrument] — *Syn.* dent, indent, strike; see **hit** 2.

**pick a fight,** *v.* — *Syn.* provoke, start, foment; see **incite.**

**pick apart,** *v.* — *Syn.* dissect, break up, break down, pick to pieces; see **break** 2, **cut** 1.

**pickax,** *n.* — *Syn.* mattock, pick, ax; see **tool** 1.

**picked,** *modif.* — *Syn.* elite, special, exclusive; see **excellent.**

**picket,** *n.* **1.** [A stake] — *Syn.* stake, pole, pillar; see **post** 1.
**2.** [A watchman] — *Syn.* patrolman, guard, union member, vedette, sentry, inlying picket.

**picket,** *v.* **1.** [To strike] — *Syn.* walk out, blockade, boycott; see **strike** 2.

**2.** [To enclose] — *Syn.* imprison, fence, corral; see **enclose** 1.

**picking,** *n.* — *Syn.* gathering, culling, separating; see **choice** 3, **preference.**

**pickings\*,** *n.* — *Syn.* profits, earnings, proceeds; see **booty.**

**pickle,** *n.* **1.** [A preservative solution] — *Syn.* solution, alcohol, formaldehyde solution; see **brine, vinegar.**

**2.** [A relish] Varieties of pickles include: cucumber, gherkin, cornichon, beet, green tomato, dill, bread-and-butter, sweet, sweet-sour, mustard, garlic, half-sour, kosher, pickled peppers, pickled beans, pickled apricots, pickled cherries, pickled peaches, pickled pears, pickled quince, pickled pineapple, pickled watermelon rind, ginger tomatoes, piccalilli, chowchow, chutney, corn relish, cranberry-orange relish, spiced currants, spiced gooseberries, beet relish, mango relish, chili sauce; see also **flavoring, herb, relish** 1, **spice.**

**3.** [\*A troublesome situation] — *Syn.* plight, impasse, dilemma, bind\*; see **difficulty** 1, 2, **predicament.**
*See Synonym Study at* PREDICAMENT.

**pickle,** *v.* — *Syn.* keep, cure, can; see **preserve** 3.

**pick-me-up,** *n.* — *Syn.* highball, whiskey, eye-opener\*; see **cocktail, drink** 1.

**pick off\*,** *v.* — *Syn.* snipe, get, shoot; see **kill** 1, **remove** 1.

**pick one's way,** *v.* — *Syn.* move cautiously, find one's way, work through; see **find** 1, **sneak, walk** 1.

**pick out,** *v.* — *Syn.* select, make a choice of, notice; see **choose.**

**pickpocket,** *n.* — *Syn.* thief, purse snatcher, mugger; see **criminal, robber.**

**pickup\*,** *n.* — *Syn.* loose woman, streetwalker, trick\*, number\*, mark\*, easy mark\*; see also **date** 3.

**pick up,** *v.* **1.** [To acquire incidentally] — *Syn.* happen upon, find, secure; see **obtain** 1.

**2.** [To take up in the hand or arms] — *Syn.* lift, uplift, cuddle; see **raise** 1.

**3.** [To receive] — *Syn.* get, take, acquire; see **receive** 1.

**4.** [\*To increase] — *Syn.* pay better, swell, swell out; see **increase** 1.

**5.** [\*To improve] — *Syn.* get better, get well, recover health; see **recover** 3.

**6.** [\*To call for] — *Syn.* call for, go for, stop for, drop in for, bring along, go to get, accompany, get, apprehend, invite; see also **arrest** 1, **invite** 1.

**7.** [\*To make a casual acquaintance] — *Syn.* fall in with, take up with, encounter, give the glad eye, offer oneself, proposition\*; see also **solicit** 3.

**pickup truck,** *n.* — *Syn.* van, autotruck, pickup; see **truck** 1, **vehicle** 1.

**picnic,** *n.* **1.** [A meal] — *Syn.* barbecue, cookout, wiener roast, clambake, fish fry; see also **meal** 2.

**2.** [\*An easy time] — *Syn.* party, good time, lark, child's play, short work, light work, smooth sailing, joy ride, sure thing, no trouble, piece of cake, cakewalk, cinch, snap.

**pictorial,** *modif.* **1.** [Having the quality of a picture] — *Syn.* graphic, scenic, striking; see **picturesque** 1.

**2.** [Making use of pictures] — *Syn.* decorated, embellished, adorned; see **illustrated.**

**picture,** *n.* **1.** [A scene before the eye or the imagination] — *Syn.* spectacle, panorama, pageant; see **view** 1.

**2.** [A human likeness] — *Syn.* portrait, representation, photo, photograph, snapshot, cartoon, image, effigy, icon, statue, statuette, figure, figurine, close-up.

**3.** [A pictorial representation] — *Syn.* illustration, engraving, etching, woodcut, cut, outline, cartoon, hologram, draft, crayon sketch, pastel, water color, aquarelle, poster, graph, oil, mezzotint, chart, map, plot, trademark, mosaic, blueprint, tapestry, showcard, advertisement, aquatint, aquatone, facsimile, animation, tracing, photograph, lithograph, zinc etching, photoengraving, collotype, halftone, rotogravure, print, ad\*, pix\*, still\*, commercial\*; see also **design** 1, **drawing** 2, **painting** 1.

Types of pictures, as works of art, include: landscape, seascape, cityscape, farmscape, snowscape, skyscape, genre painting, chiaroscuro, historical work, religious work, madonna, ascension, annunciation, Last Judgment, crucifixion; birth of Christ, battle scene, triumphal entry, detail, veronica, vernicle, icon, illumination, cameo, miniature, portrait, silhouette, self-portrait, illustration, *danse macabre* (French), nude, fresco, mural, collage, pin-up, figure, still life, center spread, animal picture, hunting print, fashion plate, diorama, panorama, photomural, photomontage, *papier collé* (French).

**4.** [A motion picture] — *Syn.* cinema, film, cartoon; see **movie.**

**5.** [A description] — *Syn.* depiction, delineation, portrayal; see **description** 1.

**6.** [\*Adequate comprehension; *usually with the*] — *Syn.* idea, understanding, survey; see **knowledge** 1.

**in the picture\*** — *Syn.* involved, concerned, part of; see **considered** 1.

**out of the picture\*** — *Syn.* immaterial, not considered, unimportant; see **irrelevant.**

**picture,** *v.* **1.** [To depict] — *Syn.* sketch, delineate, portray; see **draw** 2.

**2.** [To imagine] — *Syn.* portray, create, conceive; see **imagine** 1.

**picturesque,** *modif.* **1.** [Having the qualities of a picture] — *Syn.* pictorial, scenic, graphic, striking, arresting.

**2.** [Romantic and striking, but lacking depth and power] — *Syn.* pretty, charming, unusual; see **pleasant** 2.

**piddle,** *v.* — *Syn.* loaf, delay, idle; see **loiter.**

**piddling,** *modif.* — *Syn.* insignificant, petty, trifling; see **trivial, unimportant.**

**pie,** *n.* Varieties of pies include — *meat pies:* chicken, turkey, lamb, pork, beef, steak-and-kidney, shepherd's, cottage, pot, fish, empanada (Spanish); *dessert pies:* apple, pumpkin, pecan, rhubarb, banana cream, chocolate cream, Boston cream, chiffon, apricot, peach, pear, raisin, custard, coconut cream, rice custard, caramel nut, chocolate, lemon meringue, key lime, orange, mince, mince meat, prune, cherry, gooseberry, huckleberry, blueberry, strawberry, raspberry, blackberry, black bottom, ice cream; see also **dessert, pastry.**

**as easy as pie\*** — *Syn.* not difficult, simple, uncomplicated, a snap\*; see **easy** 2.

**piebald,** *modif.* — *Syn.* pied, mottled, dappled, varicolored; see **multicolored.**

**piece,** *n.* **1.** [Part] — *Syn.* portion, share, section, bit, slice, division, part, item, lump, hunk, scrap, interest, lot, cut, allotment, end, remnant, quota, percentage, dole; see also **part** 1.

**2.** [Work of art] — *Syn.* study, composition, creation; see **art** 2.

**3.** [Musical, literary, or theatrical composition] — *Syn.* suite, orchestration, production, opus, song, aria, harmonization, study, arrangement, treatise, exposition, sketch, play, novel, thesis, dissertation, discourse, discussion, treatment, essay, causerie, article, paper, memoir, descant, homily, poem, theme, monograph, commentary, review, paragraph, criticism, play, drama, melodrama, pageant, monologue, opera, ballet; see also **composition** 2, 4.

**4.** [Theatrical role] — *Syn.* part, lines, bit*; see **part** 3.

**go to pieces** — *Syn.* **1.** come apart, fall apart, break up, fail; see **break down** 3.

**2.** *quit, collapse, lose control; see **cry** 1, **stop** 2, **worry** 2.

**speak one's piece** — *Syn.* air one's opinions, talk, reveal; see **tell** 1.

*See Synonym Study at* PART.

**piecemeal,** *modif.* — *Syn.* piece by piece, by degrees, bit by bit, step by step; see **gradually.**

**piece together,** *v.* — *Syn.* combine, make, create; see **assemble** 3.

**pied,** *modif.* — *Syn.* piebald, dappled, varicolored, spotted; see **multicolored.**

**pier,** *n.* — *Syn.* wharf, landing, quay; see **dock** 1.

**pierce,** *v.* — *Syn.* go through, go into, pass through, pass into, break through, break into, enter, stab, intrude; see also **penetrate** 1.

**piercing,** *modif.* **1.** [Shrill] — *Syn.* deafening, earsplitting, sharp; see **loud** 1, **shrill.**

**2.** [Penetrating] — *Syn.* entering, boring, puncturing; see **penetrating** 1.

**piety,** *n.* **1.** [Devotion to duty] — *Syn.* fealty, filial allegiance, application; see **loyalty.**

**2.** [Devotion to the service of God] — *Syn.* reverence, duty, zeal; see **devotion, holiness** 1.

**3.** [Pious remarks] — *Syn.* lecture, preachment, preaching; see **sermon.**

**pig,** *n.* — *Syn.* piglet, swine, shoat; see **animal** 2, **hog** 1.

**buy a pig in a poke*** — *Syn.* take a chance, buy something sight unseen, gamble; see **risk.**

**pigeon,** *n.* — *Syn.* dove, culver, *columba* (Latin), squab; see **bird** 1.

Types of pigeons include: mourning dove, ground dove, rock dove, turtledove, ringdove, stock dove; carrier, pouter, homing, fantail, rock, wood, passenger, Cape, bronze-wing, crowned, fruit, red-billed, tooth-billed pigeon.

**pigeonhole,** *n.* — *Syn.* niche, slot, compartment; see **hole** 2, **place** 2.

**pigeonhole,** *v.* — *Syn.* classify, categorize, group, define; see **classify.**

**piggery,** *n.* — *Syn.* pigsty, stockyard, pigpen; see **enclosure** 1, **pen** 1.

**piggish,** *modif.* — *Syn.* selfish, dirty, ravenous; see **greedy** 1.

**pigheaded,** *modif.* — *Syn.* recalcitrant, insistent, stubborn; see **obstinate** 1.

**pigment,** *n.* — *Syn.* paint, oil paint, dye, coloring matter, orpiment, artist's material; see also **color** 1.

**pigpen,** *n.* **1.** [Pigsty] — *Syn.* pen, hogpen, piggery (British); see **enclosure** 1, **pen** 1.

**2.** [A messy place] — *Syn.* hovel, dump, disaster area, mess.

**pigskin*,** *n.* — *Syn.* regulation football, ball, the oval*; see **football** 2.

**pigtail,** *n.* — *Syn.* plait, hairdo, twine; see **braid.**

**pike,** *n.* — *Syn.* roadway, drive, turnpike; see **highway, road** 1.

**piker*,** *n.* — *Syn.* tightwad*, skinflint*, cheapskate*; see **miser** 2.

**pilaster,** *n.* — *Syn.* prop, pillar, minaret; see **column** 1,

post 1.

**pile,** *n.* **1.** [A heap] — *Syn.* collection, mass, quantity; see **heap.**

**2.** [*Money] — *Syn.* affluence, riches, dough*; see **wealth** 2.

**pile,** *v.* **1.** [To amass] — *Syn.* hoard, store, gather; see **accumulate** 1.

**2.** [To place one upon another] — *Syn.* rank, stack, bunch; see **heap** 1.

**piled,** *modif.* **1.** [Heaped] — *Syn.* joined, accumulated, collected; see **gathered.**

**2.** [Ranked] — *Syn.* stacked, heaped, arranged; see **organized, ranked.**

**pilfer,** *v.* — *Syn.* rob, embezzle, appropriate; see **steal.**

**pilgrim,** *n.* — *Syn.* wayfarer, wanderer, sojourner, pioneer, hajji; see also **traveler.**

**pilgrimage,** *n.* — *Syn.* travel, wayfaring, trip, hajj; see **journey.**

**pill,** *n.* **1.** [A tablet] — *Syn.* capsule, pilule, pellet; see **medicine** 2, **tablet** 3.

**2.** [*A contraceptive tablet; *usually with* "the"] — *Syn.* contraceptive pill, oral contraceptive, prophylactic; see **contraceptive.**

**pillage,** *n.* **1.** [The act of pillaging] — *Syn.* robbery, stealing, rapine; see **destruction** 1, **theft.**

**2.** [That which is pillaged] — *Syn.* booty, plunder, loot, spoils; see **booty.**

*See Synonym Study at* BOOTY.

**pillage,** *v.* — *Syn.* plunder, loot, rob; see **destroy** 1, **ravage, rob, steal.**

*See Synonym Study at* RAVAGE.

**pillar,** *n.* **1.** [A column] — *Syn.* pedestal, mast, shaft; see **column** 1, **post** 1.

**2.** [A support] — *Syn.* mainstay, dependence, guider; see **support** 2.

**from pillar to post*** — *Syn.* back and forth, fluctuating, vacillating; see **undecided.**

**pillow,** *n.* — *Syn.* cushion, feather pillow, down pillow, pneumatic cushion, foam rubber cushion, bolster, pad, padding, rest, bag, support, headrest; see also **cushion.**

**pillowcase,** *n.* — *Syn.* pillow slip, pillow casing, pillow cover, pillow sham, pillow tie; see also **cover** 1.

**pilot,** *n.* **1.** [Flier] — *Syn.* aviator, airman, fighter pilot, commercial pilot, bomber pilot, automatic pilot, mechanical pilot, aeronaut, aerial navigator, navigator, aerialist, jet jockey*, birdman*; see also **aviator.**

**2.** [One who conducts ships] — *Syn.* helmsman, steersman, navigator, man at the wheel, man at the controls, wheelman, coxswain.

**3.** [Guide] — *Syn.* scout, leader, director; see **guide** 1.

**pilot,** *v.* — *Syn.* guide, conduct, steer, manage; see **lead** 1.

**pilot program,** *n.* — *Syn.* experimental program, model program, test case, trial run; see **model** 2, **experiment** 2.

**pimp,** *n.* — *Syn.* procurer, whoremonger, pander, white-slaver, runner, hustler*, flesh-peddler*; see also **criminal.**

**pimple,** *n.* — *Syn.* pustule, papule, papula, swelling, acne, whitehead, blackhead, inflammation, blemish, bump, lump, boil, furuncle, carbuncle, blister, excrescence, caruncle, zit*; see also **blemish.**

**pin,** *n.* **1.** [A device to fasten goods by piercing or clasping] — *Syn.* clip, catch, needle, bodkin, quill, clasp, nail; see also **fastener.**

Kinds of pins include: common, safety, straight, hat, knitting, hair, clothes, bobby, toggle, cotter, push.

**2.** [A piece of jewelry] — *Syn.* tiepin, stickpin, brooch, fibula, ouch, badge, stud, sorority pin, fraternity pin, school pin; see also **jewelry.**

**3.** [A rod inserted through a prepared hole] — *Syn.* bolt, bar, dowel; see **brace** 1.

**pin,** *v.* — *Syn.* close, clasp, bind; see **fasten** 1.

**pinafore,** *n.* — *Syn.* smock, frock, overskirt; see **apron.**

**pince-nez,** *n.* — *Syn.* bifocals, eyepieces, spectacles; see **glasses.**

**pincers,** *n.* — *Syn.* pinchers, pair of pincers, wrench, pliers, nippers, tongs, instrument, tweezers, grippers, wire cutters; see also **tool** 1.

**pinch,** *n.* — *Syn.* squeeze, compression, nip, nipping, grasp, grasping, pressure, cramp, contraction, confinement, limitation, hurt, torment.

**pinch,** *v.* **1.** [To squeeze] — *Syn.* nip, crimp, cramp, tweak, compress, press, grasp.

**2.** [*To steal] — *Syn.* take, filch, rob; see **steal.**

**3.** [*To arrest] — *Syn.* apprehend, detain, hold; see **arrest** 1.

**pinchbeck,** *modif.* — *Syn.* imitation, fake, deceptive; see **false** 3.

**pinchers,** *n.* — *Syn.* pliers, pair of pincers, wrench; see **pincers, tool** 1.

**pinch-hit*,** *v.* — *Syn.* replace, act for, succeed; see **substitute** 2.

**pinch hitter*,** *n.* — *Syn.* replacement, substitute, successor; see **agent** 1, **delegate, representative** 1.

**pine,** *n.* Varieties of pine include: white, stone, mugo, whitebark, foxtail, bristlecone, nut, singleleaf, piñon, Weymouth, Scots, ponderosa, limber, Aleppo, Jeffrey, sugar, longleaf, loblolly, western yellow, pond, Arizona, Monterey, digger, Chihuahua, jack, gray, lodgepole, Georgia pitch, yellow, Torrey, bull, imou, red, Corsican; Scotch fir, balsam fir, Frasier fir; see also **tree, wood** 2.

**ping,** *n.* — *Syn.* ting, clink, sonar echo; see **sound** 2.

**pinion,** *n.* — *Syn.* feather, wing, pin feather; see **feather.**

**pinion,** *v.* — *Syn.* bind, shackle, confine, fetter; see **bind** 1.

**pink,** *modif.* — *Syn.* rosy, reddish, pinkish, flushed, dawn-tinted.

**pink,** *n.* — *Syn.* rose, red, roseate, blush-rose, salmon, flesh, flesh-colored; see also **color** 1.

**in the pink*** — *Syn.* in good health, well, fit; see **healthy** 1.

**pinnacle,** *n.* **1.** [A tower] — *Syn.* belfry, spire, steeple; see **tower.**

**2.** [An apex] — *Syn.* zenith, crest, summit; see **climax.**

*See Synonym Study at* SUMMIT.

**pinup,** *n.* — *Syn.* calendar girl, playmate, centerfold girl, gatefold girl; see **nude.**

**pioneer,** *modif.* — *Syn.* pioneering, initial, untried; see **brave** 1, **early** 1, **experimental.**

**pioneer,** *n.* **1.** [One who prepares the way] — *Syn.* pathfinder, scout, explorer; see **guide** 1.

**2.** [One in the vanguard of civilization] — *Syn.* settler, colonist, pilgrim, immigrant, colonizer, halutz, homesteader, squatter, frontiersman, backwoodsman.

**3.** [A military engineer] — *Syn.* fortification engineer, member of demolition squad, bridge builder, road builder, miner, sapper, bridge monkey*, road monkey*; see also **engineer** 1.

**pioneer,** *v.* — *Syn.* discover, explore, found; see **colonize, establish** 2, **settle** 1.

**pious,** *modif.* **1.** [Religious] — *Syn.* religious, divine, holy, devout; see **religious** 2.

**2.** [Divine] — *Syn.* hallowed, sacred, holy; see **divine** 2.

**3.** [Related to those who profess piety] — *Syn.* religious, clerical, priestly, ecclesiastical; see **religious** 1.

*See Synonym Study at* RELIGIOUS.

**pipe,** *n.* **1.** [A tube] — *Syn.* pipeline, drain pipe, sewer, waterpipe, aqueduct, trough, passage, duct, cloaca, tubular runway, canal, vessel; see also **channel** 1, **conduit, tube** 1.

**2.** [A device for smoking] — *Syn.* nosewarmer*, hayburner*, hod*, boiler*, smokestack*.

Varieties of smoking pipes include: meerschaum, corncob (*also*: Missouri meerschaum*); bulldog, brier, clay, churchwarden, narghile, hookah, Turkish, hubblebubble, opium, calabash, calumet, peace pipe, water pipe, hashish pipe, hash pipe*.

**3.** [A musical instrument] — *Syn.* wind instrument, flageolet, piccolo; see **flute, musical instrument.**

**pipe down*,** *v.* — *Syn.* become quiet, hush, speak lower; see **stop** 2.

**piper,** *n.* — *Syn.* flute player, flautist, fifer, tooter*; see **musician.**

**pay the piper** — *Syn.* take the consequences, suffer the consequences, be responsible, settle for; see **pay** 1.

**pipe up*,** *v.* — *Syn.* speak up, volunteer, shout; see **say, talk** 1.

**piquancy,** *n.* — *Syn.* seasoning, relish, zest; see **flavoring.**

**piquant,** *modif.* **1.** [Stimulating the interest] — *Syn.* charming, sparkling, enticing; see **exciting, interesting.**

**2.** [Stimulating the taste] — *Syn.* tangy, zesty, spicy; see **delicious** 1, **savory.**

**pique,** *n.* — *Syn.* umbrage, resentment, offense; see **anger, annoyance** 1, **offense.**

*See Synonym Study at* OFFENSE.

**pique,** *v.* **1.** [To anger] — *Syn.* irritate, fret, nettle; see **anger** 1, **bother** 2.

**2.** [To excite] — *Syn.* arouse, rouse, stimulate; see **excite** 1, **provoke.**

*See Synonym Study at* PROVOKE.

**piqued,** *modif.* — *Syn.* bothered, irritated, annoyed; see **angry, troubled** 1.

**piracy,** *n.* **1.** [Larceny] — *Syn.* robbery, highway robbery, privateering, hijacking, skyjacking; see also **crime** 2, **theft.**

**2.** [Plagiarism] — *Syn.* copying, lifting, cheating; see **forgery.**

**piranha,** *n.* — *Syn.* serrosalmo, caribe, man-eating fish; see **fish.**

**pirate,** *n.* — *Syn.* thief, freebooter, plunderer, pillager, marauder, privateer, soldier of fortune, corsair, buccaneer, ranger, sea rover, sea-robber, Barbary pirate, plagiarist; see also **criminal, robber.**

**piratical,** *modif.* — *Syn.* plundering, stealing, marauding; see **lawless** 2, **rebellious** 2, 3.

**piscatorial,** *modif.* — *Syn.* piscine, angling, fishing, piscatory, piscatorian, piscatorious.

**pistol,** *n.* — *Syn.* revolver, automatic pistol, automatic, six-shooter, side arm, heater*, gat*, rod*, Saturday night special, cannon, six-gun, pepper pot*, barker*, pill shooter*, iron*, forty-five, thirty-eight; see also **gun** 2, **weapon** 1.

Types of pistols include: automatic, repeating, Magnum, revolver, six-shooter, seven-shooter, Derringer, pocket, .22-caliber, .32-caliber, .38-caliber, .44-caliber, .45-caliber, 9-millimeter, Colt, Webley, Smith and Wesson, Ladysmith, Mauser, Nagant, Steyr, Browning, *modèle d'ordonnance* (French), *Luger, Parabellum* (*both* German).

**piston,** *n.* — *Syn.* plunger, ram, disk, cylinder, sucker; see also **device** 1.

**pit,** *n.* — *Syn.* abyss, cavity, depression; see **hole** 2.

**pitch,** *n.* **1.** [Slope] — *Syn.* slant, incline, angle; see **grade** 1, **inclination** 5.
**2.** [A throw] — *Syn.* toss, fling, hurl, heave, cast, pitched ball, ball, strike, delivery, offering★, the old apple★.
**3.** [Musical frequency] — *Syn.* frequency of vibration, rate of vibration, tone; see **sound** 2.
Standards of pitch include: concert, classic, high, low, international, French, Stuttgart, philharmonic, philosophical.
**4.** [A viscous liquid] — *Syn.* resin, gum resin, rosin; see **gum, tar** 1.
**make a pitch for★** — *Syn.* urge, promote, aid; see **support** 2.

**pitch,** *v.* **1.** [To throw] — *Syn.* hurl, fling, toss; see **throw** 1.
**2.** [To fall forward] — *Syn.* plunge, flop, vault; see **dive, fall** 1.
**3.** [To slope abruptly] — *Syn.* rise, fall, ascend; see **bend** 2, **lean** 1, **tilt** 1.
*See Synonym Study at* THROW.

**pitcher,** *n.* **1.** [A utensil for pouring liquid] — *Syn.* cream pitcher, milk pitcher, water pitcher, jug, vessel, amphora; see also **container.**
**2.** [In baseball, one who pitches to the batter] — *Syn.* right-hander, left-hander, southpaw★, hurler★, ace hurler★, fireball hurler★, twirler★, pill feeder★, tosser★, heaver★, chucker★; see also **player** 1.

**pitchfork,** *n.* — *Syn.* fork, hayfork, three-tined fork, header fork; see **tool** 1.

**pitch in,** *v.* — *Syn.* volunteer, work, aid; see **help** 1.

**pitch into,** *v.* — *Syn.* assault, blame, scold; see **attack** 1, **fight** 2.

**pitchy,** *modif.* — *Syn.* shadowy, gloomy, black; see **dark** 1.

**piteous,** *modif.* — *Syn.* pitiful, wretched, miserable; see **pitiful** 1.
*See Synonym Study at* PITIFUL.

**pitfall,** *n.* — *Syn.* trap, snare, meshes, deadfall; see **trap** 1.
*See Synonym Study at* TRAP.

**pith,** *n.* — *Syn.* center, stem, medulla; see **fiber** 1.

**pithy,** *modif.* — *Syn.* succinct, terse, cogent, meaty, pointed, forcible, trenchant, pregnant, weighty, substantial, sententious, epigrammatic, aphoristic, gnomic, pungent, crisp, in a nutshell; see also **concise, short** 2, **terse, trenchant** 2.
*See Synonym Study at* CONCISE.

**pitiful,** *modif.* **1.** [Affecting] — *Syn.* pathetic, pitiable, piteous, affecting, miserable, mournful, sad, sorrowful, woeful, distressed, distressing, cheerless, comfortless, lamentable, deplorable, joyless, dismal, touching, moving, stirring, arousing, poignant, heartbreaking, human, dramatic, tearful, heart-rending, depressing, afflicting, afflicted, suffering, poor, forlorn, wretched; see also **sad** 2. — *Ant.* HAPPY, cheerful, joyful.
**2.** [Contemptibly inadequate] — *Syn.* wretched, pathetic, paltry, contemptible; see **inadequate** 1, **poor** 2, **sorry** 2.

---

**SYN.** — **pitiful** applies to that which arouses or deserves pity because it is sad, pathetic, etc. /the suffering of the starving children was *pitiful*/ , but is often used now to imply contemptible inadequacy /a *pitiful* amount/; **pitiable** emphasizes the deserving, rather than the arousing, of pity, and may also suggest a greater or

lesser degree of contempt mingled with commiseration /their situation was *pitiable*/; **piteous** stresses the nature of the thing calling for pity rather than its influence on the observer /*piteous* groans/

---

**pitiless,** *modif.* — *Syn.* unfeeling, merciless, obdurate, unpitying, callous, soulless, heartless, cold, frigid, stony, insensible, uncaring, iron-hearted, unsympathetic, unmerciful, hardhearted, austere, cold-blooded, inhuman, brutal, ruthless, remorseless, relentless; see also **cruel** 2, **indifferent** 1, **remorseless** 1, **ruthless** 1, 2. — *Ant.* KIND, kindly, compassionate.
*See Synonym Study at* CRUEL.

**pitman,** *n.* — *Syn.* miner, excavator, tunneler, laborer; see **miner, worker.**

**pittance,** *n.* — *Syn.* wage, pension, pay; see **allowance** 2.

**pitter-patter,** *n.* — *Syn.* thump, patter, tap; see **noise** 1.

**pity,** *n.* **1.** [Compassionate feeling] — *Syn.* sympathy, compassion, charity, commiseration, condolence, softheartedness, tenderness, pathos, compunction, understanding, mercy, forbearance, ruth, warmheartedness, kindliness, fellow feeling, brotherly love, unselfishness, benevolence, favor, philanthropy, largeheartedness, clemency, humanity; see also **kindness** 1. — *Ant.* HATRED, severity, ferocity.
**2.** [Anything that might move one to pity, sense 1] — *Syn.* mishap, mischance, ill luck; see **catastrophe, disaster, misfortune** 1.
**have** or **take pity on** — *Syn.* show pity to, spare, pardon; see **forgive** 1, **pity** 2.

---

**SYN.** — **pity** implies sorrow felt for another's suffering or misfortune, sometimes connoting slight contempt because the object is regarded as weak or inferior /he felt *pity* for a man so ignorant/; **compassion** implies sorrow for another's sufferings or trouble accompanied by an urge to help or spare /moved by *compassion*, they did not press for payment/; **commiseration** implies openly expressed feelings of pity or sympathetic sorrow /she wept with her friend in *commiseration*/; **sympathy,** in this connection, implies such kinship of feeling as enables one to really understand or even to share the sorrow, trouble, etc. of another /a friend I can always turn to for *sympathy*/; **condolence** now usually implies a formal expression of sympathy with another in deep sorrow /a letter of *condolence*/

---

**pity,** *v.* **1.** [To feel pity for] — *Syn.* feel sorry for, feel for, sympathize with, commiserate, be sorry for, condole, be sympathetic to, show sympathy, express sympathy for, feel with, bleed for, grieve with, weep for; see also **comfort, sympathize.** — *Ant.* CENSURE, rebuke, become angry.
**2.** [To be merciful to] — *Syn.* spare, take pity on, show pity to, show forgiveness to, have mercy on, pardon, give quarter, put out of one's misery, reprieve, grant amnesty to; see also **forgive** 1. — *Ant.* DESTROY, condemn, accuse.

**pitying,** *modif.* — *Syn.* tender, compassionate, sympathetic; see **kind.**

**pivot,** *n.* — *Syn.* axle, shaft, swivel; see **axis.**

**pivot,** *v.* — *Syn.* whirl, swivel, rotate; see **turn** 1.

**pivotal,** *modif.* — *Syn.* focal, crucial, middle; see **central** 1, **crucial.**

**pixilated,** *modif.* — *Syn.* eccentric, daft, whimsical, puckish, impish, pixyish, capricious; see also **naughty, silly.**

**pixy,** *n.* — *Syn.* imp, elf, sprite, leprechaun; see **fairy** 1.

**placard,** *n.* — *Syn.* circular, bulletin, notice; see **poster.**

**placard,** *v.* — *Syn.* publicize, declare, announce; see **advertise** 1.

**placate,** *v.* — *Syn.* pacify, mollify, appease; see **pacify** 1, **quiet** 1, **satisfy** 1, 3.

*See Synonym Study at* PACIFY.

**place,** *n.* **1.** [Position] — *Syn.* station, point, spot; see **position** 1.

**2.** [Space] — *Syn.* room, compass, stead, void, distance, area, seat, volume, berth, reservation, accommodation; see also **extent.**

**3.** [Locality] — *Syn.* spot, locus, site, community, district, suburb, country, section, habitat, home, residence, abode, house, quarters; see also **area** 2, **neighborhood, region** 1.

**4.** [Rank] — *Syn.* status, position, station; see **rank** 3.

**5.** [An office] — *Syn.* position, situation, occupation; see **job** 1, **profession** 1, **trade** 2.

**6.** [A courtlike space] — *Syn.* square, park, plaza; see **court** 1, **yard** 1.

**give place (to)** — *Syn.* make room for, move over for, surrender to; see **yield** 3.

**go places\*** — *Syn.* attain success, achieve, advance; see **succeed** 1.

**in place** — *Syn.* in order, arranged, fitting, timely, appropriate; see also **fit** 1, 2.

**in place of** — *Syn.* as a substitute for, instead, taking the place of; see **instead of.**

**know one's place** — *Syn.* adapt, accept one's station, remain acquiescent, remain in one's position; see **conform.**

**out of place 1.** [Lost] — *Syn.* mislaid, displaced, gone; see **lost** 1.

**2.** [Improper] — *Syn.* inappropriate, unsuitable, not fitting; see **improper** 1.

**put someone in his place** — *Syn.* humiliate, reprimand, derogate; see **humble.**

**take place** — *Syn.* occur, come into being, be; see **happen** 2.

**take the place of** — *Syn.* replace, act in one's stead, serve as proxy for; see **substitute** 2.

**place,** *v.* **1.** [To put in a place] — *Syn.* locate, dispose, allot, allocate, settle, assign, deposit, distribute, put, plant, lodge, quarter, store, stow, set, situate, fix in, put in place, consign to a place, lay; see also **install.** — *Ant.* REMOVE, displace, dislodge.

**2.** [To put in order] — *Syn.* fix, arrange, group; see **order** 2.

**3.** [\*To be among the winners] — *Syn.* conquer, overwhelm, gain victory; see **defeat** 1, **win** 1.

**placed,** *modif.* — *Syn.* established, settled, fixed, located, based, allotted, rated, allocated, deposited, lodged, quartered, planted, set, arranged, stowed, stored, installed, situated, implanted, set up, ordered; see also **resting** 2.

**place mat,** *n.* — *Syn.* cloth, cover, doily; see **mat.**

**placement,** *n.* **1.** [Installation] — *Syn.* induction, employment, placing; see **installation** 1.

**2.** [An arrangement] — *Syn.* situation, position, deployment, arrangement; see **organization** 1.

**placement service,** *n.* — *Syn.* employment service, job placement, appointing occupations; see **employment** 1.

**placid,** *modif.* — *Syn.* calm, composed, quiet, unruffled; see **calm** 1, 2, **tranquil** 1, 2.

*See Synonym Study at* CALM.

**placing,** *n.* — *Syn.* putting, setting, laying, arranging, depositing, fixing, allocating, allotting, lodging, quartering, locating, installing, establishing, settling.

**plagiarism,** *n.* **1.** [Forgery] — *Syn.* appropriation, literary theft, falsification, counterfeiting, piracy, fraud.

**2.** [Something forged] — *Syn.* copy, fraud, counterfeit; see **forgery, imitation** 1.

**plagiarist,** *n.* — *Syn.* counterfeiter, imitator, forger, literary vandal, plagiarizer, pirate, copier; see also **cheat** 1, **impostor.**

**plagiarize,** *v.* — *Syn.* forge, paraphrase, appropriate, steal; see **copy** 2.

**plague,** *n.* — *Syn.* epidemic, Black Death, influenza; see **disease.**

**plague,** *v.* — *Syn.* disturb, trouble, irk, torment; see **bother** 2.

*See Synonym Study at* BOTHER.

**plaguy,** *modif.* — *Syn.* annoying, vexatious, disagreeable; see **disturbing.**

**plaid,** *n.* — *Syn.* tartan, crossbarred cloth, checkered cloth, Highland plaid, Scotch Highland plaid, kilt, filibeg; see also **check** 5, **cloth.**

**plain,** *modif.* **1.** [Obvious] — *Syn.* open, manifest, clear; see **definite** 1, 2, **obvious** 1, 2, **understandable.**

**2.** [Simple] — *Syn.* unadorned, unostentatious, unpretentious; see **modest** 2.

**3.** [Ordinary] — *Syn.* everyday, average, commonplace; see **common** 1, **conventional** 1, 3, **dull** 4, **traditional** 2.

**4.** [Homely] — *Syn.* plain-featured, coarse-featured, unattractive; see **ugly** 1.

**5.** [In blunt language] — *Syn.* outspoken, candid, frank, plain-spoken, impolite; see also **abrupt** 2, **frank, rude** 2.

*See Synonym Study at* OBVIOUS.

**plain,** *n.* — *Syn.* prairie, steppe, pampas, champaign, reach, expanse, open country, lowland, flat, level land, mesa, savanna, llano, moorland, moor, heath, wold, steppe, tundra, playa, veldt, downs, peneplain, the High Plains; see also **field** 1, **meadow.**

**plainly,** *modif.* — *Syn.* manifestly, evidently, visibly; see **clearly** 1, 2.

**plainsong,** *n.* — *Syn.* plainchant, chant, Gregorian chant, melody; see **song.**

**plain-spoken,** *modif.* — *Syn.* candid, direct, artless; see **frank.**

**plaint,** *n.* **1.** [Lamentation] — *Syn.* lament, moan, sorrow; see **cry** 3.

**2.** [Grievance] — *Syn.* complaint, grumble\*, gripe\*, demur; see **objection** 2.

**plaintive,** *modif.* — *Syn.* melancholy, pitiful, mournful; see **sad** 2.

**plait,** *n.* — *Syn.* braid, weaving, pleat, pleating, plaiting, crease, tuck; see also **fold** 1, 2.

**plait,** *v.* — *Syn.* braid, weave, interweave, pleat; see **fold** 2, **weave** 1.

**plan,** *n.* **1.** [A preliminary sketch] — *Syn.* draft, diagram, map, chart, delineation, time line, design, blueprint, outline, representation, form, drawing, view, projection, rough draft, road map\*; see also **design** 1, **sketch** 1.

**2.** [A proposed sequence of action] — *Syn.* scheme, project, design, outline, program, idea, conception, flow chart, projection, undertaking, method, system, tactics, procedure, treatment, intention, purpose, proposal, policy, course of action, plot, conspiracy, strategy, stratagem, arrangement, way of doing things, itinerary, prospectus, blueprint, schema, scenario, game plan\*; see also **program** 2, **purpose** 1.

**3.** [Arrangement] — *Syn.* layout, method, disposition; see **order** 3.

---

**SYN.** — **plan** refers to any detailed method or program, formulated beforehand, for doing or making something /vacation *plans*/; **design** stresses an intention to achieve a desired effect and implies the use of skill or craft, sometimes in an unfavorable sense, in arranging this /it was his *design* to separate us/; **project** suggests an ambitious or extensive plan calling for enterprise or effort, and may refer either to the proposal or to the final outcome/a research *project*/; **scheme** often connotes either an impractical, visionary plan or an underhanded intrigue /a *scheme* to embezzle the funds/

---

**plan**, *v.* 1. [To plot an action in advance] — *Syn.* prepare, scheme, devise, invent, outline, project, contrive, shape, design, map, plot, form a plan, think out, engineer, figure on, figure for, intrigue, conspire, frame, concoct, steer one's course, set guidelines, establish parameters, work up, work out, line up, plan an attack, come through, calculate on, be at, make arrangements, put up a job, reckon on, ready up, take measures, lay in provisions, bargain for, cook up★, fix to★, fix for★, pack the deal★, bore from within★, dope out★, put on ice★.
**2.** [To arrange in a preliminary way] — *Syn.* outline, draft, sketch, lay out, map out, organize, prepare a sketch, chart, map, draw, trace, design, illustrate, depict, delineate, represent, shape, preprint, chalk out, rough in, block out, block in.
**3.** [To have in mind] — *Syn.* propose, think, purpose; see **intend** 1.
**plane**, *modif.* — *Syn.* even, flush, level; see **flat** 1, **level** 2, 3, **smooth** 1.
*See Synonym Study at* LEVEL.
**plane**, *n.* 1. [A plane surface] — *Syn.* level, extension, horizontal, flat, sphere, face, stratum, dead level★.
**2.** [A tool for smoothing wood]
Types of planes include: jack, smoothing, jointing, block, circular, reed, rabbet, grooving, routing, toothing, thumb, match, dovetail, sash, beading, scraper, dado, bullnose, trying, chamfer; electric planer, jointer, foreplane; see also **tool** 1.
**3.** [An airplane] — *Syn.* aircraft, airliner, aeroplane, airship, heavier-than-air craft, *avion* (French), jet, bird★, ship★, boat★, crate★, heap★, hack★, taxi★, bus★.
Kinds of planes include: propeller, turboprop, propjet, jet, turbojet, jumbojet, rocket, scout, observation, reconnaissance, transport, supersonic transport, SST, pursuit, passenger, commuter; biplane, triplane, monoplane, dirigible, blimp, racer, glider, bomber, clipper, seaplane, hydroplane, fighter, fighter-bomber, interceptor, turbojet, stratojet, gyroplane, amphibian, zeppelin, sailplane, ultralight, hang glider.
Commonly recognized makes and models of airplanes include— *United States commercial:* Boeing 707, 727, 737, 747, 757, 777; McDonnell Douglas DC-8, DC-9, DC-10, MD-11, MD-80; Lockheed L-1001; Gulfstream; Cessna; Learjet; Beechcraft; Piper; *military:* E-3 Sentry, AWACS, F-4G Wild Weasel, F-5, F-5E Tiger, F-20 Tigershark, YF-17 Cobra, B-2 Bomber; T-34; C-135, B-52; Stratofortress; V-22 Osprey; 15 Eagle, F/A-18 Hornet, F-4 Phantom, YF-23; E-2 Hawkeye, F-14 Tomcat; F-16 Fighting Falcon, F-111 Aardvark; F-22, C-5B Galaxy, F-104 Starfighter, F-117A Stealth Fighter, A-10 Thunderbolt, AV-88 Harrier; *European commercial:* Airbus A-3400-600, A310, A320, A330, A340; Concorde; *France commercial:* Avions de Transport Regional ATR 42, ATR

52, ATR 72, Super ATR; Caravelle Super 8; *Military:* Mirage 2000; *Israel military:* Kfir-C7; *Netherlands commercial:* Fokker F-27, F-28, F-100, F-140; *Sweden commercial:* SAAB 340A, 340B, 2000; *United Kingdom commercial:* BAe 125-800, 146, 1000, Viscount 843, Vickers Vanguard 953, Jetstream 31, Jetstream Super 31, Jetstream 41, Jetstream 51; Shorts 330-200, 360; *military:* Hawk, Sea Harrier, Tornado, Lightning F.Mk3; Trident 1; *Russian Federation commercial:* Antonov, Ilyushin, Tupolev, *military:* Tu-16 Kipper, TU20 Bear, Backfire, MiG-17, MiG-21 Fishbed, Mig-23 Flogger, MiG-AT, MiG-29 Falcrum, Sn-17/20/22 Fitter.
**plane**, *v.* — *Syn.* finish, smooth, level, dress; see **flatten**.
**planet**, *n.* — *Syn.* celestial body, heavenly body, luminous body, wandering star, planetoid, asteroid.
The known planets are: Mercury, Venus, Earth, Mars, Jupiter, Saturn, Uranus, Neptune, Pluto.
**planetary**, *modif.* 1. [Nomadic] — *Syn.* vagrant, gypsy, restless; see **traveling** 2, **wandering** 1.
**2.** [Earthly] — *Syn.* tellurian, terrestrial, sublunar, mundane; see **worldly** 1, 2.
**plangent**, *modif.* — *Syn.* roaring, pounding, thundering, beating, dashing, butting, smashing, striking, throbbing, buffeting, resonant, loud; see also **hitting** 1.
**plank**, *n.* 1. [Lumber] — *Syn.* board, planking, strake; see **lumber**.
**2.** [A principle] — *Syn.* program, plan, policy, campaign promise; see **platform** 2.
**planned**, *modif.* — *Syn.* projected, on the drawing board, programmed, in the making, under consideration, on the docket, prospective, cut out, cut and dried, under advisement, prelogisticated, prepared; see also **outlined** 2.
**planner**, *n.* — *Syn.* executive, member of the executive committee, board member, member of the planning commission, director, detailer, long-range planner; see also **administrator**.
**planning**, *modif.* — *Syn.* devising, arranging, preparing, preparatory, plotting, shaping, scheming, contriving, considering, designing, laying down guide lines, developing a plan, thinking of, looking into, masterminding★.
**planning**, *n.* — *Syn.* preparation, devising, outlining; see **plan** 2.
**plans**, *n.* — *Syn.* outline, expectations, planned procedure(s); see **plan** 2, **program** 4, **sketch** 1.
**plant**, *n.* 1. [Vegetable] — *Syn.* shrub, weed, corn, bush, siip, shoot, cutting, sprout, seedling, plantlet; see also **bulb, cactus, flower** 1.
**2.** [Factory] — *Syn.* shop, mill, manufactory; see **factory**.
**plant**, *v.* — *Syn.* put in the ground, sow, set, set out, pot, start, transplant, seed, stock, colonize, settle, establish, locate, be in; see also **farm**.
**plantation**, *n.* — *Syn.* estate, ranch, manor, hacienda; see **farm**.
**planted**, *modif.* — *Syn.* cultivated, sown, seeded, stocked, implanted, strewn, drilled.
**planter**, *n.* — *Syn.* rancher, agriculturist, cultivator; see **farmer**.
**planting**, *n.* — *Syn.* sowing, seeding, drilling; see **farming**.
**plaque**, *n.* — *Syn.* plate, slab, tablet, award; see **decoration** 2, **prize**.
**plash**, *n.* — *Syn.* plop, drop, drip; see **splash**.
**plash**, *v.* — *Syn.* trickle, burble, splatter; see **splash**.
**plaster**, *modif.* — *Syn.* plaster of Paris, imitation, sham, cardboard, lath and plaster, plastered.

**plaster,** *n.* — *Syn.* mortar, binding, coat, Portland cement, gypsum, lime, plaster of Paris; see also **cement.**

**plaster,** *v.* — *Syn.* coat, bind, cement; see **cover** 1, **face** 3.

**plastic,** *modif.* **1.** [Pliant] — *Syn.* pliable, supple, impressionable; see **flexible** 1, **pliable** 1.
**2.** [Made from plastics] — *Syn.* substitute, synthetic, *ersatz* (German), molded, cast, cellulose; see also **chemical.**
*See Synonym Study at* PLIABLE.

**plastic,** *n.* — *Syn.* synthetic, synthetic compound, substitute, plastic material, processed material, polymerized substance.
Common plastics include: thermoplastic, epoxy, furane, latex, synthetic rubber, butadiene, diolefin, chloroprene, polysulfide, polyethylene, nylon, acetate, acrylic, polyester, polystyrene, PS, polypropylene, PP, polyurethane, ABS, acrylonitrile butodiene styrene, PETE, polyethylene terephthalate, HDPE, LDPE, high density polyethylene, low density polyethylene, cellophane, vinylidene chloride, phenolic, phenolformaldehyde, phenolfurfura, ethyl cellulose, urea, cellulose nitrate, acrylic, methyl methacrylate, styrene, vinyl chloride, polyvinyl chloride, PVC, melamine, copolymer vinyl, polyvinyl butyral, lignocellulose, artificial shellac.
The following are trademarked plastics: Perbunan, Buna N, Chemigum, Buna S, Methyl Rubber, SKA, SKB, Sovprene, Neoprene, Thiokil, Aralac, Velon, Saran, Orlon, Bakelite, Durez, Phenolite, Textolite, Lumarith, Ethocel, Celluloid, Nitron, Lucite, Plexiglas, Styron, Lustron, Vinylite, Zinlac, Fortisan, Formica, Mylar, Teflon, Styrofoam, Lexan, Delrin, Perspex.

**plasticity,** *n.* — *Syn.* mobility, pliancy, resilience; see **flexibility** 1.

**plate,** *n.* **1.** [Domestic utensils] — *Syn.* service, silver service, tea service; see **silverware.**
**2.** [A flat surface] — *Syn.* lamina, slice, stratum; see **plane** 1.
**3.** [A full-page illustration] — *Syn.* photograph, lithograph, etching, woodcut, electrotype, cut, engraving, mezzotint, photoengraving; see also **illustration** 2, **picture** 3.
**4.** [A flattish dish] — *Syn.* dinner plate, soup plate, salad plate, casserole, *patera* (Latin), dessert plate, platter, trencher; see also **china, dish** 1.
**5.** [Food served on a plate, sense 4] — *Syn.* helping, serving, course; see **meal** 2.
**6.** [*In baseball, the base immediately before the catcher] — *Syn.* home base, home plate, home; see **base** 5.

**plate,** *v.* — *Syn.* laminate, stratify, layer, scale, flake, overlay, gild, nickel, bronze, chrome, silver, enamel, encrust, platinize; see also **cover** 1.

**plateau,** *n.* **1.** [A plateau] — *Syn.* tableland, mesa, elevation; see **hill, plain.**
**2.** [A level] — *Syn.* degree, step, grade, interval, period, rung.

**platform,** *n.* **1.** [A stage] — *Syn.* dais, pulpit, speaker's platform, rostrum, stand, floor, staging, terrace, belvedere; see also **stage.**
**2.** [A program] — *Syn.* principles, policies, the party planks*; see **program** 4.

**platitude,** *n.* **1.** [A trite expression] — *Syn.* cliché, truism, proverb, triviality; see **cliché, motto, proverb.**
**2.** [Triteness] — *Syn.* flatness, boredom, evenness; see **dullness** 1, **monotony** 1.

*See Synonym Study at* CLICHÉ

**platitudinous,** *modif.* — *Syn.* commonplace, common, trite; see **dull** 4, **trivial, unimportant.**

**platonic,** *modif.* — *Syn.* idealistic, utopian, quixotic, spiritual, intellectual, dispassionate, nonphysical, nonsexual; see also **visionary** 1.

**platoon,** *n.* — *Syn.* detachment, military unit, company; see **army** 2.

**platter,** *n.* — *Syn.* tray, serving platter, well-and-tree platter, meat platter, silver platter, salver, trencher; see also **dish** 1, **plate** 4.

**plaudit,** *n.* — *Syn.* applause, approval, acclamation; see **praise** 2.

**plausible,** *modif.* — *Syn.* believable, probable, credible, supposable; see **likely** 1, **specious.**
*See Synonym Study at* SPECIOUS.

**plausibly,** *modif.* — *Syn.* understandably, believably, with good reason; see **reasonably** 1, 2.

**play,** *n.* **1.** [Amusement] — *Syn.* enjoyment, diversion, pleasure; see **entertainment** 1.
**2.** [Recreation] — *Syn.* relaxation, game, sport; see **entertainment** 2.
**3.** [Fun] — *Syn.* frolic, happiness, sportiveness; see **fun.**
**4.** [A drama] — *Syn.* piece, musical, theatrical; see **drama** 1, **performance** 2, **show** 2.
**5.** [Sport] — *Syn.* exhibition, match, tryout; see **sport** 1, 3.
**6.** [Action] — *Syn.* activity, movement, working; see **action** 1.
**make a play for** — *Syn.* make advances to, court, try for; see **try** 1.

**play,** *v.* **1.** [To amuse oneself] — *Syn.* entertain oneself, revel, make merry, carouse, play games, rejoice, have a good time, idle away, horse around*. — *Ant.* MOURN, grieve, sulk.
**2.** [To gambol] — *Syn.* frisk, sport, cavort, joke, dance, romp, frolic, play games, make jokes, be a practical joker, jump, jump about, skip, frolic, caper, cut capers*, cut up*, show off*, be the life of the party*, play the fool*, carry on*. — *Ant.* DRAG, mope, droop.
**3.** [To produce music] — *Syn.* perform, execute, operate, work, cause to sound, finger, pedal, bow, plunk, tinkle, pipe, toot, mouth, pump, fiddle, sound, strike, saw, scrape, twang, pound, thump, tickle.
**4.** [To display light, erratic movement] — *Syn.* waltz, spout, flicker; see **dance** 1, 2.
**5.** [To act in a play] — *Syn.* impersonate, present, represent; see **act** 3, **perform** 2.
**6.** [To engage in sport] — *Syn.* participate, engage, rival; see **compete, contest** 2.
**7.** [To pretend] — *Syn.* imagine, suppose, think; see **pretend** 1.
**8.** [To gamble] — *Syn.* chance, risk, hazard; see **gamble** 1.

**play around*,** *v.* — *Syn.* fool around, take lightly, philander; see **flirt** 1, **trifle** 1.

**play ball*,** *v.* — *Syn.* collaborate, work together, stand together; see **cooperate** 1, 2.

**playbill,** *n.* — *Syn.* program, notice, placard; see **advertisement** 2, **poster.**

**play down*,** *v.* — *Syn.* belittle, hold down, hold back, minimize; see **restrain** 1.

**played,** *modif.* — *Syn.* presented, produced, interpreted; see **given.**

**player,** *n.* **1.** [One who takes part in a game] — *Syn.* member, athlete, sportsman, sportswoman, amateur, professional, gymnast, acrobat, swimmer, diver, trackman, phenom\*, flash\*, champ\*, pro\*, semipro\*, nonpro\*, jock\*, sweat\*; see also **contestant, opponent** 1.

**2.** [An actor] — *Syn.* performer, vaudeville performer, ham\*; see **actor** 1, **actress.**

**3.** [A reproducing device] — *Syn.* record player, tape player, tape deck, video cassette recorder, VCR, compact disk player, CD player, home music center; see also **record player, tape recorder.**

**play fair,** *v.* — *Syn.* be good, be civil, mind, obey; see **behave** 2.

**playful,** *modif.* **1.** [Humorous] — *Syn.* joking, whimsical, comical; see **funny** 1.

**2.** [Frolicsome] — *Syn.* gay, merry, spirited; see **happy** 1, **jaunty.**

**playgoer,** *n.* — *Syn.* one who frequents the theater, play attender, habitué; see **frequenter.**

**playground,** *n.* — *Syn.* playing field, park, school ground, municipal playground, yard, school yard, diamond, gridiron; see also **lot** 1.

**playing,** *modif.* — *Syn.* sportive, sporting, gamboling; see **active** 1, 2.

**playmate,** *n.* — *Syn.* comrade, neighbor, companion; see **friend** 1.

**plaything,** *n.* — *Syn.* gadget, amusement, trinket; see **doll, game** 1, **toy** 1.

**playtime,** *n.* — *Syn.* vacation, holiday, recess, freedom; see **leisure.**

**playwright,** *n.* — *Syn.* scriptwriter, screenwriter, tragedian; see **author** 2, **dramatist, writer.**

**plaza,** *n.* — *Syn.* square, town square, public square; see **court** 1.

**plea,** *n.* **1.** [An appeal] — *Syn.* overture, request, supplication; see **appeal** 1.

**2.** [A form of legal defence] — *Syn.* pleading, argument, case; see **defense** 3.

**plead,** *v.* **1.** [To beg] — *Syn.* implore, beseech, solicit; see **appeal** 1, **ask** 1, **beg** 1.

**2.** [To enter a plea] — *Syn.* present, allege, cite; see **declare** 1.

**3.** [To discuss in court] — *Syn.* defend, advocate, allege, give evidence, prosecute, argue, debate, answer charges, respond, vouch, avouch, examine, cross-examine, cross-question, question.

*See Synonym Study at* APPEAL.

**plead guilty,** *v.* — *Syn.* confess, repent, concede; see **admit** 3.

**pleading,** *modif.* — *Syn.* imploring, supplicating, desirous; see **begging.**

**pleasant,** *modif.* **1.** [Affable] — *Syn.* agreeable, attractive, obliging, charming, pleasing, affable, mild, amusing, kindly, mild-mannered, gracious, genial, amiable, polite, urbane, cheerful, sympathetic, civil, cordial, genteel, engaging, social, bland, diplomatic, civilized, convivial, good-humored, good-natured, soft, fun, delightful, jovial, jolly; see also **friendly** 1, **kind.** — *Ant.* SULLEN, unsympathetic, unkind.

**2.** [Giving pleasure; *said of occasions, experiences, and the like*] — *Syn.* gratifying, pleasurable, agreeable, pleasing, enjoyable, cheering, amusing, welcome, appealing, attractive, congenial, harmonious, refreshing, satisfying, nice, all right, satisfactory, adequate, acceptable, comfortable, diverting, droll, delightful, sociable, lively, exciting, convivial, festive, cheerful, entertaining, relaxing, joyous, joyful, merry, happy, favorable, bright, sunny, melodious, mellifluous, dulcet, catchy, sparkling, enlivening, colorful, light, humorous, comforting, to one's taste, to one's liking, not half bad\*, not bad\*. — *Ant.* unpleasant, disagreeable, SAD.

**3.** [Encouraging pleasure; *said of climate*] — *Syn.* temperate, agreeable, balmy; see **fair** 3, **mild** 2.

---

*SYN.* — **pleasant** and **pleasing** both imply the producing of an agreeable effect upon the mind or senses, but the former word stresses the effect produced [a *pleasant* smile] and the latter, the ability to produce such an effect [a *pleasing* personality]; **agreeable** is used of that which is in accord with one's personal likes, mood, etc. [an *agreeable* odor]; **enjoyable** implies the ability to give enjoyment or pleasure [an *enjoyable* picnic]; **gratifying** implies the ability to give satisfaction or pleasure by indulging wishes, hopes, etc. [a *gratifying* response]

---

**pleasantly,** *modif.* **1.** [Agreeably] — *Syn.* pleasingly, charmingly, welcomely; see **agreeably.**

**2.** [Courteously] — *Syn.* gallantly, civilly, thoughtfully; see **politely.**

**pleasantry,** *n.* **1.** [Humor] — *Syn.* comedy, joking, merriment; see **humor** 1.

**2.** [A joke] — *Syn.* game, quip, jest; see **joke** 2.

**please,** *interj.* — *Syn.* if you please, if it please you, may it please you, by your leave, *bitte* (German), *s'il vous plait* (French), *por favor* (Spanish), *se v'è grato* (Italian).

**please,** *v.* **1.** [To give pleasure] — *Syn.* gratify, satisfy, make up to; see **entertain** 1.

**2.** [To desire] — *Syn.* wish, demand, command; see **want** 1.

**if you please** — *Syn.* if you will, if I may, by your leave; see **please** *interj.*

**pleased,** *modif.* — *Syn.* gratified, satisfied, charmed; see **happy** 1.

**pleasing,** *modif.* — *Syn.* charming, agreeable, gratifying, delightful; see **pleasant** 1, 2.

*See Synonym Study at* PLEASANT.

**pleasure,** *n.* **1.** [Enjoyment] — *Syn.* delight, enjoyment, happiness, joy, contentment, satisfaction, gratification, fulfillment, bliss, felicity, rapture, ease, comfort, gladness, delectation, relish, kicks\*; see also **happiness** 2, **satisfaction** 2.

**2.** [Will] — *Syn.* want, preference, wish; see **desire** 1.

**3.** [Amusement] — *Syn.* hobby, game, diversion; see **entertainment** 1, 2, **fun.**

**4.** [Gratification] — *Syn.* revelry, self-indulgence, gluttony; see **indulgence** 3.

---

*SYN.* — **pleasure** is the general term for an agreeable feeling of satisfaction, ranging from a quiet sense of gratification to a positive sense of happiness; **delight** implies a high degree of obvious pleasure, openly and enthusiastically expressed [a child's *delight* with a new toy]; **joy** describes a keenly felt, exuberant, often demonstrative happiness [their *joy* at his safe return]; **enjoyment** suggests a somewhat more quiet feeling of satisfaction with that which pleases [our *enjoyment* of the recital]

---

**pleat,** *n.* — *Syn.* pleating, tuck, crease; see **fold** 1, **plait.** Types of pleats include: box, knife, accordion, inverted, unpressed, machine, umbrella, trouser.

**pleat,** *v.* — *Syn.* ruffle, crease, gather; see **fold** 2.

**pleated,** *modif.* — *Syn.* plaited, box-pleated, knife-pleated, accordion-pleated, fluted, tucked, folded.

**plebeian,** *modif.* — *Syn.* vulgar, ordinary, coarse; see **common** 1, **conventional** 1, 3, **traditional** 2.

**plebiscite,** *n.* — *Syn.* poll, referendum, ticket; see **election** 2, **vote** 1.

**pledge,** *n.* — *Syn.* guarantee, promise, token, pawn, earnest, hostage, security, collateral, surety, warrant, warranty, guaranty, gage, agreement, oath, word, word of honor, assurance, vow, solemn word, commitment, obligation, covenant, compact, contract, bail, bond, escrow; see also **promise**.

**take the pledge** — *Syn.* vow, swear off, go on the wagon; see **promise** 1.

---

**SYN.** — **pledge**, in this comparison, applies to anything given as security for the performance of an act or contract or for the payment of a debt /he gave her a ring as a *pledge*/; **earnest** applies to anything given or done as an indication, promise, or assurance of more to follow /her early triumphs are an *earnest* of her success/; **token** is used of anything serving or given as evidence of authority, genuineness, good faith, etc. /this watch is a *token* of our gratitude/; **pawn** now usually refers to an article left as security for the money lent on it by a pawnbroker; **hostage** is applied to a person handed over as a pledge for the fulfillment of certain terms or one seized and kept to force others to comply with demands

---

**pledge,** *v.* **1.** [To give security] — *Syn.* sign for, pawn, give bond; see **guarantee** 2.

**2.** [To promise] — *Syn.* swear, vow, vouch; see **promise** 1.

**pledged,** *modif.* — *Syn.* plighted, bound, enforced; see **guaranteed, promised.**

**plenary,** *modif.* — *Syn.* entire, complete, inclusive, full; see **whole** 1.

**plenipotentiary,** *n.* — *Syn.* diplomat, spokesman, emissary; see **agent** 1.

**plenitude,** *n.* — *Syn.* wealth, excess, abundance; see **plenty.**

**plentiful,** *modif.* **1.** [Having or yielding plenty] — *Syn.* prolific, fruitful, profuse, lavish, bountiful, bounteous, plenteous, unstinted, unstinting, liberal, prodigal, unsparing, inexhaustible, bottomless, replete, generous, abundant, productive, liberal, extravagant, overliberal, overflowing, flowing, chock-full, teeming, well-provided, well-stocked, full, flush, lush with, pouring, swarming, swimming, abounding, opulent, rich. — *Ant.* STINGY, niggardly, skimpy.

**2.** [Existing in plenty] — *Syn.* abundant, copious, profuse, ample, sufficient, lavish, luxuriant, lush, exuberant, plenteous, bountiful, bumper, numerous, unlimited, abounding, prevalent, superabundant, excessive, superfluous, a dime a dozen*; see also sense 1. — *Ant.* POOR, scant, scanty.

---

**SYN.** — **plentiful** implies a large or full supply /a *plentiful* supply of food/; **abundant** implies a very plentiful or very large supply /a forest *abundant* in game/; **copious,** now used chiefly with reference to quantity produced, used, etc., implies a rich or flowing abundance /a *copious* harvest, a *copious* discharge/; **profuse** implies a giving or pouring forth abundantly or lavishly, often to excess /*profuse* in his apologies/; **ample** applies to that which is large enough to meet all demands /our savings are *ample* to see us through this crisis/

---

**plenty,** *n.* — *Syn.* abundance, lot, lots, fruitfulness, profuseness, fullness, lavishness, deluge, torrent, sufficiency, bounty, profusion, adequacy, plethora, plentifulness, plenitude, copiousness, great plenty, God's own plenty, flood, avalanche, good store, limit, capacity, adequate stock, enough and to spare, everything, *Hülle und Fülle* (German), all kinds of, all one wants, all one can eat, all one can drink, more than one knows what to do with, too much of a good thing, a good bit, all one needs, all one can use, a great deal, bonanza, a bunch*, loads*,

oodles and gobs*, full house*, egg in one's beer*; see also **excess** 1.

**pleonasm,** *n.* — *Syn.* redundancy, verbiage, circumlocution; see **repetition, wordiness.**

**pleonastic,** *modif.* — *Syn.* repetitious, wordy, redundant; see **oratorical, verbose.**

**plethora,** *n.* — *Syn.* surplus, overabundance, plenty; see **excess** 1.

**plethoric,** *modif.* — *Syn.* swollen, grown, filled; see **full** 1, **inflated.**

**plexus,** *n.* — *Syn.* net, mesh, web; see **network** 1.

**pliability,** *n.* **1.** [Flexibility] — *Syn.* facility, elasticity, mobility; see **flexibility** 1.

**2.** [Adaptability] — *Syn.* susceptibility, passivity, obedience; see **docility.**

**pliable,** *modif.* **1.** [Flexible] — *Syn.* flexible, pliant, plastic, ductile, malleable, limber, supple, elastic, bending, bendable, workable; see also **flexible** 1.

**2.** [Tractable] — *Syn.* tractable, pliant, docile, compliant, persuadable, persuasible, receptive, manipulable, adaptable, flexible, malleable, yielding, acquiescent, manageable, impressionable, irresolute, like putty*; see also **docile, obedient** 1.

---

**SYN.** — **pliable** and **pliant** both imply a capability of being easily bent, suggesting the suppleness of a wooden switch and, figuratively, a yielding nature or adaptability; **plastic** is used of substances, such as plaster or clay, that can be molded into various forms which are retained upon hardening, and figuratively suggests an impressionable quality; **ductile** applies to that which can be finely drawn or stretched out, as copper, and figuratively suggests being easily led; **malleable** is used of that which can be hammered, beaten, or pressed into various forms and figuratively suggests a readiness to be trained, changed, molded, etc. /copper is *malleable* as well as ductile; at a *malleable* age/

---

**pliant,** *modif.* **1.** [Yielding under influence] — *Syn.* tractable, yielding, pliable; see **docile, obedient** 1, **pliable** 2.

**2.** [Yielding under physical pressure] — *Syn.* limber, supple, plastic, pliable; see **flexible** 1, **pliable** 1.

*See Synonym Study at* PLIABLE.

**pliers,** *n.* — *Syn.* pinchers, forceps, tweezers; see **pincers.**

**plight,** *n.* — *Syn.* impasse, dilemma, situation, tight situation; see **difficulty** 1, **predicament.**

*See Synonym Study at* PREDICAMENT.

**plod,** *v.* — *Syn.* trudge, hike, plug; see **walk** 1.

**plop,** *v.* — *Syn.* thump, thud, bump; see **sound** 1.

**plot,** *n.* **1.** [An intrigue] — *Syn.* conspiracy, scheme, intrigue, machination, cabal, stratagem, plan, design, designs, counterplot, covin; see also **intrigue** 1, **trick** 1.

**2.** [The action of a story] — *Syn.* plan, scheme, outline, design, development, progress, unfolding, movement, story line, climax, denouement, events, incidents, enactment, suspense, structure, build-up, scenario.

**3.** [A piece of ground] — *Syn.* parcel, land, division; see **area** 2, **lot** 1.

---

**SYN.** — **plot** is used of a secret, usually evil, project or scheme, the details of which have been carefully worked out /the *plot* to deprive him of his inheritance failed/; **intrigue,** implying more intricate scheming, suggests furtive, underhanded maneuvering, often of an illicit nature /the *intrigues* at the royal court/; **machination** stresses deceit and cunning in devising plots or schemes intended to harm someone /the *machinations* of the villain/; **conspiracy** suggests a plot in which a number of people plan and act together secretly for an unlawful or harmful purpose /a conspiracy to seize the throne/; **cabal** suggests a small group of political intriguers

---

**plot,** v. **1.** [To devise an intrigue] — Syn. frame, contrive, scheme; see **plan** 1.
**2.** [To plan] — Syn. sketch, outline, draft; see **plan** 2.
**3.** [To determine a course] — Syn. map out, put forward, propose, outline, consider, plan.
**plow,** n.
Types of plows include: moldboard, gang, steam, tractor, double, straddle, sulky, wheel, mole, skim, hillside, shovel, sod, paring, bullnose, hand; lister, hoe plow, horse-hoe, garden plow, wheel hoe, harrow, cultivator, corn-hoe★; see also **tool** 1
**plow,** v. **1.** [To use a plow] — Syn. break, furrow, cultivate, harrow, turn, plow up, turn over, till, list, ridge, break ground, do the plowing, start the spring work, turn it over★, give it the gang★; see also **farm.**
**2.** [To act like a plow] — Syn. smash into, rush through, shove apart; see **dig** 1, **push** 1.
**3.** [★To fail; British, usually spelled "plough"] — Syn. suspend, send home, dismiss; see **fail** 5.
**plowed,** modif. — Syn. cultivated, turned, tilled, furrowed, broken.
**plowing,** n. — Syn. tilling, furrowing, cultivating, breaking, turning, listing; see also **farming.**
**plowman,** n. — Syn. cultivator, farm laborer, planter; see **farmer.**
**pluck,** n. — Syn. bravery, boldness, fortitude, determination; see **courage** 1.
See Synonym Study at FORTITUDE.
**plucky,** modif. — Syn. brave, spirited, game, spunky★; see **brave** 1.
See Synonym Study at BRAVE.
**plug,** n. **1.** [An implement to stop an opening] — Syn. cork, stopper, stopple, filling, stoppage, bung, spigot, river, wedge.
**2.** [An electrical fitting] — Syn. attachment plug, fitting, connection, wall plug, floor plug, plug fuse.
**3.** [A large pipe with a discharge valve] — Syn. water plug, fire hydrant, fire plug; see **hydrant.**
**4.** [Tobacco prepared for chewing] — Syn. cake of tobacco, chewing tobacco, twist, cut, baccy★, chew★, chaw★, chawin'★, chewin'★, pack of scrap★; see also **tobacco.**
**5.** [★An inferior horse] — Syn. hack, nag, plowhorse, scrub; see **horse** 1.
**plug,** v. — Syn. stop, fill, obstruct, secure, ram, make tight, drive in; see also **close** 2.
**plugging,** modif. — Syn. deterring, holding back, closing; see **block** 1, **stopping.**
**plug in,** v. — Syn. connect, make a connection, hook up; see **join** 1, 3.
**plum,** n. Varieties of plums and plumlike fruits include: freestone, Damson, Satsuma, Duarte, Elephant Heart, greengage, Reine Claude, Sugar plum; European, American, Oriental, Japanese; red, blue, yellow; French prune, Italian-Fellemberg prune, Stanley prune; see also **fruit** 1.
**plumage,** n. — Syn. down, mantle, feathers; see **feather.**
**plumb,** modif. — Syn. erect, straight, perpendicular; see **upright** 1, **vertical.**
**plumb,** v. — Syn. fathom, explore, search; see **measure** 1.
**plumber,** n. — Syn. steam fitter, tradesman, metal worker, handy man; see **worker.**

**plumbing,** n. — Syn. pipes, water pipes, sewage pipes, heating pipes, bathroom fixtures, sanitary provisions; see also **pipe** 1.
**plume,** n. — Syn. quill, crest, tuft; see **feather.**
**plummet,** v. — Syn. plunge, fall, nosedive; see **dive, fall** 1.
**plump,** modif. **1.** [Somewhat fat; said of persons] — Syn. obese, stout, fleshy; see **fat** 1.
**2.** [Filled so as to be rounded; said of things] — Syn. plethoric, round, filled; see **full** 1.
**plunder,** n. — Syn. booty, loot, winnings, spoil; see **booty.**
See Synonym Study at BOOTY.
**plunder,** v. — Syn. loot, rob, despoil, pillage; see **raid, ravage, rob.**
See Synonym Study at RAVAGE.
**plunge★,** n. — Syn. dive, leap, fall; see **dive** 1, **fall** 1.
**take the plunge★** — Syn. start, commence, attempt; see **begin** 1.
**plunge,** v. — Syn. fall, throw oneself, rush; see **dive, jump** 1.
**plural,** modif. **1.** [Concerning more than one] — Syn. few, a number of, abundant; see **many.**
**2.** [Concerning plural marriage] — Syn. bigamous, digamous, polygamous, polyandrous, morganatic.
**plurality,** n. — Syn. majority, more than half, greater amount, lion's share, favorable returns; see also **majority** 2, **lead** 1.
**plus,** modif. & prep. — Syn. added to, additional, additionally, increased by, with the addition of, surplus, positive; see also **extra.** — Ant. LESS, minus, subtracted from.
**plush★,** modif. — Syn. elegant, luxurious, sumptuous; see **rich** 2.
**plush,** n. — Syn. rayon plush, silk plush, wool plush, cotton plush, mohair plush, velvet, velveteen, plushette; see also **cloth.**
**plutocrat,** n. — Syn. magnate, tycoon, capitalist; see **aristocrat.**
**ply,** n. **1.** [A sheet] — Syn. thickness, fold, overlay; see **layer.**
**2.** [An inclination] — Syn. tendency, bent, bias; see **inclination** 1.
**ply,** v. **1.** [To use] — Syn. utilize, employ, handle, wield; see **use** 1.
**2.** [To practice] — Syn. work at, exercise, pursue; see **practice** 2.
**3.** [To supply] — Syn. replenish, equip, furnish; see **provide** 1.
**4.** [To beat] — Syn. hurt, whip, strike; see **beat** 2.
See Synonym Study at HANDLE.
**pneumatic,** modif. — Syn. breezy, atmospheric, ethereal; see **airy** 1.
**pneumonia,** n. — Syn. lung fever, pneumonitis, lobar pneumonia, croupous pneumonia; see **disease.**
**poach,** v. **1.** [To steal] — Syn. filch, pilfer, smuggle; see **steal.**
**2.** [To blend] — Syn. mash, mingle, stir; see **mix** 1.
**3.** [To cook] — Syn. steam, boil, coddle, parboil; see **cook.**
**pock,** n. — Syn. flaw, hole, mark; see **blemish, scar.**
**pocket,** modif. — Syn. small, tiny, miniature; see **little** 1, **minute** 1.
**pocket,** n. **1.** [A cavity] — Syn. hollow, opening, airpocket; see **hole** 2.
**2.** [A pouch sewed into a garment] — Syn. pouch, poke, sac, pod.
Kinds of pockets include: patch, slash, inset, watch,

coin, invisible, shirt, pants, jacket, coat, vest, side, front, back, rear, inner, outer, inside, outside.

**3.** [Small area] — *Syn.* isolated group, secluded section of persons, separated group.

**in one's pocket\*** — *Syn.* controlled, under control, regulated; see **managed.**

**in pocket\*** — *Syn.* gained, usable, ready, at hand; see **available.**

**out of pocket** — *Syn.* suffering a loss, spent, out of money, at one's own expense; see **wasted.**

**pocket,** *v.* — *Syn.* conceal, hide, enclose; see **steal.**

**pocketbook,** *n.* — *Syn.* wallet, pouch, coin purse; see **bag, purse.**

**pocketknife,** *n.* — *Syn.* jackknife, blade, penknife; see **knife.**

**pockmark,** *n.* — *Syn.* pit, smallpox scar, mark; see **blemish, scar.**

**pod,** *n.* — *Syn.* seed vessel, bean pod, pea pod; see **seed** 1.

**poem,** *n.* — *Syn.* poetry, verse, lyric, sonnet, edda, ballad, quatrain, blank verse, free verse, song, composition, creation; see also **writing** 2.

**poet,** *n.* — *Syn.* writer, poemwriter, bard, versifier, dilettante, minstrel, troubadour, jongleur, verse maker, maker of verses, scribbler of verses, metrist, lyrist, parodist, author, lyricist, librettist, dramatic poet, dramatist, lyric poet, writer of lyrics, rhymester, poetaster; see also **artist** 1, **writer.**

Major poets include — *British:* Geoffrey Chaucer, Edmund Spenser, William Shakespeare, John Donne, John Milton, John Dryden, Alexander Pope, Samuel Johnson, Robert (Bobbie) Burns, William Blake, William Wordsworth, Samuel Taylor Coleridge, Lord Byron (George Gordon), John Keats, Percy Bysshe Shelley, Alfred Lord Tennyson, Robert Browning, Gerard Manley Hopkins, William Butler Yeats, Thomas Stearns Eliot, Dylan Thomas; *American:* Edward Taylor, Edgar Allan Poe, Walt Whitman, Emily Dickinson, Edwin Arlington Robinson, Robert Frost, Carl Sandburg, Edna St. Vincent Millay, Ezra Pound, Wallace Stevens, e. e. cummings, Marianne Moore, Archibald MacLeish, Robert Lowell, Robert Penn Warren, James Schuyler, Sylvia Plath; *Classical Greek:* Homer, Sappho, Pindar, Aeschylus, Sophocles, Euripides; *Latin:* Virgil, Lucretius, Ovid, Horace, Catullus, Juvenal; *Italian:* Dante Alighieri, Petrarch, Ludovico Ariosto, Gabriele d'Annunzio; *French:* Voltaire, François Villon, Jean de La Fontaine, Charles Baudelaire, Stéphane Mallarmé, Paul Verlaine, Arthur Rimbaud, Victor Hugo, Guillaume Apollinaire; *Spanish:* St. John of the Cross, Pedro Calderón de la Barca, Federico Garcia Lorca, Pablo Neruda; *Portuguese:* Luis Vaz de Camoëns; *German:* Wolfgang von Goethe, Friedrich Schiller, Heinrich Heine, Rainer Maria Rilke, Bertolt Brecht; *Russian:* Mikhail Yurievich Lermontov, Alexander Pushkin, Vladimir Mayakovski, Boris Pasternak, Yevgeni Yevtushenko.

**poetic,** *modif.* — *Syn.* poetical, lyric, lyrical, metrical, idyllic, rhythmical, tuneful, melodious, epodic, elegiac, odic, epic, epical, romantic, dramatic, iambic, dactylic, spondaic, trochaic, anapestic, Heliconian, Parnassian, Pierian, Ionic, Sapphic, Alcaic, Pindaric, Dircaean, imaginative, rhapsodic, dipodic. — *Ant.* unpoetical, unimaginative, prosaic.

**poetize,** *v.* — *Syn.* score, sing, versify; see **compose** 3.

**poetry,** *n.* — *Syn.* poem, paean, song, versification, metrical composition, rime, rhyme, poesy, stanza, rhythmical composition, poetical writings; see also **verse** 1.

Types of poetry include: idyllic, lyric, pastoral, epic,

heroic, dramatic, erotic, elegiac, ballad, narrative, symbolic, light, humorous, satiric, didactic.

Forms of poetry include: sonnet, Shakespearean sonnet, Italian sonnet, Miltonic sonnet, Wordsworthian sonnet; Chaucerian stanza, Spenserian stanza; heroic couplet, rocking-horse couplet\*, Alexandrine, iambic pentameter, rhyme royal, ottava rima, couplet, triplet, sextet, septet, octet, distich, ode, epode, triolet, rondeau, rondel, rondelet, tanka, haiku, kyrielle, quatrain, quinzain, ballad, sestine, sloka, triad, gazel, shaped whimsey, villanelle, limerick, parody; blank verse, free verse, stopshort, stichic verse, strophic verse, stanzaic verse, accentual verse, alliterative verse.

**pogrom,** *n.* — *Syn.* slaughter, carnage, mass murder, massacre; see **carnage, murder.**

*See Synonym Study at* CARNAGE.

**poignancy,** *n.* **1.** [Intensity] — *Syn.* concentration, sharpness, piquancy; see **intensity** 1.

**2.** [Emotion] — *Syn.* feeling, pathos, sadness, sentimentality; see **emotion, feeling** 4, **pathos.**

*See Synonym Study at* PATHOS.

**poignant,** *modif.* **1.** [Sharp] — *Syn.* piquant, bitter, acute; see **sarcastic.**

**2.** [Touching] — *Syn.* moving, touching, emotional, piercing; see **moving** 2, **pitiful** 1, **sad** 2.

*See Synonym Study at* MOVING.

**point,** *n.* **1.** [A position having no extent] — *Syn.* location, spot, locality; see **position** 1.

**2.** [A sharp, tapered end] — *Syn.* end, pointed end, apex, needle point, pin point, barb, prick, spur, spike, tine, nib, snag, spine, claw, tooth, calk, rowel, stabber, sticker, prickler; see also **thorn, tip** 1.

**3.** [Anything having a point, sense 2] — *Syn.* sword, dagger, stiletto; see **knife, needle** 1.

**4.** [Purpose] — *Syn.* aim, object, intent; see **purpose** 1.

**5.** [Meaning] — *Syn.* subject, main idea, force, drift, import, gist; see also **meaning.**

**6.** [A time] — *Syn.* period, limit, duration; see **time** 1.

**7.** [A detail] — *Syn.* case, feature, point at issue; see **circumstance, detail** 1.

**8.** [A tally] — *Syn.* count, notch, mark; see **score** 1.

**at the point of** — *Syn.* on the verge of, close to, almost; see **near** 1.

**beside the point** — *Syn.* immaterial, not pertinent, not germane; see **irrelevant.**

**come to the point** — *Syn.* be brief, speak plainly, cut the matter short, get to the particulars, make a long story short\*, get down to brass tacks\*, not mince words\*, cut to the chase\*; see also **compress, contract** 2, **explain.**

**in point** — *Syn.* apt, pertinent, germane; see **relevant.**

**in point of** — *Syn.* in the matter of, as concerns, as relevant to; see **about** 2.

**make a point of** — *Syn.* stress, emphasize, do as a rule, do on principle, insist upon; see also **emphasize.**

**stretch** or **strain a point** — *Syn.* allow, make an exception, concede; see **yield** 1.

**to the point** — *Syn.* pertinent, apt, exact; see **relevant.**

**point,** *v.* **1.** [To indicate] — *Syn.* show, name, denote; see **designate** 1.

**2.** [To direct] — *Syn.* guide, steer, influence; see **lead** 1.

**3.** [To face] — *Syn.* look, aim, tend; see **face** 4.

**4.** [To sharpen] — *Syn.* taper, whet, barb; see **sharpen** 1.

**point-blank,** *modif.* — *Syn.* straight, plainly, directly, at close range; see **frank.**

**pointed,** *modif.* **1.** [Sharp] — *Syn.* fine, keen, spiked; see **sharp** 2.

**2.** [Biting or insinuating] — *Syn.* caustic, tart, trenchant; see **sarcastic.**

**pointer,** *n.* 1. [A pointing instrument] — *Syn.* hand, rod, indicator, dial, gauge, director, index, mark, arrow, signal, needle, register.
2. [A variety of dog] — *Syn.* hunting dog, gun dog, game dog; see **dog** 1.
3. [*A hint] — *Syn.* clue, tip, warning; see **hint** 1.

**pointing,** *modif.* 1. [Indicating] — *Syn.* showing, signifying, denoting, evidencing, designating, evincing, manifesting, declaring, specifying, revealing, disclosing, displaying, placing, spotting, directing to, guiding, steering, marking.
2. [Directed] — *Syn.* looking, fronting, turned, stretched toward, headed toward, facing.

**pointless,** *modif.* 1. [Dull] — *Syn.* uninteresting, prosaic, not pertinent; see **irrelevant, trivial, unnecessary.**
2. [Blunt] — *Syn.* worn, obtuse, rounded; see **dull** 1.
3. [Ineffective] — *Syn.* useless, powerless, impotent; see **incompetent, weak** 1, 2.

**point off,** *v.* — *Syn.* separate, group, detach; see **divide** 1.

**point of no return,** *n.* — *Syn.* last chance, extremity, turning point; see **end** 4.

**point of view,** *n.* — *Syn.* outlook, position, approach; see **attitude** 2.

**point out,** *v.* — *Syn.* indicate, show, denote, mention, note; see also **designate** 1, **say.**

**point up,** *v.* — *Syn.* accent, stress, make clear; see **emphasize.**

**poise,** *n.* — *Syn.* balance, gravity, equilibrium, tact; see **composure, dignity** 1.
*See Synonym Study at* TACT.

**poison,** *n.* — *Syn.* virus, bane, toxin, infection, germ, bacteria, oil, vapor, gas; see also **venom** 1.
Types of poisons include: rattlesnake, copperhead, black-widow-spider, tarantula venom; poison oak, poison ivy, death angel mushroom, hemlock, foxglove, nightshade, carbon monoxide gas, cooking gas, arsenic, lead, strychnine, oxalic, sulphuric, hydrochloric, nitric, carbolic, prussic, hydrocyanic acid; cyanide, cantharides, caustic soda, lye, belladonna, curare, aconite, Paris green, lead arsenate, blue vitriol, copper sulfate, nicotine, DDT, Agent Orange, radiation, radon gas, botulin.

**poison,** *v.* — *Syn.* infect, injure, kill, murder, destroy, vitiate, corrupt, pervert, undermine, defile, harm, taint, envenom, make ill, cause violent illness. — *Ant.* benefit, HELP, purify.

**poisoned,** *modif.* 1. [Suffering from poisoning] — *Syn.* infected, indisposed, diseased; see **sick.**
2. [Dying of poison] — *Syn.* fatally poisoned, beyond recovery, succumbing; see **dying** 1.
3. [Polluted with poison] — *Syn.* contaminated, tainted, defiled, corrupted, venomous, virulent, impure, malignant, noxious, deadly, toxic, pernicious; see also **poisonous.** — *Ant.* PURE, fresh, untainted.

**poisoning,** *n.*
Varieties of poisoning include: blood poisoning, septicemia, food poisoning, ptomaine, toxemia, lead poisoning, systemic poisoning, corrosive poisoning, irritant poisoning.

**poisonous,** *modif.* — *Syn.* noxious, hurtful, dangerous, pestiferous, baneful, malignant, infective, venomous, virulent, peccant, vicious, corrupt, deleterious, noisome, morbid, morbific, morbiferous, fatal, pestilential, miasmatic, toxic, toxiferous, deadly, destructive, bad; see also **harmful.** — *Ant.* HEALTHY, wholesome, nourishing.

**poke,** *n.* — *Syn.* jab, thrust, punch; see **blow** 1.

**poke,** *v.* — *Syn.* jab, punch, crowd; see **push** 1.

**poker,** *n.* 1. [A fire iron] — *Syn.* fireplace implement, fire-stirrer, metal bar, iron rod; see **iron** 1.
2. [A gambling game]. Varieties of poker include: draw, straight, bluff, stud, five-card stud, lowball, blind, whisky, jack pot, table stake, strip; see also **gambling, game** 1.

**polar,** *modif.* 1. [Concerning polar regions] — *Syn.* extreme, terminal, farthest; see **arctic.**
2. [Cold] — *Syn.* glacial, frozen, frigid; see **cold** 1.

**polarity,** *n.* — *Syn.* duality, contradiction, contrariety, antithesis; see **opposition** 1, 2.

**pole,** *n.* — *Syn.* shaft, flagpole, flagstaff; see **post** 1.

**polemic,** *modif.* — *Syn.* polemical, discursive, argumentative, contestable, disputatious; see also **controversial, quarrelsome** 1, **questionable** 1, **uncertain** 2.

**polemics,** *n.* — *Syn.* debate, contention, argument; see **discussion** 1.

**polestar,** *n.* — *Syn.* Polaris, guide, north star; see **star** 1.

**police,** *n.* — *Syn.* police force, law enforcement body, FBI, police officers, policemen, custodians of the law, detective force, military police, M.P.'S*, Royal Canadian Mounted Police, RCMP*, Mounties*, the law*, the fuzz*, the heat*, the man*, canine corps, New York's Finest*.

**police,** *v.* — *Syn.* watch, control, patrol; see **guard** 2.

**police officer,** *n.* — *Syn.* policeman, police woman, patrolman, patrolwoman, officer of the law, magistrate, process server, constable, bluecoat*, beat pounder*, cop, copper*, flatfoot*, the fuzz*, the man*, John Law*, the heat*, bull*, speed cop*, bobby*, redneck*.
Types of police include: mounted, military, motorcycle, traffic, city, state, highway patrol, state trooper, patrolman, sheriff, detective, SWAT, Special Weapons and Tactics team, federal agent, federal investigator, fed*, narc*, F.B.I. man*, G-man*, T-man*.

**police state,** *n.* — *Syn.* dictatorship, authoritarian government, military dictatorship, fascist government; see **autocracy.**

**policy,** *n.* — *Syn.* course, procedure, method, system, strategy, tactics, administration, management, theory, tenet, doctrine, behavior, scheme, design, arrangement, organization, plan, order.

**polish,** *n.* — *Syn.* shine, burnish, glaze; see **finish** 2.

**polish,** *v.* — *Syn.* burnish, buff, shine, brighten, rub, wax, clean, smooth, scour, furbish, finish, varnish, gloss; see also **glaze, shine** 3.

SYN. — **polish** implies rubbing, as with a cloth or tool and, often, an abrasive, paste, etc., to produce a smooth or glossy surface [to *polish* silver, glass, furniture, etc.]; **burnish** specifically suggests the rubbing of metals to make them bright and lustrous [*burnished* steel]; **buff** implies polishing with a stick or tool covered with specially treated leather (originally buffalo hide) or with a soft cloth or pad [to *buff* the fingernails]; **shine** implies making bright and clean by polishing [to *shine* shoes]

**polished,** *modif.* 1. [Bright] — *Syn.* glossy, shining, gleaming; see **bright** 1.
2. [Refined] — *Syn.* polite, well-bred, cultured; see **refined** 2.
3. [Referring to writing or speech] — *Syn.* perfected, elaborate, ornate; see **elegant** 3.
4. [Well executed] — *Syn.* flawless, masterly, masterful, accomplished, impeccable.

**polite,** *modif.* 1. [Courteous] — *Syn.* courteous, civil, obliging, thoughtful, mannerly, attentive, pleasant, gentle, mild, nice, considerate, solicitous, conciliatory, conciliative, bland, honey-tongued, amiable, gracious, cordial, good-natured, sympathetic, interested, smooth, chivalrous, gallant, diplomatic, tactful, politic, benign, propitiatory, kindly, kind, courtly, benignant, affable, agreeable, complaisant, respectful, amenable, courtly, well-bred, genteel, gentlemanly, well-mannered, well-spoken, ceremonious, formal, proper, punctilious, sociable, ingratiating, neighborly, friendly. — *Ant.* RUDE, impolite, insolent.

**2.** [Refined] — *Syn.* polished, well-bred, cultured, urbane; see **refined** 2.

---

*SYN.* — **polite** suggests a positive observance of etiquette in social behavior [it is not *polite* to interrupt]; **courteous** suggests a still more positive and sincere graciousness toward others that springs from an inherent thoughtfulness [always *courteous* to strangers]; **civil** implies merely a refraining from rudeness [keep a *civil* tongue in your head]; **chivalrous** implies disinterested courtesy toward women or devotion to the cause of the weak; **gallant** suggests a dashing display of courtesy, esp. to women [her *gallant* lover]

---

**politely,** *modif.* — *Syn.* thoughtfully, considerately, attentively, solicitously, concernedly, cordially, graciously, amiably, kindheartedly, compassionately, gently, benignantly, urbanely, affably, agreeably, civilly, gallantly, complacently, sociably, elegantly, gracefully, charmingly, ingratiatingly, winningly, blandly, tactfully, in good humor, with good grace, with old-fashioned courtesy, with easy graciousness; see also **respectfully.**

**politeness,** *n.* — *Syn.* courtesy, refinement, culture, civility; see **courtesy** 1.

**politic,** *modif.* — *Syn.* diplomatic, expedient, urbane, judicious, shrewd, crafty, sensible, sagacious, suave, bland; see also **discreet, judicious.**

*See Synonym Study at* SUAVE.

**political,** *modif.* — *Syn.* legislative, partisan, executive, administrative, concerning public affairs, having to do with politics, pertaining to government affairs, civic, state, federal; see also **governmental.**

**political science,** *n.* — *Syn.* political economy, science of government, politics, political theory, study of government, government science; see also **social science.**

**political scientist,** *n.* — *Syn.* political researcher, political observer, professor of political science, Kremlinologist, sovietologist.

**politician,** *n.* **1.** [One who follows politics professionally] — *Syn.* officeholder, office seeker, party man, partisan, legislator, lawmaker, lawgiver, congressman, member of parliament, MP, bureaucrat, politico.

**2.** [A statesman] — *Syn.* diplomat, lawmaker, governmental leader; see **statesman.**

**3.** [One who plays politics] — *Syn.* agitator, demagogue, timeserver, political panderer, poser, rabble rouser, baby-kisser*, arm-waver*, spoilsmonger*, Man on Horseback*.

**politics,** *n.* **1.** [Political science] — *Syn.* government, statesmanship, diplomacy, practical government, functional government, domestic affairs, internal affairs, foreign affairs, matters of state, *Realpolitik* (German), political realism.

**2.** [The business of obtaining public office] — *Syn.* campaigning, getting votes, seeking nomination, electioneering, being up for election*, running for office*, standing to run*, throwing one's hat in the ring*, stumping the country*, taking the stump*.

**polity,** *n.* — *Syn.* republic, commonwealth, country; see **nation** 1.

**poll,** *n.* **1.** [A census] — *Syn.* vote, consensus, survey, ballot; see **census.**

**2.** [A voting place; *usually plural*] — *Syn.* ballot box(es), voting machines, polling place, polling area.

**poll,** *v.* — *Syn.* question, register, enroll, survey; see **examine** 1, **list** 1.

**pollen,** *n.* — *Syn.* microspores, powder, fine particles; see **dust.**

**pollinate,** *v.* — *Syn.* fertilize, pollenate, cross-fertilize, breed; see **fertilize** 2.

**pollute,** *v.* — *Syn.* contaminate, dirty, befoul, defile; see **contaminate, dirty, poison.**

*See Synonym Study at* CONTAMINATE.

**polluted,** *modif.* — *Syn.* contaminated, noxious, foul, fouled, soiled, corrupted, defiled, poisoned, filthy, smelly; see also **dirty** 1.

**pollution,** *n.* — *Syn.* contamination, corruption, defilement, adulteration, blight, soiling, fouling, foulness, taint, tainting, polluting, decomposition, desecration, profanation, abuse, deterioration, rottenness, spoliation, impairment, misuse, infection, besmearing, besmirching, smirching; see also **contamination.**

Common environmental pollutants include: sewage, garbage, radiation, carbon monoxide, automobile exhaust, pesticides, chloroflurocarbons, CFCs, polychlorinated biphenyls, PCBs, hydrocarbons, carbon dioxide, dioxin, ethylene dibromide, EDB; tobacco smoke, wood smoke, coal smoke; asbestos, lead, chlorine, mercury; noise, nuclear waste, solid waste.

**poltergeist,** *n.* — *Syn.* spirit, spook, supernatural visitant; see **ghost** 1, 2.

**poltroon,** *n.* — *Syn.* deserter, dastard, recreant; see **coward, weakling.**

**polygamy,** *n.* — *Syn.* polyandry, polygyny, plural marriage, bigamy; see **marriage** 1.

**polyglot,** *modif.* — *Syn.* bilingual, multilingual, polyglottic, polylingual, learned in languages, diglottic, diglot, hexaglot, Panglossian.

**polyphonic,** *modif.* — *Syn.* harmonic, contrapuntal; two part, three part, etc.; choral, orchestral; see also **harmonious** 1.

**polytechnic,** *n.* — *Syn.* technological institute, vocational school, occupational school, trade school; see **school** 1.

**polytheism,** *n.* — *Syn.* tritheism, ditheism, pantheism, paganism, henotheism; see also **religion** 2.

**pomade,** *n.* — *Syn.* hair oil, hair cream, hair dressing, hair lotion, styling gel, ointment, balm, salve; see also **cosmetic.**

**pomade,** *v.* — *Syn.* make up, anoint, oil; see **grease.**

**pommel,** *n.* — *Syn.* saddle horn, handle, hilt, knob, ball, horn.

**pomp,** *n.* — *Syn.* grandeur, pageantry, ceremony, magnificence, affectation, splendor; see also **glory** 2, **grandeur, ostentation** 2.

**pompom,** *n.* — *Syn.* tuft, plume, tassel, topknot, knob, crest, cockade; see also **decoration** 2.

**pomposity,** *n.* **1.** [Pretension] — *Syn.* presumption, conceit, overconfidence; see **arrogance.**

**2.** [Grandiloquence] — *Syn.* balderdash, pretension, bombast; see **nonsense** 1.

**pompous,** *modif.* — *Syn.* pretentious, self-important, arrogant, haughty, proud, conceited, grandiose, bombastic, theatrical, inflated, high-flown, grandiloquent, overblown, ostentatious, showy, pontifical, stuffy*, highfalutin*, stuffed-shirted*; see also **egotistic** 2, **proud** 2.

**pompously,** *modif.* — *Syn.* pretentiously, conceitedly, boastfully, snobbishly, imperiously, insolently, autocratically, disdainfully, magisterially, overbearingly, proudly, ostentatiously, bombastically, theatrically, spectacularly, flamboyantly, gaudily; see also **arrogantly, egotistically.** — *Ant.* QUIETLY, humbly, modestly.

**pond,** *n.* — *Syn.* fishpond, millpond, lily pond; see **lake, pool** 1.

**ponder,** *v.* — *Syn.* meditate, deliberate, consider, reflect; see **think** 1.

**ponderable,** *modif.* — *Syn.* substantial, weighty, massive; see **heavy** 1.

**ponderous,** *modif.* — *Syn.* heavy, dull, weighty, lifeless; see **heavy** 1, **indifferent** 1.

*See Synonym Study at* HEAVY.

**poniard,** *n.* — *Syn.* dagger, blade, sword; see **knife.**

**pontiff,** *n.* — *Syn.* prelate, cardinal, His Holiness; see **pope.**

**pontifical,** *modif.* — *Syn.* papist, apostolic, ecclesiastical; see **papal.**

**pontificate,** *n.* — *Syn.* popedom, bishopric, the Vatican; see **papacy.**

**pontoon,** *n.* — *Syn.* barge, float, craft; see **boat, raft.**

**pony,** *n.* — *Syn.* Shetland pony, Welsh pony, Galloway horse, bronco, cayuse, mustang, Indian pony, Russian pony; see also **horse** 1.

**poodle,** *n.* — *Syn.* French poodle, French barbet, fancy dog; see **dog** 1, **pet** 3.

**pool,** *n.* 1. [Small body of liquid, usually water] — *Syn.* puddle, mudpuddle, pond, lake, fishpond, millpond, swim tank, natatorium, tarn; see also **lake.**
2. [Supply] — *Syn.* funds, provisions, amount available; see **equipment, supply** 2.
3. [Game] — *Syn.* billiards, pocket billiards, straight pool, 8-ball, 9-ball, snooker, slop, lag.

**pool,** *v.* — *Syn.* combine, merge, blend; see **join** 1.

**poop,** *n.* — *Syn.* deck of a ship, stern, back end; see **deck** 1.

**poor,** *modif.* 1. [Lacking worldly goods] — *Syn.* indigent, impoverished, impecunious, destitute, needy, necessitous, penniless, poverty-stricken, underprivileged, disadvantaged, deprived, starved, starving, straitened, penurious, pinched, distressed, in reduced circumstances, beggared, famine-stricken, underdeveloped, empty-handed, insolvent, beggarly, ill-provided, ill-furnished, in want, in penury, suffering privation, in need, feeling the pinch, unable to make ends meet, poor as a church mouse*, broke*, hard up*, strapped for money*, down and out*, out at the elbows*; see also **insolvent, ruined** 4, **wanting** 1. — *Ant.* WEALTHY, well-to-do, affluent.
2. [Lacking excellences] — *Syn.* pitiful, paltry, contemptible, miserable, pitiable, dwarfed, insignificant, diminutive, ordinary, common, mediocre, trashy, shoddy, worthless, sorry, base, mean, coarse, vulgar, inferior, imperfect, smaller, lesser, below par, subnormal, under average, second-rate, reduced, defective, deficient, lower, subordinate, minor, secondary, humble, second-hand, pedestrian, beggarly, homely, homespun, fourth-rate, tawdry, petty, unimportant, bad, cheap, flimsy, threadbare, badly made, less than good, unwholesome, lacking in quality, dowdy, undergrade, second-class, shabby, shoddy, valueless, easy, gaudy, mass-produced, gimcrack, squalid, catchpenny, trivial, sleazy, trifling, unsuccessful, second-best, tasteless, insipid, barbarous, vile, disgusting, despicable, rustic, crude, outlandish, odd, rock-bottom, garish, flashy, showy, inelegant, loud, unsightly, inartistic, affected, ramshackle, pretentious, tumble-down, glaring, artificial, flaunting, newfangled, out-of-date, old-fashioned, crummy*, junky*, two-bit*, schlock*, third-rate*, kitschy*, raunchy*, corny*,

cheesy*; see also **faulty, inadequate** 1, **unsatisfactory.**
3. [Inadequate] — *Syn.* meager, scanty, sparse; see **inadequate** 1, **scanty, wanting** 1.
4. [Lacking vigor or health] — *Syn.* feeble, puny, infirm, indisposed; see **sick, weak** 1.
5. [Lacking fertility] — *Syn.* infertile, unproductive, barren; see **sterile** 1, 2, **worthless** 1.
6. [Worthy of pity] — *Syn.* unfortunate, pitiable, hapless, wretched; see **unfortunate** 2.

---

*SYN.* — **poor** is the simple, direct term for one who lacks the resources for reasonably comfortable living; **impoverished**) is applied to one who having once had plenty is now reduced to poverty /an *impoverished* aristocrat/; **destitute** implies such great poverty that even the means for subsistence, such as food and shelter, are lacking /left *destitute* by the war/; **impecunious** applies to one who habitually lacks money and often suggests that this results from personal practices /an *impecunious* gambler/; **indigent** implies such relative poverty as results in a lack of comforts or luxuries and the endurance of hardships /books for *indigent* children/

---

**poor,** *n.* — *Syn.* needy, forgotten man, the unemployed, underdogs, the underprivileged, beggars, the impoverished masses, second-class citizen, have-nots*; see also **pauper, people** 3.

**poorhouse,** *n.* — *Syn.* poverty, retreat, debtor's prison, asylum, harbor, house for paupers, almshouse; see also **poverty** 1, **shelter.**

**poorly,** *modif.* 1. [In an inferior manner] — *Syn.* defectively, crudely, unsuccessfully; see **badly** 1, **inadequately.**
2. [*Ill] — *Syn.* indisposed, ailing, unwell; see **sick.**

**poorness,** *n.* — *Syn.* want, need, destitution; see **poverty** 1, **starvation.**

**poor-spirited,** *modif.* — *Syn.* abject, timorous, wretched, miserable, mean; see also **afraid** 1, **cowardly** 1.

**pop,** *n.* 1. [A slight explosive sound] — *Syn.* report, burst, shot; see **noise** 1.
2. [A carbonated drink] — *Syn.* soda pop, tonic, soda, cola, Coke (trademark), ginger pop, soda water, beverage, soft drink; see also **drink** 3.

**pop,** *v.* — *Syn.* dart, leap, protrude; see **jump** 1, **rise** 1.

**pope,** *n.* — *Syn.* Pontiff, Supreme Pontiff, head of the Roman Catholic Church, bishop of Rome, Primate of Italy, Roman Pontiff, vicar of Jesus Christ on earth, Metropolitan of the Roman Province, successor to Peter in the See of Rome, Patriarch of the West, His Holiness, the Holy Father, *Servus servorum Dei* (Latin); see also **father** 5, **master** 1, **priest.**

**poppy,** *n.* — *Syn.* bloom, blossom, herb; see **drug** 2, **flower** 1, 2.
Varieties of poppies include: opium, corn, Iceland, black, California, field, garden, yellow-horned, long-headed, Mexican, Oriental, prickly, red, Shirley, seaside, dwarf.

**poppycock*,** *n.* — *Syn.* humbug, gibberish, foolishness; see **nonsense** 1, **stupidity** 2.

**populace,** *n.* — *Syn.* masses, commonality, multitude; see **man** 1, **people** 3.

**popular,** *modif.* 1. [Generally liked] — *Syn.* favorite, well-liked, approved, well-received, sought-after, fashionable, stylish, beloved, attractive, praised, promoted, acclaimed, recommended, in the public eye, in demand, celebrated, noted, admired, famous, in favor, in high favor, favored, successful, in vogue, all the rage★, in★, hot★, big★, trendy★, on everybody's lips★; see also **fashionable, modern** 1. — *Ant.* UNKNOWN, in disrepute, out of favor.

**2.** [Cheap] — *Syn.* low-priced, popular-priced, marked down; see **cheap** 1, **economical** 2.

**3.** [Commonly accepted] — *Syn.* general, familiar, prevalent, prevailing, current, common, accepted, rife, in use, widespread, ordinary, adopted, embraced, having caught on, in the majority, having caught the popular fancy; see also **common** 1, **conventional** 1, 2, **traditional** 2.

**4.** [Appealing to or intended for the general public] — *Syn.* accessible, lay, popularized, simplified, commercial, bourgeois, vulgar, pop★, geared-down★, dumbed-down★, kitschy★.

**5.** [Pertaining to ordinary people] — *Syn.* mass, public, grass-roots★; see **democratic, republican**.

*See Synonym Study at* COMMON.

**popularity,** *n.* **1.** [Approval] — *Syn.* general esteem, widespread acceptance, following, prevalence, universality, demand, fashionableness.

**2.** [Fame] — *Syn.* reputation, repute, notoriety, acclaim; see **fame** 1, 2.

**popularize,** *v.* — *Syn.* familiarize, catch on, cheapen, give currency to, spread, universalize, produce in quantity, gear down★; see also **generalize** 1, **simplify**.

**popularly,** *modif.* — *Syn.* commonly, usually, ordinarily; see **regularly** 1.

**population,** *n.* — *Syn.* inhabitants, dwellers, people, citizenry, natives, group, residents, culture, community, state, populace; see also **society** 2.

**populous,** *modif.* — *Syn.* peopled, crowded, populated, thickly settled, serried, dense, thronged, thick, swarming, teeming, crawling with people★.

**porcelain,** *n.* — *Syn.* earthenware, ceramic(s), enamel, enamelware; see **china**.
Varieties and makers of porcelain include: Alcora, Amstel, Arita, Berlin, Brandenburg, bone, Bow, Bristol, Burslem, Chelsea, Cookworthy, Crown Derby, Meissen, Dresden, Belleek, Mayflower, Royal Worcester, Swansea, Lowestoft, Budweis, Caen, Chantilly, Wedgwood, Royal Doulton, Lladro, Lenox, Spode, Limoges, Rosenthal, Luneville, Sèvres, Royal Copenhagen, Dresden, Imari, Hizen, Imperial yellow, Kouan-Ki, Mandarin, rose, Capodimonte, Medici, cast, fusible, ironstone, chemical, majolica, eggshell, embossed, hybrid.

**porch,** *n.* — *Syn.* veranda, piazza, portico, breezeway, entrance, doorstep, stoop, gallery, entrance platform, carriage porch, galilee, stoa; see also **balcony, veranda**.

**porcine,** *modif.* — *Syn.* hoggish, rapacious, piggish; see **greedy** 2.

**pore,** *n.* — *Syn.* opening, foramen, orifice, vesicle; see **hole** 1, 2.

**pork,** *n.* Common cuts of pork include: ham, shank, tenderloin, loin, bacon, back, spareribs, back ribs, baby back ribs, side meat, shoulder, loin roast, crown roast, loin chops, shoulder chops, hock, Boston butt, plate, jowl, pig's feet, fat back; see also **meat**.

**pork barrel★,** *n.* — *Syn.* appropriations, graft, favoritism, government funds; see **corruption** 2.

**porker★,** *n.* — *Syn.* swine, pig, boar; see **animal** 2, **hog** 1.

**pornographic,** *modif.* — *Syn.* prurient, immoral, dirty, obscene; see **lewd** 1.

**pornography,** *n.* — *Syn.* obscene literature, prurience, salaciousness, vulgarity, quadriliteral, obscenity, gross-

ness, erotica, sexploitation, smut, cheesecake★; see also **indecency** 2.

**porous,** *modif.* — *Syn.* pervious, permeable, acceptable, pory; see **penetrable**.

**port,** *modif.* — *Syn.* lefthand, to the left, toward the left, larboard; see **left** 1.

**port,** *n.* — *Syn.* haven, anchorage, gate; see **harbor** 1, 2.

**portable,** *modif.* — *Syn.* transportable, conveyable, transferable, easily transported, manageable, compact; see also **movable**.

**portage,** *n.* — *Syn.* transport, hauling, carriage, conveyance; see **transportation**.

**portal,** *n.* — *Syn.* entrance, gateway, opening, ingress; see **door** 1, **entrance** 2, **gate**.

**portend,** *v.* — *Syn.* forecast, predict, herald; see **hint, warn** 1.

**portent,** *n.* — *Syn.* omen, clue, token, caution; see **sign** 1, **warning**.

**portentous,** *modif.* **1.** [Ominous] — *Syn.* ominous, foreboding, prophetic, momentous; see **important** 1, **ominous, sinister**.

**2.** [Unusual] — *Syn.* rare, extraordinary, significant; see **unusual** 2.

*See Synonym Study at* OMINOUS.

**porter,** *n.* **1.** [A gatekeeper] — *Syn.* doorkeeper, doorman, lodgekeeper, gamekeeper, caretaker, ostiary, janitor; see also **watchman**.

**2.** [A person, who carries another's things] — *Syn.* carrier, transporter, bellboy, pullman porter, redcap, skycap, buttons★, bellhop★, hop★.

**portfolio,** *n.* **1.** [A flat container] — *Syn.* briefcase, attaché case, folder; see **bag, case** 7, **container**.

**2.** [A collection, especially of stocks and bonds] — *Syn.* holdings, selection, documents, securities; see **collection** 2.

**3.** [An assignment] — *Syn.* office, responsibility, duties; see **duty** 2, **job** 1, 2.

**porthole,** *n.* — *Syn.* peephole, hole, opening; see **window** 1.

**portico,** *n.* — *Syn.* covered wall, colonnade, arcade; see **patio, porch**.

**portion,** *n.* **1.** [A division] — *Syn.* share, piece, part, serving; see **division** 2, **helping, part** 1, **share**.

*See Synonym Study at* PART.

**2.** [Fate] — *Syn.* fate, destiny, lot; see **fate**.

*See Synonym Study at* FATE.

**portly,** *modif.* **1.** [Fat] — *Syn.* corpulent, heavy, stout; see **fat** 1.

**2.** [Dignified] — *Syn.* majestic, grand, remarkable; see **impressive** 1, **striking**.

**portrait,** *n.* — *Syn.* likeness, portraiture, representation; see **painting** 1, **picture** 2.

**portraiture,** *n.* — *Syn.* representation, portrait, painting; see **art** 3, **picture** 2.

**portray,** *v.* **1.** [To represent] — *Syn.* depict, characterize, reproduce; see **define** 2, **describe, represent** 2.

**2.** [To imitate] — *Syn.* copy, simulate, mimic; see **imitate** 2, **impersonate, parody**.

**portrayal,** *n.* — *Syn.* depiction, replica, likeness; see **copy, description** 1, **imitation** 2.

**pose,** *n.* — *Syn.* artificial position, affectation, mannerism, airs, pretense, posture, stance, attitude, bearing, posturing, attitudinizing, act, façade, front, show, playacting; see also **fake, pretense** 1.

---

**SYN.** — **pose** refers to an attitude or manner that is assumed for the effect that it will have on others /her generosity is a mere *pose*/; **affectation** is used of a specific piece of artificial behavior intended obviously to impress others /an *affectation* of speech/; a **mannerism** is a peculiarity, as in behavior or speech, (often originally an affectation) that has become habitual and unconscious /his *mannerism* of raising one eyebrow in surprise/; **airs** is used of an affected pretense of superior manners and graces /stop putting on *airs*/ See also Synonym Study at POSTURE.

**pose,** *v.* **1.** [To pretend] — *Syn.* profess, feign, make believe; see **act** 1, **pretend** 1.
   **2.** [To assume a pose for a picture] — *Syn.* sit, model, strike an attitude, adopt a position, posture; see also **model** 3.
**posed,** *modif.* — *Syn.* formal, stiff, unnatural; see **awkward** 1, **conventional** 2, 3.
**poser,** *n.* **1.** [A pretender] — *Syn.* mimic, hypocrite, pretender; see **cheat** 1, **impostor.**
   **2.** [A mystery] — *Syn.* problem, enigma, perplexity; see **puzzle** 2, **riddle** 1.
**posh\*,** *modif.* — *Syn.* elegant, deluxe, opulent; see **rich** 2.
**posit,** *v.* **1.** [To place] — *Syn.* set, fix, secure; see **fasten** 1, **place** 1.
   **2.** [To state] — *Syn.* postulate, announce, assert, pronounce; see **declare** 2, **say.**
**position,** *n.* **1.** [A physical position] — *Syn.* location, locality, spot, seat, ground, environment, post, whereabouts, bearings, station, point, place, stand, space, surroundings, situation, site, topography, chorography, geography, region, tract, district, scene, setting; see also **area** 2, **place** 3.
   **2.** [An intellectual position] — *Syn.* view, belief, attitude; see **judgment** 3, **opinion** 1.
   **3.** [An occupational position] — *Syn.* job, situation, office; see **job** 1, **profession** 1, **trade** 2.
   **4.** [A social position] — *Syn.* station, state, status; see **rank** 3.
   **5.** [Posture] — *Syn.* pose, carriage, bearing, deportment, stance, stand, condition, situation, status, state, mien, form, manner, habit; see also **attitude** 1, **posture** 1.
*See Synonym Study at* JOB.
**position,** *v.* — *Syn.* put, locate, settle in; see **place.**
**positive,** *modif.* **1.** [Definite] — *Syn.* decisive, actual, concrete; see **definite** 1, **real** 2.
   **2.** [Emphatic] — *Syn.* peremptory, assertive, obstinate; see **emphatic** 1, **resolute** 2.
   **3.** [Certain] — *Syn.* sure, convinced, confident; see **accurate** 1, **certain** 1, 3.
*See Synonym Study at* SURE.
**positively,** *modif.* **1.** [In a positive manner] — *Syn.* peremptorily, assertively, uncompromisingly, dogmatically, arbitrarily, stubbornly, obstinately, emphatically, dictatorially, imperatively, oracularly, decidedly, absolutely, insistently, authoritatively, assuredly, confidently, unhesitatingly, with conviction, with emphasis; see also **boldly** 1.
   **2.** [Without doubt] — *Syn.* undoubtedly, unmistakably, undeniably; see **surely.**
**posse,** *n.* — *Syn.* vigilantes, search party, civilian police, detachment, lynch mob, force armed with legal authority, armed band, group of deputies, police force, posse comitatus; see also **law** 6, **police.**
**possess,** *v.* — *Syn.* hold, occupy, control; see **maintain** 3, **own** 1.
**possessed,** *modif.* **1.** [Insane] — *Syn.* mad, crazed, violent; see **insane** 1.
   **2.** [Owned] — *Syn.* kept, enjoyed, in one's possession; see **held, owned, retained** 1.

**3.** [Poised] — *Syn.* self-possessed, self-assured, confident, secure; see **calm** 1.
**possessing,** *modif.* — *Syn.* holding, occupying, owning; see **retaining.**
**possession,** *n.* **1.** [Ownership] — *Syn.* proprietary rights, hold, mastery; see **ownership.**
   **2.** [Property] — *Syn.* personal property, real estate, something possessed; see **property** 1, 2.
   **3.** [A colony] — *Syn.* settlement, territory, dependency; see **colony** 1.
**possessions,** *n.* — *Syn.* belongings, goods, effects; see **estate** 1, 2, **property** 1.
**possessor,** *n.* — *Syn.* owner, holder, proprietor, proprietress, inheritor, occupant, occupier, retainer, master, buyer, purchaser, sharer, partner, landlord, landowner, lessee, legatee, landlady, mistress, lord of the manor, laird, trustee, beneficiary, inheritor, heir, heiress; see also **owner.**
**possibility,** *n.* **1.** [The condition of being possible] — *Syn.* plausibility, feasibility, potentiality, likelihood; see **chance** 1, **probability.**
   **2.** [A possible happening] — *Syn.* hazard, chance, contingency, occasion, circumstance, hope, occurrence, fortuity, hap, happening, outside chance, incident, instance; see also **accident** 2, **event** 1, **opportunity** 1.
**possible,** *modif.* **1.** [Within the realm of possibility] — *Syn.* conceivable, imaginable, thinkable, plausible, reasonable, probable, likely; see also **likely** 1.
   **2.** [That may happen or be done] — *Syn.* feasible, practicable, workable, viable, attainable, achievable, permissible, potential, within reach; see also **likely** 1.
   **3.** [\*Acceptable] — *Syn.* tolerable, expedient, desirable, welcome; see **pleasant** 2.

---

*SYN.* — **possible** is used of anything that may exist, occur, be done, etc., depending on circumstances /a *possible* solution to a problem/; **practicable** applies to that which can readily be effected under the prevailing conditions or by the means available /a *practicable* plan/; **feasible** is used of that which is likely to be carried through to a successful conclusion and, hence, connotes the desirability of doing so /a method that is not economically *feasible*/

---

**possibly,** *modif.* — *Syn.* perhaps, by chance, mayhap; see **likely** 1, **maybe, probably.**
**post,** *n.* **1.** [An upright in the ground] — *Syn.* prop, support, pillar, pedestal, stake, stud, upright, doorpost; see also **column** 1, **mast.**
   **2.** [The mails] — *Syn.* mail service, postal service, post office, P.O.; see **mail.**
   **3.** [A position to which a person is appointed or assigned] — *Syn.* office, station, appointment, assignment; see **job** 1, **profession** 1.
*See Synonym Study at* JOB.
**postal,** *modif.* — *Syn.* post office, mail, messenger, carrier, epistolary, airmail, express, special delivery, registered, insured.
**post-bellum,** *modif.* — *Syn.* postwar, after the war, Reconstruction.
**postcard,** *n.* — *Syn.* postal card, note, letter card; see **letter** 2.
**postdate,** *v.* **1.** [To anticipate] — *Syn.* assume, overdate, date after; see **anticipate** 1.
   **2.** [To succeed] — *Syn.* replace, ensue, follow; see **succeed** 2.
**poster,** *n.* — *Syn.* placard, bill, sign, banner, *affiche* (French), sheet, billboard, signboard, handbill, broadside, flier, notice; see also **advertisement** 1, 2.

**posterior,** *modif.* **1.** [Subsequent] — *Syn.* later, coming after, succeeding, next; see **following.**
**2.** [Behind] — *Syn.* at the rear, dorsal, in back of, last, after; see also **back.** — *Ant.* anterior, preceding, AHEAD.
**posterity,** *n.* — *Syn.* progeny, descendants, seed, breed, children, issue, heirs, rising generation, new generation, younger generation, successors, lineage, future time; see also **family** 1, **offspring.**
**posthaste,** *modif.* — *Syn.* swiftly, speedily, hastily; see **quickly** 1.
**posthumous,** *modif.* — *Syn.* after death, continuing, future; see **post-mortem.**
**postlude,** *n.* — *Syn.* epilogue, finale, close; see **end** 2.
**postman,** *n.* — *Syn.* letter carrier, mail carrier, carrier; see **letter carrier.**
**post-mortem,** *modif.* — *Syn.* after death, posthumous, subsequent, post-obit, future, more recent, later, following, post-mortal, postmundane.
**post mortem,** *n.* — *Syn.* dissection, examination after death, coroner's examination; see **autopsy, examination** 3.
**post office,** *n.* — *Syn.* mail office, postal service, P.O.; see **mail, post** 2.
**postpone,** *v.* — *Syn.* defer, put off, delay, take a rain check; see **delay** 1, **suspend** 2.
*See Synonym Study at* SUSPEND.
**postponed,** *modif.* — *Syn.* deferred, delayed, retarded, put off, set for a later time, to be done later, withheld, staved off, shelved, tabled, prorogued, adjourned, intermitted, suspended; see also **late** 1, **withheld.**
**postponement,** *n.* — *Syn.* respite, suspension, adjournment; see **delay** 1, **pause** 1, 2.
**postscript,** *n.* — *Syn.* P.S., note, supplement, appendix, appendage; see also **addition** 2.
**postulate,** *v.* — *Syn.* posit, hypothesize, presume, predicate; see **assume** 1, **guess** 1, **propose** 1.
*See Synonym Study at* ASSUME.
**posture,** *n.* **1.** [Stance] — *Syn.* pose, carriage, bearing, stance, attitude, demeanor, aspect, presence, condition; see also **carriage** 1, **position** 5.
**2.** [Attitude] — *Syn.* way of thinking, feeling, sentiment; see **attitude** 2.

---

**SYN.** — **posture** refers to the habitual or assumed disposition of the parts of the body in standing, sitting, etc. *[erect posture]*; **attitude** refers to a posture assumed either unconsciously, as in manifesting an emotion or state of mind, or intentionally for a particular purpose *[an attitude of watchfulness, to kneel in an attitude of prayer]*; **pose** suggests a posture assumed, usually deliberately, as for artistic effect *[to hold a pose for a photographer]*; **stance** refers to a particular way of standing, esp. with reference to the position of the feet, as in certain sports *[the stance of a golfer]*

---

**posture,** *v.* — *Syn.* sit, display, attitudinize; see **pose** 2.
**postwar,** *modif.* — *Syn.* post-bellum, after the war, peacetime, peaceful.
**posy,** *n.* — *Syn.* corsage, garland, nosegay, spray, boutonniere, bouquet; see also **flower** 1, **wreath.**
**pot,** *n.* **1.** [Container] — *Syn.* vessel, kettle, pan, jug, jar, mug, tankard, cup, can, crock, canister, receptacle, bucket, urn, pitcher, bowl, cauldron, mortar, melting pot, crucible; see also **container.**
**2.** [*Marijuana] — *Syn.* cannabis sativa (Latin), cannabis, reefer, dope, joint*, grass*, weed*, maryjane*, boo*; see also **drug** 2, **marijuana.**
**go to pot** — *Syn.* deteriorate, go to ruin, fall apart; see **decay.**

**potable,** *modif.* — *Syn.* fit for drinking, uncontaminated, drinkable, potulent, clean, unpolluted, fresh; see also **pure** 2, **sanitary.**
**potato,** *n.* — *Syn.* tuber, white potato, sweet potato, yam, rhizome, spud*, tater*; see also **root** 1, **vegetable.**
Varieties of potatoes include: Irish Cobbler, Early Ohio, Green Mountain, Rural, Burbank, Epicure, Great Scot, Kerr's Pink, Yukon Gold, Yellow Finn, Kennebec, King Edward VII, Arran Chief, Bliss Triumph, Idaho Russet, red, white, new.
**potbellied,** *modif.* — *Syn.* obese, paunchy, bloated, beerbellied*; see **fat** 1.
**potency,** *n.* **1.** [Strength] — *Syn.* power, energy, vigor; see **manhood** 2, **strength** 1.
**2.** [Authority] — *Syn.* influence, control, dominion; see **command** 2, **power** 2.
*See Synonym Study at* STRENGTH.
**potent,** *modif.* **1.** [Strong] — *Syn.* vigorous, robust, sturdy; see **strong** 1.
**2.** [Powerful] — *Syn.* mighty, great, influential; see **dominant** 2, **powerful** 1.
**3.** [Convincing] — *Syn.* effective, swaying, cogent; see **impressive** 1, **persuasive.**
**4.** [Effective] — *Syn.* useful, stiff, efficient; see **effective.**
**potentate,** *n.* — *Syn.* monarch, sovereign, overlord; see **king** 1, **master** 1, **ruler** 1.
**potential,** *modif.* — *Syn.* possible, implied, inherent, dormant; see **latent, likely** 1.
*See Synonym Study at* LATENT.
**potentiality,** *n.* — *Syn.* capacity, possibility, energy; see **ability** 1, 2, **probability.**
**potentially,** *modif.* — *Syn.* conceivably, imaginably, possibly; see **likely** 1, **maybe, probably.**
**potion,** *n.* — *Syn.* drink, dose, tonic, elixir, draft, liquor, dram, nip, cordial, stimulant, libation, restorative, philter, spirits, aromatics, remedy; see also **drink** 2, 3, **liquid, medicine** 2.
**potpourri,** *n.* — *Syn.* medley, hodgepodge, blend; see **mixture.**
**pottery,** *n.* — *Syn.* ceramics, porcelain, crockery, earthenware, stoneware, clay ware; see also **utensil.**
Varieties of pottery include: Abruzzi, Etruscan, Apulian, Cypriote, Cambrian, Assyrian, Anatolian, Awata, Damascus, Persian, Bizen, Bendigo, Amstel, Faenza, Castelli, Sicilian, Broussa, Celtic, Chartreuse, Cognac, Sèvres, Varges, Rouen, Dresden, Burslem, Quimper, Upchurch, Mexican, Indian, peasant, inlaid, hard, soft, unglazed, glazed, roughcast, faience, majolica, bisque, biscuit.
**pouch,** *n.* — *Syn.* sack, receptacle, poke*; see **bag, container.**
**poultice,** *n.* — *Syn.* plaster, application, dressing; see **medicine** 2, **treatment** 2.
**poultry,** *n.* — *Syn.* fowl, domesticated birds, pullets, barnyard fowls; see **chicken** 1, **fowl, turkey.**
**pounce,** *v.* — *Syn.* swoop down, spring on, leap on; see **dive** 1, **jump** 1.
**pound,** *n.* **1.** [Measure of weight] — *Syn.* sixteen ounces, Troy pound, avoirdupois pound, commercial pound, pint; see also **measure** 1, **weight** 1.
**2.** [Kennel] — *Syn.* coop, doghouse, cage; see **pen** 1.
**pound,** *v.* — *Syn.* hammer, pulsate, crush, pulverize; see **beat** 1, 2, 3, **hit** 1.
*See Synonym Study at* BEAT.
**pour,** *v.* **1.** [To flow] — *Syn.* discharge, emit, issue; see **drain** 3, **flow** 2.
**2.** [To allow to flow] — *Syn.* replenish with, spill, splash; see **empty** 2.

**3.** [To rain heavily] — *Syn.* stream, flood, drench; see **rain.**

*pourboire* (French), *n.* — *Syn.* present, gratuity, tip; see **gift** 1.

**pouring,** *modif.* — *Syn.* streaming, gushing, spouting, rushing, raining, flooding, showering, discharging, emitting, issuing, escaping, emanating, welling out, spurting, spilling, shedding, draining, running, running out; see also **flowing.**

**pour it on★,** *v.* — *Syn.* overwork, overburden, add to; see **burden, increase** 1.

**pout,** *v.* — *Syn.* sulk, mope, brood, be sullen; see **frown, sulk.**

**poverty,** *n.* **1.** [Want of earthly goods] — *Syn.* destitution, want, indigence, penury, need, beggary, pennilessness, neediness, mendicancy, pauperism, insufficiency, starvation, famine, hunger, underdevelopment, dearth, privation, reduced circumstances, insolvency, impoverishment, impecuniousness, broken fortune, straits, financial distress, hardship, deficiency, meagerness, aridity, exiguity, stint, depletion, deficit, debt, poorness, hand-to-mouth existence, wolf at the door★, deep water★, hard spot★, pinch★, bite★, crunch★, tough going★; see also **lack** 1.— *Ant.* WEALTH, prosperity, comfort.
**2.** [Want of any desirable thing] — *Syn.* shortage, shortness, insufficiency, inadequacy, exigency, scarcity, incompleteness, failing, defect; see also **lack** 2.

*SYN.* — **poverty,** the broadest of these terms, implies a lack of the resources for reasonably comfortable living; **destitution** and **want** imply such great poverty that the means for mere subsistence, such as food and shelter, are lacking; **indigence,** a somewhat euphemistic term, implies a lack of comforts that one formerly enjoyed; **penury** suggests such severe poverty as to cause misery or a loss of self-respect

**poverty-stricken,** *modif.* — *Syn.* penniless, broke, bankrupt; see **poor** 1, **wanting** 1.

**powder,** *n.* — *Syn.* particles, film, pulverulence, powderiness, explosive powder, medicinal powder, cosmetic powder; see also **cosmetic, explosive, medicine** 2.

**keep one's powder dry★** — *Syn.* be ready, be prepared, alert oneself; see **prepare** 1.

**take a powder★** — *Syn.* run away, abandon, desert; see **leave** 1.

**powdery,** *modif.* — *Syn.* sandy, gravelly, dusty; see **gritty.**

**power,** *n.* **1.** [Strength] — *Syn.* vigor, energy, stamina; see **strength** 1.
**2.** [Controlling sway] — *Syn.* authority, command, jurisdiction, dominion, control, sway, ascendancy, superiority, domination, dominance, mastery, leadership, predominance, preponderance, sovereignty, prerogative, hegemony, suzerainty, prestige, influence, reign, regency, omnipotence, puissance, supreme authority, the last word, rule, law, first strike capability, warrant, rule of law, law of the jungle, brute force, authorization, supremacy, legal sanction, government, absolutism, carte blanche, say-so★, clout★, clutches★; see also **influence** 2, **leadership** 1.— *Ant.* powerlessness, subservience, collapse.
**3.** [Ability; *often plural*] — *Syn.* skill, endowment, capability; see **ability** 1, 2.
**4.** [Force] — *Syn.* compulsion, coercion, duress; see **pressure** 2, **restraint** 2.
**5.** [Energy] — *Syn.* horsepower, potential, dynamism; see **energy** 3.

**in power** — *Syn.* ruling, authoritative, commanding; see **powerful** 1.

**the powers that be★,** *n.* — *Syn.* the higher authorities, boss, bosses, the higher-ups★.

*SYN.* — **power,** as compared here, denotes the inherent ability or the admitted right to rule, govern, and determine /the limited *power* of a president/; **authority** refers to the power, because of rank or office, to give commands, enforce obedience, and make decisions /the *authority* of a teacher/; **jurisdiction** refers to the power to rule or decide within certain officially defined limits /the *jurisdiction* of the courts/; **dominion** implies sovereign or supreme authority /*dominion* over a dependent state/; **sway** stresses the predominance or sweeping scope of power /the Romans held *sway* over much of the ancient world/; **control** implies power to direct, regulate, restrain, or curb /to have no *control* over one's feelings/; **command** implies such authority that enforces obedience to one's orders /in *command* of a regiment/ *See also Synonym Study at* STRENGTH.

**powerful,** *modif.* **1.** [Wielding power] — *Syn.* mighty, all-powerful, almighty, superhuman, omnipotent, overpowering, great, invincible, dominant, indomitable, influential, authoritative, overruling, potent, puissant, forceful, forcible, compelling, ruling, prevailing, preeminent, commanding, supreme, highest, important, authoritarian, charismatic, paramount, ruthless, in the saddle, having the upper hand, in control; see also **predominant** 1.— *Ant.* WEAK, incompetent, impotent.
**2.** [Strong] — *Syn.* robust, stalwart, sturdy; see **strong** 1, 2.
**3.** [Effective] — *Syn.* efficacious, effectual, convincing; see **persuasive.**

**powerfully,** *modif.* — *Syn.* forcibly, forcefully, effectively, severely, intensely, with authority; see also **vigorously.**

**powerhouse,** *n.* — *Syn.* central station, generating plant, electric-power station, substation, dynamo station.

**powerless,** *modif.* — *Syn.* impotent, feeble, infirm; see **weak** 1, 2.

**powwow★,** *n.* — *Syn.* council, meeting, conference; see **discussion** 1.

**pox,** *n.* — *Syn.* smallpox, measles, chicken pox; see **disease.**

**practicability,** *n.* — *Syn.* potentiality, possibility, feasibility; see **probability.**

**practicable,** *modif.* — *Syn.* usable, doable, workable, functional; see **likely** 1, **possible** 2, **practical.**
*See Synonym Study at* POSSIBLE, PRACTICAL.

**practical,** *modif.* — *Syn.* matter-of-fact, pragmatic, unimaginative, solid, practicable, feasible, workable, functional, useful, sound, sound-thinking, down-to-earth, unromantic, unsentimental, unidealistic, hardheaded, realistic, sensible, sane, reasonable, rational, to one's advantage, operative, utilitarian, possible, usable, serviceable, efficient, effective, working, nuts-and-bolts★, with both feet on the ground★.— *Ant.* IMPRACTICAL, visionary, impracticable, unserviceable.

*SYN.* — **practical,** when used of things, stresses usefulness and effectiveness as tested by actual experience, and when used of people, stresses a sensible, realistic approach to life or to the particular circumstances; **practicable** is used of something that appears to be capable of being done or put into effect, but has not yet been developed or tried /before the era of electronics, television did not seem *practicable*; today it is but one of the *practical* applications of the science/

---

**practically**, *modif.* **1.** [In a practical manner] — *Syn.* unimaginatively, pragmatically, efficiently, functionally, sensibly, rationally, reasonably, realistically, with regard to use, considered as to service, from a workable standpoint; see also **effectively**.
**2.** [Virtually] — *Syn.* substantially, essentially, nearly, just about; see **almost**.
**practical nurse**, *n.* — *Syn.* attendant, nurse's helper, nursemaid; see **nurse** 1, 2, **servant**.
**practice**, *n.* **1.** [A customary action] — *Syn.* habit, usage, use, wont; see **custom** 2, **tradition** 1.
**2.** [A method] — *Syn.* mode, manner, fashion; see **method** 2, **system** 2.
**3.** [Educational repetition] — *Syn.* exercise, drill, repetition, iteration, rehearsal, recitation, preparation, study, discipline, application, training, workout, prepping*.
**4.** [A practitioner's custom] — *Syn.* work, patients, clients, clientele, professional business.
*See Synonym Study at* HABIT, PRACTICE, *v.*
**practice**, *v.* **1.** [To seek improvement through repetition] — *Syn.* drill, train, exercise, study, rehearse, repeat, recite, iterate, go over, run through, keep in practice, work at, accustom oneself, habituate oneself, prepare, warm up, work out, polish up*, sharpen up*, woodshed*, build up*.
**2.** [To employ one's professional skill] — *Syn.* function, work at, follow, put into effect, hang out one's shingle, employ oneself in, practice medicine, practice law.

---

*SYN.* — **practice** implies repeated performance for the purpose of learning or acquiring proficiency /he *practiced* on the violin every day, *practice* makes perfect/; **exercise** implies putting into active use /to *exercise* one's wits/ and often refers to activity, esp. of a systematic, formal kind, that trains or develops the body or mind /gymnastic *exercises*/; **drill** suggests disciplined group training in which something is taught by constant repetition /to *drill* a squad, an arithmetic *drill*/

---

**practiced**, *modif.* — *Syn.* trained, expert, exercised; see **able** 1, 2.
**praenomen**, *n.* — *Syn.* first name, given name, Christian name, cognomen; see **name** 1.
**pragmatic**, *modif.* — *Syn.* realistic, utilitarian, philistine, extensional, logical; see also **practical**.
**prairie**, *n.* — *Syn.* steppe, savanna, grassland; see **field** 1, **meadow**, **plain**.
**praise**, *n.* **1.** [The act of praising] — *Syn.* applause, applauding, adulation, blandishment, esteem, laud, commendation, approval, approbation, appreciation, cheering, advocacy, acclamation, adoration, acclaim, recognition, obeisance, sycophancy, homage, extolling, magnifying, glorifying, celebrating, exalting, giving thanks, saying grace, crying up, singing the praises of; see also **admiration**. — *Ant.* HATRED, contempt, dislike.
**2.** [An expression of praise] — *Syn.* laudation, eulogy, encomium, laud, kudos, regard, applause, panegyric, recommendation, hand-clapping, hurrahs, huzzah(s), bravos, ovation, cheers, cries, whistling, tribute, compliment, elogium, acclaim, flattery, plaudit, paean, blessing, benediction, boost*, rave*, a big hand*, chit*, puff*. — *Ant.* censure, BLAME, condemnation.
**sing someone's praise(s)** — *Syn.* commend, acclaim, congratulate; see **praise** 1.

**praise**, *v.* **1.** [To commend] — *Syn.* commend, recommend, laud, acclaim, extol, eulogize, applaud, cheer, endorse, sanction, admire, adulate, elevate, aggrandize, smile on, hail, salute, give an ovation to, clap, pay tribute to, give credit to, put in a good word for, say a good word for, make much of, bestow honor upon, bow down and worship, pay homage to, sing the praises of, panegyrize, advocate, compliment, appreciate, admire, celebrate, honor, congratulate, flatter, puff, rave about, boost, root for*, give a big hand*, build up*, tout*, talk up*, cry up*; see also **admire** 1, **approve** 2, **compliment** 1, 2.
**2.** [To speak or sing in worship] — *Syn.* glorify, adore, reverence; see **worship** 2.

---

*SYN.* — **praise** is the simple, basic word implying an expression of approval, esteem, or commendation /to *praise* a student's work/; **laud** implies great, sometimes extravagant praise /the critics *lauded* the actor to the skies/; **acclaim** suggests an outward show of strong approval, expressed by or as if by loud applause, cheering, etc. /he was *acclaimed* the victor; a widely *acclaimed* novel/; **extol** implies exalting or lofty praise /to *extol* the virtues of a new drug/; **eulogize** suggests lofty, formal praise in speech or writing, as on a special occasion /the minister *eulogized* the exemplary life of the deceased/

---

**praised**, *modif.* — *Syn.* admired, aided, helped, flattered, worshiped, lauded, belauded, extolled, glorified, exalted, blessed, celebrated, paid tribute to, magnified.
**praiseworthy**, *modif.* — *Syn.* select, worthy, admirable; see **excellent**.
**prance**, *v.* — *Syn.* cavort, frisk, gambol; see **dance** 2.
**prank**, *n.* — *Syn.* game, escapade, caper; see **joke** 1.
**prankish**, *modif.* — *Syn.* playful, capricious, mischievous; see **naughty**.
**pranks**, *n.* — *Syn.* antics, capers, frolics; see **trick** 1.
**prattle**, *n.* — *Syn.* twaddle, drivel, chatter; see **nonsense** 1.
**prattle**, *v.* — *Syn.* gush, jabber, chatter; see **babble**.
**pray**, *v.* **1.** [To ask or beg] — *Syn.* entreat, petition, plead; see **appeal** 1, **beg** 1.
**2.** [To call upon God] — *Syn.* hold communion with God, supplicate, implore, petition, entreat, invocate, commend someone to God, recite the rosary, tell one's beads.
*See Synonym Study at* APPEAL.
**prayer**, *n.* **1.** [An earnest request] — *Syn.* entreaty, request, intercession, thanksgiving, praise, petition; see also **appeal** 1.
**2.** [An address to the deity] — *Syn.* orison, invocation, act of devotion, supplication, devotions, benediction, litany, rogation, *brocho*, *berakah* (Hebrew).
Prayers, sense 2, include: Lord's Prayer, Pater Noster, Our Father, Hail Mary, Doxology, the Jesus prayer, Trisagion, Glory Be, Ave Maria, grace at meals, *Kiddush*, *Kaddish*, *shma Yisroel*, *amidah* (all Hebrew); matins, vespers, Angelus, Miserère, Kyrie eleison, Te Deum, collects, hours, rosary, novena, devotions, stations of the cross, evensong, compline.
**prayer book**, *n.* — *Syn.* liturgy, mass book, missal, service book, breviary, hymnal, holy text, guide; see also **bible** 2.
**prayerful**, *modif.* — *Syn.* devout, orthodox, pious; see **religious** 2.
**pray for**, *v.* — *Syn.* ask earnestly, invoke, invocate, recite the rosary; see **pray** 2.
**preach**, *v.* — *Syn.* exhort, discourse, moralize, teach, lecture, talk, harangue, inform, address.

**preacher,** *n.* — *Syn.* missionary, parson, evangelist; see **minister** 1.

**preaching,** *n.* — *Syn.* moralizing, teaching, exhortation, doctrine, instruction, homily.

**preachy,** *modif.* — *Syn.* sanctimonious, holier-than-thou, monitory; see **moral** 3.

**preamble,** *n.* — *Syn.* introduction, prelude, preface, introductory part; see **introduction** 1.
*See Synonym Study at* INTRODUCTION.

**precarious,** *modif.* — *Syn.* doubtful, uncertain, dubious; see **dangerous** 1.

**precaution,** *n.* — *Syn.* anticipation, forethought, regard; see **care** 1.

**precautionary,** *modif.* — *Syn.* prudent, discreet, alert; see **careful.**

**precede,** *v.* — *Syn.* go before, come first, be ahead of, take precedence over, preface, introduce, usher in, ring in, herald, forerun, antecede, head, lead, run ahead, go ahead, scout, light the way, go in advance, come before, antedate, come to the front, forge ahead, head up★. — *Ant.* SUCCEED, come after, come last.

**precedence,** *n.* — *Syn.* preference, precession, the lead★; see **priority.**

**precedent,** *n.* — *Syn.* authoritative example, exemplar, pattern; see **criterion, example** 1, **model** 2.

**preceding,** *modif.* — *Syn.* antecedent, precedent, previous, other, prior, aforesaid, ahead of, earlier, former, forerunning, past, foregoing, above-mentioned, above-named, above-cited, *supra* (Latin), afore-mentioned, before-mentioned, above, before, precursory, prefatory, front, forward, anterior, preliminary, preparatory, introductory, preexistent, aforeknown, already indicated, previously mentioned.
*See Synonym Study at* PREVIOUS.

**precept,** *n.* — *Syn.* doctrine, statute, rule; see **law** 3.
*See Synonym Study at* DOCTRINE.

**preceptor,** *n.* — *Syn.* instructor, mentor, lecturer; see **teacher** 1.

**pre-Christian,** *modif.* — *Syn.* before Christianity, before Christ, pagan, Old Testament, Mosaic; see also **heathen.**

**precinct,** *n.* — *Syn.* limit, confine, boundary; see **area** 2.

**precious,** *modif.* **1.** [Valuable] — *Syn.* high-priced, costly, dear; see **expensive, valuable** 1.
**2.** [Beloved] — *Syn.* cherished, inestimable, prized; see **beloved, favorite.**
**3.** [Refined and delicate] — *Syn.* overrefined, overnice, fragile, fastidious, affected, studied; see also **dainty** 1, **refined** 2.

**precious metal,** *n.* — *Syn.* silver, platinum, pewter; see **gold** 2, **metal.**

**precious stone,** *n.* — *Syn.* emerald, diamond, ruby, sapphire; see **gem** 1.

**precipice,** *n.* — *Syn.* crag, cliff, bluff; see **hill, mountain** 1.

**precipitate,** *v.* — *Syn.* accelerate, press, hurry; see **hasten** 2, **speed.**

**precipitately,** *modif.* — *Syn.* hastily, speedily, swiftly; see **immediately, quickly** 1.

**precipitation,** *n.* **1.** [Carelessness] — *Syn.* rashness, presumption, impetuosity; see **carelessness, rudeness.**
**2.** [Condensation] — *Syn.* rainfall, rain, shower, drizzle, cloudburst, downpour, snow, sleet, hail, hailstorm; see also **storm** 1.

**precipitous,** *modif.* — *Syn.* abrupt, craggy, dizzying, steep; see **abrupt** 1, **sharp** 2.
*See Synonym Study at* ABRUPT.

**précis,** *n.* — *Syn.* condensation, abridgement, abstract; see **summary.**

**precise,** *modif.* **1.** [Exact] — *Syn.* accurate, correct, well-defined, explicit; see **accurate** 1, 2, **definite** 1, 2.
**2.** [Being that and no other] — *Syn.* exact, very, specific; see **definite** 1.
**3.** [Fussily or prudishly careful] — *Syn.* fastidious, finicky, rigid, inflexible; see **careful, severe** 1.
*See Synonym Study at* ACCURATE, EXPLICIT.

**precisely,** *modif.* — *Syn.* correctly, exactly, definitely; see **accurately, specifically** 2.

**precision,** *n.* — *Syn.* exactness, correctness, sureness; see **accuracy** 2.

**preclude,** *v.* — *Syn.* prevent, impede, rule out; see **hinder, prevent, restrain** 1.
*See Synonym Study at* PREVENT.

**precocious,** *modif.* — *Syn.* gifted, bright, advanced, developed, forward, presumptuous; see also **intelligent** 1, **mature** 1.

**pre-Columbian,** *modif.* — *Syn.* before the discovery of America, old-world, pre-American, Mayan, Aztecan, Indian, Eskimo; see also **ancient** 2.

**preconception,** *n.* — *Syn.* predisposition, prejudice, bias, assumption; see **inclination** 1.

**precursor,** *n.* **1.** [A messenger] — *Syn.* forerunner, herald, vanguard; see **forerunner, messenger.**
**2.** [A predecessor] — *Syn.* ancestor, forebear, antecedent, parent; see **ancestor, forerunner.**

**precursory,** *modif.* — *Syn.* previous, prior, preliminary; see **preceding.**

**predatory,** *modif.* **1.** [Preying on other animals] — *Syn.* voracious, carnivorous, omnivorous, rapacious, predacious, raptorial, ravening, wolfish, bloodthirsty; see also **greedy** 2, **hungry, rapacious** 2.
**2.** [Plundering] — *Syn.* marauding, pillaging, looting, rapacious.

**predecessor,** *n.* — *Syn.* antecedent, forerunner, ancestor; see **ancestor, forerunner.**

**predestination,** *n.* **1.** [A forecast] — *Syn.* prediction, intention, predetermination; see **forecast.**
**2.** [Fate] — *Syn.* doom, fortune, decree; see **destiny** 1.

**predetermine,** *v.* — *Syn.* destine, predestine, fate, doom, decide.

**predetermined,** *modif.* — *Syn.* calculated, deliberate, fated; see **planned, proposed.**

**predicament,** *n.* — *Syn.* quandary, plight, dilemma, strait, puzzle, perplexity, scrape, corner, hole, impasse, tight situation, state, condition, position, circumstance, mess, muddle, imbroglio, exigency, deadlock, pinch, crisis, difficulty, fix★, pickle★, bind★, hot water★, pretty kettle of fish★, jam★, spot★; see also **difficulty** 1, 2.

---

*SYN.* — **predicament** implies a complicated, perplexing situation from which it is difficult to disentangle oneself; **dilemma** implies a predicament necessitating a choice between equally disagreeable alternatives; **quandary** emphasizes a state of great perplexity and uncertainty as to what to do; **plight** implies a distressing or unfortunate situation; **fix** and **pickle** are both colloquial terms loosely interchangeable with any of the preceding, although more precisely **fix** is equivalent to **predicament** and **pickle**, to **plight**

---

**predicate,** *n.* — *Syn.* verb, verbal phrase, part of speech, word; see **verb.**

**predicate,** *v.* — *Syn.* assert, declare, state, signify; see **mean** 1.

**predict,** *v.* — *Syn.* prophesy, prognosticate, divine; see **foretell.**

**predictable,** *modif.* — *Syn.* anticipated, foreseen, prepared for; see **expected** 2, **likely** 1.

**prediction,** *n.* — *Syn.* prophecy, foresight, prognostication; see **forecast.**

**predictive,** *modif.* — *Syn.* portentous, forbidding, auspicious; see **imminent, ominous, sinister.**

**predilection,** *n.* — *Syn.* partiality, bias, preference, liking; see **inclination** 1.
*See Synonym Study at* PREJUDICE.

**predispose,** *v.* 1. [To stimulate] — *Syn.* urge, inspire, activate; see **animate** 1.
2. [To prepare] — *Syn.* make expectant, make susceptible, influence, bias, indoctrinate; see also **teach** 1.

**predisposed,** *modif.* — *Syn.* willing, inclined, eager; see **enthusiastic** 1.

**predisposition,** *n.* 1. [A tendency] — *Syn.* leaning, bent, predilection; see **inclination** 1.
2. [A preference] — *Syn.* option, partiality, liking; see **choice** 3, **preference.**

**predominance,** *n.* — *Syn.* reign, supremacy, control; see **administration** 1, **command** 2, **power** 2.

**predominant,** *modif.* 1. [Supreme in power] — *Syn.* mighty, almighty, supreme, omnipotent, all-powerful, ascendant, reigning, ruling, overruling, prevailing, prevalent, controlling, supervisory, directing, influential, dominant, dominating, authoritative, arbitrary, paramount, preponderant, preeminent, imperious, absolute, executive, official, potent, weighty, effective, efficacious, overpowering, governing, holding the reins; see also **powerful** 1. — *Ant.* INCOMPETENT, submissive, inferior.
2. [Of first importance] — *Syn.* transcendent, surpassing, superlative; see **principal.**

---

SYN. — **predominant** refers to that which is at the moment uppermost in importance or influence /the *predominant* reason for his refusal/; **dominant** refers to that which dominates or controls, or has the greatest effect /*dominant* characteristics in genetics/; **paramount** is applied to that which ranks first in importance, authority, etc. /of *paramount* interest to me/; **preeminent** implies prominence because of surpassing excellence /the *preeminent* writer of his time/; **preponderant** implies superiority in amount, weight, power, importance, etc. /the *preponderant* religion of a country/

---

**predominate,** *v.* — *Syn.* dominate, prevail, rule; see **command** 2, **govern, manage** 1.

**preeminent,** *modif.* — *Syn.* dominant, incomparable, superior; see **predominant** 1.
*See Synonym Study at* PREDOMINANT.

**preeminently,** *modif.* — *Syn.* conspicuously, notably, incomparably; see **very.**

**preempt,** *v.* — *Syn.* acquire, seize, appropriate; see **obtain** 1.

**preen,** *v.* — *Syn.* spruce, trim, primp; see **dress** 1, **dress up.**

**prefab★,** *n.* — *Syn.* prefabricated building, mass-produced building, temporary structure, standardized housing; see **building** 1.

**prefabricate,** *v.* — *Syn.* fabricate, perform, set up, coordinate, pre-assemble; see also **assemble** 3.

**preface,** *n.* — *Syn.* introduction, prelude, prolegomenon, preliminary; see **explanation** 2, **introduction** 4.
*See Synonym Study at* INTRODUCTION.

**preface,** *v.* — *Syn.* introduce, commence, precede; see **begin** 1.

**prefatory,** *modif.* — *Syn.* opening, initiative, preliminary; see **introductory** 1.

**prefect,** *n.* — *Syn.* official, consul, regent; see **administrator.**

**prefecture,** *n.* 1. [Presidency] — *Syn.* officials, directorship, directors; see **administration** 2.
2. [Jurisdiction] — *Syn.* area, consulate, embassy; see **office** 3.

**prefer,** *v.* — *Syn.* lean toward, like better, fancy; see **favor** 1.

**preferable,** *modif.* — *Syn.* favored, better, superior; see **excellent.**

**preferably,** *modif.* — *Syn.* by preference, by choice, by selection, in preference, first, sooner, before, optionally, at pleasure, willingly, at will; see also **rather** 2.

**preference,** *n.* 1. [Something preferred] — *Syn.* choice, favorite, first choice, decision; see **choice** 3.
2. [Inclination] — *Syn.* partiality, liking, inclination, bent; see **inclination** 1.
*See Synonym Study at* CHOICE.

**preferential,** *modif.* — *Syn.* favored, special, advantageous; see **favorite, preferred, unusual** 1.

**preferment,** *n.* 1. [Promotion] — *Syn.* elevation, raise, advancement; see **promotion** 1.
2. [Priority] — *Syn.* attention, precedence, station; see **rank** 3.

**preferred,** *modif.* — *Syn.* chosen, selected, fancied, adopted, picked out, taken, elected, liked, favored, set apart, culled, handpicked, singled out, endorsed, settled upon, sanctioned, decided upon; see also **approved, named** 2. — *Ant.* NEGLECTED, unpreferred, overlooked.

**prefigure,** *v.* — *Syn.* symbolize, signify, indicate; see **mean** 1.

**prefix,** *n.* 1. [An addition] — *Syn.* affix, adjunct, preflex, prefixture.
2. [A designation] — *Syn.* title, cognomen, designation; see **name** 1.

**pregnancy,** *n.* — *Syn.* reproduction, fertilization, gestation, gravidity, propagation, parturiency, germination, fecundation, productivity, fertility.

**pregnant,** *modif.* 1. [With child] — *Syn.* gestating, gravid, fruitful, *enceinte* (French), with child, big with child, parturient, hopeful, anticipating★, in a family way★, expecting★.
2. [Meaningful] — *Syn.* significant, consequential, weighty; see **important** 1.

**prehistoric,** *modif.* — *Syn.* preceding history, very early, ancient, Stone Age, unknown; see also **old** 3.

**prejudge,** *v.* — *Syn.* presuppose, forejudge, presume, jump to conclusions★; see **decide.**

**prejudice,** *n.* — *Syn.* bias, partiality, unfairness, preconception, predilection, leaning, bent, bigotry, intolerance, prejudgment, prepossession, presupposition, discrimination, racism, sexism, ageism, anti-Semitism, homophobia, chauvinism, male chauvinism, misogyny, misandry, xenophobia, one-sidedness, favoritism, partisanship, narrow-mindedness, narrowness, parochialism, small-mindedness, illiberality, littleness, enmity, dislike, antagonism, antipathy, aversion, resentment, coolness, contempt, bad opinion, misjudgment, blinders, jaundice, jaundiced eye, tunnel vision, segregation, apartheid, detriment, disadvantage, slant, warp, twist; see also **hatred** 1, 2, **inclination** 1, **objection** 2, **spite.** — *Ant.* impartiality, tolerance, admiration.

**without prejudice** — *Syn.* 1. unbiased, objective, unprejudiced, disinterested; see **fair** 1.

**2.** not damaged, not discredited, unaltered, without implied comment; see **unchanged.**

---

*SYN.* — **prejudice** implies a preconceived and unreasonable judgment or opinion, usually an unfavorable one marked by suspicion, fear, or hatred /a crime motivated by racial *prejudice]*; **bias** implies a mental leaning in favor of or against someone or something that interferes with impartial judgment /few of us are without *bias* of any kind/; **partiality** implies an inclination to favor a person or thing because of strong fondness or attachment /the conductor's *partiality* for the works of Brahms/; **predilection** implies a preconceived liking, formed as a result of one's background, temperament, etc., that inclines one to a particular preference /a *predilection* for murder mysteries/

---

**prejudiced,** *modif.* — *Syn.* biased, preconceived, prepossessed, directed against, influenced, inclined, leaning, conditioned, presupposing, predisposed, dogmatic, doctrinaire, pedantic, opinionated, partisan, extreme, intransigent, hidebound, narrow, intolerant, bigoted, canting, illiberal, racist, sexist, xenophobic, blind, partial, narrow-minded, wedded to an opinion, insular, parochial, provincial, one-sided, not seeing an inch beyond one's nose, squint-eyed, intolerant of, disliking, having a predilection, closed against, judging on slight knowledge, smug. — *Ant.* GENEROUS, open-minded, receptive.
**prejudicial,** *modif.* — *Syn.* unjust, unfavorable, biased; see **prejudiced.**
**prelacy,** *n.* **1.** [Hierarchy] — *Syn.* rank, episcopacy, prelatism; see **ministry** 2.
**2.** [Episcopate] — *Syn.* diocese, pontificate; see **bishopric.**
**prelate,** *n.* — *Syn.* bishop, cardinal, pope; see **minister** 1, **priest.**
**preliminary,** *modif.* — *Syn.* preparatory, preceding, prefatory; see **introductory** 1.
**prelude,** *n.* **1.** [Introduction] — *Syn.* preface, preliminary preparation, prelusion; see **introduction** 1.
**2.** [Musical piece] — *Syn.* fugue, toccata, overture, voluntary; see **music** 1.
**premarital,** *modif.* — *Syn.* before the vows, before marriage, during courtship; see **before** 1.
**premature,** *modif.* — *Syn.* unanticipated, precipitate, rash; see **early** 2, **untimely.**
**prematurely,** *modif.* — *Syn.* too early, rash, precipitately; see **early** 2, **untimely.**
**premeditate,** *v.* — *Syn.* propose, aim, plot; see **intend** 1.
**premeditated,** *modif.* — *Syn.* intentional, conscious, contrived, willful; see **deliberate** 1, **planned.**
**premeditation,** *n.* — *Syn.* intention, intent, plot, design; see **plan** 2, **purpose** 1.
**premiere,** *n.* — *Syn.* debut, opening night, beginning, opening; see **performance** 1.
**premise,** *n.* — *Syn.* proposition, axiom, assumption; see **basis** 1, **proof** 1.
**premise,** *v.* **1.** [To introduce] — *Syn.* preface, commence, start, announce; see **begin** 1.
**2.** [To assume] — *Syn.* presuppose, suppose, postulate; see **assume** 1.
*See Synonym Study at* ASSUME.
**premises,** *n.* **1.** [Evidence] — *Syn.* testimony, reason, support; see **basis** 1, **proof** 1.
**2.** [Real estate] — *Syn.* bounds, limits, land; see **property** 2.
**premium,** *modif.* — *Syn.* prime, superior, select, selected; see **excellent.**

**premium,** *n.* — *Syn.* bonus, prize, gift, reward, award, bounty, something extra, rebate, incentive, added, incentive, dividend, remuneration, installment, come-on\*, freebie\*; see also **prize.**
**at a premium** — *Syn.* costly, expensive, rare; see **valuable** 1.

---

*SYN.* — **premium,** as compared here, implies a reward or prize offered as an inducement to buy, sell, or compete /a toy given as a *premium* with each package/; **bonus** refers to anything given over and above the regular wages, salary, or other remuneration. /a Christmas *bonus,* a soldier's *bonus]*; a **bounty** is a reward given by a government for a specific undertaking considered in the public interest, as the production of certain crops or the destruction of certain harmful animals; **dividend** refers to a prorated share in an amount distributed among stockholders or policyholders from profits or surplus *See also Synonym Study at* PRIZE.

---

**premonition,** *n.* — *Syn.* omen, portent, forewarning; see **sign** 1, **warning.**
**premonitory,** *modif.* — *Syn.* threatening, portentous, indicative; see **imminent, ominous, sinister.**
**prenatal,** *modif.* — *Syn.* before birth, during pregnancy, fetal.
**preoccupation,** *n.* — *Syn.* absorption, daydreaming, amusement; see **distraction** 2.
**preoccupied,** *modif.* — *Syn.* distracted, absorbed, engrossed; see **absent-minded, rapt** 2.
*See Synonym Study at* ABSENT-MINDED.
**preordain,** *v.* — *Syn.* appoint, doom, set; see **bless** 3, **predetermine.**
**prepaid,** *modif.* — *Syn.* shipped paid, with charges paid, settled for\*; see **paid.**
**preparation,** *n.* **1.** [The act of preparing] — *Syn.* preparing, fitting, making ready, manufacture, readying, putting in order, establishment, compounding, adapting, rehearsal, incubation, gestation, building, construction, formation, maturing, anticipation, founding, foreseeing, development, homework, spadework, groundwork, evolution, furnishing, build-up\*.
**2.** [The state of being prepared] — *Syn.* preparedness, readiness, fitness, adaptation, suitability, capacity, qualification, background, ripeness, mellowness, maturity, training, education, equipment.
**3.** [Something that is prepared] — *Syn.* arrangement, product, compound; see **mixture** 1.
**preparatory,** *modif.* — *Syn.* preliminary, prefatory, previous; see **introductory** 1.
**prepare,** *v.* **1.** [To make oneself ready] — *Syn.* get ready, foresee, arrange, make preparations, make arrangements, fit, adapt, qualify, put in order, adjust, set one's house in order, prime, fix, settle, fabricate, appoint, furnish, elaborate, perfect, develop, prepare the ground, lay the foundations, block out, roughhew, smooth the way, man, arm, set for, cut out, warm up, lay the groundwork, contrive, devise, lay by, lay in, make provision, put in readiness, build up, provide, provide for, provide against, make snug, clear the decks, hold oneself in readiness, be prepared, be ready; see also **anticipate** 2, **plan** 1.
**2.** [To make other persons or things ready] — *Syn.* outfit, equip, fit out; see **provide** 1.
**3.** [To cook and serve] — *Syn.* fix, make, cook, concoct, dress, brew; see also **cook, serve** 4.
**prepared,** *modif.* **1.** [Fitted] — *Syn.* adapted, qualified, adjusted; see **able** 2, **fit** 1, 2.
**2.** [Subjected to a special process or treatment] — *Syn.*

treated, frozen, pre-cooked, ready-to-eat, processed; see also **preserved** 2.

**3.** [Ready] — *Syn.* combat-ready, on the drawing board, instant, programmed, systems "go"*; see also **ready** 2.

**preparedness,** *n.* — *Syn.* readiness, mobility, zeal; see **preparation** 2, **willingness.**

**preparing,** *n.* — *Syn.* fitting, adapting, qualifying; see **preparation** 1.

**preponderance,** *n.* — *Syn.* supremacy, superiority, dominance; see **advantage** 2, **command** 2, **power** 2.

**preponderant,** *modif.* — *Syn.* predominant, overpowering, significant, dominant; see **predominant** 1, **powerful** 1.

*See Synonym Study at* PREDOMINANT.

**preponderate,** *v.* — *Syn.* excel, outdo, predominate; see **exceed, surpass.**

**preposition,** *n.* — *Syn.* part of speech, word of relationship, conjunctive word, copulative element, prefixed element, function word, form word; see also **grammar, word** 1.

**prepossessed,** *modif.* — *Syn.* biased, predisposed, inclined; see **prejudiced.**

**prepossessing,** *modif.* — *Syn.* handsome, captivating, attractive; see **charming, pleasant** 1.

**prepossession,** *n.* **1.** [Preoccupation] — *Syn.* dreaming, pastime, problem; see **distraction** 2.

**2.** [Bias] — *Syn.* tendency, aversion, partiality; see **inclination** 1, **prejudice.**

**preposterous,** *modif.* — *Syn.* absurd, outrageous, impossible; see **absurd, unusual** 2.

*See Synonym Study at* ABSURD.

**preposterousness,** *n.* — *Syn.* extravagance, ridiculousness, absurdity; see **impossibility, nonsense** 1, 2, **stupidity** 2.

**prepotent,** *modif.* — *Syn.* potent, effective, dynamic; see **powerful** 1, **strong** 8.

**prerequisite,** *modif.* — *Syn.* essential, required, expedient; see **important** 1, **necessary** 1.

**prerequisite,** *n.* — *Syn.* essential, necessity, need; see **requirement** 1.

**prerevolutionary,** *modif.* — *Syn.* before a revolution, pre-American Revolution, before the war; see **before** 1.

**prerogative,** *n.* — *Syn.* privilege, advantage, exemption; see **right** 1.

**presage,** *v.* — *Syn.* augur, forecast, predict; see **foretell.**

**presbyter,** *n.* — *Syn.* pastor, priest, clergyman; see **minister** 1.

**Presbyterian,** *n.* — *Syn.* Calvinist, Christian, non-Catholic, churchgoer; see **Protestant.**

**presbytery,** *n.* **1.** [Parsonage] — *Syn.* manse, rectory, vicarage; see **parsonage.**

**2.** [Clergy] — *Syn.* the pulpit, clerics, priesthood; see **ministry** 2.

**prescience,** *n.* — *Syn.* foresight, prediction, anticipation; see **acumen.**

**prescient,** *modif.* — *Syn.* perceptive, cautious, foresighted; see **discreet, judicious.**

**prescribe,** *v.* **1.** [To give directions] — *Syn.* guide, order, appoint; see **command** 2.

**2.** [To give medical directions] — *Syn.* designate, direct, write a prescription, write directions to a pharmacist.

**prescription,** *n.* — *Syn.* direction, prescript, medical recipe, formula, prescribed remedy; see also **medicine** 2.

Abbreviations commonly used in writing prescriptions include: aa (of each), a.c. (before meals), ad lib (freely as desired), aq. (water), b.i.d. (twice a day), c. (with),

caps. (capsule), dil. (dilute), elix. (elixir), ext. (extract), fld. (fluid), g (gram), gr (grain), gt (a drop), gtt (drops), h (hour), noct. (in the night), O (pint), ol. (oil), os (mouth), oz (ounce), p.c. (after meals), per (through or by), pil. (pill), p.r.n. (when required), q.d. (every day), q.h. (every hour), q.2 h. (every 2 hours), q.3 h. (every three hours), q.4 h. (every four hours), q.i.d (four times a day), Sig. (write on label), sp. (spirits), ss (a half), stat (immediately), syr. (syrup), t.i.d (three times a day), ung. (ointment).

**prescriptive,** *modif.* — *Syn.* authoritarian, rigid, prescribed, customary, cut and dried; see also **authoritative** 2, **determined** 1.

**presence,** *n.* **1.** [The fact of being present] — *Syn.* occupancy, occupation, residence, inhabitance, habitancy, ubiquity, ubiety; see also **attendance** 1.

**2.** [The vicinity of a person] — *Syn.* proximity, propinquity, nearness, closeness; see **neighborhood.**

**3.** [One's appearance and behavior] — *Syn.* carriage, port, demeanor, bearing; see **appearance** 1, **behavior** 1.

**presence of mind,** *n.* — *Syn.* sensibility, alertness, composure, confidence; see **acumen, watchfulness.**

**present,** *modif.* **1.** [Near in time] — *Syn.* now, existing, being, in process, in duration, begun, started, commenced, going on, under consideration, at this time, contemporary, contemporaneous, coeval, ad hoc, immediate, instant, prompt, at this moment, at present, today, nowadays, already, even now, but now, just now, for the time being, for the nonce, for the occasion; see also **modern** 1, **now** 1. — *Ant.* PAST, over, completed.

**2.** [Near in space] — *Syn.* in view, at hand, within reach; see **near** 1.

**present,** *n.* **1.** [The present time] — *Syn.* instant, this time, present moment, now; see **today.**

**2.** [A gift] — *Syn.* gift, grant, donation; see **gift** 1.

*See Synonym Study at* GIFT.

**present,** *v.* **1.** [To introduce] — *Syn.* make known, acquaint with, give an introduction; see **introduce** 3.

**2.** [To display] — *Syn.* exhibit, show, manifest; see **display** 1.

**3.** [To suggest] — *Syn.* imply, infer, intimate; see **hint.**

**4.** [To submit] — *Syn.* donate, proffer, put forth, sponsor; see **offer** 1.

**5.** [To give] — *Syn.* grant, bestow, confer; see **give** 1.

**6.** [To give a play, etc.] — *Syn.* put on, do, impersonate; see **act** 3, **perform** 2.

*See Synonym Study at* GIVE.

**presentable,** *modif.* — *Syn.* attractive, prepared, satisfactory; see **fit** 1, 2.

**presentation,** *n.* **1.** [The act of presenting] — *Syn.* bestowal, donation, delivering; see **giving.**

**2.** [Something presented] — *Syn.* present, offering, remembrance; see **gift** 1.

**3.** [A performance] — *Syn.* show, portrayal, exhibition, display; see **performance** 2, **show** 1.

**presented,** *modif.* — *Syn.* bestowed, granted, conferred; see **given.**

**presentiment,** *n.* — *Syn.* expectation, apprehension, intuition, premonition; see **anticipation** 2.

**presently,** *modif.* — *Syn.* directly, without delay, shortly; see **immediately, soon** 1.

**preservation,** *n.* — *Syn.* security, safety, protection, conservation, maintenance, saving, keeping, upkeep, storage, curing, tanning, freezing, sugaring, pickling, evaporation, canning, refrigeration.

**preservative,** *modif.* — *Syn.* saving, conservative, protective, preservatory, conservatory, precautionary.

**preservative,** *n.*— *Syn.* hygienic preserver, chemical, preserving agent, prophylaxis.

**preserve,** *v.* **1.** [To guard]— *Syn.* protect, shield, save; see **defend** 2.

**2.** [To maintain]— *Syn.* keep up, care for, conserve; see **maintain** 3.

**3.** [To keep]— *Syn.* can, conserve, process, save, put up, put down, souse, store, cure, bottle, do up, season, salt, pickle, put in brine, put in vinegar, pot, tin, dry, sundry, smoke, corn, dry-cure, smoke-cure, freeze, quick freeze, keep up, cold-pack, refrigerate, dehydrate, seal up, kipper, marinate, evaporate, embalm, mummify, mothball, fill.— *Ant.* WASTE, allow to spoil, let spoil.

**preserved,** *modif.* **1.** [Saved]— *Syn.* rescued, guarded, secured; see **saved** 1.

**2.** [Prepared for preservation]— *Syn.* conserved, dried, freeze-dried, sun-dried, dehydrated, evaporated, smoked, seasoned, pickled, canned, salted, brined, jerked, put down, put up, kippered, cured, corned, marinated, tinned, potted, bottled, cyanized, embalmed, mummified.

**preserves,** *n.*— *Syn.* jam, jelly, spread, sweet, conserve, marmalade, jell, pickles, extract, gelatin, pectin; see also **jam** 1, **jelly** 1.

**preside,** *v.*— *Syn.* direct, lead, control; see **advise** 1, **manage** 1.

**presidency,** *n.*— *Syn.* office of the president, chairmanship, position; see **administration** 2.

**president,** *n.* **1.** [Head of state]— *Syn.* chief executive, chief of state, commander-in-chief, the White House.

**2.** [Presiding officer]— *Syn.* chief executive officer, CEO, director, leader, premier, chairman, moderator; see also **administrator.**

**presidential,** *modif.*— *Syn.* official, regulatory, of the chief executive; see **administrative.**

**presiding,** *modif.*— *Syn.* supervising, controlling, directing; see **managing.**

**press,** *n.* **1.** [The pressure of circumstances]— *Syn.* rush, confusion, strain; see **haste** 2.

**2.** [Publishing as a social institution]— *Syn.* the Fourth Estate, publishers, publicists, newsmen, newspapermen, journalists, journalistic writers, editors, correspondents, political writers, columnists, periodicals, print media, periodical press, papers, newspapers; see also **reporter.**

**3.** [A printing press]
Types of presses include: rotary, web, automatic, hand, unit-type, multicolor, twelve cylinder, twenty-four cylinder, universal-unit multi-color, flatbed, high-speed, rotogravure; see also **machine** 1.

**press,** *v.* **1.** [To subject to pressure]— *Syn.* thrust, crowd, bear upon, bear down on, squeeze, hold down, pin down, screw down, force down, throng, crush, drive, weight, urge; see also **compress, push** 1.— *Ant.* RAISE, release, relieve.

**2.** [To smooth, usually by heat and pressure]— *Syn.* finish, mangle, roll; see **iron, smooth** 1.

**3.** [To embrace]— *Syn.* clasp, encircle, enfold; see **caress, hold** 1, **hug, touch** 1.

*See Synonym Study at* URGE.

**press agent,** *n.*— *Syn.* publicizer, advertiser, publicist; see **reporter.**

**press conference,** *n.*— *Syn.* interview, public report, public statement, briefing; see **announcement** 1, **hearing.**

**pressed,** *modif.*— *Syn.* rushed, in a hurry, pushed, rushing, closely timed, fast, urged, urged on, short, limited, pressured.

**pressing,** *modif.*— *Syn.* importunate, constraining, grave; see **important, urgent** 1.

**pressman,** *n.* **1.** [A printer]— *Syn.* compositor, linotypist, typesetter; see **printer.**

**2.** [A reporter]— *Syn.* journalist, newspaperman, correspondent; see **reporter.**

**pressure,** *n.* **1.** [Physical pressure]— *Syn.* force, burden, mass, load, encumbrance, stress, thrust, tension, shear, squeeze*; see also **strength** 1, **weight** 1.— *Ant.* RELEASE, relief, deliverance.

**2.** [Social pressure]— *Syn.* compulsion, constraint, urgency, demand, persuasion, stress, affliction, coercion, trouble, hardship, humiliation, misfortune, necessity, requirement, repression, confinement, unnaturalness, obligation, discipline; see also **influence** 1, **oppression** 1, **restraint** 2, **urging.**— *Ant.* AID, assistance, encouragement.

**pressure,** *v.*— *Syn.* press, compel, constrain; see **urge** 2, 3.

**pressure group,** *n.*— *Syn.* special interest group, special interests, lobby, coalition, clique; see also **organization** 3.

**presswork,** *n.*— *Syn.* typography, publishing, copying; see **printing.**

**prestige,** *n.*— *Syn.* renown, éclat, influence; see **fame** 1. *See Synonym Study at* INFLUENCE.

**presumable,** *modif.*— *Syn.* seeming, probable, apparent; see **likely** 1.

**presumably,** *modif.*— *Syn.* reasonable, credible, likely; see **probably.**

**presume,** *v.*— *Syn.* consider, suppose, take for granted; see **assume** 1. *See Synonym Study at* ASSUME.

**presuming,** *modif.*— *Syn.* arrogant, proud, presumptuous; see **egotistic** 2.

**presumption,** *n.* **1.** [An assumption]— *Syn.* conjecture, guess, hypothesis; see **assumption** 1.

**2.** [Impudence]— *Syn.* arrogance, audacity, effrontery; see **rudeness.**

**presumptive,** *modif.*— *Syn.* assumptive, circumstantial, possible; see **hypothetical** 1, **likely** 1.

**presumptuous,** *modif.*— *Syn.* arrogant, insolent, bold; see **egotistic** 2, **rude** 2.

**presuppose,** *v.*— *Syn.* presume, suppose, take for granted; see **assume** 1. *See Synonym Study at* ASSUME.

**pretend,** *v.* **1.** [To feign]— *Syn.* feign, affect, simulate, claim falsely, profess, make a pretense, imitate, assume, counterfeit, fake, sham, make as if, make as though, dissimulate, dissemble, mislead, pass oneself off, pose, impersonate, bluff, be hypocritical, purport, allege, make a show of, put on airs, put on*, let on*, make like*, go through the motions*, sail under false colors*, keep up appearances*, put up a front*, put on an act*, play possum*; see also **deceive.**

**2.** [To make believe]— *Syn.* mimic, fill a role, take a part, represent, portray, make out like, play, make as if, make as though, make believe, create, imagine, invent, act the part of, act a part, playact, put on an act*; see also sense 1, **act** 3, **imitate** 2, **impersonate, reproduce** 2.

---

**SYN.** — **pretend** and **feign** both imply a profession or display of what is false, the more literary **feign** sometimes suggesting an elaborately contrived situation /to *pretend* not to hear, to *feign* deafness/; **assume** implies the putting on of a false appearance but suggests a harmless or excusable motive /an *assumed* air of bravado/; to **affect** is to make a show of being, having, using, wearing, etc., usually for effect /to *affect* a British accent/; **simulate** emphasizes the imitation of typical signs involved in assuming an appearance or characteristic not one's own [to *simulate* interest]

---

**pretended,** *modif.* — *Syn.* feigned, counterfeit, assumed, affected, shammed, bluffing, simulated, dissimulated, lying, falsified, put on, concealed, covered, masked, cheating; see also **false** 3.

**pretender,** *n.* — *Syn.* fraud, hypocrite, rogue; see **cheat** 1.

**pretending,** *n.* — *Syn.* feigning, assumption, shamming, bluffing, dissembling, counterfeiting, simulation, dissimulation, concealment, covering, masking, cheating, screening.

**pretense,** *n.* **1.** [The act of pretending] — *Syn.* affectation, misrepresentation, falsification, act, deceit, fabrication, trickery, double-dealing, misstatement, shuffling, falsifying, simulation, excuse, insincerity, profession, ostentation, assumption, dissembling, dissimulation, evasion, equivocation, prevarication, egotism, brazenness, arrogance, dandyism, foppery, servility, toadyism, obsequiousness, sycophancy, cringing, truckling, timeserving, complacency, smugness, priggishness, prudishness, coyness, formality, stiffness, blind*, smoke screen*; see also **dishonesty, imitation** 1. — *Ant.* HONESTY, candor, sincerity.
**2.** [Something pretended] — *Syn.* gloss, falsehood, lie, falseness, affectedness, affectation, mask, cloak, show, excuse, subterfuge, pretext, fraud, appearance, seeming, semblance, wile, ruse, sham, airs, claim, mannerism; see also **deception** 1, **imitation** 2, **trick** 1.

**pretension,** *n.* **1.** [A claim] — *Syn.* assertion, demand, declaration; see **claim.**
**2.** [A pretense] — *Syn.* allegation, pretext, maintenance; see **ostentation** 2.

**pretentious,** *modif.* — *Syn.* gaudy, ostentatious, conspicuous; see **affected** 2, **ornate** 1, **pompous.**

**preterit,** *modif.* — *Syn.* past time, past action, preceding; see **past** 1.

**preternatural,** *modif.* — *Syn.* ghostly, irregular, unnatural; see **mysterious** 2, **supernatural.**

**pretext,** *n.* — *Syn.* appearance, affection, guise; see **pretense** 1.

**prettily,** *modif.* — *Syn.* pleasingly, gently, quietly; see **politely.**

**pretty,** *modif.* **1.** [Attractive] — *Syn.* attractive, comely, lovely, good-looking; see **beautiful** 1.
**2.** [Pleasant] — *Syn.* delightful, cheerful, pleasing; see **pleasant** 2.
**3.** [*Considerable] — *Syn.* ample, sizeable, notable; see **large** 1, **much** 1, 2.
**4.** [Somewhat] — *Syn.* rather, tolerably, a little; see **moderately.**
**sitting pretty*** — *Syn.* in a favorable position, prospering, thriving; see **successful.**
*See Synonym Study at* BEAUTIFUL.

**prevail,** *v.* — *Syn.* predominate, preponderate, control; see **command** 2.

**prevailing,** *modif.* — *Syn.* prevalent, general, current, rife, popular, common, regular, steady, predominant, dominant, universal, worldwide, sweeping, comprehensive, widespread, rampant, ruling, chief, principal, usual; see also **common** 1.

---

*SYN.* — **prevailing** applies to that which leads all others in acceptance, usage, belief, etc. at a given time and in a given place [a *prevailing* practice]; **current** refers to that which is commonly accepted or in general usage at the time specified or, if unspecified, at the present time [a pronunciation *current* in the 18th century]; **prevalent**

implies widespread occurrence or acceptance but does not now connote the predominance of **prevailing** [a *prevalent* belief]; **rife** implies rapidly increasing prevalence and often connotes excitement or alarm [rumors about war were *rife*]

---

**prevail upon,** *v.* — *Syn.* convince, sway, persuade; see **influence.**

**prevalence,** *n.* — *Syn.* predominance, pervasiveness, currency; see **ubiquity.**

**prevalent,** *modif.* — *Syn.* widespread, accepted, frequently met; see **common** 1, **prevailing.**
*See Synonym Study at* PREVAILING.

**prevaricate,** *v.* — *Syn.* equivocate, evade the truth, distort, falsify; see **lie** 1.
*See Synonym Study at* LIE.

**prevarication,** *n.* — *Syn.* deception, dishonesty, falsehood; see **lie** 1.

**prevaricator,** *n.* — *Syn.* perjurer, hypocrite, deceiver; see **liar.**

**prevent,** *v.* — *Syn.* preclude, obviate, forestall, avert, anticipate, block, arrest, stop, thwart, debar, repress, interrupt, halt, hinder, impede, check, frustrate, balk, foil, retard, obstruct, counter, countercheck, counteract, inhibit, restrict, limit, hold back, hold off, stop from, deter, intercept, override, circumvent, bar, ward off, keep from happening, nip in the bud, put a stop to, stave off, fend off, draw off, turn aside, rule out; see also **hinder, restrain** 1. — *Ant.* permit, aid, ENCOURAGE.

---

*SYN.* — **prevent** is to stop or keep from happening or doing, as by some prior action or by interposing an obstacle or impediment [to *prevent* disease, to *prevent* them from leaving]; **forestall** suggests advance action to stop something in its course or make it ineffective [try to *forestall* their questions]; **preclude** implies making impossible by shutting off every possibility of occurrence [locked doors *precluded* my escape]; **obviate** suggests the preventing of some unfavorable outcome by taking necessary anticipatory measures [her frankness *obviated* objections]; **avert** suggests a warding off of imminent danger or misfortune [hoping that diplomacy would *avert* war]

---

**preventative,** *n.* — *Syn.* safeguard, remedy, protection; see **medicine** 2.

**prevented,** *modif.* — *Syn.* obviated, stopped, interfered with; see **interrupted.**

**prevention,** *n.* — *Syn.* stoppage, forestalling, arrest, arresting, preclusion, obviating, bar, debarring, halt, impeding, foil, retardation, repression, restraint, restriction, inhibition, interception, overriding, circumvention, hindering, counteraction, obstruction, opposition, warding off, staving off, drawing off, keeping off, stopping, thwarting, blocking; see also **refusal.** — *Ant.* AID, encouragement, help.

**preventive,** *modif.* — *Syn.* deterrent, precautionary, tending to prevent; see **defensive.**

**preview,** *n.* — *Syn.* preliminary showing, preliminary viewing, presurvey, preliminary view, research, prior examination, preliminary study; see also **show** 1.

**previous,** *modif.* **1.** [Earlier] — *Syn.* preceding, prior, antecedent, former, foregoing, earlier, past; see also **former, preceding.**
**2.** [*Too early] — *Syn.* premature, unfounded, unwarranted; see **early** 2.

---

*SYN.* — **previous** generally implies a coming before in time or order [a *previous* encounter]; **prior** adds to this a connotation of greater importance or claim as a result of being first /a *prior* commitment/; **preceding**, esp. when used with the definite article, implies a coming immediately before /the *preceding* night/; **antecedent** often adds to the meaning of **previous** a connotation of direct causal relationship with what follows /events *antecedent* to the war/; **foregoing** applies specif. to something previously said or written /the *foregoing* examples/; **former** always connotes comparison, stated or implied, with what follows or is latter /the *former* owner/

---

**previously,** *modif.* — *Syn.* long ago, earlier, beforehand; see **before** 1.

**prewar,** *modif.* — *Syn.* before a war, prerevolutionary, time of peace.

**prey,** *n.* — *Syn.* spoil, pillage, loot; see **victim** 1.

**prey on,** *v.* **1.** [To destroy] — *Syn.* seize, raid, pillage; see **destroy** 1.

**2.** [To eat] — *Syn.* feed on, devour, consume; see **eat** 1.

**price,** *n.* — *Syn.* charge, expense, cost, expenditure, outlay, value, worth, figure, impost, dues, tariff, valuation, appraisement, quotation, fare, hire, wages, exactment, return, disbursement, rate, appraisal, reckoning, equivalent, payment, demand, barter, consideration, amount, marked price, asking price, wholesale price, list price, retail price, discount price, sticker price, estimate, output, exaction, ransom, reward, carry charge, pay, prize, return, guerdon, par value, requital, money's worth, price ceiling, ceiling; see also **charge** 1.

**at any price** — *Syn.* whatever the cost, expense no object, anyhow; see **regardless.**

**beyond price** — *Syn.* invaluable, inestimable, without price, priceless; see **valuable** 1.

**price,** *v.* — *Syn.* put a price on, fix the price of, appraise, assess, estimate a price, mark up, mark down, reduce, sticker*; see also **rate, value** 1.

**priced,** *modif.* — *Syn.* valued, estimated, worth; see **costing.**

**priced out of the market,** *modif.* — *Syn.* high-priced, unreasonable, not competitive; see **expensive.**

**priceless,** *modif.* — *Syn.* invaluable, inestimable, without price; see **valuable** 1.

**prick,** *n.* — *Syn.* tap, stab, puncture, nick, prickle; see also **cut** 1.

**prick,** *v.* — *Syn.* pierce, puncture, spur; see **cut** 1, **hurt** 1.

**prickle,** *n.* **1.** [A needle] — *Syn.* pin, spine, spike; see **needle** 1, 2.

**2.** [A sensation] — *Syn.* chill, tingling, tickle; see **feeling** 1.

**prickly,** *v.* — *Syn.* prick, sting, tingle; see **tickle** 1.

**prickly,** *modif.* — *Syn.* thorny, pointed, spiny; see **sharp** 2.

**prick up one's ears,** *v.* — *Syn.* pay attention (to), notice, listen to; see **listen** 1.

**pride,** *n.* **1.** [The quality of being vain] — *Syn.* conceit, vanity, vainglory, egoism, egotism, narcissism, ego, self-love, self-importance, self-exaltation, self-glorification, self-admiration, self-esteem, smugness, complacency, immodesty, swellheadedness*, bigheadedness*, cockiness*. — *Ant.* HUMILITY, self-effacement, modesty.

**2.** [Conduct growing from pride, sense 1] — *Syn.* haughtiness, arrogance, disdain, hubris; see **arrogance.**

**3.** [Proper respect for oneself] — *Syn.* self-esteem, self-respect, self-satisfaction, self-sufficiency, self-content, self-reliance, self-confidence, *amour-propre* (French), dignity.

**4.** [A feeling of satisfaction] — *Syn.* enjoyment, repletion, contentment; see **satisfaction** 2.

**5.** [A source of satisfaction] — *Syn.* treasure, jewel, pride and joy.

**6.** [A group of animals, especially lions] — *Syn.* pack, drove, bunch; see **herd** 1.

---

*SYN.* — **pride** refers either to a justified or excessive belief in one's own worth, merit, superiority, etc. /she takes *pride* in her accuracy/; **conceit** always implies an exaggerated opinion of oneself, one's achievements, etc. /blinded by her overweening *conceit*/; **vanity** suggests an excessive desire to be admired by others for one's achievements, appearance, etc. /his *vanity* is wounded by criticism/; **vainglory** implies extreme conceit as manifested by boasting, swaggering, arrogance, etc. /the *vainglory* of a conquering general/; **self-esteem** may suggest undue pride, but more usually implies belief in oneself and proper respect for one's worth as a person

**pride oneself on,** *v.* — *Syn.* take pride in, flatter oneself, be proud of; see **boast** 1.

**priest,** *n.* — *Syn.* clergyman, cleric, minister, man of the cloth, reverend.

Names for priests in various sects include: father, father confessor, spiritual father, priest-vicar, high priest, minor canon, pontiff, vicar, care of souls, clergyman, hieromonk, clergywoman, woman of the cloth, man of the cloth, minister, parson, pastor, chaplain, bishop, rector, preacher, presbyter, elder; *kohen* (Hebrew), rabbi; brahman, guru, lama, monk, friar; see also **minister** 1.

**priestcraft,** *n.* — *Syn.* priesthood, clergy, monasticism; see **ministry** 2.

**priesthood,** *n.* — *Syn.* clergy, Holy Orders, monasticism; see **ministry** 2.

**priestly,** *modif.* — *Syn.* ecclesiastic, episcopal, ministerial; see **clerical** 2.

**prig,** *n.* — *Syn.* prude, puritan, formalist, snob, fussbudget.

**priggish,** *modif.* — *Syn.* vain, proud, pompous; see **egotistic** 2.

**priggishness,** *n.* — *Syn.* prudishness, prudery, snobbery, puritanism, affectation; see also **hypocrisy, pretense** 1.

**prim,** *modif.* — *Syn.* stiff, formal, precise, demure, decorous, nice, orderly, tidy, cleanly, trim, spruce, pat; see also **polite** 1.

**primacy,** *n.* — *Syn.* supremacy, prelacy, authority; see **power** 2.

**prima donna,** *n.* — *Syn.* diva, star, actress, vocalist; see **singer.**

**prima facie,** *modif.* — *Syn.* at first sight, before further examination, superficial, seemingly, by all appearances; see also **apparently.**

**primarily,** *modif.* — *Syn.* originally, fundamentally, in the first place; see **essentially, principally.**

**primary,** *modif.* **1.** [Earliest] — *Syn.* primitive, initial, first; see **original** 1.

**2.** [Fundamental] — *Syn.* elemental, basic, central; see **fundamental** 1.

**3.** [Principal] — *Syn.* chief, prime, main; see **principal.**

**primary school,** *n.* — *Syn.* elementary school, lower school, lower grades, kindergarten; see **school** 1.

**primate,** *n.* **1.** [Order of mammals] — *Syn.* gorilla, chimpanzee, orangutan, gibbon, great ape, cercopithecoid, anthropoid, hominoid, brachiator; see also **hominid, man** 1.

**2.** [Archbishop] — *Syn.* cardinal, metropolitan, suffragan, patriarch; see **pope, priest.**

**prime,** *modif.* **1.** [Principal] — *Syn.* earliest, beginning, original; see **principal.**
**2.** [Excellent] — *Syn.* top, choice, superior; see **best** 1, **excellent.**
**primed,** *modif.* — *Syn.* qualified, prepared, educated; see **able** 2, **fit** 1, 2.
**prime minister,** *n.* — *Syn.* executive, leader, PM*; see **administrator.**
**prime mover,** *n.* — *Syn.* supreme being, creator, author; see **god** 2, 3.
**primer,** *n.* — *Syn.* beginner's book, textbook, preparatory book, hornbook; see **introduction** 3, 5.
**primeval,** *modif.* — *Syn.* ancient, primitive, primal, prehistoric; see **old** 3.
**primitive,** *modif.* **1.** [Simple] — *Syn.* rudimentary, embryonic, first; see **fundamental** 1.
**2.** [Ancient] — *Syn.* primeval, archaic, primordial; see **old** 3.
**3.** [Uncivilized] — *Syn.* crude, rough, simple, rude, atavistic, uncivilized, savage, uncultured, natural, barbaric, barbarous, barbarian, fierce, untamed, uncouth, Gothic, ignorant, undomesticated, wild, animal, brutish, raw, untaught, aboriginal, green, unlearned, untutored, underdeveloped; see also **fierce** 1, **savage** 1, 3.
**primp*,** *v.* — *Syn.* make one's toilet, paint and powder*, get dressed up*; see **dress** 1, **groom, prepare** 1.
**prince,** *n.* — *Syn.* sovereign, ruler, monarch, potentate; see **royalty.**
**princely,** *modif.* — *Syn.* sovereign, regal, august; see **royal** 1.
**princess,** *n.* — *Syn.* female ruler, sovereign, monarch, dauphiness, czarina, infanta; see also **royalty.**
**Princeton,** *n.* — *Syn.* Princeton University, Princeton College, College of New Jersey, Nassau Hall, Orange and Black*, one of the Big Three*, Old Nassau*, Tiger*; see also **university.**
**principal,** *modif.* — *Syn.* leading, chief, first, head, primary, prime, main, foremost, cardinal, key, major, essential, capital, important, preeminent, highest, supreme, premier, prominent, dominant, predominant, predominating, supereminent, controlling, ruling, superior, prevailing, paramount, greatest, front rank, highest-ranking, top-ranking, ranking, starring, star, stellar, incomparable, peerless, matchless, transcendent, unequaled, unrivaled, unsurpassed, maximum, crowning, sovereign, second to none, ultimate, mainline, world-class, number one*. — *Ant.* UNIMPORTANT, secondary, accessory.

---

**SYN.** — **principal** is applied to the thing or person having precedence over all others by reason of size, position, importance, etc. *[the principal rivers of Africa]*; **chief** is applied to a person or thing first in rank, authority, importance, significance, etc., and usually connotes subordination of all others *[chief executive officer, the chief advantages]*; **main,** in strict usage, is applied to the thing, often part of a system or an extensive whole, that is preeminent in size, power, importance, etc. *[the main line of a railroad]*; **leading** may stress capacity for guiding, conducting, or drawing others as well as implying a position first in importance or rank *[a leading light of the community]*; **foremost** suggests being first by having moved ahead to that position *[the foremost statesman of our time]*; **capital** is applied to that which is ranked at the head of its kind or class because of its importance or its special significance *[the capital city]*

---

**principal,** *n.* — *Syn.* chief, head, chief party, master; see **administrator.**

**principality,** *n.* — *Syn.* realm, country, state; see **territory** 2.
**principally,** *modif.* — *Syn.* chiefly, mainly, essentially, substantially, materially, eminently, pre-eminently, superlatively, supremely, vitally, especially, particularly, peculiarly, notably, importantly, fundamentally, dominantly, predominantly, basically, largely, first and foremost, in large measure, first of all, to a great degree, prevailingly, prevalently, generally, universally, mostly, above all, cardinally, in the first place, to crown all, for the most part, for the greatest part, before anything else, in the main. — *Ant.* SLIGHTLY, somewhat, tolerably.
**principle,** *n.* **1.** [A fundamental law] — *Syn.* origin, source, postulate; see **law** 4.
**2.** [A belief or set of beliefs; *often plural*] — *Syn.* system, opinion, teaching; see **belief** 1, **faith** 2, **policy.**
**in principle** — *Syn.* in theory, ideally, in essence; see **theoretically.**
**principles,** *n.* — *Syn.* ideals, standard of conduct, beliefs; see **attitude** 2, **character** 1, 2.
**print,** *n.* **1.** [Printed matter] — *Syn.* impression, reprint, issue; see **copy, edition.**
Forms of print include: line, galley proof, page proof, color proof, computer proof, author's proof, slip, pull, trial impression, foundry proof, page, sheet, spread, throwaway, first printing, second printing, letterpress, offset, inkjet, laser proof, dot matrix, thermographic.
**2.** [A printed picture] — *Syn.* engraving, lithograph, photograph, reproduction, photocopy; see also **picture** 3, **sketch** 1.
**in print** — *Syn.* printed, available, obtainable; see **published.**
**out of print** — *Syn.* O.P., unavailable, remaindered; see **sold** 1.
**print,** *v.* **1.** [To make an impression] — *Syn.* impress, imprint, indent; see **mark** 1.
**2.** [To reproduce by printing] — *Syn.* run off, print up, issue, reissue, reprint, disseminate, bring out, go to press, set type, compose, see through the press, pull proof, start the presses, take an impression, put to bed*, machine off*, let them roll*; see also **publish** 1. — *Ant.* TALK, write, inscribe.
**3.** [To simulate printing] — *Syn.* letter, do lettering, calligraph; see **write** 2.
**printed,** *modif.* — *Syn.* impressed, imprinted, engraved, stamped, lithographed, multilithed, Xeroxed (trademark), printed by offset, printed by photo-offset, silkscreened; see also **reproduced.**
**printer,** *n.* Workers in print shops include: typesetter, typographer, compositor, linotype operator, pressman, proofreader, stereotyper, mat man, printer's devil, graphic designer, paste-up artist; see also **worker.**
**printing,** *n.* **1.** [A process of reproduction] — *Syn.* typography, composition, type-setting, presswork.
**2.** [Printed matter] — *Syn.* line, page, sheet; see **print** 1.
**3.** [Publication] — *Syn.* issuing, issuance, distribution; see **publication** 1.
**printing press,** *n.* — *Syn.* rotary press, cylinder press, machine; see **press** 3.
**prior,** *modif.* — *Syn.* previous, earlier, antecedent; see **former, preceding.**
*See Synonym Study at* PREVIOUS.
**priority,** *n.* — *Syn.* superiority, preference, precedence, antecedence, precedency, previousness, pre-existence, preterition, earliness, preclude, pre-eminence, right of way; see also **advantage** 1, 2.

**priory,** *n.* — *Syn.* convent, monastery, hermitage; see **cloister** 1.

*See Synonym Study at* CLOISTER.

**prism,** *n.* **1.** [A stone] — *Syn.* crystal, pebble, gem; see **rock** 2, **stone.**

**2.** [A refractor] — *Syn.* optical instrument, kaleidoscope, spectroscope, spectrometer; see **crystal.**

**prismatic,** *modif.* — *Syn.* chromatic, kaleidoscopic, colorful; see **bright** 1, 2, **multicolored.**

**prison,** *n.* — *Syn.* penitentiary, reformatory, prison house, panopticon, guardhouse, stockade; see also **jail.**

**prisoner,** *n.* — *Syn.* captive, convict, culprit, inmate, jailbird*, detainee, the legally retarded, escapee, hostage, con*; see also **defendant.**

**prisoner of war,** *n.* — *Syn.* captive, captured personnel, POW*; see **prisoner.**

**prison ward,** *n.* — *Syn.* maximum security, pen, confinement area; see **cell** 3, **room** 2.

**pristine,** *modif.* — *Syn.* primitive, initial, primary; see **fundamental** 1, **natural** 1.

**privacy,** *n.* — *Syn.* seclusion, solitude, retreat, isolation, sequestration, separateness, aloofness, separation, concealment; see also **retirement** 2, **secrecy.**

**private,** *modif.* — *Syn.* special, separate, sequestered, retired, secluded, withdrawn, removed, not open, behind the scenes, off the record, privy, *in camera* (Latin), clandestine, single; see also **hidden** 2, **individual** 1, **isolated, own, secret** 1, **solitary.** — *Ant.* PUBLIC, open, exposed.

**in private** — *Syn.* privately, personally, not publicly; see **secretly.**

**private,** *n.* — *Syn.* enlisted man, infantryman; private first class; see **sailor, soldier.**

**privateer,** *n.* **1.** [Pirate ship] — *Syn.* private vessel, armed vessel, freebooter; see **ship.**

**2.** [Pirate] — *Syn.* buccaneer, corsair, freebooter; see **pirate.**

**privately,** *modif.* — *Syn.* confidentially, clandestinely, alone; see **personally** 1, **secretly.**

**private parts,** *n.* — *Syn.* genital organs, organs of reproduction, privates; see **genitals.**

**privation,** *n.* — *Syn.* want, destitution, penury; see **poverty** 1.

**privilege,** *n.* **1.** [A customary concession] — *Syn.* due, perquisite, prerogative; see **right** 1.

**2.** [An opportunity] — *Syn.* chance, fortunate happening, event; see **opportunity** 1.

**privileged,** *modif.* — *Syn.* free, vested, furnished; see **exempt.**

**privy,** *modif.* — *Syn.* confidential, personal, separate; see **private.**

**privy,** *n.* — *Syn.* outhouse, backhouse, outdoor toilet, latrine, outside privy; see also **toilet** 2.

**privy to,** *modif.* — *Syn.* conscious of, acquainted with, aware of; see **conscious** 1.

**prize,** *n.* — *Syn.* reward, award, honor, premium, accolade, medal, decoration, laurel, trophy, palm, crown, garland, cup, blue ribbon, citation, scholarship, fellowship, inducement, carrot, advantage, privilege, winnings, jackpot, purse, windfall, bounty, bonus, spoils, booty, plunder, loot, recompense, feather in one's cap, title, championship, first place, mark of honor, treasure, gem, meed, guerdon, payoff*, gravy*, plum*, haul*, take*; see also **booty.**

---

*SYN.* — **prize** applies to something won in competition or, often, in a lottery or game of chance /she won first *prize* in the golf tournament/; **award** implies a decision by judges but does not connote overt competition /we

received an *award* for the best news story of the year/; **reward** usually refers to something given in recompense for a good deed or for merit /a *reward* was offered for the return of the lost briefcase/; **premium**, in this connection, applies to a reward offered as an inducement to greater effort or production /to pay a *premium* for advance delivery/

---

**prize,** *v.* — *Syn.* value, esteem, cherish; see **appreciate** 2, **like** 1, 2.

*See Synonym Study at* APPRECIATE.

**prize fight,** *n.* — *Syn.* boxing match, fight, ring*; see **boxing, sport** 3.

**prize fighter,** *n.* — *Syn.* boxer, pugilist, contender; see **fighter** 2.

**prize ring,** *n.* — *Syn.* the ring, gymnasium, arena; see **ring** 5.

**probability,** *n.* — *Syn.* likelihood, possibility, contingency, hazard, plausibility, reasonableness, conceivability, prospect, likeliness, promise, possibility, chance, credibility, expectation, presumption, anticipation, practicability, feasibility, odds; see also **chance** 1, **possibility** 2. — *Ant.* DOUBT, improbability, doubtfulness.

**probable,** *modif.* — *Syn.* likely, seeming, presumable, feasible; see **likely** 1.

**probably,** *modif.* — *Syn.* presumably, seemingly, apparently, believably, reasonably, imaginably, feasibly, practicably, expediently, plausibly, most likely, everything being equal, as like as not, as the case may be, one can assume, like enough, no doubt, to all appearance, in all probability. — *Ant.* UNLIKELY, doubtfully, questionably.

**probation,** *n.* — *Syn.* period of trial, ordeal, moral trial; see **punishment.**

**probe,** *n.* — *Syn.* exploration, scrutiny, inquiry; see **examination** 1.

**probe,** *v.* — *Syn.* investigate, pierce deeply, penetrate; see **examine** 1.

**probity,** *n.* — *Syn.* fidelity, honor, integrity; see **honesty** 1.

**problem,** *n.* **1.** [A difficulty] — *Syn.* dilemma, quandary, obstacle; see **difficulty** 1, 2, **predicament.**

**2.** [A question to be solved] — *Syn.* query, intricacy, enigma; see **puzzle** 2.

**problematic,** *modif.* — *Syn.* problematical, unsettled, doubtful; see **doubtful** 1, **uncertain** 2.

*See Synonym Study at* DOUBTFUL.

**procedure,** *n.* **1.** [Method] — *Syn.* fashion, style, mode; see **method** 2, **system** 2.

**2.** [Plan] — *Syn.* course of action, idea, scheme; see **plan** 2.

**proceed,** *v.* — *Syn.* move, progress, continue; see **advance** 1.

**proceeding,** *n.* [*Often plural*] — *Syn.* process, transaction, deed, experiment, performance, measure, step, course, undertaking, venture, adventure, occurrence, incident, casualty, circumstance, happening, movement, operation, procedure, exercise, maneuver; see also **action** 2.

**proceedings,** *n.* — *Syn.* documents, minutes, account; see **records.**

**proceeds,** *n.* **1.** [Product] — *Syn.* result(s), reward, income; see **profit** 2.

**2.** [A return] — *Syn.* gain, interest, yield; see **return** 3.

**process,** *n.* — *Syn.* means, rule, manner; see **method** 2.

**in the process of** — *Syn.* during, while, when, in the course of; see **during.**

**process,** *v.* — *Syn.* treat, make ready, concoct; see **prepare** 1.

**processed,** *modif.* — *Syn.* treated, handled, fixed; see **prepared** 2.

**procession,** *n.* — *Syn.* train, advance, cavalcade; see **parade** 1.

**proclaim,** *v.* — *Syn.* declare, announce, give out, blazon; see **declare** 1.
*See Synonym Study at* DECLARE.

**proclamation,** *n.* — *Syn.* promulgation, official publication, advertisement; see **announcement** 1.

**procrastinate,** *v.* — *Syn.* defer, pause, gain time; see **delay** 1, **hesitate.**

**procreation,** *n.* — *Syn.* reproduction, conception, impregnation, generation, breeding, propagation; see also **reproduction** 1.

**proctor,** *n.* — *Syn.* appointee, minister, representative; see **agent** 1, **delegate.**

**procurable,** *modif.* — *Syn.* attainable, obtainable, on the market, for sale, purchasable, on sale; see also **available.**

**procure,** *v.* — *Syn.* obtain, get, secure, gain; see **obtain** 1.
*See Synonym Study at* OBTAIN.

**procurement,** *n.* — *Syn.* obtainment, acquirement, appropriation; see **acquisition** 1.

**procurer,** *n.* — *Syn.* pander, whoremonger, bawd\*, runner\*; see **pimp.**

**procuress,** *n.* — *Syn.* whoremonger, whore, madam; see **prostitute.**

**procuring,** *n.* — *Syn.* obtaining, acquiring, gaining; see **acquisition** 1.

**prod,** *v.* — *Syn.* provoke, crowd, shove; see **push** 1.

**prodigal,** *modif.* — *Syn.* lavish, extravagant, squandering; see **wasteful.**
*See Synonym Study at* PROFUSE.

**prodigality,** *n.* **1.** [Affluence] — *Syn.* money, profusion, abundance; see **plenty, wealth** 2.
**2.** [Wastefulness] — *Syn.* dissipation, lavishness, extravagance; see **waste** 1.

**prodigious,** *modif.* — *Syn.* huge, immense, monstrous; see **large** 1.

**prodigy,** *n.* **1.** [A marvel] — *Syn.* portent, miracle, monster, enormity, spectacle, freak, curiosity; see also **wonder** 2.
**2.** [An extraordinary person] — *Syn.* genius, child genius, *Wunderkind* (German), whiz kid\*, walking encyclopedia\*.

**produce,** *n.* — *Syn.* product, fruitage, harvest, result, resultant, crop, return, effect, consequence, amount, profit, ingathering, outcome, outgrowth, aftermath, gain, emolument, realization; see also **butter, cheese, cream** 1, **food, fruit** 1, **grain** 1, **milk, vegetable.**

**produce,** *v.* **1.** [To bear] — *Syn.* yield, bring forth, give forth, give birth to, propagate, bring out, come through, blossom, flower, deliver, generate, engender, breed, contribute, give, afford, furnish, return, render, show fruit, fructify, fetch, bring in, present, offer, provide, contribute, sell for, bear, bear fruit, accrue, allow, admit, proliferate, be delivered of, bring to birth, reproduce, foal, lamb, drop, be brought to bed, calve, fawn, whelp, cub, kitten, hatch, farrow, throw, usher into the world, spawn; see also **yield** 2.
**2.** [To create by mental effort] — *Syn.* originate, author, procreate, bring forth, conceive, engender, effectuate, write, design, fabricate, imagine, turn out, devise, hammer out, crank out\*, churn out\*, grind out\*; see also **compose** 3, **create** 2, **invent** 1, 2.
**3.** [To cause] — *Syn.* effect, occasion, bring about; see **begin** 1.

**4.** [To show] — *Syn.* exhibit, present, unfold; see **display** 1.
**5.** [To make] — *Syn.* assemble, build, construct; see **manufacture** 1.
**6.** [To present a performance] — *Syn.* present, play, put on the stage; see **act** 3, **perform** 2.

**produced,** *modif.* **1.** [Created] — *Syn.* originated, composed, made; see **formed.**
**2.** [Presented] — *Syn.* performed, acted, put on, shown, staged, brought out, offered, presented, imparted, rendered.
**3.** [Caused] — *Syn.* occasioned, propagated, begot, bred, engendered, generated, hatched, induced.

**producer,** *n.* — *Syn.* raiser, yielder, generator; see **farmer.**

**producing,** *modif.* — *Syn.* bearing, bringing forth, generating; see **fertile** 1, 2.

**product,** *n.* **1.** [A result] — *Syn.* output, outcome, produce; see **result.**
**2.** [*Often plural;* goods produced] — *Syn.* stock, goods, merchandise, manufactured product; see **commodity.**

**production,** *n.* **1.** [The act of producing] — *Syn.* origination, creation, authoring, reproduction, yielding, giving, bearing, rendering, giving forth, increasing, augmentation, accrual, return, procreation, occasioning, generation, engendering, fructification, fruiting, blooming, blossoming; see also **making.**
**2.** [The amount produced] — *Syn.* crop, result, stock; see **product** 2.
**3.** [Something produced] — *Syn.* product, composition, theatrical performance, motion picture, movie.
**make a production out of\*** — *Syn.* fuss over, elaborate, exaggerate; see **overdo** 1.

**productive,** *modif.* — *Syn.* rich, fruitful, prolific; see **fertile** 1, 2.

**productivity,** *n.* — *Syn.* richness, potency, fecundity; see **fertility** 1.

**profanation,** *n.* — *Syn.* profanity, impiety, abuse, sacrilege; see **blasphemy, heresy, sin.**
*See Synonym Study at* SACRILEGE.

**profane,** *modif.* **1.** [Worldly] — *Syn.* temporal, transitory, transient; see **worldly** 2.
**2.** [Irreverent] — *Syn.* godless, irreligious, sacrilegious; see **atheistic, impious.**

**profane,** *v.* — *Syn.* despoil, commit sacrilege, befoul, revile, commit sin, be irreligious, scorn, mock, indulge in vice, be evil, do wrong, blaspheme, swear, curse, cuss\*.

**profanity,** *n.* — *Syn.* abuse, cursing, swearing, obscenity; see **blasphemy, curse** 1.
*See Synonym Study at* BLASPHEMY.

**profess,** *v.* — *Syn.* avow, confess, pretend; see **declare** 1.

**professed,** *modif.* — *Syn.* avowed, declared, pledged; see **announced, told.**

**professedly,** *modif.* — *Syn.* slyly, deceptively, basely; see **falsely.**

**profession,** *n.* **1.** [A skilled or learned occupation] — *Syn.* calling, business, avocation, vocation, employment, occupation, job, engagement, office, situation, position, lifework, chosen work, billet, role, service, pursuit, undertaking, concern, post, berth, craft, sphere, field, specialty, walk of life; see also **church** 3, **education** 3, **journalism, law** 5, **medicine** 3, **trade** 2.
**2.** [A declaration] — *Syn.* pretense, avowal, vow; see **declaration** 1, **oath** 1.

**professional,** *modif.* **1.** [Skillful] — *Syn.* expert, learned, adept; see **able** 1, **trained.**

**2.** [Well-qualified] — *Syn.* acknowledged, known, licensed; see **able** 2.

**professional,** *n.* — *Syn.* expert, experienced personnel, specially trained person; see **specialist.**

**professor,** *n.* — *Syn.* teacher, schoolmaster, pedagogue, educator, faculty member, dominie, pundit, don (British), savant, sage; see also **teacher** 2.
Types of professors include: full, associate, assistant, professor emeritus, professor emerita, visiting, instructor, lecturer, tutor, fellow, teaching fellow, master docent.

**professorial,** *modif.* — *Syn.* academic, scholastic, scholarly; see **learned** 1, 2.

**proficiency,** *n.* — *Syn.* learning, skill, knowledge; see **ability** 1, 2.

**proficient,** *modif.* — *Syn.* skilled, expert, skillful; see **able** 2.

**profile,** *n.* **1.** [A view in outline] — *Syn.* contour, side view, silhouette; see **form** 1, **outline** 4.
**2.** [A biographical sketch] — *Syn.* portrait, biography, characterization, sketch; see **biography.**
*See Synonym Study at* OUTLINE.

**profit,** *n.* **1.** [Advantage] — *Syn.* avail, good, value; see **advantage** 3.
**2.** [Excess of receipts over expenditures] — *Syn.* gain, return(s), proceeds, receipts, take*, gate, emolument, acquisition, rake-off*, accumulation, saving, aggrandizement, augmentation, interest, remuneration, earnings. — *Ant.* LOSS, debits, costs.

**profit,** *v.* **1.** [To be of benefit] — *Syn.* benefit, assist, avail; see **help** 1.
**2.** [To derive gain] — *Syn.* benefit, capitalize on, cash in on, realize, clear, gain, reap profits, make a profit, recover, thrive, prosper, harvest, make money. — *Ant.* LOSE, lose out on, miss out on.

**profitable,** *modif.* — *Syn.* lucrative, useful, sustaining, self-sustaining, aiding, remunerative, beneficial, gainful, advantageous, paying, successful, favorable, assisting, productive, serviceable, valuable, contributive, conducive, instrumental, practical, pragmatic, effective, to advantage, effectual, sufficient, paying its way, bringing in returns, making money, paying well, paying out*, in the black*; see also **helpful** 1. — *Ant.* UNPROFITABLE, unsuccessful, unproductive.

**profitably,** *modif.* — *Syn.* lucratively, remuneratively, gainfully, usefully, advantageously, successfully, favorably, for money, productively, practically, effectively, effectually, sufficiently, sustainingly.

**profiteer,** *n.* — *Syn.* exploiter, cheater, chiseler*; see **cheat** 1.

**profitless,** *modif.* — *Syn.* vain, futile, ineffectual; see **useless** 1, **worthless** 1.

**profligate,** *modif.* — *Syn.* dissolute, abandoned, depraved; see **lewd** 2, **wicked** 1.

**profound,** *modif.* **1.** [Physically deep] — *Syn.* fathomless, bottomless, subterranean; see **deep** 1.
**2.** [Intellectually deep] — *Syn.* learned, recondite, heavy, erudite, scholarly, abstruse, mysterious, sage, serious, sagacious, penetrating, discerning, knowing, wise, reflective, knowledgeable, intellectual, enlightened, thorough, informed, of great learning, immensely learned; see also **intelligent** 1, **learned** 2, **solemn** 1. — *Ant.* SUPERFICIAL, shallow, flighty.
**3.** [Emotionally deep] — *Syn.* heartfelt, deep-felt, great; see **intense.**

**profoundly,** *modif.* — *Syn.* deeply, extremely, thoroughly; see **very.**

**profundity,** *n.* **1.** [Depth] — *Syn.* pitch, deepness, lowness; see **depth** 1.

**2.** [Perception] — *Syn.* acuity, sagacity, authority; see **acumen.**

**profuse,** *modif.* — *Syn.* abundant, extravagant, lavish, liberal, prodigal, bountiful, overflowing, luxuriant, lush, plentiful, copious, prolific, in profusion, generous, free, munificent, unstinting, profligate, wasteful, overliberal, overgenerous, excessive; see also **plentiful** 1, 2, **wasteful.**

---

*SYN.* — **profuse** implies a pouring or giving forth freely, often to the point of excess *[profuse* thanks*]*; **lavish** implies an unstinted, generous, sometimes unreasonably liberal, giving *[lavish* attentions*]*; **extravagant** always suggests unreasonably excessive, wasteful spending or giving *[extravagant* living*]*; **prodigal** implies such reckless extravagance as to suggest eventual impoverishment *[the prodigal* heirs to a fortune*]*; **luxuriant** suggests production in great and rich abundance *[luxuriant* foliage*]*; **lush** implies such great luxuriance as my seem excessive *[lush* tropical vegetation, *lush* prose*] See also Synonym Study at* PLENTIFUL.

---

**profusely,** *modif.* — *Syn.* extensively, lavishly, richly; see **much** 1, 2.

**profuseness,** *n.* **1.** [Plenty] — *Syn.* abundance, surplus, affluence; see **plenty.**
**2.** [Verbosity] — *Syn.* prolixity, verbiage, grandiloquence; see **wordiness.**

**profusion,** *n.* — *Syn.* abundance, lavishness, prodigality; see **plenty.**

**progenitor,** *n.* — *Syn.* forebear, begetter, ancestor; see **ancestor, parent.**

**progeny,** *n.* — *Syn.* issue, descendants, children; see **offspring.**

**prognosis,** *n.* — *Syn.* forecast, prophecy, prediction, diagnosis; see **guess.**

**program,** *n.* **1.** [A list of subjects] — *Syn.* schedule, memoranda, printed program; see **list, record** 2.
**2.** [A sequence of events] — *Syn.* happenings, schedule, agenda, order of business, calendar, plans, business, affairs, details, arrangements, catalog, curriculum, order of the day, series of events, appointments, things to do, chores, preparations, necessary acts, meetings, getting and spending*, all the thousand and one things*; see also **plan** 2.
**3.** [An entertainment] — *Syn.* performance, show, presentation; see **performance** 2.
**4.** [A sequence of coded instructions for a computer] — *Syn.* computer language, coded instructions, application; see **computer language.**

**program,** *v.* **1.** [To schedule] — *Syn.* slate, book, bill, budget, poll, register, list, draft, empanel, line up.
**2.** [To work out a sequence to be performed] — *Syn.* feed through, feed in, activate a computer, compute, reckon, figure, calculate, estimate, enter, compile, feed, edit, process, prioritize, concatenate, extend, delete, add.

**programmed,** *modif.* — *Syn.* scheduled, slated, lined up*; see **planned.**

**programmed learning,** *n.* — *Syn.* instruction, audiovisual learning, learning with the use of a teaching machine.

**progress,** *n.* **1.** [Movement forward] — *Syn.* progression, advance, headway, impetus, velocity, pace, momentum, motion, rate, step, stride, current, flow, tour, circuit, transit, journey, voyage, march, expedition, locomotion, ongoing, passage, course, procession, process, lapse of time, march of events, course of life, movement of the stars, motion through space. — *Ant.* STOP, stay, stand.

**2.** [Improvement] — *Syn.* advancement, development, growth, promotion; see **improvement** 1.

**in progress** — *Syn.* advancing, going on, under way, continuing; see **moving** 1.

**progress,** *v.* **1.** [To move forward] — *Syn.* proceed, move onward, move on; see **advance** 1.

**2.** [To improve] — *Syn.* advance, become better, grow; see **improve** 2.

**progression,** *n.* **1.** [Improvement] — *Syn.* progress, rise, change; see **improvement** 1.

**2.** [Sequence] — *Syn.* order, succession, series; see **sequence** 1.

**progressive,** *modif.* **1.** [In mounting sequence] — *Syn.* advancing, mounting, rising, increasing, growing, continuous, successive, following, adding, multiplying, consecutive, gradual, serial, unbroken, uninterrupted, endless, regular, methodical, uniform; see also **moving** 1. — *Ant.* FIRM, stationary, immovable.

**2.** [Receptive to new ideas] — *Syn.* tolerant, lenient, openminded, reformist, revisionist; see also **liberal** 2.

**prohibit,** *v.* **1.** [To forbid] — *Syn.* interdict, ban, outlaw, put under the ban, obstruct; see also **forbid, halt** 2, **prevent.**

**2.** [To hinder] — *Syn.* obstruct, impede, inhibit; see **hinder, prevent, restrain** 1.

**prohibited,** *modif.* — *Syn.* forbidden, restricted, not approved; see **illegal, refused.**

**prohibition,** *n.* **1.** [The act of prohibiting] — *Syn.* forbiddance, interdiction, prescription, ban, repudiation; see also **refusal.**

**2.** [Restrictions placed upon the handling or consumption of liquor; *often capital*] — *Syn.* Volstead Act, temperance, Eighteenth Amendment, Prohibition Amendment; the Noble Experiment\*, the Lost Cause\*, the Eighteenth Amusement\*.

**prohibitionist,** *n.* — *Syn.* temperance advocate, abstinent, teetotaler, nondrinker; see **abstainer.**

**prohibitive,** *modif.* — *Syn.* limiting, preventing, restrictive, restraining; see **conditional.**

**project,** *n.* — *Syn.* outline, design, scheme; see **plan** 2.

**project,** *v.* **1.** [To thrust out] — *Syn.* protrude, hang over, extend, jut, bulge, beetle, stretch out, push out, stand out, stick out, hang out, jut out, be prominent, be conspicuous, be convex. — *Ant.* WITHDRAW, regress, revert.

**2.** [To throw] — *Syn.* pitch, heave, propel; see **throw** 1.

**3.** [To propose] — *Syn.* predict, forecast, calculate, set forth; see **propose** 1.

**projectile,** *n.* — *Syn.* bullet, shell, missile; see **bullet, weapon** 1.

**projecting,** *modif.* — *Syn.* jutting, protruding, protuberant; see **prominent** 1.

**projection,** *n.* **1.** [Bulge] — *Syn.* prominence, jut, protuberance, step, ridge, rim; see also **bulge.**

**2.** [Forecast] — *Syn.* prognostication, prediction, guess; see **forecast.**

---

**SYN.** — **projection** implies a jutting out abruptly beyond the rest of the surface /the *projection* of the eaves beyond the sides of a house/; **protrusion** suggests a thrusting or pushing out that is of an abnormal or disfiguring nature /*protrusion* of the eyeballs/; **protuberance** suggests a swelling out, usually in rounded form /the tumor on his arm formed a *protuberance*/; **bulge** suggests an

outward swelling of a kind that may result from internal pressure /the *bulge* in the can resulted from the fermentation of its contents/

---

**proletarian,** *modif.* — *Syn.* low, humble, destitute; see **poor** 1.

**proletariat,** *n.* — *Syn.* the masses, commonality, working class, the rank and file; see **people** 3.

**proliferate,** *v.* — *Syn.* increase, engender, procreate, generate; see **propagate** 1, **reproduce** 3.

**proliferation,** *n.* — *Syn.* increase, conception, propagation, generation; see **procreation, reproduction** 1.

**prolific,** *modif.* — *Syn.* productive, yielding, rich, fecund; see **fertile** 1, 2.

**prolix,** *modif.* — *Syn.* diffuse, wordy, tedious; see **verbose.**

**prologue,** *n.* — *Syn.* preface, preamble, proem; see **introduction** 4.

**prolong,** *v.* — *Syn.* continue, hold, draw out; see **increase** 1, **lengthen** 1.

**prolonged,** *modif.* — *Syn.* extended, lengthy, lengthened, continued; see **dull** 4.

**prom,** *n.* — *Syn.* ball, dance, gala, promenade, class dance, junior prom, senior prom; see also **dance** 2.

**promenade,** *n.* **1.** [A walk] — *Syn.* ramble, saunter, hike, stroll; see **walk** 3.

**2.** [A dance] — *Syn.* reception, ball, prom; see **dance** 2, **prom.**

**promenade,** *v.* — *Syn.* stroll, saunter, hike, pace; see **walk** 1.

**prominence,** *n.* **1.** [A projection] — *Syn.* jut, protrusion, bump; see **bulge, projection.**

**2.** [Notability] — *Syn.* renown, influence, distinction; see **fame** 1.

**prominent,** *modif.* **1.** [Physically prominent] — *Syn.* protuberant, extended, jutting, beetling, conspicuous, protruding, projecting, noticeable, rugged, rough, hummocky, obtrusive, extrusive, shooting out, salient, hilly, raised, embossed, relieved, bossy, convex, rounded. — *Ant.* HOLLOW, depressed, sunken.

**2.** [Socially prominent] — *Syn.* notable, pre-eminent, leading; see **famous.**

**3.** [Conspicuous] — *Syn.* conspicuous, outstanding, striking, noticeable; see **conspicuous** 1, **noticeable, obvious** 1.

*See Synonym Study at* NOTICEABLE.

**promiscuity,** *n.* — *Syn.* lechery, looseness, indiscrimination; see **evil** 1, **lewdness.**

**promiscuous,** *modif.* **1.** [Mixed] — *Syn.* confused, jumbled, diverse; see **mixed** 1.

**2.** [Morally lax] — *Syn.* libertine, licentious, unrestricted; see **lewd** 2.

**promise,** *n.* **1.** [A pledge] — *Syn.* assurance, agreement, pact, oath, engagement, covenant, consent, avowal, warrant, asseveration, affirmation, swearing, plight, word, troth, vow, profession, guarantee, insurance, obligation, stipulation, commitment, betrothal, affiance, espousal, plighted faith, marriage contract, giving one's word, gentleman's agreement, attestation, word of honor, parole, warranty, foretaste.

**2.** [Hope] — *Syn.* outlook, sign, good omen, good appearance; see **encouragement** 2, **hope** 2.

**promise,** *v.* **1.** [To give one's word] — *Syn.* plight, engage, declare, agree, vow, swear, espouse, consent, asseverate, affirm, profess, undertake, pledge, covenant, contract, bargain, affiance, betroth, assure, guarantee, warrant, give assurance, give warranty, insure, cross one's heart, keep a promise, live up to, plight one's faith, plight one's troth, bind oneself, commit oneself, obligate

oneself, make oneself answerable, secure, give security, underwrite, subscribe, lead one to expect, answer for, pledge one's honor, cross one's heart and hope to die*. — *Ant.* DECEIVE, deny, break faith.
**2.** [To appear promising] — *Syn.* ensure, insure, assure; see **encourage** 2.

**promised,** *modif.* — *Syn.* pledged, sworn, plighted, vowed, agreed, covenanted, as agreed upon, undertaken, professed, consented, affirmed, asseverated, insured, warranted, vouched for, underwritten, subscribed, stipulated, assured, ensured; see also **guaranteed.**

**promising,** *modif.* — *Syn.* likely, assuring, encouraging; see **hopeful** 2.

**promontory,** *n.* — *Syn.* projection, foreland, point; see **land** 1, **peninsula.**

**promote,** *v.* **1.** [To further] — *Syn.* forward, further, advance, encourage, support, help, aid, abet, assist, develop, back, uphold, champion, patronize, propagandize, advertise, publicize, urge, advocate, cultivate, improve, strengthen, push, bolster, boost, foster, nourish, nurture, subsidize, second, befriend, benefit, subscribe to, favor, expand, serve, subserve, better, avail, sell, lobby for, get behind*, plug*, tout*, hype*. — *Ant.* DISCOURAGE, weaken, enfeeble.
**2.** [To advance in rank [ — *Syn.* raise, advance, elevate, graduate, move up, exalt, aggrandize, magnify, prefer, favor, increase, ascend, better, ennoble, dignify; kick upstairs*, up*. — *Ant.* HUMBLE, demote, reduce.

***SYN.*** — **promote** is to help in the establishment, development, or success of something [to *promote* good will]; **advance** implies assistance in hastening the course of anything or in moving toward an objective [to *advance* a project]; **forward** emphasizes the idea of action as an impetus [concessions were made to *forward* the pact]; **further** emphasizes assistance in bringing a desired goal closer [to *further* a cause]

**promotion,** *n.* **1.** [Advancement in rank] — *Syn.* preferment, elevation, raise, improvement, advance, lift, betterment, ennobling, favoring. — *Ant.* REMOVAL, demotion, lowering.
**2.** [Improvement] — *Syn.* advancement, progression, development; see **improvement** 1, **increase** 1.
**3.** [Publicity] — *Syn.* public relations, PR, advertising, notice; see **advertisement** 1, **publicity** 3.

**prompt,** *modif.* — *Syn.* timely, punctual, instantaneous, quick; see **immediate** 1, **punctual, ready** 1.
*See Synonym Study at* QUICK.

**prompt,** *v.* **1.** [To instigate] — *Syn.* arouse, provoke, inspire; see **incite, urge** 2.
**2.** [To suggest] — *Syn.* bring up, indicate, imply; see **hint** 1, **mention, propose** 1.
**3.** [To help] — *Syn.* aid, assist, advise; see **help** 1.

**prompted,** *modif.* — *Syn.* moved, incited, suggested; see **inspired** 1, **urged** 2.

**prompter,** *n.* — *Syn.* playreader, cue card, TelePrompTer (trademark).

**promptly,** *modif.* — *Syn.* on time, punctually, hastily; see **immediately, quickly** 1, 2.

**promptness,** *n.* — *Syn.* preparedness, agility, readiness; see **preparation** 2.

**promulgate,** *v.* — *Syn.* publish, declare, proclaim; see **advertise** 1.

**prone,** *modif.* **1.** [Inclined] — *Syn.* inclined, predisposed, apt; see **likely** 4.
**2.** [Lying down] — *Syn.* lying, recumbent, prostrate, face down; see **lying** 4, **supine** 1.

*See Synonym Study at* LIKELY, SUPINE.

**prong,** *n.* — *Syn.* spine, spur, spike; see **fastener.**

**pronoun,** *n.*
Types of pronouns include: personal, possessive, demonstrative, relative, definite, indefinite, interrogative, substantive, intensive, reflexive, reciprocal.

**pronounce,** *v.* **1.** [To speak formally] — *Syn.* proclaim, say, assert; see **declare** 1.
**2.** [To articulate] — *Syn.* enunciate, articulate, vocalize; see **utter.**

**pronounced,** *modif.* — *Syn.* conspicuous, notable, noticeable, clear; see **definite** 2, **obvious** 1, 2, **unusual** 1.

**pronouncement,** *n.* — *Syn.* report, declaration, statement; see **announcement** 1, 2.

**pronunciation,** *n.* — *Syn.* articulation, utterance, intonation, elocution, voicing; see also **diction.**

**proof,** *n.* **1.** [Evidence] — *Syn.* demonstration, verification, evidence, testimony, case, exhibit, reasons, documentation, credentials, data, warrant, confirmation, substantiation, attestation, corroboration, affidavit, facts, witness, deposition, trace, record, criterion, grounds; see also **confirmation** 1.
**2.** [Process of proving] — *Syn.* test, attempt, assay; see **trial** 2.
**3.** [A printed proof sheet] — *Syn.* trial proof, pull, slip, revise, trial impression, galley proof, page proof, stereo proof, foundry proof.

***SYN.*** — **proof**, as compared here, applies to facts, documents, etc. that are so certain or convincing as to demonstrate the validity of a conclusion beyond reasonable doubt; **evidence** applies to something presented before a court, as a witness's statement, an object, etc., that bears on or establishes a point in question; **testimony** applies to verbal evidence given by a witness under oath; **exhibit** applies to a document or object produced as evidence in a court

**proofread,** *v.* — *Syn.* improve, scan, proof; see **correct** 1.

**prop,** *n.* — *Syn.* aid, assistance, strengthener; see **post** 1.

**propaganda,** *n.* — *Syn.* promotion, publicity, advertisement, publication, announcement, evangelism, proselytism, promulgation, ballyhoo*, handout*.

**propagandist,** *n.* — *Syn.* disseminator, advocate, devotee, pamphleteer, advocator, indoctrinator, proselytizer, evangelist, missionary, catechizer, teacher, salesman, zealot.

**propagandize,** *v.* — *Syn.* instill, indoctrinate, instruct; see **teach** 1.

**propagate,** *v.* **1.** [To beget] — *Syn.* breed, engender, create, originate, father, sire, procreate, multiply, generate, produce, reproduce, deliver, give birth.
**2.** [To spread] — *Syn.* disseminate, diffuse, develop; see **scatter** 1, 2.

**propagation,** *n.* **1.** [Procreation] — *Syn.* reproduction, breeding, multiplication, generation, proliferation; see also **procreation, reproduction** 1.
**2.** [Diffusion] — *Syn.* spread, circulation, dispersion; see **distribution** 1.

**propel,** *v.* — *Syn.* impel, move, launch, thrust; see **drive** 3.

**propellant,** *n.* — *Syn.* charge, gunpowder, combustible; see **explosive, fuel.**

**propeller,** *n.* Types of propellers include: screw, Archimedean, fishtail, variable-pitch, feathering, marine, airplane, twin, two-bladed, three-bladed, four-bladed, weedless, pusher, pulling; propeller-wheel.

**propensity,** *n.* — *Syn.* talent, capacity, competence, inclination; see **ability** 1, 2.
See Synonym Study at INCLINATION.

**proper,** *modif.* **1.** [Suitable] — *Syn.* fit, just, decent, fitting; see **fit** 1, 2.
**2.** [Conventional] — *Syn.* customary, usual, decorous; see **conventional** 1, 2.
**3.** [Prudish] — *Syn.* prim, precise, strait-laced; see **prudish.**
**4.** [Personal] — *Syn.* private, own, peculiar; see **individual** 1.
See Synonym Study at FIT.

**properly,** *modif.* — *Syn.* correctly, fitly, suitably; see **accurately, well** 3.

**property,** *n.* **1.** [Possession] — *Syn.* belongings, lands, assets, holdings, inheritance, capital, equity, investments, goods, chattel, earthly possessions, real property, personal property, taxable property, resources, private property, public property, wealth; see also **business** 5, **estate** 1, **farm, home** 1.
**2.** [A piece of land] — *Syn.* lot, section, quarter section, estate, tract, part, realty, real estate, subdivision, farm, park, ranch, homestead, yard, grounds, frontage, acres, acreage, premises, campus, grant, landed property, field, claim, holding, plot, leasehold, freehold; see also **lot** 1.
**3.** [Characteristic] — *Syn.* attribute, quality, feature, trait; see **characteristic, quality** 1.
See Synonym Study at QUALITY.

**prophecy,** *n.* — *Syn.* prediction, prognostication, prescience, augury; see **divination.**

**prophesy,** *v.* — *Syn.* predict, prognosticate, forecast, divine; see **foretell.**

**prophet,** *n.* — *Syn.* seer, seeress*, oracle, soothsayer, clairvoyant, wizard, augur, sibyl, sorcerer, sorceress*, predictor, forecaster, prognosticator, diviner, haruspex, evocator, medium, witch, palmist, fortuneteller, palmist, tea-leaf reader, reader of the future, weather forecaster, meteorologist, ovate, bard, druid, *vates sacer* (Latin), magus, astrologer, horoscopist.

**prophetess*,** *n.* — *Syn.* seeress*, sorceress*, Cassandra; see **prophet.**

**prophetic,** *modif.* — *Syn.* predictive, foreshadowing, portentous; see **oracular** 2.

**prophylactic,** *modif.* — *Syn.* protective, preventive, preventative; see **contraceptive.**

**prophylactic,** *n.* — *Syn.* condom, rubber, sheath, Trojan (trademark); see **contraceptive.**

**prophylaxis,** *n.* — *Syn.* precaution, sanitation, prevention; see **treatment** 2.

**propinquity,** *n.* **1.** [Proximity] — *Syn.* nearness, contiguity, concurrence; see **proximity.**
**2.** [Kinship] — *Syn.* affiliation, connection, consanguinity; see **relationship.**

**propitiate,** *v.* — *Syn.* conciliate, appease, atone; see **pacify** 1, **satisfy** 1, 3.
See Synonym Study at PACIFY.

**propitious,** *modif.* **1.** [Favorable] — *Syn.* favorable, auspicious, encouraging, promising; see **hopeful** 2.
**2.** [Kindly] — *Syn.* benignant, helpful, generous; see **kind.**
See Synonym Study at FAVORABLE.

**proponent,** *n.* — *Syn.* defender, advocate, enthusiast, champion; see **protector.**

**proportion,** *n.* — *Syn.* balance, symmetry, relationship, dimension; see **balance** 2.
See Synonym Study at SYMMETRY.

**proportional,** *modif.* — *Syn.* proportionate, equivalent, comparable; see **comparative, equal.**

**proposal,** *n.* **1.** [Offer] — *Syn.* overture, recommenda-

tion, proposition, offer, suggestion, bid, motion, nomination; see also **suggestion** 1.
**2.** [Plan] — *Syn.* scheme, program, prospectus, project, proposition, plan, outline, design; see also **plan** 2.
**3.** [An offer of marriage] — *Syn.* offer, overture, proposition, asking of one's hand, betrothal; see also **engagement** 2.

---

*SYN.* — **proposal** refers to a plan, offer, etc. presented for acceptance or rejection /the *proposal* for a decrease in taxes was approved/; **proposition** specifically applies to a statement, theorem, etc., set forth for argument, demonstration, proof, etc. /the *proposition* that all men are created equal/, but it is also used similarly to **proposal** with reference to business dealings and the like

---

**propose,** *v.* **1.** [To make a suggestion] — *Syn.* suggest, offer, put forward, move, set forth, come up with, state, proffer, advance, propound, introduce, put to, contend, assert, tender, recommend, advise, counsel, lay before, submit, adduce, affirm, volunteer, press, urge (upon), hold out, make a motion, lay (something) on the line. — *Ant.* OPPOSE, dissent, protest.
**2.** [To mean] — *Syn.* purpose, intend, aim; see **mean** 1, **intend.**
**3.** [To offer marriage] — *Syn.* offer marriage, ask in marriage, make a proposal, ask for the hand of, press one's suit, pop the question*, fire the question*.
See Synonym Study at INTEND.

**proposed,** *modif.* — *Syn.* projected, prospective, advised, scheduled, expected, arranged, advanced, suggested, moved, proffered, put forward, submitted, recommended, urged, volunteered, pressed, intended, determined, anticipated, designed, schemed, purposed, considered, referred to, contingent; see also **planned.**

**proposition,** *n.* **1.** [A proposal] — *Syn.* proposal, scheme, project, suggestion; see **plan** 2, **proposal** 1, 2, **suggestion** 1.
**2.** [A statement set forth] — *Syn.* premise, thesis, theorem, position, resolution, statement; see also **declaration** 1, 2, **doctrine** 1, **hypothesis.**
See Synonym Study at PROPOSAL.

**proposition,** *v.* **1.** [To propose] — *Syn.* offer, recommend, suggest; see **propose** 1.
**2.** [To make sexual advances] — *Syn.* make overtures, make an indecent proposal, make a pass; see **solicit** 3.

**proprietary,** *modif.* — *Syn.* fashionable, restrictive, established; see **exclusive.**

**proprietor,** *n.* — *Syn.* owner, titleholder, master, proprietary; see **owner, possessor.**

**propriety,** *n.* **1.** [Suitability] — *Syn.* aptness, suitability, advisability, accordance, agreeableness, recommendability, compatibility, correspondence, consonance, seemliness, appropriateness, congruity, modesty, good breeding, dignity, concord, harmony, expedience, convenience, pleasantness, welcomeness; see also **fitness** 1. — *Ant.* INCONSISTENCY, incongruity, inappropriateness.
**2.** [Conventional conduct] — *Syn.* decorum, good manners, good behavior, correctness; see **behavior** 1, **decorum.**
See Synonym Study at DECORUM.

**propulsion,** *n.* — *Syn.* push, impulsion, impetus, momentum, drive; see also **thrust** 3.

**prorate,** *n.* — *Syn.* allocate, divide, allot; see **distribute** 1.

**prosaic,** *modif.* — *Syn.* common, mundane, trite; see **dull** 4.

**proscribe,** *v.* — *Syn.* banish, outlaw, exile; see **forbid.**

**prose,** *n.* fiction, non-fiction, composition; see **exposition** 2, **literature** 2, **story, writing** 2.

**prosecute,** *v.* **1.** [To pursue] — *Syn.* follow up, put through, execute, finish; see **continue** 1.
**2.** [Involve in a legal action] — *Syn.* contest, indict, involve in litigation, bring to justice; see **sue.**

**prosecution,** *n.* **1.** [The act of furthering a project] — *Syn.* pursuit, pursuance, undertaking; see **achievement** 2, **performance** 1.
**2.** [The prosecuting party in a criminal action] — *Syn.* state, government, prosecuting agent, prosecuting attorney, state's attorney, district attorney, DA*; see also **accuser, lawyer.**

**proselyte,** *n.* — *Syn.* neophyte, disciple, convert; see **follower.**

**prosody,** *n.* — *Syn.* versification, metrics, poem; see **poetry.**

**prospect,** *n.* **1.** [A view] — *Syn.* sight, landscape, vista; see **view** 1.
**2.** [Probability; *usually plural*] — *Syn.* likelihood, chance; see **possibility** 2, **probability.**
**3.** [A probable future] — *Syn.* expectancy, promise, presumption, hope; see **anticipation** 1, **forecast, outlook** 2.
**4.** [A possible candidate] — *Syn.* possibility, likely person, interested party; see **candidate, recruit.**
**in prospect** — *Syn.* hoped for, planned, in the offing, anticipated; see **expected** 2.

**prospective,** *modif.* — *Syn.* considered, hoped for, promised; see **planned, proposed.**

**prospectus,** *n.* — *Syn.* outline, design, scheme; see **plan** 1.

**prosper,** *v.* — *Syn.* become rich, become wealthy, be enriched, thrive, turn out well, fare well, do well, be fortunate, have good fortune, flourish, get on, rise, fatten, batten, increase, bear fruit, bloom, blossom, flower, make money, make a fortune, benefit, advance, gain, make good*, do right by oneself*, make one's mark*, roll in the lap of luxury*, feather one's nest*, come along*, catch on*, come on*, do wonders*; see also **succeed** 1.

**prosperity,** *n.* **1.** [Good fortune] — *Syn.* accomplishment, victory, successfulness; see **success** 2.
**2.** [Inflation] — *Syn.* expansion, exorbitance, affluence; see **increase** 1.

**prosperous,** *modif.* — *Syn.* flourishing, wealthy, well-off, well-to-do; see **rich** 1.

**prostitute,** *n.* — *Syn.* whore, call girl, hustler, harlot, strumpet, lewd woman, bawd, streetwalker, loose woman, fallen woman, courtesan, abandoned woman, concubine, vice girl, *fille de joie* (French), tramp, slut, lady of assignation, tart*, hooker*, lady of the evening*, bimbo*, pro*, white slave*, *poule* (French)*; see also **criminal.**

**prostitution,** *n.* — *Syn.* whoredom, hustling, harlotry, adultery, fornication, wantonness, hooking*; see also **lewdness.**

**prostrate,** *modif.* **1.** [Defenseless] — *Syn.* open, overcome, beaten; see **weak** 1, 3, 6.
**2.** [Submissive] — *Syn.* given in, obedient, subservient; see **docile.**
**3.** [Lying on the ground] — *Syn.* prone, flat, laid low; see **lying** 4, **supine** 1.
*See Synonym Study at* SUPINE.

**prostrate,** *v.* **1.** [To submit] — *Syn.* give in, obey, surrender; see **bow** 2, **yield** 1.
**2.** [To overthrow] — *Syn.* wreck, destroy, ruin; see **defeat** 2.
**3.** [To bow down] — *Syn.* fall on one's knees, bow and

scrape, kowtow, do obeisance; see **bow** 1.

**prostration,** *n.* **1.** [Submission] — *Syn.* surrender, downfall, destruction; see **docility.**
**2.** [Exhaustion] — *Syn.* tiredness, weariness, collapse; see **lassitude.**

**prosy,** *modif.* — *Syn.* stale, trite, common, prosaic; see **dull** 4.

**protagonist,** *n.* — *Syn.* leading character, lead, exemplar, hero, heroine, warrior, combatant; see also **hero** 1, **idol** 2.

**protean,** *modif.* — *Syn.* mutable, variable, unsettled; see **changeable** 2.

**protect,** *v.* — *Syn.* shield, guard, preserve; see **defend** 1, 2.

**protected,** *modif.* — *Syn.* shielded, safeguarded, cared for, watched over, preserved, defended, guarded, secured, kept safe, sheltered, harbored, screened, under the aegis of, fostered, cherished, ensconced, curtained, shaded, disguised, camouflaged; see also **covered** 1, **safe** 1. — *Ant.* WEAK, insecure, unsheltered.

**protection,** *n.* **1.** [A covering] — *Syn.* shield, screen, camouflage; see **shelter.**
**2.** [A surety] — *Syn.* certainty, safeguard, safekeeping, assurance, invulnerability, impregnability, reassurance, security, stability, strength; see also **guaranty** 2. — *Ant.* insecurity, weakness, frailty.

**protective,** *modif.* — *Syn.* protecting, emergency, as a last resort, having built-in protection, guarding, shielding.

**protector,** *n.* — *Syn.* champion, defender, patron, sponsor, safeguard, benefactor, supporter, advocate, partisan, guardian angel, guard, shield, bulwark; guide, philosopher, friend; Maecenas, abettor, savior, stand-by, promoter, mediator, friend at court, counsel, second, backer, upholder, sympathizer, tower of strength in time of need, tutelary, genius, big brother*, big sister*, angel*, cover*, front*; see also **guardian.**

**protectorate,** *n.* **1.** [Protection] — *Syn.* surety, guidance, jurisdiction; see **protection** 2.
**2.** [Province] — *Syn.* mandate, colony, dominion; see **territory** 2.

**protein,** *n.* — *Syn.* proteid, amino acid, nitrogenous matter.

**protest,** *n.* **1.** [Objection] — *Syn.* remonstrance, exception, denial, compliant; see **objection** 1.
**2.** [Public demonstration] — *Syn.* mass meeting, rally, demonstration, peace demonstration, draft demonstration, peace rally, race riot, clamor, tumult, turmoil, moratorium, sit-in*, teach-in*, study-in*, mill-in*, love-in*; see also **objection** 2.

**protest,** *v.* — *Syn.* demur, disagree, object, speak out against; see **complain** 1, **object, oppose** 1.
*See Synonym Study at* OBJECT.

**Protestant,** *n.* Protestant denominations include: Evangelist, Adventist, Baptist, Congregational, Episcopal, Lutheran, Methodist, Unitarian, Anglican, Presbyterian, Pentecostal.

**protestant,** *modif.* — *Syn.* evangelical, reformed, reform, non-Catholic, new; Adventist, Baptist, Congregational, Congregationalist, etc.; see also **Protestant,** *n.*

**protester,** *n.* — *Syn.* demonstrator, heckler, dissident, militant, rebel, reformer; see also **agitator, liberal** 2, **radical.**

**protocol,** *n.* **1.** [Contract] — *Syn.* obligation, compact, treaty; see **contract.**
**2.** [Standards] — *Syn.* order, rules, etiquette; see **custom** 1, 2.

**prototype,** *n.* — *Syn.* criterion, ideal, archetype; see **model** 1.

**protract,** *v.* — *Syn.* postpone, defer, extend, procrastinate; see **delay** 1.
*See Synonym Study at* EXTEND.

**protrude,** *v.* — *Syn.* come through, stick out, jut out, swell, point, obtrude, project, extrude, stick up, distend, pop out★.

**protrusion,** *n.* — *Syn.* bulge, projection, protuberance; see **bulge, projection** 1.
*See Synonym Study at* PROJECTION.

**protuberance,** *n.* — *Syn.* bump, knob, jutting; see **bulge, projection** 1.
*See Synonym Study at* PROJECTION.

**proud,** *modif.* **1.** [Having a creditable self-respect] — *Syn.* self-respecting, self-sufficient, self-reliant, independent, honorable, principled, dignified, stately, noble, lordly, aristocratic, lofty, exalted, impressive, imposing, fine, splendid, mettlesome, spirited, high-spirited, self-esteeming, looking one in the face, looking one in the eye, having no false modesty, pleased with oneself, holding up one's head.
**2.** [Egotistic] — *Syn.* arrogant, haughty, supercilious, conceited, egotistical, vain, vainglorious, insolent, overbearing, disdainful, imperious, self-important, snobbish, superior, grand, lordly, aristocratic, magisterial, cavalier, overweening, overbearing, high-handed, pompous, immodest, boastful, self-satisfied, complacent, smug, standoffish, aloof, stuck-up★, snooty★, on one's high horse★, high and mighty★, high-hat★, uppity★, hoity-toity★, puffed up with pride★, swell-headed★, proud as a peacock★; see also **egotistic** 2. — *Ant.* HUMBLE, unpretentious, unassuming.
**3.** [Feeling satisfaction] — *Syn.* satisfied, pleased, gratified, exultant; see **happy** 1, **satisfied.**
**do one proud**★ — *Syn.* entertain lavishly, treat well, provide for; see **entertain** 2.
**do oneself proud**★ — *Syn.* achieve, prosper, advance; see **succeed** 1.

---

**SYN.** — **proud** is the broadest term in this comparison, ranging in implication from proper self-esteem or pride to an overweening opinion of one's importance [too *proud* to beg, *proud* as a peacock]; **arrogant** implies an aggressive, unwarranted assertion of superior importance or privileges [the *arrogant* colonel]; **haughty** implies such consciousness of high station, rank, etc. as is displayed in scorn of those one considers beneath one [a *haughty* dowager]; **insolent**, less commonly used now with this meaning, implies both haughtiness and contempt, esp. as manifested in behavior or speech that insults or affronts others [she showed an *insolent* disregard for the servant's feelings]; **overbearing** implies an oppressively or haughtily domineering manner [an *overbearing* supervisor]; **supercilious** stresses an aloof, scornful manner toward others [a *supercilious* intellectual snob]; **disdainful** implies even stronger and more overt feelings of scorn for that which is regarded as beneath one

---

**proudly,** *modif.* — *Syn.* boastfully, haughtily, insolently, contemptuously, like a lord; see also **arrogantly.**

**provable,** *modif.* — *Syn.* inferable, deductible, testable, demonstrable, in evidence; see also **certain** 3, **conclusive.**

**prove,** *v.* — *Syn.* justify, substantiate, authenticate, corroborate, testify, explain, attest, show, warrant, uphold, determine, settle, fix, certify, back, sustain, validate, bear out, affirm, confirm, make evident, convince, evidence, be evidence of, witness, declare, testify, betoken, have a case, manifest, demonstrate, document, estab-

lish, settle once and for all, (just) go to show★; see also **verify.** — *Ant.* DISPROVE, break down, disqualify.

**proved,** *modif.* — *Syn.* confirmed, established, demonstrated; see **establish** 3.

**provenance,** *n.* — *Syn.* birthplace, derivation, home; see **origin** 2.

**proverb,** *n.* — *Syn.* maxim, adage, aphorism, precept, saw, saying, motto, dictum, text, witticism, repartee, axiom, truism, apothegm, byword, catch phrase, mot, epigram, moral, folk wisdom, platitude.
*See Synonym Study at* SAYING.

**proverbial,** *modif.* — *Syn.* commonplace, axiomatic, current, general, unquestioned; see also **common** 1, **dull** 4, **familiar** 1.

**proverbially,** *modif.* — *Syn.* as the saying is, as they say, as the story goes, aphoristically, axiomatically, epigrammatically, platitudinously, traditionally; see also **customarily.**

**provide,** *v.* **1.** [To supply] — *Syn.* furnish, equip, grant, replenish, provide with, accommodate, care for, indulge with, favor with, contribute, give, proffer, outfit, fit, stock, store, minister, administer, render, procure, afford, present, bestow, purvey, cater, rig, rig up, fit out, fit up, provision, ration, implement. — *Ant.* REFUSE, take away, deny.
**2.** [To yield] — *Syn.* render, afford, give; see **produce** 1.

**provided,** *conj.* — *Syn.* on the assumption that, in the event, in the case that; see **if, supposing.**

**provided that,** *conj.* — *Syn.* on condition, in the event, with that understood; see **if, supposing.**

**provide for** *or* **against,** *v.* — *Syn.* make provision, make ready, prepare for, arrange, care for, support, plan ahead; see also **prepare** 1.

**providence,** *n.* — *Syn.* divine government, divine superintendence, Deity; see **god.**

**provident,** *modif.* — *Syn.* cautious, prepared, prudent, thrifty; see **judicious.**
*See Synonym Study at* THRIFTY.

**providential,** *modif.* — *Syn.* fortunate, timely, opportune; see **hopeful** 2.

**providing,** *conj.* — *Syn.* provided, in the event *or* the case that, on the assumption that; see **if, supposing.**

**providing,** *n.* — *Syn.* provision, supplying, furnishing, equipping, replenishing, replenishment, contributing, outfitting, stocking, filling, procurement, affording, presenting, preparing, preparation, arrangement, planning, putting by, laying by, laying in, putting in readiness, granting, bestowing, giving, offering, tendering, accumulating, storing, saving.

**province,** *n.* — *Syn.* area, region, dependency; see **territory** 2.

**provincial,** *modif.* — *Syn.* rude, unpolished, countrified; see **rural.**

**provincialism,** *n.* **1.** [Dialect] — *Syn.* vernacular, localism, idiosyncrasy; see **dialect.**
**2.** [Narrow-mindedness] — *Syn.* bias, intolerance, xenophobia; see **inclination** 1, **prejudice.**

**proving,** *n.* — *Syn.* trying, examining, justifying, verifying; see **testing.**

**provision,** *n.* **1.** [Arrangement] — *Syn.* preparation, outline, procurement; see **plan** 2.
**2.** [Supplies; *usually plural*] — *Syn.* stock, store, emergency; see **equipment, reserve** 1.
**3.** [A proviso] — *Syn.* stipulation, prerequisite, terms; see **requirement** 1.

**provisional,** *modif.* — *Syn.* temporary, transient, passing, ephemeral; see **temporary.**

*See Synonym Study at* TEMPORARY.

**provisionally,** *modif.* — *Syn.* conditionally, on these conditions, on certain conditions, for the time being; see **temporarily.**

**proviso,** *n.* — *Syn.* provision, clause, conditional stipulation; see **limitation** 2, **requirement** 1.

**provocation,** *n.* — *Syn.* incitement, stimulus, inducement; see **incentive.**

**provocative,** *modif.* — *Syn.* alluring, arousing, intriguing; see **interesting, stimulating.**

**provoke,** *v.* **1.** [To vex] — *Syn.* irritate, put out, aggravate; see **bother** 2.
**2.** [To incite] — *Syn.* stir, rouse, arouse, excite, stimulate, pique, incite, spur, evoke, prompt, prod, motivate, inspire, instigate, kindle, foment, stir up, whip up, galvanize; see also **incite.**
**3.** [To cause] — *Syn.* make, produce, bring about; see **begin** 1.
*See Synonym Study at* IRRITATE.

---

**SYN.** — **provoke,** in this connection, implies rather generally an arousing to some action or feeling /thought-*provoking*/; **excite** suggests a more powerful or profound stirring or moving of the thoughts or emotions /it *excites* my imagination/; **stimulate** implies arousing to increased activity as if by goading or pricking and often connotes bringing out of a state of inactivity or indifference /to *stimulate* one's enthusiasm/; **pique** suggests stimulating as if by irritating mildly /to *pique* one's curiosity/

---

**provoked,** *modif.* — *Syn.* exasperated, incensed, enraged; see **angry.**

**provoking,** *modif.* — *Syn.* vexing, annoying, tormenting; see **disturbing.**

**provost,** *n.* — *Syn.* executive, supervisor, officer; see **administrator.**

**prow,** *n.* — *Syn.* stem, head, bowsprit, fore; see **bow** 1.

**prowess,** *n.* — *Syn.* bravery, valor, intrepidity; see **courage** 1.

**prowl,** *v.* — *Syn.* slink, lurk, rove; see **sneak.**

**proximity,** *n.* — *Syn.* contiguity, concurrence, closeness, vicinity; see **nearness** 1.

**proxy,** *n.* — *Syn.* substitute, representative, deputy, surrogate; see **agent** 1, **delegate** 1.
*See Synonym Study at* AGENT.

**prude,** *n.* — *Syn.* prig, puritan, old maid, prudish person, prune*, priss*, sourpuss*, Mrs. Grundy*, stick-in-the-mud*, spoilsport*, wet blanket*, bluenose*, goody-goody*, tattletale*.

**prudence,** *n.* — *Syn.* caution, circumspection, judgment, providence, considerateness, judiciousness, sagacity, deliberation, wisdom, foresight, forethought, care, carefulness, frugality, watchfulness, precaution, heedfulness, heed, economy, husbandry, concern, conservatism, conservation, discrimination, cunning, vigilance, coolness, calculation, presence of mind; see also **discretion** 1, **tact.** — *Ant.* CARELESSNESS, imprudence, rashness.

**prudent,** *modif.* **1.** [Cautious and careful] — *Syn.* cautious, circumspect, provident, frugal; see **careful, discreet.**
**2.** [Sensible and wise] — *Syn.* discerning, sound, reasonable; see **judicious.**
*See Synonym Study at* CAREFUL.

**prudery,** *n.* — *Syn.* stuffiness, primness, priggishness, strictness; see **behavior** 1, **courtesy** 1.

**prudish,** *modif.* — *Syn.* overnice, stilted, mincing, precise, narrow-minded, illiberal, bigoted, prissy, priggish,

over-refined, fastidious, stuffy, conventional, offish, stiff, smug, strait-laced, demure, narrow, puritanical, blue-nosed*, affected, artificial, scrupulous, overexact, pedantic, pretentious, strict, rigid, rigorous, simpering, finical, finicking, finicky, squeamish, schoolgirlish, oldmaidish, like a maiden aunt, prudish as an old maid; see also **prim.** — *Ant.* SOCIABLE, broad-minded, genial.

**prune,** *n.* Varieties of prunes include: French, Stanley, Italian-Fellemberg, St. Julien, myrobalan, Bosnian; see also **fruit** 1.

**prune,** *v.* — *Syn.* lop, clip, dock; see **cut** 1.

**pry,** *v.* **1.** [To move with a lever] — *Syn.* push, lift, raise, pull, prize, move, tilt, hoist, heave, uplift, upraise, elevate, turn out, jimmy*; see also **force** 2, **open** 2.
**2.** [To endeavor to discover; *often used with* into] — *Syn.* search, ferret out, seek, ransack, reconnoiter, peep, peer, peek, snoop, gaze, look closely, spy, stare, gape, nose, be curious, inquire, stick one's nose in*, rubber*, rubberneck*; see also **hunt** 2, **meddle** 1.

**prying,** *modif.* — *Syn.* intrusive, meddlesome, nosy*; see **inquisitive, meddlesome.**
*See Synonym Study at* INQUISITIVE.

**psalm,** *n.* — *Syn.* sacred song, praise, verse; see **song.**

**psalter,** *n.* — *Syn.* the Psalms, book of psalms, psaltery; see **book** 1.

**pseudo,** *modif.* — *Syn.* imitation, counterfeit, quasi, sham; see **false** 3.

**pseudonym,** *n.* — *Syn.* pen name, anonym, assumed name; see **alias.**
*See Synonym Study at* ALIAS.

**psyche,** *n.* — *Syn.* subconscious, mind, ego, inner self, individuality, personality; see also **character** 2.

**psychedelic,** *modif.* — *Syn.* hallucinatory, mind-expanding, mind-changing, experimental, consciousness-expanding, psychotomimetic, hallucinogenic, mind-bending*, mind-blowing*, trippy*, freaky*.

**psychedelic,** *n.* — *Syn.* stimulant, mind-expanding drug, hallucinogen; see **drug** 2.

**psychiatrist,** *n.* — *Syn.* analyst, therapist, shrink*; see **doctor** 1, **psychoanalyst.**

**psychiatry,** *n.* — *Syn.* psychopathology, psychotherapeutics, psychotherapy, psychoanalysis, alienism*, mental hygiene, mental health, psychiatrics, neuropsychiatry; see also **medicine** 1, **science** 1.

**psychic,** *modif.* **1.** [Mental] — *Syn.* analytic, intellectual, psychological; see **mental** 2.
**2.** [Spiritual] — *Syn.* telepathic, mystic, immaterial; see **supernatural.**

**psycho*,** *modif.* — *Syn.* mad, crazy, psychopathic, loony*, crazed*, screwy*; see also **insane** 1.

**psychoanalysis,** *n.* — *Syn.* therapy, analysis, psychotherapy, depth psychiatry, depth psychology, dream analysis, interpretation of dreams, depth interview, psychoanalytic therapy, group therapy; see also **therapy.**

**psychoanalyst,** *n.* — *Syn.* psychiatrist, analyst, neuropsychiatrist, psychoanalyzer, alienist*, psychopathist, psychopathologist, psychometrician, headshrinker*, shrink*; see also **doctor** 1.

**psychological,** *modif.* **1.** [Mental] — *Syn.* cerebral, psychical, subconscious, subjective; see **mental** 1, 2.
**2.** [Emotional] — *Syn.* affective, irrational, psychical; see **emotional** 2.

**psychological moment,** *n.* — *Syn.* the best time, the most propitious time, the critical moment.

**psychologist,** *n.* — *Syn.* analyst, psychiatrist, clinician; see **doctor** 1, **psychoanalyst.**

**psychology,** *n.* — *Syn.* science of mind, study of personality, medicine, therapy; see **science** 1, **social science**.

Branches and varieties of psychology include: rational, applied, developmental, clinical, existential, functional, structural, self, dynamic, organismic, motor, physiological, abnormal, experimental, educational, differential, Gestalt, Freudian, Adlerian, Jungian, genetic, applied, academic, popular, introspective, analytical, comparative, child, animal, group, individual, social, behaviorism, psychotherapy, psychometrics, psychodynamics, psychodiagnosis, parapsychology.

**psychopath,** *n.* — *Syn.* psychopathic personality, sociopath, lunatic, mental case, bedlamite★, maniac; see also **fool** 1, **madman**.

Types of psychopathic disorders include: psychotic, paranoid, schizoid, schizophrenic, manic-depressive, hysterical, cyclothymic, compulsive, obsessive-compulsive, addictive, passive-aggressive.

**psychopathic,** *modif.* — *Syn.* psychotic, deranged, (mentally) unbalanced; see **insane** 1.

**psychotic,** *modif.* — *Syn.* insane, mad, psychopathic; see **insane** 1.

**pub,** *n.* — *Syn.* public house, bar, drinking establishment; see **saloon** 3.

**puberty,** *n.* — *Syn.* boyhood, pubescence, adolescence; see **youth** 1.

**public,** *modif.* **1.** [Open to the public] — *Syn.* free to all, without charge, unrestricted, not private, known; see also **free** 4.

**2.** [Owned by the public] — *Syn.* governmental, government, civil, civic, common, communal, publicly owned, municipal, metropolitan, state, federal, country, city, township, deeded in perpetuity. — *Ant.* PRIVATE, personal, restricted.

**public,** *n.* — *Syn.* people, society, the community, populace, citizens, the nation; see also **people** 3.

**in public** — *Syn.* candidly, plainly, above board; see **openly** 1.

**publication,** *n.* **1.** [The act of making public] — *Syn.* writing, printing, broadcasting, announcement, notification, promulgation, issuing, statement, divulgation, ventilation, acquaintance, advisement, advertisement, communication, revelation, disclosure, discovery, dissemination, making current, making available.

**2.** [Something published] — *Syn.* edition, organ, printing, paper; see **book** 1, **magazine** 2, **newspaper**.

**publicist,** *n.* — *Syn.* publicity agent, press agent, publicity person, agent, public relations consultant, PR person★, publicizer, advance man, flack★.

**publicity,** *n.* **1.** [Public distribution] — *Syn.* notoriety, currency, publicness; see **distribution** 1.

**2.** [Free advertising] — *Syn.* public relations copy, release, report; see **advertising** 1, **reporting**.

**3.** [Activity intended to advertise] — *Syn.* promotion, promoting, publicizing, advertising, announcing, broadcasting, pushing, billing, making use of media, clout★, puff★, boost★, plug★; see also **advertisement** 1, 2.

**publicize,** *v.* — *Syn.* announce, broadcast, make public, promulgate; see **advertise** 1.

**publicly,** *modif.* — *Syn.* candidly, plainly, aboveboard; see **openly** 1.

**public opinion,** *n.* — *Syn.* public pressure, power of the press, popular pressure; see **force** 3, **influence, opinion** 1.

**public relations,** *n.* — *Syn.* promotion, public image, favorable climate (of opinion); see **advertising** 1, **propaganda**.

**public-spirited,** *modif.* — *Syn.* altruistic, humanitarian, openhanded; see **generous** 1.

**public utility,** *n.* — *Syn.* public service, natural monopoly, light and power; see **utilities**.

**publish,** *v.* **1.** [To print and distribute] — *Syn.* reprint, issue, reissue, distribute, bring out, write, do publishing, bring into the open, get off, get out, put to press, put forth, put about, enter the publishing field, own a publishing house, send forth, give out, give forth; see also **print** 2.

**2.** [To make known] — *Syn.* announce, promulgate, declare, proclaim; see **advertise** 1, **declare** 1.

*See Synonym Study at* DECLARE.

**published,** *modif.* — *Syn.* written, printed, made public, circulated, broached, proclaimed, promulgated, propagated, pronounced, ventilated, divulged, made current, made known, broadcast, circulated, spread abroad, disseminated, got out, appeared, released, coming forth, seeing the light, presented, offered, voiced, blazoned, noised abroad, given to the world, given publicity, brought before the public; see also **advertised, announced, issued, reported**. — *Ant.* UNKNOWN, unpublished, unwritten.

**publisher,** *n.* — *Syn.* publicist, businessman, administrator; see **journalist**.

**puck,** *n.* — *Syn.* fay, sprite, elf; see **fairy** 1.

**pucker,** *n.* — *Syn.* pleat, tuck, crease, furrow; see **fold** 1, **wrinkle**.

**pucker,** *v.* — *Syn.* pleat, gather, shirr, condense, squeeze, purse; see also **contract** 1, **wrinkle** 1.

**puckish,** *modif.* — *Syn.* impish, mischievous, playful; see **naughty**.

**pudding,** *n.* — *Syn.* mousse, custard, junket, tapioca; see **dessert**.

Kinds of pudding include: blanc mange, floating island, flan, prune whip, charlotte russe, tapioca, custard, apple snow, fruit cobbler, rice, bread, batter, cornstarch, fig, plum, banana cream, Christmas, chocolate, vanilla, butterscotch, Indian, fruit sago, graham pudding.

**puddle,** *n.* — *Syn.* plash, mud puddle, rut; see **pool** 1.

**pudgy,** *modif.* — *Syn.* chubby, chunky, stout, plump; see **fat** 1.

**puerile,** *modif.* — *Syn.* boyish, young, inexperienced, immature; see **childish** 1, **naive, young** 2.

*See Synonym Study at* YOUNG.

**puerility,** *n.* — *Syn.* absurdity, frivolity, rubbish; see **nonsense** 2, **stupidity** 2.

**puff,** *n.* — *Syn.* whiff, sudden gust, quick blast; see **wind**.

**puff,** *v.* **1.** [To flatter] — *Syn.* commend, admire, congratulate; see **praise** 1.

**2.** [To inflate] — *Syn.* distend, enlarge, swell; see **fill** 1.

**3.** [To blow] — *Syn.* exhale, pant, whiff; see **blow** 1.

**4.** [To smoke] — *Syn.* inhale, draw, drag, pull; see **smoke** 2.

**puffed,** *modif.* — *Syn.* expanded, swollen, bloated; see **full** 1, **increased, inflated**.

**puffy,** *modif.* **1.** [Windy] — *Syn.* airy, gusty, breezy; see **windy** 1.

**2.** [Conceited] — *Syn.* egocentric, pompous, mettlesome; see **egotistic** 2.

**3.** [Swollen] — *Syn.* distended, expanded, blown; see **full** 1, **increased, inflated**.

**pugilism,** *n.* — *Syn.* boxing, fighting, sparring, fisticuffs; see **boxing, sport** 3.

**pugilist,** *n.* — *Syn.* boxer, prize fighter, contender; see **fighter** 2.

**pugnacious,** *modif.* — *Syn.* belligerent, defiant, antagonistic, combative; see **quarrelsome** 1, **rebellious** 2, 3.

*See Synonym Study at* BELLIGERENT.

**puke,** *v.* — *Syn.* throw up, retch, barf★; see **vomit**.

**pull,** *n.* **1.** [The act of pulling] — *Syn.* tow, drag, haul, jerk, twitch, wrench, extraction, drawing, rending, tearing, uprooting, weeding, row, paddle; snake*, yank*.

**2.** [Exerted force] — *Syn.* work, strain, tug; see **strength** 1.

**3.** [*Influence] — *Syn.* leverage, sway, weight, authority; see **influence** 2.

**pull,** *v.* **1.** [To exert force so as to move] — *Syn.* draw, drag, tug, haul, tow, lug, trail, attract, lure, stretch, strain, wrench, yank, tear, rend; see also **draw** 1.

**2.** [To remove by pulling] — *Syn.* pick, extract, uproot, pluck out; see **draw** 1, **remove** 1.

**3.** [To incline] — *Syn.* slope, tend, move toward; see **lean** 1.

---

*SYN.* — **pull** is the broad, general term of this list, meaning to exert force so as to cause to move toward or after the source of the force; **draw** suggests a smoother, more even motion than **pull** /he *drew* his sword from its scabbard/; **drag** implies the slow pulling of something heavy, connoting great resistance in the thing pulled /she *dragged* the desk across the floor/; **tug** suggests strenuous, often intermittent effort in pulling but does not necessarily connote success in moving the object /I *tugged* at the rope to no avail/; **haul** implies sustained effort in transporting something heavy, often mechanically /to *haul* furniture in a truck/; **tow** implies pulling by means of a rope or cable /to *tow* a stalled automobile/

---

**pull apart,** *v.* — *Syn.* separate, split, force apart; see **divide** 1.

**pull away,** *v.* — *Syn.* depart, pull off, go; see **leave** 1.

**pull down,** *v.* — *Syn.* raze, wreck, remove; see **destroy** 1.

**pullet,** *n.* — *Syn.* young hen, fowl, rooster; see **bird** 1, **chicken** 1.

**pulley,** *n.* — *Syn.* sheave, block, lift, lifter, crowbar, crow, pry; see also **tool** 1.

**pulling,** *n.* — *Syn.* plucking, shaking, contesting, twitching, struggling, towing, stretching.

**pull into,** *v.* — *Syn.* come in, land, make a landing; see **arrive** 1.

**Pullman,** *n.* — *Syn.* sleeping car, chair car, sleeper; see **car** 2, **train** 2.

**pull off,** *v.* **1.** [To remove] — *Syn.* detach, separate, yank off, wrench off; see **remove** 1.

**2.** [*To achieve] — *Syn.* accomplish, manage, succeed; see **achieve** 1.

**pull oneself together,** *v.* — *Syn.* recover, revive, compose oneself, get on one's feet*; see **improve** 2.

**pull out,** *v.* — *Syn.* go, depart, stop participating; see **leave** 1, **stop** 2.

**pull over,** *v.* — *Syn.* drive or turn to the side, pull up, park; see **stop** 1, **turn** 6.

**pull rank*,** *v.* — *Syn.* order, demand, bid; see **command** 1.

**pull through*,** *v.* — *Syn.* get better, get over, triumph; see **recover** 3, **survive** 1.

**pull up,** *v.* **1.** [To remove] — *Syn.* dislodge, elevate, pull out, dig out; see **remove** 1.

**2.** [To stop] — *Syn.* arrive, come to a halt, come to a stop, get there; see **stop** 1.

**pulmonary,** *modif.* — *Syn.* of the lungs, pneumonic, lunglike, affecting the lungs, consumptive, lobar.

**pulp,** *n.* **1.** [Fleshy fruit] — *Syn.* flesh, marrow, sarcocarp, pith, pap, mash, sponge, paste, pomace, dough, batter, curd, grume, jam, poultice; see also **flesh** 2.

**2.** [A ground mixture] — *Syn.* mash, paste, wood pulp,

paste.

**3.** [Sensational writing] — *Syn.* tabloid, yellow journalism, romance, thriller, pornography, soft porn*.

**pulpit,** *n.* **1.** [The ministry] — *Syn.* priesthood, clergy, ecclesiastics; see **ministry** 2.

**2.** [A platform in a church] — *Syn.* lectern, rostrum, stage; see **platform.**

**pulpy,** *modif.* — *Syn.* smooth, thick, fleshy; see **soft** 2.

**pulsate,** *v.* — *Syn.* throb, quiver, vibrate; see **beat** 3.

**pulsation,** *n.* — *Syn.* quiver, shiver, throb; see **beat** 2.

**pulse,** *n.* — *Syn.* pulsation, vibration, oscillation, throb; see **beat** 2.

**pulverize,** *v.* — *Syn.* grind, crush, smash, comminute, triturate, levigate; see also **grind** 1.

**pummel,** *v.* — *Syn.* beat, pound, trounce; see **beat** 1, 2, **hit** 1.

*See Synonym Study at* BEAT.

**pump,** *n.* Types of pumps include: air, chain, force, Geissler, lift, mercury, sand, shell, Sprengel, suction, sump, fuel, oil, heat, vacuum, oscillating, rotary displacement, piston, centrifugal, volute centrifugal, turbine centrifugal, jet, bucket; pulsometer, hydraulic ram; see also **machine** 1, **tool** 1.

**pump,** *v.* — *Syn.* elevate, draw out, draw up, tap; see **draw** 1.

**pun,** *n.* — *Syn.* conceit, witticism, quip, quibble, double-entendre, play upon words; see also **joke** 2.

**punch,** *n.* **1.** [A blow] — *Syn.* thrust, knock, stroke; see **blow** 1.

**2.** [An instrument for denting or perforating]. Types of punches include: blacksmith's, cooper's, nail, leather, ticket, duplex, center, drift, belt, blanking, culling, forming, drawing, redrawing, bending, coining, embossing, extruding, curling, seeming, trimming, doming, tracer, grounder, planisher, perloir, beading; see also **tool** 1.

**punch,** *v.* **1.** [To hit] — *Syn.* strike, knock, thrust against; see **hit** 1.

**2.** [To perforate] — *Syn.* pierce, puncture, bore; see **penetrate** 1.

**punched,** *modif.* — *Syn.* perforated, dented, pierced, pricked, punctured, needled, stamped, embossed, imprinted, bored, dinted, wounded, bitten, tapped, transpierced, impaled, pinked, spiked, gored, speared, stabbed, spitted, stuck.

**punctilious,** *modif.* — *Syn.* formal, particular, exact; see **careful.**

**punctual,** *modif.* — *Syn.* prompt, precise, particular, on time, on schedule, exact, timely, seasonable, expeditious, periodic, regular, cyclic, dependable, recurrent, constant, steady, scrupulous, punctilious, meticulous, under the wire*, on the nose*; see also **accurate** 2, **reliable** 2. — *Ant.* UNRELIABLE, careless, desultory.

**punctuality,** *n.* — *Syn.* readiness, promptness, steadiness; see **preparation** 2, **regularity.**

**punctuation,** *n.* Marks of punctuation include: period, colon, semicolon, comma, question mark, exclamation point, parentheses, dash, brackets, apostrophe, hyphen, quotation marks, quote marks, brace, ellipsis dots, virgule, slash, asterisk.

**puncture,** *n.* **1.** [Hole] — *Syn.* cut, break, perforation; see **hole** 1.

**2.** [A flat tire] — *Syn.* flat, leak, slow leak.

**puncture,** *v.* — *Syn.* prick, perforate, pierce; see **penetrate** 1.

**punctured,** *modif.* — *Syn.* deflated, let down, no longer inflated; see **damaged, reduced** 2.

**pundit,** *n.* — *Syn.* intellectual, savant, thinker, mavin, theorist, pedant, high-brow, know-it-all*; see also **scholar** 2.

**pungent,** *modif.* — *Syn.* sharp, acid, tart; see **sour** 1.

**punish,** *v.* — *Syn.* discipline, correct, chastise, chasten, castigate, penalize, sentence, train, reprove, scold, lecture, fine, incarcerate, imprison, immure, expel, execute, exile, behead, hang, electrocute, dismiss, disbar, disbench, defrock, whip, masthead, keelhaul, smite, spank, paddle, beat, thrash, trounce, flog, birch, switch, cuff, inflict penalty, visit punishment, blacklist, blackball, make an example of, give it to*, come down hard on*, attend to*, crack down on*, make it hot for*, pitch into*, give a dressing-down*, light into*, lick*, bring to book*, teach one a lesson*, lower the boom*, ground*, throw the book at*, give one one's comeuppance*, give what for*, fix*; see also **banish** 1, **beat** 2, **censure, imprison, kill** 1, **scold.**

*SYN.* — **punish** implies the infliction of some penalty on a wrongdoer and generally connotes retribution rather than correction /to *punish* a murderer by hanging/; **discipline** suggests punishment that is intended to control or to establish habits of self-control /to *discipline* a naughty child/; **correct** suggests punishment for the purpose of overcoming faults /to *correct* unruly pupils/; **chastise** may imply severe rebuke or, more usually, corporal punishment and connotes both retribution and correction; **castigate** now implies punishment by severe public criticism or censure /to *castigate* a corrupt official/; **chasten** implies the infliction of tribulation in order to make obedient, meek, subdued, etc./"He *chastens* and hastens His will to make known", a *chastening* experience/

**punishable,** *modif.* — *Syn.* culpable, criminal, condemned; see **guilty** 1.

**punished,** *modif.* — *Syn.* corrected, disciplined, chastened, penalized, sentenced, trained, reproved, chastised, castigated, lectured, scolded, imprisoned, incarcerated, immured, expelled, exiled, transported, dismissed, debarred, disbenched, defrocked, whipped, spanked, trounced, flogged, birched, switched, cuffed, cracked down on*, given the deuce*, pitched into*, grounded*, licked*, given one's deserts*; see also **beaten** 1, **confined** 3, **executed** 2.— *Ant.* CLEARED, exonerated, released.

**punishment,** *n.* — *Syn.* correction, discipline, reproof, penalty, infliction, suffering, deprivation, unhappiness, trial, penance, retribution, deserts, just deserts, mortification, sequestration, disciplinary action, amercement, fine, mulct, reparation, forfeiture, forfeit, confiscation, dose of strap oil*, carrot-and-stick treatment*, bit of one's mind*, rap on the knuckles*; see also **execution** 2, **sentence** 1.— *Ant.* FREEDOM, exoneration, release.

**punitive,** *modif.* — *Syn.* punitory, vindictive, disciplinary; see **penal.**

**punk*,** *modif.* — *Syn.* bad, inadequate, not good; see **poor** 2.

**punk*,** *n.* — *Syn.* hoodlum, hood*, juvenile delinquent, JD*, brat, hooligan, ruffian, bully; see also **criminal, rascal.**

**puny,** *modif.* — *Syn.* feeble, inferior, diminutive; see **weak** 1.

**pup,** *n.* — *Syn.* puppy, whelp, young dog; see **animal** 2, **dog** 1.

**pupa,** *n.* — *Syn.* nymph, chrysalis, cocoon; see **cover** 2, **insect.**

**pupil,** *n.* — *Syn.* student, schoolchild, disciple, protegé; see **follower, student.**

See Synonym Study at STUDENT.

**puppet,** *n.* **1.** [A marionette] — *Syn.* manikin, figurine, moppet; see **doll.**

**2.** [An instrument] — *Syn.* follower, pawn, creature, servant; see **victim** 2.

**puppetry,** *n.* — *Syn.* exhibition, mummery, play; see **act** 2, **performance** 2, **show** 1.

**puppy,** *n.* — *Syn.* pup, whelp, young dog; see **animal** 2, **dog** 1.

**purchasable,** *modif.* **1.** [Marketable] — *Syn.* salable, on sale, for sale; see **commercial** 1, **retail.**

**2.** [Corrupt] — *Syn.* bribable, having one's price, on the take*; see **corrupt** 1, **dishonest** 1, **mean** 3.

**purchase,** *n.* **1.** [The act of buying] — *Syn.* acquirement, procurement, getting, obtaining, shopping, installment plan, bargaining, marketing, investing; see also **acquisition** 1, **buying.**

**2.** [Something bought] — *Syn.* property, possession, gain, booty, acquirement, investment; see also **acquisition** 2, **bargain** 2.

**purchase,** *v.* — *Syn.* obtain, acquire, buy up; see **buy** 1.

**purchaser,** *n.* — *Syn.* shopper, obtainer, customer; see **buyer.**

**purchasing,** *n.* — *Syn.* obtaining, procuring, acquiring; see **buying.**

**pure,** *modif.* **1.** [Not mixed] — *Syn.* unmixed, unadulterated, unalloyed, unmingled, simple, clear, genuine, undiluted, classic, real, true, fair, bright, unclouded, transparent, limpid, lucid, straight, pellucid, neat; see also **clear** 2, **genuine** 1, **simple** 1, **transparent** 1.— *Ant.* MIXED, mingled, blended.

**2.** [Clean] — *Syn.* immaculate, spotless, stainless, unspotted, germ-free, unstained, unadulterated, unblemished, untarnished, unsoiled, disinfected, sterilized, pasteurized, uncontaminated, sanitary, unpolluted, unsullied, purified, refined.— *Ant.* DIRTY, sullied, contaminated.

**3.** [Chaste] — *Syn.* virgin, continent, celibate, chaste; see **chaste** 3.

**4.** [Innocent] — *Syn.* sinless, spotless, unsullied; see **chaste** 2, **innocent** 4.

**5.** [Theoretical] — *Syn.* unproved, tentative, philosophical; see **theoretical.**

**6.** [Absolute] — *Syn.* sheer, utter, complete; see **absolute** 1.

See Synonym Study at CHASTE.

**purebred,** *modif.* — *Syn.* pedigreed, registered, full-blooded; see **thoroughbred.**

**purely,** *modif.* **1.** [Entirely] — *Syn.* totally, essentially, wholly, thoroughly; see **completely.**

**2.** [Simply] — *Syn.* merely, plainly, genuinely, solely.

**purgative,** *n.* — *Syn.* physic, emetic, purge; see **laxative.**

**purgatory,** *n.* — *Syn.* limbo, hell, torture, penance, hell on earth, place of the dead, hereafter; see also **hell** 1.

**purge,** *n.* **1.** [Cleansing] — *Syn.* abstersion, clarification, expurgation; see **cleaning, purification.**

**2.** [Excretion] — *Syn.* defecation, evacuation, catharsis; see **excretion** 1.

**3.** [Elimination] — *Syn.* eradication, disposal, murder, removal, liquidation, extermination, annihilation, extirpation, assassination, abolition, extinction, disposition, expulsion, ejection; see also **destruction** 1.

**purge,** *v.* **1.** [To cleanse] — *Syn.* clear, purify, clarify; see **clean, excrete.**

**2.** [To eliminate] — *Syn.* liquidate, exterminate, dispose of; see **abolish, forbid, kill** 1, **prevent.**

**purification,** *n.* **1.** [Cleansing] — *Syn.* purifying, ablution, lustration, purgation, catharsis, refinement, laving, washing, bathing, lavation, disinfection; see also **cleaning**. — *Ant.* POLLUTION, defilement, contamination.

**2.** [Absolution] — *Syn.* redemption, pardoning, sanctification; see **forgiveness**.

**purify,** *v.* **1.** [To cleanse] — *Syn.* chasten, clear, refine, wash, disinfect, fumigate, deodorize, depurate, clarify, deterge, rarify, sublimate, edulcorate, purge, filter; see also **clean**.

**2.** [To absolve] — *Syn.* redeem, pardon, hallow, beatify; see **excuse, forgive** 1, 2.

**puritan,** *modif.* — *Syn.* puritanical, strict, proper; see **prejudiced**.

**puritanical,** *modif.* — *Syn.* strict, rigid, prudish; see **severe** 2.

**puritanism,** *n.* — *Syn.* austerity, prudishness, strictness; see **severity**.

**purity,** *n.* **1.** [The state of being pure] — *Syn.* pureness, cleanness, cleanliness, immaculateness, stainlessness, whiteness, clearness, untaintedness, immaculacy, unsulliedness.

**2.** [Innocence] — *Syn.* artlessness, guilelessness, blamelessness; see **innocence** 2, **simplicity** 2, **sincerity**.

**3.** [Chastity] — *Syn.* abstemiousness, continence, self-command; see **chastity, virtue** 1.

**purlieu,** *n.* **1.** [Border] — *Syn.* fringe, outskirts, periphery; see **boundary, edge** 1.

**2.** [Environment] — *Syn.* vicinity, locale, district; see **area** 2, **neighborhood**.

**purple,** *modif.* — *Syn.* purplish, purply, purpled, reddish blue, bluish red; see also **red, blue** 1.

Hues of purple include: lilac, violet, mauve, heliotrope, magenta, plum, lavender, orchid, grape, puce, pomegranate, royal purple, Tyrian purple, Indian purple, dahlia purple, wine, solferino.

**purport,** *n.* — *Syn.* import, significance, intent; see **meaning**.

**purport,** *v.* — *Syn.* indicate, imply, claim to be; see **mean** 1.

**purpose,** *n.* **1.** [Aim] — *Syn.* intention, end, goal, mission, objective, object, idea, design, hope, resolve, meaning, view, scope, desire, dream, expectation, ambition, intent, destination, direction, scheme, prospect, proposal, target, aspiration; see also **plan** 2.

**2.** [Resolution] — *Syn.* tenacity, constancy, persistence; see **confidence** 2, **determination** 2, **faith** 1.

**on purpose** — *Syn.* purposefully, intentionally, designedly; see **deliberately**.

**to good purpose** — *Syn.* profitably, usefully, advantageously; see **helpfully**.

**to little (or no) purpose** — *Syn.* profitlessly, uselessly, worthlessly; see **unnecessarily**.

**to the purpose** — *Syn.* to the point, pertinent, apt; see **relevant**.

*SYN.* — **purpose** connotes a defined or specific resolution or determination in the plan had in mind /I have a *purpose* in writing you/; **intention** is the general word implying a having something in mind as a plan or design, or referring to the plan had in mind; **intent**, a somewhat formal term common in legal usage, connotes more deliberation /assault with *intent* to kill/; **aim** refers to a specific intention and connotes a directing of all efforts toward this /his *aim* is to become a doctor/; **goal** suggests laborious effort in striving to attain something /the presidency was the *goal* of his ambition/; **end** emphasizes the final result one hopes to achieve as distinct from the process of achieving it /does a desirable *end* ever justify the use of immoral means?/; **object** is

used of an end that is the direct result of a need or desire /the *object* of the discussion was to arouse controversy/; **objective** refers to a specific end that is capable of being reached /her immediate *objective* is to pass the course/

---

**purpose,** *v.* — *Syn.* intend, aim, plan, propose; see **intend** 1.

*See Synonym Study at* INTEND.

**purposeful,** *modif.* **1.** [Determined] — *Syn.* obstinate, stubborn, persistent; see **resolute** 2.

**2.** [Worthwhile] — *Syn.* deliberate, profitable, useful; see **helpful** 1.

**purposely,** *modif.* — *Syn.* intentionally, designedly, advisedly; see **deliberately**.

**purr,** *v.* — *Syn.* hum, drone, sigh, sing, mutter; see also **sound** 1.

**purse,** *n.* — *Syn.* pouch, pocketbook, handbag, bag, clutch bag, clutch, receptacle, *portemonnaie* (French), moneybag, wallet, pocket, coin purse, billfold, reticule, money belt, sack, vanity case, vanity bag, halfpenny-purse, belt-purse, sporran, bursa, saccule, *poche, pochette* (*both* French).

**hold the purse strings★** — *Syn.* be in control of money, finance, manage a household, manage a business; see **manage** 1.

**tighten the purse strings★** — *Syn.* scrimp, be sparing, hoard; see **save** 3.

**purser,** *n.* — *Syn.* ship's treasurer, treasurer, banker, bursar; see **accountant**.

**pursuant,** *modif.* — *Syn.* compatible, following, agreeable; see **harmonious** 2.

**pursue,** *v.* **1.** [To chase] — *Syn.* seek, hound, track, track down, dog, shadow, search for, search out, give chase, stalk, run after, search after, get after, go after, send after, prowl after, gun down, hunt down, trail, tag with, direct one's steps, camp on the trail of, follow close upon, move behind, hunt out, fish out, scout out, nose around, poke around, fasten oneself upon, keep on foot, follow up, attach oneself to, ask for, dig for, go running for, gun for, delve for, look about for.

**2.** [To seek] — *Syn.* strive for, try for, aspire to, attempt; see **try** 1.

**3.** [To continue] — *Syn.* persevere, proceed, follow up, carry on; see **continue** 1.

**pursuing,** *modif.* — *Syn.* out for, out to, in pursuance of, in the market for, on the lookout for.

**pursuit,** *n.* — *Syn.* chase, race, pursuance; see **hunt** 2.

**purvey,** *v.* — *Syn.* furnish, serve, supply; see **provide** 1.

**pus,** *n.* — *Syn.* purulence, discharge, fluid; see **matter** 5.

**push,** *n.* — *Syn.* shove, force, bearing, propulsion, drive, exertion, weight, straining, putting forth one's strength, shoving, thrusting, forcing, driving, exerting of pressure, lean, inducement, kinetic energy, mass, potential, reserve, impact, blow; see also **pressure** 1, **thrust** 3.

**push,** *v.* **1.** [To press against] — *Syn.* thrust, shove, butt, crowd, gore, ram, crush against, bear against, jostle, push out of one's way, bear on, lie on, shoulder, elbow, struggle, strain, exert, contend, set one's shoulder to, rest one's weight on, put forth one's strength; see also **force** 1.

**2.** [To move by pushing] — *Syn.* impel, accelerate, drive onward, launch, start, set in motion, put in motion, actuate, push forward, shift, start going, start rolling, budge, stir, inch along, shove along; see also **drive** 3, **propel**.

**3.** [To promote] — *Syn.* advance, expedite, urge; see **promote** 1.

**4.** [*To sell illegally] — *Syn.* deal in, sell under the counter, blackmarket, bootleg, moonshine; see also **sell** 1.

**pushcart,** *n.* — *Syn.* handcar, trolley, wheelbarrow; see **cart.**

**pushed★,** *modif.* — *Syn.* crowded, in trouble, in difficulty; see **embarrassed.**

**pusher★,** *n.* **1.** [Intruder] — *Syn.* pest, meddler, interrupter; see **intruder.**

**2.** [A seller of drugs] — *Syn.* dealer, black-market salesman, dope peddler, connection★; see **criminal.**

**pushing,** *modif.* — *Syn.* aggressive, forward, ambitious, pushy★; see **aggressive** 1.

*See Synonym Study at* AGGRESSIVE.

**push off,** *v.* — *Syn.* depart, start, take off; see **leave** 1.

**push on,** *v.* — *Syn.* keep going, go, make progress; see **continue** 1, 2.

**pushover,** *n.* — *Syn.* sucker, easy pickings, fool; see **victim** 2.

**pussyfoot★,** *v.* — *Syn.* evade, avoid, dodge, sidestep, hedge; see also **avoid, evade** 1.

**put,** *v.* **1.** [To place] — *Syn.* set, seat, settle; see **place** 1.

**2.** [To establish] — *Syn.* install, quarter, fix; see **establish** 2.

**3.** [To deposit] — *Syn.* invest in, insert, embed; see **plant.**

**put about,** *v.* — *Syn.* vary, veer, turn; see **change** 1.

**put across** *or* **over★,** *v.* — *Syn.* succeed, fulfill, complete; see **achieve** 1.

**put aside,** *v.* — *Syn.* deposit, save, table, put out of the way; see **store** 2.

**putative,** *modif.* — *Syn.* presumed, supposed, accepted, alleged; see **assumed** 1.

**put away,** *v.* — *Syn.* deposit, save, put out of the way; see **store** 2.

**put back,** *v.* — *Syn.* bring back, make restitution (for), put in (its) place; see **replace** 1, **return** 2.

**put by,** *v.* — *Syn.* secure, keep, save; see **preserve** 3.

**put-down★,** *n.* — *Syn.* suppression, indignity, cut★; see **insult.**

**put down,** *v.* — *Syn.* silence, repress, crush; see **defeat** 1, 2.

**put emphasis on,** *v.* — *Syn.* stress, dramatize, make clear; see **emphasize.**

**put forth,** *v.* — *Syn.* produce, form, constitute; see **compose** 3, **create** 2, **invent** 1.

**put forward,** *v.* — *Syn.* further, urge, present; see **propose** 1.

**put in,** *v.* — *Syn.* sail for, move toward, land; see **approach** 2.

**put off,** *v.* — *Syn.* postpone, defer, retard; see **delay.**

**put-on,** *modif.* — *Syn.* feigned, simulated, calculated; see **pretended.**

**put-on★,** *n.* **1.** [A trick] — *Syn.* deception, device, job★; see **trick** 1.

**2.** [A joke] — *Syn.* hoax, satire, pretense; see **fake, joke** 1, 2.

**put on,** *v.* **1.** [To pretend] — *Syn.* feign, sham, make believe; see **pretend** 1.

**2.** [*To deceive] — *Syn.* trick, confuse, confound; see **deceive.**

**put on airs,** *v.* — *Syn.* brag, show off, make pretensions; see **strut.**

**put one over on,** *v.* — *Syn.* dupe, hoodwink, pull the wool over someone's eyes; see **deceive.**

**put one's cards on the table,** *v.* — *Syn.* say, display, show; see **reveal** 1, **tell** 1.

**put one through his paces,** *v.* — *Syn.* test, try, try out; see **examine** 1.

**put out,** *v.* — *Syn.* discard, throw away, turn adrift; see **eject** 1.

**put over★,** *v.* — *Syn.* manage, do, get done; see **achieve** 1.

**putrefy,** *v.* — *Syn.* decay, rot, putresce, decompose; see **decay.**

*See Synonym Study at* DECAY.

**putrid,** *modif.* — *Syn.* corrupt, putrified, decayed; see **rotten** 1.

**put someone in his place,** *v.* — *Syn.* tell off, reprimand, correct; see **censure.**

**putter,** *v.* — *Syn.* dawdle, fritter, poke; see **loiter.**

**put through,** *v.* — *Syn.* do, manage, finish; see **achieve** 1.

**put to sleep★,** *v.* — *Syn.* destroy, subject to euthanasia, murder; see **kill** 1.

**put up,** *modif.* — *Syn.* canned, pickled, tinned; see **preserved** 1.

**put up,** *v.* **1.** [To preserve] — *Syn.* can, smoke, pickle; see **preserve** 3.

**2.** [To build] — *Syn.* erect, fabricate, construct; see **build** 1.

**3.** [To bet] — *Syn.* speculate, wager, put one's money on; see **gamble** 1.

**4.** [To entertain] — *Syn.* house, provide bed and board, make welcome; see **entertain** 2.

**put up with,** *v.* — *Syn.* undergo, tolerate, stand; see **endure** 2.

**puzzle,** *n.* **1.** [The state of being puzzled] — *Syn.* bewilderment, bafflement, perplexity, puzzlement; see **confusion** 2.

**2.** [A problem] — *Syn.* enigma, mystery, riddle, problem, question, conundrum, tangle, dilemma, quandary, issue, intricacy, maze, labyrinth, query, oracle, cabala, muddle, esoterica, secret, ambiguity, difficulty, perplexity, confusion, entanglement, frustration, paradox, puzzler, poser, teaser, brain teaser, stumper, question mark, stickler★, sixty-four dollar question★; see also **difficulty** 1, **riddle** 1. — *Ant.* ANSWER, solution, development.

**3.** [A problem to be worked for amusement]. Kinds of puzzles include: riddle, conundrum, cryptogram, logogram, crossword, jigsaw, anagram, palindrome, brain teaser, acrostic, charade, rebus, puzzle-ring, Chinese puzzle.

---

*SYN.* — **puzzle** is a situation, problem, or, often, a contrivance, that requires some ingenuity to solve or explain; **mystery** is applied to something beyond human knowledge or understanding, or may refer merely to any unexplained or seemingly inexplicable matter; **enigma** specifically applies to something whose meaning is hidden by cryptic or ambiguous allusions, or generally, to anything baffling and often mysterious; a **riddle** is a problem or enigma (usually in the form of a question in guessing games) that involves paradoxes; **conundrum** is specifically applied to a riddle whose answer is a pun, or generally, to any puzzling question or problem

---

**puzzle,** *v.* **1.** [To perplex] — *Syn.* baffle, bewilder, perplex, mystify; see **confuse.**

**2.** [To wonder] — *Syn.* marvel, be surprised, be astonished; see **wonder** 1.

*See Synonym Study at* CONFUSE.

**puzzled,** *modif.* — *Syn.* perplexed, bewildered, mystified; see **doubtful** 2.

**puzzle out,** *v.* — *Syn.* figure out, work out, decipher; see **solve.**

**puzzle over,** *v.* — *Syn.* think about, consider, debate; see **think** 1.

**puzzling,** *modif.* **1.** [Obscure] — *Syn.* uncertain, ambiguous, mystifying; see **obscure** 1.

**2.** [Difficult] — *Syn.* perplexing, abstruse, hard; see **difficult** 2.

**pygmy,** *n.* — *Syn.* bantam, pixy, dwarf; see **midget, runt.**

**pylon,** *n.* **1.** [Arch] — *Syn.* span, entrance, door; see **arch.**

**2.** [Pillar] — *Syn.* shaft, tower, post; see **column** 1.

**pyramid,** *n.* — *Syn.* tomb, shrine, remains; see **monument.**

**pyre,** *n.* — *Syn.* pile to be burned, combustible material, fuel; see **fire** 1.

**pyromaniac,** *n.* — *Syn.* arsonist, incendiary, firebug\*; see **arsonist.**

**pyrotechnics,** *n.* — *Syn.* combustible devices, rockets, sparklers; see **fireworks.**

# Q

**quack,** *modif.* — *Syn.* unprincipled, pretentious, dissembling; see **dishonest** 1, 2, **false** 1.

**quack,** *n.* — *Syn.* charlatan, mountebank, impostor, humbug, fraud, rogue, quacksalver, fake★, faker★, phony★; see also **cheat** 1, **impostor.**

---

**SYN.** — **quack** and **charlatan** both apply to a person who unscrupulously pretends to knowledge or skill he or she does not possess, but **quack** almost always is used of a fraudulent or incompetent practitioner of medicine; **mountebank,** in modern use, suggests a self-promoting person who resorts to cheap methods or trickery in his or her work, etc.; **impostor** applies esp. to a person who fraudulently assumes the identity or character of another; **fake** is a colloquial term for a person who practices deception or misrepresentation

---

**quackery,** *n.* — *Syn.* charlatanism, pretense, misrepresentation, imposture; see **deception** 1, **dishonesty.**

**quadrangle,** *n.* **1.** [A four-sided figure] — *Syn.* quadrilateral, parallelogram, rhombus, square; see **rectangle.**

**2.** [A court] — *Syn.* courtyard, forum, square, quad★; see **court** 1, **yard** 1.

**quadrangular,** *modif.* — *Syn.* rectangular, quadrilateral, plane; see **angular** 1, **square** 1.

**quadruped,** *n.* — *Syn.* four-legged animal, domestic animal, mammal; see **animal** 2.

**quadruple,** *modif.* — *Syn.* fourfold, quadruplicate, four-way, four times as great, four times as many, four-part, quadruplex, four-ply, four-cycle, quadripartite, biquadratic.

**quaff,** *v.* — *Syn.* gulp, swallow, guzzle; see **drink** 1, **swallow.**

**quagmire,** *n.* **1.** [Swamp] — *Syn.* marsh, bog, mire; see **swamp.**

**2.** [Dilemma] — *Syn.* perplexity, entanglement, quandary, morass; see **difficulty** 1, 2, **predicament.**

**quail,** *v.* — *Syn.* shrink, cower, tremble; see **wince.**

**quaint,** *modif.* **1.** [Unusual] — *Syn.* odd, strange, singular, eccentric; see **unusual** 2.

**2.** [Old-fashioned but charming] — *Syn.* picturesque, archaic, fanciful, curious, cute, pleasing, captivating, ancient, antiquated, whimsical, affected, baroque, Victorian, Gothic, Early American, Colonial; see also **charming, old-fashioned.** — *Ant.* MODERN, up-to-date, fashionable.

*See Synonym Study at* STRANGE.

**quake,** *n.* — *Syn.* temblor, tremor, shock; see **earthquake.**

**quake,** *v.* — *Syn.* tremble, shrink, cower; see **shake** 1.

**qualification,** *n.* **1.** [Prerequisite] — *Syn.* need, requisite, essential, criterion; see **requirement** 1.

**2.** [Competence] — *Syn.* capacity, skill, fitness, eligibility; see **ability** 2, **fitness** 1.

**3.** [A limiting condition] — *Syn.* modification, restriction, stipulation, reservation; see **limitation** 2.

**qualifications,** *n.* — *Syn.* endowments, acquirements, attainments; see **ability** 2, **experience** 3.

**qualified,** *modif.* **1.** [Limited] — *Syn.* conditional, modified, with reservations; see **conditional, restricted.**

**2.** [Competent] — *Syn.* adequate, equipped, fitted; see **able** 1, 2.

*See Synonym Study at* ABLE.

**qualify,** *v.* **1.** [To limit] — *Syn.* reduce, restrain, temper; see **change** 1, **restrict** 2.

**2.** [To fulfill requirements] — *Syn.* fit, suit, pass, be eligible, be equipped, be capacitated, have the requisites, meet the demands, measure up, meet the specifications, pass muster, make the grade★, fill the bill★. — *Ant.* FAIL, become unfit, be unsuited.

**quality,** *n.* **1.** [A characteristic] — *Syn.* attribute, trait, property, characteristic, character, feature, mark, point, endowment; see also **characteristic.**

**2.** [Essential character] — *Syn.* nature, essence, spirit, tone; see **character** 2.

**3.** [Grade] — *Syn.* class, kind, state, condition, caliber, merit, worth, excellence, stage, step, variety, standing, status, rank, group, place, position, repute; see also **degree** 2.

---

**SYN.** — **quality,** the broadest in scope of these terms, refers to a characteristic (physical or nonphysical, individual or typical) that constitutes the basic nature of a thing or is one of its distinguishing features /the *quality* of mercy/; **property** applies to a quality that belongs to a thing by reason of the essential nature of the thing /elasticity is a *property* of rubber/; **character,** in this connection, is the scientific or formal term for a distinctive or peculiar quality of an individual or of a class, species, etc. /a hereditary *character*/; an **attribute** is a quality assigned to a thing, esp. one that may reasonably be deduced as appropriate to it /omnipotence is an *attribute* of God/; **trait** specif. applies to a distinguishing quality of a person's character /enthusiasm is one of his outstanding *traits*/

---

**qualm,** *n.* **1.** [Doubt] — *Syn.* scruple, misgiving, doubt, compunction, reservation, uneasiness, apprehension, hesitation, hesitancy, indecision, pang, twinge, twinge of conscience, equivocalness, second thought, funny feeling★; see also **doubt** 2.

**2.** [Nausea] — *Syn.* faintness, dizziness, queasiness; see **illness** 1.

---

**SYN.** — **qualm** implies a painful feeling of uneasiness arising from a consciousness that one is or may be acting wrongly /I had *qualms* about leaving the children alone in the house/; **scruple** implies doubt or hesitation arising from difficulty in deciding what is right, proper, just, etc. /to break a promise without *scruple*/; **compunction** implies a twinge of conscience for wrongdoing, now often for a slight offense /to have no *compunctions* about telling a white lie*]*; **misgiving** implies a disturbed state of mind resulting from a loss of confidence as to whether one is doing what is right *[misgivings* of conscience*]*

**quandary,** *n.* — *Syn.* dilemma, plight, puzzle, perplexity; see **difficulty** 1, 2, **predicament.**
*See Synonym Study at* PREDICAMENT.

**quantity,** *n.* — *Syn.* amount, number, sum, bulk, mass, measure, extent, abundance, volume, capacity, lot, batch, deal, pile, magnitude, multitude, amplitude, portion, profusion, mountain, load, barrel, shipment, consignment, bushel, supply, ton, ocean, flood, spate, sea, flock, score, swarm, quite a few, army, legion, host, pack, crowd, bunch*, heap*, mess*, peck*, slew*, gob*, scads*, all kinds of*, all sorts of*; see also **plenty, size** 2.

**quarantine,** *v.* — *Syn.* isolate, hospitalize, detain, put in isolation, seclude, segregate, interdict, restrain, cordon off, put under quarantine, place in quarantine, ostracize; see also **separate** 2.

**quarantined,** *modif.* — *Syn.* isolated, confined, shut up, shut away, in quarantine, under quarantine, hospitalized, detained, restrained, separated, cordoned off, sealed off; see also **isolated.**

**quarrel,** *n.* **1.** [An angry dispute] — *Syn.* argument, wrangle, squabble, altercation, dispute, disagreement, dissension, falling-out, feud, spat*; see also **disagreement** 1, **dispute, fight** 1.
**2.** [Objection] — *Syn.* complaint, disapproval, disagreement; see **objection** 1, 2.

**quarrel,** *v.* — *Syn.* argue, wrangle, dispute, contend, fight, squabble, bicker, clash, altercate, dissent, struggle, strive, contest, object, complain, disagree, differ, fall out, break with, be at loggerheads, be at odds, charge, allegate, feud, battle, brawl, row, spar, have words with, mix it up with*, pick a bone with*, tread on one's toes*, get tough with*, lock horns*, fall foul of*, have a brush with*, have it out*, make the fur fly*, kick up a row*, scrap*, hassle*; see also **fight** 2, **oppose** 1. — *Ant.* AGREE, accord, harmonize.

**SYN.** — **quarrel** implies heated verbal strife marked by anger and resentment and often suggests continued hostility as a result; **wrangle** suggests a noisy dispute in which each person is vehemently insistent on his or her own views; **altercation** implies verbal contention that may or may not be accompanied by blows; **squabble** implies undignified, childish wrangling over a small matter; **spat** is a colloquial term for a petty quarrel and suggests a brief outburst that does not have a significant effect on a relationship

**quarreling,** *modif.* — *Syn.* disagreeing, bickering, squabbling, at odds, at loggerheads, at swords' points, not on speaking terms, at variance, out of line with, differing, in disagreement, out of accord, discordant, inharmonious, at each other's throats*.

**quarrelsome,** *modif.* **1.** [Inclined to fight] — *Syn.* factious, combative, pugnacious, contentious, disputatious, argumentative, litigious, belligerent, bellicose, truculent, unruly, passionate, violent, fiery, impassioned, hotheaded, hot-tempered, excitable, hasty, tempestuous, bickering, squabbling, with a chip on one's shoulder*, scrappy*. — *Ant.* CALM, peaceful, conciliatory.
**2.** [Bad-tempered] — *Syn.* fractious, cross, cross-grained, irascible, snappish, waspish, peevish, petu-

lant, churlish, cantankerous, thin-skinned, touchy, testy, huffy, pettish, peppery; see also **irritable.** — *Ant.* AGREEABLE, good-natured, unruffled.
*See Synonym Study at* BELLIGERENT.

**quarry,** *n.* **1.** [A mine] — *Syn.* excavation, shaft, vein, lode; see **mine** 1.
**2.** [The hunted] — *Syn.* game, chase, prey; see **victim** 1.

**quart,** *n.* — *Syn.* two pints, thirty-two ounces, one-fourth gallon; see **measure** 1.

**quarter,** *n.* **1.** [One of four equal parts] — *Syn.* fourth, one-fourth part, portion, fraction, division, span, three months, 90 days, semester, school term, quarter of an hour, fifteen minutes, quarter section, quadrant; see also **part** 1.
**2.** [One quarter of a dollar] — *Syn.* twenty-five cents, coin, two bits*; see **money** 1.
**3.** [Direction] — *Syn.* bearing, region, point; see **direction** 1.
**4.** [A section of a community] — *Syn.* neighborhood, district, section; see **area** 2.
**5.** [Mercy] — *Syn.* clemency, compassion, indulgence; see **mercy** 1.
**at close quarters** — *Syn.* at close range, close together, cramped, restricted; see **near** 1.

**quarter,** *v.* **1.** [To divide into quarters] — *Syn.* quadrisect, cleave, dismember, cut up; see **cut** 1, **divide** 1.
**2.** [To provide living quarters] — *Syn.* lodge, shelter, assign to lodgings, settle, establish, accommodate, house, put up, billet, station, post.

**quarterback,** *n.* — *Syn.* back, Q.B., quarter, gridironer*, signal caller*, field general*, barker*; see also **football player.**

**quarterly,** *modif.* — *Syn.* by quarters, once every three months, once a quarter, periodically; see **regularly** 1, 2.

**quartermaster,** *n.* — *Syn.* commissioned officer, petty officer, supply officer; see **officer** 3.

**quarters,** *pl.n.* — *Syn.* lodgings, housing, living quarters, accommodations, house, apartment, rooms, room, barracks, tent, lodge, cabins, cottage, trailer; see also **apartment, home** 1.

**quartet,** *n.* — *Syn.* four people, four voices, four musicians, string quartet, principals, ensemble, foursome.

**quartz,** *n.* Types of quartz include: amethyst, false topaz, rock crystal, rose quartz, smoky quartz, bloodstone, agate, onyx, sardonyx, carnelian, chrysoprase, citrine, chalcedony, prase, flint, jasper; see also **rock** 1.

**quash,** *v.* **1.** [To crush] — *Syn.* quell, squash, subdue, repress; see **defeat** 1, 2, **suppress.**
**2.** [To revoke] — *Syn.* nullify, repeal, revoke; see **cancel** 2.

**quasi,** *modif.* — *Syn.* supposedly, to a certain extent, seemingly; see **almost, apparently.**

**quaver,** *v.* — *Syn.* tremble, vibrate, quiver; see **shake** 1.

**quay,** *n.* — *Syn.* landing, wharf, pier; see **dock** 1.

**queasy,** *modif.* — *Syn.* nauseous, squeamish, sick to one's stomach, uneasy; see **sick, uncomfortable** 1.

**queen,** *n.* — *Syn.* ruler, monarch, female ruler, female sovereign, queen mother, regent, wife of a king, empress, czarina, consort, queen consort, queen dowager, queen regent, fairy queen, May Queen, matriarch, goddess, diva, prima donna, grande dame.

**queenly,** *modif.* — *Syn.* regal, imperial, grand, noble; see **royal** 1, 2.

**queen-size,** *modif.* — *Syn.* medium large, outsize, smaller than king-size; see **broad** 1, **large** 1.

**queer,** *modif.* **1.** [Odd] — *Syn.* peculiar, singular, strange, eccentric; see **unusual** 2.

**2.** [Slightly ill] — *Syn.* queasy, qualmish, faint; see **dizzy** 1, **sick.**

**3.** [*Suspicious] — *Syn.* strange, questionable, doubtful, irregular; see **questionable** 2, **suspicious** 2.

*See Synonym Study at* STRANGE.

**quell,** *v.* **1.** [To subdue] — *Syn.* put down, stop, silence; see **defeat** 1, 2, **quiet** 2, **suppress.**

**2.** [To allay] — *Syn.* reduce, calm, check; see **quiet** 1.

**quench,** *v.* **1.** [To satisfy] — *Syn.* slake, allay, hit the spot*; see **drink** 1, **relieve** 2, **satisfy** 1, 3.

**2.** [To smother] — *Syn.* stifle, dampen, put out, douse; see **extinguish, moisten.**

**querulous,** *modif.* — *Syn.* fretful, irascible, peevish, complaining; see **irritable.**

**query,** *n.* — *Syn.* question, inquiry, doubt; see **question** 1.

**query,** *v.* — *Syn.* ask, question, inquire about, call into question; see **ask** 1, **doubt** 1, **question** 1.

*See Synonym Study at* ASK.

**quest,** *n.* — *Syn.* journey, search, crusade; see **examination** 1, **hunt** 2.

**question,** *n.* **1.** [A query] — *Syn.* inquiry, inquiring, interrogatory, interrogative, interrogation, inquisition, feeler, catechism, inquest, rhetorical question, burning question, crucial question, leading question, catch question, academic question, vexed question, sixty-four dollar question*. — *Ant.* ANSWER, solution, reply.

**2.** [A puzzle] — *Syn.* enigma, mystery, problem; see **puzzle** 2.

**3.** [A subject] — *Syn.* proposal, topic, issue; see **issue** 1, **subject** 1.

**beside the question** — *Syn.* not germane, beside the point, immaterial; see **irrelevant.**

**beyond question** — *Syn.* beyond dispute, without any doubt, undoubtedly; see **surely, unquestionably.**

**in question** — *Syn.* being considered, under discussion, under consideration, under advisement, at issue, controversial, in dispute, up for discussion, on the floor, on the agenda; see also **controversial, questionable** 1, **uncertain** 2.

**out of the question** — *Syn.* not to be considered, by no means, unthinkable; see **impossible** 1.

**question,** *v.* **1.** [To ask] — *Syn.* inquire, interrogate, examine, query, quest, seek, search, sound out, petition, solicit, ask about, catechize, show curiosity, pry into, ask a leading question, challenge, raise a question, pick one's brains, make inquiry, quiz, cross-examine, probe, investigate, interview, debrief, put to the question, bring into question, grill*, pump*, give the third degree*; see also **ask** 1.

**2.** [To doubt] — *Syn.* distrust, suspect, dispute; see **doubt** 1, 2.

*See Synonym Study at* ASK.

**questionable,** *modif.* **1.** [Justifying doubt] — *Syn.* doubtful, dubious, uncertain, undefined, equivocal, disputable, arguable, obscure, inconclusive, controversial, vague, unsettled, open to doubt, indeterminate, debatable, moot, unconfirmed, problematic, cryptic, occult, apocryphal, hypothetical, mysterious, oracular, enigmatic, ambiguous, indefinite, contingent, provisional, paradoxical, under advisement, under examination, open to question, up for discussion, in question, to be voted on, to be decided, hard to believe, incredible, iffy*; see also **uncertain** 2. — *Ant.* DEFINITE, undoubted, certain.

**2.** [Having a poor appearance or reputation] — *Syn.* dubious, suspicious, suspect, disreputable, of doubtful character, irregular, notorious, of ill repute, unsatisfactory, unsound, thought ill of, under a cloud, unesteemed, ill-favored, unpopular, disagreeable, evil-looking, illegitimate, discreditable, disrespectable, unreliable, untrustworthy, dishonest, fly-by-night, shady*, fishy*, queer*; see also **suspicious** 2. — *Ant.* HONORED, esteemed, reputable.

*See Synonym Study at* DOUBTFUL.

**questioner,** *n.* **1.** [An examiner] — *Syn.* quizzer, interrogator, interviewer, analyst; see **examiner, investigator.**

**2.** [A skeptic] — *Syn.* doubter, scoffer, agnostic; see **cynic, skeptic.**

**questioning,** *n.* — *Syn.* interrogation, catechism, inquest; see **examination** 1.

**questionless,** *modif.* — *Syn.* without doubt, indisputable, unquestionable; see **certain** 3.

**questionnaire,** *n.* — *Syn.* inquiry, survey, poll, canvass, set of questions, application, outline, census, sampling, public-opinion poll, Gallup poll.

**queue,** *n.* **1.** [A braid] — *Syn.* pony tail, plait, pigtail; see **braid.**

**2.** [A series] — *Syn.* tail, chain, file; see **line** 1.

**quibble,** *n.* **1.** [Evasion] — *Syn.* equivocation, shift, dodge; see **avoidance, lie** 1.

**2.** [A petty objection] — *Syn.* cavil, complaint, quiddity, nit-picking; see **objection** 2.

**quibble,** *v.* — *Syn.* dodge, cavil, beat about the bush, split hairs; see **complain** 1, **evade** 1.

**quibbling,** *modif.* — *Syn.* carping, niggling, hair-splitting, nit-picking; see **critical** 2, **trivial.**

**quick,** *modif.* **1.** [Rapid] — *Syn.* fast, swift, expeditious, fleet; see **agile, fast** 1.

**2.** [Almost immediate] — *Syn.* posthaste, prompt, instantaneous; see **immediate** 1.

**3.** [Hasty] — *Syn.* impetuous, mercurial, quick-tempered; see **rash.**

**4.** [Alert] — *Syn.* ready, prompt, apt, sharp, keen, clever, smart, agile, nimble, lively, responsive, on the ball*; see also **active** 2, **clever** 1.

*See Synonym Study at* AGILE, FAST.

---

*SYN.* — **quick,** in this comparison, implies ability to respond rapidly as an innate rather than a developed faculty [*a quick mind*]; **prompt** stresses immediate response to a demand as resulting from discipline, practice, etc. or from willingness [*prompt* to obey, a *prompt* acceptance]; **ready** also implies preparation or willingness and, in another sense, connotes fluency, expertness, etc. [*a ready* sympathy, *ready* wit]; **apt,** in this connection, implies superior intelligence or a special talent as the reason for quickness of response [*an apt* pupil]

---

**quicken,** *v.* **1.** [To hasten or cause to hasten] — *Syn.* accelerate, speed up, hurry; see **hasten** 1, 2.

**2.** [To come or bring to life] — *Syn.* animate, revive, stir, arouse, stimulate, enliven, awaken, kindle, spring, grow, rise, spring up, be revived, be resuscitated, become animated, activate, revitalize, energize, strengthen, show signs of life, return to life; see also **animate** 1, **revive** 1.

*See Synonym Study at* ANIMATE.

**quickie*,** *n.* **1.** [A hasty action] — *Syn.* brief attempt, hurried encounter, short operation, quick one; see **action** 2.

**2.** [A quick drink] — *Syn.* short shot*, one for the road*, short snort*; see **drink** 2.

**quickly,** *modif.* **1.** [Rapidly] — *Syn.* speedily, swiftly, fast, briskly, fleetly, flying, with dispatch, scurrying, hurrying, rushing, shooting, bolting, darting, flashing, dashing, suddenly, expeditiously, hastily, hurriedly, in haste, in great haste, in a hurry, by forced marches, at a great rate, without delay, under press of sail, in full sail, against the clock, racing, galloping, loping, sweeping, light-footedly, wingedly, like a bat out of hell*, on the double*, like all forty*, in a flash*, in a jiffy*, to beat the band*, at full blast*, in full sail*, hellbent for leather*, like mad*, at one jump*, by leaps and bounds*, like a house afire*, double-time*, like crazy*, like fury*, full steam ahead*, in high gear*. — *Ant.* SLOWLY, sluggishly, creepingly.

**2.** [Soon] — *Syn.* at once, instantly, promptly, on the nail*, pronto*; see also **immediately, soon** 1.

**quickness,** *n.* — *Syn.* swiftness, haste, agility; see **speed.**

**quicksand,** *n.* — *Syn.* snare, trap, quagmire; see **swamp.**

**quicksilver,** *n.* — *Syn.* mercury, ore, liquid mercury; see **metal.**

**quick-tempered,** *modif.* — *Syn.* temperamental, quarrelsome, irascible, excitable; see **irritable.**

**quick-witted,** *modif.* — *Syn.* sharp, humorous, clever, alert; see **clever** 1, **intelligent** 1.

*quid pro quo* (Latin), *n.* — *Syn.* return, retaliation, remuneration, tit for tat; see **compensation, exchange** 1, 2, **revenge** 1.

**quiescence,** *n.* — *Syn.* repose, quiet, calm; see **rest** 1, 2.

**quiescent,** *modif.* — *Syn.* quiet, still, inactive, dormant; see **calm** 2, **latent.**

*See Synonym Study at* LATENT.

**quiet,** *modif.* **1.** [Calm] — *Syn.* peaceful, tranquil, untroubled, retired; see **calm** 1, 2, **withdrawn.**

**2.** [Silent] — *Syn.* hushed, muffled, noiseless, still, stilled, mute, muted, low, soft, inaudible, soundless, dumb, quieted, speechless, unspeaking, mum, quiescent, taciturn, reserved, reticent, unuttered, unexpressed, close-mouthed, close, tight-lipped, uncommunicative, secretive.

**3.** [Motionless] — *Syn.* unruffled, still, placid, level; see **calm** 2, **smooth** 1.

**4.** [Unostentatious] — *Syn.* subdued, unobtrusive, unpretentious, understated; see **modest** 2.

**quiet,** *n.* **1.** [Rest] — *Syn.* calm, tranquillity, relaxation; see **peace** 2, **rest** 1.

**2.** [Silence] — *Syn.* hush, stillness, speechlessness; see **silence** 1.

**quiet,** *v.* **1.** [To make calm] — *Syn.* calm, cool, relax, compose, tranquilize, soothe, comfort, satisfy, pacify, mollify, placate, assuage, console, subdue, reconcile, gratify, calm down, soften, moderate, smooth, ameliorate, allay, quell, becalm, lull, appease, restrain, palliate, sober, slacken; see also **comfort, ease** 1, 2. — *Ant.* EXCITE, irritate, agitate.

**2.** [To make silent] — *Syn.* hush, still, deaden, silence, soften, mute, tone down, lower the sound level, muffle, stifle, smother, gag, muzzle, stop, check, restrain, suppress, break in, cut short, preclude, confute, repress, refute, confound, answer, quell, insulate, dampen, shush, shut up*, stop the mouth*, floor*, put the lid on*, button up*, choke off*, put the kibosh on*, put the stopper on*, squelch*. — *Ant.* SOUND, ring, cause to sound.

**quiet down,** *v.* — *Syn.* grow silent, be hushed, hush, be subdued, be suppressed, become speechless, fall silent, break off, be answered, shut up*, clam up*.

**quietly,** *modif.* **1.** [Calmly] — *Syn.* peacefully, tranquilly, unconcernedly, composedly; see **calmly.**

**2.** [Almost silently] — *Syn.* noiselessly, speechlessly, inaudibly, softly; see **silently.**

**3.** [Without attracting attention] — *Syn.* unobtrusively, unostentatiously, simply; see **modestly** 1.

**quietus,** *n.* **1.** [Death] — *Syn.* decease, end, dissolution; see **death** 1.

**2.** [Defeat] — *Syn.* overcoming, final blow, overthrow; see **defeat** 2.

**quill,** *n.* — *Syn.* down, plume, pinion, shaft; see **feather.**

**quilt,** *n.* — *Syn.* comforter, bed covering, coverlet, duvet, feather bed, puff, down puff, down comforter, eiderdown, batt, patchwork quilt, pieced quilt, bedspread, pad; see also **bedding.**

**quintessence,** *n.* — *Syn.* core, pith, spirit, embodiment; see **epitome** 1, **essence** 1.

**quip,** *n.* **1.** [A witticism] — *Syn.* jest, repartee, bon mot, one-liner; see **joke** 2, **pun.**

**2.** [A jeer] — *Syn.* gibe, mockery, wisecrack*, crack*; see **insult, ridicule.**

**quirk,** *n.* — *Syn.* vagary, whim, caprice, turn, twist, peculiarity, foible, idiosyncrasy, mannerism, eccentricity, oddity, kink, crotchet, fancy, whimsy, conceit, humor, bee in the bonnet*; see also **caprice, characteristic, irregularity** 2.

**quisling,** *n.* — *Syn.* fifth columnist, turncoat, secret agent; see **traitor.**

**quit,** *v.* **1.** [To cease] — *Syn.* stop, discontinue, leave off, desist, give up, halt, end, knock off*, lay off*, pack it in*; see also **stop** 2.

**2.** [To resign] — *Syn.* leave, stop work, walk out, give notice, change jobs, step down, drop out*; see also **resign** 2.

*See Synonym Study at* ABANDON, STOP.

**3.** [To leave] — *Syn.* go away from, depart, vacate; see **leave** 1.

**4.** [To abandon] — *Syn.* give up, relinquish, renounce; see **abandon** 1.

**quite,** *modif.* **1.** [Completely] — *Syn.* entirely, wholly, totally; see **completely.**

**2.** [Really] — *Syn.* truly, positively, actually; see **really** 1.

**3.** [To a considerable degree] — *Syn.* pretty, more or less, considerably; see **very.**

**quitter,** *n.* — *Syn.* defeatist, shirker, dropout, deserter, goldbrick*, goldbricker*, piker*, ratter*, slacker*, wimp*.

**quiver,** *n.* — *Syn.* shudder, shiver, tremble; see **vibration.**

**quiver,** *v.* — *Syn.* vibrate, shudder, shiver; see **shake** 1, **wave** 3.

**quivering,** *modif.* — *Syn.* shuddering, shivering, shaking, quavering, tremulous, fluttering, trembling, vibrating.

**quixotic,** *modif.* — *Syn.* impractical, idealistic, chivalrous, daring; see **impractical, romantic** 1, **visionary** 1.

**quiz,** *n.* — *Syn.* test, questioning, exam*; see **examination** 2.

**quiz,** *v.* — *Syn.* question, test, cross-examine; see **examine** 2.

**quiz program** *or* **show,** *n.* — *Syn.* question-and-answer game, question-and-answer program, panel, battle of brains, game show, College Bowl, Jeopardy (*both* trademark).

**quizzical,** *modif.* — *Syn.* perplexed, puzzled, questioning, inquiring; see **bewildered, inquisitive.**

**quondam,** *modif.* — *Syn.* former, past, onetime; see **former, preceding.**

**quorum,** *n.* — *Syn.* majority, legal minimum, plenum; see **attendance** 2, **bulk** 2.

**quota,** *n.* — *Syn.* portion, allowance, ration; see **share.**

**quotation,** *n.* **1.** [Quoted matter] — *Syn.* excerpt, quote, passage, citation, citing, extract, selection, recitation, repetition, sentence, line, reference, plagiarism.

**2.** [A quoted price] — *Syn.* market price, current price, published price, stated price, bid; see also **price.**

**quote,** *v.* **1.** [To repeat verbatim] — *Syn.* recite, excerpt, extract; see **cite** 2.

**2.** [To state a price] — *Syn.* name a price, request, demand; see **price, rate** 1, **value** 2.

**quoted,** *modif.* **1.** [Repeated from another] — *Syn.* recited, excerpted, extracted, cited, paraphrased, echoed, instanced, copied, plagiarized.

**2.** [Offered or mentioned at a stated price] — *Syn.* asked, stated, announced, published, named, marked, given, priced, price-marked, ticketed, tagged.

**quotient,** *n.* — *Syn.* outcome, remainder, computation; see **result.**

**quoting,** *modif.* — *Syn.* repeating, reciting, citing, excerpting, copying, instancing, announcing, stating, naming, publishing.

# R

**rabbi,** *n.* — *Syn.* Jewish teacher, Jewish minister, graduate of a rabbinical school, Hebrew doctor of laws, rebbe, master, teacher, preacher, expounder of the law, Talmudist, religious functionary, Hebrew theologian; see also **priest.**

**rabbit,** *n.* — *Syn.* cony, hare, pika, leveret, lagomorph, *lapin* (French), *Sylvilagus, Lepus* (*both* Latin), bunny, cottontail, Easter bunny; see also **animal** 2, **rodent.**
Kinds of rabbits include: jack, cottontail, snowshoe, brush, pygmy, swamp, Angora, Ostend, Polish, Flemish, Siberian, Silver, Normandy, Patagonian; Belgian hare, Arctic hare, European hare, snowshoe hare, Chinchilla hare, tapeti, pika.

**rabble,** *n.* — *Syn.* mob, masses, riffraff; see **crowd** 1, **people** 3.

**rabid,** *modif.* **1.** [Fanatical] — *Syn.* obsessed, zealous, keen, extreme; see **enthusiastic** 2, 3, **fanatical, radical** 2.
**2.** [Violent] — *Syn.* mad, raging, frenzied, deranged; see **violent** 2.
**3.** [Affected with rabies] — *Syn.* hydrophobic, mad, poisoned, bitten, attacked by a mad dog, violent, frothing at the mouth, foaming at the mouth, frenzied, raging, virulent; see also **sick.**

**rabies,** *n.* — *Syn.* hydrophobia, canine madness, lyssa; see **disease.**

**race,** *n.* **1.** [A physical division of humankind] — *Syn.* species, stock, variety, type, kind, strain, breed, family, color; see also **man** 1.
The general divisions of the human race are: Caucasoid, Caucasian, white, Negroid, black, Mongoloid, yellow.
**2.** [Roughly, people united by blood or custom] — *Syn.* nationality, culture, cultural group, ethnic group, caste, variety, type, a people, humankind, mankind, tribe, sect, group, ethnic stock, human race, class, population connected by common descent, kind, nation, folk, gene pool, pedigree, lineage, community, inhabitants, population, populace, clan, breeding population; see also **culture** 2, **heredity, society** 2.
**3.** [A contest, usually of speed] — *Syn.* competition, run, dash, sprint, relay, marathon, clash, meet, event, engagement, competitive trial of speed, scurry, spurt, clip, pursuit, rush, footrace, horse race, dog race, automobile race, road race, road rally, drag race, motocross, steeplechase, handicap, round pace, chase, match, heat, lap, *concours* (French), derby, regatta, sweepstakes, turf, track, speedfest*; see also **sport** 3.
Famous races include — *automobile:* Indianapolis 500, Daytona 500, World Grand Prix, New Zealand Grand Prix, Australian Grand Prix, Sebring 12-Hour Endurance Race, Pan Formula Two Grand Prix, Targa Florio Road Race, Grand Prix of Monaco, Monte Carlo Rally, Nürburgring Sports Car Race, Grand Prix of Belgium, Le Mans 24-Hour Race, Grand Prix of France, European Grand Prix, Dutch Grand Prix, Grand Prix of Italy, British Grand Prix, German Grand Prix, United States Road Racing Championship; *horse:* Kentucky Derby, Grand National, Derby, Belmont Stakes, Aqueduct Stakes, Preakness Stakes, Breeders' Cup, Hambletonian (harness), Man O'War Stakes, San Juan Capistrano Handicap, American Derby, Arlington Classic; *yacht:* America's Cup, Admiral's Cup, Bacardi Cup Sailing Championship, St. Petersburg-Fort Lauderdale Race, Lipton Cup Race, Newport-Bermuda Yacht Race, One Ton Cup; *bicycle:* Tour de France, World Road Race Championship, Tour d'Italie, New York Six-Day, Tour of Marin, Montreal Six-Day, U.S. National Championships, Tour de St. Laurent, Tour de Mexico; *marathons:* Boston Marathon, New York City Marathon, London Marathon.
Famous racetracks include: *horse:* Epsom Downs, Churchill Downs, Belmont Park, Pimlico Track, Hialeah Park, Aintree, Saratoga, Leopardstown, Longchamp Racecourse, Gavea, Ascot, Siena; *automobile:* Sebring, Monza, Le Mans, Indianapolis, Bonneville, Brands Hatch, Silverstone.

**race,** *v.* **1.** [To move at great speed] — *Syn.* speed, hurry, run, pursue, chase, tear, tear around, bustle, spurt, press on, dash, run swiftly, hasten, trip, fly, flit, hustle, hie, scud, scorch, rush, sprint, swoop, scuttle, scurry, dart, scamper, hurtle, plunge ahead, whiz, zoom, bolt, scramble, whisk, shoot, post, skim, bowl along, ride hard, hotfoot it*, high-tail it*, make tracks*, barrel*, run like mad*, crowd sail*, wing one's way*, outstrip the wind*, burn up the road*, gun the motor*, step on it*, get the lead out*, skedaddle*, scoot*.
**2.** [To compete] — *Syn.* run a race, compete in a race, contend, follow a course, engage in a contest of speed, enter a competition, run, sprint, race-walk, gallop.

**racecourse,** *n.* — *Syn.* course, path, turf; see **racetrack.**

**racer,** *n.* **1.** [A competitor in a race] — *Syn.* runner, sprinter, marathoner, trackman; see **athlete, runner** 1.
**2.** [A vehicle designed for racing] — *Syn.* racing car, racing bike, racing model, model stripped for racing, formula car, stock car, hot rod*, dragster, speedboat, yacht, flying coffin*, motor bullet*, bronco*, sea flea, scow*.

**racetrack,** *n.* — *Syn.* racecourse, track, speedway, raceway, track circuit, course, turf, path, drive, runway, cinder path, drag strip, the cinders*, oval*, speed oval*, ring*, platter*.

**racial,** *modif.* — *Syn.* lineal, hereditary, ancestral, genetic, ethnic, national, genealogical, phyletic, phylogenic, phylogenetic, ethnological, parental, family.

**raciness,** *n.* **1.** [Sharpness] — *Syn.* tang, pungency, piquancy; see **bitterness** 1, **flavor** 1.
**2.** [Vigor] — *Syn.* vitality, liveliness, spirit; see **action** 1, **vitality.**
**3.** [Indecency] — *Syn.* suggestiveness, indelicacy, ribaldry; see **indecency** 2, **lewdness.**

**racing,** *modif.* — *Syn.* speeding, running, galloping, rushing, hurrying, sailing, whizzing, darting, dashing, flying, tearing, shooting, whisking, zooming, hastening, at full speed, bowling along, burning up the road*, making time*, with the throttle wide open*, going full tilt*. — *Ant.* CRAWLING, creeping, going at a snail's pace.

**racing,** *n.* — *Syn.* track, horse racing, automobile racing, dog racing, harness racing, sporting, the turf, running, galloping, sprinting, trotting, pacing, race-walking, rushing, hurrying, dashing, sailing, whizzing, darting, flying, tearing, competing; see also **competition** 1.

**racism,** *n.* — *Syn.* racial prejudice, racial bias, bigotry, intolerance, bias, racial discrimination, racialism, race hatred, apartheid, segregation, color line, Jim Crow*; see also **prejudice.**

**racist,** *modif.* — *Syn.* bigoted, prejudiced, white supremacist, black supremacist, antiblack, antiwhite, racialist, discriminatory; see also **prejudiced.**

**racist,** *n.* — *Syn.* bigot, white supremacist, racialist; see **bigot.**

**rack,** *n.* 1. [A frame] — *Syn.* holder, receptacle, framework, stand, shelf, ledge, perch, bracket, whatnot, arbor, trivet, box, counter, trestle, scaffold, stretcher, hatrack, clothes rack, hat tree, clothes tree, cake rack, bottle rack, wine rack, baker's rack, pen rack, gun rack, tie rack, towel rack; see also **frame** 1.
2. [An engine of torture] — *Syn.* instrument of torture, wheel, iron heel, wooden horse, thumbscrew, iron maiden, boot, water rack, bed of Procrustes, *peine forte et dure* (French), Oregon boot*; see also **torture.**

**racket,** *n.* 1. [Disturbing noise] — *Syn.* uproar, clatter, din; see **noise** 2, **uproar.**
2. [Confusion accompanied by noise] — *Syn.* disturbance, uproar, squabble, scuffle, fracas, clash, row, wrangle, agitation, babel, pandemonium, turbulence, vociferation, clamor, outcry, hullabaloo, tumult, hubbub, commotion, blare, turmoil, stir, noisy fuss, clatter, charivari, babble, roar, shouting, rumpus, riot, squall, clangor, brawl, fight, pitched battle, free-for-all*, to-do*, great-to-do*, fuss*; see also **confusion** 2, **disturbance** 2.
*See Synonym Study at* NOISE.
3. [*A means of extortion] — *Syn.* illegitimate business, illegal operation, confidence game, con game*, conspiracy, plot, intrigue, underworld activity, systematic cheating, numbers pool, policy racket, protection, swindling, fraud, illegitimate undertaking, extortion, embezzlement, bootlegging, organized crime, illicit scheme, graft, trick, dishonest game, lawlessness, scam*, shakedown*, game*, push*, lay*, dodge*, the squeeze*; see also **corruption** 2, **crime** 2, **theft.**
4. [A web and frame used as a bat]
Types of rackets include: tennis racket, squash racket, racquetball racket, fivesbat, lacrosse net, badminton racket.

**racketeer,** *n.* — *Syn.* gangster, mobster, extortionist, bootlegger; see **criminal.**

**racy,** *modif.* 1. [Full of zest] — *Syn.* rich, pungent, piquant, spicy, sharp, spirited, saucy, appetizing, smart, clever, witty, exhilarating, vigorous, forcible, strong, lively, vivacious, animated, exciting, sprightly, buoyant, playful, sportive, forceful, energetic, keen, bright, stimulating, fiery, gingery, peppery, snappy. — *Ant.* DULL, doughy, flat.
2. [*Not quite respectable] — *Syn.* indecent, erotic, suggestive, risqué; see **lewd** 1, **risqué.**

**radar,** *n.* — *Syn.* radio detecting *and* ranging, radio locator (British), radiolocation, AWACS, Loran, teleran, Missile Site Radar (MSR), Multi-Function Array Radar (MAR); see also **detector, electronics.**

**radial,** *modif.* — *Syn.* branching, branched, outspread, spoked; see **spiral, spreading.**

**radiance,** *n.* — *Syn.* brightness, brilliance, effulgence, joy; see **happiness** 1, 2, **light** 1.

**radiant,** *modif.* — *Syn.* shining, luminous, radiating, beaming; see **bright** 1, **happy** 1.
*See Synonym Study at* BRIGHT.

**radiate,** *v.* 1. [To send forth from a center] — *Syn.* shed, diffuse, spread, disperse, shoot in all directions, irradiate, emit, emit in rays, transmit, disseminate, broadcast, dispel, strew, scatter, sprinkle, circulate, send out in rays from a point, throw out, branch out, expand, widen; see also **scatter** 2, **spread** 3.
2. [To shed light or heat] — *Syn.* beam, shine, light up, illumine, heat, warm, circulate, brighten, illuminate, irradiate, glitter, glisten, glow, glare, gleam, glimmer, flare, blaze, flicker, sparkle, flash, scintillate, shimmer, coruscate, reflect, fulgurate; see also **light** 1, **shine** 1.

**radiation,** *n.* 1. [Dissemination] — *Syn.* propagation, dissipation, divarication, polarization, scattering, spread, diffraction, transmission, broadcast, emission, ramification, diffusion, dispersion, circulation, divergence, dispersal; see also **distribution** 1.
2. [Fallout] — *Syn.* nuclear particles, radioactive particles, radioactivity, radiant energy; see **fallout, pollution, X-rays.**

**radical,** *modif.* 1. [Fundamental] — *Syn.* basic, original, primitive, underlying; see **fundamental** 1, **organic.**
2. [Advocating extreme change] — *Syn.* extremist, revolutionary, fanatical, militant, rabid, insurgent, iconoclastic, advanced, forward, insurrectionary, progressive, revisionist, abolitionist, leftist, communistic, left-wing, uncompromising, intransigent, recalcitrant, mutinous, rebellious, recusant, subversive, seditious, riotous, lawless, ultraconservative, racist, white supremacist, insubordinate, anarchistic, nihilistic, Bolshevistic, Communist, socialist, liberal, immoderate, heretical, freethinking, avant-garde, Jacobinic, ultraist, ultraistic, ultra, red*, pink*; see also **fanatical, rebellious** 2, **revolutionary** 1. — *Ant.* CONSERVATIVE, reformist, gradualist.
3. [Thoroughgoing] — *Syn.* extreme, drastic, thorough, complete; see **comprehensive, extreme** 2.
*See Synonym Study at* LIBERAL.

**radical,** *n.* — *Syn.* extremist, militant, revolutionary, fanatic, insurgent, objector, revolutionist, insurrectionist, leftist, anarchist, socialist, communist, pacifist, syndicalist, nihilist, ultraist, ultra, subversive, rebel, revolter, mutineer, firebrand, Jacobin, sans-culotte, Bolshevik, Bolshevist, anarcho-syndicalist, renegade, crusader, individualist, fascist, Nazi, racist, white supremacist, misfit, iconoclast, member of the lunatic fringe, eccentric, freethinker, rightist, yippie, hippie, Black nationalist, demonstrator, peace marcher, rioter, fifth columnist, nonconformist, left-winger, right-winger, ultraconservative, John Bircher, pinko*, red*; see also **agitator, rebel** 1.

**radically,** *modif.* 1. [Completely] — *Syn.* wholly, thoroughly, entirely; see **completely.**
2. [Originally] — *Syn.* basically, fundamentally, primitively, firstly; see **essentially.**

**radio,** *n.* 1. [The study and practice of wireless communication] — *Syn.* radio transmission, radio reception, signaling, radio engineering, radiotelephony, radiotelegraphy, television, radio work, radio operation, radionics; see also **broadcasting, communication** 1, **communications.**
2. [A receiving device] — *Syn.* receiver, tuner, AM-FM radio, shortwave radio, clock radio, transistor radio, transistor, portable radio, pocket radio, car radio, Walkman (trademark), home radio, radio set, console, wireless, ship's radio, ship-to-shore radio, CB radio,

walkie-talkie, two-way radio, crystal set, ghetto blaster\*, boom box\*, squawk box; see also **communications.**

**radioactive,** *modif.* — *Syn.* active, energetic, contaminated, irradiated, dangerous, hot\*; see also **poisonous.**

**radioactivity,** *n.* — *Syn.* radiant energy, radiation, radioactive particles, Roentgen rays; see **energy** 3, **fallout.**

**radiogram,** *n.* — *Syn.* telegram, cablegram, message; see **telegram.**

**radiograph,** *n.* — *Syn.* negative, roentgenogram, gamma-ray picture; see **photograph, X-rays.**

**radio wave,** *n.* — *Syn.* FM (frequency modulation), AM (amplitude modulation), sound wave; see **frequency** 2.

**radius,** *n.* — *Syn.* space, sweep, range, semidiameter, spoke, compass, reach, span, interval, limit, scope, extent; see also **boundary, expanse.**

**raffle,** *n.* — *Syn.* sweepstakes, pool, lottery, drawing, sweeps, lots, stake, wager, flier, wagering, game of chance, bet, betting, toss-up, speculation, gaming, long odds, random shot; see also **gambling.**

**raft,** *n.* — *Syn.* flatboat, barge, float, pontoon, lighter, catamaran, life raft, swimming raft, rubber raft, balsa; see also **boat.**

**rafter,** *n.* — *Syn.* beam, timber, crossbeam, roof beam, rib, common rafter, hip rafter, jack rafter, valley rafter; see also **beam** 1, **timber** 2.

**rag,** *n.* — *Syn.* cloth, remnant, wiper, dishrag, dustcloth, discarded material, hand rag, tatter, shred, scrap, chamois cloth; see also **cloth.**

**chew the rag\*** — *Syn.* chat, converse, have a talk; see **talk** 1.

**rag\*,** *v.* — *Syn.* tease, taunt, nag, scold; see **bother** 2, **ridicule.**

**ragamuffin,** *n.* — *Syn.* beggar, waif, urchin; see **orphan, tramp** 1.

**rage,** *n.* 1. [Violent anger] — *Syn.* fury, wrath, ferocity; see **anger.**

2. [A fit of anger] — *Syn.* frenzy, tantrum, uproar, paroxysm, hysterics, explosion, storm, outburst, spasm, convulsion, fit, eruption, furor, passion, excitement, extreme agitation, madness, vehemence, fury, rampage, huff, wrath, raving, towering rage, choler, spleen, ire, resentment, bitterness, acerbity, gall, ferment, acrimony, irritation, animosity, exasperation, indignation, heat, temper, umbrage, squall, blowup\*, apoplexy\*, fireworks\*, conniption\*, conniption fit\*, hemorrhage\*; see also **fit** 2.

3. [The object of enthusiasm and imitation] — *Syn.* fad, trend, style, mode, fashion, vogue, craze, mania, the last word, the latest, the latest thing\*, the in thing\*, the newest wrinkle\*; see also **fad.**

**all the rage** — *Syn.* modish, in style, in vogue, much in demand; see **fashionable, popular** 1.

*See Synonym Study at* ANGER, FASHION.

**rage,** *v.* 1. [To give vent to anger] — *Syn.* rant, fume, rave, storm, yell, scream, rant and rave, lose one's temper, foam, splutter, flame, roar, rail, boil, boil over, shake, quiver, fulminate, seethe, shout, scold, have a tantrum, explode, run amok, run riot, rampage, fly apart, flare up, blow up, blaze up, flame up, fire up, bristle up, carry on, go on, show violent anger, act with fury, be violently agitated, bluster, be furious, get mad, get sore, anger, be livid, fret, chafe, work oneself into a sweat\*, go berserk\*, go through the roof\*, hit the ceiling\*, go into a tailspin\*, have a fit, have a conniption fit\*, blow one's top\*, breathe fire and fury\*, go on the warpath\*, go on the rampage\*, put one's fur up\*, gnash one's teeth\*, raise Cain\*, raise the devil\*, take on\*, throw a fit\*, go into orbit\*, fly out\*, fly off the handle\*,

fly into a passion\*, vent one's spleen\*, stamp with rage, look black, snap at, run mad, raise a storm, bridle up, blow a fuse\*, get hot under the collar\*, fly off at a tangent\*, cut loose\*, have a hemorrhage\*, get one's gorge up\*, get one's back up\*, foam at the mouth\*, make a fuss over\*, kick up a row\*, have a nervous breakdown\*, let off steam\*, look daggers\*, get oneself into a lather\*, lose one's head\*, flip out\*, flip one's lid\*. — *Ant.* be calm, calm down, pout.

2. [To be out of control] — *Syn.* storm, overflow, break out, erupt, explode, flare, roar; see also **burn** 1, **run** 1.

3. [To become insane] — *Syn.* go crazy, go insane, go mad, become mentally ill, take leave of one's senses, run amok, crack up\*, go nuts\*, go haywire\*, go balmy\*, go loony\*, break down\*, go off the deep end\*, flip out\*; see also **crack up** 2.

**ragged,** *modif.* — *Syn.* tattered, in shreds, patched, shabby, rough-edged, worn, badly worn, rough, worn-out, broken, worn to rags, frayed, frazzled, threadbare, shoddy, out at the seams, shredded, battered, the worse for wear, worn to a thread, down at the heels, motheaten, full of holes, torn, rent, unpressed, poorly made, badly dressed, beat-up\*; see also **shabby** 1, **worn** 2. — *Ant.* WHOLE, new, unworn.

**run ragged\*,** — *Syn.* exhaust, harass, wear out; see **tire** 2.

**raging,** *modif.* — *Syn.* furious, irate, enraged; see **angry.**

**ragout,** *n.* — *Syn.* stew, hash, *pot-au-feu* (French), goulash; see **stew.**

**ragpicker,** *n.* — *Syn.* junk dealer, scavenger, ragman; see **beggar** 2, **junk dealer.**

**rags,** *n.* — *Syn.* old clothes, patched clothing, tatters, torn garments, shreds and patches, scraps, castoff clothes, castoffs, hand-me-downs, shreds, frazzles, patches, remnants; see also **clothes.**

**ragtime,** *n.* — *Syn.* jazz, swing, Dixieland; see **jazz, music** 1.

**raid,** *n.* 1. [A predatory attack] — *Syn.* invasion, assault, forced entrance, sortie, sweep, reconnaissance in force, incursion, foray; see also **attack** 1.

2. [An armed investigation] — *Syn.* seizure, surprise entrance, police raid, roundup, bust\*, shootup\*; see also **arrest** 1, **capture.**

**raid,** *v.* — *Syn.* attack, assail, storm, fire on, march on, bomb, shell, bombard, rake, torpedo, strafe, strike at, charge, loot, assault, forage, pirate, maraud, sack, ransack, despoil, invade, force an entrance, make away with, besiege, plunder, pillage, blockade; see also **attack** 1. — *Ant.* surrender, DEFEND, protect.

**raider,** *n.* 1. [A person who makes raids] — *Syn.* bandit, thief, robber, plunderer, looter, pillager, rifler, assaulter, highwayman, brigand, privateer, invader, commando, guerrilla, cavalryman, marauder, hijacker, cattle lifter, rustler, predator, wrecker, depredator, pirate, freebooter, holdup man, sharper, pilferer, poacher, viking, bushranger, spoiler, corsair, filibuster, picaroon, filcher, buccaneer, despoiler, sacker, abductor; see also **criminal, pirate, robber.**

2. [A vessel engaged in raiding] — *Syn.* privateer, pirate ship, brigantine, corsair, submarine, U-boat, mosquito boat, torpedo boat; see also **ship.**

**rail,** *n.* 1. [A polelike structure] — *Syn.* bar, post, railing, barrier, picket, rail fence, siding, balustrade, banister, paling, rest, handrail, guardrail, grab bar, brass rail; see also **bar** 1, **fence** 1.

2. [A track; *often plural*] — *Syn.* railway, monorail, railroad track; see **railroad, track** 1.

**go off the rails\*** — *Syn.* go crazy, run amok, become insane; see **rage** 3.

**ride on a rail** — *Syn.* drive away, exile, run out of town; see **banish** 1.

**rail at,** *v.* — *Syn.* thunder against, rant, inveigh against; see **censure, denounce, rage** 1.

**railing,** *n.* — *Syn.* balustrade, fence, banister; see **rail** 1.

**raillery,** *n.* — *Syn.* banter, badinage, joking, teasing; see **fun, parody, ridicule, teasing.**

**railroad,** *n.* — *Syn.* track, line, railway, railway, trains, rails, elevated, underground, subway, *métro* (French), tube (British), commuter line, cable railway, monorail, cog railway, sidetrack, siding, passing track, loading track, feeder line, main line, double track, single track, trunk line, transcontinental railroad, system, el★, iron horse★; see also **train** 2.

**railway,** *n.* — *Syn.* track, line, route; see **railroad.**

**raiment,** *n.* — *Syn.* attire, garments, clothing; see **clothes.**

**rain,** *n.* **1.** [Water falling in drops] — *Syn.* drizzle, mist, sprinkle, sprinkling, rainfall, shower, precipitation, wet weather, downpour, torrent, pouring rain, driving rain, damp day, spring rain, cat-and-dog weather★, liquid sunshine★, mizzle★, Scotch mist★.
**2.** [A rainstorm] — *Syn.* thunderstorm, thundershower, tempest, cloudburst; see **storm** 1.

**rain,** *v.* — *Syn.* pour, drizzle, drop, fall, shower, sprinkle, precipitate, mist, mizzle★, come down, teem, spit, set in, lay the dust, patter, rain cats and dogs★, come down in buckets★, rain pitchforks★; see also **storm.**

**rainbow,** *n.* — *Syn.* iris, prism, colors; see **spectrum.**

**raincoat,** *n.* — *Syn.* trench coat, slicker, oilskin, mackintosh, mac★, London Fog (trademark), Burberry (trademark), rain poncho, waterproof, waterproof coat, water-repellent coat, Gore-Tex jacket (trademark), rubber coat, protector, sou'wester, windbreaker, parka, shell, reversible, overcoat; see also **clothes, coat** 1.

**raindrop,** *n.* — *Syn.* drop, sprinkle, dewdrop; see **rain** 1.

**rainfall,** *n.* — *Syn.* precipitation, rain, moisture; see **rain** 1.

**rain gauge,** *n.* — *Syn.* hyetometer, hyetograph, ombrometer, instrument for measuring rainfall, udomograph, ombrograph, pluviograph, udometer, pluviometer, hyetometrograph; see also **gauge.**

**rain or shine★,** *modif.* — *Syn.* without fail, regardless, whatever may happen; see **inevitable, regular** 1, 2.

**rainproof,** *modif.* — *Syn.* watertight, impermeable, waterproof, water-repellent; see **waterproof.**

**rainy,** *modif.* — *Syn.* moist, wet, coastal, drizzly; see **stormy** 1, **wet** 2.

**raise,** *n.* — *Syn.* increase, salary increment, advance; see **addition** 2, **promotion** 1.

**raise,** *v.* **1.** [To cause to rise] — *Syn.* lift, uplift, upraise, upheave, elevate, erect, hoist, run up, pull up, set up, lift up, pick up, stand up, tilt up, take up, bring up, move up, put up, hold up, cock up, heave, set upright, put on its end, boost, upcast, lever, exalt, rear, mount, pry, prize, heighten, hike★, up★, jack up★. — *Ant.* LOWER, bring down, take down.
**2.** [To nurture] — *Syn.* bring up, rear, care for, parent, nurse, suckle, nourish, wean, breed, cultivate, grow, train, foster; see also **grow** 3, **support** 5.
**3.** [To collect or make available] — *Syn.* gather, amass, allocate, procure, solicit, bring together, borrow, have ready; see also **accumulate** 1, **appropriate** 2.
**4.** [To erect] — *Syn.* build, construct, establish, put up; see **build** 1.
**5.** [To ask] — *Syn.* bring up, suggest, put; see **ask** 1, **propose** 1.
**6.** [To advance in rank] — *Syn.* elevate, exalt, dignify, honor; see **promote** 2.

**7.** [To increase] — *Syn.* advance, boost, inflate, jack up★; see **increase** 1.
*See Synonym Study at* LIFT.

**raise Cain★,** *v.* — *Syn.* create a disturbance, cause trouble, storm; see **rage** 1.

**raised,** *modif.* **1.** [Elevated] — *Syn.* lifted, hoisted, built high, heightened, set high, in relief, embossed, built, erected, constructed, set up, jerry-built; see also **built** 1. — *Ant.* REDUCED, lowered, taken down.
**2.** [Nurtured] — *Syn.* reared, brought up, trained, prepared, educated, fostered, bred, nourished, nursed.
**3.** [Produced] — *Syn.* grown, harvested, cultivated, bred, made, mass-produced, assembly-lined★.

**raise hell★,** *v.* — *Syn.* carry on, celebrate, carouse, create an uproar; see **celebrate** 3, **rage** 1.

**rajah,** *n.* — *Syn.* Indian monarch, ruler, maharajah; see **chief** 2, **king** 1, **ruler** 1.

**rake,** *n.* **1.** [A debauched person] — *Syn.* lecher, roué, libertine, playboy, profligate, sensualist, seducer, philanderer, womanizer, gigolo, Don Juan, Casanova, Lothario; see also **rascal.**
**2.** [A pronged implement]
Types of rakes include: refuse, clam, lawn, garden, York (trademark), gleaning, moss, hay, buck, stubble, weeding, oyster, horse, revolving, sweep, dump, side-delivery; leaf sweeper; see also **tool.**

**rake,** *v.* **1.** [To use a rake] — *Syn.* clear up, collect, scratch, gather, scrape, scrape together, clean up, furrow, comb, weed, clear, grade, level, smooth; see also **clean, smooth** 1, **sweep.**
**2.** [To sweep with gunfire] — *Syn.* strafe, machine-gun, blister; see **shoot** 1.

**rake-off★,** *n.* — *Syn.* illegal fee, illegitimate commission, cut★, kickback★; see **booty, commission** 5, **pay** 1, **profit** 2.

**rakish,** *modif.* — *Syn.* smart, dashing, raffish; see **fashionable, jaunty.**

**rally,** *n.* — *Syn.* mass meeting, demonstration, gathering, assembly; see **gathering.**

**rally,** *v.* **1.** [To return to the attack] — *Syn.* unite against, reassemble, renew, redouble, counterattack, come together, charge, come around, come about, surge forward; see also **attack** 1, **gather** 1, **return** 1, **revenge.** — *Ant.* disperse, SCATTER, disintegrate.
**2.** [To urge others to rally, sense 1] — *Syn.* call to arms, inspirit, rouse; see **encourage** 2, **urge** 2.
**3.** [To summon for a common purpose] — *Syn.* marshal, mobilize, muster, unite; see **assemble** 2, **gather** 2.
**4.** [To regain strength] — *Syn.* surge, recuperate, revive, grow stronger; see **recover** 3, **revive** 2.
*See Synonym Study at* STIR.

**ram,** *n.* **1.** [An object used to deliver a thrust] — *Syn.* plunger, pump, beam, prow, hammerhead, arm piece, weight, pole, shaft, lever, spike, battering ram, pile driver, tamping iron, punch, sledge hammer, rammer, tamper, monkey, bat, maul, hydraulic ram, spar, piston, drop weight, bow; see also **bar** 1, **hammer.**
**2.** [A male sheep] — *Syn.* tup, wild ram, buck, bucksheep; see **sheep.**
Breeds of rams include: Leicester, Rambouillet, Merino, Lincoln, Jacob, Scottish blackface, Wensleydale, Oxforddown, Hampshire, Cotswold, Southdown, Suffolk, Shropshire, Cheviot.

**ram,** *v.* **1.** [To strike with force] — *Syn.* bump, slam, collide, hook; see **butt** 1, **crash** 4, **hit** 1, 2.
**2.** [To thrust or pack forcibly] — *Syn.* drive, cram, jam, stuff; see **drive** 4, **pack** 2.

**ramble,** *v.* **1.** [To saunter] — *Syn.* stroll, promenade, roam, wander; see **roam, walk** 1.

**2.** [To speak or write aimlessly] — *Syn.* drift, stray, diverge, meander, blather, talk nonsense, chatter, babble, digress, maunder, get off the point, get off the subject, go off on a tangent, go on and on, talk discursively, write without sequence of ideas, expatiate, protract, enlarge, descant, be diffuse, prose, dwell on, harp on, dilate, amplify, go astray, wander, gossip, drivel, rant and rave, talk at random, talk off the top of one's head, beat around the bush.

**3.** [To go in various directions; *said especially of vines*] — *Syn.* twist, twine, wander, roam, branch off, climb, spread, fork, straggle, stray, extend, grow, clamber, trail; see also **turn** 6, **wind** 3.

**rambler,** *n.* **1.** [One who rambles] — *Syn.* rover, wanderer, globe-trotter, nomad; see **traveler, walker.**

**2.** [A rambling flower or vine] — *Syn.* rambling rose, climber, climbing shrub; see **rose, vine.**

**rambling,** *modif.* **1.** [Strolling] — *Syn.* roaming, sauntering, roving, wandering, walking, hiking, promenading, taking a walk, moving about, wandering about aimlessly, perambulatory, straggling, wayfaring, nomadic, meandering, taking an irregular course, vagrant, zigzagging, itinerant, migratory, ambulatory, peripatetic; see also **walking, wandering** 1.

**2.** [Incoherent] — *Syn.* discursive, disconnected, long-winded, diffuse; see **incoherent** 2, **verbose.**

**3.** [Covering considerable territory without much plan] — *Syn.* spread out, strewn, straggling, trailing, random, here and there, at length, widely thrown, unplanned, sprawling, gangling; see also **scattered.** — *Ant.* closely formed, PLANNED, compact.

**rambunctious,** *modif.* — *Syn.* boisterous, noisy, obstreperous; see **loud** 2, **rude** 2, **turbulent, unruly.**

**ramification,** *n.* **1.** [The process of branching] — *Syn.* forking, divarication, bifurcation, radiation, breaking, branching, dividing, subdividing, shooting off, partition; see also **division** 1. — *Ant.* CONCENTRATION, centralization, uniting.

**2.** [A result of ramification, sense 1] — *Syn.* offshoot, bough, river; see **branch** 2, **division** 2.

**3.** [A derived effect] — *Syn.* consequence, repercussion, outgrowth, implication; see **result.**

**ramp,** *n.* — *Syn.* incline, slope, grade; see **grade** 1, **inclination** 5.

**rampage,** *n.* — *Syn.* turmoil, uproar, ferment; see **disturbance** 2, **violence** 1.

**rampageous,** *modif.* — *Syn.* boisterous, uncontrollable, wild; see **turbulent, unruly, violent** 4.

**rampant,** *modif.* — *Syn.* raging, uncontrolled, growing without check, wild, violent, vehement, impetuous, turbulent, rank, luxuriant, exuberant, profuse, blustering, tumultuous, boisterous, furious, unruly, rife, prevalent, widespread, dominant, predominant, prevailing, excessive, clamorous, fanatical, exceeding all bounds, impassioned, unrestrained, unbridled, unchecked, epidemic, pandemic, extravagant, overabundant, out of control, sweeping the country, like wildfire*; see also **plentiful** 2, **wild** 3. — *Ant.* restrained, mild, scarce.

**rampart,** *n.* — *Syn.* barricade, embankment, earthwork, bulwark; see **barrier, fortification** 2, **support** 2, **wall** 1.

**ramshackle,** *modif.* — *Syn.* crumbling, rickety, dilapidated, tumbledown; see **decaying, unsteady** 1, **weak** 2.

**ranch,** *n.* — *Syn.* farm, cattle farm, sheep farm, plantation, grange, farmstead, ranchland, ranch house, ranch buildings, hacienda, dude ranch, rancho, spread*, holdout*; see also **farm, property** 2.

**rancher,** *n.* — *Syn.* ranch owner, ranchman, stockman, breeder, cattle farmer, cowkeeper, cowherder, shepherd,

drover, grazier, stock breeder, horse trainer, herdsman, herder, ranchero, broncobuster, granger, cattleman, cowboy, cattle baron, cattle king; see also **farmer.**

**rancid,** *modif.* **1.** [Decaying] — *Syn.* rotten, spoiled, tainted, turned, stale, sour, bad, contaminated, polluted, unhealthy, noxious, moldy, carious, putrescent, impure, decomposing, putrefied, musty, rank, fetid, foul. — *Ant.* FRESH, fragrant, sweet.

**2.** [Having a rank taste and odor] — *Syn.* foul, fetid, rank, stinking, reeking, putrid, offensive, smelly, sour, disagreeable, malodorous, strong-smelling, saprogenous, cloacal, feculent, mephitic, sharp, pungent, nasty, disgusting, evil-smelling, gamy, high, strong, putrefactive, turned, musty, reeky, noisome; see also **rank** 2.

**rancor,** *n.* — *Syn.* malice, spite, hatred, malignity, enmity, ill will, malevolence, ill feeling, animosity, animus, hostility, bitterness, resentment, unfriendliness, antagonism, variance, antipathy, aversion, uncharitableness, vindictiveness, hardness of heart, acrimony, harshness, venom, mordacity, acerbity, ruthlessness, umbrage, pique, bile, spleen, virulence, spitefulness, vengeance, grudge, dudgeon, vengefulness, revengefulness, retaliation; see also **hate.** — *Ant.* FRIENDSHIP, love, good will.

**random,** *modif.* — *Syn.* haphazard, chance, casual, arbitrary, desultory, aimless, indiscriminate, irregular, unsystematic, undirected, unplanned, planless, purposeless, orderless, accidental, fortuitous, blind, hit-or-miss, stray, erratic, aleatory, stochastic; see also **aimless, haphazard, irregular** 1.

**at random** — *Syn.* haphazardly, by chance, aimlessly; see **accidentally, haphazardly.**

---

*SYN.* — **random** applies to that which occurs or is done without careful choice, aim, plan, etc. *[a random remark]*; **haphazard** applies to that which is done, made, or said without regard for its consequences, relevance, etc. and therefore stresses the implication of accident or chance *[a haphazard selection of books]*; **casual** implies happening or seeming to happen by chance without intention or purpose and often connotes nonchalance, indifference, etc. *[a casual glance at the newspaper]*; **desultory** suggests a lack of method or system, as in jumping from one thing to another *[her desultory reading in the textbook]*; **chance** emphasizes accidental occurrence without prearrangement or planning *[a chance encounter]*

---

**range,** *n.* **1.** [Distance] — *Syn.* limit, reach, span, horizontal projection; see **expanse.**

**2.** [Extent] — *Syn.* scope, compass, reach, gamut, scale, continuum, area, purview, realm, sphere, expanse, sweep, spectrum, register, series, variety, assortment, array, gradation, progression; see also **extent.**

**3.** [A series of mountains] — *Syn.* highlands, sierras, chain; see **mountain** 1.

**4.** [Land open to grazing] — *Syn.* pasture, grazing land, field, meadow, lea, plain, grassland, prairie land; see also **country** 1.

**5.** [A kitchen stove] — *Syn.* gas range, electric range, portable range; see **appliance, stove.**

**out of range** — *Syn.* beyond reach, safe, out of earshot; see **distant** 1.

---

*SYN.* — **range** refers to the full extent over which something operates or is perceivable, effective, etc. and may suggest variation within those limits *[the range of one's influence, a wide range of interests]*; **reach** refers to the furthest limit of effectiveness, influence, etc. /beyond the *reach* of my understanding/; **scope** refers to the extent of action, inquiry, etc. and suggests considerable room and freedom of range, but within prescribed limits /does it fall within the *scope* of this investigation?/; **compass** suggests completeness within limits regarded as a circumference /he did all within the *compass* of his power/; **gamut** refers to the full range of shades, tones, etc. between the limits of something /the full *gamut* of emotions/

---

**range,** *v.* **1.** [To vary] — *Syn.* differ, fluctuate, extend; see **change** 4, **reach** 1, **vary** 1.
**2.** [To traverse wide areas] — *Syn.* encompass, reach, spread over, pass over, sweep over, cover, stray, cruise, stroll, wander, ramble, explore, scour, search, reconnoiter, traverse, roam, rove; see also **cross** 1, **travel** 2.
**3.** [To place in order] — *Syn.* line up, classify, arrange, rank; see **order** 3.
**ranger,** *n.* **1.** [Forester] — *Syn.* forest ranger, fire warden, game warden, woodsman; see **watchman.**
**2.** [Trooper] — *Syn.* mounted police officer, patrolman, guard; see **police officer, soldier.**
**ranging,** *modif.* **1.** [Grazing] — *Syn.* feeding, nibbling grass, browsing, chewing cud, pasturing; see also **grazing** 1, 2.
**2.** [Varying] — *Syn.* fluctuating, differing, shifting, extending; see **changing, extending.**
**3.** [Moving over wide areas] — *Syn.* roaming, roving, covering, traversing, flying over, sweeping, spanning, overrunning, stretching through; see also **traveling** 2.
**rangy,** *modif.* — *Syn.* skinny, lanky, gangling; see **thin** 2.
**rank,** *modif.* **1.** [Having luxurious growth] — *Syn.* wild, dense, lush, vigorous, tall of growth, tropical, semitropical, overabundant, jungly, fertile, rich, productive, high-growing, fructiferous, coarse, overgrown, luxuriant, exuberant, profuse, prolific, lavish, excessive, rampant, extreme; see also **green** 2, **thick** 1. — *Ant.* sparse, THIN, barren.
**2.** [Having a foul odor] — *Syn.* smelly, fetid, putrid, stinking, rancid, disagreeable, smelling, offensive, sour, foul, fusty, noisome, noxious, stale, tainted, gamy, musty, strong, putrescent, rotten, moldy, high, ill-smelling, turned, nauseating, obnoxious, disgusting, reeking, mephitic, malodorous, ordurous, nasty, feculent, strong-smelling, graveolent. — *Ant.* fragrant, SWEET, fresh.
**3.** [Corrupt] — *Syn.* gross, coarse, indecent; see **outrageous, wicked** 1.
**4.** [Utter] — *Syn.* complete, outright, flagrant; see **absolute** 1.
**rank,** *n.* **1.** [A row] — *Syn.* column, file, series, string; see **line** 1.
**2.** [Degree] — *Syn.* seniority, standing, station, authority, status, grade, class, order, level, sphere; see also **degree** 2.
**3.** [Social eminence] — *Syn.* station, position, status, distinction, note, nobility, class, caste, privilege, standing, reputation, quality, situation, esteem, condition, state, place, place in society, circumstance, footing, grade, blood, family, pedigree, ancestry, stock, parentage, birth.
**pull rank on\*** — *Syn.* take advantage of, exploit, abuse subordinates; see **abuse** 1, **command** 1, 2.
**rank,** *v.* **1.** [To arrange in a row or rows] — *Syn.* array, put in line, line up, place in formation; see **line** 4, **order** 3.
**2.** [To evaluate comparatively] — *Syn.* rate, grade, sort,

order, arrange, dispose, place, put, regard, judge, assign, classify, give precedence to, fix, establish, settle, estimate, value, valuate, list, prioritize; see also **classify.**
**3.** [To possess relative evaluation] — *Syn.* be worth, stand, have a place, head, go ahead of, go before, be anterior to, come first, forerun, antecede, have supremacy over, have the advantage of, precede, outrank, take the lead, take precedence, belong, count among, be classed, stand in relationship.
**rank and file,** *n.* **1.** [Soldiers] — *Syn.* infantry, enlisted personnel, privates; see **ranks, soldier, troops.**
**2.** [The common people] — *Syn.* general membership, general public, commonalty, masses; see **commoner, member** 1, **people** 3.
**ranked,** *modif.* — *Syn.* ordered, arranged, graded, grouped, piled, stacked, neatly stacked, corded, heaped; see also **organized, rated.** — *Ant.* DISORDERED, disarranged, strewn.
**rankle,** *v.* — *Syn.* annoy, bother, pain, rile, nettle, mortify, chafe, fret, hurt, gall, irritate, inflame, fester, gnaw at, lie embedded; see also **anger.**
**rankling,** *modif.* — *Syn.* festering, galling, irritating; see **disturbing.**
**ranks,** *pl.n.* — *Syn.* rank and file, soldiers, lower strata, common soldiery, men, enlisted personnel; see also **army** 1, **soldier.**
**ransack,** *v.* **1.** [To search thoroughly] — *Syn.* rummage, scour, comb, rake, explore, turn upside down, turn inside out, look all over, look high and low, leave no stone unturned, seek everywhere, ferret out, nose out, hunt out, overhaul, sound, spy, peer, look around, pry, scan, probe, look into, investigate, scrutinize; see also **hunt** 2, **search.**
**2.** [To loot] — *Syn.* pillage, plunder, strip, despoil, rifle, forage, maraud, raid, sack, burglarize, burgle, spoil, poach, gut, rustle, thieve, ravage, lay waste, pilfer, rob; see also **raid, rob, steal.**
**ransom,** *n.* — *Syn.* redemption money, price, payment, payoff\*; see **bribe.**
**ransom,** *v.* — *Syn.* release, rescue, deliver, recover, regain, emancipate, unchain, unfetter, buy off, extricate, reprieve, liberate, save; see also **free** 1, **redeem** 1, **rescue** 1, 2.
*See Synonym Study at* RESCUE.
**rant,** *n.* — *Syn.* bombast, tirade, raving, rhetoric; see **nonsense** 1.
**rant,** *v.* — *Syn.* rave, fume, rail, harangue; see **bluster, rage** 1.
**ranting,** *modif.* — *Syn.* raging, raving, mad; see **angry, insane** 1.
**rap,** *n.* — *Syn.* knock, thump, slap; see **blow** 1.
**beat the rap\*** — *Syn.* avoid punishment, evade, be acquitted; see **escape.**
**bum rap\*** — *Syn.* unfair sentence, blame, frame\*; see **injustice** 2, **punishment.**
**take the rap\*** — *Syn.* be punished, suffer, take the blame; see **pay for.**
**rap,** *v.* **1.** [To tap sharply] — *Syn.* knock, strike, whack; see **beat** 1, 2, **hit** 1.
**2.** [\*To talk] — *Syn.* chat, discuss freely, speak, converse; see **discuss, talk** 1.
**rapacious,** *modif.* **1.** [Greedy] — *Syn.* grasping, avaricious, insatiable; see sense 2; **greedy** 1, 2.
**2.** [Living on prey] — *Syn.* ravening, ravenous, predatory, predacious, carnivorous, devouring, voracious, omnivorous, depredatory, extortionate, murderous, raptorial, vulturous, wolfish, lupine; see also **greedy** 2, **savage** 2.

**rapacity,** *n.* **1.** [Greed]— *Syn.* avarice, covetousness, voracity; see **greed.**
**2.** [Plunder]— *Syn.* thieving, thievery, marauding; see **theft.**

**rape,** *n.*— *Syn.* violation, sexual assault, seduction, deflowering, criminal assault, abduction, statutory offense, statutory rape, defilement, abuse, molestation, devirgination, defloration, ill-usage, maltreatment, ravishment, date rape, acquaintance rape, forcible violation, gangbang★; see also **crime** 2.

**rape,** *v.*— *Syn.* violate, assault, seize, outrage, compromise, force, molest, ravish, attack, defile, deflower, wrong, despoil, devirginate, debauch, ruin, corrupt, seduce, maltreat, abuse, bang★, take advantage of★.

**raped,** *modif.*— *Syn.* assaulted, ravished, abused; see **ruined** 3.

**rapid,** *modif.* **1.** [Swift]— *Syn.* fast, speedy, accelerated, hurried; see **fast** 1.
**2.** [Quick]— *Syn.* nimble, light-footed, fleet, mercurial, brisk, expeditious, winged, lively, ready, prompt, spry; see also **active** 2, **agile.**— *Ant.* LISTLESS, sluggish, languid.
*See Synonym Study at* FAST.

**rapidity,** *n.*— *Syn.* swiftness, celerity, dispatch; see **speed.**

**rapidly,** *modif.*— *Syn.* fast, swiftly, posthaste; see **immediately, quickly** 1.

**rapier,** *n.*— *Syn.* cutlass, epee, blade; see **sword.**

**rapist,** *n.*— *Syn.* attacker, raper, ravager, ravisher, defiler, seducer, despoiler, betrayer, debaucher, deceiver, sex criminal; see also **criminal, rascal.**

**rapport,** *n.*— *Syn.* harmony, compatibility, affinity; see **agreement** 2.

**rapprochement** (French), *n.*— *Syn.* reconciliation, understanding, accommodation, friendliness; see **agreement** 2, 3, **friendship** 1.

**rapscallion,** *n.*— *Syn.* scoundrel, scamp, rogue; see **rascal.**

**rapt,** *modif.* **1.** [Enraptured]— *Syn.* transported, entranced, enchanted, bewitched, charmed, hypnotized, mesmerized, captivated, fascinated, ecstatic, enthralled, spellbound, overwhelmed, beguiled, delighted, enamored, ravished, taken, held, caught; see also **happy** 1.— *Ant.* unaffected, IMPASSIVE, unconcerned.
**2.** [Engrossed]— *Syn.* absorbed, occupied, intent, engaged, preoccupied, immersed, wrapped up in, gripped, riveted, lost, unconscious, employed, involved, inattentive, dreaming, oblivious, abstracted, absent, absent-minded, caught up in, hung up★; see also **absent-minded, busy** 1.— *Ant.* UNCONCERNED, uninterested, indifferent.

**rapture,** *n.* **1.** [Delight]— *Syn.* happiness, pleasure, joy, satisfaction, enjoyment, felicity, exhilaration, contentment, gladness, gratification, enchantment, bewitchment, elation, euphoria, ecstasy, transport, rhapsody, jubilation, buoyancy, altitudes★, seventh heaven★, cloud nine★; see also **happiness** 2.— *Ant.* PAIN, grief, affliction.
**2.** [An ecstatic state]— *Syn.* ecstasy, bliss, transport, beatitude, exaltation, enchantment, passion, glory, elysium, paradise, inspiration, enthusiasm, divine communion, mystical trance, at-oneness; see also sense 1.

*SYN.* — **rapture** now generally suggests the mental exaltation experienced when one's entire attention is captured by something that evokes great joy or pleasure; **ecstasy** implies extreme emotional exaltation, now usually intense delight, that overpowers the senses and lifts one into a trancelike state; **bliss** implies a state of great

happiness and contentment, often suggesting heavenly joy; **transport** applies to any powerful emotion by which one is carried away

**rapturous,** *modif.*— *Syn.* ecstatic, enchanted, delighted; see **happy** 1.

**rare,** *modif.* **1.** [Uncommon]— *Syn.* unusual, singular, extraordinary; see **unusual** 1, 2.
**2.** [Scarce]— *Syn.* sparse, few, scanty, meager, limited, short, expensive, precious, out of circulation, off the market, in great demand, occasional, uncommon, isolated, scattered, infrequent, deficient, almost unobtainable, few and far between★; see also **unique** 1.— *Ant.* profuse, CHEAP, abounding.
**3.** [Choice]— *Syn.* exceptional, select, matchless, superlative; see **excellent, unique** 1.
**4.** [Thin]— *Syn.* tenuous, light, rarefied; see **thin** 1, 5.
**5.** [Not completely cooked]— *Syn.* undercooked, underdone, not cooked, not done, lightly cooked, nearly raw, red, bloody, *saignant, bleu* (both French), not thoroughly cooked; see also **raw** 1.

**rare bird,** *n.*— *Syn.* rarity, *rara avis* (Latin), phenomenon, curiosity; see **irregularity** 2, **wonder** 2.

**rarefied,** *modif.* **1.** [Not dense]— *Syn.* light, thin, tenuous; see **refined** 1, **thin** 1, 5.
**2.** [Exalted]— *Syn.* lofty, select, refined, esoteric; see **grand** 2, **obscure** 3.

**rarely,** *modif.*— *Syn.* unusually, on rare occasions, once in a great while; see **infrequently, seldom.**

**rarity,** *n.* **1.** [Infrequency]— *Syn.* rareness, scarcity, uncommonness; see **irregularity** 2, **lack** 1, 2.
**2.** [A phenomenon]— *Syn.* curiosity, one of a kind, collector's item; see **gem** 2, **wonder** 2.

**rascal,** *n.*— *Syn.* scoundrel, rogue, rake, knave, villain, robber, fraud, scamp, devil, imp, hypocrite, double-dealer, sneak, shyster, cad, trickster, charlatan, swindler, grafter, cardsharp, cheat, black sheep, ruffian, tough, rowdy, bully, scalawag, mountebank, liar, blackguard, wretch, quack, tramp, beggar, bum, idler, wastrel, prodigal, hooligan, ne'er-do-well, scapegrace, miscreant, reprobate, misdoer, felon, sinner, delinquent, rakehell, recreant, malfeasor, malefactor, profligate, loafer, rapscallion, renegade, beachcomber, mendicant, urchin, gamin, impostor, opportunist, vagrant, pretender, gambler, mischief-maker, sharper, faker, louse★, skunk★, bastard★, fink★, rat★, rotten egg★, bad egg★, con man★, con artist★, flimflammer★, dirty dog★, good-for-nothing★, worm★, two-timer★, stool pigeon★, phony★, four-flusher★, slicker★; see also **criminal.**— *Ant.* HERO, nice guy, philanthropist.

**rascality,** *n.*— *Syn.* roguery, villainy, baseness, meanness, knavery, wickedness, culpability, guile, profligacy, chicanery, treachery, trickery, worthlessness, blackguardism, double-dealing, ruffianism, improbity, disreputability; see also **crime** 1, **dishonesty.**

**rascally,** *modif.*— *Syn.* base, dishonest, vicious, vile; see **dishonest** 1, 2, **mean** 3, **wicked** 1, 2.

**rash,** *modif.*— *Syn.* precipitate, impetuous, impulsive, foolish, hotheaded, thoughtless, reckless, headstrong, bold, careless, determined, audacious, heedless, madcap, unthinking, headlong, incautious, wild, precipitant, hasty, overhasty, unwary, injudicious, venturous, foolhardy, imprudent, venturesome, adventurous, daring, daredevil, jumping to conclusions, insuppressible, breakneck, irrational, fiery, furious, frenzied, passionate, immature, hurried, aimless, excited, feverish, indomitable, tenacious, frantic, indiscreet, quixotic, uncalculating, ill-advised, inadvisable, unconsidered, without thinking, unadvised, irresponsible, brash, precipitous, premature, sudden, burning one's fingers, harebrained, hotblooded, harum-scarum, game to the last, devil-may-care, rushing in where angels fear to tread. — *Ant.* CALM, cautious, level-headed.

**rash,** *n.* **1.** [A skin eruption] — *Syn.* hives, dermatitis, redness, prickly heat; see **blemish, disease.**
**2.** [A sudden large number of instances] — *Syn.* outbreak, spate, wave; see **fit 2, plenty.**

**rasher,** *n.* — *Syn.* slice, piece, portion; see **part 1, piece 1.**

**rashly,** *modif.* — *Syn.* brashly, impulsively, unwisely, abruptly, foolishly, impetuously, incautiously, carelessly, precipitately, precipitantly, precipitously, imprudently, recklessly, boldly, indiscreetly, inadvisedly, ill-advisedly, thoughtlessly, unthinkingly, furiously, hurriedly, heedlessly, boldly, daringly, headstrongly, unpreparedly, excitedly, hastily, overhastily, wildly, frantically, irrepressibly, unwarily, without thinking, without due consideration, without forethought, without planning, without investigation, in a rash manner, with great indiscretion, with bad judgment, irresponsibly, passionately, fiercely, feverishly, indomitably, headily.

**rashness,** *n.* — *Syn.* recklessness, foolhardiness, haste; see **carelessness, indiscretion 1.**

**rasp,** *v.* — *Syn.* grate, irritate, scratch; see **rub 1.**

**rasping,** *modif.* — *Syn.* hoarse, grating, grinding; see **harsh 1, hoarse, raucous 1.**

**rat,** *n.* **1.** [A rodent] — *Syn.* mouse, muskrat, vermin; see **pest 1, rodent.**
Varieties of rats include: white, black, brown, house, laboratory, longtailed, water, swamp, desert, marsh, tree, giant, field, bamboo, cotton, kangaroo, jerboa, river, pack, big-eared, short-eared, red-nosed.
**2.** [*A deserter or betrayer] — *Syn.* informer, turncoat, fink*; see **deserter, traitor.**

**ratchet,** *n.* — *Syn.* catch, sprocket, sprocket wheel, cogwheel; see **cog, wheel 1.**

**rate,** *n.* **1.** [Ratio] — *Syn.* proportion, degree, standard, scale, fixed amount, quota, relation, relationship, comparison, relative weight, measure, percentage, numerical progression, diagrammatic estimate, frequency, incidence; see also **incidence, measure 1, 2.**
**2.** [Price] — *Syn.* valuation, allowance, charge, cost per unit; see **price.**
**3.** [Speed] — *Syn.* velocity, pace, flow, motion, movement, tempo, clip, gait, tread, time, meter; see also **speed.**

**rate,** *v.* **1.** [To rank] — *Syn.* judge, estimate, evaluate, grade, relate to a standard, fix, tag, calculate, assess, deem, consider, class, determine, appraise, assay, guess at; see also **measure 1, price, rank 2.**
**2.** [*To have value or status] — *Syn.* count, rank, be a favorite, be accepted, be welcome, deserve, be deserving, merit, earn; see also **deserve, succeed 1.**
*See Synonym Study at* ESTIMATE.

**rated,** *modif.* — *Syn.* ranked, classified, graded, classed, put, placed, thought of, considered, given a rating, weighted, measured, evaluated, appraised, estimated.

**rather,** *interj.* — *Syn.* I should say, certainly, of course, by all means, most assuredly, no doubt about it, and how!* you're telling me*.

**rather,** *modif.* **1.** [To some degree] — *Syn.* fairly, somewhat, a little; see **moderately, slightly, very.**
**2.** [By preference] — *Syn.* first, by choice, in preference, sooner, more readily, willingly, much sooner, just as soon, as a matter of choice; see also **preferably.**

**ratification,** *n.* — *Syn.* acceptance, confirmation, sanction; see **permission.**

**ratify,** *v.* — *Syn.* confirm, approve, sanction, substantiate; see **approve 1, enact, endorse 2.**
*See Synonym Study at* APPROVE.

**rating,** *n.* — *Syn.* grade, relative standing, evaluation, number; see **class 1, degree 2, rank 2.**

**ratio,** *n.* — *Syn.* proportion, quota, quotient; see **degree 1, rate 1.**

**ration,** *n.* — *Syn.* allotment, portion, quota; see **division 2, share.**
*See Synonym Study at* FOOD.

**ration,** *v.* — *Syn.* proportion, allot, apportion; see **distribute 1.**

**rational,** *modif.* **1.** [Acting in accordance with reason] — *Syn.* reasonable, logical, sensible, stable, calm, cool, deliberate, discerning, discriminating, level-headed, collected, ratiocinative, thoughtful, knowing, of sound judgment, showing good sense, impartial, exercising reason, intelligent, wise, reasoning, prudent, circumspect, intellectual, reflective, philosophic, objective, farsighted, enlightened, well-advised, judicious, analytical, deductive, synthetic, perspicacious, conscious, balanced, sober, systematic, all there*, together*; see also **reasonable 1.** — *Ant.* irrational, absurd, RASH.
**2.** [Of a nature that appeals to reason] — *Syn.* intelligent, sensible, wise; see **judicious, reasonable 1, 2.**
**3.** [Sane] — *Syn.* normal, lucid, responsible, clearheaded; see **sane 1.**

---

**SYN.** — **rational** implies the ability to reason logically, as by drawing conclusions from inferences, and often connotes the absence of emotionalism /a *rational* explanation for the mysterious events/; **reasonable** suggests the use of practical reason in making decisions, choices, etc. that are fair or show good judgment /a *reasonable* solution to a problem/; **sensible** implies the use of common sense or sound judgment /you made a *sensible* decision/

---

**rationale,** *n.* — *Syn.* explanation, basis, grounds, motive; see **justification, reason 3.**

**rationalism,** *n.* — *Syn.* humanism, realism, reasoning; see **logic, reason 2.**

**rationalize,** *v.* **1.** [To justify] — *Syn.* explain away, vindicate, reconcile; see **excuse, justify 2.**
**2.** [To reason] — *Syn.* think, deliberate, intellectualize; see **reason 2.**

**rationally,** *modif.* — *Syn.* sensibly, logically, lucidly, intelligently; see **reasonably 1.**

**rattle,** *n.* — *Syn.* clatter, shaking, patter, noise, racket, rattling, din, knock, clack, clank, roll, rumble, drumming, pitapat, ratatat; see also **noise 1.**

**rattle,** *v.* **1.** [To make a rattling sound] — *Syn.* clatter, drum, clack, knock; see **sound 1.**
**2.** [*To talk rapidly and incessantly] — *Syn.* chatter, run on, prattle; see **babble.**
**3.** [*To disconcert] — *Syn.* confuse, discompose, put out, unnerve; see **confuse, disturb 2, embarrass 1.**
*See Synonym Study at* EMBARRASS.

**rattlebrained,** *modif.* — *Syn.* giddy, irrational, scatterbrained; see **silly, stupid 1.**

**rattlesnake,** *n.* — *Syn.* rattler, diamondback, sidewinder, prairie rattler, timber rattler, copperhead, water moccasin, belltail, pit viper; see also **snake.**

**rattletrap,** *modif.* — *Syn.* tottery, rickety, makeshift; see **unstable 1, weak 2.**

**rattletrap,** *n.* — *Syn.* old car, jalopy, heap*; see **automobile, wreck 2.**

**raucous,** *modif.* **1.** [Harsh] — *Syn.* strident, rough, grating, hoarse, loud, gruff, dissonant, jarring, rasping, ca-

cophonous, squawking, earsplitting, ear-piercing, blatant, sharp, acute, blaring, dry, braying, atonal, grinding, unharmonious, unmusical, piercing, shrill, penetrating, husky, discordant, stertorous; see also **harsh** 1.
**2.** [Disorderly] — *Syn.* boisterous, rowdy, loud, drunk; see **loud** 2, **unruly.**
**ravage,** *v.* — *Syn.* pillage, overrun, devastate, destroy, despoil, lay waste, plunder, sack, desolate, wreck, waste, disrupt, disorganize, demolish, annihilate, overthrow, overwhelm, break up, pull down, smash, shatter, scatter, batter down, exterminate, extinguish, prostrate, trample, trample down, dismantle, stamp out, lay in ruins, sweep away, raze, ruin, strip, impair, damage, consume, spoil, harry, ransack, maraud, wrest, prey, forage, crush, foray, violate, rape, rob, raid, pirate, seize, spoliate, capture, gut, loot; see also **damage** 1.— *Ant.* build, IMPROVE, rehabilitate.

---

*SYN.* — **ravage** implies violent destruction, usually in a series of depredations or over an extended period of time, as by an army, plague, or natural disaster; **devastate** stresses the total ruin and desolation resulting from ravaging; **plunder** refers to the forcible taking of loot by an invading or conquering army; **sack** and **pillage** both specifically suggest violent destruction and plunder by an invading or conquering army, **sack** implying the total stripping of all valuables in a city or town; **despoil** also implies the stripping of valuables but is typically used with reference to buildings, institutions, regions, etc.

---

**rave,** *v.* **1.** [To talk incoherently] — *Syn.* rant, jabber, ramble, wander; see **babble.**
**2.** [To rage] — *Syn.* storm, splutter, rail; see **rage** 1.
**3.** [To talk with great enthusiasm] — *Syn.* gush, rhapsodize, enthuse*; see **praise** 1.
**ravel,** *v.* — *Syn.* untwist, come apart, smooth out, untangle, disentangle, unsnarl, unbraid, untwine, unweave, untwist, unravel, fray, make plain; see also **loosen** 2.
**ravenous,** *modif.* — *Syn.* voracious, omnivorous, starved; see **hungry, rapacious** 2.
**ravine,** *n.* — *Syn.* gully, gorge, canyon, gulch, arroyo, valley, gap, chasm, abyss, break, crevice, crevasse, coulee.
**raving,** *modif.* — *Syn.* delirious, frenzied, shouting, wildly irrational; see **insane** 1.
**ravish,** *v.* **1.** [To charm] — *Syn.* delight, please, enchant, enrapture, bewitch, captivate, attract, allure, enthrall, hold, draw, mesmerize, magnetize, hypnotize, transport; see also **charm** 1, **fascinate.**
**2.** [To rape] — *Syn.* abduct, violate, deflower, seduce; see **rape.**
**raw,** *modif.* **1.** [Not cooked] — *Syn.* uncooked, fresh, rare, hard, unprepared, undercooked, underdone, fibrous, coarse-grained, unpasteurized, unbaked, unfried; see also **rare** 5.— *Ant.* cooked, BAKED, fried.
**2.** [Unfinished] — *Syn.* natural, untreated, rough, newly cut, unprocessed, crude, unrefined, unstained, untanned, coarse, newly mined, uncut, virgin, unedited, unevaluated; see also **unfinished** 2.— *Ant.* manufactured, REFINED, processed.
**3.** [Untrained] — *Syn.* inexperienced, immature, new, fresh; see **inexperienced.**
**4.** [Cold] — *Syn.* biting, windy, bleak; see **cold** 1.
**5.** [Without skin] — *Syn.* peeled, skinned, dressed, galled, scraped, blistered, cut, wounded, pared, uncovered, chafed, bruised, sore, irritated, inflamed.— *Ant.* coated, COVERED, healed.

**6.** [*Nasty] — *Syn.* coarse, crude, brutally frank; see **coarse** 2, **rude** 2, **vulgar** 1.
**in the raw*** — *Syn.* nude, bare, unclothed; see **naked** 1.
**rawboned,** *modif.* — *Syn.* gaunt, lean, lanky; see **thin** 2.
**ray,** *n.* — *Syn.* beam, flash, light, stream, gleam, blaze, sunbeam, wave, moonbeam, radiation, flicker, spark, irradiation, emanation, radiance, streak, shaft, pencil, patch, blink, glimmer, glitter, glint, sparkle.
Types of rays include: Roentgen, cosmic, ultraviolet, infrared, gamma, beta, alpha; X-ray, visible light, microwave, radio wave.
**rayon,** *n.* — *Syn.* cellulose fiber, synthetic fabric, semisynthetic; see **cloth, fiber** 1.
**raze,** *v.* — *Syn.* destroy, wreck, demolish, dismantle, tear down, level, ruin, scatter, overthrow, tumble, pull down, knock down, break down, mow down, blow down, batter down, cast down, reduce, fell, break up, tear up, annihilate, exterminate, overturn, flatten, topple, dynamite, bomb, bulldoze, subvert, smash, crash; see also **destroy** 1.— *Ant.* BUILD, raise, erect.
*See Synonym Study at* DESTROY.
**razor,** *n.* — *Syn.* shaver, shaving instrument, cutting edge, blade, scraper*, mower*, cutter*; see also **knife.**
Types of razors include: double-edged, single-edged, straight, pivoting, disposable, cartridge, safety, hollow-ground, electric, electric shaver*, dry-shave*, blade*.
**reach,** *n.* — *Syn.* compass, range, scope, grasp, ken, influence, extent, limit, stretch, extension, orbit, horizon, gamut; see also **ability** 1, **expanse, extent.**
*See Synonym Study at* RANGE.
**reach,** *v.* **1.** [To extend to] — *Syn.* touch, span, encompass, pass along, continue to, get to, go to, roll on, go on, stretch, go as far as, attain, equal, approach, lead, stand, terminate, end, overtake, join, come up to, penetrate to, spread, sweep; see also **spread** 3.
**2.** [To extend a part of the body to] — *Syn.* stretch, lunge, strain, move, reach out, feel for, come at, make contact with, shake hands, throw out a limb, make for, put out, touch, strike, seize, grasp; see also **stretch** 1.
**3.** [To arrive] — *Syn.* get to, get as far as, come to, enter; see **arrive** 1.
**4.** [To give an object to another] — *Syn.* hand over, relinquish, give over, give away, carry to, turn over, transfer; see also **give** 1.
**5.** [To communicate with] — *Syn.* contact, get in touch with, get through to, make an impression on; see **communicate** 2, **influence.**
**reaching,** *modif.* **1.** [Extending to a point] — *Syn.* touching, meeting, going up to, ending at, stretching, encompassing, taking in, spanning, spreading to, penetrating to, embracing, joining, sweeping on to.
**2.** [Arriving] — *Syn.* coming to, landing, touching down, entering, disembarking, making port, getting off at, alighting, putting in, getting to, stopping at, making it to*; see also **arrival** 1, **landing.**
**3.** [Extending a part of the body] — *Syn.* stretching, straining, making for, lunging, feeling for, putting out, outstretching, touching, grasping, seizing, striking; see also **extending.**
**react,** *v.* **1.** [To act in response] — *Syn.* reciprocate, respond, answer, counter, reply, behave, give back, act; see also **answer** 1.
**2.** [To feel in response] — *Syn.* be affected, respond, take, be struck, be impressed, be moved, be involved, find, catch the infection*, catch the flame*; see also **feel** 2.
**reaction,** *n.* **1.** [An answer] — *Syn.* response, reply, rejoinder, reception, receptivity, return, feedback, feeling,

opinion, reflection, counteraction, resistance, backlash, attitude, retort, reciprocation, repercussion, effect, reflex; see also **answer** 1, **opinion** 1, **result**.

Reactions to stimuli include: contraction, expansion, dilation, constriction, jerk, knee jerk, tropism, heliotropism, phototropism, cognition, shock, exhaustion, stupor, anger, disgust, revulsion, fear, joy, laughter, wonder.

**2.** [A backward tendency, especially in politics] — *Syn.* conservatism, backlash, status quo, rightism, toryism, retrenchment, regression, relapse, retrogression, retreat, withdrawal, backsliding, return to normalcy, return to the good old days; see also **conservatism, stability** 1.

**reactionary,** *modif.* — *Syn.* rigid, retrogressive, regressive, ultraconservative; see **conservative**.

**reactionary,** *n.* — *Syn.* right-winger, die-hard, ultraconservative; see **conservative**.

**read,** *modif.* — *Syn.* examined, gone over, checked over, scanned; see **investigated, understood** 1.

**read,** *v.* **1.** [To understand by reading] — *Syn.* comprehend, go through, peruse, study, pore over, scan, skim, browse, glance over, go over, examine, gather, see, know, perceive, apprehend, grasp, learn, flip through the pages, thumb through, wade through, dip into, scratch the surface, run the eye over, bury oneself in, have one's nose in a book*, crack a book*; see also **understand** 1.

**2.** [To interpret] — *Syn.* view, render, translate, decipher, decode, make out, unravel, express, explain, expound, construe, perceive, paraphrase, restate, put; see also **interpret** 1.

**3.** [To contain when read] — *Syn.* state, hold, indicate, register, record, show, express, assert, affirm.

**4.** [To utter printed matter aloud] — *Syn.* present, deliver, recite, sound out; see **address** 2, **recite** 1.

**readable,** *modif.* **1.** [Capable of being read] — *Syn.* clear, legible, coherent, distinct, intelligible, lucid, comprehensible, plain, unmistakable, decipherable, regular, orderly, fluent, neat, tidy, flowing, precise, graphic, understandable, unequivocal, explicit, straightforward, simple. — *Ant.* ILLEGIBLE, unintelligible, undecipherable.

**2.** [Likely to be read with pleasure] — *Syn.* interesting, absorbing, fascinating, engrossing, gripping, satisfying, amusing, entertaining, enjoyable, rewarding, stimulating, gratifying, pleasing, worth reading, pleasant, inviting, engaging, eloquent, well-written, smooth, exciting, compelling, riveting, suspenseful, pungent, clever, brilliant, ingenious, relaxing, appealing; see also **interesting, trenchant** 2. — *Ant.* dreary, tedious, DULL.

**reader,** *n.* **1.** [One who reads habitually] — *Syn.* bookworm, bibliophile, editor, book reviewer, literary critic, proofreader, editorial assistant, scholar, bibliomaniac, person of learning, savant, walking encyclopedia*; see also **bibliophile**.

**2.** [One who makes a profession of reading aloud] — *Syn.* lecturer, announcer, elocutionist, reciter, rhetorician, soliloquist, monologist, *diseur, diseuse* (*both* French), lector, instructor; see also **announcer**.

**3.** [Anyone admitted to a library] — *Syn.* library patron, user, browser, research worker, scholar, grind*; see also **student**.

**4.** [A book intended for the study of reading] — *Syn.* primer, storybook, graded text, companion volume, selected readings, anthology, collection, omnibus, models; see also **book** 1, **collection** 2, **text** 1.

**5.** [A grader of papers] — *Syn.* teaching assistant, T.A.,

lab assistant, professor; see **teacher** 1, 2.

**read for,** *v.* — *Syn.* try out, go out for, audition; see **perform** 2, **try out for**.

**readily,** *modif.* — *Syn.* willingly, quickly, promptly; see **eagerly, easily** 1, **immediately, willingly**.

**readiness,** *n.* — *Syn.* aptness, predisposition, eagerness; see **willingness, zeal** 2.

**reading,** *n.* **1.** [The act of interpreting written matter] — *Syn.* perusal, study, browsing, skimming, examination, scrutiny, presentation, expression, utterance, delivery, recitation, recital, rendition, enactment.

**2.** [Interpretation] — *Syn.* construction, treatment, version, commentary; see **interpretation** 2, **translation**.

**3.** [A selection from written matter] — *Syn.* brief, excerpt, digest, extract, passage, text, quotation, section, installment; see also **recitation** 3.

**4.** [A version] — *Syn.* account, paraphrase, rendering; see **interpretation** 1, **version** 1.

**readjust,** *v.* — *Syn.* rearrange, reconcile, methodize, reacclimate; see **adjust** 1, 3, **rearrange, regulate** 2.

**readjustment,** *n.* — *Syn.* rearrangement, adaptation, rehabilitation, reconstruction; see **adjustment** 1.

**read the riot act to*,** *v.* — *Syn.* rebuke, reprimand, warn, lay down the law*; see **censure, scold**.

**read up on,** *v.* — *Syn.* prepare, investigate, research, learn about; see **study** 1.

**ready,** *modif.* **1.** [Prompt] — *Syn.* quick, spontaneous, alert, attentive, wide-awake, swift, fleet, fast, sharp, immediate, instant, animated; see also **active** 2, **observant** 2, **punctual, quick** 4. — *Ant.* SLOW, dull, dilatory.

**2.** [Prepared] — *Syn.* fit, apt, set, all set, equipped, primed, skillful, ripe, handy, available, in readiness, waiting, on call, in line for, in position, on the brink of, equipped to do the job, open to, inclined, disposed, fixed for, on the mark, in harness, in the saddle, equal to, at one's beck and call, expectant, available, at hand, on hand, anticipating, in order, all systems go*, all squared away*, on tap*, on deck*; see also **able** 1, **intelligent** 1. — *Ant.* UNPREPARED, unready, unavailable.

**3.** [Enthusiastic] — *Syn.* eager, willing, unhesitant, game*; see **enthusiastic** 1, 2, **willing** 1, 2.

*See Synonym Study at* QUICK.

**at the ready** — *Syn.* in position, poised, available, at hand; see **ready** 2.

**make ready** — *Syn.* prepare, get in order, arrange, equip; see **prepare** 1.

**ready,** *v.* — *Syn.* prepare, make ready, get ready, gear up*; see **prepare** 1.

**ready-made,** *modif.* **1.** [Prepared] — *Syn.* instant, prefabricated, ready-to-wear, off-the-rack, store-bought*, built; see also **instant, prepared** 2, **preserved**.

**2.** [Trite] — *Syn.* unoriginal, commonplace, stock; see **common** 1, **conventional** 1, **dull** 4.

**real,** *modif.* **1.** [Genuine] — *Syn.* true, authentic, original, sincere; see **genuine** 1, 2.

**2.** [Having physical existence] — *Syn.* actual, solid, firm, substantive, material, live, substantial, existent, tangible, existing, present, palpable, factual, sound, concrete, corporal, corporeal, bodily, incarnate, embodied, physical, sensible, stable, in existence, *de facto* (Latin), perceptible, evident, undeniable, irrefutable, practical, true, true to life. — *Ant.* UNREAL, unsubstantial, hypothetical.

**3.** [*Very] — *Syn.* extremely, exceedingly, exceptionally, uncommonly; see **very**.

**for real*** **1.** — *Syn.* really, actually, in fact, in earnest; see **really** 1.

**2.** — *Syn.* real, actual, genuine, sincere; see **genuine** 1, 2.

---

*SYN.* — **real**, **actual**, and **true** are often used interchangeably to imply correspondence with fact, but in discriminating use, **true** implies conformity with a standard or model *[a true democrat]* or with what actually exists *[a true story]*, **actual** stresses existence or occurrence as opposed to what is possible, likely, or abstract *[actual and hypothetical examples]*, and **real** highlights a distinction between what something is and what a substitute, counterfeit, etc. seems or pretends to be *[real rubber, real courage]*

---

**real estate,** *n.* — *Syn.* land, property, lots, realty, houses, landed interests, freehold, ground, acres, messuage, holdings; see also **building** 1, **estate** 1, **farm, home** 1.

**realism,** *n.* — *Syn.* authenticity, naturalness, verisimilitude, verism; see **reality** 1.

**realist,** *n.* — *Syn.* pragmatist, naturalist, scientist, rationalist, pessimist, cynic, defeatist, hardhead*.

**realistic,** *modif.* **1.** [Practical] — *Syn.* pragmatic, sensible, sober, hardheaded; see **practical.**
**2.** [Naturalistic] — *Syn.* lifelike, true-to-life, faithful, vivid; see **genuine** 1, **graphic** 1, 2.

**reality,** *n.* **1.** [The state of being real] — *Syn.* authenticity, factual basis, truth, actuality, realness, substantiality, existence, substance, materiality, being, presence, actual existence, entity, sensibility, corporeality, solidity, perceptibility, true being, absoluteness, tangibility, palpability, verity.
**2.** [Anything that is real] — *Syn.* fact, actuality, certainty, actual state of things; see **fact** 1, 2.
**in reality** — *Syn.* in fact, in truth, actually; see **really** 1.

**realization,** *n.* **1.** [Comprehension] — *Syn.* understanding, recognition, consciousness, cognizance; see **awareness.**
**2.** [Achievement] — *Syn.* fulfillment, accomplishment, consummation; see **achievement** 1, 2, **success** 1.

**realize,** *v.* **1.** [To bring to fulfillment] — *Syn.* accomplish, actualize, effectuate, make good; see **achieve** 1, **complete** 1.
**2.** [To understand] — *Syn.* recognize, apprehend, discern; see **understand** 1.
**3.** [To receive] — *Syn.* clear, make a profit from, obtain; see **earn** 2, **profit** 2, **receive** 1.

**realized,** *modif.* **1.** [Fulfilled] — *Syn.* completed, accomplished, done, finished, concluded, actualized, come true, materialized, executed, achieved, performed, effected, consummated, substantiated, made real. — *Ant.* UNFINISHED, unfulfilled, unsubstantiated.
**2.** [Earned] — *Syn.* gained, gotten, acquired, received, accrued, made, reaped, harvested, gathered, inherited, profited, taken, cleared, obtained, gleaned, netted.

**realizing,** *modif.* **1.** [Achieving] — *Syn.* accomplishing, performing, completing, consummating, effecting, fulfilling, doing, coming through, attaining, reaching, perfecting, discharging, rounding out, bringing to fulfillment, actualizing.
**2.** [Earning] — *Syn.* making, netting, gaining, getting, acquiring, obtaining, receiving, inheriting, clearing, being paid, accruing, taking in, being allowed.
**3.** [Understanding] — *Syn.* recognizing, discerning, comprehending, appreciating, knowing, being aware, finding, suspecting, grasping, apprehending, perceiving, seeing through.

**really,** *modif.* **1.** [In fact] — *Syn.* actually, in reality, indeed, genuinely, certainly, surely, absolutely, in effect, positively, veritably, authentically, as a matter of fact, in point of fact, in actuality, upon my honor, legitimately, precisely, literally, indubitably, unmistakably, undoubtedly, categorically, I assure you, I'll answer for it, be assured, believe me, of course, honestly, truly, admittedly, nothing else but, beyond a doubt, unquestionably, as sure as you're alive*, no buts about it*, without the shadow of a doubt*, you said it*, you bet*.
**2.** [To a remarkable degree] — *Syn.* surprisingly, remarkably, extraordinarily, especially; see **very.**

**really,** *interj.* — *Syn.* indeed? honestly? for a fact? yes? is that so? what? are you sure? no fooling? no kidding?* cross your heart and hope to die?* on your honor?* you don't say?* the deuce you say!* blow me down!* ain't it the truth?* you said it!* do tell?*

**realm,** *n.* — *Syn.* domain, area, sphere; see **department** 1, **field** 4, **kingdom, range** 2, **region** 1.

**real McCoy*,** *n.* — *Syn.* the real thing, the genuine article, the original.

**realtor,** *n.* — *Syn.* real estate agent, broker, dealer; see **salesperson** 2.

**reanimate,** *v.* — *Syn.* restore, invigorate, resuscitate; see **animate** 1, **renew** 1, **revive** 1.

**reap,** *v.* **1.** [To harvest] — *Syn.* cut, mow, glean, gather, pick, produce, crop, take the yield, gather the fruit, strip the fields, pluck, cull; see also **harvest.** — *Ant.* PLANT, sow, seed.
**2.** [To gain] — *Syn.* get, acquire, procure, collect, glean, realize, draw, derive, secure, recover, retrieve, take in, profit, obtain, make capital of, pick up, receive, come to have. — *Ant.* LOSE, relinquish, give up.

**reaper,** *n.* — *Syn.* harvester, binder, grain harvester, picker; see **farmer, harvester** 1.

**reappear,** *v.* — *Syn.* come again, reenter, crop up again; see **appear** 1, **repeat** 2.

**reapportion,** *v.* — *Syn.* redistribute, redistrict, resection, reallocate, distribute, divide, allot.

**rear,** *n.* — *Syn.* hind part, back, back seat, rear end, tail end, stern, posterior, rump, butt*; see also **back** 1, 2, **rump.**

**rear,** *v.* **1.** [To raise upright] — *Syn.* lift, elevate, raise, hold up; see **raise** 1.
**2.** [To nurture] — *Syn.* bring up, raise, parent, care for; see **raise** 2, **support** 5.
*See Synonym Study at* LIFT.

**rearrange,** *v.* — *Syn.* do over, reorganize, reposition, reset, replace, reconstruct, shift, reshuffle, redistribute, rework, revamp, readjust; see also **order** 3, **prepare** 1.

**reason,** *n.* **1.** [The power of reasoning] — *Syn.* understanding, intelligence, mind, sanity; see **acumen, judgment** 1.
**2.** [A process of reasoning] — *Syn.* logic, intellection, dialectics, speculation, generalization, rationalism, argumentation, inference, induction, deduction, discernment, analysis, ratiocination, rationalization.
**3.** [A basis for rational action] — *Syn.* end, object, rationale, intention, motive, ulterior motive, basis, wherefore, aim, intent, cause, design, ground, impetus, idea, motivation, root, incentive, goal, purpose, the why and wherefore; see also **cause** 1, **purpose** 1.
**4.** [The mind] — *Syn.* brain, mentality, intellect; see **mind** 1.
*See Synonym Study at* CAUSE.

**by reason of** — *Syn.* because of, on account of, for, by way of; see **because.**

**in reason** — *Syn.* in accord with what is reasonable, rationally, understandably; see **reasonably** 1.

**out of all reason** — *Syn.* unreasonable, irrational, irresponsible; see **extreme** 2, **illogical.**

**stand to reason**— *Syn.* be plausible, be logical, be feasible, seem all right; see **convince.**

**with reason**— *Syn.* understandably, justifiably, soundly, plausibly; see **reasonably** 1, **rightly.**

**within reason**— *Syn.* within reasonable limits, justifiable, acceptable, within bounds; see **reasonable** 2.

**reason,** *v.* **1.** [To think logically]— *Syn.* reflect, deliberate, contemplate; see **think** 1.

**2.** [To seek a reasonable explanation]— *Syn.* suppose, infer, deduce, gather, draw from, conclude, generalize, adduce, rationalize, think through, study, analyze, examine, figure out, thresh out\*; see also **assume** 1, **infer** 1.

**3.** [To discuss persuasively]— *Syn.* argue, trace, contend, dispute, debate, demonstrate, point out, prove, establish, discourse, justify; see also **argue** 1, **discuss.**
*See Synonym Study at* THINK.

**reasonable,** *modif.* **1.** [Amenable to reason]— *Syn.* rational, sensible, sane, level-headed, intelligent, common-sense, common-sensical, tolerant, endowed with reason, conscious, cerebral, capable of reason, thoughtful, reflective, percipient, reasoning, ratiocinative, cognitive, perceiving, consistent, broad-minded, liberal, generous, unprejudiced, unbiased, persuasible, malleable, flexible, agreeable; see also **rational** 1. — *Ant.* unreasonable, foolish, prejudiced.

**2.** [Showing reason or sound judgment]— *Syn.* fair, right, just, judicious, prudent, sound, wise, equitable, rational, moderate, temperate, within reason, impartial, sensible, humane, politic, sapient, discreet, analytical, objective, circumspect, making sense, standing to reason, common-sense; see also **judicious, moderate** 2. — *Ant.* excessive, IMMODERATE, extreme.

**3.** [Likely to appeal to the reason]— *Syn.* feasible, sound, plausible, logical; see **understandable.**

**4.** [Moderate in price]— *Syn.* inexpensive, reduced, fair, worth the money; see **cheap** 1.
*See Synonym Study at* RATIONAL.

**reasonably,** *modif.* **1.** [In a reasonable manner]— *Syn.* rationally, sanely, logically, understandably, plausibly, sensibly, soundly, persuasively, fairly, justly, honestly, wisely, judiciously, plainly, intelligently, soberly, unaffectedly, agreeably, in reason, in all reason, within reason, within the bounds of reason, as far as possible, as far as could be expected, as much as good sense dictates, within reasonable limitations, within the bounds of possibility, with due restraint.

**2.** [To a moderate degree]— *Syn.* mildly, prudently, fairly, moderately, inexpensively, temperately, evenly, calmly, gently, leniently, sparingly, frugally, indulgently, tolerantly, within bounds.

**reasoning,** *modif.*— *Syn.* rational, logical, inductive, analytical; see **judicious, rational** 1.

**reasoning,** *n.*— *Syn.* thinking, rationalizing, argumentation, drawing conclusions; see **logic, thought** 1.

**reassure,** *v.*— *Syn.* convince, console, hearten, give confidence; see **comfort, encourage** 1, 2.

**rebate,** *n.*— *Syn.* allowance, deduction, partial refund; see **discount.**

**rebel,** *n.* **1.** [A person engaged in a political revolution] — *Syn.* insurrectionist, revolutionary, revolutionist, agitator, insurgent, insurrectionary, traitor, seditionist, mutineer, subversive, subverter, anarchist, overthrower, nihilist, guerrilla, freedom fighter, member of the uprising, rioter, demagogue, revolter, separatist, malcontent, dissident, schismatic, deserter, dissenter, seceder, apostate, sectarian, turncoat, counterrevolutionary, renegade, secessionist, Sinn Feiner, Trotskyite, underground worker, Third Worlder, refusenik; see also **radical.**

**2.** [A person of independent opinions]— *Syn.* independent, individualist, iconoclast, nonconformist, maverick, innovator, experimenter, experientialist, malcontent.

**rebel,** *v.* **1.** [To resist or endeavor to overthrow a government or other authority]— *Syn.* rise up, rise, resist, revolt, turn against, defy, resist authority, resist lawful authority, fight in the streets, strike, boycott, break with, overturn, mutiny, riot, take up arms against, start an uprising, start a confrontation, secede, renounce, combat, oppose, be insubordinate, be treasonable, upset, overthrow, dethrone, disobey, raise hell\*, kick up a row\*, run amok\*. — *Ant.* submit, OBEY, be contented.

**2.** [To object]— *Syn.* dispute, resist, shrink from, be repelled; see **oppose** 1, **recoil.**

**rebellion,** *n.*— *Syn.* insurrection, revolt, defiance, resistance; see **disobedience, revolution** 2.

**rebellious,** *modif.* **1.** [Engaged in armed rebellion] — *Syn.* revolutionary, insurgent, counterrevolutionary, warring, insurrectionary, attacking, rioting, mutinous, rebel; see also sense 2, 3.— *Ant.* BEATEN, overwhelmed, loyal.

**2.** [Inclined toward rebellion]— *Syn.* dissident, factious, seditious, fractious, disobedient, treasonable, refractory, defiant, resistant, restless, restive, riotous, insubordinate, quarrelsome, bellicose, sabotaging, subversive, disloyal, disaffected, alienated, ungovernable, unruly, threatening.— *Ant.* DOCILE, peaceful, acquiescent.

**3.** [Apt to oppose authority]— *Syn.* anarchistic, iconoclastic, individualistic, radical, pugnacious, quarrelsome, independent-minded, stubborn, contemptuous, insolent, contumacious, alienated, scornful, uncontrollable, intractable, unyielding, recalcitrant, disobedient, feisty\*; see also **lawless** 2.— *Ant.* dutiful, tractable, YIELDING.

**rebirth,** *n.*— *Syn.* resurrection, rejuvenation, renaissance, rehabilitation; see **recovery** 2, **renewal, restoration** 1, **revival.**

**rebound,** *v.*— *Syn.* reflect, ricochet, spring back; see **bounce** 1.

**rebuff,** *n.*— *Syn.* repulse, snub, reprimand, rejection; see **insult, rebuke, refusal.**

**rebuff,** *v.* **1.** [To reject]— *Syn.* refuse, repel, check, snub, dismiss, repudiate, spurn, send away, turn away, ignore, slight, disregard, put in one's place, reprove, rebuke, oppose, chide, repulse, cross, decline, resist, keep at a distance, keep at arm's length, disallow, turn down, give the cold shoulder\*, give the go-by\*, cut\*, slam the door in one's face\*, not hear of\*, put off\*, brush off\*, lash out at\*, tell where to get off\*, put down\*, give the brushoff\*, send packing\*, tell to get lost\*; see also **deny, neglect\*, refuse.**

**2.** [To beat back]— *Syn.* drive back, push back, ward off, fend off, stave off, hold off, keep off, beat off, fight off, keep at bay; see also **repel** 1, **resist** 1.

**rebuild,** *v.* **1.** [To repair]— *Syn.* touch up, patch, build up; see **repair.**

**2.** [To restore]— *Syn.* refurbish, make restoration, reconstruct, reassemble; see **reconstruct, restore** 3.

**rebuilt,** *modif.*— *Syn.* remodeled, restored, reconstructed, reorganized; see **built** 1, **repaired.**

**rebuke,** *n.*— *Syn.* condemnation, reproof, reprimand, rebuff, snub, refusal, repulse, disapproval, scolding, censure, criticism, chiding, admonition, ostracism, blame, upbraiding, reprehension, berating, reproach, reproval, expostulation, lecture, punishment, rating, objurgation, correction, affliction, castigation, admonishment, remonstrance, tongue-lashing\*, dressing-down\*, chewing-out\*, put-down\*, slap in the face\*; see also **blame** 1, **insult**. — *Ant.* COMPLIMENT, congratulations, applause.

**rebuke,** *v.* — *Syn.* reprove, reprimand, admonish; see **censure, scold.**

**rebut,** *v.* — *Syn.* confute, counter, prove false, invalidate; see **deny, disprove, refute.**

*See Synonym Study at* DISPROVE.

**rebuttal,** *n.* — *Syn.* reply, return, confutation, rejoinder; see **answer** 1, **refusal.**

**recalcitrant,** *modif.* — *Syn.* resistant, stubborn, unmanageable, refractory; see **obstinate, rebellious** 3.

**recall,** *v.* **1.** [To call to mind] — *Syn.* recollect, think of, revive, evoke; see **remember** 1.

**2.** [To remove from office] — *Syn.* discharge, disqualify, suspend; see **dismiss** 2.

**3.** [To summon again] — *Syn.* call back, reconvene, reassemble; see **assemble** 2, **summon** 1.

**recalled,** *modif.* **1.** [Remembered] — *Syn.* recollected, brought to mind, summoned up; see **remembered.**

**2.** [Relieved of responsibility] — *Syn.* brought back, stripped of office, dismissed, discharged, displaced, fired, laid off, made redundant (British), replaced, ousted, cast out, suspended, pensioned off, made emeritus, let out, let go, sent home, removed from office, removed, retired, superannuated, cashiered, kicked upstairs\*, canned\*, busted\*, washed out\*, put out to pasture\*; see also **discharged** 1.

**recant,** *v.* — *Syn.* retract, revoke, renounce, disavow, disclaim, abjure, deny, take back, cancel, back down, back out, withdraw, rescind, abrogate, forswear, contradict, repudiate, abnegate, annul, void, countermand, recall, call back, disown, unsay, nullify, repeal, draw in one's horns\*, eat crow\*, be of another mind\*, eat humble pie\*, eat one's words\*, eat one's hat\*; see also **abandon** 1. — *Ant.* ACKNOWLEDGE, maintain, proclaim.

**recapitulate,** *v.* — *Syn.* restate, sum up, reiterate, recap\*; see **repeat** 3, **summarize.**

*See Synonym Study at* REPEAT.

**recapture,** *v.* — *Syn.* regain, retake, recollect, reexperience; see **recover** 1, **remember** 1.

**recede,** *v.* **1.** [To go backward] — *Syn.* fall back, draw back, shrink, withdraw; see **retreat** 1.

**2.** [To sink] — *Syn.* ebb, drift away, lower, turn down, abate, decline, decrease, die away, go away, drop back, wash back, drop, fall, fall off, lessen, subside; see also **decrease** 1, **fall** 1. — *Ant.* RISE, flow, increase.

**receipt,** *n.* **1.** [The act of receiving] — *Syn.* receiving, acquisition, accession, acceptance, taking, arrival, recipience, getting, admitting, admission, intake, acquiring, reception; see also **admission** 2. — *Ant.* shipment, DELIVERY, giving.

**2.** [An acknowledgment of receipt, sense 1] — *Syn.* letter, voucher, release, cancellation, slip, sales slip, signed notice, stub, discharge, quittance, declaration, paid bill, chit\*; see also **certificate.**

**receipted,** *modif.* — *Syn.* certified, marked paid, stamped, signed, approved, acknowledged, attached with a receipt.

**receipts,** *pl.n.* — *Syn.* income, proceeds, gate, take\*; see **profit** 2.

**receive,** *v.* **1.** [To take into one's charge] — *Syn.* accept, be given, admit, take, get, obtain, gain, inherit, acquire, gather up, collect, reap, procure, derive, appropriate, seize, take possession, redeem, pocket, pick up, hold, come by, earn, take in, assume, draw, arrogate, win, secure, come into\*, come in for\*, catch\*, corral\*; see also **obtain** 1. — *Ant.* DISCARD, give, refuse.

**2.** [To endure] — *Syn.* undergo, experience, suffer; see **endure** 2.

**3.** [To support] — *Syn.* bear, sustain, prop; see **support** 1.

**4.** [To make welcome] — *Syn.* accommodate, greet, initiate, induct, install, make welcome, shake hands with, admit, permit, welcome, welcome home, accept, entertain, host, invite in, let in, show in, bring in, usher in, let through, make comfortable, be at home to, bring as a guest into, introduce, give a party, give access to, allow entrance to, roll out the red carpet for, give the red-carpet treatment to, put out the welcome mat for, greet with open arms; see also **entertain** 2, **greet.** — *Ant.* VISIT, be a guest, call.

---

**SYN. — receive** means to get by having something given, told, or imposed, and may or may not imply the consent of the recipient /to *receive* a gift, to *receive* a blow/; **accept** means to receive willingly or favorably, but it sometimes connotes acquiescence rather than explicit approval /he was *accepted* as a member, to *accept* the inevitable/; **admit** stresses permission or concession on the part of the one that receives /I will not *admit* them to my home/; **take,** in this connection, means to accept something offered or presented /we can't *take* money from you/

---

**received,** *modif.* — *Syn.* taken, gotten, acquired, accepted, standard, conventional, obtained, honored, brought in, signed for, admitted, collected, gathered, earned, derived; see also **accepted, acknowledged.** — *Ant.* GIVEN, disbursed, delivered.

**receiver,** *n.* **1.** [One who receives] — *Syn.* recipient, consignee, customer, heir, beneficiary, grantee, acceptor, teller, collector, object, target, victim, subject, trustee, assignee, creditor, guinea pig\*.

**2.** [A device for receiving] — *Syn.* telephone, handset, headphone, television, radio, receiving set, mission control, control center, detection device, listening device, bug\*, transceiver, hydrophone; see also **radio** 2.

**receiving,** *modif.* — *Syn.* taking, getting, acquiring, accepting, being given, inheriting, collecting, gathering, making, drawing, earning, gaining, bringing in. — *Ant.* GIVING, disbursing, awarding.

**be on the receiving end\*** — *Syn.* be the recipient, be the target, get, take; see **receive** 1.

**recension,** *n.* — *Syn.* revision, reprint, new version, reexamination; see **edition, review** 2, **revision.**

**recent,** *modif.* **1.** [Lately brought into being] — *Syn.* fresh, novel, new, newly born; see **fresh** 1, **modern** 1, **original** 3.

**2.** [Associated with modern times] — *Syn.* contemporary, up-to-date, current; see **modern** 1, 3.

**recently,** *modif.* — *Syn.* lately, in recent times, just now, just a while ago, not long ago, a short while ago, of late, latterly, newly, freshly, the other day, just yesterday, within the recent past. — *Ant.* ONCE, long ago, formerly.

**receptacle,** *n.* — *Syn.* box, wastebasket, holder, repository; see **container.**

**reception,** *n.* **1.** [The act of receiving] — *Syn.* acquisition, acceptance, accession; see **receipt** 1.

**2.** [The manner of receiving] — *Syn.* greeting, reaction, response, meeting, encounter, introduction, welcome, salutation, induction, admission, disposition, treatment; see also **greeting** 1, **reaction** 1.

**3.** [A social function] — *Syn.* gathering, party, soiree, opening, tea, matinee, cocktail party, dinner, buffet, levee, wedding party; see also **party** 1.

**receptive,** *modif.* — *Syn.* responsive, open, amenable, perceptive; see **impressionable, sensitive** 3.

**recess,** *n.* **1.** [An intermission] — *Syn.* respite, rest, pause, hiatus, interlude, break, timeout, time off, downtime, lull, breathing spell, cessation, stop, suspension, interregnum, interval, interim, halt, coffee break, breather*.
**2.** [An indentation] — *Syn.* break, dent, corner, niche, pigeonhole, mouth, opening, embrasure, hollow, crutch, fork, angle; see also **hole** 2.
**3.** [A recessed space] — *Syn.* cell, cubicle, carrel, alcove, nook, niche, cranny, oriel, hiding place, ambush, apse, closet, crypt, cove, bay; see also **hole** 3.

**recession,** *n.* **1.** [A retreat] — *Syn.* withdrawal, collapse, return, reversal; see **retreat** 1.
**2.** [An economic decline] — *Syn.* slump, economic downturn, slowdown; see **bankruptcy, depression** 3.

**recessive,** *modif.* — *Syn.* passive, latent, inactive, not dominant, receding, regressive, suspended, refluent, relapsing, dormant; see also **latent.** — *Ant.* DOMINANT, prevailing, overbalancing.

**recharge,** *v.* — *Syn.* charge again, restore, put new life into; see **renew** 1, **revive** 1.

**recipe,** *n.* — *Syn.* formula, receipt, instructions, prescription, directions, cooking directions, ingredients, compound, method, procedure.

**recipient,** *modif.* — *Syn.* on the receiving end, getting, taking; see **receiving.**

**recipient,** *n.* — *Syn.* heir, object, legatee, winner; see **beneficiary, receiver** 1.

**reciprocal,** *modif.* — *Syn.* mutual, complementary, two-sided, correlative; see **exchangeable, mutual** 1.
*See Synonym Study at* MUTUAL.

**reciprocate,** *v.* **1.** [To respond in kind] — *Syn.* return, retaliate, repay, requite; see **answer** 3, **react** 1, **revenge.**
**2.** [To exchange] — *Syn.* interchange, alternate, give and take; see **alternate** 1, **exchange** 2.

**reciprocation,** *n.* — *Syn.* return, trade, mutual exchange, quid pro quo; see **exchange** 2.

**reciprocity,** *n.* — *Syn.* interchange, exchange, mutuality, back-scratching*; see **exchange** 2.

**recital,** *n.* **1.** [A concert] — *Syn.* solo performance, program, presentation, musicale; see **concert** 2, **performance** 2, **show** 2.
**2.** [A narration] — *Syn.* account, recounting, narrative; see **recitation** 1, **report** 1, **story.**

**recitation,** *n.* **1.** [The act of reciting] — *Syn.* delivery, speaking, playing, narrating, reading, recounting, declaiming, discoursing, soliloquizing, discussion, holding forth, performance, recital, narration, rehearsal, monologue, discourse.
**2.** [A class meeting for recitation of answers] — *Syn.* quiz period, recitation period, examination, oral questioning, schoolroom exercise, discussion hour, class discussion; see also **class** 3.
**3.** [A composition used for recitation, sense 1] — *Syn.* soliloquy, monologue, speech, address, oration, talk, proclamation, poetry, reading selection, sermon, appeal, report, performance piece; see also **speech** 3, **writing** 2.

**recite,** *v.* **1.** [To repeat formally] — *Syn.* declaim, address, read, render, quote, discourse, hold forth, enact, dramatize, deliver from memory, interpret, soliloquize, chant.
**2.** [To report on a lesson] — *Syn.* answer, give a report, explain, reel off, reply to questions, give a verbal account; see also **discuss, report** 2.
**3.** [To relate in detail] — *Syn.* report, narrate, relate, recount, expatiate, enumerate, enlarge on, describe, account for, give an account of, explain, impart, convey, quote, communicate, utter, state, tell, mention, retell, picture, delineate, portray; see also **describe, narrate, tell** 1.

**reckless,** *modif.* — *Syn.* thoughtless, heedless, breakneck, wild; see **rash.**

**recklessly,** *modif.* — *Syn.* dangerously, heedlessly, with abandon; see **boldly** 1, **carelessly, rashly.**

**reckon,** *v.* — *Syn.* compute, consider, figure, calculate, enumerate, count, evaluate, judge, regard; see also **estimate** 1, 2.
*See Synonym Study at* CALCULATE.

**reckoning,** *n.* **1.** [An estimate] — *Syn.* computation, calculation, count, tally; see **calculation** 1, **estimate** 1.
**2.** [Charge] — *Syn.* account, bill, cost, debt; see **bill** 1, **charge** 1, **statement** 3.
**3.** [A settling of accounts] — *Syn.* settlement, adjustment, judgment, retribution; see **adjustment** 2, **judgment** 2, 4.

**reclaim,** *v.* **1.** [To bring into usable condition] — *Syn.* rescue, restore, work over, regenerate, redeem, recondition, recover, recover from refuse, recycle, convert, enhance, remodel, develop; see also **recover** 1, **restore** 3.
**2.** [To reform] — *Syn.* rehabilitate, mend, improve; see **reform** 1, 2.
*See Synonym Study at* RECOVER.

**reclamation,** *n.* — *Syn.* restoration, recycling, redemption, repossession; see **improvement** 1, **recovery** 3, **restoration** 1.

**recline,** *v.* — *Syn.* sprawl, lean, lounge; see **lie** 3, 4, **rest** 1.

**recluse,** *n.* — *Syn.* hermit, troglodyte, anchorite, eremite; see **ascetic, hermit.**

**recognition,** *n.* **1.** [The act of recognizing] — *Syn.* recalling, remembering, identifying, perceiving, perception, verifying, apprehending, acknowledgment, acknowledging, noticing, recollection, memory, identification, recall, reidentification, recognizing, remembrance, mental recurrence, cognizance, realization.
**2.** [Tangible evidence of recognition, sense 1] — *Syn.* greeting, acknowledgment, identification, perception, admission, verification, comprehension, appreciation, renown, esteem, notice, attention, acceptance, regard, honor, credit, token of appreciation.

**recognize,** *v.* **1.** [To know again] — *Syn.* identify, recollect, know, recall, remember, place, be familiar, make out, distinguish, verify, sight, diagnose, espy, descry, see, perceive, realize, understand, admit knowledge of, notice; see also **know** 1.
**2.** [To acknowledge] — *Syn.* appreciate, realize, concede, accept; see **acknowledge** 2, **admit** 3.
**3.** [To acknowledge the legality of a government] — *Syn.* exchange diplomatic representatives, have diplomatic relations with, sanction, approve, extend formal recognition to, extend de jure recognition to, extend de facto recognition to; see also **acknowledge** 2, **approve** 1.

**recognized,** *modif.* — *Syn.* acknowledged, accepted, identified, sighted, caught, perceived, realized, known, appreciated, admitted, recalled, remembered; see also **acknowledged.**

**recoil,** *v.* — *Syn.* withdraw, turn away, shrink from, draw back, step back, pull back, start back, flinch, start, demur, blink, shirk, falter, dodge, swerve, wince, cringe, duck, quail; see also **retreat** 1.

**recollect,** *v.* — *Syn.* recall, bring to mind, look back on; see **remember** 1.

**recollection,** *n.* — *Syn.* remembrance, recall, reminiscence, retrospection; see **memory** 1, **remembrance** 1.

**recommend,** *v.* **1.** [To lend support or approval] — *Syn.* agree to, sanction, approve, hold up, commend, extol, compliment, applaud, celebrate, praise, speak well of, speak highly of, acclaim, eulogize, confirm, laud, second, favor, back, advocate, stand by, magnify, glorify, exalt, think highly of, be satisfied with, esteem, value, prize, uphold, justify, endorse, vouch for, promote, go on record for★, be all for★, front for★, go to bat for★; see also **approve** 1, **support** 2. — *Ant.* CENSURE, disesteem, denounce.
**2.** [To make a suggestion or prescription] — *Syn.* advise, prescribe, suggest, counsel; see **advise** 1, **urge** 1.
**recommendation,** *n.* **1.** [The act of recommending] — *Syn.* advocacy, guidance, order, advice, counsel, direction, suggestion, tip, proposal, instruction, judgment, sanction, commendation, endorsement, support, approbation, charge, injunction, esteem, eulogy, praise; see also **advice, suggestion** 1. — *Ant.* disapproval, OPPOSITION, antagonism.
**2.** [A document that vouches for character or ability] — *Syn.* certificate, testimonial, reference, character, character reference, letter of recommendation, letter in support, credentials; see also sense 1.
**recommended,** *modif.* — *Syn.* urged, sanctioned, mentioned, praised, commended, endorsed, supported, suggested, advocated, counseled; see also **approved.** — *Ant.* discouraged, disapproved, discredited.
**recompense,** *n.* — *Syn.* return, repayment, reward; see **payment** 1.
**recompense,** *v.* — *Syn.* compensate, remunerate, repay; see **pay** 1, **repay** 1.
*See Synonym Study at* PAY.
**reconcile,** *v.* **1.** [To adjust] — *Syn.* adapt, arrange, regulate, square; see **adjust** 1, 3.
**2.** [To bring into harmony] — *Syn.* conciliate, assuage, pacify, propitiate, mitigate, make up, mediate, arbitrate, intercede, bring together, accustom oneself to, harmonize, restore harmony, settle, accord, dictate peace, accommodate, appease, reunite, make peace between, bring to terms, bring into one's camp, win over, bury the hatchet★, patch up★, kiss and make up★; see also **settle** 9. — *Ant.* BOTHER, irritate, alienate.
**reconciled,** *modif.* — *Syn.* settled, regulated, arranged, adjusted, accustomed, resigned, agreed to, adapted, conciliated, propitiated, harmonized, reunited, brought to conclusion; see also **determined** 1, **resigned.** — *Ant.* OPPOSED, alienated, antagonized.
**reconciliation,** *n.* — *Syn.* conciliation, settlement, rapprochement; see **adjustment** 2, **agreement** 1, 2, 3.
**reconnaissance,** *n.* — *Syn.* observation, survey, reconnoitering, surveillance; see **examination** 1.
**reconnoiter,** *v.* — *Syn.* inspect, survey, scout out; see **examine** 1.
**reconsider,** *v.* — *Syn.* reevaluate, think over, rethink, reexamine, go over, work over, rearrange, consider again, recheck, reinquire, correct, amend, revise, retrace, emend, rework, replan, review, withdraw for consideration, reweigh, amend one's judgment; see also **consider** 1, 3.
**reconstruct,** *v.* — *Syn.* rebuild, remodel, construct again, make over, revamp, recondition, reconstitute, reproduce, re-create, piece together, reestablish, restore, refashion, reorganize, replace, overhaul, renovate, modernize, rework, construct from the original, copy, remake, reassemble; see also **build** 1, **repair.**
**reconstruction,** *n.* — *Syn.* rebuilding, resetting, remodeling, modernization, reorganization, reformation, regeneration, rehabilitation, restoration,

replotting, replanning, reestablishment, remaking; see also **repair.**
**record,** *n.* **1.** [Documentary evidence] — *Syn.* manuscript, inscription, transcription, account, report, history, legend, story, writing, written material, document. Types of records include: register, catalog, list, inventory, file, database, ledger, itinerary, narration, memo, memorandum, registry, schedule, chronicle, docket, scroll, archive, note, contract, statement, will, testament, petition, calendar, log, logbook, letter, memoir, reminiscence, dictation, confession, deposition, inscription, official record, sworn document, evidence, license, bulletin, gazette, newspaper, magazine, annual report, journal, Congressional Record, transactions, debates, bill, annals, presidential order, state paper, white paper, blue book, budget, report, entry, book, publication, autograph, signature, vital statistics, deed, paper, diary, stenographic notes, ledger, daybook, almanac, proceedings, minutes, description, affidavit, certificate, muniment, memorabilium, transcript, dossier, roll, audiotape, videotape, computer disk, computer diskette, floppy disk, hard disk, CD-ROM, mag tape, magnetic tape.
**2.** [One's past] — *Syn.* career, experience, work, accomplishment, background, case history, studies, credentials, way of life, past behavior, past performance, reign, administration, official conduct, track record★; see also **life** 2, **résumé** 2.
**3.** [A device for the reproduction of sound] — *Syn.* recording, disk, album, compact disk, CD, phonograph record, LP, laser disk, single, release, wax cylinder, wax plate, recording wire, transcription, canned music, cut★, take★, platter★; see also **cassette.**
**go on record** — *Syn.* assert, attest, state, issue a public statement; see **declare** 1.
**off the record** — *Syn.* confidential, unofficial, secret, not for publication; see **private, secret** 1, 3.
**on record** — *Syn.* recorded, stated, official, on the record; see **public** 1, **recorded.**
**record,** *v.* **1.** [To write down] — *Syn.* register, write, write in, put down, mark down, jot down, set down, note down, take down, put on record, transcribe, list, note, file, mark, inscribe, log, catalog, tabulate, put in writing, put in black and white, chronicle, keep accounts, keep an account of, make a written account of, put on paper, preserve, make an entry in, chalk up, write up, enter, enroll, matriculate, report, book, post, journalize, copy, document, insert, enumerate, spill ink; see also **write** 1, 2.
**2.** [To indicate] — *Syn.* point out, point to, register, show; see **designate** 1, **read** 3.
**3.** [To record electronically] — *Syn.* tape, cut, make a record of, make a tape, tape-record, videotape, film, photograph, cut a record.
**recorded,** *modif.* — *Syn.* written, listed, filed, noted, on file, on record, in black and white, in writing, inscribed, put down, registered, documented, entered, published, noted down, described, reported, cataloged, mentioned, certified, kept, chronicled, taped.
**recorder,** *n.* — *Syn.* tape recorder, cassette, dictaphone, recording instrument; see **tape recorder.**
**recording,** *n.* **1.** [The act of one that records] — *Syn.* documentation, recounting, record-keeping; see **registration** 1, **reporting.**
**2.** [A record] — *Syn.* disk, tape, cassette; see **record** 3.
**record player,** *n.* — *Syn.* phonograph, compact disk player, CD player, stereo, hi-fi, Victrola, music box, juke box, gramophone; see also **stereo, tape recorder.**
**records,** *pl.n.* — *Syn.* documents, chronicles, archives,

public papers, registers, annals, memorabilia, memoranda, lists, returns, diaries, accounts, statistics.

**recount,** *v.* — *Syn.* relate, narrate, give an account of, convey; see **describe, narrate, report** 1.

**recoup,** *v.* — *Syn.* regain, make up for, get back; see **recover** 1.

*See Synonym Study at* RECOVER.

**recourse,** *n.* — *Syn.* appeal, support, refuge; see **aid** 1, **resort** 1.

**recover,** *v.* **1.** [To obtain again] — *Syn.* regain, get back, retrieve, recoup, reclaim, redeem, salvage, rescue, find again, recapture, repossess, bring back, win back, reacquire, rediscover, resume, catch up, replevin, replevy, seize; see also **obtain** 1. — *Ant.* LOSE, let slip, forfeit.
**2.** [To improve one's condition] — *Syn.* gain, increase, better, realize, make up for, reach, grow, collect, forge ahead, pick up, bounce back, produce, make money, make a comeback, become something*, make a name*; see also **improve** 2, **profit** 2. — *Ant.* FAIL, go bankrupt, give up.
**3.** [To regain health] — *Syn.* rally, get better, get well, recuperate, improve, convalesce, mend, heal, get over, come around, come back, come to, be restored, be oneself again, come out of it, get out of danger, get the better of, overcome, perk up, gain, gain strength, revive, be reanimated, get back, get back on one's feet, get back in shape, feel like a new person, sober up, snap out of it, pull through*, get through*, be out of the woods*, return to form*; see also **improve** 2. — *Ant.* DIE, fail, relapse.

---

**SYN.** — **recover** implies finding or getting back something that one has lost in any manner [to *recover* stolen property, to *recover* one's self-possession]; **regain** more strongly stresses a deliberate winning back of something that has been lost or taken from one [to *regain* confidence, to *regain* a military objective]; **retrieve** suggests diligent effort in regaining something that is beyond each reach [he was determined to *retrieve* his honor]; **recoup** implies recovery of an equivalent in compensation [I tried to *recoup* my losses]; **reclaim** implies recovery or restoration to a better or useful state [to *reclaim* wasteland]

---

**recovered,** *modif.* — *Syn.* renewed, found, replaced, reborn, rediscovered, reawakened, retrieved, redeemed, reclaimed, regained, revived, returned, resumed, recuperated, rehabilitated; see also **discovered, well** 1. — *Ant.* LOST, missed, dropped.

**recovering,** *modif.* — *Syn.* getting better, improving, on the mend*; see **convalescent**.

**recovery,** *n.* **1.** [The act of returning to normal] — *Syn.* reestablishment, resumption, restoration, reinstatement, rehabilitation, reconstruction, return, reformation, recreation, replacement, readjustment, improvement, improving, getting back to normal, getting back to normalcy; see also sense 2, **improvement** 1.
**2.** [The process of regaining health] — *Syn.* convalescence, recuperation, revival, rebirth, renaissance, renascence, reanimation, resurgence, resurrection, regeneration, cure, improvement, reawakening, renewal, reinvigoration, resuscitation, rejuvenation, revivification, rehabilitation, post-operative care, return to health, physical improvement, healing, betterment, comeback.
**3.** [The act of regaining possession] — *Syn.* repossession, retrieval, reclamation, redemption, indemnification, reparation, compensation, recapture, rescue, replevin, return, recouping, restoration, remuneration, reimbursement, retaking, recall, replevy.

**recreant,** *modif.* — *Syn.* cowardly, craven, false, base, low, mean-spirited, faithless, cowering, yielding, afraid, hesitant, timorous, unfaithful, disloyal, traitorous, apostate, renegade, erring, timid, fearful, dastardly, skulking, sneaking, weak-minded, pigeonhearted, unmanly, spiritless, falsehearted, arrant, perfidious, defecting, treacherous, vile; see also **cowardly** 1, 2, **false** 1. — *Ant.* BRAVE, courageous, loyal.

**recreation,** *n.* — *Syn.* amusement, relaxation, diversion, play, fun, entertainment, enjoyment, festivity, hobby, holiday, vacation, pastime, pleasure, game, avocation, refreshment; see also **entertainment** 1, **sport** 1.

**recruit,** *n.* — *Syn.* new man, new woman, novice, tyro, beginner, selectee, draftee, conscript, inductee, trainee, volunteer, enlistee, enlisted person, serviceman, soldier, sailor, marine, raw recruit, rookie*, boot*, Johnny Raw*, greenie*, G.I. Joe*; see also **soldier.**

**recruit,** *v.* **1.** [To raise troops] — *Syn.* draft, call up, enlist, select, supply, muster, deliver, sign up, induct, take in, find manpower, call to arms, call to the colors, augment the army, bring into service, seek to enroll, seek to hire; see also **enlist** 1, **hire** 1.
**2.** [To gather needed resources] — *Syn.* restore, store up, replenish, strengthen, revive, recuperate, recover, fill up, round up, recoup, improve, better, gain, regain, reanimate; see also **obtain** 1, **raise** 3.

**recruited,** *modif.* — *Syn.* inducted, called up, accepted into the armed forces; see **enlisted, initiated** 3.

**rectangle,** *n.* — *Syn.* geometrical figure, square, box, oblong, four-sided figure, quadrilateral, right-angled parallelogram; see also **form** 1.

**rectangular,** *modif.* — *Syn.* oblong, square, four-sided, quadrilateral, right-angled, orthogonal, foursquare, boxy, quadrangular, quadrate.

**rectify,** *v.* — *Syn.* redress, reform, amend; see **correct** 1, **improve** 1, **revise.**

**rectitude,** *n.* — *Syn.* integrity, honesty, uprightness; see **honesty** 1.

**rector,** *n.* — *Syn.* pastor, vicar, parson; see **minister** 1.

**rectory,** *n.* — *Syn.* vicarage, parsonage, manse; see **parsonage.**

**recumbent,** *modif.* — *Syn.* reclining, prostrate, lying down; see **lying** 4, **supine** 1.

*See Synonym Study at* SUPINE.

**recuperate,** *v.* — *Syn.* heal, pull through*, get back on one's feet; see **recover** 3.

**recur,** *v.* — *Syn.* return, reappear, crop up again; see **happen** 2, **repeat** 2.

**recurrent,** *modif.* — *Syn.* repeated, reoccurring, repetitive, habitual; see **chronic, intermittent.**

*See Synonym Study at* INTERMITTENT.

**recycle,** *v.* — *Syn.* reuse, recover, salvage, convert; see **reclaim** 1.

**red,** *n.* Hues of red include: scarlet, carmine, vermilion, crimson, cerise, cherry-red, beet-red, ruby, garnet, maroon, brick-red, infrared, far infrared, near infrared, claret, rust, red-gold, magenta, pink, damask, coral-red, blood-red, solferino, fuchsia, russet, terra cotta, bittersweet, geranium lake, nacarat, nacarine, Harvard crimson, hyacinth red, Chinese red, Morocco red, caldron, Turkey red, Alizarin red, aniline red, aurora red, Bengal red, Congo red, Venetian red, Indian red, Indian ocher, chrome-red, carthamus red, rose, rose de Pompadour, rose blush, rose du Barry, old rose, Tyrian purple, fire engine red, candy apple red; see also **color** 1, **pink.**

**in the red** — *Syn.* in debt, losing money, operating at a loss, going broke*; see **indebted.**

**see red** * — *Syn.* become angry, lose one's temper, get mad; see **rage** 1.

**red-blooded,** *modif.* — *Syn.* vigorous, high-spirited, robust; see **healthy** 1, **strong** 1.

**redden,** *v.* 1. [To grow red] — *Syn.* blush, color, flush, crimson, turn red, bloody, rust; see also **blush.**
   2. [To make red] — *Syn.* color, rouge, apply lipstick, tint, dye, paint, put paint on, ruddle, reddle, rubricate, flush, tint, encarmine, encarnadine.

**reddish,** *modif.* — *Syn.* flushed, somewhat red, rose; see **red,** *n.*

**redecorate,** *v.* — *Syn.* refurbish, refresh, renew, paint, restore, recondition, remodel, renovate, revamp, redo, rearrange, touch up, patch up, plaster, refurnish, readorn, wallpaper, clean up, carpet, do over*, fix up*; see also **decorate.**

**redeem,** *v.* 1. [To recover through a payment] — *Syn.* buy back, repay, ransom, purchase, repurchase, reclaim, retrieve, regain, recover, settle, replevy, discharge, cash in, buy off, get back, take in, call in, cover, defray, make good, restore, reinstate, recapture, replevin, recoup, repossess, buy off, pay off; see also **obtain** 1.
   2. [To save] — *Syn.* deliver, set free, reclaim, reform; see **ransom, reclaim** 1, **rescue** 1, 2.
*See Synonym Study at* RESCUE.

**redeemed,** *modif.* — *Syn.* recovered, reclaimed, gotten back; see **recovered.**

**redeemer,** *n.* — *Syn.* rescuer, deliverer, liberator; see **liberator, savior** 1.

**redeem oneself,** *v.* — *Syn.* atone, expiate, remedy, redress, propitiate, reform, keep faith, apologize, do penance, appease, give satisfaction, vindicate oneself, clear oneself, absolve oneself, prove oneself innocent, beg pardon, express regrets, make amends, make restitution, make up for; see also **pay for.**

**redemption,** *n.* 1. [Recovery] — *Syn.* retrieval, reclamation, reparation; see **recovery** 3.
   2. [Salvation] — *Syn.* regeneration, sanctification, rebirth; see **improvement** 1, **salvation** 3.

**red-handed*,** *modif.* — *Syn.* caught in the act, *in flagrante delicto* (Latin), while one is at it, in a compromising position, blatantly, with one's hand in the cookie jar*; see also **guilty** 2, **openly** 2.

**redheaded,** *modif.* — *Syn.* auburn-haired, red-haired, sandy-haired, titian-haired, strawberry blonde, carrot-topped*, brick-topped*.

**red-hot,** *modif.* 1. [Burning] — *Syn.* heated, sizzling, scorching; see **burning** 1, **hot** 1.
   2. [Zealous] — *Syn.* heated, impassioned, fanatical, eager; see **enthusiastic** 2, **excited.**
   3. [Raging] — *Syn.* vehement, violent, furious; see **extreme** 2, **intense.**
   4. [Newest] — *Syn.* latest, most recent, hippest*; see **fresh** 1, **modern** 1.

**redo,** *v.* — *Syn.* start over, redesign, rethink, go back to the drawing board, revamp, revise, redecorate, remodel, do over again; see also **repeat** 1.

**redolent,** *modif.* 1. [Fragrant] — *Syn.* sweet-smelling, perfumed, aromatic, smelling of; see **odorous** 2.
   2. [Suggestive] — *Syn.* evocative, reminiscent, recollective; see **suggestive.**

**redone,** *modif.* — *Syn.* done over, refinished, fixed up*; see **improved** 1, **revised.**

**redouble,** *v.* — *Syn.* reinforce, intensify, raise, magnify; see **increase** 1, **intensify, strengthen.**

**redoubt,** *n.* — *Syn.* breastwork, bulwark, stronghold, fortress; see **fortification** 2.

**redoubtable,** *modif.* — *Syn.* formidable, fearful, imposing; see **frightful** 1, **impressive** 1, **terrible** 1.

**redress,** *n.* 1. [Correction] — *Syn.* revision, amendment, remedy, setting right, change, reformation, renewal, remodeling, reworking, reestablishment, rectification, relief, rehabilitation, repair.
   2. [Amends] — *Syn.* compensation, satisfaction, payment, indemnity, retribution, requital, return, reparation, recompense, allowance, atonement, propitiation, adjustment, correction, conciliation, remission, indemnification, restitution, restoration; see also **pay** 2, **reparation** 2.
*See Synonym Study at* REPARATION.

**redress,** *v.* — *Syn.* set right, remedy, rectify; see **correct** 1.

**red tape,** *n.* 1. [Delay] — *Syn.* wait, inaction, roadblock, holdup; see **impediment** 1.
   2. [Bureaucracy] — *Syn.* officialism, paperwork, inflexible routine, officialdom; see **bureaucracy** 1, 2.

**reduce,** *v.* 1. [To make less] — *Syn.* decrease, lessen, diminish, cut down; see **decrease** 2.
   2. [To defeat] — *Syn.* conquer, overcome, subdue; see **defeat** 1, 2.
   3. [To lower in rank or position] — *Syn.* degrade, demote, abase; see **disgrace, humble, humiliate.**
*See Synonym Study at* DECREASE.

**reduced,** *modif.* 1. [Made smaller] — *Syn.* lessened, decreased, diminished, shortened, abridged, abbreviated, condensed, miniaturized, scaled down, transistorized, compressed, foreshortened, economized, cut down, downsized, shrunk, subtracted, contracted, melted, boiled down. — *Ant.* enlarged, stretched, SPREAD.
   2. [Made lower] — *Syn.* lowered, abated, sunk, deflated, leveled, discounted, marked down, cheapened, taken down, weakened, debilitated, humbled, demoted, degraded. — *Ant.* heightened, RAISED, elevated.
   3. [Made orderly] — *Syn.* standardized, classified, regulated, controlled, ordered, formulated, systematized, unified; see also **organized.**

**reducing,** *n.* — *Syn.* lowering, lessening, decreasing, diminishing, cutting down, shortening, foreshortening, condensing, compressing, paring down, marking down, discounting, contracting, downsizing, shrinking, shriveling, dieting, slimming down; see also **contraction** 1, **reduction** 1.

**reduction,** *n.* 1. [The process of making smaller] — *Syn.* decrease, contraction, diminution, lowering, lessening, shortening, abatement, discount, reducing, conversion, deoxidation, refinement, attenuation, atrophy, condensation, loss, decline, compression, depression, subtraction, retrenchment, downsizing, cutback, shrinkage, miniaturization, concision, constriction, modification, minimization, curtailment, abbreviation, abridgment, decrescence, syncope, ellipsis, elision, assuagement, modulation, moderation, mitigation, remission, decrement. — *Ant.* INCREASE, increasing, enlargement.
   2. [An amount that constitutes reduction, sense 1] — *Syn.* decrease, rebate, cut; see **discount.**

**redundancy,** *n.* — *Syn.* verbosity, tautology, superfluity; see **excess, repetition, wordiness.**

**redundant,** *modif.* 1. [Needless] — *Syn.* superfluous, irrelevant, excess; see **excessive, superfluous, unnecessary.**
   2. [Repetitious] — *Syn.* verbose, wordy, repetitive, tautological; see **verbose.**
*See Synonym Study at* VERBOSE.

**reduplicate,** *v.* — *Syn.* double, duplicate, ditto*; see **copy** 2, **repeat** 1, **reproduce** 2.

**reecho,** *v.* — *Syn.* reverberate, reiterate, resound; see **repeat** 3, **sound** 1.

**reed,** *n.* — *Syn.* cane, stalk, grass; see **grass** 1, **plant, weed** 1.

**reeducate,** v. — *Syn.* reinstruct, readjust, rehabilitate; see **improve** 1, **teach** 1.

**reedy,** *modif.* — *Syn.* piping, thin, piercing, sharp; see **shrill.**

**reef,** n. — *Syn.* ridge, shoal, bar, sand bar, rock, bank, beach, coral reef, atoll, ledge, rock barrier.
*See Synonym Study at* SHOAL.

**reefer\*,** n. — *Syn.* marijuana cigarette, joint\*, roach\*, stick\*; see **marijuana.**

**reek,** n. — *Syn.* stench, stink, smell; see **smell** 2.

**reek,** v. — *Syn.* smell, give off an odor, stink; see **smell** 1, **stink.**

**reel,** n. — *Syn.* spool, bobbin, windlass, spindle, wheel, wound strip, roll of film.

**reel,** v. — *Syn.* sway, stagger, lurch, weave, feel dizzy, feel giddy, bob, waver, flounder, walk drunkenly, totter, stumble, careen, pitch, roll, whirl, spin, rock, falter, fall back.

**reel off,** v. — *Syn.* rattle off, recite, enumerate; see **list** 1, **recite** 3, **specify.**

**reenter,** v. — *Syn.* reappear, come back, reemerge; see **enter** 1, **return** 1.

**reestablish,** v. — *Syn.* restore, put in place again, go back to; see **organize** 2, **renew** 1.

**reexamine,** v. — *Syn.* go back over, review, check thoroughly; see **examine** 1, **reconsider.**

**refer,** v. **1.** [To concern] — *Syn.* regard, relate, have relation, have to do with, apply, be about, answer to, involve, connect, be a matter of, have a bearing on, correspond with, bear upon, comprise, include, belong, pertain, have reference, take in, cover, appertain, point, hold, encompass, incorporate, touch, deal with; see also **concern** 1.
**2.** [To mention] — *Syn.* allude to, bring up, direct a remark, make reference to, make an allusion to, advert, ascribe, direct attention to, call attention to, attribute, cite, quote, hint at, point out, point to, note, notice, indicate, speak about, suggest, touch on, give as an example, associate, adduce, exemplify, instance, excerpt, extract; see also **mention.**
**3.** [To direct] — *Syn.* send to, put in touch with, transfer, relegate, commit, submit to, assign, give a recommendation to, introduce; see also **designate** 1, **lead** 1.

---

*SYN.* — **refer** implies deliberate, direct, and open mention of something /he *referred* in detail to their corrupt practices/; **allude** implies indirect, often casual mention, as by a hint or a figure of speech /although she used different names, she was *alluding* to her family/

---

**referee,** n. — *Syn.* judge, arbitrator, conciliator, ref\*; see **judge** 2, **umpire.**
*See Synonym Study at* JUDGE.

**reference,** n. **1.** [The act of referring] — *Syn.* indicating, pointing out, mentioning, citing, bringing up, stating, attributing, connecting, associating, relating.
**2.** [An allusion] — *Syn.* mention, citation, hint, implication; see **allusion, quotation** 1.
**3.** [A source] — *Syn.* text, original text, book, article, writing, standard work, reference book, dictionary, encyclopedia, thesaurus, directory, guidebook, footnote, eyewitness, informant, evidence; see also **dictionary, source** 2.
**4.** [A person or statement giving testimony as to someone's character, abilities, etc.] — *Syn.* friend, employer, patron, associate, backer, booster\*, recommendation, endorsement, testimonial; see also **recommendation** 2.

**referendum,** n. — *Syn.* election, poll, choice, plebiscite; see **election** 2, **vote** 2.

**referred to,** *modif.* **1.** [Mentioned] — *Syn.* brought up, alluded to, spoken about; see **mentioned, suggested.**
**2.** [Directed] — *Syn.* recommended, sent on, introduced; see **proposed, transferred.**

**referring,** *modif.* — *Syn.* alluding, suggesting, hinting, indicating, attributing, mentioning, citing, quoting, bringing up, touching on, remarking, implying, imputing, ascribing.

**refine,** v. **1.** [To purify] — *Syn.* rarefy, strain, filter, clarify; see **clean, filter** 2, **purify.**
**2.** [To improve] — *Syn.* perfect, polish, cultivate, hone; see **civilize, improve** 1, **sharpen** 2.

**refined,** *modif.* **1.** [Purified] — *Syn.* cleaned, cleansed, aerated, strained, filtered, washed, clean, rarefied, boiled down, distilled, clarified, tried, drained, elutriated, processed; see also **pure** 2. — *Ant.* RAW, crude, unrefined.
**2.** [Genteel] — *Syn.* cultivated, civilized, polished, elegant, urbane, well-bred, gracious, enlightened, free from coarseness, courtly, mannerly, suave, gentlemanly, ladylike, restrained, gentle, mannerly, high-minded, cultured, subtle, discriminating, polite, courteous; see also **polite** 1.

**refinement,** n. **1.** [The act of refining] — *Syn.* cleaning, cleansing, purification, distillation, clarification, clarifying, draining, elutriation, depuration, detersion, cracking, filtration.
**2.** [Culture] — *Syn.* civilization, cultivation, erudition, sophistication, breeding, enlightenment, wide knowledge, lore, subtlety, science, artistic attainments, scholarship, learning; see also **culture** 3.
**3.** [Genteel feelings and behavior] — *Syn.* elegance, politeness, polish, good manners, good breeding, suavity, courtesy, grace, gentleness, tact, cultivation, graciousness, civility, gentility, taste, discrimination, fineness, delicacy, dignity, urbanity, savoir-faire; see also **courtesy** 1, **elegance** 1.

**refinery,** n. — *Syn.* smelting works, oil refinery, sugar refinery; see **factory.**

**refining,** *modif.* — *Syn.* cleansing, purifying, clarifying, improving, cultivating, civilizing, elevating, perfecting, polishing, honing, sharpening, focusing, subtilizing, making purer, making cleaner, making more precise, making more subtle; see also **cleaning.**

**refinished,** *modif.* — *Syn.* restored, resurfaced, fixed up\*; see **clean** 1, **finished** 2, **repaired.**

**reflect,** v. **1.** [To contemplate] — *Syn.* speculate, muse, ponder, consider; see **consider** 3, **think** 1.
**2.** [To throw back] — *Syn.* echo, reecho, repeat, match, take after, return, resonate, reverberate, resound, copy, reproduce, reply, repercuss, be resonant, emulate, imitate, follow, catch, rebound; see also **bounce** 1, **sound** 1.
**3.** [To throw back an image] — *Syn.* mirror, shine, reproduce, show up on, flash, glare, give back, cast back, return, give forth.
**4.** [To make apparent] — *Syn.* show, indicate, reveal, exhibit; see **display** 1.
**5.** [To bring discredit] — *Syn.* cast blame on, dishonor, disgrace; see **depreciate** 2, **disgrace.**

**reflected,** *modif.* — *Syn.* mirrored, repeated, reproduced, echoed, followed, derived from, returned, thrown back, sent back, cast back, emulated, imitated, brought to mind.

**reflection,** n. **1.** [Thought] — *Syn.* consideration, pensiveness, thinking, contemplation, rumination, speculation, musing, deliberation, study, pondering, medita-

tion, concentration, absorption, cogitation, observation, weighing, mulling over; see also **thought** 1.
**2.** [An image] — *Syn.* impression, rays, light, glare, shine, glitter, appearance, idea, reflected image, likeness, shadow, duplicate, picture, echo, representation, reproduction; see also **copy, image** 2.
**3.** [Discredit] — *Syn.* censure, reproach, disesteem, imputation; see **blame** 1, **disgrace** 1.
**reflective,** *modif.* — *Syn.* contemplative, studious, pensive; see **pensive, thoughtful** 1.
*See Synonym Study at* PENSIVE.
**reflector,** *n.* — *Syn.* shiny metal, glass, reverberator; see **mirror.**
**reflex,** *modif.* — *Syn.* mechanical, unthinking, habitual, involuntary; see **automatic** 2, **spontaneous.**
**reform,** *n.* — *Syn.* reformation, betterment, amelioration, new law; see **change** 2, **improvement** 1, 2.
**reform,** *v.* **1.** [To change to a new or better form] — *Syn.* reorganize, reconstruct, rearrange, transform, ameliorate, redeem, rectify, better, rehabilitate, improve, correct, cure, remedy, convert, mend, emend, amend, restore, remodel, revise, repair, rebuild, reclaim, revolutionize, regenerate, refashion, renovate, renew, rework, reconstitute, make over, remake; see also **change** 1. — *Ant.* degrade, CORRUPT, botch.
**2.** [To correct evils] — *Syn.* amend, clean out, give a new basis, abolish, repeal, uplift, ameliorate, rectify, regenerate, redeem, rehabilitate, give new life to, remedy, stamp out, make better, standardize, bring up to code, set straight; see also sense 1; **improve** 1.
**3.** [To change one's conduct for the better] — *Syn.* resolve, mend, mend one's ways, regenerate, make amends, have a new conscience, make a new start, make resolutions, turn over a new leaf, see the error of one's ways, change one's ways, straighten out, go straight*, clean up one's act*, shape up*, get religion*, put on the new man*, swear off*; see also sense 2.
**Reformation,** *n.* — *Syn.* Lutheranism, Protestantism, Puritanism, Calvinism, Anglicanism, Evangelicalism, Unitarianism, Counter-Reformation, Protestant Movement; see also **revolution** 2.
**reformation,** *n.* **1.** [The act of reforming] — *Syn.* reform, improvement, amendment, reorganization, reconstruction, renewal, rehabilitation, rearrangement, renovation, transformation, reworking, shifting, realignment; see also **change** 1, **improvement** 1.
**2.** [The state of being reformed] — *Syn.* reawakening, repeal, abolition, rebirth, remaking, reestablishment; see also **recovery** 1, **restoration** 1.
**reformatory,** *n.* — *Syn.* reform school, house of correction, penal institution, penitentiary, school for young delinquents, borstal (British), kids' pen*, young-stir*, little house*, Junior College*; see also **jail, school** 1.
**Reformed,** *modif.* — *Syn.* denominational, unorthodox, nonconforming, sectarian, dissenting, heterodox, enlightened, Protestant, Calvinist, Zwinglian.
**reformed,** *modif.* **1.** [Changed] — *Syn.* altered, transformed, improved, ameliorated, amended, rectified, reconstructed, reconstituted, reorganized, shuffled, revised, reestablished, revolutionized, reset, reworked, renewed, regenerated; see also **changed** 2, **improved** 1. — *Ant.* preserved, degenerated, deteriorated.
**2.** [Changed for the better in behavior] — *Syn.* converted, improved, redeemed, rehabilitated, gone straight*, made a new man of, turned over a new leaf, reborn, born-again, regenerated, regenerate, sworn off; see also **righteous** 1.
**refractory,** *modif.* **1.** [Stubborn] — *Syn.* obstinate,

headstrong, willful, disobedient; see **contrary** 4, **naughty, obstinate.**
**2.** [Inflexible] — *Syn.* hard, impliable, rigid; see **firm** 2, **stiff** 1.
**refrain,** *n.* — *Syn.* chorus, undersong, theme, strain; see **chorus** 2, **music** 1, **song.**
**refrain,** *v.* — *Syn.* cease, avoid, forbear; see **abstain.**
*See Synonym Study at* ABSTAIN.
**refresh,** *v.* — *Syn.* invigorate, stimulate, restore, freshen up; see **renew** 1, **revive** 1.
*See Synonym Study at* RENEW.
**refreshing,** *modif.* **1.** [Bracing] — *Syn.* invigorating, rousing, exhilarating; see **stimulating.**
**2.** [Novel] — *Syn.* fresh, delightful, extraordinary, like a breath of fresh air; see **original** 2, **unusual** 1, 2.
**refreshment,** *n.* — *Syn.* snack, light meal, treat, drink; see **drink** 1, **food.**
**refrigerate,** *v.* — *Syn.* chill, cool, keep cold, freeze; see **cool** 2.
**refrigeration,** *n.* — *Syn.* cooling, chilling, freezing, keeping cold, preservation by cold, glaciation, glacification, regelation; see also **preservation.**
**refrigerator,** *n.* — *Syn.* fridge*, icebox, Frigidaire (trademark), cooler, cold-storage box, locker, refrigerator car, electric refrigerator, cooling apparatus, refrigeration equipment, freezer, deep freezer, quick freezer, deepfreeze.
**refuge,** *n.* **1.** [A place of protection] — *Syn.* shelter, retreat, sanctuary, asylum, haven, safe haven, home, safe house, hiding place, ambush, cover, covert, coverture, sanctum, sanctum sanctorum, den, game preserve, nature preserve, bird sanctuary, harbor, harbor of refuge, anchorage, port, port in a storm, cloister, convent, monastery, ashram, hermitage, poorhouse, orphanage, safe place, fortress, stronghold, fallout shelter, storm cellar, hideaway*, hide-out*.
**2.** [A means of resort] — *Syn.* alternative, escape, resource, recourse, last resort, outlet, way out, retreat, exit, opening.
*See Synonym Study at* SHELTER.
**refugee,** *n.* — *Syn.* exile, expatriate, fugitive, emigrant, émigré, foreigner, political refugee, expellee, evacuee, defector, castaway, homeless person, derelict, foundling, pariah, outlaw, Ishmael, prodigal, displaced person, D.P.*, alien, outcast, fugitive, renegade.
**refund,** *n.* — *Syn.* return, reimbursement, repayment, remuneration, compensation, allowance, payment for expenses, rebate, discount, settlement, discharge, acquittance, satisfaction, consolation, money back; see also **payment** 1.
**refund,** *v.* **1.** [To return] — *Syn.* pay back, reimburse, remit, repay, relinquish, indemnify, make good, balance, recoup, adjust, reward, restore, redeem, make repayment to, compensate, recompense, make up for, make amends, redress, remunerate, give back, settle, honor a claim, kick back*; see also **pay** 1, **return** 2.
**2.** [To put financial obligations on a new basis] — *Syn.* borrow, redeem, discharge, transmit, transfer, make over, resubscribe, commit, undertake, tax, renegotiate, renew, compensate, sell bonds, raise revenue, increase the public debt, issue securities.
**refunded,** *modif.* **1.** [Returned] — *Syn.* repaid, acquitted, reimbursed, discharged; see **paid, repaid, returned.**
**2.** [Placed on a new financial basis] — *Syn.* renewed, reestablished, redeemed, resubscribed, borrowed, renegotiated, reissued, revised, reconstituted.
**refurbish,** *v.* — *Syn.* renovate, restore, fix up*; see **redecorate, renew** 1, **repair.**

**refusal,** *n.* — *Syn.* rejection, repudiation, renunciation, rebuff, snub, turndown, nonacceptance, denial, disavowal, noncompliance, forbidding, veto, interdiction, proscription, ban, writ, enjoinment, exclusion, discountenancing, disallowance, negation, refutation, renouncement, repulse, withholding, disclaimer, nonconsent, unwillingness, regrets, abnegation, declination, repulsion, reversal, dissent, prohibition, disfavor, disapproval, curb, restraint, thumbs down*; see also **opposition** 2. — *Ant.* CONSENT, approval, acceptance.

**refuse,** *n.* — *Syn.* rubbish, litter, waste, leavings; see **trash** 1, 3.

**refuse,** *v.* — *Syn.* decline, reject, repudiate, deny, spurn, resist, repel, scorn, pass up, disallow, forbid, have no plans to, not anticipate, demur, protest, withdraw, hold back, withhold, shun, evade, dodge, ignore, turn down, turn from, recoil, balk, beg to be excused, send regrets, beg off, make one's excuses, regret, send off, not budge, cut out of the budget, not budget, not care to, refuse to receive, dispense with, not be at home to, disaccord with, dissent, say no, make excuses, disapprove, set aside, turn away, brush off*, not buy*, turn thumbs down*, hold out*, hold off*, turn one's back on*, turn a deaf ear to*; see also **deny.** — *Ant.* ALLOW, admit, consent.

---

*SYN.* — **refuse** is a direct, sometimes even blunt term, implying an emphatic denial of a request, demand, etc. *[to refuse a person money, to refuse permission]*; **decline** implies courtesy in expressing one's nonacceptance of an invitation, proposal, etc. *[he declined the nomination]*; **reject** stresses a negative or antagonistic attitude and implies positive refusal to accept, use, believe, etc. *[they rejected the damaged goods]*; **repudiate** implies the disowning, disavowal, or casting off with condemnation of a person or thing as having no authority, worth, validity, truth, etc. *[to repudiate the claims of faith healers]*; to **spurn** is to refuse or reject with contempt or disdain *[she spurned his attentions]*

---

**refused,** *modif.* — *Syn.* declined, rejected, rebuffed, spurned, vetoed, repudiated, forbidden, denied, disowned, disavowed, forsaken, blocked, repelled, closed to, dismissed, turned down, unbudgeted, not budgeted, not in the budget, cut from the budget, removed from the budget. — *Ant.* PERMITTED, allowed, consented to.

**refutation,** *n.* — *Syn.* rebuttal, confutation, contradiction; see **denial** 1, **refusal.**

**refute,** *v.* — *Syn.* disprove, confute, show up, rebut, explode, expose, prove false, overthrow, show the weakness in, discredit, provide refutation for, argue against, oppose, tear down, demolish, squelch, take a stand against, invalidate, cancel, cancel out, belie, give the lie to, repudiate, contradict, negate, dispute, contravene, parry, contend, debate, disclaim, convict, reply to, quash, crush, gainsay, dispose of, knock holes in*, not leave a leg to stand on*; see also **answer** 3, **confute, deny.** — *Ant.* SUPPORT, uphold, stand by.

*See Synonym Study at DISPROVE.*

**regain,** *v.* — *Syn.* recapture, retrieve, reacquire; see **recover** 1.

*See Synonym Study at RECOVER.*

**regal,** *modif.* — *Syn.* sovereign, noble, majestic; see **royal** 1, 2.

**regale,** *v.* **1.** [To entertain with something pleasing or amusing] — *Syn.* delight, please, amuse; see **amuse, entertain** 1.

**2.** [To entertain with a feast] — *Syn.* feast, treat, wine and dine*; see **celebrate** 3, **entertain** 2, **feed.**

**regalia,** *n.* **1.** [Finery] — *Syn.* best clothes, dress clothes, best bib and tucker*; see **finery.**

**2.** [A symbol of royalty] — *Syn.* insignia, decorations, crown, scepter; see **emblem, symbol.**

**regard,** *n.* **1.** [Attention] — *Syn.* gaze, look, glance, notice, view, scrutiny, concern, consideration, thought, once-over*; see also **look** 3.

**2.** [A favorable opinion] — *Syn.* esteem, respect, honor, favor, liking, interest, fondness, attachment, deference, opinion, sympathy, estimation, admiration, appreciation, reverence, homage, consideration, love, affection, value, devotion; see also **admiration.**

**in regard to** — *Syn.* as to, concerning, with regard to; see **about** 2, **regarding.**

**without regard to** — *Syn.* despite, without considering, regardless of; see **notwithstanding, regardless** 2.

**regard,** *v.* **1.** [To look at] — *Syn.* observe, notice, mark, view, watch, heed, look on, mind, give attention to, attend, gaze, note, stare at, see, witness, contemplate, scrutinize. — *Ant.* disregard, overlook, turn away.

**2.** [To have an attitude] — *Syn.* consider, think of, view, look upon, judge, deem, rate, reckon, perceive, contemplate; see also **consider** 2, **think** 1.

**3.** [To hold in esteem] — *Syn.* respect, esteem, value, admire, appreciate, honor, look up to, revere; see also **admire** 1.

**as regards** — *Syn.* concerning, with respect to, with reference to; see **about** 2, **regarding.**

---

*SYN.* — **regard** is the most neutral of the terms here, in itself usually implying evaluation of worth rather than recognition of it *[the book is highly regarded by authorities]*; **respect** implies high valuation of worth, as shown in deference or honor *[a jurist respected by lawyers]*; **esteem,** in addition, suggests that the person or object is highly prized or cherished *[a friend esteemed for her loyalty]*; **admire** suggests a feeling of enthusiastic delight in the appreciation of that which one views as superior *[one must admire such courage]*

---

**regarding,** *modif. & prep.* — *Syn.* concerning, with respect to, with reference to, with regard to, in relation to, as regards, as to, in regard to; see also **about** 2.

**regardless,** *modif.* **1.** [Heedless] — *Syn.* negligent, careless, unobservant, unheeding, inattentive, reckless, inconsiderate, inadvertent, blind, unfeeling, deaf, neglectful, unmindful, mindless, insensitive, lax, indifferent, listless, uninterested, unconcerned. — *Ant.* ALERT, attentive, watchful.

**2.** [In spite of; *usually used with of*] — *Syn.* despite, aside from, distinct from, without regard to, without considering, at all costs, at any cost, leaving aside; see also **although, but** 1, **notwithstanding.**

**regards,** *pl. n.* — *Syn.* best wishes, compliments, greetings, salutations, remembrances, respects, love, best regards, one's best, commendations, love and kisses*; see also **greeting** 1.

**regatta,** *n.* — *Syn.* boat race, rowing competition, yacht race; see **race** 3.

**regency,** *n.* — *Syn.* regime, rule, authority; see **dominion** 1, **power** 2.

**regenerate,** *v.* — *Syn.* re-create, restore, revive, reform; see **reconstruct, reform** 1, 2, **renew** 1, **revive** 1.

**regeneration,** *n.* **1.** [Reconstruction] — *Syn.* rebuilding, rehabilitation, restoration; see **reconstruction, renewal.**

**2.** [Conversion] — *Syn.* revival, redemption, rebirth,

reformation; see **improvement** 1, **recovery** 2, **salvation** 3.

**regent,** *n.* — *Syn.* governor, minister, director; see **agent** 1, **ruler** 1.

**regime,** *n.* — *Syn.* administration, management, political system; see **administration** 2, 3, **government** 1, 2.

**regiment,** *n.* — *Syn.* corps, soldiers, military organization; see **army** 2, **troops**.

**regiment,** *v.* — *Syn.* order, systematize, control, discipline; see **classify, organize** 1.

**regimentation,** *n.* — *Syn.* discipline, strict discipline, strictness, rigidity, standardization, methodization, regulation, uniformity, massing, collectivization, organization, planned economy, arrangement, mechanization, institutionalization, classification, division, lining up, adjustment, harmonization, grouping, ordering, overorganization, tight ship*; see also **command** 2, **discipline** 2, **regulation** 1, **restraint** 2.

**regimented,** *modif.* — *Syn.* disciplined, controlled, rigid; see **governed** 1, 2, **severe** 1, 2.

**region,** *n.* **1.** [An indefinite area] — *Syn.* country, district, territory, section, sector, province, zone, realm, vicinity, quarter, locale, locality, environs, precinct, county, neighborhood, terrain, domain, range.

**2.** [A limited area] — *Syn.* precinct, ward, quarter; see **area** 2.

**3.** [Scope] — *Syn.* sphere, province, realm; see **field** 4.

**regional,** *modif.* — *Syn.* provincial, territorial, local, zonal, environmental, positional, regionalistic, geographical, parochial, sectional, topical, localized, locational, insular, topographic; see also **local** 1.

**register,** *n.* **1.** [A list] — *Syn.* file, registry, roll, catalog, record, ledger, annals, entry, guest book, roster, membership, personnel; see also **list, record** 1.

**2.** [A heating regulator] — *Syn.* grate, hot-air opening, vent, radiator, heating unit.

*See Synonym Study at* LIST.

**register,** *v.* **1.** [To record] — *Syn.* check in, enroll, file, make an entry; see **list** 1, **record** 1.

**2.** [To indicate] — *Syn.* point out, point to, record; see **designate** 1, **read** 3.

**3.** [To show] — *Syn.* express, disclose, manifest; see **display** 1.

**4.** [To enlist or enroll] — *Syn.* go through registration, check into, sign up for, check in, sign in, join.

**registered,** *modif.* **1.** [Recorded] — *Syn.* enrolled, cataloged, certified, noted down; see **enrolled, recorded**.

**2.** [Pedigreed] — *Syn.* purebred, thoroughbred, blooded, pure-blooded, full-blooded.

**registrar,** *n.* — *Syn.* recorder, register, receiving clerk, registering clerk, university administrator, director of admissions, admissions officer, dean; see also **clerk** 2.

**registration,** *n.* **1.** [The act of registering] — *Syn.* enrollment, enrolling, signing up, certification, matriculation, recording, listing, filing, cataloging, booking, keeping records, noting down, stamping, authorizing, notarization; see also **enrollment** 1.

**2.** [Those who have registered] — *Syn.* enrollment, turnout, registrants, voters, hotel guests, students, matriculants, student body, delegation; see also **enrollment** 2.

**regress,** *v.* — *Syn.* backslide, relapse, revert; see **relapse, retreat** 1, **sink** 1.

**regressive,** *modif.* — *Syn.* retrogressive, reverse, reactionary; see **backward** 1, **conservative**.

**regret,** *n.* **1.** [Remorse] — *Syn.* concern, compunction, worry, repentance, self-reproach, self-condemnation,

self-disgust, misgiving, regretfulness, nostalgia, self-accusation, contrition, qualm, scruple, penitence, bitterness, disappointment, dissatisfaction, uneasiness, conscience, discomfort, annoyance, spiritual disturbance; see also **care** 2, **repentance**. — *Ant.* COMFORT, satisfaction, ease.

**2.** [Grief] — *Syn.* sorrow, pain, anxiety; see **grief** 1.

*See Synonym Study at* REPENTANCE.

**regret,** *v.* **1.** [To be sorry for] — *Syn.* mourn, bewail, lament, cry over, rue, grieve, repent, repine, have compunctions about, feel remorse for, look back upon, feel conscience-stricken, bemoan, moan, have a bad conscience, have qualms about, weep over, be disturbed over, feel uneasy about, rue the day, laugh out of the other side of one's mouth*, kick oneself*, bite one's tongue*, cry over spilt milk*. — *Ant.* CELEBRATE, rejoice, be satisfied with.

**2.** [To disapprove of] — *Syn.* deplore, be opposed to, deprecate; see **censure, disapprove** 1, **dislike**.

**regretful,** *modif.* — *Syn.* penitent, remorseful, conscience-stricken, frustrated; see **apologetic, sorry** 1.

**regrettable,** *modif.* — *Syn.* unfortunate, deplorable, lamentable, pitiful; see **unfavorable** 2.

**regular,** *modif.* **1.** [In accordance with custom] — *Syn.* customary, usual, routine; see **conventional** 1, 2, **natural** 2, **normal** 1.

**2.** [In accordance with accepted rules] — *Syn.* proper, established, legitimate, lawful; see **conventional** 1, 2, **legal** 1.

**3.** [In accordance with an observable pattern] — *Syn.* orderly, methodical, routine, symmetrical, precise, exact, systematic, punctual, steady, uniform, even, arranged, organized, patterned, constant, congruous, consonant, accordant, consistent, invariable, formal, regulated, rational, rhythmic, periodic, measured, classified, in order, unconfused, harmonious, normal, natural, cyclic, cyclical, successive, momentary, alternating, probable, recurrent, habitual, general, usual, expected, frequent, serial, automatic, mechanical, pulsating, rotational, alternate, hourly, daily, monthly, weekly, annual, seasonal, yearly, quarterly, semiannual, diurnal, quotidian, tertian, quartan, hebdomadal, menstrual, anticipated, looked for, hoped for, counted on, relied on, fixed, generally occurring, in the natural course of events, regular as clockwork*. — *Ant.* IRREGULAR, sporadic, erratic.

*See Synonym Study at* NORMAL, STEADY.

**regularity,** *n.* — *Syn.* evenness, steadiness, uniformity, routine, constancy, consistency, invariability, predictability, rhythm, recurrence, system, congruity, homogeneity, punctuality, periodicity, swing, rotation, conformity, proportion, symmetry, balance, cadence, harmony, orderliness.

**regularly,** *modif.* **1.** [As a matter of usual practice] — *Syn.* customarily, habitually, punctually, systematically, unchangingly, right along, as a rule, routinely, usually, commonly, as a matter of course, tirelessly, conventionally, ordinarily, repeatedly, recurrently, frequently, orthodoxly, faithfully, religiously, mechanically, automatically, without once missing.

**2.** [With little or no deviation] — *Syn.* normally, periodically, evenly, methodically, exactly, monotonously, rhythmically, steadily, unbrokenly, typically, continually, like clockwork, mechanically, cyclically, seasonally, day in and day out, constantly, always, ceaselessly, time and time again, day after day, invariably, redundantly, hourly, incessantly, daily, perpetually, over and over again, weekly, monthly, annually, quarterly, diurnally, at regular intervals. — *Ant.* IRREGULARLY, unevenly, erratically.

**regulate,** *v.* **1.** [To control] — *Syn.* rule, direct, govern, monitor; see **command 2, manage 1.**

**2.** [To adjust] — *Syn.* arrange, set, methodize, dispose, classify, systematize, put in order, order, fix, settle, adapt, standardize, coordinate, allocate, readjust, reconcile, rectify, correct, improve, temper, control; see also **adjust 1, order 3, organize 1.**

**regulated,** *modif.* — *Syn.* fixed, adjusted, set, arranged, directed, controlled, supervised, managed, methodized, systematized, ordered, settled, adapted, coordinated, reconciled, improved, standardized, tempered, ruled, governed, monitored; see also **classified, managed 2, organized.** — *Ant.* CONFUSED, disarranged, upset.

**regulation,** *n.* **1.** [The act of regulating] — *Syn.* handling, direction, control, administration, supervision, superintendence, governing, regimentation, classification, coordination, disposition, settlement, systematization, arrangement, organization, reorganization, management, guidance, adjustment, moderation, reconciliation, standardization, codification; see also **administration 1.**

**2.** [A rule] — *Syn.* law, statute, ordinance; see **command 1, law 3.**

*See Synonym Study at* LAW.

**regulator,** *n.* — *Syn.* damper, adjuster, transformer, thermostat, clock, lever, governor, index, valve, knob, button, dial, control, pressure valve, safety device, switch; see also **control 3, dial.**

**regulatory,** *modif.* — *Syn.* supervisory, managerial, governing, regulative; see **administrative.**

**regurgitate,** *v.* **1.** [To vomit] — *Syn.* bring up, spit up, disgorge; see **vomit.**

**2.** [To repeat unassimilated information] — *Syn.* give back, feed back, reel off, parrot; see **repeat 3.**

**rehabilitate,** *v.* — *Syn.* restore, reestablish, recondition, reeducate; see **improve 1, reform 1, 2, renew 1, restore 3.**

**rehabilitation,** *n.* — *Syn.* restoration, reclamation, reformation, reestablishment; see **improvement 1, reconstruction, recovery 1, 2, repair, restoration 1.**

**rehash,** *v.* — *Syn.* go over, rework, restate, reiterate; see **repeat 1, 3.**

**rehearsal,** *n.* — *Syn.* practice, practice performance, trial performance, exercise, drill, dry run, run-through, dress rehearsal, walk-through, reading, recitation, recital, repetition, experiment, test flight, preparation, warm-up, readying, prep\*, trial balloon\*; see also **performance 2, practice 3.**

**rehearse,** *v.* **1.** [To tell] — *Syn.* describe, recount, relate; see **narrate.**

**2.** [To repeat] — *Syn.* tell again, retell, do over, go over, recapitulate, reenact; see also **perform 1, repeat 3, talk 1.**

**3.** [To practice for a performance] — *Syn.* drill, exercise, test, experiment, hold rehearsals, speak from a script, go through, run through, hold a reading, learn one's part; see also **practice 1, try out for.**

**reheat,** *v.* — *Syn.* rewarm, recook, warm; see **heat 1.**

**reign,** *v.* — *Syn.* rule, govern, hold power, hold sovereignty, occupy the throne, wear the crown, wield the scepter, dominate, be supreme, hold sway over, prevail, predominate, administer; see also **command 2, govern, manage 1.**

**reigning,** *modif.* — *Syn.* powerful, authoritative, ruling, in power, governing, dominating, supreme, prevailing, regnant.

**reimburse,** *v.* — *Syn.* repay, compensate, make reparations; see **pay 1, refund 1.**

*See Synonym Study at* PAY.

**reimbursed,** *modif.* — *Syn.* repaid, satisfied, paid off; see **paid.**

**reimbursement,** *n.* — *Syn.* compensation, restitution, recompense; see **payment 1.**

**rein,** *n.* — *Syn.* bridle strap, line, control; see **halter 1, restraint 2.**

**draw rein** *or* **draw in the reins** — *Syn.* slow down, cease, come to a stop, pull up; see **halt 2, stop 1.**

**give free rein to** — *Syn.* authorize, permit, indulge, give carte blanche; see **allow 1.**

**keep a rein on** — *Syn.* control, check, have authority over; see **manage 1, restrain 1.**

**reincarnation,** *n.* — *Syn.* incarnation, transmigration of souls, rebirth; see **metempsychosis, renewal, resurrection.**

**reindeer,** *n.* — *Syn.* caribou, European reindeer, *Rangifer tarandus* (Latin); see **deer.**

**reinforce,** *v.* — *Syn.* buttress, bolster, augment; see **strengthen.**

**reinforced,** *modif.* — *Syn.* supported, assisted, strengthened, augmented, buttressed, bolstered, fortified, pillowed, banded, backed, braced, built-up, stiffened, thickened, cushioned, lined, shored up, beefed up\*; see also **strong 2.**

**reinforcement,** *n.* **1.** [Support] — *Syn.* coating, prop, brace, pillar; see **support 2.**

**2.** [Military aid; *usually plural*] — *Syn.* fresh troops, additional matériel, reserves; see **aid 1, army 1, 2.**

**reinstate,** *v.* — *Syn.* reinstall, put back, reelect, return, reinvest, reappoint, reestablish, put in power again, reclassify, restore, replace, rehire, redeem, rehabilitate.

**reinstated,** *modif.* — *Syn.* rehired, reinstalled, back on the payroll, back in office, returned, restored, reelected, reappointed, reinaugurated, reestablished, replaced, reinvested, reclassified.

**reiterate,** *v.* — *Syn.* restate, repeat, iterate, reemphasize; see **repeat 3.**

*See Synonym Study at* REPEAT.

**reiteration,** *n.* — *Syn.* repetition, recapitulation, restatement, redundancy; see **repetition.**

**reject,** *v.* **1.** [To refuse] — *Syn.* repudiate, decline, renounce; see **deny, rebuff 1, refuse.**

**2.** [To discard] — *Syn.* cast off, cast out, throw out, expel; see **discard.**

*See Synonym Study at* REFUSE.

**rejected,** *modif.* — *Syn.* returned, denied, rebuffed, forsaken; see **abandoned 1, refused.**

**rejection,** *n.* — *Syn.* denial, dismissal, rebuff, brushoff\*; see **refusal.**

**rejoice,** *v.* — *Syn.* exult, enjoy, revel; see **celebrate 3, exult.**

**rejoicing,** *n.* — *Syn.* exhilaration, triumph, festivity; see **celebration 2, happiness 1, 2.**

**rejoin,** *v.* **1.** [To join again] — *Syn.* go back to, reenlist, sign up again, re-up\*; see **join 2.**

**2.** [To answer] — *Syn.* respond, retort, reply; see **answer 1.**

*See Synonym Study at* ANSWER.

**rejoinder,** *n.* — *Syn.* response, retort, reply; see **answer 1.**

**rejuvenate,** *v.* — *Syn.* reinvigorate, restore, breathe new life into, make youthful; see **renew 1, strengthen.**

*See Synonym Study at* RENEW.

**rejuvenation,** *n.* — *Syn.* reinvigoration, stimulation, recharging, revitalization; see **renewal, revival 1.**

**relapse,** *n.* — *Syn.* reversion, recidivism, backsliding, regression, recurrence, decline, deterioration, reverse, reversal, setback; see also **decay** 1, **loss** 3.

**relapse**, *v.* — *Syn.* lapse, retrogress, fall, backslide, become a backslider, revert, regress, suffer a relapse, deteriorate, degenerate, retrovert, fall from grace, fall back, fall off, weaken, sink back, fall into again, slide back, slip back, be overcome, succumb, give in to again.

**relate**, *v.* **1.** [To tell] — *Syn.* recount, recite, retell; see **describe, narrate, report** 1.
**2.** [To connect] — *Syn.* associate, correlate, link; see **compare** 1.

**related**, *modif.* **1.** [Told] — *Syn.* narrated, described, recounted, explained, recorded, mentioned, stated, recited, detailed, said, communicated; see also **told**.
**2.** [Connected] — *Syn.* associated, allied, affiliated, linked, tied up, knit together, complementary, analogous, correspondent, akin, alike, like, kindred, cognate, enmeshed, parallel, correlated, intertwined, interrelated, similar, mutual, dependent, interdependent, interwoven, of that ilk, in the same category, reciprocal, interchangeable, relevant.
**3.** [Akin] — *Syn.* kindred, of the same family, german, fraternal, cognate, consanguine, of common ancestry, of one blood, agnate; see also sense 2.

---

*SYN.* — **related**, applied to persons, implies close connection through consanguinity or, less often, through marriage /we are *related* through our mothers/; applied to things, close connection through common origin, interdependence, similar character, etc. /*related* subjects/; **kindred** suggests blood relationship or, in extension, close connection because of similar nature, tastes, goals, etc. /we are *kindred* souls/; **cognate** now usually applies to things and suggests connection because of a common source /*cognate* languages/; **allied**, applied to persons, suggests connection through voluntary association; applied to things, connection through inclusion in the same category /*allied* sciences/; **affiliated** usually suggests alliance of a smaller or weaker party with a larger or stronger one as a branch or dependent /several companies are *affiliated* with this corporation/

---

**relate to**, *v.* **1.** [To have a connection to] — *Syn.* be associated with, be connected with, have a relation to, have reference to, affect, be joined with, concern, bring to bear upon, correspond to, tie in with*; see also **concern** 1, **refer** 1.
**2.** [To have a sympathetic relationship with] — *Syn.* identify with, empathize with, understand, interact with; see **communicate** 2, **empathize, react** 2.

**relation**, *n.* **1.** [Relationship] — *Syn.* connection, association, similarity; see **relationship**.
**2.** [A relative] — *Syn.* family connection, family member, kinsman; see **relative**.
**in relation to** — *Syn.* concerning, with reference to, about; see **about** 2, **regarding**.

**relationship**, *n.* — *Syn.* relation, connection, tie, association, consanguinity, affinity, likeness, link, kinship, blood tie, bond, dependence, interdependence, relativity, proportion, rapport, contact, appositeness, analogy, similarity, homogeneity, interrelation, correlation, nearness, alliance, involvement, attachment, affiliation, relevance, accord, hookup*; see also **similarity**. — *Ant.* DIFFERENCE, dissimilarity, separation.

**relative**, *modif.* **1.** [Related] — *Syn.* dependent, contingent, pertinent, applicable; see **related** 2, **relevant**.
**2.** [Comparative] — *Syn.* comparable, corresponding, relativistic, near; see **comparative**.

**relative**, *n.* — *Syn.* relation, family member, kin, family

connection, member of the family, blood relation, next of kin, sibling, sib, kinsman, kinswoman, in-law; see also **family** 1.
Relatives include: mother, father, parent, grandmother, grandfather, great-grandmother, great-grandfather, grandson, grand-daughter, ancestor, aunt, uncle, great-aunt, great-uncle, cousin, first cousin, second cousin, third cousin, fourth cousin, cousin once removed, distant cousin, wife, husband, spouse, daughter, son, child, nephew, niece, brother, sister, sibling, kinsman, kinswoman, clansman, step-father, step-mother, step-brother, step-sister, step-daughter, step-son, half-brother, half-sister, son-in-law, daughter-in-law, kissin' cousin, mother-in-law, father-in-law, brother-in-law, sister-in-law, aunt by marriage, cousin by marriage, in-law*.

**relatively**, *modif.* — *Syn.* comparatively, proportionately, comparably, approximately, nearly; see also **almost, moderately**.

**relativity**, *n.* **1.** [The physical theory of the relativity and interdependence of matter, time, and space] — *Syn.* restricted relativity, special relativity, theory of general relativity, the curvilinear universe, the denial of the absolute, time as space, fourth dimension; see also **physics**.
**2.** [The state of being dependent] — *Syn.* dependence, pertinency, relevancy, interdependence, comparability, proportionality, interconnection, contingency, conditionality, relativism; see also **relationship**.

**relax**, *v.* **1.** [To rest] — *Syn.* unwind, repose, recline, settle back, make oneself at home, breathe easy, take it easy, take one's time, take a break, sit around, sit back, stop work, lie down, unbend, be at ease, loaf, cool one's heels*, take a breather*, ease off*, take five*, slack off*, decompress*, let one's hair down*; see also **rest** 1.
**2.** [To make less rigid] — *Syn.* loosen, slacken, bend, ease up on; see **decrease** 2, **ease** 2.

**relaxation**, *n.* — *Syn.* repose, amusement, leisure, R&R; see **recreation, rest** 1.

**relaxed**, *modif.* — *Syn.* untroubled, carefree, at ease; see **comfortable** 1, **informal** 1.

**relay**, *v.* — *Syn.* communicate, transfer, convey, send forth, transmit, hand over, hand on, hand down, turn over, deliver, pass on, pass along; see also **carry** 1, **send** 1.

**release**, *n.* **1.** [Freedom] — *Syn.* liberation, discharge, deliverance; see **freedom** 1, 2, **freeing, relief** 1, 3.
**2.** [That which has been released; *usually, printed matter*] — *Syn.* announcement, statement, press release, news story, publicity, news flash, public notice, new song, new movie, latest publication, recent stock, propaganda.

**release**, *v.* — *Syn.* free, liberate, deliver, discharge, let go, acquit, loose, exempt, open up, give out for circulation, issue, publish, set free, let out, get out, bail out, hand over, let off, rescue, let loose, clear, untie, loosen, emancipate; see also **free** 1, **publish** 1. — *Ant.* imprison, confine, suppress.
*See Synonym Study at* FREE.

**released**, *modif.* **1.** [Freed] — *Syn.* discharged, set free, liberated; see **free** 1, 2.
**2.** [Announced] — *Syn.* broadcast, issued, distributed, made public; see **issued, published**.

**relegate**, *v.* **1.** [To assign] — *Syn.* commit, consign, transfer; see **assign** 1, **commit** 2.
**2.** [To remove] — *Syn.* banish, exile, expel; see **banish** 1, **dismiss** 1, 2.
*See Synonym Study at* COMMIT.

**relent,** *v.* — *Syn.* yield, soften, comply, relax; see **soften** 1, **yield** 1.
*See Synonym Study at* YIELD.

**relentless,** *modif.* — *Syn.* implacable, unmerciful, harsh, unremitting; see **constant** 1, **cruel** 2, **remorseless** 2, **ruthless** 1, 2.

**relevance,** *n.* — *Syn.* connection, significance, pertinence; see **importance** 1.

**relevant,** *modif.* — *Syn.* pertinent, applicable, germane, apropos, suitable, appropriate, apposite, fit, proper, becoming, pertaining to, apt, important, fitting, congruous, related, material, conforming, concerning, conformant, compatible, accordant, referring, harmonious, correspondent, consonant, congruent, consistent, correlated, associated, allied, relative, affinitive, connected, to the point, to the purpose, bearing on the question, having direct bearing, having to do with, *ad rem* (Latin), pat, on the nose*. — *Ant.* irrelevant, extraneous, immaterial.

---

*SYN.* — **relevant** implies close logical relationship with, and importance to, the matter under consideration *[relevant* testimony]; **germane** implies such close natural connection as to be highly appropriate or fit *[your reminiscences are not truly germane to this discussion]*; **pertinent** implies an immediate and direct bearing on the matter at hand *[a pertinent* suggestion]; **apposite** applies to that which is both relevant and happily suitable or appropriate *[an apposite* analogy]; **applicable** refers to that which can be brought to bear upon a particular matter or problem *[your description is applicable to several people]*; **apropos** is used of that which is opportune as well as relevant *[an apropos* remark]

---

**reliability,** *n.* — *Syn.* dependability, trustworthiness, constancy, loyalty, faithfulness, sincerity, devotion, honesty, authenticity, steadfastness, fidelity, safety, security.

**reliable,** *modif.* **1.** [Having a sound character] — *Syn.* dependable, trustworthy, firm, unimpeachable, trusty, sterling, strong, positive, stable, dependable, solid, staunch, decisive, unequivocal, steadfast, conscientious, constant, steady, faithful, loyal, true, sure, devoted, tried, honest, honorable, veracious, candid, true-hearted, principled, responsible, sincere, reputable, careful, proved, respectable, righteous, decent, incorruptible, truthful, upright, unfailing, unswerving, to be trusted, as good as one's word, regular*, all right*, OK*, kosher*, on the up and up*, square-shooting*, true blue*, tried and true*, straight-shooting*. — *Ant.* FALSE, irresponsible, unfaithful.
**2.** [Worthy of trust] — *Syn.* safe, honest, sound, stable, solid, steady, guaranteed, sure, certain, substantial, secure, unquestionable, conclusive, irrefutable, incontestable, credible, dependable, good, firm, strong, solvent, unfailing, infallible, authentic, competent, assured, workable, foolproof, sure-fire*. — *Ant.* DANGEROUS, insecure, undependable.

---

*SYN.* — **reliable** is applied to a person or thing that can be counted upon to do what is expected or required *[a reliable* assistant, a *reliable* car]; **dependable** refers to a person or thing that can be depended on, as in an emergency, and often connotes levelheadedness or steadiness *[a dependable* friend]; **trustworthy** applies to a person, or sometimes a thing, whose truthfulness, integrity, discretion, etc. can be relied on *[a trustworthy* source of information]; **trusty** applies to a

person or thing that continued experience has shown to be highly trustworthy or dependable *[my trusty* steed]

---

**reliably,** *modif.* — *Syn.* dependably, assuredly, presumably, certainly; see **probably, surely.**

**reliance,** *n.* — *Syn.* confidence, trust, dependence; see **faith** 1.

**relic,** *n.* **1.** [Something left from an earlier time] — *Syn.* vestige, trace, survival, heirloom, antique, keepsake, memento, curio, curiosity, token, souvenir, testimonial, evidence, monument, memorial, trophy, remains, artifact, remembrance, reminder, bric-a-brac.
**2.** [Ruins; *usually plural*] — *Syn.* remains, remnants, fragments, residue, shards, potsherds, bones, broken stones; see also **ruins.**

**relief,** *n.* **1.** [The act of bringing succor] — *Syn.* mitigation, easing, easement, alleviation, assuagement, softening, comforting, remission, deliverance, release, extrication, amelioration.
**2.** [Aid] — *Syn.* assistance, support, maintenance, welfare; see **aid** 1.
**3.** [A relieved state of mind] — *Syn.* satisfaction, relaxation, ease, comfort, release, happiness, contentment, cheer, restfulness, a load off one's mind*; see also **comfort** 1, **ease** 1.
**4.** [The person or thing that brings relief] — *Syn.* diversion, relaxation, consolation, solace, reinforcement, supplies, food, shelter, clothing, release, break, respite, remedy, nursing, medicine, medical care, redress, reparations, indemnities, variety, change, palliative, drug, painkiller, anodyne, analgesic, hypodermic, balm, cure; see also **aid** 1.
**5.** [The raised portions of a sculptural decoration or map] — *Syn.* embossment, projection, *rilievo* (Italian), high relief, half relief, bas-relief, low relief, hollow relief, intaglio, frieze, contour, configuration; see also **decoration** 1.

**relieve,** *v.* **1.** [To replace] — *Syn.* release, remove, take over for, cover for, spell*, discharge, force to resign; see also **dismiss** 1, 2, **substitute** 2.
**2.** [To lessen] — *Syn.* assuage, alleviate, soothe, comfort, allay, lighten, mitigate, ease, divert, free, soften, diminish, reduce, console, cure, aid, assist; see also **decrease** 2, **help** 1.

---

*SYN.* — **relieve** implies the reduction of misery, discomfort, or tediousness sufficiently to make it bearable *[they played a game to relieve the monotony of the trip]*; **alleviate** implies temporary relief, suggesting that the source of the misery remains unaffected *[drugs to alleviate* the pain]; **lighten** implies a cheering reduction of the weight of oppression or depression *[nothing can lighten* the burden of our grief]; **assuage** suggests a softening or pacifying influence in lessening pain or distress, calming anger or passion, etc. *[her kind words assuaged* his resentment]; **mitigate** implies a moderating or making milder of that which is likely to cause pain *[to mitigate* a punishment]; **allay** suggests an effective, although temporary or incomplete, calming or quieting *[we've allayed* their suspicions]

---

**relieved,** *modif.* **1.** [Eased in mind] — *Syn.* comforted, solaced, consoled, reassured, satisfied, allayed, soothed, relaxed, put at ease, restored, reconciled, appeased, placated, alleviated, mollified, disarmed, pacified, adjusted, propitiated, breathing easy*; see also **comfortable** 1. — *Ant.* SAD, worried, distraught.
**2.** [Deprived of something, or freed from it] — *Syn.*

replaced, released, removed, dismissed, separated from, disengaged, made free of, freed, rescued, delivered, supplanted, superseded, succeeded, substituted, interchanged, exchanged; see also **discharged** 1.
**3.** [Lessened; *said especially of pain*] — *Syn.* mitigated, palliated, softened, assuaged, eased, abated, diminished, allayed, salved, soothed, lightened, alleviated, drugged, anesthetized.
**relight,** *v.* — *Syn.* light again, reillumine, refire, reignite; see **burn** 2, **ignite, light** 1.
**religion,** *n.* **1.** [Belief in or relationship to a superior being or beings] — *Syn.* belief, faith, creed, devotion, piety, spirituality, persuasion, godliness, morality, religiosity, theology, faithfulness, devoutness, myth, superstition, supernaturalism, doctrine, confession, cult, mythology, communion, religious conscience, fidelity, spiritual-mindedness, religious bent, ethical standard; see also **faith** 2.
**2.** [Organized worship or service of a deity] — *Syn.* veneration, adoration, consecration, sanctification, prayer, ritual, rites, liturgy, ceremonial, holy sacrifice, incantation, holiday, observance, pietism, orthodoxy, reformism; see also **ceremony** 2.
**3.** [A specific system of belief and worship] — *Syn.* faith, denomination, sect; see **church** 3, **faith** 2.
Religions include: Christianity, Mormonism, Christian Science, Zen Buddhism, Buddhism, Hinduism, Islam, Sunni Islam, Sunnite Islam, Shi'a Islam, Shiite Islam, Sikhism, Jainism, Judaism, Theosophy, Zoroastrianism, Shintoism, Taoism, Bahai, Gnosticism, deism, theism, polytheism, dualism; see also **church** 3.
**get religion\*** — *Syn.* be converted, believe, change, be born again; see **reform** 3.
**religious,** *modif.* **1.** [Pertaining to religion] — *Syn.* sacred, spiritual, holy, divine, theological, ethical, moral, ecclesiastical, clerical, canonical, supernatural, sacrosanct, churchly, liturgical, theistic, deistic, monotheistic, polytheistic, pantheistic, sacerdotal, priestly, pontifical, ministerial. — *Ant.* secular, WORLDLY, earthly.
**2.** [Adhering to a religion] — *Syn.* devout, pious, godly, sanctimonious, pietistic, God-fearing, orthodox, puritanical, reverent, reverential, believing, faithful, spiritual-minded, observant, practicing, church-going, evangelistic, born-again, revivalistic, fanatic, unworldly; see also **Christian, holy** 2. — *Ant.* ATHEISTIC, agnostic, nonbelieving.
**3.** [Scrupulous] — *Syn.* methodical, minute, thorough; see **careful.**

*SYN.* — **religious** stresses faith in a particular religion and constant adherence to its tenets /to lead a *religious* life/; **devout** implies sincere, worshipful devotion to one's faith or religion; **pious** suggests scrupulous adherence to the forms of one's religion but may, in derogatory usage, connote hypocrisy /the *pious* burghers who defraud their tenants/; **sanctimonious** in current usage implies a hypocritical pretense of piety or devoutness and often connotes smugness or haughtiness /his *sanctimonious* disapproval of dancing/

**relinquish,** *v.* — *Syn.* renounce, surrender, give up; see **abandon** 1, **waive.**
*See Synonym Study at* WAIVE.
**relish,** *n.* **1.** [A condiment] — *Syn.* pickle, salsa, chutney, accent; see **appetizer, flavoring, pickle** 2.
Varieties of relish include: catsup, ketchup, piccalilli, mustard; Indian, corn, beet, horseradish, cucumber, pepper, pickle, onion, tomato, green bean, orange,

mango, pear; chowchow, spiced currants, spiced gooseberries, spiced grapes, ginger tomatoes, mincemeat, pear mincemeat, pepper hash, pickled pears, pickled peaches, pickled apricots, pickled pineapple, pickled watermelon rind, chili, chutney, bardo, cranberry sauce, pickled beets.
**2.** [Obvious delight] — *Syn.* gusto, joy, great satisfaction; see **zest** 1.
**relish,** *v.* — *Syn.* enjoy, take pleasure in, savor; see **enjoy** 1, **like** 1.
**reluctance,** *n.* — *Syn.* disinclination, qualm, hesitation; see **doubt** 2, **objection** 1.
**reluctant,** *modif.* — *Syn.* disinclined, loath, hesitant, unwilling, averse, opposed, backward, laggard, remiss, slack, squeamish, demurring, grudging, involuntary, uncertain, hanging back, hesitating, diffident, with bad grace, indisposed, unenthusiastic, resistant, wary, leery, queasy; see also **unwilling.** — *Ant.* WILLING, eager, disposed.

*SYN.* — **reluctant** implies an unwillingness to do something, as because of distaste or irresolution /I was *reluctant* to join/; **disinclined** suggests a lack of desire for something, as because it fails to suit one's taste or because one disapproves of it /I feel *disinclined* to argue/; **hesitant** implies a refraining from action, as because of fear, indecision, or doubts /don't be *hesitant* about asking this favor/; **loath** suggests strong disinclination or a decided unwillingness /I am *loath* to depart/; **averse** suggests a sustained, although not extreme, disinclination /not *averse* to borrowing money/

**reluctantly,** *modif.* — *Syn.* under protest, unwillingly, unenthusiastically, grudgingly, squeamishly, involuntarily, slowly, hesitantly, with a heavy heart.
**rely on** or **upon,** *v.* — *Syn.* depend on, have faith in, count on; see **count on, trust** 1.
*See Synonym Study at* TRUST.
**remade,** *modif.* — *Syn.* rebuilt, redone, made over, overhauled; see **improved** 1, **revised.**
**remain,** *v.* **1.** [To stay] — *Syn.* abide, dwell, reside, inhabit, sojourn, stop, live, tarry, wait, linger, pause, stay behind, stay over, rest, rest with, make camp, sit through, stick around, sit out, stay in, hold over, spend one's days; see also **settle** 7. — *Ant.* LEAVE, be off, depart.
**2.** [To endure] — *Syn.* keep on, go on, persist, prevail; see **continue** 1, **endure** 1.
**3.** [To be left] — *Syn.* remain standing, outlive, outlast; see **endure** 1, **survive** 1.
*See Synonym Study at* WAIT.
**remainder,** *n.* — *Syn.* remaining portion, balance, remnant, residue, residuum, leftovers, rest, remains, relic, vestige, dregs, surplus, leavings, excess, overplus, overage, scrap, fragment, small piece, carryover, residual portion, whatever is left, salvage, remaindered portion; see also **excess** 4.

*SYN.* — **remainder** is the general word applied to what is left when a part is taken away /the *remainder* of a meal, the *remainder* of one's life/; **residue** and **residuum** apply to what remains at the end of a process, as after the evaporation or combustion of matter or after the settlement of claims, bequests, etc. in a testator's estate; **remnant** is applied to a fragment, trace, or any small part left after the greater part has been removed /*remnants* of cloth from the ends of bolts/; **balance** may be used in place of **remainder**, but in strict use it implies the amount remaining on the credit or debit side

**remaindered**, *modif.* — *Syn.* discontinued, dropped, discounted; see **discarded, reduced** 2, **sold out.**

**remaining**, *modif.* **1.** [Staying] — *Syn.* tarrying, waiting, stopping, halting, resting, sojourning, pausing, passing the night.

**2.** [Surplus] — *Syn.* surviving, vestigial, left, leftover, unused, spare, residual, lingering, outstanding.

**remains**, *n.* — *Syn.* corpse, cadaver, relics, fossil; see **body** 2.

*See Synonym Study at* BODY.

**remake**, *v.* — *Syn.* make over, transform, revise, alter; see **change** 1, **reconstruct, renew** 1.

**remark**, *n.* — *Syn.* comment, observation, commentary, statement, saying, utterance, annotation, note, mention, reflection, illustration, point, bon mot, conclusion, talk, word, expression, assertion, aside, *obiter dictum* (Latin), witticism, crack*.

**SYN.** — **remark** applies to a brief, more or less casual statement of opinion, thought, etc. as in momentarily directing one's attention to something /a snide *remark* about his clothes/; an **observation** is an expression of opinion on something to which one has given some degree of special attention and thought /the warden's *observations* on prison reform/; a **comment** is a remark or observation made in explaining, criticizing, or interpreting something /*comments* on a novel/; **commentary** is usually applied as a collective noun to a series of written notes or spoken comments explaining or interpreting something /a *commentary* on Aristotle's *Politics*, a running *commentary* on the game/

**remark**, *v.* — *Syn.* comment, mention, observe, note; see **comment** 1, **say.**

**remarkable**, *modif.* — *Syn.* exceptional, extraordinary, uncommon, striking; see **conspicuous** 1, **striking, unusual** 1.

*See Synonym Study at* NOTICEABLE.

**remarkably**, *modif.* — *Syn.* exceptionally, singularly, notably; see **especially** 1, **very.**

**remedial**, *modif.* — *Syn.* healing, therapeutic, corrective, medicinal, curative, recuperative, restorative, tonic, health-giving, antidotal, purifying, reformative, reparative, restitutive, invigorating, soothing, alleviative, antiseptic; see also **healthful.**

**remedy**, *n.* **1.** [A medicine] — *Syn.* antidote, medication, cure, drug; see **medicine** 2, **treatment** 2.

**2.** [Effective help] — *Syn.* relief, cure, corrective, redress, support, improvement, solution, plan, panacea, cure-all, assistance, antidote, counteractive, counteraction, countermeasure; see also **relief** 4.

**remedy**, *v.* — *Syn.* cure, solve, heal, help, aid, assist, correct, right, renew, rectify, set right, redress, relieve, treat, attend, change, revise, amend, palliate, mitigate, alleviate, ameliorate; see also **heal** 1.

*See Synonym Study at* HEAL.

**remember**, *v.* **1.** [To recall] — *Syn.* recollect, recognize, summon up, relive, think of, bring to mind, refresh one's memory, be reminded of, revive, call to mind, think back, look back, go back, brood over, dwell upon, conjure up, call up, bring back, recapture, retrieve, carry one's thoughts back, look back upon, have memories of, commemorate, memorialize, reminisce, dig into the past, identify, spot*, dig up*, dredge up*. — *Ant.* LOSE, forget, neglect.

**2.** [To bear in mind] — *Syn.* keep in mind, retain, memorize, know by heart, learn, master, get, be impressed on one's mind, fix in the mind, treasure, hold dear, cherish, enshrine in the memory, carry in one's thoughts, keep a memory alive. — *Ant.* NEGLECT, ignore, disregard.

**remembered**, *modif.* — *Syn.* thought of, recalled, recollected, summoned up, brought to mind, kept in mind, retained, memorized, borne in mind, memorialized, haunting one's thoughts, commemorated, rewarded, evoked, dug up*. — *Ant.* forgotten, LOST, overlooked.

**remembering**, *n.* — *Syn.* recalling, recollecting, bringing back, summoning up, thinking of, thinking back, looking back, reminiscing, reliving, recognizing, memorializing, commemorating, celebrating.

**remembrance**, *n.* **1.** [Memory] — *Syn.* recall, recollection, afterthought, hindsight, retrospection, reminiscence, recognition, reconstruction, mental image; see also **memory** 1.

**2.** [An object that calls someone or something to mind] — *Syn.* keepsake, memento, token, reward; see **gift** 1, **memorial, souvenir.**

**remind**, *v.* **1.** [To bring into the memory] — *Syn.* bring back, make one thing of, call to mind, put one in mind of, call up, recall, suggest, evoke, ring a bell*; see also **hint.**

**2.** [To call the attention of another] — *Syn.* prompt, cue, prod, tell, suggest, caution, point out, refresh the memory, jog the memory, mention, call attention to, bring up, give a cue, stress, emphasize, nag, note, stir up; see also **hint, warn** 1.

**reminded**, *modif.* — *Syn.* warned, cautioned, prompted, put in mind of, made aware, advised, forewarned, notified, awakened, prodded.

**reminder**, *n.* — *Syn.* prompt, cue, warning, notice, admonition, note, memorandum, memo, hint, suggestion, tickler file, mnemonic device, memento, token, keepsake, trinket, remembrance, souvenir.

**reminisce**, *v.* — *Syn.* recollect, think back, look back, live in the past; see **remember** 1.

**reminiscence**, *n.* — *Syn.* account, anecdote, memory, memoirs, chronicle, recollection, firsthand account, primary source, eyewitness account, oral history, old-timer's version, personal history, nostalgia, anecdotage*; see also **remembrance** 1, **story.**

**reminiscent**, *modif.* — *Syn.* evocative, implicative, recollective, nostalgic; see **suggestive.**

**remiss**, *modif.* — *Syn.* negligent, neglectful, derelict, lax, slack, inattentive, careless, indifferent, unmindful, forgetful, uninterested, delinquent, dilatory, asleep at the switch*; see also **careless** 1, **unconcerned.**

**SYN.** — **remiss** implies the culpable omission or the careless or indifferent performance of a task or duty /*remiss* in one's obligations/; **negligent** and **neglectful** both imply failure to attend to something sufficiently or properly, but **negligent** often stresses inattentiveness or carelessness as a habit or trait /*negligent* in dress/, and **neglectful** carries an implication of intentional and culpable disregard /a mayor *neglectful* of pledges made to the voters/; **derelict** implies flagrant neglect of a duty or obligation; **lax** implies looseness in satisfying or enforcing requirements, observing standards or rules, etc. /*lax* discipline/; **slack**, in this connection, implies lack of necessary diligence, efficiency, etc. as because of laziness or indifference /*slack* service in a restaurant/

**remission**, *n.* **1.** [An alleviation] — *Syn.* abatement, lessening, release; see **reduction** 1, **relief** 1.

**2.** [An interruption] — *Syn.* pause, lull, break; see **delay** 1, **respite.**

**3.** [Pardon] — *Syn.* forgiveness, mercy, discharge; see **acquittal, forgiveness, pardon** 1.

**remit,** *v.* **1.** [To send] — *Syn.* make payment, forward, dispatch; see **pay** 1, **send** 1.

**2.** [To pardon] — *Syn.* absolve, exonerate, release; see **forgive** 1, **pardon** 1.

**remittance,** *n.* — *Syn.* payment, transmittal, money sent, enclosure; see **payment** 1.

**remitted,** *modif.* — *Syn.* made less, commuted, not strictly enforced; see **reduced** 1, 2.

**remnant,** *n.* **1.** [A remaining part] — *Syn.* remains, residue, relic, trace; see **remainder.**

**2.** [The last of a bolt of goods] — *Syn.* strip, scrap, piece, part, portion, surplus, shred, endpiece.
*See Synonym Study at* REMAINDER.

**remnants,** *pl.n.* — *Syn.* scraps, odds and ends, leftovers, leavings, particles, surplus, endpieces, remains, relics, vestiges, survivals; see also **remainder.**

**remodel,** *v.* — *Syn.* renovate, refurnish, refurbish, readjust, reconstruct, readapt, rearrange, redecorate, refashion, improve, reshape, recast, rebuild, repair, modernize, redo, repaint; see also **change** 1.

**remodeled,** *modif.* — *Syn.* renovated, refurnished, redecorated, rebuilt, repaired, modernized, altered, improved, reconstructed, readjusted, rearranged, made over; see also **changed** 2.

**remodeling,** *n.* — *Syn.* rearrangement, readjustment, reconstruction, reshaping, recasting, refurnishing, refurbishing, restoration, modernization, renovation, regeneration, redecoration; see also **improvement** 1, 2.

**remonstrance,** *n.* — *Syn.* protest, complaint, rebuke, reproach; see **objection** 2.

**remonstrate,** *v.* — *Syn.* protest, expostulate, demur, criticize, find fault, pick flaws, animadvert, censure, scold, nag, deprecate, recriminate, decry, frown upon, disparage, disapprove, object, argue, reason with; see also **complain** 1, **object, oppose** 1. — *Ant.* APPROVE, favor, support.
*See Synonym Study at* OBJECT.

**remorse,** *n.* — *Syn.* compunction, contrition, self-reproach, guilt; see **regret** 1, **repentance, shame** 2.
*See Synonym Study at* REPENTANCE.

**without remorse** — *Syn.* cruel, pitiless, relentless; see **remorseless** 1, 2.

**remorseful,** *modif.* — *Syn.* contrite, penitent, repentant; see **sorry** 1.

**remorseless,** *modif.* **1.** [Lacking remorse as a quality of character] — *Syn.* shameless, hardened, obdurate, pitiless, merciless, harsh, cruel, barbarous, inhuman, unfeeling, indurate, tyrannical, hard-hearted, impenitent, unregenerate, uncontrite, unrepenting, ruthless, fierce, savage, unchristian, hard, intolerant, insensitive, greedy, avaricious, bloody, murderous, sanguinary. — *Ant.* SORRY, remorseful, apologetic.

**2.** [Relentless] — *Syn.* implacable, inexorable, unrelenting, unyielding, unforgiving, vindictive, avenging, stern, harsh, exacting, bitter, hard-bitten, sour, grim, adamant, inflexible, perverse, intractable, strict, rigorous, tough, forbidding, crazed; see also **severe** 1, 2. — *Ant.* yielding, forgiving, indulgent.

**remote,** *modif.* **1.** [Distant] — *Syn.* far-off, faraway, far, out-of-the-way, removed, outlying, secluded, inaccessible, isolated, unknown, alien, foreign, undiscovered, off the beaten track, over the hills and far away, in a backwater, Godforsaken; see also **distant** 1, **isolated.** — *Ant.* NEAR, close, accessible.

**2.** [Ancient] — *Syn.* forgotten, past, hoary, aged, antiquated, timeworn, archaic, prehistoric, primitive, antediluvian, immemorial, antique, olden, unrecorded, primeval; see also **old** 3.

**3.** [Distant in connection, relation, etc.] — *Syn.* unrelated, irrelevant, unconnected, obscure, abstracted, indirect, inappropriate, farfetched, exclusive, alone, extraneous, apart, detached, aloof; see also **separated.** — *Ant.* RELEVANT, related, connected.

**4.** [Unlikely] — *Syn.* slight, faint, improbable; see **doubtful** 1, **unlikely.**
*See Synonym Study at* FAR.

**remote control,** *n.* — *Syn.* remote, electrical control, radio-circuit control, hand-held control, mechanization, electric eye.

**removable,** *modif.* — *Syn.* detachable, demountable, loose; see **movable.**

**removal,** *n.* **1.** [The state of being removed] — *Syn.* dismissal, discharge, expulsion, exile, deportation, banishment, elimination, extraction, dislodgment, eviction, evacuation, ejection, transference, eradication, extermination, extirpation, replacement, translocation, the boot*, the gate*, the bounce*, the chuck*, the old heave-ho*. — *Ant.* ENTRANCE, induction, introduction.

**2.** [The act of moving] — *Syn.* change of residence, relocation, move, change of address; see **departure** 1.

**remove,** *v.* **1.** [To move physically] — *Syn.* take away, cart away, clear away, carry away, tear away, brush away, transfer, transport, dislodge, uproot, displace, dislocate, evacuate, unload, discharge, lift up, doff, take off, shed, raise, shift, switch, lift, push, draw away, draw in, withdraw, separate, extract, detach, amputate, cut out, excavate, dig out, dip out, skim, tear out, pull out, take out, burn out, smoke out, rip out, take down, tear off, draw off, carry off, cart off, clear off, strike off, cut off, rub off, scrape off, take in, pull in.

**2.** [To eliminate] — *Syn.* get rid of, do away with, exclude; see **eliminate** 1.

**3.** [To kill] — *Syn.* assassinate, murder, liquidate; see **kill** 1.

**4.** [To dismiss] — *Syn.* discharge, displace, discard, expel; see **dismiss** 1, 2.

**removed,** *modif.* **1.** [Taken out] — *Syn.* extracted, eliminated, withdrawn, evacuated, dislodged, ejected, pulled out, amputated, detached, excised, expunged, extirpated. — *Ant.* left, ignored, established.

**2.** [Distant] — *Syn.* faraway, disconnected, separate; see **distant** 1, **remote** 1, 3.

**3.** [Dismissed] — *Syn.* ousted, relieved of office, retired; see **discharged** 1, **recalled** 2.
*See Synonym Study at* FAR.

**remunerate,** *v.* — *Syn.* compensate, recompense, reward; see **pay** 1.
*See Synonym Study at* PAY.

**remuneration,** *n.* — *Syn.* payment, compensation, reward, commission; see **pay** 2, **profit** 2.

**remunerative,** *modif.* — *Syn.* profitable, lucrative, gainful, moneymaking; see **profitable.**

**renaissance,** *n.* — *Syn.* rebirth, renewal, reawakening, renascence; see **resurrection, revival** 1.

**rend,** *v.* — *Syn.* tear, rip, sever, sunder; see **break** 1, **divide** 1.
*See Synonym Study at* TEAR.

**render,** *v.* **1.** [To give] — *Syn.* present, hand over, distribute; see **give** 1.

**2.** [To perform, especially a service] — *Syn.* do, execute, carry out; see **perform** 1.

**3.** [To interpret] — *Syn.* play, perform, depict; see **draw** 2, **interpret** 1, **represent** 2.

**4.** [To provide] — *Syn.* furnish, contribute, administer; see **provide** 1.

**5.** [To state formally] — *Syn.* pass, state, deliver, hand down; see **declare** 1.

**6.** [To translate] — *Syn.* transliterate, paraphrase, reword, transpose; see **translate** 1.

**rendered,** *modif.* **1.** [Performed] — *Syn.* carried out, concluded, effected; see **done** 2.

**2.** [Interpreted] — *Syn.* played, executed, performed, enacted, delivered, translated, depicted, demonstrated, delineated, represented, presented.

**rendezvous,** *n.* — *Syn.* assignation, tryst, meeting place; see **appointment** 2, **meeting** 1.

**rendezvous,** *v.* — *Syn.* meet secretly, meet privately, meet behind closed doors, assemble; see **gather** 1, **meet** 2.

**rendition,** *n.* — *Syn.* interpretation, version, reading, performance; see **interpretation** 1, 2, **translation.**

**renegade,** *modif.* — *Syn.* disloyal, treacherous, dissident; see **false** 1, **rebellious** 1, 2, **recreant.**

**renegade,** *n.* **1.** [A rebel] — *Syn.* recreant, apostate, heretic; see **deserter, rebel** 1, **traitor.**

**2.** [A fugitive] — *Syn.* escapee, exile, runaway; see **refugee.**

**renew,** *v.* **1.** [To make new or as if new] — *Syn.* restore, refresh, revive, rejuvenate, renovate, reawaken, regenerate, reestablish, rehabilitate, gentrify, reinvigorate, replace, rebuild, reconstitute, remake, refinish, refurbish, redo, revitalize, recharge, invigorate, exhilarate, resuscitate, reconceive, recondition, overhaul, recodify, replenish, go over, cool, brace, freshen, stimulate, recreate, remodel, revamp, redesign, modernize, give new life to, recover, reintegrate, make a new beginning, bring up to date, do over, make like new, bring up to code, rehab*; see also **revive** 1.

**2.** [To repeat] — *Syn.* resume, reiterate, recommence, take up again; see **repeat** 1, **resume.**

**3.** [To replace] — *Syn.* replenish, restock, refill; see **replace** 1, **replenish.**

---

**SYN.** — **renew,** the broadest term here, implies making new, fresh, or strong again by replacing or revitalizing what is old, worn, exhausted, etc. /to *renew* a stock of goods, with *renewed* faith/; to **renovate** is to clean up, replace or repair worn parts, etc. so as to bring back to good condition /to *renovate* an old apartment/; to **restore** is to bring back to an original or unimpaired condition after exhaustion, illness, dilapidation, etc. /to *restore* paintings damaged in the flood/; **refresh** implies a restoring of depleted strength, vigor, etc. by furnishing something needed /a *refreshing* sleep/; **rejuvenate** implies a restoring of youthful appearance, vigor, etc. /I felt *rejuvenated* after the heart surgery/

---

**renewal,** *n.* — *Syn.* recurrence, resumption, resurrection, rebirth, recommencement, new start, renovation, rehabilitation, gentrification, reissue, revival, comeback, reopening, redoubling, reconditioning, recharging, regeneration, restoration, reestablishment, reversion, rejuvenation, revitalization, reformation, rearrangement, replacing, replenishment, revision; see also **revival** 1. — *Ant.* DESTRUCTION, exhaustion, impoverishment.

**renewed,** *modif.* — *Syn.* refreshed, restored, revived, reborn; see **fresh** 10, **recovered, repaired, returned.**

**renounce,** *v.* **1.** [To abandon] — *Syn.* relinquish, forswear, forsake, quit; see **abandon** 1.

**2.** [To repudiate] — *Syn.* disown, disavow, give up; see **deny, discard, recant.**

**renovate,** *v.* — *Syn.* refurbish, rehabilitate, fix up*, give a face lift*; see **renew** 1, **restore** 3.

*See Synonym Study at* RENEW.

**renovated,** *modif.* — *Syn.* refurbished, remodeled, redone, modernized; see **changed** 2, **remodeled, repaired.**

**renovation,** *n.* — *Syn.* remodeling, repair, face lift*; see **improvement** 1, **remodeling, renewal, restoration** 1.

**renown,** *n.* — *Syn.* distinction, prestige, eminence; see **fame** 1.

**renowned,** *modif.* — *Syn.* famous, notable, celebrated, distinguished; see **famous.**

*See Synonym Study at* FAMOUS.

**rent,** *v.* **1.** [To sell the use of property] — *Syn.* lease, lend, let, make available, allow the use of, take in roomers, sublet, put on loan.

**2.** [To obtain use by payment] — *Syn.* hire, pay rent for, charter, contract, sign a contract for, engage, borrow, pay for services; see also **pay** 1.

*See Synonym Study at* HIRE.

**for rent** — *Syn.* available, on the market, renting, for hire, offered, advertised, to let.

**rental,** *n.* — *Syn.* rent, renting price, amount paid for rent, apartment, rental unit, rental car, leased car.

**rented,** *modif.* — *Syn.* leased, hired, contracted, engaged, let, chartered, taken, sublet, lent, on lease, off the market, occupied, tenanted.

**renter,** *n.* — *Syn.* tenant, leaseholder, roomer, lessee, rentee, occupant, sublessee, subtenant.

**renunciation,** *n.* **1.** [A voluntary giving up] — *Syn.* forswearing, sacrifice, abnegation, self-denial; see **denial** 1.

**2.** [Denial] — *Syn.* repudiation, disavowal, disclaimer, repeal; see **denial** 1, **refusal.**

**reopen,** *v.* — *Syn.* revive, reestablish, begin again; see **open** 2, **resume.**

**reorganization,** *n.* — *Syn.* rearrangement, restructuring, reestablishment, reconstitution; see **change** 1, 2, **improvement** 1.

**reorganize,** *v.* — *Syn.* restructure, revamp, reorient, reshuffle; see **organize** 2, **rearrange, reconstruct.**

**repaid,** *modif.* — *Syn.* reimbursed, remunerated, compensated, recompensed, requited, refunded, indemnified, paid back, restored, returned; see also **paid.**

**repair,** *n.* — *Syn.* reconstruction, adjustment, improvement, renovation, restoration, substitution, reformation, rehabilitation, servicing, new part, patch, restored portion, replacement, brazure, soldering; see also **improvement** 2, **repairing.** — *Ant.* BREAK, tear, fracture.

**repair,** *v.* — *Syn.* fix, mend, adjust, improve, correct, emend, put into shape, reform, patch, recondition, restore, service, overhaul, rejuvenate, refurbish, retread, touch up, put in order, revive, refresh, renew, darn, sew, revamp, rectify, right, remedy, ameliorate, caulk, cobble, renovate, reshape, rebuild, tinker, work over*, fix up*, dirty one's hands with*; see also **mend** 1, **reconstruct, restore** 3. — *Ant.* break, damage, smash.

*See Synonym Study at* MEND.

**repaired,** *modif.* — *Syn.* fixed, adjusted, mended, rearranged, adapted, settled, remodeled, rectified, corrected, righted, restored, renewed, remedied, improved, renovated, retouched, refinished, reconditioned, rebuilt, refurbished, in order, in working order, patched up, caulked, put together, put back into shape, sewn, reset, stitched up. — *Ant.* DAMAGED, worn, torn.

**repairing,** *n.* — *Syn.* mending, fixing, servicing, sewing, patching, adjusting, caulking, remodeling, cobbling, retouching, renovating, remedying, restoring; see also **improvement** 1.

**reparable,** *modif.* — *Syn.* remediable, fixable, improvable, restorable, curable, rectifiable, recoverable, emendable, redeemable, corrigible; see also **curable.**

**reparation,** *n.* **1.** [The making of amends] — *Syn.* atonement, expiation, apology, penance, propitiation, satisfaction, self-condemnation.
**2.** [Whatever is given in reparation, sense 1; *often plural*] — *Syn.* compensation, restitution, redress, indemnification, indemnity, amends, requital, atonement, satisfaction, repayment, payment, emolument, remuneration, recompense, reward, settlement, adjustment, reimbursement; see also **redress** 2.

*SYN.* — **reparation** refers to the making of amends, specif. the paying of compensation, for some wrong or injury [war *reparations*]; **restitution** implies return to the rightful owner of something that has been taken away, or of an equivalent [he made *restitution* for the libel]; **redress** suggests retaliation or resort to the courts to right a wrong [to seek *redress* for an injury]; **indemnification** refers to reimbursement, as by an insurance company, for loss, damage, etc.

**repartee,** *n.* — *Syn.* retort, quip, banter, sparring; see **answer** 1, **joke** 2, **wit** 1, 2.
*See Synonym Study at* WIT.

**repay,** *v.* **1.** [To pay back] — *Syn.* reimburse, recompense, refund, return, indemnify, give back, make amends, requite, compensate, square oneself*, settle up*; see also **pay** 1.
**2.** [To retaliate] — *Syn.* get even with, square accounts, reciprocate; see **revenge.**
*See Synonym Study at* PAY.

**repayment,** *n.* — *Syn.* compensation, indemnity, restitution; see **payment** 1, **reparation** 2.

**repeal,** *n.* — *Syn.* abrogation, annulment, cancellation, revocation, reversal, withdrawal, abolition; see also **cancellation.**

**repeal,** *v.* — *Syn.* revoke, annul, abolish; see **cancel** 2, **revoke.**
*See Synonym Study at* ABOLISH.

**repeat,** *v.* **1.** [To do again] — *Syn.* redo, remake, do over, play over, rehash, reciprocate, return, rework, reform, refashion, recast, duplicate, reduplicate, reproduce, replicate, renew, reconstruct, reerect, revert, hold over, go over again and again.
**2.** [To happen again] — *Syn.* reoccur, recur, revolve, reappear, occur again, come again, return, crop up again; see also **happen** 2.
**3.** [To say again] — *Syn.* reiterate, iterate, restate, recapitulate, reissue, republish, reutter, echo, recite, reecho, parrot, regurgitate, rehearse, retell, rehash, go over, play back, read back, quote, copy, imitate, perseverate, harp on, drum into*, come again*, sing the same old song*; see also **paraphrase.**

*SYN.* — **repeat** is the common, general word meaning to say, do, make, present, etc. over again [will you *repeat* that question, please?]; **reiterate** and the less common **iterate** both imply repeating either once or several times, but **reiterate** more strongly suggests insistent repetition over and over again [he kept *reiterating* his innocence]; **recapitulate** suggests a concise repetition of the main points in a discourse in summarizing [to *recapitulate* last week's lecture]

**repeated,** *modif.* **1.** [Done again] — *Syn.* redone, remade, copied, reproduced, imitated, reworked, refashioned, recast, done over, reciprocated, returned, duplicated, reduplicated, replicated.
**2.** [Said again] — *Syn.* reiterated, restated, recapitulated, reannounced, reuttered, recited, seconded, echoed, quoted, paraphrased, reworded, retold, rehashed.
**3.** [Happening again] — *Syn.* recurring, recurrent, periodic; see **frequent, habitual** 1.

**repeatedly,** *modif.* — *Syn.* again and again, many times, time and again; see **frequently, regularly** 1, 2.

**repeating,** *modif.* — *Syn.* recurrent, repetitious, reiterative, imitating, copying, echoing, reechoing, duplicating, reduplicating, reproducing; see also **perpetual** 2, **verbose.**

**repel,** *v.* **1.** [To throw back] — *Syn.* rebuff, resist, deflect, withstand, stand up against, oppose, check, repulse, put to flight, keep at bay, knock down, drive away, chase away, drive back, beat back, hold back, force back, push back, beat off, ward off, chase off, stave off, fight off, hold off. — *Ant.* FALL, fail, retreat.
**2.** [To cause aversion] — *Syn.* nauseate, offend, revolt; see **disgust.**
**3.** [To reject] — *Syn.* dismiss, cast aside, spurn; see **refuse.**

**repellent,** *modif.* — *Syn.* repulsive, repugnant, odious, off-putting; see **offensive** 2.

**repelling,** *n.* — *Syn.* repulsing, scattering, dispersing; see **refusal.**

**repent,** *v.* — *Syn.* be sorry, be penitent, lament, atone; see **apologize, regret** 1.

**repentance,** *n.* — *Syn.* sorrow, remorse, regret, penitence, contrition, compunction, contriteness, attrition, self-denunciation, self-abasement, self-reproach, self-condemnation, self-humiliation, penance, prick of conscience. — *Ant.* complacency, contentment, impenitence.

*SYN.* — **repentance** implies full realization of one's sins or wrongs and a will to change one's ways; **penitence** implies sorrow over having sinned or done wrong; **contrition** implies a deep, humble sorrow for one's sins, with a true purpose of amendment; **compunction** implies a pricking of the conscience and therefore suggests a sharp but passing feeling of uneasiness about wrongdoing; **remorse** implies a deep and torturing sense of guilt; **regret** may refer to sorrow over any unfortunate occurrence as well as over a fault or act of one's own

**repentant,** *modif.* — *Syn.* penitent, regretful, contrite; see **apologetic, sorry** 1.

**repercussion,** *n.* — *Syn.* consequence, result, effect, reverberation; see **result.**

**repertoire,** *n.* — *Syn.* stock, store, repertory; see **collection** 2, **supply** 1.

**repetition,** *n.* — *Syn.* recurrence, reoccurrence, reappearance, return, rerun, reproduction, replication, copy, rote, routine, duplication, renewal, recapitulation, reiteration, restatement, rehash, perseveration, redundancy; see also **wordiness.**

**repetitious,** *modif.* — *Syn.* boring, tedious, wordy, redundant; see **dull** 4, **verbose.**

**repetitive,** *modif.* — *Syn.* repetitious, repeated, monotonous; see **constant** 1, **dull** 4, **verbose.**

**replace,** *v.* **1.** [To supply an equivalent] — *Syn.*

reestablish, reconstitute, replenish, refund, reimburse, repay, redress, compensate, mend, patch, redeem, make good; see also **rearrange, reconstruct, renew** 1, **repair**. — *Ant.* LOSE, damage, injure.

**2.** [To take the place of] — *Syn.* take over, supplant, displace, supersede, substitute for, succeed, follow, oust; see also **substitute** 2.

**3.** [To put back in the same place] — *Syn.* restore, reinstate, put back; see **return** 2.

*SYN.* — **replace** implies a taking, or putting in, the place of someone or something that is now lost, gone, destroyed, worn out, etc. /to *replace* defective tubes/; **displace** suggests the ousting or dislodgment of a person or thing by another that replaces it /he had been *displaced* in her affections by another man/; **supersede** implies a replacing with something superior, more up-to-date, etc. /the steamship *superseded* the sailing ship/; **supplant** suggests a displacing that involves force, fraud, or innovation /the prince had been *supplanted* by an impostor/

**replaced,** *modif.* **1.** [Returned to the same place] — *Syn.* restored, reinstated, reintegrated, recovered, recouped, reacquired, regained, repossessed, resumed, rewon, retrieved, reestablished, put back.

**2.** [Having another in one's place; *said of people*] — *Syn.* dismissed, cashiered, dislodged; see **discharged** 1, **recalled** 2.

**3.** [Having another in its place; *said of things*] — *Syn.* renewed, interchanged, replenished; see **changed** 1.

**replacing,** *n.* — *Syn.* replacement, substitution, restoration, rearrangement, rehabilitation, reconstitution, renewal, reinstatement.

**replenish,** *v.* — *Syn.* renew, restock, refill, replace, supply, provision, refresh, recharge, refuel, top off; see also **provide** 1, **renew** 1.

**replete (with),** *modif.* **1.** [Full] — *Syn.* filled, stuffed, packed; see **full** 1.

**2.** [Abundant] — *Syn.* complete, well-supplied, plenteous; see **full** 3.

**replica,** *n.* — *Syn.* reproduction, copy, likeness, model; see **duplicate, imitation** 2.

**reply,** *n.* — *Syn.* response, return, retort; see **answer** 1.

**reply,** *v.* — *Syn.* answer, respond, rejoin, return; see **answer** 1.

*See Synonym Study at* ANSWER.

**replying,** *modif.* — *Syn.* answering, acknowledging, in response to, responding, in answer, in return, in rejoinder, reacting.

**report,** *n.* **1.** [A transmitted account] — *Syn.* description, statement, story, rumor, tale, narration, narrative, announcement, article, paper, wire, cable, telegram, recital, broadcast; see also **exposition** 2, **news** 1, 2, **story**.

**2.** [An official summary] — *Syn.* pronouncement, statement, proclamation, address, résumé, précis, outline, brief, digest, opinion, release, bulletin, write-up*; see also **record** 1, **summary**.

Types of reports include: bank statement, account statement, case study, press release, bulletin, notice, dispatch, communiqué, court decision, inventory, treasurer's report, annual report, census report, brief, proceedings, news report, broadcast, telecast, special report.

**3.** [A loud, explosive sound] — *Syn.* detonation, bang, blast, shot; see **noise** 1.

**report,** *v.* **1.** [To deliver information] — *Syn.* describe, recount, narrate, provide details, give an account, write an account, detail, set forth, inform, advise, communicate, retail, relay, wire, cable, telephone, radio,

broadcast, notify, relate, tell, state, recite; see also **tell** 1.

**2.** [To make a summary statement] — *Syn.* summarize, publish, proclaim, announce, enunciate, promulgate, make known, list, itemize, account for, give the facts, write up, present a paper, read an address.

**3.** [To present oneself] — *Syn.* be at hand, arrive, come, get to, reach, show up, check in, account for oneself; see also **arrive** 1.

**4.** [To record] — *Syn.* take minutes, inscribe, note down; see **record** 1.

**reported,** *modif.* — *Syn.* stated, recited, recounted, narrated, described, set forth, announced, broadcast, rumored, reputed, noted, expressed, proclaimed, made known, according to rumor, revealed, communicated, disclosed, imparted, divulged, recorded, in the news, in the air, all over town*. — *Ant.* UNKNOWN, secret, verified, certain.

**reporter,** *n.* — *Syn.* journalist, newspaperman, newspaperwoman, news writer, columnist, newsman, newsperson, newscaster, anchor, anchorperson, anchorman, anchorwoman, correspondent, interviewer, cub reporter, star reporter, investigative reporter, newsgatherer, stringer, member of the press, member of the fourth estate, legman*, newshound*, newshawk*; see also **writer**.

**reporting,** *modif.* — *Syn.* filing a report, sending a story, wiring a story, broadcasting; see **saying**.

**reporting,** *n.* — *Syn.* newsgathering, recounting, describing, writing up, recording, noting down, narrating, publicizing, making public, summarizing, newscasting, covering a beat; see also **broadcasting, journalism, writing** 1, 3.

**repose,** *n.* — *Syn.* rest, relaxation, inaction, peace; see **rest** 1.

**repose,** *v.* — *Syn.* lie, recline, loll, loaf; see **lie** 3, 4, **relax** 1, **rest** 1, sleep.

**repository,** *n.* — *Syn.* receptacle, locker, treasury; see **closet, container, depository, storehouse**.

**reprehend,** *v.* — *Syn.* rebuke, reprove, reprimand; see **censure, scold**.

*See Synonym Study at* CENSURE.

**reprehensible,** *modif.* — *Syn.* objectionable, culpable, blameworthy; see **guilty** 2, **wicked** 1, 2.

**represent,** *v.* **1.** [To act as a delegate] — *Syn.* be an agent for, serve, speak for, act for, hold office, be deputy for, be attorney for, act in place of, stand in for, substitute for, factor, steward, act as broker, be sent to a convention, sell for, buy for, be proxy for, do business for, be spokesperson for, be ambassador for, exercise power of attorney for.

**2.** [To present as a true interpretation] — *Syn.* render, depict, enact, realize, delineate, set forth, describe, draw, outline, portray, design, mirror, picture, body forth, interpret, stage. — *Ant.* misinterpret, DISTORT, falsify.

**3.** [To serve as an equivalent] — *Syn.* stand for, symbolize, designate, express, exemplify, typify, embody, epitomize, personify, signify, denote, reproduce, imitate, copy, impersonate.

**representation,** *n.* — *Syn.* description, narration, delineation, reproduction, copy, design, imitation, exhibition, enactment, personification, impersonation, setting forth, delegation, adumbration, depiction, portrayal, illustration, pictorialization, image, likeness, symbol.

**representative,** *modif.* **1.** [Characteristic] — *Syn.* typical, symbolic, illustrative, emblematic; see **characteristic, illustrative, typical**.

**2.** [Characterized by representation by elected delegates] — *Syn.* democratic, elected, representational; see **democratic, republican.**

**representative,** *n.* **1.** [An emissary] — *Syn.* deputy, spokesperson, sales agent; see **agent** 1, **delegate, diplomat** 1.
Diplomatic and consular representatives include: envoy, ambassador, consul, deputy, emissary, legate, minister, plenipotentiary, nuncio, attaché, diplomatic agent, chancellor, commissioner.
**2.** [One who is elected to the lower legislative body] — *Syn.* congressman, congresswoman, assemblyman, assemblywoman, councilman, councilwoman, councilperson, member of congress, member of parliament, deputy, legislator, councilor, Speaker of the House; see also **legislator, senator.**

**represented,** *modif.* **1.** [Depicted] — *Syn.* portrayed, interpreted, delineated, drawn, pictured, illustrated, defined, revealed, sketched, personified, symbolized, mirrored, characterized, brought out, described, expressed.
**2.** [Presented] — *Syn.* rendered, exhibited, enacted; see **displayed, shown** 1.

**representing,** *modif.* **1.** [Purporting to depict] — *Syn.* depicting, portraying, delineating, picturing, presenting, illustrating, showing, exhibiting, bringing out, characterizing, reproducing, describing, defining, mirroring, interpreting, symbolizing, reporting, revealing, personifying, limning. — *Ant.* MISREPRESENTATION, distorting, misrepresenting.
**2.** [Acting as an agent] — *Syn.* serving, acting for, speaking for, substituting for, being deputy for, acting by authority of, attorney for, factoring for, stewarding for, selling for, buying for, acting as broker for.

**repress,** *v.* — *Syn.* control, curb, check, inhibit; see **hinder, restrain** 1, **suppress.**

**repression,** *n.* — *Syn.* constraint, control, suppression; see **oppression** 1, **restraint** 1, 2.

**repressive,** *modif.* — *Syn.* oppressive, restrictive, authoritarian; see **autocratic** 1, **difficult** 1, **severe** 2.

**reprieve,** *n.* — *Syn.* postponement, stay, respite, release; see **acquittal, freeing, pardon** 3, **respite.**

**reprieve,** *v.* **1.** [To postpone punishment of] — *Syn.* pardon, spare, grant a stay of execution; see **delay** 1, **excuse.**
**2.** [To alleviate] — *Syn.* comfort, lessen, soothe; see **relieve** 2.

**reprimand,** *v.* — *Syn.* rebuke, reproach, admonish, criticize; see **censure, scold.**

**reprint,** *n.* — *Syn.* republication, facsimile, second edition, reissue; see **copy, edition.**

**reprint,** *v.* — *Syn.* republish, reproduce, bring out a new edition; see **print** 2.

**reprisal,** *n.* — *Syn.* retribution, retaliation, paying back, counterattack; see **revenge** 1.

**reproach,** *n.* — *Syn.* discredit, censure, rebuke; see **blame** 1, **objection** 2.
**above reproach** — *Syn.* blameless, flawless, impeccable; see **innocent** 1, 4, **perfect** 2.

**reproach,** *v.* — *Syn.* condemn, blame, chide, reprove; see **censure.**

**reproachful,** *modif.* — *Syn.* censorious, scolding, disapproving; see **critical** 2.

**reprobate,** *modif.* **1.** [Wicked] — *Syn.* unprincipled, corrupt, depraved, immoral, amoral, lewd, vicious, dissolute, profligate, vile, demoralized, vitiated, degraded, disreputable, worthless, base, despicable, repellent; see also **wicked** 1. — *Ant.* good, HONEST, fine.
**2.** [Rejected by God] — *Syn.* sinful, blasphemous,

diabolical, unregenerate, iniquitous, malevolent, God-forsaken, damned, cursed, accursed; see also **damned** 1. — *Ant.* virtuous, MORAL, God-fearing.

**reprobate,** *n.* — *Syn.* wretch, sinner, transgressor, rake, scoundrel, viper, debauchee, scamp, degenerate, seducer, sot, drunkard, toper, guzzler, sneak, libertine, scapegrace, ne'er-do-well, good-for-nothing, waster, spendthrift, hellhound, devil, rogue, bastard*, varmint*; see also **rascal.**

**reproduce,** *v.* **1.** [To make an exact copy] — *Syn.* copy, photocopy, photograph, photostat, xerograph, Xerox (trademark), print, run off, mimeograph, multigraph, type, reprint, duplicate, clone, record, portray, transcribe, electrotype, stereotype, reimpress, restamp; see also **copy** 2.
**2.** [To make a second time] — *Syn.* repeat, duplicate, replicate, re-create, recount, revive, reenact, redo, reawaken, relive, remake, reflect, follow, mirror, echo, reecho, represent.
**3.** [To multiply] — *Syn.* procreate, engender, breed, generate, propagate, fecundate, hatch, father, beget, impregnate, progenerate, sire, repopulate, multiply, proliferate, give birth, spawn.

**reproduced,** *modif.* — *Syn.* copied, printed, traced, duplicated, transcribed, dittoed, recorded, multiplied, photocopied, Xeroxed (trademark), repeated, replicated, cloned, typed, set up, set in type, reprinted, in facsimile, transferred, photographed, blueprinted, photostated, mimeographed, multigraphed, electrotyped, electroplated, engraved, photoengraved; see also **manufactured.**

**reproduction,** *n.* **1.** [The process of reproducing] — *Syn.* propagation, procreation, breeding, generation, proliferation, multiplication, duplication, copying, printing, reprinting, reduplication, replication, transcription, photocopying, photographing, photography, xerography, mirroring, reenactment, re-creation, revival, renewal, portrayal, imitation; see also **generation** 2, **procreation.**
**2.** [A copy] — *Syn.* imitation, duplicate, print, offprint; see **copy.**
**3.** [A photographic reproduction] — *Syn.* photograph, photocopy, photostat, photoengraving, rotograph, photogram, rotogravure, Xerox (trademark), xerograph, telephoto, wirephoto, blowup, X-ray, radiograph, radiogram, skiagraph, skiagram, shadowgraph, shadowgram, pic*, roto*, pix*; see also **photograph.**
*See Synonym Study at* COPY.

**reproductive,** *modif.* — *Syn.* generative, procreative, creative, conceptive; see **sexual** 1.

**reproof,** *n.* **1.** [Censure] — *Syn.* disapproval, disapprobation, blame; see **objection** 1.
**2.** [An oral or written statement intended to censure] — *Syn.* rebuke, reprimand, admonition; see **blame** 1, **objection** 2.

**reprove,** *v.* — *Syn.* admonish, rebuke, criticize, blame; see **censure.**

**reptile,** *n.* — *Syn.* reptilian, serpent, snake, lizard, saurian, dinosaur, sauropod, crocodile, alligator, crocodilian, turtle, tortoise, one of the Reptilia, amphibian; see also **lizard, snake, turtle.**

**republic,** *n.* — *Syn.* democracy, democratic state, constitutional government, commonwealth, self-government, representative government, government by popular sovereignty; see also **government** 2.

**republican,** *modif.* — *Syn.* democratic, constitutional, popular, electoral, autonomous, sovereign, representative; see also **democratic.** — *Ant.* authoritarian, AUTOCRATIC, fascist.

**republican,** *n.* — *Syn.* democrat, Jacobin, liberal, progressive, socialist, constitutionalist, Rousseauist; see also **democrat.**

**Republican,** *n.* — *Syn.* registered Republican, member of the G.O.P., Young Republican, Old Line Republican, elephant*, member of the Old Guard*; see also **conservative.**

**repudiate,** *v.* 1. [To disown] — *Syn.* disinherit, banish, renounce; see **discard, oust.**
2. [To refuse] — *Syn.* demur, decline, spurn; see **refuse.**
3. [To disavow] — *Syn.* retract, repeal, revoke; see **recant.**
*See Synonym Study at* REFUSE.

**repudiated,** *modif.* — *Syn.* rejected, thrown out, discredited; see **disgraced, refused.**

**repudiation,** *n.* — *Syn.* denial, disavowal, cancellation, abrogation; see **denial** 1, **refusal.**

**repugnance,** *n.* — *Syn.* aversion, antipathy, disgust, distaste; see **aversion, hatred** 1, **objection** 1.
*See Synonym Study at* AVERSION.

**repugnant,** *modif.* 1. [Basically opposed] — *Syn.* antagonistic, antipathetic, inimical, hostile, opposite, contrary, adverse, counter, conflicting, unconformable, contradictory, against, unfitted, incompatible, in opposition, alien; see also **different** 1, **opposed, opposing** 2, **unfriendly** 1. — *Ant.* HARMONIOUS, agreeable, conformable.
2. [Disgusting] — *Syn.* offensive, repulsive, distasteful, disagreeable; see **offensive** 2.
*See Synonym Study at* OFFENSIVE.

**repulse,** *n.* — *Syn.* rebuff, setback, snub; see **defeat** 2, **refusal.**

**repulse,** *v.* 1. [To drive back] — *Syn.* repel, set back, overthrow, resist; see **repel** 1.
2. [To rebuff] — *Syn.* spurn, reject, snub; see **rebuff** 1, **refuse.**
3. [To disgust] — *Syn.* nauseate, offend, revolt; see **disgust.**

**repulsion,** *n.* 1. [Rejection] — *Syn.* repellence, rebuff, denial, snub; see **refusal.**
2. [Aversion] — *Syn.* distaste, repugnance, disgust; see **aversion, hatred** 1, **objection** 1.

**repulsive,** *modif.* 1. [Disgusting] — *Syn.* repugnant, odious, forbidding, horrid; see **offensive** 2.
2. [Capable of repelling] — *Syn.* resistant, repellent, offensive, unyielding, stubborn, opposing, retaliating, insurgent, counteracting, attacking, counterattacking, defensive, combative, aggressive, pugnacious, obstinate. — *Ant.* YIELDING, surrendering, capitulating.

**reputable,** *modif.* 1. [Enjoying a good reputation] — *Syn.* distinguished, celebrated, honored, noted, notable, renowned, prominent, esteemed, well-known, illustrious, favored, famous, popular, acclaimed, in high favor, well-thought-of, conspicuous, eminent, high-ranking, famed; see also **important** 2. — *Ant.* DISGRACED, ignominious, infamous.
2. [Honorable] — *Syn.* respectable, trustworthy, dignified, estimable, worthy, creditable, decent, conscientious, truthful, honest, sincere, fair, reliable, dependable, just, high-principled, righteous, upright, straightforward, legitimate, on the level*. — *Ant.* DISHONEST, dishonorable, shady.

**reputation,** *n.* 1. [Supposed character] — *Syn.* estimation, repute, name, reliability, trustworthiness, respectability, dependability, credit, esteem, rep*; see also **character** 2, **fame** 2.
2. [Good name] — *Syn.* standing, prestige, stature, status, regard, favor, account, respect, privilege, distinc-

tion, honor, acceptability, social approval; see also **admiration, honor** 1.
3. [Fame] — *Syn.* prominence, eminence, notoriety; see **fame** 1.

**repute,** *n.* — *Syn.* name, good name, standing, high standing; see **fame** 1, **reputation** 1, 2.

**reputed,** *modif.* — *Syn.* supposed, alleged, presumed, putative; see **likely** 1, **reported.**

**request,** *n.* — *Syn.* call, inquiry, application, petition, question, invitation, offer, solicitation, requisition, supplication, plea, prayer, recourse, suit, entreaty, demand, behest; see also **appeal** 1.
**by request** — *Syn.* asked for, sought for, wanted, in response to a request; see **requested** 1, 2.

**request,** *v.* 1. [To ask] — *Syn.* demand, inquire, call for; see **ask** 1.
2. [To solicit] — *Syn.* beseech, entreat, petition, sue; see **beg** 1.

**requested,** *modif.* 1. [Wanted] — *Syn.* asked, demanded, wished, desired, sought, hunted, needed, solicited, petitioned, appealed, requisitioned, in demand; see also **popular** 1, **wanted.**
2. [Called for] — *Syn.* summoned, paged, asked for, called up, called in, called back, phoned, telephoned, in request, sought out, drafted; see also sense 1.

**requesting,** *modif.* — *Syn.* asking, calling for, demanding, wanting, wishing, soliciting, petitioning, requisitioning, appealing for, seeking.

**requiem,** *n.* — *Syn.* dirge, Mass for the dead, threnody; see **funeral** 1, **hymn, mass.**

**require,** *v.* 1. [To need] — *Syn.* want, lack, feel the necessity for, have need for; see **need.**
2. [To insist upon] — *Syn.* demand, oblige, necessitate, obligate, claim, exact, requisition, command, order, dictate, challenge, expect, compel, entail, look for, push for, assert oneself, call for, take no denial; see also **ask** 1.

---

**SYN.** — **require** suggests a pressing need, often one inherent in the nature of a thing, or the binding power of rules or laws /voters are *required* to register/; **demand** implies a calling for as due or necessary, connoting a peremptory exercise of authority or an imperative need /to *demand* obedience/; **claim** implies an assertion of one's right to possess something /to *claim* a throne/; **exact** implies a demanding and the enforcing of the demand at the same time /to *exact* a promise of help from her friends, to *exact* payment by the end of the week/ See also *Synonym Study at* LACK.

---

**required,** *modif.* — *Syn.* requisite, imperative, essential; see **necessary** 1.

**requirement,** *n.* 1. [A prerequisite] — *Syn.* condition, preliminary condition, essential, imperative, element, requisite, provision, indispensable provision, terms, necessity, stipulation, fundamental, first principle, precondition, reservation, specification, proviso, qualification, vital part, *sine qua non* (Latin), desideratum, must*; see also **basis** 1.
2. [A need] — *Syn.* necessity, necessary, lack, want, demand, call, claim, obsession, preoccupation, prepossession, engrossment, stress, extremity, exigency, pinch, obligation, pressing concern, urgency, compulsion, exaction, requisition.

**requiring,** *modif.* — *Syn.* needing, demanding, calling for, necessitating, involving, compelling, forcing, exacting, enjoining; see also **urgent** 1.

**requisite,** *modif.* — *Syn.* imperative, demanded, essential, needed; see **important** 1, **necessary** 1.
*See Synonym Study at* ESSENTIAL.

**requisite,** *n.* — *Syn.* necessity, prerequisite, essential; see **necessity** 2, **requirement** 1.
*See Synonym Study at* NEED.

**requisition,** *n.* — *Syn.* order, demand, call, authorization; see **command** 1, **order** 5, **request.**

**requisition,** *v.* — *Syn.* call for, order, request, press into service; see **buy** 1, **require** 2.

**requite,** *v.* — *Syn.* remunerate, repay, recompense, compensate, reward, satisfy, pay off, settle with, retaliate, revenge, quit, return; see also **pay** 1. — *Ant.* PARDON, slight, overlook.

**reread,** *v.* — *Syn.* reexamine, study again, go over; see **read** 1.

**rescind,** *v.* — *Syn.* revoke, repeal, cancel; see **abolish, cancel** 1, 2, **revoke.**
*See Synonym Study at* ABOLISH.

**rescue,** *n.* **1.** [The act of rescuing] — *Syn.* deliverance, saving, release, extrication, liberation, ransom, redemption, salvation, reclamation, reclaiming, emancipation, disentanglement, disembarrassment, recovering, heroism; see also **freeing.**
**2.** [An instance of rescue] — *Syn.* deed, feat, performance, exploit, accomplishment, heroics; see also **achievement** 2.

**rescue,** *v.* **1.** [To save from danger or evil] — *Syn.* save, preserve, recover, redeem, recapture, salvage, reclaim, retain, keep back, safeguard, protect, retrieve, withdraw, take to safety, come to the aid of, relieve, bail out*; see also **save** 1. — *Ant.* abandon, let slip from one's hands, relinquish.
**2.** [To free] — *Syn.* deliver, liberate, extricate, release, emancipate, ransom, set free, unloose, put at liberty, unleash, manumit; see also **free** 1, **ransom.** — *Ant.* IMPRISON, capture, jail.

---

*SYN.* — **rescue** implies prompt action in freeing someone or something from imminent danger or destruction or in releasing someone from captivity /the lifeguard *rescued* the drowning child/; **deliver** implies a setting free from confinement or from some restricting situation /*deliver* me from those interminable sermons/; **redeem** suggests a freeing from bondage or from the consequences of sin, or a reclaiming, as from pawn or deterioration /how can I *redeem* my good name?/; **ransom** specifically implies the payment of what is demanded in order to free one held captive; **save,** in this connection, is a general, comprehensive synonym for any of the preceding terms

---

**research,** *modif.* — *Syn.* investigating, investigative, factfinding, scientific, exploratory, planning, analytic, specialized, involved in research.

**research,** *n.* — *Syn.* investigation, analysis, inquiry, experimentation; see **examination** 1, **study** 2.

**research,** *v.* — *Syn.* read up on, do research, look into, investigate; see **examine** 1, **study** 1.

**resemblance,** *n.* — *Syn.* likeness, correspondence, coincidence; see **similarity.**
*See Synonym Study at* LIKENESS.

**resemble,** *v.* — *Syn.* look like, be like, seem like, sound like, follow, take after, parallel, match, correspond to, coincide, relate, mirror, bear analogy, approximate, remind one of, bring to mind, bear a likeness, have all the signs of, be the very image of, be similar to, come close to, appear like, bear a resemblance to, favor, come near, pass for, have all the earmarks of, echo, compare with, be comparable to, smack of*, be the spit and image of*, be a dead-ringer for*; see also **agree.** — *Ant.* DIFFER, contrast, vary.

**resent,** *v.* — *Syn.* harbor resentment, feel indignant, be annoyed, begrudge; see **dislike, envy.**

**resentment,** *n.* — *Syn.* bitterness, indignation, pique, offense, displeasure, rancor, animus, antagonism, hurt, perturbation, acrimony, acerbity, exacerbation, umbrage, grudge, envy, jealousy, spite, outrage, hostility, ill will, hard feelings, anger, ire, malice, vexation, exasperation, choler, annoyance, irritation, rankling, discontent, gall, bile; see also **anger, hate.** — *Ant.* friendship, contentment, delight.
*See Synonym Study at* OFFENSE.

**reservation,** *n.* **1.** [The act of reserving] — *Syn.* restriction, limitation, isolation, withholding, setting aside, exclusive possession, booking, bespeaking, retainment, retaining, arranging, engagement.
**2.** [An instrument for reserving] — *Syn.* ticket, pass, license, badge, stipulation, card, twofer*.
**3.** [The space reserved] — *Syn.* seat, table, car, room, bus, train, box, stall, place, parking spot, berth, compartment.
**4.** [Qualification] — *Syn.* misgiving, qualm, hesitancy, exception; see **doubt** 2, **limitation** 2, **qualm** 1.

**reserve,** *n.* **1.** [A portion kept against emergencies] — *Syn.* savings, insurance, resources, reserved funds, store, stock, provisions, assets, supply, hoard, backlog, nest egg, cache, stockpile, something for a rainy day*.
**2.** [Calmness] — *Syn.* reticence, restraint, constraint, backwardness, modesty, unresponsiveness, uncommunicativeness, caution, inhibition, coyness, demureness, aloofness, formality, remoteness, guardedness.
**3.** [A reserve player] — *Syn.* substitute, secondstring player, alternate, sub*, second-stringer*, bench polisher*, scrub*.
**4.** [Unexpected fund] — *Syn.* sinking fund, funded reserve, government securities, negotiable bonds, floating assets; see also **resources, wealth** 1.
**5.** [Land set apart for a special purpose] — *Syn.* preserve, reservation, sanctuary; see **park** 1, **refuge** 1.

**in reserve** — *Syn.* reserved, withheld, set aside, kept back, withdrawn, out of circulation, in stock, in store, in readiness, waiting, ready, kept back, kept aside, saved; see also **kept** 2, **reserved** 2.

**reserve,** *v.* **1.** [To save] — *Syn.* store up, set aside, put away; see **maintain** 3, **save** 3, **store.**
**2.** [To retain] — *Syn.* keep, possess, have; see **hold** 1, **own** 1.
**3.** [To engage ahead of time] — *Syn.* book, bespeak, arrange for; see **hire** 1, **maintain** 3.

**reserved,** *modif.* **1.** [Held on reservation] — *Syn.* appropriated, preempted, claimed, private, booked, engaged, spoken for, set apart, roped off, taken, arrogated, held, retained; see also **saved** 2. — *Ant.* PUBLIC, free, unreserved.
**2.** [Held in reserve] — *Syn.* saved, withheld, kept aside, preserved, conserved, stored away, funded, put in a safe, in storage, on ice*. — *Ant.* USED, spent, exhausted.
**3.** [Restrained] — *Syn.* reticent, withdrawn, shy, modest, backward, secretive, private, quiet, composed, retiring, guarded, uncommunicative, taciturn, unforthcoming, controlled, self-restrained, constrained, selfcontained, mild, gentle, soft-spoken, collected, aloof, distant, formal, cool. — *Ant.* LOUD, ostentatious, boisterous.

**reserves,** *pl.n.* — *Syn.* reinforcements, enlisted reserves, militia, auxiliaries; see **army** 1, 2, **troops.**

**reservoir,** *n.* — *Syn.* storage, storage place, tank, reserve, store, pool, cistern, lake, water supply, repository.

**reside,** *v.* — *Syn.* dwell, live, occupy, tenant, lodge, inhabit, populate, remain, continue, stay, sojourn, take up residence; see also **dwell**.

**residence,** *n.* 1. [A dwelling] — *Syn.* house, habitation, living quarters; see **apartment, home** 1.

2. [An official seat] — *Syn.* headquarters, residency, cantonment.

Distinguished residences include: capital, royal palace, presidential home, vicarage, bishop's palace, deanery, governor's mansion, White House, Camp David, Vatican, Buckingham Palace, Elysée, Castel Gandolfo, Escorial.

**resident,** *n.* — *Syn.* inhabitant, occupant, tenant, denizen, native, citizen, suburbanite, inmate, householder, homeowner, renter, boxholder, dweller, house-dweller; see also **citizen, inhabitant**.

**residential,** *modif.* — *Syn.* home-owning, living, suburban, domestic, private, household.

**residual,** *modif.* — *Syn.* leftover, remaining, surplus, continuing, extra, enduring, lingering; see also **remaining** 2.

**residue,** *n.* — *Syn.* residual, residuum, remainder, leavings, scraps, scourings, parings, raspings, shavings, dregs, debris, sewage, silt, slag, soot, scum, deposit, sediment; see also **excess** 4, **remainder, trash** 1.

*See Synonym Study at* REMAINDER.

**resign,** *v.* 1. [To relinquish] — *Syn.* surrender, capitulate, give up; see **abandon** 1, **yield** 1.

2. [To leave one's employment] — *Syn.* quit, leave, retire, step down, drop out, stand down, stand aside, end one's services, walk out, hand in one's resignation, give notice, leave office, abdicate, cease work, sign off, ask for one's time*, chuck one's job*, toss up one's job*.

**resignation,** *n.* 1. [Mental preparation for something unwelcome] — *Syn.* submission, humility, passivity, patience, deference, docility, submissiveness, renunciation, self-abnegation, resignedness, acquiescence, endurance, compliance, yieldingness, unresistingness. — *Ant.* RESISTANCE, unsubmissiveness, unwillingness.

2. [The act of resigning] — *Syn.* retirement, departure, leaving, quitting, giving up, abdication, surrender, withdrawal, relinquishment, abandonment, vacating, tendering one's resignation, giving up office, termination of one's connection.

**resigned,** *modif.* — *Syn.* submissive, acquiescent, docile, tractable, yielding, relinquishing, gentle, obedient, manageable, willing, agreeable, ready, amenable, pliant, compliant, easily managed, well-disposed, satisfied, quiescent, quiet, patient, unresisting, uncomplaining, tolerant, calm, reconciled, adjusted, adapted, accommodated, tame, biddable, nonresisting, passive, philosophical, renouncing, unassertive, subservient, deferential, long-suffering. — *Ant.* REBELLIOUS, recalcitrant, resistant.

**resign oneself,** *v.* — *Syn.* submit, become reconciled, accept, acquiesce; see **agree to, yield** 1.

**resilience,** *n.* — *Syn.* elasticity, snap, recoil; see **flexibility** 1.

**resilient,** *modif.* — *Syn.* flexible, rebounding, elastic, springy; see **flexible** 1.

*See Synonym Study at* FLEXIBLE.

**resin,** *n.* — *Syn.* gum, pitch, mastic, copal; see **gum**.

**resinous,** *modif.* — *Syn.* pitchy, lacquered, gummy; see **adhesive, sticky**.

**resist,** *v.* 1. [To stand firm against] — *Syn.* withstand, hold, remain, maintain, endure, bear, continue, persist, obtain, stay, brook, suffer, weather, abide, tolerate, be unalterable, be immune, be unsusceptible, be strong, persevere, last, oppose change, bear up against, stand up

to, put up a struggle, hold off, repel, remain firm, hold one's ground, be proof against, keep from yielding to, refrain from, abstain from, fight to the last ditch*, die hard*, arch one's back*, not take lying down*. — *Ant.* submit, yield, succumb.

2. [To oppose] — *Syn.* combat, fight back, counter; see **oppose** 1, 2.

**resistance,** *n.* 1. [A defense] — *Syn.* parrying, stand, holding, withstanding, warding off, rebuff, obstruction, defiance, striking back, coping, check, halting, protecting, protection, safeguard, shield, screen, cover, fight, impeding, blocking, opposition, obstinacy; see also **defense** 1, **objection** 1, **opposition** 1. — *Ant.* WITHDRAWAL, acceptance, submission.

2. [The power of remaining impervious to an influence] — *Syn.* unsusceptibility, immunity, immovability, unalterableness, hardness, imperviousness, endurance, unyieldingness, fixedness, fastness, stability, stableness, permanence, invulnerability. — *Ant.* VACILLATION, susceptibility, variability.

3. [The power of holding back another substance] — *Syn.* retardation, nonconduction, friction, nonpromotion, attrition, reserve, surface resistance, detention, volume resistance, impedance.

4. [An opposition] — *Syn.* underground movement, partisans, *maquis* (French), insurgency, uprising, boycott, strike, walkout, slowdown, front, stand, guerrilla movement; see also **revolution** 2.

**resistant,** *modif.* 1. [Antagonistic] — *Syn.* contrary, defiant, unyielding; see **opposing** 2, **rebellious** 2.

2. [Impervious] — *Syn.* immune, repellent, proof against; see **immune, tight** 2.

**resister,** *n.* — *Syn.* obstructor, staller, obstructionist, saboteur, opponent, adversary, activist, antagonist, opposition, die-hard, bitter-ender, last-ditcher, objector, conscientious objector, CO, passive resister, noncooperator, dissenter, disputer, contender, militant, guerrilla, combatant, wet blanket, damper, spoilsport, killjoy.

**resolute,** *modif.* 1. [Brave] — *Syn.* courageous, intrepid, valiant; see **brave** 1.

2. [Strong-minded] — *Syn.* determined, resolved, unwavering, steady, steadfast, firm, true, set, serious, decided, unshaken, persevering, unflagging, unfaltering, persistent, persisting, constant, set upon, intent upon, unchanging, bent on, immutable, fixed, settled, loyal, staunch, strong, stubborn, obstinate, faithful, knowing one's own mind, uncompromising, unyielding, strong-willed, tenacious, dogged, self-reliant, enduring, indefatigable, purposeful, single-minded, established, adamant, adamantine, inflexible, independent, irreconcilable, immovable, unshakable, intransigent, inveterate, obdurate, pertinacious, die-hard, gritting one's teeth*, out for blood*, putting one's foot down*, putting one's heart into*, having one's heart set on*, hellbent*. — *Ant.* UNSTEADY, vacillating, wavering.

*See Synonym Study at* FAITHFUL.

**resolutely,** *modif.* — *Syn.* with all one's heart, bravely, with a will; see **firmly** 2, **obstinately**.

**resolution,** *n.* 1. [Fixedness of mind] — *Syn.* fortitude, perseverance, resolve; see **determination** 2.

2. [A formal statement of opinion] — *Syn.* verdict, formal expression, decision, recommendation, analysis, elucidation, interpretation, exposition, presentation, declaration, recitation, assertion, determination; see also **judgment** 3.

3. [A decision as to future action] — *Syn.* resolve, commitment, intention; see **promise** 1, **purpose** 1.

**resolve,** *v.* 1. [To reach as a decision or intention] — *Syn.* determine, decide, settle, conclude, fix, pur-

pose, propose, choose, fix upon, make up one's mind, take a firm stand, take one's stand, take a decisive step, make a point of, pass upon, decree, elect, remain firm, burn one's bridges*, take the bull by the horns*, put one's foot down*; see also **decide**.
2. [To find the solution to] — *Syn.* solve, clear up, work out; see **solve**.
*See Synonym Study at* DECIDE.

**resonance**, *n.* — *Syn.* reverberation, sonority, fullness, vibration; see **depth** 2, **noise** 1.

**resonant**, *modif.* — *Syn.* resounding, reverberating, sonorous, booming; see **loud** 1.

**resort**, *n.* 1. [A relief in the face of difficulty] — *Syn.* expedient, shift, makeshift, stopgap, substitute, surrogate, resource, device, refuge, recourse, hope, relief, possibility, opportunity, option.
2. [A place for rest or amusement] — *Syn.* vacation spot, hotel, retreat.
Resorts include: seaside, mountain, curative-bath, spa, health camp, rest, camping, skiing, sports, winter, lake, summer, gambling, amusement park, night club, restaurant, dance hall, club, watering place*; see also **hotel, lodge, motel**.
**as a last resort** — *Syn.* in desperation, lastly, in the end; see **finally** 2.

---

*SYN.* — **resort**, qualified as by *last*, is usually used of a final resource toward which one turns for aid in time of need or emergency /we'll take the bus as a last *resort*/; **expedient** refers to something used to effect a desired end, specif. to something used as a substitute for the usual means /the daybed served as a useful *expedient* for unexpected guests/; **makeshift** applies to a quick expedient and, as a somewhat derogatory term, connotes an inferior substitute, carelessness, etc. /we used a crate as a *makeshift* for a table/; **stopgap** refers to a person or thing serving as a temporary substitute or expedient, to be replaced when the usual agent is available again /he's just a *stopgap* until a new manager is appointed/

---

**resort to**, *v.* — *Syn.* turn to, refer to, apply, go to, use, try, employ, utilize, have recourse to, fall back on, benefit by, put to use, make use of, recur to, repair to, take up.

**resound**, *v.* — *Syn.* reverberate, echo, ring, vibrate; see **sound** 1.

**resounding**, *modif.* — *Syn.* reverberating, ringing, thunderous, booming; see **loud** 1.

**resource**, *n.* — *Syn.* reserve, supply, support, source, stock, store, means, expedient, stratagem, relief, resort, recourse, artifice, device, refuge.

**resourceful**, *modif.* — *Syn.* inventive, ingenious, enterprising, capable; see **active** 2, **clever** 1, **intelligent** 1, **original** 2.

**resources**, *pl.n.* — *Syn.* means, money, property, stocks, bonds, products, revenue, riches, wealth, natural resources, assets, belongings, effects, collateral, capital, income, savings, wherewithal; see also **property** 1, **reserve** 1, 4, **wealth** 1.

**respect**, *n.* — *Syn.* esteem, honor, regard, deference; see **admiration, honor** 1, **reverence** 1.
**in all respects** — *Syn.* entirely, outright, wholly, thoroughly, altogether, totally, utterly, at all points, in every respect, on all counts, quite, throughout; see also **completely**.
**pay one's respects** — *Syn.* wait upon, show regard, be polite; see **visit** 4.
**with respect to** — *Syn.* concerning, in reference to, in

regard to, in respect of; see **about** 2, **regarding, respecting**.

**respect**, *v.* 1. [To esteem] — *Syn.* regard, value, look up to; see **admire** 1.
2. [To treat with consideration] — *Syn.* heed, appreciate, consider, note, recognize, defer to, show consideration for, show regard for, do honor to, be kind to, show courtesy to, spare, take into account, attend, uphold, refrain from intruding upon; see also **regard** 1. — *Ant.* RIDICULE, mock, scorn.
*See Synonym Study at* REGARD.

**respectability**, *n.* — *Syn.* integrity, decency, propriety, reputability; see **honesty** 1, **virtue** 1.

**respectable**, *modif.* — *Syn.* estimable, worthy, presentable, upright, virtuous, modest, honorable, reputable, above reproach, admirable, decorous, decent, correct, seemly, proper, *comme il faut* (French), fair, moderate, tolerable, passable, acceptable, sizable; see also **decent** 2, **honest** 1, **reputable** 2. — *Ant.* DISHONEST, indecorous, dissolute.

**respected**, *modif.* — *Syn.* esteemed, appreciated, valued; see **honored, important** 2.

**respectful**, *modif.* — *Syn.* deferential, considerate, attentive, appreciative, courteous, polite, civil, admiring, reverent, revering, reverencing, attending, upholding, regarding, valuing, venerating, taking thought for, recognizing, deferring to, showing respect for, regardful, dutiful; see also **polite** 1. — *Ant.* RUDE, impudent, contemptuous.

**respectfully**, *modif.* — *Syn.* deferentially, regardfully, reverentially, decorously, ceremoniously, attentively, courteously, politely, considerately, with all respect, with due respect, with the highest respect, in deference to; see also **politely**. — *Ant.* RUDELY, disrespectfully, impudently.

**respecting**, *modif.* — *Syn.* regarding, concerning, in relation to, relating to, pertaining to, relevant to, pertinent to, in respect to, with reference to, referring to, in connection with, anent, about, as for, as to, with regard to, in the matter of.

**respective**, *modif.* — *Syn.* particular, separate, individual, several, each separately, each to each, own, corresponding.

**respectively**, *modif.* — *Syn.* severally, each, by lot, each to each, in particular, individually, distributively, sequentially, apiece.

**respects**, *pl.n.* — *Syn.* deference, courtesies, kind wishes, best wishes, greetings, cordial regards, salaam, kowtow; see also **greeting** 1, **regards**.

**respiration**, *n.* — *Syn.* inhalation, exhalation, expiration; see **breath** 1.

**respite**, *n.* — *Syn.* reprieve, suspension, commutation, postponement, pause, interval, stop, intermission, recess, rest, break, lull, hiatus, halt, stay, deferment, acquittal, exculpation, pardon, forgiveness, discharge, immunity, deliverance, truce, cessation, interregnum, interruption, adjournment, release, surcease, remission, letup*, breather*; see also **delay** 1, **recess** 1. — *Ant.* PUNISHMENT, condemnation, penalty.

**resplendent**, *modif.* — *Syn.* shining, dazzling, splendid, radiant; see **bright** 1, **glorious** 1.

**respond**, *v.* — *Syn.* answer, reply, rejoin, rebut, return, counter, react, react favorably, acknowledge, write back, R.S.V.P.; see also **answer** 1, 3, **react** 1, 2.
*See Synonym Study at* ANSWER.

**response**, *n.* — *Syn.* rejoinder, reply, acknowledgment; see **answer** 1.

**responsibility**, *n.* 1. [State of being reliable] — *Syn.* trustworthiness, reliability, trustiness, dependability, de-

pendableness, loyalty, faithfulness, capableness, capacity, efficiency, competency, uprightness, firmness, steadfastness, stability, ability; see also **honesty** 1.
**2.** [State of being accountable] — *Syn.* answerability, accountability, liability, culpability, amenability, blame, onus, burden, subjection, boundness, obligatoriness, incumbency, engagement, pledge, contract, constraint, restraint; see also **duty** 1, **guilt.** — *Ant.* FREEDOM, exemption, immunity.
**3.** [Anything for which one is accountable] — *Syn.* obligation, trust, charge; see **duty** 2.
**responsible,** *modif.* **1.** [Charged with responsibility] — *Syn.* accountable, answerable, liable, amenable, subject, bound, incumbent on, devolving on, under obligation, constrained, tied, fettered, bonded, censurable, chargeable, culpable, to blame, at fault, guilty, obligated, obliged, compelled, contracted, held, pledged, sworn to, under contract, engaged; see also **bound** 2. — *Ant.* FREE, unconstrained, exempt.
**2.** [Capable of assuming responsibility] — *Syn.* trustworthy, trusty, reliable, capable, efficient, loyal, faithful, dutiful, dependable, conscientious, tried, self-reliant, able, competent, qualified, effective, upright, honest, firm, steadfast, steady, stable, rational, mature. — *Ant.* IRRESPONSIBLE, capricious, unstable.

---

*SYN.* — **responsible** applies to one who has been delegated some duty or responsibility by one in authority and who is subject to penalty in case of default /who is *responsible* for filing the reports?/; **answerable** implies a legal or moral obligation for which one must answer to someone sitting in judgment /not *answerable* for the crimes of one's parents/; **accountable** implies liability for which one may be called to account /you will be held *accountable* for anything you may say/

---

**responsive,** *modif.* — *Syn.* receptive, responding, reacting, answering, acknowledging, respondent, impressionable, sympathetic, understanding, sensitive, warm, warmhearted, compassionate, tender; see also **active** 2, **conscious** 1, **impressionable.** — *Ant.* INDIFFERENT, COLD, cool.
**rest,** *n.* **1.** [Repose] — *Syn.* sleep, ease, quiet, quietude, quietness, tranquillity, slumber, calm, calmness, peace, peacefulness, relaxation, recreation, refreshment, leisure, break, respite, recess, rest period, siesta, nap, doze, somnolence, dreaminess, comfort, breathing spell, vacation, holiday, time off, lull, lounge, lounging period, loafing period, R&R, decompression; see also sense 2; **sleep.** — *Ant.* STRAIN, restlessness, sleeplessness.
**2.** [State of inactivity] — *Syn.* intermission, cessation, stillness, stop, stay, halt, stand, standstill, lull, discontinuance, interval, hush, silence, dead calm, stagnation, stagnancy, fixity, immobility, inactivity, quiescence, motionlessness, inertia, catalepsy, caesura, pause, full stop, deadlock, recess, noon hour; see also sense 1; **peace** 2. — *Ant.* CONTINUANCE, activity, bustle.
**3.** [Anything upon which an object rests] — *Syn.* support, prop, stay, seat, trestle, pillar, pedestal, base, bottom, pediment; see also **foundation** 2.
**4.** [The remainder] — *Syn.* balance, residue, surplus, the others; see **excess** 4, **remainder.**
**5.** [Death] — *Syn.* release, demise, eternal rest; see **death** 1.
**at rest** — *Syn.* in a state of repose, immobile, inactive; see **resting** 1.

**lay to rest** — *Syn.* inter, assign to the grave, entomb; see **bury** 1.
**rest,** *v.* **1.** [To take one's rest] — *Syn.* sleep, slumber, doze, repose, lie down, retire, relax, unwind, lounge, let up, ease off, recuperate, rest up, take a rest, take a break, catch one's breath, refresh oneself, break the monotony, lean, recline, unbend, settle down, compose oneself for sleep, dream, drowse, take one's ease, be comfortable, stretch out, nap, nod, snooze*, take it easy*; see also **relax** 1, **sleep.**
**2.** [To be still] — *Syn.* be quiet, lie still, stand still, pause, halt, stop, stop short, hold, cease, pull up, lie to, come to rest, rest on one's oars.
**3.** [To depend upon] — *Syn.* be supported, be upheld, hang on, lie upon, be seated on, be propped by, be founded on, be based on; see also **depend** 2.
**restaurant,** *n.* — *Syn.* eating place, eating house, dining room, establishment, eatery*, greasy spoon*, hash house*, beanery*.
Types of restaurants include: café, hotel, dining room, inn, coffee shop, sandwich shop, tavern, pub, steakhouse, coffee house, chophouse, tearoom, luncheon, luncheonette, lunch-wagon, hamburger stand, fast-food outlet, fast-food joint, fast-food place, *trattoria, ristorante* (*both* Italian), *estaminet, bistro, brasserie* (*all* French), creamery, dining car, dining coach, dining saloon, diner, lunch bar, soda fountain, milk bar, hot-dog stand, snack bar, raw bar, sushi bar, automat, rathskeller, rotisserie, cabaret, night club, cafeteria, grill, grillroom, oyster house, barbecue, spaghetti house, deli, pizzeria, canteen.
**rested,** *modif.* — *Syn.* restored, refreshed, relaxed, strengthened, renewed, unwearied, unfatigued, untired, awake, revived, recovered, brought back, revivified, reanimated, revitalized, reintegrated, unworn; see also **fresh** 10. — *Ant.* TIRED, wearied, fatigued.
**restful,** *modif.* — *Syn.* soothing, relaxing, tranquilizing, untroubling, untroubled, tranquil, calm, peaceful, quiet, reposeful, calming, lulling, serene, pacific, halcyon, comforting, comfortable, easy, mild, still, soft, refreshing, restoring, hypnotic, soporific. — *Ant.* LOUD, irritating, agitating.
*See Synonym Study at* COMFORTABLE.
**resting,** *modif.* **1.** [Taking rest] — *Syn.* relaxing, unbending, unwinding, reposing, reclining, lying down, sleeping, stretched out, composing oneself, at ease, at rest, quiet, quiescent, dormant, comfortable, lounging, loafing, taking a break, taking a breathing spell, enjoying a lull, sleeping, dozing, drowsing, napping, taking a siesta, recessing, taking a vacation, having a holiday, resting up, taking it easy*, take a breather*; see also **asleep.**
**2.** [Situated] — *Syn.* located, based on, established, set on, settled on, seated, standing on, propped on, supported by, held by, reposing, lying; see also **placed.**
**rest in peace,** *n.* — *Syn.* prayer, R.I.P., *requiescat in pace* (Latin), may the earth rest light on thee, here lies, **hic jacet** (Latin); see also **epitaph.**
**restitution,** *n.* — *Syn.* compensation, return, restoration; see **payment** 1, **reparation** 2.
*See Synonym Study at* REPARATION.
**restive,** *modif.* **1.** [Restless] — *Syn.* unsettled, impatient, fidgety; see **restless** 1.
**2.** [Contrary] — *Syn.* balky, unruly, refractory, stubborn; see **contrary** 4, **obstinate.**
*See Synonym Study at* CONTRARY.
**restless,** *modif.* **1.** [Not content when still] — *Syn.* fidgety, skittish, feverish, sleepless, fitful, disturbed, jumpy,

nervous, unquiet, uneasy, unsettled, flurried, restive, impatient, agitated, fretful, flustered, twitching, trembling, tremulous, rattled, jittery\*, antsy\*; see also **active** 2, **excited.** — *Ant.* QUIET, relaxed, calm.

**2.** [Not content with conditions] — *Syn.* disturbed, uneasy, disquieted, anxious, up in arms, discontented, vexed, excited, agitated, angry, disaffected, malcontented, estranged, alienated, resentful, refractory, recalcitrant, fractious, insubordinate, contumacious, perverse; see also **rebellious** 2, 3. — *Ant.* CALM, content, satisfied.

**3.** [Not content with a settled life] — *Syn.* roving, transient, wandering, discontented, unsettled, roaming, nomadic, footloose, peripatetic, itinerant, moving, straying, ranging, rambling, gadding, gallivanting, meandering, traipsing; see also **rambling** 1. — *Ant.* settled, fixed, immovable.

**restlessness,** *n.* — *Syn.* uneasiness, disquiet, fidgetiness, excitability; see **anxiety, excitement, uneasiness, unrest** 1.

**restoration,** *n.* **1.** [The act of restoring] — *Syn.* revival, healing, return, cure, remaking, renovation, renewal, rehabilitation, reclamation, reformation, recreation, alteration, replacing, remodeling, rejuvenation, rebuilding, reestablishment; see also **recovery** 1.

**2.** [The act of reconstructing] — *Syn.* rehabilitation, reconstruction, reparation, refurbishment; see **repair.**

**restorative,** *modif.* — *Syn.* medicinal, corrective, therapeutic; see **healthful, remedial.**

**restore,** *v.* **1.** [To give back] — *Syn.* make restitution, replace, put back; see **return** 2.

**2.** [To re-create] — *Syn.* reestablish, revive, recover; see **renew** 1.

**3.** [To rebuild in a form supposed to be original] — *Syn.* rebuild, reconstruct, renovate, refurbish, repair, recondition, put back, alter, make restoration, reclaim, rehabilitate, rehab\*; see also **reconstruct, repair.**

**4.** [To reinstate] — *Syn.* reinstall, put back, reerect; see **reinstate.**

**5.** [To bring back to health] — *Syn.* revive, cure, make healthy; see **heal** 1.

*See Synonym Study at* RENEW.

**restored,** *modif.* — *Syn.* rebuilt, reestablished, revived; see **built** 1, **repaired, replaced** 1, **returned.**

**restrain,** *v.* **1.** [To hold in check] — *Syn.* check, control, curb, bridle, rein in, inhibit, suppress, keep in, handle, regulate, keep in line, guide, direct, keep down, keep from, repress, harness, muzzle, tether, chain, fetter, keep a rein on, hold in leash, govern, hold, bind, deter, hold in, hold back, hamper, constrain, restrict, stay, gag, limit, impound, bottle up, tie down, pin down, crack down, choke back, pull back, contain, stifle, sit on\*, come down on\*, put a lid on\*.

**2.** [To restrict] — *Syn.* limit, circumscribe, delimit; see **restrict** 2.

**SYN.** — **restrain,** the term of broadest application in this list, suggests the use of strong force or authority either in preventing, or in suppressing and controlling, some action /try to *restrain* your zeal/; **curb, check,** and **bridle** derive their current implications from the various uses of a horse's harness, **curb** implying a sudden, sharp action to bring something under control /to *curb* one's tongue/, **check** implying a slowing up of action or progress /to *check* inflationary trends/, and **bridle** suggesting a holding in of emotion, feelings, etc. /to *bridle* one's envy/; **inhibit** implies a suppressing or repressing of some action, im-

pulse, thought, or emotion to *inhibit* free discussion, often also by the operation of psychological constraints/

**restrained,** *modif.* — *Syn.* controlled, constrained, disciplined, understated, moderate, temperate, reasonable, cautious, subdued, under control, in check, in leading strings, under restraint, on a leash; see also **chaste** 1, **moderate** 2, 5, **reserved** 3.

**restraining,** *modif.* — *Syn.* controlling, constraining, restrictive, coercive; see **governing.**

**restrain oneself,** *v.* — *Syn.* hold back, hold aloof, forgo, desist from, show restraint, curb oneself, discipline oneself, limit oneself, efface oneself, get hold of oneself, exercise self-restraint; see also **abstain.**

**restraint,** *n.* **1.** [Control over oneself] — *Syn.* self-restraint, control, self-control, reserve, reticence, constraint, artistic economy, withholding, caution, coolness, forbearance, silence, secretiveness, stress repression, self-government, undemonstrativeness, stiffness, formality, abstinence, moderation, temperance, self-denial, self-repression, unnaturalness, constrained manner, inhibition, abstemiousness, abstention, self-discipline, self-censorship. — *Ant.* slackness, laxity, demonstrativeness.

**2.** [An influence that checks or hinders] — *Syn.* repression, deprivation, limitation, hindrance, abridgment, reduction, decrease, prohibition, confinement, check, barrier, obstacle, obstruction, restriction, bar, curb, rein, blockade, order, command, instruction, coercion, impediment, compulsion, duress, force, violence, deterrence, deterrent, discipline, assignment, definition, prescription, moderation, tempering, qualifying, lid\*; see also **limitation** 1, 2. — *Ant.* LIBERTY, license, incitement.

**3.** [A device that restrains; *often plural*] — *Syn.* bonds, fetters, straitjacket; see **chains, handcuffs.**

**restrict,** *v.* **1.** [To restrain] — *Syn.* curb, check, bind; see **restrain** 1.

**2.** [To hold within limits] — *Syn.* limit, confine, delimit, circumscribe, contain, assign, contract, shorten, narrow, decrease, enclose, keep in bounds, demarcate, define, encircle, surround, shut in, hem in, box in, diminish, reduce, moderate, modify, temper, qualify, set limits, regulate, pin down; see also **limit.** — *Ant.* INCREASE, extend, expand.

*See Synonym Study at* LIMIT.

**restricted,** *modif.* — *Syn.* limited, confined, restrained, circumscribed, curbed, bound, prescribed, checked, bounded, inhibited, hampered, marked, defined, delimited, encircled, surrounded, shut in, hitched, tethered, chained, fastened, secured, bridled, held in, held back, held down, reined in, controlled, governed, deterred, impeded, stayed, stopped, suppressed, repressed, prevented, trammeled, fettered, deprived, blocked, barred, obstructed, dammed, clogged, manacled, frustrated, embarrassed, baffled, foiled, shrunken, narrowed, straitened, cramped, shortened, decreased, diminished, reduced, moderated, tempered, modified, qualified, out of bounds, off-limits; see also **bound** 1, 2.

**restriction,** *n.* — *Syn.* constraint, limitation, stipulation; see **confinement** 1, **limitation** 1, 2, **restraint** 2.

**restrictive,** *modif.* **1.** [Contrary] — *Syn.* prohibitory, prohibitive, confining; see **confining, opposed.**

**2.** [Provisional] — *Syn.* definitive, limiting, qualificatory; see **conditional.**

**result,** *n.* — *Syn.* consequence, issue, event, effect, outcome, end, finish, termination, consummation, completion, conclusion, aftereffect, aftermath, upshot, sequel, sequence, fruit, fruition, eventuality, proceeds, emanation, outgrowth, outcropping, ensual, returns, backwash, backlash, repercussion, fallout, settlement, determination, decision, arrangement, denouement, payoff*; see also **end** 2.— *Ant.* ORIGIN, source, root.

---

*SYN.* — **result** stresses that which is finally brought about by the effects or consequences of an action, process, etc.; **effect** is applied to that which is directly produced by an action, process, or agent and is the exact correlative of *cause*}; **consequence** suggests that which follows something else on which it is dependent in some way, but does not connote as direct a connection with *cause*}; **issue** suggests a result in which there is emergence from difficulties or conflict; **outcome** refers to the result of something that was in doubt

---

**result**, *v.*— *Syn.* issue, grow from, spring from, rise from, proceed from, emanate from, germinate from, flow from, accrue from, arise from, derive from, come from, originate in, become of, spring, emerge, rise, ensue, emanate, effect, produce, fruit, follow, succeed, happen, occur, come about, come of, pan out, fall out, work out, appear, end, finish, terminate, conclude. *See Synonym Study at* FOLLOW.

**result from**, *v.*— *Syn.* proceed from, spring from, emerge, start; see **begin** 2, **result**.

**result in**, *v.*— *Syn.* end in, terminate in, conclude, finish; see **achieve** 1, **end** 1, **result**.

**resulting in**, *modif.*— *Syn.* leading to, having the result that, having the effect that, eventuating in, becoming.

**resume**, *v.*— *Syn.* take up again, reassume, begin again, continue, recommence, reoccupy, go on, go on with, renew, reopen, recapitulate, return, keep on, carry on, keep up, pick up; see also **continue** 2.— *Ant.* STOP, cease, discontinue.

**résumé**, *n.* **1.** [A summary]— *Syn.* abstract, synopsis, précis; see **summary**.
**2.** [A summary of personal and professional history] — *Syn.* curriculum vitae, work history, biography, CV, vita, bio*.

**Resurrection**, *n.* **1.** [Christ's rising from the tomb] — *Syn.* Easter, Rising from the Dead, Rolling Away the Stone, Reappearance on Earth, Overcoming Death.
**2.** [The rising of souls]— *Syn.* the Last Judgment, the Harrowing of Hell, the Second Coming of Christ, Judgment Day; see **salvation** 3.

**resurrection**, *n.*— *Syn.* return to life, reanimation, transformation, restoration, resuscitation, revival, revivifying, rebirth, renewal, renaissance, renascence, reincarnation, transmigration, transmogrification.

**resuscitate**, *v.*— *Syn.* revive, bring around, restore, restore to life; see **revive** 1.

**retail**, *modif.*— *Syn.* direct, in small lots, by the piece, by the pound, singly, local, to the consumer, in small quantities, by the package.— *Ant.* WHOLESALE, in large amounts, in quantity.

**retail**, *v.*— *Syn.* distribute, dispense, dispose of; see **sell** 1.

**retain**, *v.* **1.** [To hold]— *Syn.* cling to, grasp, clutch; see **hold** 1.
**2.** [To keep]— *Syn.* preserve, put away, husband; see **maintain** 3.
**3.** [To reserve services]— *Syn.* employ, hire, engage; see **hire** 1.
**4.** [To remember]— *Syn.* keep in mind, learn, recall; see **remember** 1, 2.

**retained**, *modif.* **1.** [Kept]— *Syn.* had, held, possessed, owned, enjoyed, secured, preserved, husbanded, saved, maintained, restrained, confined, curbed, detained,

contained, received, admitted, included, withheld, held back, put away, treasured, sustained, remembered, kept in mind, commemorated; see also **kept** 2.— *Ant.* LOST, wasted, refused.
**2.** [Employed]— *Syn.* hired, engaged, contracted, promised, chosen, selected, given a position, taken on, secured, bespoken; see also **employed**.— *Ant.* UNEMPLOYED, disengaged, let go.

**retainer**, *n.* **1.** [A person who serves another]— *Syn.* attendant, lackey, valet; see **attendant, servant**.
**2.** [A fee paid to engage services]— *Syn.* advance, deposit, money up front; see **payment** 2.

**retaining**, *modif.*— *Syn.* maintaining, sustaining, securing, saving, preserving, holding, keeping, owning, possessing, having, withholding, taking, seizing, confining, suppressing, curbing, arresting, restraining, holding back, keeping back, receiving, admitting, comprehending, accommodating, embracing, remembering, treasuring, cherishing, commemorating, employing, engaging, hiring, reserving.

**retaliate**, *v.*— *Syn.* counter, strike back, requite, repay; see **revenge**.

**retaliating**, *modif.*— *Syn.* taking revenge, getting back, turning the tables, getting even, paying off, reciprocating.

**retaliation**, *n.*— *Syn.* vengeance, reprisal, punishment; see **revenge** 1.

**retard**, *v.*— *Syn.* hinder, delay, impede, slow down; see **delay** 1, **hinder**.

**retardation**, *n.* **1.** [Something that retards]— *Syn.* obstacle, delay, hindrance; see **impediment** 1.
**2.** [Mental disability]— *Syn.* mental retardation, slowness, backwardness; see **insanity** 1.

**retarded**, *modif.* **1.** [Said of people]— *Syn.* backward, slow, developmentally disabled; see **disabled, dull** 3.
**2.** [Said of activities]— *Syn.* delayed, slowed down, slowed up, held back; see **slow** 1, 2, 3.
*See Synonym Study at* STUPID.

**retch**, *v.*— *Syn.* heave, gag, throw up; see **vomit**.

**retention**, *n.* **1.** [Custody]— *Syn.* holding, withholding, reservation, detention; see **custody** 1, **maintenance** 1, **preservation**.
**2.** [Memory]— *Syn.* recall, recognition, recollection; see **memory** 1, **remembrance** 1.

**reticence**, *n.*— *Syn.* silence, closeness, hesitation; see **reserve** 2, **shyness**.

**reticent**, *modif.*— *Syn.* reserved, uncommunicative, hesitant, quiet; see **quiet** 2, **reserved** 3, **taciturn**.

**retinue**, *n.*— *Syn.* entourage, train, suite, procession; see **escort, following**.

**retire**, *v.* **1.** [To draw away]— *Syn.* separate, withdraw, part, leave, recede, retreat, regress, draw back, seclude oneself, secede, keep aloof, keep apart, shut oneself up, deny oneself, rusticate; see also **leave** 1.— *Ant.* JOIN, accompany, take part in.
**2.** [To go to bed]— *Syn.* lie down, turn in, rest; see **lie** 4, **sleep**.
**3.** [To cease active life]— *Syn.* resign, give up work, leave active service, step down, make vacant, hand over, reach retirement age, be pensioned off, lead a quiet life, sequester oneself, get the golden handshake*, be put on the shelf*, be put out to pasture*; see also **resign** 2.
**4.** [To remove]— *Syn.* revoke, rescind, scrap; see **eliminate** 1, **withdraw** 2.

**retired**, *modif.* **1.** [Having withdrawn from active life] — *Syn.* in retirement, resigned, having reached retirement age, emeritus, emerita, superannuated, on a pension, on Social Security, leading a quiet life, secluding oneself, rusticating, on the shelf*; see also **dis-**

charged 1, **recalled** 2.— *Ant.* ACTIVE, WORKING, employed.

**2.** [Having been withdrawn] — *Syn.* removed, withdrawn, secluded, sequestered, isolated, separated, apart, drawn back, gone, gone away, drawn away, evacuated, retreated, departed.

**retirement,** *n.* **1.** [The act of retiring] — *Syn.* relinquishment, resignation, abandonment, vacating, evacuation, separation, removal, handing over, laying down, egressing, exiting, retreating, withdrawal, going away, leaving, secession, departure, recession, retreat, regression, abdication, severance.— *Ant.* ARRIVAL, entrance, taking up.

**2.** [The state of being retired] — *Syn.* seclusion, sequestration, aloofness, apartness, separateness, privacy, concealment, solitude, solitariness, isolation, remoteness, loneliness, quiet, retreat, tranquillity, refuge, serenity, inactivity, superannuation.— *Ant.* EXPOSURE, activity, association.

**retiring,** *modif.* — *Syn.* shy, quiet, self-effacing; see **humble** 1, **modest** 2, **reserved** 3.

**retort,** *n.* — *Syn.* counter, rejoinder, response, comeback*; see **answer** 1.

**retort,** *v.* — *Syn.* rejoin, riposte, snap back, shoot back*; see **answer** 1.

*See Synonym Study at* ANSWER.

**retouch,** *v.* — *Syn.* touch up, amend, modify, revise; see **correct** 1, **improve** 1, **repair.**

**retrace,** *v.* — *Syn.* reverse one's steps, go back over, backtrack, reinspect; see **reconsider, return** 1.

**retract,** *v.* **1.** [To draw in] — *Syn.* withdraw, draw back, take in; see **remove** 1, **retreat** 1.

**2.** [To disavow] — *Syn.* countermand, take back, withdraw; see **recant, revoke.**

**retraction,** *n.* — *Syn.* recantation, disowning, disavowal, abjuration, denial, revocation, recall, withdrawal, annulment, forswearing, unsaying, repudiation, nullification, quashing, abrogation, reversal, rescindment, renouncing, disclaimer, negative, contradiction, abnegation, setting aside, contraversion, gainsaying, backing down, backpedaling, reneging, stand-down*, about-face*; see also **cancellation, denial** 1.— *Ant.* CONFIRMATION, reaffirmation, corroboration.

**retreading*,** *n.* — *Syn.* renewing, updating, improving; see **improvement** 1.

**retreat,** *n.* **1.** [The act of retreating] — *Syn.* retirement, removal, evacuation, departure, escape, withdrawal, drawing back, reversal, retrogression, backing out, flight, recession, retraction, going, running away, eluding, evasion, avoidance, recoil.— *Ant.* ADVANCE, progress, progression.

**2.** [A place to which one retreats] — *Syn.* seclusion, solitude, privacy, shelter, refuge, asylum, safe place, defense, sanctuary, security, cover, ark, harbor, port, haven, place of concealment, hiding place, hideaway*, resort, haunt, habitat, hermitage, cell, convent, cloister; see also **refuge** 1.— *Ant.* FRONT, exposed position, van.

*See Synonym Study at* SHELTER.

**beat a retreat**— *Syn.* evacuate, abandon, withdraw; see **leave** 1, **retreat** 2.

**retreat,** *v.* **1.** [To retire] — *Syn.* recede, withdraw, draw back, retrograde, back out, retract, leave, go, depart, recoil, shrink, quail, run, reel, start back, pull back, reverse, seclude oneself, keep aloof, keep apart, hide, separate from, regress, resign, relinquish, lay down, hand over, sequester oneself, retrocede, backtrack, back off, back down, chicken out*.— *Ant.* STAY, continue, advance.

**2.** [In battle, to execute a forced retirement] — *Syn.*

evacuate, abandon, leave, withdraw, back out, vacate the position, retire, remove, pull out, march out, disengage, turn back, fall back, draw back, move back, give ground, move behind, beat a retreat, back down, escape, decamp, fly, run away, turn tail, be routed, give way, flee, flee in disorder, execute a strategic withdrawal, shorten one's lines, avoid, evade, elude.— *Ant.* ATTACK, progress, drive forward.

**retrench,** *v.* — *Syn.* save, conserve, scrimp, curtail; see **economize.**

**retrenchment,** *n.* **1.** [A reduction] — *Syn.* abatement, decrease, deduction; see **reduction** 1.

**2.** [Thrift] — *Syn.* curtailing, thriftiness, frugality; see **economy** 2.

**retribution,** *n.* — *Syn.* requital, reprisal, retaliation, just deserts; see **punishment, revenge** 1.

**retrieve,** *v.* — *Syn.* regain, bring back, reclaim; see **recover** 1.

*See Synonym Study at* RECOVER.

**retrograde,** *modif.* **1.** [Backward] — *Syn.* retrogressive, regressive, recessive; see **backward** 1, **reversed.**

**2.** [Degenerate] — *Syn.* crumbling, decrepit, rotting; see **decaying.**

**retrogression,** *n.* **1.** [Regression] — *Syn.* retroaction, recession, regression, throwback, backward movement, retirement; see also **retreat** 1.

**2.** [Deterioration] — *Syn.* decline, degeneration, decadence; see **decay** 1, 2.

**retrospect,** *n.* — *Syn.* hindsight, remembering, recollection, looking back; see **memory** 1, **review** 1.

**retrospective,** *modif.* — *Syn.* backward-looking, recollective, reflective, pensive; see **historical, thoughtful** 1.

**return,** *modif.* — *Syn.* coming back, repeat, repeating, repetitive, recurring, intermittent, reappearing, sent back, answering, replying, retorting, rotating, turning, rebounding, recurrent, round-trip; see also **repeated** 1.

**return,** *n.* **1.** [The act of coming again] — *Syn.* entrance, homecoming, entry, reentry, revisitation, arrival, coming, appearance, reappearance, occurrence, recurrence, reoccurrence, repetition, reversion, renewal, resurgence, bounding back, recovery, reemergence, resurfacing, recoiling, rotating; see also sense 2.— *Ant.* DEPARTURE, exit, going out.

**2.** [The act of being returned] — *Syn.* restoration, restoring, restitution, replacement, giving back, recompense, recompensing, reimbursement, repayment, acknowledgment, answer, rejoinder, reaction, reciprocation, reversion, reverberation, rebound, recoil, reconsideration; see also sense 1; **answer** 1, **reparation** 2. — *Ant.* disappearance, taking, LOSS.

**3.** [Proceeds] — *Syn.* profit, income, results, gain, avail, revenue, advantage, yield, accrual, accruement, interest. — *Ant.* FAILURE, loss, disadvantage.

**4.** [Report; *often plural*] — *Syn.* account, statement, tabulation; see **record** 1, **records, statement** 3.

**in return**— *Syn.* in exchange, back, as payment, as repayment, in compensation, as a reward, in response, in retaliation.

**return,** *v.* **1.** [To go back] — *Syn.* come back, come again, go again, recur, reappear, reoccur, repeat, revert, reconsider, reenter, reexamine, reinspect, bounce back up, resurface, turn back, retrace one's steps, turn, rotate, revolve, renew, revive, recover, regain, rebound, circle back, double back, backtrack, reverse, move back, reel back, reverberate, repercuss, recoil, retrace, hark back to, revisit, retire, retreat.— *Ant.* leave, advance, go forward.

**2.** [To give back] — *Syn.* put back, send back, restore, replace, bring back, take back, restitute, render, reseat, reestablish, reinstate, react, recompense, refund, repay, make restitution, reciprocate, requite, retaliate, exchange, hand back, roll back, toss back, thrust back. — *Ant.* HOLD, keep, hold back.

**3.** [To answer] — *Syn.* reply, respond, retort; see **answer** 1.

**4.** [To repay] — *Syn.* reimburse, recompense, refund; see **repay** 1.

**5.** [To yield a profit] — *Syn.* pay off, show profit, pay dividends; see **pay** 2, **yield** 2.

**6.** [To speak formally] — *Syn.* deliver, pass, state; see **declare** 1.

**7.** [To reflect] — *Syn.* echo, sound, mirror; see **reflect** 2, 3.

**returned,** *modif.* — *Syn.* restored, restituted, given back, gone back, sent back, brought back, turned back, come back, reappeared, recurred, reoccurred, repeated, renewed, reverted, reentered, rotated, revolved, rebounded, reverberated, refunded, exchanged, acknowledged, answered, rejoindered, repaid, yielded; see also **refused.** — *Ant.* KEPT, held, retained.

**returning,** *n.* **1.** [The act of coming back] — *Syn.* return, reappearance, repetition, reoccurrence, reoccurring, recurrence, reverberation, reentrance, retracing, revolving, revolution, rotation, rotating, rebound, reversion, retreat, turning back, homecoming; see also **return** 1.

**2.** [The act of sending back] — *Syn.* restoring, bringing back, repayment, recompensing, giving back, answering, responding, replying; see also **return** 2.

**reunion,** *n.* — *Syn.* gathering, meeting, homecoming, get-together, reuniting, meeting again, rejoining, reconciliation, restoration, harmonizing, bringing together, healing the breach, rapprochement; see also **gathering.**

**reunite,** *v.* — *Syn.* meet, meet again, reassemble, reconvene, join, rejoin, become reconciled, have a reconciliation, be restored to one another, remarry, heal the breach, make peace, get together, patch things up★, make up★. — *Ant.* SEPARATE, go separate ways, be disrupted.

**revamp,** *v.* — *Syn.* renovate, revise, overhaul, redo; see **reconstruct, renew** 1, **repair.**

**reveal,** *v.* **1.** [To make known] — *Syn.* disclose, divulge, tell, betray, betray a confidence, confess, confide, impart, publish, expose, lay bare, avow, admit, acknowledge, give utterance to, let out, give out, bring out, make public, leak, unfold, unveil, bring to light, communicate, announce, declare, inform, notify, utter, make plain, break the news, unbosom, broadcast, concede, come out with, explain, bring into the open, affirm, report, share, give away★, let the cat out of the bag★, blab★, talk★, spill★, spill the beans★, make a clean breast of★, put one's cards on the table★, let slip★, show one's true colors★, get out of one's system★, give the low-down★, blow the whistle★, let on★, open up★, spill one's guts★; see also **inform** 2, **notify** 1, **tell** 1.

**2.** [To expose] — *Syn.* show, exhibit, unveil; see **expose** 1.

---

**SYN.** — **reveal** implies a making known of something hidden or secret, as if by drawing back a veil /to *reveal* one's identity/; **disclose** suggests a laying open, as to inspection, of what has previously been concealed /she refuses to *disclose* her intentions/; **divulge** suggests that what has been disclosed should properly have been kept secret or private /do not *divulge* the contents of this letter/; **tell** may also imply a breach of confidence /kiss and *tell*/, but more commonly suggests the making known

of necessary or requested information /*tell* me what to do/; **betray** implies either faithlessness in divulging something /*betrayed* by an informer/ or inadvertence in revealing something /a blush that *betrayed* his embarrassment/

**reveille,** *n.* — *Syn.* signal, bell, bugle; see **alarm** 1.

**revel,** *n.* — *Syn.* carousal, frolic, festivity; see **celebration** 2, **entertainment** 1.

**revel,** *v.* **1.** [To make merry] — *Syn.* frolic, carouse, rejoice, party; see **celebrate** 3, **play** 1.

**2.** [To take pleasure; *used with* in] — *Syn.* indulge, delight, relish, luxuriate in; see **enjoy** 1, **like** 1.

**revelation,** *n.* **1.** [Divulgence] — *Syn.* disclosure, discovery, announcement, admission, confession, divulgement, betrayal, telling, showing, publication, exposure, exposé, bombshell. — *Ant.* SECRECY, hiding, refusal to tell.

**2.** [The act of revealing divine truth] — *Syn.* prophecy, vision, apocalypse, inspiration, sign, foreshadowing, shadowing forth, adumbration, oracle, divine manifestation; see also **divination.**

**3.** [Divine truth revealed] — *Syn.* divine word, God's word, apocalypse, cabala; see **doctrine** 1, **faith** 2.

**revelry,** *n.* — *Syn.* spree, festivity, carousing; see **celebration** 2, **entertainment** 1, **party** 1.

**revenge,** *n.* **1.** [The act of returning an injury] — *Syn.* vengeance, requital, reprisal, getting even, measure for measure, an eye for an eye, blow for blow, tit for tat, repayment, return of evil for evil, counterattack, sortie, counterinsurgency, retaliation, retribution, avenging, paying back, settling accounts; see also **attack** 1. — *Ant.* PARDON, forgiveness, excusing.

**2.** [The desire to obtain revenge] — *Syn.* vindictiveness, rancor, implacability, ruthlessness, malevolence, vengefulness, spitefulness, ill-will, animus, vendetta; see also **hate, malice.**

**revenge,** *v.* — *Syn.* avenge, retaliate, vindicate, requite, get even with, take revenge, have one's revenge, breathe vengeance, wreak one's vengeance, exact retribution, pay back, pay off, make reprisal, punish, repay, repay in kind, return like for like, return blow for blow, give tit for tat, reciprocate, settle accounts, square accounts, settle up, pay back in one's own coin, take an eye for an eye, turn the tables on, get back at, fight back, be out for blood, give an exchange, give and take, give someone their just deserts, get satisfaction, even the score, get★, fix★, give someone their comeuppance★, pay off old scores★, settle a score★, return the compliment★, pay back in spades★, fix one's wagon★, give a taste of one's own medicine★, give as good as one gets★. — *Ant.* FORGIVE, condone, pardon.

---

**SYN.** — **revenge** implies the infliction of punishment as an act of retaliation, usually for an injury against oneself, and connotes personal malice, bitter resentment, or vindictive spirit as the moving force; **avenge** implies the infliction of deserved or just punishment for wrongs or oppression

---

**revengeful,** *modif.* — *Syn.* vindictive, spiteful, malevolent, hateful; see **cruel** 1, **vindictive.**
*See Synonym Study at* VINDICTIVE.

**revenue,** *n.* **1.** [Income] — *Syn.* return, earnings, result, yield, wealth, receipts, proceeds, resources, funds, stocks, credits, dividends, interest, perquisites, salary, profits, means, fruits, emoluments, annuity, acquirements, rents; see also **income, pay** 1, 2. — *Ant.* EXPENSES, outgoes, obligations.

2. [Governmental income] — *Syn.* wealth, revenue, taxation; see **income, tax** 1.

Types of revenue include: direct tax, indirect tax, bonds, loans, customs, duties, tariff, tax surcharge, excise, property tax, income tax, sales tax, inheritance and death tax, land tax, poll tax, gasoline tax, school tax, franchise, license, grants, rates, bridge and road tolls, harbor dues, countervailing duties, differential duties, special taxation, patent stamps, stamp duties, registration duties, internal revenue, tax on spirits, tobacco tax, lease of land, sale of land, subsidy, capital gains, dividends.

**reverberate,** *v.* — *Syn.* resound, echo, reflect; see **reflect** 2, **sound** 1.

**reverberation,** *n.* — *Syn.* vibration, echo, repercussion; see **noise** 1.

**revere,** *v.* — *Syn.* reverence, venerate, worship, respect, adore, idolize, exalt, glorify, honor, admire, esteem, worship the ground someone walks on\*; see also **admire** 1.

---

**SYN.** — **revere** implies regarding with great respect, affection, honor, or deference [a poet *revered* by all]; **reverence,** more or less equivalent to **revere,** is usually applied to a thing or abstract idea rather than to a person [they *reverence* the memory of their parents]; **venerate** implies revering because of great age, dignity, or character and may suggest regarding as sacred or holy [he was *venerated* as a saint]; **worship,** in strict usage, implies the use of ritual or verbal formula in paying homage to a divine being, but broadly suggests intense, often uncritical love or admiration [he *worshiped* his wife]; **adore,** in strict usage, implies a personal or individual worshiping of a deity, but in broad usage, suggests a great love for someone and, colloquially, a great liking for something [I *adore* your hat]

---

**reverence,** *n.* 1. [A reverential attitude] — *Syn.* respect, veneration, awe, admiration, love, regard, esteem, devotion, adoration, worship, deference, honor, glorification, exaltation, idolization, obsequiousn~ss, fear, dread. — *Ant.* HATRED, contempt, disdain.

2. [The expression of reverence] — *Syn.* honor, veneration, worship, devotion, obeisance, homage, prostration, genuflection, bow, piety, devoutness, religiousness; see also **praise** 1, 2, **worship** 1. — *Ant.* RIDICULE, scoffing, mockery.

*See Synonym Study at* HONOR.

---

**SYN.** — **reverence** is applied to a feeling of deep respect mingled with love for someone or something one holds sacred or inviolable and suggests a display of homage, deference, etc.; **veneration** implies worshipful reverence for a person or thing regarded as hallowed or sacred and specifically suggests acts of religious devotion; **awe** refers to a feeling of fearful or profound respect or wonder inspired by the greatness, superiority, grandeur, etc. of a person or thing and suggests an immobilizing effect; **dread,** as it comes into comparison here, suggests extreme fear mixed with awe or reverence [a *dread* of divine retribution]

---

**reverend,** *modif.* — *Syn.* revered, respected, venerated; see **divine** 2, **religious** 2.

**reverend,** *n.* — *Syn.* divine, clergyman, minister, priest; see **minister** 1.

**reverent,** *modif.* — *Syn.* venerating, worshipful, solemn; see **respectful.**

**reverential,** *modif.* — *Syn.* pious, devout, reverent; see **religious** 2, **respectful.**

**reverie,** *n.* — *Syn.* meditation, musing, daydream, woolgathering; see **dream** 1, **fancy** 2, **reflection** 1.

**reversal,** *n.* — *Syn.* repudiation, repeal, turnabout; see **about-face, cancellation, refusal, withdrawal.**

**reverse,** *modif.* — *Syn.* opposite, contrary, backward, mirror; see **opposite** 1, **reversed.**

*See Synonym Study at* OPPOSITE.

**reverse,** *n.* 1. [The opposite] — *Syn.* converse, other side, contrary; see **opposite.**

2. [A change from good fortune to bad] — *Syn.* vanquishment, catastrophe, setback, check; see **defeat** 2, **misfortune** 1, 2.

**reverse,** *v.* 1. [To turn] — *Syn.* go back, shift, invert; see **turn** 2.

2. [To alter] — *Syn.* turn around, modify, convert; see **change** 1.

3. [To annul] — *Syn.* nullify, invalidate, repeal; see **cancel** 2.

4. [To exchange] — *Syn.* transpose, rearrange, shift; see **exchange** 1.

**reversed,** *modif.* — *Syn.* turned around, turned back, turned, backward, transposed, end for end, back to front, inverted, contrariwise, out of order, everted, inside out, regressive, retrogressive, undone, unmade. — *Ant.* ORDERED, ESTABLISHED, in order.

**reversion,** *n.* 1. [Reversal] — *Syn.* reversing, inversion, rotation, reaction; see **return** 2.

2. [Return to a former state] — *Syn.* reverting, regression, throwback, atavism; see **relapse, renewal.**

**revert,** *v.* — *Syn.* go back, recur to, regress; see **relapse, return** 1.

**reverted,** *modif.* — *Syn.* unclaimed, confiscated, seized; see **returned.**

**review,** *n.* 1. [A reexamination] — *Syn.* reconsideration, reevaluation, second thought, revision, retrospection, second view, reflection, study, survey, inspection, retrospect; see also **examination** 1, **study** 2.

2. [A critical study] — *Syn.* survey, critique, criticism, analysis, commentary, dissertation, study, investigation, discourse, theme, thesis, essay, monograph, critical review, article, report, treatise, book review, exposition, discussion, canvass, evaluation, appraisal.

3. [A summary] — *Syn.* synopsis, abstract, outline; see **summary.**

4. [A formal inspection] — *Syn.* parade, inspection, dress parade, march, procession, cavalcade, column, file, military display, march past, the once-over\*; see also **display** 2.

**review,** *v.* 1. [To criticize] — *Syn.* evaluate, critique, comment on; see **examine** 1, **interpret** 1.

2. [To examine] — *Syn.* analyze, reexamine, check thoroughly; see **correct** 1, **examine** 1, **reconsider.**

3. [To study] — *Syn.* go over, look over, bone up\*; see **study** 1.

**reviewed,** *modif.* — *Syn.* inspected, examined, reconsidered, studied, surveyed, analyzed, judged, abstracted, outlined, summarized, commented on, criticized, critiqued; see also **considered** 1.

**reviewer,** *n.* — *Syn.* critic, commentator, analyst, inspector; see **critic** 2.

**reviewing,** *n.* — *Syn.* criticizing, inspecting, examining, surveying, studying, going over, analyzing, judging, evaluating, abridging, abstracting, outlining, summarizing, commenting on, critiquing.

**revile,** *v.* — *Syn.* abuse, berate, vilify, vituperate; see **censure, denounce, scold, slander.**

*See Synonym Study at* SCOLD.

**revise,** *v.* — *Syn.* reconsider, rewrite, redraft, edit, correct, reexamine, review, look over, change, alter, rework, improve, amend, develop, compare, scan, scrutinize, overhaul, revamp, update; see also **edit** 1.

**revised,** *modif.* — *Syn.* corrected, edited, redacted, amended, updated, overhauled, improved, altered, changed, rectified, polished, redone, rewritten, reorganized, restyled, reworked, emended.

**revision,** *n.* — *Syn.* revisal, correction, editing, redaction, reediting, updating, update, overhauling, amendment, emendation, improvement, alteration, change, reconsideration, reexamination, review, rectifying, rectification, polishing, restyling, rewriting, rewrite, revised version, new edition.

**revisit,** *v.* — *Syn.* visit again, stay, call on; see **return** 1, **visit** 2, 4.

**revival,** *n.* 1. [The act of reviving] — *Syn.* renewal, renascence, renaissance, refreshment, arousal, awakening, rebirth, return, reversion, resurrection, enkindling, restoration, resumption, invigoration, vivification, resuscitation, reawakening, improvement, freshening, recovery, cheering, consolation.
2. [That which is revived] — *Syn.* life of a past era, ancient customs, former success, forgotten masterpiece, dated work, old movie, old play.
3. [An evangelical service] — *Syn.* meeting, service, revival service, evangelistic meeting, preaching, tent meeting, camp meeting; see also **ceremony** 2.

**revivalist,** *n.* — *Syn.* preacher, missionary, evangelist; see **minister** 1.

**revive,** *v.* 1. [To give new life] — *Syn.* reawaken, awaken, resuscitate, refresh, renew, enliven, enkindle, rekindle, vivify, revivify, revitalize, animate, reanimate, recondition, rejuvenate, bring to, bring around, wake up, rouse, arouse, resurrect, bring back, exhilarate, energize, freshen, invigorate, breathe new life into, reproduce, reshow, restage, regenerate, restore, activate, reactivate. — *Ant.* weary, suppress, extinguish.
2. [To take on new life] — *Syn.* come around, come to, recover, improve, flourish, awake, reawake, strengthen, gain strength, overcome, come to life, regain consciousness, rally, get better, pick up, perk up; see also **recover** 3. — *Ant.* DIE, faint, weaken.
3. [To hearten] — *Syn.* cheer, comfort, brighten, encourage, inspirit, solace, console, relieve, divert, gladden, raise the spirits, soothe, please, make joyful, delight, rejoice.

**revived,** *modif.* — *Syn.* restored, reinstituted, reestablished; see **recovered, returned.**

**revocation,** *n.* — *Syn.* annulment, repeal, repudiation; see **cancellation, retraction.**

**revoke,** *v.* — *Syn.* recall, retract, cancel, annul, repeal, rescind, abrogate, disclaim, renounce, repudiate, withdraw, take back, nullify, void, invalidate, declare null and void, abolish, negate, remove, undo, erase, expunge, obliterate, wipe out, quash, vacate, disown, dismiss, deny, abjure, reverse, countermand, counterorder, recant, eat one's words★; see also **cancel** 2. — *Ant.* APPROVE, endorse, ratify.
*See Synonym Study at* ABOLISH.

**revolt,** *n.* — *Syn.* uprising, mutiny, sedition; see **revolution** 2.

**revolt,** *v.* 1. [To rebel] — *Syn.* mutiny, rise up, resist; see **rebel** 1.
2. [To repel] — *Syn.* sicken, offend, nauseate; see **disgust.**

**revolting,** *modif.* — *Syn.* disgusting, loathsome, repulsive; see **offensive** 2.

**revolution,** *n.* 1. [A complete motion about an axis]

— *Syn.* rotation, spin, turn, revolving, circuit, orbit, round, whirl, gyration, circumvolution, cycle, roll, reel, twirl, swirl, pirouette.
2. [An armed uprising] — *Syn.* revolt, rebellion, uprising, mutiny, insurrection, anarchy, coup, coup d'état, destruction, overturn, upset, overthrow, reversal, rising, riot, outbreak, violence, bloodshed, turbulence, insubordination, disturbance, reformation, plot, cabal, junta, putsch, underground activity, guerrilla activity, unrest, upheaval, tumult, disorder, foment, turmoil, uproar, row, strife, strike, subversion, breakup, secession, convulsion, throe; see also sense 3. — *Ant.* LAW, order, control.
Important revolutions include: Protectorate, 1653, Glorious Revolution, 1688, England; Revolutionary War, American Revolution, 1775, United States; French Revolution, 1789; War of Independence, 1821, Greece; Polish Revolt Against Russia, 1830, Poland; Rise of the Young Turks, 1908; Overthrow of the Manchus, 1911, China; Mexican Revolution, 1911; Russian Revolution, October Revolution, 1917; Rise of the German Republic, 1918; March on Rome of Fascisti, 1920, Italy; Overthrow of Alphonso XIII, 1931, Spain; Nazi Seizure of Government, 1933, Germany; Chinese Communist Revolution, 1949; Revolt Against the Netherlands, 1949, Indonesia; Revolt of the French Indo-Chinese States, 1954; Cuban Revolution, 1959; Great Proletarian Cultural Revolution, 1966, China; Iranian Revolution, 1979; Opening of the Berlin Wall, 1989; Dissolution of the Soviet Union, 1991; Velvet Revolution, 1993, Czechoslovakia.
3. [A reversal] — *Syn.* change, radical change, metamorphosis, substitution, end of an era, epoch, reconstruction, overturn, upset, overthrow, debacle, cataclysm, revolution in ideas, political upheaval, disintegration, falling apart; see also sense 2; **change** 2.

**revolutionary,** *modif.* 1. [Concerned with a revolution] — *Syn.* rebellious, revolting, mutinous, insurrectionary, insurgent, destructive, anarchistic, radical, extremist, reformist, subversive, subverting, overturning, upsetting, destroying, cataclysmic, sweeping, convulsive, seceding, riotous, agitating, disturbing, working underground, working beneath the surface, seditious, factious, treasonable, traitorous. — *Ant.* PATRIOTIC, loyal, moderate.
2. [New and unusual] — *Syn.* unprecedented, novel, advanced, innovative; see **unusual** 2.

**revolutionary,** *n.* — *Syn.* revolutionist, insurgent, insurrectionist; see **rebel** 1, **resister.**

**revolutionize,** *v.* — *Syn.* transform, recast, remodel, refashion; see **change** 1, **reform** 1.

**revolve,** *v.* — *Syn.* spin, rotate, twirl; see **orbit** 1, **turn** 1.

**revolver,** *n.*
Types of revolvers include: forty-five caliber, forty-four caliber, thirty-eight caliber, thirty-two caliber, twenty-two caliber, Colt, .45★, .44★, .38★, .32★, .22★, Dewey★, pepper pot★, blue lightning★, six-shooter★; see also **gun** 2, **pistol.**

**revolving,** *modif.* 1. [Rotating] — *Syn.* turning, spinning, whirling, gyrating, rolling, reeling, twirling, swirling, pirouetting, circling, orbiting, circulating, encircling.
2. [Capable of rotating] — *Syn.* rotatory, rotary, rotational, rotative, trochilic, whirling, gyral, gyratory, gyrational, vertiginous, vortical, vorticose, circumvolutory, circumgyratory, circumrotatory.

**revulsion,** *n.* — *Syn.* disgust, distaste, repugnance; see **aversion, objection** 1.
*See Synonym Study at* AVERSION.

**reward,** *n.* **1.** [Payment] — *Syn.* compensation, remuneration, recompense; see **pay** 1, 2.

**2.** [A prize] — *Syn.* premium, bonus, award; see **prize**. See Synonym Study at PRIZE.

**reward,** *v.* — *Syn.* compensate, repay, remunerate; see **pay** 1.

**rewarded,** *modif.* — *Syn.* paid, repaid, recompensed, compensated, satisfied, remunerated, requited, given an award, awarded a prize.

**rewarding,** *modif.* — *Syn.* satisfying, fulfilling, gratifying, worthwhile; see **pleasant** 2, **readable** 2, **worthwhile**.

**rework,** *v.* — *Syn.* revise, rewrite, do over, touch up; see **edit** 1, **redo, revise**.

**rewrite,** *v.* — *Syn.* revise, recast, rework, redraft, write, edit, fill out, pad, cut, reword, rephrase, rehash, doctor*; see also **edit** 1, **revise**.

**rhapsody,** *n.* — *Syn.* fantasia, improvisation, instrumental composition; see **composition** 4, **fantasia**.

**rhetoric,** *n.* **1.** [Speech] — *Syn.* composition, discourse, oratory, oration; see **eloquence** 1, **speech** 3.

**2.** [Grandiloquence] — *Syn.* bombast, high-flown language, empty talk; see **euphuism, flatulence, wordiness**.

**rhetorical,** *modif.* — *Syn.* oratorical, bombastic, eloquent; see **verbose**.

**rhetorician,** *n.* — *Syn.* orator, soliloquist, lecturer; see **speaker** 1.

**rheumatism,** *n.* — *Syn.* rheumatoid arthritis, bursitis, stiff joints, rheumatic fever, inflammation of the joints, painful joints, rheumatiz*; see also **disease**.

**rhyme,** *n.* — *Syn.* verse, rhyming verse, vowel-chime; see **poetry**.

**rhythm,** *n.* — *Syn.* beat, cadence, swing, rise and fall; see **beat** 2, 3.

**rhythmic,** *modif.* — *Syn.* cadenced, measured, balanced; see **musical** 1, **regular** 3.

**rib,** *n.* **1.** [One part of the bony frame of the thorax] — *Syn.* true rib, false rib, floating rib, slat*, slab*, rod*, floater*; see also **bone**.

**2.** [A rod] — *Syn.* girder, bar, strip; see **rod** 1, **support** 2.

**3.** [A ridge] — *Syn.* fin, nervure, vaulting; see **ridge** 1.

**ribald,** *modif.* — *Syn.* earthy, obscene, lewd, bawdy, lascivious, vulgar, salacious, indecorous, unbecoming, coarse, ungentlemanly, unladylike, foul-mouthed, spicy, racy, risqué, indecent, dirty*, hot*, fast*, blue*, juicy*, raunchy*; see also **lewd** 1. — *Ant.* REFINED, decent, decorous.
See Synonym Study at COARSE.

**ribaldry,** *n.* — *Syn.* pornography, vulgarity, smuttiness, obscenity; see **humor** 1, **indecency** 2.

**ribbon,** *n.* — *Syn.* band, fillet, trimming, decoration, fabric, strip.

**rich,** *modif.* **1.** [Possessed of wealth] — *Syn.* wealthy, affluent, well-to-do, moneyed, prosperous, opulent, comfortable, well-off, well provided for, in easy circumstances, worth a bundle*, well-fixed*, well-heeled*, loaded*, made of money*, rolling in dough*, in clover*, on easy street*, flush*, in the money*, in the chips*. — *Ant.* POOR, poverty-stricken, destitute.

**2.** [Sumptuous] — *Syn.* luxurious, opulent, lavish, costly, elegant, magnificent, resplendent, elaborate, embellished, ornate, expensive, deluxe, chic, smart, stylish, fancy, splendid, superb, gorgeous, valuable, precious, extravagant, grand, lush, posh*, plush*, classy*, ritzy*, swank*, swanky*, snazzy*, swell*, high-class*, spiffy*, sharp*, tony*, high-toned*, upscale*. — *Ant.* CHEAP, plain, simple.

**3.** [Fertile] — *Syn.* exuberant, lush, productive, copious, plentiful, generous, fruitful, profuse, luxuriant, teeming, abundant, prolific, fecund, fruit-bearing, bearing, propagating, yielding, breeding, superabounding, prodigal; see also **fertile** 1. — *Ant.* STERILE, unfruitful, barren.

**4.** [Abounding in butter, cream, sugar, spices, etc.] — *Syn.* heavy, luscious, sweet, creamy, buttery, fatty, oily, juicy, succulent, fattening, satisfying, filling, oversweet, cloying, spicy, savory, piquant; see also **delicious** 1. — *Ant.* light, plain, low-fat.

**5.** [Laughable] — *Syn.* absurd, preposterous, ridiculous, funny, amusing, entertaining, queer, odd, strange, diverting, droll, comical, ludicrous, farcical, humorous, incongruous, foolish, killing*, sidesplitting*.

**6.** [Full; *said of sounds or voices*] — *Syn.* deep, mellow, sonorous; see **harmonious** 1, **loud** 1.

**7.** [Vivid; *said of colors*] — *Syn.* deep, intense, vibrant, strong; see **bright** 2.

---

**SYN.** — **rich** is the general word for one who has more money, possessions, or income-producing property than is necessary to satisfy normal needs; **wealthy** adds to this connotation of grand living, influence in the community, a tradition of richness, etc.; **affluent** suggests a continuing increase of riches and a high standard of living [an *affluent* suburb]; **opulent** suggests the possession of great wealth as displayed in luxurious or ostentatious living [an *opulent* mansion]; **well-to-do** implies sufficient prosperity for easy living

---

**rich,** *n.* — *Syn.* the wealthy, the well-to-do, the affluent, capitalists, upper class, plutocrats, plutocracy, the haves*.

**riches,** *n.* — *Syn.* fortune, possessions, money; see **wealth** 2.

**richly,** *modif.* — *Syn.* sumptuously, lavishly, opulently; see **largely** 2, **well** 2, 3.

**richness,** *n.* — *Syn.* copiousness, bounty, abundance; see **plenty**.

**rich person,** *n.* — *Syn.* millionaire, person of substance, capitalist, moneybags*; see **financier, millionaire**.

**rickety,** *modif.* **1.** [Liable to collapse] — *Syn.* shaky, fragile, unsteady, wobbly; see **weak** 2.

**2.** [Weak in the joints] — *Syn.* infirm, tottering, rachitic; see **sick, weak** 1.

**ricochet,** *v.* — *Syn.* reflect, rebound, skip, glance off; see **bounce** 1.
See Synonym Study at SKIP.

**rid,** *modif.* — *Syn.* relieved, quit, delivered; see **free** 2.

**be rid of** — *Syn.* be freed, be relieved of, evade, have done with; see **escape**.

**get rid of** — *Syn.* shed, eliminate, dispose of; see **discard, free** 2.

**rid,** *v.* — *Syn.* clear, relieve, shed; see **discard, free** 2.

**riddance,** *n.* — *Syn.* release, liberation, discharge; see **freedom** 2, **freeing**.

**riddle,** *n.* **1.** [A difficult problem] — *Syn.* problem, puzzle, question, knotty question, doubt, quandary, entanglement, dilemma, embarrassment, perplexity, enigma, confusion, complication, complexity, intricacy, strait, labyrinth, predicament, plight, distraction, bewilderment; see also **puzzle** 2. — *Ant.* SIMPLICITY, clarity, disentanglement.

**2.** [An obscure question to be solved for amusement] — *Syn.* mystery, conundrum, puzzle, enigma, charade, rebus, brain teaser, brain twister. — *Ant.* ANSWER, solution, explanation.
See Synonym Study at PUZZLE.

**ride,** *n.* — *Syn.* drive, trip, spin, transportation; see **journey.**

**take for a ride**★ — *Syn.* murder, abduct, trick, shoot, machine gun, slay; see also **deceive, kill** 1.

**ride,** *v.* **1.** [To be transported] — *Syn.* travel in, take, be carried, be conveyed, tour, journey, drive, motor, go for a ride, go for a spin, go for an airing, go by car, go by bicycle, bike★, cycle, pedal, go by motorcycle, go by train, go by bus; see also **drive** 3, **travel** 1.

**2.** [To control a beast of burden by riding] — *Syn.* go on horseback, manage, guide, mount, sit, sit well, have a good seat, post, direct, curb, restrain, urge on, handle, handle well, ride hard.

**3.** [To allow oneself to be dominated by circumstances] — *Syn.* drift, float, go with the current, go with the tide, move aimlessly, be without ambition, take the line of least resistance; see also **drift.**

**4.** [★To treat with unusual severity] — *Syn.* harass, persecute, domineer over, dominate, intimidate, tyrannize over, hound, hector, harry, badger, bait, tease, treat overbearingly, disparage, criticize, reproach, berate, upbraid, scold, afflict, annoy, pester, nag, deride, rag★, hassle★, razz★, roast★, needle★; see also **bait** 2, **bother** 2.

**5.** [To move as a carrier] — *Syn.* perform, perform well, ride well, ride evenly, remain stable, corner well, hold on the curves, give evidence of good design, show good engineering, hold the road, hug the road, keep an even keel, maintain balance, maintain equilibrium.

*See Synonym Study at* BAIT.

**rider,** *n.* **1.** [One who rides] — *Syn.* passenger, driver, motorist, hitchhiker, cyclist, motorcyclist, biker★, horseback rider, equestrian, horseman, horsewoman; see also **horseman, jockey.**

**2.** [An additional clause or provision, usually not connected with the main body of the work] — *Syn.* addition, amendment, addendum, appendix, supplement, adjunct, appendage, codicil.

**ridge,** *n.* **1.** [A long, straight, raised portion] — *Syn.* rib, seam, rim, backbone, spinal column, ridgepole, parapet, crest.

**2.** [Land forming a ridge, sense 1] — *Syn.* mountain ridge, range, elevation, hill, moraine, terminal moraine, medial moraine, esker, kame, hogback, arête.

**ridged,** *modif.* — *Syn.* crinkled, furrowed, ribbed; see **corrugated.**

**ridicule,** *n.* — *Syn.* derision, mockery, scorn, contempt, disdain, jeer, leer, disparagement, sneer, rally, flout, fleer, twit, taunt, taunting, making fun of, poking fun, burlesque, caricature, satire, parody, travesty, irony, sarcasm, persiflage, chaff, raillery, badinage, farce, buffoonery, horseplay, foolery, needle★, razz★, rib★, ribbing★, joshing★, ragging★, roast★, raspberry★, horse laugh★. — *Ant.* PRAISE, commendation, approval.

**ridicule,** *v.* — *Syn.* make fun of, deride, mock, taunt, gibe at, scoff at, sneer at, laugh at, point at, grin at, banter, mimic, jeer, tease, twit, chaff, disparage, belittle, flout, scorn, make sport of, poke fun at, fleer, rally, burlesque, caricature, show up, unmask, expose, satirize, parody, lampoon, cartoon, travesty, run down, make a laughing stock of, deflate, put down★, send up★, take off on★, josh★, rag★, razz★, rib★, guy★, ride★, give the Bronx cheer★, pull someone's leg★, point the finger of scorn, have a fling at★, roast★, pan★. — *Ant.* honor, APPROVE, applaud.

---

**SYN.** — **ridicule** implies making fun of someone or something but does not necessarily connote malice or hostility [he *ridiculed* her attempts to speak Greek]; **deride** suggests scorn or malicious contempt in ridiculing

[to *deride* another's beliefs]; **mock** implies contemptuous ridiculing, esp. by caricaturing another's peculiarities [it is cruel to *mock* his lisp]; **taunt** implies insulting ridicule and often an attempt to provoke, esp. by jeering and repeatedly calling attention to some humiliating fact [they *taunted* him about his failure]

---

**ridiculous,** *modif.* — *Syn.* ludicrous, absurd, laughable; see **absurd, funny** 1.

*See Synonym Study at* ABSURD.

**ridiculously,** *modif.* — *Syn.* absurdly, laughably, preposterously, foolishly, insanely, extremely, inanely; see also **humorously.**

**riding,** *modif.* — *Syn.* traveling, astride, mounted, on horseback, driving, touring, bicycling, cycling, biking★, in transit; see also **moving** 1.

**riding,** *n.* — *Syn.* traveling, journeying, horseback riding; see **journey, travel** 1.

**rife,** *modif.* **1.** [Widespread] — *Syn.* prevalent, extensive, common; see **prevailing, widespread.**

**2.** [Abundant] — *Syn.* plentiful, abounding, replete, profuse; see **full** 1, **plentiful** 1.

*See Synonym Study at* PREVAILING.

**riffraff,** *n.* — *Syn.* mob, masses, rabble; see **people** 3.

**rifle,** *n.* Types of rifles include: Albini-Braendlin, Berdan, Berthier, Chassepot, Francini-Martini, Lebel, Martini-Henry, Mannlicher, Schulhof, Sober, Peabody-Martini, Lee-Metford, Remington, Krag-Jorgensen, Sharps, Johnson, Springfield, Winchester, Garrand, Enfield, breech-loading, double-barrelled, repeating, Mauser, high-powered, low-powered, Lee straight-pull, Browning automatic (BAR), recoilless, match, Minie, muzzle-loading, rook and rabbit, saloon, Schneider repeating, carbine, M-1, M-14, M-16, AK-47, automatic, semi-automatic, stick★, iron★; see also **gun** 2, **machine gun.**

**rifleman,** *n.* — *Syn.* shooter, sharpshooter, marksman, crack shot, dead shot, huntsman, musketeer, trooper, carabineer, dragoon, shot, sniper; see also **gunner, hunter** 1.

**rift,** *n.* **1.** [An opening caused by splitting] — *Syn.* fissure, cleft, split, crack; see **break** 1, **fracture** 2, **hole** 1.

**2.** [A break in a friendly relationship] — *Syn.* breach, rupture, estrangement; see **disagreement** 1, **divorce.**

**rig,** *n.* — *Syn.* tackle, apparatus, gear; see **equipment.**

**rigging,** *n.* — *Syn.* gear, apparatus, implements; see **equipment.**

**right,** *modif.* **1.** [Correct] — *Syn.* true, precise, correct; see **accurate** 1, **valid** 1.

**2.** [Just] — *Syn.* lawful, legitimate, honest, ethical; see **fair** 1, **moral** 1, **upright** 2.

**3.** [Suitable] — *Syn.* apt, proper, appropriate; see **fit** 1, 2.

**4.** [Sane] — *Syn.* reasonable, rational, sound, wise, normal, discerning, discreet, enlightened, circumspect, penetrating, judicious, far-sighted; see also **sane** 1, 2. — *Ant.* INSANE, unreasonable, unsound.

**5.** [Justly] — *Syn.* fairly, evenly, equitably, honestly, decently, sincerely, legitimately, lawfully, conscientiously, squarely, impartially, objectively, reliably, dispassionately, without bias, without prejudice; see also **justly** 1.

**6.** [Straight] — *Syn.* directly, undeviatingly, immediately; see **direct** 1.

**7.** [Opposite to left] — *Syn.* right-hand, dextral, dexter, righthanded, clockwise, on the right, starboard. — *Ant.* LEFT, sinistral, counterclockwise.

**8.** [Designating the side intended for show] — *Syn.* outward, outer, top, finished, decorated, ornamented, trimmed, best, in good condition, unworn, best-looking, clean. — *Ant.* INNER, bottom, unfinished.

**right,** *n.* **1.** [A privilege] — *Syn.* prerogative, power, license, immunity, exemption, benefit, advantage, favor, franchise, claim, title, preference, priority, perquisite, freedom, liberty, natural expectation; see also **freedom** 1, 2.

**2.** [That which is right or just] — *Syn.* goodness, justice, morality, equity; see **fairness, fitness** 1, **honesty** 1, **virtue** 1.

**3.** [The conservative element] — *Syn.* right wing, conservatives, reactionaries, traditionalists, Old Guard, Republicans, Republican Party, Tories. — *Ant.* left, left wing, liberals.

**4.** [The part opposite the left] — *Syn.* right hand, dexter, right side, strong side, starboard, recto.

**by rights** — *Syn.* properly, justly, in fairness; see **rightfully, rightly.**

**in one's own right** — *Syn.* individually, acting as one's own agent, by one's own authority; see **independently.**

**in the right** — *Syn.* correct, accurate, just, blameless; see **fair** 1, **innocent** 1, valid 1.

**right,** *v.* **1.** [To make upright] — *Syn.* set up, set upright, put up, straighten, make straight, bring around, turn up, turn right side up, put in place, balance; see also **straighten, turn** 2. — *Ant.* UPSET, turn upside down, capsize.

**2.** [To repair an injustice] — *Syn.* adjust, correct, repair, restore, vindicate, do justice, make amends, recompense, remedy, rectify, redress, avenge, mend, amend, set right; see also **remedy, repair, revenge.** — *Ant.* WRONG, hurt, harm.

**right away,** *modif.* — *Syn.* directly, without delay, at once; see **immediately.**

**righteous,** *modif.* **1.** [Virtuous] — *Syn.* just, upright, good, honorable, honest, worthy, exemplary, noble, right-minded, goodhearted, dutiful, trustworthy, equitable, scrupulous, conscientious, ethical, moral, fair, impartial, fairminded, commendable, praiseworthy, guiltless, blameless, sinless, peerless, sterling, meritorious, deserving, laudable, punctilious, creditable, morally justifiable, charitable, philanthropic, having a clear conscience; see also **moral** 1, **reliable** 1. — *Ant.* CORRUPT, sinful, immoral.

**2.** [Religiously inclined] — *Syn.* devout, pious, religious, holy, saintly, godly, godlike, angelic, devoted, reverent, reverential, faithful, fervent, strict, rigid, devotional, zealous, spiritual; see also **holy** 2, **religious** 2. — *Ant.* IMPIOUS, irreligious, profane.

**3.** [Conscious of one's own virtue] — *Syn.* self-righteous, sanctimonious, hypocritical; see **egotistic** 2. *See Synonym Study at* MORAL.

**righteousness,** *n.* **1.** [Justice] — *Syn.* uprightness, fairness, justness, rectitude; see **fairness, honor** 1, **virtue** 1.

**2.** [Devotion to a sinless life] — *Syn.* piety, saintliness, devoutness, devotion, reverence, religiousness, godliness, spirituality, zeal, worship; see also **holiness** 1. — *Ant.* BLASPHEMY, irreverence, impiety.

**rightful,** *modif.* — *Syn.* proper, just, legitimate; see **fair** 1, **lawful, legal** 1, **permitted.**

**rightfully,** *modif.* — *Syn.* lawfully, legally, legitimately, justly, fairly, properly, truly, equitably, honestly, impartially, fittingly, in all conscience, as is fitting, in equity, by right, by rights, in reason, dispassionately, objectively, according to one's due, fair and square★, on the level★; see also **legally** 1.

**rightly,** *modif.* — *Syn.* uprightly, justly, fairly, with reason, in justice, properly, fitly, correctly, appropriately,

suitably, exactly, truly; see also **accurately, well** 2. — *Ant.* WRONGLY, without reason, erroneously.

**right-wing,** *modif.* — *Syn.* conservative, reactionary, hidebound; see **conservative.**

**rigid,** *modif.* **1.** [Stiff] — *Syn.* unyielding, inflexible, hard; see **firm** 2, **stiff** 1, **unbreakable.**

**2.** [Strict] — *Syn.* exact, rigorous, stern, stringent; see **definite** 1, **severe** 1, 2.

**3.** [Fixed] — *Syn.* set, unmoving, unyielding; see **determined** 1, **firm** 1, **resolute** 2.

**rigmarole,** *n.* — *Syn.* drivel, red tape, formalities, inanity; see **bureaucracy** 2, **nonsense** 1.

**rigor,** *n.* — *Syn.* rigidity, stiffness, inflexibility, hardness, sternness, harshness, hardship, difficulty, austerity, severity, strictness, stringency, inexorability, obduracy, exactitude, preciseness, precision, intolerance, obstinacy, freedom from deviation, uncompromisingness, inclemency, tenacity, traditionalism, conventionalism, relentlessness, rigorousness; see also **stubbornness.** — *Ant.* leniency, lenity, mildness. *See Synonym Study at* DIFFICULTY.

**rigorous,** *modif.* **1.** [Severe] — *Syn.* harsh, austere, uncompromising; see **severe** 1, 2.

**2.** [Exact] — *Syn.* precise, meticulous, dogmatic; see **accurate** 1, 2, **definite** 1.

**rile,** *v.* — *Syn.* irritate, provoke, annoy; see **anger** 1, **bother** 2.

**rim,** *n.* — *Syn.* edge, border, verge, brim, lip, brink, top, margin, line, outline, frame, band, ring, strip, brow, curb, ledge, skirt, fringe, hem, limit, confine, end, terminus, periphery; see also **edge** 1, **side** 2. — *Ant.* CENTER, middle, interior.

---

SYN. — **rim** is applied to the edge of a circular or curved surface; **brim** refers to the inner rim at the top of a cup, glass, bowl, etc. or to the projecting rim of a hat; **brink** refers to the edge at the top of a steep slope; **border** refers to the boundary of a surface and may imply the limiting line itself or the part of the surface immediately adjacent to it; **margin** implies a bordering strip more or less clearly defined by some distinguishing feature [the *margin* of a printed page]; **edge** refers to the limiting line itself or the terminating line at the sharp convergence of two surfaces [the *edge* of a box]: all of these terms have figurative application [the *rim* of consciousness, a mind filled to the *brim*, the *brink* of disaster, the *border* of good taste, a *margin* of error, an *edge* on one's appetite]

---

**rime,** *n.* — *Syn.* snow, hoarfrost, icicle; see **frost** 2, **ice.**

**rind,** *n.* — *Syn.* skin, peel, hull, shell, surface, coating, crust, bark, cortex, integument; see also **skin.** — *Ant.* INSIDE, center, interior. *See Synonym Study at* SKIN.

**ring,** *n.* **1.** [A circle] — *Syn.* loop, hoop, circlet, link; see **circle** 1, **rim.**

**2.** [A circular band of metal] — *Syn.* hoop, band, circlet, collar; see **bracelet, jewelry.**

Types of rings include: wedding, engagement, diamond, graduation, class, guard, signet, organization, umbrella, finger, pinkie, ankle, nose, key, harness, napkin, bracelet, earring, ear drop.

**3.** [A close association, often corrupt] — *Syn.* cabal, junta, combine, party, bloc, faction, group, gang, band, clique, monopoly, cartel, corner, pool, trust, syndicate, confederacy, tong, racket★, mob★, string★; see also **organization** 3.

**4.** [Pugilism] — *Syn.* prizefighting, boxing, fighting,

professional fighting, prize ring, boxing game*, fistic sport*, fight racket*; see also **boxing, sport** 3.

**5.** [The area roped for a fight] — *Syn.* arena, prize ring, boxing ring, canvas, ropes*, battle box*, P. R.*, square*, resin*.

**6.** [A ringing sound] — *Syn.* chime, peal, toll, knell, tinkle, clang, jingle, tintinnabulation, jangle, ding-dong; see also **noise** 1.

**give someone a ring***— *Syn.* call, call up, phone, speak to; see **telephone.**

**run rings around***— *Syn.* excel, outdo, surpass, overtake; see **exceed.**

**ring,** *v.* **1.** [To encircle] — *Syn.* circle, rim, surround, encompass, girdle, enclose, move around, loop, gird, belt, confine, hem in; see also **circle, surround** 1.

**2.** [To cause to sound] — *Syn.* clap, clang, bang, beat, toll, strike, pull, punch, buzz, play, sound the brass*; see also **sound** 1.

**3.** [To give forth sound by ringing] — *Syn.* resound, reverberate, peal, chime, toll, knell, tinkle, jingle, jangle, vibrate, chime, clang, bong, ding, tintinnabulate; see also **sound** 1.

**4.** [To call by ringing] — *Syn.* summon, call out, ring up, buzz for, press the buzzer, give a ring.

**ring in,** *v.* — *Syn.* start, usher in, open; see **begin** 1.

**ringleader,** *n.* — *Syn.* leader, rabble-rouser, demagogue, instigator; see **agitator, chief** 1, **leader** 2.

**ringlet,** *n.* — *Syn.* lock of hair, curl, twist, spiral; see **curl, lock** 2.

**ring out,** *v.* **1.** [To resound] — *Syn.* thunder, boom, reverberate; see **sound** 1.

**2.** [To stop] — *Syn.* halt, close, shut down; see **stop** 2.

**ring the changes on,** *v.* — *Syn.* vary, elaborate upon, reiterate; see **change** 1, **repeat** 1, 3.

**rink,** *n.* — *Syn.* ice rink, skating rink, course; see **arena.**

**rinse,** *v.* — *Syn.* clean, flush, dip in water; see **flush** 1, **soak** 1, **wash** 2.

**riot,** *n.* — *Syn.* confusion, uproar, tumult, public disturbance; see **disorder** 2, **disturbance** 2, **protest.**

**run riot** — *Syn.* run wild, run amok, revolt, riot; see **rebel** 1.

**riot,** *v.* — *Syn.* revolt, stir up trouble, fight in the streets; see **rebel** 1.

**rioter,** *n.* — *Syn.* rebel, mutineer, resister, brawler; see **agitator, radical, rebel** 1.

**riotous,** *modif.* **1.** [Rebellious] — *Syn.* tumultuous, brawling, disorderly; see **rebellious** 2, **unruly.**

**2.** [Wanton] — *Syn.* reveling, roistering, dissolute, excessive; see **lewd** 2.

**rip,** *n.* — *Syn.* rent, cleavage, split; see **cut** 2, **tear.**

**rip,** *v.* — *Syn.* tear, rend, split, cleave, rive, shred; see also **cut** 1.

*See Synonym Study at* TEAR.

**ripe,** *modif.* **1.** [Ready to be harvested] — *Syn.* fully grown, fully developed, ruddy, red, yellow, plump, filled out, matured, ready, ripened; see also **mellow** 1. — *Ant.* GREEN, undeveloped, half-grown.

**2.** [Improved by time and experience] — *Syn.* mature, mellow, wise, sweetened, increased, perfected, matured, aged, adult, experienced, discerning, sagacious, discreet, judicious, informed, versed, skilled, skillful, subtle, enlightened, sound, tolerant, forbearing, understanding, sympathetic, enriched, full; see also **mature** 1.

**3.** [Ready] — *Syn.* prepared, seasoned, consummate, perfected, finished, usable, fit, conditioned, prime, avail-

able, on the mark, completed; see also **ready** 2. — *Ant.* UNFIT, unready, unprepared.

**SYN. — ripe,** in its basic application, implies readiness to be harvested, eaten, used, etc. /ripe apples, a *ripe* cheese/ and, in extended use, full readiness to do or undergo something /ripe for change/; **mature** implies full growth or development, as of living organisms or the mind /a *mature* tree, *mature* judgment/; **mellow** suggests the qualities typical of ripe fruit, such as softness, sweetness, etc. and therefore stresses the absence of sharpness, harshness, etc. /a *mellow* flavor, a *mellow* mood/; **adult** is applied to a person who has reached complete physical or mental maturity, or legal majority, and to ideas, behavior, etc. that show mature thinking

**ripen,** *v.* **1.** [To mature] — *Syn.* grow up, come of age, mellow, reach perfection; see **mature** 1.

**2.** [To grow] — *Syn.* develop, evolve, advance; see **grow** 2.

**ripple,** *v.* — *Syn.* wave, undulate, curl, break; see **wave** 4.

*See Synonym Study at* WAVE.

**rise,** *n.* **1.** [The act of rising] — *Syn.* ascent, ascension, climb, mounting, soaring, towering, surge, upsurge, lift, upward sweep, ascent stage, reach, going up, coming up, pushing up. — *Ant.* FALL, sinking, drop.

**2.** [An increase] — *Syn.* augmentation, growth, enlargement, multiplication, heightening, intensifying, distention, stacking up, piling up, addition, accession, inflation, acceleration, doubling, advance; see also **increase** 1. — *Ant.* REDUCTION, decrease, lessening.

**3.** [Source] — *Syn.* beginning, commencement, start, emergence; see **appearance** 3, **origin** 1.

**get a rise out of*** — *Syn.* tease, bait, provoke, annoy; see **anger** 1.

**give rise to** — *Syn.* produce, initiate, begin; see **cause** 2.

**rise,** *v.* **1.** [To move upward] — *Syn.* ascend, mount, climb, scale, surmount, soar, tower, rocket, levitate, surge, sweep upward, lift, get up, bob up, move up, push up, reach up, come up, go up, sprout, grow, rear, uprise, rise up, fly up, take off, blast off, curl upward; see also **fly** 1. — *Ant.* FALL, drop, come down.

**2.** [To get up after sleeping, lying, sitting, etc.] — *Syn.* arise, awake, get out of bed, stand up; see **arise** 1, **stand** 1.

**3.** [To increase] — *Syn.* grow, swell, intensify, mount, enlarge, spread, expand, extend, augment, heighten, enhance, distend, inflate, escalate, build, pile up, stack up, multiply, accelerate, speed up, add to, wax, advance, raise, double; see also **increase** 1. — *Ant.* DECREASE, lessen, contract.

**4.** [To begin] — *Syn.* spring, emanate, issue; see **arise** 3, **begin** 2.

**5.** [To improve one's station] — *Syn.* advance, prosper, flourish, thrive, succeed, progress, be promoted, be elevated, be lifted up, better oneself, rise in the world; see also **improve** 2. — *Ant.* FAIL, go down in the world, deteriorate.

**6.** [To be built] — *Syn.* stand, be erected, be placed, be located, be put up, go up, rise up, uprise, be founded, have foundation, be situated.

**7.** [To swell; *said usually of dough or batter*] — *Syn.* inflate, billow, bulge, puff up; see **swell.**

*See Synonym Study at* ARISE.

**rising,** *modif.* — *Syn.* climbing, ascending, mounting, soaring, increasing, skyrocketing, advancing, growing, on the rise, on the increase, spiraling, going up, moving up, surging up, sloping upward, slanting up, taking off, going aloft, gaining altitude, upsurging, in the ascendant, up-and-coming, upswinging, on the upswing, upcoming, scandent, levitating, topping out*, heading for the stars*; see also **growing, increasing** 1, 2.

**rising,** *n.* — *Syn.* climbing, ascension, gaining altitude; see **increase** 1, **rise** 1.

**risk,** *n.* **1.** [Danger] — *Syn.* hazard, peril, jeopardy; see **danger.**

**2.** [The basis of a chance] — *Syn.* chance, gamble, venture, good risk, fortuity, contingency, opportunity, prospect; see also **chance** 1, **uncertainty** 3.

*See Synonym Study at* DANGER.

**run a risk** — *Syn.* take a chance, gamble, venture; see **chance** 2, **risk.**

**risk,** *v.* — *Syn.* chance, gamble, gamble on, venture, hazard, imperil, endanger, jeopardize, run the risk, take a chance, trust to chance, do at one's own peril, expose oneself to, lay oneself open to, stick one's neck out, take the liberty, defy danger, speculate, make an investment, hang by a thread, play with fire, carry too much sail, go out of one's depth, beard the lion in his den, bell the cat, double the blind, sit on a barrel of gunpowder, go through fire and water, leap before one looks, take a leap in the dark, throw caution to the wind, fish in troubled waters, skate on thin ice, sleep on a volcano, live in a glass house, go to sea in a sieve, sail too near the wind, buck the tiger; see also **chance** 2.

**risky,** *modif.* — *Syn.* perilous, precarious, hazardous; see **dangerous** 1, **endangered, unsafe.**

**risqué,** *modif.* — *Syn.* indecent, erotic, ribald, off-color, indelicate, salty, earthy, racy, spicy, suggestive, lewd, sophisticated, adult, naughty, having a double meaning, with a double-entendre, bawdy, improper, coarse, broad, daring, provocative, offensive, salacious, unprintable, not for mixed company, not for Sunday school, obscene, smutty, indiscreet, immoral, sexy*, dirty*, raunchy*, juicy*, hot*, blue*, sizzling*, choice*, raw*, strong*, warm*; see also **lewd** 1. — *Ant.* RESPECTABLE, decorous, proper.

**rite,** *n.* — *Syn.* ceremony, observance, service, ritual; see **ceremony** 2, **custom** 2, **sacrament** 1.

*See Synonym Study at* CEREMONY.

**ritual,** *n.* — *Syn.* observance, rites, routine; see **ceremony** 2, **custom** 2.

*See Synonym Study at* CEREMONY.

**ritualistic,** *modif.* — *Syn.* formal, reverent, ceremonial; see **conventional** 2, 3.

**ritzy*,** *modif.* — *Syn.* elegant, luxurious, stylish; see **rich** 2.

**rival,** *modif.* — *Syn.* competing, competitive, striving, combatant, emulating, vying, opposing, disputing, contesting, contending, conflicting, battling, antagonistic, equal. — *Ant.* HELPFUL, cooperating, assisting.

**rival,** *n.* — *Syn.* competitor, emulator, antagonist; see **contestant, opponent** 1.

**rival,** *v.* — *Syn.* equal, emulate, match, compare with, even off, approximate, near, come near to, approach, resemble, challenge, contend with, compete. — *Ant.* CO-OPERATE, aid, be unequal.

**rivalry,** *n.* — *Syn.* competition, emulation, striving, contest, vying, struggle, battle, contention, opposition, dispute; see also **competition** 1, **fight** 1. — *Ant.* COOPERATION, alliance, conspiracy.

*See Synonym Study at* COMPETITION.

**river,** *n.* **1.** [Flowing water] — *Syn.* stream, flow, course, current, tributary, branch, estuary, rivulet, river system, creek, brook, watercourse, waterway.

Famous rivers include: Seine, Rhône, Loire, Thames, Severn, Avon, Clyde, Danube, Rhine, Elbe, Don, Volga, Yenisei, Dnieper, Vistula, Nile, Euphrates, Mekong, Tigris, Ganges, Indus, Irrawaddy, Yellow, Yangste-Kiang, Niger, Congo, Zambesi, St. Lawrence, Saskatchewan, Mississippi, Missouri, Ohio, Platte, Delaware, Connecticut, Mohawk, Columbia, Gila, Colorado, Snake, Hudson, Rio Grande, Yukon, Amazon, Orinoco, La Plata, Murray.

**2.** [Anything likened to a river, sense 1] — *Syn.* wave, swell, outpouring; see **flood** 1, **plenty.**

**sell down the river*** — *Syn.* betray, cheat, desert; see **betray** 1, **deceive.**

**up the river*** — *Syn.* imprisoned, jailed, in jail; see **confined** 3.

**rivet,** *v.* — *Syn.* nail, bolt, fix; see **fasten** 1.

**riveting,** *modif.* — *Syn.* gripping, engrossing, arresting; see **interesting.**

**rivulet,** *n.* — *Syn.* brook, stream, creek; see **river** 1.

**roach,** *n.* **1.** [An insect] — *Syn.* cockroach, bug, *cucaracha* (Spanish); see **insect.**

**2.** [*The butt end of a marijuana cigarette] — *Syn.* butt, joint*, last hit*; see **marijuana, reefer.**

**road,** *n.* **1.** [A strip prepared for travel] — *Syn.* path, way, highway, roadway, street, avenue, thoroughfare, boulevard, highroad, drive, terrace, parkway, artery, byway, lane, alley, alleyway, crossroad, viaduct, underpass, overpass, causeway, paving, slab, towpath, throughway, thruway, freeway, expressway, turnpike, toll road, divided highway, superhighway, trace, trackway, trail, post road, secondary road, shunpike, market road, national highway, state highway, interstate, *Autobahn* (German), *autostrada* (Italian), drag*, main drag*.

Types of roads include: tar, blacktop, macadam, Tarvia (trademark), asphalt, concrete, brick, gravel, oiled gravel, dirt, graded earth, wood block, cobblestone, clay and sand, graded and drained, corduroy.

**2.** [A course] — *Syn.* scheme, way, path; see **plan** 2, **way** 2.

**on the road** — *Syn.* on tour, traveling, on the way; see **en route, traveling** 2.

**one for the road*** — *Syn.* cocktail, nightcap, quickie*; see **drink** 2.

**take to the road** — *Syn.* go, get underway, set out; see **leave** 1, **travel** 2.

**roadbed,** *n.* — *Syn.* crushed rock, gravel, ballast; see **foundation** 2.

**roam,** *v.* — *Syn.* wander, ramble, range, stroll, rove, walk, hike, traverse, stray, straggle, meander, prowl, tramp, saunter, peregrinate, knock around, bat around, scour, straggle, gallivant, gad, struggle along, traipse*; see also **travel** 2.

**roar,** *n.* — *Syn.* bellow, shout, boom, thunder, howl, bay, bawl, yell, bluster, uproar, din, clamor, clash, detonation, explosion, barrage, reverberation, rumble; see also **cry** 1, 2, **noise** 1. — *Ant.* SILENCE, whisper, sigh.

**roar,** *v.* — *Syn.* bellow, shout, boom, thunder, howl, bay, bawl, yell, clamor, rumble, drum, detonate, explode, reverberate, resound, reecho; see also **cry** 3, **sound** 1.

**roast,** *n.* Cuts of meat used as roasts include: shoulder, breast, rib, cross rib, rump, chuck, brisket, crown, leg, top round, bottom round, blade; Kinds of meat used for roasts include: lamb, beef, pork, veal, venison; see also **meat.**

**roast,** *v.* — *Syn.* broil, barbecue, bake; see **cook.**

**rob,** *v.* — *Syn.* thieve, take, burglarize, strip, plunder, loot, deprive of, withhold from, defraud, cheat, swindle, pilfer, break into, hold up, stick up, mug, purloin, filch, lift, abscond with, embezzle, defalcate, peculate, shoplift, despoil, pillage, sack, burgle\*, snitch\*, pinch\*, push over\*, knock over\*, roll\*, swipe\*, cop\*, rip off\*; see also **steal.**

**robber,** *n.* — *Syn.* thief, burglar, housebreaker, pickpocket, mugger, shoplifter, cheat, crook\*, bandit, holdup man, cat burglar, second-story worker, sneak thief, bank robber, swindler, embezzler, peculator, pilferer, kleptomaniac, looter, despoiler, plunderer, pillager, brigand, freebooter, pirate, marauder, shanghaier, raider, forager, thug, desperado, forger, corsair, privateer, buccaneer, highwayman, footpad, hijacker, cattle thief, cutpurse, purse snatcher, sharper, safecracker, fence\*, grafter\*, rustler\*, con artist\*, ripoff artist\*, cracksman\*, yegg\*, clip artist\*, come-on\*, chiseler\*, paper hanger\*, stick-up man\*; see also **cheat** 1, **criminal.**

**robbery,** *n.* — *Syn.* burglary, larceny, thievery; see **crime** 2, **theft.**

*See Synonym Study at* THEFT.

**robe,** *n.* — *Syn.* gown, dress, garment, vestment, cassock, mantle, draperies, covering, cape, caftan, dressing gown, bathrobe, kimono, negligee, peignoir, wrapper, tea gown, *robe-de-chambre* (French), housecoat, housedress; see also **clothes.**

**robot,** *n.* — *Syn.* automaton, android, Frankenstein, mechanical monster, humanoid, thinking machine, mechanical man, cyborg.

**robust,** *modif.* **1.** [Healthy] — *Syn.* hale, hearty, sound; see **healthy** 1.

**2.** [Strong] — *Syn.* sturdy, muscular, hardy; see **strong** 1.

**rock,** *n.* **1.** [A solidified form of earth] — *Syn.* stone, mineral mass, dike, mineral body, earth crust; see also **metal, mineral, ore.**

Types of rocks include: igneous, sedimentary, stratified, metamorphic; concretion, gypsum, alabaster, limestone, freestone, lodestone, sandstone, conglomerate, marble, dolomite; chalk, soapstone, slate, shale, mica; granite, lava, pumice, basalt, felsite, peridot, quartz, obsidian, porphyry, rhyolite, ironstone, gneiss, tufa, schist.

**2.** [A piece of rock, sense 1] — *Syn.* stone, boulder, cobblestone, pebble, fieldstone, cliff, crag, promontory, scarp, escarpment, reef, chip, flake, sliver, building stone, paving block, slab.

**3.** [Anything firm or solid] — *Syn.* defense, support, Rock of Gibraltar; see **foundation** 2.

**4.** [Rhythmic popular music] — *Syn.* rock-and-roll, heavy metal, hard rock, punk rock, progressive rock, acid rock, country rock, folk rock, rhythm and blues, soul music, Motown, funk, house music, dance music, disco, pop; see also **dance** 1, **music** 1.

**on the rocks\*, 1.** bankrupt, destitute, impoverished; see **poor** 1, **ruined** 4.

**2.** in ruins, foundered, in a shambles; see **ruined** 2.

**3.** over ice cubes, on ice, undiluted, straight.

**rock,** *v.* — *Syn.* sway, vibrate, reel, totter, swing, move, push and pull, agitate, roll, pitch, shake, shove, jolt, jiggle, quake, convulse, tremble, undulate, oscillate, quiver, quaver, wobble; see also **wave** 3.

**rock-bottom,** *modif.* — *Syn.* low, lowest, inferior; see **lowest, poor** 2.

**rocket,** *n.* — *Syn.* projectile, missile, retrorocket, spacecraft, guided missile, ballistic missile, flying missile; see also **spacecraft.**

Kinds of rockets include: liquid-fuel, solid-fuel, space, long-range, air-to-air (ATA), air-to-ground (ATG), ground-to-air (GTA), ground to ground (GTG), bar-

rage rocket, high velocity aircraft rocket (HVAR), ship-to-shore (STS), ship-to-ship, multiple re-entry vehicle (MRV), multiple independently targetable re-entry vehicle (MIRV); space shuttle.

**rocket,** *v.* — *Syn.* fly, climb, shoot up, skyrocket, ascend, soar, spring up, zoom.

**rocking chair,** *n.* — *Syn.* rocker, easy chair, armchair, Boston rocker, swing rocker, platform rocker; see also **chair** 1, **furniture, seat** 1.

**rocky,** *modif.* **1.** [Rocklike] — *Syn.* stony, flinty, hard, inflexible, solid, petrified, unfeeling, pitiless, obdurate, ragged, jagged, rugged, craggy, rockbound; see also **stone.**

**2.** [Shaky] — *Syn.* unsteady, uncertain, wobbly, chancy; see **uncertain** 2, **unsteady** 1.

**rococo,** *modif.* — *Syn.* extravagant, embellished, baroque, florid; see **ornate** 1.

**rod,** *n.* **1.** [A rodlike body] — *Syn.* staff, bar, pole, wand, stave, baton, spike, pin, rodule, cylinder, bacillus, bacillary body, bacilliform body, cylindrical object, scepter, mace, stick, twig, switch, whip, stock, stalk, trunk; see also **stick.**

**2.** [A fishing rod] — *Syn.* pole, bamboo, rod and reel, tackle.

Kinds of fishing rods include: steel, jointed, bamboo, willow, bait, trolling, casting, fly, trout, salmon, bass, deep-sea, tarpon, swordfish.

**rodent,** *n.* Common varieties of rodents include: rat, mouse, squirrel, chipmunk, beaver, porcupine, rabbit, muskrat, weasel, prairie dog, gopher, marmot, ground hog, woodchuck, spermophile, ground squirrel, chinchilla, capybara, vole, mole, hare, pika, little chief hare, paca, agouti, guinea pig, gerbil, hamster.

**rodeo,** *n.* Rodeo events include: broncobusting, steer wrestling, bulldogging, calf roping, cutting out steers, saddle bronc riding, bareback riding, bull riding.

**rodomontade,** *n.* — *Syn.* bluster, pretension, grandiloquence, exaggeration; see **bravado.**

**rogue,** *n.* — *Syn.* scoundrel, scamp, miscreant; see **criminal, rascal.**

**roguery,** *n.* — *Syn.* trickery, villainy, fraud, rascality; see **deception** 1, **dishonesty, mischief.**

**roguish,** *modif.* **1.** [Dishonest] — *Syn.* unscrupulous, sly, corrupt; see **dishonest** 1, **false** 1.

**2.** [Mischievous] — *Syn.* playful, impish, arch; see **jaunty, naughty.**

**roil,** *v.* — *Syn.* irritate, annoy, agitate, stir up; see **bother** 2, 3, **disturb** 2.

**roily,** *modif.* — *Syn.* murky, turbid, mucky; see **muddy** 1, **turbid.**

**role,** *n.* — *Syn.* function, part, character, title role, cameo, bit part, supporting role, impersonation, performance, presentation, acting, lines, characterization, guise, capacity, position, office, task, use, purpose; see also **actor** 1.

**roll,** *n.* **1.** [The act of rolling] — *Syn.* turn, turning over, throw, toss, revolution, rotation, wheeling, trundling, whirl, gyration.

**2.** [A rolled up object] — *Syn.* scroll, volute, spiral, coil, whorl, convolution, cartouche, fold, shell, cone, tube, cylinder, cornucopia.

**3.** [A long, heavy sound] — *Syn.* thunder, rumble, roar, drumbeat; see **noise** 1.

**4.** [A small, fine bread]. Types of rolls include: Parker House, potato, egg, water, hard, butter, finger, cinnamon, sweet, crescent, croissant, French, clover-leaf, poppy-seed, biscuit, danish, brioche, dinner; bagel, hot cross bun; see also **bread** 1, **pastry.**

**5.** [A list] — *Syn.* register, roster, muster roll, list of names; see **list, record** 1.

*See Synonym Study at* LIST.

**strike from the rolls** — *Syn.* expel, reject, cast out; see **dismiss** 1, **oust.**

**roll,** *v.* **1.** [To move by rotation, or in rotating numbers] — *Syn.* rotate, come around, swing around, wheel, come in turn, circle, alternate, follow, succeed, be in sequence, follow in due course; see also sense 3; **move** 1, **turn** 1.

**2.** [To cause to roll] — *Syn.* drive, push, impel, propel, throw, toss, twirl, trundle.

**3.** [To revolve] — *Syn.* turn, turn over, pivot, wind, spin, spiral, reel, gyrate, gyre, whirl, twirl, swirl, swivel, eddy, pirouette; see also sense 1; **rock.**

**4.** [To make into a roll] — *Syn.* twist, fold, curve, bend, arch, bow, furl, coil, spiral, curl, wind. — *Ant.* SPREAD, stretch, flatten.

**5.** [To smooth with a roller] — *Syn.* press, level, flatten, spread, roll out, pulverize, grind.

**6.** [To flow] — *Syn.* undulate, run, wave, surge, glide, billow; see also **flow** 1.

**7.** [To produce a relatively deep, continuous sound] — *Syn.* rumble, ruffle, drum, reverberate, cannonade, resound, echo, thunder, roar; see also **roar, sound** 1.

**8.** [To travel] — *Syn.* drive, coast, bowl, make time; see **drive** 3, **travel** 2.

**9.** [To function] — *Syn.* work, go, start production; see **operate** 2.

**rolled,** *modif.* **1.** [Made into a roll] — *Syn.* twisted, folded, furled, curved, bent, bowed, coiled, spiraled, curled, arched, voluted, convoluted, wound. — *Ant.* SPREAD, unrolled, opened out.

**2.** [Flattened] — *Syn.* pressed, leveled, evened; see **flat** 1.

**roller,** *n.* — *Syn.* wave, billow, breaker, surge; see **wave** 1.

*See Synonym Study at* WAVE.

**rollick,** *v.* — *Syn.* romp, frolic, revel; see **play** 1, 2.

**rollicking,** *modif.* — *Syn.* jolly, exuberant, high-spirited, carefree; see **jaunty.**

**roll in,** *v.* — *Syn.* arrive, appear, show up, pour in; see **accumulate** 1, **arrive** 1.

**roll out,** *v.* — *Syn.* unroll, unfurl, spread out, flatten; see **roll** 5, **unfold** 1.

**Roman,** *modif.* **1.** [Referring to the culture centered at Rome] — *Syn.* Latin, classic, classical, late classic, Augustan, ancient, Italic; see also **ancient** 2, **classical** 2.

**2.** [Referring to the city of Rome] — *Syn.* imperial, papal, eternal; see **catholic** 3, **Italian.**

**Romance,** *modif.* — *Syn.* Romanic, Latinic, Latin, Italic; see **French** 2, **Italian, Spanish.**

Languages descended from Latin include: Portuguese, Spanish, Catalan, Provençal, Rhaeto-Romanic, Italian, French, Romansh.

**romance,** *n.* **1.** [Experiences that excite the imagination] — *Syn.* fancy, fantasy, the picturesque, adventure, excitement, love, passion, romanticism, idealization, allure, fascination, enchantment, exoticism, glamour, thrill, daring enterprise, bold venture.

**2.** [A love affair] — *Syn.* affair, courtship, amour; see **affair** 2, **love** 1.

**3.** [A tale of love and adventure] — *Syn.* novel, romantic novel, fiction, love story, historical romance, Gothic novel, bodice-ripper, picaresque tale, adventure story, ballad, lyric tale, metrical romance, Arthurian romance, *chanson de geste* (French), romaunt; see also **story.**

**romantic,** *modif.* **1.** [Referring to love and adventure]

— *Syn.* fanciful, visionary, quixotic, idealistic, impractical, passionate, adventurous, daring, romanticized, idealized, unrealistic, extravagant, wild, dreamy, idyllic, lyric, poetic, chivalrous, courtly, knightly.

**2.** [Sentimental or loving] — *Syn.* amorous, tender, ardent, lovey-dovey\*; see **passionate** 2, **sentimental.**

**3.** [Referring to the Romantic Movement; *often capital*] — *Syn.* Rousseauistic, Byronic, Wordsworthian, *Sturm und Drang* (German).

**romanticist,** *n.* — *Syn.* romantic, utopist, sentimentalist; see **idealist.**

**Rome,** *n.* **1.** [Leading city in the Italian peninsula] — *Syn.* city of the Caesars, the Eternal City, city on seven hills, imperial city.

**2.** [The Catholic Church] — *Syn.* the Vatican, Catholicism, the Pope, Holy See, Mother Church; see also **church** 3.

**Romeo,** *n.* — *Syn.* lover, beau, philanderer, Lothario; see **lover** 1, **rake** 1.

**romp,** *n.* — *Syn.* frolic, play, gambol, caper, frisk, dance, skip, hop, rollicking, cavorting, sport.

**romp,** *v.* — *Syn.* gambol, celebrate, frolic; see **play** 1, 2.

**rompers,** *pl.n.* — *Syn.* jumpers, play suit, overalls; see **pants** 1.

**roof,** *n.* — *Syn.* rooftop, housetop, cover, shelter, tent, awning, house, habitation, home.

Styles of roofs include: gable, gambrel, jerkinhead, hip, break, dome, flat, spire, cupola, mansard, French, pyramidal, dormer-windowed, penthouse; see also **roofing.**

**roofing,** *n.* Varieties of roofing material include: felt, composition, roll roofing, shingles, wood shingles, composition shingles, asbestos, slate shingles, tile, asphalt, tar, shake, copper, tin, galvanized iron, thatch, straw, sod.

**rook,** *v.* — *Syn.* trick, swindle, cheat; see **cheat, deceive.**

**rookery,** *n.* — *Syn.* colony, breeding ground, breeding place, communal nest, haunt.

**room,** *n.* **1.** [Space] — *Syn.* vastness, reach, sweep, scope; see **capacity** 1, **extent, leeway.**

**2.** [An enclosure] — *Syn.* chamber, apartment, salon, cabin, cubicle, compartment, alcove, niche, vault.

Kinds of rooms include: living, sitting, drawing, dining, reception, bed, music, play, game, bath, guest, family, furnace, waiting, boudoir, cupboard, foyer, vestibule, study, library, den, recreation room, rec room, kitchen, hall, master bedroom, parlor, wardrobe, closet, press, scullery, pantry, basement, utility, laundry, sewing, cellar, attic, garret, anteroom, dormitory, alcove, ward, nacelle, barrack, office, breakfast nook, nursery, studio, schoolroom, loft, porch, sun room; see also **dining room.**

**3.** [The possibility of admission] — *Syn.* opening, place, opportunity; see **vacancy** 1.

**4.** [A rented sleeping room; *often plural*] — *Syn.* lodgings, chambers, quarters, studio, one-room apartment, bed-sitting room (British), efficiency apartment, flat, bachelor apartment\*, digs\*, pad\*; see also **apartment, bedroom.**

**roomer,** *n.* — *Syn.* lodger, occupant, dweller, paying guest; see **renter, tenant.**

**rooming house,** *n.* — *Syn.* lodging house, boardinghouse, family hotel, hotel, quarters, chambers, *pension* (French), *pensione* (Italian), bunkhouse, digs\*; see also **home** 1.

**roommate,** *n.* — *Syn.* companion, friend, flatmate, bunkmate, bedfellow, tentmate, roomie\*, bunky\*; see also **friend** 1.

**roomy,** *modif.* — *Syn.* spacious, capacious, extensive, ample; see **large** 1.

**roost,** *n.* — *Syn.* perch, roosting place, birdhouse, henhouse, resting place, landing place.

**rooster,** *n.* — *Syn.* cock, chanticleer, cockerel; see **chicken** 1.

**root,** *n.* **1.** [An underground portion of a plant] — *Syn.* radix, rootlet, root hair, tuber, taproot, radicle, rhizome, rootstock; see also **bulb.**
Types of roots include: conical, napiform, fusiform, fibrous, moniliform, nodulose, tuberous, adventitious, prop, aerial, tap; rhizome, radix, tuber, bulb, taproot.
**2.** [The cause or basis] — *Syn.* source, reason, motive, heart; see **origin** 2, 3.
*See Synonym Study at* ORIGIN.
**take root** — *Syn.* begin growing, start, become established; see **begin** 2, **grow** 1.

**rooted,** *modif.* — *Syn.* implanted, grounded, based on, fixed in; see **established** 1, **firm** 1.

**rope,** *n.* — *Syn.* cord, cordage, braiding, string, thread, strand, line, tape, lace, noose, longe.
Kinds of rope include: ratline, shroud, halyard, lanyard, stay, brace, rope ladder, painter, cable, hawser, halter, lariat, lasso; braided rope, wire rope, twine.
**at the end of one's rope** — *Syn.* desperate, despairing, in despair; see **frantic, hopeless** 2.
**give someone enough rope**★ — *Syn.* permit, give freedom, give free rein; see **allow** 1.
**know the ropes**★ — *Syn.* be experienced, understand, know the score★; see **know** 1.
**on the ropes**★ — *Syn.* near collapse, close to ruin, in danger; see **endangered.**

**roped,** *modif.* — *Syn.* tied, fast, fastened; see **firm** 1.

**roped off,** *modif.* — *Syn.* segregated, private, restricted; see **reserved** 1, **restricted.**

**ropy,** *modif.* — *Syn.* gelatinous, glutinous, stringy; see **adhesive, fibrous.**

**rosary,** *n.* — *Syn.* prayers, beads, series of prayers, string of beads.

**rose,** *modif.* — *Syn.* deep pink, reddish, rose-colored, rosy, dawn-tinted, flushed; see also **pink, red.**

**rose,** *n.* Kinds of roses include: wild, tea, miniature, climbing tea, hybrid tea, hybrid perpetual, rugosa, hybrid rugosa, polyantha, sweet briar, shrub, multiflora, floribunda, chinensis, noisette, musk, moss, climbing, bush, cabbage, cinnamon, eglantine, rambler; see also **flower** 2.
Varieties of roses include: Jacqueminot, jack★, American Beauty, Rubrifolia, Crimson Glory, Etoile de Hollande, Duquesa de Penaranda, President Hoover, Talisman, Condesa de Sastago, Santa Anita, Mlle. Cecile Brunner, Grand Duchess Charlotte, Heart's Desire, Kaiserin Auguste Viktoria, Christopher Stone, McGredy's Yellow, McGredy's Ivory, Rouge Mallerin, Mrs. Pierre Dupont, Frau Karl Druschki, Soeur Therese, Golden Dawn, King Midas, Betty Prior, Pink Aachen, White Aachen, Charlotte Armstrong, Paul Neyron, La Jolla Rohan.

**roseate,** *modif.* — *Syn.* cherry, blushing, rosy; see **pink, red, rose.**

**roster,** *n.* — *Syn.* roll, slate, membership, program; see **catalog, list, record** 1, **register** 1.

**rostrum,** *n.* — *Syn.* platform, stage, pulpit; see **lectern, platform** 1.

**rosy,** *modif.* **1.** [Rose-colored] — *Syn.* deep pink, pale cardinal, roseate; see **blushing, pink, red, rose.**
**2.** [Promising] — *Syn.* bright, pleasing, alluring, optimistic, favorable, cheerful, glowing; see also **hopeful** 2.

**rot,** *interj.* — *Syn.* humbug, nonsense, tush, twaddle, bosh★.

**rot,** *n.* **1.** [The process of rotting] — *Syn.* decomposition, corruption, disintegration; see **decay** 1, 2.
**2.** [Nonsense] — *Syn.* trash, silliness, foolishness; see **nonsense** 1.

**rot,** *v.* — *Syn.* decay, spoil, disintegrate, decompose; see **decay.**
*See Synonym Study at* DECAY.

**rotary,** *modif.* — *Syn.* rotating, whirling, encircling, turning; see **revolving** 1, 2.

**rotate,** *v.* **1.** [To turn around an axis] — *Syn.* pivot, twist, wheel, revolve; see **turn** 1.
**2.** [To alternate] — *Syn.* interchange, switch, take turns; see **alternate** 1, **exchange** 1.

**rotation,** *n.* — *Syn.* turn, circumrotation, circle; see **revolution** 1.

**rote,** *n.* — *Syn.* learning, routine, memorization; see **memory** 1, **repetition.**

**rotten,** *modif.* **1.** [Having rotted] — *Syn.* bad, rotting, putrifying, decaying, putrescent, putrified, spoiled, decomposed, decayed, offensive, disgusting, rancid, sour, feculent, purulent, pustular, rank, foul, corrupt, polluted, infected, loathsome, overripe, bad-smelling, putrid, tainted, crumbled, disintegrated, stale, noisome, smelling, fetid, mephitic, noxious. — *Ant.* FRESH, unspoiled, good.
**2.** [Not sound] — *Syn.* unsound, defective, rotted, crumbling, corroded, rusted, diseased, marred, impaired, bruised, injured, shaky, tottering, deteriorated, wasted, withering; see also **crumbly, weak** 2. — *Ant.* STRONG, sound, healthy.
**3.** [Corrupt] — *Syn.* dishonest, vitiated, base, low, contemptible, hateful, despicable, detestable, mean, nasty, scurvy, crooked, unscrupulous, unethical, immoral, vile, lowdown★, good-for-nothing★; see also **dishonest** 1, 2, **wicked** 1. — *Ant.* honest, ethical, scrupulous.
**4.** [★Very bad] — *Syn.* unsatisfactory, unpleasant, disagreeable, lousy★; see **offensive** 2, **poor** 2, **unsatisfactory.**

**rotting,** *modif.* — *Syn.* crumbling, decaying, wasting away; see **decaying, rotten** 1, 2.

**rotund,** *modif.* **1.** [Round] — *Syn.* circular, spherical, globular, plump; see **fat** 1, **round** 1.
**2.** [Full-toned] — *Syn.* resounding, vibrant, resonant, sonorous; see **loud** 1.

**rotunda,** *n.* — *Syn.* arcade, cupola, dome; see **building** 1, **dome** 1.

**roué,** *n.* — *Syn.* sensualist, playboy, reprobate; see **lecher, rake** 1.

**rouge,** *n.* — *Syn.* blusher, reddener, dye, paint, red, carmine, eosin, war paint★, drugstore complexion★; see also **cosmetic, makeup** 1.

**rough,** *modif.* **1.** [Not smooth] — *Syn.* unequal, broken, coarse, choppy, ruffled, uneven, ridged, rugged, scabrous, irregular, unsanded, needing sanding, needing finishing, needing smoothing, not sanded, not smoothed, not finished, unfinished, lacking the finishing touches, bumpy, rocky, stony, jagged, grinding, knobby, sharpening, cutting, sharp, crinkled, crumpled, rumpled, scraggly, scraggy, hairy, shaggy, hirsute, bushy, tufted, bearded, woolly, nappy, unshaven, unshorn, gnarled, knotty, nodose, bristly. — *Ant.* smooth, LEVEL, even.
**2.** [Not gentle] — *Syn.* harsh, strict, stern; see **severe** 2.
**3.** [Crude] — *Syn.* boorish, uncivil, uncultivated; see **coarse** 2, **rude** 1.
**4.** [Not quiet] — *Syn.* buffeting, stormy, tumultuous; see **stormy** 1, **turbulent.**

**5.** [Unfinished] — *Syn.* incomplete, imperfect, unpolished; see **crude** 1, **unfinished** 1.

**6.** [Approximate] — *Syn.* inexact, imprecise, estimated; see **approximate**.

**rough,** *n.* **1.** [Any roughness] — *Syn.* unevenness, irregularity, bumpiness; see **roughness** 1.

**2.** [In golf, any unkempt part of the course] — *Syn.* tall grass, weeds, brush, stoniness, off the fairway, fog★, jungle★.

**in the rough** — *Syn.* unfinished, unrefined, rough; see **crude** 1, **unfinished** 1.

**rough draft,** *n.* — *Syn.* outline, blueprint, first draft; see **plan** 1.

**roughhouse,** *n.* — *Syn.* roughness, rowdiness, horseplay; see **confusion** 2, **fight** 1, **joke** 1.

**roughly,** *modif.* **1.** [Approximately] — *Syn.* about, in round numbers, by guess; see **approximately**.

**2.** [In a brutal manner] — *Syn.* coarsely, cruelly, harshly; see **brutally**.

**3.** [In an uneven manner] — *Syn.* irregularly, bumpily, stumblingly; see **unevenly**.

**roughness,** *n.* **1.** [The quality of being rough on the surface] — *Syn.* unevenness, coarseness, brokenness, bumpiness, break, crack, ragged edge, scarification, irregularity, scratch, nick, raggedness, jaggedness, crinkledness, wrinkledness, shagginess, bushiness, beardedness, hairiness, bristling, woolliness; see also **hole** 2. — *Ant.* REGULARITY, smoothness, evenness.

**2.** [The quality of being rough in conduct] — *Syn.* harshness, severity, hardness, coarseness, rudeness, brusqueness, incivility, crudity. — *Ant.* KINDNESS, gentility, courtesy.

**round,** *modif.* **1.** [Having the shape of a globe] — *Syn.* spherical, globular, spheroid, orbed, orbicular, orbiculate, globe-shaped, globose, ball-shaped, domical, rotund.

**2.** [Having the shape of a disk] — *Syn.* circular, cylindrical, ringed, annular, oval, disk-shaped.

**3.** [Curved] — *Syn.* arched, arced, rounded, bowed, looped, whorled, recurved, incurved, coiled, curled.

**4.** [Approximate] — *Syn.* rough, in tens, in hundreds; see **approximate**.

**5.** [Large] — *Syn.* liberal, generous, expansive, extensive; see **large** 1.

**6.** [Complete] — *Syn.* rounded, done, accomplished; see **finished** 1.

**7.** [Around] — *Syn.* about, near, in the neighborhood of, close to; see **approximately**.

---

*SYN.* — **round,** the most inclusive of these words, applies to anything shaped like a circle, sphere, or cylinder, or like a part of any of these; **spherical** applies to a round body or mass having the surface equally distant from the center at all points; **globular** is used of things that are ball-shaped but not necessarily perfect spheres; **circular** is applied to round lines, or round flat surfaces, in the shape of a ring or disk, and may or may not imply correspondence in form with a perfect circle; **annular** applies to ringlike forms or structures, as the markings in a cross section of a tree

---

**round,** *n.* **1.** [A round object] — *Syn.* circle, ring, orb, globe; see **circle** 1.

**2.** [A period of action] — *Syn.* bout, course, whirl, cycle, circuit, routine, performance, tour, beat; see also **sequence** 1, **series**.

**3.** [A unit of ammunition] — *Syn.* cartridge, charge, load; see **ammunition, bullet, load** 3, **shot** 2.

**4.** [A rung] — *Syn.* crosspiece, step, stair, tread; see **rung**.

**go the rounds** — *Syn.* circulate, make the rounds, spread, be passed on; see **circulate** 1.

**round,** *v.* **1.** [To turn] — *Syn.* whirl, wheel, spin; see **turn** 1.

**2.** [To make round] — *Syn.* curve, convolute, bow, arch, bend, loop, whorl, shape, form, recurve, coil, fill out, curl, mold. — *Ant.* STRAIGHTEN, flatten, level.

**roundabout,** *modif.* — *Syn.* indirect, circuitous, devious, deviating; see **indirect**.

**rounder★,** *n.* — *Syn.* carouser, wastrel, vagrant; see **drunkard**.

**roundly,** *modif.* — *Syn.* thoroughly, soundly, wholly; see **completely**.

**roundness,** *n.* — *Syn.* fullness, completeness, circularity, oneness, inclusiveness, wholeness.

**round off,** *v.* — *Syn.* approximate, give a rough figure for, express as a round number; see **estimate** 1.

**round out,** *v.* — *Syn.* expand, fill out, enlarge; see **grow** 1.

**roundup,** *n.* — *Syn.* gathering, corralling, herding, wrangling, assembly; see also **collection** 1.

**round up★,** *v.* — *Syn.* collect, gather, bring in; see **assemble** 2.

**rouse,** *v.* **1.** [To waken] — *Syn.* arouse, wake up, awaken; see **wake** 1.

**2.** [To stimulate] — *Syn.* stimulate, urge, stir, provoke; see **animate** 1, **excite** 1, 2.

*See Synonym Study at* STIR.

**roustabout,** *n.* — *Syn.* laborer, stevedore, longshoreman, roughneck★; see **laborer, worker**.

**rout,** *n.* — *Syn.* flight, retreat, confusion; see **defeat** 2, **loss** 1.

**rout,** *v.* — *Syn.* overcome, overthrow, scatter, hunt, beat, defeat, conquer, discomfit, overpower, overmaster, overmatch, outmaneuver, vanquish, drive off, put to flight, repulse, subjugate, subdue; see also **defeat** 1, 2, 3.

*See Synonym Study at* DEFEAT.

**route,** *n.* **1.** [A course being followed] — *Syn.* way, course, road, highway, path, track, beat, circuit, round, rounds, run, range, tour, direction, tack, trajectory, line of passage, detour; see also **road** 1.

**2.** [A projected course] — *Syn.* itinerary, plans, map, layout, plot, diagram, chart, journey; see also **plan** 2, **program** 2.

**routed,** *modif.* **1.** [Provided with a route] — *Syn.* directed, laid out, ordered; see **sent**.

**2.** [Moved along a route] — *Syn.* forwarded, conveyed, carried; see **moved** 1, **transported**.

**routine,** *modif.* — *Syn.* usual, customary, everyday, methodical; see **conventional** 1, **habitual** 1, **regular** 3.

**routine,** *n.* — *Syn.* round, cycle, habit; see **custom** 1, **method** 2, **system** 2.

**rove,** *v.* — *Syn.* walk, meander, wander; see **roam**.

**roving,** *n.* — *Syn.* wayfaring, traveling, moving, floating; see **rambling** 1, **wandering** 1.

**row,** *n.* — *Syn.* series, line, rank, file; see **line** 1.

**hard row to hoe** — *Syn.* dilemma, problem, difficult task; see **difficulty** 1.

**in a row** — *Syn.* in succession, successively, in a line; see **consecutively**.

**row,** *n.* — *Syn.* squabble, quarrel, commotion; see **dispute, disturbance** 1, **fight** 1.

**rowboat,** *n.* — *Syn.* vessel, skiff, dinghy; see **boat**.

**rowdy,** *modif.* — *Syn.* boisterous, disorderly, rough; see **loud** 2, **unruly**.

**rowdy,** *n.* — *Syn.* roisterer, brawler, hooligan, tough, ruffian, thug, hoodlum, hood*, roughneck*; see also **rascal.**

**royal,** *modif.* **1.** [Pertaining to a sovereign or a sovereign's family] — *Syn.* kingly, queenly, princely, regal, imperial, high, elevated, highborn, noble, monarchic, reigning, regnant, ruling, authoritative, dominant, absolute, sovereign, paramount, supreme, born to the purple*; see also **noble** 3. — *Ant.* HUMBLE, common, lowborn.

**2.** [Having qualities befitting royalty] — *Syn.* noble, regal, great, grand, stately, lofty, illustrious, eminent, superior, worthy, honorable, dignified, kingly, queenly, princely, chivalrous, courteous, great-hearted, largehearted, majestic, magnificent, splendid, courtly, impressive, commanding, aristocratic, lordly, august, imposing, superb, glorious, resplendent, gorgeous, sublime; see also sense 1; **noble** 1, 2. — *Ant.* MEAN, ignoble, base.

**royally,** *modif.* — *Syn.* magnanimously, liberally, munificently, bounteously, lavishly; see also **generously** 1.

**royalty,** *n.* — *Syn.* kingship, queenship, sovereignty, nobility, authority, eminence, distinction, blood, birth, high descent, rank, greatness, power, supremacy, primacy, the crown, suzerainty; see also **aristocracy.**

Degrees of royalty include: czar, czarina, czarevitch, czarevna, grand duke, grand duchess, shah, emperor, empress, king, queen, prince of Wales, princess of Wales, margrave, margravine, archduke, archduchess, princess royal, queen mother, prince consort, prince, prince regent, dauphin, princess, duke, duchess.

**rub,** *n.* **1.** [A rubbing action] — *Syn.* massage, rubdown, brushing, stroke, smoothing, scraping, scouring, buffing, rasping, friction, attrition; see also **touch** 2.

**2.** [A difficulty] — *Syn.* hindrance, obstacle, dilemma; see **difficulty** 1, 2, **impediment** 1. — *Ant.* ANSWER, solution, aid.

**rub,** *v.* **1.** [To subject to friction] — *Syn.* stroke, scrape, smooth, abrade, scour, grate, grind, wear away, graze, rasp, knead, fret, massage, rub down, polish, shine, burnish, buff, brush, curry, scrub, swab, erase, rub out, file, chafe, clean.

**2.** [To apply by rubbing] — *Syn.* brush, daub, bedaub, paint, smear, spread, cover, coat, plaster, anoint, slather*.

**rubber,** *modif.* — *Syn.* elastic, rubbery, soft, stretchable, stretching, stretchy, rebounding, flexible, ductile, lively, buoyant, resilient.

**rubber,** *n.*

Types of rubber include: India, native, wild, raw, crude, crepe, vulcanized, hard, reclaimed, synthetic, butyl, methyl.

**rubbish,** *n.* **1.** [Trash] — *Syn.* litter, debris, waste; see **trash** 1.

**2.** [Nonsense] — *Syn.* drivel, twaddle, rot; see **nonsense** 1.

**rubicund,** *modif.* — *Syn.* ruddy, rosy, reddish; see **red.**

**rub out,** *v.* **1.** [To cancel] — *Syn.* eradicate, erase, delete; see **cancel** 1, **eliminate** 1.

**2.** [*To kill] — *Syn.* murder, slay, shoot; see **kill** 1.

**ruddy,** *modif.* — *Syn.* rosy, reddish, bronzed; see **red.**

**rude,** *modif.* **1.** [Boorish] — *Syn.* coarse, rough, uncouth, gauche, rustic, ungainly, awkward, lubberly, crude, vulgar, gross, crass, unrefined, uncultivated, uncultured, unpolished, uncivilized, blunt, rugged, barbarous, lumpish, ungraceful, hulking, loutish, oafish, antic, rowdy, disorderly, rowdyish, brutish, clownish, stupid, untrained, indecorous, unknowing, untaught, slovenly, ill-bred, inelegant, ignorant, inexpert, illiterate, clumsy, gawky, slouching, graceless, ungraceful, lumbering,

green, unacquainted, unenlightened, uneducated, indecent, ribald, homely, common, outlandish, disgraceful, inappropriate, hayseed*, hick*. — *Ant.* CULTURED, urbane, suave.

**2.** [Not polite] — *Syn.* impolite, discourteous, ill-mannered, uncivil, churlish, sullen, surly, sharp, harsh, gruff, brusque, blunt, abrupt, tactless, curt, short, snappish, snarling, ungracious, unkind, ungentle, truculent, crabbed, sour, disdainful, unmannerly, improper, shabby, ill-chosen, ungentlemanly, fresh, abusive, forward, loud, loud-mouthed, boorish, bold, brazen, audacious, brash, arrogant, supercilious, blustering, crass, raw, saucy, impudent, pert, unabashed, contumelious, sharp-tongued, mocking, barefaced, insolent, impertinent, offensive, uncalled-for, vituperative, naughty, hostile, insulting, nasty, disrespectful, scornful, flippant, presumptuous, sarcastic, defiant, outrageous, imperious, swaggering, disparaging, contemptuous, unfeeling, insensitive, scoffing, scurrilous, disagreeable, domineering, overbearing, high-handed, self-assertive, brutal, severe, hard, cocky, bullying, cheeky, nervy, assuming, dictatorial, magisterial, officious, meddling, intrusive, meddlesome, acrimonious, bitter, uncivilized, ill-tempered, bad-tempered, snippy*, sassy*, flip*, snotty*, snooty*, brassy*, uppity*, crusty*, bold as brass*. — *Ant.* POLITE, courteous, mannerly.

**3.** [Harsh] — *Syn.* rough, violent, stormy; see **turbulent.**

**4.** [Approximate] — *Syn.* guessed, surmised, imprecise; see **approximate.**

**5.** [Coarse] — *Syn.* rough, roughhewn, unpolished, ill-proportioned; see **crude** 1.

**6.** [Primitive] — *Syn.* ignorant, uncivilized, barbarous; see **primitive** 3.

---

**SYN.** — **rude,** in this comparison, implies a deliberate lack of consideration for others' feelings and connotes, especially, insolence, impudence, etc. /it was *rude* of you to ignore your uncle/; **ill-mannered** suggests ignorance of the amenities of social behavior rather than deliberate rudeness /a well-meaning but *ill-mannered* fellow/; **boorish** now connotes insensitivity and is applied to one who is rude or ill-mannered in a coarse, loud, or overbearing way; **impolite** implies merely a failure to observe the forms of polite society /it would be *impolite* to leave so early/; **discourteous** suggests a lack of dignified consideration for others /a *discourteous* reply/; **uncivil** implies a disregarding of even the most elementary of good manners /her *uncivil* treatment of the waiter/

---

**rudely,** *modif.* — *Syn.* impolitely, discourteously, impudently, crudely, coarsely, indecently, barbarously, roughly, harshly, sharply, bluntly, curtly, boorishly, ungraciously, uncivilly, tactlessly, uncouthly, vulgarly, indecorously, insolently, contemptuously, disrespectfully, brutally, dictatorially, churlishly, sullenly, gruffly, impishly, saucily, loudly, brazenly, blusteringly, crassly, unabashedly, mockingly, sassily*, snootily*, snippily*. — *Ant.* POLITELY, civilly, suavely.

**rudeness,** *n.* — *Syn.* discourtesy, bad manners, vulgarity, incivility, impoliteness, impudence, disrespect, misbehavior, barbarity, unmannerliness, ill-breeding, crudity, brutality, barbarism, tactlessness, boorishness, unbecoming conduct, lack of courtesy, crudeness, gaucherie, *brusquerie* (French), grossness, coarseness, bluntness, effrontery, impertinence, insolence, audacity, boldness, shamelessness, presumption, officiousness, intrusiveness, brazenness, sauciness, defiance, bumptiousness, contempt, back talk, ill temper, irritability, disdain, asperity, harshness, sharpness, acrimony, unkindness, ungraciousness, social breach, conduct not becoming a gentleman, gall*, sass*, lip*, nerve*, brass*, crust*, cheek*.

**rudimentary,** *modif.* **1.** [Primary] — *Syn.* basic, elemental, initial; see **fundamental** 1, **original** 1.

**2.** [Immature] — *Syn.* undeveloped, embryonic, simple, uncompleted; see **crude** 1, **unfinished** 1.

**rudiments,** *pl.n.* — *Syn.* nucleus, first principles, beginning, source; see **elements, origin** 2.

**rue,** *v.* — *Syn.* deplore, lament, be sorry; see **mourn** 1, **regret** 1.

**rueful,** *modif.* **1.** [Penitent] — *Syn.* contrite, remorseful, regretful; see **ashamed, sorry** 1.

**2.** [Pitiful] — *Syn.* pathetic, sorrowful, despondent; see **pitiful** 1, **sad** 2.

**ruffian,** *n.* — *Syn.* miscreant, hoodlum, bully; see **rascal, rowdy.**

**ruffle,** *n.* — *Syn.* flounce, furbelow, frill, edging; see **decoration** 2, **fringe** 2.

**ruffle,** *v.* **1.** [To disarrange] — *Syn.* rumple, tousle, dishevel; see **confuse, tangle.**

**2.** [To anger] — *Syn.* irritate, fret, nettle; see **anger** 1.

**rug,** *n.* — *Syn.* carpet, carpeting, floor covering, runner, area rug, scatter rug, straw mat, floor mat, woven mat, kilim, drugget; see also **carpet.**

Types of rugs include: Axminster, velvet, Wilton velvet, fiber, rya, mohair, wool-and-fiber, skin, bearskin, sheepskin, goatskin, numdah, Navajo, Persian, paper fiber, rag, chenille, twist, shag, braided, sisal, hand-hooked, Cambodia, camel's hair, tapestry, dhurrie, prayer, Chinese, Oriental, Smyrna, Finnish, India drugget.

**rugged,** *modif.* **1.** [Rough; *said especially of terrain*] — *Syn.* hilly, broken, mountainous; see **rough** 1.

**2.** [Strong; *said especially of persons*] — *Syn.* hale, sturdy, hardy; see **healthy** 1, **strong** 1.

**ruin,** *n.* **1.** [The act of destruction] — *Syn.* extinction, demolition, overthrow; see **destruction** 1, **wreck** 1.

**2.** [A building fallen into decay] — *Syn.* wreck, vestige, remains, rubble; see **ruins, wreck** 2.

**3.** [The state of destruction] — *Syn.* dilapidation, waste, wreck; see **destruction** 2.

*See Synonym Study at* DESTRUCTION.

---

**SYN.** — **ruin** implies a state of decay, disintegration, etc. especially through such natural processes as age and weather /the barn is in a state of *ruin*/; **destruction** implies annihilation or demolition, as by fire, explosion, flood, etc. /the *destruction* of the village in an air raid/; **havoc** suggests total destruction or devastation, as following an earthquake or hurricane /the storm wreaked *havoc* along the coast/; **dilapidation** implies a state of ruin or shabbiness resulting from neglect /the *dilapidation* of a deserted house/

---

**ruin,** *v.* **1.** [To destroy] — *Syn.* injure, overthrow, demolish; see **destroy** 1, **ravage.**

**2.** [To cause to become bankrupt] — *Syn.* impoverish, bankrupt, beggar, reduce, pauperize, fleece, make penniless, bring to destitution, bring to want, drain, exhaust, wreck, break, bust*, clean out*, cook one's goose*, do in*, do for*, wipe out*. — *Ant.* HELP, pay, fund.

**3.** [To destroy chastity] — *Syn.* rape, despoil, ravish; see **rape.**

**ruined,** *modif.* **1.** [Destroyed] — *Syn.* demolished, overthrown, torn down, extinct, abolished, exterminated, annihilated, subverted, wrecked, desolated, ravaged, smashed, crushed, crashed, extinguished, extirpated,

dissolved, totaled*, screwed up*; see also **destroyed.** — *Ant.* PROTECTED, saved, preserved.

**2.** [Spoiled] — *Syn.* pillaged, harried, robbed, plundered, injured, hurt, impaired, defaced, harmed, marred, past hope, mutilated, botched, broken, gone to the dogs*, gone to the devil*, gone to pot*, on the rocks*, done for*; see also **spoiled.** — *Ant.* repaired, RESTORED, mended.

**3.** [Rendered unchaste] — *Syn.* violated, defiled, ravished, raped, forced, despoiled, deflowered.

**4.** [Bankrupt] — *Syn.* poverty-stricken, pauperized, beggared, reduced, left in penury, penniless, fleeced, brought to want, out of business, gone under*, sold up*, busted*, broke*; see also **insolvent.** — *Ant.* RICH, prosperous, successful.

**ruinous,** *modif.* **1.** [Destructive] — *Syn.* pernicious, calamitous, disastrous; see **destructive** 2, **harmful.**

**2.** [Leading to bankruptcy] — *Syn.* unfortunate, rash, speculative, suicidal, fatal, impoverishing, pauperizing, exhausting, draining, depleting, bringing to want, reducing to penury.

**ruins,** *pl.n.* — *Syn.* remains, traces, foundations, debris, walls, wreckage, vestiges, remnants, relics, residue, wreck, rubble, detritus; see also **wreck** 2.

**rule,** *n.* **1.** [Government] — *Syn.* control, dominion, jurisdiction; see **government** 1.

**2.** [A regulation] — *Syn.* edict, dictate, precept; see **command** 1, **law** 3.

**3.** [The custom] — *Syn.* habit, course, practice; see **custom** 1, 2.

*See Synonym Study at* LAW.

**as a rule** — *Syn.* ordinarily, generally, habitually; see **customarily, regularly** 1.

**rule,** *v.* **1.** [To govern] — *Syn.* conduct, control, dictate; see **govern.**

**2.** [To regulate] — *Syn.* order, decree, direct; see **command** 2, **manage** 1.

**ruled,** *modif.* **1.** [Governed] — *Syn.* administered, controlled, managed; see **governed** 1.

**2.** [Having lines] — *Syn.* lined, marked, marked off, squared, graphed, prepared for graphs; see also **linear.**

**rule of thumb,** *n.* — *Syn.* approximation, estimate, general guideline; see **guess, hypothesis.**

**rule out,** *v.* — *Syn.* eliminate, reject, prevent, preclude; see **eliminate** 1, **exclude** 1, **prevent.**

**ruler,** *n.* **1.** [One who governs] — *Syn.* governor, leader, head of state, president, prime minister, premier, chief executive, chancellor, monarch, sovereign, emperor, prince, crowned head, potentate, dictator, commander, chief, manager, adjudicator, regent, director; for types of rulers, see also **dictator, king** 1, **leader** 2, **queen.**

**2.** [A straightedge] Types of rules include: foot rule, yardstick, carpenter's rule, slide rule, parallel rule, stationer's rule, T-square, try square, steel square, compositor's rule, compositor's ruler.

**ruling,** *n.* — *Syn.* decision, decree, verdict; see **judgment** 3, **law** 3.

**rum,** *n.*
Types of rum include: light, dark, spiced, West Indian, Jamaican, Puerto Rican, Bacardi (trademark), arrack, Cape Horn rainwater; see also **drink** 2.

**rumble,** *n.* — *Syn.* reverberation, resounding, thunder, roll, drumbeat; see also **noise** 1.

**rumble,** *v.* — *Syn.* resound, growl, thunder; see **sound** 1.

**ruminate,** *v.* **1.** [To chew the cud] — *Syn.* rechew, masticate, regurgitate; see **chew.**

**2.** [To ponder] — *Syn.* meditate on, contemplate, cogitate; see **consider** 3, **meditate** 1, **think** 1.

**rummage,** *n.* — *Syn.* odds and ends, miscellany, used goods, second-hand goods, antiques, stuff, frippery, old clothes, hand-me-downs, jumble.

**rummage,** *v.* — *Syn.* search through, ransack, search high and low, look all over, scour, turn inside out; see also **hunt** 2, **ransack** 1, **search.**

**rumor,** *n.* **1.** [Common talk] — *Syn.* hearsay, gossip, report, news, tidings, intelligence, dispatch, scandal, tittle-tattle, word of mouth, grapevine, talk, noise, cry, popular report, fame, repute, bruit, scuttlebutt*, buzz*.
**2.** [An unsubstantial story] — *Syn.* canard, hoax, fabrication, suggestion, supposition, innuendo, story, tale, invention, fiction, falsehood; see also **lie** 1.

**rumored,** *modif.* — *Syn.* reported, told, said, reputed, spread abroad, gossiped, bruited, given out, noised abroad, broadcast, it is said, as they say, all over town, current, circulating, in circulation, rife, prevailing, prevalent, persisting, general, in everyone's mouth, on everyone's lips, going around*, going the rounds*, buzzed*; see also **reported.**

**rump,** *n.* — *Syn.* posterior, buttocks, rear end, hind end, tail end, butt end, bottom, backside, behind, croup, crupper, rear, back, seat, breech, hunkers, hurdies (Scotch), fundament, derrière, hindquarters, sacrum, butt*, fanny*, ass*, buns*, can*, bum*, duff*, tush*.

**rumple,** *v.* — *Syn.* crumple, crush, fold; see **wrinkle** 1.

**rumpus*,** *n.* — *Syn.* uproar, disturbance, tumult; see **confusion** 2, **fun.**

**run,** *n.* **1.** [The act of running] — *Syn.* sprint, dash, jog, race, pace, bound, trot, gallop, canter, lope, spring, dart, rush, flight, escape, break, charge, swoop, scamper, tear, whisk, scuttle, scud, flow, fall, drop.
**2.** [A series] — *Syn.* continuity, succession, sequence, spell; see **period** 1, **series.**
**3.** [In baseball, a score] — *Syn.* point, tally, count; see **home run, score** 1.
**4.** [The average] — *Syn.* par, norm, run of the mill; see **average.**
**5.** [A course] — *Syn.* way, route, field; see **route** 1, **track** 1.
**in the long run** — *Syn.* in the final outcome, finally, eventually; see **ultimately.**
**on the run 1.** busy, in a hurry, running; see **hurrying.**
**2.** retreating, routed, escaping, on the lam*; see **beaten** 1, **runaway.**

**run,** *v.* **1.** [To move, usually rapidly] — *Syn.* flow, stream, pour, cut along, chase along, fall, roll, course, tumble, drop, leap, spin, whirl, whiz, scud, sail.
**2.** [To go swiftly by physical effort] — *Syn.* rush, hurry, race, dash, dart, bolt, shoot, tear, bound, scurry, skitter, scramble, scoot, travel, run off, run away, flee, escape, put on a burst of speed, go on the double, hasten, hasten off, light out, make tracks, dart ahead, gallop, canter, lope, jog, spring, trot, single-foot, amble, pace, speed, sprint, spurt, swoop, whisk, scamper, scuttle; see also **race** 1.
**3.** [To function] — *Syn.* move, work, go; see **operate** 2.
**4.** [To cause to function] — *Syn.* control, drive, govern, administer; see **command** 2, **manage** 1.
**5.** [To extend] — *Syn.* encompass, cover, spread; see **reach** 1, **surround** 1, 2.
**6.** [To continue] — *Syn.* last, persevere, go on; see **continue** 1.
**7.** [To read] — *Syn.* be worded, be written, appear; see **mean** 1.
**8.** [To compete] — *Syn.* oppose, contest, contend with; see **compete, race** 2.

**run after,** *v.* — *Syn.* follow, chase, hunt; see **pursue** 1.

**run amok,** *v.* — *Syn.* go wild, go berserk, run wild, run riot, go on a rampage, go crazy, go insane, lose one's head, go haywire*, go nuts*, go off the deep end*; see also **crack up** 2, **rage** 3.

**runaround,** *n.* — *Syn.* postponement, evasion, diversion, bureaucratic inertia; see **avoidance, delay** 1.

**runaway,** *modif.* — *Syn.* fleeing, running, escaping, escaped, fugitive, loose, out of control, out of hand, beyond restraint, delinquent, wild, on the loose, on the run, on the lam*; see also **disorderly** 1.

**runaway,** *n.* — *Syn.* fugitive, deserter, juvenile offender, truant; see **delinquent, fugitive.**

**run away,** *v.* — *Syn.* escape, flee, depart, steal away; see **escape, leave** 1, **retreat** 2.

**run-down,** *modif.* **1.** [Exhausted] — *Syn.* debilitated, weary, worn-out; see **tired, weak** 1.
**2.** [Dilapidated] — *Syn.* broken-down, shabby, rickety, beat-up*; see **crumbly, old** 2.

**rundown,** *n.* — *Syn.* report, outline, review; see **summary.**

**run down,** *v.* **1.** [To chase] — *Syn.* hunt, seize, apprehend; see **catch** 2, **pursue** 1.
**2.** [To speak slightingly of] — *Syn.* disparage, belittle, depreciate; see **depreciate** 2.

**run dry,** *v.* — *Syn.* dry up, stop running, cease to flow; see **dry** 1.

**(a) run for one's money,** *n.* — *Syn.* one's money's worth, satisfaction, keen competition, challenge; see **pay** 1, **satisfaction** 1.

**rung,** *n.* — *Syn.* tread, round, crosspiece, bar, rod, crossbar, level, board.

**run into,** *v.* **1.** [To collide with] — *Syn.* bump into, crash, have a collision; see **crash** 4, **hit** 2.
**2.** [To encounter] — *Syn.* come across, see, bump into*; see **find** 1, **meet** 6.
**3.** [To blend with] — *Syn.* mingle, combine with, osmose; see **merge, mix** 1.

**runner,** *n.* **1.** [One who runs] — *Syn.* racer, entrant, contestant, sprinter, distance runner, long distance runner, marathoner, middle distance runner, 220-man*, dasher, cross-country runner, jogger, trackman, hurdler, messenger, courier, postrider, post, express, dispatch bearer, cinder man*, cinder artist*, century man*; see also **athlete.**
**2.** [A vine] — *Syn.* tendril, branch, offshoot; see **vine.**

**running,** *modif.* **1.** [In the act of running] — *Syn.* racing, speeding, jogging, pacing, galloping, cantering, trotting, scuttling, scudding, scampering, fleeing, bounding, whisking, sprinting.
**2.** [In the process of running] — *Syn.* producing, operating, working, functioning, proceeding, moving, revolving, guiding, conducting, administering, going, in operation, in action, executing, promoting, achieving, transacting, wielding, determining, bringing about.
**3.** [Extending] — *Syn.* spreading, reaching, encompassing; see **extending.**
**4.** [Flowing] — *Syn.* pouring, tumbling, falling, dashing, coursing, streaming, swamping, washing over, laving, watering; see also **flowing.**

**runoff,** *n.* — *Syn.* spring runoff, drainage, surplus water; see **flow, river** 1, **water** 1.

**run off,** *v.* **1.** [To pour out] — *Syn.* empty, flow off, wash; see **drain** 3.
**2.** [To abandon] — *Syn.* depart, flee, go; see **escape, leave** 1.
**3.** [To produce] — *Syn.* turn out, duplicate, publish; see **manufacture** 1, **print** 2, **reproduce** 1.

**run-of-the-mill,** *modif.* — *Syn.* average, commonplace, ordinary; see **common** 1.

**run on,** *v.* — *Syn.* chatter, maunder, gabble; see **gossip, ramble** 2.

**run out,** *v.* **1.** [To be used up] — *Syn.* give out, dry up, fail, be exhausted, peter out\*; see also **waste** 3.

**2.** [To stop] — *Syn.* expire, finish, end; see **stop** 2.

**3.** [To become exhausted] — *Syn.* weaken, wear out, run out of gas\*; see **tire** 1.

**4.** [To go away] — *Syn.* go, depart, desert, run away; see **abandon** 2, **escape, leave** 1.

**5.** [To pour out] — *Syn.* flow, empty, leak; see **drain** 3.

**6.** [To pass] — *Syn.* elapse, slip by, glide; see **pass** 2.

**7.** [To remove physically] — *Syn.* drive out, expel, throw out; see **eject** 1.

**run out of,** *v.* — *Syn.* use up, exhaust, consume; see **consume** 2, **waste** 2.

**run over,** *v.* — *Syn.* drive over, strike, run down, knock down, trample on, kill, hurt, injure, hit and run\*.

**runt,** *n.* **1.** [A dwarf] — *Syn.* pygmy, mannikin, midget, scrub, homunculus; see also **midget.**

**2.** [A mediocrity] — *Syn.* whippersnapper, nonentity, punk\*; see **nobody** 2.

**run through,** *v.* **1.** [To examine] — *Syn.* check, read through, look at; see **examine** 1.

**2.** [To spend] — *Syn.* waste, squander, lose; see **spend** 1, **waste** 2.

**run together,** *v.* — *Syn.* blend, mingle, combine; see **merge, mix** 1.

**run up bills,** *v.* — *Syn.* squander money, throw money away, incur debts; see **spend** 1.

**rupture,** *n.* — *Syn.* breach, separation, crack; see **break** 1, **fracture** 1, 2, **tear.**

**rupture,** *v.* — *Syn.* crack, tear, burst; see **break.**

**rural,** *modif.* — *Syn.* rustic, country, farm, agricultural, pastoral, bucolic, backwoods, provincial, Arcadian, sylvan, agrarian, georgic, agronomic, ranch, exurban. — *Ant.* URBAN, industrial, commercial.

---

*SYN.* — **rural** is the comprehensive, nonspecific word referring to life on the farm or in the country as distinguished from life in the city *[rural* schools*]*; **rustic** stresses the contrast between the supposed crudeness and unsophistication of the country and the supposed polish and refinement of the city *[rustic* humor*]*; **pastoral,** often used in literary contexts, suggests a highly idealized primitive simplicity of rural life, originally among shepherds; in contrast, **bucolic,** also a literary term, suggests a down-to-earth rustic simplicity or artlessness *[her bucolic* suitor*]*

---

**ruse,** *n.* — *Syn.* artifice, stratagem, ploy, deceit; see **device** 2, **trick** 1.

*See Synonym Study at* TRICK.

**rush,** *n.* — *Syn.* haste, dash, charge; see **hurry** 1, **race** 1.

**with a rush** — *Syn.* suddenly, forcefully, rushing; see **fast** 1, **unexpectedly.**

**rush,** *v.* — *Syn.* hasten, speed, hurry up; see **hurry** 1, **race** 1.

**rushed,** *modif.* — *Syn.* hurried, driven, pressured; see **pressed.**

**rush in,** *v.* — *Syn.* take chances, hurry things, act precipitately; see **risk.**

**rushing,** *modif.* **1.** [Hurrying] — *Syn.* hastening, bestirring oneself, losing no time; see **hurrying.**

**2.** [Moving with great speed] — *Syn.* driving, darting, flying, running, dashing, scurrying, pushing, racing, galloping, plunging; see also **racing.**

**russet,** *modif.* — *Syn.* reddish-brown, yellowish-brown, chestnut; see **brown, red.**

**Russia,** *n.* — *Syn.* Russian Federation, *Rossiya*

(Russian), Union of Soviet Socialist Republics, Soviet Union, U.S.S.R., Great Russia, Little Russia, White Russia, Muscovy, Rus, Ruthenia, Siberia, the Soviets, Reds\*, Russian Bear\*; for divisions of Russia, see **Europe.**

**Russian,** *modif.* — *Syn.* Russ, *russskiy* (Russian), Great Russian, Slavic, Slav, Muscovite, Siberian.

**rust,** *modif.* — *Syn.* reddish, red-yellow, reddish-brown; see **brown, red.**

**rust,** *n.* — *Syn.* corrosion, oxidation, decomposition, corruption, decay, rot, dilapidation, breakup, wear.

**rust,** *v.* — *Syn.* oxidize, become rusty, corrode, degenerate, decay, rot, erode.

**rustic,** *modif.* **1.** [Rural] — *Syn.* agricultural, pastoral, agrarian; see **rural.**

**2.** [Boorish] — *Syn.* countrified, provincial, unsophisticated, rude, uncouth, unpolished, inelegant, awkward, coarse, rough, dull, loutish, lubberly, clownish, ungainly, lumpish, ignorant, uneducated. — *Ant.* CULTURED, refined, sophisticated.

**3.** [Suggesting the idyllic qualities of rural places or people] — *Syn.* sylvan, verdant, unadorned, idyllic, bucolic, artless, simple, plain, honest, unsophisticated, pleasing, charming, picturesque, pastoral, natural, unaffected, sturdy; see also **pleasant** 2. — *Ant.* COMPLEX, urbane, sophisticated.

*See Synonym Study at* RURAL.

**rustle,** *n.* — *Syn.* stir, whisper, ripple, swish, friction, crackle, purl, patter, susurrus; see also **noise** 1.

**rustle,** *v.* — *Syn.* stir, whisper, swish, crackle, purl, patter, ripple, crepitate, tap, sough, sigh, murmur, susurrate; see also **sound** 1.

**rustler\*,** *n.* **1.** [A robber] — *Syn.* cattle thief, horse thief, outlaw; see **robber.**

**2.** [\*An industrious person] — *Syn.* worker, driver, pusher, hustler\*, humper\*.

**rustle up\*,** *v.* — *Syn.* round up, collect, gather, forage for; see **assemble** 2.

**rustling,** *modif.* — *Syn.* murmuring, swishing, stirring; see **whispering.**

**rusty,** *modif.* **1.** [Decayed] — *Syn.* corroded, unused, neglected, worn; see **crumbly, old** 2, **rotten** 2.

**2.** [Unpracticed] — *Syn.* out of practice, soft, out of shape; see **weak** 6.

**rut,** *n.* **1.** [A deeply cut track] — *Syn.* hollow, trench, furrow; see **groove.**

**2.** [Habitual behavior] — *Syn.* custom, habit, course, routine, practice, round, circuit, circle, pattern, wont, usage, grind, treadmill, rat race\*. — *Ant.* CHANGE, variety, mutation.

**ruthless,** *modif.* **1.** [Without pity; *said of persons*] — *Syn.* pitiless, unpitying, merciless, unmerciful, tigerish, feral, ferine, ferocious, stony-hearted, heartless, obdurate, cold-blooded, remorseless, vindictive, vengeful, revengeful, rancorous, implacable, unforgiving, malevolent, hardhearted, hard, cold, unsympathetic, unforbearing, vicious, sadistic; see also sense 2; **cruel** 2. — *Ant.* MERCIFUL, forgiving, compassionate.

**2.** [Showing little evidence of pity; *said of actions, policies, etc.*] — *Syn.* savage, brutal, cruel, tyrannical, relentless, barbarous, inhuman, callous, grim, atrocious, flagrant, terrible, abominable, outrageous, inexorable, unrelenting, fiendish, oppressive, bloodthirsty, venomous, galling, dog-eat-dog; see also **cruel** 1. — *Ant.* KIND, helpful, civilized.

*See Synonym Study at* CRUEL.

**rye,** *n.* — *Syn.* cereal, grass, grain, feed; see **grain** 1.

Varieties of rye grass include: fall, spring, winter, spurred, Wallachian, Michel.

# S

**Sabbath,** *n.* — *Syn.* seventh day, Lord's day, day of rest, *dies non* (Latin), Saturday, Sunday; see also **weekend.**

**sabbatical,** *n.* — *Syn.* leave, time off, holiday; see **vacation.**

**sable,** *modif.* — *Syn.* ebony, raven, dark; see **black** 1, **brown.**

**sabotage,** *n.* — *Syn.* demolition, overthrow, subversion, treason; see **destruction** 1, **revolution** 2.

**sabotage,** *v.* — *Syn.* subvert, wreck, undermine; see **attack** 1, **destroy** 1.

**sac,** *n.* — *Syn.* welt, pouch, cellblister; see **cyst, sore.**

**saccharine,** *modif.* — *Syn.* sugary, honeyed, candied; see **sweet** 1, 2.

**sacerdotal,** *modif.* — *Syn.* priestly, ministerial, apostolic; see **clerical** 2, **divine** 2.

**sachet,** *n.* — *Syn.* fragrance, scent-bag, potpourri; see **perfume, smell** 1.

**sack,** *n.* **1.** [A bag] — *Syn.* sac, pouch, pocket; see **bag, container.**

**2.** [*Dismissal from a job; *used with "the"*] — *Syn.* notice, discharge, pink slip*, the can*; see **removal** 1.

**hit the sack*** — *Syn.* go to bed, to rest, go to sleep, retire; see **sleep.**

**sack,** *v.* **1.** [To raid] — *Syn.* pillage, plunder, loot; see **raid, ravage, rob.**

*See Synonym Study at* RAVAGE.

**2.** [*To dismiss from a job] — *Syn.* fire, discharge, lay off, can*; see **dismiss** 1.

**sackcloth,** *n.* — *Syn.* canvas, burlap, hopsacking, denim, cloth, homespun.

**in sackcloth and ashes** — *Syn.* in mourning, penitent, remorseful; see **sorry** 1.

**sacrament,** *n.* **1.** [Christian rites] — *Syn.* holy observance, ceremonial, ritual, liturgy, act of divine worship, mystery, the mysteries; see also **ceremony** 2.

In the Roman Catholic, Orthodox, and Anglican churches the seven sacraments are: baptism; confirmation; confession *or* reconciliation *or* penance; Holy Communion *or* the Eucharist; anointing of the sick *or* the laying on of hands *or* sacrament of the sick *or* extreme unction; holy orders; matrimony.

**2.** [The Eucharist and the bread and wine used in it] — *Syn.* the body and the blood of Christ, holy wafer, the Host, the elements; see **communion** 2.

**3.** [A sacred symbol or token] — *Syn.* pledge, bond, vow; see **oath** 1, **promise** 1.

**sacramental,** *modif.* — *Syn.* sacred, pure, solemn; see **religious** 1.

**sacred,** *modif.* **1.** [Holy] — *Syn.* pure, pious, saintly, divine; see **holy** 1.

**2.** [Dedicated] — *Syn.* consecrated, ordained, sanctioned; see **divine** 2.

*See Synonym Study at* DIVINE.

**sacred cow*,** *n.* — *Syn.* idol, person above criticism, thing above criticism, elite; see **favorite, pet** 3.

**sacrifice,** *n.* **1.** [An offering to a deity] — *Syn.* offering, tribute, oblation, expiation, atonement, reparation, penance, propitiation, libation, sacrificial lamb, burnt offering.

**2.** [A loss] — *Syn.* discount, deduction, reduction; see **loss** 1.

**3.** [In baseball, a play that advances a runner at the expense of the batter] — *Syn.* fielder's choice, sacrifice fly, bunt, noble deed*.

**sacrifice,** *v.* **1.** [To offer to a deity] — *Syn.* consecrate, immolate, dedicate, give up, devote, offer up, hallow, worship, make an offering of; see also **bless** 3.

**2.** [To give up as a means to an end] — *Syn.* forfeit, forgo, relinquish, yield, suffer the loss of, permit injury to, renounce, spare, give up, let go, resign oneself to, endure the loss of, sacrifice oneself, abandon oneself to, surrender, part with, waive, go astray from.

**3.** [To sell at a loss] — *Syn.* cut, reduce, sell out, sell at a bargain, have a fire sale, mark down, take shrinkage, take a beating, incur a loss, sell for a song*; see also **decrease** 2, **lose** 2.

**sacrificed,** *modif.* — *Syn.* gone, given up, thrown to the wolves*; see **abandoned, lost** 1.

**sacrificial,** *modif.* — *Syn.* atoning, conciliatory, sacrificing, expiatory, propitiatory; see also **divine** 2.

**sacrilege,** *n.* — *Syn.* profanation, desecration, blasphemy, impiety, curse, violation; see also **blasphemy, heresy.**

---

**SYN.** — **sacrilege** implies a violation of something sacred, as by appropriating to oneself or to a secular use something that has been dedicated to a religious purpose; **profanation** suggests a lack of reverence or a positive contempt for things regarded as sacred; **desecration** implies a removal of the sacredness of some object or place, as by defiling or polluting it

---

**sacrilegious,** *modif.* — *Syn.* sinful, blasphemous, profane; see **impious, wicked** 1.

**sacristy,** *n.* — *Syn.* vestry, vestibule, church room, vestry room.

**sacrosanct,** *modif.* — *Syn.* sacred, reverent, blessed, inviolable; see **divine** 2, **religious** 1.

**sad,** *modif.* **1.** [Afflicted with sorrow] — *Syn.* unhappy, sorry, sorrowful, downcast, dismal, gloomy, glum, pensive, heavy-hearted, dispirited, dejected, depressed, desolate, troubled, melancholy, morose, grieved, pessimistic, melancholic, crushed, brokenhearted, heartbroken, heartsick, despondent, careworn, rueful, anguished, disheartened, lamenting, mourning, grieving, weeping, bitter, woebegone, doleful, spiritless, joyless, heavy, crestfallen, discouraged, moody, low-spirited, *mesto* (Italian), despairing, languishing, hopeless, worried, downhearted, cast down, in heavy spirits, morbid, oppressed, blighted, grief-stricken, foreboding, apprehensive, horrified, anxious, dolorous, *triste* (French), wretched, miserable, mournful, disconsolate, forlorn, saturnine, atrabilious, jaundiced, out of sorts, distressed, afflicted, bereaved, repining, harassed, dreary, bilious, lugubrious, woeful, in the doldrums*, down*, down in the dumps*, gone into mourning*, in bad humor*, out of humor*, cut up*, in the depths*, blue*, in grief*, making a long face*, bathed in tears*, feeling like hell*, down in the mouth*. — *Ant.* HAPPY, gay, cheerful.

**2.** [Suggestive of sorrow] — *Syn.* pitiable, unhappy, dejecting, saddening, disheartening, discouraging, dispiriting, joyless, dreary, dark, dismal, gloomy, poignant, moving, touching, mournful, lachrymose, disquieting, disturbing, dimming, somber, doleful, oppressive, funereal, discomposing, lugubrious, pathetic, tragic, pitiful, piteous, woeful, rueful, sorry, unfortunate, hapless, heart-rending, dire, distressing, depressing, grievous.

**3.** [*Inferior] — *Syn.* cheap, bad, second-class; see **common** 1, **poor** 2.

---

*SYN.* — **sad** is the simple, general term, ranging in implication from a mild, momentary unhappiness to a feeling of intense grief; **sorrowful** implies a sadness caused by some specific loss, disappointment, etc. /her death left him *sorrowful*/; **melancholy** suggests a more or less chronic mournfulness or gloominess, or, often, merely a wistful pensiveness /*melancholy* thoughts about the future/; **dejected** implies discouragement or a sinking of spirits, as because of frustration; **depressed** suggests a mood of brooding despondency, as because of fatigue or a sense of futility /the novel left him feeling *depressed*/; **doleful** implies a mournful, often lugubrious, sadness /the *doleful* look on a lost child's face/

---

**sadden,** *v.* — *Syn.* oppress, dishearten, discourage, cast down, deject, depress, dispirit, get one down*, bum out*, make one's heart bleed*, cast a gloom upon*, break one's heart*.

**saddle,** *n.* — *Syn.* seat, montura, *aparejo* (Spanish), hack, hull, leather.
Types of saddles include: English, English cavalry, U.S. cavalry, Western, cowboy, stock, camel, Cossack, sidesaddle, packsaddle, pillion, cacolet, mule-chair.

**sadism,** *n.* — *Syn.* perversion, cruelty, malice, sexual abnormality, sexual aberration, *psychopathia sexualis* (Latin), masochism, sadomasochism.

**sadistic,** *modif.* — *Syn.* cruel, brutal, vicious; see **cruel** 1, 2.

**sadly,** *modif.* — *Syn.* unhappily, morosely, dejectedly, wistfully, sorrowfully, dolefully, grievously, gloomily, joylessly, dismally, cheerlessly, in sorrow.

**sadness,** *n.* — *Syn.* sorrow, dejection, melancholy, depression, grief, despondency, sorrowfulness, oppression, downs*, gloom*, blues*, dumps*.

**safe,** *modif.* **1.** [Not in danger] — *Syn.* out of danger, secure, in safety, in security, free from harm, free from danger, unharmed, unscathed, safe and sound, protected, guarded, housed, screened from danger, unmolested, unthreatened, entrenched, impregnable, invulnerable, under the protection of, saved, safeguarded, secured, defended, supported, sustained, maintained, upheld, preserved, vindicated, shielded, nourished, sheltered, fostered, cared for, cherished, watched, impervious to, patrolled, looked after, ministered to, supervised, tended, attended, kept in view, kept in order, surveyed, regulated, with one's head above water*, undercover*, out of harm's way*, on the safe side*, on ice*, in free*, at anchor*, in harbor*, snug*, snug as a bug in a rug*, out of the meshes*, under one's wing*, bearing a charmed life*, under lock and key*. — *Ant.* DANGEROUS, UNSAFE, risky.

**2.** [Not dangerous] — *Syn.* innocent, innocuous, innoxious; see **harmless** 2.

**3.** [Reliable] — *Syn.* trustworthy, dependable, competent; see **reliable** 1, 2.

---

*SYN.* — **safe** implies freedom from or escape from damage, danger, or injury or from the risk of damage, etc. /reached the fort *safe* and sound/; **secure**, often interchangeable with **safe**, is now usually applied to something about which there is no need to feel apprehension /he feels *secure* in his job/

---

**safe,** *n.* — *Syn.* strongbox, coffer, chest, repository, vault, case, reliquary, safe-deposit box, safety-deposit box.

**safe-conduct,** *n.* **1.** [Permit] — *Syn.* license, safeguard, permit, ticket, pass; see also **guaranty** 2, **passport.**

**2.** [Protection] — *Syn.* guard, convoy, consort; see **escort, guide** 1.

**safeguard,** *n.* **1.** [Protection] — *Syn.* guard, shield, surety; see **defense** 1, **protection** 2.

**2.** [License] — *Syn.* pass, safe-conduct, passport; see **escort, permission.**

**safekeeping,** *n.* — *Syn.* supervision, care, guardianship; see **custody** 1, **protection** 2.

**safely,** *modif.* — *Syn.* securely, with safety, with impunity, without harm, without risk, without mishap, without danger, harmlessly, carefully, cautiously, reliably.

**safety,** *n.* **1.** [Freedom from danger] — *Syn.* security, protection, impregnability, surety, sanctuary, refuge, shelter, invulnerability.

**2.** [*A lock] — *Syn.* lock mechanism, safetycatch, safety lock; see **fastener, lock** 1.

**safety pin,** *n.* — *Syn.* shield pin, lingerie pin, clasp, diaper pin; see **fastener, pin** 1.

**sag,** *n.* — *Syn.* depression, settling, sinking, droop, tilt, list, cant, dip, slant, fall, distortion, slump*; see also **hole** 2.

**sag,** *v.* **1.** [To sink] — *Syn.* stoop, hang down, become warped; see **bend** 2, **lean** 1.

**2.** [To lose vigor] — *Syn.* droop, decline, fail; see **hesitate, weaken** 1.

**saga,** *n.* — *Syn.* epic, legend, adventure; see **story.**

**sagacious,** *modif.* **1.** [Intellectually keen] — *Syn.* perceptive, acute, astute, shrewd; see **intelligent** 1, **witty.**

**2.** [Understanding and judicious] — *Syn.* discriminating, wise, sensible; see **judicious, rational** 1.
*See Synonym Study at* SHREWD.

**sagacity,** *n.* — *Syn.* perspicacity, discernment, shrewdness, wisdom; see **acumen, judgment** 1, sense 2.

**sage,** *modif.* — *Syn.* prudent, philosophic, discerning; see **judicious, learned** 2.

**sage,** *n.* — *Syn.* philosopher, savant, wise man, man of learning; see **master** 3, **scientist.**

**sagely,** *modif.* — *Syn.* learnedly, in an informed manner, shrewdly; see **wisely.**

**said,** *modif.* — *Syn.* pronounced, aforesaid, forenamed; see **preceding, spoken.**

**sail,** *n.* **1.** [Means of sailing a vessel] — *Syn.* sheet, sheets, canvas, muslin, cloth, rag*.
Sails include: mainsail, foresail, topsail, jib, spanker, ringsail, skysail, spritsail, staysail, fisherman staysail, topgallant, mizzen, fore topsail, fore staysail, fore trysail, fore royal, studdingsail, storm trysail, flying jib, outer jib, inner jib, working sails, light sails, kites, mizzen topsail, main topsail, upper main topsail, main staysail, fore skysail, mizzen topgallant, fore topgallant, trysail, mizzenroyal, balloon sail, spinnaker, spanker, balloon jib, crossjack, Genoa.

**2.** [A journey by sailing vessel] — *Syn.* voyage, cruise, trip; see **journey.**

**set sail** — *Syn.* go, depart, set out; see **leave** *v.* 1, **sail** *v.* 1, 2.

**sail,** *v.* **1.** [To embark] — *Syn.* take ship, put to sea, put out to sea, make sail, get under way, set sail, weigh anchor, leave, begin a voyage.

**2.** [To travel by sailing] — *Syn.* cruise, voyage, bear in with the land, go alongside, bear down on, bear for, direct one's course for, set sail, put on sail, crowd sail, put to sea, sail away from, navigate, travel, make headway, mis-stay, lie in, make at, make for, heave to, lay in, lay for, fetch up, bring to, bear off, double a point, close with, back and fill, bear up for, run down, run in, put off, put in, gather way, hug the shore, plow the waves*, hang out the washing*, plow the deep*.

**3.** [To fly] — *Syn.* float, soar, ride the storm, skim, glide.

**sailing,** *modif.* **1.** [In the act of sailing] — *Syn.* under sail, under full sail, on the high seas, under way, at sea, under canvas*; see also **boating, traveling** 2.

**2.** [Having to do with sailing, or intended for sailing] — *Syn.* rigged for sail, full-rigged, masted, square-rigged, fore-and-aft rigged, cutter-rigged, sloop-rigged, cat-rigged, three-masted, four-masted, sailed, provided with sails.

**sailor,** *n.* **1.** [A seafaring man] — *Syn.* seaman, mariner, seafarer, pirate, navigator, pilot, boatman, *matelot* (French), yachtsman, able-bodied seaman, A.B.*, Jack Tar*, tar*, hearty*, sea-dog*, limey*, shellback*, lascar*, salt*, bluejacket*.

Kinds and ranks of sailors include — *crew:* deck hand, stoker, bakehead*, boilerman, cabin boy, yeoman, purser, ship's carpenter, cooper, tailor, steward, navigator, signalman, gunner, torpedoman, watch, afterguard; *officers:* captain, commander, skipper*, navigating officer, deck officer, officer of the deck (OD), watch officer, first mate, second mate, third mate, boatswain's mate, boatswain, bos'n*.

**2.** [A member of the sailing or naval forces] — *Syn.* navy man, marine, midshipman, naval cadet, coastguardsman, Navy Seal, frogman, seabee*, bluejacket*, gob*, leatherneck*, middy*.

**sail under false colors,** *v.* — *Syn.* misrepresent, feign, sham; see **deceive.**

**saint,** *n.* **1.** [An exceptionally virtuous person] — *Syn.* paragon, salt of the earth, godly person, unworldly person, altruist, philanthropist, benefactor, angel, the pure in heart, a believer; see also **philanthropist.**

**2.** [A holy person, especially one canonized by a church] — *Syn.* martyr, Christian martyr, religious exemplar, child of god, canonized saint.

Familiar Christian saints include: St. Mary, St. Joseph, St. Matthew, St. Mark, St. Peter, St. Paul, St. Luke, St. John, St. Nicholas, St. Francis, St. Anne, St. Christopher, St. James, St. George, St. Thomas, St. Andrew, St. Patrick, St. Valentine, St. Stephen, St. Anthony, St. Denis, St. Thomas à Becket.

**saintly,** *modif.* — *Syn.* virtuous, full of good deeds, angelic, righteous, worthy, pious, holy, divine, godly, virtuous, sainted.

**sake,** *n.* **1.** [Purpose] — *Syn.* reason, cause, score, motive, principle; see also **purpose** 1, **reason** 3.

**2.** [Welfare] — *Syn.* benefit, behalf, advantage, interest, well-being; see also **advantage** 3, **welfare** 1.

**salable,** *modif.* — *Syn.* marketable, popular, suppliable; see **commercial** 2, **profitable.**

**salacious,** *modif.* — *Syn.* lascivious, wanton, lustful, lecherous; see **lewd** 2, **wicked** 1.

**salad,** *n.* — *Syn.* salad greens, slaw, mixture, combination, *mélange* (French).

Common salads include: green, tossed, garden, vegetable, fruit, tomato, cucumber, mixed, rice, potato, macaroni, bean, combination, chef's, seafood, tuna, shrimp, lobster, crab, chicken, ham, egg, Waldorf, Caesar, Greek, Niçoise, pineapple, banana, gelatin, molded, frozen; cole slaw.

**salamander,** *n.* — *Syn.* eft, newt, triton; see **lizard, reptile.**

**salary,** *n.* — *Syn.* wage, wages, recompense, payroll; see **pay** 2.

*See Synonym Study at* WAGE.

**sale,** *n.* **1.** [The act of selling] — *Syn.* commerce, business, traffic, exchange, barter, commercial enterprise, marketing, vending, trade; see also **economics.**

**2.** [An individual instance of selling] — *Syn.* deal, transaction, negotiation, turnover, trade, purchase, auction, disposal; see also **buying, selling** 1.

**3.** [An organized effort to promote unusual selling] — *Syn.* bargain sale, clearance, stock reduction, fire sale, unloading, dumping, remnant sale, going out of business sale, bankruptcy sale, yard sale, lawn sale, tag sale, garage sale, closeout*, sellout*.

**for** or **on** or **up for sale** — *Syn.* on the market, available, up for sale, on sale, offered for purchase, to be sold, marketable, saleable, advertised, listed, selling, on auction, under the hammer, on the auction block, on the block.

**on sale** — *Syn.* marked down, reduced, at a bargain, cut, at a cut rate, discounted; see also **cheap** 1, **reduced** 2.

**sales,** *n.* — *Syn.* receipts, business, take*; see **income.**

**salesman,** *n.* **1.** [A sales clerk] — *Syn.* salesperson, seller, counterman; see **clerk** 1.

**2.** [A commercial traveler] — *Syn.* sales representative, agent, solicitor; see **salesperson** 2.

**salesperson,** *n.* **1.** [A sales clerk] — *Syn.* salesman, saleswoman, saleslady; see **clerk** 1.

**2.** [A traveling sales representative] — *Syn.* salesman, saleswoman, saleslady, seller, canvasser, businessperson, traveler, traveling salesman, traveling saleswoman, Fuller Brush man, Avon lady, itinerant, drummer*, runner*, rep*, sales rep*, gentleman of the road.

**sales talk,** *n.* — *Syn.* promotion, sales patter, presentation, sales pitch; see **advertising** 1, **publicity** 3.

**saleswoman,** *n.* — *Syn.* saleslady, salesgirl, shopgirl, counter-girl, *vendeuse* (French); see also **clerk** 1, **salesperson** 2.

**salient,** *modif.* **1.** [Prominent] — *Syn.* remarkable, notable, striking; see **conspicuous** 1, **famous.**

**2.** [Projecting] — *Syn.* jutting, swelling, bowed; see **hilly, prominent** 1.

**saline,** *modif.* — *Syn.* briny, brackish, alkaline; see **salty.**

**saliva,** *n.* — *Syn.* water, spittle, salivation, excretion, phlegm, enzyme, spit.

**sallow,** *modif.* — *Syn.* wan, pallid, ashy, ashen, colorless, waxy, yellow, olive, jaundiced, muddy complexioned; see also **dull** 2, **pale** 1.

**sally,** *v.* — *Syn.* rush out, march out, go forth; see **hurry** 1.

**salmon,** *n.* **1.** [A fish]. Varieties of salmon include: Atlantic, Pacific, Alaskan, quinnat, chinook, redback, blueback, humpback, silver, coho, sockeye, chum, pink, king, dog; salmon trout, steelhead trout, red fish.

**2.** [The flesh of salmon, sense 1, used as food] — *Syn.* salmon steak, salmon filet, smoked salmon, kippered salmon, canned salmon, salmon salad, lox, goldfish*, deep-sea turkey*; see also **food.**

**salon,** *n.* — *Syn.* showroom, hall, reception room; see **gallery** 3, **room** 2.

**saloon,** *n.* **1.** [A large social room] — *Syn.* salon, apartment, ballroom; see **hall** 1, **lounge** 2.

**2.** [A dining hall, especially on a ship] — *Syn.* dining cabin, *salle à manger* (French), dining car; see **dining room.**

**3.** [A public drinking house] — *Syn.* bar, alehouse, tavern, publichouse, night club, cocktail lounge, roadhouse, grog shop*, pub*, beer parlor*, poor man's club*, joint*, hangout*, watering hole*, place*.

**salt,** *modif.* **1.** [Tasting of salt] — *Syn.* alkaline, saline, briny; see **salty.**

**2.** [Preserved with salt] — *Syn.* salted, brined, cured, pickled, corned, marinated, dilled, salt-pickled, preserved, soused*.

**salt,** *n.* **1.** [A common seasoning and preservative] — *Syn.* sodium chloride, common salt, table salt, savor, condiment, flavoring, spice, seasoning, sea salt, road salt.

Common types of flavoring salts include: garlic, sea, celery, onion, herb, barbecue, salad, seasoning, smoked, hickory smoked; salt substitute.

**2.** [A chemical compound]. Common chemical salts include: Epsom, Glauber's, Rochelle, mineral, smelling; saltpeter, sal ammoniac, salts of tartar, baking soda.

**3.** [Anything that provides savor] — *Syn.* relish, pungency, smartness; see **humor** 1, **wit** 1.

**below the salt** — *Syn.* disfavored, not in favor, not socially acceptable; see **unpopular.**

**not worth one's salt** — *Syn.* good-for-nothing, bad, worthless; see **poor** 2.

**salt of the earth** — *Syn.* a good person, solid citizen, one of nature's noblemen*; see **gentleman** 1, **lady** 2.

**with a grain** (or **pinch**) **of salt** — *Syn.* doubtingly, skeptically, *cum grano salis* (Latin); see **suspiciously.**

**salt,** *v.* **1.** [To flavor with salt] — *Syn.* season, make tasty, make piquant; see **flavor.**

**2.** [To scatter thickly] — *Syn.* pepper, strew, spread; see **scatter** 1, 2.

**salt a mine,** *v.* — *Syn.* misrepresent, fix up to sell, deceive, mislead, plant, doctor.

**salt away*,** *v.* — *Syn.* invest, put away, put in the bank, accumulate, save, set aside, hoard.

**salt down,** *v.* — *Syn.* pack in salt, cure, keep, preserve, put down, pickle.

**salty,** *modif.* — *Syn.* briny, brackish, pungent, alkaline, well-seasoned, flavored, well-flavored, highly flavored, sour, acrid.

**salubrious,** *modif.* — *Syn.* sanitary, healthy, wholesome; see **healthful.**

**salutary,** *modif.* **1.** [Healthful] — *Syn.* salubrious, healthy, wholesome, good, nutritious, health-giving; see also **healthful.**

**2.** [Beneficial] — *Syn.* tonic, helpful, remedial, bracing, advantageous, curative, restorative, invigorating; see also **helpful** 1.

**salutation,** *n.* — *Syn.* salute, address, welcome; see **greeting** 1, **regards.**

**salutatory,** *n.* — *Syn.* address, recitation, lecture; see **speech** 3.

**salute,** *n.* — *Syn.* tribute, act of respect, salutation, fanfare, salaam.

**salute,** *v.* **1.** [To address] — *Syn.* speak, recognize, hail, accost, greet; see also **address** 2.

**2.** [To recognize with respect] — *Syn.* welcome, pay one's respects to, receive, bow, greet with a bow, greet with a kiss, congratulate.

**3.** [To perform a military salute] — *Syn.* present arms, snap to attention, dip the colors, fire a salute, touch one's cap, do honor to, break out a flag; see also **praise** 1.

**salvage,** *v.* — *Syn.* retrieve, recover, regain, rescue, restore, redeem, get back, glean.

**salvation,** *n.* **1.** [The act of preservation] — *Syn.* deliverance, extrication, liberation, emancipation, rescue, release, conservation, exemption, reprieve, pardon.

**2.** [A means of preservation] — *Syn.* buckler, safeguard, assurance; see **aid** 1, **protection** 2.

**3.** [Deliverance from sin] — *Syn.* redemption, regeneration, rebirth, new birth, second birth, work of grace, forgiveness, mercy, justification, sanctification, entire sanctification.

**salve,** *n.* — *Syn.* ointment, cerate, unguent, lubricant, balm, medicine, emollient, unction, counterirritant, remedy, help, cure, cream.

Common salves include: camphor ice, zinc oxide, menthol ice, aloe, calamine, coal tar, lanolin; Vaseline, Mentholatum, Ben-Gay, Vicks Vaporub (*all* trademarks).

**same,** *modif.* **1.** [Like another in state] — *Syn.* equivalent, identical, corresponding, selfsame, very, alike, equal, equivalent; see also **alike** 1, 2, **equal.**

**2.** [Like another in action] — *Syn.* similarly, in the same manner, likewise; see **alike** 3, **related** 2.

---

*SYN.* — **same,** in one sense, agrees with **selfsame** and **very** in implying that what is referred to is one thing and not two or more distinct things /that is the *same,* or *selfsame* or *very,* house we once lived in/ and, in another sense, implies reference to things that are really distinct but without any significant difference in kind, appearance, amount, etc. /I eat the *same* food every day/; **identical,** in one sense, also expresses the first idea /this is the *identical* bed where he slept/ and, in another, implies exact correspondence in all details, as of quality, appearance, etc. /the signatures are *identical*/; **equal** implies the absence of any difference in quantity, size, value, degree, etc. /*equal* weights, an *equal* advantage/; **equivalent** implies of things that they amount to the same thing in value, force, meaning, etc. /$5 or its *equivalent* in merchandise /

---

**same,** *pron.* — *Syn.* the very same, identical object, no other, no different, substitute, equivalent, similar product, synthetic product, just-as-good*.

**sameness,** *n.* — *Syn.* uniformity, unity, resemblance, analogy, similarity, alikeness, identity, standardization, equality, unison, no difference.

**sample,** *n.* — *Syn.* specimen, unit, individual; see **example** 1, **representation.**

**sample,** *v.* — *Syn.* taste, test, inspect; see **examine** 1, **experiment** 2.

**sanatorium,** *n.* — *Syn.* resort, health resort, hospital, sanitarium, asylum, spa, watering place, retreat, pump room; see also **sanitarium.**

**sanctified,** *modif.* — *Syn.* pure, anointed, hallowed; see **blessed** 2, **divine** 2.

**sanctify,** *v.* — *Syn.* deify, glorify, dedicate, consecrate; see **bless** 3, **worship** 2.

**sanctimonious,** *modif.* — *Syn.* self-righteous, pietistic, hypocritical, holier-than-thou*, goody-goody*; see also **hypocritical.**

*See Synonym Study at* RELIGIOUS.

**sanction,** *n.* **1.** [Approval] — *Syn.* consent, acquiescence, assent; see **permission.**

**2.** [A coercive measure] — *Syn.* decree, command, writ, sentence, ban, embargo, injunction, loss of reward, penalty, punishment, punitive sanctions, civil sanctions, remuneratory sanctions.

**sanction,** *v.* — *Syn.* confirm, authorize, countenance; see **allow** 1, **approve** 1, 2, **endorse** 2.

*See Synonym Study at* APPROVE.

**sanctity,** *n.* — *Syn.* sanctification, sacredness, piety; see **holiness** 2, **virtue** 1.

**sanctuary,** *n.* **1.** [A sacred place] — *Syn.* chancel, Holy of Holies, shrine, sanctum, church, temple; see also **church** 1, **temple.**

**2.** [A place to which one may retire] — *Syn.* asylum, resort, haven, convent, screen, defense, shield, protection, refuge, retreat, shelter, den.

**3.** [A refuge for wild life] — *Syn.* shelter, game refuge, park, national park.

*See Synonym Study at* SHELTER.

**sand,** *modif.* — *Syn.* beach, chip, beige, sand beige, desert sand, ecru, natural, tan.

**sand,** *n.* **1.** [Rock particles] — *Syn.* sandy soil, sandy loam, silt, dust, grit, powder, gravel, rock powder, silica, rock flour, debris, detritus, dirt; see also **earth** 2.

**2.** [The beach] — *Syn.* strand, *plage* (French), seaside, seashore, coast, seaboard, sea bank, shingle (British).

**sandal,** *n.* — *Syn.* slipper, low shoe, evening slipper, thong, *huarache* (Spanish), wedgie, loafer, strapped pump; see also **shoe.**

**sand lot★,** *n.* — *Syn.* amateur, pickup, Little League, Twilight League; see **baseball.**

**sandstone,** *n.* Varieties of sandstone include: arkrose, freestone, brownstone, flagstone, bluestone, grit, novaculite, Triassic brownstone, Berea sandstone, Medina sandstone, Potsdam quartzite, Old Red Sandstone, New Red Sandstone; see also **mineral** 1, **rock** 1.

**sandstorm,** *n.* — *Syn.* dust storm, high wind, Mormon rain★; see **storm** 1, **wind** 1.

**sandwich,** *n.* — *Syn.* lunch, light lunch, quick lunch, wich★.

Kinds of sandwiches include: hamburger, hamburg, burger★, cheeseburger, wiener, dog★, hot dog★, red hot★, pup★, chili dog, Denver, Western, sloppy Joe, club, Dagwood, tuna fish, ham, chicken, roast beef, bologna, salami, turkey, corned beef, pastrami, ham and egg, cheese, deviled meat, steak, submarine, sub, grinder, lobster roll, clam roll, hero, poorboy, hoagie, bacon and cheese; bacon, lettuce and tomato (BLT); toasted cheese, tomato, egg salad, cucumber, watercress, peanut butter and jelly, jelly, fruit and nut, pinwheel, ribbon, checkerboard, rolled; gyro, Reuben, fajita, taco, burrito, open face.

**sandy,** *modif.* **1.** [Containing sand; *said especially of soil*] — *Syn.* light, loose, permeable, porous, easy to work, easily worked, friable, granular, powdery, gritty, sabulous, arenose.

**2.** [Sand colored; *said especially of the hair*] — *Syn.* fairhaired, fair, blond, light, light-haired, towheaded, reddish, carrot-red, carroty, sandy-red, sandy-flaxen, sunbleached, faded.

**sane,** *modif.* **1.** [Sound in mind] — *Syn.* rational, normal, lucid, right-minded, sober, sound-minded, sound, in one's right mind, self-possessed, with a healthy mind, mentally sound, balanced, healthy-minded, reasonable, having a head on one's shoulders★, having all one's marbles★, all there★, in possession of one's faculties★. — *Ant.* INSANE, irrational, delirious.

**2.** [Sensible] — *Syn.* reasonable, fair-minded, open to reason, endowed with reason, sagacious, judicious, wise, logical, intelligent, steady, with good judgment, discerning, well-advised. — *Ant.* ILLOGICAL, unreasonable, senseless.

**San Francisco,** *n.* — *Syn.* City by the Golden Gate, City of St. Francis, Frisco★, Queen City★, Golden City★, the City Cosmopolitan★, Port o' Missing Men★.

**sang-froid,** *n.* — *Syn.* equanimity, composure, coolness; see **composure.**

*See Synonym Study at* COMPOSURE.

**sanguinary,** *modif.* — *Syn.* gory, cruel, bloodthirsty; see **ferocious, savage** 2.

**sanguine,** *modif.* — *Syn.* cheerful, confident, enthusiastic, expectant, optimistic; see also **hopeful** 1, 2.

**sanitarium,** *n.* — *Syn.* health resort, sanatorium, spa, watering place, pump room, asylum, convalescent home, hospital, nursing home; see also **sanatorium.**

**sanitary,** *modif.* — *Syn.* hygienic, sanative, uncontaminated, wholesome, unpolluted, purified, sterile, healthful; see also **clean** 1.

**sanitation,** *n.* — *Syn.* sanitary science, science of public cleanliness, hygiene, asepsis, disinfection, cleanliness.

**sanity,** *n.* **1.** [Freedom from mental disease] — *Syn.* sound mind, rationality, healthy mind, *mens sana* (Latin), saneness, a clear mind, clearmindedness, wholesome outlook.

**2.** [Good sense] — *Syn.* common sense, intelligence, reason, reasonableness, prudence, good judgment, sagacity, acumen, understanding, comprehension.

**sap,** *n.* **1.** [The life fluid of a plant] — *Syn.* fluid, secretion, essence; see **juice.**

**2.** [A vital fluid] — *Syn.* lifeblood, precious fluid, substance; see **blood** 1.

**3.** [★A dupe] — *Syn.* dolt, gull, simpleton; see **fool** 1.

**sap,** *v.* — *Syn.* weaken, undermine, exhaust, subvert; see **drain** 1, 2, 3, **weaken** 2.

*See Synonym Study at* WEAKEN.

**sapience,** *n.* — *Syn.* intelligence, erudition, insight; see **knowledge** 1, **wisdom** 2.

**sapient,** *modif.* — *Syn.* sagacious, discriminating, wise; see **judicious.**

**sapless,** *modif.* **1.** [Dry] — *Syn.* shriveled, dehydrated, decayed; see **dry** 1, **withered.**

**2.** [Insipid] — *Syn.* spineless, ineffectual, lazy; see **dull** 4, **weak** 3.

**sapling,** *n.* — *Syn.* scion, seedling, slip, sprig, sprout, young tree; see also **tree.**

**sapphire,** *modif.* — *Syn.* sapphirine, greenish-blue, deep blue; see **blue** 1.

**sappy,** *modif.* **1.** [Juicy] — *Syn.* lush, succulent, watery; see **juicy.**

**2.** [Forceful] — *Syn.* potent, effectual, dynamic; see **active** 2, **powerful** 1.

**3.** [★Idiotic] — *Syn.* foolish, silly, illogical; see **stupid** 1.

**sarcasm,** *n.* — *Syn.* satire, irony, banter, derision, contempt, scoffing, flouting, superciliousness, ridicule, burlesque, disparagement, criticism, cynicism, invective, censure, lampooning, aspersion, sneering, mockery. — *Ant.* flattery, fawning, cajolery.

**sarcastic,** *modif.* — *Syn.* scornful, mocking, ironical, snide, satirical, taunting, severe, derisive, sardonic, bitter, saucy, hostile, sneering, snickering, quizzical, arrogant, Rabelaisian, Hudibrastic, disrespectful, scurrile, scurrilous, chaffing, twitting, offensive, irascible, carping, cynical, disillusioned, snarling, unbelieving, corrosive, acid, cutting, contemptuous, scorching, captious, sharp, acrimonious, pert, brusque, caustic, biting, harsh, austere, contumelious, grim.

*SYN.* — **sarcastic** implies intent to hurt by taunting with mocking ridicule, veiled sneers, etc. /a *sarcastic* reminder that work begins at 9:00 A.M./; **satirical**, or **satiric**, implies as its purpose the exposing or attacking of the vices, follies, stupidities, etc. of others and connotes the use of ridicule, sarcasm, etc. /Swift's *satirical* comments/; **ironic**, or **ironical**, applies to a humorous or sarcastic form of expression in which the intended meaning of what is said is directly opposite to the usual sense /"My, you're early" was his *ironic* taunt to the latecomer/; **sardonic** implies sneering or mocking bitterness in a person, or, more often, in his expression, remarks, etc. /a *sardonic* smile/; **caustic** implies a cutting, biting, or stinging wit or sarcasm /a *caustic* tongue/

**sarcastically,** *modif.* — *Syn.* scornfully, caustically, maliciously, sneeringly.

**sardines,** *n.* — *Syn.* young herring, menhaden, sprats, *brisling* (Norwegian), pilchard, anchovy, *Sardinia pilchardus* (Latin).

**sardonic,** *modif.* — *Syn.* sarcastic, cynical, scornful; see **sarcastic.**
*See Synonym Study at* SARCASTIC.

**sash,** *n.* — *Syn.* scarf, cincture, girdle, cummerbund; see **band** 1, 2.

**Satan,** *n.* — *Syn.* Mephistopheles, Lucifer, Beelzebub; see **devil** 1.

**satanic,** *modif.* — *Syn.* malicious, vicious, evil, devilish; see **sinister, wicked** 2.

**satchel,** *n.* — *Syn.* handbag, traveling bag, reticule; see **bag, purse.**

**sate,** *v.* — *Syn.* satiate, surfeit, glut; see **satiate.**
*See Synonym Study at* SATIATE.

**satellite,** *n.* **1.** [A small planet that revolves around a larger one] — *Syn.* moon, planetoid, minor planet, secondary planet, inferior planet, asteroid.
**2.** [A man-made object put into orbit around a celestial body] — *Syn.* space satellite, robot satellite, unmanned satellite, space station, orbital rocket, artificial moon, spacecraft, man-made moon, communications satellite, spy satellite, weather satellite, relay satellite, sputnik, satellite station, spy-in-the-sky.
Well known man-made satellites include: Tiros, Discoverer, Sputnik, Syncom, Early Bird, Echo, Telstar, Relay, Nimbus, Secor, Skylab, Soyuz, Mir, Ranger, Comstar, Voyager, Explorer, Intelsat, GOES, Viking, Landsat, NAVSTAR.
**3.** [A smaller country dependent upon a larger one] — *Syn.* protectorate, dependency, former colony, buffer state, mandate.

**satiate,** *v.* — *Syn.* sate, surfeit, cloy, glut, fill, gratify; see also **satisfy** 1.

*SYN.* — **satiate** and **sate** in their basic sense mean to satisfy to the full, but in current use **satiate** almost always implies, as **sate** often does, a being filled or stuffed so full that all pleasure or desire is lost /*satiated*, or *sated*, with food, success, etc./; **surfeit** implies a being filled or supplied to considerable or overindulgent excess /*surfeited* with pleasure/; **cloy** stresses the distaste one feels for something that is, or becomes through excessive indulgence, too sweet, saccharine, rich, etc.

/*cloying*, sentimental music/; **glut** implies an overloading by filling or supplying to excess /to *glut* the market/

**satin,** *n.* — *Syn.* silk, glossy silk, cloth, fabric of royalty.
Types of satin include: satin de chine, royal weave, satin de laine, satin de Lyon, crèpe satin, slipper satin.

**satiny,** *modif.* — *Syn.* sericeous, glossy, smooth; see **silken.**

**satire,** *n.* **1.** [The exposing of vice or folly, especially by wit] — *Syn.* mockery, irony, ridicule, caricature; see **irony, parody.**
**2.** [A work containing satire, sense 1] — *Syn.* burlesque, parody, lampoon, caricature; see **parody.**
*See Synonym Study at* WIT.

**satirical,** *modif.* — *Syn.* mocking, abusive, paradoxical; see **ironic** 1, **sarcastic.**
*See Synonym Study at* SARCASTIC.

**satirist,** *n.* — *Syn.* comedian, caricaturist, critic; see **author** 2, **writer.**

**satirize,** *v.* — *Syn.* mimic, mock, deride; see **ridicule.**

**satisfaction,** *n.* **1.** [The act of satisfying] — *Syn.* gratification, fulfillment, achievement, reparation, atonement, settlement, recompense, compensation, amends, indemnification, redemption, conciliation, propitiation, indulgence, liquidation, amusement.
**2.** [The state or feeling of being satisfied] — *Syn.* comfort, pleasure, well-being, content, contentment, gladness, delight, bliss, joy, happiness, relief, comfort, complacency, peace of mind, ease, heart's ease, serenity, contentedness, cheerfulness. — *Ant.* DISSATISFACTION, unhappiness, discontent.
**3.** [Something that satisfies] — *Syn.* treat, entertainment, refreshment, remuneration, meed, prize, reward, prosperity, good fortune; see also **aid** 1, **blessing** 2.
**4.** [Reparation] — *Syn.* reimbursement, repayment, compensation; see **reparation** 2.

**satisfactorily,** *modif.* **1.** [In a satisfactory manner] — *Syn.* convincingly, suitably, competently; see **adequately** 1, 2.
**2.** [Productive of satisfactory results] — *Syn.* amply, abundantly, thoroughly; see **agreeably.**

**satisfactory,** *modif.* — *Syn.* adequate, satisfying, competent, pleasing; see **enough** 1.

**satisfied,** *modif.* — *Syn.* content, happy, contented, filled, supplied, fulfilled, paid, requited, compensated, appeased, convinced, gratified, *sans souci* (French), sated, at ease, with enough of, without care, satiated.

*SYN.* — **satisfied** implies completed fulfillment of one's wishes, needs, expectations, etc.; **content** and **contented** imply a filling of requirements to the degree that one is not disturbed by a desire for something more or different /some persons are *satisfied* only by great wealth, others are *content* (or *contented*) with a modest but secure income/

**satisfy,** *v.* **1.** [To make content] — *Syn.* content, comfort, cheer, elate, befriend, please, rejoice, delight, exhilarate, amuse, entertain, flatter, make merry, make cheerful, gladden, content, gratify, indulge, humor, conciliate, propitiate, capture, enthrall, enliven, animate, captivate, fascinate, fill, sate, be of advantage, surfeit, gorge, glut, cloy, satiate, tickle*, brighten up*.
**2.** [To pay] — *Syn.* repay, clear up, disburse; see **pay** 1, **settle** 9.
**3.** [To fulfill] — *Syn.* do, fill, serve the purpose, be enough, assuage, observe, perform, comply with, conform to, meet requirements, keep a promise, accomplish, complete, be adequate, be sufficient, provide,

furnish, qualify, answer, serve, equip, meet, avail, suffice, fill the want, come up to, content one, appease one, fill the bill*, pass muster*, get by*, go in a pinch*. — *Ant.* NEGLECT, leave open, fail to do.

**4.** [To convince] — *Syn.* induce, inveigle, win over; see **convince, persuade** 1.

**satisfying**, *modif.* — *Syn.* pleasing, comforting, gratifying; see **enough** 1, **pleasant** 2.

**saturate**, *v.* — *Syn.* soak, overfill, drench, steep; see **immerse** 1, **soak** 1.

*See Synonym Study at* SOAK.

**saturated**, *modif.* — *Syn.* drenched, full, soggy; see **soaked, wet** 1.

**saturation**, *n.* — *Syn.* fullness, soaking, superabundance, overload, plethora, engorgement, congestion.

**saturnalia**, *n.* — *Syn.* spree, revelry, bacchanalia, debauch; see **orgy**.

**saturnine**, *modif.* — *Syn.* morose, sluggish, taciturn, passive, grave; see also **dull** 4, **solemn** 1.

**satyr**, *n.* **1.** [Demigod] — *Syn.* sylvan deity, faun, Pan; see **god** 1.

**2.** [Lecher] — *Syn.* libertine, whoremonger, rake, reprobate, debaucher, lech*, dirty old man*, old goat; see also **lecher**.

**sauce**, *n.* **1.** [A condiment] — *Syn.* appetizer, gravy, seasoning; see **flavoring, food**.

Varieties of sauce, sense 1, include: barbecue, caper, pesto, béarnaise, picante, remoulade, aioli, béchamel, drawn butter, Colbert, hollandaise, tartar, horseradish, Worcestershire, Spanish, mushroom, mustard, velouté, raisin, madeira, cheese, dill, tomato, wine, soy, duck, chef's special.

**2.** [Stewed fruit] — *Syn.* cooked fruit, fruit butter, conserve, preserve.

Varieties of sauce, sense 2, include: apple, gooseberry, blueberry, blackberry, boysenberry, loganberry, raspberry, strawberry, cranberry, orange, pear, peach, plum, cherry, grape, apricot, nectarine, prune.

**saucepan**, *n.* — *Syn.* stewpan, pot, vessel, utensil; see **pan**.

**saucer**, *n.* — *Syn.* dish, small bowl, sauce dish; see **china, dish**.

**saucily**, *modif.* — *Syn.* pertly, impudently, impolitely; see **rudely**.

**saucy**, *modif.* — *Syn.* impudent, impertinent, insolent; see **rude** 2.

*See Synonym Study at* IMPERTINENT.

**saunter**, *v.* — *Syn.* roam, ramble, wander; see **walk** 1.

**sausage**, *n.* Kinds of sausage include: pork sausage, country sausage, link sausage, Vienna sausage, wienerwurst, Bologna sausage, Italian sausage, salami, liverwurst, capocola, cervelat, Braunschweiger, Thuringer, Holstein sausage, Göteborg, landjaeger, chorizo, coppa, frankfurter, knoblauch, goose-liver sausage, head cheese, blood sausage, lachsschinken, Lyons sausage, mettwurst, mortadella, pepperoni, kolbassy, kielbasa, bratwurst, knockwurst, summer sausage, andouille sausage, smoked sausage; see also **meat**.

**savage**, *modif.* **1.** [Primitive] — *Syn.* uncivilized, barbaric, barbarian, crude, simple, original, primary, earliest, primordial, fundamental, aboriginal, pristine, ancient, archaic, rustic, primeval, native, natural, in a state of nature, unchanged. — *Ant.* civilized, advanced, sophisticated.

**2.** [Cruel] — *Syn.* barbarous, inhuman, brutal, brutish, ferine, feral, heartless, cold-blooded, destructive, blood-thirsty, bloody-minded, sanguinary, murderous, atrocious, fierce, ferocious, furious, frantic, violent,

raging, malicious, malignant, malevolent, ravening, infuriate, ravenous, rapacious, merciless, remorseless, ruthless, relentless, hellish, devilish, demoniac, diabolical, infernal; see also **cruel** 1, 2. — *Ant.* KIND, generous, gentle.

**3.** [Wild] — *Syn.* untamed, uncivilized, uncultured, uncultivated, untaught, primitive, unspoiled, rude, heathenish, pagan, ungoverned, unrestrained, turbulent. — *Ant.* TAME, broken, civilized.

*See Synonym Study at* BARBARIAN.

**savage**, *n.* **1.** [Native] — *Syn.* aborigine, cannibal, troglodyte, barbarian, tribesman.

**2.** [Brute] — *Syn.* bully, ruffian, Yahoo, animal; see **beast** 2.

**savagely**, *modif.* — *Syn.* cruelly, viciously, indecently; see **brutally**.

**savant**, *n.* — *Syn.* philosopher, authority, intellectual; see **master** 3, **scholar** 2.

**save**, *v.* **1.** [To remove from danger] — *Syn.* deliver, extricate, rescue, free, set free, liberate, emancipate, ransom, redeem, come to the rescue of, snatch from the jaws of death, wrest from danger, defend; see also **rescue** 1. — *Ant.* ENDANGER, desert, condemn.

**2.** [To deliver from sin] — *Syn.* rescue from sin, reclaim, regenerate, bring into spiritual life, deliver from the power of Satan. — *Ant.* CONDEMN, damn, send to Hell.

**3.** [To hoard] — *Syn.* collect, store, lay up, lay apart, lay in, amass, accumulate, gather, treasure up, store up, pile up, hide away, cache, stow away, draw the purse strings*. — *Ant.* WASTE, spend, invest.

**4.** [To preserve] — *Syn.* conserve, keep, put up, protect; see **preserve** 3.

**5.** [To reserve] — *Syn.* lay aside, lay away, set aside; see **maintain** 3.

**6.** [To avoid] — *Syn.* spare, curtail, lessen; see **avoid**.

*See Synonym Study at* RESCUE.

**saved**, *modif.* **1.** [Kept from danger] — *Syn.* rescued, released, delivered, protected, defended, guarded, safeguarded, preserved, salvaged, reclaimed, regenerated, cured, healed, conserved, maintained, safe, secure, freed, free from harm, free from danger, unthreatened. — *Ant.* RUINED, lost, destroyed.

**2.** [Not spent] — *Syn.* kept, unspent, unused, untouched, accumulated, deposited, retained, laid away, hoarded, invested, husbanded, amassed, stored, spared. — *Ant.* WASTED, squandered, spent.

**saving**, *modif.* **1.** [Redeeming] — *Syn.* rescuing, reparatory, preserving; see **retaining**.

**2.** [Thrifty] — *Syn.* sparing, frugal, careful; see **economical** 1.

**3.** [Conditional] — *Syn.* provisional, qualificative, contingent; see **conditional**.

**saving**, *n.* **1.** [Conservation] — *Syn.* preservation, maintenance, thrift; see **conservation, economy** 2.

**2.** [Profit] — *Syn.* gain, proceeds, increase; see **addition** 2, **profit** 2.

**savings**, *n.* — *Syn.* means, property, resources, funds, reserve, competence, investment, provision, provisions, accumulation, store, riches, harvest, gleanings, hoard, cache, nest egg*, money in the bank*, anchor to windward*, sheet anchor*, provision for a rainy day*.

**savior**, *n.* **1.** [One who saves another] — *Syn.* deliverer, rescuer, preserver, hero, knight, protector, guardian, guardian angel, good genius, good Samaritan, benefactor, friend at court*, friend in need*. — *Ant.* ENEMY, seducer, murderer.

**2.** [Christ; *often capital*; *often Saviour*] — *Syn.* Redeemer, Messiah, Intercessor, Mediator, Advocate,

Surety, The Perfect Sacrifice, The Final Sacrifice; see also **Christic**. — *Ant.* DEVIL, demon, Power of Evil.

**savoir-faire,** *n.* — *Syn.* poise, courtesy, manners; see **tact.**

*See Synonym Study at* TACT.

**savor,** *n.* — *Syn.* odor, flavor, relish, tang, taste, scent, tinge, zest, smack.

**savor,** *v.* — *Syn.* enjoy, relish, appreciate; see **like** 1.

**savory,** *modif.* — *Syn.* palatable, pleasing, appetizing, piquant, pungent, spicy, tangy, rich, flavorous, tasty, tempting, delectable, delicious, gustful, luscious, dainty, toothsome, nectareous, exquisite, ambrosial, good.

**saw,** *n.* Types of saws include: annular, circular, concave, crown, mill, ice, crosscut, band, rip, hand, panel, pruning, whip, wood, buck, keyhole, back, butcher's, hack, double, jig, table, chain, power, trephine; see also **tool** 1.

**sawmill,** *n.* — *Syn.* mill, lumber mill, portable mill; see **factory.**

**saw-toothed,** *modif.* — *Syn.* serrated, dentate, jagged, nicked, toothed, notched; see also **irregular** 4.

**saxophone,** *n.* — *Syn.* horn, brass wind, sax*; see **musical instrument.**

**say,** *v.* — *Syn.* tell, speak, relate, state, announce, remark, pronounce, declare, state positively, open one's mouth, have one's say, fling off, have one's ear, break silence, find words to express, rise to the occasion, put forth, let out, assert, maintain, express oneself, opine, answer, respond, reply, suppose, assume.

**to say the least** — *Syn.* at a minimum, at the very least, to put it mildly, minimally.

**saying,** *modif.* — *Syn.* mentioning, making clear, revealing, pointing out, giving out, remarking, noting, announcing, noticing, claiming, stating, affirming, maintaining, asserting, attesting to, certifying to, testifying to, alleging, informing, phrasing, stressing, demonstrating, averring, avouching, vouching, insisting on, publicizing, advertising, making public, swearing, implying, propounding, observing, drafting a proposition, making an announcement, making a statement, making a declaration.

**go without saying** — *Syn.* be obvious, be self-evident, need no justification.

**saying,** *n.* — *Syn.* aphorism, saw, adage, maxim, apothegm, epigram, gnome, byword, motto, proverb, precept, dictum.

---

*SYN.* — **saying** is the simple, direct term for any pithy expression of wisdom or truth; a **saw** is an old, homely saying that is well worn by repetition [the preacher filled his sermon with wise *saws*]; a **maxim** is a general principle drawn from practical experience and serving as a rule of conduct (Ex.: "Keep thy shop and thy shop will keep thee"); an **adage** is a saying that has been popularly accepted over a long period of time (Ex.: "Where there's smoke, there's fire"); a **proverb** is a piece of practical wisdom expressed in homely, concrete terms (Ex.: "A penny saved is a penny earned"); a **motto** is a maxim chosen to express a guiding principle or goal of a nation, group, etc. (Ex.: "E pluribus unum") or accepted as an ideal of behavior (Ex.: "Honesty is the best policy"); an **aphorism** is a terse saying embodying a general, more or less profound truth or principle (Ex.: "He is a fool that cannot conceal his wisdom"); an **epigram** is a terse, witty, pointed statement that often gains its effect by ingenious antithesis (Ex.: "The only way to get rid of a temptation is to yield to it")

---

**scab,** *n.* **1.** [A crust over a wound] — *Syn.* eschar, slough, crust.

**2.** [*One who replaces a union worker on strike] — *Syn.* turncoat, strikebreaker, traitor, apostate, deserter, knobstick*.

**scabbard,** *n.* — *Syn.* sheath, casing, holder, covering; see **case** 7, **sheath.**

**scabby,** *modif.* — *Syn.* flaky, scurfy, scaly; see **rough** 1.

**scabrous,** *modif.* **1.** [Rough] — *Syn.* scaly, scabby, coarse, notched, blotchy, encrusted; see also **rough** 1.

**2.** [Difficult] — *Syn.* treacherous, ominous, perilous; see **dangerous, difficult** 1.

**3.** [Improper] — *Syn.* immodest, unconventional, scandalous, indecent, shocking, indiscreet; see also **improper** 1, **risqué.**

**scaffold,** *n.* — *Syn.* framework, stage, structure; see **building** 1, **platform** 1.

**scalawag,** *n.* — *Syn.* rogue, scoundrel, trickster, scamp; see **rascal.**

**scald,** *v.* — *Syn.* char, blanch, parboil; see **burn** 2.

**scale,** *n.* **1.** [A series for measurement] — *Syn.* rule, computation, system; see **measure** 2, **order** 3.

**2.** [A flake or film] — *Syn.* thin coating, covering, incrustation; see **flake, layer.**

**3.** [A device for weighing; *often plural*] — *Syn.* steelyard, stilliard, balance, scale beam, spring scale, trebuchet, Roman balance, stapel scale, Danish balance.

Varieties of scales, sense 3, include: beam, automatic indicating, counter, cylinder, drum, barrel, flexure plate, plate fulcrum, platform, spring, electronic, digital, computing, household, miner's, assayer's.

**4.** [Musical tones] — *Syn.* range, diatonic scale, chromatic scale, major scale, minor scale, whole tone scale, harmonic scale, melodic scale; see also **music.**

**on a large scale** — *Syn.* extensively, grandly, expansively; see **generously.**

**on a small scale** — *Syn.* economically, in a small limited way, with restrictions; see **inadequate** 1, **unimportant.**

**scale,** *v.* **1.** [To climb] — *Syn.* ascend, surmount, mount; see **climb** 2.

**2.** [To peel] — *Syn.* exfoliate, strip off, flake; see **peel, skin.**

**3.** [To measure] — *Syn.* compare, balance, compute, size, allow due weight, estimate, calibrate, graduate, have a weight of, make of an exact weight.

**scale down,** *v.* — *Syn.* cut back, limit, restrict; see **decrease** 2.

**scale up,** *v.* — *Syn.* advance, augment, step up*; see **increase** 1.

**scallop,** *n.* — *Syn.* serration, border, indentation; see **cut** 2, **edge** 1.

**scalpel,** *n.* — *Syn.* dissecting instrument, surgical tool, blade; see **knife.**

**scalper*,** *n.* — *Syn.* ticket salesman, dealer, sharper, speculator.

**scaly,** *modif.* — *Syn.* rough, flaky, scabby, broken, skinned.

**scamp,** *n.* — *Syn.* rogue, knave, scoundrel; see **rascal;** see also **rowdy.**

**scamper,** *v.* — *Syn.* hasten, speed, haste; see **hurry** 1, **run** 2.

**scan,** *v.* **1.** [To analyze] — *Syn.* investigate, study, inquire into; see **examine** 1.

**2.** [To glance at] — *Syn.* browse, thumb over, consider; see **browse, look** 2.

*See Synonym Study at* EXAMINE.

**scandal,** *n.* — *Syn.* shame, disgrace, embarrassment, infamy, turpitude, discredit, blot on one's escutcheon, slander, disrepute, detraction, obloquy, calumny, defamation, opprobrium, reproach, aspersion, backbiting, gossip, eavesdropping, rumor, hearsay. — *Ant.* PRAISE, adulation, flattery.

**scandalize,** *v.* — *Syn.* calumniate, detract, defame, traduce, backbite, vilify, revile, malign, slander, offend, shock, outrage, disgust, asperse, libel, disparage, run down, lampoon, hold up to scorn, severely criticize, disgrace, decry, dishonor, embarrass, belittle, sneer at, blackball, blacken, blackguard, depreciate, condemn, deprecate, speak ill of. — *Ant.* PRAISE, laud, honor.

**scandalous,** *modif.* — *Syn.* disgraceful, infamous, disreputable, ignominious; see **lewd** 1, **shameful** 2.

**scandalously,** *modif.* — *Syn.* shamefully, indecently, cruelly; see **wrongly** 1, 2.

**Scandinavian,** *modif.* — *Syn.* Norse, Viking, Nordic, Germanic, Norwegian, Swedish, Danish, Icelandic, Gutnish, Faroese, Norwego-Danish, Northern, Northern European.

**scant,** *modif.* — *Syn.* scarce, insufficient, meager, limited; see **inadequate** 1, **scanty.**
*See Synonym Study at* SCANTY.

**scanty,** *modif.* — *Syn.* scarce, scant, meager, sparse, barely sufficient, insufficient, inadequate, spare, few, pinched, little, small, bare, slender, narrow, thin, scrimp, scrimpy, tiny, diminutive, short, stingy, in short supply, skimpy\*, measly\*; see also **inadequate** 1. — *Ant.* plentiful, ample, large.

---

**SYN.** — **scanty** implies an inadequacy in amount, number, quantity, etc. of something essential *[a scanty supply of paper]*; **scant** is applied to a barely sufficient amount or a stinted quantity *[the scant attendance at the concert]*; **spare** implies less than a sufficient amount but may connote simply lack of abundance or excess rather than hardship *[to live on spare rations]*; **sparse** applies to a scanty quantity that is thinly distributed over a wide area *[his sparse hair]*; **meager** implies thinness or insufficiency and connotes a lack of that which gives something richness, vigor, strength, fullness, etc. *[meager cultural resources]*

---

**scapegoat,** *n.* — *Syn.* substitute, sacrifice, dupe; see **victim** 1.

**scapegrace,** *n.* — *Syn.* scamp, rogue, scoundrel, scalawag; see **rascal.**

**scar,** *n.* — *Syn.* cicatrix, cat-face, mark, blemish, discoloration, disfigurement, defect, flaw, hurt, wound, injury.

**scar,** *v.* — *Syn.* mark up, cramp, cut, pinch, slash, belt, hurt, maim, pierce, stab, whip, beat, injure.

**scarce,** *modif.* — *Syn.* limited, infrequent, not plentiful; see **rare** 2, **uncommon.**

**make oneself scarce\*** — *Syn.* go, depart, run off; see **leave** 1.

**scarcely,** *modif.* — *Syn.* barely, only just, scantily; see **hardly.**

**scarcity,** *n.* — *Syn.* deficiency, inadequacy, rarity, insufficiency; see **lack** 2, **poverty** 2.

**scare,** *n.* — *Syn.* fright, terror, alarm; see **fear** 1.

**scare,** *v.* — *Syn.* panic, terrify, alarm; see **frighten** 1.
*See Synonym Study at* FRIGHTEN.

**scared,** *modif.* — *Syn.* startled, frightened, fearful; see **afraid** 1, 2.

**scare off** or **away,** *v.* — *Syn.* drive off, drive out, drive away, get rid of, dispose of; see also **frighten** 2.

**scare up\*,** *v.* — *Syn.* produce, provide, get; see **find** 1.

**scarf,** *n.* — *Syn.* throw, sash, tippet, muffler, shawl, comforter, ascot, stole, wrapper, prayer shawl, tallit, chasuble, orarion, pallium; see also **clothes.**

**scarfskin,** *n.* — *Syn.* cuticle, rind, epidermis; see **skin.**

**scarlet,** *modif.* — *Syn.* red, cardinal, royal red, Chinese red, Mandarin red, Turkey red, Persian red, Indian red, Naples red, Majolica earth, Persian earth, Prussian red, scarlet ochre, vermilion, chrome scarlet, French vermilion, paprika, Dutch vermilion, Chinese vermilion, pimento, scarlet vermilion, orient red, oriental red, chrome red, Austrian vermilion, Austrian cinnabar, para vermilion, radium vermilion, antimony vermilion, English vermilion, orange vermilion; see also **red.**

**scat,** *interj.* — *Syn.* go away, be off, begone, out of the way, get out of my way, get out from under my feet, away with you, out with you, be off with you, off with you, get out of my sight, scoot\*, scram\*, git\*, bug off\*, get out\*, shoo\*, shoo-fly\*, gangway\*, beat it\*, get going\*.

**scathing,** *modif.* — *Syn.* brutal, cruel, harsh; see **severe** 1, 2.

**scathingly,** *modif.* — *Syn.* viciously, cruelly, shrilly; see **angrily, brutally.**

**scatological,** *modif.* — *Syn.* scatologic, filthy, obscene, excremental; see **dirty** 1, **lewd** 1, 2.

**scatter,** *v.* **1.** [To become separated] — *Syn.* run apart, run away, go one's own way, diverge, disperse, disband, migrate, spread, go in different directions, blow off, go in many directions, be blown to the four winds. — *Ant.* ASSEMBLE, convene, congregate.
**2.** [To cause to separate] — *Syn.* dispel, derange, dissipate, diffuse, strew, divide, disband, shed, distribute, intersperse, disseminate, separate, disunite, sunder, scatter to the wind, sever, set asunder. — *Ant.* UNITE, join, mix.
**3.** [To seed] — *Syn.* disseminate, set, strew.
**4.** [To waste] — *Syn.* spend, expend, dissipate, fritter away, squander, lavish, be prodigal with one's substance, spend prodigally, sow, broadcast, pour out like water, exhaust, throw around\*, scatter to the birds\*; see also **spend** 1, **waste** 2.

---

**SYN.** — **scatter** implies a strewing around loosely *[to scatter seeds]* or a forcible driving apart in different directions *[the breeze scattered the papers]*; **disperse** implies a scattering which completely breaks up an assemblage and spreads the individuals far and wide *[a people dispersed throughout the world]*; **dissipate** implies complete dissolution, as by crumbling, wasting, etc. *[to dissipate a fortune]*; **dispel** suggests a scattering that drives away something that obscures, confuses, troubles, etc. *[to dispel fears]*

---

**scatterbrained,** *modif.* — *Syn.* silly, giddy, irrational; see **illogical, stupid** 1.

**scattered,** *modif.* — *Syn.* spread, strewed, rambling, sowed, sown, sprinkled, spread abroad, separated, disseminated, dispersed, strung out, distributed, widespread, diffuse, diffused, all over the place, separate, shaken out. — *Ant.* GATHERED, condensed, concentrated.

**scattering,** *modif.* — *Syn.* uneven, some, not many; see **few, irregular** 1.

**scatteringly,** *modif.* — *Syn.* unevenly, not regularly, not evenly, sometimes; see **irregularly.**

**scavenger,** *n.* — *Syn.* forager, scrounge, scrounger, hunter, freeloader, collector; see also **junk dealer.**

**scenario,** *n.* — *Syn.* plot, outline, synopsis, situation; see **summary.**

**scene,** *n.* **1.** [Spectacle] — *Syn.* exhibition, display, picture; see **view** 1.
**2.** [A disturbance] — *Syn.* fuss, commotion, uproar; see **disturbance** 1, 2.
**behind the scenes** — *Syn.* surreptitiously, quietly, deviously; see **secret** 1, 3.
**make the scene★** — *Syn.* come, get there, make it★, show up; see **arrive** 1.

**scenery,** *n.* — *Syn.* landscape, prospect, spectacle; see **view** 1, 2.

**scenic,** *modif.* — *Syn.* beautiful, spectacular, dramatic; see **picturesque** 1.

**scent,** *n.* — *Syn.* odor, fragrance, redolence; see **perfume, smell** 1, 2.
*See Synonym Study at* PERFUME, SMELL.

**scepter,** *n.* **1.** [Rod] — *Syn.* baton, stick, staff, fasces; see **wand.**
**2.** [Authority] — *Syn.* supremacy, jurisdiction, authority; see **command** 2, **power** 2.

**schedule,** *n.* **1.** [List] — *Syn.* catalogue, inventory, registry; see **list, record** 1.
**2.** [Program] — *Syn.* agenda, order of business, calendar; see **plan** 2, **program** 2.
**on schedule** — *Syn.* on time, not lagging behind, being pushed along; see **punctual.**

**schedule,** *v.* — *Syn.* record, register, catalogue; see **list** 1, **program** 1.

**scheduled,** *modif.* — *Syn.* listed, stated, arranged; see **planned, proposed.**

**scheme,** *n.* — *Syn.* project, design, plot, stratagem; see **plan** 2, **system** 2.
*See Synonym Study at* PLAN.

**scheme,** *v.* — *Syn.* intrigue, contrive, devise, plot; see **plan** 1.

**schemer,** *n.* — *Syn.* conniver, rogue, deceiver; see **rascal.**

**scheming,** *modif.* — *Syn.* tricky, cunning, crafty; see **sly** 1.

**schism,** *n.* — *Syn.* split, section, cabal, sect; see **division** 2, **faction** 1.

**schismatic,** *modif.* — *Syn.* discordant, heretical, dissident; see **atheistic, rebellious** 2.

**schismatic,** *n.* — *Syn.* heretic, rebel, dissenter; see **protester, skeptic.**

**scholar,** *n.* **1.** [A pupil] — *Syn.* student, schoolboy, schoolgirl, learner; see **student.**
**2.** [An expert in humanistic studies] — *Syn.* philosopher, savant, pundit, authority, sage, professor, academic, teacher, doctor, litterateur, learned person; see also **critic** 2, **intellectual, scientist.**
Scholars include: editor, textual critic, lexicographer, historian, biographer, bibliographer, comparativist, linguist, philologist, semanticist, paleographer, historiographer, archaeologist, demographer, geographer, geopolitician, political scientist, sociologist, philosopher, folklorist, anthropologist, economist, ethnologist, cartographer, classicist, humanist, behaviorist, dialectologist, rhetorician, grammarian, etymologist, musicologist, literary historian, theologian, orientalist.
*See Synonym Study at* STUDENT.

**scholarly,** *modif.* — *Syn.* erudite, cultured, studious; see **educated** 1, **learned** 1.

**scholarship,** *n.* — *Syn.* research, wisdom, scientific approach, learning, pedantry, accomplishments, intellectualism, erudition, bibliography, bibliomania, studentship; see also **knowledge** 1.

**scholastic,** *modif.* — *Syn.* academic, literary, lettered; see **learned** 1, 2.

**school,** *n.* **1.** [An institution of learning] — *Syn.* acad-

emy, grammar school, *lycée* (French), *Gymnasium* (German).
Varieties of schools include: preschool, nursery school, elementary school, middle school, grade school, grammar school, junior high school, high school, secondary school, private school, public school, day school, night school, parochial school, boarding school, military school, seminary, normal school, conservatory, trade school, vocational school, technical school, graduate school, professional school, divinity school, art school, business school, medical school, dental school, veterinary school, law school, law college, college of law, preparatory school, junior college, community college, the grades★; see also **academy** 1, **college, university.**
**2.** [Persons or products associated by common intellectual or artistic theories] — *Syn.* class, party, adherents, following, circle; see also **academy** 2.
**3.** [A building housing a school, sense 1] — *Syn.* schoolhouse, hall, establishment, institution; see **building** 1.
**go to school** — *Syn.* attend school, take classes, study, matriculate; see **learn** 1, **register.**

**school-age,** *modif.* — *Syn.* youthful, old enough to go to school, of school age; see **childish** 1, **young** 1.

**schoolbook,** *n.* — *Syn.* text, primer, textbook, assigned reading; see **book** 1, **text** 1.

**schoolboy,** *n.* — *Syn.* lad, learner, pupil, youth; see **student.**

**schoolhouse,** *n.* — *Syn.* structure, institution, house; see **building** 1, **school** 3.

**schooling,** *n.* — *Syn.* teaching, nurture, discipline; see **education** 1.

**schoolmate,** *n.* — *Syn.* roommate, comrade, classmate, chum★; see **friend** 1.

**schoolteacher,** *n.* — *Syn.* educator, lecturer, instructor; see **teacher** 1, 2, **professor.**

**school year,** *n.* — *Syn.* academic year, from September to June, term, semester; see **year.**

**schooner,** *n.* — *Syn.* clipper, yacht, vessel; see **boat, ship.**

**science,** *n.* **1.** [An organized body of knowledge] — *Syn.* classified information, department of learning, branch of knowledge, system of knowledge, body of fact; see also **anthropology, archaeology, astronomy, biology, botany, chemistry, cybernetics, geography, geology, mathematics, medicine** 3, **physics, physiology, psychology, social science, sociology, zoology** for commonly recognized sciences.
**2.** [A highly developed skill] — *Syn.* craftsmanship, art, deftness; see **ability** 1, 2.

**scientific,** *modif.* **1.** [Objectively accurate] — *Syn.* precise, exact, clear; see **accurate** 2, **objective** 1.
**2.** [Concerning science] — *Syn.* experimental, observable, systematic, controlled, deductive, methodically sound; see also **logical** 1.

**scientifically,** *modif.* — *Syn.* reliably, accurately, dependably; see **carefully** 1, 2, **exactly.**

**scientist,** *n.* — *Syn.* expert, specialist, investigator, laboratory technologist, laboratory technician, savant, natural philosopher, student of natural history, student of natural phenomena, explorer, research worker, research assistant, learned person, serious student, seeker after knowledge, Doctor of Science, Ph.D., scientific thinker, pure scientist, applied scientist, a Pasteur, an Einstein, a regular Einstein★.
Scientists include: anatomist, astrologist, cosmologist, astronomer, botanist, zoologist, biologist, chemist, biochemist, geneticist, embryologist, meteorologist, geologist, geographer, mathematician, physicist, psychiatrist, psychologist, astrophysicist, spectroscopist, spec-

tral analyst, ecologist, biophysicist, bacteriologist, marine biologist, oceanographer, geopolitician, systematic botanist, industrial chemist, manufacturing chemist, chemurgist, pharmacist, chemical engineer, nuclear engineer, nuclear physicist, sanitary engineer, agronomist, entomologist, ornithologist, endocrinologist, radiologist, audiologist, histologist, immunologist, oncologist, toxicologist, pathologist, graphologist, geophysicist, cartographer, neurologist, neurophysicist, paleontologist, paleobotanist, seismologist, volcanologist, structural geologist, oil geologist, mineralogist, metallurgist, anthropologist, ethnologist, comparative anatomist, Egyptologist, archaeologist, ethnobiologist, sociologist, linguist, dialectologist, folklorist; see also **dentist, doctor, professor.**

**scintillate,** *v.* — *Syn.* twinkle, glimmer, sparkle, glitter; see **shine** 1, 2.

**scion,** *n.* — *Syn.* descendant, heir, progeny; see **child, offspring.**

**scissors,** *n.* — *Syn.* shears, pair of scissors, pair of shears, cutting instrument.

**scoff,** *v.* — *Syn.* mock, deride, jeer; see **ridicule.**

**scold,** *v.* — *Syn.* admonish, chide, berate, chasten, asperse, expostulate with, rebuke, censure, reprove, upbraid, reprimand, taunt, cavil, criticize, denounce, disparage, recriminate, rate, revile, rail, abuse, objurate, vituperate, reprobate, vilify, find fault with, nag, lecture, have on the carpet*, rake over the coals*, give one a talking to*, preach*, tell off*, chew out*, bawl out*, get after*, chew down*, dress down*, call down*, lay down the law*, blow up at*, jump down one's throat*, jump on*, call*, keep after*, burn up*, light into*, take the wind out of one's sails*, put down*; see also **punish.** — *Ant.* PRAISE, commend, extoll.

---

*SYN.* — **scold** is the common term meaning to find fault with or to rebuke in angry, irritated, often nagging language *[a mother scolds a naughty child]*; **upbraid** implies bitter reproach or censure and usually connotes justification for this *[she upbraided me for my carelessness]*; **berate** suggests continuous, heated, even violent reproach, often connoting excessive abuse *[the old shrew continued berating them]*; **revile** implies the use of highly abusive and contemptuous language and often connotes deliberate defamation or slander *[he reviled his opponent unmercifully]*; **vituperate** suggests even greater violence in the attack *[vituperating each other with foul epithets]*

---

**scoop,** *v.* — *Syn.* ladle, shovel, bail; see **dip** 1.

**scoot,** *v.* — *Syn.* dart, speed, rush; see **hasten** 1, **hurry** 1.

**scooter*,** *n.* — *Syn.* motor scooter, bike*, motorbike*; see **motorcycle.**

**scope,** *n.* — *Syn.* reach, range, field; see **expanse, extent, range** 2.
*See Synonym Study at* RANGE.

**scorch,** *v.* — *Syn.* singe, roast, parch, shrivel; see **burn** 2, 6.
*See Synonym Study at* BURN.

**scorching,** *modif.* 1. [Hot] — *Syn.* fiery, searing, sweltering; see **burning** 1, **hot** 1.
2. [Harsh] — *Syn.* caustic, derisive, curt; see **sarcastic, scornful** 1, 2.

**score,** *n.* 1. [A tally] — *Syn.* stock, counterstock, countertally, reckoning, record, average, rate, account, count, number.
2. [The total of the scores, sense 1] — *Syn.* summation, aggregate, sum, addition, summary, amount, final tally, final account; see also **number** 1, **whole.**

3. [Written music] — *Syn.* transcript, arrangement, orchestration; see **arrangement** 5, **composition, music** 1.

**know the score*** — *Syn.* grasp the situation, be aware, comprehend; see **know** 1, **understand** 1.

**score,** *v.* 1. [To make a single score] — *Syn.* make a goal, gain a point, win a point, rack up*, chalk up*.
2. [To compute the score] — *Syn.* total, calculate, reckon, tally, enumerate, count, add.
3. [To damage] — *Syn.* deface, mar, mark; see **damage** 1, **maim.**
4. [To compose a musical accompaniment] — *Syn.* orchestrate, arrange, adapt; see **arrange** 3, **compose** 3.
5. [*To purchase legally or illegally] — *Syn.* get, procure, secure; see **buy** 1, **obtain** 1.
6. [*To copulate] — *Syn.* have intercourse with, sleep with, lie with, fornicate; see **copulate.**

**scorn,** *v.* 1. [To treat with scorn] — *Syn.* hold in contempt, despise, disdain; see **despise, hate** 1.
2. [To refuse as a matter of principle] — *Syn.* ignore, flout, defy, spurn, repudiate, reject, turn the back upon, avoid, shun, renounce; see also **confute, refuse, refute.** — *Ant.* ACKNOWLEDGE, accept, welcome.
*See Synonym Study at* DESPISE.

**scornful,** *modif.* 1. [Given to scorning] — *Syn.* contemptuous, disdainful, haughty, supercilious, overbearing, arrogant, insolent, cynical, sneering, hypercritical, with the nose in the air*, toplofty*, snooty*; see also **egotistic** 2. — *Ant.* RESPECTFUL, admiring, gracious.
2. [Characterized by scorn] — *Syn.* derisive, opprobrious, contumelious, scurrilous, abusive, insulting, offensive, rude, sarcastic, malicious, jeering, mocking, sneering, ironical. — *Ant.* POLITE, respectful, flattering.

**scornfully,** *modif.* — *Syn.* contemptuously, rudely, sneeringly; see **proudly, sarcastically.**

**scotch,** *v.* — *Syn.* thwart, stop, block; see **hinder.**

**scot-free,** *modif.* — *Syn.* uncontrolled, footloose, liberated; see **free** 2.

**Scotland,** *n.* — *Syn.* Scotia, the Highlands, Caledonia; see **Britain, England.**

**Scots,** *modif.* — *Syn.* Scotch, Scottish, Caledonian, highland, from north of the border, Gaelic, highland, lowland, Lallan; see also **Anglo-Saxon.**

**Scotsman,** *n.* — *Syn.* Gael, Highlander, clansman, Scotchman, Scot.

**scoundrel,** *n.* — *Syn.* rogue, scamp, villain; see **rascal.**

**scour,** *v.* 1. [To cleanse] — *Syn.* scrub, cleanse, rub; see **clean, wash** 1, 2.
2. [To search] — *Syn.* seek, look for, inquire; see **hunt** 2, **search.**

**scourge,** *n.* 1. [A whip] — *Syn.* strap, cord, stick, switch; see **whip.**
2. [Punishment] — *Syn.* correction, penalty, infliction; see **punishment.**

**scourge,** *v.* 1. [To whip] — *Syn.* flog, hit, thrash; see **beat** 2.
2. [To punish] — *Syn.* chastise, castigate, penalize; see **punish.**

**scouring powder,** *n.* — *Syn.* cleaner, scrubbing powder, detergent; see **cleanser, soap.**

**scout,** *n.* 1. [One who gathers information] — *Syn.* explorer, pioneer, outpost, runner, advance guard, precursor, patrol, reconnoiterer.
2. [*A Boy Scout]. Degrees of scouts, sense 2, include: Cub, Tenderfoot, Second Class, First Class, Star, Life, Eagle, Queen's (British), bronze palm, gold palm, silver palm.
3. [*A Girl Scout] — *Syn.* explorer, young adventurer, Bluebird, Campfire Girl, pioneer.

Girl Scout ranks include: Brownie, Junior, Cadette, Senior.

**scow,** *n.* — *Syn.* barge, cargo ship, freighter; see **boat, ship.**

**scowl,** *v.* — *Syn.* glower, disapprove, grimace; see **frown, glare** 2.

**scramble,** *v.* **1.** [To mix] — *Syn.* combine, blend, interfuse, jumble; see **mix** 1.
**2.** [To climb hastily] — *Syn.* clamber, push, struggle; see **climb** 2.

**scrap,** *n.* **1.** [Junk metal] — *Syn.* waste material, chips, cuttings; see **trash** 3.
**2.** [A bit] — *Syn.* fragment, particle, portion; see **bit** 1, **piece** 1.
**3.** [*A fight] — *Syn.* quarrel, brawl, squabble; see **fight** 1.

**scrap,** *v.* **1.** [To discard] — *Syn.* reject, forsake, dismiss; see **abandon** 2, **discard.**
**2.** [*To fight] — *Syn.* wrangle, battle, squabble; see **fight** 1, **quarrel.**

**scrapbook,** *n.* — *Syn.* portfolio, memorabilia, clippings, notebook; see **album, collection** 2.

**scrape,** *v.* — *Syn.* abrade, scour, rasp; see **irritate** 2, **rub** 1.

**scraper,** *n.* — *Syn.* grater, grader, rasp, eraser, abrasive; see also **hoe, tool** 1.

**scratch,** *n.* — *Syn.* hurt, cut, mark; see **injury** 1, **scar.**
**from scratch*** — *Syn.* from the start, from the beginning, without preparation, without a predecessor, solely; see also **alone, original** 1.

**scratch,** *v.* — *Syn.* scrape, scarify, prick; see **damage** 1, **hurt** 1.

**scratching,** *modif.* — *Syn.* grating, abrading, abrasive, attritive, rasping, erosive, scratchy, scarifying; see also **rough** 1.

**scratch the surface*,** *v.* — *Syn.* be superficial, analyze superficially, inspect superficially, touch on, touch upon, mention, skim, scan, brush; see also **begin** 1, 2.

**scrawl,** *n.* — *Syn.* scribbling, scratch, chicken tracks, *barbouillage* (French); see **handwriting.**

**scrawl,** *v.* — *Syn.* scribble, scratch, doodle; see **write** 2.

**scrawled,** *modif.* — *Syn.* scribbled, scratched, inscribed; see **written** 2.

**scrawny,** *modif.* — *Syn.* lanky, gaunt, lean, skinny; see **thin** 2.

**scream,** *n.* — *Syn.* screech, outcry, shriek; see **cry** 1, **yell** 1.

**scream,** *v.* — *Syn.* shriek, screech, squeal; see **cry** 3, **yell.**

**screaming,** *modif.* — *Syn.* shrieking, screeching, squealing; see **yelling.**

**screech,** *n.* — *Syn.* shriek, yell, outcry; see **cry** 1.

**screech,** *v.* — *Syn.* scream, shout, shriek; see **yell.**

**screen,** *n.* **1.** [A concealment] — *Syn.* cloak, cover, covering, curtain, shield, envelope, veil, mask, shade.
**2.** [A protection] — *Syn.* partition, netting, shelter, guard, security; see also **cover** 1, **protection** 2.
**3.** [A surface on which images are projected] — *Syn.* silver screen, movie screen, film screen, television screen, tube, TV screen.

**screen,** *v.* **1.** [To hide] — *Syn.* veil, conceal, mask; see **hide** 1.
**2.** [To choose] — *Syn.* select, eliminate, sift; see **choose** 1.

**screened,** *modif.* — *Syn.* hidden, sheltered, concealed; see **secret** 3.

**screw,** *n.* — *Syn.* spiral, worm, bolt, pin; see also **fastener.**
Types of screws include: jack, lead, leveling, dowel, dou-

ble, drive, Hindley's, lag, worm, male, outside, female, inside, Phillips (trademark), right-handed, left-handed, metric, milled, endless, reciprocal, tapping, carriage, drill, regulating, set, winged, thumb, rigger's, right-and-left, setting up, society, spiral, triple, feed, wood, machine, dry wall, sheet metal.

**have a screw loose*** — *Syn.* be crazy, be touched in the head, be off one's rocker*, be off one's nut*; see **insane** 1.

**put the screws to*** — *Syn.* compel, coerce, give the treatment*; see **force** 1.

**screw,** *v.* — *Syn.* twine, wind, contort; see **turn** 1, **twist.**

**screw-up*,** *n.* — *Syn.* mistake, confusion, mess; see **error** 1, **confusion.**

**screw up*,** *v.* — *Syn.* bungle, foul up, mishandle; see **botch.**

**screwy*,** *modif.* — *Syn.* odd, crazy, inappropriate; see **insane** 1, **wrong** 2, 3.

**scribble,** *n.* — *Syn.* scrawl, scrabble, scratch; see **handwriting.**

**scribble,** *v.* — *Syn.* scrawl, scratch, scrabble; see **write** 2.

**scribe,** *n.* **1.** [One who transcribes professionally] — *Syn.* copyist, clerk, secretary, keeper of accounts, copier, transcriber, scrivener.
**2.** [A writer] — *Syn.* reporter, correspondent, penman; see **author** 1, **editor, writer.**

**scrimmage,** *n.* — *Syn.* struggle, confusion, scramble, scuffle, scrap*; see also **fight** 1.

**scrimp,** *v.* — *Syn.* conserve, cut corners, pinch pennies, pinch, skimp; see also **economize, save** 3.

**script,** *n.* **1.** [Handwriting] — *Syn.* writing, characters, chirography; see **handwriting.**
**2.** [Playbook] — *Syn.* lines, text, dialogue, book, scenario.

**scriptural,** *modif.* **1.** [Authoritative] — *Syn.* recorded, accepted, standard, textual; see **authoritative** 2, **written** 2.
**2.** [Biblical] — *Syn.* ecclesiastical, canonical, divine; see **religious** 1.

**scripture,** *n.* **1.** [Writing] — *Syn.* document, manuscript, inscription; see **writing** 2.
**2.** [Truth] — *Syn.* reality, verity, final word; see **truth** 1.
**3.** [*Capital;* the Bible] — *Syn.* the Word, Holy Writ, the Book; see **Bible** 2.

**scroll,** *n.* **1.** [A rolled sheet, especially a manuscript] — *Syn.* parchment, scripture, document; see **manuscript, writing** 2.
**2.** [A curved ornament] — *Syn.* volute, spiral, convolution; see **decoration** 2.

**scrub,** *modif.* **1.** [Inferior] — *Syn.* second-rate, unimportant, mediocre; see **poor** 2.
**2.** [Dwarf] — *Syn.* stunted, puny, diminutive; see **little** 1.

**scrub*,** *n.* — *Syn.* runt, mongrel, cur, cull, dwarf, an undesirable, inferior example; see also **runt** 1.

**scrub,** *v.* — *Syn.* rub, cleanse, scour; see **clean, wash** 1, 2.

**scrubbed,** *modif.* — *Syn.* cleaned, polished, immaculate; see **clean** 1.

**scrubbing,** *n.* — *Syn.* rubbing, washing, cleansing; see **cleaning.**

**scrubby,** *modif.* — *Syn.* inferior, stunted, scrawny; see **inadequate** 1, **poor** 2.

**scrumptious,** *modif.* — *Syn.* appetizing, tasty, delectable; see **delicious** 1, **rich** 4.

**scruple,** *n.* — *Syn.* compunction, qualm, uneasiness; see **doubt** 2, **qualm** 1.
*See Synonym Study at* QUALM.

**scruples,** *pl. n.* — *Syn.* overconscientiousness, conscience, scrupulousness; see **attention** 2, **care** 1.

**scrupulous,** *modif.* **1.** [Exact] — *Syn.* punctilious, strict, conscientious; see **careful.**

**2.** [Principled] — *Syn.* ethical, upright, honorable, circumspect, moral.

*See Synonym Study at* CAREFUL.

**scrupulously,** *modif.* — *Syn.* exactly, precisely, devotedly; see **carefully** 1.

**scrutinize,** *v.* — *Syn.* view, study, pore over, stare; see **examine** 1, **watch** 1.

*See Synonym Study at* EXAMINE.

**scrutiny,** *n.* — *Syn.* analysis, investigation, inspection; see **examination** 1.

**scuff,** *n.* — *Syn.* clamor, sound, scrape; see **noise** 2.

**scuffle,** *n.* — *Syn.* struggle, shuffle, strife; see **fight** 1.

**sculptor,** *n.* — *Syn.* artist, modeler, carver, stone carver, wood carver, worker in bronze, worker in metal, worker in stone.
Major sculptors include: Phidias, Ghiberti, Donatello, Luca della Robbia, Leonardo da Vinci, Michelangelo, Giovanni da Bologna, Benvenuto Cellini, Gian Lorenzo Bernini, Auguste Rodin, Constantin Brancusi, Henry Moore, Jacques Lipchitz, Aristide Maillol, Giovanni Pisano, Augustus Saint-Gaudens, Pablo Picasso, Daniel Chester French, Frederic Remington, Louise Nevelson.

**sculpture,** *n.* **1.** [The art of sculpting] — *Syn.* carving, modeling, carving in stone, modeling in clay, kinetic sculpture, op art, casting in bronze, woodcutting, stone carving, plastic art; see also **art** 2, **image** 2.

**2.** [A sculpted work] — *Syn.* statue, statuette, figure, figurine, carving, model, relief, bas-relief, marble, stone carving, woodcarving, bronze, bust.

**sculptured,** *modif.* — *Syn.* formed, cast, molded, engraved, carved, in relief, chiseled.

**scum,** *n.* — *Syn.* froth, film, impurities; see **residue,** **trash** 1, 3.

**scurrility,** *n.* — *Syn.* coarseness, indecency, vulgarity, slander, sarcasm, defilement; see also **abuse** 1.

**scurrilous,** *modif.* — *Syn.* indecent, coarse, vulgar, foulmouthed, obscene, shameless, ribald; see also **lewd** 1, 2.

**scurry,** *v.* — *Syn.* race, scamper, rush; see **hasten** 1, **run** 2.

**scutcheon,** *n.* — *Syn.* shield, insignia, crest, device; see **decoration** 3.

**scuttle,** *v.* **1.** [To destroy] — *Syn.* submerge, abandon, dismantle; see **destroy** 1, **sink** 2.

**2.** [To hurry] — *Syn.* scurry, scramble, sprint; see **hasten** 1, **run** 2.

**scuttlebutt\*,** *n.* — *Syn.* gossip, talk, inside information, straight dope\*; see **facts, gossip** 1, **rumor** 1.

**scythe,** *n.* — *Syn.* cutter, sickle, machete; see **hoe, knife.**

**sea,** *n.* Major seas of the world include: Bering, Caribbean, Baltic, North, Irish, Mediterranean, Adriatic, Ionian, Aegean, Norwegian, Tyrrhenian, Black, Caspian, Azov, Red, Dead, White, Barents, Tasman, Okhotsk, Japan, Yellow, Philippine, South China, Arabian, East China, Java, Timor, Sulu, Celebes, Coral; see also **ocean.**

**at sea\*** — *Syn.* confused, puzzled, upset; see **bewildered, uncertain** 2.

**put (out) to sea** — *Syn.* embark, go, start out; see **leave** 1, **sail** 1.

**sea bottom,** *n.* — *Syn.* ocean floor, deep-sea floor, bottom of the sea, ocean bottom, abyssal depths, ocean depths, continental shelf, undersea topography, undersea park, marine farm, tidewater, the briny deep\*; see

also **ocean.**
Structures of the sea bottom include: bank, sands, seamount, submarine mountain, ridge, guyot, hill, tablemount, escarpment, plateau, reef, basin, canal, province, shoal, sill, channel, deep, depth, plain, trench, trough, fracture zone, rift.

**seacoast,** *n.* — *Syn.* seashore, seaboard, seaside; see **shore.**

**seafaring,** *modif.* — *Syn.* naval, oceanic, marine; see **maritime** 2, **nautical.**

**sea food,** *n.* — *Syn.* fish, halibut, mollusk, marine life; see **fish, lobster, shellfish.**

**seal,** *n.* **1.** [Approval] — *Syn.* authorization, permit, allowance; see **permission.**

**2.** [Fastener] — *Syn.* adhesive tape, sticker, tie; see **fastener, tape.**

**sealed,** *modif.* — *Syn.* secured, fixed, held together, closed, airtight; see also **firm** 1, **tight** 2.

**seal off,** *v.* — *Syn.* quarantine, close, segregate; see **forbid, restrict** 2.

**seam,** *n.* — *Syn.* joint, line of joining, union, stitching, line of stitching, closure, suture.

**seaman,** *n.* — *Syn.* seafarer, A.B., navigator, tar; see **marines, sailor** 1, 2.

**seamstress,** *n.* — *Syn.* sewer, needleworker, designer, *couturière* (French); see **dressmaker, tailor.**

**seamy,** *modif.* — *Syn.* unpleasant, bad, sordid, disagreeable; see **disappointing, disturbing.**

**séance,** *n.* — *Syn.* divination, ritual, session, meeting; see **gathering.**

**seaplane,** *n.* — *Syn.* hydroplane, airplane, amphibian; see **plane** 3.

**seaport,** *n.* — *Syn.* port, haven, town; see **dock** 1, **harbor** 2.

**sea power,** *n.* — *Syn.* navy, naval strength, naval forces, task force; see **navy.**

**sear,** *v.* **1.** [To cook by searing] — *Syn.* brown, char, burn, toast; see **burn** 2, **cook.**

**2.** [To dry by searing] — *Syn.* parch, tan, harden, cauterize; see **burn** 2, **dry** 2.

*See Synonym Study at* BURN.

**search,** *n.* — *Syn.* exploration, quest, research; see **hunt** 2.

**in search of** — *Syn.* looking for, seeking, on the lookout for; see **searching** 2.

**search,** *v.* — *Syn.* explore, examine, rummage, comb, ransack, look up and down, smell around, track down, look for, go through, cast about, beat about, poke into, grope in the dark\*, scrutinize; see also **hunt** 2, **seek** 1.

**searching,** *modif.* **1.** [Careful] — *Syn.* exploring, scrutinizing, examining; see **careful.**

**2.** [Seeking] — *Syn.* hunting, looking for, seeking, pursuing, in search of, ready for, in the market for, in need of, needing, wanting, on the lookout for\*, looking out for\*, crazy about\*, all hot for\*.

**searchlight,** *n.* — *Syn.* arc light, beam, flashlight; see **light** 3.

**search me\*,** *interj.* — *Syn.* I don't know, who knows?\*, how should I know?\*, that's not my affair, that's not in my department; see also **uncertainty** 1.

**seashell,** *n.* Common sea shells include: conch, periwinkle, abalone, ammonite, ram's horn, clam, mussel, oyster, starfish, sea urchin, sand dollar, sea snail, nautilus, scallop, cowrie, limpet, cockle, whelk; see also **shell** 3.

**seashore,** *n.* — *Syn.* seaboard, seaside, seacoast; see **shore.**

**seasick,** *modif.* — *Syn.* nauseated, miserable, suffering from *mal de mer*; see **sick.**

**seaside,** *n.* — *Syn.* seaboard, seashore, seacoast; see **resort** 2, **shore.**

**season,** *n.* — *Syn.* period, term, a while, division, certain months of the year; see also **fall** 5, **spring** 2, **summer, winter.**

**in good season** — *Syn.* not late, on time, fairly soon; see **early** 2.

**in season** — *Syn.* seasonable, on the market, (readily) available; see **available.**

**seasonable,** *modif.* — *Syn.* appropriate, opportune, convenient; see **timely.**

*See Synonym Study at* TIMELY.

**seasonal,** *modif.* — *Syn.* once a season, out of season, periodically, biennial, depending on the season, with the times, once in a while; see also **annual, yearly.**

**seasoned,** *modif.* **1.** [Spicy] — *Syn.* tangy, sharp, aromatic, salty, salted; see also **spicy** 1.

**2.** [Experienced] — *Syn.* established, settled, mature; see **able** 2, **experienced.**

**seasoning,** *n.* — *Syn.* sauce, relish, spice, herbs, pungency; see also **flavoring, pickle** 2.

**seat,** *n.* **1.** [A structure on which one may sit] — *Syn.* bench, settee, sofa, couch, settle, pew, chair, stool, bleacher, thwart; see also **furniture.**

**2.** [Space in which one may sit] — *Syn.* situation, chair, accommodation; see **place** 2.

**3.** [*The buttocks] — *Syn.* rear, rear end*, behind, breech; see **rump.**

**4.** [An official situation] — *Syn.* post, position, office, chair, place; see also **job** 1, **profession** 1, **trade** 2.

**5.** [A place of support, usually a surface] — *Syn.* bed, fitting, bottom; see **foundation** 2, **support** 2.

**have** or **take a seat** — *Syn.* be seated, sit down, occupy a place; see **sit** 1.

**seated,** *modif.* — *Syn.* situated, located, settled, installed, established, rooted, set, fitted in place, placed, arranged, accommodated with seats.

**seating,** *n.* — *Syn.* places, reservations, chairs, seats, room, accommodation, arrangement, seating space.

**seaward,** *modif.* — *Syn.* offshore, fresh, fresh from the sea, out to sea, over the sea, over the ocean; see also **coastal, maritime** 1, 2.

**seaweed,** *n.* — *Syn.* kelp, tangle, sea tangle, sea meadow, algae, marine meadow; see also **plant.**

Types of seaweed include: sea moss, Irish moss, Sargasso weed, dulse, rockweed, sea lettuce, kelp, giant kelp, agar-agar, gulfweed, hempweed, laminaria, sea cabbage.

**seaworthy,** *modif.* — *Syn.* fit for sea, navigable, secure; see **safe** 1.

**secede,** *v.* — *Syn.* withdraw, retract, leave, break away from; see **retire** 1, **retreat** 1.

**secession,** *n.* — *Syn.* withdrawal, seceding, retraction, severance; see **retirement** 1.

**seclude,** *v.* **1.** [To isolate] — *Syn.* quarantine, ostracize, evict; see **separate** 2.

**2.** [To hide] — *Syn.* screen out, conceal, cover; see **hide** 1.

**secluded,** *modif.* — *Syn.* screened, removed, sequestered; see **isolated, withdrawn.**

**seclusion,** *n.* — *Syn.* solitude, aloofness, privacy; see **retirement** 2.

*See Synonym Study at* SOLITUDE.

**second,** *modif.* — *Syn.* secondary, subordinate, inferior, next, next in order, following, next to the first, next in rank, another, other; see also **unimportant.**

**on second thought** — *Syn.* on further consideration, on mature consideration, in reality, on the other hand, as an afterthought; see also **incidentally.**

**play second fiddle to** — *Syn.* defer to, be inferior to, be less successful than, get less attention than; see **fail** 1.

**second,** *n.* — *Syn.* flash, trice, flash of an eyelid; see **moment, instant.**

**secondary,** *modif.* **1.** [Derived] — *Syn.* dependent, developed, consequent, subsequent, proximate, subordinate, subsidiary, auxiliary. — *Ant.* ORIGINAL, primary, basic.

**2.** [Minor] — *Syn.* inconsiderable, petty, small; see **trivial, unimportant.**

**seconded,** *modif.* — *Syn.* backed, favored, supported; see **approved.**

**secondhand,** *modif.* — *Syn.* used, not new, reclaimed, renewed, re-used, old, worn, borrowed, hand-me-down, pre-owned, derived, not original.

**secondly,** *modif.* — *Syn.* in the second place, furthermore, also, besides, next, on the other hand, in the next place, for the next step, next in order, further, to continue; see also **including.**

**second-rate,** *modif.* — *Syn.* mediocre, inferior, common; see **poor** 2.

**secrecy,** *n.* — *Syn.* concealment, confidence, hiding, seclusion, privacy, retirement, solitude, mystery, dark, darkness, isolation, reticence, stealth, surreptitiousness.

**secret,** *modif.* **1.** [Not generally known] — *Syn.* mysterious, ambiguous, hidden, unknown, arcane, cryptic, esoteric, abstruse, occult, mystic, mystical, classified, dark, veiled, enigmatical, enigmatic, strange, deep, buried in mystery, obscure, clouded, recondite, shrouded, unenlightened, unintelligible, cabalistic. — *Ant.* KNOWN, revealed, exposed.

**2.** [Hidden] — *Syn.* latent, secluded, concealed; see **hidden** 2.

**3.** [Operating secretly] — *Syn.* clandestine, covert, underhand, underhanded, stealthy, sly, surreptitious, close, in ambuscade, in ambush, furtive, disguised, undercover, hush-hush*, backdoor, confidential, backstairs, incognito, camouflaged, cryptographic, enigmatic, under false pretense, unrevealed, undisclosed, dissembled, dissimulated, *in camera* (Latin), under wraps*; see also **secretive, sly** 1, **taciturn.** — *Ant.* OPEN, aboveboard, overt.

---

**SYN.** — **secret,** the general term, implies a concealing or keeping from the knowledge of others, for whatever reason */my secret opinion of him/*; **covert** implies a concealing as by disguising or veiling */a covert threat/*; **clandestine** suggests that what is being kept secret is of an illicit, immoral, or proscribed nature */their clandestine meetings in the park/*; **stealthy** implies a slow, quiet secrecy of action in an attempt to elude notice and often connotes deceit */the stealthy advance of the panther/*; **furtive** adds to this connotations of slyness or watchfulness and suggests a reprehensible objective */the furtive movement of his hand toward my pocket/*; **surreptitious** connotes a feeling of guilt in the one who is acting in a furtive or stealthy manner */she stole a surreptitious glance at him/*; **underhanded** implies a stealthiness characterized by fraudulence or deceit */underhanded business dealings/*

---

**secret,** *n.* — *Syn.* mystery, deep mystery, something veiled, something hidden, confidence, private matter, code, personal matter, privileged information, top secret, enigma, intrigue, puzzle, something forbidden, classified information, an unknown, magic number, the unknown.

**in secret** — *Syn.* slyly, surreptitiously, quietly; see **secret** 3.

**secretariat,** *n.* — *Syn.* bureau, department, council; see **administration** 2, **committee.**

**secretary,** *n.* **1.** [A secondary executive officer] — *Syn.* director, manager, superintendent, cabinet member, cabinet officer, bureau chief, head of a department, department manager, administrator.
**2.** [An assistant] — *Syn.* administrative assistant, executive secretary, personal secretary, clerk, typist, stenographer, copyist, amanuensis, scribe, scrivener, recorder, confidential clerk, correspondent.

**secrete,** *v.* **1.** [To hide] — *Syn.* conceal, cover, seclude; see **disguise, hide** 1.
**2.** [To perspire] — *Syn.* discharge, swelter, emit; see **sweat** 1.
*See Synonym Study at* HIDE.

**secretion,** *n.* — *Syn.* discharge, issue, movement; see **excretion** 1, **flow.**

**secretive,** *modif.* — *Syn.* reticent, taciturn, tight-lipped, furtive, undercover, with bated breath, in private, in the dark, in chambers, by a side door, under the breath, in the background, between ourselves, in privacy, in a corner, under the cloak of, reserved.

**secretly,** *modif.* — *Syn.* privately, covertly, obscurely, darkly, surreptitiously, furtively, stealthily, clandestinely, underhandedly, slyly, behind one's back, intimately, personally, confidentially, between you and me, in strict confidence, in secret, behind the scenes, on the sly, behind closed doors, quietly, hush-hush*; see also **secretive.** — *Ant.* OPENLY, obviously, publicly.

**sect,** *n.* — *Syn.* denomination, following, order; see **church** 3, **faction** 1.

**sectarian,** *modif.* — *Syn.* denominational, narrow-minded, limited, parochial, prejudiced, bigoted; see also **dogmatic** 2.

**sectarian,** *n.* — *Syn.* dissenter, nonconformist, partisan, zealot, rebel; see also **protestant, skeptic.**

**section,** *n.* **1.** [A portion] — *Syn.* subdivision, slice, segment; see **division** 2, **part** 1, **share.**
**2.** [An area] — *Syn.* district, sector, locality; see **region** 1.
*See Synonym Study at* PART.

**sectional,** *modif.* — *Syn.* partial, exclusive, narrow, selfish, local, regional, separate, divided. — *Ant.* WHOLE, in one piece, united.

**sector,** *n.* — *Syn.* division, area, quarter; see **area** 2, **division** 2.

**secular,** *modif.* — *Syn.* temporal, profane, earthly; see **materialistic, worldly** 1.

**secure,** *modif.* **1.** [Firm] — *Syn.* fastened, adjusted, bound; see **firm** 1, **tight** 1.
**2.** [Safe] — *Syn.* guarded, unharmed, defended; see **protected, safe** 1.
**3.** [Self-confident] — *Syn.* assured, solid, determined, confident, strong, stable, sound, steady, steadfast, reliable, able, resolute.
*See Synonym Study at* SAFE.

**secure,** *v.* **1.** [To fasten] — *Syn.* settle, adjust, bind; see **fasten** 1, **tighten** 1.
**2.** [To obtain] — *Syn.* achieve, acquire, grasp; see **obtain** 1.
**3.** [To protect] — *Syn.* guard, make safe, ensure; see **defend** 1, 2.
*See Synonym Study at* OBTAIN.

**securing,** *n.* — *Syn.* acquiring, procuring, attaining; see **acquisition** 1.

**security,** *n.* **1.** [Safety] — *Syn.* protection, shelter, safety, refuge, retreat, defense, safeguard, preservation, sanctuary, ward, guard, immunity, freedom from harm, freedom from danger, redemption, salvation. — *Ant.* DANGER, risk, hazard.
**2.** [A guarantee] — *Syn.* earnest, forfeit, token, pawn, pledge, surety, bond, collateral, assurance, gage, bail, certainty, promise, warranty, pact, compact, contract, covenant, agreement, sponsor, bondsman, hostage; see also **protection** 2. — *Ant.* DOUBT, broken faith, unreliability.
**3.** [Stability] — *Syn.* soundness, assurance, surety; see **confidence** 2.

**sedan,** *n.* **1.** [Chair] — *Syn.* saddle, place, carriage; see **chair** 1.
**2.** [Vehicle] — *Syn.* car, limousine, passenger car, touring car; see **automobile, vehicle** 2.

**sedate,** *modif.* — *Syn.* composed, unruffled, serious, sober; see **calm** 1, **dignified.**
*See Synonym Study at* SERIOUS.

**sedately,** *modif.* — *Syn.* quietly, slowly, formally; see **deliberately, proudly.**

**sedative,** *modif.* — *Syn.* tranquilizing, calming, soothing; see **remedial.**

**sedative,** *n.* — *Syn.* tranquilizer, medication, narcotic; see **drug** 2, **medicine** 2.

**sedentary,** *modif.* — *Syn.* inactive, stationary, settled, quiet; see **idle** 1.

**sediment,** *n.* — *Syn.* settlings, residue, lees, dregs, dross, grounds, solids, silt, powder, sand, alluvium, loess, grit, gritty matter, soot, deposit, debris, precipitate, trash.

**sedition,** *n.* — *Syn.* treason, revolt, mutiny, insurrection; see **revolution** 2, **treason.**
*See Synonym Study at* TREASON.

**seditious,** *modif.* — *Syn.* violent, dissident, subversive, insurgent; see **lawless** 2, **rebellious** 2.

**seduce,** *v.* — *Syn.* allure, inveigle, entice, decoy, abduct, attract, tempt, bait, bribe, lure, induce, captivate, draw in, corrupt, deprave, lead astray, violate, debauch, rape, ravish, deflower, defile, ruin, sweet-talk*, vamp*, make a play for*, come on to*; see also **fascinate, tempt.** — *Ant.* PRESERVE, protect, repel.
*See Synonym Study at* TEMPT.

**seducer,** *n.* — *Syn.* debaucher, corrupter, tempter, temptress, seductress, rake; see also **lecher.**

**seduction,** *n.* — *Syn.* enticement, temptation, bewitchment, subjugation, corruption; see also **rape, violation** 2.

**seductive,** *modif.* — *Syn.* alluring, beguiling, tempting; see **charming.**

**seductress,** *n.* — *Syn.* siren, enchantress, vamp, Jezebel; see **siren** 2.

**sedulous,** *modif.* — *Syn.* attentive, assiduous, unremitting, active, desirous, unwearied, industrious, diligent, busy, hustling, keen, eager, brisk, painstaking, sleepless, avid, anxious, persevering, persistent, alert, ardent; see also **busy** 1, **careful, diligent, observant** 1, 2. — *Ant.* CARELESS, indifferent, unconcerned.
*See Synonym Study at* DILIGENT.

**see,** *v.* **1.** [To perceive with the eye] — *Syn.* observe, look at, behold, descry, examine, inspect, regard, espy, view, look out on, gaze, stare, eye, lay eyes on, mark, perceive, pay attention to, heed, mind, detect, notice, take notice, discern, scrutinize, scan, spy, survey, contemplate, remark, clap eyes on, be apprized of, make out, cast the eyes on, direct the eyes, catch sight of, cast the eyes over, get a load of*.
**2.** [To understand] — *Syn.* perceive, comprehend, discern; see **recognize** 1, **understand** 1.
**3.** [To witness] — *Syn.* look on, be present, pay attention, notice, observe, regard, heed; see also **witness.**

**4.** [\*To accompany] — *Syn.* escort, attend, bear company; see **accompany** 1.

**5.** [\*To equal, especially to equal a bet in poker] — *Syn.* meet a bet, cover a bet, match a wager; see **equal.**

**6.** [To have an appointment (with)] — *Syn.* speak to, speak with, have a conference with, get advice from; see **consult, discuss.**

---

*SYN.* — **see**, the most simple and direct of these terms, is the basic term for the use of the organs of sight; **behold** implies a directing of the eyes on something and holding it in view, usually stressing the strong impression made /he never *beheld* a sight more beautiful/; **espy** and **descry** both imply a catching sight of with some effort, **espy** suggesting the detection of that which is small, partly hidden, etc. /he *espied* the snake crawling through the grass/ and **descry** the making out of something from a distance or through darkness, mist, etc. /he *descried* the distant steeple/; **view** implies a seeing or looking at what lies before one with a defined purpose or perspective /the jury *viewed* the evidence/

---

**see about,** *v.* — *Syn.* attend to, look after, look to, provide for; see **perform** 1.

**seed,** *n.* **1.** [A botanical ovule]. Seeds and fruits commonly called seeds include: grain, kernel, berry, ear, corn, nut.

**2.** [Something to be planted] — *Syn.* grain, bulbs, cuttings, ears, tubers, roots; seed corn, seed potatoes, etc. **go** or **run to seed** — *Syn.* decline, worsen, run out; see **decay, waste** 3.

**seed,** *v.* — *Syn.* scatter, strew, broadcast; see **plant, sow.**

**seeding,** *n.* **1.** [The act of planting seed] — *Syn.* sowing, broadcasting, implanting, strewing, scattering, spreading, propagating; see also **farming.**

**2.** [Ground on which seed has been sown] — *Syn.* planting, garden, cultivated ground, cultivated field, seeded ground, garden spot, lawn, grass plot, garden plot, sod, small grain, hay.

**see fit to,** *v.* — *Syn.* decide to, be willing to, be determined to, determine to; see **want, wish** 2.

**seeing,** *modif.* — *Syn.* observing, looking, regarding, viewing, noticing, surveying, looking at, observant, wide awake, alert, awake, perceiving, inspecting, beholding, witnessing.

**seek,** *v.* **1.** [To look for] — *Syn.* investigate, explore, search for, delve for, gun for, bob for, dig for, ransack for, fish for, go gunning for, look around for, look about for, look up, hunt up, sniff out, dig out, hunt out, root out, smell around, go after, run after, see after, prowl after, go in pursuit of, go in search of.

**2.** [To try] — *Syn.* endeavor, strive for, attempt; see **try** 1.

**3.** [To find out] — *Syn.* query, inquire, solicit; see **ask** 1.

**seeking,** *modif.* — *Syn.* hunting, searching, looking for; see **pursuing.**

**seem,** *v.* — *Syn.* appear, have the appearance, create the impression, give the impression, convey the impression, impress one, appear to one, produce the reaction, induce the reaction, look, look like, resemble, make a show of, show, have the qualities of, resemble superficially, lead one to suppose something to be, have all the evidence of being, be suggestive of, have the expression, have the mien, have the deport, have the demeanor, give the effect of, give the feeling of, sound like, take on the aspect, take on the manner, make out to be\*, give the idea\*, have all the earmarks of\*, make a noise like\*.

**seemingly,** *modif.* — *Syn.* ostensibly, obviously, professedly; see **apparently.**

**seemly,** *modif.* **1.** [Suitable] — *Syn.* timely, appropriate, suitable; see **fit** 1, 2.

**2.** [Attractive] — *Syn.* pleasing, good-looking, comely; see **beautiful** 1, 2, **charming.**

**seen,** *modif.* — *Syn.* manifest, evident, viewed; see **observed** 1, **obvious** 1.

**see off,** *v.* — *Syn.* go with, bid farewell, wish bon voyage, go to the point of departure with; see **accompany** 1.

**seep,** *v.* — *Syn.* leak, flow gently, trickle; see **drain** 3, **flow** 2.

**seepage,** *n.* — *Syn.* infiltration, leakage, percolation; see **drainage, flow.**

**seer,** *n.* — *Syn.* predictor, soothsayer, vaticinator, sage, fortune teller; see also **prophet.**

**seesaw,** *n.* — *Syn.* alternation, teeterboard, hickey horse; see **teeter-totter.**

**seethe,** *v.* **1.** [To boil or be agitated] — *Syn.* bubble, churn, ferment, smolder; see **boil** 1, 2, **bubble.**

**2.** [To be angry] — *Syn.* fume, boil, steam; see **fume.**

*See Synonym Study at* BOIL.

**see through,** *v.* **1.** [To complete] — *Syn.* finish, bring to a conclusion, wind up\*; see **complete** 1, **end** 1.

**2.** [To understand] — *Syn.* comprehend, penetrate, detect; see **understand** 1.

**see to,** *v.* — *Syn.* do, attend to, look to, look after; see **understand** 1.

**segment,** *n.* — *Syn.* section, portion, fragment; see **division** 2, **part** 1, **share.**

*See Synonym Study at* PART.

**segregate,** *v.* — *Syn.* isolate, sever, split up; see **divide** 1, **separate** 2.

**segregated,** *modif.* — *Syn.* divided into racial groups, divided along racial lines, excluded, isolated, according to Jim Crow restrictions, ghettoized; see also **separated.**

**segregation,** *n.* **1.** [The act of separating] — *Syn.* dissociation, disconnection, separation; see **division** 1.

**2.** [The separation of racial groups] — *Syn.* exclusion, discrimination, racial segregation, apartheid, Jim Crowism, Jim Crow.

**seignior,** *n.* — *Syn.* Mr., master, *Herr* (German); see **mister, sir** 2.

**seize,** *v.* **1.** [To grasp] — *Syn.* take, take hold of, lay hold of, lay hands on, catch up, catch hold of, hang on, hang onto, catch, grip, clinch, clench, clasp, embrace, compass, grab, clutch, grapple, snag, pluck, appropriate, snatch, swoop up, enfold, enclose, pinch, squeeze, make fast, hold fast, possess oneself of, envelope. — *Ant.* LEAVE, pass by, let alone.

**2.** [To take by force] — *Syn.* capture, rape, occupy, win, take, take captive, pounce, conquer, take by storm, take by assault, subdue, overwhelm, overrun, overpower, ambush, snatch, incorporate, exact, extend protection to, retake, carry off, apprehend, arrogate, arrest, secure, commandeer, force, gain, take, recapture, appropriate, take possession of, confiscate, take over, pounce on, usurp, overcome, impound, intercept, steal, purloin, expropriate, abduct, seize upon, snap up, nab, trap, throttle, lay hold of, lift, snap up, hook, collar, fasten upon, wrench, claw, snare, bag, catch up, jerk, freeze onto, batten on, wring, cull, get one's clutches on\*, get one's fingers on\*, get one's hands on, hijack, skyjack\*, carjack\*, kidnap, rustle, stick up\*, hold up, swipe, clap hands on, scramble for, help oneself to, jump a claim.

**3.** [To comprehend] — *Syn.* perceive, see, know; see **understand** 1.

---

*SYN.* — **seize** is to get hold of or get control of suddenly and forcibly /he *seized* the gun from the robber; to *seize* power/; **take** is the general word meaning to get hold of by or as by the hands /to *take* a book, the opportunity, etc./; **grasp** implies holding firmly /to *grasp* a rope, an idea, etc./; **clutch** implies a tight or convulsive grasping of that which one is eager to take or keep hold of /she *clutched* his hand in terror/; **grab** implies a roughness or unscrupulousness in seizing /the child *grabbed* all the candy; to *grab* credit/; **snatch** stresses an abrupt quickness and, sometimes, a surreptitiousness in seizing /she *snatched* the letter from my hand; to *snatch* a purse/

---

**seized,** *modif.* — *Syn.* confiscated, annexed, clutched; see **beaten** 1, **captured** 1.
**seizure,** *n.* **1.** [Capture] — *Syn.* seizing, taking, apprehending; see **capture.**
**2.** [A spasm] — *Syn.* spell, convulsion, breakdown; see **fit** 1, **illness** 1.
**seldom,** *modif.* — *Syn.* rarely, unusually, in a few cases, a few times, at times, seldom seen, on divers occasions, sporadically, irregularly, inhabitually, whimsically, sometimes, when occasion permits, from time to time, infrequently, not often, not very often, occasionally, uncommonly, scarcely, hardly, hardly ever, scarcely ever, when the spirit moves, on and off, once in a while, once in a blue moon, once in a lifetime, every now and then, in a coon's age★, not in a month of Sundays★, once in a blue moon★. — *Ant.* FREQUENTLY, often.
**select,** *modif.* — *Syn.* elite, picked, preferred; see **excellent.**
**select,** *v.* — *Syn.* decide, pick, elect; see **choose** 1.
**selected,** *modif.* — *Syn.* picked, chosen, elected; see **named** 2.
**selecting,** *modif.* — *Syn.* appointing, choosing, electing, recruiting, nominating.
**selecting,** *n.* — *Syn.* choosing, selection, choice, picking, culling, electing, election, sifting, gleaning, segregating, indicating, appointing, denominating, denomination, segregation, appointment, determining, determination, winnowing, separation, separating, isolation, isolating, marking off, marking out, winnowing the wheat from the chaff★, separating the sheep from the goats★.
**selection,** *n.* **1.** [The act of selecting] — *Syn.* choice, election, determination, choosing, preference, co-optation, appropriation, adoption, reservation, separation.
**2.** [Anything selected] — *Syn.* pick, collection, excerpt; see **choice** 3, **reading** 3.
**3.** [An evolutionary process] — *Syn.* survival of the fittest, natural selection, sexual selection, unconscious selection, methodical selection, modification, change by sport, adaptation, Darwinian process, biogenesis, Mendelian fitness.
**4.** [A variety from which to choose] — *Syn.* choice, assortment, range, variety; see **choice** 2.
*See Synonym Study at* CHOICE.
**selective,** *modif.* — *Syn.* discriminating, scrupulous, particular; see **careful, judicious.**
**self,** *modif.* — *Syn.* of one's self, by one's self, by one's own effort; see **alone** 1, **individual** 1.
**self,** *n.* — *Syn.* oneself, one's being, inner nature, ego, individual, person; see also **character** 2.
**self-abuse,** *n.* — *Syn.* self-destruction, masochism, self-

murder; see **abuse** 3, **suicide.**
**self-acting,** *modif.* — *Syn.* mechanical, self-propellent, automated; see **automatic** 1.
**self-admiration,** *n.* — *Syn.* pomposity, vanity, egotism, conceit, narcissism; see also **arrogance, pride** 1.
**self-amortizing,** *modif.* — *Syn.* self-liquidating, paying for itself, funded.
**self-assurance,** *n.* — *Syn.* security, self-reliance, morale, self-confidence; see **confidence** 2.
**self-assured,** *modif.* — *Syn.* self-confident, assured, certain; see **confident** 2.
**self-centered,** *modif.* — *Syn.* self-indulgent, self-conscious, egotistical, narcissistic; see **egotistic** 1, 2, **selfish** 1.
**self-confidence,** *n.* — *Syn.* assurance, confidence, self-assurance, self-reliance; see **confidence** 2.
*See Synonym Study at* CONFIDENCE.
**self-confident,** *modif.* — *Syn.* fearless, secure, self-assured; see **confident** 2.
**self-conscious,** *modif.* — *Syn.* unsure, diffident, uncertain, shy; see **doubtful** 2, **humble** 1.
**self-consciously,** *modif.* — *Syn.* bashfully, affectedly, upset; see **ashamed, modestly** 1.
**self-contained,** *modif.* **1.** [Austere] — *Syn.* reticent, taciturn, constrained, uncommunicative; see **reserved** 3.
**2.** [Independent] — *Syn.* self-sustaining, complete, independent; see **free** 1, **whole** 1.
**self-control,** *n.* — *Syn.* poise, restraint, aplomb, self-government, discipline, self-discipline, reserve, reticence, self-restraint, discretion, balance, stability, sobriety, abstemiousness, dignity, repression, constraint, self-constraint, self-regulation. — *Ant.* NERVOUSNESS, timidity, talkativeness.
**self-defense,** *n.* — *Syn.* self-protection, self-preservation, putting up a fight; see **fight** 1, **protection** 2.
**self-denial,** *n.* **1.** [Abstemiousness] — *Syn.* asceticism, selflessness, self-sacrifice; see **moderation** 1, **restraint** 1, **temperance.**
**2.** [Privation] — *Syn.* suffering, self-neglect, torment; see **martyrdom, sacrifice** 1.
**self-destruction,** *n.* — *Syn.* suicide, self-extinction, hara-kiri, masochism; see **death** 1, **suicide.**
**self-determination,** *n.* — *Syn.* privilege, spontaneity, initiative; see **will** 3.
**self-esteem,** *n.* — *Syn.* self-respect, self-confidence, self-conceit; see **pride** 1, 3.
*See Synonym Study at* PRIDE.
**self-evident,** *modif.* — *Syn.* plain, visible, apparent; see **obvious** 2.
**self-explanatory,** *modif.* — *Syn.* plain, clear, distinct, certain, easy to understand, comprehensible, understandable, obvious, open, visible, easy to see, easily seen, manifest, self-evident, unmistakable, unequivocal, plain as the nose on one's face★, clear as crystal★, plain as day★. — *Ant.* OBSCURE, vague, uncertain.
**self-government,** *n.* **1.** [Autonomy] — *Syn.* home rule, republic, independence, self-determination; see **freedom** 1.
**2.** [Self-control] — *Syn.* self-restraint, conduct, character, stability; see **discipline** 2, **restraint** 1.
**self-important,** *modif.* — *Syn.* proud, egotistical, conceited; see **egotistic** 2.
**self-imposed,** *modif.* — *Syn.* accepted, self-determined, self-inflicted, done willingly; see **deliberate** 1, **voluntary.**
**self-indulgence,** *n.* — *Syn.* incontinence, excess, intemperance, hedonism; see **greed, indulgence** 3.
**selfish,** *modif.* **1.** [Centered in self] — *Syn.* self-seeking,

self-centered, self-indulgent, indulging oneself, wrapped up in oneself, narrow, narrow-minded, prejudiced, egotistical, egoistical, egoistic, egotistic, looking out for number one*.

**2.** [Niggardly] — *Syn.* miserly, stingy, parsimonious; see **greedy** 1.

**selfishly,** *modif.* — *Syn.* egotistically, miserly, stingily, greedily, in one's own interest, meanly, cannily, ungenerously, illiberally, unchivalrously, to gain private ends, lacking in generosity, lacking in magnanimity, lacking in consideration; see also **wrongly** 1, 2.

**selfishness,** *n.* — *Syn.* self-regard, self-indulgence, self-worship; see **greed.**

**self-liquidating,** *modif.* — *Syn.* self-amortizing, paying for itself, to be written off, funded, provided for; see also **paid.**

**self-love,** *n.* — *Syn.* vanity, conceit, self-esteem; see **arrogance, egotism.**

**self-made,** *modif.* — *Syn.* competent, self-reliant, audacious; see **able** 1, 2, **confident** 2.

**self-possessed,** *modif.* — *Syn.* placid, reserved, aloof, cool, unperturbed; see also **calm** 1, **reserved** 3.

**self-possession,** *n.* — *Syn.* self-assurance, poise, presence of mind; see **confidence** 2, **restraint** 1.
*See Synonym Study at* CONFIDENCE.

**self-regulating,** *modif.* — *Syn.* mechanical, self-adjusting, motorized; see **automatic** 1.

**self-reliance,** *n.* — *Syn.* self-trust, self-confidence, independence; see **confidence** 2.

**self-reliant,** *modif.* — *Syn.* determined, resolute, independent; see **able** 1, 2, **confident** 2.

**self-renunciation,** *n.* — *Syn.* altruism, heroism, magnanimity, self-denial; see **generosity** 1, **temperance.**

**self-reproach,** *n.* — *Syn.* remorse, contrition, repentance, guilt; see **regret** 1.

**self-respect,** *n.* — *Syn.* morale, worth, pride; see **confidence** 2, **dignity** 1.

**self-restraint,** *n.* — *Syn.* patience, endurance, control; see **restraint** 1.

**self-righteous,** *modif.* — *Syn.* sanctimonious, pious, pietistic, holier-than-thou*; see **egotistic** 2, **hypocritical.**

**self-righteously,** *modif.* — *Syn.* smugly, pompously, boastfully; see **proudly.**

**self-sacrifice,** *n.* — *Syn.* altruism, free-giving, benevolence; see **generosity** 1, **kindness** 1, 2.

**self-sacrificing,** *modif.* — *Syn.* big-hearted, helpful, self-effacing; see **generous** 1, **noble** 1, 2.

**selfsame,** *modif.* — *Syn.* same, equivalent, similar; see **alike** 1, 2, **equal.**
*See Synonym Study at* SAME.

**self-satisfaction,** *n.* — *Syn.* complacency, smugness, conceit; see **egotism.**

**self-satisfied,** *modif.* — *Syn.* smug, vain, conceited; see **egotistic** 2.

**self-seeking,** *modif.* — *Syn.* self-indulgent, rapacious, avaricious; see **greedy** 1.

**self-styled,** *modif.* — *Syn.* soi-disant (French), immodestly called, boastfully called, so-called, would-be, said to be, by one's own admission; see also **egotistic** 1, 2, **egotistically.**

**self-sufficient,** *modif.* — *Syn.* independent, competent, self-confident, efficient; see **confident** 2.

**self-taught,** *modif.* — *Syn.* self-made, self-educated, amateur, nonprofessional; see **educated** 1, **learned** 1, **local** 1.

**self-willed,** *modif.* — *Syn.* willful, opinionated, contrary, stubborn; see **obstinate** 1.

**sell,** *v.* **1.** [To convey for a consideration] — *Syn.* mar-

ket, vend, auction, dispose of, put up for sale, barter, exchange, trade, bargain, peddle, retail, merchandise, sell at the market, sell on the curb, sell over the counter, sell futures on, contract, wholesale, give title to, give a deed for, put in escrow; see also **exchange** 2. — *Ant.* BUY, OBTAIN, get.

**2.** [To betray] — *Syn.* sell out*, fail, violate; see **betray** 1, **deceive, disappoint.**

---

*SYN.* — **sell** implies the transferral of ownership of something to another for money /to *sell* books, a house, etc./; **barter** implies an exchange of goods or services without using money /to *barter* food for clothes/; **trade**, in transitive use, also implies the exchange of articles /let's *trade* neckties/, and, intransitively, implies the carrying on of a business in which one buys and sells a specified commodity /to *trade* in wheat/; **auction** implies the public sale of items one by one, each going to the highest of the competing bidders /to *auction* off unclaimed property/; **vend** applies especially to the selling of small articles, as by peddling, coin-operated machine, etc. / to *vend* souvenirs at the parade, *vending* machines/

---

**seller,** *n.* — *Syn.* dealer, peddler, tradesman, salesman, retailer, agent, vender, merchant, auctioneer, shopkeeper, trader, marketer, storekeeper; see also **businessperson.**

**selling,** *n.* **1.** [The act of selling] — *Syn.* sale, auction, bartering, trading, vending, auctioning, transfer, transferring, commercial transaction, transacting, disposal, scoring, disposing, merchandising. — *Ant.* BUYING, acquiring, purchasing.

**2.** [The occupation of selling] — *Syn.* commercial enterprise, traffic, merchandising; see **business** 1.

**sell off,** *v.* — *Syn.* trade, bargain, get rid of; see **sell** 1.

**sell-out*,** *n.* — *Syn.* betrayal, deception, deal; see **trick** 1.

**sell out*,** *v.* **1.** [To betray] — *Syn.* thwart, trick, turn in, cop out*; see **betray** 1, **deceive, disappoint.**

**2.** [To get rid of completely] — *Syn.* be bought out, be depleted, run out of; see **sell** 1.

**sell short*,** *v.* — *Syn.* denigrate, derogate, belittle; see **depreciate** 2, **insult, ridicule.**

**selvage,** *n.* — *Syn.* edge, skirting, border; see **hem, rim.**

**semantic,** *modif.* — *Syn.* semiotic, connotative, denotative; see **grammatical** 1.

**semantics,** *n.* — *Syn.* meaning, semiotics, study of meaning, general semantics, symbolic logic, semiology, connotation, denotation, exposition, explanation, explication, glossology, exegetics, symbolism, symbiology; see also **definition** 1, **interpretation** 1.

**semblance,** *n.* — *Syn.* air, guise, likeness, resemblance; see **appearance** 2, **similarity.**
*See Synonym Study at* APPEARANCE.

**semester,** *n.* — *Syn.* term, six-month period, eighteen weeks, four and one-half months; see **term** 2.

**semiannual,** *modif.* — *Syn.* twice a year, half-yearly, biannual, every six months, semiyearly; see also **biannual, seasonal.**

**semicircle,** *n.* — *Syn.* arc, semicircumference, half a circle, 180 degrees, half-moon; see also **arch, curve** 1.

**semicircular,** *modif.* — *Syn.* crescentlike, bowed, curved; see **bent, round** 1.

**semiconscious,** *modif.* — *Syn.* half-conscious, half-awake, comatose; see **asleep, dying** 1.

**semifinal,** *n.* — *Syn.* next to the last, next to the final, just before the final, preliminary to the final, elimination test, elimination round; see also **round** 2.

**semiliquid,** *modif.* — *Syn.* semifluid, pasty, gelatinous, gummy; see **liquid** 2, **thick** 3.

**seminal,** *modif.* — *Syn.* generative, primary, original, crucial, critical; see also **fundamental** 1.

**seminar,** *n.* — *Syn.* research, study, lesson, workshop; see **class** 3, **course** 4.

**seminary,** *n.* — *Syn.* secondary school, institute, theological school; see **academy** 1, **school** 1.

**semiprofessional,** *modif.* — *Syn.* amateur, not professional, highly skilled; see **able** 1, **trained.**

**sempiternal,** *modif.* — *Syn.* unchanging, incessant, everlasting; see **constant** 1, **eternal** 2.

**Senate,** *n.* — *Syn.* legislative body, United States Senate, State legislature, the lawgivers, upper branch of Congress, the Upper House; see also **legislature.**

**senate,** *n.* — *Syn.* legislative body, lawgiving body, assembly, council, deliberative body; see also **legislature.**

**senator,** *n.* — *Syn.* legislator, politician, member of the senate, statesman, elder statesman, Solon*; see also **representative** 2.

**send,** *v.* **1.** [To dispatch] — *Syn.* transmit, forward, convey, advance, express, ship, mail, send forth, send out, send in, delegate, expedite, hasten, accelerate, entrain, post, address, rush off, hurry off, get under way, put under sail, give papers, provide with credentials, send out for, address to, commission, consign; see also **export.**
**2.** [To deliver] — *Syn.* convey, transfer, pack off, give, bestow, grant, confer, entrust, assign, impart, utter, give out; see also **sense** 1.
**3.** [To project] — *Syn.* propel, fling, hurl; see **throw** 1.
**4.** [To broadcast, usually electronically] — *Syn.* transmit, relay, wire, cable, broadcast, emit, televise, conduct, communicate; see also **carry** 2.

**send about one's business,** *v.* — *Syn.* send away, discharge, get rid of, dispatch; see **dismiss** 1.

**send around,** *v.* — *Syn.* circulate, send to everybody, make available; see **distribute** 1.

**send back,** *v.* — *Syn.* reject, mail back, ship back, decide against; see **return** 2.

**send for,** *v.* — *Syn.* send away for, order, request, write away for; see **ask** 1, **obtain** 1.

**send in,** *v.* — *Syn.* submit, mail, deliver; see **offer** 1, **ship.**

**sending,** *n.* — *Syn.* shipping, posting, dispatching; see **mailing, transportation.**

**send-off,** *n.* — *Syn.* going-away party, auspicious beginning, good start; see **celebration** 2, **encouragement.**

**send packing*,** *v.* — *Syn.* send away, banish, reject, throw out*, eject; see also **dismiss** 1.

**send word,** *v.* — *Syn.* get in touch, communicate, report; see **telegraph, telephone, write** 1.

**senile,** *modif.* — *Syn.* aged, infirm, feeble, declining; see **old** 1, **sick.**

**senility,** *n.* — *Syn.* old age, dotage, anecdotage*, feebleness, anility, infirmity, decline, senile dementia, Alzheimer's disease, senescence, second childhood*, sere and yellow leaf*; see also **age** 2, **weakness** 1. — *Ant.* YOUTH, infancy, childhood.

**senior,** *modif.* — *Syn.* elder, older, higher in rank, more advanced, of greater dignity, of advanced standing, next older, next higher in rank; see also **superior.**

**senior,** *n.* — *Syn.* superior, elder, upperclassman, dean, master, oldest, first born.

**seniority,** *n.* — *Syn.* precedence, priority, status, rank, ranking, station; see also **advantage** 1, 2, **preference.**

**señor,** *n.* — *Syn.* gentleman, Mr., monsieur; see **mister, sir** 2.

**señorita,** *n.* — *Syn.* young lady, girl, maid, lass; see **girl** 1, **woman** 1.

**sensation,** *n.* **1.** [The sense of feeling] — *Syn.* sensibility, susceptibility, sensitiveness, consciousness, awareness, perception, impression; see also **emotion, thought** 1. — *Ant.* STUPOR, apathy, torpor.
**2.** [A feeling] — *Syn.* response, sentiment, passion, excitement; see **feeling** 1.

**sensational,** *modif.* **1.** [Fascinating] — *Syn.* exciting, agitating, marvelous, moving, incredible, astonishing, superb, breathtaking, eloquent, surprising, thrilling, spectacular, dramatic, stirring; see also **impressive** 1, **interesting.**
**2.** [Melodramatic] — *Syn.* exaggerated, excessive, lurid, emotional, startling, stimulating.

**sensationalism,** *n.* — *Syn.* emotionalism, melodrama, photism, McCarthyism, sentimentality, yellow journalism; see also **drama** 2, **emotion.**

**sense,** *n.* **1.** [One of the powers of physical perception] — *Syn.* kinesthesia, function, sensation; see **hearing** 3, **sight** 1, **smell** 3, **taste** 1, **touch** 1, 4.
**2.** [Mental ability] — *Syn.* intellect, understanding, reason, mind, spirit, soul, brains, judgment, wit, imagination, common sense, cleverness, reasoning, intellectual ability, mental capacity, knowledge; see also **thought** 1. — *Ant.* DULLNESS, idiocy, feeble wit.
**3.** [Reasonable and agreeable conduct] — *Syn.* reasonableness, fairmindedness, discretion; see **fairness.**
**4.** [Tact and understanding] — *Syn.* insight, discernment, social sense; see **feeling** 4, **judgment** 1.

**in a sense** — *Syn.* in a way, to a degree, somewhat; see **somehow.**

**make sense** — *Syn.* be reasonable, be logical, look all right, add up*; see **appear** 1, **seem.**

**senseless,** *modif.* — *Syn.* ridiculous, silly, foolish, pointless; see **illogical, stupid** 1.

**senses,** *n.* — *Syn.* consciousness, mental faculties, feeling, sanity, clearheadedness; see also **awareness, sense** 1, 2.

**bring to one's senses** — *Syn.* restore, bring to reason, persuade; see **convince.**

**sensibility,** *n.* — *Syn.* responsiveness, perceptivity, keenness; see **awareness, judgment** 1, **sensitivity.**

**sensible,** *modif.* **1.** [Showing good sense] — *Syn.* reasonable, rational, prudent, practical; see **judicious, rational** 1, **reasonable** 1, 2, **sane** 2.
**2.** [Aware] — *Syn.* cognizant, conscious, alive to; see **conscious** 1.
**3.** [Perceivable] — *Syn.* perceptible, discernible, material; see **appreciable, physical** 1, **tangible.**
*See Synonym Study at* CONSCIOUS, PHYSICAL, RATIONAL, TANGIBLE.

**sensitive,** *modif.* **1.** [Tender] — *Syn.* delicate, sore, raw, painful; see **tender** 6.
**2.** [Touchy] — *Syn.* high-strung, tense, nervous; see **irritable, unstable** 2.
**3.** [Sensory] — *Syn.* sentient, impressionable, sensible, perceptive, susceptible, receptive, psychic, sensorial, sensatory, tuned in*, soulful*, turned on to*; see also **sympathetic.**
**4.** [Responsive] — *Syn.* fine, delicate, fine-tuned, readily affected.

**sensitivity,** *n.* **1.** [Susceptibility] — *Syn.* allergy, irritability, ticklishness; see **irritation** 1.
**2.** [Emotional response or condition] — *Syn.* delicacy, sensibility, sensitiveness, nervousness, acute awareness, consciousness, acuteness, subtlety, feeling, sympathetic response, responsiveness, sympathy, impressionability, affectability; see also **sensation** 1.

**sensitize,** *v.* — *Syn.* stimulate, refine, sharpen; see **animate** 1, **excite** 2.

**sensory,** *modif.* **1.** [Neurological] — *Syn.* sensible, relating to sensation, relating to the senses, neural, conscious, afferent, receptive, sensatory, acoustic, auditory, aural, auricular, sonic, phonic, audio-visual, visual, ocular, optic, ophthalmic, olfactory, olfactive, gustatory, gustative, lingual, glossal, tactile, tactual; see also **sensitive** 3.
**2.** [Conveyed by the senses] — *Syn.* audible, perceptible, discernible, auricular, distinct, clear, plain, hearable; see also **obvious** 1, 2, **tangible.**

**sensual,** *modif.* **1.** [Sensory] — *Syn.* tactile, sensuous, stimulating, sharpened, pleasing, dazzling, feeling, being, heightened, enhanced, appealing, delightful, luxurious, fine, arousing, stirring, moving; see also **beautiful** 1, **emotional** 2, **exciting.**
**2.** [Carnal] — *Syn.* voluptuous, fleshly, bodily, physical, animal, erotic, sexual, pleasure-loving, pleasure-seeking, hedonistic, lewd, lustful, lascivious, earthy, unspiritual, self-indulgent, epicurean, sybaritic, sensuous, intemperate, gluttonous, rakish, debauched, orgiastic, hedonic, Corybantic, Cyrenaic, hoggish, bestial, gross. — *Ant.* CHASTE, ascetic, self-denying.

*SYN.* — **sensual** stresses relation to or preoccupation with gratifying the bodily senses and may imply grossness or lewdness /*sensual* lips/; **animal** is applied to the physical nature of humankind as distinguished from intellectual and spiritual nature, and now often does not carry a derogatory implication /*animal* appetites, sheer *animal* courage/; **carnal** implies relation to the body or flesh as the seat of basic physical appetites, now esp. sexual appetites, and usually stresses absence of intellectual or moral influence /*carnal* pleasures/; **fleshly,** expressing less censure, stresses these appetites and their gratification as natural to the flesh /*fleshly* frailty/ See also Synonym Study at SENSUOUS.

**sensuality,** *n.* — *Syn.* sensationalism, appetite, ardor, voluptuousness, sexuality; see also **desire** 3, **emotion, love** 1.
**sensuous,** *modif.* — *Syn.* sensual, passionate, physical, exciting, sumptuous, luscious, voluptuous, luxurious, epicurean; see also **sensual** 1, 2.

*SYN.* — **sensuous** suggests the strong appeal of that which is pleasing to the eye, ear, touch, etc. and, of a person, implies susceptibility to the often aesthetic pleasures of sensation /soft, *sensuous* music/; **sensual** refers to the operation or gratification of the physical senses or appetite /a *sensual* element in her sculptures, a life of *sensual* excess/; **voluptuous** implies a tending to excite, or giving oneself up to the gratification of, sensuous or, more often, sensual desires /her *voluptuous* charms/; **luxurious** implies a reveling in that which lavishly provides a high degree of physical comfort or satisfaction /a *luxurious* feeling of drowsiness/; **epicurean** implies delight in luxury and sensuous pleasure, esp. that of eating and drinking

**sent,** *modif.* — *Syn.* shipped, mailed, posted, commissioned, appointed, ordained, delegated, dispatched, directed, issued, transmitted, discharged, gone, on the road, in transit, emitted, uttered, sent forth, driven, impelled, forced to go, consigned, ordered, committed; see also **shipped.** — *Ant.* KEPT, restrained, held back.
**sentence,** *n.* **1.** [A pronounced judgment] — *Syn.* judgment, edict, dictum, decree, order, doom, determination, decision, pronouncement, considered opinion, censure, penalty, condemnation; see also **judgment** 3, **punishment, verdict.**
**2.** [An expressed thought]
Kinds of sentences, sense 2, include: simple, complex, compound, compound-complex, kernel, transformed, declarative, interrogative, imperative, exclamatory, statement, question, command, exclamation.
**sentence,** *v.* — *Syn.* pronounce judgment, adjudge, adjudicate, send up, confine, impound, incarcerate, jail, judge, doom, send to prison, send up the river★; see also **condemn** 1, **convict, imprison, punish.**
**sententious,** *modif.* **1.** [Compact] — *Syn.* concise, aphoristic, pointed; see **obvious** 2.
**2.** [Pompous] — *Syn.* bombastic, pretentious, turgid, fustian, showy; see also **oratorical, ornate** 1.
**sentient,** *modif.* — *Syn.* conscious, aware, alert, perceptive; see **observant** 1, **sensitive** 3.
**sentiment,** *n.* **1.** [Emotion] — *Syn.* sensibility, predilection, tender feeling; see **emotion, feeling** 4, **thought** 2.
**2.** [An opinion; *often plural*] — *Syn.* view, attitude, way of thinking; see **opinion** 1, **viewpoint.**
*See Synonym Study at* FEELING, OPINION.
**sentimental,** *modif.* — *Syn.* emotional, romantic, romantical, dreamy, idealistic, visionary, mawkish, maudlin, bathetic, artificial, sickish, unrealistic, susceptible, silly, overemotional, affected, simpering, languishing, artificial, insincere, overacted, schoolgirlish, sappy★, gushy★, mushy★, tear-jerking★, corny★.
**sentimentality,** *n.* — *Syn.* sentimentalism, sentiment, melodramatics, bathos, melodrama, maudlinness, triteness, mawkishness, emotionalness, mushiness★, gushiness★; see also **emotion, romance** 1.
**sentinel,** *n.* — *Syn.* lookout, sentry, watchman; see **guard.**
**sentry,** *n.* — *Syn.* sentinel, watch, protector; see **guard.**
**separable,** *modif.* — *Syn.* breakable, severable, detachable; see **divisible.**
**separate,** *v.* **1.** [To cause to part] — *Syn.* part, divide, undo, distribute, sever, sunder; see also **divide** 1.
**2.** [To keep apart] — *Syn.* isolate, insulate, single out, sequester, seclude, rope off, segregate, intervene, stand between, draw apart, split up, break up.
**3.** [To part company] — *Syn.* take leave, go away, depart; see **leave** 1.
**4.** [To classify] — *Syn.* assign, distribute, group; see **classify, order** 3.

*SYN.* — **separate** implies the putting apart of things previously united, joined, or assembled /to *separate* machine parts, a family, etc./; **divide** implies a separation into parts, pieces, groups, etc. by or as by cutting, splitting, branching, etc., often for purposes of apportionment /to *divide* the profits into equal shares/; **part** is now usually applied to the separation of persons or things that have been closely connected or associated /refused to *part* with his teddy bear/ **sever** implies a forcible and complete separation, as by cutting off a part from a whole /to *sever* a branch from a tree, *severed* all relations with her brother/; **sunder,** now largely a literary term, implies a violent splitting, tearing, or wrenching apart

**separated,** *modif.* — *Syn.* divided, parted, apart, disconnected, abstracted, apportioned, partitioned, distinct, disunited, disjointed, sundered, disembodied, cut in two, cut apart, set apart, distant, disassociated, removed, distributed, scattered, set asunder, put asunder, divorced, divergent, marked, severed, far between, in halves. — *Ant.* UNITED, together, whole.

**separately,** *modif.* — *Syn.* singly, definitely, distinctly, independently; see **clearly** 1, 2, **individually.**

**separation,** *n.* **1.** [The act of dividing] — *Syn.* disconnection, severance, division, cut, disjoining, detachment.

**2.** [The act of parting] — *Syn.* leave-taking, farewell, embarkation; see **departure** 1.

**3.** [Marital estrangement] — *Syn.* divorce, break up, parting, bust-up*; see **divorce.**

**September,** *n.* — *Syn.* fall month, autumn month, summer month, Indian summer, harvest, back-to-school season, opening of the football season.

**septic,** *modif.* — *Syn.* unsanitary, toxic, putrefactive; see **rotten** 2, **unwholesome.**

**septic tank,** *n.* — *Syn.* sewage disposal system, sanitary provisions, cesspool; see **sewer.**

**sepulcher,** *n.* — *Syn.* tomb, vault, crypt; see **grave** 1.

**sepulchral,** *modif.* — *Syn.* funereal, burial, somber; see **dismal** 1.

**sequel,** *n.* — *Syn.* consequence, continuation, progression; see **sequence** 1, **series.**

**sequence,** *n.* **1.** [Succession] — *Syn.* order, continuity, continuousness, concatenation, continuance, successiveness, progression, graduation, consecutiveness, flow, consecution, perpetuity, unbrokenness, catenation, subsequence, course.

**2.** [Arrangement] — *Syn.* placement, distribution, classification; see **order** 3.

**3.** [A series] — *Syn.* chain, string, array; see **series.**

*See Synonym Study at* SERIES.

**sequential,** *modif.* **1.** [Next] — *Syn.* subsequent, succeeding, later; see **consecutive, following.**

**2.** [Continuous] — *Syn.* incessant, steady, persistent; see **constant** 1, **regular** 3.

**sequester,** *v.* **1.** [To set apart] — *Syn.* separate, isolate, set off, segregate; see **separate** 2.

**2.** [To take over] — *Syn.* confiscate, seize, appropriate; see **seize** 2.

**3.** [To seclude] — *Syn.* withdraw, draw back, take leave; see **retire** 1, 3, **retreat** 1.

**sere,** *modif.* — *Syn.* dried up, scorched, burned; see **dry** 1, **withered.**

**serenade,** *n.* — *Syn.* melody, compliment, nocturne; see **music** 1, **song.**

**serene,** *modif.* — *Syn.* calm, tranquil, clear, pellucid, limpid, unruffled, translucent, undisturbed, undimmed, peaceful, halcyon, idyllic, smooth, quiet, still, composed, imperturbable, cool, cool-headed, sedate, level-headed, content, satisfied, patient, reconciled, easygoing, placid, comfortable, cheerful; see also **calm** 1, 2, **tranquil** 1, 2. — *Ant.* agitated, disturbed, ruffled.

*See Synonym Study at* CALM.

**serenity,** *n.* — *Syn.* composure, quietness, calmness, tranquility; see **composure, patience** 1, **peace** 2.

*See Synonym Study at* COMPOSURE.

**serf,** *n.* — *Syn.* land-slave, bondman, thrall, villein; see **servant, slave** 1.

**serge,** *n.* — *Syn.* twill, wool serge, silk serge; see **cloth.**

**sergeant,** *n.* Kinds of sergeants include: master sergeant, staff sergeant, technical sergeant, first sergeant, top sergeant, platoon sergeant, gunnery sergeant, lance sergeant, acting sergeant, sergeant first class, sergeant major, sergeant-at-arms, police sergeant, top kick*, sarge*; see also **officer** 3, **soldier.**

**serial,** *modif.* — *Syn.* consecutive, successive, ensuing, following, continued, continual, continuing, ongoing.

**serial,** *n.* — *Syn.* installment, serial picture, continued

story, series, weekly program; see also **movie.**

**series,** *n.* — *Syn.* rank, file, line, row, set, train, range, list, string, chain, order, sequence, succession, group, procession, continuity, column, cordon, progression, suite, category, classification, tier, suit, scale, array, gradation.

**SYN.** — **series** applies to a number of similar, more or less related things following one another in time or place [a *series* of concerts]; **sequence** emphasizes a closer relationship between the things, such as logical or casual connection, numerical order, etc. [the *sequence* of events]; **succession** merely implies a following of one thing after another, without any necessary connection between them [a *succession* of errors]; **chain** refers to a series in which there is a definite relationship of cause and effect or some other logical connection [a *chain* of ideas]

**serious,** *modif.* **1.** [Involving danger] — *Syn.* grave, severe, pressing; see **dangerous** 1, 2.

**2.** [Involving earnestness] — *Syn.* solemn, grave, earnest, sedate, sober; see also **solemn** 1.

**SYN.** — **serious** implies absorption in deep thought or involvement in something really important as distinguished from something frivolous or merely amusing [he takes a *serious* interest in the theater]; **grave** implies the dignified weightiness of heavy responsibilities or cares [a *grave* expression on his face]; **solemn** suggests an impressive or awe-inspiring seriousness [a *solemn* ceremony]; **sedate** implies a dignified, quiet or composed, sometimes even prim seriousness [a *sedate* clergyman]; **earnest** suggests a seriousness of purpose marked by sincerity and enthusiasm [an *earnest* desire to help]; **sober** implies a seriousness marked by temperance, self-control, emotional balance, etc. [a *sober* criticism]

**seriously,** *modif.* **1.** [In a manner fraught with danger] — *Syn.* dangerously, precariously, perilously, in a risky way, threateningly, menacingly, grievously, severely, harmfully, in a dangerous manner. — *Ant.* SAFELY, harmlessly, in no danger.

**2.** [In a manner that recognizes importance] — *Syn.* gravely, soberly, solemnly, earnestly, solemnly, thoughtfully, sternly, sedately, with forethought, with sobriety, with great earnestness, all joking aside; see also **sincerely.** — *Ant.* LIGHTLY, thoughtlessly, airily.

**seriousness,** *n.* **1.** [The quality of being dangerous] — *Syn.* gravity, weight, enormity; see **importance** 1.

**2.** [The characteristic of being sober] — *Syn.* earnestness, sobriety, solemnity, gravity, calmness, thoughtfulness, coolness, sedateness, sober-mindedness, staidness; see also **sincerity.** — *Ant.* FUN, gaiety, jollity.

**sermon,** *n.* — *Syn.* discourse, address, exhortation, lesson, doctrine, lecture; see also **speech** 3.

*See Synonym Study at* SPEECH.

**serpent,** *n.* — *Syn.* reptile, viper, ophidian; see **snake.**

**serpentine,** *modif.* — *Syn.* snakelike, winding, meandering, sinuous; see **bent, twisted** 1.

**serum,** *n.* — *Syn.* antitoxin, antiserum, agglutinin, immunotoxin, blood serum, plasma, agglutinogen, agglutinoid.

**servant,** *n.* — *Syn.* servitor, attendant, retainer, helper, hireling, lackey, dependent, menial, domestic, drudge, slave, slavey*; see also **assistant.**

Servants include: butler, chamberlain, housekeeper, chef, cook, second maid, scullery maid, kitchenmaid,

maid of all work, 'tween maid, general maid, laundress, chambermaid, parlormaid, lady's maid, seamstress, nursemaid, nurse, valet, gentleman's gentleman, doorman, footman, lackey, wine steward, major-domo, squire, driver, coachman, chauffeur, groom, stableboy, stableman, equerry, gardener, yardman, kennelman, handyman.

**serve,** *v.* **1.** [To fulfill an obligation] — *Syn.* carry out, complete, hear duty's call, hearken to the call of duty, obey the call of one's country, acquit oneself of an obligation, subserve, discharge one's duty, live up to one's duty. — *Ant.* BETRAY, dishonor, disgrace.
**2.** [To work for] — *Syn.* be employed by, labor, toil, carry on a trade, be in the employ of; see also **work** 2.
**3.** [To help] — *Syn.* give aid, assist, be of assistance; see **help** 1.
**4.** [To serve at table] — *Syn.* wait on, attend, help one to food, help.
**5.** [To obey] — *Syn.* follow, accept, agree; see **obey** 2.
**served,** *modif.* — *Syn.* dressed, prepared, offered, apportioned, dealt, furnished, supplied, provided, dished up★.
**serve notice,** *v.* — *Syn.* inform, report, give word; see **notify** 1.
**serve someone right,** *v.* — *Syn.* deserve it, have it coming★, be fair, get one's dues, be rightly served, do justice to, do the right thing by, give the devil his due★; see also **deserve.**
**serve time,** *v.* — *Syn.* stand committed, serve out a jail sentence, be incarcerated, be in jail, pay one's debt to society, go to jail, do a term, be in stir, be in the joint, do time, be sent up.
**service,** *n.* **1.** [Aid] — *Syn.* co-operation, assistance, help; see **aid** 1.
**2.** [Tableware] — *Syn.* set, silver, setting; see **china, dish** 1, **pottery.**
**3.** [A religious service] — *Syn.* rite, worship, sermon; see **ceremony.**
**4.** [Military service] — *Syn.* military, army, duty, active service, stint.
**at someone's service** — *Syn.* zealous, anxious to help, ready to serve, obedient; see **helpful** 1, **ready** 1, **willing** 1.
**in service** — *Syn.* functioning, repaired, in good condition; see **working.**
**of service** — *Syn.* useful, handy, usable; see **helpful** 1.
**service,** *v.* — *Syn.* maintain, sustain, keep up, preserve, keep safe, work on; see also **repair.**
**serviceable,** *modif.* — *Syn.* practical, advantageous, beneficial; see **helpful** 1, **usable.**
**service club,** *n.* — *Syn.* luncheon club, community welfare group, business and professional society; see **organization** 3.
Service clubs include: Rotary International, Lions, Kiwanis, Civitan International, Toastmaster's, Soroptimist, Elks, Brotherly and Protective Order of Elks (B.P.O.E.), International Order of Odd Fellows (I.O.O.F.), Shriners, Masons and Eastern Star, Knights of Pythias, Knights of Columbus, American Legion, Junior League, Ruritan National, Optimist International.
**service station,** *n.* — *Syn.* filling station, gas station, shop★; see **garage** 2.
**servile,** *modif.* — *Syn.* menial, beggarly, cringing; see **humble** 1, 2, **obsequious.**
**serving,** *modif.* — *Syn.* aiding, co-operating, helping; see **helpful.**
**serving,** *n.* — *Syn.* plateful, course, portion; see **helping, meal** 2.

**servitude,** *n.* — *Syn.* confinement, bondage, subjugation; see **slavery** 1, **subjection.**
*See Synonym Study at* SLAVERY.
**session,** *n.* — *Syn.* assembly, concourse, sitting; see **gathering.**
**set,** *modif.* **1.** [Firm] — *Syn.* stable, solid, settled; see **firm** 2.
**2.** [Determined] — *Syn.* concluded, steadfast, decided; see **determined** 1, **resolute** 2.
**3.** [Obstinate] — *Syn.* immovable, stubborn, relentless; see **obstinate** 1.
**set,** *n.* **1.** [Inclination] — *Syn.* attitude, position, bearing; see **inclination** 1.
**2.** [A social group] — *Syn.* clique, coterie, circle; see **clique, faction** 1, **organization** 3.
**3.** [A collection of related items] — *Syn.* kit, assemblage, assortment; see **collection** 2.
*See Synonym Study at* CLIQUE.
**set,** *v.* **1.** [To place] — *Syn.* insert, deposit, arrange; see **place** 1.
**2.** [To establish] — *Syn.* anchor, fix, introduce; see **establish** 2, **install.**
**3.** [To become firm] — *Syn.* jell, solidify, congeal; see **harden** 2, **stiffen** 1, **thicken** 1.
**4.** [To value] — *Syn.* rate, fix a price, estimate; see **price, value** 2.
**5.** [To fasten] — *Syn.* lock, make fast, fix; see **fasten** 1.
**6.** [To start] — *Syn.* commence, initiate, put in motion; see **begin** 1.
**7.** [To brood] — *Syn.* incubate, hatch, hover; see **produce** 1.
**set about,** *v.* — *Syn.* start, begin a task, start doing; see **begin** 1.
**set apart,** *v.* — *Syn.* isolate, segregate, make separate, make distinct, set off; see also **distinguish** 1, **separate** 2.
**set aside,** *v.* **1.** [To save] — *Syn.* put away, reserve, lay up; see **maintain** 3, **save** 3.
**2.** [To discard] — *Syn.* abrogate, repeal, reject; see **cancel** 2, **discard.**
**setback,** *n.* — *Syn.* hindrance, check, reversal; see **delay** 1, **difficulty** 1, **impediment** 1.
**set back,** *v.* — *Syn.* retard, reverse, slow down; see **defeat** 1, 3, **hinder.**
**set down,** *v.* — *Syn.* put on paper, register, write out; see **record** 1, **write** 1, 2.
**set forth,** *v.* — *Syn.* begin a journey, start out, take the first steps; see **begin** 2.
**set free,** *v.* — *Syn.* liberate, discharge, give freedom to; see **free** 1, **release.**
**set in,** *v.* — *Syn.* commence, begin to grow, turn; see **begin** 2.
**set off,** *v.* **1.** [To contrast] — *Syn.* set apart, be different, appear different, be the opposite; see **contrast** 1, **offset.**
**2.** [To explode] — *Syn.* touch off, set the spark to, detonate; see **explode** 1.
**3.** [To begin] — *Syn.* start out, set forth, set out, get under way; see **begin** 2.
**set out,** *v.* — *Syn.* initiate, start, commence; see **begin** 2.
**set sail,** *v.* — *Syn.* launch, shove off, weigh anchor; see **leave** 1, **sail** 1, 2.
**set straight,** *v.* — *Syn.* revise, inform, provide the facts; see **correct** 1, **improve** 1, 2.
**settee,** *n.* — *Syn.* couch, divan, sofa; see **couch, furniture.**
**set the pace,** *v.* — *Syn.* take the lead, pace, provide a standard; see **lead** 1.
**setting,** *n.* — *Syn.* environment, surroundings, ambience, mounting, backdrop, frame, framework, back-

ground, context, perspective, horizon, shadow, shade, distance, *mise en scene* (French). — *Ant.* FRONT, foreground, focus.

**settle**, *v.* **1.** [To decide] — *Syn.* decide, resolve, conclude; see **decide.**

**2.** [To prove] — *Syn.* establish, verify, make certain; see **prove.**

**3.** [To finish] — *Syn.* end, make an end of, complete; see **achieve** 1.

**4.** [To sink] — *Syn.* descend, decline, fall; see **sink** 1.

**5.** [To cause to sink] — *Syn.* submerge, submerse, plunge; see **immerse** 1, **sink** 2.

**6.** [To quiet] — *Syn.* calm, compose, pacify; see **quiet** 1.

**7.** [To establish residence] — *Syn.* locate, lodge, become a citizen, reside, fix one's residence, abide, set up housekeeping, make one's home, establish a home, keep house; see also **dwell.**

**8.** [To take up sedentary life; *often used with "down"*] — *Syn.* follow regular habits, live an orderly life, become conventional, follow convention, buy a house, marry, marry and settle down, raise a family, forsake one's wild ways, regulate one's life, get in a groove★, get in a rut★, lead a humdrum existence★, hang up one's hat★, clear the land★, mend one's fences★; see also **improve** 1, 2, **live** 4.

**9.** [To satisfy a claim] — *Syn.* pay, compensate, make an adjustment, reach a compromise, make payment, arrange a settlement, get squared away, reconcile, resolve, rectify, pay damages, pay out, settle out of court, settle up, patch up, work out, settle the score, even the score, clear off old scores, dispose of, get quits with, account with.

*See Synonym Study at* DECIDE.

**settled**, *modif.* — *Syn.* decided, resolved, ended; see **determined** 1.

**settlement**, *n.* **1.** [An agreement] — *Syn.* covenant, arrangement, compact; see **agreement** 3, **contract.**

**2.** [A payment] — *Syn.* compensation, remuneration, reimbursement; see **adjustment** 2, **pay** 2.

**3.** [A colony] — *Syn.* principality, plantation, establishment, foundation.

**4.** [A small community] — *Syn.* village, town, hamlet; see **town** 1, **village.**

**settler**, *n.* — *Syn.* planter, immigrant, homesteader; see **pioneer** 2.

**settle up**, *v.* — *Syn.* meet one's obligations, make a settlement, pay up, pay one's bills; see **pay** 1, **settle** 9.

**setup**, *n.* **1.** [Arrangement] — *Syn.* structure, composition, plan; see **order** 3, **organization** 2.

**2.** [★A gullible person] — *Syn.* dupe, gull, easy mark, sitting duck, trusting soul, sucker, fool, goat★, butt★, dummy★, patsy★, mark★, Simple Simon★, victim★, pushover★, cat's paw★.

**3.** [Accompaniments for alcoholic beverages] — *Syn.* service, fixings, settings.

Parts of a setup include: water, mixers, glasses, ice cubes; see also **drink** 3, **glassware.**

**set up**, *v.* **1.** [To make arrangements] — *Syn.* prearrange, inaugurate, work on; see **arrange** 2.

**2.** [To finance] — *Syn.* patronize, promote, support, pay for, subsidize.

**3.** [To establish] — *Syn.* found, originate, make provisions for; see **begin** 1, **establish** 2.

**set upon**, *v.* — *Syn.* assail, fall upon, spring at; see **attack** 1.

**sever**, *v.* — *Syn.* part, split, separate, dissociate, rend, cleave; see also **cut** 1, **divide** 1.

*See Synonym Study at* SEPARATE.

**several**, *modif.* **1.** [Few] — *Syn.* some, any, a few, quite a few, not many, sundry, two or three, a small number of, scarce, sparse, hardly any, scarcely any, half a dozen, only a few, scant, scanty, rare, infrequent, in a minority, a handful, not too many. — *Ant.* MANY, large numbers of, none.

**2.** [Various] — *Syn.* manifold, multiform, plural, a plurality, a number, not a few, numerous, diverse, a lot of, quite a lot of, a good deal; see also **many, various.**

**3.** [Distinct or separate] — *Syn.* certain, different, divers, definite, single, particular; see also **individual** 1.

**several**, *n.* — *Syn.* not too many, various ones, different ones, a minority, a small number, quite a number, quite a few, quite a variety; see also **few.**

**severally**, *modif.* — *Syn.* separately, exclusively, alone, singly; see **individually, only** 1.

**severance**, *n.* — *Syn.* section, split, separation; see **division** 1, 2.

**severance pay**, *n.* — *Syn.* pittance, stipend, allotment, payoff, golden handshake★; see also **pay** 2.

**severe**, *modif.* **1.** [Stern] — *Syn.* stern, exacting, uncompromising, unbending, inflexible, unchanging, unalterable, inexorable, harsh, cruel, oppressive, close, grinding, peremptory, obdurate, resolute, austere, rigid, grim, earnest, stiff, forbidding, resolved, relentless, strait-laced, determined, unfeeling, insensate, with an iron will, strict, inconsiderate, firm, immovable, as firm as the Rock of Gibraltar, adamant, unyielding. — *Ant.* FLEXIBLE, yielding, genial.

**2.** [Difficult or rigorous] — *Syn.* overbearing, tyrannical, mordant, sharp, exacting, stringent, drastic, domineering, rigid, oppressive, despotic, unmerciful, bullying, uncompromising, obdurate, relentless, unrelenting, hard, rigorous, austere, grinding, ascetic, grim, implacable, cruel, pitiless, critical, unjust, barbarous, censorious, crusty, gruff, crabbed, unmitigated, intractable, stubborn, autocratic, Draconian, with a heart of granite, stony-hearted, hard-shell★, rock-ribbed★, hidebound★; see also **difficult** 1. — *Ant.* EASY, easygoing, indulgent.

---

*SYN.* — **severe** applies to a person or thing that is strict, uncompromising, or restrained and connotes a total absence of softness, laxity, frivolity, etc. *[a severe critic, hairdo, etc.]* and may often imply harshness *[severe punishment, a severe tornado]*; **stern** implies an unyielding firmness, esp. as manifested in a grim or forbidding aspect or manner *[a stern guardian]*; **austere** suggests harsh restraint, self-denial, stark simplicity *[the austere diet of wartime]*, or an absence of warmth, passion, ornamentation, etc. *[an austere bedroom]*; **ascetic** implies extreme self-denial and self-discipline or even, sometimes, the deliberate self-infliction of pain and discomfort, as by religious fanatics *[an ascetic hermit]*

---

**severely**, *modif.* — *Syn.* critically, harshly, rigorously; see **firmly** 2, **seriously** 1.

**severity**, *n.* — *Syn.* asperity, sharpness, acerbity, grimness, hardness, unkindness, hardheartedness, strictness, austerity, rigor; see also **cruelty.** — *Ant.* PITY, kindness, softness.

**sew**, *v.* — *Syn.* stitch, seam, fasten, work with needle and thread, tailor, tack, embroider, bind, piece, baste. — *Ant.* RAVEL, rip, undo.

**sewage**, *n.* — *Syn.* sewerage, excrement, offscum, offal, waste matter; see also **residue.**

**sewer**, *n.* — *Syn.* drain, drainpipe, drainage tube, conduit, gutter, disposal system, sewage system, septic tank, dry well, leach field, city sewer, sewage disposal, sanitary provisions; see also **trench** 1.

**sewing,** *n.* — *Syn.* stitching, seaming, backstitching, tailoring, embroidering, darning, mending, piecing, patching, dressmaking.

**sewing machine,** *n.* Varieties and types of sewing machines include: domestic, treadle, electric, cabinet, lock-stitch, portable, chainstitch, heavy duty, commercial, factory, shoemaker's, bookbinder's, luggage maker's.

**sewn,** *modif.* — *Syn.* stitched, saddle-stitched, sewed, mended, embroidered, tailored.

**sex,** *n.* **1.** [Ideas associated with sexual relationships] — *Syn.* sexual attraction, sex appeal, magnetism, sensuality, affinity, love, courtship, marriage, generation, reproduction.
**2.** [A group, either male or female] — *Syn.* men, women, males, females, the feminine world, the masculine world, androgynes.
**3.** [Gender] — *Syn.* sexuality, masculinity, femininity, womanliness, manhood, manliness.
**4.** [Sexual intercourse] — *Syn.* coitus, making love, the sexual act, going to bed with someone; see **copulation, fornication.**
**5.** [Genitals] — *Syn.* genitalia, sexual organ, private parts, member*; see **genitals.**

**sexton,** *n.* — *Syn.* warden, bell-ringer, sacristan, servant, janitor; see also **custodian** 2.

**sexual,** *modif.* **1.** [Reproductive] — *Syn.* genitive, genital, generative, reproductive, procreative, venereal, coital; see also **original** 1.
**2.** [Carnal] — *Syn.* wanton, passionate, physical, loving, sharing, between the sexes; see also **intimate** 1, **sensual** 2.

**sexuality,** *n.* **1.** [Sexual drive or interest] — *Syn.* lust, sensuality, passion; see **desire** 3.
**2.** [Sexual character] — *Syn.* femininity, masculinity, homosexuality, lesbianism, bisexuality, gender, sexual preference.

**sexy*,** *modif.* — *Syn.* sensuous, erotic, sexually attractive, suggestive, libidinous, off-color; see also **lewd** 1, 2, **sensual** 1, 2.

**shabby,** *modif.* **1.** [In bad repair] — *Syn.* ragged, threadbare, faded, ill-dressed, dilapidated, decayed, deteriorated, the worse for wear, run-down, broken-down, poor, pitiful, worn, meager, miserable, degenerated, wretched, poverty-stricken, scrubby*, seedy*, gone to seed*, down at the heel*. — *Ant.* NEAT, new, well-kept.
**2.** [Inconsiderate] — *Syn.* contemptible, low, mean, paltry, sordid, unkind, mercenary, miserly, selfish, thoughtless, stingy*, piffling*, tight-fisted*; see also **rude** 2. — *Ant.* GENEROUS, kindly, noble.

**shack,** *n.* — *Syn.* hut, shed, hovel, cabin, shanty, shotgun shack.

**shackle,** *n.* — *Syn.* manacle, fetter, leg iron, handcuff, restraint.

**shackle,** *v.* — *Syn.* hobble, fetter, chain; see **bind** 1.

**shade,** *n.* **1.** [Lack of light] — *Syn.* blackness, shadow, dimness; see **darkness** 1.
**2.** [A degree of color] — *Syn.* cast, tone, hue; see **color** 1, **tint.**
**3.** [A slight difference] — *Syn.* variation, proposal, hint; see **suggestion** 1.
**4.** [An obstruction to light] — *Syn.* covering, blind, screen; see **curtain.**
**5.** [A ghost] — *Syn.* spirit, manes, revenant; see **ghost** 1, 2.
*See Synonym Study at* COLOR.

**shade,** *v.* **1.** [To intercept direct rays] — *Syn.* screen, shelter, shadow, cast a shadow over, overshadow, eclipse.

**2.** [To make darker] — *Syn.* darken, blacken, obscure, cloud, shadow, make dim, adumbrate, tone down, nigrify, black out, make dusky, deepen the shade, overshadow, make gloomy, screen, shut out the light, befog, keep out the light.
**3.** [To become darker] — *Syn.* grow dark, grow black, become dark, grow dim, blacken, turn to twilight, deepen into night, become gloomy, be overcast, grow dusky, cloud up, cloud over, overcloud, grow shadowy.
**4.** [*To win by a narrow margin] — *Syn.* barely win, win by a hairbreadth, nose out*; see **defeat.**

**shadow,** *n.* — *Syn.* umbra, obscuration, adumbration; see **darkness** 1.
**in** or **under the shadow of** — *Syn.* threatened, in danger of, in a dangerous situation; see **endangered.**

**shadow,** *v.* **1.** [To shade] — *Syn.* dim, veil, screen; see **shade** 1, 2, **shelter.**
**2.** [To follow secretly] — *Syn.* trail, watch, keep in sight, dog*; see **pursue** 1.

**shadowy,** *modif.* — *Syn.* dim, cloudy, in a fog; see **dark** 1, **hazy** 1.

**shady,** *modif.* **1.** [Shaded] — *Syn.* dusky, shadowy, adumbral, in the shade, sheltered, out of the sun, dim, cloudy, under a cloud, cool, indistinct, vague; see also **dark** 1.
**2.** [*Questionable] — *Syn.* suspicious, disreputable, dubious, dishonest, fishy*, crooked, underhanded.

**shaft,** *n.* **1.** [Rod] — *Syn.* stem, handle, bar, cylinder, pole; see also **rod** 1.
**2.** [A weapon] — *Syn.* arrow, spear, lance, missile; see **weapon** 1.
**3.** [Light ray] — *Syn.* wave, streak, beam of light; see **beam** 2, **ray.**
**give someone the shaft*** — *Syn.* cheat, trick, mistreat; see **abuse** 1.

**shaggy,** *modif.* — *Syn.* rough, uncombed, unkempt, furry, hirsute, hairy, long-haired.

**shake,** *n.* — *Syn.* tremble, shiver, pulsation; see **movement** 1, 2.
**no great shakes*** — *Syn.* failure, mediocrity, ordinary; see **failure** 1, 2.

**shake,** *v.* **1.** [To vibrate] — *Syn.* tremble, quiver, quake, shiver, shudder, palpitate, waver, fluctuate, reel, flap, flutter, totter, thrill, wobble, stagger, waggle; see also **wave** 1, 3.
**2.** [To cause to vibrate] — *Syn.* agitate, rock, sway, swing, joggle, jolt, jounce, bounce, brandish, jar, move, flourish, set in motion, convulse.

**shakedown*,** *n.* **1.** [Extortion] — *Syn.* exhortation, blackmail, badger game*, the squeeze*; see **theft.**
**2.** [Investigation] — *Syn.* inquiry, probe, purge; see **examination** 1.

**shake hands,** *v.* **1.** [To greet] — *Syn.* meet, welcome, receive; see **greet.**
**2.** [To agree] — *Syn.* come to terms, conclude a transaction, reach agreement, strike a bargain; see **agree.**

**shaken,** *modif.* — *Syn.* unnerved, upset, overcome; see **excited.**

**shake off,** *v.* — *Syn.* lose, get rid of, drop; see **remove** 1.

**shake up,** *v.* — *Syn.* disturb, unsettle, overturn; see **upset** 1.

**shaky,** *modif.* **1.** [Not firm] — *Syn.* quivery, trembling, jellylike, all-a-quiver, unsettled, not set, yielding, unsteady, tottering, unsound, insecure, tremulous, unstable, infirm, jittery, nervous. — *Ant.* FIRM, settled, rigid.
**2.** [Not reliable] — *Syn.* uncertain, tenuous, not dependable, not to be depended on, doubtful, questionable; see also **unreliable** 2, **unsteady** 2.

**shale,** *n.* — *Syn.* schistous clay, silt rock, sedimentary rock; see **rock** 1.

**shall,** *v.* — *Syn.* be going to, be about to, intend, want to, be obliged, must; see also **will** 3.

**shallow,** *modif.* **1.** [Lacking physical depth] — *Syn.* shoal, depthless, slight, inconsiderable, superficial, with the bottom in plain sight, with no depth, with little depth, not deep, as deep as a mud puddle*, not deep enough to float a match*, no deeper than a heavy dew*. — *Ant.* DEEP, bottomless, unfathomable.
**2.** [Lacking intellectual depth] — *Syn.* superficial, simple, silly, trifling, frothy, insane, frivolous, superficial, petty, foolish, farcical, idle, unintelligent, piffling*, piddling*, namby-pamby*, lightweight*, wishy-washy*; see also **dull** 3, **stupid** 1. — *Ant.* PROFOUND, philosophic, wise.
*See Synonym Study at* SUPERFICIAL.

**sham,** *modif.* — *Syn.* misleading, lying, untrue; see **false** 3.
*See Synonym Study at* FALSE.

**sham,** *n.* — *Syn.* fakery, pretense, pretext; see **fake.**

**shaman,** *n.* — *Syn.* medicine man, witch doctor, angakok, obeah doctor, mundunugu; see also **priest.**

**shamble,** *v.* — *Syn.* hobble, dodder, shuffle; see **limp, walk** 1.

**shambles,** *n.* — *Syn.* mess, hodge-podge, confusion; see **disorder** 2.

**shame,** *n.* **1.** [A disgrace] — *Syn.* embarrassment, stigma, blot; see **disgrace** 2.
**2.** [A sense of wrongdoing] — *Syn.* bad conscience, mortification, confusion, humiliation, compunction, regret, chagrin, discomposure, irritation, remorse, stupefaction, embarrassment, abashment, self-reproach, self-reproof, self-disgust, stings of conscience, pangs of remorse; see also **guilt.**
**3.** [A condition of disgrace] — *Syn.* humiliation, dishonor, degradation; see **disgrace** 1, **scandal.**
**put to shame 1.** — *Syn.* make ashamed, humiliate, embarrass; see **shame** *v.*
**2.** — *Syn.* outdo, do better than, outclass, beat; see **defeat** 1, 3.

**shame,** *v.* — *Syn.* humiliate, mortify, dishonor, chasten, abash, put down*; see also **disgrace, humble.**

**shamed,** *modif.* — *Syn.* disgraced, embarrassed, humiliated, mortified, ashamed, chagrined, unable to show one's face.

**shamefaced,** *modif.* **1.** [*Shy] — *Syn.* modest, restrained, retiring; see **humble** 1, **reserved** 3, **resigned.**
**2.** [Embarrassed] — *Syn.* crestfallen, humiliated, perplexed; see **ashamed.**

**shameful,** *modif.* **1.** [Offensive] — *Syn.* immodest, corrupt, immoral, intemperate, debauched, drunken, profligate, villainous, knavish, degraded, reprobate, diabolical, indecent, indelicate, lewd, vulgar, impure, unclean, fleshly, carnal, sinful, wicked; see also **offensive** 2. — *Ant.* UPRIGHT, chaste, honorable.
**2.** [Causing shame] — *Syn.* dishonorable, disgraceful, contemptible, scandalous, flagrant, obscene, ribald, heinous, infamous, opprobrious, outrageous, shocking, ignominious, gross, infernal, disgusting, too bad, unworthy, evil, foul, hellish, disreputable, despicable; see also **corrupt** 1, **dishonest** 1, 2, **wrong.** — *Ant.* WORTHY, admirable, creditable.

**shamefully,** *modif.* — *Syn.* cruelly, badly, outrageously; see **wrongly** 1, 2.

**shameless,** *modif.* — *Syn.* brazen, bold, forward; see **rude** 2, **lewd** 1, 2.

**shamelessly,** *modif.* — *Syn.* brazenly, audaciously, unblushingly; see **boldly** 1, **openly** 2.

**shank,** *n.* — *Syn.* long shank, foreleg, stem; see **leg** 1, **limb** 2.

**shank of the evening*** — *Syn.* early evening, not late, not time to go, quite early; see **early, night** 1.

**shanty,** *n.* — *Syn.* cabin, hovel, cottage; see **hut, shack.**

**shape,** *n.* **1.** [Form] — *Syn.* contour, aspect, configuration; see **appearance** 1, **form** 1.
**2.** [An actual form] — *Syn.* pattern, stamp, frame; see **mold** 1, 2.
**3.** [A phantom] — *Syn.* apparition, shade, wraith; see **ghost** 1.
**4.** [Condition] — *Syn.* state, physical state, health, fitness, lack of fitness.
*See Synonym Study at* FORM.
**out of shape** — *Syn.* distorted, misshapen, battered; see **bent, broken** 1, **flat** 1, **ruined** 1, 2, **twisted.**
**take shape** — *Syn.* take on form, grow, grow up, fill out; see **develop** 1, **improve** 2.

**shape,** *v.* **1.** [To give shape] — *Syn.* mold, cast, fashion; see **form** 1.
**2.** [To take shape] — *Syn.* become, develop, take form; see **form** 4, **grow** 2.
*See Synonym Study at* MAKE.

**shaped,** *modif.* — *Syn.* made, fashioned, created; see **formed.**

**shapeless,** *modif.* **1.** [Formless] — *Syn.* indistinct, indefinite, invisible, amorphous, amorphic, vague, anomalous, without character, without shape, without form, lacking form, inchoate, unformed, unmade, not formed, not made, not created, with no definite outline; see also **uncertain** 2. — *Ant.* FORMED, distinct, molded.
**2.** [Deformed] — *Syn.* misshapen, irregular, unshapely, unsymmetrical, mutilated, disfigured, malformed, ill-formed, abnormal; see also **deformed.** — *Ant.* REGULAR, symmetrical, shapely.

**shapely,** *modif.* — *Syn.* symmetrical, comely, proportioned; see **trim** 2.

**shape up*,** *v.* **1.** [To obey] — *Syn.* mind, conform, observe; see **behave** 2, **improve** 2, **obey** 1.
**2.** [To develop] — *Syn.* enlarge, expand, refine; see **develop** 1.

**share,** *n.* — *Syn.* division, apportionment, part, portion, quota, helping, serving, piece, ration, slice, allotment, parcel, dose, fraction, fragment, allowance, pittance, dividend, percentage, heritage, commission, cut*, whack*, rake-off*.
**on shares** — *Syn.* proportionally, in proportion, on the basis of investments; see **equally.**

**share,** *v.* **1.** [To divide] — *Syn.* allot, distribute, apportion, part, partition, deal, dispense, assign, administer. — *Ant.* UNITE, combine, withhold.
**2.** [To partake] — *Syn.* participate, share in, partake, experience, receive, have a portion of, have a share in, take part in, go in with, take a part of, take a share of; see also **like** 1. — *Ant.* AVOID, have no share in, take no part in.
**3.** [To give] — *Syn.* yield, bestow, accord; see **give** 1.
**4.** [To pay half of the expenses] — *Syn.* share expenses, pay half, go Dutch, go shares, go halves, go fifty-fifty, give and take, divide with.

SYN. — **share** means to use, enjoy, or possess in common with others and generally connotes giving or receiving a part of something /to *share* expenses/; **participate** implies taking part with others in some activity or enterprise /to *participate* in the talks/; **partake** implies taking or accepting one's share, as of a meal or responsibility /to *partake* of a friend's hospitality/

**share and share alike\***, *modif.* — *Syn.* equally, fifty-fifty\*, shared.

**shareholder,** *n.* — *Syn.* stockholder, bondholder, part-owner, sharer.

**sharing,** *n.* — *Syn.* giving, dividing, communal living, partition, splitting, distribution, share and share alike, co-operative, partaking, participating, companionate.

**shark,** *n.* **1.** [Fish]. Kinds of sharks include: whale, basking, mako, angel, blue, man-eating, hammerhead, thresher, mackerel, gray, dog, bonnethead, shovelhead, dusky, Port Jackson, sharp-nose, spinous, great white, sand, nurse, sleeper, tiger; see also **fish.**
**2.** [A con artist] — *Syn.* swindler, cheat, flimflam artist.

**sharp,** *modif.* **1.** [Having a keen edge] — *Syn.* acute, edged, keen, keen-edged, razor-edged, sharpened, ground fine, honed, honed to razor sharpness, razor-sharp, sharp-edged, fine, cutting, knifelike, knife-edged. — *Ant.* DULL, unsharpened, blunt.
**2.** [Having a keen point] — *Syn.* pointed, keen, sharp-pointed, spiked, spiky, peaked, needle-pointed, keen, fine, salient, spiny, thorny, prickly, barbed, needle-like, briery, stinging, sharp as a needle, pronged, tapered, tapering, horned, unguiculate, acuate, acuminate, aculeate, muricate, aciculate, aciculated, aciculiform.
**3.** [Having a keen mind] — *Syn.* clever, astute, bright; see **intelligent** 1.
**4.** [Having the ability to wound with words] — *Syn.* caustic, biting, acrimonious; see **sarcastic.**
**5.** [Not quite honest or honorable] — *Syn.* crafty, designing, underhand; see **sly** 1.
**6.** [Distinct] — *Syn.* audible, visible, explicit; see **clear** 2, **definite** 2, **obvious** 1.
**7.** [Vigilant] — *Syn.* attentive, watchful, close; see **observant** 1, 2.
**8.** [Intense] — *Syn.* cutting, biting, piercing; see **intense.**
**9.** [Vigorous] — *Syn.* brisk, energetic, lively; see **active** 2.
**10.** [\*Excellent] — *Syn.* fine, distinctive, first-class; see **excellent.**
**11.** [\*Stylish] — *Syn.* dressy, chic, in style; see **fashionable.**

---

*SYN.* — **sharp** and **keen** both apply to that which is cutting, biting, incisive, or piercing, as because of a fine edge, but **sharp** more often implies a harsh cutting quality *[a sharp pain, tongue, flavor, etc.]* and **keen** often suggests a pleasantly biting or stimulating quality *[keen wit, delight, etc.]* or a marked enthusiasm or intensity *[a keen student]*; **acute** literally implies sharp-pointedness and figuratively suggests a penetrating or poignant quality *[acute hearing, distress, etc.]* and often connotes suddenness and severity *[an acute heart attack]*

---

**sharpen,** *v.* **1.** [To make keen] — *Syn.* grind, file, hone, put an edge on, grind to a fine edge, hone to a razor edge, make sharp, make acute, whet, strop, give an edge to, put a point on, give a fine point to. — *Ant.* FLATTEN, thicken, turn.
**2.** [To make more exact] — *Syn.* focus, bring into focus, intensify, make clear, make clearer, clarify, outline distinctly, make more distinct. — *Ant.* CONFUSE, cloud, obscure.

**sharper\*,** *n.* — *Syn.* pretender, swindler, fraud, shark; see **cheat** 1, **impostor.**

**sharply,** *modif.* — *Syn.* piercingly, pointedly, distinctly; see **clearly** 1, 2.

**sharpshooter,** *n.* — *Syn.* shooter, gunman, marksman; see **gunner, rifleman.**

**sharp-sighted,** *modif.* — *Syn.* alert, attentive, aware, observant, lynx-eyed.

**sharp-witted,** *modif.* — *Syn.* bright, smart, discriminating; see **intelligent** 1.

**shatter,** *v.* — *Syn.* smash, shiver, fragment, destroy; see **break** 2, 3.
*See Synonym Study at* BREAK.

**shattered,** *modif.* — *Syn.* splintered, crushed, in smithereens\*; see **broken** 1.

**shave,** *v.* **1.** [To remove a shaving] — *Syn.* shear, plane, graze, slice thin, cut into thin slices, skim, pare; see also **peel, skin.**
**2.** [To remove hair] — *Syn.* barber, cut, use a razor, clip closely, strip, strip the hair from, tonsure, make bare.

**shawl,** *n.* — *Syn.* stole, tucker, shoulder shawl, cloak; see **muffler, wrap.**

**she,** *pron.* — *Syn.* this one, this girl, this woman, that girl, that woman, this female animal, that female animal; see also **girl** 1, 2, 3, **woman** 1, 2, 3.

**sheaf,** *n.* — *Syn.* bundle, package, cluster, collection; see **bunch** 1.

**shear,** *v.* — *Syn.* sever, cleave, shave; see **cut** 1.

**shears,** *n.* — *Syn.* cutters, clippers, scissors, snips, nippers, snippers.
Types of shears include: lever, alligator, crocodile, barber's, blending, cuticle, dressmaker's, metal-cutting, grass, sheepshearing, revolving, rotary, pruning, pinking, buttonhole, guillotine, power; shearing machine.

**sheath,** *n.* — *Syn.* case, scabbard, cover, spathe, sheathing, cere.
Specialized sheaths include: leaf sheath, Cirrus sheath, dentinal sheath, connective tissue sheath, myelin sheath, root sheath, tendon sheath, Neumann's sheath, sheath of Schwann, primitive sheath, *neurilemma* (Latin), sheath of Henle, preputial sheath, prepuce.

**sheathe,** *v.* — *Syn.* envelop, surround, enclose, cover; see **wrap** 2.

**shed,** *n.* — *Syn.* shelter, outbuilding, hut, lean-to, woodshed.

**shed,** *v.* — *Syn.* drop, let fall, send forth, give forth, shower down, cast, molt, exuviate, slough, discard, exude, emit, scatter, sprinkle.

**shed blood,** *v.* **1.** [To bleed] — *Syn.* lose blood, spill blood, be wounded; see **bleed** 1.
**2.** [To kill] — *Syn.* slay, slaughter, murder; see **kill** 1.

**shedding,** *n.* — *Syn.* peeling, molting, casting off, losing hair, dropping, exuviating, exfoliating.

**sheen,** *n.* — *Syn.* shine, polish, gloss; see **finish** 2, **wax.**

**sheep,** *n.* — *Syn.* lamb, ewe, ram, tup, mutton.
Types and breeds of sheep include: Leicester, Cotswold, Southdown, Cheviot, Jacob, Scottish black-face, Wensleydale, Ile de France, Welsh, broadtailed, Iceland, Tartary, Astrakhan, Wallachian, Cretan, Merino, Rambouillet, Shropshire, Dorset, Corriedale, Hampshire Down, Lincoln, Oxford, Romney, Suffolk, Mouflon, mountain, big horn, Rocky Mountain, Argali, Marco Polo's, Herny, Galway, Madras; see also **animal** 2, **goat.**

**sheepish,** *modif.* — *Syn.* timid, shy, retiring, embarrassed; see **docile, tame** 4.

**sheer,** *modif.* **1.** [Abrupt] — *Syn.* steep, very steep, precipitous; see **abrupt** 1.
**2.** [Thin] — *Syn.* transparent, diaphanous, delicate, fine, smooth, pure, lucid, translucent, gauzy, pellucid, limpid, soft, fragile, flimsy, slight, clear, lacy.

**3.** [Absolute] — *Syn.* utter, altogether, quite; see **absolute** 1.

*See Synonym Study at* ABRUPT.

**sheet,** *n.* **1.** [A bed cover] — *Syn.* covering, bed sheet, bedding, bed linen; see **bedding, cloth.**

**2.** [A thin, flat object] — *Syn.* lamina, leaf, foil, veneer, layer, stratum, coat, film, ply, covering, expanse.

**shelf,** *n.* **1.** [A ledge] — *Syn.* shoal, shallow, rock, reef, mantle, sandbank; see also **ledge, ridge** 2.

**2.** [A cupboard rack] — *Syn.* counter, cupboard, mantelpiece, rack.

**shell,** *n.* **1.** [A shell-like cover or structure] — *Syn.* husk, crust, nut, pod, case, pericarp, scale, shard, theca, integument, eggshell, carapace, plastron.

**2.** [An explosive projectile] — *Syn.* bullet, projectile, casing, cartridge; see **bullet.**

Varieties include: armor-piercing, blind-loaded, high-explosive, anti-personnel, artillery shell, cannon shell, common, deck-piercing, torpedo, shrapnel, antiaircraft; see also **weapon** 1.

**3.** [A crustaceous covering] — *Syn.* carapace, sea shell, test.

Varieties include: tortoise, crustacean, conch, snail; see also **seashell.**

**shell,** *v.* — *Syn.* strip, break off, remove the kernel, shuck, shell off, peel off, exfoliate, husk.

**shellfish,** *n.* — *Syn.* crustacean, mollusk, molluscoid, crustaceous animal, invertebrate, marine invertebrate, marine animal, arthropod, gastropod, Arthropoda, molluskan type, bivalve, shell-meat.

Types of shellfish include: crab, lobster, clam, shrimp, prawn, crawfish, crayfish, mussel, oyster, scallop, quahog, whelk, piddock, cockle, abalone, snail, boxfish, isopod, laemadipod, trilobite, branchiopod, corepod, malacostran.

**shell out\*,** *v.* — *Syn.* pay for, pay out, expend, fork over\*; see **pay** 1.

**shellshocked\*,** *modif.* — *Syn.* suffering from concussion, suffering from post-traumatic stress disorder, suffering from war nerves, psychoneurotic, neurotic, psychotic, hysterical, not oneself, upset; see also **insane** 1.

**shelter,** *n.* — *Syn.* refuge, harbor, haven, sanctuary, asylum, retreat, covert, shield, screen, defense, security, safety, guardian, protector, house, roof, tent, shack, shed, hut, shade, shadow.

---

*SYN.* — **shelter** implies the protection of something that covers, as a roof or other structure that shields one from the elements or danger [to find *shelter* from the rain]; **refuge** suggests a place of safety that one flees to in escaping danger or difficulties [he sought political *refuge* in France]; **retreat** implies retirement from that which threatens one's peace, and withdrawal to a safe, quiet, or secluded place [a country *retreat*, a *retreat* for prayer and meditation]; **asylum** is applied to a refuge where one is immune from seizure or harm, as because it is beyond a particular legal jurisdiction [the convict sought *asylum* abroad]; a **sanctuary** is an asylum that has a sacred or inviolable character [the former right of *sanctuary* in churches]

---

**shelter,** *v.* — *Syn.* screen, cover, hide, conceal, guard, take in, ward, harbor, defend, protect, shield, watch over, take care of, secure, preserve, safeguard, surround, enclose, house, lodge. — *Ant.* EXPOSE, turn out, evict.

**sheltered,** *modif.* **1.** [Shaded] — *Syn.* screened, protected, shady, veiled, covered, protective, curtained.

**2.** [Protected] — *Syn.* guarded, ensured, shielded; see **safe** 1, **watched.**

**shelve,** *v.* **1.** [To arrange] — *Syn.* space, range, line up; see **file** 1, **line** 4, **order** 3, **organize** 1.

**2.** [To postpone] — *Syn.* hold, defer, prolong, table; see **delay** 1, **suspend** 2.

**shepherd,** *n.* — *Syn.* sheepherder, caretaker, protector; see **herdsman.**

**sherbet,** *n.* — *Syn.* ice, water ice, fruit ice; see **dessert, ice cream.**

**sheriff,** *n.* — *Syn.* county officer, county administrator, peace officer, reeve; see also **police officer.**

**shield,** *n.* — *Syn.* buckler, defense, absorber, buffer, bumper, protection, shelter, pavis, guard, targe\*.

**shield from,** *v.* — *Syn.* protect, conceal, screen, hide; see **cover** 1, **defend** 2.

**shift,** *n.* **1.** [A change] — *Syn.* transfer, transformation, substitution, displacement, fault, alteration, variation; see also **change** 2.

**2.** [A working period] — *Syn.* turn, spell, stint, working time; see **time** 1.

**3.** [Those who work a shift, sense 2] — *Syn.* gang, squad, relay, group, workmen; see also **team** 1.

**make shift to** — *Syn.* contrive to, find a way to, devise a means of; see **manage, succeed** 1.

**shift,** *v.* **1.** [To change position] — *Syn.* slip, budge, fault, move, move over, turn, stir; see also **change** 4.

**2.** [To cause to shift, sense 1] — *Syn.* displace, remove, substitute; see **change** 1, **exchange** 1.

**3.** [To put in gear] — *Syn.* change gears, double-clutch, downshift, split-shift, put in drive; see also **drive** 3.

**4.** [To manage] — *Syn.* get along, shift for oneself, get by; see **endure** 2.

**shiftless,** *modif.* — *Syn.* idle, inactive, indolent; see **lazy** 1.

**shifty,** *modif.* — *Syn.* tricky, cunning, sneaky; see **sly** 1.

**shilling,** *n.* — *Syn.* twelve pence, ten new pence, bob\*, bobstick\*; see **money** 1.

**shilly-shally,** *v.* — *Syn.* falter, waver, fluctuate; see **hesitate, pause.**

**shimmer,** *v.* — *Syn.* glisten, glow, gleam, flash; see **shine** 1.

*See Synonym Study at* FLASH.

**shimmering,** *modif.* — *Syn.* glimmering, sparkling, bright, scintillating, glittering, glimmery, twinkling, glistening, twinkly.

**shin,** *n.* — *Syn.* tibia, shankbone, limb, legbone; see **bone, leg** 1.

**shin,** *v.* — *Syn.* scramble, scale, ascend; see **climb** 2.

**shindig\*,** *n.* — *Syn.* party, dance, blow out\*; see **party** 1.

**shine,** *v.* **1.** [To give forth light] — *Syn.* radiate, beam, scintillate, glitter, sparkle, twinkle, glimmer, glare, glow, flash, blaze, shimmer, illumine, illuminate, blink, shoot out beams, irradiate, dazzle, bedazzle, flash, luminesce, flicker; see also sense 2, **light** 1.

**2.** [To reflect light] — *Syn.* glisten, gleam, glow, look good, be bright, grow bright, be effulgent, scintillate, have a gloss, give back, give light, deflect, mirror; see also sense 1, **reflect** 3.

**3.** [To cause to shine, usually by polishing] — *Syn.* polish, brighten, scour, brush, put a gloss on, put a finish on, finish, burnish, furbish, wax, buff, polish up, polish to a high luster, give a sheen to, make brilliant, make glitter; see also **clean, glaze, polish.**

*See Synonym Study at* POLISH.

**shingle,** *v.* — *Syn.* shear, decrease, trim; see **cut** 1.

**shingles,** *n.* — *Syn.* asbestos shingles, felt base shingles, shakes; see **roofing.**

**shining,** *modif.* **1.** [Bright] — *Syn.* radiant, gleaming, luminous; see **bright 1, shimmering.**
**2.** [Illustrious] — *Syn.* eminent, remarkable, brilliant; see **glorious 1.**
*See Synonym Study at* BRIGHT.

**shiny,** *modif.* — *Syn.* polished, sparkling, glistening; see **bright 1.**

**ship,** *n.* — *Syn.* boat, vessel, craft.
Types of ships include: dahabeah, junk, galleon, sampan, xebec, lugger, steamer, steamship, container ship, cargo ship, cruise ship, ocean greyhound, liner, freighter, landing barge, packet, ferry, clipper, square-rigged vessel, dhow, sailing ship, transport, oil tanker, supertanker, fishing smack, lightship, pilot boat, cutteryacht, pindjajap, lorcha, galiot, casco, patamar, caique, bilander, baghla, state barge, battleship, cruiser, destroyer, corvette, aircraft carrier, whaling vessel, bark, barkentine, brigantine, schooner, windjammer, yacht, hydrofoil, catamaran, trimaran, dragger, cutter, ketch, yawl, bugeye, sloop, brig, tug, trawler, three-master, four-master, billyboy, hoy, felucca, caravel; see also **boat.**

**ship,** *v.* — *Syn.* send, consign, direct, dispatch, mail, transmit, ship out, put into the hands of a shipper, export, put on board; see also **send 1.**

**shipmate,** *n.* — *Syn.* fellow, fellow sailor, comrade; see **sailor 1.**

**shipment,** *n.* — *Syn.* consignment, lot, load, goods shipped, cargo, carload, truckload, purchase; see also **freight 2, load 1.**

**shipped,** *modif.* — *Syn.* consigned, exported, delivered, transported, F.O.B., c.i.f., carried, expressed; see also **sent.**

**shipper,** *n.* — *Syn.* sender, consigner, exporter, carrier; see **merchant.**

**shipping,** *n.* **1.** [Ships] — *Syn.* steam, sailing, freight, passenger, war transport; see also **ship** *n.*
**2.** [Transportation] — *Syn.* freighting, trucking, airborne traffic; see **transportation.**

**shipwreck,** *n.* — *Syn.* destruction, loss, sinking; see **wreck 3.**

**shipwrecked,** *modif.* — *Syn.* sunk, cast away, marooned; see **destroyed, ruined 1, wrecked.**

**shirk,** *v.* — *Syn.* elude, cheat, malinger; see **avoid, evade 1.**

**shirt,** *n.* Kinds of shirts include: dress, undershirt, sport, work, cowboy, Western, lumberman's, long-sleeved, short-sleeved, Oxford, polo, button down, linen, hair, cotton, silk, flannel, T-shirt, jersey, pullover, tank top, sweatshirt, turtleneck, Mackinaw; see also **blouse, clothes.**
**keep one's shirt on** ★ — *Syn.* be calm, be patient, be quiet, show restraint, remain calm; see **calm down.**
**lose one's shirt** ★ — *Syn.* lose everything, become bankrupt, go to the wall ★; see **fail 4, lose 2.**

**shiver,** *v.* — *Syn.* be cold, vibrate, quiver, tremble; see **shake 1, wave 3.**

**shivery,** *modif.* **1.** [Shaking] — *Syn.* tremulous, trembling, fluttering; see **quivering.**
**2.** [Brittle] — *Syn.* breakable, fragile, frail; see **weak 1, 2.**

**shoal,** *n.* — *Syn.* reef, sandbank, sand bar, shallow, shallow water, underwater knoll, bank, bar, mudflat; see also **reef, shore.**

---

*SYN.* — **shoal** applies to any place in a sea, river, etc. where the water is shallow and difficult to navigate; **bank,** in this connection, applies to a shallow place, formed by an elevated shelf of ground, that is deep enough to be safely navigated by lighter vessels; a **reef** is a ridge of rock, coral, etc. lying at or very close to the surface of the sea, just offshore; **bar** applies to a submerged ridge of sand, etc. silted up along a shore or river and often hindering navigation

---

**shock,** *n.* **1.** [The effect of physical impact] — *Syn.* crash, clash, wreck, blow; see **collision 1.**
**2.** [The effect of a mental blow] — *Syn.* excitement, hysteria, emotional upset; see **confusion 2.**
**3.** [The after-effect of physical harm] — *Syn.* concussion, stupor, collapse, trauma; see **illness 1, injury 1.**

**shock,** *v.* **1.** [To disturb one's self-control] — *Syn.* startle, agitate, astound; see **disturb 2.**
**2.** [To disturb one's sense of propriety] — *Syn.* insult, outrage, horrify, revolt, offend, appall, abash, astound, anger, floor, shake up, disquiet, dismay. — *Ant.* COMFORT, humor, please.
**3.** [To jar] — *Syn.* shake, agitate, jolt; see **jar 1.**

**shocked,** *modif.* — *Syn.* startled, aghast, upset, astounded, offended, appalled, dismayed; see also **troubled.**

**shocking,** *modif.* — *Syn.* repulsive, hateful, revolting, surprising, unexpected; see also **frightful 1, offensive 2.**

**shoddy,** *modif.* — *Syn.* sham, pretentious, gaudy, tacky ★; see **poor 2.**

**shoe,** *n.* — *Syn.* footwear, foot covering.
Types of shoes include: Oxford, slipper, Turkish slipper, moccasin, high-heel shoe, platform, espadrille, boot, sandal, Roman sandal, chopine, balmoral, Crakow, blucher, patten, pump, sabot, clog, arctic, galosh, rubber shoe, leather shoe, fabric shoe, running shoe, jogging shoe, track shoe, cross-training shoe, aerobic shoe, tennis shoe, gym shoe, sneaker, loafer, heels ★, flats ★, high tops ★, wing-tip ★, toe-shoe, ballet slipper, spike-heel shoe, backless ★, fruit boots ★, tennies ★, wedgie ★.
**in another's shoes** — *Syn.* in the position or place of another, in changed *or* different *or* other circumstances, reversal of roles; see **sympathetic, understood 1.**
**where the shoe pinches** — *Syn.* source of the trouble, problem, complication; see **difficulty 1, 2, trouble 2.**

**shoemaker,** *n.* — *Syn.* cobbler, Crispin, shoe mender, shoe repairer, mender of shoes, bootmaker; see also **craftsman.**

**shoestring,** *n.* — *Syn.* lace, tie, shoelace, latchet; see **fastener.**
**on a shoestring** — *Syn.* with too little backing, with little capital, on a tight budget, from hand to mouth, impoverished, inadequately financed; see also **poor 1.**

**shoo,** *interj.* — *Syn.* get away, begone, leave, scat; see **get out.**

**shoot,** *v.* **1.** [To discharge] — *Syn.* fire, shoot off, expel, pull the trigger, set off, torpedo, explode, ignite, blast, sharpshoot, open fire, rake, gauntlet, pump full of lead ★.
**2.** [To move rapidly] — *Syn.* dart, spurt, rush; see **hasten 1, hurry 1.**
**3.** [To kill by shooting] — *Syn.* dispatch, murder, execute; see **kill 1.**
**4.** [To hunt] — *Syn.* follow the chase, go afield, go gunning; see **hunt 1.**
**5.** [★To inquire] — *Syn.* request, solicit, ask; see **question 1.**

**shoot at,** *v.* **1.** [To fire a weapon at] — *Syn.* shoot, fire at, let off, let fly, fire a shot at, fire upon, take a shot at ★; see also **attack 1.**
**2.** [★To strive for] — *Syn.* aim, endeavor, strive; see **try 1.**

**shooting,** *n.* **1.** [Firing a weapon] — *Syn.* gunning, firing, pulling the trigger, blasting, discharging, letting go, taking aim and firing, sighting a target; see also **gunfire, shot** 1.

2. [A sport]— *Syn.* pursuit of game animals, target shooting, field sport; see **hunting.**

**shooting star,** *n.* — *Syn.* meteor, falling star, fireball, bolide, meteorite.

**shoot off one's mouth★,** *v.* — *Syn.* brag, bluster, blabber; see **boast** 1, **say, yell.**

**shoot the bull★,** *v.* — *Syn.* exaggerate grossly, carry on a lengthy conversation, converse, rap; see **boast** 1, **gossip.**

**shoot up, 1.** [To grow rapidly] — *Syn.* spring up, thrive, prosper; see **grow** 1, **rise** 1, 3, **sprout.**

2. [To attack] — *Syn.* bombard, fire at, spray with bullets; see **attack** 1, 2.

**shop,** *n.* — *Syn.* store, department store, retail store, dry goods store, novelty shop, workshop, repair shop.

**set up shop** — *Syn.* go into business, start, open up business; see **begin** 1, 2.

**shut up shop★** — *Syn.* close down, close up, go out of business, cease functioning; see **close** 4, **stop** 2.

**talk shop** — *Syn.* talk business, exchange views, discuss one's work; see **gossip, talk** 1.

**shop,** *v.* — *Syn.* shop for, shop around, look for, hunt for, try to buy; see also **buy** 1.

**shopkeeper,** *n.* — *Syn.* manager, tradesman, storekeeper; see **businessperson, merchant.**

**shopper,** *n.* — *Syn.* customer, bargain hunter, professional shopper, purchaser; see **buyer.**

**shopping,** *n.* — *Syn.* looking for bargains, inspecting goods, purchasing, comparing, looking, hunting for, matching, window-shopping; see also **buying.**

**shopping center,** *n.* — *Syn.* shopping mall, shops, trading center, parking lot; see **business** 4, **mall.**

**shore,** *n.* — *Syn.* shingle, beach, strand, seaside, seashore, sand, coast, seacoast, brim, brink, bank, border, seaboard, margin, margent, sea beach, lakeside, lakeshore, river bank, riverside, raised beach, foreshore, lee shore, windward shore.

*SYN.* — **shore** is the general word applied to an edge of land directly bordering on the sea, a lake, a river, etc.; **coast** applies only to land along the sea; **beach** applies to a level stretch of sandy or pebbly seashore or lake shore, usually one that is washed by high water; **strand** is a poetic word for **shore** or **beach**; **bank** applies to rising or steep land at the edge of a stream or river

**short,** *modif.* **1.** [Not long in space] — *Syn.* low, skimpy, slight, not tall, not long, undersized, little, abbreviated, dwarfish, stubby, squat, stunted, stocky, diminutive, tiny, small, dwarf, dwarfed, close to the ground, dumpy, chunky, thickset, compact, stumpy★, sawed-off★, runty★, pint-sized★, half-pint★, pocket-sized★.

2. [Not long in time] — *Syn.* brief, curtailed, cut short, not protracted, concise, unprolonged, unsustained, laconic, condensed, terse, succinct, pithy, summary, pointed, crisp, precise, bare, abridged, abbreviated, summarized, aphoristic, epigrammatic, compressed, compact, short-term, short-lived, fleeting, quick, hasty; see also **fleeting.**

3. [Inadequate] — *Syn.* deficient, insufficient, niggardly; see **inadequate** 1.

4. [Curt] — *Syn.* abrupt, sharp, short-tempered; see **abrupt** 2, **irritable.**

**fall short** — *Syn.* not reach, be unsuccessful, be inadequate, fall down★; see **fail** 1, **miss** 3.

**for short** — *Syn.* as a nickname, familiarly, commonly.

**in short** — *Syn.* that is, in summary, to make a long story short★; see **briefly** 1, **finally** 1.

*SYN.* — **short** and **brief** are opposites of *long* in their application to duration [a *short*, or *brief*, interval], although **short** often implies incompleteness or curtailment [*short* notice, to make *short* work of it] and **brief** often emphasizes compactness, conciseness, etc. [a *brief* review]; **short** is usually used where spatial extent is referred to [a *short* way from here]

**shortage,** *n.* — *Syn.* deficit, deficiency, short fall, scant supply, curtailment; see also **lack** 1.

**shortcake,** *n.* — *Syn.* biscuit, cookie, teacake, Scottish shortbread; see **cake** 2, **pastry.**

**shortcoming,** *n.* — *Syn.* fault, deficiency, lapse; see **weakness** 2.

**shortcut,** *n.* — *Syn.* bypass, alternative, alternate route, timesaver, timesaving method, timesaving approach; see also **way** 2, 3.

**shorten,** *v.* — *Syn.* curtail, abridge, abbreviate, condense, compress, shrink, reduce, decrease, cut short, cut, pare down; see also **decrease** 2.

*SYN.* — **shorten** implies reduction in length, extent, or duration [to *shorten* a rope, a visit, one's life, etc.]; **curtail** implies a making shorter than was originally intended, as because of necessity or expediency [expenditures *curtailed* because of a reduced income]; **abridge** implies reduction in compass by condensing, omitting parts, etc. but usually connotes that what is essential is kept [to *abridge* a dictionary]; **abbreviate** usually refers to the shortening of a word or phrase by contraction or by substitution of a symbol, but also has extended, sometimes jocular applications [an abbreviated account of events, an *abbreviated* costume]

**shorter,** *modif.* — *Syn.* smaller, lower, not so long, briefer, more limited, more concise, more abrupt, lessened, diminished, reduced, curtailed. — *Ant.* HIGHER, longer, taller.

**short for,** *modif.* — *Syn.* abbreviation for, nickname for, shortening of.

**shorthand,** *n.* — *Syn.* stenography, stenotype, speedwriting, phonography.

Varieties of shorthand include: Pitman, Gregg, Fayet, Gabelsberger, Speedwriting; see also **handwriting.**

**short-handed,** *modif.* — *Syn.* understaffed, needing help, in need of help, in the market for employees; see **wanting.**

**short-lived,** *modif.* — *Syn.* brief, momentary, temporary; see **fleeting, short** 2.

**shortly,** *modif.* — *Syn.* presently, quickly, right away; see **soon** 1.

**shortness,** *n.* — *Syn.* brevity, briefness, conciseness; see **brevity.**

**short of,** *modif.* — *Syn.* in need of, lacking, missing; see **wanting.**

**shorts,** *n.* — *Syn.* underpants, briefs, athletic underwear; see **clothes, underwear.**

**shortsighted,** *modif.* **1.** [Myopic] — *Syn.* nearsighted, purblind, astigmatic, blind; see **myopic.**

2. [Foolish] — *Syn.* unthinking, headlong, unwary; see **rash, stupid** 1.

**short-tempered,** *modif.* — *Syn.* touchy, gruff, harsh; see **irritable.**

**shot,** *modif.* — *Syn.* killed, injured, struck; see **attacked.**

**shot,** *n.* **1.** [An act of shooting] — *Syn.* firing, igniting, blasting, setting off, taking aim, sighting a target, pulling the trigger, discharge, loosing, letting fly; see also **gunfire, shooting** 1.

**2.** [A flying missile] — *Syn.* bullet, ball, pellet, lead, projectile, buckshot, grapeshot.

**3.** [An opportunity to shoot] — *Syn.* range, line of fire, reach, distance, chance, turn.

**4.** [One who shoots] — *Syn.* gunner, huntsman, marksman, hunter, rifleman.

**5.** [A loud sudden noise] — *Syn.* crack, report, blast, discharge, explosion; see also **noise** 1.

**call the shots\*** — *Syn.* direct, control, supervise; see **command** 2, **manage** 1.

**have** or **take a shot at\*** — *Syn.* endeavor, attempt, do one's best at; see **try** 1.

**like a shot\*** — *Syn.* rapidly, speedily, like a bat out of hell\*; see **fast** 1, **quickly.**

**shot in the arm\*** — *Syn.* help, boost, booster, assistance; see **aid** 1, **encouragement** 2.

**shot\***, *modif.* — *Syn.* ruined, broken, worn out, exhausted, spent, kaput\*.

**shotgun**, *n.* Sizes and types of shotguns include: 10-gauge, 12-gauge, 16-gauge, 20-gauge, 26-gauge, single-barreled, double-barreled, hammerless, full-choke, modified choke, smooth bore, single shot, repeater, magazine, hand-loading, automatic, self-loading, pump, one-trigger, two-trigger, sawed-off; see also **gun** 2, **rifle.**

**shoulder**, *n.* **1.** [Juncture of the fore leg or arm and body] — *Syn.* upper arm, upper leg, shoulder cut, shoulder joint; see **arm** 1, 2, **joint** 1.

**2.** [A projection] — *Syn.* collar, protrusion, road shoulder, soft shoulder; see **ledge, ridge** 1, 2.

**cry on someone's shoulder** — *Syn.* weep, object, shed tears; see **cry** 1, **complain** 1.

**put one's shoulder to the wheel** — *Syn.* labor, attempt, strive; see **try** 1, **work** 1.

**rub shoulders with** — *Syn.* be acquainted with, be familiar with, know, see frequently; see **associate** 1.

**shoulder to shoulder** — *Syn.* side by side, beside one another, together; see **loyally, near** 1.

**straight from the shoulder\*** — *Syn.* honestly, frankly, openly; see **direct, sincerely, truly** 2.

**turn** or **give a cold shoulder to** — *Syn.* ignore, neglect, pass over, send to Coventry; see **insult.**

**shoulder**, *v.* — *Syn.* shove, jostle, push aside.

**shoulder blade**, *n.* — *Syn.* shoulder bone, omoplate, scapula; see **bone.**

**shout**, *n.* — *Syn.* yell, roar, bellow, scream; see **cry** 1, **yell** 1.

**shout**, *v.* — *Syn.* screech, roar, scream; see **yell.**

**shout down**, *v.* — *Syn.* silence, shut up, overcome; see **defeat** 1, 3, **quiet** 2.

**shouting**, *modif.* — *Syn.* jeering, screaming, raucous; see **loud** 2, **yelling.**

**shouting**, *n.* — *Syn.* cries, yelling, jeering; see **cry** 1.

**shove**, *v.* — *Syn.* jostle, push, push out of one's way, shoulder, jostle, elbow.

**shovel**, *n.* — *Syn.* spade, scoop, trowel, snow shovel. Shovels include: coal, snow, fire, miner's, irrigating, split, twisted, pronged, scoop, round-pointed; see also **tool** 1.

**shovel**, *v.* — *Syn.* dig, take up, pick up, take up with a shovel, clean out, throw, move, pass, shift, delve, muck\*, handle a muck stick\*; see also **dig** 1, **load** 1.

**shove off\***, *v.* — *Syn.* depart, go, start out; see **leave** 1.

**show**, *n.* **1.** [An exhibition] — *Syn.* presentation, exhibit, art exhibit, retrospective, showing, exposition, occurrence, sight, appearance, program, flower show, boat show, home show, dog show, cat show, bringing be-

fore the public, bringing to public view; see also **display** 2.

**2.** [A public performance] — *Syn.* film, play, musical, carnival, representation, burlesque, production, appearance, concert, act, pageant, spectacle, light show, entertainment; see also **comedy, drama** 1, **movie.**

**3.** [Pretense] — *Syn.* sham, make believe, semblance; see **pretense** 1, 2.

**for show** — *Syn.* for sake of appearances, ostensibly, ostentatiously; see **apparently, pompously.**

**get** or **put the show on the road\*** — *Syn.* start, open, get started; see **begin** 1.

**stand** or **have a show\*** — *Syn.* stand a chance, have a chance, be possible, admit of; see **allow** 1, 2.

**steal the show\*** — *Syn.* triumph, get the best of it, win out, be the focus of attention; see **defeat** 1, 3, **win** 1.

**show**, *v.* **1.** [To display] — *Syn.* display, exhibit, manifest, present, expose, flaunt; see also **display** 1.

**2.** [To explain] — *Syn.* reveal, tell, explicate; see **explain.**

**3.** [To demonstrate] — *Syn.* attest, determine, confirm; see **prove.**

**4.** [To convince] — *Syn.* teach, prove to, persuade; see **convince.**

**5.** [To grant] — *Syn.* confer, bestow, dispense; see **give** 1.

**6.** [To indicate] — *Syn.* register, note, point; see **designate** 1, **record** 1.

---

*SYN.* — **show** implies putting or bringing something into view so that it can be seen or looked at /show us the garden/; to **display** something is to spread it out so that it is shown to advantage /jewelry *displayed* on a sales counter/; **exhibit** implies prominent display, often for the purpose of attracting public attention or inspection /to *exhibit* products at a fair/; **expose** implies the laying open and displaying of something, often unpleasant or objectionable, that has been covered or concealed /this bathing suit *exposes* the scar, to expose his shady dealings/; **flaunt** implies an ostentatious, impudent, or defiant display /to *flaunt* one's riches, vices, etc./

---

**showcase**, *n.* — *Syn.* cabinet, display counter, museum case, exhibition, display case.

**showdown**, *n.* — *Syn.* confrontation, crisis, exposé, unfolding; see **climax.**

**shower**, *n.* **1.** [Water falling in drops] — *Syn.* drizzle, mist, rainfall; see **rain** 1.

**2.** [Act of cleansing the body] — *Syn.* bathing, washing, sponging; see **bath** 1.

**3.** [An enclosure for showering] — *Syn.* showerstall, bath, shower room; see **bath** 3.

**showing**, *n.* **1.** [A show] — *Syn.* exhibit, display, exhibition, production; see **show** 1.

**2.** [An appearance] — *Syn.* occurrence, sight, manifestation; see **appearance** 3, **view** 1.

**shown**, *modif.* **1.** [Put on display] — *Syn.* displayed, demonstrated, advertised, exposed, set out, presented, exhibited, delineated, laid out, put up for sale, put up\*, put on the block\*. — *Ant.* WITHDRAWN, concealed, held back.

**2.** [Proved] — *Syn.* demonstrated, determined, made clear; see **established** 3, **obvious** 2.

**show-off**, *n.* — *Syn.* boaster, exhibitionist, egotist; see **braggart.**

**show off**, *v.* — *Syn.* brag, swagger, make a spectacle of oneself; see **boast** 1.

**showpiece**, *n.* — *Syn.* masterpiece, prime example, prize; see **masterpiece.**

**show up, 1.** [To arrive] — *Syn.* appear, come, turn up; see **arrive** 1.
**2.** [To expose] — *Syn.* discredit, worst, belittle; see **defeat** 1, 3, **convict, expose** 1.
**show window,** *n.* — *Syn.* display window, store window, picture window; see **display** 2.
**showy,** *modif.* — *Syn.* flashy, glaring, gaudy, flamboyant, ostentatious; see also **ornate** 1.
**shred,** *n.* — *Syn.* fragment, piece, tatter; see **bit** 1, **rag.**
**shred,** *v.* — *Syn.* tear, strip, cut into small pieces, reduce to tatters, tear into rags, cut into slivers, destroy.
**shrew,** *n.* — *Syn.* vixen, virago, termagant, spitfire, she-devil, scold, porcupine, dragon, fury, fire-eater, Kate the Shrew, tigress, beldame, harridan, madcap, carper, defamer, detractor, calumniator, siren, reviler, back-biter, vituperator, muckraker, Xanthippe, barracker (Australian), hell cat\*, nag\*.
**shrewd,** *modif.* **1.** [Clever] — *Syn.* astute, acute, sharp, keen, quick, perceptive, canny, knowing, sagacious, perspicacious, ingenious, sharp; see also **clever** 1, **intelligent** 1.
**2.** [Cunning] — *Syn.* calculating, crafty, cagey\*; see **sly** 1.

---

*SYN.* — **shrewd** implies keenness of mind, sharp insight, and a cleverness in practical matters *[a shrewd comment, businessman, etc.]*; **sagacious** implies keen discernment and farsighted judgment *[a sagacious counselor]*; **perspicacious** suggests the penetrating mental vision or discernment that enables one clearly to see and understand what is obscure, hidden, etc. *[a perspicacious judge of character]*; **astute** implies shrewdness combined with sagacity and sometimes connotes, in addition, artfulness or cunning *[an astute politician]* See also Synonym Study at CLEVER.

---

**shrewdly,** *modif.* — *Syn.* knowingly, cleverly, slyly, foxily, trickily, sagaciously, astutely, skillfully, ably, smartly, guilefully, deceptively, cunningly, perspicaciously, intelligently, judiciously, neatly, coolly, handily, facilely, adroitly, deftly, with skill, with cunning, with shrewdness, with sagacity, in a crafty manner, in a cunning manner, with consummate skill, with the know-how\*; see also **carefully** 2, **deliberately.**
**shrewdness,** *n.* — *Syn.* astuteness, perspicacity, sharpness; see **acumen, judgment** 1.
**shrewish,** *modif.* — *Syn.* evil-tempered, petulant, peevish; see **irritable, quarrelsome** 2.
**shriek,** *n.* — *Syn.* scream, screech, howl; see **cry** 1, 3, **yell** 1.
**shriek,** *v.* — *Syn.* scream, screech, squawk; see **cry** 1, 3, **yell.**
**shrieking,** *modif.* — *Syn.* screaming, piercing, sharp; see **shrill.**
**shrill,** *modif.* — *Syn.* high-pitched, piercing, penetrating, sharp, strident, screeching, thin, piping, deafening, earsplitting, blatant, noisy, clanging, clangorous, harsh, blaring, raucous, metallic, discordant, cacophonous, acute; see also **loud** 1. — *Ant.* SOFT, low, faint.
**shrimp,** *n.* Types of shrimp include: British, common, deep-water, freshwater, California, river, rock, pink, gulf; prawn; see also **fish, shellfish.**
**shrine,** *n.* — *Syn.* sacred place, sacred object, hallowed place, reliquary, sepulcher, memorial; see also **altar, church** 1.
**shrink,** *v.* **1.** [To become smaller] — *Syn.* contract, shrivel, shorten, narrow; see **contract** 1.

**2.** [To recoil] — *Syn.* withdraw, blench, flinch, shy away; see **recoil.**
*See Synonym Study at* CONTRACT.
**shrinkage,** *n.* — *Syn.* decrease, diminution, lessening, depreciation; see **reduction** 1.
**shrive,** *v.* **1.** [To absolve] — *Syn.* redeem, purge, pardon; see **excuse, forgive** 1.
**2.** [To confess] — *Syn.* repent, atone, pray; see **confess** 3.
**shrivel,** *v.* — *Syn.* parch, dry up, shrink; see **contract** 1, **dry** 1, **shrink** 1, **wither.**
**shroud,** *n.* — *Syn.* winding sheet, covering, graveclothes, cerements, cerecloth, pall; see also **cloth, cover** 1.
**shrub,** *n.* — *Syn.* bush, scrub, fern, dwarf tree; see **bush** 1, **hedge, plant.**
**shrubbery,** *n.* — *Syn.* shrubs, bushes, thick growth, ornamental bushes, group of shrubs, hedge, arboretum, underbrush; see also **brush** 4.
**shrug off,** *v.* — *Syn.* forget, ignore, dismiss; see **disregard.**
**shrunken,** *modif.* — *Syn.* withdrawn, withered, dwindled, contracted, shriveled; see also **dry** 1, **wrinkled.**
**shuck,** *n.* — *Syn.* husk, pod, leaf; see **shell** 1.
**shudder,** *n.* — *Syn.* tremor, shuddering, shaking, trembling.
**shudder,** *v.* — *Syn.* quiver, quake, shiver; see **shake** 1, **wave** 1.
**shuffle,** *v.* **1.** [To move with a shuffling gait] — *Syn.* scuffle, scuff, scrape, hobble; see **walk** 1.
**2.** [To mix cards] — *Syn.* change, change the order, shift around, rearrange, mix-up.
**shun,** *v.* — *Syn.* dodge, evade, keep away from, ignore, neglect; see also **avoid.** — *Ant.* accept, ADOPT, take advantage of.
**shut,** *modif.* — *Syn.* closed, stopped, locked, fastened; see **tight** 2.
**shut,** *v.* — *Syn.* close up, lock, seal; see **close** 4.
**shutdown,** *n.* — *Syn.* closing, closedown, cessation, abandonment.
**shut down,** *v.* — *Syn.* close up, close down, shut up, abandon; see **stop** 1.
**shut-in,** *n.* — *Syn.* convalescent, sufferer, cripple; see **invalid, patient.**
**shut off,** *v.* — *Syn.* turn off, discontinue, put a stop to; see **close** 4, **stop** 1.
**shut out,** *v.* — *Syn.* keep out, evict, fence out, exclude; see **bar** 1, 2.
**shutter,** *n.* — *Syn.* blind, cover, shade, storm shutter; see **curtain, screen** 1.
**shuttle,** *v.* — *Syn.* seesaw, vacillate, come and go, commute; see **alternate** 2.
**shut up,** *v.* **1.** [To cease speaking] — *Syn.* be quiet, stop talking, quiet, hush, quit chattering, silence, dry up\*.
**2.** [To close] — *Syn.* padlock, close up, close down, close out, stop; see also **close** 4.
**shy,** *modif.* — *Syn.* retiring, timorous, bashful, modest, demure, diffident; see also **humble** 1, 2.
**fight shy of\*** — *Syn.* avoid, keep from, shun, evade; see **avoid.**

---

*SYN.* — **shy** implies a shrinking from the notice of others and a reticence in approaching them; **bashful** implies such shyness as is displayed in awkward behavior and embarrassed timidity; **diffident** implies a lack of self-confidence that makes one reluctant to assert oneself; **modest** implies a reserved, unassuming manner in one who, because of ability, achievements, etc. might be expected to assert himself or herself strongly and often suggests moderation in behavior, speech, dress, etc.; **demure**, in current usage, suggests a decorously modest manner, often one that is affectedly so

**shyness**, *n.* — *Syn.* bashfulness, reserve, timidity, modesty, timorousness, timidness, coyness, demureness, sheepishness, diffidence, apprehension, backwardness, nervousness, insecurity, reticence, stage fright, mike fright★; see also **restraint** 1.

**sick**, *modif.* — *Syn.* ill, ailing, unwell, disordered, diseased, feeble, weak, impaired, suffering, feverish, nauseous, nauseated, imperfect, sickly, declining, unhealthy, morbid, rabid, indisposed, distempered, infected, invalid, delicate, infirm, frail, rickety, broken down, physically run down, confined, laid up, coming down with, under medication, bedridden, in poor health, hospitalized, quarantined, incurable, on the blink★, out of kilter★, peaked★, feeling poorly★, sick as a dog★, seedy★, in a bad way★, not so hot★, at a low ebb★, under the weather★, down in the mouth★, looking green about the gills★. — *Ant.* HEALTHY, hearty, well.

*SYN.* — **sick** and **ill** both express the idea of being in bad health, affected with disease, etc., but **sick** is more commonly used than **ill**, which is somewhat formal /he's a *sick* person; he is *sick*, or *ill*, with the flu/; in British usage **sick** generally means affected with nausea; **ailing** usually suggests prolonged or even chronic poor health /she has been *ailing* ever since her operation/; **indisposed** suggests a slight, temporary illness or feeling of physical discomfort /*indisposed* with a headache/

**sicken**, *v.* 1. [To contract a disease] — *Syn.* become ill, become sick, take sick, fall ill, become diseased, fall victim to a disease, be stricken, run a temperature, run a fever, be taken with, come down with, get a disease, catch a disease, pick up a disease, acquire, incur, suffer a relapse, languish, waste away, break out, catch one's death★, be laid by the heels★, pick up a bug★.
2. [To offend] — *Syn.* repel, nauseate, revolt; see **disgust**.

**sickening**, *modif.* 1. [Contaminated] — *Syn.* sickly, tainted, diseased; see **sick**.
2. [Disgusting] — *Syn.* revolting, nauseous, putrid; see **offensive** 2.

**sickly**, *modif.* — *Syn.* ailing, weak, weakly, feeble; see **sick**.

**sickness**, *n.* — *Syn.* ill health, ailment, infirmity; see **illness** 1.

**sick of**, *modif.* — *Syn.* tired of, disgusted, fed up, sick and tired of; see **disgusted**.

**side**, *modif.* — *Syn.* to the side, indirect, not the main, off the main, roundabout, by a devious way, off to the side, lateral, sidewise, sideways, sidelong, off center, oblique, superficial. — *Ant.* MIDDLE, direct, central.

**side**, *n.* 1. [One of two opponents] — *Syn.* party, contestant, rival, foe, combatant, belligerent; see also **faction** 1, **team** 1, 2.
2. [A face] — *Syn.* facet, front, front side, rear, surface, outer surface, inner surface, top, bottom, elevation, view; see also **plane** 1.
**from side to side** — *Syn.* back and forth, unsteadily, wobblingly; see **to and fro, unevenly.**
**on the side** — *Syn.* in addition to, as a bonus, additionally; see **extra.**
**on the side of** — *Syn.* in favor of, supporting, working with; see **for, helping.**
**take sides** — *Syn.* join, fight for, declare oneself; see **help** 1, **support** 2.

**sideboard**, *n.* — *Syn.* closet, buffet, shelf; see **cupboard, table** 1.

**sideburns**, *n.* — *Syn.* burnsides, side-whiskers, face hair, facial hair.

**side by side** — *Syn.* adjacent, nearby, faithfully; see **abreast** 1, **loyally, near** 1, **next** 2.

**side dish**, *n.* — *Syn.* dish, side order, vegetable; see **entree** 2.

**side effect**, *n.* — *Syn.* influence, symptom, reaction; see **disease, result.**

**sidehill**, *n.* — *Syn.* descent, declivity, decline; see **hill.**

**sidelight**, *n.* 1. [Window] — *Syn.* opening, skylight, casement; see **window** 1.
2. [Incidental information] — *Syn.* related information, peripheral information, gossip.

**sideline**, *n.* — *Syn.* avocation, interest, trade; see **hobby.**

**sidelong**, *modif.* — *Syn.* edgeways, laterally, indirectly; see **sideways.**

**sideshow**, *n.* — *Syn.* minor attraction, adjunct, related activity, subordinate event; see **addition** 2.

**sidesplitting**, *modif.* — *Syn.* laughable, comical, absurd; see **funny** 1.

**side-step**, *v.* — *Syn.* evade, elude, shun; see **avoid.**

**sidetrack**, *n.* — *Syn.* siding, turnout, shut; see **path** 1, **track** 1.

**sidetrack**, *v.* — *Syn.* divert, distract, interrupt, mislead; see **distract** 1.

**sidewalk**, *n.* — *Syn.* footway, footpath, paved area, pavement (British), foot pavement; see also **path** 1, **track** 1.

**sideways**, *modif.* — *Syn.* indirectly, sloping, sidelong, in the lateral direction, broadside on, from the side; see also **oblique** 1.

**side with**, *v.* — *Syn.* join, aid, incline to; see **favor** 1, 2, **help** 1, **support** 2.

**siding**, *n.* — *Syn.* outside finish, outer wall, cladding, covering; see **cover** 2, **finish** 2.
Commonly used sidings include: clapboards, weatherboards, shingles, stucco, pebbledash, brick veneer, matched siding, tongue and groove siding, aluminum sheets, steel sheets, corrugated sheets, enameled sheets, vinyl, Masonite (trademark).

**sidle**, *v.* — *Syn.* veer, walk sideways, tilt; see **walk** 1.

**siege**, *n.* — *Syn.* offense, onslaught, assault; see **attack** 1.

**siesta**, *n.* — *Syn.* nap, doze, rest; see **sleep.**

**sieve**, *n.* — *Syn.* strainer, sifter, colander, screen, bolt, bolting cloth, mesh, searce, hair sieve, drum sieve, flat sieve, quarter-inch sieve, half-inch sieve, gravel sieve, flour sieve.

**sift**, *v.* 1. [To evaluate] — *Syn.* investigate, scrutinize, probe; see **examine** 1.
2. [To put through a sieve] — *Syn.* bolt, strain, screen, winnow, grade, sort, size, searce; see also **clean, filter** 2, **purify.**

**sigh**, *n.* — *Syn.* deep breath, sigh of relief, expression of sorrow, exhalation, whisper, rustle; see also **cry** 1.

**sigh**, *v.* — *Syn.* suspire, groan, lament; see **breathe** 1, **cry** 1, **gasp.**

**sight**, *n.* 1. [The power of seeing] — *Syn.* perception, apperception, eyesight, eyes for, range of vision, apprehension, ken, keen sight, clear sight, good sight; see also **vision** 1.
2. [Something worth seeing; *often plural*] — *Syn.* show, view, spectacle, display, scene, point of interest, local scene.
3. [★An unsightly person] — *Syn.* eyesore, hag, ogre, ogress, bum, scarecrow, fright; see also **slob, tramp** 1.
**a sight for sore eyes★** — *Syn.* beauty, welcome sight, delight; see **blessing** 2, **friend** 1.
**at first sight** — *Syn.* hastily, without much thought,

without due consideration, provisionally; see **quickly** 1, 2, **rashly.**

**by sight**— *Syn.* somewhat acquainted, not intimately, superficially; see **unfamiliar** 1.

**catch sight of**— *Syn.* glimpse, notice, see momentarily, catch a glimpse of; see **see** 1.

**lose sight of**— *Syn.* miss, fail to follow, slip up on*; see **forget** 2, **neglect** 1, **omit** 1.

**on sight**— *Syn.* at once, without hesitation, precipitately; see **immediately, quickly** 1, 2.

**out of sight**— *Syn.* disappeared, vanished, indiscernible; see **gone** 1, **invisible** 1.

**sighted,** *modif.*— *Syn.* seen, in sight, located; see **observed** 1, **obvious** 1.

**sightless,** *modif.*— *Syn.* blind, eyeless, visionless, unseeing; see **blind** 1.

**sightseeing,** *n.*— *Syn.* vacationing, excursion, tour; see **touring** 2, **travel** 1.

**sightseer,** *n.*— *Syn.* tourist, observer, wanderer, voyager; see **tourist, traveler.**

**sign,** *n.* **1.** [A signal]— *Syn.* indication, portent, clue, omen, prognostic, augury, token, presentiment, divination, presage, premonition, handwriting on the wall, foreshadowing, foreboding, foreknowledge, token, manifestation, foretoken, harbinger, herald, hint, symptom, assurance, precursor, prediction, mark, badge, auspice, symbol, caution, warning, beacon, flag, highball, hand signal, wave of the arm, flash, whistle, warning bell, signal bell, signal light, high sign*.

**2.** [An emblem]— *Syn.* insignia, badge, crest; see **emblem.**

**3.** [A symbol]— *Syn.* type, visible sign, token; see **symbol.**

**sign,** *v.* **1.** [Authorize]— *Syn.* endorse, confirm, acknowledge; see **approve** 1.

**2.** [Indicate]— *Syn.* express, signify, signal; see **mean** 1, **signal.**

**3.** [Consecrate]— *Syn.* dignify, hallow, ordain, sign with a cross; see **bless** 3.

**4.** [Hire]— *Syn.* engage, contract, employ; see **hire** 1.

**signal,** *n.*— *Syn.* beacon, flag, omen; see **sign** 1.

**signal,** *v.*— *Syn.* give a sign to, flag, wave, gesture, motion, semaphore, nod, beckon, warn, indicate.

**signalize,** *v.*— *Syn.* honor, acclaim, applaud, lionize; see **praise** 1.

**signature,** *n.*— *Syn.* sign, stamp, mark, name, written name, subscription, autograph, impression, indication, designation, trademark, one's John Hancock*.

**sign away,** *v.*— *Syn.* transfer, dispose of, auction; see **sell** 1.

**signed,** *modif.*— *Syn.* marked, autographed, written, undersigned, countersigned, sealed, witnessed, subscribed, registered, receipted, enlisted, signed on the dotted line*; see also **endorsed.**

**signer,** *n.*— *Syn.* cosigner, underwriter, endorser; see **sponsor, witness.**

**signet,** *n.*— *Syn.* stamp, badge, seal; see **emblem.**

**significance,** *n.*— *Syn.* weight, consequence, point; see **importance** 1.

*See Synonym Study at* IMPORTANCE.

**significant,** *modif.*— *Syn.* meaningful, notable, vital; see **important** 1.

**signification,** *n.*— *Syn.* connotation, significance, implication; see **meaning.**

**signify,** *v.*— *Syn.* imply, import, purport; see **mean** 1.

**sign off,** *v.*— *Syn.* cease, become silent, go off the air; see **stop** 1, 2.

**sign on the dotted line*,** *v.*— *Syn.* sign, notarize, countersign, underwrite; see **endorse** 1.

**sign up for,** *v.*— *Syn.* subscribe to, take, accept; see **join** 2, **volunteer** 2.

**silence,** *n.* **1.** [Absence of sound]— *Syn.* quietness, stillness, hush, utter stillness, the stillness of death, absolute quiet, calm, noiselessness, soundlessness, quiet, deep stillness, stillness of eternal night, loss of signal, cessation of all sound, quietude, hush of early dawn, radio silence, security silence, security blackout, censorship, iron curtain.— *Ant.* NOISE, din, uproar.

**2.** [Absence of speech]— *Syn.* muteness, secrecy, taciturnity, reserve, reticence, inarticulateness, golden silence, respectful silence, sullen silence.— *Ant.* talkativeness, glibness, loquacity.

**silence,** *v.*— *Syn.* overawe, quell, still; see **hush** 1, **quiet** 2.

**silenced,** *modif.*— *Syn.* quieted, calmed, stilled, restrained, repressed, held down, held back, restricted, subdued, inhibited, gagged, coerced, suppressed, censored, under duress, under restraint, made subservient, made obedient; see also **beaten.**

**silent,** *modif.* **1.** [Without noise]— *Syn.* still, hushed, soundless; see **calm** 2, **quiet** 2.

**2.** [Without speech]— *Syn.* reserved, mute, speechless; see **dumb** 1.

**silently,** *modif.*— *Syn.* without noise, without a sound, as still as a mouse, like a shadow, in utter stillness, noiselessly, stilly, calmly, quietly, soundlessly, mutely, dumbly, in deathlike silence, like one struck dumb, morosely, speechlessly, wordlessly, as silently as falling snow.

**silhouette,** *n.*— *Syn.* contour, shape, profile; see **form** 1, **outline** 4.

*See Synonym Study at* OUTLINE.

**silk,** *n.* Varieties of silks include: taffeta, moiré, watered silk, jacquard, damask, crepe, satin crepe, satin de Lyon, satin, rajah, pongee, China silk, tissue, voile, tulle, sarcenet, faille, marabou, mousseline de soie, shantung, tussah, matelassé, surah, twilled lining, crepe de Chine, georgette, chiffon, tapestry, upholstery, velvet, chiffon velvet, plush, ribbons, tie silk, silk shirting; see also **cloth.**

**silken,** *modif.*— *Syn.* soft, tender, delicate, luxurious, like silk, made of silk, resembling silk, smooth, satiny, glossy.

**sill,** *n.*— *Syn.* threshold, beam, bottom of the frame; see **ledge.**

**silly,** *modif.*— *Syn.* senseless, ridiculous, nonsensical, foolish, fatuous, unreasonable, irrational, stupid, asinine, absurd, simpleminded, harebrained, brainless, featherbrained, empty-headed, vacuous, muddleheaded, illogical, ludicrous, preposterous, inane, giddy, frivolous, trivial, shallow, puerile, birdbrained*, airheaded*, dippy*, ditzy*, sappy*, goofy*.

---

**SYN.** — **silly** implies ridiculous or irrational behavior that demonstrates a lack of common sense, good judgment, or sobriety /it was *silly* of you to dress so lightly/; **stupid** implies a slow-wittedness or lack of normal intelligence /he is *stupid* to believe that/; **fatuous** suggests stupidity, inanity, or obtuseness coupled with a smug complacency /a *fatuous* smile/; **asinine** implies the extreme stupidity conventionally attributed to an ass /an *asinine* argument/ *See also Synonym Study at* ABSURD.

---

**silo,** *n.* **1.** [Fodder storage tower]— *Syn.* granary, crib, pit; see **storehouse.**

**2.** [Underground missile site]— *Syn.* rocket launcher, pit, superhardened silo; see **defense** 2.

**silt,** *n.* — *Syn.* sediment, deposit, sand, varbe; see **residue, sediment.**

**silver,** *modif.* **1.** [Suggestive of silver] — *Syn.* silvery, pale, white, lustrous, bright, resplendent, silvern, silvery white, silverlike, white as silver; see also **shimmering.**
**2.** [Concerning the use of silver] — *Syn.* of silver, made of silver, sterling, plated with silver, silver-gilt, silver-plated.

**silver-tongued,** *modif.* — *Syn.* articulate, oratorical, mellifluous, eloquent; see **fluent** 2.

**silverware,** *n.* — *Syn.* silver, service, cutlery, flatware, hollow ware, silver plate.
Common pieces of silverware include: knife, dinner knife, fish knife, steak knife, carving knife, butter spreader, butter knife, fork, salad fork, cold meat fork, cocktail fork, dessert fork, serving fork, tablespoon, soup spoon, dessert spoon, ice-cream spoon, slotted spoon, serving spoon, bouillon spoon, iced-tea spoon, coffee spoon, teaspoon, soup ladle, gravy ladle, berry server, jelly server, sugar spoon, sugar tongs, pastry server, pickle fork, oyster fork, grapefruit spoon, demitasse spoon, salt spoon, nutpick, spatula.

**silvery,** *modif.* **1.** [Shining] — *Syn.* shiny, glittering, brilliant; see **bright** 1, **shimmering.**
**2.** [Musical] — *Syn.* melodious, resonant, sonorous; see **harmonious** 1, **musical** 1.

**simian,** *modif.* — *Syn.* anthropoid, apelike, primate; see **animal** 1.

**simian,** *n.* — *Syn.* ape, gorilla, chimpanzee, orangutan, primate; see also **monkey.**

**similar,** *modif.* — *Syn.* much the same, comparable, related; see **alike** 2.

**similarity,** *n.* — *Syn.* correspondence, likeness, resemblance, similitude, parallelism, semblance, agreement, affinity, kinship, analogy, closeness, approximation, conformity, congruity, concordance, concurrence, coincidence, harmony, comparability, identity, community, relation, correlation, relationship, proportion, parity, comparison, simile, interrelation, homogeneity, association, connection, similar form, similar appearance, like quality, point of likeness. — *Ant.* DIFFERENCE, variance, dissimilarity.
*See Synonym Study at* LIKENESS.

**similarly,** *modif.* — *Syn.* likewise, thus, furthermore, in a like manner, correspondingly, by the same token, in like fashion, in addition, then, as well, too; see also **so.**

**simile,** *n.* — *Syn.* metaphor, analogy, likeness, epic simile, explicit comparison of dissimilars; see also **comparison** 2, **figure of speech.**

**similitude,** *n.* — *Syn.* semblance, resemblance, simulation, replica; see **copy, representation.**

**simmer,** *v.* **1.** [To boil] — *Syn.* seethe, stew, cook; see **boil** 1, **cook.**
**2.** [To be angry] — *Syn.* seethe, fret, fume; see **fume, rage** 1.
*See Synonym Study at* BOIL.

**simmer down\*,** *v.* — *Syn.* cool off, be reasonable, become calm; see **calm down.**

**simmering,** *modif.* — *Syn.* broiling, heated, boiling; see **hot** 1.

**simmering,** *n.* — *Syn.* boiling, stewing, ebullition, boil.

**simon-pure,** *modif.* — *Syn.* true, authentic, real; see **genuine** 1, **pure** 1, 2.

**simper,** *v.* — *Syn.* giggle, grin, snicker; see **smile, sneer.**

**simple,** *modif.* **1.** [Not complicated] — *Syn.* single, unmixed, unblended, mere, uncompounded, unalloyed, unadulterated, not complex, uncomplicated, without confusion, simplistic, not confusing, pure.

**2.** [Plain] — *Syn.* unadorned, unaffected, homely; see **modest** 2.
**3.** [Easy] — *Syn.* easy, not difficult, mild, of little difficulty, not arduous, done with ease, with great facility, manageable, presenting no difficulty, not puzzling; see also **easy** 2. — *Ant.* OBSCURE, puzzling, DIFFICULT.
**4.** [Stupid] — *Syn.* inane, dull, ignorant; see **shallow** 2, **stupid** 1.
**5.** [Unsophisticated] — *Syn.* ingenuous, plain, artless; see **innocent** 1, **naive.**
*See Synonym Study at* EASY.

**simple-minded,** *modif.* — *Syn.* unintelligent, childish, moronic; see **dull** 3, **naive, stupid** 1.

**simpleton,** *n.* — *Syn.* clod, idiot, bungler; see **fool** 1.

**simplicity,** *n.* **1.** [The state of being without complication] — *Syn.* singleness, homogeneity, purity, uniformity, clearness, unity, integrity, monotony. — *Ant.* CONFUSION, intricacy, complexity.
**2.** [The quality of being plain] — *Syn.* plainness, stark reality, lack of ornament, unadornment, lack of sophistication, bareness, rusticity, homeliness, freedom from artificiality, severity. — *Ant.* SOPHISTICATION, ornamentation, elaboration.
**3.** [Artlessness] — *Syn.* naïveté, ingenuousness, primitiveness; see **innocence** 2.

**simplified,** *modif.* — *Syn.* made easy, abridged, made plain, uncomplicated, clear, interpreted, broken down, cleared up, reduced; see also **obvious** 1, 2.

**simplify,** *v.* — *Syn.* clear up, clarify, explain, elucidate, interpret, reduce to essentials, make clear, make plain, break down, analyze; see also **explain, order** 3. — *Ant.* MIX, complicate, confuse.

**simplistic,** *modif.* — *Syn.* simple, overly simplified, characterized by oversimplification, condensed, oversimplified; see also **childish** 1, **naive, simple** 1.

**simply,** *modif.* **1.** [With simplicity] — *Syn.* clearly, plainly, intelligibly, directly, candidly, sincerely, modestly, easily, quietly, naturally, honestly, frankly, unaffectedly, artlessly, ingenuously, without self-consciousness, commonly, ordinarily, matter-of-factly, unpretentiously, openly, guilelessly. — *Ant.* AWKWARDLY, affectedly, unnaturally.
**2.** [Merely] — *Syn.* utterly, just, solely; see **only** 2.
**3.** [Absolutely] — *Syn.* really, in fact, totally; see **completely.**

**simulate,** *v.* — *Syn.* feign, pretend, counterfeit, dissemble, imitate, mimic, misrepresent, sham, fake, assume, affect, fabricate, disguise, concoct, exaggerate, play the hypocrite, playact, invent, copy, ape, duplicate, reproduce, resemble; see also **pretend** 1.
*See Synonym Study at* PRETEND.

**simultaneous,** *modif.* — *Syn.* coincident, at the same time, concurrent, contemporaneous, synchronous, in concert, in unison, in the same breath, in chorus, at the same instant, coinstantaneous, in time, in sync\*; see also **concomitant, contemporary** 1.
*See Synonym Study at* CONTEMPORARY.

**simultaneously,** *modif.* — *Syn.* at the same time, as one, concurrently; see **together** 2.

**sin,** *n.* — *Syn.* error, wrongdoing, trespass, transgression, wickedness, evil-doing, iniquity, immorality, crime, ungodliness, unrighteousness, veniality, disobedience to the divine will, transgression of the divine law, violation of God's law.
The seven deadly *or* capital *or* mortal sins believed by some Christian denominations to lead to spiritual death are: pride, covetousness or avarice, lust, wrath or anger, gluttony, envy, sloth. — *Ant.* RIGHTEOUSNESS, godliness, virtue.

**sin,** *v.* — *Syn.* err, do wrong, commit a crime, offend, break the moral law, break one of the Commandments, trespass, transgress, misbehave, misconduct oneself, go astray, stray from the path of duty, wander from the paths of righteousness, fall, lapse, fall from grace, fall from virtue, sow one's wild oats★, kick over the traces★, let one's foot slip★, take the primrose path★, wallow in the mire★, wander from the straight and narrow★, follow the broad way★, backslide★, live in sin★, sleep around★; see also **curse** 1, **deceive, kill** 1, **steal.**

**since,** *modif. and prep.* **1.** [Because] — *Syn.* for, as, inasmuch as, considering, forasmuch as, in consideration of, after all, insomuch as, seeing that, in view of the fact, for the reason that, by reason of, on account of, in view of; see also **because.**

**2.** [Between the present and a previous time] — *Syn.* ago, from the time of, subsequent to, after, following, more recently than, until now.

**sincere,** *modif.* **1.** [Genuine] — *Syn.* real, actual, bona fide; see **genuine** 2, **serious** 2.

**2.** [Honest] — *Syn.* truthful, faithful, trustworthy, forthright, straightforward; see also **honest** 1, **reliable** 1, 2.

**sincerely,** *modif.* — *Syn.* truthfully, truly, really, honestly, genuinely, earnestly, aboveboard, seriously, ingenuously, naturally, without equivocation, in all conscience, candidly, frankly, profoundly, deeply, to the bottom of one's heart.

**sincerity,** *n.* — *Syn.* honor, earnestness, innocence, trustworthiness, guilelessness, veracity, justice, impartiality, openness, frankness, candor, truthfulness, genuineness; see also **honesty** 1, **reliability.** — *Ant.* CUNNING, guile, deceit.

**sinecure,** *n.* — *Syn.* easy job, child's play, cinch, snap★.

**sinew,** *n.* **1.** [Tendon] — *Syn.* ligament, muscle, thew; see **cord** 2, **muscle.**

**2.** [Strength; *often in plural*] — *Syn.* strength, power, force, source of power, robustness.

**sinewy,** *modif.* **1.** [Strong] — *Syn.* powerful, forceful, acute; see **strong** 2.

**2.** [Stringy] — *Syn.* elastic, threadlike, ropy; see **flexible** 1.

**sinful,** *modif.* — *Syn.* erring, immoral, corrupt, bad; see **wicked** 1, 2, **wrong** 1.

**sinfully,** *modif.* — *Syn.* unrighteously, immorally, unjustly; see **wrongly** 1.

**sing,** *v.* **1.** [To produce vocal music] — *Syn.* chant, carol, warble, vocalize, trill, croon, choir, twitter, chirp, lilt, harmonize, sing soprano, sing tenor, sing bass, sing alto, sing baritone, raise a song, lift up the voice in song, pipe up, burst into song. — *Ant.* MUMBLE, squawk, screech.

**2.** [To produce a sound suggestive of singing] — *Syn.* buzz, resound, purr; see **hum, sound** 1.

**3.** [To write poetry] — *Syn.* celebrate in song, versify, tell in verse, compose, grow lyrical; see also **write** 1.

**singe,** *v.* — *Syn.* burn, sear, scorch; see **burn** 2, 6. *See Synonym Study at* BURN.

**singer,** *n.* — *Syn.* vocalist, songster, chorister, soloist, minstrel, chanter, cantor, hazan, precentor, choir member, chanteuse, caroler, songbird★, crooner★, groaner★, voice★; see also **musician.**

**singing,** *modif.* — *Syn.* musical, humming, chanting, warbling, purring, whistling, twittering; see also **musical** 1.

**singing,** *n.* — *Syn.* warbling, crooning, chanting, intoning; see **music** 1.

**single,** *modif.* **1.** [Unique] — *Syn.* sole, original, exceptional, singular, only, uncommon, without equal,

unequaled, peerless, without a peer, without a rival, unrivaled; see also **rare** 2, **unique** 1, **unusual** 1. — *Ant.* MANY, numerous, widespread.

**2.** [Individual] — *Syn.* particular, separate, indivisible; see **individual** 1, **private.**

**3.** [Unmarried] — *Syn.* unwed, divorced, celibate, eligible, living alone, companionless, spouseless, bachelor, maiden, unattached, free, foot-loose★, unfettered★, on the loose★, freelancing★, in the market★. — *Ant.* MARRIED, UNITED, wed.

**4.** [Alone] — *Syn.* isolated, separated, deserted; see **alone** 1.

**5.** [For the use of one person] — *Syn.* private, individual, restricted, secluded, personal, one's own, not public, not general, exclusive. — *Ant.* PUBLIC, common, general.

**single-handed,** *modif.* — *Syn.* without help, without assistance, courageously, self-reliantly; see **alone** 1, **bravely, individually.**

**single-minded,** *modif.* — *Syn.* stubborn, self-reliant, bigoted, with one aim, with one purpose, devoted; see also **determined** 1, **selfish** 1.

**singly,** *modif.* — *Syn.* alone, by itself, by oneself, separately, only, solely, one by one, privately, individually, singularly, once. — *Ant.* TOGETHER, in groups, in a crowd.

**sing out,** *v.* — *Syn.* call out, cry, bellow, speak up; see **say, yell.**

**singsong,** *modif.* — *Syn.* tiresome, repetitious, monotonous; see **dull** 4.

**singular,** *modif.* **1.** [Referring to one] — *Syn.* sole, one only, single; see **unique** 1.

**2.** [Odd or strange] — *Syn.* peculiar, uncommon, extraordinary; see **rare** 2, **unusual** 2.

**singularity,** *n.* **1.** [Irregularity] — *Syn.* deviation, curiosity, abnormality; see **irregularity** 2.

**2.** [Idiosyncrasy] — *Syn.* peculiarity, propensity, manner; see **characteristic, quirk.**

**singularly,** *modif.* — *Syn.* notably, uniquely, remarkably; see **especially** 1.

**sinister,** *modif.* — *Syn.* evil, bad, corrupt, perverse, dishonest, inauspicious, menacing, foreboding, threatening, ominous, disastrous, malign, malignant, hurtful, harmful, injurious, baneful, baleful, obnoxious, dire, woeful, disastrous, pernicious, mischievous, deleterious, poisonous, adverse, unlucky, unfortunate, unfavorable, unpropitious; see also **wicked** 1, 2. — *Ant.* FORTUNATE, lucky, opportune.

---

**SYN.** — **sinister** applies to that which can be interpreted as presaging imminent danger or evil /a *sinister* smile/; **baleful** refers to that which is menacing to the degree of being deadly, destructive, pernicious, etc. /a *baleful* influence/; **malign** is applied to that which is regarded as having an inherent tendency toward evil or destruction /a *malign* doctrine/

---

**sink,** *n.* **1.** [A basin] — *Syn.* washbasin, tub, pan, ewer, bowl.

**2.** [A sewer] — *Syn.* cesspool, drain, gutter, cloaca.

**sink,** *v.* **1.** [To go downward] — *Syn.* descend, decline, fall, subside, drop, droop, regress, slump, go under, immerse, go to the bottom, be submerged, settle, go to Davy Jones's locker★, hit bottom, touch bottom, go down with the ship. — *Ant.* RISE, float, come up.

**2.** [To cause to sink, sense 1] — *Syn.* submerge, scuttle, depress, submerse, immerse, engulf, overwhelm, swamp, lower, bring down, force down, cast down, let down, send to Davy Jones's locker\*; see also **soak** 1. — *Ant.* RAISE, float, bring up.

**3.** [To incline] — *Syn.* slant, tilt, list; see **lean** 1.

**4.** [To weaken] — *Syn.* decline, fail, fade; see **weaken** 1.

**5.** [To deteriorate] — *Syn.* spoil, degenerate, rot; see **decay, waste** 3.

**6.** [To decrease] — *Syn.* lessen, diminish, wane; see **decrease** 1.

**sinker,** *n.* — *Syn.* plummet, bob, plumb; see **weight** 2.

**sink in\*,** *v.* — *Syn.* impress, penetrate the mind, take hold, make an impression; see **influence**.

**sinking,** *modif.* — *Syn.* settling in, submerging, drowning, immersing, engulfing, dropping, falling, going under.

**sinless,** *modif.* — *Syn.* pure, perfect, upright, immaculate, saintly; see also **innocent** 4, **righteous** 1.

**sinner,** *n.* — *Syn.* wrongdoer, delinquent, offender, miscreant, adulterer, adulteress; see also **criminal, rascal.**

**sinning,** *modif.* — *Syn.* sinful, immoral, erring; see **wicked** 1, 2, **wrong** 1.

**sinuous,** *modif.* **1.** [Twisted] — *Syn.* crooked, circuitous, curved; see **indirect, twisted** 1.

**2.** [Indirect] — *Syn.* devious, vagrant, oblique; see **indirect**.

**sip,** *v.* — *Syn.* taste, drink in, sup, sample; see **drink** 1.

**Sir,** *n.* **1.** [A formal title] — *Syn.* lord, knight, baron, priest, governor, master.

**2.** [A form of address; *not always capital*] — *Syn.* sire, Your Honor, Your Excellency, Your Majesty, Your Reverence, Your Grace, My Lord, my dear sir, Mister, Bud\*, Chief\*, Big Boy\*, You\*.

**sire,** *n.* — *Syn.* procreator, parent, begetter, generator, creator; see also **father** 1.

**siren,** *n.* **1.** [An alarm] — *Syn.* horn, whistle, signal; see **alarm** 1.

**2.** [Seductress] — *Syn.* temptress, vamp\*, charmer, sex symbol, sexpot\*, *femme fatale* (French), beauty, coquette, Circe, Lorelei, tease; see also **flirt.**

**sissy\*,** *modif.* — *Syn.* weak, afraid, nellie\*; see **cowardly** 1.

**sister,** *n.* **1.** [A female relative having the same parents] — *Syn.* sibling, female sibling, stepsister, half sister, foster sister, big sister, kid sister, sis; see also **relative.**

**2.** [A sister by religious profession] — *Syn.* nun, member of a sisterhood, deaconess.

**3.** [A female member of a group] — *Syn.* associate, coworker, companion.

**sit,** *v.* **1.** [To assume a sitting posture] — *Syn.* be seated, seat oneself, take a seat, sit down, sit up, squat, perch, hunker\*, park oneself\*, take a load off one's feet\*, take a load off one's mind\*. — *Ant.* RISE, stand up, get up.

**2.** [To occupy a seat] — *Syn.* have a place, have a chair, sit in, take a chair, take a seat, take a place; see also **occupy** 2. — *Ant.* STAND, give up one's seat, be without a seat.

**3.** [To lie] — *Syn.* remain, rest, bear on; see **lie** 2, **relax** 1.

**4.** [To hold an assemblage] — *Syn.* convene, come together, hold an assembly; see **assemble** 2, **meet** 2.

**sit back,** *v.* — *Syn.* ignore, relax, keep one's hands off\*; see **neglect** 1.

**site,** *n.* — *Syn.* locality, section, situation; see **place** 3, **position** 1.

**sit-in,** *n.* — *Syn.* protest, demonstration, march, display; see **protest, strike** 1.

**sit on** or **upon,** *v.* — *Syn.* sit in on, take part in, be a part of; see **cooperate** 1, **join** 2, **work** 2.

**sit out,** *v.* — *Syn.* ignore, abstain from, hold back; see **neglect** 1, 2.

**sitter,** *n.* — *Syn.* baby sitter, one who is baby-sitting, attendant, companion, day-care worker, day-care provider; see also **nurse** 2, **servant.**

**sitting,** *n.* — *Syn.* session, seance, appointment; see **gathering, meeting** 1.

**sitting room,** *n.* — *Syn.* front room, living room, reception room; see **drawing room, parlor, room** 2.

**situate,** *v.* — *Syn.* locate, take up residence, establish; see **dwell, reside, settle** 7.

**situated,** *modif.* — *Syn.* established, fixed, located; see **placed.**

**situation,** *n.* **1.** [Circumstance] — *Syn.* condition, state, state of one's affairs; see **circumstance** 1, **circumstances** 2.

**2.** [A physical position] — *Syn.* location, site, spot; see **place** 3, **position** 1.

**3.** [A social position] — *Syn.* station, status, sphere; see **rank** 2, 3.

**4.** [An economic position] — *Syn.* position, employment, post; see **job** 1, **profession** 1, **trade** 2.

*See Synonym Study at* JOB, STATE.

**sit up for** — *Syn.* wait up for, stay up for, wait for; see **wait** 1.

**sit well with\*,** *v.* — *Syn.* please, be acceptable to, be welcome to, be agreeable to, be pleasing to, gratify; see also **satisfy** 1.

**sixpence,** *n.* — *Syn.* half a shilling, half-real, picayune, tanner\*, half-a-bob\*; see also **money** 1.

**sixth sense,** *n.* — *Syn.* foresight, clairvoyance, second sight, intuition, telepathy.

**size,** *n.* **1.** [Measurement] — *Syn.* extent, area, dimension; see **measurement** 2.

**2.** [Magnitude] — *Syn.* bulk, largeness, greatness, extent, vastness, amplitude, scope, immensity, enormity, stature, capaciousness, hugeness, humongousness\*, breadth, substance, volume, bigness, highness, mass, extension, intensity, capacity, proportion; see also **extent, quantity.**

**of a size** — *Syn.* similar, matched, paired; see **alike** 1.

**sized,** *modif.* — *Syn.* stiffened, varnished, filled; see **finished** 2, **glazed.**

**size up\*,** *v.* — *Syn.* judge, survey, scrutinize; see **examine** 1.

**sizzle,** *n.* — *Syn.* hiss, hissing, sputtering; see **noise** 1.

**sizzle,** *v.* — *Syn.* brown, grill, broil; see **cook, fry.**

**skate,** *v.* — *Syn.* slide, glide, skim, slip, skid, go quickly, race, ice skate, roller skate.

**skeleton,** *n.* **1.** [Bony structure] — *Syn.* skeletal frame, axial skeleton, appendicular skeleton, osseous processes, exoskeleton, endoskeleton, support; see also **bone.**

**2.** [Framework] — *Syn.* draft, design, sketch, outline; see **frame** 1, 2, **plan** 2.

**skeptic,** *n.* — *Syn.* doubter, unbeliever, cynic, questioner, infidel, heathen, freethinker, atheist, deist, agnostic, heretic, disbeliever, Pyrrhonist, pagan, anti-Christian, dissenter, latitudinarian, misbeliever, rationalist, profaner, materialist, positivist, nihilist, somatist, scoffer, apostate, blasphemer; see also **cynic.**

**skeptical,** *modif.* — *Syn.* cynical, dubious, distrustful, unbelieving; see **doubtful** 2, **suspicious** 1.

**skeptically,** *modif.* — *Syn.* dubiously, doubtingly, not gullibly; see **suspiciously.**

**skepticism,** *n.* — *Syn.* suspicion, uncertainty, dubiousness; see **doubt** 2, **sarcasm.**

*See Synonym Study at* UNCERTAINTY.

**sketch,** *n.* **1.** [A drawing or plan] — *Syn.* portrayal, picture, draft, design, outline, adumbration, form, shape, delineation, drawing, representation, painting, skeleton, figure, figuration, configuration, depiction, illustration, copy, likeness, *croquis* (French), fashion plate, rough sketch, preliminary sketch, tentative sketch; see also **picture** 3, **plan** 1.

**2.** [A description or plan]— *Syn.* summary, survey, outline, draft; see **description** 1, **plan** 1, 2.

**sketch,** *v.* **1.** [To draw]— *Syn.* paint, describe, depict; see **draw** 2.

**2.** [To plan]— *Syn.* outline, chart, draft; see **plan** 2.

**sketchily,** *modif.* — *Syn.* hastily, patchily, roughly, incompletely; see **badly, inadequately.**

**sketchy,** *modif.* **1.** [Rough]— *Syn.* coarse, crude, preliminary; see **introductory** 1, **unfinished** 1.

**2.** [Imperfect]— *Syn.* defective, superficial, insufficient; see **faulty, inadequate** 1.

**skid,** *v.* — *Syn.* slip, glide, move; see **slide** 1.

**skid row,** *n.* — *Syn.* skid road, run-down neighborhood, the dumps\*, desolation row\*; see **slum.**

**skiff,** *n.* — *Syn.* rowboat, dinghy, tender; see **boat.**

**skill,** *n.* **1.** [Ability]— *Syn.* dexterity, facility, craft; see **ability** 1, 2, **art** 1, **experience** 3, **talent.**

**2.** [Trade]— *Syn.* occupation, work, craft; see **job** 1, **profession** 1, **trade** 2.

*See Synonym Study at* ART.

**skilled,** *modif.* — *Syn.* skillful, a good hand at, proficient; see **able** 1, 2, **experienced.**

**skillful,** *modif.* — *Syn.* skilled, practiced, accomplished; see **able** 2, **experienced.**

**skim,** *v.* **1.** [To pass lightly and swiftly]— *Syn.* soar, float, sail, dart; see **fly** 1.

**2.** [To remove the top; especially, to remove cream] — *Syn.* brush, scoop, ladle, separate; see **dip** 2, **remove** 1.

**3.** [To read swiftly]— *Syn.* look through, brush over, scan; see **browse, examine** 1, **read** 1.

**skimp,** *v.* — *Syn.* scamp, slight, scrimp, pinch, pennies, cut corners; see also **sacrifice** 2, **save** 3.

**skimpy,** *modif.* **1.** [Deficient]— *Syn.* short, scanty, insufficient; see **inadequate** 1.

**2.** [Stingy]— *Syn.* tight, niggardly, miserly; see **stingy.**

**skin,** *n.* — *Syn.* tegument, integument, epithelium, epidermis, dermis, derma, cuticle, scarfskin, trueskin, bark, peel, rind, husk, hide, pelt, fell, coat, carapace, pelage, covering, surface, parchment, vellum.

**be no skin off one's back** or **nose\***— *Syn.* not hurt one, do no harm, not affect one; see **prosper, survive** 1.

**by the skin of one's teeth\***— *Syn.* (just) barely, scarcely, narrowly; see **hardly.**

**get under one's skin\***— *Syn.* irritate, disturb, upset; see **anger** 1.

**have a thick skin\***— *Syn.* be indifferent, not care, shrug off; see **endure** 1, 2.

**have a thin skin\***— *Syn.* be sensitive *or* timid *or* readily hurt, etc., wince, cringe; see **suffer** 1.

**save one's skin\***— *Syn.* get away *or* out, evade, leave (just) in time; see **escape, leave** 1, **survive** 1.

**with a whole skin\***— *Syn.* safe, unharmed, undamaged; see **saved** 1, **unhurt.**

---

*SYN.* — **skin** is the general term for the outer covering of the animal body and for the covering, especially if thin and tight, of certain fruits and vegetables /human *skin*, the *skin* of a peach/; **hide** is used of the tough skins of certain large animals, as of a horse, cow, elephant, etc.; **pelt** refers to the skin, esp. the untanned skin, of a fur-bearing animal, as of a mink, fox, sheep, etc.; **rind** applies to the thick, tough covering of certain fruits, as of a watermelon, or of cheeses, bacon, etc.; **peel** is used

of the skin or rind of fruit that has been removed, as by stripping /potato *peel*, lemon *peel*/; **bark** applies to the hard covering of trees and woody plants

---

**skin,** *v.* — *Syn.* peel, pare, flay, scalp, slough, cast, shed, excoriate, decorticate, exuviate, strip, strip off, pull off, remove the surface from, skin alive, husk, shuck, bark, lay bare, bare.

**skin-deep,** *modif.* — *Syn.* shallow, external, surface, unsubstantial; see **superficial, trivial.**

**skin diver,** *n.* — *Syn.* scuba diver, submarine diver, deep-sea diver, pearl diver, aquanaut, frogman\*; see also **diver.**

**skin diving,** *n.* — *Syn.* underwater swimming, snorkeling, scuba diving.

Skin diving equipment includes: wet suit, dry suit, snorkel, air tanks, mask, goggles, diving helmet, diving hood, fins, air regulator, buoyancy compensator vest, BC vest, weight belt, depth gauge, spear gun.

**skinflint,** *n.* — *Syn.* scrimp, tightwad, hoarder, Scrooge; see **miser** 1.

**skinny,** *modif.* — *Syn.* lean, gaunt, slender; see **thin** 2.

**skip,** *v.* — *Syn.* jump, caper, gambol, leap, bound, hop, ricochet; see also **jump** 1.

---

*SYN.* — **skip** suggests a springing forward lightly and quickly, leaping on alternate feet, and, of inanimate things, deflection from a surface in a series of jumps; **bound** implies longer, more vigorous leaps, as in running, or by an object thrown along the ground; **hop** suggests a single short jump, as on one leg, or a series of short, relatively jerky jumps; **ricochet** is used of an inanimate object that has been thrown or shot and that bounds or skips in glancing deflection from a surface

---

**skipper,** *n.* — *Syn.* commander, leader, operator; see **captain** 3, **officer** 3, **pilot** 2.

**skirmish,** *n.* — *Syn.* engagement, encounter, clash, conflict; see **battle** 1, **fight** 1.

*See Synonym Study at* BATTLE.

**skirt,** *n.* — *Syn.* kilt, fustanella, kirtle, petticoat, dirndl, tutu, hoopskirt, harem skirt, suit skirt, broomstick skirt, culottes, miniskirt, pleated skirt, divided skirt, hobble skirt, pannier, sarong, muu-muu; see also **clothes, dress** 2.

**skit,** *n.* — *Syn.* sketch, burlesque, parody, shtick\*; see **drama** 1.

**skittish,** *modif.* **1.** [Frivolous]— *Syn.* lively, capricious, whimsical; see **changeable** 1, 2.

**2.** [Shy]— *Syn.* timid, restive, nervous; see **afraid** 2.

**skulk,** *v.* — *Syn.* prowl, slink, lurk; see **hide** 2, **sneak.**

**skull,** *n.* — *Syn.* scalp, pericranium, brain case; see **head** 1, **cranium.**

**skunk\*,** *n.* — *Syn.* knave, rogue, scoundrel; see **rascal.**

**sky,** *n.* — *Syn.* firmament, azure, the heavens, atmosphere, the blue\*, welkin, empyrean; see also **air** 1, **heaven** 1.

**out of a clear (blue) sky\***— *Syn.* without warning, suddenly, abruptly; see **quickly** 1, **soon** 1.

**to the skies\***— *Syn.* without restraint, without limit, excessively, inordinately; see **unlimited.**

**sky-blue,** *modif.* — *Syn.* azure, cerulean, *bleu céleste* (French); see **blue** 1.

**skylight,** *n.* — *Syn.* fanlight, light, bay window; see **window** 1.

**skyline,** *n.* — *Syn.* horizon, shape, profile; see **outline** 4.

**skyscraper,** *n.* — *Syn.* tall building, tower, modern building, high-rise, eyesore\*; see also **building** 1.

**slab,** *n.* — *Syn.* plate, slice, bit, chunk, lump, chip, piece, cutting; see also **part** 1.

**slack,** *modif.* **1.** [Not taut] — *Syn.* relaxed, lax, limp; see **loose** 1.
**2.** [Not busy] — *Syn.* slow, remiss, sluggish, inattentive; see **lazy** 1, **remiss.**
*See Synonym Study at* REMISS.

**slack down** or **off** or **up,** *v.* — *Syn.* slacken, decline, lessen, become slower, become quieter; see also **decrease** 1, **slow** 1.

**slacken,** *v.* — *Syn.* loosen, retard, reduce; see **decrease** 1, 2.

**slacker,** *n.* — *Syn.* shirker, loafer, goldbrick, goldbricker; see **cheat** 1, **coward.**

**slag,** *n.* — *Syn.* cinders, recrement, refuse; see **residue.**

**slain,** *modif.* — *Syn.* slaughtered, killed, destroyed, assassinated; see **dead** 1.

**slam,** *v.* **1.** [To throw with a slam] — *Syn.* thump, fling, hurl; see **throw** 1.
**2.** [To shut with a slam] — *Syn.* bang, crash, push; see **close** 4.

**slander,** *n.* — *Syn.* defamation, calumny, scandal, libel; see **lie** 1.

**slander,** *v.* — *Syn.* vilify, defame, calumniate, asperse, decry, traduce, libel, defile, detract, depreciate, disparage, revile, dishonor, blaspheme, curse, attack, sully, tarnish, besmirch, denigrate, smirch, blot, cast a slur on, scandalize, belittle, backbite, derogate, blacken, sneer at, malign, falsify, speak evil of, give a bad name*, blacken the fair name*, dish the dirt*, sling the mud*, plaster*, blackwash*; see also **lower.** — *Ant.* PRAISE, applaud, eulogize.

**slanderous,** *modif.* — *Syn.* libelous, defamatory, disparaging; see **opprobrious** 1.

**slang,** *n.* — *Syn.* cant, argot, colloquialism, dialect, neologism, pidgin English, vulgarism, vulgarity, pseudology, lingo, jargon, shoptalk, dog Latin, slanguage*, English as she is spoke*, Franglais*, Americanese*, Spanglish*; see also **dialect, jargon** 3, **language** 1.
*See Synonym Study at* DIALECT.

**slant,** *v.* — *Syn.* veer, lie obliquely, incline; see **bend** 2, **lean** 1, **tilt** 1.

**slanting,** *modif.* — *Syn.* inclining, sloping, tilting; see **bent, oblique** 1.

**slap,** *v.* — *Syn.* strike, pat, spank; see **hit** 1.

**slapdash,** *modif.* — *Syn.* hasty, perfunctory, cursory, slipshod; see **careless** 1.

**slap down*,** *v.* — *Syn.* rebuke, reprimand, worst; see **defeat** 1, **hush** 1, **quiet** 2.

**slap-happy*,** *modif.* — *Syn.* punch-drunk, dazed, confused, giddy, spacey; see also **beaten** 1, **punished, silly.**

**slapstick,** *modif.* — *Syn.* broad, physical, absurd, droll, comical; see also **funny** 1.

**slash,** *v.* — *Syn.* slit, gash, sever; see **cut** 1.

**slashing,** *modif.* — *Syn.* harsh, brutal, vicious; see **cruel** 1.

**slat,** *n.* — *Syn.* buttress, brace, lath; see **support** 2.

**slate,** *modif.* — *Syn.* dark, dark gray, slate gray; see **gray** 1.

**slattern,** *n.* — *Syn.* trollop, whore, tramp, hussy, strumpet; see also **prostitute.**

**slatternly,** *modif.* — *Syn.* messy, sloppy, untidy; see **dirty.**

**slaughter,** *n.* — *Syn.* butchery, killing, massacre; see **carnage.**
*See Synonym Study at* CARNAGE.

**slaughter,** *v.* — *Syn.* slay, murder, massacre; see **butcher** 1, **kill** 1.

**slaughterhouse,** *n.* — *Syn.* abattoir, butchery, butcher house, shambles, stockyard, aceldama.

**Slav,** *n.* Slavs include: Russian, Bulgarian, Pole, Slovene, Slovak, Ukrainian, Bohemian, Moravian, Czech, Serb, Croat, Sorb, Deniker.

**slave,** *modif.* — *Syn.* vassal, captive, enslaved; see **bound** 1, 2, **restricted.**

**slave,** *n.* **1.** [A person in bondage] — *Syn.* bondsman, bondservant, bondslave, thrall, chattel, serf, vassal, villein, captive, bondsmaid, bondwoman, victim of tyranny, one of a subject people.
**2.** [A drudge] — *Syn.* toiler, menial, worker; see **drudge, laborer.**

**slavery,** *n.* **1.** [Bondage] — *Syn.* bondage, servitude, thralldom, enthrallment, subjection, subjugation, serfdom, constraint, captivity, restraint, bond service, vassalage, involuntary servitude; see also **captivity.**
**2.** [The use of slaves as an institution] — *Syn.* owning slaves, slaveholding, slave-owning, practicing slavery, holding slaves, the peculiar institution*; see also sense 1.
**3.** [Drudgery] — *Syn.* toil, menial labor, grind; see **work** 2.

---

*SYN.* — **slavery** implies absolute subjection to another person who owns and completely controls one; **servitude** refers to compulsory labor or service for another, often, specif., such labor imposed as punishment for crime; **bondage** originally referred to the condition of a serf bound to his master's land, but now implies any condition of subjugation or captivity

---

**Slavic,** *modif.* — *Syn.* Slav, Slavophile, Slavonic, Old Slavonic, Church Slavonic.
Words referring to Slavic peoples include: Cyrillic, Glagolitic, Russian, Belorussian, Polish, Bulgarian, Czech, Ukrainian, Bohemian, Serbian, Slovenian, Slovak, Sorbian, Macedonian, Serbo-Croatian, Croatian, Croat, Bosnian, Montenegrin, Yugoslavian.

**slavish,** *modif.* **1.** [Having the qualities of a slave] — *Syn.* servile, cringing, fawning; see **docile, obsequious.**
**2.** [Lacking originality] — *Syn.* uninspired, faithful, imitative; see **dull** 4.

**slavishly,** *modif.* — *Syn.* thoughtlessly, insensitively, scrupulously, unimaginatively; see **accurately, blindly** 2, **carelessly.**

**slay,** *v.* — *Syn.* murder, slaughter, butcher, assassinate; see **kill** 1.
*See Synonym Study at* KILL.

**sleazy,** *modif.* — *Syn.* shoddy, cheap, shabby; see **shabby, poor** 2.

**sled,** *n.* **1.** [A sled intended for sport] — *Syn.* hand sled, coasting sled, coaster, child's sled, toboggan, saucer, snowboard, belly-bumper*, belly-slammer*, pigsticker*.
**2.** [A sled intended as a vehicle] — *Syn.* sledge, bob, bobsled, bobsledge, bobsleigh, sleigh, cutter, chair, drag, stone drag, boat, stoneboat; see also **vehicle** 1.

**sleek,** *modif.* — *Syn.* silken, silky, satin, svelte; see **smooth** 1.

**sleep,** *n.* — *Syn.* slumber, doze, nap, rest, repose, sound sleep, deep sleep, nod, siesta, catnap, dream, hibernation, dormancy, Morpheus, the Sandman, snooze*, shut-eye*, the down*.

**sleep,** *v.* — *Syn.* slumber, doze, drowse, rest, nap, snooze, hibernate, dream, snore, nod, yawn, languish, flag, relax, go to bed, rest in the arms of Morpheus, drop asleep, fall asleep, lose oneself in slumber, take forty winks*, catnap*, turn in*, go rockaby*, hit the hay*, hit the sack\*, saw logs\*, sack up\*, sack out\*, catch a wink\*, roll in\*.

**sleep around**\*, *v.* — *Syn.* fornicate, be promiscuous, practice adultery; see **copulate**.

**sleepily**, *modif.* — *Syn.* dully, drowsily, as though asleep; see **slowly**.

**sleepiness**, *n.* — *Syn.* torpor, lethargy, drowsiness, somnolence, tiredness, sand in the eyes\*; see also **laziness**.

**sleeping**, *modif.* — *Syn.* dormant, inert, inactive; see **asleep**.

**sleepless**, *modif.* — *Syn.* wakeful, insomnious, insomniac; see **restless** 1.

**sleeplessness**, *n.* — *Syn.* restlessness, wakefulness, alertness; see **insomnia**.

**sleep on it**, *v.* — *Syn.* think about it, consider, ponder; see **think** 1.

**sleep (something) off**, *v.* — *Syn.* get over it, improve, sober up; see **recover** 2.

**sleepy**, *modif.* — *Syn.* drowsy, tired, dozy, somnolent, slumberous, sluggish; see also **tired**.

---

SYN. — **sleepy** applies to a person who is nearly overcome by a desire to sleep and, figuratively, suggests either the power to induce sleepiness or a quiet stillness resembling or conducive to sleep *[a sleepy town, song, etc.]*; **drowsy** stresses the sluggishness or lethargic heaviness accompanying sleepiness *[the drowsy sentry fought off sleep through the watch]*; **somnolent** is a formal equivalent of either of the preceding, though it more frequently refers to the stillness of the subject or to the subject's tendency to induce drowsiness *[the somnolent voice of the speaker]*; **slumberous**, also a formal or poetic equivalent, sometimes suggests latent powers in repose *[a slumberous city]*

---

**sleet**, *n.* — *Syn.* freezing rain, sleet storm, hail, hail storm; see **storm** 1.

**sleeve**, *n.* — *Syn.* sheath, cover, jacket, envelope. Types of sleeves on clothing include: coat, tight-fitting, flowing, short, long, dolman, cap, elbow, three-quarter, bishop, raglan, leg-of-mutton, gigot, shirt, tailored, two-piece, one-piece, cape, puff, domino, kimono.

**sleigh**, *n.* — *Syn.* cutter, sledge, bobsled; see **sled** 1, 2.

**sleight**, *n.* **1.** [A trick] — *Syn.* artifice, craft, deception, hoax; see **cunning, trick** 1.
**2.** [Ability] — *Syn.* skill, dexterity, expertise; see **ability** 1, 2.

**slender**, *modif.* — *Syn.* slim, slight, spare; see **thin** 1.

**slenderize**, *v.* — *Syn.* starve oneself, lose weight, reduce; see **diet**.

**slice**, *n.* — *Syn.* thin piece, slab, wedge, collop; see **part** 1.

**slick**, *modif.* — *Syn.* slippery, suave, sleek, glossy; see **oily** 2, **smooth** 1.

**slicker**\*, *n.* **1.** [A deceptive person] — *Syn.* cheat, trickster, sharper, city slicker; see **rascal**.
**2.** [A raincoat] — *Syn.* rain gear, foul weather gear, southwester, sou'wester; see **raincoat**.

**slide**, *v.* **1.** [To move with a sliding motion] — *Syn.* glide, skate, skim, slip, coast, skid, toboggan, move along, move over, move past, pass along.
**2.** [To cause to slide, sense 1] — *Syn.* shove, thrust, ram, impel, urge, propel, drive, press against, butt, launch, start, accelerate; see also **push** 2.
**let slide** — *Syn.* ignore, pass over, allow to decline; see **neglect** 1, 2.

**sliding scale**, *n.* — *Syn.* adjusted scale, variable scale, ratio, related rates; see **rate** 1, **relationship**.

**slight**, *modif.* **1.** [Trifling] — *Syn.* insignificant, petty, piddling; see **trivial, unimportant**.
**2.** [Inconsiderable] — *Syn.* small, sparse, scanty; see **inadequate** 1.
**3.** [Delicate] — *Syn.* frail, slender, flimsy; see **dainty** 1.

**slight**, *v.* — *Syn.* disdain, snub, overlook; see **neglect** 1, **scorn** 2.
*See Synonym Study at* NEGLECT.

**slighting**, *modif.* — *Syn.* abusive, derisive, maligning; see **derogatory, opprobrious** 1, 2.

**slightly**, *modif.* — *Syn.* a little, to some extent, to a small extent, more or less, ever so little, hardly at all, scarcely any, hardly noticeable, unimportantly, inconsiderably, insignificantly, lightly, inappreciably, imperceptibly, somewhat, rather on a small scale.

**slim**, *modif.* — *Syn.* slender, narrow, lank; see **thin** 2.

**slime**, *n.* — *Syn.* fungus, mire, ooze; see **mud**.

**slimy**, *modif.* — *Syn.* oozy, miry, mucky; see **muddy** 1, 2.

**sling**, *n.* **1.** [A hanging bandage] — *Syn.* cast, bandage, compress; see **dressing** 3.
**2.** [A weapon] — *Syn.* beany, mortar, slingshot; see **catapult, weapon** 1.

**sling**, *v.* **1.** [To throw] — *Syn.* hurl, send, shoot; see **throw** 1.
**2.** [To suspend] — *Syn.* hoist, raise, weight; see **hang** 1.

**slink**, *v.* — *Syn.* prowl, cower, lurk; see **sneak**.

**slinky**\*, *modif.* — *Syn.* sleek, sinuous, serpentine; see **graceful** 1, **smooth** 1, 2.

**slip**, *n.* **1.** [Error] — *Syn.* lapse, misdeed, indiscretion; see **error** 1.
**2.** [Misstep] — *Syn.* slide, skid, stumble; see **fall** 1.
**3.** [Undergarment] — *Syn.* underclothing, lingerie, half-slip, chemise, camisole; see also **clothes, underwear**.
**4.** [Piece of paper] — *Syn.* piece, sheet, leaf; see **paper** 1.
*See Synonym Study at* ERROR.
**give someone the slip**\* — *Syn.* get away, slip away, escape (from); see **leave** 1.

**slip**, *v.* **1.** [To slide] — *Syn.* glide, shift, move; see **slide** 1.
**2.** [To err] — *Syn.* slip up, blunder, mistake, make a mistake.
**let slip, 1.** — *Syn.* miss, fail with, slip up\*; see **drop** 2, **neglect** 1, 2.
**2.** — *Syn.* tell, divulge, let out; see **reveal** 1.

**slip on**, *v.* — *Syn.* put on, don, change clothes, get on.

**slip one over on**\*, *v.* — *Syn.* get the better of, outguess, outmaneuver; see **deceive, defeat** 1, 3, **trick**.

**slipper**, *n.* — *Syn.* house shoe, sandal, pump, dancing shoe.

**slippery**, *modif.* — *Syn.* glassy, smooth, glazed, polished, oily, slick, waxy, lubricious, unctuous, soapy, greasy, slimy, icy, lustrous, satiny, silky, satin-smooth, glabrous, sleek, glistening, wet, *glacé* (French), unsafe, insecure, uncertain, untrustworthy, unreliable, tricky, shifty, slithery, slippy, skiddy, slippery as an eel\*. — *Ant.* ROUGH, sticky, tenacious.

**slipping**\*, *modif.* — *Syn.* failing, growing worse, in error; see **unsatisfactory**.

**slip-up**, *n.* — *Syn.* oversight, mishap, omission; see **error** 1.

**slip up on**\*, *v.* — *Syn.* overlook, miss, bungle; see **fail** 1.

**slit**, *n.* — *Syn.* split, cleavage, crevice; see **hole** 1, 2, **tear**.

**slit**, *v.* — *Syn.* tear, slice, split; see **cut** 1, 2.

**slither**, *v.* — *Syn.* slink, coast, glide; see **slide** 1.

**sliver**, *n.* — *Syn.* splinter, thorn, fragment; see **bit** 1, **flake**.

**sliver**, *v.* — *Syn.* rive, splinter, crush; see **break** 1, 2, **cut** 2.

**slob**★, *n.* — *Syn.* pig, hog, slattern, tramp, sloven, draggletail, yokel, ragamuffin, tatterdemalion, mudlark, street arab, dustman, chimney-sweep, wallower, leper; see also **sight** 3.

**slobber**, *v.* — *Syn.* drip, salivate, dribble; see **drool** 1.

**slog**, *v.* — *Syn.* toil, labor, perform; see **work** 1.

**slogan**, *n.* — *Syn.* catchword, rallying cry, trade-mark; see **motto, proverb.**

**slop**, *n.* **1.** [Waste] — *Syn.* slush, swill, refuse; see **trash** 1.
**2.** [A small quantity] — *Syn.* leavings, few drops, pile; see **bit** 1.

**slop**, *v.* — *Syn.* slosh, wallow, flounder, splash, drip, spill, dash, spatter, let run out, let run over.

**slope**, *n.* **1.** [A hillside] — *Syn.* rising ground, incline, grade; see **hill.**
**2.** [Inclination] — *Syn.* slant, tilt, declivity; see **inclination** 5.

**sloping**, *modif.* — *Syn.* askew, tilted, slanted; see **oblique** 1.

**slop over**, *v.* **1.** [To overflow] — *Syn.* spill, splatter, run over; see **slop.**
**2.** [★To be sentimental] — *Syn.* gush, moon, blubber.

**sloppy**, *modif.* **1.** [Poor] — *Syn.* clumsy, amateurish, mediocre; see **awkward** 1, **careless** 1, **poor** 2.
**2.** [Wet] — *Syn.* slushy, splashy, muddy; see **wet** 1.

**slot**, *n.* — *Syn.* aperture, opening, cut; see **groove, hole** 1, 2.

**sloth**, *n.* — *Syn.* lethargy, torpidity, indolence; see **laziness.**

**slothful**, *modif.* — *Syn.* sluggish, lethargic, indolent; see **lazy.**

**slouch**, *n.* — *Syn.* bungler, incompetent, bumbler, sluggard; see **failure** 2.

**no slouch** — *Syn.* expert, professional, successful person; see **success** 3.

**slouch**, *v.* — *Syn.* droop, stoop, lounge, slump; see **bow** 1, **loaf** 1.

**slough**, *n.* — *Syn.* quagmire, bog, marsh; see **swamp.**

**slovenly**, *modif.* — *Syn.* untidy, slipshod, frowzy; see **careless** 1.

**slow**, *modif.* **1.** [Slow in motion] — *Syn.* sluggish, laggard, deliberate, gradual, moderate, loitering, leaden, creeping, inactive, torpid, slow moving, ultra-slow, crawling, imperceptible, snaillike, slow-paced, leisurely, glue-footed★, as slow as molasses★, as slow as molasses in January★. — *Ant.* FAST, swift, rapid.
**2.** [Slow in starting] — *Syn.* dilatory, procrastinating, delaying, postponing, idle, indolent, tardy, torpid, lazy, apathetic, phlegmatic, inactive, fabian, sluggish, heavy, quiet, drowsy, inert, dreamy, sleepy, lethargic, stagnant, slothful, supine, passive, slack, negligent, remiss, listless, languorous, lackadaisical, disinclined, reluctant, hesitant, enervated, dormant, abeyant, potential, latent; see also **late** 1. — *Ant.* IMMEDIATE, alert, instant.
**3.** [Slow in producing an effect] — *Syn.* belated, behindhand, backward, unpunctual, overdue, delayed, long-delayed, behindtime, regarded, impeded, detained, hindered, moss-backed. — *Ant.* BUSY, diligent, industrious.
**4.** [Dull or stupid] — *Syn.* stolid, tame, uninteresting; see **dull** 3.
*See Synonym Study at* STUPID.

**slow**, *v.* **1.** [To become slower] — *Syn.* slacken, slow up, slow down, lag, loiter, quiet, relax, procrastinate, back water, back and fill, stall★, let up★, wind down★, ease

up★, ease off★; see also sense 2, **decrease** 1, **hesitate.** — *Ant.* RISE, accelerate, mount.
**2.** [To cause to become slower] — *Syn.* delay, postpone, decelerate, moderate, reduce, regulate, retard, detain, temper, qualify, decrease, diminish, hinder, impede, hold back, keep waiting, brake, curtail, check, curb, reef, shorten sail, cut down★, rein in★, cut back★; see also **sense** 1.

**slowdown**, *n.* — *Syn.* retardation, partial stoppage, slacking off; see **production** 1, **strike** 1.

**slowly**, *modif.* — *Syn.* moderately, gradually, languidly, nonchalantly, gently, haltingly, deliberately, leisurely, casually, at one's leisure, with deliberation, with procrastination, taking one's time★, taking one's own sweet time★.

**slowness**, *n.* **1.** [Dullness] — *Syn.* sluggishness, languidness, listlessness, apathy, lethargy, drowsiness; see also **indifference** 1, **stupidity** 1.
**2.** [Weakness] — *Syn.* inactivity, feebleness, impotence; see **weakness** 1.

**sludge**, *n.* **1.** [Mud] — *Syn.* muck, ooze, slop; see **mud.**
**2.** [Waste] — *Syn.* refuse, slime, filth; see **residue.**

**slug**, *n.* — *Syn.* goldbrick, laggard, idler; see **loafer** 1.

**sluggish**, *modif.* — *Syn.* inactive, torpid, indolent; see **lazy** 1, **slow** 1, 2.

**sluggishness**, *n.* — *Syn.* apathy, drowsiness, lethargy; see **fatigue, lassitude, laziness.**

**sluice**, *n.* **1.** [A gate] — *Syn.* floodgate, conduit, lock, watergate; see **gate.**
**2.** [A trough] — *Syn.* sluiceway, moat, ditch; see **channel** 1, **trench** 1.

**slum**, *modif.* — *Syn.* ghetto, tenemental, poverty-stricken, crowded; see **poor** 1.

**slum**, *n.* — *Syn.* low neighborhood, cheap housing, poor district, tenement neighborhood, tenderloin, cabbage patch, radio city, ratnest, the wrong side of the tracks, desolation row, Harlem, Watts, Hunter's Point, skid row, Tobacco Road; see also **tenement.**

**slumber**, *n.* — *Syn.* sleep, repose, nap, doze; see **rest** 1, **sleep.**

**slump**, *n.* **1.** [Decline] — *Syn.* depreciation, slip, descent; see **drop** 2, **fall** 1.
**2.** [Depression] — *Syn.* rut, routine, bad period, slowdown; see **depression** 2.

**slump**, *v.* **1.** [Fall] — *Syn.* cave in, go to ruin, collapse; see **fall** 1.
**2.** [Decline] — *Syn.* blight, depreciate, sink; see **decay.**

**slur**, *n.* **1.** [Stain] — *Syn.* blot, smear, blemish; see **stain.**
**2.** [Aspersion] — *Syn.* stigma, reproach, exposé; see **accusation** 2.

**slur**, *v.* **1.** [To discredit] — *Syn.* cast aspersions on, disparage, slander; see **accuse.**
**2.** [To pronounce indistinctly] — *Syn.* blur, garble, mumble, mispronounce, drop words, drop sounds, hurry over; see also **say.**

**slush**, *n.* — *Syn.* melting snow, mire, refuse; see **mud.**

**slut**, *n.* — *Syn.* wench, whore, hooker★; see **prostitute.**

**sly**, *modif.* **1.** [Crafty] — *Syn.* wily, tricky, foxy, shifty, insidious, artful, shrewd, designing, deceitful, guileful, scheming, deceiving, captious, intriguing, cunning, unscrupulous, deceptive, conniving, calculating, plotting, elusive, delusive, illusory, bluffing, dissembling, dishonest, mealy-mouthed, treacherous, underhanded, sneaking, double-dealing, faithless, traitorous, sharp, smart, ingenious, cagey, canny, dishonorable, crooked★, mean★, dirty★, ratty★, double-crossing★, slick★, smooth★, slippery★, shady★. — *Ant.* HONEST, fair, just.

2. [Shrewd] — *Syn.* clever, sharp, astute; see **intelligent** 1.

3. [Secretive] — *Syn.* furtive, evasive, stealthy; see **secret** 3, **secretive**.

---

*SYN.* — **sly** implies a working to achieve one's ends by evasiveness, insinuation, furtiveness, duplicity, etc. [a *sly* bargain]; **cunning** implies a cleverness or shrewd skillfulness at deception and circumvention [a *cunning* plot]; **crafty** implies an artful cunning in contriving stratagems and subtle deceptions [a *crafty* diplomat]; **tricky** suggests a shifty, unreliable quality rather than cleverness at deception [*tricky* subterfuges]; **foxy** suggests slyness and craftiness that have been sharpened by experience [a *foxy* old trader]; **wily** implies the deceiving or ensnarement of others by subtle stratagems and ruses [*wily* blandishments]

---

**slyly,** *modif.* — *Syn.* cleverly, stealthily, shrewdly, foxily, meanly, secretly, cunningly, intelligently, with downcast eyes, on the quiet, furtively.

**smack*,** *modif.* — *Syn.* precisely, just, clearly; see **exactly**.

**smack,** *n.* **1.** [A sharp noise] — *Syn.* bang, crack, snap; see **noise** 1.

**2.** [A slap] — *Syn.* pat, hit, spank; see **below** 1.

**3.** [A small amount] — *Syn.* trace, suggestion, touch; see **bit** 1, 2.

**smack,** *v.* **1.** [To hit smartly] — *Syn.* slap, spank, cuff; see **hit** 1.

**2.** [To kiss] — *Syn.* greet, press the lips to, smooch; see **kiss**.

**smack down*,** *v.* — *Syn.* rebuke, take aback, slap down, humiliate; see **defeat** 1, 3, **rebuff**.

**smack of,** *v.* — *Syn.* bear resemblance to, bring to mind, suggest; see **resemble**.

**small,** *modif.* **1.** [Little in size] — *Syn.* little, minute, tiny, diminutive, miniature, petite; see also **little** 1.

**2.** [Little in quantity] — *Syn.* scanty, short, meager; see **inadequate** 1.

**3.** [Unimportant] — *Syn.* trivial, insignificant, unessential; see **shallow** 2, **unimportant**.

**4.** [Ignoble] — *Syn.* mean, petty, base; see **mean** 1.

**5.** [Humble] — *Syn.* modest, poor, pitiful; see **humble** 2.

---

*SYN.* — **small** and **little** are often used interchangeably, but **small** is preferred with reference to something concrete of less than the usual quantity, size, amount, value, importance, etc. [a *small* man, tax, audience, matter, etc.] and **little** more often applies to absolute concepts [he has his *little* faults], in expressing tenderness, indulgence, etc. [the *little* dear], and in connoting insignificance, meanness, pettiness, etc. [of *little* importance]; **diminutive** implies extreme, sometimes delicate, smallness or littleness [the *diminutive* Lilliputians]; **minute** and the more informal **tiny** suggest that which is extremely diminutive, often to the degree that it can be discerned only by close scrutiny [a *minute*, or *tiny*, difference]; **miniature** applies to a copy, model, representation, etc. on a very small scale [*miniature* model cars]; **petite** has specific application to a girl or woman who is small and trim in figure

---

**smaller,** *modif.* — *Syn.* tinier, lesser, petite; see **less, shorter**.

**smallness,** *n.* — *Syn.* littleness, smallishness, narrowness, minuteness, diminutiveness, infinitesimalness,

small size, minute size, diminutive size, shortness, brevity, atomity, slightness, scantiness, exiguity, tininess, petiteness, dapperness, dinkiness*.

**smallpox,** *n.* — *Syn.* variola, cowpox, the pox, white man's disease*; see **disease**.

**small talk,** *n.* — *Syn.* chitchat, light conversation, banter, casual conversation, idle conversation, table talk; see also **babble**.

**smart,** *modif.* **1.** [Intelligent] — *Syn.* clever, bright, quick; see **intelligent** 1.

**2.** [Impudent] — *Syn.* bold, brazen, forward; see **rude** 2.

**3.** [Vigorous] — *Syn.* brisk, lively, energetic; see **active** 2.

**4.** [Shrewd] — *Syn.* sharp, crafty, ingenious; see **sly** 1.

**5.** [Fashionable] — *Syn.* stylish, chic, in fashion; see **fashionable**.

*See Synonym Study at* INTELLIGENT.

**smart,** *v.* — *Syn.* sting, be painful, burn; see **hurt** 1.

**smart aleck*,** *n.* — *Syn.* show-off, boaster, wise guy; see **braggart, clown**.

**smarten,** *v.* **1.** [To beautify] — *Syn.* adjust, tidy, polish; see **improve** 1.

**2.** [To stimulate] — *Syn.* educate, tutor, animate; see **teach** 1, 2.

**smartly,** *modif.* — *Syn.* in a lively manner, in a spirited manner, in a vivacious manner, gaily, spirited; see also **active** 1, 2.

**smash,** *n.* — *Syn.* crash, breakup, breaking; see **blow** 1.

**smash,** *v.* — *Syn.* crack, shatter, crush, burst, shiver, fracture, splinter, break, demolish, destroy, dash to pieces, batter, crash, wreck, disrupt, break up, overturn, overthrow, lay in ruins, raze, topple, tumble; see also **break** 2.

*See Synonym Study at* BREAK.

**smashed,** *modif.* — *Syn.* wrecked, crushed, mashed; see **broken** 1.

**smattering,** *n.* — *Syn.* superficial knowledge, some half-truths, smatter; see **introduction** 3.

**smear*,** *n.* — *Syn.* distortion, slander, put-up job*; see **deception** 1, **lie** 1, **trick** 1.

**smear,** *v.* **1.** [To spread] — *Syn.* cover, coat, apply; see **paint** 2, **spread** 4.

**2.** [To slander] — *Syn.* defame, vilify, libel; see **insult, slander**.

**3.** [*To defeat] — *Syn.* beat, conquer, trounce; see **defeat** 2, 3.

**4.** [To dirty] — *Syn.* soil, spot, sully; see **dirty**.

**smeary,** *modif.* — *Syn.* sticky, messy, smudgy, smeared; see **dirty** 1, **oily** 1.

**smell,** *n.* **1.** [A pleasant smell] — *Syn.* fragrance, odor, scent, perfume, exhalation, redolence, essence, aroma, bouquet, trail, trace, emanation.

**2.** [An unpleasant smell] — *Syn.* malodor, stench, fetidness, stink, mephitis, mustiness, rancidity, effluvium, foulness, reek, uncleanness, fume.

**3.** [The sense of smell] — *Syn.* smelling, detection, olfactory perception, nasal sensory power, olfactory sensitivity, olfaction, response to olfactory stimuli.

---

*SYN.* — **smell** is the most general word for any quality perceived through the olfactory sense [foul and fresh *smells*]; **scent** refers to the emanation from the thing smelled, often implying that it can be discriminated only by a sensitive sense of smell [the *scent* of a hunted animal]; **odor** suggests a heavier emanation and, therefore, one that is more generally perceptible and more clearly recognizable [chemical *odors]*; **aroma** suggests a pervasive, pleasant, often sharp odor *[the aroma of fine tobacco]*

---

**smell,** *v.* **1.** [To give off odor] — *Syn.* perfume, scent, exhale, emanate, stink, stench.

**2.** [To use the sense of smell] — *Syn.* scent, sniff, inhale, snuff, perceive, detect, nose out, get a whiff of*; see also **breathe** 1.

**smell out,** *v.* — *Syn.* find, detect, identify; see **discover.**

**smelly,** *modif.* — *Syn.* stinking, foul, fetid; see **odorous** 1, **rancid** 2, **rank** 2.

**smelt,** *v.* — *Syn.* refine, extract, melt; see **clean, purify.**

**smidgen*,** *n.* — *Syn.* drop, pinch, mite; see **bit** 1.

**smile,** *n.* — *Syn.* grin, smirk, simper, pleased look, amused countenance, tender look, friendly expression, delighted look, joyous look; see also **laugh.**

**smile,** *v.* — *Syn.* beam, be gracious, look happy, look delighted, look pleased, express friendliness, express tenderness, break into a smile, look amused, smirk, simper, greet, grin; see also **laugh** 1.

**smile at,** *v.* — *Syn.* grin at, snicker at, deride, poke fun at; see **ridicule.**

**smiling,** *modif.* — *Syn.* bright, with a smile, sunny, beaming; see **happy.**

**smirch,** *n.* **1.** [A smudge] — *Syn.* spot, blotch, smear; see **blemish, stain.**

**2.** [Dishonor] — *Syn.* stigma, slur, blemish; see **disgrace** 1, 2, **scandal.**

**smirch,** *v.* **1.** [To soil] — *Syn.* smudge, discolor, smear; see **dirty.**

**2.** [To degrade] — *Syn.* sully, discredit, malign; see **humble, slander.**

**smirk,** *n.* — *Syn.* leer, grin, smile; see **sneer.**

**smirk at,** *v.* — *Syn.* simper, grin at, make a face at; see **smile.**

**smite,** *v.* — *Syn.* strike, beat, belabor; see **hit** 1.

**smith,** *n.* — *Syn.* metalworker, forger, craftsman.
Types of smiths include: blacksmith, farrier, gunsmith, metalsmith, metalworker, goldsmith, silversmith, locksmith, tinsmith, whitesmith, bronzesmith, brass-smith, coppersmith, clocksmith, coachsmith, hammersmith, scissors-smith, swordsmith, firesmith, wiresmith, cooper, wheelwright, wordsmith, songsmith; see also **craftsman, worker.**

**smithereens,** *n.* — *Syn.* particles, bits, fragments; see **bit** 1.

**smock,** *n.* — *Syn.* frock, work dress, coverall; see **clothes, dress** 2.

**smog,** *n.* — *Syn.* pollution, air pollution, fog, haze, fumes, exhaust, mist, dirty fog, smoke haze, smaze; see also **fog** 1.
*See Synonym Study at* MIST.

**smoke,** *n.* — *Syn.* vapor, fume, gas, soot, reck, smother, haze, smolder, smudge, smog.

**smoke,** *v.* **1.** [To give off smoke] — *Syn.* burn, fume, vaporize, reek, smother, smoke up, smolder, smudge, reek.

**2.** [To use smoke, especially from tobacco] — *Syn.* puff, inhale, smoke a pipe, smoke cigarettes, use cigars, drag*.

**smoked,** *modif.* — *Syn.* cured, treated with smoke, dried, exposed to smoke, kippered; see also **prepared** 2, **preserved** 2.

**smoke out*,** *v.* — *Syn.* uncover, reveal, find, ferret out; see **discover.**

**smokestack,** *n.* — *Syn.* funnel, pipe, stack, flue; see **chimney.**

**smoking,** *n.* — *Syn.* using tobacco, pulling on a pipe, burning the weed, having a drag.

**smoky,** *modif.* **1.** [Smoldering] — *Syn.* fumy, vaporous, reeking; see **burning** 1.

**2.** [Sooty] — *Syn.* grimy, messy, dingy, smoggy; see **dirty** 1.

**3.** [Gray] — *Syn.* smoke-colored, silvery, neutral; see **gray** 1.

**smolder,** *v.* — *Syn.* fume, consume, steam; see **burn** 1, **smoke** 1.

**smooth,** *modif.* **1.** [Without bumps] — *Syn.* flat, plane, even, flush, horizontal, unwrinkled, unvarying, level, monotonous, unrelieved, unruffled, mirrorlike, quiet, still, tranquil, sleek, glossy, glassy, lustrous, smooth as glass. — *Ant.* ROUGH, steep, broken.

**2.** [Without jerks] — *Syn.* uniform, regular, even, invariable, undeviating, steady, stable, fluid, flowing, rhythmic, constant, equable, singsong, continuous. — *Ant.* CHANGEABLE, spasmodic, erratic.

**3.** [Without hair] — *Syn.* shaven, beardless, whiskerless, clean-shaven, smooth-faced, smooth-chinned, glabrescent, glabrous; see also **bald.** — *Ant.* HAIRY, bearded, unshaven.

**4.** [Without qualities that are socially disturbing] — *Syn.* suave, mild, genial; see **polite** 1.

**5.** [Without irritants to the taste] — *Syn.* bland, soft, creamlike; see **creamy, delicious** 1.
*See Synonym Study at* EASY, LEVEL.

**smooth,** *v.* **1.** [To remove unevenness] — *Syn.* even, level, flatten, grade, pave, macadamize, iron, burnish, polish, glaze, varnish, gloss, remove obstruction, remove roughness, sand, clear the way, smooth the path. — *Ant.* WRINKLE, roughen, corrugate.

**2.** [To mollify] — *Syn.* palliate, mellow, mitigate; see **decrease** 2, **ease** 2, **soften** 2.

**smoothly,** *modif.* — *Syn.* flatly, sleekly, placidly; see **easily** 1, **evenly** 1.

**smoothness,** *n.* — *Syn.* evenness, levelness, sleekness; see **regularity.**

**smooth over*,** *v.* — *Syn.* conceal, cover up, hush up; see **hide** 1.

**smorgasbord,** *n.* **1.** [Buffet-style food] — *Syn.* buffet, salad bar, salad course; see **food, lunch, meal** 2.

**2.** [A varied assortment] — *Syn.* collection, array, medley, choice; see **collection** 2.

**smother,** *v.* — *Syn.* stifle, suffocate, suppress; see **choke** 1, 2, **extinguish** 1.

**smothered,** *modif.* **1.** [Extinguished] — *Syn.* drenched, consumed, drowned, put out, not burning, quenched, snuffed.

**2.** [Strangled] — *Syn.* choked, asphyxiated, breathless; see **dead** 1.

**smudge,** *n.* — *Syn.* smirch, spot, soiled spot; see **blemish.**

**smug,** *modif.* — *Syn.* self-satisfied, complacent, conceited, vainglorious, pleased with oneself, priggish, snobbish, superior, egotistical, egoistic, complacent, self-righteous, stuck up*, stuck on oneself*. — *Ant.* MODEST, retiring, reserved.

**smuggle,** *v.* — *Syn.* bring in contraband, slip by the customs, get around the customs, run contraband*; see **hide** 1.

**smuggler,** *n.* — *Syn.* bootlegger, runner, dealer, pirate, crook; see also **criminal.**

**smuggling,** *n.* — *Syn.* bootlegging, stealing, hiding, running goods, clandestine importation; see also **importation, theft.**

**smut,** *n.* **1.** [Filth] — *Syn.* dirt, muck, grime; see **filth.**

**2.** [Pornography] — *Syn.* filth, indecency, obscenity, ribaldry; see **pornography.**

**smutty,** *modif.* — *Syn.* indecent, obscene, pornographic, suggestive; see **lewd** 1, 2.

**snack,** *n.* — *Syn.* luncheon, bite, slight meal, hasty repast; see **lunch, meal** 2.

**snack bar,** *n.* — *Syn.* cafeteria, lunchroom, lunch counter, hot-dog stand, luncheteria, café; see also **restaurant.**

**snafu\*,** *n.* — *Syn.* hassle, muddle, chaos; see **confusion** 2.

**snag,** *n.* — *Syn.* obstacle, hindrance, knot; see **barrier, difficulty** 1, **impediment** 1.

**snail-paced,** *modif.* — *Syn.* snaillike, sluggish, crawling; see **slow** 1, 2.

**snake,** *n.* — *Syn.* reptile, serpent, vermin\*; see **rattlesnake.**

Common snakes include: viper, asp, pit viper, moccasin, water moccasin, copperhead, rattlesnake, rattler, cottonmouth, sidewinder, black snake, bull snake, chicken snake, coachwhip snake, coral snake, fox snake, garter snake, gopher snake, king snake, milk snake, arrow snake, water snake, garden snake, green snake, rat snake, sea snake, boa, boa constrictor, cobra, aboma, adder, milk adder, puffing adder, blowing adder, puff adder, anaconda, python, death adder, krait, black mamba, green mamba, tiger snake, fer-de-lance.

**snaky,** *modif.* **1.** [Twisting] — *Syn.* twisting, serpentine, entwined; see **indirect, twisted** 1, **winding.**

**2.** [Sneaky] — *Syn.* subtle, crafty, treacherous; see **sly** 1.

**snap,** *n.* **1.** [Fastener] — *Syn.* clasp, fastening, catch; see **fastener.**

**2.** [\*Cinch] — *Syn.* easy job, ease, no problem, breeze.

**snap,** *v.* — *Syn.* catch, clasp, lock; see **close** 4, **fasten** 1.

**snap at,** *v.* — *Syn.* vent one's anger at, jump down someone's throat, take it out on; see **get angry.**

**snap back\*,** *v.* — *Syn.* get better, revive, become stronger; see **improve** 2, **recover** 2, 3.

**snap decision,** *n.* — *Syn.* snap judgment, whim, sudden inclination, rash act; see **impulse** 2.

**snap one's fingers at\*,** *v.* — *Syn.* defy, pay no attention to, have contempt for; see **dare** 2, **oppose** 1, 2.

**snap out of it,** *v.* **1.** [To recover] — *Syn.* pull through, get over, revive; see **recover** 2, 3.

**2.** [To cheer up] — *Syn.* perk up, take heart, keep one's spirits up\*; see **improve** 2, **smile.**

**snappish,** *modif.* — *Syn.* cross, angry, touchy; see **irritable.**

**snappy\*,** *modif.* — *Syn.* with style, in good style, chic, having that certain something\*; see **active** 2, **fashionable.**

**snapshot,** *n.* — *Syn.* snap, candid camera shot, action shot; see **photograph, picture** 2, 3.

**snare,** *n.* — *Syn.* trap, lure, decoy; see **trick** 1.

*See Synonym Study at* TRAP.

**snare,** *v.* — *Syn.* ensnare, trap, catch, inveigle; see **catch** 1, 2, **deceive.**

*See Synonym Study at* CATCH.

**snarl,** *n.* **1.** [Confusion] — *Syn.* tangle, entanglement, complication; see **confusion** 2.

**2.** [A snarling sound] — *Syn.* growl, grumble, gnarl, surly speech, cross words, angry words, sullen growl; see also **noise** 1.

**snarl,** *v.* — *Syn.* growl, gnarl, gnar, grumble, mutter, threaten, bark, yelp, snap, gnash the teeth, fulminate, bully, bluster, quarrel, abuse, champ the bit\*, bite one's thumb\*; see also **cry** 3.

**snatch,** *v.* — *Syn.* jerk, grasp, steal; see **seize** 1, 2.

*See Synonym Study at* SEIZE.

**snazzy\*,** *modif.* — *Syn.* desirable, modern, attractive; see **excellent, fashionable.**

**sneak,** *n.* — *Syn.* cheater, confidence man, underhanded *or* unreliable person; see **cheat** 1, **rascal.**

**sneak,** *v.* — *Syn.* skulk, slink, creep, slip away, move secretly, steal, hide, move under cover, ambush oneself, prowl, lurk, secrete oneself, cheat, delude, deceive, soft heel away\*, gumshoe\*, ooze off\*; see also **evade** 1.

**sneakers,** *pl.n.* — *Syn.* gym shoes, tennis shoes, running shoes, basketball shoes, high tops, cross-trainers, trainers (British), plimsolls (British), canvas shoes, sport shoes, tennies, boat shoes, Nikes (trademark), Keds (trademark), sneaks; see also **shoe, tennis shoes.**

**sneaking,** *modif.* — *Syn.* unscrupulous, sinister, crafty; see **sly** 1.

**sneak out of\*,** *v.* — *Syn.* evade, worm out of, escape from, squirm out of; see **avoid, escape.**

**sneaky,** *modif.* — *Syn.* tricky, deceitful, unreliable; see **dishonest** 1, 2.

**sneer,** *n.* — *Syn.* smirk, grin, curl of one's lip, leer.

**sneer,** *v.* — *Syn.* mock, scoff, jeer, gibe, taunt, disparage, slight, scorn, despise, underrate, decry, belittle, detract, lampoon, ridicule, deride, twit, flout, burlesque, caricature, travesty, laugh at, look down, insult, affront, disdain, curl one's lip, fleer, rally, satirize, condemn, give the raspberry\*, give the Bronx cheer\*; see also **doubt** 1.

**sneeze,** *n.* — *Syn.* wheezing, suspiration, sniffle; see **cold** 3, **fit** 1.

**snicker,** *n.* — *Syn.* giggle, titter, snigger; see **laugh.**

*See Synonym Study at* LAUGH.

**snicker,** *v.* — *Syn.* giggle, titter, snigger; see **laugh.**

**snide,** *modif.* — *Syn.* base, malicious, mean; see **sarcastic, scornful** 1, 2.

**sniff,** *v.* — *Syn.* snuff, scent, inhale; see **smell** 2.

**snip,** *v.* — *Syn.* clip, slice, nip off; see **cut** 1.

**snipe,** *v.* — *Syn.* ambush, shoot, murder; see **kill** 1.

**sniper,** *n.* — *Syn.* sharpshooter, gunman, hired assassin; see **killer, rifleman.**

**snippet,** *n.* — *Syn.* particle, fragment, scrap; see **bit** 1, **part** 1, **piece** 1.

**snippy,** *modif.* — *Syn.* curt, sharp, insolent; see **abrupt** 2, **rude** 2.

**snivel,** *v.* **1.** [To cry] — *Syn.* blubber, sniffle, weep; see **cry** 1.

**2.** [To complain] — *Syn.* whine, whimper, gripe\*; see **complain** 1.

**snob,** *n.* — *Syn.* elitist, highbrow, mandarin, Brahmin, stuffed shirt\*, prig; see also **braggart.**

**snobbery,** *n.* — *Syn.* presumption, pretension, pomposity, snootiness, hauteur; see also **arrogance.**

**snobbish,** *modif.* — *Syn.* ostentatious, pretentious, overbearing, haughty, snooty\*; see also **egotistic** 2.

**snooty\*,** *modif.* — *Syn.* conceited, nasty, egotistical; see **egotistic** 2.

**snooze,** *n.* — *Syn.* slumber, drowse, nap; see **rest** 1, **sleep.**

**snore,** *v.* — *Syn.* snort, wheeze, sleep, saw logs\*; see **breathe** 1.

**snort,** *v.* — *Syn.* grunt, snore, puff, blow; see **breathe** 1.

**snotty\*,** *modif.* — *Syn.* impudent, like a spoiled brat, nasty; see **rude** 2.

**snout,** *n.* — *Syn.* muzzle, proboscis, nozzle; see **nose** 1.

**snow,** *n.* **1.** [A snowstorm] — *Syn.* blizzard, snowfall, snow flurry; see **storm** 1.

**2.** [Frozen vapor] — *Syn.* snow crystal, snowflake, slush, sleet, snowdrift, snowbank, snow blanket, powder snow, snow pack, snowfall, fall of snow, snow field.

**3.** [\*A drug] — *Syn.* opium, cocaine, coke\*, heroin; see **drug** 2.

**snow,** *v.* **1.** [To fall or let fall as snow] — *Syn.* storm, whiten, blanket, spit snow, blizzard, cover, pelt, shower, sleet.
**2.** [*To mislead] — *Syn.* overawe, beguile, bamboozle*, to pull the wool over someone's eyes*; see **mislead.**
**snow-bound,** *modif.* — *Syn.* snowed in, frozen in, frozen out, blocked off; see **isolated, trapped.**
**snow job*,** *n.* — *Syn.* persuading, flattery, deceit; see **deception** 1.
**snowy,** *modif.* — *Syn.* niveous, snowlike, fluffy, fleecy, feathery, soft, icy, cold, wintry, blizzardlike, stormy, blanketing, drifting, drifted, glaring, white, gleaming, dazzling, powdery.
**snub,** *v.* **1.** [To slight] — *Syn.* ignore, turn up one's nose at, disdain; see **neglect** 1, **scorn** 2, **shun.**
**2.** [To rebuke] — *Syn.* reprimand, reproach, admonish; see **censure, insult, scold.**
**snug,** *modif.* **1.** [Cozy] — *Syn.* homelike, compact, convenient, sheltered; see **comfortable** 2.
**2.** [Close in fit] — *Syn.* tight, trim, well-built, close.
*See Synonym Study at* COMFORTABLE.
**snuggle,** *v.* — *Syn.* curl up, cuddle, grasp; see **hug, nestle.**
**so,** *modif.* **1.** [To a degree] — *Syn.* very, this much, indeterminately, so large, vaguely, indefinitely, extremely, infinitely, remarkably, unusually, so much, uncertainly, extremely, in great measure, in some measure; see also **such.**
**2.** [Thus] — *Syn.* in such wise, on this wise, and so on, and so forth, in such manner, in this way, even so, in this degree, to this extent; see also **thus.**
**3.** [Accordingly] — *Syn.* then, therefore, and so, hence, consequently; see also **accordingly, therefore.**
**4.** [Exactly right] — *Syn.* exact, correct, just so; see **accurate** 1, **fit** 1.
**(and) so much for that** — *Syn.* enough of that, that is all, having finished; see **accordingly, enough** 1.
**so,** *conj.* — *Syn.* in order that, with the purpose that, with the result that, therefore, if only, as long as, provided that; see also **therefore.**
**soak,** *v.* **1.** [To drench] — *Syn.* drench, wet, immerse, immerge, merge, dip, water, imbrue, infiltrate, percolate, permeate, drown, saturate, impregnate, pour into, pour on, wash over, flood; see also **cover** 8, **moisten.**
**2.** [To remain in liquid] — *Syn.* steep, imbue, macerate, soften, be saturated, be infiltrated, be permeated, be pervaded, infuse, sink into, waterlog.
**3.** [To absorb] — *Syn.* dry, sop, mop; see **absorb** 1.

---

*SYN.* — **soak** implies immersion in a liquid, etc. as for the purpose of absorption, thorough wetting, softening, etc. /to *soak* bread in milk/; **saturate** implies absorption to a point where no more can be taken up /air *saturated* with moisture/; **drench** implies a thorough wetting as by a downpour /a garden *drenched* by the rain/; **steep** usually suggests soaking for the purpose of extracting the essence of something /to *steep* tea/; **impregnate** implies the penetration and permeation of one thing by another /wood *impregnated* with creosote/

---

**soaked,** *modif.* — *Syn.* sodden, saturated, wet, wet through, seeping, drenched, soggy, reeking, dripping, permeated, softened, macerated, immersed, immerged, steeped, infiltrated, dipped, pervaded, infused, flooded, drowned, sunk into, waterlogged.
**soak in*,** *v.* — *Syn.* be understood, penetrate, register*, sink in*.

**soap,** *n.* — *Syn.* saponin, solvent, softener, soapsuds, detergent; see also **cleanser.**
Varieties and forms of soap include: solid soap, hard soap, bar soap, a cake of soap, soap tablet, soap chips, soap powder, soft soap, liquid soap, gel soap, cream soap, settled soap, fitted soap, soap flakes, soap papers, glycerine soap, saddle soap, wash ball, tar soap, lead soap, metallic soap, amole, green soap, brown soap, guest soap, perfumed soap, gum soap, middle soap, neat soap, soap root, Castile soap, bath soap, laundry soap, antibacterial soap, deodorant soap, moisturizing soap, naphtha soap.
**soapy,** *modif.* — *Syn.* sudsy, lathery, foamy; see **frothy** 1.
**soar,** *v.* — *Syn.* tower, sail, rise; see **fly** 1, **glide** 2.
**sob,** *n.* — *Syn.* weeping, bewailing, convulsive sigh; see **cry** 1, 3.
**sob,** *v.* — *Syn.* lament, weep convulsively, wail; see **cry** 1.
*See Synonym Study at* CRY.
**sober,** *modif.* **1.** [Solemn] — *Syn.* restrained, earnest, grave; see **solemn** 1, **serious** 2.
**2.** [Temperate] — *Syn.* abstemious, calm, pacific; see **moderate** 4.
**3.** [Not drunk] — *Syn.* abstinent, serious, sedate, clearheaded, abstaining, self-possessed, calm, ascetic, nonindulgent, steady, dry, on the wagon*; see also **moderate** 5.
*See Synonym Study at* SERIOUS.
**soberly,** *modif.* — *Syn.* moderately, temperately, solemnly, gravely, sedately, in a subdued manner, unpretentiously, quietly, abstemiously, regularly, steadily, calmly, coolly, collectedly, unimpassionedly, somberly, staidly, seriously, earnestly, dispassionately, fairly, justly. — *Ant.* hilariously, excitedly, drunkenly.
**sobersides*,** *n.* — *Syn.* prig, puritan, stick-in-the-mud*; see **prude.**
**sobriety,** *n.* **1.** [Temperance] — *Syn.* renunciation, self-denial, teetotalism; see **abstinence, temperance.**
**2.** [Gravity] — *Syn.* earnestness, serenity, placidity; see **seriousness** 2.
**so-called,** *modif.* — *Syn.* commonly named, doubtfully called, nominal, professed, thus termed, wrongly named, popularly supposed, erroneously accepted as, usually supposed, also known as, aka*; see also **allegedly.**
**sociability,** *n.* — *Syn.* social intercourse, geniality, friendliness, affability; see **cooperation** 1, **friendship** 2.
**sociable,** *modif.* — *Syn.* affable, genial, companionable; see **friendly** 1.
**social,** *modif.* **1.** [Concerning human affairs] — *Syn.* mundane, secular, worldly, human, philanthropic, cultural, eugenical, material, political, racial, humane, benevolent, charitable, altruistic; see also **common** 5, **group, universal** 2.
**2.** [Concerning polite intercourse] — *Syn.* diverting, genial, amusing, entertaining, companionable, pleasurable, informative, civil, polite, polished, mannerly, pleasure-seeking, hospitable, pleasant.
**3.** [Sociable] — *Syn.* communicative, convivial, familiar; see **friendly** 1, **pleasant** 2.
**social climber,** *n.* — *Syn.* upstart, parvenu, nouveau riche, manipulator, lickspittle, ambitious person, yuppie*, Johnny-come-lately*, brown-noser*, yes man*, puppy dog*, babbit*, fixer*, hanger-on*; see also **opportunist, status seeker.**
**socialism,** *n.* — *Syn.* Communism, Fourierism, Saint Simonianism, Marxianism, Fabianism, Marxism, Leninism, Maoism, state socialism; see also **government** 2.

**socialist,** *n.* — *Syn.* Fourierite, Marxist, communist, Fabian; see **democrat, radical.**

**socialized medicine,** *n.* — *Syn.* Medicare, Medicaid, national health care, free clinics; see **charity, medicine** 1, 3, **welfare** 2.

**socially,** *modif.* **1.** [With regard to the welfare of mankind] — *Syn.* humanly, culturally, eugenically, ethically, religiously, philosophically, psychologically, politically, anthropologically, racially.
**2.** [With regard to polite society] — *Syn.* politely, civilly, courteously, hospitably, companionably, convivially, entertainingly, amusingly, divertingly, cordially, genially, sociably.

**social science,** *n.* — *Syn.* sociology, study of people and social phenomena, study of human society, a science dealing with a certain phase or aspect of human society, science, social studies; see also **anthropology, economics, geography, history** 2, **journalism, political science, psychology, science** 1, **sociology.**

**social security,** *n.* — *Syn.* social insurance, old age insurance, disability insurance, unemployment insurance, the dole, social security payments, social security system, retirement; see also **welfare** 2.

**social service,** *n.* — *Syn.* welfare work, aid for the needy, philanthropy; see **charity** 2, **welfare** 2.

**society,** *n.* **1.** [Friendly association] — *Syn.* friendship, social intercourse, fellowship; see **organization** 3.
**2.** [Organized humanity] — *Syn.* the public, civilization, culture, nation, community, human groupings, the people, the world at large, social life.
**3.** [Those who indulge in wealth and leisure] — *Syn.* high life, élite, aristocracy, gentlefolk, polite society, wealthy class, *haut monde* (French), smart set*, the Four Hundred*, jet set*.

**sociology,** *n.* — *Syn.* synecology, autecology, social anthropology, social psychology, study of human groups, analysis of human institutions; see also **social science.** Branches of sociology include: anthropology, demography, ethnology, social theory, cultural anthropology, human ecology, collective behavior, sociometry, sociobiology.

**sock,** *n.* — *Syn.* stocking, hose, ankle-length stocking; see **clothes, hosiery.** Stockings and socks include: silk hose, pantyhose, garter stockings, sheer stockings, rayon hose, seamless hose, support hose, cotton hose, mercerized hose, nylon stockings, full-fashioned stockings, golf hose, mesh stockings, fishnet stockings, tights; bed socks, baby socks, ankle socks, tube socks, sweat socks, crew socks, athletic socks, knee socks, bobby socks.

**sock,** *v.* — *Syn.* strike, beat, punch; see **hit.**

**socket,** *n.* — *Syn.* holder, opening, standard, support, device, cavity, joint, outlet.

**sod,** *n.* — *Syn.* clod, turf, sward, peat, pasture, meadow, lawn, grassland, mead, prairie, pasturage, green, grassplot; see also **earth** 2, **grass** 1.

**soda,** *n.* — *Syn.* pop, soda pop, tonic, cola, soft drink, soda water, carbonated water, seltzer, mineral water, fizz, fizzy water, mixer; see also **drink** 3.

**sodden,** *modif.* — *Syn.* saturated, drenched, steeped; see **soaked, wet** 1.

**sodomy,** *n.* — *Syn.* pederasty, homosexuality, bestiality; see **perversion** 2.

**sofa,** *n.* — *Syn.* couch, divan, love seat; see **couch, furniture.**

**soft,** *modif.* **1.** [Pliable] — *Syn.* malleable, pliant, elastic; see **flexible** 1.
**2.** [Soft to the touch] — *Syn.* smooth, satiny, velvety, silky, delicate, fine, thin, flimsy, limp, fluffy, feathery, flocculent, downy, woolly, pulpy, mellow, pasty, doughy, spongy, pithy, punky, mushy, mashy, soppy. — *Ant.* HARSH, ROUGH, flinty.
**3.** [Soft to the eye] — *Syn.* dull, dim, quiet, shaded, pale, pallid, light, pastel, ashen, wan, faint, blond, misty, hazy, dusky, delicate, tinted; see also **gray** 1, **shady.** — *Ant.* BRIGHT, glaring, brilliant.
**4.** [Soft to the ear] — *Syn.* low, melodious, faraway; see **faint** 3.
**5.** [Soft in conduct] — *Syn.* affectionate, considerate, courteous; see **kind.**
**6.** [Lacking training] — *Syn.* untrained, flabby, out of condition; see **fat** 1, **weak** 1.
**7.** [*Easy] — *Syn.* simple, effortless, manageable; see **easy** 2.

**be soft on** — *Syn.* treat lightly, not condemn, not oppose, fail to attack; see **favor** 2, **neglect** 1.

**soft in the head** — *Syn.* foolish, dumb, not bright, not intelligent; see **dull** 3, **stupid** 1.

---

**SYN.** — **soft** implies an absence or reduction of all that is harsh, rough, too intense, etc. so as to be pleasing to the senses [*soft* colors, a *soft* voice]; **bland** implies such an absence of irritation, stimulation, pungency, etc. in something as to make it soothing, unexciting, and hence, sometimes, uninteresting [*bland* foods, climate, etc.]; **mild** applies to that which is not as rough, harsh, irritating, etc. as it might be [a *mild* cigarette, criticism, etc.]; **gentle,** often equivalent to **mild,** carries a more positive connotation of being pleasantly soothing or tranquil [a *gentle* breeze, voice, etc.]

---

**soft drink,** *n.* — *Syn.* nonalcoholic drink, soda, pop; see **soda.**

**soften,** *v.* **1.** [To become soft] — *Syn.* dissolve, lessen, diminish, disintegrate, become tender, become mellow, thaw, melt, moderate, bend, give, yield, relax, relent. — *Ant.* STIFFEN, solidify, freeze.
**2.** [To make soft] — *Syn.* mollify, mellow, assuage, moisten, modify, palliate, appease, temper, tone down, qualify, lower, tenderize, enfeeble, weaken, deliberate, mash, knead; see also **decrease** 2. — *Ant.* STRENGTHEN, increase, tone up.

**softhearted,** *modif.* — *Syn.* tender, kindhearted, humane; see **humane** 1, **kind** 1, **merciful** 1.

**softness,** *n.* — *Syn.* mellowness, impressibility, plasticity; see **flexibility** 1.

**soft spot,** *n.* — *Syn.* weak point, vulnerability, Achilles' heel; see **weakness** 2.

**soggy,** *modif.* — *Syn.* mushy, spongy, saturated; see **soaked, wet** 1.

**soil,** *n.* — *Syn.* dirt, loam, clay; see **earth** 2.

**soil,** *v.* **1.** [To dirty] — *Syn.* stain, sully, spoil; see **dirty.**
**2.** [To disgrace] — *Syn.* shame, debase, degrade; see **disgrace, slander.**

**soiled,** *modif.* — *Syn.* dirty, stained, tainted, ruined; see **dirty** 1. *See Synonym Study at* DIRTY.

**sojourn,** *n.* — *Syn.* visit, stay, stopover, respite; see **vacation, visit.**

**solace,** *v.* — *Syn.* cheer, soothe, console, comfort; see **comfort.** *See Synonym Study at* COMFORT.

**solar,** *modif.* — *Syn.* astral, stellar, celestial, heavenly, sidereal, cosmic, empyreal, zodiacal.

**solar system,** *n.* — *Syn.* the heavens, heavenly bodies; the sun, moon, and stars; see **universe.**

**sold,** *modif.* **1.** [Sold out] — *Syn.* disposed of, bargained for, gone*, taken*; see **sold out.**

**2.** [Convinced] — *Syn.* persuaded, impressed, taken with; see **satisfied.**

**solder,** *v.* — *Syn.* mend, patch, cement; see **fasten** 1, **join** 1.

**soldier,** *n.* — *Syn.* warrior, fighter, fighting man, private, officer, enlisted man, enlisted woman, volunteer, conscript, commando, mercenary, musketeer, cadet, rank and file, ranks, selectee, commissioned officer, noncommissioned officer, warrant officer, recruit, veteran, Green Beret, Tommy (British), warmonger, militant, G.I.*, Joe*, doughfoot*, dogface*, grunt*.
Types of soldiers include: marine, infantryman, foot soldier, rifleman, sharpshooter, marksman, sniper, guerrilla, scout, skirmisher, sniper-scout, guardsman, artilleryman, gunner, cannoneer, engineer, cavalryman, trooper, knight, dragon, airman, bomber pilot, fighter pilot, torpedo operator, air gunner, radio operator, signalman, paratrooper, commando, air-borne trooper, tanker, Seabee, Green Beret, Special Forces, Ranger, draftee, selectee, ski trooper, antiaircraft gunner, pioneer, machine-gunner, sepoy, Zouave, grenadier.

**soldierly,** *modif.* **1.** [Militant] — *Syn.* martial, antagonistic, combative, warlike; see **aggressive** 2, **fighting, militaristic.**
**2.** [Brave] — *Syn.* intrepid, heroic, bold; see **brave** 1.

**sold out,** *modif.* — *Syn.* out of, all sold, out of stock, not in stock, gone, depleted.

**sole,** *modif.* — *Syn.* only one, no more than one, remaining; see **individual** 1, **single** 1.

**sole,** *n.* — *Syn.* planta, tread, ball; see **bottom** 1, **foot** 2.

**solecism,** *n.* — *Syn.* misuse, barbarism, impropriety, blunder, cacology; see also **abuse** 1, **misusage.**

**solely,** *modif.* **1.** [Exclusively] — *Syn.* singly, undividedly, singularly; see **individually, only** 1.
**2.** [Completely] — *Syn.* entirely, totally, wholly; see **completely.**

**solemn,** *modif.* **1.** [Appearing serious or thoughtful] — *Syn.* grave, serious, sober, portentous, earnest, intense, deliberate, heavy, austere, somber, dignified, staid, sedate, no-nonsense, awe-inspiring, pensive, brooding, moody, grim, stern, thoughtful, reflective. — *Ant.* HAPPY, gay, lighthearted.
**2.** [Impressive] — *Syn.* imposing, ceremonious, overwhelming; see **grand** 2.
**3.** [Sacred] — *Syn.* religious, holy, hallowed; see **divine** 2.
*See Synonym Study at* SERIOUS.

**solemnity,** *n.* — *Syn.* sobriety, ceremony, gravity, impressiveness; see **seriousness** 2.

**solemnize,** *v.* — *Syn.* consecrate, celebrate, observe, solemnify; see **celebrate** 1.
*See Synonym Study at* CELEBRATE.

**solemnly,** *modif.* — *Syn.* sedately, gravely, impressively; see **seriously** 2.

**solicit,** *v.* **1.** [To ask or beg] — *Syn.* entreat, beseech, request, petition; see **ask** 1, **beg** 1.
**2.** [To tempt for sexual purposes] — *Syn.* proposition, accost, give the come-on, approach, entice, hustle, angle on*, hit on*; see also **seduce, tempt.**
*See Synonym Study at* BEG.

**solicited,** *modif.* — *Syn.* sought, asked for, requested, petitioned, approached, invited.

**soliciting,** *n.* — *Syn.* solicitation, asking, requesting, inviting, approaching, seeking, petitioning, canvassing, inducing.

**solicitor,** *n.* — *Syn.* attorney, attorney-at-law, lawyer, counselor; see **lawyer.**
*See Synonym Study at* LAWYER.

**solicitous,** *modif.* — *Syn.* devoted, tender, loving, concerned; see **kind, thoughtful** 2.

**solicitude,** *n.* — *Syn.* anxiety, watchfulness, concern; see **care** 2.
*See Synonym Study at* CARE.

**solid,** *modif.* **1.** [Firm in position] — *Syn.* stable, fixed, rooted; see **firm** 1.
**2.** [Firm or close in texture] — *Syn.* compact, hard, substantial, dense; see **firm** 2, **thick** 1.
**3.** [Reliable] — *Syn.* dependable, trustworthy, steadfast; see **reliable** 1, 2.
**4.** [Continuous] — *Syn.* uninterrupted, continued, unbroken; see **consecutive** 1, **regular** 3.
*See Synonym Study at* FIRM.

**solid,** *n.* — *Syn.* solid body, body, mass, three-dimensional shape, fixed shape.
Solids include: cube, cone, pyramid, cylinder, prism, sphere, tetrahedron, hexahedron, octahedron, pentahedron.

**solidification,** *n.* **1.** [Hardening] — *Syn.* petrification, stiffening, setting, concretion, casehardening, solidifying, crystallization, fossilization, ossification, glaciation, freezing, calcification, compression, coagulation, concentration.
**2.** [Combination] — *Syn.* coalition, affiliation, embodiment; see **union** 1.

**solidify,** *v.* **1.** [To harden] — *Syn.* set, fix, crystallize; see **compress, harden** 2, **thicken** 1.
**2.** [To make secure] — *Syn.* become solid, cause to acquire strength, make firm; see **join** 1, **thicken** 2.

**soliloquize,** *v.* — *Syn.* apostrophize, deliver a monologue, talk to oneself, think out loud, speak; see also **address** 2, **lecture.**

**soliloquy,** *n.* — *Syn.* apostrophe, aside, monologue, monology; see **speech** 3.

**solitary,** *modif.* — *Syn.* sole, lone, only, alone, single, lonely, separate, retired, individual, secluded, isolated, singular, companionless, reclusive, unsocial, unsociable, antisocial, retiring, unfrequented, hermitlike, eremitic; see also **alone** 1. — *Ant.* accompanied, attended, gregarious, social.
*See Synonym Study at* ALONE.

**solitude,** *n.* — *Syn.* isolation, seclusion, retirement; see **silence** 1.

---

*SYN.* — **solitude** refers to the state of one who is completely alone, cut off from all human contact, and sometimes stresses the loneliness of such a condition /the *solitude* of a hermit/; **isolation** suggests physical separation from others, often an involuntary detachment resulting from the force of circumstances /the *isolation* of a forest ranger/; **seclusion** suggests retirement or confinement from intercourse with the outside world, as by remaining in one's home, a remote place, etc. /lived in *seclusion* to avoid publicity/

---

**solo,** *n.* **1.** [A musical piece for one] — *Syn.* aria, *pas seul* (French), single part; see **music** 1, **song.**
**2.** [A performance by one person] — *Syn.* solo flight, unaccompanied performance, one-person show.

**solo,** *modif.* — *Syn.* alone, on one's own, singly, single, solely.

**soluble,** *modif.* — *Syn.* capable of disintegration, capable of decomposition, dissolvable, solvable*, solvent, dissoluble, emulsifiable, dispersible, resolvable, water-soluble, fat-soluble.

**solution,** *n.* **1.** [Explanation] — *Syn.* explication, resolution, clarification; see **answer** 2.
**2.** [Fluid] — *Syn.* suspension, aqueous material, water,

solvent, chemical dissolvent, extract, sap, enzyme, juice; see also **liquid.**

**solvable,** *modif.* **1.** [*Soluble] — *Syn.* dissolvable, dissoluble, solvent; see **soluble.**

**2.** [Explainable] — *Syn.* reasonable, discernible, decipherable; see **understandable.**

**solve,** *v.* — *Syn.* figure out, work out, reason out, think out, find out, make out, puzzle out, decipher, unravel, elucidate, interpret, explain, resolve, answer, decode, get to the bottom of, fathom, get right, hit upon a solution, work, do, settle up, clear up, untangle, unlock, determine, divine, dope out*, hit the nail on the head*, hit it*, make a dent in a problem*, put two and two together*, have it*.

**solvency,** *n.* — *Syn.* financial competence, freedom from financial worries, richness; see **safety** 1, **stability** 1, **wealth** 2.

**solvent,** *n.* **1.** [Dissolvent] — *Syn.* resolvent, moderator, water, alkahest, dissolvent, chemical solution, catalyst, enzyme; see also **solution** 2.

**2.** [Solution] — *Syn.* resolution, discovery, exposition; see **answer** 2, **explanation** 1.

**somatic,** *modif.* — *Syn.* physical, bodily, corporal; see **bodily** 1.

*See Synonym Study at* BODILY.

**somber,** *modif.* **1.** [Dark] — *Syn.* shady, cloudy, drab; see **dark** 1, **dull** 2.

**2.** [Gloomy] — *Syn.* melancholy, dreary, dire; see **dismal** 1.

**some,** *modif.* **1.** [Few] — *Syn.* a few, a little, a bit, part of, more than a few, more than a little, any.

**2.** [*Extraordinary] — *Syn.* fascinating, amazing, remarkable; see **unusual** 1.

**some,** *pron.* — *Syn.* any, a few, a number, an amount, a part, a portion, more or less.

**somebody,** *pron.* — *Syn.* someone, some person, a person, one, anybody, she, he, a certain person, this person, so-and-so, whoever.

**somebody,** *n.* — *Syn.* public figure, famous person, personage, notable, VIP.

**someday,** *modif.* — *Syn.* sometime, one time, one time or another, at a future time, in a time to come, anytime, one day, on a day, one of these days, after a while, one fine day, subsequently, finally, eventually.

**somehow,** *modif.* — *Syn.* in some way, in one way or another, in a way not yet known, by one means or another, by some means, somehow or other, by hook or by crook, anyhow, the best one can, by fair means or foul, after a fashion, with any means at one's disposal, any old how*, every man for himself and the devil take the hindmost*, by guess and by God*.

**someone,** *pron.* — *Syn.* some person, one, individual; see **somebody.**

**something,** *pron.* — *Syn.* event, object, portion, anything, being; see also **thing** 1.

**sometime,** *modif.* — *Syn.* one day, in a time to come, in the future; see **someday.**

**sometimes,** *modif.* — *Syn.* at times, at intervals, now and then; see **seldom.**

**somewhat,** *modif.* — *Syn.* a little, to a degree, to some extent; see **moderately, slightly.**

**somewhere,** *modif.* — *Syn.* in some place, here and there, around, in one place or another, somewhence, somewhither, in parts unknown, someplace, about, around somewhere*, kicking around*, any old place*; see also **scattered.**

**somnambulism,** *n.* — *Syn.* sleepwalking, wandering, noctambulism, noctambulation; see **insomnia.**

**somnolence,** *n.* — *Syn.* sluggishness, drowsiness, lethargy; see **fatigue, sleepiness.**

**somnolent,** *modif.* — *Syn.* drowsy, fatigued, sleepy; see **tired.**

*See Synonym Study at* SLEEPY.

**son,** *n.* — *Syn.* male child, offspring, descendant, foster son, dependent, scion, heir, boy, junior*, chip off the old block*, his father's son*, sliver*.

**song,** *n.* — *Syn.* melody, lyric, strain, verse, tune, ballad, ditty*, number, poem, musical expression; see also **hymn.**

**for a song** — *Syn.* cheaply, at a bargain, for almost nothing; see **cheap** 1.

Types of songs include: lay, aria, air, carol, ballad, hymn, cant, anthem, rondo, paean, canticle, canzonet, canzone, roundelay, madrigal, cantata, opera, operetta, oratorio, refrain, chanson, chorale, minstrelsy, virelay, dirge, elegy, pastorale, canon, spiritual, berceuse, barcarolle, round, chant, folksong, yodel, scat, nursery tune, ditty, art song, evensong, drinking song, love song, plainsong, descant, motet, chorus, lyric, chanty, sonnet, psalm, marching song, battle song, *aubade* (French), lied, lullaby, cradlesong, serenade, vesper.

**song and dance*** — *Syn.* drivel, boasting, pretense; see **lie** 1, **nonsense** 1, **talk** 5.

**songster,** *n.* — *Syn.* vocalist, crooner, warbler; see **singer, musician.**

**sonnet,** *n.* Types of sonnets include: Italian, Petrarchan, Shakespearian, Elizabethan, Miltonic, Spenserian, Meredithian, Cummings; see also **poem.**

**sonority,** *n.* — *Syn.* vibration, timbre, resonance, richness; see **noise** 1.

**sonorous,** *modif.* — *Syn.* resonant, resounding, vibrant; see **loud** 1.

**soon,** *modif.* **1.** [In the near future] — *Syn.* before long, in a short time, in a while, shortly, forthwith, presently, quickly, in a minute, in a second, in short order, in due time; see also **someday.**

**2.** [Early] — *Syn.* in time, promptly, on time; see **early** 2.

**sooner or later,** *modif.* — *Syn.* eventually, inevitably, certainly; see **someday, surely.**

**soot,** *n.* — *Syn.* carbon, smoke, grit; see **residue, sediment.**

**soothe,** *v.* — *Syn.* quiet, mollify, tranquilize, calm, relax, assuage, alleviate, allay, pacify, lull, hush, still, placate, appease, mollify, lighten, unburden, mitigate, console, comfort, relieve, ease, reassure, cheer; see also **comfort, ease** 1, 2, **relieve** 2.

*See Synonym Study at* COMFORT.

**soothing,** *modif.* — *Syn.* calming, peaceful, comforting; see **restful.**

**soothsayer,** *n.* — *Syn.* seer, oracle, diviner; see **fortune-teller, prophet.**

**sooty,** *modif.* **1.** [Dirty] — *Syn.* dingy, grimy, smeared; see **dirty** 1.

**2.** [Dark] — *Syn.* dull, greyish, murky; see **black** 1, **dark** 1.

**sophism,** *n.* — *Syn.* fallacy, sophistry, fallacious argument, absurdity; see **deception** 1.

**sophist,** *n.* — *Syn.* thinker, clever thinker, caviler, rhetorician; see **critic** 1, **pedant, philosopher.**

**sophisticated,** *modif.* **1.** [Cultured] — *Syn.* refined, adult, well-bred; see **cultured, mature** 1.

**2.** [Complex] — *Syn.* advanced, involved, complicated; see **complex** 1, **modern** 1.

**sophistication,** *n.* — *Syn.* savoir-faire, savoir-vivre, tact, poise, refinement, finesse, social grace; see also **composure, elegance** 1.

**sophistry,** *n.* — *Syn.* sophism, subtle argument, irrationality, inconsistency; see **fallacy** 1, **pedantry.**

**sophomore,** *n.* — *Syn.* second-year student, lowerclassman, underclassman, soph*; see **student.**

**sophomoric,** *modif.* — *Syn.* reckless, brash, foolish; see **inexperienced, naive, young** 2.

**soporific,** *modif.* 1. [Soothing] — *Syn.* balmy, mesmeric, sedative; see **hypnotic, tranquil** 2.

2. [Sleepy] — *Syn.* drowsy, dull, somnolent; see **tired.**

**soporific,** *n.* — *Syn.* narcotic, anesthetic, sedative; see **drug** 2.

**soppy,** *modif.* 1. [Very wet] — *Syn.* wet, drenched, soaked, drippy, drizzling, saturated, damp, muggy, watery, rainy.

2. [Sentimental] — *Syn.* romantic, mushy, schmaltzy, maudlin.

**soprano,** *n.* — *Syn.* falsetto, descant, treble; see **singer.**

**sorcerer,** *n.* — *Syn.* witch, wizard, alchemist; see **magician** 1.

**sorcery,** *n.* — *Syn.* black magic, divination, enchantment, necromancy; see **magic** 1, **witchcraft.**

*See Synonym Study at* MAGIC.

**sordid,** *modif.* — *Syn.* ignoble, corrupt, dirty, squalid; see **dirty** 1, **mean** 1, **shameful** 1, 2.

*See Synonym Study at* MEAN.

**sore,** *modif.* 1. [Tender] — *Syn.* painful, hurting, hurtful, severe, raw, aching, smarting, sensitive, irritated, irritable, vexatious, distressing, grievous, bruised, angry, inflamed, burned, unpleasant, ulcerated, abscessed, uncomfortable.

2. [*Angry] — *Syn.* offended, hurt, resentful, irritated; see **angry.**

**sore,** *n.* — *Syn.* cut, bruise, wound, boil, ulcer, hurt, abscess, gash, stab, gall, soreness, discomfort, injury; see also **pain** 2.

**sorely,** *modif.* — *Syn.* extremely, grievously, painfully, woefully, distressfully, badly, severely, sadly, heartbrokenly; see also **so** 1, **very.**

**sorority,** *n.* — *Syn.* sisterhood, club, association; see **organization** 3.

**sorrel,** *modif.* — *Syn.* tawny, roan, sandy, red; see **brown, red.**

**sorrow,** *n.* 1. [Grief] — *Syn.* sadness, anguish, pain; see **grief** 1.

2. [The cause of sorrow] — *Syn.* catastrophe, misfortune, affliction; see **difficulty** 2, **trouble** 2.

3. [Mourning] — *Syn.* weeping, grieving, lamenting; see **mourning** 1.

**sorrow,** *v.* — *Syn.* bemoan, bewail, regret; see **cry** 1, **mourn** 1.

**sorrowful,** *modif.* — *Syn.* grieved, afflicted, sad, in sorrow, in mourning, depressed, dejected; see also **sad** 1.

*See Synonym Study at* SAD.

**sorrowfully,** *modif.* — *Syn.* regretfully, weeping, in sorrow, in sadness, in dejection; see also **sadly.**

**sorry,** *modif.* 1. [Penitent] — *Syn.* contrite, repentant, conscience-stricken, remorseful, conscience-smitten, regretful, compunctious, touched, self-accusing, melted, sorrowful, apologetic, self-condemnatory, softened.

2. [Inadequate in quantity or quality] — *Syn.* poor, paltry, trifling, cheap, mean, shabby, scrubby, stunted, small, trivial, unimportant, beggarly, insignificant, dismal, pitiful, worthless, despicable; see also **inadequate** 1. — *Ant.* PLENTIFUL, adequate, enough.

3. [Sad] — *Syn.* grieved, mournful, melancholy; see

sad 1.

**sort,** *n.* — *Syn.* species, description, class; see **kind** 2, **variety** 1.

**of sorts** *or* **of a sort** — *Syn.* some, such as they are, ordinary; see **common** 1, **poor** 2.

**out of sorts** — *Syn.* irritated, upset, in a bad mood; see **angry, troubled.**

**sort,** *v.* — *Syn.* file, assort, class; see **classify, distribute** 1, **order** 3.

**sortie,** *n.* — *Syn.* foray, sally, encounter, charge; see **attack** 1, **fight** 1.

**sort of*,** *modif.* — *Syn.* somewhat, to a degree, rather, kind of*; see **moderately, slightly.**

**so-so,** *modif.* — *Syn.* ordinary, mediocre, average; see **common** 1, **dull** 4, **fair** 2.

**sot,** *n.* — *Syn.* alcoholic, inebriate, drunk; see **drunkard.**

**sottish,** *modif.* — *Syn.* inebriated, intoxicated, soused; see **drunk.**

**sough,** *v.* — *Syn.* moan, sigh, wail; see **cry** 1, **whisper.**

**sought,** *modif.* — *Syn.* wanted, needed, desired; see **hunted.**

**soul,** *n.* 1. [A disembodied spirit] — *Syn.* phantom, ghost, shade, shadow, umbra, spirit, wraith, apparition, vision, specter, phantasm, haunt*, spook*, hant*.

2. [Essential nature] — *Syn.* spiritual being, heart, substance, individuality, disposition, cause, personality, force, essence, genius, principle, ego, psyche, life, cause.

3. [Mind] — *Syn.* intellect, intelligence, thought; see **mind** 1.

4. [The more lofty human qualities] — *Syn.* courage, love, affection, honor, duty, idealism, philosophy, culture, heroism, art, poetry, reverence, sense of beauty.

5. [A person] — *Syn.* human being, man, woman, being; see **person** 1.

**soulful,** *modif.* — *Syn.* sensitive, eloquent, deep; see **profound** 2.

**soulfully,** *modif.* — *Syn.* sorrowfully, religiously, spiritually; see **intelligently, sadly.**

**soulless,** *modif.* — *Syn.* hard, callous, insensitive; see **cruel** 2.

**sound,** *modif.* 1. [Healthy] — *Syn.* hale, hearty, well; see **healthy** 1.

2. [Firm] — *Syn.* solid, stable, safe; see **reliable** 2.

3. [Sensible] — *Syn.* reasonable, rational, prudent; see **judicious.**

4. [Free from defect] — *Syn.* flawless, unimpaired, undecayed; see **whole** 2.

5. [Proper] — *Syn.* valid, allowed, fair, sanctioned, orthodox; see also **legal** 1, **valid** 1, 2.

6. [Deep] — *Syn.* deep, intellectual, thoughtful, soulful; see **profound** 2.

7. [Complete] — *Syn.* thorough, effectual, total; see **absolute** 1.

8. [Trustworthy] — *Syn.* dependable, loyal, true; see **faithful, reliable** 1.

*See Synonym Study at* VALID.

**sound,** *n.* 1. [Something audible] — *Syn.* vibration, din, racket; see **noise** 1.

2. [The quality of something audible] — *Syn.* noise, resonance, note, timbre, tone, music, pitch, intonation, accent, tonality, tenor, sonorousness, character, quality, softness, loudness, reverberating, reverberation, sonority, ringing, mournfulness, joyousness, lightness, assonance, amplification, vibration, modulation, sweetness, harshness, discord, consonance, harmony.

3. [Water between an island and the mainland] — *Syn.* strait, bay, bight; see **channel** 2.

**sound,** *v.* **1.** [To make a noise] — *Syn.* vibrate, echo, resound, reverberate, give out sound, shout, sing, whisper, murmur, clatter, clank, rattle, blow, blare, bark, ring out, detonate, explode, thunder, emit sound, spread sound, buzz, gabble, rumble, hum, jabber, jangle, jar, whine, crash, bang, reflect, burst, boom, shrill, clitter, ruckle, chatter, creak, clang, crack, crackle, snap, roar, babble, clap, patter, prattle, clink, toot, cackle, clack, thud, slam, smash, blast, thump, snort, shriek, moan, play, quaver, trumpet, croak, caw, quack, squawk.
**2.** [To measure] — *Syn.* rule, mark, gauge, fathom, plumb; see also **examine** 2, **measure** 1.
**3.** [To seem] — *Syn.* appear, give the impression, appear to be; see **seem.**
**4.** [To pronounce] — *Syn.* articulate, enunciate, verbalize; see **say, utter.**

**sounding,** *modif.* — *Syn.* ringing, thudding, bumping, roaring, calling, thundering, booming, crashing, clattering, clinking, clanging, tinkling, whispering, pinging, rattling, rumbling, ticking, crying, clicking, reverberating, echoing, pattering, clucking, chirping, peeping, growling, grunting, bellowing, murmuring, soughing, whirring, splattering, screeching, screaming, squealing, making a noise, making a sound, making a racket, making a clatter, etc.; see also **noise** *n.* 1.

**soundless,** *modif.* — *Syn.* inaudible, silent, still; see **quiet** 2.

**sound off\*,** *v.* — *Syn.* brag, shout, shoot off one's mouth\*; see **boast** 1, **say, yell.**

**sound out,** *v.* — *Syn.* probe, feel out, sound, feel, put out a feeler\*, send up a trial balloon\*, run it up the flag pole\*, see how the land lies\*, get the lay of the land\*, see which way the wind blows\*; see also **examine** 1, **experiment** 2.

**soundproof,** *modif.* — *Syn.* soundproofed, silent, soundless; see **quiet** 2.

**soup,** *n.* Kinds of soup include: *soup du jour* (French), beef broth, mutton broth, bouillon, consommé, gumbo, bisque, turkey soup, oxtail soup, chicken soup, tomato soup, mushroom soup, celery soup, cream of tomato bisque, potato soup, purée of peas, soup à la Italienne, minestrone, borscht, borsch, vichyssoise, onion soup, clam broth, clam chowder, fish chowder, gazpacho, bouillabaisse, corn chowder, egg drop soup, won-ton soup, vegetable soup, okra soup, Scotch broth, mulligatawny, turtle soup, mock turtle soup, lentil soup, mongole, navy bean soup, black bean soup, Philadelphia pepperpot, split-pea soup; see also **broth, food, stew.**

**soupçon,** *n.* — *Syn.* dash, drop, hint; see **dash** 4.

**sour,** *modif.* **1.** [Sour in taste] — *Syn.* acid, acidulated, tart, acetous, vinegary, fermented, rancid, musty, turned, acidulous, acetose, acidic, salty, bitter, acrid, caustic, cutting, stinging, peppery, harsh, irritating, unsavory, vitriolic, tangy, vinegarish, briny, brackish, astringent, dry, sharp, keen, biting, pungent, piquant, acerb\*, acerbic, acetic, curdled, foxy, sourish, subacid, green, unripe, acescent, with a kick\*. — *Ant.* SWEET, mild, bland.
**2.** [Sour in temper] — *Syn.* on edge, ill-natured, grouchy; see **irritable.**

**SYN.** — **sour** usually implies an unpleasant sharpness of taste and often connotes fermentation or rancidity *[sour milk]*; **acid** suggests a sourness that is normal or natural *[a lemon is an acid fruit]*; **acidulous** suggests a slightly sour or acid quality *[acidulous spring water]*; **tart** suggests a slightly stinging sharpness or sourness and usually connotes that this may be pleasant to the taste *[a tart cherry pie]*

**sour,** *v.* — *Syn.* turn, ferment, spoil, go bad, acidulate, acidify, acetify, envenom, make sour, acerbate, curdle, tartarize.

**source,** *n.* **1.** [The origin] — *Syn.* beginning, cause, root; see **origin** 2, 3.
**2.** [A person or work supplying information] — *Syn.* expert, specialist, authorization, source material; see **reference** 3.
**3.** [A fountain] — *Syn.* spring, reservoir, fount; see **origin** 2.
*See Synonym Study at* ORIGIN.

**sourly,** *modif.* — *Syn.* acidulously, bitterly, uncivilly, impolitely; see **angrily.**

**sourpuss\*,** *n.* — *Syn.* killjoy, gripe, curmudgeon; see **grouch.**

**souse,** *v.* **1.** [To soak] — *Syn.* drown, wet, dunk; see **dip** 1, **immerse** 1.
**2.** [To preserve] — *Syn.* pickle, marinate, brine; see **preserve** 3.

**South,** *n.* — *Syn.* the Sunny South, South Atlantic States, the Old South, Pre-Civil War South, Southern United States, the New South, the Deep South, territory south of the Mason-Dixon line, cotton belt, tobacco states, Sunbelt, Bible belt, down south\*, Dixie\*, Dixieland\*, Southland\*; see also **Confederacy, United States.**

**south,** *modif.* **1.** [Situated to the south] — *Syn.* southern, southward, on the south side of, in the south, toward the equator, southmost, southernmost, toward the south pole, southerly, austral, tropical, equatorial, in the torrid zone.
**2.** [Moving south] — *Syn.* southward, to the south, southbound, headed south, southerly, in a southerly direction, toward the equator.
**3.** [Coming from the south] — *Syn.* headed north, northbound, out of the south, from the south, toward the north pole; see also **north** 2.

**south,** *n.* — *Syn.* southland, southern section, southern region, tropics, tropical region, equatorial region, south pole, southern hemisphere, south arctic region.

**southeast,** *modif.* — *Syn.* SE, sou'east, southeastern, southeasterly, southeastward, south-south-east (SSE), southeast by east (SEbE), southeast by south (SEbS); see also **direction** 1.

**Southern,** *modif.* — *Syn.* South Atlantic, Confederate, south of the Mason-Dixon line, Gulf, Old South, New South, cotton-raising, tobacco-raising.

**southern,** *modif.* — *Syn.* in the south, of the south, from the south, toward the south, austral, meridional, southerly; see also **south** 1.

**Southwest,** *n.* — *Syn.* the West, the Wild West, the Old West, the Great Open Spaces\*, the Cow Country\*, Cactus Country\*; see also **west** 3, **United States.**

**southwest,** *modif.* — *Syn.* SW, sou'west, southwestern, southwesterly, southwestward, south-south-west (SSW), southwest by west (SWbW), southwest by south (SWbS); see also **direction** 1.

**souvenir,** *n.* — *Syn.* memento, keepsake, reminder, token, relic, remembrance; see also **memorial.**

**sovereign,** *n.* — *Syn.* monarch, autocrat, supreme ruler; see **king.**

**sovereignty,** *n.* **1.** [The power of a sovereign or state] — *Syn.* supremacy, supreme power, sway; see **government** 1.
**2.** [Independent political authority] — *Syn.* independ-

ence, autonomy, self-determination; see **freedom** 1.

**soviet,** *modif.* — *Syn.* socialist, communist, sovietized, collective, collectivized; see also **Russian.**

**soviet,** *n.* — *Syn.* assembly, congress, council; *volost, uyezd, guberniya, oblast (all* Russian); see also **legislature.**

**Soviet Union,** *n.* — *Syn.* USSR, *CCCP* (Russian), Union of Soviet Socialist Republics, Soviet Russia, Iron Curtain country*; see also **Europe, Russia.**

**sow,** *v.* — *Syn.* seed, disseminate, propagate, scatter, plant, broadcast, drill in, drill seed, use a drill seeder, use a broadcast seeder, strew, seed down, put in small grain, do the seeding.

**sowed,** *modif.* — *Syn.* scattered, cast, broadcast, spread, distributed, dispersed, disseminated, bestrewn, strewn, strewn abroad, planted.

**sox,** *n.* — *Syn.* hose, hosiery, stockings; see **sock.**

**spa,** *n.* 1. [A mineral spring] — *Syn.* baths, spring, curative bath, health resort; see **bath** 3, **resort** 2.
2. [A whirlpool bath] — *Syn.* whirlpool, hot tub, Jacuzzi (trademark).

**space,** *modif.* — *Syn.* outer-space, space-age, transearth, lunar, Martian, interplanetary, interstellar, selenological; see also **infinite.**

**space,** *n.* 1. [The infinite regions] — *Syn.* outer space, the heavens, infinite distance, infinity, interstellar space, interplanetary space, the beyond, distance beyond the farthest stars, illimitable distance, measureless miles, the void, space-age distances, area of weightlessness, where time and space are one; see also **expanse.** — *Ant.* limit, measure, definite area.
2. [Room] — *Syn.* expanse, scope, range; see **extent.**
3. [A place] — *Syn.* area, location, reservation; see **place** 3.
4. [An interval in time] — *Syn.* season, period, term; see **time** 1.

**space,** *v.* 1. [Group] — *Syn.* align, range, apportion; see **order** 3.
2. [Interspace] — *Syn.* set at intervals, interval, keep apart; see **separate** 2.

**space-age,** *modif.* — *Syn.* twentieth-century, contemporary, recent; see **infinite, modern** 1, **space.**

**spacecraft,** *n.* — *Syn.* rocket, spaceship, shuttle, space shuttle, space station, satellite, flying saucer, capsule, unidentified flying object (UFO), manned orbiting laboratory (MOL), orbiting vehicle (O.V.), re-entry vehicle (R.V.), lunar module (L.M.), command module (C.M.), service module (S.M.), repulsor, flying missile, projectile rocket, warhead, deep-space ship, reconnaissance rocket, moon messenger, remote-controlled spaceship, probe, lunar orbiter, weather satellite; see also **satellite** 2.

**spaced,** *modif.* — *Syn.* divided, distributed, dispersed; see **separated.**

**spaced-out*,** *modif.* — *Syn.* dazed, spacey, spaced, stupefied, high, weird.

**space out,** *v.* 1. [To separate] — *Syn.* distribute, disperse, divide; see **separate** 2.
2. [To become dazed] — *Syn.* daydream, stupefy, tune out, lose one's attention.

**space platform,** *n.* — *Syn.* space station, orbiting vehicle (O.V.), manned orbiting laboratory (MOL); see **spacecraft.**

**spacious,** *modif.* — *Syn.* capacious, roomy, vast; see **large** 1.

**spade,** *n.* — *Syn.* implement, trowel, garden tool, digging tool; see **shovel.**

**Spain,** *n.* — *Syn.* Hispania, *España* (Spanish), Iberian Peninsula, Spanish people, Iberia, Castile.

**span,** *n.* — *Syn.* spread, compass, measure; see **extent.**

**span,** *v.* — *Syn.* traverse, pass over, ford; see **cross** 1.

**spangled,** *modif.* — *Syn.* burning, radiant, shiny, glittering; see **bright** 1, 2.

**Spaniard,** *n.* Spaniards include: Iberian, Basque, Catalan, Castilian, Valencian, Segovian, Cordoban, Galician, Andalusian, Aragonese, Asturian, Estremaduran.

**Spanish,** *modif.* — *Syn.* Spanish-speaking, Iberian, Romance, Hispanic, Catalan, Castilian, Galician, Andalusian, Basque, Hispano-Gallican, Spanish-American, Mexican, Puerto Rican, South American, Latin American.

**Spanish,** *n.* — *Syn.* Castilian, Hispanic, Old Spanish, Modern Spanish, *el Español* (Spanish), Latin American Spanish, Mexican, Iberian dialects; see also **language** 2.

**spank,** *n.* — *Syn.* swat, whack, spanking; see **blow** 1.

**spank,** *v.* — *Syn.* whip, chastise, thrash, cane; see **beat** 2, **punish.**

**spar,** *n.* — *Syn.* sparring match, pugilism, fight, contest; see **boxing, dispute, sport** 1.

**spar,** *v.* — *Syn.* scrap, wrestle, exchange blows; see **box** 2, **fight** 2.

**spare,** *modif.* 1. [Extra] — *Syn.* superfluous, supernumerary, additional; see **extra.**
2. [Thin] — *Syn.* lean, lanky, slender; see **thin** 2, **meager** 1.
3. [Scanty] — *Syn.* meager, thin, frugal; see **inadequate** 1, **scanty.**
*See Synonym Study at* SCANTY.

**spare,** *v.* — *Syn.* forbear, forgive, be merciful; see **pity** 2, **save** 1.

**something to spare** — *Syn.* surplus, what is left over, something extra, bonus; see **excess** 1, **remainder.**

**sparing,** *modif.* 1. [Niggardly] — *Syn.* close, tight, avaricious; see **economical** 1, **stingy.**
2. [Merciful] — *Syn.* compassionate, mild, tolerant; see **humane** 1, **merciful** 1.
*See Synonym Study at* ECONOMICAL.

**spark,** *n.* — *Syn.* glitter, glow, sparkle; see **fire** 1, **flash** 1.

**sparkle,** *v.* — *Syn.* glitter, glisten, twinkle; see **shine** 1.

**sparkling,** *modif.* — *Syn.* glinting, scintillating, gleaming; see **bright** 1, 2, **shimmering.**

**sparrow,** *n.* Types of sparrows include: Belding, Bell, black-chinned, chipping, Brewer, desert, English, Fox, Gambel, golden-crowned, Lincoln, rufous-crowned, swamp, song, silver-tongue, field, house, rock, tree, vesper, western lark, white-crowned, white-throated, yellow-throated; see also **bird** 1.

**sparse,** *modif.* — *Syn.* scattered, scanty, meager; see **inadequate** 1, **rare** 2, **scanty.**
*See Synonym Study at* SCANTY.

**Spartan,** *modif.* — *Syn.* bold, fearless, warlike, hardy, stoical, severe, frugal, disciplined; see also **brave** 1.

**spasm,** *n.* — *Syn.* convulsion, seizure, contraction; see **fit** 1.

**spasmodic,** *modif.* 1. [Twitchy] — *Syn.* jerky, convulsive, spastic; see **shaky** 1.
2. [Irregular] — *Syn.* uncertain, sporadic, periodic; see **irregular** 1.

**spat*,** *n.* — *Syn.* tiff, dispute, scrap, quarrel; see **dispute.**
*See Synonym Study at* QUARREL.

**spat,** *v.* — *Syn.* punch, thump, slap; see **hit** 1.

**spatter,** *v.* — *Syn.* splash, spot, wet, soil, swash, sprinkle, scatter, stain, bespatter, splatter, dash, dot, speck, speckle, polka-dot, stipple, pebble-dash, bedew, shower, spangle, bespeckle, seed, dribble, spray, dapple, mottle, bestrew, star, star-scatter.

**spawn,** *v.* — *Syn.* generate, bring forth, issue; see **produce** 1, **reproduce** 3.

**speak,** *v.* **1.** [To utter] — *Syn.* vocalize, pronounce, express; see **utter.**

**2.** [To communicate] — *Syn.* talk, converse, discourse, articulate, chat; see also **talk** 1.

**3.** [To deliver a speech] — *Syn.* lecture, declaim, deliver; see **address** 2.

**so to speak** — *Syn.* that is to say, as it were; in a manner of speaking, as the saying goes*; see **accordingly.**

**to speak of** — *Syn.* somewhat, a little, not much, worthy of mention; see **some.**

---

*SYN.* — **speak** and **talk** are generally synonymous, but **speak** often connotes formal address to an auditor or audience [who will *speak* at the dinner?] and **talk** often suggests informal colloquial conversation [we were *talking* at dinner]; **converse** suggests a talking together by two or more people so as to exchange ideas and information [the leaders of both countries met to *converse* for several hours]; **discourse** suggests a somewhat formal, detailed, extensive talking to another or others [she was *discoursing* to us on Keats]

---

**speak-easy*,** *n.* — *Syn.* pub, illicit liquor establishment, dive*, blind pig*; see **bar** 2, **saloon** 1.

**speaker,** *n.* **1.** [One who delivers an address] — *Syn.* speechmaker, orator, lecturer, public speaker, keynote speaker, preacher, spellbinder, declaimer, rhetorician, platform orator, stump speaker, discourser, discussant, addresser, haranguer, demagogue, elocutionist, talker.

**2.** [A presiding officer; *frequently capital*] — *Syn.* chairman, spokesman, mouthpiece, presiding officer.

**speak for itself,** *v.* — *Syn.* be self-evident, be self-explanatory, vindicate; see **explain** 1, **justify** 2.

**speaking,** *modif.* **1.** [Talking] — *Syn.* oral, verbal, vocal; see **talking.**

**2.** [Expressive] — *Syn.* meaningful, eloquent, vivid, forceful; see **fluent** 2.

**speak out,** *v.* — *Syn.* insist, assert, make oneself heard; see **declare** 1.

**speak well of,** *v.* — *Syn.* commend, recommend, support; see **praise** 1.

**spear,** *n.* — *Syn.* lance, pike, javelin, gar, halberd, halfpike, partisan, bill, lancet, bayonet, fish spear, hunting spear, weapon.

**spearhead,** *v.* — *Syn.* originate, create, initiate; see **begin** 1.

**special,** *modif.* **1.** [Intended for a particular purpose] — *Syn.* specific, particular, appropriate, especial, peculiar, proper, individual, first, unique, personal, restricted, exclusive, defined, limited, reserved, specialized, determinate, distinct, select, choice, definite, marked, designated, earmarked. — *Ant.* GENERAL, unrestricted, indefinite.

**2.** [Unusual] — *Syn.* distinctive, exceptional, extraordinary; see **unusual** 1.

---

*SYN.* — **special** and **especial** both imply that the thing so described has qualities, aspects, or uses that differentiate it from others of its class, and the choice of word generally depends on euphony, but **special** is generally used to emphasize the fact of differentiation itself [he requires a *special* diet] or exceptional status or quality [there is something *special* in her paintings]; **especial** is usually preferred where preeminence is implied [a matter of *especial* interest to you]; **specific** and **particular** are both applied to something that is singled out for attention, but **specific** suggests the explicit statement of

an example, illustration, etc. [he cited *specific* cases], and **particular** emphasizes the distinctness or individuality of the thing so described [in this *particular* case]

---

**special*,** *n.* — *Syn.* dish, course, *pièce de résistance* (French); see **breakfast, dinner, lunch, meal** 2.

**specialist,** *n.* — *Syn.* expert, adept, devotee, master, veteran, ace, scholar, professional, sage, savant, authority, connoisseur, maven*, skilled practitioner, technician, virtuoso. — *Ant.* novice, AMATEUR, beginner.

**specialize,** *v.* **1.** [To study intensively] — *Syn.* concentrate on, develop oneself in, train; see **concentrate** 2.

**2.** [To practice exclusively] — *Syn.* work in exclusively, pursue specifically, go in for, limit oneself to; see **practice** 1.

**specialized,** *modif.* — *Syn.* specific, for a particular purpose, functional, for a special purpose, specially designed, technoscientific, technoscientifically.

**specially,** *modif.* — *Syn.* particularly, uniquely, specifically; see **especially.**

**specialty,** *n.* **1.** [A thing specialized in] — *Syn.* pursuit, practice, specialization, object of study, object of attention, field of concentration, work, special project, special product, hobby; see also **job** 1, **vocation** 2.

**2.** [A superior result] — *Syn. magnum opus* (Latin), *pièce de résistance* (French); see **masterpiece.**

**specie,** *n.* — *Syn.* cash, currency, coin; see **money** 1.

**species,** *n.* — *Syn.* class, variety, sort; see **kind** 2.

**specific,** *modif.* — *Syn.* particular, distinct, precise, explicit; see **definite** 1, 2, **special** 1.

*See Synonym Study at* EXPLICIT, SPECIAL.

**specifically,** *modif.* **1.** [As an example] — *Syn.* peculiarly, especially, indicatively, pointedly, particularly, specially, respectively, concretely, individually, characteristically. — *Ant.* UNIVERSALLY, generally, commonly.

**2.** [In a specific manner] — *Syn.* circumstantially, correctly, definitely, explicitly, expressly, categorically, in detail, precisely, minutely, exactly, clearly; see also **accurately.** — *Ant.* INDIRECTLY, uncertainly, vaguely.

**specification,** *n.* — *Syn.* designation, term, written requirement, particularization, stipulation, blueprint, detailed statement, spec*.

**specified,** *modif.* — *Syn.* particularized, detailed, itemized; see **named** 2.

**specify,** *v.* — *Syn.* name, point out, designate, define, stipulate, show clearly, go into detail, particularize, blueprint, come to the point, pin down.

**specimen,** *n.* — *Syn.* individual, exemplar, part, unit; see **example** 1.

**specious,** *modif.* — *Syn.* plausible, credible, colorable, beguiling, deceptive, misleading, ostensible, meretricious, sophistical, casuistic, probable, presumable, presumptive, likely, apparent, apparently right, seemingly just, hypocritical, fallacious, unsound. — *Ant.* valid, unlikely, incredible.

---

*SYN.* — **specious** applies to that which is superficially reasonable, valid, etc. but is actually not so, and it connotes intention to deceive [a *specious* excuse]; **plausible** applies to that which at first glance appears to be true, reasonable, valid, etc. but which may or may not be so, although there is no connotation of deliberate deception [a *plausible* argument]; **credible** is used of that which is believable because it is supported by evidence, sound logic, etc. [a *credible* account]

---

**speck,** *n.* — *Syn.* spot, iota, mite; see **bit** 1.

**speckled,** *modif.* — *Syn.* mottled, specked, variegated, dotted, spotted, dappled, particolored, motley, mosaic, tessellated.

**spectacle,** *n.* — *Syn.* scene, representation, exhibition; see **display** 2, **view** 1.

**make a spectacle of oneself** — *Syn.* show off, act ridiculously, act like a fool, play the fool; see **misbehave.**

**spectacular,** *modif.* — *Syn.* striking, magnificent, dramatic, panoramic; see **sensational** 1, **thrilling.**

**spectacular,** *n.* — *Syn.* play, movie, production; see **drama** 1, **show** 2.

**spectator,** *n.* — *Syn.* beholder, viewer, onlooker, witness; see **observer** 1.

**specter,** *n.* — *Syn.* apparition, phantom, spirit; see **ghost** 1, **soul** 1.

**spectral,** *modif.* — *Syn.* phantom, unearthly, ghostlike; see **frightful** 1, **ghastly.**

**spectrum,** *n.* — *Syn.* color spectrum, chromatic spectrum, hue cycle, rainbow, fundamental colors; see also **color** 1.

**speculate,** *v.* **1.** [To think] — *Syn.* contemplate, meditate, muse, reflect, conjecture, theorize, hypothesize, hazard an opinion, consider, cogitate, beat the brains\*, wear out the gray matter\*; see also **think.** — *Ant.* NEGLECT, take for granted, ignore.
**2.** [To gamble in business] — *Syn.* risk, hazard, venture, margin up\*, be long of the market\*, pour money into\*, play the market\*, take a chance\*; see also **gamble** 1.

*See Synonym Study at* THINK.

**speculation,** *n.* **1.** [Thought] — *Syn.* meditation, consideration, thinking; see **thought** 1.
**2.** [Speculative business] — *Syn.* trading in futures, speculative enterprise, financial risk, a flier in stocks\*, risky deal\*; see also **gambling.** — *Ant.* RISK, safe investment, legitimate business.

**speculative,** *modif.* **1.** [Thoughtful] — *Syn.* contemplative, meditative, pensive; see **thoughtful** 1.
**2.** [Involving risk] — *Syn.* unsafe, insecure, risky; see **dangerous** 1, **uncertain** 2. — *Ant.* SAFE, certain, sure.

**speculator,** *n.* **1.** [A stockbroker] — *Syn.* stockholder, venturer, gambler; see **businessperson.**
**2.** [An analyst] — *Syn.* theorist, philosopher, experimenter; see **critic** 2, **examiner.**

**speech,** *n.* **1.** [Language] — *Syn.* tongue, mother tongue, native tongue; see **language** 1.
**2.** [The power of audible expression] — *Syn.* talk, utterance, discourse, conversation, articulation, oral expression, diction, pronunciation, expression, locution, vocalization, enunciation, palaver, communication, prattle, parlance, intercourse, chatter.
**3.** [An address] — *Syn.* lecture, discourse, oration, address, disquisition, harangue, oratory, sermon, dissertation, homily, recitation, prelection, allocution, talk, rhetoric, tirade, panegyric, bombast, diatribe, exhortation, eulogy, commentary, declamation, appeal, invocation, salutation, travelogue, valedictory, paper, stump, keynote address, political speech, speechification\*, elocuting\*, opus\*, pep talk\*, spiel\*; see also **communication** 2.

*SYN.* — **speech** is the general word for a discourse delivered to an audience, whether prepared or impromptu; **address** implies a formal, carefully prepared speech and usually attributes importance to the speaker or the speech /an *address* to a legislature/; **oration** suggests an eloquent, rhetorical, sometimes merely bombastic speech, esp. one delivered on some special occasion /political *orations*/; a **lecture** is a carefully prepared speech intended to inform or instruct the audience /a

lecture to a college class/; **talk** suggests informality and is applied either to an impromptu speech or to an address or lecture in which the speaker deliberately uses a simple, conversational approach; a **sermon** is a speech by a clergyman intended to give religious or moral instruction and usually based on Scriptural text

---

**speechless,** *modif.* — *Syn.* aphonic, inarticulate, voiceless, mum; see **dumb** 1, **mute** 1.
*See Synonym Study at* DUMB.

**speed,** *n.* — *Syn.* swiftness, celerity, briskness, activity, eagerness, haste, hurry, promptitude, acceleration, dispatch, velocity, readiness, agility, liveliness, quickness, momentum, promptness, expedition, rapidity, alacrity, pace, precipitation, rush, precipitancy, urgency, legerity, rate, headway, breeze\*, bat\*, clip\*, snap\*, steam\*. — *Ant.* SLOWNESS, tardiness, dilatoriness.
*See Synonym Study at* HASTE.

**speed,** *v.* **1.** [To move rapidly] — *Syn.* race, rush, hurry, go fast, ride hard, put on sail, go like the wind\*, cut along\*, crowd sail, bowl along\*, cover ground\*, gun the motor\*, give her the gas\*, go all out\*, gear up\*, go it\*, break the sound barrier\*; see also **race** 1.
**2.** [To promote] — *Syn.* expedite, advance, further; see **promote** 1.

**speeded up,** *modif.* — *Syn.* accelerated, intensified, bettered; see **fast** 1, **improved** 1.

**speedily,** *modif.* — *Syn.* rapidly, fast, abruptly; see **quickly** 1.

**speeding,** *n.* — *Syn.* exceeding the speed limit, breaking the speed law, reckless driving, careless driving; see **racing.**

**speedster,** *n.* — *Syn.* speeder, reckless driver, lawbreaker; see **driver.**

**speed up,** *v.* **1.** [To accelerate] — *Syn.* go faster, increase speed, move into a higher speed, get into high gear, get into overdrive; see also **improve** 2, **race** 1.
**2.** [To cause to accelerate] — *Syn.* promote, further, get things going, get things moving; see **improve** 1, **urge** 3.

**speedway,** *n.* — *Syn.* track, course, turnpike, highway, circuit; see also **racetrack.**

**speedy,** *modif.* — *Syn.* quick, nimble, expeditious; see **fast** 1, **rapid** 2.
*See Synonym Study at* FAST.

**spell,** *n.* **1.** [A charm] — *Syn.* abracadabra, talisman, amulet; see **charm** 2.
**2.** [A period of time] — *Syn.* term, interval, season; see **time** 1.
**3.** [\*An illness or a seizure] — *Syn.* stroke, spasm, turn; see **fit** 1, **illness** 1.

**cast a spell on** *or* **over** — *Syn.* enchant, bewitch, beguile; see **charm** 1.

**under a spell** — *Syn.* enchanted, bewitched, unable to resist; see **charmed.**

**spellbinder,** *n.* — *Syn.* charismatic person, political orator, lecturer; see **actor** 1, **speaker** 2, **talker.**

**spellbound,** *modif.* — *Syn.* entranced, amazed, fascinated; see **bewildered, charmed** 1.

**speller,** *n.* — *Syn.* word book, spelling book, primer, school text; see **book** 1, **text** 1.

**spelling,** *n.* — *Syn.* orthography, orthographic study, logography; see **grammar.**

**spell out,** *v.* — *Syn.* make clear, go into great detail, simplify; see **explain.**

**spend,** *v.* **1.** [To expend] — *Syn.* consume, deplete, waste, dispense, contribute, donate, give, liquidate, exhaust, squander, disburse, allocate, pay, discharge, lay out, pay up, settle, defray, drain one's resources, empty one's purse, bestow, use up, put in, confer, misspend, absorb, prodigalize, throw away, cast away, foot the bill\*, ante up\*, open the purse\*, fork out\*, pony up\*, blow\*. — *Ant.* SAVE, keep, conserve.

**2.** [To pass time] — *Syn.* while away, let pass, idle, fritter away, misuse, occupy oneself, employ, fill, put in, squander, kill, fool away, drift, laze; see also **consume** 2, **use** 1, **waste** 2.

**spendthrift,** *n.* — *Syn.* wastrel, squanderer, high spender, waster, prodigal, prodigal son, profligate, high-roller\*, big spender\*, high roller\*.

**spent,** *modif.* **1.** [Expended] — *Syn.* used, consumed, disbursed; see **finished** 1, **gone** 2.

**2.** [Exhausted] — *Syn.* done, finished, consumed, used up, depleted, dissipated, wasted, lost.

**spew,** *v.* — *Syn.* spread, spit, blow out; see **blow** 1, **scatter** 2.

**sphere,** *n.* **1.** [A round body] — *Syn.* ball, globule, orb; see **circle** 1.

**2.** [The celestial sphere] — *Syn.* heavens, sky, planetary sphere, *primum mobile* (Latin).

**3.** [A domain] — *Syn.* province, compass, sphere of influence, walk of life, field.

**spherical,** *modif.* **1.** [Round] — *Syn.* globular, orbicular, rounded; see **round** 1.

**2.** [Stellar] — *Syn.* celestial, astronomical, heavenly; see **stellar.**

*See Synonym Study at* ROUND.

**spice,** *n.* — *Syn.* seasoning, savor, relish; see **flavoring.**
Spices include: white pepper, black pepper, red pepper, cinnamon, allspice, nutmeg, mace, ginger, cloves, turmeric, thyme, coriander, sage, curry, caraway, saffron, cardamom, basil, oregano, salt, chili pepper, cumin, anise, paprika, cayenne.

**spicy,** *modif.* **1.** [Suggestive of spice] — *Syn.* pungent, piquant, keen, fresh, aromatic, fragrant, seasoned, perfumed, distinctive, balsamic, tangy, highly seasoned, balmy, herbaceous, savory, flavory, flavorful, tasty, redolent of the South Seas, odoriferous, perfume-laden; see also **salty, sour** 1.

**2.** [Risqué] — *Syn.* racy, erotic, sophisticated; see **risqué.**

**spider,** *n.* **1.** arachnid, spinner, harvestman, daddy longlegs.
Common spiders include: tarantula, black widow, garden, diadem, grass, trapdoor, crab, water, bird, brown, hermit, wolf, jumping, burrowing, hunting, violin back, brown recluse, daddy longlegs, harvestman.

**spigot,** *n.* — *Syn.* plug, valve, tap; see **faucet.**

**spike,** *n.* **1.** [A large nail] — *Syn.* brad, peg, pin, hob, stud; see also **nail.**
Styles of spikes include: cut, wire, iron, railway, dock, forked, barbed.
Sizes of spikes include: twenty-penny, forty-penny, sixty-penny.

**2.** [A spikelike cluster] — *Syn.* raceme, inflorescence, head; see **bunch** 1, **stalk.**

**spike,** *v.* — *Syn.* nail, pin, make fast; see **fasten** 1.

**spike a rumor\*,** *v.* — *Syn.* refute, stop gossip, reveal the facts; see **deny** 1, **expose** 2.

**spill,** *v.* — *Syn.* lose, scatter, drop, spill over, run out; see also **empty** 2.

**spilled,** *modif.* — *Syn.* shed, poured out, lost, ran out, squandered; see also **gone** 2.

**spin,** *n.* — *Syn.* circuit, rotation, gyration; see **revolution** 1, **turn** 1.

**spin,** *v.* **1.** [To make by spinning] — *Syn.* twist, mold, produce, shape, twist into shape; see also **form** 1, **twist.**

**2.** [To whirl] — *Syn.* revolve, twirl, rotate; see **turn** 1, **whirl.**

**spindle,** *n.* — *Syn.* shaft, pivot, stem, axle; see **axis, rod** 1.

**spindling,** *modif.* — *Syn.* skinny, lean, flat; see **thin** 1, 2.

**spine,** *n.* **1.** [A spikelike protrusion] — *Syn.* thorn, prick, spike, barb, thornlet, spinula, quill, ray, thistle, needle; see also **point** 2.

**2.** [A column of vertebrae] — *Syn.* spinal column, ridge, backbone, chine, rachis, vertebral process; see also **bone, vertebrae.**

**spineless,** *modif.* **1.** [Flexible] — *Syn.* pliable, limber, soft; see **flexible** 1.

**2.** [Weak] — *Syn.* timid, fearful, frightened; see **cowardly** 1, **weak** 3.

**spin off,** *v.* — *Syn.* set up, provide for, establish; see **develop** 4, **produce** 2.

**spinster,** *n.* — *Syn.* unmarried woman, virgin, single woman, old maid\*, bachelor girl\*, spin\*; see also **woman** 1.

**spiny,** *modif.* — *Syn.* pointed, barbed, spiked, thorny; see **sharp** 2.

**spiral,** *modif.* — *Syn.* winding, circling, cochlear, coiled, helical, whorled, radial, screw-shaped, circumvoluted, curled, rolled, scrolled, tendrillar, wound.

**spire,** *n.* — *Syn.* steeple, cone, pinnacle, belfry; see **tower.**

**spirit,** *n.* **1.** [Life] — *Syn.* breath, vitality, animation; see **life** 1.

**2.** [Soul] — *Syn.* psyche, essence, substance; see **soul** 2.

**3.** [A supernatural being] — *Syn.* specter, vision, apparition, specter; see **ghost** 1, 2, **god** 1, **goddess.**

**4.** [Courage] — *Syn.* boldness, ardor, enthusiasm; see **courage** 1.

**5.** [A form of alcohol; *often plural*] — *Syn.* distillation, spiritous liquor, hard liquor; see **drink** 2.

**6.** [Feeling; *often plural*] — *Syn.* disposition, temper, humor, tenor; see **feeling, mood** 1.

**7.** [Intent or meaning] — *Syn.* genius, quality, sense; see **character** 1, **meaning.**

**spirited,** *modif.* — *Syn.* lively, vivacious, effervescent; see **active** 2.

**spiritless,** *modif.* — *Syn.* dull, apathetic, unconcerned; see **indifferent** 1.

**spiritual,** *modif.* — *Syn.* refined, pure, holy; see **religious** 1.

**spiritualism,** *n.* **1.** [Occultism] — *Syn.* necromancy, mysticism, cabalism, supernaturalism, theosophy.

**2.** [Idealism] — *Syn.* insubstantiality, metaphysics, immateriality; see **idealism** 2.

**spirituality,** *n.* **1.** [Immateriality] — *Syn.* otherworldliness, unearthliness, incorporeality.

**2.** [Piety] — *Syn.* piousness, devoutness, holiness, religiosity.

**spiritually,** *modif.* — *Syn.* devoutly, religiously, mystically, in a spiritual manner; piously; see also **happily** 2, **mentally, sadly.**

**spit,** *v.* — *Syn.* expectorate, splutter, eject, drivel, slobber, drool.

**spit and image\*,** *n.* — *Syn.* image, spitting image\*, replica; see **copy.**

**spite,** *n.* — *Syn.* umbrage, malice, malignity, resentment, ill will, hatred, contempt, harsh feeling, grudge, antipathy, enmity, animosity, rancor, venom, bad blood\*; see also **hate.**

**in spite of** — *Syn.* nevertheless, in defiance of, despite; see **notwithstanding.** — *Ant.* LOVE, sympathy, affection.

**spiteful,** *modif.* — *Syn.* hateful, malicious, resentful, vindictive; see **angry, cruel** 1, 2.
*See Synonym Study at* VINDICTIVE.

**spitfire,** *n.* — *Syn.* tigress, beldame, hag; see **shrew.**

**spittle,** *n.* — *Syn.* drool, rheum, mucous, spit; see **phlegm, saliva.**

**splash,** *n.* — *Syn.* plash, plop, dash, spatter, sprinkle, spray, slosh, slop.

**make a splash\*** — *Syn.* show off\*, do something big, get results\*; see **succeed 1.**

**splash,** *v.* — *Syn.* dash, splatter, bespatter, dabble, plash, get wet, throw; see also **moisten.**

**splayed,** *modif.* — *Syn.* wide, spread out, large; see **broad 1.**

**spleen,** *n.* — *Syn.* resentment, venom, wrath; see **anger, hatred 2.**

**splendid,** *modif.* **1.** [Magnificent] — *Syn.* grand, imposing, marvelous; see **beautiful 1.**

**2.** [Glorious] — *Syn.* illustrious, celebrated, distinguished; see **glorious 1.**

**3.** [\*Very good] — *Syn.* premium, great, fine; see **excellent.**

**splendidly,** *modif.* — *Syn.* brilliantly, gorgeously, grandly, beautifully, excellently, magnificently, majestically, well, radiantly, elegantly, handsomely, illustriously, wonderfully.

**splendor,** *n.* — *Syn.* luster, brilliance, brightness; see **glory 2.**

**splenetic,** *modif.* — *Syn.* peevish, cross, fretful; see **irritable.**

*See Synonym Study at* IRRITABLE.

**splice,** *v.* — *Syn.* knit, graft, mesh; see **join 1, weave 1.**

**spliced,** *modif.* **1.** [Joined] — *Syn.* tied together, fitted, united; see **joined.**

**2.** [\*Married] — *Syn.* united, joined in holy matrimony, espoused, wedded; see **married.**

**splint,** *n.* **1.** [A support] — *Syn.* prop, rib, reinforcement; see **brace 1, support 2.**

**2.** [A sliver] — *Syn.* chip, slat, reed; see **splinter.**

**splinter,** *n.* — *Syn.* sliver, shiver, fragment, piece, flake, chip, wood; see also **bit 1.**

**splinter,** *v.* — *Syn.* shiver, shatter, split; see **break 2, smash.**

*See Synonym Study at* BREAK.

**split,** *n.* **1.** [A dividing] — *Syn.* separating, separation, breaking up, severing; see **division 1.**

**2.** [An opening] — *Syn.* crack, fissure, rent; see **hole 1.**

**split,** *v.* — *Syn.* burst, rend, cleave, divide; see **break 1, cut 1, divide 1.**

*See Synonym Study at* BREAK.

**split off,** *v.* — *Syn.* separate, go one's own way, divide; see **leave 1.**

**splitting,** *modif.* **1.** [Loud] — *Syn.* deafening, shrill, acute; see **loud 1.**

**2.** [Violent] — *Syn.* severe, harsh, acute; see **intense.**

**split up\*,** *v.* **1.** [To separate] — *Syn.* part, sunder, isolate; see **divide 1.**

**2.** [To divorce] — *Syn.* separate, have a marriage annulled, have separate maintenance; see **divorce.**

**splotch,** *n.* — *Syn.* smudge, spot, blot; see **blemish, stain.**

**splurge\*,** *v.* — *Syn.* spend lavishly, go all out, be extravagant; see **celebrate 1, 3.**

**splutter,** *v.* **1.** [Stammer] — *Syn.* stutter, stumble, gabble; see **stammer.**

**2.** [To spit] — *Syn.* spew, spray, hiss; see **spit.**

**spoil,** *v.* **1.** [To decay] — *Syn.* decay, rot, decompose, become tainted; see **decay.**

**2.** [To ruin] — *Syn.* destroy, defile, plunder; see **disgrace.**

*See Synonym Study at* DECAY, INDULGE, INJURE.

**spoilage,** *n.* — *Syn.* waste, decomposition, deterioration; see **decay 1, 2.**

**spoiled,** *modif.* — *Syn.* damaged, harmed, marred, injured, corrupted; see also **ruined 2, wasted.**

**spoiling,** *modif.* — *Syn.* rotting, breaking up, wasting away; see **decaying.**

**spoils,** *n.* — *Syn.* plunder, pillage, prize; see **booty.**

*See Synonym Study at* BOOTY.

**spoils system,** *n.* — *Syn.* corruption, party politics, corrupt practices; see **corruption 2.**

**spoke,** *n.* — *Syn.* rundle, handle, crosspiece; see **part 2, rod 1, rung.**

**spoken,** *modif.* — *Syn.* uttered, expressed, told, announced, mentioned, communicated, oral, verbal, phonetic, voiced, lingual, unwritten.

**spokesman,** *n.* — *Syn.* spokesperson, spokeswoman, deputy, mediator, substitute; see also **agent 1, representative 1, speaker 1.**

**spoliation,** *n.* — *Syn.* plundering, raid, destruction; see **attack 1.**

**sponge,** *v.* **1.** [Clean] — *Syn.* wipe, wet, wash; see **clean, mop.**

**2.** [\*To use another's money] — *Syn.* leech, sponge off, freeload\*, scrounge\*, mooch\*, bum\*; see also **borrow 1.**

**sponger,** *n.* — *Syn.* dependent, freeloader, sponge, hanger-on, parasite; see also **sycophant.**

**spongy,** *modif.* — *Syn.* springy, like a sponge, porous; see **wet 1.**

**sponsor,** *n.* — *Syn.* guarantor, advocate, patron, underwriter, supporter, backer, angel, adherent, sustainer, champion.

---

*SYN.* — **sponsor** is one who assumes a certain degree of responsibility for another in any of various ways /the *sponsors* of a television program assume the costs of production/; a **patron** is one who assumes the role of protector or benefactor of an artist, an institution, etc. usually in a financial capacity; a **backer** is one who lends support, esp. financial support, to someone or something but does not necessarily assume any responsibilities /the magazine failed when it lost its *backers*/; **angel** is a colloquial term for the backer of a theatrical enterprise

---

**sponsorship,** *n.* — *Syn.* sponsoring, favor, lending one's name to; see **aid 1, support 2, 3.**

**spontaneity,** *n.* — *Syn.* inspiration, will, tendency; see **impulse 2, inclination 1.**

**spontaneous,** *modif.* — *Syn.* involuntary, instinctive, unbidden, unplanned, impromptu, ad-lib\*, casual, unintentional, impulsive, offhand, automatic, unforced, natural, inevitable, irresistible, unavoidable, resistless, unwilling, unconscious, uncontrollable. — *Ant.* DELIBERATE, willful, intended.

---

*SYN.* — **spontaneous** applies to that which is done so naturally that it seems to come without prompting or premeditation /a *spontaneous* demonstration/; **impulsive** applies to that which is prompted by some external incitement or sudden inner inclination rather than by conscious rational volition /an *impulsive* retort/; **instinctive** suggests an immediate, unwilled response to a stimulus, as if prompted by some natural, inborn tendency /he took an *instinctive* liking to her/; **involuntary** refers to that which is done without thought or volition, as a reflex action /an *involuntary* scowl, an *involuntary* flicker of the eyelid/;

**automatic** suggests an unvarying, machinelike reaction to a given stimulus or situation *[an automatic response]*

---

**spontaneously,** *modif.* — *Syn.* instinctively, impulsively, automatically, directly, at once; see also **immediately, unconsciously.**

**spoof\*,** *n.* — *Syn.* trickery, put on, satire; see **deception** 1, **parody.**

**spoof\*,** *v.* — *Syn.* fool, play a trick on, kid\*; see **parody, trick.**

**spook,** *n.* — *Syn.* visitant, spirit, disembodied spirit; see **ghost** 1.

**spook\*,** *v.* — *Syn.* alarm, startle, terrorize; see **frighten** 1.

**spooky,** *modif.* — *Syn.* weird, eerie, ominous, scary; see **mysterious** 2, **uncanny.**

**spool,** *n.* — *Syn.* bobbin, spindle, quill, cop, bottom; see also **reel.**

**spoon,** *n.* Types of spoons include: measuring, serving, iced tea, slotted, wooden, ladle, dipper, scoop, teaspoon, dessert, soup, tablespoon, salt, sugar, gravy, demitasse, grapefruit, runcible, spork; see also **silverware.**

**spoon\*,** *v.* — *Syn.* make love, fondle, pet\*, woo; see **love** 2.

**spoor,** *n.* — *Syn.* trace, trail, scent, droppings; see **path** 1, **track** 1.

**sporadic,** *modif.* — *Syn.* infrequent, occasional, uncommon; see **irregular** 1.

**sport,** *n.* **1.** [Entertainment] — *Syn.* diversion, recreation, play, amusement, merrymaking, jollification, festivity, revelry, revel, Saturnalia, carnival, pastime, pleasure, enjoyment; see also **entertainment** 2, **fun, game** 1.

**2.** [A joke] — *Syn.* raillery, pleasantry, mockery, jest, jesting, mirth, joking, mummery, antics, trifling, tomfoolery, nonsense, jollity, laughter, drollery, escapade, practical joke.

**3.** [Athletic or competitive amusement] — *Syn.* game, competition, contest, athletic event, amateur sport, professional sport.

Sports, sense 3, include: hunting, shooting, horse racing, automobile racing, running, dog racing, cockfighting, bronco busting, bullfighting, polo, horseback riding; fishing, angling, basketball, golf, bowling, billiards, pool, tennis, squash, handball, racquetball, table tennis, volleyball, soccer, gymnastics, acrobatics, football, baseball, track and field, cricket, lacrosse, ice hockey, field hockey, skating, skiing, cross-country skiing, snowboarding, snowshoeing; fencing, jumping, boxing, wrestling, hang gliding, parasailing, parachuting; windsurfing, diving, surfing, snorkeling, water skiing, swimming, canoeing, kayaking, yachting; hiking, camping, backpacking, rock climbing, ice climbing; bicycling, motorcycling, Rollerblading, in-line skating, skateboarding; weightlifting, bodybuilding, powerlifting.

**4.** [\*A person with sporting instincts] — *Syn.* gambler, irresponsible fellow, horsey person, rake, one of the fast set; see also **clown, rascal.**

**for** *or* **in sport** — *Syn.* jokingly, in fun, jestingly; see **humorously.**

**sport\*,** *v.* — *Syn.* don, have on, be dressed in; see **wear** 1.

**sporting,** *modif.* **1.** [Interested in sport] — *Syn.* gaming, showy, flashy; see **jaunty.**

**2.** [Fair or more than fair] — *Syn.* considerate, sportsmanlike, gentlemanly; see **generous** 1, **reasonable** 2.

**sportive,** *modif.* — *Syn.* gay, playful, sprightly; see **active** 2, **jaunty.**

**sportsman,** *n.* — *Syn.* huntsman, big game hunter, woodsman; see **fisherman, hunter** 1.

**sportsmanship,** *n.* **1.** [Skill] — *Syn.* facility, dexterity, cunning; see **ability** 2.

**2.** [Honor] — *Syn.* justice, integrity, truthfulness, fairness; see **honesty** 2.

**spot,** *modif.* — *Syn.* prompt, ready, instantaneous; see **immediate** 1.

**spot,** *n.* **1.** [A dot] — *Syn.* speck, flaw, pimple; see **bit** 1, **blemish.**

**2.** [A place] — *Syn.* point, locality, scene; see **place** 3.

**3.** [Small amount] — *Syn.* minute quantity, little bit, pinch; see **bit** 1.

**hit the high spots\*** — *Syn.* **1.** hurry, travel rapidly, make good time\*; see **speed.**

**2.** treat hastily, go over lightly, touch up; see **neglect** 1, 2.

**hit the spot\*** — *Syn.* please, delight, taste good, be just right; see **satisfy** 1.

**in a bad spot\*** — *Syn.* in danger, in trouble, in difficulty, threatened, in a bad situation, on the spot\*; see also **dangerous** 1, 2.

**on the spot 1.** [Quickly] — *Syn.* immediately, now, at once; see **immediately.**

**2.** [\*In trouble] — *Syn.* in danger, in difficulty, in a corner.

**spot,** *v.* **1.** [Stain] — *Syn.* blemish, blotch, splatter; see **dirty, spatter.**

**2.** [Point out] — *Syn.* find, detect, recognize; see **locate** 1.

**spotless,** *modif.* — *Syn.* stainless, immaculate, without spot, without blemish; see **clean** 1, **pure** 2.

**spotlight,** *n.* **1.** [Light] — *Syn.* limelight, floodlight, flashlight; see **lamp, light** 3.

**2.** [Publicity] — *Syn.* attention, notoriety, publicity; see **fame** 1.

**spotted,** *modif.* **1.** [Dotted] — *Syn.* marked, dappled, blotchy; see **speckled.**

**2.** [Blemished] — *Syn.* soiled, smudged, smeared; see **dirty** 1.

**spotty,** *modif.* — *Syn.* uneven, dotted, unequal; see **irregular** 4.

**spouse,** *n.* — *Syn.* marriage partner, groom, bride; see **husband, mate** 3, **wife.**

**spout,** *v.* — *Syn.* squirt, discharge, pour, spew; see **emit** 1.

**spout off\*,** *v.* — *Syn.* brag, chatter, shoot off one's mouth\*; see **boast, talk** 1, **yell.**

**sprain,** *n.* — *Syn.* twist, overstrain, strain; see **injury** 1.

**sprained,** *modif.* — *Syn.* wrenched, strained, pulled out of place; see **hurt, twisted** 1.

**sprawl,** *v.* — *Syn.* stretch out, spread out, slouch, relax, lounge; see also **lie** 3, **sit** 1.

**spray,** *n.* — *Syn.* splash, spindrift, fine mist, shower; see **fog** 1, **froth.**

**spray,** *v.* — *Syn.* scatter, diffuse, sprinkle; see **spatter.**

**spread,** *modif.* — *Syn.* expanded, dispersed, extended, opened, unfurled, sown, scattered, diffused, strewn, spread thin, disseminated, overflowed, broadcast; see also **distributed.** — *Ant.* RESTRICTED, narrowed, restrained.

**spread,** *n.* **1.** [Extent] — *Syn.* scope, range, expanse; see **extent, measure** 1.

**2.** [A spread cloth] — *Syn.* blanket, coverlet, counterpane; see **bedspread, cover** 1, **tablecloth.**

**3.** [A spread food] — *Syn.* preserve, conserve, jelly; see butter, cheese, preserves.

**4.** [*A meal] — *Syn.* feast, banquet, informal repast; see **dinner, lunch, meal** 2.

**spread,** *v.* **1.** [To distribute] — *Syn.* cast, diffuse, disseminate; see **radiate** 1, **scatter** 2, **sow.**

**2.** [To become spread] — *Syn.* lie, flatten, level, flow, even out, be distributed, settle.

**3.** [To extend] — *Syn.* open, unfurl, roll out, unroll, unfold, reach, circulate, lengthen, widen, expand, untwist, unwind, uncoil, enlarge, increase, develop, radiate, branch off, diverge, expand; see also **grow** 1, **reach** 1. — *Ant.* CLOSE, shorten, shrink.

**4.** [To apply over a surface] — *Syn.* cover, coat, smear, daub, overlay, overspread, plate, gloss, enamel, paint, spatter, spray, veneer, plaster, gild, pave, diffuse, wax, varnish.

**5.** [To separate] — *Syn.* part, sever, disperse; see **divide** 1, **separate** 2.

**6.** [To make known] — *Syn.* publish, broadcast, proclaim; see **advertise** 1, **declare** 1.

**spreading,** *modif.* — *Syn.* extended, extensive, spread out, growing, widening, ever-widening, parasitic, radial.

**spread on,** *v.* — *Syn.* coat, cover, smear on; see **spread** 4.

**spread oneself*,** *v.* — *Syn.* live lavishly, entertain extravagantly, try to make an impression, go whole hog*; see **celebrate** 3, **spend** 1.

**spread oneself thin*,** *v.* — *Syn.* expand, proliferate, do too many things at once, attempt too much; see **increase** 1, **spread** 3, **try** 1.

**spree,** *n.* **1.** [A lively frolic] — *Syn.* revel, frolic, binge; see **celebration** 1, 2, **orgy.**

**2.** [Uninhibited activity] — *Syn.* binge, bout, shopping spree, shooting spree.

**sprig,** *modif.* — *Syn.* twig, slip, shoot; see **branch** 2, **stalk.**

**sprightly,** *modif.* — *Syn.* animated, brisk, lively, light, nimble, agile, quick, jaunty, spry, dapper, bright, spirited, energetic, vivacious, lighthearted, buoyant, frolicsome, playful, coltish, cheerful, gay, jolly, blithe, saucy, cheery, bouncy, perky, airy, chipper*. — *Ant.* DULL, morose, lethargic.

*See Synonym Study at* AGILE, LIVELY.

**spring,** *n.* **1.** [A fountain] — *Syn.* flowing well, artesian well, sweet water; see **fountain** 2, **origin** 2.

**2.** [The season between winter and summer] — *Syn.* springtime, seedtime, vernal season, flowering, budding, sowing-time, vernal equinox, blackberry winter*; see also **April, June, May, season.**

**3.** [Origin] — *Syn.* source, cause, beginning, font, fountain; see also **origin** 3.

**spring a leak,** *v.* — *Syn.* start leaking, develop a leak, be perforated, be punctured; see **leak** 2.

**springy,** *modif.* — *Syn.* pliable, wiry, light; see **flexible** 1.

**sprinkle,** *v.* — *Syn.* dampen, bedew, spray; see **moisten, spatter.**

**sprinkling,** *n.* — *Syn.* handful, few, mixture; see **several** 1.

**sprint,** *n.* — *Syn.* burst of speed, dash, supreme effort; see **race** 3.

**sprint,** *v.* — *Syn.* rush, dash, work at top speed; see **race** 1, **run** 2.

**sprinter,** *n.* — *Syn.* short-distance runner, one in the dashes, one who sprints, track runner; see **runner.**

**sprite,** *n.* — *Syn.* nymph, elf, goblin; see **fairy** 1.

**sprout,** *v.* — *Syn.* germinate, take root, shoot up, bud, burgeon; see also **grow** 1.

**spruce,** *modif.* — *Syn.* trim, tidy, well-groomed; see

neat 1.

**spry,** *modif.* — *Syn.* nimble, agile, active, vigorous; see **active** 2, **agile.**

*See Synonym Study at* AGILE.

**spume,** *n.* — *Syn.* spray, foam, scum; see **froth.**

**spume,** *v.* — *Syn.* boil, ferment, foam; see **bubble** 1.

**spunk*,** *n.* — *Syn.* spirit, courage, nerve; see **courage** 1.

**spur,** *v.* — *Syn.* goad, prick, impel; see **drive** 1, 2, **encourage** 2, **push** 2.

**on the spur of the moment** — *Syn.* suddenly, without a second thought, spontaneously, impulsively; see **quickly** 2.

**spurious,** *modif.* — *Syn.* counterfeit, apocryphal, deceptive; see **artificial** 1, **false** 2, 3.

*See Synonym Study at* ARTIFICIAL.

**spurn,** *v.* — *Syn.* refuse, reject, despise, disdain, look down on, hold in contempt; see also **evade** 1, **scorn** 2, **shun.**

*See Synonym Study at* REFUSE.

**spurt,** *n.* **1.** [A stream] — *Syn.* squirt, jet, stream; see **fountain** 2.

**2.** [An eruption] — *Syn.* explosion, commotion, discharge; see **outbreak** 1.

**spurt,** *v.* — *Syn.* spout, jet, burst; see **flow** 2.

**sputnik,** *n.* — *Syn.* orbital rocket, artificial moon, unmanned satellite; see **satellite** 2, **spacecraft.**

**sputter,** *v.* — *Syn.* stumble, stutter, falter; see **stammer.**

**spy,** *n.* — *Syn.* secret agent, intelligence agent, counterintelligence agent, counterspy, operative, espionage agent, double agent, emissary, scout, detective, observer, watcher, wiretapper, intelligencer, undercover man, secret-service agent, peeping Tom, mole*, spook*, Mata Hari*.

**spy,** *v.* **1.** [To see] — *Syn.* view, behold, descry; see **see** 1.

**2.** [To act as a spy] — *Syn.* scout, observe, watch, examine, scrutinize, take note, search, discover, look for, hunt, turn over, peer, pry, spy upon, set a watch on, hound, trail, follow, gumshoe*, heel*, sleuth*, spot*, fish out*; see also **meddle** 1, 2.

**spying,** *n.* — *Syn.* overflight, watching, observing, prying, following, wiretapping, voyeurism; see also **interference** 2, **intrusion.**

**squabble,** *n.* — *Syn.* wrangle, bickering, quarrel, spat*; see **dispute.**

*See Synonym Study at* QUARREL.

**squabble,** *v.* — *Syn.* argue, disagree, fight; see **quarrel.**

**squad,** *n.* — *Syn.* company, unit, crew; see **team** 1, 2.

**squadron,** *n.* — *Syn.* unit, group, wing; see **fleet.**

**squalid,** *modif.* — *Syn.* dirty, filthy, unclean, poor, poverty-stricken, mean, grimy, soiled, foul, reeking, ordurous, nasty, abominable, slimy, slummocky, sloshy, ill-smelling, feculent, odious, repellent, gruesome, horrid, horrible, sordid, ramshackle, besmeared, sloppy, smutty, muddy, miry, lutose, dingy, reeky, fetid, moldy, musty, fusty, offensive. — *Ant.* CLEAN, pure, spotless.

**squall,** *n.* — *Syn.* blast, gust, gale, brief gale, tempest, blow*, restricted storm; see also **storm** 1.

**squall,** *v.* — *Syn.* yell, whine, whimper; see **cry** 3.

**squally,** *modif.* — *Syn.* windy, raging, turbulent; see **stormy** 1.

**squalor,** *n.* — *Syn.* ugliness, disorder, uncleanness, misery, wretchedness; see also **filth, poverty** 1.

**squander,** *v.* — *Syn.* spend, spend lavishly, throw away, fritter away; see **waste** 2.

**square,** *modif.* **1.** [Having right angles] — *Syn.* right-angled, four-sided, equal-sided, foursquare, squared, equilateral, rectangular, rectilinear.

**2.** [*Old-fashioned] — *Syn.* dated, stuffy, conventional, conformist, boring; see also **conservative, dull** 3, **old-fashioned.**

**square,** *n.* **1.** [A rectangle] — *Syn.* equal-sided rectangle, plane figure, rectilinear plane; see **rectangle.**

**2.** [A park] — *Syn.* city center, civic center, intersection, plaza, traffic circle, open space, recreational area; see also **park** 1.

**on the square** — *Syn.* just, fair, decent; see **honest** 1, **reasonable** 2.

**square deal,** *n.* — *Syn.* fair dealing, honest dealing, just dealing, justice, consideration; see also **honesty** 1, 2.

**squarely,** *modif.* — *Syn.* honestly, considerately, fairly; see **justly** 1.

**square off,** *v.* — *Syn.* take a stance, be on guard, face, box, threaten, put up one's fists; see also **fight** 2.

**squash,** *n.* **1.** [A vegetable]. Varieties of squash include: winter, Hubbard, butternut, pumpkin, turban, winter crookneck, Canada crookneck, cushaw, summer, scallop, Italian, zucchini, straightneck, summer crookneck, acorn, pattypan, spaghetti, chayote, white bush, white bush scalloped, warted Hubbard, green, banana, yellow crookneck, Danish; see also **vegetable.**

**2.** [A court game] — *Syn.* squash racquets, squash tennis, racquet ball.

**squash,** *v.* — *Syn.* mash, crush, flatten, pulverize; see **mash.**

**squashy,** *modif.* — *Syn.* soft, marshy, pulpy; see **wet** 1.

**squat,** *modif.* — *Syn.* stocky, broad, heavy, thickset, stubby; see also **fat** 1, **short** 1.

**squat,** *v.* — *Syn.* stoop, hunch, cower; see **bow** 1, **sit** 1.

**squatter,** *n.* — *Syn.* colonist, homesteader, settler, illegal tenant; see **pioneer** 2.

**squaw***,* *n.* — *Syn.* Native American woman, Indian woman, wife*; see **Indian** 1, **woman** 1.

**squawk,** *v.* — *Syn.* cackle, crow, yap; see **cry** 3.

**squeak,** *n.* — *Syn.* peep, squeal, shrill sound; see **cry** 2, **noise** 1.

**squeak,** *v.* — *Syn.* creak, screech, scritch, peep, squeal, scream, pipe; see also **cry** 3, **sound** 1.

**squeak through***,* *v.* — *Syn.* manage, survive, get by*; see **endure** 2, **succeed** 1.

**squeal,** *v.* — *Syn.* shout, yell, screech; see **cry** 1, 3.

**squeamish,** *modif.* — *Syn.* finicky, fussy, mincing, delicate, dainty, qualmish, fastidious, hypercritical, particular, exacting, oversensitive, prim, prudish, strait-laced, puritanical, priggish, easily nauseated, readily disgusted, easily shocked, queasy, persnickety*, prissy*; see also **particular** 3.

*See Synonym Study at* PARTICULAR.

**squeeze,** *n.* **1.** [Pressure] — *Syn.* influence, restraint, force; see **pressure** 1, 2.

**2.** [An embrace] — *Syn.* hug, clasp, handshake; see **hug.**

**put the squeeze on*** — *Syn.* compel, urge, extort, use force with, use pressure with, use compulsion with; see also **force** 1, **influence.**

**squeeze,** *v.* **1.** [To exert pressure] — *Syn.* clasp, pinch, clutch, compress; see **hug, press** 1.

**2.** [To extract with pressure] — *Syn.* juice, milk, press; see **remove** 1.

**squeeze through***,* *v.* — *Syn.* survive, accomplish, get by*, squeak through; see **endure** 1, **succeed** 1.

**squelch,** *v.* — *Syn.* crush, oppress, thwart; see **censure, suppress.**

**squib,** *n.* — *Syn.* satire, burlesque, spoof; see **parody.**

**squint,** *v.* — *Syn.* look askance, give a sidelong look, look asquint, cock the eye, screw up the eyes, peek, peep; see

also **glare** 2, **look** 2.

**squint-eyed,** *modif.* **1.** [Cockeyed] — *Syn.* cross-eyed, wall-eyed, cockeyed; see **blind** 1.

**2.** [Skeptical] — *Syn.* suspicious, sinister, questioning; see **prejudiced.**

**squire,** *n.* **1.** [An attendant] — *Syn.* attendant, valet, assistant; see **servant.**

**2.** [An escort] — *Syn.* chaperon, gallant, cavalier; see **companion** 2, **date** 3, **escort.**

**squire,** *v.* — *Syn.* assist, conduct, escort; see **accompany** 1.

**squirm,** *v.* — *Syn.* wriggle, twist, fidget; see **wiggle.**

**squirt,** *v.* — *Syn.* spurt, spit, eject; see **emit** 1, **flow** 2.

**stab,** *n.* — *Syn.* thrust, prick, cut, hurt, knife thrust, bayonet thrust, wound, puncture, blow, piercing, stick, transfixion.

**make a stab at** — *Syn.* endeavor, try to, do one's best; see **try** 1.

**stab,** *v.* — *Syn.* transfix, pierce, wound, stick, cut, hurt, thrust, prick, drive, puncture, hit, bayonet, saber, knife; see also **kill** 1.

**stability,** *n.* **1.** [Firmness of position] — *Syn.* steadiness, durability, solidity, endurance, substantiality, immobility, suspense, immovability, inaction, establishment, solidness, balance, permanence.

**2.** [Steadfastness of character] — *Syn.* stableness, aplomb, security, endurance, maturity, constancy, resoluteness, determination, perseverance, adherence, backbone, assurance, resistance; see also **confidence** 2.

**stabilize,** *v.* **1.** [To fix] — *Syn.* bolt, secure, steady; see **fasten** 1.

**2.** [To support] — *Syn.* maintain, uphold, preserve; see **support** 2, **sustain** 1.

**stab in the back***,* *v.* — *Syn.* double-cross, deceive, undercut, turn traitor; see **betray** 1, **trick.**

**stable,** *modif.* **1.** [Fixed] — *Syn.* steady, stationary, solid; see **firm** 1.

**2.** [Steadfast] — *Syn.* calm, firm, constant; see **resolute** 2.

**3.** [Permanent] — *Syn.* enduring, well-built, durable; see **permanent** 1.

**stable,** *n.* — *Syn.* shelter, barn, coop, corral, hutch, kennel; see also **pen** 1.

**stable,** *v.* — *Syn.* pen, corral, put up; see **tend** 1.

**stableboy,** *n.* — *Syn.* stableman, groom, hand*; see **servant.**

**stack,** *n.* **1.** [A heap] — *Syn.* haystack, rick, pile, mass, mound; see also **haystack, heap.**

**2.** [A tall chimney] — *Syn.* flue, smokestack, pipe; see **chimney.**

**stack,** *v.* — *Syn.* rick, pile, accumulate; see **heap** 1.

**stacked,** *modif.* **1.** [Put away] — *Syn.* stored, stashed, put aside; see **kept** 2, **saved** 1, 2.

**2.** [*Amply proportioned; *said of women*] — *Syn.* shapely, well-proportioned, built*; see **buxom** 1.

**stack the deck** *or* **the cards***,* *v.* — *Syn.* prearrange, deceive, set up; see **arrange** 2, **trick.**

**stack up***,* *v.* — *Syn.* become, work out, resolve into; see **result.**

**stadium,** *n.* — *Syn.* ballpark, gymnasium, strand, amphitheater; see **arena.**

**staff,** *n.* **1.** [A stick] — *Syn.* wand, pole, stave; see **club** 3, **stick.**

**2.** [A corps of employees] — *Syn.* personnel, assistants, force, help, workers, crew, team, organization, agents, faculty, cadre, cast, operatives, deputies, servants, factotums, officers.

**3.** [An officer's assistants] — *Syn.* junior officers, corps, aides-de-camp, escort, guard of honor.

**stage,** *n.* **1.** [The theater] — *Syn.* boards, scene, parascene, limelight*, spotlight*; see also **drama** 1.

**2.** [A platform] — *Syn.* frame, scaffold, staging; see **platform** 1.

**3.** [A level, period, or degree] — *Syn.* grade, plane, step; see **degree** 1.

**by easy stages** — *Syn.* easily, gently, taking one's time*, one stop at a time; see **slowly.**

**stagecraft,** *n.* — *Syn.* acting ability, histrionics, theater, dramatics; see **acting.**

**stagehand,** *n.* — *Syn.* prompter, carpenter, costumer; see **worker.**

**stagger,** *v.* — *Syn.* totter, waver, vacillate; see **reel.**

**staggering,** *modif.* — *Syn.* monstrous, huge, tremendous; see **large** 1, **unbelievable.**

**staging,** *n.* **1.** [A production] — *Syn.* presentation, preparation, adaptation; see **acting.**

**2.** [A stage] — *Syn.* enclosure, scaffold, stage; see **frame** 1, **platform** 1.

**stagnant,** *modif.* **1.** [Still] — *Syn.* inert, dead, inactive; see **idle** 1.

**2.** [Filthy] — *Syn.* putrid, foul, filthy; see **dirty** 1.

**3.** [Dull] — *Syn.* dormant, lifeless, passive; see **listless** 1.

**stagnate,** *v.* — *Syn.* deteriorate, rot, putrefy; see **decay.**

**stagy,** *modif.* — *Syn.* showy, thespian, dramatic, affected; see **theatrical** 1.

**staid,** *modif.* — *Syn.* sober, grave, steady; see **dignified.**

**stain,** *n.* — *Syn.* blot, smirch, blemish, spot, mottle, splotch, blotch, stained spot, smudge, discoloration, stigma, brand, blot on the escutcheon, something the matter, ink spot, spatter, drip, speck.

**stain,** *v.* **1.** [To soil] — *Syn.* spot, discolor, taint; see **dirty.**

**2.** [To color] — *Syn.* dye, tint, lacquer; see **color** 1, **paint** 2, **varnish.**

**stairs,** *n.* — *Syn.* stairway, staircase, flight, companionway, steps, stair, escalator, moving stair, spiral staircase, open stairway, closed stairway, ascent.

**stake,** *n.* — *Syn.* rod, paling, pale; see **post** 1, **stick.**

**at stake** — *Syn.* at issue, in danger, risked, at risk, involved, in question, concerned, implicated; see also **endangered.**

**pull up stakes*** — *Syn.* depart, move, decamp; see **leave** 1.

**stale,** *modif.* **1.** [Old or musty] — *Syn.* spoiled, dried, smelly; see **musty** 2, **old** 2.

**2.** [Dull and trite] — *Syn.* mawkish, hackneyed, fusty; see **dull** 4.

**stalemate,** *n.* — *Syn.* deadlock, standstill, check; see **delay** 1, **pause** 2.

**stalk,** *n.* — *Syn.* stem, support, axis, pedicle, petiole, peduncle, stipe, stipes, seta, upright, quill, stack, caulis, caulicle, spire, shaft, helm, bent, scape, funicle, spike, stipel, tigella, straw, boon, bennet, stock; see also **trunk** 3.

**stalk,** *v.* — *Syn.* approach stealthily, track, chase, shadow; see **hunt** 1, **pursue** 1.

**stall,** *v.* **1.** [To break down] — *Syn.* not start, not turn over, stop working, conk out*, go dead*; see also **break down** 3.

**2.** [To delay] — *Syn.* postpone, hamper, hinder; see **delay** 1.

**stallion,** *n.* — *Syn.* stud horse, stud, steed, animal, quadruped; see also **horse** 1.

**stalwart,** *modif.* **1.** [Strong] — *Syn.* sturdy, robust, vigorous; see **strong** 1.

**2.** [Brave] — *Syn.* valiant, valorous, bold; see **brave** 1.

**stamina,** *n.* — *Syn.* strength, vigor, vitality; see **endurance.**

**stammer,** *v.* — *Syn.* falter, stop, stumble, hesitate, pause, block one's utterance, stutter, repeat oneself, sputter, halt, hem and haw.

**stamp,** *n.* **1.** [An imprint] — *Syn.* emblem, brand, cast; see **impression** 1, **imprint** 1, **mark** 1.

**2.** [A postage stamp] — *Syn.* franking, seal, postage, Christmas seal, Easter seal, trading stamp.

**3.** [A machine or tool for stamping] — *Syn.* press, die, punch, mold.

**stamp,** *v.* — *Syn.* impress, imprint, brand; see **mark** 1.

**stamped,** *modif.* — *Syn.* marked, branded, imprinted, okayed*, O.K.'d*; see also **approved.**

**stampede,** *n.* — *Syn.* rush, dash, flight, rout; see **run** 1.

**stampede,** *v.* — *Syn.* bolt, rush, panic; see **run** 2.

**stamp out,** *v.* — *Syn.* eliminate, kill off, dispatch; see **destroy** 1, **kill** 1, **remove** 1.

**stance,** *n.* — *Syn.* posture, carriage, stand, attitude; see **attitude** 1, **position** 5, **posture** 1.

*See Synonym Study at* POSTURE.

**stanchion,** *n.* — *Syn.* stay, prop, bolster; see **beam** 1, **brace** 1, **support** 2.

**stand,** *n.* **1.** [Position] — *Syn.* notion, view, belief; see **attitude** 2, **opinion** 1.

**2.** [A platform] — *Syn.* stage, gantry, station; see **platform** 1.

**make** *or* **take a stand*** — *Syn.* insist, assert, take a position; see **declare** 1, **fight** 1, 2, **say.**

**take the stand** — *Syn.* bear witness, give evidence, give testimony, be sworn in; see **testify.**

**stand,** *v.* **1.** [To be in an upright position] — *Syn.* be erect, be on one's feet, stand up, come to one's feet, rise, jump up*.

**2.** [To endure] — *Syn.* last, persist, survive, hold; see **endure** 1.

**3.** [To tolerate] — *Syn.* endure, bear, withstand; see **endure** 2.

**4.** [To be of a certain height] — *Syn.* be, attain, come to; see **reach** 1.

**5.** [To be situated] — *Syn.* fill, hold, take up; see **occupy** 2.

**6.** [To oppose] — *Syn.* withstand, stand against, confront; see **compete, oppose** 1.

**7.** [*To pay for] — *Syn.* bear the cost, stand the expense, make payment; see **pay** 1.

*See Synonym Study at* ENDURE.

**stand a chance,** *v.* — *Syn.* have a chance, be a likelihood, be a possibility, be a probability, have something in one's favor, have something on one's side, be preferred.

**standard,** *modif.* — *Syn.* regular, usual, regulation, made to a standard; see **approved, conventional** 1, **official** 3.

**standard,** *n.* **1.** [Flag] — *Syn.* pennant, banner, colors; see **flag** 1.

**2.** [Emblem] — *Syn.* symbol, figure, insignia; see **emblem.**

**3.** [Measure] — *Syn.* criterion, gauge, yardstick, example, rule, test; see also **criterion, measure** 2.

**4.** [Model] — *Syn.* pattern, type, example, norm; see **model** 2.

*See Synonym Study at* MODEL.

---

**SYN. — standard** applies to some measure, principle, model, etc. with which things of the same class are compared in order to determine their quantity, value, quality, etc. [*standard* of purity for drugs]; **criterion** applies to a test or rule for measuring the excellence, fitness, or correctness of something, especially of an abstraction /mere memory is no accurate *criterion* of intelligence/; **gauge** literally applies to a standard of measurement /a wire *gauge*/, but figuratively it is equivalent to **criterion** /sales are an accurate *gauge* of a book's popularity/; **yardstick** refers to a test or criterion for measuring genuineness or value /time is the only true *yardstick* of a book's merit/

---

**standard-bearer,** *n.* — *Syn.* commander, demagogue, boss, leading light; see **leader** 2.

**standardization,** *n.* — *Syn.* uniformity, sameness, likeness, evenness, levelness, monotony; see also **regularity.**

**standardize,** *v.* — *Syn.* regulate, institute, normalize; see **order** 3, **systematize.**

**standardized,** *modif.* — *Syn.* patterned, graded, made alike; see **regulated.**

**standardizing,** *modif.* — *Syn.* normative, normalizing, regulating, regularizing, regulative, balancing, determining, controlling, shifting, directive, directing, influencing, bringing to a norm.

**stand-by,** *n.* — *Syn.* upholder, supporter, advocate; see **patron** 1, **protector.**

**stand by,** *v.* **1.** [To defend or help] — *Syn.* befriend, second, abet; see **defend** 2, 3, **help** 1, **sustain** 3.
**2.** [To wait] — *Syn.* be prepared, be ready, be near; see **wait** 1.

**stand for,** *v.* **1.** [To mean] — *Syn.* represent, suggest, imply; see **mean** 1.
**2.** [*To allow] — *Syn.* permit, suffer, endure; see **allow** 1.

**stand-in,** *n.* — *Syn.* double, second, understudy; see **assistant, substitute.**

**standing,** *n.* — *Syn.* position, status, reputation; see **rank** 3.

**standoff,** *n.* — *Syn.* stalemate, deadlock, draw, dead end; see **delay** 1, **pause** 2, **tie** 4.

**standoffish,** *modif.* — *Syn.* cool, aloof, distant; see **indifferent** 1, **reserved** 3.

**stand one's ground,** *v.* — *Syn.* oppose, fight back, resist; see **defend** 1, **fight** 1, 2.

**stand out,** *v.* — *Syn.* be prominent, be conspicuous, emerge; see **loom** 2.

**stand pat*,** *v.* — *Syn.* stay, persist, insist on no change; see **remain** 1.

**standpoint,** *n.* — *Syn.* attitude, point of view, station; see **viewpoint.**

**stand someone in good stead,** *v.* — *Syn.* give someone good use, be of advantage, be useful.

**standstill,** *n.* — *Syn.* stop, halt, cessation; see **delay** 1, **pause** 2.

**stand up for,** *v.* — *Syn.* back, protect, champion; see **defend** 3, **support** 2, 3.

**stand up to,** *v.* — *Syn.* resist, oppose, challenge; see **fight** 1, 2.

**Stanford,** *n.* — *Syn.* Leland, Stanford Junior University, The Farm*, Leland's Racehorse Farm*, Indians*, Red and White*, Hoover's Hayfield*; see also **university.**

**stanza,** *n.* — *Syn.* stave, refrain, strophe; see **verse** 2.

**staple,** *modif.* — *Syn.* standard, chief, essential; see **necessary** 1, **principal.**

**star,** *n.* **1.** [A luminous heavenly body] — *Syn.* sun, astral body, pulsar, quasar, Seyfert galaxy, quasi-stellar object, sidereal body, fixed star, variable star, lamp*, twinkler*.

Classes of stars include: fixed, binary, multiple, supergiant, red giant, medium yellow, white dwarf, supernova, neutron star, black dwarf, black hole, star cluster, star cloud, interstellar cloud, protostar, pulsar.

Familiar stars include — *individual stars:* Betelgeuse, Sirius, Vega, Spica, Arcturus, Aldebaran, Antares, Atlas, Castor, Pollux, Procyon, Cappella, Algol, North Star, Polaris; *constellations:* Great Bear, Ursa Major, Little Bear, Ursa Minor, Big Dipper, Little Dipper, Orion, Coma Berenices, Berenice's Hair, The Gemini, Castor and Pollux, Cassiopeia, Pleiades, Hyades, Andromeda, Taurus, Canis Major, the Great Dog, Canis Minor, the Little Dog, Scorpion, Sagittarius, Corona Borealis, the Northern Crown, Pegasus, Leo, Hercules, Boötes, Cetus, Aquila, the Eagle, Cygnus, the Swan, Corona Australis *or* the Southern Crown, the Southern Cross.

**2.** [A conventional figure]. Forms of stars include: asterisk, pentacle, pentagram, hexagram, etoile, mullet, six-pointed star, five-pointed star, Star of David; see also **form** 1.

**3.** [A superior performer] — *Syn.* headliner, leading lady, leading man, movie actor, movie actress, actor, actress, favorite, player, matinee idol, chief attraction, lead, starlet*, topliner*, luminary*, the flash*.

**starch,** *n.* **1.** [A laundering agent] — *Syn.* stiffening, sizing, laundry starch, cornstarch, arrowroot starch, spray starch.
**2.** [A complex carbohydrate] — *Syn.* glycogen, polysaccharide, carbohydrate; see **carbohydrate, sugar.**
**3.** [A stiff bearing] — *Syn.* stiffness, formality, ceremony, decorum.
**4.** [Vigor] — *Syn.* energy, vitality, stamina; see **vigor** 1, 2.

**starch,** *v.* — *Syn.* dip in starch, add starch, make stiff; see **stiffen** 2, **thicken** 2.

**stare,** *v.* — *Syn.* gaze, gawk, look fixedly; see **look** 2, **watch** 1.

**staring,** *modif.* — *Syn.* bald, stary, fixed; see **dull** 3.

**stark,** *modif.* — *Syn.* stiff, firm, severe; see **abrupt** 2.

**stark-naked,** *modif.* — *Syn.* nude, without a stitch of clothing, in the altogether*, in one's birthday suit*; see **naked** 1.

**starlight,** *modif.* — *Syn.* luminous, lustrous, shining; see **bright** 1, **shimmering.**

**starlight,** *n.* — *Syn.* gleam, glimmer, twinkle; see **light** 3.

**starlike,** *modif.* — *Syn.* shining, radiant, shiny; see **bright** 1, **shimmering.**

**starred,** *modif.* — *Syn.* selected, choice, designated; see **excellent, special** 1.

**starry,** *modif.* **1.** [Shiny] — *Syn.* luminous, lustrous, shining; see **bright** 1, **shimmering.**
**2.** [Stellar] — *Syn.* celestial, heavenly, astronomical; see **stellar.**

**start,** *n.* **1.** [The beginning] — *Syn.* inception, commencement, inauguration; see **origin** 1.
**2.** [The point at which a start is made] — *Syn.* source, derivation, spring; see **origin** 2.

**start,** *v.* **1.** [To begin] — *Syn.* commence, rise, spring, get under way; see **begin** 1.
**2.** [To cause to start, sense 1] — *Syn.* inaugurate, start off, originate, embark upon; see **begin** 1, **cause** 2.
**3.** [To arouse] — *Syn.* rouse, incite, light; see **excite** 2.
**4.** [To cause to ignite] — *Syn.* light, set on fire, fire; see **ignite.**
*See Synonym Study at* BEGIN.

**started,** *modif.* — *Syn.* evoked, initiated, instituted; see **begun.**

**starter,** *n.* — *Syn.* innovator, initiator, beginner, opener, master, originator, pioneer, father of, inventor, moving spirit, leading spirit, spark plug*; see also **author** 1.
— *Ant.* FOLLOWER, adherent, successor.

**start in,** *v.* — *Syn.* commence, open, make a start, make a beginning, make the first move; see also **begin** 1, 2.

**starting,** *n.* — *Syn.* offset, outset, opening; see **origin** 2.

**startle,** *v.* — *Syn.* alarm, shock, astonish, disturb, agitate; see also **frighten** 1, **surprise** 2.

**startled,** *modif.* — *Syn.* frightened, alarmed, shocked; see **surprised.**

**startling,** *modif.* — *Syn.* shocking, alarming, unexpected; see **frightful** 1.

**start off** *or* **out,** *v.* — *Syn.* depart, begin a journey, begin a trip, go; see **leave** 1.

**start up,** *v.* **1.** [To begin to rise] — *Syn.* recover, go up, shoot up; see **rise** 1, 3.
**2.** [To activate] — *Syn.* make go, make run, crank up, get a thing started; see **begin** 1.

**starvation,** *n.* — *Syn.* deprivation, belt tightening, need, want, inanition; see also **hunger.**

**starve,** *v.* **1.** [To become weak or die from hunger] — *Syn.* famish, crave, perish; see **die** 1, **weaken** 1.
**2.** [To cause to starve, sense 1] — *Syn.* underfeed, undernourish, deprive of food, kill, withhold nourishment; see also **weaken** 2.

**starving,** *modif.* — *Syn.* famished, weakening, dying; see **hungry.**

**state,** *n.* **1.** [A sovereign unit] — *Syn.* republic, land, kingdom; see **country** 3, **nation** 1.
**2.** [A condition] — *Syn.* circumstance, situation, welfare, phase, case, station, nature, estate, time, footing, status, standing, stipulation, proviso, contingency, juncture, occurrence, occasion, eventuality, element, prerequisite, imperative, essential, requirement, limitation, category, standing, reputation, environment, chances, outlook, position, event, accompaniment.
**3.** [A difficulty] — *Syn.* plight, pinch, quandary; see **difficulty** 1, **predicament.**
**4.** [Mood] — *Syn.* frame of mind, humor, disposition; see **mood** 1.

**in a state** — *Syn.* disturbed, upset, badly off; see **confused, troubled** 1, 2.

*SYN.* — **state** and **condition** both refer to the set of circumstances surrounding or characterizing a person or thing at a given time [what is his mental *state*, or *condition?*], but **condition** more strongly implies some relationship to causes or circumstances that may be temporary [his *condition* will not permit him to travel]; **situation** implies a significant set of interrelated circumstances, and a connection between these and the person involved [to be in a difficult *situation*]; **status** refers to one's position as determined by legal or customary precedent or by such arbitrary factors as age, sex, training, mentality, service, etc. [his *status* as a veteran exempts him]

**state,** *v.* — *Syn.* pronounce, assert, affirm; see **declare** 1, **say.**

**statecraft,** *n.* — *Syn.* statesmanship, diplomacy, senatorship; see **tact.**

**stated,** *modif.* — *Syn.* established, fixed, regular, aforesaid; see **told.**

**stately,** *modif.* **1.** [Said of persons] — *Syn.* lordly, dignified, proud, imperious, haughty, stiff, formal, noble, solemn, august, ceremonious, pompous, imperious, regal, royal, kingly, imperial, masterful. — *Ant.* SIMPLE, unassuming, modest.
**2.** [Said of objects] — *Syn.* large, grand, spacious, lofty, imposing, elevated, high, majestic, magnificent, sumptuous, palatial, opulent, superb, luxurious, monumental, impressive. — *Ant.* POOR, cheap, lowly.

*See Synonym Study at* GRAND.

**statement,** *n.* **1.** [The act of stating] — *Syn.* utterance, comment, allegation, declaration, observation, remark, assertion, averment, profession, acknowledgment, avowal, protestation, assurance, asseveration, affirmation; see also **announcement** 1.
**2.** [A prepared announcement] — *Syn.* description, narrative, recital; see **announcement** 2, **declaration** 2.
**3.** [A statement of account] — *Syn.* bill, charge, reckoning, account, record, receipt, report, annual report, budget, audit, affidavit, balance sheet.

**statesman,** *n.* — *Syn.* legislator, lawgiver, Solon, administrator, executive, minister, official, politician, strategist, diplomat, representative, elder statesman, veteran lawmaker.

**statesmanship,** *n.* — *Syn.* statecraft, diplomacy, legislation; see **tact.**

**static,** *modif.* — *Syn.* immobile, unvarying, inactive; see **latent, motionless** 1.

**station,** *n.* **1.** [Place] — *Syn.* situation, site, location; see **position** 1.
**2.** [Duty] — *Syn.* occupation, service, calling; see **duty** 2.
**3.** [Depot] — *Syn.* terminal, stop, stopping place; see **depot** 2.
**4.** [Headquarters] — *Syn.* main office, home office, base of operations; see **headquarters.**
**5.** [Social position] — *Syn.* order, standing, state; see **rank** 3.
**6.** [An establishment to vend petroleum products] — *Syn.* gas station, service station, filling station, petrol station (British), pumps; see also **garage** 2.
**7.** [A broadcasting establishment] — *Syn.* television station, radio station, transmitter station, radar station, broadcasting station, plant, studio, transmitter, channel; see also **communications, radio** 2, **television.**

**station,** *v.* — *Syn.* place, commission, allot, post; see **assign** 1.

**stationary,** *modif.* — *Syn.* fixed, stable, permanent; see **motionless** 1.

**stationery,** *n.* — *Syn.* writing materials, office supplies, school supplies; see **paper** 5.

**statistical,** *modif.* — *Syn.* mathematical, demographic, arithmetical, analytical.

**statistics,** *n.* — *Syn.* enumeration, figures, demography; see **data.**

**statuary,** *n.* — *Syn.* statues, carving, art; see **image** 2, **sculpture.**

**statue,** *n.* — *Syn.* statuette, cast, figure, bust, representation, likeness, image, torso, piece, sculpture, statuary, marble, bronze, ivory, simulacrum, stabile, effigy, icon; see also **art** 2.

**statuesque,** *modif.* — *Syn.* stately, beautiful, grand; see **graceful** 2.

**stature,** *n.* — *Syn.* development, growth, tallness; see **height** 1, **size** 2.

*See Synonym Study at* HEIGHT.

**status,** *n.* — *Syn.* rank, situation, standing, station, state; see also **rank** 3.

*See Synonym Study at* STATE.

**status seeker,** *n.* — *Syn.* manipulator, social climber, self-server, *nouveau riche* (French), junior executive, ambitious person; see also **opportunist.**

**statute,** *n.* — *Syn.* enactment, ordinance, law; see **law** 3.

*See Synonym Study at* LAW.

**statutory,** *modif.* — *Syn.* sanctioned, lawful, rightful; see **legal** 1.

**staunch,** *modif.* — *Syn.* steadfast, strong, constant; see **faithful, firm** 1.

*See Synonym Study at* FAITHFUL.

**stave,** *n.* — *Syn.* stick, rod, staff; see **beam** 1, **support** 2.

**stay,** *n.* **1.** [A support] — *Syn.* prop, hold, truss; see **support** 2.

**2.** [A visit] — *Syn.* stop, sojourn, halt; see **visit**.

**stay,** *v.* — *Syn.* wait, tarry, linger, sojourn; see **visit** 2, **wait** 1.

*See Synonym Study at* WAIT.

**stay put★,** *v.* — *Syn.* remain, stand still, stand fast, persist; see **endure** 1, **resist** 1.

**stand someone in good stead,** *v.* — *Syn.* give someone good use, be of advantage, be useful.

**steadfast,** *modif.* — *Syn.* staunch, stable, constant; see **faithful**.

**steadily,** *modif.* — *Syn.* firmly, unwaveringly, undeviatingly; see **regularly** 2.

**steady,** *modif.* **1.** [Showing little variation] — *Syn.* regular, even, uniform, unvarying, patterned, equable; see also **consecutive** 1, **constant** 1, **regular** 3.

**2.** [Calm and self-possessed] — *Syn.* cool, poised, steadfast; see **calm** 1, **reserved** 3.

**go steady (with)★** — *Syn.* keep company with, court, be courted, go with, go together; see also **court** 1, **love** 1.

---

*SYN.* — **steady** implies a fixed regularity or constancy, esp. of movement, and an absence of deviation, fluctuation, faltering, etc. [*a steady breeze*]; **even,** often interchangeable with **steady,** emphasizes the absence of irregularity or inequality [*an even heartbeat*]; **uniform** implies a sameness or likeness of things, parts, events, etc. often as the result of conformity with a fixed standard [*a uniform wage rate*]; **regular** emphasizes the orderliness or symmetry resulting from evenness or uniformity [*regular features, attendance, etc.*]; **equable** implies an inherent evenness or regularity and may also suggest tranquility, serenity, or an absence of extremes [*an equable temper*]

---

**steak,** *n.* Cuts of steak include: filet mignon, tenderloin, porterhouse, sirloin, strip, Delmonico, rib, T-bone, New York, Kansas City, London broil, minute, chip, club, cube, flank, chuck, Salisbury, string, rump, shell, round; see **food, meat.**

**steal,** *v.* — *Syn.* take, filch, bag, thieve, loot, rob, purloin, embezzle, defraud, keep, carry away, carry off, appropriate, take possession of, withdraw, divert, lift, remove, impress, abduct, shanghai, kidnap, hijack, spirit away, run off with, hold for ransom, rifle, sack, cheat, cozen, hold up, strip, poach, peculate, counterfeit, circulate bad money, swindle, plagiarize, misappropriate, housebreak, burglarize, blackmail, fleece, plunder, pillage, despoil, ransack, crib★, burgle★, stick up★, skyjack★, pinch★, rustle★, rip off★, liberate★, snatch★, lift★, freeze on to★, annex★, cop★, swipe★, pinch★, mooch★, gyp★, dip one's hands into★, make off with★, borrow★; see also **seize** 2.

**stealing,** *n.* — *Syn.* piracy, embezzlement, shoplifting; see **crime** 2, **theft.**

**stealth,** *n.* — *Syn.* slyness, furtiveness, underhandedness; see **secrecy.**

**stealthy,** *modif.* — *Syn.* enigmatic, clandestine, private; see **secret** 3.

*See Synonym Study at* SECRET.

**steam,** *n.* — *Syn.* vaporized water, fumes, fog; see **cloud** 1, **vapor.**

**steam,** *v.* **1.** [To cook] — *Syn.* heat, poach, brew, pressure cook; see **cook.**

**2.** [To speed] — *Syn.* rush, sail, hurry; see **drive** 1, **speed.**

**steamboat,** *n.* — *Syn.* steamer, steamship, liner; see **boat, ship.**

**steamer,** *n.* — *Syn.* steamship, steamboat, liner; see **boat, ship.**

**steaming,** *modif.* — *Syn.* piping hot, piping, boiling, just out of the oven; see **cooking** 1, **hot** 1.

**steamroller★,** *v.* — *Syn.* steamroll★, overpower, railroad through★; see **defeat** 1, **force** 1, **trick.**

**steamy,** *modif.* **1.** [Giving off vapors] — *Syn.* vaporous, gaseous, evaporating; see **volatile** 1.

**2.** [Misty] — *Syn.* hazy, fogged, humid, clouded.

**3.** [★Erotic] — *Syn.* lewd, pornographic, purple; see **lewd** 1, 2.

**steed,** *n.* — *Syn.* charger, warhorse, palfrey; see **horse** 1.

**steel,** *n.* **1.** [A hard metal] — *Syn.* iron alloy, iron, stainless steel, tempered steel.

Forms and varieties of steel include: ingot, bar, slab, billet, rod, girder, beam, I-beam, scrap, hot rolled sheet, cold rolled sheet, plate, skelp, angle, channel, round, flat, square, joist bar, Z-bar, reinforcing, steel wool, steel filings, wire rod; see also **alloy, metal.**

**2.** [A knife sharpener] — *Syn.* sharpening rod, whetstone, oilstone.

**steel oneself,** *v.* — *Syn.* brace oneself, fortify, screw up one's courage; see **prepare** 1.

**steep,** *modif.* — *Syn.* abrupt, precipitous, sheer, perpendicular; see **abrupt** 1.

*See Synonym Study at* ABRUPT.

**steeple,** *n.* — *Syn.* turret, pointed belfry, *tourelle* (French); see **tower.**

**steeplechase,** *n.* — *Syn.* sweepstakes, derby, handicap; see **race** 3.

**steer,** *n.* — *Syn.* beef, feeder, cattle; see **cow, ox.**

**steer,** *v.* — *Syn.* point, head for, direct; see **drive** 3.

**steer clear of★,** *v.* — *Syn.* keep away from, miss, escape; see **avoid.**

**steersman,** *n.* — *Syn.* helmsman, coxwain, wheelman; see **pilot** 2.

**stellar,** *modif.* — *Syn.* celestial, heavenly, astronomical, spherical, galactic, cosmic, astrological.

**stem,** *n.* — *Syn.* peduncle, petiole, pedice; see **stalk.**

**from stem to stern** — *Syn.* the full length, completely, entirely; see **everywhere, throughout.**

**stem,** *v.* — *Syn.* arise, derive, originate; see **arise** 3, **begin** 2.

*See Synonym Study at* ARISE.

**stench,** *n.* — *Syn.* odor, stink, redolence; see **smell** 2.

**stenographer,** *n.* — *Syn.* stenographist, office worker, typist, shorthand stenographer; see **clerk** 2, **secretary** 2.

**stenography,** *n.* — *Syn.* phonography, stenotype, tachygraphy; see **shorthand.**

**stentorian,** *modif.* — *Syn.* blaring, sonorous, resounding; see **loud** 1, **raucous** 1.

**step,** *n.* **1.** [A movement of the foot] — *Syn.* pace, stride, gait, footstep, footfall, tread, stepping.

**2.** [One degree in a graded rise] — *Syn.* rest, run, tread, round, rung, level.

**3.** [The print of a foot] — *Syn.* footprint, footmark, track, print, imprint, impression, footstep, trail, trace, mark; see also **track** 2.

**4.** [An action, especially a first action] — *Syn.* start, move, measure; see **action** 2.

**in step (with)** — *Syn.* in agreement with, coinciding with, similar to; see **alike** 1, 2, 3, **similarly.**

**keep step** — *Syn.* agree to, agree with, conform to, keep in line★; see **conform.**

**out of step** — *Syn.* inappropriate, incorrect, inaccurate; see **wrong** 2, 3, **wrongly** 2.

**take steps**— *Syn.* do something, start, intervene; see **act** 1.

**watch one's step\***— *Syn.* be careful, take precautions, look out; see **watch out** 2.

**step,** *v.*— *Syn.* pace, stride, advance, recede, go forward, go backward, go up, go down, ascend, descend, pass, walk, tread, march, move, hurry, move quickly, move forward, move backward, mince, hop; see also **climb** 2, **rise** 1.

**step by step,** *modif.*— *Syn.* by degrees, cautiously, tentatively; see **carefully** 2, **slowly.**

**step down,** *v.*— *Syn.* leave, go, abdicate, get out\*; see **resign** 2, **retire** 3.

**step in,** *v.*— *Syn.* come in, arrive, be invited in; see **enter** 1.

**step on it\*,** *v.*— *Syn.* go fast, travel fast, make good time, speed up; see **speed.**

**steppe,** *n.*— *Syn.* prairie, pampas, savanna; see **plain.**

**steppingstone,** *n.*— *Syn.* help, agent, factor; see **aid** 1, **means** 1, **link.**

**step up,** *v.*— *Syn.* augment, improve, intensify; see **increase** 1.

**stereo,** *n.*— *Syn.* stereo system, sound system, audio system, component set, high-fidelity system, hi-fi, stereo recorder, stereo player, stereo receiver; see also **radio** 2, **record player, tape recorder.**

**stereotype,** *n.*— *Syn.* convention, conventional notion, fashion, institution; see **average, custom** 1, 2.

**stereotype,** *v.*— *Syn.* conventionalize, methodize, pigeon-hole, define, standardize, prejudge, normalize, catalogue, institutionalize; see also **regulate** 2, **systematize.**

**stereotyped,** *modif.*— *Syn.* hackneyed, trite, ordinary; see **conventional** 1, 2, **dull** 4.

*See Synonym Study at* TRITE.

**sterile,** *modif.* **1.** [Incapable of producing young]— *Syn.* infertile, impotent, childless, infecund, barren, issueless, without issue.— *Ant.* FERTILE, productive, potent.

**2.** [Incapable of producing vegetation]— *Syn.* desolate, fallow, waste, desert, arid, dry, barren, unproductive, fruitless, unfruitful, bleak, gaunt; see also **empty** 1. — *Ant.* RICH, productive, fertile.

**3.** [Scrupulously clean]— *Syn.* antiseptic, septic, sterilized, disinfected, decontaminated, germ-free, sterilized, uninfected, sanitary, hygienic, pasteurized; see also **pure** 2.— *Ant.* DIRTY, infected, contaminated.

**4.** [Without intellectual interest]— *Syn.* uninspiring, stupid, stale; see **dull** 4, **shallow** 2.

**5.** [Unprofitable]— *Syn.* fruitless, profitless, unproductive; see **worthless** 1, **useless** 1.

SYN. — **sterile** and **infertile** imply incapability of producing offspring or fruit, as because of some disorder of the reproductive system; **barren** and **unfruitful** are specifically applied to a sterile woman or to plants or soil; **impotent** is specif. applied to a man who cannot engage in sexual intercourse, especially because of an inability to have an erection. All of these words have figurative uses [*sterile* thinking, an *infertile* mind, a *barren* victory, *unfruitful* efforts, *impotent* rage]

**sterility,** *n.*— *Syn.* infertility, incapacity, fruitlessness; see **barrenness, worthlessness.**

**sterilize,** *v.*— *Syn.* asepticize, aseptify, antisepticize, disinfect, decontaminate, boil, autoclave, incapacitate, make sterile, pasteurize; see also **clean, purify.**

**sterling,** *modif.*— *Syn.* authentic, real, true; see **genuine** 1, **pure** 1.

**sterling,** *n.*— *Syn.* flatware, silver, cutlery; see **silverware.**

**stern,** *modif.*— *Syn.* rigid, austere, strict; see **severe** 1.

*See Synonym Study at* SEVERE.

**stevedore,** *n.*— *Syn.* docker, lumper, loader; see **laborer, worker.**

**stew,** *n.*— *Syn.* ragout, goulash, Hungarian goulash, meat pie, cottage pie, steak-and-kidney pie, gallimaufry, olla-podrida, olla, olio, stroganoff, bouillabaisse, beef stew, Irish stew, slumgullion\*, casserole, mutton stew, lamb stew, veal stew, *pot-au-feu* (French), matelote; see also **food, soup.**

**stew,** *v.* **1.** [To boil]— *Syn.* simmer, braise, fricassee; see **boil** 1, **cook.**

**2.** [To fret]— *Syn.* fume, fuss, chafe; see **fume, worry** 2.

*See Synonym Study at* BOIL.

**steward,** *n.* **1.** [A manager]— *Syn.* agent, chamberlain, purser; see **administrator.**

**2.** [An attendant]— *Syn.* waiter, waitress, porter, flight attendant, stewardess, host, hostess, maitre d'\*.

**stew in one's own juice\*,** *v.*— *Syn.* endure, be punished, take one's own medicine\*; see **suffer** 1.

**stick,** *n.*— *Syn.* shoot, twig, branch, stem, stalk, rod, wand, staff, stave, walking stick, cane, matchstick, club, baton, drumstick, timber, cudgel, ferrule, pole, bludgeon, bat, birch, rule, ruler, stock, joist, shillelagh, truncheon, cue, billet, spar, mast; see also **rod** 1.

**the sticks\***— *Syn.* rural area, country, the back country, outlying districts, the boondocks\*; see also **country** 1.

**stick,** *v.* **1.** [To remain fastened]— *Syn.* adhere, cling, fasten, attach, cleave, unite, cohere, hold, stick together, hug, clasp, hold fast, stick like wax, stick like glue\*, cling like a bur, cling like ivy, stick like a leech.— *Ant.* LOOSEN, let go, fall, come away.

**2.** [To penetrate with a point]— *Syn.* prick, impale, pierce; see **penetrate** 1, **stab.**

**on the stick\***— *Syn.* busy, alert, on the ball, moving, on the move.

SYN. — **stick** is the simple, general term here, implying attachment by gluing or fastening together, by close association, etc. [to *stick* a stamp on a letter, to *stick* to a subject]; **adhere** implies firm attachment and, of persons, denotes voluntary allegiance or devotion as to an idea, cause, or leader [to *adhere* to a policy]; **cohere** implies such close sticking together of parts as to form a single mass [glue made the particles of sawdust *cohere*]; **cling** implies attachment by embracing, entwining, or grasping with the arms, tendrils, etc. [a vine *clinging* to the trellis]; **cleave** implies a very close, firm attachment [my tongue *cleaved* to the roof of my mouth, Ruth *cleaved* to Naomi]

**stick around\*,** *v.*— *Syn.* stay, continue, be present; see **remain** 1.

**stick by\*,** *v.*— *Syn.* be loyal to, stand by, believe in; see **support** 2.

**stickiness,** *n.* **1.** [Humidity]— *Syn.* mugginess, dampness, wetness; see **humidity.**

**2.** [Cohesion]— *Syn.* adhesiveness, gumminess, fusion; see **coherence** 1.

**stick it out\*,** *v.*— *Syn.* persist, endure, stay; see **remain** 1.

**stickler,** *n.* **1.** [A zealot]— *Syn.* devotee, fanatic, contender; see **follower, zealot.**

**2.** [\*A puzzle]— *Syn.* enigma, riddle, paradox; see **irony, puzzle** 2.

**stick out,** *v.* — *Syn.* jut, show, come through; see **protrude.**

**stick-up\*,** *n.* — *Syn.* burglary, robbery, stealing; see **crime** 2, **theft.**

**stick up,** *v.* — *Syn.* show, poke up, bristle up, fly up, come through; see also **protrude.**

**stick up for\*,** *v.* — *Syn.* support, aid, fight for; see **defend** 1, 2, 3, **help** 1.

**sticky,** *modif.* — *Syn.* glutinous, ropy, viscous, gluey; see **adhesive.**

**stiff,** *modif.* **1.** [Not easily bent] — *Syn.* solid, rigid, congealed, petrified, ossified, firm, tense, unyielding, inflexible, inelastic, hard, hardened, starched, annealed, cemented, stony, starchy, taut, contracted, thick, indurate, stubborn, obstinate, pertinacious, numb, unbending, thickened, wooden, steely, frozen, solidified, chilled, benumbed, refractory. — *Ant.* FLEXIBLE, softened, soft.
**2.** [Formal] — *Syn.* ungainly, ungraceful, unnatural; see **awkward.**
**3.** [Severe] — *Syn.* rigorous, exact, strict; see **severe** 1, 2.
**4.** [Obstinate] — *Syn.* stubborn, inflexible, headstrong; see **obstinate** 1.
**5.** [Potent] — *Syn.* hard, potent, powerful; see **strong** 8.
**6.** [\*Difficult] — *Syn.* arduous, hard, laborious; see **difficult** 1.
*See Synonym Study at* FIRM.

**stiffen,** *v.* **1.** [To grow stiff] — *Syn.* jellify, gel, jelly, thicken, clot, coagulate, solidify, congeal, condense, set, curdle, freeze, inspissate, cake, chill, candy, crystallize; see also **harden** 2. — *Ant.* SOFTEN, melt, liquefy.
**2.** [To cause to become stiff] — *Syn.* harden, benumb, anneal, starch, petrify, ossify, brace, prop, cement, fix, precipitate, evaporate, strengthen, invigorate, revive, bring to, inflate. — *Ant.* RELAX, moisten, limber.

**stiff-necked,** *modif.* — *Syn.* stubborn, unyielding, priggish; see **obstinate, prudish.**

**stifle,** *v.* — *Syn.* smother, suffocate, extinguish; see **choke** 1.

**stigma,** *n.* — *Syn.* reproach, brand, stain, shame; see **blame** 1, **disgrace** 2.

**stigmata,** *n.* — *Syn.* mark, blot, defect; see **blemish.**

**stigmatize,** *v.* — *Syn.* brand, defame, discredit; see **disgrace.**

**stiletto,** *n.* — *Syn.* dagger, cutter, blade; see **knife.**

**still,** *modif.* **1.** [Silent] — *Syn.* calm, tranquil, noiseless; see **quiet** 2.
**2.** [Yet] — *Syn.* nevertheless, furthermore, however; see **besides, but** 1, **yet** 1.

**stillness,** *n.* — *Syn.* quietness, tranquillity, soundlessness; see **silence** 1.

**stilt,** *n.* — *Syn.* shore, prop, post; see **brace** 1, **support** 2.

**stilted,** *modif.* — *Syn.* pompous, affected, decorous; see **egotistic** 2, **prim.**

**stimulant,** *n.* — *Syn.* tonic, bracer, energizer; see **drug** 2.

**stimulate,** *v.* — *Syn.* arouse, excite, spur, incite; see **animate** 1, **excite** 1, **incite.**
*See Synonym Study at* ANIMATE, PROVOKE.

**stimulated,** *modif.* — *Syn.* aroused, keyed up, speeded up, accelerated; see **excited.**

**stimulating,** *modif.* — *Syn.* intriguing, enlivening, arousing, high-spirited, bracing, rousing, inspiriting, energetic, refreshing, exhilarating, warming, strengthening, enjoyable, health-building, tonic, vivifying, sharp, keen, evocative, exciting, inspiring, intoxicating, provoking, animating. — *Ant.* DULL, dreary, humdrum.

**stimulus,** *n.* — *Syn.* inducement, provocation, motive; see **incentive.**

**sting,** *n.* **1.** [An injury] — *Syn.* wound, cut, sore, stab, bite; see also **injury** 1.
**2.** [Pain] — *Syn.* prick, bite, burn; see **pain** 2.

**sting,** *v.* — *Syn.* prick, prickle, tingle; see **hurt** 4.

**stingy,** *modif.* — *Syn.* parsimonious, niggardly, miserly, penurious, close, closefisted, sordid, greedy, covetous, tightfisted, tight\*, avaricious, acquisitive, grasping, curmudgeonly, penny-pinching, grudging, cheeseparing, sparing, ignoble, cheap\*, scurvy, rapacious, near, narrow, shabby, scrimping, skimping, churlish, ungenerous, selfish, meagerly, meanly, skimpy, illiberal, extortionate. — *Ant.* GENEROUS, bountiful, liberal.

**SYN.** — **stingy** implies a grudging, mean reluctance to part with anything belonging to one; **close** suggests the keeping of a tight hold on what one has accumulated; **niggardly** implies such closefistedness that one grudgingly spends or gives the least amount possible; **parsimonious** implies unreasonable economy or frugality, often to the point of niggardliness; **penurious** implies such extreme parsimony and niggardliness as to make one seem poverty-stricken or destitute; **miserly** implies the penuriousness of one who is meanly avaricious and hoarding

**stink,** *n.* — *Syn.* stench, fetor, offensive odor; see **smell** 2.

**stink,** *v.* — *Syn.* smell bad, emit a stench, reek, smell, smell to high heaven, be offensive, make an offensive odor, smell up.

**stint,** *n.* **1.** [A limit] — *Syn.* restriction, limit, limitation; see **restraint** 2.
**2.** [A task] — *Syn.* assignment, task, job, work, consignment; see also **job** 1, 2.
*See Synonym Study at* TASK.

**stint,** *v.* — *Syn.* restrain, confine, limit; see **define** 1, **restrict** 2.

**stipend,** *n.* — *Syn.* wage, gratuity, pension; see **allowance** 2, **pay** 2.
*See Synonym Study at* WAGE.

**stipple,** *v.* — *Syn.* dapple, dot, dab; see **draw** 2, **paint** 1.

**stipulate,** *v.* — *Syn.* condition, bargain, arrange; see **designate** 1, **specify.**

**stipulation,** *n.* — *Syn.* condition, designation, obligation, arrangement; see **requirement** 1, **specification.**

**stir,** *n.* — *Syn.* agitation, tumult, bustle; see **excitement.**

**stir,** *v.* **1.** [To excite] — *Syn.* rouse, arouse, waken, awaken, rally, excite, enliven, kindle, rekindle, provoke, inflame; see also **excite** 1.
**2.** [To mix by stirring] — *Syn.* move, beat, agitate; see **mix** 1.

**SYN.** — **stir** (in this sense, often **stir up**) implies a bringing into action or activity by exciting or provoking /the colonies were *stirred* to rebellion/; **arouse** and **rouse** are often used interchangeably, but **arouse** usually implies merely a bringing into consciousness, as from a state of sleep /she was *aroused* by the bell/, and **rouse** suggests an additional incitement to vigorous action /the rifle shot *roused* the sleeping guard/; **awaken** and **waken** literally mean to arouse from sleep, but figuratively they suggest the stirring into activity of latent faculties, emotions, etc. /it *awakened*, or *wakened*, her maternal feelings/; **rally** implies a gathering of the component elements or individuals so as to stir to effective action *[to rally the troops, rallied her energy and attention]*

**stirring,** *modif.* — *Syn.* stimulating, lively, animating; see **interesting.**

**stir up trouble★,** *v.* — *Syn.* cause difficulty, foment, agitate; see **bother** 2, **disturb** 2.

**stitch,** *v.* — *Syn.* join, make a seam, baste, suture; see **sew.**

**stock,** *modif.* — *Syn.* trite, hackneyed, common; see **common** 1, **dull** 4.

**stock,** *n.* **1.** [Goods] — *Syn.* merchandise, produce, accumulation; see **commodity.**

**2.** [Livestock] — *Syn.* domestic animals, barnyard animals, farm animals; see **cow, fowl, hog** 1, **horse** 1, **sheep.**

**3.** [A stalk] — *Syn.* stem, plant, trunk; see **stalk.**

**4.** [A business share] — *Syn.* funds, assets, stocks and bonds, property, capital.

**in stock** — *Syn.* not sold out, stocked, not difficult to get; see **available.**

**out of stock** — *Syn.* sold out, sold off, gone, not available; see **sold** 1.

**take stock (of), 1.** [To take inventory] — *Syn.* count up, inventory, figure; see **count, estimate** 1.

**2.** [To consider] — *Syn.* examine, study, review; see **consider** 1, **think** 1.

**take stock in** — *Syn.* invest in, purchase, take a chance on; see **buy** 1.

**stockade,** *n.* — *Syn.* barrier, protection, enclosure; see **fence** 1.

**stocking,** *n.* — *Syn.* hose, hosiery, nylons; see **sock.**

**stock market,** *n.* — *Syn.* the market, the exchange, syndicate; see **business** 1, **market** 2.

**stock-still,** *modif.* — *Syn.* motionless, stagnant, inactive; see **idle** 1.

**stock up,** *v.* — *Syn.* replenish, supply, furnish; see **buy** 1, **provide** 1.

**stodgy,** *modif.* — *Syn.* boring, uninteresting, tedious; see **dull** 4.

**stoical,** *modif.* — *Syn.* impassive, enduring, unmoved; see **indifferent** 1.

**stoicism,** *n.* — *Syn.* impassivity, patience, sobriety; see **endurance** 2, **indifference** 1, **patience** 1.

*See Synonym Study at* PATIENCE.

**stolen,** *modif.* — *Syn.* taken, kept, bagged, robbed, filched, purloined, appropriated, impressed, lifted, diverted, abducted, kidnapped, hijacked, shanghaied, spirited away, run off with, poached, sacked, cheated, rifled, plagiarized, embezzled, misappropriated, pinched★, swiped★, ripped off★; see also **captured** 1.

**stolid,** *modif.* — *Syn.* unexcitable, impassive, apathetic; see **indifferent** 1.

*See Synonym Study at* IMPASSIVE.

**stomach,** *n.* — *Syn.* paunch, belly, breadbasket; see **abdomen.**

**stomachache,** *n.* — *Syn.* indigestion, acute indigestion, gastric upset; see **illness** 1, **pain** 1.

**stone,** *modif.* — *Syn.* rock, stony, rocky, flinty, adamantine, hard, rough, cragged, craggy, petrified, petrous, calciferous, calcific, lithic, calcified, become stone, petrographic, petrographical, crystallographic, lithographic, lithological, marble, granite.

**stone,** *n.* — *Syn.* concretion, mass, crag, cobblestone, cobble, boulder, gravel, pebble, rock, sand, grain, granite, marble, flint, gem, jewel.

**cast the first stone** — *Syn.* criticize, blame, reprimand;

see **attack** 2, **scold.**

**leave no stone unturned** — *Syn.* take great pains, do everything possible, persist, try hard; see **continue** 1, **pursue** 1, **work** 1.

**stoned★,** *modif.* — *Syn.* under the influence of drugs, under the influence of alcohol, drugged, ripped out★, high★, spaced out★, tripping★, turned on★; see also **drunk, unconscious.**

**stony,** *modif.* — *Syn.* inflexible, cruel, unrelenting; see **firm** 2, **rough** 1.

**stool,** *n.* — *Syn.* seat, footstool, footrest, ottoman, hassock; see also **furniture.**

**stoop,** *v.* **1.** [To bow or bend] — *Syn.* incline, crouch, slant; see **bow** 1, **lean** 1.

**2.** [To condescend] — *Syn.* deign, patronize, look down on; see **condescend.**

*See Synonym Study at* CONDESCEND.

**stop,** *interj.* — *Syn.* cease, knock it off, cut it out, quit it, say, hey there; see also **halt** 2.

**stop,** *n.* **1.** [A pause] — *Syn.* halt, stay, standstill; see **end** 2, **pause** 1, 2.

**2.** [A stopping place] — *Syn.* station, passenger station, wayside stop; see **depot.**

**pull out all the stops★** — *Syn.* go the limit, do everything possible, give it all one has★; see **try** 1, **work** 1.

**put a stop to** — *Syn.* halt, interrupt, intervene; see **stop** 1.

**stop,** *v.* **1.** [To halt] — *Syn.* pause, stay, stand, lay over, stay over, break the journey, tarry, stand still, shut down, rest, discontinue, come to a halt, come to a standstill, pull up, reach a standstill, check, bivouac, cease marching, hold, stop dead in one's tracks★, stop short★, freeze★, freeze up★, call it a day★, stymie★, box in★, knock on the head★, cut short★; see also **end** 1. — *Ant.* CONTINUE, proceed, advance.

**2.** [To cease] — *Syn.* cease, terminate, finish, conclude, quit, withdraw, leave off, let up, pull up, fold up, fetch up, wind up, bring up, relinquish, have done with, desist, refrain, ring down, settle, discontinue, end, close, draw up, tie up, give up, call off, bring up, close down, break up, hold up, pull up, lapse, be at an end, cut out, die away, come off, go out, stay one's hand, run out, defect, surrender, close, peter out★, call it a day★, knock it off★, lay off★, throw in the towel★, belay that★, blow over★, melt away★, drop it★, run out★, write off★, pipe down★, save one's breath★, give over★, run its course★; see also **halt** 2, **suspend** 2. — *Ant.* BEGIN, start, commence.

**3.** [To prevent] — *Syn.* hinder, obstruct, arrest; see **prevent.**

**4.** [To cause to cease] — *Syn.* arrest, check, suspend; see **halt** 2.

**SYN.** — **stop** implies a suspension or ending of some motion, action, or progress *[my watch stopped]*; **cease** implies a suspension or ending of some state or condition or of an existence *[the war had ceased, the noise ceased when the train stopped]*; **quit** is equivalent to either **stop** *[she quit working for the day]* or **cease** *[he quit working at sixty-five and retired to Florida]*; **discontinue** suggests the suspension of some action that is a habitual practice, an occupation, etc. *[he has discontinued the practice of law]*; **desist** implies a ceasing of some action that is annoying, harmful, futile, etc. *[desist from further bickering]*

**stop for,** *v.* — *Syn.* get, make a stop for, go to get; see **obtain** 1, **pick up** 6.

**stopgap**, *modif.* — *Syn.* expedient, substitute, makeshift, juryrigged; see **practical, temporary.**

**stopgap**, *n.* — *Syn.* makeshift, expedient, resource; see **resort** 1, **substitute.**
See Synonym Study at RESORT.

**stopover**, *n.* — *Syn.* layover, halt, pause; see **delay** 1.

**stop over** (*or* **by** *or* **in** *or* **off**), *v.* — *Syn.* stop to see, break a journey, stay; see **visit** 1, 2, 4.

**stopped**, *modif.* — *Syn.* at a halt, cancelled, cut short; see **interrupted.**

**stopping**, *n.* — *Syn.* staying, remaining, halt, halting, holding, hesitation, pause, encumbering, wait, check, delay, block, stand-down, ending, closing, breaking off, deterring, desisting, terminating, ceasing, shutting up*.

**storage**, *n.* — *Syn.* room, area, accommodation; see **storehouse, warehouse.**

**store**, *n.* **1.** [An establishment, especially for retail sales] — *Syn.* shop, department store, specialty shop, men's furnishing store, draper's, drygoods store, storehouse, repository, emporium, chain store, market, confectionary, business house, grocery store, *étape* (French), *godown* (Oriental), *golah* (Anglo-Indian); see also **building** 1.
**2.** [Stored goods] — *Syn.* wares, reserve, stocks; see **commodity, property** 1.

**store**, *v.* — *Syn.* put, deposit, cache, stock, store away, stow away, lay by, lay in, lay up, lay down, put away, put aside, lock away, bank, warehouse, stockpile, collect, squirrel away, pack away, set aside, amass, file, stash, salt away, file and forget, put in moth balls, mothball; see also **save** 3. — *Ant.* SPEND, draw out, withdraw.

**stored**, *modif.* — *Syn.* stocked, reserved, hoarded; see **saved** 1.

**storehouse**, *n.* — *Syn.* depository, warehouse, granary, magazine, silo, store, storage place, cornhouse, corncrib, barn, depot, cache, grain elevator, safe-deposit vault, armory, arsenal, argosy, repertory, repository.

**storekeeper**, *n.* — *Syn.* small businessman, purveyor, grocer; see **merchant.**

**storied**, *modif.* — *Syn.* famed, recognized, renowned, legendary; see **famous.**

**storm**, *n.* **1.** [A violent disturbance of the elements] — *Syn.* tempest, downpour, cloudburst, disturbance, waterspout, blizzard, snowstorm, purga, squall, hurricane, cyclone, tornado, twister, gust, blast, gale, blow, monsoon; see also **rain** 1, **wind** 1.
**2.** [An outbreak suggestive of violent weather] — *Syn.* anger, agitation, annoyance, commotion, turmoil, violence, perturbation, racket, temper, hubbub, rage, fury, passion, hysteria. — *Ant.* PEACE, harmony, quiet.

**storm**, *v.* **1.** [To be stormy] — *Syn.* blow violently, howl, blow a gale, roar, set in, squall, pour, drizzle, drop, rain, mizzle, spit, lay the dust, patter, rain cats and dogs*, come down in bucketfuls*, breathe fire and fury*, rain pitchforks and hammer-handles*; see also **snow.**
**2.** [To make a violent attack] — *Syn.* attack, charge, rush, assail; see **attack** 1.
See Synonym Study at ATTACK.

**stormy**, *modif.* **1.** [Characterized by storms] — *Syn.* rainy, wet, damp, cold, bitter, raging, roaring, frigid, windy, blustery, pouring, blustering, murky, tempestuous, turbulent, tumultuous, storming, wild, boisterous, rough, torrid, squally, dark, violent, threatening, menacing, riproaring*. — *Ant.* MILD, clement, equable.
**2.** [Characterized by violent emotions] — *Syn.* savage, riotous, agitated; see **turbulent, violent** 2.

**story**, *n.* **1.** [Imaginative writing] — *Syn.* write-up, fable, narrative, tale, myth, fairy tale, anecdote, legend, account, recital, memoir, parable, apologue, fiction, novel, romance, allegory, epic, saga, fantasy, edda; see also **literature** 1.
Kinds of stories include — *Long:* novel, romance, love story, realistic novel, detective, horror, adventure, comedy of manners, historical novel, biographical fiction, novelette, satire, saga, heroic poem, epic, mythological account, narrative, chronicle, *chanson de geste* (French); *Short:* jest, *Märchen* (German), folktale, fairy tale, apologue, canard, sketch, fantasy, anecdote, short story, novella, ghost story, example, *exemplum* (Latin), fable, *conte dévot* (French), saint's life, legend, beast tale, primitive tale, idyll, pastoral, parable, fable, allegory, short short*, western*, pulp*, bodice-ripper*, technothriller*, whodunit*.
**2.** [*A lie] — *Syn.* fib*, falsehood, fabrication.

---

*SYN.* — **story**, the broadest in scope of these words, refers to a series of connected events, true or fictitious, that is written or told with the intention of entertaining or informing; **narrative** is a more formal word, referring to the kind of prose that recounts happenings; **tale**, a somewhat elevated or literary term, usually suggests a simple, leisurely story, often somewhat loosely organized, especially a fictitious or legendary one; **anecdote** applies to a short, entertaining account of a single incident, usually personal or biographical

---

**storyteller**, *n.* — *Syn.* author, relator, fabler, narrator, minstrel, teller, bard, poet, biographer, chronicler, raconteur, anecdotist, teller of tales, spinner of yarns, fabulist, fabricator, prose writer.

**stout**, *modif.* **1.** [Brave] — *Syn.* fearless, bold, undaunted; see **brave** 1.
**2.** [Heavy or fat] — *Syn.* corpulent, fleshy, portly, heavy; see **fat** 1.
**3.** [Strong] — *Syn.* sturdy, hardy, husky; see **strong** 1.

**stove**, *n.* — *Syn.* range, cooker, oven.
Varieties of stoves include: cooking, heating, circulating, potbellied, Franklin, Norwegian, airtight, galvanized-iron, cast-iron, tile, wood, coal, oil, gas, gasjet, electric, infrared, microwave, high frequency, low frequency, atomic, portable, camp, car, tinmen's, Nuremberg; range, baseburner, kiln; see also **appliance, oven.**

**stovepipe**, *n.* — *Syn.* flue, funnel, smokestack; see **chimney.**

**straddle**, *v.* — *Syn.* bestride, ride, mount, bestraddle; see **balance** 2, **sit** 1.

**strafe**, *v.* — *Syn.* bombard, storm, barrage, shell; see **attack** 1.

**straggle**, *v.* — *Syn.* ramble, stray, wander, fall behind; see **lag** 1, **loiter, roam.**

**straggly**, *modif.* **1.** [Rambling] — *Syn.* irregular, roving, hiking; see **rambling** 1.
**2.** [Untidy] — *Syn.* messy, tangled, dispersed; see **loose** 1.

**straight**, *modif.* **1.** [Not curved or twisted] — *Syn.* rectilinear, vertical, perpendicular, rectilineal, plumb, upright, erect, in line with, unbent, in a line, on a line, in a row, inflexible, undeviating, even, level. — *Ant.* BENT, curved, curving.
**2.** [Direct] — *Syn.* uninterrupted, continuous, through; see **direct** 1.
**3.** [Correct] — *Syn.* right, orderly, exact; see **accurate** 1.
**4.** [Honest] — *Syn.* good, reliable, honorable; see **decent** 2, **honest** 1, **moral** 1, **upright** 2.
**5.** [Unmixed] — *Syn.* out-and-out, undiluted, plain, neat; see **concentrated** 1, **pure** 1.

**go straight*** — *Syn.* obey the law, avoid crime, live a decent life; see **behave** 2.

**the straight and narrow path** — *Syn.* good conduct, proper behavior, righteousness, morality; see **honesty** 1, **virtue** 1, 2.

**straighten,** *v.* — *Syn.* order, compose, make straight, rectify, untwist, unsnarl, unbend, uncoil, unravel, uncurl, unfold, put straight, level, make plumb, arrange, arrange on a line, align, realign, make upright, make perpendicular, make vertical. — *Ant.* BEND, twist, curl.

**straighten out,** *v.* — *Syn.* **1.** [To settle] — *Syn.* conclude, set at rest, figure out, resolve; see **decide, govern** 1.

**2.** [To put in order] — *Syn.* tidy, clean up, arrange; see **straighten.**

**straighten up,** *v.* **1.** [To make neat] — *Syn.* tidy, arrange, fix; see **clean, straighten.**

**2.** [To stand up] — *Syn.* rise up, arise, be upright; see **rise** 6, **stand** 1.

**straightforward,** *modif.* — *Syn.* sincere, candid, outspoken; see **frank, honest** 1.

**straightway,** *modif.* — *Syn.* at once, directly, promptly; see **immediately.**

**strain,** *n.* **1.** [Effort] — *Syn.* exertion, struggle, endeavor; see **effort** 1.

**2.** [Mental tension] — *Syn.* anxiety, tension, pressure; see **stress** 3.

**3.** [A bodily injury less than a sprain] — *Syn.* wrench, twist, stretch, ache, jerk, bruise, charley horse.

**4.** [Pressure] — *Syn.* tension, force, pull; see **stress** 2.

**strain,** *v.* **1.** [To exert] — *Syn.* strive, endeavor, labor; see **try** 1.

**2.** [To wrench] — *Syn.* twist, sprain, distort; see **hurt** 1, **wrench.**

**3.** [To stretch] — *Syn.* rack, extend, draw tight; see **stretch** 2, **tighten** 1.

**4.** [To filter] — *Syn.* refine, purify, screen; see **filter** 2, **sift** 2.

**strained,** *modif.* — *Syn.* forced, constrained, tense; see **difficult** 1.

**strainer,** *n.* — *Syn.* mesh, filter, colander; see **sieve.**

**strait,** *n.* **1.** [A channel] — *Syn.* inlet, canal, sound, narrows; see **channel** 1.

**2.** [Difficulty] — *Syn.* distress, crisis, plight, emergency; see **difficulty** 1, 2.

*See Synonym Study at* EMERGENCY.

**straiten,** *v.* **1.** [Distress] — *Syn.* perplex, corner, fluster; see **confuse, embarrass** 1.

**2.** [To limit] — *Syn.* contract, confine, constrain; see **hinder, restrict** 1.

**in straitened circumstances** — *Syn.* short of money, financially embarrassed, broke*; see **insolvent, poor** 1.

**strait jacket,** *n.* — *Syn.* jacket, confining jacket, jacket for violently insane people; see **chains.**

**strait-laced,** *modif.* — *Syn.* strict, severe, stiff; see **prudish.**

**strand,** *n.* — *Syn.* beach, coast, seacoast; see **shore.**

*See Synonym Study at* SHORE.

**stranded,** *modif.* — *Syn.* aground, beached, ashore; see **abandoned** 1.

**strange,** *modif.* **1.** [Little known] — *Syn.* foreign, external, exotic, outside, outlandish, detached, apart, faraway, remote, alien, unexplored, isolated, unrelated, irrelevant; see also **unfamiliar** 2, **unknown** 1, 2, 3, **unnatural** 1. — *Ant.* FAMILIAR, present, close.

**2.** [Not acquainted] — *Syn.* ignorant of, without knowledge of, uninformed about, unfamiliar, unheard of, newfangled, new, not versed in, unaccustomed to, novel. — *Ant.* OLD, prevailing, current.

**3.** [Unusual] — *Syn.* unusual, peculiar, odd, queer, exceptional, rare, uncommon, outlandish; see also **unusual** 1, 2.

---

*SYN.* — **strange,** the term of broadest application here, refers to that which is unfamiliar, as because of being uncommon, unknown, or new *[a strange voice, idea, device, etc.]*; **peculiar** applies either to that which puzzles or to that which has unique qualities *[a peculiar smell, pattern, etc.; behavior peculiar to beavers]*; **odd** suggests that which differs from the ordinary or conventional, sometimes to the point of being bizarre *[offended by his odd behavior]*; **queer** emphasizes an element of eccentricity, abnormality, or suspicion *[a queer look on her face]*; **quaint** suggests an oddness, esp. an antique quality, that is pleasing or appealing *[a quaint costume]*; **outlandish** suggests an oddness that is decidedly, often excessively, fantastic or bizarre *[an outlandish remark]*

---

**strangely,** *modif.* — *Syn.* oddly, queerly, newly, unfamiliarly, unnaturally, uncommonly, exceptionally, remarkably, rarely, fantastically, amazingly, surprisingly, startlingly, strikingly, singularly, remarkably, unutterably, indescribably, peculiarly, ineffably, uniquely, unusually, uncustomarily, astonishingly, exotically, marvelously. — *Ant.* REGULARLY, commonly, usually.

**strangeness,** *n.* — *Syn.* newness, unfamiliarity, exoticism, novelty, abnormality, singularity, eccentricity, fantasticality, weirdness, remoteness, indescribability, esotericism, esoterism, sense of being alien, unaccustomed quality, strange nature, unfamiliar surroundings, feeling of newness. — *Ant.* FAMILIARITY, acquaintanceship, homelike quality.

**stranger,** *n.* — *Syn.* foreigner, outsider, alien, newcomer, outlander, unknown person, out-of-towner, migrant, visitor, guest, immigrant, uninvited person, intruder, interloper, new boy in town, new girl in town, new kid in town, new arrival, nonresident, out-of-stater, stranger within the gates, floater, drifter, squatter, itinerant, transient, perfect stranger, complete stranger, not one of us*, crasher*, gate crasher, party crasher*; see also **alien.** — *Ant.* INHABITANT, citizen, native, acquaintance.

*See Synonym Study at* ALIEN.

**strangle,** *v.* **1.** [To choke] — *Syn.* asphyxiate, suffocate, smother, kill; see **choke** 1.

**2.** [To suppress] — *Syn.* subdue, stifle, repress; see **restrain** 1, **suppress.**

**strap,** *n.* — *Syn.* thong, strop, leash; see **band** 1.

**strapped*,** *modif.* — *Syn.* impoverished, out of money, broke*; see **poor** 1.

**strapping*,** *modif.* — *Syn.* big, tall, powerful, muscular, husky; see also **heavy** 1, **high** 1, **strong** 2.

**stratagem,** *n.* — *Syn.* trick, deception, plot, scheme; see **method** 2.

*See Synonym Study at* TRICK.

**strategic,** *modif.* **1.** [Clever] — *Syn.* cunning, diplomatic, tricky; see **dishonest** 1.

**2.** [Crucial] — *Syn.* vital, decisive, imperative; see **important** 1, **necessary** 1.

**strategist,** *n.* — *Syn.* tactician, schemer, contriver; see **administrator.**

**strategy,** *n.* **1.** [Tactics] — *Syn.* approach, maneuvering, procedure; see **tactics.**

**2.** [Cunning] — *Syn.* plan, master plan, artifice, craft; see **policy, tact.**

**stratification,** *n.* — *Syn.* tabular structure, lamination, scaliness, delamination; see **layer.**

**stratified,** *modif.* — *Syn.* layered, flaky, laminated, stratiform, scaly, squamous.

**stratify,** *v.* — *Syn.* laminate, flake, scale; see **plate.**

**stratum,** *n.* — *Syn.* seam, tier, level, bed; see **layer.**

**straw,** *n.* — *Syn.* hay, fodder, silage.

Straws and strawlike fibers include: oat, wheat, barley, rye, rice, buckwheat, bean, pea, buri, jijipapa, jute, raffia, palm, palmetto; see also **hay.**

**grasp at straws** *or* **a straw★** — *Syn.* panic, attempt, be desperate, try anything, make a hopeless attempt; see also **try** 1.

**a straw in the wind★** — *Syn.* evidence, indication, signal; see **sign** 1.

**strawberry,** *modif.* — *Syn.* carmine, strawberry-red, rose, rose-red, deep rose; see also **red, rose.**

**strawberry,** *n.* — *Syn.* fragaria, queen of berries, the perfect berry; see **berry** 1, **fruit** 1.

**straw man,** *n.* — *Syn.* feeble argument, weak position, blind, statement to be refuted, Aunt Sally (British); see also **fake, nonsense** 2.

**straw vote,** *n.* — *Syn.* opinion poll, unofficial ballot, dry run★; see **opinion** 1, **vote** 1, 2.

**stray,** *v.* — *Syn.* rove, roam, swerve, go amiss, go astray, deviate; see also **turn** 3, **walk** 1.

**strayed,** *modif.* — *Syn.* wandered, vagrant, roaming; see **lost** 1.

**streak,** *n.* **1.** [A band] — *Syn.* stripe, strip, ridge; see **band** 1.

**2.** [A ray or flash of light] — *Syn.* bolt, flare, beam, thunderbolt, lightning bolt, burst, glint; see also **ray.**

**like a streak** — *Syn.* like lightning, swift, speedy; see **fast** 1, **rapid** 2.

**streaky,** *modif.* — *Syn.* streaked, smudgy, veined; see **striped.**

**stream,** *n.* — *Syn.* current, rivulet, brook; see **river** 1, **water** 2.

**stream,** *v.* — *Syn.* gush, run, flow; see **flow** 1, 2.

**streamer,** *n.* **1.** [Banner] — *Syn.* standard, pennant, banner; see **flag** 1.

**2.** [Headline] — *Syn.* title, screamer, caption; see **head** 9.

**streamlined,** *modif.* — *Syn.* modernized, sleek, trim, contoured; see **smooth** 1.

**street,** *n.* — *Syn.* road, highway, way, lane, path, avenue, thoroughfare, boulevard, terrace, place, mews, route, artery, parkway, court, cross street, esplanade, boardwalk, row, embankment, square, piazza, close, alley, circle, dead end, passage, mall, circus, arcade, *via* (Italian), *rue* (French), *Strasse* (German).

**streetcar,** *n.* — *Syn.* tram, tramcar, trolley car, trolley, bus; see also **vehicle** 1.

**streetwalker,** *n.* — *Syn.* whore, hustler, harlot, lady of the evening; see **prostitute.**

**strength,** *n.* **1.** [Power] — *Syn.* power, might, potency, force, vigor, brawn, energy, nerve, vitality, sinews, muscle, backbone, physique, thews, stoutness, health, toughness, fortitude, sturdiness, hardiness, stalwartness, tenacity, mana, robustness, soundness, durability. — *Ant.* WEAKNESS, feebleness, loss of energy.

**2.** [Intensity] — *Syn.* force, depth, concentration, fervor; see **force** 3, **intensity** 1.

**on the strength of** — *Syn.* reassured by, in view of, as a result of; see **because, since** 1.

---

*SYN.* — **strength** refers to the inherent capacity to act upon or affect something, to endure, to resist, etc. /the *strength* to lift something, tensile *strength*/; **power,** somewhat more general, applies to the ability, latent or exerted, physical or mental, to do something /the *power* of

the press, of a machine, etc./; **force** usually suggests the actual exertion of power, esp. in producing motion or overcoming opposition /the *force* of gravity, the rebellion was put down by *force*/; **might** suggests great or overwhelming strength or power /with all one's *might*/; **energy** specifically implies latent power for doing work or affecting something /the *energy* in an atom, campaigned with unflagging *energy*/; **potency** refers to the inherent capacity or power to accomplish something /the *potency* of a drug/

---

**strengthen,** *v.* — *Syn.* intensify, add, invigorate, fortify, encourage, confirm, increase, multiply, empower, arm, energize, harden, reactivate, steel, reinforce, brace, buttress, stimulate, sustain, nerve, animate, reanimate, restore, reman, refresh, recover, hearten, establish, toughen, temper, bear out, rejuvenate, tone up, build up, make firm, stiffen, brace up, rally, sharpen, enliven, give weight, carry weight, substantiate, uphold, back, augment, enlarge, extend, mount, rise, ascend, wax, grow, back up, beef up★. — *Ant.* WEAKEN, cripple, tear down.

**strenuous,** *modif.* — *Syn.* arduous, demanding, exhausting, vigorous; see **active** 2, **difficult** 1.

*See Synonym Study at* ACTIVE.

**strenuously,** *modif.* — *Syn.* hard, laboriously, energetically; see **industriously, vigorously.**

**stress,** *n.* **1.** [Importance] — *Syn.* significance, weight, import; see **importance** 1.

**2.** [Pressure] — *Syn.* strain, tension, force, stretch, tautness, traction, pull, tensity, distention, eulogation, draw, extension, protraction, intensity, tightness, spring; see also **pressure** 1.

**3.** [Mental tension] — *Syn.* tension, strain, pressure, burden, hardship, overexertion, agony, trial, affliction, anxiety, nervousness, fearfulness, apprehensiveness, apprehension, impatience, fear, ferment, disquiet, disquietude, tenseness, passion, intensity, fluster, expectancy, restlessness, trepidation, misgiving, mistrust, alarm, dread, flutter, trembling, pinch, urgency, jitters★, heebyjeebies★. — *Ant.* PEACE, calm, quiet.

**stress,** *v.* — *Syn.* accent, make emphatic, accentuate; see **emphasize.**

**stretch,** *n.* — *Syn.* extent, compass, range, reach; see **time** 1.

**stretch,** *v.* **1.** [To become longer] — *Syn.* grow, expand, be extended, extend oneself, spread, unfold, increase, swell, spring up, shoot up, open, burst forth. — *Ant.* CONTRACT, shrink, wane.

**2.** [To cause to stretch, sense 1] — *Syn.* tighten, strain, make tense, draw, draw out, elongate, extend, develop, distend, inflate, lengthen, magnify, amplify, spread out, widen, pull, pull out of shape, pull into shape, draw tight, make taut, tauten. — *Ant.* RELAX, let go, slacken.

**3.** [To occupy space] — *Syn.* extend across, range, extend to, spread over, cover a given distance; see also **occupy** 2, **reach** 1.

**stretcher,** *n.* — *Syn.* litter, cot, pallet, portable bed; see **bed** 1.

**strew,** *v.* — *Syn.* spread, toss, cover; see **scatter** 2.

**stricken,** *modif.* **1.** [Hurt] — *Syn.* wounded, injured, harmed; see **hurt.**

**2.** [Removed] — *Syn.* expunged, deleted, struck.

**3.** [Overwhelmed] — *Syn.* overcome, heart-stricken, heart-struck, heartsick, desolate.

**strict,** *modif.* — *Syn.* stringent, stern, austere; see **severe** 2.

**strictly,** *modif.* — *Syn.* rigidly, rigorously, stringently; see **surely.**

**stricture,** *n.* **1.** [Censure] — *Syn.* criticism, obloquy, rebuke; see **blame** 1.

**2.** [Constriction] — *Syn.* tightness, choking, strangulation, check, squeezing, astringency, binding, control, contraction, compression, shrinking; see also **restraint** 2.

**stride,** *n.* — *Syn.* walk, pace, measured step; see **gait** 1.

**hit one's stride*** — *Syn.* get up to normal, get better, arrive; see **develop** 1, **improve.**

**take in one's stride*** — *Syn.* handle, do easily, do naturally, deal with, cope; see also **manage** 1.

**stride,** *v.* — *Syn.* stamp, march, walk pompously; see **walk** 1.

**strident,** *modif.* — *Syn.* shrill, grating, vociferous; see **loud** 1.

*See Synonym Study at* VOCIFEROUS.

**strife,** *n.* **1.** [Verbal contention] — *Syn.* quarrel, discard, animosity, conflict; see **disagreement, discord.**

**2.** [Physical struggle] — *Syn.* fighting, struggle, combat; see **fight** 1.

*See Synonym Study at* DISCORD.

**strike,** *n.* **1.** [An organized refusal] — *Syn.* walkout, deadlock, work stoppage, quitting, sit-down strike, job action, work-to-rule (British), labor dispute, sickout, tie-up, *heulga* (Spanish), *brazos caidos* (Spanish), slowdown, called strike, sympathetic strike, general strike, wildcat strike, token strike, confrontation, sit-in*, teach-in*, study-in*, blue flu*, love-in*, mill-in*; see also **revolution** 2.

**2.** [A discovery] — *Syn.* gold strike, success, find, unfolding, exposure, disclosure, opening up, laying bare, bringing to light, uncovering; see also **discovery** 1.

**3.** [A blow] — *Syn.* hit, stroke, punch; see **blow** 1.

**4.** [A pitched ball] — *Syn.* ball swung at and missed, pitch over the plate, called strike; see **pitch** 2.

**have two strikes against one*** — *Syn.* be in danger, be in trouble, be uncertain, be troubled, be handicapped; see also **doubt** 2, **fear** 1.

**on strike** — *Syn.* striking, protesting, on the picket line, out on strike; see **unemployed.**

**strike,** *v.* **1.** [To hit] — *Syn.* box, punch, thump; see **beat** 2, **hit** 1.

**2.** [To refuse to work] — *Syn.* walk out, tie up, sit down, slow down, work to rule (British), go out, be on strike, sit in, arbitrate, negotiate a contract, picket, boycott, stop, quit, enforce idleness, resist, hold out for, hit the bricks*; see also **oppose** 1, 2, **rebel** 1.

**3.** [To light] — *Syn.* kindle, inflame, scratch, light up; see **burn** 1, **ignite.**

**4.** [To seem] — *Syn.* look, have the semblance, be plausible; see **seem.**

**5.** [To find] — *Syn.* uncover, open up, lay bare; see **discover.**

**strike a balance,** *v.* — *Syn.* compromise, make mutual concessions, make an adjustment, give and take, meet halfway; see also **adjust** 1, **arbitrate, negotiate** 1.

**strike a light,** *v.* — *Syn.* illuminate, strike a match, light up; see **burn** 1, **ignite, light** 1.

**strike it rich*,** *v.* — *Syn.* strike oil, strike gold, hit the jackpot*, win the lottery*, become wealthy, make money; see also **prosper.**

**strike out,** *v.* **1.** [To begin something new] — *Syn.* start, start out, initiate, find a new approach; see **begin** 1.

**2.** [To cancel] — *Syn.* obliterate, invalidate, expunge; see **cancel** 1, **remove** 1.

**3.** [In baseball, to make three strikes] — *Syn.* be struck out, be called out, make an out, fan*, whiff*, bat the breeze*, go down swinging*.

**striker*,** *n.* — *Syn.* worker on strike, holdout, turnout, walk-outer, sit-downer; see also **protester.**

**striking,** *modif.* — *Syn.* arresting, conspicuous, noticeable, attractive, impressive, surprising, astonishing, electrifying, stunning, staggering, confounding, unusual, unwonted, singular, remarkable, extraordinary, outstanding, prominent, dazzling, startling, fascinating, noteworthy, distinguished, memorable, marked; see also **beautiful** 1, 2, **unusual** 1, 2. — *Ant.* UGLY, common, insignificant.

*See Synonym Study at* NOTICEABLE.

**string,** *n.* **1.** [A sequence] — *Syn.* chain, succession, procession; see **line** 1, **order** 3, **sequence** 1, **series.**

**2.** [Twine] — *Syn.* cord, twist, strand; see **rope, twine.**

**string along,** *v.* **1.** [To follow faithfully] — *Syn.* bow to, accede to, accept, tolerate; see **agree, follow** 2.

**2.** [To deceive] — *Syn.* fool, trick, dupe, cozen; see **deceive.**

**string bean,** *n.* — *Syn.* green bean, snap bean. Varieties include: green, wax, pole, bush, Italian, Kentucky wonder, French-cut, stringless; see also **bean** 1, **food, vegetable.**

**stringent,** *modif.* **1.** [Strict] — *Syn.* acrimonious, rigorous, harsh; see **severe** 2.

**2.** [Compelling] — *Syn.* forceful, powerful, poignant; see **convincing** 2, **valid** 1, 2.

**string of beads,** *n.* — *Syn.* chain, beads, neckband, rosary; see **necklace.**

**string up*,** *v.* — *Syn.* hang, execute by hanging, hang by the neck until dead; see **kill** 1.

**stringy,** *modif.* **1.** [Fibrous] — *Syn.* wiry, ropy, threadlike; see **fibrous.**

**2.** [Viscous] — *Syn.* pasty, gluey, gummy; see **sticky.**

**strip,** *n.* — *Syn.* tape, slip, shred; see **band** 1, **layer, piece** 1.

**strip,** *v.* **1.** [Undress] — *Syn.* divest, denude, bare, disrobe, become naked; see also **undress.**

**2.** [Remove] — *Syn.* displace, bare, remove, peel, dismantle, tear, lift off; see also **peel, remove** 1, **shred.**

*SYN.* — **strip** implies the pulling or tearing off of clothing, outer covering, etc. and often connotes forcible or even violent action and total deprivation /to *strip* paper off a wall, *stripped* of sham/; **denude** implies that the thing stripped is left exposed or naked /land *denuded* of vegetation/; **divest** implies the taking away of something with which one has been clothed or invested /an official *divested* of authority/; **bare** simply implies an uncovering or laying open to view /to *bare* one's head in reverence/; **dismantle** implies the act of stripping a house, ship, etc. of all of its furniture or equipment /a *dismantled* factory/

**stripe,** *n.* — *Syn.* line, division, strip, discoloration, varicolor, contrasting color, streak, border, decoration, demarcation, ribbon; see also **band** 1, **layer.**

**striped,** *modif.* — *Syn.* lined, barred, banded; see **barred** 1, **ruled** 2.

**stripling,** *n.* — *Syn.* fledgling, youngster, minor; see **youth** 3.

**strive,** *v.* — *Syn.* endeavor, aim, attempt; see **try** 1.

*See Synonym Study at* TRY.

**stroke,** *n.* — *Syn.* box, cuff, rap; see **blow** 1.

**stroll,** *v.* — *Syn.* ramble, saunter, gallivant; see **roam, walk** 1.

**strong,** *modif.* **1.** [Physically strong; *said especially of persons*] — *Syn.* robust, sturdy, firm, muscular, sinewy, thewy, vigorous, stout, hardy, big, heavy, husky, lusty, active, potent, energetic, tough, virile, doughty, mighty, athletic, able-bodied, powerful, manly, heavy-set, stalwart, brawny, burly, wiry, strapping, having what it takes\*, hard as nails\*, made of iron\*, in fine feather\*, having the makings\*. — *Ant.* WEAK, emaciated, feeble.

**2.** [Physically strong; *said especially of things*] — *Syn.* solid, sturdy, firm, staunch, unimpaired, well-established, well-founded, well-built, secure, tough, durable, able, unyielding, steady, stable, fixed, sound, powerful, mighty, tough, well-made, rugged, substantial, reinforced. — *Ant.* UNSTABLE, insecure, tottering.

**3.** [Healthy] — *Syn.* sound, hale, hearty; see **sense** 1, **healthy** 1.

**4.** [Firm] — *Syn.* steadfast, determined, staunch; see **resolute** 2.

**5.** [Intelligent] — *Syn.* sagacious, clear-headed, perceptive; see **intelligent** 1.

**6.** [Powerful] — *Syn.* great, mighty, influential; see **powerful** 1.

**7.** [Extreme] — *Syn.* drastic, forceful, strict; see **extreme** 2.

**8.** [Potent in effect] — *Syn.* powerful, potent, high-powered, stiff, power-packed, effective, hard, high-potency, stimulating, inebriating, intoxicating, hot\*, spiked\*.

**9.** [Undiluted] — *Syn.* straight, rich, unmixed; see **concentrated** 1.

**10.** [Intense] — *Syn.* sharp, acute, keen; see **intense.**

**11.** [Distinct] — *Syn.* clear, marked, sharp; see **definite** 2, **obvious** 1, 2.

**12.** [Competent] — *Syn.* adept, proficient, skilled; see **able.**

**13.** [Financially sound] — *Syn.* stable, solid, safe; see **reliable** 2.

**14.** [Convincing] — *Syn.* cogent, potent, forceful; see **persuasive.**

**come on strong\*** — *Syn.* impose oneself, put the make on, make a strong impression, be aggressive.

**strongbox,** *n.* — *Syn.* box, coffer, cashbox, depository; see **safe, vault** 2.

**strong for\*,** *modif.* — *Syn.* approving, favorable to, supporting, in favor of; see **favorable** 3.

**stronghold,** *n.* **1.** [A fortification] — *Syn.* fortress, citadel, castle; see **fortification** 2.

**2.** [A center of interest] — *Syn.* hotbed, center, haven; see **refuge** 1.

**strongly,** *modif.* — *Syn.* stoutly, vigorously, actively, heavily, fully, completely, sturdily, robustly, energetically, firmly, staunchly, solidly, securely, immovably, steadily, heartily, forcibly, resolutely, capably, powerfully, invincibly, indomitably, influentially, greatly, richly, well.

**strop,** *v.* — *Syn.* strap, grind, hone; see **sharpen** 1.

**struck,** *modif.* **1.** [Hit] — *Syn.* smacked, pounded, hurt; see **hit** 1.

**2.** [Closed by a strike] — *Syn.* shut down, having labor trouble, idle; see **closed** 2.

**structural,** *modif.* — *Syn.* fundamental, basic, organic, formative, skeletal, anatomic, anatomical, formational, formalistic, constructural, architectural, tectonic, geotectonic. — *Ant.* TANGLED, chaotic, unorganized.

**structural linguistics,** *n.* — *Syn.* structural analysis, structure, structuralism; see **grammar, language** 2.

**structure,** *n.* **1.** [Construction] — *Syn.* arrangement, composition, fabrication; see **formation** 1.

**2.** [A building] — *Syn.* construction, edifice, house; see **building** 1.

*See Synonym Study at* BUILDING.

**struggle,** *n.* **1.** [A fight] — *Syn.* conflict, contest, strife; see **fight** 1.

*See Synonym Study at* FIGHT.

**2.** [Effort] — *Syn.* exertion, strain, travail; see **effort** 1, 2.

**struggle,** *v.* — *Syn.* strive, grapple, cope, try; see **fight** 1.

*See Synonym Study at* TRY.

**strum,** *v.* — *Syn.* tweak, pluck, pick; see **play** 3.

**strumpet,** *n.* — *Syn.* streetwalker, whore, harlot; see **prostitute.**

**strut,** *v.* — *Syn.* swagger, put on airs, stride proudly, walk with a strut; see also **walk** 1.

**stub,** *n.* — *Syn.* stump, short end, snag, root, remainder, remnant, dock, counterfoil.

**stubborn,** *modif.* — *Syn.* obstinate, unreasonable, unyielding, headstrong; see **obstinate** 1, **resolute** 2.

*See Synonym Study at* OBSTINATE.

**stubbornly,** *modif.* — *Syn.* persistently, doggedly, tenaciously; see **firmly** 2, **obstinately.**

**stubbornness,** *n.* — *Syn.* obstinacy, doggedness, inflexibility, pertinacity, indomitability, perverseness, perversity, contumacy, obduracy, adamancy, refractoriness, mulishness, sullenness, pigheadedness, stupidity, intractableness, bullheadedness, moroseness; see also **determination** 2. — *Ant.* FLEXIBILITY, amenability, good nature.

**stubby,** *modif.* — *Syn.* chubby, stout, stocky; see **fat** 1, **short** 1.

**stucco,** *n.* — *Syn.* cement stucco, plaster, concrete, pebbledash; see **cement.**

**stuck,** *modif.* **1.** [Tight] — *Syn.* fast, fastened, cemented; see **tight** 2.

**2.** [Stranded] — *Syn.* grounded, lost, high and dry\*; see **abandoned** 1.

**3.** [Perplexed] — *Syn.* at a loss, puzzled, baffled; see **doubtful** 2.

**stud,** *n.* — *Syn.* studding, framing, upright; see also **post** 1, **stick.**

**student,** *n.* — *Syn.* learner, pupil, scholar, disciple, undergraduate, coed\*, collegian, novice, graduate student, schoolchild, schoolboy, schoolgirl, docent, apprentice, registrant, trainee, tutee, autodidact, schoolmate, classmate, seminarian, preschooler, cadet, freshman, sophomore, junior, senior, lowerclassman, upperclassman, postgraduate, doctoral candidate, bookworm, grind\*, nerd\*, preppy\*, undergrad\*; see also **follower, freshman.**

---

*SYN.* — **student** is applied either to one attending an institution above the elementary level or to one who is making a study of a particular subject [*a student* of social problems]; **pupil** is applied either to a child in school or to a person who is under the personal supervision of a teacher [Heifetz was a *pupil* of Leopold Auer]; **scholar,** orig. equivalent to **pupil,** is now usually applied to one who has general erudition or who is highly versed in a particular branch of learning [a noted classical *scholar*]

---

**studied,** *modif.* **1.** [Deliberate] — *Syn.* plotted, prepared, premeditated; see **deliberate** 1, **planned.**

**2.** [Investigated] — *Syn.* thought about, thought through, examined, gone into; see **investigated, reviewed.**

**studio,** *n.* — *Syn.* workshop, atelier, workroom, salon, broadcasting room, radio station, television station, movie studio, production studio, recording studio.

**studious,** *modif.* — *Syn.* industrious, thoughtful, contemplative, busy, well-read, well-informed, scholarly, lettered, academic, learned, bookish, earnest, diligent, assiduous, attentive, sedulous, loving study, given to study. — *Ant.* LAZY, unproductive, capricious.

**study,** *n.* **1.** [A place in which to study] — *Syn.* schoolroom, library, studio; see **office** 3, **room** 2.
**2.** [The act of studying] — *Syn.* research, investigation, memorizing, learning, reading, inquiry, examination, consideration, questioning, analyzing, comparison, thought, reflection, reasoning; see also **education** 1, **learn** 1.
**3.** [That which one studies] — *Syn.* subject, branch of learning, field of knowledge, art; see **knowledge** 1.
**study,** *v.* **1.** [To endeavor to learn] — *Syn.* read, go into, refresh the memory, read up on, burn the midnight oil, bone up, go over, cram, think, go in for, inquire, bury oneself in, dive into, plunge into.
**2.** [To endeavor to understand] — *Syn.* examine, scrutinize, analyze, investigate; see **consider** 3, **examine** 1. *See Synonym Study at* CONSIDER.
**study up on\*,** *v.* — *Syn.* prepare oneself on, become conversant with, go over, go into, do one's homework\*; see also **prepare** 1, **study** 1.
**stuff,** *n.* **1.** [Material] — *Syn.* elemental part, principle, essence; see **material** 2.
**2.** [Cloth] — *Syn.* tissue, web, textile; see **cloth.**
**stuff,** *v.* — *Syn.* ram, pad, wad, shove; see **fill** 1, **pack** 2.
**stuffed,** *modif.* — *Syn.* crowded, packed, crammed; see **full** 1.
**stuffed shirt\*,** *n.* — *Syn.* phony\*, pompous person, snob, incompetent; see **braggart, fake, impostor.**
**stuffing,** *n.* **1.** [Material used to pad] — *Syn.* packing, wadding, padding, quilting, caulking, filler, packing material.
Materials used as stuffing include: wool, cotton, kapok, sisal, feathers, fur, waste, cotton waste, rags, batting, excelsior, horsehair, shredded paper, sawdust, moss, polyester fiber.
**2.** [Material used to stuff fowl, fish, etc.] — *Syn.* dressing, forcemeat, filling; see **dressing.**
**stuffy,** *modif.* **1.** [Close] — *Syn.* confined, stagnant, muggy; see **close** 5.
**2.** [\*Conservative] — *Syn.* conventional, stodgy, uninteresting; see **conservative, dull** 3, 4, **old-fashioned.**
**stultify,** *v.* **1.** [To ridicule] — *Syn.* make a fool of, make ridiculous, make absurd, mock; see **ridicule.**
**2.** [To inhibit] — *Syn.* smother, stifle, suffocate, have a dulling effect on, negate; see also **hinder.**
**stumble,** *v.* **1.** [To move in a stumbling manner] — *Syn.* blunder, flounder, lurch, falter; see **waver.**
**2.** [To trip] — *Syn.* pitch, tilt, topple; see **fall** 1, **trip** 1.
**stumbling block,** *n.* — *Syn.* obstacle, hindrance, barricade; see **barrier, difficulty** 1, 2.
**stump,** *n.* — *Syn.* butt, piece, projection; see **end** 4.
**stumped\*,** *modif.* — *Syn.* puzzled, baffled, up a stump\*, at a loss; see **bewildered** 2, **uncertain** 2.
**stumpy,** *modif.* — *Syn.* stubby, short and thick, chunky; see **fat** 1, **heavy.**
**stun,** *v.* **1.** [To render unconscious] — *Syn.* hit, put to sleep, knock out, anesthetize; see **deaden** 1, **drug.**
**2.** [To astound] — *Syn.* astonish, bewilder, amaze; see **surprise** 1.
**stunned,** *modif.* — *Syn.* dazed, astonished, amazed, dumbfounded; see **shocked.**
**stunning,** *modif.* — *Syn.* striking, astounding, marvelous, astonishing, remarkable; see also **beautiful** 1, 2, **charming, handsome** 2.
**stunt\*,** *n.* — *Syn.* feat, trick, exploit, act, skit, comic sketch; see also **performance** 2.
**stupefaction,** *n.* — *Syn.* astonishment, amazement, surprise, perplexity; see **stupor, wonder** 1.
**stupefied,** *modif.* — *Syn.* astonished, astounded, amazed, dazzled; see **bewildered, surprised.**

**stupefy,** *v.* **1.** [To stun] — *Syn.* dull, numb, benumb; see **deaden** 1.
**2.** [To amaze] — *Syn.* astound, astonish, startle; see **surprise** 1.
**stupendous,** *modif.* — *Syn.* breathtaking, marvelous, miraculous; see **grand** 2.
**stupid,** *modif.* **1.** [Foolish] — *Syn.* senseless, brainless, idiotic, simple, ignorant, shallow, ill-advised, imprudent, witless, irrational, inane, ridiculous, mindless, ludicrous, blind, muddled, absurd, half-witted, funny, comical, silly, laughable, nonsensical, daft, illogical, indiscreet, unintelligent, irresponsible, coquettish, shallow-brained, scatterbrained, crackbrained, addled, inconsistent, flirting, unwary, incautious, misguided, wild, injudicious, imbecile, addleheaded, lunatic, insane, mad, crazy, moronic, touched, freakish, comic, puerile, inexpedient, narrow-minded, incoherent, childish, anile, senile, monstrous, outrageous, far-fetched, extravagant, preposterous, unreasonable, chimerical, asinine, useless, unwise, thoughtless, careless, vain, fatuous, light, light-headed, flighty, madcap, giddy, cuckoo\*, dippy\*, not seeking for looking\*, boneheaded\*, goofy\*, cracked\*, dumb\*, half-baked\*, in the dark\*, having a block for a head\*, not knowing what's what\*, in darkness\*, dead to the world\*, in a daze\*, knowing nothing\*, groping in the dark\*, green\*, wacky\*, harebrained\*, tetched\*, damn-fool\*, block-headed\*, not seeing an inch beyond one's nose\*, screwy\*, bats\*, cock-eyed\*, loony\*, batty\*, nutty\*. — *Ant.* SANE, wise, judicious.
**2.** [Dull] — *Syn.* dense, obtuse, slow, retarded, dull-witted; see also **dull** 3, **shallow** 2. *See Synonym Study at* SILLY.

---

*SYN.* — **stupid** implies a lack of intelligence or an incapacity for perceiving or learning such as might be shown by one in a mental stupor /a *stupid* idea/; **dull** implies a mental sluggishness that may be constitutional or may result from fatigue, disease, etc. /the fever left me *dull* and listless/; **dense** suggests obtuseness, or an irritating failure to understand quickly or to react intelligently /too *dense* to take a hint/; **slow** suggests that the quickness to learn, but not necessarily the capacity for learning, is below average /a pupil *slow* in most studies/; **retarded** is applied to those behind others of the same age or class because of mental deficiency /a *retarded* pupil/

---

**stupidity,** *n.* **1.** [Dullness of mind] — *Syn.* stupor, stupefaction, apathy, slowness, inertia, heaviness, obtuseness, sluggishness, stolidity, feeble-mindedness, folly, weakness, silliness, nonsense, absurdity, imbecility, imprudence, lunacy, simplicity, idiocy, brainlessness, shallowness, weak-mindedness, fatuousness, fatuity, incapacity, short-sightedness, poverty of intellect, impracticality, addle-headedness, dullness of comprehension, puerility, senility, ineptitude, giddiness, thickheadedness, asininity, muddleheadedness, slowness, lack of judgment, injudiciousness, stupidness, slow-wittedness, bluntness, emptiness of mind, insensibility, doltishness, ignorance, lack of intelligence, mental deficiency, fatuity, boobishness\*, nitwittedness\*, dippiness\*, battiness\*, balminess\*, goofiness\*, baloney\*, nertz\*, bull\*, hooey\*, piffle\*, phooey\*, blatherskite\*. — *Ant.* WISDOM, intelligence, judgment.
**2.** [Extreme folly] — *Syn.* witlessness, senselessness, idiocy, imbecility, lunacy, nonsensicality, nonsense, indiscretion, ludicrousness, absurdity, asininity, silliness, simplicity, ineptitude, madness, infatuation, giddiness, rashness, frivolity, irrationality, damn-foolishness; see

also **carelessness.** — *Ant.* ACUMEN, shrewdness, canniness.

**3.** [A stupid act] — *Syn.* foolishness, folly, madness, imbecility, misguidedness; see also sense 2.

**stupidly,** *modif.* — *Syn.* imprudently, stubbornly, obtusely; see **foolishly, rashly.**

**stupor,** *n.* — *Syn.* insensibility, lethargy, apathy, stupefaction, asphyxia, swoon, coma, fainting, swooning, unconsciousness, numbness, torpor, syncope, narcosis, somnolence, anesthesia, trance, revery, study, brown study, hypnosis, inertness, analgesia, suspended animation, amazement, bewilderment.

**sturdy,** *modif.* — *Syn.* firm, resolute, unyielding; see **strong** 1, 2.

**stutter,** *v.* — *Syn.* stumble, falter, sputter; see **stammer.**

**sty,** *n.* — *Syn.* den, hovel, pigsty, pigpen, hole; see also **dump, pen** 1.

**Stygian,** *modif.* — *Syn.* infernal, hellish, dreary, gloomy; see **dark** 1, **dismal** 1.

**style,** *n.* **1.** [Distinctive manner] — *Syn.* way, form, technique; see **method** 2.

**2.** [Fashion] — *Syn.* vogue, habit, custom; see **fashion** 2.

**3.** [Behavior] — *Syn.* carriage, bearing, manner, tendency; see **behavior** 1, **characteristic, habit** 1.

*See Synonym Study at* FASHION.

**in style** — *Syn.* stylish, modish, current; see **fashionable, popular** 1.

**stylish,** *modif.* — *Syn.* chic, smart, in fashion; see **fashionable.**

**stylist,** *n.* **1.** [One who writes with style] — *Syn.* romanticist, impressionist, classicist; see **author** 1, 2, **composer, writer.**

**2.** [A designer] — *Syn.* couturier, couturière, fashion designer, decorator.

**stylize,** *v.* — *Syn.* conventionalize, formalize, accord; see **conform.**

**stylus,** *n.* — *Syn.* graver, stylograph, burin; see **knife, pen** 3.

**stymie\*,** *v.* — *Syn.* block, impede, obstruct, stump; see **hinder.**

**suave,** *modif.* — *Syn.* sophisticated, agreeable, urbane, diplomatic, politic, worldly, polite, bland, smooth; see also **cultured, pleasant** 1.

---

**SYN.** — **suave** suggests the smoothly gracious social manner of one who deals with people easily and tactfully [a *suave* sophisticate]; **urbane** suggests the social poise of one who is highly cultivated and has had much worldly experience [an *urbane* cosmopolite]; **diplomatic** implies adroitness and tactfulness in dealing with people and handling delicate situations, sometimes in such a way as to gain one's own ends [a *diplomatic* answer that avoided offending either party]; **politic** also expresses this idea, often stressing the expediency or opportunism of a particular policy pursued [a *politic* move]; **bland** is the least complex of these terms, simply implying a gentle or ingratiating pleasantness and a lack of irritating factors [a *bland* disposition]

---

**subaltern,** *modif.* — *Syn.* of lower rank, servile, inferior, secondary; see **subject** 1, **subordinate.**

**subaqueous,** *modif.* — *Syn.* underwater, submarine, submersed; see **undersea.**

**subconscious,** *modif.* — *Syn.* unconscious, suppressed, repressed, subliminal, innermost, inmost; see also **mental** 2.

**subconscious,** *n.* — *Syn.* subconsciousness, preconscious, inner self, mind; see **psyche, soul** 2.

**subdivide,** *v.* — *Syn.* part, redivide, partition; see **divide** 1.

**subdivision,** *n.* **1.** [A class] — *Syn.* group, subclass, smaller group, subsidiary group, minor class; see also **class** 1, **division** 2.

**2.** [A tract] — *Syn.* development, building lots, community, neighborhood; see **tract.**

**subdue,** *v.* **1.** [To vanquish] — *Syn.* conquer, overcome, subjugate; see **defeat** 1, 2.

**2.** [To bring under control] — *Syn.* put down, quash, tame, suppress; see **command** 2, **restrain** 1.

**3.** [To tone down] — *Syn.* soften, tone down, moderate, repress; see **quiet** 1.

*See Synonym Study at* DEFEAT.

**subject,** *modif.* **1.** [Under rule] — *Syn.* governed, ruled, controlled, directed, obedient, submissive, subaltern, servile, slavish, subservient, subjected, at one's feet, at the mercy of.

**2.** [Dependent] — *Syn.* liable to, contingent on, subject to, dependent on, open to, accountable to, answerable to; see also **subordinate.**

**subject,** *n.* **1.** [Matter for discussion] — *Syn.* substance, matter, theme, material, topic, thesis, text, question, problem, theorem, motion, resolution, point, case, gist, matter in hand, subject for inquiry, item on the agenda, topic under consideration, field of inquiry, head, chapter, proposition, argument, thought, discussion.

**2.** [A title] — *Syn.* head, caption, legend; see **name** 1, **title** 1.

**3.** [One owing allegiance] — *Syn.* citizen, national, vassal; see **citizen.**

*See Synonym Study at* CITIZEN.

---

**SYN.** — **subject** is the general word for whatever is dealt with in discussion, study, writing, art, etc. [math is her favorite *subject*, her son is a frequent *subject* in her paintings]; a **theme** is a subject developed or elaborated upon in a literary or artistic work, or one that constitutes the underlying motif of the work [a novel with a social *theme*]; a **topic** is a subject of common interest selected for individual treatment, as in an essay, or for discussion by a group of persons [baseball is their favorite *topic* of conversation]; **text** is specifically applied to a Biblical passage chosen as the subject of a sermon

---

**subject,** *v.* — *Syn.* control, tame, master, subdue, reduce, subjugate, enslave, vanquish, defeat, rule, enthrall, dominate, subordinate, make subservient, suppress, constrain, Finlandize, restrain, lead captive; see also **govern** 1, **hinder.** — *Ant.* LIBERATE, release, rescue.

**subjection,** *n.* — *Syn.* bondage, subservience, servitude, colonialism, servility, dependence, subordination; see also **slavery** 1.

**subjective,** *modif.* **1.** [Not objective] — *Syn.* nonobjective, biased, personal, idiosyncratic; see **individual** 1, **prejudiced.**

**2.** [Related to the mind] — *Syn.* illusory, fanciful, resulting from a mental construct; see **mental** 2.

**subjectively,** *modif.* — *Syn.* internally, intrinsically, individually, immanently, self-centeredly, egocentrically, mentally, nonobjectively, emotionally, inner, interior, inherently, introspectively; see also **personally** 2.

**subject matter,** *n.* — *Syn.* essentials, contents, essence; see **subject** 1, **topic.**

**subject of** (*or* **under**) **discussion,** *n.* — *Syn.* question, point, matter in hand; see **subject** 1, **topic.**

**subjoin,** *v.* — *Syn.* append, postfix, suffix; see **join** 1.

**subjugate,** *v.* **1.** [To subdue] — *Syn.* suppress, enslave, master; see **defeat** 1, **hinder, restrain** 1, **subject.**

**2.** [To conquer] — *Syn.* overcome, crush, triumph over; see **defeat** 2.

*See Synonym Study at* DEFEAT.

**subjugated,** *modif.* — *Syn.* ruled, controlled, directed; see **governed** 1, **subject** 1.

**sublet,** *v.* — *Syn.* sublease, underlet, lease; see **rent** 1, 2.

**sublimate,** *v.* **1.** [To purify] — *Syn.* cleanse, refine, uphold; see **clean, purify.**

**2.** [To divert] — *Syn.* redirect, transfer, control one's feelings, repress; see **suppress.**

**sublime,** *modif.* **1.** [Noble] — *Syn.* exalted, lofty, stately; see **grand** 2, **noble** 1, 2.

**2.** [Inspiring] — *Syn.* awe-inspiring, majestic, heavenly, divine, breath-taking.

**sublimity,** *n.* — *Syn.* importance, eminence, esteem, loftiness; see **grandeur.**

**submarine,** *n.* **1.** [A submersible boat] — *Syn.* underseas boat, submersible, sub*; see **ship, warship.**

**2.** [A long sandwich] — *Syn.* sub, hero, grinder, hoagie, poor boy, Cuban sandwich, Italian sandwich, Italian, bomber, wedge.

**submerge,** *v.* **1.** [To cause to sink] — *Syn.* submerse, engulf, swamp; see **immerse** 1, **sink** 2.

**2.** [To go downward] — *Syn.* descend, immerse, subside; see **sink** 1.

**submersed,** *modif.* — *Syn.* submerged, underwater, marine; see **wet** 1.

**submission,** *n.* **1.** [Resignation] — *Syn.* obedience, meekness, assent; see **docility, resignation** 1.

**2.** [Subjection] — *Syn.* prostration, servility, cringing; see **slavery** 1.

**submissive,** *modif.* — *Syn.* passive, tractable, yielding; see **docile.**

**submit,** *v.* **1.** [To offer] — *Syn.* tender, proffer, present; see **offer** 1.

**2.** [To surrender] — *Syn.* capitulate, resign, relinquish; see **obey** 1, **yield** 1.

**3.** [To suggest] — *Syn.* advise, suggest, offer, put forward; see **propose** 1.

**subnormal,** *modif.* — *Syn.* witless, inane, foolish; see **dull** 3, **stupid** 1.

**subordinate,** *n.* — *Syn.* underling, junior, subaltern, assistant, helper, aide; see also **assistant.**

**subordinate,** *modif.* — *Syn.* inferior, junior, smaller, sub, low, baser, underaverage, insignificant, subnormal, paltry, playing second fiddle, not hold a candle to, not up to snuff, below par, below the mark, unequal to, not comparable to, in the shade, nothing to brag about, at a low ebb, lower, minor, depending on, lower in rank, subject, subservient, being a satellite, submissive, subsidiary, accessory, auxiliary, ancillary; see also **secondary** 1, **under** 2, 3. — *Ant.* SUPERIOR, higher, excellent.

**subordination,** *n.* — *Syn.* subjection, submission, servitude; see **slavery** 1.

**subpoena,** *n.* — *Syn.* summons, warrant, citation; see **command** 1.

**subpoena,** *v.* — *Syn.* cite, arraign, call; see **summon** 1.

**sub rosa,** *modif.* — *Syn.* secretly, obscurely, privately, confidentially; see **secretly.**

**subscribe,** *v.* **1.** [To give personal support] — *Syn.* advocate, consent, second; see **support** 2.

**2.** [To give financial support] — *Syn.* support, give, promise; see **contribute, pay** 1.

**3.** [Suggest] — *Syn.* submit, propose, advise; see **recommend** 1.

**4.** [To obey] — *Syn.* consent, accept, acquiesce; see **obey** 1.

**subscriber,** *n.* — *Syn.* contributor, attester, signer, backer, sponsor, endorser, paying member, regular taker; see also **patron** 1, **supporter.**

**subscript,** *n.* — *Syn.* sequel, index, addendum; see **appendix.**

**subscription,** *n.* — *Syn.* consent, approval, agreement, support, acceptance, annual payment; see also **dues, recommendation** 1, **signature.**

**subsequent,** *modif.* — *Syn.* succeeding, consequent, after; see **following.**

**subsequently,** *modif.* — *Syn.* after, consequently, afterward, in the end; see **finally** 2.

**subserve,** *v.* — *Syn.* advance, support, aid; see **promote** 1, **serve** 1.

**subservient,** *modif.* **1.** [Subordinate] — *Syn.* auxiliary, subsidiary, secondary, ancillary.

**2.** [Docile] — *Syn.* submissive, obsequious, servile; see **docile.**

**subside,** *v.* — *Syn.* recede, sink, dwindle, wane; see **ebb, fall** 1.

*See Synonym Study at* WANE.

**subsidiary,** *modif.* — *Syn.* assistant, auxiliary, subject; see **helpful** 1, **secondary** 1, **subordinate.**

**subsidize,** *v.* — *Syn.* support, finance, back, subsidize; see **contribute, promote** 1.

**subsidy,** *n.* — *Syn.* premium, indemnity, honorarium, bonus, tribute, gratuity, allowance, aid, bounty, support, pension, reward, subvention, endowment, grant, bequest, scholarship; see also **fellowship** 4, **gift** 1, **grant, payment** 1.

**subsist,** *v.* — *Syn.* stay alive, remain alive, scrape by, get along, feed on, be, go it alone, eke out an existence, live on, barely exist; see also **live** 4.

**subsistence,** *n.* **1.** [The supporting of life] — *Syn.* living, sustenance, maintenance, support, keep, bread, bread and butter, necessities of life. — *Ant.* LACK, want, hunger.

**2.** [The means of supporting life] — *Syn.* means, circumstances, resources, property, money, riches, wealth, competence, capital, substance, affluence, independence, gratuity, fortune, dowry, legacy, earnings, wages, salary, income, pension; see also **funds.** — *Ant.* POVERTY, penury, penniless.

**subsoil,** *n.* — *Syn.* loam, dirt, gravel; see **clay, earth** 2.

**substance,** *n.* **1.** [Essence] — *Syn.* body, core, pith; see **basis** 1, **essence** 1, **matter** 1.

**2.** [Object] — *Syn.* matter, material, being, object, item, person, animal, something, element; see also **thing** 1.

**in substance** — *Syn.* in essence, substantially, actually; see **essentially.**

**substandard,** *modif.* — *Syn.* inferior, second-rate, not good enough, low; see **cheap** 1, **poor** 2.

**substantial,** *modif.* **1.** [Strong] — *Syn.* solid, firm, sturdy, stout; see **strong** 1, 2.

**2.** [Important] — *Syn.* valuable, extraordinary, principal; see **important** 1, 2.

**3.** [Real] — *Syn.* material, actual, visible; see **real** 2, **tangible.**

**4.** [Considerable] — *Syn.* ample, abundant, plentiful; see **large** 1, **much** 2.

**5.** [Wealthy] — *Syn.* affluent, well-to-do, opulent; see **rich** 1.

**substantiality,** *n.* — *Syn.* materiality, physicality, realness, actuality; see **reality** 1.

**substantially,** *modif.* **1.** [Essentially] — *Syn.* really, mainly, in essence, in fact, in reality; see also **essentially.**

**2.** [Heavily] — *Syn.* extensively, considerably, largely; see **heavily, much** 1, 2.

**substantiate,** *v.* **1.** [To prove] — *Syn.* confirm, verify, bear out; see **prove, verify.**

**2.** [To actualize] — *Syn.* reify, realize, incarnate; see **complete** 1.

*See Synonym Study at* VERIFY.

**substantiation,** *n.* — *Syn.* embodiment, approval, vindication; see **proof** 1.

**substantive,** *n.* — *Syn.* nominal, common noun, proper noun; see **noun.**

**substitute,** *n.* — *Syn.* deputy, double, ghost writer, dummy, relief, fill-in, stand-in, understudy, proxy, alternate, surrogate, backup, replacement, ringer*, ghost*, sub*, pinch-hitter*; see also **agent** 1, **assistant, delegate.**

**substitute,** *v.* **1.** [To exchange] — *Syn.* interchange, change, replace; see **exchange** 1.

**2.** [To take the place of] — *Syn.* act for, do the work of, replace, supplant, displace, supercede, take another's place, double for, answer for, make way for, count for, serve in one's stead, pass for, go for, go as, step up, fill another's position, take over another's duties, fill in for, pinch-hit for*, take the rap for*, sub for*, spell*, go to bat for*, ring in*, front for*, fill someone's shoes*.

**substitution,** *n.* — *Syn.* replacement, change, swap; see **exchange** 3.

**substratum,** *n.* — *Syn.* footing, base, frame, bed; see **foundation** 2, **layer.**

**substructure,** *n.* — *Syn.* base, ground, infrastructure; see **foundation** 2.

**subterfuge,** *n.* — *Syn.* deception, device, artifice, ploy; see **deception** 1, **trick** 1.

*See Synonym Study at* DECEPTION.

**subterranean,** *modif.* **1.** [Hidden] — *Syn.* secret, furtive, concealed; see **hidden** 2.

**2.** [Below ground] — *Syn.* subsurface, sunk, sunken, subterraneous; see **underground.**

**subtilize,** *v.* — *Syn.* quibble, mislead, cavil; see **deceive, evade** 1.

**subtle,** *modif.* **1.** [Delicately suggestive] — *Syn.* indirect, implied, insinuated, inferred, illusive; see also **mental, suggestive.**

**2.** [Precise] — *Syn.* definite, complex, exact; see **detailed.**

**3.** [Clever] — *Syn.* ingenious, crafty, deft, shrewd.

**subtlety,** *n.* **1.** [A fine distinction] — *Syn.* nuance, innuendo; see **distinction** 1.

**2.** [Delicacy] — *Syn.* intricacy, exquisiteness, elegance; see **delicacy** 1.

**subtract,** *v.* — *Syn.* deduct, take away, withhold; see **decrease** 2.

**subtraction,** *n.* — *Syn.* deduction, subduction, diminution; see **discount, reduction** 1.

**suburb,** *n.* — *Syn.* outlying district, residential district, suburbia, outskirts, *banlieue* (French), neighborhood; see also **area** 2.

**suburban,** *modif.* — *Syn.* provincial, in the country, rural, beyond the city limits, away from the city; see also **district, local** 1, **rural.** — *Ant.* URBAN, metropolitan, cosmopolitan.

**suburbanite,** *n.* — *Syn.* resident, commuter, traveler; see **citizen.**

**subvention,** *n.* — *Syn.* subsidy, grant, help; see **aid** 1.

**subversion,** *n.* — *Syn.* ruin, overthrow, subversive activities, un-American activities, destruction; see also **defeat** 2, **revolution** 2.

**subversive,** *modif.* — *Syn.* seditious, treasonous, underground, insurgent; see **rebellious** 2.

**subvert,** *v.* — *Syn.* overturn, overthrow, suppress, supplant, supersede, ruin, destroy, extinguish, invert, depress, upset, undermine, corrupt, pervert, demolish, tumble, topple, capsize, reverse, level, throw down, pull down; see also **defeat** 2.

**subway,** *n.* — *Syn.* Underground (British), tube, rapid transit, *Métro* (French), sub*, chute*; see also **railroad, train** 2.

**succeed,** *v.* **1.** [To attain success] — *Syn.* achieve, accomplish, get, prosper, attain, reach, be successful, fulfill, earn, secure, succeed in, score, obtain, thrive, profit, realize, acquire, flourish, be victorious, capture, wrest, reap, benefit, recover, retrieve, gain, receive, master, triumph, possess, overcome, win, win out, surmount, prevail, conquer, vanquish, distance, outdistance, avail, reduce, suppress, worst, outwit, outmaneuver, score a point, be accepted, be well-known, grow famous, carry off, pull off, go off, come off, put through, come through, make one's way, make one's fortune, carry all before one, satisfy one's ambition, make one's mark, come into money*, hit it*, hit the mark*, hit the jackpot*, live high*, gain the day*, arrive*, come out with flying colors*, beat the game*, weather a storm*, work well*, overcome all obstacles*, play one's cards well*, crown*, top*, arrive at*, do oneself proud*, make it*, die game*, make good*, do all right by oneself*, be on top of the heap*, make short work of*, break good for*, cover ground*, get places*, click*, set the world on fire*, carry out*, carry off*, gain one's end*, bear oneself with credit*, work*, cut the mustard*, make a killing*, cut a swath*, put across*. — *Ant.* FAIL, give up, go amiss.

**2.** [To follow in time] — *Syn.* follow after, come after, take the place of, ensue, supervene, supplant, supersede, replace, postdate, displace, come next, become heir to, result, be subsequent to, follow in order, bring up the rear.

*See Synonym Study at* FOLLOW.

**succeeding,** *modif.* — *Syn.* ensuing, following after, next in order; see **following.**

**success,** *n.* **1.** [The fact of succeeding] — *Syn.* achieving, gaining, prospering, attaining, accomplishing, progressing, advancing, triumphing, making a fortune, finishing, completion, consummation, doing, culmination, conclusion, termination, resolution, completion, end, attainment, realization, maturation, breakthrough, victory, triumph, accomplishment, benefiting, profiting, having good luck, being out in front*, making a noise in the world*, making a ten strike*. — *Ant.* FAILURE, disappointment, failing.

**2.** [The fact of having succeeded to a high degree] — *Syn.* fortune, good luck, achievement, gain, benefit, prosperity, victory, advance, attainment, progress, profit, prosperous issue, the life of Riley, bed of roses, favorable outcome. — *Ant.* DEFEAT, loss, disaster.

**3.** [A successful person or thing] — *Syn.* celebrity, famous person, leader, authority, master, expert, man of fortune, somebody*, star*, gallery hit*, bell-ringer*, VIP*, tops*, smash*, worldbeater*. — *Ant.* FAILURE, loser, nonentity.

**successful,** *modif.* — *Syn.* prosperous, fortunate, lucky, victorious, triumphant, auspicious, happy, unbeaten, favorable, fortuitous, strong, propitious, advantageous, encouraging, contented, satisfied, thriving, flourishing, wealthy, up in the world*, ahead of the game*, at the top of the ladder*, in luxury*, out in front*, on the track*, over the hump*, sitting in the catbird seat*, in front of the parade*. — *Ant.* UNSUCCESSFUL, poor, failing.

**successfully,** *modif.* — *Syn.* fortunately, triumphantly, victoriously, happily, favorably, fortuitously, strongly, thrivingly, flourishingly, famously, propitiously, auspiciously, prosperously, contentedly, with colors flying, beyond all expectation, swimmingly★.

**succession,** *n.* — *Syn.* continuation, suite, set; see **sequence** 1, **series.**
*See Synonym Study at* SERIES.

**in succession** — *Syn.* consecutively, successively, in sequence, one after the other; see **consecutive, repeatedly.**

**successive,** *modif.* — *Syn.* serial, succeeding, in line, continuous, progressive; see also **consecutive** 1.

**successor,** *n.* — *Syn.* heir, heir apparent, follower, replacement; see **heir.**

**succinct,** *modif.* — *Syn.* concise, brief, crisp, pithy; see **concise, short** 2, **terse.**
*See Synonym Study at* CONCISE.

**succor,** *n.* — *Syn.* sustenance, help, assistance; see **aid** 1.

**succor,** *v.* — *Syn.* aid, assist, befriend; see **help** 1.
*See Synonym Study at* HELP.

**succulent,** *modif.* — *Syn.* pulpy, tasty, lush, fleshy; see **delicious** 1, **juicy.**

**succulent,** *n.* — *Syn.* cactaceae, crassulacae (*both* Latin), ground cover, desert vegetation, desert flora, houseleek, homewort, fouet, cactus, ice plant, live-forever, semperviva, house plant, hens and chickens; see also **cactus, plant.**

**succumb,** *v.* **1.** [To yield] — *Syn.* submit, surrender, accede; see **yield** 1.
**2.** [To die] — *Syn.* expire, drop, cease; see **die** 1.
*See Synonym Study at* YIELD.

**such,** *modif.* — *Syn.* so, so very, of this kind, of that kind, of the sort, of the degree, so much, before-mentioned.

**such,** *pron.* — *Syn.* this, that, such a one, such an one, such a person, such a thing.

**as such** — *Syn.* in itself, of itself, in and of itself, by its own nature, more than in name only; see also **accordingly, essentially.**

**such as,** *conj. & prep.* — *Syn.* for example, for instance, to give an example; see **including, similarly, thus.**

**such as it is,** *modif.* — *Syn.* as is, however poor it may be, for whatever it is worth, a poor thing but mine own; see **inadequate** 1, **poor** 2.

**suck,** *v.* — *Syn.* absorb, take up, swallow up, engulf.

**sucker,** *n.* **1.** [A fish]
Common suckers include: black horse, red horse, buffalo fish, lumpfish, sand sucker, remora, shark sucker, clingfish, chub sucker, hog sucker, hog molly, quillback, gourd-seed sucker, sweet sucker, jump rock, spotted sucker, brook sucker, lamprey; see also **fish.**
**2.** [★A victim] — *Syn.* dupe, fool, cat's-paw, john★; see **victim** 2.
**3.** [Candy] — *Syn.* sweet, confectionary, lollipop; see **candy.**

**suckle,** *v.* — *Syn.* nurse, nurture, nourish; see **sustain** 2.

**suckling,** *n.* — *Syn.* infant, babe, chick; see **baby** 1.

**suction,** *n.* — *Syn.* sucking, the force of a vacuum, effect of atmospheric pressures; see **attraction, power** 2, **pull** 1.

**sudden,** *modif.* — *Syn.* precipitate, abrupt, immediate, unexpected, unforeseen, swift, impromptu; see also **immediate** 1, **unexpected.**

**all of a sudden** — *Syn.* unexpectedly, suddenly, precipitously; see **quickly** 1.

---

**SYN.** — **sudden** implies extreme quickness or hastiness and, usually, unexpectedness /a *sudden* outburst of temper/; **precipitate** adds the implication of rashness or lack of due deliberation /a *precipitate* decision/; **abrupt** implies an unexpected break coming without warning,

often unceremoniously /taken aback by his *abrupt* departure/ and it may suggest a curtness of speech /an *abrupt* dismissal/; **impetuous** implies vehement impulsiveness or extreme eagerness /an *impetuous* suitor/

---

**suddenly,** *modif.* — *Syn.* without any warning, abruptly, swiftly; see **quickly** 1.

**suds,** *n.* — *Syn.* foam, bubbles, lather; see **froth, soap.**

**sue,** *v.* **1.** [To institute legal proceedings] — *Syn.* prosecute, litigate, claim, file suit, bring suit, contest, accuse, claim damages, seek legal redress, file a claim, prefer a claim, take one to court, go to law, bring action against, enter a lawsuit, file a plea, enter a plea, haul into court, law★; see also **accuse.**
**2.** [To make an appeal] — *Syn.* petition, entreat, solicit, demand; see **appeal** 1.
*See Synonym Study at* APPEAL.

**suet,** *n.* — *Syn.* fat, lard, blubber; see **grease, oil** 1.

**suffer,** *v.* **1.** [To feel pain] — *Syn.* undergo, experience, ache, smart, be in pain, be wounded, agonize, grieve, be racked, be convulsed, languish, droop, flag, sicken, endure torture, get it in the neck, look green about the gills★, complain of, be affected with, go hard with, flinch at, not feel like anything, labor under; see also **hurt** 4.
— *Ant.* RECOVER, be relieved, be restored.
**2.** [To endure] — *Syn.* bear, sustain, put up with; see **endure** 2.
**3.** [To permit] — *Syn.* allow, acquiesce, admit, let, concede, indulge, connive at, stretch a point, authorize, sanction, yield, bow, submit, tolerate; see also **allow** 1.
*See Synonym Study at* ALLOW, ENDURE.

**sufferance,** *n.* — *Syn.* toleration, fortitude, composure; see **endurance** 2, **patience** 1.

**on sufferance** — *Syn.* allowed, tolerated, endured; see **legal** 1, **permitted.**

**sufferer,** *n.* — *Syn.* the sick, injured person, patient, martyr; see **victim** 1.

**suffering,** *n.* — *Syn.* distress, misery, affliction; see **difficulty** 1, 2, **pain** 2, **distress.**
*See Synonym Study at* DISTRESS.

**suffice,** *v.* — *Syn.* answer, avail, serve; see **satisfy** 3.

**sufficiency,** *n.* — *Syn.* adequacy, enough, supply; see **plenty.**

**sufficient,** *modif.* — *Syn.* enough, adequate, ample, satisfactory; see **enough** 1.
*See Synonym Study at* ENOUGH.

**sufficiently,** *modif.* — *Syn.* to one's satisfaction, enough, amply; see **adequately** 1.

**suffix,** *n.* — *Syn.* affix, postfix, addition; see **appendix.**

**suffocate,** *v.* — *Syn.* stifle, smother, strangle; see **choke** 1.

**suffrage,** *n.* — *Syn.* voice, ballot, testimonial, the right to vote; see **vote** 3.

**sugar,** *n.*
Common varieties and forms of sugar include: sucrose, cane sugar, corn sugar, brown sugar, confectioner's sugar, beet sugar, grape sugar, dextrose, fruit sugar, fructose, levulose, maltose, malt sugar, lactose, milk sugar, invert sugar, maple sugar, saccharose; see also **carbohydrate, food.**

**sugary,** *modif.* **1.** [Containing sugar] — *Syn.* sticky, granular, candied; see **sweet** 1.
**2.** [Cloyingly sweet] — *Syn.* cloying, mawkish, sentimental, unctuous; see **sentimental.**

**suggest,** *v.* **1.** [To make a suggestion] — *Syn.* submit, advise, recommend; see **propose** 1.

2. [To bring to mind] — *Syn.* hint, imply, infer, intimate, insinuate; see also **hint**.

*SYN.* — **suggest** implies a putting of something into the mind either intentionally, as by way of a proposal [I *suggest* you leave now], or unintentionally, as through association of ideas [the smell of ether *suggests* a hospital]; **imply** stresses a putting into the mind of something inherent in a word, remark, action, or situation, but not openly expressed, and suggests the need for inference [the answer *implied* a refusal, her novels *imply* a belief that good triumphs over evil]; **hint** connotes faint or indirect suggestion that is, however, intended to be understood [he *hinted* that he would come]; **intimate** suggests a making known obliquely by a very slight hint [she only dared to *intimate* her feelings]; **insinuate** implies the subtle hinting of something disagreeable or of that which one lacks the courage to say outright [are you *insinuating* that I am dishonest?]

**suggested**, *modif.* — *Syn.* submitted, advanced, proposed, advocated, propounded, advised, recommended, counseled, tendered, reminded, prompted, summoned up, called up, offered, laid before, put forward.
**suggesting**, *modif.* — *Syn.* indicating, suggestive of, implying; see **saying**.
**suggesting**, *n.* — *Syn.* propounding, advancing, proposing, submitting, moving, offering, proffering, tendering, recalling, prompting, summoning up; recommending, jogging the memory, laying before, putting forward, advising, with reference to, counseling.
**suggestion**, *n.* **1.** [A suggested detail] — *Syn.* hint, allusion, suspicion, intimation, implication, innuendo, insinuation, opinion, proposal, advice, recommendation, injunction, charge, instruction, submission, tender, reminder, approach, advance, bid, idea, tentative statement, presentation, proposition.
**2.** [A suggested plan] — *Syn.* scheme, idea, outline, proposal; see **plan** 2.
**3.** [A very small quantity] — *Syn.* trace, touch, taste; see **bit** 1.
**suggestive**, *modif.* **1.** [Suggesting thoughts or ideas] — *Syn.* carrying a suggestion of, suggestive, evocative, redolent, intriguing, giving an inkling of, symptomatic, indicative; see also **symbolic**.
**2.** [Suggesting something indecent or improper] — *Syn.* risqué, indecent, obscene, racy, provocative, vulgar, ribald; see also **vulgar** 1, 2.
**suicidal**, *modif.* — *Syn.* self-destructive, mortal, lethal, ruinous; see **deadly, harmful.**
**suicide**, *n.* — *Syn.* self-murder, self-slaughter, self-destruction, hara-kiri, seppuku, suttee; see also **death** 1.
**suit**, *n.* **1.** [A series] — *Syn.* suite, set, group; see **series.**
**2.** [A case at law] — *Syn.* lawsuit, action, litigation; see **trial** 2.
**3.** [Clothes to be worn together] — *Syn.* costume, ensemble, outfit, livery, uniform; see also **clothes.**
Kinds of suits include: business suit, three-piece suit, dress suit, sport suit, bathing suit, jump suit, body suit, sweat suit, running suit; *women:* tailored suit, cocktail suit, pant suit, cardigan suit, evening suit, sun suit, play suit; *men:* leisure suit, full dress, tails*, monkey suit*, soup and fish*, dinner jacket, tuxedo, tux*, zoot suit, morning dress; *children:* snow suit, sun suit, play suit, Eton suit.
**bring suit**— *Syn.* prosecute, start legal proceedings, initiate a case; see **sue.**
**follow suit***— *Syn.* accord with, regulate one's actions

by, take a cue from*; see **follow** 2, **imitate** 2.
**suit**, *v.* **1.** [To be in accord with] — *Syn.* befit, be agreeable, be appropriate to; see **agree, agree with** 2.
**2.** [To please] — *Syn.* amuse, fill, gratify; see **entertain** 1, **satisfy** 1.
**3.** [To adapt] — *Syn.* accommodate, revise, readjust; see **change** 1.
**suitability**, *n.* — *Syn.* rightness, appropriateness, agreement; see **fitness** 1, **propriety** 1.
**suitable**, *modif.* — *Syn.* fitting, becoming, proper; see **fit** 1, 2.
*See Synonym Study at* FIT.
**suitably**, *modif.* — *Syn.* well, all to the good, pleasantly; see **fit** 1, 2.
**suitcase**, *n.* — *Syn.* case, grip, satchel; see **bag.**
**suite**, *n.* **1.** [Attendants] — *Syn.* retinue, faculty, followers; see **servant, staff** 2.
**2.** [A series] — *Syn.* sequence, scale, line, set; see **order** 3, **series.**
**3.** [Matched furniture] — *Syn.* set, bedroom suite, overstuffed set; see **furniture.**
**suited**, *modif.* — *Syn.* adapted, satisfactory, fitted; see **fit** 1, 2.
**suit oneself**, *v.* — *Syn.* do as one pleases, be self-indulgent, pamper oneself; see **satisfy** 1.
**suitor**, *n.* **1.** [A lover] — *Syn.* gallant, admirer, boyfriend, beau; see **lover** 1.
**2.** [A petitioner] — *Syn.* suppliant, supplicant, beseecher, appellant.
**suit up**, *v.* — *Syn.* prepare, make ready, get ready; see **dress** 1.
**sulfa drug**, *n.* Varieties include: sulfathiazole, sulfanilamide, sulfapyridine, sulfadiazole, sulmefrin; see also **drug** 2.
**sulk**, *v.* — *Syn.* scowl, pout, frown, be sullen, be morose, be silent, glower, lower, gripe*, grouse*.
**sulkiness**, *n.* — *Syn.* sourness, glumness, grouchiness; see **anger.**
**sulky**, *modif.* — *Syn.* cross, morose, surly, petulant; see **irritable, sullen.**
**sullen**, *modif.* — *Syn.* unsociable, silent, morose, dour, glum, sulky, sour, cross, ill-humored, petulant, moody, grouchy, crabby, surly, fretful, ill-natured, ill-tempered, peevish, gloomy, gruff, querulous, churlish, saturnine, chumpish*, sourpussed*, fiddle-faced*; see also **irritable.** — *Ant.* FRIENDLY, sociable, jolly.
**sullenly**, *modif.* — *Syn.* morosely, glumly, sourly; see **angrily, silently.**
**sullenness**, *n.* — *Syn.* sulkiness, moodiness, petulance, acrimony; see **anger.**
**sully**, *v.* **1.** [To soil] — *Syn.* blot, stain, spot; see **dirty.**
**2.** [To defame] — *Syn.* shame, debase, denounce; see **disgrace.**
**sultan**, *n.* — *Syn.* soldian, grand seignior, emperor; see **king** 1, **ruler** 1.
**sultriness**, *n.* — *Syn.* mugginess, dampness, closeness; see **humidity.**
**sultry**, *modif.* — *Syn.* close, stifling, oppressive, muggy; see **hot** 1, **wet** 1.
**sum**, *n.* — *Syn.* amount, total, quantity, sum total, aggregate, gross, tally, whole, entirety; see also **whole.**

*SYN.* — **sum** refers to the number or amount obtained by adding individual units [the *sum* of 3 and 5 is 8]; **amount** applies to the result obtained by combining all the sums, quantities, measures, etc. that are involved [we paid the full *amount* of the damages]; **aggregate** refers to the whole group or mass of individual items gathered together [the *aggregate* of our experiences*]*; **total** stresses the wholeness or inclusiveness of a sum or amount *[the collection reached a total of $200]*

**summarily,** *modif.* — *Syn.* promptly, readily, speedily; see **immediately.**

**summarize,** *v.* — *Syn.* prune down, cut back, sum, cipher, abstract, skim over, review, count up, compile, shorten, paraphrase, memory up★, put in a nutshell★; see also **decrease** 2.

**summarized,** *modif.* — *Syn.* capsulated, paraphrased, decreased, diminished, outlined, shortened, summed up, reviewed.

**summary,** *n.* — *Syn.* outline, epitome, digest, synopsis, abstract, recapitulation, rundown, abbreviation, abridgment, capitulation, paraphrase, compendium, résumé, essence, précis, extract, skeleton, brief, conspectus, prospectus, reduction, version, core, report, review, minutes, sense, essentials, case, survey, sketch, syllabus, condensation, summing-up, summation, pandect, aperçu, sum and substance, roundup, recap★, the long and short of a thing★, wrap-up★. — *Ant.* expansion, amplification, elaboration.
*See Synonym Study at* ABRIDGMENT.

**summer,** *modif.* — *Syn.* summery, summertime, in summer, vacation; see **hot** 1, **warm** 1.

**summer,** *n.* — *Syn.* summertime, summer season, full summer, dog days, sunny season, harvest, haying time, vacation, picnic days, fly time★; see also **season.** — *Ant.* WINTER, cold months, snowy season.

**summer,** *v.* — *Syn.* vacation, stay for the summer, spend the summer, take a holiday at, holiday; see also **live** 2, **remain** 1.

**summerhouse,** *n.* — *Syn.* garden house, gazebo, pergola, alcove, vinery; see also **resort** 2, **retreat** 2.

**summit,** *n.* **1.** [Topmost point] — *Syn.* apex, vertex, crest, peak, point, top, crown; see also **mountain** 1, **top** 1.
**2.** [Highest state] — *Syn.* acme, zenith, climax, culmination, pinnacle, consummation.

---

*SYN.* — **summit** literally refers to the topmost point of a hill or similar elevation and, figuratively, to the highest attainable level, as of achievement; **peak** refers to the highest of a number of high points, as in a mountain range or, figuratively, in a graph; **climax** applies to the highest point, as in interest, force, excitement, etc., in a scale of ascending values; **acme** refers to the highest possible point of perfection in the development or progress of something; **apex** suggests the highest point (literally, of a geometric figure such as a cone; figuratively, of a career, process, etc.) where all ascending lines, courses, etc. ultimately meet; **pinnacle,** in its figurative uses, is equivalent to **summit** or **peak,** but sometimes connotes a giddy or unsteady height; **zenith** literally refers to the highest point in the heavens and hence figuratively suggests fame or success reached by a spectacular rise

---

**summon,** *v.* **1.** [To call] — *Syn.* request, beckon, send for, bid, ask, draft, petition, signal, motion, sign, order, command, direct, enjoin, invoke, conjure up, muster, ring, rouse, charge, recall, call in, call for, call out, call forth, call up, call away, call down, subpoena, summons★, volunteer★.
**2.** [To convene] — *Syn.* call together, convoke, gather; see **assemble** 2.
*See Synonym Study at* CALL.

**summoned,** *modif.* — *Syn.* called for, called up, paged, drafted; see **requested** 2, **wanted.**

**summons,** *n.* **1.** [Legal call] — *Syn.* subpoena, writ, warrant; see **indictment.**
**2.** [Invocation] — *Syn.* cry, bell, calling; see **call** 4.

**summon up,** *v.* — *Syn.* recall, recollect, call to mind, be reminded; see **remember** 1.

***summum bonum*** (Latin), *n.* — *Syn.* height, highest good, supreme good, contentment; see **best.**

**sumptuous,** *modif.* — *Syn.* costly, lavish, magnificent, gorgeous, imposing, opulent, impressive, beautiful, elegant, pompous, splendid, deluxe, extravagant, luxurious; see also **rich** 2.

**sum up,** *v.* — *Syn.* summarize, review, conclude; see **examine** 1, **total** 1.

**sun,** *n.* — *Syn.* star, day-star, solar disk, solar orb, eye of heaven, great luminary, light of the day, lamp of the day, source of light, giver of light, Sol, Apollo; see also **star** 1.
**a place in the sun** — *Syn.* favorable position, favorable situation, reward, prominence; see **advantage** 1, 2, **prize.**
**under the sun** — *Syn.* on earth, terrestrial, mundane; see **earthly** 1.

**sunburned,** *modif.* — *Syn.* tanned, burned, adust, sunburnt, brown, browned by the sun, suntanned, bronzed, ruddy, brown as a berry, nut-brown, baked brown, sunbaked, peeling, blistery. — *Ant.* PALE, white-skinned, pallid.

**sundae,** *n.* — *Syn.* ice cream, ice cream with topping, dish of ice cream, parfait, banana split; see also **dessert, treat.**

**Sunday,** *n.* — *Syn.* first day, day off, Lord's day; see **Sabbath.**

**sunder,** *v.* — *Syn.* separate, part, split; see **divide** 1.
*See Synonym Study at* SEPARATE.

**sundry,** *modif.* — *Syn.* divers, several, manifold; see **various.**

**sunken,** *modif.* **1.** [Submerged] — *Syn.* capsized, immersed, inundated, scuttled.
**2.** [Below the surrounding level] — *Syn.* lowered, depressed, down; see **under** 1.

**sunless,** *modif.* — *Syn.* cloudy, overcast, gloomy, rainy, gray; see also **dark** 1.

**sunlight,** *n.* — *Syn.* daylight, sunshine, light of day; see **day** 2, **light** 1.

**sunny,** *modif.* **1.** [Full of sunshine] — *Syn.* shining, brilliant, sunshiny; see **bright** 1.
**2.** [Cheerful] — *Syn.* bright, cheery, blithe, genial; see **happy** 1.

**sunrise,** *n.* — *Syn.* dawn, sunup, break of day, daybreak, aurora; see also **morning** 1.

**sunset,** *n.* — *Syn.* sundown, evening, end of the day, eve, eventide, close of the day, sunsetting, nightfall, twilight, dusk; see also **night** 1. — *Ant.* DAWN, sunrise, morning.

**sunshade,** *n.* — *Syn.* parasol, canopy, awning; see **umbrella.**

**sunshine,** *n.* — *Syn.* sunlight, the sun, sunbeams, the sun's beams, the sun's rays; see also **light** 1.

**sup,** *v.* — *Syn.* feed, munch, dine; see **eat** 1.

**superabundance,** *n.* — *Syn.* surplus, exorbitance, overflow; see **excess** 1, **remainder.**

**superabundant,** *modif.* — *Syn.* surplus, excess, excessive; see **extreme** 2.

**superannuated,** *modif.* — *Syn.* obsolete, passé, antiquated, outdated; see **old-fashioned.**

**superb,** *modif.* — *Syn.* magnificent, august, splendid, elegant, exquisite; see also **excellent, grand** 2.

**supercilious,** *modif.* — *Syn.* disdainful, haughty, contemptuous; see **egotistic** 2, **proud** 2, **scornful** 1.
*See Synonym Study at* PROUD.

**superficial,** *modif.* — *Syn.* flimsy, cursory, perfunctory, hasty, desultory, shallow, summary, short-sighted, purblind, ignorant, narrow-minded, prejudiced, warped, partial, surface, cosmetic, skin-deep, untrustworthy, outward, external, exterior, unenlightened. — *Ant.* LEARNED, deep, profound.

*SYN.* — **superficial** implies concern with the obvious or surface aspects of a thing *[superficial* characteristics*]* and, in a derogatory sense, lack of thoroughness, profoundness, significance, etc. *[superficial* judgments*]*; **shallow**, in this connection always derogatory, implies a lack of depth, as of character, intellect, or meaning *[shallow* writing*]*; **cursory**, which may or may not be derogatory, suggests a brief or hasty consideration of something without pausing to note details *[a cursory* inspection*]*

**superficiality,** *n.* — *Syn.* triviality, shallowness, lack of depth; see **indifference.**

**superficially,** *modif.* — *Syn.* lightly, at first glance, externally, on the surface, outwardly, extraneously, flimsily, partially, hastily, ignorantly, frivolously, not thoroughly, not profoundly; see also **carelessly, casually** 2. — *Ant.* CAREFULLY, thoroughly, thoughtfully.

**superfluity,** *n.* — *Syn.* surplus, abundance, plethora; see **excess** 1, **plenty.**

**superfluous,** *modif.* — *Syn.* unnecessary, excessive, superabundant, overflowing, redundant, overmuch, very great, abounding, inordinate, needless, exorbitant, on one's hands, in excess, extravagant, profuse, turgescent, supererogatory, pleonastic, lavish, overcharged; see also **extra, extreme** 2. — *Ant.* WANTING, scanty, lacking.

**superintend,** *v.* — *Syn.* supervise, oversee, conduct; see **manage** 1, **watch** 2.

**superintendence,** *n.* — *Syn.* direction, management, supervision; see **administration** 1, **command** 2.

**superintendent,** *n.* — *Syn.* overseer, supervisor, inspector, director, landlord, custodian; see also **administrator.**

**superior,** *modif.* — *Syn.* higher, better, preferred, above, exceeding, finer, of higher rank, a cut above\*, in ascendency, more exalted; see also **excellent.**

**superiority,** *n.* — *Syn.* supremacy, preponderance, advantage; see **perfection** 3.

**superlative,** *modif.* **1.** [Supreme] — *Syn.* prime, highest, greatest, preeminent; see **best** 1, **excellent.**
**2.** [Excessive] — *Syn.* exaggerated, effusive, inflated; see **extra.**

**supernatural,** *modif.* **1.** [Divine] — *Syn.* celestial, godlike, almighty, spiritual, otherworldly, holy; see also **divine** 1.
**2.** [Preternatural] — *Syn.* superhuman, spectral, ghostly, occult, paranormal, hidden, mysterious, secret, unknown, unrevealed, dark, mystic, mythical, mythological, fabulous, legendary, misty, unintelligible, unfathomable, unearthly, inscrutable, incomprehensible, undiscernible, transcendental, metempiric, psychic, obscure, unknowable, impenetrable, invisible, concealed. — *Ant.* NATURAL, plain, common.

**supernumerary,** *modif.* — *Syn.* excessive, exaggerated, effusive; see **extreme** 2, **superfluous.**

**superscription,** *n.* — *Syn.* inscription, epigraph, title; see **identification** 2, **label.**

**supersede,** *v.* — *Syn.* outmode, succeed, take the place of; see **replace** 2.
*See Synonym Study at* REPLACE.

**superseded,** *modif.* — *Syn.* out of date, outmoded, obsolete, discarded; see **old** 2, 3, **old-fashioned, poor** 2.

**supersensory,** *modif.* — *Syn.* extrasensory, telepathic, psychic; see **mental** 2, **supernatural.**

**superstition,** *n.* — *Syn.* false belief, notion, irrationality, fear, superstitious fear.

**superstitious,** *modif.* **1.** [Having superstitions] — *Syn.* fearful, apprehensive, gullible, credulous; see **careful, stupid** 1.
**2.** [Based on superstition] — *Syn.* unfounded, groundless, untrue, unproven, erroneous.

**supervene,** *v.* — *Syn.* ensue, issue, take place, occur; see **happen** 2.

**supervise,** *v.* — *Syn.* oversee, conduct, control; see **manage** 1.

**supervised,** *modif.* — *Syn.* directed, administered, superintended; see **managed** 2.

**supervision,** *n.* — *Syn.* guidance, surveillance, direction; see **administration** 1.

**supervisor,** *n.* — *Syn.* director, superintendent, executive; see **administrator.**

**supine,** *modif.* **1.** [Lying on one's back] — *Syn.* recumbent, prostrate, prone, flat, horizontal, lying, reclining; see also **lying** 4.
**2.** [Indolent] — *Syn.* listless, languid, passive; see **indifferent, listless** 1.

*SYN.* — **supine** implies a position in which one lies on one's back, and may suggest listlessness or passivity *[lying supine* on the grass, gazing lazily at the clouds*]*; **prone**, in strict use, implies a position in which the front part of the body lies upon or faces the ground *[he* fell *prone* upon the ground and drank from the brook*]*; **prostrate** implies the position of one thrown or lying flat in a prone or supine position, as in great humility or complete submission, or because laid low *[the* victim lay *prostrate* at his attacker's feet*]*; **recumbent** suggests a lying down or back in any position one might assume for rest or sleep *[she* was *recumbent* on the chaise longue*]*

**supper,** *n.* — *Syn.* evening meal, tea, late refreshments; see **dinner, meal** 2.

**supplant,** *v.* — *Syn.* displace, supersede, usurp; see **remove** 1, **replace** 2.
*See Synonym Study at* REPLACE.

**supple,** *modif.* — *Syn.* flexible, yielding, pliant, agile; see **flexible** 1, **rubber.**
*See Synonym Study at* FLEXIBLE.

**supplement,** *n.* — *Syn.* sequel, continuation, complement; see **addition** 2, **appendix.**

**supplement,** *v.* — *Syn.* add to, supply, fill up, complete, extend, augment, supply a need, reinforce, strengthen, fortify, increase, buttress, subsidize, enhance, enrich, go hand in hand with; see also **improve** 1, **increase** 1.

**supplementary,** *modif.* — *Syn.* additional, completing, supplemental; see **extra.**

**supplicate,** *v.* — *Syn.* petition, pray, beseech; see **appeal** 1, **beg** 1.
*See Synonym Study at* APPEAL.

**supplication,** *n.* — *Syn.* entreaty, prayer, suit, petition; see **appeal** 1, **request.**

**supplied,** *modif.* — *Syn.* provided, furnished, endowed; see **given.**

**supply,** *n.* **1.** [A quantity] — *Syn.* stock, hoard, accumulation, amount, number; see also **quantity.**
**2.** [Provisions; *plural*] — *Syn.* rations, food supply, groceries, raw materials, materials on hand, stores, stocks, replenishments; see also **equipment.**

**supply,** *v.* — *Syn.* furnish, fulfill, outfit; see **provide** 1, **satisfy** 3.

**supplying,** *n.* — *Syn.* furnishing, stocking, replenishing; see **providing.**
**support,** *n.* **1.** [Aid] — *Syn.* help, assistance, comfort; see **aid** 1.
**2.** [A reinforcement] — *Syn.* lining, concrete block, rib, stilt, stay, shore, supporter, buttress, pole, post, underpinning, dependence, prop, guide, backing, stiffener, flotation, collar, rampart, abutment, stave, stake, rod, pillar, column, timber; see also **brace** 1.
**3.** [Financial aid] — *Syn.* maintenance, living, provision, livelihood, subsidy, subsistence, upkeep, care, relief, allowance, sustenance, alimentation, alimony, responsibility for; see also **payment** 1.
**4.** [One who provides support] — *Syn.* backer, provider, second, preserver; see **patron** 1, **supporter.**
**in support of** — *Syn.* approving, condoning, in favor of, in defense of; see **supporting.**
**support,** *v.* **1.** [To hold up from beneath] — *Syn.* prop, hold up, keep up, bolster up, shore up, bear up, bolster, buttress, brace, sustain, shore, stay, mainstay, underpin, undergird, keep from falling, shoulder, carry, bear, be a foundation for. — *Ant.* DROP, let fall, break down.
**2.** [To uphold] — *Syn.* uphold, maintain, sustain, back, back up, abet, aid, assist, help, bolster, stay, comfort, carry, bear out, hold, foster, shoulder, corroborate, cheer, establish, buoy, put forward, promote, advance, champion, advocate, countenance, approve, throw in with, stick by, stand behind, cast in on, substantiate, lot with, verify, get back of, stick up for, go to bat for*, confirm, further, encourage, hearten, strengthen, second, preserve, recommend, take care of, stand in with, pull for, agree with, stand up for, keep up, stand back of, take the part of, rally round, give a lift to*, boost*. — *Ant.* HINDER, discourage, deter.
**3.** [To defend] — *Syn.* second, stand by, plead for; see **defend** 3.
**4.** [To continue] — *Syn.* carry on, keep up, maintain; see **continue** 1.
**5.** [To provide for] — *Syn.* take care of, keep an eye on, care for, attend to, look after, back, bring up, sponsor, underwrite, put up the money for, set up in business, finance, pay for, subsidize, guard, chaperon, nurse, pay the expenses of, grubstake*, stake*, bank-roll*, raise*, bring home the bacon*, earn one's keep*; see also **sustain** 2. — *Ant.* ABANDON, ignore, fail.

**SYN.** — **support**, the broadest of these terms, suggests a favoring of someone or something, either by giving active aid or merely by approving or sanctioning [to *support* a candidate for office]; **uphold** suggests that what is being supported is under attack [to *uphold* civil rights for all]; **sustain** implies full active support so as to strengthen or keep from failing [sustained by his hope for the future]; **maintain** suggests a supporting so as to keep intact or unimpaired [to *maintain* the law, a family, etc.]; **advocate** implies support in speech or writing and sometimes connotes persuasion or argument [to *advocate* a change in policy]; **back** (often **back up**) suggests support, as financial aid or moral encouragement, given to prevent failure [I'll *back* you *up* in your demands]

**supportable,** *modif.* — *Syn.* sustainable, endurable, tolerable; see **bearable.**
**supported,** *modif.* **1.** [Backed personally] — *Syn.* financed, promoted, sustained; see **backed** 1.
**2.** [Supported physically] — *Syn.* held up, propped up, braced, bolstered, borne up, floating on, floated, borne up, buoyed up, lifted up, based on, founded on, raised up, having a solid foundation; see also **firm** 1.

**supporter,** *n.* — *Syn.* advocate, adherent, follower, fan, sustainer, sponsor, benefactor, upholder, confederate, champion, helper; see also **patron** 1, **subscriber.**
*See Synonym Study at* FOLLOWER.
**supporting,** *modif.* — *Syn.* upholding, aiding, shielding, promoting, approving; see also **helping.**
**suppose,** *v.* — *Syn.* conjecture, surmise, deem, think, reckon*; see also **assume** 1, **guess** 1.
**supposed,** *modif.* — *Syn.* assumed, presumed, alleged, presupposed; see **likely** 1.
**supposedly,** *modif.* — *Syn.* seemingly, supposably, believably; see **apparently, probably.**
**supposing,** *conj. & modif.* — *Syn.* if, in case that, in these circumstances, under these conditions, let us suppose, allowing that, granting that, presuming, assuming, presupposing, with the supposition that, taking for granted that.
**supposition,** *n.* **1.** [A guess] — *Syn.* surmise, notion, speculation; see **guess, guessing.**
**2.** [A theory] — *Syn.* idea, thesis, likelihood; see **hypothesis, opinion** 1.
**suppositional,** *modif.* — *Syn.* conjectural, hypothetical, presumptive; see **theoretical.**
**supposititious,** *modif.* — *Syn.* counterfeit, spurious, deceptive, fictitious; see **false** 2, 3.
**suppress,** *v.* — *Syn.* crush, overpower, overcome, contain, cut off, beat down, slap down, hold down, put down, burke, subdue, keep in, quash, repress, quell, stifle, sit on*, trample out*, bottle up*, keep in ignorance*, choke off*, come down on*, clamp down on*, crack down on*; see also **defeat** 1, 2.
**suppression,** *n.* — *Syn.* abolition, obliteration, annihilation, overriding, suppressing, overthrow, elimination; see also **defeat** 2, **destruction** 1.
**suppurate,** *v.* — *Syn.* fester, gather, maturate, discharge, putrefy; see also **decay.**
**supremacy,** *n.* — *Syn.* domination, mastery, sovereignty, supreme authority; see **command** 2, **power** 2.
**supreme,** *modif.* — *Syn.* highest, greatest, paramount, chief; see **best** 1, **excellent, principal.**
**surcease,** *n.* — *Syn.* deferment, interruption, cessation; see **delay** 1, **end** 2, **pause** 1, 2.
**surcharge,** *n.* — *Syn.* additional charge, tax, overcharge, surtax.
**surcharged,** *modif.* — *Syn.* overfull, overloaded, overburdened, superfluous, replete; see also **full** 1.
**sure*,** *interj.* — *Syn.* certainly, of course, by all means, positively, absolutely, but definitely; see also **surely.**
**sure,** *modif.* **1.** [Confident] — *Syn.* positive, assured, convinced; see **certain** 1.
**2.** [Inevitable] — *Syn.* unfailing, unavoidable, indisputable; see **certain** 3, **inevitable.**
*See Synonym Study at* CERTAIN.
**for sure** — *Syn.* certainly, for certain, without doubt; see **surely.**
**make sure** — *Syn.* make certain, determine, establish; see **fix** 4, **guarantee** 2, **manage** 1.
**to be sure** — *Syn.* of course, certainly, obviously; see **surely.**
**sure-fire*,** *modif.* — *Syn.* dependable, good, infallible; see **excellent, reliable** 2.
**surely,** *modif.* — *Syn.* doubtlessly, certainly, undoubtedly, fixedly, definitely, absolutely, evidently, explicitly, without doubt, beyond doubt, beyond question, plainly, infallibly, to be sure, most assuredly, unshakably, decidedly, inevitably, indisputably, positively, unquestionably, irrefutably, unfailingly, without any doubt, admittedly, clearly, with assurance, beyond the shadow of a doubt, nothing else but, precisely, conclusively, un-

equivocally, distinctly, by all means, in all conscience, at any rate, with certainty, unerringly, unmistakably, at all events, undeniably, manifestly, indubitably, with confidence, as a matter of course, rain or shine*. — *Ant.* DOUBTFUL, with no assurance, in doubt.

**sure thing***, *n.* — *Syn.* no gamble, certainty, safe venture, safe investment; see **winner.**

**surety,** *n.* — *Syn.* pledge, bail, forfeit; see **guaranty** 2.

**surf,** *n.* — *Syn.* waves, breakers, breaking waves, foam, froth, spindrift, rollers, combers; see also **ocean, tide, wave** 1.

**surface,** *n.* — *Syn.* exterior, covering, superficies, facade; see **cover** 2, **outside** 1.

**surfeit,** *n.* — *Syn.* surplus, superfluity, profusion; see **excess** 1, **remainder.**

**surfeit,** *v.* — *Syn.* satiate, overindulge, gorge; see **eat** 1, **fill** 1, **satisfy** 3.

*See Synonym Study at* SATIATE.

**surge,** *n.* 1. [A wave] — *Syn.* swell, billow, breaker; see **surf, wave** 1, 2.

2. [A deluge] — *Syn.* rush, swell, roll; see **flood** 1.

**surge,** *v.* 1. [To rise] — *Syn.* mount, tower, arise; see **climb** 2, **rise** 1, 3.

2. [To swell] — *Syn.* billow, heave, deluge; see **grow** 1, **swell.**

**surgeon,** *n.* — *Syn.* specialist, specialist in surgery, surgical expert, operator, interventionist, consultant, sawbones*; see also **doctor** 1.

**surgery,** *n.* — *Syn.* operative surgery, cryosurgery, surgical operation; see **medicine** 3, **operation** 4.

**surgical,** *modif.* — *Syn.* healing, curative, operational, with the surgeon's knife; see **medical, remedial.**

**surly,** *modif.* — *Syn.* morose, testy, crabby; see **irritable, sullen.**

**surmise,** *n.* — *Syn.* conjecture, attempt, theory; see **guess, hypothesis, opinion** 1.

*See Synonym Study at* GUESS.

**surmise,** *v.* — *Syn.* conjecture, guess, suppose, infer; see **assume** 1.

**surmount,** *v.* — *Syn.* conquer, overcome, subdue, triumph over; see **defeat** 2.

**surmountable,** *modif.* — *Syn.* conquerable, beatable, attainable, able to be overcome.

**surname,** *n.* — *Syn.* cognomen, last name, family name, patronymic; see **name** 1.

**surpass,** *v.* — *Syn.* excel, outdo, transcend, improve upon, go beyond, better; see also **exceed.**

*See Synonym Study at* EXCEL.

**surpassing,** *modif.* — *Syn.* exceeding, excelling, dominant; see **excellent.**

**surplus,** *n.* — *Syn.* surplusage, residue, plethora, overabundance; see **excess** 1, **remainder.**

**surprise,** *n.* 1. [A feeling of amazement] — *Syn.* astonishment, wonderment, shock; see **wonder** 1.

2. [The cause of surprise, sense 1] — *Syn.* something unexpected, blow, sudden attack, unexpected good fortune, sudden misfortune, unawaited event, unsuspected plot.

**take by surprise** — *Syn.* startle, assault, sneak up on; see **attack** 1, 2, **surprise** *v.* 1, 2.

**surprise,** *v.* 1. [To amaze] — *Syn.* astonish, astound, amaze, bewilder, confound, shock, overwhelm, dumbfound, unsettle, stun, electrify, petrify, startle, stupefy, stagger, nonplus, take aback, cause wonder, strike with wonder, strike with awe, dazzle, daze, perplex, stagger one's belief, leave open-mouthed, leave aghast, make all agog, flabbergast*, floor*, bowl over*, jar*, flash upon one*, carry one off his feet*, jolt*, take one's breath away*, strike dumb*, make one's hair stand on end*,

make one's head swim*, creep up on*, catch unaware*; see also **confuse, frighten** 1.

2. [To take unaware] — *Syn.* take by surprise, catch one in the act of, burst in upon, startle, catch off-balance*, catch flat-footed*, catch one napping*, catch asleep*, nab*, pop in on*; see also **sense** 1.

---

*SYN.* — **surprise** implies an affecting with wonder because of being unexpected, unusual, etc. /I'm *surprised* at your concern/; **astonish** implies a surprising with something that seems unbelievable /to *astonish* with sleight of hand/; **amaze** suggests an astonishing that causes bewilderment or confusion /*amazed* at the sudden turn of events/; **astound** suggests such a shocking surprise that one is left helpless to act or think /I was *astounded* by the proposal/; **flabbergast** is a colloquial term suggesting an astounding to the point of speechlessness

---

**surprised,** *modif.* — *Syn.* upset, taken unaware, astounded, caught short, caught napping, astonished, bewildered, taken by surprise, shocked, struck with amazement, confounded, nonplussed, startled, staggered, not anticipating; see also **bewildered.** — *Ant.* CALM, aware, poised.

**surprising,** *modif.* — *Syn.* extraordinary, remarkable, shocking; see **unexpected, unusual** 1, 2.

**surrealistic,** *modif.* — *Syn.* bizarre, phantasmagoric, incoherent, unconnected, absurd, dadaistic; see also **fantastic** 1, **illogical, incongruous** 1, **unreal.**

**surrender,** *n.* — *Syn.* capitulation, yielding, giving up, submission, giving way, unconditional surrender, white flag, cessation, abandonment, relinquishment, acquiescence, abdication, resignation, delivery.

**surrender,** *v.* 1. [To accept defeat] — *Syn.* capitulate, quit, give in; see **yield** 1.

2. [To relinquish possession] — *Syn.* give up, let go, resign, abdicate; see **abandon** 1.

**surreptitious,** *modif.* — *Syn.* clandestine, private, covert; see **hidden** 2, **secret** 3.

*See Synonym Study at* SECRET.

**surreptitiously,** *modif.* — *Syn.* clandestinely, stealthily, privately; see **secretly.**

**surrogate,** *n.* — *Syn.* deputy, representative, proxy; see **agent** 1, **delegate, substitute.**

**surround,** *v.* 1. [To be on all sides] — *Syn.* girdle, circle, environ, gird, enclose, shut in, close in, fence in, close around, circle about, envelope, hem in, wall in.

2. [To take a position on all sides] — *Syn.* encompass, encircle, inundate, flow around, besiege, beset, invest, close in, close around, house in, hem in, compass about, go around, beleaguer, blockade; see also **circle.** — *Ant.* ABANDON, flee from, desert.

**surrounded,** *modif.* — *Syn.* girdled, encompassed, encircled, hemmed in, fenced in, hedged in, circled about, girded, enclosed, fenced about, enveloped. — *Ant.* FREE, unfenced, agape.

**surrounding,** *modif.* — *Syn.* enclosing, encircling, encompassing, neighboring; see **around** 1.

**surroundings,** *n.* — *Syn.* setting, environs, vicinity; see **environment.**

**surveillance,** *n.* 1. [Supervision] — *Syn.* monitoring, inspection, direction; see **examination** 1.

2. [Observation] — *Syn.* close watch, constant observation, scrutiny, stakeout.

**survey,** *n.* — *Syn.* study, poll, critique, outline; see **examination** 1, **questionnaire, review** 1, 2.

**survey,** *v.* 1. [To look upon] — *Syn.* look over, take a view of, view; see **see** 1.

**2.** [To examine or summarize] — *Syn.* study, scan, inspect; see **examine** 1.

**surveyor,** *n.* — *Syn.* civil engineer, measurer, land surveyor, assessor, topographer, cartographer, geodesist; see also **engineer** 1.

**survival,** *n.* **1.** [Continuation] — *Syn.* endurance, durability, continuance; see **continuation** 1.

**2.** [Something that survives] — *Syn.* remainder, remnant, relic, vestige; see **relic** 1.

**survive,** *v.* **1.** [To live on] — *Syn.* outlive, outlast, outwear, live down, live out, weather the storm, make out, persist, persevere, last, remain, keep the wolf from the door, pull through, live through, get through, come through, keep afloat, get on; see also **endure** 1.

**2.** [To endure] — *Syn.* bear, suffer through, withstand, sustain; see **endure** 2.

**survivor,** *n.* — *Syn.* one who has escaped, one still living, one spared, one left behind, relict, posterity, descendant, heir, widow, widower, orphan, derelict.

**susceptibility,** *n.* — *Syn.* susceptivity, awareness, perceptivity; see **sensitivity** 2.

**susceptible,** *modif.* — *Syn.* responsive, receptive, susceptive; see **sensitive** 3.

**suspect,** *modif.* — *Syn.* dubious, questionable, suspected; see **suspicious** 2, **unlikely.**

**suspect,** *v.* **1.** [To doubt someone] — *Syn.* distrust, disbelieve, mistrust; see **doubt** 2.

**2.** [To suppose] — *Syn.* presume, surmise, speculate; see **assume** 1.

**suspect,** *n.* — *Syn.* the accused, defendant, prisoner, alleged perpetrator.

**suspected,** *modif.* — *Syn.* doubtful, imagined, fancied; see **questionable** 1, 2, **suspicious** 2.

**suspend,** *v.* **1.** [To debar] — *Syn.* reject, exclude, omit; see **bar** 2, **eject** 1, **refuse.**

**2.** [To cease temporarily] — *Syn.* postpone, defer, put off, discontinue, adjourn, interrupt, shelve, pigeonhole, table, put aside, set aside, hold off, delay, procrastinate, waive, take a break, recess, prorogue, dissolve, break off, cease, halt, check, stay, stave off, intermit, lay over, keep pending, hold in abeyance, keep in abeyance, put on hold, put on the back burner, put on ice, put on the shelf, back-burner*. — *Ant.* CONTINUE, carry on, expedite.

**3.** [To hang] — *Syn.* dangle, swing, wave; see **hang** 2.

**4.** [To cause to hang] — *Syn.* hang up, swing, hook up; see **hang** 1.

*See Synonym Study at* EXCLUDE.

---

*SYN.* — **suspend** denotes the breaking off of proceedings, privileges, etc. for a time, sometimes for such an indefinite time as to suggest cancellation /to *suspend* train service, to *suspend* a sentence/; **postpone** implies the intentional delaying of an action or event until a later time; **adjourn** is applied to the action of a deliberative body in bringing a session to a close, with the intention of resuming at a later time; **prorogue** applies esp. to the formal dismissal of the British Parliament by the crown, subject to reassembly; to **dissolve** an assembly is to terminate it as constituted, so that an election must be held to reconstitute it

---

**suspended,** *modif.* — *Syn.* pensile, postponed, pendulous; see **hanging.**

**suspenders,** *pl.n.* — *Syn.* braces, straps, shoulder straps, garters; see **brace** 1.

**suspense,** *n.* **1.** [Uncertainty] — *Syn.* apprehension, indecisiveness, dilemma; see **doubt** 2.

**2.** [Perplexity] — *Syn.* indecision, hesitancy, hesitation, anxiety; see **confusion** 2, **uncertainty** 3.

**suspension,** *n.* **1.** [A delay] — *Syn.* postponement, deferment, stay; see **delay** 1, **pause** 1, 2, **respite.**

**2.** [An end] — *Syn.* halt, discontinuing, stoppage; see **end** 2, **stopping.**

**suspension bridge,** *n.* — *Syn.* overhead bridge, cable bridge, tower bridge, walkway; see **bridge** 1.

**suspicion,** *n.* — *Syn.* misgiving, mistrust, surmise; see **doubt** 1.

**above suspicion** — *Syn.* honorable, cleared, gentlemanly; see **honest** 1, **innocent** 1, 4, **noble** 1, 2.

**under suspicion** — *Syn.* suspected, under a cloud of suspicion, suspect; see **questionable** 1, 2, **suspicious** 2.

**suspicious,** *modif.* **1.** [Entertaining suspicion] — *Syn.* jealous, distrustful, suspecting, doubting, questioning, wary, leery, doubtful, dubious, suspect, in doubt, without faith, skeptical, unbelieving, without belief, wondering. — *Ant.* TRUSTING, trustful, without any doubt of.

**2.** [Arousing suspicion] — *Syn.* not quite trustworthy, questionable, queer, suspect, irregular, unusual, uncommon, different, peculiar, open to question, out of line, shady, equivocal, overt, debatable, disputable. — *Ant.* REGULAR, usual, common.

**suspiciously,** *modif.* — *Syn.* doubtingly, doubtfully, skeptically, dubiously, uncertainly, distrustfully, distrustingly, unbelievingly, questioningly, problematically, in doubt, in a doubtful manner, causing suspicion, encouraging suspicion, with caution, with reservation, with some reservation, not gullibly, not wholeheartedly, not without reservations, not without doubts, with a grain of salt, with a pinch of salt, *cum grano salis* (Latin), like a doubting Thomas*.

**sustain,** *v.* **1.** [To carry] — *Syn.* bear, support, bear on the shoulder, carry on the back, hold up, support the weight of, keep from falling, keep from sinking, convey, transport, transfer, put a shoulder under, pack*, tote*, lug*. — *Ant.* ABANDON, drop, desert.

**2.** [To nourish] — *Syn.* keep up, maintain, provide food for, give food to, maintain the health of, keep in health, nurture, supply food for, nurse; see also **provide** 1, **support** 2. — *Ant.* NEGLECT, injure, starve.

**3.** [To defend] — *Syn.* befriend, favor, stand by, support, comfort, side with*, back up*, stand up for*; see also **defend** 3. — *Ant.* OPPOSE, HINDER, forsake.

*See Synonym Study at* SUPPORT.

**sustained,** *modif.* — *Syn.* maintained, continued, supported; see **backed** 1.

**sustenance,** *n.* — *Syn.* nourishment, food, nutrition; see **aid** 1, **subsistence** 1, 2.

**suture,** *n.* — *Syn.* stitching, stitch, joint; see **seam.**

**svelte,** *modif.* — *Syn.* lithe, lissome, lean, slender; see **smooth** 1, **thin** 2.

**swab,** *v.* — *Syn.* wash, sweep, scrub; see **clean, mop.**

**swabbed,** *modif.* — *Syn.* mopped down, mopped up, cleaned, scrubbed; see **clean** 1.

**swacked*,** *modif.* — *Syn.* inebriated, drunken, high*; see **drunk.**

**swaddle,** *v.* — *Syn.* swathe, enwrap, sheathe; see **clothe, wrap** 1, 2.

**swag*,** *n.* — *Syn.* loot, plunder, graft; see **booty.**

**swagger,** *v.* **1.** [To strut] — *Syn.* parade, saunter, prance; see **strut.**

**2.** [To boast] — *Syn.* gloat, brag, show off; see **boast** 1.

*See Synonym Study at* BOAST.

**swain*,** *n.* — *Syn.* wooer, beau, suitor; see **lover** 2.

**swallow,** *n.* Swallows include: bank, cliff, barn, tree, eave, rough-winged; purple martin; see also **bird** 1.

**swallow,** *v.* — *Syn.* consume, engulf, gulp, take, wash down, pour, swill, bolt, take in one draught, swig, choke down, ingurgitate, imbibe, swallow up, toss off*; see also **drink** 1, **eat** 1.

**swami,** *n.* — *Syn.* lord, master, guru, pundit; see **priest, professor, teacher** 1.

**swamp,** *n.* — *Syn.* bog, fen, quagmire, morass, marsh, slough, soft ground, wet ground, mire, peat bog, holm, swale, bottoms, river bottoms, moor, spongy ground, lowland, bayou, bottomland, cattail swamp, tule swamp, fen land, boggy ground, swampy ground, polder, trembling prairie, Everglades, muskag; see also **mud.** — *Ant.* DESERT, high ground, rocky ground.

**swampy,** *modif.* — *Syn.* boggy, wet, miry; see **marshy, muddy** 2.

**swan,** *n.* — *Syn.* aquatic bird, trumpeter, whooper; see **bird** 1.

**swank*,** *n.* — *Syn.* spectacle, array, swagger; see **display** 2.

**swank*,** *modif.* — *Syn.* ostentatious, stylish, extravagant, exclusive.

**swanky*,** *modif.* — *Syn.* showy, ostentatious, swank*; see **rich** 2, **expensive.**

**swan song,** *n.* **1.** [A death song] — *Syn.* dirge, elegy, *chant du cygne* (French); see **song.**
  **2.** [*A final act or performance] — *Syn.* farewell, farewell performance, parting shot*, peroration.

**swap,** *v.* — *Syn.* interchange, trade, barter; see **exchange** 2.

**sward,** *n.* — *Syn.* turf, sod, lawn; see **grass** 1.

**swarm,** *n.* — *Syn.* throng, crowd, multitude, dense crowd, horde, pack, troop, drove, shoal, school, colony, hive, cloud, flock, mass; see also **crowd** 1.
*See Synonym Study at* CROWD.

**swarm,** *v.* — *Syn.* gather like bees, rush together, crowd, cluster, move in a crowd, throng, flock together, gather in multitudes; see also **teem.**

**swarthy,** *modif.* — *Syn.* dark skinned, brown, dusky, tawny, dark hued, dark complexioned.
*See Synonym Study at* DUSKY.

**swastika,** *n.* — *Syn.* cross, insignia, triskelion; see **emblem.**

**swat,** *v.* — *Syn.* beat, knock, slap; see **hit** 1.

**swatch,** *n.* — *Syn.* sample, pattern, fragment; see **example** 1.

**swath,** *v.* — *Syn.* strip, row, ribbon; see **stripe, track** 2.

**swathe,** *v.* — *Syn.* drape, bandage, bind; see **clothe, wrap** 1.

**sway,** *n.* **1.** [Fluctuation] — *Syn.* swaying, swinging, swing, leaning, oscillation, vibration, undulation, wave, wavering, pulsation.
  **2.** [Authority] — *Syn.* power, jurisdiction, rule; see **dominion** 1, **government** 1, **power** 2.
*See Synonym Study at* POWER.
  **hold sway**— *Syn.* rule, control, dominate; see **govern** 1, **reign.**

**sway,** *v.* **1.** [To fluctuate] — *Syn.* bend, oscillate, swagger; see **swing** 1, **wave** 3.
  **2.** [To influence] — *Syn.* persuade, affect, divert; see **affect** 1, **influence.**
*See Synonym Study at* AFFECT, SWING.

**swear,** *v.* **1.** [To curse] — *Syn.* blaspheme, utter profanity, cuss*; see **curse** 1, 2.
  **2.** [To take an oath] — *Syn.* avow, affirm, depose, testify, state, vow, attest, warrant, vouch, assert, swear by, make an affidavit, give witness, cross one's heart.
  **3.** [To declare] — *Syn.* assert, affirm, maintain; see **declare** 1, **justify** 2.

**swear by,** *v.* — *Syn.* believe in, commit, have faith in; see **trust** 1.

**swear for,** *v.* — *Syn.* guarantee, uphold, give assurance for; see **back** 2, **help** 1, **support** 2.

**swear in,** *v.* — *Syn.* bring forward, call to testify, put on the witness stand, administer an oath, put upon oath.

**swearing,** *n.* — *Syn.* cursing, profanity, blaspheming; see **blasphemy, curse** 1.
*See Synonym Study at* BLASPHEMY.

**swear off,** *v.* — *Syn.* quit, reform, resolve; see **halt** 2, **suspend** 2, **stop** 1.

**swear out,** *v.* — *Syn.* charge with, enter a charge against, obtain a warrant; see **accuse.**

**sweat,** *n.* — *Syn.* perspiration, insensible perspiration, beads of sweat, sweating, body odor, B.O., wetness, transudation, steam.
  **no sweat*** — *Syn.* no trouble, no problem, easily done.

**sweat,** *v.* **1.** [To perspire] — *Syn.* perspire, secrete, transude, swelter, wilt, exude, break out in a sweat.
  **2.** [To work hard] — *Syn.* toil, slave, exert; see **work** 1.

**sweat blood*,** *v.* — *Syn.* slave, endure, labor; see **suffer** 1, **work** 1.

**sweater,** *n.* Types of sweaters include: coat, Norwegian, Fair Isle, Aran Isle, twin set, evening, sport, ski, cashmere, wool, cotton, fisherman's, long-sleeved, short-sleeved, barrel, sleeveless, crew neck, v-neck, turtleneck; pullover, cardigan; see **clothes.**

**sweat out*,** *v.* — *Syn.* worry, agonize, be troubled, be uncertain, be doubtful, be worried, wait anxiously; see also **endure** 2, **suffer** 1.

**sweaty,** *modif.* — *Syn.* perspiring, moist, wet with perspiration, wet with sweat, glowing, drenched in perspiration, bathed in sweat, covered with sweat; see also **hot** 1.

**Swedish,** *modif.* — *Syn.* from Sweden, from the far north, from the northland, North Germanic, Norse, Scandinavian, from the land of Svea, from Svealand.

**sweep,** *n.* **1.** [Movement] — *Syn.* course, progress, stroke; see **movement** 2, **swing.**
  **2.** [Extent] — *Syn.* range, compass, scope; see **breadth** 2, **extent, length** 1, 2, 3.

**sweep,** *v.* — *Syn.* brush up, clear, clear up, tidy*, ready up*; see also **clean, mop.**

**sweeping,** *modif.* — *Syn.* extensive, complete, all-embracing; see **comprehensive, full** 3.

**sweepings,** *n.* — *Syn.* dirt, litter, refuse; see **filth, trash** 1, 2.

**sweepstakes,** *n.* — *Syn.* contest, competition, event; see **race** 3, **sport** 3.

**sweep under the rug*,** *v.* — *Syn.* conceal, ignore, put out of sight; see **hide** 1, **neglect** 1.

**sweet,** *modif.* **1.** [Having the taste of sugar] — *Syn.* toothsome, sugary, luscious, candied, sweet as honey, sweet as sugar, sugared, honeyed, syrupy, like honey, like sugar, honeyed, saccharine, cloying, like nectar, delicious; see also **rich** 4. — *Ant.* SOUR, bitter, sharp.
  **2.** [Pleasant in disposition] — *Syn.* agreeable, pleasing, engaging, winning, delightful, patient, reasonable, gentle, kind, generous, unselfish, sweet-tempered, even-tempered, good-humored, considerate, thoughtful, companionable, saccharine, mushy, gooey, soppy; see also **friendly** 1. — *Ant.* SELFISH, repulsive, inconsiderate.
  **3.** [Not salt] — *Syn.* fresh, unsalted, uncured, unseasoned, freshened. — *Ant.* SALTY, pickled, briny.
  **4.** [Dear] — *Syn.* sympathetic, loving, winsome; see **beloved.**

**sweet,** *n.* **1.** [A term of affection] — *Syn.* dear, sweetheart, dearest; see **darling** 2.

**2.** [A dessert; *British*]— *Syn.* the sweet course, final course, pudding (British), end of the meal, top-off\*, afters\* (British); see also **dessert.**

**sweeten,** *v.* **1.** [To make sweet]— *Syn.* sugar, add sugar, add sweetening, make toothsome, give a sweet flavor to, mull; see also **flavor.**— *Ant.* SOUR, make sour, make bitter.

**2.** [To make fresh]— *Syn.* purify, freshen, remove salt from, fumigate, disinfect, cleanse, revive, renew, ventilate.

**sweetheart,** *n.*— *Syn.* beloved, dear, loved one; see **darling** 2, **lover** 1.

**sweetly,** *modif.* **1.** [In a sweet manner]— *Syn.* agreeably, pleasantly, comfortably, gently, gratefully, softly, smoothly, kindly, with winsome ways, in a winning manner, charmingly, ingenuously, with naïveté.

**2.** [With a sweet sound]— *Syn.* like music, with the sound of silver bells, like a bell, musically, tunefully, melodiously, mellifluously, with the voice of an angel, like a bird, with a golden voice; see also **harmonious** 1, **lyrical, musical** 1.

**sweetness,** *n.* **1.** [Sweetness of taste]— *Syn.* freshness, sugar content, palatableness, sweet taste, a taste like honey, flavor of honey.

**2.** [Figurative sweetness]— *Syn.* mildness, gentleness, docility, unselfishness, generosity, consideration.

**sweet potato,** *n.*— *Syn. batata* (Haitian), *patata* (Spanish), *Ipomoea batatas* (Latin), potato, potato vine, yam; see also **food, vegetable.**

**sweets,** *n.*— *Syn.* bonbons, candy, confectionery, confection, sweetmeats, comfit, preserves, candied fruit, *glacé* fruit, *glacé* nuts; see also **dessert, ice cream.**

**sweet-scented,** *modif.*— *Syn.* fragrant, aromatic, perfumed; see **odorous** 2.

**sweet-sounding,** *modif.*— *Syn.* musical, resonant, melodic; see **harmonious** 1, **lyrical, melodious.**

**sweet-tempered,** *modif.*— *Syn.* good-natured, amiable, tranquil; see **calm** 1, **friendly** 1.

**swell\*,** *modif.*— *Syn.* first-rate, desirable, fine; see **excellent.**

**swell,** *v.*— *Syn.* dilate, expand, distend, increase, enlarge, grow, grow larger, puff up, be inflated, become larger, bulge, balloon, puff, inflate, bulge out, blister, plump, round out, fill out, tumefy, become tumid, become swollen.
*See Synonym Study at* EXPAND.

**swelling,** *n.*— *Syn.* welt, wale, weal, wart, pimple, wen, carbuncle, boil, pock, pustule, inflammation, growth, corn, lump, bunion, tumor, suppuration, blister, abscess, contusion, abrasion, ridge; see also **injury** 1, **sore.**

**swelter,** *v.*— *Syn.* suffocate, wilt, broil, boil, roast, perspire; see also **sweat** 1.

**sweltering,** *modif.*— *Syn.* scorching, sultry, humid; see **close** 5, **hot** 1.

**swerve,** *v.*— *Syn.* move, turn aside, veer, deviate; see **turn** 6, **deviate.**
*See Synonym Study at* DEVIATE.

**swift,** *modif.*— *Syn.* flying, sudden, speedy; see **fast** 1.
*See Synonym Study at* FAST.

**swift-footed,** *modif.*— *Syn.* nimble, fleet, speedy; see **active** 1, **agile, fast** 1.

**swiftly,** *modif.*— *Syn.* quickly, speedily, space, without warning, with breath-taking speed.

**swiftness,** *n.*— *Syn.* acceleration, velocity, rapidity; see **speed.**

**swill,** *n.*— *Syn.* slops, garbage, waste; see **trash** 1, 2.

**swill\*,** *v.*— *Syn.* gulp down, drink up, pour down one's gullet; see **drink** 1, **swallow.**

**swim,** *n.*— *Syn.* bath, dip, plunge, swimming race, aquatic contest, dive, jump, splash.

**swim,** *v.*— *Syn.* slip, bathe, float, glide, slip through the water, move, stroke, paddle, go swimming, go for a swim, take a dip, do aquatic stunts, train for the swimming team, swim freestyle, swim the breast stroke, swim the Australian crawl, etc.; see also **swimming, race** 2.

**swimming,** *n.*— *Syn.* water sport, diving, aquatics, floating, natation, bathing, summer sport; see also **sport** 3.
Strokes in swimming include: breast stroke, back stroke, side stroke, butterfly, freestyle, crawl, modified crawl, Australian crawl, American crawl, dog paddle, trudgen.

**swimmingly,** *modif.*— *Syn.* successfully, smoothly, effectively; see **easily** 1, **quickly** 1.

**swimming pool,** *n.*— *Syn.* plunge, pool, natatorium, bathing pool, public pool, tank, swimming hole\*.

**swindle,** *n.*— *Syn.* imposition, deception, knavery; see **trick** 1.

**swindle,** *v.*— *Syn.* dupe, victimize, defraud, cheat; see **cheat, deceive.**
*See Synonym Study at* CHEAT.

**swindler,** *n.*— *Syn.* cheat, cheater, thief, impostor, charlatan, mountebank, trickster, deceiver, falsifier, counterfeiter, double-dealer, forger, rogue, absconder, fraud, confidence man\*, con man\*, fourflusher\*, sharper\*, gypo\*, gyp artist\*, clip\*, grifter\*, scammer\*, black-leg\*; see also **criminal.**

**swine,** *n.*— *Syn.* pig, porker, peccary; see **hog** 1.

**swing,** *n.*— *Syn.* sway, motion, undulation, fluctuation, stroke, vibration, oscillation, lilt, beat, rhythm; see also **wave** 3.

**in full swing**— *Syn.* lively, vigorous, animated, without reserve, without restraint; see also **active** 2, **exciting.**

**swing,** *v.* **1.** [To describe an arc]— *Syn.* sway, pivot, rotate, turn, turn about, revolve, fluctuate, waver, palpitate, oscillate, vibrate, undulate, turn on an axis; see also **rock, wave** 3.

**2.** [To cause to swing, sense 1]— *Syn.* wield, flourish, brandish, whirl, twirl, wave, hurl to and fro, throw around in a circle.

---

**SYN.** — **swing** suggests the to-and-fro motion of something that is suspended, hinged, pivoted, etc. so that it is free to turn or swivel at the point or points of attachment [a *swinging* door]; **sway** describes the slow swinging motion of something flexible or self-balancing, whether attached or unattached, in yielding to pressure, weight, etc. [branches *swaying* in the wind, a drunk *swaying* as he walked]; to **oscillate** is to swing back and forth, within certain limits, in the manner of a pendulum; **vibrate** suggests a rapid, regular, back-and-forth motion, as of a plucked, taut string, and is applied in physics to a similar movement of the particles of a fluid or elastic medium [the table began to *vibrate* with the sound] **fluctuate** implies continual, irregular alternating movements and is now most common in its extended sense [*fluctuating* prices]; **undulate** implies a gentle wavelike motion or form [*undulating* hills, grass *undulating* in the breeze]

---

**swinger\*,** *n.*— *Syn.* pleasure seeker, jet setter, libertine, life of the party\*; see **clown, sport** 4.

**swinging,** *modif.* **1.** [Moving backward and forward]— *Syn.* swaying, fluctuating, waving; see **moving** 1.

**2.** [\*Lively]— *Syn.* vivacious, spirited, sophisticated; see **active** 2, **happy** 1, **modern** 1.

**swinish,** *modif.*— *Syn.* boorish, piggish, coarse; see **beastly** 1, **rude** 1.

**swirl,** *n.* **1.** [Rapid rotating motion] — *Syn.* whirl, twist, surge, spin; see **eddy, whirl** 1.
**2.** [A twisting shape] — *Syn.* coil, whorl, twist, curl, whirl.

**swirl,** *v.* — *Syn.* eddy, whirl, surge; see **roll** 3, 6, **wave** 4.

**swirling,** *modif.* — *Syn.* swirly, twisting, in turmoil; see **writhing.**

**swish,** *v.* — *Syn.* wheeze, whiz, whisper; see **sound** 1.

**switch,** *v.* — *Syn.* turnabout, shift, rearrange; see **change** 1, **turn** 2.

**switch off,** *v.* — *Syn.* turn off, cut off the current, break the connection, disconnect, douse; see also **stop** 1.

**switch on,** *v.* — *Syn.* turn on, start, hook up, complete the connection; see **begin** 1.

**swivel,** *n.* — *Syn.* caster, pivot, pin; see **axis.**

**swivel** *v.* — *Syn.* rotate, spin, revolve; see **turn** 1.

**swollen,** *modif.* — *Syn.* distended, puffed, swelled; see **enlarged, inflated.**

**swoon,** *v.* — *Syn.* pass out, lose consciousness, languish; see **faint.**

**swoop,** *n.* — *Syn.* plunge, fall, drop; see **descent** 2, **dive** 1.

**swoop,** *v.* — *Syn.* slide, plummet, plunge; see **descend** 1, **dive, fall** 1.

**sword,** *n.* — *Syn.* saber, epee, foil, rapier, scimitar, brand, cutlass, weapon, smallsword, broadsword, bilbo, bill, cavalry sword, Toledo blade, samurai sword; see also **knife.**
**at swords' points** — *Syn.* fighting, quarreling, at war; see **angry.**
**cross swords** — *Syn.* fight with, argue with, battle, differ; see **attack** 1, 2, **fight** 2.

**swordsman,** *n.* — *Syn.* gladiator, fencer, dueler, foilist; see **contestant.**

**sybarite,** *n.* — *Syn.* voluptuary, epicure, sensualist; see **glutton.**

**sybaritic,** *modif.* — *Syn.* voluptuous, luxurious, carnal; see **sensual** 2.

**sycophant,** *n.* — *Syn.* parasite, leech, toady, flatterer, fawner, hanger-on, toadeater, tufthunter, lickspittle, flunkey, adulator, timeserver, cringer, crawler, truckler, slave, puppet, cat's-paw, groveler, spaniel, lapdog, sniveler, apple polisher, gofer, yes-man, bootlicker, brown-nose*, stooge, back-scratcher, flunky, smoothie, soft-soap artist, baloneyer, apple-saucer, doormat. — *Ant.* RULER, master, dictator.

**sycophantic,** *modif.* — *Syn.* slavish, servile, subservient; see **docile, obsequious.**

**syllabus,** *n.* — *Syn.* digest, outline, synopsis, course plan; see **plan** 1, **program** 2.

**syllogism,** *n.* — *Syn.* argument, dialectic, prologism; see **logic.**

**sylph,** *n.* — *Syn.* hobgoblin, nymph, dryad; see **fairy** 1.

**sylphlike,** *modif.* — *Syn.* slender, willowy, diaphanous, charming; see **graceful** 1, 2, **gracefully.**

**sylvan,** *modif.* — *Syn.* wooded, shady, forestlike; see **rural.**

**symbol,** *n.* — *Syn.* type, representative, regalia, emblem, insignia, totem, logo, hieroglyph, number, token, figure; see also **representation.**

**symbolic,** *modif.* — *Syn.* representative, typical, indicatory, indicative, suggestive, symptomatic, characteristic, illustrative, emblematic, metaphorical, figurative.

**symbolism,** *n.* — *Syn.* typology, metaphor, analogy; see **comparison** 2, **relationship.**

**symbolize,** *v.* — *Syn.* typify, signify, express; see **mean** 1.

**symmetrical,** *modif.* — *Syn.* balanced, well-formed, shapely, proportional, well-set; see also **regular** 3.

**symmetry,** *n.* — *Syn.* proportion, arrangement, order, harmony, equality, regularity, conformity, agreement, finish, shapeliness, centrality, evenness, balance, equivalence, equilibrium, equipoise, similarity.

---

*SYN.* — **symmetry,** with reference to the interrelation of parts to form an aesthetically pleasing whole, strictly implies correspondence in the form, size, arrangement, etc. of parts on either side of a median line or plane; **proportion** implies a gracefulness that results from the measured fitness in size or arrangement of parts to each other or to the whole; **harmony** implies such agreement or proportionate arrangement of parts, as in size, color, or form, as to make a pleasing impression; **balance** suggests the offsetting or contrasting of parts so as to produce an aesthetic equilibrium in the whole

---

**sympathetic,** *modif.* — *Syn.* compassionate, pitying, loving, considerate, sympathizing, tender; see also **sensitive** 3, **thoughtful** 2.
*See Synonym Study at* TENDER.

**sympathetically,** *modif.* — *Syn.* sensitively, perceptively, responsively, harmoniously, in accord, in harmony, in concert, *en rapport* (French), understandingly, appreciatively, compatibly, feelingly, emotionally, with feeling, warmly, heartily, cordially, kindheartedly, warmheartedly, softheartedly, humanely, in tune with.

**sympathize,** *v.* — *Syn.* condole, commiserate, pity, show mercy, show tenderness, comfort, understand, be understanding, love, be kind to, show kindliness, share another's sorrow, express sympathy, feel sorry for, be sympathetic.

**sympathizer,** *n.* **1.** [A comforter] — *Syn.* condoler, solacer, consoler; see **friend** 1.
**2.** [An advocate] — *Syn.* benefactor, partisan, collaborator, ally, backer; see also **patron** 1, **supporter.**

**sympathy,** *n.* **1.** [Fellow feeling] — *Syn.* understanding, commiseration, compassion; see **pity** 1.
**2.** [An expression of sympathy, sense 1] — *Syn.* condolence, consolation, solace, comfort, cheer, encouragement, reassurance; see also **aid.**
**3.** [Connection] — *Syn.* unity, harmony, concord, alliance, close relation, accord, agreement.
*See Synonym Study at* PITY.

**symphonic,** *modif.* — *Syn.* melodic, musical, consonant; see **harmonious** 1, **lyrical.**

**symphony,** *n.* **1.** [Harmony] — *Syn.* concord, chord, consonance; see **harmony** 1.
**2.** [A musical form] — *Syn.* ritornelle, symphonic composition, orchestral sonata, major work; see **music** 1.

**symposium,** *n.* — *Syn.* parley, debate, conference, convocation; see **discussion** 1.

**symptom,** *n.* — *Syn.* mark, sign, token, indication, trait, manifestation.

**symptomatic,** *modif.* — *Syn.* indicative, characteristic, emblematic, significant; see **suggestive.**

**synagogue,** *n.* — *Syn.* place of worship, temple, Jewish synagogue, house of God; see **church** 1.

**synchronous,** *modif.* — *Syn.* simultaneous, coincident, synchronized, in sync*; see **contemporary** 1, **simultaneous.**
*See Synonym Study at* CONTEMPORARY.

**syncopate,** *v.* — *Syn.* shorten, slide, contract, shift the beat; see **decrease** 2.

**syndicate,** *n.* **1.** [An association] — *Syn.* company, union, partnership, cartel; see **business** 4, **monopoly, organization** 3.
**2.** [A council] — *Syn.* board, cabinet, chamber; see **committee.**

*See Synonym Study at* MONOPOLY.

**syndicate,** *v.* — *Syn.* regulate, direct, merge, affiliate; see **associate** 3, **join** 2.

**syndrome,** *n.* — *Syn.* set of symptoms, characteristics, diagnostic, symptoms; see **complex** 2, **sign** 1.

**synod,** *n.* — *Syn.* congress, conclave, assembly; see **committee.**

**synonym,** *n.* — *Syn.* analogue, metonym, equivalent; see **word** 1.

**synonymous,** *modif.* — *Syn.* same, like, similar, equivalent, identical, correspondent, corresponding, alike, interchangeable, synonymic, convertible, apposite, compatible, coincident; see also **equal.** — *Ant.* CONFLICTING, divergent, contrary.

**synopsis,** *n.* — *Syn.* summary, outline, abstract, digest; see **abridgment** 2, **summary.**

*See Synonym Study at* ABRIDGMENT.

**syntax,** *n.* — *Syn.* order of words, arrangement, grammatical rules; see **grammar, language** 2.

**synthesis,** *n.* **1.** [The process of putting together] — *Syn.* combination, organization, integration, unification, constructing, construction, integrating, bringing into one, building a whole, forming into unity, making one of many; see also **union** 1. — *Ant.* SEPARATION, disseminating, dissecting.

**2.** [The result of putting together] — *Syn.* organization, organism, structure, unit, union, whole, complete whole, entirety, rounded conception, assembly, the one out of many.

**synthesize,** *v.* — *Syn.* integrate, incorporate, amalgamate; see **manufacture** 1.

**synthetic,** *modif.* **1.** [False] — *Syn.* artificial, counterfeit, plastic; see **artificial** 1, **false** 3.

**2.** [Man-made] — *Syn.* chemically made, ersatz, makeshift, unnatural, polymerized; see also **manufactured.**

*See Synonym Study at* ARTIFICIAL.

**syrup,** *n.* — *Syn.* sugar solution, treacle, sorghum; see **sugar, sweets.**

Common syrups include: cane, corn, maple, simple, sugar, glucose; molasses, blackstrap, sorghum, honey, treacle; Karo (trademark); see **sugar, sweets.**

**system,** *n.* **1.** [Order] — *Syn.* orderliness, regularity, conformity, logical order, definite plan, arrangement, rule, reduction to order, systematic procedure, systematic arrangement, logical process, orderly process; see also **order** 3.

**2.** [A method] — *Syn.* mode, way, scheme, arrangement, policy, artifice, usage, custom, practice, operation, course of action, modus operandi, definite procedure; see also **method** 2.

**systematic,** *modif.* — *Syn.* orderly, methodical, precise, well-organized; see **regular** 3.

**systematically,** *modif.* — *Syn.* orderly, in order, in regular order; see **regularly** 2.

**systematize,** *v.* — *Syn.* plan, arrange, organize, order, contrive, project, devise, design, frame, establish, institute, put in order. — *Ant.* confuse*, jumble, disorder.

# T

**tab,** *n.* **1.** [A projecting piece or part] — *Syn.* loop, stop, clip, handhold, filing tab, strip, flap, bookmark, slip, holder; see also **label, marker, tag** 2.
**2.** [*A bill] — *Syn.* check, running tab, cost, price, damage*; see also **statement** 3.
**tabernacle,** *n.* — *Syn.* recess, shrine, reliquary; see **church** 1, **temple.**
**table,** *n.* **1.** [A piece of furniture] — *Syn.* desk, pulpit, stand, board, counter, slab, dresser, bureau, lectern, sideboard, washstand, sink, horse, tea wagon, trivet; see also **furniture.**
Types of tables include: writing table, secretary, dining table, kitchen table, card table, drafting table, vanity table, operating table, altar table, retable, end table, coffee table, tea table, drop-leaf table, laboratory table, library table, refectory table.
**2.** [A statement in tabulated form] — *Syn.* schedule, digest, synopsis, report, record, chart, register, spread-sheet, compendium, index, appendix, table of contents, tabular illustration, statistics; see also **summary.**
**3.** [Food] — *Syn.* meat and drink, things to eat, spread; see **food, meal** 2.
**turn the tables*** — *Syn.* reverse, alter, switch; see **change** 1.
**under the table* 1.** — *Syn.* covertly, surreptitiously, not obviously; see **secretly.**
**2.** — *Syn.* into a stupor, dead-drunk, out cold; see **drunk.**
**table,** *v.* — *Syn.* postpone, defer, put off; see **delay** 1.
**tableau,** *n.* — *Syn.* scene, picture, illustration, portrayal; see **view** 1.
**tablecloth,** *n.* — *Syn.* table-cover, covering, oilcloth, lace cloth, spread, luncheon cloth, bridge-table cloth, tea-cloth, breakfast set, place mats, luncheon set, doilies; see also **cover** 1.
**tablet,** *n.* **1.** [A thin piece of material with an inscription] — *Syn.* slab, stone, slate, monument, plate, plaque, memorial tablet, memorial stone, record, headstone, tombstone, gravestone, marker, inscription; see also **epitaph.**
**2.** [Writing paper] — *Syn.* folder, pad, sheaf, sheets, memorandum pad, memo book, correspondence paper, ream; see also **paper** 5.
**3.** [A medicinal pill] — *Syn.* pill, dose, cake, square, capsule, caplet; see also **medicine** 2.
**taboo,** *modif.* — *Syn.* sacred, forbidden, out of bounds, reserved; see **holy** 1, **illegal, restricted.**
**taboo,** *n.* — *Syn.* restriction, reservation, stricture, limitation, law, regulation, superstition, prohibition, proscription, ban, no-no*, interdiction, social convention, moral obligation, religious convention; see also **sanction** 2.
**taboo,** *v.* — *Syn.* inhibit, interdict, prohibit, proscribe, forbid, prevent, debar, disallow, exclude, circumscribe, hinder, ban, frown upon, restrict, veto; see also **hinder, restrain** 1. — *Ant.* allow, permit, sanction.
**taboret,** *n.* — *Syn.* stool, seat, table; see **bench** 1, **chair** 1, **furniture.**

**tabulate,** *v.* **1.** [To arrange systematically] — *Syn.* formulate, enumerate, arrange, index, alphabetize, grade, codify, digest, classify, register, catalogue, systematize, methodize, put in tabular form, categorize; see also **file** 1, **list** 1, **record** 1.
**2.** [To calculate] — *Syn.* count, add up, analyze, enumerate; see **calculate** 1.
**tacit,** *modif.* — *Syn.* implicit, assumed, unspoken; see **implied, understood** 2.
**taciturn,** *modif.* — *Syn.* reticent, uncommunicative, silent, mute, speechless, close, mum, curt, close-mouthed, sententious, sparing, not liking to talk; see also **quiet** 2, **reserved** 3. — *Ant.* TALKATIVE, loquacious, chatty.
**tack,** *n.* **1.** [A short, broad-headed nail] — *Syn.* thumb-tack, glazier point, push pin, carpet tack, copper tack; see also **nail, pin** 1.
**2.** [An oblique course] — *Syn.* tangent, deviation, digression, variation, alteration, sweep, swerve, zigzag, yaw, echelon, sidling, siding, switch, turn-about-face*; see also **turn** 6.
**tack,** *v.* **1.** [To fasten lightly] — *Syn.* pin, paste, baste, tie, nail, mount, sew, stitch, hem piece together; see also **fasten** 1.
**2.** [To steer an oblique course] — *Syn.* go in zigzags, zigzag, change course, turn in the wind, deviate, turn about-face, alter one's course, jibe, yaw, sheer, wear, shift, switch, shunt, bear*; see also **turn** 6, **veer.** — *Ant.* STRAIGHTEN, hold a course, take a straight course.
**tackle,** *n.* **1.** [Equipment] — *Syn.* rigging, ropes and pulleys, apparatus; see **equipment.**
**2.** [A contrivance having mechanical advantage] — *Syn.* pulleys, block-and-tackle, mechanical purchase, differential tackle, differential*, movable pulley; see also **pulley.**
**3.** [In football, an attempt to down a ball-carrier] — *Syn.* flying tackle, low tackle, shoulder tackle, running tackle, sack, plunge, lunge, shoestring tackle*; see also **block** 5.
**4.** [In football, one who plays between end and guard] — *Syn.* linesman, right tackle, left tackle, block-and-tackle man*; see **football player.**
**5.** [In fishing, equipment] — *Syn.* gear, sporting goods, fishing paraphernalia; see **equipment, net, rod** 2.
Fishing tackle includes: hook, line, fly, rod, casting rod, reel, casting reel, cut bait, live bait, minnow, grasshopper, fish eggs, salmon eggs, worm, lure, spinner, seine, fish net, landing net, pole, gaff, float, bobber, cork, sinker, creel, tackle box, fly-typing materials, swivels, shot, deep-sea tackle, leader, number four hook, number six hook, number eight hook, number ten hook, cod hook, bass hook, pike hook, stringer, fish sack, basket, trotline.
**tackle,** *v.* **1.** [*To undertake] — *Syn.* launch, embark on, work on, set about, take up in earnest, turn one's hand to, begin, turn to, plunge into, devote oneself to, make an attempt, put one's shoulder to the wheel*, dig

in★, start the ball rolling★, square off★, get going★; see also **try** 1, **undertake.** — *Ant.* AVOID, hesitate, delay.

**2.** [In football, to endeavor to down an opponent] — *Syn.* grapple, seize, throw down, catch, grab, down, throw, throw for a loss, sack, upset, bring to the ground, stop, nail★, smear★, haul to earth★, take★, put the freeze on★.

**tact,** *n.* — *Syn.* perception, discrimination, judgment, acuteness, penetration, intelligence, acumen, common sense, perspicacity, subtlety, discernment, poise, diplomacy, savoir-faire, prudence, aptness, good taste, refinement, delicacy, the ability to get along with others, finesse, horse sense★, good politics★. — *Ant.* RUDENESS, coarseness, misconduct.

---

**SYN.** — **tact** implies the skill of one who has a quick and delicate sense of what is fitting and thus avoids giving offense in dealing with persons or difficult situations /it will require *tact* to keep him calm/; **poise** implies composure in the face of disturbing or embarrassing situations /despite the taunts of the crowd, she maintained her *poise*/; **diplomacy** implies a smoothness and adroitness in dealing with others, sometimes in such a way as to gain one's own ends /his lack of *diplomacy* lost him the contract/; **savoir-faire** implies a ready knowledge of the right thing to do or say in any situation /his *savoir-faire* helped advance his career/

---

**tactful,** *modif.* — *Syn.* urbane, suave, politic, diplomatic, civil, considerate, courteous, polished, perceptive, sympathetic, understanding, adroit, poised, observant, aware, gentle, wise, cautious, careful, prudent; see also **judicious, thoughtful** 2. — *Ant.* RUDE, hasty, uncivil.

**tactician,** *n.* — *Syn.* engineer, strategist, mastermind, planner; see **administrator, diplomat** 2.

**tactics,** *n.* — *Syn.* strategy, maneuvering, military art, generalship, plan of attack, plan of defense, procedure, stratagem, approach, disposition, map work.

**tactile,** *modif.* — *Syn.* palpable, physical, tactual, substantial; see **real** 2, **tangible.**

**tactless,** *modif.* — *Syn.* undiplomatic, unperceptive, unthoughtful, insensitive, inconsiderate, discourteous, unsympathetic, misunderstanding, impolitic, rash, hasty, awkward, gauche, clumsy, imprudent, rude, rough, crude, boorish, unpolished, gruff, uncivil, vulgar. — *Ant.* TACTFUL, urbane, politic.

**tag,** *n.* **1.** [A remnant or scrap] — *Syn.* rag, piece, shred, patch, snip, chip, fragment, snatch, trifle, scrap, waste, discard, junk, remainder, remains, leavings, refuse, stubble; see also **cloth, remnant** 2.

**2.** [A mark of identification] — *Syn.* ticket, badge, card, tab, trademark, stamp, stub, voucher, slip, label, check, chip, emblem, insignia, tally, motto, sticker, inscription, laundry mark, price tag, identification number, button, pin.

**3.** [A children's game] — *Syn.* cross tag, freeze tag, squat tag; see **game** 1.

**tag,** *v.* **1.** [To fit with a tag] — *Syn.* check, hold, earmark; see **designate** 1, **mark** 2.

**2.** [★To follow closely] — *Syn.* pursue, track, chase, track down, trace, dog, follow the heels of, trail, shadow★, tail★; see also **hunt** 2.

**tail,** *n.* **1.** [The prolongation of the spinal column] — *Syn.* rear end, rear appendage, extremity, stub, hind part, caudal appendage, *cauda* (Latin), coccyx, brush, scut, flag, dock, rudder★, cue★, fly swatter★, tassel★, wagger★; see also **rear.**

**2.** [The end of anything, especially if elongated] — *Syn.*

last part, hindmost part, tailpiece; see **end** 4. — *Ant.* ORIGIN, head, beginning.

**3.** [The rear of an aircraft]. Parts in the tail of an airplane include: empennage, tail group, rudder, tail assembly, tail skid, stabilizer, diving rudder, horizontal tail fin, elevator, airfoil.

**on one's tail★** — *Syn.* behind, shadowing, trailing; see **following.**

**turn tail★** — *Syn.* run away, evade, avoid; see **escape.**

**with one's tail between one's legs★** — *Syn.* in defeat, in fear, humbly, dejectedly; see **fearfully.**

**tail end,** *n.* — *Syn.* extremity, tip, limit; see **end** 4.

**tailor,** *n.* — *Syn.* garment maker, clothier, tailoress, dressmaker, seamstress, habit-maker, modiste, pantspresser, needle-pusher, nip-and-tucker, whipstitch, sartor.

**tailored,** *modif.* — *Syn.* tailor-made, made-to-measure, simple, specially fit; see **sewn.**

**taint,** *v.* **1.** [To pollute] — *Syn.* spoil, infect, rot; see **contaminate, decay.**

**2.** [To corrupt] — *Syn.* deprave, debase, defile; see **corrupt** 1.

See Synonym Study at CONTAMINATE.

**tainted,** *modif.* — *Syn.* infected, diseased, decayed, vitiated, contaminated, fetid, smelling, stinking, rank, putrid, rancid, graveolent, rotten, polluted, impaired; see also **spoiled.** — *Ant.* CLEAN, pure, fresh.

**take,** *n.* **1.** [Something that is taken] — *Syn.* part, cut, proceeds; see **profit** 2, **share.**

**2.** [Scene filmed or televised] — *Syn.* film, shot, motion picture; see **photograph.**

**3.** [★Something that is seized] — *Syn.* catching, haul★, swag★; see **booty, catch** 1.

**on the take★** — *Syn.* corrupt, corruptible, avaricious, money-hungry; see **greedy** 1.

**take,** *v.* **1.** [To seize] — *Syn.* appropriate, pocket, carry off; see **seize** 1, 2.

**2.** [To collect] — *Syn.* gather up, accept, reap; see **receive** 1.

**3.** [To catch] — *Syn.* seize, capture, grab, get hold of; see **catch** 1.

**4.** [To choose] — *Syn.* select, decide on, prefer; see **choose** 1, **decide.**

**5.** [To acquire] — *Syn.* win, attain, secure; see **earn** 2, **obtain** 1.

**6.** [To require] — *Syn.* necessitate, demand, call for; see **need.**

**7.** [To purchase] — *Syn.* pay for, procure, gain; see **buy** 1.

**8.** [To contract; *said of a disease*] — *Syn.* get, come down with, be seized with; see **catch** 4.

**9.** [To record] — *Syn.* note, register, take notes; see **record** 1.

**10.** [To transport] — *Syn.* convey, deliver, carry, drive; see **bring** 1, **carry** 1.

**11.** [To captivate] — *Syn.* charm, delight, overwhelm; see **entertain** 1, **fascinate.**

**12.** [To win] — *Syn.* prevail, triumph, beat; see **defeat** 1.

**13.** [To rent] — *Syn.* lease, hire, charter; see **rent** 2.

**14.** [To steal] — *Syn.* misappropriate, purloin, filch; see **steal.**

**15.** [To undergo] — *Syn.* tolerate, suffer, bear; see **endure** 2, **undergo.**

**16.** [To consider] — *Syn.* regard, look upon, hold; see **consider** 2.

**17.** [To comprehend] — *Syn.* apprehend, grasp, perceive; see **know** 1, **understand** 1.

**18.** [To lead] — *Syn.* guide, steer, pilot; see **lead** 1.

**19.** [To escort] — *Syn.* conduct, attend, go with; see **accompany** 1.

**20.** [To admit] — *Syn.* let in, welcome, give access to; see **receive** 4.

**21.** [To enjoy] — *Syn.* relish, delight in, luxuriate in; see **like** 1.

**22.** [To adopt] — *Syn.* utilize, assume, appropriate; see **adopt** 2.

**23.** [To apply] — *Syn.* put in practice, exert, exercise; see **practice** 1, **use** 1.

**24.** [To travel] — *Syn.* tour, journey, trek, travel by; see **travel** 1.

**25.** [To seek] — *Syn.* look for, search for, go after; see **hunt** 2, **seek** 1.

**26.** [To experience] — *Syn.* sense, observe, be aware of; see **feel** 2.

**27.** [*To cheat] — *Syn.* defraud, trick, swindle; see **deceive.**

**28.** [To grow] — *Syn.* germinate, develop into, grow to be; see **become** 1.

*See Synonym Study at* BRING, RECEIVE, SEIZE.

**take a chance***, *v.* — *Syn.* venture, hazard, gamble; see **risk, try** 1.

**take after,** *v.* **1.** [To resemble] — *Syn.* look like, be like, seem like; see **resemble.**

**2.** [To follow] — *Syn.* follow suit, do like, emulate; see **follow** 2.

**3.** [To chase] — *Syn.* follow, trail, track; see **hunt** 1, 2, **pursue** 1.

**take a look at,** *v.* — *Syn.* inspect, check out, test; see **examine** 1.

**take amiss,** *v.* — *Syn.* bristle, bridle, grumble, misunderstand; see **complain** 1, **mistake.**

**take a picture,** *v.* — *Syn.* shoot, snap, film; see **photograph.**

**take a shot at***, *v.* **1.** [To try] — *Syn.* endeavor, risk, hazard; see **try** 1.

**2.** [To fire at] — *Syn.* shoot, fire at, fire a shot at; see **shoot at** 1.

**take at one's word,** *v.* — *Syn.* believe, regard, accept, take one's word for; see **believe** 1.

**take away,** *v.* **1.** [To subtract] — *Syn.* deduct, take from, knock off; see **decrease** 2.

**2.** [To carry off] — *Syn.* transport, cart off, carry away; see **remove** 1.

**take back,** *v.* **1.** [To regain] — *Syn.* retrieve, get back, reclaim; see **recover** 1.

**2.** [To restrict] — *Syn.* draw in, retire, pull in; see **remove** 1, **withdraw** 2.

**3.** [To disavow] — *Syn.* retract, back down, recall; see **deny, recant, withdraw** 2.

**take down,** *v.* **1.** [To dismantle] — *Syn.* disassemble, take apart, undo; see **dismantle.**

**2.** [To write down] — *Syn.* inscribe, jot down, note down; see **record** 1, **write** 2.

**take down a peg***, *v.* — *Syn.* meeken, demean, chastise, chasten; see **humble.**

**take five,** *v.* — *Syn.* take a break, break, unwind, slow down; see **relax** 1.

**take for,** *v.* **1.** [To mistake] — *Syn.* misapprehend, misunderstand, err; see **mistake.**

**2.** [To assume] — *Syn.* presuppose, infer, accept; see **assume** 1.

**take from,** *v.* — *Syn.* take, grab, appropriate; see **seize** 2.

**take heed,** *v.* — *Syn.* heed, beward, mind; see **take care** at **care, watch out.**

**take in,** *v.* **1.** [To include] — *Syn.* embrace, comprise, incorporate; see **include** 1.

**2.** [To understand] — *Syn.* comprehend, apprehend, perceive; see **understand** 1.

**3.** [*To cheat] — *Syn.* swindle, lie, defraud; see **deceive.**

**4.** [To give hospitality to] — *Syn.* welcome, shelter, accept; see **receive** 1, 4.

**5.** [To shorten] — *Syn.* reduce, lessen, cut down, reef, furl; see also **decrease** 2.

**take in good part,** *v.* — *Syn.* stand, tolerate, bear; see **endure** 2.

**take in hand,** *v.* — *Syn.* educate, instruct, exercise; see **teach** 1.

**take in (one's) stride,** *v.* — *Syn.* handle, do, manage; see **achieve** 1, **command** 2, **perform** 1, **succeed** 1.

**take it,** *v.* **1.** [To assume] — *Syn.* suppose, presume, gather; see **assume** 1.

**2.** [To endure] — *Syn.* persevere, keep on, carry on; see **endure** 2.

**take it out on***, *v.* — *Syn.* make (another) suffer, get even with, get back at, settle with; see **revenge.**

**taken,** *modif.* **1.** [Captured] — *Syn.* arrested, seized, appropriated; see **captured** 1.

**2.** [Employed or rented] — *Syn.* occupied, reserved, held, hired, contracted for; see also **rented.**

**taken aback** — *Syn.* startled, disconcerted, caught off guard; see **bewildered, surprised.**

**take-off,** *n.* **1.** [*A burlesque] — *Syn.* cartoon, comedy, caricature, satire; see **imitation** 1, **parody, ridicule.**

**2.** [The act of leaving the ground] — *Syn.* ascent, upward flight, fly-off, climb, rise, hop, jump, vertical takeoff; see also **departure** 1, **rise** 1. — *Ant.* DIVE, descent, tailspin landing.

**take off,** *v.* **1.** [To undress] — *Syn.* strip, divest, expose; see **undress.**

**2.** [To deduct] — *Syn.* lessen, subtract, take away; see **decrease** 2.

**3.** [*To mock] — *Syn.* satirize, mimic, burlesque; see **parody, ridicule.**

**4.** [To leave the earth] — *Syn.* blast off, ascend, soar; see **fly** 1, 4, **rise** 1.

**5.** [*To depart] — *Syn.* go away, split*, shove off*; see **leave** 1.

**take on,** *v.* **1.** [To hire] — *Syn.* employ, engage, give work to; see **hire** 1.

**2.** [To acquire an appearance] — *Syn.* emerge, develop, turn; see **become** 1, **seem.**

**3.** [To undertake] — *Syn.* attempt, handle, endeavor; see **try** 1, **undertake.**

**4.** [*To meet in fight or sport] — *Syn.* engage, battle, contest; see **attack** 1, 4, **compete.**

**take one's choice,** *v.* — *Syn.* pick out, discriminate between, make a decision; see **choose** 1, **decide.**

**take one's fancy,** *v.* — *Syn.* attract, allure, catch the eye of; see **fascinate.**

**take out,** *v.* **1.** [To extract] — *Syn.* cut out, pull out, draw out; see **remove** 1.

**2.** [To escort] — *Syn.* lead, chaperon, attend; see **accompany** 1.

**take out after***, *v.* — *Syn.* chase, trail, follow; see **hunt** 1, 2, **pursue** 1.

**take over,** *v.* **1.** [To take control] — *Syn.* take charge, take command, assume charge, assume control, assume the leadership of; see also **lead** 1.

**2.** [To seize control] — *Syn.* take the reins of, take the helm of, overthrow; see **seize** 2.

**3.** [To convey] — *Syn.* transport, bear, move; see **carry** 1, **send** 1, 2, **take** 10.

**take to,** *v.* — *Syn.* enjoy, be fond of, admire; see **favor** 2, **like** 1, 2.

**take up,** *v.* **1.** [To begin] — *Syn.* start, initiate, commence; see **begin** 1.

**2.** [To raise] — *Syn.* lift, elevate, hoist; see **raise** 1.

**3.** [To shorten] — *Syn.* tighten, reduce, lessen; see **decrease** 2.

**4.** [To occupy] — *Syn.* consume, engage, fill; see **occupy** 2, **use** 1.

**5.** [To adopt as a cause] — *Syn.* appropriate, become involved in, assume, embrace; see **adopt** 2.

**take up with★,** *v.* — *Syn.* associate with, befriend, become intimate with; see **associate** 1.

**taking,** *modif.* — *Syn.* engaging, refreshing, gracious; see **charming, pleasant** 1.

**taking,** *n.* — *Syn.* catching, grabbling, stealing; see **booty, catch** 1, **theft.**

**talcum,** *n.* — *Syn.* talc, talcum powder, powdered talc, baby powder, perfumed talc, toilet powder, after-shave powder, counterirritant; see also **powder.**

**tale,** *n.* **1.** [A story] — *Syn.* anecdote, fairy tale, folk tale; see **story.**

**2.** [A lie] — *Syn.* tall tale, fiction, exaggeration; see **lie** 1.

*See Synonym Study at* STORY.

**talent,** *n.* **1.** [A gift] — *Syn.* aptitude, faculty, gift, genius, facility, skill, capability, expertise, inventiveness, turn, forte, knack★; see also **ability** 1, 2.

**2.** [★A famous person] — *Syn.* celebrity, notable, find★; see **star** 3.

---

*SYN.* — **talent** implies an apparently native ability for a specific pursuit and connotes either that it is or can be cultivated by the one possessing it [a *talent* for drawing]; **gift** suggests that a special ability is bestowed upon one, as by nature, and not acquired through effort [a *gift* for making plants grow]; **aptitude** implies a natural inclination for a particular work, specif. as pointing to special fitness for, or probable success in, it [*aptitude* tests]; **faculty** implies a special ability that is either inherent or acquired, as well as a ready ease in its exercise [the *faculty* of judgment]; **knack** implies an acquired faculty for doing something cleverly and skillfully [the *knack* of rhyming]; **genius** implies an inborn mental endowment, specif. of a creative or inventive kind in the arts or sciences, that is exceptional or phenomenal [the *genius* of Edison]

---

**talented,** *modif.* — *Syn.* gifted, capable, skilled; see **able** 1.

**talisman,** *n.* — *Syn.* good luck piece, fetish, amulet; see **charm** 2.

**talk,** *n.* **1.** [Human speech] — *Syn.* utterance, locution, parlance; see **communication** 1, **speech** 2.

**2.** [A conference] — *Syn.* symposium, parley, consultation; see **conversation, discussion** 1.

**3.** [An address] — *Syn.* lecture, oration, sermon; see **speech** 3.

**4.** [Gossip] — *Syn.* report, hearsay, tittle-tattle; see **gossip** 1, **rumor** 1.

**5.** [Nonsense] — *Syn.* bombast, twaddle, cant, banter, persiflage, noise, palaver, badinage, racket, rubbish, rot, jive★, trash★, flapdoodle★, raillery★, bunk★, fudge★; see also **jargon** 3, **nonsense** 1.

*See Synonym Study at* SPEECH.

**big talk★** — *Syn.* bragging, boasting, lying; see **exaggeration** 1.

**make talk★** — *Syn.* chat, converse, gossip; see **talk** 1.

**talk,** *v.* **1.** [To converse] — *Syn.* discuss, confer, chat, interview, speak, communicate, dialogue, engage in a dialogue, have a conversation, have a meeting of the minds, chatter, gossip, remark, be on the phone with, be in contact with, talk over, reason with, visit with, parley, commune with, read, hold a discussion, confide in, argue, observe, notice, inform, rehearse, debate, have an exchange, exchange opinions, have a conference with, pop off★, talk away★, go on★, gab★, chew the rag★, chew the fat★, compare notes with★, talk an arm off of★, talk a leg off of★, go over★, pipe up★, shoot off one's mouth★, spit out★, shoot the breeze★, shoot the bull★, pass the time of day★, be closeted with★. — *Ant.* HUSH, be silent, be still.

**2.** [To lecture] — *Syn.* speak, give a talk, deliver a speech; see **address** 2, **lecture.**

**3.** [★To inform] — *Syn.* reveal, divulge, sing★; see **notify** 1, **tell** 1.

**4.** [★To persuade] — *Syn.* induce, sway, count; see **influence, persuade** 1.

**5.** [To utter] — *Syn.* pronounce, express, speak; see **utter.**

*See Synonym Study at* SPEAK.

**talk about,** *v.* — *Syn.* treat, take into consideration, deal with; see **consider** 1, **discuss.**

**talkative,** *modif.* — *Syn.* voluble, loquacious, wordy, verbose, garrulous, verbal, chattering, glib, chatty, long-winded, effusive, long-tongued, gossipy, talky★, gabbling★, windy★, crackling★, full of hot air★, yappy★, all yaw★, gassy★, big-mouthed★; see also **fluent** 2. — *Ant.* RESERVED, laconic, speechless.

---

*SYN.* — **talkative,** implying a fondness for talking frequently or at length, is perhaps the least derogatory of these words [no one in the class is very *talkative*]; **loquacious** usually implies a disposition to talk incessantly or to keep up a constant flow of chatter [a *loquacious* mood]; **garrulous** implies a wearisome loquacity about trivial matters [a *garrulous* old man told us his life story]; **voluble** suggests a continuous flow of glib talk [a *voluble* buzz of conversation]

---

**talk back★,** *v.* — *Syn.* sass, retort, defy; see **answer** 1.

**talk big★,** *v.* — *Syn.* brag, gloat, bluster; see **boast** 1.

**talk business★,** *v.* — *Syn.* be serious, talk shop, confer; see **consult, discuss.**

**talk down to,** *v.* — *Syn.* stoop, snub, be overbearing; see **condescend, humiliate, patronize** 2.

**talker,** *n.* — *Syn.* speaker, orator, speechmaker, mouthpiece, spokesman, lecturer, actor, performer, debater, story-teller, conversationalist, raconteur, barker, announcer, preacher, lawyer, reader, rhetorician, after-dinner speaker, stump speaker, gossip, windbag★, empty barrel★.

**talking,** *modif.* — *Syn.* eloquent, chattering, mouthing, repeating, echoing, pronouncing, expressing, articulating, enunciating, ranting, spouting, haranguing, waffling, speaking, vocalizing, verbalizing, declaiming, orating, conversing, discussing, holding forth; see also **fluent** 2, **verbose.** — *Ant.* LISTENING, hearing, witnessing.

**talk into,** *v.* — *Syn.* persuade, win over, sway, affect; see **convince, influence, persuade** 1.

**talk over,** *v.* — *Syn.* consider, consult, deliberate; see **discuss.**

**talk up,** *v.* — *Syn.* acclaim, extol, commend; see **exaggerate, praise** 1.

**tall,** *modif.* **1.** [Lofty] — *Syn.* big, great, towering; see **high** 1.

**2.** [Exaggerated] — *Syn.* far-fetched, outlandish, unbelievable; see **exaggerated.**

**tallow,** *n.* — *Syn.* beef fat, mutton fat, wax; see **fat, grease.**

**tally,** *n.* **1.** [Account] — *Syn.* reckoning, summation, poll, tab; see **score** 1, 2.

**2.** [Counterpart] — *Syn.* match, complement, partner, coordinate, companion, reciprocal.

**3.** [Label] — *Syn.* identification, emblem, insignia; see **tag** 2.

**tally,** *v.* **1.** [To record] — *Syn.* write down, register, mark down; see **record** 1.

**2.** [To count] — *Syn.* add up, sum, total; see **count.**

**3.** [To agree] — *Syn.* correspond, match, jibe*; see **agree.**

*See Synonym Study at* AGREE.

**talon,** *n.* — *Syn.* spur, clutches, nail, hook; see **claw.**

**tame,** *modif.* **1.** [Domesticated] — *Syn.* subdued, submissive, housebroken, housetrained, harmless, trained, overcome, mastered, civilized, broken in, harnessed, yoked, acclimatized, muzzled, bridled, busted*, gentled down*, dehorned*, halter-wise*; see also **docile.** — *Ant.* WILD, undomesticated, untamed.

**2.** [Gentle] — *Syn.* tractable, obedient, kindly; see **gentle** 3.

**3.** [Uninteresting] — *Syn.* insipid, monotonous, routine; see **conventional** 3, **dull** 4, **uninteresting.**

**4.** [Without spirit] — *Syn.* limp, flat, weak, mild, denatured, diluted, feeble, halfhearted, spiritless, bloodless, boiled down*, half-cooked*, half-baked*, without punch*. — *Ant.* ALIVE, spirited, animated.

**tamper with,** *v.* — *Syn.* alter, diversify, vary, mess with, mess around with; see also **change** 1, **destroy** 1.

**tan,** *modif.* — *Syn.* brownish, sun-tanned, bronzed, leathercolored, unbleached, weathered; see also **brown, tan, tawny.**

**tan,** *n.* — *Syn.* light-brown, red-yellow, beige, cream, ecru, natural, saddle-tan, tanbark, buff, bronze, golden, citrine, khaki, drab, olive-brown, dun, umber, sand, tawny; see also **brown, gold** 2, **yellow** 1.

**tan,** *v.* — *Syn.* brown, suntan, bronze, sunburn, burn.

**tandem,** *modif.* — *Syn.* one behind the other, back to back, single, file, behind, in back of, in sequence, sequential, ordered, in order.

**tang,** *n.* — *Syn.* zest, flavor, taste, savor, pungency, piquancy, taste, thrill*.

**tangent,** *modif.* — *Syn.* touching, tangential, in contact; see **contiguous.**

**go off on a tangent** — *Syn.* swerve, get off course, get off the subject, lose track; see **deviate.**

*See Synonym Study at* ADJACENT.

**tangential,** *modif.* — *Syn.* digressing, diverging, divergent, digressive, unrelated, extraneous.

**tangible,** *modif.* — *Syn.* perceptible, palpable, material, real, substantial, appreciable, sensible, touchable, verifiable, physical, corporeal, solid, concrete, visible, stable, graspable, incarnated, embodied, manifest, factual, objective, tactile, actual, definite, clear-cut, substantive, real live*, big as life*, big as life and twice as natural*. — *Ant.* SPIRITUAL, ethereal, intangible.

**SYN.** — **tangible** applies to that which can be grasped, either with the hand or the mind [*tangible* assets, *tangible* benefits]; **perceptible** is applied to anything that can be apprehended by the senses but often connotes that the thing is just barely visible, audible, etc. [a *perceptible* smell of coffee]; **sensible** applies to that which can clearly be perceived [a *sensible* difference in their size]; **palpable** refers to anything that can be perceived by or as if by the sense of touch [a *palpable* fog]; **appreciable** is used of that

which is sufficiently perceptible to be measured, estimated, etc. or to have significance [an *appreciable* amount]

**tangle,** *n.* — *Syn.* snarl, snag, muddle; see **confusion** 2, **knot** 2.

**tangle,** *v.* — *Syn.* involve, complicate, confuse, obstruct, hamper, derange, mix up, discompose, disorganize, upset, unbalance, unhinge, embarrass, perplex, tie up, trap, mess up. — *Ant.* ORDER, fix, unravel.

**tangled,** *modif.* — *Syn.* tied up, confused, knit together, disordered, chaotic, out of place, mixed up, snarled, knotted, trapped, entangled, twisted, raveled, muddled, messed up*, balled up*, screwy*, wires crossed*. — *Ant.* ORGANIZED, ordered, unraveled.

**tank,** *n.* **1.** [A large container for liquids] — *Syn.* tub, basin, cistern, receptacle, vat, cauldron, keg, vessel, cask, tun; see also **container.**

**2.** [An armored caterpillar vehicle]. Types of tanks include: light, medium, heavy, radio-controlled, Goliath, Mark IV, Mark V, Mark VI, M-3, M-4, Abrams M-1, Armstrong-Vickers, Royal Tiger, T-34 (Russian), *Königstiger* (German), Hunting Panther, Panzer, General Grant*, General Sherman*, General Pershing*, land cruiser*, doodle-bug*; see also **weapon** 1.

**tankard,** *n.* — *Syn.* mug, stein, flask; see **bottle, jug.**

**tanker,** *n.* — *Syn.* steel cargo boat, oiler, oil tanker, supertanker, tank trailer, tank wagon, tank truck; see also **boat, truck** 1.

**tank farming,** *n.* — *Syn.* hydroponics, agriculture, horticulture; see **farming.**

**tanned,** *modif.* — *Syn.* brown, bronzed, tan-faced; see **sunburned, tan.**

**tantalize,** *v.* — *Syn.* tease, torment, frustrate, entice, make one's mouth water; see also **fascinate.**

**tantamount,** *modif.* — *Syn.* equivalent, parallel, identical; see **equal.**

**tantrum,** *n.* — *Syn.* conniption, outburst, scene, animosity; see **anger, fit** 2.

**tap,** *n.* **1.** [A light blow] — *Syn.* pat, rap, dab; see **blow** 1.

**2.** [A spigot] — *Syn.* faucet, petcock, valve, spout; see **faucet.**

**3.** [A partial sole used for repair] — *Syn.* patch, guard, cover, reinforcement.

**on tap** — *Syn.* on draft, fresh from the barrel, in the keg, free-flowing, on hand; see also **available.**

**tap,** *v.* **1.** [To strike lightly] — *Syn.* pat, touch, rap; see **hit** 1.

**2.** [To puncture in order to draw liquid] — *Syn.* perforate, pierce, bore, drill, broach, stab, spear, riddle, spike, lance; see also **penetrate** 1. — *Ant.* CLOSE, seal, solder.

**3.** [To obtain by means of tapping] — *Syn.* draw, draw out, draw forth, pour out, drain, empty.

**tape,** *n.* — *Syn.* ribbon, line, rope, strip.

Tapes include: braid, edging, bending, tapeline, tape measure, steel tape, surveyor's chain, adhesive tape, duct tape, gummed tape, draftsman's tape, Scotch Tape (trademark), masking tape, strapping tape, Mylar tape (trademark), packaging tape, athletic tape, reinforced tape, mending tape; videotape, audiotape, cassette tape, magnetic tape; ticker tape.

**tape,** *v.* **1.** [To fasten] — *Syn.* tie up, bond, bind, rope, wire, hold together, support with tape; see also **fasten** 1.

**2.** [To record] — *Syn.* tape-record, register, make a recording, put on tape; see **record** 2.

**3.** [To bandage] — *Syn.* tie, swathe, truss; see **bind** 1, **fasten** 1.

**taper,** *v.* — *Syn.* narrow, lessen, thin out, thin down, reduce, whittle down, grow less, taper off; see also **decrease** 1, 2.— *Ant.* INCREASE, thicken, expand.

**tape recorder,** *n.* — *Syn.* recording equipment, cassette recorder, videocassette recorder, VCR, dictaphone; see also **record player.**

Types and components of tape recorders include: tape deck, cassette deck, tape head, monaural recorder, stereo recorder, stereophonic recorder, take-up wheel, reel-to-reel, tape transport, input jack, output jack, two-track, four-track, eight-track, tape cartridge, cassette, microcassette, digital audio tape, DAT, digital counter, sound-on-sound, sound-with-sound, reverse-o-matic, automatic shutoff, hysteresis-synchronous motor, voice-activated tape machine, telephone answering machine, tape eraser, demagnetizer.

**tapering,** *modif.* — *Syn.* conical, pyramidal, pointed; see **sharp** 2.

**taper off,** *v.* — *Syn.* recede, rescind, diminish; see **decrease** 2, **taper.**

**tapestry,** *n.* — *Syn.* hanging, fabric, drapery, weaving; see **cloth, curtain, decoration** 2.

**taproom,** *n.* — *Syn.* barroom, tavern, pub; see **bar** 2, **saloon** 3.

**taps,** *n.* — *Syn.* drum taps, trumpet call, bugle taps, bugle call, tribute for the dead, dirge, light-out signal; see also **call** 4.

**tar,** *n.* **1.** [A viscous liquid] — *Syn.* pitch, mineral pitch, coal tar, wood tar, lignite tar, distillate, asphalt, roofing cement, resin; see also **gum.**
**2.** [*A sailor] — *Syn.* seaman, navy man, blue jacket, mariner, seafarer, old salt*, barnacle*, Jack*, Jack Tar*, middy*, limey* (British); see also **sailor** 1, 2.

**tardiness,** *n.* — *Syn.* detention, slowness, delay; see **lateness.**

**tardy,** *modif.* — *Syn.* overdue, too late, behindhand; see **late** 1, **slow** 2, 3.

**target,** *n.* **1.** [A goal] — *Syn.* objective, aim, purpose, end, destination, mark.
**2.** [Bull's-eye] — *Syn.* point, spot, butt, mark, dummy.
**3.** [A prey] — *Syn.* quarry, game, scapegoat; see **victim** 1, 2.

**target date,** *n.* — *Syn.* goal, finish, scheduled close, deadline; see **end** 2.

**tariff,** *n.* — *Syn.* duty, rate, charge; see **tax** 1.

**tarnish,** *v.* **1.** [To stain] — *Syn.* soil, smudge, smear; see **dirty.**
**2.** [To disgrace] — *Syn.* embarrass, defame, blacken; see **disgrace, slander.**

**tarpaulin,** *n.* — *Syn.* tarp, duck, oilcloth, sailcloth; see **canvas** 1, **cloth.**

**tarry,** *v.* — *Syn.* delay, dawdle, dally, wait; see **linger** 1, **loiter.**
*See Synonym Study at* WAIT.

**tart,** *modif.* — *Syn.* bitter, acidulous, sharp; see **sour** 1.
*See Synonym Study at* SOUR.

**tartar,** *n.* — *Syn.* hun, hothead, beast; see **barbarian** 1, **savage** 1.

**tartly,** *modif.* — *Syn.* acidulously, sharply, curtly; see **angrily.**

**tartness,** *n.* — *Syn.* sourness, acidity, acridity; see **bitterness** 1.

**task,** *n.* — *Syn.* assignment, job, chore, stint, duty, responsibility, business; see also **duty** 2, **job** 2.
**take to task** — *Syn.* reprove, criticize, judge; see **censure, scold.**

---

**SYN.** — **task** refers to a piece of work assigned to or demanded of someone and usually implies that this is difficult or arduous work [he has the *task* of answering letters]; **chore** applies to any of the routine domestic activities for which one is responsible [his *chore* is washing the dishes] or to any task that is annoying or unpleasant [it was a *chore* to visit his mother every week] **stint** refers to a task that is one's share of the work done by a group and usually connotes a minimum to be completed in the allotted time [we've all done our daily *stint*]; **assignment** applies to a specific, prescribed task allotted by someone in authority [classroom *assignments*]; **job**, in this connection, refers to a specific piece of work, as in one's trade or as voluntarily undertaken for pay [the *job* of painting our house]

---

**taskmaster,** *n.* — *Syn.* overseer, monitor, inspector; see **administrator, superintendent.**

**taste,** *n.* **1.** [The sense that detects flavor] — *Syn.* tongue, taste buds, palate, gustation, *goût* (French).
**2.** [The quality detected by taste, sense 1] — *Syn.* flavor, savor, savoriness, sapidity, aftertaste, palatableness, tang, piquancy, suggestion, zip*, wallop*, ginger*, kick*, smack*, bang*, jolt*, oomph*, drive*, nuttiness*, zing*, punch*.
The four basic sensations of taste are: sweet, sour, bitter, and salty.
**3.** [Judgment, especially esthetic judgment] — *Syn.* discrimination, susceptibility, appreciation, good taste, discernment, acumen, penetration, acuteness, feeling, refinement, appreciation; see also **judgment** 1.
**4.** [Preference] — *Syn.* tendency, leaning, affection, attachment; see **inclination** 1.
**in bad taste** — *Syn.* pretentious, rude, crass; see **tasteless** 2.
**in good taste** — *Syn.* delicate, pleasing, refined; see **tasteful** 2.
**to one's taste** — *Syn.* pleasing, satisfying, appealing; see **pleasant**

**taste,** *v.* **1.** [To experience flavor] — *Syn.* relish, savor, smack one's lips, chew, eat, bite, enjoy.
**2.** [To test by the tongue] — *Syn.* sip, try, touch, sample, lick, suck, roll over in the mouth, partake of; see also **examine** 2.
**3.** [To recognize by flavor] — *Syn.* sense, savor, distinguish; see **know** 3.
**4.** [To experience] — *Syn.* feel, perceive, know; see **undergo.**

**tasteful,** *modif.* **1.** [Delicious] — *Syn.* delectable, pleasing, tasty, savory, rich; see also **delicious** 1.
**2.** [Aesthetically pleasing] — *Syn.* gratifying, delicate, elegant, nice, fine, exquisite, aesthetic, aesthetical, chaste, fastidious, classical, cultivated, refined, precise, pure, unaffected; see also **artistic** 2, **dainty** 1.— *Ant.* RUDE, coarse, vulgar.

**tasteless,** *modif.* **1.** [Lacking flavor] — *Syn.* unsavory, dull, bland, unseasoned, vapid, savorless, flat, watery, flavorless, unpleasurable, without spice; see also **uninteresting.** — *Ant.* DELICIOUS, seasoned, spicy.
**2.** [Plain] — *Syn.* homely, insipid, trite, commonplace, innocent, unaffected, simple, natural, innocuous, stereotyped, plain, homely, wholesome; see also **common** 1.— *Ant.* UNUSUAL, extraordinary, sophisticated.
**3.** [Lacking good taste] — *Syn.* pretentious, ornate, showy, trivial, artificial, florid, ostentatious, garish, clumsy, makeshift, coarse, uncouth, useless, rude, ugly, unsightly, unlovely, hideous, foolish, stupid, crass, indecent. — *Ant.* SIMPLE, effective, handsome.

**tasty,** *modif.* — *Syn.* savory, palatable, appetizing; see **delicious** 1.

**tatters,** *pl.n.* — *Syn.* scraps, patches, shreds; see **rags, remnants.**

**tattle,** *v.* — *Syn.* prattle, tell on, chatter; see **gossip.** 2, **tattletale.**

**tattler,** *n.* — *Syn.* muckraker, busybody, snoop; see **gossip** 2, **tattletale** *n.*

**tattletale,** *modif.* — *Syn.* gossipy, garrulous, revealing; see **talkative.**

**tattletale,** *n.* — *Syn.* informer, talebearer, tattler, busybody, troublemaker, blabbermouth, snitch*, fink*, squealer*, stool pigeon*, stoolie*, rat*, ratfink*.

**tattoo,** *n.* **1.** [A design on the skin] — *Syn.* design, brand, symbol; see **emblem, mark** 1.
**2.** [A continuous drumming] — *Syn.* drum signal, bugle call, rapping, tapping.

**taught,** *modif.* — *Syn.* instructed, informed, directed; see **educated** 1, **learned** 1.

**taunt,** *n.* — *Syn.* insult, mockery, gibe; see **ridicule.**

**taunt,** *v.* — *Syn.* jeer, mock, tease, insult; see **bother** 2, **ridicule.**

*See Synonym Study at* RIDICULE.

**taut,** *modif.* — *Syn.* stretched, firm, tightly drawn, tense, rigid, unyielding, set; see also **stiff** 1, **tight** 1. — *Ant.* LOOSE, slack, loosened.

*See Synonym Study at* TIGHT.

**tautological,** *modif.* — *Syn.* repetitious, redundant, reiterative, pleonastic; see **illogical.**

**tautology,** *n.* — *Syn.* redundancy, pleonasm, reiteration; see **repetition.**

**tavern,** *n.* — *Syn.* taproom, alehouse, roadhouse, inn; see **bar** 2, **saloon** 3.

**tawdry,** *modif.* — *Syn.* sleazy, showy, gaudy, garish, tacky*; see also **common** 1, **poor** 2.

**tawny,** *modif.* — *Syn.* tanned, brownish-tan, leathery, dusky, reddish-tan, browned, brownish, dusky, dark, mulatto, russet, yellowish, golden, dark-gold, brownish-yellow, *tanné* (French); see also **dusky, brown, gold** 2, **red, tan, yellow.**

*See Synonym Study at* DUSKY.

**tax,** *n.* **1.** [A pecuniary levy] — *Syn.* fine, charge, rate, obligation, price, cost, contribution, expense; see also **dues.** — *Ant.* DISCOUNT, interest, allowance.
Taxes include: processing tax, assessment tax, toll, excise, custom, levy, impost, duty, revenue tax, tariff, tribute, dues, capital gains, capitation, tithe, towage, salvage, wharfage, brokerage, freightage, poll tax, income tax, sales tax, property tax, excise tax, inheritance tax, cigarette tax, meals tax, gift tax, estate tax, gasoline tax, luxury tax, county tax, city tax, state tax, federal tax, excess-profit tax, surtax, corporation tax, single tax.
**2.** [A burden] — *Syn.* strain, task, difficulty, imposition, demand; see also **burden** 2.

**tax,** *v.* **1.** [To cause to pay a tax] — *Syn.* assess, exact from, demand, lay an impost, exact tribute, charge duty, demand toll, require a contribution, enact a tax; see also **require** 2.
**2.** [To accuse] — *Syn.* censure, charge, tax with, reprove, reproach; see also **accuse.**
**3.** [To burden] — *Syn.* encumber, weigh down, overload; see **burden.**

**taxable,** *modif.* — *Syn.* assessable, ratable, dutiable, payable, chargeable; see also **due.** — *Ant.* FREE, tax-exempt, deductible.

**taxation,** *n.* — *Syn.* laying taxes, imposing taxes, tax collection, levying, assessment, money-gathering; see also **dues, tax** 1.

**taxed,** *modif.* **1.** [Paying taxes] — *Syn.* levied upon, demanded from, required from, assessed, drawn upon, imposed upon, subjected to tax; see also **levied.**
**2.** [Burdened] — *Syn.* overtaxed, strained, harassed, fatigued; see **tired.**

**3.** [Accused] — *Syn.* ascribed, imputed, charged, arraigned, complained against; see also **accused.**

**taxicab,** *n.* — *Syn.* taxi, cab, tourist car, sightseeing car, hack*, crawler*, nighthawk*, curb cruiser*; see also **automobile.**

**taxing,** *modif.* — *Syn.* troublesome, exacting, tedious, tiring; see **difficult** 1, **disturbing.**

**tea,** *n.* **1.** [An infusion made from tea leaves] — *Syn.* beverage, brew, infusion, decoction, black tea, green tea, herb tea, herbal tea, cha*; see also **drink** 3.
Varieties of tea include: black, Congou, Keemun Congou, Souchong, Lapsang Souchong, Oolong, Formosa, Pouchong, Bohea, Darjeeling, Ceylon, China, Yerba, Assam, orange pekoe, pekoe, green, Hyson, Young Hyson, Imperial Hyson, Gunpowder, Pearl, Earl Grey, English breakfast, Irish breakfast, blackberry, bergamot, lemon balm, Moyune Gunpowder, Twankay, panfired, basket-fired, Paraguay, mixed, jasmine, blended, spiderleaf, butterfly's eyebrow, orange flower, raspberry, spiced, sassafras, sage, mint, camomile, rose hip, tansy, ginger, Abyssinian, Labrador, horehound, cambric; tea of heaven.
**2.** [A light afternoon or evening meal] — *Syn.* snack, buffet, refreshment, refection, collation, tea party, five o'clock tea, tiffin, high tea, supper; see also **lunch, meal** 2.

**teach,** *v.* **1.** [To act as teacher] — *Syn.* instruct, tutor, coach, educate, profess, explain, expound, lecture, direct, give a briefing, rear, prepare, fit, interpret, bring up, bring out, instill, inculcate, indoctrinate, brainwash, develop, form, address to, initiate, inform, nurture, illustrate, imbue, implant, break in*, give the facts*, point a moral*, put up to*, give an idea of*, improve one's mind*, open one's eyes*, knock into one's head*, bring home to*, cram*, stuff*; see also **influence, motivate.** — *Ant.* LEARN, gain, acquire.
**2.** [To drill] — *Syn.* exercise, train, discipline, rear, ground, prepare, familiarize with, school, qualify, mold, practice, prime, perfect a routine, rehearse, repeat, memorize, accustom, habituate, make familiar with, give directions, din into, pound into*, sharpen up*, lick into shape*, polish up*. — *Ant.* FOLLOW, master, cultivate.

---

**SYN.** — **teach** is the basic, inclusive word for the imparting of knowledge or skills and usually connotes some individual attention to the learner /he *taught* her how to skate, she teaches astronomy/; **instruct** implies systematized teaching, usually in some particular subject /she *instructs* us in chemistry/; **educate** stresses the development of latent faculties and powers by formal, systematic teaching /he was *educated* in European universities/; **train** implies the development of a particular faculty or skill, or instruction toward a particular occupation, as by methodical discipline, exercise, etc. /he was *trained* as a mechanic/; **school**, often equivalent to any of the preceding, sometimes specifically connotes a disciplining to endure something difficult /he had to *school* himself to obedience/

---

**teachable,** *modif.* — *Syn.* qualified, amenable, open to instructions, sympathetic, eager, willing to learn, docile, intelligent, bright, apt; see also **able** 1, **intelligent** 1, **willing** 1, 2. — *Ant.* STUPID, unteachable, dense.

**teacher,** *n.* **1.** [One who teaches, especially in the primary or secondary grades] — *Syn.* schoolmaster, schoolmistress, scholar, educator, public school teacher, high school teacher, tutor, mentor, pedagogue, coach, master, guru, swami, mistress, kindergarten teacher, pupil teacher, teacher's aide, teacher-in-training, substitute teacher, supervisor, teach\*, schoolmarm\*, wetnurse\*.

**2.** [One who teaches advanced students] — *Syn.* professor, lecturer, instructor, don, academic, academician, docent, faculty member, graduate assistant, teaching assistant, TA.

**teaching,** *n.* — *Syn.* pedagogy, instruction, schooling, normal training; see **education** 1, 3.

**teacup,** *n.* — *Syn.* china cup, drinking cup, porcelain cup; see **china, cup, dish.**

**teakettle,** *n.* — *Syn.* teapot, tea urn, samovar; see **pot** 1, **urn.**

**team,** *n.* **1.** [People working together, especially on the stage] — *Syn.* partners, combination troupe, company, duo, trio, foursome, sextette, scream-mates\*, love team\*, heart team\*, dream team\*; see also **organization** 3.

**2.** [An organization, especially in sport] — *Syn.* contingent, aggregation, outfit, unit, crew, side, club; see also **organization** 3.

**3.** [Draft animals] — *Syn.* rig, four-in-hand, pair, span, tandem, cart horses, string, matched team.

**team,** *v.* — *Syn.* pull, couple, haul; see **draw.**

**team up with,** *v.* — *Syn.* attach oneself to, join, work together with, collaborate, corroborate; see also **accompany** 1, **cooperate** 1, 2, **help** 1.

**teamwork,** *n.* — *Syn.* partisanship, collaboration, union; see **alliance** 1, **cooperation** 1, **partnership.**

**tear,** *n.* — *Syn.* teardrop, droplet, moisture, discharge, eyewash\*; see also **drop** 1.

**tear,** *n.* — *Syn.* rent, rip, hole, slit, laceration, split, break, gash, rupture, fissure, crack, cut, breach, damage, imperfection. — *Ant.* REPAIR, patch, renovation.

**tear,** *v.* — *Syn.* rend, rip, reave, split, lacerate, shred, pull apart, tear up; see also **cut** 1, 2, **rend.**

---

**SYN.** — **tear** implies a pulling apart by force, so as to lacerate or leave ragged edges /to *tear* paper wrapping/; **rip** suggests a forcible tearing, especially along a seam or in a straight line /to *rip* a hem/; **rend,** a somewhat literary term, implies a tearing with violence /the tree was *rent* by a bolt of lightning/

---

**tearful,** *modif.* — *Syn.* weeping, mournful, lamenting, bathed in tears, teary, weepy, on the edge of tears.

**tearing,** *n.* — *Syn.* ripping, slicing, rending, cutting up, slashing, slitting, breaking, lacerating, severing, bursting, cleaving, parting in two, splitting, tearing down, destroying, knocking apart, sundering.

**tears,** *n.* — *Syn.* sobbing, sob, crying, cry, weeping, lamenting, whimpering, grieving, mourning, lamentation, waterworks\*, weeps\*, sob act\*; see also **grief** 1.

**tease,** *v.* — *Syn.* taunt, tantalize, harass, kid\*; see **bother** 2, **ridicule.**

*See Synonym Study at* BOTHER.

**teasing,** *modif.* — *Syn.* plaguing, pestering, exciting, tickling, badgering, harassing, bothering, taunting, gibing, twitting, irritating, tormenting, tantalizing, exasperating, vexing, provoking, ribbing, kidding; see also **disturbing.** — *Ant.* COMFORTING, regaling, praising.

**teaspoon,** *n.* — *Syn.* kitchen utensil, measuring spoon, $^1/_{30}$ of a tablespoon, stirrer, sugar spoon, silver spoon; see also **spoon, utensil.**

**teat,** *n.* — *Syn.* nipple, mammilla, tit, pap, dug, mammary nipple, titty\*, boob\*, jug\*, knocker\*; see also **breast** 2.

**technical,** *modif.* — *Syn.* specialized, special, scientific, professional, scholarly, mechanical, methodological, re-

stricted, abstruse, highly versed, technological, industrial. — *Ant.* ARTISTIC, nontechnical, simplified.

**technician,** *n.* — *Syn.* practitioner, professional, engineer; see **craftsman, specialist.**

**technique,** *n.* — *Syn.* procedure, system, routine, manner, way; see also **method** 2.

**tedious,** *modif.* — *Syn.* slow, wearisome, tiresome; see **dull** 4.

**tediousness,** *n.* — *Syn.* tedium, dearth, dryness; see **dullness** 1.

**tedium,** *n.* — *Syn.* boredom, tediousness, dullness; see **monotony.**

**teem,** *v.* — *Syn.* abound, overflow, swell, pour, be plentiful, pour out, swarm, superabound, bristle with, swim in, roll in, wallow in, teem with, crawl with, bristle with, overflow with, creep with, abound with; see also **grow** 1, **prosper.** — *Ant.* NEED, lack, become scarce.

**teeming,** *modif.* — *Syn.* replete, crammed, swarming; see **full** 3, **plentiful** 1.

**teenage,** *modif.* — *Syn.* adolescent, immature, youthful; see **juvenile** 1.

**teenager,** *n.* — *Syn.* adolescent, teen, youngster, high school student, youth, young woman, young man.

**teens,** *n.* — *Syn.* boyhood, girlhood, adolescence, early adolescence, puberty, late adolescence, young adulthood, teen age\*, awkward age\*, age of indiscretion\*; see also **youth** 1.

**teeter,** *v.* — *Syn.* tremble precariously, seesaw, totter, wobble, sway, waver, dangle, reel, stagger, quiver, flutter, teeter-totter, weave. — *Ant.* FALL, rest, topple over.

**teeter-totter,** *n.* — *Syn.* seesaw, teeter, teeterboard, teeteringboard, hickey horse, tipitty bounce, teeterybender; see also **game** 1, **toy** 1.

**teeth,** *n.* — *Syn.* dentition, fangs, tusks; see **tooth** 1.

**teetotaler,** *n.* — *Syn.* nondrinker, prohibitionist, prude, abstinent; see **abstainer.**

**telegram,** *n.* — *Syn.* wire, cable, cablegram, message, telegraphic message, teletype copy, radiogram, call, report, summons, night message, night letter, day letter, news message, code message, signal, flash\*, buzzer\*; see also **communication** 2.

**telegraph,** *n.* — *Syn.* Morse telegraph, electric telegraph, wireless, radio telegraph, wireless telegraph, transmitter; see also **communications, radio** 2.

**telegraph,** *v.* — *Syn.* wire, send a wire, send a cable, send a radiogram, communicate by telegram, flash\*, wire\*, file\*; see also **communicate** 2.

**telegraphed,** *modif.* — *Syn.* sent by wire, wired, radioed, cabled, communicated, sent, flashed; see also **sent.**

**telegraphic,** *modif.* — *Syn.* by code, by Morse code, by International code, abbreviated, short, worded like a telegram; see also **wireless.**

**telepathy,** *n.* — *Syn.* insight, premonition, extrasensory perception, ESP, mind reading, presentiment; see also **communication** 1, **sixth sense.**

**telephone,** *n.* — *Syn.* phone, private phone, extension phone, radiophone, radio telephone, car phone, cellular phone, pay phone, public telephone, speakerphone, conference phone, wireless telephone, cordless telephone, French phone, mouthpiece, line\*, party line\*, local line\*, long distance\*, the horn\*, the blower\* (British), extension\*, booth phone\*; see also **communications, radio** 2.

**telephone,** *v.* — *Syn.* call, call up, phone, ring, ring up, make a call to, dial, call on the phone, put in a call to, phone up\*, give a ring\*, give a buzz\*, buzz\*.

**telephoned,** *modif.* — *Syn.* phoned, radiophoned, called, communicated by telephone, reached by phone.

**telescope,** *n.* — *Syn.* field glasses, binoculars, opera glass, glass, optical instrument, reflecting telescope, refracting telescope, Galilean telescope, Gregorian telescope, mercurial telescope, helioscope, equatorial telescope, polemoscope, telelectroscope, telespectroscope, telestereoscope, telengiscope, teinoscope, prism telescope; see also **glasses.**

**television,** *n.* — *Syn.* T.V., teevee, video, color television, home entertainment center, tube★, boob tube★, the eye★, box★; see also **communications, station** 7.

**tell,** *v.* **1.** [To inform] — *Syn.* communicate, explain, say, state, instruct, direct, command, order, disclose, divulge, reveal, make known, utter, speak, report, recite, announce, let know, notify, give notice, declare, acquaint, advise, confess, impart, apprise, familiarize, represent, assert, mention, relate, convey, voice, let out, acknowledge, own, let in on, give the facts, reel off, spit out, come out with, give out, release, leak out, give inside information, break it to, break the news, express, put, show, indicate, carry tales, reveal a secret, betray, tattle, leave word, assure, keep posted, expose, lay open, open up, blurt out, fill in★, let on★, let slip★, clue in★, tell all★, level with★, give away★, come across with★, shoot★, come clean★, make a clean breast of★, get something off one's chest★; see also **discuss, inform** 2, **notify** 1, **reveal** 1, **say.** — *Ant.* HIDE, keep secret, be silent.
**2.** [To narrate] — *Syn.* describe, recount, set forth; see **narrate, report** 1.
**3.** [To deduce] — *Syn.* know, understand, make out, perceive, ascertain, find out, recognize, be sure, differentiate, discriminate, determine, know for certain, clinch★.
*See Synonym Study at* REVEAL.

**teller,** *n.* — *Syn.* cashier, clerk, bank clerk, bank employee, counting clerk, bank assistant, pay-off man★; see also **worker.**

**telling,** *modif.* — *Syn.* crucial, conspicuous, devastating, significant, valid, revealing; see also **effective, important** 1.
*See Synonym Study at* VALID.

**tell off,** *v.* — *Syn.* rebuke, reprimand, chide; see **censure.**

**telltale,** *modif.* — *Syn.* tattletale, significant, revealing; see **important** 1.

**temblor,** *n.* — *Syn.* shock, quake, tremor; see **earthquake.**

**temerity,** *n.* — *Syn.* audacity, effrontery, boldness, hardihood, rashness, presumption, overconfidence, gall, nerve, cheek, recklessness, venturesomeness, precipitancy, precipitation, hastiness, heedlessness, foolhardiness, thoughtlessness, carelessness, indiscretion, imprudence, impetuosity; see also **rudeness.** — *Ant.* PRUDENCE, caution, deliberation.

---

*SYN.* — **temerity** refers to a rashness or foolish boldness that results from underrating the dangers or failing to evaluate the consequences /he had the *temerity* to criticize his employer/; **audacity** suggests either great presumption or defiance of social conventions, morals, etc. /shocked at the *audacity* of his proposal/; **effrontery,** always derogatory in usage, connotes shamelessness or insolence in defying the rules of propriety, courtesy, etc. /his *effrontery* in addressing the teacher by her first name/; **nerve, cheek,** and **gall** are colloquial equivalents of **effrontery,** but **nerve** and **cheek** usually suggest mere impudence or sauciness and **gall,** unmitigated insolence

---

**temper,** *n.* **1.** [State of mind] — *Syn.* disposition, temperament, frame of mind, humor; see **mood** 1.

**2.** [An angry state of mind] — *Syn.* furor, ire, passion; see **anger, rage** 2.
**3.** [The quality of being easily angered] — *Syn.* impatience, excitability, touchiness, sourness, sensitivity, fretfulness, peevishness, irritability, ill-humor, acerbity, petulence, irascibility, crossness, churlishness, pugnacity, sullenness, tartness, grouchiness★, huffiness★, cantankerousness★. — *Ant.* PATIENCE, calmness, equanimity.
**4.** [The quality of induced hardness or toughness in materials] — *Syn.* tensile strength, sturdiness, hardness; see **firmness** 2, **strength** 1.
**5.** [Composure] — *Syn.* equanimity, poise, tranquility; see **composure.**
**keep one's temper** — *Syn.* remain calm, control oneself, compose oneself, not become angry; see **restrain** 1.
**lose one's temper** — *Syn.* become angry, get mad, fly off the handle★, go bananas★; see **rage** 1.
*See Synonym Study at* MOOD, DISPOSITION.

**temper,** *v.* **1.** [To soften or qualify] — *Syn.* mitigate, pacify, moderate, abate, mollify, curb, restrain; see also **ease** 1, 2, **soften** 2. — *Ant.* ATTACK, violate injure.
**2.** [To toughen or harden] — *Syn.* steel, anneal, braze, bake, chill, stiffen, caseharden, cement, vulcanize, solidify, congeal, indurate, starch, petrify, mold, set, dry, toughen up★; see also **strengthen.** — *Ant.* melt, dissolve, soften.

**temperament,** *n.* — *Syn.* character, disposition, constitution, nature, inner nature, quality, temper, spirit, mood, attitude, type, structure, make-up, humor, mood, outlook, peculiarity, individuality, personality, idiosyncrasy, distinctiveness, psychological habits, mentality, intellect, intellectual capacity, susceptibility, ego, inclination, tendency, turn of mind★.

**temperamental,** *modif.* — *Syn.* moody, sensitive, touchy; see **irritable.**

**temperamentally,** *modif.* — *Syn.* emotionally, typically, by nature; see **mentally.**

**temperance,** *n.* — *Syn.* moderation, restraint, abstinence, self-control, forbearance, self-denial, self-restraint, abnegation, frugality, sobriety, soberness, abstemiousness, teetotalism, vegetarianism, water wagon★. — *Ant.* DRUNKENNESS, prodigality, inebriation.

**temperate,** *modif.* **1.** [Moderate] — *Syn.* regulated, restrained, reasonable, fair; see **moderate** 2.
**2.** [Neither hor nor cold] — *Syn.* medium, warm, balmy; see **fair** 3, **mild** 2.
**3.** [Not given to drink] — *Syn.* abstemious, abstinent, restrained; see **moderate** 5.
*See Synonym Study at* MODERATE.

**temperature,** *n.* — *Syn.* heat, warmth, cold, body heat, weather condition, climatic characteristic, thermal reading, degrees of temperature, degrees above zero, degrees below zero.

**tempest,** *n.* **1.** [A storm] — *Syn.* gale, typhoon, blizzard; see **storm** 1.
**2.** [A commotion] — *Syn.* tumult, chaos, turmoil; see **disturbance** 2.

**tempestuous,** *modif.* — *Syn.* raging, tumultuous, furious; see **stormy** 1, **turbulent.**

**tempestuously,** *modif.* — *Syn.* furiously, frantically, without restraint; see **violently** 1, 2.

**temple,** *n.* — *Syn.* house of prayer, house of worship, synagogue, *aedes* (Latin), stupa, dagoba, pantheon, pagoda, tope; see also **church** 1.
Famous temples include: Herod's Temple, Solomon's Temple, Zerabbabel's Temple, Parthenon (Athens), Greek Doric Temple (Sicily), Pantheon (Rome), Temple of Fortuna Virilis (Rome), Dilwara Temple (India),

Lama Temple (Peking), Pura Besakih (Bali), Shawe Dagon (Rangoon), Honganji Temple (Kyoto), Angkor Wat (Cambodia).

**tempo,** *n.* — *Syn.* pace, speed, meter, rate; see **speed.**

**temporal,** *modif.* **1.** [Transitory] — *Syn.* temporary, transient, ephemeral; see **temporary.**

**2.** [Worldly] — *Syn.* secular, earthly, mundane; see **worldly** 1, 2, **materialistic.**

**temporarily,** *modif.* — *Syn.* momentarily, briefly, tentatively, for a while, for the moment, for a time, provisionally, transitorily, for the time being, pro tempore, pro tem. — *Ant.* FOREVER, perpetually, perennially.

**temporary,** *modif.* — *Syn.* transitory, transient, fleeting, short, brief, ephemeral, evanescent, fugitive, volatile, shifting, passing, summary, momentary, fugacious, stopgap, makeshift, substitute, for the time being, overnight, *ad hoc* (Latin), *ad interim* (Latin), interim, impermanent, irregular, changeable, unenduring, unfixed, unstable, perishable, provisional, acting, short-lived, mortal, pro tem, on the go★, on the fly★, on the wing★, here today and gone tomorrow★; see also **momentary.** — *Ant.* PERMANENT, fixed, eternal.

**SYN.** — **temporary** applies to a post held (or to the person holding such a post) for a limited time, subject to dismissal by those having the power of appointment [a *temporary* mail carrier]; **provisional** is specifically applied to a government (or to its officers) established for the time being in a country, a newly formed nation, etc. until a permanent government can be formed; **ad interim** refers to an appointment for an intervening period, as between the death of an official and the election of a successor; **acting** is applied to one who temporarily takes over the powers of a regular official during the latter's absence [a vice-president often serves as *acting* president]

**temporize,** *v.* — *Syn.* hedge, stall, balk; see **delay** 1, **hesitate.**

**temporizer,** *n.* — *Syn.* procrastinator, conniver, hedger, schemer; see **opportunist, social climber, status seeker.**

**tempt,** *v.* — *Syn.* lure, entice, fascinate, seduce, appeal to, inveigle, decoy, beguile, induce, intrigue, incite, provoke, allure, charm, captivate, tantalize, draw on, invite, bait, stimulate, move, motivate, rouse, instigate, wheedle, coax, lead on★, make one's mouth water★; see also **fascinate, influence, seduce.** — *Ant.* DISCOURAGE, repel, dissuade.

**SYN.** — **tempt** suggests the influence of a powerful attraction that tends to overcome scruples or judgment [I'm *tempted* to accept your offer]; **lure** suggests an irresistible force, as desire, greed, or curiosity, in attracting someone, often to something harmful or evil [lured on by false hopes]; **entice** implies a crafty or skillful attracting by offering hope of reward or pleasure [he *enticed* the squirrel to eat from his hand]; **inveigle** suggests the use of deception or cajolery in enticing someone [they *inveigled* him with false promises]; **decoy** implies the use of deceptive appearances in luring into a trap [artificial birds are used to *decoy* wild ducks]; **beguile** suggests the use of subtly alluring devices in leading someone on [beguiled by her sweet words]; **seduce** implies enticement to an improper or wrongful act, esp. to loss of chastity

**temptation,** *n.* — *Syn.* lure, attraction, fascination, appeal, inducement, bait, fancy, hankering, provocation, yen.

**tempted,** *modif.* — *Syn.* desirous, desiring, inclined, bent on, allured, seduced, enticed, in the mood for, on the verge of, drawn by, on the point of, dying to; see also **charmed.** — *Ant.* INDIFFERENT, averse to, disinclined.

**tempter,** *n.* — *Syn.* seducer, charmer, prompter; see **lecher.**

**tempting,** *modif.* — *Syn.* appetizing, attractive, fascinating, intriguing, rousing, tantalizing, provoking, provocation, alluring, mouth-watering★, temptatious★; see also **charming, tasteful** 1, 2. — *Ant.* UGLY, repulsive, unwholesome.

**ten,** *modif.* — *Syn.* tenth, tenfold, decuple, denary, decimal.

**tenable,** *modif.* — *Syn.* defensible, sustainable, impregnable, trustworthy; see **reliable** 2, **strong** 2.

**tenacious,** *modif.* **1.** [Adhesive] — *Syn.* retentive, sticky, inseparable, waxy, resisting, gummy, coriaceous, viscous, viscid, glutinous; see also **adhesive, tough** 2. — *Ant.* LOOSE, lax, slack.

**2.** [Persistent] — *Syn.* determined, pertinacious, purposeful, resolute; see **obstinate, resolute** 2.

**tenacity,** *n.* — *Syn.* perseverance, obstinacy, resolution; see **determination** 2, **stubbornness.**

**tenancy,** *n.* — *Syn.* tenure, occupancy, possession, hold; see **ownership.**

**tenant,** *n.* — *Syn.* renter, lessee, householder, rent payer, dweller, inhabitant, occupant, resident, roomer, lodger, boarder, freeholder, holder, possessor, leaseholder, tenant farmer; see also **resident.** — *Ant.* OWNER, proprietor, landlord.

**tend,** *v.* **1.** [To watch over] — *Syn.* care for, manage, direct, superintend, do, perform, accomplish, guard, administer, minister to, oversee, corral, wait upon, attend, serve, nurse, mind★; see also **manage** 1.

**2.** [To have a tendency (toward)] — *Syn.* conduce, lead, point, direct, make for, result in, serve to, be in the habit of, favor, be disposed toward, be predisposed to, be biased in favor of, be prejudiced in favor of, be apt to, gravitate toward, incline to, verge on.

**tendency,** *n.* **1.** [Direction] — *Syn.* drift, aim, bent, trend, current; see also **drift** 1.

**2.** [Inclination] — *Syn.* leaning, tenor, bias, bent; see **inclination** 1.

**SYN.** — **tendency** refers to an inclination or disposition to move in a particular direction or act in a certain way, esp. as a result of some inherent quality or habit [he has a *tendency* toward exaggeration]; **trend** suggests a general direction, with neither a definite course nor goal, subject to change or fluctuation by some external force [a recent *trend* in literature]; **current** differs from **trend** in connoting a clearly defined course, but one also subject to change [the *current* of one's life]; **drift** refers either to the course along which something is being carried or driven [the *drift* toward absolute conformity] or to a course taken by something that has unstated or unclear implications [what is the *drift* of this argument?]; **tenor,** equivalent in this connection to **drift,** connotes more strongly the clarity or purport of the unstated purpose or objective [the general *tenor* of the Bill of Rights]

**tender,** *modif.* **1.** [Soft] — *Syn.* delicate, fragile, supple; see **soft** 2.

**2.** [Youthful] — *Syn.* immature, childish, childlike; see **young** 1.

**3.** [Kind] — *Syn.* kind, warm, warmhearted, sympathetic, loving, solicitous, compassionate; see also **kind.**

**4.** [Weak] — *Syn.* fragile, frail, delicate; see **weak** 1.

**5.** [Touching] — *Syn.* moving, pathetic, affecting; see **pitiful** 1.
**6.** [Sensitive] — *Syn.* delicate, dainty, touchy, ticklish, oversensitive, hypersensitive, painful; see also **raw** 5, **sore.**

---

*SYN.* — **tender** implies a softness or gentleness in one's relations with others that is expressive of warm affection, concern, etc. *[a tender caress]*; **compassionate** is applied to one who is easily affected by another's troubles or pains and is quick to show pity or mercy *[a compassionate judge]*; **sympathetic** implies the ability or disposition to enter into another's mental state or emotions and thus to share sorrows, joys, desires, etc. *[a sympathetic interest in a colleague's career]*; **warm** and **warmhearted** suggest an interest or affection characterized by cordiality, generosity, etc. *[warm, or warmhearted, hospitality]*

**tender,** *v.* — *Syn.* proffer, present, give; see **offer** 1.
**tenderfoot\*,** *n.* — *Syn.* apprentice, novice, beginner, greenhorn\*; see **amateur.**
**tenderhearted,** *modif.* — *Syn.* softhearted, tender, humane; see **humane** 1, **kind** 1, **merciful** 1.
**tenderly,** *modif.* **1.** [Softly] — *Syn.* gently, carefully, delicately; see **lightly** 1.
**2.** [Lovingly] — *Syn.* fondly, affectionately, accordingly; see **lovingly.**
**tenderness,** *n.* — *Syn.* fondness, lovingness, love, watchfulness, consideration, sympathy, courtesy, care; see also **friendship** 2, **kindness** 1. — *Ant.* HATRED, ruthlessness, brusqueness.
**tending,** *modif.* **1.** [Inclined toward] — *Syn.* apt to, leaning, disposed to, predisposed to, bent on, likely to, prone to, liable to, verging on, working toward; see also **likely** 5.
**2.** [Giving attention to] — *Syn.* caring for, managing, directing, supervising, administering, ministering to, serving, nursing, aiding, attending, playing wet-nurse to\*, babying\*. — *Ant.* OMITTING, neglecting, avoiding.
**tendon,** *n.* — *Syn.* band, ligament, tie; see **cord** 2, **muscle.**
**tenement,** *n.* — *Syn.* apartment house, tenement house, slum dwelling, project, housing project, low-income housing, eyesore\*, firetrap\*; see also **home** 1, **hotel.**
**tenet,** *n.* — *Syn.* view, conviction, belief, position, faith, trust, opinion, impression, doctrine, system, dogma, creed, principle, profession, credo, conception, self-conviction, presumption, assumption.
*See Synonym Study at* DOCTRINE.
**tennis,** *n.* — *Syn.* lawn tennis, court tennis, platform tennis, table tennis, tennis tournament, match play, professional tennis, amateur tennis, net game\*, the tennis racket\*; see also **sport** 3.
**tennis shoes,** *n.* — *Syn.* sneakers, gym shoes, canvas shoes, tennies\*, creepers\*, pussyfooters\*; see also **shoe, sneakers.**
**tenor,** *n.* **1.** [One with a high masculine voice] — *Syn.* vocalist, singer, lyric tenor, bel canto tenor, countertenor, crooner, adenoid tenor\*, bathroom tenor\*, gelatine tenor\*, whiskey tenor\*; see also **musician.**
**2.** [Tendency] — *Syn.* tone, course, trend, drift; see **inclination** 1.
*See Synonym Study at* TENDENCY.
**tense,** *modif.* **1.** [Nervous] — *Syn.* agitated, anxious, high-strung, on edge, fluttery, jumpy, jittery; see also **excited.** — *Ant.* CALM, unconcerned, indifferent.
**2.** [Stretched tight] — *Syn.* rigid, stiff, firm; see **tight** 1.

*See Synonym Study at* TIGHT.
**tension,** *n.* **1.** [Stress] — *Syn.* tautness, force, tightness; see **balance** 2, **stress** 2.
**2.** [Mental stress] — *Syn.* pressure, strain, anxiety; see **stress** 3.
**tent,** *n.* — *Syn.* shelter, canvas, canopy, tarpaulin, covering; see also **cover** 1.
Tents and tentlike coverings include: umbrella tent, A-frame tent, awning, canopy, marquee, wigwam, tepee, booth, pavilion, kibitka, khirghiz tent, tambu, yurt, pup tent, fly tent, fly, canoe tent, lean-to tent, circus tent, rag\*, top\*, big top\*, round top\*.
**tentacle,** *n.* — *Syn.* tentaculum, arm, leg; see **appendage** 2, **feeler** 1, **limb** 2.
**tentative,** *modif.* — *Syn.* provisional, probationary, unconfirmed, not final, not settled, conditional, indefinite, undecided, iffy\*, open to consideration, subject to change, trial, on trial, makeshift; see also **experimental.** — *Ant.* CONCLUSIVE, final, decisive.
**tentatively,** *modif.* — *Syn.* experimentally, conditionally, provisionally; see **temporarily.**
**tenuous,** *modif.* **1.** [Slender] — *Syn.* slim, fine, narrow; see **thin** 2, 5.
**2.** [Flimsy] — *Syn.* insubstantial, slight, gossamer; see **light** 5, **thin** 1.
**tenure,** *n.* — *Syn.* occupancy, occupation, ownership, term of office; see **security** 2.
**tepee,** *n.* — *Syn.* Indian tent, skin tent, comical tent, wigwam, wickiup, lodge; see also **tent.**
**tepid,** *modif.* — *Syn.* lukewarm, moderate, heated; see **warm** 1.
**term,** *n.* **1.** [A name] — *Syn.* expression, terminology, phrase, word, locution, indication, denomination, article, appellation, designation, title, head, caption, nomenclature, moniker\*; see also **name** 1.
**2.** [A period of time] — *Syn.* span, interval, course, cycle, season, duration, phase, official period of tenure, quarter, course of time, semester, school period, session, period of confinement; see also **time** 2.
**bring to terms** — *Syn.* coerce, pressure, reduce to submission; see **force** 1.
**come to terms** — *Syn.* compromise, arrive at an agreement, arbitrate; see **agree.**
**in terms of** — *Syn.* in reference to, about, concerning; see **regarding.**
**terminal,** *modif.* — *Syn.* final, concluding, last; see **last** 1.
**terminal,** *n.* **1.** [An end] — *Syn.* limit, extremity, terminus; see **end** 4.
**2.** [Part of a computer] — *Syn.* data terminal, keyboard, CRT, cathode ray tube, monitor, printer, output device, input device, screen; see also **computer.**
**terminate,** *v.* **1.** [To abolish] — *Syn.* eliminate, annul, stop; see **cancel** 2, **end** 1.
**2.** [To end] — *Syn.* cease, stop, conclude, finish, discontinue, break off, abort, fire; see also **achieve** 1, **dismiss** 2, **end** 1, **stop** 2.
**3.** [To dismiss] — *Syn.* fire, let go, discharge; see **dismiss** 2.
*See Synonym Study at* END.
**termination,** *n.* — *Syn.* finish, close, terminus; see **end** 2.
**terminology,** *n.* — *Syn.* nomenclature, vocabulary, technology, specification; see **jargon** 3, **language** 1.
**terminus,** *n.* — *Syn.* end, conclusion, limit; see **end** 4.
**terms,** *pl.n.* **1.** [Conditions] — *Syn.* details, items, points, particulars; see **circumstances** 2.
**2.** [An agreement] — *Syn.* understanding, treaty, conclusion; see **agreement** 3.

**terrace,** *n.* — *Syn.* patio, garden, step terrace, landscape, platform, solarium, raised bank, park strip, hanging garden, green, plot, lawn; see also **garden, yard** 1.

**terra firma,** *n.* — *Syn.* solid ground, firm earth, land, soil, ground, dry land; see also **earth** 2.

**terrain,** *n.* — *Syn.* ground, region, territory; see **area** 2.

**terra incognita,** *n.* — *Syn.* unknown land, unfamiliar territory, unexplored field of knowledge.

**terrestrial,** *modif.* — *Syn.* earthly, physical, temporal, mundane; see **earthly** 1, **worldly** 1, 2.
*See Synonym Study at* EARTHLY.

**terrible,** *modif.* **1.** [Inspiring terror] — *Syn.* terrifying, frightening, appalling, fearful, awesome, horrifying, ghastly, awe-inspiring, petrifying, revolting, gruesome, shocking, unnerving; see also **frightful** 1. — *Ant.* HAPPY, joyful, pleasant.
**2.** [Unwelcome] — *Syn.* unfortunate, disastrous, inconvenient, disturbing, atrocious\*, lousy\*; see also **offensive** 2. — *Ant.* WELCOME, good, attractive.

**terribly\*,** *modif.* **1.** [In a terrible manner] — *Syn.* horribly, frightfully, badly, notoriously, unbelievably, seriously, fatally, fearfully, drastically, staggeringly, discouragingly, disturbingly, inconveniently, unhappily, unfortunately, markedly; see also **badly** 1. — *Ant.* FAIRLY, decently, encouragingly.
**2.** [Very] — *Syn.* extremely, intensely, remarkably; see **very.**

**terrier,** *n.* Varieties and breeds of terriers include: Irish terrier, Jack Russell terrier, Yorkshire terrier, Cairn terrier, English terrier, black-and-tan terrier, Boston terrier, fox terrier, Scotch terrier, Scottish terrier, Skye terrier, toy terrier, rat terrier, bull terrier, Welsh terrier, Bedlington terrier, West Highland white terrier, Airedale, Sealyham, wire-haired terrier, Lakeland terrier, Kerry blue terrier, Manchester terrier, Dandie Dinmont, Staffordshire bull terrier, schnauzer; see also **dog.**

**terrific,** *modif.* **1.** [Causing great fear] — *Syn.* terrifying, dreadful, appalling; see **frightful** 1, **terrible** 1.
**2.** [Unusually great or intense] — *Syn.* shocking, thunderous, deafening, world-shaking, immense, tremendous; see also **great** 1, **large** 1. — *Ant.* COMMON, ordinary, conventional.
**3.** [\*A general term of approval] — *Syn.* superb, splendid, wonderful, marvellous; see **excellent.**

**terrifically,** *modif.* — *Syn.* frightfully, mightily, horribly, intensely; see **badly** 1, **terribly** 1, 2, **very.**

**terrify,** *v.* — *Syn.* shock, horrify, terrorize; see **frighten** 1.
*See Synonym Study at* FRIGHTEN.

**territorial,** *modif.* — *Syn.* regional, sectional\*, provincial; see **national** 1.

**territory,** *n.* **1.** [A specified area] — *Syn.* region, township, empire; see **area** 2.
**2.** [An area organized politically under the central government] — *Syn.* commonwealth, colony, protectorate, dominion, province, mandate; see also **nation** 1.
**3.** [An indefinite area] — *Syn.* section, area, boundary; see **region** 1.

**terror,** *n.* — *Syn.* fright, horror, panic; see **fear** 1, 2.
*See Synonym Study at* FEAR.

**terrorist,** *n.* — *Syn.* subversive, revolutionary, incendiary; see **rebel** 1.

**terrorize,** *v.* — *Syn.* coerce, intimidate, browbeat; see **threaten** 1.
*See Synonym Study at* FRIGHTEN.

**terse,** *modif.* — *Syn.* short, pithy, laconic, taut, compact, brief, concise, pointed, neat, exact, trenchant, epigrammatic, cryptic, to the point, carefully edited, precise, abrupt, curt, clipped, brusque; see also **abrupt** 2, **concise, short** 2. — *Ant.* VERBOSE, wordy, prolix.
*See Synonym Study at* CONCISE.

**test,** *n.* **1.** [A check for adequacy] — *Syn.* inspection, analysis, countdown, probing, inquiry, inquest, elimination, proving ground(s), training stable, search, dry run\*; see also **examination** 1, **experiment** 1.
Types of tests include: engineering, technical, structural, mechanical, chemical, countdown, psychological, Rorschach, mental, intelligence, intelligence quotient (IQ), aptitude, vocational, qualifying, comprehensive, written, true-false, multiple choice, essay, oral, standardized, achievement, objective, diagnostic, semester, term, Scholastic Aptitude Test (SAT), Graduate Record Examination (GRE), Law School Admission Test (LSAT), Medical College Admission Test (MCAT), association, psychiatric, toxicological, vascular, electrocardiac, urinary, metabolic, neurological, reflex, eye, blood, Pap test, drug, stress, pregnancy, human immunodeficiency virus, HIV, breaking point, burst, heat, strength, pressure, density, longitudinal, transverse, tensility, metallurgic, electronic, supersonic, ultrasonic, spectrographic, x-ray, pneumatic, hydrostatic, expansion, contraction, flattening, compression, corrosion, eddy-current, Rockwell hardness, metallographic, complex mixture.
**2.** [A formal examination] — *Syn.* quiz, questionnaire, essay; see **examination** 2.
*See Synonym Study at* EXPERIMENT.

**test,** *v.* — *Syn.* inquire, question, try out; see **examine** 2, **experiment** 2.

**testament,** *n.* — *Syn.* covenant, testimonial, evidence; see **proof** 1.

**tested,** *modif.* — *Syn.* examined, tried, essayed, assayed, processed, proved, experimented with, approved, certified, on approval, given a trial, exposed to test, measured; see also **established** 3. — *Ant.* UNUSED, untested, untried.

**tester,** *n.* — *Syn.* validator, examiner, lab assistant; see **checker, inspector.**

**testify,** *v.* **1.** [To demonstrate] — *Syn.* indicate, show, make evident; see **prove.**
**2.** [To bear witness] — *Syn.* affirm, give evidence, swear, swear to, attest, witness, give witness, give one's word, certify, warrant, depose, vouch, give the facts, stand up for, say a good word for.
**3.** [To declare] — *Syn.* assert, attest, claim; see **declare** 1.

**testimonial,** *n.* **1.** [A recommendation] — *Syn.* voucher, credential, affidavit; see **certificate, degree** 3, **recommendation** 2.
**2.** [An expression of appreciation] — *Syn.* memorial, monument, memento; see **memorial.**

**testimony,** *n.* **1.** [The act of stating] — *Syn.* attestation, statement, assertion; see **declaration** 1.
**2.** [Evidence] — *Syn.* grounds, facts, data; see **proof** 1.
**3.** [Statement] — *Syn.* deposition, affidavit, affirmation; see **declaration** 2.
*See Synonym Study at* PROOF.

**testiness,** *n.* — *Syn.* touchiness, irritability, petulance, asperity; see **annoyance** 1.

**testing,** *n.* — *Syn.* examination, examining, trying out, trial, proving, experimenting, experimentation, questioning, measuring, measurement; see also **experiment** 1.

**testy,** *modif.* — *Syn.* grouchy, touchy, peevish; see **irritable.**

**tête-à-tête,** *modif.* — *Syn.* confidential, private, familiar; see **intimate** 1, **secretive.**

**tête-à-tête,** *n.* — *Syn.* talk, parley, colloquy, private conversation; see **conversation, discussion** 1.

**tether,** *n.* — *Syn.* leash, picket, chain, harness; see **fastener, rope.**

**tether,** *v.* — *Syn.* secure, picket, bind, lash; see **fasten** 1, **tie** 2.

**Texas,** *n.* — *Syn.* Lone Star State, Jumbo State, Longhorn State; see **South, Southwest, United States.**

**text,** *n.* **1.** [A textbook] — *Syn.* course book, class book, prescribed reading, required reading, manual, handbook, study book, assigned reference, syllabus; see also **book** 1.
**2.** [A subject, especially a verse from the Bible] — *Syn.* quotation, line, paragraph, stanza, passage, extract, topic, thesis, theme; see also **subject** 1.
**3.** [Writing, considered for its authenticity] — *Syn.* lines, textual evidence, document; see **manuscript, writing** 2.
*See Synonym Study at* SUBJECT.

**texture,** *n.* **1.** [Quality] — *Syn.* character, disposition, surface, fineness, roughness, coarseness, feeling, feel, touch, sense, flexibility, stiffness, smoothness, weave, taste; see also **fiber** 2.
**2.** [Structure] — *Syn.* composition, weave, organization, arrangement, balance, strategy, intermixture; see also **construction** 2, **form** 2.

**thank,** *v.* — *Syn.* be obliged, show gratitude, give thanks, acknowledge, show appreciation, be obligated to, be indebted to, bless, praise, bow down to, kiss, smile on, show courtesy, express one's obligation to; see also **appreciate** 1. — *Ant.* NEGLECT, ignore, show indifference.

**thanked,** *modif.* — *Syn.* blessed, shown appreciation, lauded, applauded, appreciated; see also **praised.**

**thankful,** *modif.* — *Syn.* obliged, grateful, gratified, contented, satisfied, indebted to, beholden, pleased, kindly disposed, appreciative, giving thanks, overwhelmed. — *Ant.* UNGRATEFUL, insensible, thankless.

**thankfulness,** *n.* — *Syn.* warmth of feeling, appreciation, gratefulness; see **gratitude, thanks.**

**thanking,** *modif.* — *Syn.* appreciating, being grateful, giving thanks, acknowledging appreciation, being satisfied, showing contentment, admitting indebtedness. — *Ant.* CRITICAL, disparaging, finding fault.

**thankless,** *modif.* **1.** [Not returning thanks] — *Syn.* unappreciative, ungrateful, self-centered; see **cruel** 2, **rude** 2.
**2.** [Not eliciting thanks] — *Syn.* poorly paid, unappreciated, unrewarded, profitless, disagreeable, unrecognized, vain, barren, not worth it; see also **useless** 1.

**thanks,** *n.* — *Syn.* appreciation, thankfulness, acknowledgment, recognition, gratitude, gratefulness. — *Ant.* BLAME, censure, criticism.

**thanks\*,** *interj.* — *Syn.* thank you, I thank you, much obliged, ta\* (British).

**Thanksgiving,** *n.* — *Syn.* ceremony of giving thanks, day of blessing, day of worship, Thanksgiving Day, festival of plenty, last Thursday in November, turkey day\*; see also **celebration** 1, 2, **feast, holiday** 1.

**that,** *conj.* — *Syn.* in that, so, so that, in order that, to the end that, for the reason that; see also **because.**

**that,** *modif.* — *Syn.* the, this, one, a certain, a well known, a particular, such.

**that,** *pron.* — *Syn.* the one, that one, the one in question, that fact, that other, who; see also **which.**

**at that\*** — *Syn.* even so, all things considered, anyway; see **anyhow** 1.

**not all that\*** — *Syn.* not so very, not so, rather less.

**thatch,** *n.* — *Syn.* roof covering, straw roofing, thatch palm, thatching, reed thatch, rush thatch; see also **roof, roofing.**

**thaumaturgy,** *n.* — *Syn.* miracle working, alchemy, sorcery, black magic; see **magic** 1, **witchcraft.**

**thaw,** *v.* **1.** [To melt] — *Syn.* dissolve, liquefy, flow, run, deliquesce, liquate, fuse, become liquid; see also **dissolve** 1, **melt** 1. — *Ant.* FREEZE, congeal, refrigerate.
**2.** [To unbend] — *Syn.* open up, loosen, become soft, relent, relax, mollify, grow genial; see also **soften** 1. — *Ant.* STIFFEN, harden, grow cool.
*See Synonym Study at* MELT.

**the,** *modif.* **1.** [The definite article] — *Syn.* some, a few, a particular one, a special one, a specific one, a certain one, an individual one, this, that, each, every, these, those, the whole, the entire.
**2.** [Special or unique; *often italics*] — *Syn.* preeminent, outstanding, particular, unparalleled, unequaled, supreme, unsurpassed, unusual, uncommon, rare, singular, unprecedented, exceptional, one, sole, single, significant, distinguished, especial, specific, choice, individual, peculiar, exceptional, occasional, unfamiliar, strange, spectacular, phenomenal, unheard of, unknown, unattainable, invincible, impregnable, almighty, all-powerful; see also **special** 1, **unique** 1. — *Ant.* COMMON, usual, ordinary.

**theater,** *n.* **1.** [A building intended for theatrical productions] — *Syn.* playhouse, concert hall, coliseum, hippodrome, circle theater, round theater, Greek theater, odeum, theater in the round, house, opera house, amphitheater, assembly hall, movie theater, cinema, drive-in, multiplex, movies; see also **auditorium.**
**2.** [The legitimate stage] — *Syn.* stage, drama, Broadway, the boards, theatrics, footlights, legit\*, the oak\*, the deck\*; see also **comedy, movies** 2, **show** 2.
**3.** [Any place of military action] — *Syn.* arena, combat area, battleground, sphere of operations, field, sector, terrain, bridgehead, front, salient, objective, target area, no-man's-land; see also **battlefield.**

**theatrical,** *modif.* **1.** [Concerning the theater] — *Syn.* dramatic, amateur, professional, vaudeville, touring, histrionic, comic, tragic, farcical, tragi-comic, melodramatic, operatic, theater, show.
**2.** [Showy] — *Syn.* ceremonious, meretricious, melodramatic, superficial; see **affected** 2.

**theft,** *n.* — *Syn.* robbery, racket, thievery, larceny, stealing, swindling, swindle, cheating, defrauding, rapacity, fraud, piracy, burglary, pillage, pilfering, plunder, vandalism, pocket-picking, safecracking, extortion, embezzlement, credit-card misuse, deprivation, looting, appropriation, shoplifting, fleece\*, grab\*, holdup\*, reef\*, mugging\*, stickup\*; see also **crime** 2.

---

**SYN.** — **theft** is the general term and **larceny** the legal term for the unlawful or felonious taking away of another's property without his or her consent and with the intention of depriving the person of it; **robbery** is frequently used in the same general sense as **theft**, but in its strict legal sense implies the felonious taking of another's property from that person or in his or her immediate presence by the use of violence or intimidation; **burglary** in legal use implies a breaking into a house with intent to commit theft or other felony and is often restricted to such an act accomplished at night

---

**their,** *modif.* — *Syn.* belonging to them, belonging to others, theirs, of them.

**theme,** *n.* 1. [A subject] — *Syn.* topic, proposition, argument, thesis, text, subject matter, matter in hand, problem, question, point at issue, affair, business, point, case, thought, idea, line\*, rag\*, stuff\*; see also **issue** 1, **subject** 1.
2. [A recurrent melody] — *Syn.* melody, motive, motif, leitmotif, thematic, statement, strain, air, tune, melodic subject, developed melody; see also **song.**
3. [A short composition] — *Syn.* essay, report, paper, term paper, research paper, dissertation, description, statement; see also **exposition** 2.
*See Synonym Study at* SUBJECT.

**then,** *modif.* — *Syn.* at that time, formerly, before, years ago, at that point, suddenly, all at once, soon after, before long, next, later, thereupon; see also **when** 1, 2.

**but then** — *Syn.* but at the same time, on the other hand, however; see **but** 1, 2.

**what then?** — *Syn.* in that case? and then? as a result?; see **what** 1.

**thence,** *modif.* — *Syn.* therefore, from there on, from then on, from that time, thenceforth; see also **therefore.**

**theologian,** *n.* — *Syn.* divine, theologist, ecclesiastic, scholastic; see **philosopher, scholar** 2.

**theological,** *modif.* — *Syn.* religious, churchly, ecclesiastical, rabbinical, canonical, doctrinal, scriptural, patristic, apostolic, metaphysical, supernatural, theistic, deistic, scholastic, hagiographical; see also **divine** 2. — *Ant.* ATHEISTIC, scientific, positivistic.

**theology,** *n.* — *Syn.* dogma, creed, theism; see **belief** 1, **faith** 2.

**theorem,** *n.* — *Syn.* thesis, dictum, assumption; see **doctrine** 1, **hypothesis, theory** 1.

**theoretic,** *modif.* — *Syn.* assumed, speculative, ideal; see **theoretical.**

**theoretical,** *modif.* — *Syn.* ideological, ideal, imaginative, unearthly, idealized, ideational, problematical, analytical, academic, presumed, postulated, assumed, formularized, formalistic, pedantic, codified, technical, intellectual, vague, abstract, general, conjectural, unproved, tentative, suppositional, pure, unsubstantiated, speculative, transcendental, philosophical, logical, metaphysical, contingent, instanced, open to proof, stated as a premise, in theory, on paper, in the abstract, in the realm of ideas; see also **hypothetical** 1. — *Ant.* PRACTICAL, applied, factual.

**theoretically,** *modif.* — *Syn.* in theory, on paper, in a sense, in idea, in a manner, in the abstract; see also **apparently, probably.**

**theorist,** *n.* — *Syn.* theorizer, speculator, ideologist; see **philosopher, scholar** 2, **scientist.**

**theorize,** *v.* — *Syn.* speculate, conjecture, hypothesize; see **guess** 1, **think** 1.

**theory,** *n.* 1. [Principles] — *Syn.* law, principles, postulates, data, conditions, basis, plan, provision, ideas, formularization, systemization, system, codification, code, argument, plea, scheme, foundation, method, approach, outlook, doctrine, dogma, rationale, cosmology, *Weltanschauung* (German), philosophy; see also **law** 4.
2. [Something to be proved] — *Syn.* hypothesis, assumption, conjecture, speculation, opinion; see also **hypothesis, opinion** 1.

**SYN.** — **theory,** in scientific or technical use, refers to a general principle or set of principles, based on considerable evidence, formulated to explain the operation of certain phenomena [the *theory* of evolution], though it is often loosely used to mean a mere conjecture, guess, or hypothesis; **hypothesis** refers to an explanation that is tentatively inferred, often as a basis for further experimentation, but that is not fully supported by evidence [the nebular *hypothesis*]; **law** implies an exact formulation of the principle operating in a sequence of events in nature, observed to occur with unvarying uniformity under the same conditions [the *law* of the conservation of energy]

**therapeutic,** *modif.* — *Syn.* curative, healing, corrective; see **remedial.**

**therapy,** *n.* — *Syn.* therapeutics, remedy, healing, treatment, cure; see also **medicine** 3.
Types of therapy include: physical, mental, inhalation, occupational, behavior, speech, rehabilitative, child, family, group, drug, massage, electroshock, electroconvulsive, light, radiation, oxygen, heat; chemotherapy, radiotherapy, hydrotherapy, heliotherapy, electrotherapy, psychotherapy.

**there,** *modif.* — *Syn.* in that place, not here, beyond, over there, yonder, in the distance, at a distance, over yonder, just there, where I point, in that spot, at that point; see also **where** 2.

**not all there\*** — *Syn.* crazy, eccentric, demented; see **insane** 1.

**thereabouts,** *modif.* — *Syn.* thereby, alongside, next; see **near** 1, **where** 2.

**thereafter,** *modif.* — *Syn.* from there on, from that day on, after that, forever after, from that day forward, consequently; see also **following, hereafter.**

**thereby,** *modif.* — *Syn.* by way of, how, by which; see **through** 4, **whereby.**

**therefore,** *conj. and mod.* — *Syn.* accordingly, consequently, hence, ergo, wherefore, for, since, forasmuch as, inasmuch as, for this reason, on account of, to that end, and so, on the ground, in that event, in consequence, as a result; see also **thence.**

**therein,** *modif.* — *Syn.* inside, inward, internally; see **there, within.**

**thereupon,** *modif.* — *Syn.* then, at which point, on that, thereon, suddenly, at once; see also **immediately.**

**thermal,** *modif.* — *Syn.* warm, tepid, thermic, loosely knit; see **hot** 1.

**thermometer,** *n.* — *Syn.* mercury, calorimeter, oral thermometer, anal thermometer, clinical thermometer, resistance thermometer, thermoelectric, thermoscope, telethermometer, thermostat, thermo-regulator; see also **regulator.**

**thermos bottle,** *n.* — *Syn.* vacuum bottle, thermos flask, picnic jug, icy-hot\*, thermos\*; see also **bottle, container, jug.**

**thesaurus,** *n.* — *Syn.* lexicon, glossary, synonyms and antonyms, synonymy, collection of words; see also **dictionary.**

**these,** *modif.* — *Syn.* those, the indicated, the present, the aforementioned, the already stated, the referred to, hereinafter described, the previously mentioned, the well-known, the aforesaid, the above, the below; see also **certain** 6.

**thesis,** *n.* 1. [A statement to be proved] — *Syn.* principle, belief, argument; see **hypothesis, opinion** 1.
2. [A learned essay, especially for advanced academic degrees] — *Syn.* dissertation, research, requirement for graduation, master's paper, master's essay; see also **exposition** 2.

**Thespian,** *n.* — *Syn.* player, tragedian, performer; see **actor** 1, **actress.**

**they,** *pron.* — *Syn.* people, men, those people, all, others, he and she, both; see also **everybody.**

**thick,** *modif.* **1.** [Dense] — *Syn.* compact, dense, close, impenetrable, impervious, condensed, compressed, multitudinous, numerous, lush, rank, crowded, solid, packed, populous, profuse, populated, swarming, heaped, abundant, concentrated, crammed, full, congested, packed together, closely packed, inspissated, like sardines in a can*, jam-packed*; see also **full** 1, 3, **jammed** 2. — *Ant.* SCATTERED, sparse, wide-open.
**2.** [Deep] — *Syn.* high, in depth, three-dimensional, from front to back, edgewise; see also **deep** 2. — *Ant.* LONG, wide, across.
**3.** [Of heavy consistency] — *Syn.* compact, heavy, viscous, viscid, dense, syrupy, ropy, coagulated, imporous, curdled, turbid, gelatinous, grumous, glutinous, gummous, gummy, grumose, opaque, vitrified, ossified, clotted; see also **adhesive.** — *Ant.* LIGHT, porous, filmy.
**4.** [Not clear] — *Syn.* cloudy, turbid, indistinct; see **dull** 2, **muddy** 1, **obscure** 1.
**5.** [Stupid] — *Syn.* obtuse, ignorant, doltish; see **dull** 3.
**6.** [*Intimate] — *Syn.* cordial, familiar, fraternal; see **friendly** 1, **intimate** 1.
**7.** [*Presumptuous] — *Syn.* insolent, tactless, unbearable; see **rude** 2.
**through thick and thin*** — *Syn.* faithfully, devotedly, in good and bad times; see **loyally.**

---

*SYN.* — **thick,** in this connection, suggests a great number of constituent parts massed tightly together *[thick* fur*]*; **close,** in this comparison, refers to something whose parts or elements are near together with little space between *[close*-order drill*]*; **dense** suggests such a crowding together of elements or parts as to form an almost impervious mass *[a dense* fog*]*; **compact** suggests close and firm packing, esp. within a small space, and usually implies neatness and order in the arrangement of parts *[a compact* bundle*]*

---

**thicken,** *v.* **1.** [To become thicker] — *Syn.* coagulate, curdle, petrify, ossify, solidify, freeze, clot, set, congeal, gel, grow thick; see also **harden** 2, **stiffen** 1. — *Ant.* FLOW, thaw, weaken.
**2.** [To make thicker] — *Syn.* reinforce, add, expand, enlarge, buttress, widen, swell; see also **harden** 1, **stiffen** 2. — *Ant.* DECREASE, narrow down, slice off.
**thicket,** *n.* — *Syn.* bush, shrubbery, copse, brake, underbrush, chaparral; see also **brush** 4.
**thickheaded,** *modif.* — *Syn.* stupid, ignorant, idiotic; see **dull** 3.
**thickness,** *n.* **1.** [As a quality] — *Syn.* density, compactness, solidity, closeness, heaviness, stiffness, condensation, concentration, clot. — *Ant.* FRAILTY, thinness, slimness.
**2.** [As a measurement] — *Syn.* breadth, distance through, girth; see **depth** 1, **diameter, width.**
**thickset,** *modif.* — *Syn.* stout, stocky, stubby; see **fat** 1.
**thick-skinned,** *modif.* — *Syn.* callous, hardened, unfeeling; see **indifferent** 1, **obstinate.**
**thief,** *n.* — *Syn.* burglar, highwayman, holdup man; see **criminal, robber.**
**thieve,** *v.* — *Syn.* loot, rob, filch; see **steal.**
**thievery,** *n.* — *Syn.* burglary, robbery, pilfering; see **crime** 2, **theft.**
**thievish,** *modif.* — *Syn.* stealthy, furtive, cunning; see **light-fingered, secretive, sly** 1.
**thigh,** *n.* — *Syn.* thigh bone, femur, proximal segment, ham*; see **groin, leg** 1.
**thimbleful,** *n.* — *Syn.* trifle, pinch, dab; see **bit** 1.
**thin,** *modif.* **1.** [Of little thickness] — *Syn.* flimsy, slim,

slight, tenuous, attenuated, diaphanous, sheer, rare, sleazy, permeable, paper-thin, wafer-sliced; see also **transparent** 1. — *Ant.* THICK, heavy, coarse.
**2.** [Slender] — *Syn.* slim, lean, skinny, scraggy, lank, lanky, spindly, spare, gaunt, bony, wan, rangy, skeletal, scrawny, lanky, delicate, wasted, haggard, emaciated, rawboned, shriveled, wizened, rickety, spindling, pinched, starved; see also **dainty** 1. — *Ant.* FAT, obese, heavy.
**3.** [Sparse] — *Syn.* scarce, insufficient, deficient; see **inadequate** 1.
**4.** [Having little content] — *Syn.* sketchy, slight, insubstantial, weak-kneed, vapid, weak, light, feeble, flat, diluted, thinly stretched; see also **shallow** 1, 2. — *Ant.* THICK, solid, substantial.
**5.** [Having little volume] — *Syn.* faint, shrill, piping, weak, rarefied, tenuous, attenuated, fragile, small, tiny, featherweight, bodiless, disembodied, ethereal, shaky; see also **light** 7. — *Ant.* THICK, heavy, dense.
**thin,** *v.* — *Syn.* expand, thin out, disperse, weed out, dilute, edit, delete, rarefy, reduce, attenuate; see also **decrease** 2, **weaken** 2.
**thing,** *n.* **1.** [An object] — *Syn.* article, object, item, lifeless object, commodity, device, gadget, material object, conversation piece, being, entity, materiality, corporeality, body, person, something, anything, everything, element, substance, piece, shape, form, figure, configuration, creature, stuff, goods, matter, thingy*, thingamajig*, gizmo*, whatchamacallit*, doohickey*, thingamabob*; see also **substance** 2.
**2.** [A circumstance] — *Syn.* matter, condition, situation; see **circumstance** 1.
**3.** [An act] — *Syn.* deed, feat, movement; see **action** 2.
**4.** [A characteristic] — *Syn.* quality, trait, attribute; see **characteristic.**
**5.** [An idea] — *Syn.* notion, opinion, impression; see **thought** 2.
**6.** [A pitiable person] — *Syn.* wretch, poor person, sufferer, urchin; see **patient, refugee, tramp** 1.
**7.** [Belongings; *usually pl.*] — *Syn.* possessions, clothes, personals; see **property** 1.
**8.** [Something so vague as to be nameless] — *Syn.* affair, matter, concern, business, occurrence, anything, everything, something, stuff, point, information, subject, idea, question, indication, intimation, contrivance, word, name, shape, form, entity.
**9.** [Something to be done] — *Syn.* task, obligation, duty; see **job** 2.
**do one's own thing*** — *Syn.* live according to one's own principles, do what one likes, live fully; see **enjoy oneself.**
**see things** — *Syn.* have delusions, misperceive, suffer from hallucinations; see **mistake.**
**things,** *pl.n.* — *Syn.* possessions, luggage, belongings; see **baggage, property** 1.
**think,** *v.* **1.** [To examine with the mind] — *Syn.* cogitate, reason, deliberate, ideate, muse, ponder, consider, contemplate, deliberate, stop to consider, study, reflect, imagine, conceive, examine, think twice, estimate, evaluate, appraise, resolve, ruminate, scan, confer, consult, meditate, meditate upon, take under consideration, have on one's mind, brood over, speculate, weigh, have in mind, keep in mind, bear in mind, mull over*, turn over*, cudgel one's brains*, sweat over*, stew*, bone*, beat one's brains*, rack one's brains*, use the old bean*, do some tall headwork*, do some hefty headwork*, figure out*, put on one's thinking cap*, use one's head*, pick one's steps*, hammer away at*, hammer out*, bury

oneself in*; see also **analyze** 1.— *Ant.* NEGLECT, take for granted, accept.

**2.** [To believe] — *Syn.* be convinced, deem, hold; see **believe** 1.

**3.** [To suppose] — *Syn.* imagine, guess, presume; see **assume** 1.

**4.** [To form in the mind] — *Syn.* conceive, invent, create; see **imagine** 1.

**5.** [To remember] — *Syn.* recollect, recall, reminisce; see **remember** 1, 2.

---

*SYN.* — **think** is the general word meaning to exercise the mental faculties so as to form ideas, arrive at conclusions, etc. /learn to *think* clearly/; **reason** implies a logical sequence of thought, starting with what is known or assumed and advancing to a definite conclusion through the inferences drawn /he *reasoned* that she would accept/; **cogitate** is used, sometimes humorously, of a person who is, or appears to be, thinking seriously or hard /I was *cogitating*, not daydreaming/; **reflect** implies a turning of one's thoughts on or back on a subject and connotes deep or quiet continued thought /he *reflected* on the day's events/; **speculate** implies a reasoning on the basis of incomplete or uncertain evidence and therefore stresses the conjectural character of the opinions formed /to *speculate* on the possibility of life on Mars/; **deliberate** implies careful and thorough consideration of a matter in order to arrive at a conclusion /the jury *deliberated* on the case/

---

**thinkable,** *modif.* — *Syn.* conceivable, within the limits, possible; see **convincing** 2, **imaginable, likely** 1.

**thinker,** *n.* — *Syn.* mastermind, sage, savant; see **intellectual, philosopher, scholar** 2.

**thinking,** *modif.* — *Syn.* rational, reasoning, reasonable, pensive, introspective, reflective, meditative, speculative, studious, deliberating, contemplative, absorbed, engrossed, intent on, ruminating, cerebrating; see also **thoughtful** 1.— *Ant.* STUPID, vacuous, irrational.

**put on one's thinking cap**— *Syn.* begin thinking, study, examine; see **think** 1.

**thinking,** *n.* — *Syn.* thought, reasoning, reason, cogitation, ideation, rationalization, contemplation, rumination, reflection, speculation, cerebration, deliberation, study, meditation, abstraction, musing, self-absorption, introspection, retrospection, intellectual perception, noodling*, tall headwork*.

**think twice,** *n.* — *Syn.* reconsider, weigh, pause; see **hesitate.**

**thinness,** *n.* — *Syn.* slenderness, slimness, shallowness; see **lightness** 2.

**thin-skinned,** *modif.* — *Syn.* sensitive, touchy, moody; see **irritable.**

**third,** *modif.* — *Syn.* part, after the second, next but one; see **three.**

**thirst,** *n.* — *Syn.* dryness, need for liquid, longing, craving; see **appetite** 1, **desire.**

**thirsty,** *modif.* — *Syn.* dry, parched, arid, droughty, avid, eager, sharp-set, hankering for, burning for, craving, longing for, partial to, hungry for, keen, itching for, inclined to, bonedry*, dry as a bone*, dry as a gourd*, crazy for*, wild for*; see also **hungry.** — *Ant.* SATISFIED, full, replete.

**this,** *modif.* — *Syn.* the, that, the indicated, the present, here, aforementioned, already stated.

**this,** *pron.* — *Syn.* the one, this one, the one in question, the aforementioned one, this person, the thing indicated; see also **that.**

**thistle,** *n.* Thistles include: bull, Canada, Russian, common, Scotch, cotton, teazel, yellow, star, bur; see also **plant, weed** 1.

**thither,** *modif.* — *Syn.* beyond, yonder, toward; see **there.**

**thong,** *n.* — *Syn.* lace, string, strap, whip; see **rope, twine.**

**thorax,** *n.* — *Syn.* chest, trunk, breast; see **abdomen, chest** 1.

**thorn,** *n.* — *Syn.* prickle, spine, brier, briar, nettle, bramble, barb, thistle; see also **point** 2, **spine** 1.

**thorny,** *modif.* **1.** [Thick with thorns] — *Syn.* barbed, spiny, prickly, bristly, bristled, stinging, thistly, briery, spiky, setaceous, echinate; see also **sharp** 2.— *Ant.* SMOOTH, soft, glabrous.

**2.** [Troublesome] — *Syn.* bothersome, perplexing, formidable; see **difficult** 1, 2.

**thorough,** *modif.* **1.** [Painstaking] — *Syn.* exact, meticulous, precise; see **accurate** 2, **careful.**

**2.** [Complete] — *Syn.* thoroughgoing, out-and-out, total; see **absolute** 1.

**thoroughbred,** *modif.* — *Syn.* full-blooded, purebred, pedigreed, papered, of full blood, of good breed; see also **registered** 2.

**thoroughfare,** *n.* — *Syn.* freeway, boulevard, roadway; see **highway, road** 1, **street.**

**thoroughly,** *modif.* — *Syn.* fully, wholly, in detail; see **completely.**

**those,** *modif.* — *Syn.* these, the indicated, the above-mentioned, the already stated, the certain, the particular; see also **the** 1.

**thou,** *pron.* — *Syn.* thee, yourself, thyself; see **you.**

**though,** *conj.* — *Syn.* despite, even if, if; see **although, but** 1.

**thought,** *n.* **1.** [Mental activity] — *Syn.* speculation, reflection, deliberation, cerebration, ideation, meditation, rumination, perceiving, apprehending, seeing, consideration, reasoning, intuition, imagination, logical process, perception, insight, understanding, viewpoint, concept, brainwork, thinking, knowing, realizing, discerning, rationalizing, drawing conclusions, concluding, inferring, deducing, deriving, deduction, inducing, logic, judging, rationalization, ratiocination, judgment, argumentation, cogitation, contemplation, cognition, intellection, slant*, brainstorm*, twist*, wrinkle*; see also **acumen.**

**2.** [The result of mental activity] — *Syn.* idea, plan, view, fancy, notion, impression, image, understanding, appreciation, conception, observation, belief, feeling, opinion, guess, inference, theory, hypothesis, supposition, assumption, intuition, conjecture, deduction, postulate, premise, knowledge, evaluation, assessment, appraisal, estimate, verdict, finding, decision, determination, reflection, consideration, abstraction, conviction, tenet, presumption, intellectualization, ideation, surmise, doctrine, principle, drift, calculation, caprice, reverie, sentiment, care, worry, anxiety, uneasiness, dream.

**3.** [The ideas of a given time, place, people, etc.] — *Syn.* philosophy, way of life, outlook, views, principles, worldview, *Weltanschauung* (German), *Zeitgeist* (German), spirit, custom, mores.

**4.** [Care or attention] — *Syn.* heed, thoughtfulness, solicitude; see **attention** 1, 2, **care** 2.

*See Synonym Study at* IDEA.

**thoughtful,** *modif.* **1.** [Notable for thought] — *Syn.* thinking, meditative, engrossed, absorbed, rapt in, pensive, considered, seasoned, matured, studied, philosophic, contemplative, studious, cogitative, ruminative, examined, pondered, speculative, deliberative,

reflective, introspective, clear-headed, level seasoned, matured, studied, philosophic, contemplative, studious, cogitative, ruminative, examined, pondered, speculative, deliberative, reflective, introspective, clear-headed, level-headed, keen, wise, well-balanced, judged, far-sighted, reasoning, rational, calculating, discerning, penetrating, politic, shrewd, careful, sensible, retrospective, intellectual, brainy\*, deep\*. — *Ant.* THOUGHTLESS, unthinking, irrational.
2. [Considerate] — *Syn.* considerate, heedful, polite, courteous, solicitous, friendly, kind, kindly, unselfish, concerned, anxious, neighborly, regardful, social, cooperative, responsive, aware, sensitive, benign, indulgent, obliging, careful, attentive, gallant, chivalrous, charitable. — *Ant.* SELFISH, boorish, inconsiderate.

---

*SYN.* — **thoughtful**, as compared here, implies the showing of thought for the comfort or well-being of others, as by anticipating their needs or wishes /it was *thoughtful* of you to call/; **considerate** implies a thoughtful or sympathetic regard for the feelings or circumstances of others, as in sparing them pain, distress, or discomfort /*considerate* enough to extend the time for payment/; **attentive** implies a constant thoughtfulness as shown by repeated acts of consideration, courtesy, or devotion /an *attentive* suitor/

---

**thoughtfulness,** *n.* — *Syn.* understanding, helpfulness, indulgence; see **kindness** 1.
**thoughtless,** *modif.* 1. [Destitute of thought] — *Syn.* irrational, unreasoning, unreasonable, vacuous, inane, incomprehensible, witless, undiscerning, bovine, foolish, doltish, babbling, bewildered, confused, puerile, senseless, driveling, inept, dull, heavy, obtuse, feeble-minded, flighty, empty-headed\*, lame-brained\*, barmy\*, nutty\*, loony\*, rattled\*, sappy\*, dizzy\*; see also **stupid** 1. — *Ant.* RATIONAL, reasoning, shrewd.
2. [Inconsiderate] — *Syn.* heedless, negligent, inattentive, careless, indiscreet, neglectful, self-centered, egocentric, selfish, asocial, antisocial, unmindful, unheeding, reckless, deaf, blind, indifferent, unconcerned, listless, apathetic, boorish, discourteous, rude, primitive, unrefined; see also **rude** 2. — *Ant.* CAREFUL, thoughtful, unselfish.
**thoughtlessness,** *n.* — *Syn.* inattention, oversight, heedlessness, negligence; see **carelessness, neglect** 1.
**thought over** or **through,** *modif.* — *Syn.* studied, thought about, revised; see **considered** 1, **investigated.**
**thousand,** *modif.* — *Syn.* ten hundred, millenary, thousandfold, multitudinous, myriad, numerous.
**thrall,** *n.* — *Syn.* bondman, serf, vassal; see **slave** 1.
**thralldom,** *n.* — *Syn.* servitude, subjugation, bondage; see **slavery** 1.
**thrash,** *v.* 1. [To beat] — *Syn.* trounce, flog, flail; see **beat** 2, **punish.**
2. [To toss about] — *Syn.* swing, fling, flail; see **throw** 1, **toss** 2.
*See Synonym Study at* BEAT.
**thread,** *n.* — *Syn.* cotton, yarn, wool, lisle, filament, fiber, strand, wire, hair, gossamer, cobweb, twist, string, tape, ribbon, braid, strand; see also **cloth.**
**thread,** *v.* 1. [To pass thread through a needle] — *Syn.* wire, string, run through, wind through, slip through. — *Ant.* UNDO, unthread, change the thread.
2. [To connect] — *Syn.* attach, weave together, string together; see **join** 1.
**threadbare,** *modif.* 1. [Ragged] — *Syn.* shabby, seedy, frayed; see **ragged, worn** 1.

2. [Trite] — *Syn.* stale, tedious, worn, everyday; see **common** 1, **dull** 4, **poor** 2.
**threat,** *n.* — *Syn.* menace, peril, fulmination, intimidation; see **warning.**
**threaten,** *v.* 1. [To warn of punishment] — *Syn.* intimidate, menace, caution, admonish, hold over, scare, torment, push around, browbeat, forewarn, bully, terrorize, abuse, bluster, fulminate, look daggers, thunder against, bulldoze\*, draw a gun on\*, pull a gun on\*, double the fist at\*; see also **frighten** 1, **abuse** 1, **warn.** — *Ant.* HELP, mollify, placate.
2. [To impend] — *Syn.* endanger, be dangerous, be gathering, be in the offing, imperil, be brewing, be on the horizon, approach, come on, advance; see also **frighten** 1, **loom** 2. — *Ant.* HAPPEN, seize, overcome.

---

*SYN.* — **threaten** implies a warning of impending punishment, danger, evil, etc. as by words, actions, events, conditions, or signs /he *threatened* to retaliate, the clouds *threaten* rain/; **menace** stresses the frightening or hostile character of that which threatens /he *menaced* me with a revolver/

---

**threatened,** *modif.* — *Syn.* warned, endangered, imperiled, jeopardized, in bad straits, insecure, unsafe, unprotected, vulnerable, exposed, in a crucial state, in danger, besieged, surrounded, under attack, set upon, in a bad way. — *Ant.* SAFE, invulnerable, protected.
**threatening,** *modif.* — *Syn.* alarming, menacing, dangerous, aggressive, intimidating; see also **ominous, sinister, unsafe.**
**three,** *modif.* — *Syn.* triple, treble, threefold, third, triform, triune, tertiary, thrice, triply.
**threnody,** *n.* — *Syn.* dirge, requiem, lament; see **song.**
**thresh,** *v.* 1. [To free grain or seed from hulls] — *Syn.* flail, tread, separate, winnow, sift, thrash, beat, garner; see also **beat** 2.
2. [To chastise] — *Syn.* trounce, whip, hit; see **beat** 2, **punish.**
**thresher,** *n.* — *Syn.* harvest hand, harvester, pitcher, bundle-hauler, separator man, engineer, grain-shoveler; see also **laborer.**
**threshing,** *n.* 1. [The act of removing grain from hulls] — *Syn.* separating, flailing, beating, treading, garnering, winnowing, sifting, harvesting, putting it through\*, combining\*; see also **division** 1.
2. [A beating] — *Syn.* trouncing, infliction, drubbing; see **punishment.**
**threshold,** *n.* 1. [An entrance] — *Syn.* sill, doorsill, vestibule, gate, door, groundsel; see also **entrance** 1.
2. [A beginning] — *Syn.* inception, outset, start; see **origin** 1.
**thrice,** *modif.* 1. [Threefold] — *Syn.* triply, threefold, trebly; see **triple.**
2. [Very] — *Syn.* greatly, highly, amply; see **very.**
**thrift,** *n.* — *Syn.* saving, parsimony, frugality; see **economy** 2.
**thriftless,** *modif.* — *Syn.* extravagant, lavish, negligent; see **wasteful.**
**thrifty,** *modif.* — *Syn.* economical, saving, careful, frugal; see **economical** 1.
*See Synonym Study at* ECONOMICAL.
**thrill,** *n.* — *Syn.* pleasant sensation, stimulation, good feeling, refreshment, titillation, tingle, glow, flush, response, flutter, twitter, inspiration, kick\*, bang\*, boost\*, lift\*, wallop\*; see also **excitement, fun.**
**thrill,** *v.* 1. [To excite] — *Syn.* animate, inspire, rouse, charge\*; see **excite** 1, 2.

**2.** [To become excited] — *Syn.* tingle, quiver, flutter, pant, glow, vibrate, palpitate, titillate, shiver.

**thrilled,** *modif.* — *Syn.* animated, inspired, moved, touched, imbued, stirred, electrified, aroused; see also **excited, happy** 1. — *Ant.* INDIFFERENT, unmoved, blasé.

**thrilling,** *modif.* — *Syn.* overwhelming, electrifying, exciting, exquisite, wondrous, enchanting, magnificent, breathtaking, miraculous, hair-raising, blood-tingling; see also **stimulating.** — *Ant.* COMMON, CONVENTIONAL, ordinary.

**thrive,** *v.* **1.** [To grow vigorously] — *Syn.* blossom, blossom out, burgeon, wax, shoot up, flourish, mushroom, rise, bear fruit, batten, increase, radiate, shine; see also **grow.** — *Ant.* DIE, wither, sicken.
**2.** [To prosper] — *Syn.* succeed, do well, turn out well, flourish, rise up, make one's fortune, make an auspicious start, get ahead, achieve success, advance, make progress, be booming*, feather one's nest*, get places*, make it*, make a go*; see also **prosper.** — *Ant.* FAIL, lose out, go bankrupt.

**thriving,** *modif.* — *Syn.* flourishing, blooming, prolific; see **growing.**

**throat,** *n.* — *Syn.* neck, windpipe, larynx, trachea, esophagus, jugular region, gullet, gorge, jugulum.

**cut each other's throats*** — *Syn.* ruin each other, fight, feud; see **destroy** 1.

**cut one's own throat*** — *Syn.* harm oneself, damage oneself, ruin oneself, cause one's own destruction, act contrary to one's best interest; see also **commit suicide** at **commit, damage** 1.

**ram down someone's throat*** — *Syn.* impose, pressure, coerce; see **force** 1.

**stick in one's throat*** — *Syn.* be difficult to say, not come easily, be disturbing; see **disturb** 2.

**throaty,** *modif.* — *Syn.* husky, hoarse, deep; see **hoarse.**

**throb,** *n.* — *Syn.* beat, pulsation, pulse, palpitation; see **beat** 2.

**throb,** *v.* — *Syn.* beat, pulsate, palpitate; see **beat** 3.

**throne,** *n.* **1.** [The seat on which a ruler sits] — *Syn.* chair of state, royal seat, dais, cathedra, divan, gaddi, guddee, masnad, masnad, raised chair; see also **chair** 1.
**2.** [The symbol of royal power] — *Syn.* authority, sway, dominion, royal power, sovereignty, kingship, His Royal Majesty, His Royal Highness, the Crown; see also **chair** 2, **royalty.**

**throng,** *n.* — *Syn.* multitude, mass, concourse, press; see **crowd** 1, **gathering.**
*See Synonym Study at* CROWD.

**throttle,** *n.* — *Syn.* starter, gas pedal, gas, feed, gas-feed; see also **accelerator.**

**throttle,** *v.* **1.** [To choke] — *Syn.* strangle, stifle, silence; see **choke** 1.
**2.** [To censor] — *Syn.* suppress, restrict, stifle; see **censor.**

**throttled,** *modif.* — *Syn.* silenced, stopped, halted; see **managed, restrained.**

**through,** *modif. & prep.* **1.** [Finished] — *Syn.* completed, over, ended; see **done** 1, **finished** 1.
**2.** [From one side to the other] — *Syn.* straight through, through and through, clear through*; see **in** 2, **into, within.**
**3.** [During] — *Syn.* throughout, for the period of, from beginning to end; see **during.**
**4.** [By means of] — *Syn.* by, by way of, by reason of, in virtue of, in consequence of, for, by the agency of, at the hand of, through the medium of, by dint of.
**5.** [Referring to continuous passage] — *Syn.* nonstop,

free, unhindered, unbroken, opened, rapid, one-way; see also **consecutive** 1, **constant** 1, **regular** 3. — *Ant.* BROKEN, INTERRUPTED, intermittent.

**through and through,** *modif.* — *Syn.* permeating, pervasive, enduring, thoroughly, completely; see also **penetrating** 1, **throughout.**

**throughout,** *modif. & prep.* — *Syn.* all through, during, from beginning to end, from one end to the other, everywhere, all over, in everything, in every place, up and down, from top to bottom, on all accounts, in all respects, inside and out, at full length, every bit, to the end, down to the ground*, hide and hair*, head and shoulders*, from the word go*, up to the brim*; see also **completely.**

**through thick and thin*,** *modif.* — *Syn.* in the face of adversity, in good and bad weather, in rain or shine, devotedly, loyally, constantly; see also **regularly** 1, 2.

**throw,** *v.* **1.** [To hurl] — *Syn.* fling, butt, bunt, pitch, fire, let go, sling, toss, heave, lob, dash, launch, chuck, bowl, cast, heave, hurl, let fly*, shy*, deliver*, elbow*, cast off*, lay across*. — *Ant.* CATCH, receive, grab.
**2.** [To send forth] — *Syn.* propel, thrust, force, project, discharge, butt, bunt, launch, put into motion, start, push into, drive, set going, impel, stick into, pour into. — *Ant.* RECEIVE, retrieve, accept.
**3.** [To connect or disconnect] — *Syn.* pull a lever, turn a switch, unswitch, unhook, turn off, turn on.
**4.** [To force to the ground] — *Syn.* defeat, cast down, triumph over, strike down, overwhelm, pin, nail*, flatten*, buck off*, pin to the mat*; see also **defeat** 1, 3. — *Ant.* RAISE, help up, bring on to one's feet.
**5.** [*To permit an opponent to win] — *Syn.* give up, lose the game, lose deliberately, submit, yield, surrender, give in*, back down*, chuck away*, call quits*, check out*; see also **lose** 3.

---

*SYN.* — **throw** is the general word meaning to cause to move through the air by or as by a rapid propulsive motion of the arm [*throw* a ball, *throw* some light on the mystery]; **cast,** the preferred word in certain connections [to *cast* a fishing line], generally has a more archaic or lofty quality [they *cast* stones at him]; to **toss** is to throw lightly or carelessly and, usually, with an upward or sideways motion [to *toss* a coin]; **hurl** and **fling** both imply a throwing with force or violence, but **hurl** suggests that the object thrown moves swiftly for some distance [to *hurl* a javelin] and **fling,** that it is thrust sharply or vehemently so that it strikes a surface with considerable impact [she *flung* the plate to the floor]; **pitch** implies a throwing with a definite aim or in a definite direction [to *pitch* a baseball]

---

**throw away,** *v.* — *Syn.* reject, refuse, turn down; see **discard.**

**throwback,** *n.* — *Syn.* atavism, carry-over, regression; see **remainder.**

**throw down,** *v.* — *Syn.* cast down, toss, let fall; see **discard, drop** 2.

**throw in,** *v.* — *Syn.* add, expand, give, include; see **increase** 1.

**throw in the towel** or **sponge*,** *v.* — *Syn.* give up, surrender, bow to; see **yield** 1.

**thrown,** *modif.* **1.** [Hurled] — *Syn.* pitched, tossed, heaved, flung, sent forth, propelled, discharged, directed; see also **launched.**
**2.** [Beaten] — *Syn.* knocked over, sent sprawling, heaved; see **beaten** 1.

**throw off,** *v.* — *Syn.* get better, get well, improve, gain strength; see **recover** 3.

**throw off the track** or **scent,** *v.* — *Syn.* misinform, distract, trick; see **deceive.**

**throw out,** *v.* — *Syn.* discharge, throw away, reject; see **discard, oust.**

**throw together,** *v.* — *Syn.* make quickly, do in a hurry, do a rush job; see **build** 1, **manufacture.**

**throw up,** *v.* **1.** [To vomit] — *Syn.* spew out, disgorge, regurgitate, empty one's stomach, retch\*, barf\*, puke\*; see also **vomit.**
**2.** [To quit] — *Syn.* give up, cease, terminate; see **stop** 2.
**3.** [To construct, usually hastily] — *Syn.* build overnight, put together, patch up, knock together, jury-rig; see also **build** 1.

**throw up to,** *v.* — *Syn.* bring up, nag about, taunt, mention, repeat, remind of; see also **emphasize.**

**thrush,** *n.*
Thrushes include: robin, wood, hermit, dwarf hermit, olive-backed, russet-backed, willow, Wilson's, brown; see also **bird** 1.

**thrust,** *n.* **1.** [A jab] — *Syn.* punch, stab, poke, shove, wallop, smack, dig, nick, clout, cut, clip\*, lam\*, wham\*, whack\*; see also **blow** 1.
**2.** [An attack] — *Syn.* onset, onslaught, advance; see **attack** 1.
**3.** [A strong push] — *Syn.* drive, impetus, momentum, impulsion, propulsion, pressure; see also **push.**

**thrust,** *v.* **1.** [To jab] — *Syn.* poke, push, shove, stab, pierce, interject, stick, transfix, ram, punch, wallop, hang one on\*, elbow one's way\*; see also **hit** 1. — *Ant.* RETURN, fall back, retaliate.
**2.** [To attack] — *Syn.* assault, assail, push forward; see **attack** 1.

**thud,** *n.* — *Syn.* fall, dull sound, plop; see **noise** 1.

**thug,** *n.* — *Syn.* gunman, gangster, desperado, mobster, gang leader, racketeer, criminal, hoodlum, tough\*, mug\*, gorilla\*, hood\*, yegg\*; see also **robber.**

**thumb,** *n.* — *Syn.* pollex, first digit, preaxial digit; see **finger.**
**all thumbs\*** — *Syn.* fumbling, clumsy, inept; see **awkward** 1.
**under one's thumb\*** — *Syn.* under one's control, controlled, governed; see **managed.**

**thump,** *n.* — *Syn.* thud, knock, rap, wallop, blow, pounding, whack, slap, smack, crack, bop\*, plop\*; see also **noise** 1.

**thump,** *v.* — *Syn.* pound, knock, rap, wallop, slap, strike, whack; see also **beat, hit** 1.

**thunder,** *n.* — *Syn.* crash, peal, outburst, explosion, boom, booming, roar, rumble, clap, crack, discharge, thunderbolt, uproar, blast; see also **noise** 1.

**thunder,** *v.* — *Syn.* peal, boom, rumble, resound, reverberate, roll, deafen, crash, clamor, clash; see also **roar, sound** 1, **storm.**

**thunderbolt,** *n.* — *Syn.* explosion, crash, clap of thunder, flash, peal, boom, roll, crack, flash of lightning, thunderpeal, thunderclap, thunderstroke; see also **lightning.**

**thunderous,** *modif.* — *Syn.* booming, roaring, crashing; see **loud** 1, 2.

**thunderstorm,** *n.* — *Syn.* electric storm, squall, downpour; see **thunder, storm** 1.

**thunderstruck,** *modif.* — *Syn.* astonished, confounded, astounded, dumbfounded; see **bewildered.**

**thus,** *modif.* — *Syn.* in this manner, so, consequently, hence, in such a way, just like that, in kind, along these lines; see also **therefore.**

**thwack,** *n.* — *Syn.* whack, thump, hit; see **blow** 1.

**thwack,** *v.* — *Syn.* whack, thrash, thump; see **hit** 1.

**thwart,** *v.* — *Syn.* stop, impede, frustrate; see **confuse, prevent, trammel.**
See Synonym Study at FRUSTRATE.

**tiara,** *n.* — *Syn.* coronet, diadem, circlet; see **crown** 2.

**tic,** *n.* — *Syn.* twitch, spasm, jerk, contraction; see **fit** 1.

**tick,** *n.* **1.** [A light beat] — *Syn.* clock-tick, beat, tick-tock, click, tap, light rap, slight blow, metallic sound.
**2.** [An insect] — *Syn.* parasite, bloodsucker, arachnid, acarida, louse, mite; see also **insect, pest** 1.
Ticks include: cattle, sheep, bird, wood, deer.
**3.** [A mattress] — *Syn.* feather tick, straw tick, cornhusk tick, pillow, cushion; see also **bed** 1, **mattress.**

**ticket,** *n.* **1.** [A valid token] — *Syn.* check, certificate, notice, badge, label, voucher, stub, countercheck, raincheck, docket, tag, slip, note, card, pass, receipt, record, license, permit, passage, credential, visa, passport, document, paper\*, Annie Oakley\*.
**2.** [Candidates representing a political party] — *Syn.* party list, party slate, choice, schedule, ballot, machine\*, line-up\*, ring\*, combine\*; see also **candidate, faction** 1, **party** 3.
**that's the ticket\*** — *Syn.* that's correct, that's right, truly; see **surely.**

**ticketed,** *modif.* — *Syn.* ready to board, prepared, readied; see **ready** 2.

**tickle,** *v.* **1.** [To stimulate by a light touch] — *Syn.* rub, caress, stroke, vellicate, titillate; see also **touch** 1.
**2.** [To excite mentally] — *Syn.* amuse, delight, stimulate; see **excite** 1.

**tickling,** *n.* — *Syn.* stroking, caressing, titillation; see **touch** 2.

**ticklish,** *modif.* **1.** [Sensitive to tickling] — *Syn.* hypersensitive, tickly, titillative.
**2.** [Easily upset] — *Syn.* touchy, thin-skinned, prickly; see **irritable.**
**3.** [Needing careful handling] — *Syn.* precarious, delicate, awkward, intricate.

**tidbit,** *n.* — *Syn.* morsel, mouthful, bite; see **bit** 1, **delicacy** 2.

**tide,** *n.* — *Syn.* current, flow, flux, stream, course, sluice, undercurrent, undertow, drag, whirlpool, eddy, vortex, torrent, wave, tidal wave; see also **wave** 1, 2.
Tides of the sea include: low, neap, ebb, spring, full, high, flood.

**tidiness,** *n.* — *Syn.* neatness, spruceness, uniformity; see **cleanliness.**

**tidings,** *n.* — *Syn.* news, information, word, report; see **news** 1, 2.

**tidy,** *modif.* — *Syn.* orderly, trim, spruce; see **neat** 1.

**tie,** *n.* **1.** [A fastening] — *Syn.* band, bond, strap, lace, bandage, brace, tackle, zipper, yoke; see also **fastener.**
**2.** [A necktie] — *Syn.* cravat, neckerchief, bow, four-in-hand, knot, ruff, scarf, Windsor, bolo, neckcloth, Eton tie, rag\*, rope\*, choker\*; see also **necktie.**
**3.** [Affection] — *Syn.* bond, relation, kinship, link, affinity; see also **affection** 1, **love** 1.
**4.** [An equal score, or a contest having that score] — *Syn.* deadlock, draw, even game, dead heat, stalemate, drawn battle, neck-and-neck contest, even-Steven\*, level\*, nose finish\*, standoff\*.
**5.** [A railroad tie] — *Syn.* crossbeam, track support, brace, timber, toothpick\*; see also **beam** 1.

**tie,** *v.* **1.** [To fasten] — *Syn.* bind, make fast, attach; see **fasten** 1, **join** 1.
**2.** [To tie a knot in] — *Syn.* knot, make a bow, make a tie, make a knot, do up, fix a tie, make a hitch; see also **sense** 1.
**3.** [\*To equal] — *Syn.* be on a par with, match, keep up

with, even off, balance, parallel, break even, draw, come to a deadlock; see also **equal.**

**4.** [*To marry] — *Syn.* unite, unite in marriage, join in holy matrimony; see **marry** 1.

*See Synonym Study at* FASTEN.

**tied,** *modif.* **1.** [Firm] — *Syn.* cinched, fixed, bound, made firm; see **firm** 1.

**2.** [Even] — *Syn.* evenly matched, neck and neck, in a dead heat; see **alike** 2, **equal.**

**tie down,** *v.* — *Syn.* cinch, fix, attach; see **fasten** 1.

**tie in,** *v.* — *Syn.* go with, be in relationship to, be appropriate for; see **join** 1, **relate to.**

**tie into,** *v.* — *Syn.* attack, assault, fight; see **fight** 1, 2.

**tie one on,** *v.* — *Syn.* get drunk, go on a drinking spree, binge; see **drink** 2.

**tier,** *n.* — *Syn.* row, range, layer; see **line** 1.

**tie up,** *v.* **1.** [To fasten] — *Syn.* wrap, package, secure; see **close** 4, **enclose** 1.

**2.** [To obstruct] — *Syn.* hinder, stop, delay; see **hinder.**

**tiff,** *n.* — *Syn.* quarrel, spat, wrangle; see **fight** 1.

**tiger,** *n.* — *Syn.* feline, cat, tigress, tiger-cat, man-eater. Types and breeds of tigers include: Bengal tiger, Royal Bengal tiger, American tiger, Mexican tiger, jaguar, Indian tiger, Siberian tiger, Sumatran tiger, saber-toothed tiger, black tiger, red tiger, white tiger, marbled tiger, marbled tiger-cat, clouded tiger, clouded tiger-cat, margay, ocelot, serval, chati, long-tailed tiger-cat, oceloid leopard.

**tight,** *modif.* **1.** [Firm] — *Syn.* taut, secure, fast, bound up, close, clasped, fixed, steady, tense, stretched thin, established, compact, strong, stable, enduring, steadfast, unyielding, unbending, set, stuck hard, hidebound, invulnerable, snug, sturdy; see also **firm** 1. — *Ant.* LOOSE, tottery, shaky.

**2.** [Closed] — *Syn.* sealed, airtight, impenetrable, impermeable, impervious, watertight, hermetically sealed, padlocked, bolted, locked, fastened, shut tight, clamped, fixed, tied, snapped, swung to, tied up, nailed, spiked, slammed, obstructed, blocked, blind, shut, stopped up, plugged; see also **waterproof.** — *Ant.* OPEN, penetrable, unprotected.

**3.** [Closefitting] — *Syn.* pinching, shrunken, snug, uncomfortable, cramping, skintight, short, crushing, choking, smothering, cutting. — *Ant.* LOOSE, ample, wide.

**4.** [*Intoxicated] — *Syn.* drunk, inebriated, drunken, tipsy; see **drunk.**

**5.** [*Stingy] — *Syn.* miserly, parsimonious, close; see **stingy.**

**6.** [Difficult to obtain; *said especially of money*] — *Syn.* scarce, frozen, tied up; see **rare** 2.

**sit tight★** — *Syn.* do nothing, refrain from action, stay put; see **remain** 1.

---

*SYN.* — **tight** implies a constricting or binding encirclement [*a tight collar*] or such closeness or compactness of parts as to be impenetrable [*airtight*]; **taut** (and often **tight**) is applied to a rope, cord, cloth, etc. that is pulled or stretched to the point where there is no slackness [*taut sails*]; **tense** suggests a tightness or tautness that results in great strain [*tense muscles*] *See also Synonym Study at* DRUNK.

---

**tighten,** *v.* **1.** [To make tight] — *Syn.* compress, condense, squeeze, bind, contract, strangle, constrict, crush, cramp, pinch, grip more tightly, clench, screw down, add pressure; see also **stretch** 2. — *Ant.* LOOSEN, relax, unloose.

**2.** [To become tight] — *Syn.* contract, harden, con-

geal, stiffen, toughen, become more disciplined, become stricter. — *Ant.* melt, SOFTEN, liquefy.

**tightfisted,** *modif.* — *Syn.* thrifty, niggardly, frugal, penny-pinching; see **stingy.**

**tight-lipped,** *modif.* — *Syn.* taciturn, reticent, secretive; see **quiet** 2, **reserved** 3.

**tights,** *n.* — *Syn.* pantyhose, leotard, hosiery, stockings; see **clothes, pants** 1.

**tightwad,** *n.* — *Syn.* muckworm, niggard, scrimp; see **miser** 1.

**tile,** *n.* — *Syn.* baked clay, fired clay, tiled flooring, tiling, tilework, tile roofing, roofing tile, pantile, gutter tile, decorative tile, wall tile, plastic tile, linoleum tile, asphalt tile, vinyl tile, bathroom tile, ceramic tile, drainage tile, pipe, piping, terrazzo; see also **clay, flooring, roofing.**

**till,** *n.* — *Syn.* cash register, drawer, tray, box, moneybox, shelf, cabinet drawer; see also **safe, vault** 2.

**till,** *v.* — *Syn.* cultivate, work, raise crops from; see **farm.**

**tillable,** *modif.* — *Syn.* productive, cultivable, arable; see **fertile** 1.

**tiller,** *n.* — *Syn.* planter, plowman, plower; see **farmer.**

**tilt,** *n.* **1.** [An incline] — *Syn.* slant, slope, angle, dip, rake, drop, fall, slide; see also **inclination** 5. — *Ant.* FLOOR, flat land, level surface.

**2.** [An encounter] — *Syn.* joust, bout, conflict, contest, struggle, skirmish, collision, scrimmage, fracas, tussle, scuffle, meet; see also **attack** 1, **fight** 1.

**at full tilt** — *Syn.* at full speed, charging, speeding; see **moving** 1.

**tilt,** *v.* **1.** [To incline] — *Syn.* slant, tip, turn, set at an angle, lean, slope, rake, slouch, shift, dip, sway, make oblique, turn edgewise; see also **bend** 2. — *Ant.* STRAIGHTEN, level, bring into line.

**2.** [To encounter] — *Syn.* dispute, argue, contend, attack, charge, thrust, combat; see also **fight** 2.

**timber,** *n.* **1.** [Standing trees] — *Syn.* wood, lumber, timberland, wood lot, grove, standing timber, virgin forest, second growth; see also **forest.**

**2.** [A beam] — *Syn.* rib, frame, mast, boom, tie, stringer, sill, post, stake, pole, club, log; see also **beam, lumber.**

**timbre,** *n.* — *Syn.* tone, tonality, resonance, intonation, overtone; see also **pitch** 3.

**time,** *n.* **1.** [Duration] — *Syn.* continuance, lastingness, extent, chronology, past, present, future, infinity, spacetime; see also **today.**

Units of measure for time include: millisecond, age, eon, era, epoch, nanosecond, second, minute, hour, day, week, month, year, term, decade, generation, lifetime, century, millennium, aeon; moment, instant, watch, tour, tour of duty, work period, shift, swing shift★, graveyard shift★, cat-eye shift★.

**2.** [A point in time] — *Syn.* moment, incident, event, occurrence, occasion, time and tide, instant, term, season, tide, course, sequence, point, generation; see also **moment** 1.

**3.** [A period of time] — *Syn.* season, era, interval; see **age** 3, **period** 1.

**4.** [Experience] — *Syn.* background, living, participation; see **experience** 1.

**5.** [Leisure] — *Syn.* opportunity, spare time, free moment, ease, liberty, chance; see also **freedom** 1.

**6.** [Credit] — *Syn.* account, trust, terms, delayable payment; see **credit** 4, **loan.**

**7.** [Circumstances; *usually plural; used with "the"*] — *Syn.* conditions, the present, nowadays, juncture; see **circumstance** 1, **circumstances** 2.

**8.** [A measure of speed] — *Syn.* tempo, beat, rate, meter, rhythm, cadence, swing, accent, bounce★, lift★.

**9.** [A standard of measuring time]. Time zones and standards include: Greenwich, mean, sidereal, apparent, solar, Standard, Atlantic Standard, Eastern Standard, Central Standard, Mountain Standard, Pacific Standard, Yukon Standard, Alaska Standard, Hawaii Standard, Samoa Standard, daylight-savings, astronomical, nautical.

**10.** [A standard of measuring rhythm in music]. Musical times include: simple, compound, duple, two-part, triple, three-part, quadruple, four-part, quintuple, five-part, sextuple, six-part, septuple, seven-part, nonuple, nine-part, three-four, three-quarter, mixed.

**abreast of the times**— *Syn.* up-to-date, informed, aware; see **modern** 1.

**ahead of time**— *Syn.* ahead of schedule, fast, earlier than expected; see **early** 2.

**at one time 1.** simultaneously, concurrently, at once; see **together** 2.

**2.** once, once upon a time, previously.

**at the same time**— *Syn.* simultaneously, concurrently, at once; see **together** 2.

**at times**— *Syn.* occasionally, sometimes, once in a while; see **seldom.**

**behind the times**— *Syn.* out of date, archaic, antediluvian; see **old-fashioned.**

**behind time**— *Syn.* tardy, delayed, coming later; see **late** 1.

**between times**— *Syn.* now and then, occasionally, sometimes; see **seldom.**

**do time★**— *Syn.* serve a prison term, go to jail, be imprisoned; see **serve time.**

**for a time**— *Syn.* awhile, for a while, for some time; see **awhile, temporarily.**

**for some time**— *Syn.* for a while, for quite a while, for a time, for a long time; see **awhile.**

**for the time being**— *Syn.* for the present, for now, under consideration; see **temporarily.**

**from time to time**— *Syn.* occasionally, sometimes, once in a while; see **frequently.**

**in due time**— *Syn.* eventually, at an appropriate time, in the natural course of events; see **finally** 2, **ultimately.**

**in good time**— *Syn.* at the proper time, in a short time, soon; see **quickly** 1.

**in no time**— *Syn.* almost instantly, very rapidly, without delay; see **quickly** 1, **soon** 1.

**in time 1.** eventually, after the proper time, inevitably; see **finally** 2.

**2.** on time, in the nick of time, not a minute too soon, under the wire.

**3.** on the beat, simultaneously, up to tempo; see **together** 2.

**kill time**— *Syn.* fill in the time, waste time, idle; see **wait** 1.

**lose time**— *Syn.* go too slow, tarry, cause a delay; see **delay** 1.

**make time**— *Syn.* gain time, hasten; see **hurry** 1.

**make time with★**— *Syn.* attract, lure, charm; see **seduce.**

**many a time**— *Syn.* often, regularly, consistently; see **frequently.**

**on time 1.** at the appointed time, punctually, correct; see **punctual.**

**2.** by credit, in installments, on account; see **unpaid** 1.

**out of time**— *Syn.* out of pace, unreasonable, improper; see **untimely.**

**pass the time of day**— *Syn.* exchange greetings, chat, converse; see **greet.**

**take one's own (sweet) time**— *Syn.* dawdle, fool around, dilly-dally★; see **delay** 1, **loiter.**

**time,** *v.* — *Syn.* register distance, sound a bell, clock, determine timing of, measure time; see also **measure** 1.

**time and again,** *modif.* — *Syn.* often, many times, repeatedly; see **frequently, regularly** 1.

**time-honored,** *modif.* — *Syn.* revered, eminent, noble; see **immortal** 1, **venerable** 2.

**timeliness,** *n.* — *Syn.* opportuneness, occasion, chance, moment, time and tide, opportunity.

**timely,** *modif.* — *Syn.* opportune, seasonable, in good time, fitting the times, suitable, appropriate, convenient, favorable, propitious, well-timed, modern, up-to-date, newsworthy; see also **fit** 1, 2. — *Ant.* UNFAVORABLE, ill-timed, inappropriate.

---

*SYN.* — **timely** applies to that which happens or is done at an appropriate time, esp. at such a time as to be of help or service *[a timely interruption]*; **opportune** refers to that which is so timed, often as if by accident, as to meet exactly the needs of the occasion *[the opportune arrival of a supply train]*; **seasonable** applies literally to that which is suited to the season of the year or, figuratively, to the moment or occasion *[seasonable weather]*

---

**(the) time of one's life,** *n.* — *Syn.* good time, wonderful time, celebration, fiesta, ball; see also **event** 1, 2.

**time out of mind,** *modif.* — *Syn.* from time immemorial, a long time, years ago; see **old** 3, **past** 1.

**timepiece,** *n.* — *Syn.* timekeeper, chronometer, sundial; see **clock, watch** 1.

**timeserver,** *n.* — *Syn.* self-seeker, temporizer, gold digger; see **opportunist.**

**timeserving,** *modif.* — *Syn.* opportunistic, tricky, sycophantic; see **sly** 1.

**timeworn,** *modif.* **1.** [Old] — *Syn.* antiquated, antique, ancient; see **old** 2, 3.

**2.** [Trite] — *Syn.* hackneyed, clichéd, stale, overused; see **common** 1, **dull** 4.

**timid,** *modif.* **1.** [Cowardly] — *Syn.* fainthearted, fearful, timorous, hesitant, pusillanimous, apprehensive, frightened, nervous, unnerved, tremulous, overcautious, spiritless, weak, weak-kneed, poor-spirited, shaky, feeble, daunted, browbeaten, cowed, intimidated, spineless, cowering, soft★, yellow★, scared spitless★, chicken-livered★, chicken-hearted★, afraid of one's own shadow★, wimpy★; see also **cowardly** 1. — *Ant.* bold, fearless, confident.

**2.** [Reticent] — *Syn.* shy, bashful, timorous, retiring, unassertive, submissive, mousy, diffident, shrinking, withdrawn, modest, shamefaced; see also **humble** 1.

*See Synonym Study at* AFRAID.

**timidity,** *n.* **1.** [Fear] — *Syn.* fearfulness, cowardliness, softness; see **cowardice, fear** 2.

**2.** [Reserve] — *Syn.* calmness, shyness, quiet; see **reserve** 2.

**tin can,** *n.* — *Syn.* tin, can, tin box, hermetically sealed can, No. 1 can, No. 2 can, No. 10 can, vacuum can; see also **container.**

**tinder,** *n.* — *Syn.* touchwood, splinters, kindling; see **fuel, wood** 2.

**tinfoil,** *n.* — *Syn.* tinfoil paper, aluminum foil, foil, lead foil, zinc foil, silver paper★, gold paper★; see also **paper** 5.

**tinge,** *n.* — *Syn.* tincture, shade, hint, trace; see **tint, trace** 1.

*See Synonym Study at* COLOR.

**tingle,** *v.* — *Syn.* shiver, prickle, sting, itch, creep, grow excited, get goose pimples all over\*; see also **thrill.**

**tinker,** *v.* — *Syn.* try to mend, play with, take apart, potter, trifle with, botch, mess around\*, monkey with\*; see also **repair.**

**tinkle,** *v.* — *Syn.* jingle, clink, chink, ring, chime, tintinnabulate, make a thin metallic sound, make a bell-like sound; see also **sound** 1.

**tinkling,** *modif.* — *Syn.* jingling, ringing, chiming; see **sounding.**

**tinsel,** *modif.* — *Syn.* tawdry, gaudy, pretentious, fake, glossy, cheap, catchpenny, alloyed, pseudo; see also **common** 1, **poor** 2.

**tinsmith,** *n.* — *Syn.* tinker, tinman, tinsman; see **craftsman, worker.**

**tint,** *n.* — *Syn.* tinge, hue, shade, color value, cast, flush, dye, coloring, tinct, taint, glow, pastel color, luminous color, pale hue, tone, tincture, dash, touch, chroma, luminosity, coloration, pigmentation, ground color, complexion; see also **color** 1. — *Ant.* WHITENESS, flatness, colorlessness.

*See Synonym Study at* COLOR.

**tinted,** *modif.* — *Syn.* colored, shaded, dyed, tinged, painted, tinctured, washed, stained, distempered, crayoned, touched up.

**tintinnabulation,** *n.* — *Syn.* ringing, jingle, resonance; see **noise** 1.

**tinware,** *n.* — *Syn.* tinwork, plateware, kitchenware, pots and pans; see **utensil.**

**tiny,** *modif.* — *Syn.* small, miniature, diminutive; see **little** 1.

*See Synonym Study at* SMALL.

**tip,** *n.* **1.** [The point] — *Syn.* apex, peak, top, summit, cap, nip, stub; see also **point** 2. — *Ant.* BOTTOM, middle, body.
**2.** [A gratuity] — *Syn.* reward, gift, compensation, fee, small change, money, lagniappe, *pourboire* (French), baksheesh, handout\*, grease\*, Boston quarter\*; see also **pay** 2.
**3.** [\*A bit of information] — *Syn.* hint, clue, warning, pointer, suggestion, inkling, whisper, inside information, advice, a word to the wise\*, dope\*, inside wire\*, hot steer\*, in\*, bug\*, bang\*, buzz\*; see also **knowledge** 1, **news** 1.

**tip,** *v.* — *Syn.* slant, incline, shift; see **bend** 1, **lean** 1, **tilt** 1.

**tipsy\*,** *modif.* — *Syn.* intoxicated, inebriated, tight\*; see **drunk.**

*See Synonym Study at* DRUNK.

**tiptop,** *modif.* **1.** [Topmost] — *Syn.* apical, uppermost, supreme; see **highest.**
**2.** [\*Best] — *Syn.* superior, prime, choice; see **best** 1, **excellent.**

**tirade,** *n.* — *Syn.* harangue, diatribe, invective; see **anger, dispute.**

**tire,** *n.* — *Syn.* wheel, casing, tire and tube; see **wheel** 1. Varieties of tires include: tubeless, radial, steel-belted radial, snow, mud, all-terrain, studded, whitewall, puncture-proof, recapped, low-pressure, synthetic, natural rubber, solid rubber, pneumatic, oversize, airplane, automobile, motorcycle, bicycle, recap\*, retread\*, spare\*, baloney\*, doughnut\*, rubber toe\*, sneaker\*, shoe\*.

**tire,** *v.* **1.** [To become exhausted] — *Syn.* grow weary, to become fagged, break down, droop, flag, jade, pall, faint, drop, puff, sink, yawn, collapse, give out, prostrate, wilt\*, go stale\*, poop out\*, burn out\*, burn the candle at both ends\*; see also **weary** 2. — *Ant.* REST, awake, relax.

**2.** [To make a person exhausted] — *Syn.* tax, overtax, harass, fatigue, exhaust, overwork, strain, overstrain, overburden, depress, dispirit, pain, vex, worry, distress, deject, dishearten, unman, prostrate, wear out, run a person ragged\*, do up\*, do in\*, take the tuck out of\*; see also **weary** 1.
**3.** [To bore] — *Syn.* annoy, exasperate, displease; see **bother** 2, **weary** 1.

**tired,** *modif.* — *Syn.* fatigued, weary, run-down, exhausted, overworked, overtaxed, wearied, worn, spent, wasted, burned out, worn-out, jaded, narcoleptic, drooping, distressed, unmanned, drowsy, droopy, sleepy, haggard, faint, prostrated, broken-down, drained, consumed, empty, collapsing, all in\*, finished\*, stale\*, pooped out\*, fagged\*, dog-tired\*, dead on one's feet\*, pooped\*, done in, done for\*, beat up\*, worn to a frazzle\*, played out\*, tuckered out\*, fed up\*; see also **bored, weak** 1, **worn** 2. — *Ant.* ACTIVE, lively, energetic.

---

**SYN.** — **tired** is applied to one who has been drained of much of his strength and energy through exertion, boredom, impatience, etc. [*tired* by years of hard toil]; **weary** (or **wearied**) suggests such depletion of energy or interest as to make one unable or unwilling to continue [*weary* of study]; **exhausted** implies a total draining of strength and energy; **fatigued** refers to one who has lost so much energy through prolonged exertion that rest and sleep are essential [*fatigued* at the end of the day]; **fagged**, an informal word, suggests great exhaustion or fatigue from hard, unremitting work or exertion [completely *fagged* after a set of tennis]

---

**tireless,** *modif.* — *Syn.* unwearied, unwearying, untiring, indefatigable, unflagging, incessant, hard-working, strenuous, energetic, resolute, steadfast, persevering; see also **active** 2, **enthusiastic** 1, 3. — *Ant.* TIRED, weak, listless.

**tire out,** *v.* **1.** [To become tired] — *Syn.* become exhausted, be exhausted, get tired, be overcome; see **fail** 1, **weary** 2.
**2.** [To make tired] — *Syn.* overcome, exhaust, wear down; see **defeat** 1, **weary** 1.

**tiresome,** *modif.* — *Syn.* irksome, wearying, monotonous; see **dull** 4.

**tissue,** *n.* **1.** [A network] — *Syn.* web, mesh, filigree, crossing, parcel, bundle, mass, sheaf, series; see also **network** 2.
**2.** [Thin fabric] — *Syn.* gauze, gossamer, cobwebby material, chiffon, lace, silk, webbing, scarfing; see also **cloth, veil, web** 1.
**3.** [Protective layer, especially in living organisms] — *Syn.* film, membrane, intercellular substance, parenchyma, prosenchyma, adipose tissue, muscular tissue, vascular tissue, fibrous tissue, connective tissue, nervous tissue; see also **muscle.**
**4.** [A soft paper] — *Syn.* facial tissue, toilet tissue, toilet paper, Kleenex (trademark).

**tissue paper,** *n.* — *Syn.* wrapping paper, gift wrappings, sanitary paper, onionskin paper, sheet, paper handkerchief; see also **paper** 5.

**titan,** *n.* — *Syn.* colossus, Hercules, Gargantua; see **giant** 1, 2, **monster** 1.

**titanic,** *modif.* — *Syn.* huge, colossal, enormous; see **large** 1.

**tit for tat,** *n.* — *Syn.* reprisal, retribution, requital; see **exchange** 2, **revenge** 1.

**tithe,** *n.* — *Syn.* ratable tax, assessment, levy, ten-percent contribution; see **tax** 1.

**titillate,** *v.* — *Syn.* tickle, stimulate, arouse, turn on*; see **excite** 1, 2.

**titillation,** *n.* — *Syn.* tickling, thrill, stimulation; see **excitement.**

**title,** *n.* **1.** [A designation] — *Syn.* book name, indication, heading, caption, inscription, headline, subtitle, sign, appellation; see also **name** 1.
**2.** [Ownership or evidence of ownership] — *Syn.* holding, right, claim, due, power, license; see also **deed,** 2, **ownership.**
**3.** [Mark of rank or dignity] — *Syn.* honorific, appellation, form of address, epithet, commission, decoration, medal, ribbon, coat of arms, crest, cordon, order, authority, privilege, degree; see also **emblem.**
Titles include: Sir, Doctor, Mr., Mrs., Miss, Ms, Reverend, Bishop, Archbishop, Cardinal, Pope, Monsignor, Father, Rabbi, Dame, King, Prince, Baron, Viscount, Earl, Marquis, Marquise, Duke, Grand Duke, Knight, Count, Czar, Tsar, Emperor, Empress, Sultan, Khan, Emir, Pasha, Mirza, Sahib, Effendi, Queen, Duchess, Lady, Princess, Marchioness, Viscountess, Countess, Monsieur, Madame, Mademoiselle, Señor, Señorita, Señora, Don, Doña, Herr, Fräulein, Frau, General, Colonel, Major, Captain, Lieutenant, Admiral, Commander, Sergeant, Ensign, President, Vice-President, Secretary, Speaker, Governor, Mayor, Judge, Ambassador, Representative, Senator.
**4.** [A championship] — *Syn.* cup, trophy, first place.

**titter,** *n.* — *Syn.* giggle, snicker, snigger; see **laugh.**
*See Synonym Study at* LAUGH.

**titter,** *v.* — *Syn.* giggle, snicker, twitter; see **laugh.**

**tittle,** *n.* — *Syn.* iota, jot, speck, particle; see **bit** 1.

**titular,** *modif.* — *Syn.* nominal, in name only, eponymous; see **so-called.**

**to,** *prep.* **1.** [In the direction of] — *Syn.* toward, via, into, facing, through, directed toward, traveling to, along the line of.
**2.** [Indicating position] — *Syn.* over, upon, on, in front of, before.
**3.** [Until] — *Syn.* till, up to, extending to, stopping at; see **until.**
**4.** [So that] — *Syn.* in order to, so, that one may, for the purpose of.
**5.** [Indicating degree] — *Syn.* up to, down to, as far as, in that degree, to this extent.
**6.** [Indicating result] — *Syn.* becoming, until, back, ending with.

**toadstool,** *n.* — *Syn.* fungus, fungous growth, basidiomycetous fungus, sporophore, fairies'-table, frog's-stool, toad's-meat, poisonous mushroom; see also **mushroom, plant.**

**toady,** *n.* — *Syn.* parasite, flatterer, fawner; see **sycophant.**

**to and fro,** *modif.* — *Syn.* seesaw, zigzag, back and forth, backward and forward, backwards and forwards, in and out, up and down, from side to side, from pillar to post, off and on, round and round, hitch and hike, forward and back, like buckets in a well.

**toast,** *n.* **1.** [A sentiment or person drunk to] — *Syn.* pledge, proposal, celebration, ceremony, salute, compliment, commemoration, acknowledgment, thanksgiving; see also **honor** 1.
Invitations for toasts include: here's to you, good luck, lest we forget, your health, Sir; *prosit* (German), *skoal* (Scandinavian), *salud* (Spanish), *a votre santé* (French), *lekhaim* (Yiddish), *slainte* (Irish), down the hatch*, here's how*, bottoms up*, here's mud in your eye*, here's looking at you*, cheers* (British).
**2.** [Browned bread]. Varieties of toast include: white,

rye, whole-wheat, Zwieback, pumpernickel, sourdough, honey, Melba, French, milk, cinnamon, raisin; see also **bread** 1.

**toast,** *v.* **1.** [To honor by drinking liquor] — *Syn.* drink to, pay homage to, drink to someone's health, celebrate, pledge, compliment, propose a toast, name, glorify, make special mention of; see also **drink** 2, **praise** 1.
**2.** [To brown bread] — *Syn.* put in a toaster, heat, dry, cook, crisp, parch, grill.

**tobacco,** *n.* — *Syn.* weed*, nicotine, smoke, chew, filthy weed*, coffin nails*, cancer stick*, fragrant weed*.
Forms and varieties of tobacco include: cigarette, cigar, chewing tobacco, pipe tobacco, quid of tobacco, smoking tobacco, snuff; see also **smoking.**

**toboggan,** *n.* — *Syn.* sledge, sleigh, bobsled; see **sled** 1, 2.

**tocsin,** *n.* — *Syn.* alarm bell, horn, siren, signal; see **alarm** 1, **warning.**

**today,** *n.* — *Syn.* this day, the present, our time, this moment; see **now** 1.

**toddle,** *v.* — *Syn.* waddle, stalk, wobble; see **walk** 1.

**to-do,** *n.* — *Syn.* commotion, stir, fuss; see **disorder** 2, **fight** 1.

**toe,** *n.* — *Syn.* digit, phalanx, front of the foot, tip of a shoe; see **appendage** 2.
**on one's toes*** — *Syn.* alert, aware, attentive; see **careful.**
**step** or **tread on someone's toes** — *Syn.* annoy, offend, disturb, intrude; see **anger** 1.

**toe the line** or **mark,** *v.* — *Syn.* follow the rules, be good, conform, mind; see **behave** 2.

**together,** *modif.* **1.** [Jointly] — *Syn.* collectively, unitedly, commonly; see **mutually.**
**2.** [Simultaneously] — *Syn.* at the same time, concurrently, coincidentally, synchronically, contemporaneously, concomitantly, at once, in connection with, at a blow, in unison, at one jump, in sync.

**togetherness*,** *n.* — *Syn.* fellow feeling, family feeling, community of interest, affection; see **friendship** 1, 2, **love** 1, **society** 2.

**togs*,** *n.* — *Syn.* clothing, outfit, attire; see **clothes.**

**toil,** *n.* — *Syn.* labor, occupation, drudgery; see **work** 2.

**toil,** *v.* — *Syn.* sweat, labor, slave; see **work.**

**toiler,** *n.* — *Syn.* worker, apprentice, workman; see **laborer.**

**toilet,** *n.* **1.** [Grooming one's person] — *Syn.* ablutions, dressing, morning preparations, bath, haircut, shave, shower, hairdressing, applying cosmetics, wash-up*, tidy-up*, make-up*, crumb-up*.
**2.** [A room for privacy] — *Syn.* water closet, lavatory, washroom, restroom, men's room, women's room, powder room, gentlemen's room, ladies' room, comfort station, bathroom, bath, privy, latrine, garderobe, head, amenity, necessarium, little boy's room*, little girl's room*, potty*, W.C.* (British), can*, altar room*, chamber of commerce*, poet's corner*, pot*, john*, throne room*.

**toilsome,** *modif.* **1.** [Difficult] — *Syn.* laborious, strenuous, hard; see **difficult** 1.
**2.** [Dull] — *Syn.* tedious, boring, wearisome; see **dull** 4.

**token,** *n.* — *Syn.* mark, symbol, indication, keepsake; see **emblem, gift** 1, **pledge, sign** 1, **souvenir.**
**by the same token** — *Syn.* following from this, similarly, likewise, thus; see **besides, therefore.**
**in token of** — *Syn.* as evidence of, by way of, as a gesture; see **representing** 1.
*See Synonym Study at* PLEDGE.

**told,** *modif.* — *Syn.* recounted, recorded, set down, reported, known, chronicled, revealed, exposed, made known, said, published, printed, announced, released, described, stated, set forth, included in the official statement, made public property, become common knowledge, related, depicted, enunciated, pronounced, given out, handed down, telegraphed, broadcast, telecast, included in a release, told in open court, confessed, admitted, well-known, discovered; see also **known** 2, **spoken**. — *Ant.* SECRET, concealed, unknown.

**tolerable,** *modif.* **1.** [Bearable] — *Syn.* endurable, sufferable, sustainable; see **bearable**.
**2.** [Passable] — *Syn.* fairly good, adequate, mediocre, average; see **common** 1, **poor** 2.

**tolerance,** *n.* **1.** [Open-mindedness] — *Syn.* lenity, concession, liberality, permission, forbearance, indulgence, mercy, compassion, license, sufferance, grace, freedom of worship, understanding, sensitivity, charity, benevolence, humanity, endurance, altruism, patience, good will; see also **kindness** 1, **liberalism**.
**2.** [Saturation point] — *Syn.* threshold, tolerance level, end; see **limit** 2.
**3.** [Resistance] — *Syn.* immunity, susceptibility, toleration.

**tolerant,** *modif.* — *Syn.* understanding, receptive, sophisticated; see **liberal** 2, **patient** 1.

**tolerate,** *v.* **1.** [To allow] — *Syn.* permit, consent to, authorize, put up with, stand for*; see also **allow** 1.
**2.** [To endure] — *Syn.* bear, undergo, abide, stand; see **endure** 2.
*See Synonym Study at* ENDURE.

**toll,** *n.* **1.** [Charges] — *Syn.* duty, fee, customs, exaction, tollage; see also **price**.
**2.** [Loss] — *Syn.* casualties, deaths, losses; see **damage** 2.

**toll,** *v.* — *Syn.* knell, strike, ring, sound, peal; see also **ring** 3.

**tomahawk,** *n.* — *Syn.* Indian club, hatchet, ax, war ax, stone ax, poggamoggan; see also **club** 3.

**tomato,** *n.* — *Syn.* tomato vine, tomato plant, tree tomato, love-apple, *pomme d'amour* (French), *tomate* (Spanish), *jitomate* (Spanish), *Lycopersicon* (Latin); see also **plant, vegetable**.

**tomb,** *n.* — *Syn.* vault, crypt, burial chamber, mausoleum; see **grave** 1, **monument** 1.

**tomboy,** *n.* — *Syn.* rowdy girl, hoyden, spitfire*; see **girl** 1.

**tombstone,** *n.* — *Syn.* monument, gravestone, headstone, memorial, footstone, stone, marker, cross, funerary statue.

**tomcat,** *n.* — *Syn.* male cat, tom, tommy, boar cat; see **cat** 1.

**tome,** *n.* — *Syn.* book, album, portfolio, document; see **publication** 1, **writing** 2.

**tomfoolery,** *n.* — *Syn.* silliness, horseplay, frolic; see **fun**.

**tommy gun,** *n.* — *Syn.* automatic rifle, submachine gun, machine gun; see **gun** 2, **rifle**.

**tomorrow,** *n.* — *Syn.* the morrow, next day in the course of time, the future, *mañana* (Spanish); see **day** 2.

**tom-tom,** *n.* — *Syn.* tabla, taboret, tambourine; see **drum**.

**ton,** *n.* — *Syn.* twelve hundredweight, two thousand pounds, short ton, metric ton, tonne, a thousand kilograms, long ton, shipping ton, displacement ton, measurement ton, freight ton; see also **weight** 1, 2.

**tone,** *n.* **1.** [A musical sound] — *Syn.* pitch, timbre, resonance; see **sound** 2.
**2.** [Quality] — *Syn.* nature, trend, temper; see **character** 1.

**3.** [Manner] — *Syn.* expression, condition, aspect, mode, habit; see also **mood** 1.
**4.** [A degree of color] — *Syn.* hue, tint, color value, blend, tinge, cast, coloration; see also **color** 1.

**tone down,** *v.* **1.** [To dim] — *Syn.* darken, deepen, cloud; see **shade** 2.
**2.** [To soften] — *Syn.* subdue, moderate, temper; see **soften** 2.

**tongs,** *n.* — *Syn.* pinchers, pincers, pliers, forceps, pair of tongs, sugar tongs, fire tongs, ice tongs, blacksmith's tongs; see also **tool** 1, **utensil**.

**tongue,** *n.* **1.** [The movable muscle in the mouth] — *Syn.* organ of taste, organ of speech, lingua, lingula, blabber*, clacker*, lapper*; see also **muscle, organ** 2. Parts of the tongue used in speech are: tip, apex, front, center, back.
**2.** [Speech] — *Syn.* speech, utterance, discourse; see **language** 1.
**3.** [Something resembling a tongue, sense 1] — *Syn.* shoe tongue, wagon pole, neap, bell clapper, peninsula, movable pin.

**find one's tongue** — *Syn.* recover one's ability to talk, speak up, begin talking; see **talk** 1.

**hold one's tongue** — *Syn.* refrain from speaking, hold back, keep silent; see **restrain** 1.

**on the tip of one's tongue** — *Syn.* forgotten, not quite remembered, not readily recalled; see **forgotten**.

**tongue-lashing,** *n.* — *Syn.* scolding, rebuke, reprimand.

**tongue-tied,** *modif.* **1.** [Mute] — *Syn.* silent, speechless, aphonic; see **dumb** 1, **mute** 1.
**2.** [Inarticulate] — *Syn.* reticent, nervous, inarticulate; see **reserved** 3.

**tonic,** *n.* **1.** [An invigorating mixture] — *Syn.* stimulant, bracer, refresher, invigorator, medicine, conditioner, hair tonic, liver tonic, mineral water, quinine water, patent medicine; see also **drug** 2.
**2.** [*Soda] — *Syn.* pop, soda pop, soft drink; see **soda**.

**tonight,** *n.* — *Syn.* this evening, this p.m., this night, later; see **night** 1.

**tonnage,** *n.* — *Syn.* load, burden, cargo, capacity, contents.

**tonsillitis,** *n.* — *Syn.* inflammation of the tonsils, quinsy, amygdalitis; see **disease**.

**tonsured,** *modif.* — *Syn.* shaven, clipped, shorn; see **bald** 1.

**too,** *modif.* **1.** [Also] — *Syn.* as well, likewise, in addition, additionally, moreover, furthermore, further, besides; see also **also**.
**2.** [In excess] — *Syn.* excessively, over, overmuch, exceedingly, extremely, beyond measure, over and above; see also **besides**.

**tool,** *n.* **1.** [An implement] — *Syn.* implement, utensil, machine, instrument, mechanism, weapon, apparatus, appliance, engine, means, contrivance, gadget; see also **device** 1.
Common tools include: can opener, hammer, mallet, knife, adz, vise, auger, lathe, router, sander, scraper, trowel, awl, hoe, shovel, rake, spade, jack, crank, pulley, wheel, bar, crowbar, lever, sledge, winch, cam, loom, shuttle, chisel, plane, screw, brace, bit, file, saw, drill, square, chisel, shears, screwdriver, wrench, pliers, tweezers, punch, level, scissors, ax, hatchet, corkscrew, jimmy.
**2.** [One who permits himself to be used] — *Syn.* accessory, auxiliary, accomplice, hireling, dupe, intermediary, cat's-paw, medium, vehicle, agent, go-between, messenger, easy mark, stool pigeon*, jay*, hayseed*, green-

horn*, sucker*, patsy*, stooge*, come-on*, tuna*; see also **servant**.

*SYN.* — **tool** is commonly applied to manual implements such as are used in carpentry, plumbing, etc.; **implement** applies to any device used to carry on some work or effect some purpose [agricultural *implements*]; **instrument** specifically implies use for delicate work or for scientific or artistic purposes [surgical *instruments*] and may also be applied, as are **tool** and **implement**, to a thing or person serving as a means to an end; **appliance** specifically suggests a mechanical or power-driven device, esp. one for household use; **utensil** is used of any implement or container for domestic use, esp. a pot, pan, etc.

**too much,** *n.* — *Syn.* excessiveness, extravagance, fabulousness, preposterousness, overgoing, overcharge, ever so much, more than can be used, *embarras de richesses* (French), superfluity, inordinateness, vastness, prodigiousness, immensity; see also **excess** 1. — *Ant.* LACK, want, shortage.

**tooth,** *n.* 1. [A dental process] — *Syn.* fang, tusk, sabertooth, tush, ivory, snag, artificial tooth, false tooth, edontate process, calcereous process, bony appendage.
Types of human teeth include: incisor, canine, cuspid, eyetooth*, bicuspid, premolar, first bicuspid, second bicuspid, molar*, grinder*, first molar, second molar, third molar, wisdom tooth; deciduous teeth, baby teeth*, permanent teeth.
2. [A toothlike or tooth-shaped object] — *Syn.* point, stub, projection; see **gear, peg, root.**
**get** or **sink one's teeth into*** — *Syn.* become occupied with, involve oneself in, be busy at; see **act** 1.
**in the teeth of** — *Syn.* in the face of, in conflict with, defying; see **opposing** 1.
**long in the tooth*** — *Syn.* elderly, aged, ancient; see **old** 1.
**show one's teeth*** — *Syn.* show hostility, oppose, be angry; see **threaten** 1, 2.
**throw in someone's teeth*** — *Syn.* reprimand, reproach, castigate; see **attack** 2, **censure.**

*SYN.* — **tooth** is the general, inclusive word for the hard, bonelike structures in the jaws of most vertebrates used for biting and chewing; **tusk** refers to a long, pointed, enlarged tooth projecting outside the mouth in certain animals, as the elephant, wild boar, and walrus, and used for digging or as a weapon; **fang** refers either to one of the long, sharp teeth with which meat-eating animals tear their prey or to the long, hollow tooth through which poisonous snakes inject their venom

**toothache,** *n.* — *Syn.* pain in the tooth, aching tooth, swollen gums, abscessed tooth, cavity, caries, decayed tooth; see also **pain** 2.
**tooth and nail,** *modif.* — *Syn.* energetically, fervently, forcefully; see **eagerly, fiercely, vigorously.**
**tooth-shaped,** *modif.* — *Syn.* toothlike, dentoid, dentiform; see **conical, sharp** 2.
**toothsome,** *modif.* — *Syn.* palatable, tasty, appetizing; see **delicious** 1.
**top,** *modif.* 1. [Highest] — *Syn.* topmost, uppermost, highest, on the upper end; see **highest.** — *Ant.* bottommost, LOWEST, bottom.
2. [Best] — *Syn.* prime, head, first, among the first; see **best** 1.
**top,** *n.* 1. [The uppermost portion] — *Syn.* peak, summit, crown, head, crest, tip, apex, cap, crowning point,

acme, headpiece, capital, pinnacle, zenith, consummation, spire, knap, finial; see also **height** 1. — *Ant.* BOTTOM, lower end, nadir.
2. [A cover] — *Syn.* lid, roof, ceiling; see **cover** 1.
3. [A spinning toy] — *Syn.* spinner, peg top, whipping top, musical top, whistling top, teetotum, put-and-take top, dreidel; see also **toy** 1.
4. [*The leader] — *Syn.* head, captain, chief, master; see **chief** 1, **leader** 2.
**blow one's top*** — *Syn.* lose one's temper, become angry, be enraged; see **rage** 1.
**off the top of one's head*** — *Syn.* speaking offhand, chatting, casually, off the cuff; see **extemporaneous.**
**on top** — *Syn.* prosperous, thriving, superior, at the top; see **successful.**
**top,** *v.* 1. [To remove the top] — *Syn.* prune, lop off, trim, cut off, decapitate, scrape off, pare down, shave off, amputate, file off, pollard, truncate, shear; see also **cut** 1.
2. [To exceed] — *Syn.* better, beat, excel, surpass, go beyond, overrun; see also **exceed.** — *Ant.* APPROACH, approximate, come near to.
3. [To apply topping] — *Syn.* cover, dye, roof, superimpose, spread over, hood, cloak, screen, protect, reinforce, clothe, coat; see also **paint** 2.
**topcoat,** *n.* — *Syn.* overcoat, spring coat, fall coat, duster, raincoat, raglan, topper*; see also **coat** 1.
**top-drawer,** *modif.* — *Syn.* of first importance, superior, very good, best; see **excellent.**
**toper,** *n.* — *Syn.* drinker, alcoholic, lush; see **drunkard.**
**top hat,** *n.* — *Syn.* opera hat, silk hat, beaver, high hat, topper, crush hat, gibus hat, collapsible hat, stovepipe hat*, chimney pot*, skyscraper*; see also **hat.**
**top-heavy,** *modif.* — *Syn.* overweight, unstable, bulky, tottering, unbalanced, overloaded, cumbersome, disproportionate, overcapitalized; see also **shaky** 1. — *Ant.* BALANCED, equalized, ballasted.
**topic,** *n.* — *Syn.* question, theme, subject, text, thesis, theorem, material, proposition, resolution, motion, argument, field of inquiry, point, point in question, matter, matter in hand, problem, moot point, affair, division, head, issue.
*See Synonym Study at* SUBJECT.
**topical,** *modif.* 1. [Local] — *Syn.* confined, limited, insular; see **local** 1, **restricted.**
2. [Current] — *Syn.* thematic, nominal, subjective; see **modern** 1.
**topless*,** *modif.* — *Syn.* almost nude, bare to the waist, bare-breasted, exposed; see **naked** 1.
**top-level,** *modif.* — *Syn.* leading, superior, supreme; see **excellent, important** 1.
**toplofty*,** *modif.* — *Syn.* haughty, pompous, arrogant; see **egotistic** 2.
**topmost,** *modif.* — *Syn.* uppermost, first, leading; see **highest.**
**top off,** *v.* — *Syn.* finish, end, bring to a conclusion; see **complete** 1.
**topple,** *v.* — *Syn.* tumble, plunge, go down, go over, push over, overthrow; see also **fall** 1.
**top-secret,** *modif.* — *Syn.* restricted, confidential, kept quiet, hush-hush*; see **secret** 1, 2.
**topsy-turvy,** *modif.* — *Syn.* confused, upside down, disordered, disarranged, disheveled, tangled, muddled, unhinged, out of gear, disorganized, pell-mell, disjointed, out of joint, untidy, tumultuous, riotous, dislocated, jumbled, chaotic, cluttered, littered, messy*, cockeyed*; see also **disorderly** 1. — *Ant.* ORDERLY, ordered, systematic.

**torch,** *n.* — *Syn.* beacon, light, flare, firebrand; see **flashlight.**

**carry a torch for★** — *Syn.* pine for, miss desperately, love in vain; see **love** 1.

**toreador,** *n.* — *Syn.* bullfighter, picador, *torero* (Spanish); see **matador.**

**torment,** *n.* — *Syn.* agony, suffering, misery; see **pain** 1, 2, **torture.**

**torment,** *v.* — *Syn.* abuse, mistreat, torture, irritate; see **hurt** 1.

**tormentor,** *n.* — *Syn.* oppressor, persecutor, torturer; see **dictator, enemy** 1, 2, **rascal.**

**torn,** *modif.* — *Syn.* ripped, slit, split, severed, lacerated, mutilated, broken, rent, fractured, cracked, slashed, gashed, ruptured, snapped, sliced, burst, cleaved, wrenched, divided, pulled out, impaired, damaged, spoiled; see also **ruined** 1. — *Ant.* WHOLE, repaired, adjusted.

**tornado,** *n.* — *Syn.* whirlwind, cyclone, twister, hurricane, typhoon, blow; see also **storm** 1, **wind** 1.

**torpedo,** *n.* — *Syn.* projectile, underwater missile, fish★, whale★, flying pig★; see also **weapon** 1.
Types of torpedoes include: aerial torpedo, submarine torpedo, jet torpedo, mechanical torpedo, radio-controlled torpedo, projectile, missile, mine, see also **weapon** 1.

**torpid,** *modif.* **1.** [Inactive] — *Syn.* dormant, motionless, inert; see **idle** 1, **latent.**

**2.** [Apathetic] — *Syn.* heavy, sluggish, drowsy; see **dull** 3.

**torpor,** *n.* **1.** [Stupor] — *Syn.* coma, dormancy, latency, inactivity; see **stupor.**

**2.** [Apathy] — *Syn.* dullness, sluggishness, apathy, inanition; see **indifference** 1, **laziness.**

**torque,** *n.* — *Syn.* circulatory force, twist, revolving; see **energy** 3, **revolution** 1.

**torrent,** *n.* — *Syn.* overflow, rushing water, current, violent flow, deluge, downpour; see also **flood** 1, **flow.**

**torrid,** *modif.* **1.** [Tropic] — *Syn.* tropical, austral, broiling, blazing, fiery, sweltering; see also **hot** 1, **tropic** 1.

**2.** [Passionate] — *Syn.* ardent, zealous, impassioned, fervent; see **passionate** 2.

**torso,** *n.* — *Syn.* trunk, thorax, caudex; see **body** 3.

**tortuous,** *modif.* **1.** [Winding] — *Syn.* snaky, sinuous, twisting; see **crooked** 1, **winding.**

**2.** [Not straightforward] — *Syn.* deceitful, devious, perverse, tricky; see **wicked** 1, 2.

**torture,** *n.* — *Syn.* pain, anguish, agony, torment, tribulation, rack, crucifixion, cruciation, martyrdom, pang, dolor, ache, twinge, physical suffering, mental suffering, hell on earth, bed of Procrustes; see also **cruelty.** — *Ant.* COMFORT, enjoyment, delight.

**torture,** *v.* **1.** [To torment] — *Syn.* annoy, irritate, disturb; see **abuse** 1, **bother** 2.

**2.** [To injure] — *Syn.* wound, lacerate, whip; see **beat** 2, **hurt** 1.

**Tory,** *n.* — *Syn.* traditionalist, loyalist, cavalier, reactionary, extreme conservative; see also **conservative.**

**toss,** *v.* **1.** [To throw easily] — *Syn.* hurl, fling, cast; see **throw** 1.

**2.** [To move up and down] — *Syn.* bob, buffet, stir, move restlessly, tumble, pitch, roll, heave, sway, flounder, rock, wobble, undulate, swing, rise and fall; see also **wave** 3.

*See Synonym Study at* THROW.

**toss off,** *v.* — *Syn.* drink up, drink down, swallow, gulp down; see **drink** 1, 2.

**toss-up★,** *n.* — *Syn.* deadlock, bet, draw; see **tie** 4.

**tot,** *n.* — *Syn.* child, infant, toddler, youngster; see **baby** 1.

**total,** *modif.* **1.** [Whole] — *Syn.* entire, inclusive, complete, cumulative; see **whole** 1.

**2.** [Utter] — *Syn.* complete, utter, thorough; see **absolute** 1.

*See Synonym Study at* COMPLETE.

**total,** *n.* — *Syn.* sum, entirety, result; see **whole.**

*See Synonym Study at* SUM.

**total,** *v.* **1.** [To add] — *Syn.* figure, calculate, count up, ring up, tag up, sum up, add up; see also **add** 1.

**2.** [To amount to] — *Syn.* consist of, come to, add up to; see **amount to, equal.**

**totaling,** *modif.* — *Syn.* amounting to, reckoning, calculating, adding, casting, to the amount of.

**totalitarian,** *modif.* — *Syn.* fascistic, despotic, dictatorial; see **absolute** 3, **autocratic** 1, **tyrannical.**

**totalitarianism,** *n.* — *Syn.* despotism, tyranny, dictatorship; see **fascism, tyranny.**

**totality,** *n.* — *Syn.* entirety, everything, oneness, collectivity; see **whole.**

**totally,** *modif.* — *Syn.* entirely, wholly, exclusively; see **completely.**

**tote★,** *v.* — *Syn.* take, haul, transport; see **carry** 1.

**totem,** *n.* — *Syn.* fetish, symbol, crest; see **emblem.**

**totter,** *v.* **1.** [To be near falling] — *Syn.* shake, rock, careen, lurch, quake, tremble, seesaw, teeter, dodder, crumple, sway, wobble, be loose, be weak; see also **wave** 3.

**2.** [To stagger] — *Syn.* stumble, falter, trip, weave, zigzag, reel, rock, roll, walk drunkenly, wobble, waver, hesitate.

**touch,** *n.* **1.** [The tactile sense] — *Syn.* feeling, touching, feel, perception, tactility, taction.

**2.** [Contact] — *Syn.* rub, stroke, pat, petting, fondling, rubbing, stroking, licking, handling, graze, scratch, brush, taste, nudge, kiss, peck, embrace, hug, cuddling, caress.

**3.** [★The act of borrowing] — *Syn.* cadging, begging, mooching★; see **loan.**

**4.** [A sensation] — *Syn.* sense, impression, apprehension, impact, pressure; see also **feeling** 2.

**5.** [Skill] — *Syn.* knack★, technique, finish; see **ability** 2, **method** 2, **talent** 1.

**6.** [A trace] — *Syn.* suggestion, scent, inkling; see **bit** 1.

**in touch** — *Syn.* in contact, attuned, acquainted, in close communication, within reach; see also **familiar with, in contact with** 2 at **contact.**

**out of touch 1.** not in communication, estranged, out of reach.

**2.** naive, inexperienced, uninformed; see **unaware.**

**touch,** *v.* **1.** [To be in contact] — *Syn.* stroke, graze, rub, pat, pet, nudge, thumb, finger, paw, lick, taste, brush, kiss, glance, sweep, caress, fondle, smooth, massage, sip, partake; see also **feel** 1.

**2.** [To come into contact with] — *Syn.* meet, encounter, arrive at, reach, get to, come to, attain, stop at, call at, visit. — *Ant.* PASS, MISS, AVOID.

**3.** [To relate to] — *Syn.* involve, refer to, bear on, pertain to, regard, affect, belong to, be associated with, center upon; see also **concern** 1.

**4.** [To tinge] — *Syn.* tint, brush, retouch, taint, blemish, spot, color, stain.

**5.** [★To borrow from] — *Syn.* get from, obtain from, beg from; see **borrow** 1.

**6.** [To discuss] — *Syn.* touch on, touch upon, treat, go over; see **discuss.**

**7.** [To affect emotionally] — *Syn.* move, stir, affect, impress; see **move** 3.

*See Synonym Study at* AFFECT.

**touchable,** *modif.* — *Syn.* tactual, material, actual; see **real** 2, **tangible.**

**touch-and-go,** *modif.* **1.** [Hasty] — *Syn.* rapid, casual, superficial; see **shallow** 2.
**2.** [Risky] — *Syn.* ticklish, hazardous, tricky; see **dangerous** 1, 2, **uncertain** 2.

**touchdown,** *n.* **1.** [A goal in football] — *Syn.* goal, score, six points, counter\*, marker\*, touch\*.
**2.** [A landing] — *Syn.* arrival, touching down, coming in\*, approach.

**touch down,** *v.* — *Syn.* alight, descend, settle; see **arrive** 1, **land** 4.

**touched,** *modif.* **1.** [Having been in slight contact] — *Syn.* fingered, nudged, used, brushed, handled, rubbed, stroked, rearranged, kissed, grazed, licked, tasted, fondled.
**2.** [Affected] — *Syn.* moved, impressed, stirred; see **affected** 1.
**3.** [Slightly insane] — *Syn.* odd, eccentric, peculiar, neurotic, obsessed, fanatic, queer, bizarre, unhinged, singular, flighty, moonstruck, daft, giddy, nutty\*, screwy\*, tetched\*, pixilated\*; see also **insane** 1. — *Ant.* SANE, sound, normal.

**touching,** *modif. & prep.* **1.** [Referring to] — *Syn.* regarding, in regard to, in reference to, in re, reaching, as concerns, concerning; see also **about** 2.
**2.** [Affecting] — *Syn.* moving, poignant, tender; see **moving** 2, **pitiful** 1.
**3.** [Adjacent] — *Syn.* tangent, in contact, against; see **contiguous, near** 1, **next** 2.
*See Synonym Study at* MOVING.

**touch off,** *v.* **1.** [To cause to explode] — *Syn.* detonate, light the fuse, light, set off; see **explode** 1.
**2.** [To cause to start] — *Syn.* start, initiate, release; see **begin** 1, **cause** 2.

**touchstone,** *n.* — *Syn.* standard, test, criterion; see **proof** 1.

**touch up,** *v.* — *Syn.* renew, modify, rework; see **remodel, repair.**

**touchy,** *modif.* **1.** [Irritable] — *Syn.* ill-humored, testy, irascible; see **irritable.**
**2.** [Delicate] — *Syn.* harmful, hazardous, risky; see **unsafe.**
*See Synonym Study at* IRRITABLE.

**tough,** *modif.* **1.** [Strong] — *Syn.* robust, wiry, mighty; see **strong** 1, 2.
**2.** [Cohesive] — *Syn.* solid, firm, sturdy, hard, hardened, adhesive, leathery, coherent, inseparable, molded, tight, cemented, unbreakable, in one piece, dense, closely packed. — *Ant.* WEAK, fragile, brittle.
**3.** [Difficult to chew] — *Syn.* uncooked, half-cooked, gristly, sinewy, indigestible, inedible, fibrous, old, tough as shoe-leather\*; see also **raw** 1. — *Ant.* SOFT, tender, overcooked.
**4.** [Difficult] — *Syn.* unyielding, hard, resisting, troublesome, onerous, intricate, puzzling, laborious; see also **difficult** 1, **severe** 1. — *Ant.* EASY, simple, obvious.
**5.** [Hardy] — *Syn.* robust, sound, capable; see **healthy** 1.
**6.** [*Rough and cruel] — *Syn.* savage, fierce, desperate, ferocious, ruffianly, uproarious, terrible, rapacious, riotous, uncontrollable, unmanageable. — *Ant.* FRIENDLY, genial, easygoing.
**7.** [*Unfavorable] — *Syn.* bad, unfortunate, untimely; see **unfavorable** 2.
**8.** [*Excellent] — *Syn.* fine, first-class, premium; see **excellent.**

**tough it out** — *Syn.* persevere, persist, endure; see **endure** 1.

**toupee,** *n.* — *Syn.* periwig, hairpiece, peruke, rug\*; see **wig.**

**tour,** *n.* **1.** [A journey] — *Syn.* trip, voyage, travel; see **journey.**
**2.** [A circuit] — *Syn.* round, performance tour, lecture tour.
**3.** [A shift of work] — *Syn.* tour of duty, stint, assignment.
**on tour** — *Syn.* on the road, on the lecture circuit, on the talk show circuit, away, absent; see also **traveling** 2.

**tour,** *v.* — *Syn.* voyage, vacation, take a trip; see **travel** 2.

**tour de force,** *n.* — *Syn.* accomplishment, attainment, stratagem, masterpiece; see **achievement** 2.

**touring,** *modif.* **1.** [Traveling] — *Syn.* journeying, vacationing, excursioning, voyaging; see **traveling** 2.
**2.** [Traveling by automobile] — *Syn.* motoring, driving, riding, sightseeing, out for a spin\*; see also **traveling** 2.

**tourist,** *n.* — *Syn.* sightseer, vacationist, stranger, visitor; see **traveler.**

**tournament,** *n.* **1.** [A series of contests] — *Syn.* meet, games, tourney, match; see **competition** 1, 2, **sport** 3.
**2.** [A joust] — *Syn.* clash of arms, jousts, tourney, duel, knightly combat, test of prowess; see also **fight** 1.

**tousled,** *modif.* — *Syn.* disheveled, unkempt, disordered; see **dirty** 1.

**tout\*,** *v.* — *Syn.* praise, laud, plug\*, puff; see **promote** 1.

**tow,** *v.* — *Syn.* haul, pull, drag, ferry, lug, yank, tug; see also **draw** 1.
*See Synonym Study at* PULL.

**toward,** *modif. & prep.* — *Syn.* to, in the direction of, pointing to, via, on the way to, proceeding, moving, approaching, in relation to, close to, headed for, on the road to; see also **near** 1.

**towel,** *n.* — *Syn.* wiper, drier, absorbent paper, sheet, toweling, napkin, cloth, rag\*.
Kinds of towels include: linen, cotton, huckaback, terry, guest, face, Turkish, hand, fingertip, beach, bath sheet, bath, kitchen, dish, tea, paper, napkin.
**throw in the towel\*** — *Syn.* admit defeat, give in, surrender; see **yield** 3.

**tower,** *n.* — *Syn.* spire, mast, steeple, campanile, dungeon, keep, bell tower, keep, belfry, monolith, radio tower, lookout tower, skyscraper, obelisk, pillar, column, minaret, *fleche* (French), *tourelle* (French); see also **turret.**

**tower,** *v.* — *Syn.* look over, extend above, mount; see **overlook** 1.

**to wit,** *modif.* — *Syn.* namely, in particular, *videlicet* (Latin), scilicet, *id est* (Latin), i.e.; see also **following.**

**town,** *modif.* — *Syn.* civic, community, civil; see **municipal, urban** 2.

**town,** *n.* **1.** [In the United States, a small collection of dwellings] — *Syn.* hamlet, county seat, municipality, township, borough, burg\*, jerkwater\*, hick town\*, falling-off place\*, the sticks\*; see also **village.**
**2.** [In Britain, a large municipality] — *Syn.* market town, thorp, borough; see **city.**
**3.** [Urban life] — *Syn.* city life, living in town, big time\*, bright lights\*; see **center** 2.
**4.** [The people in a city, especially the prominent people] — *Syn.* townspeople, inhabitants, high life, social life, society, high circles, social register, upper crust\*, bigwigs\*, the cream\*; see also **population.**
**go to town\* 1.** do well, prosper, flourish; see **succeed** 1.

2. go in for, go on a spree, go to it.

**town hall,** *n.* — *Syn.* assembly room, courthouse, meeting hall; see **auditorium.**

**town house,** *n.* — *Syn.* urban residence, condominium, *pied-à-terre* (French); see **apartment, home** 1.

**township,** *n.* — *Syn.* town, town government, rural community, precinct; see **government** 1.

**townsman,** *n.* — *Syn.* inhabitant, dweller, householder; see **citizen, resident.**

**town talk,** *n.* — *Syn.* hearsay, scandal, grapevine*; see **gossip** 1, **rumor** 1.

**tow truck,** *n.* — *Syn.* tow rig, tow truck, service vehicle, hoist truck; see **truck** 1.

**toxic,** *modif.* — *Syn.* noxious, virulent, lethal; see **deadly, poisonous.**

**toxin,** *n.* — *Syn.* virus, vapor, contagion; see **poison, venom** 1.

**toy,** *modif.* — *Syn.* childish, miniature, small, diminutive, model-sized, babylike, on a small scale, midgetlike, tiny, undersized, doll-like; see also **little** 1. — *Ant.* LARGE, immense, oversized.

**toy,** *n.* 1. [Something designed for amusement] — *Syn.* game, plaything, pastime; see **doll, game** 1.
Toys include: dolls, games, teddy bears, stuffed animals, rattles, puppets, kites, balls, toy weapons, blocks, puzzles, jacks, yo-yos, tops, skipping ropes, model cars, trains, planes, etc., bicycles, tricycles, roller skates, ice skates, rollerblades, marbles, skateboards, hobby horses, Legos (trademark), jack-in-the-box, hula hoop, Frisbee (trademark).
2. [Anything trivial] — *Syn.* foolishness, trifle, frippery, plaything, trinket, gadget, trumpery, stuff, triviality, bauble, knickknack, gimcrack*, whimwham*, gewgaw*; see also **trinket.**

**toy (around) (with),** *v.* 1. [*To flirt] — *Syn.* dally, take lightly, treat lightly, fool with, fool around with; see also **flirt** 1, **trifle.**
2. [To consider] — *Syn.* think about, ponder, have in mind; see **think** 1.
*See Synonym Study at* TRIFLE.

**toyshop,** *n.* — *Syn.* children's store, novelty shop, department store; see **shop, store** 1.

**trace,** *n.* 1. [A very small quantity] — *Syn.* indication, fragment, dash, dab, sprinkling, tinge, nib, snick, pinch, taste, crumb, trifle, shred, drop, speck, shade, hint, shadow, nuance, iota, scintilla, particle, jot, suggestion, touch, tittle, suspicion, minimum, snippet, smidgen, smell, spot; see also **bit** 1.
2. [A track] — *Syn.* evidence, trail, footprint; see **mark** 1, **proof** 1, **track** 2.

**kick over the traces** — *Syn.* mutiny, revolt, break away, throw off restraint; see **rebel** 1.

**trace,** *v.* 1. [To track] — *Syn.* smell out, track down, run down, follow; see **hunt** 2, **pursue** 1, **track** 1.
2. [To discover by investigation] — *Syn.* ascertain, determine, investigate; see **discover.**
3. [To draw] — *Syn.* sketch, outline, copy; see **draw** 2.

**traceable,** *modif.* — *Syn.* derivative, detectable, identifiable, visible, verifiable, referable, ascribable, attributable, imputable, explainable, accountable; see also **obvious** 1, 2, **tangible.**

**traced,** *modif.* 1. [Copied] — *Syn.* outlined, drawn, sketched, delineated, etched, impressed, imprinted, superimposed, imitated, duplicated, patterned; see also **reproduced.**
2. [Tracked] — *Syn.* followed, pursued, trailed; see **hunted, tracked.**

**tracer bullet,** *n.* — *Syn.* cartridge, ammunition, munition; see **bullet.**

**tracery,** *n.* — *Syn.* mesh, gridiron, grille; see **lattice, web** 1.

**tracing,** *n.* — *Syn.* imitation, reproduction, duplicate; see **copy.**

**track,** *n.* 1. [A prepared way] — *Syn.* path, course, road, route, trail, lane, roadway, passage, towpath, pathway, clearing, cut, alley, avenue, walk; see also **railroad.**
Types of tracks include: railroad, cinder, race, turf, rail, field, cablecar, train, el, elevated train, running, bicycle, subway, trolley; monorail, third rail.
2. [Evidence left in passage] — *Syn.* footprint, trace, vestige, impression, tire track, mark, footmark, spoor, trail, imprint, remnant, record, indication, print, fingerprint, sign, remains, memorial, token, symbol, clue, scent, wake, monument; see also **step** 3.

**keep track of** — *Syn.* keep an account of, stay informed about, maintain contact with; see **track** *v.* 1.

**lose track of** — *Syn.* lose sight of, lose contact with, abandon; see **forget** 1.

**make tracks*** — *Syn.* run away, abandon, depart quickly; see **leave** 1.

**off the track** — *Syn.* deviant, variant, deviating; see **mistaken** 1.

**the wrong side of the tracks*** — *Syn.* ghetto, poor side of town, lower class neighborhood; see **slum.**

**track,** *v.* 1. [To follow by evidence] — *Syn.* hunt, pursue, smell out, add up, put together, trail, follow, trace, follow the scent, follow a clue, follow footprints, draw an inference, piece together, dog, be hot on the trail of*, tail*, shadow*.
2. [To dirty with tracks] — *Syn.* leave footprints, leave mud, muddy, stain, filth, soil, besmear, spatter, leave a trail of dirt, draggle; see also **dirty.**
3. [To follow in alignment] — *Syn.* move in a straight line, keep in a groove, keep in line, move in the same line, follow the track, run straight.

**track down,** *v.* — *Syn.* pursue, hunt down, find; see **arrest, catch** 1, 2, **discover.**

**tracked,** *modif.* — *Syn.* traced, followed, trailed, hunted, dogged, chased, pursued, tailed*, shadowed*. — *Ant.* CAPTURED, found, caught.

**tracking station,** *n.* — *Syn.* observatory, radar station, reporting station, check point; see **station.**

**trackless,** *modif.* — *Syn.* wild, untrodden, uninhabited; see **pathless.**

**tracks,** *n.* 1. [*An injection scar] — *Syn.* needlemarks, punctures, injection marks, traces; see **injection, mark** 1, **scar.**
2. [Means of passage] — *Syn.* road, way, path, railroad, railway; see also **track** 1.
3. [Evidence of passage] — *Syn.* trail, footprints, prints, marks; see **track** 2.

**tract,** *n.* — *Syn.* expanse, plot, region, stretch, piece of land, field.

**tractable,** *modif.* 1. [Obedient] — *Syn.* docile, compliant, willing; see **docile, obedient** 1.
2. [Malleable] — *Syn.* ductile, moldable, pliable; see **flexible** 1.
*See Synonym Study at* DOCILE.

**traction,** *n.* — *Syn.* friction, adhesion, partial adherence; see **stress** 2.

**tractor,** *n.* — *Syn.* traction engine, farm tractor, kerosene tractor, caterpillar tractor, cat*; see also **engine** 1.

**trade,** *n.* 1. [Business] — *Syn.* commerce, sales, enterprise; see **business** 1.
2. [A craft] — *Syn.* occupation, profession, position; see **job** 1.
Common trades include: accountant, boilermaker, baker, barber, butcher, bookbinder, bricklayer, car-

penter, chef, construction worker, cook, draftsman, cabinetmaker, cameraman, data processing technician, data entry operator, mechanic, dressmaker, electrician, embalmer, engraver, jeweler, locksmith, metallurgist, repairman, merchant, storekeeper, millwright, miner, machinist, optician, operator, painter, plumber, printer, seamstress, shoemaker, tailor, textile worker, technician, toolmaker, welder.
**3.** [An individual business transaction] — *Syn.* deal, barter, contract; see **sale** 2.
*See Synonym Study at* BUSINESS.

**trade,** *v.* **1.** [To do business] — *Syn.* patronize, shop, purchase; see **buy** 1, **sell** 1.
**2.** [To give one thing for another] — *Syn.* barter, swap, give in exchange; see **exchange** 2.
*See Synonym Study at* SELL.

**trade group,** *n.* — *Syn.* common market, commerce, traffic; see **business** 1.

**trade in,** *v.* — *Syn.* turn in, make part of a deal, get rid of; see **sell** 1.

**trademark,** *n.* — *Syn.* label, tag, commercial stamp, manufacturer's symbol, service mark, logo, brand, owner's initials, marks of identification.

**trade on,** *v.* — *Syn.* take advantage of, make use of, rely on, rely upon; see **use** 1.

**trader,** *n.* — *Syn.* salesman, dealer, tradesman, see **businessperson, merchant.**

**tradesman,** *n.* — *Syn.* storekeeper, shopkeeper, merchant, small businessman, trader, retailer; see also **businessperson.**

**trade union,** *n.* — *Syn.* union, organized labor, guild; see **labor** 4.

**trading,** *n.* — *Syn.* dealing, buying, selling, exchanging, bartering, doing business, speculation, negotiating.

**trading stamp,** *n.* — *Syn.* certificate, token, redemption slip; see **bond** 3, **coupon.**

**tradition,** *n.* **1.** [The process of preserving orally] — *Syn.* folklore, legend, fable, popular knowledge, myth, lore, wisdom of the ages, oral history; see also **story.**
**2.** [Cultural heritage] — *Syn.* ritual, mores, law; see **culture** 2, **custom** 2.
**3.** [A belief] — *Syn.* attitude, conclusion, idea; see **belief** 1, **opinion** 1.

**traditional,** *modif.* **1.** [Handed down orally] — *Syn.* folkloric, legendary, mythical, epical, ancestral, unwritten, balladic, told, handed down, fabulous, anecdotal, proverbial, inherited, folkloristic.
**2.** [Generally accepted] — *Syn.* old, acknowledged, customary, habitual, widespread, usual, widely used, popular, acceptable, established, fixed, sanctioned, universal, doctrinal, disciplinary, taken for granted, immemorial, rooted, classical, prescribed, conventional; see also **common** 1, **regular** 3.

**traduce,** *v.* — *Syn.* defame, libel, vilify, betray; see **slander.**

**traffic,** *n.* **1.** [The flow of transport] — *Syn.* travel, passage, transportation, flux, movement, transfer, transit, ferriage, passenger service, freight shipment, truckage, cartage, influx.
**2.** [Dealings] — *Syn.* business, commerce, transactions, trade associations, exchange, soliciting, intercourse, familiarity, truck, interchange.

**tragedian,** *n.* — *Syn.* dramatist, performer, tragedienne, Thespian; see **actor** 1, **actress.**

**tragedy,** *n.* **1.** [Unhappy fate] — *Syn.* lot, bad fortune, misfortune, doom, bad end, no good end. — *Ant.* HAPPINESS, fortune, success.
**2.** [A tragic event or series of events] — *Syn.* disas-

ter, catastrophe, misfortune, adversity, affliction, hardship, struggle, misadventure, curse, blight, humiliation, wreck, failure, one blow after another*, hard knocks*; see also **difficulty** 1, 2, **catastrophe.** — *Ant.* SUCCESS, prosperity, good fortune.
**3.** [An artistic creation climaxed by catastrophe] — *Syn.* novel, play, tragic poem, melodrama, tragic drama, Elizabethan tragedy, Greek tragedy, French classic tragedy; see also **drama** 1. — *Ant.* COMEDY, satire, burlesque.

**tragic,** *modif.* — *Syn.* catastrophic, fateful, fatal, calamitous, disastrous, dire, ill-fated, pitiful, terrible, dreadful, awe-inspiring, deathly, deadly, unfortunate, unhappy, sad, painful, grim, appalling, crushing, heart-rending, heartbreaking, lamentable, shocking, harrowing, desolating, ill-starred, hapless, ruinous, baleful, destructive. — *Ant.* HAPPY, joyous, rollicking.

**trail,** *n.* — *Syn.* trace, way, path, tracks.

**trail,** *v.* **1.** [To follow] — *Syn.* track, trace, follow a scent; see **hunt** 1, 2, **pursue** 1.
**2.** [To lag behind] — *Syn.* fall back, loiter, tarry, linger, dawdle, be left behind, drag along, be out of the running*, be left in the cold*. — *Ant.* LEAD, forge ahead, be leading.

**trailer,** *n.* — *Syn.* house trailer, mobile home, auto home, truck trailer, auto cart, wagon, van, container; see also **home** 1.

**trailer house,** *n.* — *Syn.* house, mobile home, recreational vehicle, RV, portable home; see also **home** 1, **trailer.**

**trailer park,** *n.* — *Syn.* mobile home park, mobile housing area, trailer parking, trailer space, trailer facilities; see also **lot** 1.

**trailing,** *modif.* — *Syn.* following, behind, endmost, tracking, hunting, swept along, lagging, dawdling, falling behind, crawling, creeping; see also **losing** 1. — *Ant.* AHEAD, leading, foremost.

**train,** *n.* **1.** [A sequence] — *Syn.* string, chain, succession; see **series.**
**2.** [A locomotive and attached cars] — *Syn.* transport train, passenger, train, freight train, local train, limited, diplomatic train, supply train, express train, excursion train, commuter train, troop train, boat train, mail train, *rapide* (French), subway, underground, elevated, electric*, diesel*, choo-choo*, gully-jumper*, rattler*, blind*; see also **railroad.**

**train,** *v.* **1.** [To drill] — *Syn.* practice, exercise, discipline; see **reach** 2.
**2.** [To educate] — *Syn.* instruct, tutor, enlighten; see **teach** 1.
**3.** [To toughen oneself] — *Syn.* prepare, inure, grow strong, get into practice, reduce, make ready, fit out, equip, qualify, bring up to standard, whip into shape*, get a workout*. — *Ant.* WEAKEN, break training, be unfit.
**4.** [To direct growth] — *Syn.* rear, lead, discipline (oneself), mold, bend, implant, guide, shape, care for, encourage, infuse, imbue, order, bring up, nurture, nurse, prune, weed; see also **raise** 1. — *Ant.* NEGLECT, ignore, disdain.
**5.** [To aim] — *Syn.* cock, level, draw a bead; see **aim** 2.
*See Synonym Study at* TEACH.

**trained,** *modif.* — *Syn.* prepared, qualified, initiated, skilled, informed, schooled, primed, graduated, disciplined, enlightened; see also **educated** 1. — *Ant.* INEXPERIENCED, untrained, RAW.

**trainer,** *n.* — *Syn.* teacher, tutor, instructor, coach, manager, mentor, officer, master, drillmaster, boss*, handler*, pilot*.

**training,** *modif.* — *Syn.* preliminary, educational, disciplinary, pedagogic, doctrinal, scholastic, preparatory.

**training,** *n.* — *Syn.* drill, practice, exercise, preparation, instruction, foundation, schooling, discipline, basic principles, groundwork, coaching, indoctrination, preliminaries, tune-up*, build-up*; see also **education.**

**trait,** *n.* — *Syn.* habit, manner, custom, feature, attribute, quality, characteristic, idiosyncrasy, peculiarity, quirk, mannerism, oddity, trick; see also **characteristic.**
*See Synonym Study at* QUALITY.

**traitor,** *n.* — *Syn.* betrayer, traducer, deserter, renegade, Judas, quisling, Benedict Arnold, Brutus, fifth columnist, informant, informer, intriguer, spy, double agent, counterspy, collaborator, collaborationist, hypocrite, imposter, plotter, conspirator, turncoat, sneak, recreant, backslider, double-crosser*, wolf in sheep's clothing*, fink*, rat*, stool pigeon*, two-timer*, copperhead*, stoolie*; see also **rebel** 1. — *Ant.* SUPPORTER, follower, partisan.

**traitorous,** *modif.* **1.** [Treacherous] — *Syn.* faithless, recreant, unfaithful; see **false** 1.
**2.** [Treasonable] — *Syn.* seditious, disloyal, unpatriotic; see **false** 1.
*See Synonym Study at* FAITHLESS.

**trammel,** *v.* — *Syn.* impede, hinder, obstruct, clog, hamper, shackle, fetter, spancel, hobble, restrain, check, encumber, cramp, retard, oppose, cumber, incommode, discommode, discompose, thwart, frustrate, circumvent, enchain, bridle, muzzle, gag, pinion, manacle, restrict, bind, tether, tie, handcuff, curb. — *Ant.* HELP, aid, assist.

**tramp,** *n.* **1.** [A vagrant] — *Syn.* vagabond, vagrant, wanderer, bum, hobo, outcast, panhandler, drifter, derelict, hitchhiker, gypsy, loafer, unemployable, yegg*, rail-rider*, knight of the road*, moocher*, bo, flipper; see also **beggar** 1.
**2.** [Heavy footfalls] — *Syn.* trample, march, stamping, stomping, treading, gallop, pounding, hoofing*, gallumphing*; see also **step** 1, **tread.**
**3.** [A long walk, often in rough country] — *Syn.* hike, ramble, tour, march, turn, stroll, saunter, excursion, expedition, walking trip, stretch*, shin*, mush*; see also **walk** 3.
**4.** [Prostitute] — *Syn.* whore, harlot, slut; see **prostitute.**

---

*SYN.* — **vagrant** refers to a person without a fixed home who wanders about from place to place, with no regular means of support, and in legal usage, implies such a person regarded as a public nuisance, subject to arrest; **vagabond,** orig. implying shiftlessness, rascality, etc., now often connotes no more than a carefree, roaming existence; **tramp, bum,** and **hobo** are informal equivalents for the preceding, but **bum** always connotes an idle, dissolute, often alcoholic person who never works, **tramp** and **hobo** connote a vagrant, whether one who lives by begging or by doing odd jobs; **hobo** now also means a migratory laborer

---

**tramp,** *v.* **1.** [To tread heavily] — *Syn.* march, stamp, gallop, pound, stomp, tread, trample, trip, hop, do a jig, hoof it*, galumph around*; see also **walk** 1.
**2.** [To wander afoot] — *Syn.* hike, stroll, ramble, tour, walk about, take a turn, go on a walking tour, explore the countryside; see also **march, walk** 1.

**trample,** *v.* — *Syn.* stamp on, crush, tread on, grind

underfoot, injure, squash, bruise, tramp over, overwhelm; see also **defeat** 2, 3, **grind** 1.

**trance,** *n.* — *Syn.* coma, daze, brown study, insensibility; see **stupor.**

**tranquil,** *modif.* **1.** [Said especially of people] — *Syn.* calm, serene, composed, agreeable, gentle, unexcited, unexcitable, placid, amicable, peaceful, pacific, untroubled, unruffled, sober, quiet, reasonable, measured, lenient, even-tempered, smooth, gentle, poised, at ease, well-adjusted, patient, cool; see also **calm** 1, **serene.** — *Ant.* agitated, perturbed, angry, hysterical.
**2.** [Said especially of weather, nature, etc.] — *Syn.* quiet, peaceful, calm, mild, soft, temperate, moderate, low, serene, halcyon, hushed, still, whispering, murmuring, pleasing, comforting, restful, tame, sedative, soothing, even, balmy, southerly, agreeable, pastoral, paradisiacal; see also **calm** 2, **fair** 3, **serene.**
*See Synonym Study at* CALM.

**tranquilize,** *v.* — *Syn.* calm, pacify, quell; see **calm down, quiet** 1, **soothe.**

**tranquilizer,** *n.* **1.** [Calmative medicine] — *Syn.* sleeping pill, depressant, sedative, downer*; see **drug** 2, **medicine** 2.
**2.** [Pacifier] — *Syn.* mitigator, moderator, temperer, assuager, alleviator, alleviative, palliative, soother, mollifier, calmative, sedative, placebo, anodyne, soporific.

**tranquillity,** *n.* — *Syn.* calmness, peacefulness, serenity, peace, quiet, quietude, order, law and order, quietness, composure, placidity, coolness, imperturbation. — *Ant.* DISTURBANCE, perturbation, chaos.

**transact,** *v.* — *Syn.* accomplish, carry on, conclude; see **buy** 1, **negotiate** 1, **sell** 1.

**transaction,** *n.* — *Syn.* doing, proceeding, business, act, affair, matter, deed, action, event, step, happening, deal, sale, selling, buying, purchase, purchasing, trade, disposal, activity, performance, execution, undertaking.

**transatlantic,** *modif.* — *Syn.* oceanic, transoceanic, across the Atlantic, nonstop, on the other side.

**transcend,** *v.* — *Syn.* rise above, transform, excel; see **exceed.**
*See Synonym Study at* EXCEL.

**transcendency,** *n.* — *Syn.* transcendence, supremacy, primacy; see **success** 1.

**transcendent,** *modif.* — *Syn.* transcending, surpassing, exceeding; see **excellent, excelling.**

**transcendental,** *modif.* — *Syn.* transcendent, primordial, original, intuitive, intellectual, beyond grasp, unintelligible, innate, vague, obscure, fantastic. — *Ant.* CLEAR, evident, obvious.

**transcontinental,** *modif.* — *Syn.* trans-American, trans-Siberian, trans-Canadian, trans-European, cross-country, intracontinental, trans-Andean, Cape-to-Cairo.

**transcribe,** *v.* — *Syn.* reprint, copy, decipher; see **reproduce** 1.

**transcriber,** *n.* — *Syn.* copyist, copier, scrivener, translator; see **scribe** 1, **secretary** 2.

**transcript,** *n.* — *Syn.* record, fair copy, reproduction; see **copy.**

**transfer,** *n.* **1.** [Ticket] — *Syn.* token, fare, check; see **ticket** 1.
**2.** [Recording] — *Syn.* variation, substitution, alteration; see **change** 2, **shift** 1.
**3.** [A document providing for a transfer, sense 2] — *Syn.* orders, instructions, assignment; see **command** 1, **directions.**
**4.** [Relocation] — *Syn.* transferal, removal, transference, change of residence.

**transfer,** *v.* **1.** [To carry] — *Syn.* transport, convey, shift; see **carry** 1.
**2.** [To assign] — *Syn.* sell, hand over, pass the buck*; see **assign** 1, **give** 1.
**transferable,** *modif.* — *Syn.* negotiable, transmittable, interchangeable, exchangeable, conveyable, assignable, consignable, movable, portable, devisable, conductible. — *Ant.* ISOLATED, nontransferable, fixed.
**transferred,** *modif.* — *Syn.* moved, removed, shifted, transported, relocated, transmitted, turned over, sent, relayed, transplanted, reassigned, transposed, restationed, conveyed, transmuted; see also **employed, shipped.** — *Ant.* FIXED, left, stationed.
**transfiguration,** *n.* — *Syn.* transmutation, alteration, permutation; see **reformation** 1.
**transfigure,** *v.* **1.** [To transform] — *Syn.* convert, transmute, modify; see **change** 1.
**2.** [To exalt] — *Syn.* glorify, dignify, signalize; see **idealize.**
*See Synonym Study at* TRANSFORM.
**transfix,** *v.* **1.** [To fascinate] — *Syn.* captivate, bewitch, hypnotize; see **fascinate.**
**2.** [To impale] — *Syn.* spear, pierce, stick; see **penetrate** 1.
**transform,** *v.* — *Syn.* convert, transmute, metamorphose, transfigure, modify, permutate, mutate, mold, reconstruct, remodel, make over, do over; see also **change** 1.

SYN. — **transform,** the broadest in scope of these terms, implies a change either in external form or in inner nature, in function, etc. /she was *transformed* into a happy girl/; **transmute,** from its earlier use in alchemy, suggests a change in basic nature that seems almost miraculous /*transmuted* from a shy youth into a sophisticated man about town/; **convert** implies a change in details so as to be suitable for a new use /to *convert* an attic into an apartment/; **metamorphose** suggests a startling change produced as if by magic or a fundamental change in form and function /a tadpole is *metamorphosed* into a frog/; **transfigure** implies a change in outward appearance which seems to exalt or glorify /his whole being was *transfigured* by love/

**transformation,** *n.* **1.** [A change] — *Syn.* alteration, transmutation, conversion; see **change** 1, 2.
**2.** [A grammatical construction] — *Syn.* transform, transformational structure, transformed construction, equivalent grammatical sequence, alternative grammatical sequence; see also **adjective, adverb, clause** 2, **phrase, sentence** 2.
**transformational grammar,** *n.* — *Syn.* generative grammar, new grammar, string grammar; see **grammar.**
**transfuse,** *v.* — *Syn.* inject, imbue, infuse; see **instill.**
**transfusion,** *n.* — *Syn.* transfer, transference, transmission, blood exchange, bleeding; see also **exchange** 1, **phlebotomy.**
**transgress,** *v.* — *Syn.* sin, offend, do wrong, overstep, rebel, disobey, infringe, take the law into one's own hands, break the law, entrench on, encroach upon, write one's own ticket*, fly in the face of the law*.
**transgression,** *n.* — *Syn.* misbehavior, trespass, infraction; see **crime** 1, **sin, violation** 1.
**transgressor,** *n.* — *Syn.* offender, sinner, rebel; see **criminal.**
**transient,** *modif.* **1.** [Temporary] — *Syn.* provisional, ephemeral, transitory, momentary, evanescent, fleeting; see also **temporary.**

**2.** [In motion] — *Syn.* migrating, emigrating, vacating; see **moving** 2.

SYN. — **transient** applies to that which lasts or stays but a short time /a *transient* guest, feeling, etc./; **transitory** refers to that which by its very nature must sooner or later pass or end /life is *transitory*/; **ephemeral** literally means existing only one day and, by extension, applies to that which is markedly short-lived /*ephemeral* glory/; **momentary** implies duration for a moment or an extremely short time /a *momentary* lull in the conversation/; **evanescent** applies to that which appears momentarily and fades quickly away /an *evanescent* image of the scene revealed by lightning/; **fleeting** suggests the swift passing movement of a thing that cannot be caught or held /a *fleeting* thought/

**transient,** *n.* — *Syn.* guest, tourist, traveler, overnight boarder, visitor, migrant worker, migrant.
**transistor,** *n.* **1.** [An electronic device] — *Syn.* electron tube, conductor, semiconductor; see **communications, electronics.**
**2.** [*Radio] — *Syn.* portable, pocket radio, battery-powered radio; see **radio** 2.
**transit,** *n.* **1.** [Passage] — *Syn.* transition, transference, conveyance, transportation, permeation, infiltration, penetration, osmosis.
**2.** [An engineer's telescope] — *Syn.* surveyor's instrument, theodolite, transit theodolite, gauge, lookstick*; see also **telescope.**
**transition,** *n.* — *Syn.* shift, passage, flux, passing, development, transformation, turn, realignment; see also **change** 2. — *Ant.* STABILITY, constancy, durability.
**transitory,** *modif.* **1.** [Fleeting] — *Syn.* brief, ephemeral, short; see **fleeting.**
**2.** [Temporary] — *Syn.* impermanent, transient, changeable; see **temporary.**
*See Synonym Study at* TRANSIENT.
**translate,** *v.* **1.** [To change into another language] — *Syn.* decode, transliterate, transcribe, interpret, decipher, paraphrase, render, transpose, turn, gloss, Anglicize, do into, put in equivalent terms.
**2.** [To interpret] — *Syn.* explain, explicate, elucidate; see **explain, interpret** 1.
**3.** [To transform] — *Syn.* transmute, alter, transpose; see **change** 1.
**translated,** *modif.* — *Syn.* interpreted, adapted, rendered, transliterated, glossed, paraphrased, reworded, transposed, transferred, transplanted, reworked, rewritten.
**translation,** *n.* — *Syn.* transliteration, version, adaptation, rendition, rendering, interpretation, paraphrase, rewording, gloss, metaphrase, reading, pony*, crib*, plug*, key*.

SYN. — **translation** implies the rendering from one language into another of something written or spoken /a German *translation* of Shakespeare/; **version** is applied to a particular translation of a given work, esp. of the Bible /the King James *Version*/; **paraphrase**, in this connection, is applied to a free translation of a passage or work from another language; **transliteration** implies the writing of words with characters of another alphabet that represent the same sound or sounds /a Greek motto *transliterated* into the English alphabet/

**translucency,** *n.* — *Syn.* translucence, transparency, sheerness; see **clarity, lightness** 2.
**translucent,** *modif.* — *Syn.* glassy, semitransparent, pel-

lucid, frosted, crystalline; see also **clear** 2, **transparent** 1.

*See Synonym Study at* CLEAR.

**transmigrate,** *v.* — *Syn.* migrate, emigrate, move; see **leave** 1.

**transmigration,** *n.* **1.** [Migration] — *Syn.* trek, pilgrimage, movement; see **emigration.**

**2.** [Reincarnation] — *Syn.* metempsychosis, rebirth, avatar.

**transmission,** *n.* **1.** [The act of transporting] — *Syn.* transference, conveyance, carrying, hauling, sending, transmittal, communication, transposal, deliverance, importation, exportation; see also **delivery** 1, **transportation.**

**2.** [The sending of radio waves] — *Syn.* conduction, passage, broadcast, telecast, simulcast, frequency, release, radiocast, hookup*.

**3.** [A mechanism for transmitting power] — *Syn.* gears, gear box, automatic transmission, fluid transmission, planetary transmission, syncromeshed, transmission, overdrive; see also **device** 1.

**transmit,** *v.* **1.** [To send] — *Syn.* dispatch, forward, convey, broadcast; see **send** 1, 4.

**2.** [To carry] — *Syn.* pass on, transfer, communicate, carry, spread, pass along, convey, impart, hand down, bequeath; see also **carry** 2, **give** 1, **send** 2.

*See Synonym Study at* CARRY.

**transmitter,** *n.* — *Syn.* conductor, aerial, wire; see **antenna, communications, electronics.**

**transmutable,** *modif.* — *Syn.* transformable, modifiable, alternative; see **changeable** 1, 2.

**transmutation,** *n.* — *Syn.* transfiguration, alteration, mutation, metathesis, catalysis, transformation; see also **change** 1, 2, **conversion** 1.

**transmute,** *v.* — *Syn.* transform, convert, adapt; see **change** 1.

*See Synonym Study at* TRANSFORM.

**transparency,** *n.* — *Syn.* transparence, clearness, glassiness; see **clarity.**

**transparent,** *modif.* **1.** [Allowing light to pass through] — *Syn.* clear, translucent, lucid, crystalline, vitreous, pellucid, gauzy, thin, sheer, see-through, permeable, hyaline, glassy, cellophane, diaphanous; see also **clear** 2, **thin** 1. — *Ant.* opaque, murky, dark, smoky.

**2.** [Obvious] — *Syn.* obvious, easily seen, easily seen through, plain, clear, manifest, patent, understandable, clear-cut, unmistakable, apparent; see also **obvious** 1. — *Ant.* OBSCURE, hidden, difficult.

**3.** [Without hidden motives or pretense] — *Syn.* frank, open, honest, candid, clean-cut, sincere, simple, guileless, artless, ingenuous, genuine, direct, unsophisticated; see also **natural** 3. — *Ant.* SLY, crafty, shrewd.

*See Synonym Study at* CLEAR.

**transpire,** *v.* — *Syn.* ensue, occur, befall; see **happen** 2.

*See Synonym Study at* HAPPEN.

**transplant,** *n.* — *Syn.* transplanting, transplantation, introducing a donated organ, skin graft; heart transplant, cardiac transplant, kidney transplant, eye transplant, etc.; see also **operation** 4.

**transplant,** *v.* — *Syn.* reset, reorient, transpose, remove, graft, recondition, emigrate, readapt, shift over, revamp.

**transport,** *n.* **1.** [Vehicle] — *Syn.* carrier, common carrier, conveyor, mover; see **transportation.**

Means of transport include: railroad, train, transcontinental railroad, airline, airplane, supersonic airplane, car, automobile, van, taxicab, limousine, truck, bus, steamship; cargo boat, freighter, tanker, troop ship, transport plane, liner, ferryboat, barge, raft, streetcar,

ship, trolley car, subway, underground railroad, elevated railroad, wagon, cart, carriage, sled, bicycle, motorcycle, motorscooter, monorail, cablecar, helicopter.

**2.** [State of ecstasy] — *Syn.* ecstasy, bliss, rapture; see **rapture.**

*See Synonym Study at* RAPTURE.

**transport,** *v.* **1.** [To carry] — *Syn.* convey, move, bring; see **carry** 1.

**2.** [To banish] — *Syn.* deport, exile, expatriate; see **banish** 1.

*See Synonym Study at* BANISH, CARRY.

**transportation,** *n.* — *Syn.* conveying, conveyance, carrying, hauling, shipping, shipment, transport, haulage, portage, carting, moving, transferring, truckage, freightage, air lift, transference, transit, passage, ferriage, telpherage; see also **transport.**

**transported,** *modif.* — *Syn.* moved, conveyed, forwarded, transferred, carried, changed, shifted, impelled.

**transpose,** *v.* — *Syn.* interchange, reverse, transfer; see **change** 1, **exchange** 1.

**transposition,** *n.* — *Syn.* transposal, changing, inversion, metathesis; see **change** 1, 2.

**transubstantiation,** *n.* — *Syn.* transformation, transmutation, mutation; see **change** 2, **conversion** 1.

**transverse,** *modif.* — *Syn.* crosswise, bent, intersecting; see **oblique** 1.

**trap,** *n.* **1.** [A device to catch game or persons] — *Syn.* net, cul-de-sac, snare, mousetrap, deadfall, spring, pit, pitfall, blind, noose, trapfall, maneuver; see also **ambush.**

**2.** [A trick] — *Syn.* prank, practical joke, snare; see **trick** 1.

---

*SYN.* — **trap,** as applied to a device for capturing animals, specif. suggests a snapping device worked by a spring, **pitfall,** a concealed pit with a collapsible cover, and **snare,** a noose which jerks tight upon the release of a trigger; in extended senses, these words apply to any danger into which unsuspecting or unwary persons may fall, **trap** specifically suggesting a deliberate stratagem or ambush *[a speed trap]*, **pitfall,** a concealed danger, source of error, etc. *[the pitfalls of the law]*, and **snare,** enticement and entanglement *[the snares of love]*

---

**trap,** *v.* — *Syn.* ensnare, catch, confine, fool; see **ambush, catch** 2, **deceive.**

*See Synonym Study at* CATCH.

**trapped,** *modif.* — *Syn.* ambushed, cornered, at bay, with one's back to the wall*; see **captured** 1.

**trapper,** *n.* — *Syn.* hunter, huntsman, poacher, ferreter, sportsman, *voyageur* (French), fur trapper, game hunter.

**trappings,** *n.* **1.** [Trimmings] — *Syn.* adornments, trim, embellishments; see **decoration** 2.

**2.** [Equipment] — *Syn.* rigging, outfit, gear; see **equipment.**

**trash,** *n.* **1.** [Rubbish] — *Syn.* garbage, waste, refuse, dregs, filth, litter, debris, dross, oddments, sweepings, rubble, odds and ends, offal, junk, sediment, leavings, droppings; see also **excess** 4, **residue.** — *Ant.* MONEY, goods, riches.

**2.** [Persons regarded as of little account] — *Syn.* beggars, thieves, outlaws, the poor, the lower class, hobos, tramps, *hoi polloi*, (Greek), *sans culottes, canaille* (both French), wastrels, poor whites, sharecroppers, guttersnipes*, varmints*, good-for-nothings*, white trash*; see also **rascal.** — *Ant.* ARISTOCRACY, the upper class, the wealthy.

**3.** [Waste matter] — *Syn.* stuff, frippery, rags, scraps, scrap, scourings, fragments, pieces, shavings, loppings, slash, rakings, slag, parings, rinsings, deads, debris, shoddy, scoria, recrement, residue; see also sense 1.

**4.** [Nonsense] — *Syn.* drivel, twaddle, prating; see **nonsense** 1.

**trashing\***, *n.* — *Syn.* rioting, vandalism, wrecking; see **destruction** 1, **violence** 2.

**trashy**, *modif.* — *Syn.* cheap, ugly, paltry, vulgar; see **useless** 1, **worthless** 1.

**trauma**, *n.* — *Syn.* shock, injury, wound, ordeal; see **injury** 1.

**travail**, *n.* — *Syn.* labor, toil, drudgery; see **work** 2.

**travel**, *n.* **1.** [The act of journeying] — *Syn.* riding, roving, wandering, rambling, sailing, touring, biking, hiking, cruising, driving, wayfaring, going abroad, seeing the world, sight-seeing, voyaging, trekking, flying, globe-trotting, space travel, rocketing, orbiting, manning a space station, interstellar travel, intercontinental travel, jet travel.

**2.** [An individual journey] — *Syn.* tour, voyage, trip; see **journey.**

**travel**, *v.* **1.** [To move at a regular pace] — *Syn.* cover ground, progress, go; see **move** 1.

**2.** [To journey] — *Syn.* tour, cruise, voyage, commute, roam, explore, jet, rocket, orbit, go into orbit, take a jet, go by jet, migrate, trek, vacation, motor, visit, jaunt, wander, junket, adventure, quest, trip, rove, inspect, make an expedition, make a peregrination, cross the continent, cross the ocean, encircle the globe, make the grand tour, sail, see the country, go camping, go abroad, take a trip, take a train, take a boat, take a plane, cover, go walking, go riding, go bicycling, make a train trip, drive, fly, traverse, set out, set forth, sight-see, scour the country\*, bat around\*; see also **walk** 1.

**traveled**, *modif.* **1.** [*Said of persons*] — *Syn.* worldly, cosmopolitan, urbane, polished, seasoned, experienced, itinerant. — *Ant.* DOMESTIC, provincial, small-town.

**2.** [*Said of roads*] — *Syn.* well-used, busy, operating, in use, frequented, widely known, sure, safe, well-trodden, accepted. — *Ant.* ABANDONED, little-used, unexplored.

**traveler**, *n.* — *Syn.* voyager, adventurer, tourist, explorer, nomad, wanderer, peddler, truant, roamer, rambler, wayfarer, migrant, displaced person, D.P., journeyer, excursionist, junketer, sight-seer, straggler, vagabond, vagrant, hobo, tramp, gypsy, wandering Jew, gadabout, itinerant, pilgrim, rover, passenger, commuter, globe-trotter.

**traveling**, *modif.* **1.** [*Said of goods*] — *Syn.* passing, en route, on board, shipped, freighted, transported, moving, carried, conveyed, consigned, being hauled.

**2.** [*Said of people*] — *Syn.* wandering, touring, roving, on tour, vagrant, migrant, nomadic, wayfaring, itinerant, cruising, excursioning, commuting, driving, flying, ranging, sailing, riding, on vacation, migrating, voyaging; see also **moving** 2.

**traveling salesman**, *n.* — *Syn.* company representative, commercial traveler, drummer\*; see **salesman** 2.

**traverse**, *v.* — *Syn.* cross over, move over, pass through; see **cross** 1.

**travesty**, *n.* — *Syn.* burlesque, spoof, mockery, perversion; see **parody.**

*See Synonym Study at* PARODY.

**tray**, *n.* — *Syn.* platter, plate, service, plate, trencher, salver, waiter, dumb-waiter, tea wagon; see also **dish** 1.

**treacherous**, *modif.* **1.** [Traitorous] — *Syn.* treasonable, falsehearted, unfaithful, faithless; see **false** 1.

**2.** [Unreliable] — *Syn.* deceptive, undependable, dangerous, risky, misleading, tricky, dissembled, untrust-

worthy, deceitful, false, twofaced, ensnaring, faulty, precarious, unstable, insecure, shaky, slippery, ticklish, difficult, ominous, alarming, menacing. — *Ant.* RELIABLE, dependable, steady.

*See Synonym Study at* FAITHLESS.

**treacherously**, *modif.* — *Syn.* unscrupulously, deceitfully, faithlessly; see **falsely.**

**treachery**, *n.* — *Syn.* faithlessness, disloyalty, betrayal; see **dishonesty, treason.**

**tread**, *n.* — *Syn.* step, gait, walk, march, footstep; see also **tramp** 2.

**tread**, *v.* — *Syn.* walk, step, step on; see **tramp** 1, **trample.**

**treason**, *n.* — *Syn.* sedition, seditiousness, disloyalty, perfidy, treachery, seditionary act, seditious act, aid and comfort to the enemy, factious revolt; see also **crime** 2, **dishonesty, deception** 1, **revolution** 2.

---

**SYN.** — **treason** implies an overt act in violation of the allegiance owed to one's state, specif. a levying war against it or giving aid or comfort to its enemies; **sedition** applies to anything regarded by a government as stirring up resistance or rebellion against it without being an overt or absolute act of treachery

---

**treasure**, *n.* — *Syn.* richness, riches, store, cache, hoard, find, abundance, reserve, nest egg, pile\*; see also **wealth** 1, 2.

**treasure**, *v.* — *Syn.* prize, value, appreciate, cherish, hold dear, set great store by, guard, hoard; see also **admire** 1, **cherish** 1, **love** 1.

*See Synonym Study at* APPRECIATE.

**treasurer**, *n.* — *Syn.* bursar, receiver, cashier, controller, comptroller, banker, paymaster, purser, curator, steward, club officer, government official, trustee; see also **accountant, teller.**

**treasury**, *n.* — *Syn.* repository, bank, storehouse, money exchange, central money office, exchequer, bursary, money box, strongbox, cash register, safe, depository.

**treat**, *n.* — *Syn.* entertainment, surprise, amusement, free passage, feast, delectable dish, source of gratification, gift, setup\*, beano\*, spree\*.

**treat**, *v.* **1.** [To deal with a person or thing] — *Syn.* negotiate, manage, have to do with, have business with, behave toward, handle, make terms with, act toward, react toward, use, employ, have recourse to. — *Ant.* NEGLECT, ignore, have nothing to do with.

**2.** [To deal with a subject] — *Syn.* talk of, write of, speak of, discourse upon, arrange, manipulate, comment, interpret, explain, enlarge upon, criticize, discuss, review, approach, tackle\*.

**3.** [To assist toward a cure] — *Syn.* attend, administer, prescribe, dose, operate, nurse, dress, minister to, apply therapy, care for, doctor\*; see also **heal** 1.

**4.** [To pay for another's entertainment] — *Syn.* entertain, indulge, satisfy, amuse, divert, play host to, escort, set up\*, blow\*, stake to\*, stand to\*.

**treatise**, *n.* — *Syn.* tract, paper, monograph; see **exposition** 2.

**treatment**, *n.* **1.** [Usage] — *Syn.* handling, processing, dealing, approach, execution, procedure, method, manner, proceeding, way, strategy, custom, habit, employment, practice, mode, *modus operandi* (Latin), line\*, angle\*.

**2.** [Assistance toward a cure] — *Syn.* operation, medical care, surgery, therapy, remedy, prescription, regimen, hospitalization, medication, nursing, doctoring\*; see also **medicine** 2.

**treaty**, *n.* — *Syn.* agreement, pact, settlement, covenant, compact, cartel, convention, alliance, concordat, charter, sanction, entente, détente, cease-fire, truce, bond, understanding, arrangement, bargain, negotiation, deal*.

**tree,** *n.* Common types of trees include: ash, elm, oak, maple, catalpa, evergreen, spruce, balsam, birch, tulip, aspen, fir, cypress, juniper, larch, tamarack, pine, cedar, beech, chestnut, eucalyptus, hickory, walnut, sycamore, ailanthus, magnolia, olive, fig, ficus, plane, palm, willow, locust, sequoia, redwood, poplar, acacia, cottonwood, beech, box elder, apple, crabapple, redbud, mulberry, cherry, peach, plum, pear, prune, banyan, baobab, bamboo, abba, calabra, betel, mahogany, ebony, bo, ironwood, dogwood, ginko, bottle; see also **wood** 1.

**up a tree***— *Syn.* cornered, in difficulty, trapped; see **in trouble** 1 at **trouble**.

**trees,** *n.* — *Syn.* wood, woods, windbreak; see **forest**.

**trek,** *v.* — *Syn.* hike, migrate, journey; see **travel** 2.

**trellis,** *n.* — *Syn.* framework, arbor, grille; see **frame** 1, **lattice**.

**tremble,** *v.* — *Syn.* quiver, shiver, vibrate; see **shake** 1.

**tremendous,** *modif.* — *Syn.* huge, enormous, great, colossal; see **large** 1, **enormous**.
*See Synonym Study at* ENORMOUS.

**tremendously,** *modif.* — *Syn.* exceedingly, amazingly, remarkably, excessively, appallingly; see also **largely** 2.

**tremor,** *n.* — *Syn.* trembling, shaking, shivering; see **earthquake**.

**tremulous,** *modif.* **1.** [Shaking] — *Syn.* trembling, quivering, palpitating; see **shaky** 1.
**2.** [Timid] — *Syn.* fearful, shy, timorous; see **cowardly** 1, **timid** 2.

**trench,** *n.* — *Syn.* ditch, rut, hollow, gully, depression, gutter, tube, furrow, drainage canal, creek, moat, dike (British), drain, channel, main, gorge, gulch, arroyo.
Military trenches include: dugout, earthwork, moat, sap, redoubt, breastwork, entrenchment, fortification, pillbox, excavation, revetment, bunker, strong point, machine-gun nest, communication trench, front-line trench, slit trench, approach trench, tank-trap, foxhole; see also **defense** 2.

**trenchant,** *modif.* **1.** [Having a cutting edge] — *Syn.* cutting, incisive, keen, biting, pungent, severe, razorfine; see also **sharp** 1. — *Ant.* DULL, blunt, flat.
**2.** [Sharp intellectually] — *Syn.* unsparing, critical, emphatic, vigorous, impressive, strong, dynamic, pointed, intense, positive, weighty, salient, significant, pithy, sententious, crushing, forcible, crisp, caustic, concise, succinct, razor-sharp, comprehensive, pregnant, neat, to the point, graphic, explicit, ponderous; see also **intelligent** 1, **profound** 2. — *Ant.* WEAK, shallow, feeble.
*See Synonym Study at* INCISIVE.

**trend,** *n.* **1.** [Tendency] — *Syn.* bias, bent, leaning; see **inclination** 1.
**2.** [Direction] — *Syn.* course, aim, bearing; see **drift** 1.
*See Synonym Study at* TENDENCY.

**trendsetter,** *n.* — *Syn.* initiator, pacesetter, manager; see **leader** 2.

**trendy***, *modif.* — *Syn.* stylish, popular, contemporary, *au courant* (French); see **fashionable**.

**trepan,** *v.* — *Syn.* trick, trap, lure; see **deceive**.

**trepidation,** *n.* **1.** [Quaking] — *Syn.* tremor, quivering, shaking, agitation, panic.
**2.** [Dread] — *Syn.* shock, alarm, terror; see **fear** 1, 2.

**trespass,** *v.* **1.** [To transgress] — *Syn.* offend, err, displease; see **misbehave, sin, transgress**.

**2.** [To intrude] — *Syn.* intrude, encroach, invade, infringe; see **meddle** 1.

*SYN.* — **trespass** implies an unlawful or unwarranted entrance upon the property, rights, etc. of another /to *trespass* on a private beach/; to **encroach** is to make inroads by stealth or gradual advances /suburbs *encroaching* on our farmland/; **infringe** implies an encroachment that breaks a law or agreement or violates the rights of others /to *infringe* on a patent/; **intrude** implies a thrusting oneself into company, situations, etc. without being asked or wanted /to *intrude* on one's privacy/; **invade** implies a forcible or hostile entrance into the territory or rights of others /to *invade* a neighboring state/

**trespasser,** *n.* **1.** [An intruder] — *Syn.* encroacher, invader, infringer; see **intruder**.
**2.** [An offender] — *Syn.* sinner, evildoer, misdoer, reprobate; see **criminal**.

**tress,** *n.* — *Syn.* shock, lock, plait; see **braid, curl, hair** 1.

**trestle,** *n.* — *Syn.* horse, stool, frame, support, approach.

**trial,** *modif.* — *Syn.* tentative, test, trial balloon, preliminary, probationary, temporary; see also **experimental**.

**trial,** *n.* **1.** [An effort to learn the truth] — *Syn.* analysis, test, examination; see **experiment** 1.
**2.** [A case at law] — *Syn.* suit, lawsuit, fair hearing, hearing, action, case, contest, indictment, legal proceedings, claim, cross-examination, litigation, counterclaim, replevin, arraignment, prosecution, citation, court action, judicial contest, seizure, assumpsit, bill of divorce, habeas corpus, court-martial, impeachment, rap*, try*, court clash*.
**3.** [An ordeal] — *Syn.* suffering, severe test, ordeal, crucible, tribulation, affliction, trying experience, misfortune, heavy blow, annoyance, bother, irritant, nuisance, headache*, pain*; see also **affliction**.
*See Synonym Study at* AFFLICTION.

**on trial 1.** in litigation, at law, before the bar, before a judge, before a jury, indicted, being tried.
**2.** on a trial basis, on approval, for a trial period, being tested, under consideration, not yet accepted; see also **experimentally**.

**trial and error (method),** *n.* — *Syn.* empiricism, empirical method, by guess and by God*; see **experiment** 1, 2, **method** 2.

**triangle,** *n.* Kinds of triangles include: equilateral, isosceles, right-angled, obtuse-angled, scalene, acuteangled; love.

**triangular,** *modif.* — *Syn.* three-cornered, three-sided, triagonal, deltoid, delta-shaped, trilateral; see also **angular** 1.

**tribal,** *modif.* — *Syn.* tribular, racial, kindred; see **common** 5, **group**.

**tribe,** *n.* — *Syn.* primitive group, ethnic group, society, phratry, clan, totemic unit, family, sib, sept, deme, horde, sorory, class, association; see also **race** 2.

**tribulation,** *n.* — *Syn.* affliction, distress, trial, ordeal; see **affliction, grief** 1.
*See Synonym Study at* AFFLICTION.

**tribunal,** *n.* — *Syn.* bench, bar, assizes; see **court** 2.

**tributary,** *modif.* — *Syn.* subordinate, subject, minor, accessory, small, supplementary, auxiliary, adjoining, affluent, subsidiary; see also **secondary** 1. — *Ant.* PRINCIPAL, main, leading.

**tributary,** *n.* — *Syn.* stream, river, branch, feeder, anabranch, affluent, sidestream, offshoot.

**tribute,** *n.* **1.** [Recognition] — *Syn.* encomium, ap-

plause, memorial service, offering, eulogy, panegyric; see also **praise** 2, **recognition** 2.
**2.** [Money paid a conqueror] — *Syn.* ransom, fee, levy; see **bribe.**

---

**SYN.** — **tribute,** the broadest in scope of these words, is used of praise manifested by any act, situation, etc. as well as that expressed in speech or writing /their success was a *tribute* to your leadership/; **encomium** suggests an enthusiastic, sometimes high-flown expression of praise /encomiums lavished on party leaders at a convention/; **eulogy** generally applies to a formal speech or writing in exalting praise, especially of a person who has just died; **panegyric** suggests superlative or elaborate praise expressed in poetic or lofty language /Cicero's *panegyric* upon Cato/

---

**trice,** *n.* — *Syn.* while, second, minute; see **instant, moment** 1.
**trick,** *n.* **1.** [A deceit] — *Syn.* wile, casuistry, fraud, deception, ruse, cheat, cover, feint, hoax, artifice, decoy, trap, stratagem, intrigue, fabrication, double-dealing, forgery, fake, illusion, invention, subterfuge, distortion, delusion, ambush, snare, blind, evasion, plot, equivocation, concealment, treachery, swindle, imposture, feigning, impersonation, dissimulation, duplicity, pretense, falsehood, falsification, perjury, disguise, conspiracy, machination, circumvention, quibble, trickery, conundrum, beguiling, chicane, chicanery, humbug, simulacrum, maneuver, sham, counterfeit, gyp*, touch*, phoney*, come-on*, fast one*, dodge*, plant*, clip*, sucker*, deal*, con game*, bluff*, shakedown*, sell-out*, con*, funny business*, dirty work*, crooked deal*, front*, fakeroo*, gimmick*, suck-in*; see also **lie** 1. — *Ant.* HONESTY, truth, veracity.
**2.** [A prank] — *Syn.* jest, sport, practical joke; see **joke** 1.
**3.** [A practical method or expedient] — *Syn.* skill, facility, know-how*; see **ability** 2, **method** 2.
**4.** [A round of cards] — *Syn.* deal, hand, round, shuffle.
**do** or **turn the trick** — *Syn.* achieve the desired result, attain success, accomplish; see **succeed** 1.

---

**SYN.** — **trick** is the common word for an action or device in which ingenuity and cunning are used to outwit others and implies deception either for fraudulent purposes or as a prank; **ruse** applies to that which is contrived as a blind for one's real intentions or for the truth /her apparent illness was merely a *ruse* to gain time/; a **stratagem** is a more or less complicated ruse, by means of which one attempts to outwit or entrap an enemy or antagonist /military *stratagems*/; **maneuver,** while specifically applicable to military tactics, in general use suggests the shrewd manipulation of persons or situations to suit one's purposes /a political *maneuver*/; **artifice** stresses inventiveness or ingenuity in the contrivance of an expedient, trick, etc. /artifices employed to circumvent the tax laws/; **wile,** often used in the plural, implies the use of allurements or beguilement to ensnare /used all his *wiles* and cunning to close the deal/

---

**trick,** *v.* — *Syn.* dupe, outwit, fool; see **cheat, deceive.**
*See Synonym Study at* CHEAT.
**trickery,** *n.* — *Syn.* deception, dupery, fraud, quackery; see **deception** 1, **dishonesty.**
*See Synonym Study at* DECEPTION.
**trickle,** *v.* — *Syn.* drip, dribble, leak, seep, stream, issue, ooze, run; see also **flow** 2.

**trickster,** *n.* — *Syn.* fraud, confidence man, impostor; see **cheat** 1, **swindler.**
**tricky,** *modif.* **1.** [Sly] — *Syn.* wily, crafty, foxy; see **sly** 1.
**2.** [Shrewd] — *Syn.* clever, sharp, keen-witted; see **intelligent** 1.
**3.** [*Delicate or difficult] — *Syn.* complicated, intricate, critical, touchy, involved, perplexing, knotty, thorny, complex, unstable, ticklish, catchy, likely to go wrong, hanging by a thread*; see also **difficult** 1, 2. — *Ant.* EASY, clear-cut, simple.
*See Synonym Study at* SLY.
**tricycle,** *n.* — *Syn.* velocipede, three-wheeled velocipede, three-wheeled chair, three-wheeled cycle, trike*, three-wheeler*; see also **bicycle.**
**tried,** *modif.* — *Syn.* dependable, proved, approved, certified, used; see also **tested.**
**trifle,** *n.* **1.** [A small quantity] — *Syn.* particle, piece, speck; see **bit** 1.
**2.** [A small degree] — *Syn.* jot, eyelash, fraction; see **bit** 3.
**3.** [Something of little importance] — *Syn.* triviality, small matter, nothing; see **insignificance.**
**trifle,** *v.* **1.** [To act without seriousness] — *Syn.* putter, potter, fribble, dip into, slur over, dawdle, dally, mock, play at, make fun, jest, act silly, loiter, idle about, lounge, fool around, indulge in horseplay, monkey with*, monkey around*, fool with*, fool around*, mess with*, mess around*, doodle*, string along*, futz around*, horse around*; see also **change** 1, **tamper with.**
**2.** [To flirt] — *Syn.* flirt, dally, coquet, toy with, wink at, play with, play around, make advances; see also **play, flirt** 1.

---

**SYN.** — **trifle** is the general term meaning to treat someone or something without earnestness, full attention, definite purpose, etc. /began to *trifle* with the notion of retirement, *trifling* with her affections/ **flirt** implies a light, transient interest or attention that quickly moves on to another person or thing /flirted with several religions before becoming a philosopher/ **dally** implies a playing with a subject or thing that one has little or no intention of taking seriously /to *dally* with painting/; **coquet** usually suggests a trifling in matters of love /she *coquetted* with several men in her department/; **toy** implies a trifling or dallying with no purpose beyond that of amusement or idling away time /toying with the idea of writing a novel/

---

**trifler,** *n.* — *Syn.* pretender, impostor, time waster, idler, lounger, humbug, waster, slacker, shirker, lazy person, ne'er-do-well; see also **loafer.**
**trifling,** *modif.* — *Syn.* petty, small, insignificant; see **trivial, unimportant.**
**trifling,** *n.* — *Syn.* dawdling, idling, loitering; see **indifference** 1.
**trill,** *v.* — *Syn.* quaver, warble, wave, shake, roll, whistle, chirp, twitter, yodel; see also **sound** 1.
**trill,** *n.* — *Syn.* warble, quaver, vibrato, tremolo.
**trim,** *modif.* **1.** [Neat] — *Syn.* orderly, tidy, spruce; see **clean** 1, **neat** 1.
**2.** [Well-proportioned] — *Syn.* shapely, clean, well-designed, streamlined, slim, slender, shipshape, delicate, fit, comely, well-formed, symmetrical, well-made, clean-cut, well-balanced, graceful, well-molded, harmonious, beautiful, classical, compact, smart; see also **handsome** 2. — *Ant.* DISORDERED, shapeless, straggly.
**trim,** *v.* **1.** [To cut off excess] — *Syn.* prune, shave, lop,

crop, clip, shear, pare down, even up, mow, snip, plane, slice off, scrape, whittle down, carve down; see also **cut** 1. — *Ant.* INCREASE, lengthen, extend.

**2.** [To adorn] — *Syn.* ornament, embellish, beautify, betinsel, deck, beribbon, spangle, gussy up*, emblazon, embroider; see also **decorate.**

**3.** [*To defeat] — *Syn.* whip, lick, trounce; see **defeat** 1, 3.

**4.** [To refuse to take a stand] — *Syn.* hedge, temporize, equivocate, dodge, vacillate, remain neutral, stand between, compromise, sit on a fence*, shilly-shally*, hem and haw*; see also **hesitate, pause.** — *Ant.* OPPOSE, antagonize, be a partisan of.

**5.** [To prepare for sailing] — *Syn.* ballast, rig, outfit, hoist the sails, touch her up*; see also **provide** 1, **sail** 1, **trim ship.**

**trimmer,** *n.* — *Syn.* temporizer, deceiver, sycophant; see **opportunist.**

**trimming,** *n.* **1.** [Ornamentation] — *Syn.* trapping, accessory, frill, embellishment, border design, embroidered hem, tassel, edging; see also **decoration** 2, **embroidery** 1.

**2.** [The act of cutting off excess] — *Syn.* shearing, lopping off, shaving off, making even, cutting away, clipping, snipping, mowing, nipping, cropping, shortening, pruning, paring down; see also **reducing.** — *Ant.* INCREASING, extending, enlarging.

**3.** [*Defeat] — *Syn.* beating, repulse, whipping, thrashing, rebuff, upset, licking, skunking*; see also **defeat.** — *Ant.* SUCCESS, victory, achievement.

**trim one's sails*,** *v.* — *Syn.* adapt, adjust oneself, accede; see **accommodate** 2.

**trim ship,** *v.* — *Syn.* break out, rig, equip, outfit, ballast, put on an even keel; see also **balance** 2, **trim** 5.

**trinity,** *n.* **1.** [Three of a kind] — *Syn.* trio, trilogy, triplet, triplicate, threesome, triad, troika, set of three, leash, trey.

**2.** [The Holy Trinity] — *Syn.* three-personed God, the Godhead; Father, Son, and Holy Ghost; the Triune God, Trinity, the Trinity in Unity, Threefold Unity, Three in One and One in Three, Trimurti; see also **god** 3.

**trinket,** *n.* — *Syn.* plaything, toy, tinsel, frippery, knick-knack, gadget, novelty, bauble, showpiece*, dazzler*, doo-dad*, pretty-pretty*, thingamajig*; see also **jewel, jewelry, pin** 2, **ring** 2.

**trio,** *n.* **1.** [A combination of three] — *Syn.* trinity, triangle, triplet, triplicate, threesome, triad, troika, set of three, leash, trey.

**2.** [Three musicians performing together] — *Syn.* string trio, vocal trio, swing trio*; see **band** 4.

**trip,** *n.* **1.** [A journey] — *Syn.* voyage, excursion, tour; see **journey.**

**2.** [*A psychedelic experience] — *Syn.* hallucinations, LSD trip, drug trip, pipe dream, being turned on; see also **drug** 2, **indulgence** 3.

---

**SYN.** — **trip** most frequently implies a relatively short course of travel, although it is also commonly used as an equivalent for **journey** [a vacation *trip*, a *trip* around the world]; **journey**, a somewhat more formal word, generally implies travel of some length, usually over land [the *journey* was filled with hardships]; **voyage**, in current use, implies a relatively long journey by water or sometimes by air or through space [a *voyage* across the Atlantic, a *voyage* to the moon]; **jaunt** is applied to a short, casual trip taken for pleasure or recreation [a *jaunt* to the city]; **expedition** is applied to a journey, march, etc. taken

by an organized group for some definite purpose [a military *expedition*, a zoological *expedition* to Africa]

**trip,** *v.* **1.** [To stumble] — *Syn.* tumble, slip, lurch, slide, founder, fall, pitch, fall over, slip upon, plunge, sprawl, topple, go head over heels*. — *Ant.* ARISE, ascend, get up.

**2.** [To cause to stumble] — *Syn.* block, hinder, bind, tackle, overthrow, push, send headlong, kick, shove, mislead. — *Ant.* HELP, pick up, give a helping hand.

**3.** [To step lightly] — *Syn.* skip, play, frolic; see **dance** 1, 2, **jump** 1, 3.

**triple,** *modif.* — *Syn.* in triplicate, by three, treble, threefold, triplex, three-ply, ternary; see also **three.**

**tripod,** *n.* — *Syn.* three-legged stand, holder, camera stand, tripe*; see **platform** 1.

**tripping,** *modif.* — *Syn.* nimble, spry, quick; see **agile.**

**trite,** *modif.* — *Syn.* hackneyed, prosaic, stereotyped; see **common** 1, **dull** 4.

---

**SYN.** — **trite** is applied to something, especially an expression or idea, which through repeated use or application has lost its original freshness and impressive force (e.g., "like a bolt from the blue"); **hackneyed** refers to such expressions which through constant use have become virtually meaningless (e.g., "last but not least"); **stereotyped** applies to those fixed expressions which seem invariably to be called up in certain situations (e.g., "I point with pride" in a political oration); **commonplace** is used of any obvious or conventional remark or idea (e.g., "it isn't the heat, it's the humidity")

---

**triumph,** *n.* **1.** [Victory] — *Syn.* conquest, mastery, achievement, ascendancy, gain, success; see also **victory** 1.

**2.** [Exultation] — *Syn.* jubilation, jubilee, reveling; see **celebration** 2, **joy** 2.

*See Synonym Study at VICTORY.*

**triumphal,** *modif.* — *Syn.* ceremonial, garlanded, laurel-crowned; see **famous, honored, praised.**

**triumphant,** *modif.* — *Syn.* exultant, victorious, successful, lucky, winning, conquering, in the lead, triumphal, jubilant, rejoicing, dominant, laurel-crowned, champion, unbeaten, prize-winning, top-seeded, out front, triumphing, victorial, elated, in ascendancy, with flying colors. — *Ant.* BEATEN, defeated, overwhelmed.

**trivial,** *modif.* — *Syn.* petty, trifling, small, superficial, piddling, wee, little, insignificant, frivolous, irrelevant, unimportant, nugatory, skin-deep, meaningless, mean, diminutive, slight, of no account, scanty, meager, inappreciable, microscopic, atomic, dribbling, nonessential, flimsy, inconsiderable, evanescent, vanishing, momentary, immaterial, indifferent, beside the point, minute, unessential, paltry, inferior, minor, small-minded, beggarly, useless, inconsequential, picayune, worthless, scurvy, mangy, trashy, pitiful, of little moment, dinky*, small-town*, rinky-dink*, two-bit*, nickle-and-dime*, piffling*, cutting no ice*, cut and dried*; see also **shallow** 2. — *Ant.* IMPORTANT, great, SERIOUS.

**triviality,** *n.* — *Syn.* unimportance, immateriality, paltriness; see **insignificance.**

**troglodyte,** *n.* **1.** [A prehistoric cave-dweller] — *Syn.* cave man, savage, aborigine; see **hominid.**

**2.** [A recluse] — *Syn.* hermit, solitary, ascetic; see **hermit.**

**troll,** *n.* — *Syn.* ogre, goblin, elf, sprite; see **fairy** 1.

**trolley car,** *n.* — *Syn.* streetcar, electric car, cable car, trackless trolley, trolley*, electric*, trolley-bus*; see also **bus.**

**trollop,** *n.* — *Syn.* whore, streetwalker, harlot; see **prostitute.**

**troop,** *n.* — *Syn.* flock, collection, number, company, troupe, band, crowd, delegation, assemblage; see also **gathering.**

---

*SYN.* — **troop** is applied to a group of people organized as a unit *[a cavalry troop]* , or working or acting together in close cooperation *[troops of sightseers]*; **troupe** is the current form with reference to a group of performers, as in the theater or a circus; **company** is the general word for any group of people associated in any of various ways *[the whole company of his detractors]*; **band** suggests a relatively small group of people closely united for some common purpose and, in a more specific sense, a group of musicians *[a band of thieves, a brass band]*

---

**trooper,** *n.* — *Syn.* cavalryman, patrolman, state trooper, highway patrol officer, dragoon; see also **police officer, soldier.**

**troops,** *n.* — *Syn.* soldiers, armed forces, rank and file, fighting men, military, regiment; see also **army** 1, **infantry.**

**troopship,** *n.* — *Syn.* transport, landing craft, landing ship, LS, landing ship medium, LSM, landing ship tank, LST; see also **boat, ship, transport, warship.**

**trope,** *n.* — *Syn.* metaphor, figure of speech, analogy; see **comparison** 2, **simile.**

**trophy,** *n.* — *Syn.* award, memorial, decoration, citation, medal, cup, crown, ribbon, memento; see also **prize.**

**tropic,** *modif.* **1.** [Related to the tropics] — *Syn.* tropical, equatorial, jungle, Amazonian, torrid, summer, rainy, wild, south, lush, tangled; see also **hot** 1, **wet** 2. — *Ant.* COOL, temperate, arctic.
**2.** [Hot] — *Syn.* thermal, torrid, burning; see **hot** 1.

**tropical,** *modif.* — *Syn.* hot, sultry, torrid; see **tropic** 1.

**tropics,** *n.* — *Syn.* torrid zone, equator, Equatorial Africa, South America, Amazon, the Congo, the Pacific Islands; see also **jungle.**

**trot,** *v.* — *Syn.* single-foot, jog, amble, canter, rack, ride, hurry, step lively, keep an even pace; see also **run** 2.

**troth\*,** *n.* **1.** [A promise] — *Syn.* word of honor, declaration, pledge; see **promise** 1.
**2.** [Faithfulness] — *Syn.* loyalty, truth, fidelity; see **loyalty.**

**trot out\*,** *v.* — *Syn.* exhibit, show, represent; see **display** 1.

**troubadour,** *n.* — *Syn.* bard, poet, musician, balladeer; see **minstrel, singer.**

**trouble,** *n.* **1.** [Difficulty] — *Syn.* strain, stress, struggle; see **difficulty** 1, 2.
**2.** [A person or thing causing trouble] — *Syn.* annoyance, difficult situation, bother, bind, hindrance, difficulty, task, puzzle, predicament, plight, problem, fear, worry, concern, inconvenience, nuisance, disturbance, calamity, catastrophe, crisis, negative function, delay, quarrel, dispute, affliction, intrusion, disquiet, irritation, trial, pain, pique, ordeal, discomfort, injury, adversity, hang-up, case, bore, gossip, problem child, pestiferous person, meddler, pest, tease, tiresome person, talkative person, inconsiderate person, intruder, troublemaker, fly in the ointment\*, monkey wrench\*, headache\*, smart aleck\*, buttinski\*, brat\*, handful\*, holy terror\*, bad news\*, botheration\*, peck of trouble\*; see also **care** 2. — *Ant.* AID, help, COMFORT.
**3.** [Illness] — *Syn.* malady, ailment, affliction; see **disease.**

**4.** [Civil disorder] — *Syn.* riot, turmoil, strife; see **disturbance** 2.
**5.** [A quarrel] — *Syn.* argument, feud, bickering; see **dispute, fight** 1.
**in trouble 1.** — *Syn.* in a quandary, in difficulty, in a predicament, out on a limb, in chancery, unfortunate, having trouble, in hot water\*, in dutch\*, in for it\*, in bad\*, up the creek\*, up a tree\*, in the doghouse\*, in a jam\*; see also **troubled** 1, **unfortunate** 2.
**2.** — *Syn.* with child, pregnant out of wedlock, expecting\*, knocked up\*; see **pregnant** 1.

**trouble,** *v.* **1.** [To disturb] — *Syn.* disconcert, annoy, irritate; see **bother** 3, **disturb** 2.
**2.** [To take care] — *Syn.* be concerned with, make an effort, take pains; see **bother** 1.

**troubled,** *modif.* **1.** [Worried] — *Syn.* disturbed, agitated, grieved, apprehensive, pained, anxious, perplexed, afflicted, confused, puzzled, in a quandary, upwrought, overwrought, chagrined, bothered, harassed, vexed, plagued, teased, annoyed, concerned, uneasy, discomposed, disquieted, harried, careworn, mortified, badgered, baited, inconvenienced, put out, upset, flurried, flustered, afflicted, bored, tortured, piqued, pricked, goaded, irritated, displeased, exacerbated, tried, roused, disconcerted, pursued, fretted, chafed, galled, rubbed the wrong way, discommoded, ragged, tired, unquiet, molested, crossed, thwarted, fashed, fazed, distressed, wounded, sickened, griped, irascible, restless, irked, pestered, heckled, beset, persecuted, frightened, alarmed, terrified, scared, anguished, harrowed, tormented, provoked, stung, nettled, ruffled, fretting, perturbed, afraid, shaky, fearful, unsettled, suspicious, in turmoil, full of misgivings, shaken, careworn, dreading, bugged\*, between the devil and the deep blue sea\*, in a stew\*, on pins and needles\*, all hot and bothered\*, worried stiff\*, in a tizzy\*, burned up\*, discombobulated\*, miffed\*, peeved\*, all in a dither\*, riled\*, aggravated\*, with ants in one's pants\*, behind the eight ball\*, floored\*, up a tree\*, hung-up\*, up the creek without a paddle\*, uptight\*, on the anxious seat\*; see also **doubtful** 2. — *Ant.* CALM, at ease, settled.
**2.** [Pathologically disturbed] — *Syn.* schizophrenic, schizoid, psychotic, psychopathic, neurotic, psychoneurotic, paranoid, devoured by\*, hung-up\*, psyched-out\*; see also **insane** 1.

**troublemaker,** *n.* — *Syn.* malcontent, agitator, rabble-rouser, rowdy, bully, hooligan, juvenile delinquent, mischief-maker; see also **rascal.**

**troubleshooter,** *n.* — *Syn.* mediator, efficiency expert, repairman, diplomat, negotiator; see also **specialist.**

**troublesome,** *modif.* **1.** [Causing anxiety] — *Syn.* upsetting, disquieting, alarming; see **disturbing.**
**2.** [Causing nuisance] — *Syn.* bothersome, inconvenient, annoying, difficult, vexing, vexatious, irritating, oppressive, repressive, distressing, upsetting, painful, dangerous, damaging.

**trough,** *n.* — *Syn.* dip, channel, ditch, gutter, eavestrough, depression between waves, hollow, cup; see also **hole** 2.

**trounce,** *v.* **1.** [To beat] — *Syn.* flog, pummel, thrash; see **beat** 2.
**2.** [To defeat] — *Syn.* conquer, beat, win, overcome; see **defeat** 1, 2, 3.

**trousers,** *n.* — *Syn.* pants, slacks, breeches, knickerbockers; see **clothes, pants** 1.

**trousseau,** *n.* — *Syn.* bride's outfit, vesture, hope chest; see **clothes.**

**trout,** *n.* Varieties of trout include: speckled, brook, rainbow, mountain, sea, river, lake, silver, black-spotted, Dolly Varden, cutthroat, lake, salmon, steelhead, blue-backed, tiger, brown, Galway, golden, Tahoe, Rocky Mountain, Yellowstone; see also **fish.**

**trowel,** *n.* — *Syn.* blade, scoop, spade, implement; see **tool** 1.
Types of trowels include: garden, gardening, transplanting, plasterer's, mason's, pointing, bricklayer's, cement finisher's, molder's, corner, London pattern, Lowell pattern, Philadelphia pattern.

**truant,** *modif.* **1.** [Lazy] — *Syn.* idle, shiftless, indolent; see **lazy** 1.
**2.** [Errant] — *Syn.* missing, straying, playing hooky*; see **absent.**

**truant officer,** *n.* — *Syn.* attendance officer, patrolman, officer, juvenile officer; see **police officer.**

**truce,** *n.* — *Syn.* armistice, peace agreement, respite, lull, amnesty, treaty of peace, terms, suspension of arms, pause, cease-fire, break, cessation, the olive branch*, white flag*; see also **peace** 1. — *Ant.* WARFARE, combat, hostilities.

**truck,** *n.* **1.** [An automotive vehicle for hauling] — *Syn.* carriage, van, lorry (British), car, autotruck, automobile truck, buggy*, semi*, eighteen-wheeler*, rig*, crate*, boat*; see also **vehicle** 1, **wagon.**
Types of trucks include: delivery wagon, moving van, police van, patrol wagon, fire truck, fire engine, laundry truck, pickup truck, forklift, tractor, freight truck, logging truck, army truck, trailer, semitrailer, piggyback*, piggyback truck, piggyback trailer, truck trailer, truck and trailer, truck train, flatbed truck, tow truck, cement mixer, refrigerator truck, panel truck, snubnose truck, one-unit truck, freighter, garbage truck, dump truck, diesel-powered truck, chain-drive truck, amphibious truck, duck*, half-track, mechanized landing craft (LCM), landing craft for vehicles and personnel (LCVP), landing vehicle track (LVT), trac*, amtrac*, water buffalo*, alligator*.
**2.** [A small vehicle for moving heavy loads] — *Syn.* cart, handtruck, warehouse truck, platform truck, wagon, wheelbarrow, dumpcart, pushcart, dray, dolly, handbarrow.
**3.** [*Rubbish] — *Syn.* trivia, snippets, junk; see **trash** 3.
**4.** [*Vegetables] — *Syn.* garden varieties, summer crops, crops, potatoes, onions, carrots, greens; see also **crop, produce, vegetable.**

**truck,** *v.* **1.** [To send by truck] — *Syn.* ship, haul, drive, transport, cart, carry, take a load, freight; see also **send** 1.
**2.** [To traffic in] — *Syn.* peddle, deal in, handle; see **exchange** 1, **sell** 1.

**truckle,** *v.* — *Syn.* cringe, submit, cower, toady; see **wince, yield** 1.

**truck trailer,** *n.* — *Syn.* van, piggyback trailer, vehicle; see **trailer, truck** 1.

**truculent,** *modif.* **1.** [Fierce] — *Syn.* barbarous, brutal, ferocious; see **cruel** 1, 2, **fierce** 1, **savage** 2.
**2.** [Rude] — *Syn.* harsh, mean, scathing; see **rude** 2.

**trudge,** *v.* — *Syn.* plod, step, tread; see **march, walk** 1.

**true,** *modif.* **1.** [Accurate] — *Syn.* precise, exact, right, correct, straight, plumb, square; see also **accurate** 1, **valid** 1.
**2.** [Loyal] — *Syn.* sure, dependable, sincere; see **faithful, reliable** 1, 2.
**3.** [Genuine] — *Syn.* authentic, actual, pure; see **genuine** 1, **real** 2, **valid** 2.
*See Synonym Study at* REAL.

**come true** — *Syn.* become a fact, be actualized, come about; see **develop** 1, **happen** 2.

**true-blue,** *modif.* — *Syn.* loyal, staunch, dependable; see **faithful, reliable** 1.

**truehearted,** *modif.* — *Syn.* loyal, sincere, honest; see **faithful, reliable** 1.

**truelove,** *n.* — *Syn.* sweetheart, beloved, love; see **lover** 1.

**true to form,** *modif.* — *Syn.* usual, customary, as expected; see **conventional** 1, **regular** 3.

**true to life,** *modif.* — *Syn.* true-life, realistic, revealing; see **accurate** 1, **genuine.**

**truism,** *n.* — *Syn.* commonplace, self-evident truth, adage; see **cliché, motto, proverb.**
*See Synonym Study at* CLICHÉ.

**truly,** *modif.* **1.** [Really] — *Syn.* actually, absolutely, positively; see **really** 1, **surely.**
**2.** [In accordance with the truth] — *Syn.* honestly, exactly, definitely, reliably, factually, correctly, unequivocally, sincerely, scrupulously, fairly, validly, rightfully, righteously, punctiliously, faithfully, worthily, scientifically, unbiasedly, without bias, without prejudice, fairly and squarely*; see also **accurately.** — *Ant.* WRONGLY, dishonestly, deceptively.

**trump card*,** *n.* — *Syn.* best play, strongest means, most effective device, trick; see **agent** 1, **device** 2, **strength** 1.

**trumped up,** *modif.* — *Syn.* falsified, concocted, magnified; see **exaggerated, false** 2.

**trumpery,** *n.* — *Syn.* rubbish, frivolity, bosh; see **nonsense** 1.

**trumpet,** *n.* — *Syn.* horn, wind instrument, bugle, cornet, brass wind; see also **musical instrument.**

**trumpet call,** *n.* — *Syn.* reveille, signal, blare; see **alarm** 1, **call** 4, **taps.**

**trump up*,** *v.* — *Syn.* think up, devise, concoct, contrive, present fraudulent evidence, misrepresent, falsify; see also **deceive, lie** 1.

**truncate,** *v.* — *Syn.* lop, mangle, prune; see **trim** 1.

**truncheon,** *n.* — *Syn.* cudgel, bludgeon, war club, nightstick; see **club** 3, **stick, weapon** 1.

**trundle,** *v.* — *Syn.* revolve, rotate, spin; see **turn** 1.

**trunk,** *n.* **1.** [A container for goods] — *Syn.* chest, case, footlocker, traveling case, baggage, luggage, suitcase, keister*, coffin*; see also **bag, container.**
**2.** [The torso] — *Syn.* body, soma, thorax; see **abdomen, back** 2.
**3.** [The stem of a tree] — *Syn.* butt, bole, block, column, stock, log; see also **stalk.**
**4.** [A proboscis] — *Syn.* prow, snoot, snout; see **beak, nose** 1.

**truss,** *n.* — *Syn.* support, supporter, reinforcement, supporting device; see **support** 2.

**truss,** *v.* **1.** [Support] — *Syn.* hold, bear, strengthen; see **hold** 8, **support** 1.
**2.** [To bind] — *Syn.* tie, tie up, constrict, bundle, bundle up; see also **pack** 2, **press** 1.

**trust,** *n.* **1.** [Reliance] — *Syn.* confidence, dependence, belief, credence; see **faith** 1.
**2.** [A trusted person] — *Syn.* mainstay, guarantee, anchor, confidant, security, support, assurance, benefactor, patron, guardian, protector, savior, good angel*.
**3.** [Responsibility] — *Syn.* guardianship, account, duty, liability, moment.
**4.** [A large company] — *Syn.* corporation, monopoly, cartel, holding company, conglomerate, combination, combine; see also **business** 4, **organization** 3.
*See Synonym Study at* BELIEF, MONOPOLY.

**in trust** — *Syn.* in escrow, on deposit, in the custody of, deposited, held, bonded, in the care of, in the keeping of, in account with, given as surety; see also **retained** 1.

**trust,** *v.* **1.** [To believe in] — *Syn.* have faith in, believe in, rely on, depend on, depend upon, count on, bank on\*, have confidence in, place confidence in, confide in, swear by, esteem, expect help from, presume upon, lean on, turn to, fall back on, have no doubt, rest assured, be sure about, have no reservations, put faith in, give credence to, look to, be persuaded by, be convinced, put great stock in\*, set great store by\*, take at one's word\*, eat up\*; see also **believe** 1, **count on.** — *Ant.* DOUBT, mistrust, disbelieve.

**2.** [To hope] — *Syn.* presume, take, imagine; see **assume** 1, **hope.**

**3.** [To place in the protection of another] — *Syn.* lend, put in safekeeping, entrust, trust to, commit, consign, commission, assign, store with, transfer, give over, place in trust of, make someone a trustee of, make someone guardian of.

**4.** [To give credit to] — *Syn.* advance, lend, loan, let out, grant, confer, let, patronize, aid, give financial aid to. — *Ant.* BORROW, raise money, pawn.

---

**SYN.** — **trust** is to have complete faith or assurance that one will not be let down by another [to *trust* in God]; to **rely on** *or* upon a person or thing is to have confidence, usually on the basis of past experience, that what is expected will be done [she can be *relied on* to keep the secret]; to **depend on** *or* upon is to place reliance on a person or thing, esp. for support or aid [a museum that *depends on* corporate contributions]; to **count on** something is to consider it in one's calculations as certain [they *counted on* my going]; to **bank on,** a colloquial term, is to have confidence like that of one who is willing to risk money on something [don't *bank on* their help]

---

**trusted,** *modif.* — *Syn.* trustworthy, dependable, reliable, credible, trusty, tried, proved, intimate, close, faithful, loyal, true, constant, staunch, devoted, incorruptible, safe, honorable, honored, inviolable, on the level\*, kosher\*, A-1\*, regular\*, right\*, sure-fire\*; see also **established** 3. — *Ant.* DISHONEST, questionable, unreliable.

**trustee,** *n.* — *Syn.* guardian, custodian, controller, lawyer, stockholder, guarantor, regent, board member, overseer, governor, appointee, administrator, member of the directorate, garnishee.

**trusteeship,** *n.* — *Syn.* management, direction, guidance, supervision; see **administration** 1, 2.

**trustful,** *modif.* — *Syn.* naive, believing, secure; see **trusting** 1.

**trusting,** *modif.* **1.** [Naive] — *Syn.* trustful, credulous, confiding, gullible, unsuspecting, unsuspicious, easygoing, open, candid, indulgent, obliging, well-meaning, good-natured, tenderhearted, green\*, suckerish\*, doughfaced\*, with a glass jaw\*; see also **naive.** — *Ant.* CRITICAL, SUSPICIOUS, skeptical.

**2.** [Hopeful] — *Syn.* in hopes, expectant, confident, assured, optimistic, presuming, depending on, counting on, relying on, reliant, relying; see also **hopeful** 1.

**trustless,** *modif.* **1.** [Unreliable] — *Syn.* treacherous, unworthy, untrustworthy, deceitful; see **dishonest** 1, 2, **unfaithful** 1.

**2.** [Skeptical] — *Syn.* distrustful, cynical, doubting; see **doubtful** 2, **suspicious** 1.

**trustworthiness,** *n.* — *Syn.* integrity, uprightness, loyalty; see **honesty** 1, **sincerity.**

**trustworthy,** *modif.* — *Syn.* dependable, accurate, honest, true; see **reliable** 1, 2.

*See Synonym Study at* RELIABLE.

**trusty,** *modif.* — *Syn.* trustworthy, dependable, good, tried and true; see **excellent, reliable** 1, 2.

*See Synonym Study at* RELIABLE.

**trusty,** *n.* — *Syn.* trusted person, trustworthy convict, prison attendant, privileged prisoner, psalmsinger\*, valet\*; see also **prisoner.**

**truth,** *n.* **1.** [Conformity to reality] — *Syn.* truthfulness, veracity, correctness, sincerity, verity, candor, openness, honesty, fidelity, frankness, revelation, exactitude, authenticity, factualism, exactness, infallibility, precision, perfection, rectitude, certainty, genuineness, accuracy, fact, the gospel truth\*, straight dope\*, inside track\*, the nitty-gritty\*, the facts\*, the case\*. — *Ant.* LIE, deception, falsehood.

**2.** [Integrity] — *Syn.* trustworthiness, honor, probity; see **honesty** 1.

**in truth** — *Syn.* in fact, indeed, really; see **truly** 1.

---

**SYN.** — **truth** suggests conformity with the facts or with reality, either as an idealized abstraction [Pilate said to him, "What is *truth?*"] or in actual application to statements, ideas, acts, etc. [there is no *truth* in that rumor]; **veracity,** as applied to persons or to their utterances, connotes habitual adherence to the truth [I cannot doubt your *veracity*]; **verity,** as applied to things, connotes correspondence with fact or with reality [the *verity* of that thesis]; **verisimilitude,** as applied to literary or artistic representations, suggests a degree of plausibility sufficient to induce audience belief [the characterizations in that novel lack *verisimilitude*]

---

**truthful,** *modif.* — *Syn.* correct, frank, just; see **accurate** 1, **honest** 1.

**truthfully,** *modif.* — *Syn.* honestly, honorably, veraciously, accurately; see **sincerely, truly** 2.

**truthfulness,** *n.* — *Syn.* integrity, frankness, accuracy; see **honesty** 1, **sincerity.**

**truthless,** *modif.* — *Syn.* lying, deceptive, inaccurate; see **dishonest** 2, **false** 1, 2.

**try,** *v.* **1.** [To endeavor] — *Syn.* attempt, essay, undertake, exert (oneself), contend, strive, make an effort, risk, have a try, contest, wrangle, labor, work, aspire, propose, seek, try to reach, do what one can, tackle, venture, struggle for, compete for, speculate, make every effort, put oneself out, vie for, aspire to, attack\*, make a bid for\*, beat one's brains\*, bear down\*, shoot at\*, shoot for\*, drive for\*, chip away at\*, do one's best\*, bend over backward\*, make a pass at\*, go after\*, go out of the way\*, give a workout\*, do all in one's power\*, go through fire and water\*, buckle down\*, lift a finger\*, break an arm\*, break a blood vessel\*, lay oneself out\*, lay to\*, do oneself justice\*, have a go at\*, make a go of it\*, go all out\*, leave no stone unturned\*, move heaven and earth\*, hump it\*, file a strong bid\*, go all lengths\*, go to market\*, knock oneself out\*, bunch the hits\*, break one's neck\*, bust a gut\*, take a crack at\*, give it a whirl\*, fight the good fight\*.

**2.** [To test] — *Syn.* assay, investigate, put to the proof; see **analyze** 1, **examine** 1, 2.

**3.** [To conduct a trial] — *Syn.* hear, judge, examine, adjudicate, decide, hear a case, sit in judgment, give a fair hearing.

---

**SYN.** — **try** is commonly the simple, direct word for putting forth effort to do something [*try* to come], but specifically it connotes experimentation in testing or proving something [I'll *try* your recipe]; **attempt,** somewhat more formal, suggests a setting out to accomplish something but often connotes failure [he had *attempted* to take his life]; **endeavor** suggests exertion and determined effort in the face of difficulties [we shall *endeavor* to recover your loss/; **essay** connotes a tentative experimenting to test the feasibility of something difficult /she will not *essay* the high jump/; **strive** suggests great, earnest exertion to accomplish something /*strive* to win/; **struggle** suggests a violent striving to overcome obstacles or to free oneself from an impediment /I *struggled* to reach the top/

---

**trying,** *modif.* — *Syn.* troublesome, bothersome, irritating, tiring; see **difficult** 1, 2, **severe** 2.

**try on,** *v.* — *Syn.* fit, have a fitting, try on for size; see **experiment** 2, **wear** 1.

**try one's hand at\*,** *v.* — *Syn.* attempt, try out, make a stab at\*; see **experiment** 2, **try** 1.

**tryout,** *n.* — *Syn.* test, demonstration, rehearsal, hearing, audition, preliminary practice, trial, practice game, test-up\*; see also **examination** 1.

**try out for,** *v.* — *Syn.* go out for, perform, test, compete for, audition, experiment, probe, practice with, read for, try, give something a try\*; see also **rehearse** 3.

**tryst,** *n.* — *Syn.* rendezvous, assignation, union; see **appointment** 2, **meeting** 1.

**tub,** *n.* — *Syn.* keg, bucket, cask, tank, receptacle, laundry tub, bathtub, hot tub, spa, cauldron, vat, cistern, butt, firkin, tun; see also **container.**

**tubby,** *modif.* — *Syn.* plump, beefy, stout; see **fat** 1, **short** 1.

**tube,** *n.* **1.** [A hollow cylinder] — *Syn.* conduit, hose, test tube, tubing, tunnel, loom, subway; see also **pipe** 1.
**2.** [A pliable container] — *Syn.* package, paste tube, squeeze tube; see **container.**
**3.** [An electronic device] — *Syn.* cell, vacuum tube, electron tube, electronic tube; see **device** 1, **machine** 1. Electronic tubes include: electric eye, electron tube, vacuum tube, neon tube, neon light, fluorescent tube, fluorescent light, radio tube, television tube, cathode ray tube, X-ray tube, photoelectric tube, photoelectric cell, thermionic tube, thermionic valve, converter, gas tube, vapor tube, focus tube, high pressure tube, low pressure tube. Specialized tubes include: Geissler tube, Crookes tube, Venturi tube, Geiger-Müller tube, Braun tube, traveling wave tube, negative grid electron tube, photomultiplier tube, X-ray diffraction tube, grid-seal tube, disk-seal tube, grid-glow tube, glow-discharge tube, multigrid tube, multiplex tube, mercury-vapor tube, triode, tetrode, thyratron, phasitron, diode, pentagrid, klystron, ignatron, magnetron, exitron.

**tuberculosis,** *n.* — *Syn.* lung disease, pulmonary phthisis, consumption, T.B.\*, lung trouble\*; see also **disease.**

**tuck,** *n.* — *Syn.* crease, folding, pleat; see **fold** 1, 2, **plait.**

**tuck in,** *v.* **1.** [To fold in] — *Syn.* insert, put in, squeeze in, add; see **embed** 1, **include** 2.
**2.** [To pull in] — *Syn.* contract, suck in\*, tighten up.
**3.** [To eat heartily] — *Syn.* eat up, chow down\*, put on the feed bag\*; see **eat** 1.

**tuft,** *n.* — *Syn.* clump, cluster, group; see **bunch** 1.

**tug,** *v.* — *Syn.* pull, haul, tow; see **draw** 1.
*See Synonym Study at* PULL.

**tugboat,** *n.* — *Syn.* tug, towboat, tugger, tender, steam tug; see also **boat.**

**tuition,** *n.* **1.** [A charge for instruction] — *Syn.* fee, cost, expenditure; see **charge** 1, **price.**
**2.** [Instruction] — *Syn.* teaching, tutoring, schooling, lessons; see **education** 1.

**tumble,** *v.* — *Syn.* drop, plunge, descend; see **fall** 1, **topple, trip** 1.

**tumbledown,** *modif.* — *Syn.* dilapidated, decrepit, rickety; see **old** 2, **shaky** 1, **unsteady** 1, **worn** 2.

**tumbler,** *n.* **1.** [An acrobat] — *Syn.* equilibrist, gymnast, trampolinist; see **acrobat, athlete.**
**2.** [A glass] — *Syn.* goblet, cup, mug; see **glass** 2.

**tumbling,** *modif.* — *Syn.* falling, rolling, pitching, plunging, whirling, turning in the air, falling head over heels.

**tumbling,** *n.* — *Syn.* acrobatics, floor exercise, mat gymnastics; see **gymnastics.**

**tumefaction,** *n.* — *Syn.* boil, bloating, enlargement; see **growth** 3, **swelling.**

**tumid,** *modif.* **1.** [Swollen] — *Syn.* bulging, distended, bloated; see **enlarged, inflated.**
**2.** [Pompous] — *Syn.* bombastic, sonorous, inflated; see **egotistic** 2.

**tumor,** *n.* — *Syn.* neoplasm, tumefaction, cyst, malignant tumor, benign tumor; see also **growth** 3, **swelling.**

**tumult,** *n.* — *Syn.* agitation, uproar, turbulence; see **confusion** 2, **disturbance** 2, **fight** 1.

**tumultuous,** *modif.* — *Syn.* agitated, disturbed, violent; see **turbulent.**

**tun,** *n.* — *Syn.* cask, tub, vessel; see **container, tank** 1.

**tune,** *n.* — *Syn.* melody, air, aria, song, harmony, strain, theme, piece, number, ditty, jingle, a few bars; see also **melody** 2, **song.**

**call the tune\*** — *Syn.* be in control, direct, manage; see **lead** 1.

**change one's tune\*** — *Syn.* change one's mind, alter one's actions, be transformed; see **change** 4,

**sing a different tune\*** — *Syn.* change one's mind, alter one's actions, be transformed; see **change** 4.
*See Synonym Study at* MELODY.

**tune,** *v.* — *Syn.* adjust the pitch, attune, put in tune, tune up, tighten the strings, use the tuning fork, set the tune; see also **harmonize** 1.

**tuneful,** *modif.* — *Syn.* melodious, symphonic, rhythmic; see **harmonious** 1, **musical** 1.

**tune in,** *v.* — *Syn.* participate, get hip\*, become part of, enter into; see **join** 1, 2, **listen** 1, **receive** 1, **see** 1.

**tune up\*,** *v.* — *Syn.* enliven, refine, make better; see **improve** 1.

**tunnel,** *n.* — *Syn.* hole, burrow, underground passage, subway, tube, crawl space, crawlway, shaft, mine, pit, crosscut, drift, adit.

**turban,** *n.* — *Syn.* headdress, headgear, topee, puggree; see **hat.**

**turbid,** *modif.* — *Syn.* foul, swollen, muddy, cloudy, sedimentary, mixed, muddled, thick, impure, unsettled, roiled, unclean, filthy, smudgy, mired, befouled, grimy, messy, reeky, murky, dirty.

**turbulence,** *n.* — *Syn.* disorder, commotion, fracas; see **confusion** 2, **disturbance** 2, **fight** 1.

**turbulent,** *modif.* — *Syn.* riotous, violent, stormy, disturbed, noisy, restless, raging, howling, buffeting, thunderous, inclement, tumultuous, excited, passionate, uncontrolled, vehement, roaring, tempestuous, rampant, rowdy, lawless, disorderly, untamed, disordered, chaotic, agitated, fierce, wild, rude, rough, blustering, obstreperous, angry, storming, uproarious, clamorous, tremulous, mutinous, rebellious, destructive, hard, stern, bitter, fiery, rabid, boisterous, perturbed, foaming, shaking, demonstrative, vociferous; see also **intense.** — *Ant.* PEACEFUL, tranquil, at ease.

**turf,** *n.* — *Syn.* earth, peat, lawn; see **grass** 1, **sod.**

**turgid,** *modif.* **1.** [Swollen] — *Syn.* bloated, distended, puffy; see **enlarged, inflated.**
**2.** [Pompous] — *Syn.* bombastic, pompous, grandiloquent, purple\*; see **bombastic.**
*See Synonym Study at* BOMBASTIC.

**turkey,** *n.* — *Syn.* turkey cock, turkey hen, bird, fowl, Thanksgiving bird, Christmas bird, gobbler, turkey gobbler, wild turkey, domestic turkey, cock of India, hen of India, *poule d'Inde* (French), *gallina de India* (Spanish), *gallo, gallina d'India* (*both* Italian), *Indianische Henn, Huhn* (*both* German).
Types and breeds of turkeys include: bronze turkey, buff turkey, black turkey, slate turkey, white turkey, reddish brown turkey, domestic turkey, Cambridgeshire turkey, Colorado turkey, crested turkey, Honduras turkey, Mexican turkey, native turkey, New England wild turkey, Norfolk turkey, ocellated turkey, wild turkey, brush turkey, water turkey.

**turmoil,** *n.* — *Syn.* agitation, turbulence, riot; see **confusion** 2, **disturbance** 2, **uproar.**

**turn,** *n.* **1.** [a revolution] — *Syn.* rotation, cycle, circle, round, circulation, pirouette, gyre, gyration, spin, round-about-face, roll, turning, circumrotation, spiral; see also **revolution** 1.
**2.** [A bend] — *Syn.* curve, winding, twist, wind, hook, shift, angle, corner, fork, branch.
**3.** [A turning point] — *Syn.* climax, crisis, juncture, emergency, critical period, crossing, change, new development, shift, twist.
**4.** [*A shock] — *Syn.* fright, jolt, blow; see **surprise** 2.
**5.** [*An action] — *Syn.* deed, accomplishment, service; see **aid** 1.
**6.** [A change in course] — *Syn.* curve, detour, deviation, corner, ground loop, stem turn, jump turn, Christiania turn, Christy*, Telemark turn, Telemark, kick turn, inside loop, outside loop, left *or* right wing spin, tight spin, tight spiral, roll, Immelmann turn, Immelmann*.
**at every turn** — *Syn.* in every instance, constantly, consistently; see **regularly** 1.
**by turns** — *Syn.* taking turns, in succession, one after another, alternately, consecutively.
**call the turn** — *Syn.* anticipate, predict, expect; see **foretell.**
**take turns** — *Syn.* do by turns, do in succession, share; see **alternate** 1.
**to a turn** — *Syn.* correctly, properly, to the right degree, to a T; see **perfectly** 1.
**turn,** *v.* **1.** [To pivot] — *Syn.* revolve, rotate, roll, spin, wheel, whirl, gyre, circulate, go around, swivel; round, twist, twirl, gyrate, ground, loop; see also **swing** 1.
**2.** [To reverse] — *Syn.* go back, tack, recoil, change, upset, retrace, face about, turn around, capsize, shift, alter, vary, convert, transform, invert, subvert, return, alternate.
**3.** [To divert] — *Syn.* deflect, veer, turn aside, turn away, sidetrack, swerve, put off, call off, turn off, deviate, dodge, twist, avoid, shift, switch, avert, zigzag, shy away, shunt, redirect, shunt aside, shunt away, draw aside.
**4.** [To become] — *Syn.* grow into, change into, pass into; see **become** 1.
**5.** [To sour] — *Syn.* curdle, acidify, become rancid; see **ferment, sour.**
**6.** [To change direction] — *Syn.* swerve, swirl, swing, bend, veer, tack, round to, incline, deviate, detour, loop, curve, ground loop*, stem turn*, ramble*, jump turn*, kick turn*, Telemark*.
**7.** [To incline] — *Syn.* prefer, be predisposed to, favor; see **lean** 1, **tend** 2.
**8.** [To sprain] — *Syn.* strain, bruise, dislocate; see **hurt** 1, **wrench.**
**9.** [To nauseate] — *Syn.* sicken, make one sick, revolt; see **disgust.**

**10.** [To bend] — *Syn.* curve, twist, fold; see **bend** 1.
**11.** [To transform] — *Syn.* transmute, remake, transpose; see **change** 1.
**12.** [To make use of] — *Syn.* apply, adapt, utilize; see **use** 1.
**13.** [To point] — *Syn.* direct, set, train; see **aim** 2.
**14.** [To repel] — *Syn.* repulse, push back, throw back; see **repel** 1.
*See Synonym Study at* BEND.

**turn about,** *v.* — *Syn.* turn around, pivot, reverse; see **turn** 1.

**turn against,** *v.* — *Syn.* revolt, disobey, defy; see **oppose** 1, 2, **rebel** 1.

**turn and turn about,** *modif.* — *Syn.* in turn, alternately; now one, now the other; see **equally.**

**turn aside,** *v.* — *Syn.* avert, deflect, divert; see **turn** 3, **veer.**

**turn back,** *v.* — *Syn.* retrogress, retrograde, revert; see **return** 1, 2.

**turncoat,** *n.* — *Syn.* traitor, renegade, betrayer, apostate, defector; see also **deserter, traitor.**

**turn down,** *v.* **1.** [To decrease in volume, etc.] — *Syn.* hush, lower, curb; see **decrease** 2.
**2.** [To refuse] — *Syn.* reject, decline, rebuff; see **refuse** 1, **scorn** 2.

**turned,** *modif.* **1.** [Revolved] — *Syn.* spun, rounded, circled, circulated, rotated, rolled, whirled, gyrated, set going.
**2.** [Deflected] — *Syn.* switched, twisted, dodged, avoided, shied, away from, shifted, shunted, changed.

**turn in,** *v.* **1.** [To deliver] — *Syn.* hand over, transfer, give up; see **give** 1.
**2.** [*To go to bed] — *Syn.* lie down, retire, hit the hay*, hit the sack*; see **rest** 1.

**turning,** *modif.* **1.** [Bending] — *Syn.* twisting, shifting, whirling, rotating, revolving, bending, curving, spinning, wheeling, shunting; see also **writhing.** — *Ant.* PERMANENT, static, fixed.
**2.** [Growing] — *Syn.* transforming, becoming, converting, changing; see **growing.**

**turning point,** *n.* — *Syn.* peak, juncture, culmination, Rubicon; see **climax, crisis.**

**turn into,** *v.* **1.** [To change] — *Syn.* transform, alter, transmute; see **change** 1.
**2.** [To become changed] — *Syn.* be converted, transform, modify; see **change** 4.

**turnip,** *n.* — *Syn.* domestic turnip, rutabaga, Swedish turnip, turnip cabbage, kohlrabi, Teltow turnip, wild turnip, Indian turnip; see also **vegetable.**

**turn loose*,** *v.* — *Syn.* liberate, emancipate, set free, let go; see **free** 1, **release.**

**turn off,** *v.* **1.** [To stop the operation of] — *Syn.* stop, shut off, douse, close, shut, extinguish, shut down, turn out, kill the light*, kill the engine*, kill the motor*, turn off the juice*, log off*, cut the light*, cut the engine*, kill the motor*, hit the switch*; see also **halt** 2.
**2.** [*To disgust] — *Syn.* repel, repulse, disinterest; see **disgust.**

**turn on,** *v.* **1.** [To start the operation of] — *Syn.* set going, switch on, set in motion, put in gear*, log on*, boat*; see also **begin** 1.
**2.** [To attack] — *Syn.* strike, assail, assault; see **attack** 1, 2.
**3.** [*To take drugs] — *Syn.* take LSD, smoke marijuana, get high*, take a trip*, smoke pot*, get stoned*, groove*, blow pot*, steamroll*, freak out*, trip out*, rock out*, tune*, fly*, get wasted*.
**4.** [*To arouse] — *Syn.* titillate, stimulate, stir up; see **excite** 1.

**5.** [*To depend on or upon] — *Syn.* hinge on, be dependent on, be based on; see **depend** 2.

**turnout,** *n.* **1.** [Production] — *Syn.* output, aggregate, volume; see **production** 1.

**2.** [A gathering] — *Syn.* assembly, attendance, group; see **gathering.**

**turn out,** *v.* **1.** [To stop the operation of] — *Syn.* extinguish, shut off, stop; see **turn off** 1.

**2.** [To dismiss] — *Syn.* discharge, evict, send away; see **dismiss** 1, 2, **oust.**

**3.** [To produce] — *Syn.* make, put out, build; see **manufacture** 1, **produce** 2.

**4.** [To get out of bed] — *Syn.* get up, rise, wake up; see **arise** 1, **wake** 2.

**5.** [To finish] — *Syn.* end, complete, perfect; see **achieve** 1.

**6.** [To result] — *Syn.* eventuate, prove to be, be discovered to be; see **become** 1.

**turn over,** *v.* **1.** [To invert] — *Syn.* overturn, reverse, subvert; see **upset** 1.

**2.** [To transfer] — *Syn.* hand over, give over, deliver; see **assign** 1, **give** 1.

**turn over a new leaf*,** *v.* — *Syn.* get better, change for the better, put the past behind one, make resolutions, make New Year's resolutions; see also **improve** 2, **reform** 1.

**turnpike,** *n.* — *Syn.* toll road, freeway, interstate; see **highway.**

**turn sour,** *v.* — *Syn.* putrefy, rot, spoil; see **decay.**

**turn the tables,** *v.* — *Syn.* reverse conditions, reverse circumstances, give one a taste of his own medicine, hoist one with his own petard*; see **change** 1, **upset** 1.

**turn to,** *v.* **1.** [To rely upon] — *Syn.* confide, appeal to, depend upon; see **trust** 1.

**2.** [To start] — *Syn.* start to work, become interested in, take up, become engrossed in, apply oneself; see also **begin** 1.

**turn traitor,** *v.* — *Syn.* break faith, inform against, give away; see **betray** 1, **deceive.**

**turn up,** *v.* **1.** [To find] — *Syn.* disclose, learn, come across; see **discover, find** 1.

**2.** [To arrive] — *Syn.* enter, come, roll in; see **arrive** 1.

**3.** [To increase the volume, etc.] — *Syn.* amplify, augment, boost*; see **increase** 1, **intensify, strengthen.**

**turpentine,** *n.* — *Syn.* oleoresin, terebinth extract, Chian turpentine, spirits of turpentine, oil of turpentine, thinner, mineral spirits, paint thinner, turps*; see also **oil.**

**turpitude,** *n.* — *Syn.* baseness, vileness, depravity; see **evil** 1, 2.

**turquoise,** *modif.* — *Syn.* blue-green, sea-green, greenish-blue, Mediterranean blue, bright blue; see also **blue** 1, **green** 1.

**turret,** *n.* — *Syn.* tower, revolving dome, watchtower, armored tank top, conical top, gun bulge, blister; see also **top** 1.

**turtle,** *n.* — *Syn.* terrapin, tortoise, chelonian, testudinate; see **reptile.**
Types of turtles include: land, sea, river, sand, mud, painted, musk, ridley, snapping, snapper*, rain, loggerhead, box, softshell, leatherback, green, hawksbill, Galapagos; matamata, slider, stinkpot.

**tusk,** *n.* — *Syn.* canine tooth, fang, incisor; see **tooth** 1.
*See Synonym Study at* TOOTH.

**tussle,** *n.* — *Syn.* scuffle, struggle, scrap; see **fight** 1.

**tutelage,** *n.* **1.** [Instruction] — *Syn.* teaching, tutoring, tutorship, schooling; see **education** 1.

**2.** [Care] — *Syn.* guardianship, charge, protection; see **custody** 1.

**tutelary,** *modif.* — *Syn.* protecting, guardian, advisory; see **protective.**

**tutor,** *n.* — *Syn.* instructor, tutorial assistant, private teacher, teaching assistant, TA; see also **teacher** 1, 2.

**tutoring,** *n.* — *Syn.* coaching, training, private teaching, instruction, tutelage, guidance; see also **education** 1.

**tuxedo,** *n.* — *Syn.* formal suit, men's evening wear, dinner clothes, black tie, tux*, tuck*, monkey suit*, formal*, straight jacket*, soup-and-fish*; see also **suit** 3.

**T.V.,** *n.* — *Syn.* video, tube*, boob tube*, idiot box*, electronic babysitter*, telly* (British); see also **television.**

**tweak,** *v.* — *Syn.* twitch, squeeze, jerk; see **pinch.**

**tweezers,** *n.* — *Syn.* forceps, nippers, tongs; see **pincers.**

**twelve,** *modif.* — *Syn.* dozen, twelvefold, twelfth, duodecimo, duodecimal, uncial.

**twenty,** *modif.* — *Syn.* twentieth, vicenary, twentyfold, vicennial.

**twice,** *modif.* — *Syn.* double, doubly, once and again, over again, once over, two time, two times.

**twig,** *n.* — *Syn.* offshoot, limb, sprig; see **branch** 2.

**twilight,** *n.* — *Syn.* dusk, gloaming, nightfall, late afternoon, early evening, sunset, dawn, break of day, owl-light*; see also **night** 1.

**twin,** *modif.* — *Syn.* identical, fellow, twofold, second, accompanying, joint, coupled, matched, copied, duplicating; see also **second, two.** — *Ant.* SINGLE, lone, solitary.

**twin,** *n.* — *Syn.* double, counterpart, doppelgänger, identical twin, fraternal twin, twin sister, twin brother, spit and image*, spitting image*.

**twine,** *n.* — *Syn.* binder twine, braid, cordage, cord, string, pack thread; see also **rope.**

**twinge,** *v.* — *Syn.* twitch, shiver, smart; see **tingle.**

**twinkle,** *v.* — *Syn.* shimmer, flicker, sparkle; see **shine** 1.

**twinkling,** *modif.* — *Syn.* sparkling, glimmering, flashing; see **bright** 1, **shimmering.**

**twirl,** *v.* — *Syn.* spin, rotate, twist; see **turn** 1, **whirl.**

**twist,** *v.* — *Syn.* wring, wrap, twine, twirl, turn, turn around, wrap around, intertwine, wind, coil, bend, curve, rotate, spiral, corkscrew, spin, wrench, sprain, contort, distort; see also **bend** 1, 2.
*See Synonym Study at* BEND.

**twisted,** *modif.* **1.** [Crooked] — *Syn.* contorted, wrenched, bent, knotted, braided, twined, wound, wreathed, vermiculate, vermiculated, vermicular, vermiform, writhing, convolute, convoluous, twisting. — *Ant.* STRAIGHT, even, regular.

**2.** [Confused] — *Syn.* erroneous, perplexing, wrongheaded, awry, puzzling, unintelligible, disorganized, perverted; see also **confused** 2, **tangled, wrong** 3. — *Ant.* CLEAR, simple, logical.

**twitch,** *n.* — *Syn.* jerk, tic, twinge, spasm; see **fit** 1.

**twitch,** *v.* **1.** [To pluck] — *Syn.* pull, tug, snatch, yank, clutch, grip, grab, seize, clasp, grasp; see also **jerk** 1.

**2.** [To jerk] — *Syn.* shiver, shudder, have a fit, kick, work, palpitate, beat, twinge, pain; see also **jerk** 1.

**twitter,** *v.* — *Syn.* sing, chirp, whistle, peep, cheep, coo.

**two,** *modif.* — *Syn.* twin, dual, binary, both, double, bifid.

**two,** *n.* — *Syn.* two of a kind, brace, couple; see **pair.**
**in two** — *Syn.* halved, divided, split; see **separated.**
**put two and two together*** — *Syn.* reason, sum up, reach a conclusion, understand; see **decide.**

**two-by-four*,** *modif.* — *Syn.* small, cramped, narrow; see **little** 1.

**two-faced,** *modif.* — *Syn.* deceitful, caviling, treacherous, Janus-faced; see **false** 1, **hypocritical.**

**twofold,** *modif.* — *Syn.* twice over, duplex, double; see **two.**

**tycoon,** *n.* — *Syn.* financier, magnate, industrialist, robber baron*, honcho*; see also **administrator, businessperson.**

**tying,** *modif.* — *Syn.* binding, confining, restricting, limiting, checking, curbing, restraining, shackling, cramping, strict.

**type,** *n.* **1.** [Kind] — *Syn.* sort, nature, character; see **kind** 2, **variety** 2.

**2.** [Classification] — *Syn.* standard, species, type genus, type species, variety; see also **class** 1.

**3.** [Representative] — *Syn.* model, sample, example, prototype, archetype, copy order; see also **representation.**

**4.** [Letter] — *Syn.* symbol, emblem, figure, character, sign, typeface, font, screen font, bitmap font; see also **letter** 1.

Fonts of type include: Gothic, black letter, old style, new style, modern, roman, script, sans serif, Times Roman, Courier, Arial, Palatino, Stymie, Bodoni, Cheltenham, Cloister, Cushing, Forum, Blado, Polifilo, Garamond, Goudy, Baskerville, Fournier, Melior, Plantin, DeVinne, Electra, Janson, Italia, Bembo, Caledonia, Bookman, Optima, Schoolbook, Helvetica, Venezia, Granjon, Caslon, Didot, Bruce, Vale, Endeavor, Wedding, Century, Century Schoolbook, Avant Garde, Futura.

Sizes of type include: Excelsior or 3-point, Brilliant or 3½-point, Diamond or 4½-point, Pearl or 5-point, Agate or 5½-point, Non-pareil or 6-point, Minion or 7-point, Brevier or 8-point, Bourgeois or 9-point, Long Primer or 10-point, Small Pica or 11-point, Pica or 12-point, English or 14-point, Columbian or 16-point, Great Primer or 18-point.

Styles of type include: standard, lightface, boldface, extrabold, italic, underline, all caps, small caps, cursive, open, extended, condensed, shaded, upright, slanted, superscript, subscript, strikethrough, redline, expanded, wide.

**type,** *v.* **1.** [To use a typewriter] — *Syn.* typewrite, keyboard, keypunch, use a word processor, copy, transcribe, teletype, touch-type, hunt and peck*.

**2.** [To classify] — *Syn.* categorize, normalize, standardize; see **stereotype.**

**typed,** *modif.* **1.** [Set down on a typewriter] — *Syn.* type-written, copied, set up, written, transcribed; see also **printed.**

**2.** [Classified] — *Syn.* labeled, characterized, analyzed, symbolized, classed, prefigured, sampled, exemplified, made out to be, patterned, standardized, stylized, cast, formalized; see also **classified, marked** 1, **regulated.**

**typewrite,** *v.* — *Syn.* type, make a typed copy, prepare a typescript, transcribe, keyboard; see also **type** 1.

**typewriter,** *n.* — *Syn.* typing machine, office typewriter, portable, electric typewriter, electronic typewriter, word processor, computer, personal computer, PC, ticker, teletypewriter, mill*, office piano*, typer*.

**typewritten,** *modif.* — *Syn.* written on a typewriter, typed on a word processor, transcribed, copied, teletyped; see also **printed.**

**typhoon,** *n.* — *Syn.* blow, hurricane, tornado, cyclone, tropical storm; see also **storm** 1, **wind** 1.

**typical,** *modif.* — *Syn.* characteristic, habitual, usual, standard, representative, symbolic, normal, exemplary, illustrative, conventional, prototypical, archetypical, ideal, quintessential, expected, standardized, patterned, ordinary, average, common, everyday, regular, par for the course*. — *Ant.* SUPERIOR, exceptional, extraordinary.

*See Synonym Study at* NORMAL.

**typify,** *v.* — *Syn.* exemplify, symbolize, embody; see **mean** 1.

**typing,** *n.* — *Syn.* typescript, typewriting, typed copy, typewritten text, teletyping; see also **writing** 1.

**typist,** *n.* — *Syn.* secretary, typewriter operator, keyboarder, word processor, teletyper, office girl, key pounder*, typer*, typewriter*.

**typographic,** *modif.* — *Syn.* typed, set, typographical; see **printed, written** 1.

**tyrannical,** *modif.* — *Syn.* dictatorial, fascistic, totalitarian, brutal, domineering, lordly; see also **absolute** 3, **autocratic** 1.

**tyrannize,** *v.* — *Syn.* despotize, domineer, dictate, intimidate, oppress; see also **dominate.**

**tyranny,** *n.* — *Syn.* oppression, cruelty, severity, reign of terror, despotism, absolutism; see also **autocracy, fascism.**

**tyrant,** *n.* — *Syn.* despot, absolute ruler, inquisitor; see **dictator.**

**tyro,** *n.* — *Syn.* beginner, learner, apprentice; see **amateur, beginner.**

*See Synonym Study at* AMATEUR.

# U

**ubiquitous,** *modif.* — *Syn.* omnipresent, universal, all over; see **everywhere.**

**ubiquity,** *n.* — *Syn.* omnipresence, all-presence, universality, pervasion, pervasiveness.

**udder,** *n.* — *Syn.* dug, pap, nipple, teat, mammilla, breast, mammary gland, milk gland.

**ugliness,** *n.* — *Syn.* unsightliness, homeliness, hideousness, repulsiveness, loathsomeness, unseemliness, uncomeliness, offensiveness, deformity, bad looks, ill looks, ill-favored countenance, plainness, disfigurement, monstrousness, grim aspect, foulness, horridness, inelegance, frightfulness, fearfulness, odiousness, unloveliness. — *Ant.* BEAUTY, fairness, attractiveness.

**ugly,** *modif.* **1.** [Ill-favored] — *Syn.* unsightly, loathsome, hideous, homely, repulsive, unseemly, uncomely, deformed, bad-looking, plain, disfigured, monstrous, foul, horrid, frightful, revolting, repellent, unlovely, appalling, haglike, misshapen, misbegotten, hard-featured, grisly, unprepossessing, horse-faced*, having a face that would stop a clock*, looking a mess*, looking a fright*, looking like the devil *or* deuce*, not fit to be seen*. — *Ant.* handsome, BEAUTIFUL, graceful.
**2.** [Unpleasant] — *Syn.* nasty, nauseous, nauseating*, noisome, disagreeable, disgusting, odious, revolting, repellent, repulsive, sorry, vile, dirty, filthy, sordid, messy, sickening, foul; see also **unpleasant.** — *Ant.* NICE, dainty, agreeable.
**3.** [Dangerous] — *Syn.* pugnacious, quarrelsome, obnoxious, bellicose, rough, disagreeable, cantankerous, violent, vicious, evil, sinister, treacherous, wicked, formidable, truculent. — *Ant.* MILD, reasonable, complaisant.

**ukase,** *n.* — *Syn.* decree, proclamation, edict; see **judgment** 3.

**ulcer,** *n.* — *Syn.* peptic ulcer, lesion, canker, boil, abscess, focal infection, fistula, open sore, running sore; see also **sore.**

**ulcerous,** *modif.* — *Syn.* ulcerative, gangrenous, cankered; see **unhealthy.**

**ulterior,** *modif.* **1.** [Future] — *Syn.* later, subsequent, further; see **future, last** 1.
**2.** [Implied] — *Syn.* undisclosed, concealed, unsaid; see **secret** 1, 3.

**ultimate,** *modif.* — *Syn.* final, terminal, latest; see **last** 1.

**ultimately,** *modif.* — *Syn.* eventually, at last, in the end, sooner or later, as a conclusion, to cap the climax, sequentially, in the sequel, after all, in consummation, at the close, at long last, in conclusion, conclusively, climactically, in due time, after a while, in after days, presently, by and by; see also **finally** 2. — *Ant.* EARLY, in the beginning, at present.

**ultimatum,** *n.* — *Syn.* demand, requirement, term, final offer.

**ultracritical,** *modif.* — *Syn.* hypercritical, fussy, exigent; see **critical** 2, **severe** 1.

**ultramodern,** *modif.* — *Syn.* modernistic, futuristic, avant-garde; see **modern** 1, 3.

**ultranationalism,** *n.* — *Syn.* extreme patriotism, chauvinism, jingoism, xenophobia; see **loyalty, patriotism.**

**ultrasonic,** *modif.* — *Syn.* shrill, high, supersonic, suprasonic, above 20,000 vibrations per second, too high for human ears *or* hearing.

**ultraviolet,** *modif.* — *Syn.* beyond violet, having wavelengths of more than 4,000 angstroms, beyond *or* out of the range of sight; see **invisible** 1, **violet.**

**umbrage,** *n.* — *Syn.* displeasure, offense, sense of injury; see **anger, offense, resentment.**
*See Synonym Study at* OFFENSE.

**umbrageous,** *modif.* — *Syn.* dim, shaded, shadowed; see **dark** 1, **shady.**

**umbrella,** *n.* — *Syn.* parasol, sunshade, beach umbrella, *parapluie* (French), bumbershoot*, brolly* (British).

**umpire,** *n.* — *Syn.* referee, arbiter, arbitrator, judge, justice, moderator, mediator, negotiator, peace-maker, compromiser, settler, inspector, assessor, ump*, ref*; see also **judge** 2.
*See Synonym Study at* JUDGE.

**umpteen*,** *modif.* — *Syn.* very many, considerable, numerous, countless; see **many.**

**unabbreviated,** *modif.* — *Syn.* unabridged, complete, whole; see **whole** 1.

**unable,** *modif.* — *Syn.* incapable, powerless, weak, incompetent, unskilled, impotent, not able, inept, incapacitated, impuissant, inefficacious, helpless, unfitted, inefficient, unqualified, inadequate, ineffectual, inoperative. — *Ant.* ABLE, capable, effective.

**unabridged,** *modif.* — *Syn.* complete, total, intact, unshortened, comprehensive, exhaustive; see also **whole** 1.

**unaccompanied,** *modif.* — *Syn.* sole, solitary, solo, deserted; see **abandoned** 1, **alone** 1.

**unaccomplished,** *modif.* **1.** [Unfinished] — *Syn.* incomplete, unperformed, frustrated; see **unfinished** 1.
**2.** [Unskilled] — *Syn.* untrained, uneducated, inexpert; see **incompetent.**

**unaccountable,** *modif.* — *Syn.* strange, odd, peculiar; see **mysterious** 2, **unusual** 1.

**unaccounted-for,** *modif.* — *Syn.* missing, missing in action, gone, not reporting; see **lost** 1.

**unaccustomed,** *modif.* **1.** [Unfamiliar] — *Syn.* strange, unknown, unusual, singular, foreign, alien, outlandish, exotic, quaint, imported, novel, bizarre, unorthodox, different, unconventional, exceptional, suprising, altered, eccentric, variant. — *Ant.* FAMILIAR, usual, ordinary.
**2.** [Unpracticed] — *Syn.* unskilled, unused, not given to, incompetent, uninstructed, untrained, unacquainted, inexperienced, novice, ignorant, uninformed, untaught. — *Ant.* skilled, trained, EXPERIENCED.

**unacquainted,** *modif.* — *Syn.* ignorant, not introduced, unfamiliar, not intimate, not on speaking terms, isolated, strange, unknown, apart, aloof, secluded, withdrawn, out of touch, incommunicado. — *Ant.* FRIENDLY, acquainted, intimate.

**unadulterated,** *modif.* — *Syn.* uncorrupted, unalloyed, undiluted; see **pure** 1, **untouched** 2.

**unadvised,** *modif.* **1.** [Careless] — *Syn.* hasty, reckless, indiscreet, ill-advised; see **careless** 1.
**2.** [Unaware] — *Syn.* uninformed, unwarned, kept in the dark*; see **ignorant** 1.

**unaffected,** *modif.* **1.** [Genuine] — *Syn.* spontaneous, natural, simple, direct, straightforward, unassuming, modest, forthright, candid, frank, guileless, ingenuous, sincere, artless, plain, plainspoken. — *Ant.* ORNATE, pretentious, foppish.
**2.** [Uninfluenced] — *Syn.* unmoved, unaltered, unchanged, untouched, unconcerned, unimpressed, impassive, steady; see also **calm** 1. — *Ant.* CHANGED, altered, modified.

**unalterable,** *modif.* — *Syn.* unchangeable, fixed, unavoidable; see **firm** 1, 2, **inevitable, resolute** 2.

**unalterably,** *modif.* — *Syn.* rigidly, unchangeably, inflexibly; see **firmly** 1, 2, **obstinately.**

**unaltered,** *modif.* — *Syn.* the same, not changed, not altered, uninfluenced; see **unaffected** 2, **unchanged.**

**un-American,** *modif.* — *Syn.* undemocratic, fascistic, subversive; see **foreign** 1.

**unanimity,** *n.* — *Syn.* accord, unity, unison, concord, consensus, harmony, concordance, sympathy, congruence, conformity, correspondence, apposition, compatibility; see also **agreement** 2. — *Ant.* DISAGREEMENT, discord, dissonance.

**unanimous,** *modif.* — *Syn.* united, single, collective, combined, unified, concerted, harmonious, concordant, concurrent, public, popular, undivided, of one accord, agreed, common, communal, shared, universal, accepted, unquestioned, undisputed, uncontested, consonant, consistent, of a piece, with one voice, homogeneous, accordant, consensual, assenting; see also **undivided** 1. — *Ant.* DIFFERENT, dissenting, irreconcilable.

**unanimously,** *modif.* — *Syn.* with one voice, with one accord, harmoniously, all together, by acclamation, universally, unitedly, consensually, singly, collectively, without a dissenting voice, by common consent, in unison, cooperatively, concertedly, concurrently, popularly, commonly, undisputedly, consonantly, consistently, in agreement. — *Ant.* DIFFERENTLY, opposite, divergently.

**unanswered,** *modif.* — *Syn.* without reply, unrefuted, not responded to, unnoticed, unchallenged, unquestioned, demanding an answer, filed, in the files, ignored, unsettled, undecided, in doubt, disputed, moot, debatable, tabled, up in the air, vexed, open, pending, under consideration, undetermined; see also **uncertain** 2. — *Ant.* DETERMINED, answered, responded to.

**unapproachable,** *modif.* **1.** [Distant] — *Syn.* withdrawn, hesitant, aloof; see **inaccessible, distant.**
**2.** [Unmatched] — *Syn.* peerless, unsurpassed, best; see **excellent, superior, unique** 1.

**unapt,** *modif.* **1.** [Not fitting or suitable] — *Syn.* unfit, out of keeping, inappropriate; see **unsuitable.**
**2.** [Not likely] — *Syn.* improbable, not inclined, doubtful; see **unlikely.**
**3.** [Not skillful] — *Syn.* slow, dull, unskillful, inept; see **dull** 3.

**unarm,** *v.* — *Syn.* debilitate, disable, deprive of weapons; see **disarm** 1, 2, **weaken** 2.

**unarmed,** *modif.* — *Syn.* weaponless, defenseless, naked, harmless, undefended, disarmed, peaceable, unfortified; see also **pacific, weak** 5, 6. — *Ant.* ARMED, armed to the teeth, equipped.

**unasked,** *modif.* — *Syn.* uninvited, not asked, not invited, unwelcome; see **neglected, unpopular.**

**unassailable,** *modif.* — *Syn.* defended, not assailable, not subject to attack, impregnable, invulnerable; see also **protected.**

**unassuming,** *modif.* — *Syn.* quiet, retiring, reserved; see **humble** 1, **modest** 2.

**unattached,** *modif.* — *Syn.* independent, unbound, unmarried; see **free** 1, 2, 3, **loose** 1.

**unattended,** *modif.* — *Syn.* left alone, ignored, disregarded, untended; see **abandoned** 1, **neglected.**

**unauthorized,** *modif.* — *Syn.* unofficial, unapproved, unlawful, proscribed; see **illegal.**

**unavailing,** *modif.* — *Syn.* pointless, without results, fruitless; see **futile** 1, **useless** 1.

**unavoidable,** *modif.* — *Syn.* inescapable, impending, sure; see **certain** 3, **inevitable.**

**unaware,** *modif.* — *Syn.* uninformed, unknowing, oblivious, ignorant, not cognizant, unmindful, heedless, negligent, careless, insensible, forgetful, unconcerned, blind, deaf, inattentive, without notice, out of it*, square*, unhip*, out to lunch*, deaf to, dead to, caught napping, in a daze, not seeing the forest for the trees*. — *Ant.* CONSCIOUS, aware, cognizant.

**unawares,** *modif.* **1.** [Unintentionally] — *Syn.* inadvertently, ignorantly, carelessly, without thinking; see **accidentally.**
**2.** [Suddenly] — *Syn.* surprisingly, suddenly, abruptly; see **quickly** 1, **unexpectedly.**

**unbalance,** *v.* **1.** [To upset] — *Syn.* capsize, overturn, tumble; see **upset** 1.
**2.** [To derange] — *Syn.* dement, craze, obsess; see **disturb** 2, **derange** 2.

**unbalanced,** *modif.* **1.** [Deranged] — *Syn.* unsound, crazy, psychotic, neurotic; see **insane** 1, **troubled** 2.
**2.** [Unwise] — *Syn.* stupid, untrustworthy, biased; see **rash, unreliable** 1.
**3.** [Unsteady] — *Syn.* wobbly, shaky, treacherous; see **unstable** 1.

**unbar,** *v.* — *Syn.* unlock, throw open, unbolt; see **open** 2.

**unbearable,** *modif.* — *Syn.* unendurable, unacceptable, too much*; see **intolerable.**

**unbeaten,** *modif.* — *Syn.* victorious, thriving, winning; see **triumphant.**

**unbecoming,** *modif.* **1.** [Indecent] — *Syn.* improper, salacious, unworthy; see **lewd** 1, 2.
**2.** [Unsuitable] — *Syn.* unsuited, unfitted, awkward; see **improper** 1.
*See Synonym Study at* IMPROPER.

**unbelief,** *n.* — *Syn.* disbelief, doubt, skepticism, incredulity, uncertainty, agnosticism; see also **doubt** 1, **uncertainty** 1.

---

SYN. — **unbelief** implies merely a lack of belief, as because of insufficient evidence, esp. in matters of religion or faith; **disbelief** suggests a positive refusal to believe an assertion, theory, etc. [she listened with *disbelief* to his ridiculous accusations]; **incredulity** implies a general skepticism or disinclination to believe

---

**unbelievable,** *modif.* — *Syn.* beyond belief, past belief, incredible, inconceivable, staggering, unimaginable, not to be credited, dubious, doubtful, improbable, questionable, implausible, palpably false, unveracious, open to doubt, a bit thick*; see also **false** 1, 2, 3, **unlikely.** — *Ant.* LIKELY, believable, probable.

**unbelievably,** *modif.* — *Syn.* remarkably, horribly, badly; see **strangely, terribly.**

**unbeliever,** *n.* — *Syn.* atheist, freethinker, agnostic; see **atheist, skeptic.**

*See Synonym Study at* ATHEIST.

**unbelieving,** *modif.* — *Syn.* doubting, skeptical, incredulous; see **suspicious** 1.

**unbend,** *v.* — *Syn.* become more natural, become more casual, be informal, be at home, relax, let one's hair down; see also **rest** 1.

**unbending,** *modif.* **1.** [Rigid] — *Syn.* inflexible, crisp, stiff; see **firm** 5.

**2.** [Resolute] — *Syn.* firm, unyielding, stubborn; see **obstinate**.

**unbiased,** *modif.* — *Syn.* just, straight, impartial; see **fair** 1, **honest** 1.

*See Synonym Study at* FAIR.

**unbind,** *v.* **1.** [To untie] — *Syn.* unfasten, disengage, unchain; see **free** 1, **liberate** 2.

**2.** [To forgive] — *Syn.* release, clear, liberate; see **excuse**.

**unblemished,** *modif.* — *Syn.* perfect, flawless, unmarked; see **perfect** 2.

**unblessed,** *modif.* **1.** [Accursed] — *Syn.* unsaved, unholy, graceless; see **damned** 1, **wicked** 1.

**2.** [Miserable] — *Syn.* wretched, unhappy, unlucky; see **unfortunate** 2, **miserable** 1.

**unblushing,** *modif.* — *Syn.* shameless, brazen, forward; see **rude** 2, **lewd** 1, 2.

**unborn,** *modif.* — *Syn.* embryonic, incipient, expected, future, prospective, potential, latent, enwombed, in utero, anticipated, awaited.

**unbosom,** *v.* — *Syn.* tell, let out, vent, get off one's chest; see **admit** 2, **confess** 3, **reveal** 1.

**unbound,** *modif.* — *Syn.* loose, untied, unstapled, unfastened, unwrapped, unstitched, ungirt; see also **free** 1, 2, 3. — *Ant.* BOUND, stapled, tied.

**unbounded,** *modif.* — *Syn.* spreading, boundless, loose; see **infinite, unlimited**.

**unbowed,** *modif.* — *Syn.* undefeated, stubborn, resisting; see **triumphant**.

**unbreakable,** *modif.* — *Syn.* indestructible, durable, everlasting, perdurable, brass-bound, cast-iron, lasting, unshakable, solid, firm, unchangeable, invulnerable, incorruptible, resistant, rugged, tight, unyielding, adamantine. — *Ant.* DAINTY, fragile, brittle.

**unbridled,** *modif.* — *Syn.* unrestrained, uncontrolled, ungoverned, unchecked; see **unruly**.

**unbroken,** *modif.* **1.** [Whole] — *Syn.* entire, intact, unimpaired; see **whole** 2.

**2.** [Continuous] — *Syn.* uninterrupted, continuous, even; see **regular** 3, **smooth** 1, 2.

**unbuckle,** *v.* — *Syn.* unfasten, undo, unloose; see **open** 2.

**unburden,** *v.* **1.** [To unload] — *Syn.* dump, dispose of, relinquish; see **lighten** 1, **relieve** 2.

**2.** [To reveal] — *Syn.* disclose, unbosom, divulge; see **admit** 2, **confess** 3.

**unbutton,** *v.* — *Syn.* undo, open up, unfasten; see **open** 2.

**uncalled for,** *modif.* — *Syn.* unjustified, redundant, not needed; see **superfluous, unnecessary**.

**uncanny,** *modif.* — *Syn.* weird, unnatural, inexplainable, supernatural, preternatural, superhuman, ghostly, mystifying, incredible, mysterious, magical, devilish; see also **magic** 1.

*See Synonym Study at* WEIRD.

**uncared-for,** *modif.* — *Syn.* unattended, not cared for, not looked after, loose; see **neglected**.

**unceremonious,** *modif.* **1.** [Informal] — *Syn.* familiar, casual, inelegant; see **careless** 1, **informal**.

**2.** [Abrupt] — *Syn.* curt, hurried, brief; see **rude** 1, **abrupt**.

**uncertain,** *modif.* **1.** [Doubtful in mind] — *Syn.* dubious, undecided, in a quandary; see **doubtful** 2.

**2.** [Not determined] — *Syn.* undecided, undetermined, unsettled, doubtful, changeable, unpredictable, improbable, unlikely, unfixed, unsure, indeterminate, haphazard, random, chance, casual, provisional, contingent, alterable, fluctuant, subject to change, possible, vague, conjectural, questionable, problematic, suppositional, supposititious, hypothetical, theoretical, open to question, equivocal, perplexing, debatable, dubious indefinite, unascertained, ambiguous, unresolved, debated, conjecturable, unknown, unannounced, imprecise, up in the air, in doubt, in abeyance, still in debate, on the knees of the Gods★.

**uncertainly,** *modif.* — *Syn.* unreliably, illegally, confusedly; see **irregularly**.

**uncertainty,** *n.* **1.** [The mental state of being uncertain] — *Syn.* perplexity, doubt, dubiety, dubiosity, skepticism, puzzlement, quandary, mystification, guesswork, conjecture, indecision, ambivalence, dilemma. — *Ant.* OPINION, BELIEF, decision.

**2.** [The state of being undetermined or unknown] — *Syn.* incertitude, questionableness, contingency, obscurity, vagueness, ambiguity, equivocalness, doubt, difficulty, incoherence, intricacy, darkness, inconclusiveness, indeterminateness, improbability, unlikelihood, low probability, conjecturability; see also **doubt** 2. — *Ant.* DETERMINATION, sureness, necessity.

**3.** [That which is not determined or not known] — *Syn.* chance, mutability, change, unpredictability, possibility, emergence, contingency, blind spot, puzzle, enigma, question, blank, vacancy, maze, theory, risk, blind bargain, leap in the dark★. — *Ant.* FACT, TRUTH, matter of record.

*SYN.* — **uncertainty** ranges in implication from a mere lack of absolute sureness *[uncertainty* about a date of birth*]* to such vagueness as to preclude anything more than guesswork *[the uncertainty* of the future*]*; **doubt** implies such a lack of conviction, as through absence of sufficient evidence, that there can be no certain opinion or decision *[there is doubt* about his guilt*]*; **dubiety** suggests uncertainty characterized by wavering between conclusions; **dubiosity** connotes uncertainty characterized by vagueness or confusion; **skepticism** implies an unwillingness to believe, often a habitual disposition to doubt, in the absence of absolute certainty or proof

**unchain,** *v.* — *Syn.* liberate, unbind, discharge; see **free** 1.

**unchangeable,** *modif.* — *Syn.* fixed, unalterable, inevitable; see **firm** 1, **resolute** 2.

**unchangeably,** *modif.* — *Syn.* fixedly, unalterably, rigidly; see **firmly** 1, 2, **obstinately**.

**unchanged,** *modif.* — *Syn.* unaltered, the same, unmoved, constant, fixed, continuing, stable, permanent, eternal, durable, unvarying, invariable, consistent, persistent, firm, unvaried, resolute, perpetual, continuous, maintained, uninterrupted, fast. — *Ant.* CHANGED, altered, modified.

**uncharitable,** *modif.* — *Syn.* unforgiving, censorious, ungenerous, mean-spirited, selfish; see also **cruel** 2, **unmerciful**.

**uncharted,** *modif.* — *Syn.* not mapped, not explored, not described, strange, undiscovered; see also **unknown** 1, 3.

**unchaste,** *modif.* — *Syn.* shameless, lascivious, lustful, lecherous, impure; see also **lewd** 2, **sensual**.

**unchristian,** *modif.* **1.** [Sinful] — *Syn.* irreligious, pagan, evil; see **impious, wicked** 1.
**2.** [Uncivil] — *Syn.* unseemly, impolite, heartless, outrageous, dreadful; see also **ruthless** 1.

**uncivil,** *modif.* **1.** [Not civilized] — *Syn.* barbarous, crude, boorish, uncultivated; see **rude** 1.
**2.** [Ill-mannered] — *Syn.* rude, impolite, disrespectful; see **rude** 2.
*See Synonym Study at* RUDE.

**uncivilized,** *modif.* — *Syn.* barbarous, uncontrolled, barbarian; see **primitive** 3, **savage** 1, 3.

**unclassified,** *modif.* — *Syn.* not classified, not ordered, not put in order, disordered, out of order; see also **confused** 2, **unknown** 1, 3.

**uncle,** *n.* — *Syn.* father's brother, mother's brother, elder, *avunculus* (Latin); see **relative.**

**unclean,** *modif.* — *Syn.* soiled, sullied, stained, spotted, filthy, bedraggled, smeared, befouled, nasty, grimy, polluted, rank, unhealthful, defiled, impure, nonkosher, muddy, fetid, feculent, stinking, rotten, vile, decayed, contaminated, tainted, rancid, putrid, putrescent, moldy, musty, mildewed, besmirched, smirched, besmutted, smutted, besmuttered, besmeared, filmed over, bleary, dusty, sooty, smudgy, draffy, scurvy, scurfy, clogged, slimy, mucky, tarnished, murky, smudged, daubed, blurred, begrimed, spattered, bespattered, maggotty, flyblown; see also **dirty** 1, **impure** 1. — *Ant.* PURE, clean, white.

**unclench,** *v.* — *Syn.* unlock, release, relax; see **unfold** 1.

**Uncle Sam,** *n.* — *Syn.* the United States, the U.S., the government, the Internal Revenue Service, the IRS.

**uncloak,** *v.* **1.** [To expose] — *Syn.* tell, disclose, uncover; see **reveal** 1, **expose** 1.
**2.** [To undress] — *Syn.* divest, uncover, disrobe; see **undress.**

**unclothe,** *v.* — *Syn.* disrobe, uncover, divest; see **undress.**

**uncomfortable,** *modif.* **1.** [Troubled in body or mind] — *Syn.* distressed, ill at ease, uneasy, embarrassed, nervous, disturbed, pained, miserable, wretched, restless, fretted, annoyed, angry, in pain, smarting, suffering, discomposed, disquieted, discomfited, upset, vexed, on pins and needles, weary, tired, fatigued, exhausted, strained, worn, aching, griped, wracked, on the wrack, sore, galled, stiff, chafed, cramped, agonized, hurt, anguished. — *Ant.* QUIET, rested, HAPPY.
**2.** [Causing discomfort] — *Syn.* ill-fitting, awkward, annoying, embarrassing, irritating, galling, wearisome, vexatious, bothersome, difficult, hard, thorny, troublesome, harsh, grievous, dolorous, bitter, excruciating, afflictive, distressing, distressful, torturing, painful, agonizing, disagreeable. — *Ant.* EASY, pleasant, grateful.

**uncomfortably,** *modif.* — *Syn.* distressfully, dolefully, uneasily, painfully, miserably, wretchedly, restlessly, sadly, fretfully, annoyingly, disturbingly, vexatiously, agonizingly, awkwardly, irritatingly, troublesomely, harshly, grievously, dolorously, bitterly, poignantly, sharply, keenly, excruciatingly, disagreeably, unhappily, dismally, in anguish.

**uncommitted,** *modif.* **1.** [Neutral] — *Syn.* unpledged, unaffiliated, free; see **nonpartisan, neutral** 1.
**2.** [Reserved] — *Syn.* evasive, reticent, shy; see **withdrawn.**
**3.** [Withheld] — *Syn.* restrained, denied, held back; see **withheld.**

**uncommon,** *modif.* — *Syn.* unusual, out of the ordinary, different, extraordinary, unheard of, unique, rare, few and far between, exceptional, out of the way, strange, exotic, arcane, remarkable, startling, surprising, fantastic,

unaccustomed, unfamiliar, anomalous, unclassifiable, freakish, irregular, uncustomary, unconventional, unorthodox, abnormal, peculiar, odd, bizarre, eccentric, original, nondescript, prodigious, fabulous, monstrous, egregious, aberrant, curious, wonderful, unaccountable, unwonted, *outré* (French), noteworthy, queer, unparalleled, unexampled, outlandish, extreme. — *Ant.* COMMON, usual, ordinary.

**uncommonly,** *modif.* **1.** [Rarely] — *Syn.* not often, unusually, in few instances; see **infrequently, seldom.**
**2.** [Strangely] — *Syn.* remarkably, oddly, peculiarly; see **strangely.**

**uncommunicative,** *modif.* — *Syn.* reticent, silent, evasive; see **quiet** 2, **reserved** 3.

**uncompromising,** *modif.* — *Syn.* strong, inflexible, firm, unyielding, determined; see also **fair** 1, **resolute** 2.

**unconcern,** *n.* — *Syn.* apathy, aloofness, coldness, disinterest; see **indifference** 1.

**unconcerned,** *modif.* — *Syn.* indifferent, careless, feckless, heedless, apathetic, insensible, oblivious, nonchalant, insouciant, inattentive, cold, phlegmatic, impassive, supine, callous, unsympathetic, hardened, insensitive, stony, neutral, reserved, self-centered, negligent, blind, deaf, forgetful, disdainful, lukewarm, cool, lackadaisical, uninterested. — *Ant.* INTERESTED, absorbed, attached.
*See Synonym Study at* INDIFFERENT.

**unconditional,** *modif.* — *Syn.* positive, definite, absolute, outright, unconstrained, without reserve, final, certain, complete, entire, whole, unrestricted, unqualified, unlimited, actual, thorough, thoroughgoing, genuine, indubitable, assured, determinate, unequivocal, full, categorical, decisive, unmistakable, clear, unquestionable. — *Ant.* RESTRICTED, contingent, partial.
*See Synonym Study at* INDIFFERENT.

**unconditionally,** *modif.* — *Syn.* absolutely, thoroughly, unreservedly; see **completely.**

**unconfined,** *modif.* — *Syn.* loose, not confined, unrestrained; see **free** 2, 3, **unlimited.**

**unconformity,** *n.* — *Syn.* nonconformity, difference, dissent, incongruity; see **inconsistency, revolution** 2.

**unconnected,** *modif.* **1.** [Separate] — *Syn.* divided, detached, disconnected; see **separated.**
**2.** [Irrelevant] — *Syn.* impertinent, unrelated, inapplicable; see **irrelevant.**

**unconscionable,** *modif.* **1.** [Dishonest] — *Syn.* knavish, sneaky, criminal; see **unscrupulous.**
**2.** [Excessive] — *Syn.* unreasonable, too much, immoderate; see **extreme** 2.

**unconscious,** *modif.* **1.** [Comatose] — *Syn.* insensible, swooning, in a state of suspended animation, torpid, lethargic, benumbed, inanimate, bereft of senses, senseless, insensate, drowsy, numb, inert, paralyzed, palsied, tranced, entranced, in a stupor, in a coma, in a trance, stupefied, raving, out of one's head, out like a light*, knocked out*; see also **motionless** 1. — *Ant.* CONSCIOUS, vivacious, awake.
**2.** [Unaware] — *Syn.* inattentive, lost, ignorant, out of it*; see **careless** 1, **oblivious.**

**unconscious,** (*usually used with* the) *n.* — *Syn.* psyche, subliminal self, instinct, motive force; see **memory** 1, **mind** 1.

**unconsciously,** *modif.* — *Syn.* abstractedly, mechanically, unthinkingly, without thinking, perfunctorily, carelessly, automatically, habitually, by rote, unintentionally, inattentively, heedlessly, without reflection, negligently, disregardfully, thoughtlessly, neglectfully, hurriedly, without calculation, unguardedly. — *Ant.* DELIBERATELY, intentionally, willfully.

**unconstitutional,** *modif.* — *Syn.* un-American, undemocratic, lawless; see **illegal.**

**unconstitutionally,** *modif.* — *Syn.* illegally, unjustly, lawlessly; see **wrongly** 1, 2.

**uncontrollable,** *modif.* — *Syn.* obdurate, obstinate, stubborn, ungovernable, lawless, insurgent; see also **unruly.**

**uncontrolled,** *modif.* — *Syn.* open, clear, free, unchecked, unhindered, boundless, ungoverned, unsuppressed, limitless, untrammeled, unbridled, unfettered, unobstructed, independent, unburdened, unbounded, unhampered, unlimited, uncurbed, unconstrained, unconfined.

**unconventional,** *modif.* — *Syn.* unorthodox, unusual, nonconformist, individualistic, original, eccentric, iconoclastic, idiosyncratic, maverick, offbeat, alternative, Bohemian, counterculture, punk, beat, beatnik, hippie, way out*, far out*; see also **unique** 1, **unusual** 2.

**uncork,** *v.* — *Syn.* open up, unseal, remove the cork from; see **open** 2, 3, 4.

**uncounted,** *modif.* **1.** [Inconceivably numerous] — *Syn.* numberless, innumerable, multitudinous; see **many.**
**2.** [Not counted] — *Syn.* unrecorded, unconsidered, unnumbered; see **unnoticed.**

**uncouple,** *v.* — *Syn.* disconnect, sever, sunder, divorce; see **divide** 1, **separate** 2.

**uncouth,** *modif.* — *Syn.* ungainly, clumsy, crude; see **awkward** 1, **rude** 1, 2.

**uncover,** *v.* — *Syn.* unseal, uncork, unscrew, pry open, lift the lid, unstopper, dig up, reveal, tap, lay open, unclose, fish up*; see also **open** 2. — *Ant.* CLOSE, cover, seal up.

**uncovered,** *modif.* — *Syn.* exposed, conspicuous, unsafe; see **open** 4.

**uncritical,** *modif.* — *Syn.* imprudent, imperceptive, indiscriminate; see **rash.**

**unction,** *n.* **1.** [Ointment] — *Syn.* oil, unguent, liniment; see **salve.**
**2.** [Sacrament] — *Syn.* anointing, laying on of hands, blessing; see **sacrament** 1.

**unctuous,** *modif.* **1.** [Oily] — *Syn.* greasy, lenitive, unguent; see **oily** 1.
**2.** [Smooth] — *Syn.* plastic, slippery, waxy; see **oily** 2, **slippery.**
**3.** [Ingratiating] — *Syn.* smooth, suave, insinuating, obsequious; see **affected** 2, **oily** 3.

**undamaged,** *modif.* — *Syn.* uninjured, unharmed, safe; see **unhurt, whole** 2.

**undaunted,** *modif.* — *Syn.* courageous, fearless, stalwart, resolute, intrepid; see also **brave** 1.

**undeceive,** *v.* — *Syn.* disillusion, disabuse, set right, inform; see **correct** 1.

**undecided,** *modif.* — *Syn.* undetermined, in the middle, in the balance, unsettled, open, of two minds, ambivalent, dubious, unfinished, unconcluded, at a loss, up in the air*; see also **doubtful** 2, **uncertain** 2.

**undecipherable,** *modif.* — *Syn.* illegible, indistinct, impenetrable; see **obscure** 1, **vague** 2.

**undefeated,** *modif.* — *Syn.* unbeaten, victorious, winning; see **triumphant.**

**undefended,** *modif.* — *Syn.* unprotected, exposed, unguarded; see **endangered.**

**undefiled,** *modif.* **1.** [Spotless] — *Syn.* unsullied, unsoiled, flawless; see **clean** 1, **pure** 2.
**2.** [Innocent] — *Syn.* virginal, sinless, holy; see **chaste** 2, 3.

**undefined,** *modif.* **1.** [Infinite] — *Syn.* limitless, boundless, forever; see **endless** 1, **infinite** 1.

**2.** [Vague] — *Syn.* dim, unclear, indistinct; see **irregular** 4, **obscure** 1.

**undemocratic,** *modif.* — *Syn.* dictatorial, communist, communistic, fascist, fascistic, un-American; see also **autocratic** 1.

**undemonstrative,** *modif.* — *Syn.* restrained, reticent, distant; see **reserved** 3, **withdrawn.**

**undeniable,** *modif.* — *Syn.* indisputable, incontestable, irrefutable, certain, ineluctable, sure, definite, positive; see also **certain** 3.

**undependable,** *modif.* — *Syn.* careless, unsound, inconstant; see **irresponsible, unreliable** 1.

**under,** *modif.* and *prep.* **1.** [Referring to physical position] — *Syn.* on the bottom of, below, on the nether side of, covered by, beneath, concealed by, held down by, supporting, pinned beneath, on the underside of, pressed down by. — *Ant.* ABOVE, over, on top of.
**2.** [Subject to authority] — *Syn.* subordinate to, reporting to, amenable to, subjugated to, under the sway of, governed by, in the power of, obeying the dictates of, obedient to, directed by.
**3.** [Included within] — *Syn.* subsumed under, belonging to, corollary to, inferred from, consequent to, subsidiary to, comprised in, subsequent to, following; see also **below** 3. — *Ant.* DIFFERENT, distinct from, apart.

**underage,** *modif.* — *Syn.* young, youthful, minor; see **juvenile** 1.

**under arrest,** *modif.* — *Syn.* arrested, caught, apprehended, taken into custody, seized, taken in, handcuffed, confined, jailed, imprisoned, detained, shut up, penned up, put in irons, sent to prison, sent to jail, busted*, pinched*, booked*, collared*, nabbed*, sent up the river*.

**underbid,** *v.* — *Syn.* bargain, negotiate, outbid; see **bid** 1.

**under bond,** *modif.* **1.** [Responsible; *said of persons*] — *Syn.* certified, cleared, accepted; see **bonded** 1, **responsible** 1.
**2.** [Insured; *said of goods*] — *Syn.* certified, warranted, bonded; see **guaranteed, protected.**

**underbrush,** *n.* — *Syn.* thicket, brush, brushwood, boscage, jungle, undergrowth, tangle, copse, coppice, hedge, dingle, cover, wold, quick, quickset, gorse, furze, whin, spinney, scrub, bush; see also **forest.**

**undercharge,** *v.* — *Syn.* charge too little, sell for too little, cut prices, sacrifice; see **charge** 2, **sell** 1.

**underclassman,** *n.* — *Syn.* lowerclassman, first-year student, second-year student, novice; see **freshman, sophomore.**

**underclothes,** *n.* — *Syn.* undergarments, lingerie, union suit, underthings, unmentionables, skivvies*; see also **clothes, underwear.**

**under construction,** *modif.* — *Syn.* in production, in preparation, being built, going up.

**undercover,** *modif.* **1.** [Secret] — *Syn.* hidden, surreptitious, clandestine; see **secret** 3.
**2.** [Secretly] — *Syn.* privately, surreptitiously, stealthily; see **secretly.**

**undercurrent,** *n.* **1.** [Backflow] — *Syn.* cross-current, ebb tide, flow; see **undertow.**
**2.** [Direction] — *Syn.* trend, tendency, propensity, direction; see **inclination** 1.
**3.** [Indication] — *Syn.* intimation, insinuation, trace; see **hint** 1.

**undercut,** *v.* **1.** [To excavate] — *Syn.* undermine, hollow, gouge; see **cut** 2.
**2.** [To undersell] — *Syn.* undercharge, underprice, sell for less; see **sell** 1.

**underdeveloped,** *modif.* — *Syn.* backward, undeveloped, poor, poorly developed, retarded, slowed down; see also **little** 1, **weak** 1, 2, 3, 5.

**underdog,** *n.* — *Syn.* loser, underling, low man on the totem pole*; see **failure** 2, **victim** 1.

**underdone,** *modif.* — *Syn.* undone, not finished, uncooked; see **rare** 5, **raw** 1.

**underestimate,** *v.* — *Syn.* miscalculate, miscarry, come short of, undervalue, disesteem, depreciate, underrate, disparage, do scant justice to, misprize, slight, minimize, think too little of, hold too lightly, make light of, deprecate, put down*, set at naught. — *Ant.* EXAGGERATE, overestimate, overpraise.

**underfed,** *modif.* — *Syn.* skinny, starving, starved; see **hungry.**

**under fire,** *modif.* — *Syn.* under attack, in action, at the front, embattled; see **fighting.**

**underfoot,** *modif.* **1.** [Beneath] — *Syn.* down, at bottom, below; see **under** 1.
**2.** [In the way] — *Syn.* annoying, tiresome, impeding; see **disturbing.**

**undergo,** *v.* — *Syn.* sustain, submit to, support, experience, feel, know, be subject to, bear, meet with, endure, go through, encounter, bear up under, put up with, share, withstand; see also **endure** 2. — *Ant.* AVOID, ESCAPE, RESIST.

**undergone,** *modif.* — *Syn.* sustained, submitted to, supported, experienced, felt, suffered, borne, met (with), known, endured, gone through, encountered, put up with, shared, seen, withstood.

**undergraduate,** *n.* — *Syn.* underclassman, upperclassman, freshman, sophomore, junior, senior.

**underground,** *modif.* **1.** [Subterranean] — *Syn.* buried, covered, subterrene, earthed over, under the sod, in the recesses of the earth, gone to earth; see also **under** 1.
**2.** [Secret] — *Syn.* hidden, undercover, clandestine; see **secret** 2, 3.
**3.** [Unconventional] — *Syn.* experimental, radical, avant-garde; see **unusual** 2.

**underground,** *n.* **1.** [A secret movement] — *Syn.* resistance, partisans, fifth column, guerillas.

**Underground,** *n.* [British] — *Syn.* subway, tube, *Métro* (French); see **subway.**

**undergrowth,** *n.* — *Syn.* underwood, tangle, scrub; see **brush** 4, **underbrush.**

**underhanded,** *modif.* — *Syn.* secret, sneaky, secretive; see **sly** 1.

See Synonym Study at SECRET.

**underlie,** *v.* — *Syn.* carry, bear, hold up; see **hold** 8.

**underline,** *v.* **1.** [Emphasize] — *Syn.* stress, mark, indicate; see **emphasize.**
**2.** [To make a line under] — *Syn.* underscore, mark, interlineate, bracket, check off, italicize.

**underling,** *n.* — *Syn.* subordinate, hireling, servant, menial, minion, flunky*; see also **assistant.**

**undermine,** *v.* **1.** [Enfeeble] — *Syn.* impair, ruin, threaten; see **weaken** 2.
**2.** [To excavate] — *Syn.* dig out, tunnel, hollow out; see **dig** 1.

See Synonym Study at WEAKEN.

**underneath,** *modif.* and *prep.* — *Syn.* beneath, 'neath*, below, lower than, covered by; see also **under** 1.

**undernourished,** *modif.* — *Syn.* underfed, mistreated, afflicted with malnutrition, starving; see **hungry.**

**underpass,** *n.* — *Syn.* bridge, culvert, cave, passage, subway (British); see also **tunnel.**

**underpinning,** *n.* — *Syn.* basis, base, supporting structure; see **bottom** 1, **foundation** 2.

**underprivileged,** *modif.* — *Syn.* poor, indigent, disad-

vantaged, deprived, unfortunate, impoverished, needy, destitute, educationally handicapped; see also **poor** 1.

**underrate,** *v.* — *Syn.* undervalue, discount, disparage; see **underestimate.**

**underscore,** *v.* — *Syn.* mark, stress, italicize; see **emphasize, underline** 2.

**undersea,** *modif.* — *Syn.* underwater, submarine, marine, sunken.

**under sedation,** *modif.* — *Syn.* quieted, tranquilized, soothed, calmed down; see **calm** 1.

**undersell,** *v.* — *Syn.* undercut, reduce, slash, cut, undercharge, mark down; see also **sell** 1.

**undershirt,** *n.* — *Syn.* shirt, T-shirt, knit shirt, turtleneck, pull-over, combination shirt, skivvy*, vest (British); see also **clothes, underwear.**

**underside,** *n.* — *Syn.* underneath, base, root; see **bottom** 1, **foundation** 2.

**undersigned,** *n.* — *Syn.* person or persons named below, those signified, signer, endorser, inditer, author, subscriber, supporter, petitioner, covenanter, bondsman, sanctioner, negotiator, testator, ratifier, signatory, underwriter, notary; see also **patron** 1.

**undersized,** *modif.* — *Syn.* miniature, small, tiny; see **little** 1, **minute** 1.

**underskirt,** *n.* — *Syn.* skirt, slip, half slip, petticoat, chemise, shimmy, bustle, hoopskirt; see also **clothes, underwear.**

**understand,** *v.* **1.** [To comprehend] — *Syn.* comprehend, apprehend, fathom, take in, grasp, figure out, seize, take (one's meaning), identify with, know, perceive, appreciate, follow, master, conceive, be aware of, sense, recognize, grow aware, explain, interpret, cognize, see through, learn, find out, ken, see (into), catch, note, be conscious of, have cognizance of, wot, ween, realize, discern, read, distinguish, infer, deduce, induce, make out, make sense of, be apprized of, become alive to, have been around, experience, have knowledge of, be instructed in, get to the bottom of, get at the root of, penetrate, possess, be informed of, come to one's senses, see the light, make out, register*, savvy*, get*, get the gist of*, catch on*, get the point of*, dig*, read between the lines*, be with it*, get the hand of*, get the idea*. — *Ant.* MISUNDERSTAND, be ignorant, go astray.
**2.** [To suppose] — *Syn.* guess, conjecture, surmise; see **assume** 1.
**3.** [To accept] — *Syn.* concede, take for granted, count on; see **agree.**

*SYN.* — **understand** and **comprehend** are used interchangeably to imply clear perception of the meaning of something, but, more precisely, **understand** stresses the full awareness or knowledge arrived at, and **comprehend**, the process of grasping something mentally [one may *comprehend* the words in an idiom without *understanding* at all what is meant]; **appreciate** implies sensitive, discriminating perception of the exact worth or value of something [to *appreciate* the difficulties of a situation]

**understandable,** *modif.* — *Syn.* comprehensible, conceivable, appreciable, expected, to be expected, natural, normal, regular, making sense, accordant, congruous, intelligible, coherent, lucid, unambiguous, in harmony with, readable, reasonable, logical, right, customary, recognizable, justifiable, imaginable, acceptable, apprehensible, credible, on all fours with*; see also **obvious** 2. — *Ant.* ILLOGICAL, irrational, obscure.

**understandably,** *modif.* — *Syn.* naturally, with good reason, sensibly; see **reasonably** 1, 2.

**understanding,** *modif.* — *Syn.* empathetic, empathic, kindly, generous; see **patient** 1, **sympathetic.**

**understanding,** *n.* **1.** [The power to understand] — *Syn.* sharpness, intelligence, comprehension; see **judgment** 1.
**2.** [The act of comprehending] — *Syn.* recognition, knowing, perception; see **judgment** 2, **thought** 1.
**3.** [That which comes from understanding, sense 2] — *Syn.* conclusion, knowledge, perception; see **belief** 1, **opinion** 1.
**4.** [Informal agreement] — *Syn.* meeting of minds, common view, harmony, compromise; see **agreement** 2, 3.
**5.** [The intellect] — *Syn.* head, brain, mentality; see **mind** 1.

**understate,** *v.* — *Syn.* undervalue, minimize, lessen; see **decrease** 2, **underestimate.**

**understatement,** *n.* — *Syn.* modest statement, restrained statement, belittlement, litotes, restraint, underestimate, underestimation, oversimplification, less than the truth, distortion, avoidance of overemphasis or exaggeration.

**understood,** *modif.* **1.** [Comprehended] — *Syn.* penetrated, realized, appreciated, known, discovered, grasped, reasoned out, rationalized, explained, experienced, discerned, distinguished, made out, learned, fathomed, searched, explored, analyzed, mastered, conned, taken to heart, dug*. — *Ant.* UNKNOWN, overlooked, uncomprehended.
**2.** [Agreed upon] — *Syn.* concerted, ratified, reciprocally approved, assumed, stipulated, pledged, covenanted, tacitly agreed upon, taken for granted, engaged for, settled, concluded, fixed upon, endorsed, subscribed to, accepted.

**understudy,** *n.* — *Syn.* alternate, double, stand-in; see **substitute.**

**undertake,** *v.* — *Syn.* endeavor, engage, set out, promise, try out, try, begin, commence, offer, set in motion, volunteer, initiate, commit oneself to, embark upon, venture, take upon oneself, answer for, hazard, stake, move, devote oneself to, pledge oneself to, shoulder, take up for, take on, set about, go into, go about, go in for, put one's hand to, have one's hands in, have in hand, launch into, launch forth, address oneself to, enter on *or* upon, busy oneself with, tackle*, pitch into*, fall into*, buckle to*, take on*, take the plunge*, fall to*, have a try at*, go for in a big way*.

**undertaken,** *modif.* — *Syn.* set in motion, begun, launched, embarked upon, initiated, pushed forward, ventured, started, endeavored, assumed, taken up, promised, offered, volunteered, hazarded, chanced, risked, pledged, tackled, essayed, tried, aimed at, attempted, striven for, engaged for.

**undertaker,** *n.* — *Syn.* mortician, funeral director, embalmer, cremator, body snatcher*.

**undertaking,** *n.* — *Syn.* enterprise, attempt, endeavor, project, effort, venture, pursuit, essay, trial, experiment, hazard, emprise, move, task, job, engagement.

**undertone,** *n.* **1.** [A low tone] — *Syn.* buzz, murmur, hum; see **whisper** 1.
**2.** [An underlying quality] — *Syn.* undercurrent, suggestion, connotation; see **meaning.**

**undertow,** *n.* — *Syn.* eddy, maelstrom, whirlpool, undercurrent, indraft, vortex, reflex, surge, turbulence, riptide; see also **flow, tide.**

**undervalue,** *v.* — *Syn.* underrate, minimize, depreciate; see **underestimate.**

**underwater,** *modif.* — *Syn.* submarine, sunken, marine; see **under** 1, **undersea.**

**underway,** *modif.* — *Syn.* moving, advancing, making progress, initiated, started, under construction; see also **begun, undertaken.**

**underwear,** *n.* — *Syn.* undergarments, balbriggans, nether garments, underclothing, unmentionables, smallclothes, lingerie, intimate things, underlinen, underclothes; see also **clothes.**
Types of underwear include — *men:* shirt, undershirt, shorts, drawers, red flannels, union suit, combination, jockey shorts, T-shirt, boxer shorts, boxers, bikini shorts, briefs, long johns, long underwear, B.V.D.'s (trademark), skivvy*; *women:* chemise, underskirt, camisole, slip, half slip, petticoat, girdle, panty girdle, brassiere, bustier, bustle, pettipants, garter belt, bra-slip, bra, panty slip, merry widow, all-in-one, corset, corselet, briefs, bodice, *cache-sexe* (French), vest, bloomer, combination, foundation garment, panties, pantyhose, bikini, body suit, body shirt, shorts, corset cover, teddy, unitard, undervest, shimmy*, knickers (British)*, snuggies*; *infants:* shirt, drawers, pants, diaper, slip, rubber pants, soakers*.

**underweight,** *modif.* — *Syn.* gaunt, skinny, undersized, scrawny, puny; see also **thin** 2.

**underworld,** *modif.* — *Syn.* criminal, concerned with organized crime, Mafialike, gangster, mob-ruled; see also **illegal, wicked** 1.

**underworld,** *n.* **1.** [Hell] — *Syn.* Hades, Inferno, netherworld, otherworld; see **hell** 1.
**2.** [Crime] — *Syn.* gangland, gangdom, rackets, organized crime, the mob, the Syndicate, the Mafia, the Cosa Nostra, the Black Hand, criminals, riffraff.

**underwrite,** *v.* **1.** [To subscribe] — *Syn.* sign, initial, seal; see **endorse** 2.
**2.** [To approve] — *Syn.* accede, consent, okay*; see **approve** 1.
**3.** [To support financially] — *Syn.* finance, help, pay, support, guarantee, subsidize, endow, fund, refund, provide security, provide capital, provide financing, put up the money for, put up the collateral for, float a stock issue, float bonds, provide subvention for.

**undesirable,** *modif.* — *Syn.* objectionable, shunned, disliked, to be avoided, unwanted, outcast, rejected, defective, disadvantageous, inexpedient, inconvenient, incommodious, troublesome, unwished for, repellent, loathed, unsought, dreaded, annoying, insufferable, unacceptable, scorned, displeasing, disliked, distasteful, loathsome, abominable, obnoxious, unpopular, bothersome, unlikable, unwelcome, unapprovable, useless, inadmissible, unsatisfactory, disagreeable, awkward, embarrassing, unfit. — *Ant.* WELCOME, proper, suitable.

**undeveloped,** *modif.* **1.** [Immature] — *Syn.* ignored, untaught, untrained, underdeveloped; see **inexperienced.**
**2.** [Latent] — *Syn.* potential, incipient, unactualized; see **latent.**

**undifferentiated,** *modif.* — *Syn.* similar, not differentiated, not distinguished, alike; see **uniform** 1, 2.

**undigested,** *modif.* — *Syn.* unabsorbed, unassimilated, unprocessed.

**undisputed,** *modif.* — *Syn.* unchallenged, uncontested, indisputable, beyond question, acknowledged, arbitrary, unquestioned, assured, tyrannous, dogmatic, authoritative, positive, final, certain, unerring, decided, indefeasible. — *Ant.* OPPOSED, disputed, challenged.

**undistinguished,** *modif.* — *Syn.* ordinary, commonplace, plain, unremarkable; see **common** 1, **conventional** 3, **dull** 4.

**undisturbed,** *modif.* — *Syn.* placid, settled, unruffled, untroubled, calm, unfretted, smooth, regular, even, uninterrupted. — *Ant.* TROUBLED, disturbed, vexed.

**undivided,** *modif.* **1.** [Unified] — *Syn.* single, united, unanimous, concerted, combined, concentrated, whole, entire, solid, complete, full, undiminished, collective. — *Ant.* SEPARATED, different, split.
**2.** [Undistracted] — *Syn.* exclusive, whole, entire, full, total, complete, concentrated, vigilant, thorough, intense, wholehearted, minute, scrupulous, careful, rigid, diligent, circumspect, profound, labored, studied, particular, considerate, deliberate, detailed, continued, unflagging, intent, absorbed, engrossed, fast, fixed, steady. — *Ant.* TEMPORARY, occasional, momentary.

**undo,** *v.* **1.** [To unfasten] — *Syn.* untie, loosen, release; see **unhitch.**
**2.** [To bring to ruin] — *Syn.* mar, destroy, ruin, wreck, break, bring to naught, subvert, injure, overthrow, unsettle, turn topsy-turvy, upset, defeat.
**3.** [To reverse] — *Syn.* annul, cancel, do away with, invalidate; see **cancel** 2.

**undoing,** *n.* **1.** [Ruin] — *Syn.* ruination, downfall, doom, reversal, destruction, misfortune, calamity, overthrow, collapse, trouble, grief, catastrophe, defeat, perdition, shipwreck, smash, wrack, subversion, discomfiture, collapse. — *Ant.* SUCCESS, accomplishment, achievement.
**2.** [The cause of ruin] — *Syn.* casualty, accident, mishap, misadventure, misstep, *faux pas* (French), bad hap, catastrophe, mischance, bad luck, adversity, reverse, blow, trial, affliction, visitation, stroke of fate, slip, blunder, fault, omission, difficulty, failure, error, miscalculation, trip, stumble, fumble, blunder, repulse, discouragement, death-blow, last straw, death knell. — *Ant.* ADVANTAGE, good omen, godsend.

**undone,** *modif.* **1.** [Unfinished] — *Syn.* left, incomplete, unperformed; see **unfinished** 1.
**2.** [*Distraught] — *Syn.* upset, disturbed, agitated; see **troubled** 1.
**3.** [Ruined] — *Syn.* betrayed, destroyed, killed, wiped out; see **dead** 1, **ruined** 1, 2.

**undoubted,** *modif.* — *Syn.* assured, sure, unquestionable, indubitable, unquestioned, irrefutable, indisputable, undisputed, unchallenged, proved, proven, established, without question, settled, fixed; see also **certain.** — *Ant.* QUESTIONABLE, disputed, refuted.

**undoubtedly,** *modif.* — *Syn.* assuredly, without doubt, of course; see **surely, unquestionably.**

**undress,** *v.* — *Syn.* strip, take off one's clothes, undrape, disrobe, unclothe, dismantle, divest, become naked, assume the altogether*, put on one's birthday suit*, strip to the buff*, peel*, climb out of one's clothes*. — *Ant.* DRESS, put on one's clothes, attire oneself.

**undue,** *modif.* — *Syn.* improper, illegal, indecorous, unfair, unseemly, unjust, underhanded, sinister, forbidden, excessive, too great, unnecessary, extreme, extravagant, inordinate, unwarranted, unjustified, disproportionate, immoderate. — *Ant.* NECESSARY, proper, requisite.

**undulant,** *modif.* — *Syn.* undulating, waving, surging; see **moving** 1.

**undulate,** *v.* **1.** [To surge] — *Syn.* billow, wave, ripple; see **move** 1.
**2.** [To sway] — *Syn.* pulsate, oscillate, swing; see **wave** 3.
*See Synonym Study at* SWING.

**undulating,** *modif.* — *Syn.* waving, surging, undulant; see **moving** 1.

**undulation,** *n.* — *Syn.* fluctuation, swaying, wave; see **sway** 1.

**unduly,** *modif.* **1.** [Improperly] — *Syn.* improperly, ille-

gally, indecorously, unfairly, unjustly, underhandedly; see also **wrongly** 1.
**2.** [To an undue degree] — *Syn.* excessively, extremely, overabundantly, inordinately, extravagantly, disproportionately; see also **unnecessarily.**

**undutiful,** *modif.* — *Syn.* slack, careless, disloyal; see **lazy** 1, **unfaithful** 1.

**undying,** *modif.* — *Syn.* everlasting, perpetual, deathless; see **eternal** 1, **immortal** 1.

**unearned,** *modif.* — *Syn.* won, gratis, unmerited; see **free** 4.

**unearned increment,** *n.* — *Syn.* profit, rise in worth *or* value, long-term capital gain; see **increase** 1.

**unearth,** *v.* **1.** [To bring to light] — *Syn.* discover, find, uncover; see **discover, learn** 1.
**2.** [To excavate] — *Syn.* exhume, disinter, unbury; see **dig** 1, **excavate.**
*See Synonym Study at* LEARN.

**unearthly,** *modif.* — *Syn.* ghoulish, frightening, ghastly, fiendish, ghostly, supernatural, preternatural, appalling, sepulchral, funereal, devilish, hair-raising, eldritch, demoniac, Satanic, eerie, spectral, uncanny, haunted, spooky. — *Ant.* common, familiar, homely.
*See Synonym Study at* WEIRD.

**uneasiness,** *n.* — *Syn.* disquiet, restlessness, agitation, tumult, turmoil, restiveness, incertitude, anguish, dilemma, indecision, perturbation, apprehension, dispiritedness, anxiety, fearfulness. — *Ant.* CONFIDENCE, assurance, calm.

**uneasy,** *modif.* **1.** [Mentally disturbed] — *Syn.* unquiet, anxious, fearful, irascible, troubled, harassed, vexed, perturbed, alarmed, upset, afraid, apprehensive, edgy, nervous, frightened, shaky, perplexed, agitated, unsettled, suspicious, peevish, irritable, fretful, worried, anguished, in turmoil, disquieted, shaken, full of misgivings. — *Ant.* calm, collected, composed.
**2.** [Restless] — *Syn.* fidgety, jittery, on edge, on the *qui vive* (French), all nerves, jumpy, snappish, agitated, restive, languishing, drooping, uncomfortable, awkward, goaded, palpitant, molested, wrung, harrowed, tormented, chafed, in distress. — *Ant.* QUIET, placid, soothed.

**uneconomical,** *modif.* — *Syn.* extravagant, unprofitable, costly; see **expensive.**

**uneducated,** *modif.* — *Syn.* illiterate, unschooled, untaught; see **ignorant** 2.
*See Synonym Study at* IGNORANT.

**unembellished,** *modif.* — *Syn.* unadorned, plain, bare, prosaic, austere; see also **modest** 2.

**unemotional,** *modif.* — *Syn.* reticent, apathetic, insensitive; see **indifferent** 1, **quiet** 2.

**unemployable,** *modif.* — *Syn.* useless, worthless, unable to work, untrained, unqualified; see also **disabled.**

**unemployed,** *modif.* — *Syn.* out of work, laid off, at liberty, between jobs, in the bread lines, receiving charity, jobless, idle, inactive, loafing, unoccupied, without gainful employment, on the dole, cooling one's heels*, on the shelf*; see also **lazy** 1. — *Ant.* BUSY, employed, at work.

**unemployment,** *n.* — *Syn.* work stoppage, lay-off, strike conditions; see **stopping.**

**unemployment compensation,** *n.* — *Syn.* the dole, unemployment benefits, monthly check; see **check** 1, **pay** 1, 2.

**unending,** *modif.* — *Syn.* interminable, everlasting, infinite, never-ending, constant, continual, eternal, ceaseless, perpetual, incessant, steady, unremitting. — *Ant.* MOMENTARY, temporary, brief.

**unendurable,** *modif.* — *Syn.* excessive, unbearable, insupportable; see **extreme** 2, **intolerable.**

**unenterprising,** *modif.* — *Syn.* indolent, listless, tired; see **lazy, slow** 2.

**unenthusiastic,** *modif.* — *Syn.* apathetic, blasé, uninterested; see **indifferent** 1, **quiet** 2.

**unequal,** *modif.* 1. [Not alike] — *Syn.* odd, ill-matched, dissimilar; see **different** 1, **unlike.**
2. [One-sided] — *Syn.* uneven, unbalanced, inequitable; see **irregular** 1.

**unequaled,** *modif.* — *Syn.* unmatched, unrivaled, supreme; see **unique** 1.

**unequally,** *modif.* — *Syn.* unfairly, not evenly, not regularly, showing favoritism; see **differently** 1, **unevenly.**

**unequivocal,** *modif.* — *Syn.* straightforward, clear, unambiguous, explicit; see **definite** 1.

**unerring,** *modif.* — *Syn.* faultless, errorless, impeccable, accurate, true, sure, certain, reliable, infallible, unfailing, trustworthy, exact, just, invariable, perfect. — *Ant.* WRONG, inaccurate, erring.

**unessential,** *modif.* — *Syn.* inessential, dispensable, minor, slight; see **irrelevant, trivial, unnecessary.**

**unethical,** *modif.* — *Syn.* unscrupulous, unprincipled, immoral, unfair; see **dishonest** 2, **wrong** 1.

**uneven,** *modif.* 1. [Rough] — *Syn.* bumpy, rugged, jagged; see **rough** 1.
2. [Irregular] — *Syn.* notched, jagged, serrate; see **irregular** 4.
3. [Variable] — *Syn.* intermittent, spasmodic, fitful; see **irregular** 1.
4. [Odd] — *Syn.* remaining, leftover, additional; see **odd** 5.

**unevenly,** *modif.* — *Syn.* roughly, intermittently, irregularly, spottily, bumpily, with friction, haphazardly, wobbling, bumping, stumbling, hopping, jumpily, jumping, as if corrugated, all up and down, staggering; see also **irregularly.**

**uneventful,** *modif.* — *Syn.* routine, monotonous, unexciting, quiet; see **dull** 4, 6.

**unexacting,** *modif.* — *Syn.* easygoing, unruffled, tolerant; see **easy** 2.

**unexampled,** *modif.* — *Syn.* unprecedented, new, unequaled; see **unique, unusual** 1.

**unexcelled,** *modif.* — *Syn.* best, superior, unrivaled, beyond criticism; see **excellent, supreme.**

**unexceptionable,** *modif.* — *Syn.* irreproachable, faultless, flawless; see **perfect** 2.

**unexpected,** *modif.* — *Syn.* unforeseen, surprising, unlooked for, accidental, fortuitous, sudden, startling, unheralded, unpredicted, coming unaware, astonishing, staggering, stunning, electrifying, amazing, not in the cards, not on the books, past conjecture, unanticipated, not bargained for, uncontemplated, wonderful, prodigious, coming without previous intimation, unprepared for, instantaneous, eye-opening, like a bolt from the blue*. — *Ant.* EXPECTED, predicted, foreseen.

**unexpectedly,** *modif.* — *Syn.* surprisingly, suddenly, startlingly, without warning, like a bolt from the blue; see also **quickly** 1. — *Ant.* REGULARLY, according to prediction, as anticipated.

**unexpressive,** *modif.* — *Syn.* inexpressive, dull, apathetic; see **indifferent** 1, **vacant** 3.

**unfading,** *modif.* — *Syn.* unchanging, lasting, constant; see **permanent** 2, **perpetual** 1.

**unfailing,** *modif.* 1. [Inexhaustible] — *Syn.* ceaseless, endless, infallible; see **eternal** 1, 2, **infallible.**
2. [Sure] — *Syn.* absolute, continual, surefire*; see **constant** 1, **certain** 3.

**unfair,** *modif.* 1. [Unjust] — *Syn.* inequitable, wrongful, wrong, unrightful, low, base, injurious, unethical, not cricket*, bad, wicked, culpable, blamable, blame-

worthy, foul, illegal, improper, unsporting, shameful, cruel, shameless, dishonorable, unreasonable, discreditable, grievous, vicious, vile, undue, unlawful, petty, mean, unwarrantable, inexcusable, unjustifiable, iniquitous, immoral, criminal, forbidden, irregular. — *Ant.* FAIR, proper, sporting.
2. [Not in accord with approved trade practices] — *Syn.* unethical, criminal, proscribed, cheating, discriminatory, illegal, forbidden, tricky, evasive, shady, punishable, actionable, improper.

**unfairly,** *modif.* — *Syn.* unjustly, unreasonably, irregularly, illegally, immorally; see also **brutally.**

**unfaithful,** *modif.* 1. [Not faithful] — *Syn.* false, untrue, deceitful, foresworn, unreliable, traitorous, treasonable, perfidious, not true to, of bad faith, treacherous, untrustworthy, shifty, unreliable. — *Ant.* FAITHFUL, constant, loyal.
2. [Having broken the marriage vow] — *Syn.* adulterous, philandering, incontinent, unchaste; see **wicked** 1.

**unfaltering,** *modif.* — *Syn.* resolute, firm, steadfast, unflagging; see **reliable** 1, 2.

**unfamiliar,** *modif.* 1. [Unacquainted] — *Syn.* not introduced, not associated, unknown, not on speaking terms, not versed in, not in the habit of, out of contact with; see also **strange** 2. — *Ant.* FRIENDLY, intimate, acquainted.
2. [Strange] — *Syn.* alien, outlandish, exotic, remote, foreign, unknown, novel, original, different, unusual, extraordinary, unaccustomed, unexplored, anomalous, uncommon. — *Ant.* COMMON, ordinary, usual.

**unfashionable,** *modif.* — *Syn.* out-of-style, outmoded, antiquated, obsolete; see **old-fashioned, unpopular.**

**unfasten,** *v.* — *Syn.* unsnap, untie, unlock; see **unhitch.**

**unfathomable,** *modif.* 1. [Infinite] — *Syn.* boundless, unending; see **eternal** 2.
2. [Profound] — *Syn.* incomprehensible, abstruse, unknowable, enigmatic; see **mysterious** 2.

**unfavorable,** *modif.* 1. [Adverse] — *Syn.* opposed, hostile, antagonistic; see **unfriendly** 1.
2. [Not propitious] — *Syn.* inopportune, untimely, unseasonable, adverse, calamitous, unpropitious, inexpedient, bad, ill-chosen, infelicitous, ill-fated, ill-suited, ill-timed, unsuitable, improper, wrong, abortive, untoward, malapropos, inauspicious, unlucky, ill, unfortunate, regrettable, premature, tardy, late, discommodious, unfit, inadvisable, objectionable, inconvenient, disadvantageous, damaging, destructive, unseemly, ill-advised, obstructive, troublesome, embarrassing, unpromising, awkward, with a jaundiced eye*, with a cold eye*; see also **ominous.**

**unfavorably,** *modif.* — *Syn.* adversely, negatively, opposingly, oppositely, conflictingly, antagonistically, obstructively, malignantly, counteractively, contrarily, untowardly, as a deterrent, in opposition to, in the negative, on the contrary, by contraries, by blackballing, by turning thumbs down*, giving the red light to*; see also **against** 3.

**unfeeling,** *modif.* 1. [Incapable of sensation] — *Syn.* insensate, insensible, unconscious, anesthetized; see **numb** 1.
2. [Incapable of sympathy] — *Syn.* hardhearted, callous, heartless, inhuman, pitiless; see also **cruel** 2, **ruthless** 1, 2.

**unfeigned,** *modif.* — *Syn.* real, sincere, heartfelt; see **genuine** 2.

**unfilial,** *modif.* — *Syn.* refractory, disobedient, insubordinate; see **rebellious** 2, 3, **unruly.**

**unfilled,** *modif.* 1. [Empty] — *Syn.* vacant, void, drained; see **empty** 1.
2. [Not attended to; *said especially of orders*] — *Syn.*

pending, awaiting action, delayed, held up, on backorder, not dispatched, unshipped, under consideration, declined, refused; see also **unfinished** 1.

**unfinished,** *modif.* **1.** [Not completed] — *Syn.* uncompleted, undone, half done, incomplete, under construction, unperformed, imperfect, unconcluded, deficient, unexecuted, unaccomplished, in preparation, in the making, not done, in the rough, sketchy, tentative, shapeless, formless, unperfected, unfulfilled, undeveloped, unassembled, defective, found wanting, cut short, immature, faulty, crude, rough. — *Ant.* DONE, completed, perfected.
**2.** [Without a finish] — *Syn.* natural, unpainted, unvarnished, unpolished, bare, raw, rough, crude, unprotected, uncovered, plain, undecorated, unadorned. — *Ant.* painted, varnished, enameled.

**unfit,** *modif.* **1.** [Incompetent] — *Syn.* unqualified, feeble, unpracticed, inexperienced, untrained, unskilled, weak, impotent, inept, clumsy, debilitated, incapacitated, badly qualified, ill-equipped, unable, unprepared, ineffective, unapt. — *Ant.* ABLE, fit, effective.
**2.** [Unsuitable] — *Syn.* improper, ill-adapted, wrong, ill-advised, unlikely, unpromising, inexpedient, inappropriate, inapplicable, inutile, useless, valueless, mistaken, incorrect, inadequate, flimsy. — *Ant.* FIT, suitable, correct.

**unflagging,** *modif.* — *Syn.* steady, dynamic, untiring, unfailing; see **active** 2, **constant** 1.

**unflappable,** *modif.* — *Syn.* collected, cool, self-possessed, imperturbable; see **calm** 1, **deliberate** 1.

**unflattering,** *modif.* — *Syn.* plain, candid, blunt; see **critical** 2, **frank.**

**unfledged,** *modif.* **1.** [Young] — *Syn.* unfeathered, youthful, adolescent; see **young** 1.
**2.** [Immature] — *Syn.* undeveloped, inexperienced, raw; see **childish** 1, **young** 2.

**unflinching,** *modif.* — *Syn.* steadfast, unfaltering, constant, courageous; see **firm** 5, **resolute** 2.

**unfold,** *v.* **1.** [Unfurl] — *Syn.* shake out, straighten, release, display, unwind, spread out, uncurl, unwrap, unroll, give to the breeze, reel out, unbend, open, flatten, loosen, unroll, uncrease. — *Ant.* FOLD, roll, lap.
**2.** [Reveal] — *Syn.* disclose, uncover, discover, elucidate, explain, make known, publish, expose, announce, particularize, explicate; see also **reveal** 1. — *Ant.* HIDE, obscure, conceal.

**unforeseen,** *modif.* — *Syn.* surprising, abrupt, sudden; see **unexpected.**

**unforgettable,** *modif.* — *Syn.* notable, exceptional, extraordinary; see **impressive** 1, **memorable** 1.

**unforgivable,** *modif.* — *Syn.* inexcusable, unpardonable, unjustifiable, indefensible, inexpiable; see also **wrong** 1.

**unforgiving,** *modif.* — *Syn.* revengeful, avenging, relentless; see **cruel** 2, **ruthless** 1.

**unformed,** *modif.* — *Syn.* not formed, formless, incomplete; see **unfinished.**

**unfortunate,** *modif.* **1.** [Not promoting good fortune] — *Syn.* unpropitious, adverse, damaging; see **unfavorable** 2.
**2.** [Not enjoying good fortune] — *Syn.* unlucky, luckless, unhappy, hapless, afflicted, troubled, stricken, unsuccessful, without success, burdened, pained, not prosperous, ill-starred, in adverse circumstances, out of fortune, forsaken by fortune, cursed, broken, shattered, ill-fated, on the road to ruin, in a desperate plight, ruined, out of luck*, in a bad way*, jinxed*, hexed*, behind the eight ball*, hoodooed*, gone to the dogs*,

down on one's luck*; see also **sad** 1. — *Ant.* HAPPY, lucky, prosperous.
**3.** [Not enjoying prosperity] — *Syn.* destitute, impoverished, bankrupt; see **poor** 1.

**unfortunately,** *modif.* **1.** [To be regretted] — *Syn.* unluckily, regrettably, lamentably, unhappily, miserably, sadly, grievously, disastrously, dismally, calamitously, badly, dismayingly, sickeningly, discouragingly, catastrophically, horribly, if worst comes to worst. — *Ant.* HAPPILY, favorably, prosperously.
**2.** [With ill fortune] — *Syn.* by ill hap, by chance, accidentally, predestinately, as luck would have it, by an evil chance, perversely.

**unfounded,** *modif.* — *Syn.* baseless, unproven, unsupported, groundless; see **untrue.**

**unfriendly,** *modif.* **1.** [Hostile] — *Syn.* opposed, alienated, disaffected, ill-disposed, against, opposite, contrary, warlike, competitive, conflicting, antagonistic, estranged, at swords' points, at drawn daggers, inimical, at variance, at loggerheads, irreconcilable, not on speaking terms, turned against, with a chip on one's shoulder*. — *Ant.* FRIENDLY, intimate, approving.
**2.** [Lacking friendly qualities] — *Syn.* grouchy, censorious, bearish, surly, misanthropic, antisocial, uncongenial, gruff, ill-disposed, envious, uncharitable, faultfinding, combative, quarrelsome, grudging, malignant, spiteful, malicious, mean, vengeful, resentful, hateful, captious, acrimonious, peevish, aloof, unsociable, inhospitable, crabbed, suspicious, sour; see also **irritable.** — *Ant.* GENEROUS, frank, open.

**unfruitful,** *modif.* — *Syn.* barren, fruitless, sterile, arid, blasted, infertile, desert, unprofitable.
*See Synonym Study at* STERILE.

**unfunded,** *modif.* — *Syn.* bankrupt, floating, insolvent; see **poor** 1.

**unfurl,** *v.* — *Syn.* unroll, unwind, loosen; see **unfold** 1.

**ungainly,** *modif.* — *Syn.* clumsy, gawky, inexpert; see **awkward** 1, **rude** 1.

**ungentlemanly,** *modif.* — *Syn.* crude, rough, uncivil; see **rude** 1.

**ungodly,** *modif.* **1.** [Not religious] — *Syn.* profane, godless, atheistic, skeptical; see **impious.**
**2.** [Sinful] — *Syn.* sacrilegious, immoral, perfidious; see **wicked** 1, 2.
**3.** [*Outrageous] — *Syn.* dreadful, atrocious, awful, god-awful.

**ungovernable,** *modif.* — *Syn.* unmanageable, wild, uncontrollable; see **rebellious** 2, 3, **unruly.**

**ungracious,** *modif.* — *Syn.* unpleasant, discourteous, impolite; see **rude** 1, 2.

**ungraciously,** *modif.* — *Syn.* unkindly, crudely, brashly, disrespectfully; see **rudely.**

**ungrammatical,** *modif.* — *Syn.* inaccurate, incorrect, solecistic, nonstandard, improper, faulty, imprecise; see also **wrong** 2.

**ungrateful,** *modif.* — *Syn.* thankless, unthankful, selfish, lacking in appreciation, unappreciative, grasping, demanding, self-centered, unmindful, forgetful, heedless, careless, insensible, dissatisfied, grumbling, unnatural, faultfinding, oblivious. — *Ant.* THANKFUL, grateful obliged.

**unguarded,** *modif.* — *Syn.* thoughtless, frank, careless, unwary, heedless, offhand, casual, imprudent, unwise, impulsive, ill-considered, candid, ingenuous, naive, unconscious, incautious, headlong, impolitic, spontaneous, unreflective, unpremeditated. — *Ant.* DELIBERATE, cautious, wary.

**unguent,** *n.* — *Syn.* emollient, ointment, cream; see **balm** 2.

**unhallowed,** *modif.* **1.** [Unholy] — *Syn.* ungodly, unsanctified, unsacred; see **wicked** 2.
**2.** [Irreverent] — *Syn.* wicked, profane, secular; see **impious**.
**unhandy,** *modif.* **1.** [Inconvenient] — *Syn.* awkward, ill-arranged, unwieldy, ill-contrived, bothersome, clumsy, ill-adapted, cumbersome, discommodious, unfit, disadvantageous, inappropriate, unsuitable, hampering, cumbrous. — *Ant.* CONVENIENT, manageable, commodious.
**2.** [Unskillful] — *Syn.* awkward, bungling, bunglesome, maladroit, clumsy, incompetent, blundering, botching, slipshod, amateur, inexpert, fumbling, inept, heavy-handed. — *Ant.* ABLE, accomplished, nimble.
**unhappily,** *modif.* — *Syn.* regrettably, lamentably, unluckily; see **badly** 1, **unfortunately.**
**unhappiness,** *n.* — *Syn.* sorrow, woe, sadness; see **depression** 2, **grief** 1.
**unhappy,** *modif.* **1.** [Sad] — *Syn.* miserable, sorrowful, wretched; see **troubled** 1.
**2.** [Unfortunate] — *Syn.* afflicted, troubled, in a desperate plight; see **unfortunate** 2.
**unharmed,** *modif.* — *Syn.* unhurt, uninjured, intact; see **safe** 1, **whole** 2.
**unharmonious,** *modif.* **1.** — *Syn.* discordant, shrill, unmelodious; see **harsh** 1.
**2.** [Opposed] — *Syn.* antagonistic, disagreeing, not in keeping (with); see **against** 3.
**unharness,** *v.* — *Syn.* unbuckle, unstrap, unfasten; see **unhitch.**
**unhealthful,** *modif.* — *Syn.* detrimental, unhealthy, toxic, noxious; see **dangerous** 2, **harmful.**
**unhealthy,** *modif.* **1.** [Sickly] — *Syn.* not well, sick, in a decline, in ill health, infirm, delicate, feeble, shaky, valetudinarian, undernourished, rickety, spindling, ailing, invalid, weak, in a run-down condition, poorly*.
**2.** [Unwholesome] — *Syn.* deleterious, harmful, injurious, noxious, hurtful, unsanitary, toxic; see also **harmful.** — *Ant.* HEALTHY, robust, hale.
**unheard,** *modif.* — *Syn.* silent, noiseless, soundless, hushed, quiet, mute, muffled, still, inaudible. — *Ant.* AUDIBLE, heard, noisy.
**unheard-of,** *modif.* — *Syn.* unprecedented, unique, new; see **unknown** 1, **unusual** 2.
**unheeded,** *modif.* — *Syn.* disregarded, neglected, overlooked, slighted, forgotten, unnoticed, abandoned, rejected, unconsidered, glossed over, slurred over, thrust aside, skimmed over, scorned, disobeyed, repudiated, put aside, winked at, ignored, uncared for, unperceived, unseen, unobserved, unnoted, unmarked, unthought of, discarded, flouted, hid under a bushel, passed by. — *Ant.* CONSIDERED, heeded, regarded.
**unheralded,** *modif.* — *Syn.* unsung, unnoticed, unrecognized; see **unknown** 2.
**unhesitating,** *modif.* — *Syn.* prompt, steadfast, unwavering, immediate; see **certain** 1.
**unhinge,** *v.* **1.** [To detach] — *Syn.* dislodge, disjoint, disunite; see **remove** 1, **unhitch.**
**2.** [To upset] — *Syn.* unbalance, disorder, derange; see **disorganize.**
**unhitch,** *v.* — *Syn.* unhook, unfasten, untie, disengage, detach, unloose, loosen, unbuckle, unstrap, release, unharness, uncouple, free, take out of the traces. — *Ant.* FASTEN, hitch, couple.
**unhoped-for,** *modif.* — *Syn.* incredible, unforeseen, unexpected; see **unbelievable, unimaginable.**
**unhurried,** *modif.* — *Syn.* leisurely, deliberate, nonchalant; see **calm** 1, **slow** 1.
**unhurt,** *modif.* — *Syn.* uninjured, all right, unblemished,

undamaged, intact, whole, unscathed, scatheless, unharmed, unwounded, unmaimed, unbroken; see also **safe** 1.
**unhygienic,** *modif.* — *Syn.* unclean, unwashed, unsanitary; see **dirty** 1.
**unidentified,** *modif.* — *Syn.* nameless, unnamed, not known, mysterious; see **anonymous, unknown** 1, 2, 3.
**unidentified flying object,** *n.* — *Syn.* UFO, flying saucer, spaceship, alien craft.
**unification,** *n.* concurrence, affinity, combination; see **alliance** 1, **union** 1.
**unified,** *modif.* — *Syn.* made one, united, joined, combined, concerted, synthesized, amalgamated, conjoined, incorporated, blended, identified, coalesced, federated, centralized, intertwined, consolidated, associated, cemented, coupled, allied, wedded, married, confederated, conjugated, compacted. — *Ant.* separated, distinct, disjoined.
**uniform,** *modif.* **1.** [Even] — *Syn.* symmetrical, regular, steady, stable, smooth, well-proportioned, normal, straight, unwarped, true, consistent, plumb. — *Ant.* CROOKED, warped, askew.
**2.** [Alike] — *Syn.* equal, unvaried, well-matched, consonant, consistent, correspondent, mated, after the same pattern, similar, identical. — *Ant.* DIFFERENT, unlike, varied.
*See Synonym Study at* STEADY.
**uniform,** *n.* — *Syn.* costume, suit, garb, dress, habit, attire, outfit, regimentals, dress uniform, khaki, livery, OD*, GI*; see also **clothes.**
**uniformity,** *n.* **1.** [Regularity] — *Syn.* steadiness, sameness, evenness; see **regularity.**
**2.** [Harmony] — *Syn.* unity, accord, concord; see **agreement** 2.
**uniformly,** *modif.* — *Syn.* without exception, with great regularity, consistently; see **evenly** 2, **regularly** 2.
**unify,** *v.* — *Syn.* consolidate, ally, conjoin; see **join** 1, **unite** 1.
**unilateral,** *modif.* — *Syn.* concerned with one side, signed by one of two factions, one-sided, not reciprocal, unipartite, single.
**unilluminated,** *modif.* — *Syn.* dim, black, shadowy, unlit; see **dark** 1.
**unimaginable,** *modif.* — *Syn.* inconceivable, incomprehensible, incredible, inapprehensible, ineffable, unbelievable, unheard of, indescribable, unthinkable, beyond comprehension, improbable; see also **impossible** 1. — *Ant.* IMAGINABLE, conceivable, comprehensible.
**unimaginative,** *modif.* — *Syn.* barren, tedious, uninspired, unoriginal; see **common** 1, **dull** 7.
**unimpaired,** *modif.* — *Syn.* uninjured, in good shape, sound; see **perfect** 2, **whole** 2.
**unimpassioned,** *modif.* — *Syn.* dispassionate, composed, sedate, rational; see **calm** 1, **reserved** 3.
**unimpeachable,** *modif.* — *Syn.* blameless, irreproachable, faultless, like Caesar's wife; see **innocent** 1, 2, **upright** 2.
**unimpeded,** *modif.* — *Syn.* unchecked, unhampered, faultless, unrestrained; see **unlimited.**
**unimportance,** *n.* — *Syn.* immateriality, triviality, worthlessness; see **insignificance.**
**unimportant,** *modif.* — *Syn.* trifling, inconsiderable, slight, worthless, inconsequential, insignificant, unnecessary, immaterial, negligible, indifferent, unnecessary, beside the point, frivolous, useless, second-rate, low-ranking, of no account, of no consequence, of no moment, worthless, trivial, paltry, picayune, piddling*, penny ante*, mickey mouse. — *Ant.* IMPORTANT, weighty, great.

**unimposing,** *modif.* **1.** [Unassuming] — *Syn.* kind, considerate, courteous, polite, quiet, modest, unobtrusive, humble, demure, simple, unpretentious, unassuming, unembellished; see also **reserved** 3.
**2.** [Insignificant] — *Syn.* slight, paltry, unimpressive; see **trivial.**
**unimproved,** *modif.* — *Syn.* ordinary, in a natural state, untutored; see **rough** 1, **wild** 1.
**uninfluenced,** *modif.* — *Syn.* unbiased, impartial, neutral; see **fair** 1.
**uninformed,** *modif.* — *Syn.* unenlightened, naive, unacquainted; see **ignorant** 1, 2, **unaware.**
**uninhabitable,** *modif.* — *Syn.* unfit to live in, unoccupiable, unlivable, untenantable.
**uninhabited,** *modif.* — *Syn.* deserted, desolate, unsettled; see **abandoned** 1, **isolated.**
**uninitiated,** *modif.* — *Syn.* uninformed, ignorant, inexperienced; see **naive, unaware.**
**uninspired,** *modif.* — *Syn.* unexcited, unmoved, unimpressed, uninspiring; see **indifferent** 1, **unconcerned.**
**uninspiring,** *modif.* — *Syn.* trite, banal, ordinary; see **common** 1, **dull** 4.
**unintelligent,** *modif.* — *Syn.* unlearned, untaught, uneducated; see **ignorant** 2, **stupid** 1.
**unintelligible,** *modif.* — *Syn.* incomprehensible, indecipherable, meaningless, indistinct; see **obscure** 1.
**unintelligibly,** *modif.* — *Syn.* indistinctly, vaguely, inaudibly; see **obscurely.**
**unintentional,** *modif.* — *Syn.* unthinking, involuntary, erratic, accidental; see **aimless, haphazard.**
**unintentionally,** *modif.* — *Syn.* involuntarily, incidentally, casually, accidentally, inadvertently, unthinkingly, haphazardly, without design.
**uninterested,** *modif.* — *Syn.* apathetic, impassive, detached; see **indifferent** 1, **unconcerned.**
**uninteresting,** *modif.* — *Syn.* tedious, boring, tiresome, dreary, wearisome, prosaic, pedestrian, fatiguing, monotonous, dull, drab, colorless, stale, trite, commonplace, irksome, stupid, humdrum, prosy, flat, soporific, depressing, insipid, jejune, unentertaining, uninspiring, dismal, banal; see also **dismal** 1. — *Ant.* INTERESTING, exciting, lively.
**uninterrupted,** *modif.* — *Syn.* continuous, unending, unbroken; see **consecutive** 1, **constant** 1.
**uninvited,** *modif.* — *Syn.* unasked, unwanted, not asked, not invited; see **neglected, unpopular.**
**uninviting,** *modif.* — *Syn.* unpleasant, disagreeable, displeasing; see **offensive** 2, **unpopular.**
**Union,** *n.* **1.** [The United States] — *Syn.* the States, Columbia, America, the land of the free and the home of the brave, God's Country, the land of opportunity, the Colossus of the North; see also **America** 2, **United States.**
**2.** [The North in the American Civil War] — *Syn.* the Free States, Anti-Slavery States, the Northern States, Federalists; see **north.**
**union,** *n.* **1.** [The act of joining] — *Syn.* unity, unification, junction, meeting, uniting, joining, coupling, embracing, coming together, merging, fusion, mingling, concurrence, amalgam, symbiosis, commixture, amalgamation, concatenation, confluence, congregation, reconciliation, conciliation, correlation, combination, connection, annexation, linking, attachment, agglutination, coalition, conjunction, abutment, consolidation, incorporation, centralization, affiliation, confederation, copulation, coition. — *Ant.* DIVORCE, separation, severance.
**2.** [A closely knit group] — *Syn.* alliance, association, federation, society; see **alliance** 3, **organization** 3.

**3.** [A marriage] — *Syn.* wedlock, conjugal ties, matrimony, cohabitation, nuptial connection, match, matrimonial affiliation, double harness★, connubial bliss★.
**4.** [A labor union] — *Syn.* laborers, workingmen, employees; see **labor** 4.
*See Synonym Study at* ALLIANCE, UNITY.
**union shop,** *n.* — *Syn.* closed shop, unionized plant, unionized factory, union house, union establishment, preferential shop, not an open shop.
**unique,** *modif.* **1.** [Existing only in one known example] — *Syn.* single, sole, peerless, matchless, incomparable, unprecedented, unparalleled, unequaled, unrivaled, unsurpassed, novel, nonpareil, unapproachable, unapproached, anomalous, individual, sole, *sui generis* (Latin), unexampled, lone, different, unequaled. — *Ant.* COMMON, frequent, MANY.
**2.** [Rare] — *Syn.* uncommon, freakish, bizarre; see **unusual** 2.
**unison,** *n.* — *Syn.* concert, unity, conjunction, harmony, union, accord, agreement, cooperation, community, common consent, concord, sympathy, *rapprochement* (French), alliance, federation, league, bonds of amity, fraternity, concordance, reciprocity, fellowship. — *Ant.* OPPOSITION, separation, discord.
**unit,** *n.* **1.** [A whole] — *Syn.* entirety, complement, total, totality, assemblage, assembly, system.
**2.** [A detail] — *Syn.* section, segment, part, fraction, piece, joint, block, square, layer, link, length, digit, member, factor.
**unite,** *v.* **1.** [To come together] — *Syn.* join, meet, ally, combine, solidify; harden, strengthen, condense, confederate, couple, affiliate, merge, band together, blend, mix, interpenetrate, become one, concentrate, interfuse, consolidate, entwine, intertwine, grapple, amalgamate, league, band, embody, embrace, copulate, associate, assemble, gather together, conjoin, keep together, tie in, pull together, hang together, join forces, coalesce, fuse, wed, marry, mingle, stick together, stay together. — *Ant.* DIVIDE, separate, part.
**2.** [To bring together] — *Syn.* fuse, couple, blend; see **consolidate** 2, **join** 1.
*See Synonym Study at* JOIN.
**united,** *modif.* — *Syn.* unified, leagued, combined, affiliated, federal, confederated, confederate, integrated, amalgamated, co-operative, consolidated, concordant, concerted, congruent, associated, assembled, linked, banded, in partnership; see also **joined, organized.** — *Ant.* SEPARATED, distinct, individual.
**United Kingdom,** *n.* — *Syn.* England, Scotland, Northern Ireland, Wales; the British Isles, Britain, Great Britain, the mother country, U.K., G.B.★; see also **Europe.**
**United Nations,** *n.* — *Syn.* UN, peace-keeping force, international society, community of nations.
Principal bodies of the United Nations are: General Assembly, Secretariat, Security Council, International Court of Justice, Economic and Social Council, Trusteeship Council. *Agencies of the United Nations include:* World Health Organization (WHO), International Atomic Energy Agency (IAEA), General Agreement on Tariffs and Trade (GATT), International Development Association (IDA), International Finance Corporation (IFC), United Nations Educational, Scientific, and Cultural Organization (UNESCO), Food and Agriculture Organization (FAO), United Nations Industrial Development Organization (UNIDO), World Meteorological Organization (WMO), International Monetary Fund (IMF), International Fund for Agricultural Development, (IFAD), International Labor Or-

ganization (ILO), United Nations Children's Fund (UNICEF).

**United States,** *n.* — *Syn.* America, US, United States of America, U.S.A., Columbia, the Union, these States, the States, the fifty states, ZI (Zone of the Interior), the land of the Stars and Stripes, US of A*, Uncle Sam*, the land of liberty*, the land of the free and the home of the brave*, God's country*, the melting pot*, the lower forty-eight states*, stateside*, the mainland*.

**unity,** *n.* **1.** [The quality of oneness] — *Syn.* homogeneity, homogeneousness, sameness, indivisibility, solidarity, identity, inseparability, singleness, similarity, uniqueness, integration, uniformity, universality, alltogetherness, ensemble, wholeness; see also **whole.** — *Ant.* DIFFERENCE, diversity, divorce.

**2.** [Union] — *Syn.* union, federation, confederation, compact, combination, correspondence, alliance, agreement, concord, solidarity, identity of purpose, unification, aggregation; see also **organization** 3.

**3.** [Harmony] — *Syn.* unison, consonance, concord, agreement, consent, tuneability, accord.

---

**SYN.** — **unity** implies the oneness, as in spirit, aims, interests, feelings, etc., of that which is made up of diverse elements or individuals /national *unity*/; **union** implies the state of being united into a single organization for a common purpose /a labor *union*/; **solidarity** implies such firm and complete unity in an organization, group, class, etc. as to make for the greatest possible strength in influence, action, etc.

---

**universal,** *modif.* **1.** [Concerning the universe] — *Syn.* cosmic, stellar, celestial, empyrean, sidereal, astronomical, cosmogonal.

**2.** [Worldwide] — *Syn.* tellurian, mundane, earthly, terrestrial, sublunary, terrene, human, worldly. — *Ant.* LOCAL, restricted, district.

**3.** [General] — *Syn.* general, entire, all-embracing, prevalent, customary, usual, whole, sweeping, extensive, comprehensive, total, unlimited, limitless, endless, vast, widespread, catholic, ecumenical, common, regular, generic, undisputed, accepted, unrestricted. — *Ant.* SPECIALIZED, limited, peculiar.

---

**SYN.** — **universal** implies applicability to every case or individual, without exception, in the class, category, etc. concerned /a *universal* practice among primitive peoples/; **general** implies applicability to all, nearly all, or most of a group or class /a *general* election/; **generic** implies applicability to every member of a class or, specif. in biology, of a genus /a *generic* characteristic of *Homo sapiens*, *aspirin* has become a *generic* term for acetylsalicylic acid/

---

**universality,** *n.* **1.** [Generality] — *Syn.* predominance, ecumenicity, catholicity, generalization; see **generality.**

**2.** [Entirety] — *Syn.* completeness, wholeness, totality; see **whole.**

**universally,** *modif.* **1.** [Concerning the universe] — *Syn.* cosmically, astronomically, celestially, zodiacally. — *Ant.* LOCALLY, terrestrially, temporarily.

**2.** [Throughout the world] — *Syn.* in all climes, everywhere, from pole to pole, terrestrially, globally. — *Ant.* HERE, there, occasionally.

**3.** [Generally] — *Syn.* entirely, prevailingly, comprehensively, customarily, extensively, totally, endlessly, unrestrictedly; see also **completely.** — *Ant.* ESPECIALLY, specifically, sometimes.

**universe,** *n.* — *Syn.* cosmos, creation, God's handiwork,

world, the visible world, astral system, universal frame, all created things, everything, nature, the natural world. *See Synonym Study at* EARTH.

**university,** *modif.* — *Syn.* professional, advanced, graduate, college, collegiate, undergraduate, freshman, sophomore, junior, senior, learned, academic, educational.

**university,** *n.* — *Syn.* college, educational institution, institution of higher learning, multiversity, megaversity, normal school, state university, provincial university; see also **academy, college, school** 1.

Famous universities of the world include: Paris (Sorbonne), Oxford, Cambridge, Padua, Bologna, Brussels, Halle, Zurich, Basle, Goettingen, London, Edinburgh, Dublin, Oslo, Leipzig, Vienna, Upsala, Lund, Copenhagen, Berlin, Heidelberg, Moscow, Leningrad (St. Petersburg), Kazan, Kiev, Charles (in Prague), Peking, Toronto, McGill, Melbourne, Harvard, Yale, Princeton, Dartmouth, Brown, Cornell, Tufts, Duke, Stanford, Columbia, Chicago, California, Pennsylvania, Virginia, Rutgers, Notre Dame, Vassar, Wesleyan, Wellesley, Purdue, Pitt, Rice, Texas A&M, Georgetown, Auburn, Bryn Mawr, Massachusetts Institute of Technology (MIT), California Institute of Technology (CIT).

**unjust,** *modif.* — *Syn.* wrong, inequitable, wrongful; see **unfair** 1.

**unjustifiable,** *modif.* — *Syn.* indefensible, inexcusable, untenable, unallowable, unforgivable, unjust; see also **wrong** 1.

**unjustifiably,** *modif.* — *Syn.* groundlessly, erroneously, without basis, illegally, unlawfully, unrightfully; see also **badly** 1, **wrongly** 2.

**unjustly,** *modif.* — *Syn.* brutally, cruelly, meanly; see **rudely, wrongly** 1.

**unkempt,** *modif.* **1.** [Dirty] — *Syn.* disheveled, uncombed, disorderly, unclean, untidy; see also **dirty** 1.

**2.** [Rough] — *Syn.* unpolished, unsophisticated, vulgar, coarse; see **crude** 1,

**unkind,** *modif.* — *Syn.* inconsiderate, unsympathetic, harsh, severe, malignant, spiteful, mean, malicious, inhuman, inhumane, sadistic, cruel, hateful, malevolent, savage, barbarous, ruffianly; see also **rude** 1, 2. — *Ant.* KIND, benevolent, helpful.

**unknown,** *modif.* **1.** [Not known; *said of information*] — *Syn.* uncomprehended, unapprehended, undiscovered, untold, unexplained, unascertained, uninvestigated, unexplored, unheard of, unperceived, concealed, hidden, unrevealed. — *Ant.* KNOWN, established, understood.

**2.** [Not known; *said of people*] — *Syn.* alien, unfamiliar, not introduced, unheard of, obscure, foreign, strange, unacknowledged, anonymous, unnamed, ostracized, outcast, friendless, private, retired, aloof, out of the world, rusticated, forgotten.

**3.** [Not known; *said of terrain*] — *Syn.* unexplored, far-off, remote, far, distant, foreign, undiscovered, exotic, hyperborean, transoceanic, transmarine, ultramontane, antipodal, at the far corners of the earth, faraway, at the uttermost ends of the earth, in parts unknown, outlandish, unheard-of, unfrequented, untraveled, desolate, desert, unvisited, legendary, strange, Atlantean.

**unladylike,** *modif.* — *Syn.* unrefined, coarse, indelicate; see **rude** 1.

**unlawful,** *modif.* — *Syn.* forbidden, illicit, outlawed, criminal; see **illegal.**

**unlawfully,** *modif.* — *Syn.* illegally, unjustly, unjustifiably; see **wrongly** 1, 2.

**unlearned,** *modif.* — *Syn.* unlettered, rude, boorish, un-

educated, ignorant, illiterate, clownish, untutored, untaught, unread, savage, uncivilized, doltish, crass, half-taught, half-educated, uninitiated, ill-bred, unversed, uninstructed, unguided, unenlightened, benighted, dull, misguided, empty, unaccomplished, backward, superficial, pedantic, low-brow*. — *Ant.* learned, educated, adept.
*See Synonym Study at* IGNORANT.

**unless,** *prep.* — *Syn.* saving, without the provision that, if not, except, except that, excepting that; see also **except.**

**unlike,** *modif.* — *Syn.* dissimilar, unalike, different, incongruous, contradictory, ill-assorted, hostile, opposed, inconsistent, heterogeneous, diverse, contrasted, conflicting, contrary, disparate, different as night and day, disharmonious, dissonant, discordant, like apples and oranges*, clashing, separate, opposite, divergent, various, variant. — *Ant.* LIKE, similar, correspondent.

**unlikelihood,** *n.* — *Syn.* improbability, doubtfulness, inconceivability, remote possibility, a ghost of a chance*, a snowball's chance in hell*; see also **impossibility, uncertainty** 2.

**unlikely,** *modif.* 1. [Not likely to happen] — *Syn.* improbable, unheard-of, incredible, implausible, not to be thought of, unbelievable, absurd, palpably false, unconvincing, not likely, scarcely possible, apparently false, contrary to expectation, inconceivable, doubtful, dubious, questionable, untoward, extraordinary, marvelous, out of the ordinary, strange.
2. [Not likely to succeed] — *Syn.* unpromising, unpropitious, questionable, dubious. — *Ant.* LIKELY, probable, credible.

**unlimited,** *modif.* — *Syn.* infinite, limitless, boundless, unending, extensive, universal, unrestricted, unconditional, unfathomable, inexhaustible, unconfined, immense, illimitable, measureless, incalculable, interminable, without number, unfathomed, unsounded, untold, countless, numberless, incomprehensible, immeasurable, endless.

**unlisted,** *modif.* — *Syn.* unrecorded, unreported, not recorded, not listed, not reported, not identified, confidential; see also **unknown** 1, 2.

**unload,** *v.* — *Syn.* disburden, void, offload, discommode, discharge, dump, slough, unship, lighten, unlade, cast, unpack, unweight, relieve, remove cargo, disgorge, empty, deplane, unburden, break bulk. — *Ant.* FILL, load, pack.

**unloaded,** *modif.* 1. [Removed] — *Syn.* unpacked, taken out, put away, uncrated, unwrapped.
2. [Empty] — *Syn.* void, vacated, discharged; see **empty** 1.

**unlock,** *v.* — *Syn.* unbar, unfasten, open the lock; see **open** 2, **unhitch.**

**unlocked,** *modif.* — *Syn.* free, unbarred, unlatched; see **open** 1, 2.

**unlooked-for,** *modif.* — *Syn.* unanticipated, unforeseen, chance; see **unexpected.**

**unloved,** *modif.* — *Syn.* disliked, unpopular, unappreciated, abhorred, detested, despised; see also **hated.**

**unlucky,** *modif.* 1. [Unfortunate] — *Syn.* luckless, unhappy, afflicted; see **unfortunate** 2.
2. [Unpropitious] — *Syn.* ill-chosen, ill-fated, untimely; see **ominous, unfavorable** 2.

**unmade,** *modif.* — *Syn.* disheveled, messy, tousled, slept-in; see **disorderly** 1, **unfinished** 1.

**unmake,** *v.* — *Syn.* ruin, depose, exterminate; see **destroy** 1.

**unmanageable,** *modif.* — *Syn.* uncontrollable, obstreperous, willful, irrepressible, ungovernable; see also **unruly.**

**unmanly,** *modif.* — *Syn.* weak, effeminate, womanish; see **cowardly** 1, 2, 3, **feminine** 2.

**unmannerly,** *modif.* — *Syn.* uncouth, discourteous, ill-mannered; see **rude** 1.

**unmarried,** *modif.* — *Syn.* celibate, unwed, single, virgin, maiden, bachelor, eligible, chaste, unwedded, spouseless, unhitched*, unspliced*, uncoupled*, footloose and fancy-free*. — *Ant.* MARRIED, wed, wedded.

**unmask,** *v.* — *Syn.* bare, reveal, uncover; see **expose** 1.

**unmelodious,** *modif.* — *Syn.* unharmonious, dissonant, discordant; see **harsh** 1.

**unmentionable,** *modif.* — *Syn.* scandalous, disgraceful, ignoble; see **offensive** 2, **shameful** 1, 2.

**unmerciful,** *modif.* — *Syn.* merciless, pitiless, unpitying, vengeful, brutal, cruel, savage, bloodthirsty, tyrannous, monstrous, sanguine, inhumane, bestial, vindictive, ravening, cold-hearted, coldblooded, heartless, atrocious, dead to human feeling, stony-hearted.

**unmindful,** *modif.* — *Syn.* forgetful, heedless, inattentive; see **careless** 1.

**unmistakable,** *modif.* — *Syn.* conspicuous, patent, distinct, evident; see **clear** 1, 2, **obvious** 1.

**unmitigated,** *modif.* 1. [Absolute] — *Syn.* out-and-out, clear-cut, unabridged; see **absolute** 1.
2. [Unlessened] — *Syn.* untempered, unalloyed, harsh, relentless, austere, unbending; see also **severe** 1.

**unmotivated,** *modif.* — *Syn.* indolent, unenterprising, unambitious, indolent; see **indifferent, lazy** 1.

**unmoved,** *modif.* 1. [Not moved physically] — *Syn.* firm, stable, motionless, static, quiescent, solid, durable, immovable, firm as a rock, staunch, fast, moveless, statuelike, rooted, steady, immobile, unshaken, changeless, unwavering.
2. [Not moved emotionally] — *Syn.* impassive, impassible, stoic, quiet, cold, cool, calm, collected, deliberate, resolute, dispassionate, calculating, unaffected, untouched, unresponsive, unemotional, dry-eyed, callous, indifferent, judicious, unflinching, nerveless, cool as a cucumber*.

**unnatural,** *modif.* 1. [Contrary to nature] — *Syn.* monstrous, phenomenal, malformed, anomalous, irregular, unaccountable, abnormal, preposterous, marvelous, uncanny, wonderful, strange, incredible, sublime, Herculean, Atlantean, freakish, unconforming, inhuman, outrageous, unorthodox, miraculous, contrary to known laws; see also **cruel** 1, 2, **savage** 2. — *Ant.* COMMON, ordinary, usual.
2. [Artificial] — *Syn.* synthetic, imitation, manufactured, ersatz, concocted, make-up, fabricated, false, pseudo, fake, put-on*, mock, spurious, phoney. — *Ant.* NATURAL, occurring, naturally.
*See Synonym Study at* IRREGULAR.

**unnaturally,** *modif.* — *Syn.* strangely, unusually, abnormally; see **crazily.**

**unnecessarily,** *modif.* needlessly, causelessly, without occasion, by chance, carelessly, fortuitously, casually, haphazardly, wantonly, accidentally, unessentially, redundantly, inexpediently, uselessly, exorbitantly, superfluously, undesirably, objectionably, disadvantageously, optionally, avoidably, without cause, without reason, gratuitously; see also **foolishly.** — *Ant.* NECESSARILY, indispensably, unavoidably.

**unnecessary,** *modif.* — *Syn.* needless, causeless, fortuitous, casual, chance, haphazard, wanton, accidental, unessential, nonessential, beside the point, irrelevant, futile, extraneous, additional, redundant, useless, exorbitant, superfluous, worthless, undesirable, optional, avoidable, objectionable, disadvantageous, noncompulsory, random, dispensable, adventitious, without compulsion, uncalled for, pleonastic, gratuitous. — *Ant.* NECESSARY, essential, required.

**unnerve,** *v.* — *Syn.* frighten, unman, dishearten, enervate, discourage; see also **weaken** 2, **frighten** 1.

**SYN.** — **unnerve** implies a causing to lose courage or self-control as by shocking, dismaying, etc. /the screams *unnerved* her/; **enervate** implies a gradual loss of strength or vitality, as because of climate, indolence, etc. /*enervating* heat/; **unman** implies a loss of manly courage, fortitude, or spirit /he was so *unmanned* by the news that he broke into tears/

**unnoticed,** *modif.* — *Syn.* unobserved, unperceived, unseen, unheeded, overlooked, inconspicuous, secret, hidden, passed by, unobtrusive, disregarded, unconsidered, unattended, neglected, unrespected, unmarked, unremembered, unscrutinized, unremarked, uncontemplated, unrecognized, slurred over, uninspected, winked at, connived at, glossed over, lost sight of, ignored, shoved into the background, undistinguished, unexamined, unwatched, unlooked at. — *Ant.* WATCHED, noticed, seen.

**unobtrusive,** *modif.* — *Syn.* inconspicuous, modest, unassuming, meek; see **humble** 1, **reserved** 3.

**unoccupied,** *modif.* **1.** [Vacant] — *Syn.* uninhabited, empty, tenantless, deserted, abandoned, unfurnished, void, voided, disfurnished, blank, untenanted. — *Ant.* FULL, inhabited, tenanted.
**2.** [Idle] — *Syn.* loitering, inactive, unemployed, unengaged, at leisure, passive, lazy, quiescent, dormant, out of work.

**unofficial,** *modif.* — *Syn.* unauthorized, personal, casual, off the record; see **informal** 1, **private.**

**unopposed,** *modif.* — *Syn.* unchallenged, uncontested, unanimous, unrestricted, unhampered; see also **free** 1, 2, 3.

**unorganized,** *modif.* — *Syn.* chaotic, random, disorganized; see **confused** 2, **disordered, haphazard.**

**unorthodox,** *modif.* — *Syn.* unconventional, irregular, eccentric; see **different** 1, 2, **unusual** 2.

**unpack,** *v.* — *Syn.* unlade, uncrate, unwrap; see **empty** 2, **remove** 1.

**unpacked,** *modif.* **1.** [Not yet packed] — *Syn.* ready for packing, not wrapped, not crated, bulk, in storage. — *Ant.* PACKED, wrapped, boxed.
**2.** [No longer packed] — *Syn.* out of its wrappings, assembled, stripped, set up; see **removed** 1, **unloaded** 1.

**unpaid,** *modif.* **1.** [Owed; *said of debts*] — *Syn.* due, payable, not discharged, past due, overdue, delinquent, unsettled, unliquidated, undefrayed, outstanding. — *Ant.* PAID, discharged, defrayed.
**2.** [Not reimbursed; *said of creditors*] — *Syn.* due, uncompensated, unindemnified, unrewarded, defrauded, unsalaried, unfed. — *Ant.* PAID, reimbursed, indemnified.
**3.** [Working without salary] — *Syn.* voluntary, volunteer, unsalaried, amateur, freewill, donated, contributed, pro bono.

**unpalatable,** *modif.* — *Syn.* unsavory, disagreeable, inedible, uneatable; see **tasteless** 1.

**unparalleled,** *modif.* — *Syn.* unmatched, unequaled, exceptional; see **rare** 2, **single** 1, **unique** 1.

**unpardonable,** *modif.* — *Syn.* reprehensible, inexpiable, inexcusable; see **unforgivable.**

**unperturbed,** *modif.* — *Syn.* composed, tranquil, placid; see **calm** 1, 2, **undisturbed.**

**unpleasant,** *modif.* **1.** [Not pleasing in society] — *Syn.*

disagreeable, obnoxious, irksome, bothersome; see **rude** 2.
**2.** [Not pleasing to the senses] — *Syn.* repulsive, obnoxious, abhorrent; see **offensive** 2.

**unpleasantness,** *n.* — *Syn.* disturbance, nuisance, bother; see **difficulty** 1, 2, **trouble** 2.

**unpolished,** *modif.* **1.** [Rough] — *Syn.* uneven, unlevel, unvarnished; see **raw** 2, **unfinished** 2.
**2.** [Vulgar] — *Syn.* unrefined, unsophisticated, rude, crude, uncouth; see also **awkward** 1.

**unpopular,** *modif.* — *Syn.* disliked, despised, out of favor, unaccepted, abhorred, loathed, shunned, avoided, ostracized, scorned, detested, execrated, unloved, unvalued, uncared for, obnoxious; see also **offensive** 2. — *Ant.* POPULAR, liked, agreeable.

**unprecedented,** *modif.* — *Syn.* unparalleled, unique, novel, original, anomalous, abnormal, freakish, untoward, unusual, out-of-the-way, uncommon, eccentric, bizarre, odd, idiosyncratic, aberrant, prodigious, unexampled, *outré* (French), exotic, preternatural, miraculous, marvelous, outlandish, newfangled, modern, fantastic; see also **single.** — *Ant.* COMMON, regular, everyday.

**unpredictable,** *modif.* — *Syn.* random, inconstant, variable; see **changeable** 1, 2, **irregular** 1.

**unprejudiced,** *modif.* — *Syn.* unbiased, impartial, just, disinterested; see **fair** 1, **liberal** 2.

**unpremeditated,** *modif.* — *Syn.* hasty, unconsidered, blundering, without forethought; see **rash, thoughtless** 1.

**unprepared,** *modif.* — *Syn.* unready, unwarned, unwary, unexpectant, surprised, taken aback, unguarded, unnotified, unadvised, unaware, unsuspecting, taken off guard, napping*, in the dark*, going off half-cocked*; see also **inexperienced.**

**unpretentious,** *modif.* — *Syn.* simple, unassuming, prosaic; see **humble** 1.

**unprincipled,** *modif.* — *Syn.* unscrupulous, unethical, corrupt; see **dishonest** 2.

**unproductive,** *modif.* **1.** [Sterile] — *Syn.* unprolific, impotent, barren; see **sterile** 1, 2.
**2.** [Dry] — *Syn.* unfruitful, bare, desert; see **empty** 1.

**unprofessional,** *modif.* — *Syn.* improper, unethical, inadequate; see **ignorant** 2, **unsuitable.**

**unprofitable,** *modif.* **1.** [Producing but little financial return] — *Syn.* unthrifty, ill-requited, ill-paid, profitless, costly, expensive, unlucrative, unremunerative. — *Ant.* PROFITABLE, gainful, productive.
**2.** [Useless] — *Syn.* fruitless, pointless, hopeless; see **useless** 1.

**unpromising,** *modif.* — *Syn.* discouraging, unfavorable, adverse; see **negative** 2, **unlikely** 2.

**unprompted,** *modif.* **1.** [Spontaneous] — *Syn.* by chance, impulsive, automatic; see **voluntary.**
**2.** [Unintentional] — *Syn.* unpremeditated, unconscious, involuntary; see **aimless, haphazard.**

**unprotected,** *modif.* — *Syn.* defenseless, unarmed, unguarded; see **unsafe.**

**unpublished,** *modif.* — *Syn.* unprinted, in manuscript, manuscript, not published, not circulated, not distributed, not printed, not in print, uncirculated, undistributed, not made public; see also **unknown** 1.

**unqualified,** *modif.* **1.** [Absolute] — *Syn.* downright, utter, outright; see **certain** 3.
**2.** [Incompetent] — *Syn.* inexperienced, unprepared, incapable; see **unfit** 1.

**unquestionable,** *modif.* **1.** [Certain] — *Syn.* indisputable, sure, obvious, clear; see **accurate** 1, **certain** 3.

**2.** [Faultless] — *Syn.* unexceptionable, superior, flawless; see **excellent, perfect** 2.

**unquestionably,** *modif.* — *Syn.* certainly, without a doubt, surely, indubitably, indisputably, definitely, reliably, absolutely, positively, incontrovertibly, indefensibly, indeed, assuredly, of course, undoubtedly, certes, undeniably, unequivocally, past a doubt, beyond doubt, beyond a shadow of a doubt, past dispute.

**unquiet,** *modif.* — *Syn.* agitated, disturbed, restless, stirred up, anxious, restive, nervous, ill at ease, uneasy, anxious, excited, palpitant, trembling, perturbed, in commotion, in turmoil, vexed, troubled, unsettled, all hot and bothered*, in a dither*, in a tizzy*, all atwitter*; see also **disturbing.**

**unravel,** *v.* **1.** [To solve] — *Syn.* clear up, disclose, resolve; see **explain, interpret** 1.

**2.** [To untangle] — *Syn.* unwind, disengage, undo; see **free** 1.

**unreadable,** *modif.* **1.** [Illegible] — *Syn.* undecipherable, indecipherable, unclear; see **obscure** 1.

**2.** [Not pleasurable to read] — *Syn.* badly written, turgid, confused; see **dull** 3, 4, **stupid.**

**unreal,** *modif.* — *Syn.* visionary, delusive, deceptive, illusory, imaginary, imagined, hallucinatory, ideal, dreamlike, insubstantial, unsubstantial, nonexistent, fanciful, misleading, fictitious, theoretical, hypothetical, fabulous, chimerical, notional, whimsical, fantastic; see also **unbelievable.** — *Ant.* GENUINE, real, substantial.

**unrealistic,** *modif.* — *Syn.* unworkable, not sensible, not practical, not workable, not applicable, nonsensical; see also **silly, unreliable** 1, 2.

**unreasonable,** *modif.* **1.** [Illogical] — *Syn.* irrational, biased, fatuous; see **illogical.**

**2.** [Immoderate] — *Syn.* exorbitant, extravagant, inordinate; see **extreme** 2.

**3.** [Senseless] — *Syn.* foolish, silly, thoughtless; see **stupid** 1, **vacant** 3.

*See Synonym Study at* IRRATIONAL.

**unreasonably,** *modif.* — *Syn.* illogically, irrationally, stupidly; see **foolishly.**

*See Synonym Study at* IRRATIONAL.

**unrecognizable,** *modif.* — *Syn.* indistinct, indefinite, undefined; see **uncertain** 2, **vague** 2.

**unrefined,** *modif.* — *Syn.* coarse, vulgar, uncouth, unpolished, boorish; see also **rude** 1, 2.

**unregenerate,** *modif.* **1.** [Wicked] — *Syn.* sinful, carnal, profane; see **unscrupulous.**

**2.** [Irreligious] — *Syn.* sacrilegious, godless, atheistic; see **impious.**

**3.** [Obstinate] — *Syn.* recalcitrant, adamant, obdurate; see **obstinate.**

**unregulated,** *modif.* — *Syn.* deregulated, uncontrolled, uncontrollable, unchecked, chaotic; see also **disorderly, tangled, unlimited.**

**unrelated,** *modif.* — *Syn.* independent, unattached, irrelative; see **irrelevant, separate.**

**unrelenting,** *modif.* — *Syn.* cruel, merciless, pitiless; see **ruthless** 1, 2.

**unreliable,** *modif.* **1.** [Not reliable; *said of persons*] — *Syn.* undependable, irresponsible, unstable, wavering, deceitful, tricky, shifty, furtive, underhanded, untrue, fickle, giddy, capricious, untrustworthy, vacillating, fallible, weak, unpredictable; see also **dishonest** 1, 2.

**2.** [Not reliable; *said of facts and objects*] — *Syn.* deceptive, delusive, hallucinatory, plausible, specious, tricky, unsound, untrue, inaccurate, erroneous, hollow, pretended, sham, pseudo, makeshift, meretricious, misleading.

**unreliably,** *modif.* — *Syn.* uncertainly, shiftily, dubiously, irresponsibly; see **irregularly, vaguely.**

**unrepentant,** *modif.* — *Syn.* shameless, impenitent, hardened; see **remorseless** 1.

**unrequited,** *modif.* — *Syn.* unthanked, unanswered, unrecompensed; see **unpaid** 2.

**unreserved,** *modif.* — *Syn.* outspoken, uninhibited, boisterous, outgoing, lusty; see also **loud** 2, **rude.**

**unresolved,** *modif.* — *Syn.* undecided, incomplete, unconcluded, unsolved; see **unfinished** 1.

**unrest,** *n.* **1.** [Lack of mental calm] — *Syn.* malaise, distress, discomfort, perturbation, agitation, worry, sorrow, anxiety, grief, trouble, annoyance, tension, ennui, disquiet, soul-searching, irritation, harassment, upset, vexation, chagrin, mortification, perplexity, unease, disease, moodiness, disturbance, bother, dither*, tizzy*.

**2.** [Social or political restlessness] — *Syn.* disquiet, agitation, turmoil, strife, disturbance, turbulence, tumult, uproar, debate, discontent, discontentment, rebellion, uprising, contention, bickering, change, altercation, crisis, confusion, disputation, contest, controversy, quarrel, sparring, uncertainty, insurrection, suspicion, dissatisfaction.

**unrestrained,** *modif.* — *Syn.* unshackled, unrepressed, untrammeled; see **free** 1, 2, **unlimited.**

**unrestricted,** *modif.* — *Syn.* allowable, not forbidden, free; see **open** 3, **permitted, unlimited.**

**unrighteous,** *modif.* — *Syn.* sinful, iniquitous, depraved; see **lewd** 2, **wicked** 1.

**unrighteousness,** *n.* — *Syn.* wickedness, immorality, sinfulness; see **blasphemy, sin.**

**unripe,** *modif.* **1.** [Raw] — *Syn.* green, tart, immature; see **raw** 1.

**2.** [Inexperienced] — *Syn.* immature, unpracticed, new; see **inexperienced.**

**unrivaled,** *modif.* — *Syn.* matchless, peerless, unequaled; see **unique** 1, **unusual** 1.

**unroll,** *v.* — *Syn.* display, uncover, present, unfurl; see **expose** 1.

**unruffled,** *modif.* — *Syn.* collected, smooth, serene, unflustered; see **calm** 1, 2, **undisturbed.**

*See Synonym Study at* COOL.

**unruly,** *modif.* — *Syn.* uncontrollable, willful, headstrong, forward, forward, violent, impulsive, uncurbed, impetuous, ill-advised, rash, reckless, dashing, heedless, perverse, intractable, recalcitrant, self-assertive, refractory, rebellious, wayward, inexorable, restive, impervious, hidebound, unyielding, incorrigible, intemperate, drunken, lawless, vicious, brawling, unlicensed, rowdy, bawdy, quarrelsome, mob-minded, immovable, unwieldy, obdurate, resolute, inflexible, forceful, dogged, mulish, fanatic, irrational, unreasonable, irrepressible, high-spirited, impudent, abandoned, profligate, truculent, stubborn, obstinate, turbulent, disorderly, contumacious, self-willed, opinionated, bullheaded, ungovernable, stiff-necked, feckless, ornery*, mean*, rarin'*, chafing at the bit*, hellbent*, skittish*, dangerous*. — *Ant.* DOCILE, tractable, responsive.

**unsafe,** *modif.* — *Syn.* hazardous, perilous, jeopardous, risky, threatening, treacherous, fearsome, unreliable, insecure, venturesome, lowering, unstable, fraught with peril, parlous*, alarming, precarious, ticklish, giddy, dizzy, slippery, uncertain, unpromising, unprepossessing, shaky, explosive. — *Ant.* SAFE, harmless, proof.

**unsaid,** *modif.* — *Syn.* unspoken, not spoken, not expressed, not uttered, unstated; see also **quiet** 2, **silenced.**

**unsatisfactorily,** *modif.* — *Syn.* poorly, crudely, inefficiently; see **badly** 1.

**unsatisfactory,** *modif. — Syn.* disappointing, below expectation, inadequate, displeasing, undesirable, regrettable, disconcerting, disquieting, vexing, distressing, upsetting, disturbing, offensive, unacceptable, disagreeable, unwelcome, shocking, deficient; see also **poor** 2. *— Ant.* EXCELLENT, satisfactory, gratifying.

**unsavory,** *modif.* **1.** [Tasteless] *— Syn.* flavorless, bland, unappetizing; see **dull** 4.
**2.** [Offensive] *— Syn.* disagreeable, objectionable, crude, unpleasant, revolting; see also **offensive** 2.

**unscathed,** *modif. — Syn.* uninjured, unhurt, unharmed, without a scratch; see **safe** 1, **whole** 2.

**unschooled,** *modif. — Syn.* uneducated, untrained, naive, amateur; see **ignorant** 2.

**unscientific,** *modif. — Syn.* unsystematic, statistically invalid, irrational, impulsive, inconclusive; see also **illogical.**

**unscrew,** *v. — Syn.* unstopper, screw out, screw off, unfasten, take out, extract, unhitch, untwist.

**unscrupulous,** *modif. — Syn.* unprincipled, unethical, immoral, base, perfidious, degraded, selfish, self-seeking, petty, dishonest, knavish, wicked, tortuous, disingenuous, slippery, Machiavellian, casuistic, improper, Jesuitic\*, perjured, recreant, rascally, pettifogging, shifty, underhanded, two-faced, double-faced, sly, conscienceless, arrant, venal, dishonorable, corrupt, roguish, illegitimate, illegal, unfair, unorthodox, questionable, unworthy, scandalous, disgraceful, degrading, shameless, shady\*. *— Ant.* HONEST, scrupulous, fair-minded.

**unscrupulously,** *modif. — Syn.* perfidiously, wrongfully, cruelly, viciously; see **wrongly** 1.

**unseal,** *v. — Syn.* unlock, free, remove, crack; see **break** 1, **open** 2.

**unseasonable,** *modif. — Syn.* out of season, inappropriate, untimely, awkward; see **improper** 1, **unsuitable.**

**unseat,** *v.* **1.** [To unsaddle] *— Syn.* dismount, expel, get down; see **eject** 1, **remove** 1.
**2.** [To oust] *— Syn.* disbar, depose, replace; see **dismiss** 1.

**unseemly,** *modif.* **1.** [In bad taste; *said of conduct*] *— Syn.* rude, improper, unbecoming, inept, ill-advised.
**2.** [In bad taste; *said of things*] *— Syn.* vulgar, tawdry, cheap; see **poor** 2.
*See Synonym Study at* IMPROPER.

**unseen,** *modif. — Syn.* imagined, imaginary, hidden, obscure, unobserved, veiled, occult, sensed, unperceived, unnoticed, unsuspected, curtained, unobtrusive, viewless, unviewed, invisible, sightless, dark, shrouded, unnoted, impalpable, imperceptible, inconspicuous, undiscovered.

**unselfish,** *modif. — Syn.* disinterested, selfless, charitable, kind, liberal, openhanded, altruistic, large-minded, magnanimous, generous, benevolent, beneficent, indulgent, chivalrous, helpful, self-denying, self-sacrificing, loving, self-effacing, devoted, incorruptible, unbought, unbribed, unbribable.

**unselfishly,** *modif. — Syn.* openhandedly, bountifully, lavishly; see **freely** 1, 2, **generously** 1, 2.

**unselfishness,** *n. — Syn.* disinterestedness, charity, generosity, liberality, openhandedness, philanthropy, altruism, magnanimity, munificence, benevolence, beneficence, helpfulness, self-denial, self-sacrifice, lovingkindness, devotion, self-effacement, incorruptibility, largesse, bounty. *— Ant.* GREED, selfishness, avarice.

**unsettle,** *v. — Syn.* disrupt, displace, disarrange; see **bother** 2, 3, **disturb** 2.

**unsettled,** *modif.* **1.** [Undetermined] *— Syn.* undecided, unfixed, unresolved; see **uncertain** 2.

**2.** [Unstable] *— Syn.* confused, agitated, troubled, changing, explosive, shifting, precarious, ticklish, unpredictable, uneasy, unbalanced, perilous, complex, complicated, fluid, kinetic, active, busy, critical. *— Ant.* SIMPLE, stable, solid.

**unshaken,** *modif. — Syn.* unmoved, unaffected, undaunted; see **firm** 1, **resolute** 2.

**unsheathe,** *v. — Syn.* open, uncover, reveal, draw; see **remove** 1.

**unsheltered,** *modif. — Syn.* unprotected, exposed, uncovered, vulnerable; see **unprepared, unsafe**

**unshrinking,** *modif. — Syn.* fearless, staunch, courageous; see **brave** 1.

**unsightly,** *modif. — Syn.* hideous, deformed, homely; see **repulsive** 1, **ugly** 1.

**unskilled,** *modif. — Syn.* untrained, uneducated, amateur; see **ignorant** 2.

**unskillful,** *modif. — Syn.* maladroit, inept, clumsy, bungling; see **awkward** 1.

**unsociable,** *modif. — Syn.* antagonistic, distant, unsocial; see **unfriendly** 1, 2.

**unsolicited,** *modif.* **1.** [Undesirable] *— Syn.* gratuitous, undesired, unrequested; see **undesirable.**
**2.** [Free] *— Syn.* volunteered, offered, gratis; see **free** 4.

**unsophisticated,** *modif.* **1.** [Naive] *— Syn.* inexperienced, ingenuous, innocent, simple, artless; see also **inexperienced, naive.**
**2.** [Uncouth] *— Syn.* unrefined, gauche, boorish; see **awkward** 1, **rude** 1, 2.
*See Synonym Study at* NAIVE.

**unsought,** *modif.* **1.** [Unwanted] *— Syn.* unrequested, unsolicited, unbidden; see **undesirable.**
**2.** [Free] *— Syn.* volunteered, offered, gratis; see **free** 4.

**unsound,** *modif.* **1.** [False] *— Syn.* ill-founded, erroneous, incongruous; see **false** 2, **illogical.**
**2.** [Insecure] *— Syn.* unreliable, unbacked, weak; see **unstable** 2.

**unsparing,** *modif.* **1.** [Profuse] *— Syn.* lavish, liberal, plentiful; see **generous** 1, 2.
**2.** [Severe] *— Syn.* relentless, rigorous, merciless.

**unspeakable,** *modif. — Syn.* marvelous, awesome, horrid, unutterable, abominable, horrible, fearful, inexpressible, ineffable, unimaginable, dreadful, dire, shocking, appalling, frightful, frightening, alarming, preternatural, beastly, inhuman, calamitous; see also **supernatural.**

**unspeakably,** *modif. — Syn.* greatly, unbelievably, terribly; see **much** 1, 2.

**unspecified,** *modif. — Syn.* general, undefined, indefinite; see **vague** 2.

**unspoiled,** *modif. — Syn.* unblemished, spotless, faultless, wholesome; see **perfect** 2, **pure** 2.

**unspoken,** *modif. — Syn.* tacit, implicit, inferred; see **implied, understood** 1.

**unsportsmanlike,** *modif. — Syn.* unfair, disgruntled, ungentlemanly; see **rude** 2.

**unstable,** *modif.* **1.** [Having a high center of gravity] *— Syn.* unsteady, wavering, unbalanced, giddy, wobbly, wiggly, weaving, shifty, precarious, top-heavy, teetering, shifting, uncertain, rattletrap, beetling, jutting, lightly balanced. *— Ant.* FIRM, steady, solid.
**2.** [Easily disturbed] *— Syn.* variable, changeable, inconstant, giddy, capricious, fluctuating, shifty, volatile, rootless, dizzy, unpredictable, uncertain, sensitive, oversensitive, thin-skinned, timid, delicate.
**3.** [Subject to fission] *— Syn.* fissionable, fissiparous, fractionable; see **weak** 2.
*See Synonym Study at* INCONSTANT.

**unstained,** *modif. — Syn.* spotless, immaculate, virgin, stainless, white, unspotted, maiden, fresh, snowy, clear, pure, unblemished, unsullied, unsoiled, clean, untainted; see also **pure** 2, 3, 4.

**unsteady,** *modif.* **1.** [Wobbly] — *Syn.* unstable, wiggly, wavering, shaky, treacherous, unbalanced, top-heavy, leaning, ramshackle, giddy, weaving, heaving, precarious, shifting, teetering, uncertain; see also **irregular** 1, **unstable** 1.
**2.** [Inconstant] — *Syn.* changeable, fluctuating, vacillating, erratic, variable, uncertain, unfixed, capricious, volatile, unreliable, tricky, shifty, shaky, jerky, fluttering; see also **changeable** 1, 2.

**unstinted,** *modif.* — *Syn.* abundant, bountiful, profuse; see **plentiful** 1, 2.

**unstructured,** *modif.* — *Syn.* unorganized, disorganized, unregulated; see **confused** 2, **disorderly** 1.

**unstrung,** *modif.* — *Syn.* unnerved, nervous, upset; see **weak** 2, 3.

**unstuck,** *modif.* — *Syn.* unfastened, unglued, rattling; see **loose** 1.

**unstudied,** *modif.* **1.** [Natural] — *Syn.* instinctive, unforced, unaffected, unpremeditated; see **spontaneous.**
**2.** [Unlearned] — *Syn.* unversed, untrained, untaught; see **ignorant** 2, **unaware.**

**unsubstantial,** *modif.* **1.** [Flimsy] — *Syn.* fragile, frail, thin; see **light** 5.
**2.** [Unreal] — *Syn.* visionary, vaporous, imaginary; see **fantastic** 1, **unbelievable.**

**unsubstantiated,** *modif.* — *Syn.* unconfirmed, unattested, unsupported, uncorroborated; see **false** 2.

**unsuccessful,** *modif.* — *Syn.* defeated, disappointed, frustrated, nonsuited, abortive, aborted, disastrous, unprosperous, unproductive, unfortunate, unlucky, futile, vain, in vain, failing, failed, fruitless, worthless, sterile, bootless, unavailing, ineffectual, ineffective, inefficacious, immature, *manqué* (French), useless, foiled, shipwrecked, overwhelmed, overpowered, broken, overborne, ruined, destroyed, thwarted, crossed, disconcerted, dashed, circumvented, premature, inoperative, of no effect, balked, duped, left holding the sack★, skunked★, stymied★, jinxed★, out of luck★, stuck★. — *Ant.* SUCCESSFUL, fortunate, lucky.

**unsuitable,** *modif.* — *Syn.* inadequate, improper, malapropos, disagreeable, discordant, incongruous, inharmonious, incompatible, clashing, out of place, jarring, dissonant, discrepant, irrelevant, uncalled-for, dissident, inappropriate, inapt, ill-suited, unseemly, conflicting, opposite, contrary, unbecoming, unfitting, unfit, disparate, disturbing, mismatched, unapt, ill-assorted, disproportionate, divergent, mismated, unmated, inapplicable, inconformable, unassimilable, inconsistent, intrusive, infelicitious, amiss, interfering, disagreeing, uncongenial, inept, unbefitting, inapposite, inadmissible, absurd, senseless, unseasonable, unfortunate, ill-timed, unsympathetic, not in keeping, out of joint, at odds, at variance, repugnant, out of kilter★, cockeyed★. — *Ant.* FIT, suitable, proper.

**unsung,** *modif.* — *Syn.* slighted, disregarded, unacknowledged, unthought of; see **neglected.**

**unsure,** *modif.* — *Syn.* unreliable, hesitant, doubtful; see **shaky** 1, 2, **uncertain.**

**unsurpassed,** *modif.* — *Syn.* unexcelled, unequaled, matchless; see **unique** 1, **unprecedented.**

**unsuspected,** *modif.* **1.** [Undisputed] — *Syn.* trusted, uncontested, approved; see **accepted.**
**2.** [Unknown] — *Syn.* inconceived, unprecedented, improbable; see **unknown** 1, 2.

**unsuspecting,** *modif.* **1.** [Gullible] — *Syn.* undoubting, confiding, credulous; see **trusting** 1.

**2.** [Naive] — *Syn.* innocent, inexperienced, heedless, simple; see **naive.**

**unswayed,** *modif.* — *Syn.* unbiased, impartial, firm, unmoved; see **fair** 1, **resolute** 2.

**unswerving,** *modif.* — *Syn.* solid, straight, unbending; see **direct** 1.

**unsymmetrical,** *modif.* — *Syn.* asymmetrical, unbalanced, unequal, askew; see **irregular** 4.

**unsympathetic,** *modif.* — *Syn.* unpitying, unmoved, apathetic, cold; see **indifferent** 1.

**unsystematic,** *modif.* — *Syn.* irregular, disorderly, disorganized, chaotic; see **careless** 1, **confused** 2.

**untangle,** *v.* — *Syn.* clear up, put in order, disentangle; see **order** 3.

**untarnished,** *modif.* — *Syn.* unblemished, shiny, unspotted; see **clean** 1, **pure** 2.

**untaught,** *modif.* **1.** [Ignorant] — *Syn.* uneducated, unlearned, unread; see **ignorant** 2, **inexperienced.**
**2.** [Natural] — *Syn.* artless, instinctive, simple; see **spontaneous.**

**untenable,** *modif.* — *Syn.* indefensible, unsupportable, unreasonable, unsound, flawed; see also **illogical.**

**unthinkable,** *modif.* **1.** [Inconceivable] — *Syn.* incredible, unbelievable, unimaginable, improbable; see **unbelievable, unlikely.**
**2.** [Impossible] — *Syn.* out of the question, absurd, illogical, contrary to reason, beyond the bounds of possibility.

**unthinking,** *modif.* **1.** [Thoughtless] — *Syn.* heedless, rude, inconsiderate; see **careless** 1.
**2.** [Foolish] — *Syn.* impulsive, unwise, vacant; see **rash.**

**untidy,** *modif.* — *Syn.* slovenly, sloppy, unkempt, disorderly; see **dirty** 1.

**untie,** *v.* — *Syn.* unlace, unknot, loosen, unfasten; see **unhitch.**

**untied,** *modif.* — *Syn.* unfastened, slack, unbound; see **free** 2, 3, **loose** 1.

**until,** *prep.* — *Syn.* till, to, up to, up till, between the present and, in anticipation of, prior to, during the time preceding, down to, continuously, before the coming of, in expectation of, as far as; see also **unto.**

**untimely,** *modif.* — *Syn.* unseasonable, awkward, ill-timed, mistimed, inauspicious, badly timed, too early, abortive, too late, unpromising, ill-chosen, improper, unseemly, inappropriate, wrong, unfit, disagreeable, unsuited to the occasion, mistimed, intrusive, badly calculated, inopportune, out-of-date, malapropos, premature, early, previous★, unpunctual, unpropitious, unlucky, unfavorable, unfortunate, inexpedient, anachronistic. — *Ant.* EARLY, timely, seasonable.

**untiring,** *modif.* — *Syn.* inexhaustible, indefatigable, powerful, unremitting, persevering, strong, unintermitted, continuing, resolute, continued, renewed, unflagging, resistless, firm, unstinted, constant, tenacious, unwearying, durable, unwearied, sedulous, steady, determined, resolute, persistent, patient, dogged, plodding, pertinacious, undeterred, unflinching, unfaltering, unwavering, unswerving, unresting, indomitable, unceasing, staunch, unfailing. — *Ant.* WEAK, spasmodic, intermittent.

**unto,** *prep.* — *Syn.* to, toward, till, until, contiguous to, against, up to, next to, beside, in the direction of, to the degree of, to the extreme of.

**untold,** *modif.* — *Syn.* uncounted, countless, unnumbered, unexpressed, many, innumerable, myriad, beyond measure, inexpressible, incalculable, undreamed of, staggering, unimaginable, multitudinous, manifold, multiple.

**untouchable,** *modif. — Syn.* taboo, forbidden, denied; see **illegal, restricted.**

**untouched,** *modif.* **1.** [Not harmed] — *Syn.* intact, whole, secure, unbroken, in good order, unharmed, unscathed, in good condition, in a good state of preservation, safe and sound, out of danger, shipshape.
**2.** [Not contaminated] — *Syn.* virgin, incorrupt, clear, pure, immaculate, unstained, unblemished, spotless, sanitary, aseptic, unsullied, unsoiled, fresh.

**untoward,** *modif.* **1.** [Inappropriate] — *Syn.* improper, unseemly, unfitting, unwarranted, uncalled-for, impolite, unladylike, ungentlemanly; see also **rude** 2, **unsuitable.**
**2.** [Not favorable] — *Syn.* not fortunate, adverse, inauspicious, contrary, inimical, unseasonable, untimely; see also **unfortunate** 2.
**3.** [*Stubborn] — *Syn.* unruly, refractory, contrary, self-willed; see **obstinate.**

**untrained,** *modif. — Syn.* green, new, novice; see **ignorant** 2, **inexperienced.**

**untrammeled,** *modif. — Syn.* unhampered, unrestrained, unfettered; see **free** 2, 3.

**untried,** *modif. — Syn.* untested, uninitiated, new; see **inexperienced.**

**untroubled,** *modif. — Syn.* composed, serene, placid; see **calm** 1, 2.

**untrue,** *modif. — Syn.* false, misleading, specious, lying, hollow, deceptive, delusive, untrustworthy, deceitful, sham, fake, spurious, meretricious, incorrect, prevaricating, dissembling, wrong.

**untrustworthy,** *modif. — Syn.* guileful, conniving, deceitful; see **irresponsible, unreliable** 1, 2.

**untruth,** *n. — Syn.* falsehood, misrepresentation, evasion, lie, prevarication, distortion, deceit, canard, trick, pretense, false appearance, gull, cheat, mistake, dissimulation, spoof*, whopper*.

**untruthful,** *modif.* **1.** [Untrue] — *Syn.* unlikely, fake, fraudulent; see **false** 1, 2.
**2.** [Dishonest] — *Syn.* insincere, crooked, deceitful; see **dishonest** 1, 2.
*See Synonym Study at* DISHONEST.

**untruthfully,** *modif. — Syn.* untruly, dishonestly, treacherously; see **falsely, wrongly** 2.

**untutored,** *modif.* **1.** [Untaught] — *Syn.* unlearned, uneducated, illiterate; see **ignorant** 2.
**2.** [Ignorant] — *Syn.* simple, unwitting, unaware; see **ignorant** 1, **naive.**
*See Synonym Study at* IGNORANT.

**unused,** *modif.* **1.** [Not used] — *Syn.* fresh, virgin, unemployed, unexhausted, remaining, good, available, usable, employable, untouched, brand-new, pristine. — *Ant.* OLD, exhausted, worn-out.
**2.** [Surplus] — *Syn.* additional, remaining, superfluous; see **extra.**

**unusual,** *modif.* **1.** [Remarkable] — *Syn.* rare, extraordinary, strange, outstanding, great, uncommon, special, distinguished, prominent, important, noteworthy, awe-inspiring, awesome, unique, fine, unheard of, unexpected, seldom met with, surprising, superior, astonishing, amazing, prodigious, incredible, inconceivable, atypical, conspicuous, exceptional, eminent, significant, memorable, renowned, refreshing, singular, fabulous, unprecedented, unparalleled, unexampled, unaccountable, stupendous, unaccustomed, wonderful, notable, superior, marvelous, striking, overpowering, electrifying, dazing, fantastic, startling, astounding, indescribable, appalling, stupefying, ineffable, *sui generis* (Latin), out of sight*. — *Ant.* COMMON, familiar, customary.

**2.** [Different] — *Syn.* unique, extreme, uncommon, particular, exaggerated, distinctive, choice, little-known, out of the ordinary, marked, forward, unconventional, radical, exceptional, peculiar, strange, foreign, outré, unnatural, puzzling, perplexing, confounding, disturbing, novel, advanced, startling, shocking, staggering, uncustomary, breaking with tradition, infrequent, mysterious, mystifying, surprising, extraordinary, unparalleled, deep, profound, aberrant, singular, unorthodox, uncomfortable, not to be expected, eccentric, unbalanced, unclassifiable, unprecedented, inconsistent, individual, original, refreshing, newfangled, new, modern, recent, late, fresh, curious, unfamiliar, irregular, odd, unaccountable, alien, queer, unwonted, off-the-wall*, quaint, freakish, bizarre, farfetched, neurotic, exotic, outlandish, old-fashioned, out of-the-way, abnormal, irrational, monstrous, anomalous, fearful. — *Ant.* COMMON, ordinary, normal.

**unusually,** *modif.* **1.** [Not usually] — *Syn.* oddly, curiously, peculiarly; see **especially** 1, **strangely.**
**2.** [To a marked degree] — *Syn.* extraordinarily, remarkably, surprisingly; see **very.**

**unutterable,** *modif. — Syn.* indescribable, incredible, remarkable; see **impossible** 1, **unbelievable, unspeakable.**

**unvarnished,** *modif. — Syn.* plain, simple, naked, unadorned; see **frank, modest** 2.

**unvarying,** *modif. — Syn.* unchanging, continuing, regular; see **constant** 1.

**unveil,** *v. — Syn.* uncover, reveal, make known; see **expose** 1.

**unverified,** *modif. — Syn.* unproven, unproved, groundless, unsubstantiated; see **false** 2, **uncertain** 2.

**unversed,** *modif. — Syn.* uneducated, illiterate, unread; see **ignorant** 2, **inexperienced.**

**unwanted,** *modif. — Syn.* undesired, rejected, outcast; see **hated, unpopular.**

**unwarlike,** *modif. — Syn.* peaceful, tranquil, amiable; see **friendly** 1, **pacific.**

**unwarranted,** *modif. — Syn.* unjust, wrong, groundless; see **unfair** 1.

**unwary,** *modif. — Syn.* unguarded, rash, careless; see **unprepared.**

**unwashed,** *modif. — Syn.* unlaundered, unscoured, dingy, soiled, unlaved, unscrubbed; see also **dirty** 1.

**unwavering,** *modif. — Syn.* unfaltering, consistent, steadfast, resolute; see **regular** 3, **steady** 1.

**unwelcome,** *modif. — Syn.* uninvited, unwished for, repellent; see **undesirable, unpopular.**

**unwell,** *modif. — Syn.* ailing, ill, diseased; see **sick.**

**unwholesome,** *modif. — Syn.* unhealthful, baneful, insalubrious, toxic, poisonous, contaminated, nauseous, destructive, harmful, deleterious, pernicious, unnutritious, noxious, septic, pestilent, contagious, dangerous, lethal, venomous, envenomed, narcotic, virulent, indigestible, tainted, inedible, germ-infested, disease-ridden, rotten, putrescent, putrid, unpalatable, spoiled. — *Ant.* HEALTHFUL, wholesome, nutritious.

**unwieldy,** *modif. — Syn.* awkward, clumsy, cumbersome, ponderous; see **heavy** 1.

**unwilling,** *modif. — Syn.* backward, resistant, reluctant, refractory, recalcitrant, unenthusiastic, doubtful, wayward, unready, indisposed, disinclined, averse, opposed, against, contrary, indifferent, indocile, intractable, demurring, shrinking, flinching, hesitating, shy, slack, evasive, loath, shy of, laggard, malcontent, slow, remiss, grudging, uncooperative, contrary, against the grain. — *Ant.* READY, willing, eager.

**unwillingly,** *modif. — Syn.* grudgingly, resentfully, involuntarily, protestingly, sulkily, objecting, protesting, complaining, fighting back, under protest, without enthusiasm, with reservations, with objections, with complaints, with animadversions, with the worst will in the world, kicking and squalling*; see also **angrily.**

**unwind,** *v.* **1.** [To undo] — *Syn.* separate, loose, undo; see **unwrap.**
**2.** [To uncoil] — *Syn.* untwist, unravel, untwine, straighten out; see **free** 1, **loosen** 2.
**3.** [To relax] — *Syn.* recline, get rid of one's tensions, calm down; see **rest** 1, 2, **relax** 1.

**unwise,** *modif.* — *Syn.* ill-considered, ill-advised, rash; see **stupid** 1.

**unwisely,** *modif.* — *Syn.* imprudently, inadvisedly, impulsively; see **foolishly, rashly.**

**unwitting,** *modif.* **1.** [Unconscious] — *Syn.* senseless, numb, comatose; see **unconscious** 1.
**2.** [Unintentional] — *Syn.* chance, inadvertent, accidental; see **haphazard.**

**unwittingly,** *modif.* — *Syn.* ignorantly, in ignorance, without knowledge, without awareness; see **unconsciously.**

**unwonted,** *modif.* **1.** [Unusual] — *Syn.* uncommon, infrequent, rare; see **unusual** 1, 2.
**2.** [Uninformed] — *Syn.* unaccustomed, unacquainted, ignorant; see **unfamiliar** 1.

**unworldly,** *modif.* **1.** [Unearthly] — *Syn.* otherworldly, ethereal, preternatural; see **fantastic** 1, **supernatural, unreal.**
**2.** [Not concerned with this world] — *Syn.* spiritual, unmaterialistic, religious, metaphysical, idealistic, impractical.
**3.** [Not worldly-wise] — *Syn.* unsophisticated, inexperienced, green; see **naive.**

**unworthy,** *modif.* — *Syn.* undeserving, reprehensible, dishonorable, contemptible, blamable, recreant, disreputable, irreclaimable, unbecoming, unseemly, inexcusable; see also **offensive** 2, **shameful** 2. — *Ant.* WORTHY, deserving, laudable.

**unwrap,** *v.* — *Syn.* untie, undo, unpack, take out of wrappings, unroll, disclose, free, uncover, strip, lay bare, divest, dismantle, uncase, peel, husk, shuck, flay, expose, lay open, unclothe, denude. — *Ant.* WRAP, pack, COVER.

**unwritten,** *modif.* **1.** [Oral] — *Syn.* unrecorded, vocal, word-of-mouth; see **spoken.**
**2.** [Traditional] — *Syn.* unsaid, unspoken, customary, generally accepted; see **traditional** 2, **understood** 2.

**unwritten law,** *n.* — *Syn.* tradition, oral code, mutual understanding; see **custom** 2.

**unyielding,** *modif.* — *Syn.* solid, hard, firm, recalcitrant; see **stiff** 1.

**unzip,** *v.* — *Syn.* unfasten, undo, free; see **open** 3.

**up,** *modif.* and *prep.* **1.** [Situated above] — *Syn.* at the top of, at the crest of, at the summit of, at the apex of, nearer the top of, nearer the head of, nearer the source of. — *Ant.* DOWN, nearer the bottom of, farther from the head of.
**2.** [Moving from the earth] — *Syn.* upward, uphill, skyward, heavenward, away from the center of gravity, perpendicularly, into the air, higher, away from the earth.
**3.** [Expired] — *Syn.* lapsed, elapsed, run out, terminated, invalid, ended, come to a term, outdated, exhausted, finished, done. — *Ant.* CONTINUING, current, valid.
**4.** [Happening] — *Syn.* under consideration, being scrutinized, moot, live, current, pertinent, timely, relevant, pressing, urgent.

**5.** [Next] — *Syn.* after, in order, prospective; see **following.**

**up,** *v.* — *Syn.* elevate, raise up, boost; see **increase** 1, **raise** 1.

**up against it*,** *modif.* — *Syn.* in trouble, badly off, facing difficulty; see **suffering, troubled.**

**up and around*,** *modif.* — *Syn.* improved, improving, getting better, ambulatory; see **better** 3, **well** 1.

**up-and-coming*,** *modif.* — *Syn.* industrious, prospering, alert, promising; see **active** 2, **busy** 1.

**upbraid,** *v.* — *Syn.* reproach, scold, vituperate, condemn, denounce, lecture, chide, reprehend, admonish, recriminate, reprove, reprimand, castigate, tongue-lash, chastise, rebuke, revile, correct, excoriate, flay, heckle, hiss, damn, flout, deprecate, disparage, asperse, dispraise, censure, reprobate, impugn, blame, disapprove, arraign, oppugn, assail, controvert, give the lie to, expostulate, bring to book, execrate, impeach, stigmatize, brand, calumniate, rake, bark at, decry, clamor against, inveigh against, rake over the coals*. — *Ant.* PRAISE, applaud, approve.
*See Synonym Study at* SCOLD.

**upbringing,** *n.* — *Syn.* rearing, bringing up, instruction; see **childhood, training.**

**upcoming,** *modif.* — *Syn.* expected, future, imminent; see **forthcoming.**

**update,** *v.* — *Syn.* modernize, bring up to date, refresh; see **renew** 1.

**up for grabs*,** *modif.* — *Syn.* ready, open to applications, not allocated; see **available, free** 4.

**upgrade,** *n.* — *Syn.* incline, ascent, slope; see **grade** 1, **rise** 1.

**upgrade,** *v.* — *Syn.* promote, improve, enhance, update; see **promote** 2, **renew** 1, 3.

**upheaval,** *n.* — *Syn.* outburst, explosion, eruption; see **change** 2, **outbreak** 1.

**upheld,** *modif.* — *Syn.* supported, maintained, advanced; see **backed** 1.

**uphill,** *modif.* **1.** [Rising] — *Syn.* up, upward, toward the summit, toward the crest, skyward, ascending, climbing. — *Ant.* DOWN, downhill, descending.
**2.** [Laborious] — *Syn.* difficult, strenuous, with difficulty.

**uphold,** *v.* **1.** [To hold up] — *Syn.* brace, buttress, prop; see **support** 1.
**2.** [To maintain] — *Syn.* confirm, sustain, back up; see **support** 2.
*See Synonym Study at* SUPPORT.

**upholster,** *v.* — *Syn.* pad, stuff, cushion, pillow, bolster, cover, drape, deck, overspread, accouter, overlay, dress.

**upholstery,** *n.* — *Syn.* padding, stuffing, cushioning, spring-filled cushions, pillows, filling.

**upkeep,** *n.* **1.** [Maintenance] — *Syn.* conservation, subsistence, repair; see **maintenance** 1.
**2.** [Cost of maintenance] — *Syn.* expense, expenses, outlay, expenditure; see **price.**

**upland,** *n.* — *Syn.* highland, hill, high ground, moor, peak, mountain, crest, summit, ridge, barrow, hogback, elevation, height, eminence, altitude, plateau, mesa, hilltop.

**uplift,** *n.* **1.** [Social service] — *Syn.* slum clearance, settlement work, rehabilitation, social guidance, slum improvement, social planning, social education, relief work; see also **welfare** 2.
**2.** [Efforts to improve the lot of mankind] — *Syn.* improvement, betterment, education, culture, enlightenment, humanitarian effort, social reform, planned economy, the Four Freedoms, social security; see also **improvement** 1.

**upon,** *modif.* and *prep.* **1.** [On] — *Syn.* on top of, in, attached to, visible on, against, affixed to, next to, located at, superimposed.

**2.** [At the time of] — *Syn.* consequent to, beginning with, at the occurrence of; see **simultaneous.**

**upper,** *modif.* — *Syn.* top, topmost, uppermost, above, higher, more elevated, loftier, overhead. — *Ant.* UNDER, lower, bottom.

**upper-class,** *modif.* — *Syn.* highbred, wellborn, genteel; see **noble** 3.

**upper hand,** *n.* — *Syn.* sway, dominion, superiority; see **advantage** 2.

**uppermost,** *modif.* — *Syn.* loftiest, topmost, culminating; see **highest.**

**upright,** *modif.* **1.** [Vertical] — *Syn.* erect, standing, standing up, on one's feet, perpendicular, sky-pointing, steep, exalted, elevated, plumb, straight, upward, end up, on end, bolt upright, upended.

**2.** [Honorable] — *Syn.* ethical, moral, virtuous, exalted, straightforward, correct, circumspect, unimpeachable, punctilious, honest, principled, fair, impartial, incorruptible, aboveboard, high-minded, respectable, manly, right.

**uprising,** *n.* **1.** [Revolt] — *Syn.* rebellion, riot, upheaval; see **revolution** 2.

**2.** [Slope] — *Syn.* ascent, upgrade, incline; see **hill.**

**uproar,** *n.* — *Syn.* tumult, commotion, confusion, turmoil, clamor, ado, disturbance, brouhaha, din, racket, hubbub, fracas, furor, bustle, babble, bickering, discord, row, hue and cry, hassle, rumpus*, ruckus*, flap*, foofooraw*; see also **confusion** 2, **noise** 1, 2.

*See Synonym Study at* NOISE.

**uproarious,** *modif.* — *Syn.* noisy, confused, disorderly; see **loud** 2.

**uproot,** *v.* — *Syn.* eradicate, extract, remove, tear up by the roots, excavate, pull up, weed out, rip up.

**ups and downs*,** *n.* — *Syn.* troubles, complications, uncertainties; see **difficulty** 1, 2.

**upset,** *modif.* — *Syn.* disconcerted, amazed, shocked; see **confused** 2, **unsettled.**

**upset,** *n.* — *Syn.* overthrow, destruction, reversion; see **defeat** 2, **subversion.**

**upset,** *v.* **1.** [To turn over] — *Syn.* overturn, upturn, subvert, turn bottom-side up, turn inside out, upend, reverse, keel over, overset, topple, tip over, turn topsy-turvy, overbalance, invert, capsize, tilt, pitch over, overthrow. — *Ant.* STAND, erect, elevate.

**2.** [To disturb] — *Syn.* agitate, fluster, perturb; see **bother** 2.

**3.** [To beat] — *Syn.* conquer, outplay, overpower; see **defeat** 1, 2, 3.

---

**SYN.** — **upset** is the ordinary word implying a toppling, disorganization, etc. as a result of a loss of balance or stability [to *upset* a glass, one's plans, etc.; emotionally *upset*]; **overturn** implies a turning of a thing upside down or flat on its side and, in extended use, connotes the destruction of something established [to *overturn* a chair, a government, etc.]; **capsize** specifically implies the overturning or upsetting of a boat

---

**upshot,** *n.* — *Syn.* conclusion, end, outcome; see **result.**

**upside-down,** *modif.* — *Syn.* topsy-turvy, tangled, bottom-side up, inverted, rear-end foremost, backward, the wrong way, wrong-side uppermost, *patas arriba* (Spanish), cart-before-the-horse*, heels-over-apple-cart*, head-over-heels*, ass-backward*, bass-ackward*. — *Ant.* UPRIGHT, right-side up, steady.

**upstage*,** *v.* — *Syn.* draw attention from, mistreat, impose upon; see **detract, distract.**

**upstairs,** *modif.* — *Syn.* in the upper story, on an upper floor, overhead, above, up the steps; see also **upper.**

**upstairs,** *n.* — *Syn.* the upper story, the penthouse, the sleeping apartments, the rooms above the ground floor; see **attic, floor** 2.

**upstanding,** *modif.* — *Syn.* honorable, upright, straightforward; see **honest** 1.

**upstart,** *n.* — *Syn.* parvenu, snob, pretender, new rich, status seeker, adventurer, opportunist, nouveau riche, *bourgeois gentilhomme* (French), would-be gentleman, newly rich, new money, bourgeois, social climber, Johnny-come-lately*.

**upswing,** *n.* — *Syn.* growth, boom, acceleration; see **improvement, increase** 1.

**uptight*,** *modif.* **1.** [Troubled] — *Syn.* worried, concerned, apprehensive; see **troubled** 1.

**2.** [Cautious] — *Syn.* conventional, strict, old-fashioned; see **conservative.**

**up to,** *prep.* and *modif.* **1.** [Occupied with] — *Syn.* doing, scheming, devising, plotting.

**2.** [Until] — *Syn.* before, preceding, previous; see **until.**

**3.** [Equal to] — *Syn.* capable of, able to, competent; see **able** 1.

**4.** [As many as] — *Syn.* as much as, to the number of, all of.

**5.** [Dependent upon] — *Syn.* incumbent upon, the responsibility of, assigned to, expected of, enjoined upon, delegated to.

**up-to-date,** *modif.* — *Syn.* in vogue, a la mode, in fashion, up-to-the-minute, fashionable, conventional, stylish, modern, modernistic, streamlined, popular, faddish, brand-new, current, according to the prevailing taste, modish, *moderne* (French), the latest*, trendy*, in*, today*, with-it*, all the rage*, styled to the minute*.

**up to the ears,** *modif.* — *Syn.* very deeply, up to here, occupied, busy, absorbed; see also **busy** 1.

**uptown,** *modif.* — *Syn.* in the upper parts of town, central, midtown, metropolitan, urban.

**upturn,** *n.* — *Syn.* upswing, upsurge, recuperation; see **improvement** 1, **recovery** 1.

**upturned,** *modif.* — *Syn.* tilted, tipped, upside-down, inclined, sloped, slanted, expectant, upward looking, turned up, extended; see also **oblique.** — *Ant.* BENT, pensive, downcast.

**upward,** *modif.* — *Syn.* up, higher, skyward, in the air, uphill, away from the earth, up the slope, on an incline, up north*.

**up with,** *modif.* — *Syn.* even with, up to, equal to; see **equal.**

**urban,** *modif.* **1.** [Concerning city government] — *Syn.* city, metropolitan, civil; see **municipal, public** 2.

**2.** [Concerning city living] — *Syn.* city, civic, municipal, metropolitan, megalopolitan, within the city limits, inner-city, central-city, downtown, zoned, planned, business-district, civil, nonrural, ghetto, shopping, residential, apartment-dwelling, oppidan.

**urbane,** *modif.* — *Syn.* suave, mannerly, courteous; see **cultured, polite** 1.

*See Synonym Study at* SUAVE.

**urbanity,** *n.* **1.** [Courtesy] — *Syn.* civility, refinement, polish; see **courtesy** 1.

**2.** [Civilities, *in plural*] — *Syn.* amenities, decorum, courtesies; see **culture** 3, **sophistication.**

**urban renewal,** *n.* — *Syn.* rebuilding the inner city, modernization, bringing up to date, gentrification; see **improvement** 1, 2.

**urchin,** *n.* — *Syn.* youngster, rogue, waif, brat, imp; see also **child.**

**urge,** *v.* **1.** [To present favorably] — *Syn.* favor, further, support, speak for, propose, plead for, advance, rationalize, aid, recommend, endorse, ratify, confirm, promote, sanction, approve, commend, countenance. — *Ant.* discourage, prohibit, impede.
**2.** [To induce] — *Syn.* charge, beg, plead, adjure, influence, beseech, implore, ask, command, entreat, desire, request, press, importune, inveigle, talk into, incite, move, allure, tempt, attract, influence, prompt, instigate, exhort, advise, solicit, inspire, stimulate, conjure, coax, wheedle, maneuver, draw, put up to, prevail upon. — *Ant.* RESTRAIN, deter, discourage.
**3.** [To drive] — *Syn.* compel, drive, propel, impel, force, coerce, constrain, press, push, make, oblige, goad, prod, spur. — *Ant.* DENY, block, withhold.

*SYN.* — **urge** implies a strong effort to persuade someone to do something, as by entreaty, argument, or forceful recommendation /he *urged* us to leave/; **exhort** implies an earnest urging or admonishing to action or conduct considered proper or right /the minister *exhorted* his flock to work for peace/; **press** suggests a continuous, insistent urging that is difficult to resist /we *pressed* her to stay/; **importune** implies persistent efforts to break down resistance against a demand or request, often to the point of being annoying or wearisome /too proud to *importune* for help/

**urged,** *modif.* **1.** [Supported] — *Syn.* favored, furthered, proposed, plead, advanced, aided, recommended, endorsed, ratified, confirmed, promoted, sanctioned, espoused, adopted, approved, commended, countenanced, praised, pushed*, boosted*; see also **backed** 1. — *Ant.* OPPOSED, prohibited, condemned.
**2.** [Pressed] — *Syn.* begged, charged, adjured, besought, implored, asked, commanded, entreated, desired, requested, inveigled, talked into, incited, moved, motivated, allured, lured, tempted, seduced, attracted, influenced, prompted, instigated, exhorted, advised, solicited, inspired, whipped up, stimulated, coaxed, wheedled, maneuvered, put up to, prevailed upon, compelled, obliged, propelled, driven, induced, impelled, coerced, forced, constrained.

**urgency,** *n.* — *Syn.* exigency, need, gravity, seriousness; see **importance** 1, **necessity** 3.

**urgent,** *modif.* **1.** [Of immediate importance] — *Syn.* pressing, critical, necessary, imperative, important, compelling, indispensable, momentous, wanted, required, called for, demanded, salient, chief, paramount, essential, primary, vital, principal, absorbing, all-absorbing, not to be delayed, crucial, instant, leading, capital, overruling, foremost, exigent, crying; see also **important** 1. — *Ant.* TRIVIAL, irrelevant, untimely.
**2.** [Insistent] — *Syn.* compelling, hortatory, persuasive, imperious, solemn, grave, weighty, impressive, earnest, importunate, clamorous, hasty, breathless, precipitate, frantic, impetuous, imperative, convincing, beseeching, seductive, commanding, imploring, eager, zealous, anxious, moving, excited, impulsive, vigorous, enthusiastic, overpowering, masterful; see also **resolute** 2. — *Ant.* APOLOGETIC, hesitant, diffident.

**urgently,** *modif.* **1.** [Critically] — *Syn.* pressingly, instantly, imperatively, necessarily, indispensably, momently, requisitely, essentially, primarily, crucially, capitally, exigently.
**2.** [Insistently] — *Syn.* compellingly, persuasively, imperiously, solemnly, gravely, weightily, impressively,

earnestly, importunately, clamorously, hastily, breathlessly, precipitately, frantically, impetuously, convincingly, beseechingly, seductively, commandingly, imploringly, eagerly, anxious, zealously, movingly, emotionally, excitedly, impulsively, vigorously, irresistibly, enthusiastically, overpoweringly, masterfully, magisterially, compulsively.

**urging,** *n.* — *Syn.* begging, persuading, pleading, beseeching, imploring, inspiring, coaxing, wheedling, inducing, nagging, driving, insistence, stimulating; see also **persuasion** 1.

**urinate,** *v.* — *Syn.* go to the restroom *or* bathroom, have to go, micturate, excrete, use the urinal, use the bedpan, make water, pee*, tinkle*, wizz*, peepee*, go to the little boy's room*, take a leak*, have a leak*, see a man about a horse*.

**urn,** *n.* — *Syn.* vessel, jar, amphora, pot, container, cinerary urn, funerary urn.

**usable,** *modif.* — *Syn.* available, utilizable, employable, at hand, useful, unused, good, serviceable, applicable, ready, subservient, helpful, utile, valuable, beneficial, profitable, advantageous, fit, desirable, efficacious, instrumental, fitting, conformable, suitable, practicable, proper, practical, convenient. — *Ant.* USELESS, worthless, no good.

**usage,** *n.* **1.** [Custom] — *Syn.* practice, wont, rule, habit, habiture, convention, way, method, mode, routine, rote, formula, acceptance, regulation, currency.
**2.** [Accepted language] — *Syn.* good usage, grammatical usage, approved diction; see **grammar, language** 2. *See Synonym Study at* HABIT.

**use,** *n.* **1.** [The act of using] — *Syn.* practice, employment, application, usage, appliance, effecting, adoption, utilization, manipulation, bringing to bear, management, handling, performance, conduct, recourse, resort, exercise, treatment, method, technique, control, resolution, realization, association. — *Ant.* NEGLECT, disuse, dismissal.
**2.** [The state of being useful] — *Syn.* utility, usefulness, usability, employment, application, value, worth, advantage, excellence, helpfulness, convenience, suitability, expedience, aid, serviceability, merit, profit, practicability, practicality, stead, fitness, subservience, effectiveness, applicability.

**use,** *v.* **1.** [To make use of] — *Syn.* avail oneself of, employ, put to use, exercise, exert, put forth, utilize, apply, bring to bear, practice, play on, do with, draw on, adopt, take advantage of, turn to account, make do, accept, work, put in practice, relate, make with, put to work, make shift with. — *Ant.* DISCARD, reject, REFUSE.
**2.** [To make a practice of; *now only in the past tense with an infinitive*] — *Syn.* be accustomed to, practice, do.
**3.** [To behave toward] — *Syn.* deal with, handle, bear oneself toward; see **manage** 1.

*SYN.* — **use** implies the putting of a thing (or, usually in an opprobrious sense, a person regarded as a passive thing) into action or service so as to accomplish an end /to *use* a pencil, a suggestion, etc.; he *used* his brother to advance himself/; **employ**, a somewhat more elevated term, implies the putting to useful work of something not in use at that moment /to *employ* a vacant lot as a playground/ and, with reference to persons, suggests a providing of work and pay /she *employs* five accountants/; **utilize** implies the putting of something to a practical or profitable use /to *utilize* chemical byproducts/

**used,** *modif.* **1.** [Employed] -- *Syn.* put to use, utilized, applied, adopted, adapted, accepted, put in service, practiced, turned to account. — *Ant.* DISCARDED, rejected, unused.

**2.** [Accustomed] — *Syn.* practiced, customary, suited; see **habitual** 1.

**3.** [Secondhand] — *Syn.* castoff, depreciated, repossessed; see **old** 2, **worn** 2.

**used to,** *modif.* — *Syn.* familiar with, comfortable with, in the habit of, habituated to, wont to; see also **accustomed to, use** *v.* 2.

**useful,** *modif.* — *Syn.* valuable, beneficial, serviceable; see **helpful** 1.

**usefulness,** *n.* — *Syn.* application, value, advantage, excellence, convenience, suitability, range, versatility, helpfulness, utility, usability, serviceability, merit, profitableness, practicality, practicability, fitness, propriety, adaptability; see also **use** 2.

**useless,** *modif.* **1.** [Unserviceable] — *Syn.* worthless, unusable, inutile, ineffectual, expendable, incompetent, of no use, ineffective, inoperative, broken, dysfunctional, counterproductive, inefficient, unprofitable, no damn good*. — *Ant.* EFFICIENT, usable, operative.

**2.** [Futile] — *Syn.* futile, vain, unavailing, fruitless; see **hopeless** 2.

*See Synonym Study at* FUTILE.

**use up,** *v.* — *Syn.* consume, exhaust, squander; see **spend** 1, **waste** 1, 2.

**usher,** *n.* — *Syn.* conductor, guide, usherette, escort, doorman, cicerone, herald, leader, precursor, page, footboy, flunkey.

**usher,** *v.* — *Syn.* show in, show out, escort, guide, receive, show around; see also **lead** 1.

**ushered,** *modif.* — *Syn.* escorted, led, guided, supervised, conducted, shown, attended, preceded, introduced, announced, presented, squired, heralded, directed, advanced, sponsored, brought forward.

**using,** *modif.* — *Syn.* employing, utilizing, applying, adopting, taking advantage of, accepting, working, practicing, manipulating, controlling, putting in service, trying out, testing, proving, wearing out.

**usual,** *modif.* **1.** [Ordinary] — *Syn.* general, frequent, normal; see **common** 1, **natural** 2, **typical.**

**2.** [Habitual] — *Syn.* wonted, accustomed, customary, routine, normal, conventional; see also **conventional** 1.

*See Synonym Study at* NORMAL.

---

**SYN.** — **usual** applies to that which past experience has shown to be the normal, common, hence expected thing *[the usual results, price, answer, etc.]*; **customary** refers to that which accords with the usual practices of some individual or with the prevailing customs of some group *[his customary mid-morning coffee, it is customary to tip a waiter]*; **habitual** implies a fixed practice as the result of habit *[her habitual tardiness]*; **wonted** is a somewhat literary equivalent for **customary** or **habitual** *[according to their wonted manner]*; **accustomed** is equivalent to **customary** but suggests less strongly a settled custom *[he sat in his accustomed place]*

---

**usually,** *modif.* — *Syn.* ordinarily, customarily, normally, habitually; see **regularly** 1, 2.

**usurp,** *v.* — *Syn.* assume, appropriate, expropriate, commandeer, lay hold of; see also **seize** 2.

**usurpation,** *n.* — *Syn.* seizure, encroachment, deposal; see **capture.**

**usury,** *n.* — *Syn.* robbery, exploitation, stealing, lending at high interest, banking; see also **theft.**

**utensil,** *n.* **1.** [An implement; *especially for the kitchen*] — *Syn.* equipment, tool, appliance, convenience, ware(s); see also **tool** 1.

*See Synonym Study at* IMPLEMENT.

Kitchen utensils include: sieve, egg beater, knife, fork, spoon, measuring cup, measuring spoon, ladle, grater, spatula, pancake turner, can opener, egg slicer, meat grinder, butcher knife, paring knife, peeler, wire whisk, skewers, shears, pastry cutter, lemon squeezer, knife sharpener, coffee grinder, blender, food processor, vegetable brush, frying pan, saucepan, cake pan, pie pan, roaster, steamer, wok, mixing bowl, pan lid, rolling pin, pastry board, coffee pot, tea kettle, bread pan, cookie sheet, colander, meat thermometer, nutcracker, pepper grinder, funnel, garlic press, cutting board; pan scourer, bottle brush, dishpan, draining pan, sink strainer, dishmop.

**utilitarian,** *modif.* — *Syn.* practical, useful, functional; see **pragmatic, practical.**

**utilities,** *n.* — *Syn.* services, public utilities, conveniences, necessities of modern life.

Utilities include: heat, light, power, gas, water, bus, street car, telephone, electricity, garbage disposal, sewage disposal.

**utility,** *n.* **1.** [Usefulness] — *Syn.* use, service, advantage, convenience, benefit, serviceableness, expediency, avail, profit, favor, efficacy, efficiency, adequacy, productiveness.

**2.** [Utility company] — *Syn.* gas company, electricity company, water company; see **business** 4, **monopoly.**

**utilize,** *v.* — *Syn.* employ, appropriate, turn to account; see **use** 1.

*See Synonym Study at* USE.

**utmost,** *modif.* **1.** [Greatest] — *Syn.* ultimate, chief, entire, whole, full, unreserved, complete, unstinted, total, absolute, unlimited, unsparing, thorough, exhaustive, highest, maximum, most, top, plenary, undiminished, undivided, thoroughgoing, unmitigated, sheer, unqualified, unconditional, all-out*.

**2.** [Last] — *Syn.* farthest, most distant, final, last; see **last** 1.

**utopia,** *n.* — *Syn.* ideal place, idealized place, wonderland, paradise, land of milk and honey*; see also **heaven** 2.

Famous utopias include: the garden of Eden, Heaven, the Celestial City, Heavenly City, Land of Beulah, the New Jerusalem, the Promised Land, Zion, paradise, new Canaan, Goshen, Shangri-La, New Atlantis, Arcadia, Happy Valley, Land of Prester John, Kingdom of Micomicon, Laputa, Cockaigne, Erewhon, Camelot, Oz, Brook Farm.

**utopian,** *modif.* — *Syn.* idealistic, ideological, quixotic, perfect; see **hopeful** 1, **visionary** 1.

**utopian,** *n.* — *Syn.* visionary, utopist, romanticist; see **idealist.**

**utter,** *modif.* — *Syn.* complete, total, thorough; see **absolute** 1.

**utter,** *v.* — *Syn.* pronounce, talk, express, come out with, articulate, voice, whisper, mutter, shout, exclaim, enunciate, air, speak, tell, declaim, phonate, disclose, declare, say, phrase, word, assert, affirm, asseverate, ejaculate, vocalize, proclaim, give tongue to, recite, broach, blurt out, let fall, announce.

---

**SYN.** — **utter** implies the communication of an idea or feeling by means of vocal sounds, such as words, exclamations, etc. *[he uttered a sigh of relief]*; **express**, the broadest of these terms, suggests a revealing of ideas, feelings, one's personality, etc. by means of speech, action, or creative work *[to express oneself in music]*; **voice** suggests expression through words, either spoken or written *[voicing one's opinions in letters to the editor]*;

**broach** suggests the utterance or mention of an idea to someone for the first time [I'll *broach* the subject to her at dinner]; **enunciate** suggests the announcement or open attestation of some idea [to *enunciate* a theory, doctrine, etc.]

---

**utterance,** *n.* — *Syn.* declaration, saying, verbalization, phonation, assertion, announcement, pronouncement, ejaculation, vociferation, talk, speech, query, expression, sentence, declamation, statement, proclamation, recitation, asseveration, spiel, rant, jargon, response, reply, oration, peroration, set speech, delivered opinion.

**uttered,** *modif.* **1.** [Spoken] — *Syn.* declared, pronounced, affirmed, asserted, expressed, announced, articulated, proclaimed, declaimed, voiced, shouted, recited, rehearsed; see also **oral.** — *Ant.* WITHHELD, suppressed, choked in.
**2.** [Given forth] — *Syn.* issued, released, emitted, verbalized, dispersed, broadcast, sown, delivered, propagated, given currency, circulated, disseminated, diffused, divulged, disclosed; see also **announced.** — *Ant.* WITHHELD, withdrawn, banned.

**utterly,** *modif.* — *Syn.* wholly, thoroughly, entirely; see **completely.**

**uttermost,** *modif.* — *Syn.* farthest, remotest, final; see **furthest, utmost** 2.

# V

**vacancy,** *n.* **1.** [A vacated position] — *Syn.* opening, vacated post, post without an incumbent, unfilled position, unheld office, job*.

**2.** [Untenanted quarters] — *Syn.* empty room, empty apartment, room to let, apartment to let, lodging, quarters, tenantless house, uninhabited house, vacant house, unoccupied house, deserted house, house for rent, house for sale.

**vacant,** *modif.* **1.** [Without contents] — *Syn.* devoid, void, unfilled; see **empty** 1.

**2.** [Without an occupant] — *Syn.* unoccupied, untenanted, tenantless, uninhabited, idle, free, deserted, abandoned, without a resident, not lived in. — *Ant.* INHABITED, occupied, tenanted.

**3.** [Without evidence of intelligence] — *Syn.* unintelligent, vacuous, empty-headed, foolish, giddy, inane, stupid, silly, witless, thoughtless. — *Ant.* INTELLIGENT, witty, understanding.

*See Synonym Study at* EMPTY.

**vacate,** *v.* **1.** [To abandon] — *Syn.* give up, quit, renounce; see **abandon** 1.

**2.** [To leave a residence] — *Syn.* go away, relinquish, depart; see **leave** 1.

**vacation,** *n.* — *Syn.* respite, rest, recreation time, intermission, recess, nonterm, holiday, R&R, leave, leave of absence, sabbatical, time off*.

**on vacation** — *Syn.* vacationing, on leave, on holiday; see **resting** 1, **traveling** 2.

**vacationist,** *n.* — *Syn.* vacationer, tourist, sightseer; see **traveler.**

**vaccinate,** *v.* — *Syn.* inoculate, immunize, prevent, treat, mitigate, protect, inject, shoot*.

**vaccinated,** *modif.* — *Syn.* immunized, inoculated, given (hypodermic) injections, given mouth vaccine, exempted; see also **protected.**

**vaccination,** *n.* **1.** [The act of administering vaccine] — *Syn.* injection, hypodermic, inoculation, pricking, scratching, scarifying, spraying, a shot*, shots*; see also **treatment** 2.

**2.** [A result of vaccination, sense 1] — *Syn.* protection, immunization, inoculation, exemption, prevention, mitigation; see also **immunity** 2.

**vacillate,** *v.* **1.** [To totter] — *Syn.* waver, sway, stagger; see **reel, totter** 2.

**2.** [To hesitate] — *Syn.* fluctuate, dawdle, falter; see **hesitate, pause.**

**vacillating,** *modif.* — *Syn.* changeable, uncertain, unreliable, fickle, inconstant, unstable, mutable, fitful, irresolute, unsettled, unsteady, capricious, shifting, volatile. — *Ant.* CONSTANT, steady, unchanging.

**vacillation,** *n.* **1.** [Swaying] — *Syn.* vibration, swing, fluctuation; see **sway** 1, **wave** 2.

**2.** [Indecision] — *Syn.* irresolution, indecision, inconstancy; see **doubt** 2, **uncertainty** 2.

**vacuity,** *n.* **1.** [Emptiness] — *Syn.* vacancy, nothingness, void; see **emptiness, vacuum.**

**2.** [Inanity] — *Syn.* fatuity, empty-headedness, disin-

terest, disregard; see **stupidity** 1, 2, 3.

**vacuous,** *modif.* **1.** [Empty] — *Syn.* void, emptied, drained; see **depleted, empty** 1.

**2.** [Dumb] — *Syn.* inane, blank, unreasoning; see **dull** 3, 4.

*See Synonym Study at* EMPTY.

**vacuum,** *n.* — *Syn.* emptiness, rarefaction, void, vacuity, space, exhaustion.

**vacuum,** *v.* — *Syn.* vacuum-clean, clean, sweep, sweep up, hoover (British).

**vacuum cleaner,** *n.* — *Syn.* vacuum, carpet sweeper, cleaning device, Hoover (*trademark*; British); see **appliance.**

**vagabond,** *modif.* — *Syn.* nomadic, migratory, migrant, foot-loose (and fancy free), wandering, roving, drifting, roaming, errant, rambling, stray, straggling, transient, tramping, moving, itinerant, peripatetic, shifting; see also **aimless, traveling** 2.

**vagabond,** *n.* — *Syn.* vagrant, gypsy, rover; see **tramp** 1, **traveler.**

*See Synonym Study at* TRAMP.

**vagary,** *n.* — *Syn.* notion, caprice, whimsy, fad; see **caprice, impulse** 2.

*See Synonym Study at* CAPRICE.

**vagrancy,** *n.* — *Syn.* itinerancy, roving, vagabondage, homelessness, shiftlessness.

**vagrant,** *modif.* **1.** [Having no home] — *Syn.* roaming, itinerant, nomadic, homeless; see **traveling** 2, **wandering** 1.

**2.** [Having no occupation] — *Syn.* begging, idling, unemployed, profligate, prodigal, loafing, beachcombing, mendicant, panhandling*, bumming*, mooching*.

**3.** [Having no fixed course] — *Syn.* wayward, capricious, erratic; see **aimless, wandering** 1.

*See Synonym Study at* ITINERANT.

**vagrant,** *n.* — *Syn.* beggar, idler, loafer; see **rascal, tramp** 1.

*See Synonym Study at* TRAMP.

**vague,** *modif.* **1.** [Not clearly expressed] — *Syn.* indefinite, unintelligible, imprecise, inexplicit; see **obscure** 1.

**2.** [Not clearly understood] — *Syn.* uncertain, undetermined, unsure, doubtful, dubious, questionable, misunderstood, enigmatic, nebulous, puzzling, inexplicable, unsettled, bewildering, perplexing, problematic. — *Ant.* CERTAIN, sure, positive.

**3.** [Not clearly visible] — *Syn.* dim, nebulous, dark; see **hazy** 1.

*See Synonym Study at* OBSCURE.

**vaguely,** *modif.* — *Syn.* uncertainly, unclearly, not clearly, not certainly, not reliably, mistily, hazily, foggily, confusedly, shiftily, unreliably, dubiously, eccentrically, unsurely, illegally, evasively, miscellaneously, unpredictably, without clear outlines; see also **indefinitely** 1, **obscurely.**

**vagueness,** *n.* — *Syn.* imprecision, ambiguity, obscurity, double entendre; see **confusion** 2, **uncertainty** 1, 2.

**vain,** *modif.* **1.** [Possessing unwarranted self-esteem] — *Syn.* proud, arrogant, haughty; see **egotistic** 2.

**2.** [Trivial] — *Syn.* trivial, unimportant, frivolous, petty, insignificant, idle, empty, hollow, otiose; see also **trivial, unimportant.**

**in vain, 1.** — *Syn.* futilely, unprofitably, to no purpose; see **vainly.**

**2.** — *Syn.* profanely, irreverently, lightly; see **casually** 2, **rudely.**

**3.** [Useless] — *Syn.* worthless, unavailing, profitless; see **futile** 1, **useless** 1.

*See Synonym Study at* FUTILE.

**SYN.** — **vain** applies to that which has little or no real value, worth, or meaning [*vain* studies, indulging in *vain* pleasures]; **idle** refers to that which is baseless or worthless because it can never be realized [*idle* hopes, *idle* talk]; **empty** and **hollow** are used of that which only appears to be genuine, sincere, worthwhile, etc. [*empty* threats, *hollow* victories]; **otiose** applies to that which has no real purpose or function and is therefore useless or superfluous [*otiose* remarks]

**vainglorious,** *modif.* — *Syn.* vain, proud, pompous; see **egotistic** 2.

**vainglory,** *n.* — *Syn.* conceit, arrogance, pomp; see **arrogance, ostentation** 1, **pride** 1.

*See Synonym Study at* PRIDE.

**vainly,** *modif.* — *Syn.* in vain, uselessly, unnecessarily, fruitlessly, purposelessly, needlessly, unprofitably, bootlessly, futilely, to no purpose, to no avail, abortively; see also **hopelessly** 1, 2.

**vale,** *n.* — *Syn.* dell, glen, dale; see **valley.**

**valediction,** *n.* — *Syn.* send-off, good-by, farewell; see **departure** 1.

**valedictorian,** *n.* — *Syn.* first speaker, best student, principal speaker; see **scholar** 2, **speaker** 2.

**valedictory,** *modif.* — *Syn.* final, parting, terminal; see **last** 1.

**valentine,** *n.* **1.** [A love note or poem] — *Syn.* Valentine's Day card, St. Valentine's Day greeting, love verse; see **card, letter** 2.

**2.** [A sweetheart] — *Syn.* beloved, lover, boyfriend, girlfriend; see **darling** 2, **lover** 1.

**valet,** *n.* — *Syn.* manservant, *valet de chambre* (French), body servant, attendant, gentleman's gentleman; see also **servant.**

**valiant,** *modif.* **1.** [Having a character notable for valor] — *Syn.* brave, courageous, unafraid, dauntless, valorous, undismayed, intrepid, steadfast, vigorous, stouthearted, high-spirited, plucky, assertive, manful, manly, lion-hearted, mettlesome, aweless, undaunted, unflinching, unshrinking, self-reliant, strong-willed, indomitable, fearless, venturous, adventurous, powerful, puissant; see also **brave** 1. — *Ant.* COWARDLY, fearful, timid.

**2.** [Performed with valor] — *Syn.* heroic, great, grand, gallant, valorous, chivalrous, audacious, venturesome, noble, magnanimous, magnificent. — *Ant.* INEFFECTIVE, feeble, contemptible.

*See Synonym Study at* BRAVE.

**valiantly,** *modif.* — *Syn.* courageously, boldly, fearlessly; see **bravely.**

**valid,** *modif.* **1.** [Capable of proof] — *Syn.* sound, cogent, logical, conclusive, solid, well-grounded, well-founded, tested, accurate, convincing, telling, correct, determinative, compelling, persuasive, potent, stringent, strong, ultimate, unanswerable, irrefutable.

— *Ant.* WRONG, erring, misleading.

**2.** [Genuine] — *Syn.* true, original, factual, real, actual, pure, uncorrupted, authentic, confirmed, authoritative, trustworthy, credible, attested, efficient, efficacious, legitimate, adequate, substantial, proved, proven, unalloyed, unadulterated. — *Ant.* FALSE, fictitious, counterfeit.

**SYN.** — **valid** applies to that which cannot be objected to because it conforms to law, logic, the facts, etc. [a *valid* criticism, a *valid* license]; **sound** refers to that which is firmly grounded on facts, evidence, logic, etc. and is therefore free from error [a *sound* method, a *sound* argument]; **cogent** implies such a powerful appeal to the mind as to appear conclusive [*cogent* reasoning]; **convincing** implies such validity as to persuade or overcome doubts or opposition [a *convincing* performance]; **telling** suggests the power to have the required effect by being forcible, striking, relevant, etc. [a *telling* rejoinder]

**validate,** *v.* — *Syn.* confirm, sanction, legalize, certify, stamp, notarize, authorize, authenticate, substantiate, verify, prove; see also **approve** 1, **endorse** 1, **prove, verify.**

*See Synonym Study at* VERIFY.

**validity,** *n.* — *Syn.* soundness, efficacy, gravity; see **legality.**

**valise,** *n.* — *Syn.* suitcase, grip, haversack; see **bag, baggage.**

**valley,** *n.* — *Syn.* vale, glen, canyon, swale, depression, hollow, trough, notch, channel, lowland, river valley, stream valley, plain, dell, coomb, cum, col, valley floor, coulee, dale, river bottom; see also **gap** 3, **ravine.** — *Ant.* MOUNTAIN, ridge, hilltop.

**valor,** *n.* — *Syn.* bravery, courage, prowess, intrepidity, boldness, gallantry, heroism, fearlessness, valiancy, chivalry, defiance, derring-do, dash, manliness, spirit, determination, hardihood, firmness, pluck*, backbone*, fight*, guts*, grit*, sand*, intestinal fortitude*. — *Ant.* COWARDICE, fear, cowardliness.

**valorous,** *modif.* — *Syn.* fearless, intrepid, courageous; see **brave** 1, **chivalrous, manly.**

**valuable,** *modif.* **1.** [Worth money] — *Syn.* salable, marketable, in demand, high-priced, commanding a good price, precious, costly, expensive, dear, of value, in great demand, hardly obtainable, scarce, priceless, invaluable, worthwhile, inestimable, worth its weight in gold*; see also **expensive.** — *Ant.* CHEAP, worthless, unsaleable, unmarketable.

**2.** [Helpful] — *Syn.* important, estimable, worthy; see **helpful** 1, **relevant.**

*See Synonym Study at* EXPENSIVE.

**valuation,** *n.* — *Syn.* cost, appraisal, judgment; see **estimate** 1.

**value,** *n.* **1.** [Monetary value] — *Syn.* price, expense, cost, profit, worth, value in exchange, equivalent, rate, amount, market price, charge, face value, assessment, appraisal.

**2.** [The quality of being desirable] — *Syn.* use, usefulness, utility, benefit, advantage, esteem, estimation, desirability, preference, exchangeability, marketability.

**3.** [Quality] — *Syn.* worth, merit, significance, consequence, goodness, condition, state, excellence, distinction, desirability, grade, finish, perfection, eminence, superiority, advantage, power, regard, importance, mark, caliber, repute.

**4.** [Precise signification] — *Syn.* significance, force, meaning, drift, import, sense, purpose, bearing, denotation, interpretation, implication, substance, content, connotation.

**value,** *v.* **1.** [To believe to be valuable] — *Syn.* esteem, prize, appreciate; see **admire** 1, **appreciate** 2, **consider** 1, 2.
**2.** [To set a price upon] — *Syn.* estimate, reckon, assess, appraise, fix the price of, place a value on, assay, rate, figure, compute, evaluate, judge, repute, consider, enumerate, account, charge, levy, ascertain, price.
**3.** [To estimate] — *Syn.* evaluate, assess, appraise; see **estimate** 1, **reckon.**
*See Synonym Study at* APPRECIATE.

---

*SYN.* — **value** and **worth** are used interchangeably when applied to the desirability of something material as measured by its equivalence in money, goods, etc. [the *worth* or *value* of a used car], but, in discrimination, **worth** implies an intrinsic excellence resulting as from superior moral, cultural, or spiritual qualities, and **value** suggests the excellence attributed to something with reference to its usability, importance, etc. [the true *worth* of a book cannot be measured by its commercial *value*]

---

**valued,** *modif.* **1.** [Priced] — *Syn.* evaluated, appraised, charged; see **marked** 2.
**2.** [Valuable] — *Syn.* prized, treasured, esteemed; see **valuable** 1.
**valueless,** *modif.* — *Syn.* useless, worthless, of no value, good-for-nothing, disesteemed, unserviceable, unsalable, not in demand, not worth a plug nickel*.
**valve,** *n.* — *Syn.* flap, lid, plug; see **device** 1, **pipe** 1.
Types of valves include: automatic, alarm, check, cutoff, side, overhead, dry-pipe, gate, lift, piston, rocking, safety, slide, reducing, shut-off, globe, heart, throttle, sleeve, intake, exhaust, butterfly.
**vamp,** *v.* **1.** [To repair] — *Syn.* fix, mend, patch; see **repair.**
**2.** [To seduce] — *Syn.* make love to, beguile, attract; see **court** 1, **seduce.**
**vampire,** *n.* **1.** [A legendary, reanimated, bloodsucking corpse] — *Syn.* Dracula, ghoul, zombie, lamia; see **monster** 1.
**2.** [One who prays on others] — *Syn.* blackmailer, thief, extortionist, con artist; see **criminal.**
**3.** [Flirt] — *Syn.* vamp, temptress, coquette; see **flirt.**
**van,** *n.* — *Syn.* truck, small truck, delivery truck, trailer, recreational vehicle, RV, lorry (British), camper*.
**vandal,** *n.* **1.** [A marauder] — *Syn.* despoiler, rapist, thief; see **destroyer** 1, **pirate.**
**2.** [One who destroys property] — *Syn.* hooligan, tough, hoodlum, hood*, punk*, delinquent, skinhead*.
**vandalism,** *n.* — *Syn.* piracy, demolition, spoliation; see **destruction** 1.
**vane,** *n.* — *Syn.* weather vane, weathercock, wind gauge, blade; see **device** 1.
**vanguard,** *n.* — *Syn.* advance guard, van, forerunners, precursors, leaders, spearhead, front, forefront, front line, front rank, avant-garde.
**vanilla,** *n.* — *Syn.* vanilla extract, *Vanilla planifolia* (Latin), wild vanilla; see **flavoring.**
**vanish,** *v.* — *Syn.* disappear, fade, fade away, fade out, go away, dissolve; see also **disappear.**
*See Synonym Study at* DISAPPEAR.
**vanished,** *modif.* — *Syn.* gone, disappeared, dissolved, faded, burned out, swallowed in the crowd*.
**vanishing,** *modif.* — *Syn.* disappearing, going, fading; see **evanescent, hazy** 1.
**vanity,** *n.* **1.** [Personal conceit] — *Syn.* conceit, narcissism, self-love, ostentation, display, show, self-

admiration, self-glorification, self-applause, pretension, vainglory, conceitedness, coxcombery, foppishness, complacency, smugness; see also **pride** 1. — *Ant.* MODESTY, diffidence, bashfulness.
**2.** [Futility] — *Syn.* idleness, emptiness, uselessness; see **futility.**
**3.** [A toilet case] — *Syn.* vanity box, vanity roll, vanity case, vanity table, compact, double compact, toilet kit, powder case, make-up case.
*See Synonym Study at* PRIDE.
**vanity case,** *n.* — *Syn.* vanity box, make-up case, toilet kit; see **compact, vanity** 3.
**vanquish,** *v.* — *Syn.* conquer, overcome, subdue; see **defeat** 1, 2, 3.
*See Synonym Study at* DEFEAT.
**vanquisher,** *n.* — *Syn.* conqueror, tyrant, subduer; see **victor, winner.**
**vantage point,** *n.* — *Syn.* position, standpoint, perspective, point of view; see **position** 1, **viewpoint.**
**vapid,** *modif.* — *Syn.* flat, insipid, boring; see **dull** 3, 4, **uninteresting.**
**vapor,** *n.* — *Syn.* mist, steam, condensation, smog, exhalation, breath, fog, gas, haze, smoke.
**vaporization,** *n.* — *Syn.* condensation, sublimation, atomization; see **evaporation.**
**vaporize,** *v.* — *Syn.* exhale, sublimate, volatize; see **evaporate** 1.
**vaporous,** *modif.* **1.** [Foggy] — *Syn.* smoggy, aerial, vapory; see **haze** 1, **misty.**
**2.** [Fanciful] — *Syn.* fleeting, wispy, unsubstantial; see **imaginary.**
**vapors,** *n.* — *Syn.* melancholy, despair, blues*; see **depression** 2.
**vapor trail,** *n.* — *Syn.* contrail, wake, condensation trail; see **track** 2.
**variable,** *modif.* — *Syn.* inconstant, fickle, mutable, shifting, unsteady, fitful; see also **changeable** 2.
**variance,** *n.* — *Syn.* change, fluctuations, deviation, modification, oscillation, mutation, variety, diversity, incongruity, disagreement; see also **variation.** — *Ant.* AGREEMENT, unity, sameness.
**variant,** *modif.* — *Syn.* varying, exceptional, differing; see **irregular** 1, **various.**
**variant,** *n.* — *Syn.* different version, alternative, alternative reading, modification, result of variation, exceptional instance, irregularity; see also **exception** 2.
**variation,** *n.* **1.** [Change] — *Syn.* modification, alteration, mutation, diversification, deviation, shift, fluctuation, deflection, aberration, departure, variety, adaptation, curve, bend, turn, divergence, veer, digression, swerve, displacement, warping; see also **change** 1. — *Ant.* STABILITY, fixity, unchangeableness.
**2.** [Disparity] — *Syn.* inequality, difference, dissimilarity, dissimilitude, distinction, disproportion, exception, contrast, contradistinction, unconformity, irregularity, aberration, abnormality, disparity. — *Ant.* SIMILARITY, conformity, likeness.
**varied,** *modif.* — *Syn.* discrete, separate, diverse; see **different** 1, 2, **mixed** 1, **various.**
**variegate,** *v.* — *Syn.* diversify, spatter, mottle; see **color** 1, 2.
**variegated,** *modif.* — *Syn.* mottled, kaleidoscopic, varicolored; see **bright** 2, **various.**
**variegation,** *n.* — *Syn.* striation, iridescence, spectrum, rainbow; see **color** 1, 2.
**variety,** *n.* **1.** [Quality or state of being diverse] — *Syn.* diversity, change, diversification, difference, variance, medley, mixture, mélange, potpourri, miscellany, disparateness, divergency, variation, incongru-

ity, fluctuation, shift, change, modification, departure, heterogeneity, many-sidedness, unlikeness.

**2.** [Sort] — *Syn.* kind, class, division, species, genus, race, tribe, family, assortment, type, stripe, nature, kidney, ilk, character, description, rank, grade, category, classification, quality. — *Ant.* EQUALITY, equalness, similarity.

**various,** *modif.* — *Syn.* different, disparate, dissimilar, diverse, diversified, diversiform, variegated, varicolored, many-sided, several, manifold, numerous, unlike, many, sundry, divers, variable, changeable, inconstant, uncertain, of any kind, all manner of, of every description, distinct; see also **multiple** 1. — *Ant.* ALIKE, undiversified, identical.

*See Synonym Study at* DIFFERENT.

**variously,** *modif.* — *Syn.* varyingly, inconsistently, unpredictably; see **differently** 1, **unevenly.**

**varlet,** *n.* **1.** [An attendant] — *Syn.* aid, page, slave, helper; see **servant.**

**2.** [A scoundrel] — *Syn.* cad, knave, blackguard; see **rascal.**

**varnish,** *n.*

Colors of varnish include: light oak, dark oak, golden oak, mahogany, walnut, cherry, dark pine, light pine, japan black, lacquer red, gold-rust, silver wire lacquer, sheet-gold lacquer, green lacquer, brown lacquer, cream lacquer; see also **coat** 3, **cover** 2, **enamel, finish** 1.

**varnish,** *v.* — *Syn.* finish, paint, shellac, lacquer, wax, size, enamel, japan, surface, coat, luster, polish, gloss, adorn, refinish, glaze, gloss over. — *Ant.* EXPOSE, remove the finish, strip.

**vary,** *v.* **1.** [To show changes] — *Syn.* dissent, diverge, differ, deviate, digress, swerve, depart, fluctuate, alternate, diverge, diverge from, divaricate from, be distinguished from, range, be inconstant, mutate, be uncertain. — *Ant.* REMAIN, be steady, hold.

**2.** [To make changes] — *Syn.* modify, alter, diversify, change; see **change** 1.

*See Synonym Study at* CHANGE.

**varying,** *modif.* — *Syn.* diverse, differing, diverging; see **changing, different** 1.

**vase,** *n.* — *Syn.* vessel, urn, jar, pottery, porcelain, receptacle, flower holder, ornament.

Types of vases include: amphora, burette, krater, lekynos, hydria, kylix, aquaemanale, oxybaphon, tazza, alabastron, bud vase, cruse, jug, pitcher, ewer, jardiniere, libation cup, funeral urn.

Styles of vases include: Etruscan, Greek black figure, Greek red figure, canopic, T'ang, Sung, Ming, Ch'ing, blue and white, *famille verte, famille rose* (both French), Samarran luster, Majolica, delft, Belleek, faience, potiche.

**vassal,** *n.* — *Syn.* thrall, serf, bondman; see **servant, slave** 1.

**vassalage,** *n.* — *Syn.* dependency, serviture, bondage; see **slavery** 1, **subjection.**

**vast,** *modif.* **1.** [Large] — *Syn.* huge, enormous, immense; see **broad** 1, **large** 1.

**2.** [Extensive] — *Syn.* broad, far-flung, wide, spacious, expansive, spread-out, ample, far-reaching, widespread, comprehensive, detailed, all-inclusive, astronomical, prolonged, stretched out, expanded. — *Ant.* NARROW, limited, confined.

**3.** [Infinite] — *Syn.* boundless, limitless, interminable; see **endless** 1, **eternal** 2.

**vastly,** *modif.* — *Syn.* greatly, much, enormously, immensely, mightily, prodigiously, extensively, tremendously, hugely; see also **largely** 2.

**vastness,** *n.* — *Syn.* hugeness, extent, enormity; see **expanse, size** 2.

**vat,** *n.* — *Syn.* vessel, cistern, tub, barrel, tank, basin, salt pit; see also **container.**

**Vatican,** *n.* — *Syn.* the Papacy, Rome, papal palace; see **Pope.**

**vaudeville,** *n.* — *Syn.* variety show, burlesque, skit, show, entr'acte, vaud*, bawdeville*.

**vault,** *n.* **1.** [A place for the dead] — *Syn.* tomb, crypt, grave, sepulcher, ossuary, catacomb, pit, tumulus, mound, barrow, cenotaph; see also **monument** 1.

**2.** [A place for preserving valuables] — *Syn.* safe-deposit box, strongroom, bank vault, time vault, time capsule, safe, burglar-proof safe.

**vault,** *v.* — *Syn.* leap over, hurdle, clear, bound, spring, jump, mount, pole-vault.

**vaulted,** *modif.* — *Syn.* domed, arched, hemispheric; see **round** 3.

**vaulting,** *modif.* — *Syn.* eager, opportunistic, avid; see **enthusiastic** 1, 2, 3.

**vaunt,** *v.* — *Syn.* boast, swagger, brag of, puff; see **boast** 1.

*See Synonym Study at* BOAST.

**veal,** *n.* — *Syn.* calf, bob veal, deaconned veal; see **beef** 1, **meat.**

Cuts of veal include: chops, leg, shank, shoulder, rump, loin, rack, neck, breast, chuck.

Veal dishes include: veal cutlet, veal stew, calf's liver, Wiener schnitzel, veal Parmigiana, veal scallopini, veal marsala, veal piccata, veal saltimbocca, veal bird, *tête de veau* (French), osso buco (Italian).

**veer,** *v.* — *Syn.* swerve, deviate, depart, digress, diverge, bend, turn, divert, deflect, sheer, avert, curve; see also **deviate.**

*See Synonym Study at* DEVIATE.

**veering,** *n.* — *Syn.* deviation, variation, detour; see **change** 1, 2.

**vegetable,** *modif.* **1.** [Concerning flora] — *Syn.* plant, plantlike, herblike, floral, blooming, blossoming, growing, flourishing.

**2.** [Without spirit] — *Syn.* dull, monotonous, stupid, passive, unthinking, stagnant, inert, comatose, humble, stationary, inactive, mild, quiet, lowly.

**vegetable,** *n.* **1.** [A plant] — *Syn.* herbaceous plant, herb, green, legume, garden produce, edible root.

Common vegetables include: cabbage, potato, turnip, bean, carrot, pea, celery, lettuce, parsnip, spinach, squash, zucchini, tomato, pumpkin, asparagus, onion, corn, lentil, leek, garlic, radish, cucumber, artichoke, eggplant, beet, scallion, pepper, okra, kohlrabi, parsley, celtuce, chard, rhubarb, cauliflower, Brussels sprouts, broccoli, celeriac, endive, Chinese cabbage, bok choy, water cress, chicory, kale, rutabaga, mushroom.

**2.** [An inert person] — *Syn.* clod, bump on a log*, couch potato*.

**vegetate,** *v.* **1.** [To germinate] — *Syn.* sprout, bud, blossom; see **bloom, grow** 1.

**2.** [To stagnate] — *Syn.* hibernate, stagnate, languish; see **decay, weaken** 1.

**vegetation** — *Syn.* plants, plant growth, trees, shrubs, saplings, flowers, wild flowers, grasses, herbage, herbs, pasturage, weeds, vegetables, crops; see also **nature** 2.

**vehemence,** *n.* — *Syn.* frenzy, fervor, impetuosity; see **intensity** 1, **violence** 2.

**vehement,** *modif.* — *Syn.* forceful, powerful, passionate, impassioned, fervent, emphatic, impetuous, fierce, furious, violent; see also **intense.**

**vehicle,** *n.* **1.** [A conveyance] — *Syn.* transportation, transport, carrier, wheels*.

Vehicles include: carriage, buggy, wagon, sleigh, cart, motor car, bus, jeep, automobile, truck, tractor, tank, station wagon, van, cablecar, train, subway, minivan, limousine, limo*, streetcar, tram, trolley, bicycle, airplane, helicopter, shuttle, monorail, motorcycle, railroad car, taxicab, cab, hack, taxi.
2. [Means of expression] — *Syn.* organ, channel, agency; see **means** 1, **medium** 2.

**veil,** *n.* 1. [A thin fabric] — *Syn.* scarf, kerchief, mask, gauze, film, cover, tissue; see also **web** 1.
2. [A curtain] — *Syn.* veiling, screen, mantilla, cover, shade; see also **curtain**.
3. [A light mist] — *Syn.* mist, fog, cloud, rain, haze, dimness, twilight, darkness, blur, obscurity, half-light.

**vein,** *n.* 1. [A deposit of ore] — *Syn.* lode, bed, mineral bed, seam, striation, streak, strike, ledge, lead, reef, dike.
2. [A blood vessel, especially leading to the heart] — *Syn.* duct, canal, vena cava, varicose vein, veinlet, venule, artery, arteriole, capillary; see also **artery** 2, **vessel** 3.
Major veins of the human body include: jugular, pulmonary, subclavian, portal, iliac, hepatic, renal, cervical, brachiocephalic, femoral, saphenous.
3. [Anything resembling a vein, sense 2] — *Syn.* hair, thread, follicle, nerve, rib, nervure, venation.
4. [A distinctive quality or mood] — *Syn.* strain, humor, temper, tenor tone, style, bent, ilk, tang, spice, dash; see also **characteristic, mood** 1, **temperament**.
*See Synonym Study at* MOOD.

**velocity,** *n.* — *Syn.* quickness, swiftness, celerity, rapidity, impetus, escape velocity, exhaust velocity; see also **speed**.

**velour,** *n.* — *Syn.* velvet, pile fabric, shag, mohair, plush, fur fabric, bolivia; see also **cloth**.

**velvet,** *modif.* — *Syn.* velvetlike, velvety, silken, shining, plushy, velourlike, fine-textured; see also **soft** 2.

**velvet,** *n.*
Types of velvet include: pile, cut, transparent, silk, silk-and-cotton, cotton, rayon, velveteen, corduroy; see also **cloth, velour.**

**venal,** *modif.* — *Syn.* mercenary, dishonorable, vicious; see **corrupt** 1, **greedy** 1.

**venality,** *n.* — *Syn.* corruptness, sordidness, vendibility; see **dishonesty, greed.**

**vend,** *v.* — *Syn.* trade, peddle, auction; see **sell** 1.
*See Synonym Study at* SELL.

**vendetta,** *n.* — *Syn.* squabble, quarrel, feud; see **dispute, fight** 1.

**vendor,** *n.* — *Syn.* vender, peddler, huckster; see **businessperson, merchant.**

**veneer,** *n.* 1. [An outer layer] — *Syn.* surface, exterior, covering; see **cover** 1.
2. [A superficial appearance] — *Syn.* façade, show, pretense, outward display.

**veneer,** *v.* 1. [To cover with a thin layer] — *Syn.* laminate, overlay, cover, plate, coat, face, glue together, surface, finish.
2. [To give a deceptive appearance of] — *Syn.* gloss over, dissemble, conceal, whitewash; see **disguise.**

**venerable,** *modif.* 1. [Old] — *Syn.* aged, hoary, ancient; see **old** 1.
2. [Having qualities becoming to age] — *Syn.* revered, reverenced, honored, honorable, noble, august, grand, esteemed, respected, dignified, imposing, grave, serious, sage, wise, philosophical, experienced. — *Ant.* INEXPERIENCED, callow, raw.

**venerate,** *v.* — *Syn.* revere, reverence, adore; see **revere, love** 1, **worship** 2.

**veneration,** *n.* — *Syn.* respect, adoration, awe; see **reverence** 1, 2, **worship** 1.
*See Synonym Study at* REVERENCE.

**vengeance,** *n.* — *Syn.* retribution, return, retaliation; see **revenge** 1.

**vengeful,** *modif.* — *Syn.* spiteful, revengeful, rancorous; see **vindictive** 1.

**venial,** *modif.* — *Syn.* excusable, pardonable, justifiable, allowable, trivial, exculpable, defensible, slight, vindicatory, warrantable, extenuatory, mild; see also **unimportant.** — *Ant.* DEADLY, mortal, SERIOUS.

**Venice,** *n.* — *Syn.* Bride of the Sea, Queen of the Sea, Queen of the Adriatic, *Venezia* (Italian), *Venedig* (German), *Venise* (French).

**venom,** *n.* 1. [An animal poison] — *Syn.* poison, virus, toxin, bane, microbe, contagion, infection. — *Ant.* REMEDY, antidote, specific.
2. [Malice] — *Syn.* virulence, ill-will, malignity, spite; see **anger, hatred** 1, 2.

**venomous,** *modif.* — *Syn.* virulent, lethal, toxic; see **deadly, destructive** 2, **poisonous.**

**vent,** *n.* — *Syn.* ventilator, vent hole, venting hole, ventiduct, liquid-vent, vent faucet, molding, touchhole, drain, smoke hole, flue, aperture; see also **chimney.**

**vent,** *v.* — *Syn.* let out, drive out, discharge; see **release.**

**ventilate,** *v.* — *Syn.* freshen, aerate, let in fresh air, circulate fresh air, vent, air cool, air out, free, oxygenate; see also **air** 1, **cool** 2.

**ventilated,** *modif.* — *Syn.* aired out, having adequate ventilation, not close, not closed (up); see **airy** 1, **cool** 1, **open** 1.

**ventilation,** *n.* 1. [The act of providing or changing air] — *Syn.* airing, purifying, oxygenating, freshening, opening windows, changing air, circulating air, air-conditioning.
2. [Fresh air] — *Syn.* pure air, purified air, freshened air, oxygenated air, mountain air, sea air, breeze, coolness, outside air, some of the outdoors*, some of the climate*.

**ventilator,** *n.* — *Syn.* cooler, air-conditioner, fan; see **vent.**

**ventriloquism,** *n.* — *Syn.* ventriloquy, gastriloquism, polyphonism; see **speech** 2.

**venture,** *n.* — *Syn.* adventure, risk, hazard, peril, stake, chance, speculation, dare, experiment, trial, attempt, essay, test, gamble, undertaking, enterprise, investment, leap in the dark*, plunge*, potluck*, flier*, crack*, fling*.

**venture,** *v.* — *Syn.* attempt, essay, experiment, try, try out, assay, grope, feel, speculate, gamble, stake, hazard, bet, wager, play for.

**ventured,** *modif.* — *Syn.* adventured, risked, hazarded, chanced, dared, experimented, tried, invested, attempted, essayed, assayed, gambled, undertaken; see also **tested.**

**venturesome,** *modif.* — *Syn.* risky, daring, adventurous; see **brave** 1, **rash.**

**veracious,** *modif.* 1. [Honest] — *Syn.* truthful, frank, trustworthy; see **honest** 1.
2. [True] — *Syn.* valid, genuine, true; see **accurate** 1.

**veracity,** *n.* 1. [Honesty] — *Syn.* truth, truthfulness, trustworthiness, integrity, honor, honesty, ingenuousness, candor, frankness, openness, fidelity, probity, plain dealing, artlessness, sincerity, impartiality, fairness; see also **truth** 1. — *Ant.* DISHONESTY, falsity, insincerity.
2. [Accuracy] — *Syn.* truth, exactness, exactitude, reality, credibility, verity, actuality, correctness, trueness, conformity, verisimilitude, precision, rightness, authenticity, genuineness, veritableness, authoritative-

ness; see also **truth** 1.— *Ant.* ERROR, inaccuracy, fallacy.
*See Synonym Study at* TRUTH.
**veranda,** *n.*— *Syn.* portico, gallery, piazza, platform, porch, terrace, stoop; see also **porch.**
**verb,** *n.* Types of verbs include: finite, active, neuter, passive, transitive, intransitive, auxiliary, linking, reciprocal, conditional, compound, action, helping, copulative, reflexive, strong, weak, regular, irregular, reduplicating, deponent, copula; see also **part of speech.**
**verbal,** *modif.* **1.** [Using words]— *Syn.* lexical, linguistic, oral; see **linguistic, oral, spoken.**
**2.** [Concerning the wording, not the content]— *Syn.* titular, verbatim, rhetorical, diplomatic, textual, lexical; see also **literal** 1, **nominal** 1.
*See Synonym Study at* ORAL.
**verbal,** *n.* Verbals in English include: infinitive, gerund, participle, gerundive, verbal noun, present participle, verbal adjective, past participle, verbal phrase, absolute construction, independent construction; see also **part of speech.**
**verbally,** *modif.*— *Syn.* orally, by word of mouth, person-to-person, word for word; see **literally, spoken.**
**verbatim,** *modif.*— *Syn.* exactly, word for word, literatim, to the letter; see **literally.**
**verbiage,** *n.*— *Syn.* repetition, verbosity, prolixity, loquacity; see **wordiness.**
**verbose,** *modif.*— *Syn.* wordy, prolix, tedious, tautologous, redundant, repetitious, circumlocutory, repetitive, periphrastic, abounding in tautology, diffuse, repeating, pleonastic, bombastic, involved, involuted, tortuous, loquacious, long-winded, garrulous, talkative, magniloquent, grandiloquent, rhetorical, voluble, flowery, over-rhetorical, fustian, characterized by redundancy, word-mongering, farsed, stuffed, gabby*, loudmouthed*, talky*, windy*, big-mouthed*, blabby*, full of air*; see also **dull** 4.— *Ant.* TERSE, precise, succinct.

---

**SYN.** — **verbose** suggests a wordiness that results in obscurity, tediousness, bombast, etc. /a *verbose* acceptance speech/; **wordy** is the general term implying the use of more words in speaking or writing than are necessary for communication /a *wordy* document/; **prolix** implies such a tiresome elaboration of trivial details as to be boring or dull /his *prolix* sermons/; **diffuse** suggests such verbosity and loose construction as to lose all force and sharpness /a rambling, *diffuse* harangue/; **redundant** implies the use of unnecessary or repetitious words or phrases /a *redundant* literary style/

---

**verbosely,** *modif.*— *Syn.* bombastically, wordily, lengthily, oratorically, talkatively, expansively, redundantly, pleonastically, tirelessly, tiresomely, grandiloquently, longwindedly, episodically, maudlinly, clumsily, crudely, extravagantly, in a verbose manner, not succinctly, not economically, not tightly, not articulately, with verbosity, with wordiness, with undue length, with pleonasm, going on and on, beating around the bush*.
**verbosity,** *n.*— *Syn.* circumlocution, loquacity, garrulity, prolixity; see **wordiness.**
**verdant,** *modif.*— *Syn.* grassy, flourishing, verdurous; see **green** 2.
**verdict,** *n.*— *Syn.* judgment, finding, decision, answer, opinion, sentence, determination, decree, conclusion, deduction, adjudication, arbitrament.
**verdure,** *n.*— *Syn.* flora, greenness, greenery, herbage;

see **vegetation.**
**verge,** *n.*— *Syn.* edge, brink, terminus; see **boundary.**
**on the verge of**— *Syn.* not quite, at the point of, almost; see **about to.**
**verge,** *v.* **1.** [To be on the brink]— *Syn.* border, end, edge, touch; see **approach** 2.
**2.** [To tend toward]— *Syn.* incline, lean, turn, swing toward; see **tend** 2.
**verifiable,** *modif.*— *Syn.* susceptible of proof, provable, correct; see **provable, valid** 1.
**verification,** *n.*— *Syn.* verifying, attestation, affirmation; see **confirmation** 1.
**verify,** *v.*— *Syn.* establish, substantiate, authenticate, prove, check, test, validate, settle, corroborate, confirm, document, support; see also **prove.**

---

**SYN.** — **verify** is to prove something to be true or correct by investigation, comparison with a standard, or reference to ascertainable facts /some of the dates given in the book could not be *verified*/; to **confirm** is to establish as true or valid that which was doubtful or uncertain /to *confirm* a rumor/; **substantiate** suggests the producing of evidence that proves or tends to prove the validity of a previous assertion or claim /the census figures *substantiate* his charge/; **corroborate** suggests the strengthening of one statement or testimony by another /the witnesses *corroborated* her version of the event/; **authenticate** implies proof of genuineness by an authority or expert /to *authenticate* a painting/; **validate** implies official confirmation of the validity of something /to *validate* a will/

---

**verifying,** *n.*— *Syn.* verification, proving, substantiating, corroborating, authenticating, validating, confirming, testing, checking; see also **confirmation** 1.
**verily,** *modif.*— *Syn.* in very truth, truly, certainly, unquestionably, undoubtedly, without question, in fact, beyond doubt; see also **surely.**
**verisimilitude,** *n.*— *Syn.* plausibility, appearance, likelihood; see **truth** 1.
*See Synonym Study at* TRUTH.
**veritable,** *modif.*— *Syn.* true, real, utter, absolute; see **genuine** 1.
*See Synonym Study at* GENUINE.
**verity,** *n.*— *Syn.* truth, verisimilitude, actuality; see **reality** 1.
*See Synonym Study at* TRUTH.
**vermilion,** *modif.*— *Syn.* vermeil, chrome-red, cinnabar, orange-vermilion, antimony, vermilion, French vermilion, Dutch vermilion, Chinese vermilion, scarlet-vermilion, orient vermilion, vermilion-red, vermilion-scarlet, vermilion-tawny; see also **red** 1.
**vermin,** *n.*— *Syn.* insects, bugs, pests, lice, rodents, cooties*.
Vermin include: fly, flea, louse, weevil, chigger, earwig, mealybug, mite, mosquito, cockroach, bedbug, clothes moth, centipede, tick, silverfish *or* fish moth, rat, mouse, weasel; see also **insect.**
**vernacular,** *modif.* **1.** [Indigenous]— *Syn.* native, ingrained, inherent, domesticated; see **native** 2, **natural** 1.
**2.** [Informal]— *Syn.* colloquial, vulgar, everyday; see **colloquial.**
**vernacular,** *n.*— *Syn.* dialect, idiom, patois, phraseology; see **dialect, language** 1.
*See Synonym Study at* DIALECT.
**versatile,** *modif.*— *Syn.* many-sided, multifaceted, all-round, adaptable, dexterous, varied, ready, clever,

handy, talented, gifted, adroit, resourceful, ingenious, accomplished; see also **able** 1, 2.

**versatility**, *modif.* — *Syn.* flexibility, utility, adjustability; see **adaptability, usefulness.**

**verse**, *n.* 1. [Composition in poetic form] — *Syn.* poetry, poem, metrical composition, versification, stanza, rhyme, lyric, sonnet, ode, heroic verse, dramatic poetry, blank verse, *vers libre* (French).
2. [A unit of verse, sense 1] — *Syn.* line, verse, stanza, stave, strophe, antistrophe, hemistich, distich, quatrain.

**versed**, *modif.* — *Syn.* skilled, trained, competent; see **learned** 2.

**version**, *n.* 1. [One of various accounts] — *Syn.* report, account, variant, tale, story.
2. [A translation] — *Syn.* paraphrase, redaction, transcription; see **translation.**
*See Synonym Study at* TRANSLATION.

**vertebrae**, *n.* — *Syn.* spine, spinal column, backbone, chine.
Parts of the vertebra include: body, neural arch, vertebral foramen, lamina, transverse process, spinous process, zygapophysis, pedicle.
Types of vertebrae in the human spinal column include: cervical, thoracic, lumbar, sacral, coccygeal.

**vertebrate**, *modif.* — *Syn.* vertebral, of the *Vertebrata,* having a spinal column.

**vertex**, *n.* — *Syn.* peak, summit, zenith, point; see **top** 1.

**vertical**, *modif.* — *Syn.* perpendicular, plumb, upright, upward, erect, on end, cocked up, straight up.

**vertiginous**, *modif.* — *Syn.* whirling, dizzying, spinning; see **turning** 1.

**vertigo**, *n.* — *Syn.* dizziness, reeling, giddiness; see **disease**.

**verve**, *n.* — *Syn.* vigor, energy, liveliness; see **strength** 1.

**very**, *modif.* — *Syn.* extremely, exceedingly, greatly, acutely, indispensably, just so, surprisingly, astonishingly, incredibly, wonderfully, particularly, certainly, positively, truly, exaggeratedly, emphatically, really, truly, pretty, decidedly, pressingly, notably, uncommonly, extraordinarily, prodigiously, highly, substantially, dearly, amply, vastly, extensively, noticeably, conspicuously, largely, considerably, hugely, excessively, imperatively, markedly, enormously, sizably, materially, immensely, tremendously, superlatively, remarkably, unusually, immoderately, quite, indeed, somewhat, rather, simply, intensely, urgently, exceptionally, severely, seriously, in a great measure, to a great degree, beyond compare, on a large scale, ever so, beyond measure, by far, in the extreme, in a marked degree, to a great extent, without restraint, more or less, in part, infinitely, very much, to no small extent, real★, right★, right smart★, pretty★, awfully★, almighty★, almightily★, good and★, powerful★, powerfully★, hell of a★, helluva★, precious★, so★, to a fault★, a bit of★, no end★; see also **much** 1. — *Ant.* HARDLY, inconsiderably, scarcely.

**vesicle**, *n.* — *Syn.* sac, utricle, cyst; see **blister, swelling.**

**vespers**, *n.* — *Syn.* orison, evening prayer, evensong, compline; see **prayer** 2.

**vessel**, *n.* 1. [A container] — *Syn.* pitcher, urn, kettle; see **container.**
2. [A ship] — *Syn.* boat, craft, bark; see **ship.**
3. [A duct; *especially for blood*] — *Syn.* blood vessel, vein, artery, capillary, canal; see also **artery** 2, **vein** 2.

**vest**, *n.* — *Syn.* waistcoat, jacket, garment, undershirt; see **clothes.**

**vestal**, *modif.* — *Syn.* celibate, virginal, virtuous; see **chaste** 3, **pure** 2.

**vested**, *modif.* 1. [Clothed] — *Syn.* dressed, robed, outfitted; see **clothed.**
2. [Absolute] — *Syn.* fixed, settled, complete; see **absolute** 1.

**vested interest**, *n.* 1. [Close involvement] — *Syn.* interest, conflict, conflict of interest, legal interest, special concern, stake.
2. [*In plural*; Those that control trade] — *Syn.* combine, cartel, combination in restraint of trade, companies (with interlocking directorates), syndicate; see also **business** 4, **monopoly.**

**vestibule**, *n.* — *Syn.* enclosed entrance, entry, entryway, lobby, foyer, narthex, anteroom, antechamber, waiting room; see also **room** 2.

**vestige**, *n.* — *Syn.* trace, remains, scrap; see **remainder.**

**vestments**, *n.* — *Syn.* garments, robes, gowns, garb, attire, raiment, official robes; see also **clothes.**

**vest-pocket**, *modif.* — *Syn.* small, reduced, miniature, tiny; see **little** 1.

**vestry**, *n.* — *Syn.* church room, vestry room, robing room; see **sacristy.**

**veteran**, *modif.* — *Syn.* seasoned, experienced, exercised, skilled, versed, hardened, weathered, inured, steady.

**veteran**, *n.* 1. [An experienced person] — *Syn.* master, expert, one long in service, sourdough★, old hand★, one of the old guard★, old bird★, old dog★, old timer★. — *Ant.* AMATEUR, new man, youngster.
2. [An experienced soldier] — *Syn.* ex-soldier, seasoned campaigner, ex-service man, reenlisted man, old soldier, war horse★, vet★, ex-G.I★.

**Veteran's Day**, *n.* — *Syn.* Armistice Day, Remembrance Day, November 11; see **holiday.**

**veterinarian**, *n.* — *Syn.* animal specialist, vet, animal doctor; see **doctor** 1.

**veto**, *n.* — *Syn.* rejection, interdiction, prohibition, declination, negative; see also **denial** 1, **refusal.**

**veto**, *v.* — *Syn.* interdict, prohibit, decline; see **deny, forbid, refuse.**

**vetoed**, *modif.* — *Syn.* declined, rejected, disapproved; see **no, refused.**

**vex**, *v.* 1. [To trouble] — *Syn.* distress, worry, plague, trouble; see **bother** 3, **disturb** 2.
2. [To annoy] — *Syn.* provoke, irritate, anger, annoy; see **bother** 2.
*See Synonym Study at* BOTHER.

**vexation**, *n.* 1. [A vexed feeling] — *Syn.* uneasiness, irritation, bother; see **annoyance** 1.
2. [A cause of vexation, sense 1] — *Syn.* worry, trouble, misfortune; see **difficulty** 2.

**vexatious**, *modif.* — *Syn.* annoying, bothersome, irritating; see **disturbing.**

**vexed**, *modif.* — *Syn.* disturbed, annoyed, irritated; see **confused** 2, **troubled** 1.

**via**, *prep.* — *Syn.* by way of, by the route passing through, on the way to, through the medium of; see **by** 2, **through** 4.

**viaduct**, *n.* — *Syn.* bridge, way, way over, elevated road, aquaduct, ramp.

**vial**, *n.* — *Syn.* flask, phial, vessel, bottle, jar.

**vibrant**, *modif.* 1. [Pulsing] — *Syn.* vibrating, throbbing, pulsing, quaking; see **quivering.**
2. [Active] — *Syn.* energetic, vigorous, lively; see **active** 1, 2.

**vibrate**, *v.* 1. [To quiver] — *Syn.* fluctuate, flutter, waver, swing; see **wave** 3.
2. [To sound] — *Syn.* echo, resound, reverberate; see **sound** 1.
*See Synonym Study at* SWING.

**vibration,** *n.* — *Syn.* quake, wavering, vacillation, fluctuation, oscillation, quiver, shake; see also **wave** 3.

**vibrato,** *n.* — *Syn.* quaver, quiver, tremolo; see **vibration**.

**vicar,** *n.* — *Syn.* cleric, ecclesiastic, clergyman; see **minister** 1, **priest**.

**vicarious,** *modif.* **1.** [Substitute] — *Syn.* substitutional, acting, delegated; see **common** 5, **pretended**.
**2.** — *Syn.* indirect, second-hand.

**vice,** *modif.* **1.** [Subordinate] — *Syn.* vice-admiral, vice-chairman, vice-consul, vice-dean, vice-general; see also **subordinate**.
**2.** [Wicked] — *Syn.* depraved, bad, pernicious; see **vicious** 1, **wicked** 1.

**vice,** *n.* **1.** [Depravity] — *Syn.* corruption, iniquity, wickedness, fault; see **evil** 1.
**2.** [A degrading practice] — *Syn.* licentiousness, lust, lewdness, profligacy, indecency, libidinousness, sensuality, carnality.
*See Synonym Study at* FAULT.

**viceroy,** *n.* — *Syn.* ruler, governor, chief executive, representative, proxy.

**vice versa,** *modif.* — *Syn.* conversely, in reverse, the other way round, turn about, *mutatis mutandis* (Latin), about face, in opposite manner, far from it, on the contrary, in reverse English★.

**vicinity,** *n.* — *Syn.* proximity, nearness, neighborhood; see **environment, region** 1.

**vicious,** *modif.* **1.** [Corrupt] — *Syn.* bad, debased, base, impious, profligate, demoralized, faulty, vile, foul, impure, lewd, indecent, licentious, libidinous; see also **wicked** 1, 2. — *Ant.* NOBLE, PURE, virtuous.
**2.** [Prone to cruelty] — *Syn.* wicked, evil, sinful; see **cruel** 1, 2.
**3.** [Not tamed] — *Syn.* wild, untamed, insubordinate; see **unruly**.

**vicious circle,** *n.* — *Syn.* vicious cycle, chain of events, cause and effect, interreliant problems; see **difficulty** 1, 2, **predicament**.

**viciously,** *modif.* — *Syn.* cruelly, spitefully, harmfully; see **brutally, wrongly** 1, 2.

**vicissitude,** *n.* — *Syn.* mutability, uncertainty, alteration, difficulty; see **change** 2.
*See Synonym Study at* DIFFICULTY.

**victim,** *n.* **1.** [One who suffers] — *Syn.* prey, sacrifice, immolation, sufferer, wretch, quarry; game, hunted, offering, scapegoat, martyr, wretch.
**2.** [One who is easily deceived] — *Syn.* dupe, gull, fool, cat's paw, tool, hireling, boob, gudgeon, sucker★, mark★, easy pickings★, pushover★, john★, softie★.

**victimize,** *v.* — *Syn.* cheat, swindle, dupe, trick, fool; see also **deceive**.

**victor,** *n.* — *Syn.* winner, vanquisher, conqueror, champion, prize winner.

**Victorian,** *modif.* **1.** [An historical designation] — *Syn.* early Victorian, mid-Victorian, late Victorian, nineteenth-century.
**2.** [Conventional] — *Syn.* stuffy, strait-laced, mawkish; see **prudish**.
**3.** [Decorated] — *Syn.* flowery, patterned, resplendent; see **ornate** 1.

**victorious,** *modif.* — *Syn.* winning, triumphant, mastering; see **successful**.

**victory,** *n.* **1.** [The overcoming of an opponent] — *Syn.* triumph, conquest, mastery, subjugation, overcoming, overthrow, master stroke, lucky stroke, winning, gaining, defeating, subduing, destruction, killing★, knockout★, ringer★, pushover★; see also **triumph** 1.
**2.** [An instance of victory, sense 1] — *Syn.* supremacy,

ascendancy, triumph, advantage, achievement, mission accomplished, success, a feather in one's cap★.

---

**SYN.** — **victory** implies the winning of a contest or struggle of any kind [a *victory* in battle, in sports, etc., her *victory* over cancer]; **conquest** implies a victory in which one subjugates others and brings them under complete control [the *conquests* of Napoleon]; **triumph** implies a victory in which one exults because of its outstanding and decisive character [the *triumphs* of modern medicine]

---

**victuals★,** *n.* — *Syn.* meals, fare, viands, sustenance, provisions, supplies; see also **food**.

**videotape,** *n.* — *Syn.* magnetic tape, video, recording; see **tape recorder, television**.

**vie,** *v.* — *Syn.* contend, strive, rival; see **compete**.

**view,** *n.* **1.** [A sight] — *Syn.* glimpse, look, panorama, aspect, show, appearance, scene, picture, tableau, spectacle.
**2.** [A vista] — *Syn.* prospect, distance, opening, stretch, outlook, way, extended view, long view, avenue; see also **sense** 1.
**3.** [A picture] — *Syn.* illustration, origination, representation, composition, landscape, diorama, reproduction, design, imitation.
**4.** [An opinion] — *Syn.* belief, judgment, viewpoint; see **belief** 1, **judgment** 3, **opinion** 1, **viewpoint**.
*See Synonym Study at* OPINION.

**in view** — *Syn.* visible, in sight, not out of sight, perceptible, perceivable; see also **obvious** 1.

**in view of** — *Syn.* in light of, in consideration of, taking into consideration; see **because, considering**.

**on view** — *Syn.* displayed, on display, exposed; see **shown** 1;

**with a view to** — *Syn.* in order that, in order to, so that, anticipating; see **to** 4.

**view,** *v.* — *Syn.* observe, survey, inspect; see **see** 1.
*See Synonym Study at* SEE.

**viewer,** *n.* — *Syn.* spectator, watcher, onlooker; see **observer** 1.

**viewpoint,** *n.* — *Syn.* point of view, perspective, standpoint, angle, slant, position, stand, aspect, light, respect, attitude, ground, point of observation, outlook.

**vigil,** *n.* — *Syn.* watch, wakefulness, sleeplessness, sentry duty, wake; see also **watchfulness**.

**vigilance,** *n.* — *Syn.* alertness, acuity, watchfulness; see **attention** 1, 2, **diligence**.

**vigilant,** *modif.* — *Syn.* alert, watchful, keenly aware; see **careful, observant** 1, 2.
*See Synonym Study at* WATCHFUL.

**vignette,** *n.* **1.** [A design] — *Syn.* sketch, engraving, headpiece; see **design** 1.
**2.** [A story] — *Syn.* scenario, anecdote, sketch, novelette, scene; see also **story**.

**vigor,** *n.* **1.** [Activity] — *Syn.* exercise, action, energy, motion, quickness, raciness, stalwartness, alertness, agility, nimbleness, liveliness; see also **vitality**. — *Ant.* SLOWNESS, sluggishness, slothfulness.
**2.** [Force] — *Syn.* strength, vim, power, intensity, urgency, lustiness, virility, manliness, violence, vehemence. — *Ant.* WEAKNESS, impotence, effeminacy.
**3.** [Health] — *Syn.* haleness, soundness, well-being, endurance, hardiness, vitality; see also **health** 1. — *Ant.* DISEASE, feebleness, ill-health.

**vigorous,** *modif.* **1.** [Showing or requiring energy] — *Syn.* energetic, lively, dynamic, strenuous; see **active** 2.

**2.** [Strong and healthy] — *Syn.* robust, strong, hardy; see **healthy** 1, **strong** 1.

**3.** [Forceful] — *Syn.* powerful, strong, potent, zealous; see **active** 1, **persuasive**.

*See Synonym Study at* ACTIVE.

**vigorously,** *modif.* — *Syn.* energetically, alertly, eagerly, quickly, nimbly, agilely, strenuously, resolutely, firmly, forcibly, forcefully, urgently, unfalteringly, purposefully, actively, boldly, adventurously, zealously, lustily, vibrantly, robustly, stoutly, hardily, wholeheartedly, earnestly, warmly, fervidly, passionately, sincerely, devoutly, appreciatively, with heart and soul, healthily, fearlessly, intrepidly, mightily, decidedly, by brute force, to good account, like blazes★; see also **powerfully**. — *Ant.* CALMLY, aimlessly, slowly.

**vile,** *modif.* — *Syn.* despicable, foul, loathsome, depraved; see **mean** 3, **offensive** 2, **shameful** 1, 2, **wicked** 1.

*See Synonym Study at* MEAN.

**vilify,** *v.* — *Syn.* defame, revile, denounce; see **censure**, **slander**.

**villa,** *n.* — *Syn.* country property, suburban residence, dwelling; see **home** 1.

**village,** *n.* — *Syn.* hamlet, small town, community, settlement, center, thorp (British).

**villain,** *n.* — *Syn.* scoundrel, knave, brute; see **rascal**.

**villainous,** *modif.* **1.** [Depraved] — *Syn.* evil, criminal, vicious; see **wicked** 1, 2.

**2.** [Disagreeable] — *Syn.* detestable, objectionable, contrary; see **offensive** 2.

**villainy,** *n.* — *Syn.* depravity, knavery, corruptness, wickedness; see **evil** 1.

**vim,** *n.* — *Syn.* energy, pep, power, lustiness, vigor, action, spirit.

**vindicate,** *v.* **1.** [To clear] — *Syn.* acquit, free, absolve; see **absolve**, **excuse**.

**2.** [To defend] — *Syn.* plead for, second, support; see **defend** 3.

**3.** [To justify] — *Syn.* prove, bear out, warrant; see **justify** 2.

*See Synonym Study at* ABSOLVE.

**vindication,** *n.* — *Syn.* defense, acquittal, clearance, justification, proof, explanation, exoneration, exculpation, support, absolution, pardon. — *Ant.* BLAME, charge, conviction.

**vindictive,** *modif.* — *Syn.* revengeful, retaliatory, unforgiving, implacable, vengeful, unrelenting, resentful, spiteful; see also **cruel** 1, **ruthless** 1, 2. — *Ant.* KIND, generous, forgiving.

---

**SYN.** — **vindictive** stresses the unforgiving nature of one who is animated by a desire to get even with another for a wrong or injury *[vindictive* feelings*]*; **vengeful** and **revengeful** more directly stress the strong impulsion to action and the actual seeking of vengeance *[a vengeful,* or *revengeful,* foe*]*; **spiteful** implies a mean or malicious vindictiveness *[spiteful* gossip*]*

---

**vindictively,** *modif.* — *Syn.* cruelly, vengefully, spitefully; see **brutally**, **wrongly** 1, 2.

**vine,** *n.* — *Syn.* creeper, climbing plant, creeping plant, trailing plant, stem climber, leaf climber, tendril climber; see also **plant**.

Vines and creeping plants include: grapevine, honeysuckle, trumpet vine, runner vine, clematis, wisteria, bittersweet, English ivy, Virginia creeper, poison ivy, blackberry, raspberry, briar, rambler, teaberry, dewberry, morning-glory, woodbine, hopvine, bougainvil-

lea, jasmine, pea vine, watermelon, canteloupe, cucumber, wild cucumber, squash, gourd, pumpkin, passion flower.

**vinegar,** *n.* Types of vinegar include: cider, white, malt, beer, wine, tarragon, raspberry, beetroot, dilute, balsamic, rice, herb, fruit; see also **acid**.

**vineyard,** *n.* — *Syn.* grapevines, vines, grapes, wine terraces, arbor, grape arbor; see also **orchard**.

**vintage,** *modif.* — *Syn.* selected, choice, saved; see **excellent**, **old** 3.

**vintage,** *n.* — *Syn.* crop, grapes, wine, year, a good wine.

**violate,** *v.* **1.** [To transgress] — *Syn.* outrage, disrupt, infringe, break, tamper with; see also **meddle** 1.

**2.** [To rape] — *Syn.* dishonor, defile, ravish, molest, debauch, attack.

**3.** [To desecrate] — *Syn.* profane, defile, despoil, lay waste.

**violation,** *n.* **1.** [Transgression] — *Syn.* infringement, infraction, negligence, misbehavior, nonobservance, violating, shattering, transgressing, forcible trespass, trespassing, contravention, breach, breaking, rupture, flouting; see also **crime** 1, **sin**.

**2.** [Rape] — *Syn.* ravishment, assault, dishonor, defilement, mistreatment, outrage, debasement, degradation, pollution, invasion, subjugation, desecration, doing violence to; see also **disgrace** 2.

**3.** [Destruction] — *Syn.* demolition, ruin, devastation; see **destruction** 1, 2.

**violence,** *n.* **1.** [Violent disturbance] — *Syn.* rampage, tumult, disorder, clash, onslaught, struggle, destruction; see also **confusion** 1, **disturbance** 2, **uproar**.

**2.** [Violent conduct] — *Syn.* fury, force, vehemence, injury, frenzy, brutality, savagery; see also **intensity** 1.

**violent,** *modif.* **1.** [Showing power] — *Syn.* strong, powerful, forceful, forcible, rough, mighty, great, potent, coercive; see also **sense** 2. — *Ant.* QUIET, peaceful, easy-going.

**2.** [Showing strong emotions] — *Syn.* furious, mad, savage, fierce, passionate, splitting, vehement, frenzied, demonic, demoniac, frantic, fuming, enraged, disturbed, agitated, impassioned, impetuous, urgent, maddened, aroused, inflamed, distraught, infatuated, hysterical, blue in the face★. — *Ant.* CALM, appeased, quieted.

**3.** [Intense] — *Syn.* great, vehement, extreme; see **intense**.

**4.** [Characterized by the use of violence] — *Syn.* destructive, destructible, murderous, homicidal, brutal, rampageous. — *Ant.* EXPECTED, deliberate, awaited.

**5.** [Harsh] — *Syn.* drastic, hard, stringent; see **severe** 2.

**violently,** *modif.* **1.** [Characterized by violent actions] — *Syn.* destructively, forcibly, forcefully, combatively, powerfully, strongly, coercively, flagrantly, outrageously, overwhelmingly, compellingly, disturbingly, turbulently, stormily, ruinously, stubbornly, with violence, in a violent manner, abruptly, noisily, with a vengeance, like fury, rebelliously, riotously; see also **fiercely**, **vigorously**. — *Ant.* PEACEFULLY, quietly, weakly.

**2.** [Characterized by violent emotions] — *Syn.* furiously, angrily, vehemently, frantically, fiercely, hysterically, hilariously, passionately, urgently, madly, frenziedly, ardently, enthusiastically, impulsively. — *Ant.* MILDLY, gently, undisturbedly.

**violet,** *modif.* — *Syn.* lavender, mauve, purplish; see **purple**.

**violet,** *n.* Varieties of violets include: purple, white, yellow, southern wood, African, Pacific coast wood, sweet, Parma, bird's foot, dog's tooth, Rouen, Russian, early blue, bog blue, arrow-leaved, striped, beaked, Canada, round-leaved, hairy yellow, prairie yellow, pine, mountain; see also **flower** 2.

**violin,** *n.* — *Syn.* fiddle, violinette, crowd, crioth, rebec, gusla; see also **musical instrument.**
Violinlike instruments include: viol, viola, violoncello, cello, double bass, string bass.
Famous violins include: Cremona, Amati, Steiner, Klotz, Vuillaume, Forrest, Stradivarius, Guarnerius.

**violinist,** *n.* — *Syn.* musician, technician, virtuoso, instrumentalist, player, performer, fiddler.

**V.I.P.\*,** *n.* — *Syn.* very important person, notable, celebrity; see **leader** 2, **personage** 2.

**viper,** *n.* Types of vipers include: adder, asp, cobra, rhinoceros viper, puff adder, tree viper, blowing viper, black viper, pit viper, rattlesnake, copperhead, water moccasin, fer-de-lance, bushmaster, cottonmouth, sidewinder; see also **reptile, snake.**

**viperous,** *modif.* — *Syn.* lethal, deadly, venomous; see **poisonous.**

**virago,** *n.* — *Syn.* scold, vixen, ogress; see **hag, shrew.**

**virgin,** *modif.* **1.** [Chaste] — *Syn.* maidenly, pure, modest, virginal; see **chaste** 2, 3.
**2.** [Original or natural] — *Syn.* undisturbed, fresh, new, untamed; see **natural** 3, **original** 1, 3.

**virgin,** *n.* — *Syn.* maiden, unmarried woman, spinster, girl, *virgo intacta* (Latin).

**Virgin,** *n.* — *Syn.* Madonna, Blessed Virgin Mary, Queen of Saints, Our Lady, Mother of God, Mary, the Queen of Heaven, Queen of Angels, Star of the Sea, The Virgin Mother, Immaculate Conception, Immaculate Mary, BVM\*; see also **saint** 2.

**virginity,** *n.* — *Syn.* maidenhood, girlhood, spinsterhood, celibacy; see **chastity, virtue** 1.

**virile,** *modif.* **1.** [Manly] — *Syn.* masculine, potent, manly, macho; see **male, manly, masculine** 2.
**2.** [Forceful] — *Syn.* vigorous, forceful, energetic, robust; see **strong** 1.
*See Synonym Study at* MALE.

**virility,** *n.* — *Syn.* potency, masculinity, manliness, machismo; see **manhood** 2.

**virtual,** *modif.* — *Syn.* in essence, in effect, tantamount to, implicit, practical, in practice, in conduct, pragmatic.

**virtually,** *modif.* — *Syn.* for all practical purposes, practically, implicitly; see **essentially.**

**virtue,** *n.* **1.** [Moral excellence] — *Syn.* ideal, ethic, morality, goodness, righteousness, uprightness, ethical conduct, ethicality, good thing, respectability, rectitude, honor, honesty, candor, merit, fineness, character, excellence, value, chastity, quality, worth, kindness, innocence, generosity, trustworthiness, faithfulness, consideration.
The cardinal virtues of ancient Greek philosophy are the following: justice, prudence, temperance, fortitude.
The cardinal *or* theological virtues of the Christian church are the following: faith, hope, charity *or* love. — *Ant.* EVIL, immorality, depravity.
**2.** [An individual excellence] — *Syn.* quality, characteristic, attribute, temper, way, trait, feature, accomplishment, achievement, property, distinction, capacity, power. — *Ant.* LACK, inability, incapacity.
**3.** [Probity in sexual conduct] — *Syn.* virginity, purity, decency; see **chastity.**

**by virtue of** — *Syn.* on the grounds of, because of, looking toward; see **because.**

**virtuoso,** *n.* — *Syn.* maestro, artiste, expert, dilettante; see **master** 3, **musician.**

**virtuous,** *modif.* — *Syn.* good, upright, moral, chaste; see **chaste** 2, **moral** 1, **noble** 1, 2, **righteous** 1, **worthy.**

*See Synonym Study at* CHASTE, MORAL.

**virulent,** *modif.* **1.** [Deadly] — *Syn.* destructive, venomous, injurious; see **poisonous.**
**2.** [Hostile] — *Syn.* antagonistic, spiteful, hateful; see **unfriendly** 1.

**virus,** *n.* **1.** [An infection] — *Syn.* sickness, communicability, illness; see **disease, infection.**
**2.** [An organism] — *Syn.* microorganism, bacillus, phage; see **germ** 3.

**visa,** *n.* — *Syn.* endorsement, permission, entry papers, signed passport; see **permit.**

**visage,** *n.* — *Syn.* face, countenance, physiognomy; see **appearance** 1.
*See Synonym Study at* FACE.

**viscera,** *n.* — *Syn.* intestines, entrails, bowels; see **insides.**

**visceral,** *modif.* — *Syn.* instinctive, intuitive, emotional, physical, gut\*.

**viscid,** *modif.* — *Syn.* viscous, cohesive, syrupy; see **adhesive, thick** 3.

**viscosity,** *n.* — *Syn.* stickiness, viscidity, mucosity, sliminess; see **coherence** 1, **thickness** 1.

**vise,** *n.* — *Syn.* clamp, holder, swivel vise, universal vise, carpenter's vise; see also **fastener.**

**visibility,** *n.* — *Syn.* perceptibility, discernibility, distinctness, range of vision; see **clarity.**

**visible,** *modif.* — *Syn.* apparent, evident, noticeable; see **obvious** 1.

**vision,** *n.* **1.** [The faculty of sight] — *Syn.* sight, perception, perceiving, range of view, optics, eyesight.
**2.** [Understanding] — *Syn.* foresight, discernment, breadth of view, insight, penetration, intuition, divination, astuteness, keenness, foreknowledge, prescience, farsightedness; see also **acumen.**
**3.** [Something seen through powers of the mind] — *Syn.* imagination, poetic insight, fancy, fantasy, image, concept, conception, ideality, idea; see also **thought** 1, 2.
**4.** [Something seen by other than normal sight] — *Syn.* revelation, hallucination, trance, ecstasy, phantom, apparition, ghost, wraith, specter, apocalypse, nightmare, spirit, warlock; see also **fantasy** 2, **illusion** 1.

**visionary,** *modif.* **1.** [Impractical] — *Syn.* ideal, idealistic, ideological, unrealistic, romantic, utopian, quixotic, in the clouds\*; see also **impractical.** — *Ant.* PRACTICAL, realistic, pragmatical.
**2.** [Imaginary] — *Syn.* not real, chimerical, delusory, dreamy; see **fantastic** 1, **imaginary.**

**visit,** *n.* — *Syn.* social call, call, appointment, interview, formal call, talk, evening, stay, holiday, visitation; see also **vacation.**

**visit,** *v.* **1.** [To call upon the sick] — *Syn.* call upon, bring comfort, bring cheer, bring help, minister; see also **attend** 2, **encourage** 2, **nurse.**
**2.** [To live with for a short time] — *Syn.* stay with, dwell with, stop with, stop by, call at, call on, call upon, come around, be the guest of, make a visit, sojourn awhile, revisit; see also **sense** 4.
**3.** [To afflict] — *Syn.* trouble, inflict, pain; see **bother** 3.
**4.** [To stop for business or pleasure] — *Syn.* call on, call upon, make one's compliments to, look in on, visit with, call for, stop off, stop in, stop over, have an appointment with, pay a visit to, tour, take in\*, drop in on\*, hit\*, look around\*, look up\*, be closeted with\*, go over to\*, look in\*, drop over\*, pop in\*, have a date\*; see also **sense** 2.

**visitation,** *n.* **1.** [An affliction] — *Syn.* calamity, trouble, adversity, misfortune, distress, pain, sorrow, sickness; see also **difficulty** 1, 2.

**2.** [A visit] — *Syn.* call, sojourn, temporary stay; see **visiting**.

**visiting,** *modif.* **1.** [On a visit] — *Syn.* staying, stopping, residing temporarily, stopping over, stopping off, wintering, summering, calling.

**2.** [Abroad in an official or a semiofficial capacity] — *Syn.* sojourning, calling upon, touring, inspecting, reviewing, traveling, itinerant.

**visiting,** *n.* — *Syn.* calling upon, staying, stopping over, sojourning, touring, viewing, reviewing, inspecting, wintering, summering, dwelling briefly.

**visitor,** *n.* — *Syn.* guest, caller, company, visitant, official inspector.

---

**SYN.** — **visitor** is the general term for one who comes to see a person or spend some time in a place, whether for social, business, or professional reasons, or for pleasure *[visitors to the Grand Canyon]*; **visitant** now generally suggests a supernatural rather than a human visitor and, in biology, is applied to a migratory bird in any of its temporary resting places; **guest** applies to one who is hospitably entertained at the home of another, as at dinner, or, by extension, to one who pays for his lodgings, meals, etc. at a hotel; **caller** applies to one who makes a brief, often formal visit, as for business or social reasons

---

**vista,** *n.* — *Syn.* sight, long view, prospect; see **view** 1, 2.

**visual,** *modif.* — *Syn.* seen, ocular, optic, beheld, optical, imaged, perceptible, viewed, of the eye, of the vision, visible; see also **observed** 1, **obvious** 1.

**visualize,** *v.* — *Syn.* see in the mind's eye, imagine, envision, picture mentally, conceive, conjure up, call up, call to mind, fancy, reflect.

**vital,** *modif.* **1.** [Necessary] — *Syn.* essential, contribute, indispensable, requisite; see **important** 1, **necessary** 1.

**2.** [Alive] — *Syn.* live, animate, animated; see **alive** 1.

**3.** [Vigorous] — *Syn.* lively, energetic, lusty; see **active** 1, 2.

*See Synonym Study at* ALIVE.

**vitality,** *n.* — *Syn.* life, liveliness, animation, vim, vigor, intensity, continuity, endurance, energy, spirit, ardor, audacity, spunk, fervor, verve, venturesomeness, pep\*, punch\*, get-up-and-go\*.

**vitalize,** *v.* — *Syn.* animate, strengthen, energize, reanimate; see **animate** 1, **heal** 1.

*See Synonym Study at* ANIMATE.

**vitals,** *pl.n.* — *Syn.* organs, intestines, entrails; see **insides.**

**vitamin,** *n.* Vitamins important in human nutrition include: vitamin A, vitamin C, ascorbic acid, vitamin D, vitamin E, tocopherol, vitamin K, vitamin B1, thiamine, vitamin B2, riboflavin, vitamin B3, niacin, vitamin B5, pantothenic acid, vitamin B6, pyridoxine, vitamin B12, folacin, frolic acid, biotin; see also **medicine** 2.

**vitiate,** *v.* **1.** [To invalidate] — *Syn.* annul, recant, cancel, rescind; see **deny, revoke.**

**2.** [To corrupt] — *Syn.* spoil, impair, degrade, contaminate; see **corrupt** 1.

**3.** [To weaken morally] — *Syn.* debase, pervert, corrupt, deprave, debauch, blight.

**vitreous,** *modif.* — *Syn.* glassy, glasslike, thin, translucent, hyaline; see also **clear** 2, **transparent** 1.

**vitriolic,** *modif.* — *Syn.* biting, bitter, burning, sharp, caustic; see also **sarcastic.**

**vituperation,** *n.* — *Syn.* censure, disapproval, scolding,

verbal abuse; see **blame** 1.

**vituperative,** *modif.* — *Syn.* insulting, trenchant, censorious; see **critical** 2, **severe** 1.

**vivacious,** *modif.* — *Syn.* spirited, lively, animated, bubbly; see **active** 2, **happy** 1, **lively** 2.

*See Synonym Study at* LIVELY.

**vivacity,** *n.* — *Syn.* sprightliness, liveliness, animation; see **enthusiasm** 1, **life** 1.

**viva voce,** *modif.* — *Syn.* orally, vocally, articulately; see **oral.**

**vivid,** *modif.* **1.** [Brilliant] — *Syn.* shining, rich, glowing; see **bright** 1, 2.

**2.** [Distinct] — *Syn.* strong, striking, lucid; see **clear** 2, **definite** 2.

**3.** [Animated] — *Syn.* expressive, lively, vigorous; see **graphic** 1, 2.

**vividly,** *modif.* **1.** [Clearly] — *Syn.* distinctly, strongly, sharply; see **clearly** 1, 2.

**2.** [With brightness and color] — *Syn.* glowingly, strikingly, flamingly; see **brightly.**

**vividness,** *n.* — *Syn.* sharpness, distinctness, distinction; see **clarity.**

**vocabulary,** *n.* — *Syn.* wordlist, dictionary, lexicon, lexis, thesaurus, stock of words, glossary, *promptorium* (Latin), scientific vocabulary, literary vocabulary, wordhoard\*; see also **diction.**

**vocal,** *modif.* **1.** [Verbal] — *Syn.* expressed, uttered, voiced; see **oral, spoken.**

**2.** [Produced by the voice; *said especially of music*] — *Syn.* sung, scored for voice, vocalized, arranged for voice, full of voice, sonant, sounding, modulated; see also **musical** 1, **singing.**

**3.** [Outspoken] — *Syn.* free speaking, vociferous, unreserved; see **frank.**

**vocalist,** *n.* — *Syn.* chorister, songstress, caroler; see **musician, singer.**

**vocation,** *n.* **1.** [The work for which one has prepared] — *Syn.* calling, mission, pursuit; see **profession** 1.

**2.** [The work at which one is engaged] — *Syn.* employment, trade, occupation, duty, undertaking; see also **job** 1.

**vociferous,** *modif.* — *Syn.* clamorous, blatant, noisy, strident, boisterous, obstreperous; see also **loud** 1, **shrill.**

---

**SYN.** — **vociferous** suggests loud and unrestrained shouting or crying out *[a vociferous crowd, vociferous cheers]*; **clamorous** suggests an urgent or insistent vociferousness, as in demand or complaint *[clamorous protests]*; **blatant** implies a bellowing loudness and, hence, suggests vulgar or offensive noisiness, clamor, etc. *[blatant heckling]*; **strident** suggests a harsh, grating loudness *[a strident voice]*; **boisterous** implies roughness or turbulence and, hence, suggests unrestrained, noisy exuberance *[boisterous revels]*; **obstreperous** implies an unruliness that is noisy or boisterous in resisting control *[an obstreperous child]*

---

**vogue,** *n.* — *Syn.* fashion, style, mode, rage, trend, custom, practice, current practice, *dernier cri* (French); the thing\*; see also **fad.**

**in vague** — *Syn.* stylish, current, á la mode; see **fashionable, popular** 1.

*See Synonym Study at* FASHION.

**voice,** *n.* **1.** [A vocal sound] — *Syn.* speech, sound, call, cry, utterance, tongue, whistle, moan, groan, song, yell, hail, howl, yowl, bark, whine, whimper, mutter, murmur, shout, bleat, bray, neigh, whinny, roar, trumpet, cluck, honk, meow, hiss, quack; see also **noise** 1.— *Ant.* SILENCE, dumbness, deaf-mutism.

**2.** [Approval or opinion]— *Syn.* decision, wish, view; see **choice** 1, **opinion** 1.

**with one voice**— *Syn.* all together, by unanimous vote, without dissent; see **unanimously.**

**voice,** *v.*— *Syn.* assert, cry, sound, utter; see **talk** 1, **tell** 1.

*See Synonym Study at* UTTER.

**voiced,** *modif.*— *Syn.* vocal, sonant, sounded; see **oral, spoken.**

**voiceless,** *modif.*— *Syn.* dumb, mute, speechless, wordless, silent; see also **dumb** 1, **mute** 1.

*See Synonym Study at* DUMB.

**void,** *modif.* **1.** [Without force or effect]— *Syn.* barren, sterile, fruitless, meaningless, useless, invalid, vain, voided, unconfirmed, unratified, null and void, worthless, unsanctioned, set aside, avoided, forceless, unenforceable, voted out, ineffectual, ineffective, voidable.— *Ant.* VALID, in force, used.

**2.** [Empty]— *Syn.* unfilled, abandoned, unoccupied; see **empty** 1, **vacant** 2.

*See Synonym Study at* EMPTY.

**voile,** *n.*— *Syn.* cotton voile, wool voile, etamine, dress material, fabric; see also **cloth.**

**volatile,** *modif.* **1.** [Having the qualities of a gas]— *Syn.* light, airy, imponderable, subtle, buoyant, gaseous, gasiform, vaporous, vapory, vaporizable, evaporable, effervescent, expansive, resilient, elastic.— *Ant.* HEAVY, dense, solid.

**2.** [Having a sprightly temperament]— *Syn.* lively, light-hearted, vivacious, gay, animated, merry, flippant, teasing, playful, sprightly; see also **active** 1, 2, **happy** 1. — *Ant.* SOLEMN, demure, quiet.

**3.** [Liable to sudden change]— *Syn.* unstable, unpredictable, explosive; see **changeable** 1, 2.

**4.** [Fickle]— *Syn.* frivolous, capricious, whimsical; see **changeable** 1, **fickle** 2.

**volatility,** *n.* **1.** [Evaporation]— *Syn.* dryness, vaporization, volatilization; see **evaporation.**

**2.** [Airiness]— *Syn.* buoyancy, weightlessness, levity; see **lightness** 2.

**volcano,** *n.* Famous volcanoes include: Vesuvius, Etna, Pelee, Ararat, Kilauea, Mauna Loa, Mauna Kea, Wrangel, Krakatoa, Paricutin, Popocatepetl, Jokullo, Izalco, Quezaltenango, Conseguina, Mount Hood, Lassen Peak, Mount Shasta, Mount Baker, Mount St. Helens, Shishaldin, Erebus, Smerin, Gowong, Lamongong, Kirunga, Stromboli, Vulcano, Fujiyama, Orizaba, Pinatubo; see also **mountain** 1.

**volition,** *n.*— *Syn.* wish, will, conation, choice, election, preference; see also **desire** 1.

*See Synonym Study at* WILL.

**volitional,** *modif.*— *Syn.* willing, voluntary, free; see **optional.**

**volley,** *n.*— *Syn.* salvo, fusillade, round, burst, discharge, broadside, barrage, enfilade, cross-fire, curtain of fire; see also **fire** 2.

**voltage,** *n.*— *Syn.* electromotive force, electric potential, potential difference, charge; see **energy** 3.

**volubility,** *n.*— *Syn.* fluency, loquacity, garrulousness; see **eloquence** 1, **garrulity.**

**voluble,** *modif.*— *Syn.* talkative, glib, loquacious; see **fluent** 2.

*See Synonym Study at* TALKATIVE.

**volume,** *n.* **1.** [Quantity]— *Syn.* bulk, mass, amount; see **extent, quantity, size** 2.

**2.** [Contents]— *Syn.* cubical size, measure, dimen-

sions; see **capacity** 1.

**3.** [A book]— *Syn.* printed document, tome, pamphlet; see **book** 1.

**4.** [Degree of sound]— *Syn.* loudness, amplification, strength, decibels; see **sound** 2.

*See Synonym Study at* BULK.

**voluminous,** *modif.* **1.** [Large or extensive]— *Syn.* bulky, swelling, roomy, full; see **large** 1.

**2.** [*Having many folds]— *Syn.* many-folded, coiled, convoluted, full, covering, expansive, many-layered, abundant; see also **plentiful** 2.

**3.** [Profuse]— *Syn.* abounding, luxuriant, overflowing, copious, bountiful.

**voluntarily,** *modif.*— *Syn.* by preference, willingly, deliberately, optionally, spontaneously, freely, intentionally, by choice, of one's own choice, on one's own, in one's own sweet way, heart in hand, of one's own free will, on one's own hook, to one's heart's content, at one's discretion, on one's own initiative, with all one's heart.

**voluntary,** *modif.*— *Syn.* willing, willed, willful, intentional, deliberate, wished, freely, spontaneous; see also **optional.**

---

**SYN.** — **voluntary** implies the exercise of one's own free choice or will in an action, whether or not external influences are at work *[voluntary* services]; **intentional** applies to that which is done on purpose for a definite reason and is in no way accidental *[an intentional* slight]; **deliberate** implies full realization of the significance of what one intends to do and of its effects *[a deliberate* lie]; **willful** implies obstinate and perverse determination to follow one's own will despite influences, arguments, advice, etc. in opposition *[a willful* refusal]

---

**volunteer,** *n.*— *Syn.* enlistee, enlisted man, voluntary soldier, unpaid worker, charity worker, missionary, aide.

**volunteer,** *v.* **1.** [To make a proposal]— *Syn.* suggest, offer, bring forward; see **propose** 1.

**2.** [To offer one's services]— *Syn.* come forward, enlist, sign up, submit oneself, avoid conscription, take the initiative, present oneself, offer oneself, do on one's own volition, do of one's own free will, do on one's own authority, take the initiative, take upon oneself, speak up, stand up and be counted, go in*, chip in*, do on one's own hook*, take the bull by the horns*, stand on one's own feet*, take the bit between one's teeth*, paddle one's own canoe*, take the plunge*; see also **join** 2.

**volunteered,** *modif.*— *Syn.* offered, proffered, signed-up; see **enlisted.**

**voluptuous,** *modif.* **1.** [Suited to rich satisfaction of the senses]— *Syn.* luxurious, rich, profuse, extravagant, excessive, indulgent, self-gratifying, pleasurable, self-indulgent, hedonic, hedonistic, Sybaritic, pleasure-loving, epicurian, opulent, sumptuous.— *Ant.* SIMPLE, plain, bare.

**2.** [Delighting in satisfying the senses]— *Syn.* wanton, sensual, sensuous, dissipated, carnal, dissolute, licentious, lascivious, libidinous, lustful, rakish, indulging, fast, lewd, salacious, bestial, erotic, ruttish, goatish. — *Ant.* SEVERE, ascetic, self-denying.

*See Synonym Study at* SENSUOUS.

**vomit,** *v.*— *Syn.* throw up, eject, bring up, spit up, dry heave, be seasick, hurl forth, retch, ruminate, regurgitate, give forth, discharge, belch forth, spew out, spew up, puke*, barf*, toss one's cookies*, lose one's lunch*, chunder* (Australian).

**voracious,** *modif.* — *Syn.* insatiable, gross, ravening; see **greedy** 1, 2.

**voracity,** *n.* — *Syn.* gluttony, edacity*, rapacity; see **greed.**

**vortex,** *n.* — *Syn.* whirlpool, eddy, whirlwind, waterspout, spiral.

**vote,** *n.* **1.** [A ballot] — *Syn.* tally, ticket, slip of paper, ball, yes or no, rising vote, Australian ballot, secret ballot, viva-voce vote.
**2.** [A decision] — *Syn.* will, wish, referendum, choice, majority, unanimous vote, plebiscite; see also **election** 2.
**3.** [The right to vote] — *Syn.* suffrage, the franchise, manhood suffrage, universal suffrage, women's suffrage; see also **right** 1.

**vote,** *v.* — *Syn.* ballot, cast a vote, cast a ballot, give a vote, enact, establish, determine, bring about, effect, grant, confer, declare*, suggest*, propose*; see also **choose** 1, **decide.**

**voted,** *modif.* — *Syn.* decided, willed, chosen; see **named** 2.

**vote down,** *v.* — *Syn.* put down, decide against, refuse, blackball, veto; see also **deny.**

**vote for,** *v.* — *Syn.* give one's vote to, give one's ballot to, cast a ballot for, second; see **support** 2.

**vote in,** *v.* — *Syn.* elect, put in, put in office; see **choose** 1.

**vote out,** *v.* — *Syn.* reject, remove from office, vote down; see **defeat** 1, **dismiss** 1, 2.

**voter,** *n.* — *Syn.* elector, balloter, registered voter, member of a constituency, member of the electorate; part of the farm vote, labor vote, urban vote, etc.; vote caster, absentee voter, native, naturalized citizen, poll-tax payer, taxpayer, resident voter, stay-at-home voter, straw voter, proxy voter, one of the folks back home, ballot-box stuffer, floater, fagot voter; see also **citizen.**

**voting,** *modif.* — *Syn.* electing, balloting, choosing, deciding; see **electoral, selecting.**

**voting,** *n.* — *Syn.* balloting, taking the yeas and nays, polling, holding the election, choosing, deciding, casting votes.

**votive,** *modif.* — *Syn.* pledged, committed, dedicated; see **promised.**

**vouch,** *v.* — *Syn.* assert, aver, attest, warrant, affirm, verify, confirm, guarantee, asseverate, declare, testify, bear testimony, corroborate, protest, assure, predicate, profess, put forth, maintain, contend, depose, avow,

swear, take affidavit, take a Bible oath, go bail on, kiss the Book; see also **endorse** 2. — *Ant.* DENY, repudiate, discard.

**voucher,** *n.* — *Syn.* declaration, affirmation, certification, statement, chit; see also **confirmation** 1, **receipt** 2.

**vow,** *n.* — *Syn.* promise, affiance, pledge, solemn assertion, asseveration.

**vow,** *v.* — *Syn.* promise, resolve, pledge, swear, declare, take a vow; see also **promise** 1, **vouch.**

**vowel,** *n.* — *Syn.* vocoid, open-voiced sound, vowel sound, glide, diphthong, digraph; see also **consonant, letter** 1.
Linguistic terms for vowel sounds include: high, mid, low, open, close, front, back, central, flat, rounded, unrounded, tense, slack, stressed, unstressed, nasal, nasalized, labial, labialized, clipped, diphthongized.
In English spelling, symbols to represent vowels include: *a, e, i, o, u, w, y.*

**voyage,** *n.* — *Syn.* tour, trip, excursion; see **journey.**
*See Synonym Study at* TRIP.

**vulcanize,** *v.* — *Syn.* subject to vulcanization, treat, weld; see **harden** 1, 3, **join** 1, **repair.**

**vulgar,** *modif.* **1.** [Lacking in refinement or taste] — *Syn.* coarse, crude, crass, unrefined, uncouth, indelicate, boorish, uncultivated, gross, low, common, tasteless, inelegant, cheap, ostentatious, overdone, pretentious, gaudy, tacky*; see also **rude** 1, **tasteless** 3. — *Ant.* refined, elegant, genteel.
**2.** [Obscene] — *Syn.* indecent, obscene, lewd; see **lewd** 1.
**3.** [Common] — *Syn.* ordinary, familiar, popular, colloquial; see **colloquial, common** 1.
*See Synonym Study at* COARSE, COMMON.

**vulgarian,** *n.* — *Syn.* parvenu, snob, boor; see **braggart.**

**vulgarism,** *n.* — *Syn.* slang, swearing, solecism; see **curse** 1.

**vulgarity,** *n.* — *Syn.* impudence, discourtesy, crudity, indecency; see **rudeness.**

**vulnerable,** *modif.* — *Syn.* unprotected, helpless, defenseless, exposed, assailable; see also **unsafe, weak** 2, 5.

**vulture,** *n.* Types of vultures include: black vulture, condor, Egyptian vulture, king vulture, lammergeier, griffon, turkey vulture; see also **bird** 1.

# W

**wad,** *n.* **1.** [A little heap] — *Syn.* bundle, pile, mass, block, gathering, lump, tuft, clump, bunch.
**2.** [Soft materials used as a stopper or padding] — *Syn.* bushing, batting, backing, upholstery, plug, stop, pad, inner lining, interlining, underlining, coating, wadding, facing.
**3.** [*A considerable amount of money] — *Syn.* fortune, purse, bankroll, mint*; see **wealth** 2.
**wad,** *v.* **1.** [To stuff] — *Syn.* pad, back, cushion, stop up, reinforce, interline, underline, face, quilt, sheathe, upholster; see also **plug.**
**2.** [To roll into a wad] — *Syn.* crimple, wrinkle, compress, rumple.
**waddle,** *v.* — *Syn.* sway, wiggle, totter; see **walk** 1.
**wade,** *v.* — *Syn.* walk in the water, paddle, get one's feet wet; see **swim.**
**wade in,** *v.* — *Syn.* start, attempt, initiate proceedings; see **tackle** 1.
**wafer,** *n.* — *Syn.* biscuit, hardtack, slice, host, Eucharist; see also **cracker.**
**waft,** *v.* — *Syn.* convey, transport, transmit, float, blow; see also **carry.**
**wag,** *n.* — *Syn.* wit, joker, comedian; see **clown.**
**wag,** *v.* — *Syn.* shake, waggle, swing, sway, shimmy, move from side to side.
**wage,** *n.* — *Syn.* wages, pay, stipend, fee, salary, earnings, payment, emolument; see also **pay** 2.

---

*SYN.* — **wage** (also often **wages**) applies to money paid an employee at relatively short intervals, often daily, or weekly, esp. for manual or physical labor; **salary** applies to fixed compensation usually paid at longer intervals, often monthly or semimonthly, esp. to clerical or professional workers; **stipend** is a somewhat lofty substitute for **salary**, or it is applied to a pension or similar fixed payment; **fee** applies to the payment requested or given for professional services, as of a doctor, lawyer, artist, etc.; **pay** is a general term equivalent to any of the preceding, but it is specifically used of compensation to members of the armed forces; **emolument** is an elevated substitute for **salary** or **wages** and may refer to additional benefits and perquisites

---

**wage,** *v.* — *Syn.* conduct, make, carry on, engage in, prosecute, pursue.
**wager,** *n.* — *Syn.* risk, hazard, challenge; see **bet.**
**waggish,** *modif.* — *Syn.* humorous, playful, jocular; see **witty.**
**waggle,** *v.* — *Syn.* wag, play back and forth, sway, shimmy; see **wiggle.**
**wagon,** *n.* — *Syn.* wain, cart, pushcart, buggy, truck, coach, carriage, caravan, car, covered wagon, prairie schooner, Conestoga wagon, cab.
**waif,** *n.* — *Syn.* homeless child, stray, ragamuffin; see **orphan.**
**wail,** *v.* — *Syn.* moan, weep, lament; see **cry** 1, **mourn** 1.
*See Synonym Study at* CRY.

**waist,** *n.* **1.** [Part of the torso] — *Syn.* waistline, middle, midriff, diaphragm, groin, waistband, waist measurement; see also **abdomen.**
**2.** [Part of an upper garment] — *Syn.* shirtwaist, bodice, bib, trunk; see **clothes.**
**waistcoat,** *n.* — *Syn.* vest, jacket, weskit; see **clothes.**
**wait,** *n.* — *Syn.* halt, interim, time wasted; see **delay** 1, **pause** 1, 2.
**wait,** *v.* **1.** [To await] — *Syn.* expect, anticipate, tarry, pause, wait for, look for, delay for, watch for, pray for, abide, dally, remain, idle, bide one's time, mark time, fill time, wait up for, sit up for, stay up for, lie in wait for, ambush, lie low*, hole up*, hang around*, stick around*, cool one's heels*. — *Ant.* LEAVE, HURRY, act.
**2.** [To attend at table] — *Syn.* serve, deliver, tend, act as waiter, act as waitress, arrange, set, ready, place on the table, help, portion, bus dishes.
**3.** [To be left] — *Syn.* have left, be on the agenda, have to do; see **remain** 3.

---

*SYN.* — **wait** suggests remaining in place in anticipation of something /*wait* for me at the library/; **stay,** a more general term, implies a continuing in a specified place /*stay* there until you hear from me/; **remain** specifically suggests a staying behind while others go /he alone *remained* at home/; **abide,** now somewhat archaic, implies a staying fixed for a relatively long period, as in a settled residence /he came for a visit and has been *abiding* here since/; **tarry** and **linger** imply a staying on after the required or expected time for departure, **linger** esp. implying that this is deliberate, as from reluctance to leave /we *tarried* in town two days, he *lingered* at his sweetheart's door/

---

**waiter,** *n.* — *Syn.* headwaiter, steward, attendant, server, footman, servant, innkeeper, host, proprietor, lackey, *garçon* (French), counterman, busboy, waitperson*, waitstaff*, tray trotter*, soup juggler*, soda jerk*.
**wait for,** *v.* — *Syn.* await, expect, stay up for, sit up for; see **remain** 1, **wait** 1.
**waiting,** *modif.* — *Syn.* standing, languishing, in line, next in turn, expecting, hoping for, marking time, in wait, cooling one's heels*. — *Ant.* MOVING, hurrying, acting.
**waiting room,** *n.* — *Syn.* salon, lounge, restroom, terminal, hall, antechamber, foyer, preparation room, depot, station.
**wait on,** *v.* **1.** [To serve] — *Syn.* accommodate, provide, attend; see **serve** 4, **wait** 2.
**2.** [To result] — *Syn.* ensue, issue, arise; see **happen** 2.
**waitress,** *n.* — *Syn.* female attendant, server, servant, hostess, counter girl, waitperson*, waitstaff*, B-girl.
**wait up for,** *v.* — *Syn.* wait for, expect, stay up for, stay awake; see **wait** 1, **worry** 2.
**waive,** *v.* — *Syn.* forgo, abandon, relinquish, give up, surrender, disclaim, sign away, set aside, put aside, dismiss,

reject, ignore, dispense with, suspend, disregard, postpone, reserve, defer, shelve, table.

---

*SYN.* — **waive** suggests a voluntary giving up by refraining from insisting on one's right or claim to something /to *waive* a jury trial/; **relinquish** implies a giving up of something desirable and connotes compulsion or the force of necessity /we will not *relinquish* our advantage/; **abandon**, in this connection, implies a complete and final relinquishment, as because of weariness, discouragement, etc. /do not *abandon* hope/; **forgo** implies the denial to oneself of something, as for reasons of expediency or altruism /I must *forgo* the pleasure of your company this evening/

---

**waiver,** *n.* — *Syn.* relinquishment, abandonment, forgoing, reservation, refusal, rejection, disclaimer, postponement, tabling.

**wake,** *n.* **1.** [A track] — *Syn.* furrow, wash, following wave; see **track** 2.

**2.** [A funeral] — *Syn.* watch, deathwatch, vigil, viewing, obsequies, funeral service, last rites; see also **funeral** 1.

**wake,** *v.* **1.** [To waken another] — *Syn.* call, rouse, bring to life, arouse, awaken, wake up, prod, shake, nudge, break into one's slumber.

**2.** [To become awake] — *Syn.* get up, awake, be roused, get out of bed, open one's eyes, rise, arise, stir, stretch oneself, tumble out of bed*.

**3.** [To begin to comprehend] — *Syn.* notice, see, grasp; see **understand** 1.

**wakeful,** *modif.* **1.** [Watchful] — *Syn.* alert, vigilant, wary; see **careful.**

**2.** [Restless] — *Syn.* sleepless, waking, insomnious; see **restless** 1.

**wakefulness,** *n.* **1.** [Watchfulness] — *Syn.* vigilance, alertness, wariness; see **attention** 1, **prudence.**

**2.** [Restlessness] — *Syn.* sleeplessness, somnambulism, pernoctation; see **insomnia.**

**wake up,** *interj.* — *Syn.* rise and shine, arise, get up, awake, awaken, get going, get cracking*.

**waking,** *modif.* — *Syn.* wakeful, awake, wakened, conscious, growing conscious, stirring, arising, getting up, rising, acting, sharpened, alert. — *Ant.* ASLEEP, sleepy, dormant.

**walk,** *n.* **1.** [Manner of walking] — *Syn.* gait, tread, stride; see **step** 1.

**2.** [Course over which one walks] — *Syn.* pavement, sidewalk, pathway, footpath, trail, track, boardwalk, pier, promenade, avenue, street, road, alley, passage, dock, esplanade, platform, gangway; see also **street.**

**3.** [A short walking expedition] — *Syn.* stroll, ramble, turn, hike, promenade, airing, saunter, peregrination, tramp, trek, constitutional, perambulation, march, circuit, jaunt, tour.

**4.** [A base on balls; *in baseball*] — *Syn.* four balls, ticket to first*, handout*, Annie Oakley*, pass*.

**5.** [A station in life] — *Syn.* occupation, sphere of activity, position, line of work.

**walk,** *v.* **1.** [To move on foot] — *Syn.* step, pace, march, tread, amble, stroll, hike, saunter, wander, ambulate, ramble, go out for an airing, go out for an outing, take a walk, promenade, trudge, tramp, trek, tour, take a turn, roam, rove, perambulate, meander, traipse about, patrol, file off, knock about*, knock around*, hoof it*, jog it*, toddle along*, shuffle*, wend one's way*, bend one's steps*, locomote*, cruise*.

**2.** [To cause to move on foot] — *Syn.* lead, drive, exercise, train, order a march, escort, accompany, take for a walk.

**3.** [To give a base on balls; *in baseball*] — *Syn.* let pass, give free passage*, give a ticket to first*, issue an Annie Oakley*.

**walk all over*,** *v.* — *Syn.* subdue, trample on, beat down, beat up*; see **censure, rebuff** 1.

**walk away*,** *v.* — *Syn.* vanish, depart, split*; see **abandon** 1, 2, **leave** 1.

**walker,** *n.* — *Syn.* pedestrian, hiker, pilgrim, wanderer, wayfarer, trekker, rover, rambler, roamer, straggler, foot passenger, passerby, hitchhiker.

**walkie-talkie,** *n.* — *Syn.* portable transmitter and receiver, field radio, two-way radio; see **radio** 2.

**walking,** *modif.* — *Syn.* on foot, afoot, strolling, rambling, trudging, hiking, ambulant, touring, ambling, sauntering, tramping, marching, promenading, passing, roaming, wandering, wayfaring, trekking*, on shank's mare*, mushing*.

**walking papers*,** *n.* — *Syn.* discharge, dismissal, pink slip, severance pay; see **removal** 1.

**walking stick,** *n.* — *Syn.* cane, crutch, staff; see **stick.**

**walk off,** *v.* — *Syn.* depart, go one's own way, stalk off; see **leave** 1.

**walk off the job,** *v.* — *Syn.* quit, leave, go on strike; see **strike** 2.

**walk off with*,** *v.* — *Syn.* take, appropriate, pick up; see **steal.**

**walkout*,** *n.* — *Syn.* sit-down, boycott, demonstration; see **protest, strike** 1.

**walk out on,** *v.* — *Syn.* desert, leave, walk off from; see **abandon** 2.

**walkover*,** *n.* — *Syn.* easy win, conquest, triumph; see **victory** 1.

**walk with God,** *v.* — *Syn.* live a good life, live a pious life, live a holy life, be good, behave oneself, obey the moral law, conform, obey, worship.

**wall,** *n.* **1.** [A physical barrier] — *Syn.* partition, divider, dam, embankment, dike, ditch, bank, levee, stockade, fence, stone wall, drywall, stone fence, parapet, retainer, rampart, bulwark, palisade, fort, cliff, barricade, floodgate, sluice gate, paling, wattle, wattling.

**2.** [An obstacle; *figurative*] — *Syn.* barrier, obstruction, bar, cordon, entanglement, hurdle, resistance, defense, snag, hindrance, impediment, difficulty, limitation, restriction, retardation, knot, hitch, drawback, stumbling block, check, stop, curb, red tape*, fly in the ointment*, bottleneck*, red herring*, detour*.

**3.** [A side; *said of a cavity or space*] — *Syn.* flank, partition, surface, brickwork, casing, bulkhead, façade, septum, precipice, cliff, bluff, outer envelope.

**wallet,** *n.* — *Syn.* billfold, purse, pocketbook, change purse, notecase, card case, container, moneybag, French purse, *portemonnaie* (French); see also **folder** 2.

**wallop,** *v.* — *Syn.* thump, thrash, strike; see **beat** 2, **hit** 1.

**wallow,** *v.* — *Syn.* grovel, welter, flounder, lie in, move around in, roll about in, bathe in, toss, immerse, be immersed in, besmirch oneself.

**wall up,** *v.* — *Syn.* close up, surround, wall in, wall out; see **enclose** 1.

**walnut,** *modif.* — *Syn.* mahogany, dark brown, reddish-brown; see **brown, red.**

**walnut,** *n.* — *Syn.* *Juglandaceae* (Latin), English walnut, black walnut, California walnut, butternut, shagbark*, hickory*, pecan*; see also **tree.**

**waltz,** *n.* — *Syn.* music in three-quarter time, dance step, box step, hesitation, Viennese waltz; see also **dance** 1.

**waltz,** *v.* — *Syn.* box step, whirl, ballroom dance, dance in three-quarter time; see **dance** 1.

**wampum*,** *n.* — *Syn.* change, cash, coins*; see **money** 1.

**wan,** *modif.* — *Syn.* colorless, sickly, blanched; see **pale** 1. *See Synonym Study at* PALE.

**wand,** *n.* — *Syn.* magic staff, rod, fairy staff, scepter, baton, divining rod, caduceus.

**wander,** *v.* **1.** [To stroll] — *Syn.* hike, ramble, saunter; see **roam, walk** 1.
**2.** [To speak or think incoherently] — *Syn.* stray, shift, digress; see **ramble** 2.

**wanderer,** *n.* — *Syn.* adventurer, voyager, gypsy, exile; see **explorer, traveler.**

**wandering,** *modif.* **1.** [Wandering in space] — *Syn.* roving, roaming, nomadic, meandering, restless, traveling, jaunting, trekking, drifting, straying, going off, strolling, ranging, prowling, ambulatory, ambulant, straggling, on the road, peripatetic, itinerant, roundabout, circuitous. — *Ant.* IDLE, home-loving, sedentary.
**2.** [Wandering in thought] — *Syn.* discursive, digressive, disconnected; see **incoherent** 2, **incongruous** 1.

**wane,** *v.* — *Syn.* decrease, decline, subside, abate, ebb, fade, fade away; see also **decrease** 1, **fade** 1.

---

SYN. — **wane** implies a fading or weakening of that which has reached a peak of force, excellence, etc. /his fame *waned* rapidly/; **abate** suggests a progressive lessening in degree, intensity, etc. /the fever is *abating*/; **ebb**, applied specifically to a fluctuating force, refers to one of the periods of recession or decline /their *ebbing* fortunes/; **subside** suggests a quieting or slackening of violent activity or turbulence /her temper had *subsided*/

---

**wangle\*,** *v.* — *Syn.* get, acquire, procure; see **obtain** 1.

**want,** *n.* **1.** [Need] — *Syn.* privation, dearth, shortage, poverty; see **lack** 1, 2, **poverty** 1.
**2.** [Desire] — *Syn.* wish, craving, demand; see **desire** 1. *See Synonym Study at* POVERTY.

**want,** *v.* **1.** [To desire] — *Syn.* desire, require, aspire, hanker after, have an urge for, incline toward, fancy, covet, crave, long for, lust for, have a fondness for, have a passion for, have ambition, thirst after, hunger after, be greedy for, ache\*, have a yen for\*, have an itch for\*.
**2.** [To lack] — *Syn.* be deficient in, be deprived of, require; see **need.** *See Synonym Study at* DESIRE, LACK.

**wanted,** *modif.* — *Syn.* needed, necessary, desired, in need of, sought after, in demand, requested, asked for. — *Ant.* SATISFIED, fulfilled, filled.

**wanting,** *modif.* **1.** [Deficient] — *Syn.* destitute, poor, in default of, deprived of, denuded of, bereft of, devoid of, empty of, bankrupt in, cut off, lacking, short, inadequate, defective, substandard, remiss, insufficient, incomplete, missing, absent, needed, unfulfilled, on the short end\*.
**2.** [Desiring] — *Syn.* desirous of, covetous, longing for; see **envious** 2, **greedy** 1.

**wanton,** *modif.* **1.** [Unrestrained] — *Syn.* extravagant, capricious, reckless, unreserved, unfettered, free, wayward, fluctuating, changeable, whimsical, fitful, variable, fanciful, inconstant, fickle, frivolous, volatile.
**2.** [Lewd] — *Syn.* libidinous, lustful, licentious; see **lewd** 1, 2.
**3.** [Deliberately malicious] — *Syn.* unprovoked, unfair, merciless, senseless, malicious, unjustifiable, unjust, malevolent.

**war,** *n.* — *Syn.* conflict, fighting, hostilities, combat; see **battle** 1; **fight** 1.
Types of wars include: air, guerrilla, shooting, ground, sea, amphibious, three-dimensional, trench, naval, aerial, land, push-button, hot, cold, total,

limited, civil, revolutionary, political, religious, preventive, world, offensive, defensive, biological, bacteriological, germ, chemical, atomic, nuclear, psychological, atomic-bacteriological-chemical, chemical-bacteriological-radiological; war of attrition, war to end all wars, war of nerves, campaign, crusade, religious, holy war, jihad, Armageddon, blitzkrieg.

**war,** *v.* — *Syn.* fight, battle, go to war, wage war against, make war on, engage in combat, take the field against, contend, contest, meet in conflict, march against, attack, bombard, shell, kill, shoot, murder.

**warble,** *v.* — *Syn.* trill, yodel, quaver; see **sing** 1.

**warbler,** *n.* — *Syn.* singer, songster, songbird; see **bird** 1.
Varieties of warblers include: bluethroat, whitethroat, black-cap, reed, sedge, wood, pine, black-throated blue, chestnut-sided, yellow, hooded, worm-eating, Cape May, arctic, prairie, blackpoll, Dartford, grasshopper, Savi's, willow, goldcrest, yellow-throat, olive-backed, golden-crowned, Cerulean; ovenbird, water thrush, redstart, wood wren.

**war cry,** *n.* — *Syn.* slogan, rallying cry, call to arms, rally, watchword, battle cry, rebel yell, war whoop\*; see also **cheer** 3.

**ward,** *n.* **1.** [A territorial division] — *Syn.* district, division, territory, canton, precinct, department, diocese, parish, arrondissement.
**2.** [A juvenile charge] — *Syn.* protégé, dependent, child, foster child, charge, orphan, godchild, adopted child.
**3.** [Hospital room] — *Syn.* convalescent chamber, infirmary, emergency ward; see **hospital, room** 2.

**warden,** *n.* — *Syn.* official, officer, overseer, superintendent, director, guardian, tutor, keeper, head keeper, gamekeeper, churchman, jailer, bodyguard, guard, governor, prison head, head screw\*, big bull\*, Father Time\*, deacon\*, Duke\*.

**ward heeler,** *n.* — *Syn.* local boss, party hack, hanger-on; see **politician** 1.

**ward off,** *v.* — *Syn.* fend off, parry, turn aside, defend against.

**wardrobe,** *n.* **1.** [A closet] — *Syn.* chest, bureau, dresser; see **chest** 1, **closet.**
**2.** [Clothing] — *Syn.* apparel, garments, vestments; see **clothes.**

**wardship,** *n.* — *Syn.* charge, guardianship, tutelage; see **custody** 1, **ownership.**

**warehouse,** *n.* — *Syn.* wholesale establishment, storehouse, stockroom, storage place, distributing center, repository, depot, shed, entrepôt, stockpile, depository, bin, elevator, storage loft; see also **barn.**

**wares,** *n.* — *Syn.* goods, lines, stock, products, commodities, manufactured articles, merchandise, range, stuff.

**warfare,** *n.* — *Syn.* armed conflict, military operations, hostilities, armed struggle, combat, counterinsurgency; see also **battle** 1, **war.**

**war games,** *n.* — *Syn.* maneuvers, military exercises, naval exercises, army exercises, navy exercises, practice, simulated combat; see also **maneuver** 3.

**warily,** *modif.* — *Syn.* cautiously, suspiciously, vigilantly; see **carefully** 2.

**wariness,** *n.* — *Syn.* caution, suspicion, alertness; see **attention** 1, **care** 1.

**warlike,** *modif.* **1.** [Belligerent] — *Syn.* hostile, truculent, attacking, pugnacious, offensive; see also **aggressive** 2.
**2.** [Military] — *Syn.* soldierly, bellicose, martial; see **fighting, militaristic, military.** *See Synonym Study at* MILITARY.

**warlock,** *n.* — *Syn.* wizard, male witch, sorcerer; see **magician** 1, **witch.**

**warlord,** *n.* — *Syn.* bandit, boss, tyrant; see **ruler** 1.

**warm,** *modif.* **1.** [Moderately heated] — *Syn.* heated, sunny, melting, hot, mild, tepid, lukewarm, summery, temperate, clement, glowing, perspiring, sweaty, sweating, flushed, warmish*, snug as a bug in a rug*. — *Ant.* COOL, chilly, chilling.

**2.** [Emotional] — *Syn.* fervent, earnest, irascible, excitable, angry, amorous, emotional, passionate, heated, hot*, turned on*.

**3.** [Sympathetic] — *Syn.* gracious, cordial, tender, empathic; see **friendly** 1, **sympathetic.**

*See Synonym Study at* TENDER.

**warm,** *v.* — *Syn.* heat up, warm up, warm over, put on the fire; see **cook, heat** 2.

**warmly,** *modif.* **1.** [Fervently] — *Syn.* passionately, emotionally, intensely; see **angrily, excitedly.**

**2.** [Amicably] — *Syn.* cordially, genially, affectionately; see **kindly** 2, **sympathetically.**

**warmth,** *n.* **1.** [Fervor] — *Syn.* fever, passion, feeling; see **emotion.**

**2.** [Affection] — *Syn.* friendliness, kindness, sympathy; see **affection** 1, **friendship** 2.

**3.** [Heat] — *Syn.* light, glow, warmness; see **heat** 1, 5, **temperature.**

**warn,** *v.* — *Syn.* forewarn, caution, give notice, put on guard, give (fair) warning, signal, advise, alert, inform, apprise, notify, remind, forearm, prepare for the worst, offer a word of caution, admonish, counsel, exhort, enjoin, reprove, threaten, forbid, predict, prepare, remonstrate, urge, recommend, suggest, hint, put on one's guard, put on the alert, sound the alarm, give the alarm, put wise, make red lights flash*, start bells ringing*, cry wolf*, tip off*, give the high sign*, put a bug in one's ear*, cry havoc*, read the riot act*.

*See Synonym Study at* ADVISE.

**warned,** *modif.* — *Syn.* informed, admonished, made aware, cautioned, advised, given warning, prepared for the worst, told, forewarned, tipped off*, put on the lookout*.

**warning,** *n.* — *Syn.* caution, admonition, caveat, notice, advice, alarum, forewarning, portent, omen, alert, intimation, premonition, notification, sign, alarm, indication, token, hint, lesson, information, example, distress signal, prediction, signal, injunction, exhortation, high sign*, word to the wise*, tip-off*, SOS*, handwriting on the wall*.

**warp,** *n.* **1.** [Lengthwise threads] — *Syn.* skeins, ties, batts; **fiber** 1, **loom, thread.**

**2.** [A distortion] — *Syn.* bend, twist, wrinkle, skew, bias.

**warp,** *v.* — *Syn.* distort, curve, twist, pervert; see **bend** 1, 2, **distort** 3.

*See Synonym Study at* DISTORT.

**warrant,** *n.* — *Syn.* authorization, certificate, credential, official document, summons, subpoena, security, pass, testimonial, passport, credentials, permit, license, permission, chit, verification, authentication.

**warrant,** *v.* **1.** [To guarantee] — *Syn.* assure, insure, vouch for; see **assert** 1, **guarantee** 1, 2, **vouch.**

**2.** [To justify] — *Syn.* bear out, call for, give grounds for; see **explain, justify** 2.

**3.** [To authorize] — *Syn.* empower, sanction, license; see **approve** 1, **delegate** 1.

*See Synonym Study at* ASSERT.

**warrantable,** *modif.* — *Syn.* permissible, covered, legitimate; see **lawful, legal** 1.

**warranted,** *modif.* — *Syn.* allowable, allowed, justified,

guaranteed, certified, authorized, attested, secured, based, feasible, supported by fact. — *Ant.* FALSE, unwarranted, unjustified.

**warranty,** *n.* — *Syn.* guaranty, guarantee, written guaranty, pledge; see **guaranty** 2.

**warring,** *modif.* — *Syn.* at war, belligerent, battling; see **fighting.**

**warrior,** *n.* — *Syn.* soldier, knight, fighter, hero, combatant, conscript, battler, enlisted personnel.

**warship,** *n.* — *Syn.* fighting ship, armored vessel, gunboat, man-of-war, frigate, ship-of-the-line; see also **boat, ship.**

Warships include: battleship, cruiser, destroyer, frigate, guided-missile frigate, guided-missile destroyer, missile cruiser, nuclear submarine, U-boat, attack submarine, minesweeper, destroyer escort, submarine, submarine chaser, aircraft carrier, escort carrier, corvette, torpedo boat, PT-boat, raider, dreadnought, superdreadnought, capital ship, flagship, landing ship, LST, LSM, LCI, LCP, LCT.

**wart,** *n.* — *Syn.* protuberance, spot, mole, projection, blemish, growth, bulge, tumor, wen.

**war whoop,** *n.* — *Syn.* shout, bellow, war cry; see **cry** 1, **yell** 1.

**wary,** *modif.* — *Syn.* circumspect, cautious, on one's guard, leery*; see **careful, suspicious** 1.

*See Synonym Study at* CAREFUL.

**wash,** *n.* **1.** [Laundry] — *Syn.* wet wash, washing, linen, family wash, soiled clothing, clean clothes, washed clothing, rough-dry wash, flat pieces, finished laundry.

**2.** [The movement of water] — *Syn.* swishing, lapping, splash, roll, swirl, rush, surging, eddy, wave, undulation, surge, heave, flow, murmur, gush, spurt.

**3.** [*A stream bed that is usually dry] — *Syn.* arroyo, gulch, canyon, gorge, ravine, valley, gap.

**4.** [A prepared liquid] — *Syn.* rinse, swab, coating; see **liquid.**

**wash,** *v.* **1.** [To bathe] — *Syn.* clean, cleanse, lave, shine, immerse, douse, soak, shower, take a bath, take a shower, soap, rub the dirt off, scour, scrub, rinse, wipe, sponge, dip, freshen up*, wash up*, clean up*, brush up*.

**2.** [To launder] — *Syn.* clean, starch, scrub, put in a washing machine, boil, soap, take the grit out of, send to the laundry, scour, rinse out, soak, sozzle, drench. — *Ant.* DIRTY, stain, smirch.

**3.** [To brush with a liquid] — *Syn.* swab, paint, whitewash, color, coat, dye, tint, stain, tinge, touch up, retouch, daub.

**4.** [To erode] — *Syn.* eat away, carry off, decrease, wear, wear down, remove, deteriorate.

**5.** [To border upon] — *Syn.* flow along, touch, lave, reach, flood, hit, run along the edge of.

**6.** [*To be convincing] — *Syn.* be plausible, be reasonable, be acceptable, stand up, endure examination; see also **convince.**

**washable,** *modif.* — *Syn.* tubfast, fast, unfading, launderable, colorfast, pre-washed, pre-shrunk, Sanforized (trademark), tubbable*, sudsable*; see also **permanent** 2.

**washed,** *modif.* **1.** [Laundered] — *Syn.* cleaned, scrubbed, bleached, boiled, put through the wash, soaped. — *Ant.* DIRTY, soiled, foul.

**2.** [Laved] — *Syn.* bathed, dipped, drenched, sponged, doused, soaked, cleansed, submerged, watered, showered. — *Ant.* DRY, scorching, desert.

**washed out*,** *modif.* — *Syn.* dismissed, let go, failed, dropped from the program; see **discharged** 1.

**washed up***, *modif.* — *Syn.* finished, defeated, done for*; see **ruined** 1, 2.

**washer,** *n.* 1. [A flat ring] — *Syn.* disk, seat, packing, collar, lock washer, shim, bushing, patent washer; see also **part** 2.

2. [A machine for washing] — *Syn.* automatic dishwasher, washing machine, laundry machine, electric washer, gasoline washer, power-driven washer; see also **appliance, machine** 1.

**washing,** *n.* — *Syn.* laundry, soiled clothes, dirty clothes; see **wash** 1.

**Washington,** *n.* — *Syn.* the Capitol, the nation's capital, the government, the President, the Presidency, the White House, the Oval Office, the Congress, the Hill, the national government, the Federal government, the Supreme Court, the Pentagon, the CIA, the Establishment*, Foggy Bottom*, the mess in Washington*, the Washington run-around, the Washington merry-go-round*, on the banks of the Potomac*; see also **administration** 1, 2, **city.**

**washout***, *n.* — *Syn.* disaster, disappointment, mess; see **failure** 1, 2.

**wasp,** *n.* Types of wasps include: common, fossorial, digging, digger, social, solitary, hunting, potter, paper, sand, wood, spider, mud, fig, gall, cuckoo, thread-waisted; (mud) dauber, yellow jacket, hornet; see also **bee** 1.

**waspish,** *modif.* — *Syn.* bad-tempered, snappish, crabby*; see **irritable.**

**wassail,** *n.* 1. [A celebration] — *Syn.* festivity, festival, carousal; see **feast.**

2. [A toast] — *Syn.* salute, salutation, cheers, pledge, acknowledgment; see also **toast** 1.

**waste,** *modif.* — *Syn.* futile, discarded, worthless, valueless, useless, empty, barren, dreary, uninhabited, desolate, profitless, superfluous, unnecessary, functionless, purposeless, pointless, unserviceable. — *Ant.* USABLE, preserved, valuable.

**waste,** *n.* 1. [The state of being wasted] — *Syn.* disuse, misuse, dissipation, consumption, uselessness, devastation, ruin, decay, dilapidation, loss, exhaustion, extravagance, squandering, wear and tear, wrack and ruin; see also **wear.** — *Ant.* USE, PROFIT, VALUE.

2. [Refuse] — *Syn.* rubbish, garbage, scrap; see **excess** 4, **trash** 1, 3.

3. [Unused land] — *Syn.* desert, wilds, wilderness, dustbowl, wasteland, tundra, marsh, marshland, badlands, bog, fen, moor, quagmire, swamp, wash.

*SYN.* — **waste,** in this connection, is the general word for any stretch of uncultivable, hence uninhabitable, land; a **desert** is a barren, arid, usually sandy tract of land; **badlands** is applied to a barren, hilly waste where rapid erosion has cut the soft rocks into fantastic shapes; **wilderness** refers to an uninhabited waste where a lack of paths or trails makes it difficult to find one's way, esp. to such a region thickly covered with trees and underbrush

**waste,** *v.* 1. [To use without result] — *Syn.* dissipate, spend, consume, lose, be of no avail, come to nothing, go to waste, misuse, throw away, use up, misapply, misemploy, labor in vain, cast pearls before swine*, send owls to Athens*, carry coals to Newcastle*. — *Ant.* PROFIT, use well, get results.

2. [To squander] — *Syn.* burn up, lavish, scatter, splurge, spend, be prodigal, indulge, abuse, empty, drain, use up, deplete, fatigue, spill, impoverish, misspend, exhaust, fritter away, fool away, ruin, be spend-

thrift, divert, go through, gamble away, throw money into a well*, run through*, hang the expense*, scatter to the winds*, blow*, burn the candle at both ends*. — *Ant.* SAVE, be thrifty, manage wisely.

3. [To be consumed gradually] — *Syn.* decay, thin out, become thin, dwindle, lose weight, be diseased, run dry, run to seed, wilt, droop, decrease, disappear, drain, empty, wear. — *Ant.* GROW, develop, enrich.

**wasted,** *modif.* — *Syn.* squandered, spent, destroyed, lost, consumed, eaten up, thrown away, shriveled, gaunt, emaciated, decayed, depleted, scattered, drained, gone for nothing, misapplied, useless, to no avail, down the drain, unappreciated, of no use, worthless. — *Ant.* PRESERVED, saved, useful.

**wasteful,** *modif.* — *Syn.* extravagant, profligate, dissipated, prodigal, liberal, immoderate, overgenerous, incontinent, thriftless, lavish, squandering, profuse, unthrifty, improvident, careless, reckless, cavalier, wild, full-handed, without stint, destructive, with money to burn*, easy come easy go*, out of bounds*. — *Ant.* STINGY, miserly, tightfisted.

**wastefully,** *modif.* — *Syn.* extravagantly, profligately, improvidently, carelessly, wildly, immoderately, thriftlessly, recklessly, prodigally, destructively, unstintedly, incontinently, foolishly, lavishly, inconsiderately, openhandedly, imprudently, ruthlessly, profusely, overgenerously, with no thought for tomorrow, without a second thought, without restraint, without good sense, without consideration.

**waster,** *n.* — *Syn.* spendthrift, prodigal, wastrel; see **beggar** 1, **loafer.**

**waste time,** *v.* — *Syn.* malinger, dawdle, drift, goof off*, skive* (British); see also **loaf** 1.

**watch,** *n.* 1. [A portable timepiece] — *Syn.* wrist watch, pocket watch, hunter, half-hunter, stopwatch, chronometer, digital watch, analog watch, ticker*; see also **clock.**

2. [Strict attention] — *Syn.* lookout, observation, observance, surveillance, awareness, attention, vigilance, guard, heed, watchfulness. — *Ant.* NEGLECT, sleepiness, apathy.

3. [A period of duty or vigilance] — *Syn.* patrol, guard duty, night watch, shift, vigil, picket duty, sentry duty, trick*, dogwatch*, graveyard watch*, graveyard shift.

4. [Those who keep a watch, sense 3] — *Syn.* guard, sentry, sentinel, picket, watchman, lookout, scout, spotter, observer, signalman, flagman, shore patrol, S.P., military police, M.P.; see also **guardian** 1.

**watch,** *v.* 1. [To be attentive] — *Syn.* observe, see, scrutinize, follow, attend, mark, regard, listen, wait, attend, take notice, contemplate, mind, view, pay attention, concentrate, look closely.

2. [To guard] — *Syn.* keep an eye on, keep (a) prisoner, patrol, picket, police; see also **guard** 2.

**watched,** *modif.* — *Syn.* guarded, spied on, followed, held under suspicion, scrutinized, observed, marked, kept under surveillance, noticed, noted, bugged*.

**watcher,** *n.* — *Syn.* lookout, guard, spectator; see **watchman.**

**watchful,** *modif.* — *Syn.* on guard, keen, vigilant, alert, prepared, wide-awake, careful, observant.

*SYN.* — **watchful** is the general word implying a being observant and prepared, as to ward off danger or seize an opportunity /under the *watchful* eye of her guardian/; **vigilant** implies an active, keen watchfulness and connotes the immediate necessity for this /a *vigilant* sentry/; **alert** implies a quick intelligence and a readiness to take prompt action /alert to the danger that confronted them/; **wide-awake** more often implies an alertness to opportunities than to dangers and connotes an awareness of all the surrounding circumstances [a *wide-awake* young salesman]

---

**watchfulness,** *n.* — *Syn.* vigilance, alertness, attention, caution, carefulness, wide-awakeness, wariness, readiness, awareness, promptness, circumspection, mindfulness, keenness, sharpness, acuteness, quickness, briskness, vigorousness, aliveness, animation.

**watching,** *modif.* — *Syn.* vigilant, wary, alert, circumspect, observant, cautious, on the lookout.

**watchman,** *n.* — *Syn.* night watchman, sentinel, sentry, caretaker; see **guard, guardian** 1.

**watch out,** *v.* — *Syn.* take care, heed, be cautious, proceed carefully, mind, go on tiptoe, take precautions, be on one's guard, make sure of, be doubly sure, look alive★, keep an eye peeled★, handle with kid gloves★.

**watch over,** *v.* — *Syn.* protect, look after, attend to; see **guard** 2.

**watchtower,** *n.* — *Syn.* fire tower, lighthouse, observatory; see **lookout** 1.

**watchword,** *n.* — *Syn.* cue, countersign, signal; see **password, sign** 1.

**water,** *n.* 1. [Water as a liquid] — *Syn.* rain, rainwater, liquid, drinking water, tap water, city water, mineral water, salt water, spa water, distilled water, limewater, $H_2O$, aqua pura.
2. [Water as a body] — *Syn.* spring, lake, ocean, dam, sea, puddle, pond, basin, pool, river, lagoon, reservoir, brook, stream, creek, waterfall, bayou.

**water,** *v.* — *Syn.* sprinkle, spray, irrigate, soak, souse, douse, wet, moisten, flood, inundate, spatter, provide moisture enough.

**water bug,** *n.* Water bugs include: skipper, skater, water beetle, walking stick, water weevil, back swimmer, giant water bug, Croton bug, gerrid, water flea, water scorpion, water mantis, water scavenger, water treader, water boatman, water strider; see also **insect.**

**water closet,** *n.* — *Syn.* lavatory, privy, john★; see **toilet** 2.

**watercourse,** *n.* 1. [A river] — *Syn.* brook, stream, tributary; see **river.**
2. [A canal] — *Syn.* waterway, spillway, aqueduct; see **channel** 2, **trench** 1.

**water down,** *v.* — *Syn.* dilute, restrict, cut, thin, make weaker, make less potent, make less effective; see also **weaken** 2.

**watered,** *modif.* 1. [Given water] — *Syn.* sprinkled, showered, hosed, sprayed, washed, sluiced, bathed, drenched, wetted, irrigated, flooded, baptized, doused, soused, sodden, slaked, quenched; see also **wet** 1. — *Ant.* DRY, arid, thirsty.
2. [Diluted] — *Syn.* thinned, weakened, adulterated, cut, lessened, contaminated, mixed, debased, impure, corrupt, blended, weakened, spread out, inflated, cheapened.

**waterfall,** *n.* — *Syn.* cataract, Niagara, fall, cascade, rapids, force fosse, watercourse, chute, shoot; see also **water** 1, 2.

**waterfowl,** *n.* — *Syn.* water bird, game bird, wild game, wild duck, wild goose, brant, mallard, teal, snipe; see also **bird** 1.

**waterfront,** *n.* — *Syn.* wharves, embarcadero, docks; see **harbor** 2.

**water hole,** *n.* — *Syn.* well, pond, puddle, *ojo* (Spanish); see **pool, well** 1.

**water lily,** *n.* Varieties of water lilies include: water

shield, floating heart, Victoria regina, Royal water Victoria cruziana, blue Egyptian lotus, East Indian tus, Formosa water lily, rice-field water lily, spo marliac, pygmy water lily, fragrant water lily, pond yellow water lily, white water lily, golden water lily, w chinquapin, wankapin; see also **plant.**

**water nymph,** *n.* — *Syn.* sprite, mermaid, sea nym kelpie; see **fairy** 1, **goddess.**

**water power,** *n.* — *Syn.* hydraulics, water works, e tricity, water pressure, mechanical energy, elec power; see also **energy** 3.

**waterproof,** *modif.* — *Syn.* impermeable, tight, airti vacuum-packed, oiled, rubber-coated, watertight, in lated, impervious, hermetically sealed.

**watery,** *modif.* — *Syn.* moist, damp, humid, soggy, s den, wet, thin, colorless, washed, waterlike. — *Ant.* r parched, BAKED.

**wave,** *n.* 1. [A wall of water] — *Syn.* comber, sv roller, heave, tidal wave, billow, tide, surge, crest, b tube, breaker, whitecap, ripple, curl★.
2. [A movement suggestive of a wave] — *Syn.* su gush, swell, uprising, onslaught, influx, tide, fl stream, come and go, swarm, drift, rush, crush, line a line, fluctuation.
3. [Undulating movement] — *Syn.* rocking, bend winding, coil, curl, roll, twirl, loop, swirl, swing, sv corkscrew, spring, lift, rippling.
4. [A line suggestive of a wave] — *Syn.* scroll, kink, c volution, meander, loop, wavy line, twist, volute, ci cue.

---

*SYN.* — **wave** is the general word for a curving ri or swell in the surface of the ocean or other bod water; **ripple** is used of the smallest kind of w such as that caused by a breeze ruffling the face of water; **roller** is applied to any of the la heavy, swelling waves that roll in to the shore during a storm; **breaker** is applied to such a w when it breaks, or is about to break, into foam u the shore or upon rocks; **billow** is a somewhat etic or rhetorical term for a great, heaving oc wave

---

**wave,** *v.* 1. [To flutter] — *Syn.* stream, pulse, fl shake, fly, dance, flap, swish, swing, tremble, wl — *Ant.* droop, FALL, hang listless.
2. [To give an alternating movement] — *Syn.* mot beckon, call, raise the arm, signal, greet, return a gr ing, hail.
3. [To move back and forth] — *Syn.* falter, waver, cillate, vacillate, fluctuate, pulsate, vibrate, wag, wag sway, lurch, bend, swing, dangle, seesaw, wobble, i quaver, quiver, swing from side to side, palpitate, m to and fro; see also **rock.**
4. [To undulate] — *Syn.* surge, roll, flow, wind, sv billow, curl, twirl, swirl, coil, ripple, twist.
5. [To set hair] — *Syn.* put up, curl, set, permanent, up, roll up.

**waver,** *v.* — *Syn.* fluctuate, vacillate, hesitate, dillyd: seesaw, deliberate, reel, teeter, totter, hem and ha pause, stagger.

**wavering,** *modif.* — *Syn.* vacillating, fluctuating, v able; see **changeable** 1, 2, **changing.**

**wavy,** *modif.* 1. [Sinuous] — *Syn.* undulating, bun crinkly, curved; see **rough** 1, **twisted.**
2. [Unsteady] — *Syn.* wavering, fluctuating, vibrat see **changeable** 1, 2.

**wax,** *n.* Waxes include: paraffin, resin, spermaceti, la lin, petrolatum, petroleum jelly, candelilla, oxocei beeswax, honeycomb, sealing wax, earwax, cerumen, carnauba, automobile wax, floor wax, furniture polish.

**wax,** *v.* **1.** [To increase] — *Syn.* become larger, swell, grow full; see **grow** 1.

**2.** [To apply wax] — *Syn.* polish, smooth, shine; see **spread** 4.

**waxen,** *modif.* — *Syn.* waxlike, wax-covered, pale, pallid, white, whitish, wan, sickly, blanched, unhealthy, ghostly, sallow. — *Ant.* ruddy, HEALTHY, robust.

**waxy,** *modif.* — *Syn.* slick, glistening, glassy; see **slippery, smooth** 1.

**way,** *n.* **1.** [Road] — *Syn.* trail, walk, byway; see **highway.**

**2.** [Course] — *Syn.* alternative, direction, progression, trend, tendency, distance, space, extent, bearing, orbit, approach, passage, route, gateway, entrance, access, door, gate, channel.

**3.** [Means] — *Syn.* method, mode, means, plan, technique, design, system, procedure, process, measure, contrivance, stroke, step, move, action, idea, outline, plot, policy, instrument.

**4.** [Manner] — *Syn.* form, fashion, gait, tone, guise, habit, custom, usage, behavior, style.

**by the way** — *Syn.* casually, by the by, as a matter of fact; see **incidentally.**

**by way of** — *Syn.* via, routed through, detoured through, utilizing; see **through** 4.

**get out of the** or **one's way** — *Syn.* go, step aside, remove oneself, retire; see **leave** 1, **remove** 1.

**go one's own way** — *Syn.* persevere, do what one pleases, do one's thing★; see **choose** 1, **continue** 1, **decide.**

**give way (to)** — *Syn.* give preference to, permit, accede to; see **allow** 1, **retire** 1, 3, **retreat** 1, 2.

**in the way** — *Syn.* obstructing, bothersome, nagging; see **disturbing, impeding, meddlesome.**

**lead the way** — *Syn.* conduct, take the lead, be the leader; see **lead** 1.

**make one's way** — *Syn.* progress, succeed, do well; see **advance** 1, **profit** 2, **win** 1, 4.

**make way 1.** draw back, pull back, give way, withdraw; see **leave** 1, **retire** 1, 3.

**2.** make headway, move right along, get somewhere.

**on the way out** — *Syn.* declining, unfashionable, no longer fashionable, going out; see **old-fashioned, unpopular.**

**out of the way 1.** disposed of, terminated, taken out; see **away** 1, **gone** 1, 2, **remove** 1.

**2.** hard to get to, off the beaten track, in the country, rural, tucked away.

**parting of the ways** — *Syn.* break-up, disagreement, agreeing to disagree, difference of opinion; see **fight** 1, **separation** 1.

**see one's way clear** — *Syn.* agree to, be able, be willing, be prepared to; see **can** 4.

**under way** — *Syn.* going, prospering, making headway; see **moving** 1.

**wayfarer,** *n.* — *Syn.* pilgrim, rambler, voyager; see **traveler.**

**wayfaring,** *modif.* — *Syn.* voyaging, rambling, vagrant; see **traveling.**

**waylay,** *v.* — *Syn.* wait for, assail, accost; see **ambush.**

**way-out★,** *modif.* — *Syn.* unconventional, experimental, nonconformist, esoteric, strange, far-out★; see also **extreme.**

**way out,** *n.* — *Syn.* means of escape, salvation, loophole; see **escape** 2, **exit** 1.

**ways,** *n.* — *Syn.* scaffolding, props, support, stays, frame, ground ways, bilge ways, sliding ways, launching ways,

platform, framework, shores, struts.

**ways and means,** *n.* — *Syn.* methods, approaches, devices; see **means** 1, 2, **resources.**

**wayside,** *modif.* — *Syn.* roadside, side, on the road, at the curb, by the way, on the way, at the edge.

**wayward,** *modif.* — *Syn.* unruly, disobedient, perverse, headstrong, unmanageable, insubordinate, capricious, delinquent, incorrigible; refractory, willful, unruly, self-indulgent, changeable, recalcitrant, stubborn. — *Ant.* OBEDIENT, stable, RESOLUTE.

**we,** *pron.* — *Syn.* you and I, he and I, she and I, they and I, us.

**weak,** *modif.* **1.** [Lacking physical strength; *said of persons*] — *Syn.* delicate, puny, flabby, flaccid, debilitated, effeminate, feeble, frail, sickly, infirm, decrepit, enervated, senile; see also **sick.** — *Ant.* STRONG, HEALTHY, robust.

**2.** [Lacking physical strength; *said of things*] — *Syn.* flimsy, makeshift, brittle, unsubstantial, jerry-built, rickety, tumbledown, sleazy, shaky, unsteady, ramshackle, rotten, wobbly, tottery, top-heavy. — *Ant.* STRONG, shatter-proof, sturdy.

**3.** [Lacking mental firmness or character] — *Syn.* weak-minded, nerveless, fainthearted, irresolute, nervous, spineless, unstrung, palsied, wishy-washy, caitiff, hesitant, vacillating, frightened. — *Ant.* BRAVE, courageous, adventurous.

**4.** [Lacking in volume] — *Syn.* thin, low, soft, indistinct, feeble, faint, dim, muffled, whispered, bated, inaudible, light, stifled, dull, pale. — *Ant.* LOUD, strong, forceful.

**5.** [Lacking in military power] — *Syn.* small, paltry, ineffectual, ineffective, inadequate, impotent, ill-equipped, insufficiently armed, limited, unorganized, undisciplined, untrained, vulnerable, exposed, assailable, unprepared.

**6.** [Lacking in capacity or experience] — *Syn.* unsure, raw, green, fresh, untrained, young, backward, insecure, immature, unsteady, handicapped, soft, shaky, uncertain, incomplete, untried. — *Ant.* EXPERIENCED, expert, TRAINED.

---

*SYN.* — **weak,** the broadest in application of these words, basically implies a lack or inferiority of physical, mental, or moral strength [a *weak* muscle, mind, character, foundation, excuse, etc.]; **feeble** suggests a pitiable weakness or ineffectiveness [a *feeble* old man, a *feeble* joke]; **frail** suggests an inherent or constitutional delicacy or weakness, so as to be easily broken or shattered [a *frail* body, conscience, etc.]; **infirm** suggests a loss of strength or soundness, as through illness or age [his *infirm* old grandfather]; **decrepit** implies a being broken down, worn out, or decayed, as by old age or long use [a *decrepit* old pensioner, a *decrepit* sofa]

---

**weaken,** *v.* **1.** [To become weaker] — *Syn.* lessen, lose, decrease, relapse, soften, relax, droop, fail, wane, crumble, halt, limp, languish, fade, decline, abate, totter, tremble, flag, faint, wilt, lose spirit, become disheartened, fail in courage, slow down, break up, crack up★, wash out★. — *Ant.* REVIVE, STRENGTHEN, straighten.

**2.** [To make weaker] — *Syn.* reduce, minimize, enervate, debilitate, exhaust, cripple, unman, emasculate, castrate, devitalize, undermine, impair, sap, enfeeble, unnerve, incapacitate, impoverish, thin, dilute, take the wind out of★, wash up★; see also **decrease** 2. — *Ant.* REVIVE, quicken, animate.

*SYN.* — **weaken**, the most general of these words, implies a lessening of strength, power, soundness, etc. *[weakened* by disease, to *weaken* an argument*]*; **debilitate** suggests a partial or temporary gradual weakening, as by disease or dissipation *[debilitated* by alcoholic excesses*]*; **enervate** implies a lessening of force, vigor, energy, etc., as through indulgence in luxury *[enervated* by idleness*]*; **undermine** and **sap** both suggest a weakening or impairing by subtle or stealthy means *[authority *undermined* by rumors, strength *sapped* by disease]*

**weakened,** *modif.* — *Syn.* tired, depleted, drained, undermined, injured, disabled, vulnerable, weak, handicapped, feeble, unsteady, groggy, limp, open to attack. — *Ant.* FORTIFIED, strengthened, invulnerable.

**weakling,** *n.* — *Syn.* puny person, feeble creature, dotard, coward, crybaby, invertebrate, mollycoddle, milksop, jellyfish*, sissy*, softie*, pushover*, namby-pamby*, puff*, punk*.

**weak-minded,** *modif.* — *Syn.* foolish, moronic, not bright; see **stupid** 1, **weak** 3.

**weakness,** *n.* **1.** [The state of being weak] — *Syn.* feebleness, senility, anility, delicacy, invalidity, frailty, faintness, prostration, anoxia, anoxemia, decrepitude, debility, effeminacy impotence, enervation, dizziness, femininity, infirmity. — *Ant.* STRENGTH, good health, vitality.
**2.** [An instance or manner of being weak] — *Syn.* fault, failing, deficiency, defect, disturbance, lapse, vice, sore point, gap, flaw, instability, indecision, inconstancy, vulnerability. — *Ant.* VIRTUE, good, strength.
**3.** [*Inclination] — *Syn.* liking, tendency, bent; see **hunger, inclination** 1.
*See Synonym Study at* FAULT.

**weak-willed,** *modif.* — *Syn.* soft, shy, backward; see **timid** 1, 2, **weak** 3.

**wealth,** *n.* **1.** [Goods or services having economic utility] — *Syn.* capital, capital stock, economic resources, stock, stocks and bonds, securities, vested interests, land, property, labor power, commodities, cash, money in the bank, money, natural resources, assets, purse strings*, dough*, long green*. — *Ant.* POVERTY, idle resources, unemployment.
**2.** [Personal riches] — *Syn.* means, money, riches, substance, affluence, belongings, property, fortune, hoard, treasure, resources, revenue, cache, cash, competence, opulence, luxury, luxuriance, prosperity, pelf, abundance, money to burn*. — *Ant.* POVERTY, pauperism, straits.

**wealthily,** *modif.* — *Syn.* richly, extensively, opulently; see **abundantly.**

**wealthy,** *modif.* — *Syn.* prosperous, moneyed, affluent; see **rich** 1.
*See Synonym Study at* RICH.

**wean,** *v.* — *Syn.* bring up, break of, stop suckling, detach, unaccustom, reconcile to; see also **remove** 1.

**weapon,** *n.* **1.** [An instrument for combat] — *Syn.* armament, protection, weaponry, deadly weapon, hardware, sophisticated hardware, lethal weapon, defense.
Weapons include: club, spear, arrow, mace, knife, catapult, bullet, dart, flechette, missile, sling, slingshot, CAM, cybernetic anthropomorphic machine, bomb, atomic bomb, nuclear bomb, rocket, torpedo, stick, ax, firearm, cannon, gun, musket, rifle, blackjack, whip, sword, pistol, revolver, bayonet, bazooka, mortar, antiaircraft gun, machine gun, warhead; airplane, tank, submarine, destroyer.

**2.** [A device thought of figuratively as a weapon] — *Syn.* argument, plea, evidence, influence, alibi, intimidation, threat, blackmail, scolding, sharp tongue.

**wear,** *n.* — *Syn.* depreciation, damage, loss, erosion, wear and tear, loss by friction, inroads of time, diminution, waste, corrosion, impairment, wearing away, dilapidation, disappearance, result of friction. — *Ant.* GROWTH, accretion, building up.

**wear,** *v.* **1.** [To use as clothing or personal ornament] — *Syn.* bear, carry, affect, put on, don, be clothed, slip on, get on, have on, dress in, attire, array, cover, wrap, harness, get into*; see also **dress** 1. — *Ant.* UNDRESS, take off, disrobe.
**2.** [To consume by wearing] — *Syn.* use up, use, consume, wear thin, wear out, waste, diminish, cut down, scrape off, exhaust, fatigue, weather down, impair.
**3.** [To be consumed by wearing] — *Syn.* fade, go to seed, decay, crumble, weather, dwindle, shrink, decline, deteriorate, decrease, waste, become threadbare.

**wear and tear,** *n.* — *Syn.* depletion, wearing, effect of use; see **damage** 1, 2, **destruction** 2, **loss** 3, **wear.**

**wear down,** *v.* **1.** [To become worn] — *Syn.* wear out, get thin, get worn out; see **decrease** 1, **waste** 3.
**2.** [To make weary] — *Syn.* exhaust, get the better of, reduce, beat; see **defeat** 1, 3, **tire** 2.

**weariness,** *n.* — *Syn.* tiredness, exhaustion, dullness; see **fatigue, lassitude.**

**wearing,** *modif.* — *Syn.* tiring, exhausting, nerve-racking, jolting, hard, difficult, long, endless, discomforting, upsetting. — *Ant.* STIMULATING, invigorating, bracing.

**wearisome,** *modif.* **1.** [Burdensome] — *Syn.* laborious, strenuous, toilsome; see **onerous.**
**2.** [Boring] — *Syn.* tedious, tiresome, vapid; see **dull** 4.

**wear off,** *v.* — *Syn.* go away, get better, decline; see **improve** 2, **stop** 2.

**wear out,** *v.* — *Syn.* become worn, be worthless, exhaust; see **decay, waste** 1, 3.

**wear the pants** or **trousers**, *v.* — *Syn.* wield authority, run things, boss, domineer; see **dominate.**

**weary,** *modif.* — *Syn.* exhausted, fatigued, overworked; see **tired.**
*See Synonym Study at* TIRED.

**weary,** *v.* **1.** [To make weary] — *Syn.* annoy, vex, distress, irk, tax, strain, overwork, exhaust, fatigue, tire, tucker out*, harass, bore, disgust, dishearten, unman, dispirit, wear out, cause ennui, leave one cold, depress, cloy, glut, jade, overstuff, burden, sicken, nauseate. — *Ant.* REVIVE, refresh, animate.
**2.** [To become weary] — *Syn.* pain, flag, be worn out, sink, droop, lose interest, fall off, tire, grow tired, drowse, doze, sicken; see also **sleep.** — *Ant.* excite, enjoy, be amused.

**weary of,** *modif.* — *Syn.* bored, disgusted, impatient, uninterested, disinclined, vexed, unmoved, upset, nauseated, sickened, bored stiff*, bored to tears*. — *Ant.* EXCITED, moved, stimulated.

**weather,** *n.* — *Syn.* climate, atmospheric conditions, clime*, air conditions, drought, clear weather, sunny weather, foul weather, tempest, calm, windiness, the elements, cloudiness, heat, cold, warmth, chilliness.

**weather,** *v.* **1.** [To expose to the weather] — *Syn.* dry, bleach, discolor, blanch, whiten, pulverize, tan, burn, patinate, expose, harden, petrify.
**2.** [To pass through adversity successfully] — *Syn.* overcome, endure, become toughened, grow hardened, stand up against, bear the brunt of, acclimate oneself, grow strong through; see also **endure.** — *Ant.* FAIL, be overcome, fall victim to.

**weather-beaten,** *modif.*— *Syn.* decayed, battered, weathered; see **decaying, old** 2, 3, **worn** 2.

**weatherman,** *n.* — *Syn.* meteorologist, weather reporter, weather forecaster, climatologist.

**weather report,** *n.* — *Syn.* weather prediction, weathercast, meteorological forecast; see **forecast.**

**weather vane,** *n.* — *Syn.* weathercock, vane, wind gauge, wind sleeve, aerometer.

**weave,** *n.* — *Syn.* pattern, design, method of weaving, knitting, crocheting, darning, texture, interlace, warp and woof.
Types of weaves include: plain, fancy, loose, basket, satin, silk, gauze, twill, twining, herringbone, tapestry, Jacquard, crepe, velvet.

**weave,** *v.* **1.** [To construct by interlacing] — *Syn.* knit, sew, interlace, spin, twine, intertwine, crisscross, interlink, wreathe, mesh, net, knot, twill, fold, interfold, ply, reticulate, loop, splice, braid, plait, twist.
**2.** [To move in and out] — *Syn.* sidle through, make one's way, twist and turn, snake, zigzag, beat one's way, insinuate oneself through, wedge through; see also **curl** 1.
**3.** [To contrive] — *Syn.* compose, fabricate, form, make, create, body forth, manufacture, spin out, turn out, construct, piece together.

**web,** *n.* **1.** [A combination of threads] — *Syn.* cobweb, lacework, netting, plait, mesh, mat, matting, wicker, weft, warp, woof.
**2.** [An intricate combination] — *Syn.* network, interconnection, reticulation, intermixture, entanglement, tracery, filigree, interweaving, trellis.

**wed,** *v.* — *Syn.* espouse, join in wedlock, give in marriage, take in marriage, receive in marriage; see also **marry** 1, 2.

**wedded,** *modif.* — *Syn.* married, espoused, in holy matrimony; see **married.**

**wedding,** *n.* — *Syn.* nuptials, wedlock, marriage ceremony, matrimony; see **marriage** 1, **union** 3.

**wedge,** *n.* — *Syn.* spearhead, prong, entering wedge, flying column, mobile force, drive; see also **machine** 1, **tool** 1.
Devices using the principles of the wedge include: keystone, chock, shim, quoin, cleat, cotter.

**wedlock,** *n.* — *Syn.* matrimony, nuptials, espousal; see **marriage** 2, **union** 3.

**wee,** *modif.* — *Syn.* small, tiny, infinitesimal; see **little** 1, **minute** 1.

**weed,** *n.* **1.** [Wild plant] — *Syn.* noxious weed, uncultivated plant, unwanted plant, prolific plant; see **plant.**
Common weeds include: ragweed, nettle, wild morning-glory, pigweed, buckthorn, dandelion, lamb's quarters, buttonweed, dog fennel, plantain, quack grass, couch grass, crab grass, jimson weed, ironweed, wild sunflower, wild hemp, horsemint, foxtail, milkweed, wild barley, wild buckwheat, mullein, cheat grass, Russian thistle, tumbleweed, burdock, wild carrot, Queen Anne's lace, wild parsley, tarweed, vervain, vetch, purslane, wild onion, wild mustard.
**2.** [*Cigarette or cigar] — *Syn.* tobacco, coffin nail*, fag*, joint*; see **tobacco.**
**3.** [*Marijuana] — *Syn.* pot*, boo*, smoke, grass, Maryjane*; see also **marijuana.**

**week,** *n.* — *Syn.* seven days, six days, forty-hour week, working week, work week.

**week after week,** *modif.* — *Syn.* incessantly, continually, right along, regularly; see **continuing.**

**weekday,** *n.* — *Syn.* working day, workday, Monday, Tuesday, Wednesday, Thursday, Friday, not a Sunday,
not the Sabbath; see also **day** 2.

**weekend,** *n.* — *Syn.* end of the week, Saturday and Sunday, short vacation, English weekend, long weekend.

**weekly,** *modif.* — *Syn.* once every seven days; every Monday, regularly every Tuesday, etc.; once a week, occurring every week, hebdomadal.

**weep,** *v.* — *Syn.* shed tears, cry, sob, grieve for; see **cry** 1, **mourn** 1.
*See Synonym Study at* CRY.

**weeping,** *modif.* — *Syn.* crying, blubbering, sobbing, lamenting, tearful, in tears, teary-eyed, lachrymose, mourning, sorrowing, wailing, howling, moaning, shrieking; see also **sad** 1, **troubled** 1.

**weepy,** *modif.* — *Syn.* lachrymose, crying, close to tears; see **weeping.**

**weigh,** *v.* **1.** [To take the weight of] — *Syn.* measure, scale, put on the scales, hold the scales, put in the balance, counterbalance, heft*; see also **balance** 2, **measure** 1.
**2.** [To have weight] — *Syn.* be heavy, carry weight, be important, tell, count, show, register, press, pull, be a load, burden, tip the beams*, tip the scales*.
**3.** [To consider] — *Syn.* ponder, contemplate, balance; see **consider** 3, **estimate** 1, 2, **think** 1.
*See Synonym Study at* CONSIDER.

**weigh down,** *v.* — *Syn.* push down, pull down, hold down, burden, oppress; see also **depress** 2.

**weighing,** *n.* — *Syn.* measuring, estimating, considering, balancing, contemplating, evaluating, judging, deciding, thinking over.

**weight,** *n.* **1.** [Heaviness] — *Syn.* pressure, load, gross weight, net weight, dead weight, molecular weight, gravity, heft, burden, mass, density, adiposity, ponderousness, tonnage, ballast, substance, G-factor*; see also **measurement** 2, **pressure** 1. — *Ant.* LIGHTNESS, buoyancy, airiness.
Common weights include: dram, grain, ounce, pound, stone (British), hundredweight, ton, long ton, gram, kilogram, centigram, kilo, gram molecule, milligram, metric ton, metric carat, carat (grain), mole, tonneau, denier, assay ton, quintal, scruple.
**2.** [An object used for its weight] — *Syn.* counterbalance, counterweight, counterpoise, ballast, paperweight, stone, rock, leadweight, sinker, anchor, plumb, sandbag.
**3.** [Importance] — *Syn.* influence, authority, sway; see **importance** 1, **power** 2.
*See Synonym Study at* IMPORTANCE, INFLUENCE.

**weird,** *modif.* — *Syn.* mysterious, uncanny, ominous, eerie, ghastly, unearthly; see also **ghastly** 1, **mysterious** 2.

---

*SYN.* — **weird** applies to that which is supernaturally mysterious or fantastically strange [a *weird* experience]; **eerie** applies to that which inspires a vague, superstitious uneasiness or dread [the *eerie* howling of a dog]; **uncanny** applies to that which is unnaturally strange or remarkable [*uncanny* insight]; **unearthly** applies to that which is so strange or extraordinary as to seem to belong to another world [an *unearthly* light]

---

**weird sisters,** *n.* — *Syn.* the Fates, the three witches, the Sisters Three; see **fate.**

**welcome,** *interj.* — *Syn.* greetings, come right in, make yourself at home, how do you do?, glad to see you, won't you come in?

**welcome,** *modif.* **1.** [Willingly received as a guest] — *Syn.* warmly received, gladly admitted, desired, appreciated, honored, esteemed, cherished. — *Ant.* UNDE-SIRABLE, unwelcome, unwanted.

**2.** [Willingly accepted] — *Syn.* desirable, agreeable, pleasant, grateful, good, pleasing, joy-bringing, delightful. — *Ant.* UNDESIRABLE, disagreeable, unpleasant.

**welcome,** *n.* — *Syn.* greetings, salute, salutation, a hero's welcome, handshake, warm reception, free entrance, entree, hospitality, friendliness, the glad hand*. — *Ant.* REBUKE, snub, cool reception.

**wear out one's welcome***— *Syn.* bore, stay too long, make others tired, make others weary, make others bored, overstay one's welcome, hang around; see also **remain** 1, **weary** 1.

**welcome,** *v.* — *Syn.* embrace, hug, take in; see **greet.**

**welcomed,** *modif.* — *Syn.* received, accepted, initiated, taken in, greeted, celebrated, honored, welcome, accommodated, appreciated, hailed, entertained, coming in. — *Ant.* UNPOPULAR, snubbed, avoided.

**weld,** *v.* — *Syn.* fuse, fix, combine, unite, spot-weld, seam-weld, acetylene-weld, electric-weld, resistance-weld, projection-weld; see also **join** 1.

**welfare,** *n.* **1.** [Personal condition] — *Syn.* health, happiness, well-being, benefit, profit, prosperity, good, good fortune, progress, state of being.

**2.** [Social service] — *Syn.* social work, public assistance, public works, social aid, unemployment benefits, child welfare, federal aid, poverty program, social insurance, Social Security, health service, the dole; see also **aid** 1, **insurance.**

**well,** *modif.* **1.** [In good health] — *Syn.* fine, sound, fit, trim, healthy, robust, strong, hearty, high-spirited, vigorous, hardy, hale, blooming, fresh, flourishing, rosy-cheeked, whole, in fine fettle, hunky-dory*, corking*, great*, fit as a fiddle*, chipper*. — *Ant.* SICK, ill, infirm.

**2.** [Satisfactorily] — *Syn.* up to the mark, suitably, adequately, commendable, excellently, thoroughly, admirably, splendidly, favorably, famously, rightly, properly, expertly, strongly, irreproachably, ably, capably, soundly, competently. — *Ant.* BADLY, poorly, unsatisfactorily.

**3.** [Sufficiently] — *Syn.* abundantly, adequately, completely, fully, quite, entirely, considerably, wholly, plentifully, luxuriantly, extremely. — *Ant.* HARDLY, insufficiently, barely.

**as well**— *Syn.* in addition, additionally, along with; see **also, including.**

**as well as 1.** alike, as much as, as high as, as good as; see **equally.**

**2.** together with, along with, plus; see **also, including.**

**well,** *n.* **1.** [A source of water] — *Syn.* spring, fountain, font, spout, geyser, wellspring, mouth, artesian well, reservoir, cenote.

**2.** [A shaft sunk into the earth] — *Syn.* pit, hole, depression, chasm, abyss, oil well, gas well, water well, gusher*.

**3.** [Any source] — *Syn.* beginning, derivation, fount, fountainhead; see **origin** 3.

**well-balanced,** *modif.* — *Syn.* steady, sensible, well-adjusted; see **reliable** 1.

**well-behaved,** *modif.* — *Syn.* mannerly, courteous, civil; see **polite** 1.

**well-being,** *n.* — *Syn.* prosperity, happiness, fortune; see **health** 1, **welfare** 1.

**well-bred,** *modif.* — *Syn.* courteous, considerate, mannerly; see **polite** 1, **refined** 2.

**well-defined,** *modif.* — *Syn.* distinct, clear, sharp; see **definite** 2, **outlined** 1.

**well-disposed to** or **toward,** *modif.* — *Syn.* willing, friendly, encouraging; see **favorable** 3.

**well-favored,** *modif.* — *Syn.* good-looking, attractive, comely; see **handsome** 2.

**well-fixed***, *modif.* — *Syn.* well-to-do, wealthy, in comfortable circumstances; see **rich** 1.

**well-founded,** *modif.* — *Syn.* true, probable, plausible; see **likely** 1, **reliable** 2.

**well-groomed,** *modif.* — *Syn.* clean, clean-cut, clean-shaven, cared for, spruce; see also **neat** 1.

**well-informed,** *modif.* — *Syn.* informed, advised, well-read; see **educated** 1, **learned** 1, 2.

**well-intentioned,** *modif.* — *Syn.* well-meaning, honorable, high-principled, good-hearted; see **moral** 1, **noble** 2, 3.

**well-known,** *modif.* — *Syn.* famous, reputable, recognized, renowned, eminent, illustrious, familiar, widely known, noted, acclaimed, popular, public, celebrated, in the public eye, notorious, infamous. — *Ant.* UNKNOWN, OBSCURE, undiscovered.

**well-nigh,** *modif.* — *Syn.* practically, nearly, almost completely; see **almost, approximately.**

**well-off,** *modif.* — *Syn.* prosperous, well-to-do, wealthy; see **rich** 1.

**well-preserved,** *modif.* — *Syn.* lively, alert, in good condition, in possession of one's faculties; see **active** 1, 2, **aging.**

**well-rounded,** *modif.* — *Syn.* well-informed, well-balanced, with broad interests, having a good background; see **balanced, excellent.**

**well-timed,** *modif.* — *Syn.* appropriate, opportune, seasonable; see **timely.**

**well-to-do,** *modif.* — *Syn.* wealthy, well-off, prosperous; see **rich** 1.

*See Synonym Study at* RICH.

**Welsh,** *modif.* — *Syn.* Celtic, Cymric, Old Welsh, Middle Welsh, Brythonic, Brittanic.

**welt,** *n.* — *Syn.* wound, bruise, weal, bump, lump; see also **injury** 1.

**welter,** *n.* — *Syn.* commotion, uproar, turmoil; see **disturbance** 2.

**wench,** *n.* [*Usually derogatory*] — *Syn.* maid, damsel, maiden, virgin, female, unmarried woman, dame*, babe*, bimbo*, bird*, chick*, broad*, skirt*, doll*; see also **girl** 1, **woman** 1.

**wend,** *v.* — *Syn.* make one's way, saunter, stroll, meander; see **ramble** 3, **walk** 1.

**werewolf,** *n.* — *Syn.* man-wolf, wolf-man, lycanthrope, changeling; see **beast** 1, **monster** 1.

**West,** *n.* **1.** [Western Hemisphere] — *Syn.* New World, the Americas, North and South America; see **America** 1, 2.

**2.** [European and American Culture] — *Syn.* Occident, Western civilization, Christian society; see **Europe.**

**3.** [Western United States; *especially the cowboy and mining culture*] — *Syn.* the range, the prairies, Rocky Mountain country, Far West, Northwest, Southwest, where men are men*, wild-and-woolly country*, the wide open spaces*, cow country*, buffalo range*.

**west,** *modif.* — *Syn.* facing west, westerly, in the west, westernmost, westerly, westward; see also **western** 1, 2, 3.

**west,** *n.* — *Syn.* occident, westward, sunset; see **direction** 1.

**western,** *modif.* **1.** [In or toward the west] — *Syn.* westward, westerly, occidental, in the west, on the west side, where the sun sets, facing west, from the east, westernly, westernmost, westbound, occidental. — *Ant.* EASTERN, easterly, oriental.

**2.** [*Usually capital;* having characteristics of Western

Civilization] — *Syn.* Grecian, Latin, Roman, American, European, Christian, Caucasian.

**3.** [*Sometimes capital;* having characteristics of the western part of the United States] — *Syn.* cowboy, middlewestern, southwestern, far-western, in the sagebrush country, on the Western plains, in the wide open spaces, in the wild west, in the Rockies, in God's country, in the wild and woolly West*, out where the men are men*.

**westward,** *modif.* — *Syn.* to the west, in a westerly direction, westbound; see **western** 1.

**wet,** *modif.* **1.** [Covered or soaked with liquid] — *Syn.* moist, damp, soaking, soaked, drenched, soggy, muggy, dewy, watery, dank, slimy, dripping, saturated, waterlogged, sodden. — *Ant.* DRY, dried, CLEAN.

**2.** [Rainy] — *Syn.* drizzly, slushy, snowy, slippery, muddy, humid, foggy, damp, clammy, showery, stormy, drizzling, cloudy, misty. — *Ant.* CLEAR, sunny, cloudless.

**3.** [*Favoring or permitting liquor] — *Syn.* open, antiprohibitionist, pro-repeal, alcoholic, serving liquor.

**4.** [*Mistaken] — *Syn.* inaccurate, misled, in error; see **mistaken** 1, **wrong** 2.

---

**SYN.** — **wet** is applied to something covered or soaked with water or other liquid *[wet* streets, clothes, etc.*]* or to something not yet dry *[wet* paint*]*; **damp** implies slight, usually undesirable or unpleasant wetness *[a damp* room*]*; **dank** suggests a disagreeable, chilling, unwholesome dampness *[a dank* fog*]*; **moist** implies slight but, unlike **damp**, often desirable wetness *[moist* air*]*; **humid** implies such permeation of the air with moisture as to make for discomfort *[a hot, humid* day*]*

---

**wet,** *v.* — *Syn.* sprinkle, dampen, soak, splash; see **moisten.**

**wetback*,** *n.* — *Syn.* illegal immigrant, scab laborer, unskilled worker, illegally imported laborer; see **laborer, worker.**

**whack,** *n.* — *Syn.* stroke, thump, wham; see **blow** 1.

**in one whack** — *Syn.* suddenly, with one stroke, instantaneously; see **quickly** 1, **soon** 1.

**out of whack*** — *Syn.* out of order, not working, out of kilter, spoiled; see **ruined** 1, 2.

**take a whack at*** — *Syn.* attempt, endeavor, do one's best; see **try** 1.

**whale,** *n.* **1.** [A marine animal] — *Syn.* cetacean, leviathan, King of the Deep; see **fish.**

Types of whales include: sperm, white, blue, right, Greenland, sulphur-bottom, killer, gray, baleen, bottlenose, beaked, toothed, pilot, narwhal, finback, finner, humpback, beluga, blackfish, rorqual, common rorqual, blue rorqual.

**2.** [*Something impressive] — *Syn.* a great deal, a lot, abundance, a great quantity, large amount, corker*, whopper*, helluva lot*.

**wham,** *n.* — *Syn.* hit, knock, whack; see **blow** 1.

**wharf,** *n.* — *Syn.* boat landing, quay, pier; see **dock** 1.

**what,** *pron.* **1.** [An indication of a question] — *Syn.* which? what sort? what kind? what thing? what means?

**2.** [Something indefinite] — *Syn.* that which, whatever, something, anything, everything, whichever, anything at all.

**and what not*** — *Syn.* etc., and so forth, etcetera, and other things too numerous to mention, and more; see also **anything, everything.**

**whatever,** *pron.* — *Syn.* anything, everything, no matter what, whatsoever.

**what for*,** *conj.* — *Syn.* why, but why, to what end, for what purpose; see **why.**

**what have you*,** *n.* — *Syn.* other things, anything else, the rest; see **anything, everything.**

**what if*,** *conj.* — *Syn.* but suppose, imagine, supposing, pretend; see **but** 1, 2, 3, **if.**

**what it takes*,** *n.* — *Syn.* capacity, competence, aptitude; see **ability** 1, 2.

**what's what*,** *n.* — *Syn.* the facts, the truth, the lowdown*; see **answer** 1, 2, **facts.**

**wheat,** *n.* — *Syn.* grain, corn, staff of life, breadstuff, wheat flour.

Kinds of wheat include: durum, durum semolina, hard, hard red spring, hard red winter, soft red winter, farina, white; buckwheat, groats, spelt, emmer, einkorn, bulgur.

**wheedle,** *v.* — *Syn.* coax, flatter, cajole; see **beg** 1, **coax, urge** 2.

*See Synonym Study at* COAX.

**wheel,** *n.* **1.** [A thin, circular body that turns on an axis] — *Syn.* disk, ratchet, ring, hoop, roller, roulette, caster, drum, ferris wheel, wheel trolley, flywheel, cogwheel, steering wheel, sprocket, wheel, chain wheel, water wheel, noria, sakieh.

**2.** [A two-wheeled vehicle] — *Syn.* bicycle, velocipede, tandem, bike*.

**3.** [Machinery; *often used figuratively*] — *Syn.* motive power, dynamo, engine, apparatus, motor, engine, controlling force, instrumentality.

**4.** [*An important person] — *Syn.* personage, big wheel*, big shot*, V.I.P.*; see **celebrity** 2.

**at the wheel** — *Syn.* driving, in control, in charge, running things; see **running** 1, 2.

**wheel and deal*,** *v.* — *Syn.* play fast and loose, take chances, cut corners*; see **operate** 2, 3.

**wheels*,** *n.* — *Syn.* car, vehicle, transportation, buggy*; see **automobile.**

**wheeze,** *v.* — *Syn.* breathe heavily, puff, pant; see **gasp.**

**whelp,** *n.* — *Syn.* puppy, young animal, youngster, pup; see **boy, youth** 3.

**when,** *conj. & modif.* **1.** [At what time?] — *Syn.* how soon?, how long ago?, in what period?, just when?, at which instant?

**2.** [Whenever] — *Syn.* if, at any time, at the moment that, just as soon as, in the event that, on the condition that; see also **if.**

**3.** [During] — *Syn.* at the same time that, immediately upon, just as, just after, at, while, meanwhile; see also **during.**

**whence,** *conj.* — *Syn.* from where, from what place, from what origin, wherefrom.

**whenever,** *conj.* — *Syn.* at any time, at any moment, at any minute, at any hour, on any occasion, at any occasion, at the first opportunity, if, when, should.

**where,** *conj. & modif.* **1.** [A question as to position] — *Syn.* in what place?, at which place?, at what moment?, whither?, in what direction?, toward what?

**2.** [An indication of position] — *Syn.* wherever, anywhere, in whatever place, at which point, in which, to which, to what end.

**whereabouts,** *n.* — *Syn.* location, spot, site; see **place** 3.

**whereas,** *conj.* — *Syn.* since, inasmuch as, insomuch as, forasmuch as, considering that, when in fact, while, while on the contrary, although, though.

**whereat,** *modif.* — *Syn.* at which, whereupon, following which, thereupon, after which; see also **so** 2, 3.

**whereby,** *modif.* — *Syn.* by which, by means of which, through which, in accordance with which, with the help of which, how.

**wherefore,** *modif.* — *Syn.* why?, for what?, for which reason?, therefore, so, accordingly, thereupon.

**wherein,** *modif.* — *Syn.* in what way?, how?, at which point?, where?, in which?

**whereon,** *modif.* — *Syn.* on which, at which point, thereupon, at the conclusion of which, upon which, consequently, whereupon.

**wheresoever,** *conj. & modif.* — *Syn.* at whatever place, at which place, wherever, where.

**whereupon,** *modif.* — *Syn.* at which, at which point, thereupon, at the conclusion of which, as a consequence of which, whereon, upon which, consequently.

**wherever,** *conj. & modif.* — *Syn.* where, in whatever place, anywhere, in any place that, wheresoever, regardless of where, in any direction.

**wherewithal,** *n.* — *Syn.* resources, money, funds; see **means** 1, **savings.**

**whet,** *v.* — *Syn.* hone, stone, finish; see **sharpen** 1.

**whether,** *conj.* — *Syn.* if, either, even if, if it follows that, in case.

**whether or not,** *conj. & modif.* **1.** [Surely] — *Syn.* in any case, certainly, positively; see **surely.**
**2.** [If] — *Syn.* whether, yes or no, whichever; see **if.**

**whetstone,** *n.* — *Syn.* grinder's stone, hone, rubstone, emery, sharpener, grindstone, oilstone, strop, grinder's wheel, carborundum wheel.

**whew,** *interj.* — *Syn.* phew, well, my goodness, golly, gosh, gee whiz, dear me, goodness, goodness gracious, for heaven's sake.

**which,** *conj.* — *Syn.* what, whichever, that, whatever, and that, and which.

**which,** *pron.* — *Syn.* what, that, one, who.

**whichever,** *conj. & modif.* — *Syn.* whatever, which, whichsoever, no matter which, whoever.

**whiff,** *n.* — *Syn.* scent, puff, fume; see **smell** 1, 2.

**whiff,** *v.* — *Syn.* inhale, sniff, scent; see **smell** 2.

**while,** *conj.* **1.** [As long as] — *Syn.* during, at the same time that, during the time that, whilst, throughout the time that, in the time that.
**2.** [Although] — *Syn.* whereas, though, even though; see **although.**
**for a while** — *Syn.* for a time, for a short time, briefly; see **awhile, temporarily.**

**whim,** *n.* — *Syn.* notion, vagary, caprice; see **caprice, impulse** 2.
*See Synonym Study at* CAPRICE.

**whimper,** *v.* — *Syn.* whine, snivel, fuss, weep; see **complain** 1, **cry** 1, **whine.**
*See Synonym Study at* CRY.

**whimsical,** *modif.* — *Syn.* playful, capricious, comical; see **funny** 1.

**whimsy,** *n.* **1.** [Quaint or fanciful humor] — *Syn.* whimsicality, fancifulness, playfulness, drollness; see **humor** 1.
**2.** [An idle or fanciful notion] — *Syn.* caprice, whim, fancy; see **caprice.**
*See Synonym Study at* CAPRICE.

**whine,** *v.* — *Syn.* sing, hum, whistle, whimper, drone, cry, mewl, moan, murmur, grumble, snivel, complain, grouse*, gripe*, beef*.

**whinny,** *v.* — *Syn.* neigh, nicker, whicker, bray, bleat, cry.

**whip,** *n.* — *Syn.* switch, strap, rod, birch rod, ruler, cane, lash, scourge, knotted cord, knout, cat-o'-nine-tails, thong, blacksnake, dog whip, ox whip, bull whip, horsewhip, buggy whip, riding whip, riding crop, quirt, taws.

**whip,** *v.* **1.** [To flog] — *Syn.* thrash, flog, lash, scourge; see **beat** 2, **punish.**
**2.** [*To defeat] — *Syn.* rout, trounce, outdo; see **defeat** 1, 3.
**3.** [To stir] — *Syn.* beat, stir, whisk; see **mix** 1.

*See Synonym Study at* BEAT.

**whip hand,** *n.* — *Syn.* advantage, control, domination; see **command** 2, **power** 2.

**whip into shape,** *v.* — *Syn.* train, finish, fix up, polish off*; see **complete** 1, **train** 3.

**whipped,** *modif.* **1.** [Hit] — *Syn.* lashed, scourged, strapped; see **punished.**
**2.** [Defeated] — *Syn.* overcome, outdone, thrashed*; see **beaten** 1.

**whipping,** *n.* — *Syn.* beating, thrashing, strapping; see **mauling, punishment.**

**whip up,** *v.* — *Syn.* stimulate, stir up, agitate; see **disturb** 2, **excite** 1, 2.

**whir,** *v.* — *Syn.* whiz, swish, vibrate; see **hum.**

**whirl,** *n.* **1.** [Rapid rotating motion] — *Syn.* swirl, turn, flurry, spin, gyration, reel, surge, whir; see also **revolution** 1.
**2.** [Confusion] — *Syn.* hurry, flutter, fluster, ferment, agitation, tempest, storm, rush, tumult, turbulence, commotion, hurly-burly, bustle, the dizzy rounds*.

**whirl,** *v.* — *Syn.* turn around, rotate, spin, gyrate, wheel, swirl, twirl, revolve, gyre, turn, turn upon itself.

**whirling,** *modif.* — *Syn.* swirling, spinning, rotating; see **revolving** 1, **turning.**

**whirlpool,** *n.* — *Syn.* eddy, vortex, swirl, maelstrom, undertow, undercurrent, rapids, Scylla.

**whirlwind,** *n.* — *Syn.* windstorm, cyclone, tornado, twister, gale, hurricane, tempest.

**whirring,** *n.* — *Syn.* whizzing, humming, hissing, buzzing; see **noise** 1.

**whisk,** *v.* — *Syn.* flit, flutter, speed; see **hurry** 1.

**whisker,** *n.* — *Syn.* facial hair, filament, bristle, cilium; see **hair** 2.

**whiskers,** *n.* — *Syn.* beard, mustache, sideburns, burnsides, mutton chops, goatee, hair, face hair, imperial, Vandyke, alfalfa*, bristles*, muff*, chin armor*, weeds*.

**whiskey,** *n.* — *Syn.* bourbon, rye, corn, Scotch, Irish, Canadian, usquebaugh, *spiritus frumenti* (Latin), hard liquor*, likker*, spirits*, aqua vitae*, firewater*, booze*, sneaky pete*, redeye*, white lightning*, rotgut*, hooch*, alky*, corn*, home-brew*, moonshine*, mountain dew*; see also **drink** 2.

**whisper,** *n.* **1.** [A low, sibilant sound] — *Syn.* rustle, noise, murmur, hum, buzz, drone, undertone, hissing, susurration.
**2.** [A guarded utterance] — *Syn.* disclosure, divulgence, confidence, aside, stage whisper, disclosure, secret, rumor, hint, secret message, underground report.

**whisper,** *v.* — *Syn.* speak softly, speak in a whisper, speak under one's breath, speak in an undertone, tell, talk low, speak confidentially, mutter, murmur, susurrate, rustle, speak into someone's ear. — *Ant.* YELL, speak aloud, shout.

**whispered,** *modif.* — *Syn.* breathed, droned, muttered; see **quiet** 2.

**whispering,** *modif.* — *Syn.* rustling, sighing, buzzing, humming, murmuring, droning, hissing; see also **sounding.** — *Ant.* YELLING, howling, screaming.

**whispering campaign,** *n.* — *Syn.* slander, dirty politics, libel; see **gossip** 1.

**whistle,** *n.* **1.** [A shrill sound] — *Syn.* cry, shriek, howl, blast, piping, siren call, fire alarm, birdcall, signal, toot, blare; see also **noise** 1.
**2.** [An instrument that produces a shrill sound] — *Syn.* fife, pipe, pipes, panpipes, tin whistle, steam whistle, mouth whistle, traffic whistle, siren, calliope.

**whistle,** *v.* **1.** [To produce a shrill blast] — *Syn.* fife, pipe, flute, trill, hiss, whiz, wheeze, shriek, howl, blare, toot, tootle; see also **sound** 1.

**2.** [To call with a whistle] — *Syn.* signal, summon, warn, command, flag, arrest, sound a whistle.

**3.** [To produce a tune by whistling] — *Syn.* warble, tootle, trill, quaver, carol, improvise.

**whistling,** *modif.* — *Syn.* fifing, piping, trilling, shrieking, hissing, calling, tooting, caroling, warbling.

**whit,** *n.* — *Syn.* jot, iota, mite; see **bit** 1, 3.

**white,** *modif.* **1.** [The color of fresh snow] — *Syn.* ivory, silvery, snow-white, snowy, frosted, milky, milky-white, chalky, pearly, blanched, bleached, ashen, pale, wan, albescent. — *Ant.* DARK, black, dirty.

**2.** [Colorless] — *Syn.* clear, transparent, clean, blank, spotless, pure, unalloyed, neutral, achromatic, achromic. — *Ant.* COLORED, chromatic, mixed.

**3.** [Concerning the white race] — *Syn.* fair-skinned, light-complexioned, Caucasian, light-skinned, ruddy-faced; see also **European, western** 2. — *Ant.* BLACK, Negro, negroid.

**4.** [*Honorable] — *Syn.* decent, splendid, kind, courageous, good-natured, considerate.

**5.** [Pale] — *Syn.* ashen, wan, pallid; see **pale** 1.

**white-collar★,** *modif.* — *Syn.* executive, professional, business; see **administrative.**

**white elephant,** *n.* — *Syn.* junk, clutter, worthless object, outmoded object; see **heirloom.**

**whiten,** *v.* **1.** [To become white] — *Syn.* grow hoary, blench, blanch, pale, turn white, turn gray, grow pale, be covered with snow, be silvered, lose color, fade.

**2.** [To make white] — *Syn.* bleach, blanch, silver, paint white, whitewash, apply powder, chalk. — *Ant.* DIRTY, smudge, blacken.

**whiteness,** *n.* — *Syn.* colorlessness, paleness, achromatism, pallidity, hoariness, snowiness. — *Ant.* DARKNESS, blackness, color.

**white paper,** *n.* — *Syn.* document, pronouncement, government report, authoritative report, official statement, in depth analysis, in depth account; see also **declaration** 2, **writing** 2.

**white slave★,** *n.* — *Syn.* call girl, hustler, harlot; see **prostitute.**

**whitewash,** *v.* **1.** [To cover with a lime wash] — *Syn.* paint, whiten, calcimine, paint white, apply a white coating, wash.

**2.** [*To give the appearance of innocence] — *Syn.* varnish, gloss over, cover up, veneer, conceal the facts of, play down, rationalize; see also **excuse.** — *Ant.* IMPLICATE, accuse, blame.

**whither,** *modif.* — *Syn.* where?, in what direction?, toward what place?

**whittle,** *v.* **1.** [To cut] — *Syn.* pare, carve, shape, fashion, shave, model, chip off.

**2.** [To reduce slowly] — *Syn.* lessen, diminish, shave, decrease, pare down.

**whiz★,** *n.* — *Syn.* clever person, prodigy, wonder, star, genius, gifted child, gifted person, marvel.

**whiz,** *v.* — *Syn.* speed, fly rapidly, dart, race, hurtle, hurry, whir, hiss, hum.

**who,** *pron.* — *Syn.* what, that, which, he, she, they, I, you, whoever, whichever.

**whoa,** *interj.* — *Syn.* stop!, wait!, halt!, stand!

**who cares?★,** *interj.* — *Syn.* never mind, no matter, it is all the same, it makes no difference, it doesn't matter.

**whoever,** *pron.* — *Syn.* he who, she who, the one who, whatever person, no matter who.

**whole,** *modif.* **1.** [Entire] — *Syn.* all, complete, entire, total, inclusive, full, undivided, uncut, full-length, unexpurgated, unabbreviated, unabridged, integral, aggregate, indivisible, organismic, inseparable,

indissoluble, gross, undiminished, utter. — *Ant.* UNFINISHED, PARTIAL, incomplete.

**2.** [Not broken or damaged] — *Syn.* thorough, mature, developed, unimpaired, unmarred, full, unbroken, undamaged, entire, in one piece, sound, solid, replete, untouched, without a scratch, intact, uninjured, undecayed, completed, preserved, perfect, complete, safe, in A-1 condition, shipshape, in good order, together, unified, plenary, exhaustive, conclusive, unqualified, fulfilled, accomplished, consummate, to the teeth★, A-OK★. — *Ant.* BROKEN, mutilated, defective.

**3.** [Not ill or injured] — *Syn.* hale, hearty, sound; see **healthy** 1, **well** 1.

*See Synonym Study at* COMPLETE.

**whole,** *n.* — *Syn.* unity, totality, everything, oneness, entity, entirety, collectivity, sum, assemblage, aggregate, aggregation, body, lump, gross, entire stock, length and breadth, generality, mass, amount, bulk, quantity, universality, combination, complex, assembly, gross amount. — *Ant.* PART, portion, fraction.

**as a whole** — *Syn.* altogether, all told, all in all; see **altogether** 2.

**wholehearted,** *modif.* — *Syn.* sincere, earnest, candid, complete, full; see also **frank, hearty** 1.

**whole-hog,** *modif.* — *Syn.* without reservation, complete, completely, enthusiastic, enthusiastically; see also **completely, enthusiastic** 1, 2, 3.

**wholesale,** *modif.* **1.** [Dealing in large lots] — *Syn.* large-scale, discount, in the mass, quantitative, in bulk, bulk, to the retailer, by the carload, loose, in quantity, in job lots; see also **commercial** 1. — *Ant.* RETAIL, to the consumer, in small lots.

**2.** [Indiscriminate] — *Syn.* sweeping, widespread, comprehensive, extensive, complete, over-all, general, total.

**wholesome,** *modif.* — *Syn.* nutritious, nutritive, nourishing, beneficial; see **healthful.**

**whole-wheat,** *modif.* — *Syn.* graham, all-wheat, all-grain, whole-grain, 100-percent-wheat.

**wholly,** *modif.* **1.** [Completely] — *Syn.* totally, entirely, fully; see **completely.**

**2.** [Exclusively] — *Syn.* solely, specifically, individually; see **only** 1.

**whom,** *pron.* — *Syn.* that, her, him; see **who, what** 2.

**whoop,** *n.* — *Syn.* hoot, shout, cry, hurrah, cheer, halloo, howl, squawk; outcry; see also **noise** 1.

**whoop,** *v.* — *Syn.* howl, bawl, shriek, cheer, scream, cry out, shout, bellow, jeer, boo, yell.

**whooping,** *modif.* — *Syn.* yelling, hooting, bawling, shouting, booing, jeering, bellowing, hollowing, hollering★, cheering, exuberant, hilarious, gay, mad, riotous, drunken, raging.

**whoop it up★,** *v.* **1.** [To raise a disturbance] — *Syn.* celebrate, riot, get drunk, get noisy, go on a spree★, go on a toot★, paint the town red★, rip out★.

**2.** [To advertise] — *Syn.* campaign for, push, propagandize.

**whoops★,** *interj.* — *Syn.* oh-oh★, uh-oh★, oops, sorry, oh, no; see also **no.**

**whopper,** *n.* — *Syn.* great lie, falsehood, fabrication, a big one★; see **lie** 1, **story.**

**whopping★,** *modif.* — *Syn.* huge, big, mountainous; see **large** 1.

**whore,** *n.* — *Syn.* call girl, harlot, streetwalker; see **prostitute.**

**whore,** *v.* — *Syn.* engage in prostitution, prostitute oneself, solicit patrons, give oneself to hire, hustle★, walk the pavement★, cruise★; see also **solicit** 3.

**whorehouse,** *n.* — *Syn.* house of prostitution, house of ill repute, stews, cat house★; see **brothel.**

**whoremonger,** *n.* — *Syn.* whoremaster, go-between, hustler\*; see **agent 1, pimp.**

**whorl,** *n.* — *Syn.* twirl, twist, spiral; see **coil.**

**whose,** *pron.* — *Syn.* to whom, belonging to what person, of the aforementioned one, from these.

**why,** *modif., conj. & interrog.* — *Syn.* for what reason?, how so?, how?, how is it that?, on whose account?, what is the cause that?, to what end?, for what purpose?, on what foundation?, how do you explain that?, how come?\*.

**whys and wherefores\*,** *n.* — *Syn.* reason, explanation, cause; see **reason 3.**

**wick,** *n.* — *Syn.* thread, cord, taper, lampwick, candle end, lantern wick, candlewick; see also **candle.**

**wicked,** *modif.* **1.** [Morally evil] — *Syn.* evil, immoral, unethical, corrupt, unprincipled, sinful, bad, base, foul, gross, dissolute, wayward, irreligious, blasphemous, profane, evil-minded, vile, degenerate, depraved, incorrigible, heartless, shameless, degraded, debauched, hard, toughened, disreputable, infamous, indecent, mean, remorseless, reprobate, salacious, iniquitous, scandalous, atrocious, contemptible, nasty, rotten\*, low-down\*, good-for-nothing\*, dirty\*. — *Ant.* GOOD, virtuous, PURE.
**2.** [Capable of doing great damage] — *Syn.* vicious, fiendish, diabolical, hellish, villainous, rascally, devilish, malevolent, malicious, plotting, conspiratorial, iniquitous, flagrant, nefarious, criminal, heinous, murderous, tricky, sinister, ignoble, monstrous, opprobrious, felonious, dangerous, cutthroat, ratty\*, slippery\*, crooked\*. — *Ant.* HONEST, just, kind.
**3.** [Naughty] — *Syn.* naughty, mischievous, roguish; see **naughty.**

---

*SYN.* — **wicked** and **evil** both connote willful violation of a moral code, but **evil** often has ominous or malevolent implications *[an evil hour]*, and **wicked** is sometimes weakened in a playful way to mean merely mischievous *[wicked wit]*; **ill,** which is slightly weaker than **evil** in its implications of immorality, is now used chiefly in certain idiomatic phrases *[ill-gotten gains]*; **naughty** today implies mere mischievousness or disobedience *[a naughty child]*; **bad,** in this comparison, is the broadest term, ranging in implication from merely unsatisfactory to utterly depraved

---

**wickedly,** *modif.* — *Syn.* sinfully, unrighteously, immorally; see **wrongly 1.**

**wickedness,** *n.* — *Syn.* evil, depravity, immorality, sinfulness; see **blasphemy.**

**wicker,** *modif.* — *Syn.* straw-plaited, straw-woven, wicker-work, roped, plaited, woven, made of withes, made of osiers.

**wide,** *modif.* **1.** [Broad] — *Syn.* extended, spacious, deep; see **broad 1, extensive 1.**
**2.** [Loose] — *Syn.* broad, roomy, full, ample, voluminous, flowing, hanging; see also **loose 1.**
**3.** [Extensive] — *Syn.* large-scale, all-inclusive, universal; see **comprehensive.**
**4.** [Inaccurate] — *Syn.* astray, off the mark, far off; see **wrong 2, 3.**
**5.** [Sparse] — *Syn.* far-flung, separated, far; see **away 1, scattered.**
*See Synonym Study at* BROAD.

**wide-awake,** *modif.* — *Syn.* alert, watchful, vigilant; see **careful.**
*See Synonym Study at* WATCHFUL.

**widely,** *modif.* — *Syn.* extensively, generally, publicly, popularly, nationally, internationally, universally, in many places, broadly, comprehensively. — *Ant.* LOCALLY, in a small circle, narrowly.

**widen,** *v.* **1.** [To make wider] — *Syn.* add to, broaden, stretch, extend, increase, enlarge, distend, spread out, give more space, augment. — *Ant.* COMPRESS, narrow, cramp.
**2.** [To become wider] — *Syn.* unfold, grow, open, stretch, grow larger, increase, swell, multiply.

**wide-open,** *modif.* — *Syn.* unrestricted, licentious, wild; see **lawless 1, 2.**

**widespread,** *modif.* — *Syn.* extensive, general, sweeping, broad, comprehensive, far-reaching, widely accepted, boundless, popular, public, unrestricted, unlimited, on a large scale, over-all. — *Ant.* SECRET, OBSCURE, limited.

**widow,** *n.* — *Syn.* surviving wife, relict, dowager, husbandless wife, dead man's wife, widow woman\*, sod widow\*, grass widow\*, mantrap\*; see also **survivor, wife.**

**widower,** *n.* — *Syn.* surviving husband, wifeless husband, dead woman's husband, grass widower\*, widowman\*; see also **husband, man 2, survivor.**

**width,** *n.* — *Syn.* breadth, wideness, girth, diameter, distance across, amplitude, cross dimension, cross measurement, expanse. — *Ant.* LENGTH, height, altitude.

**wield,** *v.* — *Syn.* handle, manipulate, exercise, hold high, brandish, shake, wave, swing, utilize, work, ply, operate, use, flourish.
*See Synonym Study at* HANDLE.

**wield power** or **authority,** *v.* — *Syn.* dictate, rule, administer; see **manage 1.**

**wiener,** *n.* — *Syn.* wienerwurst, frankfurter, hot dog, sausage, link, vienna sausage, dog\*, weenie\*, red-hot\*, footlong\*; see also **meat.**

**wife,** *n.* — *Syn.* married woman, spouse, lady, dame, madam, matron, squaw\*, helpmate, helpmeet, consort, marrow, mate, housewife, better half\*, the missis\*, the little woman\*, wifey\*, ball and chain\*, the old lady\*. — *Ant.* WIDOW, SPINSTER, old maid.

**take to wife** — *Syn.* marry, wed, espouse; see **marry 1.**

**wig,** *n.* — *Syn.* periwig, peruke, postiche, artificial hair, fall, hairpiece, toupee, rug\*, carpet\*, piece\*; see also **hair 1.**

**wiggle,** *v.* — *Syn.* wag, waggle, wriggle, squirm, shimmy, shake, flounce, dance sensually, grind, do the grind\*, juggle the hip\*.

**wigwam,** *n.* — *Syn.* wickiup, tepee, lodge; see **shelter, tent.**

**wild,** *modif.* **1.** [Not controlled] — *Syn.* unrestrained, unmanageable, boisterous; see **disorderly 1, unruly.**
**2.** [Uncivilized] — *Syn.* barbarous, savage, undomesticated; see **primitive 3.**
**3.** [Not cultivated] — *Syn.* luxuriant, lush, exuberant, dense, excessive, desolate, waste, desert, weedy, untrimmed, impenetrable, uninhabited, native, natural, untouched, virgin, overgrown, uncultivated, untilled, uncared for, neglected, overrun, free, rampant, untamed.
**4.** [Undomesticated] — *Syn.* untamed, untrained, unbroken, not housebroken.
**5.** [Inaccurate] — *Syn.* erratic, off, unsound; see **mistaken 1, wrong 2.**
**6.** [Stormy] — *Syn.* disturbed, raging, storming; see **turbulent.**
**7.** [Excited] — *Syn.* hot, eager, avid; see **excited.**
**8.** [Dissolute] — *Syn.* unbridled, loose, licentious, profligate, orgiastic; see also **lewd 2.**
**9.** [Imprudent] — *Syn.* reckless, foolish, incautious; see **careless 1, rash.**

**run wild**— *Syn.* run out of control, rage, run riot, cut loose, rampage; see also **escape.**

**wildcat,** *modif.* — *Syn.* illegal, unsound, speculative, risky, illegitimate, unsafe, unsecured, unauthorized. — *Ant.* LEGAL, legitimate, authorized.

**wildcat,** *n.* — *Syn.* mountain lion, bobcat, cougar, Canada lynx, ocelot, cerval, caracal.

**wilderness,** *n.* — *Syn.* primitive area, wastelands, waste, wastes, back country, the woods, the North woods, primeval forest, uninhabited region; see also **desert, forest.**

*See Synonym Study at* WASTE.

**wild-goose chase\*,** *n.* — *Syn.* futile search, meaningless chase, vain inquiry, foolish quest, hopeless quest; see also **failure** 1.

**wildly,** *modif.* **1.** [Without restraint] — *Syn.* hastily, rashly, fiercely, violently, ferociously, uncontrollably, carelessly, quixotically, savagely, unwittingly, recklessly, confusedly, pell-mell. — *Ant.* CAREFULLY, prudently, judiciously.

**2.** [With emotion] — *Syn.* heatedly, passionately, avidly; see **angrily.**

**wilds,** *n.* — *Syn.* uninhabited country, wasteland, wilderness, primitive country, pioneer land, bush, forest, jungle, boondocks, unexplored territory, no man's land. — *Ant.* GARDEN, MEADOW, FIELD.

**wile,** *n.* — *Syn.* trickery, deceit, cunning, stratagem, trick, chicanery, dishonesty, plot, ruse, hoax, deception, scheming, dodge, artifice, bunco\*, humbug\*, flimflam\*, scam\*, monkey business\*, horseplay\*. — *Ant.* HONESTY, frankness, sincerity.

*See Synonym Study at* TRICK.

**will,** *n.* **1.** [Desire] — *Syn.* inclination, wish, disposition, pleasure, yearning, craving, longing, hankering. — *Ant.* COMMAND, indifference, distaste.

**2.** [Command] — *Syn.* order, insistence, decree; see **command** 1, **directions.**

**3.** [Conscious power] — *Syn.* resolution, volition, intention, will power, preference, mind, determination, self-determination, decisiveness, moral strength, discretion, conviction, willfulness. — *Ant.* DOUBT, vacillation, indecision.

**4.** [Testament for the disposition of property] — *Syn.* bequest, disposition, instructions, last wishes, bestowal, dispensation, last will and testament.

**at will**— *Syn.* whenever one wishes, at any time, *ad libitum* (Latin); see **any time.**

*SYN.* — **will,** the more inclusive term here, basically denotes the power of choice and deliberate action or the intention resulting from the exercise of this power /freedom of the *will,* the *will* to succeed/; **volition** stresses the exercise of the will in making a choice or decision /he came of his own *volition*/

**will,** *v.* **1.** [To exert one's will] — *Syn.* decree, order, command, demand, authorize, request, make oneself felt, decide upon, insist, direct, enjoin.

**2.** [To wish] — *Syn.* want, incline to, prefer; see **wish** 2.

**3.** [An indication of futurity] — *Syn.* shall, would, should, expect to, anticipate, look forward to, hope to, await, foresee, propose.

**willful,** *modif.* **1.** [Deliberate] — *Syn.* intentional, voluntary, premeditated, contemplated; see **deliberate** 1.

**2.** [Obstinate] — *Syn.* stubborn, wayward, intractable; see **obstinate** 1.

*See Synonym Study at* VOLUNTARY.

**willing,** *modif.* **1.** [Zealous] — *Syn.* energetic, prompt,

reliable, active, obedient, enthusiastic, responsible, agreeable, well-disposed. — *Ant.* RELUCTANT, grudging, stubborn.

**2.** [Ready to comply] — *Syn.* prepared, voluntary, ready, compliant, amenable, tractable, feeling, like, in accord with. — *Ant.* OPPOSED, averse, UNWILLING.

**willingly,** *modif.* — *Syn.* gladly, readily, freely, obediently, voluntarily, with relish, at one's pleasure, on one's own account, of one's own accord, with open arms, with good cheer, without demur, with pleasure, cheerfully, with all one's heart, at the drop of a hat\*, like a shot\*; see also **agreeably.**

**willingness,** *n.* — *Syn.* zeal, enthusiasm, readiness, earnestness, alacrity, eagerness, cordiality, hospitality, courteousness, compliance, good will, geniality. — *Ant.* OPPOSITION, hostility, aversion.

**will-o'-the-wisp\*,** *n.* — *Syn.* fancy, ephemera, dream, pipedream, *ignis fatuus* (Latin), shadow, illusion, vision.

**willow,** *n.* Varieties of willows include: white, crack, osier, drooping, black, peach-leaved, pussy, shining, beaked, sandbar, autumn, broad-leaved, furry, silky, hoary, prairie, gray, red, yellow, arroyo, velvet, weeping, bay, goat, basket; see also **tree, wood** 2.

**willowy,** *modif.* — *Syn.* slender, graceful, lissome; see **thin** 2.

**wilt,** *v.* — *Syn.* droop, wither, weaken, flag, dry up, shrivel, fade, go limp, become flaccid, lose freshness, faint. — *Ant.* GROW, stiffen, STAND.

**wily,** *modif.* — *Syn.* crafty, sneaky, cunning; see **sly** 1.

*See Synonym Study at* SLY.

**win\*,** *n.* — *Syn.* triumph, conquest, gain; see **success** 1, **victory** 2.

**win,** *v.* **1.** [To gain a victory] — *Syn.* be victorious, prevail, get the best of, come out first, be first, conquer, overcome, overwhelm, triumph; see also **succeed** 1.

**2.** [To obtain] — *Syn.* get, acquire, gain; see **obtain** 1.

**3.** [To reach] — *Syn.* attain, accomplish, effect; see **approach** 2, 3.

**4.** [To convince] — *Syn.* win over, bring over, persuade, bring around, convert, talk into, prevail upon, sway, overcome, influence.

**wince,** *v.* — *Syn.* draw back, cower, cringe, flinch, quail, shrink back, make a wry face, grimace, blench, shy, start, back off\*, chicken out\*.

**wind,** *n.* **1.** [Air in motion] — *Syn.* draft, air current, mistral, breeze, gust, gale, blast, flurry, whisk, whiff, puff, whirlwind, flutter, wafting, zephyr, trade wind, northeaster, southwester, sirocco, tempest, blow, cyclone, typhoon, twister, hurricane, sandstorm, foehn, prevailing westerlies, stiff breeze, spanking breeze, Chinook, khamsin, Zephyrus, Boreas.

**2.** [\*Fugitive information] — *Syn.* babble, report, talk; see **gossip** 1, **rumor** 1.

**3.** [\*The breath] — *Syn.* respiration, inhalation, breathing; see **breath** 1.

**get** *or* **have wind of\***— *Syn.* hear of, hear about, hear from, have news of, trace; see also **hear** 2.

**take the wind out of one's sails\***— *Syn.* deflate, cut down to size, best, get the better of, overcome; see also **defeat** 1.

*SYN.* — **wind** is the general term for any natural movement of air, whether of high or low velocity or great or little force; **breeze** is popularly applied to a light, fresh wind and, meteorologically, to a wind having a velocity of from 4 to 31 miles an hour; **gale** is popularly applied to a strong, somewhat violent wind and, meteorologically, to a wind having a velocity of from 32 to 63 miles an hour; **gust** and **blast** apply to sudden, brief winds, **gust** suggesting a light puff, and **blast** a driving rush, of air; **zephyr** is a poetic term for a soft, gentle breeze

**wind,** *v.* **1.** [To wrap about] — *Syn.* coil, reel in, fake down, entwine, wreathe, shroud, fold, cover, bind, tape, bandage.
**2.** [To twist] — *Syn.* convolute, screw, wind up; see **bend** 2.
**3.** [To meander] — *Syn.* zigzag, weave, snake, twist, loop, turn, twine, ramble, swerve, deviate.

**windbag,** *n.* — *Syn.* talker, boaster, bore, bag of hot air; see **braggart, gossip** 2.

**windfall,** *n.* — *Syn.* boon, stroke of luck, weal, freebie\*; see **blessing** 2, **surprise** 2.

**winding,** *modif.* — *Syn.* turning, gyrating, gyring, spiraling, twisting, snaky, serpentine, convoluted, dextrorse, dextrorsal, sinistrorse. — *Ant.* STRAIGHT, DIRECT, VERTICAL.

**windmill,** *n.* — *Syn.* rotating wheel, wind-driven wheel, post mill, tower mill, wind-charger, smock mill, water pump; see also **mill** 2, **pump.**

**window,** *n.* **1.** [An architectural opening for light and air] — *Syn.* skylight, porthole, bay window, bow window, picture window, oriel, casement, fenestration, dormer, embrasure, stained-glass, rose window, show window, bull's eye, fanlight, transom, peephole, *oeil-de-boeuf, vitrail* (*both* French).
**2.** [That which fills a window] — *Syn.* lattice, shutter, glass, pane, windowpane, stained glass.

**windowpane,** *n.* — *Syn.* pane, square of glass, glass, glazing, window.

**window shade,** *n.* — *Syn.* shade, blind, Venetian blind, screen, shutter, canopy, awning, jalousie, curtain.

**windpipe,** *n.* — *Syn.* airpipe, bronchus, trachea; see **throat.**

**windshield,** *n.* — *Syn.* windscreen (British), protection against the wind, wrap-around; see **shield.**

**windup,** *n.* — *Syn.* conclusion, end, finish, finale, completion.

**wind up\*,** *v.* **1.** [To end] — *Syn.* conclude, be through with, come to the end of; see **end** 1.
**2.** [To make tense] — *Syn.* excite, energize, enthuse, overstimulate.

**windy,** *modif.* **1.** [Characterized by wind] — *Syn.* breezy, blustery, raw, stormy, wind-swept, airy, gusty, blowing, fresh, drafty, wind-shaken, tempestuous, boisterous. — *Ant.* CALM, quiet, still.
**2.** [\*Boastful] — *Syn.* talkative, long-winded, garrulous; see **verbose.**

**wine,** *modif.* — *Syn.* wine-colored, maroon, dark red, grape; see **red.**

**wine,** *n.* Varieties of wine include: fine, sparkling, still, fortified, dry, sec, brut, sweet, heavy, light, white, rosé, blush, red, blackberry, cherry, currant, elderberry, gooseberry, dandelion; sacramental, dessert, dinner, table, medicinal, aperitif, cooking; California, French, varietal, vinifera, Italian, German, South African, Chilean, Australian; *vin mousseux, vin rouge, vin rosé, vin de table, vin ordinaire* (*all* French); sherry, Tokay, port, claret, muscatel, Canary, Malaga, Burgundy, Bordeaux, Beaujolais, Beaujolais Nouveau, Madeira, Marsala, Merlot, Champagne, (Haut) Sauterne, Rhine wine, Riesling, hock, Moselle, Chablis, May wine, Folle blanche, Chardonnay, Zinfandel, Chianti, light muscat, Catawba, Sauvignon vert, Sauvignon blanc, Pinot, Pinot Noir, Gamay, Cabernet Sauvignon, Concord, Gewürztraminer, Chenin blanc, must, retsina; see also **drink** 2.

**wine and dine,** *v.* — *Syn.* feast, make welcome, entertain lavishly; see **entertain** 2.

**wing,** *n.* **1.** [An organ or instrument of flight] — *Syn.* appendage, pinion, elytron, aileron, airfoil; see also **feather.**
**2.** [An architectural unit or extension] — *Syn.* annex, ell, addition, projection, hall, section, division, part.
**3.** [An organized group of aircraft] — *Syn.* flying unit, flight, flying squad, formation, air squadron; see also **unit** 1.
**4.** [Outer portions of a line in sports or war] — *Syn.* right wing, left wing, end of the line, end, extension, flank, side, segment.
**5.** [Entrance to the stage: *usually plural*] — *Syn.* offstage, backstage, behind-stage, back, flats, green room.
**6.** [\*A pitching arm] — *Syn.* soup bone\*, glass arm\*, heave machinery\*; see **arm** 2.

**on the wing** — *Syn.* going, leaving, progressing; see **flying.**

**take wing** — *Syn.* go, depart, run off; see **leave** 1.

**take under one's wing** — *Syn.* favor, help, guarantee; see **adopt** 2.

**wing\*,** *v.* — *Syn.* wound, injure, bring down; see **hurt** 1.

**winged,** *modif.* — *Syn.* alar, feathered, pteroid; see **flying.**

**wings,** *n.* — *Syn.* commission, insignia, second lieutenancy, aircorps officership.

**wink,** *v.* **1.** [To close one eye] — *Syn.* squint, blink, nictate, nictitate, flirt, make eyes at\*, bat the eyes\*.
**2.** [To twinkle] — *Syn.* sparkle, gleam, blink; see **flash** 1.

*SYN.* — **wink** usually implies a usually deliberate movement in the quick closing and opening of one or both eyelids one or more times [he *winked* at her knowingly]; **blink** implies a rapid series of such movements, usually performed involuntarily and with the eyes half-shut [to *blink* in the harsh sunlight]

**wink at,** *v.* — *Syn.* connive, pass over, gloss over, condone, pretend not to see, excuse, permit, forgive, turn a blind eye toward. — *Ant.* CENSURE, frown upon, revile.

**winking,** *n.* — *Syn.* nictitating, blinking, squinting, flirting, flirtation, twinkling, sparkling, flashing.

**winner,** *n.* — *Syn.* victor, conqueror, prize winner, champion, winning competitor, hero, victorious contestant, successful contestant, leading entrant, grand champion, national champion, Olympic champion, contest winner, medal winner, title-holder\*, champ\*, big boy\*, front runner\*, bell-ringer\*. — *Ant.* LOSER, vanquished, defeated.

**winning,** *modif.* **1.** [Engaging] — *Syn.* attractive, charming, dazzling, courteous, agreeable, gratifying, acceptable, cute, cunning. — *Ant.* UGLY, repulsive, loathsome.
**2.** [Victorious] — *Syn.* champion, conquering, leading; see **triumphant.**

**winnow,** *v.* — *Syn.* scatter, extract, sieve, thresh; see **separate** 2, **sift** 2.

**winsome,** *modif.* — *Syn.* cute, engaging, entrancing; see **charming.**

**winter,** *n.* — *Syn.* cold season, frosty weather, wintertime, Christmastime, Jack Frost\*, King Winter\*, squaw winter\*, blackberry winter\*.

**winter,** *v.* — *Syn.* stay for the winter, go for the winter, vacation, spend the winter, hole up\*; see also **dwell, live** 2.

**wintry,** *modif.* — *Syn.* chilly, frosty, icy, snowy, frigid, cold, bleak, raw, biting, hiemal, cutting. — *Ant.* WARM, summery, balmy.

**wipe,** v. — Syn. rub, clean, dry, dust, mop, clear, wash, swab, soak up, obliterate.

**wipe out,** v. 1. [To remove] — Syn. erase, delete, eliminate; see **cancel** 1, **remove** 1.

2. [To exterminate] — Syn. slay, annihilate, eradicate; see **destroy** 1, **kill** 1.

**wire,** n. 1. [A metal strand] — Syn. line, electric wire, cable, aerial, circuit, wiring, live wire, coil, conductor, filament, musical string, wire tape, wire cord.

2. [A metal net] — Syn. barbed wire, wire fence, chicken wire, wirework, wire cage, wire basket, wire cloth, wire entanglement; see also **fence** 1, 2, **net.**

3. [*A telegraphic message] — Syn. cablegram, telegram, message, night message, night letter, code message.

**down to the wire***— Syn. to the very end, to the bitter end, at the last, eventually; see **finally** 2.

**get in under the wire***— Syn. just make it, succeed, just squeak through*; see **arrive** 1.

**pull wires**— Syn. exert influence, go to the right people, use pull*; see **influence, manage** 1.

**wire,** v. 1. [To install wire] — Syn. set up a circuit, install electricity, lay wires, connect electric cables, prepare for electrical service, pipe*, tie on the spiders*; see also **electrify** 1.

2. [*To send a message by wire] — Syn. telegraph, flash, file; see **notify.**

**wired,** modif. 1. [Connected] — Syn. lined, hooked up, circuited, furnished for electricity.

2. [*Provided with concealed listening equipment] — Syn. bugged, tapped, miked.

3. [Excited] — Syn. nervous, jazzed*, stoked*.

**wireless,** modif. — Syn. radio, radioed, on the air, broadcast, beamed, shore-to-ship, ship-to-shore, short wave, transatlantic, transpacific.

**wire service,** n. — Syn. communications system, news service, Associated Press, AP; see **telegraph, telephone.**

**wiring,** n. 1. [The process of installing wires] — Syn. electrification, electrifying, installation of wire, preparation for electric service, doing the wiring; see also **installation** 1.

2. [Installed wires] — Syn. wirework, electric line, cable work, cables, electric installations, facilities for electric power, facilities for electric light.

3. [Circuitry] — Syn. circuit system, filamentation, wireworks, electrical wire distribution, tubing, circuit pattern, circuiting, threading, process, route, line, path, pattern, trail.

**wiry,** modif. — Syn. springy, light, lean, agile, limber, supple, sinewy, strong, vibrant, strapping athletic, brawny, well-knit, energetic, muscular.

**wisdom,** n. 1. [Intellectual power] — Syn. intelligence, sagacity, perspicacity; see **sanity** 1, **sense** 2.

2. [Good sense] — Syn. prudence, astuteness, sense, reason, clear thinking, brains, good judgment, sagacity, understanding, sanity, shrewdness, experience, practical knowledge, carefulness, vigilance, tact, balance, poise, stability, caution, solidity, hardheadedness, savoir faire (French), common sense, horse sense*, savvy*. — Ant. STUPIDITY, irrationality, rashness.

3. [Learning] — Syn. erudition, enlightenment, attainment; see **knowledge** 1.

See Synonym Study at KNOWLEDGE.

**wise,** modif. 1. [Judicious] — Syn. clever, sagacious, perceptive, understanding; see **rational** 1, **thoughtful** 1.

2. [Shrewd] — Syn. calculating, cunning, crafty; see **sly** 1.

3. [Prudent] — Syn. tactful, sensible, wary; see **careful, discreet.**

4. [Erudite] — Syn. knowledgeable, scholarly, smart; see **educated** 1, **learned** 1.

5. [*Impudent] — Syn. bold, forward, offensive, cocky*, smart*; see also **rude** 2.

**wisely,** modif. — Syn. tactfully, prudently, circumspectly, sagaciously, shrewdly, judiciously, discreetly, carefully, admirably, discerningly, sagely, knowingly, reasonably, sensibly, intelligently. — Ant. FOOLISHLY, stupidly, unthinkingly.

**wise up*,** v. — Syn. become informed, get smart*, learn one's way around*, wake up and smell the coffee*; see **learn** 1.

**wish,** n. 1. [Desire] — Syn. longing, yearning, hankering, thirst, disposition; see also **desire** 1.

2. [An expression of desire] — Syn. request, hope, intention, preference, choice, want, prayer, invocation, liking, pleasure, injunction, command, order.

3. [The object of desire] — Syn. goal, dream, promise; see **choice** 3, **hope** 2.

**wish,** v. 1. [To desire] — Syn. covet, crave, envy; see **want** 1, **yearn.**

2. [To express a desire] — Syn. hope, request, entreat, prefer, want, pray for, invoke, command, order, solicit, beg, look forward to, need; see also **require** 2.

3. [To bid] — Syn. order, instruct, tell; see **command** 1.

See Synonym Study at DESIRE.

**wishbone,** n. — Syn. furculum, breastbone, clavicle, lucky bone*, pulley bone*; see also **bone.**

**wishful,** modif. — Syn. desirous, longing, eager; see **enthusiastic** 2.

**wishing,** modif. — Syn. hoping, yearning, desiring, craving, pining, thirsting, hungering, wanting, longing.

**wishy-washy,** modif. 1. [Watery] — Syn. insipid, thin, diluted, weak, bland; see also **tasteless** 1.

2. [Weak] — Syn. feeble, spineless, lily-livered, yellow-bellied; see **weak** 3.

3. [Indecisive] — Syn. vacillating, irresolute, fence-sitting, mealy-mouthed; see **doubtful** 2.

**wisp,** n. — Syn. tuft, cluster, shred, a few strands, lock, bit, shock, cowlick, stray lock, scolding locks.

**wistful,** modif. — Syn. nostalgic, melancholy, sad, longing, yearning, pensive, wishful, hopeless, half-expectant, soulful, plaintive. — Ant. HAPPY, joyous, exuberant.

**wit,** n. 1. [Clever humor] — Syn. humor, wittiness, smartness, whimsicality, jocularity, pleasantry, drollery, waggery, banter, burlesque; see also **humor** 1.

2. [An example of wit, sense 1] — Syn. satire, irony, badinage, witticism, sally, whimsy, repartee, bon mot, joke, aphorism, jest, quip, epigram, pun, wisecrack*, gag*.

3. [One who possesses wit, sense 1] — Syn. humorist, punster, epigrammatist, comedian, banterer, clever fellow, life of the party, wag, wisecracker*, wise guy*.

**at one's wits' end**— Syn. downhearted, desperate, at a loss, helpless; see **hopeless** 2, **troubled** 1.

**have** or **keep one's wits about one**— Syn. be ready, be alert, take precautions, be on one's guard, keep one's cool*; see also **watch out** 2.

**live by one's wits**— Syn. use sharp practices, live dangerously, take advantage of all opportunities; see **prosper, trick.**

---

SYN. — **wit** refers to the ability to perceive the incongruous and to express it in quick, sharp, spontaneous, often sarcastic remarks that delight or entertain; **humor** is applied to the ability to perceive and express that which is comical, ludicrous, or ridiculous, but connotes kindliness, geniality, sometimes even pathos, in the expression and a reaction of sympathetic amusement from the audience; **irony** refers to the humor implicit in the contradiction between literal expression and intended meaning or in the discrepancy between appearance and reality in life; **satire** applies to the use, especially in literature, of ridicule, sarcasm, irony, etc. in exposing and attacking vices or follies; **repartee** refers to the ability to reply or retort with quick, skillful wit or humor

---

**witch**, *n.* — *Syn.* sorcerer, sorceress, warlock, magician, enchantress, charmer, hag, crone.

**witchcraft**, *n.* — *Syn.* sorcery, wizardry, magic, black magic, devil worship, black art, necromancy, witchery, divination, enchantment, spell, bewitchment, Wicca, voodoo, shamanism, diabolism, diablerie, demonology, Satanism; see also **magic** 1.
*See Synonym Study at* MAGIC.

**with**, *prep.* — *Syn.* by, in, in association, in the midst of, among, amidst, along with, in company with, in the company of, arm in arm, hand in glove, cheek by jowl, in conjunction with, among other things, beside, alongside of, including.

**withdraw**, *v.* **1.** [To retire] — *Syn.* depart, draw back, take leave; see **retire** 1, 3, **retreat** 1, 2.
**2.** [To remove from use or circulation] — *Syn.* revoke, rescind, abolish, repeal, annul, abrogate, veto, suppress, repress, retire, stamp out, declare illegal, ban, bar, nullify, repudiate, reverse, retract, throw overboard, invalidate, quash, dissolve. — *Ant.* introduce, put on the record, ESTABLISH.
**3.** [To remove] — *Syn.* take away, draw away, pull out, pull back, switch; see also **eliminate** 1, **remove** 1.

**withdrawal**, *n.* — *Syn.* removal, retreat, retraction, resignation, alienation, abandonment, recession, revulsion, abdication, relinquishment, departure. — *Ant.* PROGRESS, advance, appearance.

**withdrawn**, *modif.* **1.** [Removed] — *Syn.* retired, secluded, isolated, departed, cloistered, recluse, drawn back, gone into retirement, taken out, absent, retreated. — *Ant.* ACTIVE, involved, progressing.
**2.** [Introverted] — *Syn.* shy, reserved, retiring, aloof, reclusive.

**wither**, *v.* — *Syn.* shrivel, shrink, droop, wilt, decay, die, grow brown, dry up, dry out, fade, lose freshness, deteriorate, fall away. — *Ant.* REVIVE, reawaken, bloom.

**withered**, *modif.* — *Syn.* shriveled, wilted, decayed, deteriorated, shrunken, dead, browned, faded, parched, dried up, drooping, wrinkled. — *Ant.* FRESH, blooming, alive.

**withering**, *modif.* — *Syn.* shriveling, shrinking, wilting; see **decaying.**

**withheld**, *modif.* — *Syn.* concealed, held back, hidden, checked, restrained, delayed, denied, kept on leash, on ice*. — *Ant.* FREE, opened, made visible.

**withhold**, *v.* — *Syn.* hold back, hold out, reserve, keep; see **delay** 1, **deny.**

**withholding**, *modif.* — *Syn.* restraining, confining, checking, prohibiting, restricting, hindering, limiting, deterring, coercive, curbing, muzzling, bridling; see also **confining.** — *Ant.* OPEN, liberating, freeing.

**withholding tax**, *n.* — *Syn.* income tax, social security tax, withholdings, federal tax; see **tax** 1.

**within**, *modif. & prep.* — *Syn.* in, inside, on the inside, indoors, not further than, not beyond, not over, in less than, in reach of, in a period of, not outside; see also **inside** 2.

**with it***, *modif.* — *Syn.* up-to-date, *au courant* (French),

contemporary, trendy, hip*, cool*; see also **modern** 1.

**without**, *modif. & prep.* **1.** [Outside] — *Syn.* out, outdoors, outwardly, externally, on the outside, standing outside, left out.
**2.** [Lacking] — *Syn.* not with, not having, in the absence of, free from, deprived of.

**withstand**, *v.* — *Syn.* face, confront, oppose, resist, endure, stand up to, stand up against, hold out*.

**with that**, *conj. & prep.* — *Syn.* and so, as a result, therefore, in consideration of that; see **accordingly, so** 1, 2, 3.

**witness**, *n.* — *Syn.* observer, onlooker, eyewitness, spectator, bystander, deponent, testifier, beholder, signatory.
**bear witness** — *Syn.* affirm, attest, give evidence; see **testify** 2.

**witness**, *v.* — *Syn.* see, observe, be a witness, be on the scene, behold, be present, testify, vouch for, stand for, look on, say under oath, depose, be on hand.

**witnessed**, *modif.* **1.** [Observed and attested] — *Syn.* sworn to, vouched for, alleged, borne out, validated, valid, established, verified, authenticated, substantiated, supported, upheld, endorsed, brought forward.
**2.** [Legally signed by a third party] — *Syn.* deposed, notarized, certified, accredited, made official, warranted, sealed, signed; see also **legal** 1.

**witticism**, *n.* — *Syn.* jest, quirk, quibble; see **joke** 2, **pun.**

**witty**, *modif.* **1.** [Cleverly amusing] — *Syn.* humorous, droll, jocose, jocular, sarcastic, facetious, amusing, funny; see also **humorous.**
**2.** [*Intelligent] — *Syn.* sparkling, keen, quick-witted, brilliant, whimsical, clever, bright; see also **intelligent** 1.

---

*SYN.* — **witty** implies sharp, amusing cleverness and spontaneity in perceiving and commenting on, esp. in repartee and sometimes sarcastically, the incongruities in life; **humorous** connotes more geniality, gentleness, or whimsicality in saying or doing something that is deliberately comical or amusing; **facetious** is now usually derogatory in suggesting an inappropriate or ill-chosen attempt to be witty or humorous; **jocular** implies a happy or playful disposition characterized by the desire to amuse others; **jocose** suggests a mildly mischievous quality in joking or jesting, sometimes to the point of facetiousness

---

**wizard**, *n.* **1.** [A sorcerer] — *Syn.* magician, soothsayer, witch, witch doctor, necromancer, fortuneteller, astrologer, medicine man, conjurer, shaman, enchanter, hypnotist, diviner, seer, clairvoyant, palmist, augurer, medium.
**2.** [*One who works wonders] — *Syn.* wonder-worker, expert, prodigy, genius, authority, marvel*, crackerjack*, seven days' wonder*.

**wizened**, *modif.* — *Syn.* shriveled, lean, dried up, dessicated; see **old** 1, **shrunken, withered.**

**wobble**, *v.* — *Syn.* shake, quaver, flounder, vacillate, tremble, quiver, move unsteadily from side to side, dodder, teeter, totter, be unsteady, waver, quake, stagger, shuffle, waggle.

**wobbling**, *modif.* — *Syn.* shaking, quaking, trembling; see **quivering.**

**wobbly**, *modif.* — *Syn.* wavering, unbalanced, precarious; see **shaky** 1, **unsteady** 1.

**woe**, *n.* — *Syn.* sorrow, pain, misery; see **distress** 1, **grief** 1.

**woebegone,** *modif.* — *Syn.* despondent, depressed, dejected; see **sad** 1, **sorrowful.**

**woeful,** *modif.* — *Syn.* full of woe, mournful, miserable; see **pitiful** 1, **sorry** 1.

**wolf,** *n.* **1.** [An animal]. Varieties of wolves include: wild dog, dingo, Eskimo dog, gray wolf, white wolf, red wolf, jackal, coyote, timber wolf, lobo, Japanese wolf, Indian wolf, thylacine, aardwolf; see also **animal** 2, **dog** 1.
**2.** [*A seducer] — *Syn.* Don Juan, Casanova, lothario, Lochinvar, suitor, wooer, pursuer, gallant, lady killer*, lover boy*, wild man*, rapist*, brute*, lecher*, flirt*, cur*, glutton*, cannibal*, killer*.

**woman,** *n.* **1.** [An adult female] — *Syn.* female, lady, dame, matron, gentlewoman, maid, spinster, debutante, nymph, virgin, girl, old woman, chick*, bird*, broad*, fem*, doll*, deb*.
**2.** [A wife or mistress] — *Syn.* love, lover, wife, old lady*; see **housewife, mistress** 2.
**3.** [A female servant] — *Syn.* companion, housekeeper, cleaning lady, charlady (British), washerwoman, laundress, cook, maid, serving lady; see also **servant, slave** 1.
**4.** [Womankind] — *Syn.* femininity, fair sex, eternal feminine, the world of women, the female of the species*, the weaker vessel*; see also **womanhood** 2.

---

*SYN.* — **woman** is the standard general term for the adult human being of the sex distinguished from *man;* **female,** referring specif. to sex, is applied to plants and animals, but is now regarded as a mildly contemptuous equivalent for **woman** /that strong-minded *female* is here again/, except in scientific, technical, or statistical use, as in population tables; **lady,** originally used specif. of a woman of the upper classes and until recently commonly used in polite or genteel reference to any woman, is now often avoided as a general substitute for *woman,* except in such formulas as "ladies and gentlemen."

---

**woman-hater,** *n.* — *Syn.* misanthrope, misogyne, gynephobe, hater of women; see **cynic, misogynist.**

**womanhood,** *n.* **1.** [The state of being a woman] — *Syn.* adulthood, maturity, majority, womanliness, sexual prime, nubility, marriageable age, maidenhood, matronhood, spinsterhood, muliebrity, puberty.
**2.** [Womankind] — *Syn.* the fair sex, womenfolk, distaff, weaker sex*, femininity, female sex, female gender, woman, women.

**womanish,** *modif.* — *Syn.* womanly, effeminate, female; see **feminine** 2, **weak** 1.
*See Synonym Study at* FEMALE.

**womanly,** *modif.* — *Syn.* effeminate, ladylike, feminine, female, gentle, modest, compassionate, wifely, sisterly, motherly, protective, womanish, weak, fair. — *Ant.* MANLY, virile, masculine.
*See Synonym Study at* FEMALE.

**womb,** *n.* — *Syn.* uterus, female cavity, prenatal chamber, organ, belly*.

**won,** *modif.* — *Syn.* gained, achieved, conquered, taken, got, triumphed, overwhelmed. — *Ant.* BEATEN, lost, failed.

**wonder,** *n.* **1.** [Amazement] — *Syn.* surprise, awe, stupefaction, admiration, wonderment, astonishment, wondering, stupor, bewilderment, perplexity, puzzlement, fascination, consternation, perturbation, confusion, shock, start, jar, jolt, incredulity.
**2.** [A marvel] — *Syn.* miracle, curiosity, oddity, rarity, freak, phenomenon, phenom*, sensation, prodigy, act of God, portent, wonderwork, *rara avis* (Latin), nonpareil,

spectacle, perversion, prodigious event, something unnatural, the unbelievable.

**wonder,** *v.* **1.** [To marvel] — *Syn.* be surprised, be startled, be fascinated, be amazed, be dumbfounded, be confounded, be dazed, be awestruck, be astonished, be agape, be dazzled, stand aghast, stand in awe, look aghast, be struck by, be unable to take one's eyes off, admire, gape, be taken aback, stare, be flabbergasted*.
**2.** [To question] — *Syn.* be curious, query, hold in doubt; see **question** 1.

**wonderful,** *modif.* **1.** [Exciting wonder] — *Syn.* amazing, astonishing, incredible; see **unusual** 1, 2.
**2.** [Worthy of admiration] — *Syn.* fine, enjoyable, pleasing; see **excellent, pleasant** 2.

**wonderfully,** *modif.* — *Syn.* well, admirably, excellently, remarkably, unusually, unexpectedly, strikingly, magnificently, marvelously, beautifully, extraordinarily, amazingly, spectacularly, uncommonly, miraculously, famously*, stunningly*, first-rate*, to a fare-thee-well*. — *Ant.* BADLY, poorly, passably.

**wondering,** *modif.* — *Syn.* marveling, admiring, fascinated, awed, struck, in awe, awestruck, wonderstruck, guessing, pondering, speculating, flabbergasted*.

**wondrous,** *modif.* — *Syn.* remarkable, unusual, extraordinary, miraculous, admirable, fascinating, awe-inspiring, awe-full, unexpected, striking, marvelous, amazing, astounding.

**wont,** *n.* — *Syn.* practice, habit, manner, use; see **custom** 1, 2.
*See Synonym Study at* HABIT.

**wonted,** *modif.* **1.** [Usual] — *Syn.* customary, conventional, familiar; see **common** 1, **habitual** 1.
**2.** [Accustomed] — *Syn.* conditioned, habituated, accustomed; see **familiar** 1, **used** 1.
*See Synonym Study at* USUAL.

**woo,** *v.* **1.** [To make love to] — *Syn.* pay suit to, court, date, address, charm, spoon, bill and coo, make an offer, propose, seek in marriage, set one's cap for, make advances, caress, hold dear, carry on with*, give the rush*, keep company*, go steady*, come on to*, put the make on*.
**2.** [To court, figuratively] — *Syn.* cultivate, pursue, beg, solicit, entreat, aim at, stick to, seek someone's support, toady, curry favor, turn to, seek intimacy with, suck up to, butter up, brownnose; see also **propose** 1.

**wood,** *modif.* **1.** [Wooden] — *Syn.* woodlike, made of wood, hard; see **wooden** 2.
**2.** [Associated with the woods] — *Syn.* in the woods, wooded, woody, wood-dwelling, sylvan, woodsy, wild, shady, copselike, grovelike, arboreal, bowery, wild-grown.

**wood,** *n.* **1.** [A forest; *often plural*] — *Syn.* grove, woodland, copse; see **forest, timber** 1.
**2.** [The portion of trees within the bark] — *Syn.* log, timber, lumber, sapwood, heartwood.
Varieties of wood include: oak, chestnut, mahogany, teak, sugar maple, red maple, cherry, cedar, hornbeam, walnut, hickory, butternut, pecan, hemlock, spruce, bass wood, linden, beech, birch, poplar, tamarack, white pine, yellow pine, gumwood, elm, cocobolo, cypress, redwood, fir, Douglas fir, ash, red oak, live oak, white oak, willow, cottonwood, sandalwood, rosewood, lignum vitae, ebony, bamboo.

**out of the woods*** — *Syn.* out of danger, better, no longer in trouble; see **safe** 1, **saved** 1, 2.

**wooded,** *modif.* — *Syn.* timbered, forested, tree-covered, wild, sylvan, tree-laden, treed, reforested, woody, jungly, having cover, with enough forestation to preserve the run-off, timber-bearing, lumbering, uncut, not lumbered, not cut over, not cut off, with standing timber, primeval, below the timberline, jungle covered.

**wooden,** *modif.* **1.** [Made of wood] — *Syn.* wood, frame, frame-built, log-built, board, boarded, clapboard, clapboarded, plank, built of slabs; pine, oak, elm, ash, mahogany, etc.
**2.** [Having the characteristics of wood] — *Syn.* flammable, inflammable, stiff, clumsy, resinous, temporary, hard, destructible, buoyant.

**woodland,** *n.* — *Syn.* wood, woods, timberland, grove, copse, forest, timber, wilds.

**woodpecker,** *n.* Types of woodpeckers include: green, spotted, red-headed, white-headed, pileated, ivory-billed, California, golden-winged, Nuttall's, hairy, downy; flicker, red-shafted flicker, log-cock, yaffle, North American sapsucker; see also **bird** 1.

**woodsman,** *n.* — *Syn.* woodman, forester, hunter, trapper, woodcutter, lumberjack, logger, sawyer, tree trimmer.

**woodwork,** *n.* — *Syn.* molding, fittings, paneling, stairway, wood finishing, doors, window frames, sashes, jambs, wood trim.

**woody,** *modif.* — *Syn.* woodlike, pithy, xyloid, ligneous, wooden, wooded.

**wooer,** *n.* — *Syn.* sweetheart, suitor, courtier; see **date** 3, **lover** 1.

**woof,** *n.* — *Syn.* weft, cross weave, texture; see **weave.**

**wool,** *n.* **1.** [Fleecy fiber, especially of sheep] — *Syn.* fleece, yarn, lamb's wool, Angora wool, Berlin wool, German wool, Shetland wool, Australian wool, Botany wool, Llama, alpaca, vicuña, glass wool, mineral wool; see also **fiber** 1, **fur.**
**2.** [Cloth made from wool] — *Syn.* tweed, flannel, gabardine, worsted, woolen, suiting, serge, broadcloth, frieze, mohair, felt, blanketing, carpeting, Botany; see also **cloth.**

**woolen,** *modif.* — *Syn.* made of wool, woven, worsted, wool-lined, sheepskin.

**woolly,** *modif.* — *Syn.* downy, fleecy, woolen, kinky, wool-bearing, soft, fluffy, flocculent.

**word,** *n.* **1.** [A unit of expression] — *Syn.* term, name, expression, designation, concept, vocable, utterance, sound, a voicing, form of speech, speech, locution, free morpheme, morpheme word, lexeme.
Classes of words include: common noun, proper noun, personal pronoun, possessive pronoun, demonstrative pronoun, relative pronoun, interrogative pronoun, indefinite pronoun, definite article, indefinite article, transitive verb, intransitive verb, phrasal verb, descriptive adjective, quantitative adjective, participial adjective, adverb, coordinating conjunction, subordinate conjunction, relative conjunction, interjection, gerund, preposition, modifier, subject, predicate, loan word, root, primitive word, parent word, source word, etymon, synonym, antonym, cognative word, analogous word, derivative, slang, colloquialism, jargon, slang word, vulgarism, four-letter word*, dialect word, provincialism, translation, native word, foreign word, idiom, connotative word, denotative word, acronym, eponym.
**2.** [Promise] — *Syn.* pledge, commitment, oath, word of honor; see **declaration** 2, **promise.**
**3.** [Tidings] — *Syn.* report, news, information, advice, message, intelligence, announcement, account.
**4.** [A brief discourse] — *Syn.* talk, introduction, statement; see **speech** 3.
**a good word** — *Syn.* favorable comment, recommendation, support; see **praise** 2.
**be as good as one's word** — *Syn.* keep faith, be faithful, fulfill one's promise, live up to a promise; see **achieve** 1, **complete** 1.
**by word of mouth** — *Syn.* orally, verbally, through the grapevine, spoken; see **oral.**
**hang on someone's words** — *Syn.* listen to, adore, look up to; see **admire** 1, **listen** 1, 2.
**have words with** — *Syn.* argue with, differ with, differ from, bicker; see **argue** 1, **fight** 1, 2.
**in so many words** — *Syn.* succinctly, cursorily, economically; see **briefly** 1.
**man** or **woman of his** or **her word** — *Syn.* honorable man, honorable woman, trustworthy person, good risk; see **gentleman** 1, **lady** 2.
**take at one's word** — *Syn.* trust in, have faith in, have confidence in, put one's trust in; see **believe** 1.
**the word*** — *Syn.* information, the facts, the lowdown*; see **knowledge** 1, **truth** 1.

**Word,** *n.* — *Syn.* the Bible, God's Word, Scripture, Holy Scripture, Logos, dogma, holy writings, Divine Wisdom.

**word-for-word,** *modif.* — *Syn.* exactly, literally, verbatim; see **accurately.**

**wordily,** *modif.* — *Syn.* redundantly, pleonastically, bombastically; see **verbosely.**

**wordiness,** *n.* — *Syn.* redundance, redundancy, diffuseness, circumlocution, repetition, verbiage, verbosity, turgidity, prolixity, tautology, indirectness, periphrasis, flow of words, rhetoric, fullness, pleonasm, copiousness, bombast, tediousness. — *Ant.* SILENCE, conciseness, succinctness.

**wording,** *n.* — *Syn.* locution, phrasing, turn of phrase, contents, expression, style, way of putting it*.

**wordplay,** *n.* — *Syn.* verbal wit, play on words, double entendre, word games; see **pun.**

**words,** *n.* **1.** [Dispute] — *Syn.* contention, argument, wrangle; see **dispute.**
**2.** [Conversation] — *Syn.* chat, conference, communion; see **conversation, discussion** 1.

**wordy,** *modif.* — *Syn.* verbose, tedious, bombastic, prolix, long-winded; see also **dull** 4, **verbose.**
*See Synonym Study at* VERBOSE.

**work,** *n.* **1.** [Something to be done] — *Syn.* commitment, task, obligation; see **job** 2.
**2.** [The doing of work, sense 1] — *Syn.* performance, endeavor, employment, production, occupation, profession, vocation, calling, practice, activity, manufacture, industry, operation, transaction, toil, labor, exertion, drudgery, functioning, stress, struggle, slavery, trial, push, attempt, effort, pains, elbow grease*, muscle*.
**3.** [The result of labor; *often plural*] — *Syn.* composition, feat, accomplishment, output, product, deed, act, finished article, achievement, end product, opus, opera; see also **drama** 1, **literature** 1, **movie, music** 1, **picture** 3.
**4.** [Occupation] — *Syn.* profession, craft, business; see **job** 1, **trade** 2.
**at work** — *Syn.* working, on the job, engaged; see **employed.**
**give someone the works*** — *Syn.* shoot, slaughter, murder; see **kill** 1.
**in the works*** — *Syn.* prepared for, budgeted, in process, approved; see **planned, ready** 2.
**make short** or **quick work of*** — *Syn.* finish off, deal with, dispose of; see **prevent, stop** 1.
**off work** — *Syn.* not at work, off duty, not on duty, gone, gone home, out of work; see also **unemployed.**
**out of work** — *Syn.* not hired, dismissed, looking for a job, redundant (British); see **unemployed.**

**shoot the works\***, risk everything, gamble, everything, go the limit, attempt; **risk, try** 1.

**work,** v. **1.** [To labor] — *Syn.* toil, slave, sweat, do a day's work, do the chores, exert oneself, apply oneself, do one's best, overexert, overwork, overstrain, get to work, work overtime, work day and night, work early and late, work one's way up, fight one's way up, tax one's energies, pull, plod, tug, chore, struggle, strive, carry on, do the job\*, punch a time clock\*, put in time\*, pour it on\*, not spare the horses\*, work one's fingers to the bone\*, buckle down\*, bear down\*, work like a horse, work like a dog, work like a slave\*, keep at it\*, stay with it\*, put one's shoulder to the wheel\*, burn the candle at both ends\*, burn the midnight oil\*; see also **fight** 1.

**2.** [To be employed] — *Syn.* earn one's living, earn a living, have a job, hold a position, occupy a post, report for work, be off the dole, be off the welfare rolls, be among the gainfully employed, be on the job, do time\*, do one's stint\*, be working on the railroad\*, be a wage slave\*.

**3.** [To function] — *Syn.* go, run, serve; see **act** 1, **operate** 2.

**4.** [To handle successfully] — *Syn.* control, accomplish, manage; see **achieve** 1, **operate** 3.

**5.** [To fashion] — *Syn.* give form to, sculpture, mold; see **form** 1.

**6.** [To ferment] — *Syn.* sour, ripen, become worky; see **ferment**.

**workable,** *modif.* — *Syn.* useful, practicable, functional; see **working, usable**.

**work at,** v. — *Syn.* attempt, endeavor, do one's best; see **try** 1.

**worked,** *modif.* — *Syn.* fashioned, wrought, processed, treated, effected, designed, created.

**worker,** n. — *Syn.* operator, mechanic, machinist, craftsman, artist, artisan, journeyman, master worker, handworker, skilled workman, white-collar worker, field workman; see also **operator** 1.

Skilled workers include: carpenter, cabinetmaker, upholsterer, paperhanger, plasterer, bricklayer, plumber, electrician, pipefitter, coppersmith, sheet-metal worker, auto sheet-metal worker, printer, pressman, linotype operator, ship fitter, platehanger, slinger, chipper, screw machine operator, glassworker, lapping machine operator, truck driver, heavy equipment operator, automobile mechanic, punch press operator, sewing machine operator, cost accountant, clerk, file clerk, stenographer, word processor, data processing technician, data entry operator, secretary, bookkeeper, salesman, packager, darkroom operator, photographer, proofreader, railroad freight clerk, division clerk, conductor, brakeman, signalman, locomotive engineer, fireman, barber, baker, chef, butcher, farm worker, cowboy, dairyman, waiter, waitress, beautician, hairdresser, cosmetologist, day care worker, laundry worker, welder, drill press operator, hydraulic press operator, automatic screw operator, jig borer operator, drill operator, die sink operator, mason, lathe operator, gear-cutting machine operator, threading machine operator, telegrapher, teletype operator, telephone operator, radio operator, radio repairer, radio assembler, radio wirer, cigar maker, pattern builder, textile worker, tool designer, postal clerk, painter, pan coating man, galvanizer, draftsman, furrier, jewelry repairman, gold stamper, jigsaw cutter.

**work in,** v. — *Syn.* introduce, find a place for, squeeze in; see **include** 1.

**working,** *modif.* **1.** [Functioning] — *Syn.* toiling, laboring, moving, in process, in good condition, in force,

in gear, in collar, in exercise, going, twitching, effective, practical, on the job, never idle, on fire\*.

**2.** [Employed] — *Syn.* with a job, having a job, engaged, on the staff; see **employed**.

**working,** n. — *Syn.* operation, performance, functioning, fashioning, manipulation.

**workings,** n. — *Syn.* innards, mechanism, parts; see **insides, works** 1.

**working with,** *modif.* — *Syn.* cooperating, collaborating, assisting; see **helping**.

**workman,** n. — *Syn.* laborer, toiler, mechanic; see **operator** 1, **worker**.

**workmanship,** n. — *Syn.* craftsmanship, skill, quality of work, performance, handicraft, working ability, handiwork, achievement, manufacture, execution.

**work off,** v. **1.** [To get rid of by exertion] — *Syn.* work out, work away, exercise, run off, sweat off, walk off, lose.

**2.** [To pay by working] — *Syn.* pay off, work in exchange for, repay in kind.

**work on** or **upon\*,** v. — *Syn.* try to dissuade, try to encourage, use one's influence with, talk to; see **influence**.

**workout,** n. **1.** [A test] — *Syn.* tryout, drill, rehearsal; see **discipline** 1, **practice** 3.

**2.** [An exercise] — *Syn.* work, conditioning, gymnastics; see **discipline** 2, **drill** 3, **exercise** 1.

**work out,** v. **1.** [To solve] — *Syn.* come to terms, compromise, reach an agreement; see **agree, resolve** 2.

**2.** [To satisfy a requirement] — *Syn.* finish, do what is necessary, get something done; see **achieve** 1, **complete** 1, **satisfy** 3.

**work over,** v. **1.** [To repair] — *Syn.* fix, fix up, go over, redo; see **repair, repeat** 1.

**2.** [\*To beat or punish] — *Syn.* thrash, beat up\*, abuse; see **beat** 2, **punish**.

**works,** n. **1.** [Working parts] — *Syn.* cogs, wheels, gears, pistons, springs, coils, chains, rods, pulleys, wires; see also **insides**.

**2.** [Fortifications] — *Syn.* breastworks, earthworks, fort; see **fortification** 2, **wall** 1.

**3.** [\*Punishment] — *Syn.* beating, thrashing, wallop; see **abuse** 3, **attack** 1.

**4.** [\*Everything] — *Syn.* totality, entirety, the whole; see **all** 1, **everything**.

**workshop,** n. **1.** [A place where manual work is done] — *Syn.* plant, works, laboratory, foundry, studio, yards, establishment, mill.

**2.** [A meeting for study or discussion] — *Syn.* seminar, discussion group, study group, class.

**work up,** v. — *Syn.* elaborate upon, refine, enhance; see **develop** 1, 4, **improve** 4.

**work wonders,** v. — *Syn.* revitalize, regenerate, make over; see **correct** 1, **improve** 1.

**world,** n. **1.** [The earth] — *Syn.* globe, wide world, terrestrial sphere; see **earth** 1, **planet**.

**2.** [The universe] — *Syn.* cosmos, nature, creation; see **universe**.

**3.** [A specific group] — *Syn.* realm, division, system; see **class** 1, 2.

**4.** [All one's surroundings] — *Syn.* environment, atmosphere, ambiance, childhood, adolescence, adulthood, experience, life, inner life, human intercourse, memory, idealization.

**5.** [Nonreligious affairs] — *Syn.* life of action, society, career, material pursuits, secular matters, worldly interests, business, *activa vita* (Latin), worldly distractions.

**bring into the world** — *Syn.* give birth to, bear, have a baby; see **produce** 1.

**for all the world** — *Syn.* **1.** seemingly, to all appearances, like; see **apparently.**

**2.** for everything and anything, no matter, what, regardless; see **anything, everything.**

**in the world** — *Syn.* anywhere at all, wheresoever, in the universe; see **anywhere, wherever.**

**on top of the world** — *Syn.* feeling fine, feeling wonderful, feeling happy, exuberant, in the catbird seat*, successful; see also **delighted, triumphant.**

**out of this world** — *Syn.* extraordinary, strange, remarkable; see **excellent, unusual** 1, 2.

*See Synonym Study at* EARTH.

**worldly,** *modif.* **1.** [Lacking spirituality or idealism] — *Syn.* mundane, earthly, ungodly, matter-of-fact, practical, secular, profane, strategic, grubbing, money-making, unprincipled, power-loving, self-centered, opportunistic, sophisticated. — *Ant.* SPIRITUAL, religious, idealistic.

**2.** [Referring to life on the earth] — *Syn.* terrestrial, earthly, sublunary, mundane, telluric, human, natural, temporal.

*See Synonym Study at* EARTHLY.

**worldly goods,** *n.* — *Syn.* possessions, assets, nest egg*; see **property** 1.

**worldwide,** *modif.* — *Syn.* global, universal, extensive; see **common** 5, **comprehensive.**

**worm,** *n.* **1.** [A small crawling animal] — *Syn.* caterpillar, grub, larva, maggot, leech, parasite, helminth.

Common worms include: angleworm, earthworm, threadworm, pinworm, hookworm, tapeworm, galleyworm, silkworm, flatworm, blindworm, roundworm, annelid worm, cutworm, inchworm, measuring worm, army worm, cotton worm, wire worm.

**2.** [A debased creature] — *Syn.* wretch, hypocrite, beggar, fraud, brute, scoundrel, reprobate, snake, low-life, shyster, trickster, sneak, devil, demon, hellhound, scum, creep*, riffraff, sharper, swindler, hoaxer.

**3.** [Helminthiasis; *usually plural*] — *Syn.* hookworm, intestinal worms, tapeworms; see **infection** 1.

**worm,** *v.* — *Syn.* inch, insinuate oneself, sidle; see **crawl** 1, **sneak.**

**wormlike,** *modif.* — *Syn.* vermicular, sinuous, convoluted; see **twisted** 1.

**worm out of**, *v.* — *Syn.* squirm out of, evade, get out of, slip out of; see **avoid, escape.**

**worn,** *modif.* **1.** [Used as clothing] — *Syn.* carried, put on, donned, displayed, exhibited, used, sported*.

**2.** [Showing signs of wear] — *Syn.* frayed, threadbare, old, secondhand, ragged, shabby, impaired, used, consumed, deteriorated, torn, patched, the worse for wear. — *Ant.* FRESH, new, whole.

**worn-out,** *modif.* — *Syn.* used up, gone, destroyed; see **ruined** 1, 2, **useless** 1.

**worried,** *modif.* — *Syn.* troubled, anxious, concerned, hung up*, uptight*; see also **bothered, troubled** 1.

**worry,** *n.* **1.** [A state of anxiety] — *Syn.* anxiety, uneasiness, apprehension, concern; see **anxiety, care** 2, **distress** 1.

**2.** [A cause of worry] — *Syn.* problem, upset, disturbance; **fear** 2, **trouble** 2.

*See Synonym Study at* CARE.

**worry,** *v.* **1.** [To cause worry] — *Syn.* annoy, trouble, bother, bug*; see **depress** 2, **disturb** 2.

**2.** [To indulge in worry] — *Syn.* fret, chafe, grieve, take to heart, break one's heart, worry oneself, have qualms, despair, wince, agonize, writhe, suffer, turn gray with worry, be anxious, become sick with worry, stew, sweat out*; see also **bother** 1.

**worrying,** *modif.* **1.** [Engaged in worry] — *Syn.* pessimistic, pained, burdened, concerned, anxious, so-

licitous, ill at ease, disquieted, disturbed, heartsick, racking one's brains; see also **bothered.** — *Ant.* HAPPY, lighthearted, gay.

**2.** [Causing worry] — *Syn.* troubling, bothersome, disquieting; see **disturbing.**

**worrying,** *n.* — *Syn.* bother, anxiety, concern; see **care** 2, **distress** 1.

**worrywart**, *n.* — *Syn.* worrier, nervous person, nervous type*, old maid*; see **neurotic.**

**worse,** *modif.* — *Syn.* more evil, not so good, less good, deteriorated; see **poor** 2.

**worsen,** *n.* — *Syn.* make worse, fall off, take a turn for the worse, exacerbate; see **depress** 2.

**worsened,** *modif.* — *Syn.* exacerbated, depressed, lowering; see **dismal** 1.

**worship,** *n.* **1.** [Adoration] — *Syn.* prayer, devotion, homage, adulation, benediction, invocation, supplication, beatification, veneration, offering, reverence, honor, Mariolatry, hagiolatry, religious ritual.

**2.** [A religious service] — *Syn.* Mass, vespers, devotions; see **church** 2.

**worship,** *v.* **1.** [To adore] — *Syn.* adore, idolize, exalt, adulate; see **admire** 1, **love** 1, **revere.**

**2.** [To perform acts of worship] — *Syn.* sanctify, pray to, invoke, venerate, glorify, praise, exalt, offer prayers to, pay homage to, return thanks, give thanks, sing praises to, reverence, celebrate, adore, revere, laud, extol, magnify, chant, bow down before, kneel before, prostrate oneself before, canonize; see also **pray** 2.

*See Synonym Study at* REVERE.

**worshiper,** *n.* — *Syn.* churchgoer, communicant, congregant, pilgrim, supplicant, devotee, devotionalist, adorer, pietist, pious person, devout person, celebrant, saint, priest, priestess. — *Ant.* SKEPTIC, atheist, agnostic.

**worshipful,** *modif.* — *Syn.* pious, reverent, devoted; see **religious** 2.

**worst,** *modif.* — *Syn.* most terrible, most harmful, poorest, lowest, least, most ghastly, most horrible, most pitiful, least meaningful, meanest, least understanding, least effective.

**worst,** *n.* — *Syn.* calamity, catastrophe, ruin; see **destruction, misfortune.**

**at worst** — *Syn.* under the worst possible circumstances, if worst comes to worst, unluckily, grievously; see **badly** 1, **unfortunately** 1, 2.

**get the worst of** — *Syn.* fail, miss, be defeated, be beaten; see **lose** 3.

**give one the worst of it** — *Syn.* overcome, get the better of one, triumph; see **beat** 2, **defeat** 1.

**in the worst way** — *Syn.* very much, greatly, so much one can taste it*.

**worst,** *v.* — *Syn.* triumph over, overcome, best; see **beat** 2, **defeat** 1, 2, 3.

**worsted,** *n.* — *Syn.* woolens, suiting, long staple, English worsted; see **wool** 2.

**worth,** *modif.* — *Syn.* deserving, meriting, equal in value to, priced at, exchangeable for, valued at, worth in the open market, pegged at, cashable for, good for, appraised at, having a face value of, reasonably estimated at, bid at, held at.

**for all one is worth** — *Syn.* greatly, mightily, hard; see **powerfully, vigorously.**

**worth,** *n.* — *Syn.* goodness, excellence, merit; see **quality** 3, **value** 1, 2, 3, 4.

*See Synonym Study at* VALUE.

**worthless,** *modif.* **1.** [Valueless] — *Syn.* profitless, counterproductive, barren, unprofitable, unproductive, unimportant, insignificant, counterfeit, bogus, cheap, sterile, waste, wasted, no good, trashy, inconsequen-

tial, petty, piddling, paltry, trivial, trifling, unessential, beneath notice, empty, good-for-nothing, no-account*, junky*, crowbait*, not worth a damn*, of no earthly use*, not worth the trouble*, not worth speaking of*, fit for the dust hole*, not able to say much for*.
**2.** [Useless] — *Syn.* ineffective, of no use, ineffectual; see **useless** 1, **waste.**
**worthlessness,** *n.* — *Syn.* uselessness, impracticality, inefficiency, inadequacy, inability, ruined *or* worthless condition, lack of use, lack of value, inapplicability, badness.
**worthwhile,** *modif.* — *Syn.* good, serviceable, useful, important, profitable, valuable, remunerative, estimable, worthy, helpful, beneficial, meritorious, excellent, rewarding, praiseworthy.
**worthy,** *modif.* — *Syn.* good, true, honest, honorable, reliable, trustworthy, dependable, noble, charitable, dutiful, philanthropic, virtuous, ethical, moral, pure, upright, righteous, decent, incorrupt, incorruptible, meritorious, creditable, deserving, laudable, praiseworthy, estimable, right-minded, worthy of, whole-souled, model, exemplary, sterling, sinless, stainless, blameless. — *Ant.* WORTHLESS, bad, evil.
**would-be,** *modif.* — *Syn.* anticipated, assuming, supposed; see **hopeful** 1, **intended.**
**wound,** *modif.* — *Syn.* twisted, coiled, covered, wreathed, wrapped, twined, tired.
**wound,** *n.* — *Syn.* bruise, hurt, scar; see **cut** 2, **injury** 1.
**wound,** *v.* **1.** [To hurt the body] — *Syn.* gash, scrape, injure; see **cut** 2, **hurt** 1.
**2.** [To hurt the feelings] — *Syn.* trouble, upset, pain; see **bother** 3, **disturb** 2.
**wounded,** *modif.* — *Syn.* injured, hurt, disabled, stabbed, cut, lacerated, shot, scratched, bitten, gashed, hit, beaten, bruised, attacked, winged*, nicked*, pipped*; see also **hurt.**
**woven,** *modif.* — *Syn.* spun, interlinked, netted, netlike, dovetailed, wreathed, sewn, intertwined, united, interlaced, interwoven, worked into.
**wow*,** *v.* — *Syn.* triumph, overcome, be a success; see **succeed** 1.
**wraith,** *n.* — *Syn.* specter, phantom, apparition; see **ghost** 1.
**wrangle,** *n.* — *Syn.* altercation, controversy, quarrel, disagreement; see **dispute, fight** 1.
*See Synonym Study at* QUARREL.
**wrangle,** *v.* — *Syn.* bicker, squabble, dispute; see **quarrel.**
**wrap,** *n.* — *Syn.* shawl, cover, blanket, fur piece, cape, jacket, coat, cloak, light outer garment.
**wrap,** *v.* **1.** [To twine or wind] — *Syn.* roll up, swathe, muffle, bind, fold about, encircle, coil, enclose, swaddle, bandage; see also **wind** 1.
**2.** [To conceal in a wrapper] — *Syn.* envelop, enwrap, protect, encase, sheathe, shroud, cover, shelter, clothe, cover with paper, enclose in a box. — *Ant.* UNWRAP, unsheathe, open up.
**wrapped,** *modif.* — *Syn.* covered, sheathed, swaddled, swathed, enclosed, papered, protected, enveloped, encased, shrouded, concealed, hidden, clothed, done up. — *Ant.* OPEN, unwrapped, uncovered.
**wrapped up in*,** *modif.* — *Syn.* devoted to, absorbed in, in love with, affectionate; see **loving.**
**wrapper,** *n.* — *Syn.* envelope, folder, covering, cover, dust jacket, book cover; see also **cover** 2.
**wrap up*,** *v.* — *Syn.* finish, bring to an end or a conclusion, polish off*; see **complete** 1.
**wrath,** *n.* — *Syn.* fury, rage, vengeance, madness; see **anger, rage** 2.

*See Synonym Study at* ANGER.
**wrathful,** *modif.* — *Syn.* furious, raging, storming; see **angry.**
**wreath,** *n.* — *Syn.* garland, chaplet, laurel, lei, crown, festoon, floral design, funeral decoration, spray, flower arrangement; see also **bouquet** 1.
**wreck,** *n.* **1.** [The act of wrecking] — *Syn.* destruction, demolition, razing, breaking up, ruination, sabotage, smash, breakdown, bust*.
**2.** [Anything wrecked] — *Syn.* junk, ruins, skeleton, hulk, stubble, collapse, bones, scattered parts, rattletrap, relic, litter, pieces, shreds, waste, wreckage, debris.
**3.** [A shipwreck] — *Syn.* sea disaster, sinking, running aground, debacle, foundering.
**4.** [An accident] — *Syn.* crash, car-crash, collision, smash-up*, pileup*, fender-bender*; see also **collision** 1.
**5.** [*A person in poor physical condition] — *Syn.* incurable, invalid, consumptive, nervous case, overworked person, cripple, mess, goner, washout, scrub, shadow, skin-and-bones, walking nightmare.
**wreck,** *v.* **1.** [To bring to ruin] — *Syn.* spoil, ruin, destroy, disfigure, mangle, smash, tear down, raze, break, split, efface, batter, torpedo, tear to pieces, put out of order, impair, injure, stave in, bash in, mess up*, play hell with*, put out of commission*. — *Ant.* REPAIR, restore, rebuild.
**2.** [To shipwreck] — *Syn.* capsize, sink, founder, split on the rocks, crash on the beach, run aground, scuttle.
**wreckage,** *n.* — *Syn.* remains, ruins, hulk, wreck, debris, flotsam and jetsam, remnants.
**wrecked,** *modif.* — *Syn.* demolished, destroyed, broken, knocked to pieces, ruined, smashed, shipwrecked, stranded, beached, grounded, scuttled, capsized, out of order, blown to bits, junked, dismantled, shattered, on the rocks*, gone to pot*, bumsquabbled*, shot to hell*, snafu*. — *Ant.* REPAIRED, fixed, rebuilt.
**wrecking,** *modif.* — *Syn.* destroying, ruining, spoiling, smashing, breaking, splitting, shattering, undoing, battering, impairing, bashing, destructive, tearing down, tearing up.
**wren,** *n.* Kinds of wrens include: house, western house, winter, western winter, Carolina, long-billed marsh, tule marsh, cactus, cañon, rock, Nevada cañon, Berwick; see also **bird** 1.
**wrench,** *n.* **1.** [A violent twist] — *Syn.* jerk, strain, sprain, tug, pull, dislodgment, extrication, dislocation.
**2.** [A tool]
Kinds of wrenches include: monkey, single-head, double-head, pipe, Stillson, crescent, sparkplug, hubcap, flat, S-socket, connecting-rod, bearing, persuader*, knuckle-buster*, breakout*, old Maud*; see also **tool** 1.
**wrench,** *v.* — *Syn.* twist, bend, distort, pervert, extract, sprain, strain, pull, tug, jerk, dislodge, wrest, dislocate, yank.
**wrestle,** *v.* — *Syn.* grapple, struggle with, contend with, scuffle, perform in a wrestling bout, wrassle*, tangle*, grunt and growl*, trade holds*, tussle*; see also **fight** 2.
**wrestler,** *n.* — *Syn.* grappler, matman, mat performer, rassler*, bone breaker*, man mountain*, torso twister*, tangler*; see also **fighter** 1, 2.
**wrestling,** *n.* — *Syn.* contention, grappling, bout; see **fight** 1.
**wrestling match,** *n.* — *Syn.* grappling, mat game, wrestling bout; see **fight** 1, **sport** 3.
**wretch,** *n.* **1.** [An unfortunate being] — *Syn.* unfortunate, poor creature, victim, sufferer.

**2.** [A scoundrel] — *Syn.* scamp, rascal, villain, brute, traitor, deceiver, liar, fraud.

**wretched,** *modif.* **1.** [Afflicted] — *Syn.* distressed, woeful, sorrowful; see **miserable** 1, **sad** 1.

**2.** [Poor in quality] — *Syn.* weak, faulty, cheap, inferior; see **flimsy** 1, **poor** 2.

**wretchedness,** *n.* — *Syn.* misery, poverty, despondency, unhappiness, distress, grief, trouble, affliction, abjection, woe, sadness, disillusionment, depression, melancholia, dejection, discomfort, discontent, tribulation, torment, desperation, despair, desolation, bitterness, blue funk*, dumps*, blues*, doldrums*. — *Ant.* HAPPINESS, joyousness, exuberance.

**wriggle,** *v.* — *Syn.* squirm, convulse, wiggle; see **twitch** 2.

**wring,** *v.* — *Syn.* press out, squeeze out, extract, compress, twist, turn, strain, contort, bleed out, draw from.

**wrinkle,** *n.* — *Syn.* crease, furrow, crinkle, ridge, fold, corrugation, line, crow's foot, pucker, pleat.

**wrinkle,** *v.* **1.** [To form into wrinkles] — *Syn.* rumple, crease, furrow, screw up, pucker, cockle, twist, crumple, compress, crinkle. — *Ant.* STRAIGHTEN, smooth out, iron.

**2.** [To become wrinkled] — *Syn.* grow old, shrivel up, become warped, dry up, wither lose shape; see also **wither.**

**wrinkled,** *modif.* — *Syn.* creased, rumpled, furrowed, puckered, warped, twisted, crumpled, cockled, crinkled, dried up, withered, unironed, unpressed, shrivelled. — *Ant.* SMOOTH, ironed, pressed.

**writ,** *n.* — *Syn.* order, decree, warrant, process, summons, replevin, command, habeas corpus.

**write,** *v.* **1.** [To compose in words] — *Syn.* set forth, record, formulate, draft, turn out, give a report, note down, transcribe, pen, put in writing, comment upon, go into, indite, typewrite, communicate, rewrite, produce poetry, produce plays, produce novels, do imaginative writings, correspond, scribble; see also **compose** 3.

**2.** [To set down in writing] — *Syn.* inscribe, sign, scrawl, address, print, letter, autograph, reproduce, knock off*, dash off*, put in black and white*.

**write off, 1.** cancel, charge off, take a loss on, recognize as a bad debt; see **lose** 2.

**2.** forget about, disregard, shelve*, eighty-six*.

**write up** — *Syn.* expand, work up, deal at length with; see **describe, develop** 1, 4.

**writer,** *n.* — *Syn.* author, journalist, reporter, newspaperman, magazine writer, contributor, poet, novelist, essayist, biographer, dramatist, playwright, librettist, scenario writer, scenarist, screenwriter, literary critic, correspondent, foreign correspondent, feature writer, copywriter, sports writer, fashion writer, advertisement writer, ad-man*, publicist, scripter, shorthand writer, stenographer, anecdotist, amanuensis, ghost writer, song writer, copyist, scribe, editor, contributing editor, war correspondent, special writer, freelance writer, representative, women's reporter, knight of the pen*, member of the Fourth Estate*, quill driver*, scribbler*, wordsmith*, pen pusher*, hack*, newshound*; see also **author** 2, **composer.**

Major writers include — *British:* Henry Fielding, Sir Walter Scott, Charlotte Brontë, Daniel Defoe, Lewis Carroll, Emily Brontë, Virginia Woolf, George Eliot, Jane Austen, Charles Dickens, Thomas Hardy, Robert Louis Stevenson, D. H. Lawrence, James Joyce, Joseph Conrad, Samuel Beckett, George Orwell; *American:* James Fenimore Cooper, Edgar Allan Poe, Ralph Waldo Emerson, Henry David Thoreau, Nathaniel Hawthorne, Herman Melville, Samuel Langhorne Clemens (Mark Twain), Henry James, Edith Wharton, Stephen Crane, Theodore Dreiser, William Faulkner, John Steinbeck, Pearl Buck, F. Scott Fitzgerald, Thomas Wolfe, Ernest Hemingway, Norman Mailer, Truman Capote, Maya Angelou, Toni Morrison, John Barth, William Styron; *French:* (François-Marie Arouet de) Voltaire, Jean Jacques Rosseau, Victor Hugo, Honoré de Balzac, Gustave Flaubert, Georges Sand, Andre Malraux, Alexandre Dumas, Jules Verne, Albert Camus; *Italian:* Niccolo Machiavelli, Giovanni Boccaccio, Alessandro Manzoni, Ignazio Silone; *German:* Thomas Mann, Franz Kafka, Herman Hesse, Günter Grass; *Russian:* Fyodor Dostoevsky, Alexander Solzhenitsyn, Leo Tolstoy, Boris Pasternak, Ivan Turgenev, Anton Chekhov; *Spanish:* Miguel de Cervantes, Jorge Luis Borges; *Yiddish:* I.B. Singer.

**write-up*,** *n.* — *Syn.* press report, written description, written eulogy, laudatory account, review, publicity story, spread*, blurb*, rave*, notice*, build-up*.

**write up,** *v.* — *Syn.* report, publicize, record, treat of, do a sketch of, make an account of, put into words, report on, interview, do an item for the newspapers, praise in the press, ballyhoo*, build up*; see also **interview.**

**writhe,** *v.* — *Syn.* contort, move painfully, squirm, distort, suffer, twist and turn, undergo agony, turn with pain, throw a fit*. — *Ant.* REST, be at ease, move easily.

**writhing,** *modif.* — *Syn.* twisting, squirming, moving painfully, twitching, groveling, laboring, convulsed, agonized, suffering. — *Ant.* RESTING, still, sleeping.

**writing,** *modif.* — *Syn.* corresponding with, in touch with, writing to; see **contact** *v.*

**writing,** *n.* **1.** [The practice of writing] — *Syn.* transcribing, inscribing, reporting, corresponding, letter-writing, copying, typewriting, penmanship, script, lettering, printing, calligraphy, graphology, grammatology, grammatography, signing, autographing, stenography; see also **shorthand, typing.**

**2.** [Anything written] — *Syn.* literature, written matter, document, composition, article, poem, prose, paper, theme, editorial, discourse, essay, thesis, dissertation, book, manuscript, novel, play, literary production, scenario, drama, piece, work, signature, letter, pamphlet, tract, treatise, disquisition, comment, commentary, review, recitation, certificate, record, bill, bit, item, piece; see also **copy.**

**3.** [The occupation of a writer] — *Syn.* journalism, reporting, literature, authorship, freelance writing, professional writing, auctorial pursuits, the pen, the fourth estate, creative writing, novel-writing, verse-writing, feature-writing, newspaper work, the writers' craft, literary artistry, ink-slinging*, pencil-pushing*, hack writing*, writing for the pulps*, writing for the slicks*, ghost-writing*.

**writing desk,** *n.* — *Syn.* writing table, escritoire, desk; see **table** 1.

**written,** *modif.* **1.** [Composed] — *Syn.* set forth, authored, penned, drafted, drawn up, reported, signed, turned out, fictionalized, arranged, rearranged, adapted, ghost-written, recorded, dictated; see also **composed** 1.

**2.** [Inscribed] — *Syn.* copied, scriptural, transcribed, printed, lettered, autographed, signed, put in writing, in black and white, under one's hand; see also **typed** 1.

**wrong,** *modif.* **1.** [Immoral] — *Syn.* evil, sinful, illegal, wicked, naughty, salacious, base, indecent, risqué, blasphemous, ungodly, amoral, dissolute, dissipated, wanton, profane, sacrilegious, depraved, corrupt, profligate, shady*, low-down*, smutty*. — *Ant.* RIGHTEOUS, virtuous, good.

**(2.)** [Inaccurate] — *Syn.* inexact, erroneous, sophistical, mistaken, in error, incorrect, fallacious, untrue, erring, astray, amiss, ungrounded, spurious, unsubstantial, unsound, erratic, deceiving one self, in the wrong, under an error, beside the mark, laboring under a false impression, out of line, at fault, to no purpose, not right, awry, faulty, mishandled, miscalculated, misfigured, misconstructed, misconstrued, misfashioned, mismade, altered, not precise, perverse, anachronistic, at fault in one's reckoning, wide of the mark, not according to the facts, abounding in error, badly estimated, beyond, the range of probable error, a mile off*, all off*, gummed up*, crazy*. — *Ant.* ACCURATE, correct, exact.

**(3.)** [Inappropriate] — *Syn.* unfitted, ill-fitting, disproportionate, out of focus, off balance, misplaced, awkward, gauche, ill-advised, improper, unsuitable, incongruous. — *Ant.* FIT, suitable, appropriate.

**(4.)** [Referring to a side to be kept from view] — *Syn.* reverse, back, obverse, opposite, inside.

**wrong,** *n.* **1.** [Injustice] — *Syn.* vice, sin, misdemeanor, crime, immorality, turpitude, indecency, transgression, misdeed, unfairness, imposition, oppression, foul play, prejudice, bias, favor, unlawful practice, villainy, delinquency, misdoing, error, miscarriage, mistake, blunder, offense, *faux pas* (French), wrongdoing, violation, tort. — *Ant.* RIGHT, justice, fairness.
**2.** [An injury] — *Syn.* hurt, persecution, injustice, malevolence, cruelty, libel, abuse, harm, damage, spite, slander, false report, slight, misusage, outrage, inhumanity, over-presumption, insult, discourtesy, raw deal*, bum steer*, dirt*. — *Ant.* KINDNESS, good deed, consideration.

**wrong,** *v.* — *Syn.* hurt, oppress, defame, persecute, abuse, aggrieve, mistreat, misuse, use, exploit, take advantage of; see also **abuse** 1.

*SYN.* — **wrong** implies the inflicting of unmerited injury or harm upon another [*he was wronged by false charges*]; **oppress** implies a burdening with harsh, rigorous impositions or the cruel or unjust use of power [*oppressed by heavy taxation*]; **persecute** suggests constant harassment or the relentless infliction of cruelty and suffering [*the persecuted minorities of Nazi Germany*]; **aggrieve** suggests just or legitimate grounds for complaint or resentment for wrongs or injuries done [*aggrieved by the company's ill-treatment of him*]; **abuse** suggests improper or hurtful treatment, as by the use of harsh punishment or insulting or coarse language [*felt abused by his father's constant haranguing*]

**wrongdoer,** *n.* — *Syn.* lawbreaker, rogue, fugitive; see **criminal, sinner.**
**wrongheaded,** *modif.* — *Syn.* stubborn, biased, perverse, narrow; see **obstinate, prejudiced.**
**wrongly,** *modif.* **1.** [Unjustly] — *Syn.* unfairly, prejudicially, wrongfully, badly, unjustifiably, illegally, disgracefully, sinfully, unreasonably, unlawfully, criminally, reprehensibly, inexcusably. — *Ant.* RIGHTLY, decently, justly.
**2.** [Inappropriately] — *Syn.* unsuitably, improperly, awkwardly, incongruously, incorrectly, unbecomingly, indecorously, out of the question, imprudently, rashly, unnaturally, illogically, quixotically; see also **inadequately.** — *Ant.* APPROPRIATELY, tastefully, prudently.
**wrought,** *modif.* — *Syn.* created, manufactured, fashioned, formed, worked, processed, shaped, beaten, molded, woven, ornamented, coated, polished.
**wrought-up,** *modif.* — *Syn.* disturbed, anxious, worked up, agog; see **excited, tense** 1.
**wrung,** *modif.* — *Syn.* twisted, squeezed out, pressed, compressed, forced, dried.
**wry,** *modif.* **1.** [Twisted] — *Syn.* distorted, askew, cockeyed, crooked; see **twisted** 1.
**2.** [Perverse] — *Syn.* ironic, twisted, satiric, mocking.

# X

**x,** *n.* — *Syn.* unknown quantity, unknown, variable, mystery, n, y; see also **quantity.**

**Xanthippe,** *n.* — *Syn.* nag, scold, virago; see **shrew.**

**xerox** (trademark), *v.* — *Syn.* photocopy, reproduce, make a copy of, ditto; see **copy** 2.

**Xmas,** *n.* — *Syn.* the Nativity, Christmas holiday, Yule; see **Christmas, holiday** 1.

**X-rays,** *n.* **1.** [Electromagnetic radiation] — *Syn.* Roentgen rays, radioactivity, radium emanation, actinic rays, actinism, exradio, encephalogram, ultraviolet rays, refractometry, radiant energy, cathode rays; see also **energy** 3, **ray.**

**2.** [A photograph made with X-rays, sense 1] — *Syn.* x-ray photograph, radiograph, radiogram, shadograph, skingraph.

**xylophone,** *n.* — *Syn.* carillon, vibraphone, vibes*, glockenspiel, marimba, gambang; see also **musical instrument.**

# Y

**yacht,** *n.* — *Syn.* pleasure boat, sloop, auxiliary racer, class boat, racing boat, sea-going taxi*, single-sticker*; see also **boat, ship.**

**yahoo,** *n.* — *Syn.* barbarian, brute, savage; see **beast** 2, **boor.**

**Yale,** *n.* — *Syn.* Yale University, old Eli*, the Quad*, the Blue*, one of the Big Three*, Bulldogs*; see also **university.**

**yammer,** *v.* — *Syn.* nag, whine, whimper; see **complain** 1.

**yank,** *n.* — *Syn.* twitch, jerk, wrench, flip, jiggle, tug, haul, drag; see also **pull** 1.

**Yank*,** *n.* — *Syn.* American, soldier, member of the A.E.F., Yankee, doughboy*, Joe*, GI*, GI Joe*, doughfoot*; see also **Yanks.**

**yank,** *v.* — *Syn.* pull, haul, tug, drag, jiggle, flip, wrench, twitch; see also **draw** 1, **jerk** 2.

**Yankee,** *modif.* **1.** [Having New England qualities] — *Syn.* homespun, individualistic, isolationist, Republican, rockbound, set, conservative, rural, clever, tricky, hard, cunning, sharp, mercantile; see also **moderate, practical.**

**2.** [Concerning the United States] — *Syn.* North American, Western, westernized, Americanized; see **American** 2.

**Yankee,** *n.* **1.** [A New Englander] — *Syn.* Northerner, Easterner, Down Easter, early settler, Abolitionist, Unionist.

**2.** [A person from the United States] — *Syn.* American, American citizen, North American, westerner, tourist*, Yank*.

**Yanks*,** *n.* — *Syn.* American Expeditionary Forces, A.E.F., Army and Navy, Americans, American soldiers, American forces, doughboys*, doughfeet*, G.I.'s*; see also **air force, army** 1, **marines, navy.**

**yap,** *v.* **1.** [To babble] — *Syn.* jabber, rant, chatter; see **babble, talk** 1.

**2.** [To bark] — *Syn.* yip, yelp, bark.

**yard,** *n.* **1.** [An enclosure, usually about a building] — *Syn.* court, courtyard, barnyard, backyard, corral, fold, patch, patio, terrace, play area, lawn, grass, garden, clearing, quadrangle, lot; see also **playground.**

**2.** [An enclosure for work] — *Syn.* brickyard, coalyard, junkyard, navy yard, dockyard, railroad yard, stockyard, lumberyard.

**3.** [*Often plural;* tracks for making up trains] — *Syn.* railroad yard, switchyard, railway yard, marshalling yard, terminal.

**4.** [A unit of measurement] — *Syn.* three feet, pace, step, arm-span, thirty-six inches; see also **measure** 1.

**yardstick,** *n.* **1.** [A rule three feet long] — *Syn.* thirty-six-inch ruler, measuring stick, molding rule, yard, yard measure; see also **ruler** 2.

**2.** [A unit for comparison] — *Syn.* criterion, basis for judgment, criterion, standard, gauge, norm, rule, model, pattern, test, arbitrary device; see also **measure** 2. *See Synonym Study at* STANDARD.

**yarn,** *n.* **1.** [Spun fiber] — *Syn.* wool, spun wool, twist, flaxen thread, cotton fiber, rug yarn, crochet thread, knitting yarn, alpaca yarn; see also **fiber** 1, **thread.**

**2.** [A tale] — *Syn.* anecdote, sea story, adventure story, fictional account; see **story.**

**3.** [A lie] — *Syn.* fabrication, tall story, alibi, fish story*, cock-and-bull story*, crock*; see also **lie** 1.

**yaw,** *v.* — *Syn.* curve, swerve, bank; see **bend** 2, **turn** 6, **veer.**

**yawl,** *n.* — *Syn.* vessel, sailboat, ketch, jolly-boat; see **boat, ship.**

**yawn,** *v.* **1.** [To open wide] — *Syn.* gape, split open, spread out, expand, give, gap, part; see also **divide** 1, **grow** 1. — *Ant.* CLOSE, shut, come together.

**2.** [To give evidence of drowsiness] — *Syn.* gape, stretch, be sleepy, make a yawning sound, show weariness; see also **sleep, tire** 1.

**yea,** *interj.* — *Syn.* okay, aye, well; see **yes.**

**yea-high★,** *modif.* — *Syn.* so high, this high, up to here, yea-big★; see **high** 1, **short** 1.

**year,** *n.* — *Syn.* twelve months, cycle, continuum of days; see **age** 3, **time** 1.

Kinds of years include: civil, legal, calendar, lunar, solar, astronomical, natural, sidereal, tropical, equinoctial, leap, school, academic, election, fiscal.

**year after year,** *modif.* — *Syn.* year by year, annually; year in, year out, continually; see **yearly.**

**yearbook,** *n.* — *Syn.* annual, almanac, yearly report book, record, graduation book, class book, annual publication; see also **catalog** 2, **journal** 1.

**yearling,** *n.* — *Syn.* suckling, nursling, weanling; see **animal** 2, **baby** 1.

**yearly,** *modif.* — *Syn.* annually, once a year, every winter, every spring, every summer, every autumn, *per annum* (Latin), year by year; see also **annual, regularly** 1.

**yearn,** *v.* — *Syn.* want, crave, long for, fret, chafe, ache, grieve, mourn, droop, pine, languish, be eager for, be desirous of, be ardent, be fervent, be passionate, wish for, thirst for, hunger for, aspire to, set one's heart upon, hanker after★, have a yen for★; see also **try** 1. — *Ant.* AVOID, be content, be indifferent.

**yearning,** *n.* — *Syn.* want, longing, craving; see **desire** 1, **wish** 1.

**years,** *n.* — *Syn.* agedness, oldness, senescense; see **age** 2, **senility.**

**yeast,** *n.* — *Syn.* leaven, zyme, ferment, barm, amylase, pepsin, diastase; see also **catalyst, enzyme, fungus.**

**yeasty,** *modif.* — *Syn.* foamy, lathery, bubbly; see **frothy** 1.

**yegg★,** *n.* — *Syn.* felon, outlaw, safecracker; see **criminal, robber.**

**yell,** *n.* **1.** [A shout] — *Syn.* bellow, cry, yelp, roar, whoop, howl, screech, shriek, squeal, holler, hoot, yawp, hubbub, hullabaloo, hue and cry, protest; see also **noise** 1.

**2.** [Organized cheering] — *Syn.* hip-hip-hurrah, rooting, cheer; see **encouragement** 2.

**yell,** *v.* — *Syn.* bellow, cry out, scream, shout, yelp, yap, bark, bawl, roar, halloo, vociferate, whoop, howl, screech, shriek, shrill, squeal, squall, ululate, yammer, hoot, cheer, call, yip, give encouragement, call down, raise one's voice, yawp, holler★, whoop it up★; see also **sound** 1.

**yelling,** *modif.* — *Syn.* boisterous, clamorous, noisy, bawling, uproarious, turbulent, drunken, aroused, riotous, cantankerous, blatant, vociferous; see also **harsh** 1, **loud** 2. — *Ant.* QUIET, subdued, silent.

**yelling,** *n.* — *Syn.* cry, scream, shout, outcry, vociferation, screeching, bawling, yowling, bellowing, howling, yelping; see also **noise** 1, 2, **yell** 1, 2.

**yellow,** *n.* **1.** [A color]

Hues of yellow include: cream, ivory, old ivory, ivory-yellow, orange-yellow, saffron, jasmine, tawny, sand, gold, sallow, buff, straw, flaxen, alizarin yellow, anilin yellow, lemon yellow, mustard yellow, canary yellow, brilliant yellow, chrome yellow, Dutch pink-yellow, Dutch yellow, gamboge yellow, golden yellow, Imperial yellow, platinum yellow, Manchester yellow *or* naphthol

yellow, yellow carmine, yellow lake, yellow madder, yellow ocher; see also **color** 1, **gold** 2, **tan.**

**2.** [Cowardly] — *Syn.* tricky, deceitful, low, cringing, sneaking, white-livered, lily-livered, chicken, craven, treacherous; see also **cowardly** 1, 2, **mean** 1.

**3.** [Sensational; *said especially of some newspapers*] — *Syn.* lurid, scandal-mongering, muckraking, tabloid, warmongering, chauvinistic, unethical, unprincipled, sexy★, lowbrow★; see also **exciting, lewd** 1, 2, **offensive** 2, **sensational.**

**yellow,** *modif.* **1.** [Having a yellowish color] — *Syn.* yellowish, golden, jaundiced-looking; see **yellow** *n.*

**yelp,** *v.* — *Syn.* howl, screech, hoot; see **cry** 3, **sound** 1.

**yen★,** *n.* — *Syn.* longing, craving, hunger; see **desire** 1.

**yeoman,** *n.* **1.** [A naval clerk] — *Syn.* commissary clerk, ship's writer, officer's assistant, scribe★, supercargo★, quill driver★; see also **clerk** 2, **secretary** 2.

**2.** [A stout fellow] — *Syn.* common man, commoner, farmer, homesteader, freeborn man, freeholder; see also **citizen, man** 2.

**yes,** *interj.* — *Syn.* surely, of course, certainly, good, fine, aye, true, granted, very well, *mais oui* (French), all right, O.K., okay, Roger, we copy, affirmative, most assuredly, by all means, agreed, oh yes!, amen, naturally, without fail, just so, good enough, even so, in the affirmative, you bet★, okey-dokey★.

**yesterday,** *modif.* — *Syn.* recently, previously, earlier, the previous; see **before** 1.

**yesterday,** *n.* — *Syn.* the other day, the day before, recently, last day, a day ago, not long ago; see also **past** 1.

**yet,** *modif.* **1.** [Nevertheless] — *Syn.* notwithstanding, however, in spite of, despite, still, but, though, although, at any rate, on the other hand.

**2.** [Thus far] — *Syn.* until now, till, hitherto, prior to, still; see also **until.**

**3.** [In addition] — *Syn.* besides, additionally, further, furthermore, still further.

**as yet** — *Syn.* up to now, thus far, still; see sense 2.

**yield,** *v.* **1.** [To surrender] — *Syn.* give up, capitulate, succumb, relent, defer, resign, abdicate, relinquish, quit, cede, bow, give in, come to terms, sue for peace, lay down arms, cease from, let go, submit, give oneself over, admit defeat, suffer defeat, forgo, humble oneself, waive, throw in the towel★, call it quits★, back down★, holler uncle★, eat crow★; see also **abandon** 1. — *Ant.* RESIST, withstand, repulse.

**2.** [To produce] — *Syn.* bring in, return, sell for, furnish, generate, bear, bring forth, blossom, bear fruit, accrue, allow, admit; see also **bloom, produce** 1, 2.

**3.** [To grant] — *Syn.* accede, concur, acquiesce, allow, accept, comply, assent, concede, defer; see also **admit** 3, **agree.**

---

**SYN.** — **yield** implies a giving way under the pressure or compulsion of force, entreaty, persuasion, etc. /to *yield* to demands/; **capitulate** implies surrender to a force that one has neither the strength nor will to resist further /to *capitulate* to the will of the majority/; **succumb** stresses the weakness of the one who gives way or the power and irresistibility of that which makes one yield /she *succumbed* to his charms/; **relent** suggests the yielding or softening of one in a dominant position who has been harsh, stern, or stubborn /he *relented* at the sight of her grief/; **defer** implies a yielding to another because of respect for his dignity, authority, knowledge, etc. /to *defer* to another's judgment/

---

**yielding,** *modif.* **1.** [Producing] — *Syn.* bounteous, fruitful, productive; see **fertile** 1, 2, **rich** 3.

**2.** [Flexible] — *Syn.* pliant, plastic, malleable; see **flexible** 1.

**3.** [In the act of giving under pressure] — *Syn.* cracking, splitting, breaking, opening, swaying, shaking, bending, creaking, budging, wavering, softening, loosening, turning, falling back; see also **soft** 2. — *Ant.* FIRM, unyielding, impervious.

**4.** [Docile] — *Syn.* submissive, pliable, tractable, obliging; see **humble** 1, **obedient** 1.

**yielding,** *n.* **1.** [Submission] — *Syn.* gentleness, compliance, acquiescence; see **docility, humility.**

**2.** [Flexibility] — *Syn.* pliability, plasticity, pliancy; see **flexibility** 1.

**yodel,** *v.* — *Syn.* trill, warble, carol; see **sing** 1.

**yogi,** *n.* — *Syn.* mystic, fakir, anchorite; see **ascetic.**

**yoke,** *v.* — *Syn.* couple, link, connect, join, conjoin, harness, splice, unite, associate, bind, attach, fix, strap, buckle, bracket, hitch, lay together, tack together, secure, mate; see also **fasten** 1. — *Ant.* SEPARATE, divorce, sever.

**yokel,** *n.* — *Syn.* rustic, bumpkin, hayseed*, hick*, hillbilly*; see also **boor.**

**yolk,** *n.* — *Syn.* yellow, egg-yellow, egg yolk, vitellum, yelk*; see also **center** 1, **egg.**

**yonder,** *modif.* — *Syn.* farther, away, faraway; see **distant** 1, **remote** 1.

**you,** *pron.* — *Syn.* yourself, you yourself, thee, thou, all of you, you too, you alone, you all*, y'all*.

**young,** *modif.* **1.** [In the early portion of life] — *Syn.* puerile, boyish, girlish, adolescent, juvenile, budding, juvenescent, in one's teens, childlike, youthful, pubescent, boylike, girllike, new-fledged, blooming, burgeoning, childish, half-grown, growing, blossoming, at the breast, (babe) in arms, knee high to a grasshopper*. — *Ant.* OLD, aged, senile.

**2.** [Inexperienced] — *Syn.* callow, green, immature, tender, raw, untutored, unlearned, junior, subordinate, inferior, unfledged, ignorant, undisciplined, tenderfoot*, not dry behind the ears*, still wet behind the ears*; see also **incompetent, inexperienced, naive.** — *Ant.* VETERAN, expert, experienced.

**3.** [New] — *Syn.* fresh, modern, recent, newborn; see **fashionable.**

---

**SYN.** — **young** is the general word for one in an early period of life and variously connotes the vigor, strength, immaturity, etc. of this period *[a young* child,

man, etc.; *young* blood*]*; **youthful** applies to one who is, or appears to be, in the period between childhood and maturity or to that which is appropriate to such a person *[a youthful* executive, *youthful* hopes*]*; **juvenile** applies to that which relates to, is suited to, or is intended for young persons *[juvenile* delinquency, behavior, books, etc.*]*; **puerile** implies reference to adults who unbecomingly display the immature qualities of a child *[puerile* petulance*]*; **adolescent** applies to one in the period between puberty and maturity and especially suggests the awkwardness, emotional instability, etc. of this period *[adolescent* yearnings*]*

---

**youngster,** *n.* — *Syn.* child, boy, girl, pupil, kid*; see also **youth** 1.

**you're welcome,** *interj.* — *Syn.* my pleasure, forget it, think nothing of it, don't mention it, it's nothing, no problem, *de nada* (Spanish), *machts nichts* (German), *il n'y a pas de quoi* (French).

**youth,** *n.* **1.** [The state or quality of being young] — *Syn.* boyhood, adolescence, girlhood, childhood, early manhood, early womanhood, early adulthood, puberty, tender age, juvenescence, minority, youthfulness, teen age, virginity, bloom, teens*, age of ignorance*, age of indiscretion*, awkward age*, salad days*, betweenities*. — *Ant.* MATURITY, old age, senility.

**2.** [Young people] — *Syn.* the younger generation, the rising generation, the next generation, juvenility, children, the young, college youth, working youth.

**3.** [A young person] — *Syn.* boy, junior, teenager, lad, youngster, stripling, minor, young man, miss, girl, maiden, fledgling, juvenile, urchin, adolescent, student, kid*, teen*, pre-teen*, gosling*, pup*, calf*; see also **child.** — *Ant.* oldster, graybeard, dotard.

**youthful,** *modif.* **1.** [Possessing youth] — *Syn.* young, childlike, adolescent; see **active** 2, **juvenile** 1.

**2.** [Suited to youth] — *Syn.* keen, enthusiastic, zestful, vigorous, active, buoyant, lighthearted, prankish, fresh, lithe, full-blooded, full of life, full of animal spirits, limber, athletic, lightfooted, bubbling over, full of the devil*; see also **modern** 1. — *Ant.* SLOW, cautious, serious.

*See Synonym Study at* YOUNG.

**yowl,** *n.* — *Syn.* howl, yelp, wail; see **cry** 1, **yell** 1.

**yule,** *n.* — *Syn.* Nativity, Christmas season, Christmastide; see **Christmas.**

# Z

**zany,** *modif.* — *Syn.* dumb, humorous, madcap, wacky★; see **funny** 1, **witty.**

**zany,** *n.* — *Syn.* comedian, simpleton, buffoon; see **clown, fool** 2.

**zeal,** *n.* **1.** [Enthusiasm] — *Syn.* ardor, eagerness, fervor; see **enthusiasm** 1.

**2.** [Industry] — *Syn.* earnestness, hustle, hustling, bustle, bustling, intensity, industry, willingness, inclination, application, determination, promptitude, dispatch, diligence, perseverance, assiduity, intentness, readiness, aptitude, enterprise, initiative, push★, hop★, what-it-takes★, stick-to-itiveness★; see also **attention** 2, **care** 1, **cooperation** 1. — *Ant.* IDLENESS, slackness, indolence.
*See Synonym Study at* ENTHUSIASM.

**zealot,** *n.* — *Syn.* partisan, fan, bigot, fanatic, enthusiast, lobbyist, devotee, dogmatist, opinionist, missionary, fighter, cultist, follower, disciple, propagandist, plugger★, bitter-ender★, crank★, addict★, bug★, faddist★, fiend★.

---

*SYN.* — **zealot** implies extreme or excessive devotion to a cause and vehement activity in its support [*zealots* of reform]; **fanatic** suggests the unreasonable overzealousness of one who goes to any length to maintain or carry out his or her beliefs [a temperance *fanatic*]; an **enthusiast** is one who is animated by an intense and eager interest in an activity, cause, etc. [a sports *enthusiast*]; **bigot** implies blind and intolerant devotion to a creed, opinions, etc. [a religious *bigot*]

---

**zealous,** *modif.* — *Syn.* fervent, devoted, ardent; see **enthusiastic** 2, 3.

**zealously,** *modif.* — *Syn.* with zeal, assiduously, fiercely; see **industriously, vigorously.**

**zenith,** *n.* — *Syn.* top, pinnacle, summit, apogee, culmination, maximum height, highest point, climax, eminence, apex, altitude, elevation, acme, tip, crest, cap, roof, peak, crown, culminating point, tiptop★. — *Ant.* BOTTOM, foundation, base.
*See Synonym Study at* SUMMIT.

**zephyr,** *n.* — *Syn.* west wind, breeze, draft; see **wind** 1.
*See Synonym Study at* WIND.

**zeppelin,** *n.* — *Syn.* airship, dirigible, blimp; see **balloon.**

**zero,** *n.* **1.** [A cipher] — *Syn.* naught, nothing, nadir, love, below freezing, the lowest point, goose egg★, zip★, zilch★, duck egg★, nix★.

**2.** [Nothing] — *Syn.* nullity, oblivion, void; see **blank** 1.

**zero hour★,** *n.* — *Syn.* appointed hour, target day, H-hour, D-day, the time★, countdown★, jump-off★; see also **attack** 1, **crisis.**

**zest,** *n.* **1.** [Relish] — *Syn.* gusto, enjoyment, pleasure, delight, good appetite, enthusiasm, cheer, delectation, satisfaction; see also **happiness** 1. — *Ant.* OBJECTION, distaste, disgust.

**2.** [Savor] — *Syn.* taste, tang, piquancy, spice, bite, nip, pungency, punch★, snap★, ginger★, kick★, guts★, body★, zing★; see also **flavor** 1, **savor.**

**zigzag,** *modif.* — *Syn.* oblique, inclined, sloping, awry, crooked, thrawn, sinuous, twisted, askew, diagonal, curved, loxic, bent, crinkled, serrated, falcated, furcal, furcated, jagged, straggling, meandering, devious, erratic, rambling, oscillating, fluctuating, waggling, undulatory, vibratory, indirect, spiral, tortuous; see also **angular** 1, **irregular** 4. — *Ant.* STRAIGHT, parallel, undeviating.

**zip★,** *n.* — *Syn.* energy, vigor, vim; see **strength** 1, **vim.**

**zip★,** *v.* — *Syn.* run, dash, rush; see **run** 2.

**zodiac,** *n.* — *Syn.* celestial meridian, signs of the zodiac, sky signs, groups of stars, groups of planets, constellations; see also **constellation, planet, star** 1.
The twelve signs of the zodiac are: Aquarius (Water Bearer), Pisces (Fish), Aries (Ram), Taurus (Bull), Gemini (Twins), Cancer (Crab), Leo (Lion), Virgo (Virgin), Libra (Scales), Scorpio (Scorpion), Sagittarius (Archer), Capricorn (Goat).

**zone,** *n.* **1.** [A band] — *Syn.* circuit, meridian, latitude; see **band** 1, **stripe.**

**2.** [An area] — *Syn.* region, district, territory; see **place** 3, **position** 1.
Specific zones include: Torrid, Frigid, Temperate, Variable, Canal, traffic, parking, danger, building, quiet, school; Tropic of Cancer, Tropic of Capricorn, Arctic Circle, Antarctic Circle.

**zoned,** *modif.* — *Syn.* subject to zoning ordinances, planned for, platted; see **restricted, urban** 2.

**zoning,** *n.* — *Syn.* city planning, urban planning, municipal planning, controlled development; see **administration, plan** 2.

**zoo,** *n.* — *Syn.* menagerie, terrarium, aquarium, aviary, vivarium, zoological garden.

**zoological,** *modif.* — *Syn.* zoologic, mammalogical, ornithological, herpetological, ichthyological, ascidiological, echinological, conchological, entomological, arachnological, crustaceological, zoophytological, spongiological, protozoological, helminthological; see also **alive** 1, **biological.**

**zoology,** *n.* — *Syn.* life science, science of organisms, biological science, natural history; see **biology, life** 1, **natural science.**
Branches of zoology include: histology, embryology, endocrinology, cytology, physiology, evolution, human anatomy, comparative anatomy, entomology, bacteriology, ornithology, ontogeny, genetics, cytology, ethnology, taxonomy, taxonomic zoology, systematic zoology, zoochemistry, biochemistry, ecology, paleontology, paleozoology, zootechnics, bionomics, thremmatology, helminthology, ascidiology, cetology, marine biology, conchology, zoophytology, ichthyology, herpetology, mammalogy, mastology, therology, vertebrate zoology, invertebrate zoology, zoogeography, zoogamy, zoodynamics, zoopathology, zoopery, zoography.

**zoom,** *v.* — *Syn.* speed, rush, streak, zip, hum, soar like an airplane, climb like a homesick angel★; see also **climb** 1, **hurry** 1, **rise** 1.

# SUPPLEMENTARY
# WORD LISTS

# –CIDE  terms for the killing or destruction of the specified thing

aborticide (a fetus)
acaricide (acarids, or mites)
algicide (algae)
amicicide (a friend)
avicide (bird) (a bird or birds)
bactericide (bacteria)
biocide (living organisms, as by chemicals)
ceticide (a whale or whales)
deicide (a god)
ecocide (destruction of life in a large area)
elephanticide
felicide (a cat)
femicide (a woman)
feticide (a fetus)
filaricide (intestinal worms)
filicide (one's son or daughter)
formicicide (ants)
fratricide (one's brother)
fungicide (fungi)
gametocide (gamete or gametocyte)
genocide (a national, racial, political, or cultural group)
germicide (germs)
gynecide (a woman)
herbicide (plants)
homicide (a person)
infanticide (a baby)
insecticide (insects)
larvicide (larvae)
liberticide (the destruction of liberty)
lupicide (a wolf or wolves)
macropicide (a kangaroo or kangaroos)

mariticide (one's spouse, especially one's husband)
matricide (one's mother)
menticide (the destruction of a person's ability to think clearly)
microbicide (germs)
mildewcide (mildew)
miticide (mites)
ovicide (egg cells)
parasiticide (parasites)
parenticide (one's parent)
parricide (a close relative, one's parent)
patricide (one's father)
pediculicide (lice)
pesticide (a pest animal)
phytocide (plants)
prolicide (one's own child)
raticide (rats)
regicide (a king)
rodenticide (rodents)
senicide (an old man)
sororicide (one's sister)
spermaticide, spermicide (spermatozoa)
suicide (oneself)
tauricide (a bull)
tyrannicide (a tyrant)
uxoricide (one's wife)
vaticide (a prophet)
vermicide (worms, especially intestinal worms)
vespacide (wasps)
vulpecide, vulpicide (a fox or foxes)

# –CRACY  types of government; nouns designating participants in these forms of government may be formed with the combining form -crat

androcracy (by men)
angelocracy (by angels)
aristocracy (by an elite class)
arithmocracy (by a numerical majority)
autocracy (by one ruler)
bureaucracy (by a bureaucratic structure)
chromatocracy (by a single race)
democracy (by the people)
doulocracy, dulocracy (by slaves)
ergatocracy (by workers)
gerontocracy (by older persons/elders)
gynecocracy (by women)
hagiocracy (by holy people)
hierocracy (by priests or clergy)
ideocracy (based on a theory or abstract idea)
isocracy (in which all have equal political power)
kakistocracy (by the worst men)
kleptocracy (by a thief or thieves)
mediocracy (by a mediocre person or group)

meritocracy (by an intellectual elite)
mobocracy (by the mob)
monocracy (by one ruler)
neocracy (by amateurs)
ochlocracy (by the mob)
pantisocracy (in which all rule equally)
plutocracy (by the wealthy)
pornocracy (by prostitutes)
ptochocracy (by the poor)
slavocracy (by slave owners)
sociocracy (in which the interests of all are served equally)
stratocracy (by the military)
technocracy (by experts and technicians)
theocracy (by persons who believe they have divine authority)
timocracy (by those motivated by a love of honor and military glory, or by those who own property)

## –IAC   people with a certain condition, obsession, or interest

amnesiac (amnesia sufferer)
Anglomaniac (one overly fascinated by England and things English)
arithmomaniac (compulsive counter)
bibliomaniac (obsessive book collector)
bulimiac (bulimia sufferer)
claustrophobiac (claustrophobia sufferer)
dipsomaniac (obsessive craver of alcoholic beverages)
erotomaniac (erotomania sufferer)
hypochondriac (excessive worrier about one's health)
insomniac (insomnia sufferer)
kleptomaniac (obsessive thief)
logomaniac (obsessive talker)
megalomaniac (deluded believer in one's own importance)

melancholiac (melancholia sufferer)
melomaniac (obsessive music listener)
metromaniac (obsessive poetry writer)
narcomaniac (obsessive user of narcotics)
necrophiliac (person erotically attracted to corpses)
neophiliac (obsessive craver of new things or novelty)
nymphomaniac (woman obsessively preoccupied with sex)
paranoiac (paranoia sufferer)
philatelomaniac (obsessive stamp collector)
satyromaniac (man excessively preoccupied with sex)
simoniac (practicer of simony)
theatromaniac (obsessive theatergoer)

## –MANCY   divination by use of a specified means

aeromancy (weather conditions)
alectoromancy, alectryomancy (a rooster)
aleuromancy (flour)
alphitomancy (barley meal)
anthracomancy (burning coal)
anthropomancy (the internal parts of dead men)
arithmancy, arithmomancy (numbers)
armomancy (the shoulders of animals)
astromancy (stars)
axinomancy (an axhead)
belomancy (arrows)
bibliomancy (books)
capnomancy (smoke)
cartomancy (playing cards)
catopromancy, catoptromancy (a crystal ball, mirrors)
ceraunomancy (thunder)
ceromancy (melted wax dropped into water)
cheiromancy, chiromancy (the palm, hand)
cleidomancy, clidomancy (keys)
cleromancy (casting lots)
coscinomancy (a sieve and shears)
crithomancy (scattering grain over sacrificed animals)
cubomancy (throwing rice)
dactyliomancy (finger rings)
demonomancy (demons)
empyromancy (fire and smoke)
geomancy (geographic features, a handful of thrown earth, lines randomly placed on paper)
gyromancy (walking in a circle)
halomancy (salt)
hieromancy (sacred objects, sacrificial remains)

hydromancy (observation of water)
ichnomancy (footprints)
ichthyomancy (the internal parts of fish)
keraunomancy (thunder)
lecanomancy (water in a basin)
lithomancy (rocks or stones)
logomancy (words)
metopomancy (the forehead, face)
molybdomancy (the motion of molten lead)
myomancy (mice)
necromancy (the dead)
nomancy (letters)
oenomancy, oinomancy (wine)
oneiromancy (dreams)
onychomancy (fingernails)
pessomancy (pebbles)
psychomancy (souls, spirits)
pyromancy (fire)
rhabdomancy (rods, wands)
rhapsodomancy (verses)
scapulimancy, scapulomancy (cracking a mammal's scapula by heat)
scatomancy (excrement)
sciomancy (spirits of the dead)
selenomancy (the moon)
sideromancy (stars)
spatulamancy (the shoulder blade of an animal)
spodomancy (ashes)
stichomancy (poetry, passages in a book)
stignomancy (writing or carving on tree bark)
uromancy (urine)
xylomancy (wood)

# –MANIA  types of mental disorder characterized by an abnormal preoccupation with the thing specified

ablutomania (bathing)
agromania (living alone)
ailuromania (cats)
Anglomania (imitating English manners and customs)
anthomania (flowers)
arithmomania (numbers, counting)
automania (solitude)
balletomania (ballet)
bibliomania (books)
cheromania (gaiety)
choreomania (dancing)
choromania (dancing)
chrematomania (money)
cleptomania (stealing)
coprolalomania (foul speech)
cynomania (dogs)
dipsomania (alcoholic beverages)
dromomania (traveling)
egomania (oneself)
eleutheromania (freedom)
entheomania (religion)
entomomania (insects)
ergomania (work)
erotomania (sexual desire)
ethnomania (ethnic or racial autonomy)
florimania (plants)
gamomania (marriage)
gephyromania (bridges)
glazomania (list making)
gymnomania (nakedness)
gynecomania (erotomania in males)
hedonomania (pleasure)
heliomania (the sun)
hippomania (horses)
homicidomania (murder)
hydromania (water)
hypnomania (sleep)
ichthyomania (fish)
kathisomania (sitting)
kleptomania (stealing)
letheomania (narcotics)
litigiomania (legal disputes)
logomania (talking)
megalomania (delusions of great wealth, power, self-importance, and goodness)

melomania (music, melody)
metromania (writing)
monomania (one idea, a single interest)
mythomania (lying, exaggeration)
narcomania (using narcotics)
necromania (the dead)
nesomania (islands)
noctimania (night)
nostomania (going back to one's home)
nymphomania (erotomania in females)
ochlomania (crowds)
oikomania (one's home)
oinomania (wine)
oniomania (buying things)
onomatomania (words or names)
ophidiomania (reptiles)
ornithomania (birds)
paramania (complaints)
parousiamania (Christ)
phagomania (food, eating)
phaneromania (a growth on one's body)
pharmacomania (medicines)
phonomania (sound)
photomania (light)
plutomania (becoming wealthy)
poriomania (traveling)
pyromania (fire)
satyromania (erotomania in males)
scribomania (writing)
siderodromomania (railroad travel)
sitomania (food)
sophomania (wisdom)
thalassomania (the sea)
thanatomania (death)
theomania (God)
timbromania (postage stamps)
tomomania (surgery)
trichomania (hair)
trichotilomania (pulling out one's hair)
tulipomania (tulips)
uteromania (erotomania in females)
xenomania (foreigners)
zoomania (animals)

# –OLOGY  field of scholarship; nouns designating scholars in these fields may be formed with the combining form *-ologist*

acanthology (spines, sea urchins)
acarology (mites, ticks)
actinology (the chemical action of light)
adenology (glands)
aerobiology (airborne microorganisms)

aerology (air in the upper atmosphere)
agriology (history, the customs of primitive people)
agrobiology (plant life, plant nutrition)
agrology (soil)

agrostology (grasses)
alethiology (truth and error)
algology (algae)
andrology (man)
anemology (winds)
angelology (angels)
angiology (blood vessels, lymphatics)
apiology (bees)
arcticology (the polar regions)
areology (Mars)
astrogeology (the geology of planets, satellites, and asteroids)
audiology (hearing disorders)
autecology (ecology of individual plants)
autonumerology (license plate numbers)
axiology (values, as in ethics, aesthetics, religion)
bacteriology (bacteria)
balneology (baths, bathing)
biocenology (biotic communities)
bioclimatology (climate in relation to health)
bioecology (environment in relation to health)
biology (animals, plants)
biometeorology (weather in relation to health)
biopsychology (psychology in relation to health)
biosociology (sociology in relation to health)
biospeleology (organisms that live in caves)
bryology (mosses)
Buddhology (Buddha, Buddhahood)
cardiology (the heart)
carpology (fruits, seeds)
cetology (whales, dolphins)
choreology (dance notation)
Christology (Jesus Christ)
chronobiology (biology and time)
chronology (time)
climatology (climate)
conchology (shells, mollusks)
cosmology (the universe)
craniology (the human skull)
criminology (criminals)
cryobiology (low-temperature biology)
cryology (snow and ice)
cryptology (secret communications)
culturology (culture)
cyclonology (cyclones)
cytology (cells of organisms)
cytopathology (pathology of cells)
demonology (demons)
dendrochronology (tree rings)
dendrology (trees, shrubs)
deontology (ethics)
dermatology (the skin)
desmidiology (desmids)
dialectology (dialects)
ecclesiology (churches)
eccrinology (secretions)
ecology (the environment)

Egyptology (ancient Egypt)
electrobiology (electricity in living beings)
embryology (embryos)
endocrinology (endocrine glands)
enigmatology (enigmas)
enterology (intestines)
entomology (insects)
enzymology (enzymes)
epidemiology (epidemics)
epistemology (knowledge)
eschatology (ultimate matters in relation to theology)
Eskimology (Eskimo peoples)
ethnoarchaeology (archaeology of a society)
ethnobiology (biology of a society)
ethnology (races and ethnic groups)
ethnomusicology (music of a culture)
ethnopsychology (psychology of a culture)
ethology (animal behavior)
etiology (causes, origins)
etymology (the history of words)
exobiology (evolution)
fetology (the fetus)
fluviology (watercourses, rivers)
fungology (fungi)
futurology (the future, forecasting trends)
galvanology (galvanism)
garbology (refuse)
gastrology (the stomach)
gemology (gemstones)
genesiology (reproduction)
geology (the earth's crust)
geomorphology (the origin of geological features)
geratology (the aging process)
gerontology (old age)
gigantology (giants)
glaciology (glaciers)
glossology (linguistics)
grammatology (systems of writing)
graphology (handwriting)
gynecology (women's health)
halology (the chemistry of salts)
hamartiology (sin)
hedonology (pleasure)
helminthology (worms)
hematology (the blood)
heortology (religious feasts and seasons)
herbology (herbs)
heresiology (heresies)
herpetology (reptiles)
hieroglyphology (hieroglyphics)
hippology (horses)
histology (animal and vegetable tissues)
horology (the measurement of time, the making of timepieces)
hydrobiology (the biology of bodies of water)
hydrology (water)
hyetology (rainfall)

hygrology (humidity)
hymnology (hymns)
hypnology (sleep, hypnotism)
ichnology (fossil footprints)
ichthyology (fish)
iconology (icons)
ideology (ideas)
immunology (immunity)
insectology (insects)
karyology (cell nuclei)
kinesiology (bodily movement)
laryngology (the larynx)
lepidopterology (butterflies, moths)
lexicology (the meanings and origins of words)
lichenology (lichens)
limnology (freshwater lakes and ponds)
lithology (stones, rocks)
logology (words)
magnetology (magnets)
malacology (mollusks)
malariology (malaria)
Mariology (the Virgin Mary)
martyrology (martyrs)
meteorology (the atmosphere, weather, climate)
metrology (weights, measures)
microbiology (microorganisms)
missiology (religious missions)
morphology (form and structure)
muscology (mosses)
museology (museum organization and management)
musicology (music)
mycology (fungi)
myology (muscles)
myrmecology (ants)
mythology (myths)
nasology (noses)
nematology (nematodes)
neonatology (recently born infants)
nephology (clouds)
nephrology (kidneys)
neurology (nerves)
noology (the mind)
numerology (numbers)
oceanology (the sea)
odontology (teeth)
ombrology (rain)
oncology (tumors)
onomasiology (names)
ontology (being; metaphysics)
oology (birds' eggs)
ophiology (snakes)
ophthalmology (the eye)
orchidology (orchids)
organology (the organs of animals and plants)
orismology (technical terms)
ornithology (birds)
osteology (bones of the body)

otolaryngology (disorders of the ear, nose, and throat)
otology (the ear)
paleology (antiquities)
paleontology (fossil animals)
palynology (pollen, spores)
papyrology (papyrus manuscripts)
parapsychology (psychic phenomena)
parasitology (parasites)
pathology (the nature of disease)
patrology (teachings of the early church fathers)
pedology (the behavior of children)
penology (the management of prisons)
petrology (rocks)
pharmacology (medicinal drugs)
pharyngology (the pharynx)
phenomenology (phenomena in relation to philosophy)
phonology (speech sounds)
phycology (algae)
physiology (the functions of organisms or their parts)
phytobiology (the biology of plants)
phytology (plants and animals)
piscatology (fishing)
pistology (religious faith)
planetology (planets)
pneumatology (spiritual beings)
pomology (the cultivation of fruits)
ponerology (evil)
posology (the administration of drugs)
potamology (rivers)
praxeology (human conduct)
primatology (primates)
proctology (the rectum and anus)
psephology (elections)
pteridology (ferns)
ptochology (pauperism, unemployment)
pyrology (fire, heat)
reactology (psychological reactions)
reflexology (reflexes and behavior)
rheology (the flow of matter)
rheumatology (rheumatism)
rhinology (the nose)
roentgenology (medical x-rays)
sarcology (the soft tissues of the body)
scatology (feces)
sedimentology (sedimentary rocks)
seismology (earthquakes)
selenology (the moon)
semasiology (word meanings)
semiology (signs, symbols)
serology (blood serum)
sexology (sex)
sindonology (the Shroud of Turin)
Sinology (China)
sitology (nutrition, dietetics)
snakeology (snakes)

sociobiology (the biologic basis for social behavior)
somatology (bodies)
spectrology (ghosts, phantoms, apparitions)
speleology (caves)
stomatology (the mouth)
suicidology (suicide)
symbology (symbols)
symptomatology (symptoms)
synecology (plant and animal communities)
systematology (systems)
teleology (final causes)
teratology (tall tales)
thanatology (death and its causes)
thaumatology (miracles)

tonology (tones, speech)
topology (surfaces)
toxicology (poisons)
traumatology (wounds)
tribology (friction, wear)
trichology (the hair)
typhlology (blindness)
ufology (UFOs)
urbanology (cities, towns)
urology (urine)
venereology (venereal disease)
vexillology (flags)
virology (viruses)
volcanology (volcanoes)
zoology (animals)

## –PHILE  lover of the specified person or thing

acrophile (mountains)
ailurophile (cats)
alcoholphile (alcoholic beverages)
Anglophile (England or English culture)
arctophile (bears)
astrophile (stars)
audiophile (high-fidelity sound reproduction)
autophile (oneself)
bibliophile (books)
cinephile (movies)
demophile (crowds)
discophile (phonograph records)
Francophile (France or French culture)
Germanophile (Germany or German culture)
gerontophile (the elderly)
hippophile (horses)

iconophile (icons)
Italophile (Italy or Italian culture)
logophile (words)
necrophile (corpses)
oenophile (wines)
pedophile (young children)
pogonophile (beards)
polygamophile (polygamy)
Russophile (Russia or Russian culture)
Sinophile (China or Chinese culture)
Turcophile, Turkophile (Turkey or Turkish culture)
videophile (television or video recordings)
xenophile (foreign people, cultures, and customs)

## –PHILIA  love of or attraction to the specified person or thing

ailurophilia (cats)
alcoholphilia (alcoholic beverages)
androphilia (males)
Anglophilia (England or English culture)
autophilia (oneself)
claustrophilia (enclosed spaces)
coprophilia (feces)
demophilia (crowds)
epistemophilia (knowledge)
Francophilia (France or French culture)
gerontophilia (the elderly)
laparotomaphilia (surgery)
mysophilia (dirt, filth)
necrophilia (corpses)

nosophilia (being sick)
nyctophilia (night)
oenophilia (wines)
osphresiophilia (smells)
pathophilia (being sick)
pedophilia (young children)
Russophilia (Russia or Russian culture)
scopophilia, scoptophilia (nude bodies or nude pictures)
taphophilia (funerals, graves, cemeteries)
xenophilia (foreign people, cultures, and customs)
zoophilia (animals)

## –PHOBIA  fear of the specified thing; nouns designating persons with such fears may be formed with the suffix -phobe

*Animal and plant phobias:*
animals: zoophobia

bacteria: bacteriophobia, microphobia
bees: apiphobia, melissophobia

birds: ornithophobia
cats: ailurophobia, gatophobia
chickens: alektorophobia
dogs: cynophobia
feathers: pteronophobia
fish: ichthyophobia
flowers: anthophobia
fur: doraphobia
horses: hippophobia
insects: entomophobia
leaves: phyllophobia
lice: pediculophobia
mice: musophobia
microbes: bacilliphobia
parasites: parasitophobia
reptiles: batrachophobia
snakes: ophidiophobia, ophiophobia
spiders: arachnophobia
trees: dendrophobia
worms: helminthophobia

*Environmental phobias:*
auroral lights: auroraphobia
clouds: nephophobia
dampness, moisture: hygrophobia
fog: homichlophobia
ice, frost: cryophobia
lakes: limnophobia
lightning: astraphobia
meteors: meteorophobia
precipices: cremnophobia
rain: ombrophobia
rivers: potamophobia
sea: thalassophobia
snow: chionophobia
stars: siderophobia
sun: heliophobia
thunder: brontophobia, keraunophobia
water: hydrophobia
wind: ancraophobia

*Food and drink phobias:*
alcohol: potophobia
drinking: dipsophobia
eating: phagophobia
food: sitophobia
meat: carnophobia

*Health and anatomical phobias:*
beards: pogonophobia
blood: hematophobia
cancer: cancerophobia, carcinophobia
childbirth: tocophobia
cholera: cholerophobia
death, corpses: necrophobia
deformity: dysmorphophobia
disease: nosophobia, pathophobia
drugs: pharmacophobia
eyes: ommatophobia

feces: coprophobia
hair: chaetophobia
heart conditions: cardiophobia
heredity: patroiophobia
illness: nosemaphobia
infection: mysophobia
inoculations, injections: trypanophobia
insanity: lyssophobia, maniaphobia
knees: genuphobia
leprosy: leprophobia
mind: psychophobia
physical love: erotophobia
poison: toxiphobia
sex: genophobia
sexual intercourse: coitophobia
skin: dermatophobia
skin disease: dermatosiophobia
surgical operations: ergasiophobia
syphilis: syphilophobia
teeth: odontophobia
tuberculosis: phthisiophobia
venereal disease: cypridophobia
vomiting: emetophobia
wounds, injury: traumatophobia

*Inanimate object phobias:*
books: bibliophobia
crystals, glass: crystallophobia
glass: nelophobia
machinery: mechanophobia
metals: metallophobia
mirrors: eisoptrophobia
missiles: ballistophobia
money: chrometophobia
needles: belonophobia
pins: enetephobia
slime: blennophobia, myxophobia
string: linonophobia

*Miscellaneous phobias:*
certain names: onomatophobia
darkness: nyctophobia
dawn: eosophobia
daylight: phengophobia
depths: bathophobia
dirt: mysophobia
disorder: ataxiophobia
drafts: anemophobia
dreams: oneirophobia
dust: amathophobia, koniphobia
electricity: electrophobia
everything: pantophobia
fall of man-made satellites: keraunothnetopho-
    bia
fears: phobophobia
fire: pyrophobia
flogging: mastigophobia
freedom: eleutherophobia
ghosts: phasmophobia

graves: taphophobia
gravity: barophobia
ideas: ideophobia
imperfection: atelophobia
jealousy: zelophobia
justice: dikephobia
marriage: gamophobia
monsters, monstrosities: teratophobia
music: musicophobia
names: nomatophobia
narrowness: anginaphobia
neglect of duty: paralipophobia
new things: neophobia
night, darkness: achluophobia
novelty: cainophobia
nudity: gymnophobia
number 13: triskaidekaphobia, terdekaphobia
one thing: monophobia
poverty: peniaphobia
ridicule: katagelophobia
ruin: atephobia
shock: hormephobia
stealing: kleptophobia
stillness: eremophobia
strong light: photophobia
weakness: asthenophobia
words: logophobia
work: ergophobia
writing: graphophobia

*Phobias concerning groups:*
children: pedoiphobia
human beings: anthropophobia
men: androphobia
robbers: harpaxophobia
women: gynophobia
young girls: parthenophobia

*Phobias concerning religion:*
churches: ecclesiaphobia
demons: demonophobia
God: theophobia
heaven: uranophobia
hell: hadephobia, stygiophobia
sacred things: hierophobia
Satan: Satanophobia
sinning: peccatophobia

*Sensory phobias:*
being cold: frigophobia
being dirty: automysophobia

being scratched: amychophobia
blushing: ereuthophobia, eyrythrophobia
body odors: osphresiophobia
color: chromatophobia, chromophobia
fatigue: kopophobia
heat: thermophobia
itching: acarophobia, scabiophobia
noise: phonophobia
odors: osmophobia
pain: algophobia, odynophobia
pleasure: hedonophobia
sleep: hypnophobia
smell: olfactophobia
sound: akousticophobia
speech: lalophobia
sourness: acerophobia
stooping: kyphophobia
taste: geumatophobia
thinking: phronemophobia
touch: haptophobia
trembling: tremophobia

*Situation phobias:*
being alone: monophobia, autophobia
being beaten: rhabdophobia
being bound: merinthophobia
being buried alive: tophephobia
being looked at: scopophobia
crowds: demophobia, ochlophobia
enclosed spaces: claustrophobia
going to bed: clinophobia
heights: acrophobia, altophobia
high places: hypsophobia
home: domatophobia, oikophobia
infinity: apeirophobia
open spaces: agoraphobia
school: scholionophobia
shadows: sciophobia
standing: stasophobia
solitude: eremitophobia, eremophobia

*Travel phobias:*
crossing a bridge: gephyrophobia
crossing streets: dromophobia
motion: kinesophobia, kinetophobia
sea swell: cymophobia
speed: tachophobia
traveling by train: siderodromophobia
walking: basiphobia

# Names for Groups of Animals

antelopes: herd
ants: colony
apes: shrewdness
asses: herd, drove

baboons: congress
badgers: cete
bass: shoal
bears: sloth

beavers: colony
bees: colony, hive, hum, swarm
birds: dissimulation, flight, volary
bison: herd, troop
boars: singular, sounder
bovines: herd
buffalo: herd
camels: herd, flock
caribou: herd
caterpillars: army
cats and dogs: rain
cats: clowder, clutter
cattle: herd, drove
chickens: brood, clutch, flock, peep
clams: bed
cows: herd
cranes: sedge, siege
crickets: orchestra
crows: murder
deer: herd
dogs: kennel, pack
doves: dole, flight
ducks: brace, flock, gaggle, paddling, raft, team
eagles: convocation
eels: knot
eggs: clutch
elephants: herd, host, parade
elk: gang, herd
falcons: cast
ferrets: business
finches: charm
fish: draught, school, shoal
foxes: leash, skulk
frogs: army, knot, colony
geese: flock, gaggle, skein, wedge
giraffes: herd
gnats: cloud, horde
goats: tribe, trip, herd
goldfinches: charm
gorillas: band
grasshoppers: cluster
grouses: covey
hares: leap
hawks: cast, kettle (in migration flight)
hedgehogs: prickle
hens: brood
herons: siege
hippopotami: huddle
hogs: drift
horses: harras, herd, pair, stable, team
hounds: cry, mute, pack
hummingbirds: hover
jays: band, party
jellyfish: smack
kangaroos: mob, troop
kittens: kindle, kendle, litter
lapwings: deceit
larks: ascension, chattering, exaltation

leopards: leap
lions: pride
locusts: host, plague
mallards: sort
mares: stud
martens: richness
mice: nest
moles: labor
monkeys: tribe, troop
mules: barren, pack, span
nightingales: watch
owls: parliament, wisdom
oxen: team, yoke, drove, herd
oysters: bed
parrots: company
partridges: covey
peacocks: muster, ostentation
penguins: colony
pheasants: bouquet, covey, nest, nye, nide
pigeons: flock
pigs: drove, litter, herd
plovers: congregation, wing
polar bears: aurora
ponies: string
porpoises: school
quails: bevy, covey
rabbits: colony, nest
racehorses: field
ravens: conspiracy, unkindness
reindeers: herd
rhinoceroses: crash
seals: pod, herd, school, trip, harem, rookery
sheep: drove, flock, herd
skunks: stench
slugs: cornucopia
snakes: bed, slither
sparrows: host
starlings: murmuration
storks: mustering
swallows: flight
swans: ballet, bevy, wedge
swines: drift, sounder
teal: spring
tigers: streak
toads: knot
trout: hover
turkeys: rafter
turtledoves: pitying
turtles: bevy
unicorns: blessing
waterfowl: plump
weasels: gam, sneak
whales: gam, herd, pod, shoal
wolves: pack, rout
woodpeckers: descent
worms: wriggle
zebras: herd, stripe

## Names of Young Animals

antelope: calf
bear: cub, whelp
beaver: kit, kitten, pup
bird: fledgling, nestling
bison: calf
bovine: calf
cat: kit, kitten, kitty, puss, pussy
cattle: calf, yearling
chicken: chick, pullet, cockerel, poult
cow: calf, heifer
deer: fawn
dog: pup, puppy, whelp
duck: duckling
eagle: eaglet, fledgling
elephant: calf
elk: calf
fish: fingerling, fry
fox: cub, kit, pup, whelp
frog: polliwog, tadpole
goat: kid
goose: gosling
grouse: cheeper, poult
hare: leveret
hawk: eyas
hen: chick, pullet
hippopotamus: calf

horse: colt, filly, foal, yearling
kangaroo: joey
lion: cub, whelp
moose: calf
owl: owlet
oyster: spat
partridge: cheeper
pig: piglet, shoat, farrow, suckling
pigeon: squab, squeaker
quail: cheeper
rabbit: bunny, kit, leveret
reindeer: fawn
rhinoceros: calf
rooster: cockerel
sea lion: pup
seal: calf, pup
shark: cub
sheep: lamb, lambkin, cosset, hog
swan: cygnet
swine: piglet, shoat, farrow
tiger: cub, whelp
turkey: poult, chick
whale: calf, pup, cub
wolf: cub, whelp, pup
zebra: colt, foal